ELEVENTH EDITION

SCHROEDER'S
ANTIQUES
PRICE GUIDE

Edited by Sharon & Bob Huxford

COLLECTOR BOOKS
A Division of Schroeder Publishing Co., Inc.

The current values in this book should be used only as a guide. They are not intended to set prices, which vary from one section of the country to another. Auction prices as well as dealer prices vary greatly and are affected by condition as well as demand. Neither the Editors nor the Publisher assumes responsibility for any losses that might be incurred as a result of consulting this guide.

On the cover, clockwise from left:

Oak Game Table with scooped out troughs for poker chips or coins at each end and applied beading, early 1900s. 36"x36", 29" high. $495.00. Courtesy of *Collector's Encyclopedia of American Furniture, Volume II*, by Robert W. & Harriet Swedberg.

Robin Woods Dolls, Romeo & Juliet, 15", 1988-1990, $225.00 each.

Sandwich Footed Tumbler, 9 oz., Desert Gold. $75.00. Courtesy of *Collectible Glassware from the 40s, 50s, 60s...* by Gene Florence.

Mickey Mouse Alarm Clock by Bayard of France, 1960s. This clock looks like a 1930s design but is actually a more modern item. Courtesy of *The Collector's Encyclopedia of Disneyana* by David Longest & Michael Stern.

Gold Dust Tobacco Tin manufactured by B. Houde Company, Quebec, Canada. Worn condition, $2,000.00. Photo courtesy of Dennis O'Brien & George Goehring.

Tankard, 12" high, purple & pink grapes on shaded orange background, artist signed 'L.M. Gleason,' $350.00. Courtesy of *Collector's Encyclopedia of Limoges Porcelain*, 2nd Edition, by Mary Frank Gaston.

Additional copies of this book may be ordered from:

COLLECTOR BOOKS
P.O. Box 3009
Paducah, Kentucky 42002-3009

@$12.95. Add $2.00 for postage and handling.

Copyright: Schroeder Publishing Co., Inc. 1993

Introduction

As the editors and staff of *Schroeder's*, our goal is to compile the most useful, comprehensive, and accurate background and pricing information possible. Our guide encompasses nearly seven hundred categories, many of which you will not find in other price guides. Our sources are varied; we use auction results, dealer lists, trade paper ads, and we consult with national collectors' clubs, recognized authorities, researchers, and appraisers. We have by far the largest Advisory Board of any similar publication on the market. Each year we add several new advisors and now have more than three hundred who cover almost five hundred categories. They go over our computer print-outs line by line, deleting listings that are misleading or too vague to be of merit; they often send background information and photos. We appreciate their assistance very much — only through their expertise and experience in their special fields are we able to offer with confidence what we feel are useful, accurate evaluations that provide a sound understanding of the dealings in the market place today. Correspondence with so large an advisory panel adds months of extra work to an already monumental task, but we feel that to a very large extent this is the foundation that makes *Schroeder's* the success that it has become.

Our Directory, which you will find in the back of the book, lists each contributor by state. These are people who have allowed us to photograph various examples of merchandise from their show booths, sent us pricing information, or in any way have contributed to this year's book. Feel free to contact them; many will be glad to ship you the merchandise you need. If you happen to be traveling, consult the Directory for shops along your way. We also list clubs who have worked with us and auction houses who have agreed to permit us the use of photographs from their catalogs. Our Advisory Board lists only names and home states, so check the Directory for addresses and telephone numbers should you want to correspond with one of our experts. Remember that when you do, if you expect an answer from either an advisor or a contributor, please send a SASE (stamped, self-addressed envelope).

We have organized our topics alphabetically, following the most simple logic, usually either by manufacturer or by type of product. If you have difficulty in locating your subject, consult the index. Our guide is unique in that much more space has been allotted to background information than any other publication of this type, and it is easier to read due to the larger-than-average print. Our readers tell us that these are features they enjoy. To be able to do this, we have adopted a format of one-line listings wherein we describe the items to the fullest extent possible by using several common-sense abbreviations; they will be easy to read and understand if you will first take the time to quickly scan through them.

The Editors

Listing of Standard Abbreviations

The following is a list of abbreviations that have been used throughout this book in order to provide you with the most detailed descriptions possible in the limited space available. No periods are used after initials or abbreviations. When two dimensions are given, height is noted first. If only one dimension is listed, it will be height, except in the case of bowls, dishes, plates, or platters, when it will be diameter. The standard two-letter state abbreviations apply.

For glassware, if no color is noted, the glass is clear. Hyphenated colors, for example blue-green, olive-amber, etc., describe a single color tone; colors divided by a slash mark indicate two or more colors, i.e. blue/white. A number following the last comma in a listing indicates how many items are included in the lot price. Teapots, sugar bowls, and butter dishes are assumed to be 'with cover.' Condition is extremely important in determining market value. Common sense suggests that art pottery, china, and glassware values would be given for examples in pristine, mint condition, while suggested prices for utility wares such as Redware, Mocha, and Blue and White Stoneware, for example, reflect the probability that since such items were subjected to everyday use in the home they may show minor wear (which is acceptable) but no notable damage. Values for other categories reflect the best average condition in which the particular collectible is apt to be offered for sale without the dealer feeling it necessary to mention wear or damage. For instance, advertising items are assumed to be in excellent condition since mint items are scarce enough that when one is offered for sale the dealer will most likely make mention of that fact. The same holds true for Toys, Banks, Coin-Operated Machines, and the like. A basic rule of thumb is that an item listed as VG (very good) will bring 40% to 60% of its mint price (a first-hand, personal evaluation will enable you to make the final judgment); EX (excellent) is a condition midway between mint and very good, and values would correspond.

Am	American
appl	applied
att	attributed to
bk	back
bsk	bisque
blk	black
b3m	blown 3-mold
bl	blue
brn	brown
bulb	bulbous
can	canister
cb	cardboard
CI	cast iron
C	century
ca	circa
compo	composition
c	copyright
cr/sug	creamer and sugar
X, Xd	cross, crossed
c/s	cup and saucer
cvd	carved
cvg	carving
dk	dark
dtd	dated
decor	decoration
Dmn Quilt	Diamond Quilted
dbl	double

dvtl	dovetail
drw	drawer
emb	embossed, embossing
embr	embroidered
eng	engraved, engraving
etch	etched,etching
EX	excellent
ft, ftd	foot, feet, footed
fr	frame, framed
Fr	French
G	good
grad	graduated
grpt	grain painted
gr	green
HP	hand painted
hdl, hdld	handle, handled
illus	illustrated
imp	impressed
ind	individual
int	interior
irid	iridescent
Invt T'print	Inverted Thumbprint
lav	lavender
ldgl	leaded glass
L	length
lt	light
litho	lithograph

mahog	mahogany
mk	mark
MIG	Made in Germany
M	mint
MIB	mint in box
MOP	mother-of-pearl
mt, mtd	mount, mounted
mc	multicolor
NE	New England
NM	near mint
NP	nickel plated
opal	opalescent
orig	original
o/l	overlay
o/w	otherwise
pnt	paint
Pat	patented
ped	pedestal
pc	piece
pk	pink
prof	professional
porc	porcelain
rfn	refinished
re	regarding
rpt	repainted
rpr	repaired
rpl	replaced

rstr	restored
rtcl	reticulated
rvpt	reverse painted
rnd	rnd
s&p	salt and pepper
sgn	signed
SP	silverplated
sz	size
sq	square
std	standard
str	straight
trn	turned, turning
turq	turquoise
uphl	upholstered
VG	very good
Vict	Victorian
wht	white
W	width
w/	with
w/o	without
yel	yellow

A B C Plates

Children's plates featuring the alphabet as part of the design were popular from as early as 1820 until after the turn of the century. The earliest English creamware plates were decorated with embossed letters and prim moralistic verses; but the later Staffordshire products were conducive to a more relaxed mealtime atmosphere, often depicting playful animals and riddles or scenes of pleasant leisure-time activities. They were made around the turn of the century by American potters as well. All featured transfer prints, but color was sometimes brushed on by hand to add interest to the design. Braille plates were made for the blind, but these are rather scarce and therefore usually more valuable. You may also find an occasional bowl or mug.

Ceramic

American Sports, Baseball Pitcher, blk transfer, 6½", EX 210.00
Blind Girl, child in doorway, mc transfer, 5¾", EX 125.00
Boy & bunnies in hutch, bl transfer, Staffordshire, 8⅜"...............165.00
Boy w/guitar by fence w/bird, mc, 8¼" 145.00
Brighton Beach Bathing Pavilion, mc, 7" 145.00
Cat in bowl w/2 cats at side, bl rim, blk transfer, 6" 170.00
Cats in cherry tree, blk transfer, dbl bl rim, 6", EX 145.00
Child in swimsuit/5 teddy bears, dbl ABC rim, 7½", EX.............195.00
Children in center w/deaf sgns at rim, Aynsley, 6"......................200.00

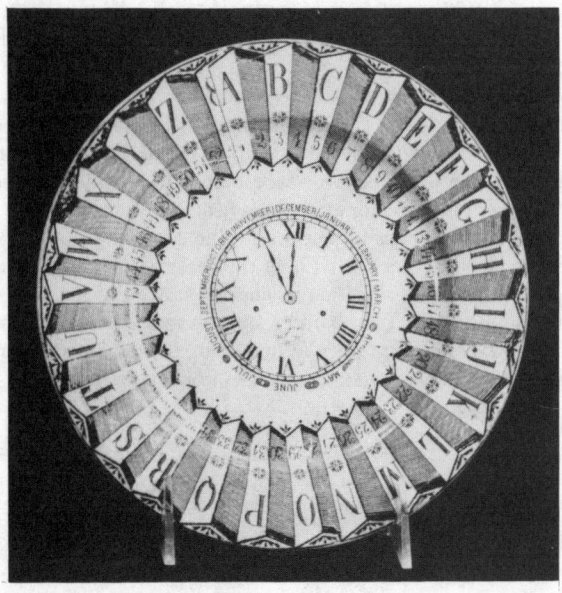

Clock face, brown transfer, RN #1752, 8", $45.00.

Crusoe building boat, transferware..110.00
Crusoe on raft, BPCo..125.00
Dandies on bucking horses, bl transfer, Staffordshire, 7⅛" 145.00
Deer & surprised hunter, bl transfer, Staffordshire, 7⅛"...............160.00
Egg, Eye, Eel, mc on blk transfer, Staffordshire, 5", NM 165.00
English newsboy w/newspapers, mc transfer, Meakin, 6", EX 120.00
Frolics of Youth, The Young Artist, mc transfer, 7¼" 100.00
Graces, 3 children in Victorian dress, mk Godwin, 5", EX 180.00
Kittens skipping rope, deaf sgns at rim, Aynsley, 6", EX 185.00
Man & child carry donkey over bridge, mc, 7¼" 85.00
Man w/basket, church at bk, mc transfer, Malkin, 7", EX 100.00
My Face Is My Fortune, transfer, emb ABC rim...........................125.00
Now I Have a Cow, mc transfer, Franklin Maxim, 5⅛" 145.00
Peacock, bl transfer, Staffordshire, 8" 160.00
Poor Richard's Way to Wealth..., mc on blk transfer, 6", NM 115.00

Seesaw Margery Daw 75.00
Silks & Satins..., Franklin's Proverbs, Meakin..............................175.00
Sioux Indian Chief, brn transfer, 7⅜" 130.00
Soldier on horsebk, bl transfer, Staffordshire, 7⅛" 150.00
Stable Yard, horses, Staffordshire, 7⅛" 160.00
Top Whipping, boys in landscape, transfer, Meakin, 5¼" 75.00
Village Blacksmith, children watching, mc transfer, 7", EX.........125.00
Zebra, mc enamel, Staffordshire, wear/stains, 6" 85.00
3 Negroes w/riddle & answer rim, mc transfer, 6", EX.................235.00

Glass

Rabbit and Alphabet, att Crystal Glass Co., 6", $50.00.

Clock w/Roman numerals, cut-out rim 75.00
Ducks w/ducklings, 6" 50.00
Elephant w/howdah & riders, 6" 70.00
Flower Bouquet, ABCs on stippled ground, frosted flowers, 6" 65.00
Old Independence Hall, stippled ABCs, scalloped, 7" 95.00
Proud Dog 50.00
Rabbit center, 6" 50.00

Tin

Brownies, ca 1893, 8⅞" 150.00
Children playing w/hoops, 2⅞" 100.00
Girl on swing, 6¼" 65.00
Peter Rabbit, animals intertwined in ABC rim, 8½" 70.00
Who Killed Cock Robin?, 8" 85.00

Abingdon

From 1934 until 1950, the Abingdon Pottery Co. of Abingdon, Ill., made a line of art pottery with a white vitrified body decorated with various types of glazes in many lovely colors. Novelties, cookie jars, utility ware, and lamps were made in addition to several lines of simple yet striking art ware. Fern Leaf, introduced in 1937, featured molded vertical feathering. La Fleur, in 1939, consisted of flowerpots and flower-arranger bowls with rows of vertical ribbing. Classic, 1939-

40, was a line of vases, many with evidence of Chinese influence. Several marks were used, most of which employed the company name. In 1950 the company reverted to the manufacture of sanitary ware that had been their mainstay before the Art Ware Division was formed.

Highly decorated examples and those with black, bronze, or red glaze usually command at least 25% higher prices.

Our advisors for Abingdon cookie jars are Joyce and Fred Roerig, authors of *The Collector's Encyclopedia of Cookie Jars*. Their address is in the Directory under South Carolina.

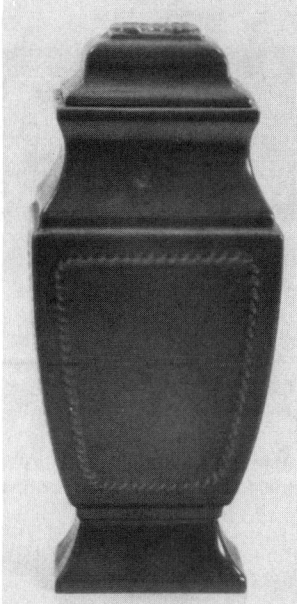

Chang jar, copper brown, 11", $275.00.

#A1, vase, red, 3½" 75.00
#G3, vase, Rope, yel, 18" 180.00
#104, vase, Delta, turq matt, 10" 28.00
#109, vase, Alpha, wht, 6" 18.00
#110, vase, Beta, lt bl, 6" 30.00
#118, vase, Classic, 10" 22.00
#142, vase, Classic, bl, mini, 5" 25.00
#200, pitcher, ice lip, red matt, 2-qt................................25.00
#266D, vase, scalloped, pk w/decor, 8"............................35.00
#305, bookend, sea gull, pk, pr 60.00
#306, ash tray..12.00
#310, vase, Chang, copper brn, 1934-36, rare................275.00
#315, vase, Athenia Classic, wht, 1934-36, 9" 36.00
#322, goblet, Swedish, gr 45.00
#351, vase, Capri, Regency gr, 5¾" 44.00
#363, bookend, colt, 5¾", pr 65.00
#375, wall pocket, dbl morning-glory, deep red 55.00
#3905b, chessman, bishop, bronze/blk, 1937, rare 235.00
#3906, shepherdess & fawn, yel w/gold traces................95.00
#400, teapot tile, geisha, turq gloss................................80.00
#402, vase, box form, wht, 1937-38, 5½"........................65.00
#404, candle holder, triple, Chain, beige 42.00
#412, vase, Volute, wht, 1937-40, lg..............................125.00
#416, peacock, wht, 1937-38 & 1942..............................35.00
#420, vase, Fern Leaf, no decor, 7¼"..............................15.00
#430, pitcher, Fern Leaf, wht, 1937-38, 8" 135.00
#441, bookend, horse head, wht, pr..................................50.00
#451, candle holder, dbl, Astor, wht, 1936-38, pr 44.00
#466, vase, wheel hdl, wht matt, 8"..................................25.00
#468, vase, sea gull, decor, wht & bl, 1946-47................35.00
#491, vase, fan form w/built-in flower holder, wht, 5x7"......22.00

#493, wall pocket, dbl, turq, 1940, 8"..............................65.00
#504, vase/planter, shell, wht, 7"....................................15.00
#516, vase, Acadia 20.00
#527, bowl, hibiscus, pk, 1941-48, sm.............................28.00
#529, bowl, Tai Leaf, bl, 16" 30.00
#543, bowl, geranium...35.00
#563, vase, urn form, bl w/decor......................................18.00
#566D, vase, scalloped, pk w/decor, 8" 35.00
#569D, cornucopia, bl w/decor 25.00
#572D, pelican, decor, scarce 40.00
#581, cornucopia, dbl, pk 20.00
#586D, wall pocket, calla lily, decor 65.00
#593, vase, bow knot, bl, 9"...25.00
#615, ash tray, blk gloss 15.00
#649, wall shelf, acanthus, wht, rare 65.00
#660, ash tray, leaf, blk & yel, 5" dia...............................35.00
#661, swan, chartreuse..35.00
#668, planter, daffodil, decor...20.00
#676D, wall pocket, cookbook 35.00
#705, vase, Modern, bl gloss..25.00
Cookie jar, #471, Old Lady, Blk, decor..........................500.00
Cookie jar, #471, Old Lady, decor 200.00
Cookie jar, #471, Old Lady, no decor 190.00
Cookie jar, #495, Fat Boy 235.00
Cookie jar, #549, Hippo, no decor, 8" 190.00
Cookie jar, #561, Baby, no decor 295.00
Cookie jar, #588, Money Sack 65.00
Cookie jar, #6021, Hobby Horse......................................180.00
Cookie jar, #611, Jack-in-the-Box, 11"...........................250.00
Cookie jar, #651, Locomotive (Choo Choo)....................135.00
Cookie jar, #653, Clock..80.00
Cookie jar, #662, Little Miss Muffet 195.00
Cookie jar, #663, Humpty Dumpty, decor 180.00

Cookie jar, Pineapple, $60.00.

Cookie jar, #665, Wigwam, minimum value 300.00
Cookie jar, #667D, Daisy..42.50
Cookie jar, #674, Pumpkin 300.00
Cookie jar, #678, Windmill 180.00
Cookie jar, #693, Little Girl 55.00
Cookie jar, #694, Little Bo Peep 235.00
Cookie jar, #695, Mother Goose.......................................285.00

Cookie jar, #696, Three Bears 85.00
Vase, what not (A); bl & wht, sm hdl, 3½" 75.00
Vase, what not (B); bl & wht, hdld, rare 85.00
Vase, what not (C); wht, medallion in center, 4½".........85.00

Adams

Wm. Adams, whose potting skills were developed under the tutelage of Josiah Wedgwood, founded the Greengates Pottery at Tunstall, England, in 1769. Many types of wares including basalt, ironstone, parian, and jasper were produced; and various impressed or printed marks were employed. Until 1800 'Adams Co.' or 'Adams' impressed in block letters identified the company's earthenwares and a fine type of jasper similar in color and decoration to Wedgwood's. The latter mark was used again from 1845 to 1864 on parian figures. Most examples of their product found on today's market are transfer-printed dinnerwares with ornate backstamps which often include the pattern name and the initials 'W.A. & S.' This type of product was made from 1820 until about 1920. After 1890 the word 'England' was included in the mark; 'Tunstall' was added after 1896. From 1914 through 1940, a printed crown with 'Adams, Estbd 1657, England' identified their products. From 1900 to 1965, they produced souvenir plates with transfers of American scenes, many of which were marketed in this country by Roth Importers of Peoria, Illinois. In 1965 the company affiliated with Wedgwood. Although there were other Adams potteries in Staffordshire, their marks incorporate either the first name initial or a partner's name and so are easily distinguished from those of this company. See also Spatter; Staffordshire; Adams Rose.

Bowl, Dr Syntax Stopt by Highwaymen, 10¼" 65.00
Bowl, vegetable; Columbus Discovers Am, gr transfer, 11" L 150.00
Cup & saucer, handleless; stick spatter w/gaudy floral, EX.............45.00
Cup plate, flock of sheep, dk bl transfer, 3⅞", NM 275.00
Muffineer, Jasper, bl 195.00
Pitcher, red spatter, paneled, stains/chips, 6⅜" 125.00
Plate, bl feather edge, floral-emb rim, mk, 6½", NM 65.00
Plate, Columbia, red transfer, mk, 10¾" 30.00
Plate, Dr Syntax Bound to a Tree, 9" 45.00
Plate, Mt Washington Steamer, bl transfer, 8" 30.00
Platter, 2 stags/3 does, bl transfer, 1850s, 16" 275.00
Soup plate, fishing/cottage scene, dk bl transfer, 10", NM 75.00

Adams Rose, Early and Late

In the second quarter of the nineteenth century, the Adams and Son Pottery produced a line of hand-painted dinnerware decorated in large, red brush-stroke roses with green leaves on whiteware, which collectors call Adams Rose. Later, G. Jones and Son (and possibly others) made a similar ware with less brilliant colors on a gray-white surface.

Bowl, early, rare sz, 9", M 750.00
Bowl, vegetable; late, 10¾", M 125.00
Creamer, early, 5¾", M 285.00
Pitcher, early, stains/minor flakes, 7" 205.00
Pitcher, late, 6¾", M 175.00
Plate, early, emb scalloped rim, 10½", NM......................125.00
Plate, early, 9", M 190.00

Plate, late, 12", EX...125.00
Plate, late, 8¾", EX...110.00
Plate, late, 9½", EX...110.00
Soup plate, early, wear/minor stains/glaze flakes, 9" 80.00
Sugar bowl, w/lid, early, M 350.00
Sugar bowl, w/lid, late, M 175.00
Tea bowl & saucer, early, M 195.00
Tea bowl & saucer, late, M 125.00
Teapot, early, dome lid, rpr, 11½" 750.00
Teapot, late, M 300.00

Washbowl, footed, hairlines, 13½" diameter; pitcher, baluster form with pulled spout and scrolled handle on flared foot, 14¼"; $350.00 for the set.

Advertising

The advertising world has always been a fiercely competitive field. In an effort to present their product to the customer, every imaginable gimmick was put into play. Colorful and artfully decorated signs and posters, thermometers, tape measures, fans, hand mirrors, and attractive tin containers (all with catchy slogans, familiar logos, and often-bogus claims) are only a few of the many examples of early advertising memorabilia that are of interest to today's collectors.

Porcelain signs were made as early as 1890 and are highly prized for their artistic portrayal of life as it was then . . . often allowing amusing insights into the tastes, humor, and way of life of a bygone era. As a general rule, older signs are made from a heavier gauge metal. Those with three or more fired-on colors are especially desirable.

Tin containers were used to package consumer goods ranging from crackers and coffee to tobacco and talcum. After 1880 can companies began to decorate their containers by the method of lithography. Though colors were still subdued, intricate designs were used to attract the eye of the consumer. False labeling and unfounded claims were curtailed by the Pure Food and Drug Administration in 1906, and the name of the manufacturer as well as the brand name of the product had to be printed on the label. By 1910 color was rampant with more than a dozen hues printed on the tin or on paper labels. The tins themselves were often designed with a second use in mind, such as canisters, lunch boxes, even toy trains. As a general rule, tobacco-related tins are the most desirable, though personal preference may direct the interest of the collector to peanut butter pails with illustrations of children, or talcum tins with irresistible babies or beautiful ladies. Coffee tins are popular, as are those made to contain a particularly successful or well-known product.

Perhaps the most visual of the early advertising gimmicks were the character logos, the Fairbank Company's Gold Dust Twins, the goose trademark of the Red Goose Shoe Company, Nabisco's ZuZu Clown and Uneeda Kid, the Campbell Kids, the RCA dog Nipper, and Mr. Peanut, to name only a few. Any example of these brings a high price on the market today.

Our listings are alphabetized by company name or, in lieu of that information, by word content or other pertinent description. When no condition is indicated, the items listed below are assumed to be in excellent condition, except glass and ceramic items, which are assumed mint. Remember that condition greatly affects value (especially true for tin items). For instance, a sign in excellent or mint condition may bring twice as much as the same one in only very good condition. On today's market, items in good to very good condition are slow to sell, unless they are extremely rare. Mint (or near-mint) examples are high.

As a general rule, beer tip trays in near-mint condition are worth $150 to $250. Spool cabinets (depending on condition) may be evaluated at $100 to $150 per drawer.

We have several advertising advisors; Allen Smith specializes in Buster Brown, Pepsi-Cola, Planters Peanuts, and Red Goose Shoes. He is listed in the Directory under Texas. Our Dr. Pepper advisor is Bill Ricketts, listed under North Carolina. Nearly all of the remaining topics and the general listings are under the advisement of Linda and Jim MacKie; they are listed in the Directory under California. For further information, we recommend *Huxford's Collectible Advertising*, available at your local bookstore or from Collector Books. See also Advertising Dolls; Advertising Cards; Automobilia; Coca-Cola; Banks; Calendars; Cookbooks; Paperweights; Posters; Sewing Items.

Key:
cb — cardboard
cl — celluloid
lcs — litho on canvas sign
pp — pre-prohibition
ps — porcelain sign
sf — self-framed
tc — tin container
ts — tin sign

Atlantic White Lead, bucket is string holder, 26", NM, $4,500.00.

Acme Quality Motor Car Finishes, ts, Model T, 14x12", G 500.00
Adam Scheidt Brewing, tip tray, bottle/glass on table, 4", G 50.00
Adams Pepsin Gum, tin display, 1920s, 3½x16x12", EX..............300.00

Adams Spearmint Gum, tc, striped, hinged lid, 5x6¾x4¾", G 135.00
Allen's Red Tame Cherry, bottle, glass label, 11", EX 200.00
Allen's Red Tame Cherry, sf tin sign, family, 18x28", EX 3,200.00
Allis Chalmers, animated dealer's sign, Baldwin Gleaner, EX 585.00
Am Lady Coffee, tin can, coffee set/lady, 1908, 3-lb..................750.00
Am Steel Farm Fences, tin match holder, 5x3½x1¼", G 65.00
Amber Soap, emb tin sign, man in moon, 19x12½", G.................70.00
Anheuser-Busch, paper sign, 5 frontier scenes, 17x8½", VG 150.00
Apache Trail Cigars, tc, Indian on horsebk, 5½x6x4", G 125.00
Armour's, cb puzzle, World's Fair Exposition, 20x28", VG 300.00
Arrow Beer, tin sign, Moran nude, 1930s, 35x23", EX................345.00
Atlantic Motor Oil, cloth banner, plane-logoed cans, 36x60".....225.00
Ayer's Cherry Pectoral, tin sign, lady w/baby, 20x14", G 1,500.00
Ayer's Hair Vigor, glass sign, sepia photo beneath, 13x11", G 170.00
Ayer's Pills, tin sign, cherubs & pill on red, 20x14", VG 2,100.00
B&L Tobacco, paper on cb sign, fire scene, 1895, 21x28", VG ...275.00
Baby Ruth Gum, tip tray, glass, EX 185.00
Bachelor Cigars, racing trotters, 1903, 24x19", EX 215.00
Baker's Breakfast Cocoa, tip tray, 1920s, 6" dia, EX 155.00
Bank Roll Cigars, tc, roll of cash, 5¼x6", VG..............................110.00
Barq's Soda, thermometer, red & blk, 1940s, 26x8", M................90.00
Bartel's Brewing, charger, flowers, 17½" dia, EX............................35.00
Bartel's Brewing, charger, lady, 17½" dia, VG 50.00
Bartel's Brewing, rvpt sign, Shonk litho, 18" dia, NM 500.00
Bartel's Brewing, tray, lady, prohibition, 12" dia, NM................130.00
Bartel's Brewing, tray, lady, 17x12", VG......................................160.00
Bartholomay Brewing, tip tray, cavalier on horse, 4" dia, NM.....150.00
Bartholomay Brewing, tip tray, lady rides winged wheel, 4", M ..125.00
Beech-Nut Chewing Gum, display rack, 1920s, 15½" H, G.........350.00
Beech-Nut Tobacco, tin bin, mc package, 10x8x8", VG..............225.00
Ben-Hur Horse Blankets, sf tin sign, products, 20x17", EX 850.00
Berry Bros Paints, emb tin sign, early, 25x13", EX 825.00
Berry Bros Varnishes, pocket mirror, kids & wagon, EX...............165.00
Big Sister Peanut Butter, witch & children, 3½", G 375.00
Billings-Chapin Paints, tin match holder, 5x3½x1¼", G..............65.00
BL Johnson Mfg Confectioneers, regulator clock, EX 995.00
Black Cat, match holder, Nonsuch Mfg, 4¼x5½x1", G...............300.00
Black Fox Cigars, tc, fox in moonlight, 5¼", G 175.00
Blue Jay Corn Plasters, display, rocking chair, '30s, 13", EX 400.00
Blue Ribbon Bourbon, oilette, hillbillies, 28x38", G...................250.00
Blue Sunoco, porc sign, logo w/arrow diecut, 22x18½", G.............80.00
Blue Tiger Tobacco, cb container, tiger, 12x8" dia, G 110.00
Blue Tiger Tobacco, cb container, tiger, 6x8x11", VG.................225.00
Borden's, paper sign, Elsie amid yel daisies, 36" 275.00
Bridal Brand Coffee, tin can, laden donkeys, oval, VG 275.00
Brockway Motor Trucks, emb ts, 1920s truck, 20x28", VG 750.00
Brookfield Rye Whiskey, tray, Meek & Beach, '05, 12x17", NM .300.00
Brownie Laundry Wax, box, cb/glass, P Cox label, 10x6x7", G 25.00
Buck's Oil, flanged porc sign, barrel, 18x28", EX 1,100.00
Budweiser Beer, cb sign, Custer's Last Fight, 32x42", VG............120.00
Budweiser Beer, cb sign, girl in red, 1907, 33x18", VG 700.00
Budweiser Beer, charger, Say When, couple, 16" dia, VG 200.00
Budweiser Beer, counter display, rvpt in plastic fr, '30s 125.00
Budweiser Beer, tin sign, goddess/bottle/girls, 15x23", NM 9,000.00
Budweiser Beer, tin sign, goddess/bottle/girls, 15x23", VG...... 2,100.00
Buffalo Brewing, tip tray, children at 1915 expo, 4¼", NM 150.00
Buffalo Salted Peanuts, tc, buffalo, 10x8" dia, 10-lb, G...............115.00
Bull Durham, regulator clock, Sessions, w/striker, NM 995.00
Bull Durham Tobacco, cb sign, bullfighting, fr, 33x52", G 450.00
Burley Boy, pocket tin, upright, 4x3½x1", G................................265.00

Buster Brown

Buster Brown was the creation of cartoonist Richard Felton; his comic strip first appeared in the *New York Herald* on May 4, 1902. Since then Buster and his dog Tige (short for Tiger) have adorned sundry commercial products but are probably best known as the trademark for the Brown Shoe Company established early in this century. Today hundreds of Buster Brown premiums, store articles, and advertising items bring substantial prices from many serious collectors.

Book, Me & My Bubble, Outcault, 1903, EX 245.00
Bowl, cereal; porc, red w/BB & Tige transfer, EX 40.00
Cigar, BB band, VG 8.50
Clock, BB Shoes, store type, M 650.00
Coat hook, orig 35.00
Cup, ceramic, MIG, 1900s, 4" 95.00
Figurine, BB & Tige, bsk, Germany, 5" 55.00
Fountain pen, 14k point 28.00
Kite, BB & Tige, G 35.00
Lunar telephone, 1960s 5.00
Magic Pad 25.00
Mannequin, baby, EX 175.00
Match safe, tin litho, BB Bread, EX 500.00
Paper doll sheet, BB Hosiery, uncut 15.00
Periscope 22.00
Plate, dessert; china, gold trim, +cup & saucer, VG 100.00
Playing cards, comic bks, complete, 1906, mini 75.00
Post card, BB & Tige, 1906, NM 25.00
Post card, Cider Days, BB/Mary Jane/Tige, Oct 1907, G 12.00
Post card, Don't Be an April Fool, Outcault, 1907 ....14.00
Rocking horse, BB & Tige, spring type, wood & hardboard, EX...225.00
Sheet music, BB color cover, 1920s, EX 55.00
Shoe horn 40.00
Shoe stretcher 35.00
Sign, BB & Tige, Authorized BB Dealer, hardboard, 14x14"........110.00
Sign, Brown's Bread, die-cut tin, 1920s, 12x14", NM 100.00
Statement wall hook 25.00
Waffle iron, BB & Tige on bk, sm 75.00
Wagon, BB Health Shoes, wood w/steel wheels, rubber tires 350.00
Wristwatch, BB Shoes, Ingersoll, 1930s, EX orig.........................300.00

C.D. Kenny

C.D. Kenny was determined to be a successful man, and he was. Between 1890 and 1934, he owned seventy-five groceries in fifteen states. He realized his success in two ways: fair business dealings and premium giveaways. These ranged from trade cards and advertising mirrors to tin commemorative plates and kitchen items. There were banks and toys, clocks and tins. Today's collectors are finding scores of these items, all carrying Kenny's name.

Doll, pnt bsk, premium, printed mk, 4", NM 85.00
Figurine, Indian in canoe, ceramic 15.00
Match holder, elephant form, gr..25.00
Plaque, George Washington, rnd, 1920s, sm, NM 50.00
Plate, Francis Scott Key, Star Spangled Banner, tin, EX...............85.00
Salt shaker, Geisha Girl..12.00
Stamp holder, celluloid, Dutch waitresses 15.00
Tape measure, retractable 45.00
Tip tray, Victorian lady, seated, 4" 100.00

Cadillac, dbl-sided porc sign, Sales & Service, rare, 42", M 1,350.00
Calabash Tobacco, pocket tin, emb, upright, 4x3½x1¼", G 225.00
California Nugget, tc, pillow shape, 3x2x2½", VG 105.00
Caloric Furnace, emb tin sign, EX color, 20x14" 85.00

Calumet Baking Powder, regulator clock, rvpt panel, 35", G.......450.00
Cascarets Wire Mesh, draped nude & moon, 12x22", G.............600.00
Ceresota Flour, match holder, tin litho, 1915, EX 200.00
Champion Spark Plugs, porc sign, early plug, 13x30", VG 950.00
Chattanooga Plows, match safe, nickel & brass w/celluloid ad 40.00
Checkers, candy tin..115.00
Chesterfield Cigarettes, door push, 1940s, EX 150.00
Chippewa Ice Cream, dbl-sided tin sign, wood fr, 20x19", EX.....445.00
Christian Feigenspan Brewing, tray, Am Can, 13" dia, EX 65.00
Chum's Liquor, tip tray, man & dog, 4¼" dia, EX 165.00
Circus Club Mallows Candy, tc, dressed dog, hat-shaped lid, EX..325.00
Circus Club Mallows Candy, tc, monkey cartoon, 7x3" dia, VG.185.00
Clabber Girl Baking Powder, tin sign, 1940s, 11x30", EX............35.00
Clark Spool Cotton, tin sign, Kellogg/Burkeley, 14x20", VG......155.00
Clark's Teaberry Gum, tip tray, vaseline glass, 1920s, EX 200.00
Cocaine for the Hair, canvas roll-down sign, 27x14", G.............550.00
Colgate's Cashmere Bouquet, flanged tin diecut, 24x15", VG . 2,700.00
Columbus Brewing, tip tray, Columbus, 1898, G 120.00
Congress Beer, corner porc sign, wht on bl, 20x14", G 175.00
Congress Beer, tin match holder, logo & case, 3x5x4½", NM ...200.00
Congress Beer, tin menu board, 13x6", EX................................150.00
Congress X-tra Fine Beer, standing ts, 1930s, 5x14", G...............55.00
Continental Cubes, cl pocket mirror, girl w/str flush, EX 250.00
Continental Insurance, sf ts, soldier, 30x20", G........................ 1,250.00
Cork Whiskey, tin sign, bottle, 1885, 14x22", EX........................75.00
Crescent Flour, tin door push, sacks, 1930s, 3¾x9½", M 110.00
Cross-Cut Cigarettes, cb box, man sawing, 3x1½x¾", EX.............75.00
Crystal Spring Brewing, stoneware match striker, 6½" dia...........300.00
Crystal Spring Brewing, tray, porc w/brass, no graphics, 12" 75.00
Crystal Spring Brewing, tray, porc w/brass rim, 12" dia, NM 300.00
Dallas Home Beer, tip tray, labeled bottle, 4" dia, NM 250.00
Dan Patch Tobacco, pail, horse & trotter, wooden bail, EX 275.00
Defiance Hot Peanuts, warmer bin, glass front, 22x19x20", G 250.00
DeLaval, match holder, woman w/separator, 4¼x5½x1", G 150.00
Detroit Stove Works, sf ts, factory panorama, 13x37", G.............150.00
Diamond Dyes, book, hardbk, 15-pg, 5x9", EX............................20.00
Diamond Dyes, cabinet, Evolution of Women, 30", G.................450.00
Diamond Dyes, cabinet, Evolution of Women, 30", NM......... 1,100.00
Diamond Dyes, cabinet, fairy/butterflies/parrot, 31", G.............800.00
Diamond Dyes, cabinet, fairy/butterflies/parrot, 31", NM 1,250.00
Diamond Dyes, cabinet, Maypole/mansion, 30", G....................600.00
Diamond Dyes, cabinet, Maypole/mansion, 30", NM.............. 1,800.00
Diamond Dyes, cabinet, Washer Woman, rfn 800.00
Diamond Dyes, cabinet, Washer Woman, 30", G 500.00

Diamond Dyes, display box, wood with sheet metal panel, G, $600.00; NM, $1,500.00.

Diamond Dyes, ts, Busy Day in Dollville, 1911, 11x17", EX **1,000.00**
Diamond Edge Tools, tin sign, bull's eye, 1940s, 10x28"................**35.00**
Diamond Matches, tin box, You Chillun..., 1½x4½x2", VG **200.00**
Dick Brothers, tip tray, bottle on blk, 4" dia, EX **70.00**
Diehl Centennial Beer, rvpt sign, 1930s, 16x8" **225.00**
Dingman's Soap, cb sign, baby crawling, 13x15", VG..................**150.00**
Dixie Boy, lunch box, EX...**425.00**
Dixie Kid Cut Plug, cb can, Blk baby label, 4½" sq, G.................**300.00**
Dobson Carpets, cb sign, factory, orig fr, 38x28", G **90.00**
Dr Chase, thermometer, man at top, bl/wht, 39x8", EX...............**400.00**
Dr Daniel's Medicines, wagon display box, 2-tiered, EX.......... **4,700.00**
Dr Green's Nervura, thermometer, EX..**95.00**
Dr Leisure's, cabinet, emb tin horse's head, 26", EX **2,000.00**
Dr McLean's...Blood Purifier, canvas sign, 16x40", EX **95.00**
Dr Miles' Nervine, cb display, girl w/dose, 3-part, 36x51", VG ...**240.00**
Dr Morse's Indian Root Pills, cb display, Indian, 27x42", G **485.00**

Dr. Pepper

A young pharmacist, Charles C. Alderton, was hired by W.B. Morrison, owner of Morrison's Old Corner Drug Store in Waco, Texas, around 1884. Alderton, an observant sort, noticed that the drugstore's patrons could never quite make up their minds as to which flavor of extract to order. He concocted a formula that combined many flavors, and Dr. Pepper was born. The name was chosen by Morrison in honor of a beautiful young girl with whom he had once been in love. The girl's father, a Virginia doctor by the name of Pepper, had discouraged the relationship due to their youth, but Morrison had never forgotten her. On December 1, 1885, a U.S. patent was issued to the creators of Dr. Pepper.

Bottle, seltzer; Cheerio-Memphis..**150.00**
Calendar, 1949, complete, NM..**50.00**
Calendar, 1951, 3-pg, 20x12", EX...**35.00**
Clock, bottle cap shape, EX...**95.00**
Clock, electric, Drink a Bite To Eat..., 15¼" dia, G.....................**450.00**
Clock, Mountain Herbs, sales executive presentation, 1982, M ..**375.00**
Clock, recent, 36x15", M..**125.00**
Dispenser, ceramic, rare, ca 1890, 21½x9", NM...................... **7,500.00**
Door pull, metal, bottle form, VG **45.00**
Post card, 10¢ coupon, M **5.00**
Sign, dbl-sided, 3-pc (has strip for store's name), rare **595.00**
Street marker, Safety First, cast brass **70.00**
Thermometer, tin, bottle shape, early, 26", NM............................**150.00**
Thermometer, tin, rnd **75.00**
Watch fob, Billiken, brass, EX..**100.00**

Dr Swett's, cl pocket mirror, shows bottle, 3" dia, VG.................**130.00**
Drum Cigarettes, cb diecut, You Can't Beat..., G.........................**200.00**
Dry Slitz Cigars, tin thermometer, mc enamel, 38x8", G.............**155.00**
Dutch Boy Paints, match holder, Dutch boy diecut, 3x7", G **165.00**
Dy-O-La Dyes, cabinet, ca 1909, 16½x11½", VG............................**450.00**
Eagle Brand Coffee, tin can, eagle logo, 4¼x6", G.......................**100.00**
Eagle Motor Oil, dbl-sided porc sign, 20¢ per Quart, 8x16".........**450.00**
Eagle Run Beer, tip tray, boy on eagle, 4¼", G **35.00**
Edelbrau Brewery, tip tray, Christopher Columbus, 4" dia, NM ..**100.00**
Educator Cakelets, tin basket, story heroes, 3x6x3¾", G.............**125.00**
Egyptienne Cigarettes, cb sign, costumed lady, 21x29", G............**250.00**
Egyptienne Cigarettes, cb sign, girls/bonnets, 31x21", EX **300.00**
EJ Larrabee Candy, tc, horse-drawn sleigh, 1880, 2x6x4", G.......**100.00**
Eldredge Brewing, ts, couple in garden, early, 22x28", G.............**300.00**
Elephant Peanuts, tin can, 10-lb, G..**100.00**

Elk Speed Pure Rye, sf tin sign, 1905, 38x25½", EX **1,200.00**
Elmira Ice Cream, tray, Cream Supreme, 1920s, 12½", EX **225.00**
Erie Brewing, tray, lady & tiger, 13½" dia, VG **125.00**
Eskimo Smoking Tobacco, canister, Husky/igloos, 6x4¼", VG ...**400.00**
Eureka, spool cabinet, 3-drw, w/thread, EX **400.00**
Even Steven Cigars, tc, man leans over banner, 5¼x3", EX **225.00**
Ever-Ready, clock, man w/razor, minor fading, 22x18"............ **1,250.00**
Fairbanks Gold Dust... Powder, wood box w/label, 32x16x8".........**200.00**
Fairy's Starch, cloth sign, 1920s, 11x30", EX **25.00**
Fatima Cigarettes, sf ts, veiled lady w/package, 23x17", G...........**250.00**
Fehr's Malt Tonic, sf ts, semi-nude/cherubs, '09, 29x23", EX .. **1,250.00**
Feinanspan Brewing, tip tray, girl's profile, 4" dia, NM **50.00**
Fencing Club Pure Rye, tin sign, Shonk, 1901, 36x23", NM .. **2,700.00**

Falstaff Bottled Beer, The Peacemaker, self-framed tin sign, 23" x 31", NM, $4,500.00.

Finck's Detroit Special Overalls, ts, 1930s, 12x9", NM...............**185.00**
Five Roses Tea, porc thermometer, red/wht, 39x8", EX...............**120.00**
Ford Batteries, porc sign, Sales & Service, 15x24", NM **575.00**
Forest & Stream Tobacco, tc, fisherman/canoe/dog, 4¼", VG.....**575.00**
Forest & Stream Tobacco, tc, man fishing, 5¼x4", VG **200.00**
Fountain Tobacco, tin canister, slip lid, 8½" dia, G.....................**150.00**
Fraser's Axle Grease, sf tin sign, Am Art Works, 25x38", G........**750.00**
Frostie Root Beer, thermometer, plastic, 18x14" **12.50**
FW Cook Brewing, bar glass, etched factory, NM **55.00**
Game Cock Rye, tin charger, dead game/bottle, 24" dia, G.........**125.00**
Game Fine Cut Tobacco, tc, birds, 8x11½x7", G.........................**275.00**
GE Radios, neon sign, bl/wht, 1943, 22½x27", NM.....................**575.00**
Gem Damaskeen Razors, clock, w/pendulum, 28x23x3½", VG.. **3,000.00**
George Zett Brewing, tray, lion logo, brass, 11½" dia, EX **70.00**
Germania Brewing, tray, lady w/eagle, 1890s, 18½x15", G..........**150.00**
Giant Peanuts, tin can, giant & castle, 10-lb, EX **650.00**
Goebel, tip tray, Delft girl w/baskets, bl/wht, 4" dia, NM..............**60.00**
Gold Dust Twins, cb box, multiple images, 12x20x14", G............**95.00**
Gold Dust Twins, cb sign, twin diecut, '12, 16½x7¾", VG **4,000.00**
Gold Medal Camp Furniture, sf tin sign, family, 14x19", VG......**650.00**
Good-Will Soap, roll-down sign, girl & kitten, 29x14", G............**145.00**
Grape-Nuts, sf tin sign, girl w/dog, 30x20", G **400.00**
Grape-Nuts, sf tin sign, girl w/dog, 30x20", NM..................... **2,000.00**
Grapette, tin sign, Grapette in oval, 1940s, 11x27", EX................**30.00**
Great West Cut Plug, lunch pail, 4½x7¾x5", VG **100.00**
Green Turtle Cigars, lunch box, turtle logo, 5x7½x4½", VG......**275.00**
Green's August Flower, mirror, beveled, 22" sq, G.......................**100.00**
Greenway Ale & Lager, tray, Canadian Mounty, 11½" dia, NM ...**60.00**
Greenway Pale Ale, tray, Canadian Mounty, 1930s, 12½", VG.....**90.00**

Greenway's Brewery, cb sign, girl's profile, 1910, 15x20", EX **325.00**
Greenway's Export Ales, tin sign, logo center, 24x17", G............**195.00**
Grow-Mo Smokers, lunch box, crowing rooster, 5x8x5", VG......**250.00**
GW Bishop Drugs & Jewelry, regulator clock, EX......................**995.00**
Haberle Brewing, etch/rvpt sign, eagle logo, 16x20", G..............**160.00**
Haberle Brewing, tap knob, NM **35.00**
Haberle Crystal Spring Brewing, convention mug, china, 1899 ..**230.00**
Hambone 5¢ Cigars, chalkboard, 13x20", EX **65.00**
Harvard Brewing, tray, Blk waiter serves couple, 1920, G............**130.00**
Harvard Peanuts, tin can, collegiate peanut, 10-lb, VG.................**60.00**
Henry Elias Brewing, tip tray, 7-sided star, 4" dia, EX **60.00**
Hershey's Superior Ice Cream, tray, w/peaches, 13" sq, G............**115.00**
Hiawatha Tobacco, wooden bucket, paper label, early, 12", G **75.00**
Hill's Bromide, cb display, flapper, 3-part diecut, 34x38", EX......**220.00**
Hinckel Brewery Lager Beer, litho-on-wood sign, 14x20", EX.....**375.00**

Hickory Garters, wooden sign, EX, $1,000.00.

Hires

Charles E. Hires, a drugstore owner in Philadelphia, became interested in natural teas. He began experimenting with roots and herbs and soon developed his own special formula. Hires introduced his product to his own patrons and soon began selling concentrated syrup to other soda fountains and grocery stores. Samples of his 'root beer' were offered for the public's approval at the 1876 Philadelphia Centennial. Today's collectors are often able to date their advertising items by observing the Hires boy on the logo. From 1891 to 1906 he wore a dress; until 1914 he was shown in a bathrobe. From 1915 until 1926, he was depicted in a dinner jacket. The apostrophe may or may not appear in the Hires name; this seems to have no bearing on dating an item.

Ad, girl w/parasol, early, 11½x9½", fr, VG....................................**145.00**
Ball, Drink Hires, rubber, bl & wht pnt, EX **17.50**
Dispenser, hourglass, orig pump, G **325.00**
Dispenser, orig pump, ca 1920, 14", M unused.......................... **1,200.00**
Glass, soda; Enjoy Nature's..., syrup line, NM..............................**45.00**
Opener, over-the-top, NM **12.00**
Sign, display, cb, creeping baby diecut, 2-pc, 11x14", EX **150.00**
Sign, paper, German peasant/Colonial man, 1890s, 18x21" **475.00**
Sign, tin, bottle illus, oval, 1950s, 24x18", M................................**85.00**
Sign, tin, It's High Time for..., 1930s, 42x14", NM.......................**65.00**

Straw dispenser..**750.00**
Thermometer, tin, bottle shape...**75.00**
Tray, girl on wood-grained ground, 10½x13", G **65.00**
Tray, Just What the Doctor..., 1914, EX...................................**400.00**

Hood's Sarsaparilla, plate, birds, testimonials on bk, 9" **75.00**
Humphrey's Veterinary, cabinet, tin front, animals, 38", EX .. **1,500.00**
Humpty Dumpty Borated Talc, tc, Great Fall, 1908, 7", EX **50.00**
Hy-Quality Coffee, cb hanger diecut, lady/coffee, 38x16", NM...**775.00**
Hyan Ginger Ale, tray, baby on bottle plane, '20s, 10x13", NM .**200.00**
Imperial Copper Polish, cb container, policeman label, 3x5", G ..**45.00**
Imperial Peanuts, tin can, devil trademk, 10-lb, G......................**175.00**
Incandescent Light & Stove, tip tray, kitchen scene, 4¼", EX **65.00**
India Wharf Brewing, bar glass, etched factory, NM...................**100.00**
Indianapolis Brewing, tray, 3 men by fire, 13x10½", VG **125.00**
Ingersoll Watches, tin & glass display case, 11x12x6", G..............**50.00**
Internat'l Tailoring, wooden thermometer, 23x7", EX.................**195.00**
Iroquois Beer, tip tray, Indian chief, 4" dia, NM **125.00**
Iroquois Beer, tray, 3 labeled bottles, 12" dia, EX......................**150.00**
Ivory Soap, cb sign, products on shelves, fr, 22x28", G...............**250.00**
J&P Coats, spool cabinet, spool figural, 4-drw, 22", G **400.00**
J&P Coats, spool cabinet, 6-drw, w/inserts, 22x26x20", G **400.00**
Jack Sprat Peanut Butter, tin can, logo, 25-lb, VG **1,000.00**
Jackie Coogan Peanut Butter, pail, Jackie in school, 3½", G **210.00**
Jackie Coogan Peanut Butter, pail, policeman, 3¼", VG.............**500.00**
John H Mann & Co Teas & Coffee, tc, scenic, 5x5x11", VG **100.00**
Jos Doelger's Beer, tin diecut, brewmeister w/mug, 27x20", G.....**400.00**
Jung Brewing, bar glass, etched factory, NM.................................**75.00**
Kansas City Brewing, tip tray, star logo, 4" dia, EX **100.00**
King Cole Coffee, tin can, king is served, ½-lb, EX **110.00**
King Edward Tobacco, pocket tin, portrait, upright, 4½" **300.00**
King's Beer, tip tray, nurse w/tray, 4½x6", NM **35.00**
Kis-Me Gum, cb diecut, early, 18½x12", EX **200.00**
Kist, tin sign, Everybody Loves To Get..., 1950s, 26x20", EX **40.00**
Konjola Medicinal, cb display, 3-part diecut, 34x47", EX............**150.00**
Krueger Brewing, tip tray, foaming mug/hops/wheat, 4¼", EX **105.00**
La Creole Hair Restorer, wooden thermometer, EX.....................**175.00**
La Raphael Liqueur Bonal, cb sign, plane, 1907, 48x36", EX **300.00**
Laflin & Rand Powder, cb sign, men & boys, 24x45", VG **450.00**
Lash's Kidney...Bitters, wood sign, girl/horse, 14x20", G **225.00**
Lemon Cola, tray, Right to the Point, 1914, 12½x16" **65.00**
Lenhert's Brewing, tip tray, dog smoking, 1910, 4" dia, NM........**250.00**
Light House Peanut Butter, pail, boat/lighthouse, 3¼", VG **500.00**
Light Sweet Cuba Tobacco, tc, 11½x8" dia, VG............................**70.00**
Lipton's Cocoa, sf ts, lady w/chocolate pot at table, 13x9", G........**35.00**

Log Cabin Syrup

Log Cabin Syrup tins have been made since the 1890s in variations of design that can be attributed to specific years of production. Until about 1914, they were made with paper labels. These are quite rare and highly prized by today's collectors. Tins with colored lithographed designs were made after 1914. When General Foods purchased the Towle Company in 1927, the letters 'GF' were added.

A cartoon series, illustrated with a mother flipping pancakes in the cabin window and various children and animals declaring their appreciation of the syrup in voice balloons, was introduced in the 1930s. A Frontier Village series followed in the late 1940s. A schoolhouse, jail, trading post, doctor's office, blacksmith shop, inn, and private homes were also available. Examples of either series today often command prices of $75.00 to $200.00 and up.

Bank, glass cabin figural, EX **32.00**

Can opener, Towle's, metal...12.00
Syrup tin, bear in door, cartoon ends, Towle's, 5-lb.....................140.00
Syrup tin, blacksmith, 33-oz..135.00
Syrup tin, boy w/lasso, 1-lb..110.00
Syrup tin, cartoon all sides, sm..110.00
Syrup tin, children, man by pump, Towle's, 33-oz..........................150.00
Syrup tin, children playing, Towle's, 33-oz, NM...........................135.00
Syrup tin, Dr RU Well, cartoon style, rare 250.00
Syrup tin, Express Office, coach, Towle's, 33-oz..........................150.00
Syrup tin, Frontier Inn, cowboys & horse, 5-lb............................220.00
Syrup tin, Frontier Jail, 12-oz...150.00
Syrup tin, hand w/finger pointing on top, Towle's, med....................165.00
Syrup tin, Home Sweet Home, 12-oz 150.00
Syrup tin, paper label, sample sz, rare, 2x1½".............................300.00
Syrup tin, red, 5-lb...50.00
Syrup tin, Stockade School, Towle's, 33-oz................................150.00
Syrup tin, Wigwam, 1-lb, very rare, 4x3¼x3½"..............................500.00
Teaspoon...17.50

Log Cabin Coffee, tin can, trappers/cabin, 5x4", VG.......................250.00
Long Tom Tobacco, tc, Blk man in checkered suit, 5x2x4", G 150.00
Lotus Salted Peanuts, tin can, lotus label, 11x7½" dia, VG 110.00
Lox Shoelaces, clock, light-up flourescent, wood/metal, NM 175.00
Lucky Strike, clock, New Haven, ca 1910, 23", EX..........................850.00
Lutten's SP Cough Drops, glass log cabin box, ftd, 7", NM 450.00
Lydia Pinkham's Vegetable Compound, diecut, 30x22", VG.....................230.00
Mahoney Whiskey, tip tray, Jefferson Memorial, 4¼", VG 45.00
Mail Pouch Tobacco, thermometer, porc, 36", EX 60.00
Mammoth Salted Nuts, tin can, elephant, 11x7½" dia, G.....................125.00
Mangus Beck, tip tray, eagle on shield, 4" dia, NM 60.00
Marx Brewing, tip tray, girl w/carnations, 4" dia, EX 60.00
Mason's Blacking, wooden box, Blk man label, 9x12x3", G 45.00
Master Guard Cigars, pail, dog w/pail in mouth, 6x6", G...................325.00
Mathieu Syrup, wood thermometer, English/French, 24x4", G 175.00
Mayo's Tobacco, roll-down sign, lady in formal, 28x13", NM 125.00
McDonald Sap Spout, tray, maple sugaring scene, 19x16", VG...............300.00
Meadow Gold Ice Cream, light-up sign, 1950s, NM 35.00
Merricks...Cotton, clock, New Haven, pendulum, 24", EX 1,200.00
Miller High Life, neon sign, 16x22", M in orig crate.......................85.00
Miller High Life Beer, charger, girl on moon, 1907, EX 1,150.00
Mission Orange, tin thermometer, w/bottle, 15" 75.00
Modox, tip tray, Indian in headdress diecut, 4¾x5", VG 275.00
Molson's Ale, table, porc top/wooden base, 26" dia, G 45.00
Monarch Peanut Butter, tin drum, Teenie Weenie, 55-lb, VG ..300.00
Monarch Popcorn, pail, Teenie Weenie on bl, 3¾", VG.......................250.00
Monarch Toffies, tin bin, Teenie Weenies/candies, 12x14½" 205.00
Monkey Brand Soap, tin sign, Missing Link, 28x20", VG 500.00
Monroe Brewing, tip tray, king w/stein, 4" dia, NM.......................100.00
Moore & Quinn, tray, dmn logo on gr, 1935, 13" dia, NM............50.00
Moses' Cough Drops, tc, portrait, orange/blk, 8x6x4", G...........115.00

Moxie

The Moxie Company was organized in 1884 by George Archer of Boston, Massachusetts. It was at first touted as a 'nerve food' to improve the appetite, promote restful sleep, and in general to make one 'feel better!' Emphasis was soon shifted, however, to the good taste of the brew, and extensive advertising campaigns rivaling those of such giant competitors as Hires and Coca-Cola resulted in successful marketing through the 1930s. Today the term Moxie has become synonymous with courage and audacity, traits displayed by the company who dared compete with such well-established rivals. For more information we recommend *The Book of Moxie* by Frank N. Potter, available at your local bookstore or from Collector Books.

Bottle, syrup; orange label, tin top, EX 200.00
Candy tin, Moxiemobile, scarce..150.00
Diecut, tin, Moxie boy, ca 1908-11, 6¾x4½", EX 290.00
Display, cb diecut, Soda Jerk, 41½x18", G 170.00
Display, wood, Moxie Maid, 28½x5½x7", G 225.00
Display, wood diecut, butler, 35x10x10", G 300.00
Fan, cb, girl & soda jerk, sm 37.00
Gravy boat, china, bird border/girl transfer, w/tray, VG...............125.00
Jacket, cloth, Moxie images in yel & gr, EX 150.00
Match holder, tin litho, bottle form, EX...............................220.00

Moxie, tin diecut with thermometer (broken), 10" x 12", NM, $2,050.00.

Mug, china, girl transfer, flared ft, 4¼x3" dia, VG 100.00
Parasol, Moxie images in yel & gr, VG 175.00
Photograph, 4 early delivery trucks, 11x14", NM 30.00
Sign, cb, man w/case of bottles, 2-sided, 24x24", G....................35.00
Sign, cb diecut, man points finger, 16¾x16¾", EX 195.00
Sign, cb stand-up, boy & girl w/parasol, 1898, 8½x6½", NM.......400.00
Sign, litho on paper, Leading Exponent..., 1898, 21x27", G........600.00
Sign, sf tin, emb bottle under Hall of Fame arch, 54x19", G 185.00
Sign, tin, Eclipse, 1920s, 19x54", VG 500.00
Sign, tin, girl on horse in speeding car, 13x19", G 200.00
Sign, tin, Moxiemobile, man on horse, 12x36", EX 975.00
Sign, tin flange, Drink Moxie, oval, 9x18", VG 100.00
Soda glass, heavy, emb logo, ca 1900s, M 45.00
Thermometer, tin, 12x6"...80.00
Thermometer, We've Got Moxie..., 16x5¾", G 50.00
Tip tray, tin, girl & violets, ca 1900-10, 5", EX 200.00
Tip tray, tin, I Just Love..., girl w/glass, 5" dia, G 110.00
Tip tray, tin, Moxie Makes You Eat..., 6" dia, G 140.00
Toy, man on horse in car, tin litho, 8½", EX...........................950.00
Tray, glass over metal, lady w/glass, 1910, 10", EX 300.00

Mrs Dinsmore's Cough Drops, tc, Somers Bros, 8x5x5", G..........140.00
Muelenbach Brewing, match safe, bottle diecut, 7x2x1", EX 255.00
Muelenbach Brewing, tip tray, labeled bottle, 5" dia, NM 35.00
Myers Pumps, flange sign, lady squirts man, 14x18", G 90.00
Nat'l Brewing, sf ts, ladies, Kaufmann/Strauss, 17x22", VG.........875.00
Nat'l Brewing, tray, 2 horse heads, Kaufmann/Strauss, 12", NM ...175.00
Nat'l Fire Insurance, rvpt sign, Liberty/flag/etc, 29x20", NM 350.00
Nat'l Oats, cup, plastic, collapsible 25.00
Nichol Kola, ts, America's Taste..., bottle, 1930s, 35x15" 50.00
Nigger Hair Tobacco, cb can, Fiji Islander lady, 5x7", G 100.00

Nigger Hair Tobacco, pail, Blk lady, 6½x5½" dia, EX 245.00
Nine O'Clock Washing-Tea, tin sign, lady & clock, 13x14", G ..250.00
Northampton Brewing, tip tray, hand/3 bottles, 4" dia, NM 100.00
Northland Ski Wax, tc, skier on front, 1940s, EX 18.00
Northwestern Mutual Life Insurance, porc sign, 20x14" 265.00
NY Enamel Paint Co, cb sign, before/after houses, 26x21", G 600.00
Ojibwa Tobacco, cb container, Indian label, 6½x8x11", G 175.00
Old Boone Distillery, sf ts, log cabin, 15x23", 1904, VG 550.00
Old Chum Tobacco, porc thermometer, 38x8", EX 175.00
Old Crow Distillery, paper/rvpt sign, fr, 27x35", EX............... 1,400.00
Old Dutch Root Beer, tin sign, windmill, 18x36", EX...................75.00
Old English Tobacco, fr cb sign, men at fire, 1900, 32x24" 185.00
Old King Cole Tobacco, tin can, Parrish label, 4¼", EX 300.00
Old Mr Boston Liquors, clock, Gilbert mechanism, 22", G 250.00
Oldsmobile, porc sign, early crest, 18" dia, M 1,000.00
Omar Cigarettes, cb sign, men smoking, orig fr, 22x15", EX........250.00
Orange Crush, tin thermometer, Crushie, EX 95.00
Orange Crush, tray, Blk man & orange, 1929, 10½x13", NM 400.00
Orange Crush, ts, red, dmn shape, 22", EX 165.00
Orange Julip, tray, Am Art, 1920s, 10½x13", NM 120.00
Pabst Blue Ribbon Beer, tray, man w/mug, 1933, 10½x13", EX ..300.00
Pabst Brewing, oilette, beer & oysters, fr, 14x18", EX.................400.00
Palmer Cigars, tin sign, That Different Smoke, 1930s, 6x20" 20.00
Pansies Salted Peanuts, tc, lady/children/flowers, 10-lb, VG 110.00
Par Ex, tray, girl rests on tiger, 1904, 12" dia, NM 225.00
Par Ex All Malt Lager, bubble tube sign, 7½x16", EX................900.00
Pard Dog Food, clock, dog w/bobbing head, electric, EX 425.00
Parrot Peanut Butter, tc, bird, press-on lid, 4x3" dia, VG 425.00
Patton's Sun-Proof Paints, cup, aluminum, collapsible 20.00
Paul Jones Whiskey, tin sign, dead game, fr, 45x32", EX 500.00
Paul Luithle's Bakery, lady w/flowers, Philadelphia, 1911, EX 150.00
Peerless Dyes, cabinet, lady & peacock, 26x18x10", G 650.00
Peerless Dyes, cabinet, train & camel caravan, 31", G 1,600.00

O'Keefe's Pilsener Lager, framed tin sign, 25" x 19", NM, $4,700.00.

Pepsi-Cola

Pepsi-Cola was first served in the early 1890s to customers of Caleb D. Bradham, a young pharmacist who touted his concoction to be medicinal as well as delicious. It was first called 'Brad's Drink,' but was renamed Pepsi-Cola in 1898.

Bottle, gr w/paper label, 1930s, 12-oz, M 55.00
Can, cone top, 1940s, rare, NM...255.00
Carrier, cb, Bigger-Better, 1930s, EX 35.00
Clock, plastic & metal, light-up, 16" dia, EX 160.00
Cooler, dbl case, 1930s, EX...365.00
Cooler, metal, bl, 1950s, EX...50.00
Cup, bottle illustration waxed paper, 1930s, M 18.00
Door push, Say Pepsi Please, NM...28.00
Fan, Pepsi Pete, 1930s, NM...75.00
Lighter, can form, 1950s...35.00
Menu board, tin, 1940s, 30x20", EX 125.00
Opener, brass, 1940s, EX...70.00
Opener, tin litho, bottle shape, 1930s, M 30.00
Pencil, mechanical, ca 1950s, EX..30.00

Pepsi Cola, dispenser, pottery, extremely rare, EX, 18½", $8,500.00.

Shakers, ceramic, Pepsi logo, 1930s, pr..165.00
Sign, cb, Big Shot, children w/bottles, 1940s, 11x24", EX 75.00
Sign, cb cutout, Pepsi & Pete, beach girl, 12x8½", EX................175.00
Sign, cb w/metal fr, 2-sided, 13x27", EX....................................225.00
Sign, celluloid & tin, 1940s, 9" dia, EX 125.00
Sign, cl/tin, bottle cap, 1940s, 9" dia, NM 75.00
Sign, sf cb, girl w/bottle, 1940s, 19x26", EX 425.00
Sign, tin, America's Biggest..., 1940, 10x35", EX 75.00
Sign, tin, Drink..., red/wht/bl, fr, 16x17", NM 250.00
Sign, tin, Pepsi-Cola Hits the Spot, 18½x27", NM.......................250.00
Thermometer, tin, yel, 1960s, 27x7", M 45.00
Thermometer, tin, 1950s, 27x7", EX 100.00
Tip tray, tin litho, girl drinks w/straw, 6⅛x4⅜", VG...................300.00
Watch fob, embossed, 1900s, 2x2" 200.00
Watch fob, enameled insert, 1900s, 2x2", NM 265.00

Peter Doelger Brewery, tray, factory/planes, 16½x13½", G..........400.00
Peter Pan Ice Cream, tin sign, 1930s, 20x16", EX 65.00
Peters Weatherbird Shoes, bag of marbles 20.00
Peters Weatherbird Shoes, mechanical pencil, EX 25.00
Peters Weatherbird Shoes, pencil box, 8½", EX 20.00
Phillips 66, porc sign, World's Finest Oil, 11x22", M 650.00
Pickwick Ale, sf tin sign, men toasting, Shonk, 28x22", VG.......675.00
Piedmont Cigarettes, folding chair, porc bk, slat seat, EX...........165.00

Piel Bros Beer, sf tin sign, elves/bottles, 13" dia, EX **425.00**
Pilsener Brewing, tip tray, bottle/glass, 4" dia, NM **45.00**
Piper Heidsieck Tobacco, sf tin sign, champagne, 18x15", VG ... **450.00**

Planters Peanuts

Mr. Peanut, the dashing peanut man with the top hat, spats, monocle, and cane, has represented the Planters Peanut Company from 1916 to 1961 when the company was purchased by Standard Brands. He promoted the company's product by appearing on premium giveaways, store displays, jars, scales, and in special promotional events. Among the favored treasures of collectors today are the glass display jars. They come in a variety of styles. Some are square, some hexagonal, some barrel-shaped, and others are round. The earliest, issued in 1926, was octagonal and is usually referred to as the 'pennant' jar. Although later reproduced, these are marked 'Made in Italy' on the bottom. The original is embossed on the back panel 'Sold Only in Printed Planters Red Pennant Bags.' In a second octagonal style, this embossed message was replaced with a paper label.

In 1930 a 'fishbowl' jar was introduced, and in 1932 a 'four-corner peanut' jar was issued. The rarest jar of all, the 'football' jar, was also used during the early 1930s. The Planters' square jar followed in the 1930s and was replaced by the 'barrel' jar. The six-sided jar with Mr. Peanut decals and the 'pickle' jar were later. All in all, more than fifteen different styles were developed.

In the late 1930s, premiums such as glass and metal figural paperweights, pens, and pencils were distributed. Post-war items were often made of plastic; Mr. Peanut salt and pepper shakers, mugs, and banks were popular. Today's collectors find a treasure trove of advertising memorabilia depicting that debonair gentleman, Mr. Peanut.

Bag, glassine, One Cent, rare **35.00**
Beach ball, inflatable bl & yel plastic, Mr Peanut **22.00**
Beach towel, Mr Peanut on wht, M **35.00**
Card, Big Game, animal, 1933 .... **10.00**
Charm, glows in the dark **6.00**
Cigarette lighter, Bic, Mr Peanut, yel, M **18.00**
Color book, American Ecology, Mr Peanut, 1972, NM **12.50**
Color book, Mr Peanut & Smokey the Bear, 1973, M **15.00**
Cookbook, Cooking the Modern Way, 1948, 40-pg, NM **22.50**
Cruet, ceramic, Mr Peanut, pr **175.00**
Dart board game, Mr Peanut on front, M **95.00**
Divet fixer, ball marker & tee set, Mr Peanut, M **10.00**
Doll, Mr Peanut, wood, jtd, EX **175.00**
Frisbee, foam, Mr Peanut, 10" dia, M **12.00**
Golf cap, Mr Peanut, M **15.00**
Jar, Barrel, running Mr Peanut, paper label **275.00**
Jar, chocolate-covered cashews, paper label, 1944, 4½-oz **25.00**
Jar, Clipper, orig lid **150.00**
Jar, Fish Bowl, rectangular label **150.00**
Jar, Fish Bowl, sq paper label **150.00**
Jar, Football, peanut finial **300.00**
Jar, frosted label, big knob, rnd **45.00**
Jar, Leap Year, orig lid **50.00**
Jar, mixed nuts, paper label, orig lid, 1950s, 4½-oz **15.00**
Jar, octagon, Pennant 5¢, 7 sides emb **250.00**
Jar, octagon, Pennant 5¢, 8 sides emb **300.00**
Jar, peanut butter, early Mr Peanut on tin lid, scarce **25.00**
Jar, Pennant 5¢, paper label **175.00**
Jar, running peanut, orig pnt, figural lid, 13x9" dia, VG **300.00**
Jar, sq, peanut finial, Planters emb ea side **150.00**
Jar, Streamline, tin lid **65.00**
Jar, 4-corner, lg blown-out peanut ea corner, M **300.00**
Jar, 6-sided, printed sq label **60.00**

Knapsack, cloth, Mr Peanut, 14x14", M **15.00**
Knife, red plastic, Mr Peanut **5.00**
Lapel pin, Planters 50th Anniversary, bl on gold-color metal **20.00**
Luggage tag, Mr Peanut, 4½x2½" **15.00**
Lunch tote, vinyl, full color, 1979, 9x10", M **25.00**
Mug, beer; ceramic, 1950s, M **50.00**
Mug, hard plastic, Mr Peanut on pk, 4" **12.00**
Nut chopper, tin, grinder at top, 4¼x3½" dia, EX **100.00**
Nut spoon, Mr Peanut, silver tone **20.00**
Pail, Mr Peanut & animals, bail hdl, 3¾x3½", VG **500.00**
Paint book, Seeing the USA, 48 states, 1950 .... **35.00**
Peanut butter maker, Mr Peanut, M in box **35.00**
Pin-bk button, cl, Mr Peanut, old, EX **15.00**
Plate, pewter, Mr Peanut, 6" dia, M **35.00**
Plate, Superbowl XIII, heavy silver-tone metal, 11" **50.00**
Poster, 1980 Winter Olympics, Mr Peanut, 18x26", M **7.50**
Radio, Mr Peanut figural, 10" **75.00**
Raft, inflatable rubberized canvas, Mr Peanut, 72x30", M **95.00**
Shakers, ceramic, Mr Peanut, rhinestone eyes, rare, pr **125.00**
Shakers, plastic, Mr Peanut, red, 3", pr **15.00**
Shoe polish, Mr Peanut & balloon, 1950s, MIB **30.00**
Straw, plastic, wht w/tan Mr Peanut at top, M **8.00**
T-shirt, Planters Potato Chips, M **15.00**
Toothbrush, Mr Peanut figural, M **10.00**
Whistle, orange plastic, Mr Peanut **8.00**

Player's Navy Mixture, ash tray, emb ships on brass, 5" **125.00**
Plexo Suspenders, cb trolly card, man bowling, 1907, 21x11" **100.00**
Plow Boy Tobacco, tc, package, bow front, 10½x8x10½", EX .. **1,350.00**
Polar Bear Chewing Tobacco, pack, 1920s, unopened **15.00**
Polar Bear Tobacco, cb hanger, bear diecut, 14x11", EX **700.00**
Polarine Motor Oil, can, touring car/mountains, 5-gal, EX **575.00**
Poll Parrot Shoes, Howdy Doody adjustable campaign hat, 18" **30.00**
Poll Parrot Shoes, mechanical pencil, EX **25.00**
Poll Parrot Shoes, tin spinner, red & yel **35.00**
Pontiac Service, porc sign, Indian silhouette, 42" dia, G **115.00**
Pony Brand Marshmallows, tc, horse logo, 5x12" dia, VG **175.00**
Popel Giller, tip tray, girl w/roses & beer, 4" dia, NM **125.00**
Postmaster Tobacco, tin container, rnd, EX **65.00**
Potosi Brewing, sf ts, picnic scene, 1905, 34x33", EX **1,200.00**
Pratt's Medicines, tin/wood cabinet, horse, 33x17x7", G **650.00**
Prestone Anti Freeze, porc thermometer, EX **95.00**

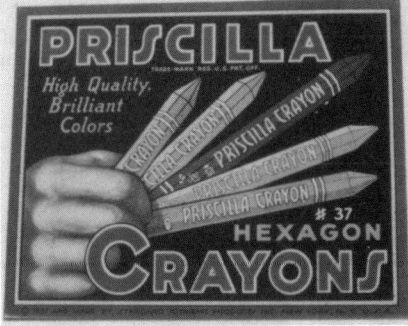

Priscilla Crayons, complete set in tin box dated 1937, MIB, $130.00.

Prost Beer, tip tray, man pours beer, 4½" dia, EX **55.00**
Prune Nuggett Tobacco, roll-down sign, girl/fruit, 30x15", NM .. **425.00**
Pulver's Cocoa, tip tray, package, 4¼", VG **300.00**

Purity Bread, display case, 1 glass shelf, 35x28x27", EX 425.00
Putnam Dyes, tin cabinet, Washington & British, 15x19x8", G....95.00
Quaker Maid Rye, tin sign, Shonk litho, 1905, 40x27", NM .. 2,000.00
Quaker Oats, tin diecut, 1920s, 15x19x7", EX 955.00

RCA Victor

Nipper, the RCA Victor trademark, was the creation of Francis Barraud, an English artist. His pet's intent fascination with the music of the phonograph seemed to him a worthy subject for his canvas. Although he failed to find a publishing house who would buy his work, the Gramaphone Co. saw its potential and adopted Nipper to advertise their product. The company eventually became the Victor Talking Machine Co. and was purchased by RCA in 1929. Nipper's image appeared on packaged accessories, in ads and brochures. If you are very lucky you may find a life-size statue of him; but all are not old, they have been reproduced! Except for the years between 1971 and 1981, Nipper has seen active duty; and, with his image spruced up only a bit for the present day, the ageless symbol for RCA still listens intently to 'His Master's Voice.'

Book, Victor Book of the Opera, 1912, EX....................................15.00
Catalog, record; performers' photos, leatherette cover, 1917 ....40.00
Figure, Nipper, hard rubber, 14x32x32", VG................................650.00
Figure, Nipper, molded plastic, 36", EX 220.00
Figure, Nipper, papier-mache, 36x18x36", G 600.00
Fold-out, Voice of Victor, 51 pictures, 4-pg, 1914, EX.................100.00
Letter & envelope, Victor Talking Machine letterhead, EX..........30.00
Needle tin, Nipper, 3-color, NM..28.00
Post card, hold-to-light, 1907..10.00
Shakers, Nipper, Lenox, 3½", pr 70.00
Sign, tin, RCA Victor Records, dbl-sided, EX 1,200.00
Snow dome, Nipper 50.00
Thermometer, porc, NM 485.00

Randolf's Nacon Cigars, sf ts, couple in reserve, 24x20" 550.00
Ranier Beer, tray, Evelyn Nesbitt, 1901, 13¼" dia 450.00
Ranier Beer, tray, girl w/arm on bear's head, 13", EX 250.00
Red Crest Tobacco, leather lunch box, rooster, 8x4x5", EX 150.00

Red Goose Shoes

Realizing that his last name was difficult to pronounce, Herman Giesceke, a shoe company owner, determined to give the public a modified, shortened version that would be better suited to the business world. The results suggested the use of the goose trademark, with the last two letters, 'ke,' represented by the key that this early goose held in his mouth. Upon observing an employee casually coloring in the goose trademark with a red pencil, Giesceke saw new advertising potential and renamed the company Red Goose Shoes. Although the company has changed hands down through the years, the Red Goose emblem has remained. Collectors of this desirable fowl increase in number yearly, as do prices. Beware of reproductions; new chalkware figures are prevalent.

Bank, goose, CI/red pnt, Red Goose School Shoes, 3¾" 225.00
Bank, Save w/Shoes...Kid, tin, worn pnt, M-1585, 5⅝" 45.00
Clicker, yel, Red Goose logo, 1950s, M 12.00
Display, goose figural, mechanical, 1930s, 22x23", EX 400.00
Figure, goose, chalkware, EX pnt, 11" 135.00
Figure, goose, papier-mache, nodder, rpr, 24" 75.00
Horn, paper, 6", EX... 4.00

Pencil box, wood, sliding top, old, 2x9", EX 85.00
Poster, Red Goose & children at schoolhouse, 1920s, EX...........275.00
Pull toy, goose, wooden, EX red pnt...70.00
Shoe bag, paper..10.00
Shoe holder, wood, 18" 200.00
Sign, tin diecut, boy holds goose by neck, 1910s, EX 300.00
String holder, goose figural, CI, VG pnt................................... 1,200.00
String holder, goose figural, tin litho, 29" 1,200.00

Red Man Cigars, tin sign, package, yel, 5x20", M...........................30.00
Red Raven Splits, tip tray, It's a Dream, bright colors, VG............85.00
Red Seal Dry Battery, porc thermometer, 1915, NM 400.00
Red Seal Dry Battery, sf ts, driver w/batteries, 19x27", G 160.00
Red Tiger Tobacco, cb containers, tiger, 5x8x11", G...................120.00
Redicut Tobacco, lunch box, hand w/package, 7x8x3½", G 125.00
Reed's Tonic, clock, miniature grandfather, 24", EX...................850.00
Reeds Tonic, regulator clock, EX.. 1,400.00
Remington, tin jack-knife stand-up display, 7½x32", G 350.00
Robert Burns Cigars, tin charger, portrait, 24" dia, G 275.00
Robert Fulton Cigars, tc, portrait medallion, 5¾x6x4", VG 155.00
Robinson Crusoe Peanuts, Crusoe/dog/peanuts, 10-lb, G 400.00

Roly Poly

The Roly Poly tobacco tins were patented on November 5, 1912, by Washington Tuttle and produced by Tindeco of Baltimore, Maryland. There were six characters in all: Satisfied Customer, Storekeeper, Mammy, Dutchman, Singing Waiter, and Inspector. Four brands of tobacco were packaged in selected characters; some tins carry a printed tobacco box on the back to identify their contents. Mayo and Dixie Queen Tobacco were packed in all six; Red Indian and U.S. Marine Tobacco in only Mammy, Singing Waiter, and Storekeeper. Of the set, the Inspector is considered the rarest and in mint condition may fetch as much as $1,000 on today's market.

Dutchman, Mayo, EX..400.00
Dutchman, Mayo, NM...550.00
Inspector from Scotland Yard, Mayo, EX 1,000.00

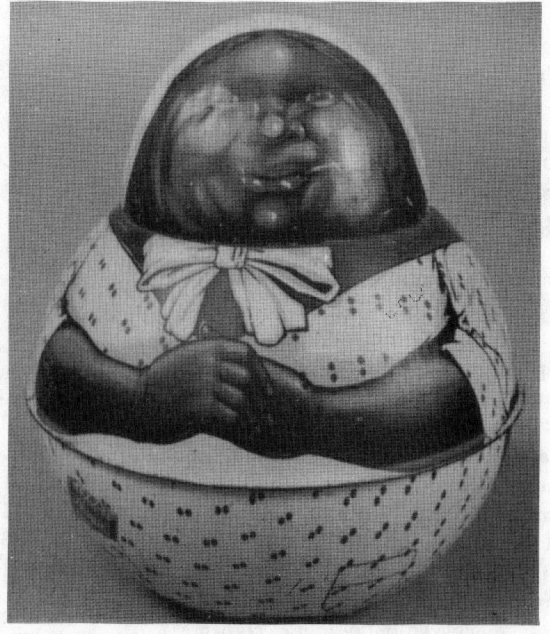

Mammy, EX, $600.00.

Satisfied Customer, VG.................................350.00
Singing Waiter, Mayo, EX............................500.00
Singing Waiter, US Marine, VG 425.00
Storekeeper, Mayo, NM 650.00
Storekeeper, VG..300.00

Royal Crown, cigarette lighter, bottle form, 1940s, sm, M 25.00
Royal Navy Tobacco, tc, sailor smoking, 5x3¾x2½"...................150.00
Ruppert Beer, neon sign, red/bl, 1930s, 10½x23", EX 475.00
Russel & Clark, spool cabinet, 9-drw, 22x29x19", EX.............1,000.00
Ryan's Brewery, growler, glass w/porc stopper, 11", EX 85.00
Sailor's Pride Tobacco, tin canister, Ilsley, 6¼x5", G 350.00
Salmon's Tea, tin container, fish, 2½" dia, G 95.00
Satin Cigarettes, tin charger, girl w/pack, 19" dia, G 350.00
Schlitz Beer, glass sign, light-up, hanging, 15x22", EX................150.00
Schlitz Beer, tap knob, enamel & brass...26.00
Schmidt's Beer, tray, Mayflower Passengers, 12½x15½", EX.........60.00
Schrafft's Chocolate, paper-on-canvas sign, girl, 24x18", G 200.00
Scottie Cigars, tc, dog, humidor lid, 5¼x4½" sq, G 150.00
Sealtest Milk, clock, light-up, EX..75.00
Seattle Brewing & Malt Co, tip tray, 1909 Expo, 4", NM............400.00
Seitz Beer, tip tray, eagle logo, 4" dia, EX 40.00
Sensation Cigars, canister, goddess, leaf over head, 5¼", EX 350.00
Sharples Cream Separators, sf tin sign, mc, 22x28", EX 4,200.00
Shaw's Malt, sf ts, lady is served/child at feet, 22x16", G 1,300.00
Sherwin-Williams Paints, cb puzzle, 2-sided, 11x16", EX...............70.00
Silver Bell Tobacco, tin container, bell & banner, 2½x3" 95.00
Singer Sewing Machines, paper sign, grandma/child, 24x14", G .375.00
Skippy Peanut Butter, can, 1½-lb, EX...150.00
Smith Bros Cough Drops, tin display, 4x11x3½", VG 155.00
Smith Bros Cough Drops, wooden box w/paper label, 39x18x10"...75.00
Smith's Ale, etched/rvpt sign, oval, 10x15½", VG.......................100.00
Snow King Baking Powder, cb diecut, ca 1900, 20x36", EX 375.00
Society King Shoes, sf ts, man w/high-button shoes, 13x9", VG ...200.00

Spidel, piano music box, closed: 6", $185.00.

Spilter's Buttermilk Talcum Powder, tc, baby on stork, EX 200.00
Squire's Pig, sf ts, JP Squire/sitting pig, 1906, 25x20", EX 2,050.00
Squirrel Brand Salted Nuts, glass jar, w/lid, 15x9", EX................150.00
Squirrel Peanut Butter, pail, orange, slip lid, 34-oz, EX 185.00
Stag Brewing, brass stencil, for barrel, 11½x17½", G 20.00

Stamper Feeds, tin sign, Full Feed Value, 1940s, 20x28", EX.........15.00
Stegmaier Brewing, tip tray, factory scene, 4¼", EX......................85.00
Stegmaier Brewing, tray, stock girl, rolled rim, 13½", EX............165.00
Stephenson's Union Suits, porc thermometer, EX colors 395.00
Sterling Pepsin Gum, cb sign, girl's face, fr, 24x35", G 500.00
Sterling Tobacco, tc, dk gr, 11½x8" dia, G 65.00
Success Manure Spreader, emb tin sign, machine, 20x28", G 500.00
Suncrest, clock, light-up, EX 175.00
Sweet Cuba Tobacco, tin bin, package, 8x8x10", VG 125.00
Sweet Cuba Tobacco, wooden pail, early labels, 11x12" dia 150.00
Sweet Girl Peanut Butter, pail, kids/sand castles, 3¾", M...........900.00
Sweet Mist Chewing Tobacco, tc, children/fountain, 11", VG ...125.00
Sweet Mist Tobacco, cb bin, children/fountain, 10½x8x5", G ...150.00
Tanlac Medicine, cb display, girl/factory, 3-pc, 34x42", VG........300.00
Teddie Peanut Butter, pail, peanut seal logo, 3¼x3½", VG.........115.00
Tetlow's Face Powder, cb diecut, girl/soldier, 14x19", G.............250.00
Texaco, porc sign, Certified Lubrication, 9x39", NM 450.00
Thomas Ryan Brewing, tray, Indian in headdress, 12" dia, VG ...100.00
Tobacco Girl Cigars, tc, girl looks through leaf, 5½", EX 1,500.00

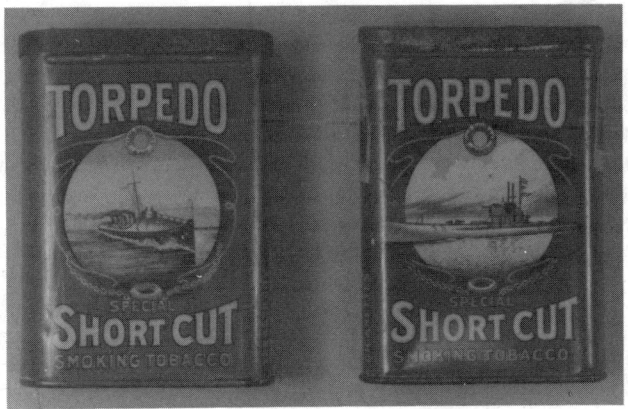

Torpedo Tobacco, pocket tins, Quebec, left: Destroyer Torpedo, $2,500.00; right: Submarine Torpedo, $4,575.00.

Tosetti, tray, Bertha, 1908, 13x13", EX 100.00
Toyland Peanut Butter, pail, toys on parade, 3½x3¾", VG 200.00
Tums, tin display, hinged bk, drw w/tins,'30, 10x7x10", G..........120.00
Tums, tin thermometer, bl/yel/red, 9x4", NM 27.50
Uncle Daniel Tobacco, tc, Webster portrait, 2x8¼", G 45.00
Uncle Green Cigars, tc, portrait over field, 5½" dia, EX 250.00
Union Beer, tray, Dutch boy w/beer & sausage, 10½x13", VG....100.00
Union Blend Tobacco, lunch box, leaf inset, 4¼x7x4½", G 200.00
Union Brewing, tip tray, labeled bottle, 4" dia, EX 70.00
Union Commander Cut Plug, pail, Washington, 4x7x5", VG.....200.00
Union Leader Tobacco, tin container, rnd, EX 45.00
Union Razors, tin sign, N America & strop, 13½x9½", G 65.00
Union Workman Chewing Tobacco, thermometer, 1940s, NM ...65.00
US Baking Co, wood box w/paper cover: Noah's Ark, 9", EX........95.00
US Marine Flake Cut, pocket tin, ca 1920, EX 150.00
US Tires, dbl-sided porc sign, 24" dia, EX 475.00
Utica Club, neon sign, 1940s, 5x15½", EX 150.00
V-B Belting, tin sign, factory/product, 13x19", G 100.00
Valley Forge Beer, tray, waitress w/tray, 10½x13", EX 100.00
Velvet Beer, tin charger, Colonials/cherubs, 24" dia, G...............150.00
Vermont Household Remedies, regulator clock, EX 1,095.00
Victor & Berliner Gramophones, tip tray, dog/machine, 4", M...155.00
Victory-V Lozenges, tc, children on sled, 2x4½x3", EX...............150.00
Walk-Over Shoes, paper sign, factory view, 26x20", G.................100.00

Water Bros Brewing, bar glass, etched factory, NM 30.00
Welcome Soap, mixed media sign, 2 girls, fr, 28x12", NM 850.00
Welsh Rabbit, tin biscuit box, dining scene, 2x10x4¼", G.........150.00
Westclox Pocket Watches, cb diecut, ...on the Dot, 24x29", VG .75.00
White Swan Coffee, cb carton, swan in pond, 25-lb, G 50.00
Wieland's Extra Pale Lager Beer, tray, Indian lady, '02, 13" 850.00
Wild West Soap, wooden box, cowboys label, 4x16x13", G.... 1,200.00
Willimantic, oak spool cabinet, 4-drw, orig pulls, VG 450.00
Winchester Potatoes, burlap sack, Conestoga wagon/rifle, VG......10.00
Wolfe's Schnapps, cb sign, early car/tavern, fr, 27x22", G.........150.00
Wrigley's Gum, cb sign, Extra Protection..., 1930s, 11x21", EX 50.00
Wrigley's Gum, tin diecut display, man w/4 boxes, 14x14x7"......550.00
Wrigley's Soap, tin sign, lg package, 14x19½", G.....................140.00
Wurzburger Beer, coaster, 4" dia, EX...................................95.00
Yankee Girl, porc sign, 1920s, 12x9", NM.............................200.00
Yellow Daisy, lunch box, flowers, 3½x7½x4½", G....................250.00
Yuengling's Ice Cream, tip tray, eagle & barrel, 4" dia, M 100.00
Zeppelin Motor Oil, tin can, blimp, 2-gal, 12", VG 200.00

7-Up

Palm press, heavy aluminum, pnt touched up, 9x3½" 95.00
Sign, cb, full color, 1960, 17x10", EX 15.00
Sign, cb, girl w/grandma, 1940s, 12x8", EX............................ 9.00
Sign, cb, Please Return, 1940s, 11x14", EX............................ 7.50
Sign, cb, Sailor Baby, 1950s, 12x15", EX..............................17.50
Sign, cb, swimmers, 1940s, 12x8", EX.................................18.00
Sign, cb, 2 bottles, 12x8", EX..10.00
Sign, plastic w/metal edge, minor scratches, 12x24".................35.00
Thermometer, porc, 4-color, 15x6", EX...............................45.00

Advertising Cards

Advertising trade cards enjoyed a heyday during the last quarter of the nineteenth century when the printing process known as chromolithography was refined and put into popular use. The purpose of the trade card was to acquaint the public with a place of business, a product, or a service. Most trade cards range in size from 2" x 3" to 3" x 5"; however, some are found in both smaller and larger sizes. Four categories of particular interest to collectors are:

Mechanical — those which achieve movement through the use of a pull tab, fold-out side, or rotating disk.

Metamorphic — cards that transform a person or a thing from a 'before' to an 'after' condition which, of course, represents a marked improvement immediately upon use of the featured product.

Hold-to-light — cards that reveal their design only when viewed before a strong light.

Diecuts — cards in figural forms such as the Heinz pickle series. Diecuts are usually in the shape of the advertised product or a theme-related object. For a more thorough study of the subject, we recommend *The Advertising Trade Card* by Kit Barry; his address can be found in the Directory under Vermont. When no condition is indicated, the items listed below are assumed to be in near-mint condition.

Adams & Westlake Stoves, 2 rats at table 10.00
Adams & Westlake Stoves, 3 monkeys at table..........................10.00
Agate Iron Ware, duck in teapot, Chinese man in pan.................12.00
Agate Iron Ware, Father Time looks at products........................12.00
Aromatic Pino-Palmine Mattress, palm trees, insert w/baby 8.00
Atkinson & Co House Furnishings, Boston, parlor scene 12.00
Bartlett's Shoe Dressing, bottle w/sunflowers.........................12.00
Beatty's Organ & Pianos, girl w/roses, bls & grs 6.00
Beatty's Pianofortes, girl writes in sand, bls & grs.................... 6.00

Bixby Blacking, gentleman, 1 shoeblack................................12.00
Bixby Blacking, king, 2 shoeblacks....................................12.00
Boss Patent Watch Case, ram charging watch case 10.00
Brooks Paints, French Cathedral, Montreal 9.00
Brooks Paints, St Peters Cathedral 9.00
Buffalo Forge Co, 4 men working at forge..............................15.00
Buttons Raven Gloss, mother, daughter, cupid, & box 8.00
Charter Oak Stoves, boy & girl at fence 6.00
Chase's Liquid Glue, sandpiper, bottle upper left 6.00
Chase's Liquid Glue, woodcock, bottle upper left...................... 6.00
Crawford Cooking Range, girl w/pk parasol 6.00
Cyclone & Household Stoves, wht-frocked girl w/doll.................. 8.00
Day & Martin Blacking, Very Free-Booters 5.00
Eagle Clock, 8th wonder, clock w/man & woman 8.00
Eagle Pencil Co, pencil, castle upper left background 12.00
Eclipse Wringer, boy in chair w/hand puppets......................... 6.00
Eclipse Wringer, boy w/flute, ducks by water 6.00
Elgin Watches, Father Time w/clock in hand...........................12.00
Empire Wringer Co, dressed foxes & sheep in wedding scene 8.00
Empire Wringer Co, 2 dressed foxes w/baby fox in cradle 8.00
Florence Oil Stoves, man reading paper at table....................... 6.00
Garitee Clothing, Phila, Old Grimes 6.00
Harlem & Westchester Clothing, man at opera 7.00
Inman Line, City of Rome...35.00
Jordan Marsh Co, Boston, 3 boys w/oversz collar 5.00
Keystone Watch Cases, keystone diecut, Father Time 8.00
Keystone Watch Cases, keystone diecut, pig w/horn 8.00
Ladies Blacking, 4 little girls...5.00
LePages Glue, man stuck in chair; parlor & woman 8.00
LePages Glue, woman stuck on park bench 8.00
Lord & Taylor Clothing, 3 frogs w/pair of shoes 8.00
Lord & Taylor Clothing, 6 frogs under mushroom 8.00
Magee Furnace Co, girl w/hourglass & butterflies...................... 6.00
Magee Furnace Co, The Magee Butler................................. 8.00
Magee Furnace Co, The Magee Cook................................. 8.00
Magee Furnace Co, The Magee Housekeeper.......................... 8.00
Mason & Hamlin Organ Co, girl, cat, dog, doll at piano 9.00
Mason & Hamlin Organ Co, girl at organ, fancy border 8.00
Michigan Stove Co, Garland Stoves, girl on beach..................... 6.00
Michigan Stove Co, Garland Stoves, lady combs girl's hair 6.00
Milwaukee Harvester Co, girl in oats w/daisy 10.00
Milwaukee Harvester Co, woman holding broken branch 10.00
Mrs Potts Sad Irons, clerk, man, interior store scene 12.00
Mrs Potts Sad Irons, man painting irons on fence 12.00
Neptune Umbrella, Hercules Against the Elements....................12.00
Paine's Furniture, Boston, child, convertible bed in parlor............. 9.00
Paine's Furniture, Boston, factory building 8.00
Putnam Nail Co, Those Horrid Boys 5.00
Roberts & Co Clothiers, Newark, statue of Kearny.................... 9.00
Round Oak Stoves, girl writing on sm chalkboard...................... 8.00
Round Oak Stoves, The Name Tells 6.00
Rutland Stove Lining, 2 girls, 1 w/hoop............................... 6.00
Sill Stove Works, girl w/dog sitting up 6.00
Stadler, Max & Co, NYC Clothiers, man, boy on horse 10.00
Stadler, Max & Co, NYC Clothiers, 3 children on toys................. 8.00
Star Paste Stove Polish, Colonial couple by stove 15.00
Sterling Piano, girl at piano, boy w/violin............................ 8.00
Swett & Co, Glenmore Base Burner, ¾ portrait of girl................. 6.00
Swett & Co, Popular Range, girl on snowshoes 8.00
Union & Web Hammock, woman in hammock, man at side 12.00
Universal Wringer, barefoot girl lying on ground 6.00
Universal Wringer, boy in sailor suit lying on ground 6.00
Walton's Linoleum, geometric design border & lettering 12.00
Waterbury Watches, man reading newspaper, woman by him 9.00

Waterbury Watches, 2 men, woman w/ostrich plume **9.00**
Waterloo Organs, 4 women around organ **8.00**
Weir Stove Co, girl w/red dress & flowers, stove **8.00**
Yates Clothiers, Phila, 2 horse riders jumping fences **9.00**

Vick's Choice Seeds, $15.00.

Advertising Dolls

Whether your interest in ad dolls is fueled by nostalgia or strictly because of their amusing, often clever advertising impact, there are several points that should be considered before making your purchases. Condition is of utmost importance; never pay book price for dolls in poor condition, whether they are cloth or of another material. Restoring fabric dolls is usually unsatisfactory and involves a good deal of work. Seams must be opened, stuffing removed, the doll washed and dried, and then reassembled. Washing old fabrics may prove to be disastrous. Colors may fade or run, and most stains are totally resistant to washing. It's usually best to leave the fabric doll as it is.

Watch for new dolls as they become available. Save related advertising literature, extra coupons, etc., and keep these along with the doll to further enhance your collection. Old dolls with no marks are sometimes challenging to identify. While some products may use the same familiar trademark figures for a number of years (the Jolly Green Giant, Pillsbury's Poppin' Fresh, and the Keebler Elf, for example) others appear on the market for a short time only and may be difficult to trace. Most libraries have reference books with trademarks and logos that might provide a clue in tracking down your doll's identity. Children see advertising figures on Saturday morning cartoons that are often unfamiliar to adults, or other ad doll collectors may have the information you seek.

Advertising dolls are still easy to find and relatively inexpensive, ranging in cost from $1.00 to $100.00, with the average price at about $10.00. They are popular with children as well as adults. For a more thorough study of the subject, we recommend *Advertising Dolls*, by Joleen Robison and Kay Sellers. Joleen is our advisor; she is listed in the Directory under Kansas.

Atlas Van Lines, Atlas Annie, cloth, 1977, 15½" **18.00**
Bell Telephones, Repair Lady, M in box **42.00**
Big Boy Restaurants, Big Boy, Dolly & Nugget, 3 for **28.00**
Blue Bonnet Margarine, Buttercup, cow puppet, M **27.50**
Bonz Dog Biscuits, dog, MIB **20.00**
Bordens, Elsie & Beauregard (calf), cloth w/vinyl face **60.00**
Breck Shampoo, Bonnie Breck, vinyl, 1971, 9", M **25.00**
British Overseas Airlines, stewardess **12.00**
Brook's Tangy Catsup, Tangyroo kangaroo, 1983, 12", M **37.50**
Budweiser Beer, turtle, beanbag, M **12.00**
C&H Sugar, Hawaiian girl, cloth, 1973, 16" **14.00**
Cadbury's Chocolate, cow's head puppet, M **15.00**

Campbell's, cheerleader, vinyl, 1957, M **42.50**
Campbell's, Scotch highlander, 1976, M **22.50**
Chicken of the Sea, mermaid, fabric, Mattel, 1974, M **30.00**
Chiffon Margarine, Mother Nature, 15", M **22.50**
Chiquita Banana, Chiquita, 1974, 16", M **20.00**
Chore Girl, girl, stuffed, 1970, 15", NM **22.50**
Close-Up Toothpaste, Dumbo the Elephant, vinyl, 1974, 8", M ... **25.00**
Coast to Coast Store, Elfy, M **25.00**
Cocoa Wheats, Gretchen, 1949, scarce, EX **37.50**
Cookie Crisp, Cookie Cop, plush, M **22.00**
Curad Bandaids, Boo Boo bear, plush, 8", M **22.00**
Diaparine Baby Wipes, baby w/diaper, vinyl, M **22.00**
Dutch Boy Paint, puppet, vinyl head, old **32.00**
Eagle Snacks Honey Roasted Peanuts, bear, MIB **27.50**
Eskimo Pie, boy, plastic, 1964, NM **17.50**
Faultless Starch Co, Miss Phoebe Prim, cloth, 1978, 12½" **42.00**
Federal Savings & Loan, Ben Franklin, M **18.00**
Fiddle Faddle Caramel Corn, bear w/fiddle, plush, M **20.00**
Fig Newton Cookies, girl w/cookie, M in box **17.50**
Franklin Life Insurance, Ben Franklin, 1970, 12" **20.00**
Friskie's Cat Food, cat, plush, MIB **22.50**
General Electric, Mr Magoo, cloth, 11" **18.00**
General Mills, Count Chocula, 1975, M **22.00**
Gillette Co, George Washington, cloth, 1974, 13" **12.50**
Hardee's, Gilbert Giddy-Up, cloth, 1971, 13½" **15.00**
Honeywell, Allergic Annie, cloth, 15" **17.50**
Hush Puppy Shoes, dog, 5", M **12.50**
John Deere Farm Machinery, stuffed gr deer, NM **32.00**
Kellogg's, Tony Tiger, cloth, 1973, 13½" **15.00**
Kellogg's, Tony Tiger, plush, 1970, 13" **30.00**
Life Savers, Mike-E-Mint, scented, w/comb, 1981, NM **17.50**

Lotta Light, Mazda Lamp Girl, uncut cloth, 17", $85.00.

Mason Mints, Peppermint Pattie, beanbag, M **12.00**
Mountain Dew, hillbilly, felt, M **27.50**
Mr Big Toilet Tissue, kitten, plush, M **17.50**
Nestles, Little Hans, cloth, 1970s, 13" **12.50**
Nestles, Quik Bunny, 1985, 8", M **17.50**
Oscar Mayer, Little Oscar, inflatable vinyl, M **16.00**
Pop's Rite Popcorn, Puffy Kernel, stuffed, M **12.00**
Procter & Gamble, Pogo Possum, vinyl, 1969, 5" **18.00**
Purex Bleach, monkey, wht plush, M in pkg **22.50**
Quaker Oats, Captain Crunch, M **20.00**

Quaker Oats, Puffy, cloth, 1930, 16"	200.00
Ralston Purina, Scarecrow, vinyl, 1965, 23"	35.00
Sambo's Restaurant, Sambo & tiger, rubber, 5", 7", pr	15.00
Shoprite, Scrunchy Bear, 1975, M	17.50
Smucker's Jam, Yogi Bear, M	25.00
Spaghetti O's, Wizard of O's, vinyl, 1978, M	17.50
Tropicana Juice, boy w/orange on hat, old, EX	25.00
Vermont Maid Syrup, Vermont Maid, vinyl, M	32.00
Vick's Vaporub, polar bear on stand, M	22.50
Wendy's, Wendy, stuffed, old, 11", NM	38.00

African Art

African art does not consist of a single class of objects. Rather, these often-powerful sculptures are carved by many varying African tribes and groups across the central continent; each item represents specific cultural and spiritual functions and meanings. Many kinds of materials are used including wood, metal, fiber, ivory, and bone. Considerable amounts of these items are now being reproduced and sold to the tourist trade, but 'authentic' African art is generally considered to consist of objects which were used in cultural and religious activities. The items listed here are authentic and considered to be of average aesthetic quality. Scott Nelson, a collector of African art, is our advisor; his address is listed in the Directory under New Mexico.

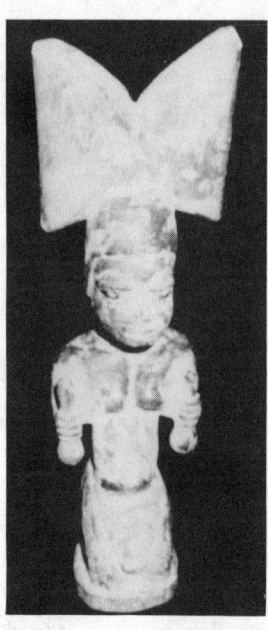

Yoruba chieftain's scepter, human figure, 12", $475.00.

Anklet, Ashanti, open wedge form, bronze, 6"	125.00
Basket, Zaire, open, cowrie shells, fiber, 15" dia	125.00
Beads, mc trade, string of 20	75.00
Bowl, Yoruba, divining, supported by 6 figures, 12" dia	675.00
Comb, Chokwe, human figural surmount, 5"	275.00
Doll, Fanti, sq head, simple design, 9"	125.00
Doll, Mossi, abstract human figure, 10"	375.00
Door, Dogon, granary, 30 human figures, 2 turtles, 26"	1,250.00
Drum, Hemba, baboon head on side, 40"	600.00
Figure, Bamana, male standing figure, sq lines, 21"	475.00
Figure, Baule, standing female, pendant, 18"	375.00
Figure, Benin, bronze, royal personage, recent, 9"	125.00
Figure, Dogon, personal fetish, bearded male, 5"	575.00
Figure, Songye, kneeling male fetish, 10"	475.00
Gold weight, Ashanti, bronze, water buffalo, 3"	125.00
Headrest, Luba, supporting human figure, 10"	475.00

Heddle pulley, Senufo, bird surmount, 7"	475.00
Ibejis, Yoruba, 10", pr	375.00
Knife, Kuba, throwing, curved decor blade, bronze hdl, 27"	175.00
Lock, Bamana, door, 2 human figural surmounts, 12"	475.00
Mask, Bamana, agricultural, hyena, 14"	275.00
Mask, Bobo, unicorn, polychrome, 25"	475.00
Mask, Dan, human face, 14"	375.00
Mask, Dogon, wolf, 18"	675.00
Mask, Marka, human face w/metal adornments	375.00
Mask, Mende, helmet, female initiation	675.00
Pendant, Pende, ivory human figure, ornate cvg, 3"	600.00
Pipe, Makonde, human head bowl, 14"	275.00
Stool, Hausa, plain legs, human head hdl, 8"	225.00
Stool, Lega, human figural supports, 13"	375.00
Wisk, Yoruba, ivory, human kneeling figure, horsehair, 11"	500.00

Agata

Agata is New England peachblow (the factory called it 'Wild Rose') with an applied metallic stain which produces gold tracery and dark blue mottling. The stain is subject to wear, and the amount of remaining stain greatly affects the value. It is especially valuable (and rare) when found on peachblow of intense color. Caution! Be sure to use only gentle cleaning methods.

Currently rare types of art glass have been realizing erratic prices at auction; until they stablize, we can only suggest an average range of values. In the listings that follow, examples are glossy unless noted otherwise. See also Green Opaque.

Creamer	1,200.00
Finger bowl, scalloped, EX mottling, 4½" dia	800.00
Plate, fluted rim, 6½"	850.00
Punch cup, EX mottling, appl hdl, 2¾x3"	650.00
Salt shaker	525.00
Sugar bowl, EX gold & mottling, 4"	1,250.00
Toothpick holder, sq top, EX color & mottling	675.00
Tumbler, EX color & mottling, 4x2½"	600.00
Vase, lily; VG color & mottling, 5¾"	900.00
Vase, 4 pinched sides, ruffled/crimped rim, 4½"	950.00

Agate Ware

Clays of various natural or artificially dyed colors were combined to produce agate ware, a procedure similar to the methods used by Niloak in potting their Mission Ware. It was made by many Staffordshire potteries from about 1740 until about 1825.

Coffee can & saucer, creamware trim, 5" saucer	350.00
Pitcher, cream; 3 lion masks & paw ft, bl/brn clay, rpr, 4½"	925.00
Pitcher, 6 vertical panels, England, 1800s, 8¾"	250.00
Plate, glazed solid agate, redware rim & base ring, late, 8"	135.00
Teapot, brn/cream, sq w/short ft, foo dog finial, rpr, 5¼"	6,300.00

Akro Agate

The Akro Agate Co. founded in 1914 primarily as a marble maker, operated in Clarksburg, West Virginia, until 1951. Their popular wares included children's dishes, powder jars, flowerpots, and novelty items along with the famous 'Akro Aggies.' Much of their glass was produced in the distinctive marbleized colors they called Red Onyx, Blue Onyx, etc.; solid opaque and transparent colors were also produced. Most of the wares are marked with their trademark, a crow flying through the letter 'A' holding an Aggie in its beak and one in each claw. Other marks include 'J.P.' on children's pieces, 'J.V. Co., Inc,' 'Braun & Corwin,' 'N.Y.C. Vogue Merc Co. U.S.A.,' 'Hamilton Match Co.,' and 'Mexicali Pickwick Cosmetic Corp.' on novelty items. In 1936 Akro obtained the moulds from the Balmer-Westite Co. of Weston, West Virginia. Westite produced a similar line of products for several years. Their ware is drab in color when compared to Akro and is generally unmarked. The embossed Westite logo does appear occasionally on the bottoms of some pieces. Westite is commonly accepted as a companion collectible of Akro.

For more information we recommend *Children's Dishes*, by Margaret and Kenn Whitmyer and *Collector's Encyclopedia of Akro Agate* by Gene Florence, available at your local bookstore. Our advisor for miscellaneous Akro Agate is Albert Morin; he is listed in the Directory under Massachusetts.

Chiquita

Creamer, baked-on colors, 1½"	8.00
Creamer, opaque gr, 1½"	5.00
Creamer, opaque turq, lav, or caramel, 1½"	16.00
Creamer, transparent cobalt, 1½"	12.00
Cup, opaque gr, 1½"	4.00
Cup, opaque turq, lav, or caramel, 1½"	12.00
Cup, transparent cobalt, 1½"	6.00
Plate, baked-on colors, 3¾"	3.00
Plate, transparent cobalt, 3¾"	7.00
Saucer, baked-on colors, 3⅛"	1.50
Saucer, gr opaque, 3⅛"	1.50
Saucer, opaque lav, caramel, or yel, 3¼"	5.00
Saucer, transparent cobalt, 3⅛"	3.00
Set, 16-pc, baked-on colors	70.00
Set, 16-pc, opaque colors other than gr	125.00
Set, 16-pc, opaque gr	47.00
Set, 16-pc, transparent cobalt	105.00
Sugar bowl, baked-on colors, open, 1½"	8.00
Sugar bowl, opaque turq, lav, or caramel, open, 1½"	16.00
Sugar bowl, transparent cobalt, open, 1½"	12.00
Teapot, baked-on colors, w/lid, 3"	18.00
Teapot, opaque gr, w/lid, 3"	12.00
Teapot, opaque turq or lav, w/lid, 3"	35.00
Teapot, transparent cobalt, w/lid, 3"	25.00

Concentric Rib

Creamer, opaque colors other than gr or wht, 1¼"	12.00
Creamer, opaque gr or wht, 1¼"	7.00
Cup, opaque colors other than gr or wht, 1¼"	7.00
Cup, opaque gr or wht, 1¼"	4.00
Plate, opaque colors other than gr or wht, 3¼"	6.00
Plate, opaque gr or wht, 3¼"	3.00
Saucer, opaque gr or wht, 2¾"	1.50
Sugar bowl, opaque colors other than gr or wht, 1¼"	12.00
Sugar bowl, opaque gr or wht, 1¼"	8.00
Teapot, opaque colors other than gr or wht, w/lid, 3⅜"	12.00
Teapot, opaque gr or wht, w/lid, 3½"	9.00

Concentric Ring

Cereal, lg, solid opaque colors, 3⅜"	20.00
Cereal, lg, transparent cobalt, 3⅜"	30.00
Creamer, lg, marbleized bl, 1⅜"	45.00
Creamer, lg, transparent cobalt, 1⅜"	30.00

Creamer, sm, marbleized bl, 1¼"	35.00
Creamer, sm, solid opaque colors, 1¼"	16.00
Cup, lg, bl marbleized	35.00
Cup, lg, opaque lav or yel, 1⅜"	30.00
Cup, lg, opaque pumpkin, 1⅜"	20.00
Cup, sm, transparent cobalt, 1¼"	27.00
Plate, lg, solid opaque colors, 4¼"	14.00
Plate, lg, transparent cobalt, 4¼"	18.00
Plate, sm, solid opaque colors, 3¼"	6.00
Plate, sm, transparent cobalt, 3¼"	18.00
Saucer, lg, solid opaque colors, 3⅛"	4.00
Saucer, lg, transparent cobalt, 3⅛"	8.00
Saucer, sm, solid opaque colors, 2¾"	3.00
Set, 16-pc, solid opaque colors, sm	105.00
Set, 21-pc, marbleized bl, lg	460.00
Sugar bowl, lg, solid opaque colors, w/lid, 1⅞"	25.00
Sugar bowl, lg, transparent cobalt, w/lid, 1⅞"	45.00
Teapot, lg, marbleized bl, w/lid, 3¾"	100.00
Teapot, lg, solid opaque colors, w/lid, 3¾"	35.00

Interior Panel

Cereal, lg, azure bl or yel, 3⅜"	27.00
Cereal, lg, marbleized gr/wht, 3⅜"	20.00
Creamer, lg, gr lustre, 1⅜"	14.00
Creamer, lg, marbleized bl/wht, 1⅜"	27.00
Creamer, lg, pk lustre, 1⅜"	20.00
Creamer, sm, azure bl or yel, 1¼"	30.00
Creamer, sm, gr lustre, 1⅜"	15.00
Creamer, sm, pk lustre, 1¼"	22.00
Cup, lg, marbleized red/wht, 1⅜"	25.00
Cup, sm, marbleized red/wht, 1¼"	25.00
Cup, sm, pk lustre, 1¼"	14.00
Cup, sm, pumpkin, 1¼"	20.00
Pitcher, sm, transparent gr or topaz, 2⅞"	14.00
Plate, lg, azure bl or yel, 4¼"	10.00
Plate, sm, marbleized bl/wht, 3¾"	12.00
Plate, sm, pk or gr lustre, 3¾"	5.00
Saucer, sm, azure bl or yel, 2⅜"	7.00
Saucer, sm, marbleized red/wht, 2⅜"	7.00
Set, lg, 21-pc, marbleized bl/wht	325.00
Set, lg, 21-pc, pk or gr lustre	225.00
Set, sm, 16-pc, marbleized red/wht, MIB	220.00
Set, sm, 16-pc, pk or gr lustre, MIB	125.00
Set, sm, 8-pc, marbleized bl/wht, MIB	105.00
Set, sm, 8-pc, transparent gr or topaz	40.00
Sugar bowl, lg, lemonade/oxblood, w/lid, 1⅞"	50.00
Sugar bowl, lg, transparent gr or topaz, w/lid, 1⅞"	22.00
Sugar bowl, sm, azure bl or yel, 1¼"	30.00
Sugar bowl, sm, marbleized bl/wht, 1¼"	25.00
Teapot, lg, lemonade/oxblood, w/lid, 3¾"	57.00
Teapot, sm, azure bl or yel, w/lid, 3⅜"	40.00
Teapot, sm, marbleized bl/wht, w/lid, 3⅜"	40.00
Tumbler, sm, opaque, 2"	40.00
Tumbler, sm, transparent gr or topaz, 2"	8.00

J.P. (Made for J. Pressman Company)

Cup, baked-on colors, 1½"	5.00
Cup, transparent cobalt w/ribs, 1½"	6.00
Cup, transparent gr, 1½"	18.00
Cup, transparent red or brn, 1½"	22.00
Plate, transparent gr, 4¼"	8.50
Plate, transparent red or brn, 1½"	15.00

Saucer, baked-on colors, 3¼" 1.50
Saucer, transparent cobalt w/ribs, 3¼" 2.50
Set, 17-pc, transparent gr 185.00
Set, 21-pc, baked-on colors 105.00
Sugar bowl, baked-on colors, w/lid, 1½" 12.00
Sugar bowl, transparent gr, w/lid, 1½" 37.00
Teapot, baked-on colors, w/lid, 1½" 18.00
Teapot, transparent gr, w/lid, 1½" 55.00

Miss America

Creamer, forest gr or marbleized orange/wht.................50.00
Creamer, wht 45.00
Cup, forest gr or marbleized orange/wht.......................40.00
Cup, wht 35.00
Plate, forest gr or marbleized orange/wht 40.00
Plate, wht 25.00
Saucer, forest gr or marbleized orange/wht..................15.00
Saucer, wht 15.00
Sugar bowl, forest gr or marbleized orange/wht, w/lid 60.00
Teapot, forest gr or marbleized orange/wht, w/lid 115.00

Octagonal

Cereal, lg, dk gr, bl, or wht, 3⅜" 9.00
Cereal, lg, lemonade/oxblood, 3⅜" 25.00
Cereal, lg, pk, other opaques, 3⅜" 10.00
Creamer, lg, beige, pumpkin, or lt bl, closed hdl, 1½" 18.00
Creamer, lg, dk gr, bl, or wht, closed hdl, 1½" 9.00
Creamer, sm, dk gr, bl, or wht, 1¼"...........................12.00

Octagonal, Play Time tea set, in various colors, MIB, $120.00.

Plate, sm, dk gr, bl, or wht, 3⅜"................................... 5.00
Saucer, sm, yel or lime gr, 3⅜".................................... 5.00
Set, lg, 21-pc, dk gr, bl, or wht 125.00
Set, lg, 21-pc, lemonade/oxblood, closed hdls, MIB....................375.00
Sugar bowl, sm, dk gr, bl, or wht, 1¼" 14.00
Teapot, lg, bl or gr..16.00
Tumbler, sm, pumpkin, yel, or lime gr, 2" 18.00

Raised Daisy

Creamer, yel, 1¾" 45.00

Cup, bl, 1¾" 42.00
Cup, gr, 1¾" 18.00
Plate, bl, 3" 10.00
Saucer, beige, 2½" 9.00
Sugar bowl, yel, 1¾" 35.00
Teapot, bl, 2⅜" 40.00
Teapot, yel, 2⅜" 40.00
Tumbler, bl (no embossed pattern), 2" 55.00
Tumbler, yel or beige, 2" 18.00

Stacked Disc

Creamer, sm, opaque colors other than gr or wht, 1¼"....................12.00
Creamer, sm, pumpkin, 1¼" 22.00
Cup, sm, opaque gr or wht, 1¼" 5.00
Pitcher, sm, opaque colors other than gr or wht, 2⅞" 14.00
Pitcher, sm, opaque gr, 2⅞" 10.00
Plate, sm, opaque bl, 3¼" 4.00
Set, 21-pc, sm, opaque colors other than gr or wht 165.00
Set, 21-pc, sm, opaque gr or wht 90.00
Sugar bowl, sm, opaque colors other than gr or wht, 1¼"................14.00
Sugar bowl, sm, pumpkin, 1¼" 22.00
Teapot, sm, opaque colors other than gr or wht, 3⅜" 14.00
Teapot, sm, opaque gr or wht, 3⅜" 12.00
Teapot, sm, pumpkin, 3⅜" 30.00
Tumbler, sm, opaque gr or wht, 2" 5.00

Stacked Disc and Interior Panel

Cereal, lg, marbleized bl, 3⅜" 40.00
Cereal, lg, transparent gr, 3⅜" 20.00
Creamer, lg, opaque solid colors, 1⅜" 20.00
Creamer, lg, transparent gr or cobalt, 1⅜" 25.00
Creamer, sm, opaque solid colors, 1¼" 16.00
Cup, lg, transparent cobalt, 1⅜" 20.00
Cup, sm, marbleized bl, 1¼" 35.00
Pitcher, sm, transparent gr, 2⅞" 15.00
Plate, lg, opaque solid colors, 4¾" 10.00
Set, lg, 21-pc, opaque solid colors, MIB......................320.00
Set, lg, 21-pc, transparent cobalt, MIB 420.00
Set, sm, 8-pc, opaque solid colors, MIB........................65.00
Set, sm, 8-pc, transparent cobalt, MIB........................115.00
Sugar bowl, lg, marbleized bl, w/lid, 1⅞" 50.00
Sugar bowl, sm, transparent gr, open, 1¼" 25.00
Teapot, lg, transparent gr, w/lid, 3¾" 45.00
Teapot, sm, transparent gr, w/lid, 2" 30.00
Tumbler, sm, opaque solid colors, 2" 40.00
Tumbler, sm, transparent cobalt, 2" 12.00

Stippled Band

Creamer, lg, transparent gr, 1½".................................18.00
Creamer, sm, transparent amber, 1¼" 27.00
Cup, lg, transparent azure, 1½".................................22.00
Cup, sm, transparent amber, 1¼" 7.00
Pitcher, sm, transparent amber, 2⅞"...........................16.00
Plate, lg, transparent amber, 4¼"............................... 7.00
Plate, lg, transparent azure, 4¼"...............................14.00
Plate, sm, transparent gr, 3¼" 4.00
Saucer, lg, transparent gr, 3¼" 5.00
Set, lg, 17-pc, transparent amber 175.00
Set, sm, 8-pc, transparent gr, MIB...............................40.00
Sugar bowl, lg, transparent amber, w/lid, 1⅞" 22.00
Sugar bowl, sm, transparent amber, open, 1¼" 27.00

Tumbler, sm, transparent amber, 1¾" 8.00
Tumbler, sm, transparent gr, 1¾" 7.00

Miscellaneous

Ash tray, bl, 'clubs' card symbol, 4" dia 45.00
Ash tray, orange, Hotel Lincoln.................................38.00
Bell, bl...75.00
Bell, orange 95.00
Bowl, bl, ivy design, #232 ....10.00
Bowl, bl onyx, 3-ftd, #340 ....18.00
Bowl, red onyx, Ribs & Flutes, #320 ....15.00
Candlestick, gr, 3¼", pr......................................80.00
Candlestick, red onyx, 3¼", pr 225.00

Candlesticks, orange, 3¼", $175.00 for the pair; Tab-handled bowl, orange, #321, $28.00.

Cornucopia, bl onyx, hand held, #766..........................12.00
Cornucopia, gr onyx, mk NYC Vogue Merc 6.00
Cup & saucer, demitasse; beige 18.00
Flowerpot, bl, Graduated Darts, #307 ....15.00
Flowerpot, bl, Ribbed Top w/Darts, #295.......................65.00
Flowerpot, bl onyx, ribbed top, #292 .... 8.00
Flowerpot, bl onyx, Stacked Disc, 2½" 5.00
Flowerpot, gr, mk Made in USA, #1309 ....65.00
Flowerpot, gr onyx, Stacked Disc, 5½" 18.00
Flowerpot, orange, mk Made in USA, #1307 ....75.00
Flowerpot, orange, ribbed top, #293 ....12.00
Flowerpot, orange, Ribs & Flutes, #296 ....10.00
Flowerpot, red onyx, Banded Dart, #300........................24.00
Flowerpot, red onyx, Ribs & Flutes, #297 .... 8.00
J Vivaudou, apothecary jar, bl 45.00
J Vivaudou, mortar & pestle, wht.............................. 8.00
J Vivaudou, powder box, bl, floral 50.00
Knife, crystal, Block, Kitchen Novelty Co NJ, orig box 35.00
Knife, gr, Grid, #739 ....75.00
Lampshade, red onyx..125.00
Powder jar, Apple, orange 150.00
Powder jar, Colonial Lady, gr 125.00
Powder jar, Colonial Lady, transparent, rare 1,200.00
Powder jar, red onyx, Concentric Ring, 3-ftd 24.00
Powder jar, Scotty dog, bl....................................65.00
Powder jar, Scotty dog, royal bl, rare.......................600.00
Tire ash tray, bl onyx, US Rubber 65.00
Vase, red onyx, Ribs & Flutes, #311, 8" 95.00
Vase, yel, Graduated Dart, #316...............................45.00
Westite, ash tray, gr transparent, hexagonal, mk 20.00
Westite, bowl, bl, mk 15.00

Westite, creamer, red onyx, hexagonal 15.00
Westite, vase, gr, 8" 18.00

Alexandrite

Alexandrite is a type of art glass introduced around the turn of the century by Thomas Webb and Sons of England. It is recognized by its characteristic shading, pale yellow to rose and blue. Although it was also produced by other companies, only examples made by Webb command premium prices.

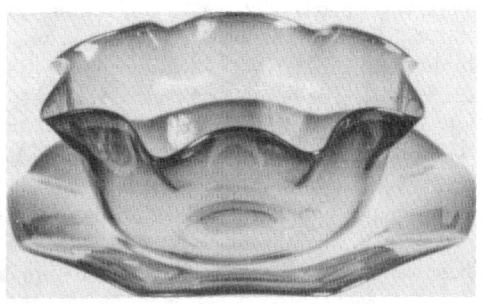

Finger bowl, 5", with underplate, $900.00.

Finger bowl, fluted, 2½x5" 650.00
Match holder, Dmn Quilt, sq top, 3x2½" 650.00
Pitcher, petal top, appl hdl, Webb, 5½" 1,700.00
Tazza, Dmn Quilt, amber ped ft, 1½x4½".................................695.00
Toothpick holder, bulbous w/sq top, Webb, 3x2¾".........................650.00
Tumbler, juice; Honeycomb, Webb, EX color, 3" 800.00

Alhambra China

A line of dinnerware made in Vienna during this century, the Alhambra pattern is strongly geometric with bold colors and gold trim. It is marked with the line name and the country of origin.

Compote, sm...85.00
Cup & saucer 55.00
Cup & saucer, bouillon; dbl hdls...................................60.00
Jam jar, Austria, w/lid & underplate 110.00
Nappy, gold loop hdl 40.00
Pitcher, 8½x4¾" 150.00
Plate, 7½" 20.00
Teapot, openwork, scalloped top, 4¾"...............................150.00
Tray, rnd, integral hdls...75.00

Teapot, 3", $75.00.

Almanacs

The earliest evidence indicates that almanacs were used as long ago as Ancient Egypt. Throughout the Dark Ages they were circulated in great volume and were referred to by more people than any other book except the Bible. *The Old Farmer's Almanac* first appeared in 1793 and has been issued annually since that time. Usually more of a pamphlet than a book (only a few have hard covers), the almanac provided planting and harvesting information to farmers, weather forecasts for seamen, medical advice, household hints, mathematical tutoring, postal rates, railroad schedules, weights and measures, 'receipts,' and jokes. Before 1800 the information was unscientific and based entirely on astrology and folklore. The first almanac in America was printed in 1639 by William Pierce Mariner; it contained data of this nature. One of the best-known editions, *Ben Franklin's Poor Richard's Almanac*, was introduced in 1732 and continued to be printed for 25 years.

By the nineteenth century, merchants saw the advertising potential in a publication so widely distributed, and the advertising almanac evolved. These were distributed free of charge by drug stores and mercantiles and were usually somewhat lacking in information, containing simply a calendar, a few jokes, and a variety of ads for quick remedies and quack cures.

Today their concept and informative, often amusing text make almanacs popular collectibles that may usually be had at reasonable prices. Because they were printed in such large numbers and often saved from year to year, their prices are still low. Most fall within a range of $4 to $15. Very common examples may be virtually worthless; those printed before 1860 are especially collectible. Quite rare and highly prized are the Kate Greenaway 'Almanacks,' printed in London from 1883 to 1897. These are illustrated with her drawings of children, one for each calendar month.

1742, Ames, complete, G 70.00
1789, Hutchins Improved, EX 40.00

Turner's Comic Almanac, two editions: 1839 and 1840, 36 pages, fraying, 8½" x 5½", $165.00 each.

1870, Ben Franklin 27.50
1872, Old Farmer's, G 8.00
1877, Maine Farmer's, EX...10.00
1878, Hostetter's US, remedies, cartoons, EX................................28.00
1882, Dr Jayne's Medical Remedies, EX 15.00
1893, Baer's Agricultural, EX 10.00
1895, Hostetter's for Merchants, Miners, Farmers..., 40-pg 7.50
1897, Old Farmer's, G 8.00

1912, Atlantic Monthly, EX... 7.50
1924, Dr Miles', 33-pg, EX.. 5.00
1934, Poor Richard's, LA Times...25.00
1937, World, 950-pg, EX 8.00
1940, Herbalistic, 1940, EX..15.00
1942, Dr Miles' New Weather Almanac & Handbook, EX............. 5.00
1949, Everson's Hi There Neighbor, Huntington IN, 142-pg 10.00

Aluminum

Aluminum, though being the most abundant metal in the earth's crust, always occurs in combination with other elements. Before a practical method for its refinement was developed in the late nineteenth century, articles made of aluminum were very expensive. After the process for commercial smelting was perfected in 1916, it became profitable to adapt the ductile, non-tarnishing material to many uses.

By the late thirties, novelties, trays, pitchers, and many other tableware items were being produced. They were often hand-crafted with elaborate decoration. Russel Wright designed a line of lovely pieces such as lamps, vases, and desk accessories that are becoming very collectible. Many who crafted the ware marked it with their company logo, and these signed pieces are attracting the most interest. Wendell August Forge (Grove City, PA) is a mark to watch for; this firm produced some particularly nice examples and upwardly mobile market values reflect their popularity with today's collectors. In general, 'spun' aluminum is from the thirties or early forties, and 'hammered' aluminum is from the fifties. Our advisor for this category is Ted Haun; he is listed in the Directory under Indiana. See also Russel Wright.

Basket, Rodney Kent, lg... 9.00
Bowl, chrysanthemums, w/lid, Continental, 11½x9", EX..............20.00
Butter dish, Buenilum 18.00
Cake saver, emb roses & leaves, mk World Hand Forged, 12" 7.50
Cake saver, plain, West Bend... 9.00
Candlestick, Buenilum, tall, pr...25.00
Celery tray, ruffled rim, twisted hdl, 18" 12.50
Cheese dish, Buenilum, w/lid 15.00
Coffee urn, Buenilum, w/stand & warmer..58.00
Console set, tulip, Farberware, bowl+pr short candlesticks 15.00
Hard-boiled egg carrier (for 4), Germany, leather strap 15.00
Martini shaker, spun 15.00
Pitcher, water; heavy strap hdl, Everlast 20.00
Tray, Deco design, Kensington, 20½x12½" 27.50
Tray, Pine Cone, Everlast, 25½x13½" 30.00
Tumbler, water; West Bend, set of 6 ....20.00

AMACO, American Art Clay Co

AMACO is the logo of the American Art Clay Co. Inc., founded in Indianapolis, Indiana, in 1919, by Ted O. Philpot. They produced a line of art pottery from 1931 through 1938 that is today beginning to interest collectors. The company is still in business but now produces only supplies, implements, and tools for the ceramic trade.

Values for AMACO have risen sharply, especially those for figurals, items with Art Deco styling, and pieces with uncommon shapes.

Our advisor for this catgory is Virginia Heiss; she is listed in the Directory under Indiana.

Bowl, #118, bl gloss w/crescent moon hdl, 6" 70.00
Candle holder, #181, bl gloss, Deco, 1¾x4", pr 95.00
Figure, #156, male dancer, wht gloss, 15" 250.00
Figure, #209, Chihuahua dog, bl gloss, 6" 110.00

Figure, seated puma, wht gloss, 4¾" ...85.00
Temple jar, #132, bl gloss, w/lid, 6" ...80.00
Vase, #S-2, gr matt, 4¾" ...30.00
Vase, #19, red matt, bulbous w/hdls, buttressed, 12" ...225.00
Vase, #2, lt bl matt, hdls, 4½" ...35.00
Vase, #74, dk bl matt, stick form, 8" ...95.00

Vase, #114, carved stylized floral reserve, dark red, $65.00.

Amberina

Amberina, one of the earliest types of art glass, was developed in 1883 by Joseph Locke, of the New England Glass Company. The trademark was registered by W.L. Libbey, who often signed his name in script within the pontil.

Amberina was made by adding gold powder to the batch, which produced glass in the basic amber hue. Part of the item, usually the top, was simply reheated to develop the characteristic deep red or fuchsia shading. Early amberina was mold-blown, but cut and pressed amberina was also produced. The rarest type is plated amberina, made by New England for a short time after 1886. It has been estimated that less than 2,000 pieces were ever produced. Other companies, among them Hobbs and Brockunier, Mt. Washington Glass Company, and Sowerby's Ellison Glassworks of England, made their own versions, being careful to change the name of their product to avoid infringing on Libbey's patent. Prices have been erratic at auction for several months; values given below are in the average range. See also Libbey.

Goblets, provenance linking these to Joseph Locke included, $800.00 for the pair.

Basket, clear rigaree at rim/ft, appl prunts, 8x4" ...300.00
Bowl, swirled ribbing & T'prints, w/lid, 5x4" ...350.00
Carafe, Hobnail, polished pontil, 8" ...295.00
Celery vase, Dmn Quilt, scalloped sq top, NE Glass, 6¾" ...500.00
Celery vase, Invt T'print, sq scalloped top, NE Glass, 6½" ...500.00
Creamer, Invt T'print, squat, amber hdl, NE Glass, 2⅝" ...395.00
Creamer, swirled bulbous body, amber hdl, 4⅞x3½" ...145.00
Finger bowl, Dmn Quilt, NE Glass, 2⅜x4½" ...275.00
Finger bowl, Dmn Quilt, trefoil rim, 4½" ...125.00
Finger bowl, 12-crimp top, faint Dmn Quilt, NE Glass, 2x4¼" ...165.00
Mug, Invt T'print, reverse color, 7½" ...425.00
Pitcher, Invt T'print, bulbous, amber hdl, 10x5⅛" ...225.00
Pitcher, Invt T'print, ruffled top, amber hdl, 9½" ...265.00
Pitcher, swirl, amber hdl, milk sz, 7⅜x4⅜" ...195.00
Pitcher, swirl, amber hdl, 7¾x5¼" ...225.00
Pitcher, swirl, cylindrical neck, amber hdl, 7½" ...175.00
Pitcher, tankard, Optic, amber hdl, NE Glass, 7" ...425.00
Punch cup, Dmn Quilt, NE Glass, 2½" ...125.00
Sauce dish, Daisy & Button, scalloped, sq, 5¾" ...110.00
Shaker, pepper; Invt T'print, NE Glass, orig pewter top, 4" ...75.00
Shot glass, HP mc florals & wht dots, 2¾" ...195.00
Sugar shaker, Invt T'print, emb butterfly on lid, bulbous, 4" ...400.00
Toothpick holder, Dmn Quilt, SP holder w/pond lilies, 4½" ...325.00
Tumbler, Dmn Quilt, NE Glass, 4x2⅝" ...120.00
Tumbler, Optic, NE Glass, 3⅝" ...95.00
Tumbler, whiskey; Dmn Quilt, NE Glass, 2¾x2" ...195.00
Vase, amber rigaree, swirled, bulbous, ftd, 10½" ...175.00
Vase, appl crystal spiral trim, 8⅛x2⅝" ...225.00
Vase, cylindrical, NE Glass, 4" ...135.00
Vase, HP orange & pk mums, amber ruffle, 9⅞x5" ...325.00
Vase, Invt T'print, cylindrical w/ruffled rim, 7" ...125.00
Vase, Invt T'print, 3-lobe top, amber petal ft, 5¼x3⅜" ...145.00
Vase, jack-in-pulpit; fuchsia to amber, 7" ...350.00
Vase, lily; ribbed, knob stem, NE Glass, 23½" ...1,250.00
Vase, lily; ribbed, NE Glass, 10" ...500.00
Vase, lily; ribbed, 15" ...500.00
Vase, lily; ribbed, 7" ...375.00
Vase, Optic Panel, cylindrical, NE Glass, 4" ...195.00
Vase, swirled cylinder shape, emb leaves at base, 8⅜" ...150.00
Vase, swirled cylinder shape, 8¾x4¾" ...125.00

Plated Amberina

Bowl, very rare, 2¾" x 4½", $2,750.00.

Butter dish, ribbed, SP base w/unicorn in center, 4¾" ... 3,400.00
Cruet, amber hdl/faceted stopper, EX color, 6½", NM ... 2,500.00
Mug, ribbed, fine color, amber hdl ... 2,100.00
Punch cup, EX ribbing & color ... 1,800.00
Punch cup, ribbed, amber pigtail hdl, fine color, 2¾" ... 2,250.00

Rose bowl, ribbed, 5½" 1,800.00
Shakers, EX ribbing & color, pr.......................................1,800.00
Tumbler, lemonade; deep ribbing, amber hdl, EX color............2,500.00
Tumbler, ribbed...1,600.00

American Encaustic Tiling Co.

A.E. Tile was organized in 1879 in Zanesville, Ohio. Until its closing in 1935, they produced beautiful ornamental and architectural tile equal to the best European imports. They also made vases, figurines, and novelty items with exceptionally fine modeling and glazes.

Advertising pc, maroon heart, 2" 65.00
Bookends, cupid & rabbit, 1926, pr 150.00
Jar, temple; blk, w/lid, 9" 150.00
Paperweight, ram figural 65.00
Tile, Alexander G Bell portrait, bl, mk, dtd 1897, 3" 65.00
Tile, Braham's portrait on gr, floral corners, 6"..........................65.00
Tile, child's portrait, circular, set of 3 ....150.00
Tile, faience, peasant lady w/flowers, bl & wht, 6x6" 65.00
Tile, faience, peasant man at table, 6x6" 65.00
Tile, knight, mc, 10x14x1"...600.00
Tile, stylized Indian in headdress holds shield, mc, 12x8"........385.00
Vase, lt gr, buttress-style arms, 8"...145.00

American Indian Art

That time when the American Indian was free to practice the crafts and culture that was his heritage has always held a fascination for many. They were a people who appreciated beauty of design and colorful decoration in their furnishings and clothing; and because instruction in their crafts was a routine part of their rearing, they were well accomplished. Several tribes developed areas in which they excelled. The Navajo were weavers and silversmiths; the Zuni, lapidaries. Examples of their craftsmanship are very valuable. Today even the work of contemporary Indian artists — weavers, silversmiths, carvers, and others — is highly collectible. For a more thorough study we recommend *North American Indian Artifacts* by our advisor, Lar Hothem; you will find his address in the Directory under Ohio.

Key:
bw — beadwork
dmn — diamond
E — Eastern
NE — Northeastern

p-h — prehistoric
S — Southern
W — Western

Apparel and Accessories

Before the white traders brought the Indian women cloth from which to sew their garments and beads to use for decorating them, clothing was made from skins sewn together with sinew, usually made of buffalo tendon. Porcupine quills were dyed bright colors and woven into bags and armbands and used to decorate clothing and moccasins. Examples of early quillwork are scarce today and highly collectible.

Early in the nineteenth century, beads were being transported via pony pack trains. These 'pony' beads were irregular shapes of opaque glass imported from Venice. Nearly always blue or white, they were twice as large as the later 'seed' beads. By 1870 translucent beads in many sizes and colors had been made available, and Indian beadwork had become commercialized. Each tribe developed its own distinctive methods and preferred decorations, making it possible for collectors today to determine the origin of many items. Soon after the turn of the century, the craft of beadworking began to diminish.

Dress, Plains, hide with fringe and 7-color pony beads, fur trim on sleeve fringe, 52" long, provenance relating to the Tiffany Foundation, $7,200.00.

Belt, Athabascan, buckskin w/4-color quilling, 1880, 31x1½".....400.00
Belt, Chippewa, full loom bw w/florals, 1910, 36x3" 225.00
Belt, Sioux, full bw/loomed geometrics, 1920, 46x2½" 150.00
Belt, Yakima, woven horse hair, mc geometrics, 1925, 36x1½" 70.00
Bonnet, Sioux baby's, full geometric bw, 1890, 8x8"....................700.00
Breech clout, Chippewa, velvet w/mc bw, 1890, 60x17" 350.00
Cap, Iroquois ceremonial, satin w/foliate bw, 1870, 11x6" 125.00
Collar, Apache woman's, mc geometrics, 1880, 10x15"...............150.00
Cuffs, Chippewa, full bw w/florals, 1890, 10x5", pr 150.00
Dress, Crow, red stroud cloth/elk teeth/cowrie shells, 1870..... 1,500.00
Dress, Iroquois, 2-pc hide w/bw & long beaded fringe, 1900........375.00
Dress, Seminole child's, ribbonwork, 1900, 15x16" 400.00
Dress, Sioux, buckskin w/yel ochre on yoke, 1930......................700.00
Gauntlets, Flathead, high-top, buckskin w/bw florals, 1930.........175.00
Gauntlets, Shoshone, full bw, Elk Dreamer's, 1880, 14x8" 900.00
Hair drop, Crow, full bw, 1870, 8" 225.00
Hat, Nez Perce, corn husk fez, 3-color sqs, 1900, 8x6" 1,350.00
Hat, Wasco, full bw w/humans & fish, 19th C, 7" 2,300.00
Headdress, Blackfoot, buffalo horn/fur/bw/hair locks, 1890..... 1,200.00
Jacket, child's, made from antique Pendleton blanket..................155.00
Legging strips, Blackfoot, full mc bw, 1900, 27x3", pr 450.00
Leggings, Cheyenne, bw/fringe, attached to trousers, 1930 ....250.00
Leggings, Cheyenne, full bw w/geometrics, tin cones, 1890 ....850.00
Leggings, Nez Perce, elk hide, pnt/bw panels, 1910, 27x24" 350.00
Leggings, Nez Perce, lg contour bw florals, #16 beads, 1880 ....600.00
Moccasins, Arapaho child's, buffalo hide w/bw toe, 1890.............175.00
Moccasins, Assiniboine, full bw sqs/triangles, 1880, 8½" 650.00
Moccasins, Athabascan child's, smoked moose hide/embr, 1910.400.00
Moccasins, Crow, hide w/fine geometric bw on toe, 1910, 9" 400.00
Moccasins, Crow woman's, floral bw on high tops, 1940, 11"......175.00
Moccasins, Crow woman's, hide w/full geometric bw toe, 1890...300.00
Moccasins, Kiowa child's, high-top, ochre/heavy bw, 1890..... 3,000.00
Moccasins, Sioux, buffalo hide, full bw Xs/triangles, 1890...........750.00
Moccasins, Sioux, buffalo hide, quillwork/bw trim, 1890.............475.00
Moccasins, Sioux, buffalo hide, vivid full bw, 1900, 10"..............500.00
Moccasins, Sioux, full bw, Xs/geometrics, hide sole, 1900 ....400.00
Moccasins, Sioux child's, mc geometric bw, 1890, 7x3" 350.00
Moccasins, Winnebago, hide, floral bw toe/side flaps, 1890.........600.00

Moccasins, Winnebago child's, yel ochre, bw lines, 1890, 8".......**700.00**
Roach, Crow, deer/porcupine quills, red/yel, 1900, 23"................**400.00**
Roach, deer hair/porcupine quills, 1885, 13x6" **200.00**
Roach, Plains, deer hair, porcupine quilled drop, 1860, 16".........**300.00**
Robe, Cheyenne, bearskin, pnt designs, 1870, 62x50" **700.00**
Robe, Sioux child's, doeskin w/red & wht bw strip, 1930 ....**500.00**
Sash, Ojibway ceremonial, bw geometrics, fringe, 1870, 35" **500.00**
Shawl, Kiowa, ribbonwork on bl trade cloth, 1920, 65x45".........**125.00**
Skirt, Kiowa, bl trade cloth w/mc ribbonwork, 1920, 28x29" **120.00**
Skirt, Kiowa, bl trade cloth w/ribbonwork, 1920, 33" L **150.00**
Vest, Cree, finely embr buckskin, 1890, lg..................................**400.00**
Vest, Hopi, full bw w/many many figures & designs, 1965 ...... **1,000.00**
Vest, Santee Sioux, trade cloth, bw/loom-bead strips, 1900.........**200.00**
Vest, Sioux, full bw, mc geometrics on wht, 1930, 20" **1,200.00**

Arrowheads and Points

Relics of this type usually display characteristics of a general area, time period, or a particular location. With study, those made by the Plains Indians are easily discerned from those of the West Coast. Because modern man has imitated the art of the Indian by reproducing these artifacts through modern means, use caution before investing your money in 'too good to be authentic' specimens.

Adena, OH, dk gray, EX color, 3⅞" **68.00**
Breckenridge Dalton, TN, off-wht, 5⅛"..**125.00**
Clovis, AR, off-wht, slight flutes, 2⅝" **88.00**
Clovis, IL, beige, classic, 4¾" **325.00**

Clovis point, early Paleo, ca 9500-9000 BC, found in Ohio in 1980s, 1¼" x 4", M, $900.00+.

Copena, TN, beige, 2" **17.50**
Dalton, AR, lt beige, 3½"..**145.00**
Dalton, MO, off-wht, fluted, 3⅛"...**65.00**
Dalton, MO, off-wht & pk, 4½"...**70.00**
Dalton, MO, tan, 4¼"...**175.00**
Dalton-Hemphill, AL, tan, 3⅛"...**50.00**
Dalton-Hemphill, AR, gray, 3½" **88.00**
Golondrina, TN, off-wht, classic, 3¼" **88.00**
Greenbrier Dalton, TN, dk gray, 1⅞"...**22.50**
Hardin, AR, brn & off-wht, 4¾"...**165.00**
Hardin, IL, gray & tan, 2⅞"...**40.00**
Hemphill, KY, tan shaded, 6"...**150.00**
Keota, AR, brn, 1¼"...**12.50**
Nodena, AR, gray, 1"...**5.00**
Pedernales, TX, beige, 4⅞"...**95.00**
Perdiz, TX, brn, classic, 1¾" **68.00**

Perdiz, TX, off-wht, classic, 1½" **45.00**
Scottsbluff, AR, beige, well made, 3⅝" **150.00**
Scottsbluff, MO, beige, classic, 3½" **160.00**
Sedalia, MO, off-wht, 3⅞"..**50.00**
Snyder, AL, sand color, 4"...**60.00**
Snyder, TN, wine, 3⅞"...**130.00**
Thebes, OH, gray, classic, 3" **180.00**

Arts and Crafts

Box, Mic Mac, quilled birchbark, chevrons, 5½x4½", VG...........**575.00**
Box, Mic Mac, quilled birchbark, dome top, 6½x5", EX.......... **1,000.00**
Box, Ojibway, bark, quillwork/sweet grass on lid, 1910, 7" **150.00**
Canteen, Navajo, silver w/hand-stamped swastikas, 1940, 6" **375.00**
Canteen, Zuni, silver w/solid shell inlay, 1940, 4x4" **300.00**
Cvg, bear, blk argellite, EX detail, 1900, 5x8" **275.00**
Drawing, ink, Navajo weaver, A Tsinajinnie, 1975, 30x18"........**200.00**
Drawing, Sioux, Ghost Dance lodges on muslin, 1890, 17x12" ...**150.00**
Painting, teepee scene, WE Rollins, 1910, 16x10" **800.00**
Painting, 2 Indians at Pueblo, Chas Damrow, 1970, 16x12"........**175.00**
Tempera painting, Pueblo Dancer, Waldo Mootzka, 1935, 11x9" .**500.00**
Watercolor, Navajo Reservation scene, R Draper, '75, 20x21"....**250.00**
Weaving, Navajo, sawtooth motif transitional, 1900, 96x58". **1,000.00**
Weaving, Navajo, Shiprock Yei/rainbow, Lily Johnson, 42x30"..**350.00**
Weaving, Scottish Rite Masonic emblems, 1890, 62x42" **2,500.00**

Bags and Cases

The Indians used bags for many purposes, and most display excellent form and workmanship. Of the types listed below, many collectors consider the pipe bag to be the most desirable form. Pipe bags were long, narrow, leather and bead or quillwork creations made to hold tobacco in a compartment at the bottom and the pipe, with the bowl removed from the stem, in the top. Long buckskin fringe was used as trim and complemented the quilled and beaded design to make the bag a masterpiece of Indian Art.

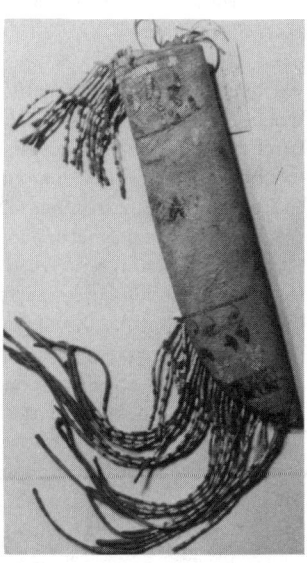

Knife sheath, 3-color quilling, quilled fringe, early, 22", $3,200.00.

Assiniboine, buffalo hide/red trade cloth/bw, 1890, 6x6" **500.00**
Blackfoot, sheath, buffalo hide/bw, sinew sewn, 1800s, 16"..... **1,200.00**
Blackfoot, sheath, tacks, 1880, 14", +lead inlay-hdld knife **4,500.00**
Cayuse, lg floral in contour bw, 1890, 8x6" **600.00**
Cheyenne, pipe, beaded hide, 2 fringed/bw tabs, 1920, 19x6" **350.00**
Cheyenne, pipe, fringed hide w/bw circle & X, 1920, 27x5" **400.00**
Cheyenne, possible, buffalo w/mc lines, 1890, 10x12", pr **2,000.00**

Chippewa, bandolier, full bw, wool fringe, 1880, 68x13" **3,750.00**
Chippewa, bandolier, full bw w/stars & leaves, 1890, 35x12".. **3,850.00**
Chippewa, bandolier, full bw/padre bead drops, 1890, 47x16".. **1,900.00**
Cree, tobacco, contour bw floral panel, fringe, 1870, 23x7" **1,000.00**
Crow, parfleche, elk hide w/VG geometrics, 1800s, 13x27".........325.00
Crow, parfleche, folded rawhide, EX pnt motif, 1880, 28x13" 500.00
Crow, parfleche, rawhide w/pnt bow ties, 1890, 26x14" 800.00
Crow, parfleche, red/bl motif, EX work, 1880, 15x12" 900.00
Crow, parfleche medicine container, pnt symbols, 1870, 5x2" 300.00
Crow, pipe, bw geometrics, quilled bottom/fringe, 1890, 41" .. **2,750.00**
Iroquois, pouch, full bw ea side w/pony beads, 19th C, 8x8".....325.00
Kiowa, bw on hide, lg tin cones on flap/bottom, 1935, 5x4".......250.00
Nez Perce, belt pouch, full bw w/palomino pony, 1890, 5x6" 275.00
Nez Perce, full bw, classic design, 1910, 11x13".........................250.00
NW Coast, pouch, full bw anthropomorphic faces, 1880, 6x4" ...450.00
Plains, knife case, bw/quills/tin cones, 20th C, 10x3" 350.00
Plateau, belt case, semi-contour bw w/cobalt, 1920, 6x6" 250.00
Plateau, belt pouch, full bw w/#16 cut beads, 1890, 6x7" 400.00
Plateau, full bw, bear/2 wolves/pine tree, 1920, 7x7" 150.00
Plateau, full bw, deer/eagle/flowers, 1920, 14x12" 300.00
Plateau, full bw, lg mare & colt, 1920, 11x9" 225.00
Plateau, full bw, 3 bl horses/eagle/Am flags, 1930, 17x14" 600.00
S Plains, strike-a-lite, seed beads/tin cones on hide, 1890.............900.00
Sioux, hide, quilled lines on Xd Am flags, 20th C, 18" 600.00
Sioux, pipe, fringed, bw geometrics/quillwork, 1920, 38x6" **1,750.00**
Sioux, purse, full bw geometrics, bk: florals, 1920, 7x7" 300.00
Sioux, strike-a-lite, full bw/quills/tin cones, 1800s, 10"...............450.00
Skokomish, carrying bag, basketry, row of dogs, 1890, 14x7" .. **1,300.00**
Ute, full bw, tin cones, fringe, 1890, 7x3" 700.00
Yakima, Elk Dreamer's, full bw w/elk & eagle, 1930s...................350.00
Yakima, Elk Dreamer's, lg full bw elk, 1920, 15x14" 300.00
Yakima, full bw w/2 natives in full dress, 1920, 12x16"...............450.00
Yakima, full floral bw, rectangular, 1940, 11x8"..........................100.00

Baskets

In the following listings, examples are basket form and coiled unless noted otherwise.

Apache, bowl, checkerbrd motif, 1910, 4x21" **1,100.00**
Apache, bowl, geometrics, ca 1900, 4x15" 990.00
Apache, bowl, geometrics, 1920, 3x12" 650.00
Apache, bowl, horses/Xs all around, w/lid, 1925, 6x10" **1,600.00**
Apache, bowl, lg star in center/dogs, 1950, 2x12" 700.00
Apache, bowl, mc geometrics/dogs, 1935, 3x4"............................700.00
Apache, bowl, star in center, 1910, 4½x20" **2,750.00**
Apache, San Carlos; burden, w/fringe & tin cones, '70, 6x3" 125.00
Apache, tray, swastikas/Xs all around, 1910, 2½x22" **2,500.00**
Apache, tray, uptrn rim, mc star/geometrics, 1930, 2x13" 550.00
Chemeuvi, olla, vertical chevron band, 1920, pristine, 8x7" ... **3,250.00**
Chemeuvi, tray, lines/geometrics, 1935, 2x6½".............................600.00
Cowlitz, hard/embricated, stairsteps, 1890, 6x5"..........................375.00
Cowlitz, hard/embricated, 2 connecting V bands, 1900, 8x6" 225.00
Cowlitz, medicine basket, human figures, w/lid, 1850, 6x10" .. **1,500.00**
Hopi, 2nd Mesa, bowl, Kachina faces, 1930, 8x6".......................175.00
Hopi, 2nd Mesa, bowl, Kachina figures, 1960, 6x12" 175.00
Hupa, bowl, blk triangles, w/lid, 1920, 7x7½".............................400.00
Hupa, bowl, finely twined, mc parallelograms, 1930, 2x2"...........150.00
Hupa, bowl, twined, mc geometrics, 1920, 3x5" 200.00
Hupa, hat, mc geometrics, 1900, 3x6½".......................................350.00
Hupa, twined, bands of line design, 1910, 6½x5"..........................200.00
Hupa, woman's hat, twined, soft geometrics, 1920, 3x7"..............275.00
Hupa, woman's hat, twined w/brn geometrics, 1910, 4x6"...........250.00
Karok, bowl, twined, blk lightning design, 1890, 5x9" 225.00

Klamath, bowl, geometrics in polychrome, 14" 375.00
Klickitat, hard/embricated, conical w/rim loops, 1930, 5x6"........275.00
Maidu, bowl, red quail topknots in V arrangement, 1890, 17"... **1,700.00**
Maidu, bowl, red/blk stairsteps, 1910, 15x18" 600.00
Mission, bowl, blk line design, 1900, 3x9" L 550.00
Mission, bowl, sidewinder rattlesnake band, 1910, 8x4" 200.00
Mission, bowl, 3 bands of design, w/hdl, 1920, 3x11".................550.00
Mono, bowl, V-design all around, 1920, 4x11" 400.00
Navajo, wedding basket, 1930, 5½x17"..325.00
Nootka, twined, w/birds & sea monsters, w/lid, 1900, 5x4" 150.00
NW Coast, Greek key in red & purple, 2⅜" H 175.00
NW Coast, stairsteps in brns/blk, 3½x6".....................................150.00
Paiute, burden basket, conical, bands of lines, 1920, 9x8" 125.00
Paiute, seed jar, twined, cord hdls, 1910, 9x6"............................250.00
Panamint, bowl, mc radiating steps, 1900, 4½x15".................. **5,500.00**
Papago, bowl, birds all around, 1965, 3x14"................................200.00
Papago, bowl, 4 lg beetles, 1940, 4x17" 250.00
Papago, olla, butterflies/eagles all around, 1960, 8x6"................250.00
Papago, olla, Grecian-shaped w/key design, 1920, 13x9" 400.00
Papago, olla, lg stylized cactus flowers, 1920, 14x11" 275.00
Papago, olla, mc human figures all around, 1935, 6x5½" 185.00
Papago, storage, Gila monsters all around, 1960, 17x13".............300.00
Papago, tightly coiled, pine trees all around, 1940, 8x6" 200.00
Papago, waterbugs/Gila monsters/horned toads, 1920, 12x15" 475.00
Pima, bowl, arrowhead design, 1910, 3x5"..................................150.00
Pima, bowl, blk fret design, 1935, 1x2½"....................................250.00
Pima, bowl, classic Pima fret design, 1910, 7x17" **1,000.00**
Pima, bowl, dmns/bl Padre beads at top, 1910, 5x3" 325.00
Pima, bowl, fret motif, 1920, 2x12"..275.00
Pima, bowl, geometrics, 1940, 3x12" 325.00
Pima, bowl, geometrics & Maltese cross in dk brn, 8½".............425.00
Pima, bowl, Padre beads at top, swastikas/Xs, 1910, 2x6"...........250.00
Pima, bowl, swastikas all around, star in bottom, 1920, 14" 400.00
Pima, child's hat, geometrics, 1920, 8x3½"..................................450.00
Pima, fine weave, birds all around, 1920, 2x3" 200.00
Pima, goblet form, mc stairsteps, 1920, 2x2½" 200.00
Pima, grain storage, swastikas all around, 1910, 15x14" 800.00
Pima, human figure (6 repeats), 1910, 5x8"................................300.00
Pima, lt on dk diagonals, w/lid, 1940, 1½x1¼" 300.00
Pima, negative fret design, w/lid, 1965, 1½x1½" 250.00
Pima, olla, EX fret design, 1920, 12x10" 700.00
Pima, olla, slanting line designs, 1900, 14x14" 450.00
Pima, plate, finely coiled, squash blossom design, 1965, 5" 275.00
Pima, tray, Greek key motif, 1920, 3x13½" 600.00
Pima, tray, lg dk turtle in center, 1965, 4x5" 125.00
Pima, tray, 4 concentric stars, 1920, 1½x12" 425.00
Pima, 6 full-length horned toads, 1800s, 14" dia..................... **1,500.00**
Pima Ghia, carrying basket, loose weave, 1870, 27" dia..............500.00
Pomo, Bam Tush tray, twined, 1900, 3x10"................................175.00
Pomo, bowl, red flame design, shells around top, 1910, 4x6".......650.00
Pomo, bowl, woven feathers in geometric design, 1950, 2½".......375.00
Pomo, bowl, 1-rod, negative stars, beads/feathers, 1910, 4" 650.00
Pomo, gift type, feathers/beads/quail topknots, 1910, 8" **5,260.00**
Pomo, 1-rod bowl, triangle motif, 1900, 1x2½".........................300.00
Skokomish, twined, dogs/terraces, rim loops, 1920, 11x6" 500.00
Tlingit, twined, mc dmns, openwork, 1900, 9x5" 125.00
Tlingit, twined, triangle design, w/lid, 1900, 9x4"......................800.00
Tlingit, twined, 2 bands of geometrics, 1900, 3x3".....................175.00
Tulare, bowl, 2 lines of rattlesnake designs, 1930, 4x7" 600.00
Tulare, bowl, 2 rattlesnake bands, 1920, 9x18" **2,600.00**
Tulare, gambling tray, classic design, 1890, 1x17" **1,000.00**
Tulare, red/blk stairsteps, bottle-neck shoulder, 1935, 8x5" **4,000.00**
Washo, bowl, flame motif, 1920, 3½x5"................................... **1,350.00**
Washo, bowl, red/blk connecting Vs, 1900, 3½x6" **1,850.00**

Washo, bowl, 1-rod, geometrics, by Tootsie Dick, 1920, 7x4".. **1,000.00**
Wintun/Pomo, bowl, V-design, clam shell disks, 1890, 6x3" **900.00**
Woodlands, woven splint w/faded gr & natural, w/lid, 3¾" **45.00**

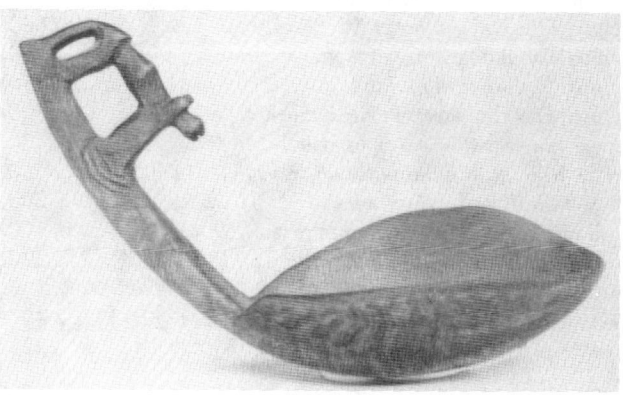

Wall basket, painted green, 1850s, minor splint loss, 27" x 12½", $3,200.00.

Blankets, Navajo

Pueblo Indians first made blankets centuries ago, but today most are made by Navajo Indians. Pendleton and Hudson's Bay blankets became widely available in the 1800s; around the turn of the century, rugs were developed because tourists were more likely to buy them as floor coverings and wall-hangings. Rugs or blankets are made in various regional styles; an expert can usually identify the area where it was made, sometimes even the individual who made it. The colors of wool are natural (gray-white, brown-black), vegetal (from plant dyes), or artificial (aniline, from synthetic chemicals.) Value factors include size, tightness of weave, artistry of design, and condition. Examples by artists whose names are well known command the higher prices.

Eye Dazzler, transitional, 1890, 51x39"..**600.00**
Eye Dazzler Sampler, Germantown, 1890, 32x22" **200.00**
Transitional, dmns/geometrics, 1910, 93x62"...............................**800.00**
Transitional, lines of parallelograms, 1910, 75x56", VG..............**300.00**
Transitional, red/brn/wht homespun, 1910, 76x54"......................**750.00**
Transitional, soft weave, striped design, 1890, 54x52".................**425.00**

Ceremonial Items

Amulet, Shaman's, Tlingit, ivory w/abalone inlay, 1910, 4½".....**275.00**
Bird stone, Mound Builder, pop-eyed, gr/gray, p-h, 4x2"..............**100.00**
Bowl, Tlingit, seal feast, wood w/ivory & abalone, 1910, 14" **550.00**
Dance wand, Plains, 2 joined horns on beaded hdl, 20th C.........**175.00**
Drum, Blackfoot, pnt symbols on hide, 1910, 3x18" **400.00**
Drum, Cheyenne, pnt bow/arrows on hide, 1920, 5x14"..............**325.00**
Drum, Chippewa, pnt hide-covered tree trunk, 1930, 4x15" **300.00**
Drum, Pueblo, hide w/pnt warrior symbol 1880, 4x16"............ **1,500.00**
Fetish, Kiowa, S Plains, umbilical, full bw, 1860, 5".....................**350.00**
Fetish, Plains, umbilical, hide w/bw & tin cones, 1890, 5" **150.00**
Fetish, Sioux, umbilical full bw lizard, 1910, 7x4".......................**100.00**
Fetish, Sioux, umbilical lizard, bw/quilled bk, 20th C, 9"............**300.00**
Fetish, Zuni, antler serpent w/beads & turq, 1900 ....**225.00**

Fetish, Zuni, human, antler, feather/bead wraps, 1930, 5" **275.00**
Hat, Iroquois, velvet w/wide bw band, 1870, 4x7" **225.00**

Horn spoon, Wasco/Wishram, animal figure on handle, decorated on back of bowl, 1800s, 7½", $2,900.00.

Human scalp, Piegan, w/orig holders & medicine sticks, 1840 ....**700.00**
Mask, Iroquois False Face, twined corn husk, 1930, 13x11" **500.00**
Mask, Kwakiutl, mask, cvd/pnt wood, somber face, 1900, 10" **300.00**
Mask, Kwakiutl, Tsonoqua, cvd/pnt/human hair, 1920, 17x10" ..**450.00**
Mask, NW Coast, hide/human hair/abalone inlay, 20th C, 9x7"..**400.00**
Mask, Tlingit, cvd & pnt w/long human hair, 1890, 11x7" **400.00**
Maskette wand, cvd & pnt wood w/teeth, 1900, 15x5"...............**300.00**
Medicine rock, excavated, Columbia River near Dalles, p-h **150.00**
Necklace, medicine; Blackfoot, buffalo teeth/beads, 1870...........**700.00**
Rattle, Blackfoot, dew claw, leather hdl w/drops, 1910, 10" **150.00**
Rattle, Comanche, gourd peyote, bw hdl/fringe, 1930, 14x3"......**300.00**
Rattle, Crow, buffalo hide, cvd, hair/feathers, 1860, 8x2"............**250.00**
Rattle, medicine; Crow, deer hoof/tinklers, bw drop, 1870 ....**600.00**
Rattle, Plains, buffalo scrotum w/pnt designs, 1870, 5" **350.00**
Spoon, Tlingit, horn w/totemic cvd hdl, 1880, 9x2"...................**500.00**
Staff, Shaman's, Tsimshian, 5 cvd figures, 1850, 9x2" **275.00**
Tabletta, Pueblo, Butterfly Dancer, 20th C, 22x13" **200.00**
Talking stick, cvd/inlaid wood, 1920, 48x2"..................................**85.00**
Wand, Plains, buffalo horn dance, full bw hdl, 20th C, 36"........**225.00**
Wand, Sioux, buffalo horn dance, fur-wrap hdl, 1890, 44" **800.00**

Dolls

Athabascan, beaded seal skin dress, 1880, 10" **250.00**
Cheyenne, hide face, bw mocs/leggings/earrings, 1880, 10x7".....**900.00**
Crow, hide face, trade cloth dress w/bw trim, 1920, 11" **125.00**

Hopi Kachinas, left: possibly 'Early Morning,' minor loss, 11", right: possibly 'Takus,' repaired, 11", $950.00 each.

Kachina, Chipmunk, old-style, cvd from 1 pc, 1950, 9x3"..........**350.00**
Kachina, Crow Mother, by F Tala Hongna, dtd 1927, 11" **450.00**
Kachina, Ogre, in dancing position, 1940, 17x5" **150.00**
Kachina, One Ear, cvd/pnt, 1890, 8½x3" **800.00**
Kachina, Pahlik Mana, tabletta/pnt cape/feathers, 1900s, 27" **350.00**
Kachina, Shalako, 1945, 27x6" **350.00**
Kachina, Shooting Star, sgn Henry Shelton, 1975, 20" **500.00**
Mojave, pottery, w/breech clout, hair, beads, 1870, 5x2"..........**400.00**
Navajo, handmade, full ceremonial dress, 1940, 14" **50.00**
Plains, bw/leather shirt & trousers, 1880, 12" **200.00**
Shoshone, EX bw dress, human scalp hair, 1890, 16"...................**500.00**
Shoshone, full costume w/bw, scalp for hair, 1890, 10x5"...........**300.00**
Sioux, bw/quilled dress, human hair, 1900, 13x5" **550.00**
Sioux, ochre/bw shirt & leggings, quilled hairpc, 1890, 13" **2,400.00**
Skookum, w/blanket & war bonnet, 1920, 18"............................**225.00**

Domestics

Bowl, Great Lakes, cvd animal w/brass tack eyes, 1900, 4x9" **125.00**
Bowl, Great Lakes, cvd wood, native rpr, 1870, 4x11".................**125.00**
Bowl, Wasco, wood w/cvd dot bands, sq rim, 1840, 4x11"...........**350.00**
Cradle, Nez Perce, bw top, holds buckskin doll, 1890, 32" **3,000.00**

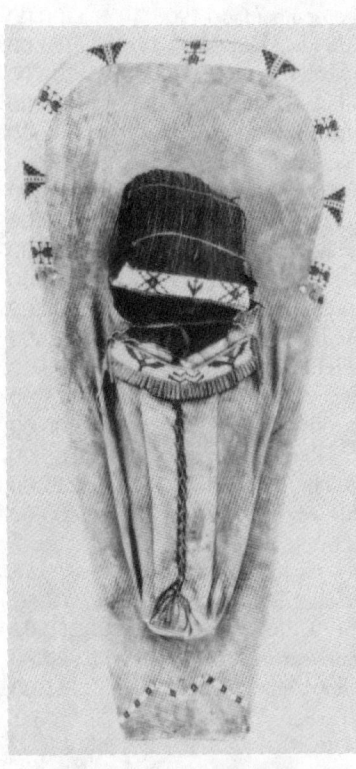

Cradleboard, Plains, beaded and fringed hide, basketry hood, yellow pigment, Ute Reservation Period, 39", $650.00.

Cradle, Sioux, full bw w/hawk bells, orig brds, 1890, 28" **4,750.00**
Ladle, Wasco/Wishram, ram's horn, 1860, 19x5" **250.00**
Mortar, Wasco, stone, cvd sunburst, Dalles OR, 1700, 6"............**300.00**
Spoon, Navajo, hand-stamped silver, 1950s, collection of 4........**225.00**
Spoon, Tlingit, cvd wood w/abalone inlay eyes, 1870, 10x3" **400.00**
Toy cradle, Menomenee, tacks/sunshade, 1890, 17x6" **150.00**
Toy cradle, Nez Perce, hide w/line bw, 1920, 24"....................**400.00**
Toy cradle, Sioux, bw/quillwork, muslin/hide top, 1890, 10".......**350.00**
Toy cradle, Sioux, hide w/bw, tacked brds, 20th C, 25" **500.00**

Jewelry

As early as 500 A.D., Indians in the Southwest drilled turquoise nuggets and strung them on cords made of sinew or braided hair. The Spanish introduced them to coral, and it became a popular item of jewelry; abalone and clam shells were favored by the Coastal Indians. Not

until the last half of the nineteenth century did the Indians learn to work with silver. Each tribe developed its own distinctive style and preferred design, which until about 1920 made it possible to determine tribal origin with some degree of accuracy. Since that time, because of modern means of communication and travel, motifs have become less distinct.

Quality Indian silver jewelry may be antique or contemporary. Age, though certainly to be considered, is not as important a factor as fine workmanship and good stones. Pre-1910 silver will show evidence of hammer marks, and designs are usually simple. Beads have sometimes been shaped from coins. Stones tend to be small; when silver wire was used, it is usually square. To insure your investment, choose a reputable dealer.

Beads, Plains, bone pipes/cowrie shells/blk beads, 1800s **75.00**
Bolo, Navajo, kite shape, very lg Bizbee turq+pc coral, 4" **300.00**
Bow guard, Navajo, silver, turq/oyster shell swastika, 1935..........**125.00**
Bracelet, Navajo, heavy, lg turq stone, 1935, 2" W **85.00**
Bracelet, Navajo, heavy, set w/lg bl gem turq, 1950, 7x2" **125.00**
Bracelet, Navajo, heavy, w/17 gr turq cabs in 3 rows, 1925..........**200.00**
Bracelet, Zuni, 3" dia top set w/100 natural turq, 1935 ....**350.00**
Concho belt, Navajo, hand hammered, w/turq & 6 butterflies....**250.00**
Concho belt, Navajo, ovals w/1 turq in ea, 1935, 40x3" **500.00**
Concho belt, Navajo, sandcast, turq in ea+1 in buckle, 1950......**150.00**
Concho belt, Navajo, stamped t'birds/butterflies, '35, 1" W **150.00**
Necklace, Chumash, shell disk beads, 1800, extra long **150.00**
Necklace, dimes/quarters, 1886 silver dollar drop, 1950, 28".......**350.00**
Necklace, Navajo, turq nuggets w/2 pr lg jacklas, 1930.................**250.00**
Necklace, Navajo, 11 turq-set silver crosses on beads, 1940 ....**350.00**
Necklace, Navajo, 12 quarters/heavy beads, naja, 1930, 26".......**300.00**
Necklace, Navajo, 3-strand turq nuggets on heishi, 1940, 30".......**70.00**
Necklace, Navajo, 5 lg turq drops, 1950, 16", +earrings...............**200.00**
Necklace, Santo Domingo, lg grad rolled turq, 1950, 20" **150.00**
Necklace, Santo Domingo, random-cut turq/wht heishi, 1935 ...**125.00**
Necklace, Santo Domingo, 2-strand shell bird fetish, 1960 ....**100.00**
Necklace, Sioux, elk teeth & trade beads, 1890, extra long.........**450.00**
Necklace, Sioux, grizzly claws/bone/quills/beads, 1890, 42"..... **3,500.00**
Necklace, Sioux, hair pipe beads w/faceted beads, 1890, 36".......**150.00**
Necklace, Zuni, 5-strand fetish, mixed stones, 20th C **200.00**
Pin, Pueblo Manta, 2 joined disks w/sm turq cabs, 1900, 4".........**500.00**
Pin, Zuni, bow tie form set w/75 sm turq cabs, 1935, 6x2" **175.00**
Squash blossom necklace, Navajo, heavy silver, 1925, 24" **550.00**
Squash blossom necklace, Navajo, 12 w/simple naja, 1930, 32" ..**200.00**
Squash blossom necklace, Navajo, 30 w/turq, 2-strand, 1935 ......**550.00**
Squash blossom necklace, Zuni, petit point, 14-plaque, '40.........**450.00**
Trade beads, red Venetian 'feather' type, 1840, 22" **50.00**
Trade beads, Venetian, various shapes, 1840, 66" **105.00**

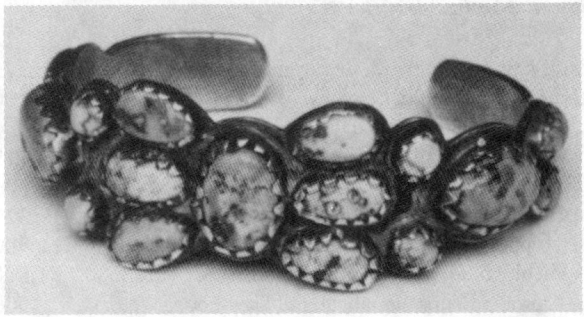

Bracelet, Navajo, early 20th century, set with 19 untreated stones, $450.00.

Knives and Chipped Blades

The knife was an indispensable tool to the Indian whether he was in battle, hunting game, or doing chores at the campsite. Before the white man's metal blades, all were made of copper, obsidian, flint, or chert. Knife cases fashioned of leather with intricate decorations of quilling or beadwork were sometimes suspended from the neck, or they were attached to the belt.

Adena, IL, off-wht, 5⅛" **75.00**
Archaic, AR, lt gray, 3¾" **17.50**
Base-tang, TX, gray, Late Archaic, 6½" **365.00**
Corner-tang, NB, beige, 4¾" **250.00**
Corner-tang, TX, brn, thin, well made, 5⅜" **195.00**
Corner-tang, TX, off-wht, 4½" **250.00**
Crooked, Great Lakes, wire-wrapped bird-form hdl, 1890, 9" **350.00**
Flake, TX, brn tones, 3¼" **12.00**
Kinney, TX, beige, 3" **22.50**
North, MO, rose, 4½x2⅞" **175.00**
Notched curved, TX, gray, 5⅞" **200.00**
Oval-ended, MO, gray, 3¾" **22.50**
Paleo, AR, gray & tan, 3¼", VG **50.00**
Sq bk, AR, brn & wine, 3¾" **22.00**
Sq bk, AR, gray & tan, 3¼" **7.50**
Sq bk, TX, gray, fine flaking, Archaic, 8⅜" **365.00**
Tlingit, copper, animal effigy hdl w/human hair, 1890, 16" **400.00**
Yurok, ceremonial, obsidian, p-h, 7x3" **125.00**
4-beveled, KS, gray, 6¼" **185.00**

Pipes

Pipe bowls were usually carved from soft stone, such as catlinite or pipestone, an argilaceous sedimentary rock composed mainly of clay. Granite was also used. Some ceremonial pipes were simply styled, while others were intricately designed naturalistic figurals, sometimes in bird or frog forms called effigies. Their stems, made of wood and often covered with leather, were sometimes nearly a yard in length.

Blk L-bowl, pewter/pipestone inlay, tacked bw stem, 20th C **275.00**
Blk stone, full bw/fringe on stem, 20th C, 23x4" **200.00**
Catlinite, pewter inlay, 5x12" **1,100.00**
Cherokee, blk stone, wolf head 1 end, raccoon opposite, 10" **300.00**
Chippewa, human face bowl, file-burned stem, 1870, 17x3" **500.00**
Clay, French trade pipe, Canadian, 1840, 3x1½" **75.00**
Hopi, pottery w/classic pnt designs, 1890, 8x3" **375.00**
Pipe tomahawk, brass, burl wood stem, 1860, 17x7" **1,200.00**
Pipe tomahawk, brass, tacked hide on stem, 20th C, 24x11" **250.00**
Pipe tomahawk, pewter inlay, brass trim, presentation, 1800 .. **3,250.00**
Plains, blk T-bowl, catlinite/pewter inlay, bw stem, 20th C **400.00**
Plains, catlinite T-bowl w/pewter inlay, 1890, 34x4" **400.00**
Plains, catlinite w/pewter inlay, hatchet head, 1890, 16x6" **200.00**
Red catlinite T-bowl, quilled wood stem, 1880, 33x5" **1,600.00**
Sioux, catlinite, cvd stem/bowl, 1880, 15" **350.00**
Sioux, catlinite T-bowl, long puzzle stem, 1870, 43x2" **6,500.00**
Tesuque, pottery, orig stem, 1880, 13x2" **100.00**

Pottery

Indian pottery is nearly always decorated in such a manner as to indicate the tribe that produced it or the pueblo in which it was made. For instance, the designs of Cochiti potters were usually scattered forms from nature or sacred symbols. The Zuni preferred an ornate repetitive decoration of a closer configuration. They often used stylized deer and bird forms, sometimes in dimensional applications.

Acoma, jar, eggshell thin, traditonal design, 1915, 9x11" **400.00**
Acoma, jar, geometrics/curvilinears, 1910, 7x6" **350.00**
Acoma, jar, geometrics/fine lines, scalloped, 1940, 9x6" **225.00**
Acoma, jar, geometrics/stylized florals, 1890, 6x5" **300.00**
Acoma, olla, curvilinears/fine lines, 1920, 10x10" **300.00**
Acoma, olla, geometrics/fine lines, 1890, 13x11" **1,900.00**
Acoma, olla, stylized bird/fine lines, 1900, 9½x7" **425.00**
Acoma, olla, thin-walled, 3-color, EX work, 1930, 10x12" **550.00**
AR, scoop, red on buff, human effigy hdl, p-h, 5" **225.00**
Bitahoochee, shoulder jar, mc geometrics, p-h, 7x4" **400.00**
Bowl, blk on blk, sgn Nita, worn, 5" **85.00**
Casas Grandes, bird effigy jar w/geometrics, p-h, 8x6" **150.00**
Casas Grandes, bird-form bowl, pnt decor, p-h, 12" **200.00**
Casas Grandes, jar, mc birds, minor wear, 8" **150.00**
Casas Grandes, jar, mc decor, human effigy on top, p-h, 7" **225.00**
Casas Grandes, jar, stylized feathers, p-h, 8x7" **175.00**
Casas Grandes, olla, blk on red, sgn Silviera, 1988, 13x8" **200.00**
Casas Grandes, snake effigy jar, blk on buff, p-h, 7x7" **250.00**
Chaco, pitcher, stylized bird effigy, blk/wht, p-h, 6x5" **850.00**
Cochiti, animal figure, blk trim, 1910, 4x6" **250.00**
Hohokam, olla, red geometrics on buff, p-h, 13x11" **500.00**
Hopi, bowl, lg Clown Kachina pnt inside, 1900, 2x6" **450.00**
Hopi, canteen, EX mc bird motif, 1920, 6x4¾" **375.00**
Hopi, jar, old Nampeyo designs, 1935, 5x6" **100.00**
Hopi, jar, 4-color, Nampeyo designs, 1930, 16x10" **2,300.00**
Hopi, pot, stylized parrots, 1930, 12" dia **550.00**
Hopi, tile, Sunface motif, 1820, 4x4½" **325.00**
Hopi, vase, stylized bird design, 1920, 9x5" **400.00**
Jeddito, bowl, blk on buff, designs w/in & w/o, p-h, 4x8" **500.00**
Laguna, olla, mc geometrics, 1880, 9½x8½" **2,700.00**
Maricopa, pot, blk on red, sgn Ida Redbird, 1955, 5x5" **125.00**
Mesa Verde, bowl, blk/wht geometrics w/in, p-h, 4x9" **200.00**
Mesa Verde, mug, blk on wht, from McElmo Canyon, p-h, 4½" .**200.00**
Mesa Verde, olla, blk bands on wht, hdls, p-h, 16x10" **400.00**
Mesa Verde, pitcher, blk stairsteps on wht, p-h, 8x9" **300.00**
Papago, bowl, Anasazi design in cream & buff, 1900, 6x7" **100.00**
Santa Clara, basket, blk w/cvd serpent, M Naranjo, 1960, 7" **200.00**
Santa Clara, blk on blk, sgn Tonita Juan, minor wear, 4x6" **175.00**
Santa Clara, jar, cvd blk ware, Margaret Tafoya, 1961, 5" **700.00**
Santa Clara, jar, cvd blk ware, sgn Belin Tapia, 1975, 8x9" **600.00**
Santa Clara, shoulder jar, blk w/imp design, 1910, 8x4" **150.00**
Santa Clara, vase, blk w/cvd serpent, Margaret Tafoya, 10" **1,250.00**
Santa Clara, wedding vase, blk clouds on blk, Pula, 1950, 9" **200.00**
Santo Domingo, bowl, geometrics, 1900, 5x8" **150.00**
Santo Domingo, jar, blk curvilinears on cream, 1920, 8x7" **200.00**
Shipibo, storage jar, geometrics, 1920, 19x20" **425.00**
Socorro, pitcher, blk on wht fine lines, p-h, 8x10" **300.00**
Zia, olla, curvilinear/foliate motif, 1890, 9½x8½" **1,500.00**
Zuni, bowl, curvilinears w/in & w/o, 1880, 4x11" **1,500.00**
Zuni, bowl, mc curvilinears w/in, 1880, 4½x9½" **350.00**
Zuni, candle holder, frog on hdl, 1920, 6½" **150.00**
Zuni, jar, florals/geometrics, 1890, 6½x5" **250.00**
Zuni, Kiva bowl, polywogs, terraced rim, 1890, 3½x6" **250.00**
Zuni, olla, heartline deer, 1990, 8" dia **600.00**
Zuni, pot, polywogs/dragonflies, terraced rim, 1950, 6x4" **75.00**

Pottery, San Ildefonso

The pottery of the San Ildefonso pueblo is especially sought after by collectors today. Under the leadership of Maria Martinez and her husband Julian, experiments began about 1918 which led to the development of the 'black-on-black' design achieved through exacting methods of firing the ware. They discovered that by smothering the fire at a specified temperature, the carbon in the smoke that ensued caused the pottery to blacken. Maria signed her work from the late teens to the 1960s; she died in 1980. Today a piece with her signature may bring prices in the $500 to $4,500 range.

Bowl, blk/blk, ascending stairsteps, sgn Carlos Dunlap, 10" 450.00
Bowl, blk/blk, geometrics, sgn Marie & Julian, wear, 4x5" 475.00
Bowl, blk/blk, incurvate, sgn Maria & Santana, 1965, 5x14" 575.00
Bowl, blk/blk, sgn Marie & Julian, 4x3" 375.00
Jar, blk/blk, serpent motif, sgn Marie, w/lid, 1935, 8x5½" **1,600.00**
Jar, polished blk, sgn Maria Poveka (Martinez), 1965, 6x6" **1,000.00**
Olla, red w/blk pnt curvilinears, 1900, 8x6" 500.00
Olla, Xs w/in triangles, 1900, 9x8" **2,600.00**

Plate, black-on-black motif of parrots and ducks, signed Marie & Julian, 12" diameter, $4,800.00.

Plate, blk/blk, serpent motif, unsgn, 1940, 12" 475.00
Plate, blk/blk, 4-part design, Maria & Julian, 1935, 1x5" 300.00
Plate, polished blk ware, sgn Marie, 1950, 10" 750.00

Rugs, Navajo

Bird pictorial w/geometrics, 1920, 58x46" 250.00
Bl-Head Yei, 4-figure, near-tapestry quality, 1960, 37x29" 350.00
Central lozenge, geometrics w/arrows, 1930, 67x52" 900.00
Coalmine Mesa, raised outlines, natural wool, 1960, 68x46" 700.00
Crystal, central geometric motif, 1930, 70x46", VG 350.00
Crystal, Xs/triangles, natural wool, 1935, 73x42" 850.00
Ganado Red, connecting X-design, 1930, 68x50" 475.00
Ganado Red, mc geometrics/feathers, 1950, 85x55" **1,400.00**
Ganado Red, old-style storm design, 1930, 40x23" 225.00
Klagetoh, sawtooth motif, 1960, 83x50" 450.00
Pictorial, birds/tree/basket, from the Gap, 1989, 44x27" 500.00
Pine Springs, vegetal dye, Laverne Begay, 1975, 50x27" 250.00
Rnd Blanket type, stylized corn stalks, 1920, 58x46" 250.00
Shiprock, Greek key motif forms dmn outline, 1950, 73x48" 850.00
Storm pattern, earth tones, from the Gap, 1965, 32x24" 225.00
Storm pattern, fine weave, 1940, 38x26" 300.00
Teec Nos Pos, mc outline motif, Nellie Kee, 1975, 75x54" **1,500.00**
Terraced central lozenge, tight weave, 1930, 112x64" **2,600.00**
Two Gray Hills, all natural wool, tight weave, 1940, 89x57" .. **2,250.00**

Two Gray Hills, central lozenge, natural wool, 1930, 50x23" 250.00
Two Gray Hills, central lozenge, natural wool, 1975, 60x41" 550.00
Two Gray Hills, fine weave, Helena Begay, 1989, 42x31" **3,500.00**
Two Gray Hills, swastikas/Xs, natural wool, 1920, 100x63" 950.00
Two Gray Hills, triangles, natural wool, 1960, 54x39" 250.00
W Reservation, geometrics, 1935, 72x43" 550.00
W Reservation, geometrics, butterfly border, 1940, 57x33" 250.00
W Reservation, geometrics/dmns/Vs, 1935, 82x41" 800.00
W Reservation, stylized water bugs, 1940, 84x42" 450.00
Wide Ruins, bands of designs, vegetal dye, 1950s, 60x35" 450.00
Yei, Rainbow Man & corn stalks, 1960, 42x35" 450.00
Yei, 3-figure, EX color, 1935, 28x28" 200.00
Yei, 9 dancers/rattlesnakes, 1900, 68x34", EX 950.00

Tools

Adz, MO, beige kaolin flint, chipped & polished, 6½" 120.00
Awl, AR, polished bone, 2¾" 35.00
Axe, IL, greenstone, ¾-grooved, 5½x3" 40.00
Axe, MO, tan, dbl bit, 5¼x2⅝" 45.00
Celt, AR, brn, ground, 3¼", EX 24.00
Celt, IL, gray, chipped & polished, 6½" 138.00
Celt, KY, chipped, 5" 45.00
Celt, KY, ground, 4¼" 40.00
Celt, MO, chipped hematite, 2¼" 20.00
Celt, MO, flint, ca 300-400 BC, 7½" 55.00
Celt, MO, off-wht flint, 5⅜" 22.00
Drill, AR, Friley, off-wht, ¾" 10.00
Drill, AR, off-wht, 1⅜" 18.00
Drill, AR, oval end, tan, 2" 12.50
Drill, AR, wine stripes, 1⅛" 12.00
Drill, MO, off-wht & rose, 2⅞" 48.00
Drill, TN, dk gray, dvtl, rare type, 3⅜" 50.00
Drill, TN, gr & blk, sq bk, 4" 22.50
Drill, TX, Angostura, ivory & tan, 2¾" 27.50
Hide scraper, elk antler, w/many mks, 1860, 14x5" 150.00
Hoe, AR, notched Mississippian style, ca 1200s, 4" 110.00
Hoe, AR, tan & gray, notched, 5x4" 115.00
Hook, halibut; Haida, yel cedar cvd as 2 seals, 1800s, 12" 350.00
Scraper, Tsimshian, slate blade, wood effigy hdl, 1860, 11" 125.00
Spade, MO, polished, 9¼" 180.00

Weapons

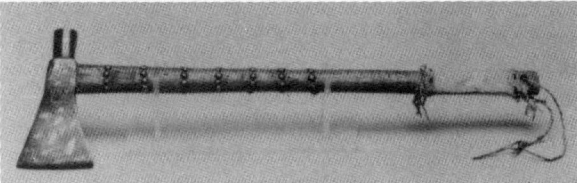

Tomahawk, Plains, engraved initials, file marks, brass tacks, and hide hand-grip beaded in dark green and sky blue, 22", $2,900.00.

Bow, Costal, horn tip, red stain, 1850, 71x1" 200.00
Bow, Plains, sinew bkd, wood w/pnt geometrics, 1870, 30x2" 200.00
Bow, Plains, wood w/red & blk pnt designs, 1850, 48x2" 300.00
Bow, Woodlands, sinew bkd, horn tips, 1850, 75x1" 400.00
Club, Plains, dbl-ended stone head, bw on hdl, 20th C, 27x5"....125.00
Club, Plains, dbl-ended stone head, full bw hdl, 20th C 200.00
Club, Plains, stone, braided horse hair over hdl, 1890, 22" 500.00
Club, Plains, stone head, wood hdl w/bw, 1890, 16x2" 125.00

Club, Plains, 3 blades made from files, tacked, 1890, 27x7".........**225.00**
Club, Plains Flop Knob, hide covered/horse hair drop, 1890 ....**300.00**
Club, Sioux, bw/quillwork, buckskin drop, 1880, 23"..................**350.00**
Club, Sioux, full bw over egg-shape head & hdl, 1880, 23x9". **1,600.00**

Miscellaneous

Axe, Plains, pipe-shape catlinite/horse hair over hdl, 1900 ....**100.00**
Blanket, Chimayo, gr w/arrows & geometrics, 1940, 84x52" **275.00**
Blanket, Kiowa, bl trade cloth w/beading, 1910, 74x59"..............**175.00**
Blanket, Pendleton, geometric stripes, 1920, 72x50" **150.00**
Blanket, Pendleton, geometrics, fringed, antique, 60x66"............**200.00**
Blanket, Pendleton, vivid stripes, 1920, 84x90" **200.00**
Box, Ojibway, quilled bark, lg star on lid, 1910, 5x3" **125.00**
Bridle, Crow, rawhide head stall w/geometric bw, 1910, 27" **600.00**
Bridle, Yakima, woven horse hair, beaded rosettes, 1960.............**250.00**
Canoe, Chippewa, birch bark, bear motif, 1920, 40", +oars **250.00**
Fire horn, cvd, w/orig flints & rag tinder, 1800, 8x3" **300.00**
Peace medal, James Madison/Peace & Friendship, 1809, 3" **300.00**
Peace medal, James Monroe, bronze w/leather thong, 1817, 3" ...**250.00**
Quirt, Apache, dk brn/wht horse hair, 1914, 32" **300.00**
Quirt, Nez Perce, antler w/tacks, horse hair drop, 1920, 10" **75.00**
Quiver, Apache, rawhide/cloth trim, 1880, 25x5", +5 arrows......**900.00**
Quiver, Cheyenne, sheep hide/bw, sinew sewn, 1870, 42" **5,750.00**
Saddle, Comanche, rawhide high-horn, tacks/fringe, 1870 .....**2,600.00**
Saddle, Plains, rawhide, dbl high-horn, tacks/fringe, 1880 ......**1,400.00**
Saddle, Yakima, buckskin, dbl high-horn, bw flap, 1975.............**350.00**
Saddle blanket, Crow, fawn hide w/hair, beads/bells, 1880 ....**200.00**
Trade silver crown, w/hallmark & provenance, 17th C, 8x4" **600.00**

Amphora

The Amphora Porcelain Works, in the Teplitz-Turn area of Bohemia, produced Art Nouveau-styled vases and figurines during the latter part of the 1800s through the first few decades of the twentieth century. They marked their wares with various stamps, some incorporating the name and location of the pottery with a crown or a shield. Because Bohemia was part of the Austro-Hungarian empire prior to WWI, some examples are marked Austria; items marked with the Czechoslovakia designation were made after the war. Our advisor for this category is Jack Gunsaulus; he is listed in the Directory under Michigan.

Basket, cherub on rim w/roses cascading down from hdl, mk **325.00**
Basket, cobalt cabochons/blown-out leaves w/gold, 4-hdl, 8" **475.00**
Bowl, rtcl lily pads at rim, gr & gold w/purple below, 8" **495.00**

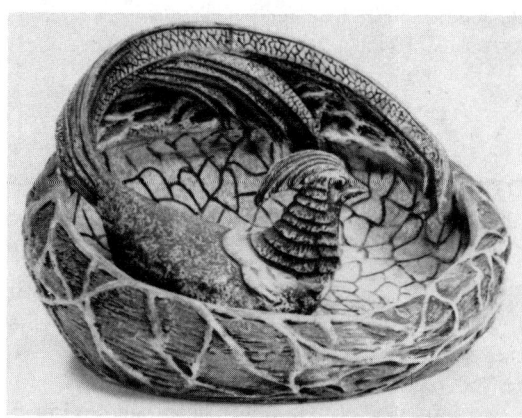

Centerpiece, Chinese pheasant in nest, 10" diameter, $1,250.00.

Ewer, group of petals form spout, twisted/8-sided, 17", EX...........**700.00**
Figurine, 3 boys pull at open baskets, mks/H, 9"..........................**495.00**
Pitcher, blown-out leaves, flower-form top, appl stems, 14".........**450.00**
Vase, appl grapes/vines, purple/irid gr, 4-hdl, RSK, 3" **275.00**
Vase, appl wolfhound & frog, bronze color, Imperial mk, 11"......**650.00**
Vase, birds/flowers, blk-lined mc on lime, 4 base hdls, 14" **250.00**
Vase, Deco flowers w/flower band at rim, mk, 9x6¼" **195.00**
Vase, emb stylized florals, hdls, 12" **355.00**
Vase, fan neck, branch-emb, 3-D pheasant at side, 16" **950.00**
Vase, floral baskets & chains, 2 salamander hdls, mk, 10x8" **350.00**
Vase, florals, mc on gr w/gold, hdls, mk, 10½x5⅝"......................**175.00**
Vase, flower-form top, emb leaves, hdls, 14" **450.00**
Vase, gr lily band on bl-gray web texture, shouldered, 9" **300.00**
Vase, iris, red & gr w/gold, serpent hdls, beading, 10¼"..............**300.00**
Vase, pearly beads allover, gold dragon hdls, crown mk, 11" **375.00**
Vase, spider webs/moths/jewels, lg integral hdls, 12½" **1,750.00**
Vase, 3-D owl perched above rim, oak branch aside, 12¾"..........**650.00**

Animal Dishes with Covers

Covered animal dishes have been produced for nearly two centuries and are as varied as their manufacturers. They were made in many types of glass (slag, colored, clear, and milk glass) as well as china and pottery. On bases of nests and baskets, you will find animals and birds of every sort. The most common was the hen.

Some of the smaller versions made by McKee, Indiana Tumbler and Goblet Company, and Westmoreland Glass of Pittsburgh, Pennsylvania, were sold to food-processing companies who filled them with prepared mustard, baking powder, etc. Occasionally one will be found with the paper label identifying the product and processing company still intact.

Many of the glass versions produced during the latter part of the nineteenth century have been recently reproduced. As late as the 1960s, the Kemple Glass Company made the rooster, fox, lion, cat, lamb, hen, horse, turkey, duck, dove, and rabbit on split-ribbed or basketweave bases. They were made in amethyst, blue, amber, and milk glass, as well as a variegated slag. It is sometimes necessary to compare items in question to verify examples of older glass in order to recognize reproductions.

For more information, we recommend *Covered Animal Dishes* by our advisor, Everett Grist, whose address is in the Directory under Illinois. In the listings below, when only one dimension is given, it is length.

Boar's head, milk glass, Atterbury, 9½"...**975.00**
Cat, milk glass, unmk McKee, 5½" **175.00**
Cat, recumbent, ribbed base, milk glass, Westmoreland, 5¼" **65.00**
Cat on lacy base, milk glass, Westmoreland...................................**95.00**
Chick on eggs on lacy base, milk glass, Westmoreland...................**90.00**
Chicken, dbl-headed, milk glass, unmk McKee, 5½" **450.00**
Cow, milk glass, 2 McKee mks, 5½" **1,050.00**
Dog, recumbent, milk glass, Westmoreland, 5¼"............................**65.00**
Dog (Chow), milk glass, 2 McKee mks, 5½"................................**500.00**
Dog (Pekinese), milk glass, att Sandwich, 4¾"............................**450.00**
Duck, milk glass w/bl head, Atterbury, 11"..................................**375.00**
Duck on cattail base, milk glass, unmk, 5½" **85.00**
Duck on wavy base, colors, Westmoreland **65.00**
Duck on wavy base, milk glass, Challinor, Taylor, & Co.............**125.00**
Elephant, milk glass, unmk McKee, 5½" **1,300.00**
Fighting cocks, chocolate, Greentown **1,500.00**
Fish, Entwined; on lacy base, milk glass, Atterbury, 6" dia **165.00**
Fish, flat; on ribbed base, bl, Fostoria, 8½"....................................**35.00**
Fox on lacy base, milk glass, mk Imperial, 6¼" **45.00**

Frog, milk glass, 1 McKee mk, 5½" 650.00
Hand & dove, dtd..110.00
Hen, str head, Indiana Glass, clear, 6" 10.00
Hen on basketweave base, Challinor, Taylor, & Co, 8"..............110.00
Hen on dmn basketweave base, bl opaque, Westmoreland, 5¼" 65.00
Hen on dmn basketweave base, milk glass, Westmoreland, 5¼" ...45.00
Hen on lacy base, milk glass w/amethyst head, Atterbury............295.00
Hen w/chicks, colors, att Wright....................................25.00
Hen w/chicks, milk glass, 2 McKee mks, 5½" 365.00
Horse, milk glass, 2 McKee mks, 5½"................................250.00
Lamb, milk glass, 2 McKee mks, 5½"................................225.00
Lamb on picket base, milk glass, Westmoreland 85.00
Lion on picket base, bl, Westmoreland 145.00
Mother eagle, colors, mk Westmoreland 75.00
Mother eagle, milk glass, Challinor, Taylor, & Co....................295.00
Pig, milk glass, 2 McKee mks, 5½"............................... 1,200.00
Quail on scroll base, milk glass......................................65.00
Rabbit, milk glass, Imperial, 9".....................................65.00
Rabbit, milk glass, mk Vallerysthal 135.00
Rabbit, milk glass, 2 McKee mks, 5½"..............................350.00
Rooster on basketweave, milk glass, Challinor-Taylor, 8" 135.00
Rooster on wide-rib base, bl opaque, Westmoreland, 5¼" 125.00
Rooster on wide-rib base, milk glass, Westmoreland, 5¼"..............65.00
Snail on strawberry, milk glass, Vallerysthal, 5¼" 85.00
Squirrel, milk glass, unmk McKee, 5½".............................145.00

Swan on knobby basketweave base, Bellmont Glass Works, 'Patent Appl'd For' inside lid, $200.00.

Swan, Black; milk glass, Challinor, Taylor, & Co, 7" 295.00
Swan, head down, milk glass, 2 McKee mks, 5½".....................335.00
Swan (closed neck) on basketweave base, bl, Westmoreland.........95.00
Turtle, amber, lg 125.00

Antiquities

The ancient Egyptians, Romans, and the early craftsmen of India and China have left us with exquisite treasures bearing mute witness of their esthetic convictions that even a water carrier, a knife, or a rug should be created a thing of beauty. Though time and the elements have taken their toll on the more fragile works of these ancient artisans, it is incredible that many remain intact to this day. The thin-walled tear and scent bottles blown by Roman artisans from the last century A.D., and examples of the red or black predynastic potteries of Egypt, though understandably quite rare, can yet occasionally be found on the market today. Jewelry, often interred with the dead, has survived the centuries well; figurines of marble and terra cotta, ceremonial masks, earthenware vessels, and other relics such as these offer us of the twentieth century the only tangible link possible to the ancient world.

Jug, Roman, 3rd/5th Century AD, network trailings, ribbed strap handle, folded rim, $2,000.00.

Bronze

Figure, Egypt, 1775-650 BC, Osiris w/crook & flail, 4⅛" 1,870.00
Figure, Egypt, 644-342 BC, Isis w/Horus, 6⅝".....................15,400.00
Finial, Greece, 700 BC, bird surmount on openwork, 3⅜" 3,000.00
Mirror, Etruscan, 200 BC, beaded rim, horse-head hdl, 11" ... 4,400.00
Pan, Etruscan, 200-100 BC, goose-head finial, 24" L............... 2,500.00

Glass

Amphorisk, 500 BC, cobalt bl, core formed, hdls, 3⅜"............ 1,320.00
Bottle, 100 AD, dk bl, globular, 2 bl-gr hdls, 3" 1,760.00
Bottle, 100 AD, wht opaque w/gr ribbon, pear form, 3" 3,575.00
Bottle, 100-200 AD, cobalt, pear shape, flared mouth, 4"............660.00
Bowl, 100 AD, gr, ribs cast in relief, 6⅝" 1,980.00
Cup, 400 AD, gr, raised ft ring, everted rim, 3⅝" dia 880.00
Jar, 400 AD, brn, pyriform w/swirling ribs, 4½" 1,100.00
Pitcher, 200 AD, amber, cylindrical, loop hdl, 2¾" 650.00

Hardstones

Bowl, Bronze Age II, 2700-2200 BC, Cycladic marble, 6¼".... 1,400.00
Cup, Egypt, 2500-2000 BC, alabaster, flared sides, 4" 1,200.00
Fragment, Egypt, 700-500 BC, king relief, limestone, 12x15".. 3,500.00
Head of girl, Graeco-Roman, 100 AD, marble, 9¾" 9,350.00
Head of man, Egypt, 380-342 BC, limestone, 3¾" 1,600.00
Jar, kohl; 12th Dynasty, 1994-1781 BC, anhydrite, 2⅜".......... 1,975.00

Jewelry

Earrings, Byzantine, 400-600 AD, gold loops w/stone dangles. **2,300.00**
Necklace, Egypt, 700-30 BC, turq faience beads, 27" **1,300.00**
Ring, Egyptian, 1550-1075 BC, gold & statite scarab............. **3,300.00**
Ring, Greek, 400 BC, gold hoop w/eng figure in oval bezel **6,000.00**
Ring, Roman, 160-180 AD, gold & carnelian w/eng head **13,000.00**

Pottery

Amphora, Campanian, 500 BC, Blk Figure, 9" **1,100.00**
Bowl, Apulian, 330-320 BC, Red Figure int, 6⅞" **660.00**
Epichysis, Apulian, 330-320 BC, Red Figure, 8⅛" **1,000.00**
Guttus, Campanian, 340-320 BC, Red Figure, shallow, 4" dia .. **1,300.00**
Jar, Myacenaean, 1400-1300 BC, buffware, hdls, 4" dia **2,200.00**
Kantharoid Skyphos, Campanian, 500 BC, Blk Figure, 5¼" ... **1,200.00**
Ushabti, 22nd Dynasty, 940-767 BC, bl-gr faience, 5¾" **4,675.00**

Terra Cotta

Figure, Greek, 500 BC, goddess w/bird, 7½" **1,500.00**
Figure, Hellenistic, 200 BC, Maenad w/fan, 13¾" **7,700.00**
Figure, Roman, 200 AD, Aphrodite w/dolphin at ft, 7⅜"........ **2,200.00**

Appliances, Electric

Electric appliances have been very collectible for quite some time with almost every type being sought after. Even larger appliances such as early washing machines and refrigerators add a finishing touch to remodeled period rooms. Smaller appliances such as toasters, coffee makers, waffle irons, fans, and other table-top items should be in working order. Check for safety before using. (Beware: old refrigerators are dangerous if their cooling units start leaking; the fluids in them are poisonous.)

Prices listed below are for appliances in very good to excellent condition and in working order. Our advisor for this category is Jim Barker; he is listed in the Directory under Pennsylvania.

Oscillating fan, Deco styling, brass blades, marked Gilbert, 12" diameter, $125.00.

Beater jar, Challenge, custard glass bottom 20.00
Beater jar, Chicago Electric, jadite bottom 30.00

Beater jar, Kenmore, crystal glass bottom 20.00
Beater jar, Vidrio, cobalt base..85.00
Blender, Universal Mixablend #B6405, EX 35.00
Blender, Waring #DL202, EX...35.00
Curling iron, Edison Electric, 1930, EX in box 28.00
Hot plate, Samson #3346N, Deco style..18.00
Iron, GE Hotpoint #113F68 ....25.00
Iron, Steam Electric, Series #S-284002, hammered aluminum 35.00
Mixer, Biltwell, w/Chalaine bl glass bowl 75.00
Popcorn popper, Fire-King, chrome, w/glass lid..............................35.00
Popcorn popper, Knap Monarch, sheet metal, red hdls, 1920, EX ...24.00
Teapot, Landers Universal #E-975, EX 30.00
Toaster, Armstrong Automatic, EX 95.00
Toaster, Bersted #78, EX 85.00
Toaster, Birtman Electric #T-14, EX..45.00
Toaster, Coleman Model #1, EX...150.00
Toaster, Dalton Electric Hearter, EX 250.00
Toaster, Dominion #1109, flip down, w/cord, EX............................35.00
Toaster, General Electric, #D-12, high sides, flowered, EX 300.00
Toaster, Manning Bowman #1208, EX 65.00
Toaster, Manning Bowman #1211, EX 150.00
Toaster, Manning Bowman #1215, EX 150.00
Toaster, Manning Bowman #1227, EX 85.00
Toaster, Mattatuck Mfg Commander #101, EX 150.00
Toaster, McGraw #1B5, EX...35.00
Toaster, Pelouze Toaster, EX...175.00
Toaster, Royal Rochester #13520, EX 45.00
Toaster, Simplex #211, EX 150.00
Toaster, Simplex #215, EX 125.00
Toaster, Star Electric, EX 85.00
Toaster, Sunbeam #T-9, EX 85.00
Toaster, Superior Electric #55, EX..100.00
Toaster, Toastmaster #1A1, EX 75.00
Toaster, Toastmaster #1B5, EX 45.00
Toaster, Universal #E79312 ....45.00
Toaster, Universal #E946, EX 65.00
Toaster, Universal #E947, EX 85.00
Toaster, Universal #7222, EX...95.00
Toaster, Universal #7732, EX..150.00
Toaster, Universal #79312, EX...50.00
Toaster, Westinghouse #TTC-43, EX..55.00

Arequipa

The Arequipa Pottery operated from 1911 until 1918 at a sanitorium near Fairfax, California. Its purpose was two-fold: therapy for the patients and financial support for the institution. Frederick H. Rhead was the originator and director. The ware, made from local clays, was often hand thrown, simply styled and decorated. Marks were varied but always incorporated the name of the pottery and the state. A circular arrangement encompassing the negative image of a vase beside a tree is most common.

Bowl, lustre, appl seashells, 2x6" 200.00
Bowl, stylized floral panels on tan, ftd, sgn R/dtd '12, 6" 500.00
Vase, cvd mermaid/fish/bubbles, dk bl matt, 4x6"................... 1,200.00
Vase, gr, bulbous, mk, #d, 5" 250.00
Vase, gr lava, early Rhead period mk, 8"..695.00
Vase, gray-plum, sq rim, vertically fluted corners, 8", EX............600.00
Vase, rose matt, sgn/dtd 1912, ovoid, 5" 250.00

Argy-Rousseau, G.

Gabriel Argy-Rousseau produced both fine art glass and quality commercial ware in Paris, France, in 1918. He favored Art Nouveau as well as Art Deco and in the twenties produced a line of vases in the Egyptian manner, made popular by the discovery of King Tut's tomb. One of the most important types of glass he made was pate-de-verre. Most of his work is signed. Items listed below are pate-de-verre unless noted otherwise.

Box, bachelor button flowers on flat lid/cylinder body, 3" **5,200.00**
Box, floral/brickwork border on lid, spade leaves, 4" dia **3,300.00**
Box, rose on lid, roses on body, pk on lt mottle, 2½" H........... **6,000.00**
Figurine, bird, azure bl w/yel ft on brn base, 3¼" **1,750.00**
Figurine, female in cloak w/flowing cape, lt/dk gr, 8"............... **1,750.00**
Figurine, kneeling nude, bird on shoulder, snake at ft, 5" **2,800.00**
Paperweight, 2 moths on cube form, yel/brn, 2⅝" **2,000.00**
Pendant, floral cluster, purple w/blk centers, 2½" dia **1,650.00**
Perfume burner, swags, red/ochre/tan/wht, ovoid, 5" **2,000.00**
Vase, paneled top on ftd base w/spider mums, gray/rose, 9" **3,800.00**
Vase, Symphorine, wht-berried branches, ovoid, 4" **5,500.00**

Art Deco

To the uninformed observer, 'Art Deco' evokes images of chrome and glass, streamlined curves and aerodynamic shapes, mirrored prints of pink flamingos, and statues of slender nudes and greyhound dogs. Though the Deco movement began in 1925 at the Paris International Exposition and lasted to some extent into the 1950s, within that period of time the evolution of fashion and taste continued as it always has, resulting in subtle variations.

The French Deco look was one of opulence — exotic inlaid woods, rich material, lush fur and leather. Lines tended toward symmetrical curves. American designers adapted the concept to cover every aspect of fashion and home furnishings from small inexpensive picture frames, cigarette lighters, and costume jewelry to high-fashion designer clothing and exquisite massive furniture with squared or circular lines. Vinyl was a popular covering, and chrome-plated brass was used for chairs, cocktail shakers, lamps, and tables. Dinnerware, glassware, theaters, and train stations were designed to reflect the new 'Modernism.'

The Deco movement made itself apparent into the fifties in wrought iron lamps with stepped pink plastic shades and Venetian blinds. The sheer volume of production during those twenty-five years provides collectors today with fine examples of the period that can be bought for as little as $10 or $20 up to the thousands. Chrome items signed 'Chase' are prized by collectors, and blue glass radios and tables with blue glass tops are high on the list of desirability in many areas.

Those interested in learning more about this subject will want to read *Collector's Guide to Art Deco* by our advisor, Mary Frank Gaston. She is listed in the Directory under Texas. See also Bronzes; Chase; Frankart; Furniture; Jewelry; Lalique; Radios; etc.

Clock, ceramic, marked St. Clements, France, ca 1925, 12" long, $125.00.

Andirons, silver-bronze cobra form, in Brandt's style, 12" **3,000.00**
Ash tray, cast metal w/chrome ball, Electrolier, 24" H, NM........**450.00**
Bar set, chrome, Zeppelin airship form, 8-pc, complete **1,200.00**
Bookend, blk/rose/wht marble in geometric configuration, 6½" **60.00**
Bottle, scent; gold circles, gr stone cap, dauber, 2x2⅝" **37.50**
Bottle, scent; Yardley, 8-point star, brass cap, Austria, 3" **27.50**
Box, cigarette; red & blk plastic, semi-circular, 5x5½"..................**45.00**
Box, jewel; nickel silver, blk velvet lining, 2½x6½" **30.00**
Candle holder, sterling floral on bronze, Heintz, 5", pr..............**200.00**
Clock, boudoir; peach-colored glass, mirrored base, Am, 7x6" **200.00**
Clock, digital; bronze case, Silvercrest, 1930s, 19" L................**200.00**
Clock, mantel; mahog/walnut, inlaid trim/#s, Germany, 8x14"...**400.00**
Coffee set, brass, Doryin Silversmith, 1930s, 5-pc **275.00**
Compact, blk enamel, gold crown & rhinestones, 8-sided, 2½".....**27.50**
Compact, chrome, geometric decor, 2x1½" **30.00**
Compact, chrome, triangular w/6" chain & finger ring, 2½"..........**50.00**
Compact, gold-pnt metal, fitted w/lipstick case, Elgin **125.00**
Compact, ivory Bakelite, blk fabric insert, 4" **45.00**
Compact, wht enameling w/gold stripes, pointed oval, 3x2½" **27.50**
Cup & saucer, demitasse; ceramic, mc dots on cream, Hancock....**15.00**
Dispenser, cigarette; plastic, sliding lid, mk Ziegfield, 6" **60.00**
Dress clip, bl rhinestones & turq beads, shield shape **30.00**
Figurine, dancer, ivory/metal, alabaster std, Battkepemy, 10" **600.00**
Figurine, lady w/2 whippets, cast plaster, Arnova, 13" **300.00**
Figurine, nude dancer, ceramic, Camden Art & Tile, 8½x11" **150.00**
Figurine, Russian wolfhounds, ceramic, Germany, 1940s, 13" L..**275.00**
Figurine, Spanish lady, pot metal/ivorene, marble base, 10" **200.00**
Flower frog, dancing nude, ceramic, Germany, 7" **55.00**
Frame, beveled glass, etched florals, 1940s, 14½x17" **85.00**
Ice bucket, chrome, cobalt glass insert, Hazel Atlas, 11x8"............**75.00**
Incense burner, CI, emb florals, geometric form, France, 6½" **125.00**
Inkwell & pen tray, sterling decor on bronze, Heintz NY **325.00**
Lamp, draped nude supports globe in hands, wht metal, 29" **395.00**
Lamp, fan-form mica-covered metal shade, metal base, 13x17"...**350.00**
Lamp, glass Saturn figural, 1939 World's Fair, 11½" **300.00**
Lamp, nude on stomach w/arms up holds light, bronzed metal **115.00**
Lamp, porc figure in gown, slag glass sphere, Argilor, 19½"..... **1,800.00**
Lamp, table; brass, slag glass panels & silk fringe shade **250.00**
Liqueur set, chrome/glass in plastic bowling-ball form, 14"...........**75.00**
Manicure kit, Bakelite, blk amoebas on gr, Germany, 3" **27.50**
Paper clip, brass, enameled butterfly, 4" **17.50**
Paperweight/cigarette lighter, chrome, elephant figural..............**100.00**
Pin, gr stone set in blk & turq enamel, silver trim..........................**35.00**
Place card holder, ceramic, girl in fur-trimmed coat, lustre..........**30.00**
Place card holder, lustreware, bird w/long beak, Germany **25.00**
Print, pk flamingo, Sterns, 12x18", pr, EX **38.00**
Purse, lg wht plastic beads, pentagon shape **25.00**
Rug, geometrics & half-moons, Davaar label, 127x106", VG **400.00**
Sconce, brass, petal-shape top, tapered base, 15", pr **265.00**
Sculpture, horse's head, wood on brass base, Hagenauer, 13" .. **1,300.00**
Stem, cocktail, nude supports pk glass bowl, unmk, 5" **55.00**
Toothpick holder, chrome, stylized swan form, unmk **20.00**
Tray, bl glass, pnt lady w/dog cameo, chrome trim, 12x9" **150.00**
Vase, blown, orange pear-shaped sections, iron fr, Czech, 11" **295.00**
Vase, copper, pk/wine arches on silver, Faure/Limoges, 6" **1,800.00**
Vase, copper, pnt w/swirled bands & waves, Sarlandie, 10" ... **1,650.00**

Art Glass Baskets

A popular novelty and gift item during the Victorian era, these one-of-a-kind works of art were produced in just about any type of art glass in use at that time. They were never marked, since these were not true production pieces but 'whimsies' made by glassworkers to relieve the tedium of the long work day. Some were made as special gifts. The more decorative and imaginative the design, the more valuable the basket.

Amber w/mc spatter & gold aventurine, cranberry int, 6½x4" ...**355.00**
Amethyst opal w/appl clear opal flower, clear hdl, 7x5" **175.00**
Bl opal, appl wht opal flower, vaseline leaf/hdl, 7¼x4½" **145.00**
Bl opal to vaseline, appl pk florals, vaseline hdl, 7x4" **145.00**
Bl w/vaseline band, wht rim, HP orange florals, 7½x7½".............**355.00**
Cream opaque, bl appl rim & flowers, loop hdl, 9½" **385.00**
Gold spangle w/mica, clear ruffle & twist hdl, 7½x7½" **175.00**
Gr opal, pk/wht appl flower, clear hdl, crimped rim, 6x4" **145.00**
Gr opal swirl, ruffled rim, appl flower, twist amber hdl, 6"..........**135.00**
Lime gr opal, ruffled, emb swirled ribs, clear hdl, 6½x6" **120.00**
Maroon & wht swirl, thorn hdl, 8" **120.00**
Mc spatter, wht int, clear twist hdl, 6⅜x4⅝".................................**110.00**
Mc spatter w/swirled ribs, ruffled rim, thorn hdl, 6½x5" **245.00**
Overshot, med bl star-shape rim on clear, twist hdl, 4" dia..........**135.00**
Pk & wht spatter w/gr aventurine, thorn hdl, hobnail rim, 7" **165.00**
Pk opal, 8-crimp rose bowl shape, 5⅜x4½"...................................**100.00**
Pk opal stripe, appl pk/wht flower+gr leaf, twist hdl, 7" **125.00**
Pk opal stripe, hobnail rim, pk thorn hdl, 8x6x8".........................**225.00**
Pk o/l, rose bowl shape, frosted hdl, 5⅛x3⅝"...............................**125.00**
Pk satin, HP florals w/gold, scalloped, triangular, 5x6x7" **295.00**
Pk/yel, deep swirls, clear hdl, English, 7½" **175.00**
Rose o/l, sq ruffled/hobnail rim, thorn hdl, 5x6½" **225.00**

Sapphire blue basket with white spatter, 8½", $165.00.

Spatter w/mica, bl int, ruffled rim, ftd, 8½" **280.00**
Vaseline opal, 2 appl flowers, vaseline hdl & ft, 8½x4x7" **245.00**
Vaseline opal Dmn Quilt, appl spatter flowers, 7½" **200.00**
Wht w/mc spatter int, ruffled edge, 6x4x5⅛" **88.00**
Wine & opal w/gold flecks, amber int, 8½" dia **150.00**
Yel opaque w/emb dmns & rib panels, clear hdl, 4¾x3¾"..............**88.00**
Yel swirl, red int, red scalloped rim, 7x5½"..................................**210.00**

Art Nouveau

From the famous 'L'Art Nouveau' shop in the rue de Provence in Paris, 'New Art' spread across the continent and belatedly arrived in America in time to add its curvilineal elements and asymmetrical ornamentation to the ostentatious remains of the Rococo revival of the 1880s. Nouveau manifested itself in every facet of decorative art. In

glassware Tiffany turned the concept into a commercial success that lasted well into the second decade of this century and created a style that inspired other American glassmakers for decades. Furniture, lamps, bronzes, jewelry, and automobiles were designed within the realm of its dictates. Today's market abounds with lovely examples of Art Nouveau, allowing the collector to choose one or several areas that hold a special interest. See also Bronzes; Jewelry; Tiffany; Silver; specific manufacturers; etc.

Bust, alabaster, young woman, sgn LG Bessi, 1900, 21" **600.00**
Candelabrum, bronze, floral cups/twisted stems, Preston, 19".....**400.00**
Candelabrum, SP, 3 floral cups, 2 nymphs as std, mk W, 20".. **1,100.00**
Candlestick, gilt bronze, nymph standing on lily pad, 10" **125.00**
Compote, gilt-bronze, rose-cast bowl, sgn Marionnet, 5½"..........**700.00**
Dish, bronze, nymph sits on rim of poppy-cast leaf, 5" H............**285.00**
Frame, gilt metal, nymph/flower in openwork border, 11x8" **220.00**
Lamp, bronze mermaid supports irid shell, Marina, 23" **1,500.00**
Lamp, cast metal, lady's upheld hand holds 3 lights, 47"............**700.00**
Mirror, hand; quadruple SP, emb florals, 11x5" **70.00**
Mirror, table; gilt bronze w/floral vines fr, 10x12" **240.00**
Plaque, lady w/flowing hair, SP over pewter, rstr, 20" **595.00**
Vase, bronze, leaf-cast decor, 4-hdl, squat baluster, 9¾" **125.00**
Vase, bronze, top as figural lady, drapery hdls, Jozon, 28" **2,400.00**
Vase, bronze, 2 appl gilt rats, sgn Hst Lerche Paris, 10" **600.00**
Vase, glass w/silvered metal base: nymph w/harp, WMF, 12" **900.00**
Vase, pearl irid glass, ftd cornucopia form, 10x6x8" **325.00**
Vase, SP pewter, maid/water nymph/frog in full relief, 22"...... **1,750.00**

Vase, polychromed terra cotta, impressed 'Made in Austria, Ernst Wahliss, Wien, #287,' 28", $4,400.00 for the pair.

Arts and Crafts

The Arts and Crafts movement began in England during the last quarter of the 19th century, and its influence was soon felt in this country. Among its proponents in America were Elbert Hubbard (see Roycroft) and Gustav Stickley (see Stickley.) They rebelled against the mechanized mass production of the Industrial Revolution and against the cumulative influence of hundreds of years of man's changing taste. They subscribed to the theory of purification of the styles: that designs be geared strictly to necessity. At the same time they sought to elevate these basic ideals to the level of accepted 'art.' Simplicity was their virtue; to their critics it was a fault.

The type of furniture they promoted was squarely built, usually of heavy oak, and so simple was its appearance that as a result many began to copy the style which became known as 'Mission.' Soon factories had geared production toward making cheap copies of their designs. In 1915 Stickley's own operation failed, forced into bankruptcy by the machinery he so despised. Hubbard lost his life that same year on the ill-fated *Lusitania*. Within the decade the style had lost its popularity.

Metal ware was produced by numerous crafts people, from experts such as Dirk Van Erp and Albert Berry to unknown novices. Prices for Arts and Crafts accessories rose dramatically in 1988, but by the beginning of 1991 appeared to have leveled off and (in some cases) were dropping. Metal items or hardware should not be scrubbed or scoured; to do so could remove or damage the rich, dark patina typical of this period. See also Furniture; Roycroft; Silver; Stickley; and specific manufacturers. Our advisor for this category is Bruce Austin; he is listed in the Directory under New York.

Ash tray, Albert Berry, copper freeform w/inlay bone, 6" 125.00
Bowl, Harry Dixon, hand-wrought copper, 5x9", EX 600.00
Bowl, Jarvie, hammered copper, incurvate, orig patina, 3x7" 500.00
Bowl, Kalo, hammered copper, VG patina (int scrubbed), 10" 210.00
Box, Apollo Studios, brass w/emb & eng landscape, sq, 3¾"..........80.00
Box, Archibald Knox, pewter w/sq motifs, MIE, 5x4½" 850.00
Box, Boston A&C Society, copper, pnt peacocks on lid, 7" dia ..600.00
Box, copper, corner strapwork, slightly domed lid, 7½" L 100.00
Box, Kalo, silver w/appl motif & letters, #3876, 5" L 650.00
Candlestick, ET Hurley, bronze, sea horse std, 13", EX 700.00
Candlestick, ET Hurley (att), bronze, sea horse std, 13" 550.00
Candlestick, Jarvie, bronze, Iota, rstr patina, 13", VG, pr 550.00
Candlestick, Jarvie, bronze, pencil std, Delta, 14", EX, pr 1,400.00
Candlestick, Jarvie, stem-like std, emb/organic cup, 14" 1,500.00
Chamberstick, Hagenauer, brass w/blk finish, 3¾", pr..................100.00
Chandelier, hammered copper sq w/4 slag lanterns, 21" 400.00
Charger, Foley, portrait, wht slip/enamel, sgn Rhead, 14" 200.00
Desk set, Buffalo A&C Shop, pnt berries on dk patina, 4-pc......900.00
Humidor, Heintz, appl silver griffins, cylindrical, 8x5" 225.00
Inkwell, ET Hurley, bronze, pointed lid, flaring base, 4x5"..........225.00
Jardiniere, D Van Erp, copper, new patina, mk/sgn, 5x7" 700.00

Lamp, 3-paneled mica shade, copper 1-light base with lightly cleaned patina, Dirk Van Erp, 11½", VG, $5,000.00.

Lamp, boudoir; Heintz, floral rtcl silk-lined 9" cone shade 600.00
Lamp, D Van Erp, copper/mica 18" shade; riveted std, 22" 20,900.00

Lamp, D Van Erp (att), 15½" copper cone shade w/mica 8,000.00
Lamp, D Van Erp, copper/mica 16" cone shade; sgn/mk std 6,600.00
Lamp, hammered copper, 19" shade w/4 mica inserts, 20"....... 2,100.00
Master salt, Kalo, hand hammered, 3-lobed, 2½", pr 260.00
Mirror, Limbert, sq glass in rectangular fr, #24, 25x44" 1,200.00
Pitcher, Jervis, gold aventurine on brn flambe, #200, 5x6" 300.00
Rug, Craftsman Drugget, Nile motif, 4-color, 120x170", VG.. 1,900.00
Rug, Drugget, geometrics, brn/rust/wht on beige, 108x140" ... 1,500.00
Runner, linen w/wht & gr floral, fringed, 45x18", G 95.00
Runner, linen w/4-color motif ea end, 16x44", G 120.00
Sconce, candle; Old Mission, hammered copper w/floral, 9x4" ...150.00
Tablecloth, linen, 4-color roses, crochet trim, 26x28", G 200.00
Tea set, Heinrichs, hammered copper w/silver trim, 6-pc........ 2,200.00
Tray, D Van Erp, copper, int border, windmill mk, 15" dia 500.00
Tray, Keswick, copper, shaped border/repousse hdls, 24x14" 350.00
Tray, Randhal, sterling, hand hammered, 4x6" 100.00
Trunk, Castle (att), sculptured hardwood dome-top, 20x45" . 6,000.00
Vase, Albert Berry, hammered copper, new patina, #37, 9".........375.00
Vase, D Van Erp, hand-wrought brass, EX patina, ovoid, 9" .. 2,700.00
Vase, hand-wrought copper, heavy, EX orig patina, 8" 1,100.00
Warming dish, D Van Erp, copper, sq w/rnd center bowl, 6" 100.00

Aurene

Frederick Carder of the Steuben Glass Works in Corning, New York, introduced Gold Aurene in 1904 and Blue Aurene a year later. Aurene is a rich, lustrous metallic iridescent glassware that also can be found in red, green, yellow, brown, and other colors, most of which are rare. It was sometimes cased on Calcite glass. Most Aurene objects are signed with an etched signature. Some had paper labels. Our advisor for this category is Thomas P. Dimitroff; he is listed in the Directory under New York.

Basket, gold w/lt gr highlights, ruffled, sgn/#455, 10" 1,200.00
Bottle, scent; gold, melon ribbed, sgn/#d, 6½x4"........................850.00

Blue Aurene bowl, 10" diameter, $500.00; Vase, 5", $600.00; Vase, 9¾", $900.00.

Bowl, gold, ring ft, sgn/#2852, 3½x9" 450.00
Bowl, gold, stretched edge, sgn/#2608, 14½" 750.00
Bowl, gold, 10-rib, incurvate, sgn/#565, 3x6" 475.00
Bowl, gr-gold, ftd, sgn/#3067, 3x6" 300.00
Bowl, mint; gold, folded-in rim, 4 appl ft, sgn/#192, 3x6" 600.00
Bowl, mint; red-gold, sgn/#1044, 6" 400.00
Candlestick, bl, twist stem, #686, 10", pr 1,500.00
Compote, bl, #2604, 6" 1,100.00
Compote, gold, sgn/#2642, 8x6" 600.00

Compote, gold, twist stem w/4 prunts, sgn/#1604, 8" dia 950.00
Decanter, gold, swirled/dimpled, w/label, 10½", +6 shots........ 1,800.00
Flower frog, gold, sgn Aurene, F Carder, 2½" dia 325.00
Salt cellar, bl, 8-rib, #564 ....400.00
Shade, gold, ribbed, orig fitter, 6½x3¼"......................................165.00
Tray, bl, stretch border, ftd, sgn Carder/#2994, 9".......................750.00
Tumble-up, gold, sgn/#3064, 5" pitcher+matching tumbler.........900.00
Tumbler, gold, #2361, 6" 175.00
Tumbler, gold, flared rim, sgn, 3⅞x3¼" 275.00
Vase, bl, rnd/squatty, sgn/#5204, 2x4" 550.00
Vase, bl, 3-stem tree-trunk form, sgn/#2744, 6½".........................950.00
Vase, gold, #312, 6" 450.00
Vase, gold, decor, #262, 8" 3,000.00
Vase, gold, EX highlights, ruffled, sgn/#723, 9x9" 950.00
Vase, gold, fan form, #6897, 11" 1,200.00
Vase, gold, hdls, #2765, 10" 1,750.00
Vase, gold, sgn, similar to #216 but thinner stem, 5¼" 550.00
Vase, gold, stick neck, sgn, 11" 800.00
Vase, gold w/gr leaves & vines w/wht flowers, #506, 7" 3,300.00
Vase, gr, decor, #884, 10".. 3,500.00
Vase, gr w/gold hearts & vines, gold int/rim, 10½" 3,500.00
Vase, jack-in-pulpit; gold, sgn/#2699, 6" 1,300.00
Wine, gold, sgn/#2828, 5" 100.00

Austrian Glass

Many examples of fine art glass were produced in Austria during
the time of Loetz and Moser that cannot be attributed to any glasshouse
in particular, though much of it bears striking similarities to the products of both artists.

Vase, crackled purple irid w/3 curling gold hdls, 7" 465.00
Vase, dk bl w/silvery oil spots, gourd form, 7"...............................250.00
Vase, gold, curled hdls, appl bl rim on trumpet neck, 7" 400.00
Vase, gold dappled/gr strings, bronze grape-cast ft, 8"...................440.00
Vase, hot pk w/gold dappling & trailing, dimpled, 11" 550.00
Vase, lt bl irid w/gr trailings, rnd w/dimpled sides, 7"...................465.00
Vase, lt gr/gold/bl dappled surface, slim ftd pear, 10" 165.00
Vase, lt pk w/pulled leaves, 8x3" 225.00

Austrian Ware

From the late 1800s until the beginning of WWI, several companies were located in the area known at the turn of the century as
Bohemia. They produced hard-paste porcelain dinnerware and decorative items primarily for the American trade. Today examples bearing
the marks of these firms are usually referred to by collectors as Austrian
ware, indicating simply the country of their origin. Of those various
companies, these marks are best known: M.Z. Austria; Victoria, Carlsbad, Austria (Schmidt and Company); and O. & E.G. (Royal) Austria.

Though most of the decorations were transfer designs which were
sometimes signed by the original artist, pieces marked Royal Austria
were often hand painted and so indicated alongside the backstamp.

Of these three companies, Victoria, Carlsbad, Austria, is the most
highly valued. Collectors should note that in our listings transfer decorations showing 'signatures' (sgn), such as 'Wagner,' 'Kauffmann,'
'LeBrun,' etc., were not actually painted by those artists but were
merely based on their original paintings.

Bowl, Blue Garden, Herend, 4x7½" 65.00
Bust, lady, rose in hair, bl/gr/gold over glaze, Wahliss, 10" 750.00
Cup & saucer, mythological scene, Kauffmann, gold hdls, pr 150.00
Ewer, floral, mc on tan/bl/ivory, gold hdl, mk, 5x7" 95.00

Ewer, lady's portrait, sgn Pompador, emb decor, rtcl hdls, 7" 150.00
Fish set, Old Man of Sea, 15" platter+12 9" plates+gravy............450.00

Plaque, cats ponder spilled ink, heavy gold rim, 12", $385.00.

Plaque, lady's portrait on dk bl: De Genlis, sgn Koller, 10"..........425.00
Plaque, mtn/lake scene, sgn Hocbe, 13" dia 75.00
Plaque, woman & Cupid, sgn A Hem, 9x6" 700.00
Plate, dog portrait, gold rococo rim, 13" 225.00
Plate, mc bird w/border of sm reserves, mk, 1890s, 10" 125.00
Urn, birds/flowers, gilt/jewels, sq base, w/lid, 1900, 12" 350.00
Urn, pk & wht flowers, rtcl top, w/lid, Alexandria Turn, 6" 75.00
Vase, Bohemian girl's portrait, florals, gold hdls, mk, 12" 275.00
Vase, clouds & Cupid w/bow, snake hdl, Carlsbad, 7½" 150.00
Vase, Royal wedding, sgn Hanke, gold floral hdls, 1920s, 17"......225.00

Autographs

Autograph collecting, also known as 'philography' or 'love of writing,' used to be a hobby shared by a few thousand dedicated collectors.
But in recent years, autograph collecting has become a serious pursuit
for more than 2,000,000 collectors worldwide. And in the past decade,
more investors are adding rare and valuable autograph portfolios to
their traditional investments. One reason for this sudden interest in
autograph investing relates to the simple economic law of supply and
demand. Rare autographs have a 'fixed' supply, meaning that unlike
diamonds, gold, silver, stock certificates, etc., no more are being produced. There are only so many Abraham Lincoln, Marilyn Monroe,
and Charles Lindbergh autographs available. In the meantime, it's estimated that more than 20,000 new collectors enter the market each
year, thus creating an ever-increasing demand. Hence, the rare autographs generally rise steadily in value each year. Because of this
scarcity, a serious collector will pay over $10,000 for a photograph
signed by both Wilbur and Orville Wright, or as much as $25,000 for a
handwritten letter of George Washington.

But by far, the majority of autograph collectors in the country do it
for the love of the hobby. A polite letter and self-addressed, stamped
envelope sent to a famous person will often bring the desired result.
And occasionally one receives not only an autograph but a nice handwritten letter thanking the fan as well!

In terms of value, there are five general types of autographs: 1)
mere signatures on an album page or card; 2) signed photographs; 3)
signed documents; 4) typed letters signed; and 5) handwritten letters.

The signatures are the least valuable, and handwritten letters the most valuable. The reasoning here is simple: with a handwritten letter, not only do you get an autograph but the handwritten message of the person as well. And this content can sometimes increase the value many times over. A handwritten letter of Babe Ruth thanking a fan for a gift might fetch a few thousand dollars. But if the letter were to mention Ruth's feelings on the day he retired, it could easily sell for $10,000 or more.

There are several major autograph collector organizations where members can exchange celebrity addresses or buy, sell, and trade their autographed wares. Philography can be a fun and rewarding hobby. And who knows! In ten or twenty years, those autographs you got for free could be worth a small fortune!

In the listings below, photos are assumed black and white unless noted color. Our advisor for autographs is Tim Anderson; he is listed in the Directory under Utah.

Key:
ADS — handwritten document signed
ALS — handwritten letter signed
ANS — handwritten note signed
AQS — autograph quotation signed
CS — counter signed
DS — document signed
ins — inscription
ISP — inscribed signed photo
LH — letterhead
LS — signed letter, typed or written by someone else
PLH — personal letterhead
sig — signature
SP — signed photo

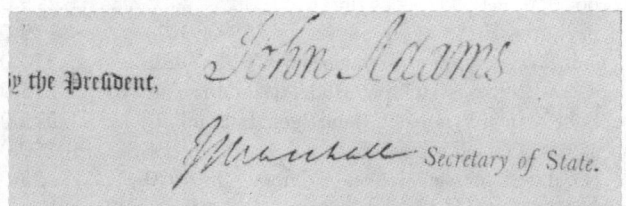

John Adams, vellum document with paper seal, 1800, $1,400.00.

Adams, Ansel; sig on card 50.00
Alpert, Herb; sig on card 7.00
Alverez, Walter Clement; sig on card 17.50
Amara, Lucine; ISP, 8x10" 25.00
Arafat, Yassir; SP, 1982, 4x7" 150.00
Astaire & Rogers, SP, full-length dancing view, 8x10" 125.00
Baez, Joan; SP, blk/wht, 3x4" 7.00
Bancroft, Dave; sig on post card 17.50
Barnard, Dr Christiaan; SP, blk/wht 25.00
Barton, Clara; sig cut from letter, EX 195.00
Benton, TH; artist, ALS 150.00
Berlin, Irving; sgn sheet music 250.00
Bohr, Niels; sig on card, Copenhagen, 1961 ....125.00
Borge, Victor; ISP, blk/wht...15.00
Borgnine, Ernest; ISP, blk/wht 18.50
Boyington, Pappy; ISP, blk/wht, ca 1945 ....95.00
Bradbury, Ray; sgn paperbk: A Treasury of Modern Fantasy 20.00
Breese, Vance; typed LS, sending autograph, Nov 30, 1940 ....195.00
Brice, Fanny; bold sig on lined paper 60.00
Bryan, William Jennings; LS, as presidential candidate 250.00
Burroughs, John; ALS, to Mrs AR West, 1-pg..................27.50
Cagney, James; SP, blk/wht, half-bust pose, M 75.00
Cantor, Eddie; sig on card...20.00

Carmichael, Hoagy; sig on card..25.00
Carroll, Madeleine; cut sig from DS 20.00
Carter, Lynda; SP, as Wonder Woman 25.00
Carter, Rosalyn; sgn US $1 bill 18.00
Castro, Fidel; sig on DC Transit Co ticket, 1959 ....375.00
Chaffee, Adna R; DS, military directive, 1899, 1-pg 25.00
Chaplin, Charles; bold SP, ca 1918, 5x7", EX 350.00
Connors, Jimmy; SP, color 18.50
Coolidge, Calvin; LS, in appreciation for book, 1929, 1-pg.........125.00
Cooper, Gladys; ALS, orders tickets, 1-pg 20.00
Crawford, Joan; ISP, vintage sepia, ca 1940........................65.00
Curtis, Ken; ISP, as Marshal Dillon's deputy, 8x10" 20.00
Daley, Richard J; bold sig on seal of city of Chicago, EX 68.50
Dean, Dizzy; sig on card 17.50
Debeck, Billy; sig on card 12.50
Domino, Fats; SP, 8x10" 30.00
Douglas, Kirk; ISP, scene from Cast a Giant Shadow, 1966...........25.00
Douglas, William O; sig on Supreme Court card, M............25.00
Dreiser, Theodore; ANS, accepting dinner invitation 50.00
Du Maurier, Daphne; sig on card, 1977................................15.00
Dumas, Alexandre; ALS, French text, 1-pg.........................125.00
Earhart, Amelia; sig on back of menu, 4½x3½" 200.00
Elam, Jack; SP, blk/wht 12.50
Elizabeth I; sig on indenture, 1597, 18x5", NM 195.00
Forsythe, John; ISP, blk/wht, 5x7" 12.50
Fosse, Bob; SP, 8x10" 25.00
Garfield, JA; calling card w/envelope, VG 475.00
Gielgud, John; SP, 5x7" 15.00
Gleason, Jackie; ISP, scene from Soldier in the Rain 65.00
Goodman, Benny; SP, 8x10" 50.00
Grable, Betty; 2-line sentiment, sig in red ink, 1951 ....55.00
Graziano, Rocky; SP, blk/wht, in business suit.....................25.00
Haley, Jack; DS, RKO contract copy, 1945, 1-pg................100.00
Hamilton, Margaret; sig on card..25.00
Hammarskjold, Dag; LS, thank you to Pearl Buck, 1955, 1-pg 450.00
Hampton, Lionel; SP, orchestra in bkground, 8x10" 30.00
Harding, Warren G; ISP, 8½x11" 300.00
Harrison, Rex; sig on playbill for Aren't We All 18.50
Hayes, Rutherford B; sig on card, as president, 3½x2¼"............100.00
Herman, Woody; SP, 8x10" 25.00
Holmes, Oliver Wendell; ANS..150.00
Hoover, Herbert; LS, personal LH, 1938, as president, M..........150.00
Hoover, J Edgar; LS, as director FBI, 1952, 1-pg..................35.00
Hubbard, Elbert; SP, in fr, 15x11".....................................550.00
Humphrey, Hubert H; sgn speech, Feb 3, 1966, 6-pg............50.00
Hurst, Fannie; sgn ink sketch, New York, 1953 ....16.00
Isroff, Lola Kovener; sgn watercolor drawing, 1971 ....37.50
James, Harry; sig on post card, 1953....................................16.00
Jefferson, Thomas; sgn manifest document, 1807, 15x10" **2,500.00**
Johnson, Andrew; cut sig from DS, with color photo, EX..........350.00
Johnson, Lady Bird; sig on Wht House LH, personal, '64, 1-pg 47.50
Karloff, Boris; sgn silver certificate....................................100.00
Kennedy, Jacqueline; sig on Wht House LH, personal, '61, 1-pg..375.00
Kennedy, Robert; sgn in book: To Seek Newer World, 1st ed 300.00
Kennedy, Rose; bold sig on Wht House card, ca 1962 ....295.00
Kipling, Rudyard; ANS 100.00
Knievel, Evil; SP, 8x10" 250.00
Krupa, Gene; ISP, 8x10" 25.00
Lombardo, Guy; sig on card..16.00
Loren, Sophia; ISP, blk/wht, ca 1955..................................35.00
Mancini, Henry; SP, seated by piano, 8x10".........................30.00
Mandrell, Barbara; SP, color..12.50
Marchesis, Blanche; AQS, 1923 ....17.50
Maxwell, Marilyn; ISP, sepia color, 8x10" 45.00

Merman, Ethel; SP, early, 5x7" 45.00
Nelson, Byron; sig on card...............................20.00
Osgood, Samuel S; ALS, sending remittance for book, '78, 1-pg ...16.00
Patterson, Floyd; SP, 8x10" 30.00
Phillips, Wendell; ALS, letter of introduction, 1881, 2-pg 20.00
Pickford, Mary; bold sig, purple ink, 1929, EX 65.00
Post, Emily; sig on card, 5x3" 16.00
Prelog, Vladimir; SP, 3½x5" 20.00
Rayburn, Sam; sig on card, as Speaker of the House.............16.00
Redford, Robert; SP, blk/wht, scene from Great Gatsby, EX 45.00
Rice, Alice Hegan; ANS, sends autograph, 1907, 1-pg 15.00
Rickenbacker, Eddie; bold sig on card, ca 1939, 3x5".............75.00
Riley, James Whitcomb; sig on wht card.........................25.00
Rivera, Graciela; SP, 5x7" 20.00
Roosevelt, Franklin Delano; LS, as president, Sept 1932, 1-pg ...175.00
Sayers, Joseph D; LS, as Gov of TX, 1902, 1-pg................25.00
Scott, George C; SP, blk/wht, scene from Patton..................75.00
Scott, Sir Walter; ALS, regrets, 3x4" 145.00
Sills, Beverly; SP, blk/wht................................25.00
Sousa, John Philip; sig on LH, 1929........................100.00
Spillane, Mickey; ISP, color, 5x7"........................27.50
Stewart, James; SP, blk/wht, ca 1960 ....45.00
Taft, Wm H; calling card, With Pleasure, dtd 1925, VG 170.00
Tiny Tim; SP, in singing pose, 8x10" 25.00
Truman, Bess; ALS, thank you, as first lady, 2-pg 95.00
Tucker, Tommy; SP, 8x10" 25.00
Tyler, John; cut sig, as president, 2x1½" 110.00
Van Dyke, Henry; sig on card, The Hague, 1916 ....15.00
Ward, Burt; ISP, blk/wht, as Robin........................45.00
Wells, Dawn; ISP, blk/wht 15.00
Westover, Russ; LS, 1930, 1-pg.........................17.50
Williams, Esther; SP, color, ca 1940, EX.......................35.00
Wilson, Nancy; SP, 8x10" 22.50
Wilson, Woodrow; DS, CS by Daniels, naval appt, 1913 ....350.00
Yeager, Chuck; SP, 10x8" 30.00
Zadora, Pia; ISP, movie scene, w/unknown Blk actor.............25.00
Zola, Emil; ALS 475.00
Zorach, William; sig on personal LH.........................17.50

Automobilia

While some automobilia buffs are primarily concerned with restoring vintage cars, others concentrate on only one area of collecting. For instance, hood ornaments were often quite spectacular. Made of chrome or nickel plate on brass or bronze, they were designed to represent the 'winged maiden' Victory, flying bats, sleek greyhounds, soaring eagles, and a host of other creatures. Today they often bring prices in the $75 to $200 range. R. Lalique glass ornaments go much higher!

Horns, radios, clocks, gear shift knobs, and key chains with company emblems are other areas of interest. Generally, items pertaining to the classics of the thirties are most in demand. Paper advertising material, manuals, and catalogs in excellent condition are also collectible.

License plate collectors search for the early porcelain-on-cast-iron examples. First year plates (e.g., Massachusetts, 1903; Wisconsin, 1905; Indiana, 1913) are especially valuable. The last of the states to issue regulation plates were South Carolina and Texas in 1917, and Florida in 1918. While many northeastern states had registered hundreds of thousands of vehicles by the 1920s making these plates relatively common, those from the southern and western states of that period are considered rare. Naturally, condition is important. While a pair in mint condition might sell for as much as $100 to $125, a pair with chipped or otherwise damaged porcelain may sometimes be had for as little as $25 to $30.

Our advisors for this category are Dennis O'Brien and George Goehring of Dennis and George Collectibles; they are listed in the Directory under Maryland. See also Gas Globes and Panels.

Advertising foldout, 1949 Ford, M, $35.00.

Ash tray, Goodrich Silvertown, tire w/gr glass insert 35.00
Badge, chauffer; Iowa, 1939, NM......................................20.00
Bell, I'm Ringing the Bell for Pontiac, 4"...............................12.00
Blotter, Amoco, Rockwell illustration, 1939, EX 20.00
Book, Dyke's Automobile & Gas Engine Encyclopedia, 1919 ....22.50
Booklet, Cadillac dealer, 1956, EX.....................................25.00
Bottle, Castrol Oil, pnt label 80.00
Bottle, Gargoyle Dmn 100.00
Box, Oldsmobile Magneto decal, dvtl wood 45.00
Brochure, Morris 850, foldout, 1960 ....27.50
Bumper sign, Pure Oil, Drive Safely, tin, old 25.00
Calendar, desk; Mobil, w/Pegasus......................................200.00
Carton, oil; Mobile Marine, cb, 4-pack, 1950s, NM 5.00
Catalog, Nash Airflyte, shows 9 models, 1951, 16-pg, NM 7.50
Extinguisher, Texaco, brass, 1930s, EX..................................50.00
Flashlight, Shamrock Oil, EX..10.00
Flower vase, carnival glass 25.00
Gear shift knob, gr & cream swirl, M....................................45.00
Grease tube, Texaco Starfak, metal, 1940s, M in cb box................20.00
Headdress, real feathers, Pontiac promotion, 1952, M 30.00
Hood ornament, swan, 1950s 45.00
Key holder, Dezol 5.00
License plate, MA, porc face, bl on wht, 1914, EX 25.00
License plate, motorcycle, GA, 1930 ....15.00
License plate, NY, 1928...30.00
Lock, gas pump; Standard Oil, brass, 1912 ....30.00
Magazine, Motor Vehicle Monthly, 1921, 84-pg, EX 7.50
Manual, Packard, 1937 ....40.00
Map rack, Sinclair, 1950s, M..25.00
Mascot, nude holding drape, opal glass, Etling France, 9" 1,500.00
Matchbox holder, Goodyear & Exide Batteries.........................50.00
Oil can, Areo Eastern Motor Oil, EX.....................................85.00
Oil can, Duplex Outboard Motor Oil, fishing boat, EX..................55.00
Oil can, Enarco Oil, 1-qt, EX 20.00
Oil can, Falcon Motor Oil, 1-qt, M......................................30.00
Oil can, Golden Leaf, 1-qt..20.00
Oil can, Hercules Motor Oil, 1-qt 15.00
Oil can, Marathon, 1-gal 20.00
Oil can, Mobil Freezone Antifreeze, 1950s, 1-qt.........................15.00

Oil can, Shell, outboard motor oil, speedboat, M 10.00
Oil can, Texaco, squirt type 15.00
Oil can, Valvoline, America's 1st, 1940s, full qt 20.00
Padlock, Sinclair, brass, 1930s, M 30.00
Photograph, 1926 gas station w/hand-operated pump & cars.........15.00
Pin-bk button, Gilmore Races...40.00
Post card, photo of 1907 Oldsmobile touring car, EX 8.00
Price list, Chevrolet parts, 1912, 84-pg, EX 27.50
Pump plate, Mobilgas 110.00
Pump plate, Mobilgas Special...295.00
Pump plate, Signal Ethyl 295.00
Radiator cap, Chevrolet, eagle, 1932 ....75.00
Radiator cap, Chevrolet Viking, 1929 ....125.00
Radiator cap, Essex Four...12.50
Radiator cap, Mack Truck, bulldog, NP, 1930s 15.00
Radiator cap, winged nude lady's torso..65.00
Sign, Go Slow! Blow Your Horn, tin, 1930s, 35".........................70.00
Sign, Sohio Gasoline, 5-color, dbl-sided, EX.............................450.00
Tie clasp, Ford logo, key shape 20.00
Tire patch kit, Texaco, 1960s, EX 8.00
Tire-holding stand, Mobile, EX...35.00
Tool check, Fordson 15.00

Reverse painting on glass, Welcome, Studebaker, ca 1920s, minor flaking, 51" long, $1,400.00.

Autumn Leaf

In 1933 the Hall China Company designed a line of dinnerware for the Jewel Tea Company, who offered it to their customers as premiums. Although you may hear the ware referred to as 'Jewel Tea,' it was officially named 'Autumn Leaf' in the 1940s. In addition to the dinnerware, frosted Libbey glass tumblers, stemware, and a melmac service with the orange and gold bittersweet pod were available over the years, as were tablecloths, plastic covers for bowls and mixers, and metal items such as cake safes, hot pads, coasters, waste baskets, and canisters. Even shelf paper and playing cards were made to coordinate. In 1958 the International Silver Company designed silverplated flatware in a pattern called 'Autumn' which was to be used with dishes in the Autumn Leaf pattern. A year later, a line of stainless flatware was introduced. These accessory lines are prized by collectors today.

One of the most fascinating aspects of collecting the Autumn Leaf pattern has been the wonderful discoveries of previously unlisted pieces. Among these items are two different bud-ray lid one-pound butter dishes; most recently a one-pound butter dish in the 'Zephyr' or 'Bingo' style; a miniature set of the 'Casper' salt and pepper shakers; coffee, tea, and sugar canisters; a pair of candlesticks; an experimental condiment jar; and a covered candy dish. All of these china pieces are attributed to the Hall China Company. Other unusual items have turned up in the accessory lines, as well, and include a Libbey frosted tumbler in a pilsner shape, a wooden serving bowl, and an apron made from the oilcloth (plastic) material that was used in the 1950s tablecloth. These latter items appear to be professionally done, and we can only speculate as to their origin. Collectors believe that the Hall items were sample pieces that were never meant to be distributed.

Hall discontinued the Autumn Leaf line in 1978. At that time the date was added to the backstamp to mark ware still in stock in the

Jewel warehouse. A special promotion by Jewel saw the reintroduction of basic dinnerware and serving pieces with the 1978 backstamp. These pieces have made their way into many collections. Additionally, in 1979 Jewel released a line of enamel-clad cookware and a Vellux blanket made by Martex which were decorated with the Autumn Leaf pattern. They continued to offer these items for a few years only, then all distribution of Autumn Leaf items was discontinued.

It should be noted that the Hall China Company has produced several limited edition items for the National Autumn Leaf Collectors Club (NALCC): a New York-style teapot (1984); a vase (1987, different than the original shape); candlesticks (1988); a Philadelphia-style teapot, creamer and sugar set (1990); a sugar packet holder (1990); a tea-for-two set and a Solo tea set (1991), a donut jug, and a large oval casserole. Other items are scheduled for production. All of these are plainly marked as having been made for the NALCC and are appropriately dated. A few other pieces have been made by Hall as limited editions for an Ohio company, but these are easily identified: the Airflow teapot and the Norris refrigerator pitcher (neither of which was previously decorated with the Autumn Leaf decal), a square-handled beverage mug, and the new-style Irish mug.

Baker, oval, Fort Pitt..90.00
Batter bowl, Saf-Hdl 2,000.00
Bean pot, 1-hdl..400.00
Bean pot, 2-hdl, 2¼-qt 135.00
Bowl, cereal; 6"..10.00
Bowl, coupe soup 12.00
Bowl, cream soup; 2-hdl...18.00
Bowl, fruit; 5½" 4.00
Bowl, metal, enamelware, set of 3 ....175.00
Bowl, mixing; set of 3: 6¼", 7½", 9".................................55.00
Bowl, Royal Glas-Bake, set of 4..45.00
Bowl, salad 14.00
Bowl, stackette; set of 3: 18-oz, 24-oz, 34-oz, w/lid 75.00
Bowl, vegetable; divided, 10½" 75.00
Bowl, vegetable; oval, w/lid, 10" 35.00
Bowl, vegetable; oval, 10½"...12.00
Bowl, vegetable; rnd, 9"...75.00
Bowl cover set, plastic, 8-pc: 7 assorted covers in pouch 50.00
Bread box, metal..175.00
Butter dish, 1-lb 275.00
Butter dish, ¼-lb 150.00
Butter dish, ¼-lb, Square Top 400.00
Butter dish, ¼-lb, Wings...600.00
Cake plate, 9½"..12.00
Cake safe, metal, motif on top & sides, 5" 35.00
Cake safe, metal, side decor only, 4½x10½" 30.00
Cake stand, metal base, orig box 150.00
Candy dish 350.00
Canister, metal, rnd, w/coppertone lid, set of 4 ....175.00
Canister, metal, rnd, w/ivory plastic lid 10.00
Canister, metal, rnd, w/matching lid, 6" 15.00
Canister, metal, rnd, w/matching lid, 7" 25.00
Canister, metal, rnd, w/matching lid, 8¼" 35.00
Canister, metal, sq, set of 4: 8½" & 4½" 135.00
Casserole, Royal Glas-Bake, deep, w/clear glass lid.........................25.00
Casserole, Royal Glas-Bake, shallow, w/clear glass lid....................20.00
Casserole, Tootsie-hdl, w/lid 22.00
Casserole/souffle, swirl, 3-pt 15.00
Casserole/souffle, 10-oz 10.00
Casserole/souffle, 2-pt..85.00
Cleanser can, metal, sq, 6"..300.00
Clock, orig works..350.00
Coaster, metal, 3⅛".. 4.00

Coffee dispenser/canister, metal, wall type, 10½x19" dia 150.00
Coffee maker, 5-cup, all china, w/china insert 250.00
Coffee maker, 9-cup, w/metal dripper, 8" 35.00
Coffee percolator, electric, all china 225.00
Coffee percolator/carafe, Douglas, w/warmer base, MIB 250.00
Cookie jar, Tootsie 165.00
Creamer, New Style 8.00
Creamer, Old Style, 4¼" 15.00
Cup & saucer 8.00
Cup & saucer, St Denis 22.00
Custard cup 4.00
Flatware, silverplate, ea 15.00
Flatware, stainless, ea 10.00
Fruit cake tin, metal 10.00
Golden Ray base, to use w/candy dish or cake plate, pr 50.00
Gravy boat 18.00
Hot pad, metal, red or gr felt-like bking, rnd 15.00
Hot pad, oval 12.00
Hurricane lamp, Douglas, w/metal base, pr 400.00
Kitchen utility chair, metal 450.00

Marmalade, 3-piece set, $55.00.

Mixer cover, Mary Dunbar, plastic 25.00
Mug, beverage 45.00
Mug, Irish coffee 85.00
Mustard jar, 3½" 55.00
Napkin, ecru muslin 25.00
Pickle dish or gravy liner, oval, 9" 18.00
Picnic thermos, metal 250.00
Pie baker, 9½" 18.00
Pitcher, utility; 2½-pt, 6" 15.00
Place mat, paper, scalloped 25.00
Place mat, set of 8, M in orig package 195.00
Plate, 10" 12.00
Plate, 6" or 7", ea 4.00
Plate, 8" 8.00
Plate, 9" 10.00
Platter, 11½" 15.00
Platter, 13½" 18.00
Playing cards, regular or Pinochle 125.00
Range set, shakers & covered drippings jar 35.00
Sauce dish, serving; Douglas, Bakelite hdl 125.00
Shakers, Casper, pr 18.00
Shakers, range, hdl, pr 18.00

Sugar bowl, New Style 12.00
Sugar bowl, Old Style, 3½" 18.00
Tablecloth, cotton sailcloth w/gold stripe, 54x54" 75.00
Tablecloth, cotton sailcloth w/gold stripe, 54x72" 85.00
Tablecloth, ecru muslin, 56x81" 150.00
Tablecloth, plastic 150.00
Teakettle, metal enamelware 150.00
Teapot, Aladdin 38.00
Teapot, long spout, 7" 45.00
Teapot, Newport 135.00
Teapot, Newport, dtd 1978 ....125.00
Toaster cover, plastic, fits 2-slice toaster 25.00
Towel, dish; pattern & clock motif 45.00
Towel, tea; cotton, 16x33" 35.00
Trash can, metal, red 100.00
Tray, glass, wood hdl, 19½x11¼" 95.00
Tray, metal, oval 55.00
Tray, red w/allover red & yel design, red border 65.00
Tray, tidbit; 2-tier 35.00
Tray, tidbit; 3-tier 55.00
Tumbler, Brockway, 13-oz 18.00
Tumbler, Brockway, 16-oz 20.00
Tumbler, Brockway, 9-oz 16.00
Tumbler, frosted, 14-oz, 5½" 12.00
Tumbler, frosted, 9-oz, 3¾" 18.00
Tumbler, gold frost etched, flat, 10-oz 30.00
Tumbler, gold frost etched, flat, 15-oz 45.00
Tumbler, gold frost etched, ftd, 10-oz 45.00
Tumbler, gold frost etched, ftd, 6½-oz 45.00
Vase, bud; 6" 175.00
Warmer base, oval 150.00
Warmer base, rnd 110.00
Warmer base, rnd, w/4 orig candles, orig mk box 125.00

Aviation

Aviation buffs are interested in any phase of flying, from early developments with gliders, balloons, airships and flying machines to more modern innovations. Books, catalogs, photos, patents, lithographs, ad cards, and posters are among the paper ephemera they treasure alongside models of unlikely flying contraptions, propellers and rudders, insignia and equipment from WWI and WWII, and memorabilia from the flights of the Wright Brothers, Lindbergh, Earhart, and the Zeppelins. See also Militaria. Our advisor for this category is John R. Joiner; he is listed in the Directory under Georgia.

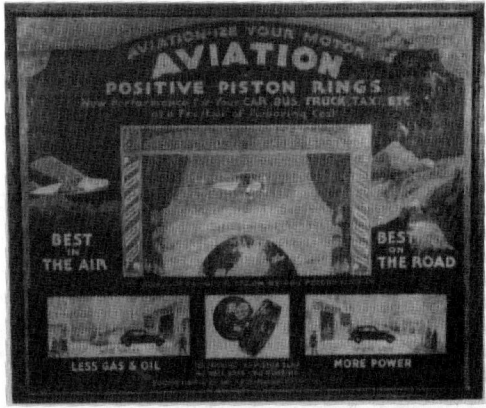

Hand-painted advertisement on hardboard, framed in wood, 53", VG, $700.00.

Ash tray, Boeing 247 airplane, metal, 1934	200.00
Bag, 1st class complimentary, Pan Am, w/toiletries	5.00
Book, Aviation History Scott Field, 1940s, EX	22.00
Book, History of Aviation, Taylor/Munson, 1972, NM	35.00
Book, Science of Preflight Aeronautics, Manley, 1942, EX	130.00
Book, Woman & Flying, Heath & Murray, London, 1929, EX	35.00
Booklet, TWA, 1935, EX	15.00
Cigarette cards, Internat'l Air Liners, 1930s, complete set	50.00
Hatpin, Eastern Airlines flight attendant	25.00
Medallion, Eastern Airlines 50th Anniversary, bronze, 1978	25.00
Plate, Pan American, Lindbergh's First Commissioned Flight	30.00
Ring, Am Airline Jr Pilot	15.00
Shot glass, Eastern Airlines	2.00
Token, Lindbergh portrait/plane, brass, 11", EX	10.00
Tumbler, Eastern Airlines, Rickenbacker, 1950, M	15.00
Wings, Eastern Airlines, plastic, child's	1.50

Avon

The California Perfume Company, the parent of the Avon Co., was founded in 1886. Although an 'Avon' line was introduced by the company in the mid-twenties, not until 1939 did it become known as Avon Products, Inc. Collectible Avon items include not only figural bottles and jars but jewelry, awards, product samples, magazine ads, and catalogs as well. Our advisor for this category is Tammy Rodrick; she is listed in the Directory under Illinois. For more information concerning the Avon Collectors Club, see the Clubs, Newsletters, and Catalogs section of the Directory. See also California Perfume Company.

In the listings that follow, unless noted MIB, prices are for bottles only.

Sonnet Toilet Water, ca 1941-'46, $22.50.

Albee Woman of Achievement Award, ceramic figure, '61, MIB	300.00
Ariel Bath Salts, clear glass, paper label, 1930	75.00
Attention Body Powder, 1943 & 1947 only, 5-oz	30.00
Bath Oil for Men, silver bottle, 1965-67, 4-oz	20.00
Bulldog Pipe, 1972	8.00
Castile Soap, paper label, 2 cakes, 1929-30	50.00
Christmas Plate, Christmas on Farm, Wedgwood, 1973, MIB	85.00
Close Harmony After Shave, in 3 fragrances, 1963, 8-oz	20.00
Cotillion Talc, 53rd Anniversary box, 1939, 2¾-oz	30.00
Decorator Cologne Mist, 4 colors & fragrances	10.00
Decorator Soap Miniatures, glass container, 9¾", MIB	25.00
Deluxe After Shave Powder, brn tin, 1961, 4-oz	15.00
Forever Spring Cologne, clear glass, flower lid, 1951, 4-oz	21.00

Fragrance Bell Cologne, clear glass, w/tag, 1965	20.00
Grape Bud Vase, amethyst glass, bath oil, 1973, 6-oz	6.00
Grecian Pitcher, milk glass, w/stopper, bath oil, 1972, 5-oz	5.00
Harvester, amber glass, 1973	5.00
Hobnail Decanter, milk glass, w/stopper, bath oil, 1972, 5-oz	5.00
Lavender Soap, 3 cakes, 1934-46	50.00
Men's Liquid Hair Lotion, clear bottle/paper label, '50s, 4-oz	15.00

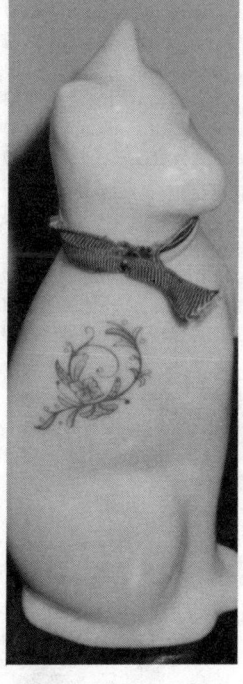

Ming Cat Cologne, milk glass with blue flower, 1971, $10.00.

Merriment Cologne, in Jolly Surprise box, 1955, 4-oz	65.00
Nearness Body Powder, satin glass, bl speckled lid, '56, 3-oz	15.00
Perfumed Pedestal Candle Container, red/wht/or amber, 1965	15.00
Period Piece Decanter, satin glass, skin softener, 1972, 50-oz	5.00
Powder Sachet, cranberry glass, silver lid, 1969, 1½-oz	10.00
Rapture Cologne, gr satin glass, 1964, 2-oz	5.00
Rose Cold Cream, milk glass, silver lid, 1932-34, 2-oz	45.00
Sapphire Swirl Skin Softener, 2 fragrances, 1973, 5-oz	5.00
Smart Move Chess Piece, 1971, MIB	10.00
Smokers Tooth Powder, gr tin, 1931-36	40.00
Spicy Talc for Men, 1962-65, 3-oz	12.00
Sterling Six, smooth top, amber glass, 1968	35.00
Strawberry Bath Foam Pitcher, red glass w/stopper, '71, 4-oz	10.00
Tiffany Lamp Cologne, in 4 fragrances, 1973, 5-oz	10.00
Victoriana Pitcher & Bowl, gr slag, 1971, MIB	13.00
Wishing set, cologne, cream & lotion sachets, 1958, MIB	55.00

Baccarat

The Baccarat Glass company was founded in 1765 near Luneville, France, and continues to this day to produce quality crystal tableware, vases, perfume bottles, and figurines. The firm became famous for the high-quality millefiori and caned paperweights produced there from 1845 until about 1860. Examples of these range from $300 to as much as several thousand. Since 1953 they have resumed the production of paperweights on a limited edition basis. Our advisors for this category are Randall Monsen and Rod Baer. Their address is listed in the Directory under Virginia. See also Paperweights.

Bottle, scent; Elizabeth Arden Cyclamen, wht & gold, 4"	500.00

Bottle, scent; Guerlain Mitsonko, label on front, 4½" 75.00
Bottle, scent; Rose Tiente Swirl, 4¼x1¾".......................................70.00
Bottle, scent; Rose Tiente Swirl, 6¾x2½" 100.00
Bottle, scent; Rose Tiente Swirl, 7½x3" 125.00
Box, Rose Tiente Swirl, lift-off lid, 2x3" **95.00**

Decanter, crystal with etching, 13", $195.00.

Decanter, cut/etched, made for JG Monnet & Co, 14" **200.00**
Decanter, smoky amber texture w/gold geese, 9½", +4 wines.......**200.00**
Hurricane lamp, amberina, bobeche w/4½" prisms, 22", pr **1,000.00**
Lamp, fairy; Rose Tiente Swirl, saucer base, 4x5⅝" **245.00**
Lamp, peg; Rose Tiente Swirl fonts & ruffled shades, 8", pr **950.00**
Shaving brush holder, Rose Tiente Swirl, mk................................**85.00**
Shot glass, millefiori paperweight base, flared rim, 2¼"................**225.00**
Tumble-up set, Rose Tiente Swirl, carafe+plate+tumbler............**225.00**
Tumbler, Rose Tiente Swirl, HP gold florals, w/label, 3¾" **230.00**
Tumbler, Rose Tiente Swirl, mk, 4x2⅞" **70.00**

Badges

The breast badge came into general usage in this country about 1840. Since most are not marked and styles have changed very little to the present day, they are often difficult to date. The most reliable clue is the pin and catch. One of the earliest types, used primarily before the turn of the century, involved a 't-pin' and a 'shell' catch. In a second style, the pin was hinged with a small square of sheet metal, and the clasp was cylindrical. From the late 1800s until about 1940, the pin and clasp were made from one continuous piece of thin metal wire. The same type, with the addition of a flat back plate, was used a little later. There are exceptions to these findings, and other types of clasps were also used. Hallmarks and inscriptions may also help pinpoint an approximate age.

Badges have been made from a variety of materials, usually brass or nickel silver; but even solid silver and gold were used for special orders. They are found in many basic shapes and variations — stars with five to seven points, shields, disks, ovals, and octagonals being most often encountered. Of prime importance to collectors, however, is that the title and/or location appear on the badge. Those with designations of positions no longer existing (City Constable, for example) and names of early western states and towns are most valuable.

Badges are among the most commonly-reproduced (and faked) types of antiques on the market. At any flea market, ten fakes can be

found for every authentic example. Genuine law badges start at $30.00 to $40.00 for recent examples (1950-1970); earlier pieces (1910-1930) usually bring $50.00 to $90.00. Pre-1900 badges often sell for more than $100.00. Authentic gold badges are usually priced at a minimum of scrap value (karat, weight, spot price for gold); fine gold badges from before 1900 can sell for $400.00 to $800.00, and a few will bring even more. A fire badge is usually valued at about half the price of a law badge from the same circa and material.

Our advisor for this category is Gene Matzke; he is listed in the Directory under Wisconsin.

New Castle Police, nickel plated, $60.00.

Austin Patrol Service, eagle atop shield, enamel/silver metal **24.00**
Chauffer, OH, 1937 ....**25.00**
Chicago Police Patrolman, 5-point star, enamel on silver..............**80.00**
Curity, PA state seal/gr enameling on wht metal, Mercer, 2½".......**12.00**
Deputy Constable, CO, brass, 6-point star, sm **40.00**
Deputy Game Warden, King Co **75.00**
Deputy Sheriff, Douglas Co NB, 6-point star, silver tone...............**45.00**
Deputy Sheriff, Laramie, 5-point star, silver metal **20.00**
Deputy Sheriff, Morgan Co IN, shield, SJ Meyer hallmk **75.00**
Game Warden, IL Dept of Conservation......................................**100.00**
NY Police Detective DEA, sunburst shield, enameling, EX...........**40.00**
Police, Stock Show, Ft Worth TX, star w/in shield, brass **55.00**
Security, eagle atop PA state seal, wht metal, Whittaker, 3" **14.00**
Special Police, Indianapolis IN, 1950, M.......................................**25.00**
TX Security Systems, eagle atop shield, Blackington hallmk.........**27.50**

Banks

Auctions continue to impact prices, especially for mechanical banks. Last year 60% of the banks sold at auction went above estimates; this year 71%. 16% were sold within the estimates, and only 13% went low. While 'auction fever' can inflate prices, it appears that the increases seen this year reflect the quality of the banks that went to auction. Quality is dominating the market. Pristine or mint condition banks consistently bring premium prices, often two or three times the amount an average bank will command. If you are interested in banks, always seek the best. They will cost more but always prove to be the best value. Banks should be complete, with all parts present, original, and in working condition (if it is mechanical). Replaced parts or retouched paint lessen a bank's value. Rarity is important, but condition is driving the market. It is becoming increasingly important that the collector carefully study the market and fully understand the factors that determine price. Go to as many shows as possible, look and feel the quality of the banks. Read all you can about the hobby, but there is nothing like hands-on experience. If you are not sure of yourself, find a good collector or dealer who can give you sound advice.

The category of mechanical banks is unique. Along with cast iron bell toys, they are among the most outstanding products of the Industrial Revolution and are recognized as some of the most successful of the mass-produced products of the nineteenth century. The earliest mechanicals were made of wood or lead; but when John Hall introduced Hall's Excelsior, a cast iron mechanical bank, it was an immediate success. J. & E. Stevens produced the bank for Hall and soon began to make their own designs. Several companies followed suit, most of which were already in the hardware business. They used newly developed iron-molding techniques to produce these novelty savings devices for the emerging toy market. Mechanical banks reflect the social and political attitudes of the times, racial prejudices, the excitement of the circus, and humorous everyday events. Their designers made the most of simple mechanics to produce banks with captivating actions that served not only to amuse but to promote the concept of thrift to the children. The quality of detail in the castings are truly fine examples of industrial art. The most collectible examples were made during the period of 1870 to 1900; however, they continued to be made until the early days of World War II. J. & E. Stevens, Shepard Hardware, and Kyser and Rex are some of the more well-known manufacturers; most made still banks as well.

Still banks are widely collected, and you can literally choose from thousands of banks. No one knows exactly how many different banks were made, but at least three thousand have been identified in the various books published on the subject. Cast iron examples still dominate the market, but the lead banks from Europe are growing in value. Tin and early pottery banks are drawing more interest as well. American pottery banks which were primarily collected by Americana collectors are becoming more important in the still bank field. This market has not been as volatile as the mechanical banks, but the number of collectors is growing. The auction market on still banks is not as extensive as with the mechanicals, but some nice examples do turn up. Collectors and dealers are still the best source.

While the cast iron banks dominate the market, there are examples made from many other materials. Combinations of tin and cardboard and banks made from tin alone are very collectible. Some of the European tin banks are quite rare; England made some fine cast iron mechanicals and many aluminum examples. The popularity of old mechanicals has created a market for reproductions and fakes. Reproductions may have minor value as such, but not as true collectibles. A few of the fakes have attained collectible status but are still not regarded as true mechanical banks.

As both value and interest continue on the increase, it becomes even more important to educate one's self to the fullest extent possible. We recommend these books for your library: *The Dictionary of Still Banks* by Long and Pitman, *The Penny Bank Book* by Moore, and *The Bank Book* by Norman. If you are primarily interested in mechanicals, *Penny Lane*, a new book by Davidson, is considered the most complete reference available. It contains a cross-reference listing of numbers from all other publications on mechanical banks.

In the listings that follow, banks are identified by L for Long, G for Griffith, M for Moore, N for Norman, D for Davidson, and W for Whiting.

Key:
CI — cast iron   NPCI — nickel-plated cast iron
EPCI — electroplated cast iron

Advertising

Amherst Stoves, buffalo, CI, EX details, 8", NM..........................850.00
Bank on John Deere Quality, mechanical blksmith, '50, 7", EX 95.00

Bank on Republic Pig Iron, M-331, CI, no pnt, modern, 7"..........25.00
Bocar Coffee, tin, M 12.50
Chevrolet Car, 1953 ....95.00
Cities Service, cb 20.00
Coca-Cola, M-1605, machine, pnt CI, 3¾", EX 3,750.00
Edison phonograph, lead, EX 165.00
Eureka Gas Heater, M-1350, tin, minor wear, 5¼"......................60.00

Left: First Federal, right: First National, $50.00 each.

Gem Furnace, M-1364, CI, worn blk pnt, 4⅝" 105.00
Howard Johnson's Restaurant, CI, dk patina, modern, 4¼" L......45.00
Ideal Stoves, stove, pnt CI, EX..475.00
James' Salt Water Taffy, compo bbl, tin lid, M............................40.00
Majestic Ice Box, M-1332, CI & sheet metal 250.00
New Heatrola, M-1354, stove, CI, worn pnt, 4½" 140.00
Old Dutch Cleanser, tin 25.00
Prudential, book, leatherette cover, no key 22.00
Radiation Stoves, L-1018, tin, minor wear, 5¼" 135.00
Red Goose Shoes, goose, CI, old worn pnt, 3¾"..........................175.00
Rival Dog Food, tin 12.50
Rochester Trust & Save, CI, 5", EX..100.00
Roper Range, M-1341, Arcade, CI, mc pnt, 4" 350.00
Sinclair, gas pump, EX...22.50
Sinclair Power X, EX...12.00
Tang Robot, plastic.. 5.00
Universal Stoves, revolving glove, tin, NM...............................250.00
Use Jumbo Soap, elephant form, CI, EX 725.00
Viking Coffee, tin, 4"...18.00
West Chemical Products, tin, M 25.00
Wolf Head Motor Oil, CI..15.00
York Stove, M-1351, stove, pnt CI, 4", EX 350.00

Mechanical

Always Did 'Spise a Mule, N-250, bench, 9¾", EX.................. 1,200.00
Artillery, D-12, J&E Stevens, rebel variant, EX pnt, 5".......... 2,100.00
Artillery, D-12, J&E Stevens, Shepard-Adams, VG pnt, 6" 1,400.00
Atlas Bank, D-13, iron/wht metal/paper on wood, 8", EX 3,300.00
Bad Accident, D-20, J&E Stevens, CI, EX pnt, 10"................. 2,860.00
Bank of Education & Economy, D-23, Proctor-Raymond, G ... 1,500.00
Bear & Tree Stump, D-20, Judd, pnt CI, 5", EX 1,200.00
Big Chief Moon, D-108, J&E Stevens, pnt CI, 10", EX........... 4,950.00
Bill E Grin, D-33, J&E Stevens, worn pnt, no trap, 4½" 600.00
Bird on Roof, D-36, J&E Stevens, CI, rare silver pnt, 6½" 2,200.00
Boy Robbing Bird's Nest, D-51, J&E Stevens, pnt CI, 6", EX . 4,500.00
Boy Scout Camp, D-52, J&E Stevens, pnt CI, 9⅞", EX 4,500.00
Boy Stealing Watermelon, Kyser & Rex, pnt CI, 1885, 6½" ... 3,400.00
Bucking Mule, D-58, Judd, CI, EX pnt, 4½" 1,100.00
Bull Tosses Boy in Well, CI, bronze pnt, later repro, EX.............880.00
Bulldog, D-64, coin on nose, J&E Stevens, pnt CI, 7", G........ 1,320.00
Butting Goat, N-1580A, Judd, pnt CI, 4½", VG......................660.00
Cabin, D-93, J&E Stevens, yel variant, no trap, 3½", EX 550.00

Calamity, D-94, J&E Stevens, pnt CI, bl sleeves, 7⅛", EX.....**18,700.00**

Cat and Mouse, Cat Balancing, D-104, painted cast iron, EX, $9,500.00.

Chimpanzee, N-1760C, Kyser & Rex, bl variant, 6", EX **5,280.00**
Circus Ticket Collector, D-115, Judd, pnt CI, 5½", EX **935.00**
Clown & Dog, D-123, Germany, tin litho, G pnt, 7" **1,870.00**
Clown on Globe, D-227, J&E Stevens, CI, faded pnt, 9" **1,980.00**
Confectionary, D-131, Kyser & Rex, pnt CI, 8½", EX **8,800.00**
Creedmoor, D-137, J&E Stevens, pnt CI, lt wear, 10", EX...... **2,600.00**
Dapper Dan, D-145, Marx, tin litho, keywind, 10", EX **660.00**
Dinah, D-153, Harper, pnt CI, short sleeves, 7", VG.................**400.00**
Dinah, N-2150B, Harper, pnt CI, long sleeves, 6½", EX **850.00**
Eagle & Eaglets, D-165, J&E Stevens, pnt CI, no trap, 8", EX **715.00**
Elephant & 3 Clowns, D-170, J&E Stevens, CI, G pnt, 5¾" .. **1,700.00**
Elephant Pull Tail, D-174, Hubley, wht variant, 5½", EX **550.00**
Elephant w/Howdah, D-173, Enterprise, bronze pnt, EX **715.00**
Frog on Rnd Base, D-204, J&E Stevens, pnt CI, 4½", EX............**750.00**
Frog on Rock, D-203, Kilgore, pnt CI, minor wear, 2¾" **700.00**
Frogs (2), D-94, J&E Stevens, CI, minor rpt/rpl eyes, 8" **2,400.00**
Gem, N-2570A, Judd, CI, gr wash, 5½", EX.................................**935.00**
Girl Skipping Rope, D-217, J&E Stevens, pnt CI, 8", EX **25,000.00**
Hall's Excelsior, D-228, J&E Stevens, tan variant, 5½", EX **495.00**
Hall's Lilliput Bank, D-230, Stevens, yel version, 4½", EX **1,980.00**

Hen and Chick, D-236, cast iron, faded paint, 10" long, $6,820.00.

Hindu, D-239, Kyser & Rex, pnt CI, minor wear, 6" **1,200.00**
Hold the Fort, D-240, bronze pattern, 6½", EX........................ **2,860.00**
Horse Race, D-247, J&E Stevens, pnt CI, flanged base, EX **4,500.00**
Humpty Dumpty, D-248, Shepard, CI/over-cleaned pnt, 7½" **880.00**
Indian Shooting Bear, D-257, Stevens, pnt CI, 10¼", EX **2,100.00**
Initiating Bank, 1st Degree; N-3000A, CI, worn pnt/lt rust **8,500.00**
Jolly Nigger, N-3370, J&E Stevens, pnt CI, 6½", EX **750.00**
Jonah & Whale, G-142, Shepard Hardware, 1890s, 10½", EX **3,200.00**
Leap Frog, D-292, Shepard Hardware, pnt CI, 5", EX **6,500.00**
Leap Frog, G-147, Shepard Hardware, pnt CI, 7½", EX **3,300.00**
Lighthouse, D-298, CI, rpt on cottage, 10½", EX **1,300.00**
Lion & 2 Monkeys, Kyser & Rex, ca 1883, pnt CI, 9", VG..... **1,100.00**
Little Jocko Musical Bank, D-303, Strauss, tin litho, EX pnt .. **3,200.00**
Magician, D-315, J&E Stevens, CI, VG pnt, 8"........................ **6,800.00**
Magician, Disappearing Hat Trick; CI w/3-color pnt, 8" **2,900.00**
Mammy & Child, D-318, Kyser & Rex, EX pnt, 9" **8,500.00**
Mason, D-321, Shepard, pnt CI, no trap, EX **6,500.00**
Memorial Money (Liberty Bell), D-322, Enterprise, EX pnt........**440.00**
Merry-Go-Round, M-1614, Grey Iron Casting, G pnt, 4½".........**350.00**
Milking Cow, Book of Knowledge repro, 9⅝"...............................**65.00**
Milking Cow, G-168, J&E Stevens, pnt CI, 10", VG **3,000.00**
Monkey, D-334, Hubley, pnt CI, 8", EX **600.00**
Monkey & Coconut, D-332, J&E Stevens, pnt CI, 8½", EX **2,500.00**
Mosque, D-340, Judd, brass figural finial, VG pnt, 9½" **850.00**
Mule Entering Barn, D-342, J&E Stevens, CI, 8½", EX **1,750.00**
National Recording, M-1062, pnt CI, 6½", EX **300.00**
New Bank, D-357, J&E Stevens, front lever, pnt CI, 5", EX .. **1,980.00**
New Creedmore, D-358, Stevens, pnt CI, rpl screw, 10", EX . **1,200.00**
Octagonal Fort, D-363, CI, VG pnt, minor crazing, 10¾" L ... **6,050.00**
Organ Bank, D-369, Kyser & Rex, cat & dog, EX pnt, 8".........**935.00**
Organ Bank, D-370, Kyser & Rex, pnt CI, yel coat, 3¾", EX **935.00**
Organ Bank, D-371, Kyser & Rex, pnt CI, minor wear, 6½" **880.00**
Owl, D-373, slot in book, Kilgore, pnt CI, 5½", EX **880.00**
Owl Turns Head, D-375, J&E Stevens, pnt CI, 7½", EX **715.00**
Paddy & Pig, N-4400B, J&E Stevens, pnt CI, flaw, 8" **3,500.00**
Panorama, D-377, J&E Stevens, gr variant, 6½", EX............... **5,200.00**
Peg-Leg Beggar, D-380, Judd, pnt CI, 5½", EX **2,500.00**
Pelican, N-4510, Trenton Lock, CI, gold pnt, 8", EX............. **4,200.00**
Picture Gallery, D-385, Shepard, CI, worn pnt, 8½" **8,250.00**
Pig in Highchair, G-210, J&E Stevens, pnt CI, 5¼", VG **660.00**

Professor Pug Frog's Great Bicycle Feat, D-400, EX, $12,000.00.

Punch & Judy, D-404, Shepard, CI, VG pnt, no base plate **1,320.00**
Quarter Century, Reynolds, complete w/ingots, NM **550.00**

Rabbit in Cabbage, D-408, Kilgore, CI, VG pnt, 4" 700.00
Rabbit Standing, Small; D-407, Lockwood, rpt, 5½" 825.00
Rooster, D-419, Kyser & Rex, pnt CI, 6½", EX.................550.00
Santa at Chimney, N-5010, Shepard, pnt CI, 6", EX 1,200.00
Snap It, D-445, Judd, CI, VG mc pnt, 4", EX.................495.00
Speaking Dog, D-447, J&E Stevens, bl dress, 7¼", EX 2,200.00
Springing Cat, G-250, Chas Bailey, lead/wood, 9", EX 23,000.00
Squirrel on Tree Stump, D-452, Mechanical Novelty ..., EX .. 1,760.00
Stump Speaker, D-453, Shepard, pnt CI, 9½", EX 2,100.00
Tabby, D-454, CI, VG pnt, rpl chick, 4¾" 240.00
Tammany, D-455, J&E Stevens, pnt CI, blk coat, 5½", EX 660.00
Teddy & Bear, D-459, J&E Stevens, pnt CI, 7", EX 3,000.00
Telephone, D-462, J&E Stevens, NPCI, minor rust, 6½" 700.00
Thrifty Tom, D-468, keywind, pnt CI, 9", EX.................715.00
Trick Buffalo, D-601, pnt CI, lever jammed, 9½", EX 3,500.00
Trick Dog, D-481, Shepard, CI, rpt, 8½", VG.................460.00
Trick Dog, D-482, Hubley, pnt CI, bl base, 8½", EX 600.00
Trick Pony, G-272, Shepard, pnt CI, 1880s, 7", EX.................2,800.00
Uncle Remus, D-492, Kyser & Rex, pnt CI, rpl trap, 4", EX .. 3,960.00
Uncle Sam, Book of Knowledge repro, 11".................75.00
Uncle Sam, D-493, Shepard Hardware, CI, worn pnt, 11½" .. 2,420.00
Watchdog Safe, D-560, J&E Stevens, CI, VG pnt, 6½" 715.00
Weeden's Plantation D-562, keywind, minor wear, 5½" 2,090.00
William Tell, D-565, J&E Stevens, pnt CI, 1896, 10½", EX... 1,875.00
World's Fair, D-573, J&E Stevens, CI, partial rpt, 8", EX 825.00
Zoo, D-576, att Kyser & Rex, pnt CI, 4¼", EX.................2,650.00

Registering

Astronaut Daily Dime.................20.00
Bean Pot 5¢ register, M-951, CI, VG pnt, 3".................270.00
Bed Post 5¢ register, M-1305.................70.00
Beehive Savings, M-681, NPCI, pnt traces, 5¼".................125.00
Beehive 10¢ register, M-681, Am Mfg, pnt CI, lt wear, 5½".................440.00
Bucket 1¢ register, CI, Japan, Pat Appl, 2¾".................90.00
Dopey 10¢ register, Disney, 1938, EX.................60.00

Five Coin Security Bank, ca 1918, 7", $135.00.

Jr Cash, M-930, worn NPCI, lt rust, 4¼".................50.00
NY World's Fair 1¢ register, M-1566, tin, M on card.................55.00
Pail 1¢ register, M-912, CI, worn pnt, 2¾".................220.00
Popeye 10¢ register, NM.................65.00
Prudential, NPCI, pat Feb 25, 1890, worn label, 7¼", EX.................425.00

Pump & Bucket 10¢ register, D-401, pnt CI, 6½", EX 2,000.00
Snow White.................185.00
Spinning Wheel, W Germany, tin litho w/2 scenes, sq, 4½".................25.00
Trunk, Phoenix 10¢ register, M-947, NPCI, worn blk pnt, 5".................95.00
World Scope 32.00

Still

$100,000 Money Bag, M-1262, pnt CI, NM.................575.00
Arabian Safe, M-882, Kyser & Rex, CI, mc wash, 4½", EX.................400.00
Aunt Jemima, M-175, w/basket, pnt wht metal, 5¼", EX.................65.00
Baseball Player on Base, M-22, lead, 5⅞", EX.................110.00
Bear Stealing Honey, M-1308, CI, japanning w/gold, 7", EX 175.00
Billiken, M-74, CI, gold pnt traces, 4⅛".................320.00
Billy Bounce, M-14, Wing, pnt CI, 4¾", EX.................650.00
Boston Bulldog, M-413, seated, CI, EX pnt, 4⅜".................235.00
Boston State House, M-1210, CI, EX pnt, 5⅛".................4,600.00
Boy Scout, M-47, w/buckle & scarf, pnt CI, 5¾", EX.................325.00
Boy w/Empty Pockets, M-274, lead, EX pnt, 3⅞".................850.00
Brementown Musicians, M-649, lead, 5⅜", EX.................1,200.00
Bulldog, M-357, CI, gold pnt, minor wear, dented, 4⅜".................65.00
Bulldog w/Collar, M-399, lead, worn pnt, 3".................275.00
Bungalow, M-999, pnt CI, 3¾", EX.................375.00
Bush-Quail, elephant, Reynolds, aluminum, M.................70.00
Camel, M-768, CI, 4¾", EX.................200.00
Capitolist, M-5, pnt CI, minor wear, 5".................1,500.00

Cat with ball, 5½", $395.00.

Cash Register Savings, M-1538, pnt CI, EX.................900.00
Church Towers, M-956, CI, worn pnt, 6¾".................625.00
Circus Elephant, M-462, pnt CI, 3⅞", EX.................350.00
City Bank w/Teller, M-1099, pnt CI, 5¼", EX.................350.00
Clown w/Crooked Hat, M-210, pnt CI, 6¾", EX.................2,000.00
Crosley Radio, M-819, Kenton, pnt CI, 5⅛", EX.................650.00
Cupola, M-1146, CI, red pnt w/mc trim, minor wear, 4".................115.00
Dog on Drum, M-359, CI, pnt traces, 4⅛".................75.00
Dolphin, M-33, Grey Iron Casting, CI, pnt traces, 4½".................450.00
Donkey, M-488, w/blanket, Kenton, pnt CI, 3⅞", EX.................750.00
Donkey, M-505, w/drum, lead & tin, worn pnt, 3½".................275.00
Dutch Boy, M-17, Grey Iron Casting, pnt CI, 6¾", VG.................575.00
Eggman, M-108, Arcade, CI, worn pnt, 4⅛", EX.................2,200.00
Eiffel Tower, M-1075, pnt CI, 10½", EX.................925.00
Elephant, M-445, seated, CI, worn pnt, 4¼", EX.................550.00
Elephant, M-463, Hoover/Curtis, CI, worn pnt, 3¾".................1,475.00
Elephant, M-479, w/chariot, Hubley, pnt CI, 4¾", EX.................2,700.00
Elephant, M-487, w/blanket, Kenton, pnt CI, 3⅛", EX.................650.00
Elephant, M-587, CI, worn red pnt, 4⅛" L.................65.00
Ferdinand the Bull, M-290, Crown, pnt compo, 5⅛", VG.................50.00
Ferris Wheel, M-1606, NPCI, lt wear, 4½".................1,025.00

Fidelity Trust Vault, M-903, JB Smith, pnt CI, 6½", EX 1,100.00
Fido on Pillow, M-443, Hubley, CI, rpt, 4" 300.00
Flatiron Building, M-1159, Kenton, pnt CI, 8¼", EX 1,250.00
Flatiron Building, M-1160, CI, silver pnt, no trap, 5¾" 65.00
Floral Safe, M-885, Kyser & Rex, CI, gold wash, 4½", EX 165.00
Flower Girl, M-1650, pnt lead, 4¾", EX 725.00
Football Player, M-11, Williams, CI, worn pnt, 5⅞" 400.00
Foxy Grandpa, M-320, Hubley, pnt CI, 5½", EX 450.00
General Butler, M-54, pnt CI, lt wear, 6½", EX 850.00
Gingerbread House, M-1029, pnt CI, 3⅞", EX 800.00
Give Me a Penny, L-733, Wing Mfg, CI, 5¾" 175.00
Globe, M-781, CI, worn red & gold pnt, 5½" 90.00
Globe on Wire Arc, M-785, Arcade, CI, 4⅝", EX 275.00
Globe Savings Fund, M-1199, pnt CI, 7⅛", EX 2,200.00
Golliwog, M-85, England, CI, EX pnt, 6¼" 475.00
Good Luck Horseshoe, M-508, pnt CI, 4¼", EX 300.00
Graf Zeppelin, M-1428, CI, worn silver pnt, 6¾" L 145.00
Gunboat Oregon, M-1463, CI, no masts, 5¼", EX 850.00
High Rise, M-1216, Kenton, pnt CI, 7", EX 825.00
Hippopotamus, M-721, CI, worn gold pnt, 5" L 200.00
Home Bank, M-1019, pnt CI, 4", EX 600.00
Horse, M-509, on tub, CI, blk & silver pnt, 5⅝", EX 125.00
House, M-922, 2-story, CI, gr & silver pnt, 4⅛", EX 110.00
Husky, M-411, CI, EX pnt, 5" 500.00
Independence Hall, M-1202, Enterprise, pnt CI, 10", EX 500.00
Indian, M-223, w/teepee, lead, worn pnt, 3¾" 275.00
Indian, M-228, w/tomahawk, CI, worn pnt, 5⅞" 320.00
Indian Bust, M-222, w/headdress, lead, EX pnt, 3⅝" 50.00
Iron Masters House, M-1027, Kyser & Rex, CI, 4¼", EX............775.00
Japanese Safe, M-1667, pnt CI, 5¾", VG 340.00
Jarmulowsky Building, M-1086, Stevens, CI, 7¾", EX 1,225.00
Jimmy Durante, M-259, wht metal, 6¾", NM 125.00
John Bull, M-1655, pnt lead, minor wear, 4½" 200.00
Jolly Nigger, N-3330, Shepard Hardware, CI, rpt, 6⅝" 125.00
Kewpie, M-292, papier-mache, worn mc pnt, no trap, 5" 35.00
King Midas, M-13, Hubley, pnt CI, 4½", EX 3,000.00
Lindbergh, M-124, w/goggles, aluminum, 6½", EX 220.00
Lindbergh, M-124, w/goggles, lead, 5⅞", EX 300.00
Mainstreet w/People, M-1471, CI, worn pnt, 3" 400.00
Man on Cotton Bale, M-37, CI, worn pnt, 4⅞" 2,500.00
Marietta Silo, M-1246, pnt CI, 5½", EX 800.00
Mary & Lamb, M-164, CI, worn pnt, 4⅜" 850.00
Mascot, M-3, Hubley 1914, pnt CI, 5¾", EX 1,800.00
Masonic Temple, M-1061, brass, 6", EX 525.00
Merry-Go-Round, M-1614, pnt CI, 4⅝", EX 1,325.00
Metropolitan, M-904, J&E Stevens, pnt CI, 6", EX 440.00
Mickey Mouse, M-202, movable head, pnt compo, EX 210.00
Monkey Smoking, M-739, pnt lead, 4½", EX........................ 1,100.00
North Pole, M-1372, brass, foundry pattern, 4¼" 375.00
Old Sleepy Eye, M-225, pnt lead, 3⅛", EX 525.00
Old South Church, M-991, pnt CI, 13", EX 6,250.00
Patriotic Hat, M-1372, tin, little wear, 2", EX 200.00
Pig w/Curly Hair, M-583, lead, worn pnt, 2⅞" 150.00
Pinocchio, M-281, Crown, compo, 5⅛", EX 80.00
Pocahontas Bust, M-226, lead, EX pnt, 3⅛" 100.00
Polar Bear, M-716, CI, worn pnt, 5¼" 340.00
Policeman, M-182, Arcade, pnt CI, 5½", EX 900.00
Porkey Pig at Barrel, M-265, pnt wht metal, 4½", MIB.............350.00
Punch & Judy, M-1299, pnt tin, 4¼", EX 200.00
Punch & Judy, M-1300, pnt tin, 2¾", EX 750.00
Rabbit, M-569, on base, CI, worn pnt, 2¼" 750.00
Reagan '85, Reynolds, aluminum, M 75.00
Rhino, M-721, Arcade, pnt CI, 2⅝", EX 625.00
Roly Poly Monkey, M-1227, tin, lt wear, 6" 300.00

Sailor Boy, M-272, lead, EX pnt, 4⅛" 750.00
Santa, M-1673, w/pack, Arcade, CI, worn pnt, 5", EX 3,600.00
Santa, M-59, Wing/Hubley, CI, worn pnt, 5⅞" 425.00
Santa, M-61, w/tree, Hubley, pnt CI, 5⅞", EX 475.00
Santa Riding Snail, Reynolds, aluminum, NM 45.00
Save...To Make Dollars, M-1545, eagle clock, CI, 3½" 165.00
Saving Sam, M-158, aluminum, EX pnt, 5¼" 525.00
Seal on Rock, M-732, CI, worn pnt, 3½" 525.00
Security Safe, Kyser & Rex, pnt CI, 6", EX 385.00
Sniffles at Barrel, M-293, pnt wht metal, 5⅛", MIB 375.00
Snowman w/Broom, M-92, Reynolds, aluminum, 4⅝", NM 70.00
Soccer Player, M-276, pnt lead, 4½", EX 575.00
Spaniel, M-361, begging, pnt lead, minor wear, 4⅜" 300.00
Statue of Liberty, M-1164, CI, worn gold pnt, 5" 115.00
Stop Sign, M-1479, Dent, pnt CI, 4½", EX 290.00
Sweet Thrift, D-550, Beverly, tin plate, 6", EX 240.00
Teddy Roosevelt, M-120, CI, pnt traces, 5" 375.00
Templetone Radio, M-826, Kenton, pnt CI, 4¼", EX................360.00
Time, N-5550, CI & glass, worn pnt, VG...............................575.00
Tower (1890), M-1198, pnt CI, 6⅞", EX 1,225.00
Turkey, M-587, CI, worn pnt, 3⅜" 160.00
US Letter Box, M-860, tin, 9¾", EX 525.00
US Mail, M-861, on Victorian base, pnt CI, EX 900.00
US Treasury, M-1053, CI, worn pnt, 3¼" 275.00
Villa, M-959, Kyser & Rex, CI, worn pnt, 5½" 400.00
Washington Monument, M-1048, CI, EX gold pnt, 6⅛" 125.00
Washington Monument, M-1049, CI, worn pnt, 7½" 275.00
Water Wheel, M-1606, CI & steel, 4½", EX 950.00
West Point Mule, M-501, pnt lead, 4⅞", EX 225.00
White City Safe #357, M-922, pnt CI, 2¾", EX 310.00
Wisconsin War Eagle, M-678, pnt CI, 2⅞", EX 1,250.00
Woolworth Building, M-1041, CI, gold pnt, minor wear, 8"..........95.00
Yellow Cab, Arcade, pnt CI, rpl driver, 8", VG 750.00

Palace, M-1116, EX finish, 8", $1,980.00.

Barber Shop Collectibles

Even for the stranger in town, the local barber shop was easy to find, its location vividly marked with the traditional red and white striped barber pole that for centuries identified such establishments. As far back as the twelfth century, the barber has had a place in recorded history. At one time he not only groomed the beards and cut the hair of his gentlemen clients but was known as the 'blood-letter' as well, hence the red stripe for blood and the white for the bandages. Many early barbers even pulled teeth! Later, laws were enacted that divided the practices of barbering and surgery.

The Victorian barber shop reflected the charm of that era with fancy barber chairs upholstered in rich wine-colored velvet; rows of bottles made from colored art glass held hair tonics and shaving lotion. Backbars of richly carved oak with beveled mirrors lined the wall behind the barber's station. During the late nineteenth century, the barber pole with a blue stripe added to the standard red and white as a patriotic gesture came into vogue.

Today the barber shop has all but disappeared from the American scene, replaced by modern unisex salons. Collectors search for the barber poles, the fancy chairs, and the tonic bottles of an era gone but not forgotten. See also Bottles; Razors; Shaving Mugs.

Blade bank, Dandy Dan, celluloid, mc, w/tool holder, 6½" 15.00
Chair, blk leather & stainless steel, Deco style, 1940s, EX...........200.00
Chair, Koch, oak, Pat 1896, EX 750.00
Chair, Koken, CI w/oak wood, rstr upholstery, 42", EX 1,100.00

Child's barber chair, porcelainized and nickel-plated cast iron, leather, and wood, with carved horse head, marked Emil J. Pidar, Chicago, 43", $1,200.00.

Display case, for brushes, glass, 11½x11½x5½"................................65.00
Mustache iron, sterling, ornate, w/brush 75.00
Neck duster, sterling scroll hdl, soft bristles, 7½"............................65.00
Pole, art glass, wall hanging, Koken.. 1,200.00
Pole, baluster trns, 3-color w/gilt ball finials, 1800s, 24"......... 1,650.00
Pole, leaded glass, Koken, 1890s, 32", VG 350.00
Pole, metal & plexiglas, 13x5½", EX..245.00
Pole, porc, red & wht stripe, 50", EX 195.00
Pole, trn wood w/mc rpt, age cracks, 90" 900.00
Pole, trn wood w/traces of pnt, base added, 77" 275.00
Pole, trn/rope cvd, red/wht rpt, 35", pr 400.00
Post card, barber shop scene, comic, 1909, EX 12.50
Razor sharpener, mechanical, Farney Model 1904, 9½x7x4" 110.00
Sterilizer, brass plated, Antiseptic, hinged top, 8" 42.50
Strop, Kriss Kross Stropper, VG in orig cb box...............................22.00
Strop, leather, sterling silver hdl w/florals, rare..............................95.00
Tool case, solid oak, compartments, brass hinges, 9x6½x3" 65.00

Barometers

Barometers are instruments designed to measure the weight or pressure of the atmosphere in order to anticipate approaching weather

changes. Those made around the turn of the century (earlier in England and on the continent) were beautifully housed in period cases of mahogany, rosewood, walnut, or cherry, often with brass trim. These quality pieces bring high prices on today's market.

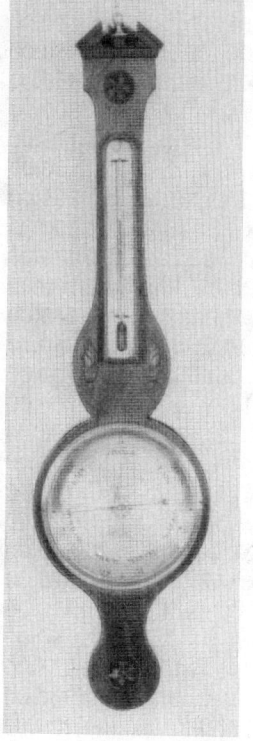

Federal inlaid mahogany barometer, dial signed A. Barnascone, Boston, MA, minor chips, 39", $4,600.00.

A Buseya, Preston, mahog veneer w/inlay, banjo form, 39" 600.00
Admiral Fitzroy's Barometer, paper bk, oak case, 42" 275.00
Chas Wilder, bird's eye walnut, brass face mk Woodruff Pat 900.00
L Meyer Coblenz, walnut w/porc face, mercury tube, 39" 250.00
P Ramos, London, mahog veneer w/inlay, needs rpr, 38".............375.00

Basalt

Basalt is a type of unglazed black pottery developed by Josiah Wedgwood and copied by many other companies during the late eighteenth and early nineteenth centuries. It was also called 'Egyptian Black.' See also Wedgwood.

Coffeepot, emb motif, dome lid w/widow Warburton, 10", VG ..300.00
Creamer, silver rim, ca 1850..75.00
Plaque, Bacchanalian motif, dk brn, E Mayer, fr, 4x6", pr 880.00
Spill vase, emb cherubs, copper lustre int, 4¾"............................200.00
Sugar bowl, ribs/cherubs, Widow Warburton finial, Mayer, 5" 165.00

Baskets

Basket weaving is a craft as old as ancient history. Baskets have been used to harvest crops, for domestic chores, and to contain the catch of fishermen. Materials at hand were utilized, and baskets from a specific region are often distinguishable simply by analyzing the natural fibers used in their construction. Early Indian baskets were made of corn husks or woven grasses. Willow splint, straw, rope, and paper were also used. Until the invention of the veneering machine in the late 1800s, splint was made by water-soaking a split log until the fibers were softened and flexible. Long strips were pulled out by hand and, while still wet and pliable, woven into baskets in either a cross-hatch or hexagonal weave.

Most handcrafted baskets on the market today were made between 1860 and the early 1900s. Factory baskets with a thick, wide splint cut by machine are of little interest to collectors. The more popular baskets are those designed for a specific purpose, rather than the more commonly-found utility baskets that had multiple uses. Among the most costly forms are the Nantucket Lighthouse baskets, which were basically copied from those made there for centuries by aboriginal Indians. They were designed in the style of whale oil barrels and named for the South Shoal Nantucket Lightship where many were made during the last half of the nineteenth century. Cheese baskets (used to separate curds from whey), herb-gathering baskets, and finely woven Shaker miniatures are other highly-prized examples of the basket weaver's art.

In the listings that follow, assume that each has a center bentwood handle (unless handles of another type are noted) that is not included in the height. Unless another type of material is indicated, assume that each is made of splint. See also American Indian; Eskimo; Sewing; Shaker.

Buttocks, EX age/color, minor damage, 7½x12x14" 95.00
Buttocks, EX color, 5x8½x8½" 175.00
Buttocks, fine wear, 12½x14" 150.00
Buttocks, late, 6½x11x12" 55.00
Buttocks, oak, cvd hdl, closely wrapped/woven, 12" 165.00
Buttocks, worn finish, 23" dia 115.00
Buttocks, 9x15x15" 165.00
Cheese, splint, minor damage, scrubbed, 16" dia 135.00
Curlicue rim, natural patina w/bl, rim hdls, ME, 11" L, EX 215.00
Egg, EX age/color, wear/damage, 16x17" 65.00
Gathering, oak, walnut dyed bands, low hdl, 13" 85.00
Gathering, sides slant to sq bottom, ca 1890s, 8x6" 175.00
Laundry, wide splint, rim hdls, 21" dia 65.00
Market, oak, sq swing dbl hdls, flat, 12½x15" 175.00
Melon rib, decorative design at hdl, 7x13" dia 100.00

Nantucket basket, oval with turned wood base and bentwood handle, 14½" wide, $990.00.

Nantucket, cane/splint, swivel hdl, worn, 7x12½" 850.00
Nantucket, swing hdl, brass fasteners, label: Ray, 6x8" 1,900.00
Nantucket, swing hdl, brass fasteners, rim damage, 7x9" 850.00

Nantucket, swing hdl, brass fasteners, 5x6½", NM 1,400.00
Nantucket, swing hdl, brass fasteners, 7½x11", EX 1,650.00
Nantucket, swing hdl, trn base, Wm Appleton, 8x12" 1,700.00
Nantucket, swing hdl, wood bottom, 10" dia...........................500.00
Nantucket, 1-egg sz, made by Sylvaro, 1900s, 3x3½", EX 650.00
Potato print, red/bl on yel, no hdl, pristine, 5x12x13" 325.00
Potato print & watercolor design in bl & red, 5x8x10" 155.00
Rye straw, conical, rim hdls, minor damage, 8½x16" 85.00
Rye straw, w/lid, 12½" 55.00
Splint, ash, bulbous, X-wrapped rim & base, ca 1850s, 8½" 175.00
Splint, bentwood rim hdls, EX worn finish, 12x17", EX 125.00
Splint, bowl shape, wrapped rim, ca mid-1800s, 4¾x10x7" 110.00
Splint, deep bowl form, 5x8½" 100.00
Splint, deep bowl form, 8x14" 125.00
Splint, EX detail/patina, oblong, 7½x16x26" 375.00
Splint, flared sides, oval rim, sq base, 11x11x20" 195.00
Splint, ftd oval, bentwood rim hdls, fabric lining, 9x13" 325.00
Splint, late, 15x22" 65.00
Splint, med patina, miniature, 2½x3¾x4¾" 85.00
Splint, natural patina w/faded red & gr, rim hdls, 15" dia 90.00
Splint, primitive, minor wear, 20x24" 100.00
Splint, rectangular, 11x12" 65.00
Splint, rnd rim, sq bottom, worn gr pnt, 7x11x12" 265.00
Splint, woven like a buttocks, 12x14" 175.00
Splint, wrapped rim hdls, oval, 13" L 105.00
Swing hdl, old finish, 7½x12½" 375.00
Swing hdl, slightly concave base, 9", EX...........................370.00
Swing hdl, well made/EX patina, 7¾x11", EX 625.00
Swing hdl, wooden bbl bottom w/metal band, bl pnt, 10x16" 700.00
Swing hdl mk WJ Rich, varnished, 9x15" 375.00

Batchelder

Ernest A. Batchelder was a leading exponent of the Arts and Crafts movement in the United States. His influential book, *Design in Theory and Practice*, was originally published in 1910. He is best known, however, for his artistic tiles which he first produced in Pasadena, California, from 1909 to 1916. In 1906 the business was relocated to Los Angeles where it continued until 1932, closing because of the Depression.

In 1938 Batchelder resumed production in Pasadena under the name of 'Kinneola Kiln.' Output of the new pottery consisted of delicately cast bowls and vases in an Oriental style. This business closed in 1951. Tiles carry a die-stamped mark; vases and bowls are hand incised.

Our advisor for this category is Jack Chipman, author of *Collector's Encyclopedia of California Pottery*; he is listed in the Directory under California.

Tile, Dutch boy, brown and blue wash, 5¾", $65.00.

Bowl, blk/brn irid, 8" 85.00
Bowl, Kinneola Kiln mk, gr, scalloped, 3x10½" 100.00
Bowl, Pasedena mk, rose, oval, 4x12x7" 135.00
Tile, castle, matt, 6x6" 85.00
Tile, florals & lion w/curly mane, 4x4" 100.00
Tile, peacocks in high relief, bl wash, mk, 12" 150.00
Tile, pomegranate panel, 4-pc 400.00
Tile, stylized flower, #443, 6x6" 80.00
Vase, lime gr, 6" 125.00

Battersea

Battersea is a term that refers to enameling on copper or other metal. Though originally produced at Battersea, England, in the mid-eighteenth century, the craft was later practiced throughout the Staffordshire district. Boxes are the most common examples. Some are figurals, and many bear an inscription. Values are given for examples with only minimal damage, which is normal. Our advisor for this category is John Harrigan; he is listed in the Directory under Minnesota.

Bodkin case, 2 panels w/mottos, pk w/gr & blk lines, 4", VG 330.00
Bonbonniere, florals/pnt-on 'hdls,' basketweave ground, 2" L 650.00
Box, bird form, bird & fruit on lid, 1½", EX 800.00
Box, Trifle from London, floral garland, 1½" L, EX 350.00
Box, Trifle from Reigate Fair, flowers, maroon base, 1½", EX......350.00
Candlestick, florals in reserves, copper mts, rpr, 9", pr 900.00
Curtain tieback, lady in garden, blk transfer, EX 75.00
Knob, Hope resting on anchor w/ship in bkground, EX..............115.00
Locket, ship, bk: clock face, EX 265.00
Needle case, floral/insects on yel, rstr, 4¾" L................550.00

Needle cases: cylindrical with floral sprays and insects on yellow, restorations, 4¾", $550.00; rectangular with figures in reserves, 7" long, $1,100.00.

Patch box, bluebird & foliage on wht lid, bl base, 1⅝x1½" 275.00
Patch box, calf form, floral lid, mirror w/in, 1⅝" L 2,400.00

Bauer

Originally founded in Paducah, Kentucky, in 1885, the J.A. Bauer Company moved to Los Angeles where it was re-established in 1909. Until the 1920s, their major products were terra cotta gardenware, flowerpots, and stoneware and yellowware bowls. During prohibition they produced crocks for home use. A more artful form of product began to develop with the addition of designer Louis Ipsen to the staff in 1915. Some of his work, a line of molded vases, flowerpots, bowls, etc., was awarded a bronze medal at the Pacific International Exposition the following year.

In 1930 the first of many dinnerware lines was tested on the market. Their initial pattern, Plain Ware, was well accepted and led the way to the introduction of the most popular dinnerware in their history and with today's collectors, Ring Ware. It was produced from 1932 into the early 1960s in solid colors of jade green, royal blue, Chinese yellow, light blue, orange-red, and (in very limited quantities) black or white. Its simple pattern was a design of closely-spaced concentric ribs, either convex or concave. Over the years, more than one hundred shapes were available. Some were made in limited quantities, resulting in rare items to whet the appetites of Bauer buffs today. Other patterns were La Linda, produced during the 1940s and 1950s, and Monterey Moderne, introduced in 1948 and remaining popular into the 1950s (made in pink, black, gray, brown, and green.)

After WWII a flood of foreign imports drastically curtailed their sales, and the pottery began a steady decline that ended in failure in 1962. Prices listed below reflect the California market. For more information, we recommend *The Complete Collector's Guide to Bauer Pottery* by Jack Chipman, our advisor for this category, and Judy Stangler. Mr Chipman's address may be found in the Directory under California.

Ring, see listings for specific values.

Ash tray, plain, sq, all colors but blk, 4" 45.00
Baking dish, Ring, yel, jade gr, or lt bl, w/lid, 4" 20.00
Bean pot, plain, blk, hdls, 4-qt 140.00
Bowl, Al Fresco, speckled, gr, or gray, 13" 22.00
Bowl, beater; Ring, orange-red, dk bl, or ivory, 1-qt 50.00
Bowl, fruit; Monterey, all colors but wht, 9" 40.00
Bowl, fruit; Monterey, wht, 6" 20.00
Bowl, fruit; Ring, orange-red, dk bl, or wht, 4" 15.00
Bowl, fruit/dessert; Contempo, all colors, 5" 6.00
Bowl, mixing; La Linda, yel, turq, or lt brn, #18, 1½-qt.................20.00
Bowl, mixing; Ring, blk, #6, 1¼-gal 200.00
Bowl, Monterey Moderne, all colors but blk, 10½" 35.00
Bowl, ramekin; Ring, blk, 4" 30.00
Bowl, salad/punch; Ring, dk bl, ivory, or burgundy, 11"............200.00
Bowl, soup; Al Fresco, coffee brn or Dubonnet, w/lid, 5½" 15.00
Bowl, vegetable; Al Fresco, speckled, gr, or gray, 7½" 12.00
Bowl, vegetable; La Linda, burgundy or dk brn, 10" 35.00
Bowl, vegetable; Monterey, all colors but wht, divided, 10½".......45.00
Butter dish, La Linda, gr, yel, or pk, oblong 50.00
Candlestick, Monterey, all colors but wht 40.00
Canister, flour; Al Fresco, speckled, gr, or gray, rare......45.00
Casserole, Al Fresco, speckled, gr, or gray, w/lid, 1½-qt..............22.00
Casserole, Ring, blk, w/lid, 6½" 150.00
Chop plate, Monterey, all colors but wht, 13" 45.00
Coffeepot, Ring, blk, 8-cup 375.00
Cookie jar, Ring, yel, jade gr, or olive 100.00
Creamer, plain, blk, midget 30.00
Cup, jumbo coffee; La Linda, lt brn, pk, or ivory 24.00
Cup & saucer, El Chico, all colors 45.00
Cup & saucer, Monterey, wht 37.50
Custard cup, La Linda, burgundy or dk brn 8.00
Flowerpot, Ring Gardenware, jade gr or lt bl, ruffled, 5" 15.00

Gravy bowl, Monterey Moderne, all colors but blk 30.00
Honey jar, Ring, all colors but black 300.00
Jardiniere, plain, blk, 6" 25.00
Marmalade, plain, blk 200.00
Mug, Ring, dk bl or burgundy, bbl form, 12-oz 45.00
Pitcher, beer; Ring, orange-red, dk bl, or wht, cylindrical............200.00
Pitcher, plain, all colors but blk, 1-qt 50.00
Plate, Al Fresco, speckled, gr, or gray, 8" 5.00
Plate, El Chico, all colors, 7½" 15.00
Plate, grill; Monterey Moderne, all colors but blk, rnd.................15.00
Plate, La Linda, burgundy or dk brn, 7½" 10.00
Plate, Monterey, wht, 9" 20.00
Plate, Monterey Moderne, blk, 9½" 25.00
Plate, salad; Ring, blk, 7½" 40.00
Platter, Monterey, all colors but wht, 12" 45.00
Platter, Monterey Moderne, blk, oval, 12" 40.00
Platter, Ring, blk, oval, 12" 75.00
Rack, oblong, holds coffee server & 6 6-oz tumblers 50.00
Relish plate, Ring, lt bl, yel, gr, sectioned, 10½" 45.00
Sherbet, Ring, orange-red, dk bl, or burgundy 40.00
Soup plate, La Linda, gr, yel or turq, 7" 22.00
Spice jar, plain, blk, 4½x3½" 200.00
Sugar bowl, Al Fresco, speckled, gr, or gray, w/lid 10.00
Sugar bowl, plain, blk, w/lid 65.00
Teapot, La Linda, burgundy or dk brn, 4-cup................................45.00
Teapot, Monterey Moderne, all colors but blk, 6-cup 60.00
Teapot, Ring, yel, lt bl, or red-brn, 2-cup......................................65.00
Tumbler, La Linda, gr, yel, or turq, 8-oz 12.00
Tumbler, Monterey, wht, 8-oz..20.00
Vase, Ring Gardenware, blk, florist stock, 10"...............................75.00
Vase, Ring Gardenware, yel, jade gr, or lt bl, cylinder, 8" 50.00

Bavaria

Bavaria, Germany, was long the center of that country's pottery industry; in the 1800s, many firms operated in and around the area. Chinaware vases, novelties, and table accessories were decorated with transfer prints as well as by hand by artists who sometimes signed their work. The examples here are marked with 'Bavaria' and the logos of some of the various companies which were located there.

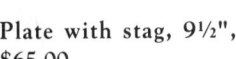
**Plate with stag, 9½",
$65.00.**

Bowl, calla lilies, gold scallops & rtcl rim, 10" 95.00
Box, floral on gr, gold trim, 4½" dia 90.00
Cake plate, floral, pk on wht w/gold medallions, sgn, 10" 25.00
Chocolate pot, floral, gold trim & hdl 90.00
Compote, mc floral sprigs, rtcl rim, 6x8" 45.00

Cookie jar, roses, pk on gr shaded w/gold, mk, 7½x5½" 100.00
Figurine, falcon, wht w/gr & gold, 10¾" 180.00
Jam jar, vintage border, hdls, sgn/dtd 85.00
Pitcher, tankard; roses, gold rim/hdl, sgn Perl, 12" 200.00
Plate, pk roses & leaves, gold border, sgn, 7½" 15.00
Teapot, pk roses w/gold, ribbed, ZS&Co, +1 c/s............................80.00
Tray, poppies, orange on cream w/gold, mk, 11½x8½"....................60.00
Vase, roses, gold trim, flaring rim, 9¾"...45.00

Beer Cans

When the flat-top can was first introduced in 1934, it came with printed instructions on how to use the triangular punch opener. Cone-top cans, which are rare today, were patented in 1935 by the Continental Can Company. By the 1960s, aluminum cans with pull tabs had made both types obsolete.

The hobby of collecting beer cans has been rapidly gaining momentum over the past ten years. Series types, such as South African Brewery, Lion, and the Cities Series by Schmit and Tucker, are especially popular.

Condition is an important consideration when evaluating market price. Grade 1 must be in like-new condition with no rust. However, the triangular punch hole is acceptable. Grade 2 cans may have slight scratches or dimples but must be free of rust. For Grade 3, light rust, minor scratching, and some fading may be acceptable. When these defects are more pronounced, a can is defaulted to Grade 4. Those in less-than-excellent condition devaluate sharply. In the listings that follow, cans are arranged alphabetically by brand name, not by brewery. Unless noted otherwise, values are for cans in Grade 1 condition.

Alt Heidelberg, flat top, 12-oz 68.00
American Dry, flat top, 12-oz 60.00
Ballantine Ale, pull top, 12-oz.. 3.00
Bavarian's Select, pull top, 12-oz...20.00
Berghoff 1887, pull top, red & gold on wht, 16-oz 18.00
Blackhawk Topping, cone top, 12-oz 95.00
Brown Derby, pull top, 12-oz... 3.00

Burkhardt's, cone top, EX, $100.00.

Busch Lager, flat top, 12-oz 65.00
Cee Bee, flat top, 12-oz..15.00
Clyde Cream Ale, cone top, orig cap, 1920s, EX.........................150.00
Colorado Imperial, pull top, 12-oz..12.50

Colt 45 Malt Liquor, pull top, 10-oz.................................. 8.00
DuBois Export, pull top, 12-oz......................................20.00
Duquesne Pilsener, cone top, 12-oz..............................42.50
Embassy Club, flat top, 12-oz..30.00
Falstaff Draft, pull top, 12-oz..22.50
Fischer, flat top, red & bl on wht, 12-oz........................32.50
Fitger's, pull top, 12-oz...10.00
Glacier, flat top, 12-oz...38.50
Grain Belt, flat top, brn & gold on wht, 12-oz.............. 5.50
Grand Prize, flat top, silver & bl, 12-oz.......................37.50
Gunther Premium Dry, flat top, 12-oz.........................35.00
Hapsburg Brand, flat top, 12-oz..................................35.00
Heritage House, pull top, 12-oz................................... 3.00
Holiday Bock, pull top, 12-oz 9.50
Hop'n Gator, pull top, wht, 12-oz 2.00
Iroquois Draft, pull top, 12-oz..................................... 5.00
Krueger Pilsner, pull top, 12-oz...................................10.00
Land of Lakes, flat top, bl & wht, 12-oz........................20.00
Old Export Brand, cone top, gold & wht, 12-oz............85.00
Old Tap, cone top, orig cap, 1920, EX.........................225.00
Old Tap Ale, cone top, orig cap, 1920, EX 300.00
Pearl Light, pull top, brn & red on wht, 12-oz............. 3.50
Pioneer, flat top, brn on wht, 12-oz.............................25.00
Primo, pull top, 12-oz.. 4.00
Regal, pull top, bl & gold on wht, 16-oz....................... 4.00
Regal Select, pull top, 12-oz.. 4.50
Rolling Rock, pull top, 12-oz.. 1.00
Schlitz Light, pull top, 12-oz.. 1.00
Schwegmann, pull top, red & wht, 12-oz......................22.50
Shell's City, pull top, 12-oz..30.00
Stag Premium Dry, cone top, 12-oz 22.50
Storz, flat top, red & gold on wht, 12-oz 12.50
Tudor Ale, flat top, gr & wht, 12-oz.............................16.00
White Label, flat top, 12-oz... 6.00

Belleek, American

From 1883 until 1930, several American potteries located in New Jersey and Ohio manufactured a type of china similar to the famous Irish Belleek soft-paste porcelain. The American manufacturers identified their porcelain by using 'Belleek' in their marks. American Belleek is considered the highest achievement of the American porcelain industry. Production centered around artistic cabinet pieces and luxury tablewares. Many examples emulated Irish shapes and decor with marine themes and other naturalistic styles. While all are highly collectible, some companies' products are rarer than others. The best-known manufacturers are Ott and Brewer, Willets, The Ceramic Art Company (CAC), and Lenox. You will find more detailed information in those specific categories. For a more thorough study of the subject, we recommend you refer to *American Belleek* by our advisor Mary Frank Gaston; you will find her address in the Directory under Texas.

Key:
AAC — American Art China   CAP — Columbian Art Pottery Works

Bowl, florals, pk on wht w/in & w/o, AAC, 2½x5"..............350.00
Cream soup, Bouquet, Coxon, w/underplate 175.00
Cup & saucer, demitasse; Tridacna, gold trim, CAP 165.00
Cup & saucer, floral reserves in red border, Morgan 220.00
Cup & saucer, morning-glories, Morgan 150.00
Mug, portrait transfer in blk tones, CAP, blk mk, 5½" 275.00
Plate, Boulevard, Coxon, 10½"......................................200.00

Plate, floral, gold rim, mk Coxon, #S-115, 10½" 200.00
Plate, peacocks & mixed florals w/gold, Gordon, 7"......55.00
Sugar bowl, pk florals, AAC, 2½" 265.00
Teapot, dragon form, gold paste leaves, CAP, 7½x9" 1,200.00
Vase, violets, salesman's sample, palette mk, 3" 110.00

Belleek, Irish

Belleek is a very thin translucent porcelain that takes its name from the village in Ireland where it originated in 1857. The glaze is a creamy ivory color with a pearl-like lustre. Tablewares, baskets, figurines, and vases have been produced; Shamrock, Tridacna, Echinus, and Lotus are but a few of the many patterns.

It is possible to date an example to within twenty to thirty years of manufacture by the mark. Pieces with an early stamp often bring prices nearly triple that of a similar but current item. With some variation, the marks have always incorporated the wolfhound, round tower, harp, and shamrock. The first three marks (usually in black) were used from 1863 to 1946. A series of green marks has been in use since 1946; the most current mark is gold, which was introduced in April, 1980. In the listings below, numbers designated with the prefix 'D' relate to the book *Belleek, The Complete Collector's Guide and Illustrated Reference.'* Portfolio Press, 170 Fifth Avenue, New York, NY 10010. Our advisor for Belleek is Richard K. Degenhardt; he is listed in the Directory under North Carolina.

Key:
A — pearl/plain	I — 1863-1890
B — cob lustre	II — 1891-1926
C — hand tinted	III — 1926-1946
D — hand painted	IV — 1946-1955
E — hand-painted shamrocks	V — 1955-1965
F — hand gilted	VI — 1965-3/31/1980
G — hand tinted and gilted	VII — 4/1/1980-current
H — hand-painted shamrocks and gilted	
I — hand painted and gilted	

Aberdeen, vase, floral, D55-II, A, lg 800.00
Artichoke Tea Ware, breakfast saucer, D1747-I, F, 7"................125.00
Bearded Mask, creamer, D1294-I, A, sm 175.00
Bird's Nest, basket, D123, 4-strand, A, 3¾"................380.00
Bust of Joy, D1129-IV, A, 11" 600.00
Calawite, candle extinguisher & stand, D1507-I, A, 3½" 750.00
Celtic, candlestick, D1511-VI, B, 4¾"..........................155.00
Celtic Tea Ware, teacup & saucer, D1437-III/D1438-III, I 125.00
Chinese Tea Ware, creamer, D486-I, D............................350.00
Chinese Tea Ware, sugar bowl, D485-I, D, 3"...............225.00
Cleary, mug, D218-III, B..60.00
Cone Tea Ware, teacup & saucer, D432-II, A 175.00
Dolphin, chamberstick, D343-VII, G 300.00
Echinus, bowl, ftd, D1521-I, B, 8¼"..............................950.00
Echinus Tea Ware, creamer, D648-I, D, 3" 350.00
Echinus Tea Ware, teapot, D659-I, A, 4" 675.00
Emerson, mug, D300-II, B...110.00
Erne Tea Ware, teacup & saucer, D445-II, D....................200.00
Fern & Flower, wall bracket, D1580-I, A, 11" 1,000.00
Figurine, Erin, D1-I, A 8,000.00
Figurine, Meditation, D20-II, A, 14½"........................ 2,000.00
Figurine, spaniel on cushion, D1555-VI, A, 3" 75.00
Five O'Clock Tea Ware, teapot, D1420-II, C, 4½" 500.00
Florence, jug, D1289-VII, G, med sz 85.00
Grass, mug, D214-V, B, 2½" 75.00

Grass Tea Ware, milk jug, D753-I, I, 6" dia................................400.00
Heart, basket, No 3, D-1258, 4-strand, D, 6½"..................455.00
Henshall, basket, D121, 4-strand, A, 8"..............................900.00
Hexagon, cake plate, D1263, 4-strand, A, 10"....................450.00
Hexagon, Tea Ware, coffee cup & saucer, D397-II, G.............150.00
Hexagon Tea Ware, teacup & saucer, D391-II, A.................130.00
Indian Corn, spill vase, D190-I, A, 6¼"..............................250.00
Institute Tea Ware, platter, D1393-I, A, 10½" dia....................375.00
Ivy, creamer, D240-III, B, med sz 75.00
Ivy Trunk, stump spill, D153-I, D, 5" 250.00
Lifford, creamer, D301-I, B, 3¼".......................................175.00
Limpet Tea Ware, dinner plate, D1375-VI, B, 10½" 70.00
Limpet Tea Ware, plate, D1372-V, A, 8" 45.00
Limpet Tea Ware, plate, D557-VI, A, 6¼"............................30.00
Limpet Tea Ware, teacup & saucer, D549-II, B, 4 sets.........340.00
Lithophane, Girl at Wall, D1538-III, A, 8x6½" 1,000.00
Lotus, creamer & sugar bowl, D244-III/D245-III, A 95.00
Mask Tea Ware, creamer, tall shape, D1483-II, A, lg............95.00
Mask Tea Ware, plate, D1491-III, B, 6¼"............................75.00
Neptune Tea Ware, plate, D423-III, B, 6¾"..........................65.00
Neptune Tea Ware, teapot, D415-unmk, A, 5"....................100.00
Neptune Tea Ware, tray, D418-II, A, 17¼x14".....................900.00
Octagon, flowerpot, D219-VI, B, 4½"...................................48.00

Oval Shamrock trinket box, D604-III, cob lustre handle,
hand-painted shamrocks, 4", $185.00.

Prince of Wales, ice pail, D3-I, A&F...................................... 8,000.00
Rathmore, vase, D1219-III, A, rstr, 7½" 60.00
Ribbon, creamer, D243(CR)-III, B, 3½"................................55.00
Ribbon, vase, flowered, D1220-III, A, 8"..............................250.00
Round Tower, vase, D1236-VI, D, 8½"..................................450.00
Shamrock Ware, basket, D109, 4-strand, A, sm......................380.00
Shamrock Ware, biscuit jar, D531-VI, E, 6½".......................130.00
Shamrock Ware, bread plate, D379-V, E, 10¼".......................85.00
Shamrock Ware, coffee cup & saucer, D372-II, E...................125.00
Shamrock Ware, coffeepot, D1319-V, H, 7"...........................275.00
Shamrock Ware, dresser tray, D1583-III, E, 10¼x5" 200.00
Shamrock Ware, kettle, D386-II, E, lg 475.00
Shamrock Ware, milk jug, rnd, D1327-III, E, sm 120.00
Shamrock Ware, plate, D377-III, H, 7" 70.00
Shamrock Ware, teacup & saucer, low shape, D366-III, E.............95.00
Shamrock Ware, teacup & saucer, tall shape, D375-III, E 95.00
Shamrock Ware, teapot, D384-VI, E, lg 250.00
Shamrock Ware, vase, pierced, D1217-II, H, 8½"...................200.00
Shell, comport, Belleek...Fermanagh, A, 3¾x9¾"..................400.00
Shell Tea Ware, teacup & saucer, D587-II, A.........................150.00

Sydenham, basket, D108, 4-strand, A, 10"............................. 1,325.00
Table centre, D56-VI, D... 1,000.00
Toy Shell, creamer & sugar bowl, D250-V, B..........................60.00
Tridacna Tea Ware, creamer, D474-II, A, 5½" 85.00
Tridacna Tea Ware, plate, D464-II, A, lg...............................85.00
Tridacna Tea Ware, shakers, D1350/D1351-unmk, A, 2¾", pr......50.00
Tridacna Tea Ware, teacup & saucer, D454-II, A.....................95.00
Tridacna Tea Ware, teapot, D475-II, B, lg............................350.00
Wall plaque, Praise Ye the Lord, D1582-I, D, 8x9" 600.00

Bells

The earliest form of bell, the crotal or closed-mouth, is most familiar to us today as the sleigh bell. Rattles, hollow forms containing stones or seed pods, are also of this type of construction. Gongs, most often associated with the Orient, have no clapper and must be struck to sound. The more common forms of bells are made with a flaring shape and a freely-moving interior clapper that causes the bell to ring as it is swung. Bells come in many shapes and serve many uses. They have been used throughout history to sound an alarm, call a congregation, announce dinnertime, or signal a victory. School bells called children in from recess, and cow bells made the herd easier to locate. Bells have been made in brass, glass, china, bronze, and cast iron; in simple as well as elaborately embossed forms; and in amusing figurals. See also Schoolhouse Collectibles.

Brass, cross figural hdl, emb figures, 7½x4" 135.00
Brass, Deco engr, cvd mutton-fat jade hdl, sm 50.00
Brass, Jacobean head hdl, emb warriors, 4x3⅛" 125.00
Brass, knight figural hdl, emb warriors, Hemony, 6½"...............135.00
Brass, lady in hoop skirt, low-cut bodice, holds fan, 7".............95.00
Brass, warrior figural hdl, emb warriors, Hemony, 6¼x3¼"..........135.00
Brass, warrior's head emb ea side, 4" 45.00
Cow bell, copper, lg, EX..12.00
Glass, bl, Rose O'Neill Cupid figural hdl, 5½" 45.00
Glass, marriage, root-beer color w/clear fancy hdl, 12"................125.00
Silver, cherub figural, hallmk...145.00
Sleigh, brass, single-throated, 42 on orig leather strap, EX 200.00
Sleigh, brass, 1⅛" dia, 23 on orig leather strap, 1890s.................125.00
Sleigh, brass, 4 on arched metal strap...40.00
Tap, SP, mushroom, CI octagonal base, Pat 1883, 6"....................55.00

Bennett, John

Bringing with him the knowledge and experience he had gained at the Doulton (Lambeth) Pottery in England, John Bennett opened a studio in New York City around 1877, where he continued his methods of decorating faience under the glaze. Early wares utilized imported English biscuit, though subsequently local clays (both white and cream-colored) were also used. His first kiln was on Lexington Avenue; he built another on East Twenty-Fourth Street. Pieces are usually signed 'J. Bennett, N.Y.,' often with the street address and date. Later examples may be marked 'West Orange, N.J.,' where he retired. The pottery was in operation approximately six years in New York. Pieces signed with other initials are usually worth less. Our advisor for this category is Robert Tuggle; he is listed in the Directory under New York.

Charger, calla lily on cobalt, sgn/1877, 17¾" 6,750.00
Charger, floral branch/5 insects on apple gr, sgn/1878, 14½" .. 4,620.00
Vase, crab apple blossoms on cobalt mottle, sgn/1880s, 10" 5,280.00
Vase, hibiscus, urn form, top missing, sgn/1879............................990.00
Vase, pk & red peonies on cobalt mottle, sgn/dtd 1882, 26" ..22,000.00

Vase, yel flowers on celadon, 10" **1,650.00**

Charger, insects and flowers on honeycomb ground, signed and dated 1878, 14½", $4,620.00.

Bennington

Although the term has become a generic one for the mottled brown ware produced there, Bennington is not a type of pottery, but rather a town in Vermont where two important potteries were located. The Norton Company, founded in 1793, produced mainly redware and salt-glazed stoneware; only during a brief partnership with Fenton (1845-47) was any Rockingham attempted. The Norton Company endured until 1894, operated by succeeding generations of the Norton family. Fenton organized his own pottery in 1847. There he manufactured not only redware and stoneware, but more artistic types as well — graniteware, scroddled ware, flint enamel, a fine parian, and vast amounts of their famous Rockingham. Though from an esthetic standpoint his work rated highly among the country's finest ceramic achievements, he was economically unsuccessful. His pottery closed in 1858.

It is estimated that only one in five Fenton pieces were marked; and although it has become a common practice to link any fine piece of Rockingham to this area, careful study is vital in order to be able to distinguish Bennington's from the similar wares of many other American and Staffordshire potteries. Although the practice was without the permission of the proprietor, it was nevertheless a common occurrence for a potter to take his molds with him when moving from one pottery to the next, so particularly well-received designs were often reproduced at several locations. Of eight known Fenton marks, four are variations of the '1849' impressed stamp: 'Lyman Fenton Co., Fenton's Enamel Patented 1849, Bennington, Vermont.' These are generally found on examples of Rockingham and flint enamel. A raised, rectangular scroll with 'Fenton's Works, Bennington, Vermont,' was used on early examples of porcelain. From 1852 to 1858, the company operated under the title of the United States Pottery Company. Three marks — the ribbon mark with the initials USP, the oval with a scrollwork border and the name in full, and the plain oval with the name in full — were used during that period.

Among the more sought-after examples are the bird and animal figurines, novelty pitchers, figural bottles, and all of the more finely-

modeled items. Recumbent deer, cows, standing lions with one forepaw on a ball, and opposing pairs of poodles with baskets in their mouths and 'coleslaw' fur were made in Rockingham, flint enamel, and occasionally in parian. Numbers in the listings below refer to the book *Bennington Pottery and Porcelain* by Barret. Our advisors for Bennington (except for parian and stoneware) are Barbara and Charles Adams; they are listed in the Directory under Massachusetts.

Key: c/s — cobalt on salt glaze

Book flask, Battle of Bennington, 5¾" **950.00**
Book flask, Bennington Companion, flint enamel, 2-qt, M **950.00**
Bowl, flint enamel, brn/yel, 1849 mk, wear/flakes, 2x7" **350.00**
Candlestick, Rockingham, B 197-C, 8", M **700.00**
Change cover, flint enamel, Swiss Lady figural, 7" **2,300.00**
Coachman, Rockingham, 1849 mk, B 419-B, M **795.00**
Cow creamer, Rockingham, EX mottle, tab broken on lid, 5½" .**350.00**
Cuspidor, flint enamel, emb dmns, B 164-A, 8½" dia **275.00**
Cuspidor, scroddled ware, emb dmns, B 186, 5x8" dia **500.00**
Cuspidor, Shell, 2 side vents, 8½" **150.00**
Foot warmer, flint enamel, B 183-2, spout rpr, 11" **400.00**
Goblet, Rockingham, w/hdl, 4½", M **475.00**
Nameplate, Rockingham fr w/parian letters, 3½x8", M **400.00**
Pitcher, bl/wht porc, Paul & Virginia, US ribbon mk, 10" **400.00**
Pitcher, flint enamel, Alternate Rib, 1849 mk, 10" **950.00**
Pitcher, flint enamel, Tulip & Heart, B 24, hairlines, 7½" **800.00**
Pitcher, graniteware, Charter Oak, US ribbon mk, 9¾" **350.00**
Pitcher, parian, Charter Oak, US ribbon mk, age line, 9½" **350.00**
Pitcher, parian, Pond Lily, US ribbon mk, 7¾" **350.00**
Pitcher, parian, Wild Rose, B 92, soiled, 10" **235.00**
Pitcher, smear glaze, Charter Oak, US ribbon mk, 9½" **400.00**
Pitcher, smear glaze, Leaf & Flower, Fenton Works mk, 9" **400.00**
Pitcher, smear glaze, Pond Lily, US ribbon mk, 8" **400.00**
Pitcher, smear glaze, Rosebud, Fenton Works mk, 9¾" **200.00**
Pitcher, smear glaze, Sunflower, US ribbon mk, 7¾" **175.00**
Pitcher, yellowware, emb floral panels, N&F mk, rpr, 10" **250.00**
Snuff jar, toby, non-flint, 4½" **850.00**
Vase, parian, boy w/sheaf of wheat figural, 7", NM **200.00**
Vase, tulip; flint enamel, 10", NM **900.00**

Swiss lady change cover, flint enamel, cream with green overglaze, 7", $2,300.00.

Stoneware

Crock, floral (delicate), c/s, Norton & Fenton, 11", EX	135.00
Crock, floral (stylized/blurred), c/s, E&LP, 13", NM	400.00
Crock, flourish/#2, quilled, c/s, 9½", NM	75.00
Crock, parrot on branch, c/s, J Norton, 7x8" NM	675.00
Crock, very lg bird/leaves, c/s, FB&Co, 13", NM	1,800.00
Jar, bird on branch, c/s, J&E, sm chips, 10"	450.00
Jar, floral spray, c/s, E&LP, ovoid, hdl chip, 14"	400.00
Jar, no decor, Julius Norton, ovoid w/hdls, 10", EX	95.00
Jar, 2 birds on branch, c/s, JN&Co, 15", EX	1,100.00
Jug, bird in brn brushed slip, L Norton & Son, 11", EX	2,700.00
Jug, bird on branch, c/s, FB Norton, 11¾"	450.00
Jug, floral (simple), c/s, Julius Norton, 14"	275.00
Jug, floral (stylized), c/s, FB Norton, chips/line, 13½"	200.00
Jug, parrot on branch, c/s, J Norton, 11"	450.00
Jug, pr lg birds in tree, tails Xd, J&E, 3-gal, EX	4,500.00

Beswick

In the early 1890s, James Wright Beswick operated a pottery in Longston, England, where he produced fine dinnerware as well as ornamental ceramics. Today's collectors are most interested in the figurines made since 1936 by a later generation Beswick firm, John Beswick, Ltd. They specialize in reproducing accurately detailed bone china models of authentic breeds of animals. Their Fireside Series includes dogs, cats, elephants, horses, the Huntsman, and an Indian figure, which measure up to 14" in height. The Connoisseur line is modeled after the likenesses of famous racing horses. Beatrix Potter's characters and some of Walt Disney's are charmingly recreated and appeal to children and adults alike. Other items, such as character Tobys, have also been produced. The Beswick name is stamped on each piece. The firm was absorbed by the Doulton group in 1973.

Figurine, Afghan, med	45.00
Figurine, Beagle, med	45.00
Figurine, cat, blk w/wht face & chest, 5"	35.00
Figurine, cat, tiger stripes, sitting, 5"	37.50
Figurine, Doberman, uncropped, med	45.00
Figurine, Jamaican lady on donkey	68.00
Figurine, King Charles Spaniel	45.00
Figurine, Scottish Terrier, med	45.00
Figurine, Siamese cat, recumbent, #1599, 7½"	47.50

Big Little Books

The first Big Little Book was published in 1933 and copyrighted in 1932 by the Whitman Publishing Company of Racine, Wisconsin. Its hero was Dick Tracy. The concept was so well accepted that others soon followed Whitman's example; and, though the 'Big Little Book' phrase became a trademark of the Whitman Company, the formats of his competitors (Saalfield, Goldsmith, Van Wiseman, Lynn, and World Syndicate) were exact copies. Today's Big Little Book buffs collect them all.

These hand-sized sagas of adventure were illustrated with full-page cartoons on the right-hand page and the story narration on the left. Colorful cardboard covers contained hundreds of pages, usually totaling over an inch in thickness. Big Little Books originally sold for 10¢ at the dime store; as late as the mid-1950s when the popularity of comic books caused sales to decline signaling an end to production, their price had risen to a mere 20¢. Their appeal was directed toward the pre-teens who bought, traded, and hoarded Big Little Books. Because so many were stored in attics and closets, many have survived. Among the super heroes are G-Men, Flash Gordon, Tarzan, the Lone Ranger, and Red Ryder; in a lighter vein, you'll find such lovable characters as Blondie and Dagwood, Mickey Mouse, Little Orphan Annie, and Felix the Cat.

In the early to mid-'30s, Whitman published several Big Little Books as advertising premiums for the Coco Malt Company, who packed them in boxes of their cereal. These are highly prized by today's collectors, as are Disney stories and super-hero adventures.

Our advisor for this category is Ron Donnelly; he is listed in the Directory under Florida.

Ace Drummond, Whitman, 1935, G	12.00
Adventures of Pete the Tramp, Saalfield, 1935, VG	32.00
Adventures of Tom Sawyer, Saalfield, Clemens, 1934, EX	48.00
Alice in Wonderland, Whitman, movie version, 1934, G	30.00
Andy Panda & Pirate Ghosts, Whitman, 1949, VG	15.00
Andy Panda & Presto the Pup, Lantz, Whitman, 1949, NM	20.00
Apple Mary & Dennie's Lucky Apples, Orr, Whitman, '39, VG	22.50
Arizona Kid, Maple, Whitman, 1936, VG	22.50
Big Chief Wahoo & Loft Pioneers, Saunders/Waggon, 1942, VG	25.00
Billy the Kid on Tall Butte, Saalfield, 1939, VG	30.00
Blaze Brandon w/Foreign Legion, DuBois, Whitman, 1938, G	12.00
Blondie, Baby Dumpling & All; Whitman, 1941, VG	25.00
Blondie & Bouncing Baby Dumpling, Whitman, 1940, VG	27.50
Boss of Chisolm Trail, Maynard, Saalfield, 1939, VG	15.00
Brenda Starr & Masked Imposter, Whitman, 1940, EX	30.00
Bronc Peeler, Lone Cowboy; Harman, Whitman, 1937, EX	30.00
Bronc Peeler, Lone Cowboy; Harman, Whitman, 1937, VG	22.50
Buck Jones in Fighting Rangers, Whitman, 1936, EX	35.00
Buck Jones in Roaring West, Repp, Whitman, 1935, VG	27.50
Buck Rogers & the Doom Comet, Nolan, Whitman, 1935, EX	50.00
Buck Rogers in 25th Century AD, Whitman, 1933, VG	80.00
Buck Rogers on Moons of Saturn, Nowlan, Whitman, 1934, VG	60.00
Buffalo Bill & Pony Express, Morgan, Whitman, 1934, VG	25.00
Bullet Benton, Saalfield, 1938, NM	25.00
Camels Are Coming, movie version, Saalfield, 1935, G	15.00
Captain Easy Behind Enemy Lines, Crane, Whitman, 1943, G	15.00
Captain Midnight & Sheik Jomak Khan, Whitman, 1946, EX	50.00
Chester Gump in City of Gold, Smith, Whitman, G	12.00
Cinderella & Magic Wand, Whitman, movie version, 1940, EX	30.00
Crimson Cloak, Endicott, Saalfield, 1939, VG	22.50
Daniel Boone, World Syndicate, 1934, VG	20.00
Dann Dunn on Trail of Counterfeiters, Whitman, 1935, VG	27.50
Death by Short Wave, Adair, Saalfield, 1938, G	15.00
Dick Tracy & Boris Arson Gang, Whitman, 1935, M	55.00
Dick Tracy & Hotel Murders, Gould, Whitman, 1937, VG	55.00
Dick Tracy Returns, Gould, Whitman, 1939, VG	25.00
Dixie Dugan & Cuddles, Saalfield, 1940, EX	25.00
Don Winslow of Navy & Great War Plot, Whitman, 1940, EX	35.00
Doomed To Die, Clinton, Edwards illus, Saalfield, 1938, VG	17.50
Down Cartridge Creek, Thompkins, Saalfield, 1938, VG	17.50
Flash Gordon & Ape Men of Mor, Dell Fast Action, 1942, EX	100.00
Flash Gordon in Jungles of Mongo, Whitman, 1938, EX	65.00
Flying Sky Clipper w/Winsie Atkins, Lee, Whitman, 1936, VG	22.50
Frank Buck Presents Ted Towers..., Whitman, 1935, EX	30.00
G-Men on the Job, Blair, Whitman, 1935, VG	20.00
Gang Busters in Action, Whitman, 1938, VG	20.00
George O'Brien in Gun Law, Packer, Whitman, 1935, VG	27.50
Green Hornet Cracks Down, Whitman, NM	75.00
Hoosier School Master, Egglestion, Five Star Library, EX	45.00
Internat'l Spy Dr Doom Faces Death at Dawn, Whitman, '37, G	20.00
Jackie Cooper in Gangster's Boy, Whitman, 1938, EX	37.50
Jane Arden & Vanished Princess, Whitman, 1938, VG	27.50
Jimmie Allen in Air Mail Robbery, Whitman, 1936, VG	22.50

Junior Nebb Joins the Circus, Hess, Whitman, 1939, VG **15.00**
Just Kids, Carter, Whitman, 1937, G **35.00**
Kay Darcy & Mystery Hideout, I Ray, Whitman, 1937, VG **22.50**
Kazan in Revenge of North, Curwood, Whitman, 1937, VG **17.50**
Kit Carson & Mystery Riders, Clinton, Saalfield, 1935, VG **27.50**
Lee Brady, Range Detective, Chambers, Saalfield, 1938, G...........**12.00**
Little Men, Packer, Whitman, 1934, oversz, G............................**15.00**
Little Orphan Annie...Treasure of Am, Whitman #1414, '39, VG .**35.00**
Mandrake the Magician, Smith, Whitman, 1935, EX **50.00**
Myra North Special Nurse & Foreign Spies, Whitman, '38, VG ...**30.00**
New Adventures of Tarzan, Burroughs, Whitman, 1935, VG........**27.50**
Og, Son of Fire; Crump, Whitman, 1935, G.................................**15.00**
Peril Afloat, Coxe, Paul illus, Saalfield, 1938, NM **35.00**
Powder Smoke Range, from RKO picture, Whitman, 1935, EX **40.00**
Riders of Lone Trails, Saxton, Whitman, 1937, EX **30.00**
Shadow & the Living Death, Hess illus, Whitman, 1940, EX **100.00**
Shirley Temple, Story of; Mack, Saalfield, 1934, VG...................**50.00**
Smilin' Jack & Stratosphere Ascent, Mosley, Whitman, '37, VG ..**32.00**
SOS Coast Guard, Engle, Whitman, 1936, G **12.00**
Spike Kelly of Commandos, Elder, Whitman, 1943, VG **22.50**
Tarzan & Journey of Terror, Burroughs, Whitman, 1950, EX........**30.00**

Texas Ranger, EX, $35.00; Radio Patrol, 1937, EX, $35.00.

Tim McCoy in the Westerner, Whitman, 1936, NM **55.00**
Tom Mix & Tony Jr in Terror Trail, Whitman, 1935, VG............**27.50**
Up Dead Horse Canyon, Gridley, Saalfield, 1940, G **12.00**
Wells Fargo, movie version, Whitman, 1938, EX **37.50**
Will Rogers, Beatty, Saalfield, 1935, VG....................................**32.00**
Wings of USA, Wyckoff, Whitman, 1940, VG **22.50**
Zane Grey's King of Royal Mounted, Whitman, 1936, EX.............**45.00**

Bing and Grondahl

In 1853 brothers M.H. and J.H. Bing formed a partnership with Frederick Vilhelm Grondahl in Copenhagen, Denmark. Their early wares were porcelain plaques and figurines designed by the noted sculptor Thorvaldsen of Denmark. Dinnerware production began in 1863, and by 1889 their underglaze color 'Copenhagen Blue' had earned them worldwide acclaim. They are perhaps most famous today for their Christmas plates, the first of which was made in 1895. See also Limited Edition Plates.

Creamer, sea gull w/gold...**40.00**
Figurine, ballerina, #2325...**180.00**
Figurine, boy kissing girl, #2162 ....**120.00**
Figurine, boy w/trumpet, #1792, 6½".....................................**170.00**
Figurine, Buttoning My Shoe, #2317.......................................**180.00**

Figurine, cat, sitting, gray & wht, #1876, 5" **98.00**
Figurine, girl feeds cat, #1745, 5½"......................................**135.00**
Figurine, girl tennis player, #2364...**165.00**
Figurine, Good Morning, #1624 ....**98.00**
Figurine, guinea pig, blk, #2499, 3½".....................................**95.00**
Figurine, Ida, #2298..**180.00**
Figurine, kingfisher, #1885, 4" **135.00**
Figurine, Little Match Girl, #1655 ....**180.00**
Figurine, Love Refused, #01614, 6¾".....................................**235.00**
Figurine, lovebird, gr, #2341, 6" L **130.00**
Figurine, parrot, bl & tan, #2019, 5¾"....................................**155.00**
Figurine, Prejudiced, #2175...**245.00**
Figurine, rabbit, recumbent, #2441, ca 1970, 4½" **55.00**
Figurine, Storyteller, #2037, 9" **185.00**
Figurine, tiger, crouched, #01712, 7½x12" **1,300.00**
Gravy boat, sea gull w/gold, attached tray **150.00**
Plate, sea gull w/gold, 9⅝" **40.00**
Platter, sea gull w/gold, 16x11"..**175.00**

Nude seated at pool tray, #1532, 8½" long, $225.00.

Birdcages

Birdcages can be found in various architectural styles and in a range of materials such as wood, wicker, brass, and gilt metal with ormolu mounts. Those that once belonged to the wealthy are sometimes inlaid with silver or jewels. In the 1800s, it became fashionable to keep birds, and some of the most beautiful examples found today date back to that era. Musical cages that contained automated bird figures became popular; today these command prices of several thousand dollars. In the latter 1800s, wicker styles came into vogue. Collectors still appreciate their graceful lines and find they adapt easily to modern homes.

House, weathered poplar w/pnt traces, wire bars, 26", EX...........**250.00**
Metal/wood, 3-story house, 4 turrets/bell tower, +stand, 58" ... **5,250.00**
Tole, made like a garden pavillion w/VG detail, 20", EX.............**475.00**
Tole, tin/wire/trn wood finial, worn orig 5-color pnt, 17"...........**125.00**
Wireware on wood fr, copper tray, blk pnt, 22x15x24" **160.00**
Wood/twisted wire, orig wht pnt w/red band, 23", EX **175.00**

Bisque

Bisque is a term referring to unglazed earthenware or porcelain that has been fired only once. During the Victorian era, bisque figurines became very popular. Most were highly decorated in pastels and gilt and demonstrated a fine degree of workmanship in the quality of their modeling. Few were marked. See also Heubach; Nodders; Dolls; Piano Babies.

Baby girl in pk w/flower baskets ea side, on plinth, 8x10¼"	**75.00**
Baby girl in yel nightgown w/puppy, unmk, 18"	**95.00**
Baby in carriage, floral spokes, facing pr, 8½" L	**450.00**
Boy carrying basket, bl shorts/lav shirt, Germany, 14"	**225.00**
Boy in lg hat w/gun, girl w/broken doll, unmk, 16", pr	**150.00**
Boy in nightshirt w/rabbit, girl in gown w/dove, 13", pr	**125.00**

Cupid and young girl by tree trunk, French, ca 1900, marked, 23", $1,500.00.

Cupids support rtcl vase, gold trim, 9"	**175.00**
Gypsies, he w/mandolin, she w/dove on her arm, 24", pr	**1,000.00**
Hen on nest, mc features on head, tan base, French, 8" L	**175.00**
Renaissance lady, Continental, 1890s, 14"	**150.00**
Romeo & Juliet, flowered clothes, holding hands, 13"	**350.00**
Vase, figure of girl w/team of horses, Germany, 7¾"	**60.00**

Black Americana

Black memorabilia is without a doubt a field that encompasses the most widely-exploited ethnic group in our history. But within this field there are many levels of interest: arts and achievements such as folk music and literature, caricatures in advertising, souvenirs, toys, fine art, and legitimate research into the days of their enslavement and enduring struggle for equality. The list is endless.

In the listings below are some with a derogatory connotation. Thankfully, these are from a bygone era and represent the mores of a culture that existed nearly a century ago. They are included only to convey the fact that they are a part of this growing area of collecting interest.

Our advisor for this category is Linda Rothe; she is listed in the Directory under Washington. Black Americana catalogs featuring a wide variety of items for sale are available; see the Directory under Clubs, Newsletters, and Catalogs for more information. See also Post Cards; Posters; Sheet Music.

Ash tray, boy eating watermelon, chalkware, EX	**65.00**
Ash tray, nude baby atop bedpan, ceramic, 3¾"	**24.00**
Ash tray, pnt metal boy nodder by metal tray, Austria, 5"	**95.00**
Banner, Aunt Jemima Pancake Jamboreee, 12" L, M	**250.00**
Bell, Mammy figural, porc, lg	**45.00**
Bonnie Bilt Bike Bobber, native w/rings in ears, 1950, 4½"	**24.00**

Book, *King Cotton*, by Charlotte Barske, 1938, 13" x 9½", M, $65.00.

Book, Little Blk Sambo, Rand McNally, 1938, M	**40.00**
Book, Little Blk Sambo, 1935, EX	**50.00**
Book, Little Brn KoKo Has Fun, Hunt, 1945, EX	**45.00**
Book, Slavery in US, Sherman, 1858	**95.00**
Book, Treasury of Stephen Foster	**30.00**
Book, Uncle Tom's Cabin, Stowe, Donohue, late 1800s, EX	**48.00**
Bottle, waiter form, frosted body, blk stopper head, 1900, 15"	**345.00**
Bottle opener, banjo player, Ideal D Pat Japan, 7"	**37.50**
Bottle opener, man w/bow tie figural, pnt CI, hanging, EX	**35.00**
Bottle opener/corkscrew, native figural, metal, EX pnt, 4"	**37.50**
Butter dish, golliwog, ceramic	**85.00**
Candy container, watermelon w/child inside, cb, EX pnt	**75.00**
Cigarette lighter, Blk Bartender, Ronson	**475.00**
Clock, Dixie Boy, tie pendulum, Lux, 1930s, EX orig	**750.00**
Coffee tin, Luzianne Mammy, bright colors, 1-lb, EX	**90.00**
Comic book, Clean Fun Starring Sugafoots Jones, 1944, EX	**125.00**
Cookbook, Diamond, Chef cover, Cream of Wheat, 1900	**30.00**
Cookbook, Fine Old Dixie Recipes, Mammy cover, 1930s, NM	**45.00**
Cookie jar, Aunt Jemima, plastic, NM	**275.00**
Crate label, Sm Blk Zinfandel, nude boy, 1930s, 4x13", EX	**15.00**
Decanter, Minstrel, pottery, Thames, Hand Painted, 9", +3 shots	**55.00**
Doll, Mammy, wood/cb incline walker, orig clothes, 1940s	**45.00**
Doll, stuffed/embr clothes, yarn hair, over bottle, 1870s	**165.00**
Egg cup, Robertson Golden Shred Golliwog, plastic, 3¼"	**75.00**
Egg timer, boy w/bow tie holds timer, 4"	**45.00**
Figurine, baby sits on potty & holds melon slice, bsk, 2¼"	**24.00**
Figurine, children, See No Evil, Hear No..., bsk, 1⅜x2¼"	**28.00**
Figurine, Christmas angel child, chalkware, HP, 2x2"	**30.00**
Figurine, chubby boy w/tummy ache, ceramic, Japan, 2½"	**30.00**
Figurine, couple in canoe, few clothes, gold trim, '40s, 6x8"	**60.00**

Figurine, Mammy w/basket, ceramic, mk Royal Crown, Germany.75.00
Figurine, 2 boys standing over potty, porc, Germany, 3" 95.00
Firecrackers, Dixie Boy, boy w/watermelon wrapper, unopened.....50.00
Game, Nodding Nancy, ring toss, ca 1900, 12" figure, EX 200.00
Grocery board, Mammy, I'se Got Ta Git, Leist, CA, 11x7" 45.00
Hat, Aunt Jemima Breakfast Club..55.00
Hotpad holder, young girl, wood, EX pnt.......................................18.00
Knocker, natural wood w/red knob, Cotton Club souvenir, EX 22.00
Lamp, lady's head, elaborate hair, brn skin, pottery, 7" 95.00
Lamp, wall; Mammy figural, ceramic, M 275.00
Lawn ornament, boy w/watermelon, CI, fine rpt, 1955, 20-lb 135.00
Letter caddy, Sambo, German porc, 3x2½" 65.00
Magazine, Negro South, 1946, EX... 6.00
Matchbook cover, Pik-A-Rib, Blk face, NM 18.00
Memo holder, Mammy, compo, Hampton Novelty, +pencil 65.00
Menu, Coon Chicken Inn, lg..150.00
Menu, Mammy cover, Halleman's Cotton Patch..., 11x17" 50.00
Pamphlet, Negro & Flag, WWI government issue, EX...................18.50
Pancake batter shaker, Aunt Jemima, yel plastic............................65.00
Paperweight, boy jockey, CI, EX pnt..125.00
Pegboard, Mammy, We Needs, 7x11", EX 75.00
Pegboard, Mammy wood diecut, EX pnt, 9x5¾" 90.00
Pencil, mechanical; Blackamoor figural, Bakelite, EX....................75.00
Pencil sharpener, man figural, metal, blade in mouth, 1" dia.......200.00
Pin-bk button, Am Negro Expo, Lincoln portrait, 1940, NM........45.00
Pitcher, man's head figural, spout at nose, 1930s, M 145.00
Planter, boy by stump w/watermelon, pottery, 6½x8" 95.00
Plaque, boy & girl eat watermelon, chalkware, 4x4" 45.00
Plaque, Mammy & Chef, HP plaster, hooks for cups, 6½", pr 45.00
Plate, Coon Chicken Inn, dinner sz...250.00
Plate, In the Evening by the Moonlight, trio, 1940s, 6¼" 50.00
Playing cards, Little Blk Sambo, 2 decks, MIB 35.00
Post card, Lena Horn, RCA Victor, M 10.00
Post card, Mammy & children, Carbon Copies, ca 1940................. 5.00
Post card, Mammy Chicken Inn, rare, NM...................................30.00
Post card, Old Slave Market, St Augustine, wht border, '40s.......... 5.00
Post card, You're Invited...Big Blow Out, boy on potty 5.00
Recipe book, Mammy w/vegetables on wooden cover....................45.00
Recipe box, Mammy on red plastic 165.00
Sack, Aunt Jemima Flour, 100-lb..100.00
Scouring pad holder, Mammy, hanging, Coventry Pottery 95.00

Shakers, Aunt Jemima & Uncle Mose, F&F, 5½", pr....................65.00
Shakers, boy & girl, brn skin, gold trim, ceramic, pr 50.00
Shakers, child & watermelon slice, blk skin, ceramic, pr 65.00
Shakers, children kissing, brn skin, ceramic, pr 55.00
Shakers, Mammy & Chef, googly eyes, redware, Japan, 4", EX.....95.00
Shakers, Mammy & Chef, very fat, chalkware, 2¼", NM, pr 70.00
Shakers, Mammy w/wash basket, ceramic, gold trim, 3", pr 75.00
Sheet music, Swingin' on the Swanee Shore, 1936, 3-pg, M 10.00
Smoking stand, butler figural, pnt CI, 34x7½x7½", VG 475.00
Spice jar, Aunt Jemima, F&F..38.00
Spice set, Aunt Jemima, on copper shelf, F&F............................280.00
Syrup, Aunt Jemima premium, F&F, 5", EX 40.00
Syrup bottle, Cotton Club, 1940s, unopened................................45.00
Syrup tin, Uncle Remus...75.00
Tablecloth, man sings I'll Never Smile Again, 53x100", EX 125.00
Tin container, Old Black Joe Axle Grease 85.00
Toby pitcher, girl figural, in wht w/orange & yel, 3½" 40.00
Towel, kitchen; Mammy serves Jell-O to child, M 45.00

Black Cats

Made in Japan during the fifties, these novelty cats may be found bearing the labels of several different importers, all with their own particular characteristics. The best known and most collectible of these cats are from the Shafford line. Even when unmarked, they are easily identified by their red bows, green eyes, and white whiskers, eyeliners, and eyebrows. Relco/Royal Sealy cats are tall and slender, and their bow ties are gold with red dots. Wales is a wonderful line with yellow eyes and gold detailing; Enesco cats have blue eyes; and there are other lines as well. When evaluating your black cats, be sure to inspect their paint and judge them accordingly. 50% paint should relate to 50% of our suggested values, which are given for cats in mint (or nearly mint) paint.

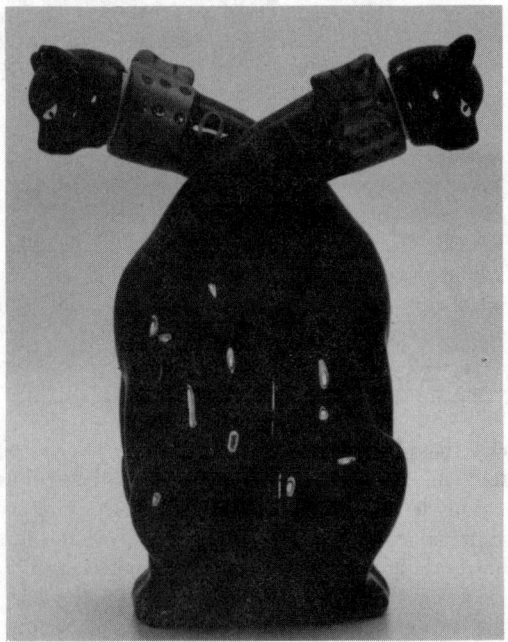

Oil and Vinegar 1-piece cruet, Royal Sealy label, $40.00.

Ash tray, face only, flat, gr eyes, Shafford, 4½"...............................20.00
Ash tray, full figure, flat, 'Ashes' in body, 2½x3¾" 7.50
Ash tray, head only, open mouth, Shafford label, 3" 18.00

Shakers, plastic, green skirt, Luzianne Coffee, F&F Mold & Die Works, $150.00 for the pair.

Condiment set, 2 heads, J&M bows, gr eyes, Shafford, 4" 50.00
Creamer, seated, paw spout, red bow, yel eyes, 6" 18.00
Creamer & sugar bowl, cat-head lids are shakers, 5⅜" 35.00
Cruet, seated, gold bow w/red dots, Relco label, 7" 12.00
Decanter, sq, upright, head stopper, 6 shots on bk, 11⅜" 50.00
Desk caddy, pen forms tail, spring body holds letters, 6½" 8.00
Funnel, w/cat face, long wood hdl, Shafford 50.00
Pincushion, cushion on bk, tongue measure 22.50
Shakers, on bk legs, paws folded, red bow, gold trim, 5", pr 18.00
Shakers, seated, bl eyes, Enesco label, 5¾", pr 15.00
Shakers, seated (3") & recumbent (1¾"), lg heads, pr...................12.00
Spice set, 6 shakers w/faces, bow tie pulls, Shafford, +rack 125.00
Sugar bowl, seated, red bow, gr eyes, Shafford, 4⅞"........................18.00
Teapot, bulbous body, head lid, gr eyes, Shafford, 6½" 45.00
Teapot, crouched, scarf/gold disk, spout through mouth, 3¾"........20.00
Teapot, w/creamer & sugar bowl, stacking.....................................50.00
Toothpick holder, arched bk, on book by vase, yel eyes, 3" 12.00
Wall pocket, gr eyes, red bow, sq pocket at bk, 5½" 65.00

Black Glass

Black glass is a type of colored glass that when held to strong light usually appears deep purple, though since each glasshouse had its own formula, tones may vary. It was sometimes etched or given a satin finish; and occasionally it was decorated with silver, gold, enamel, coralene, or any of these in combination. The decoration was done either by the glasshouse or by firms that specialized in decorating glassware. Crystal, jade, colored glass, or milk glass was sometimes used with the black as an accent. Black glass has been made by many companies since the seventeenth century. Contemporary glasshouses produced black glass during the Depression, seldom signing their product. It is still being made today.

To learn more about the subject, we recommend *A Collector's Guide to Black Glass*, written by our advisor, Marlena Toohey; she is listed in the Directory under Arkansas. Look for a newly updated value guide. See also Tiffin, L.E. Smith, and other specific manufacturers.

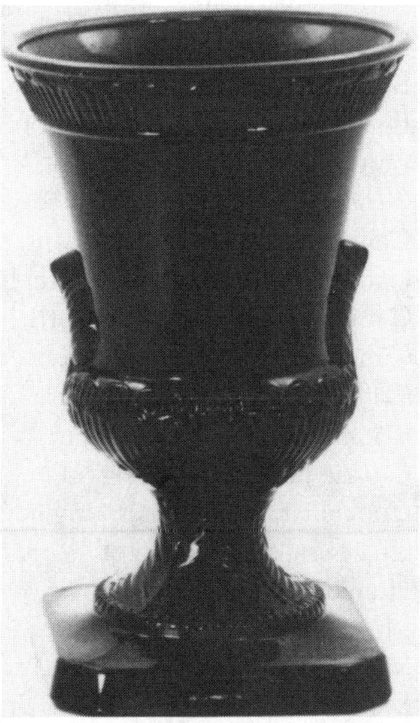

Vase, acanthus leaves on foot, 8½", $35.00.

Ash tray, elephant stands in center, Greensburg, '20s-30s, 6" 25.00
Basket, satin finish, US Glass, #9574, 1926.................................130.00
Bowl, nappy, Liberty Works, 1930, 4"..12.00
Cake plate, Do-Si-Do, hdld, LE Smith, 9½"..................................25.00
Candelabrum, 3-lite, US Glass, 1930s, 6½x7" 95.00
Candlestick, US Glass, #76, 1927-ca 1929, 9", pr 100.00
Epergne, unknown maker, ca 1915-30, 9¾x7½" 145.00
Flower cart, Viking, #772, ca 1940s 40.00
Plate, salad; Morgantown, #1517, 1932 .... 8.00
Shaker, kitchen; Lancaster Glass, #533, ca 1932, 4¾", pr 24.00
Shakers, Floral Sterling, Hazel Atlas, pr 25.00
Sherbet, Block, Hocking Glass Co, #933, ca 1930 ....12.00
Tray, tumbler; center hdl, Greensburg, #181, ca 1920s-30s 85.00
Tray, 3-ftd, Lancaster Glass, #1831/7, 10" 25.00
Vase, Florentine w/Floral Sterling, Hazel Atlas, 6"..........................18.00
Vase, jar form, att HP Sinclaire, #3354, ca 1923, 9".......................35.00
Vase, Poppy, satin finish, US Glass, #16255, 1930 ....75.00
Vase, toothpick; Bee, sq, unknown maker, ca 1887, 2½" 85.00
Vase, wht enamel dot decor, unknown maker, ca 1925-35, 3" 18.00

Blown Glass

Blown glass is rather difficult to date; eighteenth and nineteenth century examples vary little as to technique or style; it ranges from the primitive to the sophisticated. But the metallic content of very early glass caused tiny imperfections that are obvious upon examination, and these are often indicative of age.

In America, Stiegel introduced the English technique of using a patterned, part-size mold, a practice which was generally followed by many glasshouses after the Revolution. From 1820 to about 1850, glass was blown into full-size 3-part molds. In the listings below, glass is assumed clear unless color is mentioned. Numbers refer to a standard reference book, *American Glass* by Helen McKearin. See also Bottles and specific manufacturers.

Our advisor for this category is Mark Vuono; he is listed in the Directory under Connecticut.

Key: ps — pontil scar

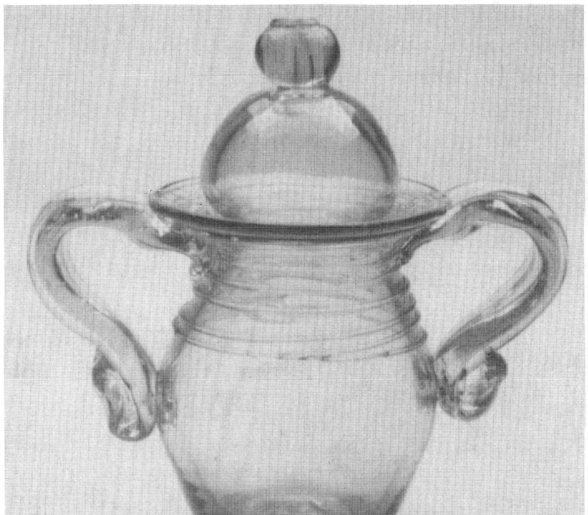

Sugar bowl, green-aqua with applied threading (minor losses), attributed to Saratoga, 1850s, 7½", $2,900.00.

Bottle, club; aqua, bulbous lip, 9" 90.00
Bowl, appl trumpet-flare ft, 13" H...175.00
Bowl, folded rim, 8x9½" 120.00
Canister, tin lid, 6" 165.00
Canister, 2 appl rings, appl knob on lid, 10½x7" 90.00
Creamer, sapphire bl, 12-rib, appl hdl, 2⅝" 50.00
Goblet, 5"..95.00

Jar, amethyst, sqd sides, flared lip, 8" 325.00
Jar, aqua, flared lip, 9¾" 125.00
Jigger, amethyst, Excelsior variant, 2½", NM 325.00
Mug, HP w/shield-shape medallion/'Remember Me,' 4¾" 220.00
Pitcher, olive-amber, tooled lip, appl hdl, pontil, 5½" 2,900.00
Salt cellar, sapphire bl, appl ft, 3¼" 225.00
Salt cellar, 20 vertical ribs, appl ft, pontil scar, 2⅝" 65.00
Vase, hyacinth; amethyst, appl ring, 7½" 225.00
Vase, trumpet; amethyst, ftd baluster stem, folded rim, 10" 475.00
Wine, emerald gr, 4⅞" 40.00
Wine, eng vintage bowl, 5", set of 4 ....90.00
Wine, peacock gr, panel-cut flared bowl, knob stem, 5" 100.00

Blown Three-Mold Glass

A popular collectible in the 1920s, '30s, and '40s, blown three-mold glass has again gained the attention of many. Produced from approximately 1815 to 1840 in various New York, New England, and Midwestern glasshouses, it was a cheaper alternative to the expensive imported Irish cut glass.

Distinguishing features of blown three-mold glass are the three distinct mold marks and the concave-convex appearance of the glass. For every indentation on the inner surface of the ware, there will be a corresponding protuberance on the outside. Blown three-mold glass is most often clear with the exception of inkwells and a few known decanters. Any colored three-mold glass commands a premium price.

The numbers in the listings that follow refer to the book *American Glass* by George and Helen McKearin.

Our advisor for this category is Mark Vuono; he is listed in the Directory under Connecticut.

Creamer, GII-21, pontiled, appl hdl, flared rim, 2¾" 100.00
Decanter, GII-20 variant, 2 appl rings, no stopper, 5½" 325.00
Decanter, GIII-24, matching stopper, minor stain, 8½" 225.00
Decanter, GV-12 (no neck detail), ribbed ball stopper, 9" 300.00
Decanter, GV-13, bulbous ribbed stopper, 8½" 175.00

Flip, GII-18, clear, open pontil, sheared and tooled rim, 5¾", $150.00.

Pan, GI-6 (type 13 base), pontiled, folded rim, 5¼" dia..............120.00
Pan, GII-18, folded rim, 1½x6" 75.00
Pan, GII-18 (type 16 base), folded rim, 5½" dia 100.00
Pan, GII-33 (type 13 base), folded rim, 5⅝" 100.00
Pan, GIII-23, folded rim, 1x4¼" 90.00
Pan, star center, folded rim, 5¾" 200.00
Pitcher, arch & fern w/snake medallion motif, 1800s, 6½" 600.00
Salt, GII-18, ftd, out of rnd, 2½" 250.00
Salt cellar, GIII-6, tooled & flared rim, 2¼", NM 130.00

Salt cellar, GV-24 variant, smooth base, 2¼", EX 70.00
Tumbler, GII-18, 3⅜" 125.00
Tumbler, GIII-6, 3" 150.00

Blue and White Stoneware

Blue and white stoneware, much of which was decorated with such in-mold designs as grazing cows and Dutch children, was made by practically every American pottery from the turn of the century until the mid-1930s. Crocks, pitchers, wash sets, rolling pins, and canisters are only a few of the items that may be found in this type of 'country' pottery that has become one of today's popular collectibles.

Roseville, Brush-McCoy, Uhl Co., and Burley Winter were among those who produced it; but very few pieces were ever signed. Naturally, condition must be a prime consideration, especially if one is buying for resale; pieces with good, strong color and fully-molded patterns bring premium prices. Normal wear and signs of age are to be expected since this was utility ware and received heavy use in busy households. In the listings that follow, crocks and jars are assumed without lids unless noted otherwise. For further information we recommend *Blue & White Stoneware* by Kathryn McNerney. See also specific manufacturers.

Bean pot, Boston Baked Beans, Flemish, w/lid 290.00
Bowl, Apricot, 9½" 85.00
Bowl, Daisy on Waffle, 10¾" 95.00
Bowl, Daisy on Waffle, 9½" 90.00
Bowl, dough; dk bl, scalloped rim, lg 85.00
Bowl, mixing; Feathers, 10½" 125.00
Bowl, plain, 11" 65.00
Bowl, Wedding Ring, 10" 125.00
Butter crock, Apple Blossom, orig lid & bail 225.00
Butter crock, Apricot, orig lid & bail 200.00
Butter crock, Apricots w/Honeycomb, orig lid & bail 225.00
Butter crock, Butterfly, orig lid & bail, 6½" 175.00
Butter crock, Cow, stenciled, orig lid & bail 150.00
Butter crock, Cows & Columns, orig lid & bail 250.00
Butter crock, Daisy & Trellis, orig lid & bail, 4½" 175.00
Butter crock, Diffused Bl, orig lid & bail, 1-lb, 4x4½" 95.00
Butter crock, Eagle, orig lid & bail 450.00
Butter crock, Indian Good Luck Sign, orig lid & bail 125.00
Butter crock, vintage, Robinson Clay Products, 10" dia, EX........105.00
Butter crock, Wildflower, orig lid & bail 150.00
Canister, Basketweave, Coffee, orig lid 195.00
Canister, Basketweave, Raisins, orig lid 225.00
Canister, Diffused Bl, Tea, orig lid 125.00
Canister, Snowflake, Rice, orig lid 150.00
Canister, Wildflower, Crackers, orig lid 175.00
Coffeepot, devil on body, emb Blanke's Coffeepot on lid, 9½" 350.00
Cookie jar, Basketweave, Put Your Fist In, orig lid, 7½" 400.00
Cookie jar, Brickers, orig lid...245.00
Cookie jar, Flying Birds, orig lid.....................................350.00
Cup & saucer, Flowerpot, deep, ca 1820................................125.00
Humidor, stippled w/bird dog on side, flower finial, w/lid 150.00
Mug, advertising 150.00
Mug, Basketweave..95.00
Mug, Cattails 125.00
Mug, Diffused Bl 75.00
Mug, Flying Bird 175.00
Mug, golfer, bl/gray, Robinson Clay Products...........................150.00
Mug, plain 65.00
Mug, Windy City (Fannie Flagg), Robinson Clay Products.........175.00
Pickle crock, Bl Bands, advertising, bail hdl, 5-gal 150.00
Pie plate, Star Mfg 145.00

Pitcher, Acorns......115.00
Pitcher, American Beauty Rose, 10"......175.00
Pitcher, Apricot, 8"......150.00
Pitcher, Barrel, +6 mugs......395.00
Pitcher, Basketweave & Flowers......175.00
Pitcher, Bl Band, plain......80.00
Pitcher, Bl Band Scroll......160.00
Pitcher, Bl Sawtooth, Wht Hall......95.00
Pitcher, Bow Tie......135.00
Pitcher, Butterfly, 4¾"......245.00
Pitcher, Butterfly, 9x7"......250.00
Pitcher, Castle & Fishscale, 8"......195.00
Pitcher, Cattails, 7½"......175.00
Pitcher, Cattails, 9"......155.00
Pitcher, Cattails & Butterfly......150.00
Pitcher, Cherry Cluster, 7½"......225.00
Pitcher, Cosmos......195.00
Pitcher, Cow, 8½"......175.00
Pitcher, Diffused Bl, 8¾", M......100.00
Pitcher, Doe & Fawn......250.00
Pitcher, Dutch Boy & Girl, 7"......160.00
Pitcher, Dutch Landscape, stenciled, tall......150.00
Pitcher, Eagle......450.00
Pitcher, Eagle w/Shield & Arrows, rare......500.00
Pitcher, Edelweiss, flower on gray bkground, M......90.00
Pitcher, Fishscale & Wild Rose, sm......95.00
Pitcher, Fishscale & Wild Rose, 10"......160.00
Pitcher, flat iron bldg/girl, Robinson Clay Products, 8½"......185.00
Pitcher, Flowers, stenciled......100.00
Pitcher, Flying Bird, 9"......550.00
Pitcher, Grape Cluster on Trellis, 8½"......165.00

Pitcher, Grapes with Rickrack, 8", $150.00.

Pitcher, Grapes on Waffle......165.00
Pitcher, Hunting Scene, rare......300.00
Pitcher, Indian Boy & Girl......225.00
Pitcher, Indian Head in War Bonnet, waffled body, 8", EX......250.00
Pitcher, Leaping Deer, 8½"......225.00
Pitcher, Lincoln w/Log Cabin......450.00
Pitcher, Lovebird, arc bands, deep color, 8½"......400.00
Pitcher, Lovebird, pale color, 8½"......275.00
Pitcher, Morning-Glory......150.00
Pitcher, Poinsettia, 6½"......250.00
Pitcher, Rose & Fishscale, 6"......165.00

Pitcher, Scroll & Leaf, advertising......250.00
Pitcher, Stag & Pine Trees, 9"......295.00
Pitcher, Swan, long beak, arched neck, deep color, 8½"......250.00
Pitcher, Swirl......155.00
Pitcher, tavern scene, Flemish Jugs...Kinney & Levan, 9"......165.00
Pitcher, Tulip......225.00
Pitcher, Wild Rose......275.00
Pitcher, Wildflower, stenciled......185.00
Pitcher, Windmill & Bush, 7"......165.00
Pitcher, 2 old men w/canes, dog's-head spout, Germany, 11"......200.00
Potty, Beaded Rose......110.00
Rolling pin, lg swirl......475.00

Rolling pin, Wildflower, $250.00.

Salt crock, Apricot, orig lid......135.00
Salt crock, Blackberry, orig lid......145.00
Salt crock, Butterfly, orig lid......185.00
Salt crock, Daisy on Snowflakes, orig lid......220.00
Salt crock, Eagle w/Arrow, orig lid......325.00
Salt crock, Flying Bird, orig lid......350.00
Salt crock, Grape on Basketweave, orig lid......150.00
Salt crock, Oak Leaf, orig lid......125.00
Salt crock, Peacock, orig lid......350.00
Salt crock, Wildflower, orig lid......175.00
Slop jar, Bow Tie......125.00
Slop jar, Fishscale & Wild Rose......150.00
Soap dish, Beaded Panels w/Open Rose......125.00
Soap dish, Beaded Rose......120.00
Soap dish, Fishscale w/Wild Rose......95.00
Soap dish, Indian in War Bonnet......195.00
Spittoon, Peacock & Fountain......275.00
Toothbrush holder, Bow Tie, stenciled flower......50.00
Toothbrush holder, Fishscale & Wild Rose......70.00
Umbrella stand, oak leaves/animals emb, 21", NM......350.00
Vase, Swirl, cone shape......300.00
Wash set, Bow Tie, 2-pc......300.00
Wash set, Fishscale & Wild Rose, 5-pc......600.00
Wash set, Rose on Trellis, 2-pc......300.00
Water cooler, Apple Blossom......500.00
Water cooler, Bl Band, orig lid......175.00
Water cooler, Cupid, orig lid......600.00
Water cooler, Polar Bear, orig lid......500.00
Water cooler, Rachel at the Well, orig lid......500.00

Blue Ridge

Blue Ridge dinnerware was produced by Southern Potteries of Erwin, Tennessee, from the late 1930s until 1956 in eight basic styles and eight hundred different patterns, all of which were hand decorated under the glaze. Vivid colors lit up floral arrangements of seemingly endless variation, fruit of every sort from simple clusters to lush assortments, barnyard fowl, peasant figures, and unpretentious textured patterns. Although it is these dinnerware lines for which they are best known, collectors prize the artist-signed plates from the forties and the limited line of character jugs made during the fifties most highly. Examples of the French Peasant pattern are valued at double the prices listed below; very simple patterns will bring 25% to 50% less.

Our advisors, Betty and Bill Newbound, have compiled a lovely book, *Blue Ridge Dinnerware, Revised Third Edition*, with beautiful color illustrations and current market values. They are listed in the Directory under Michigan. For information concerning the National Blue Ridge Newsletter, see the Clubs, Newsletters, and Catalogs section of the Directory.

Ash tray, advertising, w/rest 55.00
Ash tray, individual 13.00
Bonbon, divided, center hdls, china..................................85.00
Bowl, cereal/soup; 6" 9.00
Bowl, divided, 8" 20.00
Bowl, fruit; 5" 4.00
Bowl, mixing; 8½" 28.00
Bowl, rnd, 8" 13.00
Bowl, salad; 10½" 45.00
Bowl, soup; flat, 8" 10.00
Bowl, vegetable; divided, oval, 9"..22.50
Bowl, vegetable; oval, 9" 20.00
Box, candy; rnd w/lid 95.00
Box, cigarette..65.00
Box, cigarette; w/4 trays 110.00
Box, Mallard..400.00
Box, raised or sculptured designs 82.50
Box, Sherman Lily..550.00
Breakfast set..400.00
Butter dish, ¼-lb, w/lid...40.00
Butter pat/coaster..17.00
Cake lifter 22.50
Carafe, w/lid 60.00
Casserole, w/lid 40.00
Celery, leaf shape, china 30.00
Celery, Skyline shape 25.00
Child's cereal bowl..28.00
Child's feeding dish, deep..30.00
Child's feeding dish, divided 28.00
Child's mug...20.00
Child's plate 28.00
Child's play set...240.00
Chocolate pot, pedestal, china..150.00
Coffeepot 100.00
Creamer, china 45.00
Creamer, demitasse 50.00
Creamer, regular... 8.00
Cup & saucer, demitasse; china...30.00
Cup & saucer, regular 13.00
Dish, baking; 13x8"..27.50
Egg cup, dbl 20.00
Egg dish, deviled 32.50
Gravy boat 17.00
Gravy tray 17.00
Jug, batter; w/lid..65.00
Jug, character; china 475.00
Jug, syrup; w/lid 80.00
Lamp, china...110.00
Lazy susan...500.00
Pie baker 25.00
Pitcher, fancy, china 95.00
Plate, aluminum edge, 12" 19.00
Plate, artist sgn, china 500.00
Plate, cake; 10½" 28.00
Plate, Christmas or Turkey...60.00

Plate, dinner; 10" 17.00
Plate, dinner; 9½" 10.00
Plate, party; w/cup well & cup...22.50
Plate, salad; bird decor, 8½" 50.00
Plate, salad; 8½" 7.00
Plate, snack; 3-compartment 17.00
Plate, sq, 7½" 9.00
Plate, 11½"...28.00
Plate, 6" 3.00
Platter, artist sgn, 17½" 770.00
Platter, Thanksgiving Turkey...195.00
Platter, Turkey w/Acorns..195.00
Platter, 11"..11.00
Platter, 12½"..17.00
Platter, 13"...17.00
Platter, 15"...22.00

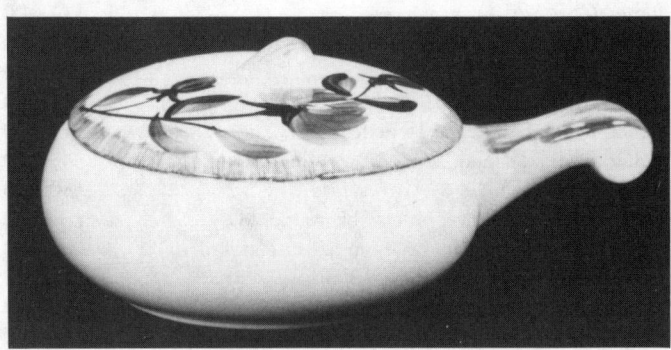

Ramekin, 7½", $25.00.

Ramekin, w/lid, 5" 20.00
Ramekin, w/lid, 7½" 25.00
Relish, deep shell, china 50.00
Relish, heart shape, sm 40.00
Relish, loop hdl, china..65.00
Relish, Maple Leaf, china 45.00
Relish, Martha, 3-compartment, china.................................80.00
Relish, T-hdl, china...40.00
Salad fork 28.00
Salad spoon 28.00
Server, center hdl..28.00
Shakers, Apple, pr..11.00
Shakers, Blossom Top, pr..32.50
Shakers, Bud Top, pr 32.50
Shakers, Chickens, pr..90.00
Shakers, ftd, china, tall, pr..45.00
Shakers, mallards, pr...150.00
Shakers, Moderne, pr...28.00
Shakers, Range, pr 32.50
Shakers, regular, short, pr 20.00
Sugar bowl, demitasse 28.00
Sugar bowl, ped or flare, china 45.00
Sugar bowl, regular, w/lid..13.00
Tea tile, rnd or sq..32.50
Teapot, china..80.00
Teapot, demitasse 80.00
Teapot, earthenware..70.00
Tidbit, 2-tier...30.00
Tidbit, 3-tier...32.50
Toast, covered..90.00
Tray, chocolate pot; china...385.00
Tray, flat shell, china..55.00

Vase, boot, 8"	70.00
Vase, bud	85.00
Vase, hdls, china, 7¼"	65.00
Vase, rnd, china, 5½"	60.00
Vase, ruffled top, 9¼"	80.00
Vase, tapered	85.00

Bluebird China

Made from 1910 to 1934, Bluebird china is lovely ware decorated with bluebirds flying among pink flowering branches. It was inexpensive dinnerware and reached the height of its popularity in the second decade of this century. Several potteries produced it; shapes differ from one manufacturer to another, but the decal remains basically the same. Among the backstamps you'll find W.S. George, Cleveland, Carrolton, Homer Laughlin, Limoges China of Sebring, Ohio; and there are others.

Bowl, fruit; Deerwood, 5½"	12.50
Bowl, fruit; Hopewell China, 5"	10.00
Bowl, gravy; w/saucer, Hopewell China	50.00
Bowl, sauce; SP Co, 4½"	10.00
Bowl, soup; PMC Co, 8"	25.00
Butter dish, 4½" holder w/in 7" dia dish, Steubenville	85.00
Casserole, w/lid, Ostro China, 10½" dia	95.00
Casserole, w/lid, SP Clinchfield, 8½" dia	85.00
Creamer & sugar bowl, w/lid, Homer Laughlin	45.00
Cup, chocolate; ftd, 3½"	35.00
Cup, coffee; unmk, 3½"	25.00
Cup, tea; unmk	15.00
Plate, dessert; Limoges, 6"	8.00
Plate, Homer Laughlin, 8½"	15.00
Plate, National China, 8"	15.00
Plate, rtcl, sq, unmk, 9"	35.00
Platter, Homer Laughlin, 15½x10½"	75.00
Platter, Hopewell China, 17½x13"	95.00
Platter, Steubenville, 12¾x9½"	55.00
Platter, unmk, 9x7"	35.00
Sauce ladle, gold scrolling	25.00
Teapot, ELP Co, 8½x8½"	125.00

Deep bowl, 5" diameter, $25.00.

Boch Freres

Founded in the early 1840s in La Louviere, Boch Freres Keramos became the foremost producer of art pottery in Belgium. Though primarily they served a localized market, in 1844 they earned worldwide recognition for some of their sculptural works on display at the International Exposition in Paris. In 1907 Charles Catteau of France was appointed head of the art department. Before that time, the firm had concentrated on developing glazes and perfecting elegant forms. The style they pursued was traditional, favoring the re-creation of established eighteenth-century ceramics. Catteau brought with him to Boch Freres the New Wave (or Art Nouveau) influence in form and decoration. His designs won him international acclaim at the Exhibition d'Art Decoratif in Paris in 1925, and it is for his work that Boch Freres is so highly regarded today. He occasionally signed his work as well as that of others who under his direct supervision carried out his preconceived designs. He was associated with the company until 1950 and lived the remainder of his life in Nice, France, where he died in 1966. The Boch Freres Keramis factory continues to operate today, producing bathroom fixtures and other utilitarian wares. A variety of marks have been used, all incorporating some combination of 'Boch Freres,' 'Keramos,' 'BFK,' or 'Ch Catteau.'

Our advisor for this category is Wayne B. Kielsmeier; he is listed in the Directory under Arizona.

Vase, blue, aqua, and turquoise with incised deer, marked Catteau, 20", $2,100.00.

Vase, crazed bright aqua, cylindrical w/tiered base, 16"	600.00
Vase, deer/geometric borders, Catteau, 14x8"	1,300.00
Vase, frieze of grazing deer, ovoid, D943/Catteau, 20"	2,100.00
Vase, mc stylized flowers on wht, bulbous, 6"	250.00
Vase, stylized prs of birds, mc on mocha matt, ovoid, 10½"	495.00
Vase, 3-color vertical floral stripes, crazed glaze, 10½"	375.00

Boehm

Boehm sculptures were the creation of Edward Marshall Boehm, a ceramic artist who coupled his love of the art with his love of nature to produce figurines of birds, animals, and flowers in lovely background settings accurate to the smallest detail. Sculptures of historical figures-sand those representing the fine arts were also made and along with many of the bird figurines, have established secondary-market values many times their original prices. His first pieces were made in the very early 1950s in Trenton, New Jersey, under the name of Osso Ceramics. Mr. Boehm died in 1969, and the firm has since been managed by his wife. Today known as Edward Marshall Boehm, Inc., the private family-held corporation produces not only porcelain sculptures but collector plates as well. Both limited and non-limited editions of their works have been issued. Examples are marked with various backstamps, all of which have incorporated the Boehm name since 1951. 'Osso Ceramics' in upper case lettering was used in 1950 and 1951.

Birds

Arctic Tern	2,600.00
Barn Owl	5,200.00
Bobolink	1,400.00
California Quail, pr	2,500.00
Canadian Geese w/Goslings, #408	695.00
Cape May Warbler	900.00
Cardinals, decor, pr	3,600.00
Eastern Bluebirds, pr	1,000.00
Fledgling Canada Warbler, #491	2,000.00
Fledgling Great Horned Owl	1,200.00
Flicker	2,400.00
Golden Crowned Kinglets, Oriental poppies, #419, 13"	2,100.00
Hooded Warbler	3,000.00
Kildeer Plover (bluebells), 1964, 10"	1,500.00
Lapwing	3,000.00
Lesser Prairie Chickens, pr	2,000.00
Mallards in Flight, ltd ed, 11"	2,055.00
Meadow Lark	2,650.00
Mergansers, pr	2,400.00
Mockingbirds	2,400.00
Mourning Doves	1,000.00
Nonpareil Buntings	875.00
Orchard Orioles	2,000.00
Parula Warblers	2,500.00

Pekin Robin, 1975, very rare, $3,000.00 at auction.

Peregrine Falcon	4,000.00
Rufous Hummingbirds	1,600.00
Winter Robin	1,350.00

Woodcock, #413, 10"	1,650.00
Yellowhammers	3,800.00

Bohemian Glass

The term 'Bohemian glass' has come to refer to a type of glass developed in Bohemia in the late sixteenth century at the Imperial Court of Rudolf II, the Hapsburg Emperor. The popular artistic pursuit of the day was stone carving, and it naturally followed to transfer familiar procedures to the glassmaking industry. During the next century, a formula was discovered that produced a glass with a fine crystal appearance which lent itself well to deep, intricate engraving, and the art was further advanced.

Although many other kinds of art glass were made there, collectors today use the term 'Bohemian glass' to most often indicate clear glass overlaid with color through which a design is cut or etched. (Unless otherwise described, the items in the listing that follows are of this type.) Red or yellow on crystal is common, but other colors may also be found. Another type of Bohemian glass involves cutting through and exposing two layers of color in patterns that are often very intricate. Items such as these are sometimes further decorated with enamel and/or gilt work. Our advisor for this category is Thomas P. Bradshaw; he is listed in the Directory under California.

Candlesticks, ruby cut to clear, stag on one, bird on the other, with label, 9", $125.00 for the pair.

Beaker, ruby, deer & trees, 5⅜"	65.00
Decanter, pk to wht opaque, cut/HP florals, 9"	295.00
Decanter, red, buildings & flowers, w/stopper	85.00
Goblet, ruby, view of Battle Monument Baltimore, 7"	450.00
Jar, amber, appl prunts, HP man w/mug, bk: verse, ftd, 13"	265.00
Pokal, lime gr w/mc shields & grapes, faceted finial, 24"	3,300.00
Pokal, red, Niagara Falls (& Capitol Bldg), 16", pr	1,900.00
Stein, red, castle in vine & scroll fr, pewter mts, 6¼"	325.00
Stein, red, Der Niagara Falls, 5"	300.00
Stein, red, dog in forest, pewter mts, 5½x3¼"	325.00
Stein, red, floral panels, pewter mts, 5⅛x3⅛"	295.00
Tumble-up, red, flowers & leaves	60.00
Tumbler, red, windmill scene, 3¾x2¾"	40.00
Vase, amber, florals, 1920s, 11"	195.00

Vase, ruby, triple dmn, scalloped top, 10" 80.00

Bookends

Though a few were produced before 1880, bookends became a necessary library accessory and a popular commodity after the printing industry was revolutionized by Mergenthaler's invention, the linotype. Books became abundantly available at such affordable prices that almost every home suddenly had need for bookends. They were carved from wood, cast in iron, bronze, or brass, or cut from stone. Today's collectors may find such designs as ships, animals, flowers, and children. Patriotic themes, art reproductions, and those with Art Nouveau and Art Deco styling provide a basis for a diverse and interesting collection.

Amish man, Amish woman, CI w/mc pnt, lt wear, 4⅝", NM 115.00
Angelus relief figure, CI 25.00
Buddha, cast metal w/bronze finish, 7¾" 65.00
Cattails/lily pads emb on bronze sq, McClelland Barclay, 4½" 275.00
Cherub as fisherman, bronze on rouge marble base, lg 380.00
Deco lady's head, bronze finish, Frankart 155.00
Deer, standing, bronze, Deco style, Frankart, 6" 140.00
Eagle sits on sphere, bronze, verde marble base 120.00
End of Trail, #169...115.00
German shepherd, brass..58.00

Griffin, French bronze, 6", $185.00.

Horse & rider, rearing, brass, Deco style, Hagenauer, 5" 375.00
Indian head w/full headdress, brass, pr 65.00
Leda & the Swan, CI, orig gold pnt, 4½x8x2¼" 85.00
Log cabin among pines, CI, mc pnt, 1920s, 6½" 45.00
Mayflower, #381 ....65.00
Owl, CI, 5¼" 40.00
Sailing ship, bronze, EX...25.00
Sailor boy, Frankart, EX pnt 95.00
Setter, standing, EX bronzing, Frankart 175.00
Setter at point, bronze, mk Atmore Bronze 150.00
Spanish man serenades lady at window, CI, 1920s, 5½"..................55.00
Whippet, recumbent, polished bronze on blk marble base 340.00

Bootjacks and Bootscrapers

Bootjacks were made from metal or wood. Some were fancy figural shapes, others strictly business! Their purpose was to facilitate the otherwise awkward process of removing one's boots. Bootscrapers were handy gadgets that provided an effective way to clean the soles of mud and such.

Bootjacks

Beetle, CI, old worn blk pnt, 1880s..35.00
Cricket, CI, 12"...35.00
Hickory, bentwood hdl, hinged/folds, use w/out bending over.......75.00
Lever action, wood & CI, EX..85.00
Naughty Nellie, CI, old gr pnt, 11x5x2½", EX.............................115.00
Raised heel holder, ornate CI, EX 65.00
Stylized fish, cvd wood, worn finish, 22" L 115.00
Try Me, CI, openwork, no pnt, ca 1890s, 12x4x1¾" 70.00

Bootscrapers

Cast steel, scottie silhouette w/edge tooling, pnt, 9"......................95.00
CI, on pan w/griffons, worn pnt, 13x17½" 215.00
Dachshund dog, CI, old worn wht pnt, 1900s, 7½x22x7" 235.00
Deco fox/hare, hammered wrought iron, Dieterich, 7x14" 1,300.00
Dragon figural, CI, early, EX 100.00
Duck, full bodied, scraper on bk, CI, 14½" L................................350.00
Lyre on oval scalloped base, CI, 9x11"..100.00
Pig silhouette, cut-out eye, CI, 8½x12" 195.00
Wrought iron, simple uprights w/scooped blade set in stone........150.00

Boru, Sorcha

Sorcha Boru was the professional name used by California ceramist Claire Stewart. She was a founding member of the Allied Arts Guild of Menlo Park (California) where she maintained a studio from 1932 to 1938. From 1938 until 1955, she operated Sorcha Boru Ceramics, a production studio in San Carlos. Her highly-acclaimed output consisted of colorful, slip-decorated figurines, salt and pepper shakers, vases, wall pockets, and flower bowls. Most production work was incised 'S.B.C.' by hand.

For further information we recommend *Collector's Encyclopedia of California Pottery*, written by our advisor, Jack Chipman. Mr. Chipman is listed in our Directory under California.

Bowl, applied lilies, 6½", $90.00.

Bowl, horse motif, 7" 37.50

Bowl, pussy willows on beige, 10" 25.00
Cup, 3 dinosaur hdls...45.00
Figurine, blue jay, bl, 6½" 165.00
Figurine, bluebird, 5x10" 95.00
Figurine, little Blk girl, 6" 375.00
Pitcher, pk lustre florals w/gold centers, beading, 6½"......65.00
Shakers, boy & girl, pr 50.00
Sugar shaker, lady figural, 6" 85.00

Bottle Openers

Around the turn of the century, manufacturers began to seal bottles with a metal cap that required a new type of bottle opener. Now the screw cap and the flip top have made bottle openers nearly obsolete. There are many variations, some in combination with other tools. Many openers were used as means of advertising a product. Various materials were used including silver and brass.

A figural bottle opener is defined as a figure designed for the sole purpose of lifting a bottle cap. The actual opener must be an integral part of the figure itself. The major producers of iron figurals were Wilton Products, John Wright Inc., Gadzik Sales, and L & L Favors. Openers may be free-standing and three-dimensional, wall hung, or flat. They can be made of cast iron (often painted), brass, bronze, or aluminum.

Those seeking additional information concerning figural bottle openers are encouraged to contact the Figural Bottle Opener Collectors, whose address can be found in the Directory under Clubs, Newsletters, and Catalogs.

Alligator, head down, CI, EX pnt.....................................70.00
Blk face, pnt CI, NM...150.00
Blk man on alligator, CI, Wilton, EX pnt.........................140.00
Bulldog's head, mouth open wide, CI w/mc pnt, lt wear, 4" 115.00
Clown, EX pnt, wall mt..150.00
Cockatoo, CI, EX pnt..155.00
Cowboy at street sign, CI, VG pnt 100.00
Dolphin, chrome..20.00
Donkey, head thrown bk, CI w/mc pnt, worn, 3⅛" 35.00
Donkey, seated, head upright, CI w/mc pnt, 3¼" 35.00
Donkey, sm body, sitting, lg head/open mouth, CI/mc, 3¾" 20.00
Drunk & palm tree, both legs down, CI w/worn mc pnt, 4" 45.00
Drunk & palm tree, CI w/mc pnt, lt wear, 4" 145.00
Drunk w/lamppost, left leg up, CI w/mc pnt, some wear, 4½" 50.00
Drunk w/sign, both legs down, CI w/mc pnt, lt wear, 4" 50.00
Drunk w/sign, right leg up, CI w/mc pnt, lt wear, 4⅜" 90.00
Elephant, seated upright, CI w/mc pnt, wear, 5"................25.00
Elephant, sitting, head bk, trunk curled, CI/mc, 3½", EX 35.00
Elephant, trunk looped over head, CI w/silver pnt, 3¼" 145.00
Flamingo, CI, Wilton, EX pnt...95.00
Horse's hind quarters, CI w/worn mc, 5½".........................50.00
Lobster, brass...28.00
Lobster, CI, worn red pnt, 3½" L..25.00
Mallard duck, brass..28.00
Monkey, CI, blk pnt...235.00
Nude, cast metal, brass plated...35.00
Parrot, CI w/worn mc pnt, lt rust, 3¼" 35.00
Parrot on perch, CI w/mc pnt, lt wear, 4⅜" 25.00
Parrot on short perch, CI w/mc pnt, 5"..............................45.00
Parrot on tall perch, CI w/worn pnt, 5"..............................40.00
Pelican, beak is opener, CI w/mc pnt, lt wear, 3⅜" 50.00
Pointer, left ft raised, CI w/mc pnt, lt wear, 4½" 40.00
Pointer, left ft raised, w/base, CI w/rpt, 4½" 35.00
Ram, sitting upright, CI w/M pnt, lt wear, 4¼" 45.00

Rooster, CI w/mc pnt, 3" 85.00
Rooster, opener in tail, mc pnt, lt wear, 3¼" 35.00
Sea gull on stump, brass 38.00
Sea horse, CI w/mc pnt, John Wright Inc, 4" 25.00
Shark, aluminum, NM pnt 40.00
Shark, brass 35.00
Tennis racket, brass 20.00
Trout, metal 50.00
4-Eyed lady, pnt CI, M 150.00
4-Eyed man, CI w/mc pnt, J Wright Co, lt wear, 3¾" 55.00

Pelican, cast iron, EX, $50.00.

Bottles and Flasks

As far back as the first century B.C., the Romans preferred blown glass containers for their pills and potions. Though you're not apt to find many of those, you will find bottles of every size, shape, and color made to hold perfume, ink, medicine, soda, spirits, vinegar, and many other liquids. American business firms preferred glass bottles in which to package their commercial products and used them extensively from the late eighteenth century on. Bitters bottles contained 'medicine' (actually herb-flavored alcohol); and, judging from the number of these found today, their contents found favor with many! Because of a heavy tax imposed on the sale of liquor in seventeenth-century England by King George, who hoped to curtail alcohol abuse among his subjects, bottlers simply added 'curative' herbs to their brew and thus avoided taxation. Since gin was taxed in America as well, the practice continued in this country. Scores of brands were sold; among the most popular were Dr. H.S. Flint & Co. Quaker Bitters, Dr. Kaufman's Anti-Cholera Bitters, and Dr. J. Hostetter's Stomach Bitters. Most bitters bottles were made in shades of amber, brown, and aquamarine. Clear glass was used to a lesser extent, as were green tones. Blue, amethyst, red-brown, and milk glass examples are rare. (Please note that color is a strong factor when pricing bottles. For example, an amber Hostetter's Bitters sells for $25.00 or less, but a green variant can bring hundreds of dollars. An aqua scroll flask may bring $50.00, but a cobalt blue variation will command over $1,000.00.)

Perfume or scent bottles were produced abroad by companies all over Europe from the late sixteenth century on. Perfume making became such a prolific trade that as a result beautifully decorated bottles were fashionable. In America they were produced in great quantities by Stiegel in 1770 and by Boston and Sandwich in the early nineteenth century. Cologne bottles were first made in about 1830 and toilet-water bottles in the 1880s. Rene Lalique produced fine scent bottles from as early as the turn of the century. The earliest were one-of-a-kind creations with silver casings. He later designed bottles for the Coty Perfume Company with a different style for each Coty fragrance. Prices for commercial perfumes vary according to condition, whether it is sealed and full, and has the original label and most of the original packaging or box. Deluxe versions bring premium prices. Example: blue flat Dans La Nuit cologne by Rene Lalique, value 6" size, $250.00. Dans La Nuit, enameled with stars by Rene Lalique, 3" round ball, $900.00.

Spirit flasks from the nineteenth century were blown in specially designed molds with varied motifs including political subjects, railroad trains, and symbolic devices. The most commonly used colors were amber, dark brown, and green.

From the twentieth century, early pop and beer bottles are very collectible, as is nearly every extinct commercial container.

Bottles may be dated by the methods used in their production. For instance, a rough pontil indicates a date before 1845. The iron pontil, used from then until about 1860, left a metallic residue on the base of the bottle, which is evident upon examination. A seam that reaches from base to lip marks a machine-made bottle from after 1903, while an applied or hand-finished lip points to an early mold-blown bottle. The Industrial Revolution saw keen competition between manufacturers; and, as a result, scores of patents were issued. Many concentrated on various types of closures; the crown bottle cap, for instance, was patented in 1892. If a manufacturer's name is present, consulting a book on marks may help you date your bottle.

Among our advisors for this category are Madeleine France (see the Directory under Florida), Mark Vuono (Connecticut), Steve Ketcham (Minnesota), and John Tutton (Virginia). In the listings that follow (most of which have been taken from auction catalogs), glass is assumed to be clear unless color is indicated. Numbers refer to a standard reference book, *American Glass*, by George and Helen McKearin. See also Advertising, various companies; Avon; Blown Glass; Blown Three-Mold Glass; California Perfume Company; Czechoslovakia; De Vilbiss; Fire Fighting; Lalique; Medical Collectibles; Steuben.

Key:
am — applied mouth	GW — Glass Works
bbl — barrel	ip — iron pontil
bt — blob top	ps — pontil scar
b3m — blown 3-mold	rm — rolled mouth
cm — collared mouth	sb — smooth base
fm — flared mouth	sl — sloping
gm — ground mouth	sm — sheared mouth
gp — graphite pontil	tm — tooled mouth

Barber Bottles

Amethyst, mc florals on ribbed body, sm/ps, 8" 160.00
Amethyst w/wht Mary Gregory-type girl, rm/ps, 7⅜" 250.00
Basketweave, milk glass w/bl opaque o/l, sm/sb, 7¼" 180.00
Citron, mc florals, rm/ps, 7¾" 125.00
Clear, mc florals on ribbed body, sm/ps, 8" 350.00
Clear w/wht opal swirled ribs, Bay Rum HP in red, 8⅛" 110.00
Cobalt, gold florals, sheared & gm/sb, 7⅝" 85.00
Cobalt, HP floral, 7", pr 175.00
Cobalt, wht Mary Gregory-type girl, rm/ps, 8¼" 250.00
Coin Spot, cranberry opal, melon ribs, rm/sb, 7" 65.00
Coin Spot, yel, melon ribs, rm/sb, 7" 40.00
Emerald gr, mc florals on ribbed body, sm/ps, 7".........................250.00
Emerald gr (bright), mc florals w/gold on ribbed body, 7" 150.00
Gr-yel, mc florals, melon ribs, tm/sb, hazy, 7⅞" 60.00
Hobnail, cranberry opal, tm, 7½", NM 70.00
Milk glass, gulls & Sea Foam in blk & gold, am/ps, 9" 125.00

Milk glass w/HP cabin & Hair Oil, gm/sb, 9⅝" 220.00
Milk glass w/yel o/l, raised enameling, sm/sb, 8⅛" 350.00
Pk satin, 8½x2¾" 100.00
Swirl, bl opal, rm/sb, 6¾" 70.00
T'print, apple gr, mc florals, rm/ps, 8¼" 80.00
T'print, lav, mc florals, rm/ps, 7⅞" 95.00
T'print, turq, rm/ps, 6¾" 50.00
Turq, mc florals on ribbed body, tm/ps, stain, 8¼" 175.00

Bitters Bottles

Aeromatic Orange Stomach, amber, am/sb, semi-cabin, 10⅛" 275.00
AR Thayer's Iron/Great Tonic, deep aqua, am/sb, 7⅛".................300.00
Atwood's Jaundice, aqua, 12-sided, am/ps, 6⅛" 65.00
Auguaer, bright yel-gr, tm/sb, orig label, 8" 70.00
Bavarian/Hoffheimer Brothers, deep olive-gr, am/sb, 9¼"...........500.00
Berkshire Amann & Co/Cincinnati O, amber, am/sb, thin, 9⅝" ..900.00
Bourbon Whiskey, deep reddish-puce, am/sb, 9⅜" 210.00
Bourbon Whiskey, grayish smoky puce, am/sb, 9¼" 375.00
Brown's Celebrated Indian Herb Pat 1868, med amber, 12⅜" 400.00
Castilian, yel-amber, am/sb, cannon form, 10" 325.00
Catawba Wine, deep olive-amber, grapes emb, 9¾" 800.00
Chartreuse Damiana NY, yel-amber, am/sb, stain, 9⅜" 90.00
Clarke's/Sherry Wine, aqua, am/sb, 8", EX 90.00
Corn Juice, aqua, am/sb, coffin form, rare, 8", EX 450.00
DeWitts Stomach, yel-amber, tm/sb, orig label, 9⅜".....................110.00
Diamond's Blood Buffalo NY, amber, am/sb, lt wear, 7½" 190.00
Dimmit's 50 Cts St Louis, amber, am/sb, strap-sided, 6½"............225.00
Doyles Hop, med amber, berries emb, am/sb, orig label, 9½" 50.00
Dr AS Hopkins Hartford Conn, amber, lady's leg, 12¼"..............450.00
Dr CW Robacks Stomach Cincinnati O, yel, am/sb, 9⅜" 325.00
Dr CW Robacks Stomach Cincinnati O, yel-amber, am/ip, 10" .275.00
Dr FFW Hogguers Detroit MI, amber, am/sb, 9¼" 325.00
Dr Geo Pierce's Indian Restorative Lowell MA, aqua, 7⅞".........55.00
Dr John Bull's Compound Louisville KY, red-amber, am/sb, 9⅝" ..275.00
Dr Lamot's Botanic, med amber, tm/sb, 8⅝" 150.00
Dr Langley's Root & Herb Boston, aqua, am/sb, 7⅛" 60.00
Dr Langley's Root & Herb Boston, dk amber, tm/sb, 6⅞" 80.00
Dr Langley's Root & Herb Boston, lt to med apple-gr, 8¾" 75.00
Dr Langley's Root & Herb Boston, med amber, am/sb, 8½".........100.00
Dr Owen's European Life Detroit, aqua, am/ps, lt wear, 7" 110.00
Dr Shepard's Wahoo, aqua, appl cm/sb, 7½" 180.00
Dr Skinner's Celebrated 25 Cent, aqua, am/ps, 8½".....................100.00
Dr Soule's Hop Bitterine 1872, yel, floral emb, am/sb, 9½" 140.00
Dr Soule's Hop 1892, olive-amber, floral emb, 9⅜" 400.00

Dr. Stephen Jewett's, olive-amber, NH back label, rare variant, 7½", $1,000.00; Kimball's, yellow-amber (scarce color), perfect back label, 6½", $475.00.

Dr Tompkins Vegetable, med gr, am/sb, orig label, 8⅝"..............750.00
Dr Wood's Sarsaparilla & Wild Cherry, aqua, am/ps, 9"............150.00
Drakes Plantation Pat 1862, med apricot-puce, 6-log, 9⅞"..........210.00
Fritz Reuter, milk glass, case gin shape, 10⅛" 375.00
Gentiana Root & Herb Boston MA, aqua, am/sb, tapered, 10" ..210.00
German Balsam...Watson Sole Agents for US, milk glass, 8¾" ...370.00
German Hop 1872 Reading MI, amber, sb, partial label, 9⅝"........65.00
Graves & Son Tonic Louisville KY, aqua, semi-cabin, 10"..........375.00
Great English Remedy/Dr Bell's Blood Purifying, amber, 9⅝" 70.00
Great Western Tonic 1868 OP Bissell, amber, orig labels, 9" 300.00
H&K Stomach Tonic, amber, am/sb, rare, 8¾" 160.00
Hagan's, amber, am/sb, triangular, 9¾" 300.00
Hartwig Kantorowicz Berlin, amber, am/sb, 9"................125.00
Hartwig Kantorowicz Pozman, milk glass, tm, NM label, 9¾" 120.00
Jackson's Aromatic Life, olive-gr, am/sb, open bubble, 9" 875.00
John W Steele's Niagara 1864, med amber, eagle/star emb, 10" ..240.00
JP Brady's Family, olive-amber, am/sb, 9⅞" 300.00
Kagy's Superior Stomach, dk amber, am/sb, 9½" 150.00
Kelly's Old Cabin Patd Mar 1870, amber, am/sb, 9⅜" 725.00
LN Kreinbrook's Mt Pleasant PA, amber, tm/sb, 8¼" 170.00
Marshall's Best Laxative & Blood Purifier, amber, 8⅝"...........65.00
Mishler's Herb Table Spoon Graduation, yel-olive, 8¾" 190.00
Nat'l, amber, am/sb, 12¼" 200.00
Nat'l, deep puce, am/sb, 12⅜" 550.00
Nat'l, yel w/amber tint, am/sb, 12½" 350.00
Nat'l, yel w/olive tint, am/sb, 12⅜" 500.00
Newman's Golden Fruit, amber, am/sb, sliver chip, 10⅞" 375.00
O'Leary's 20th Century, med amber, tm/sb, 8⅝" 75.00
Old Continental, yel w/amber striations, am/sb, 9⅞".............195.00
Old Homestead Wild Cherry Pat, med amber, am/sb, 9½" 210.00
Old Sachem & Wigwam Tonic, aqua, am/sb, 9¼" 1,600.00
Old Sachem & Wigwam Tonic, deep reddish-puce, am/sb, 9⅜"..475.00
Old Sachem & Wigwam Tonic, straw yel, am/sb, 9⅛".............550.00
Old Sachem & Wigwam Tonic, yel-puce, am/sb, 9⅜" 450.00
Oswego 25 Cents, med amber, tm/sb, 7".........................75.00
Pepsin Bitters RW Davis Drug Chicago USA, med yel-gr, 8⅛"..160.00
Rocky Mtn Tonic 1840 Try Me 1870, yel-amber, am/sb, 9¾" 275.00
Rosswinkle's Crown, amber, am/sb, G label, 9⅛" 190.00
Sazerack Aromatic (base)/PHD&Co (shoulder), milk glass, 12".350.00
Schroeder's Louisville KY, amber, tm/sb, lady's leg, 11½"..........210.00
Shurtleff's, med amber, am/sb, lady's leg, sm chip, 12⅜" 550.00
Sir Robert Edgar's English Life, amber, am/sb, 8½" 400.00
Solomon's Strengthening & Invigorating, cobalt, am/sb, 9⅝" 475.00
ST Drakes 1860 Plant'n X Pat 1862, dk red-amber, 6-log, 9¾"......95.00
ST Drakes 1860 Plant'n X Pat 1862, med amber, 6-log, 9⅞".........95.00
ST Drakes 1860 Plant'n X Pat 1862, orange-puce, 6-log, 10" 120.00
ST Drakes 1860 Plant'n X Pat 1862, yel-olive, 6-log, 9⅞"...........210.00
Star Kidney & Liver, amber, tm/sb, 8⅞" 75.00
Tip Top/HR&Co, yel-amber, am/sb, crude, 9".....................180.00
Webb's Improved Stomach, med amber, am/sb, 9"...............120.00
White's Stomach, med amber, am/sb, 9⅝" 170.00
Wm Allen's Congress, deep aqua, am/sb, 10⅛" 130.00
Wood's Tonic Wine Cincinnati OH, aqua, am/sb, crude, 9½" 150.00
Zu Zu, amber, am/sb, 8⅞" 170.00

Blown Glass Bottles and Flasks

Apothecary/utility, med gr, sm/open pontil, stain, 11"................250.00
Blacking, dk yel-amber, sm/ps, 4⅝" 130.00
Castor, GI-24, b3m, sheared & tm/ps, 4⅛" 45.00
Chestnut flask, olive-yel, rm/ps, 6⅛" 110.00
Chestnut flask, red-amber, 24-rib left swirl, ps, 5¼" 200.00
Chestnut flask, yel-amber, rm/ps, 4½" 250.00
Club, lt gr, 16-rib swirl, flattened, am/ps, 9"...................450.00

Decanter, GI-18, blue-green, b3m, Keene, lip chip, very rare, 7¾", $3,000.00.

Decanter, GI-29, b3m, purple-cobalt, tm, stopper, 5⅜" 725.00
Decanter, GII-29, b3m, flared lip, period stopper, 8⅝" 75.00
Decanter, GII-7, b3m, med to dk olive-gr, ps, 8¼" 1,350.00
Decanter, GIII-16, b3m, med olive-amber, sm/ps, 7" 350.00
Demijohn, gr, 2-pc mold, appl lip, 28" 45.00
Demijohn, olive-gr, am, 19" 75.00
Flip, GII-25, b3m, tm/ps, 5⅞"................................110.00
Globular, amber, 16 swirl ribs, irregular shape, late, 7" 55.00
Globular, med olive-yel, rm/ps, w/o flattened sides, 5¼" 150.00
Globular, med olive-yel, sm w/appl string, ps, 2⅞" 725.00
Ludlow, olive, am, 5½" 85.00
Medicine, olive-amber, rectangular w/beveled corners, 6½"........100.00
Olive gr, blown in primitive sq mold, irregular flared lip, 6" 85.00
Pitkin flask, med gr-aqua, 32 broken rib swirl, sm/ps, 6¾" 255.00
Pitkin flask, med yel w/olive tint, 36-rib swirl, 5¼"....................275.00
Pitkin flask, med yel-gr, 32 broken rib swirl, 6½"....................325.00
Pitkin flask, olive-gr, 24 broken rib swirl, 6⅞".......................150.00
Snuff, olive-amber, flared tm/ps, 4¾" 500.00
Snuff, yel-amber, flared tm/ps, flake, 4" 130.00
Storage, dk olive-amber, sm/appl string rim/ps, 12¼x9½" 235.00
Storage, med olive-yel, kickup on base, sm w/appl string, 13" 160.00
Toilet water, GI-3 type 2, b3m, cobalt, tm/ps, 5½" 125.00
Toilet water, GI-7 type 4, cobalt, tm/ps, orig stopper, 5⅜" 165.00
Utility, lt gr, fm/ps, 3" 210.00

Cologne, Perfume, and Toilet Water Bottles

Amethyst, sq w/center rib, flared tm/sb, Sandwich, 5⅝" 325.00
Amethyst, 12-sided, sl shoulders, tm/sb, 4⅞" 90.00
Amethyst (lt to med pk), 12-sided, sl shoulders, sb, 4⅝".............200.00
Amethyst (med), 12-sided, rm/sb, open bubble, 8⅝" 110.00
Aqua, 12-sided, rm/ps, 8⅞".....................................60.00
Bl w/HP florals & gold trim, bubble stopper, 6¼x1⅞" 120.00
Clear, 8-sided corset waist, tooled & rm/sb, 5⅝" 110.00
Cobalt, 12-sided, fm/sb, 6⅛" 65.00
Cobalt, 12-sided, sl shoulders, flared rm/ps, 6¼"...................300.00
Cobalt, 12-sided, tm/sb, 4¾" 110.00
Cranberry, brass Nouveau ormolu at base, cut stopper, 8¼".........195.00
Dancing Indians (emb figures), aqua, rm/ps, 4⅞"..................120.00

Deep lav-bl, 8-sided corset waist, tm/sb, 5⅞" 625.00
Gr satin, HP florals w/gold, lay-down, sterling top, 4¾" 385.00
Lamp form, clear, fm/ps, 4¾" 55.00
Milk glass, beaded rib pattern, tm/sb, 8" 55.00
Milk glass, sq w/roped corners & stars, tm/sb, 9⅛" 75.00
Milk glass, vertical ribs w/swirling stars, tm, 8" 20.00
Pearl irid lustre w/HP florals, sq form, ball stopper, 8½" 135.00
Robin's egg bl opal, 12-sided, tm/sb, 7½" 450.00
Ruby, Tree of Life w/gold, bell shape, orig top, 8½" 145.00
Ruby, 3 opal jewels w/gold, appl florals, 7¼x2⅝" 135.00
Ruby cut panels w/gold, fancy stopper, 7x3¾" 145.00

Sea horse, amethyst, 20-rib, applied ribbon, outstanding, 4", $375.00.

T'print, med amethyst, sq, rm/sb, Sandwich, 5¾" 400.00
Teal bl, 12-sided, sl shoulders, flared rm/sb, 4¾" 180.00

Commercial Perfume Bottles

Oscar de LaRenta, 8", $245.00.

A Biento, Lentheric, 1930s, 1-oz......................................60.00
Blue Grass, Elizabeth Arden, crystal, 1930s, ¼ -oz, +box 10.00
Chanel #5, Japanese market label, 1940s, sm......................10.00
Crown, Prince Matchabelli, gr enameling w/gold, 3", MIB..........150.00
Dalut de Schiaparelli, unopened, 1930s, +orig box 55.00
Danger, Ciro, unopened, 1938, +orig box..........................85.00
Early American, Shulton, unopened, 1937, +orig box 35.00
Evening in Paris, cobalt, lipstick shape, purse sz 40.00
Fete des Roses, Caron, F Bergaud, Baccarat, gilded sq, 1936........375.00

Frenzy, Cordey, unopened, 1930s, +orig box 65.00
Gigi, Saint, unopened, 1930s 45.00
It's You, E Arden, Baccarat, clear/frosted, 1939, 7½" 600.00
Je Reviens, Worth, unopened, 1940s, 4-oz..........................15.00
Jet, Cordey, unopened, 1930s, 10 drams, +orig box 45.00
Jet, Cordey, unopened, 1930s, 5 drams, +orig box..................30.00
L'Heure Bleue, Guerlain, unopened/unmk Baccarat, '30s, +box....85.00
Lady's head form, Hattie Carnegie, Wheaton, 1938.....................175.00
Mais Oui, Bourjois, unopened, 1938, +orig box 35.00
Mary Chess, Wheaton, chesspc shape, 1930s 50.00
My Sin, Lavin, Armand Rateau, blk sphere w/gilt stopper, 3¼" ..125.00
New Horizons, Ciro, 1941, +orig box................................45.00
Prince Duka, Marquay, prince figural stopper, set of 3, 3"............275.00
Risque, Leigh, unopened, 1926, 1-oz...............................35.00
Sapphire, Lynette, unopened, 1945 ....35.00
Secret de Suzanne, Suzanne, unopened, 1930s, +orig box 55.00
Sinner, unopened, 1930s 25.00
Sleeping, Schiaparelli, non-Baccarat candle version, 6½"...........95.00
Soir de Paris, Bourjois, cobalt, 1930s, lg...........................25.00
Surrender, Ciro, unopened, 1932, +orig box........................65.00
Tweed, Lentheric, unopened, 1935, +orig box 20.00
20 Carats, Dana, unopened, 1933 ....55.00
3 Musketeers, Lentheric, men's 3-pc set, 1941, +orig box 35.00
3 Silent Messengers, Lentheric, 1940, +orig box 45.00

Dairy

Clinch Haven Farms, Norton VA, bl pyro, 1-qt......................20.00
Clover Farms, Norwalk CT, gr pyro, 1-qt 18.00
Frates Dairy Inc, New Bedford on 2 sides, red pyro, qt 12.00
Hampton Dairy Mark of Quality & Service, ½-pt 3.50
Hassayampa Dairy, Prescott AZ, orange & gr pyro, 1-qt 40.00
Health Want Some, red pyro, ½-pt.................................. 8.00
Hillcrest Dairy, Cadiz OH, Steubenville OH, red pyro, 1-qt.........12.00
John Swaza Rock Highland Farms, bl pyro on clear, qt 4.00
Johnstown Sanitary Dairy, Johnstown PA, red pyro, 1-qt 12.00
Lawton's Dairy, Swansea MA, red pyro on clear, sq, 1-qt..............3.00
ML Fenton, Titusville PA, orange & gr pyro, 1-qt 25.00
Pine Grove Farm, JS Gordon, Woodsford ME, Maine I Seal, ½-pt ... 5.00
Pomeroy, Produced by..., ½-pt, EX 3.50
Sanitary Best by Test Milk, bl & red, cream top, ½-pt 20.00
Slades Dairy, Santa Fe NM, red pyro, 1-qt 25.00

Figural Bottles

Bear on lamppost, blk amethyst, Depose on base, 11⅜" 350.00
Blk waiter, blk glass head w/pnt features, frosted body, 15"..........445.00
Boot, blk bsk, leather strap & metal spur, 6½x2¼" 110.00
Clown, clear, tm/sb, 9½" 75.00
Column, milk glass base, metal Columbus top, Librowicz, 18" 300.00
Dice, clear, tm/sb, 1⅛", pr 90.00
Duck w/head up, clear, tm/sb, lt stain, 12¼" 25.00
Grant's tomb, milk glass, metal Grant bust lid, 11⅛" 275.00
Man standing, aqua, tm/ps, potstone on leg, 9¾" 50.00
Mermaid bust, curving tail, flint enamel, 8" 375.00
Monkey, milk glass, Trade Mark emb, tm/sb, 4½", EX 130.00
Pickle, med gr, gm/sb, 4½" 130.00
Pig, Rosenbaum Bros Old Ky Whiskies, unglazed pottery, 7" 275.00
Pig, Suffolk Bitters/Philbrook & Tucker Boston, yel-amber, 10" .675.00
Pig, We Trust/GAR, salt glazed, bl slip, 7" 220.00
Pitsol, amber, sm/sb, w/orig cap, 8", M..............................50.00
Skull, clear, b3m, tm, ca 1900, 4" 575.00
Uncle Sam, clear, Pat Apld For, tm/sb, 9½" 110.00

Flasks

Benjamin Franklin/TW Dyott, GI-96, aqua, sm, stain, qt............110.00
Columbia/Kensington-Eagle/Union Co, GI-118, aqua, sm, ½-pt..250.00
Corn for the World, GIV-4, bright yel-olive, sm/sb, qt...............725.00
Corn for the World, GVI-5, aqua, sm/sb, qt.................................80.00
Cornucopia/Urn, GIII-10, yel-amber, sm/ps, ½-pt 60.00
Cornucopia/Urn, GIII-12, yel-amber, sm/ps, ½-pt 140.00
Cornucopia/Urn, GIII-14a, aqua, sm/ps, ½-pt 135.00
Cornucopia/Urn, GIII-4, olive-gr, sm/ps, pt...............................70.00
Cornucopia/Urn, GIII-7, olive-yel, sm/ps, ½-pt 140.00
Dbl Eagle, GII-1, aqua, sm/ps, pt...190.00
Dbl Eagle, GII-1a, aqua, sm/ps, rare variant, pt 210.00
Dbl Eagle, GII-101, emerald gr, sm/sb, 1850s, qt.......................400.00
Dbl Eagle, GII-26, aqua, sm/ps, 1830s, qt, NM 95.00
Dbl Eagle, GII-3, aqua, sm/ps, pt 130.00
Dbl Eagle, GII-30, aqua, sm/ps, ½-pt.......................................275.00
Dbl Eagle, GII-30, lt gr, sm/ps, lt stain, ½-pt............................160.00
Dbl Eagle, GII-31, aqua, sm/ps, qt...130.00
Dbl Eagle, GII-32a, aqua, sm/ps, rare, 1840s, pt 240.00
Dbl Eagle, GII-40, aqua, sm/ps, ca 1820s, pt..............................80.00
Dbl Eagle, GII-85, yel-amber, sm/ps, 1830s, pt..........................120.00
Eagle-Coffen & Hay/Stag/Hammonton, GII-50, aqua, sm, ½-pt....140.00
Eagle/Cornucopia, GII-11a, aqua, sm/ps, lt stain, ½-pt 185.00
Eagle/Cornucopia, GII-13, aqua, sm/ps, lt wear, ½-pt 275.00
Eagle/Cornucopia, GII-6, lt gr-aqua, sm/ps, lt wear, pt................140.00
Eagle/Cornucopia, GII-73, amber, sm/ps, 1830s, pt 95.00
Eagle/Cornucopia, GII-73, med olive-gr, sm/ps, 1830s, pt.............90.00
Eagle/Flower, GII-23, deep aqua, sm/ps, pt, M............................650.00
Eagle/For Pikes Peak/Prospector, GII-21, aqua, am/sb, pt..............95.00
Eagle/Grapes, GII-56, aqua, sm/ps, 1820s, ½-pt..........................190.00
Eagle/JKB-Masonic Arch, GIV-3, gr-aqua, rm/ps, lt wear, pt.......210.00
Eagle/JP-Masonic Arch, GIV-1, lt gr, sm/ps, 1830s, pt 170.00
Eagle/JP-Masonic Arch, GIV-1a, med bl-gr, sm/ps, pt, NM.........150.00
Eagle/KCCNC/Masonic Arch, GIV-20a, olive-amber, sm/ps, pt ..130.00
Eagle/Keene/Masonic Arch, GIV-17, yel-amber, sm/ps, pt 130.00
Eagle/Masonic Arch, GIV-14, lt yel-gr, rm/ps, ½-pt....................210.00
Eagle/Masonic Arch, GIV-16, olive-gr, am/ps, pt 1,550.00
Eagle/Masonic Arch, GIV-24, olive-amber, sm/ps, ½-pt..............160.00
Eagle/Masonic Arch, GIV-7, med yel-gr, rm/ps, qt 550.00
Eagle/Masonic Arch, GIV-8a, clear flint, rm/ps, sm chip, pt 275.00
Eagle/Morning-Glory, GII-19, aqua, sm/ps, 1830s, pt 325.00
Eagle/NEG/Masonic Arch, GIV-26, olive-amber, sm/ps, ½-pt 900.00
Eagle/Pittsburgh PA-Eagle, GII-103, lt yel-aqua, sm/sb, pt 90.00
Eagle/TWD/Masonic Arch, GIV-37, aqua, sm/ps, stain, pt............90.00
Father of His Country/WA bust, GI-48, aqua, am/ps, pt 65.00

Franklin, GI-97, aqua, sm/ps, ca 1830, qt 110.00
Gen Taylor/Cannon, GX-6, pale gr, sm/ps, ½ -pt.........................220.00
Gen WA/Eagle (portrait), GI-11, aqua, sm, ca 1830s, pt 425.00
Hearts & Flowers scroll, GIX-51, aqua, sm/ps, rare, qt............. 2,100.00
Jenny Lind, GI-108, aqua, sm/ps, 7", NM 850.00
Jenny Lind, GI-110, aqua, sm/ps, lt stain, 8½".............................950.00
Jenny Lind/Glasshouse, GI-103, aqua, am, lt stain, calabash 60.00
Jenny Lind/GW/Glasshouse/S Huffsey, GI-99, aqua, calabash 80.00
Lafayette/Liberty Cap, GI-86, yel-amber, sm, ½ -pt, NM............350.00
Liberty/Eagle-Willington/Conn, GII-63, olive-amber, ½ -pt 110.00
Masonic Arch/Masonic Arch, GIV-28, deep aqua, rm/ps, ½ -pt...180.00
Rough & Ready/Taylor-Masterson/Eagle, GI-77, aqua, qt, EX ...350.00
Scroll, GIX-10, yel, flared sm, ip, 7", NM..................................625.00
Scroll, GIX-10a, deep aqua, sm/ps, pt 80.00
Scroll, GIX-10a, sapphire bl, beveled tm w/ring, ip, 7½", NM .. 1,200.00
Scroll, GIX-10b, deep olive-yel, am/ip, flake, pt 350.00
Scroll, GIX-11, amber, sm/ps, lt wear, pt 185.00
Scroll, GIX-14, aqua, sm/ps, 7½" 250.00
Scroll, GIX-14, gray tint, tm/ps, 6⅞"..375.00
Scroll, GIX-2, aqua, sm/ip, qt..60.00
Scroll, GIX-2, bright med-gr, sm/ps, qt.......................................575.00
Scroll, GIX-21, aqua, sm/ps, rare variant, pt 80.00
Scroll, GIX-26, aqua, S McKee, sm/ps, 7", NM 1,100.00
Scroll, GIX-31, amber, sm/tubular pontil, 6"...............................525.00
Scroll, GIX-31, cornflower bl, plain lip w/ring, ip, 6", NM..........550.00
Scroll, GIX-33a, amber, sm/ip, 6", NM.......................................300.00
Scroll, GIX-40, sm/fire-polished lip, ps, 2½", NM......................600.00
Scroll, GIX-41, lt emerald gr, sm/ps, 5¾"...................................600.00
Scroll, GIX-45, gr-aqua, corset waist, sm/ps, pt, NM...................350.00
Scroll, GIX-46, aqua, corset waist, sm/ps, qt 975.00
Scroll, GIX-46, aqua, sm/ps, 8½"..500.00
Scroll, GIX-51, aqua, sm/gm/ps, 8½" 1,300.00
Sheaf of Grain/8-Pointed Star, GXIII-42, aqua, calabash..............70.00
Sloop/8-Pointed Star, GX-8, lt yel-gr, sm/ps, ½ -pt, NM 170.00
Stag/Good Game/Willow Tree, GX-1, aqua, sm/ps, lt wear, pt......90.00
Success to the RR, GV-5, deep yel-amber, sm/ps, pt, EX 80.00

Success to the Railroad, GV-5, deep emerald green, pint, $275.00.

Father of His Country, Washington; A Little More Grape Captain Bragg, Taylor; deep cobalt-blue, lip chip and inside stain, quart, $475.00.

Summer Tree/Winter Tree, GX-15, aqua, am/sb, pt......................75.00
Sunburst, GVIII-1, yel-gr, sm/ps, pt 725.00
Sunburst, GVIII-16, emerald gr, sm/ps, ½ -pt 625.00
Sunburst, GVIII-16, med olive-gr, sm/ps, ½ -pt...........................235.00
Sunburst, GVIII-18, yel-amber, sm/ps, ½ -pt...............................500.00

Sunburst, GVIII-2, gr, sm/ps, mold flaw, pt 310.00
Sunburst, GVIII-28, aqua, sm/ps, ½ -pt 130.00
Sunburst, GVIII-3, bright olive-gr, sm/ps, lt wear, pt 300.00
Sunburst, GVIII-3, med olive-yel, sm/ps, pt 350.00
Sunburst, GVIII-5a, yel amber, sm/ps, bruise, pt 400.00
Sunburst/Keen-Sunburst/P&W, GVIII-8, yel-amber, sm/ps, pt ..240.00
Union/Clasped Hands/FA&Co/Cannon, GXII-40, amber, pt 180.00
Washington/Albany GW NY, GI-30, citron, sm, ½ -pt....300.00
Washington/Jackson, GI-31, yel-olive, am/ps, 1830s, pt....120.00
Zanesville/Eagle/Masonic, GIV-32, deep aqua, rm/ps, pt 180.00
Zanesville/Eagle/Masonic, GIV-32, red-amber, sm/ps, pt....385.00
Zanesville/Eagle/Masonic, GIV-32, yel-amber, sl/ps, pt, NM....210.00

Food Bottles and Jars

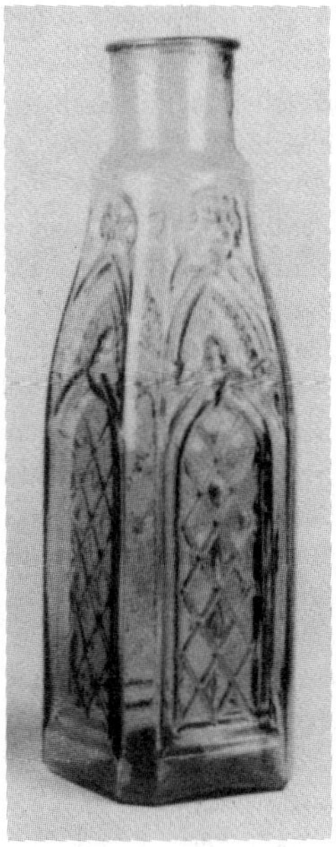

Cathedral pickle bottle, bright blue-green, three fancy arches, one plain, 14", $300.00.

Catsup, Cayuga County...NY, aqua w/yel-gr swirls, am/sb, 10" 55.00
Catsup, Pioneer, amber, 6-sided, tm/sb, 9¼", NM....160.00
Mustard, dk olive-amber, rm/sb, 3⅞" 70.00
Mustard, Giessen's Union...NY, clear, rm/ps, 4⅝" 80.00
Mustard, NW Opermann Factory, aqua, rm/ps, 4¾" 190.00
Olive, EC Hazard...NY, bright yel-gr, am/sb, 6⅞"....60.00
Peppersauce, CL Stickney, aqua, am/ps, 9", NM 80.00
Peppersauce, deep aqua, cathedral, am/ps, 9" 100.00
Pickle, aqua, cathedral, rm/ip, 11½" 350.00
Pickle, aqua, cathedral, 6-sided, rm/sb, 13⅛", NM....170.00
Pickle, bright yel, cathedral, 6-sided, rm/sb, 11⅜" 2,450.00
Pickle, citron, cathedral, 6-sided, rm/sb, 13⅛" 325.00
Pickle, deep aqua, cathedral, rm/ip, 8⅞"....400.00
Pickle, EHVG/NY, deep aqua, rm/ip, 9" 170.00
Pickle, gr-aqua, cathedral, rm/sb, 14"....275.00
Pickle, lt gr, cathedral, rm/sb, 13¾" 300.00
Pickle, lt to med gr, cathedral, rm/sb, 11⅝" 120.00
Pickle, med emerald gr, cathedral, rm/ip, 14½", EX 825.00
Pickle, WD Smith NY, deep aqua, rm/ip, 8⅝" 450.00
Pickle, Wm Underwood/Boston/32-oz, med emerald gr, 8⅜" 240.00
Pickle, WT&Co (on base), golden amber, cathedral, tm, 13⅜" .750.00
Pickle, yel-olive, unemb, am/sb, 13¾" 275.00
Preserve, Dayton Prentiss & Borden NY, aqua, rm/ps, 7" 180.00
Sauce, WM&P/NY, aqua, am/ip, inside lip chip, 9⅜" 35.00

Ink Bottles

Carter's, cobalt, cathedral, orig spout & labels, 9¾"....95.00
E Water Troy NY, aqua, am/ps, 2½" 350.00
G&R's Am Writing Fluid, aqua, rm/ps, 2⅝"....475.00
Harrison's Columbian, aqua, 8-sided, rm/ps, 1⅝" 70.00
Hover Phila, lt to med emerald gr, 12-sided, rm/ps, 1⅞" 275.00
Laughlin's & Bushfield Wheeling VA, aqua, 8-sided, 2⅞" 95.00
Pat Oct 1874 Trade Mark, aqua, locomotive, gm/sb, 2"....575.00
Petroleum PB & Co Writing Fluid, aqua, bbl form, 2⅝"....130.00
Teakettle, dk amethyst, 8-sided, gm/sb, sm chip, 2" 150.00
Teakettle, emerald gr, pnt traces, 7-sided, sb, 2"....450.00
Teakettle, fiery opal, HP/emb decor, gm/sb, 2"....350.00
Teakettle, med sapphire bl, worn gold pnt, 7-sided, 2" 250.00
Umbrella, cobalt, 8-sided, am/sb, flake, 2¾"....300.00
Umbrella, deep olive-gr, 8-sided, sm/ps, 2⅜"....130.00
Umbrella, lt to med bl-gr, 8-sided, rm/ps, 2⅜" 65.00
12-sided, lt yel-gr, rm/ps, 1⅜"....110.00

Medicine Bottles

Anderson's Dermador, aqua, am/ps, 4¼"....45.00
Brant's Indian Pulmonary Balsam, aqua, 8-sided, 6⅞"....50.00
Catalan Hair Renewer, cobalt, 5-sided, tm/sb, 6⅛"....100.00
CW Snow Druggists Syracuse NY, cobalt, eagle emb, 8¼" 190.00
ES Reed's Sons Apothecary Atlantic City NJ, milk glass, 4⅝" 110.00
Flagg's Good Samaritan's..., lt bl, 6-sided, 4" 130.00
German Fir Cough...Dillard Remedy E Bangor PA, aqua, 6⅜" 75.00
HH Warner & Co Tippecanoe, amber, am/sb, G label, 9"....130.00
Jerome's Hair Color Restorer, cobalt, fm/sb, 6⅜" 375.00
Lindsey's Blood Searcher Pittsburgh, aqua, am/sb, 8⅜" 75.00
Longley's Panacea, aqua, am/ps, lt stain, 7⅜"....90.00
Mrs E Kidder's Dysentery Cordial Boston, aqua, am/ps, 6½"....60.00
Mrs SA Allen's World's Hair Restorer...NY, med lav, 7¼" 170.00
RC&A New York (on shoulder), cobalt, am/sb, 8½" 280.00

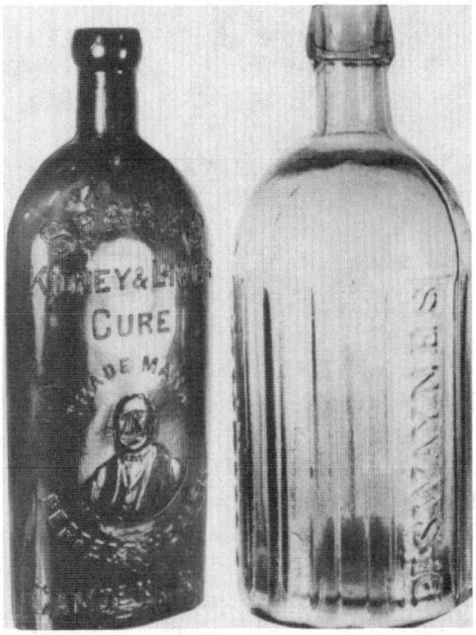

Sparks Kidney & Liver Cure, amber, 9½", rare, NM, $250.00; Dr. Swayne's Panacea, medium emerald green, rare, 7¾", $70.00.

Warner's Safe Cure (emb at neck), amber, am/sb, 9½"....110.00
Warner's Safe Diabetes Cure Melbourne, amber, am/sb, 9½" 95.00
WR Watson CH Town PEI, aqua, am/ps, 7" 95.00

Mineral Water and Soda Bottles

Boyd & Beard B Patent, yel-gr, am/ip, 6½"....210.00
C Cleminshaw Soda & Mineral...NY, sapphire bl, am/ip, 6⅞" 175.00
Chapman's Soda, aqua, rm/ps, rnd-bottom tenpin, 8"....325.00
E Bigelow & Co Springfield MA, sapphire bl, am/ip, 7⅜" 140.00

Geo Eagle, med gr, emb ribs, am/ip, 6⅞" 600.00
Geo Upp Jr, York PA, aqua, am/sb, tenpin, lt wear, 8½" 375.00
J Simonds/Boston, gr, am/ip, sm lip chip, 7⅛" 95.00
J Zerbe/Duncansville, cobalt, am/ip, chip/wear, 7½" 245.00
L Beard/Union GW/Philadelphia, yel-gr, am/ip, 6⅞"..................140.00
Phila GW/Burgin & Sons, med emerald gr, am/ip, lt wear, 7¼" 55.00
Saratoga Springs, sapphire bl, ip, 10-sided tenpin, 7⅝" 1,000.00
Sweeny & Cherry...Peerless...Water, cobalt, am/sb, 7¼" 140.00
Tweddle's Celebrated...NY, med cobalt, am/ip, 7¾" 200.00

Poison Bottles

Lattice & Dmn pattern, cobalt, tm/sb, orig label, 7½".................85.00
Lattice & Dmn pattern, cobalt, tm/sb, orig stopper, 7⅛" 135.00
Poison, Norwich 4A (on sb), amber, tm, coffin shape, 5"........ 1,450.00
Poison, skull & X-bones, cobalt, 3¼" 60.00
Poison Pat Appl'd For June 26th 1894, cobalt, skull, 3½"...........950.00
Poison/Bowman's Drug Stores/Pat Appl For, cobalt, 7½" 525.00
Poison/owl on mortar & pestle, cobalt, triangular, 9⅜"...........525.00
Poison/16-oz/Use w/Caution, cobalt, tm/sb, 8⅞" 100.00
Skull & X-bones, PD&Co (on sb), amber, tm, 2⅜" 275.00

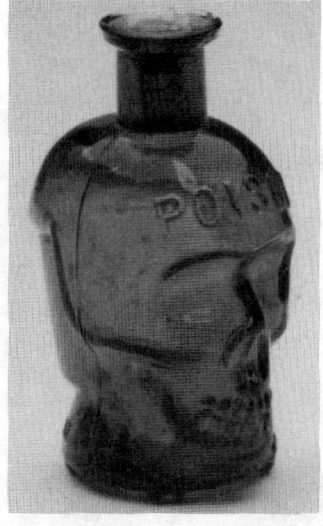

Skull figural, deep cobalt, several small lip chips, 4¼", $950.00.

Spirits Bottles

AM Bininger & Co...NY, yel-amber, cannon, sb, 12⅝" 300.00
Bininger's Old Dominion Wheat Tonic..., olive-gr, 10" 80.00
Bininger's Old KY Bourbon 1849 Reserve..., olive-gr, 9¾" 150.00
Bininger's Regulator...NY, yel-amb, clock, am/ps, 5¾" 200.00
Dip-molded case gin, olive amber, flared rm/ps, 15½"..................525.00
Dip-molded case gin, olive amber, sm/appl string rim/sb, 13" 275.00
Dip-molded case gin, olive-amber, flared am/ps, crude, 10" 100.00
Dip-molded case gin, olive-amber, flared rm/ps, 19⅝"............. 1,600.00
Distilled in 1848...AM Bininger...NY, med amber, bbl, 8" 110.00
Geo Zantinger...Phila, olive-amber, am/ps, 11⅝" 150.00
Wharton's Whiskey 1850...Glassboro NJ, amber, appl hdl, 10"...300.00

Miscellaneous

Back bar, clear, 8-sided, am, marble stopper, 10¼" 120.00
Flask, pocket; clear, label under glass, sb, 5¼" 250.00
Gargling Oil/Lockport NY, yel-amber, sb, tm, 5½" 120.00
GW Merchant/Lockport/NY, emerald gr, am, 4⅞" 120.00
Lavender Salts, Goetting & Co, see California Perfume Co
Mallet shape, dk olive-amber, appl string lip, 7⅝" 175.00

Pomade jar, Bazin/Philada, bear figural, clambroth, 3¾"..............130.00
Sweet 16, Goetting & Co, see California Perfume Co

Boxes

Boxes have been used by civilized man since ancient Egypt and Rome. Down through the centuries, specifically designed containers have been made from every conceivable material. Precious metals, papier-mache, battersea, Oriental lacquer, and wood have held riches from the treasuries of kings, snuff for the fashionable set of the last century, China tea, and countless other commodities. See also Toleware; specific manufacturers.

Amber, cvd, delicate gold filigree o/l, 2¼" 415.00
Apple, wallpaper on cb, PA newspaper w/in, 2¼x7x7" 200.00
Band, wallpaper on bentwood, Boston newspaper w/in, 9x14" ...400.00
Beech w/mc florals, hinged lid, minor wear, 10"...........................700.00
Beech w/4-color birds & flowers on dk bl, dome top 13", VG 375.00
Bentwood, bentwood hdl, indistinct label, 6x9", VG................65.00
Bentwood, blk rpt over orig gr, bentwood swivel hdl, 5x8" 300.00
Bentwood, EX patina, minor edge damage, 8" dia.......................125.00
Bentwood, laced seams, wooden spring clips, oval, 15" 150.00
Bentwood, orig bl pnt, minor age crack, 5" dia............................560.00
Bentwood, pine, 3-color floral on red stain, 1838, 9½", EX 675.00
Bentwood, pine & beech w/gr rpt, 1-finger, chip cvg, 5¾".........200.00
Bentwood, pine w/laced seams, pk pnt w/mc tulips, 15" 1,350.00
Bentwood, pnt floral decor, laced seams, 4" L 225.00
Bentwood, striped laminated wood lid, 3⅜" L 100.00
Bible, oak, geometric cvg, English, early, rpl hinges, 24" 250.00
Book shape, pine w/grpt, brn lines/red roses, 10", VG 100.00
Bride's, bentwood, orig pnt house/couple/dog, rprs, 18" 625.00
Bride's, bentwood w/mc couple & German inscription, 19", VG...850.00
Bride's, man/jumping dog/inscription in mc, 19", VG 1,150.00
Burl wood, well-figured, well made, 3" dia..................................225.00
Candle, birch w/red stain, dvtl, sliding lid, 9" L 175.00
Candle, cherry, dvtl, finger grip on slide lid, 16" L 300.00
Candle, pine w/bl pnt, slide lid, sq nails, 9½" L...........................375.00
Candle, pine w/brn over red pnt, peaked crest, primitive..............125.00
Candle, pine w/orig red pnt, dvtl, slide lid, 16" 345.00
Candle, pine/poplar, dvtl, slide lid, rfn, 15" L.............................135.00
Chip cvd florals w/folky eagle, dome top, rprs/damage, 9" 775.00
Curly maple, brass hinges & latch, 3" L 95.00
Curly maple, trn ft/dvtl case, mortised/pinned lid, 15", EX..........350.00
Inlaid, bands of colored marquetry, minor damage, 10" 125.00
Kindling, pine w/worn rpt, appl rim & end hdls, 26" L 110.00
Knife, mahog w/inlay, urn form, English, tall, pr 2,500.00
Leather-covered, brass tacks, emb brass hdl, 8"...........................45.00
Oak, cvd/pnt bird & florals, slide lid, crest, wall mt, 14".............600.00

Painted pine with 5-color freehand decoration of tulips, 1830s, minor paint wear, 12" long, $6,500.00.

Pine, bl pnt, lollipop bk, wall mt, 1800s, 26x12" **4,000.00**
Pine w/orig red, floral/bird reserves, dome top, 13" **2,300.00**
Pine w/rust flame grpt, int till, base molding, 14" **175.00**
Pine w/3-color stylized floral on red, lt wear, 12" **900.00**
Pine w/5-color stylized floral on blk, 8", EX **3,000.00**
Pine/poplar, orig red vinegar grpt, dome top, lt wear, 19" **1,150.00**
Pine/poplar w/red pnt & blk stencil decor, rpr, 10" **475.00**
Pipe, pine, dvtl drw overlaps, scalloped top w/crest, 17" **900.00**
Pipe, pine w/blk rpt, dvtl drw, cut-out rim & crest, 16" **2,200.00**
Poplar, dvtl drw, bracket fr, lift lid, 13x12x14", EX **275.00**
Poplar, worn orig blk pnt w/faded HP tulips & initials, 7" **695.00**
Poplar w/Am shield pnt on dk gr, yel/bl striping, 15" **675.00**
Poplar w/EX wht pnt, 3-color dots/zigzags/flowers, 8¾" **5,000.00**
Poplar w/red grpt, dk edge stripe, missing hasp/lt wear, 9" **275.00**
Poplar w/red-sponged yel, rpl lid finial/wear, 8x8½" dia..............**700.00**
Poplar w/traces of red, dvtl, slant lid, wallpaper w/in, 15" **275.00**
Scouring, pine, sq nail construction, 34" L **200.00**
Shoe shaped, holly wood, cvd birds/man/flowers/etc, 6" L **400.00**
Spice, bentwood w/tin edging, stenciled labels, 8 int cans **65.00**
Strong box, tin w/tooled brass trim, initials/1730, 7½", EX **270.00**
Tobacco, fish form, treenware, lt eng, minor damage, 6" **175.00**
Wallpaper on cb, florals/birds, 4-color, damage/rprs, 16" **300.00**
Wallpaper on cb, geometric/floral, 1800 newspaper w/in, 6" **350.00**
Wallpaper on cb, mc floral, 3x4" dia **230.00**
Walnut, X-hatched/anchor cvg, slide lid, dvtl, 5" L **65.00**
Walnut w/floral inlay, eng w/in: Res of..., rfn, 14" **500.00**
Walnut/cherry, dvtl, dvtl drw, arch crest, wall mt, 16x15" **1,900.00**
Walnut/poplar, scalloped w/cutout, wall mt, 1900, 19" **125.00**
Writing, brass-bound mahog, fitted, W Esser/1844, 20", VG **350.00**
Writing, brass-bound mahog, fitted int, worn/age cracks, 20"......**125.00**
Writing, pine, crest/dvtl drw & case, chip cvd, 22" **700.00**

Boyd Crystal Art Glass

Boyd Crystal Art Glass is a small but productive glass factory located in Cambridge, Ohio. It was established in 1978 when the Boyd family bought out the Degenhart factory. Over the years Boyd has produced more than 200 molds; while many were their own design, they acquired others from glasshouses no longer in business. All the Boyd pieces are marked with a distinct logo of a 'B' in diamond. Further dating is possible because a line was added under the diamond in 1983, and an additional line was added above the diamond in 1988. Boyd's glass is prized because of the colors they formulated and the fact that once a piece is produced in a particular color it will not be produced in that color again, even if that color is brought back years later. All pieces are hand pressed from glass that is from a single-day tank. Colors are made for about six weeks or less, thus limiting the number of pieces that can be produced in that color. More than 225 different colors have been used and developed by the Boyds. Much like Degenhart glass, the colors can be confusing and difficult to identify. Exceptional slags and hand-painted pieces can command up to 50% higher prices. Satin glass variations are priced 10% to 30% higher when they can be found. Our advisor for this category is Joyce Pringle; she is listed in the Directory under Texas.

Airplane, Classic Blk Carnival, new mold in 1991 ....**16.00**
Bow slipper, Furr Gr..**12.50**
Brian bunny, Oxford Gray, retired mold **7.00**
Brian bunny, Ruby, retired mold **17.50**
Bunny salt, Skytop Bl **20.00**
Bunny salt, Sunburst..**12.50**
Car, Tucker, Buckeye **10.00**
Cat slipper, Platinum Carnival..**15.00**

Chick, Bermuda, 1"..**15.00**
Chick, Enchantment, 1"... **7.00**
Chick, John's Surprise, 1"...**22.00**
Chick, Royalty, 1"...**75.00**
Duck salt, Dove Bl...**10.00**
Duck salt, Lt Peach.. **6.00**
Elizabeth mini doll, Classic Blk Satin **8.00**
Elizabeth mini doll, Lime Carnival **27.50**
Forget-me-not toothpick, Carmine (1st color in this mold) **35.00**
Forget-me-not toothpick, Teal Swirl.. **8.00**
Heart toothpick, Mint Gr...**21.00**
Hen, Carmine (1st color in this mold), 3" **60.00**
Hen, Pk Champagne, 3" **28.50**
Hen, Ruby Gold (1st color in this mold), 5".................................**50.00**
JB Scotty, Cornsilk (1st color in this mold), retired mold..............**10.00**
JB Scotty, Mulberry Mist, retired mold **18.00**
Jewel box, Cornsilk..**10.00**
Jewel box, Sam Jones Slag **40.00**
Joey the horse, Chocolate (1st color in this mold) **35.00**
Joey the horse, Zack Boyd Slag.. **9.00**
Kitten on pillow, Apricot **18.00**
Kitten on pillow, Royalty (1st color in this mold).........................**20.00**
Lamb salt, Lime Carnival.. **8.00**
Louise, Delphinium **15.00**
Louise, Impatient **12.00**
Mini vase, Candy Swirl...**13.50**
Mini vase, Dk Tangerine Slag **16.50**
Patrick, balloon bear, Enchantment..**24.50**
Patrick, balloon bear, Spinnaker Bl **7.00**
Pooche, Cobalt **10.00**
Skate boot, Heather **12.50**
Train, Teal, 6-pc set..**48.00**
Zake, elephant, Cobalt **38.00**
Zake, elephant, Flame (1st color in this mold) **37.50**
Zake, elephant, Furr Gr **22.50**

Bradley and Hubbard

The Bradley and Hubbard Mfg. Company was a firm which produced metal accessories for the home. They operated from about 1860 until the early part of this century, and their products reflected both the Arts and Crafts and Art Nouveau influence. Their logo was a device with a triangular arrangement of the company name containing a smaller triangle and an Aladdin lamp. Our advisor for this category is Daniel Batchelor; he is listed in the Directory under New York.

Bookends, monk reading at table, $100.00.

Lamps

Rvpt tulips on 18" cracked ice shade; tulip emb base **2,600.00**

Slag glass 18" 6-sided shade w/palm tree o/l; mk metal std 500.00
Store, wht shade, emb brass font, 52" 2,500.00
Table, stylized filigree on 22" slag glass shade; sq base 1,300.00

Miscellaneous

Andirons, wrought iron, inverted Y-form w/ball finial, 16" 325.00
Bookends, brass, Colonial lady & driver w/coach, 6½", pr 80.00
Bookrack, sq end panels w/windswept pine trees, 5" closed 275.00
Cigar stand, brass, tray w/3 etched cups & cutter, 30"..................225.00
Letter opener, brass, sgn 300.00
Mirror, brass easel bk w/openwork & mythological mask, 12" 200.00

Brass

Brass is an alloy consisting essentially of copper and zinc in variable proportions. It is a medium that has been used for both utilitarian items and objects of artistic merit. Today, with the inflated price of copper and the popular use of plastics, almost anything made of brass is collectible. Our advisor, Mary Frank Gaston, has compiled a lovely book, *Antique Brass and Copper*, with full-color photos; you will find her address in the Directory under Texas. See also Candlesticks.

Box, trinket; oval w/colored stones 65.00
Bucket, wrought iron rim band & bail hdl, 12½x19" 200.00
Candle sconce, S-scroll arms, good age, 10", pr..........................240.00
Coal hod, hammered, 1910, 9½" 75.00
Dipper, elongated bowl, wrought iron hdl, 20" 95.00
Figurine, fighting cock, ca 1900, 11" wide, pr............................350.00
Fireplace fender, paw ft, emb garlands, 49" L 350.00
Grater, punched, curved grating surface, steel fr, sgn, 15" 95.00
Kettle stand, EX detail, arch legs, heavy, English, 12x17" 450.00
Match box, simple punched tooling, wall mt, polished, 5½"..........70.00
Pail, iron bail hdl, Hayden's Pat, 7½x11" 150.00
Sconce, cast hand holds socket, 10", pr 900.00
Skimmer, brass w/copper rivets holding oval bowl to hdl, 20" 65.00
Skimmer, wrought iron hdl, mk FBS Canton O Pat Jan 86, 20"..135.00
Table, cast, rnd gr marble top, 22x23" dia 350.00
Taper jack, 6", EX...195.00
Wall pocket, ½-rnd w/cut-out edge, bird's head crest, 9", EX 145.00

Tray, lion in relief, United Brass Works, NY, 6½", $45.00.

Brastoff, Sascha

The son of immigrant parents, Sascha Brastoff was encouraged to develop his artistic talents to the fullest, encouragement that was well taken, as his achievements aptly attest. Though at various times he has been a dancer, sculptor, Hollywood costume designer, jeweler, and painter, it is his ceramics that are today becoming highly-regarded collectibles.

Sascha began his career in the United States in the late 1940s. In a beautiful studio built for him by his friend and mentor, Winthrop Rockefeller, he designed innovative wares that even then were among the most expensive on the market. All designing was done personally by Brastoff; he also supervised the staff which at the height of production numbered approximately 150. Wares signed with his full signature (not merely backstamped 'Sascha Brastoff') were personally crafted by him and are valued much more highly than those signed 'Sascha B.,' indicating work done under his supervision. Sascha Brastoff still resides in Los Angeles, California, at present producing 'Sascha Holograms,' which are distributed by the Hummelwerk Company.

Another medium he used in his work was resin, and such pieces are also very collectible, though extremely scarce. In the listings below, all items are signed 'Sascha B.' unless otherwise indicated (full signature). Our advisor for this category is Jack Chipman, author of *Collector's Encyclopedia of California Pottery*; Mr. Chipman is listed in the Directory under California.

Ash tray, ceramic, Eskimo in parka, lg 40.00
Ash tray, ceramic, hooded, metallic gold...30.00
Ash tray, ceramic, horse decor on gray..40.00
Bowl, ceramic, yel w/gold, 2x6"..20.00
Box, cigarette; ceramic, bird decor, wht/gold, full signature 100.00
Compote, ceramic, wht w/mc gold stripes, 10" 65.00

Compote, ivory with gold and silver dove, 9½", $65.00.

Figurine, bear, red resin, rare, 6" 150.00
Plaque, enamelled copper w/emb grapes, 17¾" 65.00
Plate, ceramic, poodle sitting up, mc, 11½" 85.00
Tray, mc abstract matt, ceramic, 17" dia...125.00
Vase, bl resin, rare, 9" 30.00
Vase, emerald gr, resin, vintage decor, 5¾" 50.00

Brayton Laguna

Durlin E. Brayton made hand-crafted vases, lamps, and dinnerware in a small kiln at his Laguna Beach, California, home in 1927. He soon married; and, with his wife, Ellen Webster Grieve, as his partner, the small business became a successful commercial venture. They are most famous for their amusing, well-detailed figurines, some of which were commissioned by Walt Disney Studios. Though very successful even through the Depression years, with the influx of imported novelties that deluged the country after WWII, business began to decline. By 1968 the pottery was closed. For more information on this as well as many other potteries in the state, we recommend *The Collectors Encyclopedia of California Pottery* by Jack Chipman; he is listed in the Directory under California.

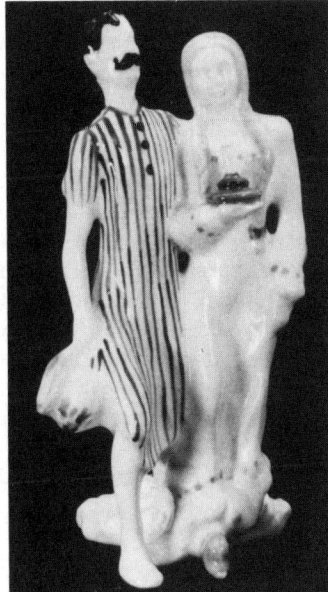

Couple in nightclothes, 8½", $50.00.

Candle holder, seated Blackamoor, pr 100.00
Figurine, Ann 45.00
Figurine, Blk choir boy, 5½" 75.00
Figurine, boy & dog 45.00
Figurine, boy & girl in matching school clothes, pr......................95.00
Figurine, couple in nightclothes, 8½" 50.00
Figurine, Dutch boy & girl, pr...90.00
Figurine, Emily 45.00
Figurine, Figaro the cat, Disney..175.00
Figurine, girl knitting sock...32.00
Figurine, Petunia & Sambo, pr 175.00
Figurine, Pluto, sniffing, Disney 165.00
Figurine, purple cow family: bull, calf & cow 165.00
Figurine, Sally, flower holder..25.00
Figurine, Siamese cat, lg, pr 200.00
Planter, baby w/pillow 35.00
Planter, lady w/shawl, 8" 35.00
Wall pocket, Blackamoor, 23", pr 250.00

Bread Plates and Trays

Bread plates and trays have been produced not only in many types of glass but in metal and pottery as well. Those considered most collectible were made during the last quarter of the nineteenth century from pressed glass with well-detailed embossed designs, many of them portraying a particularly significant historical event. A great number of these plates were sold at the 1876 Philadelphia Centennial Exposition by various glass manufacturers who exhibited their wares on the grounds. Among the themes depicted are the Declaration of Independence, the Constitution, McKinley's memorial 'It Is God's Way,' Rememberance of Three Presidents, the Purchase of Alaska, and various presidential campaigns, to mention only a few.

'L' numbers correspond with a reference book by Lindsey; 'S' refers to a book by Stuart. Our advisor for this category is Darlene Yohe; she is listed in the Directory under Arkansas.

Liberty Bell, Signers, 13½", $85.00.

American Flag, notched border, L-51 ....195.00
Balky Mule..85.00
Basketweave Motto, milk glass, Pat June 30, 1874 ....65.00
Bishop, L-201...45.00
Bunker Hill Monument, L-44, 13¼x9" 100.00
Chain & Shield 24.00
Chain Variant 25.00
Classic Warrior, 11"...100.00
Columbia, L-54...115.00
Constitution, L-43...70.00
Cupid & Venus, 10½" dia..37.50
Deer & Pine Tree, amber, old 80.00
Dewdrop w/Sheaf of Wheat, Give Us This Day..., 10" 50.00
Egyptian, Cleopatra center, 13" L 50.00
Frosted Lion, Give Us This Day..., 12" 175.00
Frosted Stork w/101 border, 11½x8" 55.00
GAR, L-505..90.00
Garfield Drape, We Mourn Our Nation's Loss, 11½"....................55.00
Garfield Memorial, L-302, 10"...65.00
Golden Rule, Do Unto Others, L-221...65.00
Horseshoe, single hdls, 13" L 55.00
Independence Hall, oval, L-29 ....95.00
It Is Pleasant To Labor for Those We Love, grapes, 12½" 55.00
Kansas, motto 48.00
Kansas, plain center...30.00
Knights of Labor 135.00
Last Supper..35.00
Liberty & Freedom, 1775, oval, 12" 50.00
Liberty Bell, John Hancock, oval, 13" 50.00
Liberty Bell, Signers, oval, 13½"..85.00
Liberty Bell, 10" dia 40.00
Lotus & Serpent...30.00
McCormick Reaper 110.00
McKinley, Gold Standard, 10½" 250.00
McKinley, It Is God's Way, L-356, 10½" L...................................60.00
McKinley, Memorial, L-350 ....50.00
McKinley, Protection, L-333..45.00
Nelly Bly, L-136, 12" L..200.00
Old State House, Philadelphia, L-32...85.00
Oregon 35.00
Polar Bear, ship, L-486, 16"...165.00
Pope Leo XIII, milk glass 50.00
Robert Burns..40.00
Rock of Ages, milk glass, oval 165.00
Rose & Snow, 11¼x8¾"...130.00
Ruth the Gleaner, Gillinder..140.00

Stippled Cherry, Our Daily Bread, 9½"..**25.00**
Stork, sapphire bl, hdls, 10" **65.00**
Tam-O'-Shanter, purple slag, L-412, 12x8½" **250.00**
Three Graces, Faith, Hope & Charity...**45.00**
Three Graces, wht opaque center, L-230.......................................**95.00**
Train, L-134..**75.00**
US Grant, L-291..**65.00**
US Grant, Let Us Have Peace, amber, 10½" **75.00**
US Grant, Let Us Have Peace, vaseline, 10½" **65.00**
Washington, 13-Star border, milk glass, old **45.00**
Washington Centennial, frosted, L-27 ....**130.00**
Westward Ho...**95.00**
William J Bryan, milk glass..**42.00**
3 Presidents, In Remembrance, oval **85.00**

Bride's Baskets and Bowls

Victorian brides were showered with gifts, as brides have always been; one of the most popular gift items was the bride's basket. Art glass inserts from both European and American glasshouses, some in lovely transparent hues with dainty enameled florals, others of Peachblow, Vasa Murrhina, satin or cased glass, were cradled in complementary silverplated holders. While many of these holders were simply engraved or delicately embossed, others such as those from Pairpoint and Wilcox were wonderfully ornate, often with figurals of cherubs or animals. The bride's basket was no longer in fashion after the turn of the century.

Watch for 'marriages' of bowls and frames. To warrant the best price, the two pieces should be the original pairing. If you can't be certain of this, at least check to see that the bowl fits snugly into the frame. Beware of later-made bowls (such as Fenton's) in Victorian holders.

In the listings that follow, if no frame is described, the price is for a bowl only.

Amethyst, HP leaves & butterflies; hdld SP fr, 6½x14" **195.00**
Apricot satin, HP ferns/tree/birds; 11" ftd/decor SP stand **350.00**
Apricot satin w/gilt decor, 4x12"; ornate/rstr Meriden fr **650.00**
Bl cased, HP florals, trumpet vase at side; SP fr, 16x11" **350.00**
Bl o/l, coralene florals, ruffled, 3½x9"...**250.00**
Bl satin o/l, HP florals & gold foliage, 5¼x11" **250.00**
Bl shaded w/HP portrait in base, HP florals, ruffled, 12" **200.00**
Clear bl to bl opal, HP enamel; ftd SP Wilcox fr w/leaves **395.00**
Cranberry cased, ruffled rim, pinched sides; Rogers fr, 7½".........**275.00**
Cranberry to mauve o/l w/HP florals, ruffled, 11½" **115.00**
Dk to lt gr satin w/HP florals, 16-scallop, 11¼" **95.00**

Enameled flowers on blue 7½" bowl cased in white, hummingbirds on frame, $475.00.

Gr satin, wht florals, pleated rim; SP fr, 3¾x10¾" **250.00**
Gr to maroon o/l, Wheeling; rstr basket fr, 14½x10" **325.00**
Pk & gr w/mica, crimped rim; 12" SP stand w/lg winged figure ...**450.00**
Pk o/l, floral w/gold, 3x11"; ornate/ftd/rstr Pairpoint fr **175.00**
Pk o/l, gold bands, HP decor; rstr SP fr, 10x10"..........................**235.00**
Pk to wht, cased, detailed enamel, Webb; 3-part std, 11x12" **400.00**
Rose satin, gold florals; SP Eagle Co base w/bird, 14" dia **1,095.00**
Verre de soie w/birds & florals, Webb; in rtcl fr, 10x13" **500.00**
Wht to pk w/mica, tri-shaped/ruffled; ornate ftd Tufts fr **450.00**
Yel satin w/gold floral; highly-decor SP ftd Derby fr **425.00**
Yel to rose satin, ruffled; intricate SP ped ft, 13x12" **425.00**

Bristol Glass

Bristol is a type of semi-opaque opaline glass whose name was derived from the area in England where it was first produced. Similar glass was made in France, Germany, and Italy. In this country, it was made by the New England Glass Company and to a lesser extent by its contemporaries. During the eighteenth and nineteenth centuries, Bristol glass was imported in large amounts and sold cheaply, thereby contributing to the demise of the earlier glasshouses here in America. It is very difficult to distinguish the English Bristol from other opaline types. Style, design, and decoration serve as clues to its origin; but often only those well versed in the field can spot these subtle variations.

Biscuit jar, tan, birds & foliage, SP rim/lid/hdl, 7½" **195.00**
Bottle, scent; gr w/gold stars & dots, gold ball stopper, 4" **88.00**
Bottle, scent; pk, gold branches & bands, gold/pk top, 10" **135.00**
Bottle, scent; turq, gold band, HP florals, ball top, 5¾"..................**75.00**
Condiment set, gray, 3-bottle, in SP fr, 5¾x4¼" **135.00**
Ewer, clambroth w/appl bl edge, 10" **65.00**
Ring tree, turq, HP florals & leaves w/gold, 2x2½" **50.00**
Salt cellar, wht, mc florals, 1⅜x1¾" **40.00**
Sweetmeat jar, cream opaque, HP florals, resilvered trim, 5" **125.00**

Vase, flowers and butterfly encircle reserve with building on blue glass, 8½", $85.00.

Vase, bl w/wht florals, cone shape, SP Webster fr, 14½" **250.00**
Vase, brn, heavy gold florals, stick neck, 6½" **75.00**
Vase, dk gr w/red & wht roses, baluster, 14½" **160.00**
Vase, gr opaque, HP boy or girl, ormolu hdls/ft, 7¼", pr **165.00**
Vase, pk, angel in horse-drawn chariot scenes, 11½", pr..............**350.00**
Vase, turq, gold bands, pk roses, wht trim, 1¾x1½".......................**30.00**
Vase, turq, gold bands & allover florals, 5¼x2¼", pr...................**135.00**
Vase, turq, gold bands & feathers, appl hdls, 2¼x3¼" **60.00**
Vase, turq, gold bands & florals w/wht dots, 3¾", pr **75.00**

British Royalty Commemoratives

While most modern-day commemorative collectors start their collections with souvenirs issued during Queen Victoria's reign, interest in royal commemorative collecting has been evident for centuries. A commemorative medal was issued for Edward VI's 1547 coronation. Ceramics are the most popular type of commemoratives. Food tins are gaining in popularity; so are glass, paper, and metal souvenirs. Since commemoratives have always been a commercial endeavor, nearly any item with room for a portrait and an inscription has been manufactured as a souvenir; thus a wide variety is available in all price ranges. Since royal events are an ongoing state of affairs, it is possible to choose almost any time in British history as a commemorative starting point. Even present-day souvenirs make a good, inexpensive beginning collection. Today's events will be tomorrow's history!

For further study we recommend *British Royal Commemoratives*, by our advisor for this category, Audrey Zeder; she is listed in the Directory under California.

Key:
anniv — anniversary
chr — christening
com — commemorative
cor — coronation
jub — jubilee
LE — limited edition
mem — memorial
wed — wedding

Baby plate, Geo V 1935 jub, Shelly, 1x7½" dia..............175.00
Beaker, Victoria scrimshaw portrait on horn.....................295.00
Bowl, Princess Charlotte 1817 death, pk lustre, 8½"..........250.00
Bust, Charles/Diana, LE (500), Royal Staffordshire, 4½"......150.00
Bust, Victoria 1887, transparent amber glass, 3x3¾x3¾"......165.00
Bust, Victoria 1897, parian, R Belt, 2¾" on blk base..........250.00
Bust, William, inscribed Jan 1, 1831, metal, Sam Parker......425.00
Covered dish, Elizabeth cor, cobalt, emb portrait, Wedgwood...75.00
Cup & saucer, Elizabeth 1953 cor, official design...............45.00
Cup & saucer, George V cor, color portrait, fluted.............150.00
Cup & saucer, Victoria/Albert 1851, pk lustre w/portraits....250.00
Dolls, Charles/Diana, wedding clothes, Goldberger, 11", pr....75.00
Ephemera, Andrew/Sarah wed, puzzle, Waddington, +tin box....45.00
Ephemera, Charles 1969 Investiture, fr 1st day cover...........60.00
Ephemera, Charles 1969 Investiture, official program..........25.00
Ephemera, Charles/Diana wed, Country Life magazine...........25.00
Ephemera, Charles/Diana wed, Illus London News magazine....20.00
Ephemera, Charles/Diana wed, puzzle w/dbl-decker bus.........20.00
Ephemera, Diana, paper dolls, Golden, 1985......................10.00
Ephemera, Edward VII cor, Collier's, Leyendecker cover........35.00
Ephemera, Elizabeth cor, Everybody's magazine..................25.00
Ephemera, Elizabeth cor, Illustrated magazine...................25.00
Ephemera, Elizabeth cor, 11 prints, Central Office Information....45.00
Ephemera, Elizabeth jub, photo, Eliz/Philip, blk/wht, 6x8".....15.00
Ephemera, Elizabeth 60th birthday, Radio Times magazine......20.00
Ephemera, George V in Scottish garb, 1911 ad calendar........35.00
Ephemera, George VI cor, booklet w/cor procession TV info....20.00
Ephemera, Princess Elizabeth, calendar, 1949, 8½x4¾".........40.00
Ephemera, Princess Margaret, Everybody's magazine, 1951.....25.00
Ephemera, Victoria, Sunkist Orange label w/portrait............15.00
Figure, Prince of Wales 1862, w/dog, Staffordshire, 14½"....1,200.00
Figure, Victoria 1840, on horse, Staffordshire, chip, 9".......350.00
Glass, Charles/Diana wed, pin dish, bl, gold portrait, 4½"....25.00
Glass, Charles/Diana wed, tankard, clear w/mc transfer........25.00
Glass, Edward VII 1902 cor, tumbler, etched portrait, 4½".....50.00
Glass, Elizabeth cor, bowl, pressed/cut, 9½"....................35.00
Glass, Elizabeth jub, pin dish, cobalt w/restaurant jub menu....45.00
Glass, Elizabeth 1959 Canada visit, tumbler, portraits.........25.00
Glass, Princess Anne, pin dish, picture as child, 4¾"..........50.00
Glass, Victoria, humidor, Victoria bust lid, milk glass........290.00
Glass, Victoria 1837, plate, pressed, chip, 3½"...............135.00
Glass, Victoria 1887, dish, pressed/cut, 4x6x2"...............125.00

Glass, Victoria 1887, dish, pressed/cut, 7½x10"...............250.00
Glass, Victoria 1887, pitcher, ornate design, 4½".............150.00
Glass, Victoria 1887 jub, plate, pressed, 10".................175.00
Medal, Victoria 1900, portrait, w/Boer War generals, 1½"......90.00
Mug, cider; Diana 30th birthday, sepia portrait, LE (250).....40.00
Mug, cider; 3 royal ladies' Aug 1990 birthday, mc portrait....40.00
Mug, Elizabeth cor, gold coat of arms, mc enameling, Myott....35.00
Mug, Elizabeth cor, sepia portrait, mc flags...................35.00
Mug, Elizabeth 1991 visit to US, mc w/Elizabeth & Bush........60.00
Mug, Elizabeth 90th birthday, mc portrait, inscription........25.00
Newspaper, Victoria 1901 death, w/pictures & narrative........45.00
Novelty, Charles/Diana wed, music box, plays Camelot, 2½".....50.00
Novelty, Charles/Diana wed, Royal Landau w/Queen, Corgi......275.00
Novelty, Elizabeth cor, hand mirror, color portrait...........25.00
Novelty, Elizabeth Ruby anniv, Lledo car w/inscription........25.00
Novelty, Victoria, brewery bottle, relief portrait, 12"......100.00
Novelty, Victoria, buckle clasp, relief/cut-out design........30.00
Novelty, Victoria, stick pin, rope bezel w/shilling...........45.00
Novelty, Victoria, velvet fr, 4 generation portraits.........250.00
Novelty, Victoria 1887, whiskey decanter, portrait, 8½"......295.00
Novelty, Victoria 1901, match safe, gutta percha, portrait...175.00
Novelty, Victoria 1901, soap bar, oval, inscr, unused.........45.00
Plaque, Victoria 1889, w/relief portrait, bronze, 7x10"......375.00
Plate, Charles/Diana 1981 wed, mc engagement portrait, 10½"..150.00
Plate, Charles/Diana 1981 wed, mc wedding portrait, 10½".....250.00
Plate, Diana, 3 portrait versions, LE Royal Doulton, 10½"....175.00
Plate, Diana 30th birthday, sepia portrait, LE (250), 8".....40.00
Plate, Duke & Duchess Cornwall 1901 Canada visit, 8½".......175.00
Plate, Edward VII 1902 cor, color portraits, Doulton, 10", pr...250.00
Plate, Edward VIII 1937 cor, Deco style w/portrait, 6½"......50.00
Plate, Elizabeth cor, official design, 6½"....................40.00
Plate, Elizabeth 1991 USA visit, mc w/Elizabeth & Bush, 10"...95.00
Plate, George VI cor, bl relief portraits, Wedgwood, pr......300.00
Plate, Prince William chr, cherub, LE Royal Crown Derby, 8"..125.00
Plate, Queen Mother 90th birthday, mc portrait, inscr, 8"....30.00
Plate, Victoria 1897 jub, brn transfer, Wagstaff & Brunt.....250.00
Plate, Victoria 1903, HP portrait, artist initials MBW.......175.00
Plate, 3 royal ladies' Aug 1990 birthday, mc portrait, 10"....60.00
Plate, 3 royal ladies' Aug 1990 birthday, mc protrait, 8"....35.00
Post card, Edward VII, in uniform, bas relief, color..........30.00
Post card, Edward VII, in uniform, color Oilette, Tuck........20.00
Post card, George V (in uniform) & Queen Mary, mc, Tuck.......20.00
Post card, George V cor, Dunbar, Delhi, blk/wht...............20.00
Post card, George VI w/teenage Princess Elizabeth in garden...10.00
Post card, Princess Diana 30th birthday, LE (500)............10.00
Post card, Queen Elizabeth 1988 Australia visit, LE (500)....10.00
Post card, Queen Elizabeth 40th wed anniv, mc, LE (1000).....10.00
Post card, Queen Elizabeth 60th birthday, blk/wht............. 6.00
Post card, Queen Mother 90th birthday, LE by Enterprise...... 5.00
Post card, Victoria 1897 jub, deco railway building..........15.00
Print, Princess Charlotte, blk/wht, 19th C, 4½x7"............25.00
Print, Victoria on throne wearing blk, 19th C, 12x17"........25.00
Print, Victoria/Albert amid oval frs of relatives, 12x17"....25.00
Spoon, Andrew/Sarah wed, mc wed day picture, SP..............12.00
Spoon, Charles/Diana wed, mc wed day picture, SP.............25.00
Spoon, Victoria, 1883 Canadian coin bowl & twist hdl.........75.00
Teapot, Queen Mother 90th birthday, mc portrait, 2-cup.......50.00
Textile, Charles/Diana, towel, mc portrait on linen..........25.00
Textile, Charles/Diana wed, scarf w/silhouettes, mc, silk....40.00
Textile, Edward VII, woven silk in oval fr, 6x5".............150.00
Textile, Elizabeth, Nottingham lace w/Elizabeth & Buckingham..25.00
Textile, Elizabeth 1977 jub, linen towel.....................20.00
Textile, Victoria 1887 jub, woven bookmk in fr...............175.00
Textile, Victoria 1897 jub, 4 generations, 28x28"...........200.00

Thimble, Queen Mother 90th birthday, enameled peepshow........30.00
Tin, Charles/Diana wed, mc portrait on plaid, Walkers 30.00
Tin, Edward VII cor, color portrait, Rowntree, 5x2¼" 65.00
Tin, Elizabeth 90th birthday, mc portrait, Walkers Shortbread 35.00
Tin, George VI cor, mc George/Elizabeth/2 princessess/events......95.00
Tin, George VI cor, on sepia-tone lid: Geo/Elizabeth/princesses ...45.00
Tin, Princess Elizabeth, Trooping Colours, Huntley & Palmer......75.00

Bowl/ash tray, maroon, ruffled...25.00
Pot, red, sgn Cecil Jones, sm 45.00
Toothpick holder...20.00
Toothpick holder, w/company label 30.00
Vase, bud; maroon, 8" 45.00
Vase, maroon, classic form, 8"...75.00
Vase, maroon, dbl rings at top, stamped PH Genter, 7" 75.00
Vase, maroon, Indian portrait emb, mk Plains Hotel/1935, 17" ..500.00
Vase, maroon, ringed, sgn Denver-JB Hunt, 7" 75.00
Vase, maroon, rings & hdls, 5" 65.00
Vase, maroon, sgn Denver-JB Hunt, 5"...50.00
Vase, maroon, squat, w/label, 5" 55.00
Vase, maroon, urn form, hdls, 7½" 70.00

Tin, St. Lawrence Seaway Opening, Harner & Co., 6",
$45.00.

Tin, Victoria w/young & old portrait & 3 generations, hinged....**195.00**
Toby mug, Diana, HP, LE, Kevin Francis **250.00**
Toby mug, George V & Queen Mary, pr **495.00**
Toby mug, Queen Mother 90th birthday, HP, LE, K Francis.......**250.00**
Tray, Charles/Diana wed, mc engagement portrait, mc, 6x7" **25.00**
Tray, Elizabeth cor, mc Elizabeth & royal residences, 12x16" **50.00**
Tray, Elizabeth cor, mc royal couple, faux wood, 13" dia **45.00**

Vase, maroon with embossed
Indian, marked Plains Hotel,
Cheyenne, Wyoming, dated 1935,
17", $500.00+.

Broadmoor

In the Spring of 1933, the Broadmoor Art Pottery was formed and space rented at 217 East Pikes Peak Avenue, Colorado Springs, Colorado. Most of the pottery produced would not be considered elaborate and only a handful was decorated. Many pieces were signed by P.H. Genter, J.B. Hunt, Eric Hellmann, and Cecil Jones. It is reported that this plant closed in 1936, and Genter moved his operations to Denver.

Broadmoor pottery is marked in several ways: a Greek or Egyptian-type label depicting two potters (one at the wheel and one at a tile-pressing machine) and the word Broadmoor; an ink-stamped 'Broadmoor Pottery, Colorado Springs (or Denver), Colorado'; and an incised version of the latter.

The bottoms of all pieces are always white and can be either glazed or unglazed. Glaze colors are turquoise, green, yellow, cobalt blue, light blue, white, pink, pink with blue, maroon red, black, and a copper lustre. Both matt and high gloss finishes were used.

The company produced many advertising tiles, novelty items, coasters, ash trays, and vases for local establishments around Denver and as far away as Wyoming. An Indian head device was incised into many of the advertising items, which also often bear a company or a product name. A series of small animals (horses, dogs, elephants, squirrels, a toucan bird, and a hippo), each about 2" high, are easily recognized by the style of their modeling and glaze treatments, though all are unmarked. Our advisors for this category are Carol and Jim Carlton; they are listed in the Directory under Colorado.

Animal figurine, ea 35.00
Bowl, snack 30.00

Broadsides

Webster defines a broadside as simply a large sheet of paper printed on one side. During the 1880s, they were the most practical means of mass-communication. By the middle of the century they had become elaborate and lengthy with information, illustrations, portraits, and fancy border designs. Those printed on coated stock are usually worth more. Our advisor for this category is Judd Caplovich; he is listed in the Directory under Connecticut.

Railroad woodcut, 1850, minor
corner damage, 18" x 11",
$600.00.

Act Concerning...Funds, Boston, 1862, EX 40.00
Carriers Address of Albion, grape border, 1824, 10x15" 40.00
Clothing Sale, No Jew-ing Business, 1879, 12x4½", VG.................50.00
Great Secret...Reduced Prices, dry goods, 1858, 13x10", VG.........25.00
Invitation to unveiling of monument in VA, 1898, sm.................25.00
Kansas Prohibition Society, ca 1890, 5x8" 15.00
Lee/Jackson celebration... VA, 1914, 32-line 27.50
Lee's Tobacco Warehouse, 1880s, 9½x12", VG 38.00
Massacre by Cherokees, monument erected, NC, 1897, EX 35.00
N Pacific...Train, St Paul MN, free land in ND, 1898, EX.............35.00
Old VA Minstrels & Cake-Walkers, VA, 1905, 17x5½" 35.00
Shareholders' Meeting at Tremont House, Boston, 1837, EX........15.00
Stark & Perfect, Dry Goods/Groceries, b/w, OH 1859, 26x20" ...200.00

Bronzes

Thomas Ball, George Bessell, and Leonard Volk were some of the earliest American sculptors who produced figures in bronze for home decor during the 1840s. Pieces of historical significance were the most popular, but by the 1880s a more fanciful type of artwork took hold. Some of the fine sculptors of the day were Daniel Chester French, Augustus St. Gaudens, and John Quincy Adams Ward. Bronzes reached the height of their popularity at the turn of the century. The American West was portrayed to its fullest by Remington, Russell, James Frazier, Hermon MacNeil, and Solon Borglum. Animals of every species were modeled by A.P. Proctor, Paul Bartlett, and Albert Laellele, to name but a few.

Art Nouveau and Art Deco influenced the medium during the twenties, evidenced by the works of Allen Clark, Harriet Frismuth, E.F. Sanford, and Bessie P. Vonnoh.

Be aware that recasts abound. While often esthetically satisfactory, they are not original and should be priced accordingly. In much the same manner as prints are evaluated, the original castings made under the direction of the artist are the most valuable. Later castings from the original mold are worth less. A recast is not made from the original mold. Instead, a rubber-like substance is applied to the bronze, peeled away, and filled with wax. Then, using the same 'lost wax' procedure as the artist uses on completion of his original wax model, a clay-like substance is formed around the wax figure and the whole fired to vitrify the clay. The wax, of course, melts away, hence the term 'lost wax.' Recast bronzes lose detail and are somewhat smaller than the original due to the shrinkage of the clay mold. For further study we recommend *Huxford's Fine Art Value Guide*, available at your local bookstore or from Collector Books

Aitken, RI; Xoros, wood nymph, gr patina/marble base, 17" .. **3,850.00**
Austrian, pnt eagle, wings wide, root base, F Bergman, 11"..... **1,500.00**

Austrian, thrush, cold pnt, 1900s, sm **260.00**
Baker, Lucy; Horse, sgn, 18x20" **1,320.00**
Ball, Thomas; Daniel Webster, dk brn patina, 30".................**7,700.00**
Bartlett, PW; mask of Marquis de Lafayette, brn patina, 4".........**715.00**
Bartlett, PW; portrait medallion of Walt Whitman, 4".............**825.00**
Benton, TH; head of Rev Jim Casy, sgn/#3, brn patina, 7"......**9,680.00**
Bissel, George; Abraham Lincoln figural, #Q438, 8".........**1,430.00**
Blum, Charles; Craftsman Carving, sgn, brn patina, 1886, 11"....**880.00**
Bolinger, Truman; Spirit of the West, #8, brn patina, 22" **990.00**
Borglum, SH; head of Sioux Indian chief, marble base, 11".......**880.00**
Bukill, G (att); George Washington w/mare & colt, 12" **5,500.00**
Bukill, G; mare nuzzling a foal, #1050, red-brn patina, 11" **1,210.00**
Chiparus, warrior fighting wild cat, blk marble base, 34" **3,080.00**
Clark, JL; Alaskan Kodiak bear, brn patina, 7" **2,475.00**
Clark, JL; Ibex, teal patina, 11" **880.00**
Clark, Sally; Gorilla, dk gray patina, 1932, 14" **5,225.00**
Coletti, Joseph; putto w/dolphin fountain, sgn, 35" **6,600.00**
Converse, Edna Tudor; running nymph, brn patina, 20".........**1,100.00**
Cooper, Alice; bacchante figure, gr-brn patina, sgn, 24" **2,200.00**
Dallin, CE; On the Warpath, dk brn patina, sgn, 9" **1,650.00**
Davidson, Jo; bust of Marshal Ferdinand Foch, 10" **2,860.00**
Farny, Henry F; Head of an Indian, #4, brn patina, 1899, 5" **825.00**
Fraser, JE; End of the Trail, dk brn patina, sgn, 12" **9,900.00**
Frishmuth, HW; Crest of the Wave, brn-gr patina, sgn, 21" .**10,450.00**
Herzel, Paul; Skyrocket, cowboy on bronco, sgn, 23" **5,500.00**
Houdon, AJ; George Washington, bust, dk brn patina, 26" ... **4,620.00**
Huntington, Jaquar Reaching, golden patina, sgn, 1899, 6" ... **2,310.00**
Jackson, Harry; One Feather, head of an Indian, sgn, 4" **1,210.00**
Jackson, Harry; Trapper Study, sgn, marble base, 20" **4,400.00**
Kauba, Carl; Running Indian, sgn/#5306, 12" **1,760.00**
Lachaise, Gaston; Standing Nude, #6, wood base, 13" **14,080.00**
Lane, Katherine; Faithful Friend, dachshund, brn patina, 5"... **2,200.00**
Laurent, GH; Doe & Her Young, dk gr patina, ca 1900, 8".........**990.00**
Macmonnies, FW; Diana, the huntress, sgn, 1890, 31" **13,200.00**
McKenzie, Robert; Shot Putter, Ready; athlete, sgn, 11".........**2,200.00**
Milles, Carl; Little Skater, gr patina, sgn, 13" **9,350.00**
Newman, Allen George; Hiker, soldier, dk gr patina, 29" **6,600.00**
Noble, William Clark; Bloodhound on Scent, sgn, 1909, 5" **550.00**
Peyrol, Indian Brave Attacking a Panther, sgn, 18"................. **1,320.00**

Austrian bronze, mouse opens to reveal nude, green marble base, 3¾", $750.00.

P.J. Mene, horse with rider, 9½", $1,800.00.

Playdays, nymph w/frogs, brn-gr patina, sgn, 23" **30,800.00**
Proctor, Alexander; Kodiak, bear's head, brn patina, 6" **3,850.00**
Putnam, Arthur; Panther, brn patina, 4"...................................**2,475.00**

Remington (after), Sargeant, cavalryman, blk-gr patina, 10" .. **4,620.00**
Roth, FGR; Chained Pig, brn patina, sgn, 3" **1,980.00**
Russell, CM; Awkward Situation, deer, brn patina, sgn, 4x7" . **2,000.00**
Russell, CM; Redbird, equestrian group, brn patina, 12x15" ... **1,500.00**
Scudder, Janet; Victory, allegorical figure, sgn, 32" **3,850.00**
Talbot, Grace; Dancing Maiden, brn patina, sgn, 1925, 14" .. **3,575.00**
Thomas, Paul; Lion Walking; golden patina, sgn/#1040, 8" **1,320.00**
Troubetszkoy, Paul; Fashionable Lady, brn-gr patina, 19" **16,500.00**
Vienna, 2 children fight over pot, orig pnt, 2½" **400.00**
Vonnoh, Bessie Potter; Good Night, sleepy child, sgn, 9" **14,300.00**
Warner, Olin Levi; bust of Daniel Cotter, 1878, 11" **880.00**
Young, MM; Listening Faun, dk gr-brn patina, sgn, 11" **2,420.00**
Zorach, William; Incarnation, sgn, Belgian marble base, 9" **3,850.00**

Brownies by Palmer Cox

Created by Palmer Cox in 1883, the Brownies charmed children through the pages of books and magazines, as dolls on their dinnerware, in advertising material, and on souvenirs. Each had his own personality, among them The Bellhop, The London Bobby, The Chairman, and Uncle Sam. But the oversized, triangular face with the startled expression, the protruding tummy, and the spindlelegs were characteristics of them all. They were inspired by the Scottish legends related to Cox as a child by his parents, who were of English descent. His introduction of the Brownies to the world was accomplished by a poem called *The Brownies Ride*. Books followed in rapid succession, thirteen in the series, all written as well as illustrated by Palmer Cox.

By the late 1890s, the Brownies were active in advertising. They promoted such products as games, coffee, toys, patent medicines, and rubber boots. 'Greenies' were the Brownies' first cousins, created by Cox to charm and to woo through the pages of the advertising almanacs of the G.G. Green Company of New Jersey. Perhaps the best-known endorsement in the Brownies' career was for the Kodak Brownie, which became so popular and sold in such volume that their name became synonymous with this type of camera. Our advisor for this category is Faye Pisello; she is listed in the Directory under New York.

Almanac, G Green Woodbury, Palmer Cox illus, 1890 ....**20.00**
Band figure, wooden, Palmer Cox, ca 1900, 8", set of 5 ....**175.00**
Basket, SP, Brownies w/chocolate advertising, Tufts....................**200.00**
Book, Another Brownie Book, Century, 1890, EX **75.00**
Book, Another Brownie Book by Palmer Cox, ca 1890, NM **65.00**
Book, Brownie Clown of Brownietown, Century, 1908, EX **200.00**
Book, Brownies Around the World, Cox illus, 1894, EX **60.00**
Book, Brownies Around the World, 1922 reprint, EX **35.00**
Book, Brownies at Home, Century Co, c 1893, 144-pg, EX.........**100.00**
Book, Brownies in Philippines, Century, 1904, EX **50.00**
Bottle, soda; emb Brownies, M **30.00**
Brownie Portrait Cubes, McLoughlin Bros, c Palmer Cox 1892 ..**300.00**
Candlestick, majolica, Irishman, EX...**175.00**
Comic sheet, 1907, lg, EX **25.00**
Creamer, Little Boy Blue verse & 4 Brownies, gold trim................**75.00**
Creamer, pottery, German Brownie **35.00**
Cup & saucer, china **50.00**
Cup & saucer, SP...**100.00**
Doll, Brownie, Palmer Cox, orig clothes & top hat, 37", EX **300.00**
Dolls, uncut cloth, dtd 1892, set of 4 ....**450.00**
Figure, papier-mache, Uncle Sam, rpr, 8" **175.00**
Game, Auto Race, tin board...**38.00**
Humidor, majolica, Brownie w/pointed bl hat................................**150.00**
Napkin ring, SP, Brownie climbs up side **165.00**
Nine Pins game, stand-up 12" figures, c 1892/Palmer Cox, EX....**250.00**

Paperweight, glass orb w/3 Brownies on bottom **125.00**
Paperweight, SP, Brownie figural **110.00**
Picture frame, paper on wood, 8x10"...**50.00**

Picture frame, silver-plated, $350.00.

Pin box, SP, 6 Brownies on lid **75.00**
Plate, china, lobster chasing Brownies **35.00**
Playing cards, Game of Brownies...**15.00**
Puzzle, jigsaw, wooden, 24-pc, c 1891, 12x10", EX **100.00**
Rubber stamp, set of 12 ....**100.00**
Ruler, Brownies & advertising, 1893, 12" **35.00**
Sheet music, Dance of the Brownies **25.00**
Sign, emb Brownies on tin, Howells Root Beer, EX....................**150.00**
Stamps, wood & rubber, orig pad & box, set of 6 ....**25.00**
Stickpin, Brownie policeman **20.00**
Table set, brass, emb Brownies, 3-pc (knife/fork/spoon)................**70.00**
Tin container, Brownie Ointment, 1924, MIB..............................**40.00**
Toothpick holder, satin glass, 3 Brownies, Mt WA.......................**400.00**
Toothpick holder, SP, Brownie on turtle, no mk **375.00**
Toothpick holder, SP, Brownie w/rifle, Pairpoint **350.00**
Tumbler game, Hand Fireworks Co, EX in box **185.00**

Brush

George Brush began his career in the pottery industry in 1901 working for the J.B. Owens Pottery Co. in Zanesville, Ohio. He left the company in 1907 to go into business for himself, only to have fire completely destroy his pottery less than one year after it was founded. Brush became associated with J.W. McCoy in 1909 and for many years served in capacities ranging from General Manager to President. (From 1911 until 1925, the firm was known as The Brush-McCoy Pottery Co.; see that section for information.) After McCoy died, the family withdrew their interests, and in 1925 the name of the firm was changed to The Brush Pottery. The era of hand-decorated art pottery had passed for the most part and would soon be completely replaced by the production of commercial lines. Of all the wares bearing the later Brush script mark, their figural cookie jars are the most collectible.

For additional information on Brush cookie jars, we recommend *The Encyclopedia of Cookie Jars* by our cookie jar advisors, Joyce and Fred Roerig; they are listed in the Directory under South Carolina. See also Brush-McCoy.

Antique Touring Car, minimum value **350.00**

Boy w/Balloons, minimum value	500.00
Chick in Nest	350.00
Cinderella Pumpkin	135.00
Circus Horse, gr, minimum value	500.00
Circus Horse, pk, minimum value	750.00
Clown, yel pants	165.00
Clown Bust	250.00
Cookie House	55.00
Cow, w/cat on bk, brn	95.00
Cow, w/cat on bk, purple, minimum value	500.00
Davy Crockett, gold trim	350.00
Davy Crockett, no gold	185.00
Dog w/Basket	275.00

Donkey with Cart, brown, #33, $265.00; Formal Pig, black, no gold, $150.00.

Donkey w/cart, #33, gray	315.00
Elephant w/Baby Bonnet	325.00
Elephant w/monkey on bk, minimum value	1,000.00
Fish	425.00
Formal Pig	165.00
Formal Pig, blk coat, no gold, mk W7	150.00
Granny, pk	185.00
Happy Bunny, wht	195.00
Hen on Basket	95.00
Hillbilly Frog, minimum value	1,000.00
Hobby Horse, minimum value	500.00
Humpty Dumpty, w/beanie & bow tie	215.00
Humpty Dumpty, w/peaked hat	185.00
Lantern, brn/cream, mk K1	55.00
Laughing Hippo	550.00
Little Angel, minimum value	750.00
Little Boy Blue, gold trim, sm, minimum value	650.00
Little Boy Blue, lg	700.00
Little Boy Blue, no gold, sm	600.00
Little Girl	250.00
Little Red Riding Hood, no gold, sm	400.00
Nite Owl	85.00
Old Clock	170.00
Old Shoe	70.00
Panda	185.00
Peter Pan, gold trim	750.00
Peter Peter Pumpkin Eater, boy/girl/pumpkin	285.00
Puppy Police	450.00
Raggedy Ann	425.00
Sitting Hippo	400.00
Sitting Pig	425.00
Smiling Bear	425.00
Squirrel on Log	75.00

Squirrel w/Top Hat	185.00
Stylized Owl	385.00
Stylized Siamese	425.00
Teddy Bear, feet apart	230.00
Teddy Bear, feet together	135.00
Treasure Chest	135.00

Miscellaneous

Bittersweet, vase, wht w/natural colors, 6"	12.00
Hanging basket, Stardust, flying saucer shape, bl w/wht	45.00
Match holder, Kolorkraft, gr, 1932, 6"	35.00
Pitcher, wht w/pk clover & gr leaves, mk K11 USA, 6½"	22.50
Planter, cowboy standing by open box, yel w/red tie, '40s	17.50
Planter, yel bird, open-top pk flower head, #246, 1957	14.00
Rose jar, blk gloss, dome lid, 1930s, 7½"	45.00
Vase, pk pagoda/floral sprigs/birds on shaded bl, #225, 8"	18.50
Vase, Princess, wht w/curving gr leaves, hdls, 12"	25.00
Vase, V form w/V, star, & eagle, 1940s, 8"	45.00
Vase, wheat heads, wht on med gr, 1939, 10"	25.00
Wall pocket, fish form, 1958	35.00

Brush-McCoy

The Brush-McCoy Pottery was formed in 1911 in Zanesville, Ohio, an alliance between George Brush and J.W. McCoy. Brush's original pottery had been destroyed by fire in 1907; McCoy had operated his own business there since 1899. After the merger, the company expanded and produced not only their staple commercial wares, but also fine artware. Lines such as Navarre, Venetian, Oriental, and Sylvan were of fine quality equal to that of their larger competitors. Because very little of the ware was marked, it is often mistaken for Weller, Roseville, or Peters and Reed.

In 1928 after a fire in Zanesville had destroyed the manufacturing portion of that plant, all production was contained in their Roseville (Ohio) plant #2. A stoneware type of clay was used there; and, as a result, the artware lines of Jewel, Zuniart, King Tut, Florastone, Jetwood, Krakle-Kraft, and Panelart are so distinctive that they are more easily recognizable. Examples of these lines are unique and very beautiful, also quite rare and highly prized!

The Brush-McCoy Pottery operated under that name until after 1925 when it became the Brush Pottery. The Brush-Barnett family retained their interest in the pottery until 1981 when it was purchased by the Dearborn Company. For more information we recommend *The Guide to Brush-McCoy Pottery*, written by Martha and Steve Stanford and edited by David P. Stanford, our advisors for this category. They are listed in the Directory under California. See also Brush.

Vases, left to right: Auniart, $475.00; King Tut, 12", $950.00; Jewel, 10", $350.00; Jetwood, 12", $1,150.00.

Bowl, Panelart, 7½"	350.00
Clock, Brn Onyx Jug Time Clock, #333, 6¾"	120.00

Jardiniere & ped, Navarre Faience, #2200 .... **1,200.00**
Jardiniere & ped, Woodland, sgn A Cusick, 28" **650.00**
Jug, Pastel Kitchenware, 7" **95.00**
Lamp, Kolorkraft, spherical, 5½" **150.00**
Pitcher, Nurock, emb peacock, #351, 5-pt **135.00**
Pitcher, Wise Bird (owl), #139, 10½" **185.00**
Spill vase, Vogue, #046, mk Vogue, 11½" **135.00**
Umbrella stand, Onyx, #71, 22½" **325.00**
Umbrella stand, Oriental, #67, 23" **1,600.00**
Vase, Brn Onyx, #050, 6" **35.00**
Vase, Cleo, 10" **375.00**
Vase, Gr Onyx, #064, 8" **25.00**
Vase, Jetwood, high gloss, #063, 12" **1,150.00**
Vase, Jewel, #045, 10" **350.00**
Vase, Jewel, #046, 12" **700.00**
Vase, King Tut, #046, 12" **950.00**
Vase, majolica Amaryllis, #082, 4" **32.00**
Vase, Sylvan, dk gr gloss, trees, bulbous top, 10" **95.00**
Vase, Vestal, cameo, 6" **75.00**
Vase, Zuniart, #062 .... **475.00**

Buffalo Pottery

The founding of the Buffalo Pottery in Buffalo, New York, in 1901, was a direct result of the success achieved by John Larkin through his innovative methods of marketing 'Sweet Home Soap.' Choosing to omit 'middle-man' profits, Larkin preferred to deal directly with the consumer and offered premiums as an enticement for sales. The pottery soon proved a success in its own right and began producing advertising and commemorative items for other companies, as well as commercial tableware. In 1905 they introduced their Blue Willow line after extensive experimentation resulted in the development of the first successful underglaze cobalt achieved by an American company. Between 1905 and 1909, a line of pitchers and jugs were hand decorated in historical, literary, floral, and outdoor themes. Twenty-nine styles are known to have been made. These have been found in a wide array of color variations.

Their most famous line was Deldare Ware, the bulk of which was made from 1908 to 1909. It was hand decorated after illustrations by Cecil Aldin. Views of English life were portrayed in detail through unusual use of color against the natural olive-green cast of the body. Today the 'Fallowfield Hunt' scenes are more difficult to locate than 'Scenes of Village Life in Ye Olden Days.' A Deldare calendar plate was made in 1910. These are very rare and are highly valued by collectors. The line was revived in 1923 and dropped again in 1925. Every piece was marked 'Made at Ye Buffalo Pottery, Deldare Ware Underglaze.' Most are dated, though date has no bearing on the value. Emerald Deldare, made with the same olive body and on standard Deldare Ware shapes, featured historical scenes and Art Nouveau decorations. Most pieces are found with a 1911 date stamp. Production was very limited due to the intricate, time-consuming detail. Needless to say, it is very rare and extremely desirable.

Abino Ware, most of which was made in 1912, also used standard Deldare shapes, but its colors were earthy and the decorations more delicately applied. Sailboats, windmills, and country scenes were favored motifs. These designs were achieved by overpainting transfer prints and were often signed by the artist. The ware is marked 'Abino' in hand-printed block letters. Production was limited; and as a result, examples of this line are scarce today. Prices only slightly trail those of Emerald Deldare Ware.

The many uncataloged items that have been found over the years indicate that Buffalo Pottery decorators were free to use their own ideas and talents to create many beautiful one-of-a-kind pieces.

Our advisors for this category are Jean and Dale Van Kuren; they are listed in the Directory under New York. Assistance was also provided by Shrader's Antiques; see California. See also Willow Ware.

Abino

Bowl, sailing scene, 9" **825.00**
Candlestick, sailing ships, 9" **500.00**
Humidor, sailing scene, 7" **900.00**
Pitcher, Portland Head Light, 7" **900.00**
Plate, sailing scene, 6½" **300.00**
Plate, windmill scene, 10" **625.00**
Powder jar, sailing scene, w/lid **650.00**
Relish tray, windmill scene, 12x6" **700.00**
Tankard, Toward the Harbor, 10" **1,150.00**
Tray, mill pond scene, 12½x9" **1,150.00**
Vase, mill pond scene, cylindrical, 7" **850.00**

Deldare

Ash tray/matchbox holder, Ye Olden Days **500.00**
Bowl, fern, w/insert **650.00**
Bowl, fruit; Fallowfield Hunt, The Death, 9" **600.00**
Bowl, fruit; Ye Village scenes, 9" **475.00**
Bowl, nut; Ye Lion Inn, 8" **495.00**
Bowl, rim soup; Ye Village Street, 9" **250.00**
Bowl, sauce; Fallowfield Hunt, Breaking Cover, 5" **160.00**
Bowl, vegetable; Ye Olden Times, 8½x6½" **375.00**
Candle holder, Emerald, Art Nouveau, shield bk **1,350.00**
Candle holder/match holder combination, untitled **500.00**
Candlestick, Fallowfield Hunt, untitled, 9" **435.00**
Candlestick, Ye Village scenes, untitled, 9" **375.00**
Chocolate pot, Ye Village scenes **1,975.00**

Chop plate, Ye Lion Inn, 14", $525.00.

Creamer, Emerald, Dr Syntax **350.00**
Creamer & sugar bowl, Ye Olden Days, w/lid **400.00**
Cup, punch; untitled **225.00**
Cup & saucer, chocolate; Ye Olden Days **410.00**
Cup & saucer, Emerald, Dr Syntax **375.00**
Cup & saucer, Fallowfield Hunt scenes **250.00**
Cup & saucer, Ye Olden Days scenes **225.00**
Egg cup, untitled **240.00**
Hair Receiver, Ye Village Street **350.00**
Humidor, Emerald, There Was an Old Sailor..., 8" **850.00**
Humidor, Ye Lion Inn, 7" **595.00**

Inkwell, Emerald, Art Nouveau, no lid	975.00
Mug, Emerald, Dr Syntax, 2¼"	500.00
Mug, Emerald, Dr Syntax, 4¼"	475.00
Mug, Fallowfield Hunt, At the 3 Pigeons, 4½"	350.00
Mug, Fallowfield Hunt, Breaking Cover, 3½"	325.00
Mug, Fallowfield Hunt, untitled, 2½"	450.00
Mug, Scenes of City Life, 2½"	325.00
Mug, Ye Lion Inn, 3½"	265.00
Mug, Ye Lion Inn, 4¼"	300.00
Pin tray, Fallowfield Hunt, untitled, 6¼x3½"	385.00
Pitcher, Emerald, Dr Syntax Bound..., 8"	800.00
Pitcher, Fallowfield Hunt, Breaking Cover, 10"	775.00
Plate, chop; Ye Lion Inn, 14"	625.00
Plate, Fallowfield Hunt, Breaking Cover, 10"	275.00
Plate, Fallowfield Hunt, The Death, 8½"	190.00
Plate, Fallowfield Hunt, untitled, 6½"	135.00
Plate, Ye Village Gossips, 10"	200.00
Tankard, Emerald, Dr Syntax scenes, 12"	1,350.00
Tankard, Fallowfield Hunt, Breakfast..., 12"	925.00
Tankard, Ye Village scenes, 12"	890.00
Tea tile, Traveling in Ye Olden Days, 6"	300.00
Teapot, Scenes of Village Life, 5¾"	395.00
Tray, calling card; Fallowfield Hunt, 7¼"	375.00
Tray, calling card; Ye Village Streets, 7¼"	335.00
Tray, dresser; Dancing Ye Minuet, 9x12"	595.00
Tray, Emerald, Art Nouveau, 9x12"	1,050.00
Tray, Fallowfield Hunt, Breakfast at 3 Pigeons	1,000.00
Tray, tea; Heirlooms, 12x10½"	695.00
Vase, untitled, 9"	345.00
Vase, untitled scenes of fashionable man & women	925.00
Vase, Ye Village Parson	925.00

Miscellaneous

Bowl, open vegetable; Bluebird, 6½x8½"	125.00
Bowl, rim soup; Bluebird	45.00
Canister, Cereal, w/lid, 7"	65.00
Canister, Pepper, w/lid, 3"	39.50
Creamer, Bluebird, 3¾"	48.00
Cup & saucer, Blue Willow	35.00
Cup & saucer, Bluebird	35.00
Dish, child's feeding; Bluebird	75.00
Dish, child's feeding; Campbell kids w/alphabet	85.00
Game set, platter+6 9" plates	485.00
Mug, Celebration, 4½"	125.00
Pitcher, Blue Willow, 8½"	235.00
Pitcher, Bluebird, 6½"	125.00

**Pitcher, Cinderella, 6",
$550.00.**

Pitcher, Cinderella, 6"	525.00
Pitcher, Fallowfield Hunt scenes on Colorido body, 7½"	455.00
Pitcher, Gaudy Willow, 8½"	595.00
Pitcher, Geranium, bl & wht, 6½"	325.00
Pitcher, Gloriana, bl & wht, 9¼"	450.00
Pitcher, Hounds & Stag, mc w/lavish gold, 6½"	585.00
Pitcher, Old Mill, bl & gold, 6½"	655.00
Pitcher, Robin Hood, mc, 8¼"	525.00
Pitcher, Whaling scene, 6"	650.00
Pitcher, Whirl of the Town, 7"	700.00
Plate, Blue Willow, 10¾"	60.00
Plate, Blue Willow, 6½"	17.50
Plate, Bluebird, 10½"	75.00
Plate, Bluebird, 9½"	50.00
Plate, commemorative; White House, bl, 10½"	68.00
Plate, fish; 9"	65.00
Plate, Gaudy Willow, 10½"	155.00
Teapot, Argyle, w/tea ball	190.00
Teapot, Geranium, 4½"	350.00
Teapot & tile, Bluebird, 6¼"	325.00
Tureen, Blue Willow, w/lid, 5½" H	350.00
Wash bowl & pitcher, Chrysanthemum	350.00

Buggy Steps

American cast iron buggy and carriage steps remain one of the important antique collecting prizes of an era long since passed. The short-lived buggy era was considered to be from 1865 through 1910. Replaced by the horseless carriage, few serviceable old steps remain. Iron buggy and carriage steps each have their own individual patented tread design features, attachment methods, size, and shape. A selected group of single steps are listed below. Our advisor for this category is John Waddell; he is listed in the Directory under Texas.

Bolt-on, Columbia Carriage Co, oval, 5½x3½"	40.00
Folding, mechanical, w/date: 16 Feb '04	28.00
Square plate, bolt-on, w/Pat date 1 Jun '86, 3x3"	18.00
Surry mt, w/wheel cover holes, 1879, 24x8⅝"	110.00
Tee, Peru, rnd, flush letters, heavy, 4¼"	45.00
Tee-mt w/rubber date pad, 19 Sept '99, 3⅝x5"	30.00
Tri-fork, checkered pad, 1930s (E) mk	25.00
Tri-fork, Deere, name brass insert, 3x4¾"	45.00
Tri-fork, Henney Buggy Co, flush letters, 3⅝x5"	40.00
Tri-fork, Moon Bro, flush letters, 3⅝x5"	40.00
Tri-fork, Studebaker, recessed letters, 3¼x5½"	40.00
Tri-fork w/date, removeable pad, 1 Feb '98, 3¾x4½"	30.00

Burmese

Burmese glass was patented in 1885 by the Mount Washington Glass Co. It is typically shaded from canary yellow to a rosy salmon color. The yellow is produced by the addition of uranium oxide to the mix. The salmon color comes from the addition of gold salts and is achieved by reheating the object (partially) in the furnace. It is thus called 'heat sensitive' glass. Thomas Webb of England was licensed to produce Burmese and often added more gold, giving an almost fuchsia tinge to the salmon in some cases. They called their glass 'Queen's Burmese,' and this is sometimes etched on the base of the object. This is not to be confused with Mount Washington's 'Queen's Design,' which refers to the design painted on the object. Both companies added decoration to many pieces. Mount Washington-Pairpoint produced some Burmese in the late 1920s and Gunderson and Bryden in the '50s and '70s, but the color and shapes are different. Our advisors for this category are Dolli and Wilfred Cohen; they are listed in the Directory under California. In the listings that follow, examples are assumed to have the satin finish unless noted shiny.

Bowl, ice cream; ruffled rim, Mt WA, 4¾" 295.00
Bowl, jelly; shiny, ruffled, appl rigaree, in SP EPNS fr 400.00
Bowl, shiny, Bryden, 2" H 45.00
Condiment set, ribbed, s&p, mustard w/spoon, in SP fr 400.00
Creamer, Mt WA, 3¾" 350.00
Creamer, wild roses, hexagonal rim, pinched spout, 2½" 350.00
Finger bowl, fluted rim, emb ribs, Webb, 2¼x4¾" 295.00
Hat whimsey, shiny, Bryden, 3" 80.00
Pitcher, HP mums, sq mouth, yel reeded hdl, Mt WA, 4¾" 650.00
Pitcher, Invt T'print, Egyptian w/bow in chariot, Mt WA, 5". 1,000.00
Pitcher, shiny, reeded hdl, ftd, Bryden, 4½" 85.00
Place setting, shiny, 8" plate, cup & saucer, Mt WA 365.00
Plate, 6" 100.00
Rose bowl, asters, Mt WA, 4½" 325.00
Rose bowl, mc florals, 8-crimp, unmk Webb, 2⅜x2⅝" 295.00
Rose bowl, mc florals, 8-crimp, Webb, 3x3" 350.00
Rose bowl, no decor, 8-crimp, unmk Webb, 3¼x3⅜" 195.00
Rose bowl, 6-sided top, 2½" 200.00
Rose jar, ovoid, dome lid, pointed hdls, Mt WA, 6½", NM........650.00
Sugar shaker, fall leaves/bl berries, globular, 4" 800.00
Sweetmeat, appl shell trim, Webb, SP basket fr, 7½x6½" 295.00
Toothpick holder, Dmn Quilt..425.00
Toothpick holder, floral in bl/wht, sq top...................................495.00
Toothpick holder, leaves & berries, 6-sided top, Webb, 2½" 495.00
Toothpick holder, shiny, collared 6-sided top, Webb, 2½" 495.00
Tumbler, lemonade; shiny, Mt WA, 3½" 350.00
Tumbler, Mt WA, 3⅞x2¾" 225.00
Vase, acorns, gold & gr, unmk Webb, 4¼x3" 325.00
Vase, acorns & leaves, gold & gr, ruffled, Webb, 3¾x2½" 325.00

Vase, acorns and oak leaves, marked Webb, 8", $895.00.

Vase, berries & leaves, fluted rim, Webb, 2⅝x3¾"......................325.00
Vase, bulbous, 3-petal folded-over rim, Mt WA, 3" 250.00
Vase, daisies/leaves, mc/gold, tapered w/narrow neck, 8" 600.00
Vase, Dmn Quilt, florals, tri-con folded-in top, 2" 300.00
Vase, florals, 2⅞x3¼" 225.00
Vase, fluted, 3 yel appl ft, unmk Webb, 3¼x2¾" 245.00
Vase, fluted base, ruffled rim, 4" 325.00
Vase, ftd, ruffled, 5" 225.00
Vase, gr ivy, bulbous, ruffled top, Webb, 3¼x3¼" 325.00
Vase, gr ivy, pinched-in sides, shield-shape top, Webb, 3⅛".......325.00
Vase, jack-in-pulpit; crimped, 9" 595.00
Vase, jack-in-pulpit; floral on stem, crimped/folded, 12" 700.00

Vase, Queen's, berries/leaves, folded-in petal rim, 3" 300.00
Vase, Queen's, folded star-shaped top, bowl form, Webb, 3x4" ...295.00
Vase, Queen's, squatty, 5-petal folded-in rim, Webb, 2½.............325.00
Vase, Queen's, star-shaped top, Webb, 3¼x2⅝"..........................335.00
Vase, scalloped, striped acid finish, Webb, 3x3½"........................225.00
Vase, shiny, mc florals amid chain bands, unmk Webb, 3¾" 275.00
Vase, shiny, trumpet form, Webb, 6x2¼" 375.00
Vase, tri-fold rim, trumpet form, 12" 375.00
Vase, vintage, 6-sided top, bowl form, Webb, 3½" 325.00
Whiskey, Dmn Quilt, Mt WA, 2½" 225.00

Butter Molds and Stamps

The art of decorating butter began in Europe during the reign of Charles II. This practice was continued in America by the farmer's wife who sold her homemade butter at the weekly market to earn extra money during hard times. A mold or stamp with a special design, hand carved either by her husband or a local craftsman, not only made her product more attractive but also helped identify it as hers. The pattern became the trademark of Mrs. Smith, and all who saw it knew that this was her butter. It was usually the rule that no two farms used the same mold within a certain area, thus the many variations and patterns available to the collector today. The most valuable are those which have animals, birds, or odd shapes. The most sought-after motifs are the eagle, cow, fish, and rooster. These works of early folk art are quickly disappearing from the market.

Butter stamp, eagle with notched details, 4½" diameter, $350.00.

Molds

Bird, 4½" dia 90.00
Cherries, elliptical form, 5½x10" L 185.00
Cow, fluted sides, rnd in oblong hinged case, rpr, 10" L.............300.00
Eagle w/emblem in breast fine cvg, 3½" dia 950.00
Fish w/water detail, EX work, 3¾", EX....................................950.00
Floral in 2 sqs, detailed, rectangular, 4½x7¾".............................65.00
Flower w/2 leaves, simple, scrubbed, 3¾" dia 50.00
Fluted sides & 'Teebutter,' 10½" L 85.00
Lamb & foliage, 3⅜" dia, EX 425.00
Pomegranate, 5" dia 75.00
Sheaf of wheat, dbl, dvtl box-type, 3⅞x6" 125.00
8 cvd designs, oblong/ftd, uncommon style, late 1800s, 2-lb.......245.00

Stamps

Acorn & 2 leaves, detailed cvg, 1-pc, 1820s, 3¼" dia..................225.00

Acorn w/stem & leaves, pie crust edge, knob hdl, 3¼" dia...........195.00
Cow, leafy sprig, trn hdl, scrubbed, age cracks, 4" dia 125.00
Cow in pasture, pie crust border, ca 1700s, 3x4½" dia.................395.00
Eagle, trn hdl, scrubbed, age cracks, 4" dia 175.00
Floral, in scalloped recess, lollipop, European, 10" 60.00
Floral, primitive, lollipop, worn finish, 8½"...............................275.00
Floral, stylized, trn hdl, minor edge chips, 4" dia 110.00
Floral w/5 petals & dot center, lollipop, ca 1790, 7" 275.00
Flower & foliage, stylized, 1-pc trn hdl, 4" dia 65.00
Geometric ea side (reversible), octagonal, 3⅞" 50.00
Geometrics w/starflowers & tulips, hdl missing, 3¼x5" 65.00
H w/dot & lines, arc design edges, ca 1800s, 3x2½" dia 85.00
Lamb & cross, concave, scrubbed, 4" dia 125.00
Pineapple, knob hdl, ca 1830, 4" dia, EX......................................90.00
Pineapple, lg X-hatching, knob hdl, 4" dia 130.00
Pineapple, rope-like border, 5½" dia...150.00
Pinwheel, detailed cvg, ca 1850, 4½" dia.....................................295.00
Sheaf of wheat, bk: starflower, lollipop w/side hdl, 7½" 150.00
Star w/5 sm stars, maple w/oak hdl, 8½".......................................135.00
Starflower, bk: sheaf of wheat, age wear/cracks, 4" dia 110.00
Starflower, lollipop, 1¼" dia, 6" L...265.00
Starflower ea side, 1 side sq, other rnd, lollipop, 10" 250.00
Strawberries, inserted hdl, scrubbed/fine age cracks, 4¾"............100.00
Sunflower w/leaves, lined border, knob hdl, 4¼" dia...................100.00
Swan on water, dmn edge, maple, 4½" dia 325.00
Thistle, 1-pc w/trn hdl, 4" dia 75.00
Thistle w/leaves & concentric lines, 4½" dia................................135.00
Tulip, deeply cvd, scrubbed, 4⅜" dia..115.00
Tulip, stylized, deeply cvd/EX detail, scrubbed, 4", VG..............145.00
Tulip (simple), worn finish, rectangular, 4x5"..............................225.00
2-Part, vintage & cherries, EX detail, scrubbed, 2¾x5½" 75.00

Butter Pats

Butter pats were most commonly used during the Victorian era, although both earlier and later examples are known to exist, including some commercial pats still in use in the 1970s. They are sometimes called by different names such as butter chips, butters, butter plates, and even butter dishes; however, 'butter pat' is the most popular colloquial name and was the term favored by manufacturers. These small plates, used at each place setting for individual 'pats' of butter, were mentioned in published material as far back as the 1850s. Their small size, availability, and affordability contribute to their collector appeal. They can be found in sterling, silverplate, pewter, glass (including pattern glass), ironstone, vitrified china, fine china, and porcelain.

There are two basic types: 1) commercial pats: used by hotels, railroads, steamships, etc. These are usually of vitrified china, but may be found in metals and fine china as well. Designs incorporating the company on the front or top side are most sought after and often have historical interest. And 2) domestic pats: those used in the household. These range from basic to ornate styles and were made in a wide variety of materials including ironstone, sterling, and fine porcelain. They were made by nearly all major manufacturers both here and abroad.

Some collectors concentrate on a particular country, producer, material, or design. Many are unmarked; but comparisons with larger, marked pieces of dinnerware patterns are often helpful in identification. Because butter pats are widely available, avoid worn or damaged examples; and don't confuse them with small plates intended for other uses such as nut and sauce dishes, salt dips, coasters, or children's toy dishes.

Some manufacturers also produced matching individual butter pat knives. These may have ceramic handles or may be all metal. When they can be found, these knives add another dimension to the collection of butter pats.

In the listings below, pats are assumed round unless noted otherwise. Those interested in learning more about butter pats may wish to subscribe to *Butter Pat Collectors' Notebook*; the address is listed in the Directory under Clubs, Newsletters, and Catalogs. Our advisor for this category is Marjorie Geddes; she is listed in the Directory under Oregon. See specific categories for other butter pats.

Key:
BS — backstamp   VC — vitrified china
TM — top mark

Royal Chelsea, 3¼" diameter, white lilies with yellow markings and green leaves, $8.00.

Commercial

Astor Hotel, VC, logo, TM, 3½" 7.50
Longfellow's Wayside Inn, Adams, TM, BS, 3¼" 8.00
Parker House, VC, logo, TM, BS, 3¼"..................................... 4.00
Restaurant, stock, gr border on wht, VC, 3¼" 2.50
RR, ATSF, California Poppy...25.00
RR, UP, Harriman Bl, VC...24.00
RR, UP, Streamliner...25.00
San Diego Hotel, VC, logo, TM, 3½" 7.50

Domestic, Ceramic

Bavaria, allover forget-me-nots, scalloped edge 6.00
Bavaria, pk rose garlands 7.50
Blue Willow, Booths..25.00
Blue Willow, Japan 12.50
Blue Willow, Ridgeway 14.00
Crown Staffordshire, allover pastel floral, w/knife....................37.50
Daffodil decal, yel ground, sq, American............................... 4.50
Flow Blue, Alaska, Grindley..30.00
Flow Blue, Argyle, Grindley..25.00
Flow Blue, Osborne, Davenport 22.50
Flower shape, HP, yel on bl, Japan..................................... 8.00
Franciscan, Desert Rose 6.50
GDA Limoges, pk roses, leaf border 7.50
Haviland Limoges, shadow leaves, pk roses 9.50
Head of bulldog, wht china, unmk 7.50
Heubach, homestead transfer, shell shape..............................12.50
Ironstone, Argosy, gr floral transfer 5.00
Ironstone, plain, square... 3.50
Ironstone, scene, bridge over stream, brn transfer..................... 8.50
Ironstone, Tea Leaf, Meakin 12.50
Majolica, pansy shape 45.00
Majolica, 2 overlapping leaves 50.00

Noritake, Azalea **65.00**
RS Germany, HP roses on gr **35.00**
Shelley, Blue Rock **25.00**
Shelley, Rose, Pansy, Forget-Me-Not.......................**30.00**
Spode, Buttercup...**12.50**
Spode, Fleur-de-lis, brn/wht.. **6.50**
Vernon Kilns, Gingham **5.00**

Domestic, Glass

Clear, etched lacy design **6.00**
Cut, Cypress...**32.50**
Cut, sgn Hawkes **27.50**
Early Am Pattern Glass, Hobbs, Daisy & Button, amber daisies....**35.00**
Early Am Pattern Glass, Tree of Life, bl **30.00**
Heisey, Ipswich, Sahara, sq..**19.00**

Domestic, Metal

Pewter, beaded edge... **7.00**
SP, acanthus leaf border **12.50**
SP, beaded edge... **8.00**
Sterling, emb shell border, sq **25.00**
Sterling, plain w/rolled edge **14.50**

Buttonhooks

Buttonhooks were made from around the mid-1800s when high-button shoes made of stiff leather became fashionable and continued to be used to some extent until 1935. They were made of bone, brass, iron, or silver — simple utilitarian no-nonsense styles, fold-up styles with jeweled gold handles, and combination styles with built-in gadgets — all designed to ease the struggle of buttoning high-top shoes, long kid gloves, and stiffly starched collars. While most do have a hook end, some were made with a wire loop instead. Study the construction; quality workmanship is an important worth-assesing factor in addition to the more obvious elements of material and design.

Brass, emb design on hdl, 4¾" **10.00**
Brn & amber marbleized celluloid hdl, 6" **12.50**
Celluloid, dk brn, shaped hdl, 9" **10.00**
Lead, lady's leg hdl, 7" **40.00**
MOP teardrop-shaped hdl, 3½" **15.00**
Pearl hdl, glove sz, 2¼" **10.00**
Plique-a-jour, HP floral, gold on silver, Shiebler, 3¼"..................**185.00**
SP, repousse, hollow hdl, 7¼".....................................**27.50**
Sterling, Indian holds Provincial flag hdl, Vancouver BC **24.00**
Sterling, Lily of the Valley, Whiting, ca 1885, 8"..........................**75.00**
Sterling, Nouveau lady's head forms hdl, 6½"..............................**75.00**
Sterling, repousse floral, mk **40.00**
Sterling, repousse scrolls **40.00**

Calendar Plates

Calendar plates were advertising give-aways most popular from about 1906 until the late twenties. They were decorated with colorful underglaze decals of lovely ladies, flowers, animals, birds and, of course, the twelve months of the year of their issue. During the late thirties they came into vogue again, but never to the extent they were originally. Those with exceptional detailing or those with scenes of a particular activity are most desirable, so are any from before 1906.

1908, flower, 8½" **35.00**
1908, mountain scene, 8¼"...**35.00**

1909, Gibson Girl, 9½" **35.00**
1909, horse's head, gold trim **30.00**

1909, portrait of a lady, 9½", $35.00.

1910, lighthouse, Pope Gosser **30.00**
1911, Old Acquaintance **25.00**
1912, lady on lily, cherubs at rim, 9¼"......................**50.00**
1913, irises, 8" **30.00**
1916, man in canoe, 7¾" **30.00**
1920, flags & club, 8¼"..**35.00**
1921, grouse **20.00**
1922, dog flushing out birds, 8¼" **45.00**
1928, deer scene, 8¾" **40.00**
1929, auto, 8½"..**32.00**
1969, God Bless Our House **10.00**

Calendars

Calendars are collected for their colorful prints, often attributed to a well-recognized artist of the period. Advertising calendars from the turn of the century often have a double appeal when representing a company whose products are themselves collectible. See also Parrish, Maxwell; Rockwell, Norman.

Theo van Hoytema, Holland, 1908, twelve color lithographs, each with a different bird, 19" x 8½", $1,000.00.

1889, Winchester, hunting vignettes, no pad, 23x15", EX...... **1,000.00**

1897, Berlin Iron Bridge, cb, multiple images, 14x11", VG **80.00**
1899, Lister's Fertilizers, lady w/wheat, 23x13", EX.....................**225.00**
1899, Ruscher & Co Lager Beer, girl framed in flowers, NM **700.00**
1903, A&P Tea Co, shopkeeper/products, cb, 19x15", EX **180.00**
1903, Hanan Shoe Co, elves, Indians, etc, EX **185.00**
1904, Dupont, EX...**465.00**
1904, Singer, Indian on die-cut animal skin, 26x22", G **75.00**
1906, Oakwood Market...Ohio, man fishing, 8½x5½", EX **90.00**
1908, Bemis Bros, US Presidents, cloth, 14x9½", VG **90.00**
1911, Firestone Tire & Rubber, 34x17", EX **1,600.00**
1911, Zett's Bavarian Beer, soldiers, 20x18", EX **155.00**
1912, Dupont, EX...**215.00**
1912, Haberle Congress Beer, men toasting girl, 23x17", EX.......**275.00**
1912, Sharples Separator, girl w/machine, cow at window, M **120.00**
1912, Zett's Bavarian Beer, soldier/friends, full pad, VG **90.00**
1913, Bartel's Brewing, girl's profile, 25x16", VG **325.00**
1913, Dr Daniels, girl feeds dogs, top only, 20x14", EX...............**200.00**
1914, Haberle Brewing, Counselors, 24x19", VG **110.00**
1914, Winchester, hunter & dogs in cornfield, 30x15", G...........**200.00**
1915, Zett's Par Ex Beer, brewery scene, 20x18", EX..................**110.00**
1917, DeLaval Separators, girl/collie, full pad, 28x17", G...........**300.00**
1918, DeLaval Separators, lady/horse, unused, 29x17", EX.........**300.00**
1919, Cream City Sash & Door, cb, elves, full pad, 16x12", EX .**500.00**
1925, Herrington's Drugs...TX, lady at dresser, 14x8½", NM **35.00**
1931, Meyers Pumps, 17x48"..**135.00**
1932, American Stores, children/flag, full pad, 25x12", VG **50.00**
1937, Centennial Beer, man w/beer, 26x13½", NM **225.00**
1943, Hercules Powder, WWI Anniv, soldier/dog, 30x13", VG...**100.00**
1948, Men of Tomorrow, Rockwell, Boy Scouts, EX......................**75.00**

Caliente

Caliente was a line of colored dinnerware made by the Paden City Pottery Company in Paden City, West Virginia. It was produced during the 1930s and 1940s in tangerine, yellow, blue, green, and cobalt blue.

Bowl, salad; 10"...**15.00**
Bowl, 9"..**12.50**
Candle holder **9.00**
Creamer...**7.00**
Cup & saucer, cobalt **8.00**
Plate, 6" **3.00**
Plate, 9½"..**6.00**
Platter, 14"..**14.00**
Shakers, pr...**16.00**
Sugar bowl, w/lid **9.50**

California Faience

California Faience was the trade name used by William V. Bragdon and Chauncy R. Thomas on vases, bowls, and other artware produced at their pottery known as 'The Tile Shop' in Berkeley, California, from 1920 to 1930. Faience tile was the principal product of the business during these years and is the favorite with today's collectors. Items in a glossy glaze are rare and therefore more valuable. Tiles were marked 'California Faience' with a die stamp.

For further information we recommend *Collector's Encyclopedia of California Pottery* by Jack Chipman; he is listed in the Directory under California.

Bookends, bear, reddish-brn, 4x4½x6", pr **300.00**
Bowl, dk bl gloss, bl int, multi-sided, 2½x6" **85.00**

Candle holders & curved bowl, bl gloss, 3-pc set.........................**125.00**
Flower holder, Oriental laundry woman, 6-color, 6" **85.00**

Tile, 6-color floral, 5" diameter, $295.00.

Tile, flower, red w/gr leaves on sky bl, mk, 5½" dia.....................**250.00**
Tile, fruit basket, 6-color, 5¼" dia...**275.00**
Tile, galleon, 5-color, 5½x5½"..**375.00**
Vase, bl alligatored matt, 5" **170.00**
Vase, rose gloss, mk, 7" **225.00**
Vase, turq crystalline, on red clay, 7½" **250.00**

California Perfume Company

D.H. McConnell, Sr., founded the California Perfume Company (C.P. Company; C.P.C.) in 1886 in New York City. He had previously been a salesman for a book company, which he later purchased. His door-to-door sales usually involved the lady of the house, to whom he presented a complimentary bottle of inexpensive perfume. Upon determining his perfume to be more popular than his books, he decided that the manufacture of perfume might be more lucrative. He bottled toiletries under the name 'California Perfume Company' and a line of household products called 'Perfection' until 1929, when 'Avon Products, Inc.' appeared on the label. In 1939 the C.P.C. name was entirely removed from the product. The success of the company is attributed to the door-to-door sales approach and 'money back' guarantee offered by his first 'Depot Agent,' Mrs. P.F.E. Albee, known today as the 'Avon Lady.'

The company's containers are quite collectible today, especially the older, hard-to-find items. Advanced collectors seek bottles and other items labeled Goetting & Co., New York; Goetting's; or Savoi Et Cie, Paris. Such examples date from 1871 to 1896. The Goetting Company was purchased by D.H. McConnell; Savoi Et Cie was a line which they imported to sell through department stores. Also of special interest are packaging and advertising with the Ambrosia or Hinze Ambrosia Company label. This was a subsidiary company whose objective seems to have been to produce a line of face creams, etc., for sale through drugstores and other such commercial outlets. They operated in New York from about 1875 until 1954. Because very little is known about these companies and since only a few examples of their product containers and advertising material have been found, market values for such items have not yet been established. Other items sought by the collector include products marked Gertrude Recordon; Marvel Electric Silver Cleaner; Easy Day Automatic Clothes Washer; pre-1930 catalogs; and California Perfume Company 1909 and 1910 calendars.

There are hundreds of local Avon Collector Clubs throughout the world that also have C.P.C. collectors in their membership. If you are interested in joining, locating, or starting a new club, contact the National Association of Avon Collectors, Inc., listed in the Directory under Clubs, Newsletters, and Catalogs. Those wanting a National Newsletter Club or price guides may contact Avon Times or Avon Collectors' Club Western World listed in the same section. Inquiries concerning California Perfume Company items should be directed toward our advisor, Dick Pardini, whose address is given under California. (Please send a large SASE; not interested in Avons or Anniversary Keepsakes.)

American Ideal Lipstick, 1929, CPC on tube, M 40.00
American Ideal Perfume, wood box, introductory sz, 1910, M.....225.00
American Ideal Perfume, 1929, gr satin box, 1-oz, MIB 140.00
Ariel Perfume, 1930, glass stopper, 1-oz, MIB 125.00
Ariel Toilet Water, 1930-35, 2-oz, M 105.00
Baby Set, 3-pc, w/box, 1916, MIB..350.00
Bandoline Hair Dressing, 1923, 4-oz, M....................................65.00
Bay Rum, 4-oz, 1908, M 100.00
Boudoir Manicure Set, 4-pc, w/booklet, 1929, M.......................100.00
California Tooth Tablet, metal lid, glass bottom, ca 1900, M........60.00
Catalog, color, w/tabs, 1920s, M...75.00
CPC Sample Case, basketweave w/label, 1915, M......................100.00
Cut Glass Perfume, 1915, 2-oz, MIB...225.00
Daphne Bath Salts, 1925, glass jar w/gold label, 10-oz, MIB 70.00
Daphne Talcum Powder, tin container, gr can, 1923, 4-oz, M.......65.00
Depilatory, 1915, 1-oz, M...100.00
Easy Day/Simplex Auto Clothes Washer, '18, zinc, 11x9", MIB..100.00
Eau De Quinine, 1923, 6-oz, M 90.00
Elite Powder, Perfect Foot Powder, oval can, 1923, sm, M.............35.00
Elite Powder, Perfect Foot Powder, tin can, 1923, 1-lb, M 75.00
Gentleman's Shaving Set, 7-pc, w/box, 1917, MIB.....................400.00
Gertrude Recordon's Introductory Facial Treatment Set, MIB....300.00
Juvenile Set, 1915, MIB 435.00
Lavender Salts, gr glass, 1910, MIB...225.00
Lemonal Cleansing Cream, jar, 1926, M 65.00
Lilac Vegetal, ribbed glass, 1925, 2-oz, M..................................65.00
Liquid Shampoo, 1923, 6-oz, M 85.00
Little Folks Set, 4 bottles, 1937, MIB 175.00
Lotus Cream, 1917, 12-oz, MIB 160.00
Lotus Cream, 1925, 4-oz, MIB..90.00
Marvel Electric Silver Cleaner, 1918, Pat Jan 11, 1910, MIB......100.00

Massage cream, 1916, $125.00.

Mission Garden Dbl Compact, brass, 1922, M 45.00
Nail Cream, tin container, 1924, M...10.00
Narcissus Perfume, 1925, 1-oz, M...120.00
Narcissus Perfume, 1929-30, mc box, 1-oz, MIB 160.00
Natoma Rose Perfume, 1914-15, glass bottle/stopper, ½-oz, M....160.00
Natoma Rose Perfume, 1916, ½-oz, M......................................150.00
Natoma Rose Talcum, Indian lady, tin, triangular, '14, 4-oz, M..120.00

Natoma Rose Talcum Powder, tin container, 1911, 3½-oz, MIB .160.00
Perfection, Auto Lustre, can, 1930, 1-pt, M 80.00
Perfection, Baking Powder, can, 1931, 1-lb, MIB........................20.00
Perfection, Coloring, bottle, 1934, ½-oz, M...............................15.00
Perfection, Coloring Set, 5 bottles in wood box, 1920, MIB........200.00
Perfection, Furniture Polish, can, 1916, 12-oz, M 70.00
Perfection, Kwick Cleaning Polish, can, 1922, 8-oz, M 50.00
Perfection, Laundry Crystals, in box, 1931, MIB........................40.00
Perfection, Liquid Shoe White, sample, 1935, ½-oz, M................30.00
Perfection, Liquid Shoe White, 1931, 4-oz, M............................20.00
Perfection, Liquid Spots Out, 1925, 4-oz, M..............................45.00
Perfection, Mending Cement, tube, 1933, MIB...........................15.00
Perfection, Mothicide, can, 1925, ½-lb, M.................................40.00
Perfection, Olive Oil, can, 1931, 1-pt, M 40.00
Perfection, Powdered Cleaner, can, ca 1934, 19-oz, M................12.00
Perfection, Prepared Starch, can, 1931, 6-oz, M 20.00
Perfection, Savoury Coloring, 1941, 4-oz, M..............................12.00
Perfection, Silver Cream Polish, can, 1931, ½-lb, M 20.00
Perfume Sample Set, 1931, MIB 180.00
Powder Sachet, bottle, ca 1915, M 45.00
Powder Sachets, 1890s, M...90.00
Powder tin, 2 nude babies play w/giant rose ea side, 1912, M 100.00
Radiant Nail Powder, tin container, 1923, M.............................25.00
Rose Pomade, jar, milk glass, 1914, M......................................65.00
Shampoo Cream, milk glass, 1908, 4-oz, M 75.00
Sweet Sixteen Face Powder, paper container, 1916, M................50.00
Tooth Tablet, aluminum lid, clear or milk wht bottom, '20s, M ...50.00
Tooth Wash, emb bottle w/label, 1915, M 105.00
Trailing Arbutus Face Powder, paper container, 1925, MIB 40.00
Trailing Arbutus Talcum, tin container, 1914, sample sz, M 70.00
Trailing Arbutus Talcum, tin container, 1925, 1-lb, M 70.00
Verna Talc, 1928, mc container, 4-oz, MIB 95.00
Vernafleur Face Powder, tin container, 1925, M 20.00
Vernafleur Perfume, 1923, 1-oz, MIB......................................140.00
Vernafleur Toilet Soap, 3 bars in paper box, 1936, MIB 60.00
Violet Almond Meal, tin container, 1923, 4-oz, M......................45.00
Witch Hazel Cream, 1904, 2-oz tube, MIB.................................50.00

Calling Cards, Cases, and Receivers

The practice of announcing one's arrival with a calling card borne by the maid to the mistress of the house was a social grace of the Victorian era. Different messages (condolences, a personal visit, or a goodby) were related by turning down one corner or another. The custom was forgotten by WWI. Fashionable ladies and gents carried their personally engraved cards in elaborate cases made of such materials as embossed silver, mother-of-pearl with intricate inlay, tortoise shell, and ivory. Card receivers held cards left by visitors who called while the mistress was out or 'not receiving.' Calling cards with fringe, die-cut flaps that cover the name, or an unusual decoration are worth about $3.00 to $4.00, while plain cards usually sell for around $1.00.

Cases

Filigree, appl butterflies/florals/beads, unmk, 3¾x2⅝".................110.00
Gold, 14k, Art Nouveau style 650.00
Ivory, cvd figures in gardens, 1800s, 3¾x2¾" 195.00
MOP, deer relief, grape & leaf cvg, hinged lid..............................85.00
Silver, eng foliage scrolls & scene of Whitley Court, 4".............145.00
Sterling, allover repousse, Birmingham England, 1902 ....325.00
Tin, vertical strap, weekdays in French on pockets, 2x11" 35.00
Tortoise shell w/ivory inlay, nacre/mc metal, 3¾" L 125.00
Tunbridge, mosaic florals, mid-1800s, EX.................................75.00

Receivers

Brass tray w/Nouveau scrolled edge, 4¼x6¼" **45.00**
CI, cupped hands w/grapes at wrist, 1865..**55.00**

Derby Silver Co. plated tray with two owls on branch, inscribed 'Should Owl'd Acquaintance Be Forgot,' 7", $450.00.

Gold-washed metal, swans hold shell-shaped dish..........................**50.00**
Hand figural, metal w/gr stone ring, Victorian styling...................**18.00**
Pewter tray, Nouveau lady at side, 4¼x7" **95.00**
Pk Dmn Quilt MOP, HP florals/butterflies, metal fr, 9½" H........**925.00**
Sterling, woodland courtship scene, Nouveau style **250.00**

Camark

The Camden Art and Tile Company (commonly known as Camark) of Camden, Arkansas, was organized in the fall of 1926 by Samuel J. 'Jack' Carnes. Using clays from Arkansas, John Lessell, who had been hired as Art Director by Carnes, produced the initial lustre and iridescent Lessell wares for Camark ('CAM'den, 'ARK'ansas) before his death in December 1926. Before the plant opened in the Spring of 1927, Carnes brought John's wife Jeanne and step-daughter Billie to oversee the art department's manufacture of Le-Camark. Production by the Lessell family included variations of J.B. Owens' Soudanese and Opalesce and Weller's Marengo and Lamar. Camark's version of Marengo was called Old English. They also made wares identical to Weller's LaSa. Pieces made by John Lessell back in Ohio were signed 'Lessell,' while those made by Jeanne and Billie in Arkansas during 1927 were signed 'Le-Camark.' By 1928 Camark's production centered on traditional glazes. Drip glazes similar to Muncie Pottery were produced, in particular the green drip over pink. In the 1930s commercial castware with simple glossy and matt finishes became the primary focus and would continue so until Camark closed in the early 1960s. Between the 1960s and 1980s the company operated mainly as a retail store selling existing inventory, but some limited production occurred. In 1986 the company was purchased by the Ashcraft family of Camden, but no pottery has yet been made at the factory.

Our advisor for this category is David Edwin Gifford. He is listed in the Directory under Arkansas. Mr. Gifford, presently examining the feasibility of starting an Arkansas Pottery Collectors Society (Camark, Niloak, and others), requests that those who are interested write and give their opinions on such an organization.

Ewer, HP irises, pk/wht/red/gr, 16" **35.00**

Figurine, cat, wht gloss, beside fish bowl, 8" **20.00**
Jug, orange & gr, ball form, clay stopper, 6½" **35.00**
Novelty, dogs, Pointer & Setter, pr...**15.00**
Planter, swans, blk, dbl neck, 8" **15.00**
Shakers, letters S&P, bl, pr...**10.00**
Shakers, steam ship, red/wht/bl, pr..**18.00**
Sign, state of Arkansas, gr, 6½" **50.00**
Vase, crackle finish, wht, gold mk, 8" **125.00**
Vase, gold lustre palm trees on bronze, sgn Lessell, 12"...............**450.00**

Vase, Old English, plum and cream, signed Le-Camark, 8½", $300.00.

Vase, orange & gr, fluted, 5" **20.00**
Wall pocket, flour scoop, pk, 8" **12.00**

Cambridge Glass

The Cambridge Glass Company began operations in 1901 in Cambridge, Ohio. Primarily they made crystal dinnerware and well-designed accessory pieces until the 1920s when they introduced the concept of color that was to become so popular on the American dinnerware market. Always maintaining high standards of quality and elegance, they produced many lines that became best-sellers; through the twenties and thirties they were recognized as the largest manufacturer of this type of glassware in the world.

Of the various marks the company used, the 'C in triangle' is the most familiar. Production stopped in 1958. For a more thorough study of the subject, we recommend *Colors in Cambridge Glass*, by the National Cambridge Collectors, Inc.; their address may be found in the Directory under Clubs. *Glass Animals and Figural Flower Frogs from the Depression Era* by Lee Garmon and Dick Spencer is a wonderful source for an in-depth view of this particular aspect of glass collecting. They are both listed in the Directory under Illinois. See also Carnival Glass.

Descriptions that contain this symbol (+) indicate items that have been reproduced; values given here are for originals.

Animals and Birds

Blue jay, flower holder...**125.00**
Blue jay, peg base **125.00**
Eagle, bookend, ea...**80.00**
Heron, lg, 12" **125.00**
Heron, sm, 9" **75.00**
Lion, bookend, ea...**110.00**
Pouter pigeon, bookend, ea...**60.00**
Scottie, bookend, pr...**150.00**

Scottie, frosted, ea..	75.00
Sea gull, flower frog	50.00
Swan, candlestick, milk glass, 4½"	175.00
Swan, carmen, 6½"	200.00
Swan, carmen, 8½"	250.00
Swan, Crown Tuscan, 3½"	40.00
Swan, Crown Tuscan, 8½"	95.00
Swan, ebony, 10½"	250.00
Swan, ebony, 12½"	300.00
Swan, ebony, 3½"	60.00
Swan, ebony, 6½"	100.00
Swan, ebony, 8½"	125.00
Swan, emerald, 3½"	35.00
Swan, emerald, 6½"	85.00
Swan, emerald, 8½"	125.00
Swan, milk glass, 3½"	60.00
Swan, milk glass, 4½"	75.00
Swan, milk glass, 6½"	125.00
Swan, milk glass, 8½"	275.00

Turkey, amber, with lid, $450.00.

Turkey, bl, w/lid	550.00
Turkey, gr, w/lid	450.00
Turkey, pk, w/lid	400.00

Apple Blossom, pk or gr; bowl, flat, 12"	55.00
Apple Blossom, pk or gr; pitcher, #3025, 64-oz	240.00
Apple Blossom, pk or gr; plate, dinner; 9½"	75.00
Apple Blossom, pk or gr; stem, #3025, 10-oz	25.00
Apple Blossom, pk or gr; stem, water; #3135, 8-oz .	25.00
Apple Blossom, pk or gr; tumbler, #3400, ftd, 2½-oz	50.00
Apple Blossom, pk or gr; vase, rippled sides, 6"	55.00
Apple Blossom, yel or amber; bowl, cereal; 6"	22.00
Apple Blossom, yel or amber; bowl, console; 12½" ..	50.00
Apple Blossom, yel or amber; bowl, low ftd, 11"	75.00
Apple Blossom, yel or amber; pitcher, ftd, 50-oz	150.00
Apple Blossom, yel or amber; pitcher, 76-oz	195.00
Apple Blossom, yel or amber; plate, dinner; sq	65.00
Apple Blossom, yel or amber; stem, water; #3130, 8-oz	22.00
Apple Blossom, yel or amber; sugar bowl, tall ftd ...	18.00
Apple Blossom, yel or amber; tumbler, #3025, 12-oz	30.00
Apple Blossom, yel or amber; tumbler, #3400, ftd, 2½-oz	40.00
Apple Blossom, yel or amber; vase, 5"	40.00
Caprice, bl; ash tray, #213, shell, 3-ftd, 2¾"	10.00
Caprice, bl; ash tray, #216, 5"	17.50

Caprice, bl; bowl, #49, 4-ftd, 8"	55.00
Caprice, bl; bowl, relish; #126, oval, 4-part, 12"	135.00
Caprice, bl; bowl, salad; #57, 4-ftd, 10"	67.50
Caprice, bl; cigarette box, #207, w/lid, 3½x2¼"	30.00
Caprice, bl; cigarette holder, #205, triangular, 2x2¼"	27.50
Caprice, bl; cup, #17	30.00
Caprice, bl; ice bucket, #201	125.00
Caprice, bl; pitcher, #183, ball form, 80-oz	250.00
Caprice, bl; plate, #30, 16"	75.00
Caprice, bl; plate, salad; #23, 7½"	20.00
Caprice, bl; saucer, #17	5.50
Caprice, bl; stem, fruit cocktail; #7, 4½-oz	65.00
Caprice, bl; stem, sherbet, low, #4, 5-oz	85.00
Caprice, bl; sugar bowl, #40, ind (+)	19.00
Caprice, bl; tumbler, #188, flat, 2-oz (+)	45.00
Caprice, bl; tumbler, #9, ftd, 12-oz	40.00
Caprice, bl; tumbler, whiskey; #300, 2½-oz	125.00
Caprice, bl; vase, #343, crimped, 8½"	150.00
Caprice, bl; vase, #345, 5½"	85.00
Caprice, crystal; ash tray, #215, 4"	7.00
Caprice, crystal; bonbon, #155, oval, ftd, 6"	15.00
Caprice, crystal; bowl, #53, crimped, 4-ftd, 10½" ..	30.00
Caprice, crystal; bowl, #62, belled, 4-ftd, 12½"	30.00
Caprice, crystal; butter dish, #52, ¼-lb	195.00
Caprice, crystal; candle reflector	150.00
Caprice, crystal; candlestick, #74, 3-light, ea	25.00
Caprice, crystal; candy dish, #168, w/lid, 6"	50.00
Caprice, crystal; compote, #136, 7"	35.00
Caprice, crystal; pitcher, #179, ball form, 32-oz ...	75.00
Caprice, crystal; plate, #30, 16"	35.00
Caprice, crystal; salver, #31, ped ft, 2-pc, 13"	140.00
Caprice, crystal; stem, wine; #301, blown, 2½-oz ...	25.00
Caprice, crystal; tumbler, #11, ftd, 5-oz	20.00
Caprice, crystal; tumbler, old fashioned; #310, flat, 7-oz	30.00
Caprice, crystal; tumbler, whiskey; #300, 2½-oz	25.00
Caprice, crystal; vase, #249, 3½"	45.00
Caprice, crystal; vase, #340, crimped, 9½"	75.00
Caprice, crystal; vase, #344, crimped, 4½"	40.00
Chantilly, crystal; bottle, salad dressing	65.00
Chantilly, crystal; bowl, bonbon, hdls, ftd, 7"	16.00
Chantilly, crystal; bowl, oval, 4-ftd, 12"	32.50
Chantilly, crystal; bowl, relish or pickle; 2-part, 7"	18.00
Chantilly, crystal; butter dish, rnd, w/lid	125.00
Chantilly, crystal; butter dish, ¼-lb	195.00
Chantilly, crystal; candy box, rnd, w/lid	52.50
Chantilly, crystal; compote, 5½"	30.00
Chantilly, crystal; cup	17.50
Chantilly, crystal; decanter, ball form	160.00
Chantilly, crystal; decanter, ftd	140.00
Chantilly, crystal; hat, sm	125.00
Chantilly, crystal; ice bucket, w/chrome hdl	65.00
Chantilly, crystal; marmalade, w/lid	55.00
Chantilly, crystal; mustard, w/lid	45.00
Chantilly, crystal; pitcher, ball form	120.00
Chantilly, crystal; plate, salad; 8"	12.50
Chantilly, crystal; shakers, hdls, pr	30.00
Chantilly, crystal; stem, claret; #3600, 4½"	30.00
Chantilly, crystal; stem, cordial; #3600, 1-oz	42.50
Chantilly, crystal; stem, cordial; #3779, 1-oz	50.00
Chantilly, crystal; stem, water; #3600, 10-oz	19.50
Chantilly, crystal; stem, water; #3625, 10-oz	25.00
Chantilly, crystal; sugar bowl	13.50
Chantilly, crystal; tumbler, iced tea; #3600, ftd, 12-oz	18.00
Chantilly, crystal; tumbler, iced tea; #3779, ftd, 12-oz	18.00

Chantilly, crystal; tumbler, juice; #3775, ftd, 5-oz 14.00
Chantilly, crystal; vase, flower; ftd, 13" 65.00
Chantilly, crystal; vase, keyhole base, 12" 50.00
Cleo, all colors but bl; basket, Decagon, hdls, 11" 30.00
Cleo, all colors but bl; bowl, Decagon, hdls, 10" 35.00
Cleo, all colors but bl; bowl, finger; #3115, w/liner 25.00
Cleo, all colors but bl; bowl, soup; tab hdls, 7½" 30.00
Cleo, all colors but bl; candy box 65.00
Cleo, all colors but bl; cup, Decagon 15.00
Cleo, all colors but bl; ice pail 60.00
Cleo, all colors but bl; pitcher, #3077, w/lid, 63-oz 225.00
Cleo, all colors but bl; pitcher, #38, 3½-pt 175.00
Cleo, all colors but bl; platter, asparagus; w/sauce & spoon 275.00
Cleo, all colors but bl; platter, 15" 155.00
Cleo, all colors but bl; server, center hdl, 12" 35.00
Cleo, all colors but bl; stem, cocktail; #3115, 3½-oz 25.00
Cleo, all colors but bl; sugar bowl, ftd 20.00
Cleo, all colors but bl; sugar cube tray 100.00
Cleo, all colors but bl; tray, wafer 175.00
Cleo, all colors but bl; tumbler, #3022, ftd, 12-oz 30.00
Cleo, all colors but bl; tumbler, #3115, ftd, 5-oz 20.00
Cleo, all colors but bl; tumbler, flat, 12-oz 30.00
Cleo, bl; basket, Decagon, hdls, 7" 30.00
Cleo, bl; bowl, console; 12" 65.00
Cleo, bl; bowl, finger; #3077, w/liner 35.00
Cleo, bl; bowl, vegetable; Decagon, oval, 9½" 75.00
Cleo, bl; creamer, ftd 30.00
Cleo, bl; ice pail 95.00
Cleo, bl; plate, Decagon, hdls, 11" 110.00
Cleo, bl; plate, 7" 15.00
Cleo, bl; stem, sherbet; #3077, tall, 6-oz 30.00
Cleo, bl; tumbler, #3022, ftd, 12-oz 60.00
Cleo, bl; tumbler, #3077, ftd, 8-oz 35.00
Crown Tuscan, bowl, seashell, #18, 3-toed, 10" 75.00
Crown Tuscan, candlestick, dolphin, shell, ftd, 4", pr 100.00
Crown Tuscan, candlestick, nude stem 110.00
Crown Tuscan, candy dish, #3500/57, 3-part, w/lid 65.00
Crown Tuscan, compote, nude stem, 7", ea 100.00
Crown Tuscan, compote, seashell, floral decor, 7" 125.00
Crown Tuscan, dish, shell, 3-ftd, 11" 75.00
Crown Tuscan, ivy ball, nude stem 225.00
Crown Tuscan, vase, centerpiece; shell, ftd, 8" 88.00
Crown Tuscan, vase, cornucopia; #3900/575, 10" 55.00
Decagon, pastels; bowl, almond; ftd, 6" 20.00
Decagon, pastels; bowl, bouillon; w/liner 7.50
Decagon, pastels; bowl, cranberry; flat rim, 3¾" 10.00
Decagon, pastels; compote, 5¾" 12.50
Decagon, pastels; cup 6.00
Decagon, pastels; mayonnaise, hdls, w/hdld liner & ladle 25.00
Decagon, pastels; plate, grill; 10" 8.00
Decagon, pastels; plate, service; 12½" 9.00
Decagon, pastels; stem, water; 9-oz 15.00
Decagon, pastels; tray, pickle; 9" 10.00
Decagon, pastels; tray, service; oval, 12" 10.00
Decagon, pastels; tumbler, ftd, 2½-oz 10.00
Decagon, red or bl; basket, upturned sides, hdls, 7" 20.00
Decagon, red or bl; bottle, oil; tall, hdl, w/stopper, 6-oz 65.00
Decagon, red or bl; bowl, bonbon; hdls, 5½" 17.00
Decagon, red or bl; bowl, cream soup; w/liner 22.00
Decagon, red or bl; bowl, fruit; flat rim, 5¾" 11.00
Decagon, red or bl; bowl, vegetable; oval, 9½" 22.00
Decagon, red or bl; bowl, vegetable; rnd, 11" 30.00
Decagon, red or bl; celery tray, 11" 20.00
Decagon, red or bl; compote, tall, 7" 30.00
Decagon, red or bl; creamer, tall, lg ft 22.00
Decagon, red or bl; gravy boat, w/liner 85.00
Decagon, red or bl; ice bucket 40.00
Decagon, red or bl; plate, 7½" 10.00
Decagon, red or bl; relish, w/6 inserts 100.00
Decagon, red or bl; saucer 2.50
Decagon, red or bl; stem, sherbet; low, 6-oz 15.00
Decagon, red or bl; sugar bowl, ftd 20.00
Decagon, red or bl; tray, service; hdls, 13" 30.00
Decagon, red or bl; tray, service; oval, 15" 25.00
Decagon, red or bl; tumbler, ftd, 12-oz 35.00
Diane, crystal; bottle, bitters 110.00
Diane, crystal; bowl, baker; 10" 40.00
Diane, crystal; bowl, berry; 5" 20.00
Diane, crystal; bowl, flared, 4-ftd, 12" 40.00
Diane, crystal; cabinet flask 165.00
Diane, crystal; cigarette urn 35.00
Diane, crystal; creamer 14.00
Diane, crystal; creamer, #3400, scroll hdl 14.00
Diane, crystal; decanter, ball form 145.00
Diane, crystal; lamp, hurricane; candlestick base 100.00
Diane, crystal; pitcher, Doulton style 250.00
Diane, crystal; pitcher, upright 150.00
Diane, crystal; plate, salad; 8" 10.00
Diane, crystal; platter, 13½" 65.00
Diane, crystal; shakers, flat, pr 28.00
Diane, crystal; stem, cordial; #1066, 1-oz 50.00
Diane, crystal; stem, cordial; #3122, 1-oz 50.00
Diane, crystal; sugar bowl, #3400, scroll hdl 14.00
Diane, crystal; tumbler, #3122, 2½-oz 22.00
Diane, crystal; tumbler, #3135, ftd, 10-oz 14.00
Diane, crystal; tumbler, ftd, 8-oz 22.00
Diane, crystal; tumbler, iced tea; #3135, ftd, 12-oz 25.00
Diane, crystal; tumbler, water; #1066, 9-oz 12.00
Diane, crystal; tumbler, 13-oz 30.00
Diane, crystal; vase, bud; 10" 32.50
Diane, crystal; vase, flower; 13" 75.00
Diane, crystal; vase, globe, 5" 25.00

Elaine, bowl, gold encrusted, 15" wide, $125.00.

Elaine, crystal; basket, hdls, upturned sides, 6" 15.00
Elaine, crystal; bowl, flared, 4-ftd, 12" 35.00
Elaine, crystal; bowl, relish; 2-part, 6" 16.00
Elaine, crystal; bowl, tab hdls, 11" 30.00
Elaine, crystal; candlestick, 5", ea 17.50
Elaine, crystal; creamer, several styles 11.00
Elaine, crystal; pitcher, ball form 100.00
Elaine, crystal; plate, salad; 8" 12.50
Elaine, crystal; plate, torte; 14" 30.00
Elaine, crystal; shakers, ftd, pr 30.00
Elaine, crystal; stem, claret; #3104, 4½-oz 60.00

Elaine, crystal; stem, claret; #3121, 4½-oz................27.50
Elaine, crystal; stem, claret; #3500, 4½-oz................27.50
Elaine, crystal; stem, sherry; #3104, 2-oz................80.00
Elaine, crystal; sugar bowl, ind................12.00
Elaine, crystal; tumbler, water; #3121, ftd, 10-oz................20.00
Elaine, crystal; tumbler, water; #3500, ftd, 10-oz................18.00
Flower frog, Bashful Charlotte, amber, 13"................180.00
Flower frog, Bashful Charlotte, bl frost, 11"................495.00
Flower frog, Bashful Charlotte, crystal, 11"................150.00
Flower frog, Bashful Charlotte, gr, 11"................250.00
Flower frog, Bashful Charlotte, gr, 6½"................145.00
Flower frog, Bashful Charlotte, lt amber, 11"................250.00
Flower frog, Bashful Charlotte, midnight bl, 11"................550.00
Flower frog, Bashful Charlotte, pk, 6½"................125.00
Flower frog, Buddha, amber................350.00
Flower frog, Draped Lady, amber, 8½"................175.00
Flower frog, Draped Lady, crystal, 12½"................150.00
Flower frog, Draped Lady, crystal frost, 13"................250.00
Flower frog, Draped Lady, dk amber, 8½"................195.00
Flower frog, Draped Lady, gr, 13"................225.00
Flower frog, Draped Lady, gr frost, 13"................225.00
Flower frog, Draped Lady, lt bl, 8½"................275.00
Flower frog, Draped Lady, lt emerald, #513, 13"................250.00
Flower frog, Draped Lady, mandarin gold, #518, 8½"................200.00
Flower frog, Draped Lady, pk, 13"................250.00
Flower frog, Draped Lady, pk, 8½"................100.00
Flower frog, Draped Lady, pk frost, 8½"................125.00
Flower frog, Geisha Girl, crystal, w/base................300.00
Flower frog, Geisha Girl, pk, w/base................450.00
Flower frog, Mandolin Lady, crystal................150.00
Flower frog, Mandolin Lady, lt gr................225.00
Flower frog, Mandolin Lady, pk................225.00
Flower frog, Melon Boy, gr................400.00
Flower frog, Melon Boy, pk................400.00
Flower frog, Rose Lady, amber, 8½"................200.00
Flower frog, Rose Lady, crystal, tall base................125.00
Flower frog, Rose Lady, crystal satin, tall base................225.00
Flower frog, Rose Lady, dk amber satin, tall base................250.00
Flower frog, Rose Lady, gr................245.00
Flower frog, Rose Lady, gr frost................230.00
Flower frog, Rose Lady, pk................200.00

Flower frog, 2 Kids, amber, $175.00.

Flower frog, 2 Kids, crystal................150.00
Flower frog, 2 Kids, gr frost................225.00
Flower frog, 2 Kids, mocha, 9"................250.00
Gloria, colors; bowl, oval, 4-ftd, 12"................65.00
Gloria, colors; bowl, salad; tab hdl, 9"................50.00
Gloria, colors; compote, fruit cocktail; 4"................20.00
Gloria, colors; ice pail, metal hdl, w/tongs................75.00
Gloria, colors; pitcher, ball form, 80-oz................225.00
Gloria, colors; plate, salad; sq................12.00
Gloria, colors; plate, 8½"................14.00
Gloria, colors; saucer, sq................3.00
Gloria, colors; shakers, ftd, w/metal tops, pr................62.50
Gloria, colors; stem, goblet; #3115, 9-oz................26.00
Gloria, colors; sugar bowl, ftd................18.00
Gloria, colors; syrup, tall, ftd................95.00
Gloria, colors; tumbler, #3120, ftd, 5-oz................20.00
Gloria, colors; tumbler, iced tea; #3135, 12-oz................25.00
Gloria, colors; vase, 11"................80.00
Gloria, crystal; basket, hdls, 6"................13.00
Gloria, crystal; bowl, cereal; 6"................9.00
Gloria, crystal; bowl, finger; ftd................12.00
Gloria, crystal; bowl, relish; 3-hdl, 3-part, 8"................20.00
Gloria, crystal; candlestick, 6", ea................17.50
Gloria, crystal; cup, rnd or sq................15.00
Gloria, crystal; plate, dinner; sq................45.00
Gloria, crystal; platter, 11½"................45.00
Gloria, crystal; tumbler, #3130, ftd, 5-oz................12.00
Imperial Hunt Scene, colors; bowl, cereal; 6"................20.00
Imperial Hunt Scene, colors; candlestick, 2-light, ea................30.00
Imperial Hunt Scene, colors; ice bucket................75.00
Imperial Hunt Scene, colors; plate, 8"................22.00
Imperial Hunt Scene, colors; sugar bowl, ftd................30.00
Imperial Hunt Scene, colors; tumbler, #3085, ftd, 12-oz................30.00
Imperial Hunt Scene, crystal; creamer, ftd................15.00
Imperial Hunt Scene, crystal; ice bucket................40.00
Imperial Hunt Scene, crystal; stem, #1402, 18-oz................60.00
Imperial Hunt Scene, crystal; stem, cocktail; #1402, 3-oz................40.00
Imperial Hunt Scene, crystal; tumbler, #1402, flat, 15-oz................35.00
Mt Vernon, amber or crystal; ash tray, #68, 4"................11.00
Mt Vernon, amber or crystal; bowl, #39, hdls, 10"................20.00
Mt Vernon, amber or crystal; bowl, fruit; #6, 5¼"................10.00
Mt Vernon, amber or crystal; box, #16, rnd, w/lid, 3"................22.00
Mt Vernon, amber or crystal; candelabrum, #38, 13½"................40.00
Mt Vernon, amber or crystal; celery, #79, 10½"................15.00
Mt Vernon, amber or crystal; celery, #79, 12"................20.00
Mt Vernon, amber or crystal; cigarette holder, #66................15.00
Mt Vernon, amber or crystal; cup, #7................6.50
Mt Vernon, amber or crystal; decanter, #47, 11-oz................50.00
Mt Vernon, amber or crystal; honey jar, #74, w/lid................30.00
Mt Vernon, amber or crystal; mug, stein; #84, 14-oz................27.50
Mt Vernon, amber or crystal; pitcher, #90, 50-oz................75.00
Mt Vernon, amber or crystal; pitcher, #91, 86-oz................100.00
Mt Vernon, amber or crystal; plate, salad; #5, 8½"................7.00
Mt Vernon, amber or crystal; relish, #200, 3-part, 11"................25.00
Mt Vernon, amber or crystal; saucer, #7................7.50
Mt Vernon, amber or crystal; shakers, #28, pr................22.50
Mt Vernon, amber or crystal; stem, cocktail; #26, 3½"................9.00
Mt Vernon, amber or crystal; sugar bowl, #8, ftd................10.00
Mt Vernon, amber or crystal; sugar bowl, #86................10.00
Mt Vernon, amber or crystal; tumbler, #14, 14-oz................20.00
Mt Vernon, amber or crystal; tumbler, #58, tall, 10-oz................12.00
Mt Vernon, amber or crystal; tumbler, whiskey; #55, 2-oz................10.00
Mt Vernon, amber or crystal; vase, #42, 5"................15.00
Mt Vernon, amber or crystal; vase, #50, ftd, 6"................25.00

Nude stem, amber; bowl, flying nude 450.00
Nude stem, amber; brandy 100.00
Nude stem, amber; candlestick, pr 550.00
Nude stem, amethyst; ash tray 200.00
Nude stem, amethyst; champagne 135.00
Nude stem, amethyst; claret 100.00
Nude stem, amethyst; cocktail 90.00
Nude stem, amethyst; compote, flared 125.00
Nude stem, carmen; ash tray 225.00
Nude stem, carmen; brandy 120.00
Nude stem, carmen; champagne 135.00
Nude stem, carmen; claret 125.00
Nude stem, carmen; cocktail 95.00
Nude stem, carmen; compote, cupped 125.00
Nude stem, carmen; goblet, water 150.00
Nude stem, carmen; ivy ball 200.00
Nude stem, carmen; ivy ball, frosted stem 250.00
Nude stem, cobalt; brandy 90.00
Nude stem, Crown Tuscan; ash tray 250.00
Nude stem, Crown Tuscan; bowl, flying nude, gold trim 225.00
Nude stem, Crown Tuscan; cocktail, amber stem 495.00
Nude stem, Crown Tuscan; compote, short ped 85.00
Nude stem, crystal; brandy 115.00
Nude stem, crystal; comport, cupped 125.00
Nude stem, crystal; goblet, water 115.00
Nude stem, crystal; ivy ball 200.00
Nude stem, dk gr; brandy 100.00
Nude stem, dk gr; claret 100.00
Nude stem, dk gr; cocktail 90.00
Nude stem, dk gr; compote, cupped 120.00
Nude stem, dk gr; goblet, water 125.00
Nude stem, dk gr; ivy ball 200.00
Nude stem, Gold Krystol; brandy 110.00
Nude stem, Gold Krystol; cocktail 100.00
Nude stem, Gold Krystol; cocktail w/Crown Tuscan stem & ft ...115.00
Nude stem, Heatherbloom Optic; brandy 185.00
Nude stem, pistachio; cocktail 95.00
Nude stem, pk & Tahoe bl; cocktail 150.00
Nude stem, royal bl; claret 125.00
Nude stem, topaz; cocktail 115.00
Nude stem, topaz; sauterne 500.00
Nude stem, Windsor bl; compote, SS-11, 7¾" 450.00
Portia, crystal; bowl, bonbon; hdls, ftd, 6" 16.00
Portia, crystal; bowl, hdls, 11" 30.00
Portia, crystal; bowl, relish; 3-part, 6½" 15.00
Portia, crystal; candlestick, 3-light, 6", ea 40.00
Portia, crystal; celery tray, 11" 22.50
Portia, crystal; cocktail shaker, w/stopper 75.00
Portia, crystal; cup, sq, ftd 18.00
Portia, crystal; ice bucket, w/chrome hdl 55.00
Portia, crystal; mayonnaise, w/liner & ladle 35.00
Portia, crystal; plate, salad; 8" 12.50
Portia, crystal; plate, sq, 8½" 15.00
Portia, crystal; plate, torte; 14" 35.00
Portia, crystal; stem, cocktail; #3130, 3-oz 17.50
Portia, crystal; stem, goblet; #3130, 9-oz 21.00
Portia, crystal; stem, sherbet; #3124, low, 7-oz 14.00
Portia, crystal; sugar bowl, ind 11.50
Portia, crystal; tumbler, bar; #3121, 2½-oz 20.00
Portia, crystal; tumbler, juice; #3130, 5-oz 16.00
Portia, crystal; tumbler, water; #3124, 10-oz 15.00
Portia, crystal; vase, bud; 10" 35.00
Portia, crystal; vase, flower; 13" 75.00
Portia, crystal; vase, globe, 5" 30.00

Portia, crystal; vase, ped ft, 11" 50.00
Rosalie, all colors but amber; bottle, French dressing 95.00
Rosalie, all colors but amber; bowl, basket; hdls, 7" 250.00
Rosalie, all colors but amber; bowl, cranberry; 3½" 20.00
Rosalie, all colors but amber; bowl, 11" 40.00
Rosalie, all colors but amber; candlestick, keyhole, 5", ea 35.00
Rosalie, all colors but amber; compote, 5¾" 30.00
Rosalie, all colors but amber; creamer, ftd 17.00
Rosalie, all colors but amber; ice bucket 65.00
Rosalie, all colors but amber; plate, dinner; 9½" 55.00
Rosalie, all colors but amber; relish, 2-part, 9" 25.00
Rosalie, all colors but amber; salt cellar, ftd, 1½" 25.00
Rosalie, all colors but amber; sugar shaker 195.00
Rosalie, all colors but amber; tumbler, #3077, ftd, 5-oz 22.00
Rosalie, amber; bowl, basket; hdls, 7" 150.00
Rosalie, amber; bowl, bouillon; hdls 15.00
Rosalie, amber; bowl, 11½" 45.00
Rosalie, amber; celery dish, 11" 20.00
Rosalie, amber; dish, nut; ftd, 2½" 30.00
Rosalie, amber; plate, hdls, 11" 20.00
Rosalie, amber; plate, hdls, 7" 7.00
Rosalie, amber; stem, cordial; #3077, 1-oz 40.00
Rosalie, amber; tumbler, #3077, ftd, 12-oz 22.00
Rosalie, amber; vase, ftd, 6½" 35.00
Rose Point, crystal; ash tray, #3500/131, oval, 4½" 60.00
Rose Point, crystal; bell, dinner; #3121 ....125.00
Rose Point, crystal; bowl, #1398, 13" 90.00
Rose Point, crystal; bowl, #1402/89, hdls, 6" 35.00
Rose Point, crystal; bowl, #3400/1, flared, 13" 65.00
Rose Point, crystal; bowl, #3400/1240, oval, 4-ftd, 12" 75.00
Rose Point, crystal; bowl, #3400/135, 4-ftd, 9" 165.00
Rose Point, crystal; bowl, #3400/168, flared, 10½" 62.50
Rose Point, crystal; bowl, #3500/28, hdls, 10" 75.00
Rose Point, crystal; bowl, bonbon; #3400/203, crimped, 6" 80.00
Rose Point, crystal; bowl, bonbon; #3900/130, tab hdls, 7" 35.00
Rose Point, crystal; bowl, fruit; #1534, blown, 5" 65.00
Rose Point, crystal; bowl, punch; Martha, #478, 15" 3,000.00
Rose Point, crystal; butter dish, #3400/52, w/lid 165.00
Rose Point, crystal; candlestick, #3400/649, 2-light, 6", ea 35.00
Rose Point, crystal; candlestick, #3900/68, 5", ea 40.00
Rose Point, crystal; candlestick, #627, 4", ea 45.00
Rose Point, crystal; creamer, #137, flat 100.00
Rose Point, crystal; creamer, #3400/68 ....20.00
Rose Point, crystal; creamer, #3900/41, ftd 20.00
Rose Point, crystal; cup, punch; #488 ....35.00
Rose Point, crystal; decanter, #1321, w/stopper, 28-oz 250.00
Rose Point, crystal; hat, #1701, 9" 450.00
Rose Point, crystal; honey dish, #3500/139, w/lid 235.00
Rose Point, crystal; ice bucket, #1402/52 ....185.00
Rose Point, crystal; ice pail, #1705 ....175.00
Rose Point, crystal; ice tub, #671 ....135.00
Rose Point, crystal; lamp, hurricane; #1601, 8" 195.00
Rose Point, crystal; marmalade, #147, 8-oz 125.00
Rose Point, crystal; mustard, #151, 3-oz 125.00
Rose Point, crystal; oil, #293, hdl, 6-oz 150.00
Rose Point, crystal; pickle dish, #3400/59, 9" 50.00
Rose Point, crystal; pitcher, #3900/118, 32-oz 250.00
Rose Point, crystal; plate, #242, 13½" 135.00
Rose Point, crystal; plate, #3400/1186, hdls, 12½" 65.00
Rose Point, crystal; plate, #3900/26, 4-ftd, 12" 65.00
Rose Point, crystal; plate, bread & butter; #3400/60, 6" 12.50
Rose Point, crystal; plate, dinner; #3400/64, 10½" 115.00
Rose Point, crystal; plate, salad; #3900/22, 8" 17.50
Rose Point, crystal; plate, service; #3900/167, 14" 70.00

Rosepoint, divided relish with center handle, 7", $125.00.

Rose Point, crystal; relish, #3500/85, hdls, 10" 65.00
Rose Point, crystal; relish, #3900/124, 2-part, 7" 37.50
Rose Point, crystal; shakers, #360, w/chrome lids, pr 55.00
Rose Point, crystal; shakers, #3900/1177, flat, w/lids, pr 40.00
Rose Point, crystal; stem, cocktail; #7966, plain ft, 1-oz 110.00
Rose Point, crystal; stem, cordial; #3500, 1-oz 65.00
Rose Point, crystal; stem, sherry; #3106, 2-oz 40.00
Rose Point, crystal; sugar bowl, #137, flat.................................100.00
Rose Point, crystal; tray, #3500/91, sq, hdls, 6" 150.00
Rose Point, crystal; tray, #3500/99, rnd, hdls, 13" 135.00
Rose Point, crystal; tray (for sugar & creamer), #3900/37 ....25.00
Rose Point, crystal; tumbler, #3106, ftd, 3-oz.............................25.00
Rose Point, crystal; tumbler, #3400/115, 13-oz............................45.00
Rose Point, crystal; tumbler, #3400/92, 2½-oz............................95.00
Rose Point, crystal; tumbler, #498, str sides, 5-oz 45.00
Rose Point, crystal; tumbler, juice; #3500, low ft, 5-oz.................30.00
Rose Point, crystal; urn, #3500/41, w/lid 425.00
Rose Point, crystal; vase, #1233, keyhole, ftd, 9½".....................65.00
Rose Point, crystal; vase, bud; #1528, 10".................................75.00
Rose Point, crystal; vase, flower; #1299, ped ft, 11" 115.00
Rose Point, crystal; vase, sweet pea; #629.................................225.00

Tally Ho, mug, ruby, $40.00.

Valencia, crystal; ash tray, #3500/124, rnd, 3¼".............................10.00
Valencia, crystal; bowl, #3500/49, hdls, 5"......................................18.00
Valencia, crystal; compote, #3500/37, 7"...40.00
Valencia, crystal; creamer, #3500/14..15.00
Valencia, crystal; finger bowl, #3500, ftd..27.50
Valencia, crystal; ice pail, #1402/52 ....50.00
Valencia, crystal; plate, sandwich; #1402, hdls, 11½".....................22.50

Valencia, crystal; relish, #3500/67, 12", 6-pc 85.00
Valencia, crystal; shakers, #3400/18, pr 50.00
Valencia, crystal; stem, claret; #1402 ....35.00
Valencia, crystal; stem, sherbet; #1402, tall 15.00
Valencia, crystal; stem, wine; #1402 ....30.00
Valencia, crystal; stem, wine; #3500, 2½-oz..................................27.50
Valencia, crystal; tumbler, #3500, ftd, 16-oz 20.00
Valencia, crystal; tumbler, #3500, ftd, 3-oz 14.00
Wildflower, crystal; bowl, #3400/4, flared, 4-ftd, 12"......................30.00
Wildflower, crystal; bowl, pickle; #477, ftd, 9½".............................25.00
Wildflower, crystal; bowl, relish; 3-part, 6½" 17.50
Wildflower, crystal; butter dish, #3900/52, ¼-lb...........................150.00
Wildflower, crystal; cocktail icer, #968, 2-pc.................................65.00
Wildflower, crystal; compote, #3121, blown, 5⅜" 40.00
Wildflower, crystal; hat, #1730, 6" 150.00
Wildflower, crystal; plate, #3400/176, 7½" 9.00
Wildflower, crystal; plate, bread & butter; #3900/20, 6½" 7.50
Wildflower, crystal; plate, salad; #3900/22, 8".............................11.00
Wildflower, crystal; plate, torte; #3900/167, 14" 35.00
Wildflower, crystal; saucer, #3900/17 or #3400/54 .... 3.50
Wildflower, crystal; shakers, #3400/77, pr....................................35.00
Wildflower, crystal; stem, cocktail; #3121, 3-oz............................22.50
Wildflower, crystal; sugar bowl, #3900/40, ind 17.00
Wildflower, crystal; tumbler, #3900/115, 13-oz.............................25.00
Wildflower, crystal; tumbler, water; #3121, 10-oz..........................17.00
Wildflower, crystal; vase, #1237, keyhole ft, 9" 40.00
Wildflower, crystal; vase, flower; #279, ftd, 13" 75.00

Cameo

The technique of glass carving was perfected 2,000 years ago in ancient Rome and Greece. The most famous ancient example of cameo glass is the Portland Vase, made in Rome around 100 A.D. After glass blowing was developed, glassmakers devised a method of casing several layers of colored glass together, often with a light color over a darker base, to enhance the design. Skilled carvers meticulously worked the fragile glass to produce incredibly detailed classic scenes. In the eighteenth and nineteenth centuries Oriental and Near-Eastern artisans used the technique more extensively. European glassmakers revived the art during the last quarter of the nineteenth century. In France, Galle and Daum produced some of the finest examples of modern times, using as many as five layers of glass to develop their designs, usually scenics or subjects from nature. Hand carving was supplemented by the use of a copper engraving wheel, and acid was used to cut away the layers more quickly.

In England, Thomas Webb and Sons used modern machinery and technology to eliminate many of the problems that plagued early glass carvers. One of Webb's best-known carvers, George Woodall, is credited with producing over four hundred pieces. Woodall was trained in the art by John Northwood, famous for reproducing the Portland Vase in 1876. Cameo glass became very popular during the late 1800s, resulting in a market that demanded more than could be produced, due to the tedious procedures involved. In an effort to produce greater volume, less elaborate pieces with simple floral or geometric designs were made, often entirely acid etched with little or no hand carving. While very little cameo glass was made in this country, a few pieces were produced by James Gillender, Tiffany, and the Libbey Glass Company. Though some continued to be made on a limited scale into the 1900s, for the most part, inferior products caused a marked reduction in its manufacture by the turn of the century. See also specific manufacturers.

Beware of new 'French' cameo glass from Romania. It is very good and is signed with 'old' signatures. Know your dealer! Our advisor for this category is Don Williams; he is listed in the Directory under Missouri.

English

Bottle, scent; floral, wht on yel, silver ball top (EX), 3" **1,200.00**
Bottle, scent; morning-glories/gold vines on bl, 1¾x1½" **950.00**

Mirrored epergne, morning-glories, white on red, English, 10½", $4,000.00.

Perfume, lay down; floral, wht on bl, Faberge cap, 3¾" **6,500.00**
Perfume, lay down; floral, wht on bl, 3¾x2" **1,500.00**
Rose bowl, wild roses, wht on rose Dmn Quilt MOP, 3½" **1,650.00**
Sweetmeat, fancy leaves, wht on sapphire, silver lid, 6" **1,800.00**
Vase, Dmn Quilt MOP w/apple blossoms, wht on bl, 5x5" **1,800.00**
Vase, floral on body/collar, wht on bl, bulbous, no mk, 9" **3,000.00**
Vase, morning-glory/foliage, wht on citron, stick neck, 9" **1,800.00**
Vase, palm-like grasses, wht on yel, sgn Woodall, 8" **3,350.00**
Vase, trumpet flowers/linear borders, wht on bl, 6" **1,800.00**
Vase, violets/leaves, wht on yel, ring-neck ovoid, 5" **1,600.00**

French

Lamp, blue, amber, and green on translucent white, signed LeMaitre, 21", $1,700.00.

Lamp, Egyptian scene on raspberry shade & base, Degue, 15". **3,300.00**
Vase, cherry branches, gray/orange/ruby, ftd, Ledoux, 15" **900.00**
Vase, foliage on purple/clear mottle, Vessiere, 6" **600.00**
Vase, grapes/leaves, brn/gr mottle on lt orange, Degue, 17"..... **1,900.00**
Vase, iris, purple/gr on lt pk, sgn Arsall, 11½" **1,800.00**
Vase, morning-glories/vines, gr on chartreuse, Arsall, 6" **1,000.00**
Vase, orchids, amethyst to clear texture, Verrerie D'Art, 3" **850.00**

Vase, pond lilies/irises, purples on yel, Arsall, 10" **1,600.00**
Vase, stylized floral, striated purple on mc, Degue, 11" **900.00**
Vase, wild roses/thorns, purple on purple to wht, Weis, 3½" **600.00**

Canary Lustre

Canary lustre was produced from the late 1700s until about the mid-nineteenth century in the Staffordshire district of England. The body of the ware was of yellow clay with a yellow overglaze; more often than not, copper or silver lustre trim was added. Decorations were usually black-printed transfers, though occasionally hand-painted polychrome designs were also used.

Jug, depicting match between Tom Cribb and Tom Molinaux, iron-red and transfer decoration, poem on back, 5", $,1900.00.

Cup & saucer, strawberries, EX..**300.00**
Mug, Harp for Elisabeth in red, leaf hdl, 2⅜", EX **375.00**
Mug, lady feeds hogs, red transfer, blk stripes, 3½", EX...............**250.00**
Mug, Lafayette & Washington, blk transfer, prof rpr, 2⅝"...........**800.00**
Mug, monkey at mirror, blk transfer, lengthy verse, EX **300.00**
Mug, poem regarding war & taxes, base chip................................**200.00**
Mug, swan, red transfer, NM..**200.00**
Pitcher, boxing transfer w/Cribb & Molinaux, red decor, 5" ... **1,900.00**
Pitcher, Charity/Faith in gray, silver lustre trim, 6½"..................**450.00**
Pitcher, emb satyr face & blown-out decor, 4½", NM **450.00**
Pitcher, English country scene ea side, blk transfer, 5½".............**400.00**
Pitcher, English country side w/shepherd & flock, transfer, EX...**200.00**
Pitcher, grapes in red/gr, brn lip/rim, swirl body, 6½"..................**650.00**
Pitcher, lg cabbage roses in red/gr/brn, 7"................................ **1,250.00**
Pitcher, mask face under spout, orange/blk pnt, 5¾", EX............**200.00**
Pitcher, silver lustre florals, 5½", EX...**175.00**
Pitcher, Wellington & Nelson, brn transfer, 5½", EX..................**450.00**
Plate, blk transfer scene, floral border, 8½", EX..........................**55.00**
Plate, lg rose in red/gr/brn, florals at rim, 6¾" **1,000.00**
Plate, red rose, emb florals at scalloped rim, 8", EX **1,000.00**
Plate, tan landscape transfer, floral border, mk, 8", NM.............**175.00**
Tea bowl & saucer, red transfer w/cherubs, Sewell, NM **130.00**
Waste bowl, mc floral w/lustre, 3x6", EX...................................**400.00**
Waste bowl, woman/children, blk transfer, hairline, 4¾" **300.00**

Candle Holders

The earliest type of candlestick, called a pricket, was constructed with a sharp point on which the candle was impaled. The socket type, first used in the sixteenth century, consisted of the socket and a short stem with a wide drip pan and base. These were made from sheets of silver or other metal; not until late in the seventeenth century were candlesticks made by casting. By the 1700s, styles began to vary from the traditional fluted column or baluster form and became more elaborate. A Rococo style with scrolls, shellwork, and naturalistic leaves and flowers came into vogue that afforded the individual silversmith the opportunity to exhibit his skill and artistry. The last half of the eighteenth century brought a return to fluted columns with neoclassic motifs. Because they were made of thin sheet silver, weighted bases were used to add stability. The Rococo styles of the Regency period were heavily encrusted with applied figures and flowers. Candelabra with six to nine branches became popular. By the Victorian era when lamps came into general use, there was less innovation and more adaptation of the earlier styles. See also Silver; specific manufacturers.

Key: QA — Queen Anne

Brass, beehive & dmn quilt, miniature, 4", pr 50.00
Brass, bold trn, wide mid drip pan, Dutch, early, 10½" 700.00
Brass, chamberstick, side push-up, 4½" 135.00
Brass, chamberstick, w/push-up, wick trimmer/snuffer, 8" 275.00
Brass, cupped base, Dutch, rprs/filled holes, 8½", pr 2,200.00
Brass, for taper, 4⅞", pr 45.00
Brass, neoclassical, w/push-up, 6¾", pr 150.00

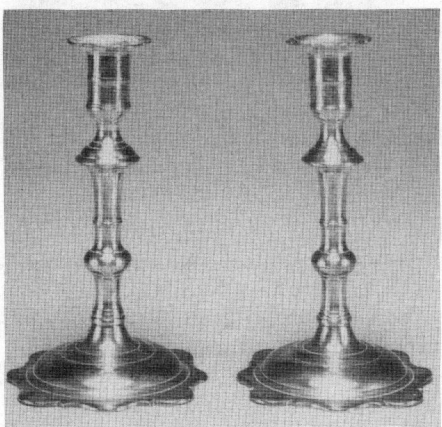

Brass, petal base, English, 1760s, 7", $800.00 for the pair.

Brass, open spiral stem, 13", pr.................................300.00
Brass, QA, resoldered base, 6¾", pr.............................410.00
Brass, QA, scalloped base, 6", pr 800.00
Brass, QA, wide quatrelobed base, 7", pr, EX....................550.00
Brass, scalloped base w/3 hoofed ft, detailed stem, 8½" 675.00
Brass, screw-in baluster stem, dome base, early, 9", pr, NM.....1,500.00
Brass, sq base w/ft, early, rpr, 8½", pr.......................1,000.00
Brass, sq base w/short ft, early, polished, 6¾"................250.00
Brass, sq base w/short ft, early, rpr, 7¾", pr 1,600.00
Brass, Victorian, w/push-up, beehive & dmn, 7½", pr............190.00
Brass, Victorian, w/push-up, King of Dmns, 12", pr.............300.00
Brass, Victorian, w/push-up, mk Solid English, 11", pr 130.00
Brass, Victorian, w/push-up, Queen of Dmns, 11½", pr 260.00
Brass, Victorian, w/push-up, 6½", pr..........................130.00
Brass, w/pan & socket, 5½" dia, 6½" hdl 165.00
Brass, wide dome base, early, 8" 1,075.00
Brass, 8-side base, EX detail, early, soldered rpr, 3", pr....1,000.00
Iron, hogscraper, w/push-up & lip hanger, polished, 5".........160.00
Iron, hogscraper, w/push-up & lip hanger, 6½" 115.00

Metal, cast as standing Egyptian, mc patina, 15" 600.00
Pewter w/brass push-up, 9", pr.............................300.00
SP, taper jack, 6½" 125.00
Wooden, sconce, primitive, sq nail construction, 16", pr....350.00
Wrought iron, adjustable socket, tripod base w/pan, 13½"....175.00
Wrought iron, spiral push-up/lip hanger, trn wood base, 7" .175.00
Wrought iron, sticking tommy, mk Russell, 12" 175.00
Wrought iron, sticking tommy, twisted detail, 9½".........125.00
Wrought iron, twist stem, spring clip, 3 ft, 8¾".............425.00

Candlewick

Candlewick crystal was made by the Imperial Glass Corporation, a division of Lenox Inc., Bellaire, Ohio. It was introduced in 1936; and, though never marked except for paper labels, it is easily recognized by the beaded crystal rims, stems, and handles inspired by the tufted needlework called candlewicking, practiced by our pioneer women. During its production, more than 741 items were designed and produced. In September 1982 when Imperial closed its doors, thirty-four pieces were still being made.

Identification numbers and mold numbers used by the company help collectors recognize the various styles and shapes. Most of the pieces are from the #400 series, though other series numbers were also used. Stemware was made in eight styles — five from the #400 series made from 1941 to 1962, one from #3400 series made in 1937, another from #3800 series made in 1941, and the eighth style from the #4000 series made in 1947. In the listings that follow, some #400 items lack the mold number because that information was not found in the company files.

A few pieces have been made in color or with a gold wash. At least two lines, Valley Lily and Floral, utilized Candlewick with floral patterns cut into the crystal. These are scarce today. Other rare items include gifts such as the desk calendar made by the company for its employees and customers; the dresser set comprised of a mirror, clock, puff jar, and cologne; and the chip and dip set.

Ash tray, #1776/1, eagle form, 6½" 40.00
Ash tray, #400/134/1, oblong, 4½" 6.00
Ash tray, #400/174, heart form, 6½" 15.00
Ash tray, nesting; 400/650, 3-pc set 36.00
Basket, #400/273, beaded hdl, 5" 165.00
Bell, #400/79, 4" 32.50
Bottle, oil; #400/121, etched Vinegar, w/stopper...........45.00
Bowl, #400/SF, rnd, 7".....................................16.00
Bowl, #400/10F, rnd, 9"....................................30.00
Bowl, #400/113A, deep, hdls, 10"...........................45.00
Bowl, #400/13F, 10"..32.00
Bowl, #400/131B, oval, flared, 14".........................150.00
Bowl, #400/17F, shallow, 12"...............................40.00
Bowl, #400/183, 3-ftd, 6"..................................37.50
Bowl, #400/231, sq, 5".....................................50.00
Bowl, #400/233, sq, 7".....................................70.00
Bowl, #400/49H, heart form, 9".............................85.00
Bowl, baked apple; #400/53X, rolled edge, 6"...............25.00
Bowl, lily; #400/74J, 4-ftd, 7"............................50.00
Butter dish, #400/144, rnd, 5½"...........................27.50
Cake stand, #400/67D, low ft, 10"..........................45.00
Candle holder, #400/100, 2-light...........................17.50
Candle holder, #400/280, flat, 3½".........................22.50
Candle holder, #400/40HC, heart form, 5"...................30.00
Candle holder, flower centerpiece; #400/196FC, 9".........125.00
Candle holder, flower; #400/40C, 5".........................20.00
Candle holder, urn; #400/129R, 6" 60.00

Candy box, #400/259, w/lid, 7" 125.00
Celery boat, #400/46, oval, 11" 45.00
Clock, rnd, 4" 100.00
Compote, #400/137, ftd, oval 95.00
Compote, #400/66B, low, plain stem, 5½" 15.00
Creamer, #400/18, domed ft 65.00
Creamer, #400/31, plain ft 6.00
Cup, after dinner; #400/77 ....15.00
Cup, tea; #400/35 .... 7.00
Decanter, cordial; #400/82/2, w/stopper, 15-oz 250.00
Finger bowl, #3800 ....13.50
Fork & spoon, salad; #400/75, 2-pc 22.00
Ice tub, #400/63, deep, 5½x8" 75.00
Knife, butter; #4000 ....150.00
Ladle, mayonnaise; #400/135, 6¼" 6.00
Ladle, punch; #400/91 ....20.00
Mayonnaise set, #400/84, divided, w/plate & 2 ladles, 4-pc 40.00
Mirror, standing; rnd, 4½" 75.00
Pickle/celery dish, 7½" 15.00
Pitcher, #400/19, low ft, 16-oz..200.00

Pitcher, #400/24, 80-oz. $120.00;
Tumbler, #400/19, 10-oz., $12.00.

Pitcher, #400/330, short, rnd, 14-oz 65.00
Pitcher, #400/424, plain, 64-oz..35.00
Pitcher, juice or cocktail; #400/419, 40-oz.........................125.00
Plate, #400/34, 4½" 4.50
Plate, #400/50, w/indent, 8" 11.00
Plate, #400/72D, hdls, 10" 15.00
Plate, birthday cake; #400/160, w/72 holes for candles, 14".........285.00
Plate, bread & butter; #400/1D, 6" 6.00
Plate, salad; #400/38, oval, 9" 25.00
Plate, salad; #400/5D, 8½" 9.00
Plate, service; #400/92D, 14" 30.00
Plate, torte; #400/75V, cupped edge, 12½" 27.50
Platter, #400/124D, 13" 65.00
Relish, #400/209, 5-part, 13½" 65.00
Salt cellar, #400/19, 2¼" 6.50
Shakers, #400/96, beaded ft, bulbous, w/chrome top, pr.............12.50
Stem, brandy; #3800 ....20.00
Stem, claret; #3800 ....30.00
Stem, sherbet; #3400, 5-oz 10.00
Stem, sherbet; #4000, tall, 6-oz 14.00
Strawberry set, #400/83, 2-pc 40.00
Sugar bowl, #400/31, plain ft 6.50
Tidbit set, #400/18TB, 3-pc 90.00

Tray, #400/29, 6½" 15.00
Tray, #400/42E, upturned hdls, 5½" 18.00
Tumbler, #3400, ftd, 9-oz 14.00
Tumbler, #3800, 12-oz 18.00
Tumbler, cocktail; #400/18, 3½" 38.00
Tumbler, iced tea; #400/18, 12-oz 40.00
Tumbler, juice; #3800, 5-oz 16.00
Tumbler, sherbet; #400/19, low, 5-oz 12.00
Vase, #400/143C, flat, crimped edge, 8" 55.00
Vase, #400/193, ftd, 10" 110.00
Vase, #400/198, 6" dia 160.00
Vase, #400/21, beaded ft, flared rim, 8½" 75.00
Vase, bud; #400/187, ftd, 7" 145.00
Vase, rose bowl; #400/132, ftd, 7½" 125.00

Candy Containers

Figural glass candy containers were first created in 1876 when ingenious candy manufacturers began to use them to package their products. Two of the first containers, the Liberty Bell and Independence Hall, were distributed for our country's centennial celebration. Children found these toys appealing, and an industry was launched that lasted into the mid-1960s.

Figural candy containers include animals, comic characters, guns, telephones, transportation vehicles, household appliances, and many other intriguing designs. The oldest (those made prior to 1920) were usually hand painted and often contained extra metal parts in addition to the metal strip or screw closures. During the 1950s these metal parts were replaced with plastic, a practice that continued until candy containers met their demise in the 1960s. While predominately clear, they are found in nearly all colors of glass including milk glass, green, amber, pink, emerald, cobalt, ruby flashed, and light blue. Usually the color was intentional, but leftover glass was used as well and resulted in unplanned colors. Various examples are found in light or ice blue, and new finds are always being discovered. Production of the glass portion of candy containers was centered around the western Pennsylvania city of Jeannette. Major producers include Westmoreland Glass, West Bros., Victory Glass, J.H. Millstein, J.C. Crosetti, L.E. Smith, Jack Stough, and T.H. Stough. While 90% of all glass candies were made in the Jeannette area, other companies such as Eagle Glass, Play Toy, and Geo. Borgfeldt Co. have a few to their credit as well.

Buyer beware! Many candy containers have been reproduced. Some, including the Camera and the Rabbit Pushing Wheelbarrow, come already painted from distributors. Others may have a slick or oily feel to the touch. The following list may also alert you to possible reproductions:

#12 Chicken on Nest
#24 Dog (clear and cobalt)
#38 Mule and Waterwagon (original marked Jeanette, PA)
#47 Rabbit Pushing Wheelbarrow (eggs are speckled on the repro; solid on the original)
#55 Peter Rabbit
#58 Rocking Horse (original in clear only)
#76 Independence Hall (original is rectangular; repro has offset base with red felt-lined closure)
#89 Happifats on Drum (no notches on repro for closure to hook into)
#90 Jackie Coogan (marked inside 'B')
#91 Kewpie (must have Geo. Borgfeldt on base to be original)
#94 Naked Child
#103 Santa (original has plastic head; repro is all glass and opens at bottom)

#114 Mantel Clock
#144 Amber Pistol (first sold full in the 1970s)
#168 Uncle Sam's Hat
#233 Santa's Boot
#242 Carpet Sweeper
#243 Carpet Sweeper
#246 Display Case
#254 Mailbox
#255 Drum Mug
#268 Safe
#289 Piano (original in only clear and milk glass, both painted)
#352 Auto
#377 Auto
#378 Station Wagon
#386 Fire Engine
Others are possible.

Our advisor for this category is Jeff Bradfield; he is listed in the Directory under Virginia. You may contact him with questions. See Clubs, Newsletters, and Catalogs for the address of the Candy Container Collectors of America. A bimonthly newsletter offers insight into new finds, reproductions, updates, and articles from over three hundred collectors and members, including all authors of books on candy containers.

Numbers used in this guide refer to a standard reference series, *An Album of Candy Containers*, Vols 1 and 2, by Jennie Long. Values are given for undamaged examples with original paint and metal parts when applicable or unless noted otherwise. Repaired pieces (often repainted) are worth only a small fraction of one that is perfect. The symbol (+) at the end of some of the following lines was used to indicate items that have been reproduced. See also Christmas; Easter; Halloween.

Acorn, #221 ....600.00
Airplane, Passenger; #323 ....275.00
Amos & Andy, #77, G pnt 450.00
Auto w/Tassels #3, #362 ....225.00
Barney Google on Pedestal, #78 ....220.00
Baseball, frosted, no decals, #222 ....25.00
Basket, flower design, #224 ....35.00
Bear on Circus Tub, orig blades, #1 ....350.00
Bear Sitting, #454 ....175.00
Bird Cage, #230 ....225.00
Bottle, Baby Dear, #64 ....10.00
Bugle or Megaphone, #278 ....22.00
Bus, Rapid Transit; G pnt #345 ....550.00
Candelabrum, #202 ....35.00
Candlestick, #201 ....300.00
Candy Cane, Mercury Glass; #613 ....80.00
Cannon, cobalt bbl, rpl carriage, #534 ....300.00
Car, Coupe, Long Hood #1, #357 ....150.00
Car, Electric Coupe #2, closure, #356 (+) 50.00
Car, Limousine, 4-door, G pnt #348 ....600.00
Car, Sedan, 4-door, orig tin wheels, w/pnt, #370 .....100.00
Charlie Chaplin, Smith, G pnt, #84 ....450.00
Charlie Chaplin by Barrel, Borgfeldt, closure, orig pnt, #83 ....150.00
Chicken in Sagging Basket, #8 ....65.00
Chicken on Oblong Basket, closure, gr, #10 ....50.00
Clock, Mantel; #2, closure, paper face, orig pnt, #116 ....140.00
Clock, Mantel; rnd top, #113 ....225.00
Coal Car on Tender, orig wheels, #396 ....300.00
Cruet, #615 ....20.00
Defense Field Gun, orig gun, #142 ....300.00
Dirigible, Los Angeles; #322 ....175.00

Dog, Mutt, #20 ....50.00
Dog w/Top Hat, #480 ....25.00
Don't Park Here, #314 ....185.00
Fairy Pups, #23 ....60.00
Fanny Farmer, Cowboy, #528 ....130.00
Fire Engine, Little Boiler, #383 ....75.00
Fish, #34 ....400.00
Flatiron, closure, orig pnt, #249 ....400.00
Flossie Fisher Chair, #128 ....300.00
Gas Pump, #316 ....225.00
Gun, cork closure, #540 ....45.00
Happifats on Drum, orig pnt & closure, #89 (+) 275.00
Horn, 3-valve, w/mouthpc, #281 ....175.00
Horns, red tubes, #621 ....22.00
Hot Doggie, clear w/pnt, #14 ....450.00
House, closure, orig pnt, #75 ....150.00
Ice Truck, #458 ....650.00
Independence Hall, #74 (+) 300.00
Jackie Coogan, #1, G pnt, #90 ....1,150.00
Kiddies' Band, complete, #277 ....200.00
Kiddies' Breakfast Bell, #18 ....45.00
Lamp, Hobnail, w/shade, #209 ....250.00
Lamp, Valentine; #556, all orig 450.00
Lantern, Barn Type #1, #177 ....95.00
Lantern, crossette-ribbed base, #198 ....15.00
Lantern, glass reflector, #185 ....18.00
Lantern, Japanese paper type, #572 ....300.00
Lantern, oval panels, #570 ....30.00
Lantern, Victory Glass #1, #191 (+Avon) 10.00

Liberty Motors Airplane, 100% paint, $2,500.00.

Little Express, #405 ....625.00
Locomotive, dbl sq windows, orig closure, #414 ....125.00
Locomotive, Little Gem, #587 ....625.00
Locomotive, screw cap, #411 ....135.00
Lucky Lindy Candy Air Mail, #666 ....250.00
Lynn Doll Nurser, #72 ....28.00
Maud Muller Milk Carrier, #69 ....175.00
Mounted Policeman, closure, orig pnt, #551 ....1,800.00
Mug, Child's Tumbler, closure, #256 ....200.00
Naked Child, Victory Glass, #94 ....65.00
Naked Child w/Derby, #95 ....45.00
Opera Glass, brass fr, #260 ....125.00
Piano, #289, w/pnt (+) 225.00
Play Nursing Set, complete, #259 ....130.00
Pocket Watch, 'Jeannette' on paper face, #457 ....450.00
Rabbit, Stough's, closure, #54 (+) 20.00

Rabbit Family, orig pnt, #43 ....750.00
Rabbit in Egg Shell, gold pnt, #48 ....75.00
Rabbit Running on Log, gold pnt, #42 ....200.00
Rabbit w/Paws Together, #52 ....55.00
Refrigerator, Victory Glass Co, #266 .... 1,800.00
Rocking Horse #1, #58 (+) 350.00
Rooster Crowing, orig pnt, #56, EX 225.00
Sand Bucket, #236 ....25.00
Suitcase, clear, #217 ....35.00
Telephone, lg glass receiver, bl glass, #580 ....85.00
Telephone, Stough's #3, #308 ....40.00
Telephone, Victory Glass #1, #298 ....200.00

Telephone, red paint, wooden receiver, Victory Glass No. 5, L-302, 5", $50.00.

Valise, #220 ....450.00
Village Buildings, no glass inserts, #76, ea 25.00
Wagon or Stagecoach, #441 ....125.00
Watch, no fob, #122 ....200.00
Watch w/Fob, complete w/fob, #122 ....375.00
Wheelbarrow, closure, #273 ....85.00
Windmill, shaker top, orig blades, #445 ....250.00

Papier-Mache

Chef on egg, pnt compo, Germany, 5", EX 250.00
Chick, mc pnt, wire legs, on cb drum, Germany, 1900s, 5" 175.00
Chick in egg, papier-mache, mc pnt, 5½" 145.00
Fish, pnt papier-mache, glass eyes, Germany, 7½", VG 235.00
Football player, jtd limbs, wooden base, lt wear, 8½" 450.00
George Washington on stump, metal axe, 4½", EX 285.00
Irish girl, flesh face, gr hat/scarf/shoes, 4", EX 110.00
Man-in-the-moon face on sphere shape, mc pnt, 3½" dia 350.00
Potato w/shamrock at top, orig pnt, 1900s, 2½x2x2" 135.00
Pug dog, standing, pnt compo, glass eyes, 3½" L, VG 260.00
Rabbit, fur, in twig cart, nests w/carrots, Germany, 12" L 1,800.00
Rabbit, glass eyes, Germany, 1900s, sm rpr, 16" 250.00
Rabbit, seated, w/glasses, pnt compo, Germany, rpr, 5" 395.00
Rabbit on accordion, papier-mache, mechanical, MIG, 10".... 1,200.00
Turkey, compo, hair wattle, head removes, Germany, 7½" 175.00

Canes

Fancy canes and walking sticks were once the mark of a gentle-man. Hand-carved examples are collected and admired as folk art from the past. The glass canes that never could have been practical are unique whimseys of the glass-blower's profession. Gadget and container sticks, which were produced in a wide variety, are highly desirable. Character, political, and novelty types are also sought after as are those with handles made of precious metals. Our advisor for this category is Bruce Thalberg.

Ash wood, man's head cvd on walnut hdl, blk pnt, 1900s, 35"....250.00
Birch w/intarsial floral inlay hdl, 35½" 60.00
Burl walnut shaft, Spanish niello silver hdl, silver ferrule 150.00
Celluloid hdl of girl feeding chickens, metal ferrule/tip 155.00
Celluloid heads of 3 bears entwined on hdl, rosewood shaft 200.00
Celluloid jockey/horse head hdl, malacca shaft 185.00
Celluloid mastif dog heads on hdl, malacca shaft 200.00
Cholla cactus, overall natural piercing, root end hdl, 36" 45.00
Ebony shaft, gutta percha dolphin hdl, horn tip, gold ferrule 110.00
Ebony shaft, horn tip, 8" horn hdl, 36½" 200.00
Glass, bl/brn swirls, 44" 80.00
Glass, bl/wht/red spiral threading, 44" 115.00
Glass, burgundy swirl stripes, baton top, 58" 175.00
Glass, latticinio w/pk & wht swirls, baton top, 36" 195.00
Hickory w/silver boar's head hdl finial, horn tip, 36" 125.00
Horn w/amber inserts, steel core, 36" 100.00
Ivory dog's head hdl, glass eyes, sterling mask, bamboo shaft 850.00
Ivory fox & eagle hdl, gold ferrule, horn tip, malacca shaft 375.00
Ivory knob (Indian w/eagle headdress) & tip, gilt ferrule 500.00
Ivory L-hdl w/stag, ebonized shank w/ivory 'knotholes,' 36"........175.00
Ivory lobster claw hdl, sterling collar/trim, rosewood shaft 450.00
Ivory w/cvg of bear attacking couple, ebonized shank, 35" 400.00
Japanese bamboo, pnt fans, stained root end w/band motif 60.00
Leather disks on steel rod, steel tip, horn hdl, 35" 90.00
Mahog, 3¼" Art Nouveau silver hdl, metal tip, 36" 150.00
Picnic type, 4 parts for utensils & flask, metal tip, 34" 250.00
Porc hdl mk Honneur et Patrie, malacca shaft, 34" 265.00
Pussy willow, 1½" sterling-capped hdl, 37½" 65.00
Rosewood, gr jadite hdl w/faceted crystal bands, bone tip 475.00
Rosewood w/cat's eye hdl, sterling ferrule w/crown bezel 275.00
Scrimshaw whalebone, whale ivory knob hdl, EX 325.00

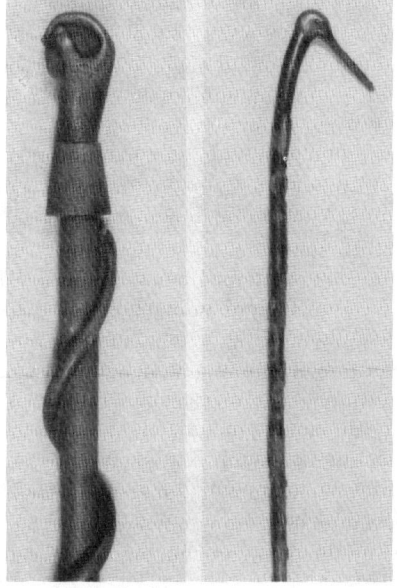

Walking sticks, maple with grip carved as a hand holding a sphere, shaft with winding serpent, 36", $950.00; the second with a carved bird grip, woodworking tools, a turtle, and a horse's leg carved on shaft, 1800s, 37", $500.00.

Stinkwood (odorless) shaft, horn tip, boar's tooth hdl, 37"..........175.00
Tortoise veneer, braided silver knob, 33" 250.00
Wood, cvd acorns & oak leaves, lady's, 35" 55.00
Wood, cvd primitive figures on shaft, knob hdl, 37½" 45.00

Wooden w/trn bone hdl & gold separator, 36", EX 75.00

Canton

Canton is a blue and white porcelain that was first exported in the 1790s by clipper ships from China to the United States, a practice that continued into the 1920s. Canton became very popular along the East coast where the major ports were located. Its popularity was due to several factors: it was readily available, inexpensive, and (due to the fact that it came in many different forms) appealing to the housewife.

The porcelain's blue and white color and simple motif (teahouse, trees, bridge, and a rain-cloud border) have made it a favorite of people who collect early American furniture and accessories. Buyers of Canton should look for pieces at large outdoor shows and up-scale antique shows. Collections are regularly sold at auction. Collectors usually prefer a rich, deep tone rather than a lighter blue. Cracks, large chips, and major repairs will substantially affect values. Prices of Canton have escalated sharply over the last twenty years, and rare forms are highly sought after by advanced collectors. Our advisor for this category is Hobart D. Van Deusen; he is listed in the Directory under Connecticut.

Basin, octagonal, 8x11" 550.00
Basket, fruit; rtcl, no hdls, 8x9" 800.00
Bidet, 14x23" 4,000.00
Bowl, salad; cut-corner style, 9" sq 900.00
Bowl, scalloped, 8" 550.00

Scalloped bowl, shallow, 9½", $650.00;
Gravy bowl, scalloped border, $200.00.

Bowl, vegetable; oval, w/lid, 8x10" 350.00
Bowl, vegetable; rectangular, w/lid, 7x8" 450.00
Candlestick, 8", pr.. 2,500.00
Creamer, helmet, 7" 450.00
Creamer, hog nose, 3½x3" 250.00
Cup, syllabub 175.00
Dish, leaf, 5x7" 300.00
Flagon, cider; foo dog finial, 6" 1,600.00
Garden seat, bbl shape, 18" H 9,000.00
Mug, 4" 450.00
Plate, butter; 6" 40.00
Plate, chop; 12"...825.00
Plate, dinner; 10" 150.00

Plate, hot water warming; 9" 350.00
Platter, octagonal, 15x12" 350.00
Platter, Well & Tree, octagonal, 18x14" 1,000.00
Salt, trencher, 2½x3½" 350.00
Shrimp dish, 9x10" 750.00
Sugar bowl, twist hdl, 4" 350.00
Tea tile, octagonal, 5x5" 325.00
Teacup & saucer 50.00
Teapot, dome top, 9" 850.00
Teapot, lighthouse, 6" 700.00
Tureen, gravy; boar's head hdls, 7" L 600.00
Tureen, soup; boar's head hdls, 12" L 1,200.00

Capo-Di-Monte

Established in 1743 near Naples and sponsored by Charles II, who was King of Naples at that time, Capo-Di-Monte produced soft-paste porcelain figurines and dinnerware usually marked with a 'crown over N' device, though a fleur-de-lis was used on occasion. The factory was closed throughout the 1760s but reopened in 1771 in the city of Naples. There both hard- and soft-paste porcelains were made, sometimes decorated with applied florals in high relief. Their technique as well as their marks were blatantly copied. As a result, this type of encrusted decoration is often referred to today as Capo-Di-Monte. The original factory closed in 1821. Some of their molds were purchased by the Docceia Porcelain factory in Florence which continues to operate to the present time. Most examples on the market today are of fairly recent manufacture. Capo-Di-Monte type wares have been made in Hungary and Germany as well as France and Italy. Many of these pieces continue to bear the 'crown over N' gold stamp. As more collectors recognize and appreciate the quality of the older ware, buyer demand drives prices higher.

Group: mother and children greet lady and gentleman, 16" x 20", $1,800.00.

Box, children & trees emb, fruit finial, paw ft, 4½x7" dia 70.00
Cache pot, lady/cherub/castle, Toulan, loop hdls, 7½x9½" 250.00
Chest, highly decorated dome top, mk R, 10" L 525.00
Chest, highly decorated medieval style w/ormolu, 15", NM.... 1,450.00
Figurine, African Crowned Crane, Armani, 14" 200.00
Figurine, boy fishing on stump, orange cap & boots, 6"................95.00
Figurine, boy photographs girl on brick wall, 10x9" 175.00
Figurine, captain w/shell & pearl, Bonalberti, 7½x9½"..............225.00
Figurine, girl by tree w/hat & parasol, 10" 125.00
Figurine, girl holds roses, flower basket at ft, sgn, 9½"..................175.00
Figurine, lady roasts chestnuts, urchin at side, Armani, 10".........250.00

Figurine, man in floral vest, bl coat, flowers in hand, 8" 160.00
Figurine, Pan seated on sq bat-emb pyramid base, 8½" 295.00
Shield, battle scene reserve, 23" L..800.00
Urn, cherub w/wreath finial, ftd floral base, 20½x8" 550.00
Urn, cherubs & grapes emb, Bacchus hdls, w/lid, 15", pr 400.00
Urn, cherubs/nymphs/florals, cherub hdls, w/floral lid, 20"..........650.00
Urn, nymphs/cherubs in dolphin boat, cherub hdls, lid, 20"........650.00
Urn, semi-nudes/grapes/jugs, gold hdls, ped base, 13½" 350.00
Urn, warrior slays man, man/lady watch, swan/mask hdls, 25" 950.00
Vase, mythological scenes, bulbous, 1830s, 8", EX, pr 575.00

Carnival Collectibles

Carnival items from the early part of this century represent the lighter side of an America that was alternately prospering and sophisticated or devastated by war and domestic conflict. But whatever the country's condition, the carnival's thrilling rides and shooting galleries were a sure way of letting it all go by — at least for an evening.

For further information on chalkware figures, we recommend *The Carnival Chalk Prize* by Thomas G. Morris, who is listed in the Directory under Oregon. Our advisors for shooting gallery targets are Richard and Valerie Tucker; their address is listed in the Directory under Texas.

Chalkware figure, Beach Flirt, mohair wig, 1919, 9½" 105.00
Chalkware figure, cat, w/glass fishbowl, ca 1930-40, 9½" 55.00
Chalkware figure, Dutch girl, standing, 1934, 11½" 55.00
Chalkware figure, flower vase, ca 1930-40, 11¾"............................27.00
Chalkware figure, Indian chief, standing, ca 1930-45, 19" 40.00
Chalkware figure, King Kong, ca 1930-40, 13¼" 35.00
Chalkware figure, lady with horse, mk Friends, 9¾x8½" 55.00
Chalkware figure, Majorette, Gittins, 1941, 12½".........................40.00
Chalkware figure, Marie, mohair wig, 1923, 13½"..........................80.00
Chalkware figure, Mexican girl, Jenkins, 1925, 14½"...................115.00
Chalkware figure, owl bank, ca 1935-45, 10¼"...............................35.00
Chalkware figure, piggy bank, Jenkins, 1949, 8x14".......................40.00
Chalkware figure, Pirate Girl, Rainwater, 1936, 14¼"....................95.00
Chalkware figure, Pluto, ca 1930-45, 7½".......................................40.00
Chalkware figure, Porky Pig, ca 1940-40, 7½" 15.00
Chalkware figure, rattlesnake ash tray, ca 1940s, 5½" 17.00
Chalkware figure, Rin Tin Tin, ca 1930-40, 10½" 20.00
Chalkware figure, Superman, ca 1940-50, 15" 125.00
Chalkware figure, Uncle Sam, ca 1935-45, 15" 50.00
Chalkware figure, US Navy Wave, Jenkins, 1944, 13".....................65.00
Chalkware figure, windmill, ca 1935-40, 10¾".................................17.00
Chalkware lamp, End of the Trail, ca 1930-45, 6½".........................65.00
Chalkware lamp, lighthouse, ca 1935-45, 15½"................................60.00
Popcorn machine, Halcomb & Hoke, wood, EX orig 2,500.00
Popcorn machine, Wood, counter-top, EX...................................375.00

Shooting Gallery Targets

Bird on rod, CI, worn, 3½x3x½" 40.00
Bird w/forked tail, worn pnt, 4" 45.00
Buffalo, standing, worn wht pnt, 6½"..85.00
Convict, pnt wood & tin, 1930s, 12"...325.00
Duck, CI, red pnt, Parker, 1900s, on base, M 175.00
Hitler head, CI, orig pnt, 10½" 225.00
Moose, CI, bl pnt, 7x5x¼" 85.00
Quail & tulip, CI, worn pnt, 10½" 85.00
Rabbit, jumping, no pnt, 8½x6½x½"...70.00
Star on rod, CI, no pnt, 4x2½x1"...45.00
Tobacco pipes, orig fr, 8x66", EX 295.00
Tom turkey, mk Evans, 7" 165.00
2 CI chicks/trigger, steel fr, 10" 50.00

Carnival Glass

Carnival glass is pressed glass that has been coated with a sodium solution and fired to give it an exterior lustre. First made in America in 1905, it was produced until the late 1920s and had great popularity in the average American household; for unlike the costly art glass produced by Tiffany, carnival glass could be mass-produced at a small cost. Colors most found are marigold, green, blue, and purple; but others exist in lesser quantities and include white, clear, red, aqua opalescent, peach opalescent, ice blue, ice green, amber, lavender, and smoke.

Companies mainly responsible for its production in America include the Fenton Art Glass Company, Williamstown, West Virginia; the Northwood Glass Company, Wheeling, West Virginia; the Imperial Glass Company, Bellaire, Ohio; the Millersburg Glass Company, Millersburg, Ohio; and the Dugan Glass Company (Diamond Glass), Indiana, Pennsylvania. In addition to these major manufacturers, lesser producers included the U.S. Glass Company, the Cambridge Glass Company, the Westmoreland Glass Company, and the McKee Glass Company.

Carnival glass has been highly collectible since the 1950s and has been reproduced for the last twenty-five years. Several national and state collectors' organizations exist, and many fine books are available on old carnival glass, including *The Standard Encyclopedia of Carnival Glass* by Bill Edwards.

#474 (Imperial), bowl, marigold, 8" 60.00
#474 (Imperial), butter dish, gr, w/lid...125.00
#474 (Imperial), pitcher, milk; gr, scarce.......................................475.00
Acanthus (Imperial), plate, smoke, 10" 290.00
Acorn (Fenton), plate, amethyst, scarce, 9" 490.00
Acorn (Millersburg), compote, marigold, rare 2,800.00
Acorn & File, compote, vaseline, rare 1,000.00
Acorn Burrs (Northwood), bowl, pastel, flat, 10"..........................420.00
African Shield (English), toothpick holder, marigold 45.00
Amaryllis (Northwood), compote, bl, sm.......................................265.00
American (Fostoria), tumbler, marigold, rare.................................600.00
Apple & Pear Intaglio (Northwood), bowl, marigold, 10" 75.00
Apple Blossom Twigs (Dugan), plate, bl...325.00
Apple Blossoms (Dugan), bowl, peach opal, 7½" 150.00
Apple Panels (English), creamer, gr..36.00
Apple Tree (Fenton), pitcher, water; bl...430.00

April Showers (Fenton), vase, pastel, $100.00.

Arched Fleur-De-Lis (Higbee), mug, marigold, rare 200.00
Arcs (Imperial), bowl, gr, 8½" 45.00
Art Deco (English), bowl, marigold, 4"...32.00
Asters, bowl, marigold, 6"..58.00

Astral, shade, marigold **45.00**
August Flowers, shade, marigold **36.00**
Aurora, bowl, amethyst, decor, 8½" **150.00**
Australian Swan (Crystal), bowl, amethyst, 9" **10.00**
Autumn Acorns (Fenton), plate, bl, rare **1,100.00**
Aztec (McKee), pitcher, marigold, rare.................. **1,300.00**
Baker's Rosette, ornament, amethyst **80.00**
Ball & Swirl, mug, marigold **90.00**
Balloons (Imperial), plate, cake; marigold **60.00**
Band (Dugan), violet hat, bl.......................................**60.00**
Banded Diamonds (Crystal), pitcher, water; amethyst, rare ... **1,200.00**
Banded Diamonds (Crystal), tumbler, marigold, rare..................**450.00**
Banded Grape (Fenton), pitcher, water; bl **400.00**
Banded Grape & Leaf (English), tumbler, marigold, rare.............**90.00**
Banded Panels (Crystal), sugar bowl, amethyst **45.00**
Banded Portland (US Glass), puff jar, marigold...........**60.00**
Banded Rib, pitcher, marigold **120.00**
Banded Rib, tumbler, marigold **20.00**
Basketweave (Fenton), vase whimsey, bl, rare............**825.00**
Basketweave & Cable (Westmoreland), creamer, wht................**210.00**
Beaded, hatpin, amethyst **24.00**
Beaded Acanthus (Imperial), pitcher, milk; gr **210.00**
Beaded Band & Octagon, lamp, kerosene; marigold **190.00**
Beaded Cable (Northwood), candy dish, amethyst.......**60.00**
Beaded Cable (Northwood), rose bowl, peach opal....................**750.00**
Beaded Hearts (Northwood), bowl, amethyst or gr **60.00**
Beaded Panels (Imperial), bowl, marigold, 8" **40.00**
Beaded Panels (Westmoreland), compote, amethyst.......**50.00**
Beaded Shell (Dugan), bowl, amethyst, ftd, 9" **95.00**
Beaded Shell (Dugan), butter dish, amethyst, w/lid **175.00**
Beaded Stars (Fenton), plate, marigold, 9" **90.00**
Beaded Swirl (English), butter dish, bl, w/lid.............**70.00**
Beaded Swirl (English), compote, marigold **45.00**
Beads (Northwood), bowl, gr, 8½".............................**60.00**
Beads & Bars (US Glass), spooner, marigold................**50.00**
Bellaire Souvenir (Imperial), bowl, marigold, scarce....**185.00**
Bells & Beads (Dugan), bowl, bl, 7½".........................**55.00**
Bells & Beads (Dugan), nappy, peach opal **70.00**
Bells & Beads (Dugan), plate, amethyst, 8" **120.00**
Big Basketweave (Dugan), basket, amethyst, sm **40.00**
Big Basketweave (Dugan), vase, aqua opal, 6".............**180.00**
Big Fish (Millersburg), bowl, amethyst, sq, very rare **1,000.00**
Big Fish (Millersburg), bowl, amethyst, tricorner **1,950.00**
Bird of Paradise (Northwood), plate, advertising; amethyst........**220.00**
Bird w/Grapes (Cockatoo), wall vase, marigold **65.00**
Birds & Cherries (Fenton), bonbon, bl **60.00**
Black Bottom (Fenton), candy jar, pastel **60.00**
Blackberry (Fenton), hat, aqua opal, open edge **150.00**
Blackberry (Fenton), plate, marigold, rare **775.00**
Blackberry (Fenton), vase whimsey, wht, rare **400.00**
Blackberry (Northwood), bowl, marigold, ftd, 9" **47.00**
Blackberry (Northwood), compote, amethyst **65.00**
Blackberry Banded (Fenton), hat shape, gr **50.00**
Blackberry Bark, vase, amethyst, rare **1,500.00**
Blackberry Block (Fenton), tumbler, wht **200.00**
Blackberry Bramble (Fenton), compote, amethyst **60.00**
Blackberry Wreath (Millersburg), bowl, amethyst, 7" ...**85.00**
Blackberry Wreath (Millersburg), bowl, ice cream; bl, 10" **950.00**
Blocks & Arches (Crystal), pitcher, amethyst, rare......**200.00**
Blocks & Arches (Crystal), tumbler, marigold, rare **70.00**
Blossom & Spears, plate, clear, 8" **40.00**
Blossoms & Band (Imperial), bowl, amethyst, 10" **42.00**
Blossomtime (Northwood), compote, gr **280.00**
Blueberry (Fenton), pitcher, pastel, scarce **1,000.00**

Blueberry (Fenton), tumbler, bl, scarce......................**95.00**
Bo Peep (Westmoreland), mug, marigold, scarce **190.00**
Bo Peep (Westmoreland), plate, ABC; marigold, rare **600.00**
Border Plants (Dugan), bowl, amethyst, ftd, 8½" **70.00**
Border Plants (Dugan), bowl, peach opal, flat, 8½".....**170.00**
Bouquet (Fenton), pitcher, bl **475.00**
Bouquet (Fenton), pitcher, marigold **250.00**
Bouquet (Fenton), tumbler, wht **85.00**
Boutonniere (Millersburg), compote, gr **260.00**
Bow & English Hob (English), nut bowl, bl **55.00**
Briar Patch, hat shape, amethyst **45.00**
Brocaded Summer Gardens, bowl, pastel **65.00**
Broken Arches (Imperial), bowl, gr, 8½" **60.00**
Broken Arches (Imperial), cup, punch; marigold **25.00**
Brooklyn Bridge (Dugan), bowl, marigold, scarce **360.00**
Bubble Berry, shade, pastel **60.00**
Bubbles, hatpin, amethyst **36.00**
Bull Dog, paperweight, marigold..............................**250.00**
Bull's Eye (US Glass), lamp, oil; marigold **185.00**
Bull's Eye & Leaves (Northwood), bowl, gr, 8½" **50.00**
Bull's Eye & Spearhead, wine, marigold.......................**48.00**
Bumblebees, hatpin, amethyst **26.00**
Butterflies (Fenton), bonbon, pastel **70.00**
Butterflies (Fenton), tray, card; bl **60.00**
Butterflies & Bells (Crystal), compote, amethyst **125.00**
Butterfly, pin tray, marigold **35.00**
Butterfly (Fenton), ornament, gr, rare **200.00**
Butterfly (Fenton), ornament, wht, rare **285.00**
Butterfly (Northwood), bonbon, amethyst, ribbed exterior **260.00**
Butterfly (Northwood), bonbon, bl, regular **75.00**
Butterfly & Berry (Fenton), bowl, amethyst, ftd, 5" **40.00**
Butterfly & Berry (Fenton), bowl, wht, ftd, 10" **375.00**
Butterfly & Berry (Fenton), pitcher, wht **1,100.00**
Butterfly & Berry (Fenton), sugar bowl, gr, w/lid **190.00**
Butterfly & Corn (Northwood), vase, vaseline, rare............... **3,000.00**
Butterfly & Fern (Fenton), pitcher, bl.......................**600.00**
Butterfly & Tulip (Dugan), bowl, marigold, whimsey shape.......**850.00**
Butterfly Bower (Crystal), compote, marigold **80.00**
Butterfly Bush (Crystal), compote, amethyst, lg **150.00**
Buttermilk (Fenton), goblet, gr, plain........................**70.00**
Button & Fan, hatpin, amethyst.................................**55.00**
Buttons & Daisy (Imperial), hat, clambroth, old only...............**60.00**
Buttons & Daisy (Imperial), slipper, clambroth, old only **70.00**
Buttress (US Glass), pitcher, marigold, rare **300.00**
Buzz Saw, shade, marigold **40.00**
Cane (Imperial), bowl, pastel, 7½" **45.00**
Cane (Imperial), dish, pickle; marigold......................**25.00**
Cane & Daisy Cut (Jenkins), basket, pastel, hdls, rare..............**190.00**
Cane & Daisy Cut (Jenkins), vase, marigold **90.00**
Cane & Scroll (Sea Thistle, English), rose bowl, bl **70.00**

Cane and Scroll (Sea Thistle, English,) creamer, marigold, $45.00.

Cannonball Vt, pitcher, marigold 250.00
Cannonball Vt, tumbler, bl 70.00
Capitol (Westmoreland), bowl, bl, ftd, sm 65.00
Capitol (Westmoreland), mug, marigold, sm 75.00
Captive Rose (Fenton), bonbon, gr 60.00
Captive Rose (Fenton), bowl, marigold, 10" 37.00
Captive Rose (Fenton), plate, bl, 9" 265.00
Carnation (New Martinsville), cup, punch; marigold 45.00
Carnival Honeycomb (Imperial), bonbon, bl 45.00
Carnival Honeycomb (Imperial), bowl, marigold, hdls, 6" 30.00
Carolina Dogwood (Westmoreland), bowl, amethyst, 8½" 90.00
Carolina Dogwood (Westmoreland), bowl, milk glass opal, 8½" .225.00
Carolina Dogwood (Westmoreland), plate, milk glass opal 290.00
Caroline (Dugan), bowl, marigold, 10" 52.00
Cathedral (Curved Star, Sweden), butter dish, marigold 185.00
Cathedral (Curved Star, Sweden), pitcher, bl, rare 2,500.00
Cathedral Arches (English), punch bowl, marigold, 1-pc 250.00
Cattails, hatpin, amethyst....................................26.00
Central Shoe Store (Northwood), bowl, amethyst, 7" 285.00
Chain & Star (Fostoria), butter dish, marigold, w/lid, rare 900.00
Chatelaine (Imperial), pitcher, amethyst, rare.................... 2,800.00
Chatelaine (Imperial), tumbler, amethyst, rare 460.00
Checkerboard (Westmoreland), cruet, clear, rare 600.00
Checkerboard (Westmoreland), goblet, amethyst, rare.............295.00
Checkerboard (Westmoreland), pitcher, amethyst, rare.......... 3,800.00
Checkerboard Bouquet, plate, amethyst, 8" 50.00
Checkers, bowl, marigold, 9"...................................32.00
Checkers, plate, marigold, 7" 50.00
Cherry (Dugan), bowl, peach opal, flat, 8" 200.00
Cherry (Dugan), cruet, wht, rare............................500.00
Cherry (Millersburg), compote, bl, lg, rare...............2,800.00
Cherry (Millersburg), pitcher, milk; marigold, rare 620.00
Cherry & Cable (Northwood), butter dish, marigold, rare 350.00
Cherry & Cable Intaglio (Northwood), bowl, marigold, 10" 36.00
Cherry & Daisies (Fenton), banana boat, marigold....................800.00
Cherry Blossoms, pitcher, bl.................................95.00
Cherry Blossoms, tumbler, bl.................................28.00
Cherry Chain (Fenton), plate, wht, 7" 150.00
Cherry Circles (Fenton), bonbon, red.................... 1,950.00
Cherry Smash (US Glass), butter dish, marigold.........................110.00
Cherry Smash (US Glass), tumbler, marigold 135.00
Cherry Stippled, tumbler, marigold..........................75.00
Cherub, lamp, pastel, rare....................................425.00
Chippendale Souvenir, sugar bowl, amethyst 80.00
Chrysanthemum (Fenton), bowl, bl, ftd, 10"..............80.00
Chrysanthemum (Fenton), bowl, red, flat, 9" 1,080.00
Chrysanthemum Drape, lamp, oil; pastel, rare..........900.00
Circle Scroll (Dugan), bowl, marigold, 5" 40.00
Circle Scroll (Dugan), butter dish, amethyst..............350.00
Circle Scroll (Dugan), vase whimsey, marigold, rare...............120.00
Classic Arts (Czech), rose bowl, marigold 460.00
Cleveland Memorial (Millersburg), ash tray, amethyst, rare ... 2,000.00
Cobblestones (Dugan), bowl, amethyst, 9" 70.00
Cobblestones (Dugan), bowl, marigold, 5" 38.00
Cobblestones (Dugan-Imperial), plate, amethyst, rare............. 1,000.00
Cobblestones (Imperial), bonbon, amber.....................75.00
Cobblestones (Imperial), bowl, amethyst, 8½" 70.00
Coin Dot (Fenton), basket whimsey, marigold, rare 60.00
Coin Dot (Fenton), bowl, amethyst, 10" 50.00
Coin Dot (Fenton), rose bowl, bl............................70.00
Coin Dot Vt (Westmoreland), compote, ice bl opal 275.00
Coin Spot (Dugan), compote, aqua opal 300.00
Colonial (Imperial), goblet, lemonade; marigold..........60.00
Colonial Lady (Imperial), vase, amethyst, rare 1,025.00

Columbia (Imperial), compote, amethyst 60.00
Columbia (Imperial), vase, gr 45.00
Columbus, plate, marigold, 8" 38.00
Concave Diamonds (Dugan), pickle castor, marigold, w/holder..450.00
Concave Diamonds (Dugan), pitcher, russet, w/lid.....................450.00
Concave Flute (Westmoreland), rose bowl, gr.............65.00
Cone & Tie (Imperial), tumbler, amethyst, rare 650.00
Connie (Northwood), pitcher, wht...........................650.00
Connie (Northwood), tumbler, wht..........................90.00
Constellation (Dugan), compote, peach opal...........160.00
Coral (Fenton), bowl, marigold, 9" 85.00
Coral (Fenton), compote, gr, rare 295.00
Corinth (Dugan), bowl, peach opal, 9" 170.00
Corinth (Dugan), dish, banana; apricot....................150.00
Corinth (Westmoreland), bowl, amethyst 50.00
Corinth (Westmoreland), bowl, teal...........................60.00
Cornucopia (Fenton), candle holder, wht, 6½", ea 100.00
Cornucopia (Fenton), candlestick, wht, 5", pr 140.00
Cosmos (Millersburg), bowl, gr, 5".............................55.00
Cosmos (Millersburg), plate, gr, 6".............................65.00
Cosmos & Cane, bowl, wht, 10" 110.00
Cosmos & Cane, chop plate, wht, rare.....................475.00
Cosmos & Cane, compote, marigold, tall, rare...........300.00
Cosmos & Cane, rose bowl, amber............................165.00
Cosmos Vt (Fenton), bowl, bl, 9".............................80.00
Cosmos Vt (Fenton), bowl, red, 9".........................425.00
Country Kitchen (Millersburg), butter dish, marigold, rare 500.00
Country Kitchen (Millersburg), vase whimsey, amethyst, rare 550.00
CR (Argentina), ash tray, bl...................................85.00
Crab Claw (Imperial), bowl, fruit; marigold, w/base.....................90.00
Crab Claw (Imperial), bowl, gr, 10"..........................60.00

Crab Claw pitcher, marigold, scarce, $395.00.

Crackle (Imperial), cup, punch; gr.............................16.00
Crackle (Imperial), pitcher, amethyst, dome base 140.00
Crackle (Imperial), spittoon, marigold, lg...................38.00
Crystal Cut (Crystal), compote, marigold...................50.00
Cut Arches (English), bowl, banana; marigold.............50.00
Cut Arcs (Fenton), compote, amethyst 48.00
Cut Arcs (Fenton), vase whimsey, wht......................70.00
Cut Cosmos (Millersburg), tumbler, marigold, rare 395.00
Cut Crystal (US Glass), bottle, water; marigold..........165.00
Cut Flowers (Jenkins), vase, marigold, 10" 150.00
Cut Flowers (Jenkins), vase, smoke, 10" 195.00
Cut Ovals (Fenton), bowl, pastel, 7"..........................70.00
Cut Sprays, vase, peach opal, 9" 95.00
Dahlia (Dugan), bowl, marigold, ftd, 5" 40.00

Dahlia (Dugan), bowl, wht, ftd, 10".................................275.00
Dahlia (Dugan), sugar bowl, amethyst.........................100.00
Dahlia (Fenton), twist epergne, marigold, 1-lily.........250.00
Dahlia & Drape (Fenton), tumble-up, ice bl, complete 185.00
Daisy (Fenton), bonbon, marigold, scarce...................185.00
Daisy & Cane (English), spittoon, bl, rare...................185.00
Daisy & Drape (Northwood), vase, gr 1,950.00
Daisy & Plume (Northwood), candy dish, amethyst 55.00
Daisy & Plume (Northwood), compote, peach opal................110.00
Daisy Block (English), rowboat, aqua, scarce................295.00
Daisy in Oval Panels (US Glass), sugar bowl, marigold 50.00
Daisy Squares, compote, amber, rare.........................500.00
Daisy Wreath (Westmoreland), bowl, milk glass opal, 8" 440.00
Dance of the Veils (Fenton), vase, marigold, rare 2,650.00
Dandelion (Northwood), vase whimsey, amethyst, rare..............650.00
Deco Lily, vase, marigold, bulbous 85.00
Deep Grape (Millersburg), compote, amethyst, ruffled top 1,850.00
Diamond & Daisy Cut (US Glass), compote, amethyst 60.00
Diamond & Daisy Cut Vt (Jenkins), punch bowl, marigold, +base.500.00
Diamond & File, bowl, marigold, 7".............................35.00
Diamond & Rib (Fenton), vase, bl, 12" 32.00
Diamond & Sunburst (Imperial), bowl, amber, 8"................55.00
Diamond & Sunburst (Imperial), cruet, oil; gr, rare 800.00
Diamond Band (Crystal), float set, amethyst..................300.00
Diamond Band & Fan (English), cordial set, marigold, complete .750.00
Diamond Checkerboard, bowl, marigold, 9"....................35.00
Diamond Checkerboard, cracker jar, marigold 75.00
Diamond Daisy, plate, marigold, 8".............................75.00
Diamond Flutes (US Glass), creamer, marigold................35.00
Diamond Fountain (Higbee), cruet, marigold, rare 675.00
Diamond Lace (Imperial), bowl, amethyst, 10" 65.00
Diamond Ovals (English), compote, marigold.................35.00

Diamond Pinwheel (English), butter dish, marigold, $65.00.

Diamond Point Columns (Imperial), bowl, marigold, 4½"............20.00
Diamond Point Columns (Imperial), butter dish, marigold...........65.00
Diamond Point Columns (Imperial), plate, marigold, 7" 35.00
Diamond Prisms (English), compote, marigold.................45.00
Diamond Ring (Imperial), bowl, amethyst....................45.00
Diamond Star, vase, marigold, 8" 60.00
Diamond Top (English), creamer, marigold...................32.00
Diamonds (Millersburg), pitcher, gr.........................265.00
Diamonds (Millersburg), pitcher oddity, gr, no spout.................350.00
Diving Dolphins (English), bowl, bl, ftd, 7".................260.00
Dogwood Sprays (Dugan), bowl, amethyst, 9".................50.00
Dolphins (Millersburg), compote, gr, rare 1,975.00

Dorsey & Funkenstein (Northwood), plate, amethyst 335.00
Dots & Curves, hatpin, amethyst..............................42.00
Dotted Daisies, plate, marigold, 8".............................65.00
Double Dolphins (Fenton), bowl, pastel, flat, 10" 60.00
Double Dutch (Imperial), bowl, gr, ftd, 9"......................60.00
Double Fan (English), tumbler, marigold, rare 100.00
Double Loop (Northwood), creamer, bl...........................100.00
Double Scroll (Imperial), bowl, red..........................185.00
Double Stem Rose (Dugan), bowl, peach opal, dome base, 8½" .225.00
Dragon & Lotus (Fenton), bowl, peach opal, ftd, 9" 680.00
Drape & Tassel, shade, wht 40.00
Drapery (Northwood), candy dish, aqua opal..................460.00
Drapery Vt (Fenton), pitcher, marigold, rare................485.00
Dugan Fan (Dugan), gravy boat, peach opal, ftd 145.00
Dutch Mill, plate, marigold, 8".................................35.00
Dutch Twins, ash tray, marigold...............................45.00
Eagle Furniture (Northwood), plate, amethyst 360.00
Elegance, bowl, amethyst, 8¼".................................190.00
Elks (Dugan), nappy, amethyst, very rare.................. 3,500.00
Elks (Millersburg), bowl, amethyst, rare.................. 1,250.00
Embroidered Mums (Northwood), bowl, bl, 9" 375.00
Enamelled Grape (Northwood), pitcher, bl....................340.00
English Button Band (English), sugar bowl, marigold 38.00
English Hob & Button (English), bowl, gr, 10"................90.00
Engraved Floral (Fenton), tumbler, gr 85.00
Engraved Grapes (Fenton), pitcher, marigold, tall 85.00
Engraved Grapes (Fenton), tumble-up, marigold 135.00
Estate (Westmoreland), mug, marigold, rare..................85.00
Exchange Bank (Northwood), plate, amethyst, 6" 200.00
Fanciful (Dugan), bowl, pastel, 8½" 60.00
Fancy Cut (English), pitcher, marigold, mini, rare.................125.00
Fans (English), cracker jar, marigold, w/metal lid............118.00
Fashion (Imperial), bowl, fruit; gr, w/base....................85.00
Fashion (Imperial), cup, punch; amethyst....................35.00
Feather & Heart (Millersburg), pitcher, gr, scarce 775.00
Feather Stitch (Fenton), bowl, bl, 8½" 60.00
Feather Swirl (US Glass), butter dish, marigold...............110.00
Feathered Arrow (English), bowl, marigold, 8½" 40.00
Feathered Serpent (Fenton), bowl, gr, 10"....................65.00
Feathers (Northwood), vase, marigold, 12" 28.00
Fenton's Arched Flute (Fenton), toothpick holder, bl 95.00
Fentonia, bowl, amethyst, ftd, 9½"..............................85.00
Fentonia, bowl, gr, ftd, 5"......................................42.00
Fern (Northwood), bowl, marigold, 6½"........................46.00
Fern Brand Chocolates (Northwood), plate, amethyst..............345.00
Fern Panels (Fenton), hat, pastel 495.00
Field Flower (Imperial), pitcher, amber 350.00
Field Thistle (US Glass), bowl, marigold, 6" 45.00
File (Imperial & English), bowl, marigold, 5" 30.00
Fine Block (Imperial), shade, gr 40.00
Fine Cut & Roses (Northwood), candy dish, amethyst, ftd...........60.00
Fine Cut Flower & Vt (Fenton), compote, marigold...............50.00
Fine Cut Rings (English), bowl, marigold, oval 40.00
Fine Prisms & Diamonds (English), vase, pastel, 14" 80.00
Fine Rib (Northwood, Fenton & Dugan), bowl, gr, 9".............75.00
Fish Net (Dugan), epergne, peach opal 525.00
Fishscale & Beads (Dugan), bowl, peach opal, 6"..............150.00
Fishscale & Beads (Dugan), plate, marigold, 7"................40.00
Five Hearts (Dugan), bowl, peach opal, dome base, 8¾"............165.00
Flannel Flower (Crystal), cake stand, marigold..................120.00
Flared Wide Panel, atomizer, marigold, 3½" 90.00
Fleur-De-Lis (Jenkins), vase, marigold 195.00
Fleur-De-Lis (Millersburg), bowl, clambroth, flat, 8½" 240.00
Flora (English), float bowl, bl..................................75.00

Floral, hatpin, amber 50.00
Floral & Grape (Dugan), hat, marigold 35.00
Floral & Grape Vt (Fenton), pitcher, amethyst, 2 variations.......285.00
Floral & Optic (Imperial), bowl, aqua opal, flat, 8" 20.00
Floral & Optic (Imperial), rose bowl, aqua, ftd 180.00
Floral & Wheat (US Glass), bonbon, amethyst, stem 45.00
Floral Oval (Higbee), creamer, marigold 65.00
Florentine (Imperial), vase, hat; pastel 85.00
Flower & Beads, plate, amethyst, 6-sided, 7½" 110.00
Flowering Dill (Fenton), hat, red 500.00
Flowering Vine (Millersburg), compote, gr, tall, very rare.......3,800.00
Flowers & Frames (Dugan), bowl, pastel, 8" 95.00
Flowers & Spades (Dugan), bowl, amethyst, 5" 30.00
Flute (British), sherbet, marigold, mk 45.00
Flute (Millersburg), vase, gr, rare 350.00
Flute (Northwood), bowl, amethyst, 5" 26.00
Flute (Northwood), salt cellar, vaseline, ftd.................75.00
Flute & Cane (Imperial), pitcher, wht, stem, rare 900.00
Flute & Cane (Imperial), tumbler, marigold, rare 350.00
Flute #3 (Imperial), bowl, custard; amethyst, 11" 285.00
Flying Bat, hatpin, gr, scarce 58.00
Folding Fan (Dugan), compote, aqua opal..................285.00
Footed Drape (Westmoreland), vase, marigold............40.00

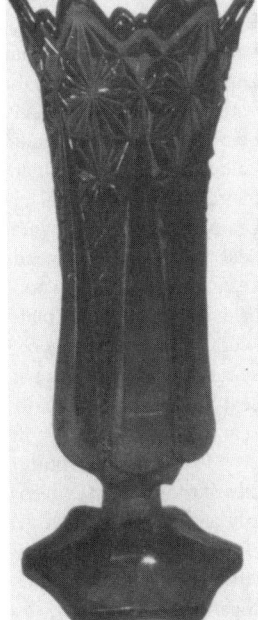

Footed Prism Panels (English), vase, blue, $85.00.

Footed Rib (Northwood), vase, advertising; aqua opal 235.00
Forget-Me-Not (Fenton), pitcher, wht 320.00
Forks (Cambridge), cracker jar, gr, rare 495.00
Formal (Dugan), hatpin holder, amethyst, rare 160.00
Forty-Niner (Imperial), decanter, marigold 125.00
Fostoria #1231 (Fostoria), rose bowl, pastel................100.00
Fostoria #600 (Fostoria), napkin ring, marigold..............75.00
Fostorial #1299 (Fostoria), tumbler, marigold 75.00
Four Flowers, bowl, bl, 6¼"....................................65.00
Four Flowers, bowl, peach opal, 10" 185.00
Four Flowers Vt, bowl, gr, ftd, 8½" 75.00
Four Flowers Vt, bowl, teal, w/metal base, rare............350.00
French Knots (Fenton), hat, peach opal 42.00
Frosted Block (Imperial), bowl, clambroth, sq, rare........52.00
Frosted Buttons (Fenton), bowl, pastel, ftd, 10" 175.00
Frosted Ribbon, pitcher, marigold 80.00

Fruit & Berries (English), bean pot, bl, w/lid, rare............275.00
Fruit & Flowers (Northwood), bonbon, wht, stem.......................575.00
Fruit Basket (Millersburg), compote, amethyst, hdld, rare 1,500.00
Fruit Lustre, tumbler, marigold...............................38.00
Gambier (Crystal), mug, marigold..............................45.00
Garden Mums (Northwood), bowl, pastel, 10"..............100.00
Garden Path (Dugan), bowl, fruit; amethyst, 10" 95.00
Garden Path Vt (Dugan), bowl, fruit; amethyst, 10".........360.00
Garland (Fenton), rose bowl, marigold, ftd...................45.00
Gay 90's (Millersburg), pitcher, gr, rare 9,500.00
Georgia Belle (Dugan), compote, gr, ftd.....................80.00
God & Home (Dugan), pitcher, bl, rare 1,000.00
Goddess Athena, epergne, amber, rare 2,800.00
Golden Flowers, vase, marigold, 7½"..........................48.00
Golden Grapes (Dugan), bowl, gr, 7".........................45.00
Golden Harvest (US Glass), wine, marigold 28.00
Golden Honeycomb (Imperial), bonbon, amber 60.00
Golden Oxen, mug, marigold..................................48.00
Good Luck (Northwood), bowl, lav, 8¾" 900.00
Gooseberry Spray, bowl, bl, 5".............................125.00
Graceful (Northwood), vase, wht............................185.00
Grand Thistle (Finland), pitcher, bl, rare 1,800.00
Grape (Imperial), cup & saucer set, gr......................85.00
Grape (Imperial), spittoon whimsey, gr..................2,050.00
Grape (Imperial), wine, gr...................................35.00
Grape (Northwood's Grape & Cable), cup, pastel.............60.00
Grape (Northwood's Grape & Cable), humidor, bl, w/lid 1,200.00
Grape & Gothic Arches (Northwood), bowl, amethyst, 10" 55.00
Grape & Gothic Arches (Northwood), bowl, gr, 5".............45.00
Grape & Gothic Arches (Northwood), creamer, bl..............80.00
Grape Arbor (Dugan), bowl, wht, ftd, 11".................110.00
Grape Arbor (Northwood), hat, marigold 60.00
Grape Arbor (Northwood), pitcher, ice gr...............3,800.00
Grape Arbor (Northwood), tumbler, bl......................260.00
Grape Delight (Dugan), bowl, nut; wht, ftd, 6".............80.00
Grape Leaves (Northwood), bowl, marigold, 8¾" 60.00
Grape Wreath (Millersburg), bowl, bl, 9"...................400.00
Grape Wreath (Millersburg), bowl, clambroth, 5"............90.00
Grapevine Lattice (Dugan), bowl, gr, 8½".....................55.00
Grapevine Lattice (Dugan), bowl, marigold, 5" 26.00
Grapevine Lattice (Fenton), pitcher, wht, rare 850.00
Greek Key (Northwood), bowl, amethyst, 8½"................90.00
Greek Key (Northwood), pitcher, gr, rare 1,085.00
Greencard Furniture (Millersburg), bowl, amethyst, rare.............800.00
Harvest Flower (Dugan), pitcher, marigold, rare.....................1,250.00
Harvest Poppy, compote, peach opal.........................160.00
Hattie (Imperial), bowl, gr...................................65.00
Hawaiian Lei (Higbee), sugar bowl, marigold................65.00
Headdress, compote, bl.......................................46.00
Heart & Horseshoe (Fenton), bowl, marigold, 8½".........800.00
Heart & Trees (Fenton), bowl, gr, 8¾".....................195.00
Heart & Vine (Fenton), plate, advertising; marigold, rare 400.00
Heart Band Souvenir (McKee), mug, marigold, lg............90.00
Hearts & Flowers (Northwood), bowl, bl, 8½"...............58.00
Heavy Diamond (Imperial), bowl, marigold, 10"............32.00
Heavy Heart (Higbee), tumbler, marigold....................75.00
Heavy Hobnail (Fenton), vase, amethyst, rare..............475.00
Heavy Hobs, lamp, peach opal, amber base.................195.00
Heavy Prisms (English), celery vase, amethyst, 6"..........90.00
Heavy Shell (Fenton), bowl, pastel, 8¼"...................150.00
Heavy Vine, lamp, marigold.................................162.00
Heisey Flute, cup, punch; marigold..........................28.00
Heron (Dugan), mug, marigold, rare........................800.00
Hexagon & Cane (Imperial), sugar bowl, marigold, w/lid............65.00

Hobnail (Fenton), vase, wht, 11" 75.00
Hobnail (Millersburg), butter dish, marigold, rare..........470.00
Hobnail (Millersburg), creamer, bl, rare..........................500.00
Hobnail (Millersburg), tumbler, bl, rare..........................950.00
Hobnail Panels (McKee), vase, clambroth, 8¾"..................65.00
Hobnail Soda Gold (Imperial), spittoon, wht, lg..................50.00
Hobnail Vt (Millersburg), jardiniere, amethyst, rare...................900.00
Hobnail Vt (Millersburg), rose bowl, marigold, rare...................850.00
Hobnail Vt (Millersburg), vase whimsey, gr, rare.....................250.00
Hobstar (Imperial), bowl, berry; marigold, 10".................35.00
Hobstar (Imperial), bowl, fruit; amethyst, w/base............85.00
Hobstar (Imperial), butter dish, gr.................................185.00
Hobstar & Arches (Imperial), bowl, smoke, 9".................52.00
Hobstar & Cut Triangles (English), plate, gr....................110.00
Hobstar & Cut Triangles (English), rose bowl, amethyst............55.00
Hobstar & Feather (Millersburg), compote, marigold, rare, 6" .. 1,500.00
Hobstar & Fruit (Westmoreland), bowl, aqua opal, rare, 6" 270.00
Hobstar Band (Imperial), celery, marigold 85.00

Hobstar Flower (Northwood), compote, blue, scarce, $75.00.

Hobstar Panels (English), creamer, marigold..................45.00
Hobstar Reversed (English), butter dish, marigold 58.00
Holly, Panelled (Northwood), bonbon, marigold, ftd..........55.00
Holly (Fenton), bowl, aqua opal, 8"..............................390.00
Holly (Fenton), hat, gr...38.00
Holly & Berry (Dugan), bowl, marigold, 7" 38.00
Holly Sprig or Whirl (Millersburg), bowl, gr, rnd, 7" 60.00
Holly Sprig Vt (Millersburg), bowl, gr, scarce.................245.00
Honeycomb (Dugan), rose bowl, peach opal....................235.00
Honeycomb & Clover (Fenton), bonbon, amber...............70.00
Honeycomb & Clover (Imperial-Fenton), spooner, marigold........90.00
Honeycomb Ornament, hatpin, bl..................................70.00
Horses Heads (Fenton), bowl, red, flat, 7½"................ 1,100.00
Horseshoe, shot glass, marigold....................................42.00
Hourglass, vase, bud; marigold......................................46.00
Humpty-Dumpty, mustard jar, marigold 75.00
Hyacinth, lamp, marigold 1,900.00
Idyll (Fenton), vase, bl, rare.......................................650.00
Illinois Daisy (English), bowl, marigold, 8"......................40.00
Illusion (Fenton), bowl, bl...90.00
Imperial #5 (Imperial), bowl, amber, 8"..........................45.00
Imperial #9 (Imperial), compote, marigold 38.00
Indiana Statehouse (Fenton), plate, bl, rare............. 3,350.00
Intaglio Daisy (English), bowl, marigold, 4½".................26.00
Intaglio Feathers, cup, marigold...................................25.00
Intaglio Ovals (US Glass), bowl, aqua opal, 7"................65.00
Interior Panels, mug, marigold......................................75.00
Interior Poinsettia (Northwood), tumbler, marigold, rare..........465.00

Interior Rays, sherbet, marigold....................................35.00
Interior Rays (Westmoreland), jam jar, marigold 40.00
Interior Swirl, spittoon, peach opal...............................95.00
Inverted Coin Dot (Northwood-Fenton), bowl, marigold........38.00
Inverted Coin Dot (Northwood-Fenton), pitcher, bl 400.00
Inverted Strawberry, bowl, amethyst, 5" 50.00
Inverted Thistle (Cambridge), butter dish, gr, rare 700.00
Inverted Thistle (Cambridge), spittoon, amethyst, rare 3,900.00
Iris (Fenton), compote, gr...58.00
IW Harper, decanter, marigold, w/stopper 75.00
Jacob's Ladder Vt (US Glass), rose bowl, marigold 52.00
Jacobean Ranger (Czech & English), pitcher, marigold..........250.00
Jacobean Ranger (Czech & English), wine, marigold 28.00
Jeweled Heart (Dugan), bowl, peach opal, 10"..............135.00
Jewels (Imperial), sugar bowl, red................................235.00
Jockey Club (Northwood), bowl, amethyst, 7"................245.00
Kangaroo (Australian), bowl, marigold, 9½"..................170.00
Kingfisher & Variant (Australian), bowl, amethyst, 9½" 190.00
Knotted Beads (Fenton), vase, gr, 4".............................40.00
Kokomo (English), rose bowl, marigold, ftd.....................45.00
Large Kangaroo (Australian), bowl, amethyst, 10"...........185.00
Lattice & Daisy (Dugan), bowl, marigold, 9".....................60.00
Lattice & Grape (Fenton), pitcher, peach opal 1,800.00
Lattice & Grape (Fenton), tumbler, gr 55.00
Lattice & Leaves, vase, marigold, 9½".............................50.00
Lattice & Points (Dugan), vase, amethyst 42.00
Lattice & Sprays, vase, marigold, 10½"...........................40.00
Lattice Heart (English), bowl, amethyst 75.00
Lattice Heart (English), compote, bl..............................85.00
Laurel & Grape, vase, marigold, 6"...............................110.00
Laurel Band, tumbler, marigold.....................................42.00
Laurel Leaves (Imperial), plate, smoke..........................60.00
Lea & Vt (English), creamer, marigold, ftd......................40.00
Leaf & Beads (Northwood-Dugan), plate whimsey, marigold......200.00
Leaf & Beads (Northwood-Dugan), rose bowl, wht, ftd 500.00
Leaf Chain (Fenton), plate, aqua opal, 9¼" 2,100.00
Leaf Column (Northwood), vase, ice bl..........................170.00
Leaf Rays (Dugan), nappy, marigold 28.00
Leaf Swirl (Westmoreland), compote, amber 60.00
Leaf Swirl & Flower (Fenton), vase, marigold 45.00
Leaf Tiers (Fenton), butter dish, marigold, ftd................175.00
Lily of the Valley (Fenton), pitcher, bl, rare 4,500.00
Lily of the Valley (Fenton), tumbler, marigold, rare..........600.00
Little Fishes (Fenton), bowl, wht, flat or ftd, 10" 850.00
Little Owl, hatpin, bl, rare..165.00
Loganberry (Imperial), vase, amber, scarce....................450.00
Long Thumbprint (Dugan), butter dish, marigold..............60.00
Long Thumbprint (Dugan), vase, peach opal, 7" 146.00
Lotus & Grape (Fenton), bonbon, red............................850.00
Lotus & Grape (Fenton), bowl, gr, flat, 7"......................50.00
Lotus Land (Northwood), bonbon, marigold....................595.00
Louisa (Westmoreland), bowl, russet, ftd.......................50.00
Louisa (Westmoreland), rose bowl, amber......................140.00
Lovebirds, bottle, marigold, w/stopper..........................400.00
Luster, tumbler, marigold 40.00
Lustre & Clear (Imperial), pitcher, marigold...................195.00
Lustre & Clear (Imperial), vase, gr, ftd, 8".....................120.00
Lustre Flute (Northwood), bowl, marigold, 5½"...............36.00
Lustre Flute (Northwood), compote, amethyst.................48.00
Lustre Rose (Imperial), bowl, clambroth, flat, 11"............60.00
Lustre Rose (Imperial), butter dish, amber...................100.00
Lutz (McKee), mug, marigold, ftd 45.00
Magnolia Drape, pitcher, marigold 240.00
Magpie (Australian), bowl, amethyst, 6"........................56.00

Maize (Libbey), celery vase, clear, rare 185.00
Many Fruits (Dugan), bowl, punch; wht, w/base 1,200.00
Maple Leaf (Dugan), bowl, marigold, stem, 9" 70.00
Maple Leaf (Dugan), pitcher, amethyst 325.00
Maple Leaf (Dugan), sugar bowl, gr.............................70.00

Marilyn (Millersburg), pitcher, green, rare, $1,300.00.

Marilyn (Millersburg), tumbler, amethyst, rare 280.00
Mary Ann (Dugan), vase, amethyst, 2 varieties, 7" 80.00
Massachusetts (US Glass), vase, marigold 150.00
Mayflower, compote, pastel.............................60.00
Maypole, vase, amethyst, 6¼" 50.00
Melon Rib (Imperial), pitcher, marigold.............................60.00
Melon Rib (Imperial), tumbler, marigold.............................24.00
Memphis (Northwood), bowl, amethyst, 10" 195.00
Memphis (Northwood), bowl, fruit; ice bl, w/base.................. 3,000.00
Mikado (Fenton), compote, red, lg 5,000.00
Milady (Fenton), pitcher, amethyst 650.00
Milady (Fenton), tumbler, marigold.............................95.00
Miniature Hobnail, cordial set, marigold, rare.............................750.00
Mirrored Lotus (Fenton), bonbon, gr.............................60.00
Mitered Diamond & Pleats (English), bowl, bl, 4½" 30.00
Mitered Ovals (Millersburg), vase, gr, rare 4,500.00
Moon & Star (Westmoreland), compote, pearl carnival.............365.00
Moonprint (English), butter dish, marigold.............................100.00
Moonprint (English), cheese keeper, marigold, rare.................135.00
Morning-Glory (Millersburg), pitcher, gr, rare.......................... 9,700.00
Morning-Glory (Millersburg), tumbler, marigold, rare 1,000.00
Mystic (Cambridge), vase, marigold, ftd, rare.............................120.00
Nautilus (Dugan-Northwood), compote, marigold, rare.......... 2,600.00
Near Cut (Cambridge), decanter, gr, w/stopper, rare.............. 2,600.00
Near Cut Souvenir (Cambridge), mug, marigold, rare.................175.00
Nell (Higbee), mug, marigold.............................65.00
Nesting Swan (Millersburg), bowl, vaseline, rnd, rare, 10"...... 2,650.00
Nesting Swan (Millersburg), rose bowl, marigold, rare 2,500.00
New Orleans Shrine (US Glass), champagne, clear......................90.00
Night Stars (Millersburg), nappy, amethyst, tricorner 1,800.00
Nippon (Northwood), bowl, ice gr, 8½" 625.00
Northern Star (Fenton), bowl, marigold, 6" 28.00
Northwood Jester's Cap, vase, peach opal.............................75.00
Northwood's Nearcut, goblet, marigold, rare.............................110.00
Northwood's Poppy, dish, pickle; aqua opal, oval.....................800.00
Nuggate, pitcher, bl, 6".............................90.00
Number 2176 (Sowerby), lemon squeezer, marigold.....................50.00
Number 270 (Westmoreland), compote, aqua............................115.00
Number 4 (Imperial), compote, marigold 30.00
Octagon (Imperial), butter dish, gr.............................126.00

Octagon (Imperial), decanter, marigold, complete.....................85.00
Octagon (Imperial), goblet, pastel.............................80.00
Octet (Northwood), bowl, marigold, 8½".............................48.00
Ohio Star (Millersburg), vase, wht, rare.............................3,500.00
Oklahoma (Mexican), pitcher, marigold, rare...........................495.00
Omnibus, tumbler, marigold, rare 375.00
Open Rose (Imperial), bowl, fruit; gr, 7" 68.00
Open Rose (Imperial), plate, amber, 9" 200.00
Optic (Imperial), bowl, amethyst, 9".............................75.00
Optic Flute (Imperial), bowl, smoke, 5".............................28.00
Optic 66 (Fostoria), goblet, marigold 45.00
Orange Tree (Fenton), bowl, red, flat, 8" 695.00
Orange Tree (Fenton), cup, marigold 28.00
Orange Tree (Fenton), pitcher, lime opal, 2 designs............. 8,000.00
Orange Tree & Scroll (Fenton), pitcher, marigold 465.00
Orange Tree Orchard (Fenton), pitcher, wht.............................675.00
Oriental Poppy (Northwood), pitcher, ice gr 1,800.00
Ostrich (Australian), cake stand, amethyst, rare 320.00
Oval & Round (Imperial), bowl, pastel, 9" 58.00
Palm Beach (US Glass), pitcher, marigold 450.00
Palm Beach (US Glass), vase whimsey, amethyst 120.00
Panama (US Glass), goblet, marigold, rare 120.00
Panelled Dandelion (Fenton), pitcher, marigold........................410.00
Panelled Hobnail (Dugan), vase, marigold, 5".............................45.00
Panelled Prism, jam jar, marigold, w/lid.............................48.00
Panelled Smocking, sugar bowl, marigold.............................65.00
Panels & Ball (Fenton), bowl, marigold, 11" 48.00
Pansy (Imperial), bowl, gr, 8¾" 45.00
Pansy (Imperial), plate, amethyst, ruffled, rare.............................90.00
Panther (Fenton), bowl, wht, ftd, 10" 675.00
Parlor Panels, vase, marigold, 4" 38.00
Pastel Panels (Imperial), creamer, pastel 60.00
Pastel Panels (Imperial), pitcher, pastel 320.00
Peach (Northwood), bowl, wht, 5" 60.00
Peach (Northwood), butter dish, wht 220.00
Peach (Northwood), spooner, marigold.............................260.00
Peach Blossom, bowl, amethyst, 7½" 70.00
Peacock, Fluffy (Fenton), pitcher, marigold 500.00
Peacock, Strutting (Westmoreland), creamer, gr, w/lid 60.00
Peacock (Millersburg), bowl, clambroth, 9" 600.00
Peacock (Millersburg), rose bowl whimsey, vaseline, rare 3,200.00
Peacock & Dahlia (Fenton), bowl, wht, 7½".............................150.00
Peacock & Grape (Fenton), bowl, red, flat or ftd, 7¾" 750.00
Peacock & Urn (Fenton), bowl, red, 8½" 3,500.00
Peacock & Urn (Fenton), goblet, marigold, rare 60.00
Peacock & Urn (Northwood), bowl, marigold, 9" 65.00
Peacock & Urn & Vts (Millersburg), bowl, gr, 9½" 260.00
Peacock at the Fountain (Dugan), pitcher, bl 395.00
Peacock at the Fountain (Northwood), bowl, gr, 9" 95.00
Peacock at the Fountain (Northwood), cup, bl 40.00
Peacock at the Fountain (Northwood), spittoon whimsey, gr ... 3,200.00
Peacock Tail (Fenton), bonbon, gr 40.00
Peacock Tail (Fenton), plate, amethyst, 9" 225.00
Peacock Tail Vt (Millersburg), compote, amethyst, scarce 100.00
Pearl & Jewels (Fenton), basket, wht, 4" 190.00
Perfection (Millersburg), pitcher, marigold, rare 4,000.00
Perfection (Millersburg), tumbler, gr, rare 650.00
Persian Garden (Dugan), bowl, fruit; peach opal, w/base.............495.00
Persian Garden (Dugan), bowl, ice cream; wht, 11" 310.00
Persian Medallion (Fenton), bonbon, ice bl 375.00
Persian Medallion (Fenton), compote, amethyst 57.00
Persian Medallion (Fenton), plate, wht, 9½" 500.00
Petal & Fan (Dugan), bowl, amethyst, 8½" 80.00
Petal & Fan (Dugan), bowl, peach opal, 10" 195.00

Petals (Dugan), compote, pastel 80.00
Pillow & Sunburst (Westmoreland), bowl, amber, 7½" 62.00
Pin-Ups (Australian), bowl, amethyst, rare, 8¾"...................110.00
Pine Cone (Fenton), bowl, gr, 6" 46.00
Pine Cone (Fenton), plate, bl, rare, 8" 96.00
Pineapple (English), bowl, amethyst, 7" 56.00
Pineapple (English), compote, bl 52.00
Pinwheel (Dugan), bowl, marigold, 6" 38.00
Pinwheel (English), vase, marigold, 8" 150.00
Plaid (Fenton), bowl, red, 8¾" 4,000.00
Plain Jane (Imperial), basket, marigold 60.00
Plain Petals (Northwood), nappy, gr, scarce 90.00
Plume Panels, vase, marigold, 7" 40.00
Poinsettia (Imperial), pitcher, milk; gr 250.00
Poinsettia (Northwood), bowl, bl, flat or ftd, 8½" 290.00
Pond Lily (Fenton), bonbon, gr...................................50.00
Pony (Dugan), bowl, aqua, 8½" 470.00
Poppy (Millersburg), compote, marigold, scarce 650.00
Poppy (Millersburg), salver, gr, rare 1,450.00
Poppy Show (Imperial), hurricane whimsey, amethyst 2,000.00
Poppy Show (Northwood), bowl, marigold, 8½" 320.00
Premium (Imperial), bowl, marigold, 8½" 45.00
Pretty Panels (Fenton), tumbler, marigold, hdld 52.00
Pretty Panels (Northwood), pitcher, gr...........................160.00
Pretty Panels (Northwood), tumbler, marigold.....................60.00
Primrose (Millersburg), bowl, bl, ruffled, 8¾" 4,000.00
Primrose (Millersburg), bowl, ice cream; marigold, 9" 110.00
Princely Plumes, candle holder, amethyst.........................260.00
Prism, hatpin, amethyst 40.00
Prism, tray, marigold, 3" 45.00
Prism & Daisy Band (Imperial), bowl, marigold, 8" 30.00
Propeller (Imperial), compote, marigold 30.00
Pulled Loop (Dugan), vase, bl 30.00
Puzzle (Dugan), compote, peach opal..............................75.00
Quartered Block, sugar bowl, marigold 50.00
Question Marks (Dugan), bonbon, ice gr...........................75.00
Quill (Dugan), pitcher, marigold, rare.........................1,400.00
Quill (Dugan), tumbler, amethyst, rare...........................450.00
Rainbow (Northwood), compote, gr.................................145.00
Raindrops (Dugan), bowl, marigold, 9" 50.00
Rambler Rose (Dugan), pitcher, bl 200.00
Rambler Rose (Dugan), tumbler, marigold 30.00
Ranger (Mexican), nappy, marigold 80.00
Ranger (Mexican), pitcher, marigold, rare 285.00
Raspberry (Northwood), bowl, marigold, 5" 28.00
Raspberry (Northwood), sauce boat, bl, ftd 160.00
Rays (Dugan), bowl, peach opal, 9" 125.00
Rays & Ribbons (Millersburg), bowl, gr, sq 135.00
Rays & Ribbons (Millersburg), plate, marigold, rare............1,100.00
Rib & Panel (Fenton), vase, marigold.............................45.00
Ribbed Elipse, mug, clambroth, rare..............................90.00
Ribbed Swirl, tumbler, gr 70.00
Ribbon & Fern, atomizer, marigold, 7" 75.00
Ribbon Tie (Fenton), bowl, bl, 8¾" 55.00
Rings, vase, marigold, 8" 55.00
Ripple (Imperial), vase, gr 40.00
Rising Sun (US Glass), butter dish, marigold.....................150.00
Rising Sun (US Glass), pitcher, bl, 2 shapes, rare.............1,850.00
Robin (Imperial), mug, smoke, old only 150.00
Rococo (Imperial), bowl, gr, 5" 140.00
Roll, tumbler, marigold..38.00
Rose Bouquet, creamer, marigold 54.00
Rose Garden (Sweden), pitcher, communion; marigold, rare..1,200.00
Rose Pinwheel, bowl, gr, rare 2,000.00

Rose Show (Northwood), bowl, custard irid, 8¾" 2,500.00
Rose Show Vt (Northwood), plate, aqua opal, 9" 1,000.00
Rose Spray (Fenton), compote, marigold...........................160.00

Rose Tree (Fenton) bowl, marigold, $350.00.

Roses & Fruit (Millersburg), bl, ftd, rare 1,000.00
Rosetime, vase, marigold 85.00
Rosettes (Northwood), bowl, marigold, dome base, 9" 58.00
Royalty (Imperial), bowl, punch; marigold, w/base 125.00
Ruffled Rib (Northwood), spittoon whimsey, marigold, rare 200.00
Ruffles & Rings (Northwood), bowl, peach opal, very rare.........900.00
Rustic (Fenton), vase, funeral; gr, 14" 220.00
S-Band (Australian), compote, amethyst...........................65.00
S-Repeat (Dugan), creamer, amethyst, sm 60.00
Sailboats (Fenton), goblet, gr...................................260.00
Sailboats (Fenton), plate, marigold..............................450.00
Saint (English), candlestick, marigold, ea.......................275.00
Salamanders, hatpin, amethyst 45.00
Scale Band (Fenton), plate, red, flat, 6½" 410.00
Scale Band (Fenton), tumbler, bl.................................35.00
Scales (Westmoreland), bonbon, teal..............................60.00
Scroll & Flower Panels (Imperial), vase, bl, old only, 10"......260.00
Scroll Embossed (Imperial), bowl, aqua, 8½"......................55.00
Scroll Embossed (Imperial), dish, dessert; gr, rnd...............120.00
Scroll Embossed Vt (English), ash tray, amethyst, hdld, 5".......60.00
Seacoast (Millersburg), tray, pin; bl, rare......................300.00
Serrated Ribs, shaker, marigold, ea..............................50.00
Shell (Imperial), plate, amethyst, 8½" 145.00
Shell & Jewel (Westmoreland), sugar bowl, wht, w/lid.............90.00
Sheraton (US Glass), butter dish, pastel.........................120.00
Sheraton (US Glass), pitcher, pastel 165.00
Ships & Stars, plate, marigold, 8"...............................30.00
Shrine (US Glass), champagne, clear 160.00
Signet (English), sugar bowl, marigold, w/lid, 6½" 70.00
Silver Queen (Fenton), pitcher, marigold.........................175.00
Singing Birds (Northwood), creamer, marigold.....................80.00
Singing Birds (Northwood), mug, aqua opal 1,800.00
Singing Birds (Northwood), pitcher, gr...........................390.00
Single Flower (Dugan), basket whimsey, bl, rare..................850.00
Single Flower (Dugan), bowl, bl, 8"..............................70.00
Six Petals (Dugan), hat, blk amethyst 125.00
Six-Sided (Imperial), candlestick, amethyst, ea..................275.00
Ski-Star (Dugan), bowl, bl, 8"...................................165.00
Ski-Star (Dugan), rose bowl, peach opal, rare 500.00
Small Rib (Dugan), compote, gr...................................40.00
Small Thumbprint, creamer, marigold 60.00
Smooth Panels (Imperial), bowl, pastel marigold, 6½".............35.00
Smooth Panels (Imperial), pitcher, gr 170.00

Smooth Rays (Imperial), bonbon, marigold 26.00
Smooth Rays (Northwood-Dugan), plate, marigold, 7" 60.00
Smooth Rays (Westmoreland), compote, amber 65.00
Soda Gold (Imperial), pitcher, marigold..210.00
Soda Gold Spears (Dugan), bowl, clear, 8½" 40.00
Soldiers & Sailors (Fenton), plate, bl, Indiana, rare 3,000.00
Sphinx (English), paperweight, amber, rare 475.00
Spiderweb (Northwood), candy dish, smoke, w/lid....................35.00
Spiderweb & Tree Bark (Dugan), vase, pastel, 6" 60.00
Spiral (Imperial), candlestick, gr, ea 75.00
Springtime (Northwood), bowl, gr, 9" 220.00
Springtime (Northwood), pitcher, amethyst, rare.................. 1,000.00
Springtime (Northwood), sugar bowl, marigold 335.00
Stag & Holly (Fenton), bowl, red, ftd, 13" 2,400.00
Stag & Holly (Fenton), plate, bl, ftd, 9" 1,800.00
Star & Diamond Point, hatpin, amethyst 50.00
Star & File (Imperial), decanter, marigold, w/stopper 110.00
Star & File (Imperial), wine, ice gr...200.00
Star Medallion (Imperial), bonbon, gr 60.00
Star Medallion (Imperial), butter dish, marigold........................100.00

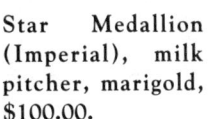

Star Medallion (Imperial), milk pitcher, marigold, $100.00.

Star Spray (Imperial), bowl, pastel, 7" 30.00
Starfish (Dugan), bonbon, peach opal, hdld, rare.........................145.00
Stars & Bars, wine, marigold 40.00
Stippled Petals (Dugan), basket, peach opal, hdld 160.00
Stippled Rambler Rose (Dugan), bowl, nut; bl, ftd 75.00
Stippled Rays (Fenton), bonbon, red..350.00
Stork & Rushes (Dugan), butter dish, amethyst, rare..................165.00
Stork & Rushes (Dugan), mug, bl 350.00
Ten Mums (Fenton), pitcher, wht, rare 1,400.00
Thin Rib (Fenton), candlestick, marigold, pr 60.00
Thistle & Lotus (Fenton), bowl, marigold, 7"..............................50.00
Thistle & Thorn (English), creamer, marigold.............................50.00
Three Diamonds (Dugan), vase, amethyst, 6" 46.00
Three Fruits (Northwood), bowl, aqua opal, 9" 1,000.00
Three Fruits (Northwood), plate, aqua opal, rnd, 9".............. 3,900.00
Three Fruits Vt (Dugan), plate, amethyst, 12-sided 200.00
Three Row (Imperial), vase, amethyst, rare 1,000.00
Three-In-One (Imperial), plate, smoke, 6½" 80.00
Tree Bark (Imperial), candlestick, marigold, 7".........................60.00
Tree of Life (Imperial), plate, marigold, 7½" 37.00
Tree Trunk (Northwood), vase, funeral; ice bl, 15" 150.00
Tulip Scroll (Millersburg), vase, marigold, rare, 6" 260.00
US Diamond Block (US Glass), compote, peach opal, rare..........75.00
Venetian (Cambridge), creamer, clambroth, rare........................500.00
Vineyard (Dugan), tumbler, wht...265.00
Vineyard & Fishnet (Imperial), vase, red, rare 600.00
Vining Leaf & Vt (English), spittoon, marigold, rare...................350.00

Vintage (Fenton), bowl, red, 8" 875.00
Vintage Banded (Dugan), tumbler, marigold, rare 500.00
Vintage Vt (Dugan), plate, marigold 295.00
Waffle Block (Imperial), pitcher, marigold...................................140.00
Waffle Block (Imperial), plate, smoke, 10" 165.00
Waffle Block (Imperial), tumbler, marigold.................................200.00
War Dance (English), compote, marigold, 5" 75.00
Water Lily (Fenton), bowl, red, ftd, 5" 750.00
Water Lily & Cattails (Fenton), spittoon whimsey, marigold . 1,600.00
Water Lily & Cattails (Fenton), toothpick whimsey, red 550.00
Water Lily & Cattails (Fenton), tumbler, marigold 95.00
Water Lily & Cattails (Northwood), pitcher, marigold 410.00
Water Lily & Cattails (Northwood), tumbler, bl, rare............. 2,700.00
Western Daisy (Westmoreland), bowl, milk glass opal 167.00
Wheat (Northwood), sweetmeat, gr, w/lid, rare 2,500.00
Whirling Hobstar (US Glass), bowl, punch; marigold, w/base.....120.00
Whirling Leaves (Millersburg), bowl, clambroth, 9" 120.00
Wild Strawberry (Dugan), bowl, peach opal, 9" 350.00
Windflower (Dugan), plate, bl, 9" 160.00
Windmill (Imperial), bowl, fruit; gr, 10½" 40.00
Windmill (Imperial), pitcher, milk; amethyst 165.00
Wine & Roses (Fenton), wine, aqua 100.00
Wishbone (Northwood), epergne, ice bl, rare 900.00
Wreath of Roses (Dugan), spittoon whimsey, amber, rare 150.00
Wreath of Roses (Fenton), bonbon, marigold..............................36.00
Zig Zag (Fenton), pitcher, bl, decor, rare 400.00
Zig Zag (Millersburg), bowl, amethyst, tricorner, 10" 550.00
Zip Zip (English), flower frog, marigold 54.00
Zipper Stitch (Czech), cordial set, marigold, 6-pc 1,200.00
Zippered Heart, bowl, amethyst, 9"..110.00

Carousel Figures

Who can forget the dazzle of the merry-go-round — lights blinking, animals prancing proudly by to the waltzes that bellowed from the band organ . . .

Gustav Dentzel, a German woodworker, created one of the first carousels in America in 1867. By the turn of the century, his animals had evolved from horses with a military bearing to fanciful creatures in various postures with garlands of flowers, exotic saddles, and other adornment. Dentzel was followed in the business by his son William, and both are noted for the exacting perfection of their carving and painting. The Philadelphia Toboggan Company, established in 1903, is famous today for its superior chariot designs. In 1901 Marcus Charles Illions formed his company, M.C. Illions and Sons. Illions' carvings became more intricate with the growth of his company, and those from the twenties are generally valued more highly than those from between 1901 and 1910. The largest carousels were produced by the Artistic Carousel Manufacturers of Brooklyn, Harry Goldstein and Solomon Stein. Charles Carmel and Daniel Muller are both exquisite carvers whose work is today very highly regarded. Other builders whose works are also very valuable (though much less intricate) are The Herschell-Spillman Company; American Merry-Go-Round and Novelty Company; Charles Dare of the New York Carousel Manufacturing Company; and Charles Parker.

Until the 1930s, carousels were found in nearly every fair and amusement park in the country. One by one, as they fell into disrepair, many have been dismantled and junked or sold at auction. Today these hand-carved creatures are respected examples of American folk art and often bring prices well into the thousands. Price is based on a number of factors, the most important of which are: carver (with Dentzel, Looff, PTC, Carmel, Illions, and Muller the most valued), type of animal (some species are rarely encountered), and intricacy of carving. Also to be considered are size, wood and paint condition, where the figure was located on the carousel, whether it stands or jumps, and in some cases its age. Because there are so many factors to consider and since no two figures are identical, exact pricing is difficult. All of these prices are from public auctions; and, where applicable, the 10% buyers premium is included. All animals listed were in good condition. Our price list was furnished by *The Carousel News & Trader*; for subscription information see the Directory under Clubs, Newsletters, and Catalogs.

Key:
IR — inside row   OR — outside row
MR — middle row   PTC — Philadelphia Toboggan
                                   Co.

Allan Herschell, half & half (wood & aluminum)	2,200.00
Allan Herschell jumper, blanket	2,310.00
Allan Herschell Trojan jumper horse, rstr	5,280.00
Anderson dbl-seater galloper	4,400.00
Anderson dragon	11,000.00
Armitage Herschell jumper, rstr	4,730.00
Armitage Herschell jumper, track machine	6,600.00
Bayol donkey	16,500.00
Bayol goat	5,500.00
Bayol rabbit	4,950.00
Carmel jumper	10,450.00
Carmel stander, IR	12,100.00
Carmel stander, OR	28,600.00
Dare horse	5,200.00

Dare, dapple gray, marble eyes, original paint (worn), minor losses, 42" long, $2,500.00.

Dentzel cat, fish in mouth, fiberglass coating	28,600.00
Dentzel deer, jumper	19,500.00
Dentzel jumper	8,000.00
Dentzel ostrich, stripped	24,200.00
Dentzel pig, w/acorn	13,000.00
Dentzel prancer	14,000.00
Dentzel rounding board, hen & rooster picture	4,000.00
Dentzel rounding board, moose picture	1,500.00
Dentzel shield	1,000.00
Dentzel stander, 'Dandy' horse	52,000.00
Dentzel stander, roached mane	29,500.00
Dentzel tiger	57,500.00
Herschell-Spillman jumper	5,280.00
Herschell-Spillman jumper, rstr	8,800.00
Herschell-Spillman mule	10,450.00
Heyn jumper	5,775.00
Illions deer, w/eagle, OR	34,000.00
Illions jumper, IR	9,000.00
Illions jumper, MR, roached mane	12,000.00
Illions jumper, OR	25,300.00

Illions rounding board	1,000.00
Looff camel	13,200.00
Looff deer, OR	15,400.00
Looff giraffe	13,200.00
Looff goat	12,300.00
Looff jumper, early	7,480.00
Looff prancer	9,900.00
Looff stander, IR	6,050.00
Muller pig	4,840.00
Muller stander, OR, rstr	42,900.00
Parker jumper, armoured	12,500.00
Parker jumper, early track machine	10,780.00
Parker jumper, Indian head, MR	5,000.00
Parker jumper, IR	3,850.00
Parker jumper, stargazer, w/bearskin & feathers	28,600.00
PTC, western-style/military, Niagara Falls carousel	36,000.00
PTC jumper, IR	5,000.00
PTC jumper, MR	7,700.00
PTC stander, w/knotted tail, OR	22,000.00
Savage cockerel	5,720.00
Savage ostrich	5,390.00
Spooner rooster	5,225.00
Stein & Goldstein jumper, IR	7,200.00
Stein & Goldstein jumper, MR	15,000.00
Stein & Goldstein stander, MR	10,500.00
Stein & Goldstein stander, OR, rstr	21,670.00

Carpet Balls

Carpet balls are glazed china spheres decorated with intersecting lines or other simple designs that were used for indoor games in the British Isles during the early 1800s. Mint condition examples are rare.

Bl intersecting lines on wht, 3½"	150.00
Blk & bl bull's eye on wht, 3", NM	112.50
Blk w/blk dots w/in frilly wht circles, 3¼"	100.00
Gold velvet, multi-pieced, late 19th C, child's, 3½"	28.00
Gr & blk stripes spanning 3 directions on wht, 3¼"	70.00
Gr dots & circles in wht frilly circles, 3⅜", EX	80.00
Pk w/pk circles w/in wht circles, 3½", EX	88.00
Wht w/bands of yel stripes spanning 3 directions, 3¼"	85.00

Cartoon Art

Collectors of cartoon art are interested in many forms of original art — animation cels, sports, political or editorial cartoons, syndicated comic strip panels, and caricature. To produce even a short animated cartoon strip, hundreds of original drawings are required, each showing the characters in slightly advancing positions. Called 'cels' because those made prior to the 1950s were made from a celluloid material, collectors often pay hundreds of dollars for a frame from a favorite movie. Prices of Disney cels with backgrounds vary widely. Background paintings, model sheets, storyboards, and preliminary sketches are also collectible — so are comic book drawings executed in India ink and signed by the artist. Daily 'funnies' originals, especially the earlier ones portraying super heroes, and Sunday comic strips, the early as well as the later ones, are collected. Cartoon art has become recognized and valued as a novel yet valid form of contemporary art.

Animation Cel, Full Color

An American Tail, Fievel, Don Bluth Studio, fr, 7x13"	825.00
Autograph Hound, Sonja Henie, blk mat, 7x4", EX	300.00

Cinderella, Lucifer, gray mat, 1950, 7x6½" 275.00
Cinderella, Stepmother, bl mat, 7½x3¼" 385.00

Goofy and Professor Von Drake in the Library, unsigned, 8" x 11", VG, $400.00.

Jetsons, Elroy & Astro on elevator pad, 5x3" 80.00
Mickey's Xmas Carol, Goofy as ghost, Disney Studio, 6x8" 600.00
Peanuts, Charlie Brown & Woodstock, Schulz, 3x3½" 125.00
Peter Pan, Mrs Darling w/Michael & John, Disney, 7x5" 275.00
Punkin Puss, w/Mush Mouse, Hanna-Barbera, 1964, 7x9"...........365.00
Road Runner, full figure, Warner Bros, 1950s, 4x6" 650.00
Star Trek, Kirk & Spock, ltd ed of 500, 6½x6½"...........................285.00
Sword in Stone, Merlin, waist up, 1963, 9x7¼" 775.00
Sword in Stone, sorcerer & owl, 8x10" 350.00
Sword in Stone, sorcerer advising Prince, 8x10" 550.00
Tom & Jerry, Tom in sword fight, hand-inked, 1950s, 6x7" 185.00
Winnie the Poo, Christopher & Eeyore, pnt ground, 6x8" 195.00
Winnie the Poo, Roo w/lunch box, pnt ground, 6x8" 165.00
101 Dalmatians, Roger & Towser, Disney, 5x5", 7x10", pr..........935.00

Animation Drawing

Bambi, full figure, pencils, 1943, 5¼x4¼" image 700.00
Black Cauldron, Orwen, pencils, finished, matted, lg 245.00
Bugs Bunny, full figure in top hat & tails, 5x3" image..................55.00
Clock Cleaners, Goofy on tower, pencils, '37, 3x2½" image........300.00
Country Cousin, mouse w/umbrella, sgn Babbit............................195.00
Dumbo, Dumbo & mother, full figure, pencil, 1942, lg..............725.00
Foghorn Leghorn, EX details, 1950s, matted fr 335.00
Hunkey & Spunky, Spunky & mom, Waldman, '38, 6x8" image .300.00
Lady & Tramp, Tramp, full figured, pencils, lg.............................450.00
Mail Pilot, Mickey Mouse in smoking plane, ca 1933, M 1,450.00
Mickey's Parrot, MM w/shotgun, pencils, '38, 7x4½" image 635.00
Mother Goose Melodies, Mother Goose/duck, '31, 4x6" image ..385.00
Orphans Fit, Donald Duck, long bill, sailor hat, 1934, rare..........775.00
Peanuts, Snoopy in grass, pen/ink, Schulz, matted/fr, 6x9" 355.00
Peter Pan, Indian lady w/papoose, pencil, finished, lg.................335.00
Pinocchio, Gideon w/cane, pencils, '40, 6¾x9½" image 725.00
Pluto's Quin-Puplets, Pluto, full figure, pencil, 1937..................300.00
Sleeping Beauty, Briar Rose, pencil, '59, 8x5" image 335.00
Sleeping Beauty, Prince Phillip, pencil, '59, 5x3" image.............265.00
Snow White & 7 Dwarfs, Dopey, full figure, pencil, 4x4" image ..265.00
Taarna, sexy costume, pen/ink/marker, early.................................300.00
Toby Tortoise Returns, Toby w/boxing gloves, 1936, lg 965.00
Why Do Birds Fly, bird-watcher, pencils, Kimball, lg...................335.00
Winnie the Poo, rabbit close-up, early, matted, 10" image 245.00

Daily Newspaper Comic Strip

Blondie, w/Dagwood & Blk delivery lady, ink, Young, 1944........250.00
Donald & Daisy Duck, mountain climbing, pen/ink, 10/28/68 ...385.00
Fritzi Ritz, India ink, E Bushmiller, 5/14/39, 14x21" 330.00
Li'l Abner, w/Daisy Mae, Al Capp, 1/26/66, 5½x19" 250.00
Li'l Abner, Wolf Trapped, India ink, 8/26/66, 2 panels................260.00
Little Orphan Annie, India ink, Gray, 1958, 6x19½" 385.00
Mickey & Minnie Mouse, Mickey & salesmen, 4/22/68, 6x21"...385.00
Mickey Mouse & Goofy on desert island, 7/23/65, 6½x21" 365.00
Steve Canyon, India ink, Milton Caniff, 1983, 6x19" 330.00
Tailspin Tommy, rustlers, India ink, H Forrest, 1931, 6x23" 400.00
Tarzan of the Apes, India ink, J Celardo, 1950s, set of 3 ....400.00
Winnie the Pooh, w/Piglet & Christopher Robin, 10/4/82...........535.00

Model Sheets

Autograph Hound, Sonja Henie, 4 full figures/6 heads, 11x14"...385.00
Betty Boop, Fearless Fred (Betty's boyfriend), full sheet 135.00
Common Cold, Goofy, 1949, 3-pg, overall: 14x17" 135.00
Dumbo, elephants posed together, 1940, 11x14" 115.00
Early to Bed, Donald Duck prepares for bed, 1940, 11x14"..........235.00
Fantasia, baby Pegasus, 6 full-figure poses, 1940, 11x14" 220.00
Jungle Book, Mowgli, 6 poses, 1967, 12½x15" 135.00
Little Hiawatha, Hiawatha & animals, 1937, 12x15"...................185.00
Mickey Mouse, many poses & notes, dtd 1937, 10x13" 425.00
Pinocchio, Jiminy Cricket, 12 poses, 1939, 11x14" 435.00
Popeye, Olive, Wimpy & Sweet Pea, compare szs, 10x14" 165.00
Popeye, Olive in various poses, sgn Waldman, 10x12" 265.00
So Dear to My Heart, various animals, 1949, 14x17" 55.00
Superman, Clark Kent, 3 full figures/5 heads, '40s, 11x13".........525.00
Tom Cat, 3 full figures, pencil, Barbera initials, rare 975.00
Who Killed Cock Robin?, 15 action sketches, 1935, 11x14" 135.00
Winnie the Pooh, Kanga & Roo, 9 images, 11x14" 265.00

Storyboard

Donald Duck, pastels, ca 1942, 8" x 8½", $550.00.

Bad Luck Duck, Donald Duck, 1959, 2-pg, ea: 8½x16½" 295.00
Fantasia, flight of Pegasus' family, 1940, 11x14" 400.00
Lone Chipmunks, Chip & Dale in western garb, 1954, 3-pg 185.00
Make Mine Music, Johnny Fedora & Alice Bl Bonnet, '46, 3-pg .200.00
One Hundred & One Dalmatians, 1961, 2-sheet, 8½x16½"........200.00
Pluto w/hat & coat, leads dog sled, ink/watercolor.....................465.00
You Can't Win, Goofy & gambling, 1949, 3-pg, 14x17" overall .300.00

Sunday Newspaper Comics

Dick Tracy, India ink, C Gould, 8/6/61, 18x27"............................550.00

Donald Duck & Uncle Scrooge, pen/ink, 4/2/78, 16x21" 545.00
Tailspin Tommy, India ink, H Forrest, 1940-41, set of 21 ....265.00
Winnie the Poo, w/Piglet at Sir Brian's, pen/ink, 7/31/83 ....565.00
Yogi Bear, India ink, H Isenberg, 1961, 17¼x24½"......................200.00

Cartoon Books

'Books of cartoons' were printed during the first decade of the twentieth century and remained popular until the advent of the modern comic book in the late thirties. Cartoon books, printed in both color and black and white, were merely reprints of current newspaper comic strips. The books, ranging from thirty to seventy pages and in sizes from 3½" x 8" up to 11" x 17", were usually bound with cardboard covers and were often distributed as premiums in exchange for coupons saved from the daily paper. One of the largest of the companies who printed these books was Cupples and Leon, producer of nearly half of the two hundred titles on record. Among the most popular sellers were *Mutt and Jeff*, *Bringing Up Father*, and *Little Orphan Annie*.

Barney Google & Spark Plug, Cupples & Leon, EX, $70.00.

Bringing Up Father, #1, Cupples & Leon, EX 80.00
Bringing Up Father, #23, Cupples & Leon, 1933, NM 35.00
Bringing Up Father, #5, McManus, EX..40.00
Bringing Up Father, 1917, Star, NM..20.00
Charlie Chaplin Comic Capers, EX 50.00
Charlie Chaplin Up in the Air, EX 50.00
Hans Und Fritz, blk/wht illus, Dirks, Saalfield, 1917, EX 60.00
Little Lulu, glossy pgs, Rand McNally, 1950, EX 35.00
Little Orphan Annie, #1, Cupples & Leon, EX.............................125.00
Little Orphan Annie, #8, Cupples & Leon, 1933, NM 70.00
Mutt & Jeff, #1, Ball, EX 110.00
Mutt & Jeff, #4, Ball, VG 45.00
Mutt & Jeff, 1929, Cupples & Leon, EX 160.00
Percy & Ferdie, 1921, Cupples & Leon, EX...................................48.00
Skeezix & Pal, 1925, Reilley & Lee, EX...40.00
Skeezix & Uncle Walt, 1927, King, NM 35.00
Skeezix Out West, 1928, Reilley & Lee, EX 20.00
Winnie Winkle, #1, Cupples & Leon, EX 35.00

Cash Registers

Cash registers are being restored, rebuilt, and used as they were originally intended, in businesses ranging from eating establishments to antique stores. Their brass and marble construction has made them almost impervious to aging, and with just a bit of polish and shine they bring a bit of the grand Victorian era into modern times.

Antique cash registers are categorized as either restored or unrestored. A restored register is one where the cabinet has been stripped, polished, and lacquered; indicators are free of dust, dirt, and visible signs of wear; key arms are rust-free, plated or painted; and key checks and rings are new, used, or originals. The drawer has been stripped and revarnished, and the rails are in good condition. All mechanisms are completely reworked; broken parts are replaced, oiled, and working perfectly. Prices for registers in unrestored condition vary greatly. Unrestored registers are classed as either working or non-working. Values for those with missing major parts are much lower. In the listings that follow, M condition refers to fully-restored cash registers; VG condition is for registers in original unrestored working condition. For further information we recommend the highly informative books *Antique Cash Registers 1880-1920*, by Bartsch and Sanchez (Mr. Bartsch's address may be found in our Directory under Oregon); and *The Incorruptible Cashier Vols.I & II*, currently available from our advisor, John Apple, who is listed in the Directory under Wisconsin.

National Cash Register Co., 'Western,' 9-key detail adder, desirable trumpeter and bellflower pattern, restored, $1,100.00.

American, 50-key register, copper plated, 212-lb, M **1,800.00**
American, 50-key register, copper plated, 212-lb, VG 900.00
McCaskey Alliance, metal, 1-drw, blk w/gold, 22x21x18", VG...100.00
Michigan #1, 22-key, M 500.00
Michigan #1, 22-key, VG..200.00
Michigan #7, 9-key, M 750.00
Michigan #7, 9-key, VG..450.00
NCR #1000 class, autographic box attachment, 1910, M........**1,200.00**
NCR #1000 class, autographic box attachment, 1910, VG 650.00
NCR #13, nickeled CI, Ionic pattern, continuous cap, M.......**1,100.00**
NCR #13, nickeled CI, Ionic pattern, continuous cap, VG.........650.00
NCR #130, barber shop, keyed from 5¢ to $1, VG....................850.00
NCR #2 or #3, inlayed wood, VG **2,200.00**
NCR #210 or #211, 11-key, fleur-de-lis pattern, M, ea **1,500.00**
NCR #210 or #211, 11-key, fleur-de-lis pattern, VG, ea **1,000.00**
NCR #226, keyed from 5¢ to $1, unplated bronze, M **1,100.00**
NCR #226, keyed from 5¢ to $1, unplated bronze, VG...............650.00
NCR #311, copper, ca 1915, VG 800.00
NCR #312 or #313, dolphin pattern, 1908-16, M, ea **1,200.00**
NCR #312 or #313, dolphin pattern, 1908-16, VG, ea 750.00
NCR #313, brass, EX..750.00

NCR #322, 15-key, extended base, M **1,600.00**
NCR #322, 15-key, extended base, VG................................... **1,100.00**
NCR #327, brass, barber shop, extended base, VG................. **1,000.00**
NCR #332 or #333, brass top, sgn, rstr **1,000.00**
NCR #332 or #333, brass top, sgn, VG................................. **500.00**
NCR #349-2-2, 2-counter, 2-drw, 1910, M............................ **1,800.00**
NCR #349-2-2, 2-counter, 2-drw, 1910, VG **1,000.00**
NCR #360 to #367, 37-key, personalized top sign, M, ea **1,050.00**
NCR #360 to #367, 37-key, personalized top sign, VG, ea **600.00**
NCR #4, 40-key 'Signature Model,' 1892, M **2,500.00**
NCR #4, 40-key 'Signature Model,' 1892, VG........................ **1,200.00**
NCR #441 or #442, crank machine, rstr **1,250.00**
NCR #441 or #442, crank machine, VG **700.00**
NCR #444, check-numbering device, 1910, M **1,400.00**
NCR #444, check-numbering device, 1910, VG...................... **800.00**
NCR #452-2, crank style, 2-drw oak base, VG.......................... **850.00**
NCR #500 Class, bronze cabinet, mahog base, ca 1908, EX.... **4,500.00**
NCR #522 Class, 2-drw, requires electricity, 1906, M............. **2,400.00**
NCR #522 Class, 2-drw, requires electricity, 1906, VG **1,500.00**
NCR #582-5E, bronze/panelled oak, 9-drw floor model, VG .. **2,800.00**
NCR #593-E-L, 9-drw, floor cabinet, 460+ lbs, 67¾", M **5,000.00**
NCR #593-E-L, 9-drw, floor cabinet, 460+ lbs, 67¾", VG **2,800.00**
NCR #71 to #99½, 79 Principle, 1892 scroll pattern, M, ea.... **1,800.00**
NCR #71 to #99½, 79 Principle, 1892 scroll pattern, VG, ea **900.00**

Cast Iron

In the mid-1800s, the cast iron industry was raging in the United States. It was recognized as a medium extremely adaptable for uses ranging from ornamental architectural filigree to actual building construction. It could be cast from a mold into any conceivable design that could be reproduced over and over at a relatively small cost. It could be painted to give an entirely versatile appearance. Furniture with openwork designs of grapevines and leaves and intricate lacy scrollwork was cast for gardens as well as inside use. Figural doorstops of every sort, bootjacks, trivets, and a host of other useful and decorative items were made before the 'ferromania' had run its course.

Our advisor for this category is J.M. Ellwood; he is listed in the Directory under Arizona. See also Kitchen, Cast Iron Bakers and Kettles; and other specific categories.

Architectural pc, eagle w/spread wings, orig pnt, 16x11x4" **225.00**
Bench, floral detail, owl head arms, pnt, early, 42" L **850.00**
Bench, 3-chair bk w/ornate crests & scrollwork, rpt, 44" **550.00**
Brace, horse-leg form, protected bldg corner from buggy, 25" **450.00**
Broiler, rotary, w/pan to collect drippings, 23½" **235.00**
Chair, Lily of Valley, W McHose & Co, OH, 33x27" **1,500.00**
Chair, vintage, bbl-bk..**200.00**
Coffeepot, wrought hdl, brass finial, 2-color pnt, 10½" **400.00**
Eagle, EX detail, 24" wingspan, gold pnt, 18" H **135.00**
Figurine, boxer dog, mc pnt, lt wear, 3" **55.00**
Figurine, cat lying on oval base, worn mc pnt, 7" L....................**150.00**
Figurine, cocker spaniel, worn blk w/red collar, 3½" **35.00**
Figurine, elephant, standing, old gold pnt, 4" **75.00**
Figurine, fly, hinged wings, gilt traces, 4½" L.............................**75.00**
Figurine, snow bird, pitted, 6" W, pr **60.00**
Finial, pineapple form, gr pnt, 21"..**300.00**
Firebk, lion's head/sunflowers, 3-panel, Vedder, 33" H, VG **850.00**
Firebk, Medusa's head/scrolls, 3-part, Vedder, 1883, 30" H..... **6,500.00**
Food mold, pig's head, 9" dia **225.00**
Garden figure, recumbent lion on sq base, pnt, 13x28", pr **2,300.00**
Gate post, ear of corn finial, scroll brace, 44", pr, VG.................**800.00**
Hitching post, cylindrical tree w/emb vintage, 43" **425.00**

Hitching posts, painted in shades of brown and blue, 1850s, 13", $1,400.00 for the pair.

Hitching post, dbl Minerva head finial on fluted post, 45".......**1,300.00**
Kettle, mk S&P Phila 3-Pt, tin lid, pnt traces, 6" dia **25.00**
Lawn ornament, rabbit, CI, orig pnt, 1900s, 10½x9½x5" **175.00**
Memo clip, duck head w/worn orig pnt & glass eyes, 5" **85.00**
Paperweight, stylized 3-D bird on flat base, 2¾" **300.00**
Plant holder, vintage, rpt, 20x22" L **100.00**
Planter, lg figure of child on plinth supports urn, 45" **2,600.00**
Plaque, horse's head relief, blk rpt, 18½" dia **100.00**
Plaque, owl holding quill pen relief, pitted, 12½x8".....................**150.00**
Plate, 1700s, 7¾" dia **120.00**
Rabbit, wht/pk pnt, Kramer Bros, 11" **200.00**
Rendering pot, 55-gal, w/cradle...**275.00**
Shelf, vining openwork floral design, rpt, 10x14" **175.00**
Shoeshine footrest, camel base, 7½" **35.00**
Stove plate, arches/tulips/SF/1756, heat crack, 21x23", VG **425.00**
Sugar nippers, spring hdls, 1 w/hand rest, ca 1800s, 8"...............**150.00**
Teakettle, wrought hdl, pitted, 9" **85.00**
Top hat whimsey, 7" **150.00**
Urn, emb swags, ftd, wht rpt, 24", pr **450.00**
Urn, foliage/mask faces, Kramer Bros, rust/losses, 53x37" **700.00**
Urn, highly ornate, mk The Urn Pat, rpt, 24" **250.00**
Urn on ped, lg scroll hdls, Kramer Bros Foundry, 37" **1,000.00**
Wafer iron, concentric rings w/flower center, iron hdl, 34" **75.00**
Washbrd, CI w/emb starflowers on rnded crest, legs, 22x12" **475.00**

Castor Sets

Castor sets became popular during the early years of the eighteenth century and continued to be used through the late Victorian era. Their purpose was to hold various condiments for table use. The most common type was a circular arrangement with a center handle on a revolving pedestal base that held three, four, five, or six bottles. Some had extras; a few were equipped with a bell for calling the servant. Frames were made of silverplate, glass, or pewter. Though most bottles were of pressed glass, some of the designs were cut; and occasionally colored glass with enameled decorations was used. To maintain authenticity and value, castor sets should have matching bottles. Prices listed below are for those with matching bottles and in frames with plating that is in excellent condition (unless noted otherwise).

Watch for new frames and bottles in both clear and colored glass; these have recently been appearing on the market.

Key: D&B — Daisy and Button

Resilvered stand with engraved bellflowers and shell-capped feet, six original bottles, plated lids, and spoon etched with foliage, HA&S, English, ca 1860s, 12", $450.00.

Breakfast, 4-bottle, cut, all orig; cranberry salt, fancy fr 195.00
3-bottle, Am Shield, pewter fr w/eagle, mini, child's sz.................95.00
3-bottle, cranberry, cut, SP tops; ornate SP fr, 5½x3¾" 200.00
4-bottle, Alabama, gr; orig glass fr...................................295.00
4-bottle, D&B (colors), orig stoppers; pressed glass fr 225.00
4-bottle, Log & Star, amber; orig ped-base fr 135.00
5-bottle, Bellflower; pewter fr, rpl period stoppers, 11" 225.00
5-bottle, cut; Geo III ftd fr mk Peter & Anne Bateman, 9" 1,500.00
5-bottle, gray cut/polished dots; rstr Tufts fr, fancy bail 165.00
5-bottle, Honeycomb; ornate Wilcox fr 185.00
6-bottle, D&B, vaseline; 19" rstr Meriden fr, w/bell....................495.00
6-bottle, gray cut decor; Rogers rstr SP fr revolves, 19" 295.00
6-bottle, pressed; 18" Simpson-Hall-Miller fr w/VG SP 125.00
6-bottle, wreath cut; 19" ftd ornate fr revolves, Cupid bail 295.00
7-bottle, cut crystal; gadrooned/shell-border Geo III fr 465.00
7-bottle+vase on figural std, Redfield & Rice SP, 1865, 21"........425.00

Catalina Island

Catalina Island pottery was made on the island of the same name, which is about twenty-six miles off the coast of Los Angeles. The pottery was started in 1927 at Pebbly Beach, by Wm. Wrigley, Jr., who was instrumental in developing and using the native clays. Its principal products were brick and tile to be used for the construction on the island. Garden pieces were first produced, then vases, bookends, lamps, ash trays, novelty items, and finally dinnerware. The ware became very popular and was soon being shipped to the mainland as well.

Some of the pottery was hand thrown; some was made in molds. Most pieces are marked Catalina Island or Catalina with a printed incised stamp, or handwritten with a pointed tool. Cast items were sometimes marked in the mold; a few have an ink stamp, and a paper label was also used.

The color of the clay can help to identify approximately when a piece was made: 1927 to 1932, brown to red clay; 1931 to 1932, an experimental period with various colors; 1932 to 1937, mainly white clay, but tan to brown were also used on occasion.

Items marked Catalina Pottery are listed in Gladding McBean. For further information we recommend *Collector's Encyclopedia of California Pottery* by Jack Chipman; he is listed in the Directory under California.

Artware

Ash tray, bear, Monterey brn 275.00
Ash tray, cowboy hat, matt gr 100.00
Ash tray, goat, matt bl..200.00
Bookends, monk design, matt gr, pr.................................750.00
Bowl, Indian design, rare 375.00

Candelabrum, 3-tier 225.00
Candle holder, yel, 5½" 95.00
Flower frog, pelican 225.00
Plate (decorative), sea horse design, mc, 12½" 500.00
Plate (decorative), Spanish galleon, mc, 12" 500.00
Tile, Spanish, mc, 6x6" 150.00
Tray, raised swordfish, wht, 14".....................................450.00
Vase, matt gr, hdls, 8" 250.00
Vase, sea foam, Deco buttress design, 6" 200.00
Vase, squat base, conical neck, 8" 225.00
Vase, stepped design w/hdls, 5" 325.00
Vase, Toyon red, bulbous base, 6" 175.00
Vase, yel, oil jar shape, 9" 275.00
Wall pocket, basketweave, 9"..200.00

Dinnerware

Catalina Island, bowl, cereal 35.00
Catalina Island, bowl, vegetable; rnd, 8½" 65.00
Catalina Island, creamer...35.00
Catalina Island, cup, coffee/tea 35.00
Catalina Island, mug, 6" 45.00
Catalina Island, pitcher, squat base...............................175.00
Catalina Island, plate, bread & butter; coupe design, 6".......15.00
Catalina Island, plate, chop; rolled rim, 12½" 65.00
Catalina Island, plate, dinner; rolled rim, 11"...................30.00
Catalina Island, plate, dinner; wide rim, 10½"..................25.00
Catalina Island, plate, salad; coupe design, 8" 20.00
Catalina Island, saucer...15.00
Catalina Island, sugar bowl, w/lid..................................45.00
Catalina Island, teapot, traditional English style..............250.00
Catalina Island, tumbler, 4"...20.00
Rope Edge, casserole, w/lid..50.00
Rope Edge, cup...20.00
Rope Edge, plate, chop; 13½".......................................60.00
Rope Edge, plate, dinner; 10½" 20.00
Rope Edge, plate, salad; 8½"...15.00
Rope Edge, saucer 10.00
Rope Edge, teapot, 4-cup...75.00

Catalogs

Catalogs are not only intriguing to collect on their own merit, but for the collector with a specific interest, they are often the only remaining source of background information available, and as such they offer a wealth of otherwise unrecorded data. The mail-order industry can be traced as far back as the mid-1800s. Even before Aaron Montgomery Ward began his career in 1872, Laacke and Joys of Wisconsin and the Orvis Company of Vermont, both dealers in sporting goods, had been well established for many years. The E.C. Allen Company sold household necessities and novelties by mail on a broad scale in the 1870s. By the end of the Civil War, sewing machines, garden seed, musical instruments, even medicine, were available from catalogs. In the 1880s, Macy's of New York issued a 127-page catalog; Sears and Spiegel followed suit in about 1890. Craft and art supply catalogs were first available about 1880 and covered such varied fields as china painting, stenciling, wood burning, brass embossing, hair weaving, and shellcraft. Today, some collectors confine their interests not only to craft catalogs in general, but often to one subject only. There are several factors besides rarity which make a catalog valuable: age, condition, profuse illustrations, how collectible the field is that it deals with, the amount of color used in its printing, its size (format and number of pages), and whether it is a manufacturer's catalog versus a jobber's catalog (the former being the most desirable). Our advisor for this category is Judd Caplovich; he is listed in the Directory under Connecticut.

Montgomery Ward Plumbing, ca 1920s, 11" x 8½", $38.00.

Adams Badges, loose cover, 1925, 44-pg, VG..............................50.00
Alco Strong Aluminum Alloys, hardcover, 1928, 60-pg, EX.........10.00
Aldens, Fall & Winter, 1952, 972-pg, EX.....................................18.00
Avon, cosmetics & toiletries, color, 1951, 230-pg, EX...............20.00
Bass Still Camera, 1939, 72-pg, EX..6.00
Belt User's Book, 1928, 70-pg, EX...5.00
Bliss & Richardson Shoe Co, 1922, 32-pg, EX.............................27.50
Boston Rubber Shoe Co, 1897, 52-pg, EX....................................17.50
Bruning, surveying & engineering supplies, 388-pg, VG 35.00
Buck Stoves, St Louis MO, 1903-04, 180-pg, VG 32.00
Busch-Sulzer Diesel Engines, many illus, 1924, 96-pg, EX 15.00
Butler Bros, hardware/home furnishings, 1920, 432-pg, EX............65.00
Carlton Mills, men's clothes, 140 fabric samples, 1932 ....80.00
Continental Products, automotive/toys, 1949, 190-pg, VG 10.00
Crane Plumbing, 1923, 104-pg, 3¼x6¼", EX 22.50
Creighton Line Women's Shoes, Lynn, MA, 1923, 20-pg, VG 22.50
Crown Overalls, 1927, 32-pg, 4x9" 20.00
Curtis Publishing, salesmen's prizes, etc, 1920, 64-pg.....................28.00
Dolly Madison Shoes, 1905, 16-pg, 7½x4½", EX...........................25.00
Elliot Co, surveying & drafting materials, 1948, 393-pg, VG.........25.00
Endicott Johnson, shoes, some color, 1913, 79-pg, EX 45.00
Frederick Herrschner Lingerie, 1920s, 24-pg, VG 12.00
Frederick's of Hollywood, lingerie, 1954, 40-pg.............................12.00
Ft Dearborn, gift & general wholesale, 1928, 612-pg, EX..............45.00
Georg Jensen, jewelry/sterling/glass, 1952, EX.............................35.00
George Brodnax, gold, silver & jewelry, 1915, 175-pg 37.50
Glass & Mirrors by National Glass Assn, 1942, 32-pg....................17.50
Goldsmith Sporting Goods, Fall & Winter, 1940, EX....................15.00
Greenlee Tools, machine illus, 1927, 68-pg, EX 10.00
Hallicrafters Radios, 1944-45, 31-pg, EX 8.00
Hammacher Schlemmer Quality Housewares, 1940, EX................18.00
Howe Fur Trappers Supplies, 1935-36, 83-pg, EX.........................15.00
Jordon Marsh, toys, 1958, EX 28.00
Krauss Cultivators, 1911, 63-pg, EX...28.00
Leedy Drums, color illus, 1930, 112-pg, EX 75.00
Leedy Drums, 1930, 112-pg, NM 75.00
Lionel Trains, all color, 1958, 54-pg 25.00
Lionel Trains, 1947, 32-pg, EX...35.00
Lord & Taylor, Christmas, 1939...17.50
Louden, farm tools & dairy equipment, 1919, 224-pg, EX.............25.00
Macy's, 15 pgs of toys, 1908, 448-pg, EX.......................................85.00

Madison Mills, men's shirts, 1915, 60-pg, EX 125.00
Marplex Wild Game Heads & Novelties, 1949, 12-pg...................10.00
McClurg Office Supplies, 1950, 305-pg, EX 12.00
McKesson's, Christmas, 1938, 147-pg, EX....................................65.00
Milton Bradley Games & Toys, 1950, 52-pg, VG.............................8.00
Montgomery Ward, Christmas, 1962, 423-pg, EX 45.00
Montgomery Ward, Fall & Winter, 1952-53, 1044-pg, EX 15.00
Montgomery Ward, machinery, furniture, etc, 1905, 64-pg 18.00
Montgomery Ward, 1914, 648-pg, EX 25.00
Nat'l Bellas Hess, Fall & Winter, 1930-31, 294-pg, EX 25.00
Nat'l Equipment, kettles for candy makers, 1913, 20-pg, M 15.00
Nat'l Mfg, Oriental & novelty fabrics, 1923, 101 samples.............45.00
Nat'l Modern Welded Pipe, many illus, 1928, 87-pg, EX 12.50
Nehi Beverages Premiums, 1930s, 12-pg, 5½x8½", VG 15.00
New Color Harmony, Dupont Paints, 1935, 43-pg 7.50
Northwestern Golf Clubs, 1962, 24-pg, EX 12.00
Parisian Fashions, lingerie, 1936, EX 20.00
Rochester Can Co, galvanized cans, 1930s, 50-pg, EX 45.00
Rodin Novelties, toys, etc, 1938, EX...24.00
Scheal Roth Violins, 1924, 32-pg, EX..55.00
Sears, Fall & Winter, 1943-44, 1072-pg, EX.................................20.00
Sears, plumbing & heating systems, 1930, 52-pg, EX 25.00
Shelly Seamless Tubes, illus, 1920, 71-pg 12.50
Spencer Fireworks, 1940s, EX..22.50
Spiegel, Spring & Summer, 1930, 112-pg, EX 25.00
SS Kresge 5 & 10¢ Stores, ca 1910, 112-pg 24.00
Studebaker, color illus, 1954, 107-pg, EX 35.00
Studebaker Color & Upholstery Selector, swatches, 1956, EX 25.00
Thomas Plant, shoes, leather bound, 1921, 80-pg, EX..................58.00
Tonk Bros, musical instruments, hardcover, 1930, 240-pg, EX 40.00
Universal Fashion Patterns, 1888, 15-pg.......................................25.00
Winchester Salesman's Gun Handbook, 79-pg, ca 1940, VG........30.00

Caughley Ware

The Caughley Coalport Porcelain Manufactory operated from about 1775 until 1799 in Caughley, near Salop, Shropshire, in England. The owner was Thomas Turner, who gained his potting experience from his association with the Worcester Pottery Company. The wares he manufactured in Caughley are referred to as 'Salopian.' He is most famous for his blue-printed earthenwares, particularly the Blue Willow pattern, designed for him by Thomas Minton. For a more detailed history, see Coalport.

Bowl, milkmaid & cow, 2x8" 220.00
Cup & saucer, handleless; blk/wht floral, bl rims, ft rpr 85.00
Cup & saucer, handleless; Britannia scene, emb ribs, mc, EX........35.00
Cup & saucer, handleless; eagle & shield, floral border, EX.........225.00
Cup & saucer, handleless; peafowl, hairlines 45.00
Cup & saucer, handleless; youth & sheep, mc, NM 50.00
Pitcher, bl floral, emb design, mask spout, 6" 500.00
Plate, deer, floral border, mfg flaw, 7" 100.00
Teapot, milkmaid & cow, prof rpr spout, 5½" 125.00
Waste bowl, Britannia scene, bl mk, 2½x5", EX 100.00

Ceramic Art Company

Jonathan Coxon, Sr., and Walter Scott Lenox established the Ceramic Art Company in 1889 in Trenton, New Jersey, where they produced fine belleek porcelain. Both were experienced in its production, having previously worked for Ott and Brewer. They hired artists to hand paint their wares with portraits, scenes, and lovely florals.

Today, artist-signed examples bring the highest prices. Several marks were used, three of which contain the 'CAC' monogram. A green wreath surrounding the company name in full was used on special-order wares, but these are not often encountered. Coxon eventually left the company, and it was later reorganized under the Lenox name. See also Lenox. Our advisor for this category is Mary Frank Gaston; she is listed in the Directory under Texas.

Box, floral, bl w/gold, oval, gr mk, 3¾x2⅜" 48.00
Chocolate pot, marine life, mermaid spout/hdl, mk, 12" 1,100.00
Creamer & sugar bowl, floral, gold on ivory, palette mk 175.00
Creamer & sugar bowl, roses, pk on bl w/gold, cr: 6"....................195.00
Cup & saucer, demi; floral, gold on bl, gold hdl, brn mk..............125.00
Ewer, tankard, monk reading on gr, mk, 14"................................395.00
Loving cup, florals w/gold, heads atop hdls (3), mk, 8½" 550.00
Pitcher, berries, maroon hdl, gold spout, palette mk, 12½" 225.00
Pitcher, dbl-spouted, florals w/gold, mk, 3"..................................165.00
Pitcher, lemonade; roses, red on gr, sgn Durr, 5½" 160.00
Pitcher, tankard; pines & full moon on dk gr, gr mk 225.00
Salt cellar, swan figural, gold trim, mk, 1¾"..................................55.00
Sherbet, gold paste florals, ped ft, mk, 3¼" 130.00

Tankard, monks under Gothic arches, $145.00.

Vase, lady's portrait, sgn Sandlers, 8"..175.00
Vase, mums, purple/pk/yel on blended ground, CAC, 10x4" 250.00
Vase, portrait, blossoms & gold trim, palette mk, 10" 375.00
Vase, purple lustre on body, bulbous, gr mk, 3¾" 110.00
Vase, spider mums, pk & yel on purple, ca 1910, 10¼"...............250.00

Ceramic Arts Studio, Madison

The Ceramic Arts Studio Company began operations sometime prior to the 1940s, but it was about then that Betty Harrington started marketing her goods through this company. Betty Harrington is the designer primarily responsible for creating the line of figurines and knick-knacks that has become so popular with collectors. There were two others — Ulli Rebus, who designed several of the animals; and Ruth Planter, who worked there for only a short time. About 65% of these items are marked, but even unmarked items become easily recognizable after only a brief study of their distinctive styling and glaze colors. Those that are marked carry either the black ink stamp or the incised mark: 'Ceramic Arts Studio, Madison, Wisc.'; a paper sticker was also used.

After the 1955 demise of the company in Madison, the owner (Ruben Sand) went to Japan where he continued production under the

same name using many of the same molds. After a short time, the old molds were retired and new and quite different items were produced. Most of the Japan pieces can be found with a Ceramic Arts Studio backstamp. The Japan identification was on a paper label and is often missing. Japan pieces are never marked Madison, Wisc., but not all Madison pieces are either. Red or blue backstamps are exclusively Japanese.

Another company that also produced figurines operated at about the same time as the Madison studio. It was called Ceramic Art (no 's') Studio; do not confuse the two.

A second and larger building in the C.A.S. complex in Madison was for the exclusive production of metal accessories. The creator and designer of this related line was Zona Liberace, Liberace's stepmother, who was Art Director for the line of figurines as well. These pieces are rising fast in value and because they weren't marked can sometimes be found at bargain prices. They were so popular that other ceramic companies bought them to complement their lines as well, so they may also be found with ceramic figures other than C.A.S.'s.

For those seeking additional information, video tapes (Series 1 and 2) are available from the author, BA Wellman, whose address can be found under Massachusetts. 1992-93 price guides are available. Mr. Wellman will also send a series of articles written for *The Daze* to those who will include an 8½" x 11½" mailer with five stamps with their requests.

Harry and Lillibeth, 6¾", $65.00 for the pair.

Ash tray, hippo 35.00
Bank, Mr Blankety-Blank, 4½" 65.00
Bell, Lillibelle, 6½" 48.00
Bowl, any Pixie series, shield shape, 5" 35.00
Bowl, shallow, scalloped, 2¼" 22.00
Candle holder, Hear No Evil Angel, 5" 42.00
Ewer, Buddha, 4"..22.00
Figurine, angel holding star 30.00
Figurine, Bali Gong, 5½" 35.00
Figurine, Balinese dance couple, 9½", pr 140.00
Figurine, Bo-Peep 25.00
Figurine, Bruce 32.50
Figurine, Cinderella & Prince Charming, pr 150.00
Figurine, Cocker Spaniel, standing/sitting, pr................................40.00
Figurine, colonial boy & girl 44.00
Figurine, Comedy & Tragedy, pr..150.00
Figurine, Friskey lamb..15.00
Figurine, frog..18.00
Figurine, Isaac & wife, 12", pr 125.00
Figurine, June & Jim, pr..25.00

Figurine, Little Boy Blue 20.00
Figurine, mother skunk...28.00
Figurine, Pensive & Blythe, pr 95.00
Figurine, Peter Pan & Wendy, pr 90.00
Figurine, Pioneer Sam 25.00
Figurine, Promenade woman, 7¾" 45.00
Figurine, shepherd & shepherdess, 9", pr 95.00
Figurine, Spanish dance man..35.00
Figurine, squirrel, bl 20.00
Figurine, Winter Willy 35.00
Flowerpot, rnd, 1" 10.00
Jug, Adam & Eve, twig hdl, 3½" 15.00
Jug, rose, 2¾" 15.00
Jug, swan body, hdl & spout, 2" 15.00
Lamp, Aphrodite & Adonis, rotating disk...................325.00
Lamp, Bali Hi & Bali Lao, rotating disk 145.00
Lamp, flutist, on base..165.00
Planter, Barbie, 7"...48.00
Planter, Lotus & Manchu, pr...90.00
Planter, Svea & Sven, 6½", pr...75.00

Planter, Svea, $40.00.

Plaque, Arabesque & Attitude, pr.....................................65.00
Plaque, Cockatoo, pr..65.00
Plaque, Harlequin & Columbine, pr 140.00
Plaque, Neptune, rare 95.00
Plaque, Shadow Dancers, 7", pr..65.00
Plaque, Zor & Zorinda, 9", pr 48.00
Shakers, Blk Sambo & tiger, 3½" & 5", pr 95.00
Shakers, chick & nest, 2¾" overall, pr 25.00
Shakers, Chinese couple, 3", pr...18.00
Shakers, Dutch boy & girl, 3", pr 20.00
Shakers, elephant, pr 20.00
Shakers, Eskimo, pr..38.00
Shakers, French boy & girl, pr...22.00
Shakers, frog & toadstool, 2" & 3", pr...............................28.00
Shakers, Santa & evergreen tree, 2¼" & 2½", pr................30.00
Shakers, snuggle bunny mother & baby, 4½", pr 25.00
Shakers, snuggle kitten & cream pitcher, 2½", pr............45.00
Shakers, snuggle mouse & cheese, 3" L, pr 32.00
Shakers, Thai & Thai Thai, pr 42.00
Shakers, Waldo & Sassy, 3¼" & 2¼", pr.............................25.00
Shelf sitter, Greg & Grace, pr 65.00
Shelf sitter, Maurice & Michele, 7", pr 65.00
Shelf sitter, Mexican boy & girl, pr..................................50.00
Shelf sitter, Tuffy & Fluffy, pr 70.00
Vase, birds, rnd, 2" 10.00
Vase, bud; Wing-Sang, 5" 35.00
Vase, duck, rnd, 2" 10.00

Metal Accessories

Arched window, for Madonna w/child............................34.00
Artist palette, left & right, 12", pr 42.00
Artist palette w/shelves, left & right, 12", pr 48.00
Beanstalk for Jack, rare 48.00
Birdcage w/perch, 14" 32.00
Diamond shadow box, for Attitude & Arabesque...........28.00
Frame w/shelf 25.00
Free-form, left & right, pr...48.00
Free-form w/shelf, left & right, pr....................................52.00
Pyramid shelves, ea 35.00
Shadow box, w/wood, sq, 13"...30.00
Sofa, for Maurice & Michele 32.00
Star, for angel trio, 9" 15.00
Triple ring shelves, ea..32.00

Chalkware

Chalkware figures were a popular commodity from approximately 1860 until 1890. They were made from gypsum or plaster of Paris formed in a mold and then hand painted in oils or watercolors. Items such as animals and birds, figures, banks, toys, and religious ornaments modeled after more expensive Staffordshire wares were often sold door to door. Their origin is attributed to Italian immigrants. Today regarded as a form of folk art, nineteenth century American pieces bring prices in the hundreds of dollars. Carnival chalkware from this century is also collectible, especially figures that are personality related. For those, see Carnival Collectibles.

Bank, cat, seated, mc pnt w/lt wear, slot added, 10", EX 200.00
Bldg w/steeple, stained glass windows, damage/rpr, 18"...............110.00
Bust of girl, arms crossed over chest, worn mc pnt, 11"...............215.00
Cat, seated, looking left, worn mc pnt, chip, 9½" 1,250.00
Chickens, kissing, 4-color, pnt darkened/wear/glued rpr, 5½"......800.00
Deer, recumbent, open front legs, traces of pnt, rprs, 10"............500.00
Dog, full body, standing, no base, worn red/blk pnt, 10x9" 300.00
Dog, seated, 3-color pnt, minor wear, sm base chips, 5½" 150.00
Dog, seated spaniel type, worn mc pnt, hairline/sm hole, 8" 75.00
Dog, standing, red/blk/gr-yel, hairline, 8" 125.00
Dog, standing, worn red & blk pnt, 7" 165.00
Dove, wht w/gr & yel pnt, lt wear, 8¾" 225.00
Dove pr, kissing, worn/faded mc pnt, 5" 300.00
Dove pr, kissing, yel/blk/yel-gr/red, lt wear, 5" 800.00
Ewe & lamb, recumbent, red/blk facial details, lt wear, 7" 300.00
Garniture, fruit compote, EX detail & color, 12½"........................900.00
Garniture, fruit/foliage, EX mc pnt, dtd 1857/name, 12½" 2,600.00
Garniture, urn w/fruit, EX detail/color, 15", EX 550.00
Horse & rider, red/blk/bl, worn/chips/possible rpr, 7"..................450.00
Owl, orig pnt, lt wear, 10½" 800.00
Parrot on ball base, yel/gr/blk, emb feathers, wear, 8" 270.00
Rabbit, nodder, red/blk pnt, wear/chip/crack, 5¾" L.....................950.00
Rabbit, sitting on haunches, gr/red/blk, 5½" 1,350.00
Rooster, yel/blk/red, EX detail, minor wear/chip, 5"....................675.00
Rooster, yel/blk/red/gr, EX color & detail, base chips, 7"......... 1,700.00
Rooster, yel/blk/red/gr, minor wear, EX color, 6½" 550.00
Squirrel, yel/blk/red, worn, 5"..500.00
Watch hutch, arched door w/cherub, worn mc pnt, rprs, 11½" ..200.00

Champleve

Champleve, enameling on brass, differs from cloisonne in that the design is depressed or incised into the metal, rather than being built up with wire dividers as in the cloisonne procedure. The cells, or depressions, are filled in with color, and the piece is then fired.

Compote, marble w/gilt bronze hdls, champleve ped ft, 12" **450.00**
Incense burner, pierced cloud top, dragon hdls, ftd, 6½" **85.00**
Jardiniere, mums/scrolls, bud hdls, 3 short ft, 10" dia **235.00**
Umbrella stand, floral scrolls, knopped cylinder, 24", EX **450.00**
Urn, geometrics on bronze, Chinese, 12" **375.00**
Urn, gilt bronze w/scroll-cast hdls, champleve base/lid, 9" **250.00**
Vase, porc w/HP cherub, champleve socle, onyx base, 8", pr **700.00**

Chase Brass & Copper Company

Americans were shocked in 1923 when an invitation to stage an exhibit at the first major post-war fair, *The 1925 Exposition des Arts Decoratifs et Industriels*, was declined by the American government because the U.S. could not comply with the exposition's requirement that only original work would be exhibited. Even though American industry produced a vast quantity of varied goods, there was very little 'original American' to show, since most design ideas were being brought in from Europe.

This blow to American prestige and the uproar that resulted prompted a dispatch of designers (among them Donald Deskey, Walter Dorwin Teague, and Russel Wright) to the Paris exhibition. They were to determine what steps would be necessary in order for U.S. designs to compete with European standards. They returned championing the new modernist style. By the mid-1930s, products were being designed and marketed that were attractive to the reluctant consumer insistent upon buying a streamline style that was uniquely American. During the decade of the thirties, the Chase Brass & Copper Company offered lamps, smoking acessories, and housewares similar to those Americans were seeing on the Hollywood screen at prices the average buyer could afford. These products are highly valued today not only because of their superior quality but also because of those who created them. Walter von Nessen, Gerth & Gerth, Rockwell Kent, Russel Wright, Laurelle Guild, and Dr. A. Reimann were some of Chase's well-known designers. Emily Post, who served as spokesperson for Chase, promoted a trend away from expensive silver and toward chromium serving pieces.

Besides chromium, Chase manufactured many products in brass, copper, nickel plate, or a combination of these metals; all are equally collectible. Some items had glass inserts which collectors also seek.

Nearly all Chase products were marked, either on the item itself or on a screw or rivet. On sets containing several pieces, the trademark may appear on only one. Be cautious. Check unmarked items to make sure they measure up to Chase's standard of quality. Lamps and lighting fixtures that are unmarked may be compared with pictures of verified examples. For safety's sake, replace both cords and internal wiring before attempting to use any electrical product. Not only will you be protected against possible loss from fire, but you will enhance the value of your collectible as well.

For more thorough study we recommend *Art Deco Chrome, The Chase Era*, and *Art Deco Chrome, Book 2, A Collector's Guide, Industrial Design in the Chase Era*. Both are authored by Richard J. Kilbride; Mrs. Kilbride is listed in the Directory under Connecticut. In the listings that follow, examples are polished unless noted satin.

Ash receiver, Globe, chrome, wht plastic knob, #17068, 4" **45.00**
Ash tray, Riviera, chrome or brass, #885, 1⅜x6¼" **20.00**
Bank, registering; Clearvue, nickel, #405002, 2x4x2" **30.00**
Bookends, Davey Jones, brass, #90142, 6x5¼", pr **60.00**
Bottle opener, Squeezit, chrome, #90086, 4½" **40.00**
Bowl, console; Compton, brass, #15007, 3x12" **45.00**

Bowl, fish; Tarpon, bronze & glass, #90125, 7⅞x7⅞" **41.00**
Bowl, ice; Antarctic, copper, plastic hdl, #17108, 7" **100.00**
Bowl, jelly; Duplex, chrome or copper, #90062, 5½" **29.00**
Bowl, sauce; Lotus, chrome & plastic, #17045, +tray & ladle **42.00**
Bowl, serving; Tulip, chrome or copper, #90095, 4¼x7⅝" **41.00**
Box, chrome or copper, 2-tray, #17106, 5¼x4¾" **30.00**
Box, cigarette; Midas, brass & blk plastic, #878, 1⅛x9x2½" **38.00**
Box, cigarette; Tamaris, chrome & plastic, #873, 1½x4¾x3¾" **33.00**
Box, powder; chrome w/Bakelite & ebony hearts on lid **55.00**
Brush set, Military, chrome or brass, #90145, 2 brushes+comb **35.00**
Candelabrum, chrome, brass or satin silver, #17114, 13½" **72.00**
Candle snuffer, Puritan, brass or satin silver, #90151, 15½" **18.00**
Candlestick, Brookfield, brass or bronze, #24012, 6¾" **25.00**
Candlestick, Bubble, chrome & bl glass, #17063, 2½" **58.00**
Casserole, chrome & plastic, #90115, electric, 6⅛x9¾" **108.00**
Coffee maker service, chrome, #90120, 8" electric pot, 4-pc **300.00**
Coffee set, Diplomat, chrome, #17029, 8" pot+cr/sug **550.00**

Coffee urn, sugar, creamer, and undertray, $300.00.

Creamer & sugar bowl, Savoy, chrome or copper, #26008, +tray ..**38.00**
Crumber, chrome or copper, half-circle form, #90147, +brush **52.00**
Cup, cocktail; Bl Moon, chrome & bl glass, #90067, 3½x2¼" **15.00**
Flashlight, Bomb, nickel, #22001, 1¾x3½" **24.00**
Hairbrush, chrome, brass or bronze, #90140, 1¼x4½x2⅛" **18.00**
Humidor, tobacco; chrome w/blk bands, #857, 6x5½" **35.00**
Ladle, chrome, wht plastic knob, #17081, 9¾" **50.00**
Lamp, Chester, brass, #6194, 11¾" **35.00**
Lamp, colonial; brass w/glass shade & prisms, #6311, 15½" **38.00**
Lamp, hurricane; Mt Vernon, brass, #16007, 9⅝", +snuffer **25.00**
Lamp, Saybrook, brass & bronze, #6304, w/reflector, 12" **75.00**
Lamp, table; Ipswich, brass or satin silver, #6313, 18¼" **43.00**
Lantern, farmer's, brass w/glass shade, #25007, 5½" **17.00**
Lighter, Fire Ball, chrome, #857, 2⅜x2⅜" **30.00**
Napkin holder, chrome or copper, plastic hdl, #90148, 3⅜" **40.00**
Newspaper rack, silver or bronze, #27027, 11⅜x8⅜x5⅛" **50.00**
Pitcher, water; Sparta, chrome or copper, #9055, 8x4½" **58.00**
Planter, hanging; Pendant, brass or bronze, #04004, 5½" **22.00**
Planter, Tom Thumb, copper or brass, #04010, 2½x2⅞", 5 for **18.00**
Relish, Savoy, chrome, glass liner, #90128, 1x8½" **30.00**
Shaker, cocktail; Gaiety, chrome w/blk trim, #90034, 11½" **45.00**
Shakers, Skyway, chrome & plastic, sq, #17095, 1¼x1⅜", pr **38.00**
Silent butler, chrome, wht plastic hdl, #17111, 11⅜" **48.00**
Spoon & fork, chrome, plastic hdls, #90076, 10⅛", pr **45.00**
Stand, smoking; Chair-Hy, chrome & plastic, #877, 17¾" **350.00**
Syrup, Jubilee, chrome & clear ribbed glass, #26004, 4¼" **40.00**
Table butler, chrome & plastic, #17100, 8⅞", +baking dish **163.00**
Tea ball, chrome, #90018, 5" **60.00**

Tray, cocktail; chrome, #09013, 15⅞x5⅜" **18.00**
Tray, Festivity, chrome & walnut, #09018, 16¾x12⅛" **55.00**
Tray, Ring, chrome, #90058, 12" dia.....................................**25.00**
Vase, Clayx, chrome or copper, #03011, 7⅞" **35.00**
Vase, Minerva, chrome or copper, #03012, 6⅜" **38.00**
Wall bracket, hurricane; brass or nickel w/mirror, #24010 ....**45.00**
Wall bracket, nickel or brass, dmn-form mirror, #04006, 14" **45.00**
Watering can, brass & copper, #05004, 8⅜x4½" **45.00**
Weathervane, brass, sailboat, #90136, 15½x9¾".........................**110.00**

Chelsea

The Chelsea Porcelain Works operated in London from the middle of the eighteenth century, making porcelain of the finest quality. In 1770 it was purchased by the owner of the Derby Pottery and for about twenty years operated as a decorating shop. Production periods are indicated by trademarks: 1745-1750 — incised triangle, sometimes with 'Chelsea' and the year added; early 1750s — raised anchor mark on oval pad; 1752-1756 — small painted red anchor, only rarely found in blue underglaze; 1756-1769 — gold anchor; 1769-84 — Chelsea Derby mark with the script 'D' containing a horizontal anchor. Many reproductions have been made; be suspicious of any anchor mark larger than ¼".

Bottle, scent; cupid at alter, appl florals, 1760s, 3", NM **2,400.00**
Bowl, florals/foliage, scalloped, swirled ribs, mk, 8¾" **575.00**
Dish, floral sprays/scattered flowers, brn rim, 6", pr.....................**375.00**
Dish, leaf form, HP veins, 1785, 11" **600.00**
Figurine, he w/basket of flowers, she w/apron full, 11", pr............**500.00**
Figurine, lady w/purple hat/apron, gold anchor, 1760, 7".............**375.00**
Figurine, man (lady) in fancy attire, gr anchor mk, 12", pr..........**125.00**

Platter, Mazarine Blue, ca 1760s, 12½", $700.00.

Seal, dog, mtd w/carnelian intaglio of Aristotle, 1¼"...................**500.00**
Tray, leaf; butterflies/leaves, gr/yel/red on wht, 9½" **550.00**
Tureen, asparagus spears w/brn raffia tie, w/lid, 7" L................ **8,000.00**
Vase, birds on branches, appl flowers, rtcl rim, hdls, 7½" **600.00**

Chelsea Dinnerware

Made from about 1830 to 1880 in the Staffordshire district of England, this white dinnerware is decorated with lustre embossings in the grape, thistle, sprig, or fruit and cornucopia patterns. The relief designs vary from lavender to blue, and the body of the ware may be porcelain, ironstone, or earthenware. Because it was not produced in Chelsea as the name would suggest, dealers often prefer to call it 'Grandmother's Ware.'

Grape, bowl, sauce; 6"... 8.00
Grape, bowl, 8"...30.00
Grape, coffeepot, 2-cup, stick hdl, 7" 65.00
Grape, creamer...35.00

Grape cup and saucer, $25.00.

Grape, egg cup **25.00**
Grape, pitcher, milk; 40-oz **50.00**
Grape, plate, 6"..**12.00**
Grape, plate, 7"..**18.00**
Grape, plate, 8"..**20.00**
Grape, sauce boat **30.00**
Grape, sugar bowl, w/lid...**40.00**
Grape, teacup **25.00**
Grape, teapot, 2-cup...**65.00**
Grape, waste bowl **40.00**
Sprig, cup & saucer...**40.00**
Sprig, plate, cake; 9"...**40.00**
Sprig, plate, dinner **25.00**
Sprig, plate, 7"..**18.00**
Thistle, butter pat **15.00**
Thistle, cup & saucer **35.00**
Thistle, plate, 7" **15.00**

Chelsea Keramic Art Works

Established in 1872 in Chelsea, Massachusetts, by several members of the Robertson family who later formed the Dedham Pottery, this firm is most noted for its experiments in attempting to re-create the ancient Oriental oxblood-red glaze. They succeeded in this in 1885 and also developed several other outstanding glazes as a result of their perseverance. One was their Oriental crackle glaze which they ultimately used in the manufacture of the very successful Dedham dinnerware. Though their very early artware utilized a redware body, by the late 1870s it was replaced with yellow- or buff-burning clay. A line called Bourgla-Reine (underglaze slip-decorated ware with primarily blue and green backgrounds) was produced, though not to any great extent. Other pieces were designed in imitation of metalware, even to the extent that surfaces were 'hammered' to further enhance the effect. Occasionally live flora was pressed into the damp vessel walls to leave a decorative impression. The pottery closed in 1889. Early wares were not marked; those made from 1875 to 1880 were marked with either two or three lines containing 'Chelsea Keramic Art Works, Robertson and Son,' the 'C-KA-W' cipher, or 'CPUS' in a 4-leaf clover. These were used up to 1889. A paper label was used for a short time on the crackleware. Our advisor for this category is Wayne B. Kielsmeier; he is listed in the Directory under Arizona. See also Dedham.

Ewer, gr/brn striations, swollen body, ftd, CKAW, 9" **300.00**
Plate, Pineapple, Robertson, bl on wht crackle, CPUS, 10" **2,100.00**
Plate, Rabbit, bl on wht crackle, CPUS, 8½" **245.00**

Plate, Upside-Down Dolphin, bl/wht crackle, CPUS, 10", NM ..**850.00**
Slipper, olive gr/brn mottle, turned-up toe, CKAW, 6" L, NM ...**300.00**
Tile, vase in relief, golden-brn gloss, 12x6", EX **160.00**
Vase, bands w/fans & flowers on bl gloss, cylindrical, 10" **1,500.00**
Vase, gr/HP floral, lion's head/ring hdls, pillow form, 13".........**250.00**
Vase, olive gr, short neck on ovoid, CKAW, mfg flaw, 6" ..**125.00**
Vase, oxblood, EX color/texture, tall slim neck, CKAW, 8" .. **2,400.00**
Vase, 2 emb bands on bl-gr w/brn, angle rim hdls, 6", NM **200.00**
Vase, 3-D squirrels, appl leafage, flat sides, 7x12", MM **1,400.00**

Vase, Japanese motif, blue gloss, signed GWF, marked CKAW, 10", $1,500.00.

Chicago Crucible

For only a few years during the 1920s, the Chicago (IL) Crucible Company made a limited amount of decorative pottery in addition to their regular line of architectural wares. Examples are very scarce today; they carry a variety of marks, all with the company name and location.

Vase, dappled lt/dk gr w/brn, 5 openings, hdls, 9" **600.00**
Vase, gr/brn mottled flambe, bulbous w/long neck, mk, 11x6" **375.00**
Vase/lamp base, frothy gr/brn flambe, akimbo hdls, 7x5" **225.00**

Children's Books

Children's books, especially those from the Victorian era, are charming collectibles. Colorful lithographic illustrations that once delighted little boys in long curls and tiny girls in long stockings and lots of ribbons and lace have lost none of their appeal. Some collectors limit themselves to a specific subject, while others may be far more interested in the illustrations. First editions are more valuable than later issues, and condition and rarity are very important factors to consider before making your purchase.

Aesop's Fables, Heritage, illus Lawson, 1941, EX **25.00**
Annie & Willie's Prayer Book, Snow, leather cover, 1885 ....**12.00**
Bobbsey Twins at Meadowbrook, 1915, EX....................................**12.00**
Boys' Sherlock Holmes, Doyle, Harper, VG **18.00**
Charlotte's Web, White, NY, 1st ed, illus, 1952, EX....................**125.00**
Children in the Wood Stories, Milton Bradley, 1st ed, 1919 ....**20.00**
Engines & Brass Bands, Doubleday Doran, 1st ed, 1933, EX..........**15.00**
Fairy Alphabet, MacKinstry, Viking, 1st ed, 1933, EX................**100.00**
Fairy Shoemaker & Other Poems, Macmillan, 1st ed, 1928, EX....**95.00**
First of May: A Fairy Tale, Crane, Boston, 1881, VG **65.00**
Flower Children, Gordon, Wise-Parslow, illus Ross, 1939, VG **30.00**
Handicraft for Boys, Collins, Stokes, 1818, 1st ed, EX **10.00**

Happy Days, linen type, 1930, EX...**15.00**
Hardy Boys' Secret of Skull Mountain, 1948, NM **15.00**
Honey Chile, Braun, Doubleday Doran, 1st ed, 1937, VG **30.00**
Hunting Snark & Other Poems, Carroll, 1st ed, 1903, VG............**35.00**
Jolly Jump-Ups Mother Goose, pop-up, Clyne, 1944, EX.............**28.00**
Little Brn Bear, color illus, Johnny Gruelle, 1920, EX.................**30.00**
Marigold Garden, Greenaway, London, 1888, VG..........................**60.00**
Merry Matchmakers, Whitman, illus Collin, 1st ed, 1940, EX.......**20.00**
Miss Bianca in the Antarctic, Little Brown, 1st ed, 1971.............**25.00**
Mother Carey's Chickens, Wiggin, library ed, 1911, EX **20.00**
Olaf the Glorious, Macmillan, illus Pitz, 1st ed, 1929, EX.............**25.00**
Old John, Cregan, Macmillan, illus Sewell, 1st ed, 1936 ....**30.00**
Only True Mother Goose, Boston, 1st ed, 1905, 100-pg, VG **37.50**
Peter Pan & Wendy, Barrie, Scribner, 1st ed, 1911, VG **40.00**
Peter Rabbit, Whitman, 1932, EX..**15.00**
Pinto Horse, Perkins, Devin-Adair, illus Borein, 1960, EX **10.00**
Pogo Party, Kelly, Simon Schuster, 1st ed, 191-pg, EX **30.00**
Prince & Pauper, Twain, Osgood, 1st Am ed, 1882, EX **175.00**
Princess & the Goblin, MacDonald, Blackie, 1924, EX **30.00**

Raggedy Ann's Wishing Pebble, by Johnny Gruelle, 1925, 25th edition, published by Volland, $20.00.

Raggedy Ann in Deep Woods, Gruelle, Volland, 1st ed, 1930 ......**35.00**
Real Mother Goose, M Winter, 33 color plates, 1930, EX.............**55.00**
Red True Storybook, Lang, Longman Green, 1st ed, EX................**60.00**
Rip Van Winkle, Irving, c 1905, EX **15.00**
Robinson Crusoe, Rhead Bros illus, 1900, EX..................................**25.00**
Selected & Illustrated Mother Goose, Tudor, Walck, 1944, VG...**30.00**
Snow White & Seven Dwarfs, Disney, NY, 1st ed, 79-pg, EX **85.00**
Song of Hiawatha, Longfellow, Boston, 1856, EX **60.00**
Story of Ferdinand the Bull, Viking, 3rd ed, illus Lawson **20.00**
Stuart Little, White, Harper, 1st ed, illus Williams, 1945 ....**50.00**
Suitable Child, Duncan, Revell, illus Green, 1909, EX **40.00**
Sunbonnet Babies ABC Book, Grover, 1939, EX...........................**35.00**
Sunny Bunny, Gruelle, Algonquin, 1918, VG **35.00**
Tales from the Storyteller's House, Boston, 1st ed, 1937................**25.00**
Tales Told in Holland, Chicago, illus Petersham, 1948, EX **30.00**
Tanglewood Tales, Hawthorne, Hampton, illus Sterrett, 1921......**50.00**
Ten Little Puppies, Tuck color illus (4), 1880, EX **35.00**
Tommy & the Indians, Cross, NY, illus, 1950, 36-pg, EX **17.50**
Visions of St Nick in Action, pop-up, Bradford illus, 1950............**38.00**
When America Was Young, Caldwell Caxton, 1st ed, 1948, EX ..**20.00**
Wind in the Willows, Heritage, illus Rackham, 1st ed, EX............**15.00**
100 Best Poems for Boys & Girls, Barrows, Whitman, 1930, G **12.50**
5 Little Pigs, muslin, Saalfield, 1909, EX **30.00**

Children's Things

Nearly every item devised for adult furnishings has been reduced to child's size — furniture, dishes, sporting goods, even some tools. All are very collectible. During the late seventeenth and early eighteenth centuries, miniature china dinnerware sets were made both in China and in England. They were not intended primarily as children's playthings, however, but instead were made to furnish miniature rooms and cabinets that provided a popular diversion for the adults of that period. By the nineteenth century, the emphasis had shifted, and most of the small-scaled dinnerware and tea sets were made for children's play.

Late in the nineteenth century and well into the twentieth, toy pressed glass dishes were made, many in the same pattern as full-scale glassware. Today these toy dishes often fetch prices in the same range as those for the 'grown-ups'!

Authorities Margaret and Kenn Whitmyer have compiled a lovely book, *The Collector's Encyclopedia of Children's Dishes*, with full-color photos and current market values; you will find their address in the Directory under Ohio. We also recommend *Children's Glass Dishes, China, and Furniture*, by Doris Anderson Lechler, available at your local bookstore or public library. See also A B C Plates; Canary Lustre; Willow Ware.

Key:
Emp — Empire   Fr — French

China

Rolled-edge plate with decals of nursery rhymes, ca 1910, 7", $125.00.

Coffee set, children in silhouette, Germany, 1902, 17-pc 275.00
Creamer, gr lustre, Merry Christmas, Germany, 2⅞".....................23.00
Cup, Bl Portrait, Germany, 1⅝" 18.00
Dinner set, Kite Flyer, ca 1860, 16-pc....................................600.00
Mug, A Mother's Affection, girl on swing, bl on wht, 2⅝" 95.00
Mug, Boys at Play, bl-gray transfer, Staffordshire, EX...................55.00
Mug, cats at play, mc transfer, 2¾".....................................60.00
Mug, hunters, mulberry transfer, Edge Malkin, 3" 90.00
Mug, Shave for a Penny, blk transfer/pk lustre trim, 2¼"............180.00
Plate, Basket, Salem China Co, 6¼" 5.00
Plate, Dutch Children, Japan 3.00
Plate, Nursery Rhyme, Germany 5.00
Plate, Pagodas, England, 3⅞"..10.00
Plate, Stick Spatter, Staffordshire, England, 5⅜"......................12.00
Plate, Tan & Gray Lustre, Japan, 3"......................................4.00
Platter, Old Curiosity Shop, Ridgway, England, 5" 25.00
Sugar bowl, Water Hen, w/lid, Staffordshire, England, 4⅜" 4.50
Tea set, bl lustre, blk trim, 15-pc...100.00
Tea set, Bl Willow, serves 4...65.00

Tea set, bone china, sm dots & florals, ca 1850, 10-pc.................250.00
Tea set, copper lustre, 21-pc 60.00
Tea set, Donald Duck, orange rims, Japan, 1940, 10-pc 165.00
Tea set, floral on ironstone, serves 4 ....75.00
Tea set, Humphrey's Clock, bl, English, 12-pc 250.00
Tea set, orchid transfer, serves 4, EX 175.00
Tea set, pk roses, Japan, serves 6, NM in box 135.00
Tea set, wht w/gold trim, Noritake, 17-pc 145.00
Teapot, Elephant Lustre, 3¼"..17.00
Teapot, Floral Medallion, Japan, 3¾" 4.00
Teapot, Gaudy Ironstone, England, 4½".................................70.00
Teapot, Sarreguemines, 5½" 95.00
Tray, Clown w/Duck & Dog on Ball, Japan, 4¼" 5.00
Tray, Floral Cabaret, Dresden, 8¼x9⅝".................................30.00
Tureen, Bl Willow, Occupied Japan, w/lid................................22.00

Tea service for four, English, $175.00.

Furniture

Examples with no dimensions given are child's size unless noted doll size.

Armchair, 3-slat bk, trn legs, rpl paper rush seat, 21"...................225.00
Armoire, lt wood, bamboo trim, 3-shelf/1-drw, Fr, 22½" 225.00
Bed, brass, ornate casting, ca 1910, ds.................................200.00
Bed, oak, Victorian, w/mattress & pillow, ds, VG......................225.00
Bed, pnt wood, high bk, primitive, ds, VG 52.00
Bed, tester; mahog, w/mattress & bedding, 1900s, 31x34" 250.00
Bed, Victorian style, ca 1875, ds, EX 275.00
Bed, walnut, trn posts, w/bedding/quilts, 1900s, 20x21", EX........300.00
Bed, wood w/ball finials, mattress/cushions, 18" L, VG.................50.00
Bed, 4-poster, EX trns, no mattress, 19" L, EX.........................125.00
Blanket chest, PA style, lift-top, bun ft, dvtl, pnt, 12" 120.00
Blanket chest, poplar w/orange grpt, molded edge, dvtl, 24"........900.00
Blanket chest, walnut, sq posts/whittled legs, 21" L, EX 450.00
Cabinet, bow front, curved glass, 2-shelf, 24x16", EX 125.00
Chair, arm; bow-bk Windsor, shaped seat/trn supports, 1890s.....525.00
Chair, arm; ladderbk, red rpt w/gold & blk striping, 19" 75.00
Chair, arm; ladderbk, simple trns, 2-slat bk, rpl seat, 18" 85.00
Chair, arm; red w/tole-style pnt, Windsor style, ds, EX...............185.00
Chair, Morris, mahog, w/cushions, EX................................325.00
Chair, paper litho w/ABCs, child's head, & frog, 8x15", EX........150.00
Chair, rabbit-ear arrow-bk, name burned in seat, rpt, 29" 145.00
Chest, ash, 3 nailed drw, porc knobs, rpr/rfn, 16x16" 150.00
Chest, curly maple, EX figure, late/wire nails, 21x24"................500.00
Chest, curly maple Emp, trn pilasters, sq nailed, 19", EX 1,300.00
Chest, lt wood w/bamboo trim, 3-drw, Fr, 7¾", EX....................210.00
Chest, mahog, 3-drw, Grand Rapids label, 26x22" 200.00
Chest, oak, 3 grad dvtl drw, scroll crest, 18x11", EX 100.00

Federal maple chest of drawers, ca 1820, 24", $1,000.00.

Chest, oak, 4-drw, w/mirror, 22½x15", G 210.00
Chest of drw, pine w/red pnt, cvd crest w/appl hearts, 12" 275.00
Chest of drw, walnut/butternut, 3 nailed drw, rfn, 16" 175.00
Commode, marble top, bamboo trim, 3-drw, Fr, 11¼" 225.00
Cradle, butternut, in swing fr w/scroll ft, dvtl, 38x24x25" 500.00
Cradle, cherry, dvtl, shaped sides/cut-out rockers, rstr 125.00
Cradle, cherry, dvtl, simple cutouts on rockers, 40", EX 350.00
Cradle, poplar w/alligatored finish, scrolled edges, 26" L 105.00
Cupboard, HP flowers on wood, 2-door, 2-shelf, 18x10", EX 150.00
Cupboard, kitchen; pine, glass knobs, losses/damage, 25" 145.00
Cupboard, step-bk style, 2 pr of doors, VG pnt, ds 240.00
Cupboard, tin, Dutch litho decor, 3-shelf/2-drw, '50s, 20" 50.00
Cupboard, wood, step-bk style, 2-door w/shelves, ds, EX 200.00
Cupboard, 2-shelf/2-door, Rogers Sunshine Toys, ds, EX.............150.00
Dresser, maple, 3-drw w/wood knobs, tilt mirror, ds, EX 130.00
Dresser, wood, 2-drw, factory made, ca 1910, ds, EX 50.00
Dry sink, 1-door, 1-drw, old grain pnt, 21x24½", G 450.00
Highchair, ladderbk, maple/hickory, 2 arch slats, rfn, EX 600.00
Highchair, ladderbk, 2-slat, rpl splint seat, 37", EX 550.00
Highchair, ladderbk, 3-slat, rabbit ear finials/trn arms 110.00
Highchair, simple crest over 4 vertical dowels, rpt, 35" 250.00
Piano, Steinway upright, litho scene w/children, 13x18", VG.....100.00
Rocker, arm; ladderbk; trn posts/arms/finials, rpt, 27" 750.00
Rocker, arm; wicker, loose weave, rpl seat, VG 75.00
Table, ice cream; metal w/wood top, 18", +2 chairs, VG 250.00
Table, oak, trn legs, 23" dia, VG- 85.00
Table, wood, folds flat, ds, EX 100.00
Trunk, dome-top, pnt w/children at play, steel straps, EX 225.00
Washstand, oak, towel bar in lyre fr, 1-drw/2-door, 15", VG 100.00
Washstand, poplar w/brn finish, gilt decor, wire nails, 9"..............45.00

Glassware

Acorn, table set, 4-pc 650.00
Amazon, creamer 40.00
Arched Panel, pitcher, cobalt 100.00
Arches, mug, 3x2¾" 45.00
Austrian, butter dish, chocolate, 2¼" 750.00
Baby Flute, bowl, berry; sm 7.00
Banded Block, mug, amber 30.00
Bead & Dart, mug, bl 18.00
Bead & Scroll, sugar bowl, crystal w/flashing, w/lid.....................150.00
Beaded Swirl VT, spooner, color..100.00
Bird & Harp, mug 40.00
Birds & Flowers, lemonade set, English, 3-pc 200.00

Braided Belt, sugar bowl, floral on milk glass.................................185.00
Button Arches, butter dish, 2⅛" 150.00
Button Panel, butter dish, clear w/gold flashing 110.00
Button Panel, sugar bowl, w/lid, 4⅝" 85.00
Buzz Saw, jug 40.00
Chimo, sugar bowl, w/lid 75.00
Clear & Diamond Panels, creamer, gr, 2¾" 45.00
Cloud Band, butter dish, milk glass w/pnt floral 155.00
Cloud Band, creamer, clear or milk glass 50.00
Colonial, creamer, gr 30.00
D&M #42, honey jug, 2⅜" 60.00
Daisy & Button, mustard, amber, ftd..35.00
Deep Stars & Octagons, pitcher, clear or milk glass 45.00
Dewdrop, spooner, bl, 2¾"..75.00
Dewdrop, table set (butter dish, spooner, cr/sug) 375.00
Diamond Band, mug, 2¼x1¼" 45.00
Diamond Ridge, creamer 65.00
Doyle's #500, butter dish, bl, 2¼" 110.00
Drape, castor set 125.00
Drape, mug, clear w/gold trim & hdl, 3x2" 12.00
Drum, butter dish 120.00
Drum, creamer 60.00
Drum, sugar bowl, w/lid, 3½" 115.00
English Hobnail, cruet 18.00
Euclid, butter dish 30.00
Fancy Cut, punch cup 25.00
Fancy Cut, spooner, 2¼" 28.00
Finecut Star & Fan, cake stand 32.00
Finecut Star & Fan, creamer 20.00
Fish, platter, oval, Federal Glass, 5¼x4½" 300.00

Floral Oval cake stand, $40.00.

Floral Twigs, mug, amber, 3¾x3" 55.00
Flower & Cherubs, mug, etched, app hdl, 3¼" 55.00
Flower Band, mug, 2½x2½" 55.00
Galloway, pitcher, clear w/gold trim, 3⅞" 32.00
Grapevine w/Ovals, creamer, amber 40.00
Grapevine w/Ovals, creamer, bl 50.00
Hawaiian Lei, creamer 20.00
Hobnail, tumble-up, bl, 3¾"...400.00
Hobnail w/T'print, creamer, bl 55.00
Hobnail w/T'print, tray, amber, 7⅜" 50.00
Hobnail w/T'print, tray, 7⅜" 35.00
Horizontal Threads, butter dish, red flashed, 1⅞"..........................100.00
Horizontal Threads, spooner 40.00
Kittens, cup & saucer, bl 200.00
Lacy Daisy, bowl, amber or mint gr, lg...70.00
Lacy Dewdrop, cake stand, 4⅛" 40.00
Lamb, sugar bowl, milk glass, lamb finial, 4⅛" 155.00
Large Block, creamer, bl opaque, 3" 45.00
Large Block, spooner, color, 3" 55.00

Leaf & Grape, decanter set, etched, 5-pc............................225.00
Liberty Bell, butter dish 180.00
Liberty Bell, mug, milk glass 165.00
Lion, creamer..60.00
Lion, cup & saucer, 1¾", 3¼"..60.00
Little Bo Peep, plate 35.00
Little Ladders, banana stand..45.00
Long Diamond #15006, sugar bowl, w/lid, 3⅞" 100.00
Menagerie, spooner, bl, 2⅝"..135.00
Michigan, spooner, clear w/flashing, 3"............................70.00
Mug, jester riding pig bkwards..45.00
Mug, Robin & Nest, bl 40.00
Nursery Rhyme, mug, Humpty Dumpty, amber, 3½".........35.00
Nursery Rhyme, mug, Little Bo Peep, 3½".......................75.00
Nursery Rhyme, pitcher..115.00
Nursery Rhyme, punch bowl, cobalt, 3¼" 425.00
Oval Star, butter dish...30.00
Oval Star, pitcher, water...65.00
Oval Star, sugar bowl, w/lid...30.00
Oval Star, tumbler 9.00
Palm Leaf Fan, banana stand...45.00
Pattee Cross, pitcher 65.00
Pattee Cross, punch cup, 1¼"...25.00
Pennsylvania, creamer, gr, 2½".......................................75.00
Pennsylvania, sugar bowl, gr w/gold, w/lid, 4".................175.00
Pert, creamer, 3¼"..85.00
Petite Hobnail, pitcher, color..235.00
Petite Square, pitcher...75.00
Plain #13, butter dish, cobalt, 1⅞" 175.00
Plain #13, sugar bowl, clear w/frosted panels, w/lid, 3¼".....120.00
Plain #13, sugar bowl, wht opal, w/lid............................125.00
Rex, creamer 25.00
Rexford, butter dish...30.00
Rooster, sugar bowl, clear or milk glass, w/lid 165.00
Rose in Snow, mug, 3½x3"..45.00
Sandwich, cup & saucer, ca 1835-50 ....300.00
Sandwich, tumbler...20.00
Sawtooth, sugar bowl, w/lid..45.00
Star, butter dish 70.00
Steigel (type), tumbler..20.00
Stippled Diamond, sugar bowl, color, w/lid 145.00
Stippled Loops, butter dish...100.00
Stippled Raindrop & Dewdrop, sugar bowl, w/lid, 3" 75.00
Stippled Rewdrop & Raindrop, creamer 65.00
Stippled Vines & Beads, butter dish, sapphire bl, 2⅜" 135.00
Stippled Vines & Beads, spooner, teal, 2⅛" 90.00
Style (Arrowhead-in-Ovals), butter dish 30.00
Sultan, butter dish, chocolate, 3¾".................................600.00
Sultan (Wild Rose w/Scrolling), spooner, color 95.00

Sunbeam, butter dish...145.00
Swirl, compote, bl opaque 45.00
Swirl, creamer..55.00
Thumbelina, creamer..15.00
Tulip & Honeycomb, creamer...20.00
Twist, butter dish...25.00
Twist, butter dish, bl opal...165.00
Twist, creamer & spooner, bl opal, pr 250.00
Two Band, sugar bowl, w/lid...55.00
Verreries De Portieux, decanter, #24070, 4½" 22.00
Wee Branches, butter dish 135.00
Wheat Sheaf, bowl, master berry.....................................45.00
Wild Rose, candlestick 95.00
Wild Rose, punch bowl 100.00

Miscellaneous

Baby carriage, lt gr w/red & blk stripes, rpl canvas top.................400.00
Basket, laundry; willow, oval, hdls, 16x12", EX 50.00
Buggy, cream/red trim, rubber tires, 22x25x13", ds, EX ...190.00
Buggy, leather top folds, spoke wheels, EX+ pnt, ds........650.00
Buggy, Victorian, reed scrolls at sides, ds, EX 250.00
Buggy, wicker, adjustable bk, ornate, 1890s, ds, EX 1,600.00
Buggy, wicker, pk & bl trim, ca 1910, 30x29", ds, EX 300.00
Buggy, wicker, simple, late 1890s, ds, EX 375.00
Buggy, wood, pnt decor, leather canopy, spoke wheels, ds ...350.00
Buggy seat, wooden plank seat/bk, wrought iron fr, 28", EX 375.00
Christening cup, eng pewter, dtd June 19, 1895, EX 75.00
Costume, Indian, brn cotton, w/headdress, handmade, 1920s, EX ..70.00
Cradle, poplar, hooded, wear, 14" L 120.00
Kaleidoscope, tin, trade beads inside, 1830s, 6½x2" dia ...195.00
Knife & fork, steel w/bone hdl, 7" 65.00
Magic set, Mysto-Magic, complete w/instructions, 1911, G 300.00
Noisemaker, hammered tin cylinder, w/pronged tool 80.00
Rattle, MOP w/emb silver cap w/bells & whistle in end 150.00
Shopping cart, litho paper on pressed brd, metal fr, 1950s...........100.00
Sled, HP top brd, brass supports, oak runners, 33", EX.....225.00
Sled, wood, welded rod fr, red/yel pnt, late, 32" 50.00
Sled, wood w/metal runners, mc floral on gr, 16" L 425.00
Sled, wood w/metal trim, CI swans head, mc floral, 37", EX.......325.00
Sleigh, push type, red pnt, yel stripes, florals, 46", VG 450.00
Stroller, wicker, wood, wire wheels, 1900, doll sz, EX 225.00
Tea set, Little Red Riding Hood, tin litho, ca '20s, 6-pc 60.00
Tea set, pewter, ornate shapes, no mk, 8-pc, sugar: 4" 375.00
Trunk, dome-top, leather covered, bombe shape, 10" L, VG.......165.00

Teddy Bears plate, children in border, $85.00.

Waffle Iron, marked Stover Jr. #8, $160.00.

Wagon, Express, stencil decor, Paris Mfg Co, EX...............650.00
Wagon, Express Coaster, stencil on red, lt rust, 36", G 175.00
Wagon, wood w/orig stencil decor, spoke wheels, 27" 850.00
Wagon seat, simple trn/pointed finals, dbl ladderbk...........650.00
Wheelbarrow, dk red pnt w/blk & yel trim, 29", EX 275.00
Wheelbarrow, walnut, rpl leg, 23" L................................85.00

Chocolate Glass

Jacob Rosenthal developed chocolate glass, a rich shaded opaque brown sometimes referred to as caramel slag, in 1900 at the Indiana Tumbler and Goblet Company of Greentown, Indiana. Later, other companies produced similar ware. Only the latter is listed here. See also Greentown. Our advisors for this category are Jerry and Sandi Garrett; they are listed in the Directory under Indiana.

Bowl, Beaded Triangle, 4½" 325.00
Bowl, File, 8"...500.00
Bowl, sauce; Rose Garland 600.00
Butter dish, Wild Rose w/Bow Knot 400.00
Celery vase, Chrysanthemum Leaf, 6" 850.00
Compote, jelly; Geneva..175.00
Compote, Melrose, 6"..200.00
Pickle dish, Aurora, violin shape 200.00
Salt dip, Honeycomb, 3½" 525.00
Shaker, Beaded Triangle 385.00
Shaker, Chrysanthemum Leaf....................................450.00
Spooner, Wild Rose w/Bow Knot 160.00
Sugar bowl, Chrysanthemum Leaf, w/lid 785.00
Toothpick holder, Geneva..450.00
Tumbler, Chrysanthemum Leaf 485.00

Christmas Collectibles

Christmas past . . . lovely mementos from long ago attest to the ostentatious Victorian celebrations of the season.

St. Nicholas, better known as Santa, has changed much since 300 A.D. when the good Bishop Nicholas showered needy children with gifts and kindnesses. During the early eighteenth century, Santa was portrayed as the kind gift-giver to well-behaved children and the stern switch-bearing disciplinarian to those who were bad. In 1822 Clement Clark Moore, a New York poet, wrote his famous *Night Before Christmas*, and the Santa he described was jolly and jovial — a lovable old elf who was stern with no one. Early Santas wore robes of yellow, brown, blue, green, red, white, or even purple. But Thomas Nast, who worked as an illustrator for Harper's Weekly, was the first to depict Santa in a red suit instead of the traditional robe, and to locate him the entire year at the North Pole headquarters.

Today's collectors prize early Santa figures, especially those in robes of fur or mohair or those dressed in an unusual color. Some early examples of Christmas memorabilia are the pre-1870 ornaments from Dresden, Germany. These cardboard figures — angels, gondolas, umbrellas, dirigibles, and countless others — sparkled with gold and silver trim. Late in the 1870s, blown glass ornaments were imported from Germany. There were over 6,000 recorded designs, all painted inside with silvery colors. From 1890 through 1910, blown glass spheres were often decorated with beads, tassels, and tinsel rope.

Christmas lights, made by Sandwich and some of their contemporaries, were either pressed or mold-blown glass shaped into a form similar to a water tumbler. They were filled with water and then hung from the tree by a wire handle; oil floating on the surface of the water served as fuel for the lighted wick.

Kugels are glass ornaments that were made as early as 1820 and as late as 1890. Ball-shaped examples are more common than the fruit and vegetable forms and have been found in sizes ranging from 1" to 14" in diameter. They were made of thick glass with heavy brass caps, in cobalt, green, gold, silver, red, and occasionally in amethyst.

Although experiments involving the use of electric lightbulbs for the Christmas tree occured before 1900, it was 1903 before the first manufactured socket set was marketed. These were very expensive and

often proved a safety hazard. In 1921 safety regulations were established, and products were guaranteed safety approved. The early bulbs were smaller replicas of Edison's household bulb. By 1910 G.E. bulbs were rounded with a pointed end, and until 1919 all bulbs were hand blown. The first figural bulbs were made around 1910 in Austria. Japan soon followed, but their product was never of the high quality of Austrian wares. American manufacturers produced their first machine-made figurals after 1919. Today, figural bulbs (especially character-related examples) are very popular collectibles. Bubble lights were popular from about 1945 to 1960 when miniature lights were introduced. These tiny lamps dampened the public's enthusiasm for the bubblers, and manufacturers stopped providing replacement bulbs.

Feather trees were made from 1850 to 1950. All are collectible. Watch for newly-manufactured feather trees that have lately been reintroduced.

For further information concerning Christmas collectibles, we recommend two highly informative books, *Christmas Collectibles* by Margaret & Kenn Whitmyer and *Christmas Ornaments, Lights, & Decorations, a Collector's Identification & Value Guide* by George Johnson. Both books are available from Collector Books or your local bookstore.

Bulbs

Clown head bulb, paper insulator, Germany, 3", $165.00.

Aviator, purple coat, pk hat, gold trim, milk glass, 3", EX 32.00
Baby in red stocking, milk glass, EX 45.00
Bear, sitting, pk, milk glass, NM 50.00
Bell w/Santa face on ea side, milk glass..35.00
Betty Boop, EX pnt 85.00
Betty Boop, pk & red dress, blk hair, milk glass, EX 60.00
Bunny, sitting, pk pnt, milk glass, NM...70.00
Candy cane, red & wht, 3", EX 25.00
Chick, mc pnt, milk glass, minor wear 22.50
Choir girl, worn pnt, milk glass, EX 40.00
Circus elephant, 3-color, celluloid, 2½", EX...................................85.00
Clown on ball, mc pnt, milk glass, 3½", EX 75.00
Clown's head, dbl-faced, mc pnt, clear glass, 2½", EX....................40.00
Cottage, mc pnt, milk glass, 2½", EX 12.50
Cross, red pnt, clear glass, EX..30.00
Darla, girl in pk dress, orange hair, milk glass, NM 135.00
Dick Tracy, EX pnt, milk glass, 3"..150.00
Dismal Desmond, polka dots, mc pnt, milk glass, M 48.00
Dog in basket, mc pnt, milk glass, EX 55.00
Dog on ball, mc pnt, clear glass, Japan, EX 50.00
Donald Duck, mc pnt, clear glass 45.00
Drama face, happy/sad, mc pnt, Germany, EX................................185.00

Duckling, mc pnt, milk glass, sm, NM 45.00
Elephant, mc pnt, milk glass, 3", EX 65.00
Father Christmas, simple pnt, clear glass, early, NM 135.00
Grapes, mc w/gr leaves, milk glass, 3¼" 25.00
Grouper fish, purple & wht, milk glass, EX 45.00
Hound, floppy ears, mc pnt, milk glass, EX 55.00
Humpty Dumpty, mc on pk wall, milk glass, 3" 45.00
Indian's head, matt face, blk hair & bonnet, milk glass 110.00
Lady w/cross, pk/brn/blk/red pnt, milk glass, 3½" 42.50
Lantern, mc pnt, mk Germany, 3", NM 30.00
Lantern, VG pnt, milk glass, Japan, lg 30.00
Lion w/tennis racket, mc pnt, milk glass, NM 60.00
Matchless Star, clear w/gr center, 2" 35.00
Matchless Star, red w/gr, plastic, 2½" 38.00
Moon Mullins, mc pnt, milk glass, EX 125.00
Orphan Annie, VG pnt, milk glass, mk c 1935, 3⅛" 110.00
Paramount shooting star, EX pnt, 4" 20.00
Parrot, mc pnt, milk glass, Japan, EX 37.50
Pear, red pnt, brass base, ivory insulator, EX 15.00
Pelican, yel & bl w/red trim, milk glass, NM 65.00
Pig, bl tie, gr jacket, yel pants, milk glsss, 3" 110.00
Pinocchio, mc pnt, milk glass, 3", VG 85.00
Rose, EX pnt, milk glass, sm 25.00
Rose, open, VG red pnt, milk glass 40.00
Sandy (dog), mc pnt, milk glass, 3", EX 110.00
Santa, flesh face, red suit, clear glass, Mazda, 2¾", EX 35.00
Santa, full figure w/pack, mc pnt, milk glass, EX 45.00
Santa, mc pnt, milk glass, 2½", EX 45.00
Santa, red/wht/gr, yel sack, clear glass, 5", NM 75.00
Santa, 2-faced, mc pnt, milk glass, 4" 50.00
Santa at door, children in window, EX pnt, milk glass 78.00
Santa in oval, mc pnt, milk glass, 3¾", NM 65.00
Snowman, red hat, bl bag, milk glass, 3", EX 32.00
Snowman w/pack on bk, mc pnt, milk glass, Japan 35.00
Student cat, fine matt pnt, clear glass, European, NM 60.00
Teddy bear, red pnt, milk glass, EX 65.00
Zeppelin, EX pnt, milk glass 65.00
3 Men in a Tub 85.00

Candy Containers

Papier-mache snowman candy container with nodding head, 7½", $35.00, by 16" feather tree in stenciled base, $150.00.

Boot, papier-mache/wood/leather, bl silk closure, 4", VG 150.00
Boy on snowball, bsk/cloth, 5½", VG 95.00
Candle, pressed paper, red w/wick & ribbon, 5½", EX 45.00
Cornucopia, crepe paper, die-cut decor, EX 88.00
Drum, Dresden, pk & wht w/gold stripe, 2⅛", EX 65.00
Drum, Dresden, red/wht/bl w/gold band & sticks, 3", NM 85.00
Drum, Dresden, red/wht/bl w/gold stripe, 2⅛", NM 55.00
Dwarf, cb, glitter, pnt face, 5" 55.00
Father Christmas, compo, fur beard & mustache, EX pnt, 5¼" 285.00
House, cb litho, 1930s, Japan, 5x3½x3" 45.00
House w/cotton Santa on cotton roof, mk Japan 85.00
Lady's shoe, Dresden, appl bow, 3½" 250.00
Piano, Dresden, blk, silver trim/pedals, wood legs, 1¼", NM 265.00
Santa, crepe paper/cotton, bsk face, 5", VG 175.00
Santa, papier-mache, felt robe, Germany, 7¾", EX 350.00
Santa, papier-mache, red coat, bl pants, 4", EX 130.00
Santa, papier-mache, red w/celluloid face, 6", EX 195.00
Santa, red flannel coat, rabbit beard, plaster pants, 7", EX 255.00
Santa on log, bsk, crepe paper clothes, 7", VG 350.00
Santa w/feather tree, pnt compo/cloth, 6½" 235.00
Santa w/mesh bag, celluloid face, compo ft, EX 135.00
Slipper, Dresden, pk crepe w/gold, 8" 265.00
Snowman, papier-mache, blk eyes, gr hat, 8" 85.00
Snowman w/top hat & pipe, celluloid, 5" 40.00
Snowman's head, musical, US Zone Germany, 6x3", EX 80.00
Star medallion, Dresden, cb/glitter, 3" 115.00
Suitcase, Dresden, labels overall, leather hdl, 1½x2½", EX 110.00
Top hat, Dresden, red silk w/silver rosettes, 2", EX 250.00
Turkey, papier-mache, EX mc pnt, 6½" 195.00
Walnut, Dresden, natural colors, 2½", M 85.00

Ornaments

Angel, Dresden, die-cut face, flat, gold hanger, 4" 350.00
Angel, wax, purple skirt, spun glass wings, 4", EX 250.00
Baby in purse, blown, pearly silver w/pk & gold, 3½", EX 65.00
Banana, spun cotton, yel/bl/wht, 3½", EX 60.00
Barometer, Dresden, very rare, 4", VG 450.00
Beet, pressed cotton, pk w/gr leaves, 2½", NM 38.00
Bell, blown, silver w/red & gr, glass clapper, 2¾", M 45.00
Bird, blown, mc w/silver, spun glass tail, clip, 4", VG 35.00
Bird, blown, silver, spun glass tail, annealed hanger, 2½" 30.00
Bird, blown, turq w/gold glitter, spun glass tail, 1950s, 4" 30.00
Butterfly, blown, pk on silver ball, 2½" 45.00
Car, blown, mc w/gold & silver, 3¼", EX 42.50
Carrot, blown, orange w/gr leaves, 5", NM 95.00
Cat in bag, blown, pearly wht/pk/bl, 4", EX 145.00
Cat in shoe, mc pnt, unsilvered, 1900s, 4", EX 145.00
Cherry, pressed cotton, red, silver wire, 1", NM 22.00
Chubby boy, blown, lt gr, pk trim on hat, 3½", EX 80.00
Circus elephant, pearly gold, red blanket, gr grass, 3", NM 110.00
Clown, blown, flesh face, pearly gold, red buttons, 4¼", NM 150.00
Cockatoo, blown, mc pnt, spun glass tail, clip, 4", M 35.00
Cuckoo clock, blown, EX pnt & details, 3" 37.50
Dachshund, Dresden, bow on collar, 4½", EX 245.00
Deer, blown, silvered amber, 4⅜" 85.00
Devil's head, blown, silver w/blk, 1920s, 3", EX 245.00
Devil's head, blown, smiling face, mc pnt, 4", EX 225.00
Doll's head, blown, mc pnt w/gold hair, 4½", NM 110.00
Eagle, Dresden, flat, gold, 2¼", EX 135.00
Elephant, blown, pearly turq, red blanket, 3", EX 135.00
Elephant, Dresden, silver, 2-sided, 4", EX 245.00
Elephant on ball, blown, yel gold w/red trim, 3½", EX 185.00
Elf in tree, blown, mc w/silver, 3", EX 100.00
Elf w/pipe, blown, gr & silver w/red trim, 3½", EX 120.00
Elf w/shovel, blown, mc w/silver, frosted beard, 3", EX 135.00

Fan, Dresden, gold hdl, silver butterfly, 4½", EX......................125.00
Father Christmas, blown, pk robe, minor wear, 5" 150.00
Fish, blown, silver, red mouth, 2½", NM......................25.00
Flapper girl, blown, mc w/silver, 2½", EX 35.00
Flounder, Dresden, silver, dbl-sided, 3½", EX......................235.00
Flower basket, blown, pk, tinsel trim, cloth flowers, 5", EX..........40.00
Girl in flower, blown, flesh face, mc pnt w/silver, 4", NM..........185.00
Goldfish, Dresden, flat, emb details, dbl sided, 3", EX................100.00
Goldilocks, blown, pearly wht, bl eyes & ribbon, 3½", EX..........200.00
Great Dane, Dresden, slight scuff, 4", VG 125.00
Happy Hooligan, blown, peach coat, yel pants, 4½", NM..........285.00
Horse w/saddle, Dresden, 3-D, silver, ornate, 3¾"......................225.00
Hummingbird, blown, turq, tinsel wings/tail, Victorian, 10" 110.00
Ice skate, Dresden, 3-D, silver, 2½"......................200.00
Icicle, pressed cotton, wht, Czechoslovakia label, 6½" 65.00
Indian, blown, pearly wht w/mc feathers, clip, 3½", M................275.00
Kugel, ball, amber, brass hanger, lt wear, 5" 65.00
Kugel, ball, bl, w/orig MIG label, rpr brass hanger, 5¾".............275.00
Kugel, ball, cobalt, Baroque cap, 2½"......................110.00
Kugel, ball, cobalt, ribbed, common hanger, 1⅝"......................250.00
Kugel, ball, cobalt, swirl leaf-end brass hanger, 4"......................165.00
Kugel, ball, cobalt, 8-petal hanger, 1½"......................110.00
Kugel, ball, gold, mercury lined, orig hanger, 8" 165.00
Kugel, ball, gr, brass hanger, Made in France, 7½" 475.00
Kugel, ball, med gr, 2½"......................110.00
Kugel, ball, red, Baroque hanger, 2"......................185.00
Kugel, ball, red, brass hanger, 4¼"......................450.00
Kugel, ball, red, brass hanger, 7"......................600.00
Kugel, ball, red, brass hanger, 9½", pr......................850.00
Kugel, ball, red/silver/wht stripes, brass cap, 1890s, 2¾" 350.00
Kugel, ball, smoky bl, emb brass cap, French, 2½"......................145.00
Kugel, grapes, bl, 6", EX 350.00
Kugel, grapes, cobalt, brass hanger, 4"......................250.00
Kugel, grapes, silver, brass clip, 5" 250.00
Kugel, grapes, silver, emb brass hanger, 7"......................285.00
Kugel, grapes, silver w/gr, 8-petal cap, ca 1890, 4"......................235.00
Kugel, pear, emerald gr, Baroque brass hanger, 3¾"......................250.00
Kugel, pear, silver, brass hanger, 9½"......................250.00
Kugel, teardrop, silver, Baroque hanger, 2¼"......................185.00
Kugel, teardrop, silver, Baroque hanger, 3½"......................225.00
Lamb, pressed cotton/stick legs, ribbon/bell, Germany, 3", EX 65.00
Lamp, blown, bl/yel/wht matt, 1950s, 3¾"......................45.00
Man on mandolin, blown, mc pnt, early, 4", NM......................235.00
Mandolin, blown, pearly wht w/mc trim, 3", EX......................30.00
Mushroom man head, blown, silver w/red hat, 1940s, 3", EX 32.00
North Pole, blown, mc w/frosted snow, ca 1950, 3½" 40.00
Ostrich, Dresden, 3-D, blk & tan, 4x3¾", EX......................200.00
Owl, blown, pearly wht w/aqua, fat, 4", EX......................45.00
Owl, Dresden, 3¾", G......................350.00
Parasol, blown, rose w/gold, tinsel & wire wrap, 7", EX.................65.00
Parasol, blown, wire wrapped, gr tassel, Victorian, 10"..................65.00
Parrot, Dresden, flat, silver w/red & gr, tinsel sprays, 7½".............125.00
Parrot, mc pnt w/silver, 4½", M......................320.00
Pear, pressed cotton, lime gr & wht, 2½", EX......................25.00
Pear, pressed cotton, yel & orange, 1"......................25.00
Pear face, pearly cream w/pk & gr, 2½", EX 95.00
Pickle, blown, pearly gr, 4", EX......................135.00
Pine cone face, blown, flesh face w/gold, 3¼", EX......................40.00
Pistol, blown, pearly wht w/aqua, silver hdl, early......................65.00
Popcorn head, blown, mc pnt, unsilvered, clip, 4½", NM..........450.00
Prince bust, mc pnt, Venetian dew trim, EX 110.00
Rose, blown, open, mc pnt, no silver, clip, 3¼", EX......................80.00
Sailboat, Dresden, flat, gold w/3 die-cut children, 3¾" 150.00
Santa, blown, gold & red suit, frosted beard, 5¼", EX.................150.00

Santa, scrap face, silver w/gold trim, 4", EX 150.00
Santa in chimney, blown, red & bl w/silver & gold trim, 3" 75.00
Santa in chimney, celluloid, red & wht, 3", VG......................60.00
Santa in pine tree, blown, mc w/gold tree, 3½", EX 110.00
Santa in sleigh, celluloid, red & wht, 2x4", EX......................50.00
Santa in stocking, blown, red & gold, worn silver, 3¾"......................70.00
Santa w/tennis racket, celluloid, EX......................50.00
Sheep, cotton, blk w/tin horns, 2½"......................55.00
Snake, blown, silver, 5½"......................95.00
Snake, blown, silver w/yel, 6", NM......................95.00
Snow angel w/feather tree, Dresden, flat, 6¾", EX......................135.00
Stork, blown, long legs, 7", EX......................95.00
Strawberry, blown, NM pnt, lg......................70.00
Sun face, blown, dbl-sided, pearly wht/pk, early, 2¾", EX...........350.00
Teapot, blown, silver w/wht matt design, 3", EX......................45.00
Tree, blown, silver w/frosted boughs, 3¼", EX......................45.00
Tree, Dresden, flat, gold w/gr candles, 6½", EX......................85.00
Trout, blown, mc w/gold, early, 3¼", VG......................65.00
Turkey, Dresden, silver w/red head & gray body, rare, 2"............185.00
Watermelon, blown, gr w/red & blk seeds, 5", NM......................165.00
Windmill, blown, mc pnt, silver Dresden blades, 2½" 75.00

Miscellaneous

Bank, pewter w/brass trim, Father Christmas in deep relief..........295.00
Bank, Santa figural, emb Merry Xmas, brn-glazed pottery, 5" 135.00

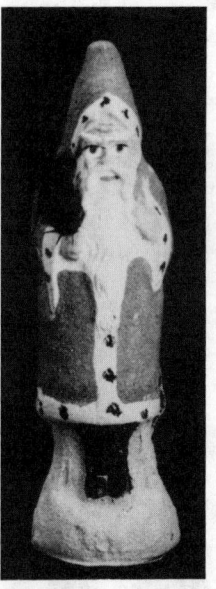

Belsnickel Santa, 11", VG, $495.00.

Bookmark, Noel & elves, woven silk, NM......................45.00
Boots, Santa's Play Boots, red plastic & wht fur, 1940s, M 48.00
Bubble light, Noma, red & gr 4.00
Cake pan, tin, Christmas tree shape, rolled rim, 10x11" 32.00
Candelabrum, Father Christmas figural, brass, English 85.00
Candle holder, cherub, gr, tin, clip-on type, 2" 85.00
Church, red cellophane windows, orig bell, electrified, 11" 65.00
Cow, Putz, brn, 2½x3½", EX......................48.00
Fence, CI w/gr pnt, 8 13½" diagonal sections+gate......................100.00
Fence, feather, Evergreen Hedge, Germany, 65", EX 525.00
Fence, gr/red pnt on wood, 4 16" sections, corner posts, M..........165.00
Fence, sheet metal w/printed gr pickets, 12 12" sections 85.00
Fence, tin w/wooden post, octagonal, 6½x28" dia......................175.00
Fence, wooden picket style, red & gr pnt, 18" sq......................165.00
Fence, wooden twigs, w/gate, Germany, 3¾x17x34"......................135.00
Garland, gr w/1½" gold beads, 96", EX......................45.00

Garland, paper bells, Father Xmas litho, '20s, Germany, 120" **65.00**
Lamb, compo w/wooden legs, 3½", NM **90.00**
Light, Dmn Point, amethyst glass, 3¾" **65.00**
Light, Dmn Quilt, bl, folded rim, 3" **65.00**
Light, Expanded Dmn, fiery opal glass, M................................**250.00**
Light, Expanded 20-Dmn, aqua...**60.00**
Light, swirl rib, aqua, folded rim, Stiegel type............................**175.00**
Lights, Noma, Mazda, string of 15, EX **35.00**
Lights, Popeye, 1930s, working **185.00**
Lights, strawberries, string of 20, EX **45.00**
Mug, Santa figural, bsk, 3"...**10.00**
Post card, Kind Wishes for Christmas, hold-to-light, EX **32.00**
Ram, wood w/metal horns, Germany, 3½", EX.........................**80.00**
Rattle, Santa figural, celluloid, mc, Occupied Japan, 4½"............**115.00**
Reindeer, lead, mk Germany, 2x1¾" **40.00**
Roly poly, Santa, celluloid, mc, Japan, 5", EX...........................**110.00**
Santa, Belsnickel, bl coat, orig feather tree, 10", EX **775.00**
Santa, Belsnickel, brn coat w/gold, 5½" **465.00**
Santa, Belsnickel, gr robe, w/feather tree, Germany, 9½" **800.00**
Santa, Belsnickel, lav robe, rare, 7" **675.00**
Santa, Belsnickel, mustard robe, 11"......................................**600.00**
Santa, Belsnickel, mustard robe, 14½", EX **900.00**
Santa, Belsnickel, red robe, 9½"..**600.00**
Santa, Belsnickel, wht robe, rpr base, 9½"...............................**400.00**
Santa, Belsnickel, wht robe, 10½", EX....................................**345.00**
Santa, bsk, red/wht/blk, Japan, 3"..**30.00**
Santa, celluloid, on metal trike, 3½x4", EX **45.00**
Santa, celluloid, red & wht, 5¼" **35.00**
Santa, felt w/rubber face, jtd body, 9", EX................................**30.00**
Santa, mechanical, waves & turns, 40" atop 5" drum..................**275.00**
Santa, plaster face, paper coat, Japan, 7"..................................**80.00**
Santa, pnt bsk face, red flannel coat, cotton beard, 8", EX............**50.00**
Santa, pressed cotton, scrap face, glass skis & poles, 5" **600.00**
Santa & Mrs Claus, celluloid, kissing, cb base, 6½", EX..............**90.00**
Santa in sleigh w/reindeer, bsk, 3", EX **115.00**
Santa suit, red cotton, cowl hood, mask face, ca 1900, EX **350.00**
Tree, feather; bl-gr w/red holly berries, Germany, 36" **215.00**
Tree, feather; gr, candle clips, wood base, 22" **195.00**
Tree, feather; gr w/red berries, German base, 24", EX **285.00**
Tree, feather; gr w/red berries, 1900s, 26", EX **265.00**
Tree, feather; gr w/red berries/poinsettias, 1900s, 36"...............**265.00**
Tree, feather; trn wood base, Germany, early, 32", EX **265.00**
Tree holder, CI, North Bros, Phila, EX orig pnt **75.00**
Tree stand, cast cement, Santa's head form, 1920s, 12" **185.00**
Tree stand, CI, 3 tripod legs, orig gr pnt, 1900s, 19x19x6"...........**70.00**
Tree stand, rotating/musical, Swill wind-up, electrified **245.00**
Tree stand, trn wood, old gr pnt, 3-legged, 18½x16", EX..............**88.00**
Tree-top angel, Dresden, 3-D, diecut w/gold wings, 6½", EX **195.00**
Tree-top star, metal w/5 candle bulbs, Noma, EX.......................**55.00**
Tree-top star, tin, gold & red pnt, Pat 1926, 8½x3" **55.00**
Wreath, pressed cb, 10½", EX **50.00**
Wreath, red chenille, red & silver foil poinsettias, 10½"..............**45.00**

Chrysanthemum Sprig, Blue

This is the blue opaque version of Northwood's popular pattern, Chrysanthemum Sprig. Though collectors often refer to it as 'blue custard,' in the strictest sense it is not. It was made at the turn of the century and is today very rare, as its values indicate.

Bowl, berry; sm **300.00**
Bowl, master fruit; 10½" W **550.00**
Butter dish **850.00**

Compote, jelly **475.00**
Condiment tray, rare, VG gold **750.00**
Creamer **385.00**

Creamer, $385.00; Sugar bowl with lid, $450.00.

Cruet **775.00**
Pitcher, water..**900.00**
Shakers, pr **450.00**
Spooner...**250.00**
Sugar bowl, w/lid **450.00**
Toothpick holder..**450.00**
Tumbler **200.00**

Circus Collectibles

The 1890s — the Golden Age of the circus. Barnum and Bailey's parades transformed mundane city streets into an exotic never-never land inhabited by trumpeting elephants with jeweled gold headgear strutting by to the strains of the calliope that issued from a fine red- and gilt-painted wagon extravagantly decorated with carved wooden animals of every description. It was an exciting experience. Is it any wonder that collectors today treasure the mementos of that golden era? See also Posters.

Key:
B&B — Barnum & Bailey   RB — Ringling Bros.

Banner, Alzora, Turtle Girl, jungle setting, 120x192" **1,100.00**
Banner, baby bear drinks from bottle, O Henry, 84x108" **550.00**
Banner, Captain Cobra, Russel, 84x108" **1,200.00**
Banner, Christy Bros, 5-Ring Wild Animal..., Erie, 78x80, EX ...**880.00**
Banner, Fat Lady, 629-lbs, Newman **880.00**
Banner, Fat Lady from Snap Wyatt, 108" **935.00**
Banner, Greatest Show on Earth, RB B&B, 1945, 108x72" ... **1,300.00**
Banner, Human Volcano, Champion Fire-Eater, 84x108"..........**935.00**
Banner, Stilt Walkers, boy & girl monkeys, 84x108" **550.00**
Banner, Waltzing Dogs, EX color, 84x108", NM **1,300.00**
Banner, 2-Headed Baby, $500 Guaranteed Real, 84x108" **1,300.00**
Book, Ringling's B&B 100th Anniversary, NM **15.00**
Button, pin-bk; Clyde Beatty & cub, Coles Bros, blk/wht, EX.......**12.50**
Magazine/daily review, RB, 1941, EX.....................................**12.50**
Magazine/program, RB, many articles, 1948, EX **25.00**
Painting, oil on canvas, clown wipes boy's tears, 26x21", EX.......**250.00**

Clarice Cliff

Between 1928 and 1935, in Burslem, England, as the director and part owner of Wilkinson and Newport Pottery Companies, Clarice Cliff and her 'paintresses' created a body of hand-painted pottery whose influence is felt to the present time.

The name for the oeuvre was Bizarre Ware, and the predominant sensibility, style, and appearance was Deco. Almost all pieces are signed and include the pattern names. There were over 160 patterns and more than 400 shapes, all of which are illustrated in *A Bizarre Affair — the Life and Work of Clarice Cliff*, published by Harry N. Abrams, Inc., written by Len Griffen and our advisors, Susan and Louis Meisel, whose address is listed in the Directory under New York.

Clarice Cliff died in 1972, shortly after the Victoria and Albert Museum showed her work in retrospect, and collectors (primarily in England) began seeking and admiring her work. In September of 1982, the Metropolitan Museum of Art in New York acquired and placed on view a selection of six pieces.

Note: Non-handpainted work (transfer printed) was produced after World War II and into the 1950s. Some of the most common names are 'Tonquin' and 'Charlotte.' These items, while attractive and enjoyable to own, have no value in the collector market.

Ash tray, Citrus Delecia, 4½" 200.00
Biscuit barrel, Autumn, 8" 1,100.00
Bowl, Geometric, octagonal, 8" 400.00
Bowl, Honolulu, 7½" 750.00
Candlestick, Melon, 2", pr 800.00
Coffeepot, Summerhouse, 7" 1,000.00
Ginger jar, Geometric, 8" 2,000.00
Isis vase, Secrets, 9½" 1,800.00
Jardiniere, Melon, 7½" 3,000.00
Lotus jug, Geometric, 12" 4,000.00
Lotus jug, Tennis, 12" 5,000.00

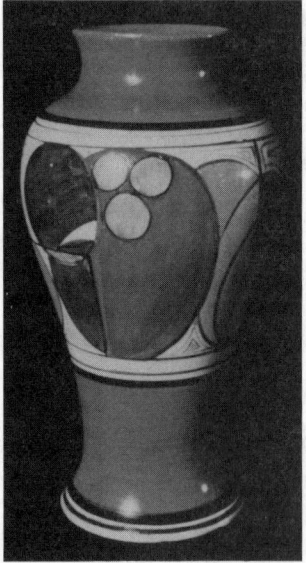

Melon pattern on shape #14 vase, ca 1930-32, 9", $1,500.00.

Sugar sifter, Windbells, conical.....................................600.00
Tea set, Cubes, conical, 7-pc 2,000.00
Vase, Bl Chintz, Yo-Yo, 9".. 3,000.00
Vase, Oranges & Lemons, cylinder, 8" 2,000.00

Cleminson

A hobby turned to enterprise, Cleminson is one of several California potteries whose clever hand-decorated wares are attracting the attention of today's collectors. The Cleminsons started their business at their El Monte home in 1941 and were so successful that eventually

they expanded to a modern plant that employed more than 150 workers. They produced not only dinnerware and kitchen items such as cookie jars, canisters, and accessories, but novelty wall vases, small trays, plaques, etc., as well. Though nearly always marked, Cleminson wares are easy to spot as you become familiar with their distinctive glaze colors. Their grayed-down blue and green, berry red, and dusty pink say 'Cleminson' as clearly as their trademark. Unable to compete with foreign imports, the pottery closed in 1963. Our advisor for this category is Jack Chipman, author of *Collector's Encyclopedia of California Pottery*; he is listed in the Directory under California.

Butter dish, Distlefink...25.00
Butter dish, lady figural 35.00
Canister, cherries on tree branch, tea sz 25.00
Cookie jar, potbellied stove.......................................75.00

Cookie jar, tulip finial, $95.00.

Cookie jar, Winter House, EX..80.00
Creamer & sugar bowl, King & Queen of Hearts 35.00
Darner, motto, 5" 15.00
Gravy boat, Distlefink, w/ladle...................................22.00
Hair receiver, girl w/hands folded, 2-pc.......................25.00
Jar, girl figural, opens at waist, 7" 25.00
Pitcher, Distlefink, 9½" 25.00
Pitcher, Gala Gray, 7"...22.50
Plaque, Let's Pay Off the Mortgage 12.00
Plaque, pear & cherries on gr 10.00
Plate, Deco fruit, red on ivory, wall hanging 14.00
Shakers, Distlefink, lg, pr...15.00
Spoon rest, leaf form 12.50
String holder, heart form, You'll Always Have Pull w/Me.............35.00
Wall pocket, coffeepot...15.00
Wall pocket, mortgage bank..12.00
Wall pocket, row of 3 red Christmas bells, gr bow 15.00

Clewell

Charles Walter Clewell was a metal worker who perfected the technique of plating an entire ceramic vessel with a thin layer of copper or bronze treated with an oxidizing agent to produce a natural deterioration of the surface. Through trial and error, he was able to control the degree of patina achieved. In the early stages, the metal darkened and, if allowed to develop further, formed a natural turquoise-blue or green corrosion. He worked alone in his small Akron, Ohio, studio from about 1906, buying undecorated pottery from several Ohio firms, among them Weller, Owens, and Cambridge. His work is usually marked. Clewell died in 1965, having never revealed his secret process to others.

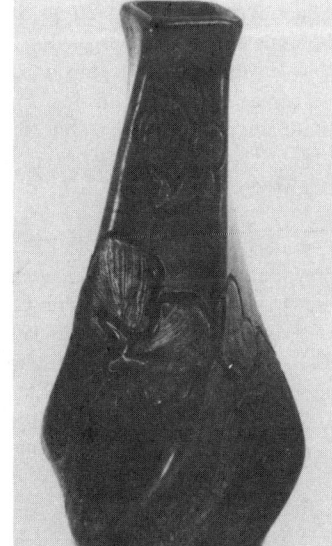

Vase, swirled with deeply carved floral, metallic patina, #115, 6", $450.00.

Candlestick, brn/gr patina, slim baluster, rnd ft, 10", pr...............**750.00**
Vase, bl/gr/orange patina, 6-sided, 9½" **900.00**
Vase, dk brn patina, elongated teardrop form, #257-2, 15x7" **650.00**
Vase, dk gr w/hint of bl, trumpet neck, #292-6, 10" **325.00**
Vase, dk gr/brn patina, ogee form, #316-46, 8" **500.00**
Vase, dk gr/rust patina, #254-2-6, sm dent in side, 6"..................**650.00**
Vase, gr/brn patina, #322-12, cylindrical w/flared lip, 8½"...........**375.00**
Vase, gr/brn patina, long can neck, bulb bottom, 10" **450.00**
Vase, gr/brn patina, ovoid w/short collar neck, 5" **300.00**
Vase, gr/orange patina, narrow rim on ogee form, 12x5" **1,600.00**
Vase, incised/tooled lg poppies, tiny neck/rim, #1118, 11" **1,100.00**

Clews

Brothers Ralph and James Clews were potters who operated in Cobridge in the Staffordshire district from 1817 to 1835. They are best known for their blue and white transfer-printed earthenwares, which included American Views, Moral Maxims, Picturesque Views, and English Views. A series called *Three Tours of Dr. Syntax* contained nearly eighty different scenes with each piece bearing a descriptive title. Two other popular series were *Don Quixote* with twenty prints and *Pictures of Sir David Wilkie* with twelve. Both printed and impressed marks were used, often incorporating the pattern name as well as the pottery. See also Staffordshire, Historical. Our advisor for this category is Richard Marden; he is listed in the Directory under New Hampshire.

Creamer, Floral Basket, dk bl transfer...**165.00**
Cup & saucer, Water Girl, dk bl transfer.......................................**185.00**
Dish, Escape of Mouse/Errand Boy, dk bl, hdls, 12", EX..............**600.00**
Plate, Christmas Eve, dk bl transfer, 8½"......................................**200.00**
Plate, Dr Syntax & Bees, dk bl transfer, 10¼" **245.00**
Plate, Dr Syntax Reading His Tour, dk bl transfer, 8¾" **195.00**
Plate, Dr Syntax Returned..., dk bl transfer, 8"............................**200.00**
Plate, Dr Syntax Star Gazing, dk bl transfer, hairline, 8" **115.00**
Plate, Dr Syntax Taking Possession..., dk bl transfer, 10¼".........**235.00**
Plate, Dr Syntax Turned Nurse, dk bl transfer, 7¾" **200.00**
Plate, Escape of the Mouse, dk bl transfer, 10" **235.00**
Plate, gaudy floral in bl/yel ochre, emb rim, 8¾", EX...................**350.00**
Plate, Hunter & Dogs, dk bl transfer, hairline, 5¾"........................**65.00**

Plate, Hunter & Dogs, dk bl transfer, 8½" **145.00**
Plate, Knighthood Confer'd on Don Quixote, dk bl, 10", NM ...**200.00**
Plate, Letter of Introduction, dk bl transfer, 5½" **220.00**
Plate, Meeting of Sancho & Dapple, dk bl transfer, 9" **195.00**
Plate, Sancho & Priest & Barber, dk bl transfer, 7½"..................**175.00**
Plate, Sancho Panza & Boar Hunt, dk bl transfer, 10" **225.00**
Plate, Sancho Panza's Debate w/Teresa, dk bl transfer, 9" **185.00**
Plate, Valentine, dk bl transfer, 8½" **200.00**
Plate, Valentine from Wilkie's Designs, dk bl, 10" **225.00**
Platter, Teresa Panza & Messenger, dk bl transfer, 14½" **465.00**
Soup, Oriental Sports, med-dk bl transfer, 8½" **185.00**
Soup, Playing at Draughts, dk bl transfer, Wilkie, 10" **200.00**
Teapot, Floral Basket, dk bl transfer, +cr/sug...............................**975.00**

Clifton

Clifton Art Pottery of Clifton, New Jersey, was organized ca 1903. Until 1911 when they turned to the production of wall and floor tile, they made artware of several varieties. The founders were Fred Tschirner and William A. Long. Long had developed the method for underglaze slip painting that had been used at the Lonhuda Pottery in Steubenville, Ohio, in the 1890s. Crystal Patina, the first artware made by the small company, utilized a fine white body and flowing, blended colors, the earliest a green crystalline. Indian Ware, copied from the pottery of the American Indians, was usually decorated in black geometric designs on red clay. (On the occasions when white was used in addition to the black, the ware was often not as well executed; so even though two-color decoration is very rare, it is normally not as desirable to the collector.) Robin's Egg Blue, pale blue on the white body, and Tirrube, a slip-decorated matt ware, were also produced.

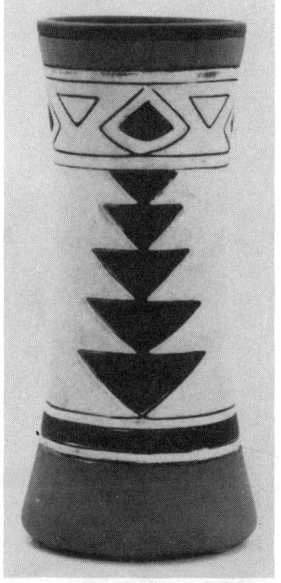

Indian Ware vase with two-color decoration, 10", $130.00.

Bowl, Indian Ware, squat/bulbous, 4 Mile Ruin AZ, 5x8" **125.00**
Jug, Indian Ware, Greek Key design, rnd, imp mk, 4½" **55.00**
Lamp, Crystal Patina base, copper/abalone shell Valk shade... **4,000.00**
Teapot, Crystal Patina, 5½" **100.00**
Teapot, imp motif on yel lustre, gold trim, 7½" **55.00**
Vase, Crystal Patina flambe, spherical w/slim neck, '06, 8"..........**350.00**
Vase, Indian Ware, geometrics, red/blk, cylinder neck, 8" **325.00**
Vase, Indian Ware, squatty, incised at shoulder, #d, 2½x3½" **50.00**
Vase, Tirrube, HP floral on red, bulbous bottom, 8½x6½" **150.00**
Vase, Tirrube, stork & foliage, #257, 12x7".................................**325.00**

Clocks

In the early days of our country's history, clock makers were influenced by styles imported from Europe and Germany. They copied their cabinets and re-constructed their movements. But needed materials were in short supply; modifications had to be made. Of necessity was born mainspring motive power and spring clocks. Wooden movements were made on a mass-production basis as early as 1808. Before the middle of the century, metal movements had been developed.

Today's collectors prefer clocks from the eighteenth and nineteenth centuries with pendulum-regulated movements. Bracket clocks made during this period utilized the shorter pendulum improvised in 1658 by Fromentiel, a prominent English clock maker. These smaller square-face clocks usually were made with a dome top fitted with a handle or a decorative finial. The case was usually walnut or ebony and was sometimes decorated with pierced brass mountings. Brackets were often mounted on the wall to accommodate the clock, hence the name. The banjo clock was patented in 1802 by Simon Willard. It derived its descriptive name from its banjo-like shape. A similar but more elaborate style was called the lyre clock.

Prices have been stable for several years. Unless noted otherwise, values are given for clocks in mint, original condition. Clocks that have been altered, damaged, or have had parts replaced are worth considerably less.

Our advisor is Bruce A. Austin; he is listed in the Directory under New York. Our novelty clock advisors are DLK Nostalgia and Collectibles; their address is given under Pennsylvania.

Note: Numbers within the line descriptions indicate movements: 1 — 8-day time and strike with pendulum; 2 — 30-hour time and strike with pendulum.

Key:
br — brass
dl — dial
esc — escapement
mcr — mercury
pnd — pendulum
reg — regulator

rswd — rosewood
T — time only
wt — weights
vnr — veneer
2nds — seconds

Brewster & Ingraham, rosewood veneer, cut glass tablet, 8-day time, strike and alarm, painted zinc dial, 20", EX, $700.00.

Banjo Clocks

Brewster-Ingraham, rswd/mahog, pnt zinc dl, 1, 32", EX..............550.00
E Howard, sq bottom, rswd grpt, paper/zinc dl, 1, 30", NM 4,600.00

EO Stennes after S Willard, presentation, 1/T w/wts, 42" **2,000.00**
Howard-Davis, #4, rswd grpt, blk/gold rvpt, 1, 32", EX........... **1,800.00**
Little-Eastman, mahog, br mts/bezel/eagle, 2 rvpt, 32"................**500.00**
New Haven, balance wheel 1/T, eagle finial (rpr), '20, 18" 80.00
New Haven, eagle finial, 2 rvpt, T&S, 1920, 36", NM 250.00
New Haven, mahog w/eagle atop, rvpt coach scene, '20s, 37" 250.00
New Haven, mahog w/octagon face, rvpt bldg, 1, 1920s, 42" 375.00
S Thomas, eagle finial missing, 2 rvpt, late, 26" 100.00
Waltham, presentation, mahog, 2 rvpt (G WA/etc), 41", EX . **1,050.00**

Beehive Clocks

Ansonia, rswd, 2, 1870s, 19", EX...**75.00**
Brewster, rswd vnr, cut glass panel, zinc dl, 1, 19", EX 450.00
Brewster-Ingraham, mahog vnr, cut glass, zinc dl, 1, 19", EX.......400.00
E&A Ingraham, rswd vnr, cut glass, pnt zinc dl, 1, 18", EX 175.00
JC Brown, rswd vnr/ripple mouldings, 1, zinc dl, 19", EX 800.00
Jerome, rswd vnr, rvpt, 1, 19", EX..210.00
Smith's, mahog vnr, detailed cut glass, wood dl, 1, 24", EX..... **1,100.00**
Terry-Andrews, pnt metal dl, bl lyre 1, rstr, 19" 285.00

Calendar Clocks

Ansonia, rswd vnr, rnd drop w/rvpt, w/date hand, 1, 25" **1,250.00**
Ansonia, Seem's dial calendar, ogee rswd vnr, 19", EX 425.00
Ansonia, Terry's calendar, rswd vnr, trn drops, 1, 26", NM..... **1,550.00**
Burwell-Carter, perpetual, zinc dl, blk/gold rvpt, 25", EX........ **1,600.00**
Davis, pressed/cvd oak, 2 rvpt, Gilbert 1, rpl finials, 28" 550.00
Gilbert, Longbranch, cvd/trn walnut, silver decor, 1, 27" 850.00
Gilbert, Maranville calendar, rswd vnr, cvd sides, 34", EX **1,750.00**
Gilbert, Owen disk calendar, rswd vnr, 1, zinc dl, 18", M **1,050.00**
Ingraham, poplar w/grpt decor, paper-on-zinc dl, 1, 24", EX........200.00
S Thomas, Column/Cornice, dbl dl, rswv vnr, mirror, rfn, 33" 950.00
S Thomas, Fashion #1, rswd vnr, 1, rpl paper dl, rprs, 29" 900.00
S Thomas, Fashion #4, walnut, 3 finials, rfn, 32", EX **1,300.00**
S Thomas, Fashion #6, walnut, 3 finials, 1, rfn, 34"................. **1,550.00**
S Thomas, sleigh-front rswd w/columns, 1, 33", VG 400.00
Welch, Arditi, Gale's calendar, pressed walnut, 1, 27", EX..........700.00

Cottage Clocks

H Sperry, pnt case, EX rvpt, sgn zinc dl, 2, 12"............................250.00
Ingraham, rswd vnr, rvpt, paper-on-zinc dl, 2, 13" 160.00
Jerome, rswd vnr, pnt zinc dl, 1/fusee, rfn/rpt, 14" 230.00
New England, Cigar Box, rvpt, pnt zinc, 2+alarm, 11", EX 475.00
Unmk, rswd vnr, 2 blk/gold tablets, 2, 14", EX.............................70.00
Unmk, rswd vnr+2 blk/gold tablets, 1875, rpt/vnr loss, 14" 70.00
Unmk, walnut, brass mts & rpl eagle finial, 1, 1890s, 20" 100.00

Crystal Regulators

France, br, bevel glass, porc dl w/florals, mercury pnd, 11" 325.00
Germany, Fr br/bevel glass case, 400 day w/pnd, 11", EX.............375.00
Gilbert, br, bevel glass, porc dl, visible esc, 10", EX 120.00
S Thomas, elliptic front, br w/Corinthian capitals, 9"..................350.00
S Thomas, Empire #10, fancy metal case, 1/faux mcr pnd, 14" 300.00
Tiffany, br, Fr 1, 1880s, 8½", NM 450.00

Kitchen Clocks

Ansonia, Kirkwood, pressed oak, 1, rpl crest/etc, worn, 23" 90.00
Ingraham, pressed oak w/free-standing columns, 1, 23", VG 150.00
Ingraham, 2 long trn spools in crest, 1, rpl door/pnd, 20"..............50.00
Kroeber, walnut, paper-on-zinc dl, 1+alarm, 18", NM 200.00

Waterbury, Belmont, pressed oak, cathedral gong, 22", NM........**150.00**
Waterbury, Feishtinger calendar, walnut, 1, zinc dl, 22", EX **450.00**

Miscellaneous Clocks

Blk Forest cuckoo, eagle crest/bird family at dl, 1880, 27" **375.00**
Carriage, Fr, 1, hr repeater, 1800s, 5½", VG.................................**475.00**
China, Fr, decorated quality case, pnd, 1880s, 8½" **200.00**
Unmk, lady lifts jeweled dl up, gilded metal, 1900s, 12" **140.00**
Waltham, br car clock, 1/T, 1930, as found, 3" dia, VG................**80.00**

Novelty Clocks

Beer barrel drinker, pendulette, non-animated **225.00**
Blessing, duck with rocking butterfly, sm letters, EX **40.00**
Enchanted Forest, pendulette, animated....................................**125.00**
GE, dog w/ball on nose, ball rolls to top of nose **160.00**
Ingraham, Roy Rogers **100.00**
Japan, wht metal elephant, 2, pnt dl, 1970, 12" **100.00**
Keebler, Martha & Geo Washington, kissing bird **100.00**
Lux, alligators & Blacks, 1936..**385.00**
Lux, Black man organ grinder, EX **200.00**
Lux, Black shoeshine boy **250.00**
Lux, mechanical bell, digital, VG **50.00**
Lux, wig wag cat, MIB **265.00**
Mastercrofter, boy & girl on swing, animated.............................**50.00**
Mastercrofter, church w/bellringer, animated.............................**45.00**
Sailor, pendulette, animated **125.00**
Tiempo, horse race, horse rocks, Brazil **60.00**
UEC, Bartender, arm moves, 1933...**125.00**
UEC, Spirit of 76 Drummer **100.00**
Woody Woodpecker, pendulette, animated **225.00**

Ogee Clocks

Ansonia, rswd vnr, rvpt, factory on label, 2, rpl, 26", EX **225.00**
E Terry, mahog vnr, EX rvpt, 2, wood dl, 23", EX **200.00**
E Terry Jr, mahog vnr/mirror, 1 att SB Terry, rpl, 34", VG..........**275.00**
Hiram Welton, mahog vnr, EX rvpt, 2+Terry's alarm, 20", G **475.00**
Jerome, mahog vnr, factory on label, rvpt, 1, rpl wt, 30" **450.00**
S Thomas, rvpt:Bengal Rose, 2, label, 1840, 26", VG **225.00**
Wm Johnson, mahog vnr w/mirror, wood dl, iron wts, 26", EX ...**200.00**

Regulators

EN Welch, mahog vnr octagon w/2 labels, 1, 1870s, 25", NM ...**250.00**
H Sperry, mahog vnr, short drop, appl cvgs, 1, rfn, 25"................**300.00**
Jerome, octagon, 1, ca 1850s, VG as found, 24" **300.00**
Juguns, walnut, 2 urns/eagle/EX trn/3 drops, 1, G orig, 38"........**250.00**
Kroeber, Vienna #51, 1, porc dl/2nds, 1880, 44", EX **450.00**
S Thomas, #1, 1/T w/2nds, 1910, 36", EX **800.00**
S Thomas, #30, mahog, 1/T w/2nds, 1900, 50", NM **1,400.00**
S Thomas, lt mahog, pnt zinc dl, 1/T w/2nds, rfn, 37", EX **700.00**
SB Terry, rswd vnr, 1/deadbeat esc/2nds, rpl dl, 38", VG............**500.00**
Sessions, #2, oak, 1/T, spring drive, 1910, 39", NM **275.00**
Sessions, Clinton, oak, 1/T, 1920, rpl bezel/hands, 28" **200.00**
Vienna, walnut, EX trn/3 urn finials, 1 w/2nds, 1900, 53" **4,150.00**
Vienna, walnut, 1/T, 3 drops/3 finials (2 rpl), 42", VG................**550.00**
Vienna, walnut w/simple cvgs (losses), 1/T, 1880s, 38" **275.00**
Waltham, oak, 1/T, rpl brd/dial/wt, rfn case, 1900s, 34" **450.00**

Shelf Clocks

Ansonia, Crystal Palace, man ea side mirror, 1, losses, 17" **275.00**
Ansonia, Wm Shakespeare, seated, porc dl, blk base, 18" L **300.00**

Atkins, rswd vnr, rvpt+mirror, 2/T, dbl-wind, rstr, 18 ....**1,200.00**
China, cvd rswd w/MOP, 1, fusee/crown wheel esc, rstr, 19".......**950.00**
E&GW Bartholomew, cvd columns/eagle splat, 2, rpl/rfn, 35" **250.00**
France, angel sits atop blk marble base w/porc dl, 22", EX...........**250.00**
Ingraham, Admiral Dewey, 1/steel plates, all orig, 23" **275.00**
Jerome, gutta percha panels, rswd vnr, 1, losses, 16" **150.00**
Jerome, rswd vnr/gutta percha panels, pnd, lacks alarm, 16".......**150.00**
Jerome-Darrow, stenciled columns/splat, Groaner 2, 35", EX **275.00**
Jerome-Darrow, stenciled/rvpt/paw ft, mvt missing, 30", VG **400.00**
S Thomas, Empire mahog/cvd fruit basket crest, 2, rpl, 37"....**1,000.00**
S Thomas, mahog vnr sleigh-front, 2 rvpt (1 rpt), 33", EX **325.00**
SB Terry, half-column, lyre/leaves in splat, 1830, 35", G **110.00**
Unmk, cvd walnut (losses), 1/calendar/paper dl, 1880, 27" **250.00**
Unmk, Eastlake case, 1, 1880s, as found, 22", EX.......................**125.00**
Welch, Venetian, rswd vnr/gilt columns, rpt/rfn, 19" **150.00**
Welch, walnut/3 trn finials, 1, pnd emb T&D Lundy, 26", EX....**300.00**

Shelf clock, mahogany, Jerome paper label, ca 1835, 39", $750.00.

Ship Clocks

Chelsea, Bakelite, 1940s, pc out of bk edge, 6½" dia **90.00**
Chelsea, br, 1/T w/2nds, 1900s, 7" dia, NM................................**250.00**
S Thomas, NP. br, br dl, 2nds, 2, bell strike, 7", EX **150.00**
Waterbury, heavy cast bronzed br, jewel lever mvt, 1930, 9".......**300.00**

Steeple Clocks

Ansonia, mahog vnr, decorated tablet, 1, rpl hands/rpr, 20"........**225.00**
Brewster-Ingraham, C Kirk CI bk, 'lyre' gong base, 20", EX **400.00**
EN Welch, rswd/walnut, brass 2, label, worn glass, 1870, 15" **110.00**
Made for export, 1 day (or 30-hour)+alarm, 1880s, re-vnr, 20" ..**110.00**
Unmk, 2/T, 1880s, rpl hands, 13½" **125.00**
Waterbury, Washington Rock rvpt, 2, 1870s, 20", EX **100.00**

Tall Case Clocks

England, fully-cvd oak w/florals etc, 1+gong, 1890, 94" **3,200.00**
Grpt Hplwht, tombstone crest w/dbl gooseneck, rpl/rprs, 82" . **1,550.00**
Quarter-sawn oak, broken arch w/3 urns atop, rpl/rst, 98" **1,400.00**
Thos Beggs, mahog, simple, 2nd hand/calendar dl, 1840, 76" . **2,000.00**

Cloisonne

Cloisonne is a method of decorating metal with enameling. Fine metal wires are soldered onto the metal body following the lines of a predetermined design. The resulting channels are filled in with enamels of various colors, and the item is fired. The final step is a smoothing process that assures even exposure of the wire pattern. The art is predominately Oriental and has been practiced continuously, except during war years, since the sixteenth century. The most excellent examples date from 1865 until the turn of the century. The early twentieth century export variety is usually lightweight and the workmanship inferior. Modern wares are of good quality and are produced in Taiwan as well as China.

Several variations of the basic art include plique-a-jour, achieved by removing the metal body after firing, leaving only the transparent enamel work; foil cloisonne, using transparent or semi-translucent enameling over a layer of embossed silver covering the metal body of the vessel; wireless cloisonne, made by removing the wire dividers prior to firing; and cloisonne executed on ceramic, wood, or lacquer rather than metal. Our advisor for this category is Donald Penrose; he is listed in the Directory under Ohio.

Apple box, clouds & peonies on bl, 3½x4" 75.00
Apple box, florals, mc on beige, 5x3½" 50.00
Bowl, cloud scrolls/peonies on wht, ped ft, 3½x10" 250.00
Bowl, clouds/peonies/birds on royal bl, 10½" 140.00
Bowl, peonies & butterfly, mc on royal bl, divided, w/lid, 8" 295.00
Brush washer, fruit group figural, mc, 4x5½" 95.00
Charger, bird & mc florals on turq w/gold, 12" dia......................395.00
Compote, floral, mc on bl, ped base, scalloped, 5½x9½"..............180.00
Duck box, male & female w/mc florals on med bl, 4½x5", pr 225.00
Egg box, girl & tree panel, clouds on 2-color ground, 8½" 90.00
Goblet, goldfish, mc on bl, stemmed, 3x2½", pr 95.00
Incense burner, lotus on Famille Noire, flame finial, 5" 80.00
Incense burner, peony on wht, cauldron type, open, 4" 40.00
Mirror, lotus, mc on bl, rnd ped base swivels, 18".........................375.00
Pencil pot, floral, mc on bl, cylindrical, 6½x3¼", pr 150.00
Teapot, floral, lt bl on bl, 3½x5" 80.00
Teapot, floral, mc on bl, 2½x4½" 80.00

Tray, temple scene, ca 1880, 18", $1,950.00.

Vase, birds in panels on lt bl, bottle form, 20"...............................325.00
Vase, cherry branches & bamboo, silver mts, ca 1880, 15"...... **1,300.00**
Vase, flowers/plants/feathers/fly whisk on beige, 15", pr 950.00
Vase, irises on leafy stems, wht/red on gr, mk Ando, 9", pr..........350.00
Vase, peonies & flowering fruit tree on bl, 24", pr........................800.00
Vase, peonies/flying birds, mc on med gr, 10", pr 225.00
Vase, prunus tree on royal bl, baluster, 12x6½", pr......................395.00
Vase, purple & wht magnolia bands, baluster, 10", pr..................250.00
Vase, stylized florals on gold-flecked ground, 1800s, 24" 550.00
Vase, 1 floral/2 deer & geese mc panels, bulbous, 7½", pr...........275.00
Vase, 2 lg carp on gray-bl, morning-glory border, mk, 15" **1,100.00**

Clothing and Accessories

'Second-hand' or 'vintage'? It's all a matter of opinion. But these days it's considered good taste (downright fashionable) to wear clothing from Victorian to styles from the sixties. Jackets with padded shoulders from the thirties are trendy. Jewelry from the Art Deco era is just as beautiful and often less expensive than current copies. But why settle for new when the genuine article can be bought for the same price with exquisite lace that no reproduction can rival! When once the 'style' of the day was so strictly obeyed, today, in New York and the larger cities of California and Texas, in particular, nothing well-designed and constructed is 'out of style.' And though costumes by such designers as Chanel, Fortuny, and Lanvin may bring four-figure prices at fine auction houses, as a general rule, prices are very modest considering the wonderful fabrics one may find in vintage clothing, many of which are no longer available. Cashmere coats, elegant furs, and sequined or beaded gowns can be bought for only a small fraction of today's retail. Though some people are strictly collectors, many do buy their clothes to wear. Care must be given to alterations, and gentle cleaning methods employed to avoid damage that would detract from their value. Our advisor for this category is Ruth Osborne; she is listed in the Directory under Ohio.

Key:

cap/s — cap sleeves	n/s — no sleeves
embr — embroidery	plt — pleated
hs — hand sewn	s/p — shoulder pads
lgth — length	s/s — short sleeves
l/s — long sleeves	/s — sleeves
ms — machine sewn	

Apron, bl/wht homespun, ms 65.00
Blouse, girl's, wht cotton, pinch plt/crochet trim, s/s, EX.............20.00
Blouse, sheer nylon, lace insert/yoke, glass buttons, '40s 15.00
Blouse, wht linen, lace-trim neck/s/hem, ca 1940s, EX 15.00
Blouse, wht linen, Peter Pan collar/silver trim, l/s, 1930s............10.00
Bonnet, child's, brn sateen & silk, worn/faded 20.00
Bonnet, christening; Battenburg lace w/ties, EX...........................35.00
Bustle, Victorian, EX 100.00
Cape, blk, heavily beaded, lace trim, Victorian, EX.....................175.00
Cape, blk silk crepe, celluloid/rhinestone closure, 1900s 75.00
Coat, child's, linen pique, lace insert collar, ca 1900s 65.00
Coat, velvet, wht fur collar, fur cuffs to elbows, 1930s, EX...........45.00
Collar & cuff set, lady's, gold linen w/scallop trim, EX.................10.00
Dress, bl-gray taffeta, rhinestone trim/plt skirt, l/s, '50s.............35.00
Dress, bl/wht cotton, sq neck, flare skirt, n/s, 1950s, EX.............25.00
Dress, blk crepe, V-front, 3-tier skirt, l/s, 1940s, EX 45.00
Dress, blk lace, sheath, jewel neck, l/s, ca 1945, EX 45.00
Dress, blk rayon crepe, sq neck, shirred waist, s/s, 1940s............35.00
Dress, blk silk crepe, A-line style, jewel neck, n/s, '20s 85.00
Dress, blk taffeta, strapless, beadwork, w/bolero jacket, EX............75.00
Dress, brn rayon print, V-neck, plt skirt, s/s, '40s.......................25.00
Dress, child's, gold linen w/embr, lace trim, 1930s, EX................40.00
Dress, child's, wht dotted Swiss, embr collar, puff/s, '20s.............28.00
Dress, child's, wht w/pk floral embr & tucks s/s, EX 35.00
Dress, christening; wht w/lace & silver trim, ca 1920-30s 80.00
Dress, cocktail; brn organdy w/embr, jewel neck, n/s, '50s...........35.00
Dress, ecru silk pongee, bow trim, jewel neck, s/s, '20s 80.00
Dress, evening; bl nylon net over satin, sq neck, '50s...................45.00
Dress, evening; yel eyelet over organdy, strapless, '50s 40.00
Dress, gr plaid silk, l/s, full skirt, 1860s, VG.............................165.00
Dress, infant's, pk linen, smocked neck, s/s, EX..........................20.00
Dress, ivory rayon w/mc floral, jewel neck, cap/s, '30s................40.00

Dress, lilac rayon print, wht collar, s/s, ca 1935, EX 40.00
Dress, red silk, overall sequin/pearl beads, l/s, 1950......................175.00
Dress, red/wht cotton stripe, kick plt w/sash, s/s, 1950s 22.50
Dress, red/wht/bl calico, high neck, 3-row flounce, l/s......................25.00
Dress, rose/blk calico, blk/ivory trim, l/s, ca 1875, EX......................160.00
Dress, teal bl, orig bustle, l/s, ruffled front, 1880s, EX......................250.00
Dress, wht cotton, embr/pearl/bead trim, plt, cap/s, 1935 ....45.00
Dress, wht cotton, tuck bodice w/embr & insert, s/s, 1940s.............45.00
Dress, wht cotton gauze, peasant style, 1940s, EX 30.00
Dress, wht lawn, smocked/lace inserts, floor lgth, ca 1908 ....250.00
Dress, yel chiffon, l/s, heavily beaded, 1920s, EX..........................250.00
Fur coat, Persian lamb, fur collar, long, EX..................................95.00
Fur muff, child's, rabbit, w/matching hat 25.00
Gloves, wht nylon, opera-lgth, 1950s, pr, up to 7.50
Gown, dressing; heavy cotton, fits over bustle, 1870s, EX 250.00
Gown, wedding; lace net, lace inserts, long train, '50s 75.00
Gown, wedding; organdy/lace, Peter Pan collar, s/s, '50s...............65.00
Hat, lady's, blk wool, wide brim, Robinson's, '40s, NM in box 40.00
Hat, lady's, cloche, blk irid feathers, 1920s, EX 45.00
Hat, top; beaver, ca 1870s, EX...85.00
Housecoat, lined brocade w/velvet trim, Mandarin style, EX.........48.00
Jacket, bed; silver-bl sateen, lace inserts, s/s, '30s..........................24.00
Jacket, flight jacket copy, leather, 1950s, EX................................150.00
Jacket, lady's, blk cut velvet, bead trim, dolman/s, 1900s.............175.00
Jacket, leather/knit, sweater look, Grais, 1950s, EX.......................60.00
Jacket, man's, buckskin, fringed sleeves, lined, 1930s, EX 88.00
Jacket, smoking; gray/red/gold on blk velvet, wht trim, EX...........55.00
Jacket, wht polka dot on peach, frog closure, peplum, '30s.............25.00
Jeans, lady's, flannel lined, 1940s, M...20.00
Knickers, boy's, wool, 1930s, M...20.00

Lady's high-top shoes, black leather with white uppers, $95.00.

Nightgown, child's, wht linen, pk trim, V-neck, n/s......................18.00
Nightgown, ecru pongee silk, bl embr/tatted trim, ca 1890 ....75.00
Nightgown, peach bias-cut satin, ecru ms trim, cap/s, '30s.............35.00
Nightgown, peach silk w/lace, long, 1950s, NM 25.00
Paisley shawl, scrolls/florals, narrow border, 1880s, 130" L 465.00
Parasol, blk silk brocade w/chenille fringe, EX...............................95.00
Parasol, child's, beaded blk silk, cvd bone hdl, VG 75.00
Parasol, wht w/ornate embr, 1910 ....95.00
Petticoat, christening; wht w/tucks & crochet trim, 30" L 45.00
Petticoat, ecru wool, ca 1900 ....35.00
Robe, man's, ecru silk pongee w/piping trim, l/s, +sash 30.00
Shawl, Kashmir, pristine, 80x72"...500.00
Shoes, baby's, wht crochet, EX...10.00
Shoes, blk fabric, 1850s, EX, pr..60.00
Shoes, brn snakeskin, high heels, open toe, EX, pr.........................60.00
Shoes, brn snakeskin, mk Ombre Tan Cobra, 1940s, MIB..........100.00
Shoes, child's boots, high-button over-the-calf style, EX 70.00
Skirt, blk taffeta, plt skirt, wide sweep hem, 1950s, EX................25.00

Skirt, blk waffle-weave crepe, floor lgth, ca 1915, EX 70.00
Skirt, wht linen, Edwardian style, 11 MOP buttons, EX 70.00
Slip, blk satin, 1920s, full-sz, EX...25.00
Slip, christening; wht w/embr eyelet hem, s/s, 32" lgth 45.00
Slip, wht cotton, punchwork trim, 1920s, full-sz, EX....................20.00
Slip, wht cotton, tucks/embr top & punchwork straps, 1916 ....60.00
Suit, boy's, wht linen, red trim, V-neck, n/s, 1930s, EX 45.00
Sweater, blk wool, pearl & rhinestone collar, bat/s, 1920s.............55.00
Sweater, infant's, lt gr knit wool w/rabbit embr, EX 18.00
Umbrella, blk silk, ruffled, Victorian, EX 120.00
Vest, man's, wht linen, lined/pockets, EX 22.00
Waist, navy silk, tucks, puff l/s, stays/bustle, ca 1895.....................75.00

Cluthra

The name Cluthra is derived from the Scottish word 'clutha,' meaning cloudy. Glassware by this name was first produced by J. Couper and Sons, England. Frederick Carder developed Cluthra while at the Steuben Glass Works, and similar types of glassware were also made by Durand and Kimball. It is found in both solid and shaded colors and is characterized by a spotty appearance resulting from small air pockets trapped between its two layers.

Vase with applied handles, 3-color, signed Kimball, 11", $425.00.

Bowl, blk to clear to wht, heavy, conical, Steuben, 8x15" 800.00
Candlestick, bl, Deco base mk Silver Crest, 8½", pr 900.00
Finger bowl, pk, hexagonal, Steuben, 2x4½" 475.00
Rose bowl, orange/bl/brn, sgn Kimball/#d, 4".............................225.00
Vase, amethyst, #2683, 10"...1,500.00
Vase, apple gr, rose jar form, Steuben, 8"...................................1,100.00
Vase, lime/wht, unsgn Steuben, 13"..400.00
Vase, orange/gray, polished pontil, Kimball, 1910-6, 7x5" 625.00
Vase, pomona gr, ovoid, sgn Steuben, 10½"............................1,000.00
Vase, wht, classic form, sgn Steuben, 6" 650.00
Vase, wht to gr, clear cased, V-form, unsgn Steuben, 6" 475.00

Coalport

In 1745 in Caughley, England, Squire Brown began a modest business fashioning crude pots and jugs from clay mined in his own fields. Tom Turner, a young potter who had apprenticed his trade at Worcester, was hired in 1772 to plan and oversee the construction of a 'proper' factory. Three years later he bought the business, which he named Caughley Coalport Porcelain Manufactory. Though the dinnerware he produced was meant to be only everyday china, the hand-painted florals, birds, and landscapes used to decorate the ware were done in exquisite detail and in a wide range of colors. In 1780 Turner introduced the Willow pattern which he produced using a newly perfected method of transfer printing. (Wares from the period between 1775 and 1799 are termed 'Caughley' or 'Salopian'; see section on Caughley.) John Rose purchased the Caughley factory from Thomas Turner in 1799, adding that holding to his own pottery which he had built two years before in Coalport. (It is from this point in the pottery's history that the wares are termed 'Coalport.') The porcelain produced there before 1814 was unmarked with very few exceptions. After 1820 some examples were marked with a '2' with an oversize top loop. The term 'Coalbrookdale' refers to a fine type of porcelain decorated in floral bas relief, similar to the work of Dresden.

After 1835 highly decorated ware with rich ground colors imitated the work of Sevres and Chelsea, even going so far as to copy their marks. From about 1895 until the 1920s, the mark in use was 'Coalport' over a crown with 'England, A.D. 1750' indicating the date claimed as the founding, not the date of manufacture. From the 1920s until 1945, 'Made in England' over a crown and 'Coalport' below was used. Later, the mark was 'Coalport' over a smaller crown with 'Made in England' in a curve below. In 1926 the Coalport Company moved to Shelton in Staffordshire and today belongs to a group headed by the Wedgwood Company. See also Indian Tree.

Box, bl studs on gilt, lid w/marbled cartouch, shaped, 4" **1,500.00**
Cup & saucer, allover gold decor on yel, miniature.....................100.00
Ewer, Loch Earn gilt cartouch on lt gr, scroll hdls, 8", EX 200.00
Figurine, Bridesmaid, bl crinoline dress, 20th C, 8".........................75.00
Flask, Japanese floral on bl, molded 3-lobe hdls, 1880s, 7"...........250.00
Plate, Banks of Dee, musical symbols, 1820s, 8" 200.00
Potpourri, appl flowers, scrolled leaf hdls, leafy lid, 8"..................750.00
Teapot, Willow Ware, fluted/rectangular, CB Dale mk, 10" W...185.00
Vase, appl florals, ftd, scroll hdls, Coalbrookdale, 7", EX.............220.00
Vase, pate-sur-pate w/flowers on pk, urn form, 8" 750.00
Vase, turq/wht beads & gilt on pk, gold scroll hdls, 7½" 700.00

Vases, artist-signed portraits on jewelled gold ground, ca 1900, 8½", $850.00 for the pair; Ewer, jewels and heraldic shields on studded ground, ca 1885, 12", $1,400.00.

Coca-Cola

J.S. Pemberton, creator of Coca-Cola, originated his world-famous drink in 1886. From its inception the Coca-Cola Company began an incredible advertising campaign which has proven to be one of the most successful promotions in history. The quantity and diversity of advertising material put out by Coca-Cola in the last one hundred years

is literally mind-boggling. From the beginning the company has projected an image of wholesomeness and Americana. Beautiful women in Victorian costumes, teenagers and schoolchildren, blue- and white-collar workers, the men and women of the Armed Forces, even Santa Claus, have appeared in advertisements with a Coke in their hands. Some of the earliest collectibles include trays, syrup dispensers, gum jars, pocket mirrors, and calendars. Many of these items fetch prices in the thousands of dollars. Later examples include radios, signs, lighters, thermometers, playing cards, clocks, and toys — particularly toy trucks.

In 1970 the Coca-Cola Company initialed a multi-million dollar 'image refurbishing campaign,' which introduced the new 'Dynamic Countour' logo, a twisting white ribbon under the Coca-Cola and Coke trademarks. The new logo often serves as a cut-off point to the purist collector. Newer and very ardent collectors, however, relish the myriad of items marketed since that date, as they often cannot afford the high prices that the vintage pieces command. For more information we recommend *Petretti's Coca-Cola Collectibles Price Guide*; you may order a copy from Nostalgia Publications, Inc., whose address is listed in under Auction Houses in the Directory.

Our advisor for this category is Gael deCourtivron; he is listed in the directory under Florida. For further information, call the Coca-holics Hotline: 813-355-COLA.

Beware of reproductions! Prices are given for the genuine original articles, but the symbol (+) at the end of some of the following lines indicate items that have been reproduced. Watch for frauds: genuinely old celluloid items ranging from combs, mirrors, knives and forks to doorknobs that have been recently etched with a new double-lined trademark. Still another area of concern deals with reproduction and fantasy items. A fantasy item is a novelty made to appear authentic with inscriptions such as 'Tiffany Studios,' 'Trans Pan Expo,' 'World's Fair,' etc. In reality, these items never existed as originals. For instance, don't be fooled by a Coca-Cola cash register; no originals are known to exist! Large mirrors for bars are being reproduced and are often selling for $10.00 to $50.00.

Key: TM — trademark

Reproductions and Fantasies

Of the hundreds of reproductions (designated 'R' in the following examples) and fantasies (designated 'F') on the market today, these are the most deceiving.

Belt buckle, no originals thought to exist (F), up to **5.00**
Bottle, dk amber, w/arrows, heavy, narrow spout (R).....................10.00
Bottle carrier, wood, yel w/red logo, holds 6 bottles (R) 10.00
Clock, mantel; brass, battery-op, Ridgway Anniv, '80, 6x9" (R) .100.00
Clock, 1981, Ridgway, dome, electric (R) 100.00
Cooler, Glascock Jr, made by Coca-Cola USA (R) 200.00
Doorknob, glass w/etched TM (F).. 3.00
Knife, bottle shape, 1970s (F)...5.00
Knife, fork, or spoon w/celluloid hdl, newly-etched TM (F) 5.00
Knife, pocket; yel & red, 1933 World's Fair (F)...............................2.00
Letter opener, stamped metal, Coca-Cola 5¢ (F)...........................3.00
Sign, cb, lady w/fur, dtd 1911, 9x11" (F) 3.00
Soda fountain glass holder, word 'Drink' not on orig (R) 5.00
Thermometer, bottle figural, DONASCO, 17" (R) 5.00
Trade card, copy of 1905 'Bathtub' foldout, emb 1978 (R) 3.00
Vanity pc (mirror/brush/etc), celluloid, newly-etched TM (F) 5.00
Watch, pocket; often old watch w/new face (R) 10.00

The following items have been reproduced and are among the most deceptive of all:
Pocket mirrors from 1905, 1906, 1908, 1909, 1910, 1911, 1916, and 1920.

Trays from 1899, 1910, 1913, 1914, 1917, 1920, 1923, 1925, 1926, 1934, and 1937.

Tip trays from 1907, 1909, 1910, 1913, 1914, 1917, and 1920.

Knives: many versions of the German brass model.

Cartons: wood versions, yellow with logo.

These items are currently being marketed:

Brass button, Taiwan, 18" (R)

Brass thermometer, bottle shape, Taiwan, 24"

Cast iron toys (none ever made)

Cast iron door pull, bottle shape, made to look old

Poster, Yes Girl (R)

Button sign, has 1 round hole while original has 4 slots, 12" (R)

Bullet trash receptacles (old cans with decals)

Paperweight, rectangular, with Pepsin Gum insert

1949 cooler radio (new)

Countless trays

Centennial Items

1986 was the year for the Coca-Cola Company to celebrate her 100th birthday; and amidst all the fanfare came many new collectible items, all sporting the 100th anniversary logo. These items are destined to become an important part of the total Coca-Cola Collectible spectrum. The following pieces are among the most popular centennial items.

Bottle, gold dipped, in velvet sleeve, 6½-oz	50.00
Bottle, Hutch, amber, Root Co, ½-oz, 3 in case	150.00
Bottle, International, set of 9 in plexiglas case	225.00
Bottle, leaded crystal, 100th logo, 6½-oz, MIB	100.00
Medallion, bronze, w/box, 3" dia	50.00
Pin set, wood fr, 101 pins	300.00
Scarf, silk, 30x30"	35.00
Thermometer, glass cover, 14" dia, M	22.00

Coca-Cola Originals

Salesman's sample cooler, 1928, 13" x 10½" x 8", in original case, NM, $7,500.00.

Ad, 1905, Lillian Nordica, +2-sided coupon, 6½x9¾", EX	225.00
Ad, 1910, Housewife magazine, ladies/dog at fountain, 22x16"	125.00
Ash tray, 1950s, porc, w/bottle lighter, NM	75.00
Ash tray, 1950s, ruby glass, card suit shape, set of 4/no box	125.00
Ash tray, 1950s, ruby glass, card suit shape, 4 in box	250.00
Ash tray, 50th Anniversary, gold bottle, 5" dia, NM	100.00
Banner, 1911, Drink a Bottle..., 11½ ft long, G	800.00
Banner, 1950s, canvas, from truck, 48x64", NM	300.00
Barrel, syrup; 1920s, w/NM label, 10-gal, EX	275.00
Blotter, 1915, CC Chewing Gum, Chew This, M	825.00
Blotter, 1915, Pure & Healthful, EX	22.50
Blotter, 1932, man reads paper, Tune In, EX	90.00

Blotter, 1940, clown, Greatest Pause on Earth, NM	50.00
Blotter, 1945, boy & girl, Canadian, NM	45.00
Book, 1925, Webster's Little Gem dictionary, NM	37.50
Book, 1960s, Touch Football Rules, M	7.50
Booklet, 1912, The Truth About CC, 16-pg, EX	35.00
Bookmark, 1900, celluloid, girl writes, 2x2¼", EX-NM	325.00
Bottle, display; 1930s, glass, Christmas, w/cap, 20", NM	250.00
Bottle, display; 1953, soft plastic, 2 halves, w/cap, 20", EX	285.00
Bottle, flavor; Big Chief, lt gr, emb Indian head	10.00
Bottle, seltzer; Carolina Club, M	75.00
Bottle, seltzer; Mt Lassen, red label, unmk top	120.00
Bottle, seltzer; 1930s, Royal Palm, NM	120.00
Bottle, str sides, Biedenham, CC script, clear, w/label, EX	150.00
Bottle, str sides, Indiana PA, lt amber, M	45.00
Bottle, str sides, Rochester NY, script logo, lt bl, 30-oz	185.00
Bottle, syrup; 1910, Drink CC in wreath, orig silver cap, EX	350.00
Bottle opener, 1950s, flat, EX	12.00
Bottle protector, 1930, paper, In Bottles, M	2.00
Bottle protector, 1942, paper, So Easy To Serve, M	2.00
Bottle rack, 1930s, Drink CC at Home, 60", NM	150.00
Bow tie, 1950s, western type, red & wht, NM	12.50
Box, CC Gum, wooden, 5¾x12¾x6¼", EX	375.00
Calendar, 1921, girl w/glass, full pad, 32x12", EX	725.00
Calendar, 1933, Village Blacksmith, full pad, 30x17", EX	375.00
Calendar, 1940, full pad, 26x14", EX	175.00
Calendar holder, 1976, tin, 9x12", NM	35.00
Can, 1960s, lg dmn, NM	60.00
Cap, soda jerk; 1920s, cloth, NM	15.00
Carrier, bottle; shopping cart (holds 2 bottles), NM	10.00
Carrier, bottle; 1930s, Christmas, cb, 7¼x8x5", G	60.00
Carrier, bottle; 1950s, cb, holds 12, NM	10.00
Case, 1940s, wood, Drink CC in Bottles on yel, EX	25.00
Case, 1950s, wood, Drink CC in Bottles, EX	15.00
Case, 1950s-60s, plastic, Drink CC in Bottles, NM	10.00
Chair, 1960, emb metal (beware of decals), folding, M	75.00
Chalkboard, 1950s, tin, red/yel/wht, 26x18", VG	75.00
Clock, 1910, leather bottle form, 8x3", EX	650.00
Clock, 1916-20, Gilbert regulator, variations exist, EX	750.00
Clock, 1941, neon, octagon shape, 18", NM	1,250.00
Clock, 1942, Drink CC Ice Cold, Sessions, 14½" sq, NM	395.00
Clock, 1942, neon, w/bottle, 16x16", EX (+)	450.00
Clock, 1950, counter top, lights up, NM	465.00
Clock, 1951, Drink CC, maroon, 17½" dia, M	75.00
Clock, 1972, plastic, schoolhouse, NM	45.00
Clock, 1974, plastic, Betty, NM	45.00
Coaster, 1940s, rubber, complete set in envelope, M	18.00
Coaster, 1950s, aluminum, M	5.00
Container, syrup; tin, emb CC, 9x6" dia, 1-gal, VG	100.00
Cooler bag, 1960, vinyl, drawstring top, M	35.00
Coupon, 1890s, 2 sided, Is the Best..., 1½x3⅜", NM	165.00
Cuff links, 1950s, sterling, pr	65.00
Cup, plastic, lights up, 12", NM	80.00
Decal, 1950s, Please Pay Cashier, M	7.50
Diecut, 1908, cb, cherub w/tray, easel bk, 14¾"	2,000.00
Diecut, 1920, cb, man in grass w/glass, 39½x28½", EX	2,500.00
Diecut, 1920s, cb, Good Company, 18x14", EX	450.00
Diecut, 1926, cb, girl w/tray, 14x11½", NM	350.00
Diecut, 1934, cb, W Beery/Jackie Cooper, 3-fold, 54", EX	1,500.00
Diecut, 1963, cb, girl w/2 6-packs, For Extra..., life sz, NM	100.00
Doll, delivery man, Buddy Lee, compo, orig uniform, 12", NM	625.00
Doll, Santa, Blk, plush, EX	100.00
Doorknob, 1910s, brass or steel, emb CC, NM	250.00
Door pull, 1930s, aluminum bottle shape (repros in iron), NM	165.00
Fan, 1911, Oriental lady in garden, EX	135.00

Fan, 1920s, cb, child picking flowers, paddle form, NM **27.50**
Fan, 1926, heavy cb, paddle form (part of display pc), rare **235.00**
Fan, 1930s, Drink CC, bottle, loop hdl, EX **32.00**
Fan, 1950s, cb foldout, flower basket, NM **28.00**
Fountain glass, 1900-04, etched, str sides, NM **575.00**
Fountain glass, 1923-27, modified flare, EX **85.00**
Fountain glass, 1929-40, TM in tail, belled sides, M **35.00**
Game, Ring Toss, EX in box **75.00**
Game, table tennis, CC logo on paddles, NM **65.00**
Game, 1938, Steps to Health, 11x26", M in orig envelope **100.00**
Jar, glass, CC Chewing Gum, w/orig lid, 10x4½x4¼" **500.00**
Lamp, 1970s, plastic, gr & wht swag, 16" dia, M **85.00**
Map, 1940s, N America, 30x36", EX **40.00**
Match holder, 1907, leather, NM **175.00**
Match striker, 1930s, porc, French, VG **80.00**
Match striker, 1930s, porc, M **365.00**
Matchbook, 1936, Delicious, Refreshing, M **5.00**
Matchbook, 1959, King Size Coke, NM **2.00**
Menu board, 1934, tin, Deco lines, NM **200.00**
Menu board, 1950, tin, Canada, M **125.00**
Menu board, 1950s, cb, Sign of Good Taste, NM **50.00**
Mug, 1920, ceramic, emb CC, rare **500.00**
Napkin, 1900s, leaves around edge, EX **60.00**
Napkin, 1920s, CC & bottle on red 'button' in center, NM **25.00**
Note pad, 1903, celluloid, Hilda Clark w/glass, 5x2½", NM **375.00**
Pencil holder, 1970s, ceramic, 75th Anniversary, M **80.00**
Pencil sharpener, 1930s, bottle form, M **28.00**
Pillow, 1950, bottle form, EX **45.00**
Pin-bk button, 1960s, Try a...Frozen CC..., M **5.00**
Pin-bk button, 1976, Happy Birthday America, M **3.50**
Pin-bk button, 1980s, Diet Coke..., M **2.50**
Plate, 1931, china, bottle & glass in center, 7¼", EX **200.00**
Playing cards, 1943, girl w/dog, NM in box **125.00**
Playing cards, 1961, girl w/bottle, M in box **35.00**
Pocket mirror, 1911, lady in lg hat, NM **225.00**
Pocket mirror, 1916, celluloid, girl w/bottle, 1¾x2¾", NM **275.00**
Post card, 1954, World's Fair, Coke Pavilion, EX **2.50**
Push bar, 1950s, metal, Refreshing New Feeling, adjustable, M **75.00**
Push bar, 1950s, porc, Iced Here, NM **85.00**
Push plate, 1930s, porc, Come In!, red/yel, oval, NM **125.00**
Push plate, 1930s, porc, oval, Have a Coke, sm, NM **165.00**
Push plate, 1930s, porc, Thanks Call Again, NM **125.00**
Push plate, 1940s, porc, French, EX **65.00**
Radiator plate, 1920s, chrome, 17", NM **325.00**
Radio, 1949, cooler form, 7x12x9½", EX to NM **500.00**
Radio, 1970s, vending machine form, NM **85.00**
Record, 1950, Learn To Dance, A Capops, 45 rpm, M **5.00**
Record, 1950s, salesman's training, 33⅓ rpm, M **10.00**
Ruler, 1950s, Refresca en Grande, Mexico, M **4.00**
Score pad, 1940s, full color, 4x7½", NM **10.00**
Shade, leaded glass, brass band/fringe, ca 1918, 16" dia, EX **4,000.00**
Sheet music, 1915, My CC Girl, rare, 10¾x13¾", EX **325.00**
Sheet music, 1940s, Rum & Coca Cola, Andrews Sisters, NM......**30.00**
Shirt, 1950s, bottle & cowboys, short sleeved, NM **85.00**
Sign, 1927, tin, Refresh Yourself!, rare, 28x29", EX **450.00**
Sign, 1927, tin, 2-sided arrow, 7¾x30", NM **400.00**
Sign, 1929, paper, man w/bottle & hot dog, 30x10", EX **375.00**
Sign, 1930s, porc, shield, sm, NM **365.00**
Sign, 1930s, porc flange, French, 18x20", EX **175.00**
Sign, 1930s, tin, Drink CC, Dasco, 5¾x17¾", EX **80.00**
Sign, 1930s, wood w/metal trim, triangular, 19x20", NM **425.00**
Sign, 1931, tin, Gas To-Day, CC Sold Here, 54x18", EX **500.00**
Sign, 1932, tin, hand holds bottle, 9x12", M **275.00**
Sign, 1933, cb, 3-D, Refresh...While Shopping, 10x22", EX **275.00**

Sign, 1933, tin, Ice Cold, vertical, 54x19", EX **275.00**
Sign, 1934, cb, bottle & hamburger, 30x14", EX **125.00**
Sign, 1934, cb, Joan Crawford, 24x14", NM **425.00**
Sign, 1934, porc, Fountain Service, 14x27", EX **325.00**
Sign, 1936, Chinatown, Oriental lady w/glass, 22x14½", NM **425.00**
Sign, 1938, porc flange, French, 18x20", EX **350.00**
Sign, 1939, porc, Fountain Service, 2-sided shield, 22x26", NM.**400.00**
Sign, 1939, tin, Delicious &..., 19x28", EX **200.00**
Sign, 1940, aluminum, cooler, circle, & arrow, EX **375.00**
Sign, 1940, cb w/wood & metal fr, girl sings, 20x36", NM..........**275.00**
Sign, 1940s, cb, Mind Reader!, girl on chaise, 29x56", EX **225.00**
Sign, 1940s, celluloid, bottle under CC, button form, 9", NM **100.00**
Sign, 1940s, flanged, Drink CC, bottle in yel dot, M **275.00**

Sign, plexiglass wall hanger, 1940s, VG, $140.00.

Sign, 1942, cb, airplane, w/string hanger, 20x22", 1 of 20, NM **35.00**
Sign, 1942, cb, girl w/umbrella by cooler, 27x16", NM **100.00**
Sign, 1948, silver glass, lights up, counter type, 12x20", NM **425.00**
Sign, 1950, cb, open burger on plate by bottle, 45x22", NM **125.00**
Sign, 1950, cb, 2-sided, girl w/bottle & party goers, 28x20".........**125.00**
Sign, 1950, glass, front lights up, 8x18", NM **250.00**
Sign, 1950, plastic, Work Safely, 12x14", NM **50.00**
Sign, 1950s, cb, Phil Rizutto, Coke's a Natural!, 12x10", EX.......**200.00**
Sign, 1950s, flange, Lunch, 2 buttons, EX **265.00**
Sign, 1950s, glass front, lights up, Drink CC, 8x18", NM **325.00**
Sign, 1950s, plastic front, Drink, lights up, 8x18", NM **125.00**
Sign, 1950s, porc, Candy & Films, 24x16", NM **325.00**
Sign, 1950s, porc, dispenser, 28x28", NM **375.00**
Sign, 1950s, porc, dispenser, 28x28", VG **175.00**
Sign, 1950s, porc, red dot, Fountain Service, 12x28", NM **175.00**
Sign, 1950s, porc, ribbon, Fountain Service, 12x28", EX.............**165.00**
Sign, 1960s, plastic, Sno-ee, lights up, 18x18", EX **50.00**
Sticker, 1930s, menu label, With Your Lunch Today, M **12.50**
Straws, 1940s, mk on ea, M in (full) box **80.00**
String holder, 1920s, 6 Pack, NM **350.00**
String holder, 1930s, Take Home CC in Cartons, 14x16", VG ..**225.00**
Telephone, Olympic Cube, NM **35.00**
Thermometer, 1915, wood, not faded, 21x5", EX **325.00**
Thermometer, 1939, porc, Silhouette Girl, 18x16", EX..............**225.00**
Thermometer, 1941, tin, dbl-bottle, 16x7", VG **150.00**
Thermometer, 1944, masonite, 17x7", NM **225.00**
Thermometer, 1950, glass front, In Bottles, 12" dia, NM..........**125.00**
Thermometer, 1950s, tin, Drink CC, 9", EX **45.00**
Thermometer, 1956, gold bottle, 7½x2¼", NM **15.00**
Thermometer, 1960s, plastic, Enjoy CC, M **30.00**

Thimble, 1920, aluminum, red enamel inlay, lt wear 25.00
Tip tray, 1913, girl w/glass, 4¼x6", EX 100.00
Tip tray, 1914, Betty, oval, 4¼x6", G 85.00
Tip tray, 1916, Elaine w/Coke, 8½x19", NM 180.00
Tip tray, 1969, Swedish smoke glass, 8x6", NM 48.00
Toy, Coke can robot transformer, Japan, rare, 5", M 80.00
Toy truck, Matchbox, yel, regular cases, EX 30.00
Toy truck, 1930s, Metalcraft, rubber wheels, 11", NM 525.00
Toy truck, 1940, Buddy L, wood, rare, 19", EX 1,850.00
Toy truck, 1940s, Smith-Miller, wood & metal, EX 550.00
Toy truck, 1950, Marx #21, Canadian Version, EX 500.00
Toy truck, 1950s, HAJI, tin litho, 4½", NM 225.00
Toy truck, 1950s, Marx, Sprite Boy, red/yel, clean, VG..............190.00
Toy truck, 1956, tin, friction, 'San' truck, NM..............................395.00
Toy truck, 1960s, Buddy L, M in box...235.00
Tray, 1904, Lillian Nordica w/glass, 10½x13¼", EX 2,350.00
Tray, 1909, St Louis Fair girl, oval, 16½x13½", NM 1,800.00
Tray, 1914, Betty, oval, 12½x15¾", EX...380.00
Tray, 1914, Betty, 10½x13¼", NM 500.00
Tray, 1920, garden girl, 10½x13¼", EX 325.00

Tray, garden girl, 1920, NM, $750.00.

Tray, 1921, autumn girl, 10½x13¼", EX 300.00
Tray, 1922, summer girl, 10½x13¼", EX 375.00
Tray, 1923, flapper girl, 10½x13¼", NM 325.00
Tray, 1925, girl w/fur, 10½x13¼", NM (+)....................................375.00
Tray, 1927, curb-side service, 10½x13¼", M.................................500.00
Tray, 1930, bathing beauty, 10½x13¼", EX 175.00
Tray, 1930, telephone girl, 10½x13¼", EX 125.00
Tray, 1933, Frances Dee, 10½x13¼", EX.......................................250.00
Tray, 1935, Madge Evans, 10½x13¼", NM....................................225.00
Tray, 1938, girl in afternoon, 10½x13¼", NM 125.00
Tray, 1941, skater girl, 10½x13¼", NM...140.00
Tray, 1950, girl w/wind in hair, 10½x13¼", VG............................25.00
Tray, 1957, birdhouse, 10½x13¼", M 85.00
Tray, 1957, rooster, 10½x13¼", EX 50.00
Tray, 1960, fishtail, Drive In for Coke, rare, NM 175.00
Tray, 1972, girl in duster, NM..10.00
Umbrella, 1920s, red & wht, EX...300.00
Visor cap, 1960s, cb, M... 6.00
Wallet, 1918, tri-fold, w/tiny calendar insert, NM 85.00
Waste paper basket, 1970s, metal, red & wht, M...........................10.00
Watch fob, ca 1907, emb brass, girl w/glass, EX............................150.00
Yard stick, Golden Rule, EX 8.00

Vendors

Though interest in Coca-Cola machines of the 1949 – 1959 era rose dramatically over the last few years, values currently seem to have leveled off and actually dropped 15% to 20%. The major manufacturers of these curved top, 5¢ and 10¢ machines were Vendo (V), Vendorlator (VMC), Cavalier (C or CS), and Jacobs. In the following listings, 'VG' values are for machines in clean, original condition.

Cavalier, model #CS72, M rstr 3,000.00
Cavalier, model #CS72, VG 650.00
Cavalier, model #C27, M rstr 3,000.00
Cavalier, model #C27, VG 850.00
Cavalier, model #C51, M rstr 2,000.00
Cavalier, model #C51, VG 500.00
Jacobs, model #26, M rstr 4,500.00
Jacobs, model #26, VG 1,250.00
Vendo, model #23, M rstr 2,000.00
Vendo, model #23, VG 450.00
Vendo, model #39, M rstr 2,500.00
Vendo, model #39, VG 650.00
Vendo, model #44, M rstr 4,000.00
Vendo, model #44, VG 1,500.00
Vendo, model #56, M rstr 3,500.00
Vendo, model #56, VG 850.00
Vendo, model #80, M rstr 2,000.00
Vendo, model #80, VG 350.00
Vendo, model #81, M rstr 3,500.00
Vendo, model #81, VG 850.00
Vendorlator, model #27, M rstr 3,000.00
Vendorlator, model #27, VG..500.00
Vendorlator, model #27A, M rstr 2,500.00
Vendorlator, model #27A, VG 600.00
Vendorlator, model #33, M rstr 2,500.00
Vendorlator, model #33, VG..600.00
Vendorlator, model #44, M rstr 3,800.00
Vendorlator, model #44, VG.. 1,350.00
Vendorlator, model #72, M rstr 3,000.00
Vendorlator, model #72, VG..750.00

Coffee Grinders

The serious collector of kitchenwares and country store items ranks coffee mills high on the list of desirable examples. A trend is developing toward preferring items whose manufacturers are easily identifiable. Names to look for include Adams, Arcade, Baldwin Bros., Daisy, Elgin National, Elma, Enterprise, Lane Bros., Parker, Regal, and Sun Mfg. Co.; there are many others. Any of these marks found on coffee mills represent companies who were in business at or before the turn of the century.

Side mills usually have a brass tag located on the tin hopper. If the hopper was made of cast iron, the name was usually cast into the metal. Some of the less expensive versions had no identification. Decals were often used on the front of lap mills and table styles, though sometimes you will find these decals on the inside of the drawer. Because decals are prone to flake off and fade, and since they are often destroyed when the mill is being refinished, lap and table mills are the most difficult types to attribute to a specific manufacturer. Canister mills had names and patent dates molded into the cast iron housing or on the canister itself. Commercial mills used in country and general stores were made of cast iron. Important information such as manufacture and patent dates was usually cast into the wheels, housing, or base of the mill. Such identification contributes considerably toward value.

Good examples of early coffee mills are rapidly becoming difficult to find. Beware of the many imported imposters that are on the market today.

Key: adj — adjustment

Enterprise Mfg., red and black paint with U.S. shield appliques in gilt, 12", $425.00.

A Kendrick & Sons No 1, lap, CI w/brass hopper, CI drw 95.00
Adams Patented, lap, pewter hopper, wood box, porc knob 105.00
AK & Sons #237707, CI, octagon base, rnd hopper, heavy 125.00
American Beauty, canister, CI & tin, orig cup & papers................55.00
Arcade, Crystal No 44, CI w/glass hopper, Arcade lid & cup 80.00
Arcade, Favorite No 27, side, CI w/orig lid...................................70.00
Arcade, Favorite No 7, side, CI, grind adj front, CI lid 65.00
Arcade, Imperial, lap, CI closed hopper, wood box, EX 80.00
Arcade, Imperial, table, closed CI hopper, wood box 85.00
Arcade, Imperial No 200, lap, CI hopper w/eagle, Pat 88, 89 ....95.00
Arcade, IXL, table, ornate CI hopper, hdl on side, 1-lb, EX 150.00
Arcade, Jewel, canister, rectangular glass hopper, w/lid, EX...........95.00
Arcade, lap, fancy CI top & hopper, wood box, EX 95.00
Arcade, Sunbeam, CI w/glass hopper, orig lid & cup, EX.............95.00
Arcade, table, w/decal, Pat 6-5-1884, 1-lb 95.00
Arcade, Telephone, canister, CI front, Pat Sept 25 '88................325.00
Arcade No 147, lap, fancy CI closed hopper, wood box, EX 85.00
Arcade No 3, canister, CI w/glass hopper, orig Arcade lid 75.00
Arcade No 4, canister, CI w/glass hopper, orig Arcade lid 75.00
Arcade No 5, side, CI, Pat June '94..65.00
Arcade No 700, lap, w/dust cover, Sears 1908 catalog, EX............90.00
Blksmith made, funnel shape, 1-hdl, open hopper, wall mt 185.00
Blksmith made, funnel shape, 2-hdl, wall mt to 2x4" 195.00
C Ibach stamp on hdl, dvtl walnut, CI hopper 145.00
Caravan, canister, CI works, tin hopper, ca 1910, VG.................65.00
Coffee Bean Roaster, tin hopper, CI trivet, wood hdl 145.00
Coles Mfg No 7, counter, CI, Pat 1887, 16" wheels, 27", EX.......545.00
Common unmk, lap, open CI hopper, orig drw, wood box, VG.....70.00
Common unmk, table, orig drw, screw cap on top, VG................75.00
Daisy No 667, miniature, CI top, wood box & drw, orig decal.......80.00
DeVe, Holland Made, lap, copper-plated hopper, decals 55.00
Elgin Nat'l No 40, counter, CI, red pnt, 2 wheels, orig, VG 425.00
Elgin Nat'l No 44, CI/red pnt, w/eagle & pan, 5" wheels, 24" 495.00
Elgin Nat'l No 48, CI w/eagle, orig lily decal, 2-wheel.................525.00
Elma, counter, CI, closed hopper, 10" single wheel, 17" 85.00
Enterprise, counter, CI, brass hopper, Pat 1873, 6" wheels, EX ...425.00
Enterprise, counter, CI, CI drw, closed hopper, Pat 1873, VG 185.00
Enterprise, counter, CI, eagle on hopper, 2-wheel, Pat 1873 ....495.00

Enterprise, floor, CI, CI hopper, Pat 1898, 39" wheels, VG 1,500.00
Enterprise, Pioneer, floor, CI, Pat 1873, 34" wheels, 65", VG .. 1,500.00
Enterprise, table clamp-on, CI w/CI cup, blk w/gold decal 55.00
Enterprise No 1, CI w/CI drw, hdl, covered hopper 185.00
Enterprise No 1, counter, open hopper, hdl, Pat 1873, 11", VG ..185.00
Enterprise No 116½, floor, Pat 1873, 39" wheels, 72", EX....... 3,500.00
Enterprise No 12, counter, w/eagle, 2-wheel, Pat 1898 ....695.00
Enterprise No 3, counter, CI w/wood drw, orig decals/pnt..........425.00
Enterprise No 7, counter, CI, w/eagle, orig pnt, 17" wheel 525.00
Enterprise No 9, CI, brass eagle, Pat 1898, 19" wheels, 28", VG .525.00
Euclid No 4, counter, aluminum hopper, 10" wheels, VG 395.00
Fairbanks Morse, floor, CI, brass hopper, 2-wheel, 72", EX 2,600.00
Golden Rule, canister, w/orig glass, CI front, wood box, EX........275.00
Grand Union Tea, canister, red pnt, orig writing, Pat 1910..........85.00
Grand Union Tea, table, CI sq base, rnd hopper, mfg Griswold ..235.00
Griswold, coffee bean roaster, rnd, CI, wood hdl, 3-pc................595.00
J Fisher, dvtl mahog, pewter hopper, handmade 155.00
J Fisher Warranted, lap, dvtl walnut, pewter hopper, unique.......155.00
Japy Freres, ornate woodwork, brass hopper, ftd 95.00
Juvenile, lap, CI, top, wood box, orig drw & decal, sm, EX..........85.00
K&M, lap, maple, aluminum closed hopper, clips on drw side.......55.00
L&S, side, CI, on orig board...65.00
L'il Tot, miniature, CI hopper & drw front, wood box 80.00
Landers, Frary & Clark, canister, CI & tin, Pat 1905, VG 70.00
Landers, Frary & Clark, lap, fancy, CI top, wood box 95.00
Landers, Frary & Clark, Regal No 44, canister, CI/tin, orig 85.00
Landers, Frary & Clark, table, CI, Pat Feb 14, 1905, EX..............75.00
Landers, Frary & Clark, Universal No 14, table, Pat 1905, VG.....65.00
Landers, Frary & Clark No 50, counter, CI, 12" wheels, EX+.......450.00
Lap, CI, brn pnt, octagon base & hopper, cup in base, 4x4x4" 80.00
Lees, canister, CI works, rnd glass hopper, EX 70.00
Lightning, canister, CI works, tin hopper, 1-lb, EX 75.00
Logan & Strobridge, Franco-American, lap, ornate CI hopper......90.00
Miniature, canister, boy & girl, 5½x1½" 85.00
Nat'l, coffee & spice counter, CI, 12" wheels, 25", VG................475.00
Nat'l, coffee & spice counter, CI, 17" wheels, 28", VG................495.00
Nat'l, counter, CI works, covered hopper, wood drw, 1-wheel.......85.00
Nat'l No 5, CI body & drw, 12" wheels, VG 425.00
Nat'l Specialty No 0, table clamp-on, CI, covered hopper............85.00
Nat'l Specialty...Philadelphia, CI, 25" wheels, VG 595.00
New Home, table, CI top, enclosed hopper, wood box, 1-lb, EX+ ..80.00
New Model, lap, CI w/CI drw, bottom opens all 4 sides 75.00
None Such, Bronson Co Cleveland OH, table, tin, pnt..................55.00
Parker, Charles; table, tall/thin, CI & tin top, hdl on top 95.00
Parker, side, Pat 1876, CI, on orig board, grind adj front 65.00
Parker (Chas) No 350, side, CI, orig lid, Pat 4/1876 ....75.00
Parker (Chas) No 5005, counter, CI, 12½" wheels, 17", EX........525.00
Parker No 2, counter, CI w/orig decals, 9" wheels, EX................425.00
Parker No 449, canister, CI works, rnd glass hopper, VG..............80.00
Parker No 5000, counter, CI, Pat 1897, 12" wheels, 17", VG......425.00
Parker No 555, Challenge Fast Grind, table, 1-lb, orig, EX...........85.00
Parker No 60, side/tin hopper, brass eagle, Parker lid 65.00
Persepolis, table, CI & brass, unique 165.00
Peugot Freres, lap, wood box, tin-covered hopper, Fr....................45.00
Primitive, lap, cherry, brass hopper, handmade/unique, 4x4" 160.00
Primitive, lap, dvtl, red buttermilk pnt, orig drw, pewter.............165.00
Primitive, lap, dvtl walnut, wrought iron, brass hopper................165.00
PS&W No 3500, side, CI, orig lid..65.00
PSW&Co No 6, side, orig CI lid, EX..65.00
Queen, miniature, CI hopper & drw front, wood box, decal..........80.00
Rock Hard, Garant-Sewaarborge, lap, imported............................45.00
Royal, side, CI w/CI cup, open hopper, Pat Apr 15, 1890, VG......65.00
RR Kreiterr, Lewisberry, York Co PA, dvtl, pewter hopper 165.00
S&H, counter, CI, w/drw, 19" wheels, 21", VG 475.00

School Bell, canister, similar to Golden Rule, CI & wood...........325.00
Simmons Hardware Co, Delmar Coffee, table, CI cover................85.00
Star, canister, tin w/CI works, Pat 1910, VG.................................65.00
Star, counter, tin drw, blk, 1-wheel, sm, VG...............................275.00
Star No 7, counter, CI, w/pan, 2-wheel, VG.................................450.00
Sun Mfg, table, cylinder style, wood, top fill, rnd, 13"...............195.00
Sun Mfg No 1080, Challenge Fast Grind, Columbus OH, table ...80.00
Swift, drug mill, CI, open hopper, Pat June 30, 1874..................495.00
Swift, side, CI, Pat 1845, Pat Aug 16, 1859, top missing..............75.00
Swift No 13, counter, orig tin drw, red pnt, 12" wheels, 19".......425.00
Swift No 15, counter, orig decals/pnt, Pat 1875, 19" wheels........875.00
Tin, lap, covered, grind caught in cup underneath.......................55.00
Turkish, brass cylinder, seal of sultan, folding hdl, old...............65.00
Turkish, primitive, table, lg sq box on 28" board, ornate, old......160.00
Universal No 109, blk tin w/gr decal, Pat 1905, EX......................65.00
W Cross & Sons, lap, CI w/orig CI drw, brass hopper & pull........85.00
Walton, Bronson, canister, tin & CI, Pat 1911...........................80.00
Walton, Clevis, canister, orig cup, Pat 7/0/1901, orig, EX............75.00
Wilson, Increase, side, CI & tin...60.00
Wrights Hdwe Co, Brighton, table, 1-lb, 8"..................................80.00
WW Weaver Warranted, dvtl walnut, pewter hopper, ca 1830...165.00
Xray, canister, CI works, tin hopper w/glass, EX..........................75.00

Coin-Operated Machines

Coin-operated machines may be the fastest-growing area of collector interest in today's market. Many machines are bought, restored, and used for home entertainment. Older examples from the turn of the century and those with especially elaborate decoration and innovative accessories are most desirable, often bringing prices in excess of $7,000.00.

Vending machines sold a product or a service. They were already in common usage by 1900 selling gum, cigars, matches, and a host of other commodities. Peanut and gumball machines are especially popular today. The most valuable are those with their original finish and decals. Older machines made of cast iron are especially desirable, while those with plastic globes have little or no collector value. When buying unrestored peanut machines, beware of salt damage.

The coin-operated phonograph of the early 1900s paved the way for the jukeboxes of the twenties. Seeburg was first on the market with an automatic 8-tune phonograph. By the 1930s, Wurlitzer was the top name in the industry with dealerships all over the country. As a result of the growing ranks of competitors, the forties produced the most beautiful machines made. Wurlitzers from this era are probably the most popularly sought-after models on the market today. The model 1015 of 1946 is considered the all-time classic, and often brings prices in excess of $6,000.

Coin-Op Newsletter; Jukebox Collectors' Newsletter; Chicagoland Antique Advertising, Slot Machine, and Jukebox Gazette; and *Loose Change Magazine* are all excellent publications for those interested in coin-operated machines; see the Clubs, Newsletters, and Catalogs section of the Directory for publishing information.

Jackie and Ken Durham are our advisors (for all but Jukeboxes); they are listed in the Directory under the District of Columbia. Our advisor for Jukeboxes is Norman Nelson; he is listed in the Directory under Ohio.

Arcade Machines

Advance 1¢ Shock, w/marque, EX orig................................325.00
Brunswick, pool table, ca 1890, EX..................................4,500.00
Buckley Treasure Chest, digger...1,950.00
Caille Cailoscope 1¢ Peep Show, EX orig..........................1,850.00

Caille Mickey Finn Strength Tester, rstr..................................4,500.00
Challenger ABT Shooting Gallery, 1950s, unused......................350.00
Chicago Coin Turf Club, upright horse race, 1 or 2 players.........600.00
Exhibit Crystal Gazer, EX...550.00
Exhibit Egyptian Mummy, EX...1,500.00
Exhibit Fist Striker, EX orig...995.00
Exhibit Iron Claw, floor model..2,500.00
Exhibit Kiss-o-Meter, EX...650.00
Exhibit Love Tester, sm, rstr..350.00
Exhibit Magic Heart, EX...750.00
Exhibit Peep Show, barrels, EX..750.00
Exhibit Whee Gee Mystic, fortune teller, EX............................750.00
Exhibit Whom Shall You Marry, EX orig...............................1,600.00
Fortune Teller, wax head & hands, oak cabinet, EX...............9,500.00
Genco Fortune Teller, EX..2,800.00
Gottlieb Bank Shot, EX...265.00
Gottlieb Lady Luck, wood rail, pinball, 1954, EX.....................650.00
Gottlieb Strength Tester, EX..300.00
Hanson Grip Machine...200.00
Love Meter 1¢, electric light-up w/bells...................................395.00
Mercury Grip Tester..250.00
Midget, movie machine, EX...750.00
Mills Bowfront 1¢ Autostereoscope Peep Show, rstr..............1,900.00
Munves Grandma's Prophecies, fortune teller, G...................3,500.00
Mutoscope Cross Country Race, EX.......................................1,250.00
Mutoscope Drivemobile, G..450.00
Mutoscope Love Analyst, fancy cabinet, EX orig.......................700.00
Mutoscope 2¢ Hockey, orig marque, early, EX........................1,250.00
Rockola World's Fair Jigsaw, pinball, EX................................1,250.00
Seeburg Chicken Sam, 1930s, VG...880.00
Seeburg Koon Hunt, M..1,700.00
Sky Chief, pinball, 1942, EX...350.00
US Marshal, gun game, EX...250.00
Visible Roulette, France, early 1900s, EX...............................2,000.00
Whiting Sculptoscope, EX..850.00
Williams Tropic Fun, pinball, rstr...375.00
Williams 10 Strike, bowling, EX..800.00
Wizard 1¢ Fortune Teller, aluminum/wood, 19x14"...............1,200.00

Jukeboxes

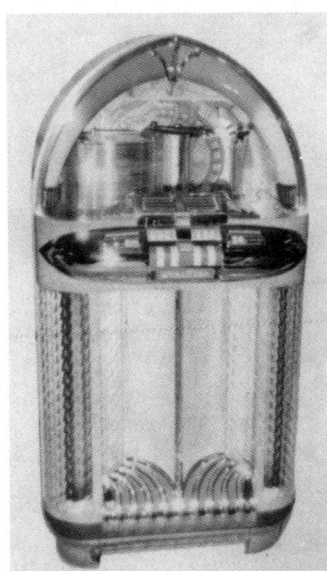

Wurlitzer #1100, restored, $6,500.00.

Airion #1200-A, EX..950.00
AMI Model #500, EX...2,700.00
AMI Model A, EX..3,000.00

Rockola #1428, EX orig	2,700.00
Rockola #1434, 78 rpm, EX orig	700.00
Rockola #1442	1,000.00
Rockola #424, EX	750.00
Rockola Empress, 1959, EX orig, +records	2,500.00
AMI Model F-80, pk, EX	1,150.00
AMI Model F-80, yel, EX	950.00
Bimbo box, animated monkeys	3,500.00
Cremona #3, rstr	6,600.00
Mills Carousel, 5¢ coin slot, 12-selection, 1933, VG orig	800.00
Ristaucrat, 100 selections, EX	500.00
Rockola #1426, rstr	5,000.00
Rockola-Gabels, oak, ca 1930, EX orig	2,500.00
Scopatone, EX orig	800.00
Seeburg #222, EX orig	1,600.00
Seeburg B, rstr	2,250.00
Seeburg C, VG orig	1,100.00
Seeburg E, rstr	12,000.00
Seeburg G, M	1,100.00
Seeburg LSI, EX	250.00
Seeburg M-100-R, EX orig	1,600.00
Seeburg Q, EX orig	675.00
Wurlitzer #1015, EX orig	7,500.00
Wurlitzer #1015, M rstr	11,000.00
Wurlitzer #1080, EX orig	6,500.00
Wurlitzer #1100, M	6,500.00
Wurlitzer #1400, complete	550.00
Wurlitzer #1500, EX	1,275.00
Wurlitzer #1900	1,500.00
Wurlitzer #2304, EX	1,175.00
Wurlitzer #24, EX orig	3,500.00
Wurlitzer #500, EX orig	3,000.00
Wurlitzer #600, VG orig	1,900.00
Wurlitzer #61, counter top, EX orig	3,500.00
Wurlitzer #616, VG	600.00
Wurlitzer #750, EX orig	6,000.00
Wurlitzer #800, G	3,000.00
Wurlitzer #800, rstr	6,500.00
Wurlitzer Peacock, M rstr	19,800.00
Wurlitzer Victory, EX	10,000.00

Slot Machines

Bally Clover Bell, M	2,000.00
Buckley Long-Shot Horse Race, EX orig	600.00
Caille Blk Cat, musical cabinet, 1902, 66", EX rstr	18,000.00
Caille Commander-Streamline, yel, 1930s, EX	700.00
Caille 10¢ Grand Prize, 4-reel	1,675.00
Caille 25¢ Superior, rstr	1,675.00
Caille 5¢ Bullfrog, floor model, 1903, NM	24,500.00
Jennings $1 Club Chief, M	3,500.00
Jennings Victoria JP, 1932, EX orig, +vendor	1,500.00
Jennings 25¢ Standard Chief, rstr	1,550.00
Jennings 5¢ Dixie Bell, console, EX	1,575.00
Jennings 5¢ Duchess, rstr	1,275.00
Jennings 5¢ Dutch Boys, EX	1,700.00
Jennings 5¢ Export Chief, M rstr	1,450.00
Jennings 5¢ Lite-Up Sun Chief, 1940s, EX rstr	1,800.00
Jennings 5¢ Today, VG	900.00
Jennings 50¢ Greyhound, 1930s, EX	1,500.00
Jewell 5¢ Bell, EX orig	1,200.00
Keeney 5¢ Super Bell, VG orig	1,250.00
Mills Castle Front, gold award, rstr	1,600.00
Mills Skyscraper, EX	1,200.00

Mills Spinner, EX orig	1,000.00
Mills 1¢ QT Dmn Front, 19x12½x13½", VG	950.00
Mills 10¢ Bursting Cherry, VG	1,800.00
Mills 10¢ Hi-Top, VG orig	1,500.00
Mills 10¢ Poinsettia, rstr	1,400.00
Mills 25¢ Golden Falls, EX orig	1,800.00
Mills 5¢ Bonus Horse Head, ca 1939, EX	2,500.00
Mills 5¢ Dewey, quarter-sawn oak, anchor motif, rstr	7,800.00

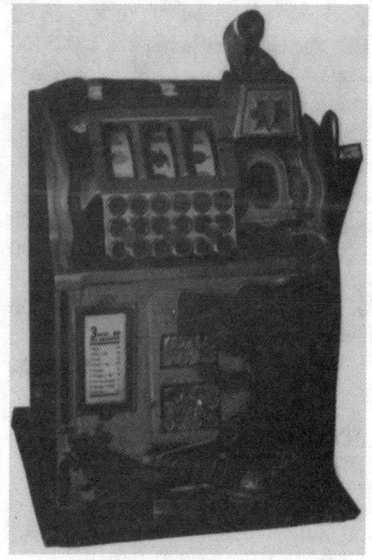

Mills 5¢ Lion's Head, 1931, VG, $1,975.00.

Mills 5¢ Owl, upright	6,500.00
Mills 5¢ Poinsettia, EX	1,350.00
Mills 5¢ QT Smoker, 1930s, scarce	1,200.00
Mills 5¢ Vest Pocket, EX orig	400.00
Mills 5¢ War Eagle, NM orig	2,000.00
Pace $1 Chrome Front, EX	1,095.00
Pace 5¢ Bantam, M display front & jackpot, G orig	995.00
Rockola 5¢ War Eagle, NM orig	2,000.00
Watling 1¢ Treasury, VG	3,200.00
Watling 25¢ Rol-A-Top, NM	3,000.00
Watling 5¢ Bird of Paradise, EX orig	3,500.00
Watling 5¢ Lincoln Deluxe, EX orig	1,700.00

Trade Stimulators

Ad-Lee Puritan Baby, fortune & 1¢ gumball, G	250.00
Bluebird 1¢ Penny Flip, w/gumball vendor, 17x12x8", EX	265.00
Buckley Bang Tail, EX orig	425.00
Caille Jumbo, EX orig	2,000.00
Daval Penny Pack, EX	375.00
Daval Puritan Baby Bell 3¢ Fortune, 1931, EX	465.00
Daval's Poker, 5-reel, 1940s, EX orig	375.00
Deval Chicago Clubhouse	550.00
Good Luck 1¢ Poker, oak & CI, 5-reel, 15x11x9", VG	325.00
Groetchen 21 Blackjack	500.00
Imp 5¢ Cigarettes, 1940s, M in box	195.00
Jennings 5¢/10¢ Cigarolla, wood case, 60x20x22", G	325.00
Line 'Em Up 1¢ Cigar, penny flip	225.00
Mills Bell Boy	1,575.00
Mills Little Perfection, 4-reel, oak cabinet, 1926, 16", EX	800.00
Mills 5¢ Target Practice, CI, NM orig	450.00
Nat'l Smokes, EX	330.00
Nat'l Target, cast aluminum, penny flip	250.00
Penny Ante Draw Poker, 1930s, EX orig	325.00
Sittman & Pot 5¢ Cards, CI, Nafew, EX	2,000.00

Skill Cards 5¢ Poker, EX orig 285.00
Skilltest 1¢, oak cabinet, EX 245.00
Superior 1¢ Baseball..500.00
Swami, fortune dispenser......................................85.00
Whiz-Ball, baseball skill game, counter top, 1930s, EX 400.00

Vendors

Abbey 5¢, peanuts, cash tray, 1930s, EX.........................70.00
Acorn, gumball, oak w/emb scrolls, late 1940s, EX 65.00
Ad-Lee E-2, gum, EX..600.00
Ad-Lee 1¢ Listerated Pepsin Gum, CI, glass globe, EX 750.00
Advance, football globe, peanuts, EX.........................175.00
Advance Big Mouth, peanuts, 1923, EX orig 185.00
Advance 1¢ Simplex Variety, peanuts, 1908, 17x7x8", VG 950.00
American Flags 1¢, gumball, 1930, EX orig 195.00
Atlas 1¢/5¢ Masters Hi Top, EX 275.00
Atlas 5¢ Bantam, peanuts, rstr 65.00
Baby Grand, golden oak, gumball, VG...........................50.00
Berkshire, gumball, orig decal 465.00
Chic-Mint 1¢ Ball Gum, CI/pressed steel, orig globe, EX 450.00
Chicago 5¢, gum/candy, metal & glass, vertical, 15x8x6", G.......100.00
Colgan's 1¢, gum, glass case, clockwork, 14½x6x8", VG 2,600.00
Columbus, matches, CI 100.00
Columbus #18, aluminum 275.00
Columbus #21, EX 350.00
Columbus B, peanuts...650.00
Columbus Bi-More, gum 550.00
Columbus M, EX orig 225.00
Dr Pepper Vendo #81, 12-oz bottles, EX rstr...................... 1,500.00
Empire 1¢, EX 295.00

Ever Ready Lunch Counter, 10¢ sandwich vendor, oak case, 1900s, 25", $600.00.

Exhibit Esco 2¢, cards, EX......................................150.00
Exhibit Rotary Merchandiser.................................. 1,950.00
Fortune 1¢, napkins, EX 80.00
Grand Dad, EX 75.00
Hawkeye, peanuts, 1940s..75.00
Hershey 5¢, candy bars, tan/brn/wht silver, 28", EX...............150.00
Jennings 5¢ Century, EX orig 1,400.00
King 1¢ Twin..250.00
Mr Cornet's US Standard 5¢, aspirin, St Louis MO, VG.............225.00
Northwestern #31 5¢ Merchandiser, EX...........................155.00
Northwestern #33, peanuts, frosted globe, EX...................185.00
Northwestern Jet, peanuts, 1950s, VG.............................40.00
Northwestern 1¢, peanuts, gr granite on CI, glass globe, EX........110.00

Northwestern 1¢ Merchandiser, porc, w/slug eliminator, 1931....165.00
Pace 5¢ Bantam, gumball, EX................................. 1,250.00
Pulver Gum, Clown, porc, 1899, NM 1,450.00
Pulver Gum, Foxy Grandpa, 4-panel 1,150.00
Pulver Gum, Policeman, clockwork, 1-pc, 20", EX orig.............700.00
Pulver Gum, Traffic Cop, clockwork, 1-pc, 20", VG orig 850.00
Pulver Gum, Yel Kid, animated, 2-panel, 24", VG orig 750.00
Shermack, dbl stamps, EX 45.00
Shipman Mfg 10¢, postage cards, 3 for 10¢, EX 95.00
Silver King, hot nuts, EX 135.00
Silver King Deluxe, peanuts, late 1930s, EX.....................85.00
Super V, gumball, EX..60.00
Topper 1¢, gumball, EX...100.00
Unique 1¢, hand lotion, all decals, 1920s, M 350.00
Vendex, gumball, EX orig.......................................125.00
Victor Baby Grand, gumball, EX..................................45.00
Victor Selectorama, early capsule machine, EX orig 90.00
Victor Universal, gumball, 1940s, EX orig 65.00
Victor Vendorama, 1950s, VG....................................25.00
Victor 1¢, gumball, oak & metal case, 7x7x11½", G...............50.00
Victor 1¢ Basketball, gumball, wooden, 1950, EX.................145.00
Victor 1¢ Halfback, gumball, 1950s, EX 50.00
Victor 1¢ Model V, peanuts, 1940s, EX 65.00
Zeno, stick gum, oak cabinet, clockwork, 1893, EX 900.00

Miscellaneous

Alarm clock, Sessions 10¢, for motel, 1940, NM..................45.00
Modern Peerless 1¢ Weighing Machine, Deco red/blk, EX orig ..200.00
Peerless 1¢ Aristocrat, lollipop scale........................ 1,000.00
Watling 1¢ President Fortune Teller, lollipop scale.............. 1,900.00
Watling 1¢ Scale, Philadelphia, 1918, 73x29x20", EX 700.00
Watling 1¢ Scale, What Is Yur Wate..., porc/CI, 1920, 71" 550.00

Comic Books

For almost sixty years, the American public has been thrilled by the monthly adventures of everyone's favorite comic book heroes such as Superman, Captain Marvel, and Spiderman. Each 10¢ comic book issue, featuring a new saga of adventure and mystery, were usually met with excitement and anticipation by the youngsters who eagerly purchased them from their neighborhood candy store or newsstand. Unfortunately, the vast majority of these comic books were eventually discarded in favor of other worldly pursuits. Due to this fact, most comic books from the '30s and '40s did not survive, making them a very scarce and desirable collectible in today's world.

First editions in high-grade condition may bring prices as high as $500 or more. Marvel Comics #1, published in October 1939, has sold for the astounding price of $35,000. Rarity, age, and quality of artwork are prime factors in determining comic book values. Condition is also very important. A good copy of Showcase #4 (the first appearance of the silver-age Flash) might sell for around $350, but a copy of the same book would sell for $6,000 in NM condition. Our advisor for this category is Steve Fishler; he is listed in the Directory under New York.

Ace Comics, #73, EX/NM 56.00
Action Comics, #239, DC Comics, VG+ 31.00
Action Comics, #248, DC Comics, EX.............................26.00
Action Comics, #267, DC Comics, G/G+ 40.00
Action Comics, #28, DC Comics, VG 150.00
Adventure Comics, #286, DC Comics, VG/EX.......................14.25
Adventures of Bob Hope, #66, DC Comics, G+ 3.00
All American Men of War, #13, DC Comics, G/VG 15.00

All Star Comics, #13, DC Comics, EX+......................................525.00
All Star Comics, #31, DC Comics, EX-.......................................220.00
Amazing Mystery Funnies, #7, Centaur, EX/NM................. 1,200.00
Amazing Spiderman, #1, Marvel, VG 925.00
Aquaman, #32, DC Comics, EX... 8.00
Avengers, #9, Marvel, EX...49.00
Baby Huey & Papa, #2, Harvey, 1962, M 55.00
Batman, #210, DC Comics, EX+.. 5.00
Battlefront, #44, Atlas, VG 2.25
Ben Hur, #1052, Dell, 1979, EX..10.00
Beware the Creeper, #1, DC Comics, EX...................................18.00
Brave & Bold, #85, DC Comics, VG 5.25
Buccaneers, #19, Quality, G/VG..36.00
Captain America, #105, Marvel, EX+.......................................26.00
Captain America Comics, #35, Timely, EX................................360.00
Captain Marvel, #1, Marvel, NM...73.00
Captain Marvel Adventures, #54, Fawcett, EX 50.00
Captain Marvel Adventures, #59, Fawcett, VG 21.00
Captain Marvel Jr, #11, Fawcett, G 28.00
Captain Marvel Jr, #75, Fawcett, G/VG 6.00
Classic Comics/Illustrated, #1, Gilberton, EX 22.00

Daredevil #5, EX, $180.00.

Detective Comics, #103, DC Comics, G 22.00
Detective Comics, #123, DC Comics, G 78.00
Detective Comics, #213, DC Comics, VG/VG- 76.00
Donald Duck, Four Color, #282, Dell, EX-................................71.00
Eighty-Page Giant, #15, DC Comics, G/VG................................ 7.00
Fantastic Four, #10, Marvel, EX...140.00
Fantastic Four, #6, Marvel, VG...150.00
Felix the Cat, #2, Dell, EX 27.50
Four Color, 2nd series, #681, Dell, EX+...................................21.00
Four Color, 2nd Series, #692, Dell, VG/EX 4.00
Ghost Rider, #3, Marvel, NM.. 5.00
Green Hornet Comics, #33, Harvey, EX+ 52.00
Harvey Hits, #10, Little Lotta, Harvey, EX...............................15.00
Honeymooners, #3, Christmas Special, Triad, NM 3.00
House of Secrets, #37, DC Comics, VG-.................................... 3.00
House of Secrets, #65, DC Comics, G.. 1.50
Iron Man, #15, Marvel, EX+...16.00
It Really Happened, #1, Kit Carson, 1944, EX 20.00
Journey Into Mystery, #117, Marvel, EX...................................20.00
Jumbo Comics, #77, Fiction House, VG 20.00
Justice League of America, #10, DC Comics, VG 31.00
Little Lulu, Four Color, #146, Dell, VG....................................50.00
Lone Ranger, #84, Dell, VG.. 6.25
Long Bow, #8, Fiction House, EX 11.00
Looney Tunes & Merrie Melodies, #100, Dell, G/G+ 3.25
Looney Tunes & Merrie Melodies, #90, Dell, VG 4.00

Mad, #19, EC Comics, EX+...45.00
Marvel Mystery, #73, Timely, EX/NM....................................275.00
Mickey Mouse, Four Color, #157, Dell, G/VG 25.00
Miss Fury Comics, #1, Timely, EX/NM 910.00
Mystery in Space, #38, Dell, VG..24.50
Mystery in Space, #81, DC Comics, VG.................................... 6.25
Rangers Comics, #5, Fiction House, G/VG 40.00
Richie Rich, #1, Marvel, VG-...135.00
Strange Adventures, #131, DC Comics, VG 7.75
Strange Tales, #160, Marvel, EX/NM 13.25
Sub-Mariner Comics, #8, Timely, VG.....................................152.00
Superboy, #79, DC Comics, G+... 6.75
Superman, #137, DC Comics, VG/EX.......................................22.75
Superman, #138, DC Comics, EX 29.00
Superman, #44, DC Comics, EX+ 133.00
Superman's Girlfriend Lois Lane, #31, DC Comics, VG+.............. 3.75
Superman's Girlfriend Lois Lane, #4, DC Comics, EX 60.00
Suspense Comics, DC Comics, #8, VG 108.00
Tales of Suspense, #69, Marvel, G/VG 4.25
Tales of Unexpected, #1, DC Comics, G+..................................66.00
Two-Fisted Tales, #28, EC Comics, EX 62.00
Uncle Scrooge, #45, Dell, G/VG.. 6.00
Walt Disney Comics & Stories, #164, Dell, VG.......................... 5.00
Walt Disney Comics & Stories, #81, Dell, G.............................. 5.00
War Against Crime, #11, EC Comics, VG-................................100.00
Whiz Comics, #45, Fawcett, VG/EX...37.00
Whiz Comics, #81, Fawcett, EX-..19.00
World's Finest Comics, #100, DC Comics, G 16.50
World's Finest Comics, #93, DC Comics, G++ 8.75
Young Allies, #8, Timely, VG..80.00

Consolidated Lamp and Glass

The Consolidated Lamp and Glass Company of Coraopolis, Pennsylvania, was incorporated in 1894. For many years their primary business was the manufacture of lighting glass such as oil lamps and shades for both gas and electric lighting. The popular 'Cosmos' line of lamps and tableware was produced from 1894 to 1915. (See also Cosmos.) In 1926 Consolidated introduced their Martele line, a type of 'sculptured' ware closely resembling Lalique glassware of France. (Compare Consolidated's 'Lovebirds' vase with the Lalique 'Perruches' vase.) It is this line of vases, lamps, and tableware which is often mistaken for a very similar type of glassware produced by the Phoenix Glass Company, located nearby in Monaca, Pennsylvania. For example, the so-called Phoenix 'Grasshopper' vases are actually Consolidated's 'Katydid' vases.

Items in the Martele line were produced in blue, pink, green, crystal, white, or custard glass decorated with various fired-on color treatments or a satin finish. For the most part, their colors were distinctively different from those used by Phoenix. Although not foolproof, one of the ways of distinguishing Consolidated's wares from those of Phoenix is that most of the time Consolidated applied color to the raised portion of the design, leaving the background plain, while Phoenix usually applied color to the background leaving the raised surfaces undecorated. This is particularly true of those pieces in white or custard glass.

Consolidated closed its doors for good in 1964. Subsequently a few of the molds passed into the hands of other glass companies that later reproduced certain patterns; one such re-issue is the 'Chickadee' vase, found in avocado green, satin-finish custard, or milk glass.

Martele Line

Bird of Paradise, candy box, milk glass, oval 75.00
Bittersweet, lamp, coral berries, aqua vines on milk glass.............130.00

Blackberry, vase, gold on milk glass, 18" 475.00
Blackberry, vase, gr wash on crystal, 18" 350.00
Chickadee, vase, bl cased, 6½" 250.00
Cockatoo, console bowl, purple wash, 13" 150.00
Cockatoo, vase, dk gr wash on crystal, 8½" 250.00
Dancing Girl w/Pan, vase, satin custard w/tan & lav, 11½"........425.00
Dogwood, vase, cased, amber wash, 10½" 250.00
Dogwood, vase, red w/gold pattern, 10½" 325.00
Dragonfly, vase, crystal w/cranberry stain on pattern, 6" 80.00
Dragonfly vase, ruby stain on crystal, 6" 85.00
Fish, vase, gr cased, 10" 300.00
Five Fruits, plate, gr wash, 6" 20.00
Five Fruits, sundae, purple wash, ftd 25.00
Floral, vase, bl & gr on wht satin, 9" 120.00
Hummingbird, puff box, bl birds & pk roses, 7" 110.00
Hummingbird, vase, gr stain on crystal, 5½" 80.00
Hummingbird & Orchids, candle holder, purple wash, 7", pr 180.00
Iris/Floral, candle holder, amber wash, low, pr 100.00
Iris/Floral, candlestick, pk wash, tall, pr 150.00
Iris/Floral, jug, gr cased, ½-gal 200.00
Iris/Floral, tumbler, sepia wash, ftd 25.00
Jonquil, vase, custard w/bl flowers, gr leaves, 6" 85.00
Katydid, ash tray, amber wash, triangular 80.00
Katydid, fan vase, custard w/gold- & ruby-accented pattern........370.00
Line 700, lamp, crystal w/cranberry stain & gold, brass base........225.00
Line 700, plate, crystal w/satin bkground, 8" 27.00
Lovebirds, banana boat in ormolu, coral/gr/brn, 15" 450.00
Lovebirds, vase, gold on opal, 10½" 400.00
Nuthatch, window box, custard w/bl birds, brn cones, 10½" 200.00
Orchids, comport, sepia wash on crystal, ftd, 10" 135.00
Screech Owl, vase, coral owls, gr reeds on satin custard, 6" 135.00
Swallows, bowl, purple wash on crystal, 9" 135.00

Pattern Glass

Bulging Loops, shakers, pigeon blood, pr 160.00
Cone, shaker, bl, tall 75.00
Cone, shaker, pk satin 35.00
Cone, toothpick holder, pk satin 65.00
Coreopsis, biscuit jar, milk glass w/gr band, 6½" 90.00
Coreopsis, cracker jar, milk glass w/pk & gr 200.00
Cosmos, tumbler, milk glass w/pk band 70.00
Criss Cross, tumbler, cranberry satin 135.00
Criss Cross, tumbler, wht 50.00
Florette, cruet, pk satin 225.00
Florette, mustard pot, pk 65.00
Florette, toothpick holder, pk cased 70.00
Guttate, mustard pot, pk 80.00
Guttate, salt shaker, pk cased, tall 50.00

Miscellaneous

Catalonian, plate, dinner; lav wash, 10" 22.00
Catalonian, tumbler, flat, pk wash, 5½" 18.00
Catalonian, tumbler, ftd cone, amber wash, 5" 15.00
Catalonian, tumbler, ftd cone, gr, 5" 18.00
Catalonian, vase, triangle 1101, red, 10" 150.00
Catalonian, whiskey, emerald gr, 2-oz 12.00
Catalonian, whiskey jug, emerald gr 80.00
Con Cora, box, milk glass heart w/gold braid 40.00
Regent Line, vase, crimped top, Ivy, 7" 45.00
Ruba Rombic, jug, jade..430.00
Ruba Rombic, perfume, jungle gr 225.00
Ruba Rombic, toilet bottle, sunshine................................250.00

Ruba Rombic, tumbler, jade, 9-oz 70.00
Santa Maria, tray, French crystal, lg 350.00
Spanish Knobs, goblet, yel, 6⅝" 30.00
Spanish Knobs, sundae, ftd, gr wash, 4⅛" 20.00
Spanish Knobs, tumbler, ftd, gr wash, 7½" 25.00

Cookbooks

Cookbooks from the nineteenth century, though often hard to find, are a delight to today's collectors both for their quaint formats and printing methods as well as for their outmoded, often humorous views on nutrition. Recipes required a 'pinch' of salt, butter 'the size of an egg' or a 'walnut,' or a 'handful' of flour. Collectors sometimes specialize in cookbooks issued as advertising premiums. Especially desirable are the figurals that were shaped like a jar, a slice of bread, or some other form relative to the product. Others with unique features such as illustrations by well-known artists or references to famous people or places are priced in accordance. Cookbooks written earlier than 1874 are the most valuable and when found command prices as high as $200; figurals usually sell in the $10 to $15 range. Our advisor for this category is Charlotte Safir; she is listed in the Directory under New York. For further information we recommend *A Guide to Collecting Cookbooks* by Col. Bob Allen and *Price Guide to Cookbooks and Recipe Leaflets* by Linda Dickinson.

Key:
CB — Cookbook   dj — dust jacket

Amy Vanderbilt's Complete CB, Doubleday, 811-pg 5.00
Art of Home Candy Making, 1915, 89-pg, G 15.00
Better Homes & Gardens CB, ring binder, ca 1950....................30.00
Betty Crocker's Guide to...Entertaining, 1st ed, '59, 252-pg 20.00
Boston Cooking School CB, Boston, 1950, dj, EX 20.00
Campbell's Great Restaurants CB, no date, paperback, G 5.00
Candies & Bonbons & How To Make Them, 1913, 275-pg..........15.00
Casserole CB, 1968, 124-pg, M 7.50
CB, Tried Recipes; ca 1925, 225-pg, G 9.50
CB for Two, 1957, 339-pg, VG 10.00
CB of the Woman's Educational Club, Toledo, 1911, 256-pg, G ..25.00
Children's Mission CB, 1920, 179-pg, VG........................12.50
Chinese Cooking w/American Meals, 1970, 228-pg 6.00
Cross Creek Cookery, 1st ed, Scribner, 1942, dj, VG 35.00
Fannie Farmer's Chafing Dish Possibilities, Boston, 1899 ....50.00
Favorite Recipes of the Movie Stars, 1931, 48-pg, VG..........35.00
Fish Cookery, 1921, 348-pg, VG......................................17.50
Fondue, Chafing Dish & Casserole Cookery; 1969, 290-pg, VG 6.00
Foods of the World, Time Life, ca 1969, 99-pg 10.00
General Foods CB, 1935, 370-pg, VG................................18.50
Good Things To Eat, 1925, 118-pg, G..............................22.50
Heloise's Kitchen Hints, 1963, 180-pg, EX 6.00
Household Discoveries, 1909, 743-pg, VG 20.00
Joy of Eating Natural Foods, 1962, 363-pg, EX 6.50
Life's Picture CB, ring binder, 1961, 292-pg, VG 25.00
Magic Chef Cooking, American Stove Co, 1935, 196-pg, VG 7.50
Marjorie Kinnan Rawlings' CB, 1st ed, London, 1960, dj, VG 28.00
Mastering Art of French Cooking, Julia Childs, 1972, 716-pg........15.00
Modern Encyclopedia of Cooking, 1959, 736-pg................20.00
My Own CB, Gladys Taber, 1st ed, 1972, dj, VG 50.00
National CB, 1932, 425-pg 12.00
New Household Discoveries, 1917, 805-pg........................20.00
Out of Alaska's Kitchens, 1951, 241-pg, 11x8", G 15.00
Pillsbury CB, Minneapolis, 1914, 125-pg, VG..................20.00
Saturday Evening Post All American CB, 1964, 257-pg............15.00

Settlement CB, 1938, 623-pg.................................20.00
Stillmeadow Kitchen, 1st ed, 1947, dj, VG 47.50
Sunset CB of Favorite Recipes, San Francisco, '49, 415-pg, G........ 8.50
Taste of Ireland, 1968, 124-pg, VG.........................12.50
Woman's Exchange CB, 1901, 511-pg, VG................45.00
Working Wives CB, ca 1963, 162-pg, VG 6.00

Cookie Cutters

Early hand-fashioned cookie cutters have recently been commanding stiff prices at country auctions, and the ranks of interested collectors are growing steadily. Especially valuable are the figural cutters; and the more complicated the design, the higher the price. A follow-up of the carved wooden cookie boards, the first cutters were probably made by itinerant tinkers from left-over or recycled pieces of tin. Though most of the eighteenth-century examples are now in museums or collections, it is still possible to find some good cutters from the late 1800s when changes in the manufacture of tin resulted in a thinner, less expensive material. The width of the cutting strip is often a good indicator of age; the wider the strip, the older the cutter. While the very early cutters were 1" to 1½" deep, by the twenties and thirties, many were less than ½" deep. Crude, spotty soldering indicates an older cutter, while a thin line of solder usually tends to suggest a much later manufacture. The shape of the backplate is another clue. Later cutters will have oval, round, or rectangular backs, while on the earlier type the back was cut to follow the lines of the design. Cookie cutters usually vary from 2" to 4" in size, but gingerbread men were often made as tall as 12". Birds, fish, hearts, and tulips are common; simple versions can be purchased for as little as $12.00 to $15.00. The larger figurals, especially those with more imaginative details, often bring $75.00 and up. The cookie cutters listed here are tin and handmade unless noted otherwise.

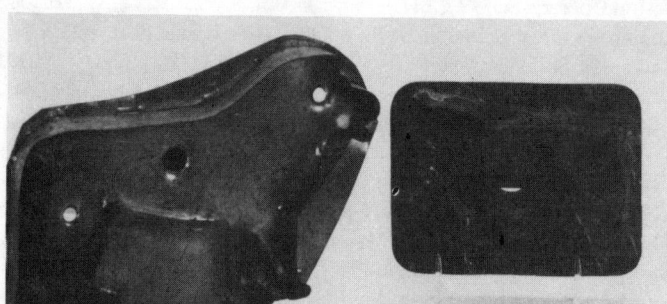

Lion, 6", $65.00; Horse, 4", $23.00.

Angel, 8" 38.00
Bird, aluminum, 4¾".. 3.00
Bunny, aluminum, red metal hdl............................ 5.00
Charlie Brown or Lucy, plastic, 1952, ea................ 6.50
Dog, sm 15.00
Dove looking bk over wing, flatbk, 1830s, 4½".......75.00
Duck, thick, late 1800s, 2½x4½x1"........................18.00
Elephant, punched on cylinder form, 4¼x1½" dia 125.00
Father Christmas, 10"...65.00
Fish, wide strap hdl, 7" L 200.00
Gabriel, lg angel, 10" 60.00
Gingerbread man, aluminum, 5" 4.00
Gingerbread man w/pointed cap, 10½x4x½"............130.00
Hand, 4¾"...175.00
Heart, flat bk, 4x4" 35.00
Heart, hdl, 4½x3½" 28.00
Heart, solid bk w/hole in center, 1800s, 3x3x½" 20.00

Horse, 8½"...200.00
Lamb, 4"..20.00
Lion, aluminum, red metal hdl 5.00
Man, very stylized, 13½x6".................................450.00
Man w/wide pants & sm hat, late 1800s, 5"............55.00
Multiple: Dutchman/woman/mouse/acorn/heart/leaf in 7" dia 75.00
Peacock, 1880s, 3½x4"..45.00
Rabbit, aluminum, 4".. 3.00
Rabbit, solid bk, appl hdl, 10½x9¾x1½" 275.00
Rabbit, standing, flat bk, 6x3½" 35.00
Santa, aluminum, deep, gr wood hdl......................12.50
Santa, 10"..38.00
Sleigh, 6" 40.00
Star, 5-pointed, solid bk, 1800s, 3½x3½"...............20.00
Turkey, minor dents, 2½" L 150.00
Woman, hands on hips, stylized, 7½".....................85.00

Cookie Jars

The appeal of the cookie jar is universal; folks of all ages, both male and female, love to collect 'em! The early thirties' heavy stoneware jars of a rather nondescript nature quickly gave way to figurals of every type imaginable. Those from the mid to late thirties were often decorated over the glaze with 'cold paint,' but by the early forties underglaze decorating resulted in cheerful, bright, permanent colors and cookie jars that still have a new look fifty years later.

Unmarked jars, unless properly identified and rare, bring the lowest prices, while cookie jars trimmed in gold are usually highly valued. The examples listed below were made by companies other than those found elsewhere in this book; see also specific manufacturers.

Our advisor for this catgory is Barry Thomsen; he is listed in the Directory under Ilinois. For further study we recommend *An Illustrated Guide to Cookie Jars* by Ermagene Westfall and *The Collector's Encyclopedia of Cookie Jars* by Fred and Joyce Roerig.

ABC Blocks Teddy Bear, Starnes.............................85.00
After School Cookies, American Bisque, EX...............75.00
Albert Apple, Pee Dee, NM 110.00
Apple, yel, unmk, lg...40.00
Ark, Treasure Craft...45.00
Aunt Jemima, soft plastic, Quaker, NM 210.00
Baby Bear, Treasure Craft, EX................................45.00
Baby Pig, Regal China 300.00
Balloon Lady, Pottery Guild..................................100.00
Bantam Rooster, California Originals.......................50.00
Barn, owl finial, Treasure Craft 40.00
Bear, sitting, 1 ear turned down, NM 30.00
Bear, wht underglazed, Gilner 50.00
Bear w/Beanie, brn, sm 20.00
Bear w/Cookie, American Bisque............................60.00
Bear w/Visor Hat, American Bisque 60.00
Black Santa Sitting, 24k gold belt buckle, Gifford, lg 225.00
Black Topsy Girl, red dots & belt, scarce 275.00
Boy Pig, American Bisque 60.00
Brown Bagger, Doranne of California, EX 35.00
Buddha, Twin Winton 125.00
Bugs Bunny, rnd...150.00
Bull, bl pants, Japan 30.00
Bulldog atop Cookie Safe......................................100.00
Canister w/Flowers, Robinson Ransbottom 25.00
Casper the Ghost, Harvey, NM 850.00
Cat on Beehive, American Bisque 50.00
Chef, Pearl China 600.00

Chef, Robinson Ransbottom, EX 68.00
Chicken, brn, Fapco, NM 40.00
Chicken, Robinson Ransbottom, EX 65.00
Chimpanzee, Treasure Craft, NM 55.00
Churn, lt red-brn w/pk flowers, American Bisque 22.50
Clown, color underglazed, American Bisque, EX 50.00
Clown, finger in mouth, cold pnt, EX 25.00
Clown, Pan American Art, VG 40.00
Clown, Sierra Vista, NM 55.00
Coffee Grinder, Japan 22.50
Coffeepot, Treasure Craft, lg 40.00
Collegiate Owl, American Bisque, NM 50.00
Cookie Boy, RW Frookie 42.50
Cookie Cola, Doranne of California 50.00
Cookie Corral 40.00
Cookie Monster, California Originals 70.00
Cookie Monster, Muppets Inc 50.00
Cookie Safe, Cardinal 65.00
Cookie Truck, American Bisque 55.00
Cookie Wagon, American Bisque 75.00
Cow, no pnt, American Bisque 50.00
Cow Jumped Over the Moon, gold trim, Robinson Ransbottom .225.00
Cupcake, Doranne of California 38.00

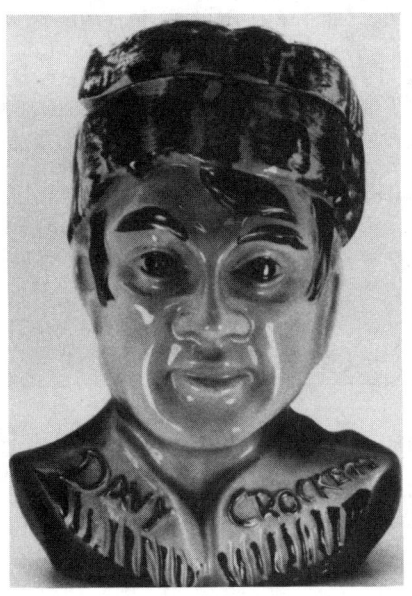

Davy Crockett, Regal China, $350.00.

Dog in Basket, Japan 32.00
Dog in Basket, no pnt, American Bisque 40.00
Dog in Wash Tub, Treasure Craft, NM 55.00
Doggie in Barrel, Treasure Craft, lg, NM 55.00
Donkey w/Milk Wagon, American Bisque 70.00
Dutch Boy, underglazed, Pottery Guild, NM 60.00
Ee-Yore, sitting, Duncan, NM 45.00
Elf, Twin Winton 35.00
Elf's Schoolhouse, California Originals, NM 60.00
Elsie in Barrel 150.00
Elsie the Cow, Pottery Guild, EX 180.00
Flintstones Dino/Golf Bag, American Bisque 750.00
Flintstones Rubles House, American Bisque 525.00
Football, Treasure Craft 30.00
Fred Flintstone w/Pebbles, NM 95.00
Garbage Can, Doranne of California 40.00
Granny Holding Spoon, Hirsch 40.00
Heating Stove, blk, American Bisque, NM 27.50
Hillbilly Clown, Morton, EX 55.00

Hobo Clown, Treasure Craft, EX 55.00
Horse, Twin Winton, EX 35.00
Hound Dog, Market Square, made for JC Penney 25.00
House, w/smiley face, Sierra Vista, EX 50.00
Howdy Doody, Vandor, NM 155.00

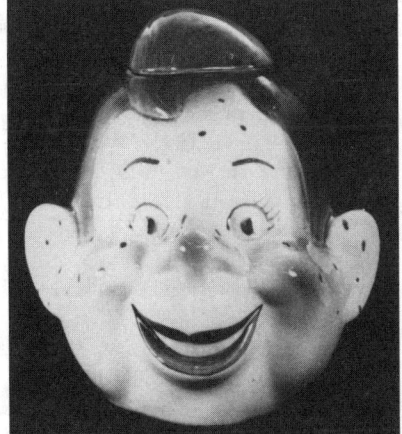

Howdy Doody, $575.00.

Ice Cream Cone, cherry on top, Japan 25.00
Ice Cream Sundae w/Cherry, Doranne of California ...50.00
Indian w/Lollipop, unmk, NM 68.00
Jukebox, silver, w/all cookie songs, unmk 90.00
Keebler Elf, plastic, F&F Mold & Die 125.00
Ken-L-Ration Pup, F&F Mold & Die 165.00
King Lion, yel w/lollipop, Japan 28.00
Kraft Marshmallow Bear, Regal China, EX 145.00
Lamb, American Bisque, EX 70.00
Lamb, Twin Winton 45.00
Leopard, Treasure Craft, HP, 12", EX 50.00
Lion, bug on nose, Doranne of California 45.00
Lion Cub Twins, Japan 32.00
Little Bo Peep, Napco 135.00
Majorette, Regal China 150.00
Mammy, bl & gray, Mosaic Tile 425.00
Mammy, hands on hips, red/wht/blk, A&T Importers ..50.00
Mammy, lid in stomach, Rockingham, scarce 275.00
Mammy, Nat'l Silver 200.00
Mammy, Nat'l Silver, sm mold separation inside 150.00
Mammy, plastic, F&F Mold & Die, M 325.00
Mammy, yel, Mosaic Tile 395.00
Mammy at Cookstove, making pancakes, Wisecarver ..150.00
Mammy w/Churn & Boy, Wisecarver 150.00
Mammy w/Cookie Jar, Wisecarver 150.00
Mammy w/Mixing Bowl, Wisecarver 140.00
Mammy w/Spoon, bl & wht Xs on dress, unmk, NM ..725.00
Mexican, napping, Treasure Craft 40.00
Mickey Mouse on Drum, California Originals 250.00
Mickey Mouse w/Flour Bag 135.00
Milano Cookies, Pepperidge Farm premium 150.00
Milk Can, Treasure Craft, EX 30.00
Monk, Treasure Craft, NM 55.00
Mushrooms w/Frog, Sierra Vista, NM 65.00
Old Woman in Shoe, Doranne of California, EX 60.00
Olive Oyl, American Bisque 1,550.00
Oreo Cookie, USA, lg 37.50
Oriental Lady, Regal China, EX 325.00
Oscar the Grouch, California Originals 80.00
Paddington Bear 100.00
Pekingese, bow in hair, Doranne of California, M 65.00

Pelican, unmk, NM 50.00
Pig w/Flowers, Los Angeles Potteries, NM.....................45.00
Pillsbury Doughboy, dtd 1973...70.00
Poodle, burgundy, American Bisque 100.00
Popeye, American Bisque..875.00
Pound Puppy...85.00
Preacher, Robinson Ransbottom, NM 115.00
Pup in Pot, plain version, American Bisque...................50.00
Quaker Oats, Regal China 150.00
Rabbit in Basket, EX pnt, unmk......................................50.00
Rabbit in Hat, American Bisque, EX 45.00
Rabbit in Magician's Hat, NM 75.00
Raccoon, Fitz & Floyd, dtd 1979....................................125.00
Raggedy Ann, Japan, EX..20.00
Rio Rita, HP, mc, Fitz & Floyd 125.00
Rocking Horse, Treasure Craft, EX 50.00
Rooster, gray underglaze, De Forrest of California, NM ...65.00
Rooster, Sierra Vista 55.00
Sack of Cookies, American Bisque, EX...........................50.00
Sailor Monkey w/Sucker & Cookie, Japan.....................37.50
Sailor Mouse, Twin Winton, EX 35.00
Santa Bust, plastic, Carolina Enterprises 1973..............35.00
Santa in Easy Chair, unmk, NM 85.00
Sheriff Pig, Robinson Ransbottom 90.00
Smokey the Bear, Twin Winton 40.00
Stagecoach, plastic windows, Sierra Vista 275.00
Stella Strawberry, Pee Dee, poor pnt..............................90.00
Strawberry Pie, a la mode, Doranne of California..........65.00
Superman, California Originals......................................400.00
Telephone, Sierra Vista, paper label 50.00
Thumper, Disney, EX..80.00
Tiger, sits, lg smile, Japan 28.00
Time for Cookies, brn, unmk 40.00
Toll House Cookies, Nestle's 120.00
Tomato Basket, Doranne of California, NM.....................50.00
Trans Formers 85.00
Treasure Chest, American Bisque 65.00
Trolley Car, Treasure Craft 55.00
Turtle, stands w/sm rabbit on bk, cold pnt, EX 50.00
Umbrella Kids, American Bisque...................................215.00
Victorian House, Treasure Craft, EX 40.00
Walnut, squirrel on top, Twin Winton, sm, NM.............35.00
Winking Owl in Overalls, California Originals 40.00
Winnie the Pooh, California Originals 125.00
Wise Bird, Robinson Ransbottom, EX..............................38.00
Yogi Bear, American Bisque..450.00

Cooper, Susie

A twentieth-century ceramic designer whose works are now attracting the attention of collectors, Susie Cooper was first affiliated with the A.E. Gray Pottery in Henley, England, in 1922 where she designed in lustres and painted items with her own ideas as well. (Examples of Gray's lustreware is rare and costly.) By 1930 she and her brother-in-law, Jack Beeson, had established a family business. Her pottery soon became a success, and she was subsequently offered space at Crown Works, Burslem. In 1940 she received the honorary title of Royal Designer for Industry, the only such distinction ever awarded by the Royal Society of Arts solely for pottery design. Miss Cooper received the Order of the British Empire in the New Year's Honors List of 1979. She was the chief designer for the Wedgwood group from 1966 until she resigned in 1972. Since 1980 she has worked on a free-lance basis.

Tulip vase, $250.00; Cubist jug, $150.00; Beechwood sugar bowl, hand painted, $30.00; Jazz Age vase, hand painted, $400.00; Meat dish, hand painted, $150.00.

Bowl, pk & blk matt, tube-line design, 6½" H.............................300.00
Coffeepot, Acorn, bl/gr wash, 7¾" 250.00
Coffeepot, Dresden Spray w/bl wash, Falcon shape, 6½" 200.00
Cup, silver lustre, Gray's, 2¼"...65.00
Dish, Peacock Feather, bl/gr, shallow, oval, 8½" L 150.00
Egg cup, brn/orange/yel flowers, Gray's, 2"..................................30.00
Jug, Cubist pattern, Paris shape, Gray's.......................................150.00
Plaque, Nosegay, w/gr-wash border, 16".......................................125.00
Plate, brn/pk-wash bands & pk dots, 8"...20.00
Plate, Corn Poppy, red/blk/brn, Wedgwood, 10½" 20.00
Punch bowl, Feather sgraffito, pk, 12"..85.00
Sauce boat, Gray Leaf w/gr wash, 3"...40.00
Teapot, Wedding Ring, 5"..50.00
Tray, hors d'oevres; bl fish, gr/red/brn bands, 9¾" 45.00
Vase, aerographed in brn/gr/yel, 7½"...125.00
Vase, sgraffito scrolls, pk, 12"..300.00

Coors

The firm that became known as Coors Porcelain Company in 1920 was founded in 1908 by John J. Herold, originally of the Roseville Pottery in Zanesville, Ohio. Though still in business today, they are best known for their artware vases and Rosebud dinnerware produced before 1939.

Coors vases produced before the late thirties were made in a matt finish; by the latter years of the decade, high-gloss glazes were also being used. Nearly fifty shapes were in production, and some of the more common forms were made in three sizes. Typical colors in matt are white, orange, blue, green, yellow, and tan. Yellow, blue, maroon, pink, and green are found in high gloss. All vases are marked with a triangular arrangement of the words 'Coors Colorado Pottery' enclosing the word 'Golden.' You may find vases (usually 6" to 6½") marked with the Colorado State Fair stamp and dated 1939. For such a vase, add $10.00 to the suggested values given below.

Our advisor for this category is Jo Ellen Winther. Advice for miscellaneous listings was provided by Jim and Carol Carlton; all are listed in the Directory under Colorado.

Apple baker, Rosebud, 4¾" dia 20.00
Baker, Rosebud, 4¾" dia 12.50
Baking pan, Rosebud, 10¾"x6¾" 17.50
Bowl, mixing; Rosebud, hdld, 3½-cup...............................15.00
Bowl, pudding; Rosebud, early, lg 20.00
Bowl, pudding; Rosebud, 2-pt, sm 12.50
Bowl, pudding; Rosebud, 3-pt, sm 14.00

Cake knife, Rosebud, 10" 22.50
Casserole, Dutch; Rosebud, 3½-cup 25.00
Casserole, Rosebud, str sides, 2-pt 20.00
Casserole, Rosebud, w/lid, 14-cup 38.00
Cookie jar, HP decor, lg 35.00
Egg cup, Rosebud, 6-oz 25.00
Jar, utility; Rosebud, 2½-pt 25.00

Rosebud, utility jar, $30.00.

Muffin set, Rosebud, 8" plate w/5½" dome lid 65.00
Planter, orange matt, 3-legged, 8¾" 25.00
Plate, Rosebud, 7¼" 7.50
Plate, soup; Rosebud, 4" 14.00
Saucer, Rosebud, 5½" 6.00
Shakers, Rosebud, str sides, 4½", pr.....................12.50
Shakers, Rosebud, 2½", pr 24.00
Teapot, Rosebud, 2-cup 45.00
Tumbler, Rosebud, ftd, no hdl, 12-oz 30.00
Tumbler, Rosebud, hdl, 8½-oz 25.00
Vase, yel, imp design, 5½" 30.00
Water server, Rosebud, Commemorative, corked stopper, 3-pt 88.00
Water server, Rosebud, corked stopper, 6-cup 40.00

Miscellaneous

Ash tray, 'Beer, Butter, Malted Milk,' rnd, flat 65.00
Ash tray, ivory, common 3.00
Bank, clown, hanging 100.00
Bank, clown, sitting..100.00
Bowl vase, scroll hdls extend above wide collar neck, 6" 40.00
Bowl vase, scroll hdls extend above wide collar neck, 7¼".............75.00
Bud vase, bulbous w/long trumpet neck, 9" 40.00
Coffee maker, porc, 4-part 75.00
Crock, malted milk; porc, w/lid 75.00
Figurine, Monks, laughing/crying, pr 500.00
Lamp, cvd leaves & berries, bulbous, 7", +shade 150.00
Mug, w/Colorado State Fair, 1934..........................45.00
Mug, w/lion decal 18.00
Shaker, bottle form 15.00
Shaker, keg form 15.00
Vase, bulbous urn form w/hdls, 12" 100.00
Vase, bulbous urn form w/hdls, 7½" 45.00
Vase, bulbous urn form w/hdls, 8½" 65.00
Vase, bulbous w/collar neck, rope hdls, 9½" 60.00
Vase, cvd leaves & berries, bulbous, 6½" 35.00
Vase, Empire State Bldg, sq w/stepped buttresses, 9" 75.00
Vase, ftd bowl form w/akimbo rim-to-shoulder hdls, #7, 6½" 40.00
Vase, ftd bowl from w/akimbo rim-to-shoulder hdls, #7, 8" 75.00
Vase, horizontal ribbing, molded ring hdls, 5" 40.00

Vase, ½-circle rim-to-base hdls, Deco shape, 5¾" 25.00
Vase, ½-circle rim-to-base hdls, Deco shape, 6¼" 35.00
Vase, ½-circle rim-to-base hdls, Deco shape, 8¼" 75.00

Copper

Hand-crafted copper was made in America from early in the eighteenth century until about 1850, with the center of its production in Pennsylvania. Examples have been found signed by such notable coppersmiths as Kidd, Buchanan, Babb, Bently, and Harbeson. Of the many utilitarian items made, teakettles are the most desirable. Early examples from the eighteenth century were made with a dovetailed joint which was hammered and smoothed to a uniform thickness. Pots from the nineteenth century were seamed. Coffeepots were made in many shapes and sizes and along with mugs, kettles, warming pans, and measures are easiest to find. Stills ranging in sizes of up to fifty-gallon are popular with collectors today.

Our advisor, Mary Frank Gaston, has compiled a lovely book, *Antique Brass and Copper*, with many full-color photos and current market values; you will find her address in the Directory under Texas.

Ale bucket, wire hdl & ring lid lifter, ca 1910, 6", EX...................85.00
Coffeepot, tinned, turned wood hdl, acorn finial, 7½" 50.00
Dutch oven, dvtl, brass bail, wrought ears, rib bands, 16" 275.00
Kettle, mk on hdl: Geo Clippinger PA, ca 1821, 7" 400.00
Kettle, tapered/bulbous, lg spout, sgn Dayton Stutsman, 10"... 1,300.00
Measure, brass rim labeled Fairbanks & Co, cylinder, 4x5" 325.00
Pail, dvtl, str sides, pouring spout, brass bail, 12x13".....................125.00
Pail, iron bail w/copper ears, riveted, ca 1800s.............................78.00
Pitcher, dvtl, mk D Bentley & Sons, battered/rpr, 9" 65.00
Pot, dvtl, cylindrical, cast brass rim hdls, V Olac, 10x9" 65.00
Saucepan, dvtl, mk J Van Range Co, 6", w/7" CI hdl.....................40.00
Saucepan, dvtl, soldered rpr, 9x13", w/12" wrought hdl 65.00
Saucepan, dvtl, 12" dia, 12" hdl, +lid w/hdl..............................75.00
Saucepan, dvtl, 7", w/8¾" CI hdl..45.00
Saucepan, dvtl, 8½" dia, 9¾" wrought copper hdl 50.00
Saucepan, dvtl, 9", w/10¾" wrought copper hdl 75.00
Saucepan, mk DH&M Co, 11½" dia, 12" CI hdl 55.00
Sieve, dvtl, 7", w/8" wrought copper hdl....................................85.00
Skillet, 8", w/8¾" CI hdl...65.00
Teakettle, dvtl, attached base fits into stove cutout, 15"..............100.00
Teakettle, dvtl, swivel hdl mk #4, PA origin, polished, 6½" 265.00
Teapot, overall fluting, wood knob/hdl, ca 1790, 11x6"..............165.00

Teakettle, dovetailed, 6½", $325.00.

Copper Lustre

Copper lustre is a term referring to a type of pottery made in Staffordshire after the turn of the nineteenth century. It is finished in a metallic rusty-brown glaze resembling true copper. Pitchers are found in abundance, ranging from simple styles with dull bands of color to those with fancy handles and bands of embossed, polychromed flowers. Bowls are common; goblets, mugs, teapots, and sugar bowls much less so. It's easy to find, but not in good condition. Pieces with hand-painted decoration and those with historical transfers are the most valuable. Our advisor for this category is Richard Marden; he is listed in the Directory under New Hampshire.

Creamer, wht vintage band, purple resist floral band, 4" **45.00**
Creamer, woman/child at desk, red/wht on yel, stains, 5" **165.00**
Pitcher, King Henry III transfer, rpr spout, 5" **150.00**
Pitcher, Lafayette/Corwallis reserve on red body, 1810, 8" **1,750.00**
Pitcher, transfer scenes in reserves on yel w/mc band, 6¾" **125.00**
Pitcher, woman/child play badminton, red/wht on yel, 8¾" **350.00**
Teapot, leaves, copper on yel band, eagle hdl, 5¾" **130.00**
Teapot, vines/flowers in bl & lustre, 6" **160.00**

Coralene Glass

Coralene is a unique type of art glass easily recognized by the tiny grains of glass that form its decoration. Lacy allover patterns of seaweed, geometrics, and florals were used, as well as solid forms such as fish, plants, and single blossoms. It was made by several glasshouses both here and abroad. Values are based to a considerable extent on the amount of beading that remains. Our advisors for this category are Betty and Clarence Maier; they are listed in the Directory under Pennsylvania.

Pitcher, peaches with rigaree, English, 8", $450.00; Tumbler, $150.00.

Pitcher, clear cased in rose, seaweed motif, amber hdl, 5" **220.00**
Pitcher, wht w/flying bird & leafy branch, mk Pat, 7" **200.00**
Rose bowl, fish/water lilies on cranberry, 4 gr ft, 5", EX **500.00**
Rose bowl, pk o/l, yel beaded motif, 6-crimp, 3¼x4¾" **375.00**
Rose bowl, pk w/yel seaweed, 5-crimp, amber ft, 3x4½" **375.00**
Tumbler, bl shaded o/l, overall yel beaded motif, 3¾" **325.00**
Vase, blossoms & butterflies, ftd, Moser **1,250.00**
Vase, cranberry, mc florals & birds, mk Pat, 4x3" **195.00**
Vase, pk MOP Dmn Quilt w/star & dmn motif, 4¾x3" **475.00**
Vase, pk MOP Dmn Quilt w/yel wheat, 10½" **1,075.00**
Vase, pk shaded Snowflake MOP, wheat motif, 6½" **650.00**
Vase, pk to bl, beaded designs in irregular panels, 11¼" **665.00**
Vase, rose o/l, yel beaded motif, 4⅝x3⅝" **450.00**

Vase, yel o/l, yel beaded motif, 5x2⅞" **295.00**

Coralene, Oriental

Ceramics decorated in the same manner as coralene glass were produced in Japan during the early 1900s. Many items are marked 'Patent Pending' or with a specific patent date.

Biscuit jar, foliage/floral on bl, SP lid **365.00**
Ewer, fruit, pk & gr on gr & gold, 4x3½" **205.00**
Plate, florals, pk on gr bsk, much gold, 7¾" **85.00**
Vase, buds & leaves w/gold on lav, Kinran, 1909, 10½" **650.00**
Vase, iris, pk/lav on gr, cobalt & gold trim, 9x3½" **455.00**

Cordey

The Cordey China Company was founded in 1942 in Trenton, New Jersey, by Boleslaw Cybis. The operation was small with less than a dozen workers. They produced figurines, vases, lamps, and similar wares, much of which was marketed through gift shops both nationwide and abroad. Though the earlier wares were made of plaster, Cybis soon developed his own formula for a porcelain composition which he called 'Papka.' Cordey figurines and busts were characterized by old-world charm, Rococo scrolls, delicate floral appliques, ruffles, and real lace which was dipped in liquified clay to add dimension to the work.

Although on rare occasions some items were not numbered or signed, the 'basic' figure was cast both with numbers and the Cordey signature. The molded pieces were then individually decorated and each marked with its own impressed identification number as well as a mark to indicate the artist-decorator. Their numbering system began with 200 and in later years progressed into the 8000s. As can best be established, Cordey continued production until sometime in the mid-1950s. Boleslaw Cybis died in 1957, his wife in 1958.

Key: ff — full figure

Lady, #302, 16", $200.00.

Ballerina, #4101, dancing position, lace trim, 10¾" **220.00**
Bird, #2037, perched on stump, 8½" **125.00**
Bird, #6004R, bl/wht, on tree stump, 10" **135.00**
Box, #6041, 3 lg roses & ruffled lace on lid, 7½" dia **65.00**
Box, trinket; #7038, roses & mixed florals, ftd **55.00**

Bust, #4172P, cream w/pk lace jabot & bonnet, 15" **195.00**
Bust, #5009, girl w/hat, 6" **65.00**
Bust, #5014, Junior Prom, ringlets, 7" **60.00**
Cat, seated, wht w/bow, pk rose, 8¾" **200.00**
Clock, mantel; #914, Rococo, Lanshire Electric, 9½" **250.00**
Lady, #300, ff, ruffles, pantaloons, holds flowers, 15½" **200.00**
Lady, #4073, ff, much lace, 13" **185.00**
Lady, #5066, Carmen, ff, lav dress, long coat, high hat, 14" **200.00**
Lady, #5071, Chinese Mandarin, ff, lace/gilt, 11" **165.00**
Lady, #5082, ringlets, lace kerchief, 10½" **135.00**
Lady, #5084, upswept hair, scrolled base, 11¾" **135.00**
Lady, #5089A, bl eyes, upswept hair, 11¼" **160.00**
Lady, #8039, 15" **200.00**
Lamp, #304/#305, Grape Harvesters, 16½", pr **300.00**
Lamp, #31386, lady w/much lace, Rococo base **250.00**
Lamp, #5041/#5084, dbl figure (man & lady), pr **250.00**
Lamp, #5084, lady, upswept gray hair, lace, bustle, 11½" **140.00**
Lamp, #5399, chicken in cattails/etc, 16" figure, +shade **335.00**
Lamp, Chinese Goddess, 12" figure on wood base, 26" **185.00**
Man, #303, plumed hat, ff, 16" **225.00**
Man, #4153, ff, much lace, 14" **185.00**
Man & lady, #304/#305, Grape Harvesters, ff, 16", pr **350.00**
Man & lady, #4129-A, man w/violin, seated lady, 11" **300.00**
Man & lady, #5041/#5049, 11", pr **300.00**
Neopolitan Boy, #5046, ff, 9½" **140.00**
Pheasant, #343, vibrant mc, very early, scarce, 17" **260.00**
Plaque, advertising, 4½x3" **100.00**
Tray, leaf form, 13" **95.00**
Vase, #7094, Orientals in relief, appl flowers, 8" **160.00**
Wall masque, #902, lady's face, 10" **200.00**
Wood Duck female, #324RG, head thrown bk, 15" **450.00**
Yorkshire Girl, #5047, ff, grapes in dress folds, 10" **150.00**

Corkscrews

The history of the corkscrew dates back to the mid-1600s, when wine makers concluded that the best-aged wine was that stored in smaller containers, either stoneware or glass. Since plugs left unsealed were often damaged by rodents, corks were cut off flush with the bottle top and sealed with wax or a metal cover. Removing the cork cleanly with none left to grasp became a problem. The task was found to be relatively simple using the worm on the end of a flintlock gun rod. So the corkscrew evolved. Endless patents have been issued for mechanized models. Handles range from carved wood, ivory, and bone to porcelain and repousse silver. Celluloid lady's legs are popular. Our advisor for this category is Roger Baker; he is listed in the Directory under California.

Belgium, Challenge, common type, 1850s, EX **25.00**
Boar's tusk hdl, sterling end w/SP worm & lifter, Pat 1906 ....**165.00**
Brown Foreman, bullet type, advertising **38.00**
Champion, CI w/emb vines overall, wood hdl, bar mt **125.00**
England, ebony wood hdl, thick disk, ca 1880, EX **25.00**
England, steel picnic screw, ca 1800, EX **150.00**
England, 2" ivory hdl, steel shaft/worm, 1850s **130.00**
Farrow & Jackson Ltd London, sq shaft, wire helix, ca 1885 ....**85.00**
Foreign Pat, golf club, NP brass, 1¼" worm inside, 7½" **50.00**
France, dbl horn hdl, octagonal fr **75.00**
Germany, Ernst Uhr Aug 15 1889, lever-operated fr, EX **125.00**
Germany, pocket style, plated lifter & worm, silver sleeve **88.00**
Germany, Saks Fifth Ave, brass fish form, mid 1900s, 5½" **75.00**
Germany, swivel-over collar type, rubber ring fr, EX **25.00**
Haff Pat, brass ring mk Pat Appl For, Apr/May 1885 ....**85.00**
Haviland & Co SF Cal, rosewood hdl, 1890s, EX **165.00**

Italy, brass rack & pinion, 1920s, EX **32.00**
John Watts Sheffield England 1909, NP, center worm, EX **37.50**
Laurent Sibet Rockport France, grapevine hdl, EX **18.00**
Lund Patentee London, rack & pinion, Pat 1855, EX **285.00**
Nifty, Vaugan of Chicago, folding worm & capper, sm **7.50**
Ram's horn hdl (7"), plain helix worm, EX **25.00**
Rapid, brass w/rosewood hdl & steel clamp, bar mt, EX **365.00**
Starr, Brn Mfg Pat'd Apr 1925, w/bottle opener, wall mt **18.00**
US, curved boar's tooth 6" hdl, silver end cap **90.00**
US, NP steel worm, cap lifter & wire breaker, EX...................**150.00**
US, stag horn hdl, sterling cap ea end, ca 1900, 8" **125.00**
US Clough Pat, wood sleeve, advertising, EX.........................**25.00**
US Clough Pat of 1904, crown cap lifter, advertising...................**32.00**
Williamson's Pat 1897, self-pulling, EX **28.00**

Cosmos

Cosmos, sometimes called Stemless Daisy, is a patterned glass tableware produced from 1894 through 1915 by Consolidated Lamp and Glass Company. Relief-molded flowers on a fine cross-cut background were painted in soft colors of pink, blue, and yellow. Though nearly all were made of milk glass, a few items may be found in clear glass with the designs painted on. In addition to the tableware, lamps were also made.

Miniature kerosene lamp, enameled flowers on milk glass, 7", $325.00.

Bottle, cologne; orig stopper, rare **150.00**
Butter dish **235.00**
Condiment set, 3-pc in fr **350.00**
Creamer **150.00**
Lamp, banquet; kerosene, 24" **475.00**
Lamp, banquet; slender base, rnd globe, all orig, 16" **525.00**
Lamp, mini, 7" **325.00**
Lamp, 10" **400.00**
Pickle castor, dbl, mk SP fr..**500.00**
Pickle castor, single, ftd SP fr **350.00**
Pitcher, milk; 5" **170.00**
Pitcher, syrup; 6" **200.00**
Pitcher, water...**250.00**
Shakers, tall, orig lids, pr **150.00**
Spooner..**125.00**
Sugar bowl, open **150.00**

Sugar bowl, w/lid 185.00
Tumbler, 3¾" 65.00

Cottageware

You'll find a varied assortment of novelty dinnerware items, all styled as cozy little English cottages or huts with cone-shaped roofs; some may have a waterwheel or a windmill. Marks will vary. English-made Price Brothers or Beswick pieces are valued in the same range as those marked Occupied Japan, while items marked simply Japan are considered slightly less pricey. Our advisor for this category is Grace Klender; she is listed in the Directory under Ohio.

Teapots, back: English, 6½", $65.00; front: Occupied Japan, 6½", $65.00.

Biscuit jar, Maruhon Ware, Occupied Japan, 6½x5¼" 65.00
Butter dish, Occupied Japan...55.00
Butter pat, emb cottage, rectangular, Occupied Japan....................17.50
Chocolate pot, English 135.00
Condiment set, pr shakers & mustard on tray, Occupied Japan 45.00
Cookie jar, Maruhon Ware, 8x6¼" 75.00
Cookie or biscuit jar, Occupied Japan 85.00
Creamer, windmill, Occupied Japan, 2⅝" 15.00
Creamer & sugar bowl, English, 2½", 4½" 45.00
Creamer & sugar bowl, w/lid, on tray, Occupied Japan 50.00
Dish w/cover, Occupied Japan, sm 35.00
Grease jar, Occupied Japan..17.50
Mug, Price Bros...50.00
Pitcher, water; English..150.00
Shakers, cottage & lighthouse, on base, Occupied Japan, pr..........30.00
Shakers, windmill, Occupied Japan, pr 20.00
Sugar bowl, windmill, w/lid, Occupied Japan, 3⅞" 25.00
Teapot, windmill, Occupied Japan, 4⅞" 45.00

Coverlets

The Jacquard attachment for hand looms represented a culmination of weaving developments made in France. Introduced to America by the early 1820s, it gave professional weavers the ability to easily create complex patterns with curved lines. Those who could afford the new loom adaptation could now use hole-punched pasteboard cards to weave floral patterns that before could only be achieved with intense labor on a draw-loom.

Before the Jacquard mechanism, most weavers made their coverlets in geometric patterns. Use of indigo-blue and brightly colored wools often livened the twills and overshot patterns available to the small-loom home weaver. Those who had larger multiple-harness looms could produced warm double-woven, twill-block, or summer-and-winter designs.

While the new floral and pictorial patterns' popularity had displaced the geometrics in urban areas, the mid-Atlantic, and the Midwest by the 1840s, even factory production of the Jacquard coverlets was disrupted by cotton and wool shortages during the Civil War. A revived production in the 1870s saw a style change to a center-medallion motif, but a new fad for white 'Marseilles' spreads soon halted sales of Jacquard-woven coverlets. Production of Jacquard carpets continued to the turn of the century.

Rural and frontier weavers continued to make geometric-design coverlets through the nineteenth century, and local craft revivals have continued this tradition through this century. All-cotton overshots were factory produced in Kentucky from the 1940s, and factories and professional weavers made cotton-and-wool overshots during the past decade.

Many Jacquard-woven coverlets have dates and names of places and people (often the intended owner — not the weaver) woven into corners or borders.

In the listings that follow, examples are blue and white unless noted otherwise.

Crib coverlet, J. Packer weaver, PA, 1839, 6-color cotton and wool, 38" x 31", $600.00.

Jacquard

Centennial bldg borders, D Pursell, OH, 78x82".........................750.00
Democrat Rooster, gr/red/bl wool+wht cotton, Klein/1849 ....800.00
Eagle corners w/1849, flags/coins in center, red/wht, sgn 1,500.00
Eagles/floral medallions, bl/wht, Hagamen, NJ/1843, 90x76" 800.00
Floral, eagle/star borders, 3-color, sgn/1836, 2-pc, NM............ 2,050.00
Floral, gr/rust/bl/wht, sgn Lorenz, dbl weave, 86x98" 350.00
Floral, red/natural/teal bl, 2-pc dbl, 76x78", EX 300.00
Floral, rooster borders, 4-color, Smith/1836, 2-pc single 600.00
Floral medallions, bird borders, 3-color, Rausher label, EX.........200.00
Floral medallions, dbl vine border, 3-color, mfg by Pursell...... 1,800.00
Floral medallions, house borders, 3-color, label/1850, rpr 700.00
Floral medallions, urn border, Lorenz/1840 ....750.00
Floral/birds, red/bl/gr/wht, sgn W&JM Cright/1855, 2-pc...........650.00
Floral/birds/fruit, Boston Town border, 1840s, 83x80", EX 850.00
Memorial Hall center, eagle spandrels, 3-color wool/linen 750.00
Roses, triple bird border, 4-color, 2-pc single, 82x92"............. 1,000.00
Star center, eagles in corners, red/wht, 1-pc single, EX...............425.00
Sunburst & Lily, red/bl/gr wool+wht cotton, Cosley/1847 ...... 1,100.00
Trees/confronting parrots, bl/red/wht cotton, Shank/1836 ....500.00

Overshot

Geometrics, dk bl/salmon/olive/wht, lt wear, 2-pc	450.00
Graphic geometrics, bl/red/wht, 2 sides fringed	300.00
Lines form sqs w/ovals at intersection, 1-pc, 86x107"	150.00
Optical, red/bl/natural, wear/stains, 88x96"	100.00
Optical, woven/tied fringe, rnd corners 1 end, 2-pc, EX	225.00
Optical sqs w/in circles, bl/red/natural, 84x96"	300.00
Sqs in sqs, bl/red/wht, 2-pc dbl, rebound, 63x83"	325.00
Sqs w/radiating spokes, 4-part sqs, openwork border, EX	250.00
9-part sqs alternate w/dotted sqs, navy/teal/red/wht, wear	225.00

Cowan

Guy Cowan opened a small pottery near Cleveland, Ohio, ca 1912, where he made tile and artware on a small scale from the natural red clay available there. He developed distinctive glazes — necessary, he felt, to cover the dark red body. After the war and a temporary halt in production, Cowan moved his pottery to Rocky River, where he made a commercial line of artware utilizing a highly fired white porcelain. Although he acquiesced to the necessity of mass-production, every effort was made to insure a product of highest quality. Fine artists, among them Waylande Gregory, Thelma Frazier Winter, and Viktor Schreckengost, molded figurines which were often produced in limited editions, some of which sell today for prices in the thousands. Most of the ware was marked 'Cowan' or 'Lakewood Ware,' not to be confused with the name of the 1927 mass-produced line called 'Lakeware.' Falling under the crunch of the Great Depression, the pottery closed in 1931.

Bowl, console; bl/gr mottled sea horse ea side, 17"	110.00
Bowl, copper lustre, flared top, 4x8"	40.00
Candle holder, ivory, sea horse base, 4", pr	30.00
Candle holder, leaping gazelle, caramel gloss, 5¾"	135.00
Candlestick, Rowfant Club, ground hog, gr, ltd ed, 9½"	1,100.00
Charger, fish/seaweed emb, lt bl on dk bl, 11½"	500.00
Cigarette holder, sea horse base, Delft bl	35.00

Congo Head, by Waylande Gregory, metallic charcoal and bronze, 15", $2,200.00.

Decanter, burnt orange, ribbed, w/stopper, 10½"	600.00
Decanter, King from Alice in Wonderland, ca 1929, 12"	600.00
Figurine, Russian Peasant Dancer, tan crackle	750.00
Figurine, Spanish Dancer, male & female, mc, pr	750.00
Jar, ginger; purple lustre, w/lid, early, 5½"	300.00
Lamp, russet, allover star-shaped flowers, ovoid, 21"	200.00
Lamp, splotchy rust matt sphere base, metal shade, 20"	1,500.00
Lamp & shade, mother deer & young emb, brn/gr matt, 19"	1,500.00
Punch bowl, Jazz, bl/blk, sgn Schreckengost, 8" H	15,000.00
Tea set, yel, melon rib, 3-pc, ea w/lid	225.00
Vase, brn crystalline, paneled fan form, 8"	60.00
Vase, lav irid over beige, ribbed, trumpet form, 9½"	125.00
Vase, purple, in metal holder, 4"	125.00
Vase, streaky peach, ruffled/ftd, sgn AB, mfg flaw, 6½"	150.00
Vase, turq gloss, hand-thrown rings, sm rim, 9x10"	200.00
Vase, underwater seascape, dk bl on lt bl gloss, ovoid, 6½"	550.00

Cracker Jack

Kids have been buying Cracker Jack since it was first introduced in the 1890s. By 1912 it was packaged with a free toy inside. Before the first kernel was crunched, eager fingers had retrieved the surprise from the depth of the box — actually no easy task, considering the care required to keep the contents so swiftly displaced from spilling over the side! Though a little older, perhaps, many of those same kids still are looking — just as eagerly — for the Cracker Jack prizes. Point of sale, company collectibles, and the prizes as well have over the years reflected America's changing culture. Grocer sales and incentives from around the turn of the century — paper dolls, post cards and song books — were often marked Rueckheim Brothers (the inventors of Cracker Jack) or Reliable Confections. The first loose-packed prizes were toys made of wood, clay, tin, metal, and lithographed paper. Plastic toys were introduced in 1946. Paper wrapped for safety purposes in 1948, subjects echo the 'hype' of the day — Yo-Yos, tops, whistles, and sports cards in the simple, peaceful days of our country, propaganda and war toys in the forties, games in the fifties, and space toys in the sixties. Few of the estimated 15 billion prizes were marked. Advertising items from Angelus Marshmallow and Checkers Confections (cousins of the Cracker Jack family) are also collectible. When no condition is indicated, the items listed below are assumed to be in excellent condition. 'CJ' indicates that the item is marked. Note: An often-asked question concerns the tin Toonerville Trolley marked 'CJ.' No data has been found in the factory archives to authenticate this item; it is assumed that the 'CJ' merely refers to its size. Our advisor for this category is Wes Johnson; he is listed in the Directory under Kentucky.

Tin wagon and horses, 2" long, $65.00.

Cast Metal Prizes

Badge, shield, CJ Jr Detective, silver, 1931, 1¼"	35.00
Badge, 6-point star, mk CJ Police, silver, 1931, 1¼"	35.00
Button, stud bk, Me for Cracker Jack, boy & dog	18.00

Button, stud bk, Xd bats & ball, CJ pitcher/etc series, 1928...........**78.00**
Chair, T (Tootsie), 3 different sectional pcs, pnt, mini, ea **12.00**
Dollhouse items: lantern, mug, candlestick, etc; no mk, ea............ **6.50**
Horse & wagon, CJ, 3-D, silver or gold, early, 2½", ea **250.00**
Pistol, soft lead, inked, CJ on barrel, early, rare, 2⅛" **180.00**
Ring, alphabet letter setting (series), unmk, ea **3.00**
Rocking horse, no rider, 3-D, inked, early, 1⅛" **9.00**
Rocking horse w/boy, 3-D, inked, early, 1½" **22.00**
Tootsie Toy series: boats, cars, animals; '31, ¾"-1½", ea **7.00**

Dealer Incentives

Blotter, CJ question mk box, yel, 7¾x3¾" **225.00**
Cart w/2 movable wheels, wood dowel tongue, CJ **33.00**
Corkscrew/opener, metal plated, CJ/Angelus, 3" **65.00**
Corkscrew/opener, metal plated, CJ/Angelus, 3¾" tube case **65.00**
Jigsaw puzzle, CJ or Checkers, 1 of 4, 7x10", in envelope **35.00**
Magic puzzle, metal, CJ/Angelus, 1 of 15, '34, ea in envelope **14.00**
Mask, Halloween; paper, CJ, 10" or 12", ea **24.00**
Match holder, hinged, eng gold-tone case, CJ, 2½x1⅞" **650.00**
Palm puzzle, mirror bk, CJ, mk Germany/RWB, 1910-14, 1½"....**110.00**
Pencil top clip, metal/celluloid, oval boy & dog logo **210.00**
Pencil top clip, metal/celluloid, tube shape w/package.................**190.00**
Post card, bear, 1 of 16, CJ, 1907..**22.00**
Tablet, school; CJ, 1929, 8x10" **195.00**

Packaging

Box, popcorn; red scroll border, CJ, ca 1920..................................**85.00**
Box, popcorn; store display, CJ, 1923, no contents **65.00**
Canister, tin, CJ Candy Corn Crisp, 10-oz **75.00**
Canister, tin, CJ Coconut Corn Crisp, 1-lb **55.00**
Canister, tin, CJ Coconut Corn Crisp, 10-oz **65.00**
Crate, shipping; wood, CJ, Reuckheim Bros Eck, 1902-22, lg......**175.00**

Paper Prizes

Baseball CJ score counter, 3⅜" L..**95.00**
Book, Animals (or Birds), to color, Makatoy, 1949, mini **35.00**
Book, Bess & Bill on CJ Hill, series of 12, 1937, mini...................**85.00**
Book, Birds We Know, CJ, 1928, mini.....................................**65.00**
Book, drawing w/tracing paper, CJ, 1920s, mini.........................**110.00**
Book, Twigg & Sprigg, CJ, 1930, mini.....................................**85.00**
Booklet, stickers/wise cracks/riddles, Borden, CJ, 1965 on **1.00**
Decal, cartoon or nursery rhyme figure, 1947-49, CJ....................**31.00**
Disguise, ears, red (punch out from carrier), 1950, pr....................**22.00**
Disguise, glasses, hinged, cellophane lenses, CJ, 1933 ....**85.00**
Disguise, glasses, hinged, w/eyeballs, 1933 .... **6.00**
Disguise, mustache, blk/brn, in carrier, CJ, 1949 ....**45.00**
Fortune wheel, 2-pc litho, turn for fortune, CJ, 1¾".......................**68.00**
Game, Midget Auto Race, wheel spins, CJ, 1949, 3⅜" H **25.00**
Game spinner, ...baseball at home, rectangle, CJ, 2¾" W **125.00**
Game spinner, ...baseball at home, unmk, 1946, 1½" dia **40.00**
Hat, fold out, More You Eat/More You Want, CJ, early.................**75.00**
Hat, Indian headdress, CJ, early 1930s, 2½" **110.00**
Hat, Indian headdress, CJ, 1950s, 5⅜" **275.00**
Magic game book, erasable slate, series of 13, 1946, ea.................**27.00**
Movie, boy at blkboard, turn wheel: draws/erases, CJ, '31, 2" **185.00**
Movie, Goofy Zoo, turn wheel(s): change animals, 1939 ....**12.00**
Movie, pull tab for 2nd picture, series, CJ, 1943, 1¼", ea **82.00**
Movie, pull tab for 2nd picture, yel, early, 3", in envelope...........**125.00**
Palm puzzle, ball(s) roll into holes, plastic dome, from 1966 .... **1.00**
Riddle card, 2 series of 20, in package/from factory, CJ, ea.............**7.00**
Sand picture, sand pours for action, series of 14, 1967, ea **9.00**

Top, golf game, wood stick center, CJ, 1933 ....**47.00**
Transfer, iron on, sport figure or patriotic, CJ, 1939, ea **26.00**
Whistle, Razz Zooka, C Carey Cloud design, CJ, 1949.................**32.00**

Plastic Prizes

Animals, standup, letter on bk, series of 26, Nosco, 1953, ea **3.50**
Animals, standup on base, assorted, Nosco or CJ, 1947 on, ea........ **1.50**
Badge, pin-bk, celluloid, pretty lady, CJ label, 1¼" **98.00**
Baseball players, 3-D, bl or gray team, 1958, 1½", ea.....................**8.00**
Disk, emb comic character, series of 12, 1954, 1½" dia **12.00**
Disk, emb fish plaque, oval, series of 10, 1956, ea........................**9.00**
Dog, 3-D, hollow base, series of 10, CJCO, 1954, ea **4.50**
Figure, circus; stands on base, 1 of 12, Nosco, 1951-54................ **1.75**
Figure on rocking base, semi-flat, 1 of 9, Cloud design, '56 .... **3.00**
Fob, alphabet letter w/loop on top, 1 of 26, 1954, 1½" **2.25**
Magnifying glass, many designs/shapes, from 1961, ea................... **1.00**
Pinball game, lever shoots ball/score in holes, 1964 to recent......... **2.00**
Signs, road; Stop, Caution, etc, yel, series of 10, 1954-60, ea.......... **3.00**
Spinner, varied colors, 10 designs, from 1948, ea **1.50**
Toys, take apart/assemble, variety, from '62, assembled, ea............ **1.00**
Toys, take apart/assemble, variety, from '62, unassembled, ea **2.25**
Whistle, tube w/animals on top, CJ, 1 of 6, 1950-53, 1⅜" **8.50**

Premiums

Bat, baseball; wood, Hillerich & Bradsby, CJ, full sz **125.00**
Book, pocket; jester on cover, CJ **62.00**
Book, pocket; riddle/sailor boy/dog on cover, RWB, CJ **35.00**
Harmonica, full scale, emb CJ, early, rare, 5⅛" **650.00**
Mirror, oval, Angelus (redhead or blond) on box........................**89.00**
Pen, ink; w/nib, tin litho bbl, CJ...**650.00**
Recipe book, Angelus, 1930s..**22.00**
Wings, air corps type, silver or blk, stud-bk, CJ, '30s, 3", ea..........**75.00**

Tin Prizes

Badge, emb/plated CJ officer, 2⅜" or 1⅝", early, ea **110.00**
Bank, 3-D book form, red/gr/or blk, CJ Bank, early, 2" **95.00**
Boy & dog, diecut, complete w/bend-over tab, CJ........................**110.00**
Boy & dog, diecut, w/o tab at top **85.00**
Boy & dog, stand-up litho rectangle, est 1916, lg or sm, ea..........**145.00**
Brooch or pin, various design on card, CJ/logo, early, ea **100.00**
Cash register, litho, More You Eat, CJ, early, 1⅞" **400.00**
Clicker, 'Noisy CJ Snapper,' pear shape, aluminum, 1949 ....**32.00**
Doll dishes, tin plated, CJ, '31, 1¾", 1⅞", & 2⅛" dia, ea **32.00**
Fortune Wheel, 2-pc litho, CJ, 1939-41, 1¾" **43.00**
Helicopter, yel propellor, wood stick, unmk, 1937, 2⅝" **18.00**
Horse & wagon, litho diecut, CJ & Angelus, 2⅛" **65.00**
Horse & wagon, litho diecut, gray/red mks, CJ, 1914-23, 3⅛".....**395.00**
Model T Ford, License: NY 1915 #999, blk/wht, CJ, rare, 2"....**410.00**
Oval standup, Am flag, 1 of 4, unmk, 1936-46 ....**14.00**
Oval standup, comic character, 1 of 10, CJ, 1936-46 ....**85.00**
Pocket watch, silver of gold, CJ as numerals, 1931, 1½".................**58.00**
Sled, tin plated, CJ, 1931, 2" L...**49.00**
Small box shape: electric alarm clock litho, unmk, 1⅛" **75.00**
Small box shape: electric stove litho, unmk, 1⅛" **90.00**
Small box shape: garage litho, unmk, 1⅛" **85.00**
Small box shape: radio litho, bl, unmk, 1⅛" **110.00**
Soldier, litho, die-cut standup, officer/private/etc, unmk, ea........**17.00**
Tall box shape: Frozen Foods locker freezer, '47, unmk, 1¾".........**65.00**
Tall box shape: grandfather clock, unmk, 1947, 1¾".....................**50.00**
Tall box shape: radio, Tune in w/CJ, brn/yel, 1939, 1¾" **115.00**
Tall box shape: Refrigerator Car, CJ 2006, 1947, 1¾" L.................**95.00**

Train, engine & tender, litho, CJ Line/512 ....145.00
Train, litho coach only, red, unmk, 1941..................22.00
Train, litho engine only, red, 1941, unmk 17.00
Tray, emb, litho w/early package, smaller version 115.00
Tray, emb, litho w/early package, 2¼x1¾" 95.00
Wagon shape: Caterpillar tractor, unmk, 1931, 1¾" L ...31.00
Wagon shape: CJ Shows, circus wagon, series of 5, ea...120.00
Wagon shape: Playtime Trailer (auto trailer), unmk, 1947 ....35.00
Wagon shape: tank, orange/red/gr camouflage, unmk 65.00
Wagon shape: Tank Corps No 57, gr & blk, 1941 ....30.00
Wheelbarrow, tin plated, bk leg in place, CJ, 1931, 2½" L 50.00

Miscellaneous

Ad, comic book, CJ, ea 9.00
Ad, Saturday Evening Post, mc, CJ, 1919, 11x14" 18.00
Hat, ball park vendor cap, CJ, 1930s.......................30.00
Medal, CJ salesman award, brass, 1939, scarce 165.00
Sign, bathing beauty, 5-color cb, CJ, early, 17x22" 185.00
Sign, boy or girl w/box of CJ, 5-color cb, early, 17x22", ea 185.00
Sign, Jack & Bingo, die-cut litho, easel standup, CJ, early.........145.00
Sign, Santa & prizes, mc cb, Angelus, early, lg...........95.00
Sign, Santa & prizes, mc cb, Checkers, early, lg............ 1,000.00
Sign, Santa & prizes, mc cb, CJ, early, lg...............165.00

Crackle Glass

Crackle glass (or craquelle) was made during the 1800s in America as well as abroad. The name is derived from the texture of the ware, achieved by first plunging the hot glass into cold water, then reheating and reblowing the vessel, thereby producing ware with a crackled appearance.

Cruet, lt bl w/HP floral, 7" 175.00
Egg, on low std, 7-pc liqueur set w/in...................125.00
Pitcher, cranberry, rnd mouth, bulbous, 7¼x5½" 175.00
Tumbler, ruby, HP purple flowers, 3¾" 50.00
Vase, amberina, clear ruffled top, appl leaves, 6⅛".......395.00
Vase, cranberry flashed, clear base, braided stem, ftd, 10" 60.00

Cranberry

Cranberry glass is named for its resemblance to the color of cranberry juice. It was made by many companies both here and abroad, becoming popular in America soon after the Civil War. It was made in free-blown ware as well as mold-blown. Today cranberry glass is being reproduced, and it is sometimes difficult to distinguish the old from the new. Ask a reputable dealer if you are unsure. See also Cruets; Salts; Sugar Shakers; Syrups.

Bottle, scent; silver o/l lilies & scrolled stems, 6½" 400.00
Box, gold decor, melon ribs, hinged lid, 3x3½" 225.00
Box, HP village scene on lid, florals around base, 4x4½" 295.00
Box, patch; HP bl flowers & wht decor 225.00
Condiment set, 3-bottle, in SP fr, 5⅜x4"..................185.00
Decanter, gold scrolls/florals, clear wafer ft, 11x4⅛" 175.00
Decanter, HP florals, clear hdl & stopper, 10½x4".......195.00
Decanter, silver scroll hdls, lift top w/cork, 10", pr......500.00
Jam dish, clear appl rigaree, SP basket fr, 6x5½" 145.00
Pitcher, HP florals, ruffled neck, clear hdl, blown, 7½".......245.00
Pitcher, Invt T'print, bulbous, rnd mouth, 5¾x3¾".......95.00
Pitcher, Optic, clear hdl, 11⅝x5".........................195.00
Pitcher, Optic, clear hdl, 12¾x6½".......................265.00

Pitcher, Optic, clear hdl, 5x3"............................68.00
Pitcher, plain & patterned panels alternate, 6¾x4⅛" 95.00
Tumbler, florals w/gold, clear low ped ft, 3⅝x2"..........55.00
Tumbler, Honeycomb, HP daisies/forget-me-nots, 4½".......60.00
Vase, crystal mat-su-noke florals, ftd/ruffled, 8x6".......595.00
Vase, crystal rigaree & leaves, ped ft, 9¼x4⅜".......195.00
Vase, emb decor, crystal ft & appl leaves, 7¼x3" 100.00
Vase, gold flowers/butterfly, silver leaves, ftd, 5¼x5½" 395.00

Creamware

Creamware was a type of earthenware developed by Wedgwood in the 1760s and produced by many other Staffordshire potteries, including Leeds. Since it could be potted cheaply and was light in weight, it became popular abroad as well as in England, due to the lower freight charges involved in its export. It was revived at Leeds in the late nineteenth century, and the type most often reproduced was heavily reticulated or molded in high relief. These later wares are easily distinguished from the originals since they are thicker and tend to craze heavily. See also Leeds.

Basket, rtcl, yel/blk design, mk Mayer, rpr rib, 3x8" 295.00
Coffeepot, brn/bl granite w/wht bands, dog finial, rpr, 10" 700.00
Creamer, King of Prussia, blk transfer, bk: angel, 4" 225.00
Mug, emb panels w/bands of yel w/bl lines, leaf hdl, 6", EX.........200.00
Pepper pot, 3-leaf clover & flowers, maroon band, 4", EX 75.00
Plate, blk transfer initials/garlands, rtcl, 9", EX 125.00
Plate, emb/rtcl rim, att Leeds, chips, 9½" 175.00
Soup dish, mk Davenport, 9½"............................65.00
Sweetmeat, lady sits above 2 5-shell tiers, Leeds type, 10"...........600.00
Tea caddy, HP florals/geometrics, early, 4x4½", EX 120.00
Teapot, lady pours tea in red, twist hdl, flower finial, 5"......... 1,350.00
Teapot, ribbed, rope hdl w/floral ends, dome lid, 9", EX 950.00
Waste bowl, mc roses, 6", EX 120.00

Crown Ducal

Earthenware marked 'Crown Ducal' and decorated by Charlotte Rhead is becoming quite collectible. This is the mark of A.G. Richardson & Co., Ltd., located in Tunstall and Ferrybridge in the Staffordshire district of England.

Biscuit jar, floral panels, gold trim, SP top, 7½x5½" 125.00
Chop plate, Byzantine, sgn C Rhead, 12¾".................195.00
Plaque, Autumn Leaves, mc leaves on tan, C Rhead, mk, 14" 225.00
Plaque, floral, mc on beige mottle, C Rhead, #4491, 12½" 225.00
Plate, Geo Washington Bicentennial, rose border, 1932, 10½" 45.00
Plate, Washington & Lafayette on porch, Mt Vernon, 10½".........45.00
Vase, Byzantine, mc Deco design on gold mottle, 5⅞x4"............145.00
Vase, florals, mc on beige mottle, C Rhead, #4491, 6⅞" 165.00
Vase, hummingbirds on beige, butterfly on bk, mk, 9¼" 95.00

Crown Milano

Crown Milano was introduced in 1884 by the Mt. Washington Glass Company. When the company merged with Pairpoint in 1894, it continued to be one of their best sellers. It is an opaque, highly decorated ware with gold or colored enamels in intricate designs on pale backgrounds. Many pieces were marked 'CM' with a crown. Since it is nearly always found in a satin finish, in the listings that follow, satin is assumed unless glossy is indicated. Our advisors for this category are

Betty and Clarence Maier; they are listed in the Directory under Pennsylvania.

Biscuit jar, flowers/gold scrolls on yel & wht, Mt WA lid 750.00
Biscuit jar, gold-lined roses/thorns on opal, EX SP lid, 6"........ 1,200.00
Biscuit jar, starfish, red/yel beads on hobnail opal, 6½"..............900.00
Biscuit jar, thistles, melon ribbed, crab-emb lid, 7½" 1,300.00
Bowl, pansies, crimped/gold rim, globular, no mk, 6" 125.00
Bowl, pansies on shiny wht, fan shape, shallow, 8" 150.00
Bowl vase, beaded pinwheels, emb swirled ribs, 4" 525.00
Box, roses on wht, melon ribs, hinged lid, 5" dia 295.00
Bride's basket, florals on wht, cut/folded rim 4x9"; SP fr............465.00
Jardiniere, mums/florals on pk w/gilt scrollwork, 6x8"................385.00
Pitcher, pr in fancy attire on shiny wht, att Guba, 12"................650.00
Rose bowl, floral & swirled gold lines on yel, no mk, 4" 220.00
Rose bowl, orchids on brn to yel, 4½x5"..................................450.00
Sugar shaker, autumn leaves on orange to yel, ribbed, 3".........525.00
Sweetmeat, appl jewels/scrolls on swirled cream, 4" 1,100.00
Sweetmeat, starfish/jewels on pnt ground w/florals, 6x6" 1,300.00
Tray, trinket; florals/medallion & gold, sq, 1½x5½" 165.00
Tumbler, gold flower garland & trim, 3¾x2¾" 550.00

Vase, allover gold roses, 10½", $2,500.00.

Vase, apple blossoms/gold beads on wht, sm hdls, 5x4", NM 600.00
Vase, cactus/foliage on cream, swirled/bulbous, 7" 3,000.00
Vase, ferns, gold & tan, scrolls at neck, globular body, 9" 900.00
Vase, ferns/gold floral medallions, egg form, label, 9"................500.00
Vase, flowers/gold scrolls, snake around stick neck, 10" 2,300.00
Vase, gold scrolls & rim, 9 lg berry prunts, 11½" 495.00
Vase, leaves/acorns w/gold on ribbed yel, no mk, 8½" 1,500.00
Vase, mums on shiny wht, stick neck w/spiral thorn hdl, 13" ...750.00
Vase, orchids on Burmese color, rnd w/long neck, no mk, 14" . 2,300.00
Vase, thistles/blossoms, pk/gr/bl on cream, no mk, 12x4" 1,400.00
Vase, winged dragons & gilt on yel, no mk, bulbous, 11" 2,500.00

Cruets

Cruets, containers made to hold oil or vinegar, are usually bulbous with tall narrow throats and a stopper. During the nineteenth century and for several years after, they were produced in abundance in virtually every type of glassware available. Those listed below are assumed to be with stopper and mint unless noted otherwise.

Amber, bl hdl & stopper, sq bulbous form, 3-petal top, 7¾" 155.00

Amberina, reeded hdl, ftd, hollow stopper 350.00
Arched Fleur-de-Lis, ruby stained, Higbee 395.00
Balder 50.00
Broken Column 65.00
Champion (Fans & Crossbar), amber stained..............................175.00
Champion (Fans & Crossbar), ruby stained..................................195.00
Clear to gr shaded, HP lav foliage & gold leaves, 9¼x2½"..........165.00
Coreopsis, HP florals 295.00
Cranberry, pewter neck/lid/ft & hdl, 8½x4" 225.00
Cupid & Venus, Maltese Cross finial stopper 140.00
Daisy & Button w/Crossbars, vaseline, lg....................................160.00
Daisy & Fern, Apple Blossom mold, wht opal, clear stopper 115.00
Dbl Circle, gr 165.00
Dewey, vaseline 165.00
Dmn Quilt, amberina, faceted amber stopper, 3-fold rim, 5½" 450.00
Empress, emerald gr w/EX gold 315.00
Feather 55.00
Flora, clear w/gold..145.00
Forget-Me-Not, gr opaque, Challinor 165.00
Herringbone, pk MOP, frosted hdl & stopper 450.00
Herringbone Buttress, emerald gr, gr stopper, rare.......................450.00
Hobnail, cranberry, clear hdl, pressed faceted stopper, 7" 350.00
Intaglio, clear opal 110.00
Invt T'print, amber, bl reeded hdl, faceted bl stopper, 7⅜" 95.00
Invt T'print, amberina, amber hdl & faceted stopper, 5" 350.00
Invt T'print, cranberry, 3-fold rim, cranberry stopper, 5½"..........300.00
Invt T'print, peacock bl, amber hdl & faceted stopper 150.00
Invt T'print, rubina, trefoil rim, clear hdl & stopper, 6" 195.00
Invt T'print, rubina verde, funnel shape 250.00
Invt T'print, rubina verde, lime hdl & faceted stopper, 6½"........250.00
Jacob's Ladder, w/orig Maltese Cross stopper................................125.00
Lacy Daisy 50.00
Leaf Mold, vaseline spatter, matching faceted stopper 395.00
Log & Star, amber 75.00
Lone Star, gr 250.00
Medallion Sprig, amethyst, amethyst stopper 300.00
Medallion Sprig, gr to clear...275.00
New Hampshire (Bent Buckle), orig Teasel stopper......................50.00
Optic Dmn Quilt, HP florals, sq form...135.00
Paddle Wheel...55.00
Panelled Thistle 75.00
Pleat & Panel, apple gr, matching acorn stopper, Heisey.............125.00
Rib Optic (Utopia Optic, Tiny Optic), gr w/HP decor 135.00
Ribbed Pillar, pk & wht spatter..235.00
Rising Sun, ruby stained..350.00
Satina Swirl, bl, cut bl stopper, very rare 650.00
Scalloped 6-Point, ruby stained, clear stopper, 6¾".....................125.00
Shoshone, ruby stained..235.00
Swag w/Brackets, bl opal, matching stopper 450.00
Swag w/Brackets, vaseline opal, rpl stopper 450.00
Thousand Eye, amber 135.00
Thousand Eye, amber, Richard & Hartley variant 185.00
Torpedo...55.00
Vesta, amber, amber stopper 195.00
Yel cased, HP florals w/gold, 3-petal top, clear stopper, 6" 85.00

Cup Plates, Glass

Before the middle 1850s, it was socially acceptable to pour hot tea into a deep saucer to cool. The tea was sipped from the saucer rather than the cup, which frequently was handleless and too hot to hold. The cup plate served as a coaster for the cup. It is generally agreed that the first examples of pressed glass cup plates were made about 1826 at the

Boston and Sandwich Glass Co. in Sandwich, Cape Cod, Massachusetts. Other glassworks in three major areas (New England, Philadelphia, and the Midwest, especially Pittsburgh) quickly followed suit.

Antique glass cup plates range in size from 2⅝" up to 4¼" in diameter. The earliest plates had simple designs inspired by cut glass patterns, but by 1829 they had become more complex. The span from then until about 1845 is known as the 'Lacy Period,' when cup plate designs and pressing techniques were at their peak. To cover pressing imperfections, the backgrounds of the plates were often covered with fine stippling which endowed them with a glittering brilliance called 'laciness.' They were made in a multitude of designs — some purely decorative, others commemorative. Subjects include the American eagle, hearts, sunbursts, log cabins, ships, George Washington, the political candidates Clay and Harrison, plows, beehives, etc. Of all the patterns, the round George Washington plate is the rarest and most valuable — only three are known to exist today.

Authenticity is most important. Collectors must be aware that contemporary plates which have no antique counterparts and fakes modeled after antique patterns have had wide distribution. Condition is also important, though it is the exceptional plate that does not have some rim roughness. More important considerations are scarcity of design and color.

Our advisor for this category is John Bilane; he is listed in the Directory under New Jersey. The book *American Glass* by George and Helen McKearin has a section on glass cup plates. A more definitive book is *American Glass Cup Plates* by Ruth Webb Lee and James H. Rose. Numbers in the listings that follow (computer sorted) refer to the latter. When no condition is indicated, the examples listed below are assumed to have only minor rim roughness as is normal. See also Staffordshire; Pairpoint.

R-102, VG	52.00
R-104, G	30.00
R-105, scarce, VG	48.00
R-109, VG	48.00
R-124A, VG	38.00
R-129, VG	38.00
R-13C, G	30.00
R-136A, rare, VG	75.00
R-145C, G	28.00
R-147A, G	38.00
R-148, VG	31.00
R-149, VG	34.00
R-151, G	35.00
R-154B, VG	35.00
R-159B, G	30.00
R-160B, VG	34.00
R-162A, G	28.00
R-162B, VG	33.00
R-174, EX	40.00
R-176A, VG	35.00
R-177, VG	44.00
R-180A, scarce, G	42.00
R-20, EX	36.00
R-203, VG	51.00
R-208, scarce, G	44.00
R-22, VG	28.00
R-232, rare, G	50.00
R-236, G	32.00
R-245, G	28.00
R-246, VG	36.00
R-255, G	18.00
R-257, VG	30.00
R-257A, VG	32.00

R-258, VG	30.00
R-269, VG	30.00
R-269B, scarce, VG	40.00
R-269C, G	25.00
R-27, G	24.00
R-271A, VG	33.00
R-28, G	24.00
R-29-X-1, VG	30.00
R-313, G	18.00
R-323, VG	18.00
R-324, VG	19.00
R-331, G	14.00
R-332A, VG	20.00
R-332B, VG	19.00
R-336, VG	25.00
R-339, VG	19.00
R-340, VG	18.00
R-341, VG	20.00
R-343B, VG	35.00
R-37, scarce, VG	42.00
R-379, VG	13.00
R-389, G	11.00
R-39, G	21.00
R-390A, G	11.00
R-392, VG	14.00
R-393, G	10.00
R-396, VG	13.00
R-397, VG	13.00
R-40, VG	28.00
R-402, VG	14.00
R-403, VG	13.00
R-433, scarce, G	22.00
R-439C, scarce, G	26.00
R-440, G	28.00
R-444, EX	37.00
R-447, G	22.00
R-447A, VG	26.00
R-449, G	45.00
R-465N, G	16.00
R-47, VG	30.00
R-48, G	28.00
R-49, G	26.00
R-501, G	14.00
R-531, G	19.00
R-56, scarce, G	45.00
R-562A, very rare, G	250.00
R-564, VG	28.00
R-565B, G	28.00
R-569, G	37.00
R-575, scarce, G	53.00
R-590, VG	35.00
R-593, scarce, VG	52.00
R-596, VG	45.00
R-605A, scarce, VG	135.00
R-610, VG	39.00
R-610A, VG	34.00
R-610C, VG	40.00
R-610D, G	35.00
R-619, G	38.00
R-619A, G	35.00
R-62A, VG	45.00
R-628, scarce, G	53.00
R-632A, G	38.00
R-636, VG	45.00

R-640, G 18.00
R-641A, G 11.00
R-642, G 18.00
R-65, scarce, VG 44.00
R-661, G 15.00
R-662, G 29.00
R-665A, G 32.00
R-666, VG 38.00
R-666A, scarce, G 40.00
R-667A, VG 36.00
R-679, VG 30.00
R-680B, VG 31.00
R-69, rare, EX 80.00
R-78, scarce, EX 65.00
R-79, VG 40.00
R-95, VG 36.00
R-97, scarce, G 42.00
R-98, rare, VG 70.00

Currier & Ives by Royal

During the 1950s dinnerware decorated with blue transfer-printed scenes taken from prints by Currier and Ives was manufactured by Royal China and given as premiums through A&P stores. In addition to the dinnerware, a line of Fire King baking pans and accessories was also available, as were vinyl placemats and various sizes of glass tumblers. Today it is readily available at reasonable prices, and it has become a very popular collectible at malls and flea markets around the country.

Ash tray..12.00
Bowl, cereal; scarce, 6⅜" 10.00
Bowl, lug soup, 6⅜"..15.00
Bowl, soup; flat, 8½" 8.00
Bowl, vegetable; oval 18.00
Bowl, 10"...16.00
Bowl, 5½"...3.00
Bowl, 9"..14.00
Butter dish, ¼-lb 20.00
Casserole, w/lid...50.00

Chop plate, 12", $15.00.

Creamer..5.00
Cup & saucer.. 4.00
Gravy boat.. 8.00
Gravy boat, w/ladle & liner.............................20.00
Mug...12.50
Pie plate, 10" 12.00
Plate, 10½" 7.50
Plate, 12"..15.00
Plate, 6" 3.00
Plate, 7⅜"...6.00
Plate, 9"...6.50
Platter, 13"...18.00
Shakers, pr...12.00
Sugar bowl, w/lid 8.00
Teapot..50.00
Tumbler, juice...10.00
Tumbler, old fashioned, 3¼".............................10.00
Tumbler, 13-oz, 5½" 10.00
Tumbler, 9-oz, 4¾" 8.00

Custard

As early as the 1880s, custard glass was produced in England. Migrating glassmakers brought the formula for the creamy ivory ware to America. One of them was Harry Northwood, who in 1898 founded his company in Indiana, Pennsylvania, and introduced the glassware to the American market. Soon other companies were producing custard, among them Heisey, Tarentum, Fenton, and McKee. Not only dinnerware patterns but souvenir items were made. Today custard is the most expensive of the colored pressed glassware patterns. The formula for producing the luminous glass contains uranium salts which imparts the cream color to the batch and causes it to glow when it is examined under a black light.

Argonaut Shell, bowl, master berry; gold & decor, 10½" L..........225.00
Argonaut Shell, butter dish, gold & decor 325.00
Argonaut Shell, butter dish, no gold..............................275.00
Argonaut Shell, compote, jelly; gold & decor, scarce..................135.00
Argonaut Shell, creamer, gold & decor 135.00
Argonaut Shell, creamer, no gold 110.00
Argonaut Shell, cruet, gold & decor................................550.00
Argonaut Shell, pitcher, water; gold & decor..............395.00
Argonaut Shell, sauce, ftd, gold & decor 65.00
Argonaut Shell, spooner, gold & decor 135.00
Argonaut Shell, sugar bowl, w/lid, gold & decor 200.00
Argonaut Shell, tumbler, gold & decor............................95.00
Bead Swag, goblet, floral & gold....................................60.00
Bead Swag, sauce, floral & gold.....................................45.00
Bead Swag, tray, pickle; floral & gold, rare 260.00
Bead Swag, wine, floral & gold......................................58.00
Beaded Circle, bowl, master berry; floral & gold 245.00
Beaded Circle, butter dish, floral & gold 400.00
Beaded Circle, creamer, floral & gold 160.00
Beaded Circle, cruet, floral & gold, rare 1,100.00
Beaded Circle, pitcher, water; floral & gold 600.00
Beaded Circle, shakers, floral & gold, pr....................750.00
Beaded Circle, spooner, floral & gold 175.00
Beaded Circle, sugar bowl, w/lid, floral & gold..................250.00
Beaded Circle, tumbler, floral & gold, very rare 100.00
Cane Insert, berry set, 7-pc..400.00
Cane Insert, table set, 4-pc..450.00
Cherry & Scales, bowl, master berry; nutmeg stain 130.00
Cherry & Scales, butter dish, nutmeg stain 225.00

Cherry & Scales, creamer, nutmeg stain........................115.00
Cherry & Scales, pitcher, water; nutmeg stain, scarce 325.00
Cherry & Scales, spooner, nutmeg stain, scarce 95.00
Cherry & Scales, sugar bowl, w/lid, nutmeg stain, scarce............125.00
Cherry & Scales, tumbler, nutmeg stain, scarce...................50.00
Chrysanthemum Sprig, bowl, master berry; gold & decor 235.00
Chrysanthemum Sprig, bowl, master berry; no gold.................175.00
Chrysanthemum Sprig, butter dish, gold & decor 300.00
Chrysanthemum Sprig, celery vase, gold & decor, rare........... 1,500.00
Chrysanthemum Sprig, compote, jelly; gold & decor 115.00
Chrysanthemum Sprig, compote, jelly; no decor 75.00
Chrysanthemum Sprig, creamer, gold & decor.....................105.00
Chrysanthemum Sprig, cruet, gold & decor, 6¾"......................290.00
Chrysanthemum Sprig, pitcher, water; gold & decor 425.00
Chrysanthemum Sprig, sauce, ftd, gold & decor 50.00
Chrysanthemum Sprig, shakers, gold & decor, pr....................250.00
Chrysanthemum Sprig, spooner, gold & decor.....................105.00
Chrysanthemum Sprig, spooner, no gold 70.00
Chrysanthemum Sprig, toothpick holder, gold & decor 275.00
Chrysanthemum Sprig, toothpick holder, no decor 165.00
Chrysanthemum Sprig, tumbler, gold & decor 55.00
Dandelion, mug, nutmeg stain...165.00
Delaware, creamer, breakfast; pk stain 70.00
Delaware, sauce, pk stain 65.00
Delaware, tray, pin; gr stain 75.00
Delaware, tumbler, pk stain...55.00
Diamond w/Peg, bowl, master berry; roses & gold....................215.00
Diamond w/Peg, butter dish, roses & gold 235.00
Diamond w/Peg, creamer, ind; no decor 30.00
Diamond w/Peg, creamer, ind; souvenir 45.00
Diamond w/Peg, creamer, roses & gold 75.00
Diamond w/Peg, mug, souvenir 50.00
Diamond w/Peg, napkin ring, roses & gold, rare.......................150.00
Diamond w/Peg, pitcher, roses & gold, 5½"............................225.00
Diamond w/Peg, sauce, roses & gold 40.00
Diamond w/Peg, shakers, souvenir, pr...................................175.00
Diamond w/Peg, sugar bowl, w/lid, roses & gold.....................160.00
Diamond w/Peg, toothpick holder, roses & gold 125.00
Diamond w/Peg, tumbler, roses & gold 55.00
Diamond w/Peg, water set, souvenir, 7-pc..............................650.00
Diamond w/Peg, wine, roses & gold 55.00
Diamond w/Peg, wine, souvenir 40.00
Everglades, bowl, master berry; gold & decor 215.00
Everglades, butter dish, gold & decor 365.00
Everglades, creamer, gold & decor 145.00
Everglades, sauce, gold & decor..60.00
Everglades, shakers, gold & decor, pr.....................................325.00
Everglades, spooner, gold & decor 145.00
Everglades, sugar bowl, w/lid, gold & decor 215.00
Everglades, tumbler, gold & decor 100.00
Fan, bowl, master berry; good gold..185.00
Fan, butter dish, good gold..210.00
Fan, creamer, good gold...110.00
Fan, ice cream set, good gold, 7-pc..500.00
Fan, pitcher, water; good gold 275.00
Fan, sauce, good gold 55.00
Fan, spooner, good gold..95.00
Fan, sugar bowl, w/lid, good gold 135.00
Fan, tumbler, good gold 75.00
Fan, water set, good gold, 7-pc...700.00
Fine Cut & Roses, rose bowl, fancy int, nutmeg stain.................100.00
Fine Cut & Roses, rose bowl, plain int....................................85.00
Geneva, bowl, master berry; floral decor, ftd, oval, 9" L 90.00
Geneva, bowl, master berry; floral decor, rnd, 9" 120.00

Geneva, butter dish, floral decor 195.00
Geneva, butter dish, no decor 125.00
Geneva, compote, jelly; floral decor.......................................85.00
Geneva, creamer, floral decor 90.00
Geneva, cruet, floral decor 395.00
Geneva, pitcher, water; floral decor.......................................225.00
Geneva, sauce, floral decor, oval..45.00
Geneva, sauce, floral decor, rnd 45.00
Geneva, shakers, floral decor, pr 250.00
Geneva, spooner, floral decor 90.00
Geneva, sugar bowl, open, floral decor....................................85.00
Geneva, sugar bowl, w/lid, floral decor 150.00
Geneva, syrup, floral decor 435.00
Geneva, toothpick holder, floral w/M gold 335.00
Geneva, tumbler, floral decor..50.00
Georgia Gem, bowl, master berry; good gold 135.00
Georgia Gem, bowl, master berry; gr opaque 115.00
Georgia Gem, butter dish, good gold 190.00
Georgia Gem, celery vase, good gold 145.00
Georgia Gem, creamer, good gold 95.00
Georgia Gem, creamer, no gold 50.00
Georgia Gem, mug, good gold 45.00
Georgia Gem, powder jar, w/lid, good gold 75.00
Georgia Gem, shakers, good gold, pr 135.00
Georgia Gem, spooner, souvenir 55.00
Georgia Gem, sugar bowl, w/lid, no gold.................................95.00
Grape (& Cable), bottle, scent; orig stopper, nutmeg stain 550.00
Grape (& Cable), bowl, master berry; nutmeg stain, ftd, 11".......295.00
Grape (& Cable), bowl, nutmeg stain, 7½"...............................50.00
Grape (& Cable), butter dish, nutmeg stain 275.00
Grape (& Cable), compote, jelly; nutmeg stain 130.00
Grape (& Cable), compote, nutmeg stain, 4½x8" 275.00
Grape (& Cable), cracker jar, nutmeg stain..............................750.00
Grape (& Cable), creamer, breakfast; nutmeg stain 75.00
Grape (& Cable), humidor, bl stain, rare 800.00
Grape (& Cable), humidor, nutmeg stain, rare..........................850.00
Grape (& Cable), nappy, nutmeg stain, rare..............................45.00
Grape (& Cable), pitcher, water; nutmeg stain 375.00
Grape (& Cable), plate, nutmeg stain, 7" 45.00
Grape (& Cable), plate, nutmeg stain, 8" 55.00
Grape (& Cable), powder jar, nutmeg stain 350.00
Grape (& Cable), punch bowl, w/base, nutmeg stain 1,650.00
Grape (& Cable), sauce, nutmeg stain, ftd 45.00
Grape (& Cable), spooner, nutmeg stain..................................145.00
Grape (& Cable), sugar, breakfast; open, nutmeg stain 75.00
Grape (& Cable), sugar bowl, w/lid, nutmeg stain 195.00
Grape (& Cable), tray, dresser; nutmeg stain, scarce, lg...............325.00
Grape (& Cable), tray, pin; nutmeg stain.................................125.00
Grape (& Cable), tumbler, nutmeg stain...................................75.00
Grape & Gothic Arches, bowl, master berry; pearl w/gold...........200.00
Grape & Gothic Arches, butter dish, pearl w/gold....................200.00
Grape & Gothic Arches, creamer, pearl w/gold, rare...................90.00
Grape & Gothic Arches, favor vase, nutmeg stain 80.00
Grape & Gothic Arches, goblet, pearl w/gold 75.00
Grape & Gothic Arches, pitcher, water; pearl w/gold.................275.00
Grape & Gothic Arches, sauce, pearl w/gold, rare......................80.00
Grape & Gothic Arches, spooner, pearl w/gold 80.00
Grape & Gothic Arches, sugar bowl, w/lid, pearl w/gold 125.00
Grape & Gothic Arches, tumbler, pearl w/gold 65.00
Grape Arbor, vase, hat form..90.00
Heart w/T'print, creamer..80.00
Heart w/T'print, lamp, good pnt, scarce, 8" 375.00
Heart w/T'print, sugar bowl, ind...75.00
Honeycomb, wine..65.00

Horse Medallion, bowl, gr stain, 7" 70.00
Intaglio, bowl, master berry; gold & decor, ftd, 9" 250.00
Intaglio, butter dish, gold & decor, scarce 300.00
Intaglio, compote, jelly; gold & decor..........................125.00
Intaglio, creamer, gold & decor..................................110.00
Intaglio, cruet, gold & decor 425.00
Intaglio, pitcher, water; gold & decor 345.00
Intaglio, sauce, gold & decor 48.00
Intaglio, shakers, gold & decor, pr 200.00
Intaglio, spooner, gold & decor 115.00
Intaglio, sugar bowl, w/lid, gold & decor 165.00
Intaglio, tumbler, gold & decor 75.00
Inverted Fan & Feather, bowl, master berry; gold & decor 215.00
Inverted Fan & Feather, butter dish, gold & decor 350.00
Inverted Fan & Feather, compote, jelly; gold & decor, rare........450.00
Inverted Fan & Feather, creamer, gold & decor 150.00
Inverted Fan & Feather, cruet, gold & decor, scarce, 6½" 900.00

Inverted Fan and Feather, pitcher, gold trim, $600.00.

Inverted Fan & Feather, punch cup, gold & decor.....................250.00
Inverted Fan & Feather, sauce, gold & decor 65.00
Inverted Fan & Feather, shakers, gold & decor, pr 550.00
Inverted Fan & Feather, spooner, gold & decor 145.00
Inverted Fan & Feather, sugar bowl, w/lid, gold & decor............225.00
Inverted Fan & Feather, tumbler, gold & decor 95.00
Jackson, bowl, master berry; good gold, ftd 125.00
Jackson, creamer, good gold..85.00
Jackson, pitcher, water; good gold.................................250.00
Jackson, pitcher, water; no decor 150.00
Jackson, sauce, good gold 45.00
Jackson, shakers, good gold, pr 165.00
Jackson, tumbler, good gold..50.00
Louis XV, berry set, w/nutmeg, 7-pc 375.00
Louis XV, bowl, master berry; good gold............................165.00
Louis XV, butter dish, good gold...................................200.00
Louis XV, creamer, good gold..80.00
Louis XV, cruet, good gold 300.00
Louis XV, pitcher, water; good gold................................225.00
Louis XV, sauce, good gold, ftd.....................................47.00
Louis XV, spooner, good gold..80.00
Louis XV, sugar bowl, w/lid, good gold 150.00
Louis XV, tumbler, good gold..65.00
Maple Leaf, bowl, master berry; gold & decor, scarce...............335.00

Maple Leaf, butter dish, gold & decor 300.00
Maple Leaf, compote, jelly; gold & decor, rare...............455.00
Maple Leaf, creamer, gold & decor 135.00
Maple Leaf, cruet, gold & decor, rare 2,500.00

Maple Leaf, pitcher, green stain and gold trim, $400.00.

Maple Leaf, sauce, gold & decor, scarce.........................95.00
Maple Leaf, shakers, gold & decor, pr 650.00
Maple Leaf, spooner, gold & decor 135.00
Maple Leaf, sugar bowl, w/lid, gold & decor 195.00
Maple Leaf, tumbler, gold & decor 95.00
Panelled Poppy, lamp shade, nutmeg stain, scarce 800.00
Peacock & Urn, bowl, ice cream; nutmeg stain, sm...............80.00
Peacock & Urn, bowl, ice cream; nutmeg stain, 10" 335.00
Punty Band, shakers, pr 165.00
Punty Band, spooner, floral decor 75.00
Punty Band, tumbler, floral decor, souvenir....................65.00
Ribbed Drape, butter dish, scalloped, roses & gold...........325.00
Ribbed Drape, compote, jelly; roses & gold, rare 200.00
Ribbed Drape, creamer, roses & gold, scarce 150.00
Ribbed Drape, cruet, roses & gold, scarce 550.00
Ribbed Drape, pitcher, water; roses & gold, rare 345.00
Ribbed Drape, sauce, roses & gold 40.00
Ribbed Drape, shakers, roses & gold, rare, pr 300.00
Ribbed Drape, spooner, roses & gold 150.00
Ribbed Drape, toothpick holder, roses & gold.................375.00
Ribbed Drape, tumbler, roses & gold............................65.00
Ribbed Thumbprint, wine, floral decor 75.00
Ring Band, bowl, master berry; roses & gold 135.00
Ring Band, butter dish, roses & gold..........................235.00
Ring Band, compote, jelly; roses & gold, scarce 165.00
Ring Band, creamer, roses & gold 115.00
Ring Band, cruet, roses & gold 400.00
Ring Band, pitcher, roses & gold, 7½" 315.00
Ring Band, sauce, roses & gold.................................40.00
Ring Band, shakers, roses & gold, pr 135.00
Ring Band, spooner, roses & gold 110.00
Ring Band, syrup, roses & gold................................415.00
Ring Band, toothpick holder, roses & gold 110.00
Ring Band, tray, condiment; roses & gold 175.00
Singing Birds, mug, nutmeg stain...............................75.00
Tarentum's Victoria, bowl, master berry; gold & decor 200.00

Tarentum's Victoria, butter dish, gold & decor, rare.................275.00
Tarentum's Victoria, celery vase, gold & decor, rare.................225.00
Tarentum's Victoria, creamer, gold & decor, scarce..................125.00
Tarentum's Victoria, pitcher, water; gold & decor, rare..............365.00
Tarentum's Victoria, spooner, gold & decor..........................125.00
Tarentum's Victoria, sugar bowl, w/lid, gold & decor................160.00
Tarentum's Victoria, tumbler, gold & decor...........................70.00
Vermont, butter dish, bl decor.....................................185.00
Vermont, toothpick holder, bl decor................................135.00
Vermont, vase, floral decor, jeweled................................75.00
Wide Band, bell, roses...175.00
Wild Bouquet, butter dish, gold & decor, rare......................650.00
Wild Bouquet, creamer, no gold.....................................145.00
Wild Bouquet, cruet, no decor, w/clear stopper.....................750.00
Wild Bouquet, sauce, gold & decor...................................60.00
Wild Bouquet, spooner, gold & decor................................145.00
Wild Bouquet, tumbler, no decor.....................................75.00
Winged Scroll, bowl, master berry; gold & decor, 11" L.............155.00
Winged Scroll, butter dish, good gold..............................185.00
Winged Scroll, butter dish, no decor...............................150.00
Winged Scroll, celery vase, good gold, rare........................400.00
Winged Scroll, cigarette jar, scarce...............................155.00
Winged Scroll, compote, ruffled, rare, 6¾x10¾".....................495.00
Winged Scroll, cruet, good gold, clear stopper.....................295.00
Winged Scroll, hair receiver, good gold............................135.00
Winged Scroll, pitcher, water; bulbous, good gold..................350.00
Winged Scroll, sauce, good gold.....................................45.00
Winged Scroll, shakers, bulbous, good gold, rare, pr...............350.00
Winged Scroll, shakers, str sides, good gold, pr...................195.00
Winged Scroll, sugar bowl, w/lid, good gold........................150.00
Winged Scroll, syrup, good gold....................................395.00
Winged Scroll, tumbler, good gold...................................75.00

Cut Glass

The earliest documented evidence of commercial glass cutting in the United States was in 1810; the producers were Bakewell and Page of Pittsburgh. These first efforts resulted in simple patterns with only a moderate amount of cutting. By the middle of the century, glass cutters began experimenting with a thicker glass which enabled them to use deeper cuttings, though patterns remained much the same. This period is usually referred to as Rich Cut. Using three types of wheels — a flat edge, a mitered edge, and a convex edge — facets, miters, and depressions were combined to produce various designs. In the late 1870s, a curved miter was developed which greatly expanded design potential. Patterns became more elaborate, often covering the entire surface. The Brilliant Period of cut glass covered a span from about 1880 until 1915. Because of the pressure necessary to achieve the deeply cut patterns, only glass containing a high grade of metal could withstand the process. For this reason and the amount of handwork involved, cut glass has always been expensive.

Bowls cut with pinwheels may be either foreign or of a newer vintage, beware! Identifiable patterns and signed pieces that are well cut and in excellent condition bring the higher prices on today's market.

Key:
dmn — diamonds   X-cut — cross-cut
strw — strawberry   X-hatch — crosshatch

Bonbon, Broadway, sq form, Huntly, 2x8"............................135.00
Bottle, scent; allover X-cut dmns, fluted, cut stopper, 6½".........120.00
Bowl, banana; florals/leaves, Harvard center, 14½" L...............175.00
Bowl, bars of cane/hobstars, serrated/scalloped, 8½"...............200.00

Bowl, berry; hobstars & fans, 8"...................................150.00
Bowl, geometrics/hobstars/fans/strw/dmns/miters, Roden, 9".........275.00
Bowl, Hobstar & Zipper, heavy, 9"..................................95.00
Bowl, hobstars, cane, fine checkering, heavily cut, 9".............140.00
Bowl, hobstars in X-hatch split vesicas, hobstar base, 8"..........225.00
Bowl, hobstars/heavy-knotched mitres, heavy, 3½x9" sq.............350.00
Bowl, hobstars/prisms/relief dmn & fans, serrated, 10".............250.00
Bowl, pinwheels/fans, serrated/scalloped, 9".......................125.00

Bowl, shields centered by feathered wreaths, 10", $650.00.

Bowl, strw/dmn/fan, 5x10"...150.00
Box, cigarette; buzz stars, oblong ash tray top, 3x4".............45.00
Box, Florence Star w/notched prism lid, SP collar.................440.00
Box, glove; floral cuttings on lid, 11" L, EX.....................400.00
Butter dish, hobstars, X-hatching, center hdl, 3¾x5".............165.00
Carafe, hobstars/X-cut dmn, notched fluted neck, 7"...............90.00
Celery, floral & Harvard w/dbl X vesicas, 11x5"...................110.00
Cheese dish, hobstar chain/arcadia X-hatches/prisms, 8"dia........450.00
Cheese dish, lg swirls, faceted knob, 10½" dia, NM...............550.00
Compote, hobstars/feathers, wide teardrop stem, 8x6".............175.00
Creamer & sugar bowl, Hobstar & Zipper...........................115.00
Creamer & sugar bowl, hobstars, cut ft...........................125.00
Creamer & sugar bowl, intaglio florals, sgn Illig Corning........150.00
Creamer & sugar bowl (open), Mary, spherical, 3x6"; 4x3".........450.00
Decanter, Berry & Leaf, amber/clear, faceted base/stopper, 10"...90.00
Decanter, dmn cuts w/clear panels, honeycomb neck, 12"...........150.00
Ferner, pinwheels/fans/Harvard variant vesicas, 3-ftd, 7½".......70.00
Finger bowl, bull's eyes, hobstars, sgn Egginton, 5" dia.........45.00
Horseradish jar, hobstars & fans, orig stopper...................125.00
Ice bucket, hobstars/curved mitres/checkering, hdls, 4x7"........325.00
Jar, hobstar/oval, flared rose-emb silver lid, 9x7"..............750.00
Knife rest, Cane & Nailhead Dmn, 6"...............................85.00
Knife rest, fans w/X-hatched dmns, tapered ends, 4" L............20.00
Knife rest, Zipper, dmns & fans, bumbbell shape, 4" L............20.00
Mayonnaise, hobstars/hobnail/X-hatches, 6¾", +underplate.........350.00
Napkin ring, intaglio flowers, heavy blank.......................65.00
Nut dish, hobstars/buttons form a star, Greek key border,........15.00
Pitcher, Fortuna w/fans, 10½", +6 4" tumblers....................650.00
Pitcher, paneled hobstars & dmn fans, 10½".......................250.00
Pitcher, Pineapple & Fan, heavy, 8½".............................350.00
Pitcher, tankard, hobstars, honeycomb hdl, sterling trim, 10"....145.00
Punch bowl, Comet, 2-pc, 12x12".................................2,400.00

Punch bowl, Horseshoe, 2-pc, 12x9" 650.00
Rose bowl, geometrics allover, 9" 500.00
Rose bowl, hobstars, 3" dia 85.00
Sugar bowl, intaglio strawberries/florals, hdls, silver lid 150.00
Sugar bowl, Russian, flared tab hdls, sgn NN, 7½" dia 500.00
Tray, dbl vesicas, hobstars, strw fans, 15x11"..............................795.00
Tray, hobstar chain/pinwheels/cane, dished octagon, 12" 425.00
Tray, hobstars/cane bars/vesicas, fan-cut hdl, 13½" 650.00
Tray, Royal by Hunt, serrated leaf shape w/hdl, 9"......................300.00
Vase, bars/circles in panels above & below hobstars, 15" 300.00
Vase, bull's eyes connected w/X-hatches, waisted, 13" 225.00
Vase, buzz stars, 3 frosted rose & leaf panels, 9½x7¼" 90.00
Vase, dmn point panels w/frosted vintage, rayed base, 8½"...........75.00
Vase, dmn point panels w/vertical ribs, frosted florals, 8½"...........80.00
Vase, dmn points w/floral & leaf bands, 9x5½" 85.00
Vase, hobstar band/bull's eye & prismatic-cut body, 11"..............145.00
Vase, hobstars/X-hatches, serrated, flaring base, 16" 450.00
Vase, leaves/birds/flowers, trumpet form, 13" 150.00
Vase, paneled hobstars & floral canes, 15x7¼" 650.00
Vase, prisms & sqs w/starred buttons, trumpet, Hoare, 12x5" 275.00
Vase, X-cut/dmn & fan, trumpet form, 12"..................................125.00
Vase, 11 columns of stars & bull's eyes, serpentine, 12x6"...........370.00
Whiskey, hobstars & English Dmn, 3⅝" 85.00
Whiskey jug, hobstars/fine checkering, hdl w/button, 9" 650.00

Cut Overlay Glass

Glassware with one or more overlying colors through which a design has been cut is called 'Cut Overlay.' It was made both here and abroad.

Compote, cobalt to clear, wild geese/turkey/etc, 11x9" 325.00
Cup & saucer, cobalt to clear, paneled, sm 65.00
Jar, dk blood red to clear, w/lid, 9" 100.00
Pitcher, red to clear, Harvard, sgn JK Berger, 6½" 750.00
Pitcher, red to clear, X-hatch/fan, bulbous, 7", NM................. 1,300.00

Vase, white cut to cranberry with floral band and gilt scrolls, 15", $300.00.

Vase, amber, wheel eng vine & flower cuts, faceted rim, 7½"........50.00
Vase, amethyst to clear, dmn points & fans, raised base, 7½" 150.00
Wine, set of 12, ea a different color, 7½" 225.00

Cut Velvet

Cut Velvet glassware was made during the late 1800s. It is characterized by the effect achieved through the execution of relief-molded patterns, often ribbing or diamond quilting, which allows its white inner casing to show through the outer pastel layer.

Vase, Diamond Quilted, blue, 6", $165.00.

Bowl, pk, appl crystal trim & ft, 4¼x6" 255.00
Celery vase, Dmn Quilt, deep bl, pleated top, Mt WA, 6½".........725.00
Pitcher, Dmn Quilt, bl, squatty, reeded hdl, sq rim, 5½"..............300.00
Pitcher, Dmn Quilt, bl, Webb, 7½" 325.00
Rose bowl, Dmn Quilt, bl, 4-crimp top, 3⅝x3⅜" 165.00
Rose bowl, Dmn Quilt, bl, 6-crimp, 3¾x3½" 175.00
Rose bowl, Dmn Quilt, pk, 4-crimp, 3⅜x3½"................................195.00
Rose bowl, Dmn Quilt, pk, 4-crimp, 4x2⅞" 175.00
Vase, Dmn Quilt, dk orange, rare color, ruffled, 6" 450.00
Vase, Dmn Quilt, pk to wht, bulbous w/ruffled rim, ftd, 7" 250.00

Cybis

Boleslaw Cybis was a graduate of the Academy of Fine Arts in Warsaw, Poland, and was well recognized as a fine artist by the time he was commissioned by his government to paint murals in the Polish Pavillion's Hall of Honor at the 1939 World's Fair. Finding themselves stranded in America at the outbreak of WWII, the Cybises founded an artists' studio, first in Astoria, New York, and later in Trenton, New Jersey, where they made fine figurines and plaques with exacting artistry and craftsmanship entailing extensive handwork. The studio still operates today producing exquisite porcelains on a limited edition basis.

Ballerina on Cue, wht 500.00
Beatrice..875.00
Bobwhite Chick 1,000.00
Bull.. 2,750.00
Calla Lily 800.00
Cat w/Bl Ribbon 1,000.00
Colonial Flower Basket... 3,250.00
Conductor's Hands 500.00
Dahlia...775.00
Deer Mouse 125.00
Duckling 150.00

Elephant	4,000.00
Elizabeth Ann	200.00
Exodus	1,350.00
Field Mouse on Clover	125.00
Folk Singer	500.00
Girl w/Bird, kneeling, 4½"	150.00
Great Wht Heron	1,500.00
Guinevere	775.00
Hamlet	1,200.00
Horse, prancing, wht, 11x14"	400.00
Horse, satin, decor	1,100.00
Jane Eyre, Portraits in Porcelain, 12"	1,250.00
Juliet	2,000.00
Karina, ballerina, 6¾"	475.00
Little Bl Heron	1,000.00
Little Princess	400.00
Madonna Queen of Angels	475.00
Mushroom Jack-O'-Lantern	275.00
Narcissus	500.00
Nefertiti	1,500.00
Noah	1,500.00
Pansies w/Butterfly	400.00
Queen Titania	1,500.00
Rapunzel, pk	400.00
Scarlett	1,300.00
Squirrel, bushy tail, holds acorn	295.00
Thoroughbred	1,000.00
Wild Duck, old	250.00
Windflower	175.00

Czechoslovakian Collectibles

Czechoslovakia came into being as a country in 1918. Located in the heart of Europe, it was a land with the natural resources necessary to support a glass industry that dates back to the mid-fourteenth century. This ware has recently captured the attention of today's collectors, and for good reason. There are beautiful vases — cased, ruffled, applied with rigaree or silver overlay — fine enough to rival those of the best glasshouses. Czechoslovakian art glass baskets are quite as attractive as Victorian America's, and the elegant cut glass perfumes made in colors as well as crystal are unrivaled. There are also pressed glass perfumes, molded in lovely Deco shapes, of various types of art glass. Some are overlaid with gold filigree set with 'jewels.' Jewelry, lamps, porcelains and fine art pottery are also included in the field.

More than thirty-five marks have been recorded, including those in the mold, ink stamped, acid etched, or on a small metal nameplate. The newer marks are incised, stamped 'Royal Dux made in Czechoslovakia' (see Royal Dux), or printed on a paper label which reads 'Bohemian Glass made in Czechoslovakia.' (Communist controlled since 1948, Czechoslovakia is once again a free country.) For a more thorough study of the subject, we recommend you refer to the book *Made in Czechoslovakia*, by Ruth A. Forsythe; she is listed in the Directory under Ohio. Another fine book is *Czechoslavakian Glass & Collectibles* by Dale & Diane Barta. In the listings that follow when one dimension is given, it refers to height; decoration is enamel unless noted otherwise.

Candy Baskets

Bl mottle, yel ruffled top, blk hdl, 8"	110.00
Blk w/silver mica, bl int, blk hdl, 8"	95.00
Gr varicolored stripes, lt gr hdl, flared rim, 8"	85.00
Gr w/dk gr streaks, red opaque o/l, gr hdl, 8½"	110.00
Mc mottle, crystal flat-top hdl, slender/incurvate, 8½"	85.00
Mc mottle, flat-top crystal thorn hdl, 6½"	110.00
Red & yel mottle, twisted crystal thorn hdl, 7"	125.00
Red w/dk streaks, clear twisted thorn hdl, 5½"	145.00
Varicolored, wide ruffled rim, squat, str Hobnail sides, 5½"	145.00

Cased Art Glass

Bowl, cameo-cut vine, dk gr on lt orange, ftd, 5½"	400.00
Bowl, red, wide flared rim, 12"	55.00
Candlestick, dk autumn mottle, 8½"	40.00
Candlestick, orange w/mc mottle at base, 10¼"	40.00
Decanter, orange, silver-deposit bird, 12"	95.00
Pitcher, exotic bird on orange, blk hdl, 11½"	125.00
Rose bowl, mc spatter, leaf decor, SP flower lid, 5x5½"	125.00
Vase, bl, pk int, ruffled top, ftd, 8½"	85.00
Vase, bl, 3 blk buttress ft, 9"	95.00
Vase, blk, silver-deposit bands & clover, squat, ftd, 7¼"	75.00
Vase, bud; mc mottle, slim w/wide base, 8¼"	45.00
Vase, bud; orange, silver-deposit florals, 6¼"	30.00
Vase, gr bullet form w/3 bl buttress ft, 8¾"	60.00
Vase, HP medallions, blk on orange, blk-lined rim/ft, 8½"	60.00
Vase, jack-in-the-pulpit; yel w/mottled base, 7½"	55.00
Vase, lt gr, 3 bl angle hdls, bl rim, 8¼"	350.00
Vase, mottled, hexagonal, ftd, short neck, 4"	60.00
Vase, mottled, metal flower arranger, 5½"	50.00
Vase, paperweight-like canes, red int, squat, 5½"	125.00
Vase, pk, canes, red o/l veins, hdls, 7"	350.00
Vase, red w/gr aventurine at base, squash form, 7¼"	125.00
Vase, shiny blk over orange, tricorn top, mk, 9"	75.00
Vase, varicolored, bulbous, flared rim, 11½"	180.00
Vase, wht, appl bl leaf at waist, 8"	65.00
Vase, wht, rose int, ruffled top, spherical, 5½"	70.00
Vase, yel, appl blk serpentine decor, shouldered form, 7¼"	85.00
Vase, yel mottle w/blk trim, ftd trumpet form, 6¾"	50.00
Vase, yel satin, mc pastoral scene, flared cylinder, 9½"	180.00
Wine, red w/blk stem, silver trim, 7½"	35.00

Cut Glass Perfume Bottles

Amber, sm neck, wide base, clear figural stopper, 5½"	225.00
Amber, tall slim form, crystal faceted stopper, 6⅛"	145.00
Amethyst, shouldered form, frosted floral stopper, 4¾"	145.00
Amethyst, sides slope to wide base, nude stopper, 6⅝"	350.00
Blk opaque, stepped Deco form, crystal stopper, 4⅝"	110.00
Crystal, dmn cuttings, red fan stopper, 3½"	60.00
Crystal, overall cuttings, figure stopper, 6¼"	250.00
Crystal, stepped sides, bl shield-form stopper, 6½"	60.00
Crystal, wide base, yel prism stopper, 4"	65.00
Crystal & frosted, dome base, frosted peacock in stopper, 8"	225.00
Crystal & frosted, waffled cuts, butterfly stopper, 5½"	110.00
Gr, flared base, gr prism stopper, 5¼"	155.00
Gr, narrow neck, wide base, gr fan stopper, 4⅞"	78.00
Gr, wide shoulders, frosted florals in stopper, 6½"	125.00
Pk, shouldered form, ftd, crystal floral stopper, 5¾"	90.00
Pk, sq cuttings, clear prism stopper, 7¼"	90.00
Red, shouldered form, crystal cut stopper, 5⅞"	400.00

Lamps

Art Deco dancer beside crystal bubble sphere on ped, 9"	450.00
Art Deco geometrics, spherical, matching Deco cone shade, 9"	500.00
Basket, bl beaded, red-beaded fruit, gold trim, 8"	450.00
Beaded crystal, basket filled w/bl flowers, 8½"	450.00
Desk, acid-cut shade, 10"	160.00

Goebel girl in glass flower dress, 10¼" 585.00
Milk glass, pk & gold pnt, kerosene, 12¾" 110.00
Mottled satin base & shade, 12½" 180.00
Perfume, HP florals, yel on clear frosted, 4" 235.00
Student, acid-cut shade, pnt metal quatrefoil base, 12" ...350.00
Wall sconce, 2-arm, prisms, 14½" 145.00

Mold Blown and Pressed Bottles

Amethyst, gold decor, tall slim ft, atomizer, 7" 110.00
Amethyst & crystal, HP daisies, 7" 95.00
Bl, nude & butterfly, bl stopper, scarce, 5¼" 385.00
Crystal, gold decor w/red jewels, 4¾" 185.00
Crystal, squat, floral ornaments on stopper, 1¾" 35.00
Gr, appl blk serpentine decor, atomizer, 8" 90.00
Mottle cased, slim neck, puff-box base, blk stopper, 6⅜" ...135.00
Orange cased, blk ft & stopper, 6½" 55.00
Topaz tinted, pillow form, jet stopper, 5" 25.00

Opaque, Crystal, Colored Transparent Glass

Bowl, pk lustre, bl lustre King Tut decor, 3½" 350.00
Candlestick, pk, appl leaf & vine decor, 8" 45.00
Decanter, amber, floral cuttings, cylindrical, 8" 55.00
Figurine, beer waiter, mc on gr mottled base, 7¾" 295.00
Figurine, entomologist w/bug, mc on mc base, Deco style, 8" ...325.00
Figurine, Henry VIII, red & gr coat, foil label, 9¼" 325.00
Figurine, obstetrician w/baby, mc on bl base, Deco style, 8" ...295.00
Figurine, Spanish soldier w/sword, bl jacket w/gold, 8½" ...325.00
Figurine, teacher, gr coat, gray pants, 7⅛x3" 295.00
Pitcher, amber, yel o/l, 11½" 125.00
Pitcher, bl bubbly glass, tall matching stopper, 8⅝" 85.00
Pitcher, orange & gr, stacked cone form, clear hdl, 12½" ...85.00
Vase, blk w/orange spiraling stripes, cylindrical, 6½" 65.00
Vase, cobalt cut to clear, floral etch, 10¼" 150.00
Vase, frosted, emb wild horses, spherical, 7" 45.00
Vase, golden topaz, orange pull-ups, fan form, 8" 95.00
Vase, orange/wht mottle, cylindrical, 5⅞" 27.50
Vase, pk lustre w/threading at top, ftd cylinder, 9⅜" 300.00
Wine, gr bubbly glass, HP riding scene, 4¼" 40.00

Pottery, Porcelain, Semi-Porcelain

Bowl, mc Deco floral band on blk, wht int, str sides, 3x7" ...55.00
Clock, faux marble w/flower basket, German works, 7" ...110.00
Coffeepot, Art Deco peasant w/HP flowers, 7" 85.00
Creamer, cow figural, tail forms hdl, 6¼" 48.00
Cup & saucer, rooster, brn on tan w/gr, child's sz 32.50
Figurine, elephant, blk w/yel saddle blanket, 4½" 45.00
Figurine, hound dog, brn & wht, 5" 35.00
Jar, Egyptian decor, gold trim, hdls, 8½" 350.00
Potato server, potato form w/butter pat finial, 5" 16.00
Teapot, girl finial, skirt forms body of pot, 8" 85.00
Teapot, pk lustre, bulbous, 6⅛" 30.00
Wall pocket, bl w/mc peacock, 7¼" 45.00

D'Argental

D'Argental cameo glass was produced in France from the 1870s until about 1920 in the Art Nouveau style. Browns and tans were favored colors used to complement florals and scenic designs developed through acid cuttings. Our advisor for this category is Don Williams; he is listed in the Directory under Missouri.

Vase, apple branches, double overlay, 12", $2,800.00; Vase, scene with cottage, double overlay, 8", $1,400.00.

Cameo

Atomizer, river scene, gr/dk gr on apricot & gray, 9" 1,750.00
Box, berry branches, wine/brn on lime, dome lid, 5½" dia 1,200.00
Perfume burner, florals/birds, orange/brn on amber, 6½" 1,200.00
Vase, allover grapevines, burgundy on amber, 17" 2,200.00
Vase, apple branches, red & wine on amber, dbl o/l, 12x7" 2,800.00
Vase, berries/leaves, dk bl on bl frost, bottle form, 6½" 750.00
Vase, lines/dots/floral band, wine on gr, bottle form, 12" 550.00
Vase, river/mtns, gr/wine on gray opal, swollen cylinder, 6" 1,000.00
Vase, roses, red/gr on lt gr to red, slim bottle form, 10" 1,500.00
Vase, scenic w/trees in foreground, red/wine on mottle, 10" ... 2,100.00
Vase, Spesbourg/Sites d'Alsace (castle), baluster, 12" 2,000.00
Vase, trees/castle/river, shades of red on yel, 14" 2,200.00
Vase, trees/fence, dk brn/gr on rust, elongated/bun ft, 13" 1,600.00
Vase, tulips/leaves, purple on bl, expanded cylinder, 9½" 1,200.00
Vase, woodland scene/cottage, dbl o/l, 8" 1,400.00

Daum Nancy

Daum was an important producer of French cameo glass, operating from the late 1800s until after the turn of the century. They used various techniques — acid cutting, wheel engraving, and handwork — to create beautiful scenic designs and nature subjects in the Art Nouveau manner. Virtually all examples are signed. Our advisor for this category is Don Williams; he is listed in the Directory under Missouri.

Cameo

Bowl, mulberries/leaves, orange/bl mottle on yel, lobed, 6" 1,000.00
Box, river scene, dbl o/l, sq w/rnd domed lid, 6" dia 2,600.00
Dish, cvd/pnt/gilt banner 'I'an Nevf Av Gfi,' 2x6" 1,100.00
Lamp, trumpet flowers, red/wine on amber base & 7½" shade. 9,000.00
Lamp base, apple blossoms, cvd/HP, 9", on gilt metal ft 1,500.00
Lamp base, lilies/slim leaves, orange/wine on amber, 11" 1,800.00
Salt cellar, floral, cut/HP on yel/rust mottle, 1x2", pr 1,600.00
Vase, berries/branches, 3 foil-bkd appl cabochons, 6½" 6,600.00
Vase, berry clusters, orange/bl mottle on yel, slim, 10" 1,600.00
Vase, ducks in groups of 3, egg form in metal ped ft, 5" 2,500.00
Vase, floral, 7-color on frost, lg appl ornaments, ftd, 8" 9,500.00
Vase, floral (long-stemmed), gr/gilt on amber, 16" 1,500.00
Vase, floral/leaves, burgundy on yel & cream mottle, 8" 2,000.00

Vase, foxglove, red/wine/blk on yel to red/wine, 13½" **2,900.00**
Vase, iris/dragonfly, gilt on amethyst, waisted, 14" **2,000.00**
Vase, mistletoe, cut/HP/gilt on acid-etched lt gr, 5" **425.00**
Vase, poppies, cvd/HP on yel/orange mottle, 3"....................... **1,100.00**
Vase, river scene, pk/burgundy dbl o/l on orange, ftd, 8" **2,500.00**
Vase, snow scene, cvd/pnt on lt amberina, 8½x3½", pr **2,300.00**
Vase, spikey flowers, cut/HP, cylindrical w/bun ft, 11" **2,500.00**
Vase, thistles, wine on striated orange, metal ft, slim, 5" **275.00**
Vase, tree/lake, blk on turq/yel mottle, flattened/rnd, 5" **1,300.00**
Vase, trees, gr/blk on yel/red/bl mottle, bulbous, 8x7" **3,000.00**
Vase, vines/lg leaves/tendrils, gr on wht/plum, hdls, 5" **1,300.00**
Vase, winter scene on orange mottle, rectangular, 3¾" **1,500.00**

Miscellaneous

Bowl, amber, etched tiers of triangles w/in panels, 12"..................**850.00**
Bowl, bl/gr matt swirl, 3-peak rim, ped ft, 8" H **600.00**
Bowl, lt gr, conical w/4 heavily-draped lobes, 8½" **550.00**
Box, gr/blk mottle w/gold foil, bowl base, 4x4½"............................**500.00**
Decanter, clear w/gray streaks & mottling, red stopper, 11".........**300.00**
Dish, bottle gr w/bubbles, crimped rim, 10" **400.00**
Vase, etched abstracts on clear, blk ft, flared rim, 19".............. **2,860.00**
Vase, etched band w/geometrics on ycl, cylindrical, 11"......... **2,500.00**
Vase, etched bands on honey-yel, spherical w/flared rim, 10" . **2,000.00**
Vase, etched lappets & polka dots on lt bl, ovoid, 4" **500.00**
Vase, etched stylized leaves on yel, ovoid, 13" **2,100.00**
Vase, gold spangled w/cvd leaves & berries, ftd, 8x6" **1,800.00**
Vase, gr w/air bubbles in thick walls, sqd form, 9½"....................**650.00**
Vase, gr w/foil flecks blown into ribbed iron frwork, 10" **2,600.00**
Vase, gray, vertical ribs, flared top, 8x8" **800.00**
Vase, lt bl to cobalt w/gold flecks, mold-blown, 9", EX **2,500.00**
Vase, red/yel spatter w/pulled gold mica motif, 18"................. **1,000.00**
Vase, scenic, brn on rust to yel, HP, 3" **1,500.00**
Vase, thick walls w/int bl streaks/mottle, flared, 12" **550.00**
Vase, yel/turq mottle w/dk amethyst ped ft, spherical, 5" **950.00**

Davenport

W. Davenport and Company were Staffordshire potters operating in that area from 1793 to 1887, producing earthenware, creamware, porcelain, and ironstone. Many different stamps, all with 'Davenport,' were used to mark the various types of ware. See also Mulberry; Flow Blue.

Pitcher, tavern scene in relief, 4½" **165.00**
Plate, fence, underglaze bl transfer w/mc enamel, 9½" **85.00**
Plate, Many a little makes..., Franklin's, dk bl on wht, 9" **195.00**
Soup plate, gr feather edge/4-color floral, 8", EX.......................**160.00**
Tureen, sauce; Flute Player, bl transfer, anchor mk, EX...............**135.00**

Davis, Lowell

Figurines, plates, bells, and ornaments painted by Lowell Davis and produced by Border Fine Arts, Schmid Sculptured Porcelain, capture the heritage of rural America.

Lowell Davis, known better as Mr. Lowell to his farm animals, is described by many as 'just a country farmer from Missouri' fulfilling his dreams of preserving rural America as he knew it in the 1930s. Mr. Lowell rebuilt Red Oak II, a 1930 village, from actual buildings he spent hours in as a child. You can visit this unique town refurbished with antiques and 'supplies' in Grandpa's General Store in Carthage, Missouri.

A Secondary Market Price Guide is published by Rosie Wells Enterprises for his collectibles. She is listed in the Directory under Clubs, Newsletters, and Catalogs. Items below are assumed to be in mint condition with box.

Blossom & Calf, #225-326, retired, ltd ed 1000, 5" **775.00**
Brer Rabbit, #225-252, retired, 4¼".. **1,600.00**
Bustin' w/Pride, lithograph, #223-007, sgn/#d, 16½x13½" **170.00**
Country Road, #225-030, retired, 5"..**675.00**
Double Trouble, #225-211, retired, 2½" **425.00**
Dry As a Bone, #225-216, retired, 3¼" **250.00**
Gossips, #225-248, retired, 3½"...**250.00**
Home from Market (w/base), #223-601, ltd ed 1200, retired .. **1,100.00**
Ignorance Is Bliss, #225-031, retired, 6" **1,100.00**
Moon Raider, #225-325, retired, ltd ed 900................................**400.00**
Peter & Wren (w/base), #223-556, ltd ed 2500, 6" **325.00**
Self Portrait, lithograph, #223-015, sgn/#d, 8½x11" **160.00**
Studio Mouse, #225-215, retired, 2½"...**295.00**
Up To No Good, #225-218, retired, ltd ed 900, 6¼"......................**85.00**
Woman's Work, #225-232, retired..**95.00**

De Vez

De Vez was a type of acid-cut French cameo glass produced by Cristallerie de Pantin in Paris around the turn of the century. Our advisor for this category is Don Williams; he is listed in the Directory under Missouri.

Cameo

Atomizer, seascape/boats, bl on lt pk, gilt-metal mts, 10"........ **1,500.00**
Compote, water/mtns/bldgs, rust/brn on yel, clear int, 4" **1,100.00**
Lamp, boudoir; island scene, gr/coral/yel, 3 cuts, 6¾" **1,800.00**
Rose bowl, trees/water, blk on gold & pk satin, 3" H.............. **1,200.00**
Vase, boats/river/mtns, pk/gr on opaline, dbl o/l, 10x3".......... **1,400.00**
Vase, lg tree/mtns/lake, gr on gray w/bl, baluster, 8" **1,500.00**
Vase, river fr w/branches, pk/bl on yel, baluster, 8" **1,300.00**
Vase, river scene fr by lg trees, rust/dk bl on yel, 6" **1,100.00**
Vase, stylized leaves/blossoms, dbl o/l, ruffled rim, 10" **550.00**
Vase, swans on mtn lake fr by trees, yel on gray, slim, 12"....... **2,000.00**
Vase, wisteria vines/leaves, lav on wht, flared rim, 6" **950.00**

De Vilbiss

Perfume bottles, atomizers, and dresser accessories marketed by the De Vilbiss Company are appreciated by collectors today for the various types of lovely glassware used in their manufacture, as well as for their pleasing shapes. Various companies provided the glass, while De Vilbiss made only the metal tops. They marketed their merchandise not only here but in Paris, England, Canada, and Havana as well. Their marks were acid stamped, ink stamped, in gold script, molded in, or on paper labels. One is no more significant than another. For more information we recommend *Bedroom and Bathroom Glassware of the Depression Years* by Margaret and Kenn Whitmyer; their address is listed in the Directory under Ohio. Our advisor for this category is Randy Monson; he is listed in the Directory under Virginia.

Atomizer, crystal w/gold-draped lady stem, 7¼" **245.00**
Atomizer, dk bl enamel w/blk decor, orig bulb & cord, 5¼" **60.00**
Atomizer, ebony, long cord, tasseled bulb, 6¼" **90.00**
Atomizer, French opal, Coin Dot, ball form, by Fenton **38.00**
Atomizer, gold crackle, beaded flower on top, mk, 4¾".................**65.00**

Atomizer, gr enamel, orig cord & bulb, 6" 70.00
Atomizer, gr enamel w/much gold, orig cord & bulb, 7¾" 120.00
Atomizer, gr hobnail, by Fenton..42.00
Atomizer, lt gr, Opalescent Windows, 5"...............................85.00
Atomizer, orange stained, on crystal base, 6" 75.00
Atomizer, orange w/gr irid lily pads & vines, no bulb, 8" 175.00

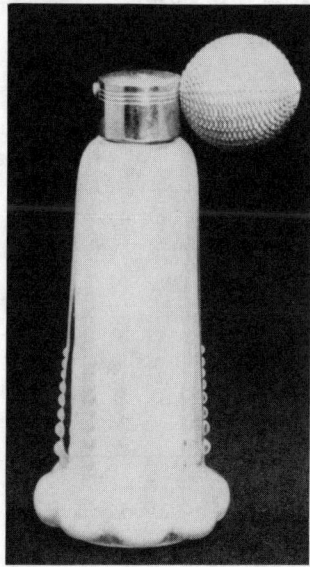

Atomizer, rose overlay, Fenton, ca 1945, 6", $125.00.

Bottle, scent; irid, blk enamel top, stemmed ft, mk 80.00
Bottle, scent; smoke gray, hand blown, sm 285.00
Lamp, perfume; nude figure on glass insert, 12"...........................285.00
Lamp, perfume; nude figure on glass insert, 7"............................235.00
Pin tray, blk matt w/gold trim..30.00
Pin tray, orange enamel w/blk & gold decor, 3¼x5⅝"........................25.00

Decanters

Ceramic whiskey decanters were brought into prominence in 1955 by the James Beam Distilling Company. Few other companies besides Beam produced these decanters during the next ten years or so; however, other companies did eventually follow suit. At its peak in 1975, at least twenty prominent companies and several on a lesser scale made these decanters.

We have tried to list those brands that are the most popular with collectors. Likewise, individual decanters listed are the ones (or representative of the ones) most commonly found. The introduction of 'wheel decanters' (specifically cars and trains with moving wheels) in the mid-1970s has caused a resurgence in the collecting of decanters. The following listing is but a small fraction of the several thousand different decanters that have been produced.

These decanters come from all over the world. While Jim Beam owns its own china factory in the U.S., some of the others import from Mexico, Taiwan, Japan and elsewhere. They vary in size from miniatures (approximately 2-oz.) to gallons. Values range from a few dollars to more than $3,000 per decanter.

A mint condition decanter is one with no chips or cracks and all labels intact. Whether a decanter is full or not has no bearing on the value, nor does a missing federal tax stamp. It is advisable to empty the contents of a ceramic decanter, otherwise the thin inner glaze could crack, allowing the contents to seep through the porous body, thus ruining the decanter. An (m) behind a listing indicates a miniature. All others are fifth or 750 ml unless noted otherwise. Our advisor for this category is Roy Willis; he is listed in the Directory under Kentucky.

Beam Model-T Ford, $50.00.

Aesthetic Specialties (ASI)

Kentucky Derby 25.00
Model-T Ice Cream Truck.....................................65.00
Model-T Telephone Truck.....................................65.00
Stanley Steamer, 1909, gr or blk...........................45.00

Beam

Centennial Series, Alaska Purchase 6.00
Centennial Series, Cheyenne 5.00
Centennial Series, Chicago Fire............................15.00
Centennial Series, Santa Fe...............................160.00
Centennial Series, St Louis Arch...........................20.00
Centennial Series, Yellowstone 5.00
Executive Series, 1961 Golden Chalice 50.00
Executive Series, 1962 Flower Basket.......................35.00
Executive Series, 1963 Royal Rose 40.00
Executive Series, 1964 Royal Gold Diamond 40.00
Executive Series, 1965 Marbled Fantasy 50.00
Organization Series, Amvets 5.00
Organization Series, Blue Goose 5.00
Organization Series, Cedars of Lebanon......................5.00
Organization Series, Ducks Unlimited #1, 1974 ....45.00
Organization Series, Ducks Unlimited #2, 1975 ....50.00
Organization Series, Ducks Unlimited #3, 1977 ....40.00
Organization Series, Elks, 1968 ....6.00
Organization Series, Kentucky Colonel 10.00
Organization Series, Marine Devil Dog......................35.00
Organization Series, Shrine, Indiana........................5.00
Organization Series, Shrine, Moila w/sword, 1972 ....25.00
Organization Series, Telephone #1, wall, 1975 ....45.00
Organization Series, Telephone #2, candlestick, 1978.......45.00
Organization Series, Telephone #3, cradle, 1979............18.00
Organization Series, Turtle (Are you a Turtle?) 18.00
Wheel Series, Ambulance....................................55.00
Wheel Series, Cable Car, 1968 ....5.00
Wheel Series, Cable Car, 1983..............................55.00
Wheel Series, Chevy Bell Air Convertible, 1957, blk........90.00
Wheel Series, Chevy Camaro, 1969, yel 65.00
Wheel Series, Chevy Corvette, 1954, bl.....................90.00
Wheel Series, Chevy Corvette, 1955, copper 85.00
Wheel Series, Chevy Corvette, 1963, blk....................90.00
Wheel Series, Chevy Corvette, 1978, Indy Pacecar..........165.00

Wheel Series, Chevy Corvette, 1984, red or wht 55.00
Wheel Series, Duesenberg, 1934, lt or dk bl 125.00
Wheel Series, Fire Chief's Car, 1928 ....110.00
Wheel Series, Fire Chief's Car, 1934..65.00
Wheel Series, Fire Engine, Ford, 1930 ....135.00
Wheel Series, Fire Engine, Mack, 1917 ....135.00
Wheel Series, Fire Engine, Mississippi Valley Pumper 125.00
Wheel Series, Ford, Mustang, blk 125.00
Wheel Series, Ford, Mustang, 1964, wht or red 50.00
Wheel Series, Ford, 1903 Model-A, red or blk 45.00
Wheel Series, Ford, 1913 Model-T, blk or gr 50.00
Wheel Series, Ford, 1928 Model-A 75.00
Wheel Series, Ford, 1929 Phaeton 60.00
Wheel Series, Jewel Tea Wagon 80.00
Wheel Series, Oldsmobile, 1904 ....40.00
Wheel Series, Racecar, Unser Olsonite Eagle...............................70.00
Wheel Series, Stutz Bearcat, gray or yel 60.00
Wheel Series, Thomas Flyer, bl or cream......................................75.00
Wheel Series, Trains, Casey Jones Boxcar 50.00
Wheel Series, Trains, Casey Jones Caboose 50.00
Wheel Series, Trains, Casey Jones Engine w/Tender 60.00
Wheel Series, Trains, Casey Jones Tank Car................................50.00
Wheel Series, Trains, Locomotive, General 85.00
Wheel Series, Trains, Locomotive, Grant.....................................70.00
Wheel Series, Trains, Locomotive, JB Turner 125.00

Brooks

Animal Series, Bear 6.00
Animal Series, Dog, Setter w/Bird 10.00
Animal Series, Horse, Man O' War 15.00
Animal Series, Lion on Rock 8.00
Animal Series, Penguin 10.00
Automotive & Transportation Series, Auburn Boat Tail, 1932.....20.00
Automotive & Transportation Series, Corvette, 1978 Pacecar......40.00
Automotive & Transportation Series, Duesenberg......................20.00
Automotive & Transportation Series, Racer, Indy #21 ....25.00
Automotive & Transportation Series, Racer, Ontario #10 ....25.00
Automotive & Transportation Series, Tank, Army 18.00
Automotive & Transportation Series, Thunderbird, '56, bl or yel ..75.00
Automotive & Transportation Series, Train, Ironhorse 6.00
Bird Series, Canadian Honker...12.00
Bird Series, Quail 6.00
Hambletonian 12.00
Institutional Series, Am Legion Convention, 1973, Hawaii 10.00
Institutional Series, Am Legion Convention, 1974, Miami 10.00
Institutional Series, Am Legion Convention, 1977, Denver..........15.00
Institutional Series, FOE Eagle, 1978 ....18.00
Institutional Series, FOE Eagle, 1979 ....20.00
Institutional Series, FOE Eagle, 1980 ....35.00
Institutional Series, Kachina #1, Morning Singer, 1971 ....110.00
Institutional Series, Kachina #2, Hummingbird, 1973 ....70.00
Institutional Series, Kachina #3, Antelope, 1974.........................65.00
Institutional Series, Shrine, Clown 15.00
Institutional Series, Shrine, Fez 12.00
Institutional Series, Shrine, Sphynx 10.00
People Series, Fireman..20.00
People Series, Keystone Cops 40.00
People Series, Pirate 6.00
Sports Series, Bareknuckle Fighter 15.00
Tennis Player 12.00

Hoffman

Aesop's Fables, 6 different, ea..18.00

Car Series, Racecar, Donahue Sunoco #66....................................110.00
Car Series, Racecar, Rutherford #3 ....75.00
Mr Lucky Series, Mr Blacksmith 45.00
Mr Lucky Series, Mr Doctor 35.00
Mr Lucky Series, Mr Fireman 70.00
Mr Lucky Series, Mr Photographer 35.00
Mr Lucky Series, Mr Policeman 35.00
No Hunting Series, Bears & Cubs 40.00
No Hunting Series, Bobcat & Pheasant 50.00
No Hunting Series, Eagle & Fox 50.00
No Hunting Series, Falcon & Rabbit 45.00
No Hunting Series, Owl & Chipmunk 40.00
No Hunting Series, Wolf & Raccoon 45.00

Lionstone

Bicentennial Series, Betsy Ross 25.00
Bicentennial Series, George Washington 25.00
Bicentennial Series, Paul Revere 25.00
Bicentennial Series, Sons of Freedom 35.00
Old West Series, Dancehall Girl...50.00
Old West Series, Indian Weaver...30.00
Old West Series, Rainmaker...30.00
Old West Series, Shootout at OK Corral, 3-pc set 375.00
Old West Series, Trapper 25.00
Old West Series, Wells Fargo Man..15.00
Sports Series, Baseball Players 70.00
Sports Series, Boxers 60.00
Sports Series, Football Players 60.00
Sports Series, Hockey Players 50.00

McCormick

Bicentennial Series, 8 different, ea..28.00
Entertainer Series, Elvis & Hound Dog 375.00
Entertainer Series, Elvis Aloha 125.00
Entertainer Series, Elvis Bust 35.00
Entertainer Series, Elvis on Rising Sun.......................................375.00
Entertainer Series, Elvis w/Teddy Bear 375.00
Entertainer Series, Louis Armstrong 85.00
Entertainer Series, Tom T Hall 75.00
King Arthur Series, Guenivere 35.00
King Arthur Series, King Arthur..50.00
King Arthur Series, Merlin..35.00
King Arthur Series, Sir Lancelot..35.00

Old Commonwealth

Coal Miner #3, w/lump of coal 50.00
Coal Miner #3, w/lump of coal, mini 25.00
Coal Miner #4, Lunchtime 40.00
Coal Miner #4, Lunchtime, mini 22.00
Coal Miner #5, Coal Shooter 40.00
Coal Miner #5, Coal Shooter, mini 22.00
Irish, Coins of Ireland 28.00
Irish, Dogs of Ireland 25.00
Irish, Horses of Ireland..28.00
Kentucky Thoroughbreds 40.00
Tennessee Walking Horse 40.00
Yankee Doodle 20.00

Ski Country

Bicentennial Series, Birth of Freedom 85.00

Bicentennial Series, Birth of Freedom, mini.................................110.00
Bicentennial Series, Birth of Freedom, 1-gal...........................2,200.00
Bird Series, Blackbird, Redwing 45.00
Bird Series, Blue Jay 65.00
Bird Series, Blue Jay, mini..45.00
Bird Series, Bluebirds wall plaque..75.00
Bird Series, Bluebirds wall plaque, mini 40.00
Bird Series, Chicadees 50.00
Bird Series, Chicadees, mini 25.00
Bird Series, Duck, wood wall plaque 350.00
Bird Series, Duck, wood wall plaque, mini 75.00
Bird Series, Eagle, Harpy 135.00
Bird Series, Eagle, Harpy, mini...90.00
Bird Series, Eagle, Hawk..150.00
Bird Series, Eagle, Hawk, mini 75.00
Bird Series, Oriole...50.00
Bird Series, Oriole, mini...25.00
Bird Series, Osprey Hawk...190.00
Bird Series, Osprey Hawk, mini...150.00
Bird Series, Woodpecker, Ivory Billed 65.00
Bird Series, Woodpecker, Ivory Billed, mini..............................30.00
Circus Series, Barnum, PT 45.00
Circus Series, Barnum, PT; mini..25.00
Circus Series, Elephant...50.00
Circus Series, Elephant, mini...35.00
Circus Series, Ringmaster 30.00
Circus Series, Ringmaster, mini...20.00
Indian Series, End of the Trail...200.00
Indian Series, End of the Trail, mini 100.00
Indian Series, Great Spirit...100.00
Indian Series, Great Spirit, mini 20.00
Indian Series, Southwest Dancers, set of 6.............................350.00
Indian Series, Southwest Dancers, set of 6, mini.....................200.00
Wildlife Series, Badger Family...35.00
Wildlife Series, Badger Family, mini..18.00
Wildlife Series, Coyote Family...50.00
Wildlife Series, Coyote Family, mini 20.00
Wildlife Series, Elk 200.00
Wildlife Series, Elk, mini..70.00
Wildlife Series, Otter..60.00
Wildlife Series, Otter, mini 25.00
Wildlife Series, Raccoon 60.00
Wildlife Series, Raccoon, mini...32.00

Wild Turkey

Baccarat Crystal w/Case 250.00
Charleston Centennial 65.00
Liggett & Meyers, 1971...300.00
Mack Truck..30.00
Series III, No 1, In Flight...100.00
Series III, No 1, In Flight, mini 32.00
Series III, No 2, w/Bobcat..125.00
Series III, No 2, w/Bobcat, mini..35.00
Series III, No 3, Fighting...125.00
Series III, No 3, Fighting, mini..35.00
Wedgewood, crystal w/case 225.00

Decoys

American colonists learned the craft of decoy making from the

Indians who used them to lure birds out of the sky as an important food source. Early models were carved from wood such as pine, cedar, balsa, etc., and a few were made of canvas or papier-mache. There are two basic types of decoys: water floaters and shorebirds (also called 'stick-ups'). Within each type are many different species, ducks being the most plentiful since they migrated along all four of America's great waterways. Market hunting became big business around 1880, resulting in large-scale commercial production of decoys which continued until about 1910 when such hunting was outlawed by the Migratory Bird Treaty.

Today decoys are one of the most collectible types of American folk art. The most valuable are those carved by such artists as Laing, Crowell, Ward, and Wheeler, to name only a few. Each area, such as Massachusetts, Connecticut, Maine, the Illinois River, and the Delaware River, produces decoys with distinctive regional characteristics. Examples of commercial decoys produced by well-known factories — among them Mason, Stevens, and Dodge — are also prized by collectors. Though mass-produced, these nevertheless required a certain amount of hand carving and decorating. Well-carved examples, especially those of rare species, are appreciating rapidly, and those with original paint are more desirable. Writer Carl F. Luckey has compiled a fully illustrated identification and value guide, *Collecting Antique Bird Decoys*; you will find his address in the Directory under Alabama. *The Collector's Guide to Decoys* by Sharon and Bob Huxford contains hundreds of photos (many in color) and gives values realized at auction during the past two years, available from your local bookstore or Collector Books. In the listings that follow, all decoys are solid-bodied unless noted hollow.

Key:
OP — original paint   RP — repaint
ORP — old repaint   WOP — worn original paint
OWP — original working paint   WRP — working repaint

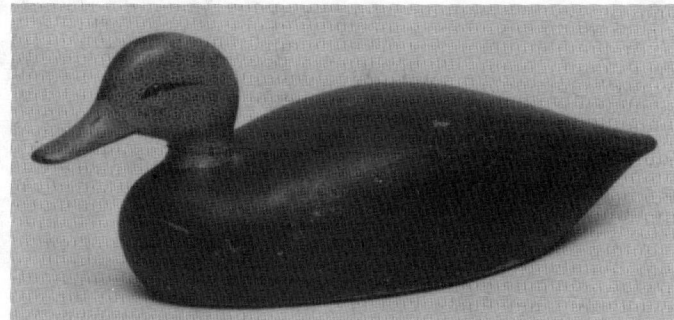

Black Duck, attributed to Keyes Chadwick, Martha's Vineyard, glass eyes, original paint, age cracks, old break in neck, paint wear, ca 1940s, 18" long, $550.00.

American Merganser pr, Frank Dobbins, hollow, sgn, M.............130.00
Blk Duck, Capt Ike Phillips, ca 1880, sm dents, G OP................600.00
Blk Duck, Charles Birch, rpr neck crack, WOP..........................400.00
Blk Duck, John English, ca 1895, hollow, EX OP, NM 7,500.00
Blk Duck, Ken Anger, hollow, NM OP, NM...............................900.00
Blk Duck, Mason's Challenge, slope-breast, rpr chip, OP...........450.00
Blk Duck, Mason's Premier, sm tail chip, NM OP...................1,950.00
Blk Duck, Peterson Co, early, neck crack/rpr, OP, VG...............325.00
Blk Duck, Ralph Welles, hollow, 1930, EX feathering, EX OP....300.00
Blk Duck, Rhodes Truex, hollow, G OP, rpr o/w EX structure....400.00
Blk-Breasted Plover, Crowell, glass eyes, NM OP, flakes.........5,400.00
Blk-Breasted Plover, Dodge Co, rstr crack/rpr bill, NM OP........500.00

Blk-Breasted Plover, Obediah Verity, cvd wings, NM OP	700.00
Bluebill drake, Harry Shourds, hollow, pnt by John Hillman	250.00
Bluebill drake, Ira Hudson, WRP, crack/age lines	700.00
Bluebill drake, Pratt's Second Grade, OP, VG	150.00
Bluebill drake, Stevens Co, age checks/rpr neck, 1880, OWP	285.00
Bluebill drake, Wildfowler Co, balsa body, WOP	125.00
Bluebill hen, Charles Wheeler, cork body, cracks/chips, OP	350.00
Bluebill hen, cork body, lt chips/cracks, OP	450.00
Bluebill hen, Mason's Premier, lt tail/bill chip, OP	475.00
Bluebill pr, Evans' Competition, OP, EX structure	400.00
Bluebill pr, Jim Currier, early, all orig, EX	1,200.00
Bluewinged Teal drake, Madison Mitchell, preening, 1981, M	800.00
Bluewinged Teal hen, Mason's Standard, glass eye, OP, VG	180.00
Bluewinged Teal hen, Victor Co, all orig, EX	90.00
Bluewinged Teal pr, Paul Gibson, NM OP, EX structure	325.00
Brant, Nathan Cobb, cvd tail/eyes, WRP, tail chip/lines, EX	6,500.00
Brant, Wildfowler Co, Harry Shourds model, sm dents, NM OP	375.00
Bufflehead drake, Herters Inc, NM OP, EX structure	140.00
Bufflehead drake, Miles Hancock, OP, lt wear, EX structure	400.00
Canada Goose, Ben Schmidt, hollow, sm tail chip, EX OP	450.00
Canada Goose, Lloyd Parker, pnt by Chris Sprague, sm dents	550.00
Canada Goose, Mason's Premier, EX feathering, EX OP	7,250.00
Canada Goose, Wildfowler Co, balsa body, rpr/split, OP	90.00
Canvasbk drake, Dick Janson, cvd feathers, OP, VG wear	1,200.00
Canvasbk drake, Jim Pierce, sleeping, stamp, NM OP, NM	100.00
Canvasbk drake, Lee & Lem Dudley, WRP, rpr crack o/w EX	6,500.00
Canvasbk drake, Sam Barnes, age splits, EX OP, lt wear	800.00
Canvasbk drake, Ward Bros, sgn/dtd 1948, sm hairlines, OP	950.00
Canvasbk drake, Wildfowler Co, hollow, RP bk o/w EX OP	225.00
Cinnamon Teal, Pratt Co, all orig, EX, rare	275.00
Coot, Evans Co, sm head separation o/w EX, OP	210.00
Coot, Mason's Challenge, mk W Barber, tail chip, NM OP	1,400.00
Curlew, Herters Inc, all orig, M	165.00
Curlew, Mason Co, early, split tail, sm chip, OWP, rare	400.00
Dowitcher, Mason Co, spring plumage, tack eyes, OP, EX	900.00
Elder Drake, Wildfowler Co, hollow, sm crack bk, EX OP	350.00
Golden Plover pr, Mark McNair, relief cvg, sgn, EX	1,600.00
Goldeneye drake, Frank Coombs, neck crack, OP, EX	1,400.00
Goldeneye hen, Davey Nichols, ca 1905, relief cvg, EX OWP	900.00
Goldeneye hen, Hays Co, filler flakes & crack o/w EX, G OP	200.00
Gray Coot, Walter Rupple, head w/some turn, sgn, orig, M	150.00
Great Horned Owl, Swisher & Soules Co, ca 1920, CI w/OP	450.00
Greenwinged Teal drake, Ken Anger, tail crack, NM OP, EX	5,000.00
Greenwinged Teal hen, Mason's Premier, age line, OP, EX	1,600.00
Gull, Dodge Co, lt age lines, ca 1880, OWP, rare	500.00
Hooded Merganser pr, H Conklin, mk, NM OP, EX structure	825.00
Mallard drake, Dodge Co, mk JH, OP, EX structure	325.00
Mallard drake, Mason's Standard, tack eyes, WOP, VG	100.00
Mallard drake, Peterson, bill rpr/rpl filler, ca 1880, OP	245.00
Mallard pr, Reynolds Co, cloth over wire, G	90.00
Merganser drake, Jay Parker, hollow, lt crazing, RP bill	150.00
Pintail drake, Mason's Premier, early, RP head, EX OP, VG	750.00
Pintail drake, Tony Bianco, rpr tail tip, OP, lt wear	200.00
Rail, Gus Wilson, raised wing tips, sm dents, OP, VG	600.00
Red-Breasted Merganser drake, Willie Ross, rstr bill, RP	500.00
Redhead drake, Chadwick, mk HMJ/WLM, EX OP/structure	1,250.00
Redhead pr, Mason's Standard, tack eyes, age line o/w NM	450.00
Snow Goose, Herters Inc, several sm body dents, NM OP	295.00
Snow Goose, Wildfowler Co, Quogue mk, sm dents, NM OP	450.00
Swan, Capt Harry Jobes, lt flakes/age splits, OP	275.00
Swan, Wildfowler Co, hollow, OP w/flaking, EX structure	500.00
Widgeon drake, Stevens Co, 1880, partial RP o/w EX OP	1,600.00
Wood Duck pr, Jim Slack, NM OP, EX structure	215.00
Yellowlegs, George Boyd, sm split/tail chip, EX OP, o/w M	1,800.00

Dedham Pottery

Originally founded in Morrisville, Pennsylvania, as the Chelsea Keramic Works, the name was changed to Dedham Pottery in 1895 after the firm relocated in Dedham, near Boston, Massachusetts. The move was effected to make use of the native clay deemed more suitable for the production of the popular dinnerware designed by Hugh Robertson, founder of the company. The ware utilized a gray stoneware body with a crackle glaze and simple cobalt border designs of flowers, birds, and animals. Decorations were brushed on by hand using an ancient Chinese method which suspended the cobalt within the overall glaze. There were thirteen standard patterns, among them Magnolia, Iris, Butterfly, Duck, Polar Bear, and the Rabbit, the latter of which was chosen to represent the company on their logo. On the very early pieces the rabbits face left; decorators soon found the reverse position easier to paint, and the rabbits were turned to the right. In addition to the standard patterns, other designs were produced for special orders. These and artist signed pieces are highly valued by collectors today.

Though their primary product was the blue-printed crackle-glazed dinnerware, two types of artware were also produced: crackle glaze and flambe. Their notable volcanic ware was a type of the latter. The mark is incised and often accompanies the cipher of Hugh Robertson. The firm was operated by succeeding generations of the Robertson family until it closed in 1943. Our advisor for this category is Dale MacLean; he is listed in the Directory under Massachusetts. See also Chelsea Keramic Art Works.

Vases, sea green, 8½", $500.00; blue and green drip on shaded red to green ground with areas of exposed clay throughout, 6", EX, $350.00; flowing olive and blue shades, 9", VG, $250.00.

Bowl, moss gr mottled drip, 4 arched ft, sgn HR, 8¾"	500.00
Vase, crackleware, blue jay on branch, stamped, 1931, 8"	1,500.00
Vase, crackleware, butterfly/flowers in bl, 1900s, 6"	2,300.00
Vase, dk brn/bl/gr/cream flambe, Oriental form, Dedham, 9"	600.00
Vase, dragon's blood/moss gr/lt bl/rust, experimental, 3"	425.00
Vase, oxblood, short neck on squat bulbous form, DP97E, 6"	1,600.00
Vase, red/burnt brn drip, short neck, sgn HR, 9", EX	2,000.00
Vase, sea gr gloss, BW/HCR/DP44D, 8½"	500.00
Vase, vegetation, bl/wht, wide mouth on cylinder, 9½"	2,200.00

Dinnerware

Bacon rasher, Elephant, stamped, 9¾x6"	1,900.00
Bowl, Grape, stamped, 4x9"	500.00
Bowl, Iris, imp/stamped registered, 3x9"	1,100.00
Bowl, Polar Bear, stamped, 2x5¼"	800.00

Bowl, Rabbit, O rebus in border, imp/stamped, 5½x11½" **1,100.00**
Bowl, Rabbit, stamped, 2x4¼" **200.00**
Bowl, Rabbit, stamped, 2x5¼" **275.00**
Bowl, Rabbit, stamped registered, 2x3½" **160.00**
Bowl, Rabbit, stamped registered, 3¼x8" **425.00**
Bowl, Rabbit, stamped registered/Tercentenary 1636-1936, 7½".**210.00**
Bowl, Rabbit, 5-sided, stamped registered, 1½x7" **650.00**
Bowl, soup; Rabbit, imp/stamped, 1¼x8½" **330.00**
Candle holder, Rabbit, stamped registered, 1½" **650.00**
Charger, Azalea, imp/stamped, 12" **575.00**
Coffeepot, no decor, experimental, imp/stamped, 8½" **1,700.00**
Creamer, Horse Chestnut, stamped, 2¼" **375.00**
Creamer, Rabbit, imp/stamped, 3½" **325.00**
Creamer, Rabbit, squat/bulbous, stamped, glaze flaws, 3½" **150.00**
Creamer & sugar bowl, Elephant, w/lid, stamped, 2", 2¾" **600.00**
Cup & saucer, bouillon; Rabbit, 2-hdl, stamped registered, 2" **400.00**
Cup & saucer, demitasse; Rabbit, stamped registered..................**275.00**
Cup & saucer, Grape, stamped, 3" **300.00**
Cup & saucer, Rabbit, O rebus in border, stamped, 3" **300.00**
Cup & saucer, Rabbit, stamped, 2½" **375.00**
Cup & saucer, Rabbit, stamped, 3" **300.00**
Cup plate, Rabbit, stamped registered, 4½" **235.00**
Egg cup, dbl; Rabbit, stamped registered, 3" **275.00**
Knife rest, Rabbit, figural, faint stamp, 2½" **700.00**
Marmalade, Swan, incised/stamped, hairline, 5" **500.00**
Mug, Elephant (w/baby), stamped registered, 3" **1,200.00**
Mug, Rabbit, imp/stamped, 4¼", NM **425.00**
Pitcher, Elephant, stamped, 8½" **1,800.00**
Pitcher, Night & Day, owl/moon, chicken/sun, registered, 5" **650.00**
Pitcher, Night & Day, stamped registered, 4½" **650.00**
Pitcher, Rabbit, cylindrical w/angle hdl, stamped, 6¾", NM **700.00**
Pitcher, Rabbit, stamped, 4½" **650.00**
Plate, Azalea, imp/stamped, 8½" **250.00**
Plate, Birds in Potted Orange Tree, stamped, 6" **425.00**
Plate, Butterfly, imp/stamped registered, 5" **550.00**
Plate, Butterfly, stamped, sm rpr, 9¾" **220.00**
Plate, Crab, stamped, 8½" **800.00**
Plate, Crab, waves at rim, 6" **650.00**
Plate, Day Lily, imp/stamped, 6", NM...............................**650.00**
Plate, Dolphin, Upside Down; scrolls, imp, 10", NM.............**850.00**
Plate, Duck, imp/stamped, 8½" **350.00**
Plate, Duck, imp/stamped, 9¾" **425.00**
Plate, Duck, O rebus in border, imp/stamped, 6" **375.00**
Plate, Elephant, imp/stamped registered, 8½"....................**950.00**
Plate, Flying Woodcock, stamped, hairline/glaze flaws, 8½" **475.00**
Plate, Grape, imp/stamped, 10" **275.00**
Plate, Grape, O rebus in border, imp/stamped, 6" **250.00**
Plate, Grape, sgn Davenport, stamped, 9¾" **350.00**
Plate, Horse Chestnut, imp/stamped registered, 7½" **285.00**
Plate, Horse Chestnut, O rebus in border, imp/stamped, 10" **400.00**
Plate, Horse Chestnut, stamped, 6" **250.00**
Plate, Iris, imp/stamped, 6" **250.00**
Plate, Iris, reverse colors, imp rabbit mk, 9¾" **350.00**
Plate, Lobster, waves at rim, stamped, 8½" **1,100.00**
Plate, Lotus Blossom, imp/stamped, 6" **1,100.00**
Plate, Magnolia, M Davenport, imp/stamped, 6" **255.00**
Plate, Mushroom, pk glazed, imp/stamped, chipped, 8½".............**200.00**
Plate, Pineapple, imp/stamped, 8½" **950.00**
Plate, Polar Bear, imp, 7¼" **600.00**
Plate, Polar Bear, O rebus in border, stamped, 8½" **3,100.00**
Plate, Pond Lily, O rebus in border, imp/stamped, 8½" **275.00**
Plate, Poppy, imp/stamped, 8½" **1,700.00**
Plate, Rabbit, child's, stamped, 7½" **700.00**
Plate, Rabbit, O rebus in border, imp/stamped, 10"....................**550.00**

Plate, Rabbit, O rebus in border, imp/stamped, 8½" 375.00
Plate, Rabbit, stamped, 8½" 300.00
Plate, Rabbit, stamped registered, 7½" 240.00
Plate, Rabbit, stamped registered/Tercentenary, 8½"............75.00
Plate, Snowtree, O rebus in border, imp/stamped, 8½" 275.00
Plate, Snowtree, stamped, 6" 230.00
Plate, Snowtree, 2 imp mks/stamped registered, 9¾" 325.00
Plate, Swan, imp/stamped, 7½" 425.00
Plate, Swan, stamped, 6½" 400.00
Plate, Swan & Cattails, dbl rabbit mk/stamped, 8½" 275.00
Plate, Tufted Duck, imp, 6" 300.00
Plate, Turkey, imp rabbit mk/stamped, 9¾" 350.00
Plate, Turkey, imp/stamped, 10" 550.00
Plate, Turkey, imp/stamped registered, 6" 300.00
Plate, Turkey, O rebus in border, imp/stamped, 8½" 750.00
Plate, Turkey, stamped, 10" 225.00
Platter, Rabbit, stamped, lt hairline, 14x8" 950.00
Shaker, Rabbit, sgn DP, cork stopper, 2½" 350.00
Shaker, Rabbit, 2¾", pr 300.00
Stein, Rabbit, imp/stamped, base chips, 5¼" 225.00
Sugar bowl, Rabbit, stamped registered, 2½x4" 300.00
Sugar bowl, Rabbit, w/lid, stamped registered, 3x4¾" 400.00
Tea tile, Rabbit, stamped registered, 5½" sq 325.00
Tea tile, Rabbit, 5-sided, stamped registered, 6" 335.00
Teapot, Rabbit, stamped registered, 7" **2,600.00**
Tray, Rabbit, stamped, 1½x13½" dia, NM.........................900.00

Scottie Dog, plate, 8½", $1,500.00; jar, $1,650.00.

Degenhart

The Crystal Art Glass factory in Cambridge, Ohio, opened in 1947 under the private ownership of John and Elizabeth Degenhart. John had previously worked for the Cambridge Glass Company and was well known for his superior paperweights. After his death in 1964, Elizabeth took over management of the factory, hiring several workers from the defunct Cambridge Company, including Zack Boyd. Boyd was responsible for many unique colors, some of which were named for him. From 1964 to 1974, more than twenty-seven different moulds were created, most of them resulting from Elizabeth Degenhart's work and creativity, and over 145 official colors were developed. Elizabeth died in 1978, requesting that the ten moulds she had built while operating the factory were to be turned over to the Degenhart Museum. The remaining moulds were to be held by the Island Mould and Machine Company, who (complying with her request) removed the familiar 'D in heart' trademark. The factory was eventually bought by Zack's son,

Bernard Boyd. He also acquired the remaining Degenhart moulds, to which he added his own logo.

In general, slags, jades, and opaques should be valued 15% to 20% higher than crystals in color.

Beaded Oval Toothpick, Bittersweet, 1976 ....35.00
Bicentennial Bell, Amethyst 11.00
Bicentennial Bell, Canary 10.00
Bicentennial Bell, Crown Tuscan 15.00
Bicentennial Bell, Crystal...6.00
Bicentennial Bell, Elizabeth's Lime Ice 15.00
Bicentennial Bell, Opal 12.00
Bicentennial Bell, Vaseline 10.00
Bird Salt & Pepper, Opal..35.00
Bow Slipper, Blue Marble Slag 25.00
Buzz Saw Wine, Cobalt 35.00
Buzz Saw Wine, Crystal 15.00
Chick, Crown Tuscan, hand stamped, 2" 45.00
Chick, Lemon Custard, 2" 50.00
Child's Mug, Apple Green 22.00
Coaster, Amber...7.00
Colonial Drape Toothpick, Sapphire 15.00
Daisy & Button Salt, Cobalt 15.00
Daisy & Button Salt, Light Amberina 12.50
Daisy & Button Toothpick, Cobalt Carnival, hand stamped........30.00
Daisy & Button Toothpick, Crown Tuscan 25.00
Daisy & Button Toothpick, Light Amberina.................16.00
Forget-Me-Not Toothpick, Bluebell 15.00
Forget-Me-Not Toothpick, Canary 12.00
Forget-Me-Not Toothpick, Caramel............................30.00
Forget-Me-Not Toothpick, Crystal 8.00
Forget-Me-Not Toothpick, Lavender Blue 25.00
Forget-Me-Not Toothpick, Periwinkle 15.00
Forget-Me-Not Toothpick, Toffee 25.00
Gypsy Pot Toothpick, Canary 12.00
Gypsy Pot Toothpick, Cobalt, hand stamped 25.00
Gypsy Pot Toothpick, Tomato.....................................35.00
Hand, Bernard's Boyd Ebony 20.00
Hand, Crown Tuscan...18.00
Hand, Honey Amber 6.00
Hand, Persimmon 10.00
Heart Box, Brown...22.00
Heart Box, Crown Tuscan...25.00
Heart Box, Elizabeth Blue 40.00
Heart Box, Milk Blue 24.00
Heart Toothpick, April Green 25.00
Heart Toothpick, Bernard Boyd's Ebony 35.00
Heart Toothpick, Caramel 35.00
Heart Toothpick, Dark Blue Jay Slag............................40.00
Heart Toothpick, Sapphire 15.00

Heart Toothpick, Seafoam Green 25.00
Hen Covered Dish, Caramel Custard, 3" 45.00
Hen Covered Dish, Sapphire, 3" 18.00
Hen Covered Dish, Sparrow Slag, 3" 40.00
Hobo Shoe, Milk Blue 16.00
Hobo Shoe, Sparrow Slag 20.00
Mini Pitcher, Opal...22.00
Owl, Amberina 50.00
Owl, Bernard Boyd's Ebony 60.00
Owl, Blue-Green Marble 72.50
Owl, Custard 40.00
Owl, Dark Elizabeth Lime Ice.....................................45.00
Owl, Fog Opaque 60.00
Owl, Heliotrope...95.00
Owl, Lemon Chiffon...35.00
Owl, Midnight Sun 35.00
Owl, Milk Blue 25.00
Owl, Pearl Gray 30.00
Owl, Pigeon Blood 40.00
Owl, Pink Lady 34.00
Owl, Tangerine, scarce 125.00
Pooch, Bittersweet Slag..66.00
Pooch, Blue Jay Slag 28.00
Pooch, Buttercup Slag 40.00
Pooch, Caramel Slag...26.00
Pooch, Charcoal 20.00
Pooch, Daffodil 18.00
Pooch, Dark Amethyst 15.00
Pooch, Dark Ivory Slag, scarce 45.00
Pooch, Gray Marble..16.00
Pooch, Green Caramel Slag 40.00
Pooch, Gun Metal 22.00
Pooch, Henry Blue 20.00
Pooch, Milk Blue 18.00
Pooch, Red...25.00
Pooch, Tangerine, scarce 50.00
Pooch, Tomato 35.00
Pooch, Tomato Slag..40.00
Priscilla, Blue & White 100.00
Priscilla, Crystal...50.00
Priscilla, Heatherbloom 100.00
Priscilla, Jade Green 100.00
Priscilla, Orchid 85.00
Priscilla, Periwinkle 75.00
Priscilla, Smoky Blue 80.00
Robin Covered Dish, Fawn..55.00
Skate Shoe, Cobalt Carnival 40.00
Skate Shoe, Sapphire..30.00
Texas Boot, Amethyst 15.00
Tomahawk, Amber 18.00
Tomahawk, Crown Tuscan, unmk 50.00
Tomahawk, Emerald Green...23.00
Turkey Covered Dish, Amberina 55.00
Turkey Covered Dish, Crown Tuscan 75.00
Turkey Covered Dish, Gray Slag..................................80.00
Wildflower Candy Dish, Crown Tuscan, unmk 35.00
Wildflower Candy Dish, Twilight Blue..........................30.00

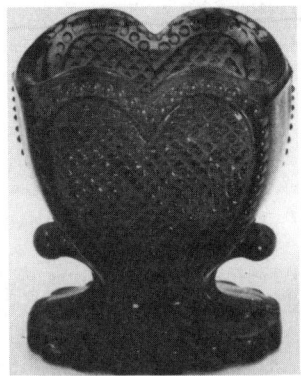

Heart toothpick holder, ruby, $35.00.

Delatte

Delatte was a manufacturer of French cameo glass. Founded in 1921, their style reflected the influence of the Art Deco era with strong color contrasts and bold design. Our advisor for this category is Don Williams; he is listed in the Directory under Missouri.

Cameo

Lamp, floral, red on butterscotch, bullet shape, 15" **2,750.00**
Vase, floral, brn to orange, 2 cuts, 9¼x3½" **750.00**
Vase, irises, bl/purple on wht, narrow neck, 8" **1,000.00**
Vase, landscape along river, maroon/rose on wht, hdls, 9" **1,200.00**
Vase, rhododendron, wine on mc mottle, metal base, 16" **2,000.00**
Vase, trees at river, pk/mauve, 2 cuts, 7½x4⅜" **1,200.00**
Vase, wisteria, bl tones on frost & bl, 10" **1,250.00**

Delft

Old Delftware, made as early as the 16th century, was originally a low-fired earthenware coated in a thin opaque tin glaze with painted-on polychrome designs. It was not until the last half of the 19th century, however, that the ware became commonly referred to as Delft, acquiring the name from the Dutch village that had become the major center of its production. English, German, and French potters also produced Delft, though with noticeable differences both in shape and decorative theme.

In the early part of the 18th century, the German potter, Bottger, developed a formula for porcelain; in England, Wedgwood began producing creamware — both of which were much more durable. Unable to compete, one by one the Delft potteries failed. Soon only one remained. In 1876 De Porcelyne Fles reintroduced Delftware on a hard white body with blue and white decorative themes reflecting the Dutch countryside, windmills by the sea, and Dutch children. This manufacturer is the most well known of several operating today. Their products are now produced under the Royal Delft label. Examples listed here are blue on white unless noted otherwise. See also specific manufacturers.

Cow creamer, late 1800s, 10½" long, $300.00.

Bottle, Dutch, man & woman, Royal Goedewaagen, 7½", pr 120.00
Charger, basket of flowers, plume border, 14", pr 750.00
Charger, Continental, allover florals, mc, 1780s, 12", VG 325.00
Charger, Holland, basket of flowers, 1700s, 16", EX 850.00
Charger, Oriental-style motif w/floral medallion, 14" 250.00
Epergne, gr/wht, 3 scroll legs (w/sm cups) lift dish, 11" 650.00
Figurine, lamb, flowers & scrolls, sgn, 4½" 170.00
Flower brick, English, coastal scenes, 1700s, 3x3x6", EX 550.00
Jug, N Europe, tulip/stars, 3-color, 1780s, 7¾", NM....................600.00
Plate, figure in landscape, 9", pr, EX 300.00
Plate, floral center/rim, 9", pr, EX 250.00
Plate, vase of flowers, polychrome, 8¾", EX 400.00

Spoon rest, Germany, sailing scene, ca 1900, 6x4½" **49.00**
Tankard, Germany, birds/sprigs, pewter lid/base, 1700s, 10"........**650.00**
Tile, house in rnd reserve, minor edge chips, 5x5" **40.00**
Tile, 2 Dutch women, sgn URK, fr, 11x11" **65.00**
Tile picture, Holland, fleet of ships, 8 tiles, 19x25"....................**700.00**
Vase, Dutch, birds/floral sprigwork, 1700s, 5½", VG....................**550.00**
Vase, florals, full decor, sq/flared, 4½" **59.00**
Vase, mill/seascape, full decor, flared top, 1930s, 4¼x2½" **35.00**
Vase, Royal Delft, floral, slender neck, 3½x2¼" **39.00**

Depression Glass

Other than coins and stamps, colored glassware produced during the Depression era is probably the most sought-after collectible in the field today. There are literally thousands of collectors in the United States and Canada buying, selling, and trading 'Depression Glass' on today's market.

Depression Glass is defined by Gene Florence, author of several best-selling books on the subject, as 'the inexpensive glassware made primarily during the Depression era in the colors of amber, green, pink, blue, red, yellow, white, and crystal.' This glass was mass produced, sold through five-and-dime stores and mail-order catalogs, and given away as premiums with gas and food products.

The listings in this book are far from being complete. If you want a more thorough presentation of this fascinating glassware, we recommend *The Collector's Encyclopedia of Depression Glass, Pocket Guide to Depression Glass; Elegant Glassware of the Depression Era;* and *Very Rare Depression Glass, Vol. II* by Gene Florence, whose address is listed in the Directory under Kentucky.

Adam, bowl, cereal; gr, 5¾"..35.00
Adam, bowl, dessert; pk, 4¾" 12.50
Adam, bowl, gr, 7¾"..19.50
Adam, bowl, pk, oval, 10" 20.00
Adam, bowl, pk, w/lid, 9" 47.50
Adam, butter dish, gr, w/lid..275.00
Adam, cake plate, pk, ftd, 10"...17.50
Adam, candlestick, delphite, 4", pr...200.00
Adam, candy jar, gr, w/lid, 2½"...85.00
Adam, coaster, pk, 3¼" 17.50
Adam, creamer, pk 15.00
Adam, cup, pk 20.00
Adam, pitcher, pk, 32-oz, 8"..45.00
Adam, plate, dinner; gr, sq, 9" 18.00
Adam, plate, grill; gr, 9" 15.00
Adam, platter, pk, 11¾"...16.50
Adam, saucer, gr, sq, 6".. 6.00
Adam, shakers, pk, ftd, 4", pr 55.00
Adam, sherbet, pk, 3" 22.50
Adam, sugar bowl, gr 16.00
Adam, sugar or candy lid, pk 18.50
Adam, tumbler, iced tea; pk, 5½"...50.00
American Pioneer, bowl, console; pk, 10¾" 45.00
American Pioneer, bowl, gr, hdls, 9"..22.50
American Pioneer, bowl, pk, hdls, 5"..13.50
American Pioneer, bowl, pk, w/lid, 8¾" 85.00
American Pioneer, candy jar, pk, w/lid, 1-lb..................................75.00
American Pioneer, cheese/cracker set, crystal, 2-pc 45.00
American Pioneer, coaster, gr, 3½"...25.00
American Pioneer, creamer, gr, 2¾" 20.00
American Pioneer, cup, crystal or pk 9.00
American Pioneer, goblet, water; pk, 8-oz, 6" 32.50

American Pioneer, ice bucket, gr, 6"	50.00
American Pioneer, lamp, pk, 8½"	80.00
American Pioneer, mayonnaise, pk, 4¼"	52.50
American Pioneer, plate, gr, hdls, 11½"	17.00
American Pioneer, plate, gr, 6"	14.00
American Pioneer, plate, pk, 8"	7.50
American Pioneer, saucer, pk	4.00
American Pioneer, sherbet, gr, 3½"	17.00
American Pioneer, sherbet, pk, 4¾"	23.00
American Pioneer, sugar bowl, gr, 3½"	20.00
American Pioneer, tumbler, juice; gr, 5-oz	30.00
American Pioneer, tumbler, pk, 12-oz, 5"	32.50
American Pioneer, tumbler, pk, 8-oz, 4"	23.00
American Pioneer, vase, gr, rnd, 9"	185.00
American Pioneer, whiskey, pk, 2-oz, 2¼"	40.00
American Sweetheart, bowl, berry; monax, rnd, 9"	50.00

American Pioneer, amber covered pitcher, 5", $250.00, 7", $300.00; 6" plate, $34.50; 8" plate, $22.50.

American Sweetheart, bowl, berry; pk, flat, 3¾"	30.00
American Sweetheart, bowl, cereal; monax, 6"	9.50
American Sweetheart, bowl, console; monax, 18"	325.00
American Sweetheart, bowl, cream soup; pk, 4½"	40.00
American Sweetheart, bowl, soup; monax, flat, 9½"	47.50
American Sweetheart, creamer, pk, ftd	9.50
American Sweetheart, lamp shade, monax	425.00
American Sweetheart, pitcher, pk, 60-oz, 7½"	475.00
American Sweetheart, plate, chop; monax, 11"	10.00
American Sweetheart, plate, dinner; pk, 9¾"	25.00
American Sweetheart, plate, luncheon; monax, 9"	9.00
American Sweetheart, plate, salad; monax, 8"	7.00
American Sweetheart, plate, salver; bl, 12"	145.00
American Sweetheart, plate, server; monax, 15½"	175.00
American Sweetheart, saucer, pk	3.50
American Sweetheart, shakers, monax, ftd, pr	225.00
American Sweetheart, sherbet, pk, ftd, 3¾"	15.00
American Sweetheart, tidbit, 2-tier, red, 8" & 12"	175.00
American Sweetheart, tumbler, pk, 10-oz, 4¾"	70.00
American Sweetheart, tumbler, pk, 5-oz, 3½"	55.00
Anniversary, bowl, fruit; pk, 9"	17.50
Anniversary, butter dish, crystal, w/lid	22.50
Anniversary, candlestick, crystal, 4⅞", pr	15.00
Anniversary, creamer, pk, ftd	8.50
Anniversary, pickle dish, crystal, 9"	4.00
Anniversary, plate, dinner; pk, 9"	8.00
Anniversary, relish, pk, 8"	8.50
Anniversary, sugar lid, crystal	5.00
Aunt Polly, bowl, berry; bl, 4¾"	12.00

Aunt Polly, bowl, berry; irid, 7⅞"	16.00
Aunt Polly, bowl, bl, oval, 8⅜"	75.00
Aunt Polly, butter dish, gr, w/lid	210.00
Aunt Polly, creamer, gr	25.00
Aunt Polly, plate, sherbet; bl, 6"	10.00
Aunt Polly, shakers, bl, pr	185.00
Aunt Polly, sugar bowl, gr or irid	20.00
Aunt Polly, tumbler, bl, 8-oz, 3⅝"	22.50
Aunt Polly, vase, gr, ftd, 6½"	25.00
Aurora, bowl, cereal; gr, 5⅜"	7.00
Aurora, bowl, cobalt, deep, 4½"	25.00
Aurora, creamer, pk, 4½"	15.00
Aurora, cup, cobalt	9.50
Aurora, tumbler, pk or cobalt, 10-oz, 4¾"	16.00
Avocado, bowl, gr, hdls, 5¼"	28.00
Avocado, bowl, pk, 3¼" deep, 9½"	80.00
Avocado, bowl, preserve; pk, 1-hdl, 7"	16.00
Avocado, bowl, salad; gr, 7½"	45.00
Avocado, cake plate, pk, hdls, 10¼"	30.00
Avocado, plate, luncheon; gr, 8¼"	17.00
Avocado, plate, sherbet; pk, 6⅜"	12.00
Avocado, saucer, gr, 6⅜"	25.00
Beaded Block, bowl, gr, 1-hdl, 5½"	7.00
Beaded Block, bowl, opal, rnd, 6¼"	15.00
Beaded Block, celery dish, irid, 8¼"	17.50
Beaded Block, creamer, amber	15.00
Beaded Block, jelly dish, gr, hdls, 4½"	7.00
Beaded Block, plate, bl, rnd, 8¾"	18.00
Beaded Block, plate, vaseline, sq, 7¾"	9.00
Beaded Block, sugar bowl, crystal	14.00
Beaded Block, vase, bouquet; pk, 6"	11.00
Block Optic, bowl, berry; gr, 8½"	21.00
Block Optic, bowl, cereal; gr, 5¼"	10.00
Block Optic, candlestick, pk, 1¾", pr	65.00
Block Optic, cup, gr or pk	6.00
Block Optic, goblet, wine; pk, 4½"	28.00
Block Optic, ice bucket, gr	30.00
Block Optic, pitcher, gr, 54-oz, 8½"	30.00
Block Optic, pitcher, pk, 80-oz, 8"	60.00
Block Optic, plate, dinner; yel, 9"	35.00
Block Optic, plate, luncheon; gr, 8"	4.00
Block Optic, plate, sherbet; yel, 6"	2.50
Block Optic, saucer, gr, 5¾"	8.50
Block Optic, shakers, pk, ftd, pr	65.00
Block Optic, sherbet, yel, 5½-oz, 3¼"	8.00
Block Optic, sugar bowl, gr	10.00
Block Optic, tumbler, pk, ftd, 3-oz, 3¼"	17.00
Block Optic, whiskey, pk, 2-oz, 2¼"	22.50
Bowknot, bowl, berry; gr, 4½"	12.00
Bowknot, cup, gr	6.00
Bowknot, plate, salad; gr, 7"	9.00
Bowknot, tumbler, gr, 10-oz, 5"	15.00
Bubble, bowl, berry; bl, 4"	12.00
Bubble, bowl, berry; gr, 8⅜"	11.00
Bubble, bowl, cereal; bl, 5¼"	10.00
Bubble, bowl, fruit; gr, 4½"	5.50
Bubble, bowl, soup; bl, flat, 7¾"	12.00
Bubble, creamer, gr	9.50
Bubble, cup, bl	3.00
Bubble, cup, red	6.00
Bubble, plate, dinner; gr, 9⅜"	12.50
Bubble, plate, grill; bl, 9⅜"	17.50
Bubble, platter, bl, oval, 12"	14.00
Bubble, saucer, red	3.00

Bubble, tumbler, iced tea; red, 12-oz 10.00
Bubble, tumbler, juice; red, 6-oz 7.00
Cameo, bowl, berry; gr, 8¼" 30.00
Cameo, bowl, cereal; pk, 5½" 50.00
Cameo, bowl, console; gr, 3-ftd, 11" 57.50
Cameo, bowl, cream soup; gr, 4¾" 55.00
Cameo, bowl, vegetable; yel, oval, 10" 35.00
Cameo, cake plate, gr, 3-ftd, 10" 17.50
Cameo, candlestick, gr, 4", pr 90.00
Cameo, candy jar, pk, low, w/lid, 4" 425.00
Cameo, cookie jar, gr, w/lid 42.50
Cameo, cup, crystal 5.00
Cameo, cup, gr 13.00
Cameo, cup, pk 65.00
Cameo, goblet, water; gr, 6" 45.00
Cameo, pitcher, water; gr, 56-oz, 8½" 42.50

Cameo, plate, dinner; yellow, 9½", $6.00.

Cameo, sherbet, gr, blown, 3⅛" 13.00
Cameo, sherbet, pk, 4⅞" 85.00
Cameo, sugar bowl, gr, 3¼" 15.00
Cameo, tumbler, gr, flat, 11-oz, 5" 23.00
Cameo, vase, gr, 8" 22.50
Cherry Blossom, bowl, berry; pk, 4¾" 12.00
Cherry Blossom, bowl, soup; gr, flat, 7¾" 45.00
Cherry Blossom, butter dish, pk, w/lid 60.00
Cherry Blossom, coaster, gr 12.00
Cherry Blossom, cup, pk 15.00
Cherry Blossom, pitcher, pk, ftd, patterned top, 36-oz 47.50
Cherry Blossom, plate, grill; gr, 10" 60.00
Cherry Blossom, plate, salad; gr, 7" 17.00
Cherry Blossom, platter, gr, oval, 11" 28.00
Cherry Blossom, platter, pk, 13" 50.00
Cherry Blossom, sugar lid, pk 12.00
Cherry Blossom, tray, sandwich; delphite, 10½" 16.00
Cherry Blossom, tumbler, gr, ftd, allover pattern, 8-oz, 4½"...28.00
Cherry Blossom, tumbler, pk, flat, patterned top, 12-oz, 5"....45.00
Cherryberry, bowl, berry; pk or gr, 4" 8.00
Cherryberry, butter dish, crystal or irid, w/lid 140.00
Cherryberry, compote, pk or gr, 5¾" 20.00
Cherryberry, creamer, crystal or irid, 4⅝" 14.00
Cherryberry, pickle dish, pk or gr, oval, 8¼" 13.00

Cherryberry, pitcher, crystal or irid, 7¾" 150.00
Cherryberry, tumbler, crystal or irid, 9-oz, 3⅝" 16.00
Chinex Classic, bowl, vegetable; brntone or ivory, 7" 13.00
Chinex Classic, butter dish, brntone or ivory 50.00
Chinex Classic, creamer, castle decal 17.00
Chinex Classic, cup, floral decal 6.00
Chinex Classic, plate, dinner; castle decal, 9¾" 15.00
Chinex Classic, plate, sandwich; floral decal, 11½"............12.50
Christmas Candy, bowl, soup; crystal, 7⅜"...................... 6.00
Christmas Candy, cup, teal 17.50
Christmas Candy, mayonnaise, crystal, w/ladle 17.50
Christmas Candy, plate, luncheon; teal, 8¼"...................15.00
Christmas Candy, plate, sandwich; teal, 11¼"..................35.00
Christmas Candy, sugar bowl, crystal 8.00
Circle, bowl, pk, 8" 11.00
Circle, decanter, gr, hdls 35.00
Circle, pitcher, gr, 60-oz 27.50
Circle, sherbet, gr, 4¾" 7.00
Circle, tumbler, water; gr or pk, 8-oz, 4" 9.00
Cloverleaf, bowl, cereal; gr, 5" 22.00
Cloverleaf, bowl, gr, 8" 47.50
Cloverleaf, candy dish, yel, w/lid 95.00
Cloverleaf, cup, blk 14.00
Cloverleaf, cup, pk 6.00
Cloverleaf, plate, luncheon; pk or gr, 8" 6.00
Cloverleaf, shakers, yel, pr 95.00
Cloverleaf, sugar bowl, gr, ftd, 3⅝" 8.50
Cloverleaf, tumbler, gr, ftd, 10-oz, 5¾" 19.00
Colonial, bowl, cream soup; pk, 4½"...........................52.50
Colonial, bowl, master berry; gr, 9" 25.00
Colonial, bowl, vegetable; crystal, oval, 10" 15.00
Colonial, butter dish, pk, w/lid 550.00
Colonial, goblet, claret; crystal, 4-oz, 5¼" 15.00
Colonial, goblet, cocktail; gr, 3-oz, 4" 23.00
Colonial, pitcher, gr, 54-oz, 7" 45.00
Colonial, plate, grill; pk, 10" 20.00
Colonial, plate, sherbet; pk, 6" 4.00
Colonial, platter, gr, oval, 12" 19.00
Colonial, sherbet, pk, 3⅜" 9.00
Colonial, sugar lid, gr 17.00
Colonial, tumbler, gr, ftd, 5-oz, 4" 23.00
Colonial, tumbler, pk, ftd, 10-oz 40.00
Colonial, tumbler, water; crystal, 9-oz, 4" 12.00
Colonial Block, bowl, gr, 7" 15.00
Colonial Block, bowl, pk, 4" 6.00
Colonial Block, candy jar, gr, w/lid 32.50
Colonial Block, creamer, pk 9.50
Colonial Block, pitcher, gr 35.00
Colonial Block, sugar bowl, gr 9.50
Colonial Fluted, bowl, cereal; gr, 6" 7.50
Colonial Fluted, bowl, master berry; gr, 7½" 14.00
Colonial Fluted, creamer, gr 5.00
Colonial Fluted, plate, luncheon; gr, 8" 4.00
Colonial Fluted, sugar bowl, gr, open 4.00
Colonial Fluted, sugar lid, gr 12.00
Columbia, bowl, salad; crystal, 8½" 14.00
Columbia, butter dish, crystal, w/lid 15.00
Columbia, plate, bread & butter; pk, 6" 10.00
Columbia, plate, luncheon; pk, 9½"............................22.00
Columbia, tumbler, juice; crystal, 4-oz, 2⅞"..................16.00
Coronation, bowl, berry; red, 4¼" 6.00
Coronation, bowl, master berry; pk, hdls, 8" 8.00
Coronation, cup, red 5.00
Coronation, nappy, pk, 6½" 4.00

Coronation, plate, luncheon; gr, 8½" 30.00
Coronation, sherbet, pk 4.00
Coronation, tumbler, pk, ftd, 10-oz, 5" 18.00
Cremax, bowl, vegetable; ivory, 9" 6.00
Cremax, cup, demitasse; ivory w/decor 20.00
Cremax, plate, dinner; ivory w/decor 8.50
Cremax, plate, sandwich; ivory, 11½" 4.00
Cremax, sugar bowl, ivory w/decal 9.50
Cube, bowl, dessert; gr, 4½" 6.00
Cube, butter dish, pk, w/lid, 6½" 50.00
Cube, coaster, gr, 3¼" 6.00
Cube, cup, pk 6.00
Cube, plate, luncheon; gr 5.00
Cube, shakers, pk, pr 30.00
Cube, sugar bowl, pk, open, 3" 6.00
Cube, tumbler, gr, 9-oz, 4" 55.00
Daisy, bowl, berry; amber, 4½" 8.00
Daisy, bowl, master berry; crystal, 9⅜" 12.00
Daisy, cup, amber 5.50
Daisy, plate, cake or sandwich; amber, 11½" 12.00
Daisy, plate, dinner; amber, 9⅜" 8.00
Daisy, plate, salad; crystal, 7⅜" 3.00
Daisy, relish dish, crystal, 3-part, 8⅜" 10.00
Daisy, tumbler, crystal, ftd, 9-oz 9.00
Diamond Quilted, bowl, bl or blk, 1-hdl, 5½" 14.00
Diamond Quilted, bowl, cream soup; pk or gr, 4¾" 7.00
Diamond Quilted, candlestick, gr, pr 22.00
Diamond Quilted, compote, pk, w/lid, 11½" 62.50
Diamond Quilted, cup, bl or blk 14.00
Diamond Quilted, ice bucket, bl 80.00
Diamond Quilted, plate, sherbet; gr, 6" 3.00
Diamond Quilted, punch bowl, gr, w/stand 375.00
Diamond Quilted, sherbet, bl or blk 13.00
Diamond Quilted, tumbler, pk or gr, ftd, 12-oz 14.00
Diamond Quilted, whiskey, gr, 1½-oz 7.50
Diana, ash tray, pk, 3½" 3.00
Diana, bowl, amber, scalloped rim, 12" 15.00
Diana, bowl, cereal; amber, 5" 10.00
Diana, bowl, salad; pk, 9" 18.00
Diana, creamer, pk 10.00
Diana, cup, amber 8.00
Diana, plate, bread & butter; pk or amber, 6" 1.50
Diana, platter, pk, oval, 12" 20.00
Diana, sherbet, amber 8.00
Diana, tumbler, crystal, 9-oz, 4⅛" 20.00
Dogwood, bowl, berry; monax or cremax 35.00
Dogwood, bowl, cereal; gr, 5½" 20.00
Dogwood, bowl, fruit; pk, 10¼" 275.00
Dogwood, cup, gr 22.00
Dogwood, plate, bread & butter; monax or cremax 20.00
Dogwood, plate, luncheon; gr, 8" 7.00
Dogwood, sherbet, gr, low ftd 85.00
Dogwood, tumbler, pk, decor, 10-oz, 4" 30.00
Doric, bowl, cereal; pk, 5½" 37.50
Doric, bowl, vegetable; gr, oval, 9" 25.00
Doric, butter dish, pk, w/lid 60.00
Doric, candy dish, pk, w/lid, 8" 27.50
Doric, plate, salad; pk, 7" 14.00
Doric, platter, gr, oval, 12" 20.00
Doric, shakers, pk, pr 27.50
Doric, sherbet, gr, ftd 11.00
Doric, tray, serving; gr, sq, 8" 15.00
Doric, tumbler, pk, ftd, 10-oz, 4" 40.00
Doric & Pansy, bowl, master berry; pk or crystal, 8" 18.00

Doric & Pansy, butter dish, ultramarine, w/lid 395.00
Doric & Pansy, plate, salad; ultramarine, 7" 27.50

Doric & Pansy, plate, dinner; ultramarine, 9", $22.00.

Doric & Pansy, sugar bowl, pk 60.00
Doric & Pansy, tumbler, ultramarine, 9-oz, 4½" 50.00
English Hobnail, bowl, pk or gr, 4½" or 5", ea 10.00
English Hobnail, candlestick, pk or gr, 3½", pr 32.00
English Hobnail, candy dish, pk or gr, w/lid, 15" 275.00
English Hobnail, cigarette box, cobalt 60.00
English Hobnail, egg cup, pk or gr 36.00
English Hobnail, goblet, cobalt, 6¼-oz 45.00
English Hobnail, goblet, cocktail; pk or gr, 3-oz 17.00
English Hobnail, goblet, wine; cobalt, 2-oz 44.00
English Hobnail, pitcher, pk or gr, 23-oz 145.00
English Hobnail, plate, dinner; pk or gr, 10" 22.00
English Hobnail, plate, pie; pk or gr, 7¼" 5.00
English Hobnail, relish, pk or gr, oval, 8" or 9", ea 18.00
English Hobnail, shakers, pk or gr, rnd or sq base, pr 77.50
English Hobnail, sherbet, pk or gr 14.00
English Hobnail, tumbler, iced tea; pk or gr, 12-oz, 5" 24.00
English Hobnail, tumbler, pk or gr, ftd, 9-oz 16.00
English Hobnail, vase, pk or gr 135.00
Fire-King Alice, cup, wht 7.50
Fire-King Alice, plate, wht, 9½" 15.00
Fire-King Jane Ray, bowl, oatmeal; jadite, 5⅞" 4.00
Fire-King Jane Ray, creamer, jadite 4.00
Fire-King Jane Ray, plate, dinner; jadite, 9⅛" 5.00
Fire-King Jane Ray, platter, jadite, 12" 10.50
Fire-King Oven Glass, baker, bl, 2-qt 12.50
Fire-King Oven Glass, bowl, utility; bl, 10⅛" 15.00
Fire-King Oven Glass, custard cup, bl, 6-oz 3.50
Fire-King Oven Glass, plate, pie; bl, 9" 8.00
Fire-King Oven Glass, roaster, bl, 8¾" 40.00
Fire-King Philbe, bowl, vegetable; bl, oval, 10" 95.00
Fire-King Philbe, cup, pk or gr 80.00
Fire-King Philbe, plate, grill; pk or gr, 10½" 40.00
Fire-King Philbe, plate, luncheon; crystal, 8" 18.00
Fire-King Philbe, plate, sandwich; pk or gr, 10" 60.00
Fire-King Philbe, platter, crystal, closed hdls, 12" 25.00
Fire-King Philbe, tumbler, iced tea; pk or gr, ftd, 6½" 65.00
Fire-King Square, bowl, dessert; all colors, 4¾" 4.50
Fire-King Square, plate, dinner; all colors, 9¼" 7.50
Fire-King Swirl, cup, jadite 3.50
Fire-King Swirl, plate, dinner; jadite, 9⅛" 5.00
Fire-King Swirl, sugar lid, jadite 3.50
Fire-King Turquoise Blue, ash tray 6.00
Fire-King Turquoise Blue, bowl, mixing; rnd, 4-qt 12.50
Fire-King Turquoise Blue, bowl, mixing; 2-qt 8.00

Fire-King Turquoise Blue, creamer 5.00
Fire-King Turquoise Blue, plate, egg; w/gold trim 12.50
Fire-King Turquoise Blue, plate, 10" 22.50
Fire-King Turquoise Blue, plate, 9" 6.50
Floral, bowl, vegetable; gr, w/lid, 8" 37.50
Floral, butter dish, gr, w/lid................................80.00
Floral, candy jar, pk, w/lid..................................30.00
Floral, coaster, pk, 3¼" 12.00
Floral, pitcher, pk, ftd cone, 32-oz, 8" 25.00
Floral, plate, sherbet; pk, 6" 4.50
Floral, sherbet, gr 13.00
Floral, sugar bowl, pk 8.00
Floral, tumbler, juice; pk, 5-oz, 4".........................15.00
Floral, tumbler, water; gr, 7-oz, 4¾".......................18.00
Floral & Diamond Band, bowl, berry; gr, 4½".............. 7.50
Floral & Diamond Band, butter dish, gr, w/lid 100.00
Floral & Diamond Band, pitcher, gr, 42-oz, 8"...........85.00

Floral & Diamond Band, plate, luncheon; pink, 8", $27.50.

Floral & Diamond Band, sugar bowl, pk or gr, 5¼" 12.00
Floral & Diamond Band, tumbler, water; pk, 4" 17.50
Florentine No 1, ash tray, gr, 5½" 20.00
Florentine No 1, bowl, berry; gr, 5" 10.00
Florentine No 1, butter dish, pk, w/lid.....................150.00
Florentine No 1, coaster, pk, 3¾"..........................22.00
Florentine No 1, pitcher, yel, flat, 48-oz, 7½"............155.00
Florentine No 1, platter, pk, oval, 11½" 17.00
Florentine No 1, sugar lid, pk or yel 17.00
Florentine No 1, tumbler, iced tea; pk, ftd, 12-oz, 5¼"....27.00
Florentine No 1, tumbler, water; gr, ftd, 10-oz, 4¾" 19.00
Florentine No 2, bowl, berry; yel, 4½".....................16.00
Florentine No 2, bowl, gr, 5½".............................27.50
Florentine No 2, butter dish, yel, w/lid 135.00
Florentine No 2, coaster, yel, 3¼" 19.00
Florentine No 2, custard cup, gr...........................52.50
Florentine No 2, pitcher, gr, 76-oz, 8¼"...................80.00
Florentine No 2, plate, dinner; gr, 10" 12.00
Florentine No 2, plate, salad; yel, 8½" 8.00
Florentine No 2, platter, pk, oval, 11" 13.00
Florentine No 2, shakers, yel, pr 45.00
Florentine No 2, sugar bowl, gr............................ 7.00
Florentine No 2, tumbler, iced tea; gr, 12-oz, 5" 27.50
Florentine No 2, tumbler, juice; yel, 5-oz, 3⅜" 18.00

Florentine No 2, tumbler, yel, ftd, 5-oz, 4"...............14.00
Flower Garden w/Butterflies, bonbon, blk, w/lid, 6⅝"....250.00
Flower Garden w/Butterflies, candlestick, amber, 8", pr....75.00
Flower Garden w/Butterflies, compote, yel, 2⅞" 25.00
Flower Garden w/Butterflies, cup, pk.......................55.00
Flower Garden w/Butterflies, plate, amber, 7" 15.00
Flower Garden w/Butterflies, powder jar, pk, ftd, 7½".....95.00
Flower Garden w/Butterflies, tray, amber, oval, 5½x10" 47.50
Flower Garden w/Butterflies, vase, blk, hdls, 10" 225.00
Flower Garden w/Butterflies, vase, pk or gr, 10½".........100.00
Forest Green, bowl, dessert; gr, 4¾" 5.00
Forest Green, bowl, salad; gr, 7⅜" 9.50
Forest Green, cup, gr, sq 4.00
Forest Green, plate, dinner; gr, 10" 20.00
Forest Green, plate, luncheon; gr, 8⅜" 5.00
Forest Green, punch bowl, gr 20.00
Forest Green, vase, gr, 9" 6.00
Fortune, bowl, dessert; pk, 4½" 4.00
Fortune, cup, pk 3.50
Fortune, tumbler, water; pk, 9-oz, 4"...................... 8.00
Fruits, bowl, berry; pk, 5" 15.00
Fruits, pitcher, gr, flat, 7" 50.00
Fruits, plate, luncheon; pk, 8" 5.00
Fruits, tumbler, juice; pk, 3½" 15.00
Fruits, tumbler, pk, 12-oz, 5" 55.00
Georgian, bowl, master berry; gr, 7½" 45.00
Georgian, creamer, gr, ftd, 4" 13.00
Georgian, platter, gr, closed hdls, 11½"...................55.00
Georgian, sugar bowl, gr, ftd, 3" 10.00
Georgian, tumbler, gr, flat, 9-oz, 4" 45.00
Harp, ash tray, crystal 4.50
Harp, cake stand, crystal, 9" 20.00
Harp, tray, crystal, hdls, rectangular......................27.50
Heritage, bowl, berry; pk, 5" 35.00
Heritage, bowl, master berry; bl or gr, 8½" 150.00
Heritage, creamer, crystal, ftd............................20.00
Heritage, plate, dinner; crystal, 9¼" 10.00
Hex Optic, bowl, mixing; pk or gr, 9" 16.00
Hex Optic, butter dish, pk or gr, w/lid, rectangular, 1-lb.....67.50
Hex Optic, dish, refrigerator; pk or gr, 4x4" 9.00
Hex Optic, pitcher, pk or gr, ftd, 48-oz 35.00
Hex Optic, tumbler, pk or gr, 7-oz, 4¾" 7.00
Hex Optic, whiskey, pk or gr, 1-oz, 2" 7.00
Hobnail, bowl, cereal; crystal, 5½" 3.50
Hobnail, cup, pk or crystal................................ 4.00
Hobnail, plate, luncheon; pk or crystal, 8½"............... 3.00
Hobnail, tumbler, iced tea; crystal, 15-oz................. 6.50
Holiday, bowl, vegetable; pk, oval, 9½" 15.00
Holiday, candlestick, pk, 3", pr...........................75.00
Holiday, cup, pk 6.00
Holiday, pitcher, pk, 52-oz, 6¾"...........................27.50
Holiday, platter, pk, oval, 11⅜".........................15.00
Holiday, sugar bowl, pk, open 8.00
Homespun, bowl, cereal; pk, 5" 16.00
Homespun, cup, pk, child's sz 25.00
Homespun, platter, pk, closed hdls, 13" 12.00
Homespun, tea set, pk, child's sz, 14-pc 250.00
Homespun, tumbler, pk, ftd, 9-oz, 6¼" 22.50
Indiana Custard, bowl, berry; ivory, 4⅞" 7.50
Indiana Custard, bowl, vegetable; ivory, oval, 9½" 24.00
Indiana Custard, cup, ivory 35.00
Indiana Custard, plate, dinner; ivory, 9¾" 18.00
Indiana Custard, plate, salad; ivory, 7½" 9.50
Indiana Custard, sugar lid, ivory 15.00

Iris, bowl, cereal; crystal, 5" 70.00
Iris, bowl, salad; crystal, ruffled, 9½" 10.00
Iris, bowl, sauce; crystal, ruffled, 5" 8.00
Iris, bowl, soup; irid, 7½" 45.00
Iris, candlestick, irid, pr 40.00
Iris, cup, crystal 12.00
Iris, goblet, cocktail; crystal, 4-oz, 4¼" 20.00
Iris, goblet, wine; irid, 4" 27.50
Iris, lamp shade, crystal, 11½" 40.00
Iris, plate, dinner; crystal, 9" 45.00
Iris, sugar bowl, crystal 9.00
Iris, tumbler, crystal, ftd, 6½" 25.00
Jubilee, bowl, yel, 3-ftd, 8" or 9", ea 195.00
Jubilee, cake tray, pk, hdls, 11" 60.00
Jubilee, cup, pk 35.00
Jubilee, plate, luncheon; yel, 8¾" 15.00
Jubilee, sherbet or champagne, yel, 4¾" 45.00
Lace Edge, bowl, cereal; pk, 6⅜" 15.00
Lace Edge, compote, pk, ftd, w/lid, 7" 40.00
Lace Edge, flower bowl, pk, w/crystal frog................20.00

Lace Edge, plate, salad; pink, 8¼", $18.00.

Lace Edge, tumbler, pk, flat, 5-oz, 3½" 20.00
Laced Edge, bowl, fruit; bl or gr, 4½" 25.00
Laced Edge, bowl, vegetable; bl or gr, 9" 85.00
Laced Edge, creamer, bl or gr 35.00
Laced Edge, plate, dinner; bl or gr, 10" 50.00
Laced Edge, tidbit, bl or gr, 2-tier, 8" & 10"...............75.00
Lake Como, bowl, cereal; wht, 6"...............................18.00
Lake Como, cup, St Denis; wht 20.00
Lake Como, plate, dinner; wht, 9¼" 20.00
Lake Como, platter, wht, 11" 50.00
Laurel, bowl, berry; bl, 5" 12.00
Laurel, bowl, master berry; gr, 9" 16.00
Laurel, bowl, vegetable; gr or ivory, 9¾" 16.00
Laurel, candlestick, gr or ivory, 4", pr.........................27.50
Laurel, cup, bl 18.00
Laurel, plate, salad; gr, 7½" 9.00
Laurel, tea set, gr, child's sz, 14-pc 250.00
Laurel, tumbler, gr, flat, 9-oz, 4½" 37.50
Lincoln Inn, ash tray, blk 11.00
Lincoln Inn, bowl, gr, ftd, 9¼"....................................18.00
Lincoln Inn, goblet, water; bl or red 23.00
Lincoln Inn, nut dish, bl or red, ftd 16.00

Lincoln Inn, plate, bl or red, 12" 30.00
Lincoln Inn, shakers, blk, pr 225.00
Lincoln Inn, vase, bl or red, ftd, 12" 130.00
Lorain, bowl, cereal; yel, 6" 50.00
Lorain, bowl, vegetable; gr, oval, 9¾" 35.00
Lorain, plate, luncheon; yel, 8⅜" 24.00
Lorain, plate, sherbet; gr, 5½"......................................6.00
Lorain, platter, gr, 11½"...22.00
Lorain, sherbet, yel, ftd 27.00
Lorain, sugar bowl, yel, ftd..19.00
Madrid, ash tray, amber, sq, 6" 180.00
Madrid, bowl, soup; gr, 7" 15.00
Madrid, bowl, vegetable; pk, oval, 10" 14.00
Madrid, butter dish, amber, w/lid................................62.00
Madrid, cookie jar, pk, w/lid 28.00
Madrid, jam dish, bl, 7" 30.00
Madrid, pitcher, amber, 80-oz, 8½" 55.00
Madrid, pitcher, juice; amber, 36-oz, 5½" 35.00
Madrid, plate, dinner; amber, 10½" 30.00
Madrid, plate, sherbet; pk or gr, 6" 3.00
Madrid, platter, bl, oval, 11½" 20.00
Madrid, sugar lid, gr 35.00
Madrid, tumbler, amber, ftd, 5-oz, 4" 22.00
Manhattan, bowl, cereal; crystal, 5½" 25.00
Manhattan, bowl, fruit; pk, closed hdls, 9½" 30.00
Manhattan, candlestick, crystal, 4½", pr.....................12.00
Manhattan, compote, pk, 5¾" 25.00
Manhattan, plate, dinner; pk, 10¼" 85.00
Manhattan, plate, salad; crystal, 8½" 16.00
Manhattan, sherbet, crystal 7.00
Manhattan, tray, relish; pk, w/5 inserts, 14" 45.00
Mayfair, bowl, bl, low/flat, 11¾" 55.00
Mayfair, bowl, cereal; bl, 5½" 40.00
Mayfair, bowl, fruit; pk, deep, 12" 45.00
Mayfair, bowl, vegetable; bl, oval, 9½" 50.00
Mayfair, bowl, vegetable; gr, 7".................................110.00
Mayfair, bowl, vegetable; pk, w/lid, 10" 85.00
Mayfair, bowl, vegetable; pk, 10" 20.00
Mayfair, cake plate, gr, ftd, 10" 90.00
Mayfair, cake plate, pk, hdls, 12"................................32.00
Mayfair, candy dish, bl, w/lid....................................225.00
Mayfair, celery dish, gr or yel, 10" 95.00
Mayfair, cookie jar, pk, w/lid 40.00
Mayfair, cup, bl 40.00
Mayfair, decanter, pk, w/stopper, 32-oz......................125.00
Mayfair, goblet, cocktail; pk, 3-oz, 4" 65.00
Mayfair, pitcher, bl, 80-oz, 8½" 150.00
Mayfair, platter, gr or yel, closed hdls, oval, 8x12½" 195.00
Mayfair, relish, pk, 4-part, 8⅜".....................................24.00
Mayfair, sherbet, bl, flat, 2¼" 75.00
Mayfair, sherbet, gr or yel, ftd, 4¾" 140.00
Mayfair, tumbler, iced tea; bl, 13½-oz, 5¼" 130.00
Mayfair, tumbler, water; pk, 9-oz, 4¼" 24.00
Mayfair (Federal), bowl, sauce; amber, 5" 7.50
Mayfair (Federal), bowl, vegetable; crystal, oval, 10" 15.00
Mayfair (Federal), cup, amber 7.50
Mayfair (Federal), plate, grill; crystal, 9½" 8.00
Mayfair (Federal), plate, salad; gr, 6¾"..........................8.00
Mayfair (Federal), platter, gr, oval, 12" 25.00
Mayfair (Federal), tumbler, crystal, 9-oz, 4½" 12.00
Miss America, bowl, berry; gr, 6¼" 10.00
Miss America, bowl, crystal, curved in at top, 8" 35.00
Miss America, cake plate, crystal, ftd, 12" 22.50
Miss America, compote, pk, 5" 20.00

Miss America, creamer, red, ftd............155.00
Miss America, cup, pk 19.00
Miss America, goblet, water; crystal, 10-oz, 5½"......20.00
Miss America, plate, salad; pk, 8½"......19.00
Miss America, sherbet, crystal 7.00
Miss America, tumbler, iced tea; pk, 14-oz, 5¾"......65.00
Miss America, tumbler, juice; pk, 5-oz, 4"......40.00
Miss America, tumbler, water; gr, 10-oz, 4½"......16.00
Moderntone, ash tray, cobalt, w/match holder center, 7¾" 115.00
Moderntone, bowl, cream soup; amethyst, ruffled, 5"......18.00
Moderntone, bowl, cream soup; cobalt, 4¾"......17.00
Moderntone, bowl, soup; amethyst, 7½"......80.00
Moderntone, butter dish, cobalt, w/metal lid......85.00
Moderntone, cup, amethyst 9.00
Moderntone, plate, salad; amethyst, 6¾" 8.00
Moderntone, plate, sandwich; cobalt, 10½"......40.00
Moderntone, shakers, cobalt, pr......35.00
Moderntone, tumbler, amethyst, 9-oz......22.00
Moderntone, tumbler, cobalt, 12-oz......80.00
Moondrops, bottle, scent; bl or red, rocket style 195.00
Moondrops, bowl, berry; bl, 5¼"......11.00
Moondrops, bowl, console; gr or pk, rnd, 3-ftd, 12"......30.00
Moondrops, bowl, soup; bl or red, 6¾"......70.00
Moondrops, butter dish lid, blk......250.00
Moondrops, candlestick, bl or red, 3-light, 5¼", pr......90.00
Moondrops, creamer, pk or gr, 3¾"......15.00
Moondrops, decanter, pk or gr, rocket style, 10¼"......200.00
Moondrops, goblet, bl or red, 8-oz, 5¾"......30.00
Moondrops, goblet, water; pk or gr, w/metal stem, 6¼"......15.00
Moondrops, goblet, wine; pk or gr, 4-oz, 4"......12.00
Moondrops, pitcher, blk, w/lip, lg, 50-oz, 8" 110.00
Moondrops, plate, luncheon; bl or red, 8½"......14.00
Moondrops, plate, sherbet; bl or red, 6⅛" 6.00
Moondrops, platter, bl or red, oval, 12"......30.00
Moondrops, powder jar, bl or red, 3-ftd......135.00
Moondrops, sherbet, pk or gr, 2⅝"......10.00
Moondrops, sugar bowl, bl or red, 4"......15.00
Moondrops, tumbler, bl or red, 8-oz, 4⅜"......15.00
Moondrops, tumbler, pk or gr, 9-oz, 4⅞"......14.00
Moondrops, vase, bl or red, flat, ruffled top, 7¾" 55.00
Moondrops, vase, blk, rocket style, 9¼"......115.00
Moonstone, bowl, berry; opal, 5½"......15.00
Moonstone, bowl, opal, flat, 7¾"......11.00
Moonstone, goblet, opal, 10-oz......17.50
Moonstone, plate, luncheon; opal, 8"......12.50
Moonstone, relish, opal, divided, 7¾" 9.50
Moonstone, sherbet, opal, ftd...... 6.50
Moroccan Amethyst, bowl, oval, 7¾"......15.00
Moroccan Amethyst, bowl, 10¾"......25.00
Moroccan Amethyst, goblet, juice; 5½-oz, 4⅜" 8.50
Moroccan Amethyst, plate, sandwich; 12"......10.00
Moroccan Amethyst, tumbler, iced tea; 16-oz, 6½"......15.00
Mt Pleasant, bowl, amethyst, deep, scalloped, ftd, 9"......25.00
Mt Pleasant, bowl, fruit; blk, sq ftd, 4"......17.50
Mt Pleasant, bowl, pk, scalloped, hdls, 8"......17.50
Mt Pleasant, cake plate, blk, hdls, 10½"......35.00
Mt Pleasant, candlestick, cobalt, dbl, pr 40.00
Mt Pleasant, cup, pk or gr...... 8.50
Mt Pleasant, shakers, pk or gr, 2 styles, pr......22.00
Mt Pleasant, sugar bowl, pk or gr 17.50
New Century, ash tray or coaster, gr or crystal, 5⅜"......27.50
New Century, bowl, master berry; gr, 8"......15.00
New Century, cup, cobalt......18.00
New Century, decanter, gr, w/stopper......45.00

New Century, pitcher, cobalt, 60-oz, 7¾"......30.00
New Century, plate, salad; gr, 8½" 8.00
New Century, sugar lid, gr......12.00
New Century, tumbler, gr, 12-oz, 5¼"......20.00
Newport, bowl, berry; amethyst, 4¼"......11.00
Newport, bowl, master berry; amethyst, 8¼"......28.00
Newport, creamer, cobalt......13.00
Newport, cup, amethyst 8.50
Newport, plate, luncheon; cobalt, 8½"......10.00
Newport, shakers, amethyst, pr......37.50
Newport, tumbler, amethyst, 9-oz, 4½"......28.00
No 610 Pyramid, bowl, berry; pk, 4¾"......16.00
No 610 Pyramid, bowl, gr, oval, 9½"......25.00

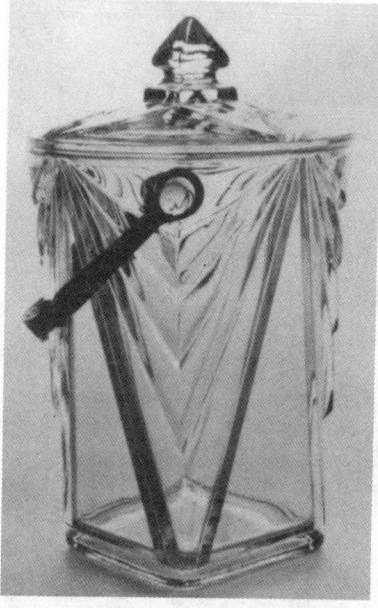

No 610 Pyramid, ice tub, crystal, $50.00.

No 610 Pyramid, pickle dish, pk, 5¾x9½"......28.00
No 610 Pyramid, pitcher, gr......195.00
No 610 Pyramid, relish tray, pk, hdls, 4-part......35.00
No 610 Pyramid, tumbler, crystal, ftd, 11-oz......55.00
No 610 Pyramid, tumbler, gr, ftd, 8-oz......30.00
No 612 Horseshoe, bowl, berry; gr, 4½"......19.00
No 612 Horseshoe, bowl, vegetable; yel, 8½"......25.00
No 612 Horseshoe, creamer, yel, ftd......14.00
No 612 Horseshoe, pitcher, gr, 64-oz, 8½"......220.00
No 612 Horseshoe, plate, sandwich; yel, 11½"......15.00
No 612 Horseshoe, plate, sherbet; yel, 6" 5.00
No 612 Horseshoe, relish, gr, ftd, 3-part 18.00
No 612 Horseshoe, sherbet, yel......14.00
No 612 Horseshoe, tumbler, yel, 12-oz, 4¾"......115.00
No 616 Vernon, creamer, gr, ftd......22.00
No 616 Vernon, plate, sandwich; crystal, 11½"......11.00
No 616 Vernon, plate, sandwich; yel, 11½"......24.00
No 616 Vernon, tumbler, crystal, ftd, 5"......13.00
No 618 Pineapple & Floral, ash tray, amber, 4½"......18.00
No 618 Pineapple & Floral, bowl, berry; crystal, 4¾"......22.00
No 618 Pineapple & Floral, bowl, cereal; crystal, 6"......22.00
No 618 Pineapple & Floral, bowl, cream soup; crystal 18.50
No 618 Pineapple & Floral, bowl, vegetable; amber, oval, 10" 18.00
No 618 Pineapple & Floral, cup, amber 8.00
No 618 Pineapple & Floral, plate, dinner; amber, 8⅜"......13.00
No 618 Pineapple & Floral, plate, salad; crystal, 8⅜" 7.00
No 618 Pineapple & Floral, relish platter, crystal, 11½"......18.00
No 618 Pineapple & Floral, sherbet, amber, ftd......17.50

No 618 Pineapple & Floral, tumbler, crystal, 12-oz, 5" 37.50
No 618 Pineapple & Floral, tumbler, crystal, 8-oz, 4¼" 32.50
No 622 Pretzel, bowl, soup; crystal, 7½" 9.00
No 622 Pretzel, creamer, crystal 4.00
No 622 Pretzel, pickle dish, crystal, hdls, 8½" 5.00
No 622 Pretzel, plate, crystal, indent, sq, 7¼" 8.50
No 622 Pretzel, tumbler, crystal, 5-oz, 3½" 20.00
No 622 Pretzel, tumbler, crystal, 9-oz, 4½" 22.00
Normandie, bowl, berry; amber, 5" 5.00
Normandie, bowl, master berry; pk, 8½" 19.00
Normandie, cup, amber 6.50
Normandie, pitcher, pk, 80-oz, 8" 100.00
Normandie, plate, dinner; pk, 11" 90.00
Normandie, plate, salad; amber, 7¾" 8.00
Normandie, platter, irid, 11¾" 11.00
Normandie, shakers, pk, pr 65.00
Normandie, sugar bowl, irid 6.50
Normandie, tumbler, iced tea; amber, 12-oz, 5" 22.00
Old Cafe, bowl, cereal; red, 5½" 9.00
Old Cafe, bowl, pk, hdls, 5" 4.00
Old Cafe, candy dish, red, low, 8" 10.00
Old Cafe, cup, red 7.00
Old Cafe, lamp, red 22.00
Old Cafe, pitcher, pk, 36-oz, 6" 60.00
Old Cafe, pitcher, pk, 80-oz 80.00
Old Cafe, tumbler, water; pk, 4" 10.00
Old Cafe, vase, red, 7¼" 15.00
Old English, bowl, fruit; any color, ftd, 9" 25.00
Old English, candy dish, any color, flat, w/lid 47.50
Old English, creamer, any color 16.00
Old English, egg cup, crystal 7.50
Old English, goblet, any color, 8-oz, 5¾" 27.50
Old English, sherbet, any color, 2 styles 18.00
Old English, sugar bowl, any color 16.00
Old English, sugar lid, any color 30.00

Old English, vase, fan-type, green, 5⅜", $45.00.

Ovide, bowl, cereal; wht w/decor, 5½" 12.00
Ovide, candy dish, blk, w/lid 40.00
Ovide, creamer, blk 6.00
Ovide, cup, gr 3.00
Ovide, plate, luncheon; wht w/decor, 8" 12.50
Ovide, shakers, gr, pr 25.00
Ovide, sherbet, blk 5.50
Ovide, sugar bowl, blk 6.00
Ovide, tumbler, wht w/decor 16.00
Oyster & Pearl, bowl, red, 1-hdl, 5½" 11.00

Oyster & Pearl, candle holder, red, 3½", pr 40.00
Oyster & Pearl, plate, sandwich; red, 13½" 35.00
Parrot, bowl, berry; gr, 5" 18.00
Parrot, bowl, master berry; amber, 8" 70.00
Parrot, bowl, vegetable; amber, oval, 10" 55.00
Parrot, butter dish, amber, w/lid 1,100.00
Parrot, cup, gr 30.00
Parrot, plate, dinner; gr, 9" 38.00
Parrot, plate, sherbet; amber, 5¾" 15.00
Parrot, platter, gr, oblong, 11¼" 35.00
Parrot, saucer, amber or gr 11.00
Parrot, tumbler, amber, heavy, ftd, 5¾" 105.00
Parrot, tumbler, gr, 10-oz, 4¼" 100.00
Patrician, bowl, cereal; amber, 6" 20.00
Patrician, bowl, cream soup; pk, 4¾" 16.00
Patrician, bowl, master berry; amber, 8½" 40.00
Patrician, bowl, vegetable; gr, oval, 10" 23.00
Patrician, butter dish, gr, w/lid 95.00
Patrician, butter dish, pk, w/lid 195.00
Patrician, cookie jar, amber, w/lid 80.00
Patrician, cup, gr 9.00
Patrician, jam dish, pk 25.00
Patrician, pitcher, amber, molded hdl, 75-oz, 8" 95.00
Patrician, plate, dinner; gr, 10½" 30.00
Patrician, plate, luncheon; amber, 9" 10.00
Patrician, plate, salad; pk, 7½" 14.00
Patrician, saucer, gr 7.50
Patrician, shakers, pk, pr 75.00
Patrician, sugar bowl, amber 7.50
Patrician, sugar lid, gr 48.00
Patrician, tumbler, gr, ftd, 8-oz, 5¼" 45.00
Patrician, tumbler, pk, 14-oz, 5½" 25.00
Patrick, bowl, console; pk, 11" 75.00
Patrick, bowl, fruit; yel, hdls, 9" 40.00
Patrick, cheese & cracker set, pk 85.00
Patrick, cup, yel 15.00
Patrick, goblet, cocktail; pk, 4" 45.00
Patrick, goblet, water; yel, 10-oz, 6" 35.00
Patrick, mayonnaise, pk, 3-pc 125.00
Patrick, plate, salad; yel, 7½" 10.00
Patrick, sugar bowl, pk, 4¾" 35.00
Patrick, tray, yel, hdls, 11" 35.00
Petalware, bowl, berry; pk, 9" 12.50
Petalware, bowl, cereal; floral w/red trim, 5¾" 27.50
Petalware, cup, pk 6.00
Petalware, pitcher, crystal, bands decor, 80-oz 22.00
Petalware, plate, salad; 8" 8.00
Petalware, plate, salver; monax, 12" 17.50
Petalware, sherbet, monax, low, ftd, 4½" 6.00
Primo, bowl, yel or gr, 7¾" 18.00
Primo, cake plate, yel or gr, 3-ftd, 10" 18.00
Primo, plate, grill; yel or gr, 10" 8.50
Primo, plate, yel or gr, 7½" 7.00
Primo, sherbet, yel or gr 8.50
Princess, bowl, berry; pk, 4½" 16.00
Princess, bowl, cereal; topaz, 5" 26.00
Princess, bowl, vegetable; pk, oval, 10" 17.50
Princess, candy dish, gr, w/lid 45.00
Princess, pitcher, pk, ftd, 24-oz, 7⅜" 425.00
Princess, pitcher, pk, 37-oz, 6" 38.00
Princess, plate, dinner; topaz, 9½" 14.00
Princess, plate, grill; gr, 9" 11.00
Princess, platter, topaz, closed hdls, 12" 50.00
Princess, relish, pk, divided, 7½" 20.00

Princess, shakers, spice; gr, 5½" 37.50
Princess, sherbet, gr, ftd 18.00
Princess, sugar bowl, topaz, open 8.00
Princess, tumbler, gr, sq, ftd, 9-oz, 4¾" 55.00
Princess, tumbler, iced tea; gr, 13-oz, 5¼" 32.00
Princess, tumbler, juice; pk, 5-oz, 3" 19.00
Princess, tumbler, pk, ftd, 10-oz, 5¼" 19.00
Princess, tumbler, water; topaz, 9-oz, 4" 20.00
Princess, vase, pk, 8" 25.00
Queen Mary, bowl, berry; pk, 5" 5.00
Queen Mary, bowl, cereal; pk, 6" 20.00
Queen Mary, butter dish, crystal, w/lid 20.00
Queen Mary, candy dish, pk, w/lid 30.00
Queen Mary, coaster, pk, sq, 4¼" 5.00
Queen Mary, compote, crystal, 5¾" 6.00
Queen Mary, creamer, pk, ftd 17.50
Queen Mary, cup, crystal 5.00
Queen Mary, pickle dish, crystal, 5x10" 8.00
Queen Mary, plate, dinner; crystal, 9¾" 12.50
Queen Mary, relish tray, pk, 3-part, 12" 12.00
Queen Mary, sugar bowl, pk, ftd, open 17.50
Queen Mary, tumbler, crystal, ftd, 10-oz, 5" 24.00
Radiance, bonbon, amber, ftd, 6" 10.00
Radiance, bonbon, bl or red, w/lid, 6" 45.00
Radiance, bowl, amber, crimped, 12" 25.00
Radiance, butter dish, bl or red 395.00
Radiance, candlestick, bl or red, 8", pr 55.00
Radiance, compote, amber, 6" 18.00
Radiance, creamer, bl or red 20.00
Radiance, cup, bl or red 15.00
Radiance, cup, punch; amber................................. 6.00
Radiance, goblet, cordial; bl or red, 1-oz 35.00
Radiance, plate, luncheon; amber, 8" 9.00
Radiance, shakers, bl or red, pr.............................75.00
Radiance, tumbler, amber, 9-oz 16.00
Radiance, vase, bl or red, flared, 10" 50.00
Raindrops, bowl, cereal; gr, 6" 6.50
Raindrops, sherbet, gr 6.00
Raindrops, sugar bowl, gr, open 6.00
Raindrops, sugar bowl lid, gr 35.00
Raindrops, tumbler, gr, 10-oz, 5" 8.50
Ribbon, bowl, cereal; gr, 5" 13.50
Ribbon, candy dish, gr, w/lid 32.50
Ribbon, cup, gr.. 4.00
Ribbon, plate, luncheon; gr, 8" 4.00
Ribbon, shakers, blk, pr.......................................37.50
Ribbon, sherbet, gr, ftd 4.50
Ring, bowl, berry; crystal w/decor, 5" 4.50
Ring, butter tub or ice tub, crystal w/decor 27.50
Ring, cocktail shaker, crystal.................................17.50
Ring, pitcher, crystal w/decor, 80-oz, 8½" 27.50
Ring, plate, luncheon; crystal w/decor, 8" 4.00
Ring, shakers, crystal w/decor, 3", pr 32.00
Ring, sherbet, crystal, ftd, 4¾" 4.50
Ring, tumbler, crystal, 10-oz, 4¾" 7.00
Ring, tumbler, iced tea; crystal, ftd, 6½" 6.50
Ring, tumbler, juice; crystal w/decor, ftd, 3½" 7.00
Ring, vase, crystal w/decor, 8" 30.00
Rock Crystal, bonbon, red, scalloped edge, 7½" 47.50
Rock Crystal, bowl, crystal, scalloped edge, 5".......13.50
Rock Crystal, bowl, salad; red, scalloped edge, 7" ...50.00
Rock Crystal, butter dish, crystal, w/lid 300.00
Rock Crystal, cake stand, red, ftd, 2¾x11" 95.00
Rock Crystal, candelabra, red, 2-light, pr 185.00

Rock Crystal, candlestick, crystal, tall, 8", pr..........60.00
Rock Crystal, cruet, oil; crystal, w/stopper, 6-oz 75.00
Rock Crystal, lamp, electric; red 500.00
Rock Crystal, pitcher, crystal, w/lid, 9" 150.00
Rock Crystal, plate, dinner; red, scalloped edge, 10½" 45.00
Rock Crystal, relish, red, 2-part, 11½" 60.00
Rock Crystal, server, sandwich; red, center hdl 90.00
Rock Crystal, shakers, crystal, 2 styles, pr 67.50
Rock Crystal, stemware, wine; crystal, 3-oz..............17.00
Rock Crystal, tumbler, old fashioned; red, 5-oz 50.00
Rock Crystal, vase, red, ftd, 11" 135.00
Rose Cameo, bowl, berry; gr, 4½" 7.50

Rose Cameo, plate, salad; green, 7", $7.50.

Rose Cameo, sherbet, gr 9.50
Rosemary, bowl, berry; gr, 5" 7.00
Rosemary, bowl, cereal; gr, 6" 25.00
Rosemary, bowl, cream soup; pk, 5" 20.00
Rosemary, bowl, vegetable; oval, 10" 12.50
Rosemary, creamer, pk, ftd 14.00
Rosemary, plate, grill; gr 12.00
Rosemary, platter, amber, oval, 12" 13.00
Rosemary, platter, pk, oval, 12" 25.00
Rosemary, sugar bowl, pk, ftd 15.00
Rosemary, tumbler, amber, 9-oz, 4¼" 25.00
Roulette, cup, crystal 35.00
Roulette, pitcher, pk or gr, 65-oz, 8" 30.00
Roulette, plate, sandwich; pk or gr, 12" 10.00
Roulette, tumbler, juice; crystal, 5-oz, 3¼" 6.50
Roulette, tumbler, old fashioned; pk or gr, 7½-oz 35.00
Roulette, tumbler, pk or gr, ftd, 10-oz, 5½" 22.00
Roulette, whiskey, crystal, 1½-oz, 2½" 6.50
Round Robin, bowl, berry; gr, 4" 4.50
Round Robin, creamer, gr, ftd 6.50
Round Robin, cup, gr, ftd 4.50
Round Robin, plate, sandwich; irid, 12"................... 6.50
Round Robin, sherbet, gr....................................... 4.50
Round Robin, sugar bowl, irid, open 5.50
Roxana, bowl, berry; yel, 5" 6.00
Roxana, bowl, yel, 4½x2⅜" 8.00
Roxana, plate, sherbet; yel, 6" 4.00
Roxana, tumbler, yel, 9-oz, 4¼" 14.00
Royal Lace, bowl, berry; bl, 5" 38.00
Royal Lace, bowl, gr, rolled edge, 3-ftd, 10" 65.00

Royal Lace, bowl, master berry; gr, rnd, 10" 25.00
Royal Lace, bowl, nut; bl 350.00
Royal Lace, butter dish, bl, w/lid...475.00
Royal Lace, candlestick, crystal, ruffled edge, pr........................25.00
Royal Lace, candlestick, pk, rolled edge, pr 45.00
Royal Lace, pitcher, bl, 64-oz, 8"...135.00
Royal Lace, plate, dinner; gr, 9⅞" 20.00
Royal Lace, shakers, pk, pr...50.00
Royal Lace, sherbet, crystal, ftd 8.50
Royal Lace, sugar lid, bl 125.00
Royal Lace, tumbler, bl, 12-oz, 5⅜"..60.00
Royal Lace, tumbler, pk, 9-oz, 4⅛"...14.00
Royal Ruby, bowl, berry; red, 3¾" 4.50
Royal Ruby, creamer, red, ftd 8.50
Royal Ruby, plate, luncheon; red, 8½" 7.00
Royal Ruby, sugar bowl, red, ftd, open 6.50
Royal Ruby, sugar lid, red 9.00
Royal Ruby, tumbler, juice; red, 3" 7.50
Royal Ruby, vase, red, 2 styles, 9"...15.00
Sandwich (Hocking), bowl, crystal, ruffled, 4⅞" 12.50
Sandwich (Hocking), bowl, Desert Gold, smooth, 6½" 12.00
Sandwich (Hocking), bowl, Forest Green, scalloped, 5¼" 18.00
Sandwich (Hocking), bowl, punch; crystal, 9¾" 15.00
Sandwich (Hocking), bowl, red, scalloped, 8" 35.00
Sandwich (Hocking), bowl, salad; Desert Gold, 9" 27.50
Sandwich (Hocking), bowl, salad; Forest Green, 7" 50.00
Sandwich (Hocking), creamer, pk..20.00
Sandwich (Hocking), pitcher, juice; crystal, 6" 50.00
Sandwich (Hocking), plate, crystal, 8".. 3.00
Sandwich (Hocking), plate, dinner; Forest Green, 9" 62.50
Sandwich (Hocking), sugar bowl, crystal, w/lid............................14.50
Sandwich (Hocking), tumbler, crystal, ftd, 9-oz 7.50
Sandwich (Hocking), tumbler, juice; Forest Green, 5-oz 3.50
Sandwich (Indiana), bowl, pk, 6" 3.50
Sandwich (Indiana), bowl, pk, 8¼" 10.00
Sandwich (Indiana), butter dish, teal, w/lid 150.00
Sandwich (Indiana), creamer, red..40.00
Sandwich (Indiana), cruet, teal, w/stopper, 6½-oz 130.00
Sandwich (Indiana), decanter, pk, w/stopper 100.00
Sandwich (Indiana), goblet, red, 9-oz 40.00
Sandwich (Indiana), pitcher, red, 68-oz 125.00
Sandwich (Indiana), plate, dinner; pk, 10½" 17.50
Sandwich (Indiana), plate, luncheon; red, 8⅜" 17.50
Sandwich (Indiana), sugar bowl, amber, lg, open 8.50
Sandwich (Indiana), tumbler, iced tea; crystal, ftd, 12-oz 9.50
Sharon, bowl, cereal; pk, 6"..18.00
Sharon, bowl, cream soup; amber, 5" 22.50
Sharon, bowl, fruit; pk, 10½"..28.00
Sharon, bowl, vegetable; gr, oval, 9½" 22.00
Sharon, butter dish, gr, w/lid...75.00
Sharon, cheese dish, amber, w/lid 175.00
Sharon, jam dish, gr, 7½" 35.00
Sharon, pitcher, gr, w/ice lip, 80-oz 325.00
Sharon, plate, cake; gr, ftd, 11½"..50.00
Sharon, plate, salad; pk, 7½" 18.00
Sharon, platter, gr, oval, 12½"...20.00
Sharon, shakers, amber, pr..37.50
Sharon, tumbler, amber, ftd, 15-oz, 6½"...85.00
Sharon, tumbler, gr, thick, 9-oz, 4⅛"..55.00
Sharon, tumbler, pk, thick, 12-oz, 5¼"...65.00
Ships, cocktail shaker, bl w/wht decor 27.50
Ships, ice bowl, bl w/wht decor 27.50
Ships, pitcher, bl w/wht decor, 86-oz 40.00
Ships, plate, dinner; bl w/wht decor, 9"...25.00

Ships, tumbler, iced tea; bl w/wht decor, 10½-oz..........................12.00
Ships, tumbler, juice; bl w/wht decor, 5-oz, 3¾"........................... 9.50
Ships, tumbler, old fashioned; bl w/wht decor, 8-oz.....................14.00
Sierra, bowl, cereal; pk, 5½" 9.50
Sierra, bowl, vegetable; gr, oval, 9¼" 80.00
Sierra, cup, pk 9.50
Sierra, plate, dinner; gr, 9" 16.00
Sierra, platter, gr, oval, 11"...37.50
Sierra, shakers, pk, pr..35.00
Sierra, sugar bowl, gr, open...20.00
Sierra, tumbler, pk, ftd, 9-oz, 4½"...37.50
Spiral, bowl, berry; gr, 4¾" 4.50
Spiral, creamer, gr, flat or ftd 7.00
Spiral, pitcher, gr, 58-oz, 7⅝"...27.50
Spiral, plate, luncheon; gr, 8" 3.00
Spiral, platter, gr, 12"...20.00
Spiral, shakers, gr, pr...27.50
Spiral, tumbler, water; gr, 9-oz, 5" 7.00
Starlight, bowl, cereal; wht, closed hdls, 5½" 6.00
Starlight, bowl, pk, closed hdls, 8½"...13.00

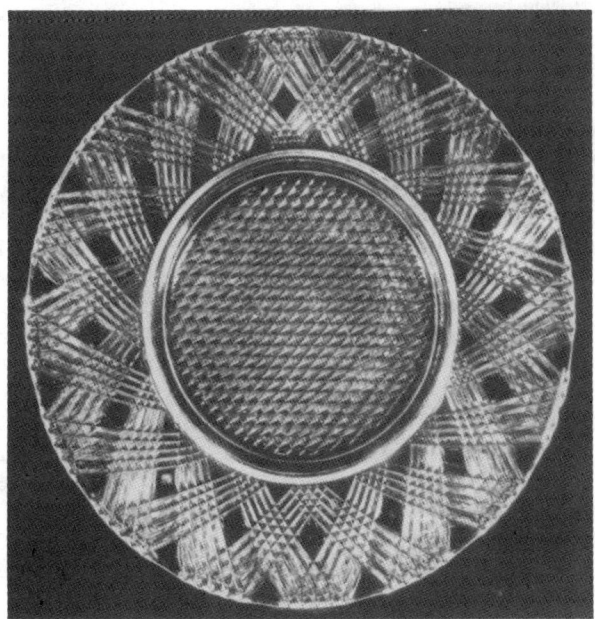

Starlight, plate, dinner; white, 9", $6.00.

Starlight, plate, luncheon; wht, 8½" 3.00
Starlight, plate, sandwich; pk, 13"..13.00
Starlight, shakers, wht, pr...20.00
Starlight, sherbet, wht 11.00
Strawberry, bowl, berry; irid, 4" 6.00
Strawberry, bowl, pk or gr, deep, 6¼"..60.00
Strawberry, butter dish, crystal, w/lid...130.00
Strawberry, creamer, pk or gr, 4⅝"..30.00
Strawberry, plate, salad; crystal, 7½" 8.00
Strawberry, sugar bowl, pk or gr, sm, open 15.00
Strawberry, tumbler, pk or gr, 8-oz, 3⅝".......................................25.00
Sunflower, ash gray, gr, center design, 5".......................................11.00
Sunflower, cup, gr 11.00
Sunflower, saucer, pk 6.00
Sunflower, sugar bowl, gr, open..16.00
Sunflower, tumbler, pk, ftd, 8-oz, 4¾"..22.00
Swirl, bowl, salad; pk, rimmed, 9" 15.00
Swirl, bowl, ultramarine, closed hdls, ftd, 10"...............................25.00
Swirl, butter dish, ultramarine, w/lid...235.00

Swirl, candle holder, delphite, 1-light, pr 100.00
Swirl, plate, sandwich; pk, 12½" 10.00
Swirl, plate, ultramarine, 7¼" 10.00
Swirl, platter, delphite, oval, 12" 30.00
Swirl, tray, delphite, hdls, 10½" 22.50
Swirl, tumbler, ultramarine, ftd, 9-oz 30.00
Tea Room, bowl, banana split; pk, flat, 7½" 72.00
Tea Room, celery dish, gr, 8¼" 27.50
Tea Room, marmalade, gr, w/lid 177.50
Tea Room, mustard, pk, w/lid 110.00
Tea Room, plate, luncheon; pk, 8¼" 25.00
Tea Room, relish, gr, divided 20.00
Tea Room, sugar bowl, gr, flat, w/lid 165.00
Tea Room, sugar bowl, pk, w/lid, 3" 95.00
Tea Room, sundae, pk, ruffled top, ftd 65.00
Tea Room, tumbler, gr, ftd, 6-oz 30.00
Tea Room, tumbler, pk, ftd, 12-oz 45.00
Tea Room, vase, gr, str sides, 9½" 55.00
Thistle, bowl, cereal; pk, 5½" 18.00
Thistle, bowl, fruit; gr, 10¼" 150.00
Thistle, plate, cake; gr, 13" 125.00
Thistle, plate, luncheon; pk, 8" 10.00
Thumbprint, creamer, gr, ftd 11.50
Thumbprint, plate, dinner; gr, 9¼" 6.00
Thumbprint, shakers, gr, pr 22.50
Thumbprint, sugar bowl, gr, ftd 11.50
Thumbprint, tumbler, 5-oz, 4" 5.00
Twisted Optic, bowl, cream soup; pk or gr, 9¾" 10.00
Twisted Optic, mayonnaise, pk or gr 18.00
Twisted Optic, pitcher, pk or gr, 64-oz 27.50
Twisted Optic, plate, pk or gr, oval w/indent, 7½x9" 4.50
Twisted Optic, plate, salad; pk or gr, 7" 2.50
Twisted Optic, preserve bowl, pk or gr, w/lid 25.00
Twisted Optic, server, sandwich; pk or gr, open center hdl 18.00
US Swirl, bowl, berry; pk, 4⅜" 6.00
US Swirl, bowl, gr, 1-hdl, 5½" 9.00
US Swirl, butter dish, gr, w/lid 62.50
US Swirl, candy dish, gr, hdld, w/lid 25.00
US Swirl, creamer, gr 10.00
US Swirl, pitcher, pk, 48-oz, 8" 40.00
US Swirl, shakers, gr, pr 40.00
US Swirl, sugar bowl, gr or pk, w/lid 27.50
US Swirl, tumbler, pk, 12-oz, 4⅝" 12.00
US Swirl, vase, gr, 6½" 15.00
Victory, bowl, cereal; bl or blk, 6½" 25.00
Victory, bowl, console; bl or blk, 12" 60.00
Victory, bowl, vegetable; pk or gr, oval, 9" 27.50
Victory, creamer, bl or blk 40.00
Victory, gravy boat, bl or blk, w/liner 280.00
Victory, plate, luncheon; pk or gr, 8" 6.00
Victory, platter, bl or blk, 12" 60.00
Victory, sherbet, pk or gr, ftd 12.00
Victory, sugar bowl, bl or blk 40.00
Vitrock, bowl, cream soup; wht, 5½" 14.00
Vitrock, bowl, vegetable; wht, 9½" 10.00
Vitrock, plate, dinner; wht, 10" 6.00
Vitrock, plate, luncheon; wht, 8¾" 4.00
Waterford, ash tray, crystal, 4" 6.50
Waterford, bowl, cereal; pk, 5½" 22.00
Waterford, butter dish, pk, w/lid 195.00
Waterford, coaster, crystal, 4" 3.00
Waterford, creamer, pk, Miss America style 8.50
Waterford, goblet, crystal, 5¼" 14.00
Waterford, goblet, pk, Miss America style, 5½" 75.00

Waterford, pitcher, pk, tilted ice lip, 80-oz 125.00
Waterford, plate, sandwich; pk, 13¾" 22.00
Waterford, saucer, pk 4.00
Waterford, shakers, crystal, 2 styles, pr 8.00
Waterford, tumbler, juice; pk, Miss America style, 5-oz 55.00
Windsor, ash tray, gr, 5¾" 42.00
Windsor, bowl, berry; crystal, 4¾" 3.00
Windsor, bowl, cereal; pk, 5⅛" 16.00
Windsor, bowl, fruit console; pk, 12½" 95.00
Windsor, bowl, vegetable; gr, oval, 9½" 20.00
Windsor, candlestick, pk, 3", pr 70.00
Windsor, candy jar, crystal, w/lid 15.00
Windsor, coaster, gr, 3¼" 15.00
Windsor, creamer, pk 9.50
Windsor, pitcher, gr, 52-oz, 6¾" 45.00
Windsor, plate, chop; gr, 13⅝" 40.00
Windsor, plate, salad; crystal, 7" 3.50
Windsor, powder jar, pk 50.00
Windsor, relish platter, pk, divided, 11½" 175.00
Windsor, sherbet, crystal, ftd 3.00
Windsor, sugar bowl, gr, w/lid 25.00
Windsor, tray, gr, 8½x9¾" 35.00
Windsor, tray, pk, 4⅛x9" 45.00
Windsor, tumbler, crystal, 5-oz, 3¼" 7.50

Derby

William Duesbury operated in Derby, England, from about 1755, purchasing a second establishment, The Chelsea Works, in 1769. During this period fine porcelains were produced which so impressed the King that in 1773 he issued the company the Crown Derby patent. In 1810, several years after Duesbury's death, the factory was bought by Robert Bloor. The quality of the ware suffered under the new management, and the main Derby pottery closed in 1848. Within a short time, the work was revived by a dedicated number of former employees who established their own works on King Street in Derby.

The earliest-known Derby mark was the crown over a script 'D'; however this mark is rarely found today. Soon after 1782, that mark was augmented with a device of crossed batons and six dots, usually applied in underglaze blue. During the Bloor period, the crown was centered within a ring containing the words 'Bloor' above and 'Derby' below the crown, or with a red printed stamp — the crowned Gothic 'D.' The King Street plant produced figurines that may be distinguished from their earlier counterparts by the presence of an 'S' and 'H' on either side of the crown and crossed batons.

In 1876 a new pottery was constructed in Derby, and the owners revived the earlier company's former standard of excellence. The Queen bestowed the firm the title Royal Crown Derby in 1890; it still operates under that name today. See also Royal Crown Derby.

Basket, flower encrusted sides/hdls, oval, 1825, 8¾" L 850.00
Box, dove on foliage-encrusted nest, purple/wht, 1800, 8" 800.00
Cup, head of nymph mold, fruiting vines in hair, 1815, 3¾" 300.00
Cup & saucer, exotic bird, Kakiemon palette, 1815 ....80.00
Cup & saucer, handleless; vines, underglaze bl, ribbed mk 215.00
Figurine, cow, recumbent calf by flowering tree, 1800, 4½" 210.00
Figurine, ewe w/suckling lamb, 1770s, 5", EX 550.00
Figurine, lady w/basket & flowers, seated, 1830, 5", EX 240.00
Figurine, recumbent cat, wht w/gold collar, 1820, 2¼" L 300.00
Flowerpot & stand, florals/gold bands/scroll hdls, 1810, VG 160.00
Plate, alternate panels of Buddhistic lions & flowers, 8¾" 180.00
Plate, exotic bird, Kakiemon palette, 7" 45.00
Plate, Imari decor, gilt w/minor wear, 7", pr 100.00

Sauce dish, bl/gilt border w/3 floral reserves, paw ft, 7" 235.00
Tray, mc floral rim w/gilt, red crown mk, 11" 65.00
Vase, campana; View in Cumberland, snake hdls, 1820s, 6½" 350.00
Vase, scenic reserves on dk bl, gilt hdls, 1850s, 7", pr 450.00

Plate, hawk center, gold and blue border, crown mark, 9½", $325.00.

Desert Sands

As early as the 1850s, the Evans family living in the Ozark Mountains of Missouri produced domestic clay products. Their small pot shop was passed on from one generation to the next. In the 1920s it was moved to North Las Vegas, Nevada, where the name Desert Sands was adopted. Succeeding generations of the family continued to relocate, taking the business with them. From 1937 to 1962 it operated in Boulder City, Nevada; then it was moved to Barstow where it remained until it closed in the late 1970s.

Desert Sands pottery is similar to Mission Ware by Niloak. Various mineral oxides were blended to mimic the naturally occuring sand formations of the American West. A high-gloss glaze was applied to add intensity to the colorful striations that characterize the ware. Not all examples are marked, making it sometimes difficult to attribute. Marked items carry an ink stamp with the Desert Sands designation. Paper labels were also used.

Bowl, swirled colors, ped base, w/lid, 8" 65.00
Bowl, swirled colors, 2½x4½" 10.00
Bowl, swirled colors, 4½" 10.00
Candle holder vase, brn & wht swirl, 5" 22.50
Cup & saucer, swirled colors 25.00
Mug, swirled colors 22.50
Plate, swirled colors, 8" 15.00

Salt and pepper shakers, $25.00 for the pair.

Tumbler, swirled colors...10.00
Vase, swirled colors, cactus ink mk, 7"......................................28.00
Vase, swirled colors, 3½x3" 15.00
Vase, swirled colors, 5" 20.00

Devon, Crown Devon

Devon and Crown Devon were trade names of S. Fielding and Company, Ltd., an English firm founded about 1879. They produced majolica, earthenware mugs, vases, and kitchenware. In the 1930s they manufactured an exceptional line of Art Deco vases that have recently been much in demand.

Box, music; Harry Lauder, couple on lid, 1930s, 2½x4x6" 175.00
Jug, musical, Auld Lang Syne, 7x5½" 195.00
Mug, musical, John Peel, tankard, 6x4½" 165.00
Mug, musical, John Peel & hunt scene, mk, 7¾x5¾"....................195.00
Mug, musical, May Dance, 6¾x5⅜" 165.00

Dickota

The Dickota Pottery, a name coined from Dickinson, North Dakota, where it was founded as a brickyard, began operations in the early 1930s. In 1934 potters formerly associated with the North Dakota School of Mines and Charles Hyten from Niloak began their own operation there. Hyten developed a line of swirled ware which was marked 'Dickota Badlands.' Vases, bowls, and ash trays in a mottled glaze were also made. A variety of marks were used, all of which contain the Dickota name. The company closed in the late 1930s. Our advisor for this category is David Gifford; he is listed in the Directory under Arkansas.

Ash tray, cowboy hat, advertising 45.00
Ash tray, horseshoe form, advertising creamery products..............38.00
Bookends, ram form, pr..90.00
Paperweight, elephant, solid form, gr 90.00
Pitcher, bl, w/ice lip, 8" 50.00

Pitcher, blue mottled, 5", $35.00.

Vase, Badlands, mc swirled clay, 5"..35.00
Vase, Badlands, mc swirls, sgn Howard Lewis, 6¾" 100.00
Vase, bud; pk, 6½" 30.00
Vase, mauve, flat fan shape w/scallops, 4½"................................33.00
Vase, pk, hdls, 3x5"...30.00

Documents

Although the word 'document' is defined in the general sense as 'anything printed or written, etc., relied upon to record or prove something. . .,' in the collectibles market, the term is more diversified with broadsides, billheads, checks, invoices, letters and letterheads, land grants, receipts, and waybills some of the most sought after. Some documents in demand are those related to a specific subject such as advertising, mining, railroads, military, politics, banking, slavery, nautical, or legal (deeds, mortgages, etc.). Other collectors look for examples representing a specific period of time such as colonial documents, Revolutionary, or Civil War documents, early western documents or those from a specific region, state, or city.

Aside from supply and demand, there are five major factors which determine the collector-value of a document. These are:

1) Age — Documents from the eastern half of the country can be found that date back to the 1700s or earlier. Most documents sought by collectors usually date from 1800 to 1900. Those with twentieth century dates are still abundant and not in demand unless of special significance or beauty.

2) Region of origin — Depending on age, documents from rural and less-populated areas are harder to find than those from major cities and heavily populated states. The colonization of the West and Mid-West did not begin until after 1850, so while an 1870s billhead from New York or Chicago is common, one from Albuquerque or Phoenix is not, since most of the Southwest was still unsettled.

3) Attractiveness — Some documents are plain and unadorned, but collectors prefer colorful, profusely illustrated pieces. Additional artwork and engravings add to the value.

4) Historical content — Unusual or interesting content, such as a letter written by a Civil War soldier giving an eye-witness account of the Battle of Gettysburg or a western territorial billhead listing numerous animal hides purchased from a trapper, will sell for more than one with mundane information.

5) Condition — Through neglect or environmental conditions, over many decades paper articles can become stained, torn, or deteriorated. Heavily damaged or stained documents are generally avoided altogether while those with minor problems are more acceptable, although their value will decrease anywhere from 20% to 50% depending upon the extent of damage. Avoid attempting to repair tears with scotch tape — sell 'as is' so that the collector can take proper steps toward restoration.

Foreign documents are plentiful; and, though some are very attractive, resale may be difficult. The listings that follow are generalized; prices are variable depending entirely upon the five points noted above. Values here are based upon examples with no major damage. Our advisor for this category is Warren Anderson; he is listed in the Directory under Utah.

Key: illus — illustrated   vgn — vignette

Annuity, sgn Young King, Seneca Indian chief, 1822, EX...........**385.00**
Appointment, to West Point, sgn WW Belknap, 1875, 3-pg.........**42.00**
Arrest warrant, PA, 1859, VG..**45.00**
Auction, NH, personal property, 1838, 8x10", VG **32.00**
Baggage report, VA & Truckee RR, gives destination, 1876 ....**12.50**
Bill of lading, MT, Ft Benton to Ft Shaw, train vgn, 1879 ....**35.00**
Bill of sale, LA, 20 slave names & ages, 8x14", VG.....................**72.50**
Billhead, Streacy & Gregg Blksmithing, service costs, 1881 ....**15.00**
Certificate, CA, Grand Circle/Women of Woodcraft, '02, 11x17" ..**30.00**
Certificate, MT brand, 1927.. **8.00**
Check, Apalachicola FL, steamship vgn, 1852, 9x4½", VG **25.00**
Check, AZ, La Fortuna Mining Co, cactus vgn, 1900, EX **15.00**
Check, CO, Bank of Ouray, Ute Indian vgn, 1904, 4x9", EX **25.00**
Check, HI, sgn by 1st governor, 1922, VG **52.00**
Check, OR & CA RR, sgn Holladay, Portland, 1870, 3x9", EX .**250.00**
Check, UT Territory, Wells Fargo Bankers, 1877 ....**30.00**
Code card, homographic signals/instructions, ca 1885 ....**15.00**
Commission, Confederate becomes corporal, 1862, 12x15", EX....**55.00**

Commission, lieutenant in air service, 1924, EX..........................**28.00**
Conviction certificate, MD, stealing & escape, 1830, 8x9" **28.00**
Deed, CO, Roseacrans Lode for $100, 1863, 8x13", 1-pg **75.00**
Deed, NH sale of property, handwritten, 1763, 12x8", EX............**27.50**
Deed, PA, script on parchment, wax seals, 17x25".........................**50.00**
Deed, property for back taxes, 1810, VG **28.00**
Deed, sale of NH land, boundaries/privileges, etc, 1783................**27.50**
Discharge papers, Civil War, 55th PA Regiment, 1865, EX **75.00**
Discharge papers, lists ailments/old age of 42, 1862......................**6.00**
Envelope, CA, Wells Fargo & Co, ca 1855-60, EX......................**30.00**
Estate inventory, handwritten, lists land/buildings/etc, 1783 ....**17.50**
General orders, exchange of prisoners of war, 1865, EX **7.50**
General orders, extension of sick leave, 1862, 1-pg......................**12.50**
Land grant, OH, parchment, Pres Polk (secretary sgn), 1848 ....**85.00**
Land grant, TX, emb land office seal, 1858, 13x15" **75.00**
Ledger, general store accounts, 1878-81, 150-pg, EX....................**25.00**
Letter, Blk Bird Mining & Milling letterhead, 1888, 1-pg **25.00**
Letter, CA Mining & Milling letterhead, 1897, 2-pg, EX............**25.00**
Letter, Civil War soldier, camp news, 4-pg, 1862 ....**22.50**
Letter, Ft Schuler, soldier's news, handwritten, 1864, 3-pg...........**30.00**
Letter, GA, guardianship of orphans, emb seal, 1863, 7x12" **42.50**
Letter, GA, soldier's war news to sister, 1862, 4-pg......................**30.00**
Letter, GA to ME, lumber purchase concerns, 1867, 3-pg, EX **10.00**
Letter, Guthrie city letterhead, to Smith & Wesson, 1928 ....**10.00**
Letter, KS Pacific RR letterhead, handwritten, 1876, 1-pg **60.00**
Letter, Mexico, tourist observations, 1888, 1-pg, EX....................**30.00**
Letter, MT, Am Ranch letterhead, 1909, M................................**12.00**
Letter, news of Lusitania & war, ca 1915, group of 4....................**25.00**
Letter, NM Territory, re mules needed at post, 1869, 1-pg **35.00**
Letter, officer war news on ship America, 1812, 1-pg, VG..........**120.00**
Letter, OR, Office Inspector Indian Supplies, 1875, 8x10" **75.00**
Letter, Paris, w/pass for free movement in city, 1919 ....**38.00**
Letter, RI, state contracts out prisoners, 1852, 3-pg, VG **38.00**
Letter, War Dept concerns of sale of arsenal, 1858, EX................**32.00**
List, cargo & prices for schooner & owners, 1879, 14x16"............**10.00**
List, VA, quartermaster's stores, 5 horses, 1864, 8x10".................... **7.50**
Membership, WA Nat'l Monument Society, 4 vgns, 1850, 7x9"..**150.00**

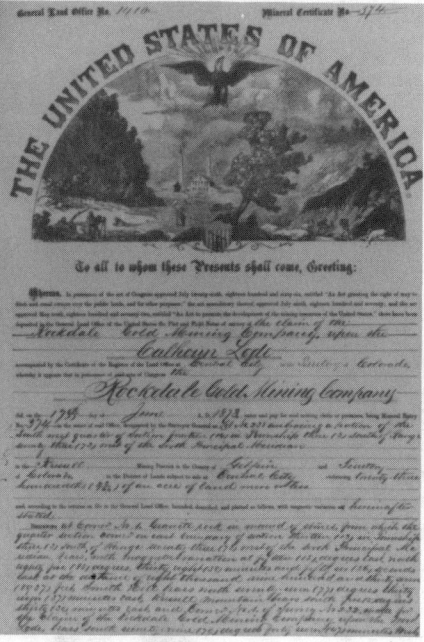

Mineral certificate, Colorado Territory, 1875, $125.00.

Muster roll, FL, confederate prisoners, 1862, 22x21" **150.00**
Notice, NY, Nat'l Banker's Express Co, 1865, 7x10", EX...............**38.00**
Order, ID Territory, Ft Laramie, handwritten, 1864, 1-pg............**45.00**

Pay voucher, NH, soldier's 60 days service, 1815, 7x6", VG 40.00
Pay voucher, officer, lists servant/pay/food/clothing, 1864 .... 5.00
Receipt, Boston, for dry goods, printed, priced, 1872, EX 5.00
Requisition, forage for horses, dtd 1862, VG 12.50
Roster, sick & wounded, 1864, 15x10", VG 100.00
Roster, Spanish Am War, lists killed/battles, 1898-99, 48-pg 35.00
Shipping order, MA, building supplies, 1858, 8x11", EX 10.00
Special order, NY, promotion of officer, 1865, EX 14.00
Statement, TX, slave possession, handwritten, 1843, 2½-pg...........70.00
Tax, NH, $2 tax duty on carriage, 1814, 8x13", VG 38.00
Trolley card, PA, plumbing advertising, ca 1920s, 11x21" 20.00
Visa, travel to Havana by steamship, 1857, 8½x14"......................70.00
Waybill, Holbrook & Ft Apache Stage Line, 1904, 7x17" 35.00

Dollhouses and Furnishings

Dollhouses were introduced commercially in this country late in the 1700s by Dutch craftsmen who settled in the East. By the mid-1800s they had become meticulously detailed, divided into separate rooms, and lavishly furnished to reflect the opulence of the day. Originally intended for the amusement of adults of the household, by the latter 1800s their status had changed to that of a child's toy. Though many early dollhouses were lovingly hand-fashioned for a special little girl, those made commercially by such companies as Bliss and Schoenhut are highly valued.

Furniture and furnishings in the Biedermeier style featuring stenciled Victorian decorations often sell for several hundred dollars each. Other early pieces made of pewter, porcelain, or papier-mache are also quite valuable. Certainly less expensive but very collectible, nonetheless, is the quality, hallmarked plastic furniture produced during the forties by Renwal and Acme, and the 1960s Petite Princess line produced by Ideal. In the listings that follow, dollhouses are litho paper on wood, unless otherwise noted. When no manufacturer or country of origin is noted, examples are German, turn of the century. Our advisor for this category is Barbara Rosen; she is listed in the Directory under New Jersey. See also Miniatures.

Furniture

Dining and bedroom sets, pink and blue paint, ca 1930s, 11 pieces, $75.00.

Andirons, brass, Tynietoy, pr, EX 20.00
Bath scales, ivory, Renwal 7.00
Bed, Jenny Lind, Tynietoy 60.00
Bed, pk, w/low headboard, Strombecker, 4⅝", EX 12.50
Bed, twin; dk wood, Strombecker, EX...17.50
Bed, youth; pk, w/pk silk mattress, Strombecker, EX.....................22.50
Blanket chest, lid opens, Strombecker, EX 12.50
Buffet, brn, Renwal 7.50
Chair, dining; Strombecker, set of 4, EX..40.00

Chair, host; Petite Princess...12.50
Chair, rocking; brn, tall bk, Little Hostess, EX 12.50
Chair, side; Chippendale w/gr seat, Tynietoy 50.00
Chair, slat bk, gr, Tootsietoy 10.00
Chair, swivel desk; red, Renwal 6.00
Chair, wing; red w/brn legs, Little Hostess, EX 12.50
China cabinet, pine w/china knobs, American, ca 1900, 19" 60.00
Clock, grandfather; dk wood, Strombecker.......................................9.50
Clock, kitchen; gr, rnd, Strombecker, EX 4.50
Corner cupboard, dk wood, Tynietoy, EX 80.00
Dresser, dbl; ivory, Little Hostess, EX 12.50
Fireplace, Petite Princess, EX...20.00
Hamper, gr, w/open top, Strombecker, EX....................................... 6.50
Icebox, w/open door, Strombecker...17.50
Ironing board, pk, Renwal 7.50
Kitchen & dinette set, Penny Brite, MIB 125.00
Lamp, floor; w/cream shade, Strombecker....................................... 7.50
Lamp, table; brass, Petite Princess...10.00
Piano & bench, Petite Princess...20.00
Refrigerator, gr, coil top, Tootsietoy, 1930s 40.00
Sink, bathroom; pk, w/bl faucets, Renwal 7.50
Sofa, red, Strombecker, EX...10.50
Sofa & chair set, dk bl, Strombecker, EX...15.00
Stove, gas range, Tootsietoy, ca 1930..35.00
Table, bedside; pk, Renwal 5.00
Table, dining; Petite Princess, in box, EX 30.00
Table, dressing; bl, w/stool & perfumes, Petite Princess 30.00
Table, drop-leaf, gate-leg, w/2 drw, Little Hostess, EX 12.50
Table, end; tier style, Petite Princess..12.50
Table, kitchen; gr, Strombecker, EX 10.00
Tricycle, red & yel, Renwal 6.50

Houses

Bliss, 3-story, lithographed paper on wood with metal railings, EX, $1,600.00.

America, farmhouse, 2-story/2-room, pnt wood, 1880s, 18", EX..800.00
America, Victorian, 2-story, paper on wood, 1890s, 17", G ... 1,000.00
Bliss, Adirondack cabin, 2-story/2-room, ca 1900, 18", EX 650.00
Bliss, farmhouse, 2-story, paper on wood, 1895, 20", EX.......... 2,250.00
Bliss, fort, tin litho, w/4 soldiers & cannon, 8½x8x4", G............450.00
Bliss, grocery, paper on wood, fold-down, 1895, 11x8x6", EX . 1,900.00
Bliss, stable, 3 stalls/loft, paper on wood, 13x10x5", EX 550.00
Bliss, Victorian, 2-story, widow's walk/stairs, 1900, EX 11,250.00
Bliss, Victorian cottage, paper on wood, 1900, 14", EX 1,300.00
Bliss, 2-story, paper on wood, no chimney, 1890s, 9x6x3" 800.00
Bliss, 2-story/2-room, paper on wood, 1900, 13", EX 1,000.00
Bliss, 2-story/2-room, paper on wood, 1910s, 17x11", EX 1,400.00

Bliss (att), 2-story/2-room, paper on wood, 1910, 13", EX 700.00
Bliss type, block style, 2-story, paper on wood, 1913, 14" 300.00
Bliss type, keyhole style, pnt wood, 1950s, 16x19x7", EX............200.00
Borgfelt, Jefferson Cottage, printed Masonite, 1920, VG............100.00
Carriage house, pnt wood, mechanical doors, '10, 20", G 300.00
Cass, cottage, printed wood, porch, ca 1912, 10x11x9", G 350.00
Continental, 2-story/4-room, paper on wood, 1890, 22", EX .. 7,250.00
Converse, cottage, pnt wood, 1913, 10", VG 200.00
England, Victorian house, 2-story/2-room, 1890s, 38", EX 500.00
France, 2-story/2-room, paper on wood, 1890s, 11", VG 600.00
Garage, paper litho/pnt wood, roof removes, 15", VG....................55.00
Germany, barn, paper on wood, 2-story/3-stall+loft, 13", VG 200.00
Germany, grocery, pnt wood, arched top, contents, 1885, 16"... 1,900.00
Germany, kitchen, Dutch scenic paper, furnished, 1900s, 17" . 1,300.00
Germany, 2-story, pnt wood, roof opens, 1910, 14x9x7", EX 400.00
Germany, 2-story/2 room, pnt wood, 1910s, 16x16x8", EX..........900.00
Germany, 2-story/2-room, pnt wood, 1885, 11x6x5", G 300.00
Grimm & Leeds, Dandy Toy House, 2-story, cb, 1903, 23", EX ..400.00
Handmade, cottage, pnt wood, shingled, '30s, 10x15x10", VG 600.00
Marx, Colonial, 2-story, tin litho, furnished, EX 100.00
Marx, Newlyweds Rooms, tin litho rooms, set of 6, 5" L..............300.00
Marx, ranch style, tin litho, w/accessories, EX...............................85.00
Marx, Suburban Colonial, tin litho, w/breezeway, EX....................85.00
McLoughlin, church, litho on wood, 15x7x8", G 450.00
McLoughlin, 2-story, pnt wood, paper litho int, 1900, 18", G 300.00
San Francisco row house, 2-story/4-room, pnt wood, 23", EX . 1,050.00
San Francisco Victorian, redwood/pine, 5-story, EX................ 2,400.00
Schlesinger, kitchen, emb tin, furnished, 1900, 18", EX 250.00
Schoenhut, Colonial, 1-room, pnt wood, orig label, 12x11x14"..400.00
Schoenhut, Colonial, 2-story, paper on wood, 1920, 27" 1,900.00
Schoenhut, Dutch colonial, 2-story, pnt wood, 1930s, 18", VG..750.00
Schoenhut, RR station, pnt wood, ca 1925, 14x9x9", VG 350.00
Schoenhut, Spanish style, 2-story/4-room, '30s, 20x28x11", VG..450.00
Schoenhut, 2 story, stucco, electrified, roof removes, 48" 200.00
Schoenhut, 2-story, pnt wood, cb roof, shutters, '20, 17", VG 300.00
Theatrical stage, paper on wood, 3 bkdrops, 20", G........................50.00
Town hall, pnt wood, glass windows, bell tower, rprs, 56" 1,800.00
Tudor manor, pnt wood, 1-story/4-room, '30s, 17x21x13", VG...200.00
Victorian cabinet house on wheels, pnt wood, 4-room, 45" 1,000.00

Dolls

Collecting dolls of any sort is one of the most rewarding hobbies in the United States. The rewards are in the fun, the search, and the finds — plus there is a built-in factor of investment. No hobby, be it dolls, glass, or anything else, should be based completely on investment; but any collector should ask: 'Can I get my money back out of this item if I should ever have to sell it?' Many times we buy on impulse rather than with logic, which is understandable; but by asking this question we can save ourselves a lot of 'buyer's remorse' which we have all experienced at one time or another.

Since we want to learn to invest our money wisely while we are having fun, we must become aware of defects which may devaluate a doll. In bisque, watch for eye chips, hairline cracks and chips, or breaks on any part of the head. Composition should be clean, not crazed or cracked. Vinyl and plastic should be clean with no pen or crayon marks. Though a quality replacement wig is acceptable for bisque dolls, composition and hard plastics should have their originals in uncut condition. Original clothing is a must except in bisque dolls, since it is unusual to find one in its original costume.

A price guide is only that — a guide. It suggests the average price for each doll. Bargains can be found for less-than-suggested values, and 'unplayed-with' dolls in their original boxes may cost more. Dealers must become aware of condition so that they do not overpay and therefore overprice their dolls — a common occurrence across the country. Quantity does not replace quality, as most find out in time. A faster turnover of sales with a smaller margin of profit is far better than being stuck with an item that does not sell because it is overpriced. It is important to remember that prices are based on condition and rarity. When no condition is noted, dolls are assumed to be in excellent condition with the exceptions of Armand Marseille, Madame Alexander, and Effanbee dolls, which are priced in mint condition. In relation to bisque dolls, excellent means having no cracks, chips, or hairlines, being nicely dressed, shoed, wigged, and ready to to be placed into a collection. For a more thorough study of the subject, we recommend you refer to the many lovely doll books written by authority Pat Smith, available at your favorite bookstore or public library.

Key :

bjtd — ball-jointed	OC — original clothes
blb — bent limb body	p/e — pierced ears
bsk — bisque	pnt — painted
c/m — closed mouth	pwt — paperweight eyes
hh — human hair	RpC — replaced clothes
hp — hard plastic	ShHd — shoulder head
jtd — jointed	ShPl — shoulder plate
MIG — Made In Germany	SkHd — socket head
NC — no clothes	str — straight
o/c — open closed	trn — turned

Armand Marseille

Armand Marseille, mold #390, sleep eyes, open mouth, fully, jointed composition body, 33", $1,000.00.

Alma, ShHd, 12" 185.00
Alma, ShHd, 15" 250.00
Alma, ShHd, 26" 550.00
AM, baby, flange neck, 1907, 16" 525.00
AM, Darling Baby, 1906, 12" 300.00
AM, Floradora, ShHd, 20" 350.00
AM, Floradora, ShHd, 23" 465.00
AM, Floradora, SkHd, 12" 185.00
AM, Floradora, SkHd, 15" 300.00
AM, Floradora, SkHd, 17" 285.00
AM, Floradora, SkHd, 27" 775.00
AM, Floradora 1374, ShHd, fur eyebrows, 21" 400.00
AM, Floradora 3748, ShHd, 21" 375.00
AM, Indian, SkHd, o/c, 1890s, 8" 450.00
AM, Kiddiejoy, ShHd, cloth body, c/m, girl, 20" 1,600.00

AM, Kiddiejoy, ShHd, 9" 225.00
AM, lady, SkHd, c/m, mk MH (Max Handwerck), 1913, 10" .. 1,000.00
AM, My Dearie, SkHd, 1908, 14" 235.00
AM, My Playmate (body), closed dome & c/m, 18" 1,600.00
AM, Rosebud, ShHd, 1902, 15" 300.00
AM, Roseland, 1910, 18" 400.00
AM, ShHd, boy, 14" 300.00
AM, SkHd, c/m, 14" 850.00
AM, SkHd, CM Bergmann, 24" 565.00
AM, SkHd, o/c eyes, 7" 125.00
AM, SkHd, o/m, blk, 12" 475.00
AM, SkHd, 16" 225.00
AM, SkHd, 17" 295.00
AM, SkHd, 26" 575.00
AM, SkHd, 8" 165.00
AM, Sunshine, ShHd, 1910, 24" 550.00
AM, trn ShHd, talks, 16" 500.00
AM 1894, ShPl, 26" 550.00
AM 1894, SkHd, blk, 12" 475.00
AM 1894, SkHd, wht, 12" 225.00
AM 1894, SkHd, wht, 16½" 325.00
AM 1894, SkHd, 14" 250.00
AM 200, SkHd, googly eyes, 11½" 2,600.00
AM 210, SkHd, googly eyes, 6" 1,600.00
AM 231, Fany, baby, c/m, 1913, 25" 9,800.00
AM 248, mk GB (Geo Borgfeldt), o/m, 1912, 10" 185.00
AM 250, mk GB (Geo Borgfeldt), SkHd, c/m, molded hair, 10½" .375.00
AM 252, SkHd, googly eyes, 10" 800.00
AM 252, SkHd, googly eyes, 1915, 9½" 800.00
AM 253, SkHd, googly eyes, 1915, 16" 2,800.00
AM 253, SkHd, googly eyes, 6½" 750.00
AM 253, SkHd, googly eyes, 8" 900.00
AM 254, SkHd, googly eyes, molded hair, 8" 950.00
AM 255, SkHd, intaglio eyes, 7½" 425.00
AM 257, baby, SkHd, 1914, 22" 550.00
AM 300n, adult, SkHd, 15½" 1,200.00
AM 315, Queen Louise, SkHd, 27" 850.00
AM 320, SkHd, c/m, googly eyes, 6½" 650.00
AM 3200, ShHd, some trn, 15" 250.00
AM 3200, ShHd, some trn, 1898, 14" 250.00
AM 3200, ShHd, some trn, 1898, 16" 265.00
AM 3200, ShHd, some trn, 22" 450.00
AM 3200, ShHd, some trn, 26" 600.00
AM 323, SkHd, googly eyes, 11" 1,200.00
AM 323, SkHd, googly eyes, 7½" 750.00
AM 324, googly eyes, 7" 465.00
AM 327, SkHd, baby, fur hair, 1914, 12" 300.00
AM 327, SkHd, 1914, 12" 250.00
AM 327, SkHd, 1914, 20" 1,200.00
AM 328, baby, SkHd, closed dome, 1922, 14" 365.00
AM 329, girl, SkHd, 9" 250.00
AM 341, My Dream Baby, flange, c/m, wht, 8" 250.00
AM 341, My Dream Baby, flange, c/m, 15" 525.00
AM 341, My Dream Baby, flange, c/m, 18" 675.00
AM 341, My Dream Baby, flange, c/m, 1924, 7" 185.00
AM 341, My Dream Baby, flange, c/m, 21" 700.00
AM 341, My Dream Baby, SkHd, c/m, 16" 600.00
AM 347, SkHd, 1909, 16" 475.00
AM 3500, ShHd, 17" 425.00
AM 351, My Dream Baby, flange, o/m, wht, 22" 850.00
AM 351, My Dream Baby, flange, o/m, 26" 1,200.00
AM 351, My Dream Baby, flange, o/m, 6" 145.00
AM 351, Wee One, rubber body, 1922, 7" 165.00
AM 352, Baby Love, flange, 1914, 19" 625.00

AM 3524, Baby Gloria, flange neck, 18" 1,000.00
AM 362, Teenie Weenie, baby, closed dome, wht, 15" 400.00
AM 370, fur eyebrows, 22½" 400.00
AM 370, 12" 175.00
AM 370, 15" 265.00
AM 370, 16½" 300.00
AM 370, 19½" 350.00
AM 370n, 12" 175.00
AM 372, Kiddiejoy, ShHd, molded hair, 1926, 9" 350.00
AM 375, Kiddiejoy, girl, SkHd, c/m, molded hair, 20" 2,600.00
AM 390, My Dearie, SkHd, 1908-22, 18½" 425.00
AM 390, My Dearie, 23" 485.00
AM 390, o/m, 7½" 150.00
AM 390, pnt bsk, 9" 145.00
AM 390, walks, 22" 625.00
AM 390, 16" 350.00
AM 390, 18" 400.00
AM 390, 21" 450.00
AM 390, 22" 485.00
AM 390, 24" 525.00
AM 390, 9½" 225.00
AM 390n, Louisa, 1915, 27" 625.00
AM 390n, Patrice, 18" 650.00
AM 390n, 1915, 11" 275.00
AM 395, Heidi, SkHd, 1920, 9" 225.00
AM 402, SkHd, pnt bsk, 14" 250.00
AM 450, SkHd, c/m, provincial attire, 19" 1,400.00
AM 500, Infant Berry, molded hair, 1908, 10" 500.00
AM 500, Infant Berry, molded hair, 1908, 5" 250.00
AM 500, Infant Berry, molded hair, 1908, 8" 300.00
AM 550, SkHd, c/m, 16" 2,400.00
AM 560a, Dorothy, 1912, 15" 475.00
AM 590, Hoopla Girl, o/c eyes & mouth, 16" 1,600.00
AM 600, SkHd, flange, c/m, 1910, 10" 1,300.00
AM 800, Baby Sunshine, 'Mama' talker in head, 1925, 16" 2,100.00
AM 917, Mobi, baby, Germany, SkHd, 1921, 16" 450.00
AM 95, trn ShHd, 20" 425.00
AM 966, baby, SkHd, flirty eyes, 14" 450.00
AM 970, Ladie Marie, Otto Gans, 1916, 20" 650.00
AM 975, Sadie, baby, Otto Gans, 1914, 17" 525.00
AM 975, Sadie, baby, SkHd, 1914, 24" 700.00
AM 975, Sadie, baby, SkHd, 1914, 9" 200.00
AM 980, baby, SkHd, 14" 350.00
AM 985, baby, SkHd, 13½" 400.00
AM 990, Happy Tot, baby, SkHd, 13" 400.00
AM 990, Happy Tot, baby, SkHd, 1910, 16" 450.00
AM 990, Happy Tot, baby, SkHd, 1910, 21" 675.00
AM 990, Happy Tot, baby, SkHd, 8" 185.00
AM 991, Kiddiejoy, baby, SkHd, 14" 400.00
AM 992, baby, SkHd, 1914, 22" 750.00
AM 995, baby, SkHd, 12" 300.00
AM 996, baby, SkHd, 15" 425.00
AM 997, Kiddiejoy, baby, SkHd, 14" 400.00
Columbia, ShHd, 1904, 24" 550.00
Lily, ShHd, 1913, 17" 350.00
Mabel, ShHd, 1898, 15" 250.00
Mabel, ShHd, 1898, 17" 300.00
Queen Louise, SkHd, 1910, 22" 450.00
Queen Louise, 100, Germany, SkHd, 1910, 12" 250.00
Queen Louise, 100, SkHd, 1910, 18½" 425.00
Wonderful Alice, SkHd, fur eyebrows, 26" 750.00

Automaton

Bimbo, 5 monkeys, 8-track tape selections, glass front, 32" 850.00

Blk dancer on box, gessoed head, clockwork, Pat 1873, 10", G ...**325.00**
Blk warrior on camel's bk, Mandaville, 1870s **4,500.00**
Girl, ShHd, brn set eyes, stands on box, sgn Jumeau, 20" **4,500.00**
Gypsy girl, bsk head, p/e, stationary eyes, OC, Spain, 20" **4,000.00**
Lady w/basket & dog, bsk head, pwt, c/m, Lambert, 19", G..... **3,500.00**
Magician, nodding bsk head, OC, McIntyre, 16", EX **3,700.00**
Mother & child in cradle, Schoenau & Hoffmeister, 1890s, 12".. **2,800.00**

Barbie Dolls and Related Dolls

Though the face has changed three times since 1959, Barbie is still as popular today as she was when she was first introduced. Named after the young daughter of the first owner of the Mattel Company, the original Barbie had a white iris but no eye color. These dolls are nearly impossible to find, but there is a myriad of her successors and related collectibles just waiting to be found. When no condition is indicated, the dolls listed below are assumed to be nude and in excellent condition unless otherwise specified. For further information we recommend *The Wonder of Barbie* and *The World of Barbie Dolls* by Paris and Susan Manos; and *The Collectors Encyclopedia of Barbie Dolls and Collectibles* by Sibyl DeWein and Joan Ashabraner.

Allan, 1963, standard doll, MIB...**65.00**
Barbie, 1959, #1, blond, swimsuit, holes in feet, MIB **2,500.00**
Barbie, 1960, #2, no holes in feet, MIB...**850.00**
Barbie, 1960, #3, bl eyes, curved brows, ivory skin, MIB.............**325.00**
Barbie, 1960, #4, vinyl plastic, tan skin **250.00**
Barbie, 1961, #4, vinyl plastic, tan skin, MIB................................**265.00**
Barbie, 1961, #5, hollow body, curly bangs, MIB..........................**200.00**
Barbie, 1962, #8, hollow body, Pat Pend, MIB..............................**95.00**
Barbie, 1964, Ponytail Swirl, no curly bangs.................................**275.00**
Barbie, 1965, Color Magic, MIB..**250.00**
Barbie, 1970, standard doll, MIB...**145.00**
Barbie, 1971, Dramatic New Living, MIB.......................................**85.00**
Barbie, 1972, Busy, long blond hair, MIB **95.00**
Barbie, 1972, Busy Barbie w/Holdin' Hands, MIB **95.00**
Barbie, 1972, Walk Lively, MIB...**125.00**
Barbie, 1974, Sun Valley, w/ski accessories, MIB **85.00**
Barbie, 1975, Free Moving, blond, MIB **70.00**
Barbie, 1976, Ballerina Barbie on Tour, MIB.................................**45.00**
Barbie, 1976, Beautiful Bride, bendable knees, w/gown, MIB **85.00**
Barbie, 1978, Fashion Photo, remote control play camera, MIB....**60.00**
Barbie, 1979, Ballerina, MIB **50.00**
Barbie, 1979, Beauty Secrets, MIB **50.00**
Barbie, 1979, Pretty Changes, MIB **50.00**
Barbie, 1983, Twirly Curls...**25.00**
Brad, 1971, bendable legs, MIB...**65.00**
Cara, 1976, Blk, blk ponytail w/wht ribbon, MIB..........................**45.00**
Cheryl Ladd, 1978, bendable knees, jtd waist, 11½", MIB **20.00**
Christie, 1976, Super Star, MIB...**55.00**
Donnie Osmond, 1968, vinyl head, bendable legs, 11¾", MIB......**45.00**
Francie, 1970, Growin' Pretty Hair, MIB..**90.00**
Francie, 1971, Twist 'N Turn, blond or brunette, MIB..................**425.00**
Grizzly Adams, 1971, plastic w/red lower torso, 10", MIB.............**30.00**
Ken, 1961, flocked hair, movable head, arms, & legs....................**125.00**
Ken, 1969, Talking Ken, MIB..**60.00**
Ken, 1971, Live Action, MIB..**65.00**
Ken, 1973, Mod Hair, MIB...**30.00**
Ken, 1976, Now Look, either version, MIB **35.00**
PJ, 1969, New 'N Groovy, MIB..**85.00**
PJ, 1971, Live Action PJ on Stage **95.00**
Ricky, 1965, red hair, str legs, freckles **125.00**
Shaun, 1979, w/guitar, OC, 12", MIB..**20.00**
Skipper, 1964, long red hair, MIB **80.00**

Skipper, 1973, Pose 'N Play, M in package **17.50**
Skipper, 1979, Super Teen, MIB..**30.00**
Skooter, 1964, MIB..**85.00**
Stacey, 1968, Twist 'N Turn, MIB **90.00**
Steffie, 1972, Busy Steffie w/Holdin' Hands, MIB.........................**95.00**
Twiggy, 1968, twist waist, bendable knees, MIB **200.00**

Barbie Gifts Sets and Related Accessories

When no condition is indicated, the items listed below are assumed to be mint and in the original box.

1976 Gold Medal Barbie Skater, MIB, $45.00.

Barbie Ballerina Fashion, Princess Aurora, MIB............................**65.00**
Barbie Car, roadster, MIB..**250.00**
Barbie Chase Lounge, MIB..**38.00**
Barbie Dune Buggy, MIB...**90.00**
Barbie Mattel-a-Phone, M **17.50**
Barbie Motor Roller, w/Funtime Barbie, MIB................................**100.00**
Barbie Round the Clock Gift Set, 1964, MIB..................................**600.00**
Barbie Sports Car, Irwin, MIB **75.00**
Barbie stand, for #1 Barbie, rnd w/2 prongs, M **75.00**
Barbie's Horse Dancer, MIB..**65.00**
Barbie's New Restyled Dream House, MIB **85.00**
Barbie's Teen Dream Bedroom, MIB...**35.00**
Clothes, Barbie Beautiful Bride, 1966, MIB...................................**150.00**
Clothes, Barbie Brunch Time outfit, 1964, MIB.............................**55.00**
Clothes, Barbie Country Club Dance outfit, MIB **22.50**
Clothes, Barbie Garden Wedding outfit, 1965, MIB.......................**40.00**
Clothes, Barbie London Tour outfit, 1965, MIB.............................**60.00**
Clothes, Barbie Patio Party outfit, 1955, MIB................................**70.00**
Clothes, Barbie Picnic Set outfit, M **70.00**
Clothes, Barbie Pk Formal outfit, Sears, MIB.................................**95.00**
Clothes, Barbie Solo in the Spotlight outfit, 1958, M **95.00**
Clothes, Barbie Sweet Dreams, 1961, M **25.00**
Clothes, Francie Clam Diggers outfit, 1965, MIB...........................**45.00**
Clothes, Francie First Formal outfit, 1965, MIB **75.00**
Clothes, Ken American Airlines Captain, 1964, MIB **50.00**
Clothes, Ken Arabian Nights outfit, 1963, MIB **65.00**
Clothes, Ken College Student outfit, 1954, MIB.............................**55.00**
Clothes, Ken Here Comes the Groom outfit, 1965, MIB.................**110.00**
Clothes, Ken Time To Turn In outfit, 1965, MIB............................**45.00**
Clothes, Midge Orange Blossom outfit, 1962, MIB.........................**40.00**

Clothes, Skipper Land & Sea outfit, 1964, MIB 30.00
Clothes, Steffie Kitty Kapers outfit, 1972, MIB.......................75.00
Ken & Allan case, vinyl, France, M...65.00
Skipper 'N Skooter Dbl Bunk Beds & Ladder, MIB 50.00
Talking Barbie Pk Premiere gift set, 1969, MIB 500.00
World of Barbie House, M...40.00

Belton

Concave head, 2 or 3 hole, EX bsk, o/c or c/m w/wig, 10" 1,600.00
Concave head, 2 or 3 hole, EX bsk, o/c or c/m w/wig, 13" 2,000.00
Concave head, 2 or 3 hole, EX bsk, o/c or c/m w/wig, 15" 2,400.00
Concave head, 2 or 3 hole, EX bsk, o/c or c/m w/wig, 16" 2,400.00
Concave head, 2 or 3 hole, EX bsk, o/c or c/m w/wig, 17" 2,600.00
Concave head, 2 or 3 hole, EX bsk, o/c or c/m w/wig, 20" 3,100.00
Concave head, 2 or 3 hole, EX bsk, o/c or c/m w/wig, 22" 3,300.00
Concave head, 2 or 3 hole, EX bsk, o/c or c/m w/wig, 23" 3,500.00
Concave head, 2 or 3 hole, EX bsk, o/c or c/m w/wig, 26" 3,800.00
Concave head, 2 or 3 hole, EX bsk, o/c or c/m w/wig, 8" 975.00

Bru

Closed mouth, all kid body, bsk lower arms; Bru, 16" 9,600.00
Closed mouth, all kid body, bsk lower arms; Bru, 18" 12,000.00
Closed mouth, all kid body, bsk lower arms; Bru, 21" 20,000.00
Closed mouth, all kid body, bsk lower arms; Bru, 26" 26,000.00
Closed mouth, kid/wood body, bsk lower arms; Bru Jne, 12" .20,000.00
Closed mouth, kid/wood body, bsk lower arms; Bru Jne, 14" .18,000.00
Closed mouth, kid/wood body, bsk lower arms; Bru Jne, 16" .20,000.00
Closed mouth, kid/wood body, bsk lower arms; Bru Jne, 20" .24,000.00
Closed mouth, kid/wood body, bsk lower arms; Bru Jne, 25" .30,000.00
Closed mouth, kid/wood body, bsk lower arms; Bru Jne, 28" .36,000.00
Closed mouth, kid/wood body, bsk lower arms; Bru Jne, 32" .42,000.00
Closed mouth, mk Bru, circle dot, 16" 23,000.00
Closed mouth, mk Bru, circle dot, 19" 25,000.00
Closed mouth, mk Bru, circle dot, 23" 29,000.00
Closed mouth, mk Bru, circle dot, 26" 34,000.00
Open mouth, comp walker's body, throws kisses, 18" 5,600.00
Open mouth, comp walker's body, throws kisses, 22" 6,400.00
Open mouth, comp walker's body, throws kisses, 26" 7,300.00
Open mouth, nursing (Bebe), high color, late SFBJ, 12" 1,900.00
Open mouth, nursing (Bebe), high color, late SFBJ, 15" 2,800.00
Open mouth, nursing (Bebe), high color, late SFBJ, 18" 3,400.00
Open mouth, nursing Bru (Bebe), early, EX bsk, 12".............. 5,600.00
Open mouth, nursing Bru (Bebe), early, EX bsk, 15".............. 7,800.00
Open mouth, nursing Bru (Bebe), early, EX bsk, 18".............. 9,700.00
Open mouth, socket head, compo body; Bru, R, 14", EX bsk .. 4,800.00
Open mouth, socket head, compo body; Bru, R, 17", EX bsk .. 6,000.00
Open mouth, socket head, compo body; Bru, R, 22", EX bsk .. 8,200.00
Open mouth, socket head, compo body; Bru, R, 25", EX bsk .. 8,200.00
Open mouth, socket head, compo body; Bru, R, 28", EX bsk .. 9,000.00

China, Unmarked

Adelina Patti, center part, curls at temples, 1860s, 14" 350.00
Adelina Patti, center part, curls at temples, 1860s, 18" 500.00
Adelina Patti, center part, curls at temples, 1860s, 22" 675.00
Biedermeier or Bald Head, takes wig, RpC, 14" 975.00
Biedermeier or Bald Head, takes wig, RpC, 20" 1,500.00
Brown Eyes (pnt), any hairstyle or date, 16"................................950.00
Brown Eyes (pnt), any hairstyle or date, 20" 1,400.00
Common Hairdo, blond or blk hair, RpC, after 1905, 12" 145.00
Common Hairdo, blond or blk hair, RpC, after 1905, 23" 200.00
Common Hairdo, blond or blk hair, RpC, after 1905, 8" 85.00

Covered Wagon Style, sausage curls, RpC, 1840s-70s, 12" 425.00
Covered Wagon Style, sausage curls, RpC, 1840s-70s, 24" 850.00
Curly Top, loose ringlet curls, RpC, 1845-60s, 16" 625.00
Curly Top, loose ringlet curls, RpC, 1845-60s, 20" 750.00
Dolly Madison, modeled ribbon & bow, RpC, 1870-80s, 14" 275.00
Dolly Madison, modeled ribbon & bow, RpC, 1870-80s, 18" 485.00
Dolly Madison, modeled ribbon & bow, RpC, 1870-80s, 21" 550.00
Flat Top, blk hair, mid-part/short curls, RpC, ca 1860, 17" 285.00
Flat Top, blk hair, mid-part/short curls, RpC, ca 1860, 20" 325.00
Glass Eyes, various hairstyles, RpC, 1840s-70s, 14" 2,000.00
Glass Eyes, various hairstyles, RpC, 1840s-70s, 22" 3,000.00
Japanese, blk or blond hair, mk or unmk, RpC, 1910-20s, 14".....145.00
Japanese, blk or blond hair, mk or unmk, RpC, 1910-20s, 17".....185.00
Man or Boy, glass eyes, side part, RpC, 14" 1,600.00
Man or Boy, pnt eyes, side part, RpC, 14", EX 1,200.00
Man or Boy, pnt eyes, side part, RpC, 16" 1,400.00
Man or Boy, pnt eyes, side part, RpC, 21½" 3,400.00
Peg Wood Body, early hairdo, 16", EX 3,800.00
Pet Name, molded shirtwaist w/name on front, RpC, 1905, 19"..350.00
Pet Name, molded shirtwaist w/name on front, RpC, 1905, 8"....125.00
Pierced Ears, various hairstyles, RpC, 14" 600.00
Pierced Ears, various hairstyles, RpC, 18" 850.00
Snood/Combs, any appl hair decor, RpC, 14" 600.00
Snood/Combs, any appl hair decor, RpC, 17" 850.00
Spill Curls, w/or w/out head band, RpC, 14" 450.00
Spill Curls, w/or w/out head band, RpC, 22" 775.00
Wood Body, articulated/slim hips, RpC, 1840s-50s, 12" 1,500.00
Wood Body, articulated/slim hips, RpC, 1840s-50s, 17" 4,600.00
Wood Body, jtd hips, covered-wagon hairdo, 1840s-50s, 12" 950.00
Wood Body, jtd hips, covered-wagon hairdo, 1840s-50s, 15" . 1,900.00

Cloth

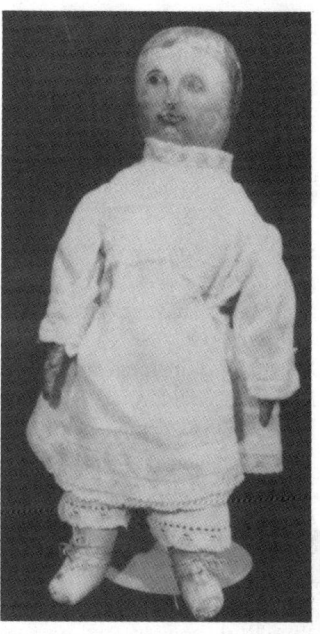

Columbian, by Emma Adams,
early stamp, 15", VG, $3,000.00.

Boy, handmade, HP face, fingers, orig clothes, 1920s, 28", EX ...150.00
Charlie Chaplin, Deans, 1915, uncut 125.00
Chase, stockinette, cotton body, pnt/molded hair, 21", EX 785.00
Chase, stockinette, molded/pnt hair, ca 1900, 15½", EX 600.00
Chase, stockinette, pnt features, OC, 19", VG 625.00
Merrie Marie, printed cloth, uncut 175.00
Palmer Cox Brownie, Sailor, printed cloth, uncut, 8" 125.00
Snow White, Dopey & Grumpy, oilcloth, '30s, OC, 15", 11" 325.00

Effanbee

Bernard Fleischaker and Hugo Baum became business partners in 1910; and, after two difficult years of finding toys to buy and a retail market to sell them in, they decided to manufacture dolls of their own. Their lovely dolls were a decided success largely because of their dedication to their work and the mutual trust and respect they held for each other. This is reflected in the Effanbee trademark — Eff stands for Fleischaker and bee for Baum. The company still exists today.

Anne Shirley, o/c eyes, hh wig, OC, 21", EX 350.00
Baby Grumpy, compo/cloth, RpC, 14" 225.00
Bubbles, flange-swivel head, compo/cloth, ca 1925, OC, 21" 325.00
Fluffy, vinyl, o/c eyes, rooted hair, 1957, OC, 10" 40.00
Gumdrop, all orig, 15", MIB...65.00
Honey Ann, hp, walker, o/c eyes, blond saran wig, OC, 24" 365.00
Lil' Darlin, vinyl/cloth, molded hair, pnt eyes, frown, 21" 85.00

Effanbee Little Lady/Fluffy marked on head, original clothes, 10", $50.00.

Little Lady, compo/cloth, pnt eyes, 1944, OC, 17" 350.00
Lovums, red molded hair, o/c mouth, orig romper/hat, 14"..........165.00
Mae Starr, compo/cloth, o/m w/tongue & 2 teeth, OC, 29" 450.00
Mae West, OC, 1982, 15", M...45.00
Martha Washington, compo, pnt eyes, bent arm, OC, 9" 85.00
Mary Lee, ShHd, compo/cloth, orig wig/OC, 31" 250.00
Mickey, SkHd, compo, bent limbs, RpC, 10" 325.00
Miss Blk America, 1977, 11", M 850.07
Miss Holland, Internat'l Collection, 1977, 11"...............................75.00
Patsy, o/c eyes, on mk Patricia body, OC, 15" 300.00
Patsy Ann, compo, tin o/c eyes, 1928, OC, 19" 400.00
Patsy Baby, compo, fully jtd, o/c eyes, caracul wig, OC, 11" 265.00
Patsy Lou, compo, bent right arm, o/c eyes, wig, 22"....................485.00
Patsy Ruth, compo/cloth, o/c eyes, rpl wig, OC, 26" 650.00
Rosemary, ShHd, compo, jtd limbs, o/m w/6 teeth, OC, 27" 400.00
Susan B Anthony, 1980, OC, 15"..200.00
Sweetie, pk christening gown, 1976, 8" 50.00

Half Dolls

Half dolls, lovely porcelain figures awaiting attachment to secure bases, were never meant to be objects of play. Most of these lovely ladies were firmly sewn into pincushion bases that were beautifully dec-orated and served as the skirt of their gown. Other skirts were actually covers for items on milady's dressing table. Some were used for parasol or brush handles or for tops to candy containers or perfume bottles. Most popular from 1900 to about 1930, they will most often be found marked with the country of their origin — Bavaria, Germany, France, and Japan. You may also find some fine quality pieces marked Goebel, Dressel and Kester, and Heubach.

For further information we recommend *The Collector's Encyclopedia of Half Dolls* by Frieda Marion and Norma Werner, available at your local bookstore or from Collector Books.

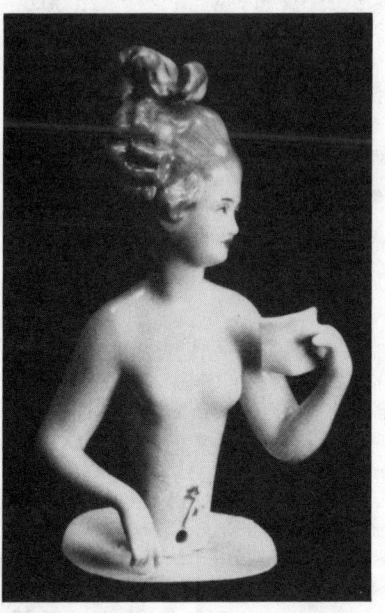

German half doll, lady holding letter, marked Dressel & Kestner, 5", $475.00.

Germany, arms & hands attached, common type, 3", up from.......30.00
Germany, arms & hands attached, common type, 5", up from.......40.00
Germany, arms & hands attached, common type, 8", up from.......55.00
Germany, arms & hands completely away, 12", up from 900.00
Germany, arms & hands completely away, 3", up from................125.00
Germany, arms & hands completely away, 5", up from................250.00
Germany, arms & hands completely away, 8", up from................425.00
Germany, arms extended, hands attached, 3", up from 65.00
Germany, arms extended, hands attached, 5", up from 75.00
Germany, arms extended, hands attached, 8", up from 95.00
Japan mk, 3", up from 20.00
Japan mk, 5", up from 30.00
Japan mk, 8", up from 50.00

Handwerck

#G9-12, bsk ShHd, o/m, o/c eyes, p/e, hh wig, RpC, 24" 475.00
#10, bsk ShHd, o/c eyes, o/m, p/e, rpl wig, 30" 700.00
#109-12, o/c eyes, o/m, p/e, rpl wig, RpC, 24", EX 475.00
#139, brn eyes, new body/wig, 28" 900.00
#3, bsk ShHd, jtd body, o/m, o/c eyes, p/e, RpC, 20", G 285.00
Child, bsk, bjtd, glass eyes, o/m, wig, after 1885, RpC, 18" 375.00
Germany Handwerk, bsk/papier-mache, o/m, rpl wig, 19" 400.00

Heubach

#111 73, character, SkHd, compo, pwt, Tiss-Me, OC, 7½" 1,400.00
#2 Heubach Germany, SkHd, o/m w/4 teeth, RpC, 11" 525.00
#2/0, character, Kathy, SkHd, o/c eyes, 1900s, OC, 9", VG 165.00
#3/0 Germany, boy, ShHd, intaglio eyes, flocked hair, 10" 425.00
#320-A, bsk head, rstr compo, o/c eyes, o/m, 15", VG 250.00
#4/0, SkHd, papier-mache body, intaglio eyes, RpC, 8", EX 265.00

#454-14/0, Blk, bsk head, sleep eyes, finger chip, 10", VG...........350.00
#5/0, SkHd, jtd compo, intaglio eyes, OC, 9½", EX.....................450.00
#9 5/8 3 2/0, Patti, SkHd, jtd compo, o/c eyes, OC, 8½"............675.00
#9 5/8 3 3/0, Gwen, SkHd, jtd compo, glass eyes, OC, 8"...........525.00
Coquette, SkHd, o/c eyes w/lids, o/m, 1912, RpC, 13", EX..........725.00

Heubach-Koppelsdorf

#250, bl o/c eyes, o/m w/4 teeth, OC, 8".......................................165.00
#250 3/0, SkHd, jtd compo, o/c eyes, o/m w/4 teeth, 18".............385.00
#250-6, bsk swivel head, o/c eyes, o/m, RpC, 25".........................495.00
#264-5/0, bsk head, jtd compo, set eyes, 14", VG...........................290.00
#275, bsk SkHd, kid body, o/c eyes, o/m w/teeth, mohair, 12".....145.00
#300 7/0, baby, bl set eyes, o/m, rpl wig, 10", G...........................65.00
#320-18, bsk ShHd, compo body, o/m, set eyes, wig, 17", G........485.00
Newborn, compo/cloth, o/c eyes, c/m, pnt hair, 16"....................600.00
Wonderful Alice, DRGM 377439, SkHd, fur eyebrows, 26".......600.00

Ideal

Bride, compo, o/c eyes, blond wig, P-90, OC, 15".......................175.00
Cinnamon, grow hair, all orig, 12"..45.00
Deluxe Kissy, all orig, ca 1962, 22", M..85.00
Fanny Brice Baby Snooks, wood compo, 12", NM......................365.00
Judy Garland, wood compo, jtd limbs, OC, 18", NM..................400.00
Kerry, grow hair, OC, 15"...55.00
Miss Revlon, blond, OC, jewelry, early, 18", NM.......................165.00
Saucy Walker, hp, flirty eyes, o/m w/teeth, OC, 23"..................100.00
Toni, strawberry blond, RpC, 15", NM.......................................225.00

Jumeau

    Emile Jumeau took over his father's doll company sometime in the 1870s. He brought many new innovations and ideas to the business. One fascination Jumeau had concerned dolls' eyes and led to the patents for eyelids that dropped over the eye itself; a second type allowed the doll to 'sleep.' Jumeau's distaste for German dolls is apparent in the booklets that were packaged with his dolls. These booklets referred to the German dolls as cheap and ugly and and as having 'stupid' faces. In reality, these less-expensive dolls were the downfall of the French doll manufacturers, and in 1899 the Jumeau company had to combine with several others in an effort to save the French doll industry from the German competition.

Bisque-head Bebe stamped depose Tete Jumeau, Bte. S.G.D.G.//3, paperweight eyes, pierced ears, closed mouth, ball-jointed composition and wood body, 12", $3,800.00.

Bsk SkHd, blond mohair, w/bottle/dog/music box, 18", VG.... 4,800.00
Closed mouth, mk EJ (incised) Jumeau, 10" 5,500.00
Closed mouth, mk EJ (incised) Jumeau, 14" 5,900.00
Closed mouth, mk EJ (incised) Jumeau, 16" 6,400.00
Closed mouth, mk EJ (incised) Jumeau, 19" 6,800.00
Closed mouth, mk EJ (incised) Jumeau, 21" 7,400.00
Closed mouth, mk Tete Jumeau, 10" 3,700.00
Closed mouth, mk Tete Jumeau, 14" 3,400.00
Closed mouth, mk Tete Jumeau, 16" 4,000.00
Closed mouth, mk Tete Jumeau, 19" 4,400.00
Closed mouth, mk Tete Jumeau, 21" 4,800.00
Closed mouth, mk Tete Jumeau, 23" 5,300.00
Closed mouth, mk Tete Jumeau, 25" 5,700.00
Closed mouth, mk Tete Jumeau, 28" 6,500.00
Closed mouth, mk Tete Jumeau, 30" 7,200.00
Depose/Tete Jumeau, swivel head, p/e, long curls, 18" 6,300.00
Depose/Tete Jumeau, swivel head, p/e, long curls, 28" 9,200.00
E 6 J/Jumeau, swivel head, inset eyes, kid body, 16"................ 5,800.00
E 6 J/Jumeau, swivel head, inset eyes, kid body, 20"................ 6,600.00
EJ/Depose Brevete, swivel head, inset eyes, 'mama/papa,' 16" . 5,800.00
Jumeau 1907, SkHd, appl ears, o/m, 18"................................ 2,400.00
Jumeau 1907, swivel head, o/m, o/c eyes, p/e, 18" 2,400.00
Jumeau 1907, swivel head, o/m, o/c eyes, p/e, 23" 2,800.00
Jumeau 1909, swivel head, o/m, inset eyes, p/e, 21" 2,800.00
Long face, c/m, 21"...23,000.00
Long face, c/m, 30"...26,000.00
Mechanical/musical, cm, p/e, pwt eyes, hh, 12" on 4" box 4,200.00
Open mouth, mk Tete Jumeau, 10" 1,400.00
Open mouth, mk Tete Jumeau, 14" 1,800.00
Open mouth, mk Tete Jumeau, 16" 2,300.00
Open mouth, mk Tete Jumeau, 19" 2,500.00
Open mouth, mk Tete Jumeau, 21" 3,000.00
Open mouth, mk Tete Jumeau, 23" 3,300.00
Open mouth, mk Tete Jumeau, 25" 3,600.00
Open mouth, mk Tete Jumeau, 28" 3,900.00
Open mouth, mk Tete Jumeau, 30" 4,200.00
Open mouth, mk 1907 Jumeau, 14" 1,400.00
Open mouth, mk 1907 Jumeau, 17" 2,200.00
Open mouth, mk 1907 Jumeau, 20" 2,600.00
Open mouth, mk 1907 Jumeau, 25" 3,300.00
Open mouth, mk 1907 Jumeau, 28" 3,500.00
Open mouth, mk 1907 Jumeau, 32" 3,600.00
Phonograph in body, o/m, 20" 3,400.00
Phonograph in body, o/m, 25" 4,800.00
Portrait Jumeau, c/m, 16" 6,000.00
Portrait Jumeau, c/m, 20" 7,700.00

Kammer and Reinhardt

#100/5, SkHD, bent leg, pnt eyes & hair, 20" 1,600.00
#101, boy or girl w/glass eyes, 12" 2,000.00
#101, boy or girl w/glass eyes, 16" 5,000.00
#101, boy or girl w/glass eyes, 20" 7,000.00
#101, boy or girl w/glass eyes, 9" 2,200.00
#101, boy or girl w/pnt eyes, 12" 1,800.00
#101, boy or girl w/pnt eyes, 16" 2,900.00
#101, boy or girl w/pnt eyes, 20" 3,600.00
#101, boy or girl w/pnt eyes, 9" 1,500.00
#109, rare, w/glass eyes, 15" 17,000.00
#109, rare, w/glass eyes, 18" 26,000.00
#109, rare, w/pnt eyes, 15" 14,000.00
#109, rare, w/pnt eyes, 18" 22,000.00
#112, rare, w/glass eyes, 15" 17,000.00
#112, rare, w/glass eyes, 18" 20,000.00

#112, rare, w/pnt eyes, 15" 10,000.00
#112, rare, w/pnt eyes, 18" 17,000.00
#114, rare, pnt eyes, 11" 3,200.00
#114, rare, w/glass eyes, 15" 6,300.00
#114, rare, w/glass eyes, 18" 7,200.00
#114, rare, w/pnt eyes, 15" 3,700.00
#114, rare, w/pnt eyes, 18" 5,500.00
#115 or #115a, closed mouth, 15" 3,400.00
#115 or #115a, closed mouth, 18" 4,600.00
#115 or #115a, closed mouth, 22" 5,200.00
#115 or #115a, open mouth, 15" 1,600.00
#115 or #115a, open mouth, 18" 2,600.00
#115 or #115a, open mouth, 22" 2,500.00
#116 or #116a, closed mouth, 15" 2,500.00
#116 or #116a, closed mouth, 18" 3,300.00
#116 or #116a, closed mouth, 22" 4,200.00
#116 or #116a, open mouth, 15" 1,600.00
#116 or #116a, open mouth, 18" 2,000.00
#116 or #116a, open mouth, 22" 2,400.00
#117, closed mouth, 18" 4,600.00
#117, closed mouth, 24" 6,400.00
#117, closed mouth, 30" 7,400.00
#117a, closed mouth, 18" 4,900.00
#117a, closed mouth, 24" 7,500.00
#117a, closed mouth, 30" 9,000.00
#126, sleeping/flirty glass eyes, open mouth, silent, 28" 2,000.00
#126, toddler, sleeping/flirty eyes, open mouth, 13½" 550.00
Buster Brown, SkHd, pnt eyes, c/m, K*R, 1900s, 23", w/Tige . 5,400.00
Dolly face, open mouth, mold #400-403-109, etc, 16" 600.00
Dolly face, open mouth, mold #400-403-109, etc, 20" 725.00
Dolly face, open mouth, mold #400-403-109, etc, 24" 850.00
Dolly face, open mouth, mold #400-403-109, etc, 28" 1,000.00
Dolly face, open mouth, mold #400-403-109, etc, 38" 2,500.00
Dolly face, open mouth, mold #400-403-109, etc, 40" 2,700.00

Kestner

Johannes D. Kestner made buttons at a lathe in a Waltershausen factory in the early 1800s. When this line of work failed, he used the same lathe to turn doll bodies. Thus the Kestner company began. It was one of the few German manufacturers to make the complete doll. By 1860, with the purchase of a porcelain factory, Kestner made doll heads of china and bisque as well as wax, worked-in-leather, celluloid, and cardboard. In 1895 the Kestner trademark of a crown with streamers was registered in the U.S. and a year later in Germany. Kestner felt the mark was appropriate since he referred to himself as the 'king of German dollmakers.'

Early closed mouth bisque shoulder head by Kestner, #8, 20", $1,250.00.

A, ShHd, o/m, MIG/Kestner, 19" 525.00
A/5, ShHd, o/c mouth, 23" 2,600.00
B/164-4, SkHd, googly eyes, 'watermelon smile,' RpC, 15" 3,800.00
B/6, ShHd, kid w/bsk ½-arms, o/m w/teeth, o/c eyes, 19" 525.00
B/6, SkHd, jtd compo, o/m w/2 teeth, set eyes, 22" 600.00
Bergmann, SkHd, made for CM Bergmann, o/m, JDK/CM, 14" ..295.00
Bergmann, SkHd, made for CM Bergmann, o/m, JDK/CM, 17" ..475.00
Bergmann, SkHd, made for CM Bergmann, o/m, JDK/CM, 20" ..575.00
Century Doll Co, flanged closed dome, c/m, 15" 650.00
C13/129, bsk SkHd, o/m, 4 teeth, o/c eys, rpl wig, RpC, 22", G..625.00
D/8, SkHd & ShHd, kid w/bsk ½-arms, c/m, 15" 1,400.00
E/9, ShHd, o/m, MIG, 26" 950.00
E/9, SkHd, o/m, 1892, 26" 950.00
Escelsior Germany, SkHd, compo, o/m w/4 teeth, OC, 32"..... 1,250.00
G/11, Hilda, SkHd, o/c eyes, o/m w/2 teeth, 1920s, 15" 3,300.00
G/11, SkHd, brn, o/m, 16" 3,300.00
G/8, trn ShHd, o/m, MI/JDK, 19" 525.00
Grace Putnam, bsk, 1-pc, pnt eyes, 10/10/COPR, 6" 650.00
Grace Putnam, bsk, 1-pc body & head, 1/COPR, 1923, 6" 650.00
Grace Putnam, Bye-Lo baby, 1360/30/COPR, RpC, 11" 750.00
Grace Putnam, Bye-Lo baby, 6 12/COPR, 1927, 16" 800.00
Grace Putnam, Bye-Lo baby, 6 12/COPR, 1927, 5" 650.00
H 1/2, ShHd, o/m, 23" 650.00
H/12, SkHd, o/c mouth, JDK, 1892, 23" 2,800.00
Handwerck, SkHd, made for Handwerck, o/m, JDK/H/12, 23"....550.00
Handwerck, SkHd, made for Handwerck, o/m, JDK/H/12, 27"....750.00
Hilda, toddler, jtd body, o/m, o/c eyes, 1914, rstr, 15" 3,800.00
I/13, SkHd, o/m, JDK, 1892, 16" 475.00
I/13, SkHd, o/m, JDK, 1892, 26" 700.00
J/13, SkHd, o/m, 1896, 27" 750.00
JDK, bsk head, c/m, glass eyes, appl ears, OC, 20", EX 3,200.00
JDK, bsk head on celluloid, R Gummi Co, turtle mk, 18"...........650.00
JDK 12, SkHd, o/m, pwt, bent limbs, RpC, 15", VG...............400.00
JDK 12, SkHd, o/m w/2 teeth, o/c eyes, orig wig, RpC, 16" 850.00
JDK 241, SkHd, jtd compo, o/m w/4 teeth, RpC, 21½", EX ... 5,400.00
K/12, ShHd, made for Century, o/c mouth, molded hair, 21" . 2,200.00
Kewpie, bsk, Rose O'Neill/10 945G, 1913, 8" 350.00
KK/14 1/2d, o/m, 1896, 26" 800.00
L 1/2/15½, SkHd, c/m, 14" 1,800.00
L/15, SkHd, bsk ShPl, c/m, 21" 2,200.00
L/15, SkHd, c/m, 21" 2,300.00
L/3, ShHd, o/c mouth w/molded teeth, 23" 2,800.00
N/17, SkHd, o/m, 1892, 17" 475.00
ShHd, o/c eyes, o/m, kid body & legs, bsk arms, 19", EX 400.00
SkHd, Oriental, o/m, JDK/Kestner, 14" 4,600.00
SkHd, pnt eyes, JDK/3 4/0, 8" 500.00
Trn ShHd, Kidoline w/bsk ½-arms, o/c eyes, G/MIG, 16" 450.00
10, SkHd, bsk ShPl, c/m, 21" 2,400.00
10, SkHd, o/c mouth w/2 teeth, JDK/MIG, 12" 450.00
10/G, SkHd, c/m, JDK, 1912, 12" 600.00
1070, SkHd, o/m, G11/237 15/JDK Jr 1914 HILDA/GES, 16".. 3,600.00
11, SkHd, o/c mouth, pnt eyes to side, JDK/MIG, 11" 600.00
12, SkHd, 5-pc baby, o/m/2 teeth, o/c eyes, JDK/MIG, 15" 650.00
13, SkHd, o/m, JDK/MIG, 18" 575.00
143, ShHd, jtd compo, o/c eyes, o/m, mohair wig, 14", EX 850.00
143, ShHd, kid w/bsk ½-arms, o/m, 17" 1,000.00
143, ShHd, kid w/bsk ½-arms, o/m/teeth, 12" 850.00
145, ShHd, kid w/bsk ½-arms, o/c mouth, 15" 2,200.00
145, SkHd, c/m, MI/O/G/18, 14"....................................1,500.00
145, SkHd, c/m, 143/4/0/JDK, 11" 700.00
146, SkHd, swivel, on ShPl, o/m, JDK, 18" 650.00
147, trn ShHd, o/m, JDK, 25" 950.00
148, ShHd, kid w/bsk ½-arms, o/m, 7 1/2, 18"......................600.00
148, ShHd, kid w/bsk ½-arms, o/m, 7 1/2, 21".......................725.00

150.1, bsk, Kestner seal on body, 8" 350.00
151, SkHd, 5-pc baby, o/m/teeth, intaglio eyes, MIG/5, 12"........425.00
151, SkHd, 5-pc baby, o/m/teeth, intaglio eyes, MIG/5, 16"........575.00
151, SkHd, 5-pc baby, o/m/teeth, intaglio eyes, MIG/5, 20"........675.00
152, character baby, compo, o/c eyes, o/m w/tongue, 11½"..........300.00
152, SkHd, made for Wolf, o/m, LW & CO 12, 1916, 20" 750.00
154, SkHd/ShHd, kid w/bsk ½-arms, o/m/teeth, DEP, 14"...........450.00
154, SkHd/ShHd, kid w/bsk ½-arms, o/m/teeth, DEP, 17"...........600.00
154, SkHd/ShHd, kid w/bsk ½-arms, o/m/teeth, DEP, 20"...........800.00
154, SkHd/ShHd, kid w/bsk ½-arms, o/m/teeth, DEP, 26" 1,000.00
16, SkHd, o/m, JDK/MIG, 21"..625.00
16/GES#1, ShHd, o/c mouth, molded boy's hair, 16" 2,600.00
167, SkHd, jtd compo, o/m, p/e, F 1/2/MI6 1/2/G, 16"...................500.00
167, SkHd, jtd compo, o/m, p/e, F 1/2/MI6 1/2/G, 20"...................600.00
168, SkHd, o/m, MID/G7, 26"..850.00
169, SkHd, jtd compo, c/m, o/c eyes, B 1/2/BI6 1/2G, 16" 2,400.00
169, SkHd, jtd compo, c/m, o/c eyes, B 1/2/BI6 1/2G, 18" 2,800.00
171, SkHd, jtd compo, o/m, o/c eyes, 'Daisy,' F/M110, 15" 465.00
171, SkHd, jtd compo, o/m, o/c eyes, 'Daisy,' F/M110, 18" 625.00
171, SkHd, jtd compo, o/m, o/c eyes, 'Daisy,' F/M110, 22" 750.00
171, SkHd, jtd compo, o/m, o/c eyes, 'Daisy,' F/M110, 32" 1,350.00
180 12/Ox/Crown seal, SkHd, o/m, 16"......................................465.00
201, ShHd, celluloid on kid, o/m, set eyes/lashes, JDK, 19".........500.00
211, SkHd, 5-pc baby, o/c mouth, o/c eyes, MI10/G/JDK, 12"...550.00
211, SkHd, 5-pc baby, o/c mouth, o/c eyes, MI10/G/JDK, 15"...725.00
215, SkHd, jtd compo, fur eyebrows, o/m, MI9/GJDK, 21"..........800.00
217A/Kestner, bsk, c/m smile, googly pnt eyes, 12" 2,400.00
221/GES/GESCH, SkHd, c/m smile, googly eyes, G/JDK, 21". 8,200.00
235, toddler, kid body, 16"..725.00
241, character, SkHd, o/c eyes, JDK, OC, 22" 6,800.00
245, SkHd, 5-pc baby, G/MIG/11/JDK Jr/1914 Hilda, 14" 3,300.00
245, SkHd, 5-pc baby, G/MIG/11/JDK Jr/1914 Hilda, 17" 3,600.00
257, SkHd, 5-pc baby, o/m, G/JDK, 10" 450.00
257, SkHd, 5-pc baby, o/m, G/JDK, 16" 675.00
257, SkHd, 5-pc baby, o/m, G/JDK, 20" 850.00
257, SkHd, 5-pc baby, o/m, G/JDK, 24" 1,400.00
26, K&Co/JDK/MIG/81, 16"..465.00
260, flirty-eyed toddler, OC, 16" 1,500.00
270, SkHd, o/m, made for Carl Trautman, CP/39, 38" 2,400.00
639, trn ShHd, closed dome, c/m, G/6, 18" 1,400.00
7 1/2/B, ShHd, kid w/bsk ½-arms, o/m w/teeth, o/c eyes, 14" 425.00

Lenci

Elena Scavini, separated from her husband who was in the service of Italy during WWI, found herself painfully alone after the death of her baby. With her brother as her partner, this talented artist began designing lovely felt-covered dolls with beautiful hand-painted features. These dolls became her children, and she regarded them as a tribute to her lost daughter.

Following the war, her husband returned and joined the firm as a partner. The Lenci firm (a name he used as a term of endearment for his wife) soon became well-known in the doll-making industry. Great care was taken in every detail. Characteristics of Lenci dolls include seamless, steam-molded felt heads, quality clothing, childishly plump bodies, and painted eyes that glance to the side. Fine mohair wigs were used, and the middle and fourth fingers were sewn together. Look for the factory stamp on the foot, though paper labels were also used. Dolls under 10" are known as mascots and usually sell for $125.00 to $150.00. The Lenci factory continues today, producing dolls of the same high quality.

Baby, jtd w/bent limbs, organdy dress/bonnet, 16", M 1,400.00
Boy, all felt, blond wig, OC, 1930s, 12".......................................400.00

Chinaman, w/opium pipe, 1920s, 12½", M 1,650.00
Flapper, long limbs, OC, 28"... 1,200.00
Girl, blond curls, organdy dress & bonnet, 21"...........................850.00
Girl, brn braids, felt dress & shoes, 20½" 850.00
Girl, glass eyes, 16" 1,800.00
Girl, jtd arms & legs, mohair wig, organdy dress, 14", M 600.00
Girl toddler, red wig, OC, 17"...850.00
Glass eyes, braided bun, canvas-type body/limbs, 18" 2,600.00
Lady, adult face, OC, 24" 1,200.00
Lady, w/cigarette, OC, 25"... 1,300.00
Old woman, gray mohair wig, opens in bk for sewing goods.... 1,200.00
Peasant girl, swivel neck/jtd body, all orig, 16", EX...................975.00
Romana, swivel head, w/labels, ca 1920s, 28", NM................. 2,200.00
Worthem, brn eyes, natural hair, OC, 1930s, 17" 385.00

Lenci, all felt, painted eyes, 18",
$1,000.00.

Madame Alexander

Beatrice Alexander founded the Alexander Doll company in 1923 using a lovely doll that was designed after her daughter Mildred. With the help of her three sisters, the company prospered; and by the late 1950s there were three factories with over six hundred employees making Madame Alexander dolls. The company still produces these lovely dolls today.

Albania, str legs, 1987 only, 8" 65.00
Alexander-kins, Wendy Ann, bend-knee walker, basic doll........175.00
Alexander-kins, Wendy Ann, organdy dress, cotton pinafore 400.00
Alexander-kins, Wendy Ann, str leg walker, nude, 1955 ....150.00
Alice in Wonderland, hp, Maggie, 14", w/trousseau 925.00
Anna Ballerina, compo, Wendy Ann, 18" 12,00.00
Antony, Mark, 1980-85, 12" 60.00
Austria Girl, hp, str legs, Wendy Ann, 8" 60.00
Babsie Skater, Princess Elizabeth, 1941, 15"................................725.00
Baby Clown, hp, pnt face, Wendy Ann, 1955, 8" 1,900.00
Baby Precious, cloth/vinyl, 1975, 14"..55.00
Ballerina, compo, Wendy Ann, 1938, 17"....................................550.00
Beau Brummel, cloth, 1930s...725.00
Binnie, hp, Cissy, 1954, 18"..200.00
Bitsey, compo, 11" 145.00

Blue Danube, hp, Margaret, 1953-54, 18" 1,200.00
Bonnie Toddler, vinyl, 1954-55, 19"..............................125.00
Brenda Starr, hp, beach clothes, 1964, 12" 250.00
Bride, bend knees, 1966-72, 8".....................................175.00
Bride, hp, Cissette, pk dotted swiss, 1957, 10"..............350.00
Brigitta, from Sound of Music, 11"................................245.00
Bunny, plastic/vinyl, Melinda, 1962, 18"........................275.00
Canada, hp, bend knees, Wendy Ann, 1968-72, 8" 125.00
Carmen Portrait, compo, pnt eyes, 9"............................275.00
China, compo, Tiny Betty, 1936, 7"................................225.00
Cinderella, plastic/vinyl, Mary Ann, pk gown, 1970-81, 14" 90.00
Clarabell Clown, 1951, 19"...450.00
Colonial, hp, bend-knee walker, Wendy Ann, 1962-64, 8" 300.00
Cookie, compo/cloth, 1938, 19"......................................465.00
Czechoslovakia, hp, bend knees, Wendy Ann, 1972, 8" 125.00
Daisy, Cissette, 1987-89, 10" 60.00
Davy Crockett Girl, hp, Wendy Ann, 1955, 8"................700.00
Dicksie & Ducksie, cloth/felt, 1930s..............................600.00
Dionne Quint, compo, toddler, 20" 600.00
Dionne Quint, compo w/cloth body, 17" 500.00
Dolly Madison, 1976, 1st set 130.00
Dr Defoe, compo, 1937, 14"..1,000.00
Dutch, bend-knee walker, Maggie Mixup, 8" 250.00
Easter Doll, hp, Wendy Ann, 1968, 8"........................ 1,200.00
Edith w/Golden Hair, cloth, 18".....................................600.00
Elise, hp/vinyl arms, street clothes, 1957-60, 16½" 165.00
Emily, cloth & felt, 1930s...600.00
English Guard, hp, bend knee, Wendy Ann, 1966-68, 8" 425.00
Estonia, str legs, 1986-87, 8"..75.00
Fairy Princess, compo, Tiny Betty, 1940, 7"...................225.00
Faith, hp, Wendy Ann, Americana Group, 1961, 8" 2,300.00
France, compo, Tiny Betty, 1936, 7"...............................200.00
Funny, cloth, 1963-77, 18"..65.00
Gainsborough, hp, Cissy, 1957, 20"............................1,200.00
Ginger Rogers, compo, Wendy Ann, 1940-45, 14" 1,200.00
Godey, compo, Wendy Ann, 1945, 21" 1,900.00
Godey Groom, hp, Margaret, 14"...................................950.00
Grandma Jane, plastic/vinyl, Mary Ann, 1970, 14"..........200.00
Greek Boy, hp, Wendy Ann, bend knee, 1965-68, 8".............345.00
Groom, hp, Wendy Ann, 1953-55, 7½"...........................425.00
Heidi, compo, Tiny Betty, 7"...245.00
Hulda, compo, Margaret, 1946, 18"................................950.00
Ice Capades, Cissy 1,400.00
Iris, Cissette, 1987-88, 10"...60.00
Isolde, Opera Series, 1985-86, 14".................................675.00
Jacqueline in Riding Habit...950.00
Jane Withers, compo, c/m, 1937, 12"..............................650.00
Joanie, plastic/vinyl, 1960, 36".......................................325.00
June Wedding, hp, Wendy Ann, 1956, 8" 375.00
Kate Greenaway, cloth, 16"...800.00
Katie, plastic/vinyl, Black Smarty, 1963, 12"..................375.00
Kelly, hp, Lissy, 1959, 12"...425.00
Kitten Mama, 1963, 18"...125.00
Lady Churchill, Margaret, 1953, 18"...........................1,100.00
Lady in Waiting, hp, Wendy Ann, 1955, 8" 1,400.00
Lila Bridesmaid, compo, Tiny Betty, 1938, 7" 195.00
Little Audrey, vinyl, 1954..200.00
Little Cherub, compo, 11" 125.00
Little Granny, plastic/vinyl, Mary Ann, 1966, 14" 200.00
Little Maid, str legs, 1987-89, 8".......................................55.00
Little Nannie Etticoat, str leg, 1986-89 ....55.00
Lively Kitten, 1962-63, 14"..145.00
Lively Pussy Cat, 1966-69, 20".......................................145.00
Lord Nelson, vinyl, 1984-86, 12"......................................70.00

Louisa Adams, President's Ladies, 1st set 130.00
Lucy Bride, compo, Wendy Ann, 1939, 14"...................375.00
Madame (Alexander), 1984, 21" 385.00
Madeline, rigid vinyl, 1961, 18"......................................700.00
Maggie Mixup, hp, 1960, 8"...400.00
Maggie Mixup, in riding habit, 8" 725.00
Maggie Walker, hp, 1949, 18"...450.00
Manet, 1982-83, 21"...300.00
Margaret O'Brien, compo, 14½" 645.00
Marie Antoinette, 1987-89, 21".......................................245.00
Marlo Thomas, plastic/vinyl, Polly, 1967, 17".................525.00
Mary Ann, plastic/vinyl, 1965 to date, 14".......................60.00
Mary Ellen Playmate, plastic/vinyl, Mary Ann, 14" 325.00
Mary Gray, plastic/vinyl, 1988, 14"..................................55.00
Mary Mine, cloth/vinyl, 14"...85.00
McGuffey Ana, cloth, 16"..700.00
Melanie, compo, Wendy Ann, 1945, 21"..................... 1,900.00
Melinda Ballerina, plastic/vinyl, 1953, 14"......................350.00
Mimi, in formal, 30"...650.00
Mimi, plastic/vinyl, 1971, 21"..600.00
Miss America, compo, holds flag, 1940, 14"...................650.00
Monet, 1984, 21"..225.00
Muffin, cloth, 1966, 19"...125.00
Napoleon, 1980, 12"...70.00
Normandy, compo, Tiny Betty, 1935-38, 7"....................245.00
Nurse, compo, Betty, 14"..400.00
Old Fashioned Girl, compo, Betty, 13" 350.00
Orchard Princess, compo, Wendy Ann, 21" 1,900.00
Parlour Maid, hp, Wendy Ann, 1956, 8" 1,800.00
Peggy Bride, hp, Margaret, 1950, 14"..............................500.00
Philippines, str legs, 1986-87, 8"......................................65.00
Pilgrim, compo, Tiny Betty, 7"..200.00
Pitty Pat Clown 400.00
Polly, plastic/vinyl, 1965, 17"..250.00
Polly Pigtails, hp, Maggie, 14½"......................................785.00
Precious, compo/cloth, 1937, 12"...................................145.00
Prince Charming, compo, Margaret, 1947, 16"...............575.00
Princess Elizabeth, compo, Tiny Betty, 7" 235.00
Princess Elizabeth, compo, 15".......................................485.00
Princess Elizabeth, w/Dionne head, 8" 235.00
Princess Margaret Rose, compo, Princess Elizabeth, 15" 750.00
Priscilla, cloth, 18"...650.00
Pussy Cat, cloth/vinyl, 1965 to date, 14"..........................95.00
Queen, hp, Margaret, 1953, 18".....................................800.00
Queen of Hearts, 1987 to date, 8"...................................55.00
Queen Scarlet, 1955, velvet robe 900.00
Rebecca, compo, Wendy Ann, 1940, 17".........................900.00
Red Boy, hp, bend knees, Wendy Ann, 1972, 8"...............60.00
Renoir, compo, Wendy Ann, 1945, 21" 1,900.00
Renoir, hp, Cissette, 1968, 10" 465.00
Renoir Child, plastic/vinyl, Nancy Drew, 1967, 12" 150.00
Rhett, 1981-85, 12"..65.00
Riley's Little Annie, plastic/vinyl, Mary Ann, 1967, 14" 200.00
Robin Hood, 1988 to date, 8"...55.00
Rodeo, hp, Wendy Ann, 1955, 8" 900.00
Romeo, compo, Wendy Ann, 18"................................1,200.00
Rosey Posey, cloth/vinyl, 1976, 14"..................................60.00
Royal Wedding, compo, 21" 1,900.00
Russian, compo, Tiny Betty, 1935-36, 7"........................175.00
Sailorette, hp, Cissette, 1988, 10".....................................60.00
Sarah Bernhardt, 1987, 21"...230.00
Scarlett O'Hara, hp, Margaret, 14"..............................1,000.00
Scottish, str legs, 1973-75, 8"..60.00
Sitting Pretty, foam body, 1965, 18"................................385.00

Madame Alexander 'Sleeping Beauty,' 9", MIB, $475.00.

Smarty, plastic/vinyl, 1962, 12"	285.00
So Big, cloth/vinyl, pnt eyes, 1968-75, 22"	125.00
Southern Belle, hp, 1955, 8"	800.00
Story Princess, Margaret, 1954-56, 15"	600.00
Sunbeam, newborn infant, 1951, 11"	80.00
Sunbonnet Sue, compo, Little Betty, 1937, 9"	80.00
Sweet Baby, cloth/latex, 1948, 18½"	50.00
Sweetie Baby, 1962, 22"	165.00
Timmy Toddler, plastic/vinyl, 1960-61, 23"	175.00
Tommy, hp, Lissy, 1962, 12"	1,200.00
Topsy-Turvy, compo, Tiny Betty heads, 1935	165.00
Turkey, hp, bend knees, Wendy Ann, 1968-72, 8"	125.00
Victoria, baby, 1966, 18"	90.00
Violetta, Cissette, 1987-89, 10"	60.00
Wendy, hp, Margaret, 1953, 15"	700.00
White Rabbit, cloth/felt	600.00
Winnie Walker, hp, Cissy, 1953, 15"	225.00
Yolanda, Brenda Starr, 1965, 12"	250.00

Papier-Mache

Papier-mache Black boy with straw hat, early, 9½", $250.00.

Blond molded hair, pnt eyes, cloth/leather body, 1870s, 24"	650.00
Gentleman, molded/pnt head, cloth, wood limbs, 1930, 13"	525.00

German ShHd, molded/pnt hair, jtd shoulders/hips, 10½"	125.00
Greiner, molded hair, pnt eyes, cloth w/kid arms, 29"	1,850.00
Molded features, hemp hair, set glass eyes, EX kid body, 20"	850.00
Motschmann type, pnt o/l, muslin body, glass eyes, 5"	150.00
Poured, ShHd, glass eyes, appl wig, cloth wire body/limbs, 12"	245.00
ShHd (thin), inset porc eyes, molded-on shoes, 16th C, 17½"	1,400.00
Trn ShHd, glass eyes, c/m, cloth/kid body, RpC, 18"	550.00
Unmk, molded/pnt clown head, cloth body, OC, 13½"	225.00

Parian

Adelina Patti, center part, 1860s, RpC, 14"	365.00
Bald head, ear details, orig wig, 1850s, RpC, 14"	750.00
Blond molded hair, glazed collar & bow tie, 1850s, 20", EX	600.00
Blond molded hair, pwt, p/e, Germany, 1860s, 15", VG	200.00
Bow at top of hair, ringlets, brn eyes, 14"	675.00
Combs modeled in hair, glass eyes, p/e, RpC, 17"	1,400.00
Hair in snood w/feather, 1863, RpC, 14"	950.00
ShHd, molded hair, cloth, pk/silver accents, bsk limbs, 9"	850.00

Schoenhut

Albert Schoenhut left Germany in 1866 to go to Pennsylvania to work as a repairman for toy pianos. He eventually applied his skills to wooden toys and later designed an all-wood doll which he patented on January 17, 1911. These uniquely jointed dolls were painted with enamels and came with a metal stand. Some of the later dolls had stuffed bodies, voice boxes, and hollow heads; some were made with heads of imitation bisque. These innovations influenced the development of the popular Bye-Lo Baby which was introduced in 1924. Due to the changing economy and fierce competition, the company closed in the mid-1930s.

Baby head, pnt hair, decal eyes, o/c mouth, jtd, 17"	700.00
Baby head, pnt hair & eyes, bent limbs, 16"	650.00
Boy, jtd body & head, intaglio eyes, blond wig, OC, 14½"	675.00
Character girl, cvd hair w/bow, intaglio eyes, jtd, OC, 14"	2,000.00
Dolly face, o/c eyes, o/m w/teeth, OC, 20"	925.00
Dolly face, pnt eyes, o/c mouth, jtd, OC, 17"	700.00
Girl, cvd hair w/comb mks, c/m, spring jtd, OC, 19"	2,300.00
Girl, cvd hair w/molded ribbon, spring jtd, OC, 19"	2,300.00
Girl, jtd body & head, intaglio eyes, blond wig, OC, 14"	650.00
Girl, jtd body & head, intaglio eyes, blond wig, OC, 17"	750.00
Girl, jtd body & head, intaglio eyes, 1911, OC, 16"	700.00
Girl, smiling o/m w/teeth, #309, OC, 21"	2,500.00
Pouty boy, jtd body, bl eyes, #1913, 1910, 11", EX	550.00
Walker, pnt decal eyes, c/ or o/c mouth, OC, 14"	875.00
Walker, pnt decal eyes, c/ or o/c mouth, OC, 17"	1,000.00

SFBJ

By 1895 Germany was producing dolls of good quality at much lower prices than the French dollmakers because of lower wages in German factories. This was a serious threat to the French companies; and, in a supreme effort to save the doll industry, several leading French manufacturers united to form one large company in the hope they could combine their strengths to save the French market. Bru, Raberry and Delphieu, Pintel and Godchaux, Fleischman and Blodel, and Jumeau united to form the company today known as SFBJ. Their dolls did well while Germany was otherwise occupied with WWII, but after the war German doll production proved to be too strongly competitive, and SFBJ closed in 1958.

Bebe Parisiana, bsk head, c/m, inset eyes, 1902, 16"	2,800.00
Celestine, bsk SkHd on papier-mache, o/m, inset eyes, 18"	950.00

SkHd, jtd papier-mache/wood body, o/m, o/c eyes, 30" 2,700.00
Tete Jumeau, p/e, o/m, o/c eyes/lashes, 18" 1,400.00
Tete Jumeau, p/e, o/m w/teeth, o/c eyes, jtd wrists, 22" 1,900.00
20, molded ptd shoes & eyes, 5-pc body, Paris/12, 10" 350.00
203, 1900 bsk head on compo, o/c mouth, inset eyes, 20" 2,800.00
215, bsk swivel on compo, c/m, inset eyes, 15" 2,000.00
223, bsk, closed dome, o/m w/8 teeth, molded hair, 17" 2,000.00
227, brn swivel closed dome head, animal skin wig, 15" 2,400.00
227, brn swivel closed dome head, animal skin wig, 18" 2,000.00
227, closed dome, o/m, inset eyes, pnt hair, 15" 1,800.00
228, toddler, papier-mache body, c/m, inset eyes, 16" 2,000.00
229, compo w/swivel head, o/c mouth, inset eyes, 18" 3,500.00
229, wood walker, o/c mouth, inset eyes, 18" 3,600.00
230, compo walker, p/e, o/m, inset eyes, 16" 1,500.00
230, SkHd, p/e, o/m, o/c eyes, 23" 2,400.00
235, closed dome, molded hair, o/c mouth & eyes, 16" 2,300.00
235, closed dome, molded hair, o/c mouth & eyes, 8" 750.00
236, laughing Jumeau, o/m, o/c eyes, dbl chin, 12" 1,600.00
236, laughing Jumeau, o/m, o/c eyes, dbl chin, 20" 2,400.00
238, compo w/swivel head, o/m, inset eyes, Paris 6, 15" 3,000.00
239, Poulbot, c/m, street urchin, red wig, 14" 16,000.00
239, Poulbot, c/m, street urchin, red wig, 17" 19,000.00
245, boy, o/c mouth, lg glass eyes, googly, pnt shoes, 12" 2,800.00
245, boy, o/c mouth, lg glass eyes, googly, pnt shoes, 8" 1,000.00
247, toddler, o/c mouth/2 inset teeth, 16" 2,600.00
247, toddler, o/c mouth/2 inset teeth, 20" 2,900.00
247, toddler, o/c mouth/2 inset teeth, 24" 3,400.00
247, Twirp, SkHd, o/c mouth & eyes/2 teeth, 21" 2,800.00
251, toddler, 25" 2,900.00
251, 1099 character baby, o/c mouth, eyes, hair lashes, 16" 1,700.00
251, 1099 character baby, o/c mouth, eyes, hair lashes, 18" 2,000.00
252, pouty, c/m, inset eyes, papier-mache body, 11" 4,500.00
252, pouty, c/m, inset eyes, papier-mache body, 18" 6,200.00
252, pouty, c/m, inset eyes, papier-mache body, 22" 7,900.00
257, 1900 toddler, o/c mouth, inset eyes, 16" 2,500.00
266, character, bsk head, closed dome, o/c mouth, 20" 3,800.00
301, bsk SkHd on compo, o/m, inset eyes, 16" 725.00
301, bsk SkHd on compo, o/m, inset eyes, 22" 1,200.00
301, bsk SkHd on compo, o/m, inset eyes, 28" 1,250.00
301, bsk SkHd on compo, o/m, inset eyes, 30" 2,000.00
60, French WWI nurse, 5-pc body, SFBJ/13/0, 8½" 400.00
60, kiss-blower, cryer/walker, 22" 2,200.00
60, o/m w/teeth, o/c eyes, jtd body & wrists, 25½" 950.00
60, SkHd, compo w/str legs, o/m, curved arms, 15" 650.00
60, SkHd, papier-mache/compo, plunger cryer, o/m, 1-pc, 11"....450.00

Shirley Temple

Bsk, Japan, 7½" 265.00
Compo, 11", cowboy outfit, orig pin, EX 825.00
Compo, 11", in trunk, EX..950.00
Compo, 13", o/c eyes, o/m, OC, Ideal 650.00
Compo, 13", o/m, o/c eyes, jtd shoulders/hips, 1936, OC............450.00
Compo, 13", tagged bl/wht dress w/pin, 1930s, all orig 650.00
Compo, 15", OC, Ideal 600.00
Compo, 16", o/c eyes, o/m, handmade clothes, 1936, EX 350.00
Compo, 16", red dotted dress, velvet coat/hat, all orig...............650.00
Compo, 18", o/c eyes, o/m, jtd, mohair wig, Ideal, '30s, VG 685.00
Compo, 20", Ideal, NM 750.00
Compo, 20", OC, NM 750.00
Compo, 20", tagged clothes, all orig, orig box........................ 1,200.00
Compo, 22", OC, rpl wig..450.00
Compo, 22", teeth, orig bl dress w/daisies, Ideal, 1934, NM 750.00
Compo, 25", sailor suit, EX..900.00

Compo, 27", flirty eyes, orig, EX 1,100.00
Compo, 30", unmk, M...450.00
Vinyl, 12", complete w/4 outfits, Ideal, 1957, MIB 285.00
Vinyl, 12", gr/wht dress, slip, complete, Ideal, 1957, MIB...........200.00
Vinyl, 12", Heidi, Ideal, 1982, MIB 200.00
Vinyl, 14", Montgomery Ward's, 1972, MIB 200.00
Vinyl, 15", flirty eyes, orig clothes, 1952, M 265.00
Vinyl, 15", Heidi outfit, w/pin & tag, 1957 ....300.00
Vinyl, 15", RpC, Ideal 245.00
Vinyl, 16", Ideal, 1973, MIB 200.00
Vinyl, 16", polka dot dress, Ideal, 1972, M 200.00
Vinyl, 16", Rebecca, Ideal, 1972 ....200.00
Vinyl, 16", red dotted dress/Captain Jan outfit, 1973, MIB...........200.00
Vinyl, 16", Stand Up & Cheer dress, 1973, MIB 200.00
Vinyl, 17", Heidi outfit, w/pin, MIB 400.00
Vinyl, 19", flirty eyes, all orig, 1957 ....450.00
Vinyl, 19", Heidi, 1957, MIB +2 extra orig outfits 500.00
Vinyl, 36", OC, EX 1,800.00
Vinyl, 36", pk pleated dress, EX.. 1,800.00
Vinyl, 8", Stowaway, Ideal, 1982..45.00

Shirley Temple Hawaiian, body marked Shirley Temple, head marked Ideal, 18", $825.00.

Simon and Halbig

Simon and Halbig was a large German doll firm that operated from ca 1870 until the 1930s. They were a popular supplier of bisque heads to French dollmakers of the 1870s and '80s. This company made dolls for such famous companies as Gimbel Bros., Jumeau, Kammer and Reinhardt, as well as many others. Halbig became the sole owner of the company in 1895 but did not register 'S&H' as his trademark until ten years later.

AW, SkHd, o/m, SH/13, 21" 675.00
Baby Blanche, SkHd, o/m baby, S&H, 16"................................800.00
Baby Blanche, SkHd, o/m baby, S&H, 21"................................950.00
CM Bergmann, SkHd, o/m, Simon & Halbig, 3 1/2, 18"...............575.00
CM Bergmann, SkHd, o/m, 1895, Halbig/S&H5, 30" 1,300.00
CM Bergmann, SkHd, o/m, 1897, S&H6, 12" 350.00
CM Bergmann, SkHd, o/m, teeth, Simon & Halbig, RpC, 32" . 1,400.00
Elenore, SkHd, o/m, CMB/Simon & Halbig, 18" 600.00
G68, SkHd, flirty eyes, 1908, S&H/K*R, 16" 550.00
Handwerck, SkHd, o/m, G/Halbig, 4, 26" 850.00

Handwerck, SkHd, o/m, S&H, 30" 650.00
Handwerck, SkHd, o/m, 1893, 16" 450.00
Handwerck, SkHd, o/m, 1895, G/S&H/1, 16" 450.00
Handwerck, SkHd, o/m, teeth, Simon & Halbig, rpl wig, 32" .. 1,045.00
S&H3, all bsk, c/m, inset eyes, molded-on shoes, 6" 285.00
10, SkHd, o/m, G/Halbig/S&H, 16" 475.00
10, SkHd, o/m, G/Halbig/S&H, 19" 575.00
10, SkHd, o/m, G/Halbig/S&H, 22" 675.00
10 1/2, SkHd, o/m, flirty o/c eyes, S&H, 18" 625.00
100, SkHd, o/m, Simon & Halbig/S&C/G, 15" 475.00
100, SkHd, o/m, Simon & Halbig/S&C/G, 22" 675.00
101, SkHd, c/m, Simon & Halbig/K*R, 16" 4,800.00
1039, SkHd, o/m w/teeth, p/e, jtd arms/wrists, hh, 22" 725.00
1078, SkHd, o/m, pwt, p/e, S&H, RpC, 18½" 800.00
109, SkHd, o/m, 1895, Handwerck/G/Halbig, 23" 675.00
114, SkHd, c/m, glass eyes, Simon & Halbig K*R/L, 14" 6,300.00
114, SkHd, c/m, glass eyes, Simon Halbig K*R/L, 20" 7,900.00
114, SkHd, c/m, Simon & Halbig K*R/L, 9" 1,200.00
115, SkHd, c/m, 1912, K*R/Simon & Halbig, 16" 3,400.00
115a, SkHd, c/m pouty, K*R/Simon & Halbig, 15" 3,400.00
1159, SkHd, adult, 1905, G/Simon & Halbig/S&H7, 14" 1,200.00
1159, SkHd, adult, 1905, G/Simon & Halbig/S&H7, 18" 1,800.00
1159, SkHd, adult, 1905, G/Simon & Halbig/S&H7, 24" 2,700.00
1159, SkHd, swivel on ShPl, wood w/kid fashion, o/m, 19" 2,000.00
116a, SkHd, c/m, K*R/Simon & Halbig, 17" 3,200.00
116a-38, SkHd, 2 teeth, tongue, K*R/Simon & Halbig, 17" ... 2,000.00
1160, Louisa May Alcott, bsk head, cloth body, 7", EX 115.00
117, SkHd, c/m, 1919, Simon & Halbig/K*R, 16" 4,000.00
117, SkHd, c/m, 1919, Simon & Halbig/K*R, 20" 4,700.00
117a, SkHd, c/m, K*R/Simon & Halbig, 16" 4,400.00
117a, SkHd, c/m, K*R/Simon & Halbig, 20" 5,000.00
117n, SkHd, o/m, Simon & Halbig/K*R, 20" 2,000.00
119, SkHd, o/m, 13/Handwerck 5/Halbig, 16" 575.00
121, SkHd, o/c mouth/teeth, flirty o/c eyes, 1920, K*R, 16" ... 1,400.00
121, SkHd, o/c toddler, 16" 1,200.00
121, SkHd, o/m, 1920, K*R/Simon & Halbig, 14" 1,000.00
121, SkHd, o/m, 1920, K*R/Simon & Halbig, 19" 1,500.00
122, SkHd, 1920, K*R/Simon & Halbig, 14" 850.00
1249 Santa, bsk head, jtd compo, o/c eyes, o/m, p/e, 20" 1,200.00
126, SkHd, o/c mouth, SH, 23" 950.00
126, SkHd, o/m, Simon & Halbig/K*R, 14" 500.00
126, SkHd, o/m, Simon & Halbig/K*R, 19" 800.00
126/36, SkHd, o/m, pwt eyes, Simon & Halbig/K*R, 17" 800.00
127, SkHd, o/m, K*R/Simon & Halbig, 18" 675.00
128, SkHd, o/m, K*R/Simon & Halbig, 14" 800.00
128, SkHd, o/m, K*R/Simon & Halbig, 19" 1,300.00
1296, SkHd, 1911, FS&Co/Simon & Halbig, 14" 475.00
1329, SkHd, o/m, olive, G/Simon & Halbig/SH, 14" 2,200.00
151, SkHd, o/c mouth, pnt eyes, S&H/1, 16" 6,500.00
156, SkHd, 1925, S&H, 18" 625.00
156, SkHd, 1925, S&H, 22" 725.00
159, SkHd, o/m, Simon & Halbig, 16" 550.00
179, SkHd, o/m, Simon & Halbig S11H DEP, 20" 700.00
1848, SkHd, o/m, Jutta Simon & Halbig, 16" 525.00
191, SkHd, o/m, Bergmann/CB, 18" 625.00
1923, SkHd, o/m, SH Sp 53/4/G, 14" 500.00
1923, SkHd, o/m, SH Sp 53/4/G, 21" 700.00
1923, SkHd, o/m, SH Sp 53/4/G, 26" 950.00
246, SkHd, o/m, 1900, K*R/Simon & Halbig, 18" 650.00
282, SkHd, o/m, SH, 14" 500.00
282, SkHd, o/m, SH, 18" 650.00
282, SkHd, o/m, SH, 22" 725.00
383, SkHd, flapper body, SH, 14" 1,200.00
402, SkHd, o/m, K*R SH, 16" 625.00

403, SkHd, o/c mouth, K*R, Simon & Halbig, 20" 2,800.00
403, SkHd, o/m, pwt, papier-mache body, RpC, 18½" 500.00
403, SkHd, o/m, walker, K*R SH, 21" 1,400.00
409, SkHd, o/m, S&H, 24" 685.00
409, SkHd, o/m, S&H, 26" 850.00
409, SkHd, o/m, S&H, 30" 1,400.00
48m SkHd, o/m, 1905, Simon & Halbig/K*R, 27" 1,000.00
50, SkHd, c/m, Simon & Halbig, 16" 1,800.00
50, SkHd, o/m, 1900, K*R/Simon & Halbig, 14" 500.00
53, SkHd, c/m, brn bsk, Simon & Halbig/K*R, 16" 1,800.00
530, SkHd, o/m, G/Simon & Halbig, 21" 675.00
540, SkHd, o/m, G/Halbig/S&H, 16" 750.00
540, SkHd, swivel on bsk ShPl, o/m, S&H, G, 16" 750.00
55, SkHd, o/m, flirty eyes, p/e, Simon & Halbig/K*R, 23" 575.00
550, SkHd, o/m, Simon & Halbig/S&H, 16" 525.00
570, SkHd, o/m, Halbig S&H/G, 18" 700.00
570, SkHd, o/m, walking, head turns, G/Halbig S&H, 18" 750.00
576, SkHd, o/m, Simon & Halbig, 16" 575.00
612, SkHd, o/m, MIG/S&H/CM Bergmann, 16" 550.00
670, SkHd, o/m, Simon & Halbig, 16" 575.00
70, SkHd, o/m, 1896, Halbig/K*R, 26" 850.00
70, SkHd, o/m w/teeth, Simon & Halbig/K*R, 28" 1,200.00
719, SkHd, bjt, o/m, S12H/Dep, rpl wig, RpC, 20", EX.......... 2,400.00
719, SkHd, c/m, S&H DEP, 16" 1,800.00
719, SkHd, swivel, ShPl, c/m, S&H, DEP, 20" 2,800.00
739, SkHd, c/m, brn, S 5 H DEP, 14" 1,800.00
739, SkHd, c/m, brn, S 5 H DEP, 18" 2,400.00
759, SkHd, o/m, brn, S 10 H DEP, 20" 800.00
769, SkHd, c/m, S&H DEP, 17" 2,300.00
905, SkHd, swivel on ShPl, c/m, SH, 21" 3,300.00
908, SkHd, swivel on ShPl, c/m, SH, 16" 2,600.00
929, SkHd, c/m, S&H, DEP, 20" 2,400.00
929, SkHd, c/m, S&H, DEP, 25" 3,200.00
939, SkHd, c/m, S 11H DEP, 17" 2,600.00
939, SkHd, c/m, S 11H DEP, 23" 3,000.00
939, SkHd, o/c eyes, o/m, S16H, 30" 3,600.00
940, SkHd, closed dome, o/c mouth, S 2 H, 26" 3,600.00
940, SkHd, swivel on ShPl, o/c mouth, S 2 H, 14" 2,000.00
945, SkHd, c/m, S 2 H DEP, 16" 2,000.00
949, ShHd, o/c eyes, o/m, S 10 H, bride clothes, 19½" 900.00
99, SkHd, o/m, 1899, 11 1/2 Handwerck/Halbig, 16" 525.00

Steiner

Jules Nicholas Steiner established one of the earliest French doll manufactories in 1855. Having been a clockmaker, he began with mechanical dolls, and his patents grew to include walking and talking dolls. In 1880 he registered a patent for a doll with moving eyes. This doll could be put to sleep by turning a rod that operated a wire attached to its eyes. Though these new innovations brought much acclaim to the Steiner company, it closed around 1910 because it could not compete with the less-expensive German dolls that were flooding the market at that time.

A Series child, c/m, o/c eyes, jtd, cb pate, RpC, 12" 3,200.00
A Series child, c/m, o/c eyes, jtd, cb pate, RpC, 20" 5,500.00
B Series, jtd, wire-eyed, o/m teeth, p/e, crier, 20½".................. 6,000.00
Bourgoin, c/m, pwt eyes, 1870s, RpC, 16" 4,800.00
Bourgoin, c/m, pwt eyes, 1870s, RpC, 20" 6,200.00
Bourgoin, c/m, wire eyes, jtd, p/e, orig wig, RpC, 18" 5,000.00
C Series, bl eyes, c/m, p/e, jtd body, RpC, 12" 2,600.00
C Series child, c/m, rnd face, pwt eyes, RpC, 16" 4,800.00
Le Parisien, A Series, 1892, 16" 4,000.00
Le Parisien, Blk, c/m, brn glass eyes, 1900, OC, 13" 2,400.00

Mechanical, key wind, kicks/cries, teeth, RpC, 18" **2,500.00**
Unmk, early wht bsk, rnd face, o/m w/teeth, jtd, RpC, 14" **4,200.00**

Vogue

Brickette, vinyl, o/c eyes, curly hair, 1978, OC, 16" **95.00**
Frolicking Fables Ballerina, pnt lashes, 1952, OC, M **300.00**
Ginny, Bo Peep, hp, o/c eyes, pnt lashes, '52, OC, 8", M **300.00**

**Vogue Ginny 'Country Fair' walker, 1958, 8",
$265.00.**

Ginny, hp, strung, pnt eyes, OC, 8" **250.00**
Ginny, Toddles, compo, OC, 7½", M **265.00**
Ginny Crib Crowd, bent-leg baby, lamb's wool wig, NM **650.00**
Ginny Queen, hp, o/c eyes, molded lashes, OC, M **1,500.00**
Jill, hp, o/c eyes, 10", MIB **95.00**
Miss Ginny, OC, 15", NM **65.00**
Star Bright, OC, 18", M **125.00**
Welcome Home Baby, OC, 20", M **75.00**

Wax, Poured Wax

Over compo, c/m, glass eyes, cloth body, wig, RpC, 29" **700.00**
Over compo, ShHd, cloth body, kid hands, RpC, 33", VG **800.00**
Over compo, ShHd, set eyes, molded hair, cloth body, 15" **350.00**
Over compo, ShHd, talker, 1890s, 19½", EX **875.00**
Over compo, ShHd, wire-eyed (blk glass), wig, kid arms, 26" . **1,200.00**
Over papier-mache, jtd wooden body, wire-eyed, all orig, 11" **550.00**
Poured, cloth body, glass eyes, inset hair, England, 21", VG ... **1,400.00**

Miscellaneous

French Huret type, flange neck, bl eyes, OC, 14" **5,000.00**
Limoges, bsk head, o/m, set eyes, orig wig, Favorite, 27" **1,600.00**
Orsini, bsk, lt bl eyes, sgn on bk, all orig, 5" **1,500.00**

Door Knockers

Door knockers, those charming precursors of the door bell, come
in an intriguing array of shapes and styles. The very rare ones come
from England. Cast iron examples made in this country were often produced in forms similar to the more familiar doorstop figures.

**Basket of flowers, multicolor
paint on cast iron, 4" long,
EX, $55.00.**

Betty Boop, pnt CI, old, EX 150.00
Betty Boop, pnt CI, reproduction 22.00
Butterfly, CI, mc pnt, EX 225.00
Cat w/arched back, brass 55.00
Couple kissing, bronze, 10½" 42.50
Girl watering flowers, CI w/MOP 175.00
Lady's head, flowers/fruit in hair, CI, 1800s, 8½x4½x2" 95.00
Lion's head, ring knocker, brass, 1880s, 4¼", EX 80.00
Owl, brass, old 35.00
Parrot, CI, EX mc pnt 75.00
Parrot in oval, CI w/mc pnt, 4½" 75.00
Sea horse & seashell, brass, EX 90.00
Woodpecker, CI, Hubley 135.00
Woodpecker on tree trunk, CI, orig pnt, Pat Appl For, 6½" 135.00

Doorstops

Although introduced in England in the mid-1800s, cast iron
doorstops were not made to any great extent in this country until after
the Civil War. Once called 'door porters,' their function was to keep
doors open to provide better ventilation. They have been produced in
many shapes and sizes, both dimensional and flat backed, and in the
past few years have become a popular, yet affordable collectible. While
cast iron examples are the most common, brass, wood, and chalk were
also used. An average price is in the $40 to $50 range, though some are
valued at more than $200. Doorstops retained their usefulness and
appeal well into the thirties.

The prices below reflect market values in the east where doorstops
are now at a premium. For other areas of the country, it may be necessary to adjust prices down about 25%. In the listings below, items are
assumed flat backed unless noted full figured and cast iron unless noted
otherwise. For further information we recommend *Doorstops, Identification and Values* by Jeanne Bertoia.

Key: ff — full figured

ABC Scottie Dog, ff, collar emb ABC, 12½x4½", EX 375.00
Ann Hathaway's Cottage, Greenblatt #114, 1927, 7½x6⅛", EX .400.00
Ann Hathaway's Cottage, Hubley, EX pnt, 6⅜x8⅜" 225.00
Art Deco Bathing Beauties w/Umbrella, Fish, orig mc pnt, VG ..285.00
Art Deco Mexican Guitar Player, worn mc pnt, 11¾" 145.00
Bassett Hound, Hubley, ff, gilt & blk pnt, 7x6½", VG 400.00
Boston Bulldog, glass eyes, Greenblatt, wedge bk, G pnt, 13" 200.00
Boston Bulldog, seated, head to right, blk/wht enamel, 7½" 85.00
Buccaneer, ff, old gold rpt, 6⅞" 45.00

Camel on Oval Base, ff, worn blk rpt, 5⅝" 45.00
Caped Man w/Book & Cane, ff, 7⅜x4½", EX 350.00
Cardinal, ff, EX pnt, 5x3½" 185.00
Castle, EX mc pnt, rare, 8x5¼" 400.00
Cat, seated, Gary Iron Works, 1925, old gold rpt, 7" 65.00
Cat, seated, old blk & wht rpt, 9½" 85.00
Cat, seated/upright, eyes shut, worn orig wht pnt, 8½" 200.00
Cat silhouette, paw lifted/tail up, blk pnt, 9½" 235.00
Chameleon, Sherwin Williams Paint Co, 1¼x8", EX 140.00
Child in Sailor Suit, traces old mc pnt, 8¾", G 285.00
Circus Elephant, ff, EX pnt, 5x8" 95.00
Cockatoo, porcelainized; #38, 12x5¾", rare, M 200.00
Cocker Spaniel, faces front, Metalcrafters, wedge, 9x7", EX 110.00
Cocker Spaniel, Hubley, ff, blk & wht pnt, 6¾x11" 250.00
Colonial Pilgrim, B&H, gilt pnt, 10½x6½", EX 275.00
Cop, standing, Le Mur, ff head, hollowed out bk, 8", G 285.00
Cornucopias, Hubley #132, EX pnt, 8½x6" 235.00
Cottage, Hubley, NM pnt, 5¾x7½" 175.00
Cottage w/Fence, National Foundry #32, gray roof variant, EX ...175.00
Covered Wagon, Hubley #375, 9½x5⅛", EX...........................190.00
Daisy Bowl, Hubley #452-1, 7½x5⅛", EX 125.00
Dog & Doghouse, mk Verona, bronze finish, sm 45.00
Dog by Fence, Albany Foundry, 6⅝x8⅝", VG..........................150.00
Dolphin, Spencer, wedge, 10x4½", EX 125.00
Double Scotties w/Handle, recumbent, 8½x9", EX 100.00
Dutch Girl, Littco #33, G pnt, 13x10" 200.00
Egyptian Camel, recumbent, old mc pnt, 4½", G 75.00
Elephant w/Raised Trunk, mk H2, 8½x11", VG 125.00
Fireside Cat, Hubley #335, ff, 5⅝x10¾", VG 165.00
Flower Oval, B&H, w/rubber knobs, 7⅝x3⅝", EX 125.00
Flowered Oval, Albany Foundry #137, 7¾x6⅜", VG..................110.00
Frog, ff, yel & gr pnt, 3½x6¾", VG 85.00
Geese, group of 3, Hubley, worn mc pnt, 8" 210.00
George Washington, bl jacket variation, 12¼x6⅜", VG 450.00
Gnome w/Keys, ff, EX pnt, 10x5⅜" 350.00
Gutter Pup, Hubley, ff, G pnt, 8½x7" 200.00
Heron, Albany Foundry, ff, 7½x5⅛", EX 125.00
Horseshoe, wedge, 5x4", VG 115.00
Hound Dog, VG pnt, 12x8⅝" 155.00
Lantern, 13x5", EX 200.00
Lion, ff, EX pnt, very heavy, 7x8" 95.00
Little Girl, ff (hollow), VG pnt, 7x4½" 250.00
Little Girl Holding Shoe, B&H #417, rubber knobs, 10x6", EX .450.00
Lobster, gr-blk pnt, 12½x6½", EX 475.00
Lobster, red & gr pnt, 12½x6½", EX 550.00
London Mail Coach, old mc pnt, 7⅜" 65.00
Lone Star of Texas, wedge, 10½x10¼", EX 375.00
Maiden, lt gr dress, EX pnt, 8⅞x3¾" 375.00
Man w/Mug & Staff, brass w/CI base insert, 13⅛x8¼", EX.........125.00
Monkey, seated, left hand under jaw, EX mc pnt, 8½" 350.00
Monkey on Barrel, Taylor Cook #3, 1930, EX pnt, 8⅜x4⅞" 450.00
Monkey w/Brass Earrings, Seated; ff, old pnt, 6¾", VG.............85.00
Mutt & His Bone, G pnt, 8¼x5½"..145.00
Old Salt, ff, EX pnt, 11x4⅛" 225.00
Organ Grinder w/Monkey, worn red & bl pnt, 10" 175.00
Owl, aluminum or pot metal, SF Taylor, wedge, 3¾x5½", EX 95.00
Owl, side view, EX pnt, 5¾" 75.00
Parrot, Albany Foundry, G pnt, 12½x7½" 125.00
Parrot in Ring, B&H, w/rubber knobs, EX pnt, 13¾x7¼"...........325.00
Parrot on Perch, old mc rpt, 6½" 40.00
Pekingese, Hubley, ff, orig pnt, 14½x9", EX 675.00
Penguin, CI w/worn blk & wht pnt, ff, lt rust, 11" 215.00
Persian Cat, Hubley, ff, blk & wht pnt, 8½x6½", VG................140.00
Pheasant, mc pnt w/minor wear, sgn Everett, Hubley, 8"..........500.00

Pineapple, brass w/CI insert, very heavy, 13x6", EX.................110.00
Pirate Girl, EX pnt, 13⅞x7¼" 300.00
Pointer, left leg raised, blk & wht pnt, 15" 85.00
Police Dog, bronze, ff, 8¾" 60.00
Polly, Hubley #180, w/sticker, 8⅛x5¼", VG 175.00
Poppy, Hubley #440, 10⅝x7⅞", NM 150.00
Pud Boston Terrier, ff, emb Pud on blanket, VG pnt, 10x9¾" 225.00
Rabbit, ff, realistic, 8⅛x6½", VG 300.00
Rabbit by Fence, Albany Foundry, EX pnt, 6⅞x8⅛" 400.00
Rabbit w/Top Hat, Albany Fountry #94, EX pnt, 9⅞x4¾" 450.00

Ram, EX paint, 7½", $135.00.

Rooster, EX pnt, 7x5½" 150.00
Saddled Horse on Base, EX pnt, 10½x7⅝" 125.00
Scottie, blk & wht dog on gr base, 7x9", VG............................150.00
Scottie, 1¾" wedge, orig yel pnt, 7⅝x8¾", VG 150.00
Southern Belle, lg flowered hat in right hand, worn, 11" 55.00
Spotted Dog, Taylor Cook, 1930, VG pnt, rare, 7¾x7¾" 575.00
Stag, CI w/worn orig mc pnt, glass eyes, no base, 19" 475.00
Steeplechase, woman on wht horse, 7¼x7½", EX 375.00
Street Singers, Hubley, old rpt, rare, 6½x7½", EX...................375.00
Swallows, Hubley #480, 8½x7½", EX 475.00
The Patrol, Renier Novelty, ff, 8¾x3¾", EX 250.00
Three Geese, Hubley, sgn Fred Everett, EX pnt, 8x8" 475.00
Twin Kittens, old mc rpt, 7½", G 75.00
Two Birds on Perch w/Berries, orig mc pnt, 8¼", VG 145.00
Two Men in Livery, Fish, worn orig pnt, 9"............................625.00
West Wind, English, no-hdl variation, 16⅛x7⅝" 475.00
Windmill, mc pnt w/minor wear, 7" 9,495.00
Wolfhound, no base, rpt, 15"...85.00

Dorflinger

   C. Dorflinger was born in Alsace, France, and came to this country when he was ten years old. When still very young, he obtained a job in a glass factory in New Jersey. As a young man, he started his own glassworks in Brooklyn, New York, opening new factories as profits permitted. During that time he made cut glass articles for many famous people including President and Mrs. Lincoln, for whom he produced a complete service of tableware with the United States Coat of Arms. In 1863 he sold the New York factories because of ill health and moved to his farm near White Mills, Pennsylvania. His health returned, and he started a plant near his home. It was there that he did much of his best work, making use of only the very finest materials. Christian died in 1915, and the plant was closed in 1921 by consent of the family.

   Dorflinger glass is rare and often hard to identify. Very few pieces were marked — many only carried a small paper label which was quickly discarded.

Water pitcher, cranberry over clear with allover brilliant cut design, 7½", $1,900.00.

Tray, cranberry/clear, cut w/cherries & peaches, 12"	2,000.00
Tray, ice cream; pinwheels, 12½"	650.00
Tray, sharp/heavy cuttings, 2½x12x10½"	650.00
Vase, hobstars & 5 lg cut bull's eyes, 10"	245.00
Vase, Kalana Pansy, ruffled, widely flared, 5"	235.00
Vase, Kalana Poppy, ftd trumpet form, 13"	350.00

Dragon Ware

An undulating moriage dragon with a fierce expression decorates shaded gray bisque backgrounds in this type of ware that was very popular as gift-shop items during the forties and fifties. It was produced in Japan and may sometimes be found with the Nippon mark. Only unmarked items are listed here.

Cup, demitasse	9.00
Cup & saucer, nude lithophane	25.00
Demitasse set, lithophane, 15-pc	150.00
Pitcher, mini, 1¾"	12.50
Plate, 7"	15.00
Saucer, brn rim	3.00
Teapot, cobalt w/gold dragons, sgn Shofar, +14 pcs	425.00
Tea set, pearlized cups, 11-pc, serves 4	65.00
Tea set, star/Lima mks, #30, 3-pc	85.00
Vase, gold trim, bulbous, 5"	85.00
Vase, slender form, 6"	50.00

Dresden

The term Dresden is used today to indicate the porcelains that were produced in Meissen and Dresden, Germany, from the very early eighteenth century well into the next. John Bottger, a young alchemist, discovered the formula for the first true porcelain in 1708 while being held a virtual prisoner at the palace in Dresden because of the King's determination to produce a superior ware. Two years later a factory was erected in nearby Meissen with Bottger as director. There fine tableware, elaborate centerpieces, and exquisite figurines with applied details were produced. In 1731, to distinguish their product from the wares of such potters as Sevres, Worcester, Chelsea, and Derby, Meissen adopted their famous crossed swords trademark. During the next century, several potteries were producing porcelain in the 'Meissen style' in Dresden itself. Their wares were marked with their own logo and the Dresden indication. Those listed here are from that era. Our advisor for this category is Donald Penrose; he is listed in the Directory under Ohio. See the Meissen section for examples with the crossed swords marking.

Basket, appl florals on bowl & loop hdl, rtcl rim, ftd, 7" W	150.00
Bowl, centerpc; pnt/appl florals, sgn, boat shape, 7½x17"	350.00
Bowl, mc florals w/gold, rtcl sides, 1860 mk, 7½x10½"	250.00
Compote, mc florals, sgn Schumann, rtcl rim, 5½x7½"	110.00
Compote, mc florals w/gold, rtcl, ped ft, 8½"	150.00
Figurine, Amour Tete-a-Tete, romantic couple w/lamb, 7x9"	550.00
Figurine, ballerina, red hair, pk & wht lace skirt, 6"	175.00
Figurine, boy feeding geese, EX color, ca 1910, 5½x2¾"	195.00
Figurine, Chess Game, couple at table, 5½x6½"	450.00
Figurine, Dame de La Corude Francois I, Thieme, 1875, 8"	350.00
Figurine, dancing couple, red coat, appl florals, 6x5"	225.00
Figurine, girl sits w/lamb, boy sits w/instrument, 7x9"	550.00
Figurine, Gypsy lady sits w/goat, 8x10½"	450.00
Figurine, lady in wht gown, red flower trim, yel hat, 8"	350.00
Figurine, lady on couch w/music, man w/violin, 10½x10"	850.00
Figurine, lady seated w/greyhound at feet, 8x8"	325.00
Figurine, man & lady at chess table, 5½x6½"	450.00
Figurine, Marquise de Vereuil, Carl Thieme, 1875, 8"	350.00
Figurine, Ring Around Rosy, 3 girls in circle, 6½x8½"	325.00
Figurine, 2 ladies at tea table, man in red coat, 8x12"	950.00
Figurine, 2 ladies sit, 1 w/book, 1 w/basket, 10x12"	950.00
Figurine, 2 men w/violins & lady at piano, 9½x11"	975.00

Plaque, portrait of a young woman, 9" x 7", $1,500.00.

Plaque, maid's portrait, sgn Graf, ornate iron fr, 5"	550.00
Tazza, mc florals, gilt, rtcl, mk, 5x6½"	75.00
Tea set, roses, molded head on pot, Carl Thieme, 1875, 15-pc	750.00
Teapot, duck figural, HP feathers, gray body, loop hdl, 6x10"	345.00
Vase, couple in panel, florals w/gold, vine hdls, 15x11½"	575.00
Vase, ladies & children, Wissman mk, ewer form, mk, 12x5½"	795.00

Vase, scenic medallion on cobalt w/much gold, old mk, 8".........**325.00**

Dresser Accessories

Dresser sets, ring trees, figural or satin pincushions, manicure sets — all those lovely items that graced milady's dressing table — were at the same time decorative as well as functional. Today they appeal to collectors for many reasons. The Victorian era is well represented by repousse silver-backed mirrors and brushes and pincushions that were used to display ornamental pins for the hair, hats, and scarves. The hair receiver — similar to a powder jar but with an opening in the lid — was used to hold the lovely strands of hair retrieved from the comb or brush. These were wound around the finger and tucked in the opening to be used later for hair jewelry and pictures, many of which survive to the present day. (See Hair Weaving.)

Celluloid dresser sets were popular during the late 1800s and early 1900s. Some included manicure tools, pill boxes, and buttonhooks, as well as the basic items. Because celluloid tends to break rather easily, a whole set may be hard to find today. (See also Plastics.) With the current interest in anything Art Deco, sets from the thirties and forties are especially collectible. These may be made of crystal, Bakelite, or silver, and the original boxes just as lavishly appointed as their contents.

Atomizer, jadite, short disk form, orig cord & bulb, 3¾"...............**60.00**
Box, blk w/emb panels, crystal seated nude finial, 4½" dia **165.00**
Box, gr frosted coach form, blk lid w/crown finial **98.00**
Box, pk frost, embracing couple form lid...**85.00**
Box, powder; Tartanware, orig puff, ca 1840, 3½x2¾" **175.00**
Compact, amber, etched florals, Cambridge **40.00**

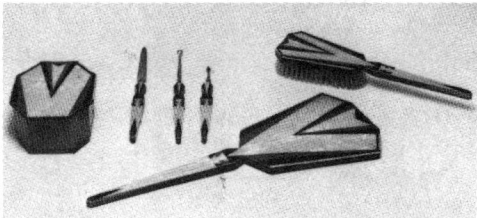

Dresser set, Art Deco with plastic handles in red, black, and pearl, ca 1920s, minor wear, $125.00.

Set, Am Pioneer, crystal, Liberty, 4-pc **125.00**
Set, cut & frosted semi-circles, chrome tops, Germany, 7-pc.......**450.00**
Set, cut crystal, 1920s, 2 bottles+jar+hair receiver......................**500.00**
Set, mc florals on gr & wht china, 5-pc on 9x12" tray **225.00**
Set, pk & yel florals w/gold, Limoges/Rosenthal, 6-pc **295.00**
Set, pk blown glass, gold trim, 2 7" bottles+powder box.................**80.00**
Set, silver w/eng circles, La Pierre, 1920s, 11-pc.........................**330.00**
Set, sterling w/emb florals, Whiting Mfg, 1895, 10-pc **770.00**
Set, vaseline, mk Shari, 4-pc on 2x7" tray **155.00**
Set, wht ironstone, Adams, octagonal 13" tray+3 pcs **125.00**
Tray, milk glass, Jenny Lind in oval, Fostoria, 11½".....................**30.00**
Tray, milk glass, Paneled Grape, Westmoreland **12.50**

Dryden

James Dryden opened his pottery company in Ellsworth, Kansas, in 1946. Within a year he was producing 2,000 pieces a week, and the company continued to grow. During the 1950s some of the pottery was subcontracted to Van Briggle. In 1956 Dryden moved to Hot Springs, Arkansas.

Ellsworth clay was dark tan, while pieces made in Hot Springs

were of white clay. This helps date the ware, most of which is marked and numbered. Expect to find pieces in nice condition with high gloss glazes in colors reflective of the period. Various marks were used, but the majority include either the words 'Dryden' or 'Ozark Frontier.' Our advisor for this category is Ralph Winslow; he is listed in the Directory under Kansas.

Bowl, gr, #44, 5x14"...**20.00**
Creamer, dk gr, #12, mini..**12.00**
Creamer, souvenir Valley Forge, #950, 4" **16.00**
Creamer & sugar bowl, gr/tan mottled, #900.................**19.00**
Cup, aqua, Brookville Hotel, #1.....................................**20.00**
Jug, maroon, KU, mini, 3¼"...**20.00**

Mug, face in relief, $25.00.

Pitcher, blk, #49, 11", +6 blk tumblers in brass carrier...................**45.00**
Pitcher, mini creamer, yel, #180,3"..................................**15.00**
Shakers, maroon, Wichita Kans, #73 ....**16.00**
Syrup, brn, Lindsborg Kans, #94, 6½" **23.00**
Vase, aqua, #104, 3"..**15.00**
Vase, boot, maroon, Mankato Kans, 5".............................**13.00**
Vase, ivy leaves, yel/gr, 5" **18.00**
Vase, deer, gr, #7x, 8½" **18.00**
Vase, leaf, gr/tan, 5" **18.00**
Vase, maroon, #6A, 6" **15.00**
Vase, maroon, sq, #17, 4" **15.00**
Vase, navy, #75, 7", pr...**26.00**

Duncan and Miller

The firm that became known as the Duncan and Miller Glass Company in 1900 was organized in 1874 in Pittsburgh, Pennsylvania, a partnership between George Duncan, his sons Harry and James, and his son-in-law Augustus Heisey. John Ernest Miller was hired as their designer. He is credited with creating the most famous of all Duncan's glassware lines, Three Face. (See Pattern Glass.) The George Duncan and Sons Glass Company, as it was titled, was only one of eighteen companies that merged in 1891 with U.S. Glass. Soon after the Pittsburgh factory burned in 1892, the association was dissolved, and Heisey left the firm to set up his own factory in Newark, Ohio. Duncan built his new plant in Washington, Pennsylvania, where he continued to make pressed glassware in such notable patterns as Bagware, Amberette, Duncan Flute, Button Arches, and Zippered Slash. The firm was eventually sold to U.S. Glass in Tiffin, Ohio, and unofficially closed in August, 1955.

In addition to the early pressed dinnerware patterns, today's Duncan and Miller collectors enjoy searching for opalescent vases in many patterns and colors, frosted 'Satin Tone' glassware, acid-etched designs, and lovely stemware such as the Rock Crystal cuttings. Milk glass was made in limited quantity and is considered a good investment. Ruby glass, Ebony (a lovely opaque black glass popular during the twenties and thirties), and, of course, the glass animal and bird figurines are all highly valued examples of the art of Duncan and Miller.

Expect to pay at least 25% more than values listed for 'color' for ruby and cobalt and as much as 50% more in the Georgian, Pall Mall and Sandwich lines. Pink, green, and amber Sandwich is worth approximately 30% more than the same items in crystal. Milk glass examples of American Way are valued up to 30% higher than color, 50% higher in Pall Mall. Add approximately 40% to listed prices for opalescent items. Etchings, cuttings, and other decorations will increase values by about 50%. For further study, we recommend *The Encyclopedia of Duncan Glass,* by Gail Krause; she is listed in the Directory under Pennsylvania. Another book of great interest is *Glass Animals and Figural Flower Frogs from the Depression Era* by Lee Garmon and Dick Spencer; they are both listed under Illinois.

Animals and Birds

Bird of Paradise	475.00
Donkey, cart & peon	475.00
Duck, ash tray, 8"	20.00
Goose, fat, 6x6"	245.00
Heron, 7"	95.00
Leaf Swan, bl or pk, 6½"	125.00
Leaf Swan, vaseline opal, 6½"	185.00
Mallard Duck, cigarette box, #30, w/lid, 3½x4½"	45.00
Ruffled Grouse	1,750.00
Swan, ash tray, crystal w/bl neck, 4"	35.00
Swan, bl opal, W&F, spreadwing, 10x12½"	245.00
Swan, crystal w/gray cut, 10½"	145.00
Swan, gr opal, W&F, spreadwing, 10x12½"	225.00
Swan, open, 7"	45.00
Swan, red w/crystal neck, 8"	50.00
Swan, solid, 3"	30.00
Swan, solid, 5"	20.00
Swan, solid, 7"	45.00
Swan, wht milk glass w/red neck, 10½"	450.00
Swordfish	145.00
Swordfish, bl opal, rare	500.00

Astaire, color; goblet, champagne	18.00
Canterbury, amber; goblet, water; 8-oz	18.00
Canterbury, amber; plate, 8"	14.00
Canterbury, amber; stem, cocktail; ftd, 3½"	10.00
Canterbury, chartreuse; goblet, water	14.00
Canterbury, color; bowl, 5"	10.00
Canterbury, color; relish, divided	20.00
Canterbury, color; relish, 3-part, 3-hdl, 9"	50.00
Canterbury, crystal; cigarette box, silver lid	40.00
Canterbury, crystal; compote, high ft	20.00
Canterbury, crystal; plate, 12"	35.00
Canterbury, crystal; sugar bowl, 9-oz	10.00
Canterbury, crystal; tray, 4-part	14.00
Canterbury, lt bl; sherbet	7.00
Canterbury, lt bl; stem, wine	12.00
Caribbean, color; bowl, fluted sides, hdls, 3¾x5"	30.00
Caribbean, color; bowl, vegetable; hdls, 9¼"	50.00

Caribbean, color; cocktail shaker, 33-oz, 9"	150.00
Caribbean, color; cup, punch	17.50
Caribbean, color; pitcher, syrup; 9-oz, 4¼"	110.00
Caribbean, color; plate, luncheon; 8½"	25.00
Caribbean, color; relish, oblong, 9½"	52.50
Caribbean, color; salt cellar, 2½"	15.00
Caribbean, color; shakers, w/metal top, 5", pr	75.00
Caribbean, color; stem, cordial; 1-oz, 3"	125.00
Caribbean, color; stem, sherbet; ftd, 4¼"	15.00
Caribbean, color; tumbler, ftd, 8½-oz, 5½"	35.00
Caribbean, color; tumbler, iced tea; ftd, 11-oz, 6½"	40.00
Caribbean, color; tumbler, shot glass; 2-oz, 2¼"	45.00
Caribbean, color; vase, ftd, 10"	110.00
Caribbean, color; vase, str sides, ftd, 8"	75.00
Caribbean, crystal; bowl, 8½"	22.50
Caribbean, crystal; candy dish, w/lid, 4x7"	35.00
Caribbean, crystal; cheese/cracker liner, hdls, 11"	15.00
Caribbean, crystal; plate, salad; 7½"	8.00
Caribbean, crystal; plate, 14"	15.00
Caribbean, crystal; relish, 2-part, rnd, 6"	10.00
Caribbean, crystal; server, center hdl, 5¾"	11.50
Caribbean, crystal; tray, rnd, 12¾"	17.50
Caribbean, crystal; vase, ruffled, 7½"	25.00
Fine Rib, color; pitcher, lg	85.00
Fine Rib, color; pitcher, sm	65.00
Fine Rib, color; tumbler, iced tea	18.00
Fine Rib, color; tumbler, juice	14.00
First Love, crystal; bowl, #6, flared, 12"	75.00
First Love, crystal; bowl, hdl, 6"	35.00
First Love, crystal; bowl, oval, scalloped, 13"	75.00
First Love, crystal; candlestick, #304, 2-lite, pr	75.00
First Love, crystal; candy dish, 3-part	32.00
First Love, crystal; compote	30.00
First Love, crystal; goblet, water; tall	35.00
First Love, crystal; plate, sandwich; 12"	65.00
First Love, crystal; relish, terrace; 4-part, hdls, 9"	60.00
First Love, crystal; stem, chamgagne	32.00
First Love, crystal; stem, cocktail	30.00
First Love, crystal; sugar bowl, hdls	20.00
First Love, crystal; vase, #117, 8"	70.00
First Love, crystal; vase, cornucopia	70.00
First Love, crystal; vase, urn; hdls, 7"	70.00
Hobnail, bl opal; candy dish, 1-lb, 9½"	65.00
Hobnail, crystal; bowl, centerpiece; crimped, 12"	25.00
Hobnail, crystal; candlestick	12.00
Hobnail, crystal; compote	24.00
Hobnail, crystal; mug, cobalt hdl, 3¾"	15.00
Hobnail, crystal; top hat, 4"	30.00
Hobnail, pk or bl; candy dish	125.00
Hobnail, pk or bl; tumbler, iced tea; flat	30.00
Language of Flowers, crystal; bowl, 11½"	35.00
Language of Flowers, crystal; candlestick, 3", pr	35.00
Mardi Gras, crystal; cake plate, ftd, 10"	75.00
Mardi Gras, crystal; cake salver	75.00
Mardi Gras, crystal; creamer, ind	25.00
Mardi Gras, crystal; cup, punch	8.00
Murano, flower arranger, milk glass, 11"	160.00
Murano, milk glass; bowl, oval, 10x7"	17.00
Murano, milk glass; crimp plate, 8" +3x6½" bowl, set	195.00
Murano, pk opal; bowl, crimped, 11½"	85.00
Nautical, crystal; anchor & rope bookends, no eagle, pr	350.00
Pall Mall, chartreuse; swan, 7"	57.00
Pall Mall, color; swan, 10½"	400.00
Pall Mall, color; swan, 7"	270.00

Pall Mall, crystal; swan, leaf cutting, 10¼" 145.00
Pall Mall, crystal; swan, silver o/l, 7" 35.00
Pall Mall, crystal; swan, 7" 30.00
Pall Mall, red; swan, 13" 110.00
Sandwich, crystal; ash tray, sq, 2⅔" 8.00
Sandwich, crystal; bonbon, heart form, w/ring hdl, 5" 15.00
Sandwich, crystal; bottle, oil; 5¾" 50.00
Sandwich, crystal; bowl, epergne; w/center hole, 12" 50.00
Sandwich, crystal; bowl, fruit; crimped, ftd, 11½" 50.00
Sandwich, crystal; bowl, fruit; 5" 14.00
Sandwich, crystal; bowl, lily; vertical edge, 10" 50.00
Sandwich, crystal; bowl, nappy, 2-part, 5" 12.00
Sandwich, crystal; bowl, salted almond; 2½" 12.00
Sandwich, crystal; butter dish, w/lid, ¼-lb 40.00
Sandwich, crystal; candelabrum, w/bobeche/prisms, 3-light 225.00
Sandwich, crystal; candlestick, w/bobeche/prisms, 1-light 30.00
Sandwich, crystal; candlestick, 2-light, 5" 25.00

Sandwich cheese set, 13" platter, 5½" x 3" compote, $50.00.

Sandwich, crystal; cigarette holder, ftd, 3" 27.50
Sandwich, crystal; compote, ftd, 4¼" 200.00
Sandwich, crystal; pitcher, ice lip, 64-oz, 8" 125.00
Sandwich, crystal; plate, hostess; 16" 90.00
Sandwich, crystal; plate, torte; 12" 55.00
Sandwich, crystal; relish, 4-part, hdls, 10" 35.00
Sandwich, crystal; shakers, w/glass top, 2½", pr 25.00
Sandwich, crystal; stem, oyster cocktail; ftd, 5-oz, 2¾"..............15.00
Sandwich, crystal; stem, wine; 3-oz, 4¼" 20.00
Sandwich, crystal; sugar shaker, w/metal top, 13-oz...................75.00
Sandwich, crystal; tray, ice cream; rolled edge, 12" 40.00
Sandwich, crystal; tumbler, iced tea; ftd, 12-oz, 5¼" 17.50
Sandwich, crystal; tumbler, juice; ftd, 5-oz, 3¾" 12.00
Sandwich, crystal; vase, epergne; threaded base, 7½" 165.00
Sandwich, crystal; vase, ftd, 10" 75.00
Sanibel, bl opal; relish, 2-part, 8¾" 35.00
Sanibel, color; nappy, fruit; 6½" 20.00
Sanibel, color; relish, 3-part, oval, 12" 40.00
Ships, amber; plate, 8" 16.00
Ships, gr; plate, 8" 18.00
Spiral Flutes, color; bottle, oil; w/stopper, 6-oz 135.00
Spiral Flutes, color; bowl, bouillon; 3¾" 15.00
Spiral Flutes, color; bowl, cereal; sm flange, 6½" 25.00
Spiral Flutes, color; bowl, cream soup; ftd, 4¾" 15.00
Spiral Flutes, color; bowl, nappy, w/lid, 6" 60.00
Spiral Flutes, color; bowl, nappy, 11" 30.00
Spiral Flutes, color; compote, 4⅜" 15.00
Spiral Flutes, color; cup, seafood sauce; 2½" 22.00
Spiral Flutes, color; cup & saucer 15.00
Spiral Flutes, color; ice tub, hdls 40.00
Spiral Flutes, color; pitcher, ½-gal 125.00

Spiral Flutes, color; platter, 11" 32.50
Spiral Flutes, color; sweetmeat, w/lid, 7½" 85.00
Spiral Flutes, color; tumbler, ginger ale; 11-oz, 5½" 50.00
Spiral Flutes, color; tumbler, soda; 7-oz, 4¾" 27.50
Spiral Flutes, color; vase, 8½" 17.50
Spiral Flutes, crystal; bowl, nappy, 8" 15.00
Sylvan, bl opal; swan, 12½" 195.00
Sylvan, crystal; plate, 7¼" 7.50
Tavern, crystal; cruet, 6-oz 16.00
Tear Drop, crystal; ash tray, 5" 8.00
Tear Drop, crystal; bottle, bar; w/stopper, 12" 95.00
Tear Drop, crystal; bottle, oil; 3-oz 20.00
Tear Drop, crystal; bowl, finger; 4¼" 7.00
Tear Drop, crystal; bowl, fruit; 7" 7.00
Tear Drop, crystal; bowl, punch; 2½-gal, 15½" 85.00
Tear Drop, crystal; bowl, salad; 12" 35.00
Tear Drop, crystal; bowl, salad; 9" 25.00
Tear Drop, crystal; bowl, sq, 4-hdl, 12" 42.50
Tear Drop, crystal; candy box, 3-part, 3-hdl, w/lid, 8" 45.00
Tear Drop, crystal; candy dish, heart form, 7½" 22.00
Tear Drop, crystal; celery, 2-part, hdls, 11" 18.00
Tear Drop, crystal; cheese & cracker set, 2-pc 42.50
Tear Drop, crystal; compote, ftd, 4¾" 12.00
Tear Drop, crystal; creamer, 6-oz 6.00
Tear Drop, crystal; marmalade, w/lid, 4" 35.00
Tear Drop, crystal; pitcher, milk; 16-oz, 5" 50.00
Tear Drop, crystal; pitcher, water; silver decor 125.00
Tear Drop, crystal; plate, canape; 6" 10.00
Tear Drop, crystal; plate, dinner; 10½" 27.50
Tear Drop, crystal; plate, torte; rolled edge, 16" 37.50
Tear Drop, crystal; plate, torte; 14" 35.00
Terrace, color; ash tray, sq, sm 28.00
Terrace, color; cup & saucer 65.00
Terrace, color; plate, dinner; sq 65.00
Terrace, color; tumbler, juice; flat 32.00
Touraine, crystal; goblet, water 8.00
Willow, crystal; sherbet or champagne, 4¾" 14.00

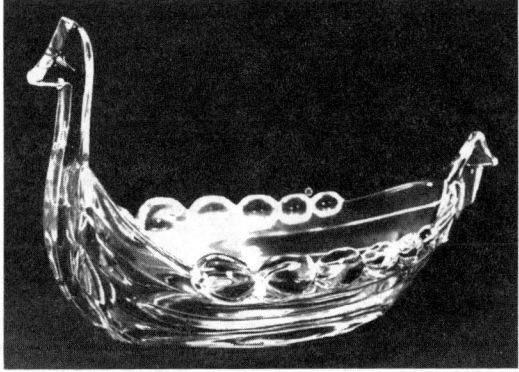

Viking boat, 12" long, $125.00.

Durand

Durand Art Glass was a division of Vineland Glass Works in Vineland, New Jersey. Created in 1924, it was geared specifically toward the manufacture of fine handcrafted artware. Iridescent, opalescent, and cased glass was used to create such patterns as King Tut, reminiscent of Tiffany and Steuben. Production halted in 1931 after the death of Victor Durand. Very few examples are signed, and unmarked pieces are often mistaken for Steuben or Quezal. Unmarked items are often hard to sell, sometimes bringing only about half the price of a similar but signed piece. Our advisor for this category is Mike Roscoe; he is listed in the Directory under Michigan.

Candlestick, feathers, bl-tip on amber, etch wheat, 9", pr 275.00
Candlestick, feathers, dk bl/wht/gr, wide bobeche, 3x5", pr........165.00
Candlestick, King Tut, 10", pr.................................... 1,225.00
Charger, ambergris w/emerald border, 10-rib, 14½" 150.00
Compote, feathers, wht on cobalt, yel base/stem, 4½x6" 750.00
Lamp, hearts/vines, gold/gr on opal irid 6" dome, tree base 2,100.00
Lamp, leaves/threading, gold/gr on opal 7" dome shade/base... 1,750.00
Lamp base, bl/gold drags on gr, trumpet vase, brass mt, 16".........600.00
Lighter, King Tut, gold plated mts, table sz, EX..........................475.00
Plate, 6-lobe pulled flower center on bl, 8"..................................300.00
Torch lamp, gr/wht crackle-cased ambergris, ornate metal ft.......600.00

Vase, cameo parrot, iridescent blue over blue mottle, signed/#1710-10, 10", $2,900.00.

Vase, bl irid w/gold threading, #1995-6, 6x5" 695.00
Vase, bl irid w/threading (losses), flared top, sgn, 9¾" 325.00
Vase, dk bl irid, trumpet neck on bulbous body, 8x7" 825.00
Vase, feathers, gold & wht w/bl tips on gold, threaded, 8" 1,550.00
Vase, feathers, gr/wht, Egyptian crackle, 8¾x4¼" 965.00
Vase, feathers, wht w/bl on gold, gold threads, ftd, 11½"......... 2,050.00
Vase, gold irid, flat base, trumpet form, sgn, 16"..........................750.00
Vase, hearts/vines, ivory on bl irid, disk ft, 12" 1,200.00
Vase, hearts/vines, wht on bl, flared/tapered, 6" 1,100.00
Vase, King Tut, wht/gold/cobalt irid on gr, unsgn, 7" 500.00
Vase, leaves/vines, gold on opal, gold int, cylinder, 11½" 900.00
Vase, leaves/vines, gr irid on gold, ruffled baluster, 6" 875.00

Elfinware

Made in Germany from about 1920 until the 1940s, these miniature vases, boxes, salt cellars, and miscellaneous novelty items are characterized by the tiny applied flowers that often cover their entire surface. Pieces with animals and birds are the most valuable, followed by the more interesting examples such as diminutive grand pianos, candle holders, etc. See also Salts, Open.

Baby buggy, 2x1½x2¾"...55.00
Bottle, cologne; appl roses, gr lustre, 8½"..................................55.00
Box, mc on gr, 1¾x2¼"...50.00
Dutch shoe, 4" 75.00
Inkwell, 3x3¾" 55.00
Place card holder, fan-shaped basket, pk & yel roses 25.00
Salt cellar, swan 55.00

Slipper, appl roses, Germany, 3"..45.00
Teapot, 2½" 55.00
Watering can, 6" 60.00

Vase, 2¾", $40.00; Swan, 2¼", $55.00.

Epergnes

Popular during the Victorian era, epergnes were fancy centerpieces often consisting of several tiers of vases (called lilies), candle holders, or dishes, or a combination of components. They were made in all types of art glass, and some were set in ornate plated frames.

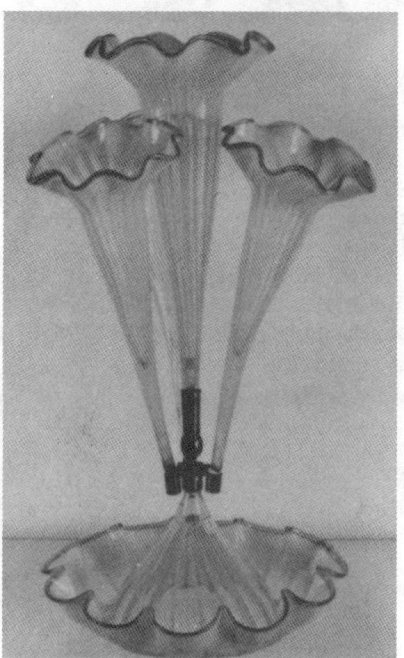

5-piece epergne in white opalescent with applied green edge, 19", $350.00.

Cranberry, 3 hanging baskets/4 lilies, vaseline trim, 21" 1,855.00
Cranberry, 3 lilies w/rigaree+2 canes in swirl bowl, 19" 250.00
Cranberry opal, 3 ruffled trumpets w/rigaree+2 canes, 12" 550.00
Cranberry opal to amber, lifted center vase+3 in leaf stand........400.00
Cranberry w/crystal applique, 3-lily, 18x9"..................................425.00
Cut glass w/panels, grad 2-tier tazza w/vase atop, 18x11" 450.00
Gr opal stripes, 4 lg lilies, 20" 750.00
Orange to vaseline overshot, 1-lily, brass mts, 14½" 375.00
Rubina center lily, NP ft, ruffled bowl, 12⅜x9½".........................325.00

Sapphire bl, HP daisies, 1 ruffled lily, 11¾x7" 245.00
Wht opal stripes/gr edge, 3 lilies in ruffled bowl, 19" 350.00

Erphila

Ebeling and Ruess, an importing company in Philadelphia, began operations in 1886. The acronym 'Erphila' was frequently substituted for the manufacturer's mark on the imported items. It appears that the Erphila mark was used through the late 1930s and then again after WW II on products from U.S. Zone Germany as well as from other areas. The company imported from factories such as Fustenberg, W. Goebel, Villeroy and Boch, Heinrich, Keramos, and Schumann, to name a few. Figurines, art pottery, and some utilitarian items can be found bearing the Erphila mark. Examples are hard to find. Early German marks (those prior to 1900) often contain the word 'Fustenberg.' After the turn of the century, a rectangular mark in green ink was used. Following WW I, porcelain items were imported from Czechoslovakia. These sometimes carried gold and silver labels. A small variety of marks were used in the 1920s and '30s, but they all contained the name Erphila. Sticker labels were also used. 'Bavaria,' 'Black Forest,' and 'Italy' are sometimes found in combination with 'Erphila.'

Ebeling and Ruess continue the importing business, but it appears that since the 1940s they are also using an 'E' and 'R' on a bell-shaped mark. Because this mark does not contain the name 'Erphila,' we do not consider it to be such. We assume that they stopped using this name sometime in the 1950s.

Covered pitcher, hand-painted poppies, 8", $80.00.

Basket, porc, brn/bl/gr, deer hdl, MIG, 3¾" 22.50
Bust, lady's head, Art Deco, Czech mk, 8" 135.00
Candlestick, red & bl flowers on wht, hdl, MIG, 5¾" 22.00
Cookie jar, coach scene, egg shape, 8¼" 300.00
Creamer, gr/wht/blk, cat hdl, MIG, 4" 45.00
Creamer, red dots on wht, 3½" 9.00
Dish, divided; tartan plaid bi-color, w/hdl 45.00
Figurine, bull terrier, MIG, 5½" L 26.00
Figurine, cat, wht w/gold ball, MIG, 10½" L 120.00
Figurine, fighting cock, wht/mc, 6½x7", pr 90.00
Figurine, German shepherd, tan/brn, MIG, 6" 42.00
Figurine, goose, wings spread, wht/gray, MIG 25.00
Figurine, pirate, parrot on shoulder, MIG, 4" 15.00
Figurine, Scottie dog, blk head, MIG, 2½" 18.00
Figurine, setter dogs (2), hunting pose, blk/brn/wht, MIG 45.00
Figurine, spaniel, sitting, brn/wht, MIG, 6" 45.00

Figurine, Victorian couple, MIG, 6" 30.00
Jelly dish, mc fruit, MIG, w/lid & short spoon 25.00
Miniature, chicken on nest, Bavaria, bl 37.50
Mug, Colonial drinking scene, #14, ½-liter 35.00
Pitcher, orange & gr flowers, 5½" 22.00
Pitcher, orange flowers on gr, w/lid & underplate, 5½" 35.00
Pitcher, orange flowers on gr, w/lid & underplate, 8½" 55.00
Pitcher, red/wht/blk rings, 9", +3 mugs 150.00
Planter, campfire silhouette, gold/brn, 5" 50.00
Planter, Oriental scene, Italy, 3x5¼" 25.00
Shakers, blk dots on wht, 5", pr 30.00
Teapot, demitasse; Cherry Chintz, +6 c/s 150.00
Toothpick holder, blk/wht dog by tub, 3½" 17.00
Vase, mc flowers, 5⅜" 35.00
Vase, mc webs, gr int, #6356/9, 4¼" 24.00
Vase, orange, bulbous, Czech Art Pottery, 10" 55.00

Eskimo Artifacts

While ivory carvings made from walrus tusks or whale teeth have been the most emphasized articles of Eskimo art, basketry and wood-working are other areas in which these Alaskan Indians excel. Their designs are effected through the application of simple yet dramatic lines and almost stark decorative devices. Though not pursued to the extent of American Indian art, the unique work of this northern tribe is beginning to attract the serious attention of today's collectors.

Basket, coiled, birds all around, 1930, 9½x9½" 225.00
Basket, coiled, no design, w/lid, 1900, 9x11" 300.00
Box, baleen, ivory bear finial, sgn Dodson/1968, 3x4" dia 550.00
Cribbage brd, walrus ivory, cvd walrus/eagle, 1900, 24" 600.00
Cvg, stone, polar bear, cvd in old style, 1900, 3x7" 250.00
Doll, hand cvd/articulated, in native costume, 1800s, 16" 225.00
Doll, handmade of hide w/fur clothing, 1930, 8x4" 50.00
Doll, wood face, complete fur outfit, boots, 1920, 13" 75.00
Mask, cvd/pnt wood, w/appendages, 1920, EX quality, 15x10"....750.00
Mask, hand; Oriental-like features, earrings, 1930, 18x11".........400.00
Mask, stylized/elongated, wood w/pnt traces, 20th C, 9" 500.00

Polychrome wood mask with carved bone teeth, fur and animal tooth suspension, 8½", $700.00.

Necklace, fossil ivory teeth/Peking glass beads, 1850, 30" 375.00
Necklace, graduated fossil ivory beads, 1910, 21" 75.00
Necklace, polished bone beads w/bone doll drop, 1910, 39" 275.00
Olla, coiled basketry w/geometrics, 1910, 12x11" 250.00

Rattle, cvd as human head, 1870, 4x2½" 200.00
Tool, etching; fossil ivory, detailed, Bering Sea culture 850.00
Toy sled, made from caribou jawbone & baleen, 1920, 12x4" 100.00
Wand, Shaman's, w/doll & beaded fur medallion, 1900, 11x4" ...275.00

Fabris Porcelain

In quality, workmanship, and design, fine Fabris porcelain sculptures might easily be confused with Meissen and Dresden pieces; only the red-iron anchor mark denotes the difference.

The French sculptor, Jean-Pierre Varion, formerly of the Vincennes factory, settled in Este, Italy, during the 1850s. He died soon after developing his own formula for porcelain. His wife, Fiorina, and a partner, Antonio Costa, formed a business and manufactured the first Fabris sculptures at Bassano del Grappa in 1875. Many of the figurines and groupings were after paintings by 18th-century artists such as the Rococo decorator Fragonard, Longhi, and the playwright Carlo Goldoni. Most of the figures and groups were of a limited production; strict attention was given to detail.

The Museum Collection, a 1980-1982 re-issue, utilized the very early molds. A gold anchor mark was used on this limited line only; after this period, they reverted back to the red-iron anchor. Items listed here bear the red mark unless noted otherwise. Our advisor for this category is Donald Penrose; he is listed in the Directory under Ohio.

Aunt, aunt on sofa chaperoning 2 lovers, 9x16" 2,000.00
Beauties, 2 ladies on flowered balcony, 8½x10" 650.00
Cecilia, girl w/wht skirt, 2 flower baskets, 4½x5¼" 300.00
Coppersmith, man sits/mends copper pot, tricorn hat, 5½x8" 350.00

Flamenco Dancer, girl in red bodice and lace dress, 13½", $950.00.

Gertrude, flowered dress, knitting bag, 6x7" 425.00
Girl in pk lace skirt, holding basket of flowers, 5x8½" 550.00
Harlequin's Love, girl & clown in costume, seated, 11x15" 2,700.00
Lady Beatrice, wht skirt, fashion magazine in lap, 7½x7½"..........550.00
Lovers, lady w/man resting head on her lap, 9x7" 750.00
Margarita, girl w/ft on bl pillow, wht skirt, 6x6"..........................350.00
Melon Vendor, brn pants, wht apron, & melons, 5½x10½" 350.00
Musical, 2 figures: man at piano, woman singing, 6½x8½" 650.00
Swing, girl on swing in floral & leaf arbor, 10x11½" 1,500.00
2-Faced Woman, young girl on 1 side, old hag on other, 9" 450.00

Fairings

Fairings, small chinaware figural groups that portray amusing (if not risque) scenes of courting couples, marital woes, and family feuds, were popular purchases and prizes at 19th-century English fairs. From 1840 through the 1850s, their bases were embossed with marks that identified the manufacturer as well as the artist who applied the polychrome enameling. From 1860 until 1870, they were no longer marked and became smaller in size. During the 1870s they retained their smaller size but once again were marked in relief, indicating manufacturer and artisan. Through the 1880s all marks were omitted; but the bases were much more shallow than those from the 1860s. About 1890 the Staffordshire potters sold the molds to German manufacturers who marked their product with the name of their country until about 1900. Examples from this period are most commonly encountered. Fairings made in Germany in the early 20th century often have two holes in their bases.

Generally, the more complex groups and those that are marked bring the higher prices. Earlier examples from the sixties and seventies are of better quality. Similar items such as small boxes and match holders with much the same type of theme and figural decoration are also listed here.

Baby & dog pull at doll, gold trim, 2¾x2½x5" 175.00
Before Marriage, couple on sofa 245.00
Box, cameo on front, musical instruments on lid, 3¾" 95.00
Box, cat w/frog, English, 3"...90.00
Box, child on bed pulls on pajama bottoms, Elbogen mk, 4" 120.00

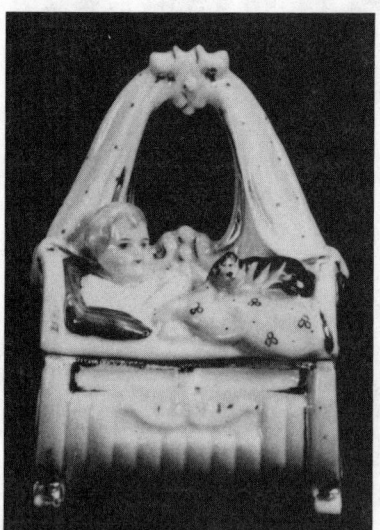

Box, child in bed with kitten, #3500, 4¼", $120.00.

Box, child w/trumpet, doll in basket, Staffordshire, 3¾" 175.00
Box, dressing table w/mirror, various adornments, 3½" 100.00
Box, reclining child w/basket of flowers, English, 3½" 90.00
Box, 2 children w/picture book, English, 4" 90.00
Box, 3 children play on oval lid, Staffordshire, 4⅝" 200.00
Did You Ring Sir?, man in tub & maid, early 135.00
Happy Father, What 2?..., couple/twins, 1880s, 3½" 110.00
Last in Bed To Put Out the Light, 3½" 225.00
Looking Down Upon His Luck, father & 3 infants 195.00
Nip on the Sly 225.00
O Do Leave Me a Drop, 2 cats at bowl 225.00
Oysters Sir, lady at bench, w/match striker...................................255.00
Power of Love, lady w/tray, 3¼x3½" 185.00
Uncle Sam figure on sm dish, Germany...200.00
Who Said Rats?, cat in bed, mouse on table, early 135.00

Will We Sleep First or How?, 5½x4" 195.00
12 Months of Marriage, unmk, 3½x3½" 265.00
3 O'Clock in the Morning, 2¾x3¾" 225.00

Fans

The Japanese are said to have invented the fan. From there it went to China, and Portuguese traders took the idea to Europe. Though usually considered milady's accessory, even the gentlemen in 17th-century England carried fans! More fashionable than practical, some were of feathers and lovely hand-painted silks with carved ivory or tortoise sticks. Some French fans had peepholes. There are mourning fans, calendar fans, and those with advertising.

Fine antique fans (pre-1900) of ivory or mother of pearl have recently escalated in value. Those from before 1800 often sell for upwards of $1,000.00. Examples with mother of pearl sticks are most desirable; least desirable are those with sticks of celluloid. Our advisor for this category is Vicki Flanigan; she is listed in the Directory under Virginia.

Birds HP on silk, Mt Fuji cvd on sticks, Japan, 1900s, 12" 990.00
Blk Chantilly lace, ornate cvd/gilt MOP sticks, 1870s, 10½".......550.00
Cherubs HP on vellum, silver/gilt MOP sticks, 1890s, 11½" 440.00
Chinese figures cvd in continuous scene on ivory, 1830s, 7½" 245.00
Classical lady HP/printed on paper, MOP sticks, 1850s, +case 440.00
Courting couples HP on vellum, bone sticks, French, 1890s 500.00
Diana & warrior HP on paper, ivory sticks, Dutch, 1850s, 12" 330.00
Duchesse lace, simply cvd MOP sticks, 1890s, 13½" 330.00
Figures HP/emb on paper leaf, cvd ivory sticks, 1760s, 11" 660.00
HP paper leaf: baby Moses, cvd floral MOP sticks, 1850s, 10" 440.00
Lace sprays on net, pierced/cvd MOP sticks, 1870s, 11" 550.00
Ladies HP on paper, ornate border/MOP sticks, Fr, 1850s, 11"....880.00
Lovers HP on silk, cvd ivory sticks, Continental, 1870s, 11".......245.00
Merchants HP on paper, cvd ivory sticks, China, 1780s, 12".......770.00
Oriental boating scene on silk, tortoise shell sticks, 1890s...........200.00
Orientals HP on paper, ivory sticks, Canton, 1850s, 11" 660.00
River landscape, ivory brise, Japan, 1870s, 8½", +case 235.00
Rosepoint lace, cvd MOP sticks, Continental, 1890s, 11½" 825.00
Rosepoint lace, cvd/gilt MOP sticks, Continental, 1900, 12" 715.00
Satin-bk ivory lace in bird pattern, MOP sticks, 1870s, 11" 330.00
Scrolling florals on wht metal filigree, China, 1850s, 7½" 660.00
Sequins on silk, ornate bone sticks, late 1800s, 7½" 250.00
Silk w/HP flowers, ivory sticks, French, in fr, 30" W 375.00

Farm Collectibles

Country living in the 19th century entailed plowing, planting, and harvesting; gathering eggs and milking; making soap from lard rendered on butchering day; and numerous other tasks performed with primitive tools of which we in the 20th century have had little first-hand knowledge. For more information on this subject, we recommend *Collecting Farm Antiques,* an identification and value guide by our advisor for this category Lar Hothem; his address is listed in the Directory under Ohio. See also Cast Iron; Woodenware; Wrought Iron.

Barn vent, star w/in triangle, iron hinges, 41x48" 450.00
Bee smoker, tin w/red leather bellows, EX 35.00
Blberry picker, wood fr/iron teeth, Makepeace/1894, 8½x9" 175.00
Cream separator, McCormick Deering, ca 1920s, 45", NM 150.00
Hames, brass knobs, orig red pnt 25.00
Implement seat, CI, openwork, no pnt, late 1800s, 14x12"...........70.00
Implement seat, Hayes, CI, EX 150.00
Implement seat, Peerless Reaper 400.00

Implement seat, Stoddard, CI, EX...65.00
Milk stool, some burl in top, irregular surface, 12x16x8" 135.00
Scoop, grain; metal w/trn wood hdl..30.00
Shovel, curly maple w/EX figure, made from 1-pc, 42" 1,000.00
Strainer, milk cooling; tin, ca 1860, 5¾x12" 28.00
Tractor, John Deere Model R diesel, EX 3,300.00
Tractor, John Deere 430T, 1959, EX.......................................2,500.00
Tractor, Twin City 27-44, lg, EX...1,750.00
Wrench, implement; American Harrow 12.50
Yoke, water carrying; ltweight wood w/2 hooks, sm 45.00

Fenton

Frank and John Fenton were brothers who founded the Fenton Art Glass Company in 1906 in Martin's Ferry, Ohio. The venture, at first only a decorating shop, began operations in July of 1905 using blanks purchased from other companies. This operation soon proved unsatisfactory, and by 1907 they had constructed their own glass factory in Williamstown, West Virginia. John left the company in 1909 and organized his own firm in Millersburg, Ohio.

The Fenton Company produced over 130 patterns of carnival glass. They also made custard, chocolate, opalescent, and stretch glass. This company has always been noted for its various colors of glass and has continually changed its production to stay attune with current tastes in decorating. In 1925 they produced a line of 'handmade' items that incorporated the techniques of threading and mosaic work. Because the process proved to be unprofitable, the line was discontinued by 1927. Even their glassware made in the past twenty-five years is already regarded as collectible. Various paper labels have been used since the 1920s; only since 1970 has the logo been stamped into the glass.

For information concerning Fenton Art Glass Collectors of America, Inc., see the Clubs, Newsletters, and Catalogs section of the Directory. See also Carnival Glass; Custard Glass; Stretch Glass.

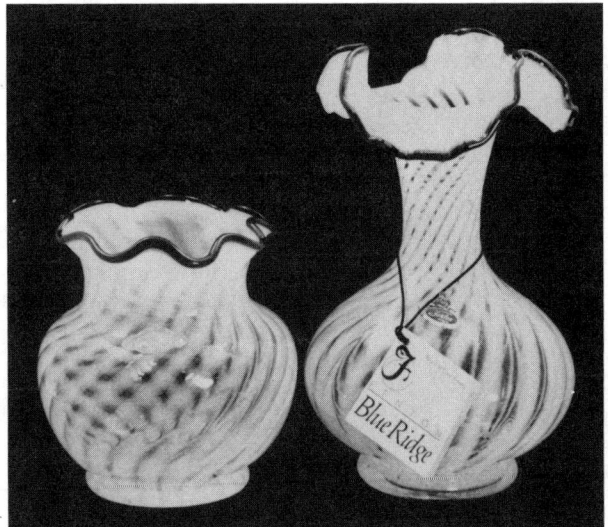

Blue Ridge, vase, 1930s, 5½", $65.00; vase, 1985 reissue, 8", $45.00.

Figurines

Bear, blk, sitting...16.00
Bear, carnival, sitting..20.00
Bear, wht, sitting...16.00
Bear, wht irid, sitting 15.00
Boy, blk, praying 12.00
Bunny, lt bl...16.00

Bunny, pale yel	16.00
Girl, jade gr, praying	10.00
Apple Tree, vase, topaz opal, #1561, 10"	150.00
Aqua Crest, basket, #1923, 10"	70.00
Aqua Crest, basket, fan form, #37, 4"	60.00
Aqua Crest, vase, #37, mini	48.00
Aqua Crest, vase, triangular, #36, 4"	25.00
Beaded Melon, basket, bl o/l, #711, 1949-51	60.00
Beaded Melon, bottle, scent; lime o/l, #711, 4½"	60.00
Beaded Melon, vase, rose o/l, #711, 8"	48.00
Bicentennial plate, bl opaque	18.00
Big Cookies, basket, jade gr, #1681	110.00
Big Cookies, basket, ruby, wicker hdl, #1681, 10½"	120.00
Black Rose, hurricane lamp, #7398, 1953-54	100.00
Block & Star, jam set, milk glass, #5603	30.00
Block & Star, jam set, turq, #5603, 1955-56	60.00
Blue Opal, plate, leaf form, #175, 8"	40.00
Blue Overlay, basket, #1924, 5" dia	48.00
Blue Overlay, jug, hdl, #192, 6"	38.00
Blue Overlay, top hat, 4"	35.00
Blue Overlay, vanity set, #192A, 3-pc	75.00
Burmese, pitcher, leaf decor, #7461	40.00
Chinese Yellow, bowl, mixing; ca 1933	32.00
Chinese Yellow, bowl, oval, #1663, 13"	110.00
Chinese Yellow, vase, #621, 6"	55.00
Coin Dot, basket, cranberry opal, #1437, 7"	85.00
Coin Dot, bowl, honeysuckle opal, #203, 1948-49, 6"	45.00
Coin Dot, lamp, student; honeysuckle opal, 21"	150.00
Coin Dot, pitcher, cranberry opal, #1924, 4"	38.00
Coin Dot, pitcher, water; cranberry opal, #1353, 9½"	115.00
Coin Dot, top hat, cranberry opal, 4"	65.00
Coin Dot, tumbler, cranberry opal, #1447, 12-oz	25.00

Coin Dot, vase, cranberry with opalescent overlay, 6", $95.00.

Coin Dot, vase, cranberry opal, #194, ca 1948-58, 8½"	48.00
Crystal Crest, vase, dbl-crimped, #192, ca 1942, 6½"	65.00
Daisy & Button, cigarette holder, bl opal, #1900, 3¾"	38.00
Daisy & Button, console set, milk glass, #1904, 3-pc	40.00
Daisy & Button, vanity set, rose, #1900, 4-pc	160.00
Daisy & Button, vase, gr pastel, #1957, 8½"	45.00
Dancing Ladies, bowl, Chinese Yel, #900, 11"	110.00
Dancing Ladies, vase, crystal, scalloped rim, #901	195.00
Dancing Ladies, vase, ruby, scalloped rim, #901	295.00

Diamond Lace, console set, flint opal, 3-pc set	65.00
Diamond Lace, epergne, aqua crest, 3-lily	125.00
Diamond Lace, salver, bl opal, 9"	60.00
Diamond Optic, jug, ruby o/l, #192, 1942-48, 6"	45.00
Diamond Optic, pitcher, mulberry, #192, 5"	145.00
Diamond Optic, vase, mulberry, #192, 9"	120.00
Diamond Optic, vase, ruby, fan form, #1502, 8½"	38.00
Diamond Optic, vase, ruby o/l, dbl-crimped, #192, 7½"	45.00
Dolphin, bonbon, jade gr, hdls, 6"	22.00
Dolphin, bowl, jade gr, hdls, 6"	22.00
Dolphin, bowl, jade gr, rolled rim, ftd, hdls, #1608	95.00
Dolphin, bowl, pk, cut decor, hdls, #1621-1703, 9"	35.00
Dolphin, bowl, royal bl, hdls, etched decor, sq, 9½"	78.00
Dot Optic, pitcher, water; cranberry opal	175.00
Dot Optic, plate, bl opal, 8"	145.00
Dot Optic, sugar shaker, bl opal	90.00
Dot Optic, sugar shaker, cranberry opal	125.00
Dot Optic, top hat, cranberry opal, smooth rim, 6"	110.00
Dot Optic, vase, cranberry opal, tulip form, #192	55.00
Ebony, bowl, cupped, #607, ca 1925, 8"	60.00
Ebony, candy jar, HP decor, #8, 9"	65.00
Emerald Crest, bowl, heart form, 2¾x5"	40.00
Emerald Crest, cake stand, low std	80.00
Emerald Crest, creamer, #680, 3¼"	30.00
Emerald Crest, flowerpot, attached saucer, #401, 4½"	45.00
Emerald Crest, vase, 4½x4"	28.00
Flame, bowl, rolled rim, 10"	95.00
Flame, candlestick, hexagonal, #449, 8¾", pr	145.00
Flame, candy container, #636, 10½"	90.00
Georgian, cup, amber, #1611	12.50
Georgian, cup, ruby, #1611, 3¼" dia	18.00
Georgian, sherbet, rose, high ft, #1611, 6-oz	15.00
Georgian, tumbler, Moonstone, #1611, ca 1933	18.00
Georgian, tumbler, royal bl, #1611, 9-oz	15.00
Gold Crest, top hat, #1924, 4"	40.00
Grape & Cable, bowl, ruby non-irid, #935, ca 1915	48.00
Green Opal, basket, #6137, ca 1960, 7"	50.00
Green Overlay, creamer, #711, 4"	15.00
Hanging Hearts, vase, bl or yel, 14"	150.00
Hobnail, ash tray, bl opal, fan form, 5½"	32.50
Hobnail, ash tray, French opal, fan form, 5½"	37.50
Hobnail, ash tray, topaz opal, fan form, 5½"	37.00
Hobnail, basket, bl opal, 1948-54, 4½"	45.00
Hobnail, basket, bl opal, 7"	65.00
Hobnail, basket, cranberry opal, #3835, 5½"	55.00
Hobnail, basket, cranberry opal, #3837, 7"	65.00
Hobnail, basket, French opal, 4"	40.00
Hobnail, bonbon, roses & gold on milk glass, hdls, 7"	40.00
Hobnail, bonbon, topaz opal	25.00
Hobnail, bone dish, topaz opal, crescent form	35.00
Hobnail, bottle, vanity; bl opal, 1953, 7½"	100.00
Hobnail, cake salver, topaz opal, 13"	135.00
Hobnail, candlestick, bl opal, cornucopia, 6", pr	90.00
Hobnail, candlestick, cranberry opal, #3870, pr	125.00
Hobnail, candlestick, French opal, dbl-crimped, 4½", pr	35.00
Hobnail, candlestick, topaz opal, #389, 4½"	25.00
Hobnail, compote, Colonial gr, lg	18.00
Hobnail, creamer & sugar bowl, bl opal, sm	45.00
Hobnail, cruet, bl opal, 4"	28.00
Hobnail, cruet, turq, #3869, ca 1955-56, 5"	35.00
Hobnail, epergne, French opal, apartment sz	110.00
Hobnail, goblet, water; bl opal	32.00
Hobnail, goblet, wine; French opal	15.00
Hobnail, jam set, bl opal, #389, 3-pc	95.00

Hobnail, jug, bl opal, 5½" 35.00
Hobnail, jug, milk glass, squat, 80-oz.............................65.00
Hobnail, marmalade set, French opal, 4-pc 110.00
Hobnail, mayonnaise set, bl opal, 3-pc...........................65.00
Hobnail, mustard set, bl opal, 3-pc.................................30.00
Hobnail, nut dish, milk glass, ftd, #3629.......................10.00
Hobnail, pitcher, water; milk glass, crimped 40.00
Hobnail, shakers, bl opal, flat, pr...................................55.00
Hobnail, shakers, French opal, flat, pr............................40.00
Hobnail, shakers, French opal, ftd, pr.............................70.00
Hobnail, slipper, bl opal 23.00
Hobnail, top hat, bl opal, 3" 24.00
Hobnail, tray, bl opal, fan form, 10½" 50.00
Hobnail, tumbler, French opal, 15-oz..............................15.00
Hobnail, tumbler, gr opal, 15-oz, 6"................................25.00
Hobnail, vase, bl opal, dbl-crimped, ftd, 8" 50.00
Hobnail, vase, bl opal, dbl-crimped, squat, 5" 28.00
Hobnail, vase, bl opal, ftd fan form, 6".............................35.00
Hobnail, vase, bl opal, sq, #389, 4½"..............................32.00
Hobnail, vase, cranberry opal, dbl-crimped, squat, 5"....55.00
Hobnail, vase, cranberry opal, dbl-crimped, 3" 38.00
Hobnail, vase, cranberry opal, fan form, mini 55.00
Hobnail, vase, cranberry opal, hat form, 3" 37.50
Hobnail, vase, French opal, conical, 6"............................14.00
Hobnail, vase, French opal, fan form, #389, 8¼"............25.00
Hobnail, vase, lime gr opal, dbl-crimped, #1949, 3" 35.00
Hobnail, vase, lime gr opal, dbl-crimped, #389, 4½" 40.00
Hobnail, vase, lime gr opal, tricornered, #389, 4"..........30.00
Hobnail, vase, plum opal, pitcher form, #3760 ....185.00
Hobnail, vase, topaz opal, fan form, 3½" 50.00
Hobnail, vase, topaz opal, fan form, 8¼".........................65.00
Hobnail, vase, topaz opal, 5" 40.00
Ivory Crest, candlestick, cornucopia, pr.........................40.00
Ivy, rose bowl, gr/wht, #711, 5".......................................55.00
Ivy, vase, gr/wht, #1925, 6¼"..40.00
Jade Green, bowl, cupped, ftd, 5¾"................................15.00
Jade Green, bowl, oval, hdls, 17"....................................95.00
Jade Green, candelabrum, #2318, 6".............................50.00
Jade Green, candle holder, 1½", pr................................15.00
Jade Green, compote, oval, #1608................................110.00
Jade Green, compote, 6x6½"..40.00
Jade Green, macaroon jar, #1681.................................110.00
Jade Green, sugar bowl 17.50
Jade Green, vase, fan form, 5½"......................................40.00
Jade Green, vase, flip; 9"..62.50
Leaf Tiers, bowl, French opal, 10"...................................40.00
Leaf Tiers, bowl, milk glass, #1790, ca 1934-36, 10".......38.00
Lilac, biscuit jar, rare...295.00
Lilac, bowl, shell form, #9020, 10".................................95.00
Lilac Overlay, jug, #6068, ca 1955-56, 6½" 55.00
Lincoln Inn, compote, lt bl...42.00
Lincoln Inn, cup & saucer, cobalt 25.00
Lincoln Inn, finger bowl, cobalt 30.00
Lincoln Inn, goblet, water; red 25.00
Lincoln Inn, goblet, wine; jade gr, 4".............................32.00
Lincoln Inn, olive dish, jade gr, hdls.............................15.00
Lincoln Inn, tumbler, ruby, ftd, 5¼"..............................28.00
Lincoln Inn, tumbler, water; red, ftd, 9-oz....................24.00
Mandarin Red, ginger jar, gold dragon, ebony lid & ft, #893.......265.00
Mandarin Red, mayonnaise, cone shape, ftd 75.00
Mandarin Red, vase, #621, 6"...60.00
Melon Rib, pitcher, bl o/l, 9"..60.00
Melon Rib, vase, rose o/l, 8½"...20.00
Melon/Silver Crest, cologne & powder set 50.00

Ming Green, bowl, oval, 12" 60.00
Ming Green, pitcher, #1653, 10"......................................90.00
Ming Rose, bowl, 3-ftd, #249, 9"....................................50.00
Ming Rose, macaroon jar, 6½"..75.00
Moonstone, basket, red decor, 10x9½x7"....................195.00
Moonstone, candlestick, ebony base, #549, ca 1924, 8" 110.00
Moonstone, vase, on 5-leg ebony base, #612, 6½".......200.00
Orange Tree, wine, rose, ca 1930, 5"..............................20.00
Peach Blow, bowl, shell form, #9020..............................75.00
Peach Crest, basket, milk glass hdl, #192, 1948, 10" 160.00
Peach Crest, basket, milk glass hdl, 1924, 7x5" 57.00
Peach Crest, bowl, sq, #203, 1940-44, 7½".....................38.00
Peach Crest, jar, powder; w/2 colognes 150.00
Peach Crest, jug, #192A, 9"..75.00
Peach Crest, rose bowl, 5"...22.50
Peach Crest, vase, #6056, 6"..45.00
Peach Crest, vase, dbl-crimped, 8½"..............................40.00
Peach Crest, vase, hand holds vase form, #193, 10¼"....95.00
Peach Crest, vase, triangular, #187, 1940-43, 5"............48.00
Peacock, vase, burmese, 8"...65.00
Pekin Blue, bowl, oval, #1663, 12½"...............................80.00
Pekin Blue, candlestick, #318, 3"...................................30.00
Periwinkle Blue, bowl, crimped, ca 1935, 8½"...............60.00
Periwinkle Blue, macaroon jar, 1935, 6½".....................155.00
Periwinkle Blue, vase, crimped, #847, 6½".....................62.50
Periwinkle Blue, vase, fan form, 5½x8½" 85.00
Pineapple, bowl, console; wht satin, #2000A, 12½" 45.00
Plymouth, bonbon, ruby...22.00
Plymouth, goblet, wine; red 20.00
Plymouth, highball, amber, #1620, 8-oz........................25.00
Plymouth, sherbet, cobalt, 4¼"......................................24.00
Polka Dot, rose bowl, cranberry opal, 5"......................110.00
Polka Dot, shakers, cranberry opal, 3", pr.....................65.00
Priscilla, bowl, emerald gr, cupped, #1890, 1951-52, 9"....32.00
Rib Optic, creamer & sugar bowl, gr opal, #1604..........85.00
Rib Optic, night set, gr opal, #401, ca 1927, 2-pc...........55.00
Rib Optic, top hat, French opal, #1923, 3½x6"...............40.00
Rib Optic, top hat, French opal, 10"..............................225.00
Ring, pitcher, water; French opal, #201, 7"....................80.00
Rose Crest, basket, #192, 10"...38.00
Rose Crest, jug, hdl...45.00
Rose Crest, plate, 12"...37.00
Rose Overlay, basket, #1924, ca 1943-48, 5"..................60.00
Rose Overlay, jug, #4516, 8½"...40.00
Rose Overlay, powder box, #711....................................22.50
Royal Blue, ash tray, 3-ftd, #848, 4"..............................22.00
Royal Blue, bowl, flower form, #848, 9".........................28.00
Royal Blue, candle holder, #848, 4" dia 15.00
Ruby, candlestick, #249, ca 1933, pr..............................65.00
Ruby, plate, sq form, hdls, #1639, 12"............................65.00
Ruby, tray, leaf form, #175, 8½"......................................40.00
Ruby, vase, eng decor, #184, 12"..................................120.00
Ruby Overlay, bottle, scent; #192A................................40.00
Ruby Overlay, ivy ball, ftd, #1021..................................60.00
Ruby Overlay, top hat, 4½"..35.00
San Toy, bowl, etched, #349, 8½"...................................40.00
San Toy, ice pail, satin, #1616.......................................35.00
San Toy, vase, etched, #898, 11½"..................................60.00
Scroll & Eye, plate, turq, openwork rim, #9015, 8½"......35.00
September Morn, nymph, lt bl, w/base.........................195.00
Sheffield, bowl, French opal, crimped, #1800, 12" 38.00
Sheffield, tumbler, amethyst, #1800, 4".........................18.00
Silver Crest, basket, 7½"..36.00
Silver Crest, bowl, banana; ftd......................................28.00

Silver Crest, cake plate, ped ft, low, 13" **32.50**
Silver Crest, cake salver, 13" **35.00**
Silver Crest, compote, nut...**21.00**
Silver Crest, compote, 6x8"...**15.00**
Silver Crest, epergne, lg **140.00**
Silver Crest, jug, #192A, ca 1943-48, 9".....................................**48.00**
Silver Crest, plate, 11½" **32.00**
Silver Crest, plate, 6" **10.00**
Silver Crest, plate, 8½"...**12.00**
Silver Crest, tray, tidbit; 3-tier **45.00**
Silver Crest, vase, dbl-crimped, #1924......................................**30.00**
Silver Turquoise, bowl, sm...**10.00**
Silvertone, pitcher, iced tea; etched, #1352.............................**68.00**
Silvertone, plate, amethyst, 3-ftd, #1009, 7½" **25.00**
Snow Crest, top hat, emerald gr, 5"...**100.00**
Spanish Lace, cake stand, milk glass, 12" **40.00**
Spiral, rose bowl, cranberry opal, crimped, #201, 5" **55.00**
Spiral, vase, cranberry opal, #3160, 6½" **50.00**
Spiral, vase, cranberry opal, #3253, ca 1955-59, 6½"............**50.00**
Spiral/Blue Ridge, vase, French opal, #186, ca 1939, 8" **50.00**
Stars & Stripes, tumbler, cranberry opal, flat, 3¾" **125.00**
Stretch, tray, bl, center hdl, 11" **30.00**
Swan, bonbon, gr or pk, #5..**20.00**
Swan, bonbon, pk **25.00**
Swan, bowl, amber, oval, #6, 11½" **80.00**
Swan, bowl, gr, sm **25.00**
Swan, bowl, pk, oval, lg **60.00**
Swan, novelty, wht satin, #4, 4" **30.00**
Swirl, ginger jar, cranberry opal, 10½" **175.00**
Swirl, vase, French opal, #1923...**25.00**
Swirled Feather, fairy lamp, cranberry opal, #2090.................**180.00**
Swirled Feather, fairy lamp, gr opal, #2092, 6" **110.00**
Teardrop, candy box, milk glass, #6985, ca 1955-56, 6" **28.00**
Vasa Murrhina, vase, Bl Mist, #6459, 14" **95.00**
Vasa Murrhina, vase, bl/gr/wht, #6454, 4" **55.00**
Vasa Murrhina, vase, bl/gr/wht, basket form, #6437, 11" **120.00**
Vasa Murrhina, vase, pk/gr/wht, #6459, 15" **115.00**
Vasa Murrhina, vase, Rose Mist, fan form, #6457, 7" **60.00**
Velvatone, vase, etched, triangular, #1934, 5" **48.00**
Vintage, bowl, bl opal, ruffled, #466, ca 1910............................**40.00**
Violet In Snow/Silver Crest, compote, 7"...................................**30.00**
Water Lily, bonbon, Pekin bl, oval, #597 ....**35.00**
Wistaria, candlestick, purple irid, ca 1924-26, 8", pr..............**110.00**
Wistaria, creamer & sugar bowl, wht satin **50.00**
Wistaria, vase, etched, #184, 11½" **40.00**
Wistaria, vase, wht satin, fan form, #349, 8" **38.00**

Fiesta

Fiesta is a line of dinnerware produced by the Homer Laughlin China Company of Newell, West Virginia, from 1936 until 1973. It was made in eleven different solid colors with over fifty pieces in the assortment. The pattern was developed by Frederic Rhead, an English Stoke-on-Trent potter who was an important contributor to the art-pottery movement in this country during the early part of the century. The design was carried out through the use of a simple band-of-rings device near the rim. Fiesta Red, a strong red-orange glaze color, was made with depleted uranium oxide. It was more expensive to produce than the other colors and sold at higher prices. Today's collectors still pay premium prices for Fiesta Red pieces. During the fifties the color assortment was gray, rose, chartreuse, and dark green. These colors are relatively harder to find and along with Fiesta Red and medium green (new in 1959) command the higher prices.

Fiesta Kitchen Kraft was introduced in 1939; it consisted of seven-

teen pieces of kitchenware such as pie plates, refrigerator sets, mixing bowls, and covered jars in four popular Fiesta colors.

As a final attempt to adapt production to modern-day techniques and methods, Fiesta was restyled in 1969. Of the original colors, only Fiesta Red remained. This line, called Fiesta Ironstone, was discontinued in 1973.

Two types of marks were used: an ink stamp on machine-jiggered pieces and an indented mark molded into the hollowware pieces.

In 1986 HLC reintroduced a line of Fiesta dinnerware in five colors: black, white, pink, apricot, and cobalt (darker and denser than the original shade). Since then yellow, turquoise, and seafoam green have been added. Collectors have found that the new line poses no theat to their investments.

In the listings below, 'original colors' indicates only four of the original six — ivory, light green, turquoise, and yellow (or those remaining after specific original colors have been priced). Red and cobalt values are listed separately. For more information we recommend *The Collector's Encyclopedia of Fiesta, Harlequin, and Riviera* by Sharon and Bob Huxford, now in its seventh edition available at your local bookstore or from Collector Books.

Dinnerware

Ash tray, '50s colors **52.00**
Ash tray, orig colors **32.00**
Ash tray, red or cobalt **40.00**
Bowl, covered onion soup; cobalt & ivory....................................**275.00**
Bowl, covered onion soup; red **300.00**
Bowl, covered onion soup; turq **1,200.00**
Bowl, covered onion soup; yel or lt gr..**225.00**
Bowl, cream soup; '50s colors **40.00**
Bowl, cream soup; med gr, minimum value **1,200.00**
Bowl, cream soup; orig colors **25.00**
Bowl, cream soup; red or cobalt..**35.00**
Bowl, dessert; '50s colors, 6" **35.00**
Bowl, dessert; med gr, 6" **190.00**
Bowl, dessert; orig colors, 6"...**25.00**
Bowl, dessert; red or cobalt, 6" **32.00**
Bowl, fruit; '50s colors, 4¾" **22.00**
Bowl, fruit; '50s colors, 5½" **26.00**
Bowl, fruit; med gr, 4¾"..**180.00**
Bowl, fruit; med gr, 5½"..**50.00**
Bowl, fruit; orig colors, 11¾"..**105.00**
Bowl, fruit; orig colors, 4¾"...**18.00**
Bowl, fruit; orig colors, 5½"...**18.00**
Bowl, fruit; red or cobalt, 11¾" **140.00**
Bowl, fruit; red or cobalt, 4¾" **22.00**
Bowl, fruit; red or cobalt, 5½" **22.00**
Bowl, ftd salad; orig colors..**22.00**
Bowl, ftd salad; red or cobalt **190.00**
Bowl, ind salad; med gr, 7½" **62.00**
Bowl, ind salad; red, turq, & yel, 7½" **50.00**
Bowl, nappy; '50s colors, 8½" **36.00**
Bowl, nappy; med gr, 8½"...**60.00**
Bowl, nappy; orig colors, 8½" **25.00**
Bowl, nappy; orig colors, 9½" **30.00**
Bowl, nappy; red or cobalt, 8½"...**35.00**
Bowl, nappy; red or cobalt, 9½"...**40.00**
Bowl, Tom & Jerry; ivory w/gold letters......................................**120.00**
Bowl, unlisted; red, cobalt, or ivory **175.00**
Bowl, unlisted; yel..**55.00**
Candle holder, bulb; orig colors, pr **52.00**
Candle holder, bulb; red or cobalt, pr **65.00**
Candle holder, tripod; orig colors, pr..**200.00**

Candle holder, tripod; red, cobalt, or ivory, pr 245.00	Pitcher, ice; orig colors 60.00
Carafe, orig colors 115.00	Pitcher, ice; red or cobalt 75.00
Carafe, red or cobalt 135.00	Pitcher, jug, 2-pt; '50s colors 70.00
Casserole, '50s colors 165.00	Pitcher, jug, 2-pt; orig colors 38.00
Casserole, French; standard colors other than yel 300.00	Pitcher, jug, 2-pt; red, cobalt, or ivory 48.00
Casserole, French; yel 160.00	Plate, '50s colors, 10" 34.00
Casserole, med gr 240.00	Plate, '50s colors, 6" 6.00
Casserole, orig colors 75.00	Plate, '50s colors, 7" 9.50
Casserole, red or cobalt 115.00	Plate, '50s colors, 9" 15.00
Coffeepot, '50s colors 150.00	Plate, cake; lt gr or yel 300.00
Coffeepot, demi; orig colors 135.00	Plate, cake; red or cobalt 365.00
Coffeepot, demi; red, cobalt, or ivory 165.00	Plate, calendar; 1954 or 1955, 10" 30.00
Coffeepot, orig colors 95.00	Plate, calendar; 1955, 9" 35.00
Coffeepot, red or cobalt 120.00	Plate, chop; '50s colors, 13" 40.00
Compote, orig colors, 12" 75.00	Plate, chop; '50s colors, 15" 45.00
Compote, red or cobalt, 12" 95.00	Plate, chop; med gr, 13" 65.00
Compote, sweets; orig colors 34.00	Plate, chop; orig colors, 13" 22.00
Compote, sweets; red or cobalt 42.00	Plate, chop; orig colors, 15" 25.00
Creamer, '50s colors 20.00	Plate, chop; red or cobalt, 13" 25.00
Creamer, ind; red 105.00	Plate, chop; red or cobalt, 15" 32.00
Creamer, ind; turq 165.00	Plate, compartment; '50s colors, 10½" 30.00
Creamer, ind; yel 42.00	Plate, compartment; orig colors, 10½" 20.00
Creamer, med gr 35.00	Plate, compartment; orig colors, 12" 30.00
Creamer, orig colors 14.00	Plate, compartment; red or cobalt, 10½" 24.00
Creamer, red or cobalt 16.00	Plate, compartment; red or cobalt, 12" 28.00
Creamer, stick hdld, orig colors 22.00	Plate, deep; '50s colors 35.00
Creamer, stick hdld, red or cobalt 25.00	Plate, deep; med gr 58.00
Cup, demi; '50s colors 150.00	Plate, deep; orig colors 24.00
Cup, demi; orig colors 35.00	Plate, deep; red or cobalt 34.00
Cup, demi; red or cobalt 40.00	Plate, med gr, 10" 55.00
Egg cup, '50s colors 85.00	Plate, med gr, 6" 10.00
Egg cup, orig colors 32.00	Plate, med gr, 7" 15.00
Egg cup, red, cobalt, or ivory 40.00	Plate, med gr, 9" 30.00
Lid, for mixing bowl #1-#3, any color 275.00	Plate, orig colors, 10" 22.00
Lid, for mixing bowl #4, any color 300.00	Plate, orig colors, 6" 3.50
Marmalade, orig colors 100.00	Plate, orig colors, 7" 6.00
Marmalade, red or cobalt 135.00	Plate, orig colors, 9" 7.50
Mixing bowl, #1, orig colors 55.00	Plate, red or cobalt, 10" 28.00
Mixing bowl, #1, red, cobalt, or ivory 78.00	Plate, red or cobalt, 6" 5.00
Mixing bowl, #2, orig colors 40.00	Plate, red or cobalt, 7" 8.00
Mixing bowl, #2, red or cobalt 52.00	Plate, red or cobalt, 9" 14.00
Mixing bowl, #3, orig colors 45.00	Platter, '50s colors 32.00
Mixing bowl, #3, red or cobalt 55.00	Platter, med gr 60.00
Mixing bowl, #4, orig colors 50.00	Platter, orig colors 20.00
Mixing bowl, #4, red or cobalt 58.00	Platter, red or cobalt 28.00
Mixing bowl, #5, orig colors 58.00	Sauce boat, '50s colors 40.00
Mixing bowl, #5, red or cobalt 62.00	Sauce boat, med gr 60.00
Mixing bowl, #6, orig colors 75.00	Sauce boat, orig colors 28.00
Mixing bowl, #6, red, cobalt, or ivory 82.00	Sauce boat, red or cobalt 38.00
Mixing bowl, #7, orig colors 128.00	Saucer, '50s colors 4.50
Mixing bowl, #7, red, cobalt, or ivory 145.00	Saucer, demi; '50s colors 34.00
Mug, Tom & Jerry; '50s colors 60.00	Saucer, demi; orig colors 10.00
Mug, Tom & Jerry; ivory w/gold letters 45.00	Saucer, demi; red or cobalt 12.00
Mug, Tom & Jerry; orig colors 36.00	Saucer, med gr 7.50
Mug, Tom & Jerry; red or cobalt 52.00	Saucer, orig colors 2.50
Mustard, orig colors 95.00	Saucer, red or cobalt 3.50
Mustard, red or cobalt 130.00	Shakers, '50s colors, pr 28.00
Pitcher, disk juice; gray 750.00	Shakers, med gr, pr 48.00
Pitcher, disk juice; red 165.00	Shakers, orig colors, pr 15.00
Pitcher, disk juice; yel 30.00	Shakers, red or cobalt, pr 20.00
Pitcher, disk water; '50s colors 150.00	Sugar bowl, ind; turq 160.00
Pitcher, disk water; med gr 365.00	Sugar bowl, ind; yel 65.00
Pitcher, disk water; orig colors 60.00	Sugar bowl, w/lid, '50s colors, 3¼x3½" 36.00
Pitcher, disk water; red or cobalt 85.00	Sugar bowl, w/lid, med gr, 3¼x3½" 55.00

Sugar bowl, w/lid, orig colors, 3¼x3½" 22.00
Sugar bowl, w/lid, red or cobalt, 3¼x3½" 30.00
Syrup, orig colors 165.00
Syrup, red or cobalt..190.00
Teacup, '50s colors 28.00
Teacup, med gr..32.00
Teacup, orig colors 20.00
Teacup, red or cobalt 25.00
Teapot, lg; orig colors 80.00
Teapot, med; '50s colors 155.00
Teapot, med; med gr 260.00

Large teapot, red or cobalt, $95.00.

Teapot, med; orig colors 70.00
Teapot, med; red or cobalt..92.00
Tray, figure-8; cobalt..45.00
Tray, figure-8; turq..135.00
Tray, figure-8; yel..150.00
Tray, relish; mixed colors, no red 130.00
Tray, utility; orig colors 22.00
Tray, utility; red or cobalt..28.00
Tumbler, juice; chartreuse, Harlequin yel or dk gr 160.00
Tumbler, juice; orig colors 20.00
Tumbler, juice; red or cobalt 28.00
Tumbler, juice; rose 30.00
Tumbler, water; orig colors..36.00
Tumbler, water; red or cobalt 40.00
Vase, bud; orig colors..38.00
Vase, bud; red or cobalt 50.00
Vase, orig colors, 10" 350.00
Vase, orig colors, 12" 425.00
Vase, orig colors, 8" 265.00
Vase, red or cobalt, 10"..425.00
Vase, red or cobalt, 12"..535.00
Vase, red or cobalt, 8"..350.00

Kitchen Kraft

Bowl, mixing; lt gr or yel, 10" 60.00
Bowl, mixing; lt gr or yel, 6" 32.00
Bowl, mixing; lt gr or yel, 8" 50.00
Bowl, mixing; red or cobalt, 10" 70.00
Bowl, mixing; red or cobalt, 6" 38.00
Bowl, mixing; red or cobalt, 8" 60.00
Cake plate, lt gr or yel..35.00

Cake plate, red or cobalt 40.00
Cake server, lt gr or yel 55.00
Cake server, red or cobalt 65.00
Casserole, ind; lt gr or yel 90.00
Casserole, ind; red or cobalt 100.00
Casserole, lt gr or yel, 7½"..65.00
Casserole, lt gr or yel, 8½"..70.00
Casserole, red or cobalt, 7½"..70.00
Casserole, red or cobalt, 8½"..75.00
Covered jar, lg; lt gr or yel 160.00
Covered jar, lg; red or cobalt 180.00
Covered jar, med; lt gr or yel 150.00
Covered jar, med; red or cobalt 165.00
Covered jar, sm; lt gr or yel 145.00
Covered jar, sm; red or cobalt 160.00
Covered jug, lt gr or yel 140.00
Covered jug, red or cobalt 160.00
Fork, lt gr or yel..45.00
Fork, red or cobalt..50.00
Metal frame for platter..20.00
Pie plate, lt gr or yel, 10" 35.00
Pie plate, lt gr or yel, 9" 30.00
Pie plate, red or cobalt, 10" 40.00
Pie plate, red or cobalt, 9" 35.00
Shakers, lt gr or yel, pr..60.00
Shakers, red or cobalt, pr 70.00
Spoon, lt gr or yel..48.00
Spoon, red or cobalt..52.00
Stacking refrigerator lid, lt gr or yel......................................40.00
Stacking refrigerator lid, red or cobalt..................................45.00
Stacking refrigerator unit, lt gr or yel....................................25.00
Stacking refrigerator unit, red or cobalt 30.00

Finch, Kay

Kay Finch and her husband, Braden, operated a small pottery in Corona Del Mar, California, from 1939 to 1963. The company remained small, employing from twenty to forty local residents who Kay trained in all but the most requiring tasks, which she herself performed. The company produced animal and bird figurines, most notably dogs, Kay's favorites. Figures of 'Godey' type couples were also made, as were tableware (consisting of breakfast sets) and other artware. Most pieces were marked. Our advisor for this category is Jack Chipman, author of *The Collector's Encyclopedia of California Pottery*; he is listed in the Directory under California.

Bunny family, 3 pieces, $175.00.

Bank, pig, floral decor, 10" 75.00
Cookie jar, Cookie Pup (dog), 12¾" 175.00
Cookie jar, Cookie Puss (cat), 11¾" 175.00
Figurine, Afghan head, 12" 150.00
Figurine, camel, 5" 85.00
Figurine, cat, Ambrosia, 10¾" 150.00
Figurine, choir boy, 7¾" 45.00
Figurine, cocker spaniel, 8" 75.00
Figurine, Dalmation, 17" 250.00
Figurine, elephant, 5" 45.00
Figurine, Godey man holding bouquet, 7½" 65.00
Figurine, Hansel & Gretel, 7", pr 85.00
Figurine, hen 45.00
Figurine, lamb, 2¼" 25.00
Figurine, nativity set, gold trim, 6-pc 350.00
Figurine, owl, 8¾" 35.00
Figurine, peasant boy, 7" 40.00
Figurine, peasant girl, 5½" 30.00
Figurine, rooster, 8¼" 65.00
Figurine, Scotty champion on base 175.00
Shakers, Pup (matches cookie jar), 6", pr 45.00
Shakers, Puss (matches cookie jar), 6", pr...................45.00

Findlay Onyx and Floradine

Findlay, Ohio, was the location of the Dalzell, Gilmore, and Leighton Glass Company, one of at least sixteen companies that flourished there between 1886 and 1901. Their most famous ware, Onyx, is very rare. It was produced for only a short time beginning in 1889 due to the heavy losses incurred in the manufacturing process.

Onyx is layered glass, usually found in creamy white with a dainty floral pattern accented with metallic lustre that has been trapped between the two layers. Other colors found on rare occasions include a light amber (with either no lustre or with gilt flowers), light amethyst (or lavender), and rose. Although old tradepaper articles indicate the company originally intended to produce the line in three distinct colors, long-time Onyx collectors report that aside from the white, production was very limited. Other colors of Onyx are very rare, and the few examples that are found tend to support the theory that production of colored Onyx ware remained for the most part in the experimental stage. Even three-layered items have been found (they are extremely rare) decorated with three-color flowers. As a rule of thumb, using white Onyx prices as a basis for evaluation, expect to pay two to three times more for colored examples.

Floradine is a separate line that was made with the Onyx molds. A single-layer rose satin glassware with white opal flowers, it is usually priced in the general range of colored Onyx.

Chipping around the rims is very common, and price is determined to a great extent by condition. Our advisors for this category are Betty and Clarence Maier; they are listed in the Directory under Pennsylvania.

Floradine

Bowl, fluted, squat bulbous base, 4" 775.00
Box, dome lid, 6" dia 1,600.00
Box, dome lid (chipped lid), 6" dia 575.00
Creamer, bulbous, fluted neck, 4⅝" 1,150.00
Mustard pot, 3¾" 1,000.00
Spooner, 4" 900.00
Sugar bowl, bulbous, w/lid, 5½" 1,200.00
Syrup pitcher, fluted neck, hinged metal cap, 7".......1,500.00
Toothpick holder, 2½" 800.00

Tumbler, slightly bulbous, 3⅝" 700.00
Vase, fluted cylinder neck, bulbous body, 6½".............900.00

Floradine syrup pitcher, 7", $1,500.00.

Onyx

Bottle, tumble-up; wht w/silver decor, no tumbler, 8¾" 500.00
Bowl, wht w/purple decor, fluted rim, squat body, 4" 1,000.00
Bowl, wht w/silver decor, 7½" 400.00
Box, dresser; wht w/silver decor, 5" dia, EX 650.00
Celery vase, wht w/silver decor, 6½", EX 350.00
Creamer, wht w/silver decor, 4½", EX 250.00
Mustard pot, wht w/lt orange decor, rare, 3½" 1,000.00
Mustard pot, wht w/silver decor, metal lid, silver spoon.............550.00
Pitcher, wht w/silver decor, polished rim chip, 7½" 800.00
Salt shaker, wht w/silver decor, 3" 275.00
Sugar bowl, wht w/silver decor, w/lid, 5½" 350.00
Sugar shaker, wht w/silver trim, NP top, 5½x3" 475.00
Syrup, wht w/silver decor, metal thumb-lift lid, 7" 850.00
Toothpick holder...375.00
Tumbler, wht w/silver decor, bbl shape, 3½x2⅞" 350.00
Tumbler, wht w/silver decor, bbl shape, 3¾x2¾" 395.00
Vase, amber w/wht decor, fluted neck, bulbous body, 4⅜"...........400.00

Fire Marks

During the early 19th century, insurance companies used fire marks — signs of insurance — to indicate to the volunteer firefighters which homes were covered by their company. Handsome rewards were promised to the brigade that successfully extinguished the blaze, so competition was fierce between rivals and sometimes resulted in an altercation at the scene to settle the matter of which brigade would be the one to fight the fire! Fire marks were originally made of cast iron or lead; later examples were sometimes tin or zinc. They were used abroad as well as in this country, and those from England tended to be much more elaborate. When municipal fire departments were organized in the mid- to late 1860s, volunteer departments and fire marks became obsolete.

CI w/traces of pnt, emb hose & FA, 11½x7½" 210.00
City Insurance Co, Cin; emb pumper w/6 firemen, CI/mc, 13" ...650.00
Eagle Ins Co, Cincinnati, OH; gold on blk, CI, 8x12" 850.00
FA, CI, emb hose & FA, pitted, 7x11" 100.00
Fire Dept Insurance, mc on CI oval, 8x12" 375.00
Firefighting tools amid hose border, CI, 19th C, 5¾" dia............185.00
Mutual Insurance, angel flying over Charleston, 9½x7½".............65.00
UF, w/pumper, CI w/pnt traces, oval, lt rust, 8½x11" 75.00

Firefighting Collectibles

Firefighting antiques from the nineteenth century reflect the feeling of pride the men had in their companies and in their role as volunteer fire fighters. Fancy dress uniforms and helmets, silver trumpets full of flowers recall the charisma of the 'Laddies' on parade. Leather buckets, bed keys, muffin bells, rattles, torches, lanterns, and riveted leather hose all serve as reminders of that era, long past.

In the 1860s the old volunteer units begrudgingly gave way to the 'paid municipal firefighter.' The politically astute and sometimes physically aggressive volunteer organizations many times went down hard and maintained group integrity many years after paid forces were in place.

With the inception of 'disciplined,' paid forces, the ascention to more sophisticated fire alarms and fire supression equipment was accelerated. Hand and horse-drawn equipment predominated until about WWI when apparatus motorization really took hold and for the most part was the dominating factor by 1920. Suspicious of the new machines, many northern fire departments kept horse-drawn sleighs in reserve well into the late 1920s.

Today there is a large, active group of collectors for fire department antiques (items over 100 years old) and an even larger group seeking related collectibles (those less than 100 years old). Note: In the extinguishers listed below, the term 'apparatus type' refers to that which is carried on or by fire apparatus; 'building type' are those found hanging on walls of buildings. Our advisors for this category are H. Thomas and Patricia Laun; they are listed in the directory under New York.

Key: s+a — soda & acid

Alarm, Gamewell Vitalarm-The Instantaneous Fire Detector, EX...**80.00**
Alarm box, Federal, aluminum, complete......................................**75.00**
Alarm box, Gamewell, aluminum type 51, complete...................**120.00**
Alarm box, Gamewell, CI, telegraph door, complete orig...........**175.00**
Alarm box, Holtzer Cabot, CI/brass, rnd bldg style....................**65.00**
Alarm box, Horni, aluminum, complete......................................**85.00**
Alarm box, Utica Fire Alarm & Telegraph, CI, Excelsior sz.......**600.00**
Alarm indicator, Gamewell, cherry flat-top case......................**1,850.00**
Alarm indicator, Gamewell, oak case, vibrating bell................**2,350.00**
Alarm indicator, Gamewell, oak flat-top case..........................**1,750.00**
Alarm indicator, Moses Crane, fancy walnut case, flat wheels.**3,200.00**
Alarm indicator, Moses Crane, fancy walnut case, rnd wheels.**2,800.00**
Axe, Viking style, red/bl pnt head, blk hdl, EX.........................**295.00**
Badge, Deputy Chief Milton FD #36, gold tone..........................**25.00**
Badge, Gloucester FD, schooner in center, silver tone................**30.00**
Badge, hat; Brookline Fire Dept, Maltese cross, silver tone...........**30.00**
Badge, Lynn FD #145, seal in center, NP..................................**25.00**
Badge, Montgomery-1-1847, shield shape, sterling.....................**85.00**
Badge, presentation; NY, gold front on gold-tone bk, EX............**180.00**
Badge, St Paul Fire Dept, w/eagle, NP, early.............................**25.00**
Badge, Woburn FD #103, silver tone...**25.00**
Bed key, CI, 19th century, 4½", EX..**150.00**
Bell, Am LaFrance, chrome, w/yoke from ladder truck, 12".......**400.00**
Bell, apparatus, locomotive style, chrome plated, 10", NM........**300.00**
Bell, apparatus, locomotive style, 10" in swing harp..................**675.00**
Bell, apparatus, locomotive style, 12", NM................................**375.00**
Bell, brass, muffin type w/wooden hdl, 6" dia, EX.....................**600.00**
Belt, parade; leather, blk w/red & wht lettering, ca 1852, EX......**95.00**
Belt, parade; leather w/metal letters, 2-pc, EX...........................**75.00**
Book, FD Utica NY, softbk, 1884, 173-pg, 6x9", EX..................**65.00**
Book, Fires & Firefighters, JV Morris, 394-pg, EX.....................**25.00**
Book, New Bedford MA FD, history, hardbk, 1890, 239-pg, EX....**60.00**
Booklet, Annual Report...Fall River FD...1909, 80-pg, EX.........**22.00**

Bucket, leather, orig pnt, hdl, EX...**210.00**
Bucket, leather, W Cotting...1830, worn pnt, EX......................**240.00**
Bucket, rubber, Franklin Hook & Ladder Co 1823, rpt, pr.........**250.00**
Bucket, rubber, SBH Co No 1 in red & blk letters, EX...............**100.00**
Button, Brooklyn Fire Dept, brass, emb lady w/axe, 1" dia...........**32.50**

Button, brass, very early, 1¼" diameter, $150.00.

Cap, dress bl w/gold FD buttons & trumpet badge, EX.................**45.00**
Cape, leather, blk pnt w/gray stripe, dtd 1821, 45" L, VG......**1,800.00**
Extinguisher, Ahrens Fox, nickel/brass, apparatus type, s+a.......**235.00**
Extinguisher, Alert, Am LaFrance, bldg type, s+a.......................**35.00**
Extinguisher, ALF Foamite, nickel/brass, apparatus, s+a, NM.....**150.00**
Extinguisher, Badgers, pnt label, pony sz...................................**65.00**
Extinguisher, Liberty, tin, dry chemicals, EX.............................**30.00**
Extinguisher, Mack, nickel/brass, apparatus type, s+a................**200.00**
Extinguisher, Rameses, Egyptian Mfg...KY, EX..........................**30.00**
Extinguisher, Richmond, tin cylinder, EX..................................**60.00**
Extinguisher, Seco, copper/brass, bldg type, s+a, 2½-gal.............**20.00**
Extinguisher, Ward LaFrance, nickel/brass, apparatus, s+a........**185.00**
Gauge, Am LaFrance, brass, beveled glass, 0-300 psi, 4" dia......**100.00**
Gauge, Providence Pipe & Sprinkler, brass, 5¾" dia....................**35.00**
Gong, Gamewell Newton Upper Falls MA, turtle style, 6", EX....**125.00**
Gong, LW Bills, brass, turtle style, w/key, 10".........................**165.00**
Gong, Star Electric, bldg type, oak case, +10" brass bell.........**1,475.00**
Grenade, Harden's, emb quilting, bl, full....................................**65.00**
Grenade, Harden's Star, bl, rnd, empty.......................................**75.00**
Grenade, Harden's Star, cobalt, emb ribs, orig contents, 6½".....**110.00**
Grenade, Harden's Star, ribbed, bl, rnd, full..............................**75.00**
Grenade, Hayward's, amber, full...**150.00**
Grenade, Hayward's...Pat Aug 8 1871, apple gr, 6¼", NM.........**235.00**
Grenade, HSN, straw color, scarce..**125.00**
Grenade, HSN, yel-amber, emb dmns, orig contents, 7¼".........**190.00**
Helmet, aluminum, high eagle w/leather frontpc, EX................**160.00**
Helmet, fiberglass, leather frontpc, EX......................................**35.00**
Helmet, leather, high eagle, jockey style, scarce.......................**550.00**
Helmet, leather, high eagle w/frontpc, Anderson & Jones, EX....**230.00**
Helmet, leather, high eagle w/frontpc, Cairns, EX....................**365.00**
Helmet, leather, high eagle w/frontpc, Comb-nation-1-MFD, EX.**280.00**
Helmet, leather, high eagle w/frontpc, HA Winship, EX...........**270.00**
Helmet, leather, high eagle w/frontpc, John Olson, EX.............**325.00**
Helmet, leather, low front w/frontpc, Cairns, NM....................**160.00**
Helmet, torch; leather, high eagle w/rpl frontpc, EX................**240.00**
Horn, alarm; Gamewell, red & wht, 29" L, EX............................**95.00**
Lamp, Orient #5 in ruby panel, 2 bl/1 clear panel, SP, 15"......**3,200.00**
Lantern, Dietz Fire King, brass, red globe, Pat 07, VG..............**160.00**
Lantern, Dietz Fire King, red globe, brass, sliding cage, EX.......**250.00**
Lantern, Dietz Fire King, Seagrave, nickel/brass, EX.................**400.00**
Lantern, Dietz Queen Fire Dept, nickel brass, hand sz...............**625.00**
Lantern, Eclipse, NP & brass, lacking cage...............................**450.00**
Nozzle, Akron Brass, foam, aluminum w/cord covering, EX.........**75.00**
Nozzle, bayonet applicator, low velocity fog, 1½".......................**25.00**

Nozzle, Blanchard Pat, brass, #2, 7½", NM..............95.00
Nozzle, brass, steamer w/copper tip, playpipe, scarce, 45"............210.00
Nozzle, brass, w/Ashworth shut-off, 26", EX..............70.00
Nozzle, Eureka, brass w/rubberized body, leather grips, 35" 80.00
Nozzle, General, brass w/leather grip hdls, 22" 80.00
Nozzle, RI Coupling Co, NP brass/cord covering, playpipe, 32" ...80.00
Nozzle, Rockwood, bayonet piercing applicator 35.00
Nozzle, UL, brass & copper, cord covering, playpipe, EX..............45.00
Nozzle, Underwriters, brass, string wrap, w/tip, 2½" 40.00
Rattle, alarm; dbl reed, walnut w/metal-weighted end, EX 105.00
Rattle, alarm; single reed, iron-weighted end, EX 110.00
Rattle, alarm; walnut wood, dbl reed, 10½" 150.00
Rattle, alarm; wooden, single reed, trn hdl, 9", EX............95.00
Salesman's sample, fire boots, Candee, miniature............95.00
Shield, presentation; leather, Protector 22..., 8"............250.00
Siren, Sireno, copper & aluminum, electrical............60.00
Telephone, alarm box; Western Electric, EX............50.00
Torch, brass, used to light boiler, suction plunger, 19" 85.00
Torch, parade; brass w/trn wooden hdl, 29", EX............275.00
Torch, parade; Water Witch, brass w/trn wooden pole, 10" 480.00
Trumpet, Adams Fire Dept, brass, 21", EX 400.00
Trumpet, brass, eng #3 on body, tassel cord, 19½", EX............420.00
Trumpet, heavy tin, 15" 225.00
Trumpet, presentation grade SP, eagle head tassel mts, 17" 1,150.00
Trumpet, Walton Bros NY, brass, 10", EX............300.00
Whistle, building type, brass, manual pull lever, 24" 300.00
Wrench, Boston Coupling Co, combination spanner, 9½", EX.....10.00
Wrench, Buffalo Fire...NY, brass, folding spanner, 9½" 300.00

Early Gamewell house gong, fancy oak case, 18", EX, $4,200.00.

Fireglow

Fireglow is a type of art glass that first appears to be an opaque cafe au lait, but glows with rich red 'fire' when held to a strong source of light.

Biscuit jar, alternate ribs, florals, SP hdl, Mt WA, 6x8½" 450.00
Creamer & sugar bowl, florals, 3" 150.00
Ewer, birds on tree branches, 7" 165.00
Garniture, 2 10" vases+13" urn, exotic florals, Sandwich 650.00
Pitcher, floral branches, 3-petal top, bulbous, 7¼x6" 395.00
Tumbler, narrow ribs 110.00
Vase, gold-traced mauve flowers & leaves, mk PK, 11"............250.00

Vase, mc florals, ornate brass holder, 7½" 150.00
Vase, stick neck, 7½"............120.00

Fireplace Implements

In the colonial days of our country, fireplaces provided heat in the winter and were used year round to cook food in the kitchen. The implements that were a necessary part of these functions were varied and have become treasured collectibles, many put to new use in modern homes as decorative accessories. Gypsy pots may hold magazines; copper and brass kettles, newly polished and gleaming, contain dried flowers or green plants. Firebacks, highly ornamental iron panels that once reflected heat and protected masonry walls, are now sometimes used as wall decorations.

By Victorian times the cookstove had replaced the kitchen fireplace, and many of these early utensils were already obsolete. But as a source of heat and comfort, the fireplace continued to be used for several more decades. See also Wrought Iron.

Andirons, brass, Baroque, urn form, lion mask/paw ft, 30" 1,000.00
Andirons, brass, belted ball finial on trn shaft, 1825, 15" 325.00
Andirons, brass, mk Whittingham NY, 19"............750.00
Andirons, brass, standing figures on bases w/mermaids, 25"........700.00
Andirons, brass, urn finials, hex bases, ball ft, 1820s, 16" 425.00
Andirons, CI, Hessian soldier, blk rpt, 20" 300.00
Andirons, CI, owl on branch, orig blk pnt, 14x8½x12½"............250.00
Andirons, CI, seated dog, mk R Clancy MA, 14", EX 850.00
Andirons, wrought iron, decorative brass leaf finials, 23" 275.00
Andirons, wrought iron, spade ft, gooseneck finial, 20" 675.00
Bellows, leather w/HP village, 1835, 18", VG............ 1,400.00

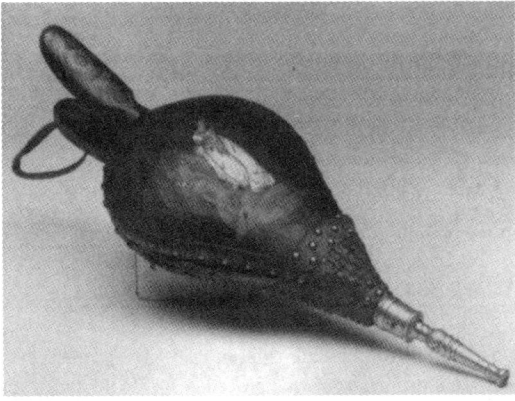

Painted and decorated bellows, 1800s, 19", EX, $550.00.

Bellows, turtle bk, dk pnt w/gilt, red beneath, 17" 200.00
Bellows, turtle bk, orig pnt/smoke gr/fruit decor, rstr, 18" 225.00
Broiler, wrought, upright, 3-leg base w/spade ft, 28" 825.00
Broiler, wrought iron, rotary, 22" 125.00
Coals carrier, sheet/wrought iron, slide lid, wood hdl, 38" 325.00
Crane, free-standing;, wrought, used in open hearth, 26x54" 450.00
Ember tongs, wrought iron, scissors shape, 1700s, 11½" 150.00
Fireboard, geometrics, 6-color, 1800s, 23x36" 2,000.00
Fork, toasting; wrought, 2-tine, ring hdl, 20" 35.00
Fork, toasting; wrought, 3-tine, flat shaft, ring hdl, 25½"............190.00
Fork, wrought, heart hdl, 25", on stand 145.00
Frame, wrought iron, for hanging pots in open fire, 16" L 150.00
Kettle stand, brass/wrought iron, trn wood hdl, 13½" 125.00
Kettle stand, wrought iron w/rtcl brass top, trn hdl, 11" 225.00
Kettle tilter, wrought iron, serpentine hdl, pitted, 19" 275.00

Larding needle, tin, used when roasting meat, 6½"..........................8.00
Roaster, game bird; wrought, Rizzler Plymouth, 1800s, 30".........375.00
Skewer, fancy hdl, sgn Plymouth Jabber 75.00
Toaster, iron w/flip-winged joint on 4 arched fr, wood hdl..........260.00
Toaster, wrought iron, well-shaped hdl, 18"..............................225.00
Toaster, wrought iron, 12½" L 150.00

Fisher, Harrison

Harrison Fisher (1875-1934), noted illustrator and creator of the Fisher Girl, was the son of landscape artist, Hugh Anoine Fisher. His career began in his teens in San Francisco where he did artwork for the Hearst papers. Later in New York, his drawings of beautiful American women attracted much attention and graced the covers of the most popular magazines of the day such as *Puck, Ladies' Home Journal, Saturday Evening Post,* and *Cosmopolitan.* He also illustrated novels, and his art books were treasured. His drawings appeared on thousands of post cards and posters. His creation of the Fisher Girl and his panel of six scenes of the *Greatest Moments in a Woman's Life* made him the most sought-after and well-paid illustrator of his day.

Art book, A Dream of Fair Women, EX 200.00
Art book, American Beauties, Bobbs Merril, 1st ed, 1909, EX 195.00
Art book, American Girls in Miniature, 1912, w/box, EX...........250.00
Art book, Hiawatha, EX 150.00
Art book, Little Gift Book, 1913..175.00
Banner, Red Cross, nurse, w/Foringer's madonna, 41½x8½", EX ..95.00
Bookplate, American Beauties, 1909, 11x8½" 65.00
Candy tin, Dancing Girl, Tindeco, 2½x7" dia.............................40.00
Magazine cover, Ladies' Home Journal, ea.................................22.00
Post card, Greatest Moments, set of 6 in orig matting & fr 95.00
Poster, Have You Answered...Red Cross Christmas Roll Call 125.00
Print, American Beauties, 1909 ....275.00
Print, American Belles, 1911 ....285.00
Print, Bachelor Bells, 1908..160.00
Print, Danger, ca 1908, old fr 85.00
Print, Dream of Fair Women, 1907...195.00
Print, Dumb Luck, matted print: 6½x10½", fr: 11x15" 25.00
Print, King of Hearts, orig fr, 11x13"..65.00

Fishing Collectibles

Collecting old fishing tackle is becoming more popular every year. Though at first most interest was geared toward old lures and some reels, rods, advertising, and miscellaneous items are quickly gaining ground. Values are given for examples in excellent or better condition and should be used only as a guide. For more information contact our advisor Randy Hilst, an appraiser and collector whose address and phone number are listed in the Directory under Illinois.

Louis Rhead Nature Lure 'Brown Frog,' rare, $600.00.

Catalog, Creek Chub, 1945 ....45.00
Catalog, Heddon, 1932 ....65.00
Catalog, Heddon, 1952 ....25.00
Catalog, South Bend, 1938 ....25.00
Fish decoy, Creek Chub, glass eyes, wood...............................300.00
Fish decoy, Heddon, glass eyes, wood....................................300.00
Lure, Al Foss Jazz Wiggler, no eyes, metal..............................10.00
Lure, Al Foss Shimmy Wiggler, no eyes, metal 8.00
Lure, Creek Chub Champ Spoon, pnt eyes, metal 22.00
Lure, Creek Chub Darter, pnt eyes, wood................................10.00
Lure, Creek Chub Dive Bomber, pnt eyes, wood.......................20.00
Lure, Creek Chub Jigger, glass eyes, wood...............................75.00
Lure, Creek Chub Pikie Minnow, glass eyes, wood....................10.00
Lure, Creek Chub Plunker, glass eyes, wood............................10.00
Lure, Creek Chub River Rustler, glass eyes, wood.....................70.00
Lure, Creek Chub Seven Thousand, bead eyes, wood................25.00
Lure, Creek Chub Wee Dee, glass eyes, wood 225.00
Lure, Heddon Crab Wiggler, glass eyes, wood..........................30.00
Lure, Heddon Game Fisher, no eyes, wood...............................20.00
Lure, Heddon Meadow Mouse, bead eyes, wood.......................25.00
Lure, Heddon Musky Crazy Crawler, pnt eyes, wood...................40.00
Lure, Heddon Punkinseed, pnt eyes, wood................................40.00
Lure, Heddon River Runt, glass eyes, wood 25.00
Lure, Heddon River Runt Spook, pnt eyes, plastic 8.00
Lure, Heddon Spoony Frog, no eyes, metal...............................25.00
Lure, Heddon Underwater Minnow, glass eyes, wood 70.00
Lure, Heddon Vamp Spook, pnt eyes, plastic 10.00
Lure, Heddon Zaragossa, glass eyes, wood...............................65.00
Lure, Helga Devil, no eyes, plastic 10.00
Lure, Paw Paw Lippy Joe, tack eyes, wood............................... 8.00
Lure, Paw Paw Mouse, tack eyes, wood...................................10.00
Lure, Shakespeare Pikie Kazoo, glass eyes, wood.....................50.00
Lure, Shakespeare Swimming Mouse, glass eyes, wood.............12.00
Lure, South Bend Fish Oreno, glass eyes, wood 12.00
Lure, South Bend Plug Oreno, glass eyes, wood 65.00
Lure, South Bend Vaccuum Bait, glass eyes, wood 50.00
Lure, Weller Simplex Minnow, glass eyes, wood 40.00
Lure, Winchester Spinner, no eyes, metal 35.00
Minnow trap, Camp, glass...50.00
Minnow trap, Orvis, glass 75.00
Reel, BF Meek, #25 Blue Grass, non-levelwind.........................150.00
Reel, Horton #3, non-levelwind...90.00
Reel, Langely Plug Cast, levelwind 12.00
Reel, Ocean City Quick-A-Part, non-levelwind 30.00
Reel, Ocean City Sea Girt, non-levelwind 15.00
Reel, South Bend #1000, levelwind 12.00
Reel, South Bend #1200, levelwind 12.00
Rod, Heddon Black Beauty, fly rod, bamboo, 9-ft.......................75.00
Rod, South Bend, fly rod, bamboo, 9-ft.....................................25.00
Tackle box, Heddon, 3-tray, metal 20.00

Flags of the United States

The brevity and imprecise language of the first Flag Act of 1777 allowed great artistic license for our early flag makers. As a result, vast and varied interpretations were produced until 1912 when stringent design standards were established for the new 48-star flag. Early patterns ranged from 'scatter' arrangements to elaborate wreaths and 'Great Stars.' Most surviving vintage flags are of the 'generic' variety, devoid of any special pedigree or proven history. Nevertheless, these cherished artifacts continue to be avidly collected on the basis of age, scarcity, configuration, craftsmanship, and aesthetic merit.

Pre-Civil War flags of 33 stars or less are very scarce and usually surface as 'big ticket' items. In those relatively uncharted waters, the terms of any given transaction are always subject to the influence of personal predisposition as well as the give-and-take of the negotiating process itself. There has also been a surging interest in Civil War-era flags of 34 and 35 stars as more Americans begin to focus on that epic period of U.S. history. That, in combination with the demands of a large and well-entrenched fraternity of Civil War collectors, has dramatically stimulated pricing into what is now clearly a seller's market.

Since 36 star flags are more likely to be post-Civil War flags, they, along with 37 star flags, have less broad-based appeal. Nevertheless, both vintages can fetch very respectable prices. Flags of 38 stars and the unofficial vintages of 39, 40, and 42 stars provide a popular, moderately priced marketplace for journeyman flag buffs and collectors of Americana, while the elusive 43 star flag is sought by nearly everyone. Flags of 44, 45, and 46 stars are production line items. Nevertheless, they are not without collecting merit and are usually available at comparatively modest prices. Ordinary 48 star flags flood the flea markets and are of little interest to most collectors, but the scarcer 49 star flag can generate occasional attention. 13 star flags, produced over a period of 200 years, surface in all forms and must be judged on a case-by-case basis. Many flag buffs favor flag sizes that are manageable for wall display, and most will make allowances for normal wear and tear. With rare exception, modern-day repros of historical flags have little or no collector appeal.

The dollar value of a flag is by no means based on age alone. The wide price swings in the listings that follow are the result of a variety of special considerations and features. Mass-printed flags, for instance, are generally not the equal of handcrafted flags, nor do unions with conventional rows of stars compare to the remarkable 'Great Star' and wreath patterns of the past. In fact, almost any special feature that stands out as unusual or distinctive is a potential asset. Imprinted flags and inscribed flags; 8-pointed stars, gold stars, and added stars; extra stripes, missing stripes, tri-color stripes, and war stripes are all part of the pricing equation. And while political and military flags may rank above all others in terms of prestige and price, any flag with a significant and well-documented historical connection has 'star' potential (pardon the pun). Our advisor for this category is Robert Banks; he is listed in the Directory under Maryland.

13 stars, Betsy Ross flag, by granddaughter, 1903, 8x12" 500.00
13 stars, Civil War boat ensign, USS Wabash, 44x64" 1,200.00
13 stars, in semi-wreath, hand sewn, 1870s, 54x102" 140.00
13 stars, printed, w/advertisement, 1880s, 4x7" 30.00
13 stars, US Navy boat ensign, dtd Sept 1904, 44x78" 75.00
13 stars, 3-2 pattern, machine sewn, 1880s, 24x48" 75.00
13 stars, 3rd MD pattern, hand sewn, 1840s, 32x45" 445.00
16 stars, naval ensign, hand sewn, CW era, 44x60" 550.00
19 stars, 16 orig+3, sewn scrap fabric, 39x66" 960.00
20 stars, hand-embr into Great Star, rare, 24x32" 900.00
23 stars, Civil War related, home-sewn muslin, 48x96" 200.00
25 stars, stenciled burlap on 24" wood tripod pole, 5x7" 170.00
26 stars, Great Star, embr on sewn silk, 30x43" 630.00
29 stars, entirely hand sewn, poor condition, 43x68" 410.00
30 stars, gold stars/fringe, silk, delicate, 52x68" 375.00
31 stars, Great Star, Lincoln related, printed, 11x14" 145.00
31 stars, Great Star, 14 stripes, hand sewn, 39x69" 600.00
32 stars, dbl wreath of inset stars, hand sewn, 36x48" 435.00
33 stars, hand-/machine-sewn wool bunting, 66x92" 475.00
33 stars, wreath pattern, printed glazed muslin, 16x22" 85.00
33 stars, wreath w/10 stripes, hand sewn, 77x127" 380.00
34 stars, dbl-wreath pattern, hand-sewn bunting, 24x36" 500.00
34 stars, dbl-wreath pattern, printed silk, 18x28" 160.00
34 stars, Great Star, mixed fabrics, sewn, 91x154" 550.00
34 stars, pattern variation, stitched cotton, 76x136" 360.00
34 stars, printed, added Garfield campaign legend, 24x48" 325.00

34 stars form shield, all hand sewn, worn, 51x66" 600.00
35 stars, hand/machine sewn, 96x180" 425.00
35 stars, recruiting flag, sewn bunting, 50x116" 500.00

Civil War-era flag of 35 stars in standard pattern, all hand-stitched bunting, 60" x 132", $500.00.

36 stars, Civil War, 8-pointed sewn wreath, 78x90" 720.00
36 stars, hand-sewn wool bunting, 68x85" 200.00
36 stars, 11 tricolor stripes, hand sewn, 51x99" 230.00
37 stars, printed silk, 32x40" 40.00
37 stars, row pattern, stitched bunting, 30x48" 150.00
37 stars, wreath pattern, hand-sewn cotton, 72x106" 290.00
37 stars, 6-pointed, hand-/machine-stitched cotton, 60x84" 325.00
38 stars, Blaine campaign, printed cotton, 17x27" 275.00
38 stars, Centennial 1886, printed cotton, 15x24" 48.00
38 stars, dbl-wreath pattern, sewn muslin, 87x128" 160.00
38 stars, Great Star, printed silk, gold fringe, 12x17" 40.00
38 stars, pattern variation, hand sewn, 96x164" 80.00
38 stars, printed glazed muslin pattern variation, 30x48" 50.00
38 stars, triple-wreath pattern, sewn bunting, 76x136" 240.00
38 stars, Union on red war stripe, homemade, 44x84" 75.00
38 stars, 1776-1876 pattern, printed linen, 27½x46" 250.00
39 stars, clamp-dye printed wool bunting, 56x117" 95.00
39 stars, originally 34 Great Star, sewn, 69x129" 360.00
39 stars, row pattern variation, printed silk, 12x24" 45.00
39 stars, scatter pattern, hand sewn, 78x120" 170.00
39 stars, triple wreath, hand-sewn bunting, 60x108" 250.00
39 stars, unofficial silk flag, printed, 12x16" 32.00
40 stars, unofficial, hand/machine sewn, 61x115" 90.00
40 stars, wreath-in-box pattern, hand sewn, 43x82" 140.00
40 stars backed by 39, hand sewn, unique, 72x114" 250.00
41 stars, unofficial, printed, rare, some damage, 16x24" 100.00
42 stars, minor pattern variation, sewn bunting, 96x138" 68.00
42 stars, printed cotton, unhemmed, 18x24" 22.00
42 stars, Union scatter pattern, hand sewn, 48x72" 134.00
43 stars, machine-sewn bunting, extremely rare, 29x70" 382.00
43 stars (1 side only), 98989 pattern, homemade, 38x48" 150.00
44 stars, hand-sewn bunting, 70x144", EX 85.00
44 stars, machine-sewn cotton bunting, 53x82" 45.00
45 stars, machine-sewn cotton bunting, 80x108" 24.00
45 stars, modified 38-star, hand sewn, 120x192" 110.00
45 stars, triple-wreath GAR flag, printed muslin, 11x16" 40.00
45 stars, Union, hand-sewn wool bunting, 92x135" 30.00
45 stars, Union Jack, machine-sewn bunting, 50x76" 37.00
46 stars, machine-sewn wool bunting, 72x138" 35.00
46 stars, printed silk, in baton-type carrying tube, 12x17" 17.00
46 stars, random pattern, machine sewn, 40x100" 55.00
47 stars, unofficial, sewn bunting, 108x137" 140.00
48 stars, machine-sewn cotton bunting, 60x96" 12.00
48 stars, modified 44-star flag, hand sewn, 60x90" 60.00
48 stars, sewn canton resting on red war stripe, 41x61" 35.00

48 stars, staggered rows (early), printed muslin, 13x23" 10.00
48 stars, Whipple Peace Flag, printed silk, 14x24" 160.00
48 stars, 10-9 pattern, printed bunting, rare, 39x61" 55.00
49 stars, embr w/sewn stripes, gold fringe, 48x72" 30.00
49 stars, machine-sewn cotton bunting, 36x60" 15.00
49 stars, Navy Jack, machine-sewn nylon, 32x48" 12.00
50 stars, Carter campaign, printed plastic, 12x18" 15.00
50 stars, flew over the capitol memento, new, 60x96"..................20.00
52 stars, Spanish Am war era, home sewn, rare, 44x84" 185.00
56 stars, printed crepe paper, Oriental, 1920s, 9x9" 18.00

Florence Ceramics

Figurines marked 'Florence Ceramics' were produced in the forties and fifties in Pasadena, California. The quality of the ware and the attention given to detail are prompting a growing interest among today's collectors. The names of these lovely ladies, gents, and figural groups are nearly always incised into their bases. The company name is ink-stamped. Because this is a relatively new area of collecting and the rarity of many items has yet to be determined, examples are evaluated by size and the intricacy of design. Our advisor for this category is Jack Chipman, author of *The Collector's Encyclopedia of California Pottery*; he is listed in the Directory under California.

Scarlett, gold trimmed, 9", $100.00.

Amber, holds parasol..175.00
Amelia, fancy metallic brocade, 8" 300.00
Annabel, 8½"...140.00
Annette, rare, 8½" 225.00
Chinese lady holding bouquet planter, 8½"...................50.00
Chinese lantern boy, 9" 50.00
Claudia, 9½"...95.00
Delia, dusty rose gown 85.00
Dolores...100.00
Elaine, gr gown, sm 45.00
Elizabeth on couch, 8¼x7"..200.00
Girl standing beside planter, 7"...45.00
Girl w/brn hair stands before book planter........................35.00
Girl w/vase in front of skirt 35.00
Jennifer, 8½"..130.00
Joy...40.00
Lady holding skirt planter, 7"..45.00
Lillian, gold trim, 8" 100.00

Lisa, rose, 6" 85.00
Louise, gr, 7½" 90.00
Madelyn, 9"...135.00
Marie Antoinette, 10" 125.00
Marilyn 135.00
Matilda, 8½" 85.00
Melanie, fancy, 7½"..85.00
Oriental couple, gr w/yel trim, 8¼", pr............................85.00
Polly, flower holder..35.00
Rhett, fancy, 9" 100.00
Sherri, 8¾"..150.00
Wendy, flower holder 30.00
Yvonne, fancy 150.00
Yvonne, plain 85.00

Florentine Cameo

Although its appearance may look much like English cameo, the decoration on this type of glass is not wheel cut or acid etched. Instead, a type of heavy paste — usually a frosty white — is applied to the surface to create a look very similar to true cameo. It was produced in France as well as England; it is sometimes marked 'Florentine.'

Pitcher, chinoiserie, yel on bl satin, basketweave cut, 8" 195.00
Tumbler, floral, wht on cranberry, 3⅞x2⅝"................................110.00
Vase, bird & foliage, wht on citron, 5"...75.00
Vase, birds & florals, wht on cranberry satin, 9" 215.00
Vase, dogwood/butterfly, wht on bl, ovoid, flanged rim, 9"..........200.00
Vase, floral, wht on bl, 4-petal top, 7¾x4¼" 185.00
Vase, morning-glories, wht on pk, 4-loop ribbon hdls, 12", pr 995.00

Flow Blue

Flow Blue ware was produced by many Staffordshire potters; among the most familiar were Meigh, Podmore and Walker, Samuel Alcock, Ridgway, John Wedge Wood (who often signed his work Wedgwood), and Davenport. It was popular from about 1825 through 1860 and again from 1880 until the turn of the century. The name describes the blurred or flowing effect of the cobalt decoration, achieved through the introduction of a chemical vapor into the kiln. The body of the ware is ironstone, and Oriental motifs were favored. Later issues were on a lighter body and often decorated with gilt.

Our advisor, Mary Frank Gaston, has compiled a lovely book, *The Collector's Encyclopedia of Flow Blue China*, with full-color illustrations and current market values; you will find her address in the Directory under Texas.

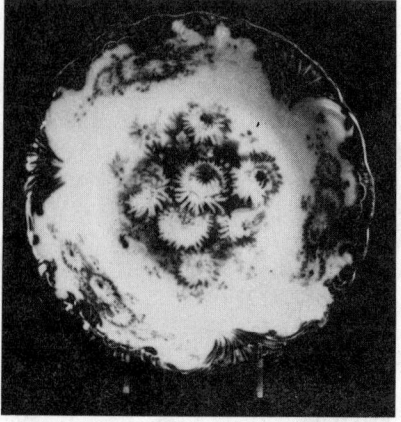

Dahlia bowl, Upper Hanley Pottery, 10", $120.00.

Abbey, relish, Geo Jones & Sons, 5½x10½"...............................120.00
Alaska, gravy boat, Grindley...95.00
Albany, bowl, vegetable; Grindley, 10¼"..................................95.00
Albany, bowl, vegetable; Grindley, 9".......................................85.00
Albany, butter dish, Grindley 235.00
Albany, cup & saucer, Grindley..65.00
Albany, gravy boat, w/underplate, Grindley............................150.00
Albany, plate, Grindley, 6¾"..35.00
Albany, plate, Grindley, 8¾"..40.00
Albany, platter, Grindley, 11¾"..125.00
Albany, sauce bowl, Grindley, 5¼"...28.00
Aldine, gravy boat, Grindley..65.00
Amoy, bowl, vegetable; Davenport, 8½"..................................265.00
Amoy, cup & saucer; handleless; Davenport 135.00
Amoy, gravy boat, Davenport...350.00
Amoy, plate, Davenport, 10½"..110.00
Amoy, plate, Davenport, 4"...45.00
Amoy, plate, Davenport, 9¼"...95.00
Amoy, platter, Davenport, 16"..400.00
Amoy, sauce bowl, Davenport..65.00
Amoy, sugar bowl, Davenport, w/lid......................................295.00
Arabesque, compote, ped ft, Mayer..725.00
Arabesque, plate, Mayer, 10¾"...125.00
Arabesque, platter, Mayer, 10¾"...195.00
Argyle, bone dish, Grindley...48.00
Argyle, platter, Grindley, 12¾x8¾"..165.00
Argyle, platter, Grindley, 15¼x10½".......................................185.00
Argyle, platter, Grindley, 17½x12"...225.00
Art Nouveau, soup ladle...225.00
Arundel, cookie jar, Doulton 150.00
Ashburton, butter pat, Grindley..22.50
Ashburton, creamer, Grindley 110.00
Ashburton, platter, Grindley, 20x15"......................................250.00
Athens, gravy boat, Meigh...200.00
Athens, honey dish, Meigh 65.00
Atlanta, bowl, 9"..80.00
Atlas, toothbrush holder..60.00
Ayr, bowl, vegetable; 8¼"...75.00
Ayr, butter pat 30.00
Basket, plate, dinner; Pratt, child's sz....................................100.00
Basket, sugar bowl, w/lid, Pratt, child's sz.............................150.00
Beatrice, plate, 10"...55.00
Beaufort, bowl, Grindley, 10" 90.00
Beaufort, platter, Grindley, 14"..150.00
Beaufort, platter, Grindley, 16¼"..175.00
Beauties of China, soup, flanged rim, MV&Co, 11"................130.00
Beauty Rose, pitcher, 6"...95.00
Belford, gravy boat..65.00
Belmont, bone dish, Meakin..45.00
Belmont, butter pat, Meakin..30.00
Belmont, plate, Meakin, 6¾"..30.00
Bentick, plate, Meakin, 10"...65.00
Blue Danube, bowl, vegetable; oval, Johnson Bros, ind 40.00
Blue Danube, soup tureen, Johnson Bros................................450.00
Blue Rose, bowl, Grindley, 6¼"..40.00
Bolingbroke, bone dish, Ridgway..45.00
Brooklyn, wash bowl & pitcher, Johnson Bros 950.00
Brussels, gravy boat...45.00
Byzantine, butter pat, Wood & Sons..30.00
Candia, compote, ped ft, Cauldon...625.00
Candia, pitcher, melon ribs, Cauldon, 5x5⅜"..........................165.00
Carlton, bowl, vegetable; rose finial, Alcock 425.00
Carnation, chamber pot, Minton..210.00
Cashmere, platter, Ridgway & Morley, 18"..............................750.00

Celia, cup & saucer..45.00
Celtic, bone dish, Grindley 40.00
Celtic, tureen, vegetable; w/lid, Grindley...............................225.00
Chain of States, plate, 9"...65.00
Chapoo, cup plate, Wedge Wood...85.00
Chapoo, teapot, Wedge Wood, 9x10".....................................600.00
Chatsworth, charger, 11"...145.00
Chatsworth, gravy boat..65.00
Chen-si, sugar bowl, w/lid..295.00
Chinese, bowl, 10"...90.00
Chinese, cup & saucer, demitasse; Wedgwood 55.00
Chinese, platter, Dimmock, 15½"...375.00
Chiswick, cup & saucer..45.00
Christine, bowl, 9"...80.00
Chusan, charger, Wedgwood 350.00
Chusan, creamer, Clementson...325.00
Chusan, platter, ca 1845, 13½x10½".......................................325.00
Chusan, sauce bowl, Fell..55.00
Circassia, soup, flanged, 10½" 115.00
Clarence, butter pat, Grindley...30.00
Clarence, pitcher, 6"...195.00
Clarence, soup bowl, Grindley, 9" 55.00
Clarence, sugar bowl, Johnson Bros...90.00
Clarissa, butter pat, Johnson Bros..30.00
Clarissa, tureen, w/lid, Johnson Bros 175.00
Clayton, cup & saucer, demitasse; Johnson Bros 58.00
Clayton, platter, Johnson Bros, 14½".......................................155.00
Clayton, waste bowl, Johnson Bros 70.00
Clover, bowl, vegetable; oval, w/lid, Grindley, 11" 250.00
Clover, cup & saucer, demitasse; Grindley 50.00
Clover, platter, Grindley, 16½"..185.00
Cluny, pitcher, 7"...140.00
Clytie, plate, Grindley, 9¾"...70.00
Coburg, platter, Edwards, 13¾" 325.00
Coburg, platter, Edwards, 17x12"...450.00
Coburg, wash bowl & pitcher, Edwards............................... 1,750.00
Colonial, bone dish, Meakin..40.00
Colonial, bowl, Meakin, 9"...80.00
Colonial, butter pat, Meakin..32.00
Colonial, gravy boat, Meakin...75.00

Togo plate, Colonial Pottery, 8¾", $45.00.

Colonial, gravy tray, Meakin..40.00
Conway, bowl, New Warf Pottery, 9" 80.00
Conway, creamer, New Warf Pottery.......................................140.00
Conway, plate, New Wharf Pottery, 10" 90.00
Conway, plate, New Wharf Pottery, 9".....................................70.00
Countess, gravy boat..65.00

Cows at Well, mug, Doulton 150.00
Cyprus, toothbrush holder, Ridgway 60.00
Dainty, bowl, vegetable; oval, w/lid, Maddock, lg 275.00
Dainty, butter pat, Maddock 30.00
Dainty, egg cup, Maddock 100.00
Daisy, bone dish 40.00
Daisy, platter, 12¼" 160.00
Davenport, creamer, Wood & Sons 85.00
Davenport, platter, Wood & Sons, 14x10" 70.00
Delamere, bowl, open hdls, Alcock, 15" 220.00
Delph, cheese dish, Wood & Sons 180.00
Doreen, pitcher, 7½" 190.00
Doreen, shaving mug 70.00
Dorothy, vase, Johnson Bros, 4½" 70.00
Dresden, sugar bowl, Villeroy & Boch, child's sz 175.00
Duchess, gravy boat & undertray, Grindley 135.00
Dudley, tureen, w/lid, Ford & Sons 210.00
Dundee, gravy boat, Ridgway 95.00
Ebor, gravy boat, Ridgway 95.00
Ellesmere, tureen, soup; Furnival 265.00
Excelsior, cup plate, Fell 100.00
Excelsior, plate, Fell, 10½" 115.00
Excelsior, plate, Fell, 9" 80.00
Fairy Villas, bowl, Adams, 10" 100.00
Ferrara, creamer & sugar bowl, Wedgwood 225.00
Florida, bowl, Grindley, 10" 125.00
Florida, bowl, oval, Grindley, 6" 35.00
Florida, bowl, vegetable; w/lid, Grindley 225.00
Florida, cup & saucer, Grindley 65.00
Florida, platter, Grindley, 10¼" 125.00
Florida, sauce dish, Johnson Bros 25.00
Formosa, bowl, potato; Mayer, 10¾" 375.00
Formosa, plate, Mayer, 9¾" 135.00
Gainsborough, pitcher, Ridgway, 2½-qt 225.00
Geisha, butter dish, orig insert, Upper Hanley, 3-pc 275.00
Geranium, soup tureen, w/lid, Ridgway 1,000.00
Gironde, bowl, vegetable; w/lid, Grindley 200.00
Gironde, butter pat, Grindley 28.00
Gironde, pitcher, Grindley, 9½" 275.00
Gironde, plate, Grindley, 6" 27.50
Gironde, relish, Grindley, sm 85.00
Glenmore, bone dish, Grindley 40.00
Glentine, creamer & sugar bowl, w/lid, Grindley 175.00
Glenwood, chamber pot, Wood & Sons, 8½" 170.00
Gothic, soup, flanged, 9" 95.00
Grace, butter pat, Grindley 30.00
Grace, plate, Grindley, 11" 70.00
Grace, tureen, vegetable; w/lid, Grindley 225.00
Grenada, cup & saucer, coffee; Alcock 75.00
Grenada, cup & saucer, tea; Alcock 65.00
Grenada, gravy boat, Alcock 100.00
Greville, crescent plate, Bishop & Stonier, 9½x6" 70.00
Greville, platter, Bishop & Stonier, 18½x15" 275.00
Hamilton, creamer, Meakin 95.00
Hamilton, gravy boat, Meakin, w/undertray 125.00
Hanley, charger, hanging holes, Meakin 135.00
Hawthorne, shaving brush holder, Dunn Bennett & Co 75.00
Hindustan, soup, flanged, John Maddock 80.00
Hofburg, bowl, open hdls, Grindley, 11" 110.00
Holland, bone dish, Meakin 40.00
Holland, bowl, vegetable; w/lid, Meakin 160.00
Holland, gravy boat, Meakin 160.00
Holland, platter, Meakin, 12½" 125.00
Holland, platter, Meakin, 16" 175.00

Holland, saucer, Meakin 25.00
Hong Kong, cup plate, Meigh 115.00
Hong Kong, pitcher, water; Meigh 365.00
Hong Kong, plate, Meigh, 10½" 125.00
Hong Kong, platter, Meigh, 16x12" 425.00
Hong Kong, platter, Meigh, 18x12" 650.00
Hudson, bowl, berry; Meakin, 5¼" 27.50
Hudson, tureen, w/lid, Meakin 165.00
Idris, bowl, vegetable; w/lid, Grindley 145.00
Indian, cup & saucer, handleless; Pratt 125.00
Indian, platter, Pratt, 13¼x10¼" 275.00
Indian, sauce bowl, Pratt 55.00
Indian Bridge, plate, red accents, 9½" 100.00
Indian Bridge, platter, 13x10" 225.00
Indian Jar, cup plate, Furnival 100.00
Indian Jar, plate, Furnival, 10¼" 110.00
Indian Jar, platter, Furnival, 22" 1,150.00
Ingeborg, sugar bowl 90.00
Iris, possett cup 65.00
Ivanhoe, plate, Rebecca Repelling the Templar, 10¼" 80.00
Ivanhoe, plate, Wedgwood, 10" 75.00
Ivy, soup, Davenport, 10½" 125.00
Janette, bowl, Grindley, 10" 90.00
Janette, bowl, oval, Grindley, 6" 35.00
Janette, plate, Grindley, 8" 60.00
Janette, sauce tureen, w/lid, Grindley 200.00
Japan, plate, Fell, 10½" 120.00
Japan, platter, Fell, 15x11" 325.00
Jaqueminot, pitcher & bowl, Ridgway 1,200.00
Jaqueminot, soap dish, Ridgway, 3-pc 225.00
Jaqueminot, toothbrush holder, Ridgway 175.00
Jesmond, pitcher, 7" 150.00
Kelvin, bowl, vegetable; oval, Meakin, 8½x6¾" 110.00
Kelvin, butter pat, Meakin 30.00
Kelvin, gravy boat & undertray, Meakin 145.00
Kelvin, plate, Meakin, 9" 57.50
Kelvin, platter, Meakin, 12½x8½" 150.00
Kenworth, bowl, berry; Johnson Bros 40.00
Kenworth, bowl, vegetable; rnd, deep, Johnson Bros 80.00
Kenworth, cup & saucer, Johnson Bros 60.00
Kenworth, gravy boat, Johnson Bros 70.00
Kenworth, plate, Johnson Bros, 9" 50.00
Kenworth, platter, Johnson Bros, 14x11" 175.00
Keswick, gravy boat 65.00
Killarny, plate, 9" 45.00
Kirkee, plate, 10½" 125.00
Kyber, bowl, Adams, 9" 75.00
Kyber, plate, Adams, 10" 110.00
Kyber, plate, Adams, 9" 90.00
Kyber, platter, Adams, 10" 120.00
La Belle, bone dish, Wheeling 45.00
La Belle, bowl, vegetable; w/lid, Wheeling, 10¼" 270.00
La Belle, charger, Wheeling, 11¼" 135.00
La Belle, charger, Wheeling, 12" 150.00
La Belle, creamer, Wheeling 120.00
La Belle, dresser tray, Wheeling 75.00
La Belle, molasses pitcher, w/catch plate, Wheeling 125.00
La Belle, plate, Wheeling, 10" 75.00
La Belle, plate, Wheeling, 9" 55.00
Lahore, bowl, vegetable; Philips, 8¼" L 250.00
Lahore, platter, Philips, 15½x12" 400.00
Lancaster, sauce dish, New Wharf Pottery 30.00
Landscape, cup & saucer, demitasse; Wedgwood 65.00
Landscape, platter, Wedgwood 145.00

Le Pavot, pitcher, milk; Grindley	265.00
Lily, coffeepot, 9"	125.00
Lincoln, plate, 9"	65.00
Linda, bowl, berry; Maddock, sm	35.00
Linda, plate, Maddock, 9"	45.00
Lois, bowl, 9"	80.00
Lorne, butter pat, Grindley	34.00
Lorne, sugar bowl, w/lid, Grindley	125.00
Lustre Band, coffeepot, Elsmore & Forster	475.00
Lustre Band, cookie plate	90.00
Madras, butter pat, Doulton	32.00
Madras, pitcher, Doulton, 5½"	195.00
Madras, platter, Doulton, 13½"	195.00
Mandarin, pitcher, water; Pountney	395.00
Mandarin, tureen, vegetable; w/lid, Maddock	450.00
Manilla, plate, Podmore Walker, 7¾"	90.00
Manilla, teapot, Podmore Walker	625.00
Marco, creamer & sugar bowl	135.00
Marechal Niel, bone dish, Grindley	40.00
Marechal Niel, bowl, berry; Grindley, sm	35.00
Marechal Niel, butter pat, Grindley	30.00
Marechal Niel, creamer, Grindley	145.00
Marechal Niel, gravy boat, Grindley	100.00
Marguerite, bone dish, Grindley	40.00
Marguerite, bowl, vegetable; w/lid, Grindley	200.00
Marlborough, platter, 14"	225.00
Martha, bone dish, Grindley	25.00
Melbourne, gravy boat & undertray	145.00
Melbourne, platter, Grindley, 18x12"	245.00
Melrose, platter, Doulton, 18x12"	245.00
Mikado, platter, Corn, 16x12"	250.00
Montana, egg cup, Johnson	80.00
Muriel, creamer, Upper Hanley	125.00
Neapolitan, creamer	125.00
Ning-Po, platter, 14½"	295.00
Non Pareil, bowl, vegetable; oval, Burgess & Leigh, 9½"	150.00
Non Pareil, creamer, Burgess & Leigh, lg	125.00
Non Pareil, cup & saucer, Burgess & Leigh	85.00
Non Pareil, soup tureen, rectangular, w/lid, Burgess & Leigh	475.00
Normandy, butter dish, Johnson Bros	295.00
Normandy, butter pat, Johnson Bros	28.00
Normandy, cup & saucer, demitasse; Johnson Bros	55.00
Normandy, cup & saucer, Johnson Bros	75.00
Oban, toothbrush holder	60.00
Olympia, bowl, Grindley, 9"	80.00
Olympia, saucer, Grindley	22.00
Oregon, teapot, Johnson Bros	400.00
Oregon, tureen, 8-ftd, hdls, w/lid, Johnson Bros, 6¼x9x5"	175.00
Oriental, creamer, Alcock	290.00
Oriental, platter, Alcock, 17"	495.00
Oriental, relish, self hdls, 8½x5"	68.00
Oriental, sauce bowl, Ridgway	35.00
Oriental, tureen, sauce; Alcock, 3-pc	650.00
Oriental, tureen, vegetable; w/lid, Ridgway	350.00
Osborne, bowl, vegetable; w/lid, Ridgway	225.00
Osborne, platter, Ridgway, 14¼"	120.00
Osborne, tureen, soup; Ridgway	400.00
Oxford, platter, Johnson Bros, 14x10¼"	175.00
Paisley, creamer, Mercer	90.00
Pansies, egg cup	35.00
Paris, plate, New Wharf Pottery, 9"	50.00
Paris, platter, Edge Malkin & Co, 14¼x11"	130.00
Pekin, platter, Wilkinson, 15"	175.00
Pelew, cup & saucer, handleless	95.00
Penang, platter, Ridgway, 13½x10½"	375.00
Persian Moss, bowl, Utzschneider, 9"	80.00
Poppy, creamer, Grindley	110.00
Portman, cup & saucer, Grindley	65.00
Progress, butter pat, Grindley	28.00
Progress, platter, Grindley, 12½"	130.00
Raleigh, bowl, berry; Burgess & Leigh	22.50
Raleigh, bowl, vegetable; w/lid, Burgess & Leigh	225.00
Raleigh, plate, Burgess & Leigh, 8¾"	30.00
Raleigh, plate, Burgess & Leigh, 9½"	45.00
Raleigh, platter, Burgess & Leigh, 13½x10¼"	125.00
Raleigh, platter, Burgess & Leigh, 17¾x13½"	195.00
Raleigh, soup, Burgess & Leigh, 8¾"	35.00
Richmond, plate, Meakin, 6"	30.00
Richmond, plate, Meakin, 9"	50.00
Rock, plate, Challinor, 7½"	60.00
Rock, platter, Challinor, 10"	125.00
Rococo, bowl, cereal; deep	40.00
Rose, bowl, Grindley, 13"	210.00
Rose, butter dish, Grindley, 2-pc	145.00
Rose, plate, Grindley, 9"	45.00
Rose & Ivy, plate, BWM & Co, 10½"	50.00
Scinde, bowl, vegetable; hdls	350.00
Scinde, plate, Alcock, 8½"	95.00
Scinde, plate, Walker, 9"	110.00
Shanghae, bowl, vegetable; w/lid, Furnival	625.00
Shanghae, soup, rimmed, Furnival	125.00
Shanghai, plate, Grindley, 9¾"	70.00
Shanghai, platter, Grindley, 12½x8¾"	150.00
Shell, plate, Challinor, 6¼"	45.00
Shell, wash bowl & pitcher, Challinor	1,150.00
Sterling, creamer	90.00
Sterling, teapot	185.00
Temple, cup & saucer, handleless; Podmore Walker	135.00
Tillenberg, tureen, soup; w/lid & undertray, Clementson	1,000.00
Tivoli, gravy boat, Furnival	160.00
Tivoli, tureen, soup; Furnival	1,950.00
Togo, plate, Winkle, 10"	50.00
Tokio, bowl, 5"	13.00
Tokio, platter, Johnson Bros, 12½x9½"	140.00
Tokio, platter, Johnson Bros, 14½x10¾"	198.00
Tonquin, plate, Heath, 10½"	135.00
Tonquin, platter, Heath, ca 1850, 13½x10½"	325.00
Touraine, bowl, vegetable; oval, w/lid, lg	250.00
Touraine, plate, Alcock, 8¾"	60.00
Touraine, plate, Alcock, 9"	55.00
Triumph, shaving mug	65.00
Turin, plate, Johnson Bros, 10"	55.00
Turin, plate, Johnson Bros, 9"	45.00
Turin, platter, Johnson Bros, 14½x10½"	135.00
Turin, platter, Johnson Bros, 16¼x12"	150.00
Turin, tureen, rnd, w/lid, Johnson Bros	155.00
Venice, plate, Grimwade, 10"	65.00
Venice, toothbrush jar, Grimwade, 4x5⅜"	80.00
Vermont, cup & saucer, demitasse; Burgess & Leigh, 6 for	275.00
Vermont, soup, Burgess & Leigh, 8¾"	45.00
Victoria, bowl, Wood & Son, 10"	90.00
Violette, cup & saucer	45.00
Waldorf, bowl, New Wharf Pottery, 9"	90.00
Waldorf, cup & saucer, Podmore Walker	70.00
Waldorf, plate, New Wharf Pottery, 8⅞"	65.00
Waldorf, platter, New Wharf Pottery, 10"	150.00
Watteau, biscuit jar, Doulton	450.00
Watteau, bowl, vegetable; Doulton, 8½"	95.00

Watteau, butter pat, Doulton..30.00
Watteau, charger, Doulton, 12¾"..................................175.00
Watteau, compote, rnd, ped ft, Doulton......................365.00
Watteau, gravy boat, Doulton...95.00
Watteau, plate, Doulton, 10½"......................................110.00
Watteau, plate, Doulton, 5½"...30.00
Watteau, plate, Doulton, 8½"...75.00
Watteau, plate, Doulton, 9"..85.00
Watteau, platter, New Wharf Pottery, 10¾".................95.00
Watteau, sauce dish, Doulton...25.00
Watteau, soup, flanged rim, Doulton, 7½".....................55.00
Watteau, soup, flanged rim, Doulton, 9".......................65.00
Waverly, pitcher, Maddock, 1½-qt...............................300.00
Wentworth, plate, 8½"...40.00
Whampoa, mug, 4⅛x4"...295.00
Whampoa, platter, 17"...395.00
Windsor Wreath, fruit bowl, tall ped...........................225.00
Woodbine, punch bowl, 10"..230.00
Woodland, plate, 9"...45.00
Yeddo, plate, 9¼"...65.00

Flue Covers

When spring housecleaning started and the heating stove was taken down for the warm weather season, the unsightly hole where the stovepipe joined the chimney was hidden with an attractive flue cover. They were made with a colorful litho print behind glass with a chain for hanging. Although scarce today, some scenes were actually reverse painted on the glass itself. The most popular motifs were florals, children, and lovely ladies. Square, rectangular, or diamond shapes are more valuable than oval or round covers, especially when Victorian ladies or children are pictured. Occasionally flue covers were made in sets of three — one served a functional purpose, while the other two were added to provide a more attractive wall arrangement. They range in size from 7"-8" to 13"-14", but 9" is the average.

Portrait of a cat, 10", $115.00.

Birds, mountains, trees, & clouds, under glass 38.00
Brass, rural winter scene, EX 15.00
Roman lady's profile, gold emb paper.......................................27.50
Victorian interior scene, under glass, 9" 48.00
Victorian maid, gold glitter trim, 12"...75.00
Vintage car, under glass..45.00

Folk Art

That the creative energies of the mind ever spark innovations in functional utilitarian channels as well as toward playful frivolity is well documented in the study of American folk art. While the average early settler rarely had free time to pursue art for its own sake, his creative energy exemplified itself in fashioning useful objects carved or otherwise ornamented beyond the scope of pure practicality. After the advent of the Industrial Revolution, the pace of everyday living became more leisurely, and country folk found they had extra time. Not accustomed to sitting idle, many turned to carving, painting, or weaving. Whirligigs, imaginative toys for the children, and whimsies of all types resulted. Though often rather crude, this type of early art represents a segment of our heritage and as such has become valued by collectors. See also Baskets; Decoys; Frakturs; Samplers; Trade Signs; Weathervanes; Wood Carvings.

Watercolor theorem painting on velvet, 1850s, 17" x 23", EX, $2,900.00.

Birdhouse, church form, pnt Gothic windows, '50s, 29x24x14" ..**400.00**
Birdhouse, wooden, shake shingles, dk gr pnt, 10x10x7" **85.00**
Calligraphy, elephant/motto on banner, blk/brn, 20x28" **475.00**
Calligraphy, kittens play w/yarn, 3-color ink, sgn, 15x18" **650.00**
Calligraphy certificate, red/blk ink, laid paper, 8x12" **175.00**
Charcoal on paper, children/lake/Indian in canoe, 18x22".........**375.00**
Cvg, mermaid, made from 1 pc, added base, dk patina, 16" **925.00**
Cvg, ocean liner, hollow, cvd portholes, pnt, 1930s, 24" **350.00**
Cvg, parrot, pnt limestone, ca 1900s, 7½x4x3½" **210.00**
Cvg, parrot on perch, wood/mc pnt/glass eyes, 1900s, 17" **350.00**
Diorama w/clipper ship, orig mc pnt, lt damage, 21x40"..............**450.00**
Diorama w/Geo WA, paper/pencil/hair/fabric/etc, 1822, 16" **750.00**
Doll, Abe Lincoln, cloth w/compo head, HP, 1930s, 12", EX **60.00**
Fish decoy, Muskie, wood/tin, worn pnt, 18"...............................**90.00**
Footstool, cloth covered w/3 horn legs, 1900s, 7½x8½" **45.00**
Jumping Jack on stick, cvd/mc pnt, plumed hat, 24", EX **250.00**
Man w/rifle, articulated sheet metal silhouette, pnt, 13" **1,000.00**
Map of US, ink/watercolor, sgn/dtd 1819, EX work, 29x35"........**750.00**
Memory jar, appl memorabilia, gold pnt, 11"................................**65.00**
Ornament, wrought iron, cross/sun/moon/ladder, tooled, 30" . **1,150.00**
Painting, oil on tin, horse, mtns beyond, 1820s, 14" dia **30.00**
Painting, pastel still life, gold-leaf fr, 1850s, 21x16"....................**135.00**
Painting, watercolor, birds & blossoms, 1900s, fr, 27x13" **75.00**
Painting on sea chest lid, ship, primitive, 16x33".........................**750.00**

Paper cutout, Family Record (unused), shadow box fr, 26x32" **200.00**
Paper cutout, 2 rnd designs, intricate, sgn, 9x12" **725.00**
Pen-work exercise, Endless Knot, inscribed/1844, 17x22", EX ..**250.00**
Shelf, wood, butterfly form, mc pnt, 12x13x5" **60.00**
Slingshot, handmade, cvd snake on grip, old bl pnt, 10" **30.00**
Theorem on velvet, basket of fruit/flowers, 12x13" **1,600.00**
Theorem on velvet, bldg/trees/deer, 5-color, 12x13" grpt fr **2,100.00**
Theorem on velvet, floral, rosewood fr w/gilt liner, 20x22" **400.00**
Theorem on velvet, hen on nest, sgn Rank, decor fr, 13x15" **325.00**
Theorem on velvet, parrot on bowl of fruit, stains, 22x36" **3,050.00**
Theorem on velvet, stylized fruit compote/butterfly, 15x18"... **3,500.00**
Tinsel picture, primitive vase of flowers, mc on wht, 13x11"......**300.00**
Totem pole, 2 Indian heads/2 trappers' heads, pnt, 1900s, 10" **90.00**
Watercolor on paper, boy in blk/wht dress w/whip, 9x7" **800.00**
Watercolor/graphite theorem, horse/flag/eagle, 20x26" **2,850.00**
Watercolor/graphite theorem, memorial/1840s dates, 21x26" **600.00**
Watercolor/graphite theorem on paper, urn/flowers, 12x10" **475.00**
Whirligig, airplane, tin/wood, propellers on wings, 1940s, 24" **165.00**
Whirligig, airplane, welded tin, detailed pnt, '30s, 25x18x9" **375.00**
Whirligig, Blk man w/suit & bow tie, pnt wood, 1920s, 20" **125.00**
Whirligig, man w/bucksaw sawing, mc pnt, 1930s, 16x15x12" ...**125.00**
Whirligig, policeman, arms rotate, blk/wht pnt, 13", EX **1,200.00**
Whirligig, surfer on surfboard, sgn J Marin '35, 16" **1,800.00**
Yard ornament, crane, pnt wood, Deco style, 39".........................**110.00**

Fostoria

The Fostoria Glass Company was built in 1887 at Fostoria, Ohio, but by 1891 it had moved to Moundsville, West Virginia. During the next two decades, they produced many lines of pressed patterned tableware and lamps. Their most famous pattern, American, was introduced in 1915 and was produced continuously until 1986 in well over two hundred different pieces. From 1920 to 1925, top artists designed tablewares in colored glass — canary (vaseline), amber, blue, orchid, green, and ebony — in pressed patterns as well as etched designs. By the late thirties, Fostoria was recognized as the largest producer of handmade glassware in the world. The company ceased operations in Moundsville in 1986.

Many items from both the American and Coin Glass lines are currently being reproduced by Lancaster Colony. In some cases the new glass is superior in quality to the old. Since the 1950s, Indiana Glass has produced a pattern called 'Whitehall' that looks very much like Fostoria's American, though with slight variations. Because Indiana's is not handmade glass, the lines of the 'cube' pattern and the edges of the items are sharp and untapered in comparison to the fire-polished originals. Three-footed pieces lack the 'toe' and instead have a peg-like foot, and the rays on the bottoms of the American examples are narrower than on the Whitehall counterparts. The Home Interiors Company currently offer several pieces of American look-alikes which were not even produced in the United States. Be sure of your dealer and study the books suggested below to become more familiar with the original line.

Coin Glass reproductions are flooding the market. Among items you may encounter are an 8" round bowl, 9" oval bowl, 8¼" wedding bowl, 4½" candlesticks, urn with lid, 6¼" candy jar with lid, footed comport, sugar and creamer; there could possibly be others. Colors in production are crystal, green, blue, and red. The red color is very good, but the blue is not the original color, nor is the emerald green. Buyer beware!

We are assisted in our listings by the Fostoria Glass Society of America, Inc., whose mailing address may be found in the Directory under Clubs, Newsletters, and Catalogs. For further information see *Elegant Glassware of the Depression Era* by Gene Florence and *Fostoria, the Popular Years, Third Edition Price Guide* by Jo Ann Schliesman. *Glass Animals and Figural Flower Frogs of the Depression Era* by Lee Garmon

and Dick Spencer offers an in-depth look at that particular aspect of Fostoria's production. Their addresses are listed in the Directory under Illinois. Items with (+) at the end of the lines are currently being reproduced; prices are for original issues.

Figurines

Chanticleer, 10¾" **200.00**
Chinese Lotus, silver mist, 12¼" **225.00**
Colts, sitting...**35.00**
Colts, standing, bl **40.00**
Deer, sitting or standing **40.00**
Deer, sitting or standing, milk glass **55.00**
Deer, sitting or standing, silver mist **40.00**
Duck, mama **25.00**
Duck w/3 ducklings, amber, set **50.00**
Duckling, head back (+) **20.00**
Duckling, head down (+) **15.00**
Duckling, walking (+) **15.00**
Eagle, bookend...**90.00**
Elephant, bookend **75.00**
Fish, horizontal, rare...**125.00**
Fish, vertical..**95.00**
Frog **35.00**
Horse, bookend...**65.00**
Madonna, silver mist, orig issue, 10" (+) **60.00**
Madonna, silver mist, w/base, orig issue, 11¾" (+) **80.00**
Madonna, 10" (+)..**60.00**
Mermaid, 10" **115.00**
Owl, bookend..**175.00**
Owl, bookend, ebony...**225.00**
Pelican **55.00**
Penguin **55.00**
Polar bear, amber...**125.00**
Polar bear, frosted **40.00**
Sea horse, bookend...**100.00**
Seal..**55.00**
Seal, frosted **45.00**
Squirrel..**25.00**
Squirrel, amber...**35.00**
Squirrel, frosted **25.00**
St Francis, silver mist, orig issue, 13½" (+)...........**325.00**
Whale **20.00**

American, ash tray, sq, 5" **55.00**
American, bowl, centerpiece; 11" **45.00**
American, bowl, fruit nappy; 4¾" **22.50**
American, bowl, nappy; 8" **35.00**
American, bowl, punch; 2-gal, 14" **275.00**
American, cake salver, rnd, 10".............................**75.00**
American, cake salver, sq, 10".................................**95.00**
American, candy dish, ftd, w/lid............................**45.00**
American, creamer, 4¼" **15.00**
American, goblet, cocktail; ftd, 3-oz, 2⅞" **15.00**
American, goblet, low, 9-oz, 5½" **11.00**
American, mustard jar, w/lid & spoon, 3¾"..............**32.50**
American, platter, oval, 10½" **55.00**
American, sauce boat, 6¾" **47.50**
American, shakers, 3½", pr **25.00**
American, tumbler, whiskey; 2-oz, 2½"....................**25.00**
American, vase, 8" **47.50**

American candle holder, 6", $80.00.

Arlington, ash tray, 7" 15.00
Arlington, candle holder, 2-lite, 5¼", pr 30.00
Arlington, compote, sq, 9½" 30.00
Arlington, marmalade set, #2694, 3-pc 32.50
Arlington, shaker, salt; 5½" 10.00
Baroque, bl; bonbon, 3-toed, 7⅜" 22.50
Baroque, bl; bowl, hdls, 10½" 65.00
Baroque, bl; candlestick, 4", pr 35.00
Baroque, bl; compote, 5½" 27.50
Baroque, bl; ice bucket, 4⅜" 110.00
Baroque, bl; plate, 9" 55.00
Baroque, bl; relish, pickle; 8" 25.00
Baroque, bl; tumbler, iced tea; flat, 14-oz, 5⅞" 95.00
Baroque, crystal; bowl, serving; hdls, 8½" 20.00
Baroque, crystal; cheese & cracker set, 2-pc 45.00
Baroque, crystal; creamer, ind 7.50
Baroque, crystal; mayonnaise set, w/liner & ladle 42.00
Baroque, topaz; bowl, nappy; hdls, 5" 20.00
Baroque, topaz; bowl, rolled edge, 11" 30.00
Baroque, topaz; candlestick, 2-lite, 4½", ea 30.00
Baroque, topaz; candlestick, 3-lite, pr.........................50.00
Baroque, topaz; plate, 7" 10.00
Betsy Ross, bowl, flared, 10½" 32.50
Betsy Ross, bowl, fruit; 10¾" 27.50
Betsy Ross, creamer, ftd, 4" 15.00
Betsy Ross, plate, 8" 9.00
Bouquet, bonbon, #2630, 3-toed, 7¼" 22.50
Bouquet, bowl, #2630, rolled edge, 11" 35.00
Bouquet, bowl, #2630, tricornered, 3-toed, 7⅛" 25.00
Bouquet, bowl, nappy; #2630, hdls, 4½" 12.00
Bouquet, bowl, serving; #2630, hdls 27.50
Bouquet, candlestick, 3-lite, 7¾", pr...........................70.00
Bouquet, candlestick, 4½", pr 30.00
Bouquet, condiment set, #2630, 3-pc 125.00
Bouquet, goblet, cocktail; #6033, 4-oz, 4¼" 15.00
Bouquet, pitcher, 3-pt, 9½" 175.00
Bouquet, plate, salad; #2630, crescent form, 7½"..........25.00
Bouquet, platter, #2630, oval, 12" 37.50
Bouquet, tidbit, #2630, w/metal hdl, 10¼" 42.50
Bouquet, tray, utility; #2630, hdls, 9⅛" 27.50
Bouquet, tumbler, #6033, ftd, 5-oz, 4½" 13.50
Bouquet, vase, bud; #2621, ftd, 6" 47.50
Bridal Wreath, bonbon, #2630, 3-toed, 7¼" 17.50

Bridal Wreath, bowl, #2630, flared, ftd, 10¾" 26.50
Bridal Wreath, candlestick, #2630, 4½", pr 30.00
Bridal Wreath, creamer, #2630, ind 12.00
Bridal Wreath, plate, cake; #2630, hdls 35.00
Bridal Wreath, plate, torte; #2630, 14" 35.00
Bridal Wreath, sugar bowl, ftd, 4" 12.00
Buttercup, bowl, salad; #2364, 10½" 30.00
Buttercup, comport, #2364, 8" 45.00
Buttercup, goblet, cordial; #6030, 3-oz, 3⅞" 37.50
Buttercup, pitcher, #6011, 53-oz, 8⅞"........................225.00
Buttercup, plate, #2337, 8" 16.00
Buttercup, plate, salad; #2364, crescent form, 7¼" 37.50
Buttercup, plate, sandwich; #2364, 11" 35.00
Buttercup, plate, torte; #2364, 14" 45.00
Buttercup, sugar bowl, #2350½, ftd, 3⅛" 17.50
Buttercup, tumbler, #6030, 5-oz, 4⅝" 18.50
Camellia, bowl, #2630, flared, 12" 40.00
Camellia, bowl, salad; #2630, 8½" 27.50
Camellia, bowl, utility; #2630, oval 35.00
Camellia, candy jar, #2630, w/lid, 7" 52.50
Camellia, condiment set, #2630, 3-pc 100.00
Camellia, goblet, parfait; #6036, 5½-oz, 5⅞" 22.50
Camellia, pitcher, cereal; #2630, 1-pt, 6⅛" 85.00
Camellia, plate, #2630, 9" 22.50
Camellia, plate, cake; #2630, hdls 25.00
Camellia, platter, #2630, oval, 12" 42.50
Camellia, shakers, #2630, w/chrome lid, pr 52.50
Camellia, tray, luncheon; #2630, center hdl, 11¼" 32.50
Camellia, tumbler, iced tea; #6036, 12-oz, 6⅛" 17.50
Camellia, vase, #2660, 8" 62.50
Camellia, vase, bud; #5092, ftd, 8" 50.00
Century, basket, reeded hdl, 10½" 75.00
Century, bonbon, 3-toed, 7¼" 17.50
Century, bowl, salad; 10½" 45.00
Century, bowl, serving; hdls, 10½" 35.00
Century, bowl, snack; ftd, 3½" 42.50
Century, bowl, vegetable; oval, 9½" 32.50
Century, candlestick, 4½", pr 35.00
Century, candy jar, w/lid 47.50
Century, mayonnaise set, w/plate & ladle, 3-pc.............47.50
Century, mustard jar, w/lid & spoon, 4" 45.00
Century, pitcher, 3-pt, 7⅛" 135.00
Century, plate, torte; 14" 27.50
Century, platter, oval, 12" 40.00
Century, shakers, 3¼", pr 17.50
Century, tray, muffin; hdls, 8½" 32.50
Century, vase, oval base, 8½" 95.00
Chatham, goblet, cordial; 1-oz, 3¼" 15.00
Chatham, goblet, 9½-oz, 6⅞" 10.00
Chatham, plate, #2337, 8" 7.50
Chatham, tumbler, iced tea; #6036, ftd, 12-oz, 6⅛" 10.00
Chintz, bowl, #2496, flared, 12" 45.00
Chintz, candlestick, #2496, 3-lite, 6", pr 90.00
Chintz, candy box, #2496, 3-part, w/lid, 6¼" 125.00
Chintz, creamer, #2496½, ind 20.00
Chintz, ice bucket, #2496 ....125.00
Chintz, pitcher, #5000, ftd, 3-pt, 9¾" 375.00
Chintz, plate, dinner; #2496, 9" 45.00
Chintz, relish, celery; #2496, 11" 37.50
Chintz, tidbit, #2496, 3-toed, flat, 8¼" 22.50
Chintz, tumbler, ftd, 5-oz, 4¾" 20.00
Christiana, goblet, #6030, 10-oz, 7⅞" 20.00
Christiana, goblet, cordial; #6030, 1-oz, 3⅞" 25.00
Christiana, goblet, oyster cocktail; #6030, 4-oz, 3¾".....18.00

Christiana, plate, #2337, 8"	10.00
Christiana, tumbler, juice; #6030, ftd, 5-oz, 4⅝"	16.00
Circlet, bowl, #2666, oval, 8¼"	15.00
Circlet, creamer, #2666, 3½"	8.50
Circlet, goblet, sherbet; #6055, 6-oz, 4½"	8.00
Circlet, plate, serving; #2364, 14"	17.50
Circlet, relish, #2364, 3-part, 10"	20.00
Circlet, shakers, #2364, w/chrome top, 3¼", pr	20.00
Circlet, tray, for sugar bowl & creamer, #2666	9.00
Circlet, tumbler, iced tea; #6055, ftd, 12¼-oz, 6⅛"	10.00
Coin, crystal; ash tray, #124	35.00
Coin, crystal; ash tray, oblong, #115	15.00
Coin, crystal; ash tray, 1-coin, #123	18.00
Coin, crystal; ash tray, 4-coin, #114	25.00
Coin, crystal; bowl, oval, #189, 9" (+)	30.00
Coin, crystal; bowl, rnd, #179, 8" (+)	55.00
Coin, crystal; cake plate, #630	100.00
Coin, crystal; candy box, rnd, #354, w/lid	40.00
Coin, crystal; candy jar, w/lid, #347 (+)	35.00
Coin, crystal; cigarette urn, #381	25.00
Coin, crystal; compote, ftd, w/lid, #212	150.00
Coin, crystal; jelly dish	15.00
Coin, crystal; pitcher, #453, 1-qt	55.00
Coin, crystal; punch bowl, w/stand & cups	500.00
Coin, crystal; shakers, pr	42.50
Coin, crystal; sugar bowl, w/lid, #673 (+)	30.00
Coin, crystal; tumbler, highball; #64	38.00
Coin, crystal; tumbler, old fashioned, 4¼"	30.00
Coin, crystal; tumbler, scotch; #73	30.00
Coin, crystal; tumbler, 4"	25.00
Coin, crystal; vase, bud; #799, 8"	20.00
Coin, crystal; wedding bowl, ftd, w/lid, #162	65.00
Coin, emerald gr; ash tray, #127, 10"	55.00
Coin, emerald gr; bowl, #179, 8"	125.00
Coin, emerald gr; bowl, oval, #187, 9"	78.00
Coin, emerald gr; candy box, w/lid, #354, 6⅜"	75.00
Coin, emerald gr; creamer, 3½"	35.00
Coin, emerald gr; decanter, w/stopper, #400	335.00
Coin, olive gr or amber; ash tray, #124	40.00
Coin, olive gr or amber; ash tray, 4-coin, #114, 7½" dia	35.00
Coin, olive gr or amber; bowl, #179, 8"	75.00
Coin, olive gr or amber; bowl, oval, #189, 9"	45.00
Coin, olive gr or amber; cake plate, #630	100.00
Coin, olive gr or amber; candle holder, #316, 4½", pr	45.00
Coin, olive gr or amber; candlestick, 8", pr	65.00
Coin, olive gr or amber; candy box, w/lid, #354, 6⅜"	35.00
Coin, olive gr or amber; candy jar, w/lid, #347	35.00
Coin, olive gr or amber; cigarette urn, #381	25.00
Coin, olive gr or amber; compote, ftd, #199 (+)	45.00
Coin, olive gr or amber; condiment set, #737	215.00
Coin, olive gr or amber; cruet	70.00
Coin, olive gr or amber; goblet, #2	45.00
Coin, olive gr or amber; jelly dish, ftd, #448, 3¾"	20.00
Coin, olive gr or amber; lamp, coach; #320	180.00
Coin, olive gr or amber; lamp, courting; #310	150.00
Coin, olive gr or amber; nappy, 1-hdl, 5⅜"	25.00
Coin, olive gr or amber; pitcher, #453, 1-qt	65.00
Coin, olive gr or amber; shakers, pr	35.00
Coin, olive gr or amber; sherbet, #7	40.00
Coin, olive gr or amber; sugar bowl, w/lid, #673	35.00
Coin, olive gr or amber; vase, bud; #799, 8"	24.00
Coin, olive gr or amber; wedding bowl, w/lid, #162	75.00
Coin, red or bl; ash tray, oblong, #115	35.00
Coin, red or bl; ash tray, 1-coin, #123	30.00

Coin, red or bl; ash tray, 4-coin, #114, 7½" dia	45.00
Coin, red or bl; bowl, console; 5½x8¾"	55.00
Coin, red or bl; bowl, oval, #189, 9"	55.00
Coin, red or bl; cake plate, rare	225.00
Coin, red or bl; candle holder, #316, 4½", pr (+)	65.00
Coin, red or bl; candlestick, 8", pr	100.00
Coin, red or bl; candy box, w/lid, #354, 6⅜"	65.00
Coin, red or bl; candy jar, w/lid, #347 (+)	50.00
Coin, red or bl; compote, ftd, #199	85.00
Coin, red or bl; compote, ftd, w/lid, #212	195.00
Coin, red or bl; creamer, #680 (+)	25.00
Coin, red or bl; goblet, water; 6⅝"	85.00
Coin, red or bl; goblet, wine; 5-oz	85.00
Coin, red or bl; lamp, coach; electric	250.00
Coin, red or bl; lamp, courting	175.00
Coin, red or bl; nappy, hdl, #499, 5⅜"	35.00
Coin, red or bl; pitcher, #453, 1-qt	100.00
Coin, red or bl; shakers, pr	50.00
Coin, red or bl; vase, bud; 8"	50.00
Coin, red or bl; wedding bowl, w/lid, #162	100.00
Colony, ash tray, rnd, 6"	15.00
Colony, bowl, fruit; low, 14"	50.00
Colony, bowl, oval, ftd, 11"	65.00
Colony, bowl, punch; 2-gal, 13¼"	375.00
Colony, bowl, rolled edge, 9"	35.00
Colony, candlestick, 7", pr	35.00
Colony, compote, low, w/lid, 6⅜"	35.00
Colony, cup, punch; 5¼-oz	20.00
Colony, goblet, cocktail; 3½-oz, 4"	15.00
Colony, pitcher, 3-pt, 8½"	185.00
Colony, plate, cake; hdls, 10"	27.50
Colony, plate, cracker; 12½"	20.00
Colony, plate, torte; 18"	95.00
Colony, platter, 12"	42.50
Colony, tray, luncheon; hdls, 11½"	27.50
Colony, tray, muffin; hdls, 8⅜"	25.00
Colony, tumbler, flat, 12-oz, 4⅞"	20.00
Colony, vase, cornucopia, 9¼"	125.00
Colony, vase, cupped, ftd, 7"	55.00
Contour, ash tray, #2666, 6½"	5.00
Contour, bonbon, #2666, 6⅞"	10.00
Contour, bottle, oil; #2666, w/stopper, 6-oz, 5⅜"	32.50
Contour, bowl, salad; #2666, 9"	15.00
Contour, candlestick, #2638, 4½", pr	20.00
Contour, goblet, sherbet; #6060, 6 ½-oz, 4½"	17.00
Contour, pitcher, sauce; #2666, 8½"	20.00
Contour, plate, canape; #2666, 7⅜"	9.50
Contour, plate, party; #2666, 8½"	15.00
Contour, relish, #2666, 2-part, 7⅜"	12.50
Contour, sugar bowl, #2666, ind	7.00
Contour, tumbler, iced tea; #6060, ftd, 14-oz, 6¼"	20.00
Coronet, bowl, flared, 12"	17.50
Coronet, bowl, salad; 10"	18.50
Coronet, candlestick, 4½", pr	25.00
Coronet, plate, tidbit; flat, 3-toed, 8¼"	10.00
Coronet, plate, 7"	5.00
Coronet, relish, 2-part, 6½"	11.00
Coronet, relish, 3-part, 10"	15.00
Coronet, tray, sugar & creamer; 7½"	9.50
Crest, goblet, #6061, 11-oz, 5⅛"	8.00
Crest, plate, #2337, 8"	8.00
Crest, tumbler, juice; #6061, ftd, 6-oz, 4¾"	6.00
Cynthia, bowl, #2560, hdls, 11"	27.50
Cynthia, bowl, relish; #2560, 3-part, 10"	27.50

Cynthia, candlestick, 2-lite, 5⅛", pr 32.00
Cynthia, goblet, 9-oz, 7⅜" 18.00
Cynthia, plate, cake; #2560, hdls, 10½" 20.00
Cynthia, plate, torte; 14" 35.00
Cynthia, tumbler, iced tea; #6017, 12-oz, 6" 15.00
Ebony, ash tray, #2667, 5" 12.50
Ebony, bowl, salad; #2666, 9" 25.00
Ebony, candlestick, #2402 or #2430, 2", pr 22.00
Ebony, candy jar, #2430, w/lid 42.50
Ebony, lamp, candle; #2545 ....37.50
Ebony, vase, Tut; #2288, hdls, 8½" 25.00
Heather, basket, #2630, reeded hdl, 10¼" 75.00
Heather, bonbon, #2630, 3-toed, 7¼" 22.50
Heather, bowl, utility; #2630, oval, hdls, 10" 42.50
Heather, butter dish, #2630, oblong, w/lid, 7½" 52.50
Heather, compote, #2630, 4⅜" 25.00
Heather, ice bucket, #2630, 4⅞" 75.00
Heather, pitcher, #2630, 3-pt, 9½" 245.00
Heather, plate, #2630, 8" 14.50
Heather, platter, #2630, oval, 12" 37.50
Heather, relish, #2630, 3-part, 11⅛" 37.50
Heather, shakers, #2630, w/chrome top, pr 50.00
Heather, tray, luncheon; #2630, center hdl, 11¼" 32.50
Heather, vase, #2470, ftd, 10" 75.00
Heather, vase, #2660, hdls, 7½" 67.50
Heirloom, bowl, #2720/168, 6½" 32.50
Heirloom, candlestick, floral; #2813/311, 3⅞", pr 45.00
Heirloom, plate, #2570/575, 17" 45.00
Heirloom, vase, #1002/833, 18" 75.00
Heirloom, vase, #2738/751, hdls, 4½" 38.50
Heraldry, bowl, lily pond; #2364, 12" 45.00
Heraldry, candlestick, #2324, 4", pr 25.00
Heraldry, goblet, #6012, 10-oz, 6⅞" 15.00
Heraldry, goblet, cordial; #6012, 1-oz, 3½" 19.50
Heraldry, goblet, oyster cocktail; #6012, 4-oz, 3½" 12.00
Heraldry, relish, #2364, 3-part, 10" 27.50
Heraldry, tray, luncheon; #2364, center hdl, 11¼" 32.50
Heraldry, tumbler, juice; #6012, ftd, 5-oz 12.00
Holiday, bowl, ice; 6⅝" 7.50
Holiday, tumbler, dbl old fashioned; 12-oz, 3¾" 5.00
Holiday, tumbler, whiskey; 1½-oz, 2⅛" 3.50
Holly, bowl, fruit; #2364, 13" 37.50
Holly, candlestick, #2324, 4", pr 35.00
Holly, goblet, sherbet or champagne; #6030, high, 6-oz 18.00
Holly, mayonnaise set, #2364, w/plate & ladle, 3-pc 52.50
Holly, pitcher, #6011, 53-oz, 8⅞" 195.00
Holly, relish, #2364, 2-part, 8¼" 32.50
Holly, sugar bowl, #2350½, ftd, 3⅛" 16.50
Holly, tumbler, iced tea; #6030, ftd, 12-oz, 6" 21.50
Horizon, bowl, cereal; #2650 ....5.00
Horizon, bowl, dessert or finger; #5650 ....4.00
Horizon, bowl, serving; #2650, hdls 11.50
Horizon, plate, sandwich; #2650 ....10.00
Horizon, tumbler, sherbet; #5650, 3⅜" 3.50
Ingrid, bowl, #2666, oval, 8¼" 16.00
Ingrid, goblet, cocktail; #6052, 3¾-oz, 3⅞" 8.00
Ingrid, goblet, cordial; #6052, 1¼-oz, 3⅛" 12.50
Ingrid, relish, #2364, 3-part, 10" 22.50
Jamestown, bl or red; butter dish, oblong, 8" 75.00
Jamestown, bl or red; plate, torte; 14" 35.00
Jamestown, bl or red; plate, 8" 15.00
Jamestown, bl or red; tumbler, juice; ftd, 5-oz, 4¾" 15.00
Lacy Leaf, bowl, #2630, flared, 12" 38.50
Lacy Leaf, bowl, tidbit; 3-toed, 7⅛" 17.50

Lacy Leaf, pitcher, #2630, 3-pt, 7⅛" 135.00
Lacy Leaf, shakers, #2630, w/chrome top, pr 37.50
Lido, bowl, bonbon; #2496, 3-toed, 7⅜" 16.50
Lido, bowl, serving; #2496, hdls, 8½" 26.50
Lido, candlestick, #2545, 2-lite, 6¾", pr 44.50
Lido, candy box, #2496, 3-part, w/lid, 6¼" 48.50
Lido, goblet, saucer champagne; #6017, 6-oz, 5½" 15.00
Mayflower, bonbon, 3-toed, 7¼" 17.50
Mayflower, bowl, fruit; #2560, 13" 35.00
Mayflower, bowl, olive; #2560, 6¾" 14.50
Mayflower, cup, #2560, ftd 16.50
Mayflower, plate, #2560, 6" 6.00
Mayflower, sugar bowl, #2560, ftd, 3½" 17.50
Mayflower, tumbler, #6020, ftd, 12-oz, 6⅜" 18.00
Meadow Rose, bowl, #2496, flared, 12" 55.00
Meadow Rose, bowl, nappy; #2496, hdls, 5" 15.00
Meadow Rose, candlestick, #2496, 5½", pr 62.50
Meadow Rose, goblet, claret; #6016, 4½-oz, 6" 42.50
Meadow Rose, mayonnaise set, #2496½, 3-pc 65.00
Meadow Rose, pitcher, #5000, ftd, 3-pt, 9¾" 395.00
Meadow Rose, plate, #2496, 9" 45.00
Meadow Rose, saucer, #2496 ....7.00
Meadow Rose, tray, sugar & creamer; #2496½, 6½" 18.50
Milkweed, bonbon, 3-toed, 7¼" 21.00
Milkweed, bowl, salad; 10½" 34.00
Milkweed, butter dish, oblong, w/lid, 7½" 38.50
Milkweed, mayonnaise set, w/plate & ladle, 3-pc 47.50
Milkweed, plate, torte; 14" 35.00
Milkweed, sugar bowl, ftd, 4" 12.50
Milkweed, tray, luncheon; center hdl, 11¼" 28.50
Minuet, bowl, relish; #2574, 3-part, 10" 19.50
Minuet, candlestick, 2-lite, 5¼", pr 25.00
Minuet, cup, ftd, 6-oz 11.00
Minuet, goblet, cocktail; #6025, 3½-oz, 3½" 10.00
Minuet, plate, torte; #2574, 14" 22.50
Minuet, sugar bowl, #2574, 3¾" 10.00
Minuet, tumbler, iced tea; ftd, 12-oz, 5⅝" 12.50
Mulberry, goblet, cocktail; #6026, 4-oz, 5" 20.00
Mulberry, goblet, cordial; #6026, 1-oz, 3⅞" 28.50
Mulberry, plate, #2337, 7" 8.50
Mulberry, tumbler, juice; #6026, ftd, 5-oz, 3¾" 12.50
Navarre, bonbon, #2496, 3-toed, 7⅜" 27.50
Navarre, bowl, #2496, flared, 12" 55.00
Navarre, bowl, nappy; 3-corner, 4⅝" 15.00
Navarre, candlestick, 3-lite, 6¾", pr 90.00
Navarre, goblet, saucer champagne; #6016, 6-oz, 5⅝" 21.50
Navarre, goblet, wine; #6016, 3¼-oz, 5¼" 32.50
Navarre, ice bucket, #2496, 4⅜" 125.00
Navarre, pitcher, ftd, 3-pt, 9¾" 275.00
Navarre, plate, #2440, 9" 45.00
Navarre, plate, torte; #2496, 14" 45.00
Navarre, sugar bowl, #2440, ftd, 3⅝" 17.50
Navarre, tumbler, #6016, ftd, 13-oz, 5⅞" 24.00
Nosegay, creamer, #2666, 3½" 8.50
Nosegay, goblet, sherbet; #6051, 6½-oz, 4⅜" 8.50
Nosegay, mayonnaise set, #2364, 3-pc 37.50
Nosegay, plate, relish; #2666, 3-part, 10¾" 25.00
Nosegay, plate, snack; #2666, 10" 15.00
Nosegay, tumbler, iced tea; #6051, ftd, 12¼-oz, 6⅛" 11.50
Pine, bowl, #2666, oval, 8¼" 35.00
Pine, butter dish, #2666, oblong, w/lid, 7" 32.50
Pine, creamer, #2666, 3½" 14.50
Pine, cup, #2666, 8-oz 12.50
Pine, goblet, #6052, 9¾-oz, 5⅞" 18.50

Pine, pitcher, #2666, 1-qt, 6⅞" 125.00
Pine, tumbler, iced tea; #6052, 13-oz, 9⅛" 18.50
Plume, bowl, #2666, oval, 8¼" 14.00
Plume, goblet, #6051, 10½-oz, 6¼" 8.50
Plume, plate, canape; #2666, 7⅜" 9.50
Plume, tumbler, iced tea; #6051, 12¼-oz, 6⅛" 8.00
Raleigh, bowl, flared, 12" 17.50
Raleigh, cup, ftd 5.00
Raleigh, plate, torte; 14" 17.50
Raleigh, relish, celery; 10½" 10.00
Raleigh, tray, muffin; hdls 15.00
Randolph, ash tray, sq, 3½" 10.00
Randolph, cup, ftd, 6-oz 12.50
Randolph, plate, 9" 10.00
Randolph, tray, 7" 17.50
Randolph, tumbler, ftd, 9-oz, 5¼" 15.00
Reflection, candlestick, #2364, 4", ea 7.50
Reflection, cup, #2666 ....6.00
Reflection, goblet, sherbet or champagne; #6033, high, 6-oz 8.00
Reflection, sugar bowl, #2666, ind 6.50
Reflection, tumbler, juice; ftd, 5-oz, 4½" 8.00
Romance, bowl, fruit; #2364, 13" 52.50
Romance, candlestick, #6023, 2-lite, 5½", pr 75.00
Romance, compote, #2364, 8" 95.00
Romance, cup, #2350½, ftd 18.00
Romance, plate, #2337, 8" 16.00
Romance, plate, cracker; #2364, 11¼" 45.00
Romance, plate, sandwich; #2364, 11" 30.00
Romance, relish, pickle; #2364, 8" 27.50
Romance, tumbler, #6017, ftd, 9-oz, 5½" 23.50
Rose, bowl, salad; #2666 ....25.00
Rose, cup, #2666, 8-oz 20.00
Rose, goblet, sherbet; #6036, low, 6-oz, 4⅛" 18.50
Rose, mayonnaise set, #2666, 3-pc 52.50
Rose, pitcher, #6011, ftd, 53-oz, 8⅞" 225.00
Rose, shakers, #2364, w/chrome top, 2⅝", pr 52.50
Rose, tumbler, juice; #6036, 5-oz, 4⅝" 18.00
Seascape, bowl, ftd, 8¾" 42.50
Seascape, creamer, 3⅜" 19.50
Seascape, plate, buffet; 14" 48.50
Seascape, plate, relish; 2-part, 9" 28.50
Seascape, tray, oval, 7½" 21.50
Shirley, bonbon, #2496, 3-toed, 7⅜" 22.50
Shirley, bowl, #2496, hdls, 10½" 37.50
Shirley, candy box, #2496, 3-part, w/lid, 6¼" 85.00
Shirley, creamer, #2496, ind 17.50
Shirley, goblet, claret; #6017, 4-oz, 5⅞" 25.00
Shirley, plate, cake; #2496, hdls, 10" 25.00
Shirley, tumbler, #6017, ftd, 12-oz, 6" 21.50
Skyflower, bowl, #2666, oval, 8¼" 15.00
Skyflower, butter dish, #2666, oblong, w/lid, 7" 37.50
Skyflower, goblet, cordial; #6061, 1-oz, 2½" 11.50
Skyflower, mayonnaise set, #2666, 3-pc 37.50
Skyflower, plate, canape; #2666, 7⅜" 11.50
Skyflower, tumbler, iced tea; #6061, 12-oz, 6" 8.00
Sonata, bowl, fruit; #2364, 13" 15.00
Sonata, candlestick, #2364, 2-lite, 5½", pr 25.00
Sonata, compote, #2364, 8" 11.50
Sonata, plate, torte; #2364, 14" 15.00
Sonata, tray, luncheon; #2364, center hdl 22.50
Spinet, goblet, oyster cocktail; #6033, 4-oz, 3¾" ...11.50
Spinet, tumbler, iced tea; #6033, 13-oz, 5⅞" 12.50
Spray, bowl, salad; #2666 ....25.00
Spray, butter dish, #2666, oblong, w/lid, 7" 32.50

Spray, creamer, #2666, ind 13.50
Spray, goblet, claret; #6055, 4¼-oz, 4⅝" 20.00
Spray, plate, #2337, 7" 8.00
Spray, plate, snack; #2666, 10" 27.50
Spray, relish, #2666, 2-part, 7⅜" 21.50
Spray, shakers, #2364, w/chrome top, 3¼", pr 37.50
Spray, tumbler, iced tea; #6055, ftd, 12¼-oz, 6⅛" ...18.50
Sprite, bonbon, #2630, 3-toed, 7¼" 12.50
Sprite, candlestick, #2630, 2-lite, 7" 40.00
Sprite, cup, #2630, ftd, 6-oz 11.50
Sprite, goblet, cocktail; #6033, 4-oz, 4¼" 13.50
Sprite, mayonnaise set, #2630, 3-pc 35.00
Sprite, plate, cake; #2630, hdls 17.50
Sprite, plate, torte; #2630, 14" 32.50
Sprite, saucer, #2630 ....3.50
Sprite, tumbler, iced tea; #6033, 13-oz, 5⅛" 15.00
Stardust, bonbon, #2666/136, 6⅞" 12.50
Stardust, goblet, cordial; #6068, 1¼-oz, 3" 15.00
Stardust, plate, torte; 2364/567, 14" 17.50
Stardust, relish, #2364/620, 2-part, 8¼" 15.00
Stardust, tumbler, iced tea; #6068, 13-oz, 5⅞" 10.00
Starflower, basket, #2630, reeded hdl, 10¼" 52.50
Starflower, bowl, #2630, rolled edge, ftd, 11" 37.50
Starflower, bowl, bonbon; #2630, 3-toed, 7¼" 22.50
Starflower, bowl, fruit; #2630, 5" 11.50
Starflower, bowl, snack; #2630 ....22.50
Starflower, bowl, vegetable; #2630, oval, 9½" 27.50
Starflower, cheese & cracker set, #2630, 2-pc 52.50
Starflower, creamer, #2630, ftd, 4½" 12.50
Starflower, cup, #2630, ftd, 6-oz 15.00
Starflower, pitcher, cereal; #2630, 1-pt, 6⅛" 75.00
Starflower, plate, #2630, 8" 9.00
Starflower, platter, #2630, oval, 12" 35.00
Starflower, sugar bowl, #2630, ftd, 4" 15.00
Starflower, tumbler, juice; #6049, 5¾-oz, 4⅞" 12.00
Starflower, vase, #2657, ftd, 10½" 70.00
Starflower, vase, bud; #5092, ftd, 8" 50.00
Sylvan, bonbon, #2666, 6⅞" 12.00
Sylvan, butter dish, oblong, #2666, w/lid, 7" 35.00
Sylvan, goblet, #6060, 10½-oz, 5⅞" 10.00
Sylvan, plate, serving; #2666, 14" 22.50
Sylvan, shakers, #2364, w/chrome lid, 3¼", pr 18.50
Sylvan, tray, sugar & creamer; #2666, ind 9.50
Thistle, bowl, #2666, oval, 8¼" 18.50
Thistle, creamer, #2666, 3½" 10.00
Thistle, goblet, #6052, 9¾-oz, 5⅞" 17.50
Thistle, plate, canape; #2666, 7⅜" 12.50
Thistle, relish, celery; #2666, 9" 18.00
Thistle, sugar bowl, #2666, 2⅝" 10.00
Thistle, tumbler, iced tea; #6052, 13-oz, 9⅛" 18.50
Thistle, vase, bud; #6021, 6" 45.00
Vesper, goblet, wine or cocktail; #6086/27, 5½-oz 8.00
Vesper, plate, #2337/549, 7" 4.00
Vesper, plate, #2337/550, 8" 5.00
Vesper, tumbler, juice; #6086/88, 5½-oz, 4½" 8.00
Wheat, bowl, salad; #2666 ....20.00
Wheat, candle holder, floral; #2666, 6", pr 30.00
Wheat, cup, #2666, 8-oz 15.00
Wheat, goblet, claret or wine; #6051, 4-oz, 4½" 18.50
Wheat, mayonnaise set, #2666, 3-pc 45.00
Wheat, plate, snack; #2666, 10" 15.00
Wheat, sugar bowl, #2666, 2⅝" 10.00
Wheat, tumbler, juice; #6051, ftd, 5-oz, 4" 12.00
Willow, bowl, fruit; #2574, 13" 25.00

Willow, dish, celery; #2574, 10½" **25.00**
Willow, goblet, sherbet; #6023, low, 6-oz, 4⅛" **10.00**
Willow, plate, cake; #2574, hdls, 10" **25.00**
Willow, plate, torte; #2574, 14" **35.00**
Willow, tumbler, #6023, ftd, 9-oz, 5⅛" **12.50**
Willowmere, bowl, fruit; #2560, 13" **47.50**
Willowmere, candlestick, #2560, 2-lite, 5⅛", pr **75.00**
Willowmere, creamer, #2560, ftd, 7-oz, 4⅛" **15.00**
Willowmere, goblet, #6024, 10-oz, 7⅛" **22.50**
Willowmere, pitcher, #5000, 3-pt, 9¾" **275.00**
Willowmere, tray, luncheon; #2560, center hdl, 11½" **42.50**
Willowmere, tumbler, #6024, ftd, 5-oz, 4⅝" **16.00**
Winburn, butter dish, w/lid, 8¼" **45.00**
Winburn, creamer, 4½" **15.00**
Winburn, pitcher, ½-gal, 8" **45.00**
Winburn, tumbler, iced tea; 10½-oz, 5¼" **16.50**

Windsor Crown footed chalice, ruby, 9½", $90.00; candy dish, gold, 6", $55.00.

Fraktur

Fraktur is a German style of black letter text type. To collectors the fraktur is a type of hand-lettered document used by the people of German descent who settled in the areas of Pennsylvania, New Jersey, Maryland, Virginia, North and South Carolina, Ohio, Kentucky, and Ontario. These documents recorded births and baptisms and were used as bookplates and as certificates of honor. They were elaborately decorated with colorful folk-art borders of hearts, birds, angels, and flowers. Examples by recognized artists and those with an unusual decorative motif bring prices well into the thousands of dollars. Frakturs made in the late 1700s after the invention of the printing press provided the writer with a prepared text that he needed only to fill in at his own discretion. The next step in the evolution of machine-printed frakturs combined woodblock-printed decorations along with the text which the 'artist' sometimes enhanced with color. By the mid-1800s even the coloring was done by machine. The vorschrift was a handwritten example prepared by a fraktur teacher to demonstrate his skill in lettering and decorating. These are often considered to be the finest of frakturs. Those dated before 1820 are most valuable.

The practice of fraktur art began to diminish after 1830 but hung on even to the early years of this century among the Pennsylvania Ger-

mans ingrained with such customs. Our advisor for this category is Frederick S. Weiser; he is listed in the Directory under Pennsylvania.

Key:
brd — board   p/i — pen and ink
lp — laid paper   wc — watercolored
pr — printed   wp — wove paper

Bookplate in watercolor and ink attributed to Johann Eyer, upper section (shown) over scrolled reserve with name and '1807,' 7½" x 5", $2,500.00.

Birth Record

P/i/wc/lined paper, hearts/birds/etc, 1824, 5-color, 9x11" **1,900.00**
P/i/wc/lp, birds/trees/data, 4-color, 1808, 12x10" **1,100.00**
P/i/wc/lp, floral wreath, att Berk's Co artist, 8x13", EX **3,500.00**
P/i/wc/lp, Flying Angel artist, 4-color, 1801, 15x20", EX **1,650.00**
P/i/wc/lp, heart/etc, 3-color, 1791, 3½x3½", EX **135.00**
P/i/wc/lp, heart/tulips/etc, 1808, 14x10", EX **425.00**
P/i/wc/lp, hearts/etc, M Brechall, 1800, 16x11½", EX **1,400.00**
P/i/wc/lp, hearts/parrots/etc, 5-color, sgn/1805, 20" W, EX **1,800.00**
P/i/wc/lp, intricate mc florals, 1777, 9x7½", EX....................... **1,300.00**
P/i/wc/lp, lg angel, 4-colors, taped rprs/tears, 17x20"....................**550.00**
P/i/wc/lp, 4 birds/flowers, 5-color, 1815, 15x19", VG **2,100.00**
P/i/wc/wp, certificate, mariner's star, 1810, 9x11", VG **400.00**
P/i/wc/wp, heart/flowers, 4-color, some English, 16x18", EX **975.00**
P/i/wc/wp, stylized flowers, 3-color, 1819, lt stain, 8x12"......... **2,950.00**
P/i/wc/wp, 3-color florals, 1786-1819 data, 17x12", VG **1,350.00**
P/i/wp, boats/bldgs/hearts/etc, sgn/1830, 14x10", EX **1,550.00**
Pr/block-printed color, angels/etc, Peters, 22x17", VG **85.00**
Pr/wc, angels/etc, A Purvelle, Reading, 1852, 21x17"...................**165.00**
Pr/wc, angels/etc, Eagle Bookstore, 1895, 18x15" **50.00**
Pr/wc, angels/etc, J Herman, 1825 birth, 18x14", EX **325.00**
Pr/wc, kneeling children/butterfly, J Herman, 1825, 20x17"........**125.00**
Pr/wc/lp, birds/data in heart, J Baumann, 1807, 14x17", VG **375.00**
Pr/wc/lp, 2 angels/heart/circle, 1824, minor stains, 15x18" **250.00**

Miscellaneous

P/i, certificate, bl-gr/blk, Empire fr w/gold rpt, 12x10" **195.00**
P/i/wc, record, angels/birds/etc, 3 entries, 17x14", VG................**500.00**
P/i/wc/lp, bookplate, bird/flowers/name/1798, 4-color, 8x6", VG...**500.00**
P/i/wc/lp, bookplate, birds/vines/name/1843, 2-pg, book intact ...**400.00**
P/i/wc/lp, bookplate, heart/flowers/name/1771, 6x3", EX............**100.00**
P/i/wc/lp, practice page w/flowering tree & hands, 9x11" **1,000.00**
P/i/wc/lp, vorschrift, vine border w/tulip, 1806, 8x13" **3,200.00**
P/i/wc/lp, vorschrift, 4-color, 11x9", EX **300.00**

P/i/wc/wp, (name) 1840 Lancaster..., 4-color, 8½x6" 500.00
P/i/wc/wp, bookmark, bird on branch, EX color, fr, 6x5" 900.00
P/i/wc/wp, bookplate, angel/heart/etc, brn/gr, 7x4¾", EX 425.00
P/i/wc/wp, bookplate, name/1837, 5-color, sgn, 6½x4" 700.00
P/i/wc/wp, floral/circle/inscription/1831, 3-color, 6½x9" **1,150.00**
P/i/wp, bookplate, blk ink, dtd 1843, 8½x6" 150.00
Wc, poem for trees, star planting diagram, sgn/1830, 9x5" 800.00
Wc/pin pricking, bookmark, parrot w/fruit in talons, 8x6" **1,100.00**
Wc/wp, basket of flowers, 4-color, sgn/1838, 11x9".....................700.00

Frames

Styles in picture frames have changed with the fashion of the day, but those that especially interest today's collectors are the deep shadow boxes made of fine woods such as walnut or cherry, those with Art Nouveau influence, and the oak frames decorated with molded gesso and gilt from the Victorian era. Our advisor for this category is Michael Hinton; he is listed in the Directory under Pennsylvania.

Pyrographic oak leaves and acorns, 8" diameter, $45.00.

Blk pnt w/floral, emb brass disks, 3¾" W, 17x13" 325.00
Brass, ornate border, metal bk, 6x5"..55.00
Brass & copper, rope design edge, rnd, easel bk, 6¼"...................60.00
CI, eagle/flags/drum/bugles/swords/etc, WWI era, 9½x6½" 85.00
Inlaid, lt & dk wood, 2" W, 15x11" 100.00
Pine w/blk pnt & gilt decor, molded, 1½" W, 21x24" 150.00
Pine w/burl grpt, beveled, 2¾" W, 22x27"................................200.00
Pine w/orig finish, gilt liner, 1¾" W, 12x14", pr.........................140.00
Pine w/orig gray smoke grpt, sq nails, 1½" W, 9x11", pr 295.00
Pine w/walnut inlaid heart/geometrics/dmns, 2½" W, 10x8" 150.00
Poplar, mortised, corner blocks, red finish, 1¾" W, 17x14" 90.00
Poplar w/red flame grpt, beveled, 3" W, 20x15", pr.....................950.00
Silver, branch/bird, eng/repousse, shaped top, English, 9" 800.00
Silver, maid picks apples, eng/repousse, WI Broadway, 14" **2,500.00**

Frances Ware

Frances Ware, produced in the 1880s by Hobbs, Brockunier and Company of Wheeling, West Virginia, is either clear or frosted with amber-stained rim bands. The most often found pattern is Hobnail, but Swirl was also made.

Hobnail, clear; bowl, 7½" 65.00
Hobnail, clear; butter dish 95.00
Hobnail, clear; creamer..60.00
Hobnail, clear; finger bowl, 4"..35.00
Hobnail, clear; pitcher, 8½"...125.00
Hobnail, clear; spooner...40.00
Hobnail, frosted; bowl, ftd, berry pontil, 6x10" 150.00
Hobnail, frosted; bowl, oblong, 8"..70.00
Hobnail, frosted; bowl, sq, 7½"...70.00
Hobnail, frosted; bowl, 2½x5½"..40.00
Hobnail, frosted; bowl, 4½"...30.00
Hobnail, frosted; bowl, 8"..75.00
Hobnail, frosted; bowl, 9"..85.00
Hobnail, frosted; butter dish...120.00
Hobnail, frosted; celery vase 75.00
Hobnail, frosted; creamer 75.00
Hobnail, frosted; finger bowl, 4"..35.00
Hobnail, frosted; marmalade..125.00
Hobnail, frosted; pitcher, milk...150.00
Hobnail, frosted; pitcher, water; sq top 175.00
Hobnail, frosted; plate, sq, 5¾"..25.00
Hobnail, frosted; sauce dish, sq, 4".......................................28.00
Hobnail, frosted; shakers, pr 75.00
Hobnail, frosted; spooner 70.00
Hobnail, frosted; sugar bowl, w/lid..80.00
Hobnail, frosted; syrup, pewter lid..165.00

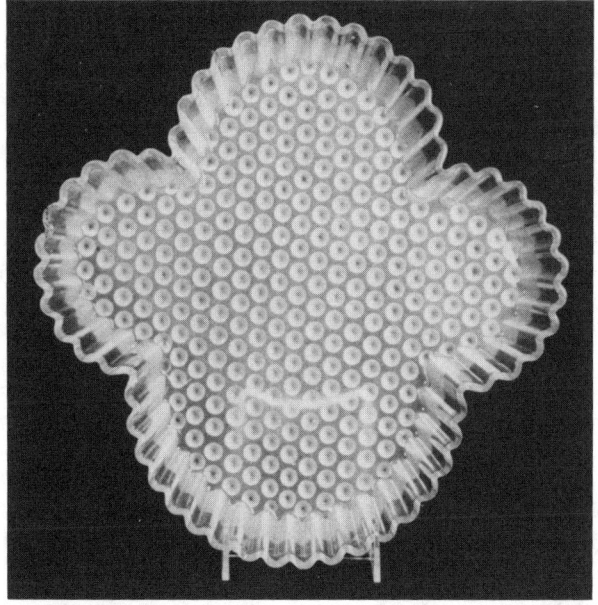

Tray, cloverleaf form, frosted with amber-stained rim, 12", $125.00.

Hobnail, frosted; toothpick holder...60.00
Hobnail, frosted; tray, oblong, 14".......................................150.00
Hobnail, frosted; tumbler, water...45.00
Swirl, clear; shakers, pr 55.00
Swirl, clear; syrup...90.00
Swirl, frosted; bowl, 3¾" H...40.00
Swirl, frosted; cruet..175.00
Swirl, frosted; cruet, orig stopper, miniature............................260.00
Swirl, frosted; mustard jar..140.00
Swirl, frosted; shakers, pr...75.00

Swirl, frosted; sugar shaker, orig lid........................125.00
Swirl, frosted; syrup, Pat dtd..................................145.00
Swirl, frosted; toothpick holder.............................110.00
Swirl, frosted; tumbler..35.00

Franciscan

Franciscan is a trade name used by Gladding McBean and Co., founded in northern California in 1875. In 1923 they purchased the Tropico plant in Glendale where they produced sewer pipe, gardenware, and tile. By 1934 the first of their dinnerware lines, El Patio, was produced. It was a plain design made in bright, attractive colors. El Patio Nouveau followed in 1935, glazed in two colors — one tone on the inside, a contrasting hue on the outside. Coronado, a favorite of today's collectors, was introduced in 1936. It was styled with a wide, swirled border and was made in pastels in both a satin and glossy finish. Before 1940 fifteen patterns had been produced. The first hand-decorated lines were introduced in 1937, the ever-popular Apple pattern in 1940, Desert Rose in 1941, and Ivy in 1948. Many other hand-decorated and decaled patterns were produced there from 1934 to 1984.

Dinnerware marks before 1940 include 'GMcB' in an oval, 'F' within a square, or 'Franciscan' with 'Pottery' underneath (which was later changed to 'Ware.') A circular arrangement of 'Franciscan' with 'Made in California USA' in the center was used from 1940 until 1949. At least forty marks were used before 1975; several more were introduced after that. At one time, paper labels were used.

The company merged with Lock Joint Pipe Company in 1963, becoming part of the Interpace Corporation. In July of 1979, Franciscan was purchased by Wedgwood Limited of England, and the Glendale plant closed in October, 1984.

Authority Delleen Enge has compiled an informative book, *Franciscan Ware*, with current values. You will find her address in the Directory under California. Our advisor for this category is Jack Chipman, author of *The Collector's Encyclopedia of California Pottery*; he is listed in the Directory under California. See also Gladding McBean.

Coronado

Bowl, cereal..10.50
Bowl, cream soup 15.00
Bowl, vegetable; serving, oval.................................28.00
Bowl, vegetable; serving, rnd 15.00
Candlesticks, pr..28.00
Candy dish, rnd, w/lid...49.00
Casserole, w/lid 28.00
Cigarette box 39.00
Coffeepot, demitasse..49.00
Creamer & sugar bowl, w/lid 31.00
Cup & saucer 12.00
Cup & saucer, demitasse...22.00
Gravy boat, w/attached plate....................................28.00
Nut cup, ftd...16.00
Plate, chop; 12"...22.00
Plate, chop; 14"...33.00
Plate, 6½" 8.00
Plate, 7½" 10.00
Plate, 8½" 11.00
Platter, 11½"...22.00
Platter, 15½"...33.00
Saucer, cream soup.. 6.50
Shakers, pr...15.00
Sherbet 10.00
Teapot...39.00

El Patio

Bowl, cereal...12.00
Bowl, fruit 11.00
Bowl, salad; 3-qt 25.00
Bowl, vegetable; oval 31.00
Butter dish...31.00
Creamer.. 9.00
Cup.. 9.00
Cup, jumbo 18.00

Gravy boat with attached underplate, $27.00.

Plate, bread & butter 7.00
Plate, 10½"..14.00
Plate, 8½" 11.50
Saucer... 3.50
Saucer, jumbo 7.00
Sherbet..10.00
Sugar bowl, w/lid...17.00
Teapot, w/lid, 6-cup...39.00

Franciscan Fine China

The main line of fine china was called Masterpiece. There were at least four marks used during its production from 1941 to 1977. Almost every piece is clearly marked. This china is true porcelain, the body having been fired at a very high temperature. Many years of research and experimentation went into this china before it was marketed. Production was temporarily suspended during the war years. More than 170 patterns and many varying shapes were produced. All are valued about the same with the exception of the Renaissance group, which is 25% higher.

Bowl, vegetable; serving, oval.................................49.00
Cup..17.00
Plate, bread & butter 17.00
Plate, dinner 28.00
Plate, salad 20.00
Saucer..11.50

Hand-Painted Embossed Earthenware

Values listed here apply to the following: Apple, Desert Rose, Ivy, Meadow Rose, Forget-Me-Not, October, Strawberry, Fresh Fruit, and other hand-painted patterns.

Ash tray, ind 11.50
Bowl, batter...49.00

Bowl, lug hdl, sm	15.50
Bowl, soup; flat	15.50
Bowl, vegetable; sm	14.00
Bowl, vegetable; w/lid	49.00
Bowl, 7½"	28.00
Bowl, 8¼"	39.00
Casserole, stick hdls, 12-oz	22.00
Coaster, 3¾"	17.00
Coffeepot	72.00
Compote, lg	39.00
Creamer, lg	15.50
Cup & saucer, demitasse, ea	22.00
Cup & saucer, jumbo	28.00
Egg cup	15.50
Goblet	25.00
Mug, lg	20.00
Pickle dish, 10¼"	31.00
Pitcher, water	57.50
Pitcher, 1-pt	25.00
Plate, chop; 14"	57.50
Plate, grill; 10¾"	35.00
Plate, 10½"	18.00
Plate, 6½"	7.50
Plate, 8½"	14.00
Plate, 9½"	16.00
Platter, 12½"	35.00
Platter, 19½"	109.00
Relish, 3-part, 11"	35.00
Shakers, Rosebud, pr	23.00
Shakers, tall, pr	35.00
Sugar bowl, open, sm	29.00
Sugar bowl, w/lid, lg	33.00
Tray, 3-tier	40.00
Tumbler, 5⅛"	18.00

Frankart

During the 1920s Frankart, Inc., of New York City, produced a line of accessories that included figural nude lamps, bookends, ash trays, etc. These white metal composition items were offered in several finishes including verde green, jap black, and gun-metal gray. The company also produced a line of caricatured animals, but the stylized nude figurals have proven to be the most collectible today. With few exceptions, all pieces were marked 'Frankart, Inc.' with a patent number or 'pat. appl. for.' All pieces listed are in very good original condition unless otherwise indicated. Our advisor for this category is Walter Glenn; he is listed in the Directory under Georgia.

Aquarium, seated nude on iron stand, aqua, rectangular, 36"	625.00
Ash tray, bk-to-bk nudes hold rack of 4 rnd inserts, 8"	385.00
Ash tray, floor model, 3 nudes hold 6" pottery ash bowl, 25"	750.00
Ash tray, nude holds 6" pottery ash bowl overhead, 13"	365.00
Ash tray, stylized pigeon holds insert in wings, 6", NM	110.00
Bookends, futuristic long-necked female heads, 7", pr	245.00
Bookends, kneeling nude, bk supports book, 6", pr	325.00
Bookends, nude sits atop metal book, 10", pr	235.00
Bookends, nudes in headstand support books, 10", pr	325.00
Bookends, seated baby reads oversz book, 6", pr	235.00
Bookends, stylized elephant w/flared ears, 5", pr	135.00
Cigarette box, 2 bk-to-bk nudes stand/hold glass box, 9"	475.00
Inkwell, seated nude w/pen tray on side, 5½"	275.00
Lamp, nude kneels before 4" bubble ball, 8"	585.00
Lamp, peek-a-boo nude peeks around candlelight bulb, 13"	390.00

Lamp, standing nude silhouettes against glass panel, 10"	385.00
Lamp, 2 nudes stand/face ea other through glass rods, 12"	900.00
Mirror, kneeling nude holds aloft 7" rnd mirror, 11"	450.00
Smoke set, standing nude holds box, tray on base, 10"	455.00
Vase, standing nude embraces 1" dia frost glass vase, 11"	345.00
Vase, 3 nudes stand/surround 5" cylindrical glass vase, 10½"	485.00

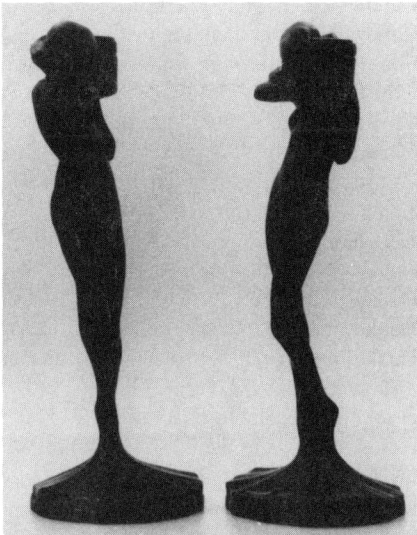

Candlesticks, symbolic of 'The Flame,' 12½", NM, $450.00 for the pair. (Also produced as lamps with parchment shades).

Frankoma

The Frank Pottery, founded in Oklahoma in 1933 by John Frank, became known as Frankoma in 1934. The company produced decorative figurals, vases, and such, marking their ware from 1936-38 with a pacing leopard 'Frankoma' mark. These pieces are highly sought. The entire operation was destroyed by fire in 1938, and new molds were cast — some from surviving pieces — and a similar line of production was pursued. The body of the ware was changed in 1954 from a honey tan to a red brick clay, and this, along with the color of the glazes (over forty have been used), helps determine the period of production. A Southwestern theme has always been favored in design as well as in color selection.

In 1965 they began to produce a limited-edition series of Christmas plates, followed by a bottle vase series in 1969. Considered very collectible are their political mugs, bicentennial plates, Teenagers of the Bible plates, and the Wildfire series. Their ceramic Christmas cards are also very popular items with today's collectors.

Frankoma celebrated their 50th anniversary in 1983. On September 26 of that same year, Frankoma was again destroyed by fire. Because of a fire-proof wall, master molds of all 1983 production items were saved, allowing plans for rebuilding to begin immediately. 'Grand Opening' was celebrated in July, 1984.

For a more thorough study of the subject we recommend that you refer to *Frankoma Treasures* by Phyllis and Tom Bess, our advisors; you will find their address in the Directory under Oklahoma.

Ash tray, Art Deco, Ada clay, #456	10.00
Ash tray, Cocker Spaniel, Desert Gold, Ada clay, unmk, 3"	50.00
Bank, dog, 7½"	40.00
Billiken, any color	75.00
Bookend, female figure, seated, w/Taylor name, #425, 5½"	350.00
Bookend, Ocelot, Ada clay, #422, 1934-38, 7¼"	200.00
Bookend, Rearing Clydesdale, #431, pr	250.00
Bookends, Dreamer Girl, gr, pr	275.00

Bowl, Gracetone, Pine Cone, Jade 30.00
Bowl, Lazybone, 11" 18.00
Bowl, Lazybone, 9" 8.00
Bowl, Plainsman, 10½" 8.00
Bowl, Plainsman, 12" 7.00
Bowl, 4-leaf clover, Clay Bl, #223 ....8.00
Candle holder, Ada clay, pacing leopard mk, #300, pr..........65.00
Candle holder, Oral Roberts.....................................10.00
Candy dish, clam shell, Prairie Gr 8.00
Carafe, w/lid, all colors 20.00
Christmas card, 1955-56...70.00
Christmas card, 1958..60.00
Christmas card, 1967-68...40.00
Christmas card, 1975, bird in hand, Grace Lee, rare 100.00
Compote, shell form, #214, 1942-50, 6" 8.00
Cornucopia, tall, Ada clay, #56, 1942-49, 7" 30.00
Cup, Wagon Wheel, w/incised hex mk, #94C.......................10.00
Donkey mug, 1975, Autumn Yel 25.00
Donkey mug, 1976, Centennial Red 25.00
Donkey mug, 1978, Woodland Moss 25.00
Elephant mug, 1972, Prairie Gr 40.00
Flower holder, Hobby Horse, #182, 3½" 150.00
Flowerabrum, Wht Sand, Ada clay 65.00
Grease jar, w/lid, #46, 1938, 3¾" 20.00
Jug, Golda's Corn, brn, dtd 1951 ....20.00
Lamp base, from Wagon Wheel sugar bowl 45.00
Mug, War God, #T-3, 1962-63, 12-oz 12.00
Mug, Wht Sand, horse decal, 18-oz 10.00
Pipe rest, #454, 2x6½x6½" 75.00
Pitcher, Fireside, #77-A.......................................65.00
Pitcher, jug form, w/stopper, 1934-35, 3-cup, 5" 50.00
Pitcher, Wagon Wheel, #94-D, 2-qt 25.00
Planter, log, #9-L, 11" 10.00
Plaque, Indian , 3¾" 10.00
Plaque, Will Rogers, w/border, Prairie Gr, Ada clay............32.50
Plate, Conestoga Wagon 50.00
Plate, Wagon Wheel, #94G, 7" 3.50
Plate, Wagon Wheel, 9" 8.00
Plate, Wht-Tail Deer, 1973 ....75.00
Plate, Wildlife, Buffalo 50.00
Plate, Will Rogers Centennial 15.00
Platter, Wagon Wheel, #94Q, 13" 20.00
Sculpture, Amazon Woman, mk Frank Potteries, #101, 6¼x8" ...350.00
Sculpture, Bucking Bronco, no stepped base, #423, 5" 165.00
Sculpture, Circus Horse, Cherokee Red, #138, 4½" 150.00
Sculpture, Cowboy Boot, mk Frankoma Pottery...................15.00
Sculpture, Donna Ruth, pacing leopard mk, #113, 7¾" 175.00
Sculpture, Fan Dancer, Ada clay, #113, 13½" 225.00
Sculpture, Flower Girl, Prairie Gr, Ada Clay, #700...........65.00
Sculpture, Greyhound, 6 petals on bk base, 1983 repro, 14" ...50.00
Sculpture, Indian Mask, Maiden, ivory, Ada clay, #138 ....38.00
Sculpture, Walking Elephant, #169, 1¾" 75.00
Shakers, Snail, Desert Gold, Ada clay, #558-H, pr 10.00
Sign, Frankoma Pottery, late 1940s-60 ....65.00
Swan, #229, 1950-63, 9"...40.00
Tray, oval, #36, 1955-64, 12" 25.00
Trivet, Lazybones, Prairie Gr, #4-TR 40.00
Tumbler, juice; #90-C, 1938-65, 3-oz, 2½" 5.00
Tumbler, Lazybone, 2⅞" 3.00
Tumbler, Wagon Wheel, #80C, 4½" 15.00
Vase, bird hdls, pacing leopard mk, #85 ....50.00
Vase, Cactus, Red Bud 40.00
Vase, Cockatoo, pacing leopard mk, 5x8" 110.00
Vase, collector; V-13, blk & Terra Cotta, 1981, 13" 40.00

Vase, collector; V-4, blk & Terra Cotta, 1972 ....65.00
Vase, collector; V-5, Flame Red, 1973, 13"....................70.00
Vase, leaf hdls, early glaze, #71, 1942, 10" 75.00
Vase, Ram's Head, pacing leopard mk, 9¼" 100.00
Vase, Wagon Wheel, #94, 1942-61, 7" 30.00
Wall pocket, boot, Robin Egg Bl, #133, 6½" 7.00
Wall pocket, Wagon Wheel, #94-Y, 1949-53, 7" 35.00

Sculpture, seated puma, Prairie Green, 7½", $85.00 (with Pacing Leopard logo, $200.00).

Fraternal Organizations

Fraternal memorabilia is a vast and varied field. Emblems representing the various organizations have been used to decorate cups, shaving mugs, plates, and glassware. Medals, swords, documents, and other ceremonial paraphernalia from the 1800s and early 1900s are especially prized. Our advisor for Odd Fellows is Greg Spiess; he is listed in the Directory under Illinois. Mike Roscoe, our Masonic advisor, is listed under Michigan.

Elks

Champagne, four tobacco leaves and two scimitars form base, 1909, 4½", $65.00.

Charm, watch; gold enameling 25.00
Flask, ceramic, emb symbols, wht w/brn, dtd 1912, 4½x2½".......120.00
Note pad & pencil, Ladies Night, 1916, EX 35.00
Plaque, cvd wood, stag w/clock & scroll, rpr, 21x24" 100.00

Plate, metal, 1907 reunion.................................32.00
Ribbon, Syracuse Lodge...1885, w/2½" bronze pin.......... 7.50

Masons

Beaker, glass, eng symbols, corset shape, 6".............70.00
Book, Low Twelve, Masonic Supply Co, 1913, EX 20.00
Decoration, CI, compass, T-sq, & C emblems, 1800s, 7x6x¼" 55.00
Display pc, cast brass, symbols on shield form, 1890s, 12x9½"...180.00
Goblet, eng schooner/'President'/eagle, cut X-hatching, 6½" 675.00
Manuscript certificate, degree of Master Mason, Nov 1800, EX ..250.00
Plate, Concordia Lodge, 110 Anniversary, 1904, 9½" 35.00
Sign, gilt wood, comass/square/'G,' 1800s, 33" 700.00
Tie clip, blk stone w/emblem on silver metal.................................12.00
Tie clip, 12k gold-filled, emblem hangs from chain, early 25.00
Wristwatch, Dudley, wht gold filled w/Bible, M 2,200.00

Odd Fellows

Apron, symbol on wht sheepskin panel, 1890s, 16x13"..................55.00
Axe, ceremonial, all wood, blk/silver head, 1880s, 41" 85.00
Banner, symbols on bl, gold braid, 30x18", EX 85.00
Sash, red/wht stripes, stars on bl at top, 1890s, 39x5".................45.00
Uniform, ceremonial, blk cloth w/shiny circles, 1900s, EX 65.00
Wristwatch, symbols on dial, silver case, Waltham 200.00

Shrine

Champagne glass, Louisville, 1909.................................65.00
Champagne, 4 tobacco leaves as base, 2 scimitars, 1909 ....65.00
Cup & saucer, glass, Los Angeles, 1906 ....70.00
Emblem, sword/moon/Egyptian, metal, orig pnt, 1920, 12x12"......85.00
Measure, dbl liquor; cranberry & clear, St Louis 1909 ....295.00
Mug, glass, Atlantic City, 1904...75.00

Fruit Jars

As early as 1829, canning jars were being manufactured for use in the home preservation of foodstuffs. For the past 25 years, they have been sought as popular collectibles. At the last estimate, over four thousand fruit jars and variations were known to exist. Some are very rare, perhaps one-of-a-kind examples which have survived to the present day. Among the most valuable are the black glass jars, the amber Van Vliet, and the cobalt Millville. These often bring prices in excess of $3,000.00 when they can be found. Aside from condition, values are based on age, rarity, color, and special features. Our advisor for this category is John Hathaway; he is listed in the Directory under Maine.

A Kemp New York, aqua, no cork closure, qt.................................48.00
AD & H Chambers Union Fruit Jar, bl, wax sealer, qt.................148.00
AG Smalley & Co Boston Mass, base: patent dates, amber, qt......33.00
Anchor Hocking (H in anchor) Mason, clear, pt 1.00
Atlas (clover) Good Luck, clear, qt.................................... 3.00
Atlas E-Z Seal, aqua, 48-oz.................................15.00
Atlas HA Mason, clear, HA glass insert, ½-pt.................. 8.00
Atlas Mason Fruit Jar, aqua, qt.................................20.00
Atlas Mason's Patent, aqua, pt 4.00
Atlas Special Mason, aqua, qt 5.00
Atlas Strong Shoulder Mason, aqua, pt 3.00
Automatic Sealer, aqua, qt.................................100.00
Ball Eclipse, clear, qt.................................... 5.00
Ball Ideal, bk: Bicentennial medallion, bl, qt.................. 2.00
Ball Ideal, bl, ½-pt.......................................35.00

American, NAG Co. Porcelain Lined on green-aqua, smooth base, sheared and ground lip, midget, M, $120.00.

Ball Mason, lt gr, Boyd form, ½-gal 14.00
Ball Perfect Mason, bl, 36-oz 20.00
Ball Perfect Mason, clear, ribbed, ½-pt 3.00
Ball Sanitary Sure Seal, bl, qt.............................. 8.00
Beaver (beaver), clear, qt..................................28.00
Brighton, clear, no closure, qt 48.00
Brockway Clear Vu Mason, clear, qt.......................... 1.00
Brockway Sur-Grip Mason, clear, qt.......................... 3.00
Calcutt's Pat Apr 11th Nov 7th 1893 (on lid), clear, qt 38.00
Canadian Mason Jar Made in Canada, clear, pt.................. 1.00
Columbia, amethyst, qt....................................28.00
Crown Crown (ring crown), aqua, ½-gal 15.00
Crystal Jar, clear, qt.....................................33.00
Curtis & Moore Trade Mark Boston Mass, clear, ½-gal 18.00
Daisy FE Ward & Co, aqua, qt 9.00
Doolittle (block letters), clear, qt...............................38.00
Doolittle (script), clear, pt 43.00
Double Safety, clear, regular mouth, ½-pt..................... 7.00
Double Safety, clear, ½-gal 4.00
Drey Improved Everseal, clear, ½-gal 5.00
Eagle, aqua, qt...125.00
EC Hazard & Co Schrewbury NJ (on base), aqua, tall qt 9.00
Electric Trademark (script in circle), aqua, pt 7.00
Empire (in stippled cross), clear, pt 5.00
Erie Lightning, amethyst, qt.............................58.00
Everlasting Jar (jar in flag), aqua, ½-gal 28.00
Excelsior, aqua, no closure, qt 40.00
Excelsior Improved, aqua, ½-gal 48.00
F&S (in circle), aqua, pt................................18.00
Favorite Trade Mark, aqua, pt 28.00
FCG Co (base), aqua, qt.................................23.00
Federal (draped flag) Fruit Jar, lt gr, qt.....................148.00
Forster Jar, clear, qt....................................15.00
Foster Sealfast, clear, pt 3.00
Foster's Sealfast, clear, ½-pt............................. 6.00
Franklin Dexter Fruit Jar, aqua, ½-gal.....................33.00
Gem, aqua, qt 7.00
Gem, aqua, ½-gal 10.00
Glassboro Trade 2 Mark Improved, aqua, ½-gal 18.00
Green Mountain C-A-Co (in fr), clear, pt....................10.00
Haines Patent March 1st 1870, aqua, qt.....................93.00
Hamilton Glass Works 1 Quart, aqua, qt....................198.00
Hazel Atlas E-Z Seal, aqua, pt 9.00
Hazel Preserve Jar, clear, ½-pt..........................38.00

Hero (over cross), aqua, qt	**48.00**
Hero Improved, aqua, qt	**22.00**
Hom-Pak Mason, clear, qt	**2.00**
HW Pettit Westville NJ (on base), aqua, pt	**10.00**
Ideal Imperial Quart, aqua, qt	**23.00**
Jeannette J (in sq) Mason Home Packer, clear, qt	**1.00**
Jos Middleby Jr Inc (vertically), lt amethyst, ½-gal	**4.00**
Kerr Economy TM, base: Sand Springs Okla, clear, pt	**2.00**
King (on banner below crown), clear, pt	**9.00**
King (on banner/crown/flags), clear, ½-pt	**38.00**
Knowlton Vacuum (star) Fruit Jar, aqua, qt	**23.00**
Knox (K in keystone) Mason, clear, w/zinc lid, qt	**1.00**
L&W, aqua, no closure, qt	**48.00**
Lafayette (script), aqua, ½-gal	**123.00**
Lamb Mason, clear, w/zinc lid, pt	**2.00**
Leotric, base: Salem NJ, aqua, pt	**7.00**
LG Co (on base), aqua, wax sealer, ½-gal	**23.00**
Longlife Mason, amber, qt	**10.00**
Lustre RE Tongue & Bros Co Phila (in circle), aqua, pt	**10.00**
Made in Canada Perfect Seal (in shield), amber, qt	**38.00**
Magic (star) Fruit Jar, amber, qt	**648.00**
Mason (in straight line), amber, pt	**73.00**
Mason (shepherd's crook), aqua, pt	**14.00**
Mason Jar of 1858 TM (in circle & sq), aqua, ½-gal	**88.00**
Mason Jar of 1872, base: Whitney Glass Works, aqua, qt	**38.00**
Mason's (cross) Improved, aqua, pt	**8.00**
Mason's (shield) Union, aqua, qt	**125.00**
Mason's IGCo Patent Nov 30th 1858, aqua, qt	**12.00**
Mason's Improved, aqua, ½-gal	**4.00**
Mason's Patent Nov 30th 1858, amethyst, qt	**10.00**
Mason's Patent 1858, aqua, qt	**10.00**
Mason's Patetn (spelling error) Nov 30th 1858, aqua, qt	**20.00**
Mason's 1 Patent Nov 30th 1858, aqua, ½-gal	**15.00**
Mason's 5 Patent Nov 30th 1858, aqua, ½-gal	**15.00**
McDonald New Perfect Seal, bl, pt	**9.00**
Motor Standard Products (in oval), clear, ½-pt	**12.00**
Mrs Chapins Mayonnaise Boston Mass, clear, pt	**3.00**
Patent Sept 18 1860, aqua, qt	**98.00**
Patented Columbia Dec 29th 1896, clear, ½-pt	**18.00**
Perfect Seal (script in circle), clear, no lid, pt	**4.00**
Pine De Luxe Jar, clear, sq, pt	**6.00**
Queen, bk: CFJ Co, aqua, ½-gal	**28.00**
Quick Seal (in circle), bl, pt	**2.00**
RE Tongue & Bros Co Inc Lustre Phil (in sq), aqua, qt	**10.00**
Reliable Home Canning Mason, clear, w/zinc lid, qt	**4.00**
Rose, clear, ½-gal	**43.00**
Safe Seal Made in Canada, clear, pt	**3.00**
Samco Super Mason, clear, w/zinc lid, ½-gal	**4.00**
Schram Automatic Sealer (in flag), clear, no lid, pt	**4.00**
Sealfast, base: Foster, clear, ½-pt	**7.00**
Silicon (in circle), aqua, qt	**12.00**
SKO Queen Trademark Wide Mouth Adjustable, clear, ½-pt	**6.00**
Smalley's Full Measure AGS Pint, aqua, qt	**12.00**
Standard (over erased mastadon), bk: W McC & Co, aqua, qt	**28.00**
Standard (shepherd's crook), aqua, wax sealer, qt	**28.00**
Star Glass Co New Albany Ind, aqua, qt	**38.00**
Sun (in circle w/radiating rays), aqua, qt	**68.00**
Superia AG Co (in circle), aqua, pt	**14.00**
Sure Seal, bl, qt	**5.00**
Sure Seal Made for L Bamberger & Co, bl, qt	**12.00**
Swayzee's Improved Mason, aqua, ½-gal	**10.00**
The Mason (The in tail of M), aqua, qt	**15.00**
TM Lightning Reg US Patent Off (on base), clear, ½-gal	**2.00**
TM Lightning Reg US Patent Office, aqua, qt	**2.00**

Trade Mark Lightning, amber, qt	**40.00**
Trade Mark Lightning Reg US Pat Off, bl, pt	**63.00**
Trade Mark The Dandy, dk amber, qt	**148.00**
Trademark Banner Registered (in banner), clear, pt	**10.00**
Trademark Banner Warranted (in circle), bl, pt	**6.00**
Veteran (bust of veteran), amethyst, pt	**28.00**
Victory (in shield), lid: The Victory Jar, clear, pt	**4.00**
Victory 1 (circled by patent dates), aqua, qt	**48.00**
Victory 1 (circled by patent dates), aqua, ½-gal	**48.00**
Wears (in circle), aqua, pt	**15.00**
Wears Jar (in stippled oval), clear, pt	**8.00**
Whitney Mason Pat'd 1858, aqua, qt	**15.00**
Winslow Jar, aqua, qt	**58.00**
Wm Frank & Sons Pittsburg (base), aqua, qt	**23.00**
Woodbury, aqua, qt	**38.00**
4 Seasons Mason, clear, qt	**2.00**

Fry

Henry Fry established his glassworks in 1901 in Rochester, Pennsylvania. There, until 1933 when it was sold to the Libbey Company, he produced glassware of the finest quality. In the early years they produced beautiful cut glass; and when it began to wane in popularity, Fry turned to the manufacture of occasional pieces and oven glassware. He is perhaps most famous for the opalescent pearl glass called 'Foval.' It was made in combination with crystal or colored trim. Because it was in production for only a short time in 1926 and 1927, it is hard to find.

Collectors of Depression-era glassware look for the opalescent reamers and opaque green kitchenware made during the early thirties. Our advisor for this category is Ron Damaska; he is listed in the Directory under Pennsylvania. For further study we recommend *The Collector's Encyclopedia of Fry Glassware* by the Fry Glass Society. See also Kitchen Collectibles.

Tankard pitcher with rose etching, $225.00.

Aquarium, amber	**100.00**
Ash tray, blk, 4 buttress ft	**20.00**
Bowl, fruit; #2200, jade trim & connector, rolled rim, 10"	**225.00**
Bowl, nappy; Wilhelm, 4-part, hdls	**165.00**
Candlestick, Foval, pearl w/bl spiral threads, 9¾"	**150.00**
Candy dish, emerald w/crystal swirl connector, petal ft	**50.00**
Coffeepot, Foval, #3000	**375.00**
Compote, #2502, Delft bl stem & trim, festooned, 9" dia	**190.00**

Compote, #2502, Delft stem, Dutch Kids silver o/l, tall..............300.00
Compote, Foval, pearl/Delft bl, knob stem, 6½x12"..................325.00
Console set, royal w/crystal swirl connector, 3-pc 250.00
Creamer & sugar, Dmn Optic, azure bl, set 40.00
Cruet, Pershing, sgn, w/stopper......................................125.00
Cup & saucer, #2000, stippled w/Delft hdl, set........................75.00
Cup & saucer, rose, HP floral, set....................................30.00
Goblet, quilted rose w/gr swirl connector, flared 15.00
Perfume, wheel etch pearl w/jade base, w/atomizer, 7" 185.00
Pitcher, Brighton, 6" 165.00
Plate, #3101, jade w/Dutch Kids silver o/l, sgn Rockwell.............150.00
Plate, cake; Sunnybrook, emerald 35.00
Plate, grill; amber...25.00
Plate, salad; #2504, pearl w/Delft trim edge, 8½"....................30.00
Sherbet, Dmn Optic, rose, twisted stem, silver o/l....................25.00
Teapot, #2002, pearl, 2-cup..155.00
Tumbler, water; De Rose etch, gold trim rim...........................15.00
Vase, #828, 3 jade ft, 5" 260.00
Vase, chalice; Geneva, 10"...200.00
Vase, De Honeysuckle etch, 811 line, 12" 40.00
Vase, Foval, pearl, ribbed, bl at rim/3 ball ft, 5x5" 225.00
Vase, Foval, pearl w/flared rim & bl ped ft, 9" 200.00
Vase, ivy; blk w/crystal swirl connector..............................40.00
Vase, pearl/Delft bl, flared/waisted/ftd, 9½"........................250.00
Vase, violet; #823, HP floral trim, Delft ft, 4" 240.00

Fulper

The Fulper Pottery was founded in 1899, after nearly a century of producing utilitarian stoneware under various titles and managements. Not until 1909 did Fulper venture into the art pottery field. Vasekraft, their first art line, utilized the same heavy clay body used for their utility ware. Although shapes were unadorned and simple, the glazes they developed were used with such flair and imagination (alone and in unexpected combined harmony) that each piece was truly a work of art. Graceful Oriental shapes were produced to complement the important 'famille rose' glaze developed by W.H. Fulper, Jr. Other shapes and glazes were developed in line with the Arts and Crafts movement of the same period.

During WWI, doll's heads and Kewpies were made to meet the demand for hard-to-find imports. Figural perfume lamps and powder boxes were made both in bisque and glazed ware. Examples prized most highly by collectors today are those made before a devastating fire destroyed the plant in 1929, resulting in an operations takeover by Martin Stangl later that same year.

Several marks were used: a vertical 'Fulper' in a line reserve, a horizontal mark, a Vasekraft paper label, 'Rafco,' 'Prang,' and 'Flemington.'

Fulper values are to a major degree determined by the desirability of the glazes and forms. And, of course, larger examples command higher prices as well. Lamps with colored glass inserts are rare and highly prized. Our advisor for this category is Douglass White; he is listed in the Directory under Florida.

Bowl, bl crystalline (lg flakes) to brn flambe, 4-ftd, 11" 300.00
Bowl, bl w/mustard flambe, bl int, ftd, 4¼x9¾"..........................250.00
Bowl, bl wisteria, widely flared, 4 cut-out ft, 7" 125.00
Bowl, brn/caramel flambe, shallow, 13"..................................250.00
Bowl, bulb; purple/pk flambe, blk rim, 11"..............................275.00
Bowl, console; turq drip on burgundy, lg, +2 candle holders.............225.00
Bowl, effigy; bl-gr flambe to caramel, figural ft, 7x11".................750.00
Bowl, gr matt, 3-part overhead hdl extends into ft, 8x5"................250.00
Bowl, gr w/ivory streaks, lobed, rtcl flower flange, 12" 250.00
Bowl, med gr runs over mahog flambe, artichoke form, 6x9" 700.00

Bowl, purple/blk flambe, lt flambe int, floriform, 3x7"..................150.00
Bowl, red matt, apple gr int, base w/4 lg ft in brn, 7x12"...............700.00
Bowl, rose matt, rolled/incised rim, 2½x13½".............................275.00
Bowl vase, bl w/gold flambe, incurvate, 5½".............................225.00
Bud vase, blk/bl/yel crystalline, knop base, 9".........................150.00
Bud vase, gr matt on bl, sq w/4-lobe petal ft, 8½" 125.00

Bulldog, dated 1917, 7¾", $1,750.00.

Candlestick, elephant's breath brn/gray flambe, 16", pr 1,900.00
Candlestick, ivory top, heavy bl on sq shaft, 10", pr 350.00
Decanter, musical, olive to leaf gr w/some crystals.....................150.00
Flower frog, fish, tan/rust/bl/gr blended, 4" 75.00
Flower frog, pelican, gr semi-crystalline, 7" 125.00
Humidor, mirror blk, w/lid, rare..625.00
Jar, cafe au lait, #195, 4½"..350.00
Lamp, gr matt w/bl, glass inserts, mushroom shape, 19" 11,000.00
Pitcher, gr matt/charcoal, coiled mold, bulbous, 5¼"...................175.00

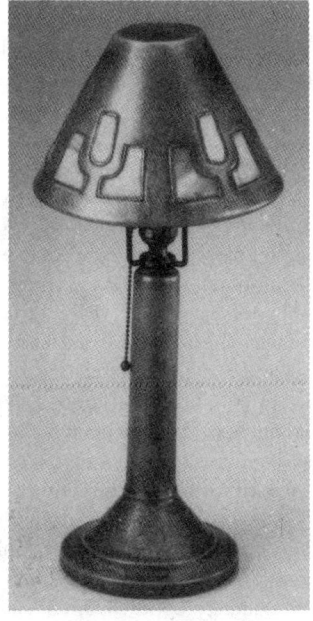

Table lamp, geometric glass inserts, #106, 14", $4,000.00.

Vase, bl crystalline, fan form, 6½" 400.00
Vase, bl crystalline flambe w/brn, can neck w/hdls, 9x6" 475.00
Vase, bl crystalline over brn & caramel flambe, ovoid, 5½".............190.00
Vase, bl flambe over rust, hdls at bulbous bottom, 8x7".................650.00

Vase, bl matt, slim cone form, cut-out rectangular hdls, 11".........300.00
Vase, bl w/silvery streaks, 4 loop shoulder hdls, 13" 2,300.00
Vase, bl/gr crystalline, fixed ring hdls, 12¾"..................................450.00
Vase, bl/gr-streaked flambe, ovoid w/sm neck, 14".......................500.00
Vase, bl/gr/yel crystalline, bracketed bar neck hdls, 9x9"......... 1,200.00
Vase, blk flambe drip on Chinese bl flambe, ovoid, 14x7"..........850.00
Vase, blk to brn/bl/cream flambe, wide top w/angle hdls, 8" 375.00
Vase, blk/gr/yel, twig neck, wide base, #98, 8½"............................100.00
Vase, brn matt, cylinder w/wide mouth, angle hdls, 4½", NM 125.00
Vase, brn/gr gloss, ribbed cylinder, lug hdls/can neck, 9" 150.00
Vase, brn/gr matt, wide mouth/can neck, angle hdls, 5" 125.00
Vase, brn/tiger's eye crystalline, hdld rose jar form, 12".......... 1,100.00
Vase, butterscotch flambe, trumpet neck/bulbous bottom, 14"...850.00
Vase, Chinese bl to gr flambe, flared collar neck, 16x7"......... 1,500.00
Vase, copper dust, gr flambe at wide base, hdls conform, 9".........500.00
Vase, cucumber gr crystalline, horizontal hdls, 13x13"............ 1,700.00
Vase, cucumber gr w/silver & blk crystals, 12x7".........................950.00
Vase, emb mushrooms, yel to brn flambe, cylindrical, 10" 700.00
Vase, famille rose over taupe matt, angle rim hdls, 7x7".............275.00
Vase, gr crystalline, short neck w/3 loop hdls, bulbous, 7½" 650.00
Vase, gr flambe on dk brn/ivory flambe, 4 openings, ftd, 8" 650.00
Vase, gr flambe w/gray crystalline, horizontal hdls, 12x10" 1,000.00
Vase, gr flambe w/rust crystalline drip, long hdls, 10x8" 650.00
Vase, gr matt, bulbous w/rim-to-width hdls, 7"............................150.00
Vase, gr matt, hammered, bulbous w/wishbone hdls, 9x9" 500.00
Vase, gr-brn on gr-bl flambe, shaped can neck w/hdls, 9x12" 850.00
Vase, gr/brn crystalline, flaring w/sq-top bar hdls, 12"..................375.00
Vase, gun metal/bl drip on famille rose, Oriental hdls, 11"...... 1,200.00
Vase, lav-bl semi-gloss over magenta, hdls, no mk, 6¾" 100.00
Vase, leopard-skin gray/gr, Oriental hdls, 5x7"...........................350.00
Vase, mahog/bl flambe on ivory, 7-sided, #445, 8½" 350.00
Vase, med gr over ivory crystalline, hammered, hdls, 12x11" 900.00
Vase, med-gr texture over ivory crystalline flambe, 16x6" 1,600.00
Vase, moss gr to rose flambe, tapered, lg ring hdls, 13x8".............500.00
Vase, mushrooms at base, streaky brn to periwinkle, 9½"..............465.00
Vase, mustard/olive-gray drip crystalline, bulbous, 7¾" 1,100.00
Vase, purple/rose streaky, pear w/Oriental-style hdls, 11"....... 1,500.00
Vase, rose in high relief, bl w/gr-tinged petals, mk, 6x6½"..........180.00
Vase, sky bl to cream, flat loop hdls at rim, ped ft, 9x9"..............500.00
Vase, turq/olive crystalline, slender w/rnd ft, 9" 175.00

Furniture

From the cabinetmaker's shop of the early 1800s with apprentices and journeymen who learned every phase of the craft at the side of the master carpenter, the trade had evolved by the mid-century to one with steam-powered saws and turning lathes and workers who specialized in only one operation. By 1870 the Industrial Revolution was in progress, and large factories in the East and Midwest turned out increasingly elaborate styles, ornately machine carved and heavily inlaid. Rococo, Egyptian, and Renaissance Revival furniture adapted well to factory production. Eastlake offered a welcome respite from Victorian frumpery and a return to quality handcrafting. All of these styles remained popular until the turn of the century.

As early as 1880, factories began using oak; early mail-order catalogs offered oak furniture, simply styled and lighter in weight, since long-distance shipping was often a factor. Mission, or Craftsman, a style introduced around 1890, was simple to the extreme. Stickley and Hubbard were two of its leading designers. Other popular Victorian styles were Colonial Revival, Cottage, Bentwood, and Windsor. Prices are as variable as the styles.

To learn more about furniture, we recommend *The Collector's Encyclopedia of American Furniture* by Robert and Harriet Swedberg.

Note: When only one dimension is given for blanket chests, dry sinks, tables, settees, and sofas, it is length.

Key:
Am — American	G — good
brd — board	Geo — Georgian
Chpndl — Chippendale	grpt — grainpainted
Co — Country	hdbd — headboard
cvd — carved	hdw — hardware
cvg — carving	Hplwht — Hepplewhite
c&b — claw and ball	NE — New England
do — door	QA — Queen Anne
drw — drawer	trn — turning
Emp — Empire	Vict — Victorian
Fed — Federal	W/M — William and Mary
Fr — French	: — over (example: 1 do:2 drw —
ftbd — footboard	1 door over 2 drawers)

Bed

Louis Phillippe rosewood day bed, ca 1840, $450.00.

Canopy, birch/pine Sheraton, tall posts, repro, single sz 450.00
Canopy, cherry w/str pine hdbd, pencil posts, full sz, EX 900.00
Canopy, mahog, trn/cvd ft posts, tapered head posts, 66" 650.00
Day, EX trn, 3-vase bk adjusts, rpl rush seat, 23x68", EX 9,000.00
Field, poplar/pine w/old red, folding, shaped hdbd, full sz.............350.00
G Nakashima, day bed, walnut Deco, burlap cushions, 84"..... 3,900.00
Majorelle, mahog, chevron panels w/floral inlay, 69" 3,850.00
Majorelle, 3-part hdbd w/rows of daffodils, ftbd same, 56"....... 1,000.00
Maple/pine Co Sheraton, sq or trn 61" posts, canopy fr, rfn.... 2,800.00
Marquetry, Nouveau florals, cvd tendrils, brass o/l, France...... 1,300.00
Mission, oak w/orig finish, 3 wide slats in hd/ftbds.......................175.00
Rope, curly maple/poplar, trn posts/paneled hdbd, rfn 300.00
Rope, red-stain poplar Co, trn posts/peaked hdbd, 42x71x53" 125.00
Rope, vinegar grpt, bulbous trn/shaped hdbrd/ball finials 4,000.00
Tall post, curly maple, EX trn, 80" 3,000.00
Tester, Southern Am mahog, scroll hdbd, 1860s, 115"........... 7,000.00

Bench

Blk worn pnt w/gold floral, 2-chair bk, rush seat, 47", VG..........900.00
Bucket, pine Co, traces of worn gray pnt, 36x46".......................550.00
Limbert, settle #558, 9 bk slats, 3 ea side, uphl, 85" 3,500.00
Limbert, settle #562, 9-slat bk/5-slat sides, mk, 76", EX 8,500.00
Limbert, settle #654½, 2-slat sides/6-slat bk, rfn 2,300.00
Mammy's, worn orig stenciling, rpl baby guard, 56" 800.00

Oak English, wainscot panel bk, scroll arms, uphl seat, 74" 900.00
Pine, primitive, weathered brn finish, cut-out legs, 61" 150.00
Poplar w/weathered patina, wire nails, 21" W 1-brd top, 60" 195.00
Settle, Co Emp, 3-slat bk/plank seat/scroll arms, rpr, 71" 325.00
Settle, PA decor, 3-seat half-spindle bk, 70" 1,600.00
Settle, pine w/re-grpt (as oak) Co English, damage, 53x72" 400.00
Settle, poplar, trn legs, plank seat, spindle bk, rfn, 121" 320.00
Water, pine w/pnt layers, cut-out ends, base shelf, 43" 225.00
Water, pine w/worn bl & wht rpt, scalloped apron, 31x61" 520.00
Water, walnut, worn/weathered, 37" 150.00
Windsor, bulbous trn, scroll arms, low bk, rprs/rpl, 48" 2,100.00
Windsor Co, bamboo cvg, plank seat, simple, rfn/rpl/rpr 575.00
Yel pine w/worn red pnt Co, cut-out ft/scalloped apron, 64" 150.00

Blanket Chest

Cherry Co, w/drw, high ft w/scroll apron & drw, rstr/rpl.............600.00
Curly maple/poplar Co, raised panels/trn ft, rpl lid, 40" 550.00
Pine, dvtl case/till, bracket ft w/rprs, rfn, 22x43" 425.00
Pine w/bl traces Co Chpndl, EX detail, 2 base drw, 52" 650.00
Pine w/mc tulips/1844, Somerset Co PA, rpl ft, 25" 5,200.00
Pine w/orig red & stylized blk grpt, 49", EX................................400.00
Pine w/red grpt & blk ft Co Chpndl, 2-drw, till, EX+ 3,850.00
Pine w/red rpt Co, 6-brd/dvtl drw, rpl brasses, 33x46" 250.00
Pine/poplar w/red & blk grpt, dtd 1904, att J&J Sala, 48" 850.00
Pine/poplar w/red grpt, dvtl, bracket ft, rprs, 50" 650.00
Pine/poplar w/red stain Soap Hollow PA, dtd 1856, 23" 13,000.00
Poplar w/old red, trn ft/dvtl/appl edge molding, till, 33".............450.00
Poplar w/red flame grpt, dvtl bracket ft/case, till, 40" 1,000.00

Bookcase

FL Wright, Heritage Henredon, glass do/shelves, 76x65" 1,900.00
Limbert, #372, 2-do, arched pane:2 upright panels, 60x48" ... 2,200.00
Mahog Chpndl, 2 do:slant lid:4 drw, MA, 1789, 76" 14,000.00
Oak, sectional, 4-unit, 1920s, rstr/rfn...500.00
Oak, 3-do, cvd trn posts, paw ft, rstr/rfn 950.00

Bureau, See Chest

Cabinet

Burlwood Deco w/lt wood inlay, glazed center section, 68" 900.00
Console, Vict, pnt floral, shaped D-form marble top, 61"........ 3,000.00
Curio, giltwood Louis XVI style, curved glass, wear, 32" 1,000.00
Curio, marquetry w/ormolu, curved glass, 1890s, 65x33"......... 1,000.00
Ebonized Renaissance Revival, marble top, German, 43x41" 450.00
Gilt:composition, Fr-style, 1900s, 52x24" 625.00
Majorelle, vitrine, rtcl floral crest/apron, inlay, 75x30".........17,500.00
P Follot, Deco w/ivory inlay, bowed 2-do front, 56x38" 7,000.00
Vernis Martin, vitrine, gold w/scene, curved glass, 58x27"..... 2,350.00
Vernis Martin, vitrine, ormolu mts, HP panels, 73x33" 2,600.00

Candlestand

Birch Hplwht, spider legs/spade ft, oval 22" top rpl, EX.............475.00
Cherry Co, tripod w/snake ft, trn column, 16" sq 1-brd top..... 1,050.00
Cherry/walnut, spider legs, 2-brd 22" shaped top w/reeding.........600.00
Mahog Chpndl, tripod w/snake ft, urn-trn std, 22" tilt top 700.00
Mahog Hplwht, birdcage, 19" dmn-form tilt top, EX 1,550.00
Mahog w/inlay Hplwht, trn column, spade ft, 16x21" tilt top . 1,600.00
Maple Co Chpndl w/ink grpt, trn column, 15" 1-brd top, EX ... 2,500.00
Maple w/some curl in snake ft, trn column, rpl 18" oval top........200.00
Walnut Hplwht, spider legs/spade ft, 22x15" tilt top, rpr 650.00
Windsor, poplar, trn/splay legs, trn column, 14" 1-brd top 350.00

Chair

William and Mary carved maple side chair, Massachusetts, ca 1700, refinished, $2,000.00.

Arm, Louis XV, uphl cartouch bk, serpentine seat, 36", pr 1,900.00
Arm, mahog Italian, scroll arms/eagle-cvd legs, needlepoint 750.00
Arm, Sheraton, red/blk grpt/striping, EX detail, rpr/rpl.............375.00
Arm, 4 lg stag horns form fr, tapestry-like uphl, sturdy 1,000.00
Bannister-bk scroll arm, trn posts/legs, rush seat, 1800s 950.00
Bannister-bk side, dk grpt over early pnt, EX trn/crest 600.00
Bannister-bk side, EX trn detail, rpl rush seat....................................425.00
Corner, Co, trn legs/posts, curved rail, rush seat, VG..................400.00
Corner, Co, trn posts/well-shaped arm rail, rush seat, EX 500.00
Corner, Co Chpndl, rpl slip seat, rfn 650.00
Corner, mahog Chpndl, c/b ft, cvd knees/slats, rpr/rpl............. 1,350.00
Ladderbk arm, cleaned down to old red, sausage trn, rpr............550.00
Ladderbk arm, maple, 5-slat, bulb-trn stretcher, rpl seat 4,250.00
Ladderbk arm, old red/VG color, 4 grad slats, rpl seat, 44" 2,000.00
Ladderbk arm, red stain, 3 str slats, mushroom caps, rpl/EX.........100.00
Ladderbk arm, 3-slat, trn finials, flat whittled arms, early 700.00
Ladderbk arm, 4 arched slats, trn ft/stretcher, paper seat 275.00
Ladderbk arm, 5 arched splats, new splint seat, rfn......................175.00
Ladderbk arm, 5 grad arched slats, trn finials/etc, rpt............. 3,700.00
Ladderbk arm Co, 4 arched slats, trn supports, rpl seat..................95.00
Ladderbk rocker, figured maple, tall 4-slat bk.............................550.00
Ladderbk side, 3-slat, trn finials, worn rush seat 85.00
Ladderbk side, 4 arch splats, trn button ft, rush seat, rpt 70.00
Limbert, rocker #676, center slat w/2 sq cutouts, brand, EX.... 1,000.00
Marjorelle, host chair, sunflowers inlaid in bk splat 4,000.00
Moravian side, W-shaped bk splats, pr 400.00
Rocker, worn red/blk grpt w/gold & yel striping, trn legs 150.00
Side, birch Co, Spanish ft/pierced slat/cvd ears, rpl seat 325.00
Side, blk rpt w/yel striping, EX trn, vase splat, rush seat 525.00
Side, Co Chpndl, maple/lt curl, ornate splat, rpl rush seat...........500.00
Side, Co QA, EX trn/duck ft/vase splat/yoke crest, rpt 1,000.00
Side, curly maple w/EX stripe, trn legs, vase splat, rfn..................775.00
Side, mahog Chpndl, cabriole legs, c/b ft, shell-cvd crest 4,500.00
Side, mahog Chpndl, cvd fan crest/ornate pierced splat, rfn 250.00
Side, mahog Hplwht, serpentine seat fr, pierced splat, rpr 200.00
Side, maple Co, shaped crest/vase splat, trn legs, rpl seat............300.00
Side, maple w/curl, sabre leg, rpl cane seat, rpr fr, pr..................170.00
Side, Shop o/t Crafters, mahog w/uphl, wide bk splat, VG 200.00
Side, stenciled fruit/foliage on brn, half-spindle bk, EX+.............150.00
Side, walnut QA, balloon seat, vase splat, yoke crest, EX 4,500.00

Side, walnut w/ivory inlay Dutch Baroque, rprs, 42" 450.00
Windsor, bow-bk arm, bamboo trn, saddle seat, rfn/rpr 550.00
Windsor, bow-bk arm, bulbous trn, saddle seat, rfn 1,400.00
Windsor, bow-bk arm, EX detail, red rpt, rpl/rpr 350.00
Windsor, bow-bk arm, EX trn/detail, bl alligatored rpt, EX..... 1,000.00
Windsor, bow-bk arm, saddle seat, trn supports/legs, rpl 850.00
Windsor, bow-bk arm, shaped seat, trn legs, sgn Hall, rpr 700.00
Windsor, bow-bk arm, shaped seat, trn legs/supports, rpl 500.00
Windsor, bow-bk side, 7-spindle, saddle seat, VG 100.00
Windsor, bow-bk side, 9-spindle, bamboo trn, saddle seat 375.00
Windsor, bow-bk side, 9-spindle, saddle seat, rpr/rfn 200.00
Windsor, bow-bk side, 9-spindle, trn legs, saddle seat, rfn 600.00
Windsor, brace-bk arm, uphl saddle seat, bulbous trn, rpt 900.00
Windsor, brace-bk side, unsgn Wallace Nutting-type, rpt 700.00
Windsor, brace-bk side, 7-spindle, saddle seat, rfn, EX 400.00
Windsor, comb-bk arm, red stain, 9-spindle, rprs/rpl/worn 500.00
Windsor, comb-bk arm, saddle seat, mismatched trn, rpr/rpt .. 3,000.00
Windsor, comb-bk continuous arm, shaped seat, trn supports 950.00
Windsor, fan-bk arm, saddle seat, bulb trn, rfn/rpr/rstr 1,150.00
Windsor, fan-bk arm, saddle seat/EX trn, cvd ears, rstr/rpr 1,000.00
Windsor, fan-bk side, 7-spindle, saddle seat, 1780s.................. 1,500.00
Windsor, high-bk rocker, 5-spindle, rfn.................................450.00
Windsor, side, bamboo trn, medallion bk, rfn 225.00
Windsor, writing arm, shaped seat, drw under seat, rpr/rpl ... 2,000.00
Windsor, writing arm, shaped seat, low comb crest, rpt/rpl..........450.00
Wingbk, mahog-fr Chpndl, sq legs/H-stretcher, worn uphl 2,900.00
Wingbk, mahog-fr Hplwht, simple inlay, sq legs, EX.............. 2,200.00
Wingbk, pine-fr Co Hplwht, braces added, rpr/re-uphl, 42" 700.00

Chair Set

Curly maple Sheraton, rope crest/pierced bk, 1 arm+5............ 6,000.00
FL Wright, dining, uphl sq bks/seats, sgn, 4 .... 1,600.00
Side, curly maple, 3 horizontal slats, worn rush seats, 4 ....750.00
Side, gr w/3-color florals, rush seats, worn, 6 ....650.00
Side, mahog Centennial Chpndl style, c&b ft, slip seat, 4 ..... 1,300.00
Side, mahog Hplwht, pierced splat/shaped bk, uphl seat, 4 .... 1,000.00
Side, mahog QA, ca 1900, slip seats re-uphl, 8.........................800.00
Side, oak Art Deco, sq uphl bl & U-shape seat, 37", 8 .... 1,500.00
Side, PA decor, roses on gray, bl/yel striping, 6 .... 1,200.00
Side, red/blk grpt w/eagle & crest on 2 bk slats, EX, 6 .... 4,200.00
Side, rpt w/floral stencil, crest:3-rod half bk, EX, 6 ....780.00
Side, half-spindle bk, flame grpt, yel bands/gilt stencil, 6 ..... 1,500.00
Windsor, bamboo trn, rfn, 4...980.00
Windsor, bamboo trn, shaped seat, rfn/minor rpr, 5 ....550.00
Windsor, bow-bk side, 9-spindle, saddle seat, 3........................ 1,650.00

Chest

Apothecary, pine/polar, 6 nailed drw w/bevel edges, 25x25" 375.00
Bachelor's, mahog, pull-out shelf, 4-drw, rpr/rpl, 33x36" 1,000.00
Birch Chpndl, shaped top, bracket ft, 4-drw, 37x38", EX........ 2,350.00
Birch/bird's eye veneer drw/mahog X-band Co Sheraton, EX . 2,000.00
Butternut Co, 2 sm step-bk drw:3, bracket ft, rpr/rfn, 42" 500.00
Cherry Chpndl bowfront, ogee ft, rpl brasses/rfn, 38x40" 2,200.00
Cherry Co QA, high scalloped dvtl ft, rpl hdw/bkbrds, 38" 1,550.00
Cherry Hplwht, cove mold, Fr ft, 3 drw:5, 63x43", EX 7,000.00
Cherry Sheraton bowfront, trn ft, rpl hdw/rfn/rprs, 39x40" 850.00
Cherry/flame veneer Emp, rope-cvd pilasters, trn ft, 52x47".......850.00
Cherry/flame veneer Sheraton bowfront w/walnut inlay, rfn .. 1,300.00
Chest on chest, cherry Co Chpndl, flutings, rpr/rpl, 70" 2,450.00
Chest on chest, walnut w/inlay Hplwht, Fr ft, rpl hdw, 71".... 4,200.00
Curly maple Emp, scroll ft/pilasters, 4-drw, wood pulls, EX 650.00
Dower, pine w/bl pnt, 4-color arches/flowers, PA, 52", EX 15,500.00

FL Wright, Heritage/Henredon, 4-drw, 28x22x20", EX 950.00
Mahog Chpndl, fluted columns, ogee ft, rpr/rstr, 35x42" 3,900.00
Mahog Chpndl, 4 dvtl drw/bracket ft, rprs/rpl, rare sz, 30" ... 1,800.00
Mahog Sheraton bowfront, reeded legs/pilasters, rfn, 41" 750.00
Mahog veneer Hplwht, rpl Fr ft & apron, rprs/damage, 39x43" ...275.00
Mahog w/inlay Hplwht, appl beading, rpl brasses, 46x44"....... 1,700.00
Mahog w/inlay Hplwht, Fr ft/scalloped apron, rpl/rfn, 35" 2,800.00
Mahog w/inlay Hplwht bowfront, Fr ft, 4 dvtl drw, rpl/rpr 1,500.00

Federal birch and bird's-eye maple veneer chest, ca 1820s, original finish, minor imperfections, 42" x 42", $3,100.00.

Maple Chpndl, molded cornice, 6 grad/dvtl/overlap drw, 52" .. 4,750.00
Maple Co Chpndl, bracket ft, 4 dvtl drw, rpl hdw, 34x39"...... 1,650.00
Maple QA, ink grpt old/not orig, orig eagle hdw, 44x38" 700.00
Maple w/lt curl Co Chpndl, 4-drw (3-drw facade), rstr, 43" ... 1,600.00
Maple w/some curl+other woods Co Emp, trn ft/pilasters, EX 700.00
Mule, cherry w/inlay Co Hplwht, 2 false drw+2, rstr/rpl 650.00
Mule, pine, orig brn vinegar grpt, 2-drw, EX detail, 40x43" 2,400.00
Mule, pine Co, cut-out ft/scalloped apron, 2 dvtl drw, VG 225.00
Mule, pine Co, scalloped apron, 2 drw, early, rpt, 36" 2,500.00
Mule, pine w/old red Co QA, 3 drw+3 false drw, rpr/rpl, 57".. 2,800.00
Poplar w/old red Co, 12 dvtl drw, rpl trn pulls, 33x35", VG 400.00
Spice, mahog Chpndl, fretwork spandrels in panel do, 34x24" .. 1,900.00
Sugar, poplar, trn legs, hinged lid, rfn, 28x33x17"....................350.00
Sugar, walnut Hplwht, eagle/fan inlay added later, rpl lid............900.00
Walnut Chpndl, dentil molding, ogee ft, rstr/rpr, 67x41"........ 5,000.00
Walnut w/inlay Hplwht, Fr ft, scrolled apron, as found, EX 3,000.00

Cupboard

Corner, cherry, 12-pane do, cove mold, serpentine int, 87" 4,000.00
Corner, cherry, 2 8-pane do, rosettes/finials on bonnet top..... 5,750.00
Corner, curly maple Co, panel do (2:3 sm:2), cove mold, 80". 2,700.00
Corner, pine, curved shelves w/spoon cutouts, rstr, 41" 600.00
Corner, pine English Co, stop-flute columns, glass top, 78" 1,300.00
Corner, pine English Co, 4 panel do w/molding, 80", EX........ 3,000.00
Corner, pine/poplar Co, 12-pane do:2 panel do, 1-pc, 78x41".. 1,200.00
Corner, poplar, cornice/4 panel do/2 butternut drw, 83" 1,150.00
Corner, poplar Co, 9-pane do:drw w/rnd front:2 panel do, EX . 1,500.00
Corner, walnut Co, cove molding, panel do (2:2), 2-pc, 80".... 1,850.00
Corner, walnut Hplwht, arched glazed do, ogee ft, 96", EX 6,250.00
Corner/hanging, pine, base/cornice molding, panel do, 37x34"...650.00

Hanging, pine, orig red flame grpt, scrolled crest, 38" 600.00
Hanging, poplar w/dk grpt, dvtl w/molding, 36", EX.................500.00
Jelly, poplar w/red rpt, simple cut-out ft, panel do, 40" 485.00
Jelly, poplar/old red, cut-out ft, drw:2 panel do, rpr, 61" 350.00
Pewter, pine, open w/3 shelves, brd/batten do, 81x38", VG ... 1,200.00
Pewter, pine Co, cut-down base w/panel do, rfn, 72x42".........1,200.00
Pine, 3 drws in high bk:2 panel do, scroll sides, 48x42"...........1,000.00
Pine Co, bl/wht pnt over red, appl trim on frieze, 84", EX...........950.00
Pine/poplar w/red flame grpt, simple, drw/2 panel do, 45" 1,000.00
Poplar w/dk stain, simple cut-out ft, panel do, 38x27" 250.00
Poplar w/red stain, open 2-shelf top w/scroll sides, 79" 600.00
Walnut Co, mortised, sq post ft, panel ends/4 do, 1-pc, 77".........950.00

Desk

Chippendale mahogany oxbow slant lid desk, Massachusetts, ca 1780, replaced brasses, prospect door, and lid, 44" x 40", $4,250.00.

Birch, Co QA, slant front, rpl brasses/rprs/rfn, 45x41" 2,000.00
Birch Chpndl oxbow slant front, bandy c&b ft, 4-drw, 46" 3,750.00
Butler's, walnut w/inlay Hplwht, fitted/drop front, rpr/rpl....... 1,500.00
Cherry Hplwht, slant front, fitted, rstr/rpl/rfn, 44x36" 1,400.00
Cherry w/inlay Chpndl-Hplwht transition, bold detail, 42" ..12,750.00
G Nakashima, rosewood/walnut Deco, Y-shape supports, 83" .. 4,000.00
Lap, mahog English, foliate brass panel inlay, 20" 500.00
Lap, mahog English, MOP inlay, 20" L....................................300.00
Lifetime, drop front #8532, 1-drw, 39x31" 350.00
Mahog Chpndl, fitted/4-drw, rstr, 37" 1,600.00
Mahog Regency, tilt-up top:3 sm drw, trn legs, 42" 1,050.00
Mahog w/inlay Hplwht lady's, fitted int:4-drw, rfn, 53x42"..... 3,000.00
Mahog/cherry Centennial kneehole slant-lid, fan cvg/c&b ft .. 2,000.00
Majorelle, walnut, leaves/flowers inlaid on drop front, 66"...... 1,700.00
Maple Co Chpndl, slant front, much rstr/rpl/rfn, 44x40" 1,800.00
Schoolmaster's, cherry w/inlaid escutcheons Hplwht, 3-drw 675.00
Walnut w/line inlay, slant lid, ca 1800, 40" 3,100.00

Dry Sink

Pine Co, 1-brd do w/battens, CI thumb pc, rfn, 30x38", EX 350.00
Pine w/red pnt, dvtl drw: 2 base drw 650.00
Poplar w/lt bl pnt Co, simple well, 2 panel do, 54".....................975.00
Poplar w/pnt layers, scalloped base, panel do, drw, 48" 650.00
Red/gr pnt, open top, 1 base drw, 1800s, 36x27"........................ 1,000.00

Highboy

Mahog Phila Chpndl-style repro, Northern Co, 82" 1,500.00

Maple Co QA, 9-drw, scroll apron, married/rpl/rfn, 70x40" ... 6,000.00
Maple w/some curl QA, scroll apron, rprs/rpl, 70" 7,500.00
Maple/curly maple QA, married top/bottom but period, 70"... 6,100.00
Tiger maple QA, flat top, rpl hdw/rpl pendants, 1750s, 70" ...25,000.00
Walnut QA, flat top, rstr/rpl hdw/rfn, 68" 15,000.00

Lowboy

Cherry QA, cabriole legs/duck ft, orig hdw, minor rpr/rpl 5,000.00
Curly maple PA QA, scroll apron, drops missing, rprs/rpl 6,750.00
Figured walnut veneer w/inlay, QA, oval pad ft, rfn/rprs......... 2,200.00
Mahog Chpndl, cvd shell, ornately cvd legs, rpl hdw, 1790s..85,000.00
Walnut/maple QA, trn drops/cvd fan, 4-drw, early brasses...... 8,000.00

Pie Safe

Butternut/poplar, 6 star-punched tin panels, 60", EX.................700.00
Hanging, pine/poplar, punched tin panels in do/ends, 19x21".. 1,250.00
Pine/poplar, bl on gray pnt, 12 tin panels, 58"..........................950.00
Poplar, 3 punched tin panels, high cut-out base, rpr/rfn..............650.00

Rack

Baker's, hardwood English, mortised, dowel shelves, 44x30" 175.00
Drying, gr-pnt pine, shoe ft, 3 mortised bars, rprs, 27x35" 145.00
Drying, pine/poplar, 3 mortised bars, primitive, 32x40", VG 95.00
Drying, poplar, 3 mortised/pinned bars, arch ft, 48x43", EX 125.00

Secretary

Cherry Co, slant lid/fitted, bookcase top, 2-pc, 80", EX 3,950.00
Mahog Sheraton Hplwht, cylinder lid/2 Gothic glazed do, 84" .. 2,300.00
Mahog w/inlay Hplwht, bookcase w/geometric mullions, 88".. 3,100.00
Maple w/red grpt:gr, pigeon-hole top:case w/drw:fr base.......... 1,700.00
Poplar Co, rfn to yel grpt, 2 glaze do:pigeonholes:2 do, EX..........550.00
Walnut Vict, burl cylinder lid, EX cvd crest/columns, 110" 2,000.00

Settee

American Rococo walnut settee, grape carvings, 68" long, $700.00.

Mahog Geo style, cvd cabriole legs w/hoof ft, 1900, 66" 350.00
Sheraton w/wht rpt & stenciling, EX detail, rush seat, 37"...... 2,300.00
Walnut Vict, floral cvd crest, scroll arms/legs, EX uphl 375.00
Walnut-fr Rococo Revival, grapes on crest rail, 66", NM........ 1,100.00
Windsor, plank seat, spindle bk, rfn, 40" 800.00

Shelf

Crock, pine w/rpt PA, 3-tier, EX detail, 30x38" 500.00
Hardwood w/red stain, very simple, 3-tier, wall mt, 23x25" 200.00
Pnt pine, corner/wall mt, 3 shaped panels, Zoar OH, 47" 1,100.00
Poplar, scalloped ends/crests, wall mt, 30x25" 400.00
Poplar w/old red, truncated sides, molded edges, 26x26" 1,050.00
Soft wood w/old red, molded/curved sides, wall mt, 28x30" 800.00

Sideboard

American Rococo rosewood sideboard, New York, ca 1850, 67" x 48", $700.00.

Leleu, att; mahog, drw ea side 2 do, brass legs, 112" 385.00
Limbert, mirrored bkbrd w/cutouts, 3 drw:3 do:drw, unsgn...... 1,600.00
Mahog Fed, marble top, ring-trn ft/acanthus capitals, 74" 1,200.00
Mahog w/inlay Fed, shaped top & case, 72" 4,000.00
Mahog w/inlay Hplwht, bowfront, 4 do (2 curved), much rstr . 1,000.00
Mahog w/inlay Hplwht, side drws bow out, rpl hdw/rfn, 68" .. 4,000.00
Mahog w/inlay Hplwht-style Centennial, well made, 66" 3,200.00
Satinwood w/inlay English Hplwht, 38", EX 850.00

Sofa

Co Hplwht, sq tapered/molded mahog legs, boxy style, 77".... 1,000.00
Mahog-fr Classical, scrolled arms/crest, elaborate ft, 88" 1,100.00
Mahog-fr Co Sheraton, open arm posts, re-uphl, 72" 2,400.00
Mahog-fr Fed, cvd reeding, ca 1800s, rpl leg/rfn, 76" 1,200.00
Mahog-fr Fed, foliate cvd armrests, paw/cornucopia ft, 90" 1,250.00
Mahog-fr Sheraton, ebony inlay, EX trn detail, 72"................ 7,000.00
Mahog-fr Sheraton, trn/reeded legs, open arms, 78", VG 1,250.00
Sheraton bowfront, reeded arms/legs, reuphl, EX....................... 2,100.00

Stand

Adirondak, corner type, blk/red/gold pnt, 4-tier, 63" 210.00
Adirondak, twisted root/burl assembly base, 16" dia top 200.00
Ash Co, trn legs, 2 dvtl drws, loose 2-brd 22x24" top, rpt............350.00
Cherry Co, trn legs, dvtl drw, 2-brd 20x21" top, rfn....................350.00
Cherry w/curly maple & burl veneer, trn legs, 3-brd rpl top 275.00
Cherry w/curly maple drw, dvtl drw, trn legs, rpl 19" top 175.00
Cherry/birch Co Hplwht, well-shaped cut-out top, rpr/rfn 850.00
Cherry/birch Co Hplwht, 1-brd 17" top:drw, rpt over red............500.00
Cherry/curly maple Co, trn legs, bowfront drw, rpl 26" top 275.00
Cherry/mahog veneer Sheraton, 2-drw/trn legs/1-brd top, rfn 350.00

Curly maple Co Sheraton, bowfront dvtl drw, rpl 2-brd top 350.00
Curly maple Co Sheraton, trn legs, dvtl drw, 1-brd 22" top.........700.00
Drop leaf, birch Co Sheraton, 2-drw, EX trn, 17x22" top 375.00
Drop leaf, cherry w/EX old red pnt Co, 2 drw/EX trn 1,000.00
Mahog Hplwht, veneer aprons, serpentine 18x24" top, rfn.........700.00
Mahog w/inlay Fr Louis XV, ormolu/marble top, 1910, 31", pr...575.00
Maple Co Sheraton, some curl, 2 dvtl drw, 1-brd 17x19" top......500.00
Maple w/3 cherry drw Co Sheraton, trn legs, altered, 30x22"......420.00
Michigan Chair Co, magazine stand, 4 open shelves, 33" 225.00
Pine Co Hplwht, pencil legs, nailed drw, 2-brd top, VG..............350.00
Pine w/red rpt Co Hplwht, sq tapered legs, 1-brd 18" top 200.00
Pine w/red traces Co Hplwht, sq legs, dvtl drw, 2-brd top 275.00
Pine/butternut/poplar Co Hplwht w/red wash over wht, drw.......250.00
Plant, Adirondak, orig gr pnt w/orange & gold, 40x52" 550.00
Plant, rosewood w/marble top, 3 lg scrolls on base w/3 ft 1,600.00
Work, mahog/flame veneer Emp, 4 opal pulls, 18" top unfolds....425.00
Work, walnut/cherry Co Sheraton, 1-drw, 21" lift lid rpl.............400.00

Stool

Footstool, pine, worn gr pnt, primitive, 18" L................................75.00
Footstool, poplar w/red & blk grpt Co Sheraton, 12" L, pr 900.00
Footstool, Windsor, bamboo trn, blk rpt, oval top, 8" H..............200.00
Footstool, Windsor, pine w/blk pnt & striping, rpt top, sgn..........225.00
Footstool, Windsor, splay base, re-uphl, not period, 7x14" 175.00
Oak, worn finish, primitive, 9" dia top, 28" 75.00

Table

Tea table, carved oak, attributed to Charles Rohlfs, unsigned, refinished, 26" diameter, $1,800.00.

Banquet, cherry w/line inlay Hplwht, 17" sq leaves rpl, pr 1,800.00
Card, cherry/mahog veneer Co Sheraton, trn legs, D-top, rfn 650.00
Card, curly maple Hplwht, drw, rpl 34" sq top 900.00
Card, mahog/flame veneer w/inlay Emp, well-cvd paw ft, EX... 1,200.00
Card, mahog w/inlay Hplwht, sq legs, damage/rprs, 40" 600.00
Center, mahog Fr Empire, 38" marble top, triangular plinth ... 2,500.00
Cherry Co, cut-out curved legs, cracked 1-brd 20x34" top..........350.00
Console, burlwood, 3-volute support on stepped base, Fr, 43" 900.00
Console, cvd dolphin base w/worn gilt, chinoiserie top, rpr 2,100.00
Console, cvd/gilt Baroque w/faux marble top, cvgs, 65" 800.00
Console, gilt/rosewood Baroque, EX cvg on apron/4 legs, pr ... 3,100.00
Dressing, yel-pnt pine, mc fruit/foliage, trn legs, 36x35" 1,100.00
Drop leaf, cherry w/inlay Hplwht, 6-leg, rpl 47" top...................600.00
Drop leaf, mahog QA, duck ft, 15x46" top+17" leaves, rstr 400.00

Drop leaf, mahog QA, rnd legs/duck ft, 42x16" leaves, rpr 700.00
Drop leaf, maple w/some curl, 6x36" leaves, rpl top/rfn 425.00
Drop leaf, rosewood veneer Regency style, bronze ft, 34"............700.00
Drum, mahog Regency, drw-set frieze, 4 legs w/brass ft, 43" 2,600.00
FL Wright, bedside, spruce, ca 1950, 20x18" top, pr................ 1,300.00
FL Wright, dining, Heritage/Henredon, 4 L-legs join, 54" 1,600.00
FL Wright, end table w/triangular top, sgn/#d, EX 700.00
FL Wright, low w/sq top on block base, sgn/#d, 13x27" 800.00
G Nakashima, walnut 37" dia top on travertine cube base 550.00
Hardwood/pine Co QA, trn legs/button ft, rpl 23x31" top...... 2,400.00
Harvest, pine w/old red, sawbuck base, 1-brn 129" top, rpl..........975.00
Hutch, birch/pine Co, sq legs, 3-brd 35x40" cut-down top 550.00
Hutch, Co pine, cut-out 1-brd base ends, 1895, top cracked 700.00
Hutch, hardwood/pine, worn red on base, sq legs, 47" dia....... 3,000.00
Hutch, pine/poplar Co, hinged seat, 2-brd 40x62" top, EX 1,100.00
Limbert, #131, 30" 8-side top, 4 panel legs w/cutouts, mk 1,600.00
Limbert, #139, 48" 8-side top, 4 slab sides w/long cutouts....... 9,000.00
Limbert, #183, 48x33" top, dbl keyed, 2 cut-out panel sides ... 2,700.00
Limbert, library #165, corbels support top, mk, rfn, 44" 900.00
Limbert, library #166, 2-drw, 3-slat sides, 48", VG 1,100.00
Mahog Geo, 3-tier, ea w/trn ped on tripod slipper ft, 43" 1,000.00
Mahog w/inlay Hplwht, 1-drw w/orig hdw, rstr/rfn, 24" 700.00
Majorelle, library, 2-tier, inlaid floral border, 31x57x35" 7,700.00
Maple/bird's eye veneer w/edge inlay Co demi-lune, 40" 750.00
Parlor, Baroque cvd base, 1900s, 23x34" oval marble top 700.00
Pembroke, birch Co Hplwht, mortised/pinned, 44x14" leaves 400.00
Pembroke, cherry Co Sheraton, trn legs, 34x9" leaves, rfn 850.00
Pembroke, cherry/birch Hplwht, 10" D-form leaves, 42" 300.00
Pembroke, mahog w/inlay English Hplwht, rprs, 30x9" leaves.....875.00
Pembroke, mahog w/inlay Hplwht, sq legs/dvtl drw, rpl hdw 700.00
Pembroke, mahog w/inlay Hplwht, 11" D-form leaves, 32" 700.00
Pembroke, mahog w/line inlay Hplwht, orig hdw, 11" leaves . 1,300.00
Pickled oak Art Deco, sq top w/leather insert, 36" sq 250.00
Pine Co English Hplwht, bl rpt w/blk lines, 2-brd 30" top 700.00
Pine sawbuck, 1-brd edge-beaded 20x30" top, rfn 450.00
Pine w/red flame grpt Co Sheraton, trn legs, drw, 36" 450.00
Pine w/red rpt Co Hplwht, sq legs/splay base, 24" top worn.........675.00
Pine/poplar/blk flame grpt Co Hplwht, sq legs/30" 1-brd top .. 2,800.00
Refectory, hardwood Fr Francis I, rprs, 122"............................ 1,700.00
Sawbuck, pine w/traces of pnt, 2-brd 66" top, drw removed 450.00
Sewing, mahog Fed, fold-over top/3-drw, cvd knees, paw ft ... 3,750.00
Tavern, birch/pine Co QA, str trn legs, oval 1-brd 28" top..... 1,900.00
Tavern, cherry/pine Co QA, trn legs/button ft, 40", VG......... 2,900.00
Tavern, hardwood/pine Co, trn legs, rpl 30x40" top/ft, rpr..........250.00
Tavern, maple w/lt curl Co QA, red grpt base, 1-brd 27" top.. 4,900.00
Tavern, maple w/red traces, 1-brd 22x26" top, losses 400.00
Tavern, maple w/curl Co QA, scalloped apron, VG 22" top........750.00
Tavern, maple/lt curl Co QA, trn legs, oval 2-brd 30" top 3,500.00
Tavern, maple/pine Co QA, red traces, trn legs, 36"...................750.00
Tavern, maple/pine Co QA, 2-brd breadbrd top rpl, rfn/rstr.......695.00
Tavern, pine/hardwood Co QA w/red rpt, EX trn, rpl top....... 2,300.00
Tea, birch Chpndl, trn column, rpl birdcage/36" tilt top 600.00
Tea, curly maple Co, birdcage, rnd 3-brd 24" tilt top, EX 775.00
Tea, mahog Chpndl, 3-leg std/c&b ft, 33" serpentine top rpl 650.00
Tea, maple QA, 32" tray top, sm duck ft, much rstr/rpr............ 1,900.00
Work, curly maple/poplar w/pnt traces, 2-brd 46x30" top............550.00
Work, walnut Co QA, trn legs/duck ft, 2-drw, rpl 58" top..........400.00
Writing, Continental 1850s pnt w/birds, cabriole legs, 44" 1,500.00
Writing, figured walnut Louis XVI, ormolu mts, 42" 5,000.00

Washstand

Cherry Co Sheraton, gallery, base shelf, 4-brd rpl top..................325.00
Mahog w/burl veneer English, 3 trn legs, EX cvg, 32" H, EX.......225.00

Poplar Co, sq posts, base drw, solid scalloped top/gallery 150.00
Poplar w/comb grpt, alligatored, scalloped crest/base, 30"............600.00
Poplar w/old red Co, spool trn, drw/gallery, 22" W, EX 200.00
Tiger maple, bk splash, drw, rpl lower shelf, EX 500.00

Painted and decorated washstand, New England, ca 1830, minor paint loss, 41" x 15", $1,500.00.

Miscellaneous

Bed steps, pine/poplar w/worn grpt, trn & sq legs, 22" 600.00
Bin, poplar w/worn red & gr pnt, 2-compartment, 27x25"...........395.00
Dough box, poplar w/rpt, trn legs, dvtl lid/box, 39" L, EX 300.00
Etagere, rosewood/marble, Am Rococo, fancy crest, 90x60" ... 3,400.00
Hall seat, Limbert #79, 'bicycle' seat, ladder-like bk, EX.............550.00
Huntbrd, yel pine Co Hplwht, sq legs/2-drw, 50" W 3,400.00
Library steps, mahog Regency style, brass rails/casters.................800.00
Pole screen, mahog w/petit-point scene, English Regency, 61"....250.00

Galena

Pottery made in the Galena, Illinois, area was generally plain utility ware with lead glaze and often in a pumpkin color with some slip decoration or splashes of other colors. The potteries thrived from the early 1830s until sometime around 1860. In the listings that follow, all items are made of red clay unless noted otherwise.

Bowl, gr mottle w/orange spots, tooled lid, 3½x10", EX 160.00
Bowl, mixing; dk gr w/orange spots, stacking rim, 6x9½"..............150.00
Figure, dog, brn splashes on cream, rpr................................... 1,100.00
Figure, dog, open front legs, red clay/brn mottle, 9", VG 650.00
Figure, spaniel-like dog, seated, dk brn................................... 1,950.00
Flowerpot, unglazed, tooled band/crimped, w/saucer, 5x8" 250.00
Jar, canning; lt gr w/orange spots, rim chip, 8" 325.00
Jar, gr glaze w/amber spots, tooled line, 11", EX 150.00
Jar, gr glaze w/orange spots, bulbous lip, hdls, 13" 250.00
Jar, gr glaze/orange spots/brn flecks, 7", EX 225.00
Jar, gr w/orange spots, well-molded neck, 9" 625.00
Jar, 2-tone, cream & orange, 8½"...400.00
Jug, brn flecks, flared lip, appl hdl, 6" 55.00
Jug, flat bottom, gr w/orange spots, sm....................................425.00
Jug, gr mottled/2 rings of wht slip, tooled lip, 8½", EX.................400.00

Jug, gr w/orange splashes, ovoid, 12" **1,000.00**
Jug, gr/orange mottle, tooled lines, sloping shoulder, 6" **150.00**
Jug, lt/dk gr mottle w/few orange spots, tooled lip, 8½"...............**250.00**
Jug, orange overall, slightly ovoid, 10" **375.00**
Jug, orange/gr mottle w/brn flecks, ovoid, chips, 10½" **350.00**
Pitcher, gr/orange mottle, side spout, tooling, 5½".....................**230.00**

Galle

Emile Galle was one of the most important producers of cameo glass in France. His firm, founded in Nancy in 1874, produced beautiful cameo in the Art Nouveau style during the 1890s, using a variety of techniques. He also produced glassware with enameled decoration, as well as some fine pottery — animal figurines, table services, vases, and other objects d' art. In the mid-1880s he became interested in the various colors and textures of natural woods and as a result began to create furniture which he used as yet another medium for expression of his artistic talent. Marquetry was the primary method Galle used in decorating his furniture, preferring landscapes, Nouveau floral and fruit arrangements, butterflies, squirrels, and other forms from nature. It is for his furniture and his cameo glass that he is best known today. All Galle is signed. In the listings below, 'fp' indicates items that have been fire polished. Our advisor for this category is Don Williams; he is listed in the Directory under Missouri.

Cameo

Vase, fuchsias on yellow over deep violet, 6¾", $1,200.00.

Bottle, scent; ferns, gr on gr mottle, frost stopper, 4½" **2,200.00**
Bowl, trees/river, brn on peach to gr, boat form, 5x7" **1,400.00**
Bowl vase, berries, fp brn on wht frost/yel-gr, 2x2½".....................**425.00**
Box, floral/vines, yel/rust on pk frost, bowl base, 2½x5" **1,000.00**
Chandelier, tulips/dragonfly, orange on lt bl, rnd, 9" **6,600.00**
Jar, snowdrop blossoms, purple on lt gray, ftd, w/lid, 8" **1,800.00**
Lamp, candle; florals, gr/brn/red/orange, rtcl std, 7"................. **2,050.00**
Lamp, vintage, wine on pk dome shade/trumpet base, 17" **12,000.00**
Lamp base, dogwood, brn on yel, baluster, 14½" **1,300.00**
Lamp base, hydrangea, bl/gr dbl o/l on frost, slim, 12" **1,500.00**
Sconce, magnolias, red on yel, half rnd, iron scroll mts........... **6,000.00**
Shot glass, maple seeds, pk & gr on frost, 2½" **600.00**
Tumbler, 4-petal flower, wht/bl/gr on clear & pk, 2¾" **600.00**
Vase, autumn leaves/seed pods on mottle, hexagonal, 11½".... **3,250.00**
Vase, berries, purple on frost to yel, banjo form, 6½" **1,200.00**
Vase, berries/leaves, red on orange/frost mottle, 2½" **1,000.00**
Vase, blown-out clematis, brn/yel, 10x7" **13,000.00**

Vase, boats/birds/trees/lake, snails cvd on base, slim, 21" **8,000.00**
Vase, branches w/buds, brn on pk/yel, stick neck/ftd, 11" **800.00**
Vase, chestnut branches, dbl o/l, cylinder w/ball base, 10" **1,400.00**
Vase, clematis, bl/purple on gray, fp, ftd 6-side ovoid, 7"........ **2,400.00**
Vase, clematis, purple on lt yel, slim, 12" **1,500.00**
Vase, clematis cluster, dbl o/l, bulbous w/hdls at neck, 8" **2,600.00**
Vase, clematis/vines, bl on frost & lt pk, ftd, 6" **2,500.00**
Vase, columbine, cvd/HP on moss gr, silver floral rim, 8½" ... **2,000.00**
Vase, ferns, dbl o/l, cylindrical, pinched rim, 10x5" **2,000.00**
Vase, floral, brn on orange frost, stick neck, 5½" **1,300.00**
Vase, floral, brn/gr on peach & wht frost, ftd, 3½x3".................**800.00**
Vase, floral, burgundy on orange frost, tapered form, 7" **1,700.00**
Vase, floral branches, orange on wht, bulb w/can neck, 4" **400.00**
Vase, floral branches, wine on pk, ovoid w/collar neck, 6" **700.00**
Vase, fuchsia, bright gr on lt pk frost, star mk, 10" **1,000.00**
Vase, hyacinth, brn on yel, slim form, 7" **600.00**
Vase, hydrangea branches, gr/brn dbl o/l on pk, 10" **2,600.00**
Vase, hydrangeas, lav & purple on pk to wht frost, 6½" **1,650.00**
Vase, lg hazelnut branches, amber on bl, flattened/ftd, 9" **2,000.00**
Vase, lilies, tan on ice bl frost, inverted cylinder, 19" **1,700.00**
Vase, mtn scene, turq/bl on wht/gold, bowling-pin form, 8".... **3,000.00**
Vase, orchids, brn on yel/gr mottle, tapered cylinder, 7" **1,300.00**
Vase, pine cones, brn on wht frost, squat w/stick neck, 4½".... **1,600.00**
Vase, pods/lg leaves, gr/brn dbl o/l on pk, slim, 16" **2,600.00**
Vase, poppies, fp rust on bl, cylindrical w/bun base, 18" **3,000.00**
Vase, poppies, orange on gray, fp, cylindrical, 9" **1,500.00**
Vase, Queen Anne's Lace, gr/brn dbl o/l on pk, slim, 12".......... **1,600.00**
Vase, roses/leaves, burgundy on amber, bbl form, 6" **3,000.00**
Vase, ships at sea, yel cased in clear/amber, fp, baluster, 5" **1,600.00**
Vase, spider mums, fp/cut/HP, rim w/yel & bl patina, 13" **4,000.00**
Vase, trees, brn/gr on peach/wht frost, scalloped, 11x6" **5,250.00**
Vase, trees/mtns, bl/purple dbl o/l on yel, pear form, 7" **1,600.00**
Vase, water lilies, bl/brn dbl o/l on amber, ftd, 7" **1,400.00**
Vase, water plants, brn on cream, flask w/crescent rim, 5" **1,200.00**
Vase, water plants, gr on gold, pinched, 9¾x5" **2,500.00**
Vase, wildflowers, purple on pk, cylinder w/bun ft, 8" **2,000.00**
Vase, wisteria on wht frost, banjo shape, 5" **1,050.00**

Enameled Glass

Bottle, scent; lake scene w/man & boat, sq form, 4¾" **1,980.00**
Cup & saucer, thistles/cross on lt amber, ftd **850.00**
Decanter, bow-tied festoons/dragonflies, 8", +7" underbowl ... **4,000.00**
Decanter, thistles, pk/wine on amber w/gilt, w/hdl, 8"............. **1,300.00**
Ewer, wildflower sprays on lt amber w/gilt inclusions, 8" **2,200.00**
Pitcher, red/brn mottle w/appl gr serpent hdl, floral, 3" **1,650.00**
Vase, prunus/strapwork, appl prunts on lt tan, sgn, 10" **1,500.00**

Marquetry, Wood

Pedestal, 2-shelf, floral inlay, 45x16"...................................... **4,500.00**
Table, bird/oak leaves on scalloped top, 4 legs, 25" dia............ **1,500.00**
Table, corners w/Oriental scene & geometrics, 28x22x17" **1,800.00**
Table, floral inlay top, floriform legs, 4: 16" to 29" **11,000.00**
Table, orchids inlay, rtcl leafy panel at base, 30x28x16" **2,750.00**
Table, tea; lake scene, lower shelf: floral inlay, 30x36" **6,500.00**
Table, tea; 2 floral/dragonfly inlaid tiers, 34x33x23" **4,000.00**
Table, 2-tier, maple leaves/floral inlay, 29x26" **2,000.00**
Vitrine, rtcl lily-pad gallery/apron, inlaid floral, 58x26".........**20,000.00**

Pottery

Centerpc, florals, gr/red/brn on wht, basket form, 7½" L **1,000.00**
Compote, unicorn on lt bl, 9" dia, pr **1,500.00**

Dish, butterfly/bamboo/gilt, mc on cream, sled form, 5¾" 770.00
Figurine, owl, brn/wht/blk/earth tones, on rnd base, 13" **4,000.00**
Gravy boat, floral/dragonflies on bl, dk bl/yel bands, 10" 385.00
Inkwell, Oriental couple pulls fabric between them, 18" L **2,000.00**

Gambling Memorabilia

Gambling memorabilia from the infamous casinos of the West and items that were once used on the 'Floating Palace' riverboats are especially sought after by today's collectors.

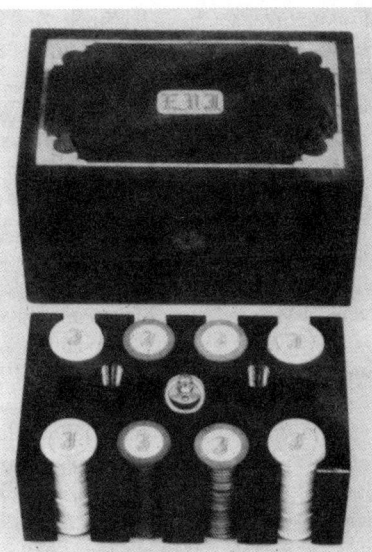

Cased set of 198 engraved ivory poker chips, red or blue and white with engraved initial, rosewood case with brass inlay, EX, $1,900.00.

Booklet, playing cards; Stanley Cohen, 1916, 31-pg 60.00
Caddy, poker chip; inlaid mahog, some damage, 12" L 275.00
Cash drawer, oak, 1800s, 5½x18x13½", EX, +3 keys 300.00
Catalog, C Caro, Paris, gambling equipment, 1902, 86-pg...........175.00
Cheating device, placed on forearm to release card, EX..............650.00
Chip, Bakelite, various colors, 18 for 12.50
Chip, compo, emb horse & jockey, red/wht/bl, 24 for 15.00
Chip, geometrics on pressed clay, 20 for 10.00
Chip, ivory, scrimshaw dmn, brn border ....·..........27.50
Chip, ivory, scrimshaw 25 ....48.00
Chip, single-wing plane on pressed clay, 15 for 5.00
Chips, Famous Jockey Club, complete set, MIB 45.00
Dice cage, NP brass post, Rott Games, NYC, 12x4½", EX...........100.00
Keno goose, oak, w/balls, EX..550.00
Marker, MOP, yel #1, lav #5, rose #20, set of 3 ....38.00
Snooker score counter, celluloid, Whitehead & Hoag, 1905 ....60.00
Visor, gr celluloid, old, EX..25.00
Wheel, hazzard; wood w/CI spokes in base & top...........................300.00
Wheel, roulette; Rottgames Co, Bakelite holder, 14", EX..............25.00
Wheel, roulette; traveling type, 1900s, EX 195.00
Wheel, roulette; w/claw-ft table, EX... **3,200.00**

Game Calls

Those interested in hunting and fishing collectibles are beginning to take notice of the finer specimens of game calls available on today's market. Our advisor for this category is Randy Hilst; he is listed in the Directory under Illinois.

Early duck calls, left: Warner Wiles, $65.00; right: Bill Willis, $50.00.

Crow, Charles Perdew, cedar...100.00
Crow, Fred Allen, wood...40.00
Crow, Irving Lohman, wood 10.00
Crow, PS Olt, V-16 Junior Model, hard rubber 30.00
Crow, Tom Turpin, wood...100.00
Crow, Yentzen, wood..10.00
Duck, Andy Bowles, wood...250.00
Duck, Bill Clifford, laminated wood 150.00
Duck, Charles Perdew, cvd ducks, wood 1,500.00
Duck, Charles Perdew, 2 silver bands, wood.............................300.00
Duck, Earl Dennison, wood 75.00
Duck, Jim Slack, ear of corn replica, wood.................................50.00
Duck, PS Olt, model D-2 (rnd hole), hard rubber 30.00
Duck, Tube Dawson, checkered wood 300.00
Duck, Wayne Meyer, cvd ducks, wood bbl...............................150.00
Goose, Charles Grubbs, wood...300.00
Goose, PS Olt, A-5 Model, hard rubber 40.00
Predator, Burnham Bros, plastic..10.00
Predator, Weems, wood 10.00
Turkey, PS Olt, F-6 Model, cedar...50.00

Gameboards

Gameboards, the handmade ones from the 18th and 19th century, are collected more for their folk art quality than their relation to games. Excellent examples of these handcrafted 'playthings' sell well into the thousands of dollars; even the simple designs are often expensive. If you are interested in this field, you must study it carefully. The market is always full of 'new' examples. Well-established dealers are often your best sources; they are essential if you do not have the expertise to judge the age of the boards yourself.

Checkers, blk/brn w/yel edge, blk appl lip, 1890s, 20x20" **1,000.00**
Checkers, maroon/yel, gilt scrolls on blk border, 1880s **1,300.00**
Checkers, peach border w/red & gr pretzels/stars, 1800s.......... **1,800.00**
Checkers, pine w/3-color pnt, lt wear, 28x16" 250.00
Checkers, pine w/4-color pnt, 17x18"..350.00
Checkers, poplar w/5-color pnt, 16" sq 375.00
Checkers, red/blk rpt, 18x31" 275.00
Checkers, red/blk sqs, gr/blk border, 1800s, 18" **1,100.00**
Checkers, red/blk w/molded gilt edge, 20th C, 11½x11½"...........125.00
Checkers, rvpt, gold leaf w/blk & mc, fr, 21x21"..........................100.00
Parchesi, orange/gr/blk, bk: checkers, 1800s, 19x20"...................850.00

Games and Puzzles

Game collectors are finding it more difficult to find their treasures at shows and flea markets. Most of the action these days seems to be through specialty dealers and auctions. The appreciation of the art on the boards and boxes continues to grow. You see many of the early games proudly displayed as art, and they should be. The period from the 1850s to 1910 continues to draw the most interest. Many of the games of that period were executed by well-known artists and illustrators. The quality of their lithography cannot be matched today. The historical value of games made before 1850 has caused interest in this period to increase. While they may not have the graphic quality of the later period, their insights into the social and moral character of the early 19th century are interesting.

20th-century games invoke a nostalgic feeling among collectors who recall looking forward to a game under the Christmas tree each year. They search for examples that bring back those Christmas morning memories. While the quality of their lithography is certainly less than the early games, the introduction of personalities from the comic strips, radio and later TV created new interest. Every child wanted a game that featured their favorite character. Monopoly, probably the most famous game ever produced, was introduced during the Great Depression. This year a Charles B. Darrow version (he later sold his game to Parker Bros.) of Monopoly, circa 1934, went for $2,400.00.

The auction market for games continues to expand. Prices remained strong for the year. 63% of the games sold at auction went well above estimates. 16% were sold within the estimate range, and 21% sold below estimate.

Jigsaw puzzles have been around almost as long as games. The first examples were handcrafted from wood, and they are extremely difficult to find. Most of the early examples featured moral subjects just as the board games did. By the 1890s jigsaw puzzles had become a major form of home entertainment. In the Depression years, jigsaw puzzles were set up on card tables in almost every home. The early wood examples are the most valuable.

Cube puzzles, or blocks, were often made by the same companies as the board games. Again, early examples display the finest quality of lithography. While all subjects are collectible, some (such as Santa blocks) often command prices higher than games from the same period.

Antique American Games by Lee Dennis provides an excellent overview of games from 1840-1940. *The Games People Played* (Collectors Showcase, January/February) by Earnie and Ida Long is an excellent review of 19th-century games and historical material on games in general. See also Personalities.

Games

At the Front, Milton Bradley, lithographed paper-on-cardboard soldiers, cast iron echo guns, wooden ammunition, VG, $900.00.

Air Raid Warden, Milton Bradley, 1943, EX	75.00
Army Air Corps, Parker Bros, 1942, EX	75.00

Beverly Hillbillies, Milton Bradley, 1963, NM	18.00
Bruce Jenner Decathlon, Parker Bros, 1979, M	15.00
Carrom, w/stand & rule book dtd 1899, +cloth bags w/pcs	125.00
Casper the Friendly Ghost, Milton Bradley, 1959, EX	20.00
Chiromagica, McLoughlin Bros, wooden box, 1870s, EX	750.00
Christmas Mail, Ottman litho, ca 1905, G	200.00
Columbo, Milton Bradley, 1973, M	30.00
Dewey's Victory, Parker Bros, wooden box, ca 1900, EX	425.00
District Messenger Boy, brd game, ca 1886, EX	175.00
Donkey Game, Milton Bradley, ca 1905, EX	60.00
Donkey Party, 1941, EX	12.00
Fairyland Game, Milton Bradley, 1880s, EX in box	150.00
Fast Mail, Milton Bradley, wooden box, ca 1900, EX	100.00
Favorite Steeple Chase, JH Singer, 1895, EX	600.00
Flying US Air Mail, brd game, Parker Bros, 1929, MIB	100.00
Fortune Teller, Milton Bradley, VG	55.00
Game of Balloon, Bliss, dvtl/hinged box, 1889, EX	500.00
Game of Bicycle Race, McLoughlin Bros, wood box, 1895, EX	850.00
Game of Bobb, McLoughlin Bros, wooden box, 1898, EX	425.00
Game of Cat, Chafee & Selchow, wooden box, 1898, EX	200.00
Game of Familiar Quotations, ca 1888, EX	25.00
Game of Golf, Clark, Tokalon Series #352, 1905, EX	475.00
Game of Golf, McLoughlin Bros, wooden box, 1896, EX	750.00
Game of Man in Moon, McLoughlin Bros, wood box, '01, EX	4,600.00
Game of Telegraph Boy, McLoughlin, wood box, 1888, EX	1,000.00
Game of US Geography, Parker Bros, 1963, NM	20.00
Game of Visit of Santa Claus, McLoughlin, ca 1899, EX	1,900.00
Game of Watermelon Patch, McLoughlin Bros, 1890, EX	2,250.00
Great American Flag Game, Parker Bros, 1940, complete	40.00
Gunfight at OK Corral, older version, EX	15.00
Hearts Dice, letter game, Parker Bros, 1914, EX	22.50
Hurdle Race, Milton Bradley, ca 1905, G	275.00
Jan Murray's Treasure Hunt, NM	40.00
Kentucky Derby Racing Game, 1938, NM	15.00
Land of the Lost	60.00
Limited Mail & Express, Parker Bros, wood box, 1894, EX	650.00
Lindy Hop-Off, Parker Bros, ca 1927, 25-pc, EX	375.00
Little Drummer, Ottman, ca 1907, VG	90.00
Little Red Schoolhouse, 1952, EX	35.00
London Game, Parker Bros, wooden box, 1898, EX	700.00
Man in Moon, brd game, McLoughlin Bros, '01, EX in box	3,500.00
Merry Christmas, Milton Bradley, ca 1905-10, G	600.00
Monopoly, Chas B Darrow, ca 1934, rules on box, EX	2,400.00
No Time for Sergeants, Parker Bros, EX	20.00
North Pole Game, Milton Bradley, ca 1905, complete, EX	475.00
Peg Baseball, Parker Bros, all orig, EX	55.00
Rival Policemen, McLoughlin Bros, wooden box, 1896, EX	1,600.00
Rough Riders, EO Clark, ca 1900, EX in box	300.00
Round the World, mc litho brd, Milton Bradley, 1912, EX	200.00
Siege of Havana, Parker Bros, 1898, wooden box, EX	475.00
Spoof, Milton Bradley, 1918, EX	28.00
Steeple Chase, EO Clark, ca 1905, EX in box	100.00
Table croquet, paper litho label, ca 1890, 12½x6½", G	25.00
Tiddly Winks, Milton Bradley, 1932	15.00
Tom Hamilton's Pigskin Game, 1935, EX	65.00
Touring, Parker Bros, 1937, EX	15.00
Tourist, A Railroad Game, Milton Bradley, G	200.00
Trip Round World, McLoughlin Bros, wood box, 1897, EX	1,200.00
Uncle Wiggily, Milton Bradley, 1961, NM	68.00
Vanderbilt Cup, Ottman, orig directions, complete, 1905	650.00
World Educator, Reed Toy Co, 1897, EX	125.00
Yankee Doodle, Parker Bros, wooden box, ca 1895, EX	650.00
Yankee Trader, 1941, EX	35.00
Zippy Zepps, Alderman Fairchild, ca 1925, EX	325.00

Puzzles

Locomotive puzzle, McLoughlin Bros., in wooden box, VG, $400.00.

Artistic Cubes Puzzle, 1892, EX in box	200.00
Aunt Louisa's Cube puzzle, Puss 'n Boots, McLoughlin, EX	135.00
Barnyard scene, Built Rite, EX	5.00
Children gargling Listerine, cb, 1930s, 11x13¾", NM	20.00
Deco lady w/parrot, litho on wood, 1930s, 8¼x5¼", EX	15.00
Fairy Tale Puzzles, Platt & Munk, ca 1963, set of 4, MIB	12.50
Gibson girls in bathing suits, litho on wood, 1909, 4x8"	32.00
Katzenjammer Kids, 4 in set, 1920s, EX in box	75.00
Map of Ohio, worn litho on wood, 12½x16"	185.00
Model Ship, cb, sailing vessel, Milton Bradley, 22x17", EX	60.00
Mother Goose Scroll Puzzle, McLoughlin Bros, 1890s, 10x8"	55.00
Pigs, Jamar, EX	5.00
Puppies Picture Puzzles, Saalfield, '41, set of 3, EX in box	10.00
Put-Together Puzzle Book, S Gabriel Sons, '20s, 8½x11", EX	15.00
United States Spelling, 1889, EX in box	120.00
Up the Heights of San Juan, McLoughlin, ca 1900, 13½x18"	250.00
White Sewing Machine, dbl sided, ca 1883, EX	150.00

G. A. R. Memorabilia

The 'The Grand Army of the Republic' was first conceived by Chaplain W.J. Rutledge and Major B.J. Stephenson early in 1864 when they were tent-mates during our own Civil War. These men vowed to each other that if they were spared they would establish an organization that would preserve friendships and memories formed during this time. Shortly after the war ended, Rutledge and Stephenson made their desires a reality. The first National Convention of the Grand Army of the Republic was held in Indianapolis, Indiana, on November 20, 1866. The purpose of the organization was to provide aid and assistance to the widows and orphans of the fallen Union dead and to care for the hospitalized veterans as needed. The last comrade of the G.A.R. died in 1949.

Many items are surfacing from the early encampments which were held on both state and national levels, resulting in a wide variety of souvenir items having been made.

Badge, membership; eagle atop pin, flag ribbon, star drop	25.00
Badge, 50th Anniversary of Gettysburg, shield drop, EX	30.00
Book, Rules & Regulations..., Heath, 1886, EX	35.00
Booklet, Abe the War Eagle, 1899, 4x5", EX	35.00
Cabinet photo, man in GAR dress w/wife, EX	15.00
Canteen, emb portraits on NP brass, 1891 reunion, M	165.00
Cup, tin, 42nd Nat'l Encampment 1903 pnt on side, 3½"	85.00
Drum, Leedy Mfg, Indianapolis, 1892, 15½" dia, EX	225.00
Flag holder, CI, bugle & drumsticks at top, 7x10"	25.00
Medal, Woman's Relief Corps membership, 1884, 4x1½"	15.00
Paperweight, State Memorial Statue at Gettysburg, glass, 3"	22.50
Post card, mother & children at cemetery w/flag, 1915, NM	3.00
Post card, photo of Lincoln Monument, 1907, M	3.50
Program, NH Veterans...15th Encampment, 1926, 9x12", EX	12.50
Ribbon, 30th Reunion, eagle at top, 1915, EX	12.50
Sheet Music, I Love the Whole United States, 1913, EX	12.50

Gas Globes and Panels

Gas globes and panels, once a common sight, have vanished from the countryside but are being sought by collectors as a unique form of advertising memorabilia. Early globes from the 1920s, now referred to as 'one-piece globes,' were made of molded milk glass and were globular in shape. The gas company name was etched or painted on the glass. Few of these were ever produced, and this type is valued very highly by collectors today.

A new type of pump was introduced in the early 1930s; the old 'visible' pumps were replaced by 'electric' models. Globes were changing at the same time. By the mid-thirties a five-piece globe consisting of a pair of inserts, two retaining rings, and a metal body was being produced in both 15" and 16½" sizes. Collectors prefer to call globes that are not one-piece or plastic 'three-piece glass' (Type 2) or 'metal body, glass inserts' (Type 3). Though metal body globes (Type 3) were popular in the 1930s, they were common in the 1920s, and some were actually made as early as 1915. Though rare in numbers, their use spans many years. In the 1930s Type 2 and Type 3 globes became the replacements of the one-piece globe. The most recently manufactured gas globes, used since the late 1940s, are made with a plastic body that contains two 13½" glass lenses.

Note: Standard Crowns with raised letters are one-piece globes that were made in the 1920s; those made in the 1950s (no raised letters), though one-piece, are not regarded as such by today's collectors. Both variations are listed below.

Our advisor for this category is Scott Benjamin; he is listed in the Directory under California.

Type 1, Plastic Body, Glass Inserts – 1931-1950s

Ashland Diesel	150.00
Champlin	125.00
D-X Marine, rare	325.00
Deeprock	125.00
Dixie, plastic band	125.00
DX Ethyl	150.00
DX Lubricating Gasoline, tan body	175.00
Falcon	350.00
Frontier Gas, Rarin' To Go, w/horse	250.00
Marathon, no runner	125.00
Marine, sea horse, EX color	325.00
Never Nox Ethyl	175.00
Shamrock, oval body	150.00
Shamrock, w/clover	150.00
Spur	125.00
Texaco Sky Chief	150.00
Viking, pictures Viking ship	250.00

Wood River	125.00
66 Flite Fuel, Phillips, shield shape	250.00

Type 2, Glass Frame, Glass Inserts – 1926-1940s

American	250.00
Atlantic Hi-Arc, glass gill body	300.00
Coltex Service Gasoline, unused	250.00
Derby	300.00
Esso	200.00
Frontier Gas, no horse	225.00
Gulf	250.00
Guyler Brand, milk glass, 18", EX	600.00
Indian Gas, Red Dot	400.00
Koolmotor, clover shape	400.00
Mobil Gas	300.00
Pure	275.00
Shell, milk glass, clam shape	350.00
Shell, shell shape, red letters	325.00
Sinclair Dino, milk glass, EX	175.00
Sinclair H-C, narrow glass body, Red Dot	300.00
Sinclair Pennant	400.00
Skelly Anomarx w/Ethyl	350.00
Skelly Powermax	300.00
Spartan	300.00
Standard Crown, bl	500.00
Standard Crown, green or orange, each	600.00
Standard Crown, wht, red, or gold, each	350.00
Texaco Diesel Chief	350.00
Texaco Ethyl	375.00
Texaco Star, blk outline on 'T'	325.00
Trophy, Our Premium Gasoline	300.00
White Flash, gill body	275.00
White Rose, glass body, 13½"	375.00
WNAX	550.00

Type 3, Metal Frame, Glass Inserts – 1915-1930s

White Star, refinished metal frame, General Ethyl face on reverse, 19", EX, $400.00.

Atlantic Ethyl, 16½"	350.00
Atlantic White Flash, 16½"	350.00
Cities Services Oils, 15" metal fr, 1929	350.00
Crown, crown figural w/red traces, 16", EX	700.00
Essolene, 16"	325.00
General Ethyl, 15" metal frame, complete	650.00
Happy Gas, metal band, 16½"	350.00
Mobil Gas, winged horse, metal fr, NM	400.00
Mobilfuel Diesel, lg horse, high profile, metal band	425.00

Pure, porc body, 15"	400.00
Purol Gasoline, w/arrow, porc body	650.00
Purol Pep, porc body	500.00
Red Crown Ethyl	425.00
Richfield	400.00
Rocor, w/eagle, metal fr	450.00
Signal, rstr metal fr, 15", VG	1,800.00
Socony, milk glass inserts	650.00
Sunland Ethyl, 15"	450.00
Sunoco, 15", pr	300.00
Texaco Leaded, glass panels, in fr, pr	2,200.00
Tidex, 16"	350.00
Tydol, cast faces, 15"	600.00
Tydol, 16½"	350.00
White Star, 15" metal fr, complete	650.00

Type 4, One-Piece Glass Globes, No Inserts, Co. Name Etched, Raised or Enameled – 1914-1931

Atlantic, chimney cap	2,200.00
Champlin Gasoline	1,000.00
Diamond	650.00
Dixie, etched, 1-pc	1,000.00
Gasoline, emb on dk gr ground, 14", NM	400.00
Iowa Gas	1,100.00
Mobil Oil Gargoyle, emb, red & blk details, 12", EX	1,200.00
Musgo	3,000.00
Pierce Pennant, etched	1,800.00
Red Crown, rnd, etched	2,500.00
Republic, 3-sided, 1-pc	750.00
Shell, rnd, etched	450.00
Sinclair, etched, milk glass	750.00
Sinclair Aircraft, etched	2,500.00
Sinclair Aircraft, pnt	1,800.00
Sinclair H-C, pnt	650.00
Skelly	600.00
Standard Red Crown Ethyl, emb letters	700.00
Super Shell, clam shape	800.00
Super Shell, rnd, etched	1,800.00
Texaco, milk glass, emb letters, brass collar	700.00
Texaco Ethyl	950.00
That Good Gulf..., emb, orange & blk letters, EX	650.00
White Eagle, eagle shape, blunt nose	800.00
White Rose, pnt	1,700.00

Gaudy Dutch

Inspired by Oriental Imari wares, Gaudy Dutch was made in England from 1800 to 1820. It was hand decorated on a soft-paste body with rich underglaze blues accented in orange, red, pink, green, and yellow. It differs from Gaudy Welsh in that there is no lustre (except on Water Lily). There are seventeen patterns, some of which are: War Bonnet, Grape, Dahlia, Oyster, Urn, Butterfly, Carnation, Single Rose, Double Rose, and Water Lily. For further information we recommend the *Collector's Encyclopedia of Gaudy Dutch & Welsh* by John Shuman.

Butterfly, bowl, 6"	600.00
Butterfly, pitcher, milk; 4", M	825.00
Butterfly, plate, butterfly on side, 8⅜", M	900.00
Butterfly, sugar bowl	1,700.00
Butterfly Variant, creamer, 3¾"	1,200.00
Butterfly Variant, deep dish, 8"	425.00
Butterfly Variant, plate, 10"	850.00

Butterfly variant, flakes on lid, 5¾", $1,200.00.

Carnation, creamer, 4¾" 550.00
Carnation, plate, 10" 1,100.00
Carnation, plate, 7¼", M 550.00
Carnation, sugar bowl 800.00
Carnation, teapot 1,350.00
Dahlia, creamer..900.00
Dahlia, plate, rare, 8½" 2,100.00
Double Rose, creamer, squat, 3½" 575.00
Double Rose, creamer, 5" 575.00
Double Rose, cup & saucer 525.00
Double Rose, jug, mask spout, dk beard, 6" 1,500.00
Double Rose, pitcher, 8" 1,300.00
Double Rose, plate, 10"....................................800.00
Double Rose, plate, 9", M 900.00
Double Rose, platter, 10½" 2,700.00
Double Rose, platter, 15" 3,300.00
Double Rose, sugar bowl, w/lid, 5" 900.00
Dove, creamer, lt stains/flaking, spout chip, 5" 450.00
Dove, creamer, pear form, 4½" 650.00
Dove, creamer, squat, 4" 375.00
Dove, plate, plain border, 6¼", M 500.00
Dove, plate, 10", M...900.00
Dove, plate, 8", M...575.00
Dove, teapot, 7½" 600.00
Dove, toddy plate 700.00
Grape, pitcher, 8" 2,200.00
Grape, plate, 10" 600.00
Grape, platter, 15" 900.00
Grape, teapot 700.00
Oyster, coffeepot, dome lid, 11½" 1,900.00
Oyster, creamer...400.00
Oyster, plate, 8½" 475.00
Primrose, 'Riley' plate, 10" 2,400.00
Primrose, sugar bowl 900.00
Single Rose, coffeepot, dome lid, 11" 5,200.00
Single Rose, creamer, 4½" 550.00
Single Rose, deep dish, 10"..............................625.00
Single Rose, plate, 10"....................................600.00
Single Rose, plate, 6½" 235.00
Single Rose, plate, 7¼", M 500.00
Single Rose, sugar bowl, rnd, age line 625.00
Single Rose, tea bowl & saucer 300.00
Strawflower, plate, 8½" 825.00
Strawflower, soup plate, EX..............................800.00
Sunflower, coffeepot, spout rstr, 9½" 1,500.00
Sunflower, creamer, bulbous, 4½" 775.00
Sunflower, plate, 10" 950.00
Urn, plate, wear/some flaking, 10" 600.00

Urn, plate, 8¼", M 625.00
Urn, tea bowl & saucer, lt stain/sm flakes............400.00
Urn Variant, plate, 10"....................................600.00
War Bonnet, creamer, 4" 550.00
War Bonnet, cup plate 650.00
War Bonnet, deep dish, 9½" 1,400.00
War Bonnet, plate, 9½" 525.00
War Bonnet, soup plate 700.00
War Bonnet, toddy plate, 8"..............................800.00
Zinnia, 'Riley' plate, 10" 1,100.00
Zinnia, plate, deep, 9¾" 1,125.00

Gaudy Ironstone

Gaudy Ironstone was produced in the mid-1800s in Staffordshire, England. Some of the ware was decorated in much the same colors and designs as Gaudy Welsh, while other pieces were painted in pink, orange, and red with black and light blue accents. Lustre was used on some designs, omitted on others. The heavy ironstone body is its most distinguishing feature.

Key:
pc — polychrome   ug bl — underglaze blue

Bowl & pitcher, floral, bl/wht, 14" dia; 12", EX............................425.00
Cup & saucer, floral, pc/purple lustre, no hdl, EX 50.00
Cup & saucer, floral, ug bl/red & gr enamel, Adams, EX 35.00
Cup & saucer, Strawberry, pc/ug bl/purple lustre, no hdl............100.00
Dish, Strawberry, copper/pk lustre, w/lid, 8-sided, 9½", EX 300.00
Pitcher, floral, dragon hdl, octagonal, 6", pr.............................350.00
Pitcher, Morning-Glory, paneled, ug bl, 8".................................210.00
Plate, toddy; Urn, ug bl/pc/lustre, 4¾" 175.00
Plate, vintage, ug bl/pc/lustre, minor stains, 8" 60.00
Platter, Morning-Glory, ug bl/gr, red/blk enamel, 14", EX 250.00
Platter, rose, 4-color, mk England, 13" 175.00
Waste bowl, floral, ug bl/pc/purple lustre, 5" 165.00

Gaudy Welsh

Gaudy Welsh was an inexpensive hand-decorated ware made in both England and Wales from 1820 until 1860. It is characterized by its colors — principally underglaze blue, orange-rust, and copper lustre — and by its uninhibited patterns. Accent colors may be yellow and green. (Pink lustre may be present, since lustre applied to the white areas appears pink. A copper tone develops from painting lustre onto the dark colors.) The body of the ware may be heavy ironstone, creamware, earthenware, or porcelain; even style and shapes vary considerably. Patterns, while usually floral, are also sometimes geometric and may have trees and birds. Beware! The Wagon Wheel pattern has been reproduced.

Columbine, cup & saucer 95.00
Daisy & Chain, creamer & sugar bowl, w/lid................................150.00
Daisy & Chain, teapot 200.00
Feather, cup & saucer 50.00
Feather, plate, 8" 65.00
Flower Basket, mug, hdl...150.00
Flower Basket, plate, 9" 150.00
Grape, creamer, 4" 50.00
Grape & Lily, cup & saucer...90.00
Morning-Glory, cheese dish 135.00
Morning-Glory, plate, 8" 85.00
Oyster, bowl, 8"..150.00

Oyster, cup & saucer..80.00
Oyster, pitcher, 3½x3¼" 90.00
Oyster, plate, dessert; 6" 60.00

Oyster mug, $145.00.

Pagoda, pitcher, 5⅝"..100.00
Strawberry, plate, 8¼" 150.00
Tulip, creamer, 5¼" 110.00
Tulip, cup & saucer..90.00
Tulip, teapot, ornate lid, 7¼" 235.00
Tulip, waste bowl, 6⅜" 110.00
Urn, tureen, 9½"..275.00
Wagon Wheel, mug, 2¾" 85.00
Wagon Wheel, pitcher, 8½"......................................225.00
Wagon Wheel, plate, 7½"..90.00

Geisha Girl

Upon the discovery of tea in China some four thousand years ago, civilization was beset with a small problem — what to use in serving this special beverage. One solution came in the form of 'Geisha Girl' porcelain. At the end of the 19th century, this lovely type of Japanese tea service found its way to the west. Produced in more than 312 patterns, this fine porcelain features geishas going about the everyday activities of Japanese life. Mt. Fuji is very often included in the background along with a wide variety of flora and fauna. Though some items were entirely hand painted and others were hand decorated over decals, most were made by the raised stencil method, embellished by hand painting. Tea sets, snack sets, table wares, children's dishes, salt and pepper shakers, and even such items as mustache cups may be found. Pieces were bordered in one of many bright colors, among them red, yellow, blue, green, or brown. (Colors mentioned in the descriptions that follow refer to border colors.) As interest continues to climb, so will the values. For further information, we recommend *The Collector's Encyclopedia of Geisha Girl Porcelain* by Elyce Litts, available at your local bookstore or from Collector Books.

Key:
#2 — Torii	#68 — SGK China, Occupied
#4 — T in Cherry Blossom	Japan
#11 — diaper mk	J #1 — Yachi
#12 — Royal Kaga	J #6 — Tashiro
#16 — SNB	J #16 — Kutani
#19 — Japan	J #19 — Ozan
#20 — Made in Japan	J #36 — Made by Kato
#35 — Plum Blossom	J #46 — Yasutera
#42 — Vantine	

Biscuit jar, Carp A, ftd, red-orange w/gold......................75.00
Bonbon, Bamboo Trellis, red w/gold..............................45.00

Bowl, Dragonboat, cobalt w/gold, 8" 35.00
Bowl, master berry; Porch, cobalt w/gold 20.00
Bowl, rice; Carp D, red 12.00
Bowl, salad; Fan A, 4-lobed, 3 reserves, red w/yel..............40.00
Box, Parasol D, egg form, red-orange, #20, 4½x3¾x3½" 28.00
Butter pat, Basket of Mums, red-orange w/gold, 3¼" 8.00

Child's plate, Long Stemmed Peony, red border, marked Made in Japan, Ryu Studio, 4⅜", $12.00.

Compote, Child Reaching for Butterfly, hdld, #20, 3½x7½" 30.00
Creamer, Garden Bench G, mc border, J#19, w/lid, 4"..............28.00
Creamer & sugar bowl, Fan B, dk gr................................25.00
Cup & saucer, cocoa; Basket B, fluted, dk apple gr w/gold 25.00
Cup & saucer, cocoa; Footbridge B, ribbed, red w/gold 25.00
Cup & saucer, demi; Chrysanthemum Garden, red, J#16...............25.00
Cup & saucer, tea; Bicycle Race, red-orange w/gold....................30.00
Cup & saucer, tea; Blue Hoo, child's sz............................15.00
Cup & saucer, tea; Kite A, brn w/gold 15.00
Egg cup, Cricket Cage, red-orange 12.00
Hair receiver, Battledore, dk apple gr w/gold......................35.00
Jar, cracker; Writing A, melon ribbed, ftd, cobalt w/gold 100.00
Mug, Bamboo Trellis, red w/gold buds, #19, 4x3" 26.00
Mustard jar, Lesson, red w/gold, J#1..............................15.00
Nut dish, Shell Game, ftd, red w/gold & tan, J#46 .... 7.00
Pitcher, water; Fishing A, red-orange w/yel, 11".....................85.00
Plate, Circle Dance, swirl fluted, red-orange w/yel, 6¼"..............18.00
Plate, Inside the Teahouse, swirl fluted, apple gr, 8½"..............35.00
Plate, Wait for Me, flower form, red-orange w/gold, 8¾" 26.00
Pot, cocoa; Parasol B, cobalt w/gold, #16 ....55.00
Pot, cocoa; Writing B, fluted, red w/gold, 9½" 65.00
Shakers, Picnic C, cobalt w/gold, red neck, pr....................22.00
Sugar bowl, Mother & Daughter, 2 reserves, red w/gold 14.00
Tea set, Cloud B, melon ribbed, red-orange w/yel, J#6, 13-pc........95.00

Georgia Art Pottery

In Cartersville, Georgia, in August 1935, W.J. Gordy first fired pottery turned from regional clays. By 1936 he was marking his wares 'Georgia Art Pottery' (GP) or 'Georgia Art Pottery' (GAP) and continued to do so until 1950 when he used a 'Hand Made by WJ Gordy' stamp (HM). Since 1970 he has signed his pottery. Known throughout the world for his fine glazes, he won the Georgia Governor's Award in 1983. Examples of his ware are on display in the Smithsonian. His father W.T.B. and brother C.X. are also well-known potters.

Bean pot, mk HM, M gold, 2-qt 80.00
Candy dish, glossy bl, 2 hdls, fluted top, mk GAP 75.00
Churn, Albany slip, mk GP, 3-gal...300.00

Cowboy hat, (GAP), 3", $100.00; Pitcher, black gloss (GAP), 4", $85.00; Pitcher, red, rare color (GP), 3", $150.00.

Creamer & sugar bowl, yel, mk HM, 3" 75.00
Flower frog, copper gr, spherical, mk GP, 4" 100.00
Jug, bl w/M gold, beehive form, 1-gal 50.00
Kettle, red, 3-leg, mk HM, 3" 40.00
Mug, brn, barrel form, mk GAP, 4" 65.00
Pitcher, brn over wht, incised Etowah Mounds, mk HM, 2" 65.00
Pitcher, dusty pk, mk GAP, 4" 75.00

German Porcelain

Unless otherwise noted, the porcelain listed in this section is marked simply 'Germany.' Products of other German manufactures are listed in specific categories. See also Bisque; Pink Pigs; Elfinware.

Figurines, each with lamb, Ludwigsburg, 1700s, 10", $1,250.00.

Bottle, scent; appl florals, pear shape, flower finial, 11" 300.00
Bowl, maidens in Grecian garden, rtcl rim, 9" 75.00
Chocolate pot, lovers in garden w/gold, Kauffman, 1882, 9½" 150.00
Cracker jar, mc flower panels on cobalt, 7¼x6" 180.00
Figurine, Bavarian boy & girl, Neiderville gold/pastel, 7", pr.........55.00
Figurine, Beggar Lady, Musical Vagabond, 7", pr 245.00
Figurine, Bust of Caesar, pk triangle mk, 9" 350.00
Figurine, dbl; boy & girl, pastels, bsk, Grafenthal, 15" 175.00
Figurine, girl in gr & red w/fan & pearls, Schierholz, 14½"..........750.00
Figurine, girl w/winged hat & butterfly wings on bk, 8" 295.00

Figurine, goose girl w/flower basket, shield mk, 4x4½" 50.00
Figurine, lady in toga cvg bust of man w/chisel, 8" 225.00
Figurine, lady w/dog in apron, man w/dish & leash, 13", pr.........395.00
Figurine, monkey orchestra, 1880s, minor rstr, 5", set of 7 ...... 2,200.00
Figurine, 17th century gentleman, well made, ca 1920, 6" 95.00
Jar, appl fruit on lid, mc decor, crown mk, 3½x6" 100.00
Plaque, Mephistopheles tempts Faustus, 9x12", tortoise fr 3,700.00
Plaque, 2 women in medieval garb walk in country, 7x5" 150.00

Gladding McBean and Company

This company was established in 1875 in Lincoln, California. They first produced only clay drainage pipes, but in 1883 architectural terra cotta was introduced, which has been used extensively in the United States as well as abroad. Sometime later a line of garden pottery was added. They soon became the leading producers of tile in the country. In 1923 they purchased the Tropico Pottery in Glendale, California, where in addition to tile they also produced huge garden vases. Their line was expanded in 1934 to included artware and dinnerware.

At least fifteen lines of art pottery were developed between 1934 and 1942. For a short time they stamped their wares with the Tropico Pottery mark; but the majority was signed 'GMcB' in an oval. Later the mark was changed to 'Franciscan' with several variations. After 1937 'Catalina Pottery' was used on some lines. (All items marked 'Catalina Pottery' were made in Glendale.) For further information we recommend *The Collector's Encyclopedia of California Pottery* by our advisor for this category, Jack Chipman. He is listed in the Directory under California.

Bowl, Capistrano Art Ware, coral satin, leaf form, 9¾x14" 21.00
Bowl, Catalina Art Ware, ivory satin, sq, 10" 23.00
Bowl, Coronado Art Ware, ivory satin, 14" 39.00
Bowl, Coronado Art Ware, 9"..21.00
Candlestick, Coronado Art Ware, coral satin, 6½" 17.25

Carafe, 8½", and four mugs, $85.00.

Compote, Coronado Art Ware, ivory satin 28.50
Cup & saucer, Ruby Art Ware 28.00
Lamp base, Ox Blood Art Ware 74.00
Pitcher, Tropico Art Ware, bl, 5¾" 14.50
Plate, sectional; Hotel Ware, ivory, 10½" 21.00
Vase, bud; Encanto Art Ware, celadon...9.50
Vase, Capistrano Art Ware, ivory satin, turq int, flat form............10.50
Vase, Catalina Art Ware, ivory satin, turq int, shell form..............23.00
Vase, Encanto Art Ware, coral satin, cylindrical, 11½" 32.00

Glass Knives

Glass knives were manufactured from about 1920 to 1950, with distribution at its greatest in the late thirties and early forties. Colors generally followed Depression glass dinnerware: crystal, light blue, light green, pink (originally called rose), and more rarely amber, forest green, and white (opal). Many glass knives were hand painted in fruit or flower designs. Knife blades were ground to a sharp edge. Today knives are usually found with blades nicked through years of use or bumping in silverware drawers, or reground, which is acceptable to collectors as long as the original knife shape is maintained.

Many glass knives were engraved for gift-giving, personalized with the recipient's name and occasionally with a greeting. Originally presented in boxes, most glass knives were accompanied by a paper flyer extolling the virtues of the knife and describing its care.

Boxes printed with world's fair logos are fun to find, though not rare. Butter knives, which are smaller than other glass knives, typically were made in Czechoslovakia and sometimes match the handle patterns of glass salad sets. Knife lengths often vary slightly from each other because the knives were snapped off the molded glass during manufacture.

Our advisor for this category is Adrienne Escoe; she is listed in the Directory under California. For information concerning the Glass Knife Collectors Club, see the Clubs, Newsletters, and Catalogs section of the Directory.

Values reflect knives with minor blade roughness or resharpening.

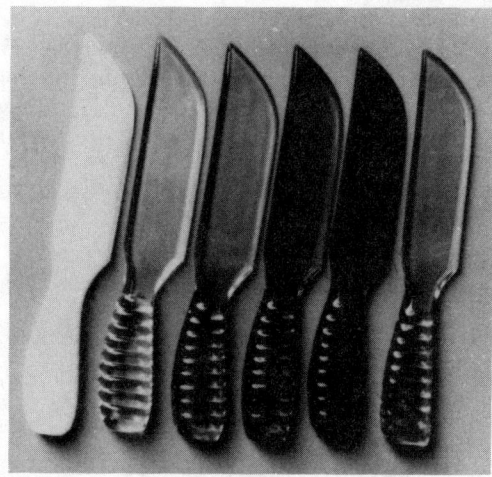

Stonex knives, see listings for specific color values.

Aer-Flo (Grid), amber, 7½"	150.00
Aer-Flo (Grid), crystal, 7½", +box	24.00
Aer-Flo (Grid), gr, 7½"	30.00
BK, crystal, HP lemons, 9¼", +box	22.00
Block, gr, 8¼", +box	22.00
Butter, crystal/amber, 5½"	18.00
Butter, gr/crystal, 6¼"	20.00
Butter, orange/crystal, 6⅜"	10.00
Butter, red/crystal, 6¼"	25.00
Candlewick, crystal, 8½"	325.00
Cryst-o-lite, crystal, 3 pinwheels, 8½"	8.00
Dagger, 9¼"	75.00
Dur-x 3 Leaf, amber, 9¼"	110.00
Dur-x 3 Leaf, bl, eng 'LM Greenbaum,' 9¼"	25.00
Dur-x 3 Leaf, bl, 8½"	17.00
Dur-x 3 Leaf, crystal, eng 'Treasure Island-1939,' 8⅜"	8.00
Dur-x 3 Leaf, crystal, 9¼", +box	10.00
Dur-x 3 Leaf, gr, eng 'Somers,' 8½"	20.00
Dur-x 3 Leaf, pk, eng 'Treasure Island-1939,' 8½"	21.00
Dur-x 5 Leaf, crystal, 9¼"	11.00
Dur-x 5 Leaf, gr, 9¼"	17.00

Dur-x 5 Leaf, pk, 9⅛", +box	15.00
ESP, gr, HP flowers, 9¼", +box	35.00
JCW, crystal, 9¼"	25.00
Plain hdl, gr, 8¼"	35.00
Plain hdl, gr, 9", +box	25.00
Plain hdl, pk, 9", +box w/printed 1933 World's Fair logo	38.00
Rose Spray, crystal, eng 'Merry Xmas-1939-Montgomery's,' 8½"	22.00
Rose Spray, pk, 8½", +box	65.00
Steel-ite, crystal, 8½"	22.00
Steel-ite, gr, 8½"	65.00
Stonex, amber, 8½"	110.00
Stonex, crystal, 8½", +box	30.00
Thumbguard, crystal, HP flowers, 9¼", MIB	25.00
Thumbguard, crystal, 9¼"	12.00
Vitex (3 Star), bl or pk, 8⅜"	20.00
Vitex (3 Star), bl or pk, 9¼", +box	20.00
Vitex (3 Star), crystal, 8½"	10.00
Vitex (3 Star), crystal, 9¼", +box	10.00

Glidden

Genius designer Glidden Parker established Glidden Pottery in 1940 in Alfred, New York, having been schooled at the unrivaled New York State College of Ceramics at Alfred University. Glidden pottery is characterized by a fine stoneware body, innovative forms, outstanding hand-milled glazes, and hand decoration, which make the pieces individual works of art. Production consisted of casual dinnerware, accessories, and artware that was distributed internationally.

In 1949 Glidden Pottery became the second ceramic plant in the country to utilize the revolutionary Ram pressing machine. This allowed for increased production and for the most part eliminated the previously used slip-casting method. However, Glidden stoneware continued to reflect the same superb quality of craftsmanship until the factory closed in 1957. Although the majority of form and decorative patterns were Mr. Parker's personal designs, Fong Chow and Sergio Dello Strologo also designed award-winning lines.

Glidden will be found marked on the unglazed underside with a signature that is hand incised, mold impressed, or ink stamped. Interest in this unique stoneware is growing as collectors discover that it embodies the very finest of Mid-Century High Style. Our advisor is David Pierce; he is listed in the Directory under Ohio.

Plate, Turn of the Century, #35, 5½", $45.00.

Ash tray, Safex, dbl rectangle, 12½x6½"	35.00
Ash tray, Teardrop, Zig-Zag, #183, 1¼x6x4½"	25.00
Baker, Feather, #22, 2x11x9"	30.00

Bottle, liquor; Alfred Stoneware, #813/#814/#815, 3 in basket **60.00**
Bowl, cobalt, sq, #23, 2x10x10" **35.00**
Bowl, Early Pk, oval, #38, 2x7¼x4¾" **30.00**
Bowl, fruit; Turq Matrix, #21, 4½" **12.00**
Bowl, Leaf, Engobe, #27, 1¼x5¾x5¾" **15.00**
Bowl, salad; Early Pk, #17, 4¼x8" **25.00**
Bowl, serving, Counterpane, #622, 7½" **15.00**
Candle bench, Mexican Cock, 2x8¾x3¾" **40.00**
Casserole, Viridian, #163, 6½x11" **35.00**
Cup, Sage & Sand, oval, #441-A **12.00**
Flowerpot, Gr Mesa, #4031, 7½x10" **150.00**
Gravy, Viridian, trigger hdl, #453, 3¼x7¾x3½" **30.00**
Ladle, Garden, hanging **25.00**
Laisy Daisy server, Celadon, complete **70.00**
Pitcher, Feather, #615, 1-qt **50.00**
Pitcher, milk; Turq Matrix, #614, 1 ½-pt **45.00**
Plate, canape; Amiable Cats, #35, 5½" **30.00**
Plate, canape; Turn of the Century, #35, 5½" **45.00**
Plate, chop; Boston Spice, #608, 17" **45.00**
Plate, dinner; Sage & Sand, sq, 10¼" **15.00**
Plate, luncheon; Flourish, sq, #33, 8" **20.00**
Plate, salad; Plaid, #65, 7x7" **15.00**
Platter, Yellowstone, #28, 15x11½" **35.00**
Spoon, Alfred Stoneware, #820, 10½" **20.00**
Teapot, Yellowstone, #240, 3½x7x5¼" **60.00**
Tray, candy/nut; Goldfish, #200, 8x6"+stand **50.00**
Vase, cobalt, ball form, #49, 7x5¾" **60.00**

Goebel

F.W. Goebel founded the Hummelwork Porcelain Manufactory in 1871, located in Rodental, West Germany. They produced porcelain figurines, plates, and novelties, the most famous of which are the Hummel figurines (these are listed in a separate section). There were many other series produced by Goebel — Disney characters, birds, animals, Art Deco figurines, and the Friar Tuck Monks that are especially popular. Our advisors for this category are Gale and Wayne Bailey; they are listed in the Directory under Georgia.

Brown Monk bank, stylized bee mark, 4", $40.00.

Cardinal Tuck (Red Monk)

Condiment set & tray, stylized bee mk **250.00**
Mustard, S183, stylized bee mk...**65.00**

Pitcher, S141 2/0, stylized bee mk, 2½" **50.00**
Pitcher, S141/0, stylized bee mk, 4" **75.00**
Shakers, P153, stylized bee mk, pr **55.00**
Sugar bowl, Z37, stylized bee mk **75.00**

Friar Tuck (Brown Monk)

Ash tray/bowl, ZF43, stylized bee mk **35.00**
Bank, SD29, stylized bee mk, 4" **40.00**
Calendar, KF55, 3-line mark **40.00**
Condiment set & tray, stylized bee mk **60.00**
Cookie jar, K29, full bee mk, 9" **150.00**
Creamer & sugar bowl, S141/0 & Z37, full bee mk **60.00**
Creamer & sugar bowl, w/tray, stylized bee mk **65.00**
Decanter, KL92, stylized bee mk, 10" **65.00**
Decanter, KL95, stylized bee mk, 10" **60.00**
Egg cup, 4 on tray, E95A&B, stylized bee mk **75.00**
Egg timer, dbl; E96, stylized bee mk **45.00**
Egg timer, single; E104, 3-line mk **45.00**
Flask, KL97, 3-line mk..**65.00**
Liquor tot, KL94, stylized bee mk, 2" **15.00**
Mug, T74/III, stylized bee mk, 8" **75.00**
Mug, T74/0, stylized bee mk, 4" **25.00**
Mug, T74/1, full bee mk, 5" **40.00**
Mustard, S183, full bee mk, 4" **30.00**
Oil & vinegar, M80, 3-line mk **75.00**
Pitcher, S141 2/0, full bee mk, 2½" **25.00**
Pitcher, S141/III, stylized bee mk, 8" **75.00**
Pitcher, S141/0, cross-eyed, full bee mk, 4" **40.00**
Pitcher, S141/0, stylized bee mk, 4" **25.00**
Pitcher, S141/1, cross-eyed, full bee mk, 5" **45.00**
Pitcher, S141/1, stylized bee mk, 5" **35.00**
Shakers, musicians, TMK6, pr **30.00**
Shakers, P153, full bee mk, pr **30.00**
Thermometer, KF56, 3-line mk **45.00**
Wine glass, monk stem **30.00**

Miscellaneous

Creamer, yel chick, child's, 1950 mk **30.00**
Figurine, bust of MI Hummel, wht, HU-2..........................**75.00**
Figurine, cat, Mitzi, fluffy, wht, 3½" **78.00**
Figurine, cat, wht w/brn spots, 3½" **35.00**
Figurine, Child's Prayer, Charlot Byj **50.00**
Figurine, Colonial couple, crown mk, 10" **275.00**
Figurine, Dumbo, mk, 1950s, 4", NM **325.00**
Figurine, Wise Owl, mk, 1950s, 4" **300.00**
Mainzelmaennchen, elf doll, vinyl, stylized bee mk, 4" **15.00**
Mug, Great Dane head figural, brn w/blk trim, mk, 1½x1" **45.00**
Pitcher, Santa Claus, full bee mk, 4" **75.00**
Shakers, Santa Claus, full bee mk, pr **50.00**
Sugar bowl, Santa Claus, full bee mk, 4½" **75.00**
Teacup & saucer, Santa Claus, full bee mk, 3" **50.00**
Toby pitcher, full bee mk, miniature, 1½" **30.00**
Toby pitcher, S129 3/0, crown mk, 4"................................**45.00**
Toby pitcher, S130/1, crown mk, 7"...................................**65.00**

Goldscheider

The Goldscheider family operated a pottery in Vienna for many generations before seeking refuge in the United States following Hitler's invasion of their country. They settled in Trenton, New Jersey, in the early 1940s where they established a new corporation and began producing objects of art and tableware items. In 1946 Marcel Goldscheider established a pottery in Staffordshire where he manufactured bone china figures, earthenware, etc., marked with a stamp of his signature. Larger artist-signed examples from either location are very valuable.

Ash tray, German Shepherd, 5½x7½" 60.00
Bust, Madonna w/crown, 7" 85.00

Butterfly Girl, signed Lorenzl, 18½", M, $2,300.00.

Figurine, dancer in full yellow dress, sgn Latour, 8¾" 300.00
Figurine, lady w/umbrella, 11½" 175.00
Figurine, nude dancer, plumed headpc, cape, Thumasch, 19" .. 2,000.00
Figurine, nude sits on blk oval base, Lorenzl, 8" 1,650.00
Figurine, reclining nude, terra cotta, Vienna 1,250.00
Figurine, Yankee Doodle Dandy, 7" 125.00
Lamp base, semi-nude, lav skirt, w/fruit & grain, rstr, 32" 2,200.00
Mask, lady, blk ringlets, orange lips, mk Wein, 10"......................500.00
Mask, lady, curly hair, red lips, yel apple, mk Wein, 8"...............450.00
Music box, Colonial girl, 7"...95.00
Plaque, Madonna & Child, sticker, 15" 750.00

Gonder

Lawton Gonder grew up with clay in his hands and fire in his eyes. Gonder's interest in ceramics was greatly influenced by his parents who worked for Weller and a close family friend and noted ceramic authority, John Herold. In his early teens Gonder launched his ceramic career at the Ohio Pottery Company, while working for Herold. He later gained valuable experience at American Encaustic Tile Company, Cherry Art Tile, and the Florence Pottery. Gonder was plant manager at the Florence Pottery until fire destroyed the facility in late 1941.

After years of solid production and management experience, Lawton Gonder established the Gonder Ceramic Art Company, formerly the Peters and Reed plant, in South Zanesville, Ohio. Gonder Ceramic Art produced quality art pottery with beautiful contemporary designs which included human and animal figures and a complete line of Oriental pottery. Accentuating the beautiful shapes were unique and innovative glazes developed by Gonder such as flambe (flame red with streaks of yellow), 24k gold crackle, antique gold, and Chinese crackle.

All Gonder is marked with the company name and mold number. They include 'Gonder U.S.A' in block letters, 'Gonder' in script, 'Gonder Original' in script, and 'Gonder Ceramic Art' in block letters. Paper labels were also used. Some of the early Gonder molds closely resemble Rumrill designs that had been manufactured at the Florence

Pottery; and, because some Rumrill pieces are found with similar (if not identical) shapes, matching mold numbers, and Gonder glazes, it is speculated that some Rumrill was produced at the Gonder plant. In 1946 Gonder started another company which he named Elgee (chosen for his initials LG) where he manufactured lamp bases until a fire in 1954 resulted in his shifting lamp production to the main plant. Operations ceased in 1957. Our advisors for this category are Marilyn and John McCormick; they are listed in the Directory under Kansas.

Ewer, shell and starfish, dark green with brown drip, #508, 13½", $40.00; Trade sign, white with purple streaking, 2" x 7", $75.00; Vase, scalloped shell, yellow with blue mottle, J-60, 8", $13.00.

Basket, no hdls, dk gr, pk int, H-36, 6¼x9¼" L 14.00
Basket, shell w/hdl, dk gr, #674, 7½" 7.50
Bowl, crescent shape, dk gr w/brn drip, J-55, 5x12½" L 10.00
Candle holder, crescent shape, bl, J-56, 6½", pr..............................22.00
Ewer, scrollwork at base, gold crackle, J-25, 11¼" 25.00
Ewer, shell w/starfish, dk gr w/brn drip, #508, 13½"......................40.00
Sign, Gonder Pottery USA, wht w/purple streaking, 2x7" 75.00
Vase, dbl lip w/ribbing, flambe, #383, 6½" 13.00
Vase, dbl-lip urn, dk gr, pk int, E-1, 7" 6.00
Vase, drape w/rope cinch, bl w/yel mottle, pk int, H-605, 9" 12.50
Vase, flower form, yel, pk int, E-3, 7½" 5.00
Vase, ribbon candy design, yel w/brn streaking, #517, 10½" 13.00
Vase, scalloped shell, yel w/bl mottle, pk int, J-60, 8¼" 13.00
Vase, sphere shaped, chartreuse w/wht drip, #746, 7" dia..............10.00
Vase, twisted body, flesh w/gr mottle, E-64, 6¼" 5.00
Vase, violet blossom, bl w/pk mottle, E-372, 6¼" 7.50
Vase, 2 swans at base, dk gr, pk int, H-47, 8½"...............................15.00

Goofus Glass

Goofus was an inexpensive type of lustre-painted pressed glassware made by many companies during the first two decades of the 20th century. Bowls and trays are most common, and red and gold combinations are found more often than blues and greens.

Bottle, scent; pk tulips, orig pnt & stopper, 3½", EX.....................20.00
Bowl, dogwood, orig pnt, 3x9½", EX 45.00
Bowl, gr poppy, sgn Northwood, 2½x7", M 30.00
Bowl, grapes on amethyst, scalloped, sq, orig pnt, 10", EX............75.00
Bowl, irises form ruffles in rim, orig pnt, 3x7", M 25.00
Bowl, pears/cherries/plums, crimped, EX orig pnt, 4x7" 35.00
Bowl, reindeer in center, EX..18.00
Cake plate, acorn & leaf, amethyst, 12"...20.00

Candy dish, figure-8 design, serrated rim, orig pnt, 8½" **55.00**
Coaster, flowers, orig pnt, rare, 3" dia, EX, set of 4 ....**40.00**
Compote & saucer, poppy, crackle glass, orig pnt, 4" **25.00**
Lamp, fairy; roses, flash-fired gr, 3 holes for smoke, 7" **35.00**
Lamp, oil; cabbage roses on amethyst, orig pnt, 15", M **100.00**
Lamp, oil; Nosegay, #2, EX orig pnt **150.00**
Lamp, oil; Roses in Snow, glass base, orig pnt, 15" **95.00**
Plate, cake; red & silver pnt, 13x13" **25.00**
Plate, monk drinking, rose edge, orig pnt, rare, 7", EX **35.00**
Plate, poppy, gr, mk N, 7" **30.00**
Plate, roses in center, 8½" **20.00**
Powder box, basketweave, milk glass, orig pnt, rare, M **50.00**
Shakers, poppy, EX orig pnt, 3", pr **35.00**
Tray, dresser; roses w/in heart form, minor rstr, 6" W **55.00**
Vase, Cabbage Rose, milk glass, remains of orig pnt, 5½" **30.00**
Vase, daisies, group of 4, molded hdls, orig pnt, 12" **40.00**
Vase, dogwood blossoms, baluster, orig pnt, 15" **50.00**
Vase, iris on bl glass, minor rstr, 6½" **28.00**
Vase, peacock, orig pnt, 10½" **145.00**
Vase, peacock in a tree, red/gr/gold, M orig pnt, 15" **100.00**
Vase, Roses in Snow, classic form, rpt, 10" **20.00**
Vase, Statue of Liberty, rare **95.00**
Water bottle, basketweave, orig wht pnt, 10" **40.00**
Water bottle, grapes on crackle, no pnt, 7½" **35.00**

Cabbage Rose and Poppy vases, 7", $45.00 each.

Goss and Crested China

William Henry Goss received his early education at the Government School of Design and as a result of his merit was introduced to Alderman William Copeland, who owned a large pottery firm. Under the influence of Copeland, Goss quickly learned the trade and soon became their chief designer. Little is known about this brief association, and in 1858 Goss left to begin his own business. After a short-lived partnership with a Mr. Peake, Goss opened a pottery on John Street, Stoke-on-Trent, but by 1870 he had moved to his business to a location near London Road. This pottery became the famous Falcon Works.

Many of the early pieces made by Goss were left unmarked and are difficult to discern from products made by the Copeland factory, but after he had been in business for about fifteen years, all of his wares were marked. Today unmarked items do not command the prices of the later marked wares.

Adulphus William Henry Goss joined his father's firm in the 1880s. He introduced cheaper lines, though the more expensive lines continued in production. Shortly after his father's death in 1906, Adulphus retired and left the business to his two younger brothers. The busi-

ness suffered from problems created by a war economy, and in 1936 Goss assets were held by Cauldron Potteries Ltd. These were eventually taken over by the Coalport Group, who retained the right to use the Goss trademark. Messrs. Ridgeway Potteries bought all the assets in 1954, as well as the right to use the Goss trademark and name. Now it remains to be seen if Goss ware will ever be produced again. Other area potters produced crested wares similar to Goss. Some of these are also listed.

Our advisor for this category is Patrick Herley; he is listed in the Directory under New York. Further assistance was given by David Taylor who is listed under England. Items below include listings of related crested ware as well as those of Goss.

Plate, $80.00; teapot stand, $35.00

Abbots cup, Fountains Abbey **15.00**
Beer barrel, Burton **18.00**
Beer bowl, dragon **25.00**
Bottle, Sutherland **10.00**
Bowl, Glastonbury **10.00**
Bucket, milk; Swiss **18.00**
Bucket, Norwegian **20.00**
Bust, Carlton, Alexandra **60.00**
Bust, Carlton, Edward VII **75.00**
Bust, Carlton, Wordsworth **50.00**
Creamer, Yarmouth, sm **22.00**
Cup & saucer, flags decor (war allies) **55.00**
Egg cup **10.00**
Ewer, Boston **22.00**
Ewer, Japan, 3½" **25.00**
Figurine, Arcadian, Colonial man **65.00**
Figurine, Carlton, Fisher girl **50.00**
Figurine, Willow, Burns at the plough **70.00**
Flask, Caerleon Tear **12.00**
Huer's House **135.00**
Irish Mather, lg **60.00**
Jug, Dorchester **12.00**
Jug, Gloucester **15.00**
Jug, Kendall, Assyrian Armor **21.50**
Jug, Litchfield **12.00**
Jug, Reading **10.00**
Jug, Scarborough **13.00**
Jug, water; Egyptian **10.00**
Kettle, Hastings **10.00**
Look Out House **110.00**
Manx Cottage **85.00**
Match holder, Blk boy figural, 1930s **100.00**
Milk can, Welsh, w/lid **15.00**
Mortar, Bideford **12.50**
Pipkin, Southampton, lg **30.00**

Pipkin, Southampton, sm 10.00
Pitcher, Devon Oak, sm..10.00
Plate, flags decor (war allies) 80.00
Porridge pot, Guy's 18.00
Pot, Manx 18.00
Pot, Roman, Painswick 15.00
Rufus Stone 20.00
Shakespeare's House, sm 100.00
St Nicholas Chapel...170.00
Teapot stand, verse, sq shape 35.00
Tobacco jar, terra cotta, 5½", EX 45.00
Trinket box, Manchester College, w/lid, rnd, sm......................23.00
Urn, Minster 15.00
Urn, Musselburg, Kirkpark 15.00
Urn, Nottingham...13.00
Vase, Doncaster 20.00
Vase, Exeter 10.00
Vase, flags decor (war allies), wide mouth, tapered 35.00
Vase, Glastonbury 10.00
Vase, Southport 15.00
Wall pocket, Christ Church, lg 30.00
Wine cooler, Bolton Abbey 45.00
Yorick's Skull, lg 135.00
Yorick's Skull, sm...65.00

Gouda

Since the 18th century the main center of the pottery industry in Holland was in Gouda. One of its earliest industries, the manufacture of clay pipes, continues to the present day. The artware so easily recognized by collectors today was first produced about 1885. It was decorated in the Art Nouveau manner. Stylized florals, birds, and geometrics were favored motifs; only rarely is the scene naturalistic. The Nouveau influence was strong until about 1915. Art Deco was attempted but with less success. Though most of the ware is finished in a matt glaze, glossy pieces in both pastels and dark colors are found on occasion and command higher prices. Decoration on the glossy ware is usually very well executed. Most of the workshops failed during the Depression, though earthenware is still being made in Gouda and carries the Gouda mark. Until very recently Regina was still making a limited amount of the old Gouda-style pottery in a matt finish. Watch for the Gouda name, which is usually a part of the backstamp of the various manufacturers.

Ash tray, floral, mc on gr, Damar, house mk, 6" dia 65.00
Ash tray, Regina, shoe form, mk, 5⅛" L 60.00

Candlesticks, signed, #921, 7", $265.00 for the pair.

Candlestick, Danier, mc florals on blk, mk, 3x5½" 95.00
Dish, foliage, 5-branch base in blk, 1921, 7x13"......................300.00
Dutch shoe, blk satin w/mc details, hole for hanging, 5½".........65.00
Ewer, florals, rust/brn/gr on cream, Orel, house mk, 8⅛" 110.00
Pitcher, mc decor on blk, Zenith, 7x3⅜" 95.00
Tray, mc Deco florals, bl & gold trim, 11⅛" dia.......................110.00

Graniteware

Graniteware, made of a variety of metals with enamel coatings, derives its name from its appearance. The speckled, swirled, or mottled effect of the vari-colored enamels may look like granite — but there the resemblance stops. It wasn't especially durable! Expect at least minor chipping if you plan to collect.

Graniteware was featured in 1876 at Phily's Expo. It was mass produced in quantity, and enough of it has survived to make at least the common items easily affordable. Color is an important consideration in evaluating an item; cobalt blue and white, green and white, brown and white, and old red and white swirled items are unusual, thus more expensive. Pieces of heavier weight, seam constructed, riveted, and those with wooden handles and tin lids are usually older.

In recent months, magazine articles featuring decorating ideas with an emphasis on the 'country look' have caused the price of graniteware to escalate — a trend which is likely to continue.

For further study we recommend *The Collector's Encyclopedia of Graniteware, Colors, Shapes, and Values* by our advisor, Helen Greguire. (Helen has a second edition in progress.) She is listed in the Directory under New York. For the address of the National Graniteware Society, see the section on Clubs, Newsletters, and Catalogs.

Baking pan, speckled gray, wire hdls, sq, 10" 24.00
Biscuit cutter, brn & wht mottled, Onyx Ware, 2¼" dia, NM.....425.00
Bowl, cereal; bl & wht relish, pewter trim, M 165.00
Bowl, soup; cobalt & wht med swirl, blk trim, M 65.00
Bread box, wht & lt bl chicken wire, rnd, brass hdl/latch, NM ...155.00
Bread raiser, gray med mottled, ftd, w/domed lid, med sz, M........195.00
Bucket, miner's dinner; gray lg mottle, 4-pc, M.........................295.00
Butter bucket, lt gray speckle, wire hdl, 8" 65.00
Butter dish, bl & wht lg mottled, seamless, spun knob, NM 400.00
Butter dish, wht w/bl decor, lg, NM..275.00
Can, cream; bl & wht fine mottle, dk bl trim, w/tin lid, M..........185.00
Can, milk; shaded deep sea gr to moss gr, Shamrock Ware, NM .325.00
Candlestick, gray med mottled, NM 175.00

Candlestick, gray large mottled, 7" diameter, beehive shape, NM , $255.00.

Canister, coffee; wht w/dk bl trim, lid w/strap hdl, M 110.00
Canister, flour; bl & wht fine mottled w/bl trim, M 225.00
Churn, bl & wht lg swirl, floor-model dasher type, 18", NM... 1,250.00
Coaster, bl & wht lg swirl, wht interior, Bl Dmn Ware, NM 165.00
Coffee biggin, bl & wht fine mottled, squat, 3-pc, NM 365.00
Coffee biggin, bl w/apple blossoms, pewter biggin & trim, 5-pc...425.00

Coffee biggin, red & wht, med swirl 'snow on mtn,' 4-pc, M 595.00
Coffee biggin, solid lt bl w/gold bands, glass lid, 3-pc, NM 210.00
Coffee boiler, cobalt & wht lg swirl, shallow pit bottom, NM 395.00
Coffee boiler, red & wht lg swirl w/dk bl trim, old, NM.............850.00
Coffee boiler, solid dk gray, Sterling Gray label, M 175.00
Coffee flask, solid bl, screw-on metal top, 5x4¾", NM.................425.00
Coffee roaster, blk & wht med mottle, sm, solid metal drum, M ..400.00
Coffee urn, wht w/florals, pewter trim, alcohol burner. M 1,250.00
Coffeepot, brn & wht med mottle, brass & wood trim, M 375.00
Coffeepot, gr & wht lg swirl, Emerald Ware, NM 395.00
Coffeepot, gr & wht relish, hinged spout, wood hdl/knob, M 235.00
Coffeepot, gray & wht mottled, acorn finial, 1880s, 9½", NM 125.00
Coffeepot, red-brn & wht fine mottle, Manning Bowman, NM ..215.00
Coffeepot, shaded dk violet to lt violet, Thistleware, M 275.00
Coffeepot, wht & gr veins lg mottle, Elite, M 200.00
Coffeepot, wht w/blackberries, pewter trim copper bottom, M 250.00
Colander, gray, strap hdls, ftd, ca 1890s, 12".............................55.00
Corn mold, Am Gray, M 125.00
Creamer, red & wht lg mottled, blk trim, squat, 1970s, M 65.00
Cuspidor, end-of-day lg swirl, salesman's sample, M....................950.00
Custard cup, lt bl & wht lg swirl, wht interior, blk trim, NM 85.00
Dipper, bl & wht speckled, 14", M...55.00
Dipper, cobalt, M...36.00
Dipper, cobalt w/wht, perforated, M 65.00
Dipper, cocoa; gray med mottle w/blk trim, wood hdl, NM 185.00
Dipper, cocoa; wht, hollow hdl, M 115.00
Dipper, gr & wht lg swirl, bl hollow hdl & trim, M.....................135.00
Dipper, pickle; solid yel w/gr trim & hdl, M 95.00
Dipper, Windsor; bl & wht lg swirl, blk trim, hollow hdl, NM 95.00
Dish, pudding; wht & bl-gray lg mottle, oblong, NM...................110.00
Dish pan, end-of-day lg swirl, blk trim & hdls, NM 135.00
Double boiler, gr & wht swirl, cobalt trim, Emerald Ware, NM ..395.00
Double boiler, wht swirls on lt bl, cobalt hdl, 2-pc, 7", NM.........135.00
Dust pan, solid bl, seamless w/appl hdl, NM...............................195.00
Egg cup, wht w/blk trim, NM...95.00
Egg pan, bl & wht lg mottle, ca 1915, 4⅞" dia, NM....................220.00
Egg pan, wht & bl chicken wire, side spout, NM..........................125.00
Egg separator, cobalt w/fine wht veining, perforated, NM 550.00
Fry pan, dk gr & wht lg swirl, blk trim & hdl, chrysolite, NM 235.00
Fry pan, gr & wht lg swirl, wht interior, blk trim & hdl, NM 165.00
Funnel, bl & wht lg swirl, squat, Columbian Ware, NM..............245.00
Funnel, mottled bl & wht, curved hdl, ca 1800, 9" 65.00
Funnel, percolator; bl & wht, lg mottle 'snow on mtn,' M...........185.00
Grater, Am Gray, Ideal, M 450.00
Gravy boat, bl & wht lg swirl, blk trim/hdl, Bl Dmn Ware, NM .895.00
Gravy boat, lt bl & wht fine mottle, cobalt trim & hdl, ftd, NM.325.00
Holder, wht w/dk bl trim, mk Swiebeln, perforated, NM 185.00
Jar filler, fruit; bl & wht lg mottle, NM 145.00
Kettle, fish or poacher; bl & wht lg mottle, Elite, NM.................295.00
Ladle, oyster; Am Gray mottled, perforated, NM 60.00
Ladle, soup; brn & wht lg swirl, wht int, blk hdl & trim, NM 155.00
Ladle, soup; gr & wht lg swirl, dk bl trim, Emerald Ware, NM 175.00
Ladle, soup; lt bl & wht swirl, M..55.00
Lavabo & basin, bl & wht lg swirl, blk trim, brass spigot, NM 450.00
Match holder, dbl pocket; gray med mottle, Kieckhefer, NM 450.00
Measure, cobalt & wht lg swirl, seamed lip, 1-qt, NM 475.00
Mold, fish, solid wht, w/ring, lg, NM 175.00
Mold, Turk's head, gray lg mottled, 6½" dia, M 85.00
Mug, cobalt & wht lg swirl, 2-cup, M..95.00
Mug, dk gr & wht lg swirl, bl trim, chrysolite, M........................135.00
Mustard jar, brn/wht/blk bands on wht, w/lid & ladle, NM 195.00
Pail, chamber; bl & wht lg swirl, blk trim, wood bail, NM 170.00
Pail, speckled cobalt, wire hdl, ca 1800, 6⅝x9", NM....................55.00
Pail, water; bl & wht lg swirl, blk trim, Columbian Ware, M 195.00

Pan, baking or stove; dk gr & wht lg swirl, chrysolite, NM..........225.00
Pan, bread; blk & wht lg mottle w/blk trim, seamed ends, NM ...155.00
Pan, jelly roll; cobalt & wht lg mottle, 1" deep, M 65.00
Pan, muffin; cobalt & wht lg swirl, blk trim, 8-cup, NM 325.00
Pan, muffin; lt bl & wht lg swirl, 6-cup, NM..............................650.00
Pan, stew; bl & wht lg mottled, blk trim & hdl, NM 120.00
Pie pan, cobalt & wht lg swirl, blk trim, 9", NM 75.00
Pie pan, dk gr & wht lg swirl, wht interior, chrysolite, NM 95.00
Pie pan, lg swirled cobalt & wht, wht int, 8½" dia, NM 65.00
Pie pan, swirl lt bl & wht, 3x9", NM...65.00
Pitcher, milk; end-of-day lg swirl, NM.......................................650.00
Pitcher, milk; gr & wht lg swirl, Emerald Ware, NM 295.00
Pitcher, water; bl & wht med mottled w/gold, collar base, NM ...225.00
Pitcher, water; gr & wht med mottled, gr trim, Elite, NM 175.00
Plate, dessert; orange & wht lg swirl, blk trim, ca 1960, M 35.00
Plate, soup; gray med mottled, Iron City label, M 85.00
Platter, wht w/blk swan & trim, 8-sided oval, M 155.00
Roaster, bl & wht lg swirl, blk hdls, w/flat-top lid, NM...............275.00
Roaster, bl & wht lg swirl w/blk trim, oval, dome lid, NM 165.00
Roaster, lt robin's egg bl & wht, mk Reed, w/lid, 9x16½", NM ...155.00
Salt box, pk & wht med mottle w/red trim, mk SEL, NM............395.00
Salt box, solid red w/blk bk & trim, NM 130.00

Salt box, gray mottled, wooden lid, 6" x 7", NM, $525.00.

Saucer, Am gray lg mottled, 6⅞", M 55.00
Scale, counter top; wht w/windmill, Eagle Trademark, VG.........340.00
Scoop, spice; Am gray lg mottled, M..290.00
Shaker, salt; lt bl & wht lg swirl, w/metal screw-on top, M.........850.00
Skimmer, bl & wht lg swirl, perforated, flat, blk hdl, NM 135.00
Soap dish, bl & wht swirl, hanging, M 125.00
Soap dish, hanging; solid bl, fluted bottom, NM 55.00
Soup tureen, wht & bl chicken wire, ftd, Elite, w/lid, NM 395.00
Spatula, Am gray solid, NM 75.00
Spoon, apple butter; wht & gr relish, 19⅜", NM 65.00
Spoon, basting; speckled bl, 14", NM..50.00
Spoon, end-of-day lg mottled, blk hdl, NM 115.00
Spoon, lt bl & wht lg swirl, NM...85.00
Spoon, mixing; bl & wht lg swirl, blk hdl, Columbian, 15", NM ..135.00
Spoon, mixing; bl & wht mottled, NM..55.00
Steamer insert, brn & wht swirl, bail hdl, M.................................35.00
Strainer, kettle; wht & bl chicken wire, hdl & hook, VG............130.00
Strainer, tea; Am gray solid, NM 65.00
Strainer, tea; bl & wht lg swirl, screen bottom, NM....................195.00
Sugar bowl, wht w/calla lilies, pewter trim, M............................295.00
Syrup, dk gr & wht lg swirl, NP copper lid, chrysolite, M 995.00
Tea steeper, chrysolite, NM 365.00
Teakettle, gray & wht relish, deep pit bottom, w/lid, VG.............270.00

Teapot, Am gray lg mottled, bell shape/pewter trim, w/lid, M.....325.00
Teapot, Am gray mottled, pewter trim/copper bottom, squat, M.325.00
Teapot, apple gr, tangerine int, squat, Vollrath Ware, M 140.00
Teapot, bl & wht fine mottle, metal ped, Elite, 2-cup, M 350.00
Teapot, bl & wht lg swirl w/blk trim, Columbian, 1-qt, NM 575.00
Teapot, cobalt & wht lg swirl, wood hdl, w/ribbed lid, M............275.00
Teapot, solid bl w/decor, mk Specter Germany 39, squat, sm 165.00
Teapot, wht, pewter trim, copper-trim bottom, squat, M.............225.00
Teapot, wht/pk/yel/wine, end-of-day chicken wire, squat, NM ...435.00
Toothbrush holder, wall type, solid wht, holds 3 brushes, NM 145.00
Tray, Am gray med mottled, sq, NM 145.00
Tray, aqua-gr & wht lg mottle, wht int, brass hanger, NM 325.00
Tray, cobalt & wht lg swirl w/blk trim, oblong, NM 295.00
Tray, wht & gr med mottle, wht int, hdld, oblong, Elite, NM 95.00
Tube cake pan, cobalt & wht lg swirl, blk trim, NM...................260.00
Tube mold, Turk's head, sm wht swirls on gray, 5⅞x9¾", M 125.00
Tube mold, wht, fluted sides, 3x5¾", M 35.00
Tumbler, bl & wht fine mottle w/blk trim, 2¾", NM..................145.00
Utensil rack, bl & wht lg mottled, w/2 orig utensils, M 450.00
Utensil rack, solid blk, w/3 matching utensils, M 300.00
Vase, wall hanging; cream & dk maroon lg swirl, NM 275.00
Wash basin, gr & wht lg swirl, w/eyelet, Emerald Ware, NM 135.00
Wash pitcher & bowl, red w/blk trim & hdl, squat, NM.............200.00
Water carrier, bl & wht lg mottled, oval, w/emb lid, NM............425.00

Green and Ivory

Green and ivory are the colors of a type of country pottery decorated with in-mold designs very similar to those of the more familiar
blue and white wares. It is unmarked and was produced from about
1910 to 1935 by many manufacturers as part of their staple line of
kitchenwares.

Bowl, Apricot, 9½" 75.00
Bowl, Daisy & Waffle, 10" 65.00
Butter crock, Apricots & Honeycomb, w/lid & bail....................125.00
Butter crock, Daisy & Waffle, w/lid..150.00
Mug, Grape 45.00
Pitcher, Basketweave & Morning-Glory, rope hdl, 9"..................160.00
Pitcher, Cow, EX color & detail, 7½".......................................160.00

**Pitcher, Cows, 7",
$160.00.**

Pitcher, Grape 125.00
Pitcher, Indian Head in war bonnet, waffle body, 8½", NM 185.00
Pitcher, Pine Cone, 9"..150.00
Spittoon, Cosmos, 6"..75.00
Toothpick holder, Swan 30.00
Umbrella stand, Irises, 20"...350.00

Green Opaque

Introduced in 1887 by the New England Glass Company, this ware
is very scarce due to the fact that it was produced for less than one year.
It is characterized by its soft green color and a wavy band of gold reserv-
ing a mottled blue metallic stain. It is usually found in satin; examples
with a shiny finish are extremely rare.

Basket, ruffled Hobnail amber rim, amber hdl, 8¾x9⅛"...............550.00
Bowl, everted lip, shallow, 7" 750.00
Bowl, scalloped gold in EX mottled border, 4" 600.00
Bowl vase, NM gold & mottling, 3x4¼"....................................850.00
Cruet, tricorn, 6".. 1,150.00
Shakers, squat form, EX mottling, 2¾", pr.................................475.00
Spooner, 3¾" 850.00
Tumbler, EX deep mottling & gold, 3¾x2½"...............................650.00
Tumbler, lemonade; w/hdl, 5" 900.00
Tumbler, Optic Ribs, fine mottling, gold border 650.00
Vase, flared mouth, M gold & mottling, 6" 900.00

Greenaway, Kate

Kate Greenaway was an English artist who lived from 1846 to
1901. She gained worldwide fame as an illustrator of children's books,
drawing children clothed in the styles worn by proper English and
American boys and girls of the very early 1800s. Her book, *Under the
Willow Tree*, published in 1878, was the first of many. Her sketches
appeared in leading magazines, and her greeting cards were in great
demand. Manufacturers of china, pottery, and metal products copied
her characters to decorate children's dishes, tiles, and salt and pepper
shakers as well as many other items. See also Almanacs; Napkin Rings.

Biscuit jar, ceramic, boy w/tinted features, w/lid........................150.00
Book, Almanack for 1884, London, VG 60.00
Book, Mother Goose, London, Routledge, 1st ed, 1881, VG.........95.00
Book, Pied Piper of Hamlin, Greenaway illus, NM 65.00
Butter pat, china, children playing...35.00
Cup & saucer, pk lustre 125.00
Engraving, Harper's Bazaar, Jan 1879, full-pg.............................25.00
Figurine, boy w/basket, porc, 1893 mk, 8½x4"...........................525.00
Match safe, SP, emb children, sm...48.00
Pickle castor, bl, 2 girls, blown-out florals, SP fr.........................455.00
Plate, ABC, girl in lg hat, Staffordshire, 7" 85.00
Plate, children at play, fruit, birds & flowers, 9"..........................100.00

**Stickpin holder, Meriden silver-
plate, 4", $125.00.**

Toothpick holder, bsk, girl sits on stump, basket on bk.................40.00
Toothpick holder, glass, 2 girls sit beside basket 85.00
Wall pocket, ceramic, 6 girls on open book form, 6x9x3"...........110.00

Greentown Glass

Greentown glass is a term referring to the product of the the Indiana Tumbler and Goblet Company of Greentown, Indiana, ca 1894 to 1903. Their earlier pressed glass patterns were #11, a pseudo-cut glass design; #137, Pleat Band; and #200, Austrian. Another line, Dewey, was designed in 1898. Many lovely colors were produced in addition to crystal. Jacob Rosenthal, who was later affiliated with Fenton, developed his famous chocolate glass in 1900. The rich shaded opaque brown glass was an overnight success. Two new patterns, Leaf Bracket and Cactus, were designed to display the glass to its best advantage, but previously existing molds were also used. In only three years, Rosenthal developed yet another important color formula, golden agate. The Holly Amber pattern was designed especially for its production. The Dolphin covered dish with a fish finial is perhaps the most common and easily-recognized piece ever produced. Other animal dishes were also made; all are highly collectible. There have been many repros — not all are marked!

Our advisors for this category are Jerry and Sandy Garrett; they are listed in the Directory under Indiana. See the Pattern Glass section for clear pressed glass, only colored items are listed here.

Animal dish, bird w/berry, emerald gr 295.00
Animal dish, bird w/berry, teal bl...270.00
Animal dish, cat on hamper, clear, low 300.00

Animal dish, cat on hamper, chocolate, 4½", $400.00.

Animal dish, cat on hamper, cobalt, tall 365.00
Animal dish, cat on hamper, wht agate, 5" 400.00
Animal dish, dolphin, beaded, cobalt 385.00
Animal dish, dolphin, beaded, emerald gr 435.00
Animal dish, dolphin, beaded, golden agate................................800.00
Animal dish, dolphin, beaded, Nile gr 1,650.00
Animal dish, dolphin, sawtooth, amber 365.00
Animal dish, dolphin, sawtooth, canary 450.00
Animal dish, dolphin, sawtooth, emerald gr.................................450.00
Animal dish, dolphin, smooth, chocolate.....................................335.00
Animal dish, hen, amber..160.00
Animal dish, hen, chocolate 650.00

Animal dish, hen, cobalt..400.00
Animal dish, hen, wht opaque 160.00
Animal dish, rabbit, amber (reproduced).....................................150.00
Animal dish, rabbit, cobalt...350.00
Animal dish, rabbit, emerald gr (reproduced)..............................175.00
Animal dish, rabbit, wht opaque (reproduced).............................150.00
Austrian, bowl, canary, 8"..200.00
Austrian, butter dish, canary 350.00
Austrian, cake stand, canary 285.00
Austrian, creamer, chocolate, 4¼"...165.00
Austrian, creamer, cobalt, child's...250.00
Austrian, punch cup, amber 185.00
Austrian, vase, Nile gr, 6"..365.00
Beehive, tumbler, chocolate..400.00
Beehive, vase, bud; amber 280.00
Brazen Shield, butter dish, bl..200.00
Brazen Shield, cake stand, bl, 10⅜" 200.00
Brazen Shield, pitcher, bl 225.00
Brazen Shield, tumbler, bl..70.00
Cactus, bowl, chocolate, 8¼"...145.00
Cactus, celery vase, chocolate, 7½"..450.00

Cactus, sweetmeat, chocolate, 9½", $675.00.

Cactus, cracker jar, chocolate 280.00
Cactus, sugar bowl, clear w/bl opal rim 350.00
Cactus, vase, chocolate, 6"...450.00
Cord Drapery, bowl, amber, 8" 160.00
Cord Drapery, bowl, cobalt, rectangular 200.00
Cord Drapery, compote, amber, w/lid, 4½" 225.00
Cord Drapery, goblet, emerald gr 250.00
Cord Drapery, pitcher, cobalt 250.00
Cord Drapery, syrup, amber...350.00
Cupid, butter dish, Nile gr...450.00
Cupid, creamer, wht opaque 90.00
Cupid, sugar bowl, chocolate, w/lid...450.00
Dewey, butter dish, canary, 4"..90.00
Dewey, creamer, Nile gr, 4"...150.00
Dewey, cruet, emerald gr, w/orig stopper 170.00
Dewey, parfait, amber 70.00
Dewey, sugar bowl, canary, w/lid, 2¼" dia....................................75.00
Dewey, sugar bowl, emerald gr, w/lid, 4" 110.00
Dewey, tumbler, emerald gr..65.00
Dewey, tumbler, Nile gr..625.00
Early Diamond, tumbler, cobalt 100.00

Fleur-de-lis, butter dish, chocolate..................................650.00
Fleur-de-lis, spooner, chocolate..180.00
Greentown Daisy, butter dish, chocolate..........................265.00
Greentown Daisy, creamer, emerald gr frost, w/lid 90.00
Greentown Daisy, sugar bowl, wht opaque, w/lid 65.00
Herringbone Buttress, bowl, emerald gr, 5¼"...................225.00
Herringbone Buttress, bowl, gr, 7¼"................................225.00
Herringbone Buttress, cordial, amber, 3"..........................350.00
Herringbone Buttress, shaker, emerald gr.........................250.00
Herringbone Buttress, syrup, emerald gr, metal lid..........365.00
Herringbone Buttress, vase, emerald gr, 10".....................295.00
Holly, tumbler, beaded decor, wht agate, rare, 4" 1,400.00
Holly Amber, bowl, oval, ped ft.....................................1,500.00
Holly Amber, butter dish..1,750.00
Holly Amber, compote, w/lid, 6½"................................1,500.00
Holly Amber, compote, w/lid, 7½", EX 1,600.00
Holly Amber, compote, w/lid, 8¼"................................2,250.00
Holly Amber, cruet 1,900.00
Holly Amber, mug, 4½"...475.00
Holly Amber, nappy, w/hdl, 4½", NM 550.00
Holly Amber, pitcher...2,500.00
Holly Amber, spooner..685.00
Holly Amber, syrup, metal lid 925.00
Holly Amber, toothpick holder (reproduced).....................450.00
Holly Amber, tumbler, beaded rim.....................................675.00
Holly Amber, vase, 6"...680.00
Leaf Bracket, butter dish, chocolate..................................165.00
Leaf Bracket, butter dish, cobalt.......................................900.00
Leaf Bracket, pitcher, chocolate..450.00
Leaf Bracket, spooner, chocolate...95.00
Leaf Bracket, toothpick holder, chocolate 290.00
Mug, Serenade, clear..75.00
Mug, Serenade, cobalt 350.00
Mug, Serenade, emerald gr 115.00
No 11, bowl, gr, rectangular, 8x6½"....................................75.00
No 11, tumbler, iced tea; chocolate 375.00
Novelty, buffalo, wht opaque, dtd 1901.............................345.00
Novelty, corn vase, amber, 4⅝"..165.00
Novelty, Dewey bust, wht opaque......................................185.00
Novelty, hairbrush, Nile gr...500.00
Novelty, Indian head, emerald gr, w/lid.............................600.00
Novelty, mitted hand, chocolate..900.00
Novelty, wheelbarrow, Nile gr (reproduced) 290.00
Pitcher, Paneled, chocolate..575.00
Pitcher, Paneled, clear...65.00
Pitcher, Ruffled Eye, canary..285.00
Pitcher, Ruffled Eye, emerald gr.......................................165.00
Pleat Band, compote, chocolate, smooth rim, plain stem, 4¼" 165.00
Pleat Band, shaker, amber 75.00
Scalloped Flange, vase, chocolate...85.00
Scalloped Flange, vase, Nile gr..300.00
Shuttle, bowl, chocolate, 8¼"...500.00
Shuttle, creamer, chocolate..550.00
Shuttle, goblet, chocolate...750.00
Shuttle, mug, amber 325.00
Shuttle, punch cup, chocolate 110.00
Shuttle, sugar bowl, chocolate, w/lid.................................650.00
Stein, Herringbone, clear 65.00
Stein, indoor drinking scene, chocolate, 5¾"....................175.00
Stein, indoor drinking scene, Nile gr, handleless 400.00
Stein, outdoor drinking scene, chocolate...........................165.00
Stein, outdoor drinking scene, clear...................................100.00
Teardrop & Tassel, bowl, cobalt, 7¼"................................130.00
Teardrop & Tassel, compote, Nile gr, w/lid, 5½" 365.00

Teardrop & Tassel, relish, amber, oval 125.00
Teardrop & Tassel, sugar bowl, emerald gr, w/lid..............190.00
Teardrop & Tassel, tumbler, bl, type 1, 3⅞x2¾" 65.00
Toothpick holder, dog head, amber frost............................300.00
Toothpick holder, sheaf of wheat, chocolate (reproduced)..........850.00
Toothpick holder, sheaf of wheat, teal bl...........................250.00
Toothpick holder, witch's head, clear (reproduced).....................165.00
Tumbler, Paneled, chocolate...475.00
Tumbler, Sawtooth, chocolate..100.00

Grueby

    William Henry Grueby joined the firm of the Low Art Tile Works at the age of fifteen; and in 1894, after several years of experience in the production of architectural tiles, founded his own plant, the Grueby Faience Company, in Boston, Massachusetts. Grueby began experimenting with the idea of producing art pottery and had soon perfected a fine glaze (soft and without gloss) in shades of blue, gray, yellow, brown, and his most successful, cucumber green. In 1900 his exhibit at the Paris Exposition Universelle won three gold medals.

    Grueby pottery was hand thrown and hand decorated in the Arts and Crafts style. Vertically-thrust stylized leaves and flowers in relief were the most common decorative devices. Tiles continued to be an important product, unique (due to the matt glaze decoration) as well as durable. Grueby tiles were often a full inch thick. Obviously incompatible with the Art Nouveau style, the artware was discontinued soon after 1910. The ware is marked in one of several ways: 'Grueby Pottery, Boston, USA'; 'Grueby, Boston, Mass.'; or 'Grueby Faience.' The artware is often artist signed. Our advisor for this category is David Rago; he is listed in the Directory under New Jersey.

Bowl, bl, 2½x6½"...275.00
Bowl, dk gr, leaves, flower-shape rim, 6" 660.00
Bowl, elephant-skin gr, tooled/appl leaves, W Post, 3x5" 990.00
Bowl, gr, raised finger ridges w/in, 3x8" 300.00
Bowl, gr gloss w/yel int, leaves, sq rim, sgn WP, 3½x6"............350.00
Bowl, gr w/lg leaves, 5x8"..1,300.00
Bowl, gr w/yel flowers & 2 rows of leaves, A Lingley, 10" 6,500.00
Bowl vase, oatmeal w/emb leaves, lime gloss int, 3½x6" 375.00
Jardiniere, dk gr, tall/wide leaves & buds, glaze line, 12" 1,200.00
Paperweight, scarab, brn matt, 4"......................................330.00
Paperweight, scarab, lt/dk ochre, 2⅝" 200.00
Paperweight, scarab, ochre on bl, minor roughness, 2½" 250.00

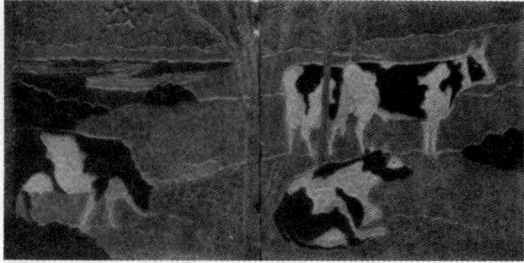

Tile frieze, cows in a landscape, in brown, cream, shades of green and blue-gray, no mark, some chips, 12", $6,250.00.

Tile, ellipse in circle, gr/terra cotta, 3x3"...........................65.00
Tile, horse w/serpent by tree, mc, artist sgn, 4x4" 375.00
Tile, mermaid w/mirror, beige & cobalt, unmk, 6x6".............225.00
Tile, rectangles in star, bl/terra cotta, mk, 3x3" 85.00
Tile, trees in hilly landscape, grs/bls/brns, MCM, 6" 935.00

Tile, tulip, yellow w/lt gr stems & leaves on dk gr, ES, 6" **465.00**
Vase, bsk w/crackled yel bottom half, spherical, 4x4" **400.00**
Vase, curdled gr, 7 tooled/appl leaves, initialed, 8x7" **3,150.00**
Vase, dk gr, leaves/buds, cylinder w/fluted rim, WP, 8½" **1,000.00**
Vase, dk gr, tooled/appl leaves, M Seaman, 9x5" **1,650.00**
Vase, dk gr, tooled/appl vertical leaves, 8x4" **1,400.00**
Vase, gr, appl leaves on bulb bottom, Erikson, rstr, 10x6"............**990.00**
Vase, gr, broad leaves, sgn Annie Lingley, kiln pulls, 6x5" **850.00**
Vase, gr, broad leaves/buds, cylindrical, 11½", EX **1,400.00**
Vase, gr, cut-bk leaves, spherical, rim rstr, 4x4" **350.00**
Vase, gr, daffodils/long leaves (3 repeats), #147, 11" **3,750.00**
Vase, gr, emb vertical lines at long can neck, mfg flaw, 7"...........**650.00**
Vase, gr, leaves tooled at bulbous bottom, sgn, 7" **800.00**
Vase, gr, leaves/buds, glaze miss at base, bulbous, 8" **1,200.00**
Vase, gr, overlapping leaves, wide-mouth cylinder, 8¾" **600.00**
Vase, gr, slim upright leaves, cylinder w/sm rim, RE, 9" **4,000.00**
Vase, gr, tooled/appl end-curl leaves & buds, W Post, 13x9" .. **2,700.00**
Vase, gr, tooled/appl leaves, flat shoulder, rstr, 9x5" **1,300.00**
Vase, gr, wide leaves on bulbous base, sgn WP, 4½" **800.00**
Vase, gr, 16 tooled/appl upright leaves, W Post, 9x5½" **3,500.00**
Vase, gr, 6 cvd leaves, gourd form, sgn Erickson, 7" **880.00**
Vase, gr w/tooled & appl leaves & yel buds, W Post, 12x6" ... **4,125.00**
Vase, gr w/yel buds between tall leaves, R Erickson, 11x9" **7,000.00**
Vase, gr w/yel trefoils, cvd leaves at bulbous base, 13½" **3,800.00**
Vase, lt bl, hand thrown, 5x5" **220.00**
Vase, lt bl, wide leaves/stems/buds, 8x5", NM **1,600.00**
Vase, yel w/wht flowers, leaves on broad base, sgn/dtd, 10"..... **6,000.00**

Gutta Percha

Gutta Percha is the plastic substance from the latex of several types of Malaysian trees. It resembles rubber but contains more resin. A patent for the use of this material in manufacturing an early type of plastic was issued in the 1850s, and it was used extensively for daguerreotype cases and picture frames. Numbers in the following listings refer to *American Miniature Case Art* by Rinhart, an excellent reference that is now out of print. When found, copies of this book usually sell for $100.00 to $150.00.

Case, Church Window, Rinhart #52, 6th-plate, EX.......................**50.00**
Case, cluster w/leaf decor, w/ambrotype, 6th-plate, VG.................**50.00**
Case, Eagle at Bay, Rinhart #70, 6th-plate, VG **70.00**
Case, geometrics, Rinhart #180, 6th-plate **55.00**
Case, goblet w/flowers, Rinhart #142, 1850s, 9th-plate, EX...........**32.00**
Case, Gypsy Fortuneteller, w/ambrotype, 4th-plate, EX..............**135.00**
Case, leafy rosette fr in inverted oval, 9th-plate, VG **45.00**
Case, Mary & Her Lamb, Littlefield/Parsons, 1861, 9th-plate **55.00**
Case, Masonic symbols, 6th-plate, EX..**75.00**
Case, Tryst, 4th-plate, EX..**85.00**
Case, US shield on cannon/flags, ca 1845, 6th-plate, EX.............**85.00**
Frame, scalloped, ca 1850s, whole plate, 8¼x6¼" **195.00**
Match safe, Queen Victoria on front, rare **125.00**
Mirror, hand; lady's portrait, dtd 1866 ....**37.50**
Necklace, lg links, 20", +2½" rose pendant **65.00**
Token, Jefferson bust, Union Coffee Co, NY, 1½" **24.00**

Hair Weaving

A rather unusual craft became popular during the mid-1800s. Human hair was used to make jewelry (rings, bracelets, lockets, etc.) by braiding and interlacing fine strands of hair into hollow forms with pearls and beads added for effect. Hair wreaths were also made, often using hair from deceased family members as well as the living. They

were displayed in deep satin-lined frames along with mementoes of the weaver or her departed kin. The fad was abandoned before the turn of the century. Our advisor for this category is Steve DeGenaro; he is listed in the Directory under Ohio. See also Mourning Collectibles.

Bar pin, gold mt w/central ball of coiled hair...................................**65.00**
Bracelet, continuous hair coil, gold mts...**50.00**
Bracelet, narrow braid w/gold clasp...**85.00**
Bracelet, openwork, seed pearls/flowers in eng gold clasp **130.00**
Bracelet, patterned band, lg gold clasp set w/bl cameo.................**100.00**
Brooch, dbl coil of hair on gold mt...**100.00**
Brooch, gold & blk enamel fr around hair weaving.........................**65.00**
Brooch, gold/blk enamel, woven garden scene, sm heart drop.....**250.00**
Brooch, weaving: United By Love memorial, hearts/birds/etc **310.00**
Cuff links **110.00**
Locket, gold & enamel mt, knots/seed pearls/monogram plaque .**360.00**
Necklace, ribbon style, gold clasp set w/moss agate......................**140.00**
Necklace, woven 'beads,' w/heart-shape drop of coiled hair.........**100.00**
Necklace, 3 twisted coils of hair, 2 in lacy weave **95.00**
Pendant, cameo in ornate fr set w/garnets, hair on reverse **130.00**
Pendant, hair cross w/gold terminals & monogram plaque, lg......**110.00**
Pin, garnet fr enclosing hair sample, sm...**35.00**
Pin, heart & anchor made of fine hair coil **45.00**
Pin, 2 shades of hair w/in rectangular gold fr **40.00**
Ring, hair woven to resemble belt w/gold buckle.............................**50.00**
Stick pin, gold (?) mt w/finely woven initial **40.00**

Hall

The Hall China Company of East Liverpool, Ohio, was established in 1903. Their earliest product was whiteware toilet seats, mugs, jugs, etc. By 1920 their restaurant-type dinnerware and cookingware had become so successful that Hall was assured of a solid future. They continue today to be one of the country's largest manufacturers of this type of product.

Hall introduced the first of their famous teapots in 1920; new shapes and colors were added each year until about 1948, making them the largest teapot manufacturer in the world. These and the dinnerware lines of the thirties through the fifties have become popular collectibles. For more thorough study of the subject, we recommend *The Collector's Encyclopedia of Hall China* by Margaret and Kenn Whitmyer; their address may be found in the Directory under Ohio.

Flare Ware cookie jar with Gold Lace decoration, $45.00.

Acacia, bowl, Radiance, 7½"..**10.00**
Acacia, bowl, Radiance, 9"..**14.00**

Acacia, bowl, salad; 12" 12.00
Acacia, teapot, Radiance 95.00
Blue Blossom, bowl, thick rim, 7½" 30.00
Blue Blossom, casserole, Thick Rim 45.00
Blue Blossom, sugar bowl, w/lid, New York 30.00
Blue Bouquet, cake plate 16.00
Blue Bouquet, platter, oval, 13¼" 18.00
Blue Bouquet, shakers, hdld, pr 18.00
Blue Garden, teapot, New York 125.00
Blue Garden, teapot, Streamline 175.00
Blue Willow, casserole, 7½" 55.00
Bouquet (Zeisel), butter dish 35.00
Cactus, ball jug, #3 ....65.00
Cactus, bowl, Five Band, 6" 18.00
Cactus, cookie jar, Five Band 125.00
Cactus, sugar bowl, w/lid, Viking 20.00
Cactus, teapot, French 75.00
Cameo Rose, bowl, vegetable; w/lid 30.00
Cameo Rose, plate, 7¼" 6.00
Cameo Rose, platter, oval, 15½" 20.00
Clover, bowl, Radiance, 6" 15.00
Clover, shakers, hdld, pr 30.00
Crocus, bowl, cereal; 6" 12.00
Crocus, coffeepot, Meltdown 50.00
Crocus, drip jar, #1188, open 45.00
Crocus, plate, 6" 5.00
Crocus, shakers, hdld, pr 18.00
Crocus, water bottle, Zephyr 200.00
Fantasy, bean pot, New England, #4 ....85.00
Five Band, carafe, Chinese red 95.00
Flamingo, creamer, Viking 18.00
Flare Ware, coffee server, 15-cup 35.00
Heather Rose, bowl, fruit; 5¼" 4.00
Heather Rose, bowl, oval, 9¼" 11.00
Heather Rose, plate, 6½" 4.00
Heather Rose, platter, oval, 13¼" 12.00
Heather Rose, teapot, London 20.00
Meadow Flower, ball jug, #3 ....45.00
Meadow Flower, casserole, Radiance 28.00
Morning Glory, bean pot, New England, #4 ....75.00
Morning Glory, bowl, Thick Rim, 8½" 16.00
Morning Glory, pretzel jar 85.00
Morning Glory, teapot, Rutherford 65.00
Mt Vernon, bowl, cereal; 6¼" 4.50
Mt Vernon, plate, 8" 5.00
Mums, bowl, soup; flat, 8½" 12.00
Mums, coffeepot, Terrace 55.00
Mums, creamer, Art Deco 12.00
Mums, creamer, Medallion 10.00
Mums, platter, oval, 13¼" 16.00
Orange Poppy, bowl, vegetable; rnd, 9¼" 20.00
Orange Poppy, coffeepot, Great American 45.00
Orange Poppy, jug, #3, ball form 38.00
Orange Poppy, plate, 7¾" 8.00
Orange Poppy, platter, oval, 11¼" 16.00
Orange Poppy, shakers, hdld, pr 18.00
Pastel Morning-Glory, bowl, soup; flat, 8½" 12.00
Pastel Morning-Glory, plate, 6" 4.00
Pastel Morning-Glory, shakers, hdld, pr 18.00
Primrose, bowl, oval, 9¼" 12.00
Red Poppy, bowl, cereal; 6" 8.00
Red Poppy, bowl, Radiance, 7½" 10.00
Red Poppy, bowl, salad; 9" 16.00
Red Poppy, cake safe, metal 20.00

Red Poppy, creamer, Daniel 8.00
Red Poppy, cutting board, wooden 30.00
Red Poppy, jug, Radiance, #5 ....16.00
Red Poppy, plate, 8¼" 6.00
Red Poppy, shakers, ea 8.00
Red Poppy, soap dispenser, metal 30.00
Red Poppy, tumbler, clear glass 18.00
Richmond, platter, oval, 13¼" 12.00
Rose Parade, bowl, str-sided, 9" 16.00
Rose Parade, shakers, Pert, pr 20.00
Rose White, bowl, Medallion, 6" 12.00
Rose White, bowl, str-sided, 9" 12.00
Rose White, jug, Pert, 5" 13.00
Rose White, sugar bowl, Pert 12.00
Royal Rose, ball jug, #3 ....30.00
Royal Rose, teapot, Aladdin 95.00
Sears' Arlington, pickle dish, 9" 5.00
Serenade, bowl, fruit; 5½" 3.00
Serenade, drip jar, w/lid, Radiance 14.00
Serenade, platter, 13¼" 14.00
Serenade, saucer 1.50
Shaggy Tulip, teapot, Radiance 95.00
Silhouette, ball jug, #3 ....65.00
Silhouette, bowl, Radiance, 7½" 14.00
Silhouette, bowl, vegetable; rnd, 9¼" 16.00
Silhouette, casserole, Medallion 30.00
Silhouette, creamer, modern 10.00
Silhouette, jug, Medallion, #3 ....16.00
Silhouette, pitcher, clear glass, Federal 95.00
Silhouette, plate, 9" 10.00
Silhouette, shakers, Five Band, pr 16.00
Silhouette, sugar bowl, w/lid, Medallion 12.00
Silhouette, teapot, New York 95.00
Silhouette, tray, rectangular, metal 32.00
Spring (Zeisel), bowl, salad; lg, 14½" 12.00
Spring (Zeisel), coffeepot, 6-cup 30.00
Springtime, cake plate 12.00
Springtime, platter, oval, 13¼" 14.00
Stonewall, casserole, Radiance 30.00
Sunglow, ash tray 4.00
Teapot, Adele, maroon 100.00
Teapot, Airflow, cobalt w/gold flowers....................35.00
Teapot, Aladdin, marine bl w/gold, 6-cup 40.00
Teapot, Apple, blk w/gold trim 250.00
Teapot, Automobile, cobalt w/platinum, 6-cup 400.00
Teapot, Automobile, maroon w/silver 350.00
Teapot, Baltimore, red 75.00
Teapot, Basket, emerald gr w/gold 145.00

Teapot, basket-ball, Chinese Red, $400.00.

Teapot, Boston, emerald gr w/gold trim, 6-cup	32.00
Teapot, Damascus, turq, 6-cup	100.00
Teapot, Donut, red	275.00
Teapot, Football, Chinese red, 6-cup	400.00
Teapot, Football, emerald gr w/gold trim	375.00
Teapot, French, Cadet bl w/gold flowers	45.00
Teapot, Hollywood, daffodil, gold net, 4-cup	28.00
Teapot, Hollywood, maroon, 4-cup	20.00
Teapot, Kansas, emerald gr w/gold trim	250.00
Teapot, Melody, canary w/wht & gold, 6-cup	175.00
Teapot, Melody, Chinese red	145.00
Teapot, Moderne, turq w/gold, 6-cup	42.00
Teapot, Murphy, turq bl, 1940s	35.00
Teapot, Nautilus, maroon w/gold	125.00
Teapot, New York, Cadet bl w/gold, 2-cup	30.00
Teapot, New York, cobalt w/gold band variant, 4-cup	35.00
Teapot, New York, cobalt w/gold trim, 6-cup	30.00
Teapot, New York, delphinium bl w/gold, 2-cup	22.00
Teapot, New York, red, 6-cup	55.00
Teapot, Ohio, blk with gold trim	250.00
Teapot, Philadelphia, marine bl w/gold, 6-cup	50.00
Teapot, Philadelphia, turq w/gold, 6-cup	45.00
Teapot, Regal, Apple gr w/gold trim	150.00
Teapot, Rhythm, Chinese red, 6-cup	150.00
Teapot, Rhythm, cobalt, 6-cup	150.00
Teapot, Star, Chinese red	125.00
Teapot, Star, cobalt w/gold	75.00
Teapot, Star, turq w/gold & stars, 6-cup	35.00
Teapot, Streamline, canary w/platinum, 6-cup	75.00
Teapot, Twinspout, marine bl w/gold, 6-cup	95.00
Teapot, Windshield, maroon, roses & gold, 6-cup	35.00
Teapot, World's Fair	275.00
Tulip, bowl, fruit; 5½"	4.00
Tulip, bowl, Radiance, 9"	14.00
Tulip, bowl, Thick Rim, 8½"	17.00
Tulip, creamer, modern	8.00
Tulip, shakers, hdld, pr	22.00
Wild Poppy, bean pot, New England, #3	75.00
Wild Poppy, coffeepot, drip; sm, Terrace	125.00
Wild Poppy, custard, Radiance	8.00
Wild Poppy, sugar bowl, w/lid, Hollywood	25.00
Wildfire, bowl, Thick Rim, 6"	12.00
Wildfire, drip jar, w/lid, Thick Rim	18.00
Wildfire, shakers, hdld, pr	18.00
Wildfire, teapot, Boston	75.00
Yellow Rose, bowl, cereal; 6"	8.00
Yellow Rose, bowl, soup; flat, 8½"	10.00
Yellow Rose, coffeepot, Dome	35.00
Yellow Rose, plate, 8¼"	4.00
Yellow Rose, shakers, hdld, pr	18.00
Yellow Rose, teapot, New York	40.00

Hallmark

Hallmark introduced a line of artplas (molded plastic) ornaments in 1973 that has quickly become popular with collectors. Also of growing interest to collectors are the small artplas party-type favors now known as Merry Miniatures. A magazine edited by Rosie Wells, our advisor for this category, is available if you want more information. Rosie also publishes a yearly official Secondary Price Guide on Hallmark ornaments. Her address is listed in the Directory under Clubs, Newsletters, and Catalogs, and again under Illinois. Items listed below are assumed to be in mint condition with the original box.

1974, Snowgoose, QX107-1, wht glass ball, 3¼" dia	77.00
1976, Nostalgia, QX222-1, Locomotive, as in '75, dtd 1976	160.00
1977, Nostalgia, QX181-5, Nativity	145.00
1979, Blk Angel, QX207-9, gold glass ball	15.00
1979, Here Comes Santa, QX155-9, Santa's Motorcar	425.00
1979, Rocking Horse, QX340-7, quilted fabric ornament	15.00
1980, Here Comes Santa, QX143-4, Santa's Express	175.00
1980, Rockwell, QX306-1, Santa's Visitors, 1st in series	215.00
1982, Frosty Friends, QX452-3, 3rd in series	125.00
1982, Holiday Wildlife, QX313-3, Cardinals, 1st in series	400.00
1983, Friendship, QMB904-7, musical ornament, 4½"	135.00
1983, Tin Locomotive, QX404-9, 2nd in series, dtd	195.00
1984, Brass Carousel, QLX707-1	70.00
1984, Heartful of Love, QX443-4, bone china	40.00
1984, 3 Kittens in Mitten, QX431-1, knitted mitten	40.00
1985, Candy Apple Mouse, QX470-5, handcrafted	45.00
1985, Frosty Friends, QX482-2, 6th in series	47.50
1986, Mr & Mrs Santa, QX705-2, lighted, 1985 reissue	75.00
1987, Tin Locomotive, QX484-9, 6th in series, dtd	40.00
1988, Country Express, QLX721-1, light & motion ornament	40.00
1989, Kringle's Toy Shop, QLX701-7, light & motion ornament	55.00
1990, Frosty Friends, QX439-6, 11th in series, 2½"	17.50
1990, Starship Christmas, QLX733-6, blinking lights	27.00
1991, Starship Enterprise, QLX719-9, average value	100.00

Halloween

The origin of Halloween can be traced back to the ancient practices of the Druids of Great Britain who began their New Year on the 1st of November. The Druids were pagans and their New Year's celebrations involved pagan rites and superstitions. They believed that as the old year came to an end the Devil would gather up all the demons and evil in the world and take them back to Hell with him. Witches were women who had sold their souls to the Devil and, with their black cat in attendance, flew up through their chimneys on brooms. When the Roman Catholic Church came into power in 700 A.D., they changed the holiday into a religious event called 'All Saints Day,' or 'Allhallow's.' The evening before, October 31, became 'Allhallow's Eve' or 'Hallowe'en.' Today Halloween is strictly a fun time, and Halloween items are fun to collect. Pumpkin-head candy containers of papier-mache or pressed cardboard, noisemakers, post cards with black cats and witches, costumes, and decorations are only a sampling of the variety available. See also Candy Containers.

Candy container, cat, mohair covered, Germany, 1920s, EX	235.00
Candy container, ghost head, papier-mache, Victorian, 3½"	250.00
Candy container, jack-o'-lantern, compo, Germany, 3"	185.00
Candy container, jack-o'-lantern, Fleischmann's label, 4½"	110.00
Candy container, vegetable man, squash body/bean legs, 2¼"	250.00
Candy container, witch, cotton batting/crepe, Japan, '30s, 5"	265.00
Clapper, wood, witch on broom, city skyline, 8¼x4½"	85.00
Decoration, bat w/honeycomb, Beistle	45.00
Decoration, blk cat w/arched bk, diecut, Germany, lg	65.00
Decoration, Dracula, pressed cb, Japan, 1950s	65.00
Decoration, jack-o'-lantern, crepe paper, Dennison, M in pkg	85.00
Decoration, owl, papier-mache, blk w/orange & gold, lg	195.00
Decoration, owl sits w/in man-in-moon, diecut, 5" dia	65.00
Decoration, witch, paper, accordion type, USA, '30s, 27"	65.00
Decoration, witch, pressed cb, orange/blk/wht, 8", EX	95.00
Fan, cat face, paper w/crepe paper trim, 12½"	85.00
Jack-o'-lantern, owl, pressed cb, blk w/orange & gold, lg	150.00
Jack-o'-lantern, pressed cb, faces both sides, 10½"	150.00
Jack-o'-lantern, pressed cb, 4½"	85.00

Jack-o'-lantern, tin, worn yel/blk pnt, w/bail, early, 6½" 650.00
Jack-o'-lantern, tin litho, owl/moon/bats, 1930s, 5x6" 95.00

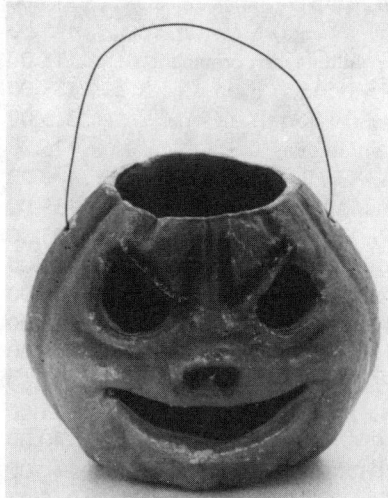

Jack-o'-lantern, 9½", $90.00.

Lantern, cat w/paper eyes & mouth, VG 95.00
Lantern, cat's face, blk pressed cb, orig insert, 6" 95.00
Lantern, skull, milk glass, metal fr, 1920s.....................................85.00
Mask, witch, paper litho, Germany 85.00
Nodder, pumpkin head on log, compo, orange/blk, 6" 485.00
Noisemaker, blk devil, litho on tin, wood hdl, 5", EX 45.00
Noisemaker, clown & girl, metal & wood, USA, EX 25.00
Noisemaker, clowns playing drums, litho on tin, USA 25.00
Noisemaker, girls in costumes, tin & wood, Barone Toy Mfg 17.50
Noisemaker, witches, tin litho, Kirckhof, 12½", EX 25.00
Noisemaker, 3 boys & girl make noise, Kirckhof USA...................25.00
Nut cup, witch diecut on blk & orange paper.................................25.00
Punch board, Japan, 3½x2½", NM...45.00
Rattle, witches/cats on tin litho, Gotham, 6x4" dia 45.00
Roly poly, scarecrow, celluloid, 3½", NM...................................120.00
Tambourine, people dance about pumpkin face, tin, 6½" dia 85.00
Tambourine, pumpkin face, Chein, EX...85.00

Hamada, Shoji

Shoji Hamada is the most famous of all Japanese potters. He was a former chemist who worked with Bernard Leach in the 1920s to rediscover the art of Oriental 'rural' pottery. All of Hamada's ceramics were fired in a wood-fired kiln. He used local clays, oxides, and ash glazes ground by hand. Hamada used a seal mark during the early 1920s when he was at St. Ives, England. After returning to Japan in 1923, his work was never signed. Instead he signed the wooden boxes he used for shipping.

Bottle, iron-pigmented brn, irregular facets, att, 10" 175.00
Bowl, iron-pigment organic forms on neutral, w/spout, 5x8" 450.00
Pitcher, salt glaze, stylized iris ea side, no mk, 7½" 200.00

Hampshire

The Hampshire Pottery Company was established in 1871 in Keene, New Hampshire, by James Scollay Taft. Their earliest products were redware and stoneware utility items such as jugs, churns, crocks, and flowerpots. In 1878 they produced majolica ware which met with such success that they began to experiment with the idea of manufacturing art pottery. By 1883 they had developed a Royal Worcester type of finish which they applied to vases, tea sets, powder boxes, and cookie

jars. It was also utilized for souvenir items that were decorated with transfer designs prepared from photographic plates.

Cadmon Robertson, brother-in-law of Taft, joined the company in 1904 and was responsible for developing their famous matt glazes. Colors included shades of green, brown, red, and blue. Early examples were of earthenware, but eventually the body changed to semi-porcelain. Some of his designs were marked with an M in a circle as a tribute to his wife, Emoretta. Robertson died in 1914, leaving a void impossible to fill. Taft sold the business in 1916 to George Morton, who continued to use the matt glazes that Robertson had developed. After a temporary halt in production during WWI, Morton returned to Keene and re-equipped the factory with the machinery needed to manufacture hotel china and floor tile. Because of the expense involved in transporting coal to fire the kilns, Morton found he could not compete with potteries of Ohio and New Jersey who were able to utilize locally available natural gas. He was forced to close the plant in 1923.

Bowl, bulb; leaves emb on gr matt, lt gr gloss int, #57, 10" 300.00
Bowl, water lilies emb on gr matt, 3x10"...90.00
Bowl vase, leaves/ribs emb on gr matt, angular body, 4" H 275.00
Cookie jar, Royal Worcester, souvenir, egg form/claw ft, 7" 125.00
Lamp base, morning-glory leaves/vines, bl gloss, 15", EX.............375.00
Pitcher, Royal Worchester, souvenir, upright top, no mk, 5½" 40.00

Stein, photographic view of Greensboro Women's College, 5½", $75.00.

Stein, Royal Worcester, souvenir (train), holly band, 5½" 85.00
Urn, gr matt, architectural hdls, 11" 435.00
Vase, bl mottle, swollen cylinder w/narrow mouth, 6½" 325.00
Vase, buds/leaves/stems emb on mauve matt, circle mk, 6¾".......225.00
Vase, gr matt, narrow neck w/looping hdls, 14"...........................425.00
Vase, leaves emb on bl mottle, bulbous, 8", NM 225.00
Vase, leaves emb on lt bl w/dk bl specks, 4" 150.00
Vase, Royal Worcester, souvenir, tree stump form, mk, 4½".........45.00
Vase, upright overlapped leaves, gr matt, ovoid, #127, 8½" 350.00
Vase, 5 leaves/buds emb on mottled gr matt, wht clay, 7"............295.00

Handel

Philip Handel was best known for the art glass lamps he produced at the turn of the century. His work is similar to the Tiffany lamps of the same era. Handel made gas and electric lamps with both leaded glass and reverse-painted shades. Chipped ice shades with a texture similar to overshot glass were also produced. Shades signed by artists such as Bailey, Palme, and Parlow are highly valued.

China and glassware decorated by Handel are rare and command high prices on today's market. Teroma is a term used to describe glassware decorated on the exterior with paint that has a sandy finish. Many of Handel's chinaware blanks were supplied by Limoges. Our advisor for this category is Daniel Batchelor; he is listed in the Directory under New York.

Leaded glass lamp with irises, Handel tag within, 24" diameter, $3,500.00.

Lamps

Base, bronze w/gr patina, simple tree-trunk design, 22".................**175.00**
Boudoir, 6-rib 7" floral shade sgn Sample #5; bl metal std.......**1,300.00**
Candle, chipped ice 8¼" shade w/pnt fruits, sgn/#7173, pr......**1,500.00**
Candle, Teroma woods shade w/irid wash int, unsgn, 15"............**600.00**
Desk, geometric-etched half-cylinder shade adjusts, 12"..........**1,300.00**
Floor, rvpt 10" scenic dome shade w/in 3-leg harp fr, 57" **4,400.00**
Hanging, strapwork mt w/4 strapwork-design shades, #3410........**950.00**
Hanging, 10" ball w/pnt parrot on branch on gold, metal mts. **1,900.00**
Hanging, 6 shaped panels, metal o/l border, sgn, 22" **550.00**
Lamp, pnt 7" frosted/orange shade w/ivy in harp std, 57"............**465.00**
Night lite, Teroma frosted crackle shade, hardwood std, 7½" **600.00**
Shade, gas chandelier; Teroma leaves, sgn RG, 6-sided, #2904 ...**275.00**
Shade, rvpt woods & birds, sgn Gubisch, sgn/#6886, 10" **2,500.00**
Table, chipped ice 15" yel shade w/gr floral; textured std............**950.00**
Table, chipped ice 18" cone shade w/pnt floral band; mk std.. **3,000.00**
Table, ldgl 14" shade w/6 bent panels, bronze forest o/l...........**1,500.00**
Table, ldgl 19" wisteria shade w/rtcl top, tree base.................**10,000.00**
Table, ldgl 20" panel/disk 7-side shade; bronzed base, EX **800.00**
Table, pnt 18" daffodil/leaves sanded shade; leaf-mold std......**4,250.00**
Table, pnt 18" dmns/tulip-panels shade sgn RC; Chinese std.. **2,600.00**
Table, rvpt 15" birch trees shade; bronze metal std, 22" **2,500.00**
Table, rvpt 15" woodland domical shade; oviform std, 22"......**1,900.00**
Table, rvpt 16" birch trees shade; sgn/#5519 std, 24" **3,000.00**
Table, rvpt 18" autumn leaf shade, sgn/#6204; 24" **3,700.00**
Table, rvpt 18" chipped ice scenic shade; Chinese vase std..... **8,000.00**
Table, rvpt 18" chipped ice scenic shade; Grueby-style std **13,000.00**
Table, rvpt 18" chipped ice shade w/trees sgn Bailey; EX **3,950.00**
Table, rvpt 18" daffodil #5648 shade; sgn baluster std **5,000.00**
Table, rvpt 18" desert/bldgs/people shade, Bailey; urn std **7,500.00**
Table, rvpt 18" dogwoods vase sgn/#6818; vase std, 23" **4,000.00**
Table, rvpt 18" exotic bird shade, sgn/#7125, scrolled std **23,000.00**
Table, rvpt 18" floral conical shade; scroll-ftd std, 24" **5,450.00**
Table, rvpt 18" landscape shade #7115; invt lily std **3,500.00**
Table, rvpt 18" landscape shade; 4-hdl/4-ftd std #7031 ....**5,250.00**

Table, rvpt 18" leaves & berries shade; quatrefoil ftd std.........**1,550.00**
Table, rvpt 18" macaws/jungle shade; urn std on rtcl base **17,600.00**
Table, rvpt 18" mtn landscape shade; baluster std, 23" **6,000.00**
Table, rvpt 18" Nile/Egyptian #6641 shade; #1853 std, 26" **7,000.00**
Table, rvpt 18" parrots & florals shade, sgn/#7023, 24" **18,000.00**
Table, rvpt 18" roses/butterflies shade #7032; leafy std...........**12,000.00**
Table, rvpt 18" scenic shade; std w/3 scroll legs on disk **6,000.00**
Table, Teroma/rvpt 18" scenic shade #5487; trunk std, 23" **5,000.00**
Table, Teroma 10" floral shade by WR; #2654, 20" **2,000.00**
Table, Teroma 15" aquatic shade sgn Palme; mermaid std **10,000.00**
Table, Teroma 18" exotic birds shade by Palme; 3-part std ...**13,500.00**
Table, 6-panel 15" slag shade w/floral o/l; #1801 std **2,750.00**
Table, 6-panel 18" slag shade w/floral o/l; unmk std **4,000.00**

Miscellaneous

Candlestick, Teroma, amber/clear frost, floral etch, 9" **300.00**
Candlestick, Teroma, windmill on pastels, sgn, 8½", pr **2,400.00**
Cigar urn, 3 Indians, ormolu, 3½", +ash tray & match urn **1,400.00**
Humidor, monk drinking wine on dk gr, mk, 6x3" **1,000.00**
Humidor, owl on branch, squat/bulbous, #4038......................**1,400.00**
Sconce, hammered copper, #5199, 11" **500.00**
Vase, Teroma, gold wheat on lt gr w/chipped ice effect, 5x4"......**400.00**
Vase, Teroma, mtns/trees on chipped ground, sgn Bailey, 10" **2,850.00**
Vase, Teroma, mtns/trees on chipped ice ground, 10" **2,000.00**

Harker

The Harker Pottery was established in East Liverpool, Ohio, in 1840. Their earliest products were yellowware and Rockingham produced from local clay. After 1900 whiteware was made from imported materials. The plant eventually grew to be a large manufacturer of dinnerware and kitchenware, employing as many as three hundred people. It closed in 1972 after it was purchased by the Jeannette Glass Company. Perhaps their best-known lines were their Cameo wares, decorated with white silhouettes in a cameo effect on contrasting solid colors. Floral silhouettes are standard, but other designs were also used. Blue and pink are the most often found background hues; a few pieces are found in yellow.

Colonial Lady batter set, $70.00.

Baker, Petit Point, 9"...**17.50**
Bowl, Amy, deep, 9"..**20.00**
Bowl, Chesterton Gray, 5½" **5.00**

Bowl, Mallow, 6" 6.00
Bowl, utility; Deco Dahlia, 9" 17.50
Cake lifter, Amy 14.00
Cake plate, Deco Dahlia, w/lid 15.00
Casserole, Petit Point, w/lid, 8½" 35.00
Creamer, Cameo Rose 8.00
Custard, Deco Dahlia 4.00
Custard, Red Apple 12.00
Jug, batter; Amy, w/lid 25.00
Pie plate, Amy 10.00
Pie plate, Cameo Rose, 9" 20.00
Plate, Mallow & Pansy, 12" 10.00
Plate, Pastel Tulip, salad sz 3.00
Plate, Springtime, tab hdls, 6¾" 3.00
Platter, Cameo Rose, 14" 15.00
Rolling pin, Fruits 75.00
Rolling pin, Kelvinator 85.00
Rolling pin, Mexican decal 75.00
Rolling pin, Pastel Tulip 80.00
Shakers, Orange Tulip, pr 6.00
Spoon, Mallow 16.00
Spoon, Red Apple 12.00
Sugar scoop, Amy 35.00
Teapot, Modern Tulip 15.00
Teapot, Orange Tulip w/Wheat 20.00

Harlequin

Harlequin dinnerware, produced by the Homer Laughlin China Company of Newell, West Virginia, was introduced in 1938. It was a lightweight ware made in maroon, mauve blue, and spruce green, as well as all the Fiesta colors except ivory (see Fiesta). It was marketed exclusively by the Woolworth stores, who considered it to be their all-time best seller. For this reason, they contracted with Homer Laughlin to reissue Harlequin to commemorate their 100th anniversary in 1979. Although three of the original glazes were used in the reissue, the few serving pieces that were made were restyled, and collectors found the new line to be no threat to their investments.

The Harlequin animals, including a fish, lamb, cat, penguin, duck, and donkey, were made during the early 1940s, also for the dime-store trade. Today these are very desirable to collectors of Homer Laughlin China.

In the listings that follow, use the values designated 'high' for all colors other than turquoise and yellow. For medium green, double the 'high' values on all items other than flat items and small bowls. *The Collector's Encyclopedia of Fiesta* by Sharon and Bob Huxford is available in its seventh edition and contains a more thorough study of this subject. Available from Collector Books or your local bookstore.

Demitasse cup and saucer, $30.00 to $50.00;

Animals, mavericks 30.00
Animals, non-standard colors 140.00
Animals, standard colors 65.00
Ash tray, basketweave, high 42.00
Ash tray, basketweave, low 30.00
Ash tray, regular, high 45.00
Ash tray, regular, low 40.00
Bowl, '36s oatmeal; high 16.00
Bowl, '36s oatmeal; low 10.00
Bowl, '36s; high 22.00
Bowl, '36s; low 15.00
Bowl, cream soup; high 16.00
Bowl, cream soup; low 12.00
Bowl, fruit; high, 5½" 8.00
Bowl, fruit; low, 5½" 5.00
Bowl, ind salad; high 20.00
Bowl, ind salad; low 15.00
Bowl, mixing; Kitchen Kraft, mauve bl, 8" 110.00
Bowl, mixing; Kitchen Kraft, red or spruce gr, 6" .. 70.00
Bowl, mixing; Kitchen Kraft, yel, 10" 110.00
Bowl, nappy; high, 9" 22.00
Bowl, nappy; low, 9" 15.00
Bowl, oval baker, high 22.00
Bowl, oval baker, low 16.00
Butter dish, high, ½-lb 82.00
Butter dish, low, ½-lb 70.00
Candle holder, high, pr 180.00
Candle holder, low, pr 150.00
Casserole, w/lid, high 80.00
Casserole, w/lid, low 50.00
Creamer, high lip, any color 70.00
Creamer, ind; high 16.00
Creamer, ind; low 12.00
Creamer, novelty, high 20.00
Creamer, novelty, low 14.00
Creamer, regular, high 12.00
Creamer, regular, low 8.00
Cup, demitasse; high 40.00
Cup, demitasse; low 25.00
Cup, lg, any color 88.00
Cup, tea; high 9.00
Cup, tea; low 7.50
Egg cup, dbl, high 18.00
Egg cup, dbl, low 12.00
Egg cup, single, high 20.00
Egg cup, single, low 16.00
Gravy boat, high 20.00
Gravy boat, low 15.00
Marmalade, any color 100.00
Nut dish, basketweave, orig color 7.50
Perfume bottle, any color 65.00
Pitcher, service water; high 45.00
Pitcher, service water; low 35.00
Pitcher, 22-oz jug, high 42.00
Pitcher, 22-oz jug, low 24.00
Plate, deep; high 18.00
Plate, deep; low 12.00
Plate, high, 10" 22.00
Plate, high, 6" 4.50
Plate, high, 7" 6.50
Plate, high, 9" 12.00
Plate, low, 10" 13.00
Plate, low, 6" 3.50
Plate, low, 7" 4.50

Plate, low, 9"	7.00
Platter, high, 11"	16.00
Platter, high, 13"	22.00
Platter, low, 11"	10.00
Platter, low, 13"	15.00
Saucer, demitasse; high	10.00
Saucer, demitasse; low	6.00
Saucer, high	3.50
Saucer, low	2.00
Saucer/ash tray, high	42.00
Saucer/ash tray, ivory	60.00
Saucer/ash tray, low	40.00
Shakers, high, pr	15.00
Shakers, low, pr	12.00
Sugar bowl, w/lid, high	16.00
Sugar bowl, w/lid, low	12.00
Syrup, any color	160.00
Teapot, high	80.00
Teapot, low	55.00
Tray, relish; mixed colors	180.00
Tumbler, high	40.00
Tumbler, low	30.00

Hatpin Holders

Most hatpin holders were made from 1860 to 1920 to coincide with the period during which hatpins were in vogue. The taller types were required to house the long hatpins necessary to secure the large hats that were in style from 1890 to 1914. They were usually porcelain, either decorated by hand or by transfer with florals or scenics, although some were clever figurals. Glass examples are rare, and those of slag or carnival glass are especially valuable.

If you are interested in collecting or dealing in hatpins or hatpin holders, you will find that authority Lillian Baker has several fine books available on the subject, including her most recent publication *Collector's Encyclopedia of Hatpins and Hatpin Holders*, complete with beautiful color illustrations and current market values. She is listed in the Directory under California. For information concerning the International Club for Collectors of Hatpins and Hatpin Holders, see the Clubs, Newsletters, and Catalogs section of the Directory. Our advisor for this category is Robert Larsen; he is listed in the Directory under Nebraska.

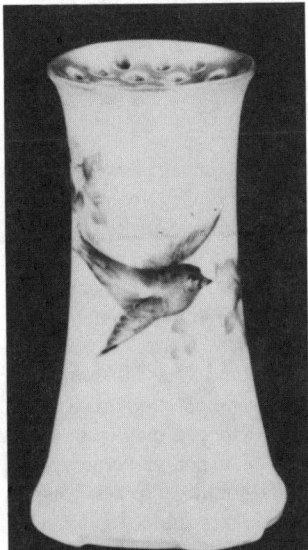

**R.S. Germany with bluebird, 4½",
$85.00.**

Admiral Perry, 13 pin holes, RS Prussia mk, 3¾"	1,200.00
Austrian, china slipper w/florals, wall mt, pr	550.00
Austrian, HP floral, w/attached trinket box	200.00
Bisque, cameo medallion on cone-form wall mt	240.00
Bisque, lg bear beside cylinder	600.00
Brass, w/pincushion, pin tray, ring holder	140.00
China, HP floral, artist sgn, wall mt	260.00
China, HP floral, saucer type	90.00
China, lady's portrait on slipper form	175.00
China, roses on obelisk form	60.00
China, slipper form, wall mt	220.00
English, butterflies, gold/cobalt on pearl lustre, 1895, 5"	295.00
English, china, Isle of Man, souvenir	45.00
Germany, china w/roses in high releif	60.00
Nippon, gold w/florals, mk Hand Painted	250.00
Royal Bayreuth, lady's portrait tapestry, bl mk	575.00
Royal Vienna, bsk lady by shell, mk Wahliss	625.00
RS Prussia, hexagonal w/floral, attached trinket box, mk	400.00
Schafer & Vater, jasperware medallion, 5"	155.00

Hatpins

A hatpin was used to securely fasten a hat to the hair and head of the wearer. Hatpins, measuring from 4" to 12" in length, were worn from approximately 1850 to 1920. During the Art Deco period, hatpins became ornaments rather than the decorative functional jewels that they had been. The hatpin period reached its zenith in 1913 just prior to World War I, which brought about a radical change in women's headdress and fashion. About that time, women began to scorn the bonnet and adopt 'the hat' as a symbol of their equality. The hatpin was made of every natural and manufactured element in a myriad of designs that challenge the imagination. They were contrived to serve every fashion need and complement the milliner's art. Collectors often concentrate on a specific type: hand-painted porcelains, sterling silver, commemoratives, sporting activities, carnival glass, Art Nouveau and/or Art Deco designs, Victorian Gothics with mounted stones, exquisite rhinestones, engraved and brass-mounted escutcheon heads, gold and gems, or simply primitive types made in the Victorian parlor. Some collectors prefer the long pin-shanks while others select only those on tremblants or nodder-type pin-shanks.

If you are interested in collecting or dealing in hatpins, see the information in the Hatpin Holders introduction concerning reference books and a national collectors' club. For further study we recommend *The Collector's Encyclopedia of Hatpins and Hatpin Holders*, available at your local bookstore. or from Collector Books. Our advisor for this category is Robert Larson; he is listed in the Directory under Nebraska.

Amethyst, kidney form, faceted, 10"	65.00
Amethyst quartz, in sterling fr, 9"	70.00
Branch coral, mt mk Gold Top, 6"	55.00
Brass claw holds pearl, 8¾"	75.00
Celluloid, amber rose bud, 6½"	65.00
Celluloid, gray pleated cone w/button top, 8"	45.00
China, ball form w/HP robins, 8½"	150.00
China, heart shape w/HP roses, 7½"	95.00
Conch shell, w/5 hanging shells, 9"	65.00
Conch shell, wire mt, 8"	45.00
Copper, crab figure, 5¼"	55.00
Coral rose, in Art Nouveau mt, 8"	110.00
Feather-covered ball mtd w/brilliants, 6"	65.00
Gilt metal, bison head, 7"	55.00
Gilt metal, lg owl head w/glass eyes, 7¾"	80.00
Gilt metal, Model T, wheels turn, rhinestone lights, 8"	260.00

Gilt metal, race car w/driver, 9½" 75.00
Gilt metal beetle, gr enamel/brilliants, spring mt, 7¾"................300.00
Gilt metal lily mtd w/fresh-water pearl, 8½" 65.00
Glass, bl ribbed heart, 8¾"...75.00
Gold tone, lantern set w/lg brilliant, 8¾" 210.00

Gold-tone metal knot with drop, $115.00; Celluloid flower, $45.00.

Gold-washed Indian head set w/agate, 8" 300.00
Gold-washed mt, cameo type, 8½"..110.00
Goldstone/gilt metal spider on movable mt, 7¾" 180.00
Ivory, button type w/cvd dragon, 12¾"....................................100.00
Ivory, cvd monkey riding on rabbit, 10", NM...............................55.00
Ivory, 3-D dog's head w/inlaid eyes, 10½"..................................140.00
Ivory, 3-D hand, 7" 40.00
MOP, barrel w/miniature view, 8¾" 80.00
MOP, fish figural, 9" 40.00
Mosaic, dome shape, 10½" 120.00
Mosaic, heart shape, 8"..185.00
Moss agate, cube shape, 9"...35.00
Plastic, acorn w/face, 7" 35.00
Plastic, wht w/faux mosaic decor, 7" 40.00
Plique-a-jour, gr, flattened dome shape....................................675.00
Porc w/HP portrait & brilliants, 11¾" 130.00
Rhinestone, lg button type, 12½"..50.00
Satsuma, geisha girls 245.00
Silver, boar figural, European, 9"..60.00
Silver lyre set w/1 pearl, English hallmks, 11" 120.00
Sterling, Charles Horner 55.00
Sterling, ear of corn, 12" 65.00
Sterling, fencing sword, ornate, 6" 40.00
Sterling, flying reptile w/colored stone, 7½" 80.00
Sterling, horse head w/horseshoe, 7½".......................................75.00
Sterling, Indian head figural, Hiawatha & Laughing Water, pr...575.00
Sterling, Louisiana Purchase Exposition, 7½".............................130.00
Sterling mt w/lg bl stone, 9½" 120.00
Sterling w/ornate monogram, 8"...45.00
Sulfide w/rooster, 10"...130.00
Tortoise shell, openwork ball, 11"..150.00
Turquoise, cushion-mt, single stone, 9¾" 40.00
Turquoise w/matrix, in gold-washed mt, 9" 40.00
Wood, button w/pnt-on snake & fruit, 6¾" 30.00
Wood, egg shape, blk finish set w/brilliants, 13" 30.00

Haviland

The Haviland China Company was organized in 1840 by David Haviland, a New York china importer. His search for a pure white, non-porous porcelain led him to Limoges, France, where natural deposits of suitable clay had already attracted numerous china manufacturers. The fine china he produced there was translucent and meticulously decorated, with each piece fired in an individual sagger.

It has been estimated that as many as 60,000 chinaware patterns were designed, each piece marked with one of several company backstamps. 'H. & Co.' was used until 1890 when a law was enacted making it necessary to include the country of origin. Various marks have been used since that time including 'Haviland, France'; 'Haviland & Co. Limoges'; and 'Decorated by Haviland & Co.' Various associations with family members over the years have resulted in changes in management as well as company name. In 1892 Theodore Haviland left the firm to start his own business. Some of his ware was marked 'Mont Mery.' Later logos included a horseshoe, a shield, and various uses of his initials and name. In 1941 this branch moved to the United States. Wares produced here are marked 'Theodore Haviland, N.Y.' or 'Made In America.'

Though it is their dinnerware lines for which they are most famous, during the 1880s and 1890s they also made exquisite art pottery using a technique of underglaze slip decoration called Barbotine, which had been invented by Ernest Chaplet. In 1885 Haviland bought the formula and hired Chaplet to oversee its production. The technique involved mixing heavy white clay slip with pigments to produce a compound of the same consistency as oil paints. The finished product actually resembled oil paintings of the period, the texture achieved through the application of the heavy medium to the clay body in much the same manner as an artist would apply paint to his canvas. Primarily the body used with this method was a low-fired faience, though they also produced stoneware.

Authority Mary Frank Gaston has compiled a lovely book, *Haviland Collectibles and Objects of Art*, with full-color illustrations and current values; you will find her address in the Directory under Texas. Numbers in the listings below refer to pattern books by Arlene Schleiger.

Gravy boat with attached undertray, pink floral and gold on white, 9" long, $45.00.

Ash tray, man in tux, Pigall's Paris-Montmartre, 4½x3" 48.00
Basket, floral/clover, gold trim/hdl, 1893-1930, 4x5¼" 130.00
Basket, HP violets, ca 1876-1930...98.00
Berry set, violets, amateur decor, 6-pc....................................80.00
Bowl, vegetable; Ganga, w/lid, octagonal 145.00
Butter pat, florals, Nenuphar form, 1876-89, 3" sq 20.00
Cake plate, Her Majesty, Satsuma form, 8½x12" 165.00
Cake stand, Marseille form, ca 1876-1930, 2x9"...........................90.00
Chocolate pot, floral/gold decor, star form, 1893-1931, 8"..........160.00
Chocolate pot, mc florals, Epi Haut form, 1876-89, 7¼" 85.00
Chocolate pot, pk florals w/gold, emb scallops, 1890s, 5¼" 95.00
Coffeepot, floral sprays, Pompador, 1888-96, 8½" 175.00
Coffeepot, scalloped spout, gold trim, 1850s-65, 8"......................100.00
Coffeepot, wide gold bands, curved hdls, 1850s-65, 9" 100.00
Compote, center medallion, ormulu mtd, 1893-1930, 7x5½" 125.00

Creamer & sugar bowl, Cannele, w/lid, 4", 3½" 145.00
Creamer & sugar bowl, wht w/gold band, 1850s-65 ....155.00
Cup & saucer, demi; birds/flowers, gold-beaded border 50.00
Cup & saucer, demi; floral w/gold, Silver form, 1893-1930 ....50.00
Cup & saucer, floral w/turq border, ca 1876-80 ....45.00
Cup & saucer, Ganga................................30.00
Cup & saucer, orchids & dragonflies, salesman's sample, mk.......100.00
Cup & saucer, Rosalinde, French....................30.00
Dish, lobster amid 2 half shells form, 1893-1930, 11½" W 255.00
Egg cup & saucer, Club Ware, US Navy emblem, 1880s-90s.........50.00
Hair receiver, florals w/gold, 4-lobed, 1893-1930, 5" 145.00
Humidor, elephant form, gold trim, 1850s-65, 8" 11,000.00
Humidor, monkey form, artist sgn, Sandoz, 1904-20s 450.00
Jardiniere, Terra Cotta, sculpted flowers, unsgn, 1873-82 ...... 1,600.00
Match box, florals, Marseille form, 1888-1896, 1x5".....................70.00
Mayonnaise dish/underplate, leaf shape, wht w/gold trim 80.00
Menu stand, florals on Marseille form, 1888-96, 6½x4"...............190.00
Pitcher, Portia form, ca 1893-1930 ....155.00
Plate, #856, dinner sz.................................22.00
Plate, Baltimore Rose, Ransom form, 1893-1930, 8½" 60.00
Plate, Greenaway-style figures, Tresse mold, 1876-80, 9½"..........175.00
Plate, huntsman on horsebk, sgn Jean Dufy, 9½" 140.00
Plate, oyster; cobalt w/gold trim, 1888-96, 8½" 90.00
Plate, oyster; shell design, HP in factory, 1876-80, 9" 110.00
Platter, floral, pk on wht, gold & wht bows, Limoges, 16x11" 65.00
Platter, Princess, 12" 45.00
Pudding dish, gold trim, hdld liner, 1904-20s 165.00
Sardine box, HP, fish form hdl, ca 1888-96, 1¼x4½" 100.00
Shaving mug, gold name & trim, 1876-78, 3¼" 100.00
Spooner, Hotel China, for J Reed Whipple, 1893, 6" 145.00
Sugar bowl, rose finial, ca 1876-89, 7" 70.00
Tea set, forget-me-not/gold medallions, 1894 mk, for 10......... 1,500.00
Teapot, emb florals, flower finial, gold trim, 1850s-65 ....85.00
Teapot, penguin figural, artist sgn, Sandoz, 1904-20s, 5¾" 500.00
Tray, Drop Rose, wht, ca 1876-1930, 15¾x10¾" 475.00
Tureen, soup; Blackberry............................150.00
Tureen, wht w/gold decor, Marseille form, 1888-96, 9x12" 250.00
Vase, Barbotine-type flowers, sgn JH, ovoid w/4 ft, 10" 275.00
Vase, gourd; Terra Cotta, floral, 1873-82, 7¼" 950.00
Vase, grapes, sgn, non-factory decor, hdls, 1893-1930, 12".........225.00
Vase, HP florals ea side, 3-hdl, 1893-1930, 11"...................... 1,100.00
Vase, scenic, appl gold w/emb floral on cobalt, 16½" 1,500.00
Vase, sculpted florals, hdls, sgn Lindeneher, 16½" 3,200.00
Vase, Terra Cotta, sculpted florals, 12", pr.......................... 1,200.00
Wash set, red bands w/gold trim, 7-pc 850.00

Hawkes

Thomas Hawkes established his factory in Corning, New York, in 1880. He developed many beautiful patterns of cut glass, two of which were awarded the Grand Prize at the Paris Exposition in 1889. By the end of the century, his company was renowned for the finest in cut glass production. The company logo was a trefoil form enclosing a hawk in each of the two bottom lobes with a fleur-de-lis in the center. Approximately one of every two pieces is marked. Our advisors for this category are Jeanette and Marvin Stofft; they are listed in the Directory under Indiana.

Basket, hobstars/fans, hobstar base, 3-t'print hdl, 9x8" 990.00
Bowl, Century, 10", NM................................275.00
Bowl, Festoon, sgn, 3½x8¼"................................550.00
Bowl, Russian & Pillar, heavy, 9¾" dia 600.00
Bowl, T'print-cut rim, oval cutting on sides, 2¾x8" 80.00

Calling card receiver, Dmn & Strawberry, ped ft, 3x7" 165.00
Candle holder, intaglio floral, hollow bulb stem, 3½", pr............150.00
Creamer & sugar bowl, hobstars, sgn 150.00

Flower center, 6" x 8", $800.00.

Ice tub, Strawberry Dmn & Fan, rayed base, trefoil mk, 5x6" 295.00
Pitcher, cocktail; cut band, silver/crystal stirrer, 16" 175.00
Pitcher, cocktail; cut/eng, w/metal stirrer, 16½"........................110.00
Pitcher, stars, strawberry dmns & fans, urn form, 9¼"................285.00
Plate, Gladys, 7" 150.00
Plate, Kensington, 13" 1,250.00
Plate, Millicent, center hdl, silver repousse, 10"..........................250.00
Plate, Venetian, Hawkes, 9"...350.00
Punch bowl, Albion, hobstars/fans/mitre cuts, 7x15" 1,600.00
Vase, cut, eng mums/leafy stems, knopped ped ft, sgn, 12" 450.00
Vase, Gravic, Thistle, sgn, 14¾" 450.00
Vase, polished iris cutting, silver flower hdls/rim/ft, 7" 425.00
Wine, Queen's pattern, sq base, sgn, 6½" 125.00

Heisey

A.H. Heisey began his long career at the King Glass Company of Pittsburgh. He later joined the Ripley Glass Company which soon became Geo. Duncan and Sons. After Duncan's death Heisey became half-owner in partnership with his brother-in-law, James Duncan. In 1895 he built his own factory in Newark, Ohio, initiating production in 1896 and continuing until Christmas of 1957. At that time Imperial Glass Corporation bought some of the moulds. After 1968 they removed the old 'Diamond H' from any moulds they put into use. In 1985 HCA purchased all of Imperial's Heisey molds with the exception of the Old Williamsburg line.

During their highly successful period of production, Heisey made fine hand-crafted tableware with simple, yet graceful designs. Early pieces were not marked. After November 1901 the glassware was marked either with the 'Diamond H' or a paper label. Blown ware is often marked on the stem, never on the bowl or foot. For information concerning Heisey Collectors of America, see the Clubs, Newsletters, and Catalogs section of the Directory. For an in-depth look at the animals and figurines Heisey produced (as well as those by many other glasshouses), we recommend *Glass Animals and Figural Flower Frogs of the Depression Era* by Lee Garmon and Dick Spencer; both are listed in the Directory under Illinois.

Animals and Birds

Airedale 450.00

Asiatic Pheasant 290.00
Bull, sgn 1,300.00
Chick, head down...65.00
Chick, head up...65.00
Clydesdale..375.00
Clydesdale, Harvey amber........................1,500.00
Colt, kicking 190.00
Colt, kicking, amber...600.00
Colt, kicking, cobalt 950.00
Colt, rearing 195.00
Colt, rearing, amber...600.00
Colt, rearing, cobalt 950.00
Colt, standing 90.00
Colt, standing, amber 550.00
Colt, standing, cobalt 900.00
Cygnet, baby swan, 2½" 185.00
Dolphin, candlestick, #110, pr 240.00
Dolphin, candlestick, moongleam, #110, pr 500.00
Donkey..250.00
Duck, ash tray 75.00
Duck, ash tray, flamingo...................................140.00
Duck, ash tray, marigold...................................195.00
Duck, flower block 110.00
Duck, flower block, hawthorne 175.00
Elephant, amber, lg 1,850.00
Elephant, amber, med 1,850.00
Elephant, amber, sm 1,600.00
Elephant, lg..350.00
Elephant, med 375.00
Elephant, sm...195.00
Fish, bookend 125.00
Fish, bowl, 9½" 425.00
Fish, candlestick 140.00
Fish, match holder 120.00
Fish, Tropical 1,400.00
Flying Mare 2,200.00
Flying Mare, amber 3,000.00
Frog, cheese plate, #1210, flamingo 125.00
Frog, cheese plate, marigold 285.00
Frog, cheese plate, moongleam 240.00
Gazelle..1,500.00
Giraffe, head bk 185.00
Giraffe, head to side 185.00
Goose, wings down 425.00
Goose, wings half 95.00
Goose, wings up 100.00
Hen...360.00
Horse head, bookend...120.00
Horse head, bookend, amber.........................2,000.00
Horse head, cigarette box, #1489, 4½x4"............55.00
Horse head, cocktail shaker................................85.00
Irish Setter, ash tray...30.00
Irish Setter, ash tray, flamingo...........................45.00
Irish Setter, ash tray, moongleam 55.00
Kingfisher, flower block, flamingo....................150.00
Kingfisher, flower block, hawthorne 200.00
Kingfisher, flower block, moongleam................175.00
Mallard, wings down...275.00
Mallard, wings half 175.00
Mallard, wings up 130.00
Piglet, sitting...75.00
Piglet, standing 75.00
Plug Horse...110.00
Plug Horse, amber 600.00

Plug Horse, cobalt 1,000.00
Pouter Pigeon 600.00
Rabbit, paperweight..135.00
Ringneck Pheasant, 11¾" 125.00
Rooster, amber, 5⅜" 2,500.00
Rooster, Fighting, 8" 160.00

Rooster vase, 6½", $85.00.

Rooster, vase, 6½" 85.00
Rooster, 5⅜" 350.00
Rooster head, cocktail 50.00
Rooster head, cocktail shaker, 1-qt 65.00
Scotty..95.00
Sea Horse, cocktail 140.00
Show Horse 1,000.00
Sow 500.00
Sparrow 80.00
Swan, ind nut, #1503...18.00
Swan, master nut, #1503 ....45.00
Swan, 7" 700.00
Wood Duck 550.00

Chintz, crystal; bowl, floral; hdls, ftd, 8½" 32.00
Chintz, crystal; compote, oval, 7".......................40.00
Chintz, crystal; finger bowl, #4107 ....8.00
Chintz, crystal; mint dish, ftd, 6".......................18.00
Chintz, crystal; pickle/olive dish, 2-part, 13" 15.00
Chintz, crystal; pitcher, dolphin ft, 3-pt 115.00
Chintz, crystal; stem, cocktail; #3389, 3-oz 15.00
Chintz, crystal; sugar bowl, 3-dolphin ft 20.00
Chintz, crystal; tumbler, iced tea; #3389, 12-oz 14.00
Chintz, sahara; bowl, mint; ftd, 6"......................30.00
Chintz, sahara; grapefruit, #3389, Duquesne, ftd 50.00
Chintz, sahara; plate, luncheon; sq, 8" 22.00
Chintz, sahara; stem, parfait; #3389, 5-oz............30.00
Chintz, sahara; tray, sandwich; sq, center hdl, 12" 65.00
Chintz, sahara; vase, dolphin ft, 9" 175.00
Crystolite, crystal; basket, hdls, 6" 375.00
Crystolite, crystal; bottle, oil; 3-oz....................40.00
Crystolite, crystal; bowl, dessert; 8" 15.00
Crystolite, crystal; candle block, 1-light, sq 12.00
Crystolite, crystal; candy, swan, 6½" 35.00
Crystolite, crystal; celery tray, rectangular, 12"....35.00
Crystolite, crystal; cigarette holder, ftd 17.50
Crystolite, crystal; cigarette lighter 10.00
Crystolite, crystal; cup 15.00

Crystolite, crystal; jam jar, w/lid.................................50.00
Crystolite, crystal; plate, salad; 8½".........................15.00
Crystolite, crystal; plate, torte; 11"..........................24.00
Crystolite, crystal; stem, cordial; #5003, 1-oz.............90.00
Crystolite, crystal; vase, ftd, 6".................................17.50
Empress, alexandrite; bowl, cream soup; +sq plate 180.00
Empress, alexandrite; celery tray, 10"........................200.00
Empress, alexandrite; creamer 250.00
Empress, alexandrite; plate, sq, 8"............................75.00
Empress, crystal; bowl, frappe; w/center 20.00
Empress, crystal; compote, sq, 6" 40.00
Empress, crystal; cup, #1401½ 25.00
Empress, crystal; plate, muffin; upturned sides, 12".....30.00
Empress, crystal; relish tray, 4-part, 16".....................30.00
Empress, crystal; stem, oyster cocktail; 2½-oz.............15.00
Empress, flamingo; bowl, floral; flared, 9"..................70.00
Empress, flamingo; bowl, lemon; oval, w/lid, 6½".........85.00
Empress, flamingo; cup, bouillon; hdls 28.00
Empress, flamingo; cup & saucer 50.00
Empress, flamingo; nappy, dolphin ft, 7½"..................60.00
Empress, flamingo; pickle/olive dish, 2-part, 13"..........25.00
Empress, flamingo; plate, sq, hdls, 12".......................55.00
Empress, flamingo; plate, 12".....................................50.00
Empress, flamingo; relish tray, 3-part, 10"...................70.00
Empress, moongleam; ash tray...................................230.00
Empress, moongleam; bowl, floral; hdls, ftd, 8½"..........65.00
Empress, moongleam; bowl, vegetable; oval, 10" 55.00
Empress, moongleam; cup & saucer 32.00
Empress, moongleam; jug, flat 250.00
Empress, moongleam; plate, sandwich; hdls, 12" 55.00
Empress, moongleam; tumbler, iced tea; 12-oz.............45.00
Empress, sahara; candlestick, dolphin ft, 6", ea............125.00
Empress, sahara; cup, custard or punch; 4-oz..............30.00
Empress, sahara; nappy, 4½"......................................10.00
Empress, sahara; plate, 8"..20.00
Empress, sahara; stem, saucer champagne; 4-oz 40.00
Empress, sahara; tumbler, dolphin ft, 8-oz..................150.00
Greek Key, crystal; bottle, water 165.00
Greek Key, crystal; candy dish, w/lid, 1-lb..................140.00
Greek Key, crystal; creamer & sugar bowl...................75.00
Greek Key, crystal; egg cup, 5-oz...............................60.00
Greek Key, crystal; jelly dish, ftd, hdls, w/lid 145.00
Greek Key, crystal; nappy, 4½"...................................20.00
Greek Key, crystal; nappy, 8"......................................37.50
Greek Key, crystal; plate, 10".....................................55.00
Greek Key, crystal; plate, 6" 12.00
Greek Key, crystal; puff box, #3, w/lid........................95.00
Greek Key, crystal; shakers, pr....................................120.00
Greek Key, crystal; spooner, lg 75.00
Greek Key, crystal; tumbler, flared rim, 10-oz..............33.00
Greek Key, flamingo; bowl, punch; ftd 750.00
Ipswich, crystal; stem, saucer champagne; 5-oz............12.50
Ipswich, crystal; tumbler, str rim, 10-oz 12.50
Ipswich, flamingo; candy jar, w/lid, ½-lb.....................250.00
Ipswich, flamingo; tumbler, ftd, 12-oz.........................50.00
Ipswich, moongleam; candlestick; 1-lite, 6".................225.00
Ipswich, moongleam; pitcher, ½-gal 350.00
Ipswich, sahara; finger bowl, w/underplate..................40.00
Ipswich, sahara; tumbler, ftd, 8-oz.............................30.00
Lariat, crystal; basket, ftd, 10" 195.00
Lariat, crystal; bowl, salad; 10½"................................30.00
Lariat, crystal; celery dish, 13" 20.00
Lariat, crystal; cigarette box.......................................22.50
Lariat, crystal; cup...12.00

Lariat, crystal; lamp & globe, candle; 8" 85.00
Lariat, crystal; plate, cookie; 11" 22.00
Lariat, crystal; plate, salad; 8" 9.00
Lariat, crystal; stem, claret; blown, 4-oz......................20.00
Lariat, crystal; stem, sherbet; low, 6-oz.......................11.00
Lariat, crystal; tumbler, iced tea; ftd, 12-oz.................22.00
Lodestar, dawn; ash tray...65.00
Lodestar, dawn; candlestick, 2-light, 5¾", pr................600.00
Lodestar, dawn; creamer 50.00
Lodestar, dawn; mayonnaise 55.00
Lodestar, dawn; plate, 8½"..65.00
Lodestar, dawn; sugar bowl...50.00
Minuet, crystal; bell, dinner 65.00
Minuet, crystal; bowl, floral; ftd, 11"...........................50.00
Minuet, crystal; candelabrum, 1-light, w/prisms..........125.00
Minuet, crystal; candlestick, #1511, 2-light, ea 175.00
Minuet, crystal; creamer, #1511..................................35.00
Minuet, crystal; ice bucket, dolphin ft 135.00
Minuet, crystal; plate, salad; 7" 12.00
Minuet, crystal; plate, torte; #1511, 14" 50.00
Minuet, crystal; stem, cocktail; #5010, 3½-oz..............40.00
Minuet, crystal; stem, water; #5010, 9-oz 35.00
Minuet, crystal; tumbler, juice; #5010, 5-oz................25.00
Minuet, crystal; vase, #5013, 5"..................................35.00
Octagon, crystal; basket, #500, 5"..............................60.00
Octagon, crystal; plate, bread & butter; 7".................. 5.00
Octagon, flamingo; bonbon, #1229, upturned sides, 6" 15.00
Octagon, flamingo; creamer, #500..............................15.00
Octagon, flamingo; plate, sandwich; #1229, 10"...........25.00
Octagon, flamingo; platter, 12¾".................................35.00
Octagon, hawthorne; bowl, #1229, ftd, 8"...................50.00
Octagon, hawthorne; plate, muffin; #1229, 12" 55.00
Octagon, marigold; ice tub, #500...............................135.00
Octagon, moongleam; ice tub, #500 ....85.00
Octagon, moongleam; jelly bowl, #1229, 5½" 20.00
Octagon, moongleam; plate, sandwich; center hdl, 10½".....45.00
Octagon, sahara; dish, frozen dessert; #500................15.00
Octagon, sahara; jelly bowl, #1229, 5½".......................10.00
Octagon, sahara; plate, hors d'oeuvre; #1229, 13" 35.00
Old Colony etch, crystal; bowl, salad; hdls, rnd, 10" 32.00
Old Colony etch, crystal; bowl, vegetable; oval, 10" 30.00
Old Colony etch, crystal; celery tray, 10" 14.00
Old Colony etch, crystal; grapefruit, 6".......................15.00
Old Colony etch, crystal; plate, rnd, 6"....................... 6.00
Old Colony etch, crystal; stem, champagne; #3390, 6-oz.....10.00
Old Colony etch, crystal; stem, cordial; #3380, 1-oz......75.00
Old Colony etch, crystal; tumbler, soda; #3380, ftd, 8-oz.....10.00
Old Colony etch, flamingo; bottle, oil; ftd, 4-oz 70.00
Old Colony etch, flamingo; bowl, 3-hdld, 9"................75.00
Old Colony etch, flamingo; cup, bouillon; hdls, ftd........18.00
Old Colony etch, flamingo; grapefruit, #3380, ftd 16.00
Old Colony etch, flamingo; mint dish, dolphin ft, 6".....22.00
Old Colony etch, flamingo; plate, muffin; sq, hdls, 13"......40.00
Old Colony etch, flamingo; plate, rnd or sq, 8"............17.00
Old Colony etch, flamingo; stem, claret; #3390, 4-oz....22.50
Old Colony etch, flamingo; stem, sherbet; #3390, 6-oz 20.00
Old Colony etch, flamingo; sugar bowl, ind..................30.00
Old Colony etch, flamingo; tumbler, bar; #3380, ftd, 1-oz 37.50
Old Colony etch, flamingo; tumbler, iced tea; #3390, ftd, 12-oz....24.00
Old Colony etch, marigold; compote, #3368, ftd, 7"......95.00
Old Colony etch, marigold; stem, soda; #3380, tall, 10-oz 32.50
Old Colony etch, marigold; tumbler, iced tea; #3380, ftd, 12-oz....35.00
Old Colony etch, moongleam; bowl, finger; #4075 ....14.00
Old Colony etch, moongleam; cigarette holder, #3390...........55.00

Old Colony etch, moongleam; decanter, 1-pt 525.00
Old Colony etch, moongleam; plate, muffin; rnd, hdls, 12" 75.00
Old Colony etch, moongleam; plate, rnd or sq, 7".........................20.00
Old Colony etch, moongleam; stem, champagne; #3380, 6-oz.......25.00
Old Colony etch, moongleam; vase, ftd, 9" 175.00
Old Colony etch, moongleam; stem, water; #3390, tall, 11-oz.......32.00
Old Colony etch, moongleam; tray, hors d'oeuvre; hdls, 13" 55.00
Old Colony etch, sahara; bowl, hdls, ftd, 5"..............................27.00
Old Colony etch, sahara; creamer, dolphin ftd 45.00
Old Colony etch, sahara; nappy, dolphin ft, 7½".........................65.00
Old Colony etch, sahara; pitcher, #3390, dolphin ftd, 3-pt 210.00
Old Colony etch, sahara; shakers, pr...110.00
Old Colony etch, sahara; stem, parfait; #3380, 5-oz 15.00
Old Colony etch, sahara; stem, water; #3390, low, 11-oz...............25.00
Old Colony etch, sahara; tray, celery; 13"...................................26.00
Old Colony etch, sahara; tumbler, dolphin ft.............................165.00
Old Colony etch, sahara; tumbler, soda; #3390, ftd, 8-oz 25.00
Orchid, crystal; basket, #1540, 8½"..400.00
Orchid, crystal; bowl, epergne; 9½" 395.00
Orchid, crystal; bowl, floral; crimped, 13".................................60.00
Orchid, crystal; bowl, floral; 11"..55.00
Orchid, crystal; bowl, gardenia; 13" 65.00
Orchid, crystal; candle holder, epergnette; deep, 6", ea...............295.00
Orchid, crystal; candy dish, bow knot finial, 6" 160.00
Orchid, crystal; cocktail icer, #3304, w/liner 165.00
Orchid, crystal; compote, blown, 5½".......................................87.50
Orchid, crystal; cup, #1509 or #1519 ....45.00
Orchid, crystal; decanter, #4036½, 1-pt...................................225.00
Orchid, crystal; ice bucket, #1519, hdls 250.00
Orchid, crystal; jelly bowl, hdls, 6"..30.00
Orchid, crystal; mayonnaise, #1519, hdl, 5½"............................40.00
Orchid, crystal; mint dish, ftd, 5½" 32.00
Orchid, crystal; pitcher, #1519, 73-oz.....................................400.00
Orchid, crystal; plate, cake; #1519, ftd, 12" 215.00
Orchid, crystal; plate, dinner; #1519, 10½" 115.00
Orchid, crystal; relish, rnd, 9"..60.00
Orchid, crystal; saucer, #1509 or #1519 ....7.50
Orchid, crystal; stem, cocktail; #5025, 4-oz...............................40.00
Orchid, crystal; stem, sherry; #5022 or #5025, 2-oz 95.00
Orchid, crystal; tray, celery; #1519, 12" 45.00
Orchid, crystal; vase, #1519, ftd, 7" 85.00
Orchid, crystal; vase, #1519, 14" 600.00

Plantation, 2-light candelabrum, $105.00; Epergne candle holder, $125.00 for the pair.

Plantation, crystal; ash tray, #1567, 3½".................................17.50
Plantation, crystal; bowl, fruit or floral; #1567, 12" 45.00
Plantation, crystal; bowl, salad; #1567, 9"................................30.00
Plantation, crystal; cake plate, #1567, ftd, 13"............................95.00

Plantation, crystal; candle holder, epergne; #1567, 5", ea............100.00
Plantation, crystal; cheese dish, #1567, w/lid, ftd, 5"....................85.00
Plantation, crystal; compote, #1567, deep, w/lid, 5"......................60.00
Plantation, crystal; jelly bowl, #1567, hdls, 6½".........................18.00
Plantation, crystal; relish, #1567, rnd, 4-part, 8".........................25.00
Plantation, crystal; stem, claret; #1567, blown, 4½-oz 25.00
Plantation, crystal; stem, sherbet; #1567, 6½-oz.........................20.00
Plantation, crystal; tumbler, pressed, 10-oz................................30.00
Pleat & Panel, crystal; bowl, bouillon; #1170, hdls, 5" 15.00
Pleat & Panel, crystal; plate, dinner; #1170, 10¾" 15.00
Pleat & Panel, crystal; stem, saucer champagne; #1170, 5-oz.......... 5.00
Pleat & Panel, flamingo; bowl, chow-chow; #1170, 4"..................18.00
Pleat & Panel, flamingo; bowl, vegetable; #1170, oval, 9" 30.00
Pleat & Panel, flamingo; marmalade, #1170, 4¾" 20.00
Pleat & Panel, flamingo; plate, sandwich; #1170, 14" 45.00
Pleat & Panel, flamingo; tumbler, iced tea; #1170, 12-oz..............15.00
Pleat & Panel, hawthorne; tray, compartment spice; #1170, 10" ...125.00
Pleat & Panel, moongleam; creamer, #1170 ....30.00
Pleat & Panel, moongleam; nappy, #1170, 8".............................30.00
Pleat & Panel, moongleam; plate, #1170, 6" 15.00
Pleat & Panel, moongleam; tumbler, #1170, 8-oz........................30.00
Provincial, crystal; bottle, oil; #1506, w/#1 stopper, 4-oz 55.00
Provincial, crystal; cup, punch; #1506 ....10.00
Provincial, crystal; nappy, #1506, 4½".....................................11.00
Provincial, crystal; mustard...25.00
Provincial, crystal; relish, 4-part, 10" 40.00
Provincial, crystal; stem, #1506, 10-oz 20.00
Provincial, crystal; vase, sweet pea; #1506, 6".............................25.00
Provincial, limelight; creamer, #1506, ftd.................................95.00
Provincial, limelight; plate, luncheon; #1506 ....50.00
Provincial, limelight; relish, 4-part, 10"...................................225.00
Provincial, limelight; tumbler, #1506, ftd, 9-oz 65.00
Ridgeleigh, crystal; ash tray, #1469, rnd, 4" 20.00
Ridgeleigh, crystal; bowl, floral; #1469, swan hdls, 14" 250.00
Ridgeleigh, crystal; bowl, salad; #1469, 9" 30.00
Ridgeleigh, crystal; decanter, #1469, w/#95 stopper, 1-pt 155.00
Ridgeleigh, crystal; jelly bowl, #1469, hdls, 6"............................20.00
Ridgeleigh, crystal; pitcher, #1469, ½-gal................................200.00
Ridgeleigh, crystal; plate, hors d'oeuvre; #1469 ....30.00
Ridgeleigh, crystal; soda, #1469, cupped or flared, 12-oz 25.00
Ridgeleigh, crystal; stem, cordial; #1469, blown, 1-oz.................125.00
Ridgeleigh, crystal; stem, sherbet; #1469, blown, 5-oz.................12.50
Ridgeleigh, crystal; tumbler, bar; #1469, 2½-oz 20.00
Ridgeleigh, crystal; tumbler, soda; #1469¾, 12-oz 25.00
Ridgeleigh, crystal; vase, #3, flared rim 27.50
Ridgeleigh, limelight; cigarette holder, #1469, w/lid 210.00
Rose, crystal; bell, dinner; #5072 ....125.00
Rose, crystal; bowl, #1519, oval, 4-ftd, 11" 175.00
Rose, crystal; bowl, fruit or salad; #1519, ftd, 9" 120.00
Rose, crystal; candlestick, #134, 2-light, 5", pr 160.00
Rose, crystal; celery tray, #1519, 13".......................................70.00
Rose, crystal; chocolate dish, #1519, w/lid, 5" 175.00
Rose, crystal; cigarette holder, #4035......................................85.00
Rose, crystal; creamer, #1519, ftd...40.00
Rose, crystal; jelly bowl, #1519, ftd, 6½"..................................50.00
Rose, crystal; mayonnaise, #1519, ftd, 5½" 50.00
Rose, crystal; mint dish, #1509, ftd, 5¾" 50.00
Rose, crystal; plate, dinner; #1519, 10½" 135.00
Rose, crystal; stem, oyster cocktail; #5072, ftd, 3½-oz 50.00
Rose, crystal; vase, #4198, 8"..120.00
Rose, crystal; vase, violet; #1519, ftd, 3½" 95.00
Saturn, crystal; bottle, oil; #1485, w/#1 stopper, 2-oz 45.00
Saturn, crystal; bowl, fruit; #1485, flared rim, 12" 32.50
Saturn, crystal; candlestick, #1485, 1-light, ftd, 3", ea 25.00

Saturn, crystal; stem, cocktail; #1485, 3-oz 15.00
Saturn, crystal; vase, violet; #1485 ....25.00
Saturn, limelight; mayonnaise, #1485 ....80.00
Saturn, limelight; shakers, #1485, pr 550.00
Saturn, limelight; stem, fruit cocktail; #1485, 4-oz 75.00
Saturn, limelight; tumbler, soda; #1485, 12-oz..................65.00
Twist, crystal; bottle, oil; #1252, w/#78 stopper, 4-oz 30.00
Twist, crystal; creamer, #1252, ftd....................................55.00
Twist, crystal; tumbler, iced tea; #1252, 12-oz 18.00
Twist, flamingo; bottle, French dressing; #1252 ....75.00
Twist, flamingo; bowl, nasturtium; #1252, oval, 8" 30.00
Twist, flamingo; mayonnaise, #1252½ 22.50
Twist, flamingo; stem, saucer champagne; #1252, 5-oz.......15.00
Twist, flamingo; tumbler, iced tea; #1252, ftd, 12-oz 30.00
Twist, marigold; cheese dish; #1252, hdls, 6" 20.00
Twist, marigold; shakers, #1252, pr 125.00
Twist, moongleam; bowl, nut; #1252, ind..........................30.00
Twist, moongleam; cocktail shaker; #1252, w/metal lid 400.00
Twist, moongleam; pitcher, #1252, 3-pt 160.00
Twist, moongleam; stem, oyster cocktail; #1252, 3-oz.........35.00
Twist, moongleam; tumbler, soda; #1252, str & flared, 8-oz ...21.00
Waverly, crystal; bowl, gardenia; #1519, 13" 20.00
Waverly, crystal; box, trinket; #1519, w/lion lid, rare 600.00
Waverly, crystal; cheese dish, #1519, ftd, 5½" 20.00
Waverly, crystal; compote, #1519, low ftd, 6" 20.00
Waverly, crystal; plate, cake; #1519, ftd, 13½" 60.00
Waverly, crystal; relish, #1519, 4-part, 9" 25.00
Waverly, crystal; shakers, #1519, pr 60.00
Waverly, crystal; stem, wine; #1519, blown, 3-oz 30.00
Waverly, crystal; vase, #1519, ftd, 7" 25.00
Yeoman, crystal; cigarette box or ash tray, #1184 ....30.00
Yeoman, crystal; plate, oyster cocktail; #1184, 9" 12.00
Yeoman, crystal; tray, #1184, center hdl, 3-part, 11" 15.00
Yeoman, flamingo; egg cup, #1184.....................................30.00
Yeoman, flamingo; sugar shaker, #1184, ftd.......................95.00
Yeoman, hawthorne; compote, #1184, shallow, high ftd, 5" ...55.00
Yeoman, hawthorne; plate, #1184, 10½" 60.00
Yeoman, hawthorne; plate, finger bowl underliner; #1184....15.00
Yeoman, marigold; bowl, baker; #1184, 9"........................100.00
Yeoman, marigold; cup & saucer, after dinner; #1184.........85.00
Yeoman, moongleam; bowl, fruit; #1184, oval, 9" 45.00
Yeoman, moongleam; cheese plate, #1184, hdls 15.00
Yeoman, moongleam; sauce boat, #1184, w/underliner.........35.00
Yeoman, moongleam; whiskey, #1184, 2½-oz......................15.00
Yeoman, sahara; bowl, vegetable; #1184, 6".......................14.00
Yeoman, sahara; platter, #1184, oval, 12" 20.00
Yeoman, sahara; tray, #1184, rectangular, 7x10" 50.00
Yeoman, sahara; tumbler, iced tea; #1184, 12-oz 25.00

Rum pot, cobalt, very rare, $2,500.00.

Heubach

Gebruder Heubach is a German porcelain company that has been in operation since the 1800s, producing quality figurines and novelty items. They are perhaps most famous for their doll heads and piano babies, most of which are marked with the circular rising sun device containing an 'H' superimposed over a 'C.'

Baby, crawling, wht gown, kicking legs, 5½x8" 535.00
Baby in brn bear costume, crawling, #5578, 3" 295.00
Baby in highchair, sm 165.00
Bear, dressed, w/flowers, waits at door, sgn 225.00
Bear on step on outhouse 185.00
Blond baby sits in tattered shoe, 12" 1,900.00
Boy & girl fishing at beach, 13", M..................................895.00

Boy in nightdress, 8", $600.00.

Child in bunny costume stands before eggshell, 9" 425.00
Dutch girl w/attached basket, flirty pose, mk, 7½" 295.00
Girl dancer in tan ruffled dress, wht collar, mk, 6½" 125.00
Girl dancing, bl dress, pk bow, wht collar, 11½" 500.00
Girl in gr bonnet leans on hoe, 11"..................................225.00
Girl in lg hat sits & pulls off socks, 5" 200.00
Girl in pk pleated skirt, gr sash, mk, 5¾" 125.00
Humidor, Jasper, gr, Indian chief on lid, 5" 165.00
Lady w/baby in arm, jug in hand, pastels, mk, 12½" 395.00
Pin dish, Indian in full dress, wht on gr jasper, mk 65.00
Planter, shepherdess w/flock figural, mk, 4x10¾x2¾" 195.00
2 sm girls dancing, EX color, beading & gold, 12½x9"........325.00

Hickman, Royal Arden

Born in Willamette, Oregon, Royal A. Hickman was a genius in all aspects of design interpretation. Mr. Hickman's expertise can be seen in the designs of the lovely Heisey figurines, Kosta crystal, Bruce Fox aluminum, Three Crowns aluminum, Vernon Kilns, and Royal Haeger Pottery (as well as handcrafted silver, furniture, and paintings).

Because Mr. Hickman moved around during much of his lifetime, his influence has been felt in all forms of the media. Designs from his independent companies include 'Royal Hickman Pottery and Lamps' (sold through Ceramic Arts, Inc., of Chattanooga, Tennessee), 'Royal Hickman's Paris Ware,' 'Royal Hickman — Florida,' and 'California

Designed by Royal Hickman.' The following listings will give examples of pieces bearing the various trademarks. Our advisor for this category is Lee Garmon and Doris Frizzell; both are listed in the directory under Illinois. See also Royal Haegar; Vernon Kilns, Melinda pattern.

Bruce Fox Aluminum

Leaf tray, 14", $25.00.

Banana leaf, mk Royal Hickman-RH 6, 22½" L 20.00
Candle snuffer, sterling, sgn Royal Hickman, 12" 35.00
Dish, lobster, lg 40.00
Dish, 3-point leaf, sgn Royal Hickman, 15½" L 20.00
Platter, fish, EX detail, sgn Royal Hickman-RH 3, 13x9" 50.00

California, Designed by Royal Hickman

Bowl, red w/blk highlights, #607, 9½" 15.00
Figurine, deer, apple gr w/wht spots, appl eyes, 15" 25.00
Figurine, giraffe & young, pk w/blk spots & base, 11x7" 35.00
Punch bowl, Tom & Jerry, w/8 mugs 300.00
Swan, red w/blk highlights, #643, 17" 40.00

Miscellaneous Signatures

Sea horse vase, sgn Royal Hickman USA, #468, 8" 25.00
Vase, fish figurine, 'petty crystal glaze,' #467 ....25.00
Vase, lg heart, sgn Royal Hickman, Italy, #3774 ....35.00

Royal Hickman – Florida

Vase, free-form, #578, 14" 40.00
Vase, horse's head, gray w/wht mane, 13¾" 75.00
Vase, pouter pigeon, blk cascade, #599, 8½" 40.00
Vase, swan, head down, blk cascade, #624-R, 14" 60.00

Historical Glass

Glassware commemorating particularly significant historical events became popular in the late 1800s. Bread trays were the most common form; but plates, mugs, pitchers, and other items were also pressed in clear as well as colored glass. It was sold in vast amounts at the 1876 Philadelphia Centennial Exposition by various manufacturers who exhibited their wares on the grounds. It remained popular well into the twentieth century.

In the listings that follow, L numbers refer to a book by Lindsey; M numbers correspond with a book by Marsh. Both are standard guides used by many collectors. Our advisor for this category is Darlene Yohe; she is listed in the Directory under Arkansas. See also Bread Plates; Pattern Glass.

Bottle, Grover Cleveland bust, clear & frosted, L-318, lg 225.00
Bowl, General Grant, Patriot & Soldier, clear/frosted, 9⅜" 65.00
Bust, Lt Richard Hobson, frosted, L-382, 5" 265.00
Bust, MJ Owens, frosted 55.00
Calabash, Roosevelt-TVA, aqua, qt 60.00
Celery, Independence Hall 65.00
Compote, Washington Centennial, ftd, open 40.00
Covered dish, Battleship Oregon, L-469, 6½" L, EX 75.00
Covered dish, kitchen stove, flatiron hdl, L-149, 7" 300.00
Creamer, Liberty Bell, reeded hdl 125.00
Cup, McKinley, w/lid, L-355 ....60.00
Cup plate, Bunker Hill 30.00
Flask, John Paul Jones 20.00
Goblet, Liberty Bell, 6" 40.00
Goblet, Shield, 1876 Centennial 50.00
Goblet, 3 Presidents, rare 325.00
Hat, He's Allright — The Same Old Hat, Harrison campaign ...150.00
Lamp, oil; Goddess of Liberty, 1876 Centennial 125.00
Lamp chimney, Columbus, etched on frosted band, L-9, 8" 250.00
Mug, Knights of Labor, L-513 ....45.00
Mug, Martyrs Lincoln & Garfield 50.00
Mug, Mephistopheles 65.00
Mug, Mephistopheles, milk glass 75.00
Paperweight, Cleveland sulfide medallion, 3½" 195.00
Paperweight, Director Goshorn, 1876, Gillinder, L-449 ....155.00
Paperweight, Lincoln, clear/frosted, Gillinder, M-166 ....250.00
Paperweight, McKinley portrait, milk glass 125.00
Paperweight, Memorial Hall 175.00
Pickle dish, Emblem, L-58 ....45.00
Pitcher, Dewey, L-400 ....55.00
Pitcher, Texas Centennial, Alamo, 9" 80.00
Plaque, Lincoln Logs, milk glass/brn flashing, L-287, 6¾" 225.00
Plate, Columbus, milk glass 35.00
Plate, George Washington, milk glass 45.00

Plate, Liberty head in shield, 13" long, $175.00.

Plate, McKinley, Protection & Plenty	48.00
Plate, Old Glory	45.00
Plate, Pope Leo, milk glass, L-240	25.00
Plate, Wm H Harrison, Tippecanoe, Fort Meigs, amber, 8"	225.00
Relish, Flaming Sword	35.00
Shaker, Benjamin Franklin, M-194	85.00
Shaker, Lighthouse	48.00
Snuff jar, Railroad Mills, amber, w/label	20.00
Statue, Ruth the Gleaner, frosted, 1876 Phila Expo, Gillinder	175.00
Sugar bowl, Liberty Bell, L-25	110.00
Syrup, Peace & Plenty, emb sailing ship & anchor, strap hdl	195.00
Toothpick holder, man w/hat, rare	225.00
Toothpick holder, Preparedness, soldier figural, L-483	145.00
Tumbler, bar; Bumper to the Flag, Civil War, L-480	110.00
Tumbler, Hobson, in laurel wreath, frosted	60.00
Tumbler, Lord's Prayer, blown & etched	35.00
Tumbler, Louisiana Purchase, L-107	35.00
Tumbler, Nelson of America, L-397	28.00
Tumbler, Our Martyred President, McKinley & flags	30.00
Tumbler, Philadelphia Sesquicentennial	18.00
Tumbler, Protection, Sound Currency, McKinley & Hobart	55.00

Hobbs, Brockunier, & Co.

Hobbs and Brockunier's South Wheeling Glass Works was in operation during the last quarter of the 19th century. They are most famous for their peachblow, amberina, Daisy and Button, and Hobnail pattern glass. The mainstay of the operation, however, was druggist items and plain glassware — bowls, mugs, and simple footed pitchers with shell handles. See also Frances Ware.

Rubena verde Hobnail bowl, in Meriden frame with applied leaves, 7½" diameter, $495.00.

Bowl, Daisy & Button, shallow, sgn, 7"	325.00
Carafe, Block, frosted w/amber flash, lg	145.00
Cheese dish, Hobnail, cranberry opal, rare	350.00
Cruet, Hobnail, bl opal, orig bl faceted stopper, M	225.00
Goblet, Block, amber frost, rare	110.00
Lamp, finger; Snowflake, cranberry opal, 3"	500.00
Pitcher, Hobnail, amber, sq mouth, bulbous, 8x6¼"	225.00
Pitcher, Hobnail, amberina rosy-fuchsia to amber, 7¾"	465.00
Tumbler, Hobnail, frosted amber, 10-row, 4x2⅝"	75.00
Vase, Invt T'print, honey amber, reeded/swirled top, 12"	100.00

Homer Laughlin

The Homer Laughlin China Company of Newell, West Virginia, was founded in 1871. The superior dinnerware they displayed at the Centennial Exposition in Philadelphia in 1876 won the highest award of excellence. From that time to the present, they have continued to produce quality dinnerware and kitchenware, many lines of which are becoming very popular collectibles. Most of the dinnerware is marked with the name of the pattern and occasionally with the shape name as well. The 'HLC' trademark is usually followed by a number series, the first two digits of which indicate the year of its manufacture. See also Fiesta; Harlequin; Riviera.

Advertising mug, 3-color decoration, $35.00 to $40.00.

Amberstone, bowl, soup	4.50
Amberstone, butter dish	35.00
Amberstone, casserole	30.00
Amberstone, plate, 10"	7.00
Amberstone, sauce boat	20.00
Amberstone, shakers, pr	12.50
Amberstone, sugar bowl, w/lid	7.50
Americana, bowl, vegetable; rnd, 8"	18.00
Americana, cup & saucer	10.00
Americana, platter, 15"	45.00
Carnival, plate, 6½"	2.00
Carnival, teacup	3.50
Casualstone, ash tray, rare	7.50
Casualstone, casserole	20.00
Casualstone, coffee server	22.00
Casualstone, creamer	4.50
Casualstone, cup & saucer	6.50
Casualstone, marmalade	30.00
Casualstone, plate, dinner	6.00
Casualstone, platter, rnd	14.00
Conchita, Hacienda or Mexicana, bowl, fruit; 5"	8.00
Conchita, Hacienda or Mexicana, cup & saucer	14.00
Conchita, Hacienda or Mexicana, egg cup, rare	20.00
Conchita, Hacienda or Mexicana, platter, 10"	15.00
Conchita, Hacienda or Mexicana, sauce boat	22.00
Conchita, Hacienda or Mexicana, sugar bowl, w/lid	18.00
Conchita, Hacienda or Mexicana, teapot, rare	90.00
Conchita or Mexicana, bowl, mixing; Kitchen Kraft, 10"	30.00
Conchita or Mexicana, pie plate, Kitchen Kraft	30.00
Conchita or Mexicana, shakers, Kitchen Kraft, pr	40.00
Conchita or Mexicana, spoon, Kitchen Kraft	40.00
Dogwood, bowl, mixing; Kitchen Kraft, 6½"	18.00
Dogwood, bowl, vegetable; 8¾"	12.00
Dogwood, platter, 13½"	15.00
Dogwood, teapot, w/gold trim	45.00
Harmony, bowl, mixing; Kitchen Kraft, 10"	30.00
Harmony, casserole, Kitchen Kraft, w/lid, 8"	25.00
Harmony, cup & saucer	7.50

Harmony, fork or spoon, Kitchen Kraft, ea 35.00
Historical American Subjects, creamer 12.00
Historical American Subjects, plate, 10" 20.00
Jubilee, bowl, fruit.. 4.00
Jubilee, casserole, w/lid 25.00
Jubilee, egg cup 6.00
Jubilee, pitcher, juice; Fiesta mk 120.00
Jubilee, plate, 10" 7.00
Jubilee, platter, 13" 10.00
Jubilee, teapot 28.00
Oven-Serve, bowl, oval baker; Embossed Line, 8½" 8.00
Oven-Serve, casserole, Embossed Line, w/lid, 10" 28.00
Oven-Serve, pie plate, Kitchen Bouquet 15.00
Oven-Serve, plate, Embossed Line, 10" 5.00
Pastel Nautilus, bowl, cream soup 10.00
Pastel Nautilus, bowl, vegetable; oval 9.00
Pastel Nautilus, cup & saucer 7.00
Pastel Nautilus, gravy boat 12.00
Pastel Nautilus, plate, 10" 8.00
Pastel Nautilus, sugar bowl, w/lid 9.00
Priscilla, coffeepot, Kitchen Kraft 60.00
Priscilla, pitcher, water; Kitchen Kraft 20.00
Priscilla, plate, 8" 6.00
Priscilla, platter, 13½" 15.00
Rhythm, bowl, fruit; 5½" 5.00
Rhythm, bowl, mixing; Kitchen Kraft, 10" 85.00
Rhythm, bowl, nappy..10.00
Rhythm, bowl, vegetable 14.00
Rhythm, cup & saucer 12.00
Rhythm, plate, calendar 10.00
Rhythm, plate, 10"..12.00
Rhythm, plate, 7" 5.00
Rhythm, platter, 11½" 12.50
Rhythm, sauce boat, cobalt 17.50
Rhythm, shakers, pr 9.00
Rhythm, spoon rest, red.......................................550.00
Rhythm, teapot..40.00
Rhythm Rose, cake plate, Kitchen Kraft, 10½" 15.00
Rhythm Rose, coffeepot, Kitchen Kraft 32.00
Rhythm Rose, cup & saucer, AD 16.00
Rhythm Rose, plate, 9" 5.00
Rhythm Rose, platter, 13" 10.00
Rhythm Rose, underplate, Kitchen Kraft, 6" 10.00
Serenade, bowl, lug soup 10.00
Serenade, creamer 7.00
Serenade, plate, chop 15.00
Serenade, sugar bowl, w/lid 10.00
Serenade, teapot 45.00
Tango, bowl, fruit; 5¾" 5.00
Tango, casserole, w/lid, colors other than red 30.00
Tango, casserole, w/lid, red...................................35.00
Tango, cup & saucer, colors other than red 6.00
Tango, cup & saucer, red 8.00
Tango, plate, 10"...10.00
Tango, shakers, red, pr...12.00
Virginia Rose, bowl, deep, 5" 8.00
Virginia Rose, bowl, mixing; Kitchen Kraft, 10" 25.00
Virginia Rose, bowl, vegetable; oval, 10" 15.00
Virginia Rose, cake server, Kitchen Kraft, scarce 25.00
Virginia Rose, egg cup, dbl 18.00
Virginia Rose, mug, coffee 20.00
Virginia Rose, pitcher, water; 7½" 75.00
Virginia Rose, plate, 9" 6.00
Virginia Rose, platter, scarce, 10½" 15.00

Virginia Rose, platter, w/gravy liner, 9" 12.00
Virginia Rose, platter, 13" 16.00
Virginia Rose, sugar bowl, w/lid 15.00
Wells Art Glaze, bowl, cream soup 10.00
Wells Art Glaze, casserole, w/lid 35.00
Wells Art Glaze, cup & saucer 7.00
Wells Art Glaze, plate, 10" 10.00
Wells Art Glaze, platter, oval, 13½" 12.00
Wells Art Glaze, syrup..60.00
Wells Art Glaze, syrup, w/decals 32.00
Wells Art Glaze, teapot...45.00

Hull

The A.E. Hull Pottery was formed in 1905 in Zanesville, Ohio, and in the early years produced stoneware specialities. They expanded in 1907, adding a second plant and employing over two hundred workers. By 1920 they were manufacturing a full line of stoneware, art pottery with both airbrushed and blended glazes, florist pots, and gardenware. They also produced toilet ware and kitchen items with a white semi-porcelain body. Although these continued to be staple products, after the stock market crash of 1929, emphasis was shifted to tile production. By the mid-thirties interest in art pottery production was growing; over the next fifteen years, several lines of matt pastel floral-decorated patterns were designed, consisting of vases, planters, baskets, ewers, and bowls in various sizes.

The Red Riding Hood cookie jar, patented in 1943, proved so successful that a whole line of figural kitchenware and novelty items was added. They continued to be produced well into the fifties. (See also Little Red Riding Hood.) Through the forties their floral artware lines flooded the market, due to the restriction of foreign imports. Although best known for their pastel matt-glazed ware, some of the lines were high gloss. Rosella, glossy coral on a pink clay body, was produced for a short time only; and Magnolia, although offered in a matt glaze, was produced in gloss as well.

The plant was destroyed in 1950 by a flood which resulted in a devastating fire when the floodwater caused the kilns to explode. The company rebuilt and equipped their new factory with the most modern machinery. It was soon apparent that the matt glaze could not be duplicated through the more modern processes, however, and soon attention was concentrated on high-gloss artware lines such as Parchment and Pine and Ebb Tide. Figural planters and novelties, piggy banks, and dinnerware were produced in abundance in the late fifties and sixties. By the mid-seventies dinnerware and florist ware were the mainstay of their business. The firm discontinued operations in 1985.

Our advisor, Brenda Roberts, has compiled a lovely book, *The Collector's Encyclopedia of Hull Pottery*, with full-color photos and current values which has been recently reprinted. You will find her address in the Directory under Missouri.

Athena, cornucopia, #608, 1960-70s, 8½" 24.00
Blossom, bowl, mixing; #20, 9½"...........................35.00
Blossom, casserole, #21, w/lid, 7½" 32.00
Blossom, creamer, #28, 4½" 22.00
Blossom Flite, basket, T-2, 6" 50.00
Blossom Flite, candle holder, T-11, 3" 28.00
Blossom Flite, teapot, T-14, 8¼" 65.00
Bouquet, bowl, brn ink stamp, sq, 9¾" 60.00
Bouquet, bowl, mixing; #20, 7½" 28.00
Bouquet, grease jar, #24, 32-oz 35.00
Bow Knot, basket, B-12, 10½" 600.00
Bow Knot, bowl, console; B-16, 13½"......................220.00
Bow Knot, candle holder, B-17, 4" 60.00

Bow Knot basket, B-29, 12", $1,250.00.

Bow Knot, cornucopia, B-5, 7½" 95.00
Bow Knot, flowerpot/attached saucer, B-6, 6½" 125.00
Bow Knot, jardiniere, B-19, 9⅜" 560.00
Bow Knot, vase, B-10, laced hdls, 10½" 275.00
Bow Knot, wall pocket, B-24, cup & saucer form, 6" ...145.00
Bow Knot, wall pocket, B-27, whisk broom form, 8" ...145.00
Bow Knot, wall pocket, unmk, iron form, 6¼" 170.00
Butterfly, ash tray, B-3, heart form, 7" 26.00
Butterfly, ewer, B-15, gold trim, 13½" 120.00
Butterfly, lavabo, top B-25, base B-24, 16" 95.00
Butterfly, tray, serving; B-23, gold trim, 11½" 45.00
Butterfly, vase, B-10, 7" 36.00
Calla Lily, cornucopia, #570/33, bl/cream, 8" 75.00
Calla Lily, ewer, #506, pk/bl, 10" 240.00
Calla Lily, vase, #530/33, pk/gr, hdld, 7" 110.00
Camellia, ewer, #105, squat, 7" 125.00
Camellia, mermaid/shell planter, #104, 10½" 850.00
Camellia, vase, #131, laced hdls, 4¾" 32.00
Camellia, vase, #139, lamp form, 10½" 160.00
Capri, vase, #48, 1961, 13¾" 25.00
Capri, vase, #50, urn form, 1961, 9" 28.00
Classic, ewer, #6, 6" 22.00
Continental, basket, #55, 12¾" 70.00
Continental, vase, bud; #66, 9½" 25.00
Crescent, casserole, B-2, w/lid, 10" 8.00
Crescent, mug, B-16, 4¼" 9.00
Crestone, coffeepot, w/lid, 1962, 11" 70.00
Debonair, cookie jar, #0-8, ca 1955, gr/yel, 8¾" 50.00
Dogwood, ewer, #519, 13½" 550.00
Dogwood, vase, #513, hdld, 6½" 60.00
Dogwood, window box, #508, 10½" 130.00
Early Art, pitcher, stoneware, emb decor, #27, 6½" 200.00
Early Art, vase, semi-porc, H in circle, turq, 4½" 32.00
Early Art, vase, stoneware, #40, H in circle, 7" 60.00
Early Art, vase, stoneware, unmk, 5½" 32.00
Early Utility, bowl, #106, H in circle, brn on tan, 6" 20.00
Early Utility, casserole, #113, gr banded, w/lid, 7½" 40.00
Early Utility, flowerpot, w/saucer, #538, gr, 4" 28.00
Early Utility, mug, emb Chocolate Soldier, brn, 3¾" 28.00
Early Utility, pitcher, semi-porc, H in circle, gr, 4¼" 38.00
Early Utility, sugar canister, block H in dmn, gr, 6½" 50.00
Early Utility, vinegar cruet, unmk, gr, 6½" 50.00
Ebb Tide, basket, E-11, 16½" 100.00
Ebb Tide, basket, unmk, 6¼" 45.00
Fantasy, window box, #74, 12½" 20.00
Fiesta, cornucopia, #49, 8½" 35.00
Fiesta, jardiniere, #43, 6" 24.00

Fiesta, vase, emb deer, #50, 9" 40.00
Floral, cookie jar, #48, ca 1952-53, 8¾" 45.00
Floral, pitcher, #46, ca 1952, 6" 30.00
Heritage Ware, grease jar, A-3, 5¾" 25.00
Heritage Ware, pitcher, A-7, 4½" 15.00
House 'N Garden, butter dish, avocado gr, ¼-lb, 7¾" 15.00
House 'N Garden, canister, mirror brn, rnd, w/lid, set of 4 ....130.00
House 'N Garden, casserole, covered hen, mirror brn, 2-qt 38.00
House 'N Garden, cookie jar, mirror brn, 9" 22.00
House 'N Garden, plate, dinner; mirror brn, 10½" 5.00
Imperial, baby planter, #5-51, 5¼" 6.00
Imperial, basket, F-38, ca 1960s, 6¾" 18.00
Imperial, planter, unmk, 6¾" 12.00
Imperial, vase, #454, urn form, 5" 5.00
Imperial, window box, #82, 12½" 25.00
Iris, basket, #408, 7" 170.00
Iris, bowl, console; #409, 12" 185.00
Iris, ewer, #401, 8" 115.00
Iris, vase, #406, hdld, 8½" 85.00
Iris, vase, #414, hdld, 10½" 165.00
Magnolia, glossy; basket, H-14, 10½" 190.00
Magnolia, glossy; candle holder, H-24, 4" 22.00
Magnolia, glossy; ewer, H-19, 13½" 210.00
Magnolia, glossy; vase, H-17, 12½" 90.00
Magnolia, matt; basket, #10, 10½" 225.00
Magnolia, matt; bowl, console; #26, 12" 120.00
Magnolia, matt; creamer, #24, 3¾" 28.00
Magnolia, matt; ewer, #18, 13½" 225.00
Magnolia, matt; ewer, #5, 7" 95.00
Magnolia, matt; lamp base, drilled, 12½" 210.00
Magnolia, matt; vase, #21, tab hdld, 12½" 130.00
Magnolia, matt; vase, #22, 12½" 210.00
Marcrest, mug, unmk, 3¼" 3.00
Mardi Gras, bowl, mixing; unmk, 10¼" 32.00
Mardi Gras, flowerpot, #91, 9½" 25.00
Mardi Gras, flowerpot, #93, 8½" 20.00
Mardi Gras, vase, #94, 10" 35.00
Mardi Gras/Granada, basket, #65, 8" 95.00
Mardi Gras/Granada, ewer, #63, ivory, 10½" 80.00
Mardi Gras/Granada, vase, #216, 1947, ivory, 9" 25.00
Mayfair, wall pocket, #84, mandolin form, 1960, 7" 24.00
Novelty, baby, #62, ca 1945, 6¼" 25.00
Novelty, Bandana Duck, #74, ca 1950s, 7x9" 40.00
Novelty, basket girl, glossy, #954, ca 1945, 8" 28.00
Novelty, clown planter, #82, ca 1950s, 6¼" 22.00
Novelty, dachshund, 6x14" 95.00
Novelty, frog bank, unmk, 3¾" 65.00
Novelty, giraffe planter, #115, ca 1950s, 8" 30.00
Novelty, leaf dish, #85, ca 1950s, 13" 22.00
Novelty, little girl planter, #90, ca 1950s, 5½" 18.00
Novelty, lovebirds planter, #93, ca 1950s, 6" 24.00
Novelty, Old Spice Shaving mug, ca 1937-44, 3" 22.00
Novelty, owl bank, unmk, 3¾" 75.00
Novelty, pheasant planter, #61, ca 1950s, 6x8" 30.00
Novelty, pig bank, #196, mirror brn, 6" 15.00
Novelty, pig bank, emb floral, mk USA, 1940, 14" 90.00
Novelty, pig bank, mirror brn, #197, 1978, 8" 20.00
Novelty, pig bank, 1958, 3½" 40.00
Novelty, pig bottle, Leeds, ca 1945, 7¾" 50.00
Novelty, pig planter, #60, ca 1945, 5" 24.00
Novelty, planter, #201, 1940, 5" 25.00
Novelty, rabbit, unmk, 2¾" 35.00
Novelty, rooster, #951, ca 1940s, 7" 35.00
Novelty, swing band accordionist, unmk, 6" 70.00

Novelty, swing band tuba player, unmk, 5¾" 70.00
Nuline, casserole, D-13, w/lid, 7½" 35.00
Nuline, cookie jar, D-20, w/lid, 8"..75.00
Orchid, bowl, console; #314, hdld, 13"..245.00
Orchid, lamp base, unmk, 10"...230.00
Parchment & Pine, basket, S-8, 16½" L...95.00
Parchment & Pine, ewer, S-7, 14¼" 100.00
Parchment & Pine, teapot, S-15, 8"...75.00
Pine Cone, vase, #55, 6½"..45.00
Poppy, basket, #601, 9"...300.00
Poppy, ewer, #610, 13½" 700.00
Poppy, ewer, #610, 4¾" 50.00
Rainbow, pitcher, gr agate, 1960-70s, 7½"...................................22.00
Rainbow, vase, bud; tangerine, 1960-70s, 9"................................15.00
Regal, planter, #301, ca 1960-70s, 3½" 5.00
Rosella, basket, R-12, 7" 115.00
Rosella, ewer, R-9, 6½"..45.00
Rosella, lamp base, L-3, 1946, 11"..210.00
Rosella, sugar bowl, R-4, 5½"...30.00
Royal Imperial, window box, #82, 12½" 15.00
Royal Woodland, basket, W-9, 8¾"...35.00
Royal Woodland, bowl, console; W-29, 14½" 55.00
Royal Woodland, ewer, W-24, 13½"..120.00
Royal Woodland, wall pocket, W-13, 7½".......................................40.00
Serenade, bowl, fruit; S-15, 7"...60.00
Serenade, candy dish, S-3, w/lid, 8½" 60.00
Serenade, sugar bowl, S-19, w/lid, 3¼" 25.00
Sueno Tulip, jardiniere, #115-33, 7"..140.00
Sueno Tulip, vase, #103-33, 6"...90.00
Sueno Tulip, vase, #110-33, laced hdls, 6"....................................45.00
Sunglow, casserole, #51, w/lid, 7½"...32.00
Sunglow, grease jar, #53, 5¼"...22.00
Thistle, vase, #51, 6½"..32.00
Tokay, basket, #11, moon form, 10½"..65.00
Tropicana, vase, #54, 12½" 275.00
Tuscany, candy dish, #9, w/lid, 7x8½" 55.00
Utility, jug, unmk, pk & bl bands on cream, 6" 40.00
Victorian, vase, B-37, gold trim, 1970s 6.00
Water Lily, basket, L-14, 10½" 145.00
Water Lily, bowl, console; L-21, 13½"..125.00
Water Lily, cornucopia, L-7, 6½"...60.00
Water Lily, creamer, L-19, 5" 30.00
Water Lily, dbl cornucopia, L-27, 12" 120.00
Water Lily, jardinier, L-23, 5½"...90.00
Water Lily, vase, L-11, 9½" 80.00
Wildflower, basket, W-16, 10½" 210.00
Wildflower, ewer, W-19, 13½"...240.00
Wildflower, lamp base, W-17, drilled, 12½" 170.00
Wildflower, vase, W-13, 9½"..95.00
Wildflower, vase, W-20, 15½"...300.00
Wildflower (Number Series), cornucopia, #58, 6¼" 95.00
Wildflower (Number Series), creamer, #73, 4¾" 45.00
Wildflower (Number Series), teapot, #72, 8".................................325.00
Woodland, glossy; basket, W-22, 10½"...100.00
Woodland, glossy; jardiniere, W-8, 5½"...38.00
Woodland, glossy; teapot, W-26, 6½"..65.00
Woodland, matt; basket, hanging; W-12, 7½" 400.00
Woodland, matt; bowl, console; W-29, 14" 230.00
Woodland, matt; vase, dbl bud; W-15, 8½"...................................110.00

Hummel

Hummel figurines were created through the artistry of Berta Hum-

mel, a Franciscan nun called Sister M. Innocentia. The first figures were made about 1935 by Franz Goebel of Goebel Art Inc., Rodental, West Germany. Plates, plaques, and candy dishes are also produced; and the older, discontinued editions are highly sought collectibles. Generally speaking, an issue can be dated by the trademark. The first Hummels, from 1934-1950, were either incised or stamped with the 'Crown WG' mark. The 'full bee in V' mark was employed with minor variations until 1959. At that time the bee was stylized and represented by a solid disk with angled symmetrical wings completely contained within the confines of the 'V.' The three-line mark, 1964-1972, utilized the stylized bee and included a three-line arrangement, 'c by W. Goebel, W. Germany.' Another change in 1970 saw the 'stylized bee in V' suspended between the vertical bars of the 'b' and 'l' of a printed 'Goebel, West Germany.' Collectors refer to this mark as the 'last bee' or 'Goebel bee.' The current mark in use since 1979 omits the 'bee in V.' For a more thorough study of the subject we recommend *Hummel Figurines and Plates, A Collector's Identification and Value Guide* by Carl Luckey, available at your local book dealer. Idiosyncrasies in the numerical order of the following listings are due to computer sorting. See also Limited Edition Plates.

Key:
ce — closed edition	GB — Goebel bee
CM — crown mark	SB — stylized bee
FB — full bee	LB — last bee

Blessed Event, #333, last bee mark, 5¼", $265.00.

#10/I, Flower Madonna, color, LB, 8¼"...............................195.00
#106, Merry Wanderer, plaque, CM, wooden fr, 5⅛x4¾" 7,750.00
#109/II, Happy Traveler, SB, 8"...350.00
#11/2/0, Merry Wanderer, FB, 4¼" 130.00
#110/I, Let's Sing, SB, 3⅞"...135.00
#111/110, Let's Sing, candy box, 3-line mk, 6"......................255.00
#111/3/0, Wayside Harmony, LB, 3¾" 80.00
#112/I, Just Resting, FB, 5"...180.00
#113, Heavenly Song, candle holder, LB, 3½x4¾"................. 1,850.00
#114, Let's Sing, ash tray, SB, 3½x6¾".................................125.00
#12/II, Chimney Sweep, FB, 7¼" 115.00
#123, Max & Moritz, 3-line mk, 5¼" 120.00
#124/I, Hello, LB, 7" 135.00
#125, Vacation Time, plaque, SB, 4¾x4" 185.00
#126, Retreat to Safety, plaque, FB, 5x4¾" 265.00
#127, Doctor, FB, 4¾" 165.00
#129, Band Leader, LB, 5¼" 125.00
#130, Duet, FB, 5¼" 265.00
#132, Star Gazer, 3-line mk, 4¾" 135.00
#135, Soloist, FB, 4¾" 145.00
#136/V, Friends, SB, 10¾" 925.00
#140, Mail Coach, plaque, FB, 4½x6¾" 325.00

#141/3/0, Apple Tree Girl, LB, 4" 80.00
#143/I, Boots, SB, 6¾" 185.00
#145, Little Guardian, 3-line mk, 3¾" 90.00
#15/0, Hear Ye Hear Ye, FB, 5" 215.00
#152/B/II, Umbrella Girl, SB, 8" 1,100.00
#153/0, Auf Widersehen, LB, 7" 185.00
#16/2/0, Little Hiker, CM, 4¼" 365.00
#163, Whitsuntide, FB, 7¼" 485.00
#164, Worship, font, FB, 4¾x2¾" 65.00
#165, Swaying Lullaby, plaque, SB, 5¼x4½" 140.00
#166, Boy w/Bird, ash tray, LB, 3¼x6¼" 110.00
#168, Standing Boy, plaque, FB, 5½x4⅛" 725.00
#169, Bird Duet, SB, 4" 125.00
#172/II, Festival Harmony, 3-line mk, 10¾" 285.00
#173/II, Festival Harmony, SB, 11" 395.00
#176/0, Happy Birthday, 3-line mk, 5½" 165.00
#177/III, School Girls, 3-line mk, 9½" 1,350.00
#180, Tuneful Goodnight, SB, 4¾x4" 265.00
#182, Good Friends, LB, 4" 115.00
#183, Forest Shrine, FB, 7x9" 1,200.00
#184, Latest News, 3-line mk, 5¼" 185.00
#192, Candlelight, candle holder (long), FB, 6¾" 500.00
#195/I, Barnyard Hero, SB, 5¾" 225.00
#196/0, Telling Her Secret, LB, 5¼" 185.00
#2/III, Little Fiddler, FB, 11" 1,350.00
#20, Prayer Before Battle, LB, 4¼" 110.00
#200/0, Little Goat Herder, 3-line mk, 4¾" 145.00
#201/I, Retreat to Safety, FB, 5½" 300.00
#206, Angel Cloud, font, LB, 4¾x2¼" 32.00
#21/0, Heavenly Angel, LB, 4¼" 65.00
#217, Boy w/Toothache, 3-line mk, 5½" 130.00
#22/I, Angel w/Birds, FB, 4x3¼" 465.00
#224, Wayside Harmony, table lamp, SB, 7½" 295.00
#235, Happy Days, table lamp, SB, 7¾" 435.00
#243, Madonna & Child, font, 3-line mk, 4x3¼" 35.00
#248, Guardian Angel, font, LB, 5½x2¼" 38.00
#25, Angelic Sleep, candle holder, SB, 3½x5" 150.00
#255, Stitch in Time, SB, 6¾" 265.00
#26/I, Child Jesus, font, LB, 5x1½" 30.00
#29, Guardian Angel, FB, 5⅝x2½" 1,975.00
#3/I, Bookworm, SB, 5½" 235.00
#32/1, Little Gabriel, FB, 5" 175.00
#33, Joyful, ash tray, LB, 3½x6" 88.00
#35/0, Good Shepherd, 3-line mk, 4¾x2¼" 32.00
#36/I, Child w/Flowers, FB, 4½x3½" 265.00
#37, Herald Angels, candle holder, LB, 2¼x4" 110.00
#42/0, Good Shepherd, FB, 6¼" 180.00
#45/0, Madonna w/Halo, SB, 10½" 65.00
#46/0, Madonna w/o Halo, FB, 10¼" 115.00
#48/V, Madonna, plaque, SB, 8¼x10½" 1,400.00
#49/0, To Market, SB, 5½" 200.00
#5, Strolling Along, LB, 4¾" 100.00
#50/I, Volunteers, LB, 6½" 275.00
#51/0, Village Boy, CM, 6" 535.00
#52/0, Going to Grandma's, SB, 4¾" 185.00
#55, St George, 3-line mk, 6¾" 245.00
#6/II, Sensitive Hunter, LB, 7½" 220.00
#65, Farewell, LB, 4¾" 165.00
#66, Farm Boy, FB, 5¼" 250.00
#67, Doll Mother, FB, 4¾" 265.00
#68/0, Lost Sheep, SB, 5½" 145.00
#70, Holy Child, 3-line mk, 6¾" 98.00
#71, Stormy Weather, LB, 6¼" 275.00
#72, Spring Cheer, 3-line mk, 5" 80.00

#73, Little Helper, SB, 4¼" 110.00
#78/I, Infant of Krumbad, SB, 2½" 40.00
#81/0, School Girl, LB, 5¼" 100.00
#82/0, School Boy, FB, 5½" 185.00
#83, Angel Serenade, SB, 5" 195.00
#9, Begging His Share, w/hole, SB, 5½" 235.00
#91/A&B, Angel at Prayer, SB, 4¾x2", pr 65.00
#92, Merry Wanderer, plaque, LB, 5⅛x4¾" 95.00
#93, Little Fiddler, plaque, 3-line mk, 5⅛x4¾" 115.00
#94/I, Surprise, 3-line mk, 5½" 155.00
#95, Brother, FB, 5½" 175.00
#96, Little Shopper, 3-line mk, 4¾" 120.00
#97, Trumpet Boy, SB, 4¾" 75.00
#98/2/0, Sister, SB, 4¾" 100.00
#99, Eventide, 3-line mk, 4¾" 235.00

Valentine Gift, first club piece, 1972, German market, $400.00.

Hutschenreuther

The Porcelain Factory C.M. Hutschenreuther operated in Bavaria from 1814 to 1969. After the death of the elder Hutschenreuther in 1845, his son Lorenz took over operations, continuing there until 1857 when he left to establish his own company in the nearby city of Selb. The original manufactory became a joint stock company in 1904, absorbing several other potteries. In 1969 both Hutschenreuther firms merged, and that company still operates in Selb; they have distributing centers in both France and the United States. Our advisor for this category is Jack Gunsaulus; he is listed in the Directory under Michigan.

Kneeling nude, 7", $350.00.

Bowl, cardinals on ivory, sgn Granget, 4½" **75.00**
Bowl, floral, mc on bl w/silver, Baroque ft, w/lid, 7½x8"............**150.00**
Figurine, hunting dog, wht w/brn spots, sgn Diller, 7x12" **375.00**
Figurine, nude, wht w/gold shot put, 1936 Olympics, mk, 11".....**275.00**
Figurine, nude boy on frisky colt, mk, 7¾x7½" **275.00**
Figurine, running girl w/fawn, sgn Tutter, 20" **770.00**

Imari

Imari is a generic term which covers a broad family of wares. It was made in more than a dozen Japanese villages, but the name is that of the port from whence it was shipped to Europe. There are several types of Imari. The most common features a design with panels of birds, florals, or people surrounding a central basket of flowers. The colors used in this type are underglaze blue with overglaze red, gold, and green enamels. The Chinese also made Imari wares which differ from the Japanese type in several ways — the absence of spur marks, a thinner-type body, and a more consistent control of the blue. Imari-type wares were copied on the continent by Meissen and by English potters, among them Worcester, Derby, and Bow.

Bottle vase, floral, gold trim, 1850s, 9", EX, pr **400.00**
Bottle vase, flowers/dragons/bldgs, 1850s, mfg flaw, 12"...............**300.00**
Bowl, figure & landscape reserves, mc w/gold, 1900s, 11x8"........**550.00**
Bowl, florals around underglaze bl medallion, 1900s, 11".............**225.00**
Bowl, garden scene w/birds, brass lion mask hdls/base, 12"...... **1,800.00**
Charger, central bouquet w/paneled border, late 1800s, 19" **350.00**
Jar, floral & landscape, baluster, pierced metal lid, 8¾"..............**400.00**
Jardiniere, floral panels, fluted body, 1850s, hairline, 6" **475.00**

Punch bowl, flying phoenix, vines and flowers, 1800s, 15" diameter, $3,600.00.

Punch bowl, garden scenes, paneled borders, 1850s, 11"..............**550.00**
Punch bowl, peacocks/geometrics, gold trim, 1880s, 12", NM.. **1,400.00**
Soup plate, florals & pagoda, 10½" **75.00**
Tobacco jar, floral, gold trim, melon finial, 1880s, 5" **300.00**
Tray, arms of Horsemonden, floral rim, ca 1716, rpr, 6" sq **800.00**
Tray, birds/leaves/flowers, leaf hdls, 1880s, 15" L **330.00**
Vase, dragons/bldgs/etc, bottle form, 1850s, mfg flaws, 12".........**325.00**

Imperial Glass Company

The Imperial Glass Company was organized in 1901 in Bellaire, Ohio, and started manufacturing glassware in 1904. Their early products were jelly glasses, hotel tumblers, etc., but by 1910 they were mak-

ing a name for themselves by pressing quantities of Carnival Glass, the iridescent glassware that was popular during that time. In 1914 NuCut was introduced to imitate cut glass. The line was so popular that it was made in crystal and colors and was reintroduced as Collector's Crystal in the 1950s. From 1916 to 1920, they used the lustre process to make a line called Imperial Jewels, now referred to as stretch glass. Free-Hand ware, art glass made entirely by hand using no molds, was made from 1922 to 1928.

The company entered bankruptcy in 1931 but was able to continue operations and reorganize as the Imperial Glass Corporation. In 1936 Imperial introduced the Candlewick line, for which it is best known. In the late thirties, the Vintage Grape Milk Glass line was added, and in 1951 a major ad campaign was launched making Imperial one of the leading milk glass manufacturers.

In 1940 Imperial bought the molds and assets of the Central Glass Works of Wheeling, West Virginia; in 1958 they acquired the molds of the Heisey Company and in 1960 the molds of the Cambridge Glass Company of Cambridge, Ohio. Imperial used these molds, and since '51 they have marked their new glassware with an 'I' superimposed over the 'G' trademark. The company became a subsidiary of Lenox in 1973; subsequently an 'L' was added to the 'IG' mark. In 1981 Lenox sold Imperial to Arthur Lorch, a private investor (who modified the L by adding a line at the top angled to the left). He in turn sold the company to Robert F. Stahl, Jr., in 1982. Mr. Stahl filed for Chapter 11 to reorganize, but in mid-1984 liquidation was ordered, and all assets were sold. The few items that had been made in '84 were marked with an 'N' superimposed over the 'I' for 'New Imperial.' See also Candlewick; Carnival Glass; Stretch Glass.

Animals and Birds

Asiatic pheasant, amber **325.00**
Champ Terrier, caramel slag, 5¾" **95.00**
Chick, head down, milk glass **10.00**
Chick, head up, milk glass **10.00**
Clydesdale, amber **325.00**
Clydesdale, salmon **325.00**
Clydesdale, Verde Gr...**150.00**
Colt, balking, aqua, dtd 1979 ....**70.00**
Colt, balking, Ultra Bl..**45.00**
Colt, kicking, Ultra Bl **50.00**
Colt, standing, caramel slag..**45.00**
Colt, standing, milk glass..**75.00**
Cygnet, blk **55.00**
Cygnet, lt bl **25.00**
Dog, Airedale, caramel slag **95.00**
Dog, Airedale, Ultra Bl...**65.00**
Dog, Airedale, Ultra Bl satin **80.00**
Donkey, caramel slag **55.00**
Donkey, Meadow Gr Carnival **95.00**
Elephant, caramel slag, med **55.00**
Elephant, Meadow Gr Carnival, #674, med...................................**95.00**
Elephant, pk satin, sm...**70.00**
Filly, head bkward, Verde Gr **145.00**
Filly, head forward, satin...**75.00**
Fish, candle holder, Sunshine Yel **45.00**
Fish, match holder, Sunshine Yel satin...**20.00**
Gazelle, Ultra Bl **125.00**
Horse head, bookend, pk, rare **300.00**
Mallard, wings down, caramel slag **190.00**
Mallard, wings down, lt bl satin..**22.50**
Mallard, wings half, caramel slag **35.00**
Mallard, wings half, lt bl satin...**22.50**
Mallard, wings up, caramel slag **35.00**

Mallard, wings up, lt bl satin 22.50
Owl, hootless, milk glass, Doeskin.......................50.00
Piglet, sitting..45.00
Piglet, standing, ruby, hole between legs 95.00
Piglet, standing, Ultra Bl 45.00
Plug Horse, pk, HCA, 1978 ....40.00
Rabbit, paperweight, milk glass 25.00
Rooster, amber..425.00
Rooster, fighting, pk 175.00
Sow, amber...325.00
Swan, nut dish, dtd..35.00
Tiger, paperweight, blk......................................65.00
Tiger, paperweight, jade 85.00
Wood duck, caramel slag....................................45.00
Wood duck, Sunshine Yel satin 45.00
Wood duck, Ultra Bl satin 45.00
Wood duckling, floating, Sunshine Yel satin..........15.00
Wood duckling, standing, Sunshine Yel 15.00
Wood duckling, standing, Sunshine Yel satin..........15.00

Cathay Crystal

Cathay Crystal was conceived and designed by Virginia B. Evans in 1949. Representative of China's history, this line consisted of thirty-eight designs which were produced in a satin/frosted combination. Except for items too small to accomodate it, each piece bears the script signature of its designer. The line was lavishly introduced at the National China and Glass Show in Pittsburgh in 1949. Items from the line were presented in boxes lined with green suede and lettered in gold, each piece having its own number. But as was often true for unusual art glass lines, Cathay Crystal did not meet sales expectations, and the line was manufactured for only two years; sales halted in 1957. For a short time and in limited amounts, some designs were produced in color; but the Evans name was removed from the molds.

Candle servant, $350.00 for the pair.

#5001, pagoda 550.00
#5002, Shang candy jar 250.00
#5004, Yang & Yin ash tray 175.00
#5006, butterfly ash tray 25.00
#5007, plum blossom ash tray.............................25.00
#5008, peach blossom mint or nut set 20.00
#5009, dragon candle holder, pr.........................400.00
#5010, junk flower bowl 250.00
#5011, Wu Ling ash tray 125.00
#5012, Ku ribbon vase 750.00
#5013, pillow candle base 50.00

#5014, bamboo urn 400.00
#5016, Fu wedding vase 200.00
#5017, egrette 300.00
#5018, pillow cigarette set, 3-pc 550.00
#5019, Ming jar...80.00
#5020, Shen console set 300.00
#5022, fan sweetmeat box 175.00
#5024, scolding bird..175.00
#5026, phoenix bowl 175.00
#5029, empress book stop, pr.............................250.00
#5030, Lu-Tunb book holder, pr 350.00
#5033/34, candle servants, pr 350.00
#5038, Celestial centerpc 350.00
#5085, Pavillion tray 350.00

Ash tray, purple slag satin...................................17.00
Basket, Daisy, milk glass, Doeskin 25.00
Basket, Monticello...25.00
Bowl, baked apple; Tradition................................10.00
Bowl, Collector's Crystal, 10".............................15.00
Bowl, console; Cape Cod, rolled rim, 13".............40.00
Bowl, nappy, Cape Cod, Azalea, 5".....................15.00
Bowl, Rose Design, milk glass, glossy, 9".............20.00
Bowl, swan, milk glass, Doeskin, 8"....................35.00
Bowl, swan, purple slag, glossy, 4".....................20.00

Crochet Crystal cake plate, $25.00.

Cake plate, Cape Cod, 72-candle 200.00
Cake plate, Tradition, crystal, 72-candle 75.00
Creamer & sugar bowl, Cape Cod, #160/30..........17.50
Cruet, purple slag satin 36.00
Decanter, Collector's Crystal, gold trim.................45.00
Decanter, grape design, Peacock Carnival 60.00
Decanter, Peachblow..150.00
Goblet, Cape Cod, Azalea, 11-oz.........................20.00
Lamp, Dew Drop opal...90.00
Mug, Dumbo, gr, 1974.......................................50.00
Mug, Storybook, milk glass, glossy.......................23.00
Mustard, Cape Cod, #160/156, w/lid & spoon, 3-pc....17.50
Nest, Swan, milk glass, Doeskin...........................25.00
Oyster cocktail, Cape Cod 8.00
Parfait, Cape Cod, #1602, 6-oz..........................12.00
Pitcher, Cape Cod, #160/24, 2-qt........................85.00
Pitcher, water; Tradition, crystal...........................35.00
Plate, Cape Cod, dinner sz.................................35.00
Plate, Monticello, sq, 12"...................................18.00
Plate, Tradition Bl, 8"..10.00
Punch set, Cape Cod, 15-pc..............................175.00

Server, Cape Cod, #160/93, ftd, 12"	65.00	Decanter, #100, outhouse, man, & bird	75.00

Server, Cape Cod, #160/93, ftd, 12" 65.00
Shakers, Cape Cod, #160/109, sq, pr..................................18.00
Shakers, Cape Cod, #160/116, pr..16.00
Shakers, Salz & Pfeffer, Carnival..42.00
Sundae, Cape Cod, #1602, 6-oz 7.00
Tumbler, Bambu, 14-oz 5.00
Tumbler, dbl old fashioned; Cape Cod, #160, 14-oz 20.00
Tumbler, iced tea; Cape Cod, cobalt, ftd 25.00
Tumbler, Little Shot, red, 2½-oz 12.50
Vase, Cape Cod, #160/21, ftd, 11" 55.00
Vase, Daffodil design, milk glass, glossy, 6" 10.00
Vase, Free-Hand, bl-blk w/wht drag looping, 11½x5" 200.00
Vase, Free-Hand, butterflies, bl irid on wht, 7¼" 395.00
Vase, Free-Hand, heart leaves, gr irid on wht, gold int, 6¾" 395.00
Vase, Genie, bl opal, ftd, 5" 25.00

Imperial Porcelain

The Blue Ridge Mountain Boys were created by cartoonist Paul Webb and translated into three-dimension by the Imperial Porcelain Corporation of Zanesville, Ohio, in 1947. These figurines decorated ash trays, vases, mugs, bowls, pitchers, planters, and other items. The Mountain Boys series were numbered 92 through 108, each with a different and amusing portrayal of mountain life. Imperial also produced American Folklore miniatures, twenty-three tiny animals under two inches in size, and the Al Capp Dogpatch series. Because of financial difficulties, the company closed in 1960.

Ash tray, baby knocks on outhouse, 8", $125.00.

American Folklore Miniatures

Cat, 1½" 40.00
Cow, 1¾" 35.00
Hound dogs...35.00
Plaque, store ad, Am Folklore Porcelain Miniatures, 4½" 300.00
Sow..30.00

Blue Ridge Mountain Boys by Paul Webb

Ash tray, #101, man w/jug & snake 75.00
Ash tray, #103, hillbilly & skunk 75.00
Ash tray, #105, baby, hound dog, & frog..............................110.00
Ash tray, #106, Barrel of Wishes, w/hound 75.00
Ash tray, #92, 2 men by tree stump, for pipes 125.00
Box, cigarette; #98, dog atop, baby at door, sq.....................115.00

Decanter, #100, outhouse, man, & bird 75.00
Decanter, #104, Ma leaning over stump, w/baby & skunk 95.00
Decanter, man, jug, snake, & tree stump, Hispch Inc, 1946 ....75.00
Figurine, #101, man leans against tree trunk, 5" 90.00
Figurine, man on hands & knees, 3" 95.00
Figurine, man sitting, 3½" 95.00
Figurine, man sitting w/chicken on knee, 3" 95.00
Jug, #101, Willie & snake 75.00
Mug, #94, Bearing Down, 6" 95.00
Mug, #94, dbl baby hdl, 4¼" 95.00
Mug, #94, ma hdl, 4¼" 95.00
Mug, #94, man w/bl pants hdl, 4¼" 95.00
Mug, #94, man w/yel beard & red pants hdl, 4¼" 95.00
Mug, #99, Target Practice, boy on goat, farmer, 5¾" 95.00
Pitcher, lemonade 200.00
Plaque, store ad, Handcrafted Paul Webb Mtn Boys, rare, 9" 500.00
Planter, #100, outhouse, man, & bird 75.00
Planter, #105, man w/chicken on knee, washtub 110.00
Planter, #110, man, w/jug & snake, 4½" 65.00
Planter, #81, man drinking from jug, sitting by washtub 75.00
Shakers, Ma & Old Doc, pr 95.00

Miscellaneous

Items in this section that are designated 'IP' are miscellaneous novelties made by Imperial Porcelain; the remainder are of interest to Paul Webb collectors, though made by an unknown manufacturer. Prints on calendars and playing cards are signed 'Paul Webb.'

Calendar, 1954, 12 sgn scenes, Brown & Bigelow, complete 35.00
Figurine, cat in high-heeled shoe, 5½" L.............................40.00
Hot pad, Dutch boy w/tulips, rnd, IP....................................30.00
Ink blotters, sgn scenes, ea 8.00
Mug, #29, man hdl, sgn Paul Webb, 4¾" 25.00
Planter, #106, dog sitting by tub, IP 75.00
Planter, #26, man & tree stump, sgn Paul Webb, bl 25.00
Planter, #27, man, jug, & barrel, sgn Paul Webb.................25.00
Playing cards, ad: Rafe Oiling Gun, Brown & Bigelow, MIB 45.00
Shakers, pigs, 5", pr 95.00
Shakers, standing pigs, IP, 8", pr 95.00

Indian Tree

Indian Tree was a popular dinnerware pattern produced by various potteries since the early 1800s to recent times. Although backgrounds and borders vary, the Oriental theme is carried out with the gnarled, brown branch of a pink-blossomed tree. Among the manufacturers' marks, you may find represented such notable firms as Coalport, S. Hancock and Sons, Soho Pottery, and John Maddock and Sons.

Bowl, cereal; Johnson Bros 8.00
Bowl, soup; Johnson Bros..10.00
Bowl, soup; Spode-Copeland, flat..15.00
Bowl, vegetable; oval, Johnson Bros......................................20.00
Cup & saucer, Johnson Bros..10.00
Plate, bread & butter; Johnson Bros......................................5.00
Plate, dinner; Johnson Bros 8.00
Plate, salad; Johnson Bros..7.00
Platter, Johnson Bros, 10"..22.50

Inkwells and Inkstands

Receptacles for various writing fluids have been used since ancient times. Through the years they have been made from countless materials — glass, metal, porcelain, pottery, wood, and even papier-mache. During the 18th century, gold or silver inkstands were presented to royalty; the well-known silver inkstand by Philip Syng, Jr., was used for the signing of the Declaration of Independence, and impressive brass inkstands with wells and a pounce pot (sander) were proud possessions of men of letters. When literacy vastly increased in the 19th century, the dip pen replaced the quill pen; and inkwells and inkstands were widely used and produced in a broad range of sizes in functional and decorative forms from ornate Victorian to flowing Art Nouveau and stylized Art Deco designs. However, the acceptance of the ballpoint pen literally put inkstands and inkwells 'out of business.' But their historical significance and intriguing diversity of form and styling fascinate today's collectors.

Art glass, Loetz type, brass figural lid, 4½" sq.................................950.00
Blown, dk cobalt, squatty, w/lid, 2x2¾" dia...............................130.00
Blown, olive gr, GII-2, sm rim flake, 1¾x2⅜" 150.00
Blown, olive-amber, GIII-24, bruise on top, 1½x2¼"..................100.00
Brass, devil's head form, porc insert, England..............................100.00
Brass, raised center holds crystal bottle, hinged lid, 1800s...........120.00
China, HP bird & florals, w/undertray, Am, 1890s, 2½x4⅛" 95.00
China, HP bird & florals w/gold, 1890s, 2⅝x4⅝" 85.00
China, HP mc florals, Am, 1890s, 3⅛x3⅞" 85.00
CI, Pat June 4 1861 Nov 16 64, Am, ca 1860s, 5½x5" 120.00
CI, revolving, w/clear snail well, Am, 1880s, 4½"........................125.00
Copper, hammered, Arts & Crafts type, Apollo Studios, 4½"........75.00
Crystal & sterling, Truncated Pyramid, 2" sq 235.00
Cut glass, brass partner's lid, 2½" sq 250.00
Cut glass, vaseline, octagonal, hinged lid, 3" H...........................550.00
Glass, Daisy & Button, sapphire bl, cat figural finial...................150.00
Glass, emerald gr, clear appl ft, SP cap, 2¾" 150.00
HR Quimper, Breton lady, oblong, 5"...545.00
Iron, w/pen rack & candle socket, pitted, 7½", EX.......................200.00
Metal, elephant w/monkey on top, mc pnt, EX.............................125.00
Metal, helmet w/metal strap form, 2x3", EX.................................110.00
Nalsea, bl & wht, hinged lid, 3½" dia...650.00
Nippon, Phoenix Bird, loose lid, 4" sq 250.00
Porc, Oriental boy figural, hat is lid 85.00
Porc, sq form on attached saucer 95.00
Pot metal, dog beside tree trunk, 2½" H..125.00
Pottery, lady reclines on couch form, Rockingham, 3¼x4½".......250.00
Pottery, man reclining on couch, brn Rockingham, 3¾x5⅜" 250.00
Pressed glass, Dmn pattern, cobalt, SP loose lid 345.00

Sevres Empire porcelain inkwell, cobalt ground, gilt leafage, 8", NM, $550.00.

Staffordshire, bird's nest, 3" dia..225.00
Stoneware, Perry & Co London on salt glaze, 1870s, 3⅝x2⅝".......80.00
Tin, floral emb, milk glass well, desk top, 3¼x5¼" 75.00
Traveler's, golden oak, brass int, 2" sq..65.00
Traveler's, rnd, brn-leather covered, 2" dia...................................75.00
Wood, cvd poodle head, cobalt insert...350.00
Wood, 4 cvd chickens on grassy base, 2 are lids, 9x16" 350.00

Insulators

The telegraph was invented in 1844. The devices developed to hold the electrical transmission wires to the poles were called insulators. The telephone, invented in 1876, intensified their usefulness; and, by the turn of the century, thousands of varieties were being produced in pottery, wood, and glass of various colors. Even though it has been rumored that red glass insulators exist, none have ever been authenticated. Many insulators are embossed with patent dates.

Of the more than 3,000 types known to exist, today's collectors evaluate their worth by age and rarity of color. Aqua and green are the most common colors in glass, dark brown the most common in ceramic. Threadless insulators (for example, CD #737) made between 1850 and 1870, bring prices well into the hundreds, if in mint condition.

In the listings that follow, the CD numbers are from an identification system developed in the late 1960s by N.R. Woodward.

Those seeking additional information about insulators are encouraged to contact the National Insulator Association (whose address may be found in the Directory under Clubs, Newsletters, and Catalogs) or attend a club-endorsed show. (For information see Directory under Florida for Jacqueline and Len Linscott).

Key:
CB — corrugated base   SDP — sharp drip points
CD — Consolidated Design   RB — rough base
SB — smooth base   RDP — round drip points

CD 101, Brookfield, bk: No 9, SB, aqua.. 3.00
CD 112, B, SDP, aqua.. 2.00
CD 115, Armstrong's No 3, bk: Made in USA A, SB, clear............ 1.00
CD 121, Am Tel & Tel Co, SB, aqua 2.00
CD 121, Brookfield, Crown-12, SB, aqua 2.00
CD 121.4, AU, bk: B, SB, aqua 30.00
CD 128, Pyrex/TM Reg US Pat Off, bk: CSA...USA, SB, clear..... 1.00
CD 131, Crown Arc, LG Tillotson & Co, Brooks Pat, SB, aqua .100.00
CD 131.4, LGT Co, SB, aqua...45.00
CD 133, California, SB, smoke 30.00
CD 133, City Fire Alarm, SB, aqua 40.00
CD 133, HG Co, bk: No 7 Standard, SB, amber 250.00
CD 134, Am Ins Co Patd Sept 13 81, SB, aqua...........................15.00
CD 136, Crown, B&O Pat Jan 25th 1870, SB, gr..........................12.00
CD 140, Jumbo, SB, aqua...140.00
CD 143, Canadian Pacific Ry Co, SB, lt purple 12.00
CD 143, GNW Dwight, bk: Pattern, SB, Canadian, aqua..............50.00
CD 145, B, bk: B, SB, amber 55.00
CD 145, B, bk: B, SB, aqua 4.00
CD 145, Hemingray, bk: No 21, SDP, aqua................................... 2.00
CD 145, Lynchburg/L w/in oval, bk: No 43, SDP, aqua 10.00
CD 145, Postal, SB, purple 11.00
CD 150, Brookfield/Pat Oct 8, 1907, SB, aqua 60.00
CD 152, emb Diamond, SB, lt lime, Canadian............................... 8.00
CD 152.9, Agee, cross-cut, lt purple, Foreign 25.00
CD 154, Agee, RDP, sage gr, Foreign..70.00
CD 154, Dominion 42, P (w/in emb dmn), SB, lt gr 4.00
CD 154, Hemingray 42, bk: Made in USA, RDP, aqua.................. 1.00

CD 154, Whitall Tatum Co No 1/No, bk: Made in USA, SB, aqua . **1.00**
CD 155, Armstrong's DP-1, bk: Made in USA A, SB, clear **2.00**
CD 155, Hemingray-45, bk: Nos Made in USA, SB, clear............. **1.00**
CD 156.1, base emb: Sept 13, 1881, aqua...............................**30.00**
CD 160, California, SB, smoke..**5.00**
CD 160, L (w/in oval)/Lynchburg, bk: No 32...USA, SDP, gr **13.00**
CD 161, emb star, SB, gr **6.00**
CD 162, Hemingray 19, bk: Made in USA, RDP, Hemingray Bl.... **3.00**
CD 162, Hemingray 19, bk: Made in USA, RDP, lt cobalt **50.00**
CD 164, HG Co PATENT MAY 2, 1893, SDP, amber **70.00**
CD 190/191, California, SB, purple **600.00**
CD 196, HG Co, bk: Pat May 2, 1893, SDP, aqua **30.00**
CD 200, no name, no embossing, SB, aqua............................**50.00**
CD 203, Armstrong's TW, bk: Made in USA A, SB, clear............. **2.00**
CD 203, HEMINGRAY 56, bk: Made in USA, CB, lt gr **15.00**
CD 217, Armstrong's 51-C3 Made in USA A, SB, amber **5.00**
CD 231, Kimble-820 Tempered, bk: Made in USA, CB, clear **4.00**
CD 252, Gayner, bk: 620, SB, aqua **35.00**
CD 254, M&E Co, bk: No 58, SB, aqua...............................**100.00**
CD 257, Hemingray 60, bk: Made in USA, RDP, aqua................. **5.00**
CD 269, Jumbo, SB, aqua...**225.00**
CD 270, no embossing, SB, gr..**100.00**
CD 280, NO 135, SB, gr...**30.00**
CD 296, Brookfield, SB, aqua...**12.00**
CD 318, Fred M Locke Victor NY, bk: 19, SB, aqua **90.00**
CD 470, ESA, bk: N 95, SB, aqua..**25.00**

Irons

Iron collections represent centuries of civilization and history through the diversity of these implements used to smooth and press clothing. Terra cotta irons were used during the period of the Roman Empire. The Hong Kong Museum of Arts has a pan iron from the Han Dynasty. Excavations reveal mysterious primitive glass irons in Viking graves. More recent history is rich with cast iron, charcoal, box, and fuel irons.

Joining an iron-collectors' club where you can see and handle old irons is a wonderful way to gain the knowledge and experience you need to become a wise iron collector. A novice must learn to avoid the temptation to buy cheap irons; experienced collectors avow they never overpay by buying quality. Condition is of the utmost importance. Common irons should grade very good or better. Only for scarce items should the condition be relaxed. Remember that it is the top-level pieces whose values tend toward rapid appreciation. Because good old irons have been passed down through several generations, by now it is unusual to find a 'sleeper'; and, as the ranks of iron collectors continue to swell, supplies diminish and values increase. Buy fine workmanship, design, style, and quality; a well-chosen iron collection could be one of today's best investments.

In the listings that follow, prices are given for examples in very good to excellent condition. Damage, repairs, excessive wear, rust, and missing parts can dramatically reduce value. Our advisor for this category is The Iron Lady (Carol and Jimmy Walker), whose address is listed in the Directory under Texas. See also Appliances.

Box, American, Bless & Drake Salamander, w/slug.......................**75.00**
Box, Belgian, w/slug & trivet **800.00**
Box, English, w/slug..**140.00**
Box, German, brass single post, w/slug.............................**350.00**
Charcoal, American, Ne Plus Ultra, dbl chimney....................**125.00**
Charcoal, French, single post **350.00**
Charcoal, German, Max Elb Dresden **1,100.00**
Charcoal, German, monster head chimney..........................**1,095.00**
Combination, charcoal/fluter **125.00**

Combination, sadiron/fluter, wire latch **90.00**
Detachable hdl, Colebrookdale **25.00**
Detachable hdl, Ober, dbl-point..**50.00**
Detachable hdl, Potts..**30.00**
Detachable hdl, Universal Thermo-Cell, w/3 bases.................**90.00**
Fluter, Erie, w/detachable hdl..**95.00**
Fluter, Geneva, Pat 1866 ....**50.00**
Fluter, Shepard, rolling, w/heater.....................................**135.00**
Fluter, Star, crank type **125.00**
Fluter, The Original Knox, w/picture..................................**180.00**
Fuel, American, Diamond, triangle tank...............................**45.00**
Fuel, American, Peerless, rnd tank on face **75.00**
Fuel, Canadian, Coleman #4, blk.......................................**95.00**
Fuel, Canadian, Coleman #4, red or beige, ea **295.00**
Little, Dutch, iron-shaped chocolate mold **135.00**
Little, Enterprise Star, w/ventilated hdl, 2⅝".......................**100.00**
Little, French, boar on face, 4"..**200.00**
Little, French, lady ironing on face, 4" **225.00**
Little, French, oval CF & anchor on face, 4"..........................**85.00**
Little, Ober, dbl-point, 4"..**125.00**
Little, Portuguese, chimney, charcoal, 3⅝" **1,000.00**
Little, Potts type, w/trivet & detachable hdl, 3½" **75.00**
Little, Swan, 2¾" **95.00**
Natural gas, American, 'I Want U' Comfort **40.00**
Natural gas, American, Imperial **60.00**
Natural gas, English, OK on face..**95.00**
Natural gas, German, ox tongue on gas stove **85.00**
Sadiron, Enterprise Star, dbl-point.....................................**25.00**
Sadiron, Enterprise Star, sq bk **30.00**
Sadiron, French, bl porc **140.00**
Sadiron, French, LeGaulois #5 ....**35.00**
Sadiron, Laclede **15.00**
Sleeve, Asbestos...**30.00**
Sleeve, Hub..**25.00**
Sleeve, Sensible #1 ....**35.00**
Sleeve, Sweeney #4..**95.00**
Travel, English, boudoir, meta fuel **85.00**
Travel, English, Fuluse, meta fuel, w/heating stand.................**140.00**
Travel, German, Feldmeyer, alcohol....................................**290.00**
Travel, Hot Point, w/trivet, curling iron, pan, hdl & lid **90.00**

Ironstone

During the last quarter of the 18th century, English potters began experimenting with a new type of body that contained calcinated flint and a higher china clay content, intent on producing a fine durable whiteware — heavy, yet with a texture that would resemble porcelain. To remove the last trace of yellow, a minute amount of cobalt was added, often resulting in a bluish-white tone. Wm. and John Turner of Caughley, and Josiah Spode II were the first to manufacture the ware successfully. Others, such as Davenport, Hicks and Meigh, and Ralph and Josiah Wedgwood, followed with their own versions. The latter coined the name 'Pearl' to refer to his product and incorporated the term into his trademark. In 1813 a 14-year patent was issued to Charles James Mason, who called his ware Patented Ironstone. Francis Morley, G.L. Asworth, T.J. Mayer, and other Staffordshire potters continued to produce ironstone until the end of the century. While some of these patterns are simple to the extreme, many are decorated with in-mold designs of fruit, grain, and foliage on ribbed or scalloped shapes. In the 1830s transfer-printed designs in blue, mulberry, pink, green, and black became popular; and polychrome versions of Oriental wares were manufactured to compete with the Chinese trade. See also Mason's Ironstone. Our advice for this category comes from Home Place Antiques, whose address is listed in the Directory under Illinois.

Teapot, Meakin #38,
9", $140.00.

Athens, cup & saucer, handleless; Wedgwood.....................28.00
Baker, Gothic, 8-sided rectangle, Edwards 45.00
Basket, fruit; Shaw...85.00
Bone dish, Crescent, Meakin, 6⅝x3⅛" 38.00
Bone dish, Crescent, Wilkinson, 6¼x3", EX 45.00
Bowl, soup; Nocho (Little Palm), T&R Boote, 8⅝" 7.50
Bowl, vegetable; Nacho (Little Palm), T&R Boote, 5" dia 10.00
Bowl, vegetable; Prairie, Clementson, 8¼x6⅝x1¾" 25.00
Bowl, vegetable; Sharon Arch, w/lid, Wedgewood.............87.50
Bowl, vegetable; Sq Ridged, Wilkinson, 7⅝x7⅝" 25.00
Bowl, vegetable; Star Flower, w/lid, JW Pankhurst 80.00
Bowl, vegetable; 1851 Octagon, T&R Boote, 9⅛x7⅛" 60.00
Butter dish, Daisy, sq, w/lid & liner, Shaw, EX................165.00
Chamber pot, Corn & Oats, Wedgewood, w/lid, 8½" 135.00
Chamber pot, Panelled Thistle, Bridgwood & Clarke 47.50
Coffeepot, Lily, Burgess 185.00
Compote, Sunburst, rnd, 6-sided/ftd, Shaw, 4x9½".......125.00
Creamer, Bamboo, Meakin, 5⅛", VG 65.00
Creamer, Grenade..50.00
Cup & saucer, handleless; Laurel Wreath, Elsmore & Forster........40.00
Cup & saucer, handleless; Lily 45.00
Cup & saucer, handleless; Pomegranate Variant, 2⅝x3⅞".....40.00
Cup & saucer, handleless; Sydenham, T&R Boote 50.00
Cup & saucer, handleless; Vintage (Grape & Medallion), 3⅛" 45.00
Cup & saucer, handleless; Wheat, Cochran 40.00
Cup & saucer, Morning-Glory, Elsmore & Forster, EX 80.00
Cup plate, Chinese, Shaw, 4½"..57.50
Cup plate, Nacho (Little Palm)...35.00
Cup plate, Niagara Fan, Shaw, 3⅞", EX............................60.00
Dish, relish; St Louis, John Edwards................................42.00
Dish, relish; Vintage, Challinor 42.50
Food mold, eagle, mk Meakin, oval, 5¼x7", EX 165.00
Food mold, floral w/fluted sides, mk Copeland, 6x7".....295.00
Food mold, man milking in relief, oval, fluted sides, 8" 45.00
Food mold, 3 fish, heart border, unmk, rare, 5¾x7½" 525.00
Gravy boat, Ceres, Elsmore Forster, 5¼"..........................55.00
Gravy boat, Fuchsia, bulbous, 1860s, 5¼" 45.00
Gravy boat, Paris, Henry Alcock & Co 60.00
Gravy boat, President, John Edwards 60.00
Pitcher, Civil War scenes commemorate Ellsworth/etc, 9", EX ...295.00
Pitcher, milk; Royal, John Edwards, 8⅝" 60.00
Pitcher, syrup; Panelled Columbia, 5", EX 65.00
Plate, Bow Knot & Clover, 8¾".......................................20.00
Plate, bread & butter; Chinese, Shaw, 6¾".......................40.00
Plate, cream soup; Sydenham, T&R Boote, 8⅜" 12.50
Plate, dessert; Prairie, Clementson, 6⅝", EX....................12.50
Plate, dinner; Bellflower, Edwards, 9¾" 18.00

Plate, dinner; Ceres, orange lustre, 9½" 35.00
Plate, dinner; New York, Clementson, 10¾" 32.00
Plate, dinner; Niagara, Walley, 9⅝".................................26.00
Plate, dinner; Sydenham, T&R Boote, 9½".......................22.50
Platter, Nosegay, Baker & Co, 13½" 35.00
Platter, Sharon Arch, Wedgwood, 16½"............................47.50
Platter, Wheat, Meakin, 16½"...65.00
Sauce bowl, Sydenham, w/undertray & ladle, T&R Boote 225.00
Shaving mug, Athens, 3¼x3⅛", EX 72.50
Shaving mug, Berlin Swirl 70.00
Shaving mug, Ceres, 3¾x3⅝" 70.00
Shaving mug, Wild Flower, 3⅜x3⅜"................................80.00
Soap dish, Bordered Hyacinth, w/insert & lid, 4¼"........145.00
Soap dish, Cable & Ring, oval, w/lid & drain, Shaw, EX............200.00
Soup plate, plain, Meakin, 9" 12.50
Soup plate, Sydenham, rnd, 10-sided, T&R Boote, 8⅜" 24.00
Sugar bowl, Ceres, w/lid, Elsmore & Forster, 7¼"...........65.00
Sugar bowl, Pomegranate Variant, Niagara, Walley, 6¾" 165.00
Sugar bowl, Walled Octagon, w/lid 70.00
Teapot, Tuscan, w/lid, John Edwards...............................160.00
Tureen, sauce; Columbia, w/underplate & ladle, Clementson 215.00
Tureen, sauce; Lily of the Valley, w/lid & underplate 180.00
Tureen, sauce; Split Pot, w/underliner & lid, Edwards 145.00
Tureen, soup; Plain Uplift, w/underliner & ladle 300.00
Tureen, vegetable; Octagon, w/lid, Boote........................85.00
Tureen, vegetable; Sq Ridged, Wedgwood, w/lid, 5¼" 100.00
Tureen, vegetable; Sunburst, rectangular, 6-sided, w/lid.............180.00
Wash bowl, Sharon Arch, Wedgewood, 13¾"..................100.00
Wash bowl, Victory, John Edwards.................................110.00
Wash bowl & pitcher, Octagon, Boote............................195.00
Wash pitcher, Ceres, Elsmore & Foster, 11", EX 125.00
Wash pitcher, Corn & Oats 150.00
Wash pitcher, Teaberry Variant, NY, Clementson, 12", EX 235.00
Wash pitcher, Vintage, Challinor....................................130.00
Waste bowl, Ceres, Elsmore & Forster 90.00

Ivory

Technically, true ivory is the substance composing the tusk of the elephant; the finest type comes from Africa. However, tusks and teeth of other animals — the walrus, the hippopotamus, and the sperm whale, for instance — are similar in composition and appearance and have also been used for carving. The Chinese have used this substance for centuries, preferring it over bone because of the natural oil contained in its pores, which not only renders it easier to carve but also imparts a soft sheen to the finished product. Aged ivory usually takes on a soft caramel patina, but unscrupulous dealers sometimes treat new ivory to a tea bath to 'antique' it! A bill passed in 1978 reinforced a ban on the importation of whale and walrus ivory. All examples listed here are Oriental in origin unless noted otherwise.

Basket seller, draped w/wares, sgn Matsuyama, 6" 550.00
Belt buckle, cvd heart shape, 1⅞".................................135.00
Bookmark, cvd dog's head, 5" L......................................45.00
Candlestick, Egyptian caryatid stem, 9", pr 160.00
Deity dances, lotus base w/turq & coral, Sino-Tibetan, 11" 1,000.00
Dragon-headed tortoise supports cvd/inscribed stele, 12½" 1,500.00
Emperor & Empress in battle armor astride horse, 20", pr 2,400.00
Emperor in elaborate dragon robe stands, holds scepter, 14"........450.00
God of War, Kuan Ti, 14" 550.00
Goddess sits on dbl lotus base, holds sm Buddha, 13".................950.00
Grape harvester & little boy, Japan, 7" 600.00
Joss standing w/arms raised, 7".......................................90.00
Joss w/group of boys around him, figs cvd on dome base, 6" 800.00

Carved Japanese group, two boys and a fruit seller, signed, 12½", $700.00.

Kuan Ti, God of War, 6" 300.00
Kuan Yin holds peony & prunus branch, 10" 300.00
Man w/2 boys, monkey on hurdy-gurdy, Japan, 1900, 5½"..........395.00
Plaque, Roman battle scene, Germany, 1800s, 5½x13" L, +fr. 3,000.00
Plaque, 3 ladies/putti/herm, Germany, 1800s, 5½x7", +fr 550.00
Quan Yin, seated dhyansana w/well-detailed robes, 5½"............300.00
Quan Yin w/peach & longevity symbols stands by sm deer, 12" ..900.00
Sage holds staff, stands by table w/teapot, 13".........................1,000.00
Shou Lao w/staff & peach, 12" 550.00

Jack-in-the-Pulpit Vases

Popular novelties at the turn of the century, jack-in-the-pulpit vases were made in every type of art glass produced. Some were simple, others elaborately appliqued and enameled. They were shaped to resemble the lily for which they were named.

Amberina, HP decor, swirled body, amber 3-leg base, 12" 445.00
Clear opal w/vaseline ft, cranberry rim, HP decor, 6" 145.00
Cranberry w/red rim, vaseline stem w/rigaree, 6"............................95.00
Cranberry w/spatter, ruffled rim, 5¼x3½" 85.00
Gr overlay, crystal petal ft, 5⅜x5⅝"...110.00
Lime gr opal, 7¾x4¾"...65.00
Maroon opal to vaseline, 6½x4¼" 75.00
Mc spatter, wht int, appl wishbone ft, 8x3¾"...............................110.00
Oxblood & wht spatter, vaseline opal petal top, 11⅛x5⅞" 100.00
Pk & yel opal stripes, bulbous, 5½x3¼" 75.00
Purple shaded o/l, flower top, petal ft, 7x5½"...............................110.00

Jackfield

Jackfield has come to be a generic term used to refer to wares with a red clay body and a high-gloss black glaze. It originated at Jackfield, in Stropshire, England; however, it was produced in the Staffordshire district as well. While some pieces are decorated with relief motifs or painted-on florals and gilding, many are unadorned. Teapots produced in the 18th century were known locally as 'black decanters.' These pots and figural dogs and roosters are the items most often found.

Coffeepot, elongated ovoid w/dome lid, long spout, 11", NM......850.00
Creamer, 3 lion-mask ft, cut-out rim, 5", EX 60.00
Figurine, spaniel, glass eyes, gold trim, 13", pr 200.00
Teapot, spherical, flat lid, 5x8" 135.00

Japanese Lustreware

Imported from Japan during the 1920s, novelty tableware items, vases, ash trays, etc. — often in blue, tan, and mother-of-pearl lustre glazes — were sold through five-and-dime stores or given as premiums for selling magazine subscriptions. The Occupied Japan Club is listed in the Directory under Clubs, Newsletters, and Catalogs.

Ash tray, clown w/card suite decor, bridge set of 4 ....10.00
Ash tray, donkey pulling cart mk Ashes, 2½" W 5.00
Ash tray, plunger in opening..12.50
Clothes brush w/flapper half-doll, ribbon waistband 25.00
Condiment set, bl & tan, 2 cruets+shakers+mustard jar 30.00

Creamer and sugar bowl on tray, Deco florals, $40.00.

Creamer & sugar, mc floral on orange, child's sz 22.50
Cup & saucer, pagoda on orange, red mk..12.50
Lamp, bird/leaves/lily base, rose decor on paper shade, 10" 30.00
Lemon dish, lemon decor, hdld 12.50
Shakers, bbl form, floral, orange top, pr on oval tray.....................12.50
Shakers, house, bl & tan, pr on rectangular tray............................10.00
Shakers, yel chick in shell, hdl, 1929, pr..12.00
Tea set, bl & tan, pot+cr+sug+6 c/s+6 cake plates 50.00
Tea set, bluebird decor, child's sz, 13-pc, serves 4 ....50.00
Toothpick holder, grotesque bird w/wings wide, open mouth, 5" ..12.00
Vase, HP sailing vessel, 4½", pr...20.00

Jewelry

Jewelry as adornment has always been regarded with special affection. Whether it be a trinket or a costly ornament of gold, silver, or enameled work, jewelry has personal significance to the wearer. The art of the jeweler is valued as is any art, and the names Lalique or Faberge on collectible pieces bring prices demanded by the signed works of Picasso. Once the province of kings and noblemen, jewelry now is a legacy of all strata of society. The creativity reflected in the jeweler's art has resulted in a myriad of decorative adornments for men and women, and the modern usage of 'lesser' gems and base metals has elevated the value and increased the demand for artistic merit, so that now it is considered by collectors to be on a par with intrinsic value. Luxuriously appointed pieces of Victorian splendor and Edwardian grandeur now compete with the unique, imaginative renditions of jewelry produced in the exciting Art Nouveau period as well as the adventurous translation of jewelry executed in man-made materials versus natural elements. Today prices for gems and gemstones crafted into antique and collectible jewelry are based on artistic merit, personal appeal, pure sentimentality, and intrinsic value. Note: Diamond prices vary greatly depending on color, clarity, etc. Values given here are for diamond jewelry with a standard commercial grade of diamonds that are most likely to be encountered.

Our advisor for this category is Rebecca Dodds; her address may be found in the Directory under Florida. If you are interested in collecting or dealing in jewelry, you will find that authority Lillian Baker has several fine books available on the subject — *100 Years of Collectible Jewelry: 1850-1950; Art Nouveau and Art Deco Jewelry;* and *Fifty Years of Collectible Fashion Jewelry: 1925-1975.* These books are complete with beautiful full-color illustrations and current market values. Mrs. Baker is listed in the Directory under California. See also Plastics.

Key:

A/C — Arts and Crafts	gf — gold filled
AD — Art Deco	grad — graduated
AN — Art Nouveau	gp — gold plated
cab — cabochon	gw — gold washed
cl — clear	k — karat
comp — complementary	m/c — mine cut
ct — carat	plat — platinum
dmn — diamond	r/c — rose cut
dwt — penny weight	r/stn — rhinestone
Euro — European cut	rdm — rhodium
fl — filigree	stn — stone
g'el-plt — gold electroplate	tw — total weight
g-stn — gemstone	wg — white gold
g-t — gold toned	yg — yellow gold

Bar pin, plat fl, 2 Euro dmn 2.50 & .65ct+20 sapphires 7,000.00
Bar pin, plat fl, 5 Euro dmn tw 3.63+9 emeralds 3,200.00
Bar pin, yg/plat AD w/6x5mm oval sapphire+24 sm r/c dmn .. 1,500.00
Bar pin, 10k yg fl, 3 lg garnets, 2½" 195.00
Bar pin, 14k wg fl on yg w/cab bl stone, ½x1¼" 75.00
Belt, Wm Spratling, silver, 20 rope-trim disks, sgn, 32" 1,100.00
Bracelet, bangle; 14k yg, eng decor, sm..125.00
Bracelet, bangle; 14k yg, flower & leaf emb, ⅜" W 225.00
Bracelet, bangle; 3 rows rose-cut Bohemian garnets, hinged........550.00
Bracelet, charm; 14k yg, dbl-strand, pearl/gold/dmn charms........550.00
Bracelet, charm; 14k yg, 3 gold coins, 4 misc charms 480.00
Bracelet, charm; 14k yg links, 12 dwt 240.00
Bracelet, Georg Jensen, lg cabs & silver florets alternate 800.00
Bracelet, Georg Jensen, 3 bird plaques+3 w/dyed onyx cabs ... 1,100.00
Bracelet, Georg Jensen, 6 bud-emb ovals, beaded links, 7" 300.00
Bracelet, Jo Michaels, 5 silver floral & amethyst plaques 150.00
Bracelet, Kalo, sterling bangle, ¾" W..550.00
Bracelet, Mary Gage, sterling, openwork w/lg quartz cab, 2½".....600.00
Bracelet, plat w/center mtd .35ct dmn+74 tw 2.5ct 2,500.00
Bracelet, 14k wg fl, center dmn, 2 sapphire baguettes..................575.00
Brooch, crescent moon & star, Bohemian garnets........................150.00
Brooch, Georg Jensen, silver openwork leaf mt w/7 coral cabs 460.00
Brooch, German silver, 2 HP swans on lake, many marcasites.......65.00
Brooch, Mary Gage, beaded silver mum w/shaped turq pc, 4" 350.00
Brooch, Mary Gage, lg turq w/in leafy openwork fr, 3" dia 175.00
Brooch, Mary Gage, sterling sword w/turq & coral stones, 5" 275.00
Brooch, onyx w/floral millefiori design in gold fr.........................325.00
Brooch, plat fl bow w/1.25ct Euro dmn+2 at .40+6 sm dmn ... 1,500.00
Brooch, yg/plat rtcl crown w/pearl+72 Euro dmn tw 3.5 .... 2,000.00
Brooch, 10k yg fl, blk onyx w/5 sm dmns+2 pearls......................150.00
Brooch, 14k yg, HP flower bouquet 80.00
Brooch, 14k yg twist mt w/36 dmn tw 1.6ct, +earrings tw .6... 1,400.00
Brooch/pendant, wg flower/ribbon mt+pear drop, 136 dmn.... 1,400.00
Cameo, shell, ornate 800 silver fr, 1¼" 75.00
Cameo, 14k fl mt, lady, flower in hair, dmn necklace, 2¼" 1,100.00
Charm, cat, ivory celluloid, ruffled collar, 1½" 18.00
Clip/pin, Georg Jensen, malachite w/in floral mt, 2"....................250.00
Earrings, Georg Jensen, 2 curled silver leaves ea, mk 180.00
Earrings, plat sunburst w/23 dmn tw 2.5ct 1,300.00
Earrings, plat/yg, ea mtd w/.30ct Euro dmn+8.5mm pearl............700.00
Earrings, 14k, 1" cultured pearls in cage, screw bks.......................40.00

Earrings, 14k wg w/dmns tw .70cts, swirl & leaf shape, pr 700.00
Earrings, 14k yg flower w/5 sm rubies & 7 seed pearls 300.00
Earrings, 9x14mm teardrop blk onyx, gold scroll mt, 1890s, 2" ..550.00
Lavalier, Bohemian garnet w/drop on 28" 14k yg chain...............185.00
Lavalier, 14k yg, .12ct emerald..150.00
Necklace, Baroque pearls, 23" 2-strand 7.5mm, stn-set yg mt......500.00
Necklace, choker, 49 7mm pearls w/oval 10k wg clasp 375.00
Necklace, Deco chrome links w/pk stn trim & pear drop, 11" 95.00
Necklace, Dior, pearls, 2-strand, amethyst in clasp, 25" 95.00

Necklace by Georg Jenson, marked GJ in square, Denmark, 1915, $600.00.

Necklace, Georg Jensen, pillow heart on solid chain, 18"............500.00
Necklace, ivory beads, 11mm, 40"...88.00
Necklace, Kalo, sterling leaf-&-cherry emb plaques, 16" 600.00
Necklace, Kalo, stylized acorns/oak leaves, no mk, 16" 175.00
Necklace, melon-style blk jet satin glass, 9½" 90.00
Necklace, plat, seed pearl fl-mt pendant w/tassel+.4 tw dmn .. 1,200.00
Necklace, Venetian beads w/embedded foils/roses/etc, 28" 95.00
Necklace, 14k yg, flat weave w/11 dmn tw .9ct 900.00
Necklace, 18k yg, hollow beads on 16" chain................................250.00
Pendant, cloisonne leaves w/gr cab stn in brass fr, ¾x1¼" 30.00
Pendant, Georg Jensen, deep slots top & bottom, 2⅜" dia............150.00
Pendant, Kalo, link chain w/drop: Baroque pearl/appl flower 650.00
Pendant, plat, aqua 21x40mm briollett/mt: aqua+6 sm dmn .. 1,200.00
Pin, blk jet glass, cvd, circle arrangement, 1¾"...............................48.00
Pin, Georg Jensen, blk onyx bead rests on center curl, #336........125.00
Pin, Gorham, silver dragonfly, 2½x1½"...150.00
Pin, Kalo, sterling, bead flanked by scroll, #237, 2¼" 400.00
Pin, Kalo, sterling dog cutout, 1" 280.00
Pin, plat, Am flag w/baguette & rnd dmn/ruby/sapphires, sm.. 1,000.00
Pin, 14k wg, flower w/in circle, brn dmn+59 dmn tw 3.75ct ... 2,200.00
Pin, 14k yg, openwork w/hearts, lg oval citrine, 1½"...................325.00
Pin, 18k yg rooster set w/many sm rnd dmn, 3-color enamel... 2,000.00
Pin/pendant, brn gutta percha knot w/gold trim, 1¼" 75.00
Ring, Georg Jensen, 2 joined disks, #130 ....85.00
Ring, Oakes, yg rtcl leaf & acorn mt w/amethyst 475.00
Ring, plat, dmn 1.65ct Euro cut+4 sm dmn in fl....................... 3,600.00
Ring, plat, dmn 2.10ct flanked by 2 sm baguettes 5,800.00
Ring, plat, emerald-cut 3.15ct emerald fr by sm emeralds.......15,000.00
Ring, plat, m/c dmn 1.1ct in fl mt w/2 synthetic sapphires 1,400.00
Ring, plat, zircon 11mm centered by 53 tiny dmns/sapphires 550.00
Ring, plat, 2 dmn .70ct ea+10 sm tw .65 in fl, 1920 .... 2,200.00
Ring, plat fl w/1.30ct Euro dmn+12 tw .80, ca 1920................. 2,800.00
Ring, yg, synthetic 16x22mm sapphire in branch mt w/sm dmn..500.00
Ring, yg, 4 cushion emeralds (1.45ct)+20 m/c dmns tw 1.5 .... 3,100.00
Ring, 10k yg, classical cameo in fl mt 225.00
Ring, 10k yg, 9x17mm opal in fl mt...225.00
Ring, 10k yg fl, sm ruby 125.00

Ring, 12k yg, oval opal 16x11mm..350.00
Ring, 14k rose gold, pearl amid bl turq on wide emb band.............85.00
Ring, 14k rose gold, 4 tiers Bohemian garnets, heavy mt............145.00
Ring, 14k wg, 8x11mm oval cut bl sapphire+16 dmns tw .33ct...575.00
Ring, 14k wg fl, .8ct dmn+2 bl sapphires....................................275.00
Ring, 14k wg fl w/sm dmn...125.00
Ring, 14k yg, angel skin coral cameo, openwork 125.00
Ring, 14k yg, center opal encircled w/6 .20 sapphires 375.00
Ring, 14k yg, emerald-cut 12x10mm tourmaline in wire mt........125.00
Ring, 14k yg, fire opal in flower setting 125.00
Ring, 14k yg, leopard, ruby eyes+18 sapphire spots+4 sm dmns...350.00
Ring, 14k yg, lg central opal+dmns tw .9cts...............................600.00
Ring, 14k yg, lg synthetic alexandrite in ornate mt.....................175.00
Ring, 14k yg, marquise aquamarine, lg fl mt...............................175.00
Ring, 14k yg, scissors-cut 16x22mm amethyst.............................190.00
Ring, 14k yg leaf & branch w/tw 1ct dmns.................................850.00
Ring, 14k yg thunderbird set w/1 sm dmn...................................225.00

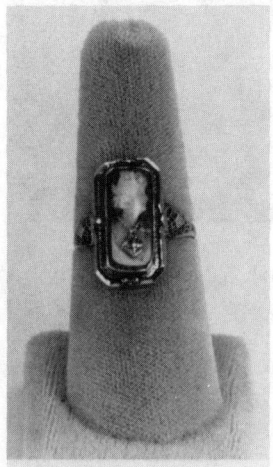

Ring, cameo reverses to red stone, 18k white gold, $495.00.

Ring, 18k yg, pearl encircled by 18 brilliant-cut rubies 475.00
Ring, 18k yg, 6 sm Euro cut dmns+2 .6ct rubies in 1" oval mt....850.00
Ring, 18k yg fl, eng hinged top opens for photo 300.00
Scarf pin, 14k yg flower form w/Bohemian garnet center.............100.00
Stickpin, 14k yg, angel skin coral cab..50.00
Stickpin, 14k yg/plat, Euro dmn .94ct in 8-side fl mt 1,100.00
Tie tack, 14k eng clip-on 65.00

Costume Jewelry

Bar pin, gp Etruscanwork, knot center w/r'stns, 1¾x½" 30.00
Bracelet, bangle; Danecraft, Greek key design, ⅜" W 45.00
Bracelet, bangle; Whiting & Davis, diagonal stripes, hinged 40.00
Bracelet, Coro, bl moonstone links w/r'stns between, ½" W..........32.00
Bracelet, Eisenberg, lg r'stns w/3 lg oval r'stn centers..................165.00
Bracelet, Mexican silver peacock w/fl feathers, 2½" 75.00
Bracelet, slave; brass fl flower w/attached ring, '20s.....................75.00
Bracelet, tennis; bl sq r'stns 40.00
Bracelet, Trifari, gp w/lg marquise r'stn center, 1" W 38.00
Bracelet, Weiss, dbl-row sq r'stns 50.00
Bracelet+earrings, Whiting-Davis, MOP claw set in gold metal..150.00
Earrings, Hobe, mc beads, fl set, pk r'stn trim, 1".........................40.00
Earrings, Jomaz, g'el-plt flower, 1½" dia......................................45.00
Earrings, Kenneth Lane, r'stn crescents, clip, 2" 125.00
Earrings, Kenneth Lane, starfish w/pearl+2 rows r'stns, 1½".......125.00
Earrings, Kramer, aurora borealis r'stns on ball, ¾" dia................22.50
Earrings, Marvella, faux gr jade, oval, ¾"......................................25.00
Earrings, Marvella, lg gray Baroque pearls on gold leaf, ⅞" 20.00
Earrings, Matisse, enamel on copper 25.00

Earrings, Weiss, r'stn flower w/faux emerald, clip, ⅞"...................25.00
Necklace, bl foiled glass beads, fl spacers, short 35.00
Necklace, Coro, wht metal chevron links w/r'stns in ea................45.00
Necklace, Georg Jensen, sterling leaves & berries, 2-oz 475.00
Necklace, Haskell, pearl choker w/butterfly pendant...................150.00
Necklace, Monet, long & short beads, choker style 20.00
Necklace, Van Dell, dbl-leaf sterling links, short 48.00
Pendant, Emmons, faux topaz in ornate circle, 1¼"+chain...........27.50
Pin, Carnegie, unicorn head, r'stns on silvertone, lg 125.00
Pin, Coro, 3 lg amethysts on sterling spray, 4½" 80.00
Pin, Danecraft, sterling flower wreath, 1¼" 42.50
Pin, Eisenberg, bow, turq/pk/wht cabs, dk metal, 1930s.............225.00
Pin, Eisenberg, emerald gr stn flower w/r'stn accents 90.00
Pin, Francois, entwined circles tied w/gold-tone mesh, lg 20.00
Pin, Gerry, gp German shepherd, 1¼"...17.50
Pin, Kim, copper Art Moderne cat, 3" 22.50
Pin, Kramer, gp horn of plenty w/hanging pearls, 3" 45.00
Pin, Monet, gp star, ornate openwork, 2½"....................................20.00
Pin, Schiaparelli, gr r'stns w/lg dangling pearl drop 350.00
Pin, Sterlingcraft by Coro, pelican, gold on sterling, 1⅝" 45.00
Pin, Truart, sterling, red-stone florals, 4½"...................................30.00

Judaica

The items listed below are representative of objects used in both the secular and religious life of the Jewish people. They are evident of a culture where silversmiths, painters, engravers, writers, and metal workers were highly gifted and skilled in their art. Most of the treasures shown in recently-displayed exhibits of Judaica were confiscated by the Germans during the late 1930s up to 1945; by then eight Jewish synagogues and fifty warehouses had been filled with Hitler's plunder.

Candlestick, Bezalel silver, Tuscan style, ca 1920, 8", pr.............500.00
Candlestick, Polish silver, grapes, 1-lite, 1900, 14", pr 1,250.00
Candlestick, Russian silver, grape/leaf supports, 12", pr 1,000.00
Celebratory plate, silver, The Struggle, by Lipchitz, 1974...........400.00
Charity box, Palestinian, pnt metal, sq, early 1900s, 5" 165.00
Clock, alarm; Palestine General Insurance, sq, 1930s, 5".............145.00
Desk blotter, Bezalel bound leather, Jerusalem, '20s, 10x13" 250.00
Ethrog box, Russian silver, family crest on lid, 6" W 1,045.00
Goblet, Austro-Hungarian silver, cartouch, 1881, 8"...................600.00
Hanukkah lamp, Am brass, stylized baluster/dome base, 12" 230.00
Hanukkah lamp, Bezalel brass, lions/stylized, ca 1920, 9" 1,760.00
Hanukkah lamp, Continental brass, Moses/Aaron, ca 1910, 10"..100.00
Hanukkah lamp, Continental brass, Star of David, ca 1920, 12" .360.00
Hanukkah lamp, Continental silver, grape/fan, ca 1910, 4" 625.00
Lap desk, wood, cvd Holy scenes, w/inkwell, 1890s, 14" L 1,100.00
Letter opener, wood, bust profile T Herzl, ca 1950, 10" 600.00
Mezuzah case, Bezalel silver, Jerusalem, ca 1920, 4" L.................360.00
Mezuzah case, Palestinian ivory, mt on wood, ca 1910, 4" L........600.00
Napkin ring, Bezalel SP, ca 1920, 2"..195.00
Sabbath lamp, Italian brass, bird's head, ca 1890s, 20" 1,100.00
Sabbath lamp, Moroccan brass, pierced bkplate, ca 1890, 17".....500.00
Sampler, German-Hebrew New Year's greeting, 1904, 9x11".......275.00
Snuff box, Continental silver, book form, Star of David, 3" L 500.00
Spice container, Continental brass, ca 1900, 2" dia 175.00
Spice tower, Bezalel silver, sq base/pennant top, 1930, 6"...........220.00
Spice tower, filigree silver, bells/pennants, 14" 990.00
Tablecloth, Persian cotton, festival use, ca 1950 ....120.00
Torah mantle, Israeli velvet, mc icons, 1949, 28" L 250.00
Wall hanging, German linen, commemorative, 1870, 27x27" ...1,100.00
Wall sconce, Polish brass, eagle/lion, ca 1910, 3-lite, pr 400.00

Jugtown

The Jugtown Pottery was started about 1920 by Juliana and Jacques Busbee, in Moore County, North Carolina. Ben Owen, a young descendant of a Staffordshire potter, was hired in 1923. He was the master potter, while the Busbees experimented with perfecting glazes and supervising design and modeling. Preferred shapes were those reminiscent of traditional country wares and classic Oriental forms. Glazes were various: natural-clay oranges, buffs, 'tobacco-spit' brown, mirror black, white, 'frog-skin' green, a lovely turquoise called Chinese blue, and the traditional cobalt-decorated salt glaze. The pottery gained national recognition; and, as a result of their success, several other potteries were established. Jugtown is still in operation; however, they no longer use their original glaze colors which are now so collectible.

Bowl vase, sugar glaze, 6" x 8", $150.00.

Bowl, redware, orange glaze, hand-thrown, mk, 2¼x6¼" 28.00
Bowl, redware, 7½" 32.00
Inkwell/vase, Chinese bl...120.00
Pitcher, brn speckled, incised decor, 8½" 58.00
Pitcher, gr w/bl, bulbous w/pinched spout, 5½" 55.00
Vase, Chinese bl, bulbous, 5" 175.00
Vase, Chinese red/bl, 4" 125.00
Vase, cobalt, bulbous w/rim-to-width hdls, mk, 8" 195.00
Vase, gr/red thick gloss on red clay, imp mk, 4½".................115.00
Vase, metallic glaze, 4 appl hdls, 8½" 75.00
Vase, tobacco-spit brn, jug form, 4½" 50.00

K. P. M. Porcelain

Under Frederick the Great, King of Prussia, porcelain manufacture was instituted in Berlin in 1751 by William K. Wegeley. In jealous competition with Meissen, hard-paste porcelain was produced (dinnerware, figurines, vases, etc.) some of which were undecorated while other pieces were hand painted in Watteau scenes, landscapes, or florals. It soon became evident that the factory was unable to offer serious competition. The King withdrew his support, and the factory failed in 1757. In 1761 Johann Ernst Gotzkowsky bought the rights and attempted a similar operation which soon failed due to financial difficulties. Still determined to gain the same recognition enjoyed by Meissen, the King bought the plant in 1763 and ruled the operation with an iron hand, often assuring his success by taking advantage of his position. The King died in 1786, but production has continued and quality tableware and decorative porcelains are still being made on a commercial basis. Earliest marks were simply 'G' or 'W,' followed by the sceptre mark. After 1830 'K.P.M.' with an orb or eagle was adopted. Our advisor for this category is Don Williams; he is listed in the Directory under Missouri.

Coffeepot, Roman Key w/florals & gold, 9", +13x13" tray..........345.00
Cup & saucer, classical decor on bl/gilt, winged figure hdl 140.00

Porcelain plaque of a young woman, inscribed Madime, by Shultz, 10" x 7½", $7,000.00.

Plaque, Christ kneeling by rock, 5¾x8½" 1,750.00
Plaque, Daphne, bust portrait, after Wagner, oval, 11" 4,750.00
Plaque, lady sits by pool/watches cockatoo, fr, 12x8" oval....... 1,600.00
Plaque, lake scene w/houses etc, 4x6", +fr 650.00
Plaque, Madime, seated semi-nude, by Shultz, 10x8" 7,000.00
Plaque, Madonna & Child, 8x6" 8,000.00
Plaque, Magdalene w/book, after Batoni, 11x19", +gilt fr 8,000.00
Plaque, party of Arabs attacked by 3 leopards, 11x9", +fr 6,500.00
Plaque, portrait of a lady, Louis XVI fr, 7x5"............................ 1,300.00
Plaque, urchins eat fruit, dog, Morillo, 10x12", +fancy fr 5,000.00
Plaque, Vestalin, after Kauffmann, 8x6", +gilt fr 3,100.00
Plaque, woman w/2 cherubs, sgn JG, after Bougereau, 10x8" 750.00
Plateau mirror, 16-pc scrollwork sides remove, 1850s, lg......... 1,000.00
Vase, Chinese style, bl/wht/gilt, 1900, 12½", pr 800.00

Kayserzinn Pewter

J.P. Kayser Sohn produced pewter decorated with relief-molded Art Nouveau motifs in Germany during the late 1800s and into the twentieth century. Examples are marked with 'Kayserzinn' and the mold number within an elongated oval reserve. Items with dimensional animals, insects, and birds, etc. are valued much higher than bowls, plates, and trays with simple embossed florals, which are usually priced at $100.00 to about $200.00, depending on size.

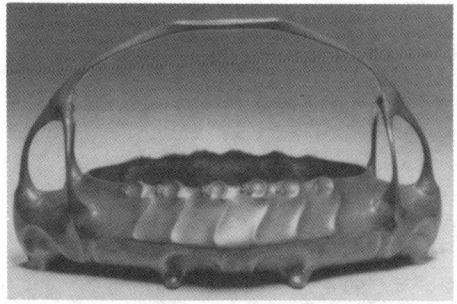

Basket, #4529, 17" long, $2,500.00.

Bowl, nut; simple style, flat, #4366, sm, pr.........................55.00
Bowl, serving; sunflowers & dragonfly, oval, #4120, 10¼x6" **120.00**
Candelabrum, 2-lite, cylinder cups on T-form std, #4531, 10"... **1,100.00**
Candlestick, Nouveau style, #4465, 12½" 160.00
Chamberstick, stylized sunflowers, 2-pc, #4144.................**225.00**
Platter, domed leaf-emb lid, sgn JA, #4413, 21x8" **400.00**

Keen Kutter

Keen Kutter was a brand name of E.C. Simmons Hardware, used from about 1870 until the mid-1930s. In 1923 Winchester merged with Simmons but continued to produce Keen Kutter marked knives and tools. The merger dissolved, and in 1940 the Simmons Company was purchased by Shapleigh Hardware. Older items are very collectible. For further study we recommend *Keen Kutter*, an illustrated price guide by Jerry and Elaine Heuring, available at your favorite bookstore or public library. Our advisor for this category is Jim Calison; he is listed in the Directory under New York.

Tableware (knives and forks), service for 8, $80.00.

Awl, scratch; KK #100, VG 12.50
Axe, broad; KK #78, EX 65.00
Axe, freighters; KK #88 ....35.00
Axe, hand; KK #2, VG 20.00
Bevel, sliding T; KK #12510, 10", EX 22.50
Bit, countersink; KK #120, EX 12.50
Bit, expansive; 9", EX 17.50
Bit brace, KK #16, 6", VG 35.00
Calipers, inside; KK #28, EX 38.00
Chisel, cold; KK #10, 1" sz, EX 12.50
Chisel, firmer; KK #8, set of 8, EX 145.00
Dividers, KK #110, EX 42.50
Drill, breast; KK #600, 16", EX 65.00
Drill brace, KK #10, EX 125.00
Drill brace, KK #14, EX 25.00
Hammer, brick; KK #15, 24-oz, EX 42.50
Hammer, KK #85, 8-oz, EX 25.00
Hammer, saw setting; 7-oz, EX 42.50
Hammer, 28-oz, EX 22.50
Hatchet, flooring; KK #1, EX 28.00
Hatchet, lathing; KK #401, EX 27.50
Hatchet, shingling; KK #1, EX 22.50
Hedge shears, KK #8½, EX 17.50
Hoe, mortar; KK #10, EX 25.00
Horse clippers, KK #920, EX 18.00
Knife, pocket; KK #2884, wht celluloid hdl, 3¼", NM...................58.00
Knife, pocket; KK #793, yel hdl, 3-blade, VG 50.00
Knife, pruning; KK #105, cocobolo hdl, 4⅜", EX 30.00
Level, iron, KK #612, 12", EX 80.00

Level, wood, KK #3/26, EX 28.00
Mallet, KK #306, VG 20.00
Mitre box, KK #528, EX 125.00
Nail apron, EX 70.00
Oil stone, KK #72, EX 18.00
Pipe cutter, KK #2, EX 70.00
Plane, circular; KK #115, 10", EX 225.00
Plane, jack; KK #5C, 14", EX 28.00
Plane, jointer; mk, 26", EX 35.00
Plane, smooth; KK #36, 10", EX 40.00
Pliers, channel lock; KK #507, 6½", EX 22.50
Pliers, combination; KK #150, EX 26.00
Pliers, combination; KK #180, NM 20.00
Pliers, slim nose; KK #25, EX 22.50
Plumb bob, KK #60, EX 48.00
Punch, revolving; KK #44, EX 22.50
Razor, straight; KK #7423, wht celluloid hdl, EX 35.00
Razor hone, KK #20, in metal box w/instructions, NM...........35.00
Razor strop, Automatic Safety; KK #600, w/orig box, M 45.00
Reamer, KK #126, EX 12.50
Rule, folding; KK #320, w/caliper, EX 42.00
Rule, zigzag; KK #506, 72", M 27.50
Saw, coping; KK #50, M 28.00
Saw, flooring; mk, EX 38.00
Saw, hand; KK #88, EX 22.50
Saw, stair builder; KK #6, M 65.00
Saw set, KK #10, VG 15.00
Scraper, cabinet; KK #212, 6½", EX 47.50
Screwdriver, KK #40, 2", EX 6.00
Screwdriver, KK #50, 8" blade, EX 17.50
Shovel, KK #2B, wood hdl, EX 28.00
Spoke shave, KK #95, EX 22.50
Square, combination; KK #60, 6", EX 85.00
Square, try; KK #1226, 6", EX 22.50
Tap & die set, KK #30, EX 52.00
Tin snips, KK #7, EX 22.50
Vise, bench; KK #500, VG 45.00
Vise, pipe; KK #212, EX 42.50
Wagon, KK #98, 15½x34", EX 195.00
Wrench, adjustable; KK #404, 4", NM 72.50
Wrench, alligator; KK #40, EX 60.00
Wrench, automobile; KK #96, EX 37.50
Wrench, monkey; KK #18, EX 45.00

Kelva

Kelva was a trademark of the C.F. Monroe Company of Meriden, Connecticut; it was produced for only a few years after the turn of the century. It is distinguished from the Wave Crest and Nakara lines by its unique Batik-like background, probably achieved through the use of a cloth or sponge to apply the color. Large florals are hand painted on the opaque milk glass; and ormolu and brass mounts were used for the boxes, vases, and trays. Most pieces are signed. Our advisors for this category are Dolli and Wilfred Cohen; they are listed in the Directory under California.

Box, Crown mold w/scenic panels, ormolu ft, 6½" dia.............. **1,200.00**
Box, floral, pk on bl-gray, mirror in lid, 4½" dia 515.00
Box, floral, pk on gr, brass ft/mts, 6-sided, 3½x3½" 395.00
Box, floral on gr, oval, 2¾x5" L 425.00
Box, metal openwork w/florals & beading on glass lid, 3x3" 425.00
Box, roses, pk on gr, fuchsia trim, 3½x6" dia 690.00
Box, roses in wht reserves on bl, 8" dia 850.00
Box, wild roses on bl mottle, 3½x8" L 895.00

Humidor, Cigars/floral on rare brn, str sides, 4¾x3½" 550.00
Humidor, Cigars/florals on bl, oval form.......................575.00
Planter, daisies, pk on gray mottle, metal rim, 8" dia 400.00
Shakers, floral on moss gr, 3", pr 350.00
Tray, Crown mold, floral on moss gr, 6" dia 275.00
Tray, floral, 3" bowl form, metal bail hdl.......................275.00
Vase, floral on rose, trumpet form w/4 ormolu ft, 6x2"...............450.00
Vase, lg floral on lt gr, cylindrical, ormolu ft/hdls, 14" 750.00

Box, pink wild roses on mottled green ground,
6" diameter, $600.00.

Kentucky Derby Glasses

Since the 1940s souvenir glasses have commemorated the famous
Kentucky Derby; recently these have become popular collectibles, especially among race fans. Among the most valuable is the plastic Beetleware tumbler from the forties, the shorter version made in 1945, and
the 1950 tumbler which is now valued at around $175.00. On the Gold
Cup glass from 1952, current winners are shown along with those from
the previous year. There were two from 1958; one was the Gold Bar
tumbler, and the other was called the Iron Liege. Both were simply left-
over '57 glasses with the 1958 winners added at the top.

1964, $22.00.

1940s, aluminum 165.00
1940s, plastic Beetleware 300.00
1945, short 400.00

1945, tall 175.00
1948 ....65.00
1949, He Has Seen Them All 65.00
1950 ....175.00
1951 ....150.00
1952, Gold Cup 65.00
1953 ....50.00
1954 ....45.00
1955 ....40.00
1956 ....40.00
1957 ....35.00
1958, Gold Bar..45.00
1958, Iron Liege 50.00
1959-60, ea...30.00
1961 ....25.00
1962-65, ea...22.00
1966 ....18.00
1967-68, ea...16.00
1969 ....15.00
1970 ....14.00
1971-72, ea...12.00
1973 ....10.00
1974..8.00
1975 ....7.00
1976 ....6.00
1977-78, ea. 5.00
1979-80, ea...5.00
1981-82, ea...4.00
1983..3.00
1984-86, ea...3.00
1987-88, ea...3.00
1989-92, ea..2.00

Kew Blas

Kew Blas was a trade name used by the Union Glass Company of
Summerville, Massachusetts, for their iridescent, lustered art glass produced from 1893 until about 1920. The glass was made in imitation of
Tiffany and achieved notable success. Some items were decorated with
pulled leaf and feather designs, while others had a monochrome lustre
surface. The mark was an engraved 'Kew-Blas' in an arching arrangement.

Decanter, gold, ribbed/pnt stopper, 15" 900.00
Dish, gold, slightly shaped rim, shallow, 5½".................................200.00
Finger bowl, gold, ribbed, 5", +6½" plate 400.00
Pitcher, feathers in gr, gold int & swirl hdl, 4½" 700.00
Tumbler, gold, pinched-in sides, 5x3⅛" 295.00
Vase, feathers, gr w/gold, gold int, 5½" 535.00
Vase, gold, trumpet form, flaring undulating rim, 10" 750.00

King's Rose

King's Rose is a soft-paste ware that was made in Staffordshire,
England, from about 1820 to 1830. It is closely related to Gaudy Dutch
in body type as well as the colors used in its decoration. The pattern
consists of a full-blown, orange-red rose with green, pink, and yellow
leaves and accents. When the rose is in pink, the ware is often referred
to as Queen's Rose. Our advisor for this category is Richard Marden; he
is listed in the Directory under New Hampshire.

Coffeepot, dome lid, minor wear, 11¾" 950.00
Coffeepot, spout rstr, 10½"...300.00

Creamer, solid border, minor wear, 4½" 450.00
Cup & saucer, vine border, minor wear 200.00
Plate, Queen's, 8½", NM...95.00
Plate, solid border, 6", NM.......................................150.00
Plate, vine border, stains, 6½".................................100.00
Plate, 7½", M...175.00
Teapot, prof rpr, 7"..650.00
Teapot, sectional border, lt wear, 5⅞".......................400.00
Teapot, solid border, lid rpr/hairlines, 6½" 225.00
Waste bowl, Oyster pattern, stains/chips, 6⅜"............225.00

Kitchen Collectibles

During the last half of the 1850s, mass-produced kitchen gadgets were patented at an astonishing rate. Most were ingeniously efficient. Apple peelers, egg beaters, cherry pitters, food choppers, and such were only the most common of hundreds of kitchen tools well designed to perform only specific tasks. Today all are very collectible. Our advisor for Cast Iron Bakers and Kettles is Denise Harned, who is the author of *Griswold Cast Collectibles*. She is listed in the Directory under Connecticut. We also recommend *Kitchen Glassware of the Depression Years* by Gene Florence and *Kitchen Antiques 1790-1940* by Kathryn McNerney. See also Appliances; Molds; Primitives; Tinware; Wooden Ware.

Cast Kitchen Ware

Santa Claus cake mold, Griswold, 12", $395.00.

Bundt pan, Griswold #965 for Frank Hay 400.00
Candy mold, Griswold #100, star & hearts, 7¾" dia 145.00
Cornstick pan, Griswold #262, mini, M 95.00
Cornstick pan, Griswold #273, 13¼" 115.00
Cornstick pan, Griswold #283, 1x14x7⅝" 150.00
Cornstick pan, Griswold #955, 22 sticks, 1¼x14¼x7½" 125.00
Danish cake pan (aebleskiver), Griswold #31, rimless, early.....125.00
Danish cake pan (aebleskiver), Griswold #32..................75.00
Deep fat fryer, Griswold #1003, 2½-qt..........................60.00
Dutch oven, Griswold #10 Chuck Wagon, w/lid, 8-qt 145.00
Dutch oven, Griswold #12, Tite Top, 15-qt 95.00
Dutch oven, Griswold #6, w/trivet 160.00
Dutch oven, Griswold #9, Tite-Top, lg emblem, 6-qt 55.00
Griddle, Griswold #609A, lg emblem, 10½" dia 65.00
Griddle, Griswold #8, dmn mk, bail hdl, 19x9⅛" 88.00

Griddle, Griswold #8, rectangular 50.00
Griddle, Griswold #9, rnd..100.00
Griddle, Wagner #6..70.00
Hibachi grill, Griswold #903, mk G, 30x18x12" 95.00
Kettle, Griswold #8, Erie, Maslin shape, 6-qt................65.00
Kettle, service; Griswold #000, sm emblem, chrome finish.....40.00
Kettle, Wagner #0, 3" 50.00
Meat loaf pan, Griswold #877, Erie, 2¾x10⅛x5½".........85.00
Popover pan, Griswold #18, Erie, 1⅝x9½x5½" 100.00
Pot warmer/grill, Griswold #803, Erie, 8" dia 115.00
Roaster, Griswold #3, Erie, lg emblem, w/trivet, 12¾" ...125.00
Roaster, Griswold #95, sm 125.00
Skillet, fish; Griswold #15, Erie PA emblem, w/lid, 15" L ...165.00
Skillet, Griswold #0 Toy, ⅞x4⅛" 75.00
Skillet, Griswold #10, Erie, w/smoke ring, 3x12¼".........100.00
Skillet, Griswold #12, Erie, w/smoke ring, 13¼".............150.00
Skillet, Griswold #5, sm emblem, no smoke ring............24.00
Skillet, Odorless; Griswold #8 ....110.00
Skillet, snack; Griswold #42, Erie, 1⅛x7½" 85.00
Skillet, Wagner #3 ....22.00
Skillet, Wagner #9 ....32.50
Skillet griddle, Griswold #110, Erie, lg emblem, 12¾"....115.00
Teakettle, Griswold #6, Erie, 4-qt...............................80.00
Teakettle, Griswold #7 Safety Fill, Erie, 5-qt................55.00
Vienna roll pan, Griswold #6, Erie PA 95.00
Waffle iron, Griswold #12, Erie, 9⅜x4" pans 130.00
Waffle iron, Griswold #19 Heart & Star, 8½" pans.........165.00
Waffle iron, Griswold #6 ....185.00
Waffle iron, Griswold #8, American, later version, w/stand....115.00
Waffle iron, Griswold #8, 8½" pans 185.00
Waffle iron, Wagner, Pat Feb 22 1910, wood hdl, +stand....132.00
Wheat stick pan, Griswold #28, Erie, 7 sticks, 13½x7" ...150.00

Glassware

Baker, opal, oval, Fry, 1917, 6"...................................17.50
Batter jug, crystal w/cobalt lid, Paden City..................40.00
Batter jug, dk gr, New Martinsville.............................50.00
Batter jug, gr transparent, Liberty, American Pioneer 150.00
Batter jug, pk, Jenkins 100.00
Bean pot, opal, Fry, 1924, 2-pt...................................50.00
Bottle, water; crystal, Beveragette, Pat 1919 ....12.00
Bottle, water; crystal, General Electric, shows refrigerator.....15.00
Bottle, water; gr transparent, flat sided, metal lid, Hocking 40.00
Bottle, water; gr transparent, w/tin lid, Hocking, 32-oz.....20.00
Bottle, water; royal ruby, Hocking..............................50.00
Bowl, batter; gr transparent, ribbed, Anchor Hocking 25.00
Bowl, batter; Mayfair bl, ribbed, Anchor Hocking.........100.00
Bowl, batter; turq bl, Anchor Hocking 30.00
Bowl, beater; delphite base, w/hand beater. 45.00
Bowl, mixing; amethyst, Hazel Atlas, 9⅝".....................20.00
Bowl, mixing; gr transparent, JE Marsden, 5-pt, 10"......37.50
Bowl, mixing; milk glass, Hocking, 9½".........................10.00
Bowl, mixing; pk, Hazel Atlas, 10⅝".............................17.50
Butter dish, cobalt, Crisscross, oblong, w/lid, ¼-lb.......70.00
Butter dish, delphite, emb Butter, oblong, Jeannette, ¼-lb.....145.00
Butter dish, gr transparent, oblong, Hazel Atlas, ¼-lb....35.00
Butter dish, yel opaque, oblong, McKee, w/lid...............60.00
Canister, coffee; jadite, Jeannette 30.00
Canister, Red Circle, w/screw-on lid, Hocking, set of 3....30.00
Canister, tea; milk glass, dot decor, McKee, 48-oz.........35.00
Casserole, Fry, 1941, rnd, w/lid, 6" 32.50
Casserole, gr, Fry, 1938, w/lid 75.00
Casserole, opal, etched floral lid, Fry, 1954 ....32.50

Casserole, opal, etched lid, Fry, 1954, w/silver fr 32.50
Cocotte, str sides, Fry, 1926, 4½" 22.50
Cruet, yel, Lancaster Glass, w/faceted stopper 65.00
Custard cup, etched leaves, Fry, 1927 ....15.00
Dish, hot roll; oval, Fry, 1953, 6" 27.50
Dish, meatloaf; emb grapes on lid, Fry, 1928, 9" 25.00
Gravy boat, red, Imperial, w/underliner..150.00
Grease jar, wht w/red flowerpots, w/lid..18.00
Grease jar, yel opaque, Hocking...35.00
Hot fudge warmer, Fry, w/metal lid...32.50
Ice bucket, amber, Cambridge, etch grapes 35.00
Ice bucket, frosted gr, Hocking, mk Frigidaire Ice Server 10.00
Ice bucket, frosted gr, HP polar bear, Fostoria 30.00
Ice bucket, yel transparent, Fenton 85.00
Juice extractor, crystal, Handy Andy, w/metal crank hdl 30.00
Ladle, crystal w/red hdl...35.00
Ladle, wht, Imperial...35.00
Measure, caramel, 1-spout, hdl, McKee, 4-cup 450.00
Measure, crystal, advertising, Health Club Baking Powder 25.00
Measure, crystal, 1-spout, hdl, Fry, 1933, 1-cup.............................30.00
Measure, crystal, 1-spout, ribbed sides, Heisey, 1-cup..................175.00
Measure, crystal, 1-spout, Tufglas, 4-cup 55.00
Measure, crystal, 2-spout, no hdl, Pyrex, 1-cup................................22.00
Measure, delphite, pitcher form, McKee, 2-cup 55.00
Measure, fired-on gr, pitcher form, McKee, 2-cup 10.00
Measure, fired-on gr, 2-cup...10.00
Measure, fired-on red, Hazel Atlas, 1-cup 35.00
Measure, gr, 3-spout, Hazel Atlas, 1-cup...17.50
Measure, gr transparent, pitcher form, Jeannette, 2-cup 75.00
Measure, gr w/wht dots, pitcher form, Hazel Atlas, 2-cup 40.00
Measure, jadite, Jeannette, 1-cup...12.00
Measure, mk Rochester Glass Co, ca 1902, 1-spout, 1-cup 40.00
Measure, ultramarine, Jeannette, 1-cup...35.00
Measure, yel, 3-spout, Hazel Atlas, 1-cup 175.00
Mixer, crystal, emb measure, Silver & Co, w/chrome top 20.00
Napkin holder, gr transparent, Fan Fold 85.00
Napkin holder, milk glass, emb Fort Howard Handi-Nap Napkins ..35.00
Napkin holder, wht, Nar-O-Fold...30.00
Pan, cake; opal, sq, Fry, 1935, 8" 18.00
Pitcher, batter; red, McKee..75.00
Pitcher, gr transparent, Jenkins 40.00
Pitcher, milk; pk, Hazel Atlas...17.50
Platter, meat; opal, Fry, 1918, in copper holder, 13" 17.50
Refrigerator dish, cobalt, rnd, Hazel Atlas, 5¾"...............................50.00
Refrigerator dish, delphite, McKee, 4x5" 22.50
Refrigerator dish, fired-on bl, oval, Hocking, 7" 15.00
Refrigerator dish, gr, Vitrock, 8x8" 22.00
Refrigerator dish, gr transparent, mk Tuflas Hydrator #1 ....60.00
Refrigerator dish, gr transparent, sq, w/lid, Tufglas, 6" 20.00
Refrigerator dish, pk, Federal, 8x8" 30.00
Refrigerator dish, pk, sq, Jennyware, 4½" 18.00
Refrigerator dish, yel transparent, Hazel Atlas.................................30.00
Relish, bl opaque, divided, Pyrex 15.00
Rolling pin, amethyst, blown..85.00
Rolling pin, Chalaine bl, blown..275.00
Rolling pin, crystal w/screw-on cobalt hdls.....................................175.00
Rolling pin, delphite, smooth end opposite lid end, McKee 325.00
Rolling pin, jadite, circle band opposite lid end, McKee.............225.00
Rolling pin, pk, w/screw-on wood hdls 275.00
Salad set, crystal, Cambridge, w/label, 2-pc 35.00
Salad set, lt bl, Imperial, 2-pc..65.00
Salt box, amber, oblong, w/glass lid, Sneath...................................125.00
Salt box, gr, emb Salt on lid, rnd, Jeannette 150.00
Shakers, dk jadite, sq, Jeannette, ea 12.00

Shakers, fired-on bl, ribbed, Hocking, ea 8.00
Shakers, fired-on bl, ribbed, Hocking, w/metal lid, ea....................8.00
Shakers, ultramarine, ftd, Jennyware, w/label, ea 20.00

Salt and pepper shakers, Jadite, 5", $30.00 for the pair.

Straw holder, crystal, Heisey, w/glass lid.......................................225.00
Sugar bowl, gr, Crisscross, w/lid 50.00
Sugar shaker, amber, horseshoe pattern 35.00
Sugar shaker, crystal, Beehive..25.00
Sugar shaker, gr, Hex Optic..85.00
Syrup, amber, Cambridge, w/lid 50.00
Syrup, amber, Tally Ho, metal lid, Cambridge 40.00
Syrup, gr transparent, Hazel Atlas...22.50
Syrup, pk, Cambridge, hinged metal lid..50.00
Syrup, pk, Hazel Atlas 40.00
Tray, sugar cube; yel transparent, Cambridge 65.00
Trivet, red, rnd, ftd 40.00

Miscellaneous

Food chopper, Queen Anne, mid-1800s, Albany, NY, $800.00.

Apple peeler, handmade, walnut, 21" L 175.00
Apple peeler, Little Star, EX 85.00
Apple peeler, maple, pewter ferrule, belt driven, 1800s, 22" L.....225.00
Apple peeler, pine, iron fittings, trough form, ca 1790 25x7½" ..200.00
Apple peeler, Reading Hardware Co, pnt traces, Pat 1877, EX......80.00
Apple peeler, White Mountain, Goodell Co, CI, EX 45.00
Bread maker, Universal, bucket type, tin, emb directions 45.00
Can opener, cow figural, tail curls on hdl, CI, Victorian 35.00
Can opener, Peerless, CI, 1903, EX...12.50
Can opener, tan & brn marbleized Catalin hdl.................................7.50
Candy dipper, copper, riveted hdl, ca 1900, 10" dia bowl 50.00
Cheese drainer, wood, twisted wire bottom, 1800s, 12" dia 75.00

Cheese slicer, Handi-Kraft, gr pnt metal, 5½x5½" **18.00**
Cheese slicer, sm slot, brass hdl, 3-tooth pickup **8.00**
Cherry seeder, Rollman Mfg Co No 8, ca 1900s, 12" **35.00**
Churn, Dazey, #10, high-top, 1-qt, M......................**950.00**
Churn, Dazey, #40, 4-qt...**95.00**
Churn, Dazey, #80, 2-gal...**80.00**
Churn, Dazey, 3-qt..**100.00**
Churn, unmk, emb jar, 1-qt......................................**150.00**
Cookie crimper, tin w/wood hdl, ca 1800s, 4½" **50.00**
Cookie roller, maple, concentric rings, ca 1860, 12"........**35.00**
Cookie roller, wood, 10 corrugated rings, bulb hdl, ca 1875, 12" ...**48.00**
Cream whip, Andirock..**22.00**
Cutter, biscuit; tin, arched rolled-edge strap hdl, 1890s **12.00**
Cutter, biscuit; tin, scalloped, gr pnt wood hdl, 1930s....................**6.00**
Cutter, doughnut; Rumford.....................................**22.00**
Cutter, doughnut; tin, wide arched hdl, ca 1900s, 2½" **12.00**
Cutter, kraut; ash w/dvtl cherry hopper, rfn/damage, 41".............**75.00**
Cutter, kraut; wooden, heart cutout in tombstone crest, 20" **350.00**
Cutter, kraut; 2 blades in scalloped pine brd, 5¾x15" **180.00**
Dipper, bronze, decorative cut-out hdl, 17½" **55.00**
Dough scraper, wrought iron, 4½" **75.00**
Egg beater, Taplin's Dover Pattern Improved, Pat 1903, 12½" **30.00**
Egg beater, United Royalties, Pat 1929, pnt gr wood hdl **22.00**
Egg beater, 2-speed, Deco style, blk & wht pnt, EX.................**17.50**
Egg whisk, blk tin & coiled wire, ca 1880s, 7½" **12.00**
Fork, stainless, gr pnt hdl w/wht stripe, ca 1930, 14½" **8.00**
Funnel, tin, copper tipped, rolled edge, ca 1800s, 20" **28.00**
Grapefruit corer, pumpkin Catalin hdl **8.00**
Grater, brass, half rnd, 1-pc fr, early 1800s, rare, 13"..................**225.00**
Grater, cornmeal; punched tin on pine brd, ca 1700s, 30"..........**85.00**
Grater, mk All In One Pat Pend, ca 1904, 10⅝".......................**25.00**
Grater, Norlund Corn, 2 metal-toothed blades, wood fr, 12" **15.00**
Grater, nutmeg; tin, curved front, str bk, 1890s.....................**15.00**
Grater, sleeve; blk tin & wire, sq arched hdl, 1901, 7½" **30.00**
Grinder, food; Griswold #0, CI, EX.............................**75.00**
Grinder, food; 2 curved blades, upright wood hdls, sgn, 10"..........**65.00**
Grinder, poppy seed; spun aluminum, hopper......................**37.50**
Grinder, spice; blk CI, ca 1890, wall mt.........................**38.00**
Ice cream scoop, red Catalin hdl **15.00**
Ice crusher, Dazey **10.00**
Ice crusher, Lightning...**15.00**
Ice pick, steel, metal ferrule, sq wood hdl, 1900s **5.00**
Juicer, Griswold #9 ....**135.00**
Juicer, Vitorio Deluxe #2, metal, clamp-on, ca 1900.................**35.00**
Knife, butcher; steel, walnut hdl w/copper rivets, ca 1890 .... **9.00**
Lard can, tin, rnd, w/lid, ca 1900s, 5x5" **8.00**
Lemon squeezer, galvanized iron, hinged, 2-pc, ca 1890s, 8".........**50.00**
Lemon squeezer, LF&C, CI, 2-hdl................................**22.50**
Lemon squeezer, Newman's The Drum Squeezer, Pat 1883, 9" **75.00**
Masher, twisted iron, blk pnt wood hdl, ca 1890, 9½"...............**22.00**
Meat cleaver, steel, wood hdl w/copper rivets, ca 1890 ....**24.00**
Meat pounder, CI half-circle w/frets, wood hdl, 1800s **95.00**
Meat pounder, toothed yel stoneware, Pat Dec 25, 1877 ....**85.00**
Muffin pan, Ekco, tin, 6 fluted cups, ca 1900s.................... **8.00**
Pasta/noodle roller, CI/wood, John Taber, rare **165.00**
Pastry blender, nickeled iron, gr pnt hdl, ca 1900s, 9½".................**18.00**
Pie crimper, blk Bakelite middle grip, wht plastic wheel **15.00**
Pie crimper, brass/wrought iron, well made/EX detail, 7½".............**325.00**
Pie crimper, eng wrought iron, wooden hdl, 8" **85.00**
Pie crimper, Vaughn's, gr Catalin hdl, 1920 ....**17.50**
Pineapple corer/peeler, tinned metal, ca 1930s, 5" **18.00**
Pot scrubber, chain link, open loop iron hdl.......................**30.00**
Pricker, biscuit; metal spikes, mushroom knob hdl, 4x4" dia..........**95.00**
Rice baller, aluminum **10.00**

Ricer, plated tin, hinged CI hdl, ca 1925, 10¾" **18.00**
Rolling pin, clear glass, Roll Rite cap............................**22.00**
Rolling pin, dk amber blown glass, 13½" **65.00**
Rolling pin, milk glass, wooden hdls **55.00**
Rolling pin, solid brass...**85.00**
Shredder/slaw cutter, Wonder Grater, dtd 1930s, 8½" **8.00**
Sifter, tin, Bromwell, ca 1925, 5-cup **18.00**
Sifter, tin & wire, Pat Made in USA, ca 1900s, 3½" **15.00**
Skimmer, brass bowl w/flower piercing, wrought hdl, 18", VG **55.00**
Tongs, tan marbleized Catalin hdls **6.00**
Turner, galvanized tin, grooved hdl, ca 1890, 12½" **9.00**
Turner, metal, trn wood hdl, ca 1890, 14" L **20.00**
Whip, cream; wire & tin, Horlick Cream Whipper, ca 1920, 9½".**32.00**

Knives

Knife collecting as a hobby began in earnest during the 1960s when government regulations required for the first time that knife companies mark their product with the country of origin. The few collectors and dealers cognizant of this change at once began stockpiling the older knives made before this law was enacted. Another impetus to the growing interest in this area came with the Gun Control Act of 1968, which severely restricted gun trading. Frustrated gun dealers transferred their attention to knives. Today there are collectors clubs in many of the states.

The most sought-after pocket knives are those made before WWII. However, Case, Schrade, and Primble knives of a more recent manufacture are also collected. Most collectors prefer knives 'as found.' Do not attempt to clean, sharpen, or in any way 'improve' on an old knife.

The prices quoted here are for knives in mint condition (except for those in the Miscellaneous section). If a knife has been used, sharpened, or blemished in any way, its value decreases. The newer the knife, the greater the reduction in value. Our advisor for this category is Charles D. Stapp; he is listed in the Directory under Indiana. For futher information refer to *The Standard Knife Collector's Guide* by Ron Stewart and Roy Ritchie.

Key:
bd — blade   p/b — push button
Cut — Cutlery

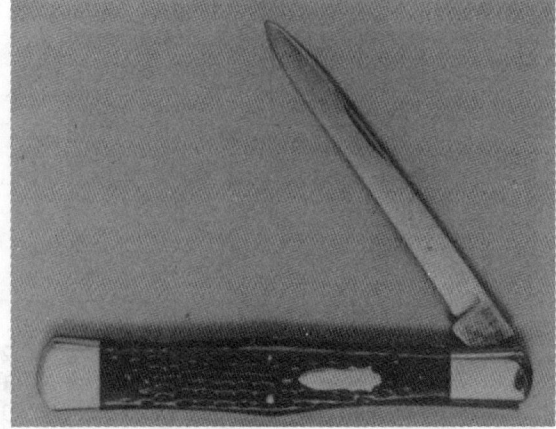

Case, #61213, Tested XX, 5¾", M, $450.00.

Case, B1048, Christmas tree hdl, tested XX, 1930s, 4⅛" **300.00**
Case, B151L, faux onyx hdl, 1-bd, tested XX, 1930s, 5¼"............**585.00**
Case, C31050, yel compo hdl, 1-bd, tested XX, 1930s, 5⅛".........**590.00**
Case, G100, celluloid hdl, tested XX, EX **140.00**

Case, M279SS, metal hdl, 2-bd, XX, 1940-64, 3⅛", M 32.00
Case, RM1093, mottled red hdl, tested XX, 1930s, 5", M............300.00
Case, 1116SP, bone hdl, 1-bd, USA, 1965-70, M 38.00
Case, 2136B, blk hdl, 1-bd, XX, 1940-65, M 150.00
Case, 2138LSS, slick blk hdl, Dots, 1970, 5⅝", EX 30.00
Case, 22087, slick blk hdl, 2-bd, USA, 1965-69, 3¼", M 20.00
Case, 23087, slick blk hdl, 3-bd, tested XX, 1920-40, 3¼", M 100.00
Case, 2345½, slick blk hdl, XX, 1940-64, 3⅝", M.......................85.00
Case, 31048SP, florist's, yel hdl, 1-bd, XX, 1940-65, 4⅛", M.........35.00
Case, 3185, yel compo hdl, tested XX, 1930s, 3⅝", M 170.00
Case, 32098, yel comp hdl, 2-bd, tested XX, 1920-40, 5½"............180.00
Case, 33092, yel compo hdl, 3-bd, USA, 1965-69, 4", M 48.00
Case, 4200SS, wht compo hdl, USA, 1965-69, 5½", M...............100.00
Case, 5111½LSSP Cheetah, stag hdl, 1-bd, 4½", M 135.00
Case, 5197LSSP, stag hdl, 1-bd, Lightning, 1980-85, 5", M 70.00
Case, 5347SHSP, stag hdl, 3-bd, USA, 1965-69, 3⅞", M 55.00
Case, 61011, gr bone hdl, 1-bd, tested XX, 1930s, M 120.00
Case, 6116, gr bone hdl, 1-bd, tested XX, 1930s, 3⅜", M 180.00
Case, 6185, doctor's, stag hdl, 1-bd, Dots, 1971-75, 3¾", M 50.00
Case, 62009, gr bone hdl, XX, 1940-55, 3¼", M 130.00
Case, 6202½, gr bone hdl, 1940s, XX, 3⅜", M...........................80.00
Case, 62024, gr bone hdl, 2-bd, XX, 1940-64, 3", M 80.00
Case, 6214½, gr bone hdl, 2-bd, XX, 1940s, 3⅜", M...................87.50
Case, 6225½, bone hdl, 2-bd, Dots, 1970, 3", M 30.00
Case, 6225½, rough blk hdl, tested XX, 1930s, 3", M 170.00
Case, 6231½, red bone hdl, 2-bd, XX, 1940-64, 3¾", EX.............65.00
Case, 6251, knife-fork combo, gr bone hdl, Tested XX, 5¼", M ..525.00
Case, 6299, rough blk hdl, 2-bd, XX, 1940-50, 4⅛", M...............120.00
Case, 63047, bone hdl, 3-bd, 10 Dot, 1970, 3⅞", M....................32.00
Case, 6332, bone hdl, 3-bd, USA, 1965-69, 3⅝", M 30.00
Case, 640045R, blk plastic hdl, USA, 1965-69, 3¾", M 28.00
Case, 7106, tortoise hdl, tested XX, 2⅝", M.............................250.00
Case, 82079½, pearl hdl, 2-bd, tested XX, 1920-40, 3¼", M........180.00
Case, 9201, faux pearl hdl, Dots, 1970, 2⅝", M 25.00
Case, 9279, faux pearl hdl, 2-bd, XX, 1940-64, 3⅛", M 78.00
Primble, Belknap, 4861, jack, bone hdl, 2-bd, 3¾", M 45.00
Primble, Belknap, 5222, Congress, bone hdl, 2-bd, 3", M 35.00
Primble, Belknap, 5380, stockman's, bone hdl, 3-bd, 3½"............45.00
Primble, Belknap, 5514, brn bone hdl, 4-bd, 3¾", M 58.00
Primble, Belknap, 5517, Congress, bone hdl, 4-bd, 4⅛", M........50.00
Primble, Belknap, 7022, bone hdl, 2-bd, 2⅝", M 25.00
Primble, Belknap, 703, Rogers bone hdl, 3-bd, 3¼", M..............35.00
Primble, Belknap, 902, Rogers bone hdl, 2-bd, 2⅞", M..............32.00
Primble, Belknap, 903, faux peachseed bone hdl, 2⅞", M 25.00
Queen, 15, Rogers bone hdl, 2-bd, 3½", M..............................40.00
Queen, 24, trapper's, winterbottom bone hdl, 2-bd, 4", M..........38.00
Queen, 3, sleeveboard, winterbottom bone hdl, 3¼", M.............28.00
Queen, 38, jigged bone hdl, 1-bd, 5¼", M 190.00
Queen, 57, pearl hdl, 3-bd, 3⅜", M 32.00
Queen, 6120, stag hdl, 2-bd, 4½", M 38.00
Queen, 6155, winterbottom bone hdl, 1-bd, 3½", M 55.00
Queen Stainless, 35, rough blk hdl, 3-bd, 2⅝", M 25.00
Queen Steel, 11, winterbottom bone hdl, 1-bd, 4⅛", M 30.00
Queen Steel, 38, winterbottom bone hdl, 2-bd, 3", M 50.00
Queen Steel, 46, fisherman's, winterbottom bone hdl, 5", M........40.00
Queen Steel, 55, gr Rogers bone hdl, 3-bd, 3¼", M.....................35.00
Remington, RB040, brn bone hdl, 1-bd, 3⅜", M........................88.00
Remington, RH73, brn bone hdl, 2-bd, 3⅛", M........................100.00
Remington, R1723, bone hdl, 2-bd, 3½", M.............................155.00
Remington, R182, blk hdl, 2-bd, 3¾", M 145.00
Remington, R205, jack, redwood hdl, 2-bd, 3⅝", M 125.00
Remington, R219, brass hdl, 2-bd, 3⅝", M.............................165.00
Remington, R3059, stockman's, metal hdl, 3-bd, 4", M.............240.00
Remington, R3493, bone hdl, 3-bd, 3⅜", M............................200.00

Remington, R3655, stockman's, pyremite hdl, 3-bd, 3⅞", M........280.00
Remington, R3714, pearl hdl, 3-bd, 3⅞", M............................380.00
Remington, R4053, bone hdl, 2-bd, 3⅝", M............................200.00
Remington, R433, bone hdl, 3-bd, 3⅜", M..............................180.00
Remington, R4375, girl scout's, pyremite hdl, 3⅜", M.................200.00
Remington, R4593, muskrat, brn bone hdl, 2-bd, 4", M.............265.00
Remington, R55, pyremite hdl, 2-bd, 3⅜", M...........................165.00
Remington, R555, candy stripe hdl, 2-bd, 3¼", M....................160.00
Remington, R6133, bone hdl, 3-bd, 3½", M.............................140.00
Remington, R6956, stag hdl, 2-bd, 3", M 300.00
Remington, R698, cocobolo hdl, 1-bd, 4", M.............................85.00
Remington, R7363, corkscrew, bone hdl, 2⅝", M 95.00
Remington, R8034, bartender's, pearl hdl, 2-bd, 2⅞", M 200.00
Schrade Cut, C2154¾AP, pearl hdl, 2-bd, 3⅜", M......................70.00
Schrade Cut, C2533¾Q, celluloid hdl, 2-bd, 3", M.....................48.00
Schrade Cut, R2974W, ivory celluloid hdl, 2-bd, 4¼", M 115.00
Schrade Cut, 115, peachseed blk compo hdl, 1-bd, 5¼", M........125.00
Schrade Cut, 136, lineman's, cocobolo hdl, 1-bd, 4½", M 28.00
Schrade Cut, 151, switchbd, mottled celluloid hdl, 4", M 100.00
Schrade Cut, 181, bark loosener, faux ivory hdl, 1-bd, 4", M........32.00
Schrade Cut, 2064W, ivory celluloid hdl, 2-bd, 3⅝", M 85.00
Schrade Cut, 225, hunter's, jigged brn hdl, 2-bd, 5¼", M 125.00
Schrade Cut, 242, blk peachseed bone hdl, 2-bd, 3⅛", M............30.00
Schrade Cut, 2424SEO, tortoise celluloid hdl, 2-bd, 3⅛" 45.00
Schrade Cut, 708, yel compo hdl, 2-bd, 2¾", M.........................40.00
Schrade Cut, 716, grafting, faux ivory, 2-bd, 3¾", M 38.00
Schrade Cut, 7236, MOP hdl, 2-bd, 2½", M.............................42.50
Schrade Cut, 778RB, stainless steel hdl, 2-bd, 2⅞", M 27.50
Schrade Cut, 8564, Christmas tree hdl, 3-bd, 3⅜", M................220.00
Schrade Cut, 884, stag hdl, 3-bd, 4", M..................................135.00
Schrade Cut, 8963, bone hdl, 3-bd, 3½", M...............................80.00
Winchester, 1703, Barlow, bone hdl, 1-bd, 5", M......................240.00
Winchester, 2070, jack, celluloid hdl, 1-bd, 3½", M..................115.00
Winchester, 2306, Senator, pearl hdl, 2-bd, 2⅝", M 110.00
Winchester, 2368, sleeveboard, pearl hdl, 2-bd, 3", M.................95.00
Winchester, 2842, Senator, stag hdl, 2-bd, 3¼", M...................115.00
Winchester, 2931, jack, stag hdl, 2-bd, 3¼", M 155.00
Winchester, 3009, cattleman's, celluloid hdl, 3-bd, 3⅝"............275.00
Winchester, 3904, whittler's, brn bone hdl, 3-bd, 3⅝", M..........600.00
Winchester, 3963, stockman's, stag hdl, 3-bd, 4", M.................225.00
Winchester, 4950, scout's, bone hdl, 3⅝", M 200.00

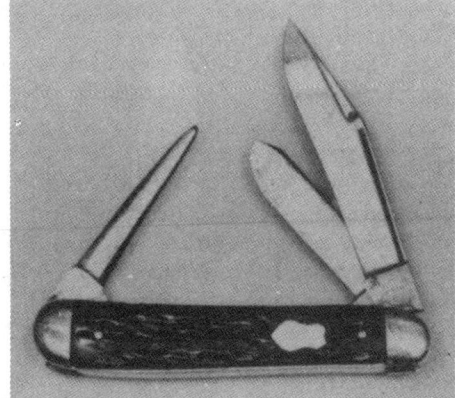

Remington, R100R,
3⅜", $125.00.

Miscellaneous

Bowie, Confederate D, walnut grip, brass guard, 15", EX.............300.00
Bowie, NP crossguard, blk compo grips, sq pommel, 1900, 16"....195.00
Bowie, Rodgers, Sheffield, NP grip & crossguard, 1860s, 14".......350.00
Bowie, SC Wragg, silver crossguard, NP hilt, 1860s, 11" 265.00

Bowie, Sheffield, NP crossguard, ebony girps, 1870s, 13" 135.00
Bowie, 2-pc stag grips w/silver inlay, 1850s, 13½", EX 500.00
Dirk, German silver pommel & X-guard, 5" dbl-edge blade, EX..125.00
Dirk, Hart Bros, Prussia, florals on pommel, 1880s, 10", G 40.00
Farrier's, stag grips, Sheffield, 1850s, 4" closed, VG.....................35.00
Fishing, J Russell Gr River, sawtooth bk, 8½", +scabbard............100.00
Hunting, J Russell Gr River, wood hdl, 8¾", +scabbard...............150.00
US Marine Corp Hospital, Briddell, wood hdl, 11¼" bd, EX.......150.00

Kosta

Kosta glassware has been made in Sweden since 1742. Today they are one of that country's leading producers of quality art glass. Two of their most important designers were Elis Bergh (1929-1950) and Vicke Lindstrand, artistic director from 1950 to 1973. Lindstrand brought to the company knowledge of important techniques such as Graal, fine figural engraving, Ariel, etc. He influenced new artists to experiment with these techniques and inspired them to create new and innovative designs. Today's collectors are most interested in pieces made during the 1950s and '60s. Our advisor for this category is Abby Malowanczyk; she is listed in the Directory under Texas.

Bowl, bl crystal, flared cylinder, B Vallien Boda, 5¼x3" 500.00
Bowl, cranberry w/wht gridwork, flared/bulbous, sgn/#d, 5x3½" ..150.00
Bowl, gr-cased, int gr/brn streaks, Lindstrand/#56675, 5x6¼"......325.00
Bowl, indigo & clear, Warff, #25973, 2x6" 225.00

Vase, crystal cased to green with internal green and brown striations, signed Lindstrand, #56675, 5" X 6¼", $325.00.

Vase, cut in twist, int blk line, att Lindstrand, #602, 13" 600.00
Vase, gl-on gr spiral stripes, flattened oval, sgn/#d, 6¾" 425.00
Vase, heavy/clear, seaweed w/in, Lindstrand/LU2007, 14" 600.00
Vase, Manhattan (skyline), V Lindstrand/LG #163, '55, 15" .. 3,000.00
Vase, red & clear, elongated teardrop form, LH #1336, 12" 275.00

Kutani

Kutani, named for the Japanese village where it originated, was first produced in the seventeenth century. The early ware, Ko Kutani, was produced for only about thirty years. Several types were produced before 1800, but these are rarely encountered. In the nineteenth century, kilns located in several different villages began to copy the old Kutani wares. This later, more familiar type has large areas of red with

gold designs on a white ground decorated with warriors, birds, and flowers in controlled colors of red, gold, and black.

Chocolate pot, bird/floral panels, people in gardens, 9" 135.00
Chocolate pot, birds/peonies/people, red/gold, 1870s, 8½" 125.00
Incense burner, bird in garden panels, firing lines, 9"..................800.00
Jardiniere, mtn villages in panels, 1880s, 10x12" 650.00
Platter, dragon, scholar on horned animal, fish form, 17" 400.00
Vase, festival scene, foliate borders, 1800s, 18" 2,100.00
Vase, figural scenes, cicada hdls, baluster, 1900, now lamp..........525.00
Vase, peacock in garden panels, dbl gourd, w/lid, 1800s, 18" .. 1,000.00

L. E. Smith

Perhaps best known for their line of black glass vases and novelty items, this twentieth-century American glass company also made several patterns of colored Depression-type dinnerware.

Serving tray in black glass with four footed tumblers, $85.00.

Animals and Birds

Elephant, ash tray, blk, #2 ....35.00
Elephant, ash tray, pk 45.00
Horse, bookends, amber, rearing, ea..38.00
Horse, bookends, bl, ritz, rearing, ea...38.00
Horse, bookends, blk, rearing, ea 55.00
Horse, bookends, cobalt, rearing, ea...40.00
Horse, bookends, crystal, rearing, ea 20.00
Horse, bookends, emerald, rearing, ea 38.00
Horse, bookends, ruby, rearing, ea..40.00
King fish aquarium, gr...250.00
Queen fish aquarium..150.00
Rooster, butterscotch slag, Ltd Ed, #208 ....85.00
Scottie, crystal, lg, 5" 30.00
Swan, cobalt, lg 65.00
Swan, milk glass, lg 45.00

Bean pot, Greek Key, w/lid, 1920s-30s 45.00
Bonbon, blk, hdld, ftd, #2400, 3" 25.00
Bonbon, cobalt, ftd, hdl...13.00

Bonbon, gr, #81	7.00
Bowl, blk, bulbous, #50, 5¾"	7.50
Bowl, blk, ftd, #515, 7" dia	20.00
Bowl, mayonnaise; blk w/silver decor, #635, 1930s	12.00
Cake salver, blk, ftd, 4½x10"	35.00
Candy dish, Dresden floral, wht, rolled rim	17.50
Compote, blk, crimped rim, 7x9"	35.00
Cookie jar, gr transparent	65.00
Cup, Romanesque, aqua	9.00
Flower arranger w/attached candles, Romanesque, amber, 11"	20.00
Jardiniere, Greek Key, blk, 3-ftd, #23, 1930s	22.00
Tray, cordial; blk, #381	10.00
Tray, cordial; gr or pk, #381	9.00
Vase, blk, #1900, 7¼"	20.00
Vase, blk, #49, 6"	13.00
Vase, blk, fan form, 8-sided ft, #1000, ca 1925-30s	35.00
Vase, blk w/silver decor, tab hdls, #102, 1930s, 6"	18.00
Vase, cobalt, stippled t'print, 5¾"	7.50
Vase, dancing girls, blk, #433, 7"	20.00
Window box, blk, #405, 7¾"	22.00
Window box, Pan & dancing girls, milk glass, 6¼"	10.00

Labels

Before the advent of the cardboard box, wooden crates were used for transporting products. Paper labels were attached to the crates to identify the contents and the packer. These labels often had colorful lithographed illustrations covering a broad range of subjects. Eventually the cardboard box replaced the crate, and the artwork was imprinted directly onto the carton. Today these paper labels are becoming collectible — primarily for the art, but also for their advertising appeal. Our advisor for this category is Cerebro; their address is listed in the Directory under Pennsylvania.

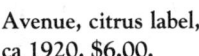
Avenue, citrus label, ca 1920, $6.00.

Apple, Bird Valley, lg crow, 1920, 9x10½", M	4.50
Apple, Buffalo, buffalo w/lg horns, 1930, 9x10½", M	8.00
Apple, Falls, wht waterfall, 1930, 9x10½"	2.00
Apple, Lucky Trail, prospector & horse, 1915, 9x10½", EX	15.00
Apple, Merry Christmas, Santa & sleigh, 1940s, 5x8", M	2.00
Apple, Snow Owl, wht owl, 1920, 9x10½", M	3.50
Asparagus, King of Hearts, half of card/lg red heart, 1940	2.00
Asparagus, Pride of River, Mississippi riverboat, 1930, M	6.50
Asparagus, River Lad, Dutch boy/windmills, 1930, 9x10½"	4.00
Bread, American Biscuit Co, w/wheat sheaf, ca 1910, 9x9"	21.50
Cigar, America's Pride, Washington on Delaware, 6x9", M	6.50
Cigar, Blush Rose, lady/sunset/flowers, 4½x4½", M	15.00
Cigar, El Frison, eagle perched on top of world, 6x9", M	9.00

Cigar, Greeting, Krueger & Braun, 1900, 6x9", M	75.00
Cigar, Mozart, portrait of composer, 4½x4½", M	12.00
Cigar, New York, New York City skyline, 5x8", M	7.00
Cigar, Rose of Roses, lady w/flowers, 6x9", VG	10.00
Cigar, Supporter, soccer player kicks ball, 4½x4½", M	9.00
Citrus, Azalea, orange-pk flowers, 1940, 9x9", M	65.00
Citrus, Blue Bird, bird in flight, 7x7", EX	3.00
Citrus, Booty, pirate on trunk of fruit, 1930, 9x9", EX	22.00
Citrus, Fellowship, clasped hands, 1930, 9x9", M	3.00
Citrus, Moonbeam, moon over orchard, 1930, 9x9", M	4.00
Citrus, Piney Woods Belle, fruit grove/fruit, 9x9", M	6.50
Citrus, Poinsettia, flower w/ornament, 1930s, 10x11", M	15.00
Citrus, Wren, bird on branch in swamp, 9x9", M	8.00
Cotton spool, Aneuk Seudati, boy & girl/fan	3.00
Cotton spool, Wide Awake, lg bl eyes, EX	6.00
Cranberry, Clipper Brand, ships at sea, 1927, 7x10", M	5.00
Cranberry, Harvard Brand, Harvard Square at Cape Cod, 7x10"	7.00
Cranberry, Silver Medal, Pan-Am Expo medals, 7x10", M	2.00
Hotel, Waldorf Astoria, NY, 1930s, 4" dia, EX	10.00
Lemon, Basket, basket full of lemons, 1940, 8¾x12½", M	1.50
Lemon, Fallbrook, rushing water/forest, 1930, 8¾x12½"	2.00
Lemon, Leader, brn horse, 1930, 8¾x12½", EX	3.00
Lemon, Morning Sun, mission w/sunrise, 1930, 8¾x12½"	4.00
Lemon, Terrier, dog, 8¾x12½", EX	22.00
Orange, Bronco, cowboy on horseback, 1920, 10x11¾", M	5.00
Orange, Polo, polo player, 1920, 10x11¾", M	5.00
Orange, Santa, portrait w/rosy cheeks, 1930s, 10x11", M	12.00
Orange, Ta-Che, Indian, 1930, 10x11¾", M	18.00
Orange, Venice Cove, rooster, 1930, 10x11¾", EX	3.00
Paint, Automobile Enamel, Art Deco design, 1916, 4x7½"	8.50
Peach, Fresh Carolina Peaches, peaches on gr & bl, 7x8", M	4.00
Peach, Star Brand, lg peach & sm Indian head, 7x8", EX	15.00
Pear, Broadway, red letters on gold, 7½x11", M	2.00
Pear, Foothills, view of valley, 1920, 7½x11", M	4.75
Pear, Lady of the Lake, maiden eating pear, 1940, M	4.00
Pear, Pansy Brand Bartlett, ca 1915, 4½x10"	10.00
Pear, Round Robin, lg robin on bl ground, 1930, M	3.75
Pear, Statue, Statue of Liberty, 1940, 7½x11", M	1.00
Strawberry, Borden-Pekin Fruit, strawberries, M	1.50
Vegetable, Hot Brand, cowboys branding, 1940, 9x6", M	1.00
Vegetable, Lion, lion on red ground, 1928, 9x6", M	3.00
Vegetable, Santa Maria, speeding train, 1930, 9x6", M	3.00
Vegetable, Up N' Atom, rabbit wears boxing gloves, 1930, M	2.50
Yam, Champ, football player/sweet potato, 9x9", M	4.00
Yam, La Grande Sweets, map of LA w/capital building, 9x9"	2.00
Yam, Mary Agnes, girl w/straw hat full of yams, 9x9", M	2.00
Yam, Vitamin, mother feeding vitamins to child, 9x9", M	3.00

Labino

Dominick Labino was a glass blower who until mid-1985 worked in his studio in Ohio, blowing and sculpting various items which he signed and dated. A ceramic engineer by trade, he was instrumental in developing the heat-resistant tiles used in space flights. His glassmaking shows his versatility in the art. While some of his designs are free-form and futuristic, others are reminiscent of the products of older glasshouses. Because of problems with his health, Mr. Labino became unable to blow glass himself; he died January, 10, 1987. Work coming from his studio since mid-1985 has been signed 'Labino Studios, Baker,' indicating ware made by his protegee, E. Baker O'Brien. In addition to her own compositions, she continues to use many of the colors developed by Labino.

Bowl, amber, horse-head prunts, sgn/1981, 4" **525.00**
Bowl, appl cobalt & cadmium prunts, sgn/1975, 5½x5"..........**700.00**
Bowl, bl w/yel & bl swags forming star, sgn/1975, 7"........**800.00**
Bowl, gold ruby, sgn/1968, 7½" **850.00**
Nut dish, bl/yel, ftd, sgn/1972, 5½" **400.00**
Paperweight, Moss Scrape, mc in bl irid, sgn/1983, 2½" dia **475.00**
Sculpture, Emergence, clear/encased pk-amber, sgn/1972, 11".. **3,100.00**
Sculpture, Fountain, amber/pk/lav in crystal, lobed, 9½" **4,200.00**
Sculpture, Iris, cobalt, sgn/1975, 7½"..........................**800.00**
Sculpture, Rende-vous VII, bl w/encased amber, sgn/1970, 7"... **2,600.00**
Vase, amber-gr, slim form, sgn/11-1970, 21".................**850.00**
Vase, bl w/red vertical bands, oviform, sgn/1981, 12" **850.00**
Vase, bl-gr opal, cylindrical w/free-form base, sgn/1965, 7"..........**800.00**

Vase, clear with interior yellow and gold swag, 1975, 5½", $1,150.00.

Vase, copper red, mc embedded florals, sgn/1984, 4½" **800.00**
Vase, copper ruby, continuous prunts, sgn/2-1971, 11½" **950.00**
Vase, Harlequin, red/wht/blk/yel stripes, ovoid, 1982, 7" **800.00**
Vase, Sappherin, ovoid w/air traps, sgn/1968, 8" **900.00**
Wine, lt bl, twisted air trap stem, sgn/1966, 9¾" **450.00**

Lace, Linens, and Needlework

It has been recorded that lace was found in the tombs of ancient Egypt. Lace has always been a symbol of wealth and fashion. Italian laces are regarded as the finest ever produced, but the differences between them and the laces of France are nearly indistinguishable. Needlework was revived during the 18th century and became the favorite of feminine pastimes. Examples of many forms (tatting, embroidery, needlepoint, and crochet, for instance) are available today; and, though fragile in appearance, have withstood the ravages of time with remarkable durability.

Key:
embr — embroidered   ms — machine sewn
hs — hand sewn

Bedspread, Battenburg draped sides, lined, 106x94", NM **450.00**
Bedspread, crochet, Popcorn Star & Sq, 81x100+3" fringe, M **450.00**
Bolster cover, homespun, bl/wht checks, ms, stains, 31x64" **95.00**
Bolster cover, Irish linen, floral embr, scalloped, 32x86" **85.00**
Centerpiece, Battenburg, floral, 11"...**85.00**
Centerpiece, Battenburg, Grape & Leaf, 10" dia **85.00**

Centerpiece, Battenburg, vintage, 10" dia **85.00**
Centerpiece, Battenburg, 38" sq...**85.00**
Centerpiece, Battenburg 4" border, 16" dia **50.00**
Centerpiece, crochet, initial A in center, 10x17"........................**65.00**
Centerpiece, crochet, 2 cats, 12x18"..**85.00**
Handkerchief, wedding; Battenburg **55.00**
Handkerchief, wht linen w/lace trim..**12.00**

Needlework picture with printed silk portrait of George Washington, sequins, ribbons, and gem-like stones on natural silk ground, 36" x 32", VG, $900.00.

Needlepoint, 3 figures in Biblical costumes, 17x15"....................**195.00**
Needlework, birds in bird bath, Splish Splash, 20x26" **125.00**
Needlework, sunbonnet girl & October, 8½" sq **65.00**
Piano scarf, lg embr florals w/long fringe....................................**150.00**
Pillowcase, red embr birds in heart wreath, 32x17", NM, pr **65.00**
Runner, Cluny 4" border, 8" at corners, 17x42" **125.00**
Runner, crochet, A in center w/flowers, 10x17".........................**65.00**
Runner, crochet, cat center, 7½x13" **85.00**
Runner, crochet, cherubs pattern, wht, 12½x38" **85.00**
Runner, filet lace, Grecian women & cherubs ea end, 18x34".......**65.00**
Runner, linen, ecru, +8 napkins & place mats **150.00**
Sham, pieced/appliqued, red/gr floral, initials, pr **135.00**
Sham, red embr roses, bees in corners, EX **65.00**
Show towel, embr floral/birds/lady, sgn/1821, fringe, 62" **110.00**
Show towel, homespun, dmn pattern/embr initials, 51x19"..........**65.00**
Show towel, homespun, 4-color embr, rows of fringe, 62"..........**220.00**
Show towel, pk X-stitch peacocks/flowers/sgn/1849, 63" **700.00**
Show towel, red/bl X-stitch flowers/birds/sgn/1833, 58", EX.......**400.00**
Show towel, wool needlepoint/embr mc flowers/sgn/1851, 56"....**300.00**
Tablecloth, Battenburg 4" border, 8" flower corners, 22" sq.........**195.00**
Tablecloth, Cluny inserts, medallion center, 64x68", EX **145.00**
Tablecloth, damask, scalloped crochet edges, M **150.00**
Tablecloth, homespun, gold/wht checks, hs, lt wear, 38x54".......**145.00**
Tablecloth, Italian pointe de Venice, figural bands, 1900s **400.00**
Tablecloth, linen, allover cutwork, 52x46", +6 napkins **195.00**
Tablecloth, linen, appliqued flowers, 48x52", EX.......................**95.00**
Tablecloth, linen, ecru, 60x94", +12 napkins, EX......................**185.00**
Tablecloth, linen, mc embr flowers, scalloped, 104x70" **125.00**
Tablecloth, linen, monogram, 72x108", M................................**120.00**
Tablecloth, linen, red X-stitch lilies & border, 58x74" **145.00**
Tablecloth, machine lace, wht, 62" dia.......................................**85.00**

Lalique

Beginning his lengthy career as a designer and maker of fine jewelry, Rene Lalique at first only dabbled in glass, making small panels of pate-de-verre (paste-on-paste) and cire perdue (wax casting) to use in his jewelry. He also made small flacons of gold and silver with his glass inlays, which attracted the attention of M.F. Coty, who commissioned Lalique to design bottles for his perfume company. The success of this venture resulted in the opening of his own glassworks at Combs-la-Ville in 1909. In 1921 a larger factory was established at Wingen-sur-Moder in Alsace-Lorraine. By the thirties Lalique was world renowned as the most important designer of his time.

Lalique glass is lead based, either mold blown or pressed. Favored motifs during the Art Nouveau period were dancing nymphs, fish, dragonflies, and foliage. Characteristically the glass is crystal in combination with acid-etched relief. Later some items were made in as many as ten colors (red, amber, and green among them) and were occasionally accented with enameling. These colored pieces, especially those in black, are highly prized by advanced collectors.

During the twenties and thirties, Lalique designed several vases and bowls reminiscent of American Indian art. He also developed a line in the Art Deco style decorated with stylized birds, florals, and geometrics. In addition to vases, clocks, automobile mascots, stemware, and bottles, many other useful objects were produced. Items made before his death in 1945 were marked 'R. Lalique'; later the 'R' was deleted even though some of the original molds were still used. Numbers found on the bases of some pieces are catalog numbers. Beware of fraudulent pieces that have began to surface in increasing numbers. Our advisor for this category is John Danis; he is listed in the Directory under Illinois.

Key:
cl/fr — clear and frosted   RL — signed R. Lalique
L — signed Lalique   RLF — signed R. Lalique, France

Luminaire, Gros Poisson Algues, RLF, 12" x 15", $8,500.00.

Ash tray, fish surrounded w/bubbles, fr, LF, 5½" 225.00
Ash tray, mouse figural center, yel, RLF, 1920s...........................395.00
Atomizer, Le Provencal, procession of women, fr, RL/MIF, 4" 385.00
Bottle, scent; Ambre Antique, for Coty, brn wash, RL, 6" 1,200.00
Bottle, scent; Coeurs, 4-heart vial, RLF, 3¾", orig case................175.00
Bottle, scent; Deux Fleurs, fr, RLF, 3½".....................................400.00
Bottle, scent; Enfants, band of figures, bl wash on fr, RLF 800.00
Bottle, scent; for Nina Ricci, disk form, ball stopper, 8" 230.00
Bottle, scent; L'Or, patinated stopper, for Coty, w/box, 3" 1,100.00
Bottle, scent; Le Parfum, blk enamel, for Forvil, RLF, 7" 800.00
Bottle, scent; Roses, cl/fr, ftd, stopper, LF, 6" 700.00
Bottle, scent; Dans la Nuit, dk bl washed w/emb stars, 3" 600.00

Bowl, Chiens #1, dogs/leafage, ftd, RLF, 9½" 900.00
Bowl, Coquilles, scalloped shell, opal, RLF, 5" 165.00
Bowl, Dahlias, opal, RLF, 9½"..880.00
Bowl, Dauphins, fish/waves, opal, RLF, 9½".................................900.00
Bowl, formed as if from lg leaves, fr, LF, 3¾x8" L 150.00
Bowl, Gui, mistletoe, cl w/gray wash, berry ft, RL, 8"...................300.00
Bowl, Nemours, blk-centered flowers, amber wash, RLF, 10".. 1,000.00
Bowl, peacock feathers, opal, RLF, ca 1925, 10" 900.00
Bowl, Volubilis, 3 flowers form ft, RL/etched F, 8½"....................880.00
Box, Clones, beetles, opal, 6½"... 1,850.00
Box, Coq, rooster/wheat, blk, sgn L, 4" dia, in orig box.......... 6,600.00
Box, Coq, rooster/wheat, blk, sgn L, 4" dia, no box 4,000.00
Box, Roger, cl, molded L, 5½" dia..880.00
Brooch, Sauterelles, gr, sgn L, 3¼" 5,500.00
Carafe, Pouilly, +6 glasses, patinated, RLF............................. 1,100.00
Chandelier, Charmes, cl/fr, bowl form w/4 chains, RL, 14" 2,750.00
Clock, Morneaux, lovebirds, cl/fr, dome top, 7x9" 2,450.00
Clock, pendulet; Naiads, nudes, opal, RL, 4½" sq.................... 2,250.00
Collector plate, 1965 .... 1,000.00
Collector plate, 1966 ....325.00
Collector plate, 1967 ....200.00
Collector plate, 1968 ....100.00
Collector plate, 1969 ....100.00
Collector plate, 1970 ....80.00
Collector plate, 1971 ....80.00
Collector plate, 1972 ....75.00
Collector plate, 1973 ....100.00
Collector plate, 1974 ....100.00
Collector plate, 1975 ....100.00
Collector plate, 1976 ....150.00
Figurine, Hirondelles, flying birds, cl/fr, RL, 12" 2,500.00
Figurine, nude girl w/goat, LF, 4" 300.00
Figurine, Thais, nude w/drapery, amber, RL, 8x9" 7,500.00
Inkwell, Serpents, entwined snakes, fr, RL, 6" dia 3,250.00
Mascot, Chrysis, kneeling nude bends bkward, fr, RLF, 5" 3,700.00
Mascot, Falcon, cl/fr, RL/#1124, 6"..935.00
Mascot, rooster, cl/fr, RLF/#1133, 8" 660.00
Menu holder, lovebirds, cl/fr, RL, ca 1925................................225.00
Paperweight, Tete D'Aigle, eagle head, amber, RL, 4½" 1,100.00
Pendant, Lys, amber, eng L, 2" L...600.00
Pitcher, orangeade; Blidah, cl/fr, sgn, 8".................................. 1,295.00
Plate, Chiens, hunting dog, patinated, eng L, 8" 550.00
Toilet set, Epines, bl patina, atomizer+3 bottles, RL 1,300.00
Vase, Ajaccio, band of ibex/floral ground, gr wash, RLF, 8" 1,600.00
Vase, Archers, fr, ovoid, no mk, ca 1932, 10" 4,100.00
Vase, Avallon, grapevines/birds, fr, cylindrical, LF, 6" 650.00
Vase, Bacchantes, nudes, fr, tumbler form, RLF, 10x8" 3,000.00
Vase, Bacchantes, nudes, fr/brn wash, L/Cristal/F, 9½" 3,500.00
Vase, Bacchus, fr/polished, RLF, 7" 1,100.00
Vase, Beautrelillis, jeweled base, gray wash, RLF, 6x7"............ 1,500.00
Vase, Bellis, patinated opal, RLF, 5¾" 1,100.00
Vase, body formed by 2 doves, fr, LF/label, 8" 325.00
Vase, Camaret, stylized fish, fr, bulbous, RLF/#d, 5" 800.00
Vase, Caudebec, oversz flower-emb hdls w/bl wash, RL, 6"..........700.00
Vase, Ceylon, lovebirds, fr/gray patina, RLF, 9½" 3,300.00
Vase, Ceylon, 4 prs lovebirds, opal, RLF/#d, 9½"..................... 3,500.00
Vase, Druides, mistletoe, gr opal, RLF/#d, 7¾x7½" 2,250.00
Vase, Escargot, snail shell mold, opal w/bl wash, RLF, 8½" 2,200.00
Vase, Font-Romeu, 12 notched spears, cl/fr, RLF, 8½" 1,045.00
Vase, Grizes, birds/branches, cl/fr, cylindrical, RLF, 7" 880.00
Vase, Gros Scarabees, beetles, amber, spherical, RL, 11½".....13,200.00
Vase, Ibis, fr/patinated, RLF, 9" 1,100.00
Vase, Laiterons, leaves, pnt on tan wash, ovoid, RLF, 3¼"....... 1,925.00
Vase, Lievres, band of rabbits w/blk wash on opal, RL, 6" 1,400.00

Vase, Milan, notched leaves, gr fr, bulbous, RLF, 11", NM ...**12,100.00**
Vase, Mon Naie du Pape, leafage, opal, cylindrical, RLF, 9" ... **4,400.00**
Vase, Ormeaux, elm leaves, bl wash, spherical, RLF, 6" **1,300.00**
Vase, Ormeaux, elm leaves, opal cased, RLF/#984, 6¾" **1,300.00**
Vase, Oursin, as sea urchin, cl/fr w/bl, spherical, RLF, 7" **1,100.00**
Vase, Poissons, lg fish, dk gr, spherical, RL, 9½" **20,900.00**
Vase, Rampillon, leaves/dmn shapes, fr, RLF, 5" **1,200.00**
Vase, Ronces, briars, opal, unsgn, 9½" **1,650.00**
Vase, Saint-Francois, high-relief buds, cl/fr, RL, 7" **825.00**
Vase, Serpent, coiled snake, amber, bulbous, RL, 10".............**17,600.00**
Vase, stylized fern fronds, cl/fr, spherical, RLF, 7" **425.00**
Vase, 3 grapevine-relief bands, cl, bulbous, RL, 5" **700.00**

Lamps

The earliest lamps were simple dish containers with a wick that hung over the edge or was supported by a channel or tube. Grease and oil from animal or vegetable sources were the first fuels used. Ancient pottery lamps, crusie, and Betty lamps are examples of these early types. In 1784 Swiss inventor Ami Argand introduced the first major improvement in lamps. His lamp featured a tubular wick and a glass chimney. During the first half of the 19th century, whale oil, burning fluid (a highly explosive mixture of turpentine and alcohol), and lard were the most common fuels used in North America. Many lamps were patented for specific use with these fuels.

Kerosene was the first major breakthrough in lighting fuels. It was demonstrated by Canadian geologist Dr. Abraham Gesner in 1846. The discovery and drilling of petroleum in the late 1850s provided an abundant and inexpensive supply of kerosene. It became the main source of light for homes during the balance of the 19th century and for remote locations until the 1950s.

Although Thomas A. Edison invented the electric lamp in 1879, it was not until two or three decades later that electric lamps replaced kerosene household lamps. Millions of kerosene lamps were made for every purpose and pocketbook. They ranged in size from tiny night or miniature lamps to tall stand or piano lamps. Hanging varieties for homes commonly had one or two fonts (oil containers), but chandeliers for churches and public buildings often had six or more. Wall or bracket lamps usually had silvered reflectors. Student lamps, parlor lamps (now called Gone-with-the-Wind lamps), and patterned glass lamps were designed to complement the popular furnishing trends of the day. The Angle Lamp Company of New York City developed a unique type of kerosene lamp that was a vast improvement over those already on the market; they were sold from about 1889 until 1929 and were expensive for their time. From about 1910 Aladdin lamps with a mantle became the mainstay of rural America, providing light that compared favorably with the electric light bulb. Gaslight, introduced in the early 19th century, was used mainly in homes of the wealthy and public places until the early 20th century. Most fixtures were wall or ceiling mounted, although some table models were also used.

Few of the ordinary early electric lamps have survived. Many lamp manufacturers made the same or similar styles for either kerosene or electricity, sometimes for gas. Top-of-the-line lamps were made by Pairpoint, Phoenix, Tiffany, Bradley and Hubbard, and Handel. See also these specific sections.

Currently values of peg lamps are up by about 30% to 40%, and pattern glass lamps in some of the standard lines have jumped from 25% to 100%. When buying lamps that have been converted to electricity, inspect them very carefully for any damage that may have resulted from the alterations; such damage is very common, and when it does occur, the lamp's value may be lessened by as much as 50%.

For those seeking additional information on Aladdin Lamps, we recommend *Aladdin — The Magic Name in Lamps*; *Aladdin Electric*

Lamps; and *A Collector's Manual and Price Guide*, all written by our advisor for Aladdins, J. W. Courter; he is listed in the Directory under Illinois. Another of our lamp advisors is Ruth Osborne; she is listed under Ohio. See also specific manufacturers.

Key:
ac — acorn burner   nb — nutmeg burner
hb — hornet burner   Vb — P&A Victor burner

Aladdin Lamps

Aladdin lamp B-25, original 14" Whip-O-Lite shade, NM, $450.00.

Bed, #2305SS, whip-o-lite flocked & fluted shade, electric, EX ..**125.00**
Bedroom, P-54, ceramic, electric, NM **30.00**
Bedroom, P-68, ceramic, electric, EX **20.00**
Beehive, B-83, ruby crystal, NM **310.00**
Boudoir, G-22, alacite, electric, 1952, EX..**50.00**
Boudoir, G-24, Cupid, alacite, electric, NM...................................**125.00**
Boudoir, G-32, moonstone, electric, 1935, EX **50.00**
Boudoir, G-48, alacite, raised leaf, electric, 1951, EX.....................**35.00**
Boudoir, M-158, metal, electric, EX...**35.00**
Bracket, #12, 4-arm, complete w/burner, EX **135.00**
Bridge, #7072, swing arm, reflector, electric, NM **175.00**
Bridge, B-131, electric, EX..**150.00**
Caboose, #23, complete w/shade, EX **50.00**
Cathedral, #109, amber crystal, EX..**80.00**
Cathedral, B-112, rose moonstone, EX...**200.00**
Contemporary, M-454, ceramic w/metal base, electric, NM..........**20.00**
Contemporary, M-475, ceramic, blk iron base, electric, EX **20.00**
Corinthian, B-101, amber crystal, NM **70.00**
Corinthian, B-124, wht moonstone font, gr moonstone ft, EX....**165.00**
Desk, G-202, alacite, electric, EX **110.00**
Figural, G-16, Lady, alacite, electric, EX **300.00**
Figural, G-24, Cupid, tall base, electric, NM **125.00**
Floor, #1005, MOP glass bowl, electric, EX..................................**250.00**
Floor, #1255, w/shade, EX **125.00**
Floor, #3348-B, electric, NM **125.00**
Floor, torchier; #3761, electric, EX..**225.00**
Florentine, #1220, gr moonstone, 8½", EX **1,175.00**
Hanging, #12, w/plain glass shade, kerosene, EX..........................**250.00**
Hanging, #2, w/#203 shade, EX **400.00**
Lincoln Drape, Short; B-61, amber crystal, EX **1,400.00**
Lincoln Drape, Tall; B-75, alacite, scallop ft, EX **300.00**
Lounge, #1050, candle arms, swan base, electric, NM **210.00**
Majestic, B-121, rose moonstone, NM...**275.00**

Orientale, B-130, ivory, EX 100.00
Orientale, B-132, rose gold, NM 200.00
Pin-up, G-355C, Hoppy Gun in Holster, alacite, electric, EX 150.00
Queen, B-96, wht moonstone, NM 310.00
Queen, B-98, rose moonstone, EX 325.00
Quilt, B-85, wht moonstone, NM 230.00
Quilt, B-90, wht moonstone font, blk moonstone ft, EX 240.00
Ranch house, G-378C, alacite, illuminated urn, electric, EX 170.00
Simplicity, B-27, alacite w/gold lustre, EX 200.00
Simplicity, B-29, gr, EX 90.00
Table, #1, complete w/burner, NM 500.00
Table, #21C, brass font, complete w/burner, EX 70.00
Table, #7, compete w/burner, EX 225.00
Table, E-203, Vogue Pedestal, orange, electric, EX 350.00
Table, E-302, Vogue Vase, peach, electric, EX 275.00
Table, G-12, moonstone, electric, EX 150.00
Table, G-140, moonstone, electric, EX 60.00
Table, G-167, moonstone, electric, EX 75.00
Table, G-300, alacite, tall harp, electric, EX 40.00
Table, G-84, Velvex, electric, EX 350.00
Table, M-1, bronze, electric, NM 85.00
Table, P-427, ceramic, electric, EX 30.00
Table, P-438, ceramic, electric, EX 25.00
Touch, MT-518, Genie, ceramic base, electric, NM 350.00
Treasure, B-137, bronze, EX 110.00
TV, #384, Shell, ceramic, electric, EX 35.00
TV, M-469, metal w/shade, electric, NM 20.00
Urn, G-375, Dancing Ladies, alacite, electric, NM 700.00
Urn, G-378C, Hoppy Bullet, alacite, electric, EX 170.00
Venetian, A-100, wht, EX 80.00
Vertique, B-87, rose moonstone, EX 290.00
Vertique, B-92, gr moonstone, EX 200.00
Victoria, B-25, china w/decor, EX 350.00
Washington Drape, B-41, amber crystal, rnd base, EX 90.00
Washington Drape, B-48, gr crystal, bell stem, EX 220.00
Washington Drape, B-51, gr crystal, filigree stem, NM 100.00
Washington Drape, B-54, gr crystal, plain stem, EX 75.00

Angle Lamps

Angle lamp, embossed grape design, etched elbows, colored chimneys, very rare. (Value with plain white chimneys and clear elbows, $600.00.)

Hanging, dbl, plain can, polished brass 275.00
Hanging, 4-burner, emb fleur-de-lis, antique copper finish 975.00

Wall, dbl, emb grapes, antique brass 875.00
Wall, emb grapes, nickel finish 275.00
Wall, plain can, nickel finish 125.00

Chandeliers

Brass, brass swags/glass beads, 22x20" 525.00
Brass, 4-arm, portraits on 15" milk glass shades, EX 675.00
Brass, 4-arm, Steuben shades, 13" dia ceiling plate, 28" L..........985.00
Brass, 8-lite (4 gas/4 electric), 4 ribbed opal shades, 47" 1,550.00
CI, 4-arm, clear fonts, #2 burners, pearl-top chimneys, EX..........450.00
Crystal, 9-arm, prisms/beads on gilt fr, 18½" dia 400.00
Crystal beads/ormolu, Louis XVI style, 18" 1,700.00
Cut crystal, 35-lite, faceted bead drapes, Rococo, 50"............ 1,200.00
Gilt bronze, Empire style, 8-lite, scrolls, 1800s, 21" H 2,600.00
Ormolu, 15 scroll/flower branches, female busts, 54" 5,800.00

Decorated Kerosene Lamps

Cranberry flashed w/eng vintage, marble base, 11" 400.00
Cut o/l, bl/wht/clear, dbl marble base 1,200.00
Cut o/l, cranberry/clear, milk glass stem, gold trim, 10" 275.00
Cut o/l, red/wht/clear, opal base w/gilt, 14", EX 900.00
Cut o/l, wht/cranberry, marble base, brass stem/collar, 11" 400.00
Lime gr frost w/HP florals, metal base, 17¼" 500.00
O/l (red/wht marbleized), clear/frosted acid cut-bk shade, 18".....495.00
Ruby stain cut to clear, brass stem, marble base, 18" 800.00
Wht w/red & bl loops, flat hand.. 1,625.00

Fairy Lamps

Aqua Dmn Quilt, orig Clarke porc insert, brass hdl 225.00
Bl Dmn Quilt MOP, Clarke's...Cricklite, 7" 675.00
Bl Dmn Quilt MOP, mk Clarke pressed glass base, 4¾x3⅞".......195.00
Bl frost, clear & wht stripes, emb ribs, Clarke base, 4¾" 195.00
Bl frost to clear, HP florals w/gold, Clarke base, 5¾" 195.00
Bl opal, emb ribs, mk Clarke base, 3¾x2⅞" 85.00
Bl opaque, emb beading, clear Clarke base, 5¼x2⅞"...............110.00
Bl Swirl MOP, ruffled base, 5⅛x5¼" 450.00
Bl verre moire, wht loopings, Clarke cup, 3⅝x5¾" 400.00
Burmese, HP florals, clear base mk Will of Wisp, 4" 265.00
Burmese, no decor, mk Clarke base, 3½" 160.00
Burmese, ruffled base, Clarke insert, mk Pat, 5½" 1,100.00
Burmese, Webb, clear mk Clarke base, 3¾x2⅞" 250.00
Canary yel satin, ruffled shade & base, 6", M 595.00
Chartreuse frost, clear & wht swirls, Clarke base, 4½x4" 195.00
Clear opal overshot, crown figural, mk Clarke base, 4⅜" 175.00
Cranberry overshot, crown figural, Clarke base, 4½x3" 195.00
Cranberry overshot, crown figural for 1887 Jubilee, 4½".............225.00
Cranberry verre moire, Clarke insert, 5½x6½" 495.00
Cranberry verre moire, pyramid sz, 3¾x2¾" 165.00
Cranberry w/mica & irregular gr threading, Clarke base, 3¾"......145.00
Gr spangle (similar to silveria), clear Clarke base, 3¾" 145.00
Nailsea, bl w/wht loops, tricorner base, 7x8" 775.00
Nailsea, pk w/wht loops, Clarke base in cranberry/clear fr, 4".....335.00
Orange frost w/clear swirls; gold-wash metal stand, 4½" 275.00
Peachblow, mc leaves, Webb, clear Clarke cup, 4¾" 500.00
Pk, gold, & wht spatter, emb ribs, 3-part, 5⅜x4¼" 395.00
Pk Dmn Quilt MOP, matching cup base, 4⅞x3½" 345.00
Rose Dmn Quilt MOP, clear mk Clarke base, 3½x3"................145.00
Rose Dmn Quilt MOP, mk Clarke base, 3¾x2⅞" 145.00
Sapphire frost, Drape, clear Clarke base, 4¾x4" 150.00
Teal bl & wht swirl o/l, emb swirl, Clarke base, 4⅞" 195.00
Vaseline frost w/emb puffy Dmn Quilt, Clarke base, 4" 125.00

Wht frosted verre moire, clear mk Clarke base, 4⅜x4" 165.00
Wht opal overshot, crown figural, Clarke base, 4½x3" 195.00
Wht satin emb swirl, rose lining, matching cup base, 4¾" 325.00
Yel satin, lacy blk garlands, Webb; gold metal stand, 5" 295.00
Yel satin w/emb swirled ribs on dome shade & can base, 3½" 200.00

Gone-with-the-Wind and Banquet

Bow Tie & moth etched on frost, adjustable, mk Gladstone 275.00
Florals emb on pk satin; brass base, 26" 1,470.00
Milk glass pnt gr w/pk & wht carnations; Handel base, 19" 800.00
Optic Panels on cranberry, Kosmos Brenner burner, 25" 250.00
Roses emb on clear satin, electrified, 24" 645.00
Windmills & sailboats, bl on wht, Parker, 29" 995.00
Wreath Pillar & Pebble on red satin, drop-in font, 25½" 850.00

Hanging Lamps

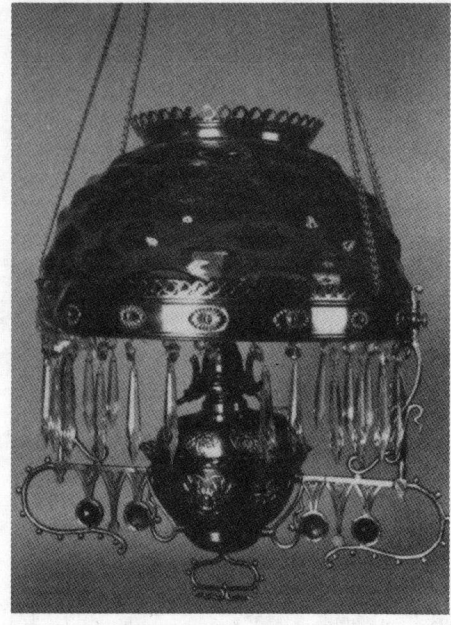

Parlor lamp, cranberry thumbprint shade, red brass frame, $1,000.00.

Larkin, lg roses on shade/font shell; brass fr w/fringe 275.00
Milk glass shade/ribbed font; counterbalance brass fr 250.00
Parlor, pnt scenic on milk glass shade, clear font; brass fr 275.00
Pk shaded to clear opal; brass fr, EX 250.00
Ribbed, cranberry 7½" shade; brass fr, EX....................................185.00
Sailing scene HP on milk glass 16" shade; brass fr, VG 260.00

Lanterns

Barn, mortised pine fr, triangular, 11", VG...................................175.00
Barn, wood fr, tin top/bottom, 4 glass sides, 13½", EX 275.00
Brass, sq w/3 red glass sides, 1800s, 6½" 70.00
Campaign, pierced tin w/colored glass sides, wrought fr, pr 175.00
Camping, tin, mk Stonebridge Folding...Nov 20 1906, 10", G 60.00
Candle, tin, 3-corner shape w/turret top, 18½", VG 235.00
Dietz, Buggy, bulbous, Pat 1904-1908-1914, 7½" 66.00
Dietz & Smith, Pat Mar 1864, 10", EX...70.00
Dietz #10 Brass Tubular, polished brass, 9½" 70.00
Dietz #13 Satellite, unpnt tin, brass cap/top, bail hdl, 12" 100.00
Dietz #7-G Ship & Lake Shore, unpnt tin, gr globe, 12", VG 100.00
Dietz #8 Gem, Pat Jan 28 1868, kerosene model, VG 80.00
Dietz #9 Champion, burner mk Dietz & Smith, 11" 80.00
Dietz Crystal emb on tin & on glass font, Fitall on globe 130.00
Dietz Dmn, brass w/clear globe, 7¾" 95.00

Dietz Farm, unpnt tin, sq w/convex burner, 10", VG 150.00
Dietz Little Star, NP brass, globe emb US Tublar...........................75.00
Dietz Navy Standard Deck, dtd '08, cobalt globe, 11" 175.00
Dietz Pocket Pat Sept 7th 1875, litho of man/newspaper, 6" 180.00
Dietz Racket, brass w/clear globe, 8" 65.00
Isinglass & iron, conical hood/cylinder body, 15" 155.00
Policeman's, tin, ca mid-1600s, 6", EX...50.00
Ribbed onion font w/tin hdl, twin-tube burner, 13½", EX...........150.00
Ship's, tin w/removable fonts, red reflector, 10¼", pr 80.00
Skater's, brass w/clear globe, emb Baby, 4½" 500.00
Skater's, brass w/clear globe, high ft, 7", NM 175.00
Skater's, brass w/sandy ruby globe, 7", EX 225.00
Skater's, Dietz Boy NY USA emb on brass font, 6" 195.00
Tin, glass globe, imp J Fleming, 10" 80.00
Tin, punched cylinder, hinged door, removable base, pnt, 11" 260.00
Tin, punched cylinder, 3 openings w/glass, hinged door, 12".......225.00
Tin, punched cylinder w/cone top, rpr ring hdl, pnt, 12" 185.00
Tin, punched half-cylinder, open front, crimped hood, 14" 425.00
Tin, punched pyramid top, 4 sides glass, Parker's Pat, 7" 140.00
Tin w/pressed glass globe, blk pnt, ring hdl, 11" 275.00
Tin w/shield-shaped cutouts over glass, 4-sided, 8", EX................75.00

Lard Oil/Grease

Betty, iron, brass heart finial mk 1848 (split), 4½" 375.00
Betty, iron, open font, hanger, simple...125.00
Betty, iron, tooled/sgn JS/1835/#106 (Schmidt), 5½" 1,700.00
Betty, pnt iron, X-hammer mk on brass finial, rpl latch, 4½" 125.00
Betty, tin, tray-like base, Ipswich, 11¾", EX.................................275.00
Crusie, dbl, wrought, ram horn finial, pitted, 6½" 325.00
Kettle, brass, heavy iron gimbal hanger, 6½" 200.00
Kettle, brass, in harp support, 3-leg ft eng FMO 1857, 7" 115.00
Kettle, iron, cylinder font w/uneven plating, 8¾" 225.00
Kettle, iron w/brass gimbal font, 4-ftd base, 7" 525.00
Pan, iron, hanging, orig sawtooth trammel, 27½" 350.00
Pan, iron, twisted hanger, 1700s, 20" 200.00
Pan (triangular), iron, hanging, sawtooth trammel, 28"...............425.00
Rush, iron, candle socket counterbalance, rpr, 8" 300.00
Rush, iron, candle socket counterbalance, 7¾" 325.00
Rush, iron, scrolled counterbalance, 3 slipper ft, 11" 325.00
Rush, iron, socket counterbalance, 3-leg crown base, 10" 500.00
Rush, iron, twist stem, wood base, 8¾" 125.00
Tin, cylinder font, tall stem, saucer base, chain w/pick, 8" 100.00

Miniature Lamps, Kerosene

Amber Picket, finger lamp, nb, 3½", NM 150.00
Amber w/emb fishscales, stem lamp, disk base, nb, 5" 95.00
Artichoke, lav & gr on milk glass, nb, 8", EX 200.00
Artichoke, pk satin, nb, 7⅜", EX 600.00
Bl, emb swirl rib & 'Sun Light,' finger lamp w/tin base, 3".............75.00
Bl, stem lamp, 4-lobed w/emb rings, scalloped base, ab, 5" 100.00
Bl opaque w/floral decal, ball shade/can base, rpl/b, 8½".............400.00
Bl w/swirl-emb font on brass stem & ft, nb, 4½" 65.00
Bl Waffle, stem lamp, nb, 4½" 90.00
Bl-gr font on brass saucer, finger lamp, ab, 2⅞" 175.00
Brass font w/NP reflector, ab, 5½", pr 100.00
Capo-di-Monte, owl figure on log, glass eyes, rpl/b, 5" 7,250.00
Chimney only, cranberry w/emb swirls, 6"....................................350.00
Cobalt Little Duchess font on brass saucer, ab, 2⅛", EX 205.00
Cranberry, clear shell ft, umbrella top/ovoid base, 9", EX 375.00
Cranberry w/beaded swirl, sm top/wide base, hb, 8" 200.00
Cranberry w/emb swirl, ball top/bottom, nb, 6", NM...................425.00
Cranberry-flashed w/beaded swirls, sm top/wide base, hb, 9" 70.00

Cranberry in diamond pattern, applied clear feet, acorn burner dated 1877, 9", $1,000.00.

Dbl Acorn, pnt milk glass; Pat Jan 1872 Aug 1875, 10¼" **4,250.00**
Dk amber w/appl hdl, finger lamp, hb, 3"................................**95.00**
Emerald gr, ball shade & base w/gold flowers & trim, hb, 9".......**200.00**
Gothic Arch, gold/gr trim, ball top/can base, ab, 7", EX.............**100.00**
Gothic Arch, wht w/gr pnt, mug form w/chimney, ab, 7¾" **150.00**
Gr Bull's Eye, stem lamp, ab, 4¾", pr.....................................**160.00**
Gr opaque w/emb flowers & netting, ball shade/base, nb, 8".......**300.00**
Gr w/Beaded Heart, stem lamp, ab, 5½"...................................**350.00**
Gr w/emb floral, stem lamp, ab, 5⅜", EX.................................**100.00**
Little Buttercup, bl, finger lamp, ab, 2¾".................................**175.00**
Little Buttercup, dk amethyst, finger lamp, ab, 2¾" **70.00**
Milk glass, emb daisies, balls around base, rare **395.00**
Milk glass w/aqua trim, paneled, sm ball top/vase bottom, 6½" ...**175.00**
Milk glass w/emb flowers, umbrella top/jar-like base, 7".............**200.00**
Owl face in 3-color pnt on wht ball shade, body on base, 8" ... **1,200.00**
Pineapple in Basket, milk glass w/brn pnt, 7" **400.00**
Pk cased satin, puffed Dmn Quilt, umbrella shade, nb, 8"...........**450.00**
Pk cased/shiny, emb lappets on shade/sqd-off base, nb, 7" **105.00**
Porc base/wht glass ball shade, gr w/romantic decal, Vb, 9".........**275.00**
Quilted amberina w/clear base petals, ball top/can base, 9" **250.00**
Red satin w/emb plumes, ball shade, shaped base, nb, 8¾" **500.00**
Santa Claus, EX **2,700.00**
Skeleton, bsk, gr eyes, NM... **7,000.00**
Twinkle, amethyst, ball top/onion base, ab, 7", NM **225.00**
Wht w/emb flowers, pk/bl/yel pnt, ball top/flared base, 8" **125.00**
Wht w/pk+bl+yel & emb flowers, ball top/flared base, nb, 9"......**125.00**
Wht w/yel & pk pnt, emb swirls/acanthus, ball top/base, 8" **175.00**
Yel cased shade w/gold fleur-de-lis, iron scroll legs, 11" **400.00**
Yel cased w/dmn puffs, umbrella top/ball bottom, 8", NM...........**625.00**
Yel Raindrop MOP, ruffled 4-lobe bowl top/ftd base, 8", EX **600.00**

Pattern Glass Lamps

Apollo, bl, #1 burner, stem lamp, 8" **175.00**
Aquarius, lt bl, stand lamp, 10"..**110.00**
Aquarius, vaseline, ftd finger lamp, 4¾", NM..................................**130.00**
Atterbury Loop, clear font/milk glass stem & ft, 9" **100.00**
Bloxam, bl & wht spatter font, clear stem & ft, 7½" **300.00**
Bull's Eye, emerald, ftd finger lamp, safety hdl, 5½" **150.00**
Cable in Ring, Atlantic Cable commemorative, 1860s, 4⅛" **125.00**
Canadian Drape, stand lamp, 7½"...**75.00**
Coolidge Drape, cobalt, finger lamp, 6", EX **275.00**
Daisy & Button Panel, med bl, ftd finger lamp, w/hdl, 5" **125.00**
Dmn Base (Fostoria), cobalt font/clear ft & hdl, 5¾", EX............**450.00**

Dmn w/Oval Window, pewter collar, 2-tube burner, 8¾"............**300.00**
Empress, gr, finger lamp, 5¼", EX **125.00**
Erin Fan, emerald gr, ftd finger lamp, 5", pr **175.00**
Eyebrows, finger lamp, 5¼"..**70.00**
Frosted Artichoke, finger lamp, EX..**65.00**
Hobb's Snowflake, bl, finger lamp, 3" **60.00**
Invt Dmn & T'print, flint, hexagonal base, 10½", EX **125.00**
Lyre, finger lamp, pewter 2-tube burner, 4" **250.00**
Moon & Star, hand lamp, early, 3⅞"..**180.00**
Princess Feather, apple gr, stem lamp, #2, 9½" **135.00**
Princess Feather, bl, stem lamp, 10", NM **135.00**
Princess Feather, cobalt, stem lamp, 8½", EX...............................**225.00**
Princess Feather, orange satin on clear stem & ft, #2, 9½" **750.00**
Prisms w/Plain Band, milk glass, #1 Queen Anne burner, 3½" **95.00**
Sheldon Swirl, clear opal, clear stem/ft, #1, 7¾", EX **200.00**
Sheldon Swirl, clear opal, stem lamp, 8", EX................................**200.00**
Sheldon Swirl, cranberry opal, clear stem/ft, 7¾", NM **400.00**
Sheldon Swirl, vaseline opal, clear stem/ft, #1, 9" **350.00**
Shield & Star font on milk glass stem & ft, 8½" **95.00**
Snowflake, bl opal, flat finger lamp...**375.00**
Snowflake, cranberry opal w/gold, #2 burner, stem lamp, 9⅛".....**450.00**
Wild Rose, clear font on caramel slag base, 8" **300.00**
Windows, cranberry opal, oil burner, 10" **450.00**
Zippered Loop, finger lamp, 4¾" **68.00**

Peg Lamps

Bl Dmn Quilt MOP, brass ped base, 10½", EX **325.00**
Bl Dmn Quilt MOP, ruffled shade, brass base, complete, 12".. **1,020.00**
Bl Swirl MOP, ruffled shade, 16½" **750.00**
Cranberry w/optic ribs, onion form, on 11" brass sticks, pr **335.00**
Dmn Quilt, pk o/l, brass fr w/sq base, complete, 14½"..................**700.00**
Rainbow Dmn Quilt MOP, 6x3⅝"...**825.00**
Ruby to clear o/l w/gold, 2-tube fluid burner, lt wear **275.00**
Swirled fonts, brass kero burners, 6½", pr **190.00**
Yel o/l, mushroom shade, brass candlestick, 15" **525.00**

Reverse-Painted Lamps

Reverse-painted scenic shade attributed to Pittsburgh, 16" diameter, $1,200.00.

Cottage scene 16" shade; leaf-mold base, Jefferson, 21" **800.00**
Lighthouse/birds 16" pebbly shade; Jefferson, 21", EX **600.00**
Mtn scene on 14" sgn Jefferson shade; slim 2-lite base, EX **800.00**
River scene on 14" shade; Aladdin metal base, Jefferson **800.00**
Scenic 16" dome shade; pnt metal std w/HP glass inserts.............**465.00**

Swans/trees on 16" chipped ice shade; leaf-cast std, 21" **2,200.00**
Village pastoral scene on 14" shade; sgn Pittsburgh std **1,900.00**
Water/sailboats on 19" Handel-style shade; pnt ribbed std **550.00**
Windmill w/metal squirrel-motif o/l on 16" shade; emb base.......**495.00**

Student Lamps, Kerosene

Brass, dbl, gr o/l wht-cased shades, 20" **400.00**
Brass, dbl, rpl wht shades, electrified, Kaiser, 22", pr...................**500.00**
Brass, milk glass shade, Kosmos Brenner, 18" **285.00**
Brass, vertical canister font, orig wht shade, 12" **455.00**
Brass, w/chimney & wht shade, Welsbk burner, 20", EX **175.00**
Brass, 10" gr cased shade, Manhattan Brass Co 1883, 23", EX **375.00**
Brass w/pk-pnt wht shade, mk Oct 28 '79, nb, 9½", EX...............**800.00**
Miller syphon-style, wht shade, cut/frosted font, NP, 21" **1,100.00**

Whale Oil/Burning Fluid

Acanthus Leaf, milky bl on clambroth std, Sandwich, 12", VG ..**300.00**
Atterbury Reed font, cranberry/wht, brass/marble base, 10" **1,200.00**
Blown, ball font on candlestick-form base, 11", NM...................**195.00**
Blown, elongated conical font on pressed base w/lg knop, 9".......**500.00**
Blown, panel-cut font, hollow stem, stepped base, chips, 11" **315.00**
Blown, pear font on 6-sided stem & floral-emb ft, 7", pr.............**275.00**
Blown, shouldered font on ribbed stem & stepped ft, 6½" **120.00**
B3m loop-emb shouldered font on 6-sided stem/ft, rpl/b, 6" **125.00**
Circle & Ellipse, canary font, hexagonal base, 9" **475.00**
Flint, bull's eye/fleur-de-lis font, scalloped base, 9", EX **145.00**
Flint w/smocking & bull's-eye dmn, orig tin insert, 9¾" **700.00**
Floral-cut cylindrical font, bronze stem on onyx ft, 10" **185.00**
O/l, pk cut to wht/clear w/butterflies, cut shade, Sandwich **2,900.00**
O/l, wht cut to cranberry w/grapes, metal/marble stem, 12".........**750.00**
Paneled salt-shaker form, 1-tube burner, 2½", pr.....................**100.00**
Paneled/shouldered font, 6-sided stem/ft, pewter mts, 5½" **200.00**
Petticoat, lyre/star, appl hdl, brass burner w/cap, 6¾" **285.00**
Plain font, stem & ft, brass collar, 2-tube burner, 6½" **125.00**
Ripley marriage, clear clambroth on wht base, 11½", NM **1,300.00**
Star & Punty, pewter collar, 2-tube burner, 8¾" **175.00**

Miscellaneous

Architect's, Emeralite, w/Daylite screen....................................**275.00**
Auto, tin, Dietz Beacon Dash Lamp NY USA, 13", VG **40.00**
Bracket, pressed/frosted fonts in ornate CI fr, pr........................**175.00**
Bracket, Wheeler Reflectory Co, fancy pressed font **150.00**
Brass font on sled runners, wht shade w/bl pnt, Pat 79, NM.... **1,125.00**
Dietz #2 tubular beach lamp, hinged side reflectors, rpt..............**225.00**
Dietz #3 globe street lamp, CI bracket, worn pnt, 25" **250.00**
Dietz #4 tubular wall lamp, triangular, rnd reflector, 22" **200.00**
Dietz #60 beacon light, pnt tin, lg reflector, 21"............................**250.00**
Dietz Bestov Hand Lamp, unpnt tin, lock-on chimney, 9".............**95.00**
Lacemaker's, blown, cut circles around font, 10"...........................**325.00**
Lacemaker's, cranberry Invt T'print shade, brass base, 17"...........**500.00**
Lacemaker's, cranberry overshot, brass base, kerosene, 16½".......**395.00**
Miner's, iron, chicken finial, wick pick, 8" **250.00**
Spice, brass, log pig-type mk Oct 28 '79, nb, 7"..............................**850.00**
Watch Pocket, NP brass, Folmer & (?) Mfg NY Pat 91, 2" dia **350.00**

Le Verre Francais

Le Verre Francais was produced during the 1920s by Schneider at Epinay-sur-Seine in France. It was a commercial art glass in the cameo style composed of layered glass with the designs engraved by acid.

Favored motifs were stylized leaves and flowers or geometric patterns. It was marked with the name in script or with an inlaid filigrane. Our advisor for this category is Don Williams; he is listed in the Directory under Missouri.

Chandelier, trumpet blossoms and buds, burgundy to brown on yellow and orange mottle, conical, 13", $2,800.00.

Cameo

Bowl, flower clusters, wine to rust on rust, bun ft, 13½" **2,000.00**
Chandelier, trumpet flowers on elongated cone shade, 13" H. **2,800.00**
Lamp, long leaves, gr to bl on tangerine shade/base, 12" **3,500.00**
Lamp, perfume; floral, purple-brn on peach, metal lid, 4" **1,000.00**
Lamp, roses, pk to gr on pk dome shade/base, 13"................... **3,500.00**
Lamp, sunflowers on shade/base, red/amethyst on pk, 14"....... **3,000.00**
Vase, balloon-type flowers, dk on lt bl, cushion base, 15" **1,800.00**
Vase, butterflies, red on bl/yel mottle, hdls, 17"...................... **2,700.00**
Vase, Deco floral, dk bl on lt bl & wht, ftd, 12½x5" **1,200.00**
Vase, Deco floral, mc on yel/rust, angular body, ftd, 18" **1,500.00**
Vase, exotic blossoms/berries vines, purple/pk on pk, 13" **1,700.00**
Vase, floral, purple on pk mottle, cylinder w/bun base, 14" **1,400.00**
Vase, floral, purple on pk mottle, ovoid w/bun base, 12" **1,100.00**
Vase, floral top, orange on lt gr, cylinder, Charder, 22" **3,000.00**
Vase, flower clusters, wine to red on rust ftd U-form, 12" **1,500.00**
Vase, garlands, orange on wht, baluster, sgn Charder, 14" **1,300.00**
Vase, geese, brn on yel mottle, wide shoulder, ftd, 19" **2,500.00**
Vase, geese, brns/bls on yel/amber mottle, ftd, 13¾"................ **1,500.00**
Vase, Japanese lanterns, brn/orange/yel, 16" **1,500.00**
Vase, long-stem flowers, wine on orange, bun base, 22" **1,650.00**
Vase, morning-glories, rust to bl on yel, goblet form, 16" **1,600.00**
Vase, roses/leafage, red/purple on gray mottle to turq, 16"....... **2,000.00**
Vase, swags, purple on pk/orange mottle, ftd urn form, 9½" **900.00**

Leeds, Leeds Type

The Leeds Pottery was established in 1758 in Yorkshire and under varied management produced fine creamware, often highly reticulated and transfer printed, shiny black-glazed Jackfield wares, polychromed pearlware, and figurines similar to those made in the Staffordshire area. Little of their early ware was marked; after 1775 the impressed 'Leeds Pottery' mark was used. From 1781 to 1820, the name 'Hartley Greens & Co.' was added. The pottery closed in 1898.

Today the term 'Leeds' has become generic and is used to encompass all polychromed pearlware and creamware, wherever its origin. Thus similar wares of other potters (Wood for instance) is often incorrectly called 'Leeds.' Unless a piece is marked or can be definitely attributed to Leeds by confirming the pattern to be authentic, 'Leeds-Type' would be a more accurate nomenclature.

Key:
sp — soft paste

Basket, creamware, lattice sides, 10", +undertray	150.00
Charger, sponged tree w/peafowl, bl feather edge, sp, 12"	900.00
Compote, bl Oriental motif, rtcl ft/oval bowl, mk, 11" L	800.00
Cradle, brn/bl/yel stippling on basketweave, 5" H	475.00
Creamer, bl Oriental motif, stains/sm flakes, 3½"	225.00
Creamer, 3-color floral, slim form, sm chips, 3⅝"	150.00
Creamer, 4-color decor, flakes/base chip, 3⅝"	125.00
Creamer, 4-color tulip, 3⅜", VG	500.00
Creamer, 5-color peafowl in tree, 4¼", EX	500.00
Mug, 4-color gaudy floral, emb leaf hdl, sp, 5", EX	285.00
Pitcher, farmers' tools/horse/cow/J Farr/1803, sp, 8", EX	2,600.00
Pitcher, 3-color, gaudy floral, emb leaf hdl, 7", EX	525.00
Pitcher, 4-color, gaudy floral, prof rpr/edge wear, 7½"	345.00
Pitcher, 5-color, sheaf/farm tools, rpr, 6⅝", VG	400.00
Plate, toddy; 5-color eagle/stars, gr feather edge, 5½"	800.00
Plate, 4-color floral, brn stripe on scalloped rim, 8", EX	150.00
Plate, 4-color gaudy swag/basket, bl feather edge, 9½", NM	345.00
Plate, 4-color simple gaudy floral, sp, 8½", EX	65.00
Plate, 5-color eagle, bl feather edge, pearlware, 7", NM	410.00
Plate, 5-color floral, gr feather edge, 8-sided, stains, 6½"	40.00
Plate, 5-color gaudy tulip, sp, 7", NM	325.00
Plate, 5-color peafowl/sponged tree, gr feather edge, 8", EX	400.00
Sugar bowl, 3-color gaudy floral, pearlware, 4½", VG	180.00
Tea bowl & saucer, 3-color gaudy floral, sp, EX	185.00
Tea bowl & saucer, 5-color gaudy floral, ribbed, sp, EX	235.00
Teapot, bl chinoiserie, flower finial, twist hdl, rpr, 5"	350.00
Teapot, bl chinoiserie, str sides, sp, rpr, 6¾"	500.00
Teapot, 5-color floral, sp, hairlines/edge chips, 6"	200.00
Teapot, 5-color gaudy floral, sm chips, mini, 4⅜"	750.00
Vase, quintal; bl/wht floral, 6¾", pr, EX	1,800.00
Vase, quintal; 4-color gaudy floral, prof rpr/chips, 7½"	275.00

Legras

Legras and Cie was founded in St. Denis, France, in 1864. Production continued until about 1914. In addition to their enameled wares, they made cameo art glass decorated with outdoor scenes and florals executed by acid cuttings through two to six layers of glass. Their work is signed 'Legras' in relief. Our advisor for this category is Don Williams; he is listed in the Directory under Missouri.

Cameo

Vase, grape leaves in burgundy, bottle form, 9"	500.00
Vase, grapevines, cut/pnt on gray, bulbous w/long neck, 16"	1,650.00
Vase, landscape, cut/pnt in fall colors, waisted, 4¼"	900.00
Vase, landscape, cvd/pnt on clear brn, 8"	450.00
Vase, leaves/berries, citron on orange to citron, 12"	1,400.00
Vase, leaves/berries, cut/pnt, orange on cream, 8"	750.00
Vase, leaves/vines, wine stain on textured frost, 8½"	550.00
Vase, maple branches/pods, triple o/l, flat-sided oval, 6½"	825.00
Vase, maple leaves/pods, gr on lt yel, pear form, 5"	330.00
Vase, mtns/trees, cvd/pnt, bl/gr on yel & orange, 8"	800.00
Vase, sailboat/mtns/lg trees, cut/pnt, 13"	1,200.00

Miscellaneous

Box, snowy trees/birds pnt on orange sky, cylindrical, 2¾"	750.00
Vase, band of scrolled design etched on wht/turq mottle, 6"	385.00
Vase, berry vine, etched/pnt on pk, bulbous rim, 26"	880.00
Vase, bluebird/reeds pnt on yel to orange, sgn Leg, 11", pr	770.00
Vase, floral, mc on coral to yel frost, sgn, 9"	275.00
Vase, flowers, bl/wht pnt on orange/yel mottle, 9"	500.00
Vase, orange mottled/cased, pnt interwoven foliage, 14"	700.00
Vase, Star of David medallion pnt on orange mottle, 14½"	825.00

Lenox

Walter Scott Lenox, former art director at Ott and Brewer, and Jonathan Coxon founded The Ceramic Art Company of Trenton, New Jersey, in 1889. By 1906 Coxon had left the company and to reflect the change in ownership, the name was changed to Lenox, Inc. Until 1930 when the production of American-made Belleek came to an end, they continued to produce the same type of high-quality ornamental wares that Lenox and Coxon had learned to master while in the employ of Ott and Brewer. Their superior dinnerware made the company famous, and since 1917 Lenox has been chosen the official White House China. Our advisor for this category is Mary Frank Gaston; she is listed in the Directory under Texas. See also Ceramic Art Company.

After dinner coffeepot, sugar and creamer, silver overlay, Belleek mark, $375.00.

Ash tray, gold ship, American Export 1960, 5½"	40.00
Bookends, Blk lady's torso, Deco, gr mk, pr	275.00
Bouillon set, Empress	45.00
Bowl, Collector's Club Fruit of Life, sculpted band, 9"	92.50
Bowl, fruit; Montclair	18.00
Bowl, Lotus Leaf, wht, shape #37	95.00
Bowl, vegetable; Lace Point, oval	50.00
Bowl, vegetable; Orchard, w/lid	70.00
Bowl, vegetable; Temple Blossom, oval	55.00
Bowl, wht ware, dragon hdls, Belleek mk, 13" dia	160.00
Cake plate, Orchard	40.00
Cake stand, Ming, low ped	75.00
Candlestick, wht ware, raised scalloped base, Belleek mk, pr	165.00
Coffee set, Blue Wreath, silver o/l, 3-pc	325.00
Coffeepot, floral garlands, silver o/l, Belleek mk, 11"	660.00
Creamer, Ming	60.00
Creamer & sugar bowl, Colonial, gold trim	95.00
Creamer & sugar bowl, Lace Point	75.00
Cup, Ming, blk mk	40.00
Cup, Terrace	15.00
Cup & saucer, Country Garden	40.00
Cup & saucer, demitasse; Engagement, wht	95.00
Cup & saucer, Fairfield	40.00
Cup & saucer, Montclair, old style	30.00
Cup & saucer, Temple Blossom	35.00

Cup & saucer, Tuxedo...40.00
Cup & saucer, Wyndcrest..35.00
Figurine, First Waltz, ltd ed, 1984............................125.00
Figurine, flapper's head, 4"..95.00
Figurine, Floradora, no decor...................................265.00
Figurine, seal on ledge, ivory, 6x4"..........................150.00
Figurine, vase, blue jay in tree, 5-color, ink stamp.....300.00
Lamp, boudoir; Deco lady w/hoop skirt & fan forms shade, 9".....265.00
Lamp, nude figural, 1929, 12½".................................800.00
Leaf dish, contemporary style, gold trim, 7½"..............50.00
Mug, bl florals w/gold, lily pads at rim/base, gold hdl.....55.00
Mug, grapes, mc on gr shaded, sgn, dtd 1914, 7x4".....110.00
Mug, Harvard College, 1910, gr mk, 5¼"...................125.00
Mug, HP berries & leaves, sgn, Belleek mk, 4½".........110.00
Pitcher, pk textured w/wht hdl, girl's mask spout, 7½".....110.00
Pitcher, silver o/l w/floral cameo, palette mk, 8".........500.00
Plate, bread & butter; Lace point...............................10.00
Plate, bread; Lenox Rose..20.00
Plate, dinner; Mystic..30.00
Plate, fuchsia border w/heavy silver o/l border, 10".....135.00
Plate, mallard duck among rushes, gold trim, sgn Nosek, 10".....175.00
Plate, Montclair, salad sz..15.00
Plate, salad; Caribee..20.00
Plate, salad; Country Garden....................................25.00
Plate, salad; Lenox Rose...20.00
Platter, Empress, lg..150.00
Platter, Lace Point, oval, 16".....................................80.00
Relish plate, dbl, leaf-emb rim & int, center hdl, 15½".....75.00
Salt cellar, swan figural, 24k gold palette mk, NM.........45.00
Shaker, talcum; HP roses (non-factory decor), Belleek mk, 6".....140.00
Shakers, Rhodora, pr...80.00
Swan, bl mk, 8½"...75.00
Swan, gold mk, 2"...25.00
Swan, wht ware, open, Belleek wreath mk, 1¾x2"..........35.00
Tea set, gold florals surround pastel roses, sgn/mk, 3-pc.....335.00
Tea set, Virginian, gold hdls, 11" pot, 3-pc................350.00
Teapot, gold bands, 1930s, 2x3"................................85.00
Teapot, Waldorf Astoria, pk w/silver bands, silver top, 1937.....95.00
Toby, William Penn, Indian hdl...............................225.00
Vase, bl-gray, wht int, platinum rim, 5½x6¾"...............50.00
Vase, bud, multiflorals on porc, 6".............................35.00
Vase, Empire, swan hdls, 1930 gr mk, 10½"..................85.00
Vase, floral cameos, silver o/l, Belleek mk, 10"...........550.00
Vase, portrait medallions/florals, gold rim, palette mk, 10".....350.00
Vase, portrait reserve, allover silver o/l, ftd, 9".........1,700.00
Vase, swan on lake on gr, gr palette mk, 12x9"............575.00
Vase, wht, urn form, claw ft, gr wreath mk, 9⅜".........250.00

Letter Openers

Made in a wide variety of materials and designs, letter openers make for an interesting collection that is easy to display and easy on the budget as well. Our advisor for this category is Ron Damaska; he is listed in the Directory under Pennsylvania.

Brass, lion hdl, Victorian...45.00
Brass, ship eng on hdl, 9"...22.50
Brass, Victor Evans, EX...12.00
Brass dagger, 9½", in red leather scabbard.................15.00
Bronze, Mechanics Savings Bank, Manchester NH.......18.00
Celluloid, relief violets & leaves w/some color, 10".......15.00
Chromed steel, Irwin Auger Bit, Wilmington, auger hdl.....25.00
Ivory, cvd to represent a dagger, Oriental, 12"............35.00

Ivory blade w/rosewood hdl, 7½", EX.........................50.00
Metal, arrowhead figural, Anaconda Copper & Brass, EX.....15.00
Metal, nail figural, AS&W Co....................................12.50
MOP, sterling hdl, 3"..7.50
Silverplate, figural horse head hdl, Reed & Barton.......85.00
Sterling, floral relief, Jacobi & Jenkins, 7"................125.00
Whalebone w/rosewood hdl, 7", EX............................75.00

Brass letter openers, Indian, 8¾"; Gargoyle, 9", $25.00 each.

Libbey

The New England Glass Company was established in 1818 in Boston, Massachusetts. In 1892 it became known as the Libbey Glass Company. At Chicago's Columbian Expo in 1893, Libbey set up a ten-pot furnace and made glass souvenirs. The display brought them worldwide fame. Between 1878 and 1918, Libbey made exquisite cut and faceted glass, considered today to be the best from the brilliant period. The company is credited for several innovations — the Owens bottle machine that made mass-production possible and the Westlake machine which turned out both electric light bulbs and tumblers automatically. They developed a machine to polish the rims of their tumblers in such a way that chipping was unlikely to occur. Their glassware carried the patented Safedge guarantee. Libbey also made glassware in numerous colors, among them cobalt, ruby, pink, green, and amber. In 1935 it was bought by Owens-Illinois and remains a division of that company. See also Amberina and other specific types.

Bowl, cut, lovebirds/wisteria, octagonal, 8"...............900.00
Bowl, cut, Russian Ambassador, 4½x11½"..................875.00
Bowl, fruit; cut, hobstars w/fan & dmn panels, sgn, 8½".....250.00
Claret, Lucerne, 5½"..14.00
Cocktail, kangaroo stem in opal................................110.00
Compote, amberina, hdls, ped ft w/ring under bowl, 5x6½".....1,050.00
Compote, amberina, Invt T'print, sgn, 4x6"................800.00
Compote, cut/eng florals, hollow stem, sq base, 6¼x5¼".....225.00
Creamer & sugar bowl (open), cut, lovebirds/wisteria, 3".....650.00
Decanter, cut amberina, Russian, no stopper, 7½".....1,100.00
Goblet, water; cat stem in opal................................125.00
Maize, bowl, gr husks, 8"..200.00
Maize, carafe, custard w/gold husks.........................300.00
Maize, celery vase, clear w/amber irid, bl husks, 6½".....200.00

Maize, celery vase, custard w/bl husks, 6½"....................................**165.00**
Maize, cruet, clear w/bl husks, maize stopper, rare......................**350.00**
Maize, pickle castor, custard w/gr husks, SP fr..........................**500.00**
Maize, pitcher, clear w/amber irid, bl husks, clear hdl, 9"...........**585.00**
Maize, pitcher, custard w/gr husks, strap hdl, 8½x5½".................**485.00**
Maize, shakers, custard w/bl husks, pr......................................**350.00**
Maize, sugar shaker, custard w/gold-traced yel husks, 6"..............**235.00**
Maize, syrup, clear, amber irid, bl husks, 6".............................**385.00**
Maize, syrup, custard w/gr husks, scarce, 6"..............................**350.00**
Maize, toothpick holder, custard w/gold-traced gr husks.............**400.00**
Maize, tumbler, custard w/gold-traced yel husks, bbl, 4¼".........**165.00**
Pickle castor, amberina swirl, sgn, ornate ftd fr........................**245.00**
Pitcher, cut, Buzz Star & Fan, rayed base, thumb-cut hdl, 8".......**250.00**
Pitcher, cut, Corinthian, 8½"...**390.00**
Pitcher, cut, Kingston, 13"...**550.00**
Pitcher, cut, Kingston, 9"..**395.00**
Pitcher, cut amberina, Russian, tapered cylinder, 12", EX......**2,000.00**
Plate, cut, Kimberly, 7"...**190.00**
Punch bowl, cut, hobstars/thistles/fans, on stand, 10" dia...........**800.00**
Punch bowl, cut, strawbery dmn/hobstar & fan, sgn, +24 cups..**1,000.00**
Vase, allover brilliant cut, faceted neck ring, 8x12"..............**1,500.00**
Vase, amberina, ribbed, ruffled, ftd trumpet form, 11"...........**1,500.00**
Vase, amberina, scalloped/flared, 4½x5"...............................**525.00**
Vase, cut, ferns & bull's eyes, sawtooth rim, 1905 mk, 5½".......**150.00**
Vase, cut, hobstars/hobnails, 2 lg notch-cut hdls, sgn, 18"......**2,800.00**
Vase, flower center; cut, Empress, no mk, 7x12"...................**1,050.00**
Vase, frosted intaglio thistles, serrated rim, ftd, mk, 12"..........**395.00**
Vase, intaglio florals, 3-fold rim, 5".......................................**400.00**

Compote, opalescent elephant stem, signed, rare, 11" diameter,
$550.00.

Limited Edition Plates

Currently, values of some limited edition plates have risen dramatically while others have drastically fallen. Prices charged by plate dealers in the secondary market vary greatly; we have tried to suggest an average.

Bing and Grondahl

1895, Behind the Frozen Window......................................**5,500.00**
1896, New Moon..**1,700.00**

1897, Christmas Meal of Sparrows..**990.00**
1898, Roses & Star...**610.00**
1899, Crows Enjoying Christmas..**1,175.00**
1900, Church Bells Chiming...**975.00**
1901, 3 Wise Men..**375.00**
1902, Gothic Church Interior...**325.00**
1903, Expectant Children..**330.00**
1904, View of Copenhagen from Fredericksberg Hill.............**130.00**
1905, Christmas Night...**130.00**
1906, Sleighing to Church...**80.00**
1907, Little Match Girl..**95.00**
1908, St Petri Church..**60.00**
1909, Yule Tree..**75.00**
1910, Old Organist...**70.00**
1911, Angels & Shepherds...**65.00**
1912, Going to Church..**65.00**
1913, Bringing Home the Tree...**70.00**
1914, Amalienborg Castle..**65.00**
1915, Dog on Chain Outside Window....................................**105.00**
1916, Prayer of the Sparrows...**60.00**
1917, Christmas Boat..**60.00**
1918, Fishing Boat..**60.00**
1919, Outside the Lighted Window...**55.00**
1920, Hare in the Snow...**55.00**
1921, Pigeons..**45.00**
1922, Star of Bethlehem..**45.00**
1923, Hermitage...**50.00**
1924, Lighthouse..**50.00**
1925, Child's Christmas...**50.00**
1926, Churchgoers..**50.00**
1927, Skating Couple..**70.00**
1928, Eskimos...**45.00**
1929, Fox Outside Farm..**55.00**
1930, Christmas Train...**70.00**
1931, Tree in Town Hall Square..**65.00**
1932, Lifeboat at Work..**65.00**
1933, Korsor-Nyborg Ferry..**50.00**
1934, Church Bell in Tower..**50.00**
1935, Lillebelt Bridge..**50.00**
1936, Royal Guard..**50.00**
1937, Arrival of Christmas Guests...**60.00**
1938, Lighting the Candles..**120.00**
1939, Old Lock-Eye, The Sandman...**115.00**
1940, Delivering Christmas Letters...**125.00**
1941, Horses Enjoying Meal...**190.00**
1942, Danish Farm on Christmas Night....................................**135.00**
1943, Ribe Cathedral..**135.00**
1944, Sorgenfri Castle..**70.00**
1945, Old Water Mill...**90.00**
1946, Commemoration Cross..**50.00**
1947, Dybbol Mill...**70.00**
1948, Watchman...**55.00**
1949, Landsoldaten...**55.00**
1950, Kronborg Castle at Elsinore...**85.00**
1951, Jens Bang..**70.00**
1952, Old Copenhagen Canals & Thorsvaldsen Museum...........**60.00**
1953, Snowman..**55.00**
1954, Royal Boat..**65.00**
1955, Kaulundorg Church...**70.00**
1956, Christmas in Copenhagen..**90.00**
1957, Christmas Candles...**105.00**
1958, Santa Claus...**75.00**
1959, Christmas Eve..**95.00**
1960, Village Church..**125.00**

1961, Winter Harmony 90.00
1962, Winter Night 50.00
1963, Christmas Elf..65.00
1964, Fir Tree & Hare 35.00
1965, Bringing Home the Tree....................................35.00
1966, Home for Christmas..30.00
1967, Sharing the Joy 30.00
1968, Christmas in Church 25.00
1969, Arrival of Guests..20.00
1970, Pheasants in Snow 17.00

M. I. Hummel

1971, Heavenly Angel..525.00
1972, Hear Ye, Hear Ye 50.00
1973, Glober Trotter 95.00

M.I. Hummel, Goose Girl, 1974, $50.00.

1975, Ride into Christmas 50.00
1976, Apple Tree Girl 50.00
1977, Apple Tree Boy...60.00
1978, Happy Pastime 45.00
1979, Singing Lesson 30.00
1980, School Girl 45.00

Royal Copenhagen

Royal Copenhagen, Christmas Night, 1959, $90.00.

1908, Madonna & Child 2,900.00
1909, Danish Landscape 125.00
1910, Magi...100.00
1911, Danish Landscape 125.00
1912, Christmas Tree 125.00
1913, Frederik Church Spire 105.00
1914, Holy Spirit Church 115.00
1915, Danish Landscape 115.00
1916, Shepherd at Christmas 80.00
1917, Our Savior Church 70.00
1918, Sheep & Shepherds 70.00
1919, In the Park 75.00
1920, Mary & Child Jesus...75.00
1921, Aabenraa Marketplace...70.00
1922, 3 Singing Angels...60.00
1923, Danish Landscape 60.00
1924, Sailing Ship..85.00
1925, Christianshavn 75.00
1926, Christianshavn Canal 70.00
1927, Ship's Boy at Tiller..115.00
1928, Vicar's Family...70.00
1929, Grundtvig Church 70.00
1930, Fishing Boats..85.00
1931, Mother & Child...85.00
1932, Frederiksberg Gardens...80.00
1933, Ferry & Great Belt...120.00
1934, Hermitage Castle...97.00
1935, Kronborg Castle 155.00
1936, Roskilde Cathedral 125.00
1937, Main Street of Copenhagen 140.00
1938, Round Church of Osterlars.................................230.00
1939, Greenland Pack Ice 240.00
1940, Good Shepherd..330.00
1941, Danish Village Church.......................................260.00
1942, Bell Tower..305.00
1943, Flight into Egypt...390.00
1944, Danish Village Scene...180.00
1945, Peaceful Scene 320.00
1946, Zealand Village Church......................................135.00
1947, Good Shepherd..190.00
1948, Nodebo Church 165.00
1949, Our Lady's Cathedral...165.00
1950, Boeslunde Church 160.00
1951, Christmas Angel 275.00
1952, Christmas in Forest 105.00
1953, Frederiksberg Castle 105.00
1954, Amalienborg Palace..105.00
1955, Fano Girl 160.00
1956, Rosenborg Castle 145.00
1957, Good Shepherd..75.00
1958, Sunshine Over Greenland 115.00
1959, Christmas Night 90.00
1960, Stag 105.00
1961, Training Ship...125.00
1962, Little Mermaid...150.00
1963, Hojsager Mill 65.00
1964, Fetching the Tree 45.00
1965, Little Skaters 53.00
1966, Blackbird..26.00
1967, Royal Oak 28.00
1968, Last Umiak...27.00
1969, Old Farmyard..27.00
1970, Christmas Rose & Cat 29.00

Limoges

From the mid-eighteenth century, Limoges was the center of the porcelain industry of France, where at one time more than forty companies utilized the local kaolin to make a superior quality china, much of which was exported to the United States. Various marks were used; some included the name of the American export company (rather than the manufacturer) and 'Limoges.' After 1891 'France' was added. Pieces signed by factory artists are more valuable than those decorated outside the factory by amateurs. For a more thorough study of the subject, we recommend you refer to *The Collector's Encyclopedia of Limoges Porcelain* by our advisor Mary Frank Gaston, who is listed in the Directory under Texas. Her book has beautiful color illustrations and current market values.

Chocolate pot, floral w/gold, Coronet, 10", +4 c/s 325.00
Chocolate pot, gold ribbons & bl floral sprays, mk, 10" **195.00**
Chocolate pot, red poppies & gr buds in panels, HC&S, 9½" 250.00
Chocolate pot, roses on melon ribs, red-brn hdl, H&Co, 9" 170.00
Dresser set, pastel florals w/gold, 6-pc 325.00
Jar, powder; pate-sur-pate, Greek in chariot, sgn, 4½" 225.00
Jardiniere, mc florals, 4 Baroque ft, mk, 5x9" dia.........................250.00
Jardiniere, roses/wht scrolls on mc, 7½x11" 300.00
Pitcher, cider; grapes on gr shaded, mk, 5¾x6" 145.00
Pitcher, tankard; allover grapes & vines, 15" 200.00

Plaque, peasant couple, marked Flambeau, 12½",
$800.00.

Plaque, lady's portrait, sgn Dussou, 15" dia 650.00
Plaque, lady's portrait, waist-length, 1900, 11x8", +fr.................475.00
Plaque, mc roses on gr to yel, T&V, 16" dia 450.00
Plate, birds scene, sgn Dubois, gold Rococo rim, 12¼"..................295.00
Plate, boars in snow, sgn Pradet, Coronet, 10" 225.00
Plate, duck, sgn Max, gold Rococo rim, Coronet, 10" 125.00
Plate, florals, sgn Stafford, 9¼"..40.00
Plate, fox & birds, gold Rococo rim, artist sgn, 12½" 135.00
Plate, game bird, heavily emb/scalloped, pierced, B&H, 10" 250.00
Plate, game birds, sgn Dubois, gold Rococo rim, mk, 12¼"..........275.00
Plate, holly, heavy gold Rococo rim, T&V, 12½" 185.00
Plate, pastoral scene, sgn, gold Rococo rim, mk, 10¼" 145.00
Plate, quail, sgn Day, gold Rococo rim, mk, 13¾"........................225.00
Plate, Wm Henry Harrison service, T&V, 8½" 550.00
Platter, lg fish/vegetation, sgn Defer, 26", +insert 700.00
Platter, wild fowl, sgn Barbarin, 19", +12 plates 1,500.00

Punch bowl, birds & flowers, vintage int, T&V, 1915, 12½".......350.00
Punch bowl, grapevines, ftd stand, 15", +rnd tray & 10 cups.......900.00
Punch bowl, grapevines w/in & w/out, scroll ft, 15" 400.00
Teapot, malachite w/silver, +cr/sug & 16" hdld tray 880.00
Tray, couple plays music, sgn Malerband/dtd, metal mts, 16" 900.00
Vase, angels & roses on bl, sgn Ryland, ruffled/hdls, 9½".............350.00
Vase, roses, sgn Perl, 2 gold ring hdls/4 gold ft, 12x9" 550.00

Lithophanes

Lithophanes are porcelain panels with relief designs of varying degrees of thickness and density. Transmitted light brings out the pattern in graduated shading, lighter where the procelain is thin and shaded in the heavy areas. They were cast from wax models prepared by artists and depict views of life from the 1800s, religious themes, or scenes of historical significance. First made in Berlin about 1803, they were used as lampshade panels, window plaques, or candle shields. Later steins, mugs, and cups were made with lithophanes in their bases. Japanese wares were sometimes made with dragons or geisha lithophanes. See also Dragon Ware; Steins.

Candlestand, crystal ft, 4¾" dia cone shade w/children, 8" 425.00
Lamp, student; dbl, 4-panel, brass base, mk Germany, 24" 1,800.00
Lamp, 4-panel (children/animals), bronze base, rtcl lid, 5"..........750.00
Panel, hunters in forest, mk PPM, 4½x5¼" 135.00
Panel, Maguerite praying among ruins, 9x7", in bronze stand......900.00
Shade, 5-panel, bldgs, Niagara, monument, etc, 9" dia 600.00
Shade, 5-panel, scenics, mother/child, etc, 7x9½" dia 500.00
Shade, 6 trapezoid panels, scenic, sgn/#d, 6¼x12" 750.00
Stein, couple dancing, deer transfer, ½-L.......................................95.00
Tea set, peacock, 3-pc, +5 c/s...165.00

Little Red Riding Hood

Though usually thought of as a product of the Hull Pottery Company, research has shown that a major part of this line was actually made by the Regal Company. The idea for this popular line of novelties and kitchenware items was developed and patented by Hull, but records show that to a large extent Hull sent their whiteware to Regal to be decorated. Little Red Riding Hood was produced from 1943 until 1957. Values have risen sharply over the past several months. For further information we recommend *Collecting Hull Pottery's Red Riding Hood* by Mark Supnick. Watch for the announcement of another book on this subject by Joyce and Fred Roerig, authors of *The Collector's Encyclopedia of Cookie Jars*.

Match holder, Regal, $800.00.

Butter dish	350.00
Canister, salt	1,000.00
Canister, spice	625.00
Creamer & sugar bowl, head pour, w/lid	700.00
Creamer & sugar bowl, side pour	250.00
Jar, cracker; skirt held wide, 8½"	500.00
Mug, wht, no decor, minimum value	1,000.00
Mug, decor	2,000.00
Pitcher, milk; ruffled skirt, w/apron, rare, 8½"	1,500.00
Pitcher, milk; standing, 8"	235.00
Planter, standing, wall hanging	450.00
Shakers, standing, rare, 4½", pr	850.00
Shakers, standing, 3¼", pr	50.00
Shakers, standing, 5¼", pr	150.00
Sugar bowl, crawling	225.00
Teapot	350.00

Liverpool

In the late 1700s, Liverpool potters produced a creamy ivory ware, sometimes called Queen's Ware, which they decorated by means of the newly perfected transfer print. Made specifically for the American market, patriotic inscriptions, political portraits, or other States themes were applied in black with colors sometimes added by hand. (Obviously their loyalty to the crown did not inhibit the progress of business!) Before it lost favor in about 1825, other English potters made a similar product. Today Liverpool is a generic term used to refer to all ware of this type. Our advisor for this category is Richard Marden; he is listed in the Directory under New Hampshire.

Platter, Liberty and Washington's tomb, marked Herculaneum Pottery, minor wear, 15", $4,000.00.

Bowl, ship w/British flag, verses/humorous scenes, 5", NM	425.00
Coffeepot, Portobello, brn w/yel chinoiserie transfer, 11"	300.00
Creamer, Portobello, brn w/yel chinoiserie transfer, 5½"	150.00
Jug, Am Militia/Proscribed Patriots/Seal of US, mc, 10", NM	3,600.00
Jug, Am ship/rural scene, Purinton under spout, 9", NM	1,600.00
Jug, Apotheosis of Washington/US ship, bulbous, 11", EX	2,800.00
Jug, British ship/couple/verse, gilt trim/name, 8½"	500.00
Jug, Commodore Perry/We have met..., bk: 2nd view, 9", EX	3,200.00
Jug, farm scene & fisherman/mill & waterfall, 10½", EX	435.00
Jug, Farmers Arms/Flower Girl/verse, red, rpr, 7"	450.00
Jug, hunt scenes/intellectual arts, mc, 10"	475.00

Jug, Map of E Coast/Independence, eagle under spout, 10"	2,700.00
Jug, Map of Ireland/Hibernia, hairline, 8¾"	925.00
Jug, Napoleon Bonaparte & numerals, sm rpr, 5½"	575.00
Jug, Peace/Prosperity to Am, blk, old rprs, 8"	300.00
Mug, True Blooded Yankee, ship w/flag, blk, 6", EX	800.00
Plate, ship w/Am flag, 9¾", VG	350.00

Lladro

Lladro porcelains are currently being produced in Labernes Blanques, Spain. Their retired and limited edition figurines are popular collectibles.

Girl with balloons, #5141, 11", $195.00.

Arabian knight w/peacock, #1310, 14"	265.00
Couple w/dog, #4563, 19"	165.00
Idyll, Perriot & Columbine by stump, #1017, 13"	225.00
Judge seated in chambers, sgn J Ruiz, #1281, LL mk, 13"	900.00
Lady reclining against rock, #1271, 12x12"	265.00
Lady stands beside chair, #4703, 19"	265.00
Lady w/child & basket, #4993, 9"	85.00
Lady wearing shawl & holding parasol, #4914, 17"	250.00
Lord & lady on wood plinths, bookends, #1382/#1382, 11"	400.00
Man playing mandolin, Gres glaze, #1247, 14"	325.00
Mother & 2 children, #4864, 15"	300.00
Old Folks, 19th-C couple, #1033, 20"	225.00
Old man & troubador w/mandolin, #4652, 14"	185.00
Peddler, man w/burro, #4859, 10"	175.00
Poet, man beside terrace wall, #5397, 12"	265.00
Satyr w/cymbals seated on plinth, #1007, 10"	250.00
Shakespeare, sgn J Ruiz, #1338, LL mk, 13" +matching plaque	600.00
Shepherd & shepherdess (courting) w/sheep, #4903, 15"	265.00
Spanish lady w/baby, bsk, #4822, 9"	150.00
Spring Breeze, lady w/wide-rimmed bonnet, #4936, 14"	145.00
Young Harlequin w/cat, boy in clown suit, #1229, 9"	265.00

Locke Art

Joseph Locke already had proven himself many times over as a master glass maker, working in leading English glasshouses for more than seventeen years. He came to America where he joined the New England Glass Company. There he invented processes for the manufacture of several types of art glass — amberina, peachblow, pomona, and agata among them. In 1898 he established the Locke Art Glassware Co. in Mt. Oliver, Pittsburgh, Pennsylvania. Locke Art Glass was produced using an acid-etching process by which the most delicate designs were produced on crystal blanks. Most examples are signed simply 'Locke Art,' often placed unobtrusively near a leaf or a stem. Other items are signed 'Jo Locke,' some are dated, and some are unsigned. Most of the work was done by hand. The business continued into the 1920s. For further study we recommend *American Art Glass* by Shuman, available at your local bookstore.

Pitcher, etched vintage, sgn, 8" **495.00**
Pitcher, Grape & Line, ornate hdl, tankard form, 8½" **950.00**
Pitcher, Nouveau poppies & leaves, flared base, unsgn, 8½" **155.00**
Tumbler, Vintage, ribbed, unsgn, 5¼" **150.00**
Vase, etched ferns, ribbed, folded/crimped rim, unsgn, 10½" **115.00**
Vase, frosted camphor, stork/reeds, 6" **500.00**
Whiskey, wheat sheaves, sgn, 2⅝" **150.00**

Locks

The earliest type of lock in recorded history was the wooden cross bar used by ancient Egyptians and their contemporaries. The early Romans are credited with making the first key-operated mechanical lock. The ward lock was invented during the Middle Ages by the Etruscans of Northern Italy; the lever tumbler and combination locks followed at various stages of history with varying degrees of effectiveness. In the 18th century, the first precision lock was constructed. It was a device that utilized a lever-tumbler mechanism. Two of the best-known of the early 19th century American lock manufacturers are Yale and Sargent, and today's collectors value Winchester and Keen Kutter locks very highly. Factors to consider are rarity, condition, and construction. Brass and bronze locks are generally priced higher than those of steel or iron. Our advisor for this section is Joe Tanner; he is listed in the Directory under Washington.

Key:
bbl — barrel   st — stamped

Pin tumbler push key lock marked Reg'D US Mail, $125.00.

Brass Lever Tumbler

Ames Sword Co, Perfection stamped on shackle, 2¾" **50.00**
Bingham's Best Brand, BBB emb on front, 3¼" **150.00**
Cleveland 4 Way, Cleveland 4 Way emb on front, 3⅝" **90.00**
Crusader, shield, swords emb on body, 2¾" **45.00**
Eagle Lock Co, word Eagle emb on front, scrolled, 3" **60.00**
Jackson's, stamped Jackson's on front, 2½" **25.00**
Keen Kutter, shape of KK emblem, KK emb on front, 4¾" **115.00**
Mercury, Mercury emb on body, 2¾" **25.00**
Motor, Motor emb on body, 3¼" **35.00**

Our Very Best, OVB emb on body, 2⅞" **150.00**
Roeyonoc, Roeyonoc stamped on body, 3¼" **40.00**
Romer & Co, Romer & Co stamped on dust cover, 3" **55.00**
Ruby, Ruby emb in scroll on front, 2¾" **25.00**
Safe, Safe emb in scroll on front, 2⅜" **20.00**
Siberian, Siberian emb on shackle, 2½" **90.00**
Sphinx, sphinx & pharaoh head emb on front, 2¾" **35.00**
W Bohannan & Co, SW emb in scroll on front, 2⅜" **30.00**
Winchester, Winchester emb on front, 3" **160.00**

Combinations

Chicago Combination Lock Co, stamped on front, brass, 2¾" **60.00**
Corbin Sesamee 4-Dial Brass Lock, stamped Sesamee, 2¾" **12.00**
Edwards Mfg Co No-Key, stamped on lock, brass, 2¾" **60.00**
Junkunc Bros Mfrs, all stamped on bk, brass, 1⅞" **25.00**
Karco stamped on body, 2½" **50.00**
Number or letter disk type (4 disks), brass, 2¾" **130.00**
Sq lock case of steel, stamped Pat Germany, 4-wheel, 3¼" **110.00**
Sutton Lock Co stamped on body, 3" **200.00**
Your Own stamped on body, 3⅞" **325.00**

Eight-Lever Type

Armory, brass, Armory 8-Lever stamped on front **25.00**
Electric, steel, Electric stamped on front **25.00**
Goliath, steel, Goliath 8-Lever stamped on front **20.00**
Miller, steel, Miller 8-Lever stamped on front **15.00**
Samson, brass, 8-Lever stamped on front **18.00**

Iron Lever Tumbler

Bull, word Bull emb on front, 2⅝" **30.00**
Bulldog, word Bulldog & face of dog emb on front, 2¾" **30.00**
Dan Patch, Dan Patch emb on front, horseshoe on bk, 2¾" **130.00**
Dragon, word Dragon & dragon emb on front, 2⅞" **25.00**
Eagle, word Eagle emb on body, 4⅜" **40.00**
Indian Head, Indian head emb on front, 3" **80.00**
Jupiter, word Jupiter/star & moon emb on front, 3¼" **18.00**
Karo, word Karo emb on front, CI, 3⅛" **25.00**
King Korn, words King Korn emb on body, 2⅞" **20.00**
Nineteen O Three, 1903 emb on front, iron, 3⅞" **90.00**
Red Chief, words Red Chief emb on body, 3¾" **80.00**
Rugby, football emb on body, 3" **20.00**
Unique, word Unique emb on front, 3¼" **90.00**
Yale & Towne, lion face emb on front, shackle mk Y&T, 3" **110.00**

Lever Push Key

Champion, emb Champion 6-Lever, brass push-key type, 2¼" **25.00**
Climax, emb Climax 6-Lever, iron push-key type, 2¼" **35.00**
Columbia, emb Columbia 6-Lever, brass push-key type, 2¼" **35.00**
Dash, emb Dash 6-Lever, iron push-key type, 2¼" **25.00**
Excelsior, emb Excelsior 6-Lever, brass push-key type, 2¼" **25.00**
Harvard, emb Harvard 4-Lever, brass push-key type, 2" **60.00**
IXL, emb IXL on body, 2¼" **60.00**
Keystone, emb Keystone 6-Lever, brass push-key type, 2¼" **40.00**
McIntosh, emb McIntosh on body, 2¼" **90.00**
SB Co, emb SB Co on body, 3¼" **60.00**
Smith & Egge Mfg Co, Smith & Egge stamped on front, 3" **75.00**
Ten Star, emb Ten Star 6-Lever, 2¼" **45.00**

Logo — Special Made

Brass pancake push key emb US Internal Revenue, 2¼" **185.00**

Heart-shape brass lever type emb Shults Co, bbl key, 2¾" **45.00**
Heart-shape brass lever type st Board Education, bbl key, 3½" **50.00**
Sq brass pin-tumbler case st Regd US Mail, int counter, 2¾" **120.00**
Sq Yale-type brass pin tumbler, emb w/Texaco & star, 3" **25.00**
Sq Yale-type brass pin tumbler, st Shell Oil Co on body, 3⅛" **20.00**
Sq Yale-type brass pin tumbler, st US/A/tree/Forest Svc, 2⅞" **125.00**

Pin-Tumbler Type

Corbin, brass, Corbin in oval stamped on body, 3⅝" **30.00**
Eagle, brass, Eagle stamped on body, 2⅞" **20.00**
Fulton, emb Fulton on body, 2⅝" **30.00**
Hope, brass, emb Hope on body, 2½" **18.00**
Il-A-Noy, emb Il-A-Noy on body, 2½" **40.00**
Pearl, brass, emb Pearl on body, 2⅛" **16.00**
Sargent, brass, emb Sargent on body, 3" **15.00**
Segal, iron, emb Segal on shackle, 3¾" **40.00**
Shapleigh, emb Shapleigh on body, 2⅝" **35.00**
Yale, brass, emb Yale on body, Made in England on shackle, 3" ...**50.00**
Yale, brass, emb Yale on body, Yale & Towne on shackle, 2⅝" **25.00**

Scandinavian (Jail House) Type

JHW Climax Co, iron, 2⅞" **50.00**
Star, emb line on bottom, iron, 3¾" **90.00**
Star, iron, 2½" **70.00**
99 Miller, emb 99, brass, 1¾" **90.00**
999 Miller, emb 999, brass, 2½" **75.00**

Six-Lever Type

Eagle, brass, Eagle Six Lever stamped on body **15.00**
Edwards, iron, Edwards stamped on body......................................**15.00**
Safe, brass, Safe stamped on body **18.00**
Yale, brass, Yale emb on front **12.00**

Story and Commemorative

AYPEX Seattle (Alaska Yukon Pacific Expo), emb tin/iron, 3" ..**200.00**
Canteen, US emb on lock, lock: canteen shape, 2"......................**500.00**
CI, emb ornate scroll motif throughout body of lock, 3½" **170.00**
CI, emb skull/X-bones w/florals, NH Co on bk, 3¼" **250.00**
CQD/sinking ship Titanic & SOS waves emb on brass, 2¾" **120.00**
Eagle/stars/shield & stars, emb CI, Eagle Liberty, 2½" **300.00**
Mail Pouch, emb on lock, lock in shape of a mail pouch, 3⅛" **200.00**
1901 Pan Am Expo, brass, emb w/buffalo, 2⅝" **175.00**

Warded Type

Army, iron pancake ward key, emb letters, 2½"............................**35.00**
Globe, iron sq lock case, emb US on bk, 2⅜" **20.00**
Hex, iron, sq lock case, emb US on bk, 2⅛" **95.00**
Navy, iron pancake ward key, bk: scrolled emb letters, 2½" **30.00**
Red Cross, brass sq case, emb letters, 2" **10.00**
Rex, steel case, emb letters, 2⅝"..**18.00**
Safe, brass sq case, emb letters, 1⅞" **8.00**
Safety First, brass pancake type, emb letters, 2¾" **15.00**
Secure, iron pancake type, emb letters, 2⅝" **20.00**
Sprocket, brass oval shape, emb letters, 2⅛" **55.00**
Try Me, iron pancake type, emb letters, 2½" **25.00**
Winchester, brass sq case, stamped letters, 2¾" **125.00**

Wrought Iron Lever Type (Smokehouse Type)

DM&Co, bbl key, 4¼" **15.00**

MW&Co, bbl key, 2⅝"..**10.00**
MW&Co, flat key, 3½" **20.00**
S&Co, bbl key, 3" **8.00**

Loetz

The Loetz Glassworks was established in Klostermule, Austria, in 1840. After Loetz's death the firm was purchased by his grandson, Johann Loetz Witwe. Until WWII the operation continued to produce fine artware, some of which made in the early 1900s bears a striking resemblance to Tiffany's, with whom Loetz was associated at one time. In addition to the iridescent Tiffany-style glass, he also produced threaded glass and some cameo. Our advisor for this category is Don Williams; he is listed in the Directory under Missouri.

Key: att — attributed   o/l — overlay

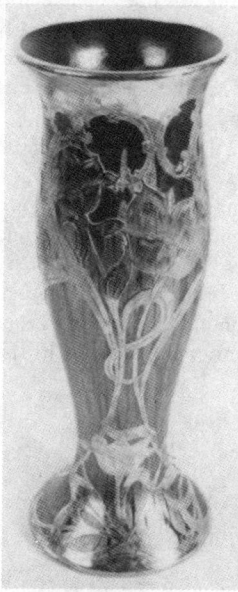

Vase, iridescent raindrops on lt amber-green, silver overlay with irises, 15", M, $3,750.00.

Basket, amber w/irid bl string-like design, prunt hdl, 10"............**850.00**
Bowl, burgundy/opal irid mottle, ruffled, shallow, 9" **500.00**
Bowl, gold w/loops, appl gold leaves on scalloped rim, 9½" **500.00**
Bowl, wine irid w/T'prints, 7"; metal 4-leaf ftd hdld base............**500.00**
Candle lamp, red/gr leaves on gold-spotted shade/base, 12".......**650.00**
Conch shell, pk w/silvery crackling, seaweed ft, 7½" **1,650.00**
Inkwell, dk bl threading, pyramid shape, 3½"..............................**450.00**
Lamp, threaded gr irid ball shade, bronze snake base, 20" **4,400.00**
Pitcher, wht irid/crackled o/l, sqd top, ribbed hdl, 5½" **350.00**
Rose bowl, gr irid/wine threading, 4½", in staghorn base **350.00**
Shade, feathers, wht/gr on yel irid, sm rim flakes, 4½" **80.00**
Syrup, cobalt w/mc free-style designs, silver mts, 8" **650.00**
Vase, amber irid w/oil spots, bl/silver o/l, dbl gourd, 9" **700.00**
Vase, amber w/lt bl & silver oil spots, flared/ruffled, 6".................**350.00**
Vase, amber w/rose & gold, slim neck/wide base, 13"..................**250.00**
Vase, bl w/bl & platinum spots, trumpet neck/bulb base, 7" **500.00**
Vase, bl w/oil spots, dbl gourd w/in appl 4-leg frwork, 9".........**1,800.00**
Vase, bl/gold irid w/pk highlights, pinched cylinder, 9" **500.00**
Vase, cameo butterfly/floral, lilac/gr on gray, 14"....................**1,400.00**
Vase, clear w/bl & purple spots, trefoil top, dimples, 8" **160.00**
Vase, drapes/swirls, gr irid w/EX irid, sqd/dimpled, 6½" **800.00**
Vase, feathers, bl irid on dk ruby, baluster body, 12" **2,600.00**
Vase, feathers, gold on red w/much bl irid, shouldered, 9".......**1,650.00**
Vase, gold w/waves, ruffled; bronze Nouveau holder, 9" **1,700.00**

Vase, gold w/bl & platinum texture, pinched sides, 5" **250.00**
Vase, gr irid, pinched, twisted, ribbed, unmk, 9¾" **700.00**
Vase, gr irid w/appl snake, cylindrical/ftd, 13" **400.00**
Vase, gr irid w/purple appl teardrops, dimpled, 6x4" **250.00**
Vase, gr irid w/random threads, bottle form, 9¾" **145.00**
Vase, gr irid w/silver dappling, gourd form, 4¾" **495.00**
Vase, gr w/purple & bl irid, emb rings, hdld tub form, 5½" **210.00**
Vase, gr/bl irid w/droplets, 4-lobe top, pinched sides, 8" **350.00**
Vase, gr/mulberry ribbons on lime+opal spots, ftd, 10" **900.00**
Vase, purple w/threading, 3-point folded top, dimpled, 9" **325.00**
Vase, rainbow irid w/gr edge, 3 appl drops, ribbed, 4" **500.00**
Vase, rainbow irid w/purple arches, pinched sides, 12" **900.00**
Vase, rainbow irid w/purple trailings, gourd form, 11" **1,000.00**
Vase, red to gold w/bl irid oil spots, dimpled shoulder, 4" **500.00**
Vase, rust irid shaded to gr, crimped fan form, 9" **275.00**
Vase, salmon irid w/overlapped gr irid leaves, 4-spout, 4x7" **500.00**
Vase, silver o/l Nouveau iris, gr waves on lime w/spots, 7" **3,600.00**
Vase, swirls/spots, gr/silver/bl irid, 3-lobe lip, 7x13" **1,300.00**
Vase, yel w/gold, bl/platinum pulled waves, dbl gourd, 6½" **1,800.00**

Lomonosov Porcelain

Founded in 1744, the Lomonosov porcelain factory produced exquisite porcelain miniatures for the Czar and other Russian nobility. One of the first factories of its kind, Lomonosov pieces consisted largely of vases and delicate sculptures. In the 1800s Lomonosov became closely involved with the Russian Academy of Fine Arts, a connection which has continued to this day, as the company continues to supply the world with these fine artistic treasures.

Afghan hound, lg...**38.50**
Airdale terrier **23.00**
Dachshund, miniature **4.00**
Donkey, recumbent **17.50**
Great Dane...**28.50**
Leopard cub...**15.50**
Moose...**98.00**
Otter...**37.00**
Penguin #2 ....**21.00**
Polar bear, lg...**145.00**
Rabbit, gray, miniature **12.50**
Snowbird..**11.00**
Terrier **22.00**
Wild cat **40.00**
Yakut woman **59.00**

Longwy

The Longwy workshops were founded in 1798 and continue today to produce pottery in the north of France near the Luxembourg-Belgian border. The ware for which they are best known was produced during the Art Deco period, decorated in bold colors and designs. Earlier wares made during the first quarter of the nineteenth century reflected the popularity of Oriental art, cloisonne enamels in particular. The designs were executed by impressing the pattern into the moist clay and filling in the depressions with enamels. Examples are marked 'Longwy,' either impressed or painted under glaze. Our advisor for this category is Wayne Kielsmeier; he is listed in the Directory under Arizona.

Plaque, earthenware, jungle scene w/elephants, 15" dia **1,700.00**
Tile, Deco lady & flowers, Primavera, 8" sq...................................**850.00**
Trivet, Primavera, woman w/exotic foliage, after Mattise, 8" **850.00**
Vase, Deco flowers, some w/in sqs, on crazed cream, 12½" **990.00**

Vase, florals, mc on bl, tubular shape, 9" **325.00**
Vase, pnt/emb fowl, base w/4 elephant-head legs, 11", pr **600.00**

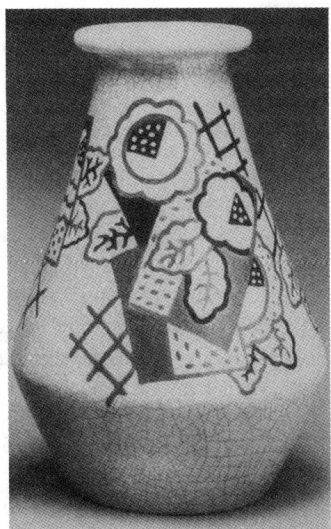

Vase, rectilinear and floral designs, marked Primavera, signed Lesieutre, 12½", $1,050.00.

Lonhuda

William Long was a druggist by trade who combined his knowledge of chemistry with his artistic ability in an attempt to produce a type of brown-glazed slip-decorated artware similar to that made by the Rookwood Pottery. He achieved his goal in 1889 after years of long and dedicated study. Three years later he founded his firm, the Lonhuda Pottery Company. The name was coined from the first few letters of the last name of each of his partners, W.H. Hunter and Alfred Day. Laura Fry, formerly of the Rookwood company, joined the firm in 1892, bringing with her a license for Long to use her patented airbrush-blending process. Other artists of note, Sarah McLaughlin, Helen Harper, and Jessie Spaulding, joined the firm and decorated the ware with nature studies, animals, and portraits, often signing their work with their initials. Three types of marks were used on the Steubenville Lonhuda ware. The first was a linear composite of the letters 'LPCO' with the name 'Lonhuda' impressed above it. The second, adopted in 1893, was a die-stamp representing the solid profile of an Indian, used on ware patterned after pottery made by the American Indians. This mark was later replaced with an impressed outline of the Indian head with 'Lonhuda' arching above it. Although the ware was successful, the business floundered due to poor management. In 1895 Long became a partner of Sam Weller and moved to Zanesville where the manufacture of the Lonhuda line continued. Less than a year later, Long left the Weller company. He was associated with J.B. Owens until 1899, at which time he moved to Denver, Colorado, where he established the Denver China and Pottery Company in 1901. His efforts to produce Lonhuda utilizing local clay were highly successful. Examples of the Denver Lonhuda are sometimes marked with the LF (Lonhuda Faience) cipher contained within a canted diamond form.

Bowl, banana boat; tiny blossoms, 4-ftd, hdls, 5½x9½"...............**165.00**
Bowl, floral, 3-ftd, sgn Jessie Spaulding, mk/1899, 7" **275.00**
Vase, apple blossoms, #810, 7¼" **150.00**
Vase, grapes, gray-bl w/gr & rust vine on brn bsk, 9½" **275.00**
Vase, spider mums, artist sgn, long neck/bulbous, 10¾" **425.00**
Vase, thistles/leaves, bk: flower, mk Denver-Lonhuda, 7½".........**255.00**

Lotton

Charles Lotton is a contemporary glass artist, living and working in Lansing, Illinois. Examples of his glass are much in demand and are on display in many major museums and other collections of distinction, among them the Smithsonian, The Art Institute of Chicago, The Corning Museum of Glass, and the Chrysler Museum. For further information concerning this subject, we recommend *Lotton Art Glass,* co-authored by Charles Lotton and Tom O'Conner; see the Directory under Illinois.

Bowl, verre de soie dbl multiflora, 13" dia 4,000.00
Lamp, amber multiflora w/pk blossoms, 28" 3,000.00
Lamp, boudoir; neodymium sunset multiflora, 10" 950.00
Paperweight, neodymium dbl mini-magnum w/leaf & vine 350.00
Sculpture, free-form, gold ruby, pk & bl pulled through, 10"... 1,100.00
Vase, bl lustre zippers on wht opal, 11" 450.00
Vase, cypriot; cobalt w/bl lustre lava, 6" 500.00
Vase, gold ruby multiflora, crystal cased, closed mouth, 7" 1,200.00
Vase, King Tut on selenium red, bulbous, 7" 400.00
Vase, mandarin red, rolled-out lip, 6" 700.00
Vase, mandarin yel, classic form, 5" 350.00
Vase, opal multiflora on mottled ground, gourd shape, 10" 1,200.00
Vase, pk multiflora on gr aventurine, 11" 800.00
Vase, pulled feathers on lav, bulbous, 5" 550.00
Vase, ruby wisteria, rolled-out lip, 9" 550.00
Vase, selenium red multiflora, orange blossoms, 8½" 1,000.00
Vase, selenium red w/bl lustre leaf & vine, 7½" 400.00
Vase, sunset multiflora, 6" 3,400.00

Lotus Ware

Isaac Knowles and Issac Harvey operated a pottery in East Liverpool, Ohio, in 1853 where they produced both yellowware and Rockingham. In 1870 Knowles brought Harvey's interests and took as partners John Taylor and Homer Knowles. Their principal product was ironstone china, but Knowles was confident that American potters could produce as fine a ware as the Europeans. To prove his point, he hired Joshua Poole, an artist from the Belleek Works in Ireland. Poole quickly perfected a Belleek-type china, but fire destroyed this portion of the company. Before it could function again, their hotel china business had grown to the point that it required their full attention in order to meet market demands. By 1891 they were able to try again. They developed a bone china, as fine and thin as before, which they called Lotus. Henry Schmidt from the Meissen factory in Germany decorated the ware, often with lacy filigree applications or hand-formed leaves and flowers to which he added further decoration with liquid slip applied by means of a squeeze bag. Due to high production costs resulting from so much of the fragile ware being damaged in firing and because of changes in tastes and styles of decoration, the Lotus Ware line was dropped in 1896. Some of the early ware was marked 'KT&K China'; later marks have a star and a crescent with 'Lotus Ware' added. For further study, we recommend *American Belleek* by our advisor, Mary Frank Gaston. She is listed in the Directory under Texas.

Bowl, appl jeweled medallion ea end, ruffled/beaded rim, 6¼" 400.00
Bowl, appl pcs & 'leaves,' twig hdl, scalloped, 9", NM.................700.00
Bowl vase, appl chains/medallions, 7½" 1,000.00
Bowl vase, appl fish net, 4½" 350.00
Bowl vase, molded prunus branches, ruffled/beaded rim, 4½" 350.00
Bowl vase, rtcl scrolling gadroons, ruffled/beaded rim, 4½"..........300.00
Bowl vase, rtcl/scrolling lacy panels, 4½" 300.00
Bowl vase, ruffled/beaded rim, 4½" 100.00
Creamer, daisies, wht on lt gr, gr/gold twig hdl.........................275.00
Ewer, gilt leafy sprigs/purple & pk flowers, 9½" 450.00
Ewer, pastel flowers/gilt, beadwork, 9¾" 500.00
Jar, appl fish net panels, 6½" 450.00

Jar, potpourri; rtcl scrolling gadroons, ftd, 7½" 800.00
Jug, milk; pk roses on pk w/gr neck, sgn McMasters/1900 ....225.00
Pitcher, apple blossoms, gold twig hdl, squatty, 5" 300.00
Shell dish, gilt floral on pk, 8" 400.00
Tea set, mc wildflowers, sgn Ferber, pot: 4½", +sug/cr 450.00
Teapot, pastel florals/gilt, sgn Ferber, tapered body, 9" 225.00
Vase, appl/raised/jeweled designs, ftd/hdld, 15" 4,200.00
Vase, bottle form w/lg scrolled hdls, 9" 250.00
Vase, floriform; yel lily w/pk & gr leaf base, 8" 425.00

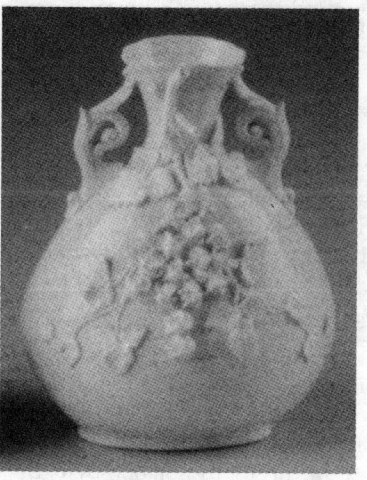

Vase, applied white flowers, light green handles, KTK Lotus Ware mark, 8", $950.00.

Vase, gr w/appl wht flowers, slender neck w/sm hdls, 8", NM......900.00
Vase, gr w/appl wht flowers, sm neck hdls, 6" 500.00
Vase, transfer of Psyche/gilt borders, lg hdls, 15" 2,400.00

Lu Ray Pastels

Lu Ray Pastels dinnerware was introduced in the early 1940s by Taylor, Smith, and Taylor of East Liverpool, Ohio. It was offered in assorted colors of Persian Cream, Sharon Pink, Surf Green, Windsor Blue, and Gray in complete place settings as well as many service pieces. It was a successful line in its day and is once again finding favor with collectors of American dinnerware.

Bowl, cream soup 24.00
Bowl, fruit; 5½" 4.50
Bowl, mixing; lg 45.00
Bowl, salad; lg 30.00
Bowl, soup; 8" 8.50
Bowl, tab hdl, 6" 10.00
Bowl, vegetable; oval 12.50
Bowl, vegetable; 9" 10.00
Bowl, 36's 25.00
Butter dish, w/lid, ¼-lb 25.00
Casserole, w/lid 60.00
Coffeepot, demi; ovoid, w/lid 95.00
Coffeepot, demi; str sides, w/lid 150.00
Creamer.. 5.00
Creamer, demi; ovoid 22.00
Creamer, demi; str sides 40.00
Cup & saucer 7.50
Cup & saucer, demi 16.00
Cup & saucer, demi; str sides 25.00
Egg cup 12.00
Egg cup, Chatham Gray, rare color 15.00
Epergne 60.00
Nut dish 22.50

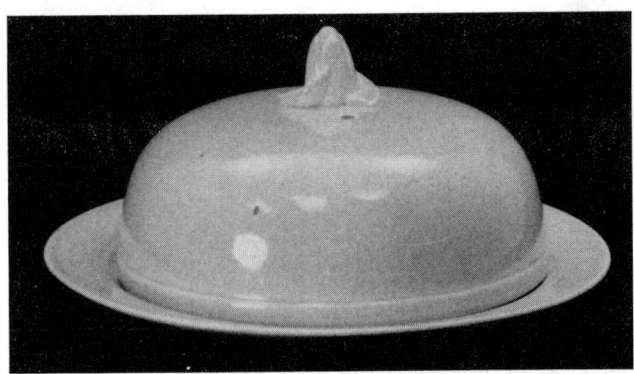

Muffin cover with 8" underplate, $80.00.

Pitcher, bulbous w/flat bottom	40.00
Pitcher, ftd	45.00
Pitcher, juice; ovoid	110.00
Pitcher, syrup	40.00
Plate, cake	25.00
Plate, Chatham Gray, rare color, 7"	6.00
Plate, chop; 14"	18.00
Plate, grill	15.00
Plate, serving; tab hdl	25.00
Plate, very rare, 8"	15.00
Plate, 10"	10.00
Plate, 6"	2.00
Plate, 7"	4.00
Plate, 9"	5.00
Platter, #1040, 9½"	6.00
Platter, oval, 11½"	8.00
Platter, oval, 12"	9.00
Platter, oval, 13"	10.00
Relish, 4-part	60.00
Sauce boat, fast-stand	17.50
Sauce pitcher	18.00
Saucer, cream soup	12.50
Shakers, pr	8.50
Sugar bowl, demi; ovoid, w/lid	24.00
Sugar bowl, w/lid	9.00
Sugar bowl, w/lid, demi; str sides	40.00
Teapot, w/lid, curved spout	40.00
Teapot, w/lid, flat-top spout	45.00
Tidbit, 2-tier	18.00
Tray, pickle	15.00
Tumbler, juice	22.50
Tumbler, water	37.50
Vase, bud; 2 styles, ea	150.00

Lunch Boxes

Early twentieth-century tobacco companies such as Union Leader, Tiger, and Dixie sold their products in square, steel containers with flat, metal carrying handles. These were specifically engineered to be used as lunch boxes when they became empty. (See Advertising, specific companies.) By 1930 oval lunch pails with colorful lithographed decorations on tin were being manufactured to appeal directly to children. These were made by Ohio Art, Decoware, and a few other companies. In 1950 Aladdin Industries produced the first 'real' character lunch box — a Hopalong Cassidy decal-decorated steel container now considered the beginning of the kids' lunch box industry. The other big lunch box manufacturer, American Thermos (later King Seely Thermos Company) brought out its 'blockbuster' Roy Rogers box in 1953, the first fully lithographed steel lunch box and matching bottle.

Other companies (ADCO Liberty; Landers, Frary & Clark; Ardee Industries; Okay Industries; Universal; Tindco; Cheinco) also produced character pails. With the publication of the book *Official Price Guide to Lunch Box Collectibles* by Scott Bruce in 1988, the hobby has skyrocketed. Today's collectors often tend to specialize in those boxes dealing with a particular subject. Western, space, TV series, Disney movies, and cartoon characters are the most popular. There are well over five hundred different lunch boxes available to the astute collector. Our advisor for this category is Alan Smith; he is listed in the Directory under Texas.

Alice in Wonderland, wht vinyl, w/thermos, 1974, EX	90.00
Astronauts, dome top, 1960, M	300.00
Betsey Clark, w/thermos, 1977, EX	30.00
Bionic Woman, w/thermos, 1977, EX	35.00
Blondie, 1969, EX	75.00

Brave Eagle, with thermos, $180.00.

Bonanza, gr, 1963, M	200.00
Chuck Wagon, dome top, w/thermos, 1958, EX	250.00
Davy Crockett at Alamo, Adco, 1955, EX	140.00
Davy Crockett Indian Fighter, 1955, EX	140.00
Dick Tracy, w/thermos, 1977, EX	175.00
Disney School Bus, dome top, w/thermos, EX	55.00
Disney World, w/thermos, 1972, VG	38.00
Emergency, dome top, w/thermos, 1977, EX	75.00
Get Smart, w/thermos, 1966, VG	70.00
Gomer Pyle, w/thermos, 1966, VG	75.00
Hogan's Heroes, dome top, 1966, VG	240.00
Holly Hobbie, wht vinyl, w/thermos, 1978, EX	30.00
Hong Kong Phooey, EX	25.00
Hopalong Cassidy, red tin, 1951, EX	100.00
Hot Wheels, w/thermos, 1970, EX	40.00
How the West Was Won, w/thermos, 1979, EX	47.50
It's a Small World, wht vinyl, w/thermos, 1969, VG	95.00
King Kong, w/thermos, 1977, EX	45.00
Kiss, w/thermos, M	65.00
Land of the Giants, EX	80.00
Liddle Kittles, vinyl, w/thermos, 1969, EX	90.00
Linus the Lion Hearted, gr vinyl, w/thermos, 1965, EX	200.00
Lost in Space, dome top, w/thermos, 1967, EX	300.00
Mickey Mouse Club, w/thermos, 1976, VG	35.00
Mork & Mindy, w/thermos, 1979, VG	30.00
Pele, M	38.00
Popeye, w/thermos, 1962, EX	155.00
Raggedy Ann & Andy, w/thermos, 1973, EX	20.00
Rocky & Bullwinkle, w/thermos, 1962, EX	300.00

Six Million Dollar Man, w/thermos, 1978, EX 35.00
Smokey the Bear, blk vinyl, w/thermos, 1965, VG.....................160.00
Snow White, w/thermos, 1975, VG 45.00
Waltons, 1974, VG 30.00
Welcome Back Kotter, w/thermos, 1977, EX.............................85.00
Wonder Woman, bl vinyl, w/thermos, 1978, EX 70.00
Woody Woodpecker, 1972, EX 100.00

Lutz

From 1869 to 1888, Nicholas Lutz worked for the Boston and Sandwich Glass Company where he produced the threaded and striped art glass that was popular during that era. His works were not marked; and, since many other glassmakers of the day made similar wares, the term Lutz has come to refer not only to his original works but to any of this type.

Bowl, clear w/wht threads, yel/gold stripes, rolled rim, 5" 85.00
Compote, lav/pk/opal swirl, entwined snake stem, 7" 275.00
Finger bowl, pk/gold stripes, wht latticinio, baby-face hdl 165.00
Tazza, cranberry/clear threads, ribbon candy ft/bowl, 3x6" 165.00
Tumbler, yel-gr w/wht streaks, appl prunts, 3¼" 55.00
Wine, wht opaque/bl/clear swirl, att 135.00

Maastricht

Maastricht, Holland, was the site of the De Sphinx Pottery, founded in 1836 by Petrus Regout. They made earthenware decorated with transfer prints as well as dinnerware with gaudy hand-painted designs. Potteries are still working in this area today.

Bowl, stick spatter, gaudy floral, 6" 27.50
Bowl, stick spatter, gaudy floral, 9", NM 38.00

Cup and saucer, dark blue transfer, $40.00.

Pitcher, milk; Canton, mc Oriental motif.....................................45.00
Plate, Abe Lincoln, Petrus Regout, 9" 50.00
Plate, parakeets, bl transfer, Petrus Regout & Co, 8" 35.00
Plate, stick spatter, mc floral, mk, 9" 45.00
Plate, stick spatter, mc floral, 7½" 30.00

Maddux of California

One of the California-made ceramics now so popular with collectors, Maddux was founded in the late 1930s and during the years that followed produced novelty items, TV lamps, figurines, planters, and tableware accessories. Our advisor for this category is Doris Frizzel; she is listed in the Directory under Illinois.

Cats, black matt, 12½", $32.00 for the facing pair.

Console set, #1067, pk 16" shell bowl+pr Early Birds.....................15.00
Flamingo, flying, natural, #970, 11" 25.00
Flamingo, winging, natural, #971, 12" 25.00
Horse, prancing, #982 ....15.00
Mallards, natural, #928 male/#929 female, 9½", pr.......................30.00
TV lamp, Colonial ship, #892, 10½" 20.00
TV lamp, dbl deer, running, natural, #829, 10½" 25.00
TV lamp, Malibu shell, Pearltone, #889, 10¼" 20.00
TV lamp, nativity scene, 3-D planter, #846, 12" 25.00
TV lamp, prairie schooner (covered wagon), #844, 11" 30.00
TV lamp, stallion, prancing, on base, #810, 12" 25.00
TV lamp, swan planter, porc wht, #828, 12½".............................15.00
Vase, horse head, aqua, #225, 12½" 18.00

Magazines

Magazines are collected for their cover prints and for the information pertaining to defunct companies and their products that can be gleaned from the old advertisements. In the listings that follow, items are assumed to be in very good condition unless noted otherwise. Our advisor for this category is Asa Forbes, Jr.; he is listed in the Directory under New York. See also Movie Memorabilia; Parrish, Maxfield.

Key:
  M — mint condition, in original wrapper
  EX — excellent condition, spine intact, edges of pages clean and
       straight
  VG — very good condition, the average as-found condition

American Girl, 1966, Dec, Coke bk cover.......................................4.00
American Weekly, 1957, Jan 20, DD Eisenhower cover, VG 8.00
Antiques, 1922, Mar, Boston State House cover, EX 10.00
Band Leaders, 1944, Mar, Georgia Carrol cover, EX 20.00
Baseball Digest, 1948, Stan Musial cover, EX...............................24.00
Boy's Life, 1965, Feb, BSA/Rockwell cover, VG 15.00
Broadcast Weekly, 1930, Feb 15, radio personalities cover 15.00
Broadcast Weekly, 1930, Feb 22, Rudy Seiger cover, EX 15.00

Coronet, 1954, June, homemaker w/appliances cover, VG 2.00
Down Beat, 1941, Apr 1, Dale Evans cover, EX 30.00
Esquire, 1955, Nov, Petty Girl fold-out, VG................................25.00
Fortune, 1930, Feb, 1st issue 50.00
Harper's Weekly, 1901, Sept, McKinley memorial, EX.................20.00
House Beautiful, 1959, Oct, Frank Lloyd Wright feature 10.00
Ladies' Home Journal, 1901, Nov, lady golfer cover, EX.............14.00
Ladies' Home Journal, 1924, Nov, NC Wyeth illus, EX...............20.00
Ladies' World, 1895, June 1, 11x14", VG 10.00
Laugh Book, 1959, Dec, Kim Novak cover, EX 6.00
Life, 1938, Mar 21, Hitler follows Army into Austria, EX.............. 5.00
Life, 1938, May 23, Errol Flynn cover, EX 25.00
Life, 1940, Feb 5, Swedish aviators cover, EX 3.50
Life, 1941, Mar 10, German war news, EX 5.00
Life, 1941, Sept 1, Rita Hayworth cover, M 15.00
Life, 1942, July 6, Am flag cover, M... 8.00
Life, 1942, Sept 14, Japan war news, EX 5.00
Life, 1945, Feb 12, Russian soldier cover, M 5.00
Life, 1945, May 21, Churchill cover, M..................................... 7.00
Life, 1948, Jan 19, war in Holy Land, EX 5.00
Life, 1948, Oct 4, Dewey & Truman campaign news, M............. 5.00
Life, 1949, Apr 18, Mary Martin cover, VG 5.00
Life, 1950, Jackie Robinson cover, NM 50.00
Life, 1950, July 3, Washington color cover, NM........................ 3.50
Life, 1951, Apr 9, Omar Bradley in uniform, EX 4.00
Life, 1955, Aug 8, Ben Hogan cover, EX 8.00
Life, 1955, freshwater game fish photos, VG............................. 6.00
Life, 1964, May 1, New York World's Fair, M 10.00

Life, May 7, 1965, John Wayne cover, $30.00.

Life, 1965, May 7, John Wayne cover, EX...................................15.00
Look, 1939, May 23, Mrs Roosevelt cover, VG 12.50
Look, 1948, Apr 13, Brooklyn Dodgers' 50 Years cover 10.00
Magazine Digest, 1951, Dec, Mario Lanza cover, VG 6.00
Magazine Digest, 1951, Jan, Douglas MacArthur cover.................. 6.00
Master Detective, 1934, Apr, Dillinger & gang cover, EX 20.00
Motor Age, 1910, Jan 1913, Madison Sq Garden, EX 20.00
Needlecraft, 1925, Oct, needlework/leaf sprays cover, EX.............. 6.00
Penthouse, 1969, Sept, No 1, Vol 1, EX 18.00
People, 1954, Jane Russell cover, NM...20.00
People Today, 1950, Ava Gardner cover, EX 20.00
Playboy, 1964, Jan, Marilyn Monroe/Vargas girls, EX 22.50

Ramparts, 1966, Jan, Bogart & Bergman cover, EX.....................18.00
Redbook, 1957, Oct, Ernie Kovack cover, VG 6.00
Saturday Evening Post, 1942, May 10, Agatha Christy story 6.00
Saturday Evening Post, 1943, Rosie the Riveter, Rockwell, EX....35.00
Sports, 1950, Stan Musial cover, NM 30.00
Sports, 1967, May, Koufax & Clemente cover, EX......................10.00
Sports Illustrated, 1965, Mickey Mantle cover, EX 35.00
Sports Illustrated, 1968, Pete Rose cover, EX 24.00
Sports Illustrated, 1979, Aug 13, Silver Anniversary, EX............... 7.50
Tempo, 1957, Anita Ekberg cover, NM......................................15.00
Tempo, 1958, Jayne Mansfield cover, NM..................................25.00
Time, 1937, Dec 27, Disney cover, NM.....................................40.00
Time, 1939, July 24, Edda Ciano cover, EX 12.00
Time, 1939, Picasso cover, EX...20.00
Time, 1941, Mussolini cover, EX..20.00
Time, 1942, Mountbatten of the Commandos cover, EX..............20.00
Time, 1942, Shostakovich cover, Artzybasheff, EX.....................20.00
Time, 1945, Gen Patton cover, EX 28.00
Time, 1946, Apr 8, Laurence Olivier cover, EX 12.50
Time, 1947, Leo Durocher cover, EX 25.00
Time, 1948, Betty Grable cover, EX 24.00
True Detective, 1933, Dec, Pretty Boy Floyd cover, VG 15.00
TV Digest, 1949, Oct 29, Lone Ranger cover, M 35.00
TV Digest, 1953, Jan 3, Jackie Gleason cover, EX......................22.50
TV Guide, 1952, Mar 7, Arthur Godfrey cover, VG 25.00
TV Guide, 1952, May 17, Gene Autry cover, EX.........................37.50
TV Guide, 1960, May 21, Bat Masterson cover, VG 12.50
TV Guide, 1966, Dec 3, Rat Patrol cover, VG 22.50
TV Radio Mirror, 1955, Sept, McGuire Sisters cover, EX............... 7.50
Venus, 1973, Nov, No 1, Vol 1, EX 17.00
Wisdom, 1956, Jonas Salk cover & feature, EX...........................30.00
Woman's Home Companion, 1917, Feb, Cheerups by Rush, VG..10.00

Majolica

   Majolica is a type of heavy earthenware, design-molded and decorated in vivid colors with either a lead or tin type of glaze. It reached its
height of popularity in the Victorian era; examples from this period are
found in only the lead glazes. Nearly every potter of note, both here
and abroad, produced large majolica jardinieres, umbrella stands, pitchers with animal themes, leaf shapes, vegetable forms, and nearly any
other design from nature that came to mind. Few, however, marked
their ware. Among those who did were Minton, Wedgwood, and
George Jones in England; Griffin, Smith and Hill (Etruscan) in
Phoenixville, Pennsylvania; and Chesapeake Pottery (Avalon and
Clifton) in Baltimore.
   For further information we recommend *The Collector's Encyclopedia of Majolica Pottery* by Mariann Katz-Marks (see Directory, Pennsylvania). Our advisor for this category is Hardy Hudson; he is listed in
the Directory under Florida.

Basket, basketweave w/vining trim & hdl, Minton, 1865, 6½" ...800.00
Basket, floral on basketweave, dbl hdls, G Jones, 8¾x11¼".........700.00
Bouquet holder, fish form, arched tail, G Morley, 9¾"................225.00
Bowl, basketweave, scalloped, Wedgwood, 1875, 8½x9¾"...... 1,000.00
Bowl, chestnut leaf on folded napkin int, G Jones, 2¾x9"...........350.00
Bowl, lattice band, lg ribbon/floral garland, Wedgwood, 12" 750.00
Bowl, salad; floral & scroll ea corner, sq, Wedgwood, 9¾"..........500.00
Bowl, vining leaves border, twig ftd, Holdcroft, 10½" 300.00
Bowl, 2 children supports at base, G Jones, 1875, 4¼" 800.00
Box, sardine; fish on leaves, basket-form base, G Jones, 8"...... 1,000.00
Box, sardine; swan finial, cobalt ground, dolphin ft, 6" 600.00
Box, trunk form w/sailor appl to lid, Continental, 6½" 550.00

Bracket, shelf; suit of armor form, Schiller, 1870s, 15½" 1,000.00
Butter dish, musical cartouches, 3-part, Minton, 5½" 7,000.00
Butter dish, Shell & Seaweed, Etruscan.......................................900.00
Butter pat, horseshoe form w/turq center, Wedgwood, 3" 60.00
Cake stand, Cauliflower, Etruscan, Griffin-Smith-Hill, 9" 350.00
Candlestick, Happy Hooligan by lamppost figural, 7", EX 100.00
Charger, appl snake & frog, Palissy type, 1900s, rstr, 17"......... 2,000.00
Cheese dish, lilies of valley w/rope fr, Stilton, 1880s, 11"........ 1,400.00
Cheese keeper, Daisy & Fence on cobalt, G Jones, 11" H 3,500.00
Cheese keeper, florals, basketweave base, Wedgwood, 10" H . 2,000.00
Cheese keeper, florals/bark, 12" 1,400.00
Cheese keeper, Rose & Picket Fence, G Jones, 7x10" 2,800.00
Cistern, quadrefoil form, merman hdls, Minton, 1856, 15x21" . 1,000.00
Coffeepot, Daisy, mc on wht, Etruscan, 5x9"................................600.00
Colander, 16 holes, 3 ft, ca 1890s, 2½x11½" 400.00
Compote, Daisy, Etruscan, ped ft, lg 350.00
Compote, overlapping begonia leaves, Etruscan, tall 325.00
Creamer, Wild Rose, Etruscan, 4½"..125.00
Cup & saucer, Water Lily, 6½" saucer 160.00
Cuspidor, Sunflower, Etruscan, 7" 600.00
Ewer, Neptune scene, dolphin hdl, European, 1850s, 33" 950.00
Ewer, swan form top, grassy rock base, 1880s, 17¼" 800.00
Figurine, Bacchus w/thyrsus, Wedgwood, 1860s, 16" 1,500.00
Figurine, bird on leafy perch, 4-color, Continental, 12".............375.00
Figurine, elephant w/howdah on rocky oval, Continental, 8"......700.00
Figurine, lion & 2 cubs, Brn-Westhead-Moor, 15x11" 1,800.00
Figurine, magpie, tail up, trunk base, Minton, 22" 1,200.00
Figurine, setter dog, blk spots on wht, Minton, 6⅛".....................800.00
Game dish, vintage swags, rabbit on lid, Wedgwood, 8½" 1,500.00
Humidor, pipe finial, Germany 110.00
Humidor, pug dog form, head forms lid, England, 7¾".................400.00
Jardiniere, berries on wood-look, sq, England, 8½" 450.00
Jardiniere, blkberries on bark, Wedgwood, 1882, 11"...................800.00
Jardiniere, florals emb on bulbous form, 1880s, rstr, 10½" 600.00
Jardiniere, grotesque masks on intersecting bands, 8" 500.00
Jardiniere, Lily, leaves & flower, 7½x6¼", +pedestal 500.00
Jug, Washington & Lincoln, Wedgwood, ca 1876, 5½", EX 300.00
Match holder, monkey in loincloth before holder, 7¾" 300.00
Mug, trailing ivy on cobalt, lav int, unmk, 4"...............................225.00
Mustache cup & saucer, Bamboo & Fern, Wardle, 7" 400.00
Mustache cup & saucer, Bow & Floral, mc on ivory, English 400.00
Mustache cup & saucer, Shell & Seaweed, Etruscan, 8" 600.00
Nut dish, bird beside dish, Geo Jones, 10½" 1,400.00
Nut dish, squirrel beside dish, G Jones, 1875, 10½" 1,500.00
Oyster plate, 5 gr shells on mc fr, Minton, 1874, 9⅛"..................400.00
Oyster stand, 4 fish atop, 4-tier, base turns, Minton, 11"......... 4,000.00
Pedestal, florals on cobalt, French, 1880s, wear, 26" 700.00
Pitcher, basketweave, hound hdl, pewter lid, Wedgwood, 5¾" ...425.00
Pitcher, bird & squirrel cartouches, Fielding, 1880s, 9¾"............700.00
Pitcher, butterfly on cobalt w/in bamboo fr, 3".............................150.00
Pitcher, cat form, tail hdl, mouse on paw, Minton, 1875, 10" . 1,200.00
Pitcher, cat w/banjo form, tail hdl, 1880s, 9⅛"..............................600.00
Pitcher, cherubs at sides, mermaid hdl, Minton, 1869, 8" 1,200.00
Pitcher, chickens w/wheat sheaf figural, English, 7".....................285.00
Pitcher, Corn, Etruscan, Griffin-Smith-Hill, 6" 325.00
Pitcher, dancing figures on tower body, Minton, 1861, 9⅜" 800.00
Pitcher, dbl fish form, Brownfield & Son, 1879, 11½".............. 1,100.00
Pitcher, ear of corn form, England, 1869, hairline, 8½" 250.00
Pitcher, Egyptian Lotus, cobalt trim, Copeland, 6½"...................500.00
Pitcher, fish form, tail hdl/mouth spout, 1880s, 12½" 400.00
Pitcher, fish jumps from water, cobalt ground, JRL mk, 7" 295.00
Pitcher, goose form, monkey hdl, Brownfield, 14" 1,000.00
Pitcher, ivy on tree bark, brn/gr, English, 8"..................................250.00
Pitcher, nautilus shell figural, waves at base, Fielding, 8".............375.00

Pitcher, owl figural, wht ironstone, Morley, 8¼" 350.00
Pitcher, parrot form, mc, St Clement, France, 12" 150.00
Pitcher, pug dog form, Continental, ca 1880, rstr, 10½".............295.00
Pitcher, rooster form, bright colors, France, 12" 150.00
Pitcher, rose on cobalt, twig hdl, English, 6" 160.00
Pitcher, shell form, Fielding, 8" 400.00
Pitcher, soccer players, mc, Etruscan, 7¾" 2,000.00
Pitcher, wheat & leaves, rope trim, G Jones, 1870s, 7" 650.00
Pitcher & bowl, lily pads on bl, Minton, 1859, 12", 15¼" 2,500.00

**Pitcher, zinnias, dragon handle, 10½",
$400.00.**

Planter, cherubs amid tall grass, Continental, 1880s, 3¼" 400.00
Planter, Picket Fence & Raspberry, lav int, 8" 400.00
Planter, trunk form w/birds & leaves, Keene, 1880s, 10" 500.00
Plate, Bird & Fan, Wedgwood, ca 1870, 9"....................................250.00
Plate, bird in flight on turq, att Holdcroft, 8½" 175.00
Plate, Dogwood, simple branches at rim, Holdcroft, 8" 175.00
Plate, fish & daisy on cobalt, Holdcroft, 9" 175.00
Plate, Morning-Glory, red/gr on med bl, shaped rim, 9" 175.00
Plate, napkin on basketweave, mc Morley, 8¾" 250.00
Plate, portrait, floral swags on 8-sided rim, Wedgwood, 9" 300.00
Plate, Water Lily, gr, Minton, 9" 300.00
Platter, appl fish amid sea creatures, France, rpr, 13½" 500.00
Platter, Banana Leaves & Bows, unmk, 14½" 300.00
Platter, cherries & butterflies on turq, Germany, 11" 85.00
Platter, roses on basketweave, cobalt rim, 13" 250.00
Platter, strawberry & flower border, Wedgwood, 1883, 13" 400.00
Salt cellar, stag's head supports dish, Minton, 1880s, 4½" 900.00
Sardine box, Sardinia, boat form, gr stripes, Wedgwood, 8"........800.00
Sardine box, 2 lg Xd fish on lid, Etruscan, 6" W...........................800.00
Shaker, gold stippled, gr ferns at base, rare 195.00
Spooner, Shell, albino, unmk Etruscan, 3½" 140.00
Strawberry dish, berries & flowers, Minton, 1868, 8½" 1,000.00
Sugar bowl, cottage form, 3-color w/lav int, 4"..............................200.00
Sweetmeat centerpc, dk-skin boy w/bowl stands on rocks, 20" .. 1,500.00
Syrup, Sunflower, cobalt, Etruscan...400.00
Tazza, leaves on trunk base, Griffin-Smith-Hill, 1885, 9½" 400.00
Teapot, cat on hdl, mouse finial, iron form, Minton, 7½" 6,000.00
Teapot, chick on nest form, twig hdl, 6"...275.00
Teapot, Chinaman holding coconut, Holdcroft, 7".......................500.00
Teapot, Fan & Bird, mc on cream, England, 5", +cr/sug 500.00

Teapot, fish swallowing fish form, tail hdl, England, 11" **600.00**
Teapot, floral, branch hdl/acorn finial, England, 1860s, 7¼".......**300.00**
Teapot, Holly & Berries on bl lattice, bark spout/hdl, 6" **250.00**
Teapot, monkey holding melon form, tail hdl, Minton........... **2,400.00**
Teapot, monkey on bk of snake form, Portugal, rstr, 9" **900.00**
Teapot, Oriental man form, queue hdl, Minton, rpr, 5" **1,200.00**
Teapot, Oriental village scenes, rectangular, 1880s, 9½" **500.00**
Tile, birds at nest, brass fr, Minton-Hollins-Co, 7¼"..................**300.00**
Toby jug, lady w/fan, hair forms hdl, Minton, 1862, 11¼" **1,500.00**
Toby jug, Quaker man & lady, Minton, 1868, 11¼", pr.......... **1,700.00**
Tray, bread; basketweave, rope border, England, 1880s, 10"........**300.00**
Tray, bread; X-hatching w/in rope trim, Wedgwood, 1883, 13"...**400.00**
Tray, fruit; acorns & oak leaves, Etruscan, 12" **400.00**
Tray, relish; Onion & Pickle, cobalt ground, Wedgwood, 8" **300.00**
Trivet, iris on lt bl, sq, ftd, late 1800s, 12" **300.00**
Tureen, dead rabbit & bird on lid, Minton, 1860s, 14½" L **2,500.00**
Umbrella stand, bird/butterfly/etc, Fielding, 1878, rpr, 23" **1,200.00**
Umbrella stand, floral/bamboo, unmk Holdcroft, 1880, 24".... **1,200.00**

Vase, applied grapes and leaves, Thomas Shirley, 12", $295.00.

Vase, bird & morning-glories, Holdcroft, 1885, rstr, 17¼" **1,200.00**
Vase, bird among bullrushes, G Jones, 1874, rstr, 9¼" **1,100.00**
Vase, heron on lt bl, cylindrical, Holdcroft, 11¼" **1,000.00**
Vase, lady w/fan by tree trunk form, Continental, 12" **400.00**
Vase, mermaids mtd ea side, dbl loop hdls, Minton, 1865, 16". **1,400.00**
Vase, Pineapple & Hand figural, cuff at wrist, 7¼" **600.00**
Vase, pond lilies on shell shape, Continental, 1880s, 19¼" **600.00**
Vase, ram's head relief, Thomas Shirley, 6" **500.00**
Vase, songbird beside trumpet flower form, 5", pr **800.00**
Wall pocket, basket form w/panels & vines, Minton, rstr........ **1,000.00**
Wash basin, Secessionist ware, w/lid, Minton, 10½" **600.00**

Malachite Glass

Malachite is a type of art glass that exhibits strata-like layerings in shades of green, similar to the mineral in its natural form. Some examples have an acid-etched mark of Moser/Carlsbad, usually on the base. However, it should be noted that in the past fifteen years there have been reproductions from Czechslovakia with a paper label. Our advisor for this category is Donald Penrose; he is listed in the Directory under Ohio.

Ash tray, Zodiac animals, Moser/Carlsbad, 2x5½"..........................**85.00**

Basket, woman & cherubs, loop hdl, 6x6½" **150.00**
Box, nude women on lid, Moser/Carlsbad, 3x4" dia....................**125.00**
Box, turtle form, ridged bk (lid), 4x8"..**75.00**
Buddha on lotus base, beaded headdress, 6x7½"...........................**90.00**

Basket, woman and cherubs, loop handle, 6x6½", $150.00.

Cat seated, tail around paw, 4½"..**45.00**
Vase, nude woman & grapes, Moser/Carlsbad, 9½" **175.00**
Vase, nude women & flowers, Moser/Carlsbad, 5", pr.................**150.00**
Vase, semi-nude woman ea corner, 7x10½" **750.00**

Mantel Lustres

Mantel lustres are decorative vases or candle holders made from all types of glass, often highly decorated, and usually hung with one or more rows of prisms. In the listings that follow, values are given for a pair.

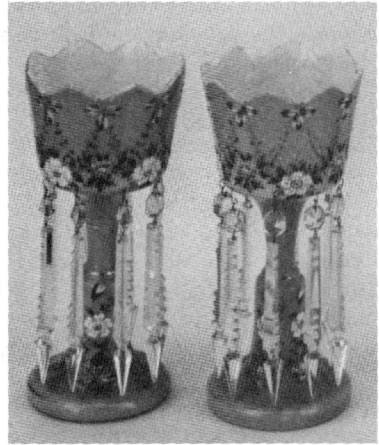

Cased pink Bristol lustres with florals and gold, faceted prisms, 11½", $350.00 for the pair.

Cranberry w/HP floral, scalloped, long prisms, 14" **540.00**
Gr/wht o/l, HP floral, tulip-form top, prisms, Bohemian, 12" **750.00**
Gr/wht o/l, out-trn petal top, long prisms, Bohemian, 13" **900.00**
Lead crystal, cut, w/prisms, 14" **450.00**
Pk cased in wht w/gilt florals, 2 rows of prisms, 15" **400.00**
Pk w/HP flowers & gold panels, teardrop prisms, 12"...................**450.00**
Pk w/wht fleur-de-lis/bl dots/gold scrolls, prisms, 15" **750.00**
Ruby glass w/HP floral & gilt, Bohemian, 1800s, 14"...................**475.00**

Maps and Atlases

Maps are highly collectible, not only for historical value but also for their sometimes elaborate artwork, legendary information, or data that since they were printed has been proven erroneous. There are many types of maps including geographical, military, celestial, road, and railroad. The most valuable are those made before the mid-1800s. Our advisor for this category is Judd Caplovich; he is listed in the Directory under Connecticut.

Key: hc — hand colored   p — publisher

Atlases

Asher & Adams Atlas, 1871, lg folio, VG 150.00
Burritt's Atlas, hc, 1835, lg folio, VG 250.00
Colton's Atlas of the World, 47 sm & lg folio maps, 1856..........350.00

German adaptation of the Bellin mapping of Canada, ca 1755, hand colored, 28x23", EX, $250.00.

Handy Royal Atlas of Modern Geography, 1886, 45 maps, EX ...250.00
J Olney's New & Improved School Atlas, ca 1830, folio, EX 125.00
J Olney's New Illustrated Family Atlas..., 1865, lg folio 425.00
Melish's US, Carey, lg folio w/leather covers, 1821, EX..............625.00
Mitchell's Ancient Atlas, E Butler, 1844, sm folio 25.00
Mitchell's New Gen, 147 maps & plans, Bradley, 1886, VG 200.00
Philco Radio Atlas of World, 1934-35, EX 7.50
Royal Atlas of...Geography, 1895, Edinburgh, 56 maps, EX 400.00

Maps

Asia, hc, HS Tanner, 1823, 18½x21½", EX 200.00
Australia, fancy border, Tallis, London, 1851, 14x10", VG 135.00
Bohemia, figures/views in borders, eng, John Speed, 1626...........200.00
British Empire in N Am, Gibson, 1762, 9¾x8¼" 150.00
CA, hc, fancy border, Colton, NY, 1860, 13x16", EX..................115.00
CA/San Francisco inset, fancy border, Colton, 1860, 13x16"......100.00
Canada w/New Brunswick, Bradford & Goodrich, 1842, 12x14" .85.00
Choctaw Nation, Indian Territory; Bien, ca 1900, 36x32" 50.00
DE & MD, fancy border, Johnson & Browning, 1861, 13x16".......65.00
Delaware Bay & River, Fisher, Phila, 1776, 7½x9½" 150.00
Emigrant Indians W of AR & MO, Bowen & Co, 19x18" 50.00
Europe, eng, Robert Wilkinson, London, 1790s, 8½x11"..............35.00
FL w/inset FL Keys, fancy border, AJ Johnson, 1867, 13x16".........65.00
GA w/RR & canals, hc, Bradford & Goodrich, 1842, 14½x12" ..110.00
Geology of the Globe, hc, Hitchcock, 1853, 19x23", VG 155.00
Great Plains, N TX & NM; Morse & Breese, 1844, 14x11", EX .400.00

HI & HI Islands in 1885, EX detail, GPO, 1906, 50x40", VG 85.00
Indian Reservations...US; litho, H Price, 1883, 18x30", EX 75.00
Indian Reservations...US; Sackett/Wilhelms, 1898, 23x32½" 50.00
Indian Territory & OK, litho, Bien, 1890, 25x29" 60.00
KY, hc, Bradford & Goodrich, Boston, 1842, 12x14½" 115.00
LA, full color, fancy border, Colton, 1860, 13x16", EX................65.00
MN & Dakota, fancy border, Mitchell, 1860, 12x13" 65.00
MS, Morse & Breese, 1842, 14x11", VG 75.00
MS & Province of LA, JB Homann, ca 1687, 19½x23" 300.00
N Am, eng, hc, D Burgess, 1839, 8½x10½", VG 85.00
N Am, hc, W Marshall, 1835, 10½x8½", EX 100.00
N Am, Radefeld, Hildburghausen, 1847, 12x14".........................75.00
N Am w/pre-LA Purchase borders, Harisson, Paris, 7¼x8½" 85.00
NE, Dakota, ID & MT; hc, Johnson & Ward, 1866, 18x26" 90.00
New Zealand, Tallis, London, 1851, 14x10", EX 90.00
Niagara, Eye Sketch of the Falls; Stockdale, 1798, 6½x9"..............60.00
Nova Anglia Septentronali Americae..., Homann, 1740, 19x23"..600.00
OH, eng, John Melish, Phila, 1815, lt stain, 14x12" 175.00
OH, hc, Greenleaf, Boston, 1842, 12x13", EX 130.00
OH, hc/eng, p John Kilborne, Columbus, 1822, 32x31" 650.00
OH, hc/eng, 1838, 19x16"..225.00
OH Dept of Int, hc/eng, Major & Knapp, 1866, 18x20", EX 150.00
OK Indian Territory, hc, GPO, Washington, 1889, 27x33", EX....95.00
Richmond VA in 1864, hc, Washington, ca 1893, 17x28", EX...140.00
S Pole & S Hemisphere, Greenleaf, 1842, 10½" dia, EX.............125.00
SW Mexico, Mawman, London, 1827, 7x9", EX 130.00
TN, hc, Bradford & Goodrich, Boston, 1842, 12x14½" 100.00
US, eng w/vignettes, Tallis, London, 1851, 11x13½", EX 180.00
US w/FL inset, eng, hc, detailed, Greenleaf, 1842, 13x15" 145.00
US w/Indian locations, Wilkinson, London, 1790s, 8¾x11" 100.00
US w/16 states, E Harisson, Paris, 1807, 7¼x8½", EX 100.00
VA & FL, eng, orig margins, Jansson, 1639, 15¼x19¾" 400.00
W Fl...Pensacola...Iberville River, Lodge, ca 1760, 8x14" 150.00
W Indies, hc, detailed, Greenleaf, 1842, 11x13", EX 100.00
WA & OR, hc, fancy border, Colton, 1860, 13x16", EX..............125.00
World, full color, EX detail, DuFour, Paris, 1864, 22x32" 475.00
World in hemispheres, Robert Wilkinson, 1790s, 11x17½" 125.00
World w/Cook's voyages, Tallis, London, 1851, 11x13½" 95.00

Marblehead

What began as therapy for patients in a sanitarium in Marblehead, Massachusetts, has become recognized as an important part of the Arts and Crafts movement in America. Results of the early experiments under the guidance of Arthur E. Baggs in 1904 met with such success that by 1908 the pottery had been converted to a solely commercial venture. Simple vase shapes were often incised with stylized animal and floral motifs or sailing ships. Some were decorated in low relief; many were plain. Simple matt glazes in soft yellow, gray, wisteria, rose, tobacco brown, and their most popular, Marblehead blue, were used alone or in combination. The Marblehead logo is distinctive — a boat with full sail and the letters 'M' and 'P.' The pottery closed in 1936.

Bowl, bl, 3x9" 300.00
Bowl, bl w/gray int, 3¾x9" 325.00
Bowl, bright yel semigloss, incurvate, 1½x3" 270.00
Bowl, flower/leaf border, 3-color on ochre, shallow, 7" 650.00
Bowl, leafy band, dk bl on slate bl, ftd, HT, 2½x6½" 450.00
Bowl, pk, conical, 4x6"...270.00
Bowl vase, florals at incurvate rim, 3-color, 3¼" H................. 1,100.00
Bowl vase, stylized floral devices, 4-color, 3¼" H 1,000.00
Candlestick, lav, step-down styling, 2x4", pr.............................210.00
Creamer, purple, 3"..100.00

Hanging basket, bl, 3 hdls at rim, 5" W 175.00
Hanging basket, gr w/brn flecks, 3 rim hdls, 6" 195.00
Hanging basket, lav matt, 3 rim hdls, paper label, 4x5" 225.00
Plaque, trees, 7-color, Baggs (?), screwed to fr, rpr, 6x10" 3,750.00
Rose bowl, lilac, 3½" 185.00
Tile, flowers in vase, lav/gr/bl on wht w/bl border, 6", VG 175.00
Tile, sailing ship, bl/brn/wht, wht border, 7" dia, EX 450.00
Tile, sailing ship, bl/gr/brn, in metal fr, 4¾" 450.00
Vase, Arts & Crafts floral, dk gray on gray speckle, HT, 9" 3,500.00
Vase, bl, ribbed w/finger ridges, fan form, 6" 250.00
Vase, bl, stick neck, low wide base, 6" 195.00
Vase, bl, wide body, 5"...225.00
Vase, bl, wide trumpet form, 4x8", NM 225.00
Vase, checked bands top/base, gray/brn/gr, sgn HT, 8½", EX . 1,600.00
Vase, dk bl, 8x3½" 475.00
Vase, floral clusters w/long stems, 2-color, H Tutt, 7x4" 4,200.00
Vase, flowers/arched branches, cvd/pnt, 5-color, 3¾" 2,000.00
Vase, geometric top/base band, sage on moss gr, HT, 11"........ 7,500.00
Vase, gray, bl int, expanded cylinder, 7" 295.00
Vase, gray, bulbous shoulder, slender base, 4"..........................210.00
Vase, lav, flaring rim, sm ft, 2½x4" 110.00
Vase, lav, glossy int, ftd bowl form w/flared top, 5x7" 325.00
Vase, leaves/berries, cvd/pnt, yel on brn/dk brn, 3½" 750.00
Vase, leaves/berries top to base, blk over bl, ovoid, 5½".............850.00
Vase, moth band, slate bl on stippled lt bl, artist sgn, 7" 1,900.00
Vase, parrots on branches, 4-color on mustard, sgn B, 7" 3,750.00
Vase, phoenix, bl-gray on gray, Baggs design, cylinder, 9"....... 4,000.00
Vase, pk semigloss w/tan specks, concave cylinder, 5" 250.00
Vase, poppy pods/leaves, dk gray on pebbly lt gray, MT, 7"..... 1,000.00
Vase, primitive trees/circles, 4-color, mfg flaw, 6¾" 1,200.00

Vase, stylized shoulder decoration in blue on dove gray, Hannah Tutt's monogram, 9½", $3,850.00.

Vase, stylized trees, 4-color, sgn HT, cylindrical, 4x4" 1,500.00
Vase, vertical panels w/sea horses, 5-color, wide base, 6"......... 5,500.00
Vase, wide stylized shoulder band, bl on gray, HT/#31, 9½" ... 3,850.00
Wall pocket, dk bl, hemispherical, 4½" 275.00
Wall pocket, gr, flared at top, 5x7" 300.00
Wall pocket, tan to rust semigloss, acorn form, 5".......................260.00

Marbles

Marbles have been popular with children since the mid-1800s. They've been made in many types from a variety of materials. Among some of the first glass items to be produced, the earliest marbles were made from a solid glass rod broken into sections of the proper length which were placed in a tray of sand and charcoal and returned to the fire. As they were reheated, the trays were constantly agitated until the marbles were completely round. Other marbles were made of china, pottery, steel, and natural stones.

Below is a listing of the various types, along with a brief description of each. When size is not otherwise indicated, prices are listed for mint condition marbles of average size, ½" to 1".

Agates: stone marbles of many different colors — bands of color alternating with white usually encircle the marble; most are translucent.

Ballot Box: handmade (with pontils), opaque white or black, used in lodge elections.

Bloodstone: green chalcedony with red spots, a type of quartz.

China: with or without glaze, in a variety of hand-painted designs — parallel bands or bull's-eye designs most common.

Clambroth: opaque glass with outer evenly spaced swirls of one or alternating colors.

Clay: one of the most common older types; some are painted while others are not.

Comic Strip: a series of twelve machine-made marbles with faces of comic strip characters, Peltier Glass Factory, Illinois.

Crockery: sometimes referred to as Benningtons; most are either blue or brown, although some are speckled. The clay is shaped into a sphere, then coated with glaze and fired.

End of the Day: single-pontil glass marbles — the colored part often appears as a multicolored blob or mushroom cloud.

Goldstone: clear glass completely filled with copper flakes that have turned gold-colored from the heat of the manufacturing process.

Indian Swirls: usually black glass with a colored swirl appearing on the outside next to the surface, often irregular.

Latticinio Core Swirls: double-pontil marble with an inner area with net-like effects of swirls coming up around the center.

Lutz Type: glass with colored or clear bands alternating with bands which contain copper flecks.

Micas: clear or colored glass with mica flecks which reflect as silver dots when marble is turned. Red is rare.

Onionskin: spiral type which are solidly colored instead of having individual ribbons or threads, multicolored.

Peppermint Swirls: made of white opaque glass with alternating blue and red outer swirls.

Ribbon Core Swirls: double-pontil marble — center shaped like a ribbon with swirls that come up around the middle.

Rose Quartz: stone marble, usually pink in color, often with fractures inside and on outer surface.

Solid Core Swirls: double-pontil marble — middle is solid with swirls coming up around the core.

Steelies: hollow steel spheres marked with a cross where the steel was bent together to form the ball.

Sulfides: generally made of clear glass with figures inside. Rarer types have colored figures or colored glass.

Tiger Eye: stone marble of golden quartz with inclusions of asbestos, dark brown with gold highlights.

Vaseline: machine-made of yellowish-green glass with small bubbles.

For a more thorough study of the subject, we recommend *Antique and Collectible Marbles, Third Edition*, an identification and value guide by Everett Grist; you will find his address in the Directory under Illinois.

Agate, contemporary, carnelian, 1¾"..175.00
Banded Opaque, gr & wht, 2" 375.00
Banded Opaque, red & wht, 1¾" 500.00
Banded Opaque, red & wht, ¾" 75.00
Banded Transparent Swirl, bl, ¾" 40.00
Banded Transparent Swirl, lt gr, 1¾" 300.00
Bennington, bl, 1¾"...15.00

Bennington, bl, ¾"	1.00
Bennington, brn, 1¾"	10.00
Bennington, fancy, 1¾"	20.00
Bennington, fancy, ¾"	2.00
China, decorated, glazed, apple, 1¾"	350.00
China, decorated, glazed, rose, 1¾"	400.00
China, decorated, glazed, wht w/geometrics, 1¾"	65.00
China, decorated, unglazed, geometrics & flowers, ¾"	250.00
Clambroth, opaque, bl & wht, 1¾"	1,800.00
Clambroth, opaque, bl & wht, ¾"	150.00
Clambroth Swirl, red/wht, Germany, 1900, ⅞"	275.00
Clear Swirl Lutz-type, clear w/wht & gold swirls, 1¾"	375.00
Clear Swirl Lutz-type, clear w/wht & gold swirls, ¾"	85.00
Cloud, w/mica, red & wht, 1¼"	450.00
Comic, Cotes Bakery, advertising	250.00
Comic, Kayo, rare	125.00
Comic, Little Orphan Annie	85.00
Comic, Moon Mullins	150.00
Comic, set of 12	1,000.00
Comic, Skeezix	100.00
Cork Screw, machine-made	3.00
End of Day, bl & wht, 1¾"	400.00
Goldstone, ¾"	35.00
Indian Swirl, 1¾"	700.00
Indian Swirl Lutz-type, gold flakes, ¾"	300.00
Line Crockery, clay, wht w/zigzag gr & bl lines, ¾"	25.00
Mica, bl, ¾"	25.00
Mica, gr, 1¾"	200.00
Onionskin, w/mica, 1¾"	500.00
Onionskin, w/mica, ¾"	75.00
Onionskin, 16-lobe, unusual, 2"	700.00
Onionskin, 2"	400.00
Onionskin, ¾"	50.00
Onionskin, 4-lobe, 1¼"	175.00
Onionskin Lutz-type, gold flakes, 1¾"	800.00
Opaque Swirl, gr, ¾"	35.00
Opaque Swirl Lutz-type, bl, yel, gr, or vaseline, ¾"	225.00
Peppermint Swirl, opaque, red, wht, & bl, 1¾"	450.00
Peppermint Swirl, opaque, red, wht, & bl, ¾"	85.00
Pottery, tan w/purple lines, 1¾"	35.00
Ribbon Core Lutz-type, red, 1¾"	800.00
Slag, machine-made, sm	1.00
Slag, machine-made, 1½"	85.00
Solid Opaque, bl, ¾"	75.00
Solid Opaque, gr, 1¾"	300.00
Sulfide, aardvark, 1⅜"	100.00
Sulfide, alligator, 1¾"	160.00
Sulfide, baboon, 2⅛", NM	230.00
Sulfide, bear, sitting, 1⅝", EX	80.00
Sulfide, bear, standing, 1¾", M	140.00
Sulfide, bear, standing, 2¼"	250.00
Sulfide, bear, walking, 1", M	110.00
Sulfide, bird, flying, surface wear, 2 int bubbles, 1¼"	80.00
Sulfide, bird w/long feathers, 1½", M	150.00
Sulfide, bust of Geo Washington, 2⅜", NM	650.00
Sulfide, camel, 2"	250.00
Sulfide, cat, 1¼"	75.00
Sulfide, cat reclining, many bubbles, 1½", EX	60.00
Sulfide, child, seated, 1½", NM	260.00
Sulfide, child w/ball & mallet, 1¼"	250.00
Sulfide, child w/sailboat, 1¾"	650.00
Sulfide, coin w/number 7, 2"	350.00
Sulfide, cow, grazing, 2⅛", NM	225.00
Sulfide, cow, 1⅛"	100.00

Sulfide, dbl eagle, very rare, 1¾"	675.00
Sulfide, dog, begging, 2", NM	160.00
Sulfide, dog, bird in mouth, 2"	600.00
Sulfide, dog, long haired, 1¼", NM	135.00
Sulfide, donkey, 1⅝", NM	125.00
Sulfide, dove, 1⅝", M	160.00
Sulfide, dove on post, 1⅛"	175.00
Sulfide, eagle, 1⅝"	185.00
Sulfide, eagle on post, 2", EX	285.00
Sulfide, elephant, 1⅝", M	160.00
Sulfide, fish, 2", NM	150.00
Sulfide, fish, 2⅛", M	200.00
Sulfide, fox, 1½", EX	130.00
Sulfide, goat, 1¾", M	150.00
Sulfide, goat, 2", M	225.00
Sulfide, hen, 1⅛"	100.00
Sulfide, hen on nest, 1½", M	300.00
Sulfide, horse, rearing, 2", NM	250.00
Sulfide, jackal, 1", EX	150.00
Sulfide, Jenny Lind bust (pnt), 1⅜"	900.00
Sulfide, lady in dress (pnt), 1¼", M	700.00
Sulfide, lamb, 1¼", EX	100.00
Sulfide, lamb, 1¾", M	140.00
Sulfide, lion, 1⅝", NM	85.00
Sulfide, lion, 2", NM	175.00
Sulfide, man & lady, 2⅜", NM	1,500.00
Sulfide, monkey, 1⅛"	95.00
Sulfide, otter, 1½"	135.00
Sulfide, papoose, 1⅝"	300.00
Sulfide, papoose, 2"	450.00
Sulfide, pelican, 1¼"	275.00
Sulfide, pig, 1¼"	90.00
Sulfide, pig, 1⅝", NM	120.00
Sulfide, pig, 2", M	180.00
Sulfide, rabbit, running, 2"	180.00
Sulfide, rabbit, 1¼"	80.00
Sulfide, raccoon, 2"	200.00
Sulfide, ram, 2"	175.00
Sulfide, rooster, 2", M	180.00
Sulfide, Santa Claus, 2"	350.00
Sulfide, squirrel on bk legs, 1½", EX	75.00
Sulfide, squirrel w/nut, 1½", M	100.00
Sulfide, squirrel w/nut, 2", EX	200.00
Sulfide, steer, 1⅝", M	125.00

Marine Collectibles

See also Steamship Collectibles; Telescopes; Scrimshaw; Tools.

Bell, brass, 6" dia, w/bracket, EX	30.00
Binnacle, brass top w/dry card compass, wooden base, 55" H	995.00
Book, Am Coast Pilot, Blunt, 17th edition, 1854, EX	65.00
Book, Art of Rigging, Biddlecombe, 1925, G	40.00
Book, log; India to England, 1789-92, worn	350.00
Book, record; ship's carpenter, leather cover, 1853, 8x13"	95.00
Bucket, tar; reinforced leather w/orig rope hdl, 12x9", EX	150.00
Cask, water; orig pnt, ca 1900, 11"	40.00
Chronometer, T Merser, EX in orig case	1,100.00
Chronometer, Ulysse Nardon, EX in brass-bound mahog case	950.00
Circumfercenter, iron w/brass vanes, Wadsworth 1877, 8½"	110.00
Clock, brass, strikes 8 bells, Waterbury, 4½" dial, EX	200.00
Depth recorder, brass, John Lilley, Pat 1821, 15" L, EX	115.00
Funnel, lamp-filling; copper, brass tag: Poop Deck, Aft..., 7"	25.00
Gimbal, brass, dolphin terminals, complete, pr	75.00

Gun, harpoon; muzzle-loading percussion, 1850s, 52" L **1,800.00**
Harpoon, dbl flue head, iron shaft, 1860s, 30", EX........................**195.00**
Harpoon, dbl flue head, steel shaft, 1860s, 24", EX **140.00**
Harpoon, wrought, single toggle type, wood shaft, 1830s, 35" **250.00**
Inclinometer, brass bezel Oman mk on dial face, G **90.00**
Lamp, hanging, brass, Perkins, electric, 17" **35.00**
Lance, fish killing; wrought w/steel shaft, 1840s, 26" **130.00**
Lantern, cabin, Viking brass w/grillwork, 15", pr **75.00**
Lantern, copper, brass label: Wm Harvie, Glasgow, 22", EX **95.00**
Lantern, copper, emb brass label: Seahorse, no burner, 22" **75.00**
Lantern, mast head; galvanized, mustard pnt, w/burner, 12" **50.00**
Lantern, officer's inspection, brass, oil burner, 12" **50.00**
Light, anchor; brass, electric, EX...**50.00**
Light, deck; solid brass, w/guard & socket from Liberty ship..........**25.00**
Light, mast head; brass w/port & starboard lenses, EX **60.00**
Light, Rushmore...Lens Mirror...NJ, NP brass, 8" dia **100.00**
Light, search; electric, w/bracket & yoke, 14" dia, EX **100.00**
Octant, ebony/brass/ivory, Spencer-Brning-Rust, 14", +case.......**560.00**
Octant, mahog w/ivory scales, brass fittings, complete, 18"..... **1,250.00**
Porthole, solid brass, 17" dia, EX...**85.00**
Pouch, document; gr canvas w/printed ship information **35.00**
Prism, azimuth, all brass fittings, well made, EX **50.00**
Propeller, bronze, mk Vaughn, 9" dia...**65.00**
Quadrant, bk staff; ebony w/boxwood, A Newel, 1750s, EX.... **3,000.00**
Rudder, brass, 44" L, EX **100.00**
Rule, parallel; brass, TS&JD Negus, 18", pr....................................**35.00**
Salinometer, cased brass, 10¼", EX in mahog box.........................**60.00**
Sector, solid ivory, ca 1900, 12" (opened) **100.00**
Sextant, dbl fr, brass w/silver scales, +orig case **1,250.00**
Sextant, Pillar Delux, platinum/gold scales, Heath, 1991........ **1,000.00**
Sextant, Spencer Browning, brass w/silver scales, EX..................**750.00**
Sextant, telescopic, Throughton & Simms London, pocket sz ...**500.00**
Ship's figure head, Indian princess, cvd wood, rpt, 56" **1,700.00**
Spade, blubber; wrought, hollow haft, 19" **60.00**
Thermometer, sea water; solid brass, mtd on teak panel.................**75.00**
Voice tube, heavy brass, hinged lid, 7x3" dia **20.00**
Watch, deck; Waltham US Maritime Commission, mahog case .**250.00**
Wheel, ship's; CI, brass-capped wooden spokes, mk, 90-lb **235.00**

Ship's telegraph, Chadburns of Liverpool, all brass, for twin screw vessel, 38", $800.00.

Martin Bros.

The Martin Bros. were studio potters who worked from 1873 until 1914, first at Fulham and later at London and Southall. There were four brothers, each of whom excelled in their particular area. Robert, known as Wallace, was an experienced stonecarver. He modeled a series of grotesque bird and animal figural caricatures. Walter was the potter, responsible for throwing the larger vases on the wheel, firing the kiln, and mixing the clay. Edwin, an artist of stature, preferred more naturalistic forms of decoration. His work was often incised or had relief designs of seaweed, florals, fish, and birds. The fourth brother, Charles, was their business manager. Their work was incised with their names, place of production, and letters and numbers indicating month and year.

Seated demon playing flute, wooden base, signed, 5½", $1,650.00.

Bird, heavily textured, head removes, rpr flaws, 16½" **16,500.00**
Bird, silver covered, winking, sgn/1897, 11".............................. **6,000.00**
Figurine, demon, seated, playing flute, wood base, 5½" **1,650.00**
Figurine, imp musician, seated X-legged, cream/lt brn, 5", EX **360.00**
Pitcher, bl foliage, monogram, 5" **88.00**
Pitcher, floral cvg, wht on brn, 4-sided w/hdl atop, 7½" **275.00**
Vase, blk-brn metallic bark texture, sq cylinder, 3½"....................**350.00**
Vase, fish/seaweed incising, brn tones/wht/blk, ftd, 8½" **995.00**
Vase, grotesque, 4-necked, claw ft, 13" **650.00**
Vase, poppies/dragonfly, HP/cvd, ftd, 1892/Southall, 8½" **400.00**
Vase, squash on red lustre, 7" W **185.00**

Mary Gregory

Mary Gregory glass, for reasons that remain obscure, is the namesake of a Boston and Sandwich Glass Company employee who worked for the company for only two years in the mid-1800s. Although no evidence actually exists to indicate that glass of this type was even produced there, the fine colored or crystal ware decorated with figures of children in white enamel is commonly referred to as Mary Gregory. The glass, in fact, originated in Europe and was imported into this country where it was copied by several eastern glasshouses. It was popular from the mid-1800s until the turn of the century. It is generally accepted that examples with all-white figures were made in the U.S.A., while gold-trimmed items and those with children having tinted faces or a small amount of color on their clothing are European. Though amethyst is rare, examples in cranberry command the higher prices. Blue ranks next; and green, amber, and clear items are worth the least. Watch for new glass decorated with screen-printed children and a minimum of hand painting. The screen effect is easily detected with a magnifying glass.

Bottle, amber, boy, cut faceted amber stopper, 9" **195.00**

Bottle, clear, girl w/flower, w/stopper, 9"........................60.00
Box, amber, lady w/necklace, hinged lid in brass fr, 6"................650.00
Box, bl, boy & dot decor, 3⅞x4" dia.........................250.00
Box, bl, boy w/hat, lift-off lid, 2½x3½" dia.........................195.00
Box, lime gr, boy, brass ft, hinged lid, 3¾x3¾"......................225.00
Box, lime gr, boy w/hat, 3⅜x5" dia.........................195.00
Brooch, blk, lady in plumed hat, oval, 1¾x1¼"......................295.00
Cruet, amber, boy, 3-petal top, amber stopper, 9½"..............265.00
Cruet, sapphire bl, boy w/flower, clear hdl & stopper, 8"............325.00
Decanter, cranberry, man w/watch, mushroom stopper, 9½".......375.00
Flask, lady's, gr, boy, brass collar/lid, 3¾x2¼"......................250.00
Goblet, cranberry, girl w/hat, clear ped ft, 4¾x2½"..............110.00
Lamp, bl/wht swirl font, bl base, girl fishing, 16¼".................1,375.00
Mug, amber, boy, bbl shape, 4x2½"........................65.00
Mug, bl, boy w/balloons, 4".........................75.00
Mug, bl, girl w/arms out, 4".........................75.00
Mug, clear, boy w/flowers, 2 gold leaves, 4½".........................50.00
Pitcher, tankard, olive-amber, girl, gold trim, 10¾".................375.00
Pitcher, tankard, sapphire bl, shepherdess, 10"......................250.00
Sugar bowl, clear, girl on ground, flesh tones, w/lid, 5".............85.00
Tumbler, cranberry, girl w/hat, 4x2"........................85.00
Tumbler, gr, 2 girls, 1 boy, 3 trees, 3½".........................75.00

**Vases, amberina, 10",
$850.00 for the facing pair.**

Vase, amber, girl w/balloon, scalloped rim, 10½x3¾".............225.00
Vase, amethyst, boy w/berry, 12"........................395.00
Vase, bl, boy, Optic pattern in glass, ruffled, 8⅝".................175.00
Vase, bl, boy on knee offers heart to girl, 11¾"......................460.00
Vase, bl, boy w/butterfly, 10x4"........................235.00
Vase, bl, girl picking apples, pnt rim, 12"......................255.00
Vase, bl, girl w/flowers, 6¾x3"........................165.00
Vase, bl, heron in flight, 11", pr.........................395.00
Vase, bl, lady in knee pants, flesh tones, rigaree, 10½".............250.00
Vase, blk amethyst, boy w/fishing pole, 11¾"......................245.00
Vase, blk amethyst, dbl figure, 11⅜x6⅛"......................450.00
Vase, cobalt, girl sitting w/flower basket, 4¾x4"......................195.00
Vase, cobalt, girl w/balloon, 4½x2½"........................85.00
Vase, cobalt, sailor boy or girl blow bubbles, ftd, 10", pr.............545.00
Vase, cranberry, boy blowing bubbles, ped ft, 9"......................295.00
Vase, cranberry, boy or girl, bottle form, 9x3½", pr.................375.00
Vase, cranberry, boy or girl reading, 4", pr.........................150.00
Vase, cranberry, girl, stick form, 5¾x2"......................125.00
Vase, cranberry, girl w/flower basket, 11".........................350.00
Vase, cranberry, girl w/umbrella, 9⅛"......................250.00
Vase, gr, girl w/flower basket, 12"........................300.00
Vase, gr, lady w/birds & hoop, 12½"........................320.00
Vase, gr, lady w/lilies, 2-pc, 21"........................1,500.00

Vase, gr opaque, boy w/bowl of flowers, ruffled, 11x4½".............225.00
Vase, lime gr, girl by shore, gold trim snail hdls, 11½"...............295.00
Vase, lime gr, lady w/fruit basket, 10"........................140.00
Vase, pk opaque, girl sitting on branch, 12x5½"......................225.00
Vase, royal bl, Alpine man, 11"........................365.00

Mason's Ironstone

In 1813 Charles J. Mason was granted a patent for a process said to 'improve the quality of English porcelain.' The new type of ware was in fact ironstone which Mason decorated with colorful florals and scenics, some of which reflected the Oriental taste. Although his business failed for a short time in the late 1840s, Mason re-established himself and continued to produce dinnerware, tea services, and ornamental pieces until about 1852 at which time the pottery was sold to Francis Morley. Ten years later, Geo. L. and Taylor Ashworth became owners. Both Morley and the Ashworths not only used Mason's molds and patterns but often his mark as well. Because the quality and the workmanship of the later wares do not compare with Mason's earlier product, collectors should take care to distinguish one from the other. Consult a good book on marks to be sure.

Cup & saucer, demitasse; Oak........................25.00
Cup & saucer, handleless; rose, 4-color, mk......................27.50
Jar, Willow Ware, bl transfer on wht, w/dome lid, 16".............275.00
Jug, Chrysanthemum, bl/orange, mk, 1860, 5¼", M.................235.00
Pitcher, Japan pattern, ca 1815, 6½"......................295.00
Platter, chinoiserie, mc, 1820-30, 17", M 155.00
Platter, Imari, mk, 15½" L........................300.00
Platter, Mandalay, Ashworth, 11½"........................42.50
Soup tureen, chinoiserie on gr & wht, floral finial, +stand.........800.00
Vase, chinoiserie, mc on bl, pagoda finial, 1840, rpr, 61"........1,200.00

Massier

Clement Massier was a French artist-potter who in 1881 established a workshop at Golfe Juan, France, where he experimented with metallic lustre glazes. (One of his pupils was Jacques Sicardo, who brought the knowledge he had gained through his association with Massier to the Weller Pottery Company in Zanesville, Ohio.) The lustre lines developed by Massier incorporated nature themes with allover decorations of foliage or flowers on shapes modeled in the Art Nouveau style. The ware was usually incised with the Massier name, his initials, or the location of the pottery. Massier died in 1917.

**Jug, handle formed as Nouveau maiden,
purple lustre with foliage design, signed,
24", $3,000.00.**

Ewer, purple irid, mask spout/crouching nude hdl, 10", EX **1,100.00**
Ewer, purple irid w/foliage, Nouveau maid as hdl, rstr, 24"...... **2,000.00**
Vase, butterflies, purple/gold on bl, turq int, sgn CM, 5¾" **700.00**
Vase, flowing colors of brn/gold/bl, cylindrical, 12", VG **125.00**
Vase, 2 dragonflies/cattails HP on gray-bl w/gilt, 7½" **450.00**

Match Holders

Before the invention of the safety match in 1855, matches were kept in matchboxes and carried in pocket-size match safes because they ignited so easily. John Walker, an English chemist, invented the match more than one hundred years ago — quite by accident. Walker was working with a mixture of potash and antimony, hoping to make a combustible that could be used to fire guns. The mixture adhered to the end of the wooden stick he had used for stirring. As he tried to remove it by scraping the stick on the stone floor, it burst into flames. The invention of the match was only a step away! From that time to the present, match holders have been made in amusing figural forms as well as simple utilitarian styles and in a wide range of materials. Both table-top and wall-hanging models were made — all designed to keep matches conveniently at hand. Our advisor for this category is Ron Damaska; he is listed in the Directory under Pennsylvania. See also Advertising.

Blk boys (2) hold basket, bronze-finished metal, French..............**185.00**
Boots on striker base, lacquerware, England **95.00**
Box holder on tray, bronze, Gorham...**95.00**
Box holder on tray, Hall China...**20.00**
Boy w/butterfly net, bsk..**45.00**
Bucket, bl opal, cut pattern, tab hdls, 2⅞x2⅝"..............................**48.00**
Cat, wood figural, tail is hanger, 10½" **25.00**
Clothing drying on line (figural), Japan..**18.00**
Cone shape on tray, decal decor, Haviland **95.00**
Cone shape on tray, stoneware **50.00**
Elephant, crackle glaze, holder in bk, striker on head....................**45.00**
Elephant head, milk glass, wall type...**165.00**
Hand holding container, amber glass **75.00**
Indian chief, mc bsk figural, 5x3"...**85.00**
Log cabin, hinged roof, CI figural, orig pnt, 1860s, 4x2½" **135.00**
Monkey in bow tie, hat at ft, striker on head, bsk, Germany **150.00**
Pipes & florals, unmk RS Prussia, dbl, rare **145.00**
Pockets (dbl), floral decor, porc, Heubach, wall type **125.00**
Punch, Go to Bed, brass figural, 6½"..**350.00**
Rooster finial, ped base, claw ft, CI **145.00**
Sled (work type), carries 2 sap buckets, brass...............................**150.00**
Urns (dbl), lacy CI, dtd 1867, 7½" **75.00**

Match Safes

Match safes, aptly-named cases used to carry matches in the days before cigarette lighters, were used during the last half of the 19th century until about 1920. Some incorporated added features (hidden compartments, cigar cutters, etc.) some were figural, and others were used by retail companies as advertising giveaways. They were made from every type of material, but silverplated styles abound.

Our advisor for this category is Ron Damaska; he is listed in the Directory under Pennsylvania. See also Advertising.

Advertising, leather, w/cigar cutter, NM **45.00**
Advertising, Red Top Rye, gutta percha, 2-pc................................**75.00**
German silver, florals & ornate scrolling along edge, M **35.00**
Gutta percha, 'hammered' motif, M **30.00**
Gutta percha, initials amid scrolling, lt discoloration....................**28.00**

Metal, cowboy roping buffalo emb, EX **75.00**
Metal, lady's face in man's smoke on mc celluloid insert **175.00**
Nickel & brass, Nouveau florals & swags, lt wear, EX...................**32.00**
Silver, enameled nude on shaped unemb form, 1¼" L **100.00**
Silveroine, Nouveau florals in relief, M **25.00**
SP, mermaid relief, Columbian 1893/Uncle Sam, Whiting **155.00**
Steel, 7 sm rose-cut dmns+sm cabochon sapphire, 1⅞" L **140.00**

Embossed sterling, fleur-de-lis and ribbons, $55.00; Nouveau scrolls, $65.00.

Sterling, fishing scene in relief, EX **32.00**
Sterling, floral eng, monogram, 1902, 1¾x2"................................**80.00**
Sterling, Nouveau lady's head relief, ornate...................................**95.00**
Sterling, nude/foliage repousse, shaped rectangle, 2½" **125.00**
Sterling, plain, B'ham 1899, w/ring for attachment, EX...............**75.00**
Sterling, scroll/floral repousse, free-form, 2¾"..............................**65.00**
Sterling, stripes, eng initials w/in circle, ca 1915, EX **65.00**

McCoy

The third generation McCoy potter in the Roseville, Ohio, area was Nelson, who with the aid of his father, J.W., established the Nelson McCoy Sanitary Stoneware Company in 1910. They manufactured churns, jars, jugs, poultry fountains, and foot warmers. By 1925 they had expanded their wares to include majolica jardinieres and pedestals, umbrella stands and cuspidors, and an embossed line of vases and small jardinieres in a blended brown and green matt glaze. From the late twenties through the mid-forties, a utilitarian stoneware was produced, some of which was glazed in the soft blue and white so popular with collectors today. They also used a dark brown mahogany color and a medium to dark green, both in a high gloss. In 1933 the firm became known as the Nelson McCoy Pottery Company. They expanded their facilities in 1940 and began to make the novelty artware, cookie jars, and dinnerware that today are synonomous with 'McCoy.' To date more than two hundred cookie jars of every theme and description have been produced. It should be noted that the cookie jar market is in an unparalleled state of flux at this time. Prices are extremely volatile; and the rarest, most desirable jars are commanding record prices. It's impossible to determine how much longer this upward spiral will continue.

More than a dozen different marks have been used by the company; nearly all incorporate the name 'McCoy,' although some of the older items were marked 'NM USA.' For further information consult *The Collector's Encyclopedia of McCoy Pottery* by Sharon and Bob Huxford, available at your local bookstore or public library. Our McCoy cookie jar advisor is Judy Posner; she is listed in the Directory under Pennsylvania.

Cookie Jars

Animal Crackers 95.00
Apollo Age, minimum value 400.00
Apple, 1950-64 ....35.00
Apple on Basketweave 45.00
Astronauts...200.00
Bananas 75.00
Barnum's Animals 200.00
Baseball Boy...150.00
Bear, cookie in vest 55.00
Betsy Baker 175.00
Black Kettle, w/immovable bail, HP flowers 25.00
Bobby Baker 45.00
Bugs Bunny, cylinder 185.00
Caboose...125.00
Cat on Coal Scuttle......................................150.00
Chairman of the Board, minimum value 300.00
Chef 110.00
Chiffoniere, Early American Chest 60.00
Chinese Lantern 55.00

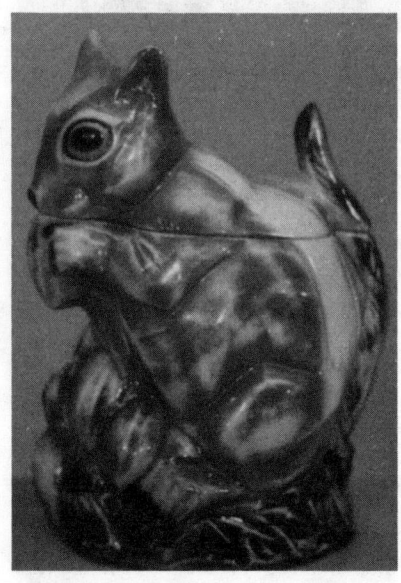

Chipmunk, $95.00.

Christmas Tree, minimum value 400.00
Circus Horse 150.00
Clown Bust 55.00
Clown in Barrel...95.00
Clyde Dog 125.00
Coalby Cat, minimum value 200.00
Coffee Grinder 30.00
Coffee Mug...30.00
Colonial Fireplace...85.00
Cookie Barrel 25.00
Cookie Boy 150.00
Cookie Cabin..75.00
Cookie Jug, dbl loop 25.00
Cookie Jug, single loop, 2-tone gr rope 22.00
Cookie Jug, w/cork stopper, brn & wht 18.00
Cookie Log...35.00
Cookie Safe..65.00
Cookstove 40.00
Corn..95.00
Covered Wagon 55.00
Cylinder, w/red flowers 25.00

Dalmations in Rocking Chair, minimum value 275.00
Dog on Basketweave.......................................50.00
Drum...55.00
Duck on Basketweave 45.00
Dutch Boy 45.00
Dutch Girl, boy on reverse, rare......................125.00
Dutch Treat Barn...55.00
Elephant..125.00
Elephant w/Split Trunk, rare, from 250.00
Engine, blk..125.00
Football Boy...150.00
Forbidden Fruit 65.00
Friendship...125.00
Frontier Family...45.00
Fruit in Bushel Basket 45.00
Gingerbread Boy..40.00
Globe 175.00
Grandfather Clock..65.00
Granny...75.00
Hamm's Bear..125.00
Happy Face...40.00
Hen on Nest 85.00
Hillbilly Bear, rare, minimum value..................350.00
Hobby Horse 110.00
Honey Bear 60.00
Indian...225.00
Jack-O'-Lantern, minimum value 300.00
Kangaroo, bl...225.00
Kettle, jumbo sz...30.00
Kissing Penguins 65.00
Kitten on Basketweave 65.00
Kittens on Ball of Yarn 85.00
Kookie Kettle, blk..30.00
Lamb on Basketweave......................................45.00
Leprechaun, minimum value 450.00
Liberty Bell..40.00
Little Clown 65.00
Lollipop...55.00
Mac Dog 65.00
Mammy 185.00
Mammy w/Cauliflower, G pnt, minimum value 550.00
Modern...35.00
Monk...40.00
Mother Goose..95.00
Mr & Mrs Owl 85.00
Oaken Bucket..25.00
Old Churn 25.00
Pears on Basketweave 35.00
Pelican...95.00
Pepper, yel..25.00
Picnic Basket 65.00
Pineapple 55.00
Pineapple, Modern...45.00
Pirate's Chest 55.00
Popeye Cylinder..185.00
Potbelly Stove, blk...35.00
Puppy, w/sign 75.00
Quaker Oats, from 300.00
Red Barn, cow in door, rare, minimum value 250.00
Rooster, 1955-1957...95.00
Rooster, 1970-1974...55.00
Round w/HP Leaves 30.00
Sad Clown 55.00
Snoopy on Doghouse......................................200.00

Snow Bear 65.00
Stagecoach, minimum value 350.00
Strawberry, 1955-57..35.00
Strawberry, 1971-75..30.00
Teapot..25.00
Tepee 225.00
Tilt Pitcher, blk w/roses 26.00
Tomato...25.00
Touring Car 75.00
Tudor Cookie House..95.00
Tulip on Flowerpot 95.00
Turkey..150.00
Two Kittens on Low Basket, minimum value..............300.00
Upside Down Bear, panda 55.00
WC Fields 165.00
Wedding Jar 85.00
Windmill..85.00
Wishing Well..40.00
Woodsy Owl 175.00
Wren House 95.00
Yosemite Sam, cylinder 185.00

Miscellaneous

Basket, oak leaf & acorn decor 25.00
Bean pot, Suburbia Ware, mk #7, 1964, 2-qt.............10.00
Beverage jug, Sunburst Gold, w/lid 40.00
Bowl, shoulder; bl, ringed, rectangular base, 9".........22.00
Bowl, shoulder; shield mk, #11 ....14.00
Churn, salesman's sample, 1½".................................35.00
Coffeepot, Grecian, gr & gold, w/creamer & sugar bowl 55.00
Creamer, dog figural, mk, 1950s...............................22.50
Jardiniere, flying birds, no mk, 1935, 7½" 24.00
Jardiniere & pedestal, Butterfly, no mk, 1940, 21" 125.00
Lamp base, horse figural...40.00
Mug, grape motif, no mk, 1926 ....10.00
Mug, Willow ware..10.00
Pitcher, chicken form, ivory, no mk, 1943 ....12.50
Pitcher, floral on brn, tilt style, 1939 ....25.00
Pitcher, tankard, Buccaneer, no mk 40.00
Pitcher, tankard, Indian Peace Sign, no mk, 1926........28.00
Pitcher, Water Lily, fish hdl, no mk, 1935................35.00
Planter, pear figural, mk #7, 1954............................10.00
Shakers, together form cabbage, 1954, pr..................30.00
Table, no mk, late 1930s, 20"...................................75.00
Vase, emb florals, lizard hdls, no mk 38.00

McCoy, J. W.

The J.W. McCoy Pottery Company was incorporated in 1899. It operated under that name in Roseville, Ohio, until 1911 when McCoy entered into a partnership with George Brush, forming the Brush-McCoy Company. During the early years, McCoy produced kitchenware, majolica jardinieres and pedestals, umbrella stands, and cuspidors. By 1903 they had begun to experiment in the field of art pottery and, though never involved to the extent of some of their contemporaries, nevertheless produced several art lines of merit. Their first line was Mt. Pelee, examples of which are very rare today. Two types of glazes were used, matt green and an iridescent charcoal gray. Though the line was primarily mold formed, some pieces evidence the fact that while the clay remained wet and pliable it was pulled and pinched with the fingers to form crests and peaks in a style not unlike George Ohr.

The company rebuilt in 1904 after being destroyed by fire, and

other artware was designed. Loy-Nel Art and Renaissance were standard brown lines, hand decorated under the glaze with colored slip. Shapes and artwork were usually simple but effective. Olympia and Rosewood were relief-molded brown-glaze lines decorated in natural colors with wreaths of leaves and berries or simple floral sprays. Although much of this ware was not marked, you will find examples with the die-stamped 'Loy-Nel Art, McCoy' or an incised line identification.

Loy-Nel-Art, jardiniere, mk, 1905, 6" 160.00
Loy-Nel-Art, vase, cylindrical, mk, 9" 135.00
Loy-Nel-Art, vase, integral hdls, no mk, 8" 135.00

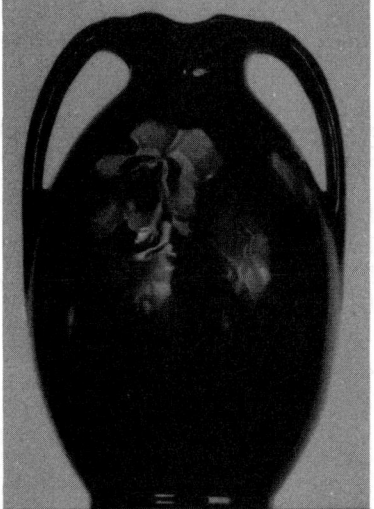

Loy-Nel-Art vase, 8", $135.00.

Olympia, punch bowl, 1905 ....550.00
Olympia, vase, integral hdls, ftd, 12" 250.00
Rosewood, ewer, 1905, 10" 275.00

McKee

McKee Glass was founded in 1853 in Pittsburgh, Pennsylvania. Among their early products were tableware of both the flint and non-flint variety. In 1888 the company relocated to avail themselves of a source of natural gas, thereby founding the town of Jeannette, Pennsylvania. One of their most famous colored dinnerware lines, Rock Crystal, was manufactured in the 1920s. During the thirties and forties, colored opaque dinnerware and kitchenware, Sunkist reamers, and 'bottoms up' cocktail tumblers were produced as well as a line of black glass vases, bowls, and novelty items. All are popular items with today's collectors. The company was purchased in 1916 by Jeannette Glass, under which name it continues to operate. See also Animal Dishes with Covers; Depression Glass; Kitchen Collectibles; Reamers.

Bottoms Up, butterscotch, opal, 3¼" 70.00
Bottoms Up, jadite, no coaster 50.00
Bowl, centerpc; Honeycomb, pk, ftd.........................45.00
Bowl, Red Ships, 9" 25.00
Canister, coffee; Red Ships......................................30.00
Clock, Tambour Art, amber or pk.............................300.00
Egg cup, custard 14.00
Egg cup, Red Ships, 1930s 15.00
Lamp, Danse de Lumiere, pk....................................600.00
Lamp, nude, gr 150.00
Lamp, Torchiere, crystal frost w/blk top 150.00
Measure, custard, 2-cup...30.00

Measure, jadite, 4-cup..**37.00**
Reamer, lemon; jadite **27.00**
Refrigerator dish, custard, red dots, 4x5"........................**20.00**
Shaker, Red Ships, blk top **12.00**

Medical Collectibles

The field of medical-related items encompasses a wide area from the primitive bleeding bowl to the X-ray machines of the early 1900s. Other closely related collectibles include apothecary and dental items. Many tools that were originally intended for the pharmacist found their way to the doctor's office, and dentists often used surgical tools when no suitable dental instrument was available. A trend in the late 1700s toward self-medication brought a whole new wave of home-care manuals and 'patent' medical machines for home use. Commonly referred to as 'quack' medical gimmicks, these machines were usually ineffective and occasionally dangerous. Our advisor for this category is Jim Calison; he is listed in the Directory under New York.

Book, Dr Minder's Anatomical Manikin of Female Body, EX **175.00**
Book, Sajou's Analytic Cyclopedia...Medicine, '23, 11-vol set ...**110.00**
Book, Textbook of Pathology, Wood, 1932, 1354-pg, EX..............**22.00**
Breast pump, brass extractor, Young, Edinburgh, VG **395.00**
Conversation tube, wht metal, horn-shaped silk-covered tube **235.00**

Cresolene lamp, complete, $95.00; box containing Cresolene inhalant, $20.00.

Ear scoop, ivory, ca 1860, in leather case..**88.00**
Ear scoop, silver, ebony hdl, hallmk 1804 ....**275.00**
Ear trumpet, aluminum, segmented, collapsible, 11", EX **295.00**
Eye cup, cobalt, 8-panel..**17.50**
Eyelid retractor, ivory hdl, mk Hills King St Borough, 1850s **125.00**
Fleam, brass, Greaves, ca 1840, +3 blades **100.00**
Infuser, porc, Berlin Germany **22.50**
Mouth gag, steel, 1700s, EX **195.00**
Needle, suturing; dbl, Savigny, 1850s, M in sheath.....................**185.00**
Opthalmoscope, Curry & Paston, ca 1890, +case **125.00**
Opthalmoscope, Dezeng, 1920s, EX in wood box **55.00**
Optometer, NP brass, Pat 1875, EX **75.00**
Quack machine, Glo-Pax, ultra violet rays, 1912, MIB.................**42.00**
Spoon, medicine; pewter, Gibson **335.00**
Spoon, medicine; sterling, dbl ended, mk 1881 ....**365.00**
Tongue depressor, brass, folding, unmk, ca 1890...........................**150.00**
Tooth extractor, bone hdl, 5½" **130.00**
Tooth key, ebony, X-hatched hdl, Weiss, London, ca 1850.........**395.00**

Meissen

The Royal Saxon Porcelain Works was established in 1710 in Meissen, Saxony. Under the direction of Johann Freidrick Bottger, who in 1708 had developed the formula for the first true porcelain body, fine ceramic figurines with exquisite detail and tableware of the highest quality were produced. Although every effort was made to insure the secrecy of Bottger's discovery, others soon began to copy his ware; and in 1731 Meissen adopted the famous crossed swords trademark to identify their own work. The term 'Dresden ware' is often used to refer to Meissen porcelain, since Bottger's discovery and first potting efforts were in nearby Dresden. See also Onion Pattern.

Bowl, figure of maid (or lad) aside, mk, 8x12", pr, EX **1,100.00**
Bowl, vines/flowers on yel & wht, vine-emb rim, 1900, 11" **200.00**
Bust of child, appl corsage, appl feather on hat, rpr, 6" **400.00**
Bust of child, appl floral corsage, gilt, 1880s, 6", EX....................**450.00**
Candelabra, 3-lite, figure by flower-encrusted std, 21", pr ...**1,000.00**
Candelabrum, 3-lite, appl flowers/HP bugs, 1880s, 12", EX **440.00**
Candlestick, florals w/gold, 6-sided top, Xd swords, 5½"..............**150.00**
Chandelier, 12-lite, 3 cherubs hold swags of flowers, 22½" **1,500.00**

Children working a wine press, 1890s, repairs, 13", $2,500.00.

Clock, allover appl florals+3 figures, scrolled case, 13" **1,000.00**
Compote, floral reliefs, gold trim, Xd swords, 6½x12"................**550.00**
Creamer, floral, magenta/gilt on wht, w/lid, mk, 5¾", EX............**225.00**
Cup & saucer, mc florals/bldgs/gilt, Xd swords.............................**65.00**
Figurine, Athena, owl & Medusa-head shield aside, rstr, 5½"......**400.00**
Figurine, boy in striped trousers/vest feeds ducks, rpr, 5".............**395.00**
Figurine, cherub gardener, mk, 4¾", NM **300.00**
Figurine, cherub on skull, mk, 8" **1,000.00**
Figurine, cherubs (2) lay brick, rpr, 3¾" **400.00**
Figurine, child kneels by dog eating from bowl, mk, 6" L............**650.00**
Figurine, child kneels by fish trap, lobster in bag, 4¼" **475.00**
Figurine, child w/horse toy, newspaper hat dtd 1905, 6½" **650.00**
Figurine, children (6) by wine press, rprs, 13" **2,500.00**
Figurine, couple, fancy 1700s garb, he w/bird, 28", pr, EX **700.00**
Figurine, cupid as St Geo stands on dragon, rpl weapon, 8".........**950.00**
Figurine, cupid blacksmith works on heart at anvil, 7½" **850.00**
Figurine, cupid w/spoon & bowl sits on brick oven, rpr, 6" **650.00**
Figurine, dog drinks from bowl, little girl sits beside, 3½" **450.00**
Figurine, flower girl, seated on oval scrollwork base, 4½" **250.00**

Figurine, girl w/mandolin, seated boy w/sickle, rstr, 6" 650.00
Figurine, group of 4 dancers, hands joined, mk 1910, 6", VG 250.00
Figurine, Harlequin family, 1880s, 7" 1,700.00
Figurine, Jes les unis, cupid by fluted column, 5½", NM 400.00
Figurine, lady gathers flowers in skirt 'bowl,' mk, 7½" 650.00
Figurine, lady in lacy attire lays cards on table, 6", VG 450.00
Figurine, lady in lacy winter clothing w/muff & tablet, 8" 1,300.00
Figurine, lady sits by table, sorts flowers, 1880s, 5½", EX 600.00
Figurine, lady w/grapes in apron, lg hat, 1880s, rprs, 6¾" 475.00
Figurine, man & lady, stylish attire, w/urn on plinth, 9" 925.00
Figurine, seated lady w/letter, standing man, 1880s, 5½" 550.00
Figurine, Turk by rearing horse, appl flowers, rprs, 10" 300.00
Figurine, Wind allegorical holds bird, cage aside, rpr, 5" 600.00
Figurine, youth/maid/child by urn, mk, rpr, 7¾" 950.00
Plate, lady in robe holds club, 1900, 9½" 300.00
Plate, mc floral/gilt, scalloped, Xd swords, 10½" 145.00
Shoe, w/cherub atop, decor, mk, lt wear, 6" L 500.00
Sweetmeat, figure seated by scalloped dish, wht, 10" L, pr...........300.00
Teapot, floral, magenta/gilt on wht, ovoid, mk, 4¼" 275.00
Tray, tea; floral, gold scroll/shell band w/open hdls, 16" 465.00
Urn, floral reserve/gilt on cobalt, serpent hdls, 12" 550.00

Mercury Glass

Mercury glass was popular during the 1850s and enjoyed a short revival at the turn of the century. It was made with two thin layers, either blown with a double wall or joined in sections, with the space between the walls of the vessel filled with a mixture of tin, lead, bismuth, and mercury. The opening was sealed to prevent air from dulling the bright color. Though most examples are silver, blue and gold can be found on occasion. Remember that the value of this type of glass hinges greatly upon condition of the mercury lining. In the listings that follow, all examples are silver unless noted another color.

Candlestick, gold, dome base, 6", pr..78.00
Goblet, gold, wht enamel floral band, 5" 38.00
Pitcher, eng floral, clear hdl, early, water sz.............................235.00
Tie backs, emb flowers, pewter fittings, 3½" dia, pr.....................65.00
Vase, floral sprays in panel, mc on silver, 10", pr.......................225.00
Vase, silver w/wht enamel birds, 7½" 50.00
Witch ball, 18", +stand 165.00

Merrimac

Founded in 1897 in Newburyport, Massachusetts, the Merrimac Pottery Company primarily produced tile and gardenware. In 1901, however, they introduced a line of artware that is now attracting the interest of collectors. Marked examples carry an impressed die-stamp or a paper label, each with the firm name and the outline of a sturgeon, the Indian word for which was Merrimac.

Bowl, blossoms/lily pads cvd on dk feathered gr, 5x8½" 1,400.00
Bowl, crackled pk mottle, incurvate, 2x5", NM 175.00
Bowl, gr, brn int, flared cone form w/hdls, 3x7½" 175.00
Bowl, gr matt & speckled blk, angled shoulder, 2¾x6" 250.00
Vase, gr glaze, bulbous, imp sturgeon mk, 9½x9½" 475.00
Vase, lt gr/gray mottle on dk gr, compressed sphere, 6" 650.00
Vase, orange-red clay w/clear overglaze, imp mk, 4½x8" 135.00
Vase, stylized leaves/buds, feathered gr matt, 6x5", NM.............800.00

Metlox

The Metlox Manufacturing Company was founded in 1927 in Manhattan Beach, California. Before 1934 when they began producing the ceramic housewares for which they have become famous, they made ceramic and neon outdoor advertising signs. The company went out of business in 1989.

Well-known sculptor Carl Romanelli designed artware in the late 1930s and early 1940s (and again briefly in the 1950s). His work is especially sought after today. For further information we recommend *The Collector's Encyclopedia of California Pottery* by our advisor, Jack Chipman; he is listed in the Directory under California.

Antique Grape, bowl, cereal 6.00
Antique Grape, bowl, divided, rnd, 9½" 15.00
Antique Grape, bowl, vegetable; oval......................................20.00
Antique Grape, cup & saucer..6.00
Antique Grape, gravy boat, w/liner 15.00
Antique Grape, plate, 10½" 8.50
Antique Grape, plate, 6½" 4.00
Antique Grape, plate, 7½" 5.00
Antique Grape, platter, 12" 15.00
California Ivy, bowl, berry; 5¼" 6.00
California Ivy, bowl, cereal; 6¾" 8.00
California Ivy, bowl, vegetable; divided...................................20.00
California Ivy, bowl, vegetable; 9" 18.00
California Ivy, butter dish..25.00
California Ivy, casserole, w/lid..35.00
California Ivy, chop plate, 13" 25.00
California Ivy, cream soup 10.00
California Ivy, creamer & sugar bowl......................................15.00
California Ivy, cup, demitasse...10.00
California Ivy, cup & saucer 8.00
California Ivy, gravy boat 16.00
California Ivy, plate, 10" 10.00
California Ivy, plate, 6¼" 4.00
California Ivy, plate, 8" 7.00
California Ivy, plate, 9¼" 9.00
California Ivy, platter, 11" 18.00
California Ivy, shakers, pr 8.00
California Ivy, tumbler, 6" 18.00
California Provincial, coffeepot..40.00
California Provincial, creamer...7.00
California Provincial, sugar bowl 8.00
Delphinium, bowl, vegetable; 8¾" 20.00
Delphinium, bowl, 6"..8.00
Delphinium, bowl, 9¾"..18.00
Delphinium, creamer 7.00
Delphinium, cup & saucer...10.00
Delphinium, plate, 9"..9.00
Fruit Basket, creamer 6.00
Fruit Basket, platter, 13¾"..12.50
Fruit Basket, platter, 9½"..8.50
Fruit Basket, shakers, pr 8.50
Homestead Provincial, chop plate...15.00
Homestead Provincial, creamer 8.00
Homestead Provincial, cup & saucer.......................................10.00
Homestead Provincial, plate, 10" 6.00
Homestead Provincial, plate, 6" 4.00
Homestead Provincial, plate, 7½" 5.00
Homestead Provincial, platter, 11" 15.00
Homestead Provincial, platter, 13" 20.00
Homestead Provincial, server, 2-part.......................................25.00
Homestead Provincial, shakers, hdl, pr 8.00
Homestead Provincial, soup, flat...10.00
Peach Blossom, bowl, vegetable; 8⅞".......................................10.00
Peach Blossom, pitcher, twig hdl...25.00

Peach Blossom, plate, sq, 10¼" 8.00
Peach Blossom, plate, 6" 4.00
Provincial Fruit, bowl, tab hdl, 5" 6.00
Provincial Fruit, bowl, vegetable; divided, stick hdl 20.00
Provincial Fruit, canister, sugar 20.00
Provincial Fruit, pitcher, ice lip 25.00
Red Rooster, creamer...10.00
Red Rooster, cup & saucer 10.00
Red Rooster, plate, 10" 10.00
Red Rooster, plate, 7½" 6.00
Red Rooster, server, 3-part, 9x13" 40.00
Sculptured Daisy, bowl, cereal; 7" 4.50
Sculptured Daisy, bowl, 6" 4.00
Sculptured Daisy, bowl, 8½" 5.00
Sculptured Daisy, canisters, set of 3 ....75.00
Sculptured Daisy, cookie jar 45.00
Sculptured Daisy, creamer & sugar bowl, w/lid 10.00
Sculptured Daisy, cup & saucer 6.00
Sculptured Daisy, gravy boat 20.00
Sculptured Daisy, plate, 10½" 6.00
Sculptured Daisy, platter, 11" 12.50
Sculptured Daisy, platter, 14¼" 22.00
Sculptured Daisy, shakers, pr 12.50
Sculptured Zinnia, bowl, salad; ind 6.00
Sculptured Zinnia, bowl, vegetable; oval 12.50
Sculptured Zinnia, bowl, 7" 3.00
Sculptured Zinnia, butter dish 15.00
Sculptured Zinnia, creamer & sugar bowl 8.00
Sculptured Zinnia, cup & saucer 6.50
Sculptured Zinnia, plate, dinner 10.00
Sculptured Zinnia, plate, 7½" 5.00
Sculptured Zinnia, shakers, pr 7.50
Sculptured Zinnia, teapot 35.00

Cookie Jars

Barrel of Apples 50.00
Basket of Fruit..50.00
Bear, bl coat...55.00
Bear, roller skates 60.00
Bear, sombrero..60.00
Bear, sweater & cookie 50.00
Beau Bear 40.00
Black Topsy Girl, bl skirt, red belt 185.00
Clown 80.00
Cow, crier in lid 195.00
Drum, bsk, mk 30.00
Dutch Boy 80.00
Fido 65.00
Frog 68.00
Humpty Dumpty 70.00
Lamb's Head..70.00
Mammy w/Mixing Bowl, bl dots 175.00
Mammy w/Mixing Bowl, red dots 175.00
Owl, gr 70.00
Puddles Duck 65.00
Raccoon 135.00
Rose 120.00
Uncle Sam Bear...250.00

Romanelli Artware

Figurine, cowgirl, mc (HP), #1819, 9½" 195.00

Figurine, rooster, satin wht, 8¼".................................55.00
Figurine, water bird, satin wht, #1824, 9½" 75.00
Figurine, 2 birds on branch, satin bl, #1826................45.00
Miniature, alligator, satin bl, 9"..................................65.00
Miniature, donkey, brn, 3"..35.00
Miniature, flamingo, satin bl, 6¼"...............................25.00
Miniature, monkey on all 4s, turq/brn, 4½" 65.00
Miniature, sea horse, satin wht, 4½" 45.00
Vase, nude woman & cornucopias, satin wht, #1805 ....150.00
Vase, sea horse, satin bl, #1809, 9¼" 125.00
Vase, water-bearer woman, satin wht, #1816, 9¼".......95.00

Figure of a fish, Romanelli design, $75.00.

Mettlach

In 1836 Nicholas Villeroy and Eugene Francis Boch, both of whom were already involved in the potting industry, formed a partnership and established a stoneware factory in an old restored abbey in Mettlach, Germany. Decorative stoneware with in-mold relief was their specialty, steins in particular. Through constant experimentation, they developed innovative methods of decoration. One process, called chromolith, involved inlaying colorful mosaic designs into the body of the ware. Later underglaze printing from copper plates was used. Their stoneware was of high quality, and their steins won many medals at the St. Louis Expo and early world's fairs. Most examples are marked with an incised castle and the name 'Mettlach.' The numbering system indicates size, date, stock number, and decorator. Production was halted by a fire in 1921; the factory was not rebuilt. Our advisor for this category is Ron Fox; he is listed in the Directory under New York.

Key:
L — liter   PUG — print under glaze
POG — print over glaze   tl — thumb lift

#1005, stein, relief: tavern scenes/verse, 1-L, M 400.00
#1028, stein, relief: couple at harvest/verse, ½-L, M 165.00
#1044/1452, plaque, PUG: man's portrait, sgn Holbein, 17½" ...800.00
#1044/411, plaque, PUG: barmaid, 15", M..................................500.00
#1091/2368, beaker, PUG: waiter serving wine, ¼-L, M...............75.00
#1121, stein, glazed, mosaic, inlaid lid, .3-L, NM........................400.00
#1146, stein, etched: drinking scene, inlaid lid, ½-L, M 525.00
#1179/2327, beaker, PUG: Gesang, ¼-L, M 80.00
#1233/2327, beaker, PUG: boy & dog, ¼-L, M...........................140.00
#1290/3225, plaque, PUG: Hamburg, shield form, 13x11", M.....600.00
#1370, stein, relief: couple & verse, ½-L, M 198.00

#752, jester, 2-liter, minor flakes, $1,500.00; #738, student fox, 2-liter, minor chips repair, tang split, $825.00.

#1403, stein, etched: bowling scene, pin finial, ½-L, M 400.00
#1453, stein, etched: portrait, eagle finial, ½-L, M....................745.00
#1467, stein, relief: harvest scenes, ½-L, M 145.00
#1475, stein, etched: gnomes, grapes on lid, gnome tl, ½-L 635.00
#1476, stein, etched: gnomes, grapes inlay lid, ½-L, NM 400.00
#1526, stein, PUG: knight & verse, pewter lid, 1-L, M 300.00
#1526/1076, stein, PUG: man drinking, bird lid, ½-L, M 300.00
#1526/1078, stein, PUG: cavalier, pewter lid, ½-L, M 265.00
#1526/1114, stein, PUG: Munich Child, ½-L, M........................285.00
#1526/1218, stein, PUG: Heidelberg, shield on lid, ½-L, M 300.00
#1526/599, stein, PUG: knight blowing horn/verse, 1-L, M 325.00
#1526/644, stein, PUG: couple & verse, pewter lid, 3-L, M 500.00
#1530/593, stein, PUG: XII Mitteldeutches...1889, SP lid, ½-L..775.00
#1537, vase, etched: cupids as 4 seasons, 14⅛", M 700.00
#1566, stein, etched: highwheeler, ½-L, M...................................825.00
#1577, stein, etched: tavern scene, pewter tang/lid, 4½-L, M......950.00
#1856, stein, etched: eagle, inlaid lid, ½-L, M 2,000.00
#1909/1097, stein, PUG: drunks & night watchman, ½-L, M 325.00
#1909/1350, stein, PUG: portrait reserve, rpr strap, ½-L 450.00
#1909/673, stein, PUG: dwarfs, pewter lid, ½-L, M.....................275.00
#1909/715, stein, PUG: Perkeo & cavaliers drink, ½-L, M 375.00
#1914, stein, etched: man w/flag, inlaid lid, ½-L, M 600.00
#1932, stein, etched: cavaliers, bronze inlaid lid, ½-L, M 550.00
#1995, stein, etched: man drinking, inlaid lid, ½-L, M 500.00
#1997, stein, PUG/etched: portrait in shield, ½-L, M...................275.00
#2005, stein, etched: interior scene, inlaid lid, ½-L, M 550.00
#2024, stein, etched/glazed: Berlin, prof rpl lid, ½-L 265.00
#2025, stein, etched: cherubs, inlaid lid, .3-L, M.........................300.00
#2035, stein, etched: Bacchus scene, inlaid lid, .3-L, M..............300.00
#2035, stein, etched: Bacchus scene, inlaid lid, ½-L, M 360.00
#2050, stein, etched: couple & verse, inlaid lid, ½-L, M 1,650.00
#2051, stein, etched: students, inlaid lid, ½-L, M........................600.00
#2052, stein, etched: Munich Maid, cherub inlay lid, ¼-L, M 365.00
#2074, stein, etched: caged bird, inlaid lid, ½-L, M.................. 2,500.00
#2098, stein, floral mosaic, inlaid lid, 4.4-L, M 650.00
#2099, stein, floral mosaic, inlaid lid, .3-L, M 385.00
#2132, pokal, relief: figure, stoneware lid, rpr, .9-L 500.00
#2133, stein, etched: gnome, inlaid lid, ½-L, M 2,000.00
#2140/763, stein, PUG: Kur Regt Nr 6, pewter lid, ½-L, NM......525.00
#2169, loving cup, etched: cavalier scenes, 3-hdl, 5", EX 255.00
#2176/1055, stein, PUG: men drinking in interior, 2.1-L, M 770.00
#2181/958, stein, PUG: cavaliers, pewter lid, ¼-L, M.................250.00
#2182, stein, relief: bowling scene, pin finial, ½-L, M 245.00
#2211, stein, relief: bowling scene, sgn HF, .3-L, M....................235.00

#2262/1054, stein, PUG: surrealistic scene, 4.2-L, M 1,200.00
#2268/1047, humidor, PUG: gnomes, 7", M.........................600.00
#2271/955, stein, PUG: maid serves man, ½-L, M 385.00
#2282, stein, etched: cavaliers, inlaid lid, ½-L, M 660.00
#2327/1288, beaker, PUG: fox, ¼-L, M...................................165.00
#2368/1140, beaker, PUG: cavaliers, ¼-L, M............................80.00
#2388, stein, character: pretzels, pretzel hdl, ½-L, M 365.00
#24, stein, relief: cavaliers, inlaid lid, ½-L, M............................350.00
#24, stein, relief: cavaliers, relief pewter lid, 1-L, M..................450.00
#2448, pitcher, cameo: dancers, 3-L, M 285.00
#2632, stein, etched: drinking scene, inlaid lid, ½-L, M 500.00
#2634, stein, cameo: cavaliers/jester, inlaid lid, 2½-L, M 1,500.00
#2715, stein, cameo: dancers in panels, pewter lid, ½-L, M 525.00
#2761, stein, cameo/etched: couple, rpl tl, 2.3-L 1,850.00
#2767, stein, etched: Munich Maid, ½-L, M 825.00
#2781, beaker, cameo: couple reserve, bl/wht, ¼-L, M.................350.00
#2789/6134, stein, Rookwood-type portrait, pewter lid, ½-L, M .500.00
#280/678, stein, PUG: men w/barrel, pewter lid, ½-L, M............200.00
#2815, beaker, cameo: dancers, ¼-L, M......................................295.00
#2818, coaster, etched: smoker toasting, 4½", M........................215.00
#2819, coaster, etched: drinking/smoking, 4½" 100.00
#2833, stein, etched: student drinking, brick base, ½-L, M..........555.00
#284, stein, HP: fraternal crest, strap rpr, ½-L...........................400.00
#2869, stein, relief: Munich, Hofbrauhaus finial, 2.9-L, M......9,000.00
#2909, vase, etched: Nouveau flowers, mc/wht, wavy lip, 17". 1,700.00
#2922, stein, etched: hunters at fire, ¼-L, M..............................275.00
#2935, stein, etched: hops & barley, rpr, ½-L.............................265.00
#2958, stein, etched: bowling scene, inlaid lid, 2.8-L, M............550.00
#3005, stein, etched: man in oval, sgn F Ringer, 1-L, M.............650.00
#3085, stein, tapestry/etched: man drinking, ½-L, M..................365.00
#3085, stein, tapestry/etched: postman, pewter lid, 1-L, M.........650.00
#3087, stein, tapestry/etched: lady drinking, ½-L, M..................440.00
#3090, stein, etched: guitarist & lady, ½-L, M 700.00

#3090, signed Heina Schlitt, 1-liter, EX, $650.00.

#3140/883, stein, PUG: Ulan Regt Nr 13, pewter lid, ½-L, M 465.00
#3142, stein, etched: dancers, Munich Maid on lid, ½-L, M........625.00
#3328, stein, transfer: man drinking, inlay lid, ½-L, M 345.00
#3364, sugar bowl, etched: Nouveau decor, 3x4½", +spoon 500.00
#3366, mug, etched: Nouveau decor, 2", M................................250.00
#402, stein, relief: knight, pewter lid, ½-L, M 600.00
#406, stein, relief: crest, pewter lid, ½-L, M...............................300.00
#5003, stein, faience: Nuremburg scene, rpl tl, 5-L 650.00
#6140/2784, Rookwood type, portrait, int glaze, 2.2-L, M 750.00
#7074, plaque, relief: cupid & lady, wht on gr, 1907, sq, 8" 400.00

Microscopes

The microscope has taken on many forms during its 250-year evolutionary period. The current collectors' market primarily includes examples from England, those surplused from institutions, and continental beginner and intermediate forms which sold through Sears Roebuck & Company and other retailers of technical instruments. Earlier examples have brass maintubes which are unpainted. Later, more common examples are all black with brass or silver knobs and horseshoe-shaped bases. Early and more complex forms are the most valuable; these always had hardwood cases to house the delicate instrument and its accessories. Instruments were never polished during use, and those that have been polished to use as decorator pieces are of little interest to most avid collectors. Our advisor for this category is Dale Beeks; he is listed in the Directory under Idaho.

Acme, brass & iron, EX, +14" case 250.00
Bausch & Lomb, 1876, brass, tripod base, 16", EX, +case 375.00
Bausch & Lomb, 1885, brass, tripod base, 16", EX, +case 350.00
Bausch & Lomb, 1897, all brass, horseshoe base, 14", EX............350.00
Bausch & Lomb, 1897, brass tube, blk base, 14", EX....................175.00
Bausch & Lomb, 1915, blk, horseshoe base, EX 95.00
Bulloch, Chicago, 1880, brass, Y base, complex, 15", +case.........650.00
English, Watson, 1880, binocular form, 18", EX, +case 750.00
English, 1870s, student form, brass, 12", case/accessories 265.00
English, 1876, professional form, brass, 18", case/accessories 775.00
French, drum or furnace form, 5", EX, +case 55.00
French, 1910s, student form, 9", G, +case 65.00
German, 1860s, student form, rnd base, G, +case 125.00
Grunow, New Haven, iron & brass, 15", EX, +case 450.00
Grunow, New York, iron & brass, 15", EX, +case 325.00
Gundlach, Manhattan, student form, all brass, 11", EX 165.00
Gundlach, 1879, brass, Y base, 14", EX..225.00
Magnifier, brass, on 3-leg stand w/screw-type focus, 1x1¾" 40.00
Magnifier, etymologist's, brass w/ivory hdl, 1850s 135.00
Manheld, 1890s, simple form, 3", G 45.00
McAllister, chain-drive focus, brass, 14", G, +case 325.00
McIntosh Battery & Optical, brass & iron, 12", G.........................225.00
Queen, brass & iron, Y base, 14", G, +case..................................325.00
Spencer Lens Co, brass, horseshoe base, 13", EX...........................155.00
Stamp magnifier, brass, 3-leg, 1½" H, G 20.00
Tighe, brass, 12", +case, EX 225.00
Tolles, Boston, 1880s, brass, Y base, 16", G, +case......................325.00
Zentmeyer, tripod base, brass, dbl pillar, complex, 18", G............950.00

Midwestern Glass

As early as 1814, blown glass was made in Ohio. By 1835 glasshouses in Michigan were producing similar pattern-molded types that have long been highly regarded by collectors. During the latter part of the 19th century, all six of the states of the Northwest Territory were mass-producing the pressed glass tableware patterns that were then in vogue. Various types of art glass were made in the area until after the turn of the century. Items listed here are attributed to the Midwest by certain physical characteristics known to be indigenous to that part of the country. See also Findlay Onyx; Greentown Glass; Libbey; Zanesville Glass. Our advisor for this category is Mark Vuono; he is listed in the Directory under Connecticut.

Bottle, club, aqua, broken blisters/lt stain, 7¾".................................65.00
Bottle, club, aqua, 19 swirl ribs, 8⅜" 70.00
Bottle, globular, aqua, 18-rib, appl collar, pontil, 7"......................195.00
Bottle, gold-amber, left swirl, rolled mouth, globular, 8"...............400.00

Flask, chestnut; bright gr, 24 vertical ribs, pontil, 5½"............. 1,100.00
Flask, chestnut; citron to amber, 18-dmn, minor wear, 6⅜" 1,600.00
Paperweight, gold-amber, solid free-form bird on dome, 2¾" 130.00
Vase, gold-amber, folded rim, 6¾" 150.00

Militaria

Because of the wide and varied scope of items available to collectors of militaria, most tend to concentrate mainly on the area or areas that interest them most or that they can afford to buy. Some items represent a major investment and because of their value have been reproduced. Extreme caution should be used when purchasing Nazi items. Every badge, medal, cap, uniform, dagger, and sword that Nazi Germany issued is being reproduced today. Some repros are crude and easily identified as fakes, while others are very well done and difficult to recognize as reproductions. Purchases from WWII veterans are usually your safest buys. Reputable dealers or collectors will normally offer a money-back guarantee on Nazi items purchased from them. There are a number of excellent Third Reich reference books available in bookstores at very reasonable prices. Study them to avoid losing a much larger sum spent on a reproduction. Our advisor for this category is Ron Willis; he is listed in the Directory under Oklahoma.

Imperial German

Badge, Bavarian Veterans Assoc, gilt medal, EX 50.00
Badge, wound; WWI, navy, stamped, blk pnt, EX 27.50
Badge, 50 assault tank; pierced silver w/skull & Xd bones, EX 550.00
Brooch, mourning; 1914 Iron Cross, silver, EX 20.00
Buckle, enlisted man, brass w/silver inset, EX................................30.00
Buckle, Wurttemberg General, brass/enameling, EX....................135.00
Epaulets, Army Medical Hauptmann, gilt on bl, pr......................75.00
Helmet, WWI, Prussian General, spike, brass fittings, EX 300.00
Letter opener, WWI, trench art, cartridge hdl w/crest, 7" 17.50
Medal, Hannover Langensalza, bronze, dtd 1866, w/ribbon 20.00
Medal, WWI, Iron Cross, 2nd class, tarnished, 1914......................20.00
Medal, WWI, sharpshooting, eagle center, blk enameling, 2" 35.00
Post card, Bismark commemorative, portrait, EX 5.00
Shoulder boards, WWI, enlisted, field gray, EX, pr 50.00
Tunic, Model 1915, General, gray wool w/red, EX 1,200.00
Watch fob, Kaiser Wilhelm, brass, ca 1915, EX.............................18.00

Third Reich

Armband, Deutsche Wehrmacht, blk on yel cotton, EX...............20.00
Armband, Veteran's Assoc, Iron Cross on dk bl wool, EX 50.00
Armband, WWII, Hitler Youth, complete w/RZM tag, M.............15.00
Badge, combat; WWII, Luftwaffe Observer, cloth w/embr eagle....20.00
Badge, Kriegsmarine U-Boat, brass, swastika, early, EX 135.00
Badge, Nazi, Navy Destroyers, wreath & eagle, EX 80.00
Badge, WWII, Luftwaffe Glider Pilot, silver wreath/eagle 165.00
Badge, WWII, Luftwaffe Paratrooper, diving eagle on brass, EX .125.00
Badge, WWII, propeller entwined w/swastika, silver, EX..............50.00
Badge, WWII, Tank Assault, bronze, EX 25.00
Banner, WWII, Nazi swastika & cross, 15 ½-ft 100.00
Bar, WWII, Close Combat, gilt medal, hallmk, rare, EX 200.00
Boots, riding; Army officer, blk leather, pull-on straps, EX...........65.00
Canteen, Afrikakorps officer, felt cover, web strap........................27.50
Cap, visor; Army Panzer officer, crush type, gr/pk trim, EX 325.00
Cap, visor; WWII, Waffen SS M43, camouflage cotton, NM......200.00
Chevrons, WWII, Luftwaffe Gefreiter, silver on gray wool, pr.......12.50
Collar tab, WWII, SS Panzer, gray on blk wool, EX 35.00
Compass, march; Hitler Youth, locking needle, 2x2" 55.00

Compass, WWII, Luftwaffe, wrist type, blk Bakelite, EX 37.50
Dagger, Kriegsmarine officer, Eickhorn, brass scabbard, EX.........250.00
Dagger, Nazi Youth, EX, +blk metal sheath 55.00
Disc, Concentration Camp ID, stamped tin, scarce.......................45.00
Driver's permit, WWII, Army vehicle, ink stamps, dtd 1940 ....25.00
Flying suit, WWII, Luftwaffe, blk leather, zip front, EX..............195.00
Goggles, WWII, desert vehicle driver, NM in tin canister.............15.00
Helmet, Army, M35 pattern, snow camouflage, EX 150.00
Helmet, Army Luftwaffe transitional, field gray, NM..................135.00
Helmet, Army M35/40 pattern, field gray, eagle decal, EX..........125.00
Helmet, Fire Police, pnt aluminum, decals, strap, EX...................35.00
Helmet, WWII, Luftwaffe Paratrooper, gray pnt, EX 750.00
Helmet cover, WWII, Paratrooper, camouflage, EX....................135.00
Insignia, sleeve; Hitler Youth, wht on gr, EX 20.00
Insignia, visor hat; Luftwaffe, metal wreath w/prongs, EX 10.00
Jacket, WWII, Army, camouflage, summer cotton, EX 165.00
Knee pads, Paratrooper, gray cotton w/elastic, pr 85.00
Manual, WWII, Army, drills, weapon use, etc, dtd 1941, NM 17.50
Map, German streets, eagle/swastika, Hitler on bk......................32.00
Medal, WWII, Police 1st Class Long Service, gold, 25 yrs............50.00
Mess kit, Army, utensils & can opener, eagle/41 on hdls 15.00
Mess plate, wht porc, eagle mk on bottom, 1939 ....10.00
Pants, Waffen SS Assault Gunner, gr herringbone, EX...............145.00
Plaque, Hitler profile, silver finish, fr, 10x8", EX.......................40.00
Sextant, swastika & eagle mk on dvtl box, EX 250.00
Shoulderboards, German Youth, red piping on bl wool, pr 20.00
Shoulderboards, SS Concentration Camp Unterscharfuhrer, pr..135.00
Shoulderboards, WWII, SS Artillery, silver/blk/red, pr................32.00
Telegram, Reichstag Buro eagle stamp, EX................................22.50
Uniform, Hitler Youth Athlete, shirt & shorts, EX 50.00
Wallet, Army, Solduch, eagle emb on leather, EX 22.50
Whip, 8-thong, leather w/wood shaft, 13", EX 25.00

Japanese

Backpack, WWII, Army, khaki canvas, webbed straps 20.00
Badge, breast; Frogman officer, gilt ship, wht metal wreath 12.50
Badge, Reserve, gilt star, anchor/Xd swords, lg, EX 18.00
Banner, WWII, mum/sun/flag, going into service, 9x33", EX 32.50
Bowl, Army, star on inside rim, 2x7", EX 17.50
Cape, WWII, Army officer, waterproof, w/hood & collartabs, EX ..55.00
Dagger, Navy officer, gilt wash, sharkskin grip, +scabbard...........145.00
Gas mask, WWII, civilian, complete w/straps & filter, 1943 ....12.50
Gloves, WWII, olive drab wool, fur lined, EX 22.50
Grenade, WWII, ceramic, spherical w/brn glaze, EX 35.00
Hachimaki, WWII, Navy, silkscreened anchor, 15x32", EX..........18.00
Helmet, Marine Landing Forces, mum emblem, camouflage, EX ..165.00
Helmet, WWII, khaki cotton, wht int, star insignia, EX...............60.00
ID tag, WWII, brass oval w/Japanese characters, EX...................12.50
Insignia, helmet; WWII, Naval Landing Forces, mum & anchor ..15.00
Jacket, WWII, Army, tanker cadet, wool, type 5, dtd 1944, EX.....45.00
Medal, China Incident, complete w/ribbon & case, M 27.50
Mess kit, WWII, gr-brn finish, int tray, NM..............................32.00
Muzzle cover, brass, for Ariska rifle 27.50
Scope, WWII, Navy Artillery Spotters, brass, 2-tube, EX............425.00
Socks, WWII, Army, wht cotton, unissued, 2 pr..........................12.50
Spurs, WWII, officer's, w/leathers & khaki pnt, M 35.00
Sword, WWII, Army Showa blade, 39", +metal scabbard............100.00
Sword, WWII, Naval officer, Showa machined blade, EX............225.00
Telescope, artillery spotting, 25x2 power, Nikko, +case 265.00
Tunic, WWII, Army, tropics, olive drab cotton, EX 75.00
Uniform, WWII, Army, khaki cotton, wood buttons, EX..............60.00
Wings, WWII, pilot, yel/silver embr on bl, VG 32.00

United States

Armband, WWII, Air Raid Warden, red/wht/bl, EX.................... 5.00
Badge, Spanish Am War Veteran, eagle atop flag, 1898 ....20.00
Badge, WWI, Armistice Day reunion, celluloid, NM.................... 8.00
Badge, WWI, Ship Building Identification, bronze, EX 15.00
Badge, WWII, Army Air Force Bombadier, sterling, EX..............30.00
Badge, WWII, Balloon Observer, cloth, wht on khaki, EX...........15.00
Badge, WWII, Technical Observer, cloth, wht wings on khaki 8.00
Banner, WWI, In Service, silk, 58x34", EX 25.00
Belt, Civil War, Naval officer, brass eagle/anchor buckle 75.00
Book, Collier's Photographic History of WWI, EX 25.00
Book, History of Civil war, Brady photos, 510-pg, EX.................75.00
Book, History of Transport Service, Gleaves, c 1921, EX 15.00
Book, Memoirs of Gen Sherman, 1875, 2-volume set, EX 55.00
Book, Peace Negotiations, Lansing, 1921, EX 7.50
Book, WWII 5th Armored Division Pocket History, illus, EX 32.50
Boots, Indian War, Cavalry, blk leather, ca 1870, EX..................50.00
Bugle, presentation; Spanish-Am War, gold-plated, ornate, NM ..135.00
Cannon ball, Civil War, Gettysburg pnt on side, 7", EX...............75.00
Canteen, Civil War Confederate, tin, pnt traces, 7½" 65.00
Card, Am Legion Life Membership, eng brass, NM.....................20.00
Chair, Civil War, folding, Bartholomew's Pat 1863, EX 75.00
Chevron, pre-WWI, Cavalry Sergeant, wool/cotton, ca 1900 ....22.50
Chronometer, WWII, US Navy, Hamilton Watch Co, '41, EX ..265.00

Civil War commemorative mirror, carved with bust of Lincoln, Black man, torch of Liberty and Bible, large eagle atop, ca 1870, 43" x 29", $4,750.00.

Coat, Civil War, Naval officer, 10 eagle buttons, VG...................50.00
Collar insignia, WWI, Army Headquarters, enlisted, bronze 7.50
Collar insignia, WWI, Cavalry, bronze, crossed sabers, EX 17.50
Collar insignia, WWI, Field Artillery, bronze, cannons, EX 7.50
Coveralls, flight; Navy, M-700, khaki nylon, EX.........................27.50
Flag, Civil War, Confederate, thin cloth, 12x18", G....................30.00
Fork, Civil War, bone or ivory, 2-tine, 5¼", EX 17.50
Graduation program, Officer candidate school, 1945, 32-pg 15.00
Haversack, Spanish Am War, tan canvas, stencil, 13x13", VG 22.00
Helmet, flight; WWII, Army Air Force pilot, khaki twill, EX 15.00
Helmet, WWI, 3rd Division patch, EX.......................................30.00
Helmet liner, WWII, Airborne, khaki, no sweatband or strap.......58.00
Ink blotter, Army/Navy insignia charts, 1942, 4x9", M 7.50
Insignia, hat; WWI Chief Petty Officer, anchor w/overlay 8.00
Jacket, field; Vietnam War, camouflage fatigue, EX 12.50
Knife, pocket; WWII, US Army, 2-blade, wood grip, EX..............22.50
Knife, trench; WWII, M3 pattern, Camillus, dtd 1943, NM..........75.00
Leaflet, propaganda; WWII, dropped on Japanese, EX.................32.00

Life vest, WWII, Navy, Mae West style, EX 35.00
Manual, field; WWI, engineer's, 1917, 528-pg, EX 17.50
Manual, Mexican Border 1916 Signal Corps, 64-pg, EX 17.50
Manual, WWI, Lewis machine gun, Savage Arms Model '17, EX .32.00
Map, WWII, 2-sided, Western Europe, cloth, 27x27", EX 22.50
Map case, WWII, khaki canvas, 4-pocket int, dtd 1942, EX..........20.00
Medal, WWI, Welcome Home, bronze, laurel wreath, 1919, EX ..25.00
Medal, WWII, Marine Good Conduct, bronze w/ribbon, M..........22.50
Navigation kit, WWII, Army Air Corps pilot, NM in case............48.00
Pants, WWII, US Air Force, fleece lined, VG.................................25.00
Parka, WWII, khaki cotton w/fur trim, reversible, EX 45.00
Pass, San Diego Electric RR, Insure Victory, 1944, 2x4"................ 7.50
Ration book, red leatherette, 8x7", M 12.50
Saddle bags, motorcycle; WWI, heavy leather, 6x11", EX 22.00
Shirt, Vietnam War, Navy Seabees, khaki, 2 flap pockets, EX 10.00
Shirt, WWII, Marine Corps, khaki twill wool, M...........................10.00
Shoulderboards, WWI, Navy Dental Corps Commander, EX, pr ..10.00
Spoon, apothecary; Civil War, wood, mk US on hdl 17.50
Spurs, WWI, Cavalry officer, NP fr, complete, EX, pr...................25.00
Stove, field; Vietnam War, gas burners, khaki pnt, 1963, EX 20.00
Trousers, WWII, Army Infantry, dress bl, gold side stripes, EX......22.50
Tunic, Coastal Artillery private, bl wool, ca 1895, VG...................95.00
Tunic, Korean War, Navy Petty Officer, tan khaki, EX 15.00
Tunic, WWII, Navy Commodore, bl twill, gold buttons, EX.........55.00
Uniform, Civil War drummer boy, NY, bl w/brass buttons, EX ...125.00
Uniform, Indian War, bl wool, brass buttons, EX.........................350.00
Uniform, Spanish War, 4-pocket wool tunic & visor cap, EX 95.00
Uniform, West Point cadet, swallow-tail, gray/bl, 1890s, EX 65.00
Uniform, WWI, Infantry private, khaki wool, EX.........................35.00
Uniform, WWII, desert camouflage, 2-pc, M 35.00
Wings, WWII, Army Air Force Glider Pilot, sterling, EX..............75.00

Milk Glass

Milk glass is the current collector's name for milk-white opaque glass. The early glassmaker's term was Opal Ware. Originally attempted in England in the 18th century with the intention of imitating china, milk glass was not commercially successful until the mid-1800s. Pieces produced in the U.S.A., England, and France during the 1870-1900 period are highly prized for their intricate detail and fiery, opalescent edges.

Our advisor for this category is Rod Dockery; he is listed in the Directory under Texas. In our listings, B stands for Belknap, F for Ferson, and M for Millard, all standard reference books. See also Animal Dishes with Covers; Bread Plates; Historical Glass; Westmoreland.

Bottle, Bunker Hill, sphere-shape closure, F-440, 14¾" 150.00
Bottle, Klondike Nugget, B-238b..65.00

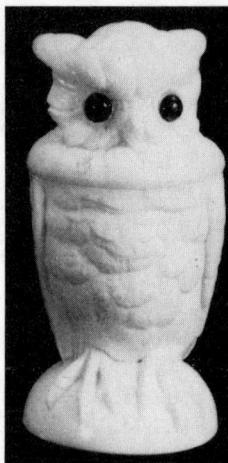

Jar, owl with glass eyes, 6½", $135.00.

Bowl, Blackberry, 5½" 12.00
Compote, Atlas, scalloped rim, B-103 ....100.00
Compote, Crossed Fern, scalloped, M-79b, 8½" 50.00
Compote, Jenny Lind, F-380/B-122 ....100.00
Compote, scrolling, 6-sided, Challinor & Taylor, F-383..............110.00
Covered dish, Baby Moses on cattail base, unmk, B-160, 6¼" 200.00
Covered dish, Baseball..22.00
Covered dish, Battleship Oregon, att Flaccus, 6⅜" L.....................55.00
Covered dish, Football, 5" 65.00
Creamer, Blackberry, F-251 ....45.00
Creamer, Paneled Wheat, F-255 ....50.00
Goblet, Strawberry...20.00
Jar, Queen Victoria, M-259a...100.00
Mug, Bleeding Heart, 3½"...60.00
Mustard, bull's head, dtd, F-53, w/ladle.......................................180.00
Pin dish, Star of David w/bl florals & gold trim, 4" 20.00
Plate, Anchor & Belaying Pin, old pnt, F-683, M-42a 30.00
Plate, Anchor & Yacht, B-17a 25.00
Plate, Beaded Loop Indian, B-8f 35.00
Plate, Block Border, fancy, deep, B-10a 20.00
Plate, California Bear, F-543 ....105.00
Plate, Chrysanthemum, B-14e, orig pnt, 6½" 25.00
Plate, heart shape, 6" 28.00
Plate, Horseshoe, Easter Greetings, PL Co 35.00
Plate, Jefferson Davis, F-554 ....48.00
Plate, Niagara Falls, B-8e...30.00
Plate, Woof Woof, B-13f...45.00
Plate, 3 Bears, F-473 ....35.00
Plate, 3 Kittens, B-14c, 7½" 35.00
Plate, 3 Owls, dtd 1901, F-500 ....35.00
Platter, Liberty Bell, Hancock, F-572, 13⅜" 260.00
Platter, Retriever (after bird), lily pad border, B-53......................95.00
Relish dish, Blackberry, 9½" L...20.00
Salt cellar, master; Strawberry, ftd..20.00
Spooner, Blackberry, F-253 ....38.00
Sugar bowl, Blackberry, berry finial, dtd, F-250 ....55.00
Sugar bowl, Ribbed Lacy Edge, M-134, b......................................35.00
Sugar bowl, Wild Iris, orig gold pnt, F-300 ....55.00
Sugar shaker, Grape, w/top...45.00
Tray, floral sprays in center, loop hdls, M-33b, 11x7" 30.00
Tumbler, Louisiana Purchase, M-193b..20.00

Millefiori

Millefiori was a type of art glass produced during the late 1800s. Literally, the term means 'thousand flowers,' an accurate description of its appearance. Canes, fused bundles of multicolored glass threads such as are often used in paperweights, were cut into small cross sections, arranged in the desired pattern, refired, and shaped into articles such as cruets, lamps, and novelty items. It is still being produced, and many examples found on the market today are of fairly recent manufacture. See also Paperweights.

Bowl, 2x3"..60.00
Creamer, 4" 65.00
Cup & saucer, 2¼" H...95.00
Lamp, 9" dome shade, bottle-form base, 19".................................725.00
Slipper, camphor ruffle & heel, 5" 145.00
Vase, stick neck, 8" 95.00

Miniatures

There is some confusion as to what should be included in a listing of miniature collectibles. Some feel the only true miniature is the salesman's sample; other collectors consider certain small-scale children's toys to be appropriately referred to as miniatures, while yet others believe a miniature to be any small-scale item that gives evidence to the craftsmanship of its creator. For salesman's samples see specific category; other types are listed below. See also Dollhouses and Furnishings; Children's Things.

Ranking at the top of today's leading collectibles, scaled 1:12" miniatures represent the work of hundreds of artisans who supply local shops with highly prized one-of-a-kind articles and specialties, all scaled one inch to the foot. Many leading producers and distributors of collectibles have entered the field as well. Clubs for miniature enthusiasts have sprung up throughout the United States, Canada, and abroad. Authority Lillian Baker has compiled a lovely book, *Creative and Collectible Miniatures*, with many full-color photos; you will find her address in the Directory under California.

Bed warmer, brass w/tooled lid, trn wood hdl, EX detail, 10".......100.00
Bed warmer, copper w/brass ferrule, trn hdl, 9" 200.00
Bench, oak Gothic style, cvd drapery motif, 21" 225.00
Blanket chest, pine w/red pnt, 6-brd, 10" L 475.00
Blanket chest, pine w/rust vinegar grpt, pristine, 18" L 3,350.00
Blanket chest, poplar, dvtl bracket ft, till, 20" L, VG..................275.00
Blanket chest, poplar, gr pnt/mc floral, sgn/PA, 1861, 13" 4,900.00
Blanket chest, poplar w/wht pnt & smoke grpt, 6-brd, 8" L 2,175.00
Blanket chest, walnut, dvtl/base molding, rpl, 16" L 195.00
Bucket, copper, cylindrical, w/bail hdl, 2⅜".................................60.00
Candle mold, tin, 6-tube, minor soldering, 4½" 500.00
Candlestand, mahog, trn ped, rnd trn ft, 7" 60.00
Candlestand, walnut, tilt-top, handmade, some age, rfn, 19".......150.00
Castor set, 4 pressed glass pcs in pewter fr, 4⅝" 125.00
Chest, walnut, cvd surfaces/scrolls/fretwork, 1900, 9½" 150.00
Chest, walnut, 5 dvtl drw, orig brass pulls, 14x12" 325.00
Chest of drw, pine, red/blk grpt, trn ft, sm drw atop, 14" 600.00
Cupboard, maple w/burl, bird's-eye veneer, cvd moldings, 19" 400.00
Fireside broiler, tin, semicircular hood, 3¼" 200.00
Footstool, floral on grpt gold & yel, bootjack ft, 1840, 6" 600.00
Iron, CI, swan shaped, worn red pnt, w/trivet, 2¾" 65.00
Jug, redware w/brn brushing, tooled lines, ribbed hdl, 4⅜" 225.00
Jug, stoneware, cvd bird/ME/basket/star in bl, 3⅝" 3,300.00
Kettle stand, brass, fancy rtcl top, 3¼".......................................155.00
Lamp, toleware, tubular, worn red pnt, 2" 95.00

Ormolu miniature coach, 1800s, 9½" x 22", $550.00.

Pickle castor, cranberry Invt T'print, 3½", in rstr fr 300.00
Saucepan, tin, brass lid, minor pitting/rprs, 3" dia, 4" hdl 65.00
Table, curly maple, 3 tripod legs, trn ped, 9½" 750.00
Table, tilt-top, poplar w/old red, trn column/tripod, 9"................875.00
Taster, copper w/tooled wrought iron hdl & brass rivets, 6" 125.00
Teakettle, brass, gooseneck spout, rings at shoulder, 4¾"............135.00
Teakettle, cast brass, wood hdl, wrought iron trivet, 4" 100.00

Teakettle, copper, gooseneck spout, 4" 125.00
Teakettle, copper, handmade, EX detail, 2¾" 150.00
Teakettle, tin w/wooden knob, 4½" 85.00

Minton

Thomas Minton established his firm in 1793 at Stoke on Trent and within a few years began producing earthenware with blue-printed patterns similar to the ware he had learned to decorate while employed by the Caughley Porcelain Factory. The Willow pattern was one of his most popular. Neither this nor the porcelain made from 1798 to 1805 was marked (except for an occasional number series), making identification often impossible.

After 1805 until about 1816, fine tea services, beehive-shaped honey pots, trays, etc. were hand decorated with florals, landscapes, Imari-type designs, and Neoclassic devices. These were often marked with crossed 'L's. It was Minton that invented the acid gold process of decorating, which is now used by a number of different companies. From 1816 until 1823, no porcelain was made. Through the twenties and thirties, the ornamental wares with colorful decoration of applied fruits and florals and figurines in both bisque and enamel were usually left unmarked. As a result, they have been erroneously attributed to other potters. Some of the ware that was marked bears a deliberate imitation of Meissen's crossed swords. From the late twenties through the forties, Minton made a molded stoneware line (mugs, jugs, teapots, etc.) with florals or figures in high relief. These were marked with an embossed scroll with an 'M' in the bottom curve. Fine parian ware was made in the late 1840s, and in the fifties Minton perfected and produced a line of quality majolica for which they gained widespread recognition. Leadership of the firm was assumed by Minton's son Herbert sometime around the middle of the 19th century. Working hand in hand with Leon Arnoux, who was both a chemist and an artist, he managed to secure the company's financial future through constant, successful experimentation with both materials and decorating methods. During the Victorian era, M.L. Solon decorated pieces in the pate-sur-pate style, often signing his work; these examples are considered to be the finest of their type. After 1862 all wares were marked 'Minton' or 'Mintons,' with an impressed year cipher.

Many collectors today reassemble the lovely dinnerware patterns that have been made by Minton. Perhaps one of their most popular lines was Minton Rose. The company itself once counted forty-seven versions of this pattern being made by other potteries around the world. In addition to less expensive copies, elaborate hand-enameled pieces were also made by Aynsley, Crown Staffordshire, and Paragon China.

Dinnerware values given in the following listings are for items that were produced from 1870-1950. Current production pieces bring lower prices on the resale market. Our advisor for this category is Glenn Roe (Old China Patterns Ltd.); he is listed in the Directory under New York. See also Majolica; Pate-Sur-Pate.

Bowl, vegetable; Gold Rose (gold leaf decor), w/lid.....................400.00
Bowl, vegetable; Minton Rose, w/lid..490.00
Cup & saucer, Delft underglaze bl w/gold, G-1613, 1874-1911 ...110.00
Cup & saucer, HP birds/jungle on turq enamel, G-2536, 1878-81 .300.00
Cup & saucer, Minton Rose, A-4807 ....96.00
Cup & saucer, Persian Rose, B-838 ....90.00
Plate, dinner; Essex Birds, earthenware, octagonal, ca 1881 ....49.50
Plate, dinner; Minton Rose 94.50
Plate, dinner; Persian Rose, B-838 ....88.00
Plate, salad; Cockatrice, turq..56.00
Teapot or coffeepot, Persian Rose, B-838, ea...............................365.00
Urn, Egyptian pattern, majolica, 37", pr................................... 7,500.00

Mirrors

The first mirrors were made in England in the 13th century of very thin glass backed with lead. Reverse-painted glass mirrors were made in this country as early as the late 1700s and remained popular throughout the next century. The simple hand-painted panel was separated from the mirrored section by a narrow slat, and the frame was either the dark-finished Federal style or the more elegant, often-gilded Sheraton.

Mirrors changed with the style of other furnishings; but whatever type you purchase, as long as the glass sections remain solid, even broken or flaking mirrors are more valued than replaced glass. Careful resilvering is acceptable if excessive deterioration has taken place. Our advisor for this category is Michael Hinton; he is listed in the Directory under Pennsylvania.

Key:
Emp — Empire   QA — Queen Anne
Fed — Federal

Baroque style, cvd face/scrolls/flowers, gilt, 1800s, 61" **1,200.00**
Bird's-eye fr, gilt liner, 21x16" **150.00**
Centennial mahog, lg gesso eagle/garlands, rpt, 37x21" **275.00**
Cherry fr, trn sides w/corner blocks, 12x10" **450.00**
Chpndl mahog scroll, gilt liner/phoenix, rpr/re-gild, 36" **1,575.00**
Chpndl mahog scroll, VG orig glass, rpr/glued, 43x22" **750.00**
Chpndl mahog scroll veneer, gilt liner, crest cvg, 37", VG **550.00**
Convex, gilt/ebony liners, ball detail, candle arms, 21" **650.00**
Convex Fed, w/lg spreadwing eagle crest, 1820, 28"....................**950.00**
Courting, pine, inset rvpt stripes/crest, orig case, 16x11" **1,600.00**
Emp 2-part mahog, rope-cvd pilasters, rpl glass/rpr, 46" **325.00**
Emp 2-part w/rvpt house, red/yel grpt, 21x13", EX **500.00**
Emp 2-part w/rvpt house, rpl mirror, bkbrd damage, 21x12" **225.00**
Emp 2-part w/rvpt landscape, blk/gold half-column fr, 20" **425.00**
Heritage Henredon, designed by FL Wright, #2002, 20x15".......**750.00**
Hplwht mahog veneer/inlay scroll, rpl ear, orig glass, 28" **550.00**
Louis XVI, gilt/cvgs: musical items/flowers, 1800s, 66x43" **600.00**
Mahog Chpndl scroll, composition decor, rfn, 31x13", EX..........**850.00**
Plateau, SP fleur-de-lis, fancy ft, 14", EX.................................**115.00**
Plateau, SP floral sides, beaded top, ftd, 14", EX **125.00**

Queen Anne, walnut facings on white pine, original glass, minor losses to facing, lower Hudson Valley, NY, 1750s, 18", $2,100.00.

Plateau, SP scrolls & cutouts, floral ft, 10" **95.00**
QA mahog veneer/pine, gilt liner, worn orig glass, 17x10" **675.00**

QA walnut veneer, ogee fr, rpr/rpl glass, 37x13" **425.00**
Shaving, hardwood, EX trn, worn orig glass, rprs, 8x12" **150.00**
Shaving, mahog, ball ft, drw, plain posts, rpr/rpl, 19"..................**200.00**
Shaving, mahog veneer on pine w/line inlay, drw, 16x14" **150.00**
Shaving, mahog veneer w/inlay bowfront, ogee ft, 2-drw, EX......**275.00**
Traveling, 2 octagonal glasses in walnut fr, folds, 2½x3" **110.00**

Mocha

Mocha Ware is utilitarian pottery made principally in England (and to a lesser extent in France) between 1780 and 1840 on the then prevalent creamware and pearlware bodies. Initially, only those pieces decorated in the seaweed pattern were called 'Mocha,' while geometrically decorated pieces were referred to as 'Banded Creamware.' Other types of decorations were called 'Dipped Ware.' During the last thirty to forty years the term 'Mocha' has been applied to the entire realm of 'Industrialized Slipware' — pottery decorated by the turner on his lathe using coggle wheels and slip cups.

Mocha was made in numerous patterns — Tree, Seaweed or Dandelion, Rope (also called Worm or Loop), Cat's-eye, Tobacco Leaf, Lollypop or Balloon, Marbled, Marbled and Combed, Twig, Geometric or Checkered, Banded, and slip decorations of rings, dots, flags, tulips, wavy lines, etc. It came into its own as a collectible in the latter half of the 1940s and has become increasingly popular as more and more people are exposed to the rich colorings and artistic appeal of its varied forms of abstract decoration.

The collector should take care not to confuse the early pearlware and creamware Mocha with the later kitchen yellowware, graniteware, and ironstone sporting mocha-type decoration that was produced in America by such potters as J. Vodrey, George S. Harker, Edwin Bennett, and John Bell. This type was also produced in Scotland and Wales and was marketed well into the twentieth century.

Bowl, earthworm on gray, emb gr rim, brn stripes, 3x5", NM **700.00**
Bowl, earthworm on wht, bl/brn stripes, minor wear, 3x6" **800.00**
Bowl, seaweed, blk on gray, emb gr band, 3x6", EX **450.00**
Bowl, seaweed on rust, rim w/gr ribs, blk/wht lines, 7", EX **250.00**
Bowl, 4-color marbleizing, emb gr band, 2x4½", NM...................**650.00**
Chamber pot, cat's eye/leaves on emb gr band, 8x9", EX **500.00**
Cup & saucer, seaweed, blk on tan, wht int, EX...........................**400.00**

Double water jug, earthworm, cat's eye, and twig decoration, extremely rare, EX, 14½", $8,000.00.

Mug, earthworm, checkerbrd rim band, 6" **700.00**
Mug, seaweed, blk on rust, brn/blk lines, w/lid, 4½", EX..............**700.00**
Mug, wht dots on blk/wht/bl/yel bands, leaf hdl, 4¾", EX...........**275.00**
Mustard, cat's eye bands/stripes, emb leaf hdl, 4", VG **1,200.00**
Mustard, earthworm on bl, brn/rust bands, leaf hdl, 2¼", EX......**375.00**

Pepper castor, blk/wht checked band, bl/wht rings, 5", EX 500.00
Pepper castor, emb gr stripe, wht/brn/rust bands, 4", EX 700.00
Pepper castor, leaves on orange, gr/bl/wht/brn stripes, 4"............800.00
Pepper castor, seaweed on gray, blk/wht lines, VG dome top 200.00
Pitcher, cat's eye/earthworm on herringbone bands, 7", EX ... 1,450.00
Pitcher, cat's eye/leaf garland, leaf spout/hdl, 8", VG.................875.00
Pitcher, dk brn w/wht stripes, gr rib bands, 6¾", EX 525.00
Pitcher, dots in brn/wht on gray, bl bands, bulbous, 7" 1,000.00
Pitcher, dots/waves in wht, bl/blk bands, bulbous, 7", EX 350.00
Pitcher, earthworm on bl, band w/3-line wht waves, 6¾" 800.00
Pitcher, earthworm on wide rust band, bulbous, 6¾" 800.00
Pitcher, seaweed on gray, blk lines, leaf hdl, rpr, 7", VG.............400.00
Pitcher, seaweed on yel, gr neck ribs/leaf hdl, 7½", EX 1,100.00
Pitcher, trees/dots, 5-color, imp patterns, bulbous, 8" 2,300.00
Teabowl & saucer, seaweed, blk on orange, emb bl rim, EX.... 1,300.00

Molds

Food molds have become a popular collectible — not only for their value as antiques, but because they also revive childhood memories of elaborate ice cream Santas with candy trim, or barley sugar figurals adorning a Christmas tree. Ice cream molds were made of pewter and came in a wide variety of shapes and styles. Chocolate molds were made in fewer shapes but were more detailed. They were usually made of tin, copper, and occasionally of pewter. Hard candy molds were usually metal, although primitive maple sugar molds (usually simple hearts, rabbits, and other animals) were carved from wood. (Unless otherwise indicated, those in our listings are cast aluminum or stainless steel.) Cake molds were made of cast iron or cast aluminum and were most common in the shape of a lamb, a rabbit, or Santa Claus. Our advisors for this category are Dale and Jean Van Kuren; they are listed in the Directory under New York.

Chocolate Molds

Army truck, row of 4 in fr..157.50
Asian girl w/fan, row of 8 in fr..72.50
Barrel, 2 rows of 6 ....40.00
Bars (24), japanned tin, ca 1890s, 11".......................................45.00
Beetles, 2 rows of 5 in fr...72.50
Boy in sailor suit, row of 4 in fr..147.50
Boy w/pail & shovel, row of 5 in fr...110.00
Cactus w/star, row of 7 in fr 77.50
Chick w/umbrella, row of 4 in fr...110.00
Chicken, EX detail, 2-part w/clips, 4½" 70.00
Cigar, row of 9 in fr 70.00
Clown, pig decor on pants, 1¾x3¾" 45.00
Cyclist on racing bike, 4x3½"...95.00
Dog, begging, row of 5 in fr..110.00
Dog, row of 4 in fr..110.00
Duckling, 2 rows of 5 in fr 95.00
Easter egg, 2-pc w/clips, ca 1920, 7" 40.00
Easter egg, 3 in mold, 2-pc, ca 1925, 9½"................................110.00
Easter rabbit, sitting, 2 rows of 3 in 12¾" L fr...........................52.50
Easter rabbit w/basket, 12-part, 12"..65.00
Fish, row of 7 in fr..95.00
Fish, 2-part, 5x10¼x2½" 85.00
Fish, 4x7½x2" 65.00
Frog, row of 5 in fr..95.00
Girl w/watering can, row of 5 in fr..110.00
Goldfish, detailed, 2¼x6¼" 57.50
Kangaroo, row of 4 in fr..170.00
Kewpie, row of 4 in fr...127.50

Kris Kringle, 2¼x6"...95.00
Lighthouse, row of 5 in fr..95.00
Lighthouse, row of 8 in fr..110.00
Lion, #41, 2¼x6¼" 57.50
Locomotive, #25454, 2x5¼"...110.00
Man in crescent-shaped moon, row of 5 in fr.............................95.00
Man in moon, 2 rows of 10 in fr..87.50
Motorcycle, row of 4 in fr..110.00
Negro girl, standing, row of 4 in fr..110.00
Pig, smiling, #8325, 1¾x3½"...50.00
Rabbit, dbl, hinged w/3 clips, ca 1900s, 5½"..............................55.00
Rabbit, recumbent, ears laid bk, 2-part, 8".................................145.00
Rabbit, row of 5 in fr...85.00
Rabbit, running, 2-part w/3 joiners, 8½".......................................88.00
Rabbit, smoking pipe, row of 5 in fr..110.00
Rabbit, standing, 2-part, 6¼x3¼x1½"..55.00
Rabbit in auto, row of 4 in 17" L fr..67.50
Rabbit w/basket, dbl, 9½"..147.50
Rabbit w/basket, paw up, sitting, #8218, 12" 95.00
Rabbit w/gun & pouch, row of 6 in fr..145.00
Rabbit w/pack, row of 2 in 8x9" fr..82.50
Rabbit w/pack, 4 in mold, hinged 2-pc, 7"..................................55.00
Rabbit w/pack, 4 in mold, wht metal w/tin plate, 7" 55.00
Race car w/driver, 1 row of 4 in fr...160.00
Rooster, #8080, 7½"..67.50
Santa w/bag, 3-part, clip missing, 10½" 225.00
Sheep, standing, row of 5 in fr..127.50
Skippy Skimmer, 2-part, ca 1925, 6½"...85.00
Stork, row of 4 in fr 157.50
Swan, row of 5 in fr...127.50

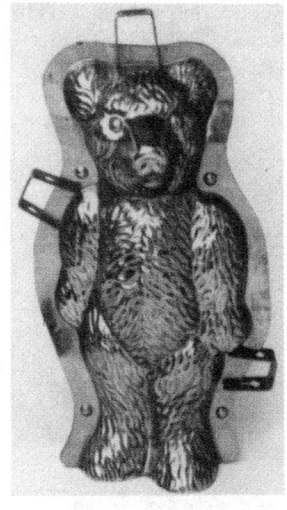

Teddy bear, #2644, 11", $200.00.

Tennis racket, row of 6..60.00
Thermometer, row of 6 in fr..95.00
Turtle, 1 row of 5 in fr..110.00

Hard Candy Molds

Battleship in waves, TM-256, groove for stick, 2½x1¼" 55.00
Castle w/flag, groove for stick, 1¾x1½" 75.00
Hand, TM-31, groove for stick, 1¾x1¼".....................................42.50
Mary w/lamb, TM-244, groove for stick, 2x2" 80.00
Mouse, TM-37, groove for stick, 2x1"..90.00
Paddle wheel, TM-217, groove for stick, 2¼x1¼" 87.50
Pipe, TM-88, groove for stick, 3½x¾"..42.50
Rabbits w/baby in cart, T-41, groove for stick, 4½x3½".............100.00

Rat, TM-238, groove for stick, 2½x1" **80.00**
Ship cannon, TM-255, groove for stick, 2½x1¼" **55.00**

Ice Cream Molds

Abraham Lincoln portrait, pewter, hinged, E&CO NY, 4½" **110.00**
Apple, E-240 ....**25.00**
Bell, #605 ....**32.00**
Bicycle, lady rider, K-431 ....**60.00**
Boat, S&Co, 5" L **25.00**
Champagne bottle in cooler, S-206 ....**65.00**
Christmas bells, 5 in mold, hinged 2-pc, ca 1900s **45.00**
Cupid sits on rose, full figure, E-959 ....**55.00**
Easter egg, E-906 ....**22.50**
Easter lily, E-354, 3-pc **55.00**
Football, #381, 3-pc **30.00**
Football, E-1159 ....**25.00**
Goat, rearing, S-346 ....**80.00**
Goose egg, #298 ....**25.00**
Grape cluster, E-278 ....**20.00**
Harp, aluminum, K-361, 1940s **32.00**
Kiwanis emblem, E-1111 ....**28.00**
Log, K-626 ....**25.00**
Medallion, passion flower relief, E-270 ....**32.00**
Mum, E-355 ....**22.00**
Peach, E-233 ....**25.00**
Peach half w/stone, #160 ....**25.00**
Pear, E-248 ....**30.00**
Penguin, 3½" **40.00**
Potato, K-154 ....**35.00**
Rose, E-295 ....**30.00**
Rotary Club emblem, E-1110 ....**27.50**
Santa, E-961 ....**85.00**
Shriner emblem, E-1081 ....**30.00**

Snowman, #601, 5", $95.00.

Soldier, 5⅝" **45.00**
Stork w/baby, standing, E-1151 ....**55.00**
Waffle, E-842 ....**55.00**
Wedding ring, E-1142 ....**30.00**
Wolf, 3-part, K-428 ....**80.00**

Maple Sugar Molds

Cow in 2 parts, varnished, 4½x7" **65.00**
Heart, spade, dmn; pine, deep cvg, ca 1835, 16x4x2" **240.00**

Heart, wood, iron hinge, pouring hole at top, 1890s, 5" **85.00**
Heart & clover, primitive, 5x17½" **50.00**
Rooster, primitive, 6x12" **295.00**

Miscellaneous

CI, chicken, 2-pc, hdls, for cake, 7x8½" **65.00**
CI, hearts & stars, Pat 1870, 16½x9" **175.00**
CI, pig's head, 9" dia..**225.00**
CI, Turk's head, ca 1800s, 3¼x9" **65.00**
Copper, emb ear of corn in oval top, ca 1800s, 6x5" **350.00**
Copper, emb lion in oval top, ca 1800s, 6x5", EX **350.00**
Copper/tin, emb eagle in oval top, 6" L **275.00**
Copper/tin, Turk's head, 8¼" dia **85.00**
Stoneware, dbl lion, British Blanc-Mange Jelly, 10⅝" **145.00**
Tin, fish, late 1800s, 3x13x6"...**100.00**
Tin, fruit, corrugated sides, 3x4x6" **50.00**
Tin, melon top w/ring hdl, ca late 1800s, 9x6¼" **40.00**
Tin, 3 fruits w/leaves emb in sq, lid/base removes, 6x6" **95.00**

Monmouth

The Monmouth Pottery Company was established in 1892 in Monmouth, Illinois. Their primary products were salt-glazed stoneware crocks, churns, and jugs, Bristol, spongeware, and brown glaze. In 1906 they were absorbed by a conglomerate called the Western Stoneware Company. Monmouth became their #1 plant and until 1930 continued to produce stoneware marked with their maple leaf logo. Items marked 'Monmouth Pottery Co.,' were made before 1906; after the merger, 'Co.' was dropped and 'Ill.' was substituted.

Jardiniere, Egyptian motif, brown-glazed interior, 7", $75.00.

Ash tray, advertising, 3 sets of ftprints, 9" **10.00**
Jardiniere, Aztec, 7" **75.00**
Jug, beehive; 5-gal...**125.00**
Mug, short, squat, band around center, mk **7.50**
Pitcher, brn, horizontal ribs, 5½" **9.00**
Pitcher, cobalt, water sz **17.50**
Platter, brn, oval, lg **9.00**
Vase, brn, rope-trimmed hdls, 12" **65.00**
Vase, rust, 8" **12.00**

Mont Joye

Mont Joye was a type of acid-cut French cameo glass produced by

Cristallerie de Pantin in Paris around the turn of the century. It is accented by enamels. Our advisor for this category is Don Williams; he is listed in the Directory under Missouri.

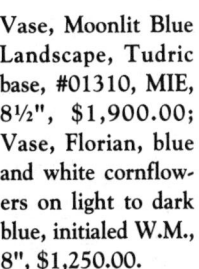

Vase, cranberry with gold floral, 4-sided cylinder, unsigned, 12", $975.00.

Planter, gold decor on gr frost, 7½" 275.00
Vase, chestnuts/leaves, gold on crackle, mk France, 5" 225.00
Vase, floral, burgundy on frost, gold trim, 6½" 400.00
Vase, floral, red/gr on chipped ice, mk, 9½" 750.00
Vase, florals w/gold in panels, unmk, 11" 350.00
Vase, mums/leafage, gold on gr, flattened/bulbous/ftd, 16" 935.00
Vase, poppies on frost, cylindrical neck, 11" 465.00
Vase, spider mums, gold on gr texture, 13½" 1,200.00

Moorcroft

William Moorcroft was an English potter who worked for MacIntyre Potteries from 1897 to 1913, signing his pieces with his last name or 'W. M.' In 1913 he established a workshop in Burslem, England, where he produced tablewares and a line of fine Art Nouveau vases, bowls, etc., which until 1916 were marked with the impressed mark 'Burslem,' either with or without his initials or signature. After 1916 an impressed 'England' was added, and from 1918 to 1929 the mark was 'Moorcroft' and 'Made in England,' with or without initials or signature. For the period from 1928 until 1945, the impressed mark read 'Moorcroft — Potter to HM the Queen,' with or without initials or signature; it was sometimes accompanied by a paper label. A second version of this mark was used from 1945 until 1949. At that time 'Moorcroft' and 'Made in England was reinitiated and is the mark still in use today; a paper label (Potter to the Late Queen Mary) was added from 1953 until 1979. The latest variation may contain the initials of William's son, Walter, or Walter's signature. Note: Except for pieces with a salmon-pink background, all of William's work was signed. Those he refused to sign because he personally did not like them.

William Moorcroft died in 1945, and Walter continued in the business. Walter soon created his own designs, but he signed only the larger examples. Today W. Moorcroft Ltd. continues to use many of the same methods of hand-applied, slip-trailed decoration that William developed. Walter recently retired, and his brother William John is presently in charge of the company. He is developing his own designs that are introducing a new look to the Moorcroft line. Our advisor for this category is Bob Haynes. He is listed in the Directory under Washington.

Key:
#1 — Potter to Her Majesty the Queen, Made in England

#2 — MacIntyre
#3 — W. Moorcroft
#4 — Burslem England
#5 — Florian (brown)
#6 — WM Moorcroft, Des

Vase, Moonlit Blue Landscape, Tudric base, #01310, MIE, 8½", $1,900.00; Vase, Florian, blue and white cornflowers on light to dark blue, initialed W.M., 8", $1,250.00.

Basket, pomegranates, mc on bl, SP hdl, #3/MIE/104, 4" 425.00
Bowl, hibiscus, red on gr, #3, lg paper label, 5½" 125.00
Bowl, Landscape, bl/yel on gr, #6, R-397964, 2x6" 600.00
Bowl, poppies, gr/bl on wht, #2, 2½x3½" 575.00
Bowl, sailboats on lt gr & bl, hdls, #1/3, 4" 250.00
Charger, berries, red/yel on dk red, bl mk, 11¾"..........................400.00
Chocolate pot, floral, bl/gr on ivory, pitcher form, #2, 6" 675.00
Cookie jar, Florian, poppies in bl tones, #5/6, 6x7", NM 750.00
Cookie jar, Florian, poppies/gold on gr w/bl & wht, #2, 7" 950.00
Cookie jar, wisteria, mc on bl to wht, SP lid, #4/sgn, 6" 1,100.00
Cup & saucer, Claremont, toadstools, #3/Schreve & Co, 3" 475.00
Inkwell, Moonlit Bl Landscape, bl script sgn, 2" 550.00
Inkwell, orange lustre, silver lid, #3/4, 2½" 350.00
Inkwell, pomegranates, Tudric lid, onion form, #3/4, 2x4½" 800.00
Lamp base, orchids, mc on dk bl, MIE Royal Warrant/#3, 12" 800.00
Match holder, Landscape, red/rose on sand/gr, #2, 3" 375.00
Match striker, Florian, poppies, brn/bl on mustard, #2, 3x4" 400.00
Match striker, pomegranates, mc on gr, spherical, #3/4, 2" 375.00
Pitcher, Dura Ware, floral, gr/bl on pk, gr stripe, #2, 7" 475.00
Tea set, cornflowers, mc on lt gr, #2, sgn/dtd 1912, 3-pc 1,500.00
Tea set, orchids, mc on lt gr to bl, #1, pot: 6x9", 3-pc.................900.00
Vase, anemone, 3-color on lt to med bl, #3/dk bl WM, 6" 350.00
Vase, Aurelian, transfer w/enamel & gilt, #2, ftd/slim, 12" 1,000.00
Vase, Aurelian, transfer w/gilt, tall slim neck, #2, 6" 575.00
Vase, Aurelian, transfer w/gold on dk bl, #2, 7½" 650.00
Vase, Aurelian, transfer w/red & gold, ogee w/hdls, #2, 9" 900.00
Vase, Claremont, toadstools, imp mk, gr initials, 3"......................500.00
Vase, Claremont, toadstools, EX art/form, #4/3, 1914, 8½" 3,500.00
Vase, Damsen, fruit on gr/bl, wide trumpet form, MIE, 10" 750.00
Vase, Eventide Landscape, #3, 10" 1,500.00
Vase, Eventide Landscape, slim form, imp mks/WM in bl, 6" 950.00
Vase, Florian, bl/wht, slim form, #2/6/W-701, 12" 1,400.00
Vase, Florian, bl/wht on lt bl, #2/4/6, slim ogee form, 12" 1,200.00
Vase, Florian, cornflowers in bl/gr, gourd form, #6, 3" 475.00
Vase, Florian, gr/gold/pk, EX artwork, wide body, #2, 6" 1,200.00
Vase, Florian, gr/gold/pk, slim w/hdls, #2, 1903, 12", NM 850.00
Vase, Florian, irises, med/lt bl on dk bl, #5/6, 9" 1,000.00
Vase, Florian, leaves, gr on bl & gr, bottle form, #2, 9" 1,000.00

Vase, Florian, lt/dk bl, sm neck, #2/initials, 3" 500.00
Vase, Florian, orchids on bl tones, #5/3, 8½" 800.00
Vase, Florian, peacock feathers, 5-color, hdls, #5/WM, 5" 700.00
Vase, Florian, poppies, yel/gr/bl on lt bl, slim, #5, 12" 2,500.00
Vase, Florian, tulips, EX art, slim/hdld, #5/6, 14".................... 1,800.00
Vase, Florian, yel/gr on bl & wht, slim neck, #2/6, 5" 550.00
Vase, Florian Lilac, heavy gold, dbl gourd, #3/4, 1905, 9"............850.00
Vase, Florian Lilac, mc/gold band at shoulder, #2/3, 9"............950.00
Vase, forget-me-nots on wht, urn form w/hdls, #2/3/4, 7" 950.00
Vase, freesia on bl-gr, #3, 5" 350.00
Vase, Moonlit Bl Landscape, bottle form, #3/MIE, 6" 900.00
Vase, Moonlit Bl Landscape, bulbous shoulder, #3/MIE, 6" .. 1,200.00
Vase, Moonlit Bl Landscape, imp mk/bl initials, bulbous, 3½" 395.00
Vase, Moonlit Bl Landscape, slim ovoid, #3/imp mks, 5" 750.00
Vase, peacock feathers, red/bl on muted red, #3/MIE, 11"....... 3,250.00
Vase, plums, red/yel on dk bl, MIE/script initials, 3½" 295.00
Vase, plums, silver rim, imp mk, MIE, 4"................................350.00
Vase, plums, yel/purple/gr on dk bl, lg hdls, #2/MIE, 11" 950.00
Vase, pomegranates, gr initials, bulbous, 2½" 225.00
Vase, pomegranates, red/grs on dk bl, bulbous, #1/3, 3x3½" 350.00
Vase, pomegranates, red/wine/dk bl/gr mottle, #3, 3x4"..............350.00
Vase, pomegranates, red/yel on gr/bl, onion form, #3/4, 4" 350.00
Vase, pomegranates, red/yel/bl on gr mottle, #3, 2x2" 225.00
Vase, pomegranates, WM initials, 2" 225.00
Vase, poppies, wide body, MIE/initials, 4" 500.00

Moravian Pottery & Tile Works

Dr. Henry Chapman Mercer was an author, anthropoligist, histo-
rian, collector, and artist. One of his diversified interests was pottery. In
1898 he established the Moravian Pottery and Tile Works in
Doylestown, Pennsylvania, the name inspired by his study and collection of decorative stove plates made by the early Moravians. Because
the red clay he used there proved unfit for tableware, he turned to the
production of handmade tile which he himself designed. Though never
allowing it to become more than a studio operation, the tile works was
nevertheless responsible for some important commercial installations,
one of which was in the capitol building at Harrisburg.

Mercer died in 1930. Business continued in the established vein
under the supervision of Mercer's assistant, Frank Swain, until his
death in 1954. Since 1968 the studio has been operated by The Bucks
County Commission, and tiles are still fashioned in the handmade tradition. They are marked 'Mercer' and are dated.

Mosaic, Indian chipping flint, cement bking, 32x38" 500.00
Tile, Aves ship, 4x4" 65.00
Tile, bird, Mercer, 4" 75.00
Tile, deer, Mercer, 4"..75.00
Tile, human figure, mk Doctor, 4" 75.00
Tile, Mayflower, Mercer, 4"...75.00
Tile, Priscilla, spinning wool 55.00
Tile, Santa Maria, 4" 75.00
Tile, Stoveplate, Trinity series, 9x9"..245.00
Tile, Vicar of Stowe...60.00
Tile, Zodiac series, Scorpio...55.00

Morgan, Matt

From 1883 to 1885, the Matt Morgan Art Pottery of Cincinnati,
Ohio, produced fine artware, some of which resembled the pottery of
the Moors with intense colors and gold accents. Some of the later wares
were very similar to those of Rookwood, due to the fact that several
Rookwood artists were also associated with the Morgan pottery. Some

examples were marked with a paper label, others with either a two- or
three-line impression: 'Matt Morgan Art Pottery Co.,' with 'Cin. O.'
sometimes added.

**Plaque, central profile of a young woman, irides-
cent glaze, paper label, 14", $425.00.**

Jug, bamboo/flying bird, dk gr on gr, red clay, MAD, 4½" 400.00
Plaque, profile of lady, hair bound by scarf, irid, 13" dia 425.00
Vase, floral, pk/wht on celadon, dbl gourd w/lid, label, 6" 500.00
Vase, forest/bridge/people, Hirschfeld, pillow form, 14x12" 4,250.00

Morgantown Glass

The Morgantown Glass works, incorporated in 1899, experienced
many name changes over the years. Today 'Morgantown Glass' is a generic
term used to indicate all glass produced there. Purchased by Fostoria in
1965, the factory was permanently closed in 1971. Our advisors for this
category are Jerry Gallagher and Randy Supplee, both long-time
researchers of Morgantown Glass. They are presently preparing for publication a listing of all known company etchings. Both are listed in the Directory under Minnesota. See Clubs, Newsletters, and Catalogs for information concerning Morgantown Collectors of America (a research society
founded by Mr. Gallagher) and The Morgantown Newsletter, a quarterly
M.A.C. journal with research updates and reports of current trends.

 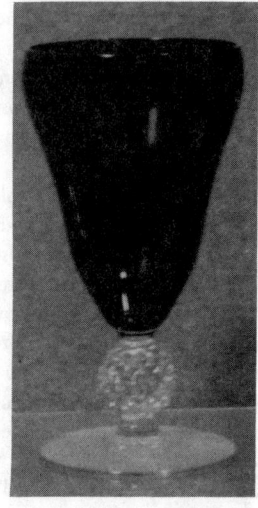

**Footed tumblers, left: Golf Ball, #7643, cobalt, 9-oz.,
$35.00; right: Old English, #7678, cobalt, 10-oz., $37.50.**

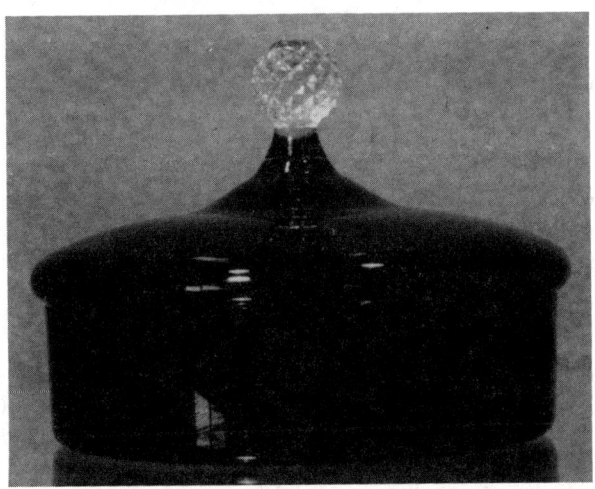

Candy box, Golf Ball, #7643, ruby with crystal finial, $160.00.

Figurals

Chanticleer, amber bowl/ft; crystal stem; cocktail, 4-oz **38.00**
Chanticleer, cobalt bowl; crystal stem/ft; cocktail, 4-oz **60.00**
Chanticleer, crystal; stem, cocktail, 4-oz................................**20.00**
Chanticleer, pastel bowl/ft; crystal stem; cocktail, 4-oz **32.00**
Chanticleer, ruby bowl; crystal stem/ft; cocktail, 4-oz **42.50**
Jockey, crystal bowl/ft; amber stem; champagne, 6-oz **60.00**
Jockey, crystal; stem, champagne; 6-oz..................................**35.00**
Mai Tai, crystal; amber stem; cocktail, peacock optic, 5-oz............**55.00**
Mai Tai, crystal; amber stem; cocktail, 3½-oz **42.50**
Mai Tai, crystal; amber stem; sherbet, lg, 10-oz **50.00**
Mai Tai, crystal; topaz stem; cocktail, 3½-oz **48.00**
Old Crow, crystal; stem, cocktail; 6⅛", 5½-oz.........................**65.00**
Owl, amber or gr; tumbler, highball; 15-oz................................**52.00**
Summer Cornucopia, crystal; stem, champagne; 7-oz **110.00**
Top Hat, cobalt bowl; crystal stem/ft; cocktail, 4½-oz **65.00**
Top Hat, pastel bowl/ft; crystal stem; cocktail, 4½-oz **48.00**
Top Hat, ruby bowl; crystal stem/ft; cocktail, 4½-oz.................**57.50**
Top Hat, Steigel gr bowl; crystal bowl/ft, cocktail, 4½-oz **47.50**

Adonis etch, crystal; gr stem; goblet, #7606½ Athena, 9-oz **95.00**
Adonis etch, crystal; jug, wide optic; #37 Barry, 48-oz................**185.00**
Adonis etch, crystal; tumbler, ftd; #7654 Treasure, 9-oz **22.00**
Adonis etch, gr; stem, cafe parfait; #7604½ Heirloom, 5-oz **52.00**
Adonis etch, rose; stem, cordial; #7604½ Heirloom, 1-oz **110.00**
Adonis etch, rose; tumbler, ftd, #7654 Treasure, 12-oz **38.00**
Adonis etch, topaz; plate, salad; #1500, 7¼"................................**25.00**
Adonis etch, topaz; stem, goblet; #7604½ Heirloom, 9-oz **48.00**
Adonis etch, topaz; stem, wine; #7604½ Heirloom, 3-oz..............**55.00**
Am Beauty etch, crystal; stem, cocktail; #7565 Astrid **28.00**
Am Beauty etch, crystal; tumbler, bar; #8107, 2¾-oz **45.00**
Am Beauty etch, crystal; tumbler, flat, #9701, 9-oz.......................**28.00**
Am Beauty etch, rose; finger bowl, #2927, 4¼" **58.00**
Am Beauty etch, rose; liner plate, #2927, 6"................................**20.00**
Am Beauty etch, rose; stem, goblet; #7565 Astrid, 10-oz **55.00**
Am Beauty etch, rose-amber; jug, w/lid, #2 Arcadia, 54-oz **235.00**
Art Moderne, cobalt bowl/crystal stem; sherbet, #7640, 5½-oz......**42.00**
Art Moderne, cobalt w/crystal stem; candlestick, #7640½, pr......**230.00**
Art Moderne, cobalt w/crystal stem; cordial, #7640, 1½-oz............**85.00**
Art Moderne, crystal bowl/blk stem; champagne, #7640, 5½-oz **36.00**

Art Moderne, crystal bowl/blk stem; goblet, #7640, 9-oz **58.00**
Art Moderne, rose bowl/crystal stem; wine, #7640, 3-oz **58.00**
Barry #37, azure w/crystal hdl & ft; jug, needle etch, 48-oz..........**160.00**
Barry #37, crystal w/jade gr hdl & ft; jug, 48-oz **195.00**
Candle holder, burgundy; #110 Sonata, 5", 7", 9", set of 3...........**115.00**
Candle holder, peacock bl; slant, #82 Cosmopolitan, 7", pr...........**65.00**
Candle holder, ruby; #9935 Barton, 3¾", pr **45.00**
Candle holder, steel; #9931 Florentine, 5½", pr **48.00**
Carlton, crystal w/blk stem; goblet, #7606½, 9-oz **85.00**
Carlton, crystal w/blk stem; wine, #7606½ Athena, 3-oz **98.00**
Carlton, platinum Marco; bowl, console; #4355, 13" **135.00**
Carlton, platinum Marco; stem, cocktail; #7653, 3½-oz................**38.00**
Carlton, platinum Marco; stem, goblet; #7653 Cantata, 9-oz **68.00**
Carlton, platinum Marco; tumbler, ftd, #7642 Comet, 12-oz **40.00**
Carlton, platinum Marco; tumbler, ftd, #7642 Comet, 2½-oz.......**32.00**
Carlton etch, crystal; stem, champagne; #7668 Galaxy, 6-oz **28.00**
Carlton etch, crystal; stem, cordial; #7668 Galaxy, 1½-oz **48.00**
Carlton etch, crystal; stem, goblet; #7668 Galaxy, 10-oz................**32.00**
Carlton etch, crystal; stem, sherbet; #7668 Galaxy, 6-oz **22.00**
Carlton etch, crystal; tumbler, ftd, #7668 Galaxy, 11-oz **28.00**
Carlton etch, crystal; tumbler, ftd, #7668 Galaxy, 9-oz **20.00**
Cathay etch, crystal; stem, goblet; #7590 Kingswood, 9-oz **55.00**
Cathay etch, lt amber; vase, bud; ftd, #305 Luanna, 10" **95.00**
Cathay etch, rose; vase, bud; ftd, #305 Luanna, 10" **125.00**
El Mexicano, Hyacinth; jug, 54-oz **265.00**
El Mexicano, Ice; cigarette box, w/lid....................................**120.00**
El Mexicano, Ice; ice tub **110.00**
El Mexicano, Ice; jug, liquor, w/stopper..................................**145.00**
El Mexicano, Ice; sherbet, ftd, 7-oz **24.00**
El Mexicano, Ice; tumbler, beer; flat, 8-oz **20.00**
El Mexicano, Ice; tumbler, iced tea; ftd, 13-oz............................**28.00**
El Mexicano, Ice; tumbler, lemonade/tea; flat, 14-oz **28.00**
El Mexicano, Ice; tumbler, liquor; flat, 3-oz **22.50**
El Mexicano, Ice; tumbler, orange juice; flat, 6½-oz **22.50**
El Mexicano, Rose Quartz; sherbet, ftd, 7-oz.............................**48.00**
El Mexicano, Rose Quartz; tumbler, iced tea; ftd, 13-oz................**58.00**
El Mexicano, Roze Quartz; jug, 54-oz....................................**190.00**
El Mexicano, Seaweed, ice tub **98.00**
El Mexicano, Seaweed & Ice; flower bowl, 13", 120.00 up to......**145.00**
El Mexicano, Seaweed & Ice; jug, fat, 2 styles, 140.00 up to **195.00**
El Mexicano, Seaweed & Ice; jug, 54-oz, from 125.00 up to **165.00**
El Mexicano, Seaweed & Ice; plate, 6½", from 24.00 up to **30.00**
El Mexicano, Seaweed & Ice; plate, 7½", from 24.00 up to **36.00**
El Mexicano, Seaweed & Ice; plate, 9¼", from 48.00 up to **65.00**
El Mexicano, Seaweed & Ice; vase, 5" to 7", from 45.00 up to **95.00**
El Mexicano, Seaweed; jug, liquor; w/stopper.............................**165.00**
El Mexicano, Seaweed; relish, 3-part **97.50**
El Mexicano, Seaweed; tumbler, liquor; flat, 3-oz **27.50**
Elizabeth etch, azure; stem, cocktail; #7664, 3½-oz.....................**55.00**
Elizabeth etch, azure; stem, goblet; #7630 Ballerina, 9-oz **67.50**
Elizabeth etch, azure; stem, goblet; #7664, 10-oz **85.00**
Elizabeth etch, azure; stem, wine; #7630 Ballerina, 2¾-oz............**75.00**
Elizabeth etch, crystal; plate, salad; #1500, 7¼".........................**27.50**
Elizabeth etch, crystal; stem, goblet; #7630 Ballerina, 9-oz **55.00**
Fernlee, crystal w/blk stem; comport, #7672 Octette, 6" **148.00**
Fernlee, crystal w/blk stem; wine, #7672 Octette, 3-oz................**75.00**
Fernlee, crystal; cup & saucer, #1511 ....**42.50**
Fernlee etch, crystal; stem, goblet; #7966 Trumpet, 10-oz **47.50**
Floret etch, crystal; stem, champagne; #7684 Yale, 5½-oz.............**52.50**
Floret etch, crystal; stem, cocktail; #7684 Yale, 2-oz **58.00**
Floret etch, crystal; stem, goblet; #7684 Yale, 9-oz **65.00**
Floret etch, crystal; stemmed icer & insert; unknown # **95.00**
Flower Light, Bristol Bl; vase, 5½"; candle/frog; #9938 ....**67.50**
Flower Light, Gypsy Fire, bowl, 6"; candle/frog; #9922 Sharon **40.00**

Flower Light, Thistle; bowl, candle/frog; #9941½ Vesta **48.00**
Fontinelle etch, #7620 blk stem; candlestick, low, pr **195.00**
Fontinelle etch, #7620 Fontanne blk stem; champagne, 6-oz **110.00**
Fontinelle etch, #7620 Fontanne blk stem; comport, 6" **160.00**
Fontinelle etch, #7620 Fontanne blk stem; goblet, 9-oz............**135.00**
Golf Ball #7643, cobalt w/crystal stem & hdl; Irish coffee **95.00**
Golf Ball #7643, cobalt w/crystal stem; candlestick, 4", pr...........**130.00**
Golf Ball #7643, cobalt w/crystal stem; comport, low, 6" **145.00**
Golf Ball #7643, pastel w/crystal; cocktail, 3½-oz **27.50**
Golf Ball #7643, pastel w/crystal; cordial, from 48.00 up to **60.00**
Golf Ball #7643, rose w/crystal stem; goblet, 9-oz....................**39.00**
Golf Ball #7643, rose w/crystal stem; wine, 3-oz **44.00**
Golf Ball #7643, ruby w/crystal finial; candy box, 7" **160.00**
Golf Ball #7643, ruby w/crystal stem; champagne, 5½-oz **28.00**
Golf Ball #7643, ruby w/crystal stem; claret, 4½-oz **55.00**
Golf Ball #7643, ruby w/crystal stem; cocktail, 3½-oz **34.00**
Golf Ball #7643, ruby w/crystal stem; cordial, 1½-oz **48.00**
Golf Ball #7643, ruby w/crystal stem; goblet, 9-oz **32.00**
Golf Ball #7643, ruby w/crystal stem; parfait, 5-oz.................**60.00**
Golf Ball #7643, ruby w/crystal stem; sherbet, 5½-oz **24.00**
Golf Ball #7643, ruby w/crystal stem; wine, 3-oz **46.00**
LeMons, gold on cobalt; stem, champagne; #7640, 5½-oz **110.00**
LeMons, gold on cobalt; stem, goblet; #7640, 9-oz **185.00**
LeMons, platinum on cobalt; stem, wine; #7640, 3-oz **115.00**
Mayfair etch, crystal; stem, champagne; #7668 Galaxy, 6-oz **27.00**
Mayfair etch, crystal; stem, goblet; #7668 Galaxy, 10-oz **34.00**
Mayfair etch, crystal; stem, sherbet; #7668 Galaxy, 6-oz **22.00**
Mayfair etch, crystal; tumbler, ftd, #7668 Galaxy, 11-oz **25.00**
Mayfair etch, crystal; tumbler, ftd, #7668 Galaxy, 9-oz **18.50**
Melon Rib, alabaster w/cobalt ft; tumbler, #20069, 11-oz **75.00**
Melon Rib, alabaster; jug, cobalt hdl, #20069 ....**285.00**
Morgantown Sq, crystal; open stem, champagne; #77942, 5½-oz .**100.00**
Morgantown Sq, crystal; open stem, goblet; #77942, 8½-oz.........**130.00**
Old Bristol, cobalt w/opal disk-node; candlestick, 4", pr **235.00**
Old Bristol, cobalt w/opal trim; compote, crimped, #7956, 6" **265.00**
Old English #7678, cobalt w/crystal stem; goblet, 10-oz................**48.00**
Old English #7678, ruby w/crystal stem; comport, 6" **185.00**
Old English #7678, ruby w/crystal stem; goblet, 10-oz **55.00**
Old English #7678, Steigel gr w/crystal ft; candlestick, pr............**165.00**
Old English #7678, Steigel gr w/crystal ft; tumbler, 13-oz **45.00**
Old English #7678, Steigel gr w/crystal ft; tumbler, 2½-oz **45.00**
Old English #7678, Steigel gr w/crystal stem; champagne..............**33.00**
Old English #7678, Steigel gr w/crystal stem; claret, 5-oz...........**47.50**
Old English #7678, Steigel gr w/crystal stem; claret, 5-oz...........**47.50**
Old English #7678, Steigel gr w/crystal stem; cocktail **34.00**
Old English #7678, Steigel gr w/crystal stem; cordial **50.00**
Old English #7678, Steigel gr w/crystal stem; goblet, 10-oz............**38.00**
Old English #7678, Steigel gr w/cyrstal stem; oyster.....................**45.00**
Old English #7678, Steigel gr w/crystal stem; parfait, 5-oz...........**55.00**
Old English #7678, Steigel gr w/crystal stem; sherbet **30.00**
Old English #7678, Steigel gr w/crystal stem; wine, 3-oz............**44.00**
Paragon #77943½, crystal bowl/blk stem; goblet, 9-oz................**120.00**
Paragon #77943½, crystal bowl/blk stem; sherbet, 5½-oz **67.50**
Punch bowl, crystal; Frostie (Carlton) decor, #21, 12".................**395.00**
Pygon #77943, crystal/frosted; stem, wine; Thorpe, 3½-oz...........**110.00**
Pygon #77943, frosted; wine, sgn Thorpe HP decor, 3½-oz **235.00**
Richmond etch, crystal; stem, champagne; #7570 Horizon, 5-oz ...**20.00**
Richmond etch, crystal; stem, champagne; #7589, 10-oz **22.00**
Richmond etch, crystal; stem, goblet; #7570 Horizon, 5-oz **20.00**
Richmond etch, crystal; stem, goblet; #7589 Laurette, 9-oz..........**29.00**
Richmond etch, crystal; stem, grapefruit; #7804, 21-oz...............**25.00**
Richmond etch, crystal; tumbler, ftd, #9701, 12-oz **20.00**
Saranac etch, crystal; stem, cordial; #7690 Monroe, 1-oz.............**67.50**
Saranac etch, crystal; stem, goblet; #7690 Monroe, 9-oz **62.50**

Silk-Screen Color Printing on Crystal

Manchester Pheasant, champagne, #7664 Queen Anne, 6½-oz ..**138.00**
Manchester Pheasant, finger bowl, ftd, #2940 ....**95.00**
Manchester Pheasant, goblet, #7664 Queen Anne, 10-oz............**185.00**
Manchester Pheasant, jug, ftd, #37 Barry, 48-oz **495.00**
Queen Louise, rose stem; champagne, 37614 Hampton, 6-oz **130.00**
Queen Louise, rose stem; goblet, #7614 Hampton, 9-oz.............**165.00**
Queen Louise rose stem; sherbet, #7614 Hampton, 6-oz.............**110.00**

Sunrise Medallion Etch

#37 Barry, azure; jug, 48-oz...**385.00**
#37 Barry, crystal; jug, 48-oz...**300.00**
#45 Catherine, azure; vase, bud; 10" **195.00**
#53 Serenade, rose; vase, bud; 10".......................................**325.00**
#7630 Ballerina, azure; stem, cordial; 1½-oz **95.00**
#7630 Ballerina, azure; stem, goblet; 9-oz **50.00**
#7630 Ballerina, azure; stem, wine; 2¾-oz...............................**68.00**
#7630 Ballerina, crystal w/blk ft; stem, goblet; 9-oz **75.00**
#7630 Ballerina, crystal w/blk ft; stem, parfait; 5-oz **75.00**
#7630 Ballerina, crystal; stem, goblet; 9-oz **48.00**
#7630 Ballerina, gr; stem, cocktail; 3-oz **48.00**
#7630 Ballerina, gr; stem, goblet; 9-oz **67.50**
#7630 Ballerina, gr; stem, sherbet/sundae; 6-oz.........................**52.50**
#7630 Ballerina, rose; stem, champagne; 6½-oz **45.00**
#7630 Ballerina, rose; stem, goblet; 9-oz **58.00**
#7654½ Legacy, crystal w/moonstone stem; cocktail, 3-oz...........**100.00**
#7654½ Legacy, crystal w/moonstone stem; goblet, 9-oz.............**145.00**
#7664 Queen Anne, azure; stem, champagne/sherbet; 6½-oz.........**54.00**
#7664 Queen Anne, azure; stem, goblet; 10-oz..........................**65.00**
#7664 Queen Anne, azure; stem, wine; 2¾-oz **72.50**

Tinker Bell etch, crystal; night/medicine set, 4-pc **345.00**
Tinker Bell etch, crystal; stem, champagne; #7631, 7½-oz............**52.50**
Tinker Bell etch, gr; vase, bud; #53 Serenade, 10" **295.00**
Virginia etch, amber; stem, champagne; #7614 Hampton, 6-oz.....**47.50**
Virginia etch, amber; stem, goblet, #7614 Hampton, 9-oz **85.00**
Virginia etch, crystal; stem, champagne; #7587, 5½-oz.................**22.00**
Virginia etch, crystal; stem, goblet; #7587 Hanover, 9-oz **27.50**
Virginia etch, crystal; tumbler, ftd, #90074 Belton, 9-oz..............**18.50**
Yale #7684, cobalt; stem, champagne, 5½-oz **70.00**
Yale #7684, cobalt; stem, goblet; 9-oz....................................**80.00**
Yale #7684, crystal; stem, cocktail; 2-oz **45.00**
Yale #7684, ruby; stem, champagne; 5½-oz................................**72.50**
Yale #7684, ruby; stem, goblet; 9-oz......................................**87.50**

Moriage

The term 'moriage' refers to certain Japanese wares decorated with applied slipwork designs. There are several methods used to achieve the characteristic relief effect. The decorative devices may be designed separately and applied to the vessel, piped on in narrow ribbons of clay (slip-trailed), or built up by brushing on successive layers of liquified slip. See also Dragon Ware; Nippon.

Chocolate pot, 4 floral medallions on gr, much slipwork, 9".....**245.00**
Ewer, floral medallions, mc slipwork, bulbous bottom, 12" **365.00**
Ewer, rose panels, beading/floral slipwork, 6x5½" **200.00**
Sugar shaker, roses on gr, barrel form **95.00**
Urn, florals/bird/leaves/buds, gold slipwork, Japan, 10" **200.00**

Vase, mc slipwork on aqua, unmk, 2¾x1½" **48.00**
Vase, slipwork trail florals, mc bird-on-limb panels, 12½" **250.00**

Ewer, Nouveau florals, 13½",
$400.00.

Pomeranian, #768-A, 4½", $70.00; Collie, 6½", $75.00.

Boston Terrier, ivory markings on blk, standing, 6x6", M..............**75.00**
Boxer, ivory & blk details on med brn, standing, 5½x5½" **75.00**
Bulldog, tan & charcoal, standing, 5x6½" **88.00**
Chow pup, tan & brn, recumbent, 3x3"...**50.00**
Cocker Spaniel, #763D **55.00**
Cocker Spaniel pup, #820B **35.00**
Collie, tan & ivory, standing, 6x7", M...**75.00**
Dalmatian, #812, sm...**45.00**
English Spaniel, ivory w/blk, standing, 5½x6½" **80.00**
German Shepherd, standing, 7" **85.00**
German Shepherd pup, gray & charcoal, 3x3½" **40.00**
Great Dane, blk details on tan, recumbent, 7½x6½".....................**75.00**
Horse, #701D, lg **68.00**
Pekingese, blk details on tan, standing, 3½x4½" **80.00**
Persian cat..**48.00**
Spaniel pup, ivory & golden tan, recumbent, 3¼x3½"..................**40.00**
Springer Spaniel, 5" **65.00**
St Bernard, 6½x8½"..**95.00**

Mortar and Pestle

Mortars are bowl-shaped vessels used for centuries for the purpose of grinding drugs to a powder or grain into meal. The masher or grinding device is called a pestle.

Brass, early, 4¾", +pestle **75.00**
Burl, EX figure, soft finish, 7", +pestle **320.00**
Burl, good figure, 8", +curly maple trn pestle...............................**675.00**
CI, ca 1870, 5½", +flared pestle **65.00**
CI, inverted bell form, ftd, ca 1870, 6¾", +pestle **95.00**
Lignum vitae, minor age cracks, 8" **200.00**
Stoneware, ftd base, 4 rests, early 1800s, +turq pestle **125.00**
Wood, crescent form, 13½" L, +roller pestle **325.00**
Wood, trn, 1800s, 6", +pestle **180.00**

Mortens Studio

Oscar Mortens was already established as a fine sculptural artist when he left his native Sweden to take up residency in Arizona. During the 1940s he developed a line of detailed animal figures which were distributed through the Mortens Studios, a firm he co-founded with Gunnar Thelin. Thelin hired and trained artists to produce Mortens' line, which he called Royal Designs. More than two hundred dogs were modeled and over one hundred horses. Cats and wild animals such as elephants, panthers, deer, and elk were made, but on a much smaller scale. Bookends with sculptured dog heads were shown in their catalogs, and collectors report finding wall plaques on rare occasions. The material they used was a plaster-type composition with wires embedded to support the weight. Examples were marked 'Copyright by the Mortens Studio' either in ink or decal. Watch for flaking, cracks, and separations. Crazing seems to be present in some degree in many examples. When no condition is indicated, the items listed below are assumed to be in near-mint condition, allowing for minor crazing.

Afghan, tan/charcoal face, 7x7", M..**90.00**
Beagle pup, #555 ....**38.00**

Morton Pottery

Six potteries operated in Morton, Illinois, at various times from 1877 to 1976. Each traced its origin to six brothers who immigrated to America to avoid military service in Germany. The Rapp brothers established their first pottery near clay deposits on the south side of town where they made field tile and bricks. Within a few years, they branched out to include utility wares such as jugs, bowls, jars, pitchers, etc. During the ninety-nine years of pottery operations in Morton, the original factory was expanded by some of the sons and nephews of the Rapps. Other family members started their own potteries where artware, gift-store items, and special-order goods were produced. The Cliftwood Art Pottery and the Morton Pottery Company had showrooms in Chicago and New York City during the 1930s. All of Morton's potteries were relatively short-lived operations with the Morton Pottery Company being the last to shut down on September 8, 1976. For a more thorough study of the subject, we recommend *Morton's Potteries: 99 Years* by Doris and Burdell Hall; their address can be found in the Directory under Illinois.

Morton Pottery Works – Morton Earthenware Co. (1877-1917)

Bank, acorn, brn Rockingham w/acorn stove advertising, 2½" **70.00**
Bank, acorn, cobalt, rare, 2½" **75.00**
Bowl, yel ware, 4 narrow wht slip bands, waffled bottom, 15½".....**95.00**
Bowl, yel ware w/wide center wht band, #9s, 10¼" **65.00**
Chamber pt, yel ware, infant sz **30.00**

Crock, brn Rockingham, reversed N&S in mk, 1-gal **65.00**
Mug, coffee; brn Rockingham, 3½" **50.00**
Paperweight, buffalo, brn, advertising Rock Sand Co, 2½" **50.00**
Pie baker, yel ware, 9¼" dia......................................**75.00**
Rice nappy, yel ware, fluted, 11" **75.00**
Rice nappy, yel ware, fluted, 6½" **40.00**
Teapot, Rebecca at the Well, brn Rockingham, #24s, 4-pt...........**80.00**

Cliftwood Art Potteries, Inc. (1920-1940)

Ash tray, jade gr, ind, 2½" dia...................................**10.00**
Bean pot, old rose, ind..**10.00**
Bookends, lion & lioness on rocky base, natural colors, pr **100.00**
Bowl, burgundy, nested set w/lids, 4½", 3¾", 3½" **35.00**
Bowl, sweetmeat; yel/gr drip, w/lid, 2x4¾x4¾".....................**30.00**

Cliftwood Art Potteries, vase, snake with fish in mouth as handles, cobalt blue, 18", $80.00. (As a lamp, $120.00.)

Creamer, orchid/pk drip, w/lid, 1-pt..............................**30.00**
Planter, crane, open bk, turq matt, 6½" **18.00**
Planter, elephant, open bk, brn chocolate drip, 7x5" **40.00**
Planter, elephant w/bk pack, dk brn/jade gr, 5¾" **50.00**
Planter, police dog, open bk, wht matt, 5".......................**20.00**
Reamer, Herbage gr, rare **55.00**
Teapot, bl/mulberry, 8-cup, +matching ftd trivet **60.00**
Vase, brn chocolate drip, cone shape, 18" **75.00**
Vase, cobalt, Egyptian tomb, #125, 18" **200.00**
Vase, dk bl/dk yel drip, bulbous, 6½" **45.00**
Vase, turq matt, ewer form, 8"...................................**25.00**
Vase, turq/pk drip, fan form, hdl, 9" **35.00**
Vase, wht matt/old rose spray, dolphin base, 9" **50.00**

Midwest Potteries, Inc. (1940-1944)

Ash tray/ring holder, flat tray w/attached hand, wht w/gold **20.00**
Bowl, flower; deep turq matt, 2½x11" **18.00**
Bowl, flower; nest w/attached bird, bl spray, 6½".................**15.00**
Bowl, flower; 2 semicircular pcs, brn/yel drip, 4½" H **18.00**
Creamer, cow standing on 4 legs, wht w/gold **25.00**
Ewer, wht w/pk int, 8" **18.00**
Figurine, bird of paradise, bl/brn spray, 12" **25.00**
Figurine, deer w/antlers, rearing stance, wht w/gold, 12" **30.00**
Figurine, elephant, trumpeting, wht, GOP in gold, 9".............**18.00**
Figurine, gull in flight, wht w/gold, 12" **35.00**
Figurine, spaniel, wht w/gold, 6" **18.00**
Figurine, squirrel, brn drip, 7½"................................**35.00**
Figurine, swan, 14k gold, 10" **22.00**
Planter, broken egg, tripod base, gr, 6".........................**10.00**
Planter, clown holding pants legs out, wht w/cold pnt, 6"..........**14.00**

Planter, kingfisher on stump, bl matt, 4" **8.00**
Planter, sea shell w/attached bl heron, gold trim, 11½" **30.00**
Plaque, African native, female, blk, glossy, 8" **30.00**
Plaque, African native, female w/gold neck rings & ear bones.......**40.00**
Plaque, African native, male, blk, glossy, 9" **30.00**

Morton Pottery Company (1922-1976)

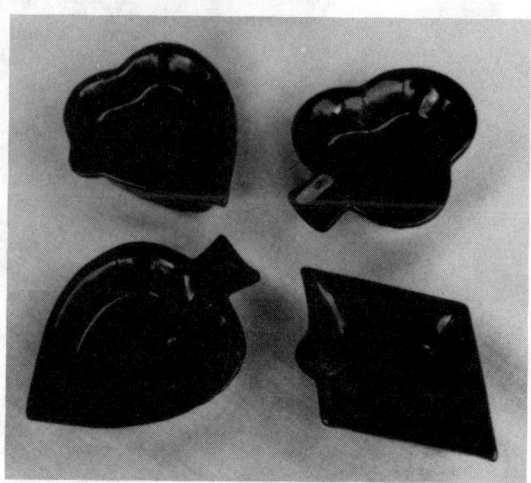

Bridge ash trays, red glaze, $25.00 for the four-piece set.

Bookend, bald eagle, brn & wht, pr **30.00**
Bookend, books w/baby shoe planters, wht matt, pr **18.00**
Bookend, parrot planter, mc, pr..................................**25.00**
Bowl, pastel, str sides, nested set of 5 ....**45.00**
Cookie jar, basket of fruit, gr w/natural-color fruit **35.00**
Cookie jar, bl bird, yel breast, lg eyes **35.00**
Cookie jar, circus animals, cylindrical, yel & orange **35.00**
Cookie jar, harlequin emb on sq form, gr........................**25.00**
Cookie jar, panda, mk AFK Industries **30.00**
Deviled egg plate, 15 egg shapes w/rooster center **18.00**
Deviled egg tray, 12 egg shells w/chick finial **22.00**
Lamp, calla lily dbl planter, yel/gr, mk Morton USA **35.00**
Lamp, Davy Crockett, adult figure w/mini bear **40.00**
Lamp, Davy Crockett, boy figure w/mini bear **35.00**
Lamp, horse & colt by pump w/water barrel, natural colors **50.00**
Mug, beer; Happy Days Are Here Again, brn, bbl shape.............**22.00**
Mug, beer; Milwaukee Tent & Awning, brn Rockingham.............**24.00**
Mug, milk; cow & calf, Sunshine Dairy Products **25.00**
Night light, Teddy bear, wht w/bl or pk paws, brn ears **30.00**
Planter, baby's highchair, bl **10.00**
Planter, camel, wht...**10.00**
Planter, lovebirds on nest, mc **14.00**
Planter, steam locomotive, blk **15.00**
Planter, touring car, top down, brn **16.00**
Water fountain figure, fish, pk..................................**20.00**

American Art Potteries (1947-1961)

Figurine, hen & rooster, gray/wht spray, 8", pr **30.00**
Flower bowl, bullet form, blk/gray spray, 3½x12" **12.00**
Flower bowl, octagonal, elongated, yel/gr spray, 2x10" **8.00**
Flower bowl, oval/scalloped, purple/yel spray, 3x8½", +plate........**14.00**
Flower bowl, S shape, yel/wht, 2x10" **10.00**
Flower frog, frog, gr/yel spray, 2½"............................**12.00**
Flower frog, titmouse on raised disk, mauve/yel spray, 8" **16.00**

Flower frog, turtle, gr/yel spray, 3¾" **14.00**
Lamp, gnarled tree trunk, gr/blk spray, 12" **20.00**
Lamp, pillar of 8 flat sqs on lg sq base, wht/gold, 16" **30.00**
Lamp, poodle sits in begging position, blk/pk, 15" **25.00**
Lamp, TV; cardinals on planter, mauve/gray spray, 12" **25.00**
Lamp, TV; fish pr on rectangular base, gr/yel spray, 6" **22.00**
Vase, bl/lav spray, mini, 4" **8.00**
Vase, dbl cornucopia, bl/rose spray, 10½" **20.00**
Vase, pitcher, bl/gray spray w/gold, 7" **18.00**
Vase, swan w/elongated neck, gr/yel spray w/gold, 11" **20.00**
Wall pocket, tree trunk w/appl bird, brn/gray spray, 5" **14.00**

Mosaic Tile Co.

The Mosaic Tile Company was organized in 1894, in Zanesville, Ohio, by Herman Mueller and Karl Langenbeck, both of whom had years of previous experience in the industry. They developed a faster, less-costly method of potting decorative tile, utilizing paper patterns rather than copper molds. By 1901 the company had grown and expanded with offices in many major cities. Faience tile was introduced in 1918, greatly increasing their volume of sales. They also made novelty ash trays, figural boxes, bookends, etc., though not to any large extent. Until they closed during the 1960s, Mosaic used various marks that included the company name or their initials — 'MT' superimposed over 'Co.' in a circle.

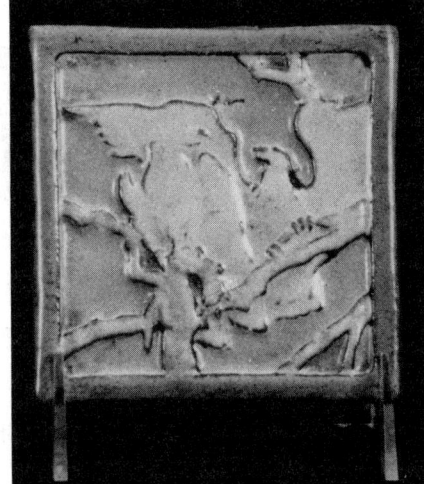

Tile, eagle pair in tree limbs, violet and green, 4½", $60.00.

Brush holder, lav, fireplace form, mk **55.00**
Figurine, blk bear, 6x9" **125.00**
Figurine, German Shepherd, tan, 10½" **125.00**
Paperweight, wht shield; NY, Rotary Internat'l seal, 3" **25.00**
Tile, Lincoln's profile, wht on bl, 3½" **30.00**
Tile, Mary & Lamb **25.00**

Moser

Ludwig Moser began his career as a struggling glass artist, catering to the rich who visited the famous Austrian health spas. His talent and popularity grew and in 1857 the first of his three studios opened in Karlsbad, Czechoslovakia. The styles developed there were entirely his own; no copies of other artists have ever been found. Some of his original designs include grapes with trailing vines, acorns and oak leaves, and richly enameled, deeply cut or carved floral pieces. Sometimes jewels were applied to the glass as well. Moser's animal scenes reflect his careful attention to detail. Famed for his birds in flight, he also designed stalking tigers — even elephants — all created in fine enameling.

Moser died in 1916, but the business was contined by his two sons who had been personally and carefully trained by their father. The Moser company bought the Meyr's Neffe Glassworks in 1922, and continued to produce quality glassware.

When identifying Moser, look for great clarity in the glass; deeply carved, continuous engravings; perfect coloration; finely applied enameling (often covered with thin gold leaf); and well-polished pontils. Our advisor for this category is Don Williams; he is listed in the Directory under Missouri. Items described below are enameled unless noted otherwise.

Vase, rubena verde with applied prunts, gilt and enamel oak leaves and acorns, signed/#606, D180, 11", $2,300.00; Pitcher, bright blue with applied salamander handle, gilt and enamel fern fronds, a bird, and several insects, 12", $2,300.00. (Both at auction.)

Bottle, scent; clear w/heavy gold, tall stopper, 10", NM **500.00**
Box, cameo/gold Amazon warriors on cobalt, ball ft, sgn, 5" **395.00**
Box, cranberry w/gold scrolling vines, hinged, sq, 5¾" **150.00**
Candy dish, facet-cut alexandrite, 5¾" dia **495.00**
Chalice, amethyst to clear, gold vintage, appl leaves, 6¾" **650.00**
Cup & saucer, clear to gr tint, gold/wht enameling......................**350.00**
Decanter, cranberry w/gold grapes, 12½", +6 3" glasses **900.00**
Decanter, prunts/appl jewels ea side, unsgn, 16"...........................**400.00**
Pitcher, gr, mc/gold florals & scrolls, 4 high gilt ft, 10" **525.00**
Spa mug, sapphire, gnomes, #s eng down side, sgn, 4¾".............**400.00**
Toasting glass, dmn-cut base, gold floral eng, unmk, 7¼" **145.00**
Tumbler, 6 szs fit inside ea other, gilt scenes , VG box **330.00**
Urn, wht cut to cranberry, HP floral reserves w/gold, 14" **650.00**
Vase, acid-cut scene, amethyst/clear, sgn MK, 8" **600.00**
Vase, amber, gold band/reserve: maid by stream, paneled, 9".......**400.00**
Vase, amethyst, bird/lily pads, gold trim, 10" **475.00**
Vase, amethyst, intaglio tulips, gold rim, slim neck, 6½" **400.00**
Vase, cameo fuchsias, gr/amethyst on amber/burgundy, 9" **3,000.00**
Vase, cameo poppies, rubena w/appl flower, 10x3" **2,500.00**
Vase, clear to gr w/lg intaglio florals, flared, 15".........................**700.00**
Vase, cobalt, etched elephants/palm trees, gold trim, 11" **1,750.00**
Vase, cobalt w/acid-cut gilt Roman soldiers, 12-panel, 15" **1,800.00**
Vase, emerald w/gold leaves, Dutchman in reserve, hdls, 22".. **1,300.00**
Vase, gold Baroque scrolls w/bl florals, ftd/4-lobed, 8x6" **990.00**
Vase, gr, gilt reserve w/lady's portrait, ftd, 12½" **325.00**
Vase, gr opal to clear, poppies w/gold, ribbed baluster, 11" **600.00**
Vase, gr to clear, dmn cut top, serrated, star base, 12"..................**225.00**
Vase, lav w/HP nude, gilt border/ft, trumpet form, sgn, 20".........**650.00**
Vase, red w/appl portrait medallion, mtd on gilt stand, 15" **1,000.00**

Vase, smoke crackle, appl orchid, heavy enameling, 8¾" **675.00**

Moss Rose

Moss Rose was a favorite dinnerware pattern of many Staffordshire and American potters from the mid-1800s. In America the Wheeling Pottery of West Virginia produced the ware in large quantities, and it became one of their bestsellers, remaining popular well into the nineties.

Bone dish, unmk, gold edge...**32.00**
Bowl, vegetable; unmk, w/lid...**50.00**
Butter pat, Meakin, EX...**15.00**
Coffee mug & saucer, Meakin...**60.00**
Coffeepot, EC&Co, 9"...**80.00**
Creamer & sugar bowl, unmk..**22.50**
Cup & saucer, handleless; gilt trim, Tucker, undersize, EX..........**275.00**
Gravy boat, Meakin...**35.00**
Plate, dinner; unmk, 10"...**15.00**
Plate, Meakin, 7" **12.50**
Platter, rectangular, Meakin, 14x10".....................................**30.00**
Shaving mug, unmk...**22.00**
Soap dish, Delaware...**45.00**
Tea set, American, 14-pc...**125.00**
Tea set, demitasse; fancy hdls & ft, American, 15-pc.................**150.00**
Tray, tiered, unmk...**20.00**
Tray, unmk, 8"..**15.00**
Wash set, unmk, 11" pitcher+13½" bowl **295.00**

Mother-of-Pearl Glass

Mother-of-Pearl glass was a type of mold-blown satin art glass popular during the last half of the 19th century. A patent for its manufacture was issued in 1886 to Frederick S. Shirley, and one of the companies who produced it was the Mt. Washington Glass Company of New Bedford, Massachusetts. Another was the English firm of Stevens and Williams. Its delicate patterns were developed by blowing the gather into a mold with inside projections that left an intaglio design on the surface of the glass, then sealing the first layer with a second, trapping air in the recesses. Most common are the Diamond Quilted, Raindrop, and Herringbone patterns. It was made in several soft colors, the most rare and valuable is rainbow — a blend of rose, light blue, yellow, and white. Occasionally it may be decorated with coralene, enameling, or gilt. Our advisors for this category are Betty and Clarence Maier; they are listed in the Directory under Pennsylvania.

Bottle, scent; Dmn Quilt, bl, w/stopper, 5"....................................**355.00**
Bowl, Dmn Quilt, bl shaded, bird & flowers, brass fr, 9x7½" **995.00**
Bowl, Dmn Quilt, pk, sq ruffled & frosted rim, 2x8"....................**275.00**
Bowl, Flower & Acorn, bl, gold florals, SP rim, 4x9¼".............. **1,025.00**
Bowl, Herringbone, orange, 6-crimp, 3⅜x5¼" **295.00**
Bowl, Ribbon, pk, chartreuse int, 3½x4" **675.00**
Creamer, Coin Spot, gold, appl frost hdl, 3-corner top, 5½".........**325.00**
Creamer, Coin Spot, gold to wht, dimpled sides, 5½"...................**325.00**
Creamer, Dmn Quilt, bl, bulbous, frosted hdl, sgn Webb, 5" **350.00**
Creamer, Dmn Quilt, rainbow to wht, str/flaring, 4¾"..................**550.00**
Creamer, Ribbon, bl, frosted hdl, wafer ft, 8-crimp, 3x3" **265.00**
Ewer, Dmn Quilt, bl, bulbous, lobed top, camphor hdl, 6½"........**300.00**
Ewer, Dmn Quilt, bl, thorny camphor hdl, 7½", pr **565.00**
Finger bowl, Herringbone, rose, cloverleaf top, 3x4¼".................**185.00**
Lamp, Dmn Quilt, bl, orig brass mts, 18x8"................................**895.00**
Lamp, Swirl, brn, brass ft/mts, 20½"..**995.00**
Mug, Dmn Quilt, pk to wht, flowers, frosted hdl, 3½" **275.00**

Pitcher, Dmn Quilt, MOP body, pk/bl/yel at sq neck, 7¾" **850.00**
Pitcher, Dmn Quilt, rainbow to wht, bulbous, 6" **850.00**
Rose bowl, Dmn Quilt, rainbow, ftd, mk Patent, 3½x4¼"....... **1,395.00**
Rose bowl, Dmn Quilt, rose, egg shape, mk Patent, 3½x2¾".......**275.00**
Rose bowl, Ribbon, bl, frosted wafer ft, 8-crimp, 2½x3⅛"...........**210.00**
Rose bowl, Ribbon, bl, 7-crimp, 1⅞x2⅜" **195.00**
Rose bowl, Ribbon, bl, 8-crimp, 2⅝x4" **225.00**
Rose bowl, Ribbon, rose-red, 11-crimp, 2⅞x3¾".........................**245.00**
Shade, Dmn Quilt/Melon Rib, rose to melon, fluted, 4⅜x6¼" **265.00**
Shade, Melon Ribbed Swirl, pk, ruffled, 4⅞x7⅝".........................**265.00**
Shade, Swirl, pk, ruffled, 6¾x9" **375.00**
Sugar shaker, Invt T'print, cranberry, stork/flowers, 5" **800.00**
Sweetmeat, Herringbone, pk, gold enameling, SP trim.................**565.00**
Tumbler, Dmn Quilt, apricot, 3⅞x3" **125.00**
Tumbler, Dmn Quilt, pk, HP daises & foliage, 3¾" **265.00**
Tumbler, Dmn Quilt, pk, pastel coralene florals, HP bugs, 4"......**495.00**
Tumbler, Dmn Quilt, vivid rainbow w/pk & wht blossoms **1,050.00**
Tumbler, Herringbone, apricot shaded, 3¾x2¾".........................**125.00**
Tumbler, Herringbone, yel, HP mc florals, 3⅞x2¾".....................**225.00**
Vase, bud; Dmn Quilt, bl, card plate in ornate brass fr, 10"...**650.00**
Vase, Coin Spot, pk shaded, bl HP florals w/gold, 5⅞x3½" **395.00**
Vase, Dmn Quilt, apricot shaded, sq top, thorn hdl, 8"................**250.00**
Vase, Dmn Quilt, bl, bottle form, 7¼x3½" **135.00**
Vase, Dmn Quilt, bl, HP bees, Webb, 4", pr...............................**575.00**
Vase, Dmn Quilt, bl, HP florals, 4¾x3" **195.00**
Vase, Dmn Quilt, bl, ruffled rim, 6½x4" **210.00**
Vase, Dmn Quilt, bl, wht int, fluted, 7¼x2½" **165.00**
Vase, Dmn Quilt, butterscotch shaded, ribbed, ruffled, 9x5" **550.00**
Vase, Dmn Quilt, peach, bottle form, triple-ring neck, 9" **175.00**
Vase, Dmn Quilt, pk, ruffled, 7x3½"...**160.00**
Vase, Dmn Quilt, pk, 4 pinched sides, ruffled/ftd, 7", pr **400.00**
Vase, Dmn Quilt, pk w/vaseline satin overcasing, 10½"..............**495.00**
Vase, Dmn Quilt, rainbow, fluted/frilly neck, hdls/4 ft, 9" **950.00**
Vase, Dmn Quilt, rainbow, frosted ball ft, 5¼x4¼"....................**995.00**
Vase, Dmn Quilt, rainbow shaded, bulb w/cylinder neck, 7" **550.00**
Vase, Drape, cream, amber rigaree at neck, 4-crimp, 5" **225.00**
Vase, Drape, gr, bowl form, 5½x6⅛" **300.00**
Vase, Drape, pk, ruffled rim, 5¾x3⅜" **225.00**
Vase, Drape, rose, ruffled rim, 5⅞x3½" **495.00**
Vase, Federzeichnung, brn w/bl & wht dots, stick neck, 10" ... **2,250.00**
Vase, Federzeichnung, brn w/pk int, EX gold, 6" **2,125.00**
Vase, Flower & Acorn, chartreuse, 3-petal top, 4¼x5" **425.00**
Vase, Herringbone, bl, frosted ft & hdls, 9¾x4½".......................**750.00**

Vase, Herringbone, white shaded to pink, 11", $250.00.

Vase, Herringbone, bl, ruffled rim, 5¾x3⅛" 185.00
Vase, Herringbone, pk, ruffled, ribbed, frosted hdls, 7½" 225.00
Vase, Herringbone, rose, ruffled ewer form, 6¾x4" 245.00
Vase, Hobnail, bl, folded-in sq top, 5½" 615.00
Vase, Loop & Teardrop, bl, ruffled rim, 11½" 350.00
Vase, Ribbon, bl, rstr SP fr w/deer, 8¾" 295.00
Vase, Ribbon, bl, SP holder, 7⅞x3½" 165.00
Vase, Swirl, pk shaded, reeded hdls, ruffled rim, 11½" 355.00

Mourning Collectibles

During the 18th and early 19th centuries, ladies made needlework pictures, samplers, paintings on ivory plaques, watercolor drawings, etc. to commemorate the death of a loved one. Elements contained in nearly all examples are the tomb, mourners, a weeping willow tree, and data relating to the deceased. Often plaits of hair were included. Today these are recognized and valued as a valid form of folk art. Our advisor for this category is Steve DeGenaro; he is listed in the Directory under Ohio. See also Hair Weaving.

Watercolor and ink memorial on paper, early 1800s, tears, varnished, 13" x 15", $450.00.

Brooch, gold w/enameled urn & tree, hair sample, sgn, 1⅛" 65.00
Locket on chain, containing hair pc, gold mts, 1860-80 ....150.00
Needlework picture, mourning theme, ca 1840s, 10x28", G ... 1,600.00
Paper cutout, tombs/trees/silhouettes of faces, emb, 6x7" 325.00
Photograph, post-mortem, cabinet card, 5x8", VG........................25.00
Watercolor/ink, willows/tomb, dtd 1822, 25x18", VG 750.00
Watercolor/ink, willows/tomb, unsgn, 1800s, 7x10", NM 3,000.00

Movie Memorabilia

Movie memorabilia covers a broad range of collectibles, from books and magazines dealing with the industry in general to the various promotional materials which were distributed to arouse interest in a particular film. Many collectors specialize in a specific area — posters, pressbooks, stills, lobby cards, or souvenir programs (also referred to as premiere booklets). In the listings below, a one-sheet poster measures approximately 27" x 41", three-sheet: 41" x 81", and six-sheet: 81" x 81". See also Autographs; Cartoon Art; Personalities.

Lobby card, Barbarian & Geisha, John Wayne, 11x14" 25.00
Lobby card, Belles on Their Toes, scene card, 1952, 11x14"..........15.00
Lobby card, Check Your Guns, Eddie Dean, 11x14" 15.00
Lobby card, Day the Earth Stood Still 300.00
Lobby card, Gateway, Ameche/Whelan, 1938, 11x14", set 250.00
Lobby card, Going My Way, scene card, 1944, 11x14", EX 50.00
Lobby card, Goodbye Mr Chipps, scene card, 1939, 11x14" 85.00
Lobby card, I'll See You in My Dreams, D Day, 11x14" 25.00
Lobby card, Little Miss Broadway, Temple, 11x14", set, EX ... 1,500.00
Lobby card, Rainmaker, scene card, 1956, 11x14", EX................10.00
Lobby card, Range Law, Johnny Mack Brown, 11x14"................25.00
Lobby card, Snow White, 1975 re-release, full set, M 100.00
Lobby card, Star for Night, Trevor/Darwell, '36, 11x14", set 150.00
Magazine, Big Song Hit, Bob Hope cover, 1944, 16-pg, 9x14" 16.00
Magazine, Cine Revue, Jayne Mansfield cover, May, 1958, VG ...50.00
Magazine, Cinemacabre, issue #7, VG 15.00
Magazine, Dig, Bobby Rydell cover, EX 15.00
Magazine, Film Careers, Judy Garland cover, 1964, EX 30.00
Magazine, Mid-Week Pictorial, Garbo cover, EX 20.00
Magazine, Modern Screen, Garland/Rooney cover, 1940, EX........40.00
Magazine, Motion Picture, Debbie Reynolds cover, 1956, EX 20.00
Magazine, Motion Picture, Jane Russell cover, 1949, EX 30.00
Magazine, Motion Picture, Pat Boone cover, June 1960, M...........15.00
Magazine, Movie Life, Tuesday Weld cover, Oct 1961, EX 7.50
Magazine, Movie Mirror, Gene Autry cover, 1940, EX.................30.00
Magazine, New Movie, Gloria Swanson cover, Sept 1930, EX 50.00
Magazine, Photoplay, Debbie Reynolds cover, Sept 1963, EX 7.50
Magazine, Photoplay, Doris Day cover, Monroe story, 1953 ....38.00
Magazine, Photoplay, Shirley Temple cover, Dec 1936, VG 80.00
Magazine, Picture Play, Lombard cover, 1932, EX.......................35.00
Magazine, Radio-TV Mirror, Eve Arden cover, Monroe ad, 1953 .45.00
Magazine, Screen Land, Veronica Lake cover, 1948, EX 18.00
Magazine, Screen Romances, Shirley Temple cover, 1936, EX 40.00
Magazine, Silver Screen, Shirley Temple cover, 1936, EX............18.00
Magazine, Silver Screen, T Power/N Shearer cover, 1938, EX 32.00
Magazine, Starland, Fess Parker cover, 1955...............................9.50
Magazine, Tempo, Mamie Van Doren cover, 1953, EX................22.50
Magazine, TV Star Parade, Eddie & Liz cover, Feb 1954, EX 7.50
Poster, Annie Get Your Gun, 1950, 14x36", EX 60.00
Poster, Barbarian & Geisha, John Wayne, 14x36", EX 40.00
Poster, Big Jake, John Wayne, 1-sheet 30.00
Poster, Black Trail, Johnny Mack Brown, 27x41", EX..................35.00
Poster, Bus Stop, M Monroe, Deco colors, 27x41", EX 550.00
Poster, Cahill, John Wayne, 27x41", EX......................................25.00
Poster, Call of the Wild, 1953, 41x81" 185.00
Poster, Castle on Hudson, J Garfield/A Sheridan, 14x36", EX ...125.00
Poster, Chaser, D O'Keefe, MGM, Tooker Litho, '38, 27x41" ...100.00
Poster, Cincinnati Kid, 1965, 22x28" 40.00
Poster, Circus World, John Wayne, 1-sheet 45.00
Poster, Curse of Werewolf, 1961, 81x80", NM 125.00
Poster, Deep Blue Sea, Vivien Leigh, 27x41", EX 45.00
Poster, Dial M for Murder, 1954, 63x47", VG...........................100.00
Poster, Facts of Life, Bob Hope/Lucille Ball, 14x36", EX.............65.00
Poster, Fantasia, Litho in USA, 1950, 57x40", NM 150.00
Poster, Fish Hooky, Little Rascals, 1952, 41x27", EX.................137.50
Poster, Four's a Crowd, Errol Flynn, 1938, 27x41", EX 800.00
Poster, Gentlemen Prefer Blondes, 1953, 22x28", EX.................275.00
Poster, Godzilla, Paul Anthony Enterprises, 1956, 41x27" 195.00
Poster, Gone w/Wind, purple/blk/wht, 1943, 27x41", EX...........800.00
Poster, I Thank a Fool, Susan Hayward, 14x36", EX 25.00
Poster, In the Good Old Summer Time, 1949, 41x81", EX 225.00
Poster, King Kong, 1956, 41x27", NM......................................680.00
Poster, Life w/Father, 1947, 14x36", VG...................................85.00
Poster, Little Miss Broadway, Temple, 1938, 27x41", NM 1,100.00

Poster for *Laramie*, featuring Charles Starrett, Smiley Burnette, and others, 20" x 26", $35.00.

Poster, Mame, Lucille Ball, 27x41", EX 25.00
Poster, Mummy's Curse, Lon Chaney Jr, 14x36", EX 40.00
Poster, Niagara, Marilyn Monroe, 22x28", NM...........................575.00
Poster, Painted Desert, G O'Brien, Morgan Litho, '38, 1-sheet ..150.00
Poster, Pinocchio, Disney Production, Buena Vista, 77x39", EX ..300.00
Poster, Rage of Paris, Darriux/Fairbanks, 1938, 27x41", EX.........100.00
Poster, Red Badge of Courage, 1951, 41x81", EX 90.00
Poster, Return of Vampire, Bela Lugosi & girl, 14x36", EX 175.00
Poster, Riders of Deadline, Wm Boyd as Hoppy, 27x41", EX.........40.00
Poster, River of No Return, Marilyn Monroe, 1954, 22x28", EX.100.00
Poster, Rollover, Fonda/Kristofferson, 1981, 1-sheet 17.50
Poster, Room Service, Marx Bros, 22x28" 500.00
Poster, Rooster Cogburn, John Wayne, 1-sheet..............................40.00
Poster, Saratoga Trunk, 1945, 14x36", EX.....................................70.00
Poster, Sky Grant, Dix/Fontaine, Morgan Litho, '38, 27x41" 100.00
Poster, Snake Pit, 1948, 14x36", VG 85.00
Poster, Speedway, Elvis Presley/Nancy Sinatra, 27x41", EX 100.00
Poster, Stalag 17, 1953, 27x41", EX 65.00
Poster, State Fair, 1962, 22x28", VG 10.00
Poster, Stick to Your Guns, Wm Boyd as Hoppy, 1941, 27x41" ..100.00
Poster, Streetcar Named Desire, Brando/Leigh, 22x28", EX 100.00
Poster, Till the Clouds Roll By, 1946, 27x41", EX 100.00
Poster, Tom Mix Circus & Wild West, 42x28"...........................200.00
Poster, True Grit, John Wayne, 1-sheet...60.00
Poster, Winning Team, Ronald Reagan/Doris Day, fr, 14x36" ...200.00
Poster, You Only Live Twice, 1967, 14x36", EX 150.00
Poster, Young Tom Edison, 1940, 22x28", EX.............................100.00
Poster, Ziegfeld Girl, 1944, 27x41", EX 150.00
Poster, 2001: A Space Odyssey, 1968, 14x36", VG.....................100.00
Pressbook, An American in Paris, 1951, EX 125.00
Pressbook, Gone w/the Wind, 1954, EX.......................................100.00
Pressbook, Guilty of Treason, 1949, EX..15.00
Pressbook, Little Lord Fauntleroy, 1935, EX..................................85.00
Pressbook, South Sea Woman, Lancaster/Mayo, 1955, 11x17"......17.50
Pressbook, Yellow Submarine, 1967, EX 100.00
Program, Beau Geste, loose cover...35.00
Program, Fantasia, Disney Productions, 32-pg, 40", EX 60.00
Program, Hunchback of Notre Dame, Lon Chaney, EX................65.00
Still, Lon Chaney/Sam De Grasse, ca 1915, 6½x8½", EX 35.00
Still, Swing, Sister, Swing, Ted Weems & Orchestra......................17.50
Trailer, By the Light of the Silvery Moon, theater, 16mm.............10.00
Trailer, Bye Bye Birdie, theater, 16mm..12.50

Trailer, Camelot, 30-second, 16mm 7.00

Mt. Washington

The Mt. Washington Glass Works was founded in 1837 in South Boston, Massachusetts, but moved to New Bedford in 1869 after purchasing the facilities of the New Bedford Glass Company. Frederick S. Shirley became associated with the firm in 1874. Two years later the company reorganized and became known as the Mt. Washington Glass Company. In 1894 it merged with the Pairpoint Manufacturing Company, a small Brittania works nearby, but continued to conduct business under its own title until after the turn of the century. The combined plants were equipped with the most modern and varied machinery available and boasted a working force with experience and expertise rival to none in the art of blowing and cutting glass. In addition to their fine cut glass, they are recognized as the first American company to make cameo glass, an effect they achieved through acid-cutting methods. In 1885 Shirley was issued a patent to make Burmese, pale yellow glassware tinged with a delicate pink blush. Another patent issued in 1886 allowed them the rights to produce Rose Amber, or amberina, a transparent ware shading from ruby to amber. Pearl Satin Ware and Peachblow, so named for its resemblance to a rosy peach skin, were patented the same year. One of their most famous lines, Crown Milano, was introduced in 1893. It was an opal glass either free-blown or pattern-molded, tinted a delicate color and decorated with enameling and gilt. Royal Flemish was patented in 1894 and is considered the rarest of the Mt. Washington art glass lines. It was decorated with raised, gold-enameled lines dividing the surface of the ware in much the same way as lead lines divide a stained glass window. The sections were filled in with one or several transparent colors and further decorated in gold enamel with florals, foliage, beading, and medallions.

Our advisors for this category are Betty and Clarence Maier; they are listed in the Directory under Pennsylvania. See also Amberina, Cranberry; Salt Shakers; Burmese; Crown Milano; Royal Flemish; etc.

Atomizer, HP pansies, melon shape, rpl bulb 150.00
Biscuit jar, floral, pk on wht, crab motif on lid sgn MW 650.00
Box, blown-out florals on lid & corners, gr w/gold, 7" sq 1,200.00

Box, portrait of a man on lustreless ivory, 5" diameter, $465.00.

Box, pastel florals & gold on lustreless wht, 4½x6" dia 550.00
Condiment set, roses, red on yel, 3-bottle; Wilcox fr, 7½" 225.00
Lamp base, cameo urn/bird band, wht to pk, metal mts, 8"..........375.00
Pitcher, gold fish/coral/sea plants on clear, 6x5½".........................950.00
Pitcher, mc mums/leaves on clear, 6x5½"......................................450.00

Shakers, cranberry satin w/floral, fig form, 2¾", pr.......................550.00
Shakers, floral on egg shape, metal chicken head lid, pr 450.00
Shakers, opal w/floral, fig form, 2¾", pr.......................250.00
Shakers, pnt Burmese w/floral, ribbed cylinder, 4½", pr.......140.00
Sugar shaker, asters, bl/pk on peach, ribbed fig form, 4".......650.00
Sugar shaker, daisies, wht on shaded yel, egg form, 4½"............175.00
Sugar shaker, floral, bl/wht on yel satin, egg form, 4"...............170.00
Sugar shaker, floral, pastel on lt bl, egg form, 4½x3" 200.00
Sugar shaker, floral on opal ware, 5".......................100.00
Toothpick holder, autumn leaves/bl berries on satin.................175.00
Vase, chrysanthemums on yel opal, 9x7½".......................575.00
Vase, Lava, mc chips w/wht outlines, 3¾"........................ 1,750.00
Vase, Napoli, frog/bulrushes, gold trim, bulbous base, 9" 975.00
Vase, seaweed on brn to gold satin, long-neck gourd, 11"...........495.00

Mulberry China

Mulberry china was made by many of the Staffordshire area potters from about 1830 until the 1850s. It is a transfer-printed earthenware or ironstone named for the color of its decorations, a purplish-brown resembling the juice of the mulberry. Some pieces may have faded out over the years and today look almost gray with only a hint of purple. (Transfer printing was done in many colors; technically only those in the mauve tones are 'mulberry'; color variations have little effect on value.) Some of the patterns (Corean, Jeddo, Pelew, and Formosa, for instance) were also produced in Flow Blue ware. Others seem to have been used exclusively with the mulberry color. Our advisor for this category is Mary Frank Gaston; she is listed in the Directory under Texas.

Athens, bowl, vegetable; nut finial 375.00
Athens, cup plate, Adams 50.00
Athens, plate, 10".......................40.00
Avon, teapot, lg.......................350.00
Bochara, platter, 14" 95.00
Bochara, soup, shallow, John Edwards, 8½".......................45.00
Bochara, wash bowl, 14".......................150.00
Bryonia, sauce dish, 5" 10.00

Castle, teapot, $325.00.

Bryonia, soup tureen, rnd, w/lid 95.00
Chusan, plate, Podmore Walker, 8¼" 25.00
Chusan, platter, 18".......................200.00
Corea, plate, 12-sided, Clementson, 9½" 65.00
Corea, sugar bowl, Clementson 175.00
Corea, teapot, Clementson 295.00
Corean, cup.......................40.00
Corean, cup plate 50.00

Corean, plate, 7¾" 35.00
Corean, sugar bowl, lion hdls 128.00
Corean, toothbrush box, w/lid 200.00
Cyprus, plate, Davenport, 7½".......................35.00
Cyprus, platter, Davenport, 15½".......................195.00
Cyprus, teapot, Davenport 350.00
Cyprus, tureen, vegetable; Davenport, w/lid.......................175.00
Delhi, plate, 7¾".......................32.00
Delhi, soap box, w/lid.......................125.00
Foliage, cup & saucer, handleless; Walley 65.00
Foliage, plate, 9".......................25.00
Hong Kong, platter, 13¼".......................110.00
Jeddo, bowl, vegetable; Adams & Sons, 8".......................125.00
Jeddo, creamer, Adams & Son, 7¼".......................135.00
Jeddo, pitcher, milk; Adams & Son, 8¼" 155.00
Jeddo, plate, Adams & Son, 10¼".......................65.00
Jeddo, plate, Adams & Son, 7½" 35.00
Jeddo, plate, Adams & Son, 9¼" 45.00
Jeddo, sauce bowl, Adams & Son.......................35.00
Jeddo, teapot, Adams & Sons.......................375.00
Jeddo, wash bowl & pitcher, Adams & Son, ca 1845 ....575.00
Marble, toothbrush holder, w/lid.......................45.00
Marble, wash pitcher, Alcock 175.00
Nankin, bowl, vegetable; w/lid, Davenport, lg 325.00
Nankin, creamer, Davenport.......................135.00
Nankin, sugar bowl, Davenport.......................150.00
Nankin, waste bowl, Davenport 85.00
Neva, pitcher, Challinor, 9".......................200.00
Neva, teapot, Challinor.......................250.00
Panama, creamer, Challinor.......................175.00
Panama, gravy boat, Challinor 150.00
Pelew, cup & saucer, handleless; Challinor 65.00
Pelew, plate, Challinor, 9¾".......................45.00
Pelew, plate, 8".......................35.00
Pelew, sugar bowl, Challinor 50.00
Pelew, teapot, 6-sided.......................325.00
Pelew, waste bowl 95.00
Peruvian, plate, Wedgwood, 7¼" 30.00
Peruvian, teapot.......................275.00
Rhone Scenery, bowl, vegetable; w/lid, Mayer, ca 1855 ....185.00
Rhone Scenery, coffeepot, Podmore 375.00
Rhone Scenery, gravy boat 120.00
Rhone Scenery, plate, 9½".......................45.00
Rhone Scenery, platter, 13½".......................100.00
Rhone Scenery, platter, 15¾".......................125.00
Rose, cup & saucer, handleless.......................55.00
Rose, platter, 14".......................140.00
Susa, bowl, fluted rim, 9¼".......................85.00
Temple, plate, Podmore Walker, ca 1850, 8¾".......................42.00
Temple, tea bowl & saucer, Podmore Walker 75.00
Temple, tea tile, Podmore Walker, ca 1850 ....75.00
Tonquin, cup & saucer, Heath.......................80.00
Washington Vase, creamer.......................175.00
Washington Vase, cup & saucer 65.00
Washington Vase, pitcher, 8".......................295.00
Washington Vase, plate, Podmore Walker, 8½".......................55.00
Washington Vase, platter, 16" 190.00
Washington Vase, relish.......................88.00
Washington Vase, sugar bowl, w/lid, Podmore Walker, 9½".......265.00
Washington Vase, teapot 325.00

Muller Freres

Henri Muller established a factory in 1900 at Croismare, France.

He produced fine cameo art glass decorated with florals, birds, and insects in the Art Nouveau style. The work was accomplished by acid engraving and hand finishing. Usual marks were 'Muller,' 'Muller Croismare,' or 'Croismare, Nancy.' In 1910 Henri and his brother Deseri formed a glassworks at Luneville. The cameo art glass made there was nearly all produced by acid cuttings of up to four layers with motifs similar to those favored at Croismare. A good range of colors was used, and some pieces were gold flecked. Handles and decorative devices were sometimes applied by hand. In addition to the cameo glass, they also produced an acid-finished glass of bold mottled colors in the Deco style. Examples were signed 'Muller Freres' or 'Luneville.' Our advisor for this category is Don Williams; he is listed in the Directory under Missouri.

Cameo

Bowl, poppies, pk on lt gray, mk Croismare, 4¾x9" 7,000.00
Box, floral, reds on frost to lt red, dome lid, 4x5" 1,100.00
Vase, birds/foliage/geometrics, dbl o/l, 3-ftd sphere, 8" 1,700.00
Vase, iris, red/wine on frost w/mc flecks, bun ft, 16" 1,850.00
Vase, lamb attacked by wolf, dbl o/l, spherical, 4¾" 1,950.00
Vase, mums, amber/brn on wht, dbl o/l, baluster, 18" 4,500.00
Vase, poppies (detailed), wine on bl to yel, ovoid, 9" 2,700.00
Vase, river/trees, brn/gr on wht/rust, hdld flask form, 5" 950.00
Vase, trees by river, dbl o/l, ovoid w/flared rim, 8" 1,800.00

Miscellaneous

Chandelier, bl/orange mottle, ivy motif hdw, 14" shade+3 sm . 1,500.00
Lamp, orange/brn mottle 'lily' in wrought branch std, 19" 1,500.00
Lamp, yel/rust mottle helmet shade; 3-strap/leafy std, 15" 1,200.00
Lamp, 16" peach shade w/emb floral panels; metal base, 35"... 1,650.00
Scarab night light, base cast as beetle's legs, 7½" L 3,000.00
Vase, birch trees, mc/HP on yel & orange mottle, 13" 1,650.00
Vase, int decor of red/bl glass & silver foil, 5" 165.00
Vase, int silver specks, orange/gr/bl swirls & streaks, 9" 525.00
Vase, orange/bl-blk int decor, ovoid, 3" 330.00
Vase, red/bl mottle w/silver inclusions, spherical, 9¾" 375.00

Muncie

Muncie Pottery, established in Muncie, Indiana, by Charles O. Grafton, was produced from 1922 until about 1935. It is made of a heavier clay than most of its contemporaries; the styles are sturdy and simple. Early glazes were bright and colorful. In fact, Muncie was advertised as the 'rainbow pottery.' Later most of the ware was finished in a matt glaze. The more collectible examples are those modeled after Phoenix Glass vases — sculptured with lovebirds, grasshoppers, and goldfish. Their line of Art Deco-style vases bear a remarkable resemblance to the Consolidated Glass Company's Ruba Rombic line. Vases, candlesticks, bookends, ash trays, bowls, lamp bases, and luncheon sets were made. A line of garden pottery was manufactured for a short time. Items were frequently impressed with MUNCIE in block letters. Letters such as A, K, E, or D and the numbers 1, 2, 3, 4, or 5 often found scratched into the base are finishers' marks.

Bookend, orange/blk flambe, emb owls, pr..90.00
Jug, refrigerator; orange peel, ball form, w/stopper, 7" 85.00
Lamp, wht drip over pk, swan head hdls, Aladdin..........................185.00
Vase, bl matt, Ruba Rhombic, 7" 75.00
Vase, bl/cream drip, gloss, cylinder w/emb, 10" 135.00
Vase, blk gloss, trumpet, 12" 150.00
Vase, lt gr matt, hand trn, ruffled top, hdls, 6"................................35.00
Vase, rose/gr (matt) airbrush, ribbed pillow form, 6" 45.00

Vase, rose/gr airbrush, hand trn, ruffled top, 4"..............................25.00
Vase, yel gloss, ribbed pillow form, 6" 60.00
Wall pocket, gr/rust matt, fan form, 7" 85.00

Musical Instruments

The field of automatic musical instruments covers many different categories ranging from tiny dolls and trinkets concealing musical movements to huge organs and orchestrions which weigh many tons. Music boxes, first made in the late 18th century by Swiss watchmakers, were produced in both disk and cylinder models. The latter type employs a cylinder studded with tiny projections. As the cylinder turns, these projections lift the tuned teeth in the 'music comb,' and the melody results. The value of the instrument depends upon the length of the cylinder and the quality of workmanship, though other factors must also be considered. Those in ornate cabinets or with extra features such as bells, mechanical birds, etc. often sell for much more. Units built into matching tables sell for about twice the amount they would bring otherwise. While small and medium size units are still being made today, most of the larger ones date from the 19th century. Disk-type music boxes utilize interchangeable steel disks with projecting studs, which by means of an intervening 'star wheel' cause a music comb to play. There are many different variations and mechanisms. Most were made in Germany, but some were produced in the United States. Among the most popular makes are Polyphon, Symphonion, and Regina. The latter was made in Rahway, New Jersey, from about 1894 through 1917.

Player pianos were made in a wide variety of styles. Early varieties consisted of a mechanism which pushed up to a piano and played on the keyboard by means of felt-tipped fingers. These use sixty-five note rolls. Later models have the playing mechanisms built in. At first these also used sixty-five note rolls, but those produced from about 1908 until 1940 use eighty-eight note rolls.

Coin-operated electric pianos are deluxe versions of player pianos. These incorporate expression mechanisms so that by using special-made rolls they can play the hand-recorded rolls of famous pianists. Popular makes include Ampico, Duo-Art, and Welte. Roll-operated organs were made in many forms, ranging from table-top models to large foot-pumped versions. Of the latter the Aeolian Orchestrelle is considered to be one of the best.

Unless noted, prices given are for instruments in fine condition, playing properly, with cabinets or cases in well-preserved or refinished condition. In all instances, unrestored instruments sell for much less, as do pieces with broken parts, damaged cases, and the like. On the other hand, particularly superb examples in especially ornate case designs and pieces which have been particularly well restored often will command more.

Key:
c — cylinder   d — disk

Mechanical

Accordion, Tanzabar, roll-operated, EX.................................... 1,200.00
Box, Capitol Cuff Box A, EX orig 2,800.00
Box, Criterion, 20½" dbl c, oak upright, rstr 9,800.00
Box, Ducommiun Giroux, 4-tune, 13⅛" c, inlaid lid, EX 2,200.00
Box, Empress, 9¼" d, mahog, EX 1,100.00
Box, Kalliope #60 Style, 13¼" d, inlaid case, +10 disks........... 2,000.00
Box, L'epee, 8-tune, 13" c, key wind, rstr 1,600.00
Box, L'Universal, interchangable c, VG.................................... 1,100.00
Box, Lecoultre, 4-tune, 13⅛" c, inlaid lid, rstr 2,200.00
Box, Lecoultre, 8-tune, 13" c, lever wind, fruitwood, EX......... 2,850.00
Box, Lepee, 6-tune, 10½" c, key wind, rstr/rnf 1,400.00

Box, Lepee, 8-tune, 13" c, key wind, rstr 1,800.00
Box, Lochman Original, 24½" d, saucer bells, EX orig 21,500.00
Box, Longdorf, 4-tune, 13¼" c, rstr cabinet 3,800.00
Box, Mira, 15¾ d, console, dbl comb, VG 5,800.00
Box, Mira, 18½" console, mahog 10,000.00
Box, New Century, 18½" d, single comb, +15 disks, EX......... 4,000.00
Box, Nicole, 3-tune, wire hinges, early, rare, rstr 3,850.00
Box, Nicole, 4-tune, 8⅛" c, key wind, EX orig 2,650.00
Box, Nicole, 6-tune, 10½" c, key wind, early, EX orig 2,500.00
Box, Nicole Freres, 8-tune, 13⅛" c, inlaid lid, rstr 2,800.00
Box, Nicole Mandolin, 8-tune, 17¾" c, lever wind, NM........ 6,600.00
Box, Nicole Overture, 4-overture, 12⅛" c, key wind, rstr........ 9,500.00
Box, Nicole Piano Forte, 13" c, key wind, NM 3,000.00
Box, Paillard Longe Marche Piccolo Zither, 8-tune, rstr.......... 4,000.00
Box, Paillard Mandolin Basse, 8-tune, 21½" c, 2 combs, EX .. 5,500.00
Box, Polyphon, 14⅛" d, 12 bells, rstr, +12 disks, NM............. 5,500.00
Box, Polyphon, 24½" d, w/gambling mechanism, rstr 1,250.00
Box, Regina, 15½" d, automatic changer, mahog, EX.............17,000.00
Box, Regina, 15½" d, oak table model, EX............................. 3,500.00
Box, Regina, 15½" d, serpentine, mahog 4,500.00
Box, Regina, 27" d, automatic changer, cvd dragons, EX 19,500.00
Box, Regina, 27" d, folding top, serpentine case, rstr 8,000.00
Box, Regina Corona #36, 15½" d, flat front, EX orig.............14,000.00
Box, Regina Style II, 15½" d, w/base cabinet 5,800.00

Stella disk music box, #3415, 17¼" disks, single comb, mahogany case with oak leaf carving, 13" x 29", $4,800.00.

Box, Stella, 14" d, mahog 2,800.00
Box, Stella, 17¼" d, console floor model, EX.......................... 5,800.00
Box, Stella, 17¼" d, table model, inlaid case, VG.................... 4,500.00
Box, Stella #84, 17½" d, mahog 6,200.00
Box, Symphonion, 17⅝" d, ornate base cabinet...................... 5,500.00
Box, Symphonion #192, upright, w/base, 25¼".................... 9,000.00
Box, Symphonion #30A, 13⅝" d, M 2,500.00
Caliola, Wurlitzer, wood pipes, roll or hand play, EX 14,500.00
Calliope, Cossette, on cart, EX.. 2,500.00
Calliope, Tangley, hand & roll play, +23 A rolls, EX.............. 9,500.00
Desk, Regina, 20¾" d, short bedplate mvt, EX.......................11,500.00
Nickelodeon, Capitol by N Tonawanda, w/violin pipes, EX ... 6,500.00
Nickelodeon, Coinola, 1915, EX... 8,500.00
Nickelodeon, Seeburg E, w/xylophone, oak, rstr..................... 8,500.00
Nickelodeon, Seeburg L, EX orig.. 5,500.00
Nickelodeon, Seeburg L, M rstr.. 6,000.00
Nickelodeon, Seeburg L, VG.. 3,900.00
Nickelodeon, Wurlitzer D, rstr...10,000.00
Nickelodeon, Wurlitzer I, keyboard style, 1912, EX 7,500.00
Orchestrelle, Aeolian #40, 116-note, EX 4,800.00

Orchestrelle, Aeolian F, oak case, rstr, 96" 8,500.00
Orchestrelle, Aeolian V, oak case, rstr..................................... 4,500.00
Orchestrelle, Aeolian W, mahog, rstr....................................... 7,500.00
Organ, band; Artisan C-1, EX 14,000.00
Organ, band; Artisan C-2, EX 18,000.00
Organ, band; Wurlitzer #103, oak case, EX 13,000.00
Organ, band; Wurlitzer #150, golden oak facade, rstr.............39,500.00
Organ, Celestina, paper roller, NM, +spools 750.00
Organ, console; Wilcox & White, 46-key, golden oak, EX 3,750.00
Organ, Hammond BC/V, w/tone cabinet 750.00
Organ, Mollanari, crank style 5,800.00
Organ, player; Aeolian #1500, oak case, fretwork, rstr 2,300.00
Organ, pumper-player; Wilcox & White, walnut, 1886, EX.... 4,500.00
Organ, reed pump; Estey, rstr 200.00
Organ, Reproduco, w/chimes, rstr.. 6,500.00
Pianino, Wurlitzer, oak case, 2 ranks of pipes, leaded glass....11,000.00
Piano, grand; Boston Mason-Hamlin RA, 68", EX orig........... 8,000.00
Piano, grand; Electrova, 5 orig leaded glass panels................. 3,200.00
Piano, grand; Hallet & Davis, art case, 68", EX orig 2,500.00
Piano, grand; Knabe Ampico A, mahog, rstr, 68" 10,000.00
Piano, grand; Mason-Hamlin, pianocorder, 1973, 68", NM ...12,500.00
Piano, grand; Mason-Hamlin Ampico RBB, 1927, rstr, 84" ...25,000.00
Piano, grand; Steinway Duo-Art AR, rstr 25,000.00
Piano, grand; Steinway Duo-Art Louis XVI XR, walnut, '26, EX .23,500.00
Piano, grand; Steinway Duo-Art XR, mahog, rstr, EX 7,950.00
Piano, grand; Steinway Duo-Art XR, satin blk, rstr................14,000.00
Piano, grand; Weber Duo-Art, Mediterranean case, rstr, 73".14,500.00
Piano/organ, Seeburg MO, 52 wooden/37 lead pipes, EX 1,800.00
Rolmonica, 1920s, +14 rolls..110.00
Violano, Mills Virtuoso, EX orig 18,000.00

Non-Mechanical

Accordion, Hohner, by Beshe Ge Toors, EX, +VG case.............125.00
Accordion, Monarch, 10-key, 1880s, in damaged box 100.00
Accordion, Trafficanty, MOP inlay, Italy, EX in orig case 135.00
Banjo, 5-string; Gibson, w/resonator, EX...................................165.00
Bugle, US Navy, ca 1918, VG...65.00
Cello, stamped & labeled: Ehrmann-Albany, 1870s, EX.............150.00
Clarinet, McClellan Universal, #34N-81-4260L, +case...............150.00
Cornet, all brass, shepherd's crook design, ca 1870, VG 45.00
Cornet, York, B flat, fingertip key change to A, NP.....................30.00
Drumsticks, curly maple w/leather-covered heads, 13" L, EX.........85.00
Fife, rosewood w/brass ends, Civil War era, EX 40.00
Guitar, Fender, inlay on neck, electric/dbl pickups, '60s, VG 30.00
Harmonica, Echo Harp, 96-hole, EX in orig box 22.50
Harmonica, Herb Shriner's Hoosier Boy, Hohner, MIB................75.00
Harmonica, Hohner's Best, MIB...25.00
Horn, H Durand-Paris, E flat alto, all brass, 1920s, G 45.00
Mandolin, Stella, label, inlaid butterfly, early, VG......................35.00
Piano, grand; Steinway Hplwht-style case, 66" 4,500.00
Piccolo, blk wood, 6-key, Austria, ca 1900, EX 40.00
Saxophone, Beuscher, B flat tenor, #88511, EX in worn case 80.00
Trumpet, Barclay, Czech, brass, EX, +case 195.00
Violin, Antonio Stradivarious Cermonesis...1737, EX................190.00
Violin, Carlo Ferdinando Landolfi Milano, 2-pc bk, 15", VG........45.00
Violin, De Salzasrd, French, 1-pc maple bk & sides, EX...............50.00
Violin, John Juzek, 14", +bow & case 85.00
Violin, Paris, 2-pc maple bk, machine head, spruce top, EX 70.00
Zither, Anton Heimeyer, rosewood front, MOP tuners, 22x12" 75.00
Zither, rosewood top, marquetry, teardrop shape, 10x11", EX 220.00

Mustache Cups

Mustache cups were popular items during the late Victorian

period, designed specifically for the man with the mustache! They were made in silverplate as well as china and ironstone. Decorations ranged from simple transfers to elaborately applied and gilded florals. To properly position the 'mustache bar,' special cups were designed for the 'lefties.' These are the rare ones!

Blue floral on white with pink handle, triangular form, 3", $125.00.

Blue Onion, 1800s	90.00
Floral, bl on wht w/gold trim, Germany	60.00
Floral, gold X-hatching & hdl, Limoges, ca 1908	95.00
Floral, mc w/gold on wht, #d, 3¾"	70.00
Oriental motif, HP, 2¾x3", +5½" saucer	55.00
Pk lustre w/floral band, Germany, 4½"	40.00
Poppies, ornate hdl, Bavaria, +saucer	42.50
Roses, red on gr, Germany	55.00
SP, cut/beaded decor, Eureka Silver, 1901, +saucer	115.00
SP, eng monogram/florals, gilt int, Meriden	135.00
SP, floral eng, Barbour, EX	80.00

Nailsea

Nailsea is a term referring to clear or colored glass decorated in contrasting spatters, swirls, or loops. These are usually white but may also be pink or blue. It was first produced in Nailsea, England, during the late 1700s but was made in other parts of Britain and Scotland as well. During the mid-1800s a similar type of glass was produced in this country. Originally used for decorative novelties only, by that time tumblers and other practical items were being made from Nailsea-type glass. See also Lamps.

Bottle, bellows; clear w/pk & wht loopings, rough lip, 11" L	100.00
Bottle, bellows; fiery opal w/red loopings, rigaree, 9", EX	100.00
Bottle, dbl gemel, clear w/cranberry & wht loopings, 9½"	55.00
Bottle, gemel, clear w/cranberry & wht loopings, 10¼"	135.00
Bottle, gemel, clear w/maroon & wht loopings, 10⅝"	160.00
Finger bowl, chartreuse w/wht loopings, 4-fold rim, 4½"	75.00
Flask, clear w/milk glass & cranberry loopings, 7¼"	110.00
Flask, cobalt w/wht loopings, pontiled, 7⅜"	130.00
Flask, milk glass w/citron loopings, tooled lip, 6⅝"	95.00
Flask, milk glass w/dk bl loopings, 6½"	130.00
Flask, pocket; cranberry w/wht loopings, 7¾"	185.00
Powder horn whimsey, 2 shades of bl w/wht loopings, 12", EX	165.00
Rolling pin, clear w/pk loopings, 1800s, 19"	110.00

Nakara

Nakara was a line of decorated opaque milk glass produced by the C.F. Monroe Company of Meriden, Connecticut, for a few years after the turn of the century. It differs from their Wave Crest line in several ways. The shapes were simpler; pastel colors were deeper and covered more of the surface; more beading was present; flowers were larger; and large transfer prints of figures, Victorian ladies, cherubs, etc. were used. Ormolu and brass collars and mounts complemented these opulent pieces. Most items were signed; however, this is not important since the ware was never reproduced. Our advisors for this category are Dolli and Wilfred R. Cohen; their address is listed in the Directory under California.

Ash tray, floral on gr hexagonal bowl, ormolu mts, sm	200.00
Box, appl ceramic flowers, octagonal, 7" dia	825.00
Box, Bishop's Hat w/floral & beading, 4" dia	475.00
Box, blown-out pansy on lid, unemb bottom, 3¾" dia	500.00
Box, cherubs in wht reserve on antique gold, 6" dia	575.00
Box, Collars & Cuffs/lady's portrait/beading, unemb	1,000.00
Box, Crown mold, peonies on moss gr, 8½" dia	800.00
Box, floral in bl reserve on wht lid, oval, 5¼" L	450.00
Box, Kate Greenaway figures/beading, unemb form, 6" dia	800.00
Box, mirror in lid, floral on moss gr, 4½" dia	475.00
Box, ring; portrait on lid, 2x2¼"	550.00
Hair receiver, floral on moss gr, metal lid	425.00
Humidor, Cigars on lid, lady in shaped reserve, 9x7"	1,000.00
Humidor, Cigars/floral/beading on rust, unemb, 5½x4"	800.00
Match holder, floral on pk, ormolu rim/hdls	325.00
Plaque, Queen Louise in wht reserve on bl, ormolu mt	1,500.00
Tray, floral/beading, 3¾" dia, rnd ormolu-fr mirror above	525.00
Tray, pin; floral on pk, ormolu rim & hdls, sm	200.00
Vase, bl w/Burmese shading, HP orchids, 11¼"	965.00

Napkin Rings

Napkin rings became popular during the late 1800s. They were made from various materials. Among the most popular and collectible today are the large group of varied silverplated figurals made by American manufacturers.

When no condition is indicated, the items listed below are assumed to be all original and in very good to excellent condition. A timely warning: inexperienced buyers should be aware of excellent reproductions on the market, especially the wheeled pieces. However, these do not have the fine detail and patina of the originals and tend to have a more consistent, soft pewter-like finish. Recently the larger figurals in excellent condition have appreciated considerably. Only those with a blackened finish, corrosion, or broken and/or missing parts have maintained their earlier price levels.

Key:
gw — gold washed   SH&M — Simpson, Hall, & Miller
R&B — Reed & Barton

Bear reaches for bee on ring, tiered oval base, R&B #1470	195.00
Bird on branch, open wings, oval base, Meriden #291	90.00
Bird perched on leaves beside ring, logs base, Meriden #248	90.00
Bird pulling ring, ball-ftd base, sgn Meriden, EX	195.00
Boy leans on ring, whistle in mouth, Tufts #1622	295.00
Boy offers cookie to begging dog, Rogers Bros #199	295.00
Boy on fence, hands out, rectangular base	295.00
Boy w/admiral's hat & sword rides turtle, Middletown #71	235.00
Boy w/drumsticks, crawls w/ring on bk, Meriden #248	265.00
Boy w/sleeves rolled pushes ring, Meriden #161	225.00
Bud vase atop ring, circular floral base, Webster #168	135.00
Bull on oval base by flower-etched ring, Knickerbocker	185.00
Cat about to pounce, fly on ring, rnd base	120.00
Cat w/glass eyes, eng ring is body, #4310	350.00
Cat w/glass eyes guards mouse, rnd base, Rogers #4377	235.00

Chair of tree limbs holds ring, rstr...............................125.00
Cherries & stems, leaf base, Acme 135.00
Cherub in cap w/feather, clenched fist raised, Pairpoint 165.00
Cherub in top hat kneels on rnd base, Meriden #222 ....175.00
Cherub kneels & holds rope on alligator's neck 335.00
Cherub leans on ring beside vase, sq base 200.00
Cherub w/oar rides astride dolphin, rstr, Meriden #157 ....295.00
Cherubs sit ea side of ring, R Smith #147 ....135.00
Chick sits on wishbone, circular base, Meriden #552 ....75.00
Chick w/wings spread, perched on limb base 65.00
Cockatoo on curved hdl of sulky-type base, SH&M #9 ....295.00
Cow on grassy ftd rectangular base, sgn 295.00
Crane pulls at worm on ring, oval base, R&B #1126 ....195.00
Cupid (wings), sits X-legged, ftd base, vase, Pairpoint #10 ....395.00
Cupid blowing horn, floral rectangular base, SH&M #051 ....185.00
Cupid climbs ladder to ring, rectangular base, Acme #736 ....110.00
Cupid on ring, reins on reindeer, oblong base, Toronto #10........295.00
Cupid sharpening arrow, rnd base, Meriden 195.00
Cupid w/ring on bk, scrolled ball base, Barbour #10....................165.00
Doe on rnd raised base, ring at side, Toronto #1106 ....155.00
Dog climbing to reach bird atop ring, Meriden 125.00
Dog howls w/head up, lg oval floral base, Barbour #49 ....285.00
Dog reaches for cat on ring, raised base, Meriden #275 ....235.00
Dog w/curly hair, glass eyes, no base 225.00
Dog w/glass eyes sits, ring forms body, Wilcox #4311...................300.00
Dog w/long nose sits on oval ring, R&B #1485 ....105.00
Dog w/ring on bk, rnd base, Hall-Elton #0152 ....200.00
Eagle perches on bar, eng ring on wings, Rogers Bros #203 ....295.00
Egyptian kneels, holds ring behind him, R&B #1508 ....225.00
Fans arched over to form ring, butterfly atop, Derby....................125.00
Flintlock rifles Xd on ea side of filigree ring, Meriden #355 ....175.00
Fox w/ring on bk, grapes overhead 225.00
Foxes ea side of ring, no base....................................100.00
French nobleman & butterfly, ped ft, Derby #3520.....................415.00
Frog w/glass eyes on jack-in-pulpit leaf w/ring, R&B #1475.........400.00

Gentleman stands before
ruffled ring, 3¼", $395.00.

Giraffe nibbles vine tied to ring, Manhattan #239 ....285.00
Giraffe under palm tree, rectangular base, Racine #145 ....395.00
Girl w/stick, dog w/paws up, Babcock #207 ....225.00
Goat on rectangular base beside ring, Knickerbocker #181............85.00
Goat pulls wheeled cart, EX 350.00
Greenaway baby w/bonnet on chair, Middletown #98.................295.00
Greenaway boy by fence on textured/ftd base, Tufts #1593 ....295.00
Greenaway girl & boy w/pail on hill, inscr Jack & Jill, Tufts 450.00

Greenaway girl on stomach, ring on bk, Wilcox #01548 ....300.00
Greenaway girl w/fawn, arm on ring, oval base, Meriden............425.00
Greenaway girl w/rifle on sq ftd base 325.00
Horse prancing w/ring on bk, leaf base w/ball ft 160.00
King Neptune kneels on oval base, ring on head......................165.00
Lady holds ring on bk, barking dog, R&B #1175 ....200.00
Lady w/parasol, boy rolling ring, Tufts #1597 ....450.00
Leaves over ring, sq carpet-like base, Toronto #1168 ....85.00
Lion on bk legs, paws on ring, Meriden 275.00
Lions resting on sawhorses ea side of ring 95.00
Monkey dressed as man, rectangular base 130.00
Owl & violin on ruffled sheet-music base, Wilcox....................235.00
Parakeet on branch, leafy base, Toronto #1108 ....90.00
Peacock on rnd repousse base, ornate ring, NM 325.00
Pheasant leans on branch, flat octagonal base, Meriden #246 .....150.00
Pig caught in fence beside ring, Meriden #309 ....100.00
Rabbits (lg) on grassy sq base, Pairpoint 450.00
Ring in wheelbarrow w/emb flowers & scrolls, Pairpoint #10 ......155.00
Robin, chain looped around neck, fancy open base.....................220.00
Roses & leaves on oval ring, Rogers #4......................45.00
Sheep rests beside ring, octagonal base, Aurora #35...................195.00
Shepherd dog sits on base beside bbl-shaped ring, Tufts 250.00
Squirrel w/nut beside ring, rectangular base, 3x2" 195.00
Stag w/ring on bk, rectangular base, Meriden #204 ....350.00
Swan pulls wheeled ring, Meriden #334 ....295.00
Swords Xd on triangular ring, Meriden #642 ....75.00
Turkish dancer ea side of ring, Strictland #107 ....75.00
Turtle on circular base holding up ring, Meriden #216 ....85.00
Winged cherubs, dancing, hold ring aloft, Meriden #200 ....350.00

Nash

A. Douglas Nash founded the Corona Art Glass Company in Long Island, New York. He produced tableware, vases, flasks, etc. using delicate artistic shapes and forms. After 1933 he worked for the Libbey Glass Company.

Perfume, gold iridescent, unusual
form, signed/#523, 7½", with 7"
stopper inside, $935.00.

Bonbon, Chintz, bl, ped ft, 2⅞x5" 225.00
Bottle, scent; gold irid, stick neck, blown-out bottom, 8" 935.00
Bowl, gold w/floral intaglio under rim, sgn/#12, 8½" 325.00
Champagne, Bl Grotto, 7¼"......................110.00
Compote, Chintz, gr, flange rim in red w/gray spirals, 5x8" 485.00
Goblet, pk, threaded, clear twist stem, mk Libbey, 7" 145.00
Pitcher, Chintz, lt gr on clear crackle, 5½", +4 tumblers 265.00

Sherbet, gold irid, vein-textured, sgn, 2x3½" 100.00
Sherbet, pulled concentric lines, gr & bl on clear, +plate............250.00
Vase, gold, curving sq rim, sgn/#539, 6¾", pr 500.00

Natzler, Gertrude and Otto

The Natzlers came to the United States from Vienna in the late 1930s. They settled in Los Angeles where they continued their work in ceramics, for which they were already internationally recognized. Gertrude created the forms; Otto formulated a variety of interesting glazes, among them volcanic, crystalline, and lustre. Our advisor for this category is Abby Malowanczyk; she is listed in the Directory under Texas.

Bowl, yellow-green with brown at the edges, square form with drawn-in sides, signed, 2½" x 4¾", $750.00.

Bowl, bl/purple mottled gloss, thin-walled, bulbous, 3x4½" 950.00
Bowl, frothy wht matt on red clay, mk/#546, 2¼x4¾" 475.00
Bowl, orange/rust drip, thin walled, sgn in ink, K112, 6" 2,400.00
Bowl, thick wht over dk brn, hemispherical, pnt sgn, 5½" 2,000.00
Bowl, yel w/gray to brn streaks, oval rim, flared/ftd, 8" 2,200.00
Vase, dk bl/blk crystalline, wide cylinder/sm cone neck, 4"..... 2,500.00
Vase, lt turq/lav bubbled lava on cylinder, 8"...........................1,900.00

New England Glass Works

Founded in 1818 by Deming Jarves in Boston, Massachusetts, the New England Glass Company produced cut, blown three-mold, free-blown, and pressed glass of the highest quality. They were recognized for their fine decorative accomplishments, using etching, gilding, and engraving to emphasize their wares. For more than fifty years, they produced prize-winning pressed glass dinnerware sets. Because they refused to compromise the quality of their product by using the cheaper lime-based glass that flooded the market in the 1860s, the company fell into financial trouble and by 1877 was forced to close. However, William Libbey, who had been the sales manager there since 1870, leased the premises and resumed operations with his father, Edward Drummond Libbey, as full partner. In 1892 the firm became known as The Libbey Glass Company. See also Amberina; Libbey.

Champagne, Pineapple, flint, 5x2½" 165.00
Goblet, Dmn Point w/Flutes...60.00
Sugar shaker, floral, pk on lime opal, ribbed fig form, 4".............800.00
Tumbler, bar; Pineapple, flint, 3¾"..135.00
Vase, amethyst, circle/ellipse mold, ftd trumpet form, 7" 175.00
Vase, frosted camphor w/stork, Locke design, 4½" 200.00
Whiskey, Pineapple, flint, 3x2¾"...135.00
Wine, Pineapple, flint, 4x2"..110.00

New Geneva

In the early years of the 19th century, several potteries flourished in the Greensboro, Pennsylvania, area. They produced utilitarian stoneware items as well as tile and novelties for many decades. All failed well before the turn of the century.

Flowerpot, attached base, 2 names/floral in brn, 8", EX 550.00
Jar, red clay w/brn floral/foliage, appl hdls, 10", NM 795.00
Pitcher, gray clay w/brushed floral, 6½", NM 525.00
Pitcher, red clay w/brn-brushed floral, 9⅝".................................650.00
Pitcher, red clay w/detailed brn-brushed floral, 5¾"....................675.00

New Hall

The New Hall Company was established in the early 1780s in the Shelton district of England. In the early years, they produced hardpaste dinnerware typically decorated with simple floral sprays, often assigning a number rather than a name to their patterns. By 1812 a bone china body was favored and styles revised to suit the fashion. Decorations became more elaborate. Much of the ware was unmarked and is often attributed to Worcester. Occasionally a piece was marked 'New Hall' within a double circle. Production ceased by 1835.

Bowl, mc floral, 2½x5", EX 45.00
Cup & saucer, mc floral & brn King's roses, pk border 110.00
Plate, mc floral, N 241, 8½" 90.00
Teapot, mc floral springs, lobed body, +underplate, 6", VG 500.00
Teapot, pearlware, mc floral, lion finial, rpr, 5¾"..........................275.00
Waste bowl, floral sprigs, ribbed, 4½" 75.00

New Martinsville

The New Martinsville Glass Company took its name from the town in West Virginia where it began operations in 1901. In the beginning years, pressed tablewares were made in crystal as well as colored and opalescent glass. Considered an innovator, the company was known for their imaginative applications of the medium in creating lamps made entirely of glass, vanity sets, figural decanters, and models of animals and birds. In 1944 the company was purchased by Viking Glass, who continued to use many of the old molds, the animals molds included. They marked their wares 'Viking' or 'Rainbow Art.' Viking recently ceased operations and has been purchased by Kenneth Dalzell, President of the Fostoria Company. They, too, are making the bird and animal models. Although at first they were not marked, future productions are to be marked with an acid stamp. Dalzell/Viking animals are in the $50.00 to $60.00 range. Values for cobalt and red items are two to three times higher than for the same item in clear. See also Depression Glass.

For further information concerning Fostoria animals, we recommend *Glass Animals and Figural Flower Frogs of the Depression Era,* by Lee Garmon and Dick Spencer; both authors are listed in our Directory under Illinois.

Figurines

Bear, baby, head turned or head str 45.00
Bear, mama 195.00
Bear, papa 225.00
Chick 20.00
Crow, cocktail 15.00
Duck, dk teal, Viking's Epic Line, 9" 30.00

Duck, fighting, head up or head down, Viking's Epic Line.............35.00
Duck, fighting, standing, Viking's Epic Line................................35.00
Duck, orange, Viking's Epic Line, 13½" 40.00
Elephant, bookend 75.00
Gazelle...65.00
German Shepherd...65.00
Hen 65.00
Horse, head up 95.00
Nautilus shell 35.00
Pig, mama 300.00
Piglet, standing 125.00
Pony, long-legged, bl, Viking's Epic Line 75.00
Porpoise, orig 450.00
Rooster, lg 85.00
Seal, candlestick, lg, pr 150.00
Seal w/ball, bookends, lg, pr 130.00
Seal w/ball, candle holder, sm, ea......................................55.00
Seal w/ball, sm, ea 45.00
Squirrel, flat or on base 40.00
Starfish, ea...65.00
Tiger 175.00
Tiger, head down 195.00
Wolfhound 75.00
Woodsman...95.00

Basket, Janice, cobalt or ruby, 8¼", ea 110.00
Basket, Janice, crystal, 8¼" 55.00
Bonbon, Janice, #4524, hdls 11.00
Bookends, ship, pr...125.00
Bottle, scent; Geneva, w/blk stopper 30.00
Bowl, console; Janice, apricot, ftd 45.00
Bowl, Prelude, crimped, 12" 50.00
Candy dish, Florentine, #44/29, 3-part 23.00
Cocktail, Prelude 18.00
Cordial, Prelude...30.00
Old fashioned, Prelude, 3¼" 25.00
Plate, Janice, Canterbury etch, 13½" 35.00
Plate, Janice, ruby, 8½" 22.00
Plate, sandwich; Prelude, 14" 42.00
Relish, basket etch, 3-part, 12"..30.00
Relish, Janice, silver overlay, 2-part, 6"................................18.00
Relish, Janice, 2-part, 6" 14.00
Relish, Prelude, 3-part 35.00
Swan, bonbon, cobalt, 6"...45.00
Swan, bowl, amber, 10½" 35.00
Swan, Janice, crystal w/red neck, 10" 50.00
Swan, rnd, 7x6"...30.00
Tumbler, Addie, blk, ftd, 4¾" 10.00
Tumbler, Oscar, amber, platinum trim................................. 4.00
Vanity set, 1 bottle & rnd puff box, amethyst 72.50
Vanity set, 2 bottles, puff box & rnd tray, pk or gr 90.00
Vanity set, 2 bottles, puff box & triangular tray, bl 115.00

Newcomb

The Newcomb College of New Orleans, Louisiana, established a pottery in 1895 to provide the students with first-hand experience in the fields of art and ceramics. Using locally dug clays — red and buff in the early years, white-burning by the turn of the century — potters were employed to throw the ware which the ladies of the college decorated. Until about 1910 a glossy glaze was used on ware decorated by slip painting or incising. After that a matt glaze was favored. Soft blues and greens were used almost exclusively, and decorative themes were chosen to reflect the beauty of the South. 1930 marked the end of the matt-glaze period and the art-pottery era.

Various marks used by the pottery include an 'N' within a 'C,' sometimes with 'HB' added to indicate a 'hand-built' piece. The potter often incised his initials into the ware, and the artists were encouraged to sign their work. Among the most well-known artists were Sadie Irvine, Henrietta Bailey, and Fannie Simpson.

Newcomb pottery is evaluated to a large extent by two factors: design and condition. In the following listings, items are assumed matt unless noted otherwise. Our advisor for this category is Dave Rago; he is listed in the Directory under New Jersey.

Bowl, daffodils cvd/pnt at flaring rim, H Bailey, 3½x8" 1,000.00
Bowl, moon/moss, S Irvine, 3¾x5½" 1,300.00
Bowl, squirrel/branch band on bl, H Bailey, 3x8¾" 1,800.00
Bowl vase, gardenias on bl, S Irvine, 3½x 4½" 950.00
Candlestick, hdld cup w/motto, floral tray, Irvine, rpr, 4" 1,000.00
Jar, 3-line incised poem, lt/med/dk bl & wht, EH Elliot, 8"..... 7,150.00
Jardiniere, trees, bl on yel to cream, LeBlanc, rpr, 9x7" 4,500.00
Mug, band of flowers at top, glossy, A Roman/JM, 4x5" 1,800.00
Mug, dandelions on cream gloss, cvd motto, SB Levy, 6"........ 2,500.00
Mug, face of devil/2-line motto, glossy, GR Smith, 5" 2,500.00
Pitcher, floral, wht/gr on ivory & blk gloss, Roman, 7x5" 5,200.00
Pitcher, jonquils, cvd/pnt on gloss, Ada Lonnegan, 6" 2,400.00
Plaque, moon/moss/pond, cvd/pnt on gloss, S Irvine, 8" dia.... 5,500.00
Plaque, pine trees, gr on dk bl, S Irvine, 5¾" dia 1,200.00

Plaque, high-glaze scenic, signed Sadie Irvine, CM-67, Q, paper label with title 'Moonlight,' 8" diameter, $5,500.00.

Plate, stylized flower border, L Nichols, 7½", NM 1,300.00
Tile, birds in maple tree, C Littlejohn, 4" 1,100.00
Vase, band with bats & crescent moons, sgn FP, Xd, 7x4" 4,400.00
Vase, clematis, yel/bl on lt bl, S Irvine, wide base, 5x5" 1,650.00
Vase, cypress trees against yel sky, AF Simpson, 1913, 5½" 1,500.00
Vase, daffodils, yel/wht on dk bl, sgn CL, wide base, 9"........... 1,200.00
Vase, daisies pnt on lt bl gloss, H Joor/J Meyer, 1902, 12"....... 2,200.00
Vase, detailed tree band cvd on gloss, LeBlanc, 5x6", NM...... 4,950.00
Vase, floral at shoulder on dk bl, sgn Bailey, 4x5"................... 1,250.00
Vase, floral band, pk/gr on bl, S Irvine, 8x3½"........................ 1,400.00
Vase, floral band, red/yel/gr on dk bl, H Bailey, '20, 3x2½".........750.00
Vase, florals drip from sqd rim on lt bl, J Hunt, 5½x6" 1,300.00
Vase, geometric leaf band/incised lines, Charlaron, 4x6" 1,000.00

Vase, gr crystalline, red clay, bracket hdls, sgn FR, 6" 700.00
Vase, gr to bl gloss on red clay, sgn KR, 3x4" 290.00
Vase, gr/brn gloss, onion form w/tiny opening, 4x4" 350.00
Vase, grapes, cvd/pnt on gloss, SB Levy/JM, 5x5" 1,100.00
Vase, iris blossoms (A&C), cvd/pnt on gloss, SE Wells, 10" ..18,700.00
Vase, jonquils, wht w/gr leaves on bl, AF Simpson, 3x3" 700.00
Vase, lg blossoms, pk/gr on bl, S Irvine, 11x5" 3,300.00
Vase, lg iris on bl gloss, Ameile Roman, 8x4" 8,000.00
Vase, long-stem florals on gr & bl, AF Simpson, 5x5" 2,850.00
Vase, long-stem poppies, cylindrical, M Summey/JM, '10, 8".. 4,750.00
Vase, lt gr/brn gloss on red clay, label, 6" 425.00
Vase, moon/lg royal palm trees, S Irvine, 11x5", NM 3,600.00
Vase, moon/moss, bl/lt gr, H Joor, 5½x3" 1,100.00
Vase, moon/moss/trees, Aurelia Arbo, 6½x4½" 1,900.00
Vase, moon/moss/trees on lt bl, A Simpson, 5½x4½" 1,870.00
Vase, moon/very heavy moss, EX art, A Simpson, 11x4½" 6,300.00
Vase, mossy trees in bayou scene, S Irvine, 6½x8½" 4,000.00
Vase, oak tree band cvd/pnt on bl gloss, LeBlanc, 13x9"........16,000.00
Vase, pine cones, pk on bl, H Bailey, cylindrical, 7x5" 1,540.00
Vase, roses, red on dk bl, Sadie Irvine, 2x3" 475.00
Vase, stylized band, cvd/pnt on bl gloss, CR/W/NC/ZZ20, 10".. 2,600.00
Vase, stylized organic motif on gloss, K Kopman, 7x5", NM .. 1,870.00
Vase, 3 V-shape panels w/tree tops & flowers, sgn CNC, 7½" 750.00

Newspapers

In addition to historic content, there are other factors that can add or take away from the value of an old newspaper. These factors are: whether or not the account is a 'first report' (the first time that the news appeared — a 'later-report' is a subsequent reporting); location of articles on the event (those with front-page articles are more highly valued); displayability (size of headlines, presence of photos or graphics to illustrate the event, etc.); whether the paper is from a small or large town; a daily or weekly; and charisma of the paper or event. Prices listed here are for a typical mid-sized town paper with front-page coverage and medium-size headlines.

Papers that do not cover a specific event are called 'atmosphere' newspapers. While these are not as valuable, they offer interesting insight into a particular era through ads for runaway slaves, ships' schedules, jobs wanted, etc. Many have interesting articles on topics such as mermaids, hangings, sea voyages, and a host of other topics.

For a more complete price guide and information on how to determine values as well as how to grade historic newspapers, detect reprints, where to buy and sell originals, and much more, the Newspaper Collectors Society of America offers a *Free Mini-Course About Historic Newspapers*. To obtain your copy of the 32-page primer and extensive price guide, send $2.00 to NCSA, Box 19134-S, Lansing, MI 48901. From it you will learn, for instance, how to recognize the original April 15, 1865, *New York Herald* version of the report of Lincoln's assassination from among the thousands of reprints which abound today. This booklet could save collectors from making bad investments and prevent dealers from losing their honest reputation. Our advisor for this category is Rick Brown; he is listed in the Directory under Michigan.

Key:
lr — letter   pub — publisher

1784-1799, Atmosphere papers.......................................25.00
1800-1859, Atmosphere papers....................................... 7.00
1861, Civil War opens, first reports 250.00
1861, Civil War opens, later reports 100.00
1861-1865, Atmosphere papers, Confederate 125.00
1861-1865, Atmosphere papers, Union 10.00

1861-1865, Major battles of Civil War, Confederate titles 225.00
1861-1865, Major battles of Civil War, first reports...................150.00
1861-1865, Major battles of Civil War, later reports 75.00
1862, Emancipation Proclamation..200.00
1863, Battle of Gettysburg, first reports 225.00
1863, Battle of Gettysburg, later reports 175.00
1863, Gettysburg address..250.00
1865, Capture & death of J Wilkes Booth 125.00
1865, End of Civil War, first reports 200.00
1865, End of Civil War, later reports 100.00
1865, Fall of Richmond 125.00
1865, Harper's Weekly, Apr 29 edition.......................................225.00
1865, Leslie's Illustrated Newspaper, Apr 29 edition...................300.00
1865, Lincoln assassination, NY Herald, Apr 15, 10 AM ed .. 2,000.00
1865, Lincoln assassination, NY Herald, Apr 15, 2 AM ed 700.00
1865, Lincoln assassination, NY Herald, Apr 15, 3 AM ed 600.00
1865, Lincoln assassination, other titles, first reports...................200.00
1865, Lincoln assassination, other titles, later reports..................100.00
1866-1900, Atmosphere papers 3.00
1871, Chicago fire, Chicago paper, 1st reports 500.00
1871, Chicago fire, later reports 175.00
1871, Chicago fire, other first reports 100.00
1872, Grant elected 2nd term 12.00
1876, Custer's Last Stand, first reports..250.00
1876, Custer's Last Stand, later reports...175.00
1876, Tilden defeats Hayes, lg graphics...115.00
1876, Tilden defeats Hayes, no graphics...35.00
1877, Hayes declared president 17.00
1880, Garfield elected..18.00
1881, Billy the Kid killed 400.00
1881, Garfield assassinated 40.00
1881, Gunfight at OK Corral 400.00
1882, Jesse James killed, first reports...400.00
1882, Jesse James killed, later reports..250.00
1884, Grover Cleveland elected...12.00
1885, Ulysses S Grant dies...40.00
1889, Johnstown flood 30.00
1892, Grover Cleveland re-elected 2nd term...................................17.00
1892, Lizzie Borden crime & trial 15.00
1898, Sinking of Maine, NY Journal or World................................250.00
1898, Sinking of Maine, other titles...50.00
1898, Spanish American War begins 35.00
1898, Spanish American War ends..35.00
1900, James Jeffries defeats Jack Corbett to retain title 12.00
1900, McKinley elected 2nd term..17.00
1900-1945, Atmosphere papers.. 2.00
1901, McKinley assassinated 70.00
1903, Wright Brother's flight 550.00
1904, Teddy Roosevelt elected 17.00
1906, San Francisco earthquake, other titles 85.00
1906, San Francisco earthquake, San Francisco paper 200.00
1908, Taft elected 10.00
1912, Sinking of Titanic, first reports 325.00
1912, Sinking of Titanic, later reports 100.00
1912, Wilson elected 15.00
1914, WWI begins...40.00
1915, Lusitania sunk, first reports..85.00
1916, Woodrow Wilson elected 12.00
1917, US declares war 27.00
1918, November 11 Armistice 25.00
1920, Harding elected 12.00
1920, Prohibition takes effect...22.00
1920, Women's Suffrage, 19th amendment 22.00
1924, Coolidge elected 12.00

1925, Scopes 'Monkey' trial verdict 22.00
1926, Tunney defeats Jack Dempsey 25.00
1927, Babe Ruth hits 60th home run.........................250.00
1927, Lindbergh in Paris, first reports 100.00
1927, Lindbergh in Paris, later reports 40.00
1928, Hoover elected...12.00
1929, Byrd flies to South Pole 15.00
1929, St Valentine's Day Massacre 210.00
1929, Stock Market crash 85.00
1931, Al Capone found guilty 45.00
1932, FDR elected 1st term 12.00
1932, Lindbergh baby found dead 20.00
1933, Prohibition repealed 18.00
1934, Bonnie & Clyde killed.....................................110.00
1934, Dillinger killed, Chicago title 185.00
1934, Dillinger killed, other titles............................95.00
1936, FDR elected 2nd term......................................10.00
1936, King Edward renounces crown 13.00
1937, Amelia Earhart vanishes 15.00
1937, Hindenburg explodes, first reports 85.00
1937, Hindenburg explodes, later reports 45.00
1939, Gone w/Wind, Atlanta Constitution/Journal, Dec 15-16 ....75.00
1939, Gone w/Wind, either Atlanta title, Dec 17-19.....................17.00
1939-1945, Major battles in the war 18.00
1940, FDR elected 3rd term.......................................12.00
1941, Pearl Harbor attacked, Honolulu Star-Bulletin 600.00
1941, Pearl Harbor attacked, Dec 8 issues, first reports 25.00
1941, Pearl Harbor attacked, other titles w/lg headlines 40.00
1944, D-Day..20.00
1944, FDR elected 4th term.......................................12.00
1945, FDR dies...12.00
1945, First atomic bomb dropped 25.00
1945, Japan surrenders..25.00
1945, VE-Day or VJ-Day 30.00
1948, Babe Ruth's death...100.00
1948, Dewey Defeats Truman, Chicago Daily Tribune 500.00
1950, US enters Korean War......................................12.00
1953, Truce signed to end Korean War.......................17.00
1956, Eisenhower elected 2nd term 8.00
1957, Soviets launch Sputnik....................................15.00
1958, Alaska joins Union, Alaska title........................35.00
1959, Hawaii joins Union, Honolulu title 35.00
1960, JFK elected 8.00
1961, Alan Shepard, 1st American in space 12.00
1961, Roger Maris hits 61st home run, breaks Ruth's record..........85.00
1962, Death of Marilyn Monroe 30.00
1962, John Glenn orbits the earth 12.00
1963, JFK assassination, Nov 22, Dallas title 70.00
1963, JFK assassination, Nov 22, other titles 10.00
1963, JFK assassination, papers dtd Nov 23 to Nov 26.................. 3.00
1964, LBJ elected 7.00
1967, Superbowl I...12.00
1968, Bobby Kennedy assassination 18.00
1968, Martin Luther King assassination......................18.00
1968, Nixon elected 1st term 5.00
1969, Moon landing...25.00
1973, Vietnam peace pacts signed.............................. 7.00
1974, Nixon resigns 12.00
1976, Carter elected.. 3.00
1977, Death of Elvis, Memphis paper..........................40.00
1977, Death of Elvis, other titles 7.00
1980, Chicago Sun-Times error: It's Reagan & Ford 2.00
1980, Death of John Lennon, NY title.........................18.00
1986, Challenger explodes 7.00

Nicodemus

Chester Nicodemus began making pottery items in 1937 in Columbus, Ohio, using local red clay containing a large amount of iron and known for durabilty. From this clay he makes animal and bird sculptures, Christmas cards, nativity sets, and many other items as well. The line he produces is called Ferro-Stone. Many colors are used, some of which are turquoise, antique ivory, green mottle, and golden yellow — all shaded with the warm brown tones of the clay which he allows to show through the glaze. Examples are usually marked with his name incised into the clay, but paper labels are also in use. Our advisors for this category are James Riebel and Terry Krause; they are listed in the Directory under Ohio.

Ash Tray, fraternity 10.00
Bookends, camel, pr...200.00
Bookends, Dryad (kneeling nude), pr 180.00
Christmas decoration..25.00
Coffeepot, ind..100.00
Figurine, bird..50.00
Figurine, bull, 7"...125.00
Figurine, cat, 3"...50.00
Figurine, Madonna of the Flowers.............................85.00
Figurine, St Francis...150.00
Nativity set, 9-pc..300.00
Vase, sm..100.00

Niloak

During the latter part of the 1800s, there were many small utilitarian potteries in Benton, Arkansas. By 1900 only the Hyten Brothers Pottery remained. Charles Hyten, a second generation potter, took control of the family business around 1902. Shortly thereafter he renamed it the Eagle Pottery Company. In 1909 Hyten and former Rookwood potter Arthur Dovey began experimentation on a new swirl pottery. Dovey previously worked for the Ouachita Pottery Company of Hot Springs and produced a swirl pottery there as early as 1906. In March 1910 the Eagle Pottery Company introduced Niloak, kaolin spelled backwards. During 1911 Benton businessmen formed the Niloak Pottery corporation. Niloak, connected to the Arts and Crafts Movement and known as 'mission' ware, had a national representative in New York by 1913. Niloak's production centered on art pottery characterized by accidental, swirling patterns of natural and artificially colored clays. Many companies through the years have produced swirl pottery, yet none achieved the technical and aesthetic qualities of Niloak. Hyten received a patent in 1928 for the swirl technique. Although most examples have an interior glaze, some early pieces have an exterior glaze as well; these are extremely rare. Swirl/Mission Ware production continued steadily until the Depression when hard times and sagging sales caused Hyten to produce more traditional wares. In 1931 Niloak introduced Hywood Art Pottery, a glazed ware (sometimes similar in shape to Weller's Nile) of mostly hand-thrown vases. Soon thereafter, Niloak introduced castware as its primary production and renamed the line Hywood by Niloak. Throughout its existence, the company produced utilitarian items as well as artware. In 1934 Hyten's company found itself facing bankruptcy. Hardy L. Winburn, along with other Little Rock businessmen, raised the necessary capital and were able to provide the kind of leadership needed to make the business profitable once again. Both lines (Eagle and Hywood) were renamed 'Niloak' in 1937 to capitalize on this well-known name. The pottery continued in production until 1947 when it was converted to the Winburn Tile Company, which exists to this day in Little Rock. Be careful not to confuse the swirl production of the Evans Pottery of Missouri with Niloak. The significant difference is the dark brown matt interior glaze of Evans pottery.

Our co-advisors for this category are Lila and Fred Shrader (see the Directory under California) and David Edwin Gifford (see Arkansas). Gifford is currently considering the prospects of starting an Arkansas Pottery Collectors Society. He invites all interested parties to contact him for more information.

Mission Ware vase, 9", $140.00.

Mission Ware

Ash tray, w/match holder, 6½" 125.00
Bowl, cuspidor form, 3x5" 65.00
Bowl, rtcl inverted lip, 4x5" 79.00
Bowl, str sides, 2x4" 50.00
Bowl, tab hdls, 8½x2½" 95.00
Bowl, w/paper label, 3½" 50.00
Candlestick, flared base, 9" 145.00
Candlestick, 4¾" dia 78.00
Flower frog, overall glaze, 1½x3½" 50.00
Ginger jar, w/lid, 8" 175.00
Jardiniere, w/1" banded collar, 10x12" 285.00
Lamp base, w/old fittings, 8" 225.00
Mug, barrel form, 5½" 90.00
Pitcher, bulbous, 8" 155.00
Pitcher, ice lip, w/paper label, 7" 185.00
Stein, str sides w/flared base, 6" 110.00
Tumbler, shot; 2" 45.00
Tumbler, slightly flared rim, 4½" 40.00
Vase, baluster, brn, bl & cream, 10" 130.00
Vase, bulbous, 3½" 54.00
Vase, bulbous, 8½" 130.00
Vase, cone form, w/3" W ft, 10" 135.00
Vase, cylindrical w/flare at base, 14" 165.00
Vase, fan form, 7½" 110.00
Vase, inverted cone form, 4" 75.00
Vase, pear form, 5½" 65.00
Vase, rose bowl, 6" 85.00
Vase, teardrop form w/narrow neck, 10½" 145.00
Vase, waisted form, 6" 90.00

Miscellaneous

Basket, woven texture, 5" 35.00
Bowl, canoe form 38.00
Bowl, petal form, flat, 8" 35.00

Candlestick, cornucopia form, pr 50.00
Chocolate pot, mauve to gray, 7½" 45.00
Cookie jar, w/lid, 8" 75.00
Creamer, mauve to gray, 3½" 15.00
Creamer, stylized florals, 3½" 15.00
Cup & saucer, mauve to gray 22.00
Figurine, fawn, mauve to gray, 6½" 15.00
Figurine, seated Colonial lady, 5½" 22.50
Mug, pk gloss, 3½" 10.00
Pitcher, ball form, mauve to gray, w/stopper, 8½" 65.00
Planter, elephant, wht matt, 5" 25.00
Planter, polar bear, wht matt, 5½" 35.00
Planter, seated colonial lady, 5½" 22.50
Planter, squirrel, tan matt, 5½" 35.00
Teapot, Aladdin form, pk gloss 50.00
Tumbler, woven texture, pk gloss, 5½" 10.00
Vase, cylindrical w/ruffled edge, 6" 28.00
Vase, 3-cylinder on ped, w/paper label, 6" 45.00

Nippon

Nippon generally refers to Japanese wares made during the period from 1891 to 1921, although the Nippon mark was also used to a limited extent on later wares (accompanied by 'Japan'). Nippon, meaning Japan, identified the country of origin to comply with American importation restrictions. After 1921 'Japan' was the acceptable alternative. The term does not imply a specific type of product and may be found on items other than porcelains. For further information we recommend *The Collector's Encyclopedia of Nippon Porcelain* by our advisor, Joan Van Patten; you will find her address in the Directory under New York. In the following listings, items are assumed hand painted unless noted otherwise. Numbers included in the descriptions refer to these specific marks:

Key:
#1 — China E-OH   #5 — Rising Sun
#2 — M in Wreath   #6 — Royal Kinran
#3 — Cherry Blossom   #7 — Maple Leaf
#4 — Double T Diamond in   #8 — Royal Nippon, Nishiki
     Circle   #9 — Royal Moriye Nippon

Ash tray, moriage dragon, tricornered, #2, 5½" 125.00
Ash tray, seal figure beside odd-shaped tray, #2, 3½x7" 550.00
Bowl, cobalt & gold, scalloped rim, #7, 7½" 175.00
Bowl, florals, gold rim, 6-sided, 3-ftd, gr #2, 7¼" 85.00
Bowl, florals, pk on gr shaded, 3 ring hdls, #2, 7" 75.00
Bowl, gold o/l on wht, beaded scalloped rim, #7, 9¾" 120.00
Bowl, Gouda-type florals, hdls, gr #2, 8" 120.00
Bowl, lg pastel roses, ornate gold scalloped rim, #7, 12" 230.00
Bowl, peanuts in relief, brn rim & hdls, gr #2, 7" 125.00
Bowl, roses, yel on wht, tub hdls, unmk, 8" 115.00
Bowl, yel florals, river scene beyond, gold hdls, #2, 7¾" 110.00
Box, cigarette; Champion Katerfelto, #2, 5½" L 300.00
Box, trinket; stork w/baby, gold trim, gr #2, 4" 150.00
Butter dish, yel roses, gold rims & hdl, gr #2, 7½" 145.00
Cake set, florals, cobalt w/gold rim, bl #7, 5-pc 425.00
Candlestick, florals on cobalt w/gold, #2, 8", pr 325.00
Candy dish, gold o/l on wht, bl #7, 7" 65.00
Cheese dish, Wedgwood, cream on bl, slant top, #2, 7¾" 400.00
Chocolate pot, florals on wht w/gold, ornate hdl, #2, 9¾" 115.00
Chocolate pot, moriage dragon, HP mk, 10½", +4 c/s 400.00
Chocolate pot, silver o/l w/cobalt on wht, mk, 11", +4 c/s 350.00
Compote, Wedgwood, cream on bl, ftd, gr #2, 5¼" H 365.00
Cookie jar, gold o/l on wht, w/underplate, RC mk, 8" 300.00

Cookie jar, red mark, $250.00.

Cookie jar, moriage dragon on brn, ftd, #2, 7"	325.00
Cookie jar, swan scenic w/cobalt & gold, ftd, #7, 8½"	600.00
Cracker jar, florals, bl & pk on wht, Greek key rim, #2, 9½"	175.00
Creamer & sugar bowl, gold o/l swags on wht, RC mk	65.00
Cup, bouillon; roses & gold swags on wht, ftd, mk, 3¾"	20.00
Cup & saucer, bouillon; bl bird/florals on wht, 2 hdls, #7	40.00
Cup & saucer, doll face, #5, child's sz, 2⅛", 5"	65.00
Demitasse pot, US Capitol Building reserve w/gold, #7, 6¾"	175.00
Doll, policeman w/club in hand, incised mk, 3¾"	115.00
Dresser set, florals w/heavy gold o/l, #7, 3-pc	400.00
Dresser set, roses on wht w/gold, child's, Torii mk, 3-pc	200.00
Ewer, floral reserve on gold, bl #7, 9½"	350.00
Ewer, fox hunt tapestry, Greek key border, #7, 7"	825.00
Ewer, heavy gold o/l on cobalt, bl #7, 10"	600.00
Ewer, mc florals on blk, cobalt top, angle hdl, #6, 10"	250.00
Ewer, portrait banded reserve on cobalt w/gold, #7, 6½"	425.00
Ewer, swan scenic w/moriage top, ornate hdl, HP mk, 10"	345.00
Ferner, camel scenic, geometric border, 4-ftd, hdls, #2, 5¾"	365.00
Ferner, floral band, relief-molded hdls, gr #2, 3¾x8½"	275.00
Ferner, gold o/l on wht, scalloped top, 4-ftd, #7, 7¼"	175.00
Ferner, Indian rider in relief, brn tones, ftd, #2, 6¾"	750.00
Ferner, Wedgwood, cream on bl, relief-molded hdls, #2, 8½"	600.00
Hair receiver, pk florals w/gold o/l on wht, #7, 4½" dia	60.00
Humidor, bridge scenic, bl water & earth tones, #2, 5½"	450.00
Humidor, chariot scene in relief, earth tones, mk, 6¼"	1,200.00
Humidor, children in landscape relief, gr #2, 6¾"	2,000.00
Humidor, devil & cards on brn, #2, 6"	600.00
Humidor, dogs in relief, geometric border, #3, 6"	900.00
Humidor, elk scenic, geometric borders, gr #2, 5½"	525.00
Humidor, figures/animals in relief, gr/tan borders, #7, 7½"	1,300.00
Humidor, florals on gold w/much beading, #7, 5½"	700.00
Humidor, fox hunt scenic band on gr, bl #7, 6½"	575.00
Humidor, horse racing scenic, geometric border, #2, 7"	575.00
Humidor, moriage pipes on shaded ground, bl #7, 7"	650.00
Humidor, playing cards on bl, brn finial & rim, #2, 6½"	450.00
Humidor, sampan scenic on earth tones, #2, 5"	350.00
Humidor, tiger in relief, earth tones, #2, 7"	1,100.00
Incense burner, geisha figural, mk, 5"	225.00
Inkwell, floral reserves on brn, gr #2, 3" sq	185.00
Jug, whiskey; river reserve, keg form, gr #2, 5½"	685.00
Jug, wine; English coach scene reserve on gr, bl #7, 9½"	750.00
Jug, wine; sampan reserve, floral band w/gold, gr #2, 9½"	725.00
Lamp, sampan scenic banded reserve on cobalt, mk, 17"	275.00
Lemon dish, gulls, bl on wht, hdls, bl #5, 5½"	25.00
Mug, Egyptian figures, geometric border, gold #2, 5"	250.00
Mug, man on camel, earth tones, moriage trim, #2, 4¾"	250.00
Plaque, Blk man w/banjo, narrow gold band, gr #2, 7¾"	350.00

Plaque, buffalo in relief, gr #2, 10½"	800.00
Plaque, exotic bird on grape branch, bl #7, 11"	275.00
Plaque, Indian chief reserve, geometric borders, #7, 10½"	900.00
Plaque, Indian fishing from canoe, gr #2, 11"	400.00
Plaque, man on camel relief, geometric border, #2, 10½"	1,100.00
Plaque, planting scene in relief, gr #2, 12"	1,600.00
Plaque, sheep herding scene, thin gold rim, gr #2, 10"	300.00
Plate, fishing scenic, cobalt w/gold rim, gr #2, 10"	225.00
Plate, pk rose border w/gold, plain wht center, mk, 5"	12.50
Shakers, woodland scene, earth tones, #2, 2½", pr	75.00
Smoke set, phoenix bird, mc on tan, gr #2, 7" tray, 3-pc	300.00
Snack set, cranes, wht on lt bl w/gold, mk, 8½" tray+cup	60.00
Spittoon, floral, mc on wht, #7, 3¼" dia	175.00
Stein, landscape scenic, gr #2, 7"	500.00
Stein, monk drinking, vintage decor, gr #2, 7"	500.00
Stein, woodland scene, shields in borders, cylinder, #7, 11"	575.00
Sugar shaker, roses, pk on wht w/gold, #7, 4"	125.00
Tea set, butterflies, bl & yel on wht, child's, #5, 15-pc	250.00
Tea strainer, florals on cream w/gold, gr #2, 6" L	110.00
Teapot, scenic reserve, cobalt w/gold, gr #2, 6"	275.00
Tile, Tree in Meadow	28.00
Tray, dresser; portrait reserves, gold o/l on wht, #7, 12"	275.00
Trivet, river scenic, sq, canted corners, #2, 5"	55.00
Urn, cattle at river scenic, gold hdls, gr #2, 16½"	1,400.00
Urn, fruit & blossoms, gold beading, w/lid, #7, 13"	700.00
Urn, portrait reserve, red & wht bands w/gold, #7, 12"	1,200.00
Urn, river scenic reserve, gr bands, gold trim, #7, 10½"	700.00
Urn, wide scenic band, gold beads, 3-ftd, hdls, unmk, 9¼"	450.00
Vase, acorns & leaves in relief, brns, bulbous, #7, 7"	600.00
Vase, Anna Potacka reserve, gold o/l on wht, hdls, #7, 7½"	500.00
Vase, bird on moriage branch, ornate hdls, ftd, #7, 9¼"	350.00
Vase, cloisonne on porc, bulbous, gold mk, 4"	275.00
Vase, Dutchman reserve on brn, angle hdls, #2, 5½"	200.00
Vase, elephant & florals in relief, angle hdls, ftd, #2, 8"	900.00
Vase, exotic bird reserves, geometrics, hdls, bl #2, 14"	475.00
Vase, florals, red on bl, gold angle hdls, bl #7, 10"	145.00
Vase, florals in relief, gold beaded top, hdls, #7, 8½"	550.00
Vase, florals on cobalt, integral hdls at base, #7, 9½"	175.00
Vase, florals on wht, 4 up-turned gold hdls, ftd, #2, 9¼"	220.00
Vase, florals w/cobalt & gold, cylindrical, #7, 14¼"	450.00
Vase, florals w/lav Wedgwood trim, hdls, #2, 8¾"	500.00
Vase, geishas in landscape, geometric border, hdls, #7, 8"	175.00
Vase, gold o/l landscape (heavy), lg hdls, bl #2, 7½"	265.00
Vase, gold o/l scenic reserve on cobalt, hdls, #7, 7½"	500.00
Vase, gold on cobalt, basket form, gr #2, 7¾"	350.00
Vase, Gouda-style decor, basket form, gr #2, 7"	160.00
Vase, grapes tapestry, bulbous, bl #7, 6"	550.00
Vase, hyacinths, classic form, hdls, bl #7, 10¾"	285.00

Vase, lady's portrait reserve on cobalt with gold beading, blue maple leaf mark, 5", $425.00.

Vase, man on camel, buttressed ft, angle hdls, #2, 18" 650.00
Vase, man on camel, much gold, integral hdls, bl #7, 8" 400.00
Vase, moriage butterflies w/jewels, hdls, #7, 9" 375.00
Vase, moriage gulls on earth tones, hdls, bl #7, 4½" 225.00
Vase, moriage landscape, integral hdls, bl #7, 7" 425.00
Vase, moriage landscape, up-turned hdls, #7, 13½" 450.00
Vase, moriage owl on branch, hdls, ftd, #7, 8½" 400.00
Vase, mums, gold o/l (heavy) on cobalt, hdls, #7, 10" 525.00
Vase, open roses on gold, shouldered, bl #7, 8½" 175.00
Vase, orchids, gold band at rim, classic form, #7, 10½" 300.00
Vase, Oriental man in landscape, angle hdls, mk, 9½" 175.00
Vase, pk roses, landscape beyond, cylindrical, #7, 12" 360.00
Vase, portrait reserve, roses, gold ring hdls, #7, 6¾" 325.00
Vase, portrait reserve w/cobalt & gold, cylindrical, #7, 12" 600.00
Vase, river reserve, scalloped top, ring hdls, gr #2, 6¾" 145.00
Vase, river reserve on cobalt w/gold, angle hdls, #2, 9½" 325.00
Vase, rose tapestry, bottle form, bl #7, 8½" 550.00
Vase, rose tapestry w/gold, bulbous, bl #7, 6" 525.00
Vase, roses, mc on gold, bulbous, ornate hdls, #6, 8¾" 275.00
Vase, roses, pk on bl, classic form, gold hdls, #7, 6¾" 65.00
Vase, roses reserve on gold w/turq dots, gr #7, 9¼" 400.00
Vase, scenic sponge tapestry, cylindrical, hdls, unmk, 8½" 425.00
Vase, sunset scenic, earth tones, hdls, gr mk, 7½" 175.00
Vase, swan reserve tapestry, integral hdls, #7, 6" 500.00
Vase, swan scenic w/moriage trim, ornate hdls, #7, 9" 345.00
Vase, water scene reserves w/gold o/l, hdls, #7, 11¼" 250.00
Vase, Wedgwood, bird on floral branch, hdls, #2, 9" 350.00
Vase, Wedgwood, cream on bl, classic form, hdls, gr #2, 8" 500.00
Vase, windmill scenic, earth tones, loving-cup form, #2, 5½" 100.00

Nodders

So called because of the nodding action of their heads and hands, nodders originated in China where they were used in temple rituals to represent deity. Early in the 18th century, the idea was adopted by Meissen and by French manufacturers who produced not only china nodders but bisque as well. Most nodders are individual; couples are unusual. The idea remained popular until the end of the 19th century and was used during the Victorian era by toy manufacturers.

Blk child, seated, fist raised, bsk, 5" 235.00
Boy w/2 dogs, bsk, 6" 285.00
Clown, bsk, Lennile China for Ardalt in Japan, 1950s, 5¾" 45.00
Clown, flow bl, 7" 175.00
Dickens character sitting on chair, porc, 3" 130.00
Dutch girl, porc, 6" 175.00
Eskimo kissing couple, papier-mache, unmk 25.00
Girl w/skirt up, legs swing, porc, Made in Japan 95.00
Hobo in chair, bsk, EX mc pnt, 3½" 210.00
Indian girl pounds grain, wood, EX pnt.......................................45.00
Lady seated on wooden chair, papier-mache, 4" 365.00
Man w/chicken, lady w/vegetables & spoon, bsk, 6", pr 180.00
Monkey, nodding head & tail, clay, 3" 95.00
Monkey trio playing cards, bsk, EX details, 5" 565.00
Native w/shield & spear, bsk, 3" 95.00
Oriental girl w/book, clay, 6" 135.00
Oriental lady sitting, nods & fans, bsk, 5¼" 165.00
Oriental lady w/musical instrument, bsk, 5" 165.00
Oriental man w/2 pk baskets, bsk, EX mc pnt, 4½" 150.00
Parrot on perch beside ash tray, metal 120.00

Noritake

The Noritake Company was first registered in 1904 as Nippon

Gomei Kaisha. In 1917 the name became Nippon Toki Kabushiki Toki. The 'M' in wreath mark is that of the Morimura Brothers, distributors with offices in New York. It was used until 1941. The tree crest mark is the crest of the Morimura family.

The Noritake Company has produced fine porcelain dinnerware sets and occasional pieces decorated in the delicate manner for which the Japanese are noted. Their Azalea pattern was produced exclusively for the Larkin Company, who gave the lovely ware away as premiums to club members and their home agents. From 1916 through the thirties, Larkin distributed fine china which was decorated in pink Azaleas on white with gold tracing along edges and handles. Early in the thirties, six pieces of crystal hand painted with the same design were offered: candle holders, a compote, a tray with handles, a scalloped fruit bowl, a cheese and cracker set, and a cake plate. All in all, seventy different pieces of Azalea were produced. Some, such as the fifteen-piece child's set, bulbous vase, china ash tray, and the pancake jug, are quite rare. Marks varied over the years; the earliest was the blue rising sun Nippon mark, followed by the Noritake M in wreath with variations. Later the ware was marked 'Noritake, Azalea, hand painted, Japan.' Authority Joan Van Patten has compiled a lovely book, *The Collector's Encyclopedia of Noritake*, with many full-color photos and current prices; you will find her address in the Directory under New York. In the following listings, examples are hand painted unless noted otherwise. Numbers refer to these specific marks:

#1 — Komaru   #2 — M in Wreath
#3 — N in Wreath

Azalea

Basket, mint; Dolly Varden, #193 ....195.00
Bonbon, #184, 6¼" 50.00
Bowl, #12, 10" 42.50
Bowl, deep, #310 ....68.00
Bowl, fruit; shell form, #188, 7¾" 385.00
Bowl, oatmeal; #55, 5½" 28.00
Bowl, vegetable; divided, #439, 9½" 295.00
Bowl, vegetable; oval, #101, 10½" 60.00
Bowl, vegetable; oval, #172, 9¼" 58.00
Butter chip, #312, 3¼" 145.00
Butter tub, w/insert, #54 ....48.00
Cake plate, #10, 9¾" 40.00
Candy bowl, #185 ....195.00
Candy jar, #313 ....695.00
Casserole, gold finial, w/lid, #372 ....540.00
Casserole, w/lid, #16 ....125.00
Celery tray, closed hdls, #444, 10" 330.00
Celery/roll tray, #99, 12" 55.00
Cheese/butter dish, #314 ....135.00
Child's set, #253, 15-pc..2,500.00
Coffeepot, AD; #182 ....595.00
Compote, #170 ....98.00
Condiment set, #14, 5-pc...65.00
Creamer & sugar bowl, #122 ....158.00
Creamer & sugar bowl, #449, ind..395.00
Creamer & sugar bowl, #7 ....45.00
Creamer & sugar bowl, AD; open, #123 ....140.00
Creamer & sugar bowl, gold finial, #401 ....155.00
Cruet, #190 ....195.00
Cup & saucer, #2 ....17.50
Cup & saucer, AD; #183 ....150.00
Cup & saucer, bouillon; #124, 3½" 24.50
Egg cup, #120 ....60.00
Jam jar set, #125, 3-pc...155.00

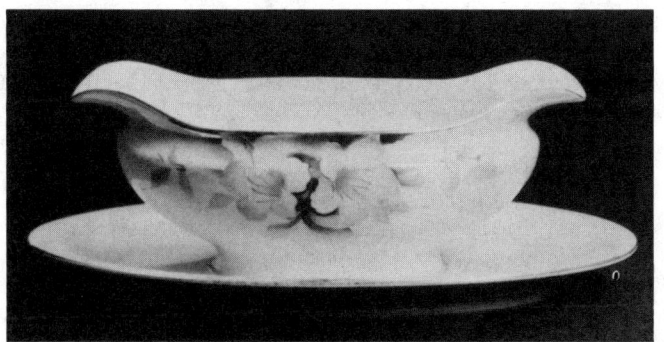

Azalea gravy boat, #40, $48.00.

Mayonnaise set, scalloped, #453, 3-pc	495.00
Mustard jar, #191	60.00
Pickle/lemon set, #121	24.50
Pitcher, milk jug; #100, 1-qt	195.00
Plate, #4, 7½"	10.00
Plate, bread & butter; #8, 6½"	10.00
Plate, breakfast; #98, 8½"	24.00
Plate, cream soup; #363	175.00
Plate, dinner; #13, 9¾"	28.00
Plate, grill; 3-compartment, #338, 10¼"	165.00
Plate, scalloped sq, salesman's sample	950.00
Plate, soup; #19, 7⅛"	25.00
Plate, sq, #315, 7⅝"	85.00
Platter, #17, 14"	60.00
Platter, #186, 16"	475.00
Platter, #56, 12"	58.00
Platter, cold meat; #311, 10¼"	215.00
Refreshment set, #39, 2-pc	48.00
Relish, #194, 7⅛"	85.00
Relish, loop hdl, 2-part, #450	425.00
Relish, oval, #18, 8½"	20.00
Relish, 2-part, #171	58.00
Relish, 4-part, #119, rare, 10"	150.00
Saucer, fruit; #9, 5¼"	10.00
Shakers, #126, ind, pr	27.50
Shakers, bell form, #11, pr	30.00
Shakers, bulbous, #89, pr	30.00
Spoon holder, #189, 8"	115.00
Spoon holder, #339, 2-pc	35.00
Syrup, #97, w/underplate	135.00
Tea tile, #169, 6"	48.50
Teapot, #15	110.00
Teapot, gold finial, #400	495.00
Toothpick holder, #192	130.00
Vase, bulbous, #452	1,150.00
Vase, fan form, ftd, #187	185.00
Whipped cream set, #3, 3-pc	38.50

Ash tray, Deco lady w/floral skirt, orange lustre, #2, 4¼"	125.00
Ash tray, Indian portrait, geometric rim, gr #2, 6½"	125.00
Ash tray, nude perched at rim of flower form bowl, #2, 7"	260.00
Basket, red w/floral int, gold hdl, #2, 5½"	125.00
Bowl, floral, gold lustre, 3-ftd, gr #2, 6¾"	45.00
Bowl, floral center, orange lustre rim, hdls, red #2, 9½"	30.00
Bowl, floral medallion, bl & gold lustre, hdls, #2, 9¼"	60.00
Bowl, floral medallions, much gold, hdls, oval, #2, 6"	35.00
Bowl, fruit; Tree in Meadow, shell form, #210, 6½x7¾"	235.00
Bowl, house in snow scene, 5-lobe, 3-hdl, red #2, 6½"	50.00

Bowl, parakeets, gold lustre rim, hdls, gr mk, 7"	40.00
Bowl, parrot on branch, blk rim w/gold edge, gr #2, 10"	55.00
Bowl, river scene, gold rim & angular hdls, gr #2, 7"	35.00
Box, powder; bl w/cat finial, gr #2, 4¼" H	190.00
Box, powder; river scene on lid, gr #1, 3¾"	50.00
Box, puff; Deco lady on orange lustre, gr #2, 4"	225.00
Box, puff; lady figural, base forms skirt, #2, 5¾"	260.00
Box, trinket; Deco lady & whippet on lid, gr #2, 3"	55.00
Bread & butter set, grape cluster at rim, blk trim, #2, 7-pc	80.00
Butter tub, Tree in Meadow, #139	60.00
Cake plate, river scene, hdls, gr #2, 10½", +6 sm plates	125.00
Candlestick, bird on branch, geometric rim/base, #2, 8¼"	95.00
Celery set, vegetables, bl lustre, #2, 12½", +6 salts	115.00
Celery tray, Tree in Meadow	40.00
Chamberstick, Egyptian band, orange lustre, gr #2, 6½", pr	155.00
Chamberstick, floral, orange lustre, ring hdls, #2, 2¼", pr	90.00
Cheese & cracker dish, lady finial, #2, 9"	215.00
Cheese dish, Deco florals, blk trim & hdl, slant top, #2, 8"	85.00
Chip & dip set, river scene, 2-tier, gr #2, 9¾"	80.00
Chocolate set, florals on wht w/gold, #2, 9-pc	225.00
Chocolate set, pyramid scene, bl/yel, #2, 13-pc	225.00
Coaster, sailboat, orange & bl lustre, #2, 4"	12.50
Compote, floral to side, bl lustre rim, gold hdls, #2, 8½"	60.00
Compote, gold rose panels/mc florals on bl, mk, 7x10"	225.00
Condiment set, Deco parrots on red, #2, 3-pc on 6¾" tray	95.00
Condiment set, river scene, red #2, 3-pc on 7½" tray	75.00
Cracker jar, man on camel scene, cobalt & gold trim, #1, 7"	250.00
Demitasse set, river scene, earth tones, #2, 16-pc	295.00
Flower holder, tropical bird figural on base, gr #2, 4¾"	190.00
Humidor, floral reserve on red, gr #2, 4¼"	200.00
Humidor, silhouette-style figures, gr #2, 6¾"	375.00
Jam jar, gold lustre, blk trim, strawberry finial, #2, 3½"	70.00
Jar, potpourri; bl & wht w/gold, rose finial, #2, 6"	80.00
Lemon dish, lemons at center, gold lustre, hdl, #2, 5¾"	30.00
Lemon dish, Tree in Meadow	17.50
Match holder, Deco lady smoking, #2, 1¾"	75.00
Match holder, horses on tan, bell form, #2, 3½"	105.00
Mustard jar, river scene, gold trim, gr #2, 2½"	32.00
Napkin ring, lg open roses on ivory, gr #2, 2¼"	42.50
Nappy, floral, scalloped gold rim & hdl, #2, 6½"	35.00
Plaque, silhouette-style figure on couch, gr #2, 8½"	250.00
Punch bowl, floral rim & int, turq w/gold, #2, 13", +8 cups	800.00
Sauce dish, flower form, petal underplate, #2, 6¼", +ladle	70.00
Smoking set, butterflies, gold trim, #2, 3-pc on 7½" tray	400.00
Smoking set, florals on red, wht int, #2, 2-pc on 7" tray	275.00
Syrup, river scene, earth tones, w/underplate, #2, 4¼"	60.00
Teapot, exotic florals on cobalt w/gold, #2, 6", +cr/sug	125.00

Tea tile, red mark, 6½" diameter, $80.00.

Tile, Tree in Meadow, 5" 47.50
Toothpick holder, Spanish dancer, gold rim, 3-hdl, #2, 2¼" 65.00
Urn, floral on wht w/much gold, angle hdls, w/lid, #2, 10¼" 225.00
Urn, river medallion on red w/gold, w/lid, #2, 12" 275.00
Vase, floral on wht w/cobalt & gold, hdls, #2, 10½" 175.00
Vase, florals along rim, gr body & ft, fan form, #2, 6½" 95.00
Vase, jasper, bl & wht, angle hdls, #1, 9½" 350.00
Vase, peacock feathers on tan, ruffled, mk, 8" 110.00
Vase, river scene medallion on turq w/gold, hdls, #2, 7¼" 170.00
Vase, roses, gold at rim & hdls, classic form, #2, 8½" 120.00
Vase, wide floral band on gr, ftd fan form, #2, 6½" 90.00

North Dakota School of Mines

The School of Mines of the University of North Dakota was established in 1890; but due to a lack of funding it was not until 1898 that Earle J. Babcock was appointed as Director, and efforts were made to produce ware from the native clay he had discovered several years earlier. The first pieces were made by firms in the east from the clay Babcock sent them. Some of the ware was decorated by the manufacturer; some was shipped back to North Dakota to be decorated by native artists. By 1909 students at the University of North Dakota were producing utilitarian items such as tile, brick, shingles, etc. in conjunction with a ceramic course offered through the Chemistry Department. By 1910 a ceramic department had been established, supervised by Margaret Kelly Cable. Under her leadership, fine artware was produced. Native flowers, grains, buffalo, cowboys, and other subjects indigenous to the state were incorporated into the decorations. Some pieces have an Art Nouveau/Art Deco style easily attributed to her association with Frederick H. Rhead, with whom she studied in 1911. During the twenties the pottery was marketed on a limited scale through gift and jewelry stores in the state. From 1927 until 1949 when Miss Cable announced her retirement, a more widespread distribution was maintained with sales branching out into other states. The ware was marked in cobalt with the official seal — 'Made at School of Mines, N.D. Clay, University of North Dakota, Grand Forks, N.D.' in a circle. Very early ware was sometimes marked 'U.N.D.' in cobalt by hand.

Vase, carved scene with mountain goat, signed Cable and C.K., blue and green gloss, 8", $1,100.00.

Bowl, sky bl, Mattson, 7" 115.00
Bowl vase, bl gloss, vertically ribbed, artist sgn, 2x4" 150.00
Cup, tooled lineation, gr gloss, brn body, 3x4" 195.00
Lamp base, bl/violet, sgn Smith, 1936, 7" 265.00
Paperweight, Rebekkah, gr gloss, sgn 65.00

Pitcher, gr, dolphins/fish/shell, sgn, #d, mk, 7¼" 195.00
Vase, floral, lt bl w/gun metal center on dk bl, Huck, 4¾" 415.00
Vase, roosters/etc, brn/yel on sienna, Barr, UND, 5x6" 325.00
Warming base, gr, openwork side w/cowboy, sgn Winge, 6½" 335.00

Northwood

The Northwood Company was founded in 1896 in Indiana, Pennsylvania, by Harry Northwood, whose father, John, was the art director for Stevens and Williams, an English glassworks. Northwood joined the National Glass Company in 1899 but in 1901 again became an independent contractor and formed the Harry Northwood Glass Company of Wheeling, West Virginia. He marketed his first carnival glass in 1908, and it became his most popular product. His company was also famous for its custard, goofus, and pressed glass. Northwood died in 1923, and the company closed. See also Carnival; Custard; Goofus; Opalescent; Pattern Glass.

Bowl, Leaf Medallion, clear w/gold, 9" 35.00
Bowl, master berry; Cherry T'print, +6 ind 135.00
Bowl, master berry; Leaf Umbrella, mauve, +6 ind 385.00
Butter dish, Memphis, gr w/gold 150.00
Butter dish, Panelled Holly 125.00
Butter dish, Royal Oak, rubena, acorn finial 225.00
Butter dish, Royal Oak, rubena frost 225.00
Creamer, Grape & Gothic Arches, gr w/gold 25.00
Creamer, Jeweled Heart, clear/frost, HP decor 40.00
Creamer, Memphis, gr w/gold 65.00
Creamer, Panelled Holly, gr w/gold 35.00
Creamer, Strawberry & Cable, clear w/red & gold 75.00
Cruet, Leaf Mold, cased spatter, orig stopper 325.00
Cruet, Leaf Mold, cased spatter w/mica 375.00
Cruet, Parian Swirl, cranberry 195.00
Pickle castor, Leaf Mold, cased spatter w/gold mica, Tufts fr 345.00
Pitcher, water; Barbella, cobalt w/gold, +6 tumblers 195.00
Pitcher, water; Cherry & Lattice, clear/frosted, HP decor 95.00
Pitcher, water; Cherry & Plum, clear w/red pnt, +6 tumblers 275.00
Pitcher, water; Cherry T'print, +6 tumblers 225.00
Pitcher, water; Dmn & Clubs, gr w/gold, +5 tumblers 195.00
Pitcher, water; Grape & Cable, ruby stained, gold trim 150.00
Pitcher, water; Invt Fan & Feather, gr w/gold, +6 tumblers 175.00
Pitcher, water; Lattice & Cherry, ruby stained, gold trim 125.00
Pitcher, water; Leaf Mold, cased spatter 395.00
Pitcher, water; Leaf Mold, vaseline, 7-pc 665.00
Pitcher, water; Leaf Umbrella, bl frosted, +6 tumblers 725.00
Pitcher, water; Leaf Umbrella, cranberry, +6 tumblers 595.00
Pitcher, water; Leaf Umbrella, mauve, +6 tumblers 735.00
Pitcher, water; Leaf Umbrella, yel, wht int, clear hdl 250.00
Pitcher, water; Peach, gr w/gold, +6 tumblers 355.00
Pitcher, water; Plum & Cherry, ruby stained, gold trim 125.00
Pitcher, water; Royal Ivy, clear/frosted, +6 tumblers 295.00
Pitcher, water; Royal Oak, clear/frosted 110.00
Pitcher, water; Royal Oak, rubena, +6 tumblers 595.00
Pitcher, water; Venus & Cupid 75.00
Punch cup, Cherry & Cable, stemmed 25.00
Rose bowl, bl & gr pull-ups, 8-crimp, thorn ft, 3¼x3½" 295.00
Rose bowl, bl & lime pull-ups on cream, 8-crimp, 3¼x3¼" 295.00
Rose bowl, gr/chartreuse/bl pull-ups on wht, ftd, 3x2⅞" 295.00
Rose bowl, pull-up, pk w/lav feather swirls, bl int, 4x4½" 1,200.00
Spooner, Memphis, gr w/EX gold 65.00
Spooner, Peach, gr 70.00
Sugar bowl, Strawberry & Cable, w/lid 110.00
Sugar shaker, Leaf Mold, bl frosted 185.00

Sugar shaker, Leaf Mold, cased spatter in clear............................125.00
Sugar shaker, Leaf Umbrella, clear/frosted....................................295.00
Sugar shaker, Parian Swirl, turq opaque.......................................110.00
Syrup, Leaf Mold, milk glass, rare...255.00
Toothpick holder, Leaf Umbrella, bl cased 275.00
Toothpick holder, Pillar Ribbed, pk & wht spatter 65.00
Toothpick holder, Royal Ivy, cranberry & frosted.........................90.00
Toothpick holder, Royal Ivy, rubena frost 125.00

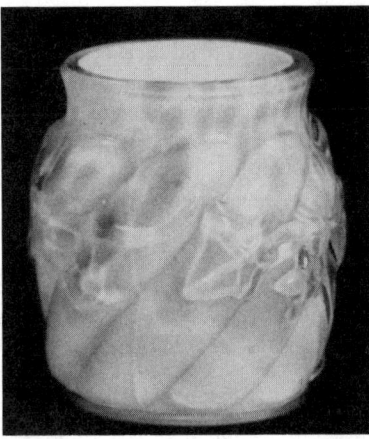

Toothpick holder, Royal
Oak, cased spatter, 2½",
$80.00.

Toothpick holder, rubena, threaded 250.00
Tumbler, Grape & Leaf, wht opaque, decor......................................40.00
Tumbler, Memphis, gr w/gold..35.00
Tumbler, Strawberry & Cable 35.00
Vase, feathers, brn on peach, robin's egg bl int, 5½x3" 775.00
Vase, pull-up, pk/wht swags on lime satin, bulbous, 4" 400.00

Nutcrackers

The nutcracker, though a strictly functional tool, is a good example of one to which man has applied ingenuity, imagination, and engineering skills. Though all were designed to accomplish the same end, hundreds of types exist in almost every material sturdy enough to withstand sufficient pressure to crack the nut. Figurals are popular collectibles, as are those with unusual design and construction. Patented examples are also desirable. Our advisor for this cateogry is Earl MacSorley; he is listed in the Directory under Connecticut.

Alligator figural, brass, mk China, 9½" 40.00
Bearded elf, CI, 10" 285.00
Blk boy in straw hat, cvd wood, mc pnt, rare 1,000.00
Blk pirate, Germany, cvd wood, mc pnt, glass eyes, EX 475.00
Clamp-on style, CI, mechanical, Enterprise Pat 1914 ....30.00
Dog, CI, blk pnt, Harper Supply, 13x6x2½"...............................130.00
Dog, gilded CI, tail opens/closes mouth, ca 1800s, 11½"..............75.00
Elephant, CI, old red pnt, twine tail, 5x9¾" 125.00
Mythological birds, for betel nuts, brass, old................................50.00
Parrot, tail lever, mc pnt on CI, 10" 35.00
Punch & Judy, brass, full figure, 5" 78.00
Squirrel on branch, bronze 25.00
Squirrel up on bk legs, CI, orig silver pnt, 1890s, 8½"................235.00

Occupied Japan

Items marked 'Occupied Japan' have become popular collectibles in the last few years. They were produced during the period from the end of World War II until April 18, 1952, when the occupation ended.

By no means was all of the ware exported during that time marked 'Occupied Japan'; some was marked 'Japan' or 'Made In Japan.' It is thought that because of the natural resentment felt by the Japanese toward the occupation, only a fraction of these wares carried the 'Occupied' mark. Even though you may find identical 'Japan'-marked items, because of its limited use, only those with the 'Occupied Japan' mark are being collected to any great extent. Values vary considerably, based on the quality of workmanship. Generally, bisque figures command much higher prices than porcelain, since on the whole they are of a finer quality.

For those wanting more information, we recommend *The Collector's Encyclopedia of Occupied Japan Collectibles* by Gene Florence; he is listed in the Directory under Kentucky. Our advisor for this category is Florence Archambault; she is listed in the Directory under Rhode Island. She represents the Occupied Japan Club, whose mailing address may be found in the Directory under Clubs, Newsletters, and Catalogs. All items in the listings that follow are assumed ceramic unless noted otherwise.

Ash tray, Indian, wht on bl 'Wedgwood' type, 2⅝" 8.00
Ash tray, metal w/emb Statue of Liberty, NY City souvenir 10.00
Ash tray, N Carolina souvenir, state shape....................................10.00
Ash tray, NY City souvenir, emb scenes on metal, oval 6.00
Atomizer, bl glass, dmn pattern, MIOJ mk 20.00
Binoculars, Prismex coated lens, 8x30, Field 850, #2013 ....65.00
Bookends, Dutch boy & girl, bright pnt, red mk............................35.00
Bookends, penguins, blk/bl & orange on wht, 4"...........................35.00
Bowl, florals emb on gold metal, 3 angel ft, emb mk 15.00
Bowl, Livonia (Dogwood), Mieto Norleans China, 8⅞" 8.00
Box, floral medallion on lacquerware, Maruni, 9x5½" 60.00
Bracelet, gold expansion style w/bl stones, emb MIOJ mk 20.00
Bracelet, rhinestones in stretch metal band, Lady Patricia............40.00
Bracelet, 3 rows of graduated pearls on wire, paper label 18.00
Brooch & earrings, cvd florals, celluloid, incised mk 25.00
Butter dish, gr basketweave, rectangular, T in Circle mk..............18.00
Candle holder, Colonial lady between 2 holders, 4".......................20.00
Cigarette box, exotic flowers on blk, T over M mk 20.00
Cigarette lighter, elephant w/howdah, gold-pnt metal, emb mk....17.00
Cigarette lighter, fish form, Continental NY SP, MIOJ mk...........15.00
Cigarette lighter, Indian chief's head figural, metal 20.00
Corner shelf, blk lacquerware, 2-shelf, folds flat, 13¾"................50.00
Corner shelf, lacquerware, folds flat, 9¼" 40.00
Cup & saucer, floral, mc on wht swirled body, Gold China...........10.00
Cup & saucer, floral, pk on blk, scalloped rim, MIOJ mk..............15.00
Cup & saucer, floral medallions on bl, yel int, Saji China 17.50
Cup & saucer, floral on wht, gold trim, ornate hdl, red mk...........15.00
Cup & saucer, heavy gold trim at rim & hdls on wht, MIOJ mk ...15.00
Cup & saucer, river scene, gold trim, Auger design, MIOJ mk 20.00
Cup & saucer, roses, pk on wht, scalloped rim, Ucagco 12.00
Cup & saucer, tomato figural, child sz..8.00
Demitasse pot, floral w/gold, Nasco, MIOJ mk, +6 c/s................135.00
Demitasse set, autumn branch on wht, red mk, 15-pc.................165.00
Doll, baby boy, celluloid, crochet clothes, 7"...............................35.00
Doll, Dutch girl w/instrument, celluloid, mk, 8⅝".......................45.00
Doll, feather dancer, celluloid, emb mk, 4½"................................15.00
Doll, feather dancer, feathers at waist, celluloid, 13"....................45.00
Doll, Kewpie, celluloid, 2¾"..20.00
Doll, quints, celluloid, 2¾", set of 5, MIB....................................95.00
Fan, florals on bl, paper & wood, 8¾" spine.................................15.00
Figurine, Aborigine man & lady, comic, red mk, 4¾", pr 45.00
Figurine, accordion player, red hat, bl pants, bl mk, 4" 12.50
Figurine, angel on butterfly, bsk, 3⅜x3".......................................32.00
Figurine, Balinese boy & girl dancers, bl mk, 7½", pr..................70.00
Figurine, Balinese lady dancer, gold hat, MIOJ mk, 8¾" 37.50
Figurine, Blk fiddler, bl hat, red pants, 6" 50.00

Figurine, boy & girl on fence, 4", pr 20.00
Figurine, boy w/boxing gloves, blk mk, 4½" 12.00
Figurine, boy w/saxophone, bl pants, red hair, 4⅝" 10.00
Figurine, boy w/skis over shoulder, 3¾" 10.00
Figurine, Colonial lady, brn & wht, red mk, 8¼" 37.50
Figurine, Colonial lady, hands away, ornate gown, 7½" 25.00
Figurine, couple at piano, red MIOJ mk, 4" 12.50
Figurine, couple in plumed hats, bsk, MIOJ mk, 9¾", pr ...135.00
Figurine, dancing lady, orange gown, 3¼" 8.00
Figurine, Deco lady dancer, mc, bsk, 6½" 55.00
Figurine, Dutch girl, bl & wht, 3¼" 8.00
Figurine, elephant, gr, trunk up, Ucagco, w/emblem, 3¾" ...15.00
Figurine, girl w/dog, red mk, 4⅛" 10.00
Figurine, girl w/pitcher, blond hair, striped apron, 4" 8.00
Figurine, lady, feathers in hair, ornate gown, red mk, 10½" ...45.00
Figurine, lady w/fan, many ruffles, red mk, 10½" 45.00
Figurine, lady w/lute, seated, bsk, 6" 22.00
Figurine, lady w/2 baskets, Delft style, bl mk, 6¼" 32.50
Figurine, man w/hands in pockets, bsk, 2½" 7.50
Figurine, Mexican w/sombrero & serape, 5¼" 18.00
Figurine, Nouveau lady holds dress wide, red mk, 5" 17.50
Figurine, Oriental, hands folded/head bowed, Moriyama, 7½" ...15.00
Figurine, Oriental lady w/fan, gr trousers, 5" 15.00
Figurine, Oriental man w/instrument, lady dancer, 10½", pr ...100.00
Figurine, Oriental religious symbol, brn/ivory, 4" 6.50
Figurine, peacock, bright colors, 7" 25.00
Figurine, pups in basket, 3" 10.00
Figurine, rooster & hen on base, 5" 20.00
Figurine, spaniel, sitting, blk & wht, 4½x5½" 15.00
Figurine, villain & lovely lady, bl MIOJ mk, 7½" 60.00
Fishbowl decoration, mermaid reclining, gr tail, bsk, 4⅜" ...20.00
Fishbowl decoration, pagoda on rocky base, tree at side ...12.00
Flag, US 48-star, silk, paper label, 1½x2" on 3½" stick ... 5.00
Incense burner, elephant w/howdah lid, gold trim, Ucagco ...32.00
Jar, powder; windmill scene on heart form, 2¾" 15.00
Lamp, Colonial couple in bl & yel, 7⅛", pr 70.00
Lamp, lady's head figural, 4-ftd, 10" 50.00
Leaf dish, florals on wht w/gold trim, bl mk, 2½" 4.00
Magnifying glass, celluloid................................12.00
Miniature, coffeepot, HP floral on wht w/gold, 2" 5.00
Miniature, pitcher, yel flower on wht, red mk, 3⅛" 5.00
Miniature, water can, HP floral, 1¾" 3.00
Mug, elephant figural, brn, trunk forms hdl, 4¾" 18.00
Mug, Santa figural, cap forms hdl, red mk 32.00
Necklace, miniature beads, single strand, paper label 15.00
Pin, bird in flight, bl wings & tail, celluloid, incised mk ...12.50
Pin, Scottie dog in bl sweater, red bow, celluloid 12.50
Pin, Scottie head, red bow at neck, celluloid, incised mk ...12.50
Planter, baby buggy, mk, 5¼" 15.00
Planter, bird aside house figural, MIOJ mk, 3" 7.00
Planter, couple w/rabbits, Paulux, bsk, 5¼x7½" 150.00
Planter, elephant w/trunk up, open howdah, arch emblem ...12.00
Planter, kitten on slipper, MIOJ mk, 2½x5¼" 12.50
Planter, Mexican in sombrero naps before vase, MIOJ mk, 3½" ...12.00
Planter, Mexican w/guitar beside basket vase, MIOJ mk, 4¼" ...16.00
Planter, zebra, blk & wht, MIOJ mk, 6¼x5¼" 15.00
Plaque, Dutch boy figural, chalkware, Yomake, 7½" 22.00
Plaque, mallard in flight, 6½" 22.50
Plate, Hibiscus, Rosetti, Chicago USA, 8¼" 20.00
Plate, mc roses, sgn, gold trim, Gold China, 7"............32.00
Relish, red lacquerware, 3-part, Bafuri HP..., 15x5¾".......55.00
Shakers, bride & groom, MIOJ mk, pr 20.00
Shakers, chicks in dbl basket holder, MIOJ mk, pr 20.00
Shakers, coffeepot, metal w/emb florals, pr 15.00

Shakers, cowboy boots w/spurs, metal, mk inside heel, pr ...15.00
Shakers, penguin, shiny metal, emb mk, pr 20.00
Shakers, strawberry, red w/gr leaves, pr on gr leaf tray 20.00
Shelf sitter, ballerina, net tutu, 5" 24.00
Shelf sitter, boy fishing, red & gr clothes, bl hat, bsk, 5" ...20.00
Shelf sitter, musician girl, unglazed pottery, 4½", pr 20.00
Shell dish, violets on wht, gold trim, red mk, 3" 4.00
Sugar bowl, corn figural, yel & gr, w/lid 12.50
Sugar bowl, Livonia (Dogwood), Mieto Norleans China, w/lid ...18.00
Sugar bowl, mum, pk on ivory w/gold, w/lid 15.00
Tablecloth, red plaid w/yel & bl, sewn-in tag, 48" sq, M 45.00
Tea set, floral on wht w/orange lustre, 15-pc 95.00
Teapot, tomato figural, Maruhon Ware, MIOJ mk, 4½" 30.00
Toy, dog, celluloid, w/squeaker............................20.00
Tray, red lobster at center of 3 lg gr leaves 30.00
Tumbler, tomato figural, Maruhon Ware, MIOJ mk, 3".......10.00
Umbrella, paper & wood, 18" before opening, MIOJ mk 25.00
Vase, clown child beside egg, 2½" 10.00
Vase, daffodil on wht, ftd, angle hdls, MIOJ mk, 4" 10.00
Vase, floral on brn, ewer form, 3¾" 7.50
Vase, island scene, cylindrical, 8" 30.00
Wall pocket, iris figural, bl/gr/wht 12.50
Wall pocket, parrot figural, bright pnt 32.50
Water lily, celluloid, MIB.................................15.00

Girl with goose, boy with dog, 8", $50.00 for the pair.

Ohr, George

George Ohr established his pottery around 1893 in Biloxi, Mississippi. The unusual style of the ware he produced and his flamboyant personality earned him the dubious title of 'the mad potter of Biloxi.' Though acclaimed by some of the critics of his day to be perhaps the most accomplished thrower in the history of the industry, others overlooked the eggshell-thin walls of his vessels, each a different shape and contortion, and saw only that their 'tortured' appearance contradicted their own sedate preferences.

Ohr worked alone. His work was typically pinched and pulled, pleated, crumpled, dented, and folded. Lizards and worms were often applied to the ware, each with detailed, expressive features. He was well recognized, however, for his glazes, especially those with a metallic patina. The ware was marked with his name, alone or with 'Biloxi' added. Ohr died in 1918. Our advisor for this category is Fer-Duc, Inc.; whose address is listed in the Directory under New York.

Vase, brown, purple and green dappled bottom; green and gun powder on waisted portion; claret neck with rough beige splotches, some with burst surfaces; olive and purple mottled rim with gun powder spots, 8", $19,000.00.

Bowl, gun metal over brn, pleated/manipulated rim, 5" 475.00
Bowl, med brn w/blk metal flakes, folded/crimped rim, 2x5" 600.00
Creamer, dk brn metallic, pinched sides, loop hdl, 3" 850.00
Cup, gr gloss, cvd toast, mk 3-18-18966 #61 w/note, 3" 650.00
Goblet, ochre gloss, wide body, 3¼" 150.00
Jardiniere, moss gr w/pk dappling, pie-crimped rim, 8" 1,980.00
Jug, puzzle; brn mottle, early script signature, rare 1,100.00
Mug, dk brn/gray metallic, tiered mid-section, 6" 800.00
Penholder, panther head, cobalt on gr-glazed scroddled sq 550.00
Pitcher, dk brn metallic, deep in-body twist, 3" 750.00
Pitcher, gun metal w/gr & bl, folded rim, dimpled base, 6"......2,090.00
Pitcher, textured gun metal, gr int, simple hdl, 4"......................750.00
Pitcher, 1 side dk red/1 pk, pumpkin int, 2-spout/2-hdl, 3" 1,500.00
Teapot, bl/pk mottle, snake appl at shoulder & as spout, 5"....4,180.00
Teapot, gun-metal crystalline, flat lid, cylindrical, 7" 3,800.00
Vase, bl-blk, pointed dbl hdls, twist neck, ftd, rpr, 10x7" 6,000.00
Vase, blk metallic, pocked, part bsk, shoulder twist, 8x5" 3,500.00
Vase, blk semigloss metallic, mid-body twist, 2½x4"....................900.00
Vase, brick/moss mottle, pinched/pleated/dimpled sides, 5" 935.00
Vase, dk gray, severely folded/compressed, 3½x7"...................2,640.00
Vase, gun metal, ovoid, 3½" 175.00
Vase, maroon over mustard, in-body twist, can neck, 5x5" 4,950.00
Vase, midnight bl over cobalt gloss, rim w/lg flutes, 5" 850.00
Vase, olive mottle, thin w/5 dimples in 1 side, 4x4"....................880.00
Vase, olive-gr irid mottle, ftd cylinder, 1898, 4"..........................400.00
Vase, pk/purple w/blk, t'print neck band, 6x3¾" 2,400.00
Vase, redware w/brn splashes, pleated rim on can neck, 5" 1,200.00
Vase, rose/gr/wine/dk bl/yel flambe, can neck, 7x5"................2,400.00
Vase, speckled dk gr, looped/intricate hdls, neck twist, 9".......4,500.00
Vase, spotted mauve/orange, pinched sides, crumpled rim, 5". 2,960.00
Vase, 1 side red/gr/bl, 1 pk/wht/bl/gr, folded neck, 7x5" 7,500.00

Old Ivory

Old Ivory dinnerware was produced during the late 1800s by Herman Ohme, of Lower Salzbrunn in Silesia. The patterns are referred to by the numbers stamped on the bottom of many items. (Though not every piece is numbered, the vast majority bears the tiny blue fleur-de-lis/crown mark with Silesia or Germany beneath.) Patterns #16 and #84 are the easiest to find and come in a wide variety of table items. Values are about the same for both patterns. Other floral designs include pink, yellow, and orange roses; holly; and lavender flowers — all on the same soft ivory background. The ware was not widely distributed; its two main distribution points were in Maine and, to a lesser extent, Chicago. Our prices are intended to represent a nationwide average, though you may have to pay a little more in some areas. Novice collectors should be aware of copy-cat versions from the turn of the century that are much heavier and of a coarser material. They are marked 'Old Ivory' without the blue trademark. They are not included in this listing.

Bowl, #10, 9½" 125.00
Bowl, #118, brn/cream roses, 9" 115.00
Bowl, #15, gr/brn/pk poppies, 9½" 150.00
Bowl, #16 or #84, 6½" 40.00
Bowl, #16 or #84, 9½" 150.00
Bowl, #22, Holly Berry, 9" 225.00
Bowl, #32, 9½" 120.00
Bowl, #73, 9½" 125.00
Bowl, oyster; #15, 3x5¼" 110.00
Bowl, oyster; #16 or #84 ....175.00
Butter pat, #74, 3" 100.00
Cake plate, #12, yel/pk roses, w/hdls, 10", +6 6" plates ...350.00
Cake plate, #15, w/hdls, 10¾" 150.00
Cake plate, #16 or #84, +6 plates 250.00
Cake plate, #16 or #84, hdls, 10" or 11".......................150.00
Cake plate, #21, w/hdls, 10" 195.00
Cake plate, #22, Holly Berry, w/hdls, 10" 200.00
Cake plate, #7, 9½" 125.00
Cake plate, #75, hdls, 10½", 7-pc 150.00
Candy dish, #200, brn roses w/rust buds, arched hdl, 8" L ...145.00
Candy dish, #200, cloverleaf shape, 5¾x5¼" 95.00
Celery, #200, 11½" 100.00

Chocolate pot, rare mold, 11", $400.00.

Chocolate pot, #16 or #84 ....400.00
Chocolate set, #16 or #84, 13-pc..................................800.00
Chop plate, #11, 12"...145.00
Cracker jar, #11, bbl shape, Clarion Ohme, 8" 350.00
Creamer & sugar bowl, #12 ....165.00
Creamer #11..60.00
Cup & saucer, #16 or #84 ....85.00
Cup & saucer, chocolate; #16 or #84 ....75.00
Cup & saucer, chocolate; #75 ....75.00
Muffineer, #16 or #84 ....350.00
Mustard pot, #16 or #84, w/lid & hdls, 3½", +MOP spoon 275.00
Nappy, #12..90.00

Nappy, #15 ....75.00
Nappy, #73, hdl extends from rim to center, 6" 75.00
Plate, #11, rare, 9½" 165.00
Plate, #12, 7½" 85.00
Plate, #124, 6-sided, 8¾" 85.00
Plate, #16 or #84, rare, 9½" 195.00
Plate, #16 or #84, 7½" 15.00
Plate, #7, Clarion, rare, 9¾", EX 200.00
Platter, #15, 11½", oval 150.00
Relish dish, #22, 6½" 125.00
Sugar bowl, #28 ....100.00
Tea tile, #11, 6" dia, EX 160.00
Tea tile, #15 ....185.00
Teapot, #16 or #84 ....350.00
Toothpick holder, #15 ....250.00
Tray, bread; #73, lg open brn roses, 12" L 115.00
Tray, dresser; #15, pk/gr/brn flowers, 11½" L 115.00
Tray, dresser; #16 or #84, worn gold, 11¾" L 115.00
Tureen, #15, w/lid & hdls, 6x10" L 750.00

Old McDonald's Farm by Regal

Located in Antioch, Illinois, the Regal China Company has been in business since 1938. Products of interest to collectors are James Beam Decanters, cookie jars, salt and pepper shakers and similar novelty items. The Old McDonald's Farm series listed below is becoming especially collectible. Our advisor for this category is Joyce Roerig, author of *The Collector's Encyclopedia of Cookie Jars*; she is listed in the Directory under South Carolina.

Creamer, $90.00; Sugar bowl, $95.00.

Butter dish, cow's head 200.00
Canister, flour; med 225.00
Canister, pretzels, peanuts, popcorn, chips, tidbits, lg, ea 300.00
Canister, spice; sm 125.00
Cookie jar, barn figural 250.00
Creamer, rooster 90.00
Grease jar, pig 175.00
Pitcher, milk; cow's head, gold bell, tankard form 325.00
Shakers, churn, pr 50.00
Shakers, feed sacks w/sheep's head, pr 165.00
Shakers, son & daughter, pr 80.00
Sugar bowl, hen 95.00
Teapot, duck's head 250.00

Old Paris

Old Paris porcelains were made from the mid-18th century until about 1900. Seldom marked, the term refers to the area of manufacture rather than a specific company. In general, the ware was of high quality; characterized by classic shapes, colorful decoration, and gold application.

Bottle, scent; dk bl & gold w/lg floral panels, sq, 5", EX 250.00
Candy dish, florals, sm 50.00
Coffee/tea set, chinoiserie figural motif, 2 pots, 10 c/s 1,900.00
Compote, lattice sides w/rose band, paw ft, 1830, 10" L, pr..... 1,000.00
Cornucopia, eagle head terminal, scenic reserve, 9", EX, pr 225.00
Jar, apothecary; w/lid, mk, 6" 225.00
Pitcher, florals, 'Souvenir' in gold under lip, 9½" 550.00
Saucer, hdls cast as heads, 1815 ....120.00
Scent/bouquet holder, lad playing pipes on lid, sgn MD 350.00
Tazza, center reserve w/HP swans, ornate ft, oval 1,200.00
Tureen, sauce; gilt rim, ca 1850s, miniature 100.00
Vase, bldgs/people on pk/gold, ftd U-form/sq base, 17", pr 3,600.00
Vase, cameo reserve, ornate lion head hdls, ftd, 13", pr 650.00
Vase, HP floral, elaborate appl floral rim & hdls, 24", pr..... 1,100.00
Vase, lg appl flowers, gold trim, ftd cornucopia form, 10" 225.00
Vase, lg floral panels, ornate bird head hdls, 18", EX, pr 475.00
Vase, ruffled fan w/lg 3-D figural group in bsk, 23", EX................950.00
Vase, scenes w/ruins, winged sphinx hdls, now lamp, 14", pr.......850.00
Vase, tulips in vertical panel, fan form, 14x9" 350.00
Vase, Venus/Cupid, gold trim, griffin hdls, now lamp, 14" 1,000.00

Old Sleepy Eye

Old Sleepy Eye was a Sioux Indian chief who was born in Minnesota in 1780. His name was used for the name of a town as well as a flour mill. The Sleepy Eye Milling Company of Sleepy Eye, Minnesota, contracted the Weir Pottery Company of Monmouth, Illinois, to make steins, vases, salt crocks, and butter tubs which the company gave away to their customers in each bag of their flour. A bust profile of the old Indian and his name decorated each piece of the blue and gray stoneware. In addition to these four items, the Minnesota Stoneware Company of Red Wing made a mug with a verse which is very scarce today.

In 1906 Weir Pottery merged with six others to form the Western Stoneware Company in Monmouth. They produced a line of blue and white ware using a lighter body, but these pieces were never given as flour premiums. This line consisted of pitchers (five sizes), steins, mugs, sugar bowls, vases, trivets, and mustache cups. These pieces turn up only rarely in other colors and are highly sought by advanced collectors.

Advertising items such as trade cards, pillow tops, thermometers, paperweights, letter openers, post cards, cookbooks, and thimbles are considered very valuable.

The original ware was made sporadically until 1937. Brown steins and mugs were produced in 1952.

Bowl with Indian head, 6½", $550.00.

Barrel, flour; orig paper label, 1920s............................**935.00**
Barrel, grapevine-effect banding...............................**1,500.00**
Butter crock, Flemish **625.00**
Calendar, 1904 ....**375.00**
Cookbook, EX **185.00**
Cookbook, Indian on cover, Sleepy Eye Milling Co, 4¾x4" **70.00**
Cookbook, loaf of bread shape, NM **310.00**
Coupon, for ordering cookbook **60.00**
Dough scraper, tin/wood, To Be Sure, EX.........................**435.00**
Fan, Indian chief, die-cut cb, 1900.............................**220.00**
Flour sack, cloth, mc Indian, red letters **345.00**
Flour sack, paper, Indian in blk, blk lettering, NM **125.00**
Ink blotter..**125.00**
Label, barrel end; mc Indian portrait, 16", NM **160.00**
Label, egg crate; Indian chief in color, 1930s, 9x11" **32.00**
Label, egg crate; unused...**22.50**
Letter opener, bronze **1,050.00**
Match holder, pnt **1,875.00**
Match holder, wht **1,050.00**
Milk carton..**22.50**
Mirror, advertising, 1935 ....**45.00**
Mug, bl & wht, 4¼" **220.00**
Mug, verse, Red Wing, EX......................................**1,625.00**
Paperweight, bronzed company trademk............................**560.00**
Pillow cover, Sleepy Eye & tribe meet Pres Monroe **750.00**
Pillow cover, trademk center w/various scenes, 22", NM..........**750.00**
Pitcher, #1 ....**185.00**
Pitcher, #2 ....**250.00**
Pitcher, #3, rare **315.00**
Pitcher, #3, w/bl rim **1,375.00**
Pitcher, #4 ....**400.00**
Pitcher, #5 ....**435.00**
Pitcher, bl on cream, 8", M **345.00**
Pitcher, bl/gray, 5" **235.00**
Pitcher, gold & brn, 1981 ....**160.00**
Pitcher, standing Indian, good color, #5 size **1,560.00**
Post card **110.00**
Post card, colorful trademk, 1904 Expo Winner **185.00**
Ruler, wooden **500.00**
Salt crock, Flemish **560.00**
Sign, tin, Sleepy Eye Flour & Cereal Products, 14x10", EX **2,750.00**
Spoon, demitasse; emb roses in bowl, Unity SP **105.00**
Spoon, Indian-head hdl..**125.00**
Stein, bl & wht, 7¾" **625.00**
Stein, brn, 1952, 22-oz **435.00**
Stein, brn & wht **1,125.00**
Stein, brn & yel, Western Stoneware **1,125.00**
Stein, cobalt **1,000.00**
Stein, Flemish..**595.00**
Stein, ltd edition, 1979-84, ea..................................**125.00**
Sugar bowl, bl & wht, 3" **750.00**
Tumbler, etched, 1979 commemorative **32.00**
Vase, bl & wht, good color, 9" **530.00**
Vase, brn on yel, rare color **1,000.00**
Vase, Indian & cattails, Flemish, 8½" **470.00**
Watch fob, Sleepy Eye Mills, Indian, M **62.50**

O'Neill, Rose

Rose O'Neill's Kewpies were introduced in 1909 when they were used to conclude a story in the December issue of *Ladies' Home Journal*. They were an immediate success, and soon Kewpie dolls were being produced worldwide. German manufacturers were among the earliest and also used the Kewpie motif to decorate chinaware as well as other items. The Kewpie is still popular today and can be found on products ranging from Christmas cards and cake ornaments to fabrics and wallpaper.

In the following listings, 'sgn' indicates that the item is signed Rose O'Neill. Unsigned items are of little interest to collectors. Items marked 'Germany' are sometimes reproductions.

Five-piece dresser set, signed O'Neill, marked Royal Rudolstadt, Prussia, $1,500.00.

Book, Lady in Wht Veil, O'Neill illus, 1909, VG **40.00**
Kewpie, bean-bag body, 10", M **45.00**
Kewpie, Blk Hottentot, bsk, w/sticker, 3½" **345.00**
Kewpie, bsk, jtd arms, 1-pc body, w/sticker, 1½" **95.00**
Kewpie, bsk, jtd arms, 1-pc body, w/sticker, 12"......................**1,400.00**
Kewpie, bsk, jtd arms, 1-pc body, w/sticker, 6" **195.00**
Kewpie, bsk, jtd arms & hips, w/sticker, 12"..........................**1,200.00**
Kewpie, bsk, jtd arms & hips, w/sticker, 9".............................**875.00**
Kewpie, bsk head, jtd, glass eyes, chubby toddler, sgn, 10" **4,200.00**
Kewpie, bsk head, pnt eyes, cloth body, w/sticker, 12" **2,200.00**
Kewpie, bsk shoulder head, cloth body, sgn, 6" or 7"..................**600.00**
Kewpie, celluloid, jtd arms, w/sticker, 9" **175.00**
Kewpie, celluloid, w/sticker, 2"..**45.00**
Kewpie, cloth, mask face, Kreuger, orig clothes, 15" **385.00**
Kewpie, cloth, mask face, Kreuger, 12", M **185.00**
Kewpie, cloth, mask face, Kreuger, 21", M **485.00**
Kewpie, compo, jtd arms, 9", M **135.00**
Kewpie, Gardener, bsk, w/sticker, 4"..................................**495.00**
Kewpie, Guitar Player, bsk, w/sticker, 3½" **365.00**
Kewpie, hard plastic, fully jtd, 12", M................................**385.00**
Kewpie, hard plastic, 1-pc body & head, 8", M **95.00**
Kewpie, plush w/vinyl face mask, Knickerbocker, 6", M **60.00**
Kewpie, Traveler, bsk, blk or tan suitcase, w/sticker, 3½" **300.00**
Kewpie, vinyl, jtd arms, 9", M **55.00**
Kewpie, vinyl, not jtd, 9", M **35.00**
Kewpie baby, 1-pc stuffed body & limbs, 15", M **145.00**
Kewpie holding cat, bsk, w/sticker, 4"................................**500.00**
Kewpie in basket w/flowers, bsk, w/sticker, 3½" **650.00**
Kewpie w/dog Doodle, bsk, w/sticker, 3½" **1,500.00**
Kewpie w/drawstring bag, bsk, w/sticker, 4½".........................**600.00**
Kewpie w/rabbit, bsk, w/sticker, 2½"..................................**365.00**
Kewpie w/rose, bsk, w/sticker, 2" **350.00**
Kewpie w/turkey, bsk, w/sticker, 2"...................................**365.00**
Kewpie w/umbrella & dog, bsk, w/sticker, 3½" **1,400.00**
Magazine cover, Woman's Home Companion, Jan 1924, EX **10.00**
Mold, ice cream; Kewpie, Pat 1913, 6" **150.00**
Pincushion, Kewpie, bsk, sgn, 2½"......................................**300.00**
Post card, I'd Like to Travel w/You, Kewpie/suitcase, VG.............**30.00**

Post card, Valentine Kewpies, sgn O'Neill, EX 35.00
Post card, We Wish You an Easter, 3 Kewpies, sgn, p/Gibson........25.00
Sign, Santa Claus Kewpie, cb, 1913, 11½" H 65.00
Talcum container, Kewpie figural, tin or celluloid, 7" or 8".........195.00

Onion Pattern

The familiar pattern known to collectors as Onion acquired its name through a case of mistaken identity. Designed in the early 1700s by Johann Haroldt of the Meissen factory in Germany, the pattern was a mixture from earlier Oriental designs. One of its components was a stylized peach, which was mistaken for an onion; as a result, the pattern became known by that name. Usually found in blue, an occasional piece may also be found in pink and red. The pattern is commonly associated with Meissen, but it has been reproduced by many others including Villeroy and Boch and Royal Copenhagen.

Blue Danube is a modern line of Onion-patterned dinnerware produced in Japan and distributed by Lipper International of Wallingford, Connecticut. 125 items are available in porcelain; it is sold in most large stores with china departments.

Sugar bowl, Crossed Swords mark, $190.00.

Basket, rtcl, shallow, Meissen, 1890s, 7", pr 300.00
Bowl, berry; Xd swords, 5¼" 40.00
Bowl, Meissen in oval, 8½" 100.00
Bowl, notched corners, Xd swords, sq, 9"................................275.00
Bowl, scalloped, Xd swords, 3¼x4¾" dia 120.00
Bowl, sq, Meissen in oval, #19, 8½", pr..................................200.00
Butter chip 25.00
Cache pot, gilt borders, Meissen, 1890s, 5½"..........................225.00
Cake plate, rnd, 10" 150.00
Canister, Reis, barrel form, w/lid..75.00
Canister, Zucker, stenciled, ped base 65.00
Cheese board, unmk 75.00
Cheese grater 250.00
Chop plate, Meissen, 12"..185.00
Coffeepot, 1800s, 9½" 375.00
Compote, twisted knopped stem, Meissen, 8¾x9" 375.00
Cruet, Meissen, 5½", pr..300.00
Cup & saucer 25.00
Dish, leaf shape, w/hdl, Xd swords, 3½" 75.00
Dish, shell shape, Meissen, 1900, 7¾", pr...............................220.00
Funnel, loop hdl, unmk Germany...95.00
Letter opener, brass blade, Germany 35.00
Masher, lg 165.00
Masher, sm 135.00

Meat tenderizer, German..135.00
Plate, dinner; 1900s, 10½" 70.00
Plate, fruit grouping, ca 1850, 9½" 150.00
Plate, Meissen, 8¼"..55.00
Plate, sq, Meakin, 7" 30.00
Plate, Xd swords, 9¾" 60.00
Platter, oval, 17" 295.00
Platter, oval w/tab hdls, Meissen, 20" 400.00
Platter, scalloped oval, 1880s, Xd swords, 23x18" 500.00
Platter, Xd swords, 1850s, 21" 425.00
Reamer, red, old, unmk Germany 100.00
Rolling pin, heavy porc, unmk Germany, 18" 270.00
Salt box, rnd, wooden lid, hanging, Made in Japan, 7" H 95.00
Salt box, stenciled 120.00
Sauce boat, Hutschenreuther 30.00
Sauce boat, w/attached undertray, Xd swords, 3½x4⅞x8"...........190.00
Shaving mug, w/matching brush 75.00
Spoon, 10¼"...85.00
Spoon holder, wall mt, early, rare 275.00
Sugar bowl, w/lid, mk Thurn, Kloesterle, Meissen-Form, 3" 100.00
Tea set, doll's sz, 10-pc 165.00
Tray, scroll/leaf rim, gilt, quatrefoil, Meissen, 10½" L.............550.00
Tureen, leaf finial & hdls, Meissen, w/lid, 13½".......................600.00
Tureen, shell hdls, dome lid, 1900, 10½" H 650.00
Utensil holder, hanging, 15-slot, 5½x12x10" 495.00
Vase, ftd, Xd swords, 5" 125.00
Whisk 100.00

Opalescent Glass

First made in England in 1870, opalescent glass became popular in America around the turn of the century. Its name comes from the milky-white opalescent trim that defines the lines of the pattern. It was produced in table sets, novelties, toothpick holders, vases, and lamps.

Alaska, banana boat, bl 175.00
Alaska, berry set, bl, 7-pc 275.00
Alaska, bowl, bl, sq, 8" 95.00
Alaska, butter dish, bl or vaseline 260.00
Alaska, butter dish, bl w/HP floral 250.00
Alaska, celery tray, bl 155.00
Alaska, celery tray, vaseline 145.00
Alaska, creamer, bl 70.00
Alaska, creamer, vaseline 60.00
Alaska, creamer, vaseline w/HP floral 70.00
Alaska, cruet, bl, w/stopper 235.00
Alaska, cruet, vaseline 225.00
Alaska, cruet, vaseline w/HP floral 265.00
Alaska, pitcher, water; bl..350.00
Alaska, pitcher, water; bl w/HP floral......................................400.00
Alaska, pitcher, water; clear 175.00
Alaska, pitcher, water; vaseline...350.00
Alaska, sauce, bl 25.00
Alaska, sauce, gr w/HP floral 30.00
Alaska, shakers, bl or vaseline, pr..65.00
Alaska, spooner, bl..65.00
Alaska, spooner, vaseline 45.00
Alaska, sugar bowl, bl, w/lid...150.00
Alaska, sugar bowl, vaseline, w/lid..130.00
Alaska, tumbler, vaseline 60.00
Arabian Nights, pitcher, water; cranberry 600.00
Arabian Nights, tumbler, bl..60.00
Arabian Nights, tumbler, cranberry 110.00

Argonaut Shell, berry set, clear, 7-pc 225.00
Argonaut Shell, butter dish, bl 275.00
Argonaut Shell, compote, jelly; vaseline 75.00
Argonaut Shell, creamer, bl 75.00
Argonaut Shell, cruet, bl 275.00
Argonaut Shell, pitcher, water; bl 350.00
Argonaut Shell, spooner, bl 150.00
Argonaut Shell, sugar bowl, bl, w/lid 200.00
Argonaut Shell, tumbler, vaseline 100.00
Astro, bride's bowl, bl, ruffled, 8" 35.00
Beaded Ovals in Sand, butter dish, gr 250.00
Beaded Ovals in Sand, creamer, bl 70.00
Beatty Rib, creamer, ind; clear 20.00
Beatty Rib, sugar bowl, bl, w/lid 95.00
Beatty Rib, table set, bl, 4-pc 265.00
Beatty Rib, toothpick holder, clear 24.00
Beatty Swirl, butter dish, bl 150.00
Beatty Swirl, celery vase, bl 75.00
Beatty Swirl, pitcher, water; bl 130.00
Beatty Swirl, syrup, bl, rare 200.00
Beatty Swirl, tray, water; vaseline 75.00
Bubble Lattice, pitcher, water; cranberry 325.00
Bubble Lattice, sugar bowl, bl, w/lid 160.00
Buttons & Braids, pitcher, water; bl 165.00
Buttons & Braids, pitcher, water; cranberry...........350.00
Buttons & Braids, tumbler, bl 35.00
Buttons & Braids, tumbler, cranberry.....................85.00
Chrysanthemum Base Reverse Swirl, mustard, bl 135.00
Chrysanthemum Base Reverse Swirl, sugar shaker, cranberry 245.00
Chrysanthemum Base Swirl, butter dish, cranberry...300.00
Chrysanthemum Base Swirl, spooner, bl 75.00
Chrysanthemum Base Swirl, syrup, bl....................175.00
Chrysanthemum Base Swirl, toothpick holder, cranberry 125.00
Chrysanthemum Base Swirl, tumbler, cranberry.........85.00
Circled Scroll, butter dish, bl 295.00
Circled Scroll, compote, gr 125.00
Circled Scroll, cruet, bl 350.00
Circled Scroll, shakers, bl, pr 190.00
Circled Scroll, sugar bowl, bl, w/lid 225.00
Circled Scroll, tumbler, gr 70.00
Coin Spot, celery vase, cranberry 150.00
Coin Spot, compote, peach 35.00
Coin Spot, creamer, bl 50.00
Coin Spot, pitcher, water; bl, 9" 120.00
Coin Spot, pitcher, water; clear 85.00
Coin Spot, pitcher, water; cranberry 250.00
Coin Spot, sugar shaker, bl, bulbous base 85.00
Coin Spot, sugar shaker, cranberry, ring neck 120.00
Coin Spot, tumble-up, cranberry..........................250.00
Coin Spot, tumbler, cranberry 45.00
Contessa, basket, amber, 4¼x7" 100.00
Criss Cross, finger bowl, cranberry 95.00
Daisy & Fern, cruet, Netted Blossom mold, bl........110.00
Daisy & Fern, pitcher, water; bl 165.00
Daisy & Fern, pitcher, water; clear........................95.00
Daisy & Fern, pitcher, water; cranberry, solid hdl ...275.00
Daisy & Fern, syrup, bl 120.00
Daisy & Fern, tumbler, cranberry 45.00
Daisy in Criss Cross, pitcher, water; bl.................400.00
Daisy in Criss Cross, syrup, bl............................245.00
Daisy in Criss Cross, syrup, cranberry 400.00
Diamond Spearhead, butter dish, gr......................225.00
Diamond Spearhead, butter dish, vaseline 195.00
Diamond Spearhead, celery vase, bl......................110.00

Diamond Spearhead, compote, bl 95.00
Diamond Spearhead, compote, jelly; vaseline, rare 75.00
Diamond Spearhead, creamer, cobalt 125.00
Diamond Spearhead, cup, cobalt 75.00
Diamond Spearhead, goblet, bl 150.00
Diamond Spearhead, mug, bl 75.00
Diamond Spearhead, pitcher, water; cobalt 450.00
Diamond Spearhead, pitcher, water; gr 325.00
Diamond Spearhead, sugar bowl, cobalt, w/lid 175.00
Diamond Spearhead, sugar bowl, gr, w/lid 150.00
Diamond Spearhead, syrup, cobalt 450.00
Diamond Spearhead, tumbler, vaseline....................45.00
Dolly Madison, butter dish, bl............................290.00
Dolly Madison, creamer, bl 75.00
Dolly Madison, pitcher, water; gr 350.00
Dolly Madison, spooner, gr...................................75.00
Dolly Madison, sugar bowl, gr, w/lid 125.00
Dolly Madison, tumbler, bl 75.00
Double Greek Key, butter dish, bl 300.00
Double Greek Key, celery vase, bl 115.00
Double Greek Key, creamer, bl 65.00
Double Greek Key, shakers, bl, pr 250.00
Double Greek Key, spooner, bl 70.00
Double Greek Key, sugar bowl, bl, w/lid 150.00
Double Greek Key, toothpick holder, bl 300.00
Double Greek Key, tumbler, bl 65.00
Drapery, pitcher, water; bl 165.00
Drapery, rose bowl, aqua......................................75.00
Drapery, rose bowl, bl 65.00
Drapery, water set, bl, 7-pc 375.00
Drapery, water set, clear, 7-pc 200.00
Everglades, butter dish, bl w/gold 225.00
Everglades, butter dish, vaseline 275.00
Everglades, compote, jelly; bl w/gold 85.00
Everglades, compote, jelly; vaseline 110.00
Everglades, creamer, bl 80.00
Everglades, cruet, vaseline 350.00
Everglades, pitcher, water; bl 350.00
Everglades, pitcher, water; vaseline 325.00
Everglades, spooner, vaseline 85.00
Everglades, sugar bowl, bl w/gold 150.00
Everglades, sugar bowl, vaseline, w/lid 150.00
Everglades, tumbler, bl 65.00
Everglades, tumbler, bl w/gold 75.00
Fern, shaker, cranberry 50.00
Fern, spooner, cranberry 120.00
Flora, bowl, master berry; vaseline.........................75.00
Flora, butter dish, bl..245.00
Flora, butter dish, vaseline 175.00
Flora, butter dish, vaseline w/gold........................210.00
Flora, celery vase, bl 110.00
Flora, compote, jelly; bl, rare 135.00
Flora, creamer, vaseline 80.00
Flora, cruet, vaseline..375.00
Flora, pitcher, water; vaseline.............................400.00
Flora, shakers, bl, pr 350.00
Flora, shakers, vaseline, pr 300.00
Flora, spooner, vaseline..70.00
Flora, sugar bowl, vaseline, w/lid 110.00
Flora, toothpick holder, bl..................................450.00
Flora, toothpick holder, vaseline 400.00
Flora, tumbler, vaseline..75.00
Fluted Scrolls, bowl, master berry; bl.....................65.00
Fluted Scrolls, butter dish, bl w/HP decor..............185.00

Fluted Scrolls, butter dish, vaseline 165.00
Fluted Scrolls, creamer, bl 55.00
Fluted Scrolls, creamer, vaseline 60.00
Fluted Scrolls, cruet, vaseline, orig stopper 175.00
Fluted Scrolls, dresser jar, vaseline, w/lid 55.00
Fluted Scrolls, pitcher, water; bl opal 195.00
Fluted Scrolls, pitcher, water; vaseline 195.00
Fluted Scrolls, puff box, bl 45.00
Fluted Scrolls, puff box, vaseline 40.00
Fluted Scrolls, spooner, bl 50.00
Fluted Scrolls, sugar bowl, vaseline, w/lid 88.00
Fluted Scrolls, water set, clear, 5-pc 225.00
Frosted-Leaf & Basketweave, butter dish, bl............................250.00
Frosted-Leaf & Basketweave, creamer, bl 135.00
Frosted-Leaf & Basketweave, sugar bowl, bl, w/lid 165.00
Frosted-Leaf & Basketweave, sugar bowl, vaseline, w/lid 145.00
Hobnail, bowl, bl, scalloped, 11" 95.00
Hobnail, box, vaseline, Hobnail finial, 5x5" dia 90.00
Hobnail, creamer, vaseline, bulbous, 4" 225.00
Hobnail, pitcher, bl, bl hdl, bulbous w/ruffled rim, 8x8" 250.00
Hobnail, pitcher, bl, clear threaded hdl, 5½" 75.00
Hobnail, pitcher, cranberry, sq mouth, lg 185.00
Hobnail, pitcher, rubena, clear hdl, +6 tumblers......................750.00
Hobnail, pitcher, vaseline, clear reeded hdl, milk sz 115.00
Hobnail, pitcher, yel, 7" 225.00
Honeycomb & Clover, butter dish, bl..300.00
Honeycomb & Clover, pitcher, water; bl 300.00
Honeycomb & Clover, sugar bowl, bl, w/lid 175.00
Honeycomb & Clover, tumbler, bl..85.00
Horse Chestnut, bowl, vaseline, twisted stem, 4½x5½" 230.00
Idyll, butter dish, bl 325.00
Idyll, butter dish, gr 350.00
Idyll, creamer, clear 36.00
Idyll, creamer, gr 85.00
Idyll, spooner, gr, 4½x3½" 70.00
Idyll, sugar bowl, bl, w/lid..200.00
Idyll, toothpick holder, bl..230.00
Idyll, tumbler, bl 90.00
Intaglio, bowl, master berry; bl..100.00
Intaglio, butter dish, bl 350.00
Intaglio, compote, jelly; bl..30.00
Intaglio, compote, jelly; vaseline 39.00
Intaglio, creamer, bl w/HP decor..55.00
Intaglio, creamer, clear 20.00
Intaglio, creamer, vaseline..45.00
Intaglio, cruet, bl, w/bl stopper 135.00
Intaglio, pitcher, water; bl 165.00
Intaglio, sugar bowl, vaseline, w/lid 90.00
Intaglio, tumbler, bl 100.00
Inverted Fan & Feather, creamer, bl 135.00
Inverted Fan & Feather, pitcher, water; bl 495.00
Inverted Fan & Feather, sugar bowl, bl, w/lid 200.00
Inverted Fan & Feather, tumbler, bl 75.00
Iris w/Meander, berry set, vaseline, 6-pc 220.00
Iris w/Meander, bowl, bl, 8½" 85.00
Iris w/Meander, bowl, master berry; bl, 10" 90.00
Iris w/Meander, butter dish, bl 240.00
Iris w/Meander, compote, jelly; bl..45.00
Iris w/Meander, creamer, vaseline 95.00
Iris w/Meander, cruet, vaseline..350.00
Iris w/Meander, pitcher, water; bl 325.00
Iris w/Meander, pitcher, water; vaseline 275.00
Iris w/Meander, plate, bl, 7" 40.00
Iris w/Meander, shakers, bl, pr..200.00

Iris w/Meander, spooner, bl 75.00
Iris w/Meander, sugar bowl, bl, w/lid 150.00
Iris w/Meander, sugar bowl, gr, w/lid 125.00
Iris w/Meander, toothpick holder, clear....................................45.00
Iris w/Meander, toothpick holder, gr..55.00
Iris w/Meander, toothpick holder, vaseline................................75.00
Iris w/Meander, tumbler, bl 75.00
Jackson, butter dish, bl 215.00
Jackson, butter dish, vaseline 215.00
Jackson, cruet, clear 95.00
Jackson, cruet, vaseline..165.00
Jackson, pitcher, water; vaseline 350.00
Jackson, powder box, bl 55.00
Jackson, shakers, vaseline, pr..175.00
Jackson, spooner, vaseline 60.00
Jackson, sugar bowl, bl, w/lid 110.00
Jackson, tumbler, vaseline 80.00
Jewel & Flower, butter dish, clear 95.00
Jewel & Flower, butter dish, vaseline 225.00
Jewel & Flower, creamer, vaseline 85.00
Jewel & Flower, cruet, bl 300.00
Jewel & Flower, pitcher, water; bl 450.00
Jewel & Flower, shakers, vaseline, pr 180.00
Jewel & Flower, sugar bowl, vaseline, w/lid 145.00
Jewel & Flower, tumbler, bl 90.00
Jeweled Heart, compote, bl 125.00
Jeweled Heart, cruet, bl 350.00
Jeweled Heart, nappy, clear, ruffled, 6" 22.00
Jeweled Heart, spooner, bl 110.00
Jeweled Heart, sugar bowl, bl, w/lid 175.00
Jeweled Heart, toothpick holder, bl 250.00
Jeweled Heart, water set, bl, 7-pc 625.00
Leaf Chalice, rose bowl, gr, ped ft 45.00
Leaf Chalice, sugar bowl, gr, ped ft, w/lid................................55.00
Lustre Flute, butter dish, bl 245.00
Lustre Flute, creamer, bl 85.00
Lustre Flute, pitcher, water; bl..295.00
Lustre Flute, spooner, bl 85.00
Lustre Flute, sugar bowl, bl, w/lid 175.00
Lustre Flute, tumbler, bl 65.00
Palm Beach, butter dish, bl..275.00
Palm Beach, compote, vaseline 175.00
Palm Beach, creamer & sugar bowl, bl, w/lid............................195.00
Palm Beach, pitcher, water; bl..385.00
Palm Beach, pitcher, water; vaseline..350.00
Palm Beach, sauce, bl 25.00
Palm Beach, spooner, bl..85.00
Palm Beach, tumbler, bl..85.00
Paneled Holly, berry set, bl opal, 6-pc......................................350.00
Paneled Holly, butter dish, bl..300.00
Paneled Holly, creamer, bl..75.00
Paneled Holly, pitcher, water; bl w/gold..................................500.00
Paneled Holly, sauce bowl, bl w/gold 45.00
Paneled Holly, spooner, bl..65.00
Paneled Holly, sugar bowl, bl, w/lid 225.00
Paneled Holly, tumbler, bl..75.00
Paneled Sprig, toothpick holder, clear 45.00
Poinsettia, bowl, clear, ruffled, 3-ftd..40.00
Poinsettia, pitcher, water; bl, tankard form..............................275.00
Poinsettia, sugar shaker, bl 150.00
Poinsettia, syrup, bl 300.00
Poinsettia, tumbler, bl..50.00
Queen's Crown, creamer, yel, 5" 80.00
Regal, butter dish, clear 75.00

Regal, butter dish, gr w/gold 200.00
Regal, celery vase, bl 125.00
Regal, cruet, bl 400.00
Regal, pitcher, water; bl 250.00
Regal, pitcher, water; clear 95.00
Regal, spooner, gr 55.00
Regal, sugar bowl, bl, w/lid 145.00
Reverse Swirl, butter dish, bl opal 125.00
Reverse Swirl, creamer, bl 125.00
Reverse Swirl, pitcher, water tankard; cranberry 425.00
Reverse Swirl, shakers, cranberry, cylindrical, ring neck, pr 250.00
Reverse Swirl, spooner, bl 95.00
Reverse Swirl, spooner, cranberry 110.00
Reverse Swirl, sugar bowl, bl, w/lid 175.00
Reverse Swirl, syrup, vaseline 135.00
Ribbed Spiral, butter dish, bl 350.00
Ribbed Spiral, compote, bl 47.00
Ribbed Spiral, creamer, bl 65.00
Ribbed Spiral, plate, vaseline 35.00
Ribbed Spiral, shakers, vaseline, pr 185.00
Ribbed Spiral, sugar bowl, bl, w/lid 225.00
Ribbed Spiral, tumbler, bl 75.00
Scottish Moor, pitcher, water; cranberry 375.00
Scottish Moor, tumbler, cranberry 90.00
Scroll w/Acanthus, butter dish, bl 350.00
Scroll w/Acanthus, creamer, bl 60.00
Scroll w/Acanthus, cruet, bl, w/clear stopper 190.00
Scroll w/Acanthus, cruet, vaseline 350.00
Scroll w/Acanthus, pitcher, water; vaseline ...350.00
Scroll w/Acanthus, spooner, bl 65.00
Scroll w/Acanthus, sugar bowl, vaseline, w/lid 125.00
Scroll w/Acanthus, tumbler, bl 75.00
Seaweed, cruet, bl 245.00
Seaweed, rose bowl, vaseline, lg 95.00
Shell, butter dish, bl 450.00
Shell, compote, bl 110.00
Shell, cruet, bl 425.00
Shell, pitcher, water; bl 500.00
Shell, sauce, clear, 6 for 150.00
Shell, spooner, bl 95.00
Shell, toothpick holder, bl 400.00
Shell, tumbler, bl 75.00
Spanish Lace, pitcher, water; bl 150.00
Spanish Lace, pitcher, water; clear 95.00
Spanish Lace, pitcher, water; cranberry 375.00
Spanish Lace, rose bowl, clear 35.00
Spanish Lace, shakers, cranberry, pr 175.00
Spanish Lace, sugar bowl, bl, w/lid 175.00
Spanish Lace, sugar shaker, bl 135.00
Spanish Lace, sweetmeat, cranberry, SP rim/lid/hdl, M ..375.00
Spanish Lace, tumbler, cranberry 75.00
Squirrel & Acorn, compote, gr 75.00
Stars & Stripes, bud vase, lt bl, 7" 150.00
Stars & Stripes, bud vase, red, 7" 200.00
Stars & Stripes, pitcher, red, tapered cylinder, 8" 1,300.00
Stars & Stripes, pitcher, turq, 8" 550.00
Stippled Leaf & Basketweave, spooner, bl 75.00
Sunburst on Shield, creamer, bl 125.00
Sunburst on Shield, cruet, vaseline 650.00
Sunburst on Shield, pitcher, water; bl 500.00
Sunburst on Shield, spooner, vaseline 85.00
Sunburst on Shield, sugar bowl, clear, w/lid ...135.00
Sunburst on Shield, sugar bowl, vaseline, w/lid ...175.00
Sunburst on Shield, tumbler, bl 100.00

Swag w/Brackets, berry set, gr, 7-pc 200.00
Swag w/Brackets, butter dish, gr 135.00
Swag w/Brackets, compote, gr 30.00
Swag w/Brackets, pitcher, water; vaseline 250.00
Swag w/Brackets, sauce, vaseline 25.00
Swag w/Brackets, shakers, bl, pr 190.00
Swag w/Brackets, spooner, gr 45.00
Swag w/Brackets, sugar bowl, gr, w/lid 75.00
Swag w/Brackets, toothpick holder, bl 300.00
Swag w/Brackets, tumbler, bl 60.00
Swag w/Brackets, tumbler, clear 30.00
Swag w/Brackets, water set, vaseline, 7-pc 495.00
Swirl, hat, clear, lg 75.00
Swirl, pitcher, water; bl 125.00
Swirl, pitcher, water; clear 60.00
Swirl, sugar shaker, cranberry 150.00
Swirl, toothpick holder, cranberry, scarce tumbler shape 65.00

Tokyo master berry bowl in green, $50.00.

Tokyo, compote, gr 33.00
Tokyo, creamer, bl 65.00
Tokyo, cruet, bl, w/clear stopper 115.00
Tokyo, pitcher, water; bl, rare 300.00
Tokyo, shakers, bl, pr 180.00
Tokyo, sugar bowl, clear, w/lid 50.00
Tokyo, water set, gr, 7-pc 595.00
War of Roses, boat dish, vaseline, 3x7½x2½" 50.00

Water Lily and Cattails in blue, Spooner, $45.00; Creamer, $45.00.

Water Lily & Cattails, bowl, gr, 9" 50.00
Water Lily & Cattails, bowl, master berry; clear, ruffled 35.00

Water Lily & Cattails, butter dish, bl	375.00
Water Lily & Cattails, creamer, bl	45.00
Water Lily & Cattails, pitcher, water; bl	295.00
Water Lily & Cattails, sugar bowl, bl, w/lid	175.00
Water Lily & Cattails, tumbler, bl	50.00
Wild Bouquet, berry set, clear, 6-pc	145.00
Wild Bouquet, butter dish, bl	400.00
Wild Bouquet, compote, jelly; bl	125.00
Wild Bouquet, compote, jelly; clear	45.00
Wild Bouquet, cruet, bl	325.00
Wild Bouquet, cruet, clear	125.00
Wild Bouquet, pitcher, water; bl	250.00
Wild Bouquet, sugar bowl, bl, w/lid	200.00
Wild Bouquet, toothpick holder, bl	300.00
Wild Bouquet, tumbler, bl	100.00
Wild Bouquet, tumbler, gr	60.00
Wreath & Shell, bowl, master berry; bl	85.00
Wreath & Shell, butter dish, bl	225.00
Wreath & Shell, celery vase, bl	165.00
Wreath & Shell, cracker jar, bl	695.00
Wreath & Shell, creamer, bl	110.00
Wreath & Shell, creamer, vaseline	75.00
Wreath & Shell, pitcher, water; bl	350.00
Wreath & Shell, rose bowl, bl	75.00
Wreath & Shell, salt dip, bl	135.00
Wreath & Shell, sauce, vaseline	18.00
Wreath & Shell, spittoon, lady's, vaseline	90.00
Wreath & Shell, spooner, bl	75.00
Wreath & Shell, spooner, vaseline	65.00
Wreath & Shell, sugar bowl, vaseline, w/lid	130.00
Wreath & Shell, toothpick holder, bl	250.00
Wreath & Shell, toothpick holder, vaseline w/decor	250.00
Wreath & Shell, tumbler, bl	70.00

Opaline

A type of semi-opaque opal glass, opaline was made in white as well as pastel shades and is often enameled. It is similar in appearance to English bristol glass, though its enamel or gilt decorative devices tend to exhibit a French influence.

Basket, green with gold and jewels, 8", $95.00.

Bottle, scent; bl, red/wht/gold decor, orig stopper, 5"	60.00
Bottle, scent; pk w/cream & gold feathers, 8½x3¼"	175.00
Box, pk, gold scrolls, scenic hinged lid, 1¾x2½"	95.00
Ring tree, bl, gold & wht trim, 2½" dia	45.00

Vase, pk, exotic bird & flowers, no mk, 10"	235.00
Vase, wht, bird among flowers, English mk, 10½"	435.00

Orientalia

The art of the Orient is an area of collecting currently enjoying strong collector interest, not only in those examples that are truly 'antique' but in the 20th-century items as well. Because of the many aspects involved in a study of Orientalia, we can only try through brief comments to acquaint the reader with some of the more readily available examples and suggest specialized reference sources for detailed information. Our advisor for this category is Clarence Bodine; he is listed in the Directory under Pennsylvania. See also Canton; Champleve; Cloisonne; Coralene, Oriental; Dragon Ware; Geisha Girl; Imari; Ivory; Kutani; Moriage; Nippon; Noritake; Peking Cameo Glass; Rose Medallion; Satsuma; Soapstone.

Key:
Ch — Chinese	FV — Famille Verte
ctp — contemporary	E — export
cvg — carving	hdwd — hardwood
do — door	Jp — Japan
drw — drawer	Ko — Korean
Dy — Dynasty	lcq — lacquer
FJ — Famille Juane	rswd — rosewood
FN — Famille Noire	tkwd — teakwood
FR — Famille Rose	

Nanking-type blue and white hexagonal garden seat, pierced sides, 1820s, 19", NM, $2,200.00.

Blanc de Chine

Figure, female deity w/flowers beside a deer, 1700s, 16", pr	1,500.00
Figure, Guanyin seated on rockwork base, 1800s, 13"	1,100.00
Vase, hu-form w/mask & ring hdls, incised decor, 1880s, 14"	600.00

Blue and White Porcelain

Bottle, arabesques, cylindrical, Arita, 1800s, 8"	300.00
Bowl, dragon in clouds, spear/dot border, 1800s, w/lid, 9"	425.00
Bowl, E, hawthorne branch, 1800s, hairline, 10"	275.00
Brush box, floral, emb/wht on bl, 1880s, 7", E	250.00
Charger, florals overall, Ming Dy, rim rpr, 12"	300.00

Charger, peonies/landscapes/diapering, 1800s, Jp, 17" **200.00**
Charger, peony blossoms, Jp, 1800s, 15" **300.00**
Dish, 3 friends central motif, octopus border, Arita, 12" **200.00**
Garden seat, village, Nanking type, hexagonal, 19", EX........ **2,200.00**
Ginger jar, birds/florals, sgn, 1800s, wood lid, 11", EX **200.00**
Ginger jar, hawthorn decor, teak lid, Kangxi, 1800s, 8½"............**250.00**
Jar, birds, bamboo, cherry blossoms, globular, Yi Dy, 5½"........ **1,500.00**
Jar, prunus blossoms, ovoid, Kangxi, Ch, 5" **600.00**
Jar, shou characters medallion, globular, Ko, 1700s, 7" **600.00**
Jardiniere, birds/florals, hexagonal, 1880s, 7¾" H **385.00**
Plaque, crane on gnarled tree, Arita, hdwd fr, 15½x10½" **325.00**
Umbrella stand, cylindrical, Jp, late 1800s, 24⅝" **325.00**
Vase, dragon in clouds ingests fish, 1800s, 24" **300.00**
Vase, dragon/phoenix/peonies, copper accents, 24" **275.00**

Bronze

Vase with dragons and fish relief, signed, 10", $250.00.

Bowl, everted rim, ring hdls, Han Dy, 2¼x6" **300.00**
Box, gilt lcq figures, diapering, heart form, Jp, 1800s, 4" **300.00**
Brazier, low cylindrical body w/3 cabriole legs, Jp, 7x13" **600.00**
Cache pot, 2 creatures hold oval vessel w/waves, 1800s, 13" **350.00**
Figure, Bodhisattva w/hands in vitarka mudra, 1800s, 25" **525.00**
Figure, deity stands in flowing robe w/scroll, Jp, 20"....................**600.00**
Figure, elephant, ivory tusks, sgn Seikoku, 1800s, 14"..................**600.00**
Figure, Guanyin seated on lotus throne, gilt, 1800s, 14".......... **1,500.00**
Figure, official stands in Tang-style dress, 1700s, 12" **600.00**
Incense burner, archaic style, foo dog finial, 18" **400.00**
Jar, mc metal inlay, foo dog finial, EX work/detail, 12" **725.00**
Lamp, dragons/birds in relief, glass shade, electric, 74" **575.00**
Mirror, cast figurals & florals, ca 1600, Yi Dy, 12" dia.................**650.00**
Mirror, pine relief, rtcl crane, minor pitting, 4¾" dia...................**300.00**
Plaque, lady's portrait in relief, Jp, 1900s, 17½x13"......................**175.00**
Umbrella stand, dragons in relief, cylindrical, 1800s, 24" **350.00**
Vase, bird & turtle reliefs, appl dragon, 1900s, 24" **250.00**
Vase, spherical, low relief decor, kirin finial, 1800s, 15" **550.00**
Vase, 9 scholars/sages among bamboo in frieze, mc pnt, 18" **550.00**

Celadon

Celadon, introduced during the Ching Dynasty, is a green-glazed ware developed in an attempt to imitate the color of jade. Designs are often incised or painted on over glaze in heavy enamel applications.

Bowl, barbed rim, cvd peonies int, scroll frieze, Ming, 15" **1,200.00**
Box, soap; Rose Canton, gilt, 1850s, w/lid & underdish................**150.00**

Dish, Rose Canton, birds/butterflies/etc, 1850s, 9½" W **250.00**
Fruit basket, rtcl border, Rose Canton motif, 10", +tray **935.00**
Jar, FR landscapes w/bldgs, foo dog finial, metal mts, 18" **1,100.00**
Plate, int landscape, cvd foliage rim, Ch, 1800s, 11½" **300.00**
Platter, Rose Canton, bird/butterflies/etc, 1850s, 13", EX............**250.00**
Vase, molded dragon, inverted/squat cylinder, 7x10"..................**285.00**

Furniture

Armchair, cracked ice pattern, cane seat, fretwork arms, sm... **1,250.00**
Armchair, softwd, horseshoe bk, panel seat, 1800s, pr **4,400.00**
Desk, Ch, cvd/lcq, highly ornate, 2-part, 56x42" **1,100.00**
Desk, 3-drw top on 2 peds w/2 drws ea, 1800s, 33x62" **2,750.00**
Etagere, hdwd, pierced/cvd crest, 2 doors, Ch, 1800s, 81" **650.00**
Etagere, lion head in galley, 2 cvd drws, 2 shelves, 51x35" **750.00**
Settee, Ch, tkwd, dragons/flowers/birds/etc, 50" L **1,000.00**
Settee, hdwd, spindle-bk, solid panel seat, 38" L **1,400.00**
Stand, Ch, cvd w/eagle legs, dk lacquer, 30"...............................**350.00**
Stand, Ch, tkwd, cvd apron, 2-shelf, marble top, 36" **375.00**
Stand, Ch, tkwd, highly cvd, soapstone insert, 18x16" dia **300.00**
Stand, Ch, tkwd, marble insert, 32", EX **260.00**
Stand, shelf, cvd apron/legs, marble top, Huanghuali, 32x15" **275.00**
Table, altar; elmwood, 3-drw/2 doors, brass mts, 35x71x19" ... **1,000.00**
Table, Ch, tkwd, highly cvd w/dragons, serpentine, 45" **1,100.00**
Table, cvd frieze/legs, sq top, pnt/parcel gilt, 9½x20" **500.00**
Table, elm, scroll apron, brackets at legs, 1800s, 33x49x25" ... **2,750.00**
Table, hdwd, cvd cabriole legs, Jp, 13x46" **450.00**

Chinese two-tier table, teakwood with marble insert, 24" x 21", $400.00.

Table, rswd/cloisonne, 5-leg, ring base, Ming style, 16x13" **185.00**
Table, Zitan, pierced apron/sq legs, Ch, 1800s, 32x45" **2,000.00**
Work table, E, gilt/lcq scenes, workbag, gold claw ft **650.00**

Hardstones

Amethyst, court lady seated w/fan & flower, 5¼x4¼"..................**170.00**
Amethyst, court lady w/fly whisk & flower, 5" **130.00**
Amethyst, court lady w/peony in raised hands, 5½" **140.00**
Amethyst, incense burner, foo lion hdls/finial, 4x5½" **175.00**
Amethyst, phoenix in peony bush, 7½x5½" **325.00**
Amethyst, vase, floral cvg, peony lid, 6x6" **350.00**
Coral, pk; God of Longevity, long ears, pear in hand, 2¼" **150.00**
Coral, red; God of Longevity w/bottle of Elixer of Life, 3"..........**250.00**
Coral, red; goddess w/gourd bottle of Elixer of Life, 2"..............**180.00**
Coral, red; lady w/peonies in 1 hand, cloth on other, 3" **190.00**
Goldstone, 3 fairies in prunus tree, inlaid base, 6½".....................**250.00**
Jade, bl-gr; court lady w/flowers & fan, 8x4½" **350.00**

Jade, burmese w/red skin; Kwan Yin w/sceptre & bottle, 9" 250.00
Jade, dk gr w/brn wht; floral cvg w/dbl inset, w/lid, 5½".............250.00
Jade, dk gr w/tan flecks; magpie on floral branch, 7x4"...............275.00
Jade, gr w/wht; vase, floral cvg, ring hdls, w/lid, 6" 250.00
Jade, lt gr; phoenix bird in tree, magpie below, 9½"...................350.00
Jade, lt gr; vase, stylized dragons, hdls, w/lid, 8½".....................250.00
Jade, med gr; court lady w/peonies & scarf, 8½x5".....................350.00
Jade, spinach; urn, dragons, ring hdls, w/lid, 12x7½" 750.00
Tigereye, duck (box), standing, cvd base, 5½" L, pr....................650.00
Tigereye, Tang Horse, front ft raised, 4x5" 175.00
Turq, unicorn, reclining, w/matrix, 3x4" 350.00

Inro

Ivory, cvd/inlay, warrior/lady as warrior, 4-case, 3½" 2,200.00
Lcq, gold, branches w/semi-precious stones, 3-case, 2¼".............600.00
Lcq, gold & silver, autumn flowers, rtcl ivory ojime, 3⅝"........ 1,320.00
Lcq, gold & silver, insects, 4-case, 1800s, 2⅝" 1,750.00
Lcq, gold & silver, shrine by stream, 4-case, 1800s, 2¾"....... 1,875.00
Lcq, monkey & mosquito, sgn Koma, 1800s, 5-case, 3" ... 1,100.00
Lcq, peonies & butterfly, ojimi+netsuke, 4-case, 4¾"............650.00
Lcq, takamakie figures, ojimi+netsuke, 3-case, 1½" 300.00

Lacquer

Lacquerware is found in several colors, but the one most likely to be encountered is cinnabar. It is often intricately carved, sometimes involving hundreds of layers built one at a time on a metal or wooden base. Later pieces remain red, while older examples tend to darken.

Japanese gold lacquer footed tray, samurai in battle, 18th century, 18", NM, $1,900.00.

Box, blk w/gilt figural scenes, scalloped form, Jp, 9" L................675.00
Box, ivory landscape/floral inlay, 1700s, Ming Dy, 4½x12" 400.00
Box, leafy vines, gold on blk, octagonal, on ftd stand, 18" 400.00
Cabinet, animals/much gilt, pewter mts, 1800s, 18x18x12".........625.00
Cabinet, gold on nashiji, wood inlay, Meiji Period, 17x14x7" 850.00
Figure, Amida Buddha on lotus throne, worn gilt, 1800s, 30" . 3,000.00
Figure, hooded monks on platform, Jp, 1800s, 10x16" 750.00
Lap desk, E, fitted int, 1800s, 6x16x10", on later stand................300.00
Screen, Mt Fuji scenes, MOP birds, shrine shape, 1800s, 36" 500.00
Sewing box, gold chinoiserie, w/ivory sewing aids, 14", EX 300.00
Sewing box, red w/gilt & blk genre scenes, 8-sided, 9x16" 700.00
Shonada, butterflies/scenic, shelves/doors, 1800s, 42" 3,600.00
Stand, cinnabar, cvd foliate decor, rectangular, 5½x10½"...........300.00
Stand, landscapes/birds, arched legs, Jp, 1800s, 16x25" 1,100.00
Table, MOP inlay, tilt-top, Jp, late 1800s, 28x23½" dia 265.00

Tea caddy, flowers/birds in MOP inlay 125.00
Tray, kimono; floral spray on blk, sq, 1800s, 23½", EX 750.00

Netsukes

A netsuke is a miniature Japanese carving made with a hole called a *himitoshi*, either channeled or within the carved design, that allows it to be threaded onto a waist cord and worn with the kimono. Because the kimono had no pockets, the Japanese man hung his tools, pipe, tobacco pouch, and other daily necessities from his sash. The netsuke was the toggle that secured them all. Although most are of ivory, others were made of bone, wood, metal, porcelain, or semi-precious stones. Some were inlaid or lacquered. They are found in many forms, but figurals are the most common and desirable. They range in size from 1" up to 3", which was the maximum size allowed by law. Most netsukes represented the religion, mythology, and the habits of the average person. There was no written word, hence carvers depicted the daily life of their people.

Careful study is required to recognize the quality of the netsuke. Many have been made in Hong Kong in recent years; and, even though some are very well carved, these are considered copies and avoided by the serious collector. There are many books that will help you learn to recognize quality netsukes, and most reputable dealers are glad to assist you. Use your magnifying glass to check for repairs. In the listings that follow, netsukes are ivory unless noted otherwise; 'stained' indicates a color wash.

Boy in brimmed hat, bone, stain details, Gyokuzan, 1800s, 2"... 1,200.00
Dancer & drummer, wood, ivory/ebony inlay, sgn/1800s, 1¾" . 1,320.00
Dancer w/Okina mask, stained details, Kaneaki, 1800s, 1¾" 660.00
Daruma, seated, hooded robe, sgn Shumin, 1800s, 1½" 770.00
Deer, recumbent, lcq, Kajikawa Bunryusai, 1800s, 2¼" 3,000.00
Drummer crouching, stained details, Rakumin, 1800s, 1½" 1,540.00
Hotei & baby, stained details, Mosatomo, 1800s, 1¼"............ 1,100.00
Old man w/boy, stained details, Ono Ryomin, 1800s, 1½" 1,320.00
Ox, recumbent, silver, incised hairwork, 1800s, 2⅛" 1,650.00
Puppeteer w/puppet on box, wood, stone inlay, 1880s, 1⅜" 1,320.00
Puppy & monkey, wooden, inlaid eyes, Josui, 1800s, 1½" 1,200.00
Rakan seated w/legs Xd, wood, sgn Masayuki, 1800s, 1½" 2,090.00
Sambaso dancer w/Okina mask, wood, Hironobu, 1800s, 1¾" . 2,475.00
Tiger on haunches, dbl-inlay eyes, 1800s, 1½" 1,100.00
Tiger w/bamboo shoot, inlaid eyes, Rantei, 1800s, 1¼" 3,300.00

Porcelain

Chinese export ware was designed to appeal to Western tastes and was often made to order. During the 18th century, vast amounts were shipped to Europe and on westward. Many of these lines of dinnerware were given specific pattern names. Rose Mandarin, Fitzhugh, Armorial, Rose Medallion, and Canton are but a few of the more familiar.

Bowl, E, courtyard scenes, 1780, lt wear, 9" 770.00
Bowl, E, European hunt scenes, 1775, rstr, 11" 1,100.00
Bowl, FV, Hundred Antiques, Kangxi, 8¼"................................770.00
Bowl, salad; Nanking, 1800s, mfg flaw, 9½" 650.00
Bowl, swan scene, 2 gold-leaf loop hdls, Jp, 4½x12"......................90.00
Bowl, wht prunus & mc butterfly, oblong, Ch, 1900, 6½x8½".......75.00
Brushpot, FV, dragon & demon among waves, Kangxi, 5¼"........660.00
Candlestick, Cabbage & Moth, 1875, 10½", EX, pr....................900.00
Candlestick, vines/birds w/gilt on wht, Jp, 1880s, 7", pr 350.00
Charger, hawk portrait, geometric border, 1800s, 21", EX 400.00
Chocolate pot, E, coat of arms, str sides, 7½" 1,980.00
Chop plate, Fitzhugh, red-orange, eagle/banner w/BLP, 16¼" 850.00
Coffeepot, E, str sides, branch hdl, gold monogram, 9½" 400.00
Compote, FR, mixed florals on wht, 1800s, 5", pr 425.00

Chinese export porcelain armorial-decorated chocolate pot, 7½", $2,000.00.

Creamer, Bl Fitzhugh, helmet form, 5½"	450.00
Creamer, E, mc floral, helmet form, 5½"	175.00
Creamer, E, Oriental figures, mc on wht, pear form, 4"	275.00
Cup & saucer, Bl Fitzugh, set of 5, NM	850.00
Dish, Bl Fitzhugh, fluted, scalloped rim, 9½" sq	850.00
Dish, Rose Canton, floral/butterfly panels, 1850s, 11" L	375.00
Figurine, gods of good fortune, Ch, 12", set of 3	125.00
Figurine, Siamese god, seated, bl jacket & vase, 10x7½"	95.00
Fruit basket, Bl Fitzhugh, rpr hdls, 11", +undertray	1,500.00
Garden seat, Bl Fitzhugh, hexagonal, 19"	5,000.00
Ginger jar, Mandarin-style figures/inscriptions, 1880s, 9"	220.00
Jar, ladies in kimonos, Imari-style, w/lid, Ch, 11½", pr	175.00
Lamp, boudoir; pk & blk fish on gr seaweed, Ch, 12x6"	75.00
Mug, E, 'Chicken Skin,' courtyard scene, dragon hdl, EX	950.00
Pitcher, floral shield/border, sepia/gilt/bl, 1800, 5"	220.00
Plate, Bl Fitzhugh, 10"	110.00
Plate, E, peasants farming, Rose Canton border, wear, 10"	500.00
Plate, Orange Fitzhugh, 8", pr	650.00
Platter, Bl Fitzhugh, X-shaped gravy trap & well, 17"	400.00
Platter, E, figural courtyard scene, gilt, 1780s, 15"	750.00
Platter, E, floral in mc, pk rim, 12¾", NM	300.00
Platter, E, floral in mc/gilt, orange-peel texture, 11"	275.00
Platter, Nanking, spearhead/lattice border, w/strainer, 16"	700.00
Punch bowl, E, armorial/florals, 1800, int hairline, 12"	1,100.00
Punch bowl, E, European hunt scene, gilt, 1780, 12¾", EX	6,000.00
Punch bowl, E/FR, people/flowers in medallions, 1850s, 16"	2,200.00
Punch bowl, Rose Canton, butterflies/flowers, 1850s, 15"	990.00
Punch bowl, Rose Canton, 1800s, gilt wear, 13"	500.00
Screen, FR, immortals on wht, wood stand, 1900, 23x18½"	325.00
Soup plate, E, armorial crest, spearhead border, 1765, 8½"	350.00
Sugar bowl, Bl Fitzhugh, gold trim, w/lid & tray, NM	750.00
Sugar bowl, Bl Fitzhugh, w/lid, 5", NM	550.00
Tankard, E, Western-style Sailor's Farewell, 1780, rstr, 7"	700.00
Tea caddy, E, eagle w/shield, brn/gilt, prof rpr, 5⅜"	425.00
Teapot, Bl Fitzhugh, 6½", EX	350.00
Teapot, mandarin figural, orange hdl/spout, Ch, ca 1874, 7"	150.00
Teapot, Rose Canton, shouldered, dome lid, 11", EX	300.00
Teapot, Shou Lao in gr/yel robe, twig hdl, Ch, ca 1874, 3½"	150.00
Tray, fruit basket; Bl Fitzhugh, rtcl rim, oval, 11"	450.00
Tureen, E, armorial, bl/gilt on wht, flower finial, 14", NM	2,200.00
Umbrella stand, Rose Canton, butterflies/bugs/etc, 29"	1,500.00
Vase, dragons & clouds on turq, men in panels, Dy mk, 19"	350.00
Vase, E/FR, Greek key frames, bulb w/can neck, 1800s, 15"	935.00
Vase, floral, Makuzu Kozan style, Jp, 1880s, 18"	165.00
Vase, FN, gr foliage w/mc accents on blk, Ch, 24½"	2,000.00
Vase, FR, birds among prunus blossoms, late 1800s, 16"	500.00
Vase, FR, scenic panels, flower stand in bk, hdls, Ch, 16"	350.00
Vase, FV, birds/florals/insect panels, 1800s, 20"	2,750.00

Vase, FV, deer in landscape, bottle form, 1800s, 21½"	500.00
Vase, FV, dragons & florals, dbl-gourd, Kangxi, 17"	14,300.00
Vase, FV, phoenix/butterfly/peony, underglaze bl, Kangxi, 10"	880.00
Vase, God of Longevity/Kwan Yin/bird/poem, 1861, Ch, 23"	350.00
Vase, peonies/deer/trees/poem/script, Ch, ca 1861, 23"	350.00
Vase, roses w/gold on red, bl/wht floral base, 3-hdl, Jp, 9"	150.00
Vase, temple; Rose Canton, peacocks/garden, 1830, rstr, 32"	1,500.00

Rugs

The Oriental and Eastern rug market has enjoyed a renewal of interest in recent years as collectors have become aware of the fact that some of the semi-antique rugs (those sixty to one hundred years old) may be had at a price within the range of the average buyer.

Key:
comp — complimentary	mdl — medallion
dmn — diamond	s/a — semi-antique
gb — guard border	

Baluch, overall mc octagons, rust boat border, 73x39", VG	700.00
Baluch prayer, tree of life, flowerhead border, 51x30", VG	500.00
Bordjalou Kazak prayer, lt bl mdl on red, 1850s, 54x47", EX	750.00
Boukara, 3 columns of octagonal gul motifs on red, 90x108"	2,500.00
Hamadan, floral lattice/ivory mdl on rose, 1880s, 96x49"	500.00
Hamadan, rose/dk bl dmn mdl on navy cartouch, 1910, 75x48"	500.00
Heriz, overall palmets on red, navy turtle border, 144x144"	4,500.00
Karabagh, 3 lg mdl on dk brn, crab border, 1900s, 84x52"	1,000.00
Karabagh prayer, rows of plants, mc on rose, bl gb, 48x31"	475.00
Kazak, navy mdl w/floral, dragon's tooth border, 72x44", EX	700.00
Khamseh, 4 mdl column, red/bl/gr on red, even wear, 74x48"	700.00
Kuba, dmn med, red/bl/tan/gold on bl, 1800s, 62x41", EX	900.00
Sarouk, intricate floral on red, multiple gb, 26x50", EX	600.00
Shirvan, red/dk bl mdl+6 sm royal bl on red, 1900s, 87x58"	2,500.00

Snuff Bottles

The Chinese were introduced to snuff in the 17th century, and their carved and painted snuff bottles typify their exquisite taste and workmanship. These small bottles, seldom measuring over 2½", were made of amber, jade, ivory, and cinnabar; tiny spoons were often attached to their stoppers. By the 18th century, some were being made of porcelain, others were of glass with delicate designs tediously reverse painted with minuscule brushes sometimes containing a single hair. Copper and brass were used but to no great extent.

Cloisonne, mc florals & flying bird panels on red-brn, 3"	150.00
Cloisonne, mc florals/butterfly in bl panels on blk, 3"	150.00
Cloisonne/enamel, floral, ovoid, 1800s, 4" H	85.00
Hornbill, cvd figural scenes, chain & hdwd stand, Ch, 8"	900.00
Rock crystal, int pnt landscape, sgn Zhou Leyuan, 1800s, 2¼"	1,100.00
Rvpt, battle scenes on bl, sgn, 6½"	150.00
Tigereye, fantail fish/foo lion cvg ea side, 3"	120.00

Sumida

Bowl, boy on rim, 5"	200.00
Bowl, 3 ladies in kimonos on rim, gr int, sqd, 6x7"	400.00
Brush pot, 2 appl monkeys, seal signature, 4"	230.00
Figurine, monk gathers celadon robe about him, 5"	365.00
Mug, appl figure makes offering to bird, 5"	190.00
Mug, boy after nest of eggs, imp mks, 4⅝x3⅛"	195.00
Tankard, appl children, seal signature, 12½", +3 5" mugs	925.00
Teapot, lady & flowers, Art Deco shape	365.00

Vase, child on limb on side, red rope-like bottom half, 8" 265.00
Vase, geisha relief, bl on red, 4¾x4½" 175.00
Vase, man w/basket of rocks in relief, brn/gray, 6¾"...................220.00
Water pot, Gama Sennin seated on toad, 6¾" L 230.00

Textiles

Robe, embroidered and couched with a large dragon on blue ground, 1800s, light wear, 60" long, $1,320.00.

Hanging scroll, ink/color on silk, Buddha/Lohans, 1800s, 23" 900.00
Kimono, wht silk, bl/mc/gold embr bands, wear/damage, 59" 110.00
Panel, boys in activities woven on silk, Ch, fr, 56x46"................700.00
Panel, embr scholar/mule+attendant, bridge/pavilion, 44x9" 225.00
Panel, prunus & bird embr on blk silk, 1800s, 58x23", pr 450.00
Robe & skirt, florals & birds embr on bl silk, ca 1900, EX...........400.00

Woodblock Prints, Japanese

Actor, sgn Toyokuni I, 1800s, 15x10" 250.00
Beauties, sgn Eisen ga, Oban, 2 prints......................................275.00
Fishermen, sgn K Ohmayagashi, 1830, matted, unfr, 11x15".......175.00
Kamezaki at Night, Hasui, ca 1928, orig ed, 15x10"...................200.00
Landscape, sgn Kiyochika, 1847-1915, matted/fr, 17x12", pr.......230.00
Night view, sgn Hiroshige, 1820, matted, unfr, 9x14"................245.00
Roof Tops, Hasui, 1st ed, 6x8" 250.00
Suno village in winter, sgn Hokusai, 1820, unfr, 11x15"..............300.00

Miscellaneous

Brush pot, ivory, cvd boys & deer in landscape, wood base, 6" 425.00
Hibachi, figured wood/copper, 1900, 19x13"................................950.00
Model of English frigate, E, bone, rosewood base w/MOP, 23" .. 9,000.00
Ojime, soft metal, iroe-takazogan insects, sgn, 1800s, 5⅝" 250.00
Tsuba, copper inlay, mythical beasts, Meiji, 4" 3,000.00
Tsuba, Jp, iron, dragon in clouds, warrior & poetess, 3⅛"........ 1,300.00
Tsuba, Jp, iron, scattered torn fans, 1600s, 3¾" 990.00
Tsuba, Jp, iron, Uba & her broom inlay, sgn, oval, 3½" 3,300.00
Vase, florals/landscapes, lcq on papier-mache, 13", pr 1,500.00
Vase, mixed metal, birds & incised flowers, 1800s, 3½" 100.00
Vase, sang de boeuf, bottle form, Ch, 1800s, 16".......................275.00
Vase, stoneware, appl figures, long neck, Song Dy, 14"...............300.00
Vermeil, bird, 24k gold on silver, enamel, MOP inlay, 4¼" 75.00
Vermeil, kingfisher, 24k gold on silver, pnt/filigree, 5" 80.00
Vermeil, pheasant, 24k gold on silver, mc pnt, 5x3½" 180.00
Vermeil, phoenix, 14k gold on silver, carnelian inlay, 4x2"..........90.00
Vermeil, phoenix, 24k gold on silver, 3 carnelians, 6x5" 260.00
Vermeil, rooster, 24k gold on silver, mc pnt/coral stones, 5" 150.00

Orrefors

Orrefors Glassworks was founded in 1742 in the Swedish province of Smaaland. Utilizing the expertise of designers such as Simon Gate, Edward Hald, Vicki Lindstrand, and Edwin Ohrstrom, it produced art glass of the highest quality. Various techniques were used in achieving the decoration. Some were wheel engraved; others were blown through a unique process that formed controlled bubbles or air pockets resulting in unusual patterns and shapes. Our advisor for this category is Abby Malowanczyk; she is listed in the Directory under California.

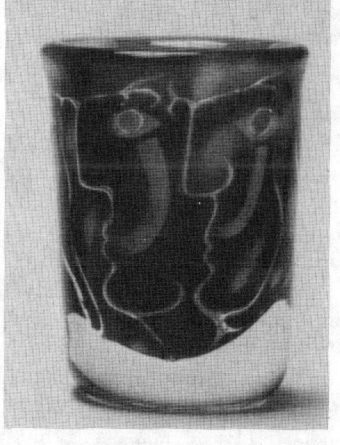

Ariel glass vase with profiles in deep aubergine and powder blue, signed Ingebord Lundin, #505-F2, 1981, 6¾", $2,400.00.

Bowl, Ariel, bubbles in gray, Ingeborg Lundin/#8010, 8"............440.00
Rabbit, #4287-111, Olle Alberius, 6x7½".....................................200.00
Vase, cased geometric bl panels, Ravenna #236/Palmqvist, 5" 825.00
Vase, clear over bl, sq, NU3736, 9" 175.00
Vase, etched boy/waterfall/geese, Palmqvist, 1941, 6½" 425.00
Vase, Graal, fish/aquatic plants, E Hald, bulbous, 4¾" 425.00
Vase, Graal, fish/seaweed, sq form, E Hald, #d, 6½" 750.00
Vase, paperweight; intaglio girl, Ohrstrom, 5".............................350.00
Vase, Poseidon/mermaid/sailboat, Landberg Expo #3541, 12" .. 7,000.00
Vase, rectangular w/eng hatch mks, 10-59/Lundin, 12½" 400.00
Vase, Romeo/Juliet on balcony, sgn/#d, 7¾" 150.00
Vase, vertical reeds eng below stars, #38328/CH, 6x3" 135.00
Vase, 3 eng female bathers, Simon Gate/38/1863, 7x10" 1,300.00

Ott and Brewer

The partnership of Ott and Brewer began in 1865 in Trenton, New Jersey. By 1876 they were making decorated graniteware, parian, and 'ivory porcelain' — similar to Irish belleek though not as fine and of different composition. In 1883, however, experiments toward that end had reached a successful conclusion, and a true belleek body was introduced. It came to be regarded as the finest china ever produced by an American firm. The ware was decorated by various means such as hand painting, transfer printing, gilding, and lustre glazing. The company closed in 1893, one of many that failed during that depression. In the listings below, the ware is belleek unless noted otherwise. Our advisor for this category is Mary Frank Gaston; she is listed in the Directory under Texas.

Basket, crisscross indents, gold leaves, twig hdl, mk, 4" 475.00
Bowl, Cactus, gold thistles inside & out, mk, 3¼x10½".............900.00
Bowl, dessert; bl int, shell ft, rare, 2x4"......................................195.00
Cake plate, Tridacna, gold decor, rare, 9½".................................300.00
Chocolate pot, floral, bl on wht, ca 1866 mk 185.00

Cup & saucer, gold paste flowers, 2½", 5½" dia............................220.00
Cup & saucer, Tridacna, lavender luster int, gold rim 95.00
Ewer, gold stylized leaves, cactus hdl, 8½"................................ 1,000.00
Humidor, wht w/brn staves, gold hdl, Tiffany & Co/mk..............500.00
Pitcher, cherries, 6" 125.00
Pitcher, irises etc, bamboo spout/neck, cactus hdl, 8" 1,200.00
Pitcher, mc morning-glories, gold leaves, mk, 6¼x10½" 1,800.00
Pitcher, Tridacna, wht w/gold, mauve lustre int, mk, 1¾" 75.00
Plate, flowers, pk & gold paste, ruffled, 9" 190.00
Ram's horn, wht lustre, red mk... 1,800.00
Shell dish, purple lustre int, ftd, 2½x5¼" 220.00
Teapot, Tridacna, yel w/gold, wht loop hdl, mk, 4" 300.00
Tray, gold paste orchid, sq, ruffled rim, 8¼" 395.00
Tray, pin; bl/wht florals, gr/brn leaves, ruffled, 4¼" 145.00
Vase, leaves & butterfly, gold paste on matt, hdls, 5½"................550.00

Overbeck

The Overbeck Studio was established in 1911 in Cambridge City, Indiana, by four Overbeck sisters. It survived until the last sister died in 1955. Early wares were often decorated with carved designs of stylized animals, birds, or florals with the designs colored to contrast with the background. Others had tooled designs filled in with various colors for a mosaic effect. After 1937, Mary Frances, the last remaining sister, favored handmade figurines with somewhat bizarre features in fanciful combinations of color. Overbeck ware is signed 'OBK.' Large vases from 8" to 12" usually command prices from $1,000 to $3,000 on today's market. Our advisor for this category is Wayne Kielsmeier; he is listed in the Directory under Arizona.

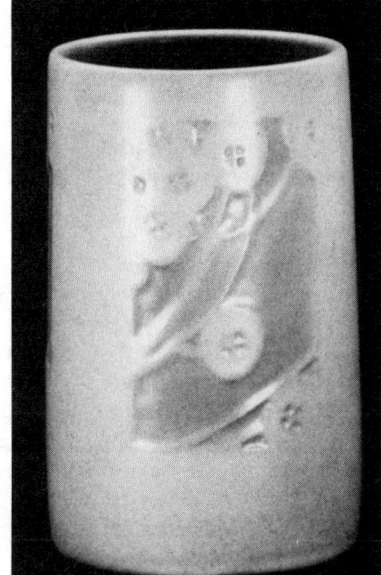

Vase, stylized floral panels, green on beige, signed EF, 9", $1,000.00.

Figurine, Colonial girl, hoop skirt, mc 310.00
Figurine, elephant, pk...425.00
Figurine, robin w/wings spread, feeding 4 chicks in nest.......... 1,100.00
Vase, bl semi-gloss speckle, sgn, 4"...175.00
Vase, floral, gr on tan, sgn EF, 9" 1,050.00
Vase, pine cones cvd in panels, pk-brn ground, sgn EF, 4¾" .. 1,075.00

Overshot

Overshot glass is characterized by the beaded or craggy appear-

ance of its surface. Earlier ware was irregularly textured, while 20th-century examples tend to be more uniform. Our advisor for this category is Mike Roscoe; he is listed in the Directory under Michigan.

Basket, royal bl star-shape rim, crystal bowl/hdl, 4" dia 135.00
Bowl, bl, ruffled, ornate brass holder, 6⅝x8⅝" 195.00
Bowl, cranberry to crystal, tricornered w/rolled edge, 10" 175.00
Bowl, rubena, on figured wht metal ped ft, 6⅜x8½".....................165.00
Custard cup, rose, Sandwich, set of 8 ....150.00
Decanter, cranberry, w/ice bladder, bubble stopper, 11¾"...........325.00
Jam jar, cranberry, appl gr & gold snake, w/underplate................125.00
Pitcher, cranberry, clear reeded hdl, wafer ft, early, 9" 245.00
Pitcher, cranberry, emb swirls, clear reeded hdl, 9x5⅛" 195.00
Pitcher, tankard, cranberry, reeded hdl, hinged metal lid, 9" 185.00
Vase, cranberry, appl pk flower, ruffled top, 11x3½" 295.00

Owen, Ben

Ben Owen worked at the Jugtown Pottery of North Carolina (see Jugtown) in 1959; he continued in the business in his own pottery until 1972. His ware was stamped 'Ben Owen, Master Potter.'

Vase, blk-flecked gr gloss, high shoulder w/4 loop hdls, 5"..........250.00
Vase, Chinese bl curdled w/wht, 7"...210.00

Owens Pottery

J.B. Owens founded his company in Zanesville, Ohio, in 1891, and until 1907, when the company decided to exert most of its energies in the area of tile production, made several quality lines of art pottery. His first line, Utopian, was a standard brown ware with underglaze slip decoration of nature studies, animals, and portraits. A similar line, Lotus, utilized lighter background colors. Henri Deux, introduced in 1900, featured incised Art Nouveau forms inlaid with color. (Be aware that the Brush McCoy Pottery acquired many of Owens' molds and reproduced a line similar to Henri Deux, which they called Navarre.) Other important lines were Opalesce, Rustic, Feroza, Cyrano, and Mission, examples of which are rare today.

The factory burned in 1928, and the company closed shortly thereafter. Values vary according to the quality of the artwork and subject matter. Examples signed by the artist bring higher prices than those that are not signed.

Vase, leaves on Aurelian-type background, marked Sunburst, signed HH, 13½", $400.00.

Aborigine, vase, 5" 225.00
Aqua Verdi, vase, incised decor, 5".......................295.00
Art Nouveau, jardiniere, 7"...................................295.00
Henri Deux, vase, lady's profile, #1307 shape, mk, 8" 350.00
Lotus, vase, floral, wht on pk shaded, 10½" 295.00
Lotus, vase, gr to ivory shaded, 11¼" 400.00
Matt Utopian, umbrella stand, florals on brn, Pillsbury, 20"........650.00
Matt Utopian, vase, floral, sgn ST, cylinder w/sm neck, 15"........495.00
Matt Utopian, vase, grapes, artist sgn, long slim neck, 18" 850.00
Utopian, floral, sgn Ferrell, cylindrical, #1178, 13", EX 250.00
Utopian, pitcher, silver o/l, clover, sgn Bell, 4½".................... 1,500.00
Utopian, vase, mushrooms, 2 lg hdls, 5x7¾" 250.00
Utopian, vase, pansies, artist initialed, 3-ftd, 3½" 125.00
Utopian, vase, silver o/l w/ornate florals, 5" 1,650.00

Pacific Clay Products

The Pacific Clay Products Company got its start in the 1920s as a consolidation of several smaller southern California potteries. The main Los Angeles plant had been founded in 1890 to make kitchen stoneware, ollas, and similar items. Terra cotta and brick were later produced.

In 1932 Hostess Ware, a vividly-colored line of dinnerware, was introduced to compete with Bauer's Ring Ware. Coralitos, a lighter-weight, pastel-hued dinnerware line was first marketed in 1937, and a similar but less expensive line called Arcadia soon followed. Art ware including vases, figurines, candlesticks, etc. was produced from 1932 to 1942, at which time the company went into war-related work and pottery manufacture ceased. A limited amount of hand-decorated dinnerware was also made. For further information we recommend *The Collector's Encyclopedia of California Pottery* by our advisor, Jack Chipman; he is listed in the Directory under California.

Bean pot, no rings, 1-hdl, 6¼" 30.00
Carafe, Ring-style, w/lid 27.50
Casserole, Ring-style, w/lid, sm 20.00
Chop plate, Ring-style, 12" 30.00
Coaster, Ring-style, 4" 7.50
Coffee cup, Ring-style, lg......................................15.00
Coffee cup & saucer, AD; Ring-style 30.00
Cup & saucer, demitasse; Ring-style 12.50
Figurine, nude holds feather, 15½".........................55.00
Figurine, pan, seated/playing pipes, very rare...............250.00
Gravy bowl, Ring-style, hdl....................................22.00
Pitcher, ice lip, tilt-type jug....................................35.00
Pitcher, syrup; Ring-style 32.50
Plate, dinner; Ring-style, 11"..................................10.00
Plate, luncheon; Ring-style, 9" 9.00
Plate, salad; Ring-style, 7½" 8.00
Relish tray, Ring-style, 4-part, wood hdl 40.00
Shakers, Ring-style, dk bl, pr.................................10.00
Teapot, Ring-style, ftd, lg 75.00
Teapot, Ring-style, low, sm 45.00
Tray, Ring-style, 15" dia 45.00
Tumbler, Plain, orange, bulbous.............................15.00
Tumbler, Ring-style..15.00
Vase, cobalt, 9⅝"...35.00
Vase, gr, #417, 4" 15.00
Vase, gr, slender, 8" 35.00
Vase, turq, 4"...15.00

Paden City

The Paden City Glass Company began operations in 1916 in Paden City, West Virginia. The company's early lines consisted largely of the usual pressed tablewares, but by the 1920s production had expanded to include colored wares in translucent as well as opaque glass in a variety of patterns and styles. The company maintained its high standards of handmade perfection until 1949, when under new management much of the work formerly done by hand was replaced by automation. The Paden City Glass Company closed in 1951; its earlier wares, the colored patterns in particular, are becoming very collectible.

Paden City Glass is not always easily recognized by collectors or dealers, as it was almost never marked. It is believed this was so the glass could be sold to decorating companies. The company assigned both line numbers and names to many of its blanks or sets of glassware. Colors were sometimes given more than one name, and etchings were named as well. All this makes identification of items offered for sale through mail order difficult, and labels prepared by dealers are often confusing.

A review of literature available on Paden City reveals the following names for the company's plate etchings: Ardith; California Poppy; Cupid; Delilah Bird (Peacock Reverse); Frost; Gazebo; Gothic Garden; Lela Bird; Nora Bird; Orchid (three variations); Peacock and Rose (Peacock and Wild Rose); Samarkand; Trumpet Flower; Utopia. Names given to cuttings made on Paden City blanks are Yorktown and Lazy Daisy. It is not clear whether the names originated with Paden City or with secondary decorating companies.

Our advisors for this category are George and Mary Hurney; they are listed in the Directory under Illinois. For further information concerning Paden City animals, we recommend *Glass Animals and Figural Flower Frogs from the Depression Era* by Lee Garmon and Dick Spencer; they are listed under Illinois as well.

This list gives company line numbers with corresponding line names:

#69, #69½ — Georgian
#191 — Party
#210 — Regina
#220 — Largo
#221 — Maya
#411 — Mrs B
#412 — Crow's Foot Square
#890 — Crow's Foot Round
#895 — Lucy
#991 — Penny
#994 — Popeye and Olive

And, finally, a listing of colors with alternate names or descriptive phrases:

Amber — (dull)	Mulberry — amethyst
Cheriglo — (delicate) pink	Opal — opaque white
Cobalt Blue — Royal Blue	Primrose (amber with reddish tint)
Crystal — (clear, no tint)	Red — Ruby
Dark Green — (forest green)	Rose — (dark pink)
Dark Amber — (honey color)	Yellow — (pale, soft)
Light Blue — Copen, Neptune	

Animals and Birds

American eagle head, bookends, 7½", pr 250.00
Bunny, cotton-ball dispenser, ears bk, bl frosted 90.00
Bunny, cotton-ball dispenser, ears bk, crystal frosted 60.00
Bunny, cotton-ball dispenser, ears bk, milk glass 95.00
Bunny, cotton-ball dispenser, ears bk, pk frosted 70.00
Bunny, cotton-ball dispenser, ears up, pk frosted 150.00
Goose, bl, 5" 100.00
Pheasant, head turned, 12" L 90.00
Pheasant (Chinese), 13¾"......................................85.00
Pony, 12"..90.00
Pouter pigeon, bookends, 6½", ea............................75.00

Rooster, frosted 65.00
Rooster, head down, 8¾" 75.00
Rooster (Barn Yard), 8¾" 80.00
Rooster (Chanticleer), crystal, 9¼" 85.00
Rooster (Elegant), bl, 11" 175.00
Squirrel on curved log, 5¾" 65.00
Swan (Dragon), 9¾" L 125.00

Bowl, Blk Forest, crystal, 3-ftd...............................60.00
Bowl, console; Cupid, pk or gr, 11" 95.00
Bowl, Crow's Foot, red, ftd, 12" 55.00
Bowl, fruit; Peacock & Wild Rose, color, oval, ftd, 8½" 75.00
Bowl, Gothic Garden, yel, sq...................................38.00
Bowl, Orchid, red or bl, hdls, 8½" 75.00
Bowl, Peacock & Wild Rose, color, ftd, 10½" 80.00
Bowl, Peacock Reverse, color, sq, hdls, 8¾"..............75.00
Cake plate, Ardith, yel w/cherry etch, ftd, 11½" 60.00
Candle holder, Cupid, pk, pr................................125.00
Candlestick, #300 Line, amber, rolled top, 5", pr 14.00
Candlestick, Blk Forest, crystal, 2-lite, pr 50.00
Candlesticks, Orchid, red or bl, 5¾", pr..................100.00
Candy dish, Cupid, gr, ftd, w/lid, 4¾" 150.00
Candy dish, Nora Bird, pk or gr, 3-part, w/lid, 6½" 85.00
Compote, Ardith, yel w/cherry etch, high std............55.00
Compote, Crow's Foot, red 25.00
Compote, Cupid, pk or gr, 6¼" 65.00
Compote, Peacock Reverse, pk, 6" 35.00
Cream soup, Crow's Foot, amber.............................10.00
Creamer, Mrs B, amber 5.50
Creamer, Orchid, yel or gr......................................25.00
Cup, Peacock Reverse, color 65.00
Cup & saucer, Blk Forest, gr, 3 styles, ea..................75.00
Cup & saucer, Crow's Foot, amber 9.50
Cup & saucer, Crow's Foot, red...............................15.00
Cup & saucer, Lucy, red 20.00
Cup & saucer, Penny Line, ruby...............................10.00
Cup & saucer, Wotta Line, red.................................20.00
Goblet, Penny Line, gr..12.00
Goblet, Penny Line, ruby, 6"...................................20.00
Goblet, wine; Futura, red, 3-oz 9.00
Ice bucket, Orchid, red or bl, 6" 100.00
Ice bucket, Peacock & Wild Rose, color, 6" 110.00
Ice tub, Cupid, pk or gr, 4¾" 135.00
Ice tub, Party Line, pk...22.00
Mayonnaise, Nora Bird, pk or gr, w/liner 75.00
Plate, cheese & cracker; SS Dreamship, bl, w/lid, 12 ......60.00
Plate, Crow's Foot, amber, 9" 10.00
Plate, Crow's Foot, red, sq, 6" 3.50
Plate, Cupid, pk or gr, 10½" 75.00
Plate, luncheon; Blk Forest, blk, 8" 25.00
Plate, luncheon; Peacock Reverse, color, 8½" 35.00
Plate, Nora Bird, pk or gr, 8" 20.00
Plate, Popeye & Olive, red, 8" 12.00
Plate, Wotta Line, 9½" 8.00
Relish, Peacock & Wild Rose, color, 3-part................50.00
Server, Blk Forest, amber, center hdl 50.00
Server, Mrs B, amber, center hdl.............................18.00
Server, Orchid, red or bl, center hdl 65.00
Server, Peacock & Wild Rose, color, center hdl, 10½" 70.00
Shakers, Party Line, amber, pr..................................9.00
Shakers, Party Line, ruby, pr...................................45.00
Sherbet, Peacock Reverse, color, 4⅞" 40.00

Sherbet, Popeye & Olive, red, 3¼" 12.00
Soup, Crow's Foot, red, hdls...................................19.00
Sugar bowl, Blk Forest, red, 2 styles 50.00
Sugar bowl, Crow's Foot, red 12.50
Sugar bowl, Cupid, pk, 4" 75.00
Sugar bowl, Nora Bird, pk or gr, 4½"........................37.50
Sugar bowl, Orchid, yel or gr 25.00
Tumbler, Blk Forest, flat, 5-oz 25.00
Tumbler, Nora Bird, pk or gr, ftd, 4¾" 50.00
Vase, Blk Forest, cobalt, 6½"..................................100.00
Vase, Cupid, pk or gr, elliptical, 8¼" 250.00
Vase, Lela Bird, gr, 12" 100.00
Vase, Orchid, red or bl, 10" 95.00
Vase, Peacock Reverse, color, 10" 85.00
Vase, Popeye & Olive, red, ruffled, 7" 40.00
Vase, Utopia, blk, 10½"..175.00

Paintings on Ivory

Miniature works of art executed on ivory from the 1800s are assessed by the finesse of the artist, as is any fine painting. Signed examples and portraits with an identifiable subject are usually preferred.

Lady, elaborate hairdo/veil, 1780s, 2⅜" dia 350.00
Lady, fleur-de-lis mk, gilt Florentine fr, 8½x7" 195.00
Lady, sgn Weiss, in gold case, 4½x3½" 100.00
Lady, sgn/inscribed Geo Hete, 1850, orig case, 6x5" 275.00
Lady draped in wht, w/an oil lamp, label, 7x6", 16x14" fr 325.00
Lady w/plumed hat, sgn Thumerelle, tintype liner fr, 4x3" 125.00
Madonna & Child, gilt Florentine fr, 7x6" 250.00
Marie Antoinette (& Josephine), sgn, eng ivory fr, 5½x5", pr.....260.00

Napoleon Bonaparte, gilt-metal mat in ebonized wooden frame, signed Bernard, 5", $1,400.00.

Mother & child dressed in Empire style, sgn Savy, 5½" 500.00
Orpheus, after Geo de Forest Bush, 1880s, 3¾x6" 325.00
Taj Mahal, Indian cvd fr w/easel bk, 5x4½" 100.00
Young girl w/bl sash, emb brass fr, 2½x1¾" 225.00
Young man, eng brass case w/lock of hair, 2⅝x2¼" 520.00
Young man, rectangular gold-colored case, 2¾x2¼" 250.00

Pairpoint

The Pairpoint Manufacturing Company was built in 1880 in New

Bedford, Massachusetts. It was primarily a metalworks whose chief product was coffin fittings. Next door, the Mt. Washington Glassworks made quality glasswares of many varieties. (See Mt. Washington for more information concerning their artware lines.) By 1894 it became apparent to both companies that a merger would be to their best interest.

From the late 1890s until the 1930s, lamps and lamp accessories were an important part of Pairpoint's production. There were three main types of shades, all of which were blown: puffy — blown-out reverse-painted shades (usually floral designs); ribbed — also reverse painted; and scenic — reverse painted with scenes of land or seascapes (usually executed on smooth surfaces, although ribbed scenics may be found occasionally). Cut glass lamps and those with metal overlay panels were also made. Scenic shades were sometimes artist signed; and, although many are unmarked, some are stamped 'Pairpoint Corp.' Blown-out shades may be marked 'Pat July 9, 1907.' Bases were made from bronze, copper, brass, silver, or wood and are always signed.

Because they produced only fancy, handmade artware, the company's sales lagged seriously during the Depression; and, as time and tastes changed, their style of product was less in demand. As a result, they never fully recovered; consequently part of the buildings and equipment was sold in 1938. The company reorganized in 1939 under the direction of Robert Gunderson and again specialized in quality hand-blown glassware. Isaac Babbit regained possession of the silver departments, and together they established Gunderson Glassworks, Inc. After WWII, because of a sharp decline in sales, it again became necessary to reorganize. The Gunderson-Pairpoint Glassworks was formed, and the old line of cut, engraved artware was reintroduced. The company moved to East Wareham, Massachusetts, in 1957. But business continued to suffer, and the firm closed only one year later. In 1970, however, new facilities were constructed in Sagamore under the direction of Robert Bryden, sales manager for the company since the 1950s.

In 1974 the company began to produce lead glass cup plates which were made on commission as fund raisers for various churches and organizations. These are signed with a 'P' in diamond and are becoming quite collectible. Our advisor for Pairpoint lamps is Daniel Batchelor; he is listed in the Directory under New York. See also Napkin Rings.

Key: pwt — paperweight

Glass

Bowl, cobalt, ftd, 4½x10½" 75.00
Bowl, med gr, eng vintage, 2x15" 225.00

Console set in canaria (vaseline), 21" candlesticks wired for electricity, $375.00.

Box, Delft, mc florals/sailboat/etc, att Guba, 7½" L 565.00
Compote, amber, eng vintage 150.00
Flip vase, lt amethyst, eng vintage, lt ribbing, 10" 150.00

Hudidor, mums, gold on apricot satin, metal mts, mk, 7" 400.00
Shaker, red w/blk ft, metal lid, Gunderson, 10", EX, +6 martinis...275.00
Swan, ruby w/clear head & neck, 12x13" 450.00
Vase, amber, clear knop & stem, 11½", pr...................................115.00
Vase, amethyst, etched floral, horn-of-plenty shape, 11" 200.00
Vase, bud; clear body on bl swirl bubble-ball base, 9"...................75.00
Vase, floral, bl/gold on opal cylinder; SP cherub std, 15" 330.00
Vase, ruby, trumpet form on clear bubble-ball base, 13", pr.........300.00

Lamps

Puffy boudoir lamp with pansies, roses, and asters against latticework, signed, 14½" x 9½" diameter, $2,800.00.

Boudoir, puffy 8" shade w/4 flower groups; #3047½ std 2,750.00
Puffy 12" Orange Tree/butterfly shade; tree std, 25" 27,500.00
Puffy 12½" azalea bouquet shade; 3-leg std #3060, 22" 16,500.00
Puffy 14" butterfly/roses shade; sgn petal-mold std, 21" 5,200.00
Puffy 14" Devonshire floral shade; sgn 21" slim std................. 5,500.00
Puffy 14" Stratford floral shade; lion heads on std................... 7,000.00
Puffy 16" Devonshire roses/hummingbird shade; #3088 std, EX.. 9,900.00
Puffy 8" Caprilon floral shade; 4-paw-ftd std 4,000.00
Puffy 9" floral/stylized tree shade (NM); sgn std 1,950.00
Puffy 9" roses/butterflies sqd shade; twist std 3,000.00
Puffy 9" Stratford dogwood-border shade; #3064 std, 14" 5,000.00
Puffy 9" Stratford shade w/mum clusters; #3056 std................. 3,300.00
Rvpt 12" Directorie trees shade sgn Gorham; glass-ball std 1,850.00
Rvpt 14" Florence 8-section shade; sgn #3086 base, 20".......... 2,500.00
Rvpt 15" ocean w/ship & dolphin shade sgn Ona M, EX; 20". 2,000.00
Rvpt 16" Directorie blk/mc floral shade; 3-arm std, 27"........... 4,400.00
Rvpt 18" Carlisle shade, exotic flowers/parrots; #3070 std....... 6,500.00
Rvpt 18" Exeter exotic birds/trees shade; #3070 SP std 6,000.00
Rvpt 18" Exeter stylized floral shade (NM); sgn urn std 1,800.00
Rvpt/emb reeding 14" Malta shade w/lg tulips; trumpet std 7,150.00

Pairpoint Limoges

Limoges china blanks were imported from France in strict accordance with Pairpoint specifications. They were decorated by Pairpoint in designs that ranged from simple to elaborate florals and scenics. These are easily identified. Look for the Pairpoint name over a crown with the Limoges name below. You may also find similar ware marked 'Pairpoint Minton.'

Bowl, mums, gold on eggshell, fish finial, hdls/lid, 8" W 535.00

Gravy boat, Dresden, mc flowers on wht, w/undertray **175.00**
Platter, poppies w/gold, scalloped/rtcl rim, sgn/#d, 14x10" **225.00**
Tureen, mums foliage, fish finial, 8x6½x6" **500.00**
Vase, barefoot maid dances on Oriental rug, hdls, 15" **1,375.00**
Vase, gladiolus, cherub w/peonies, w/gilt, cobalt hdls, 15" **1,325.00**
Vase, mums, 8¼" **350.00**

Paper Dolls

No one knows quite how or when paper dolls originated. One belief is that they began in Europe as 'pantins' (jumping jacks) and were frequently worn as part of the costume. By the late 1790s, they were being mass-produced. During the 19th century, most paper dolls portrayed famous dancers and opera stars such as Fanny Elssler and Jenny Lind. In the late 1800s, the Raphael Tuck Publishers of England produced many series of beautiful paper dolls; retail companies used them as advertisements to further the sale of their products. Around the turn of the century, many popular women's magazines began featuring a page of paper dolls.

Most familiar to today's collectors are the books with dolls on cardboard covers and clothes on the inside pages. These made their appearance in the late 1920s and early thirties. The most collectible (and the most valuable) are those representing celebrities, movie stars, and comic-strip characters of the thirties and forties.

Authority Mary Young has compiled an informative book, *Collector's Guide to Paper Dolls*, with current prices; you will find her address in the Directory under Ohio. When no condition is indicated, the dolls listed below are assumed to be in mint, uncut, original condition. Cut sets will be worth about half price if all dolls and outfits are included and pieces are in very good condition. If dolls were produced in die-cut form, these prices reflect such a set in mint condition with all costumes and accessories.

Little Henry paper dolls, in original envelope with six outfits, S.& F. Fuller, London, 1810, EX, $550.00.

Ann & Joe, MA Donohue & Co, #80C, EX **20.00**
Ann Sothern, cut, w/folder, EX **30.00**
Baby Secret, Mattel, uncut **20.00**
Ballet Dancers, Merrill, 1947, M **30.00**
Barbara Britton, Saalfield #1596, uncut, 1954, NM **65.00**
Bedknobs & Broomsticks, uncut, M **25.00**
Bette Davis, Merrill #4816, 1942, NM **35.00**

Betty & Dick Tour the USA, Standard Toykraft, 1940, NM **22.00**
Betty Grable, cut, 3 dolls+clothes, Merrill #1558, 1951, EX **45.00**
Birthday Party Cutouts, Whitman #2084, uncut, 1961, M **20.00**
Blondie, Whitman, #993, family figures+dogs, 1945, uncut, EX **88.00**
Carol Lynley, Whitman uncut, 1950, NM **22.50**
Chatty Cathy, Whitman #1961, c Mattel, uncut, 1964, NM ...."**25.00**
Claudette Colbert, Saalfield #322, uncut, 1943, EX **125.00**
Deanna Durbin, Merrill #3480, cut clothes, 1940, EX **30.00**
Debby Reynolds, Whitman, partially cut, complete, 1950, EX **45.00**
Dennis the Menace, Whitman #1991, uncut, 1960, M **35.00**
Dollies To Dress Like Father & Mother, Platt & Munk #225, EX ...**22.50**
Dolly Dingle Gives a Thanksgiving Dinner, uncut, EX **27.50**
Dolly Dingle Welcome Home Party, uncut, NM **28.00**
Doris Day, Whitman #1952, 1955, NM **30.00**
Dorothy, Playtime House #313, NM in VG box **8.00**
Dotty & Danny on Parade, Burton #875, 1935, EX **25.00**
Elizabeth Taylor, Whitman, 6 uncut pgs, 1957, NM **60.00**
Elly May of Beverly Hillbillies, uncut, M **35.00**
First Family (Reagans), Dell #52644, 1981, M **8.00**
First Ladies of Wht House, Saalfield #2164, uncut, 1937, M **55.00**
Gone w/the Wind, Merrill #3404, 14 figures w/clothes, 1940......**175.00**
Gulliver's Travels, uncut, 1939, NM **35.00**
Hedy Lamarr, Merrill #3482, 2 dolls+10 outfits, VG **40.00**
Hello I'm Adeline, Animated Book Co, 1944, EX **18.00**
Jackie & Caroline Wonderful Paper Dolls, Magic/Wand, 1960s....**65.00**
Jane Fonda, Saalfield #1369, 1965, M **30.00**
Janet Lennon, uncut, M...**30.00**
Jeanette MacDonald, Merrill #3460, 1941, EX **45.00**
Joan's Wedding, Whitman #990, 1942, EX **8.00**
Joanne Woodward, cut, w/orig folder, EX **40.00**
Judy Garland, Whitman #999, complete, 1940, EX **50.00**
Lana Turner, Whitman #964, 2 cut/6 uncut pgs, EX **48.00**
Lana Turner, Whitman #988, 2 dolls+32 outfits, 1942, EX **50.00**
Let's Play Paper Dolls, McLoughlin, 1938, EX...........................**22.00**
Little Darling Dressing Dolls, Am Colortype, 6 dolls, EX **42.50**
Little Women, Lowe, #L-1030, 4 figures+clothes, 1941, EX..........**45.00**
Lucille Ball, Saalfield, 1945, M **40.00**
Magic Doll, Parker Bros, ca 1948, EX **12.00**
Magic Marry, Milton Bradley #4132-B, 1948, EX in box **10.00**
Mary Frances Housekeeper, JC Winston, ca 1914, EX **135.00**
Mary Poppins Magic..., stay-on clothes, 62-pc, unused, M **45.00**
Military Wedding, Samuel Lowe #L-529, 1943, EX **65.00**
My Dolly Sister Nan, Sam Gabriel Sons #D-90, EX **27.50**
Natalie Wood, Whitman #2086, uncut, 1958, NM **55.00**
Patty's Party, Stephen's Publishing #175, NM **10.00**
Rhonda Fleming, Saalfield, 1954, M **50.00**
Ricky Nelson, Whitman #2081, uncut, 1959, M........................**125.00**
Rita Hayworth, Saalfield #2712, 1948, NM...............................**70.00**
Rosemary Clooney, cut, w/orig folder, EX.................................**35.00**
Roy Rogers & Dale Evans, Whitman, 1954, EX **35.00**
Shirley Temple, 2 dolls+clothes, Saalfield #1787, 1940, EX **35.00**
Shirley Temple Magnetic Doll, Gabriel #303, NM **32.00**
Storyland Paper Dolls, Saalfield #2798, 6 children, complete **6.00**
Tina the Talking Paper Doll, Colorforms #5550, NM **10.00**
War Girls, Samuel Lowe #l-529, 1943, EX **65.00**

Paperweights

All paperweights listed here are made totally of glass (including the lampwork flowers, fish, birds, snakes, lizards, and millefiori rods). The only elements that are not glass are the clay sulfides encased within some of the Baccarat and St. Louis weights. Today, antique weights (1845 to ca 1870s) and those made by contemporary artists attract the most attention and are the most expensive. Lower-priced 'gift' weights come from American glasshouses and studios, China, Murano, Italy, and Scotland. But because of the expenses involved in their manufacture (fuel, material, and labor), even they are not cheap. There is an international association of paperweight collectors with many state and regional chapters. (For information see Clubs, Newsletters, and Catalogs in the Directory.) Many books are currently available on the subject of paperweights. For the beginner we recommend *All About Paperweights* by L.H. Selmen.

Probably inspired by the work of Pierre Bigaglia (Venice), the French factories of Baccarat, Clichy, and St. Louis turned their attention to paperweight-making in the 1840s. They first made millefiori paperweights, the technique a revival of methods used in Alexandria, Damascus, Rome, and Byzantium before the time of Christ. (This art form had faded out but had been revived in 16th-century Venice.) The French Classic period was 1845 to 1860; English and American (Sandwich and New England) glasshouses followed their lead about ten years later. Gradually, as the paperweight's popularity declined, production began to wane; Clichy closed in the 1880s. Baccarat made weights as late as 1910; in the '20s and '30s, a worker by the name of Dupont revived the art. Then in the 1950s St. Louis and Baccarat sparked a renewal of interest in weight-making that is still going strong today. Some of the most desirable weights from American artists were made by the Banfords, Randall Grubb, Rick Ayotte, Chris Buzzini, Ken Rosenfeld, Gordon Smith, Paul Stankard, Charles Kaziun (d), Del (d) and Debbie Tarsitano, and the Trabuccos. From Scotland, Paul Ysart (d) was also well known.

Note: Prices do not reflect the usual 10% buyer's fee charged by most auction houses. Furthermore, there are many factors which determine value, particularly of antique weights. Auction-realized prices of contemporary weights are usually other than issue price; 'list price' may be for weights issued earlier and reduced for clearance or influenced by market demand and other factors. The dimension given at the end of the description is diameter.

Key:
A — antique	latt — latticinio
cl — clear	mill — millefiori
con — concentric	o/l — overlay
fct — faceted	pm — pastry mold
gar — garland	pwt — paperweight
grd — ground	sil — silhouette
jsp — jasper	

Ayotte, Rick

Cabbage Rose, 3¾"	600.00
Cedar waxwings on fall foliage, 3¾"	800.00
Christmas 1991, wht & red flowers, 3¾"	600.00
Ducks on pond, 3¾"	1,450.00
Pond Life, frog w/tadpoles under water, 4"	1,200.00
Poppy bouquet w/bl & wht flowers, 3¾"	850.00

Baccarat, Antique

Antique Baccarat double clematis weight, 3⅛", $1,700.00.

Ben Franklin, sulfide, 2½"	1,200.00
Close mill, horse/rooster/monkey/devil sils, 1847 cane, 2½"	1,650.00
Close mill, rooster/horse/dog/hen/shamrock sils, 1848, 2⅜"	1,600.00
Close mill, tightly packed, mc canes, 2⅞"	800.00
Close mill w/in torsade of wht bl-threaded cable, 3"	1,650.00
Dbl 10-petal red-striped star-center clematis w/bud, 3"	1,700.00
Garlanded butterfly w/marbled wings, star base, 2⅝"	3,000.00
Lg pompon w/cane center w/in cane gar, star base, 3"	1,700.00
Peach pompon w/yel & wht stardust cane center, 1¾", EX	1,100.00
Primrose, 6 bl-edged wht petals+11 leaves, star base, 3¼"	2,000.00
Queen Victoria, sulfide (cracks), Victoria Reine..., 3¼"	425.00
6-petal bl/wht primrose w/star center, fct, star base, 3¼"	1,500.00

Baccarat, Modern

Abe Lincoln, dbl o/l sulfide, fct, sgn GP/1953, 3"	400.00
Close pack mill, Zodiac sils, 1971, 3"	450.00
Frog/wht flower on dk gr pebbly grd, sgn/1974, 2⅞"	450.00
Gridel rooster sil cane+row of all 18 in series, 1971, 3½"	400.00
Mt Rushmore, dbl o/l sulfide, Jean Goy, fcts, 1976, 4" L	400.00
Pattern mill, dbl o/l, top fct+7, 18-fct base, 1970, 3", NM	475.00
Pattern mill, lg ring w/in 5 sm, muslin grd, 1973, 3¼"	400.00
Pope Pius XII, sulfide, dmn base, sgn David/1959, 2¾"	100.00
Queen Elizabeth II, sulfide, outer cane gar, fct, 1977, 3¼"	275.00
Robert E Lee, dbl o/l sulfide, top fct+10, sgn/1955, 3"	300.00
Salamander on pebbly yel+3 silvery rocks, 1973 cane, 3¼"	550.00
12-petal pk dahlia/leaves on teal grd, 1971 cane, 3"	350.00
3 strawberries/blossom on dk bl grd, 1974 cane, 2¾"	400.00

Banford, Bobby

Compound buckeyes, 3¼"	600.00
Violet bouquet w/star-cut base	450.00
Yel flower w/purple buds, 3" dia	450.00

Banford, Bob

Bl morning-glories on wht trellis, pk grd, 3¼"	750.00
Purple/yel pansy, buds/leaves, wht base, columnar fcts, sgn, 2¾"	600.00
Triple pansy bouquet, 3"	800.00

Banford, Ray

Iris/roses in cut-out basket, dmn-cut base, cane sgn, 3"	1,000.00
Roses in basket cut as wicker, dbl o/l, cane sgn, 3¼"	1,200.00
Triple rose bouquet on bl grd, 3"	800.00

Buzzini, Chris

Desert, 3 orange blossoms & rocks on sandy grd, ltd ed 25, 3"	675.00
Fct bouquet w/apple blossoms, heather, etc, ltd ed 25, 3¼"	950.00
Pk & wht crown vetch, ltd ed 40, 3"	475.00
Purple asters (2) & yel China rose, ltd ed 40, 3"	550.00

Clichy, Antique

Barber pole chequer, 18 canes/latt twists/filigree rods, 2⅝"	2,600.00
Con mill, complex 8-point star cane, in stave basket, 3"	1,750.00
Con mill, rose center+6 more, cane gar, 3¾", NM	700.00
Con mill, 4 rows in bl/wht stave basket, 2¼"	1,400.00
Con mill cane gar w/florets on turq, 2½"	675.00
Macedoine, whole/scrambled mc mill canes+pk/gr rose, 2¾"	800.00
Pattern mill, rose+5 sm rings ea w/complex cane, fct, 2¾"	800.00
Pattern mill, 5 rings around pastry mold on lt bl grd, 3"	950.00
Pinwheel, 44 amethyst rods/wht latt tubes+turq floret, 3"	1,300.00

Scattered mill, central pk rose, 3" 800.00
Spaced con mill, 3 rings about star cane cluster w/rose, 3" 1,100.00
Swirl, 30 pk/wht threads around lg pastry mold, lt wear, 2¼".. 1,150.00
6 cane loops swirl about pastry mold cane, apple gr grd, 3" 1,100.00

Grubb, Randy

Branch of wht plum blossoms, 3" 425.00
Cluster of purple grapes, 3" dia 250.00
Compound triple clusters of gr grapes, 3" 375.00
Rose over wht dbl o/l enhances mauve plum blossoms, 3" 800.00

Kaziun, Charles

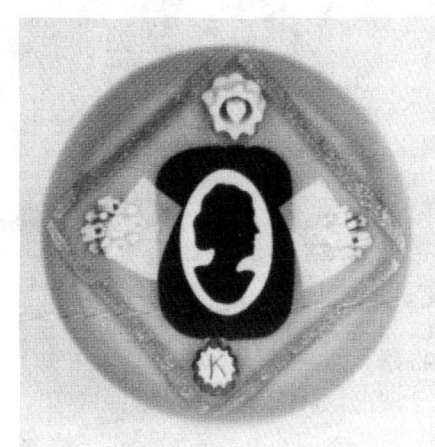

Charles Kaziun silhou-
ette weight, black and
white with millefiori,
1¼" x 2", $950.00.

Bottle, 6-petal yel spider lily w/red & yel stamen, fct, 3¼" 900.00
Pansy set on purple grd, mini, 2⅛" 1,045.00
Perfume bottle w/red crimp rose in base & stopper, 4½" 3,500.00
Pk crimp rose, yel over wht o/l, fct, 2¼" 1,760.00
Pk shaded tulip, upright type w/ped, 3½" 1,100.00
6-petal mauve-to-yel tulip, 4 leaves, K cane, ped ft, 3" 1,000.00

New England Glass

Blown glass pear on cl rnd base, 2⅞" 1,200.00
Close conc mil w/central cane in pastel colors, 2¾" 400.00
Nosegay w/3 complex mil flowers on wht latt grd, 2½" 550.00
5 pears & 4 cherries on wht latt grd, 2½" 650.00

Perthshire

Carpet grd w/central bl flower, 1983, 3" 300.00
Giant panda in hollow fct translucent bl o/l, ltd ed 300, 3" 645.00
Mill heart on red grd w/2 rows of spaced mill, 2⅞" 175.00
Pattern mill w/center cane, ribbon twist & gar of canes, 3" 95.00
Sea horse+2 fish/pk seaweed, crab/shell, fct, P 1981, 3½" 300.00
2-layer cushion w/central rooster sil, 1977, 3" 375.00
5-flower bouquet, wht cushion grd, blk cut o/l, P cane, 3" 400.00
86-petal dahlia, top fct+4, sgn P 1972 in canes, 3⅛" 600.00

Rosenfeld, Ken

Fall bouquet on orange grd, 3½" 600.00
Yel corn & red chiles, 3" 400.00
Yel daffodils/lilacs/wild rose spring bouquet, 3" 450.00
3 pumpkins w/stems & leaves, 3" 350.00
6 orange orchids on bl grd, 3" 500.00

Smith, Gordon

Lipstick Tang w/coral, 3" 600.00

Snake w/rocks & flowers & buds on sand grd, 3" 650.00
Triple wht dogwood blossoms, 3" 600.00
3 strawberries, wht blossom, & bud, 3" 650.00

St. Louis, Antique

Crown, twisted red/gr ribbons alternate w/latt, 2⅝" 2,400.00
Dbl 15-petal bl clematis, red/wht jsp grd, 2½" 1,600.00
Dbl 15-petal pk clematis, top fct+2 rows of 6, 3" 1,800.00
Macedoine, many pcs twist filigree on upset muslin, 3" 450.00
Purple+2 red+2 wht turnips in dbl swirl wht latt basket, 2¾" . 1,400.00
2 woods strawberries+5 blossoms, 2⅝" 1,400.00
3 pears+3 apples in wht latt 'bowl,' 3⅛" 1,800.00
4 mill cane flowers w/in cane gar, upset muslin grd, 2¾" 1,800.00
4 mill cane flowers/leaves on dmn-cut amber grd, fct, 2⅝" 900.00
45-petal pk dahlia, bl/amber stamen cane, star base, 2¾" 3,250.00

St. Louis, Modern

Bouquet, red/wht cut o/l, 1977, 3" 550.00
Camomile w/52 bl petals, cane center, latt grd, 1975, 2¾" 400.00
Dbl pk clematis, dbl swirl wht latt grd, cane sgn, '71, 2¾" 300.00
Gen De Gaulle in 1940, fct sulfide, latt base, 1977, 3" 750.00
Handcooler, 8 twist red/bl ribbons+wht latt, SL/1976, 2¾".........300.00
Hourglass, floret+7 rows mill canes, latt body, 1979, 6" 900.00
Marquis de Lafayette, sulfide, cane gar, fct, 1967, 3" 200.00
Penholder, scattered mill 16-cane base on upset muslin, '77........600.00
Plaque, King Edward VIII, sulfide, experimental, 1¾x2" 250.00
Pope John Paul II, sulfide, GP Jean Paul II, fct, '81, 3" 175.00
Upright 3-color bouquet on wht latt mushroom, fct, 1978, 3" 550.00
Yel pear on 'cookie' base, A Bourlard, 1 of 3, '69, 3¾" 600.00

Stankard, Paul

Allium, 2 bl blossoms w/roots on cl, 3" 2,500.00
Bl Bottle Gentians, 9-flower spray, Experimental/S, 3¼" 1,650.00
Field Pansy, 3-flower, on dk bl over wht grd, S/1978, 2¾" 850.00
Full pk rose/2 buds/many leaves, Experimental/S/1979, 3" 1,000.00
Goat's beard, bouquet over purple-pk grd, sgn/1989, 3¼" 1,500.00
Goat's beard, earth spirit in root system, sgn/1989, 3" 2,200.00
Meadowreath, 5-petal yel flower/buds/etc on cl, S cane, 2¾" 800.00
Nature's Splendor bouquet, pk/wht/yel/violet, S/1978, 3¼" 1,800.00
Oriental floral, curved tan floral branch on cl, S/1978, 3" 950.00
St Anthony's Fire, 7 red flowers on lt bl, s/1980, 3¼" 1,500.00
3 5-petal pk wild roses on lt bl grd, S cane/1978, 2¾" 1,200.00

Tarsitano, Debbie

Bee w/in 10-petal pk flower, bl buds, star base, sgn, 3" 750.00
Bl dahlia, star base, 2⅜"...900.00
Flowers in basket, top fct+6, star base, sgn w/cane, 3¼" 750.00
4-flower yel/orange bouquet, sgn, 2¾" 475.00

Tarsitano, Delmo

Earth Life, snake/pebbles/wood on sand grd, cane sgn, 3⅞"..... 1,100.00
Earth Life, spider/flowers on sand grd, cane sgn, 3⅜" 875.00
Honeycomb w/bee & flower, top fct+2 rows of 8, cane sgn, 3¼".850.00
Honeycomb/bee/flower, 3¼".. 1,700.00
Spider/flower/4 lg leaves/web eng by Erlacher, cane sgn, 3½"......850.00
2 peaches on branch, star base, sgn w/cane, 3" 800.00
2-berry sprig w/blooms on cl, sgn w/cane, 2¾"................................550.00

Trabucco, David and Jon

Acorns & berries on branch, frosted surface w/cl leaves, 3½".......450.00

Bouquet of bl/yel/wht blossoms, 3¼" **400.00**
Bouquet of red blossoms, red berries, wht buds, 3" **300.00**
Rose w/bud & foliage, 3" **300.00**

Trabucco, Victor

Lt bl ribbed morning-glory, 3¼" **600.00**
Magnum strawberries w/foliage & stem, 3¼" **950.00**
Orchid w/foliage, cvd/frosted ext w/clear design, magnum **1,200.00**
Red camellia & bud on branch, 3¼" **600.00**

Whitefriars

Whitefriars 1976 faceted patterned millefiori weight with American flag, signed and dated cane, 3⅛", $245.00.

Con mill w/butterfly sil in center, fct, 1977, 3" **350.00**
Inkwell, 6 rings of canes, 5 in stopper, red/wht/bl, 6" **350.00**
Pattern mill, 3 Wisemen in center, 1/5 fct, sgn/1976, 3⅛" **300.00**
Vase, mill weight base, 8" **300.00**

Ysart, Paul

Aventurine dragonfly & 6 complex canes on upset muslin, 2¾" .**675.00**
Dbl pk clematis in wht latt basket, cane sgn, 3" **550.00**
Fish over sandy grd w/shells & rocks, 2¾" **850.00**
Gr aventurine/goldstone fish over rocky grd, cane sgn, 2⅞" **700.00**
Parrot on branch w/leaves on bl jsp grd, 3" **900.00**
2 ducks & pk water lily on pond, 2¾" **825.00**

Miscellaneous

Bacchus, close con mill, 5 rings about red/wht setup, 3" **500.00**
Boston & Sandwich, dbl red clematis, 3" **750.00**
Boston & Sandwich, pk 10-petal poinsettia, 3" **850.00**
Boston & Sandwich, 4 red cherries/5 leaves, 2¾" **950.00**
Erlacher, Max; spread-wing eagle, sgn/#16, 3½" **250.00**
Erlacher, Max; tiger lily eng, sgn/#8, ltd ed, 3½" **300.00**
Hacker, Harold; blk snake on spatter grd, sgn, 2¼" **325.00**
Hacker, Harold; grape gluster on granular wht, sgn, 2¾" **1,750.00**
Pantin, 4 purple Damson plums on pk stems+4 lg leaves, 3" .. **3,600.00**
Whittemore, FD; hummingbird on bluebell stalk, red grd, 2½" ...**350.00**

Papier-Mache

The art of papier-mache was mainly European. It originated in Paris around the middle of the 18th century and became popular in America during Victorian times. Small items such as boxes, trays, inkwells, frames, etc. as well as extensive ceiling moldings and larger articles of furniture were made. The process involved building layer upon layer of paper soaked in glue, then coaxed into shape over a wood or wire form. When dry it was painted or decorated with gilt or inlays. Inexpensive 20th-century 'notions' were machine processed and mold pressed. See also Christmas; Candy Containers.

Tea board, gilt pineapples and acanthus leaves on black, 32", EX, $1,500.00.

Bonnet stand, gessoed, pnt lady's face, early, EX **850.00**
Rabbit, sponged coat, 4" L **95.00**
Shaving stand, gilt decor/MOP inlay, 1850, EX **240.00**
Squeak toy, 2-sided w/comic faces, Germany, 1900, 2½" dia **350.00**

Parian Ware

Parian is hard-paste unglazed porcelain made to resemble marble. First made in the mid-1800s by Staffordshire potters, it was soon after produced in the United States by the U.S. Pottery at Bennington, Vermont. Busts and statuary were favored, but plaques, vases, mugs, and pitchers were also made.

Bust, May Queen, Ceramic/Crystal Palace, 1868, Copeland, 13" ..**110.00**
Bust, Schiller, Germany, 9½" **175.00**
Bust, Wagner, mk Robinson & Leadbeater, 7⅞x2¼x3½" **145.00**
Figurine, seated whippet, mk, 4⅜" **45.00**
Group, nude man embracing draped woman, 19th C, 13½", pr ...**750.00**
Pitcher, allover emb figures, dtd 1842, Jones & Walley, 8" **95.00**
Pitcher, 3 eagles form spouts, WA Father of Co/etc, rpr, 9" **375.00**

Parrish, Maxfield

Maxfield Parrish was a painter and illustrator who began his career in the last decade of the 19th century. His work remained prominent until the early 1940s. His most famous painting, *Daybreak*, was published in print form and sold nearly two thousand copies between 1910 and 1930. All prices are for framed prints except for those from the 1960s.

Ad, Oneida Silver Co, 1918, 11x15" **50.00**
Ad, Peter Piper Picked Pickled Peppers, Ferry Seed, 15x10½" **75.00**
Book, Arabian Nights, 1930, Scribner **125.00**
Book, Dream Days, 1st edition, EX **195.00**
Book, Early Years, sketches **260.00**
Book, Emerald Storybook, 1924, Duffield **75.00**
Book, Golden Age, 1905, Dodd Mead **95.00**
Book, Golden Treasury of Songs & Lyrics, 1926, Duffield...........**150.00**
Book, Knave of Hearts, 1925, spiral bound edition **350.00**

Book, Knave of Hearts, 1925, 1st edition, Scribner......................800.00
Book, Poems of Childhood, 1904, 1st edition, Scribner 95.00
Book, The Golden Age, 1899, 1st edition, John Lane Co 125.00
Calendar, Autumn Afternoon, 1956, complete, 17x10", EX 125.00
Calendar, Cadmus Sowing the Dragon's Teeth, 1923, MIB 130.00
Calendar, Contentment, Edison/Mazda, 1928, complete, fr, lg....550.00
Calendar, Ecstacy, Edison/Mazda, 1930, complete, fr, lg..............625.00
Calendar, Golden Hours, Edison/Mazda, '29, fr, 40x19", NM ...1,250.00
Calendar, Jason & His Teacher, 1953, complete, 15½x9½" 80.00
Calendar, Reveries, Edison/Mazda, 1927, complete, fr, sm 250.00
Calendar, Solitude, Edison/Mazda, 1932, complete, fr, sm..........250.00
Calendar print, Canyon, complete, fr, 12x16",..........................150.00
Calendar print, Early Autumn, Brown/Bigelow, 1939 ....225.00
Calendar print, Golden Hours, Edison Mazda, '29, fr, 15x21" 575.00
Card, greeting; Sheltering Oaks, M.....................................20.00
Card, greeting; Twilight Hour 17.50
Catalog cover, Nash Books, The Prospector, complete 40.00
Catalog cover, Santa Barbara Museum, Flyaway Horse, complete .30.00
Cigar box label, Old King Cole, 6x10", M 67.50
Magazine, Collier's, Pirate w/Sword, June 1909, VG.....................95.00
Magazine, Harper's, Oneida Silver Co ad, Dec 1918, EX 85.00
Magazine, LH Journal, Sweet Nothings, April 1921, complete......80.00
Magazine, Life, A Dark Futurist, March 1923, VG.....................120.00
Magazine, Life, Easter, April 1922, EX 150.00
Magazine cover, Collier's, Jack Frost, fr 135.00
Magazine cover, LH Journal, Bubbles, Sept 1904, complete 55.00
Magazine cover, Life, Good Mixer, Jell-O ad bk, Jan 1924 ....130.00
Menu cover, The Broadmoor Hotel, 21x14½", M.....................270.00
Playing cards, In the Mountains, Brown/Bigelow, M 165.00
Post card, The Broadmoor, 1921, 7x9", M 45.00
Print, Air Castles, 16x12" 185.00
Print, Aladdin in the Cave, 6¾x9" 35.00
Print, Atlas, 1909, 11x13" 145.00
Print, Autumn, 1905, 14x18" 190.00
Print, Cadmus Sowing the Dragon's Teeth, 8¼x6½" 20.00
Print, Canyon, Reinthal/Newman, 12x15"...........................200.00
Print, Centaur, 1910, scarce, 12x13½"................................165.00
Print, Circe's Palace, maiden, 1908, 15½x12½" 110.00
Print, Cleopatra, 12x13¾"..375.00
Print, Daybreak, gesso fr, 6x10".......................................125.00
Print, Dinkey Bird, 1905, 13x18" 200.00
Print, Dreaming, Reinthal/Newman, 18x30".........................650.00
Print, Dreaming, 12½x14½", NM 325.00
Print, Early Autumn, Brown/Bigelow, 16x13" 125.00
Print, Easter, 1922, 7x10" 60.00
Print, Enchantment, Edison/Mazda, 8x26", NM 500.00
Print, Evening Shadows, 1953, 11x9".................................210.00
Print, Falls by Moonlight, 11x8".......................................100.00
Print, Frog Prince, 1925, orig fr, 8x12".................................75.00
Print, Garden of Allah, 12x21"...195.00
Print, Golden Hours, Edison/Mazda, 1929, 16x23".................475.00
Print, Harvest, 1911, 7x9"...50.00
Print, Hilltop, Reinthal/Newman, 10x14".............................250.00
Print, Hilltop, 12x20"...350.00
Print, Hilltop, 34x23", NM 575.00
Print, Interlude, 11x14", EX...195.00
Print, King's Entrance, Knave of Hearts 85.00
Print, Lady Ursula, 1925, 12x14" 80.00
Print, Land of Make Believe, 11x8½", EX 70.00
Print, Lantern Bearers, sm..210.00
Print, Lute Players, 11x7"..150.00
Print, Lute Players, 1924, 22x34" 680.00
Print, Lute Players, 6x9" 525.00
Print, Moonlight, 12x15" 200.00

Print, New Hampshire, 11x8½" 35.00
Print, Night Is Fled, Edison/Mazda, 1918, 17x14".................900.00
Print, Old Glen Mill, Brown/Bigelow, 14x21"........................325.00
Print, Peaceful Valley, Reinthal/Newman, 1955, 16x12" 180.00
Print, Prince Agib, 11x9" 90.00
Print, Queen Gulnare, 1906, scarce, 11x13".........................150.00
Print, Reveries, 10½x16", EX..425.00
Print, Royal Gorge, 21x17"..360.00

Rubiyat, copyright 1917, $395.00.

Print, Sea Nymphs, 6x8" 80.00
Print, Shuffle-Shoon & Amber Locks, 9x7" 30.00
Print, Sleeping Giant, 7x9"...100.00
Print, Solitude, Edison/Mazda, 11x14", M...........................325.00
Print, Spirit of Night, 18x30", EX 1,025.00
Print, Spring, 1905, orig fr, 14x18" 200.00
Print, Stars, 20x12" 500.00
Print, Stars, 30x18" 850.00
Print, Sunrise, 16x22", NM 295.00
Print, Three Wise Men, 9¼x6"..50.00
Print, Tranquility, 29⅜x24"...200.00
Print, Venetian Lamplighter, 12x18"..................................250.00
Print, When Day Is Dawning, 1954, orig fr, 13x17" 200.00
Print, Wild Geese, Reinthal/Newman, 1924, 12x15" 200.00
Print, Wynken, Blynken, & Nod; unfr, 15x11"..........................150.00

Pate-Sur-Pate

Pate-sur-pate, literally paste-on-paste, is a technique whereby relief decorations are built up on a ceramic body by layering several applications of slip, one on the other, until the desired result is achieved. Usually only two colors are used, and the value of a piece is greatly enhanced as more color is added. See also Rousseau, Argy; Walter, A.

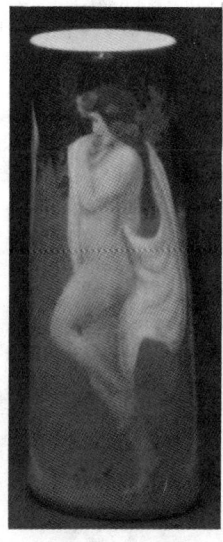

Vase, three female bathers, natural colors, Meissen #133-116, 9", $1,050.00.

Box, 2 putti on dolphins on lid, bombe form, Limoges, 8" 200.00

Plaque, girl w/basket picks flowers from tree, mk, 10x6" 275.00
Plate, cherub w/in rtcl shell & scroll border, Minton, 9" 385.00
Vase, cupid in relief, wht on blk, pillow form, G Jones, 6".........525.00
Vase, lady on ped/vase emits cherubs, wht/gr, Minton, 14" 1,500.00

Pattern Glass

Pattern Glass was the first mass-produced fancy tableware in America and was much prized by our ancestors. From the 1840s to the Civil War, it contained a high lead content and is known as 'Flint Glass.' It is exceptionally clear and resonant. Later glass was made with soda lime and is known as non-flint. By the 1890s pattern glass was produced in great volume in thousands of patterns, and colored glass came into vogue. Today the highest prices are often paid for these later patterns flashed with rose, amber, canary, and vaseline; stained ruby; or made in colors of cobalt, green, yellow, amethyst, etc. Demand for pattern glass declined by 1915, and glass fanciers were collecting it by 1930. No other field of antiques offers more diversity in patterns, prices, or pieces than this unique and historical glass that represents the Victorian era in America.

Our advisor for this category is Darlene Yohe; she is listed in the Directory under Arkansas. For a more thorough study on the subject, we recommend *The Collector's Encyclopedia of Pattern Glass* by Mollie Helen McCain, available from Collector Books. See also Bread Plates; Cruets; Historical Glass; Salt and Pepper Shakers; Salts, Open; Sugar Shakers; Syrups; specific manufacturers such as Northwood.

Note: Values are given for open sugar bowls and compotes unless noted 'w/lid.'

Actress, bottle, scent; 11" **48.00**
Actress, cake stand, 10" **150.00**
Actress, celery vase, HMS Pinafore scene...................**165.00**
Actress, compote, high std, 10" **95.00**
Actress, dresser tray **55.00**
Actress, mug, HMS Pinafore scene **55.00**
Actress, sauce bowl, ftd, frosted **45.00**
Actress, shakers, orig tops, pr......................................**90.00**
Admiral Dewey, see Dewey; See Also Greentown, Dewey
Alabama, honey dish **65.00**
Alabama, spooner..**37.50**
Alabama, toothpick holder, ruby stained......................**135.00**
Albany, celery vase..**27.50**
Albany, spooner..**25.00**
Almond Thumbprint, champagne, flint...........................**55.00**
Almond Thumbprint, goblet, non-flint **15.00**
Amazon, banana stand..**68.00**
Amazon, bowl, scalloped rim, 4½" **12.00**
Amazon, cordial, etched..**38.00**
Amazon, tumbler, etched...**22.50**
Amazon, wine, etched **24.00**
Amberette, see Klondike
Anthemion, pitcher, water; 8¼" **45.00**
Anthemion, plate, 10" **50.00**
Anthemion, sugar bowl, w/lid **37.50**
Apollo, cake stand, 10"...**55.00**
Apollo, compote, sawtooth rim, 9½" **50.00**
Apollo, salt cellar...**20.00**
Apollo, sugar bowl, w/lid **48.00**
Arched Grape, goblet **22.50**
Arched Grape, sugar bowl, w/lid **47.50**
Argus, bottle, bitters **65.00**
Argus, champagne...**55.00**
Argus, compote, open, 4½x6"...**45.00**

Argus, egg cup...**25.00**
Argus, tumbler, ale; ftd, 5"..**32.00**
Argus, whiskey...**65.00**
Art, biscuit jar, ruby stained **200.00**
Art, compote, w/lid, 9x9½" **50.00**
Art, sugar bowl, w/lid **35.00**
Art, tumbler...**38.00**
Art, vinegar jug, 3-pt **65.00**
Ashburton, decanter, canary yel, flint, orig stopper.......**950.00**
Ashburton, goblet, flint **35.00**
Atlas, cake stand, 8" **35.00**
Atlas, jelly compote, ruby stained, w/lid, 5" **60.00**
Atlas, salt cellar, ind **15.00**
Atlas, whiskey **22.50**
Aurora, celery vase..**32.50**
Aurora, goblet, ruby stained **40.00**
Aurora, mug, ruby stained **67.50**
Aurora, wine..**25.00**
Austrian, creamer, emerald gr **110.00**
Austrian, nappy...**35.00**
Austrian, punch cup, amber **135.00**
Austrian, rose bowl **48.00**
Austrian, wine...**32.00**
Baby Thumbprint, see Dakota
Balder, see Pennsylvania
Baltimore Pear, cake stand, high std **50.00**
Baltimore Pear, goblet **32.00**
Baltimore Pear, plate, 8½" **32.00**
Baltimore Pear, sauce bowl, flat......................................**12.50**
Banded Portland, butter pat **20.00**
Banded Portland, candlestick, pr.....................................**85.00**
Banded Portland, sugar bowl, ind....................................**25.00**
Banded Portland, toothpick holder **25.00**
Banded Portland, tumbler, pk stained **42.50**
Bar & Diamond, bread tray **32.00**
Bar & Diamond, compote, high std, 6"............................**28.00**
Bar & Diamond, creamer..**32.00**
Bar & Diamond, goblet, ruby stained..............................**48.00**
Bar & Diamond, sugar bowl, w/lid..................................**50.00**
Bar & Diamond, tumbler..**22.50**
Barberry, butter dish, shell finial **65.00**
Barberry, cake stand, 9½" **37.50**
Barberry, syrup, orig lid **95.00**
Barberry, tumbler, ftd...**22.50**
Barberry, wine...**30.00**
Barley, cordial...**48.00**
Barley, creamer..**25.00**
Barley, pickle castor, orig SP fr, +tongs **87.50**
Barley, pitcher, water; pressed hdl...................................**75.00**
Barley, sugar bowl, w/lid **30.00**
Barred Forget-Me-Not, sugar bowl, w/lid **40.00**
Barrel Huber, see Huber
Basket Weave, butter dish **32.00**
Basket Weave, egg cup, apple gr......................................**28.00**
Basket Weave, pitcher, milk; gr..**70.00**
Basket Weave, pitcher, water; amber **50.00**
Basket Weave, tumbler, vaseline, ftd **22.00**
Beaded Band, compote, low std, w/lid, 9" **50.00**
Beaded Band, spooner...**25.00**
Beaded Band, wine..**28.00**
Beaded Grape, cake stand, gr, sq, 6x9".............................**88.00**
Beaded Grape, cordial **17.50**
Beaded Grape, creamer **37.50**
Beaded Grape, sauce dish, hdls..**15.00**

Beaded Grape Medallion, goblet, buttermilk 32.00
Beaded Grape Medallion, plate, 6" 28.00
Beaded Medallion, butter dish 42.50
Beaded Medallion, celery vase 37.50
Beaded Medallion, plate, 8" 25.00
Beaded Medallion, sugar bowl 25.00
Beaded Mirror, see Beaded Medallion
Beaded Tulip, creamer 88.00
Beaded Tulip, goblet 38.00
Beaded Tulip, pitcher, water 70.00
Bearded Head, see Viking
Bellflower, bowl, scalloped, 8" 75.00
Bellflower, butter dish, vine lid, flint 98.00
Bellflower, castor set, 5-bottle, pewter fr 215.00
Bellflower, champagne, bbl form, single vine 100.00
Bellflower, decanter, dbl vine, 1-qt 235.00
Bellflower, egg cup, single vine 40.00
Bellflower, honey dish, single vine, 3" 30.00
Bellflower, sauce bowl, single vine 17.50
Bellflower, syrup, single vine, David Baker Pat lid 500.00
Bellflower, tumbler, bar; fine rib, single vine 85.00
Bellflower, wine, single vine, bbl form, knop stem, flint ...100.00
Bent Buckle, see New Hampshire
Bevelled Diamond & Star, shakers, pr 17.50
Bigler, decanter, bar lip, 1-pt 60.00
Bigler, tumbler, ale 60.00
Bigler, tumbler, water 80.00
Bird & Fern, see Hummingbird
Bird & Strawberry, bowl, 5½" 32.00
Bird & Strawberry, cake stand 65.00
Bird & Strawberry, creamer 55.00
Bird & Strawberry, creamer, w/color stains 100.00
Bird & Strawberry, goblet 185.00
Bird & Strawberry, tumbler 50.00
Bleeding Heart, bowl, 8" 37.50
Bleeding Heart, butter dish 60.00
Bleeding Heart, egg cup 42.50
Bleeding Heart, pitcher, water; appl hdl 155.00
Bleeding Heart, wine, knob stem 165.00
Block & Fan, bowl, berry; ftd, 8" 22.50
Block & Fan, butter dish, ruby stained 75.00
Block & Fan, celery vase 32.50
Block & Fan, creamer, ruby stained, sm 60.00
Block & Fan, goblet, ruby stained 98.00
Block & Fan, pickle dish 18.00
Block & Fan, sugar shaker 55.00
Block & Fan, wine 48.00
Blue Jay, see Cardinal Bird
Bouquet, sugar bowl, w/lid 32.00
Bow Tie, bowl, 8" 40.00
Bow Tie, creamer 55.00
Bow Tie, pitcher, milk; 5½" 45.00
Bow Tie, punch bowl 95.00
Broken Column, banana stand 115.00
Broken Column, bowl, ruby stained, 6" 40.00
Broken Column, cake stand, 9" 75.00
Broken Column, finger bowl 32.00
Broken Column, pitcher, water 90.00
Broken Column, plate, ruby stained, 4" 32.00
Broken Column, relish, oval, 11x5" 25.00
Broken Column, spooner, ruby stained 120.00
Buckle, butter dish, acorn finial, flint 72.50
Buckle, creamer, non-flint 35.00
Buckle, egg cup, flint 35.00

Buckle, goblet, flint 40.00
Buckle, tumbler 30.00
Buckle, wine 45.00
Buckle w/Star, bowl, oval, 7" 17.50
Buckle w/Star, cake stand, 9" 38.00
Buckle w/Star, sauce dish, ftd 10.00
Buckle w/Star, spill holder 50.00
Bull's Eye, salt cellar, ftd, flint, master 35.00
Bull's Eye, sugar bowl, w/lid 125.00
Bull's Eye, tumbler, bar 32.00
Bull's Eye & Daisy, decanter, emerald gr 100.00
Bull's Eye & Daisy, spooner 18.00
Bull's Eye & Daisy, tumbler, emerald gr 15.00
Bull's Eye & Daisy, tumbler, water; clear w/gold 17.50
Bull's Eye & Fan, custard cup 10.00
Bull's Eye & Fan, pitcher, lemonade; ftd 50.00
Bull's Eye & Fan, relish, bl stained 32.00
Bull's Eye Band, see Reverse Torpedo
Bull's Eye in Heart, see Heart w/Thumbprint
Bull's Eye w/Diamond Point, decanter, orig stopper, 1-qt 185.00
Bull's Eye w/Diamond Point, salt cellar, master, w/lid 95.00
Bull's Eye w/Diamond Point, sauce 22.00
Bull's Eye w/Diamond Point, wine 125.00
Bull's Eye w/Fleur-de-Lis, compote, 8" 50.00
Bull's Eye w/Fleur-de-Lis, creamer 65.00
Bull's Eye w/Fleur-de-Lis, goblet 80.00
Bull's Eye w/Fleur-de-Lis, sugar bowl, w/lid 140.00
Button Arches, goblet, ruby stained 38.00
Button Arches, plate, 7" 9.00
Button Arches, punch cup 12.50
Button Arches, syrup 72.50

Broken Column.

Cabbage Rose, bottle, bitters; 6½" 115.00
Cabbage Rose, bowl, w/lid, 7½" 32.50
Cabbage Rose, champagne 45.00
Cabbage Rose, egg cup 38.00
Cabbage Rose, pitcher, 3-pt 150.00
Cabbage Rose, spooner 25.00
Cable, cake stand, 9" 95.00
Cable, champagne, rare 215.00
Cable, compote, high std, 5½" 60.00
Cable, pitcher, water 525.00
California, see Beaded Grape
Canadian, butter dish 88.00
Canadian, celery vase 50.00
Canadian, goblet 55.00
Cane, cordial 20.00
Cane, goblet, vaseline 40.00
Cane, honey dish 15.00
Cane, slipper, bl 24.00
Cane, waste bowl, amber, 7½" 30.00
Cardinal Bird, butter dish 85.00

Cardinal Bird, cake stand 70.00
Cardinal Bird, pitcher, water 135.00
Carnation, pitcher, water; ruby stained, gold trim.......265.00
Cathedral, bowl, amethyst, 8" 68.00
Cathedral, creamer, bl, tall 45.00
Cathedral, goblet, vaseline 55.00
Cathedral, relish tray, fish shape, vaseline 50.00
Centennial, see Liberty Bell
Chain, bread plate 28.00
Chain, relish, oval, 8" 12.50
Chain, sugar bowl, w/lid 35.00
Chain w/Diamonds, see Washington Centennial
Chain w/Star, creamer 25.00
Chain w/Star, goblet 22.50
Chain w/Star, sauce bowl 12.00

Chain with Star.

Champion, celery vase, amber stained 48.00
Champion, pitcher, water 65.00
Chandelier, cake stand, etched, 10" 80.00
Chandelier, creamer 32.00
Checkerboard, compote, 8" 27.50
Checkerboard, goblet 25.00
Cherry & Cable, pitcher, water 82.00
Classic, creamer, clear & frosted 130.00
Classic, pitcher, water; collared style 225.00
Classic, plate, President Cleveland 185.00
Coin, see US Coin
Colorado, banana stand, gr 35.00
Colorado, cake stand 65.00
Colorado, calling card tray 27.50
Colorado, mug 18.00
Colorado, vase, 12" 42.50
Columbian Coin, celery vase, clear w/gold coins 90.00
Columbian Coin, goblet, clear w/gold 62.50
Columbian Coin, spooner, frosted coins 60.00
Columbian Coin, syrup, frosted coins 185.00
Comet, butter dish 185.00
Comet, goblet, flint 120.00
Comet, tumbler, water 115.00
Compact, see Snail
Connecticut, celery vase 25.00
Connecticut, tumbler, lemonade; hdl 20.00
Cord & Tassle, compote, low, 8" 27.50
Cord & Tassle, egg cup 37.50
Cord & Tassle, pitcher, water 88.00
Cord Drapery, butter dish 60.00
Cord Drapery, compote, w/lid, 9" 68.00
Cord Drapery, creamer, 5" 55.00
Cordova, creamer, ind 37.50
Cordova, punch cup, emerald gr 28.00
Cordova, tumbler 17.50

Croesus, bowl, gr, 8" 95.00
Croesus, cake stand, gr 125.00
Croesus, creamer, regular, purple w/gold 140.00
Croesus, sauce bowl, flat 17.50
Crow's Foot, see Yale
Crown Jewels, see Chandelier
Cryptic, see Zippered Block
Crystal Wedding, compote, high std, ruby stained, 7x13" ...135.00
Crystal Wedding, pitcher, water; sq, ruby stained 235.00
Crystal Wedding, plate, ruby stained, 10" 47.50
Crystal Wedding, tumbler 37.50
Cube w/Fan, see Pineapple & Fan
Cupid & Venus, cake plate 47.50
Cupid & Venus, celery vase 42.50
Cupid & Venus, compote, w/lid, high std, 8" 95.00
Cupid & Venus, marmalade jar, w/lid 80.00
Cupid & Venus, wine 90.00
Currant, cake stand, 4¼x9¼" 68.00
Currant, goblet, buttermilk 35.00
Currant, relish 14.00
Currier & Ives, creamer 32.00
Currier & Ives, plate, 10" 18.00
Currier & Ives, sauce bowl, oval 12.50
Currier & Ives, syrup, bl 185.00
Curtain, butter dish 55.00
Curtain, sugar bowl, w/lid 38.00
Curtain Tie-Back, goblet, flat base 25.00
Cut Log, butter dish 60.00
Cut Log, compote, w/lid, 7½x5½" 48.00
Cut Log, tumbler 47.50
Dahlia, butter dish 50.00
Dahlia, compote, high std, w/lid, 7" 52.50
Dahlia, egg cup, bl, single 42.50
Dahlia, pitcher, water 48.00
Dahlia, pitcher, water; vaseline 90.00
Daisy & Button, butter dish, rnd 60.00
Daisy & Button, celery vase 32.00
Daisy & Button, creamer, gr 38.00
Daisy & Button, finger bowl, vaseline 40.00
Daisy & Button, tumbler, water; amber 24.00
Daisy & Button w/Crossbar, creamer, regular 32.00
Daisy & Button w/Crossbar, goblet 27.50
Daisy & Button w/Crossbar, goblet, bl 40.00
Daisy & Button w/V Ornament, pitcher, water; amber 95.00
Daisy & Button w/V Ornament, sauce bowl 12.00
Daisy & Button w/V Ornament, tumbler, amber 30.00
Dakota, basket, ruby stained 250.00
Dakota, bottle, etched, 5½" 42.50
Dakota, compote, 9x8" 58.00
Dakota, waste bowl 60.00
Dakota, water tray, 13" dia 88.00
Dart, goblet 25.00
Dart, jelly compote 18.00
Dart, sugar bowl, w/lid 35.00
Deer & Dog, goblet 22.50
Deer & Dog, spooner 60.00
Deer & Pine Tree, cake stand, bl 115.00
Deer & Pine Tree, creamer, apple gr 90.00
Deer & Pine Tree, finger bowl 55.00
Deer & Pine Tree, sauce bowl, ftd 22.50
Delaware, butter dish, rose w/gold 145.00
Delaware, finger bowl, rose w/gold 70.00
Delaware, marmalade, rose w/gold, SP fr 90.00
Delaware, tumbler 22.50

Dew & Raindrop, bowl, berry; 8" 40.00
Dew & Raindrop, bud vase, 6" 25.00
Dew & Raindrop, cordial 12.50
Dew & Raindrop, punch cup 8.00
Dewdrop, egg cup, dbl 22.00
Dewdrop, goblet, vaseline 28.00
Dewdrop, relish 15.00
Dewdrop Band, goblet 12.50
Dewey, butter dish, amber 32.00
Dewey, see also Greentown, Dewey
Dewey, tumbler 48.00
Diagonal Band, goblet 27.50
Diagonal Band w/Fan, celery 22.50
Diagonal Band w/Fan, plate, 8" 12.50
Diagonal Band w/Fan, sugar bowl, w/lid 35.00
Diamond Cut w/Leaf, butter dish 22.50
Diamond Cut w/Leaf, creamer 23.00
Diamond Horseshoe, see Aurora
Diamond Medallion, see Grand
Diamond Point, celery, flint 75.00
Diamond Point, claret, flint 110.00
Diamond Point, honey dish, flint 18.00
Diamond Point, pitcher, water; tankard form, flint, qt 175.00
Diamond Point, whiskey, appl hdl, flint 92.50
Diamond Quilted, champagne 22.00
Diamond Quilted, compote, low std, amber, 5½" dia 15.00
Diamond Quilted, creamer, amber 38.00
Diamond Quilted, tumbler, vaseline 24.00
Diamond Thumbprint, cake stand, 3x8⅜" 190.00
Diamond Thumbprint, decanter, orig stopper, 1-qt 235.00
Diamond Thumbprint, finger bowl 98.00
Diamond Thumbprint, tumbler, bar 135.00
Diamond Thumbprint, wine 245.00
Doric, see Feather
Double Leaf & Dart, see Leaf & Dart
Drapery, butter dish 38.00
Drapery, compote, low std 60.00
Drapery, pitcher, water; appl hdl 78.00
Drapery, spooner 30.00
Egg in Sand, creamer 28.00
Egg in Sand, dish, swan center 45.00
Egg in Sand, relish 12.50
Egg in Sand, water tray 42.50
Egg in Sand, wine 32.00
Egyptian, compote, sphinx base, 12x7" 200.00
Egyptian, goblet 45.00
Egyptian, pitcher, water 195.00
Elephant, see Jumbo
Emerald Green Herringbone, see Florida
Empress, butter dish, emerald gr w/gold 98.00
Empress, sugar bowl 37.50
Empress, tumbler, emerald gr w/gold 50.00
English Hobnail Cross, see Klondike
Esther, butter dish, ruby stained 125.00
Esther, cracker jar, amber stained 235.00
Esther, goblet, amber stained w/enamel decor 150.00
Esther, ice cream tray, gr w/gold 150.00
Esther, pitcher, water 60.00
Esther, pitcher, water; amber stained 200.00
Esther, sugar bowl, w/lid 45.00
Esther, syrup, gr w/gold 200.00
Etched Dakota, see Dakota
Eureka, butter dish 78.00
Eureka, egg cup 32.00

Eureka, salt cellar, ftd 37.50
Eureka, tumbler, ftd 28.00
Excelsior, bottle, bar; flint, 1-qt 88.00
Excelsior, cake stand, flint, 9¼" 165.00
Excelsior, cordial, flint 45.00
Excelsior, platter, 9¼" L 27.50
Eyewinker, banana boat, flat, 8½" 82.50
Eyewinker, banana stand, high std 150.00
Eyewinker, creamer, mini 55.00
Fairfax Strawberry, see Strawberry
Fan w/Crossbars, see Champion
Fan w/Diamond, pitcher, water 55.00
Feather, bowl, 7" 25.00
Feather, jelly compote, w/lid, 8¼" 135.00
Feather, plate, 10" 40.00
Feather, tumbler, water 45.00
Festoon, cake stand, high std, 9" 42.50
Festoon, plate, 8" 32.50
Festoon, relish dish, 9x5½" 36.00
Fine Cut, goblet, bl 50.00
Fine Cut, water tray 30.00
Fine Cut & Block, champagne, amber 68.00
Fine Cut & Block, cruet, bl, faceted stopper, 5½" 78.00
Fine Cut & Block, pitcher, water; amber 88.00
Fine Cut & Diamond, see Grand
Fine Cut & Feather, see Feather
Fine Cut & Panel, bowl, oval, 8" 17.50
Fine Cut & Panel, plate, bl, 7" 30.00
Fine Cut & Panel, waste bowl, vaseline 37.50
Fine Rib, cordial, flint 90.00
Fine Rib, wine, flint 45.00
Fine Rib w/Cut Ovals, goblet, flint 235.00
Fingerprint, see Almond Thumbprint
Fishscale, butter dish 45.00
Fishscale, creamer 25.00
Fishscale, plate, sq, 9" 30.00
Flamingo Habitat, compote, 6" 42.50
Flamingo Habitat, creamer 42.50
Flamingo Habitat, tumbler 32.00
Florida, bowl, 9" 22.00
Florida, goblet, gr 42.00
Florida, plate, 7½" 12.00
Florida, relish, sq, 6" 12.00
Flower Pot, creamer, vaseline 88.00
Flower Pot, pitcher, milk 45.00
Flower Pot, sugar bowl 40.00
Flute, bottle, bar; flint, 1-qt 75.00
Flute, egg cup, flint 32.00
Flute, tumbler, ale; flint 48.00
Frosted Circle, butter dish 50.00
Frosted Circle, spooner 30.00
Frosted Circle, syrup, spring lid 100.00
Frosted Circle, tumbler 25.00
Frosted Leaf, compote, w/lid, flint 265.00
Frosted Leaf, egg cup, flint 80.00
Frosted Leaf, wine, flint 175.00
Frosted Lion, see Lion
Frosted Roman Key, goblet 45.00
Frosted Roman Key, sugar bowl, w/lid 85.00
Frosted Stork, celery vase 65.00
Frosted Stork, pickle castor, orig fr 200.00
Frosted Stork, sauce bowl 28.00
Frosted Stork, waste bowl 42.00
Galloway, basket, twisted hdl 78.00

Galloway, cake stand, rose stained 88.00
Galloway, olive dish, clear w/gold, 6" 22.00
Galloway, pitcher, rose stained, water sz 175.00
Galloway, sherbet, clear w/gold 25.00
Galloway, tumbler, ruby stained 55.00
Garfield Drape, compote, 6" 88.00
Garfield Drape, goblet 37.50
Garfield Drape, pitcher, milk 60.00
Garfield Drape, tumbler 36.00
Gem, see Nailhead
Good Luck, see Horseshoe
Gothic, goblet 55.00
Gothic, sauce bowl, flat, 4" 10.00
Grand, celery vase, ftd 25.00
Grand, sugar bowl, w/lid 38.00
Grape & Festoon w/Shield, compote, 10½" 62.50
Grape & Festoon w/Shield, spooner 25.00
Grape & Festoon w/Stippled Leaf, goblet 27.50
Grape & Festoon w/Stippled Leaf, sugar bowl, w/lid 60.00
Grape Band, sugar bowl 20.00
Grasshopper, bowl, ftd, 7" 22.00
Grasshopper, butter dish, amber 95.00
Grasshopper, pitcher, water 70.00
Grasshopper, sugar bowl, w/insect, w/lid 75.00
Guardian Angel, see Cupid & Venus
Hairpin, celery vase 60.00
Hairpin, pitcher, 8" 180.00
Halley's Comet, celery vase 32.00
Halley's Comet, pitcher, tankard 95.00
Halley's Comet, relish 18.00
Halley's Comet, salt cellar 22.00
Hamilton, butter dish 70.00
Hamilton, cake stand 150.00
Hamilton, tumbler, water 75.00
Hamilton w/Leaf, compote, scalloped, frosted leaf, 8" ...137.50
Hamilton w/Leaf, tumbler, clear leaf 50.00
Hamilton w/Leaf, whiskey, hdl, clear leaf 95.00
Hand, celery vase 50.00
Hand, tumbler 88.00
Hartley, celery 22.50
Hartley, creamer, vaseline 42.50
Hartley, tumbler 28.00
Hawaiian Lei, cake stand, 9¼" 30.00
Hawaiian Lei, sauce bowl, ftd, 3¼" 7.50
Heart w/Thumbprint, card tray 22.00
Heart w/Thumbprint, cruet 80.00
Heart w/Thumbprint, goblet, gr w/gold 85.00
Heart w/Thumbprint, syrup 98.00
Hearts & Spades, see Medallion
Heavy Panelled Finecut, goblet, vaseline 32.00
Heavy Panelled Finecut, salt cellar, ind 10.00
Herringbone, goblet 22.00
Herringbone, jelly compote, gr 42.50
Herringbone Band, see Ripple
Herringbone Buttress, see Greentown, Herringbone Buttress
Hexagon Block, sauce dish, flat, etched, amber stained, 4¼" 12.50
Hickman, cake stand 30.00
Hickman, creamer, gr w/gold 35.00
Hickman, goblet, gr w/gold 42.50
Hickman, relish, gr 17.50
Hickman, rose bowl 25.00
Hidalgo, celery vase, flat base, amber stained 40.00
Hidalgo, sugar shaker 48.00
Hidalgo, tumbler 27.50

Hidalgo, waste bowl 27.50
Hinoto, egg cup 38.00
Hinoto, tumbler, ftd 40.00
Holly, butter dish 165.00
Holly, compote, 7½" 100.00
Holly, egg cup 70.00
Holly, goblet 95.00
Holly, pitcher, water 235.00
Holly, salt cellar, flat base 68.00
Holly Amber, see Greentown Holly Amber
Honeycomb, cake stand, non-flint, 10½" 32.00
Honeycomb, champagne, flint 48.00
Honeycomb, goblet, non-flint 17.50
Honeycomb, tumbler, lemonade; flint 42.50
Honeycomb, whiskey, hdl, flint 132.00
Honeycomb w/Flower Rim, bowl, berry; gr 46.00
Hops & Barley, see Wheat & Barley
Horn of Plenty, butter dish, acorn finial, flint 130.00
Horn of Plenty, celery, flint 180.00
Horn of Plenty, cordial, flint 135.00
Horn of Plenty, goblet, flint 70.00
Horn of Plenty, mug, appl hdl, flint, sm 135.00
Horn of Plenty, spill holder 80.00
Horseshoe, bowl, vegetable; oval 35.00
Horseshoe, butter dish 95.00
Horseshoe, plate, 10" 55.00
Horseshoe, salt cellar, ind 20.00
Horseshoe, waste bowl 42.50
Huber, champagne, flint 32.00
Huber, salt cellar, ftd, flint 32.00
Huber, wine, flint 15.00
Hummingbird, creamer 45.00
Hummingbird, pitcher, milk 50.00
Hummingbird, pitcher, water; bl 140.00
Hummingbird, waste bowl, 5¼" 37.50
Idaho, see Snail
Illinois, cheese dish, sq 70.00
Illinois, olive dish 15.00
Illinois, pitcher, milk; rnd, SP trim 180.00
Illinois, sugar shaker 62.00
Illinois, toothpick holder 30.00
Inverted Fern, compote, 8" 60.00
Inverted Fern, goblet 22.50
Inverted Fern, salt cellar, master 30.00
Inverted Fern, sugar bowl, w/lid 80.00
Invincible, sugar bowl, w/lid 55.00
Iris Column, see Broken Column
Iris w/Meander, see Opalescent Glass
Iris w/Meander, sugar bowl, w/lid, clear w/gold 55.00
Ivy in Snow, goblet 68.00
Ivy in Snow, mug, ruby stained 47.50
Ivy in Snow, relish 20.00
Ivy in Snow, syrup 72.50
Ivy in Snow, wine, ruby stained 65.00
Jacob's Ladder, cake stand, 12" 55.00
Jacob's Ladder, castor bottle 22.50
Jacob's Ladder, compote, low std, 9" 55.00
Jacob's Ladder, creamer 35.00
Jacob's Ladder, goblet, water; amber 40.00
Jacob's Ladder, sauce dish, ftd, 4½" 15.00
Jersey Swirl, creamer 28.00
Jersey Swirl, goblet, buttermilk 32.00
Jersey Swirl, goblet, water 48.00
Jersey Swirl, salt cellar, bl, ind 22.00

Jersey Swirl, wine..18.00
Jewel Band, bread platter 42.50
Jewel Band, egg cup..22.50
Jewel Band, pitcher, milk.......................................42.00
Jewel Band, sugar bowl, w/lid 37.50
Jewel w/Dewdrop, mug..15.00
Jewel w/Dewdrop, sugar bowl, w/lid.....................72.50
Jewel w/Dewdrop, whiskey, hdl 7.50
Jewel w/Moondrop, cake plate..............................48.00
Jewel w/Moondrop, tumbler 42.50
Jewelled Moon & Star, butter dish........................72.50
Jewelled Moon & Star, celery, frosted, amber & bl stained 95.00
Jewelled Moon & Star, goblet................................30.00
Jewelled Moon & Star, platter 45.00
Jewelled Moon & Star, wine 24.00
Job's Tears, see Art
Jumbo, creamer..235.00
Jumbo, pitcher, elephant in base..........................700.00
Jumbo, spoon rack 500.00
Kentucky, cruet...40.00
Kentucky, sauce bowl, ftd 8.00
Kentucky, sugar bowl, w/lid...................................35.00
Kentucky, toothpick holder....................................28.00
King's Crown, butter dish 40.00
King's Crown, castor bottle 20.00
King's Crown, claret, ruby stained..........................55.00
King's Crown, cordial 40.00
King's Crown, creamer, clear w/gold, ind..............30.00
King's Crown, mustard jar 60.00
King's Crown, pitcher, water; etched....................125.00
King's Crown, punch bowl, ftd..............................265.00
King's Crown, tumbler, bl.......................................78.00
King's Crown, wine..20.00
Klondike, bowl, sq, frosted, amber stained, 8".....135.00
Klondike, goblet, amber stained...........................135.00
Klondike, shakers, frosted, amber stained, orig top, pr 120.00
La Clede, see Hickman
Lace, see Drapery
Ladder w/Diamonds, toothpick holder, gold trim 22.00
Lady Hamilton, butter dish.....................................35.00
Lady Hamilton, sauce dish, flat, 4".......................... 6.00
Lawrence, see Bull's Eye
Leaf, see Maple Leaf
Leaf & Dart, bowl, 6x9"...18.00
Leaf & Dart, pitcher, water; appl hdl 88.00
Leaf & Dart, relish...17.50
Leaf & Dart, sugar bowl, w/lid................................45.00
Leaf Bracket, see Greentown, Leaf Bracket
Leaf Medallion, see Northwood, Leaf Medallion
Liberty Bell, butter dish 135.00
Liberty Bell, goblet..55.00
Liberty Bell, pitcher, water.....................................750.00
Liberty Bell, spooner, mini....................................300.00
Liberty Bell, sugar bowl, w/lid................................98.00
Lily of the Valley, creamer, ftd...............................75.00
Lily of the Valley, egg cup.......................................45.00
Lily of the Valley, relish..22.50
Lincoln Drape, creamer...150.00
Lincoln Drape, egg cup...55.00
Lincoln Drape w/Tassel, salt cellar, master..........120.00
Lion, cheese dish, frosted......................................185.00
Lion, cheese dish, rampant lion finial, frosted..........................385.00
Lion, compote, low ft, frosted, 5x7¾" dia 65.00
Lion, cordial, frosted...165.00

Lion, goblet...55.00
Lion, pickle dish 50.00
Lion, salt cellar, frosted, master...........................145.00
Log Cabin, compote, 10½"....................................285.00
Log Cabin, creamer..125.00
Log Cabin, marmalade...250.00
Log Cabin, pitcher, water 350.00
Long Spear, see Grasshopper
Loop, compote, w/lid, flint, 9x7".............................80.00
Loop, goblet, flint 18.00
Loop, pitcher, water; flint......................................145.00
Loop, wine, flint..32.00
Loop & Dart, butter dish...48.00
Loop & Dart, creamer..32.00
Loop & Dart, pitcher, water....................................75.00
Loop & Dart, tumbler, ftd.......................................32.50
Loop & Dart w/Round Ornament, creamer 38.00
Loop & Moose Eye, egg cup, flint...........................30.00
Loop w/Stippled Panels, see Texas
Louisiana, cake stand 48.00
Louisiana, match holder 37.50

Magnet and Grape.

Magnet & Grape, champagne, clear leaf 42.50
Magnet & Grape, cordial, frosted leaf, 4" 145.00
Magnet & Grape, pitcher, milk; clear leaf 70.00
Magnet & Grape, whiskey, frosted leaf 135.00
Maine, creamer...28.00
Maine, tumbler, gr...40.00
Maine, wine, gr..70.00
Manhattan, basket, lg..235.00
Manhattan, carafe, water; pk stained 72.50
Manhattan, vase, 7"...15.00
Manhattan, violet bowl...22.50
Maple Leaf, bowl, vaseline, oval, flat, 6x10" 48.00
Maple Leaf, compote, jelly; amber, 9"....................58.00
Maple Leaf, plate, bl, 9"...38.00
Maryland, butter dish, ruby stained.......................90.00
Maryland, goblet, clear w/gold...............................30.00
Maryland, pitcher, milk...55.00
Maryland, relish, ruby stained 50.00
Mascotte, cheese dish, etched 75.00
Mascotte, compote, etched, 7x5"...........................30.00
Mascotte, pitcher, water...50.00
Mascotte, shaker, etched 25.00
Massachusetts, cordial...55.00
Massachusetts, creamer, breakfast sz.....................17.50
Massachusetts, pitcher, water 75.00
Massachusetts, plate, sq, 8".....................................30.00
Massachusetts, punch cup......................................12.50
Medallion, cake stand 28.00
Medallion, cake stand, amber.................................48.00

Medallion, pitcher, water 22.50
Medallion, sugar bowl, w/lid........................32.50
Michigan, carafe, water 135.00
Michigan, goblet 32.00
Michigan, goblet, gr stained, enameled........................45.00
Michigan, pickle dish 10.00
Minerva, bowl, rectangular, 9" 42.50
Minerva, butter dish 95.00
Minerva, relish, oval 37.50
Minerva, salt cellar, master 30.00
Minnesota, basket 62.50
Minnesota, carafe 40.00
Minnesota, creamer, clear w/gold 60.00
Minnesota, tumbler, water 20.00
Minnesota, wine 24.00
Minor Block, see Mascotte
Mirror, see Galloway
Missouri, butter dish, gr 58.00
Missouri, spooner 24.00
Missouri, syrup 70.00
Moon & Star, bowl, berry; 8¼" 32.00
Moon & Star, claret........................48.00
Moon & Star, creamer 50.00
Moon & Star, tray, water 75.00
Moon & Star, tumbler, ftd 65.00
Morning Glory, salt cellar, flint, ind 200.00
Nail, cordial 65.00
Nail, decanter 35.00
Nail, goblet, etched........................42.50
Nail, pitcher, water 80.00
Nail, sauce dish, ftd, 3½" 12.00
Nailhead, bowl, 6" 17.50
Nailhead, butter dish 45.00
Nailhead, relish 10.00
Nailhead, tumbler 40.00
New England Pineapple, champagne 185.00
New England Pineapple, creamer, appl hdl 175.00
New England Pineapple, decanter, w/bar lip, 1-qt........................188.00
New England Pineapple, sauce dish 18.00
New England Pineapple, tumbler, bar........................120.00
New Hampshire, bowl, clear w/gold, 8" 16.00
New Hampshire, goblet, clear w/gold........................20.00
New Hampshire, sugar bowl, rose stained, 3"........................27.50
New Jersey, compote, high std, clear w/gold, 8"........................72.50
New Jersey, olive dish, clear w/gold........................22.50
New Jersey, sugar bowl, clear w/gold 55.00
New Jersey, vase, gr, 8" 28.00
Notched Rib, see Broken Column
O'Hara Diamond, cup & saucer, ruby stained........................58.00
O'Hara Diamond, pitcher, water tankard........................40.00
O'Hara Diamond, pitcher, water tankard; ruby stained................175.00
O'Hara Diamond, sugar shaker........................55.00
Oak Leaf Band, celery 35.00
Oak Leaf Band, relish 12.00
Oaken Bucket, see Wooden Pail
One Hundred & One, compote, low std 62.50
One Hundred & One, pitcher, water; appl hdl........................115.00
One Hundred & One, sugar bowl, w/lid........................45.00
One-O-One, see One Hundered & One
Open Rose, goblet 20.00
Open Rose, sugar bowl, w/lid........................42.50
Oregon #1, jelly compote 25.00
Oregon #1, toothpick holder 55.00
Oregon #1, tumbler, water 28.00

Oregon #1, water carafe........................38.00
Orion, see Cathedral
Ostrich Looking at Moon, goblet........................125.00
Palmette, bread plate, hdls, 9" 32.00
Palmette, creamer, appl hdl 60.00
Palmette, cup plate 45.00
Palmette, tumbler, water; ftd 42.50
Panelled Daisy, bowl, berry; master 22.50
Panelled Daisy, bowl, oval, 5¾x8¼" 18.00
Panelled Daisy, butter dish 65.00
Panelled Daisy, plate, sq, 9" 28.00
Panelled Daisy, water tray 35.00
Panelled Dewdrop, bowl, oval, 8¼" 30.00
Panelled Dewdrop, goblet 27.50
Panelled Dewdrop, wine 22.50
Panelled Forget-Me-Not, butter dish, bl 65.00
Panelled Forget-Me-Not, goblet 28.00
Panelled Forget-Me-Not, marmalade 50.00
Panelled Forget-Me-Not, relish, amber 50.00
Panelled Herringbone, see Florida
Panelled Nightshade, goblet, bl........................68.00
Panelled Star & Button, creamer 35.00
Panelled Star & Button, spooner........................25.00

Panelled Thistle.

Panelled Thistle, cake stand, 9" 32.00
Panelled Thistle, champagne, w/bee, flared 40.00
Panelled Thistle, goblet........................38.00
Panelled Thistle, pitcher, milk 48.00
Panelled Thistle, vase, 9¼" 25.00
Pavonia, celery vase, ruby stained 70.00
Pavonia, compote, 7" 45.00
Pavonia, pitcher, lemonade 115.00
Pavonia, plate, etched, 6½" 15.00
Pavonia, sugar bowl, w/lid 60.00
Pavonia, waste bowl........................68.00
Peerless, see Lady Hamilton
Pennsylvania, butter dish, clear w/gold 60.00
Pennsylvania, decanter, clear w/gold 125.00
Pennsylvania, goblet, clear w/gold........................25.00
Pennsylvania, sauce dish, flat, clear w/gold, 5¼" 10.00
Pennsylvania, toothpick holder, clear w/gold 32.00
Pennsylvania, tumbler, water; clear w/gold........................25.00
Pennsylvania, wine, gr 40.00
Pillow Encircled, mug 32.00
Pillow Encircled, pitcher, water tankard; ruby stained 110.00
Pineapple & Fan, celery tray 32.00
Pineapple & Fan, creamer, gr w/gold........................42.50
Pineapple & Fan, vase, trumpet form, 10" 32.00
Pineapple Stem, see Pavonia
Pioneer, see Westward Ho
Pleat & Panel, box, 5x8" 45.00

Pleat & Panel, butter dish, ftd 50.00
Pleat & Panel, plate, canary 28.00
Pleat & Panel, shakers, orig top, pr 70.00
Pleat & Panel, sugar bowl 25.00
Plume, bowl, 9¼" 22.00
Plume, butter dish 45.00
Plume, pitcher, water; ruby stained 175.00
Plume, sugar bowl 20.00
Pointed Jewel, custard cup 20.00
Polar Bear, goblet...110.00
Polar Bear, pitcher, water; frosted 345.00
Polar Bear, waste bowl, frosted 100.00
Polar Bear, water tray, frosted 140.00
Popcorn, cake stand, 11" 55.00
Popcorn, wine 32.00
Portland, creamer, clear w/gold 32.00
Portland, goblet, pk stained 70.00
Portland, pitcher, water; str sides, clear w/gold 60.00
Portland, punch cup, pk stained 38.00
Portland, syrup, clear w/gold 85.00
Portland, toothpick holder 24.00
Portland, vase, 9" 32.50
Powder & Shot, creamer, flint 98.00
Powder & Shot, egg cup, flint 55.00
Powder & Shot, goblet, buttermilk; flint 38.00
Powder & Shot, salt cellar, master; flint 40.00
Prayer Rug, see Horseshoe
Pressed Leaf, cordial 18.00
Pressed Leaf, goblet 25.00
Pressed Leaf, sugar bowl, w/lid 40.00
Primrose, card tray, amber, wire fr, 4½" dia 35.00
Primrose, creamer 30.00
Primrose, pickle dish, amber............................20.00
Primrose, sugar bowl, w/lid 45.00
Primrose, wine...20.00
Princess Feather, butter dish 50.00
Princess Feather, cake plate 32.00
Princess Feather, nappy 25.00
Princess Feather, pitcher, water........................78.00
Princess Feather, plate, amber, flint, 7" 175.00
Princess Feather, relish 18.00
Priscilla, banana stand 98.00
Priscilla, cracker jar 185.00
Priscilla, goblet 38.00
Priscilla, syrup, orig pewter lid 130.00
Prism, compote, scalloped rim, 7" 22.50
Prism w/Diamond Points, tumbler.....................40.00
Psyche & Cupid, goblet 38.00
Psyche & Cupid, pitcher, water........................80.00
Pygmy, see Torpedo
Raindrop, syrup 32.50
Recessed Pillared Red Top, see Nail
Red Block, decanter, 12" 165.00
Red Block, mug 35.00
Red Block, pitcher, water; 8" 155.00
Red Block, sugar bowl, w/lid............................80.00
Red Block, wine 38.00
Red Top, see Button Arches
Regal Block, wine 18.00
Reverse Torpedo, bowl, 6" 12.50
Reverse Torpedo, cordial................................48.00
Reverse Torpedo, honey dish, sq, w/lid...............165.00
Reverse Torpedo, mug....................................32.00
Reverse Torpedo, relish, oval, ruby stained, 9" 38.00

Ribbed Ivy, butter dish 98.00
Ribbed Ivy, egg cup.......................................30.00
Ribbed Ivy, tumbler, bar 95.00
Ribbed Palm, butter dish 95.00
Ribbed Palm, goblet.......................................37.50
Ribbed Palm, pitcher, water 285.00
Ribbed Palm, spooner.....................................35.00
Ribbon, cheese dish, frosted 155.00
Ribbon, creamer, frosted 40.00
Ribbon, goblet, frosted 37.50
Ribbon, goblet, frosted 50.00
Ribbon, salt cellar, frosted, master......................10.00
Ribbon, waste bowl, frosted 40.00
Ribbon Candy, butter dish, ftd 65.00
Ribbon Candy, goblet......................................35.00
Ribbon Candy, mug..24.00
Ribbon Candy, spooner 30.00
Ribbon Candy, wine..50.00
Ripple, goblet...20.00
Ripple, sugar bowl...15.00
Ripple Band, see Ripple
Rising Sun, goblet, purple trim...........................25.00
Rochelle, see Princess Feather
Roman Key, champagne, frosted 75.00
Roman Key, compote, frosted, low std, 7"..............50.00
Roman Key, sugar bowl, frosted, w/lid..................80.00
Roman Key, wine, frosted.................................65.00
Roman Rosette, bread plate, ruby stained 75.00
Roman Rosette, celery vase 32.00
Roman Rosette, creamer...................................35.00
Roman Rosette, mug, lemonade 32.50
Roman Rosette, sugar bowl, w/lid........................42.50
Roman Rosette, tumbler, lemonade 34.00
Rose in Snow, butter dish, bl 145.00
Rose in Snow, cake stand, bl, 9" 165.00
Rose in Snow, goblet, amber 45.00
Rose in Snow, mug, In Fond Remembrance 35.00
Rose in Snow, pitcher, water.............................135.00
Rose in Snow, platter, oval..............................135.00
Rose in Snow, spooner, sq 38.00
Rose in Snow, sugar bowl, rnd, w/lid....................50.00
Rose in Snow, tumbler 42.00
Rose in Snow, tumbler, bar 65.00
Rose Sprig, compote, yel, 5x7" 42.50
Rose Sprig, creamer, yel...................................38.00
Rose Sprig, pitcher, water; amber 75.00
Rose Sprig, sauce dish, ftd, bl 18.00
Rose Sprig, tumbler, appl hdl 50.00
Rosette, compote, 4½" 12.50
Rosette, pickle dish..15.00
Rosette, tumbler, 5".......................................22.00
Rosette, waste bowl..27.50
Rosette & Palms, celery...................................22.50
Rosette & Palms, plate, 10" 18.00
Royal Ivy, see Northwood, Royal Ivy
Royal Oak, see Northwood, Royal Oak
Ruby Thumbprint, see King's Crown
Sandwich Star, decanter, bar lip, 1-pt...................65.00
Sandwich Star, spill holder 60.00
Sawtooth, butter dish, flint...............................75.00
Sawtooth, champagne, knob stem, flint 60.00
Sawtooth, creamer, flint...................................85.00
Sawtooth, pitcher, water; appl hdl, flint 28.00
Sawtooth, plate, flint, 6½"................................42.50

Sawtooth, spooner, non-flint.............................25.00

Sawtooth, wine, flint 38.00

Sawtooth Band, see Amazon

Scalloped Daisy Red Top, see Button Arches

Scroll w/Flowers, cordial 38.00

Scroll w/Flowers, egg cup 16.00

Scroll w/Flowers, spooner 25.00

Sedan, see Panelled Star & Button

Sequoia, see Heavy Panelled Finecut

Shell & Jewel, bowl, 8" 32.00

Shell & Jewel, pitcher, water 35.00

Shell & Jewel, pitcher, water, bl 85.00

Shell & Jewel, sauce bowl, amber 15.00

Shell & Jewel, spooner 24.00

Shell & Jewel, tumbler 20.00

Shell & Tassel, bowl, oval, 12" 78.00

Shell & Tassel, butter dish, dog finial.................110.00

Shell & Tassel, celery vase, sq 50.00

Shell & Tassel, oyster plate, 9½" 235.00

Shell & Tassel, salt cellar, shell form 27.50

Sheraton, butter dish 42.50

Sheraton, goblet, bl...45.00

Sheraton, pitcher, water 48.00

Sheraton, spooner, amber 32.00

Sheraton, wine 20.00

Shoshone, butter dish, clear w/gold....................65.00

Shoshone, carafe 35.00

Shoshone, plate, 7½" 20.00

Shoshone, relish dish 12.50

Shoshone, salt cellar, ind..................................22.00

Shoshone, toothpick holder, ruby stained.............90.00

Shovel, compote 18.00

Shrine, mug 20.00

Shrine, pickle dish 18.00

Shrine, sugar bowl, w/lid 50.00

Shrine, tumbler, 4" 42.00

Shuttle, champagne 40.00

Shuttle, see also Greentown, Shuttle

Shuttle, shaker 55.00

Shuttle, spooner, scalloped rim 35.00

Shuttle, wine 22.00

Skilton, celery vase, ruby stained 88.00

Skilton, creamer...32.00

Skilton, pitcher, water 45.00

Skilton, water tray 50.00

Skilton, wine 30.00

Smocking, creamer, ind....................................110.00

Snail, basket, ruby stained, 8" 55.00

Snail, cheese dish..110.00

Snail, pickle dish..30.00

Snail, plate, 7" 50.00

Snail, rose bowl, 5" 55.00

Snail, shakers, ruby stained, pr 98.00

Snail, sugar bowl, w/lid, ruby stained, regular 95.00

Snail, wine 68.00

Snakeskin & Dot, goblet 32.00

Spades, see Medallion

Spirea Band, butter dish, bl 50.00

Spirea Band, cordial, amber 40.00

Spirea Band, goblet, vaseline 38.00

Spirea Band, pitcher, water; amber 62.50

Spirea Band, relish 17.50

Spirea Band, sugar bowl, amber.........................30.00

Spirea Band, wine 25.00

Spirea Band, wine, amber 32.00

Sprig, creamer 32.00

Sprig, pitcher, water 50.00

Sprig, sugar bowl, w/lid 45.00

Squirrel, creamer, rare.....................................85.00

Star Rosetted, butter dish 45.00

Star Rosetted, sugar bowl, w/lid 45.00

Stars & Stripes, creamer 22.00

Stars & Stripes, tumbler, bl 72.50

States, butter dish 68.00

States, cocktail, flared, clear w/gold 24.00

States, pitcher, water; clear w/gold 48.00

States, plate, clear w/gold, 10" 27.50

States, shakers, clear w/gold, pr 38.00

States, tumbler 27.50

Stedman, egg cup 22.00

Stedman, goblet 30.00

Stedman, spooner 15.00

Stippled Chain, cake stand 48.00

Stippled Chain, goblet......................................22.50

Stippled Chain, goblet, purple 25.00

Stippled Double Loop, butter dish 45.00

Stippled Double Loop, sugar bowl, w/lid 35.00

Stippled Double Loop, tumbler 25.00

Stippled Double Loop, wine 50.00

Stippled Forget-Me-Not, bread platter 42.00

Stippled Forget-Me-Not, cup & saucer 40.00

Stippled Forget-Me-Not, sugar bowl, w/lid 36.00

Stippled Forget-Me-Not, tumbler.........................32.00

Stippled Grape & Festoon, celery vase 40.00

Stippled Grape & Festoon, goblet........................32.00

Stippled Grape & Festoon, salt cellar, master 25.00

Stippled Grape & Festoon, spooner 24.00

Stippled Ivy, egg cup 25.00

Stippled Ivy, goblet 20.00

Stippled Ivy, sugar bowl, w/lid 37.50

Stippled Panelled Flower, see Maine

Strawberry, goblet, 6" 18.00

Strawberry, wine 98.00

Strawberry & Currant, goblet.............................24.00

Strawberry & Currant, mug 36.00

Strawberry & Currant, pitcher, milk 42.00

Strigil, goblet...42.50

Strigil, punch cup 12.50

Sunk Honeycomb, cracker jar 32.00

Sunk Honeycomb, cup & saucer, ruby stained.......32.00

Sunk Honeycomb, mug, ruby stained, souvenir 42.00

Sunk Honeycomb, tumbler, etched......................25.00

Sunk Honeycomb, wine, ruby stained 35.00

Sunken Primrose, see Florida

Swan, compote, swan finial, 8" 195.00

Swan, creamer 45.00

Swan, goblet, canary 75.00

Swan, spooner 48.00

Swan, sugar bowl, bl.......................................55.00

Teardrop, tumbler, water; etched 22.50

Teardrop & Diamond Block, see Art

Teardrop & Tassel, celery vase...........................40.00

Teardrop & Tassel, sauce dish 13.00

Teardrop & Tassel, see also Greentown

Tennessee, compote, low std, 7" 32.00

Tennessee, mug..38.00

Tennessee, wine, colored jewels 88.00

Texas, cake stand, pink stained, 9½" 78.00

Texas, cruet, clear w/gold, orig stopper 70.00
Texas, pickle dish, clear w/gold, 8½" 32.00
Texas, pitcher, water; clear w/gold 120.00
Texas, spooner, clear w/gold 30.00
Texas, toothpick holder, rose stained 90.00
Texas, wine, clear w/gold 55.00
Theatrical, see Actress
Thousand Eye, butter dish, 7½" 50.00
Thousand Eye, cake stand, 3-knob stem, gr 60.00
Thousand Eye, cordial, amber 32.00
Thousand Eye, goblet, vaseline 40.00
Thousand Eye, mug, 3½" 18.00
Thousand Eye, pitcher, water; apple gr, ½-gal 90.00
Thousand Eye, pitcher, water; ½-gal 50.00
Thousand Eye, plate, vaseline, 10" 35.00

Thousand Eye.

Thousand Eye, platter, amber, oval, 11" 72.50
Thousand Eye, string holder, bl 42.50
Thousand Eye, tumbler, apple gr 32.00
Three Face, biscuit jar 900.00
Three Face, butter dish 145.00
Three Face, celery vase 125.00
Three Face, champagne, saucer type 150.00
Three Face, claret 125.00
Three Face, compote, 7½x6" 75.00
Three Face, creamer 125.00
Three Face, marmalade jar 225.00
Three Face, pitcher, water 325.00
Three Face, spooner 80.00
Three Face, sugar bowl, w/lid 120.00
Three Face, wine 175.00
Three Panel, bowl, amber, 7" 25.00
Three Panel, butter dish, bl 50.00
Three Panel, goblet, amber 32.00
Three Panel, sugar bowl, vaseline, w/lid 75.00
Three Panel, tumbler 15.00
Thumbprint, see Argus
Thumbprint Band, see Dakota
Thunderbird, see Hummingbird
Torpedo, compote, high std, 13¾" 150.00
Torpedo, cup & saucer 60.00
Torpedo, pitcher, milk; ruby stained 140.00
Torpedo, tumbler, water; ruby stained 45.00
Torpedo, wine 88.00
Tree of Life, celery dish 40.00
Tree of Life, salt cellar, ftd, gr opaque 98.00
Tree of Life, shakers, pr 45.00
Tree of Life, sugar bowl, w/lid, in SP fr 95.00
Triple Triangle, butter dish 60.00
Triple Triangle, goblet, ruby stained 32.00
Triple Triangle, wine, ruby stained 48.00

Truncated Cube, celery vase, ruby stained 50.00
Truncated Cube, decanter, 12" 60.00
Truncated Cube, goblet 28.00
Truncated Cube, pitcher, water tankard 55.00
Truncated Cube, tumbler, ruby stained 38.00
Tulip w/Sawtooth, compote, flint, 7½x9" 88.00
Tulip w/Sawtooth, creamer, flint 85.00
Twin Snowshoes, creamer 25.00
Two Panel, butter dish, vaseline 60.00
Two Panel, compote, high std, apple gr, w/lid 132.00
Two Panel, marmalade 35.00
Two Panel, salt cellar, amber, master 24.00
Two Panel, spooner, amber 36.00
US Coin, bowl, frosted, 6" 225.00
US Coin, butter dish 400.00
US Coin, cake stand, 10" 350.00
US Coin, champagne, frosted 375.00
US Coin, compote, frosted, 6½x8½" 255.00
US Coin, compote, high std, 7" 325.00
US Coin, compote, w/lid, high std, frosted, 8" 450.00
US Coin, spooner 225.00
US Coin, sugar bowl, w/lid 325.00
US Coin, toothpick holder, frosted 175.00
US Coin, tumbler 145.00
US Coin, tumbler, frosted 225.00
US Coin, wine 235.00
Utah, goblet 25.00
Utah, jelly compote, low std, w/lid, 6" 22.50
Valencia Waffle, cake stand, amber 75.00
Valencia Waffle, compote, low std, w/lid, 7" 60.00
Valencia Waffle, creamer 40.00
Valencia Waffle, salt cellar, amber, master 25.00
Valencia Waffle, salt cellar, master 24.00
Valencia Waffle, sauce bowl, ftd 15.00
Valencia Waffle, water tray 30.00
Vermont, butter dish 42.50
Vermont, creamer, gr w/gold, 4" 50.00
Vermont, see also Custard Glass
Vermont, spooner, gr w/gold 70.00
Vermont, tumbler, clear w/gold 18.00
Viking, apothecary jar 60.00
Viking, butter dish 68.00
Viking, celery vase 40.00
Viking, egg cup 32.50
Viking, mug 60.00
Viking, spooner 32.00
Viking, sugar bowl, w/lid 65.00
Waffle, champagne 150.00
Waffle, creamer, appl hdl 135.00
Waffle, tumbler, bar 70.00
Waffle, waste bowl 70.00
Waffle & Thumbprint, bowl, 5x8¼" 52.50
Waffle & Thumbprint, decanter, orig stopper, 1-qt 225.00
Waffle & Thumbprint, salt cellar, master 42.00
Waffle & Thumbprint, sugar bowl, w/lid 165.00
Waffle & Thumbprint, whiskey 90.00
Waffle & Thumbprint, wine 70.00
Washington, bottle, bitters 88.00
Washington, claret 140.00
Washington, cordial 145.00
Washington, honey dish, 3½" 32.00
Washington, salt cellar, master; rnd 30.00
Washington, tumbler 78.00
Washington Centennial, butter dish, ftd 95.00

Washington Centennial, champagne	72.50
Washington Centennial, compote, 6½x8"	42.00
Washington Centennial, pickle dish	36.00
Washington Centennial, salt cellar, master	35.00
Washington Centennial, wine	50.00
Wedding Bells, goblet	45.00
Wedding Bells, pitcher, water; clear w/gold	48.00
Wedding Bells, wine	25.00
Wedding Ring, pitcher, milk	88.00
Wedding Ring, syrup	97.50
Wedding Ring, tumbler	80.00
Westward Ho, butter dish	185.00
Westward Ho, compote, low std, 6" dia	110.00
Westward Ho, goblet	75.00
Westward Ho, marmalade	195.00
Westward Ho, sauce bowl, ftd, 4½"	32.00
Westward Ho, spooner	80.00
Westward Ho, sugar bowl, w/lid, 4½"	175.00
Wheat & Barley, cake stand, bl, 8"	42.50
Wheat & Barley, mug	22.50
Wheat & Barley, pitcher, milk	42.50
Wheat & Barley, plate, closed hdls, vaseline, 9"	42.50
Wheat & Barley, salt cellar, bl	37.50
Wheat & Barley, shakers, pr	37.50
Wheat & Barley, syrup, amber	185.00
Wheat & Barley, tumbler, vaseline	32.00
Wildflower, butter dish, flat, amber	32.50
Wildflower, cake stand	48.00
Wildflower, creamer, vaseline	50.00
Wildflower, pitcher, water; amber	70.00
Wildflower, relish	20.00
Wildflower, tumbler	27.50
Willow Oak, bowl, w/lid, 7"	40.00
Willow Oak, bowl, 7"	15.00
Willow Oak, bread plate, 11"	37.50
Willow Oak, cake stand	42.00
Willow Oak, goblet, amber	48.00
Willow Oak, shaker, amber	70.00
Willow Oak, waste bowl	32.00
Windflower, creamer	32.00
Windflower, goblet	42.00
Windflower, tumbler, bar	38.00
Wisconsin, butter dish	88.00
Wisconsin, celery tray	42.00
Wisconsin, creamer	50.00
Wisconsin, cup & saucer	48.00
Wisconsin, relish	22.50
Wisconsin, toothpick holder	40.00
Wisconsin, wine	65.00
Wooden Pail, creamer	32.00
Wooden Pail, pitcher, water; amethyst	135.00
Wooden Pail, spooner, vaseline	52.00
Wooden Pail, sugar bowl, amethyst, mini	24.00
Wooden Pail, tumbler	18.00
Wooden Pail, tumbler, bar; amethyst	38.00
Wyoming, cake plate	50.00
Wyoming, goblet	67.50
Wyoming, wine	85.00
X-Ray, bowl, berry; beaded rim, 8"	27.50
X-Ray, butter dish, amethyst w/G gold	175.00
X-Ray, creamer, ind	18.00
X-Ray, cruet, emerald gr	135.00
X-Ray, sugar bowl, w/lid, regular	37.50
X-Ray, toothpick holder	30.00

X-Ray, tumbler	14.00
Yale, celery vase, emerald gr	48.00
Yale, compote, w/lid, 7"	70.00
Yale, goblet	32.00
Yale, shakers, emerald gr, pr	50.00
Yale, spooner	25.00
Yale, tumbler	20.00
Zipper, butter dish	48.00
Zipper, cheese dish	60.00
Zipper, goblet	35.00
Zipper, pitcher, water	42.50
Zipper, spooner	25.00
Zipper Slash, champagne	30.00
Zippered Block, carafe	40.00
Zippered Block, creamer, lg	37.50
Zippered Block, pitcher, water	125.00
Zippered Block, tumbler	35.00
Zippered Block, wine	32.00

Paul Revere Pottery

The Saturday Evening Girls were a social group of young Boston ladies who met to pursue various activities, among them pottery making. Their first kiln was bought in 1906, and within a few years it became necessary to move to a larger location. Because their new quarters were near the historical Old North Church, they chose the name Paul Revere Pottery. With very little training, the girls produced only simple ware. Until 1915 the pottery operated at a deficit; then a new building with four kilns was constructed on Nottingham Road. Vases, miniature jugs, children's tea sets, tiles, dinnerware, and lamps were produced, usually in soft matt glazes often decorated with incised, hand-painted designs from nature. Occasional examples in a dark high gloss may also be found.

Several marks were used: 'P.R.P.'; 'S.E.G.'; or the circular device, 'Boston, Paul Revere Pottery' with the horse and rider.

The pottery continued to operate; and, even though their product sold well, the high production costs of the handmade ware caused the pottery to fail in 1946.

Tea set, blue irises with green leaves carved and painted on light blue and tan with white border and dark blue base (creamer has minor damage), SEG/AM, $2,400.00.

Bowl, chick in center on dk yel, flanged, PRP/FL/2-26, 6½"	200.00
Bowl, floral border on wht, SEG/6-16, 2½x4½"	230.00
Bowl, lotus band, cvd/pnt on bl, SEG/SG, 2½x6"	450.00
Bowl, mc bands w/motto 'Best Laid Schemes...,' SEG/FL, 6"	400.00

Bowl, swan/flower band cvd/pnt on teal, SEG/FL, 2¼x5½" 700.00
Bowl, tree band, 3-color on med gr, SEG/SG/2-14, 5x12" 2,000.00
Bowl vase, tree band, cvd/pnt on teal, SEG/AM, 4¼" 950.00
Dish, band w/5 mice, cream w/blk outlines, SEG/TB/7-09, 5½" ..350.00
Lamp base, bl/wht drip on gray-bl speckled, cylinder, 11" 275.00
Mug, 'In the Forest Must Always Be...,' SEG/AM/dtd, 4", NM ...800.00
Pitcher, facing rooster band/motto on turq, SEG/sgn, 9¾" 2,200.00
Pitcher, milk; turq, ovoid, SEG/FL/5-23 ....75.00
Pitcher, tulip band, cvd/pnt on navy, PRP/11-23, 4½" 225.00
Plate, 'Monroe His Plate,' duck center on wht, PRP/26, 7½" 250.00
Teapot, iris band on bl, SEG/AM/1912, 8", +cr (EX)/sug 2,400.00
Tile, cottage/landscape, 4-color on yel, PRP, 5¾" dia 375.00
Tile, landscape, yel/gr/bl on navy, PRP/FL, 5½" dia 250.00
Tile, landscape band, cvd/pnt on yel, SEG/FL, 5½" dia 200.00
Vase, aqua mottle on gr, bulbous, 7" 155.00
Vase, dk bl, swollen cylinder, SEG/LS/1-16, 8½", NM 175.00
Vase, floral band, mc on turq gloss, ovoid, PRP, 4" 325.00
Vase, floral band on yel & wht, SEG/7-26, 10" 700.00
Vase, lotus band on lt bl, ovoid, 4¾" 200.00
Vase, sea gull band on yel, PRP/JMD/8-25, 10½" 850.00
Vase, tree border, 4-color on brn, PRP, 8½" 2,300.00
Vase, tree/hill band, brn/bl on yel, PRP/11-26, 8½" 700.00
Vase, tulip band on teal, ovoid, SEG/12-22, 6¾" 325.00

Peachblow

Peachblow, made to imitate the colors of the Chinese Peachbloom porcelain, was made by several glasshouses in the late 1800s. Among them were New England Glass; Mt. Washington; Webb; and Hobbs, Brockunier, and Company. Its pink shading was achieved through action of the heat on the gold content of the glass. While New England's peachblow shades from deep crimson to white, Mt. Washington's tends to shade from pink to blue-gray. Although usually glossy, a satin (or acid) finish was also produced, and many pieces were enameled and gilded. In the 1950s Gunderson-Pairpoint Glassworks initiated the reproduction of Mt. Washington peachblow using an exact duplication of the original formula. Though of recent manufacture, this glass is very collectible. In the listings that follow, the finish is glossy unless noted acid. Our advisors for this category are Betty and Clarence Maier; they are listed in the Directory under Pennsylvania.

Bowl, gold pine needles/prunus/butterfly, Webb, 2½x3¾" 295.00
Celery vase, scalloped rim, NE Glass, 6½" 300.00
Celery vase, sq top, NE Glass, 6½" 400.00
Creamer, Mt WA, rare, 3½" 2,150.00
Creamer, sq top, name etched on shoulder, Wheeling, 4" 700.00
Creamer & sugar, ribbed, World's Fair 1893, NE Glass 1,100.00
Creamer & sugar (open), ribbed, wht hdls, NE Glass, 3", 2¾" 450.00
Cruet, ruffled 3-sided rim, clear hdl, orig stopper, NE Glass 600.00
Pear, NE Glass, 4¾x3" 165.00
Pitcher, sq top, EX color, amber hdl, Wheeling, 5" 850.00
Powder jar, flowers/autumn leaves, emb SP lid, 4x4½" 150.00
Rose bowl, acid, World's Fair 1893 in gold, NE Glass, 2½" 325.00
Rose bowl, 8-crimp, Webb, 2¾x3" 225.00
Shaker, rnd, Wheeling, 2½" 395.00
Sugar shaker, NE Glass, 5½" 900.00
Sugar shaker, ringed neck, Wheeling, 5½" 550.00
Tumbler, EX color, Wheeling, 3¾" 450.00
Vase, acid-cut texture, pinch sides, stick neck, Webb, 8" 800.00
Vase, appl clear florals & ft, Webb, 11¾x5¾" 650.00
Vase, draped mold, ruffled, Wheeling, 7" 600.00
Vase, EX color, bulbous, Wheeling, 6½" 1,125.00
Vase, floral in gold & purple, sgn PK, English, 7½" 150.00

Vase, gold florals & bug, Webb, 5¾x3" 275.00
Vase, gold prunus, stick neck, Webb, 7¼x3¼" 265.00
Vase, gold prunus, Webb, 3¾x2¾" 365.00
Vase, gold prunus, Webb, 7x4" 325.00
Vase, gold prunus & bee, Webb, 6½x3½" 450.00
Vase, gold prunus & dragonfly, propeller mk, 5x2½", pr 475.00
Vase, gourd form, Wheeling, 8" 750.00
Vase, heavy gold prunus, Webb, 10x6" 495.00
Vase, lily; acid, tricorner rim, NE Glass, 8" 650.00
Vase, lily; tricorner top, Gunderson, 9" 250.00
Vase, Morgan; acid, satin griffin base, Wheeling, 10" 1,400.00
Vase, Morgan; shiny, Wheeling, 8", in griffin base 1,600.00
Vase, ribbed, squat/bulbous, scalloped/flared, Mt WA, 4½" 2,500.00
Vase, ruffled folded-over rim, 5 frosted ft, Sandwich, 4½" 250.00
Vase, stick neck, amber rigaree, Wheeling, 8¼x3⅜" 750.00
Vase, stick neck, Wheeling, 10½" 825.00

Wheeling pitcher, square mouth, 8", $1,000.00; Wheeling vase, 11", $825.00.

Peking Cameo Glass

The first glasshouse was established in Peking in 1680. It produced glassware made in imitation of porcelain, a more desirable medium to the Chinese. By 1725 multi-layered carving that resulted in a cameo effect led to the manufacture of a wider range of shapes and colors. The factory was closed from 1736 to 1795, but glass made in Po-shan and shipped to Peking for finishing continued to be called Peking glass. Only the cameo-type glassware is listed here. Our advisor for this category is Donald Penrose; he is listed in the Directory under Ohio. See also Orientalia.

Bowl, bird on floral branches, red on wht, w/lid, 6½x7½" 385.00
Bowl, hibiscus flowers, bl on wht, 2x7" 195.00
Vase, bird in peony tree, bl on wht, 10", pr 615.00
Vase, birds & pine tree, red on wht, 9", pr....................................495.00
Vase, butterflies & peonies, red on wht, 12" 475.00
Vase, ducks & lotus flower, red on wht, bulbous, 8½", pr 600.00
Vase, floral panels, red on wht, hexagonal, 10¼", pr....................715.00
Vase, lotus bushes, bl on wht, 10¼" 365.00
Vase, monkey in pine tree, red on wht, 9¼" 360.00
Vase, peonies, red on wht, dbl-gourd shape, 9", pr 615.00
Vase, peony & butterflies, red on wht, 6", pr 275.00
Vase, peony & butterfly, yel on wht, 9¼" 300.00
Vase, peony flowers, red on wht, gourd shape, 10", pr 715.00

Vase, pine tree & raven, gr on wht, 9" 275.00

Peloton

Peloton glass was first made by Wilhelm Kralik in Bohemia in 1880. This unusual art glass was produced by rolling colored threads onto the transparent or opaque glass gather as it was removed from the furnace. Usually more than one color of threading was used, and some items were further decorated with enameling. It was made with both shiny and acid finishes.

Pitcher, clear and white threading with enameled leaves and flowers, 7½", $375.00.

Rose bowl, lav, mc strings, clear ft, 6-crimp, 2¾x2½" 225.00
Rose bowl, pk cased, mc strings, wishbone ft, 6-crimp, 3x2½" 225.00
Rose bowl, wht opaque cased, mc strings, 6-crimp, 2¼x2⅜" 200.00
Vase, clear over lav shaded, mc strings, crimped, 6x4½" 450.00
Vase, pk shaded, pastel strings, bulbous, ribbed, 4" 600.00
Vase, wht, mc strings, ribbed, 5 wishbone ft, 7x4" 450.00
Vase, wht opaque, mc strings, folded tricorner top, 4x5" 350.00

Pennsbury

Established in the 1950s in Morrisville, Pennsylvania, by Henry Below, the Pennsbury Pottery produced dinnerware and novelty items, much of which was sold in gift shops along the Pennsylvania Turnpike. Henry and his wife, Lee, worked for years at the Stangl Pottery before striking out on their own. Lee and her daughter were the artists responsible for many of the early pieces, the bird figures among them. Pennsbury pottery was hand painted, some in blue on white, some in multicolor on caramel. Pennsylvania Dutch motifs, Amish couples, and barber shop singers were among their most popular decorative themes. Sgraffito, or hand incising, was used extensively. The company marked their wares 'Pennsbury Pottery' or 'Pennsbury Pottery, Morrisville, PA.'

In October of 1969 the company closed. Contents of the pottery were sold in December of the following year; and, in April of 1971, the buildings burned to the ground. Items marked Pennsbury Glenview or Stumar pottery (or these marks in combination) were made by Glenview after 1969. Pieces manufactured after 1976 were made by the Pennington Pottery. Several of the old molds still exist, and the original Pennsbury Caramel process is still being used on novelty items, some of which are produced by Lewis Brothers, NJ. Production of Pennsbury dinnerware was not resumed after the closing. For those wishing to learn more, we recommend *Pennsbury Pottery Video Book 1* and accompanying 1987-88 price guide offered by our advisor Shirley Graff and BA Wellman. He is listed in the Directory under Massachusetts; Mrs. Graff is in Ohio. Prices may be higher in some areas of the country, particularly on the East Coast, the southern states, and Texas.

Ash tray, Camden & Amboy RR, John Bull, 5¾x7¾" 38.00
Ash tray, Doylestown Trust 25.00
Ash tray, Dreadnaught, ship series, oval, sm 45.00
Ash tray, Hex, rnd, 5" 15.00
Ash tray, Outen the Light 20.00
Ash tray, pk tulip, octagonal, 3¼x5" 12.00
Ash tray, Rooster, scalloped, 8" 15.00
Ash tray, Rotary Club, Levittown, 8" 15.00
Ash tray, What Giffs? 20.00
Bird, Barn Swallow, 6x4½" 125.00
Bird, bookend, Eagle, 8¼", pr 125.00
Bird, Nuthatch, 3¼x3" 125.00
Bowl, cereal; Hex, 5½" 12.00
Bowl, Dutch Talk, 9" 65.00
Bowl, Folkart, rnd, 11" 30.00
Bowl, pretzel; Amish 45.00
Bowl, pretzel; Quartet, 8x11" 45.00
Bowl, Revere, ftd, 9" 30.00
Bowl, salad; Black Rooster, 6¼" 35.00
Bowl, soup; Red Rooster, ruffled rim 35.00
Bread plate, Wheat 30.00
Butter dish, Hex 18.00
Candlestick, Tulip, 2x5", pr 40.00
Candy dish, Bird Over Heart, heart form 18.00
Canister, Black Rooster, wooden lid, 4-pc set, minumum value ..385.00
Casserole, Black Rooster, rnd, w/lid, 7" 35.00
Cheese & cracker set, Hex, 3½x11" 60.00
Cigarette box, Red Rooster, 2½x4¼" 25.00
Coaster, Doyletown Nat'l Bank & Trust 12.00
Coaster, Fish, pretzel form 15.00
Coaster, Schultz 30.00
Coffeepot, Red Rooster, 2-cup, 6½" 50.00
Compote, Hex, ftd, 5" 18.00
Cookie jar, Red Rooster or Red Barn, ea 100.00
Creamer, Black Rooster, 4" 25.00
Creamer & sugar set, Amish, 2-pc, lg 30.00
Cruet, oil or vinegar; Black Rooster, pr 125.00
Cup & saucer, Black Rooster 30.00
Cup & saucer, Hex or Folkart 20.00
Cup & saucer, Red Rooster 30.00
Desk basket, Red Rooster, 5x5¼x3¼" 30.00
Egg cup, Hex 18.00
Figurine, Liberty Bell, 3½" 25.00
Gravy boat, Black Rooster 25.00
Hot plate, harvest scene, electric, w/cord, EX 80.00
Hot plate, Hex, 6x6" tile in metal fr, electric 75.00
Mug, beer; Eagle or Fisherman, 4½" 20.00
Mug, coffee; Coast Guard, 3¼" 15.00
Mug, coffee; Olson or Schultz, Barbershopper 18.00
Pitcher, Amish man, 2" 20.00
Pitcher, Barbershop Quartet, 7¼" 45.00
Pitcher, Eagle, 6¼" 20.00
Pitcher, Folkart, 3¾" 20.00
Pitcher, Red Rooster, 6" 30.00
Plaque, Amish Sayings, 7x5" 25.00
Plaque, Colt Wells Fargo Gun 45.00
Plaque, Nat'l Newark & Essex 30.00
Plaque, Outen the Light, 4" 35.00
Plaque, Railroad, General 45.00
Plate, Black Rooster, 10" 40.00
Plate, Boy & Girl, in factory fr, 11" 45.00
Plate, Courting Buggy, 8" 20.00
Plate, dinner; Folkart or Hex, 10" 22.00
Plate, Red Rooster, 10" 40.00

Plate, Yuletide, 1970 ....30.00
Platter, Fish, lg 40.00
Platter, Folkart or Hex, oval, 11x14" 25.00
Shakers, Black Rooster, pitcher form, pr...............25.00
Silent butler, Hex, bellows form, w/lid...................40.00
Snack set, Red Rooster, 2-pc 18.00
Teapot, Hex, 4-cup 40.00
Tile, Come in Without Knocking, 6" dia..................20.00
Tile, Hex, 6x6", in factory fr...................................25.00
Tureen, Folkart, w/ladle hook & ladle 150.00
Wall pocket, bird 50.00
Wall pocket, God Bless Our Mortgaged Home, sq, 6½" 40.00

Pens and Pencils

The first metallic writing pen was patented in 1809, and soon machine-produced pens with steel nibs gradually began replacing the quill. The first fountain pen was invented in 1830; but, due to the fact that a suitable metal for the tips had not yet been developed, they were not manufactured commercially until the 1880s. The first successful commercial producers were Waterman in 1884 and Parker with the Lucky Curve in 1888.

The self-filling pen of 1890 featured the soft, interior sack which filled with ink as the metal bar on the outside of the pen was raised and lowered. Variations of the pumping mechanism were tried until 1932 when Parker introduced the Vacumatic, a sackless pen with an internal pump. Our advisors for this category are Judy and Cliff Lawrence; they are listed in the Directory under Florida. For those seeking additional information, a magazine is published monthly by the Pen Fancier's Club, whose address can be found in the Directory under Clubs, Newsletters, and Catalogs. In the listings that follow, all pens are lever-filled unless otherwise noted.

Key:
AF — aeromatic filler	GPT — gold-plated trim
BF — button filler	HR — hard rubber
CF — cartridge filler	NPT — nickel-plated trim
CPT — chrome-plated trim	PF — plunger filler
ED — eyedropper filler	TD — touchdown filler
GFT — gold filled trim	VF — vacumatic filler
GFM — gold-filled metal	

Ballpoint Pens

Eberhard Faber, 1946, brn/GF cap, EX..65.00
Eversharp, CA, 1946, bl/GF cap, M 95.00
Eversharp, CA, 1947, GFM, EX...150.00
Eversharp, Skyline, CA, 1944, maroon w/striped cap, EX..............75.00
Eversharp, Skyline, CA, 1948, brn w/gold striped cap, M 75.00
Reynold's Internat'l, 1945, aluminum, GF clip, EX 250.00
Sheaffer, Stratowriter, 1946, GFM, M 95.00

Fountain Pens

Aiken Lambert, 1919, blk HR, NPT, EX..100.00
Arthur A Waterman, #103, 1909, blk chased HR, ED, EX..........100.00
Byer & Hayes, 1921, blk chased HR, NPT, EX 69.00
Conklin, 25P Crescent Filler, 1917, blk chased HR, GFT, EX 225.00
Eversharp, Gold Seal Doric, 1932, Kashmir, EX 1,200.00
Eversharp, Skyline, 1942, blk, GFT, EX...60.00
Eversharp, Skyline, 1945, bl, silver striped cap, M..........................90.00
Eversharp, Skyline, 1946, blk, GFM cap & derby, GFT, EX........100.00
Eversharp, Skyline Presentation, lady's, 1945, bl, GFM cap, M 90.00

Faber Castell, 1954, blk, GFT, twist filler, EX 125.00
Gold Bond, Stonite, 1929, gr marbleized, GFT, EX........................90.00
Ingersoll, 1925, NP metal, EX 100.00
Mont Blanc, #22, 1963, blk, GFT, twist filler, EX 200.00
Mont Blanc, #3-42G, 1942, blk, GFT, twist filler, EX 250.00
Parker, Bl Dmn Vacumatic, 1945, gr stripes, GFT, VF, M..........110.00
Parker, Bl Dmn 51, 1945, brn, GFT, GFM cap, VF, NM..............100.00
Parker, Duofold, 1941, pk/silver stripes, GFT, BF, EX.................100.00
Parker, Duofold Deluxe Big Red, 1926, wide band, GFT, BF, EX..995.00
Parker, Duofold Jr, 1926, blk, GFT, BF, EX..................................140.00
Parker, Duofold Jr, 1928, Mandarin yel, gold trim, BF, EX 250.00
Parker, Duofold Sr, 1926, blk, GFT, BF, EX..................................295.00
Parker, Duofold Sr, 1927, lapis bl, GFT, EX.................................895.00
Parker, Duofold Sr, 1930, blk, gold trim, BF, EX.........................295.00
Parker, Duofold Jr, 1928, gr marbleized, GFT, BF, G 100.00
Parker, Parkette (Canada), 1938, gr marbleized, GFT, EX............70.00
Parker, Parkette Deluxe, 1936, red pearl, GFT, EX 90.00
Parker, Royal Challenger, 1937, gold marbleized, BF, EX............180.00
Parker, Senior Maxima Vacumatic, 1937, blk w/gold, VF, EX 895.00
Parker, Signet 61, 1961, GFM, capillary filler, EX.......................190.00
Parker, Special 51, 1950, maroon w/chrome cap, CPT, AF, EX.....50.00
Parker, True Blue, 1932, GFT, BF, EX...125.00
Parker, Vacumatic, 1935, blk, GFT, VF, EX...................................195.00
Parker, Vacumatic, 1935, silver pearl, NPT, VG, EX....................250.00
Parker, Vacumatic, 1947, blk, GFT, VF, M 90.00
Parker, VP, 1962, red, Lustraloy cap, AF, EX...............................250.00
Parker, 51, 1950, gr w/Lustraloy cap, CPT, AF, EX 55.00
Parker, 51, 1950, maroon, Lustraloy cap, CPT, AF, M..................80.00
Pelican, DRP #100, 1932, blk, GFT, twist filler, EX 395.00
Sheaffer, #3, 1935, silver-red streaked pearl, CPT, EX 70.00
Sheaffer, #3-25, 1925, blk, GFT, EX...125.00
Sheaffer, #5-30, 1933, blk, GFT, EX..90.00
Sheaffer, Imperial III, 1967, blk, GFT, TD, EX 60.00
Sheaffer, Imperial V, 1967, bl, GFM cap, GFT, TD, M.................80.00
Sheaffer, Junior, 1935, silver pearl, CPT, EX 60.00
Sheaffer, Lifetime, 1928, gr jade, EX...250.00
Sheaffer, Lifetime, 1934, blk, GFT, EX..115.00
Sheaffer, Lifetime, 1939, blk, solid gold trim, EX 250.00
Sheaffer, Lifetime Feathertouch 1000, 1939, blk, EX....................250.00
Sheaffer, Lifetime Triumph, 1942, blk, gold cap/clip, PF, EX 550.00
Sheaffer, PFM I Snorkel, 1959, maroon, CPT, alloy nib, TD, M.125.00
Sheaffer, PFM II, 1959, bl, Lustraloy cap, CPT, TD, M 150.00
Sheaffer, Self-Filling #2, 1924, gold trim, GFM, EX.....................250.00
Sheaffer, Wht Dot Sentinel Snorkel Triumph, blk, GFM cap, M..85.00
Sheaffer, Wht Dot Snorkel Triumph, 1953, blk, GFT, TD, M 85.00
Sheaffer, Wht Dot TM Triumph, 1951, GFM, TD, M..................185.00
Swan, #46 ETN, 1927, red mottled, GFT, G...................................300.00
Swan, 1932, pk pearl marbleized, GFT, EX 100.00
Wahl, Signature, 1922, blk chased HR, GFT, EX 575.00
Wahl, 1927, blk chased HR, GFT, G 100.00
Wahl-Eversharp, Gold Seal, 1929, bl marbleized, GFT, EX........375.00
Wahl-Eversharp, Gold Seal, 1929, coral, GFT, EX 125.00
Waterman, Demonstrator, 1948, clear plastic, GFT, M 250.00
Waterman, Emblem, 1947, blk, GFT, M 325.00
Waterman, Hundred Year, 1939, blk, GFT 395.00
Waterman, Ideal #0552½V, 1924, gold filigree, GFT, EX 175.00
Waterman, Ideal #0754, 1926, blk chased HR, GFT, EX..............180.00
Waterman, Ideal #52V, 1920, blk chased HR, NPT, EX 100.00
Waterman, Ideal Continental #42, 1924, GFM, ED, EX......... 1,750.00
Waterman, Ideal 12PSF, 1916, blk chased HR, NPT, M 150.00
Waterman, 1974 (France), silver moire, CPT, cartridge, M 100.00

Mechanical Pencils

Eversharp, Big Boy, 1927, GFM, EX 150.00

Eversharp, Big Boy, 1927, red HR, EX 140.00
Eversharp, Skyline Repeater, 1942, brn, GFT, M 50.00
Eversharp, 1926, GFM, M 50.00
Eversharp, 1926, red chased HR, EX 60.00
Parker, Duofold, 1928, lapiz bl, EX 112.00
Parker, Duofold Big Bro, 1926, blk, GFT, EX 250.00
Parker, Duofold Sr, 1926, red, GFT, EX 165.00
Parker, Pastel, 1929, apple gr moire, EX......................................89.00
Sheaffer, Lifetime, 1926, blk, G 90.00
Sheaffer, 1922, cherry red, rare, EX...130.00
Wahl-Eversharp, Colonnade, 1926, GFM, EX 140.00
Wahl-Eversharp, Golf, 1930, blk, EX 90.00
Wahl-Eversharp, 1920, SP, M 40.00
Wahl-Eversharp, 1922, blk chased HR, GFT, EX 50.00
Wahl-Eversharp, 1929, bl marbleized, GFT, EX 90.00
Wahl-Eversharp, 1929, red HR, M..70.00
Waterman, Ideal Ripple, 1927, bl-gr HR, GFT, EX 135.00
Waterman, Pansy Panel Sterling, 1924, EX.................................150.00

Sets

Eversharp, Bantam, 1932, bl swirl, GFT, AF, EX 90.00
Eversharp, Silver Seal Doric, 1936, silver pearl, CPT, EX 795.00
Parker, Custom 21, blk w/gold, GFM caps, AF, M 80.00
Sheaffer, #875, 1946, red stripes, GFT, PF, EX 90.00
Sheaffer, Lifetime Triumph 2000, 1946, blk, gold clips/bands 535.00
Sheaffer, PFM III Snorkel, 1959, maroon, GFT, TD, M 225.00

Personalities, Fact and Fiction

One of the largest and most popular areas of collecting today, if trade-paper ads and articles be any indication, is character-related memorabilia. Everyone has favorites, whether they be comic-strip personalities or true-life heroes. The earliest comic strip dealt with the adventures of the Yellow Kid, the smiling, bald-headed Oriental boy always in a nightshirt. He was introduced in 1895, a product of the imagination of Richard Fenton Outcault. Today, though very hard to come by, items relating to the Yellow Kid bring premium prices.

In 1902 Buster Brown and Tige, his dog and constant companion (more of Outcault's progenies), made it big in the comics as well as in the world of advertising. Shoe stores appealed to the younger set through merchandising displays that featured them both. Today items from their earlier years are very collectible.

Though her 1923 introduction was unobtrusively made through only one newspaper, New York's *Daily News*, Little Orphan Annie, the vacant-eyed redhead in the inevitable red dress, was quickly adopted by hordes of readers nationwide; and, before the demise of her creator, Harold Gray, in 1968, she had starred in her own radio show. She made two feature films, and in 1977 'Annie' was launched on Broadway.

Other early comic figures were Moon Mullins, created in 1923 by Frank Willard; Buck Rogers by Philip Nowlan in 1928; and Betty Boop, the round-faced, innocent-eyed, chubby-cheeked Boop-Boop-a-Doop girl of the early 1930s. Bimbo was her dog and KoKo her clown friend.

Popeye made his debut in 1929 as the spinach-eating sailor with the spindly-limbed girlfriend, Olive Oyl, in the comic strip *Thimble Theatre*, created by Elzie Segar. He became a film star in 1933 and had his own radio show that during 1936 played three times a week on CBS. He obligingly modeled for scores of toys, dolls, and figurines, and especially those from the thirties are very collectible.

Tarzan, created around 1912 by Edgar Rice Burroughs, and Captain Midnight, by Robert Burtt and Willfred G. Moore, are popular heroes with today's collectors. During the days of radio, Sky King of the Flying Crown Ranch (also created by Burtt and Moore) thrilled boys

and girls of the mid-1940s. Hopalong Cassidy, Red Rider, Tom Mix, and the Lone Ranger were only a few of the other 'good guys' always on the side of law and order.

But of all the fictional heroes and comic characters collected today, probably the best loved and most well known is Mickey Mouse. Created in the late 1920s by Walt Disney, Micky (as his name was first spelled) became an instant success with his film debut, Steamboat Willie. His popularity was parlayed through wind-up toys, watches, figurines, cookie jars, puppets, clothing, and numerous other products. Items from the 1930s are usually copyrighted 'Walt Disney Enterprises'; thereafter, 'Walt Disney Productions' was used.

Mickey Mouse's dog pal Goofy celebrated his 60th birthday in 1992. Originally known as Dippy Dawg, he first appeared in a 1932 cartoon, 'Mickey's Revue.' Soon Goofy emerged as a star in his own right and in the fifties was featured in many films in which he attempted very unsuccessfully to demonstrate his skiing skills, driving abilities, etc.

For those interested in Disneyana, we recommend *Stern's Guide to Disney Collectibles*, available from Collector Books. Our advisors for this category are Cathy and Norm Vigue; they are listed in the Directory under Massachusetts. See also Autographs; Banks; Big Little Books; Cartoon Books; Children's Books; Comic Books; Cookie Jars; Dolls; Lunch Boxes; Movie Memorabilia; Paper Dolls; Pin-Back Buttons; Posters; Rock 'N Roll Memorabilia; Toys.

Addams Family, Thing bank, NM in box 85.00
Alice in Wonderland, paint box, tin, Page of London, 20x9" 20.00
Alice in Wonderland, record album, G Rogers, Disney, 1944 ....35.00
Alice in Wonderland, school bag...60.00
Alice in Wonderland, tile, British, 1930s 175.00
Amos & Andy, table clock, 1935...245.00
Annie Oakley, Little Golden Book, AO Sharpshooter, 1956, EX .10.00
Art Linkletter, House Party Game, M...39.00
Arthur Godfrey, ukelele, Emenee, w/song book, 1950, MIB 50.00
Babe Ruth, wristwatch, Exact Time 275.00
Babes in Toyland, fr-tray puzzle, Whitman, 1965, M 12.00
Bambi, Gadabout Jr suitcase...50.00
Bambi, shakers, ceramic, unmk, 1940s, pr...................................30.00
Batman, Batmobile, red tin litho, battery op, '70s, 11½", M........125.00
Batman, cave lamp, EX 75.00
Batman, sticker book, Whitman, 1966, M....................................28.00
Beatles, Band-Aid dispenser, dtd 1966 ....12.50
Beatles, hairbrush, M in unopened pkg 15.00
Beatles, tray, 4 autographed pictures, England, 1960s 35.00

Betty Boop tea set in original box, lustreware, service for four, $375.00.

Betty Boop, dbl flip book, 1930s, EX..38.00
Betty Boop, figure, jtd wood, orig blk dress, Kallus, EX...............850.00

Betty Boop, shirt decal, 1950s 12.00
Betty Boop, socks, 1930s, orig label, rare, pr 95.00
Betty Boop, tip tray, tin litho, Spanish wording, 6½", EX 35.00
Betty Boop, wall vase, figural, Fleischer Studios 125.00
Beverly Hillbillies, card game, 1963, NM 15.00
Beverly Hillbillies, jigsaw puzzle, 1960s, MIB 12.50
Big Bad Wolf, metal charm, Disney, early, NM 45.00
Billy West, BW Club ring..20.00
Bing Crosby, game, Call Me Lucky, 1954, MIB................45.00
Blondie, cookie cutters, NM in box 100.00
Blondie, Cookie figure, Syrocco, 1944, M....................30.00
Blondie, game, ...Goes to Leisureland, Westinghouse, 1935 ....20.00
Blondie, paint book, Whitman #605, NM 25.00
Blondie, stationery set, 1950s, EX 26.00
Blondie & Dagwood, interchangeable wood blocks, 1951, MIB ...45.00
Blue Fairy, valentine, animated, 1939, M in envelope 25.00
Bobbie Benson's B-Bar-B Riders, color book, Whitman, 1950, M .20.00
Bozo the Clown, Stitch-a-Story, M 10.00
Buck Rogers, Chief Explorer badge, M 200.00
Buck Rogers, pencil box, yel & blk on gr, 1935, EX 75.00
Buck Rogers, pocket watch, Ingraham, w/illus box & insert ... 1,000.00
Buck Rogers, Solar Scout badge, M 75.00
Buffalo Bill, cap gun, CI, EX 65.00
Buffalo Bill Jr, belt buckle, Mars candy premium, EX...................15.00
Bugs Bunny, mug, full-color graphic, Warner Bros, 1960s, M 39.00
Bugs Bunny, talking alarm clock, 1974, MIB................35.00
Bugs Bunny, toothbrush holder, plastic figural, Warner Bros.........39.00
Captain America, Sentinels of Liberty badge, NM 330.00
Captain Gallant, game, 1955, EX....................................35.00
Captain Marvel, Shazam paper game, 1944, M in envelope..........45.00
Captain Midnight, Cod-O-Graph, 1947 radio premium 45.00
Captain Midnight, decoder, no key, 1949........................65.00
Captain Video, press book, toys & merchandise shown, EX 75.00
Charlie McCarthy, egg cup, lustreware, 1930s.............185.00
Charlie the Tuna, pencil sharpener, MIB 25.00
Charlie the Tuna, wristwatch, 1977, M in flat box 45.00
Cinderella, wristwatch, 1955, MIB 100.00
Cisco Kid, face mask, paper 30.00
Cisco Kid, hobby horse..85.00
Cisco Kid, photo card, Tip Top Bread 12.50
Cisco Kid, scarf slide, radio premium, M 30.00
Cisco Kid & Pancho, cereal bowl, blk on milk glass, M 20.00
Cisco Kid & Pancho, masks, Tip Top Bread, pr 40.00
Colonel Sanders, figure, compo, 1954, 6½", M.............65.00
Dale Evans, Hartland figure, w/Buttercup, M 165.00
Dale Evans, wash mit, cloth 20.00
Dale Evans, wristwatch, orig band, 1951, NM 95.00
Darth Vader, bank, ceramic, 1977, rare, M 95.00
Darth Vader, helmet, Don Post, 1977, MIB..................150.00
Darth Vader, lamp, ceramic, bust figural, lg................90.00
Darth Vader, telephone, 1-pc standing unit, M 65.00
Davy Crockett, bedspread, chenille, EX 195.00
Davy Crockett, game, Rescue, EX 50.00
Davy Crockett, jacket, vinyl, fringed, w/coonskin cap, EX 65.00
Davy Crockett, lamp, chalkware figural, dtd 1955, EX...............55.00
Davy Crockett, mug, red Fire-King 14.00
Davy Crockett, pitcher, brn on frosted glass, 1955, 8"...............45.00
Davy Crockett, tie clip, copper-tone metal, MIB 15.00
Davy Crockett, tumbler, red graphics on clear, 5⅞" 15.00
Dennis the Menace, hand puppet, w/stand & ft 20.00
Dick Tracy, kit, Crimestoppers Club, 1961 giveaway, MIB............25.00
Dick Tracy, membership certificate, Secret Service, 1939 ....25.00
Dick Tracy, Secret Detective Methods & Magic Tricks, 1939, M ..30.00
Dionne Quintuplets, hair ribbon, 1936, M on card 75.00

Knickerbocker Donald Duck cloth doll fitted with music box (overwound), 16", $1,760.00.

Donald Duck, game, cards, Disney, 1949, EX in box 20.00
Donald Duck, puppet, unpunched, from DD Bread, M 14.50
Donald Duck, ring toss game, DD/nephews standing target, MIB..75.00
Donald Duck, valentine card, dtd 1939, M....................25.00
Dopey, bank, compo figural, WDE, dtd 1938 ....100.00
Dopey, lamp, ceramic figural, dtd 1938, w/orig shade, 7" 200.00
Dr Kildare, game, 1963, EX 20.00
Dr Kildare, Thumpy the Heart Beat stethoscope, M in pkg 20.00
Dr Seuss Cat in the Hat, alarm clock, NM 165.00
Elmer Fudd, wristwatch, Sheraton, 1972, M in pkg.....................85.00
Elsie the Cow, charm, gold-tone plastic, ¾" dia 12.00
Elsie the Cow, cookbook, hard-cover, 1952, 1st ed, 374-pg 30.00
Elsie the Cow, creamer, pottery, 6x6" 45.00
Elsie the Cow, figure, jtd wood, leather ears, 7x6", NM 65.00
Elsie the Cow, pin-bk button, tin litho 18.00
Elsie the Cow, place mat, paper, M 15.00
Elsie the Cow, Zippo lighter, EX graphics, 2⅛", EX 55.00
Elvira, spray hair color 2.50
Elvis Presley, Anniversary photo album, 1978, M 35.00
Elvis Presley, calendar, 1986, M 8.00
Elvis Presley, Christmas tree ornament 15.00
Elvis Presley, handkerchief, dtd 1956, M......................20.00
Elvis Presley, mug, plastic, thermal, 1977, M 10.00
Elvis Presley, pennant, 1977, M 10.00
Elvis Presley, shakers, ceramic, pr.................................55.00
Elvis Presley & Priscilla, paper dolls, 1st ed, uncut 40.00
Farina, post card, sepia tones, Hal Roach, M 15.00
Felix the Cat, pencil case, w/orig rulers, 1934, NM 95.00
Ferdinand the Bull, game, 1938, EX...............................38.00
Flintstones, Bam Bam bubble pipe, 1963, M in pkg.....................22.00
Flintstones, Betty & Barney Rubble spoon rest, ceramic, 1961 ......38.00
Flintstones, Pebbles bank, vinyl 25.00
Flintstones, snow dome, Hanna Barbera, 1975, M.......................39.00
Frank Buck, Official Handbook for Members 35.00
Frankenstein, mask, rubber, full head, EX 35.00
Fred Astaire, dance studio trophy, 1960.........................38.00
Frosty the Snowman, puzzle, F Winship, Whitman, NM 7.50
G-Man, Radio Club ring...20.00
Gabby Hayes, cannon ring, complete 250.00
Gene Autry, boots, rubber, EX in orig box 150.00
Gene Autry, dbl gun & holster set, MIB........................375.00
Gene Autry, Dude Ranch game, MIB.............................95.00
Gene Autry, guitar, Emenee Professional, MIB 75.00

Gene Autry, gun & holster, Flying A, NM 190.00
Gene Autry, photo post card, M 10.00
Gene Autry, record, Peter Cottontail, 78 rpm, NM 12.00
Gene Autry, sheet music, Red River Valley, EX 20.00
Gene Autry, wristwatch, rpl hands, 1951, EX 150.00
Gene Autry, wristwatch, 1951, MIB 450.00
GI Joe, color book, M 10.00
Goofy, figure, wooden, Goofy playing basketball, 1950s, MIB 27.50
Goofy, snack tray, Goofy as golfer, 1950s, M 25.00
Green Hornet, compartment ring, premium 750.00
Happy Hooligan, bank, pottery figural, dtd 1920, NM 225.00
Hopalong Cassidy, bedspread 185.00
Hopalong Cassidy, binoculars, metal, NM 35.00
Hopalong Cassidy, button, Saving Club Teller, M in pkg 18.00
Hopalong Cassidy, Chinese Checkers, EX 100.00
Hopalong Cassidy, clothes hamper, EX 250.00
Hopalong Cassidy, compass hat ring 195.00
Hopalong Cassidy, display, Butternut Bread, M 85.00
Hopalong Cassidy, face mask, latex, MIB 200.00
Hopalong Cassidy, floor mat, chenille, 45" 95.00
Hopalong Cassidy, guitar, w/Topper, EX 75.00
Hopalong Cassidy, gun, Zoomerang, red, MIB 125.00
Hopalong Cassidy, gun & holster school box, complete 85.00
Hopalong Cassidy, hair trainer 25.00
Hopalong Cassidy, hat, gray felt, rare, EX 175.00
Hopalong Cassidy, ice cream container, EX 35.00
Hopalong Cassidy, jewelry, Anson, MIB 125.00
Hopalong Cassidy, plate, sgn Ivan Anderson, rare 120.00
Hopalong Cassidy, puzzle, Milton Bradley, 1950s, NM 22.50
Hopalong Cassidy, radio, blk, EX 600.00
Hopalong Cassidy, radio, red, working 500.00
Hopalong Cassidy, rug, 24x48", EX 125.00
Hopalong Cassidy, scarf, w/Topper, lg 45.00
Hopalong Cassidy, stationery, Buzza Cardoza, EX in box ...175.00
Hopalong Cassidy, tumbler, blk graphics on milk glass, 4¾" 25.00
Hopalong Cassidy, Western Ranch Playhouse set, NM 200.00
Hopalong Cassidy, wristwatch, 1950, NM 75.00
Howdy Doody, bandana, sgn Bob Smith, NM 50.00
Howdy Doody, Doodler kit, electric 45.00
Howdy Doody, flashlight ring 145.00
Howdy Doody, Fudge Bar wrapper, 1950 ....3.00
Howdy Doody, HD's TV Game, missing spinner, NM 25.00
Howdy Doody, ice cream spoon, Kayran, M 10.00
Howdy Doody, Magic Trading Card 10.00
Howdy Doody, marionette, compo head & hands, 19", EX 150.00
Howdy Doody, night light, ceramic, Leadworks 20.00
Howdy Doody, pin, full-figure plastic 18.00
Howdy Doody, puppet mitten kit, M on orig sealed box 45.00
Howdy Doody, record player, MIB 250.00
Howdy Doody, slipper sock kit, VG orig pkg 45.00
Howdy Doody, spinning top, 1970s, M 22.00
Howdy Doody, wall walker 35.00
Huckleberry Hound, china cup, Screen Gems, 1¾" dia, M 25.00
Huckleberry Hound, cuff links & tie clip, 1959, M on card ...25.00
Huckleberry Hound, shooting gallery, 1959, EX 40.00
Jack Armstrong, Answer Box, radio premium 45.00
Jack Armstrong, Egyptian ring, radio premium 45.00
Jack Armstrong, Explorer's telescope, 1938 radio premium 40.00
Jack Armstrong, propeller gun, EX in box 65.00
Jackie Gleason, Away We Go bus, 1955, EX 350.00
Jackie Gleason, song folio, 1954 ....28.00
James Bond, game, Secret Agent, NM 30.00
James Bond, ring, thin metal, adjusts, 1950s, M 10.00
Jiminy Cricket, tin clicker, ...United Way, 1940s, M 45.00

Joe Palooka, Little Max's bank/candy container, 1950s, MIB 25.00
John Glenn, astronaut puzzle, cb, Japan, 1960s, 8x6", NM 5.00
Kayo, figure, HP lead, 1930s, 1¼", M 35.00
Keystone Cop, doll, bubble head, EX 48.00
Lady & Tramp, tape dispenser, heavy metal, 1950s, NM 32.00
Little Audrey, doll, vinyl, 13" 28.00
Little Orphan Annie, board game, Treasure Hunt, 1930s, EX 25.00
Little Orphan Annie, cane top, ceramic, pnt wear, 1930s, EX ...45.00
Little Orphan Annie, decoder, 1940 ....24.00
Little Orphan Annie, game, Rummy, 1935, EX in orig box ...20.00
Little Orphan Annie, mask, premium, full color, ca 1933 .....35.00
Little Orphan Annie, puzzle, 1930s, MIB 30.00
Little Orphan Annie, wall pocket, lustreware, EX 175.00
Little Orphan Annie, wristwatch, Harold Gray 125.00
Little Orphan Annie & Sandy, pull toy, wooden, 1930s, EX ...115.00
Little Orphan Annie & Sandy, shakers, 1930s, pr 38.00
Lone Ranger, badge, Chief Scout shield, tin, 1941, sm, EX 25.00
Lone Ranger, badge, Safety Club, Bond Bread, 1938, M 30.00
Lone Ranger, badge, secret compartment 45.00
Lone Ranger, ballpoint pen, Silver Bullet Secret Code, '50s, M 75.00
Lone Ranger, board game, premium, EX 30.00
Lone Ranger, bolo tie, 50 Years, 1933-83 ....12.00
Lone Ranger, cap pistol, CI, EX 250.00
Lone Ranger, cap rifle, Winchester, 1963, M on orig cb 195.00
Lone Ranger, cork gun, long barrel, EX 125.00
Lone Ranger, cup, Clayton Moore, 1961, M 95.00
Lone Ranger, Deputy kit, Cheerios premium, 1980, M 25.00
Lone Ranger, first-aid kit, tin litho, hinged lid, 1½x6x4" 35.00
Lone Ranger, game, tin litho target, Marx, 1938, EX 110.00
Lone Ranger, hairbrush, wooden hdl, 1939, M in box 75.00
Lone Ranger, pattern, Simplicity, complete, EX 15.00
Lone Ranger, Peace Patrol membership card, EX 16.00
Lone Ranger, pedometer, premium, M 30.00
Lone Ranger, pencil, Silver Bullet, M on card 45.00
Lone Ranger, pin, Betty Gardenia Glow flower, rare 275.00
Lone Ranger, poster, 50th anniversary 22.00
Lone Ranger, push puppet, plastic & wood, 6", EX 85.00
Lone Ranger, ring, Atom Bomb, Kix premium, EX 65.00
Lone Ranger, ring, flashlight, EX 50.00
Lone Ranger, ring, saddle, w/filmstrip, EX 135.00
Lone Ranger, ring, 6-Shooter, premium 95.00
Lone Ranger, rocking horse, VG 225.00
Lone Ranger, shoe brush, 1950s, NM in box 55.00
Lone Ranger, Silver Bullet w/compass & silver ore 50.00
Lone Ranger, snow dome, LR lassoing calf, M 95.00
Lone Ranger, tent, 1958, NM in orig box 225.00
Lone Ranger, toothbrush holder, compo figural, 1938, EX 68.00
Lone Ranger, Victory Corps pin, 1942, EX 18.00
Lone Ranger, watch fob, metal, 1938 ....50.00
Lone Ranger & Tonto, guitar, Jefferson, MIB 50.00
Lone Wolf, watch fob 40.00
Ludwig Von Drake & D Duck, shakers, ceramic, WDP, '61, pr ...35.00
Maggie & Jiggs, shakers, ceramic, pr 45.00
Magilla Gorilla, cannon, 1964, MIB 115.00
Mary Poppins, manicure kit, unopened, M 35.00
Mary Poppins, paint & crayon set, Disney, 1964, MIB 30.00
Mary Poppins, SP spoon, dtd 1964, child's, EX 15.00
Maverick, dbl gun & holster set, MIB 185.00
Mickey & Minnie Mouse, creamer, bl lustre, 1930s 35.00
Mickey & Minnie Mouse, toothbrush holder, WDE, 1930s, 4½" ...225.00
Mickey Mouse, buttons (4), WDE, 1930s, M on decorated card ...75.00
Mickey Mouse, figure, bsk, playing saxophone, WD, 1940s ...75.00
Mickey Mouse, fountain pen, Inkograph, '36, EX color, 5½" ...175.00
Mickey Mouse, game, Canasta Jr, EX in orig box 28.00

Mickey Mouse alarm clock, US Time, $675.00, MIB.

Mickey Mouse, game, Coming Home, Marx, 1934, EX in box 195.00
Mickey Mouse, game, Old Maid cards, WDE, MIB......................85.00
Mickey Mouse, game, Scatterball, NM in box........................295.00
Mickey Mouse, game, target, complete, 1935, NM 275.00
Mickey Mouse, iron applique, Bondex, 1946 ....35.00
Mickey Mouse, kaleidoscope, EX...35.00
Mickey Mouse, Mouseketeer ears, 1950s, M on card 25.00
Mickey Mouse, napkin ring, Bakelite figural, '30s, 2¾x2¾".........60.00
Mickey Mouse, night light/music box, plastic, Schmid, 5x6".........55.00
Mickey Mouse, penny book, Uphill Fight, 1934, EX...................17.50
Mickey Mouse, pitcher, MM figural, WD, early, milk sz 115.00
Mickey Mouse, planter, Leeds China, 1947.............................125.00
Mickey Mouse, pocket watch w/fob, MIB 750.00
Mickey Mouse, puppet form, Colorforms, MIB...........................55.00
Mickey Mouse, sheet music, Wedding Party, 1931, EX.................30.00
Mickey Mouse, shoe polish, Scuffy, liquid, MIB 20.00
Mickey Mouse, Stardust paint-by-number, M 16.50
Mickey Mouse, swim ring, inflatable, 1950s, M in pkg.................35.00
Mickey Mouse, switchplate, plastic, 1950s, 5", M in pkg 22.00
Mickey Mouse, telephone, Western Electric 95.00
Mickey Mouse, tie rack, wooden, 1930s, EX 110.00
Mickey Mouse, wall pocket, lustreware, sgn Disney, Japan 235.00
Mickey Mouse, wristwatch, Bradley, 1978-79, M 100.00
Mickey Mouse, wristwatch, Ingersoll, gold-plated case, 1947 ......200.00
Mickey Mouse, wristwatch, MM in bellbottoms, Remex, '50s, EX ...25.00
Mickey Mouse Club, hat, 1950s 40.00
Mickey Mouse Club, pocket flashlight..20.00
Minnie Mouse, bank, heavy CI, EX pnt, 1930s, 8¼".................155.00
Minnie Mouse, egg cup, ceramic, unmk, 1930s, 3".....................95.00
Minnie Mouse, figure, jtd wood, w/label, 1935, 4" 145.00
Minnie Mouse, figure, jtd wood, 1930s, 5½"...........................110.00
Minnie Mouse, tumbler, blk graphics on clear glass, WD, 4¾" 25.00
Monkees, Mike Nesmith doll, M on card 12.50
Moon Mullins, figure, HP lead, 1930s, 2", M.............................35.00
Moon Mullins, figure, jtd wood, 4", NM...................................95.00
Mother Hubbard, game, Parker Bros, complete w/instructions 120.00
Munsters, board game, 1964, MIB..55.00
Munsters, movie poster, 3-sheet, M 145.00
Olive Oyl, tile, ceramic, wall hanging, 3x4" 45.00
Our Gang, book, Story of Our Gang, full color, 1939, EX.............35.00
Our Gang, calendar, 1943, EX...85.00
Our Gang, Jean Darling plate, ceramic, 1920s, M 50.00
Our Gang, post card, sepia, M 12.00
Perry Mason, Missing Suspect game, Parker Bros, 1959, EX 40.00
Pete Rose, Wheaties cereal box, M 15.00
Pinky Lee, paint set, MIB...70.00
Pinocchio, figure, jtd wood & papier-mache, WDP, 10" 85.00

Pinocchio, pail, tin, 2 lg faces, colorful, 1930s, 5" dia, NM 150.00
Pinocchio, Playing Xylophone, battery op, 1961, EX in box 125.00
Pinocchio, record album, 3 records in sleeve, WDE, 1939, EX 95.00
Pinocchio, scatter rug, M 75.00
Pluto the Pup, book, linen type, WDE, EX 85.00
Popeye, book, Choose Your Weppins, Saalfield, EX.....................10.00
Popeye, book, House That Popeye Built, Wonder Book, '60, NM.10.00
Popeye, bubble set, King Features, 1936, NM in orig box 25.00
Popeye, chalk, 1953, MIB...18.00
Popeye, figure, celluloid, 3", M..225.00
Popeye, game, Popeye the Juggler, tin litho, 1929, EX 55.00
Popeye, pencil sharpener, amber or gr Bakelite, ea......................60.00
Popeye, popcorn tin, rectangular, 1949, NM 75.00
Popeye, wallpaper, 1930s, 10-ft roll, M 195.00
Porky Pig, wristwatch, Sheraton, 1972, M in pkg......................200.00
Prince Valiant, pin-bk button, rare 25.00
Raggedy Ann, music box, Schmid...65.00
Ramar of the Jungle, game, EX 40.00
Ramar of the Jungle, puzzle, 1955, boxed set of 4 ....30.00
Rawhide, canteen, M in pkg...35.00
Red Riding Hood, hand puppet, 1950s, MIB 35.00
Red Riding Hood, paint book, Ohio Art, EX 20.00
Red Riding Hood, tin plate 18.00
Red Ryder, BB gun, plastic stock, Plymouth MI 70.00
Red Ryder, mittens, unopened in orig pack 40.00
Red Ryder, salesman's case for gloves 250.00
Reddy Kilowatt, figure, jtd wood, 14", EX 90.00
Richard Nixon, clicker, tin, pear shape, M 20.00
Rifleman, rifle, MIB...295.00
Rin Tin Tin, rifle, plastic, 5¼" 8.00
Rocky Graziano, boxing gloves, MIB......................................145.00
Roy Rogers, alarm clock, animated, working, EX 250.00
Roy Rogers, annual, 1954...39.00
Roy Rogers, badge, 5-point star, EX 25.00
Roy Rogers, bank, tin litho, w/Trigger, wall mt 85.00
Roy Rogers, bedspread, embr figures, EX 175.00
Roy Rogers, booties, blk felt w/wht fringe, RR & Trigger, M.......100.00
Roy Rogers, camera, box style, w/Trigger, EX............................35.00
Roy Rogers, chaps, vinyl, w/Trigger, 1950s, pr..........................35.00
Roy Rogers, crayon set w/stencils, NM 195.00
Roy Rogers, guitar, Jefferson, MIB..65.00
Roy Rogers, gun, Crackin' Good, paper premium 22.00
Roy Rogers, gun & holster set, NM 165.00
Roy Rogers, harmonica, Rider's, NM 15.00
Roy Rogers, Hartland figure, w/Trigger, sm, M on card 120.00
Roy Rogers, horse trailer & jeep, MIB.....................................200.00
Roy Rogers, horseshoe set, MIB..85.00
Roy Rogers, lamp, compo, w/Trigger, sgn, M...........................250.00
Roy Rogers, Magic Playaround set, complete 250.00
Roy Rogers, modeling clay set, NM 125.00
Roy Rogers, mug, plastic figural, F&F Mold & Die, M................15.00
Roy Rogers, neckerchief 35.00
Roy Rogers, pencil box 35.00
Roy Rogers, photo, w/Trigger, color, 1940s, 8x10", M 12.50
Roy Rogers, plate, ceramic, w/Trigger, dinner sz, M 38.00
Roy Rogers, raincoat w/hat, vinyl 425.00
Roy Rogers, ring, branding iron 125.00
Roy Rogers, ring, magnifier 75.00
Roy Rogers, saddle, EX tooled leather 650.00
Roy Rogers, shirt, yel w/blk yoke & embr, 1950s, M 45.00
Roy Rogers, telephone 350.00
Roy Rogers, tent, EX 225.00
Roy Rogers, toothbrush, M in pkg...30.00
Roy Rogers, wristwatch, orig band, ca 1951, NM......................110.00

Rudolph the Red-Nosed Reindeer, snow dome, 1950s, M............45.00
Scarlett O'Hara, game, One of Her Problems, NM 45.00
Scarlett O'Hara, perfume bottle, Pinaud, 1940s 145.00
Schmoo, planter, 1948 ....30.00
Schmoo, tumbler, orange on clear glass, Al Cap, 1949, M...........20.00
Shirley Temple, book, Little Princess, #1783, 1939, M 45.00
Shirley Temple, candy mold, scarce 150.00
Shirley Temple, cereal box, 1930s, EX 225.00
Shirley Temple, cigar bands, 1930s 75.00
Shirley Temple, color book, Bluebird, 1930s, all orig, EX 95.00
Shirley Temple, creamer, cobalt glass, M 35.00
Shirley Temple, doll pin, Ideal, 1930s, rare 95.00
Shirley Temple, figurine, Happy Birthday, 1930s, 5½", NM..........75.00
Shirley Temple, mannequin, compo, 1930s, 13½", EX 450.00
Shirley Temple, mug, cobalt glass, M.......................................35.00
Shirley Temple, paper dolls, Saalfield #440, uncut...................95.00
Shirley Temple, slipper box, EX photo, 1930s, EX 155.00
Sky King, ring, Magni-Glow...60.00
Sky King, ring, radar, M 200.00
Sky King, ring, Tele-blinker, EX 90.00
Sky King, Spy Detecto Writer, NM in box...............................175.00
Sleeping Beauty, fr-tray puzzle, Whitman, 1959, NM.....................8.00
Smokey the Bear, furry slipper socks, head on ea, pr..................65.00
Smokey the Bear, shakers, ceramic figural, M, pr 35.00
Snoopy, bank, Snoopy on doghouse figural................................35.00
Snoopy, figure, vinyl, 1960s, 8½" 30.00
Snoopy, light switch cover, 1965 ....12.50
Snoopy, music box, Schmid, lg, M...20.00
Snoopy, wristwatch, playing tennis, NM...................................35.00
Snow White, cake tin, Denmark, 1948, 4x8x8", VG 250.00
Snow White, ironing board, metal, Wolverine, 21x27x8" 45.00
Snow White, program, Radio City Hall, 1938 ....75.00
Snow White, puzzle, Whitman, Disney, 1938, set of 2, MIB.........65.00
Snow White, suitcase, doll's, 1940s 45.00
Snow White, toothbrush holder, china, 1938, 5" 150.00
Snow White, wristwatch, 1957, NM...60.00

Snow White and the Seven Dwarfs Christmas ornaments, boxed set, EX, $250.00.

Snow White & 7 Dwarfs, chewing gum pack, 1938, EX 85.00
Snow White & 7 Dwarfs, chocolate tin, Belgium, 1938, 8x12"...110.00
Snow White & 7 Dwarfs, sticker book, 1967, M 13.50
Snow White & 7 Dwarfs, throw rug, 1940s, lg, EX.....................125.00
Space Patrol, diplomatic pouch, complete, NM 125.00

Space Patrol, rocketship balloon w/illus envelope, M 195.00
Spike Jones, Sax-o-Fun, EX in VG box......................................40.00
Straight Arrow, bandana, Nat'l Biscuit premium, 1949 ....50.00
Straight Arrow, color book, NM 45.00
Straight Arrow, ring, Good Luck, radio premium 50.00
Straight Arrow, target game 55.00
Superboy, color book, Whitman, 1967, M 18.00
Superman, bicycle siren, MIB...30.00
Superman, birthday cake candle set, Wilton, MIB 5.00
Superman, check, Daily Planet, for $1, Sunnyland premium 75.00
Superman, Colorforms, 1964, NM..36.00
Superman, coloring cloth, vinyl, +crayons/eraser, M in pkg 25.00
Superman, comic book, Sugar Smacks premium, 1955, EX............25.00
Superman, Crazy Foam can 25.00
Superman, figure, vinyl, inflatable, 72", MIB 20.00
Superman, fork & spoon, Imperial, M on card...........................25.00
Superman, game, Presto Magic, dry transfers, EX 3.50
Superman, game, Speed, 1940s, EX 118.00
Superman, gun, Krypto Ray, w/film, NM 185.00
Superman, noise balloon, 1966 ....10.00
Superman, pistol, Cinematic Picture, Daisy, EX in box 250.00
Superman, pistol, water; Multiple Toymakers, M on card............125.00
Superman, puzzle, fr-tray, 1966...12.50
Superman, record player, M...65.00
Superman, ring, airplane 195.00
Superman, shoelaces, MIB...8.00
Superman, Super Plants planter, Nat'l Periodical Pub, 1975, M ...12.00
Superman, telephone, rotary, complete, red base, EX 950.00
Sweet Pea, bank, ceramic figural, 1980, M................................35.00
Tom Corbett, binoculars, metal, NM in orig box 95.00
Tom Corbett, Modeling & Coloring set, VG in box....................45.00
Tom Corbett, school bag..100.00
Tom Mix, badge, Dobie County, radio premium 20.00
Tom Mix, boot box, TM & horse graphics, 1930s, EX 50.00
Tom Mix, bracelet, ID; premium, 1947, EX...............................35.00
Tom Mix, cowboy boots, MIB...350.00
Tom Mix, fob, Goldore, radio premium 35.00
Tom Mix, manual, 1941, EX 45.00
Tom Mix, movie makeup kit, M in mailer.................................175.00
Tom Mix, periscope, M in mailer..75.00
Tom Mix, photograph, premium, silver fr 95.00
Tom Mix, pocket knife, w/Tony 250.00
Tom Mix, ring, Mystery, radio premium 200.00
Tom Mix, ring, sliding whistle 75.00
Tom Mix, Rocket parachute, M in mailer 125.00
Tom Mix, rocking horse, w/Tony, NM 250.00
Tom Mix, rodeo rope, M in mailer...150.00
Tom Mix, shooting gallery, dbl, Parker Bros, '35, NM in box......265.00
Tom Mix, signal arrowhead, Lucite, radio premium, M in mailer .70.00
Tom Mix, telegraph, M in mailer..75.00
Tom Mix, telescope & whistle, Ralston, NM 35.00
Tom Mix, telescope w/birdcall, EX 135.00
Tonto, color book, Whitman, 1957, NM...................................15.00
Tonto, color book, Whitman #114815, 1953, M.......................25.00
Uncle Wiggily, mug, Ovaltine premium, 1934, EX 55.00
Wanted Dead or Alive, game, tin litho target, EX in box............275.00
Wanted Dead or Alive, rifle, EX 40.00
Wile E Coyote, wristwatch, Sheraton, 1972, M in pkg 250.00
Winnie the Pooh, bank, Pooh's Honey, Enesco/WDP, '60s, 4½" .35.00
Wizard of Oz, game, 1974, M 12.50
Woody Herman, toy clarinet, MIB...28.00
Woody Woodpecker, game, Travel w/WW, 1956, EX 40.00
Wyatt Earp, Hartland figure, on horse, M................................165.00
Wyatt Earp, wallet, vinyl, w/Hugh O'Brien signature, EX..............28.00

Yellow Kid, cigar box, EX **400.00**
Yellow Kid, ice cream mold...**125.00**
Yellow Kid, ladder, Bliss **200.00**
Yellow Kid, mask, papier-mache, 1920s, 22x24x10", G **300.00**
Yellow Kid, store receipt, 8¼x4¼", EX **35.00**
Zorro, costume, Ben Cooper #233, 1950s, MIB **45.00**
Zorro, costume, WD, EX in orig box **28.00**
Zorro, handkerchief, Disney, M **20.00**
Zorro, puzzle, fr-tray, Disney, M **15.00**
Zorro, wristwatch, cellophane on hat, 1957, MIB **185.00**
3 Stooges, Moe costume, Ben Cooper, MIB **145.00**
3 Stooges, Moe ventriloquist doll, Horsman, EX................**110.00**
3 Stooges, photo, full color, giveaway, ca 1960, 8x10" **10.00**
3 Stooges, ring, Curly flicker, 1950s **9.00**

Peters and Reed

John Peters and Adam Reed founded their pottery in Zanesville, Ohio, just before the turn of the century, using the local red clay to produce a variety of wares. Moss Aztec, introduced about 1912, has an unglazed exterior with designs molded in high relief and the recesses highlighted with a green wash. Only the interior is glazed to hold water. Pereco (named for Peters, Reed and Company) is glazed in semi-matt blue, maroon, or cream. Orange was also used very early, but such examples are rare. Shapes are simple with in-mold decoration sometimes borrowed from the Moss Aztec line. Wilse Blue is a line of high-gloss medium blue with dark specks on simple shapes. Landsun, characterized by its soft matt multicolor or blue and gray combinations, is decorated either by dripping or by hand brushing in an effect sometimes called Flame or Herringbone. Chromal, in much the same colors as Landsun, may be decorated with a realistic scenic, or the swirling application of colors may merely suggest one. (Brush-McCoy made a very similar line called Chromart. Neither will be marked; and, due to the lack of documented background material available, it may be impossible make a positive identification. Collectors nearly always attribute this type of decoration to Peters and Reed.) Shadow Ware is a glossy, multicolor drip over a harmonious base color. When the base is black, the effect is often iridescent.

Perhaps the most familiar line is the brown high-glaze artware with the 'sprigged'-type designs. Although research has uncovered no positive proof, it is generally accepted as having been made by Peters and Reed. It is interesting to note that many of the artistic shapes in this line are recognizable as those made by Weller, Roseville, and other Zanesville area companies. Other lines include Mirror Black, Persian, and an unidentified line which collectors call Mottled Colors. In this high-gloss line, the red clay body often shows through the splashed-on multicolors.

In 1922 the company became known as the Zane Pottery. Peters and Reed retired, and Harry McClelland became president. Charles Chilcote designed new lines, and production of many of the old lines continued. The body of the ware after 1922 was light in color. Marks include the impressed logo or ink stamp 'Zaneware' in a rectangle.

Bookends, Pereco, Arts & Crafts upright sq on sq base, 5" **80.00**
Candlestick, Brn Ware, trailing leaves, 14½" **125.00**
Flowerpot, Florentine, cvd geometrics, 4" **40.00**
Flowerpot, Moss Aztec, pine cones/needles, #200, 5" **50.00**
Hanging basket, Moss Aztec, basketweave, #105, 5" **55.00**
Jar, ginger; Marbleized, mc swirls on brn, 5½" **95.00**
Jardiniere, Moss Aztec, floral, #226, 8½" **125.00**
Jug, Brn Ware, cavalier, floral band, 5" **95.00**
Letter holder, Brn Ware, floral, rectangular, 4½x8" **85.00**
Loving cup, Brn Ware, lion's head & florals, 3-hdld **175.00**
Medallion, Moss Aztec, commemorative, rare, 2½" dia.................**95.00**

Pitcher, Brn Ware, sprigged-on cavalier, 5" **80.00**
Planter, Brn Ware, wreath, hdl across top, 5½x8" **55.00**
Vase, Brn Ware, cherry sprigs, pinched neck, hdls, 5" **65.00**
Vase, Brn Ware, floral, donut shape, 10½" **145.00**
Vase, bud; Landsun, brn/beige/bl/gr, 14" **60.00**
Vase, Chromal, mtns & foliage scene, #5, 10" **350.00**
Vase, Landsun, gr/brn/bl, #37, 6" **45.00**
Vase, Matt Green, #19, 12" **50.00**
Vase, Mirror Ware, blk irid/gr drips, #777, 9" **175.00**
Vase, Moss Aztec, floral, 12" **115.00**
Vase, Shadow Ware, bl & brn drips on tan, bulbous, 12" **150.00**
Wall pocket, Egyptian Ware, profile portrait, #83, 8" **125.00**
Wall pocket, Moss Aztec, floral, sgn Ferrell, 10" **90.00**

Pewabic

The Pewabic Pottery was formally established in Detroit, Michigan, in 1907 by Mary Chase Perry Stratton and Horace James Caulkins. The two had worked together since 1903, firing their ware in a small kiln Caulkins had designed especially for use by the dental trade. Always a small operation which relied upon basic equipment and the skill of the workers, they took pride in being commissioned for several important architectural tile installations.

Some of the early artware was glazed a simple matt green; occasionally other colors were added, sometimes in combination, one over the other in a drip effect. Later Stratton developed a lustrous crystalline glaze. The body of the ware was highly fired and extremely hard. Shapes were basic, and decorative modeling, if used at all, was in low relief. Mary Stratton kept the pottery open until her death in 1961. In 1968 it was purchased and reopened by Michigan State University.

Several marks were used over the years: a triangle with 'Revelation Pottery' (for a short time only), 'Pewabic' with five maple leaves, and the impressed circle mark.

Lamps, hand thrown, matt orange glaze, stamped mark, 29", $1,600.00 for the pair.

Bowl, brn-rose lustre, turq int, rolled rim, 3x9" **300.00**
Bowl, cream/brn, shallow, loop hdls, 5¼" **200.00**
Bowl vase, lt bl-gray on med dk bl w/irid, 4½x5½".......................**700.00**
Box, imp peacock on bl-gr irid, canted corners, mk, 5" W **250.00**
Box, lid: incised fish, gold on turq, irid bottom, 5" L.................**325.00**
Pin, cornucopia, tan w/mc fruit, label, 3"....................................**160.00**
Plate, dragonfly, early, 11"...**800.00**
Plate, running rabbit border, gr/bl/neutral, 10½" **750.00**
Vase, bl drip over irid, 2½"..**295.00**

Vase, feathered bl/gold lustre over royal bl, 12x9" 1,800.00
Vase, gold w/turq drip, spherical, 3" 850.00
Vase, gold w/turq drip, wide ovoid w/flared rim, 4½" 935.00
Vase, golden lustre, 5x3½" 475.00
Vase, gray irid w/turq drip, ovoid, 3½"...450.00
Vase, lt matt gr, maple leaf mk, 5½" 385.00
Vase, silver/lav matt, gr/turq dripping from shoulder, 13"........ 2,600.00

Pewter

Pewter is a metal alloy of tin, copper, very small parts of bismuth and/or antimony, and sometimes lead. Very little American pewter contained lead, however, because much of the ware was designed to be used as tableware, and makers were aware that the use of lead could result in poisoning. (Pieces that do contain lead are usually darker in color and heavier than those that have no lead.) Most of the fine examples of American pewter date from 1700 to the 1840s. Many pieces were melted down and recast into bullets during the American Revolution in 1775; this accounts to some extent why examples from this period are quite difficult to find. The pieces that did survive may include buttons, buckles, and writing equipment as well as the tableware we generally think of.

After the Revolution makers began using antimony as the major alloy with the tin in an effort to regain the popularity of pewter, which glassware and china was beginning to replace in the home. The resulting product, known as britannia, had a lustrous silver-like appearance and was far more durable. While closely related, britannia is a collectible in its own right and should not be confused with pewter.

Key: tm — touch mark

Basin, eagle tm for Thos D Boardman (faint), lt wear, 2x8" 205.00
Basin, HN Rust, rare, rpr/wear, 2x8" 650.00
Basin, Joseph Belcher tm, wear/pitting/scratches, 2x8" 650.00
Basin, no mk, wear/battering, 3x13" 175.00
Basin, Samuel Hamlin tm (faint), pitted, 2x7¾" 100.00
Beaker, unmk, ftd, 2⅜" 95.00
Beaker, unmk Am, 3⅛" 100.00
Bowl, baptismal; unmk, ftd, pitted, 5x3".......................................135.00
Bowl, unmk, ftd, lt battering, 2¼x4¾"...150.00
Bowl, unmk, ftd, pitting/old rpr, 2x4¾" 45.00
Candlestick, att Homan, Cincinnati OH, lip rpr, 10" 150.00
Candlestick, unmk, removable bobeche, 10¾", pr 300.00
Candlestick, unmk, 7¾", pr 250.00
Candlestick, unmk, 9¾", pr 270.00
Chalice, communion; Reed & Barton, 7" 120.00
Charger, H&R Joseph tm, wear/pitting, 12" 115.00
Charger, Samuel Ellis tm, corroded surface, 17" 295.00
Charger, Samuel Ellis tm, wear/pitting/scratches, 18" 225.00
Charger, Samuel Hamlin tm, wear/pitting/scratches, 11½"..........300.00
Charger, Thos Danforth II tm, wear/pitting/scratches, 12" 400.00
Charger, Thos Danforth III+2 eagles w/TD, 1800, 18"........... 2,000.00
Charger, Thos Swanson tm/Sam Ellis hallmarks, SP, 15", EX 245.00
Charger, Townsend & Compton tm, wear/scratches, 13½" 120.00
Charger (shallow bowl), eagle tm for W&S Yale, scarce, 13" 625.00
Coffeepot, Homan & Co, eng floral, floral finial, dents, 8"..........170.00
Coffeepot, James Dixon, English, 12" 120.00
Deep dish, Thos Danforth II (lt), hammered booge, 13", EX 250.00
Flagon, Smith & Feltman, Albany, 12" 350.00
Inkwell, HB Ward, dents/sm splits, 2⅝x4" dia..............................100.00
Lamp, sparking; unmk, single spout, brass burner w/cap, 4" 85.00
Lamp, sparking; unmk, single spout w/snuffer, wear, 4½".............125.00
Lamp, time; unmk, clear blown font, 11"......................................350.00
Lamp, whale oil; Morey & Smith, petticoat form, 4", EX 155.00
Lamp, whale oil; unmk Am, minor dents, 6½", pr 450.00
Measure, James Yates, bellied, Quart, wear/rpr, 6" 85.00
Measures, some mk J Yates, assembled set of 8 up to 10", EX .. 1,600.00
Pitcher, JD Locke tm, ovoid, strap hdl, dome lid, 9¾" 550.00
Pitcher, Sellew & Co, ovoid, acanthus, dome lid, 9¾" 400.00
Plate, B Barns tm, lt wear/scratches, 8" 200.00
Plate, Bush & Co tm, lt wear, 8" 105.00
Plate, crowned rose tm for Jacob Whitmore, lt wear, 8"..............275.00
Plate, eagle tm for Blakeslee Barns, 8" 300.00
Plate, eagle tm for Nathaniel Austin, lt wear, 8" 275.00
Plate, eagle tm for Thos Boardman, wear/scratches, 7¾" 325.00
Plate, eagle tm for Thos Danforth III, minor wear, 7¾" 325.00
Plate, F Bassett NY, scarce, 9", VG 350.00
Plate, Gershom Jones tm, minor wear, 8½" 375.00
Plate, indistinct tm, English, wear/scratches, 9¾" 65.00
Plate, indistinct tm, wear, 8½" 125.00
Plate, John Shorey tm, English, wear/corrosion, 9" 55.00
Plate, John Skinner tm, smooth brim w/initials, 9", EX 400.00
Plate, Joseph Belcher tm, wear/pitting, rare, 8" 650.00
Plate, lion tm for Thos Danforth I, minor wear, 8" 550.00
Plate, Love tm, lt wear/scratches, 8" 225.00
Plate, Norwich scroll tm of J Danforth, wear/pitting, 8" 375.00
Plate, Richard Austin tm, minor pitting/scratches, 8½" 200.00
Plate, Samuel Ellis tm, English, minor pitting/battered, 9" 75.00
Plate, Thos Danforth I tm, wear/scratches, 8" 95.00
Plate, Townsend & Compton tm, lt wear/scratches, 8½"............100.00
Plate, unmk Am, wear/scratches, 8"..130.00
Porringer, bkwards R tm on cast heart hdl, battered, 4" dia 175.00
Porringer, eagle tm (partial)/S Danforth, rpr/split, 5"...................425.00
Porringer, eagle tm for Wm Calder, flower hdl, rpr, 5"................450.00
Porringer, Lee/Gleason-type hdl w/hearts & crescent, 3", EX......100.00
Porringer, SG mk on cast crown hdl, wear, 5½" 125.00
Porringer, unmk, heart & crescent Lee-type hdl, 3⅜" 150.00
Porringer, unmk Am, cast crown hdl, 5"......................................175.00
Porringer, unmk Am, cast hdl, 5"..100.00

Rare lighthouse-shaped flagon by Boardman & Co., ca 1825, $900.00.

Sugar bowl, Sellew & Co, ornate scroll hdls, rpr hdls, 7" 400.00
Sugar bowl, unmk/att Sellew, cast ear hdls, 6"............................200.00
Syrup, Homan & Co, cast floral finial, 7¾" 250.00
Tankard, mk Bell in Hand, Boston, cast ear hdl, late, 4" 35.00
Tankard, unmk, tulip shape, Half Pt, wear/lt battering, 4" 55.00
Tankard measure, English tm, eng monogram/crown, rpr, 8".......325.00
Teapot, G Richardson, rpt hdl, 7½" 350.00
Teapot, J Danforth #4 tm, minor battering/soldered rpr, 7" 300.00

Teapot, J Danforth #5, squat/bulbous, ftd, wood finial, 7"	325.00
Teapot, J Danforth tm, well shaped, 9⅜", EX	600.00
Teapot, JB Woodbury tm, rpt hdl/lt battering, 7"	250.00
Teapot, Morey & Smith Warranted, Boston, 7½"	100.00
Teapot, Roswell Gleason, paneled, wood hdl/finial, 10"	200.00
Teapot, scroll tm for C Curtiss, wishbone hdl, 7"	300.00
Teapot, Sellew & Co, flower finial, scroll hdl, 9⅜"	300.00
Teapot, unmk Am, ornate hdl, 8"	175.00

Phoenix Bird

Blue and white Phoenix Bird china has been produced by various Japanese potteries from the early 1900s. With slight variations the design features the Japanese bird of paradise and scroll-like vines of Kara-Kusa, or Chinese grass. Although some of their earlier ware is unmarked, the majority is marked in some fashion. More than one hundred different stamps have been reported, with 'Made in Japan' the one most often found and Morimura's wreath or crossed stems (both having the letter 'M' within) coming in second. The cloverleaf with 'Japan' below very often indicates an item having a high-quality transfer print design. Newer items, if marked at all, carry a paper label. Compared to the older ware, the coloring of the new is whiter and the blue more harsh; the design is sparse with more ground area showing. Although collectors buy even 'new' pieces, the older is of course more highly prized and valued. For further information we recommend *Phoenix Bird Chinaware, Books I — IV* by Joan Collett Oates, privately published by our advisor, Joan Oates; her address is in the Directory under Michigan. Join Phoenix Bird Collectors of America (PBCA) and receive the *Discoveries* newsletter, an informative publication that will further your appreciation of this chinaware.

Bowl, cereal; 6"	11.50
Butter pat, old	9.00
Butter tub & drain, hdls, 2¾x5"	65.00
Candy/nut tub, hdls, 2"	25.00
Chamberstick, #1, old	135.00

Chamberstick, scalloped ring handle, no mark, 2" x 5" diameter, $135.00.

Condensed milk container, #2, w/underplate	125.00
Creamer, #6, bell form	20.00
Creamer & sugar bowl, w/lid, #20, mk 4	45.00
Cup, bouillon; inside border, w/hdls & underplate	22.00
Cup & saucer, demitasse; Occupied Japan	18.00
Custard cup, inside border	15.00
Egg cup, dbl, 3¼"	16.50
Egg cup, single, 2¼" H	10.00
Ladle, gravy; 6"	45.00
Plate, dinner; 9¾"	48.00
Plate, HP, scalloped rim, 7¼"	35.00

Plate, transfer print, plain edge, 7¼"	9.00
Shakers, #2, 2", pr	30.00
Shakers, globular, #2, 2", pr	30.00
Shakers, mushroom form, #9, pr	20.00
Sugar bowl, w/lid, Nippon, #10	22.00
Tureen, vegetable; oval, w/lid	135.00

Phoenix Glass

Founded in 1880 in Monaca, Pennsylvania, the Phoenix Glass Company became one of the country's foremost manufacturers of lighting glass by the early 1900s. They also produced a wide variety of utilitarian and decorative glassware, including art glass by Joseph Webb, colored cut glass, Gone-with-the-Wind style oil lamps, hotel and bar ware, and pharmaceutical glassware. Today, however, collectors are primarily interested in the 'Sculptured Artware' produced in the 1930s and 1940s. These beautiful pressed and mold-blown pieces are most often found in white milk glass or crystal with various color treatments or a satin finish.

Phoenix did not mark their 'Sculptured Artware' line on the glass; instead, a silver and black or gold and black foil label in the shape of the mythical phoenix bird was used.

Quite often glassware made by the Consolidated Lamp and Glass Company of nearby Coraopolis, Pennsylvania, is mistaken for Phoenix's 'Sculptured Artware.' Though the style of the glass is very similar, one distinguishing characteristic is that perhaps 80% of the time Phoenix applied color to the background leaving the raised design plain in contrast, while Consolidated generally applied color to the raised design and left the background plain. Also, for the most part, the patterns and colors used by Phoenix were distinctively different from those used by Consolidated. The glassware of both firms is of equal quality and comparable value.

In 1970 Phoenix Glass became a division of Anchor Hocking which in turn was acquired by the Newell Group in 1987. Phoenix has the distinction of being one of the oldest continuously operating glass factories in the United States. For more information, see the section on Consolidated Glass.

Key: MG — milk glass

Lighting

Oil lamp, GWTW, MG, bl & pk flowers, filigree base	300.00
Shade, crystal w/acid-etched design, 2" fitter, 5" H	18.00

Reuben Line

Catalonian, sugar bowl, dk bl on crystal, triangular	30.00
Catalonian, vase, amber on crystal, cylindrical, label, 7"	60.00
Catalonian, vase, fan; dk bl on crystal, 7"	50.00
Philodendron, vase, Reuben line bl on opal, 11"	150.00
Wild Geese, vase, amber on crystal, satin pattern, label	200.00

Sculptured Artware

Ash tray, coral bkground/MOP flowers on MG, 5½" L	65.00
Ash tray, slate gray bkground/MOP flowers on MG, 3" L	35.00
Aster, vase, cadet bl bkground on satin MG, 7"	90.00
Bachelor Button, vase, gr bkground on satin MG, 7"	150.00
Bluebell, vase, taupe bkground on satin MG, 7"	115.00
Candy box, lt bl bkground, wht violets on crystal, 6½" dia	150.00
Cigarette box/lid, wht satin bkground, bl flowers/gr leaves	100.00
Cosmos, vase, aqua bkground, wht flowers on crystal, 7½"	125.00

Daisy, vase, bl bkground on MG, glossy figures, 9¼" dia 190.00
Dancing Girl, vase, gr bkground on MG, satin figures, 12" 350.00
Diving Girl, bowl, pk bkground/wht figures on crystal, oval 200.00
Fern, vase, pk ferns, gr grass, pale bl bkground on MG, 7" 90.00
Freesia, vase, cedar rose bkground on crystal, 8" 140.00
Jewel, vase, lt bl bkground, MOP pattern on MG, 5" 65.00
Jonquil, platter, lt bl bkground on crystal satin, 14" dia 250.00
Lily, vase, sea gr bkground on crystal satin, tri-crimp, 8"..............120.00
Madonna, vase, burgundy bkground on MG, MOP figure, 10" 175.00
Philodendron, vase, amber, 1960s...40.00
Pine Cone, vase, no cones, aqua on crystal satin, 6½" 200.00
Primrose, vase, cedar rose on crystal, 8¾" 275.00
Strawberry, bowl, 3-part, tan on MG, 10½" 375.00
Strawberry, candle holders, tan on MG, 4¼", pr 130.00

Sunflowers vase, clear-cased white, 10",
$200.00.

Thistle, vase, orchid bkground on crystal, wht pattern, 18".........375.00
Tiger Lily, bowl, wht bkground, crystal satin flowers, 11½".........200.00
Water Lily, bowl, gr bkground on crystal, satin pattern, 14".......300.00
Water Lily, candle holders, gr on crystal, 4¾", pr 115.00
Wild Geese, vase, flint opal, satin finish, 9¼" 200.00
Wild Rose, vase, taupe bkground on MG, shaded pattern, 10½" .150.00

Miscellaneous

Anniversary, vase, 1880-1980, crystal sprayed ivory.....................40.00
Bicentennial, vase, crystal w/red, wht, & bl pattern.....................40.00
Blackberry, creamer & sugar bowl, pearl luster on MG, w/lid 50.00
Blackberry, goblet, caramel lustre on MG, 7-oz 20.00
Ivy & Snow, bowl, crystal, oval, 9" 15.00
Ivy & Snow, celery, crystal, 7¾" 25.00
Lace Dew Drop, bowl, pk on MG, 8" sq..35.00
Lace Dew Drop, jam jar, caramel lustre on MG, w/lid, 4½" 20.00
Lace Dew Drop, server, bl on MG, ftd, 11" 45.00
Moon & Star, comport, pearl lustre on MG, lg, 8" dia 40.00
Queen Anne, Jell-O mold, crystal, star shaped 2.50

Phonographs

The phonograph, invented by Thomas Edison in 1877, was the first practical instrument for recording and reproducing sound. Sound wave vibrations were recorded on a tinfoil-covered cylinder and played back with a needle that ran along the grooves made from the recording, thus reproducing the sound. Other companies further improved Edi-

son's invention, and by 1900 three phonograph companies were in business. Early models had morning-glory horns; these are especially desirable. The early cylinder players are all of special interest, because after 1910 nearly all models were made to play disk records. By 1925 the hand-cranked players were discontinued and were replaced by electric phonographs.

Key:
mg — morning-glory   rpd — reproducer
NP — nickel plated

Amberola #75, cylinder, built-in record storage, EX 320.00
Brunswick, EX rpd, lg mahog floor model, complete 125.00
Brunswick Cortex Model, upright, EX...275.00
Busy Bee Grand, front mt, oak case, red mg horn, EX................300.00
Carola, floor model, upright, child's, in wooden case 210.00
Columbia AA, rear tone arm cylinder rpd, sm, EX.....................900.00
Columbia AB Graphophone, cylinder player w/2 mandrels ... 1,150.00
Columbia AJ Graphophone, disk player.......................................650.00
Columbia AK, disk player 850.00
Columbia AT Graphophone, 2-min, lg mg horn, 1901...............375.00
Columbia AZ Graphophone, cylinder player, EX.........................325.00
Columbia BA, disk player, EX..900.00
Columbia BC Graphophone, 20th-C type, 54" brass horn 2,100.00
Columbia BK Graphophone, cylinder player, w/lyre rpd, EX.......425.00
Columbia BQ, lg NP mg horn, EX...750.00
Columbia Grafonola, mahog case, upright, EX.............................200.00
Columbia Grafonola, oak case, table model 120.00
Columbia P, rear mt, mg horn, EX..625.00
Columbia QQ Graphophone, oak base/lid, key wind, 14" horn...275.00
Decca, disk player, portable, wood case w/horn in lid 250.00
Edison Amberola #20, 4-min, oak cabinet, EX............................275.00
Edison Amberola I-A, cylinder player, upright 1,800.00
Edison Amberola X 395.00
Edison B-19, dmn disk, mahog case, table model 330.00
Edison B-80, dmn disk, mahog case, table model 225.00
Edison BV-1, mahog table-top cylinder player 270.00
Edison C-19, dmn disk, oak case, upright 325.00
Edison Concert, 43" brass horn, EX 2,250.00
Edison Fireside, 2/4-min, C rpd, metal cygnet horn 550.00
Edison Gem, oil-pan model, orig rpd, sm blk horn 675.00
Edison Gem, unusual gear-change attachment, EX......................475.00
Edison Gem B, banner decal, C rpd, sm horn...............................375.00
Edison Gem D, Maroon; cylinder player 1,250.00
Edison Home, ribbon decal on oak, brass bell horn, EX 425.00
Edison Home, suitcase model, 14" blk bell horn, C rpd, M.........525.00
Edison Home, 2/4-min, cylinder player, w/mg horn.....................850.00
Edison Laboratory Model C-19, mahog dmn disk, upright 175.00
Edison S-19, dmn disk, mahog case, floor model 135.00
Edison S-19, dmn disk, oak case, upright......................................175.00
Edison Standard, banner front 395.00
Edison Standard, cylinder player, brass bell horn 475.00
Edison Standard, K rpd, red mg horn, suitcase model.................475.00
Edison Standard, S rpd, brass bell horn..400.00
Edison Standard, 2/4-min, cylinder player, w/horn 500.00
Edison Standard, 4-min, ribbon decal, lg mg horn 325.00
Edison Triumph, O rpd, repeater attachment, cygnet horn..... 4,300.00
Edison VI, internal horn, cylinder player, mahog table top 300.00
Fontenelle A, oak upright, roll-type doors, NM 180.00
Kalamazoo Duplex, EX decals, orig 2 horns, rpd, NM............. 3,300.00
Little Wonder, iron base, horn w/rpd in middle, EX 600.00
Pathe, cylinder box, 14" aluminum horn, EX 475.00
US Banner type, complete, rare... 1,500.00
US Junior, complete, rare 1,000.00

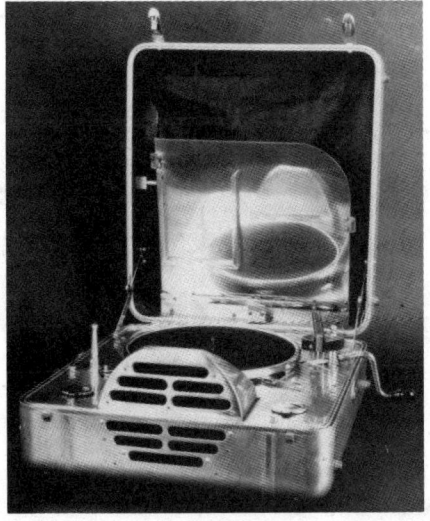

RCA Victor special, aluminum and various metals, ca 1935, 8" x 16" x 17", $3,100.00 at auction.

Victor D, silk-jacketed brass bell horn, EX	1,850.00
Victor II, disk player, oak horn, EX	2,000.00
Victor Monarch Special, 24" front mt brass bell horn, 1901	800.00
Victor R, wood tone arm, EX	1,100.00
Victor Schoolhouse #8-7, oak, EX	775.00
Victor Schoolhouse XXV, disk player, wood horn, upright, EX	1,700.00
Victor VE 4-3X, floor model	120.00
Victor Victrola XVII, mahog, EX	950.00
Victor VV-I-70, table model	150.00
Victor VV-VI, internal horn, disk player, oak table top	90.00
Victor VV-XII, mahog case, table model	550.00
Victor VV-50, oak case, portable	150.00
Victrola VV-IX, oak case, table model	175.00
Zonophome Concert, disk player, brass horn, rare	1,200.00

Photographica

Photographic collectibles include not only the cameras and equipment used to 'freeze' special moments in time but also the photographic images produced by a great variety of processes that have evolved since the daguerrean era of the mid-1800s. Among the earliest cameras was the sliding box-on-a-box camera. It was focused by sliding one box in and out of the other, thus adjusting the distance of the lens to the ground glass. This was replaced on later models with leather bellows. These were the forerunners of the multi-lens cameras developed in the late 1870s, which were capable of recording many small portraits on a single plate. Double-lens cameras produced stereo images which, when viewed through a device called a stereoscope, achieved a 3-dimensional effect. In 1888 George Eastmann introduced his box camera, the first to utilize roll film. This greatly simplified the process, making it possible for the amateur to enjoy photography as a hobby. Detective cameras, those disguised as books, handbags, etc., are among the most sought after by today's collectors.

Many processes have been used to produce photographic images: daguerreotypes — the most-valued examples being the full-plate which measures 6½" x 8½"; ambrotypes, produced by an early wet-plate process whereby a faint negative image on glass is seen as positive when held against a dark background; and tintypes, contemporaries of ambrotypes but produced on japanned iron and not as easily damaged. Other collectible images include carte de visites, known as CDVs, which are portraits printed on paper and produced in quantity. The CDV fad of the 1800s enticed the famous and the unknown alike to pose for these cards, which were circulated among the public to the extent that they became known as 'publics.' When the popularity of

CDVs began to wane, a new fascination developed for the cabinet photo, a larger version measuring about 4½" x 6½". Note: A common portrait CDV is worth only about 50¢ unless it carries a revenue stamp on the back; those that do are valued at about $1.00 each.

Stereo cards, photos viewed through a device called a stereoscope, are another popular collectible. The glass stereo plates of the mid-1800s and photo prints produced in the darkroom are among the most valuable. In evaluating stereo views, the date and condition are all-important. Some views were printed over a thirty- to forty-year period; 'first generation' prices are far higher than later copies. Right now, quality stereo views are at a premium.

For the most part, good quality images have either maintained or increased in value. Poor quality examples (regardless of rarity) are not selling well. Interest in cameras and stereo equipment is down, and dealers report that often average-priced items that were moving well are often completely overlooked. Though rare items always have a market, collectors seem to be buying only if they are bargain priced.

Our advisor for this category is John Hess; he is listed in the Directory under Massachusetts. For more information on the market values of collectible photographs, we recommend *Huxford's Fine Art Value Guide*, available at your local bookstore or from Collector Books. See also Gutta Percha.

Key: CW — Civil War

Ambrotypes

4th plate, curly-haired girl in gingham dress, +case, EX	55.00
4th plate, Union soldier w/hand in jacket, EX	75.00
6th plate, drummer boy in plumed hat, ca 1862, +case, EX	55.00
6th plate, man w/blk dog, +case, VG	20.00
6th plate, man w/dog on chair before building, +case, EX	50.00
6th plate, political marcher w/fancy breast sash, +case, EX	65.00
6th plate, post mortem of child holding flowers, +case, EX	50.00
6th plate, post mortem of newborn triplets, EX	300.00
6th plate, Union sergeant w/musket, +case, EX	125.00
6th plate, violinist, +case, VG	50.00
9th plate, button & lace salesman w/sales case, +case, EX	49.00
9th plate, sheriff w/5-point star in rnd disk badge, +case	50.00
9th plate, soldier w/eagle-hilt sword at chest, +case, VG	80.00

Cabinet Photos

Admiral Dewey, Hero of Manila, ca 1899, VG	20.00
Blk woman college graduate w/glasses, Bridle, Phila PA, VG	10.00
Calendar Stone Used by Aztec Indians, Parlors, VG	12.50
Che-Mah, Chinese dwarf, Wendt, Boonton NJ, VG	19.50
Cowboy on horsebk, Parsons, Ainsworth NE, ca 1900, EX	35.00
CW map of Port Hudson LA, troop movement, EX	12.50
Fairview, Wm J Bryan's home, Keystone, VG	8.00
Fire Lt in full uniform, O'Neil, N Bedford MA, VG	12.50
Four-horse drawn hook & ladder fire wagon, VG	25.00
Ft Popham ME, cannons & balls, Spanish Am War era, EX	17.50
George Kiowa Commanche Warrior, Irwin, 1890s, EX	50.00
Girl (about 2 yrs old) w/pet cat, 1880s, EX	8.00
JF Hines, fireman in bib-fireshirt, Carr, Webster MA, EX	22.50
John T Trowbridge, author, half-length pose, EX	6.50
Lady hunter w/single-shot rifle & dog, EX	45.50
Lookout Mt, Chattanooga TN, JB Linn, ca 1860s, EX	16.00
MA officer in full dress w/sword, dtd 1890, EX	15.00
Madam Price, 520 Lbs & Charles Price, Albino, Eisenmann, VG	15.00
Old Gypsy woman seated on donkey, J Laurent, Madrid, EX	10.00
Republican Headquarters, Great Falls NH, 1888, EX	22.50
Steamer Gov Andrew at Hull MA, brn mt, ca 1883, VG	16.00

Steamer Monhansett at pier w/passengers, G.................10.00
Triplet Boys of Mr & Mrs CR Bacon...Aged 9 Years, 1881 ....16.50
US Cruiser Charleston, San Francisco, April 1890 ....15.50
Washington Monument, Cap Stone Set, Dec 6, 1884, CS Cudlip...10.00
Wht man w/2 Indian women at Rosebud Agency, Shaw, VG 50.00
Young cowboy w/2 guns on nearby chair, VG 50.00
6 Spanish Am War sailors of USS Brooklyn, EX.................22.50

Cameras

Bosley C22, ca 1953, 35mm, VG 50.00
Brownie Cresta, box type, ca 1958, MIB.................20.00
Brownie Flash Six-20, box type, ca 1940s, NM.................. 8.00
Brownie 127, 1965-67, +case, EX.................15.00
Canon IVS, ca 1950s, VG.................95.00
Coronet Ambassador, box type, ca 1955, EX 18.00
EKC Instamatic Reflex, 126 film, ca 1968, EX.................70.00
Graphic 35, ca 1957, VG.................30.00
Hawkette #2, folding type, 120 film, ca 1930s, M.................60.00
Kodak Gift #1A, 1930, MIB 300.00
Kodak Instamatic 304, 126 film, ca 1965, VG 8.00
Kodak Jr Six-16, folding type, ca 1935, VG.................20.00
Minolta A, 1955-57, EX.................45.00
Olympus 35I, 24 exposure, 1948, VG.................60.00
Petri Color 35E, fully automatic, 1970, EX.................40.00
Polaroid Pathfinder 110, 1952-57, VG.................48.00

Carte De Visites

Albino lady holds wht cockatoo, Bogardus, NY, EX.................16.00
Alexander Stephen, facing front, Anthony, Brady Studio, EX 70.00
Anna Swan, 413-Lb Giant Woman, VG 25.00
Ashbury Benjamin, the Leopard Boy, EX 35.00
Benjamin Franklin w/glasses, CD Fredricks, EX 10.00
Brig Gen Lewis Blenker, Brady, ca 1860, EX.................60.00
Brig Gen Thomas J Rodman, Maj Ordnance USA, scarce, EX......26.00
Chang & Eng, Siamese Twins, ca 1865, VG.................35.00
Chippewa Indian wedding group, Martin's Gallery, EX 50.00
Civil War amputee missing left leg, EX.................95.00
Civil War Libby Prison, Richmond VA, exterior view, EX............14.50
Crystal Palace, View at London; 1869, G 15.00
Dudly Foster, Age 4 Years, Weight 5 Lbs, Eisenmann, VG............ 9.50
Edwin Bates, seated, Brady, VG 40.00
Egyptian Temple, Interior View..., ca 1860, VG 30.00
Entrance to Washington's Tomb, Mt Vernon, VA, 1860s, VG...... 8.50
Gen AM McCook, seated ¾-pose, VG 15.00
Gen George A Custer w/long hair, Brady, ca 1865, EX.................275.00
Gen George Thomas, Morse Gallery, ca 1862, EX 50.00
Gen Sheridan, half-length, facing front, EX 30.00
Girl w/snake, circus performer, ca 1870s, EX.................30.00
Horace Greeley, half-length pose, EX 12.50
Jefferson Davis, ¾-pose, Brady, ca 1860s, VG.................60.00
Jewish headstone in Prag cemetery, EX 12.50
Keddy's Photographic & Ambrotype Gallery, 1860s, EX 140.00
Lady gymnast working out w/weights, full length, ca 1870.............10.00
Les Quatres Napoleons, ca 1870.................15.00
Louisa May Alcott & Friends, Marshall & Co, EX.................18.00
Lucia Zarate, the Mexican Liliputian, Wood, scarce, EX 20.00
Maj Gen Ambrose Burnside, looking to left, Gurney, EX 15.00
Marie Antoinette of France, France, ca 1868 ....16.50
Military Wedding, group scene, VG 35.00
Miss Rebecca Myers, Age 20 Years, Height 23"..., VG.................12.50
Mrs JC Fremont, seated before landscape bkdrop, EX 35.00
Mrs Jefferson Davis, Anthony, VG.................22.00

Nina, a Common Prostitute, ca 1905, EX.................35.00
Post mortem of baby in coffin, Bly, Hanover NH, ca 1865 ....20.00
Prince of Wales, Brady, 1860, VG.................20.00
Rock of Gibraltar, ca 1860, VG.................20.00
Tom Thumb's wedding party, VG 20.00
Union officer in frock coat w/shoulder boards, Currier, G 15.00
Waino & Plutano, Wild Men of Borneo, Eisemann, NY, VG 25.00

Daguerreotypes

Half plate, George Mumford, ca 1850, +case, EX.................100.00
Half plate, John Buckingham, +case, EX 90.00
4th plate, seated lady holds wht fan, +case, EX 30.00
6th plate, chemist at work, octagonal mat, +case, EX 625.00
6th plate, husband & wife (identified), +leather case, EX 15.00
6th plate, lady ill in bed, EX.................650.00
6th plate, lady in linsey-woolsey blanket, ca 1845, +case 20.00
6th plate, lady w/guitar, ca 1858, +floral emb case, EX 110.00
6th plate, MA militia soldier w/tall peaked cap, +case, EX.................150.00
6th plate, man in farmer's jacket smoking cigar, EX.................130.00
6th plate, plantation overseer, +case, EX 70.00
6th plate, post mortem of elderly lady in bonnet, +case, EX.........80.00
6th plate, Quaker man, seated, VG 39.50
6th plate, sad little girl w/book, ca 1848, +case, EX 26.00
6th plate, seaman, ca 1845, octagonal mat, case, EX.................135.00
6th plate, wallpaper hanger w/paper & scissors, +case, G 130.00
6th plate, 2 sisters w/matching dresses, +half case, EX.................20.00
9th plate, bearded man in straw bowler hat w/cigar, +case 15.00

Photos

Albumen, Cass Durham, W Point grad, Brady, 1865, 8x10", EX ...20.00
Albumen, Co (Infantry), Regimental Nat'l Colors, 1862, 7x9"...200.00
Albumen, Dr Jonathan Letterman...in Field, ca 1862, 8x9½"......425.00
Albumen, Edison Jumbo No 1 Dynamo, 1881, 11½x17", EX 650.00
Albumen, Edison Machine Works, NYC; 1881, 12x16" 700.00
Albumen, Lt Gen US Grant, on horsebk, Reed, ca 1870s, EX.......50.00
Albumen, Mount Pleasant Mills, PA, 7x10", VG 17.00
Albumen, Passenger Engine Built at Portland..., 1860s, 5x7", EX .50.00
Albumen, Petersburg Gas Works, Gardner, 1865, 7x9", VG 35.00
Albumen, Ruins of Stone Bridge at Bull Run, 7x9", VG.................50.00
Albumen, train & 7 giant redwood logs, Webb, 1890, 7x10"......22.50
Albumen, 4 Blk apple pickers & wht overseer, 5¾x8", VG 22.50
Bromide, Brewer's 1912 baseball team, mtd, Moore, 6x8".................55.00
Bromide, Flying Hutchinsons & Plane, Barrows, 1920s, 8x10" 37.50
Bromide, War Weary Huns, German prisoners, 6½x8½" 15.00

Edward S. Curtis orotone,
Prayer to Great Mystery,
gesso damage to frame,
image size 13½" x 10",
$3,100.00.

Photogravure, In the Land of the Apsaroke, 1908, 8x4", VG 25.00
Photogravure, Lone Chief Otto, ES Curtis, lg folio, VG 75.00
Photogravure, Washerwoman on the Dunes, Kuehn, 1906, 7x9" .38.00
Silverprint, Gambling Casino Interior, CA, 1920s, 7½x9½" 50.00
Silverprint, Graf Zeppelin, interior, 1928, 6x8½", EX................120.00
Silverprint, mother & child on gang plank, Hine, 1905, 5x4" 425.00

Stereoscopic Views

Am soldier repairs field phone during gas attack, WWI 3.00
Am soldiers on Philippine island w/carbines, 1899, VG 8.50
Am troops wading Norzogaray River, Spanish Am War, 1899........ 4.00
Baldwin Dirigible in Flight, Ashbury Park, NJ, ca 1905, EX 47.50
Balloon ascension w/17 persons about, Paris, 1860s, VG 32.50
Beached Steamer on Rocks, orange mt, VG 20.00
Blackfeet Indians, Ingersoll, 1898, VG 15.00
Chaplain Brown of Rough Riders speaks to regiment, EX 4.00
Chicago River Harbor View from Randolph Street, VG................15.00
Congregational Church, Emporia KS, 1870s, VG 6.50
Flat Bottom Riverboat in Flint River, GA, yel mt, VG..................20.00
Gen Fitzhugh Lee entering Havana w/Army, mtd, EX 4.00
German machine guns inspected by French, WWI era 2.50
Great Eastern, at NY Harbor, wht mt, J Cremer, Phila, EX 70.00
Indians before trading post in ID, EX 8.00
Japanese in trenches at Port Arthur, Russo-Japanese War, '05........ 3.00
Josh Billings (pen name of Henry W Shaw), Gurney, EX 15.50
Lindbergh & Spirit of St Louis, Keystone, ca 1928, EX 32.00
Little girl & her 4 dolls & Blk Mammy, #312, Weller, VG............. 9.50
Officer w/field glasses, S African Boer War, ca 1900 .... 4.00
President Wilson, Lloyd George & Clemencea at Versailles........... 3.00
PT Barnum's Party at Yosemite Falls, #556, Woodward, G............. 6.50
San Francisco earthquake & fire, Mission district, 1906 .... 3.50
Sioux warrior on horsebk w/children, Ingersoll, 1899, EX............12.50
Sitting Bull, Ingersoll, EX...17.50
Soldier reading letter, equipment around him, 1898, EX 5.00
Steamer Martha's Vineyard, VG 18.00
Steamer Transport Richmond, orange mt, VG 35.00
Storefront of #58-60 AC Skinner Hosiery & Lace Store, VG......... 6.50
Tornado, June 17, 1882, Grinnell, IA; Bierstadt, NY...................18.50
Train wreck, Hartford CT, DS Camp, 1870s 10.50
VA Creeper Wagon, pulled by cow, JA Palmer, VG 8.50
13th US Infantry in Tampa preparing for Cuba, EX....................... 4.00

Tintypes

6th Plate tintype of Zouave soldier, $550.00.

Half plate, boy w/cat, VG 35.00
Half plate, farmhouse & family outside, VG.................................25.00

4th plate, bearded pioneer w/Indian wife & daughter, VG 45.00
4th plate, 4 Repatriated POW Union Soldiers, EX 110.00
6th plate, armed bear hunters, VG 50.00
6th plate, butcher w/meat saw, +case, EX....................................40.00
6th plate, cooper w/tools, VG 40.00
6th plate, CW artillery soldier w/Hardee hat on knee, EX...........29.50
6th plate, CW corporal seated, full length, EX 32.00
6th plate, jockey in full dress, seated, 1870s, EX..........................25.00
6th plate, lady holds concertina in lap, +case, VG 35.00
6th plate, Union officer w/sword held aloft, +case, EX.................65.00
6th plate, 3 Indian War soldiers in kepis, 1 is Blk, EX.................25.00
9th plate, CW soldier in greatcoat & cape, +case 30.00
9th plate, CW soldier w/M1849 Colt revolver, +case, EX 140.00
9th plate, NH Volunteer Soldier of A Co, seated, +case, VG........30.00
9th plate, 6 CA gold miners next to sluice, +case, EX 145.00

Viewers and Slides

Brewster, ebonized eye pcs, mirrored top flap, EX 195.00
Brewster, walnut, scalloped mirror flat, in fitted box, EX.............300.00
Graphoscope, for stereo/cabinet card photos, 1870s, EX..............275.00
Magic lantern, Atlas support lens, red pnt w/blk/gold, 13" 175.00
Magic lantern, pnt tin/brass, w/12 slides, Plank, EX in box 100.00
Magic lantern, tin w/brass plaque, wood hdl, AT Tompson...........95.00
Stereopticon, SP w/flying bird decor, EX....................................198.00
Viewmaster Stereoscope, +80 Viewmaster reels, 1950s, EX 75.00
Witte Moviescope, 4-in-1, cb, Zeotrope design, w/strips, VG......275.00

Miscellaneous

Book, Way to Better Pictures, ca 1830, 80-pg, 5x8" 8.50
Catalog, Kodaks & Kodak Supplies, ca 1915, VG 6.00
Mutescope card, Wm Franum w/gun, ca 1929, 3½x5½"................. 8.50
Stanhope, pen/letter opener, souvenir of Niagara Falls 75.00

Picasso Art Pottery

Pablo Picasso created some distinctive pottery during the 1950s, marking the ware with his signature.

Bowl, bird on branch, partially glazed, Madoura, 1952, 6" 1,600.00
Bowl, Blkbird, ed of 500, mk Edition Picasso, 1952, 7"............ 1,320.00
Charger, clock w/tongue, fauns w/flower, Madoura, 17" 7,150.00
Jug, woman's face, partially glazed, Madoura, 12" 5,500.00
Pitcher, rider & horse, glazed, Madoura, 1952, 8" 7,700.00
Pitcher, woman, glazed int, beige slips, Madoura, 1955, 13".... 4,400.00
Plate, dancers, partially glazed, Madoura, 1957, 12x15" 7,150.00
Plate, goat's head in profile, glazed, Madoura, 1950, 11" 3,080.00
Plate, owl, unglazed, Madoura, 1955, 15x13" 7,150.00
Platter, eng bull, glazed, Madoura, 1947, 12x15" 4,950.00
Platter, still life w/spoon, glazed, blk slip, Madoura, 13" 4,180.00
Vase, owl, unglazed, Madoura, 1958, 11" 7,150.00
Vase, woman, unglazed, Madoura, 1955, 12" 5,775.00

Pickard

Founded in 1897 in Chicago, Illinois, the Pickard China Company was originally a decorating studio, importing china blanks from European manufacturers. Some of these early pieces bear the name of those companies as well as Pickard's. Trained artists decorated the wares with hand-painted studies of fruit, florals, birds, and scenics and often signed their work. In 1915 Pickard introduced a line of 23k gold over a dainty floral-etched ground design. In the 1930s they began to experiment with the idea of making their own ware and by 1938 had succeeded in developing a formula for fine translucent china. Since 1976 they have issued an annual limited edition Christmas plate. They are now located in Antioch, Illinois.

The company has used various marks: 'Pickard' with double circles; the crown mark; 'Pickard' on a gold maple leaf; and the current mark, the lion and shield. Work signed by Challinor, Marker, and Yeschek is especially valued by today's collectors. Our advisor for this category is Milt Steinfeld; he is listed in the Directory under New Jersey.

Basket, mauve w/gold tracery, gold int/hdl, 4x5¼" 75.00
Bowl, allover gold on etched floral, hdls/ped ft, 3x9½" 55.00
Bowl, cake; violets, trees & lake, Felix, shallow, hdls..................350.00
Bowl, fruit; artist sgn, dbl hdl, 5" 95.00
Bowl, poppies w/gold, gold rim & hdls, sgn Yeschek, 7½"............275.00
Candy dish, allover gold on etched floral, hdls/divided, 6½" 50.00
Chocolate pot, carnations & florals w/gold, ca 1908 mk, 9" 235.00
Coffeepot, demitasse; Modern Conventional, 9", +cr/sug............495.00
Creamer & sugar bowl, pk dogwood w/gold, mk 72.50
Cup & saucer, violets w/gold, sgn James, Bavaria mk 85.00

Nut bowl, hand-painted walnuts, scalloped gold rim and foot, 6½" diameter, $65.00.

Pitcher, lemonade; mixed florals, Challinor, 6½"..........................595.00
Pitcher, lemonade; peaches, Seidel, 6½"....................................575.00
Plate, poppies, E Challinor, scalloped, 8½" 200.00
Sugar shaker, allover gold on etched floral 45.00
Tea set, gold, gilt/floral on cream band, Rosenthal, 3-pc 275.00
Tray, bluebells, gold scalloped rim, 1910 mk, 8½x7"....................275.00
Vase, bud; allover gold on etched floral, mk, 8" 35.00
Vase, harbor scene, 4 sailboats on MOP, sgn Gifford, 7½"...........425.00
Vase, moonlight scene w/palms, artist sgn, gold hdls, 21" 550.00
Vase, palms in moonlight scenic, 6½" 350.00
Vase, poppies, gold on pearlized ground, gold rim, mk, 8" 225.00

Pickle Castors

Pickle castors, which were both functional and decorative, became popular after the Civil War, reaching their peak about 1885. By 1900 they had virtually disappeared from factory catalogs. Numerous styles were available. They consisted of a decorated, silverplated frame that held either a fancy clear pressed-glass insert or one of decorated colored art glass — the latter being popular in the more affluent Victorian households and more desirable with collectors today.

In the listings below, the description prior to the semi-colon refers to the jar (insert), and the remainder of the line describes the frame.

Where no condition is indicated, the silverplate is assumed to be in very good to excellent condition; glass jars are assumed mint.

Aquamarine with hand-painted floral, 11", $395.00.

Aqua to rose w/HP florals; rstr Southington fr 395.00
Bl w/HP forget-me-nots; Aurora SP fr, 7¾x5¼" 395.00
Block, dbl inserts; rstr Meriden fr, orig set 1886 ....350.00
Block, vaseline; ftd Reed & Barton fr 395.00
Canes (5 rows), deep amber; eng/emb SP fr, +tongs 265.00
Clear frost bbl jar w/leaf finial; orig sq ftd fr w/pickles..................395.00
Clear frost pumpkin jar; leafy base, fr w/pickles & leaves.............395.00
Clear scenic medallions on textured glass; Wilcox fr, worn 250.00
Cranberry vertical ribs, bulbous; rstr fancy fr, +tongs..................595.00
Daisy & Button, bl; orig ftd SP fr 275.00
Daisy & Button, gr pressed glass; ftd SP fr 275.00
Dmn Point Fan; ftd Meriden SP fr, G, +tongs...............................85.00
Dmn Quilt MOP, bl; rstr Rogers fr w/shells, 12½", +tongs...........765.00
Dmn Quilt MOP, pk; ftd rstr Reed & Barton fr, +tongs...............395.00
Dmn Quilt rubena w/bleeding hearts, Mt WA; Pairpoint fr, 13" .450.00
Fine Cut, assorted colors; triple rstr ftd fr w/figurals/etc........... 1,200.00
Fine Cut, bl; rstr Meriden fr, 10¾x4" 225.00
Herringbone MOP, pk shaded; ornate ftd Tufts fr, EX................450.00
Hobnail, vaseline; Viking ft on rstr Webster fr, stork finial 550.00
Invt T'print, amberina, HP decor; fancy bail, ftd rstr SHM fr 695.00
Invt T'print, amberina, lg HP bird; ornate Tufts fr.......................650.00
Invt T'print, amethyst, corset shape; orig SP fr 375.00
Invt T'print, bl, HP daisies/cut flowers; Meriden fr 425.00
Invt T'print, bl w/HP florals; ornate ftd fr, rstr, 11½"..................485.00
Invt T'print, coffee, HP decor; cupids emb on Meriden fr, EX.....450.00
Invt T'print, cranberry; simple Wilcox fr, 9" 195.00
Invt T'print, rubena, HP; stand w/butterfly, Pairpoint fr, EX 495.00
Melon Swirl, clear & frosted; Rogers tree bark fr, +tongs 150.00
Paneled Sprig, cranberry, HP decor; claw-ftd Reed & Barton fr .425.00
Pk satin cased, HP flowers; ornate fretwork on rstr fr, +fork 695.00
Reverse Swirl, clear opal; ball-ftd Reed & Barton fr.....................255.00
Sapphire bl craquelle; ornate Tufts fr.......................................325.00
Strawberry, Dmn Point & Fan Near Cut; sgn SP fr, +tongs.........105.00
Yel to peach satin, gilt oak leaves; Mt WA stand, Pairpoint fr 950.00

Pie Birds

Pie Birds (also known as pie vents and pie funnels) have been in use since Victorian times. Placed in the middle of a pie, they serve the dual purpose of supporting the pastry and allowing steam to escape from the pie so that it does not boil over. They come in various, interesting forms, are hollow and glazed inside and out. Beware of clay-like incense burners tagged as pie vents — some may even carry a tag: 'Pie Bird — Do Not Wash.' Our advisor for this category is Alan Pedel; he is listed in the Directory under England.

Teddy Bear in chef's hat, vents from hat, $35.00.

Benny the Baker, mk Pat Pending, Cardinal China	68.00
Bird, big mouth, blk, ceramic	28.00
Bird, Morton Pottery	20.00
Bird, wht, big mouth, ceramic	30.00
Blk Chef holding rolling pin, ceramic	55.00
Elephant, brn, ceramic	55.00
Humpty Dumpty, mk England	52.00
Owl, stylized, pottery	45.00
Rooster, Bl Willow	17.50

Pierce, Howard

Howard Pierce opened a studio in Claremont, California, in the mid-1940s where he produced small ceramic models of birds and animals, figurines, and vases, making his molds and decorating his ware with no outside help except for his wife and more recently his daughter. He is best known for his skill at sculpting his models, which he decorates entirely with the airbrush. Early items were incised 'Howard Pierce, Claremont, California' or stamped 'Howard Pierce Porcelain.' Not all of his ware is marked, however, and some pieces carry only his initials. For more information we recommend *The Collector's Encyclopedia of California Pottery* by Jack Chipman, whose address may be found in the Directory under California.

Figurine, antelope's head, 16½"	48.00
Figurine, bobwhite hen, standing, stylized form	22.50
Figurine, cat, seated, sandstone, 14"	45.00
Figurine, duck decoy, gray/wht	25.00
Figurine, Eskimo, stylized, brn, 7", pr	40.00
Figurine, gander & 2 geese, brn/wht, 3-pc set	50.00
Figurine, monkey, seated, stylized, gray, rare, 9½"	65.00
Figurine, rabbit, long ears, brn agate, 10½"	36.00
Figurine, raccoon, brn/wht, pr	32.00
Figurine, roadrunner, brn & wht, lg	24.00
Figurine, squirrel, gray, 4"	12.00
Flower frog, quail w/2 young, 6½"	37.50
Flower frog, St Francis, 12x7"	50.00
Planter, deer in central opening, gr gloss, rectangular, 8"	62.50

Pietra-Dura

From the Italian Renaissance period, Pietra-Dura is a type of mosaic work used for plaques, table tops, frames, etc. that includes small pieces of gemstones, mother-of-pearl, and the like.

Brooch, florals/malachite leaves, 14k gold fr, 1860s, 2x1½"	400.00
Panel, birds & leaves, 2x4"	75.00
Pedestal, ebonized, fruit/flower inlay, bronze mts, 53"	1,650.00
Plaque, birds on branches, bl sky, Florentine, 12x10"	2,200.00
Plaque, country int: man at table talks w/girl, 10x13"	2,200.00
Plaque, elderly couple & child, giltwood fr, 10x8"	1,045.00

Pigeon Blood

Pigeon blood glass, produced in the late 1800s, may be distinguished from other dark red glass by its distinctive orange tint.

Celery vase, Torquay pattern, SP trim	140.00
Creamer, Venecia, HP decor	160.00
Cruet, Invt T'print, orig stopper	230.00
Pitcher, melon ribs, milk sz	145.00
Shakers, Flower Band, orig tops, pr	165.00
Sugar Shaker, Bulging Loops	245.00
Toothpick holder, Bulging Loops	150.00
Toothpick holder, Fine Rib	65.00
Vase, HP florals, 10½"	180.00

Pillin

Polia Pillin was born in Poland in 1909; many of her family were artisans and craftsmen. Except for a few weeks of formal instruction at the Hull House in Chicago, Pillin is self-taught in the arts. Her work has been shown in many exhibits, and she has received awards from the Los Angeles County Art Institute, Syracuse Museum, Los Angeles County Fair, and the California State Fair. First interested in oils and watercolors, she has carried the same Byzantine quality over to her pottery. All of her work is signed 'Pillin' or 'W&P Pillin,' both with the loop of the P extended in an arc over the remaining letters of her name.

Plate, ochre tones, 9", $250.00.

Bowl, bust portraits & birds on bl, 5½x10½"	375.00
Bowl, bust portraits on blk, 6½x5½"	325.00
Bowl, punch; mc yel, rare, 16"	1,500.00
Bowl, red abstract, 3¾x5½"	175.00
Charcoal, Southwest scene, fr, 19x12"	475.00

Lamp base, 12 figurals, rare, 14" 1,500.00
Painting, abstract, paper, fr, 15x11" 750.00
Pendant, horse on bl, 2" 55.00
Plaque, farm scene, 12x12" 900.00
Plaque, HP scene, 11x10" 950.00
Plate, children w/balloons on yel, 7½" 100.00
Plate, frolicking horses on gr, 7½" 110.00
Vase, Bentonite, abstract, 6" 250.00
Vase, Bentonite, fish decor, 4" 425.00
Vase, birds on gr w/pastels, 5¼" 150.00
Vase, birds on yel, 1½" 50.00
Vase, bust portraits on blk, bulbous, 9½" 395.00
Vase, bust portraits on gr, bulbous, 8½" 325.00
Vase, figural, blk, 11" 900.00
Vase, fish, pk & gr, squat, 2" 75.00
Vase, gr/pastel, bottle form, 11½" 140.00
Vase, horses on pastels, 5¾" 195.00
Vase, nudes on red, 12x6", NM 1,000.00
Vase, 3 nudes on bl, 9¼" 425.00
Vase, 3 nudes on pastels, 4½" 195.00

Pin-Back Buttons

Most of the advertising buttons made until the 1920s were top-quality, full-color, celluloid-covered buttons termed 'cellos.' Many were issued in sets on related topics featuring historical people and events, animals and birds, and other themes. Several cigarette, gum, and candy companies used buttons as inserts in their products. Usually the name of the company or product was printed on a paper placed in the back of the button and held securely by the pin. Most of the back papers are still in place today, aiding in the identification of the button. Beginning in the 1920s, a large number of buttons were lithographed (printed on metal); these buttons are referred to as 'lithos.' Nearly all advertising buttons are collected today with perhaps these exceptions: common buttons picturing flags of various nations, general labor union buttons denoting the payment of dues, and similar buttons with clever sayings.

Following is a listing of some of the most popular non-political buttons. Values reflect buttons which have designs centered, colors aligned, no fading or yellowing, no spots or stains, and no cracks, splits, or dents. See also Personalities; Political.

Buy American, eagle on shield, red/wht/bl, 1930s, NM................... 8.00
Chew Bulldog Twist, dog's portrait, mc, ca 1900, EX...................... 8.00
Darkies' Dream, lg watermelon slice, mc, ca 1910, EX 7.50
Detroit Electric 1910, early auto, blk/wht, EX 27.50
For the Boys Over There, United War Work Campaign 25.00
Fordson Tractors To Help w/War, tractor, 1910s, EX 27.50
Happy New Year, The Bulletin, Phila, celluloid, 1920s 30.00
I Chew Rex Pepsin Gum Do You, bl & wht, ca 1900, VG............. 3.00
I Have Visited Gerber Baby, baby portrait, 1930s, NM..................10.00
I Like Elvis, red & wht, 1950s, EX 12.50
Jersey Central Lines, Statue of Liberty silhouette, 1930s, M 3.00
Let's Be Friends Sunbeam Bread, girl w/slice on bl, 1930s, M 4.00
Queen Victoria Dmn Jubilee 1837-1937, portrait, mc, EX.............. 7.50
Support Blk Liberation, John Brown portrait on gr, 1960s, M 2.50
To Hell w/the Kaiser...25.00
Union Beer, keg w/in wreath, mc, ca 1910, NM........................20.00
Vote Yes for Sunday Movies, bl & wht, 1930s, EX 7.00
Welcome Lindy, portrait, red/wht/bl/blk, 1920s, NM.................... 8.00

Pink Lustre Ware

Pink lustre was produced by nearly every potter in the Stafford-shire district in the 18th and 19th centuries. The application of gold lustre on white or light-colored backgrounds produced pinks, while the same over dark colors developed copper. The wares ranged from hand-painted plaques to transfer-printed dinnerware.

Three-piece set with stylized lustre florals, $65.00.

Creamer, lg roses/grapes/tendrils, 4½" 275.00
Cup & saucer, Cadmus & Chancelor Livingston, red transfer 165.00
Cup & saucer, handleless; church decor, minor wear 95.00
Cup & saucer, resist vintage w/in wide pk band 50.00
Figurine, couple, silver lustre/mc enamel, minor wear, 4½" 425.00
Pitcher, house pattern, emb ribs, floral rim, 4¾", EX....................60.00
Pitcher, Pike/bk: Capt Hull (transfers), 6¾" 3,100.00
Pitcher, Queen Victoria/Prince Albert on bl, 7", EX 200.00
Pitcher, woman/child, brn transfer w/mc, urn form, 6⅜" 150.00
Plaque, He That Believes Shall Be Saved, 7¾x8¾", EX 85.00
Plate, Shepherd Boy, center transfer, deep, 1830s, 7¾" 60.00
Punch bowl, florals/house scene, scenic int, 11" 435.00
Teapot, Cadmus & Chancelor Livingston, w/blk transfers, rpr....450.00
Teapot, pk/purple florals, minor stains, 7½" 100.00
Wash bowl & pitcher, lg red roses, miniature, pitcher: 2¾" 100.00

Pink Pigs

Pink Pigs on cabbage green were made in Germany around the turn of the century. They were sold as souvenirs in train depots, amusement parks, and gift shops. 'Action pigs' (those involved in some amusing activity) are the most valuable, and prices increase with the number of pigs. Though a similar type of figurine was made in white bisque, most serious collectors prefer only the pink ones. They are marked in two ways: 'Germany' in incised letters, and a black ink stamp 'Made in Germany' in a circle.

1 beside gr drum, wall-mt match holder...60.00
1 beside stump, camera around neck, toothpick holder..................95.00
1 coming out of cup 65.00
1 coming out of suitcase...85.00
1 coming through gr fence, post at sides, open for flowers..............95.00
1 in case looking through binoculars..85.00
1 in gr Dutch shoe...50.00
1 in gr suitcase bank, head 1 side, bk other, gold trim 75.00
1 in Japanese submarine, Japan imp on both sides.........................125.00
1 in jaws of trap, rare, unmk, 5" L 110.00

1 in money sack bank 85.00
1 lg pig sitting behind 3" trough 75.00
1 napping on side, Schlite Patent, 5" L............................98.00
1 on binoculars, gold trim..95.00
1 on gr trinket dish, leg caught in lobster claw 65.00
1 on horseshoe-shaped dish w/raised 4-leaf clover 75.00
1 on keg playing piano..125.00
1 on shoulder of gr ink bottle 75.00
1 reclining on horseshoe ash tray 70.00
1 riding train, 4½" 125.00
1 sits, holds orange Boston Baked Beans pot match holder 65.00
1 sits by high-top boot 70.00
1 sitting in bathtub 95.00
1 sitting on log, mk Germany 80.00
1 standing in gr tub 95.00
1 w/attached toothpick holder 65.00
1 w/front ft in 3-part dish containing 3 dice, 1 ft on dice 75.00
1 w/tennis racket stands beside vase, Lawn Tennis, 3¾" 88.00
1 wearing chef's costume, holds frypan, w/basket..........................95.00
2, mother & baby in bl blanket in tub, rabbit on board atop..........85.00
2, mother in tub gives baby a bottle, lamb looks on, 4x3½" 85.00
2, 1 at telephone booth, 1 inside, 4½" 70.00
2 at confession, 4½" 88.00

Two pigs behind trough, $65.00.

2 by eggshell 80.00
2 dancing, in top hat, tux & cane 95.00
2 holding hands in roadster, 4½" L 130.00
2 in basket, Merry Squeelers, 3½x3" 90.00
2 in bed, Good Night on footboard, 4x3x2½" 145.00
2 in carriage 95.00
2 in love sit on lg log, 2 openings on tree stump, 7" L 75.00
2 in open trunk, 3¾" 95.00
2 in purse..75.00
2 on basket, head raising lid, plaque on front..................80.00
2 on binoculars, gold trim..115.00
2 on cotton bale, 1 peers from hole, 1 over top................90.00
2 on gr tray 50.00
2 on seesaw on top of pouch bank 75.00
2 on top hat..95.00
2 on tray hugging, 3x4½"..65.00
3, 1 on lg slipper playing banjo, 2 dancing on side 125.00
3 at trough, 4½" L 98.00
3 dressed up on edge of dish..80.00
3 sm pigs behind oval trough, mk, 2¾x2½x1¾" 90.00
3 w/baby carriage, father & 2 babies, Wheeling His Own 95.00
3 w/carriage, mother & 2 babies, Germany......................95.00

Pisgah Forest

The Pisgah Forest Pottery was established in 1920 near Mount Pisgah in Arden, North Carolina, by Walter B. Stephen, who had worked in previous years at other locations in the state — Nonconnah and Skyland (the latter from 1913 until 1916). Stephen, who was born in the mountain region near Asheville, was known for his work in the Southern tradition. He produced skillfully executed wares exhibiting an amazing variety of techniques. He operated his business with only two helpers. Recognized today as his most outstanding accomplishment, his Cameo line was decorated by hand in the pate-sur-pate style (similar to Wedgwood Jasper) in such designs as Fiddler and Dog, Spinning Wheel, Covered Wagon, Buffalo Hunt, Mountain Cabin, Square Dancers, Indian Campfire, and Plowman. Stephen is known for other types of wares as well. His crystalline glaze is highly regarded by today's collectors.

At least nine different stamps mark his wares, several of which contain the outline of the potter at the wheel and 'Pisgah Forest.' Stephen died in 1961, but the work was continued by his associates. Our advisor for this category is R.J. Sayers; he is listed in the Directory under North Carolina.

Creamer & sugar bowl, Cameo, wagon train, dtd 1955................100.00
Jug, bl glaze, w/drip spout, 7½" 45.00
Pitcher, bl w/red stripes throughout, 8"..60.00
Pitcher, Cameo type, Indian shoots buffalo, half glaze, 12"..........200.00
Sugar bowl, brn, dtd 1934 ....20.00
Teapot, Cameo, bl, wagon train..150.00
Teapot, yel glaze 35.00
Vase, bl w/pk int, dtd 1937, 7" 20.00
Vase, Cameo, bl, child running & trees, dtd 1950, 10" 200.00
Vase, Cameo, half gr/half brn, sailing ships, dtd 1949................250.00
Vase, crystalline, bl w/wht crystals, bulbous, dtd 1950 ....75.00
Vase, crystalline, wht w/bl fleck, pk int, dtd 1950......................100.00
Vase, purple, vertical glaze runs, dtd 1955, 7"................................30.00

Pittsburgh Glass

As early as 1797, utility window glass and hollowware were being produced in the Pittsburgh area. Coal had been found in abundance, and it was there that it was first used instead of wood to fuel the glass furnaces. Because of this, as many as 150 glass companies operated there at one time. However, most failed due to the economically disastrous effects of the War of 1812. By the mid-1850s those that remained were producing a wide range of flint glass items including pattern-molded and free-blown glass, cut and engraved wares, and pressed tableware patterns. Our advisor for this category is Mark Vuno; he is listed in the Directory under Connecticut.

Bottle, amber, 24 swirl ribs, globular, 2nd period/att, 6"................95.00
Candlestick, flint, petal cup, scalloped base, 9", EX, pr 150.00
Candlestick, hollow sockets w/pewter inserts, 9½", pr, EX..........350.00
Canister, 2 appl rings, dome lid w/finial, 12" 175.00
Compote, appl ft/rim, baluster stem, 6¾x8½" 350.00
Compote, knop stem, appl ft, cone lid w/appl finial, 12" 425.00
Compote, Pillar Mold, wide flat lip, knop baluster, 9x10" 375.00
Compote (open sugar), appl ft/wafer stem/folded rim, 4½x5" 575.00
Food cover, folded edge, appl knob, 14½" dia..............................175.00
Jar, ftd urn form w/cut panels, also on dome lid, 11", pr 350.00
Jar, urn form, dome lid, appl finial, 15½", pr, EX 500.00
Tumbler, cobalt, 6 panels/6 arches, sm base flake, 3⅜" 70.00
Vase, Pillar Mold, appl rim, 10¾"..375.00

Vase, Pillar Mold, wide ft, flared lip, 9½" 250.00
Vase, ribbed ogee body, scalloped flared lip, 8" 100.00

Decanter with Bull's-Eye and Panel cutting, att Robert Curling & Sons, ca 1830-40, pint-plus, NM, $350.00.

Plastics

The term 'collectible plastics' is defined as those types produced between 1868 (when synthetic plastics were invented) and the period immediately following WWII. There are several, and we shall mention each one and attempt briefly to acquaint you with their characteristics:

1) Pyroxylin (Celluloid, Loalin, French Ivory, Pyralin). Chemical name: cellulose nitrate. Earliest form, invented in 1868 by John Wesley Hyatt; highly flammable; yellows with age; much used in toiletry articles. Fairly lightweight, many articles of pyroxylin were made by heating and molding thin sheets.

2) Cellulose Acetate (Tenite, Similoid). Made in attempt to produce a product similar to cellulose nitrate but without the flammability. Had limited use in the costume jewelry trade; most often encountered as car knobs and handles of the thirties and forties. Surfaces tend to crack with age and exposure to light. Always molded, never cast. Colors varied; imitation horn and marble were most popular.

3) Casein Plastics (Ameroid, Galalith, Dorcasine, Casolith). Invented in 1904 using milk proteins. Use limited to buttons and buckles due to warping and lengthy curing time. Made in a wide range of colors; very easy to laminate or to carve from stock rods or sheets, but never molded.

4) Phenol Formaldehyde (Bakelite, Catalin, Marblette, Agatine, Gemstone, Durite, Durez, Prystal). Invented by L.H. Baekeland in 1908; used extensively in the thirties. There are two major types: cast and molded. Molded types include Durez and Bakelite, dark-toned, wood-flour filled plastics that were used extensively for early telephones (still used when non-conductivity of heat and electricity is vital). The most popular name in cast phenolics was Catalin, trade name of the American Catalin Corporation of New York. Made in a wide range of colors; widely used for costume jewelry, cutlery handles, decorative boxes, lamps, desk sets, etc. Heavyweight material with a slightly 'greasy' feel; very hard but can be carved with files, grinding tools, and abrasive cutters. Buffs to high, durable polish. Cast phenolics were used primarily from 1930 to around 1950 when they proved too labor-intensive to be economical.

5) Urea Formaldehyde (Beetleware, Plaskon, Duroware, Hemocoware, Uralite). Invented around 1929, this was lighter in color than phenol formaldehyde, thus used for injection-molded products in pastel colors. Lightweight, not strong; shiny rather than glossy. It cannot be carved and was used mainly for cheap radio and clock cases, never for jewelry.

The period between the two World Wars produced acrylic resins such as Lucite and vinyl. Polystyrene made its appearance then, and furfural-phenols were in use in industrial applications. Though a great future was predicted for ethyl cellulose, by the late thirties it was still in the experimental phase. For most purposes the field of decorative plastics from the first half of the century can be narrowed down to the five major types listed above. Of these, cellulose acetate is rarely encountered. Casein is limited to button and belt buckle manufacture; urea is easily identifiable as a cheap, brittle material. Pyroxylin is the celluloid of which so many vanity sets were made. Molded phenolics such as Bakelite were dark in color and used for utilitarian objects; cast phenolics such as Catalin were used most notably for jewelry (please don't call it Bakelite), cutlery handles, desk sets, and novelties.

Dealers and collectors should be aware of '70s reproduction Marblette animal napkin rings (they have no eye rods and no age patina) and molded acrylic bracelets in imitation of carved Catalin ones (look for a seam line or lack of definition in 'carved areas'). As prices rise, copies become more common. 1986 saw the mass-production of inlaid polka-dot bracelets using old-stock findings but without the precision fit (or patina) of the originals. In 1988 and continuing to the present, a large number of 'collage' pieces appeared in vintage clothing and antique stores on the West and East Coasts. These are over-sized, glued-together assemblages of old Catalin stock parts including buttons with the shanks filed off, poker chips, etc. made into brooches or pendants, sometimes hung on necklaces of re-strung Catalin beads. They can be recognized by their aesthetically jumbled, 'put-together' look; and although some may claim they are 'old,' they are not.

Our advisor for this category is Catherine Yronwode, who also publishes an informative newsletter, *The Collectible Plastics*; she is listed in the Directory under California. Our thanks to Benjamin Rose for help with radio prices.

Bakelite

Catalin five-color advertising pen with dice, $20.00.

Cigarette box, half-cylinder, rotates open, dk brn 40.00
Clock, electric, alarm, Deco design, blk or dk brn 60.00
Clock, mantel, wind-up alarm, Deco design, dk brn 50.00
Inkwell, streamlined, blk, w/lid 25.00
Penholder, streamlined, blk...22.50
Radio, Majestic #55, dk brn, 1939 ....250.00
Radio, Silvertone Compact, Sears, dk brn, 1936-1937.................250.00
Radio, Stewart Warner Varsity College, dk brn, 1938-1939........250.00
Roulette wheel, dk brn, 1930s..80.00
Roulette wheel, mc Catalin chips, wood rack, w/box, 1930s 200.00
Watch, lady's handbag; Westclox, blk, 2¾" dia.............................70.00

Catalin

Ash tray, marbleized lt gr, sq, 4½" 30.00
Barometer, Taylor, amber & dk gr, rectangular, 4" 40.00
Bottle opener, chrome plate, red, gr, or amber hdl 8.00
Bracelet, bangle; apple-juice clear, figural bk-cvg.......................175.00
Bracelet, bangle; apple-juice clear, floral bk-cvg 150.00
Bracelet, bangle; apple-juice clear, geometric bk-cvg 130.00
Bracelet, bangle; deep cvg, w/rhinestones 80.00
Bracelet, bangle; elaborate floral cvg, narrow 40.00

Bracelet, bangle; elaborate floral cvg, wide 65.00
Bracelet, bangle; lt geometric cvg, narrow 28.00
Bracelet, bangle; lt geometric cvg, wide 45.00
Bracelet, bangle; novelty, mc, figural or animal cvg 250.00
Bracelet, bangle; scratch cvd, narrow 18.00
Bracelet, bangle; scratch cvd, w/rhinestones 25.00
Bracelet, bangle; scratch cvd, wide 25.00
Bracelet, bangle; stylized floral cvg, narrow 28.00
Bracelet, bangle; stylized floral cvg, wide 45.00
Bracelet, bangle; uncvd, narrow 6.00
Bracelet, bangle; uncvd, wide 10.00
Bracelet, bangle; 12 inlaid polka dots, wide 180.00
Bracelet, bangle; 2-color stripes 70.00
Bracelet, bangle; 3-color stripes 90.00
Bracelet, bangle; 4-color (or more) stripes 125.00
Bracelet, bangle; 6 inlaid polka dots, narrow 180.00
Bracelet, cellulose acetate chain, 7 cvd figural charms 200.00
Bracelet, clamper; figural, animal, or novelty applique 225.00
Bracelet, clamper; inlaid geometric designs 150.00
Bracelet, clamper; stylized floral cvg 52.00
Bracelet, clamper; w/inlaid rhinestones 40.00
Bracelet, curved/flat links, deeply cvd 60.00
Bracelet, curved/flat links, uncvd 45.00
Bracelet, stretch; orig elastic, Catalin & metal 48.00
Bracelet, stretch; orig elastic, deeply cvd 60.00
Bracelet, stretch; orig elastic, mc, uncvd 50.00
Buckle, latch type, mc, novelty or figural applique 40.00
Buckle, latch type, mc, stylized floral or geometric, cvd 40.00
Buckle, latch type, mc, uncvd 25.00
Buckle, latch type, 1-color, novelty or figural applique 25.00
Buckle, latch type, 1-color, stylized floral or geometric 10.00
Buckle, latch type, 1-color, uncvd 5.00
Buckle, latch type, 1-color w/rhinestones, Deco 25.00
Buckle, slide type, mc, stylized floral or geometric, cvd 35.00
Buckle, slide type, mc, uncvd 12.50
Buckle, slide type, 1-color, stylized floral or geometric, cvd 8.00
Buckle, slide type, 1-color, uncvd 4.00
Butter mold, gr/amber/brn, floral cvg, 2½" 32.00
Buttons, card of 6, red or blk laminated, 1½" rod 18.00
Buttons, card of 6, scotty, fruit, or cvd floral figural 28.00
Buttons, card of 6, uncvd octagonal, amber, 1" dia 10.00
Cake breaker, CJ Schneider, red, gr, or amber hdl 3.00
Carving set, knife, fork, steel 30.00
Carving set, 3-pc w/wood wall rack 40.00
Checkers, red & blk, full set, in box 32.00
Cheese slicer, scotty hdl, wood & chrome base 15.00
Chess set, hand cvd, red & blk, leather box 250.00
Chopsticks, ivory, pr 3.00
Cigarette box, chrome inserts, cylindrical, 4½" 40.00
Cigarette box, lt gr, wood bottom, rectangular, 5½x3¾" 30.00
Cigarette holder, imitation amber, sterling tip, orig case 25.00
Cigarette holder, long, mc or w/rhinestones 25.00
Cigarette lighter, Arco-Lite devil's head, red or blk 150.00
Cigarette lighter, mc stripes or inlay 30.00
Clock, New Haven, wind-up alarm, amber, Deco, 3⅝" 52.00
Clock, Sessions, electric alarm, scalloped case, 4¼" dia 52.00
Clock, Seth Thomas, wind-up alarm, maroon case, 3½" 42.00
Clock, Westclox, Moonbeam, electric flashing light alarm 60.00
Clothesline, Jigger, red anchors, 10 pins, metal box 10.00
Cocktail recipes, Ben Hur, mtd on drunk, red w/blk base 40.00
Cocktail recipes, Ben Hur, mtd on fighting roosters 40.00
Cork, Ben Hur, w/red fighting roosters, blk base 20.00
Corkscrew, chrome, red, gr, or amber hdl 12.50
Corn holder, Kob Knobs, dmn shape or lathe trn, 8 +box 40.00

Crib toy, Tykie Toy, boy, girl, clown, kitten, etc, ea 100.00
Crib toy, Tykie Toy, clown, loalin head/Catalin body 60.00
Crib toy, Tykie Toy, elephant, laolin head/Catalin body 60.00
Crib toy, Tykie Toy, 11 mc spools on string, 1940s 50.00
Crib toy, Tykie Toy, 12-1½" rings on 2⅞" ring, 1940s 50.00
Crib toy, Tykie Toy catalogue, 1946 ....25.00
Crib toy, Tykie Toy Tales (book about these toys), 1946........35.00
Dice, ivory or red, 2½", pr 15.00
Dice, ivory or red, ¾", pr 2.00
Dice cage, metal/red Catalin, blk Lucite base, w/dice 75.00
Dice cup, leather or cork lined 30.00
Dominoes, ivory or blk, full set, w/wood box 30.00
Dominoes, red or gr, full set, w/wood box 40.00
Drawer pull, 1-color, w/pnt inlay stripe 2.00
Drawer pull, 2-color, octagon, w/inlaid dot 3.00
Dress clip, mc inlaid Deco design 20.00
Dress clip, novelty, figural, animal, or vegetable 50.00
Dress clip, scratch cvd 14.00
Dress clip, stylized floral cvg 20.00
Dress clip, 1-color, w/rhinestones, Deco design 20.00
Earrings, lg drop style, pr 10.00
Earrings, novelty, figural, animal, or vegetable, pr 35.00
Earrings, stylized floral cvg, pr 15.00
Earrings, uncvd disks, pr 6.00
Egg beater, red, gr, or amber hdl 16.00
Flatware, chrome plate, 1-color hdl 1.50
Flatware, chrome plate, 3-pc matched place setting 6.00
Flatware, stainless, 1-color hdl 2.00
Flatware, stainless, 1-color hdl, leatherette box, 36-pc 180.00
Flatware, stainless, 1-color hdl, 3-pc matched place setting 7.50
Flatware, stainless, 2-color hdl 3.50
Flatware, stainless, 2-color hdl, wood box, 36-pc 225.00
Flatware, stainless, 2-color hdl, 3-pc matched place setting 12.00
Gavel, lathe turned, ivory 18.00
Gavel, lathe turned, red, blk, & ivory 25.00
Gavel, lathe turned, red, w/presentation box, dtd 1946 ....28.00
Ice cream scoop, stainless, red hdl 19.00
Inkwell, Carvacraft Great Britain, amber, dbl well 75.00
Inkwell, Carvacraft Great Britain, amber, single well 50.00
Knife, cvd red, gr, or amber hdl 6.00
Lamp base, brass & amber, Deco design, 10" 30.00
Lamp base, red, amber, & blk, Deco design, 8" 44.00
Letter opener, blk & amber stripes, Deco design 20.00
Letter opener, chrome/Catalin, Deco design 14.00
Letter opener, marbleized gr, dagger shape 20.00
Mah-Jong set, tiles, rails, 6-color, complete, w/box 45.00
Memo pad, Carvacraft Great Britain, amber 35.00
Nail brush, Ducky, duck shape, translucent eye rod 32.00
Nail brush, marbleized lt gr, 2½x1½" 8.00
Nail brush, Masso, amber octagon, 2" dia 8.00
Nail brush, turtle shape, dark amber, 3½" 16.00
Napkin ring, amber, red, or gr, 2" dia band 5.00
Napkin ring, animal or bird, no inlaid eye or ball on head........25.00
Napkin ring, elephant w/ball on head 30.00
Napkin ring, lathe turned, amber, red, or gr, 1¾" dia 5.00
Napkin ring, Mickey Mouse or Donald Duck shape w/decal........58.00
Napkin ring, rabbit w/inlaid eye rod 32.00
Napkin ring, rocking horse or camel w/inlaid eye rod 66.00
Napkin ring, scotty, w/inlaid eye rod 38.00
Napkin ring set, 6-colors, 2" band, orig box 30.00
Necklace, cellulose acetate chain, animal figurals 185.00
Necklace, cellulose acetate chain, Deco dangling pcs 100.00
Necklace, cvd red & amber beads, 18" 65.00
Necklace, uncvd gr beads, 20" 40.00

Ozone generator, Air-Clear, dk amber, streamlined case 70.00
Pencil sharpener, Disney character decal, silhouette shape...........38.00
Pencil sharpener, gun, tank, or plane shape w/decal....................30.00
Pencil sharpener, orange, no decal, ¾x1".................................. 8.00
Pencil sharpener, red, Mickey Mouse decal, ¾x1" 30.00
Pencil sharpener, scotty, red, cvd details, blk base....................30.00
Pencil sharpener, scotty, yel, silhouette shape 20.00
Pencil sharpener, Trylon & Perisphere, 1939 World's Fair 50.00
Penholder, amber & blk striped, Deco design............................35.00
Penholder, marbleized amber, Deco design...............................25.00
Penholder, scotty, red w/blk base 45.00
Picture frame, amber & red Deco design, 6x7" 45.00
Picture frame, red, gr, or amber, sq, 6" 25.00
Pin, animal, resin wash w/glass eye, lg....................................95.00
Pin, animal, resin wash w/glass eye, sm..................................75.00
Pin, animal or vegetable, inlaid or appl in several colors, lg........170.00
Pin, animal or vegetable, inlaid or appl in several colors, sm 95.00
Pin, animal or vegetable, 1-color, lg......................................80.00
Pin, animal or vegetable, 1-color, sm.....................................60.00
Pin, mc Deco design, lg..60.00
Pin, mc Deco design, sm...40.00
Pin, novelty or patriotic figural, resin wash/inlay/appl, lg 185.00
Pin, novelty or patriotic figural, resin wash/inlay/appl, sm...........120.00
Pin, novelty or patriotic figural, 1-color, lg.............................95.00
Pin, novelty or patriotic figural, 1-color, sm............................65.00
Pin, stylized floral cvg, lg..40.00
Pin, stylized floral cvg, sm...32.00
Pin, w/danglers, animal or vegetable, resin wash/inlay/appl 175.00
Pin, w/danglers, animal or vegetable, 1-color 100.00
Pin, w/danglers, geometric form, mc.....................................60.00
Pin, w/danglers, geometric form, 1-color................................45.00
Pin, w/danglers, novelty or patriotic, resin wash/inlay/appl 210.00
Pin, w/danglers, novelty or patriotic, 1-color...........................110.00
Pipe, amber & gr, bowl lined w/clay......................................28.00
Pitcher, glass, red, gr, or amber hdl, syrup size 18.00
Pocket watch, Debonaire, yel Deco case, 1⅞" dia.......................60.00
Poker chip rack, cylindrical, w/50 chips, 2½" 85.00
Poker chip rack, rectangular, w/200 chips, 4" 120.00
Powder box, amber & blk fluted cylinder, 2½"...........................45.00
Powder box, amber & gr fluted cylinder, 4".............................56.00
Radio, AMC 'Peaktop,' amber, maroon trim.......................... 2,500.00
Radio, Emerson Cathedral (AU190), amber........................... 1,200.00
Radio, Emerson Cathedral (AU190), bright red, very rare.....13,000.00
Radio, Emerson Cathedral (AU190), gr marbled................... 2,200.00
Radio, Emerson College model, amber or gr, 1938......................900.00
Radio, Emerson College model, red, 1938........................... 1,200.00
Radio, Fada Streamliner, amber, amber knobs/bezel, 1941 ....900.00
Radio, Fada Streamliner, amber, red knobs/bezel, 1941 .... 1,000.00
Radio, Fada Streamliner, red, amber knobs/bezel, 1941, rare... 9,800.00
Radio, Kadette Klockette, amber, gr, or maroon, 1937........... 1,200.00
Radio, Kadette Klockette, red, 1937................................. 1,500.00
Ring, inlaid Deco stripe design, 2-color 45.00
Ring, stylized floral cvg, 1-color 35.00
Ring, uncvd, 1-color...15.00
Ring, uncvd, 2-color...25.00
Ring case, hinged-lid style, amber or maroon 100.00
Ring case, open-top style, amber, red, or blk, Deco design............85.00
Safety razor, Schick Injector, amber hdl 12.00
Safety razor, Schick Injector, extra blades, orig box, 1939 ....40.00
Salad servers, Chase chrome, ivory, blk, or brn, pr......................30.00
Salad servers, chrome, red, gr, or amber hdls, pr 12.00
Shakers, ball shape or half-cylinder shape, 1½", pr.....................25.00
Shakers, glass, in 3⅛" Catalin holder, pr.................................19.00
Shakers, mushroom shape, amber & ivory, 1⅞", pr 25.00

Shakers, stepped cylinder shape, 3½", pr.................................25.00
Shakers, Washington Monument, 3¼", pr................................25.00
Shaving brush, red, gr, or amber...18.00
Shaving brush, red, gr, or amber, w/holder..............................30.00
Spatula, stainless, red, gr, or amber hdl 4.50
Spoon, iced tea, chrome, w/Catalin knob, 6-pc set 18.00
Spoon, slotted, stainless, red, gr, or amber hdl 4.50
Steering knob, chrome clamp...18.00
Stirrer, iced tea; Chase, chrome ball/mint leaf, 6-pc set 26.00
Stirrer, iced tea; shovel blade, Catalin hdl, 6-pc set...................36.00
Strainer, red, gr, or amber hdl, 2¾" dia.................................. 4.00
Strainer, red, gr, or amber hdl, 5" dia................................... 6.00
Swizzle stick, baseball-bat shape, amber or red......................... 4.00
Swizzle stick holder, amber or red, Rheingold Lager decal 70.00
Thermometer, BT Co, amber & blk, 2¾" dia 38.00
Thermometer, Taylor, amber & dk gr, rectangular, 4" 45.00
Writing set, blk, amber, or gr marble, Deco, 5-pc, orig box..........150.00

Celluloid

Bracelet, imitation tortoise w/inlaid rhinestones 40.00
Bracelet, snake w/inlaid rhinestones 48.00
Bridge marker, pnt ivoroid animal or figure, France 20.00
Bridge pencil holder, animal, pearlescent ivory on blk.................60.00
Buttons, ivoroid or pearlescent, ¾" dia, card of 6...................... 8.00
Carving set, ivoroid, knife/fork/steel, eng blade 30.00
Clock, Greek temple facade, wind-up alarm, ivoroid 45.00
Dresser set, amberoid & gr marbleized, 7-pc 70.00
Dresser set, ivoroid, 10-pc, w/9" bevel glass mirror....................100.00
Dresser set, ivory pearlescent or amberoid, 5-pc 50.00
Flatware, gr pearl on blk hdl, 3-pc set................................... 9.00
Flatware, ivoroid hdl, table knife, fork, or spoon, ea.................... 1.00
Hair receiver, ivoroid, pearlescent or amberoid, w/2-part lid 10.00
Manicure set, ivoroid, pearlescent or amberoid, 10-pc, +case 30.00
Manicure set, ivoroid, 18-pc, roll-up leather case 25.00
Manicure set, 4 mini-tools in coral-color tube, Germany..............22.00
Manicure set, 4 mini-tools in tube holder w/pnt florals................35.00
Mirror, dresser; ivoroid, cut-out hdl, bevel glass, 8"..................18.00
Mirror, dresser; ivoroid, oval bevel glass, 13"..........................28.00
Mirror, dresser; pearlescent or amberoid, bevel glass, 12"............20.00
Picture frame, easel bk, ivoroid, 2" dia..................................12.00
Powder box, ivoroid, pearlescent or amberoid 10.00
Shaving stand, ivoroid, 5-pc, w/razor 75.00

Lucite

Bottle, perfume; w/atomizer, rose inclusion..............................10.00
Bracelet, stretch, orig elastic, clear, bk-cvd.............................25.00
Picture frame, Deco, clear, sq, 6"..14.00
Purse, box style, clear or tortoise 42.00
Shakers, translucent red, 4", pr...12.00

Playing Cards

Playing cards can be an enjoyable way to trace the course of history. Knowledge of the art, literature, and politics of an era can be gleaned from a study of its playing cards. When royalty lost favor with the people, Kings and Queens were replaced by common people. During the periods of war, generals, officers, and soldiers were favored. In the United States, early examples had portraits of Washington and Adams as opposed to Kings, Indian chiefs instead of Jacks, and goddesses for Queens.

Tarot cards were used in Europe during the 1300s as a game of chance, but in the 18th century they were used to predict the future and were regarded with great reverence.

The backs of cards were of no particular consequence until the 1890s. The marble design used by the French during the late 1800s and the colored wood-cut patterns of the Italians in the 19th century are among the first attempts at decoration. Later the English used cards printed with portraits of royalty. Eventually cards were decorated with a broad range of subjects from reproductions of fine art to advertising.

Although playing cards are becoming popular collectibles, prices are still relatively low. Complete decks of cards printed earlier than the first postage stamp can still be purchased for less than $100.

Key:
C — complete   OB — original box
cts — courts   sz — size
hc — hand colored   XC — extra card
J — joker

Dr. Van Dykes Holland Bitters, complete set of 52, damage to card holder, ca 1900, $130.00.

Advertising

Big Ben Roll Cut Smoking Tobacco, wide, 52+J, M 10.00
CA Wine Depot, special aces/photo J, ca 1900, 52+J-XC, M 75.00
Gordon's Dry Gin, wide, special aces/photo J, '09, 52+J, M...........25.00
Hamart Promotions, ads cts, M 7.00
New England Telephone, wide, special aces/photo J, XC, M.........75.00
Reddy Kilowat, photo bk, dbl pinochle, M 15.00
Rolls-Royce, Universal, gold edges, ca 1960, 52+JJ, M 10.00
Saks 34th St, wide, special aces/photo J, XC, M............................50.00
Smirnoff Vodka, special cts/Js, 52+JJ, M.....................................12.00
Wickuler Beer, cts drinking beer, 1975, 32C, M................................ 8.00

France and Belgium

Banque Nat'l, Mundi, 1970, 52+J, EX... 8.00
Dynastie Royale, Belgian royalty cts, 1934, 52+XC, M..................35.00
Le Jeu de la Vme, Pino Zac, caricature cts/Js, M.............................20.00
Malmenayde, Paris pattern/gold edges, ca 1860, 52C, M 75.00
Mesmaeker Freres, Turnhout, ca 1890, M....................................25.00
Peacock Brand, Brepols, peacock aces, 52+JJ, M 5.00
Union Fait la Force, bomb on Hitler J, ca '40, 52+J, OB, NM.......75.00

Germany, Austria, and Czechoslovakia

Dondorf Shakespeare #192, gold edges, M.....................................160.00
Famous people, Heilmeier, caricature cts, 1985, 32+JJ, M 55.00
Italian suited, Piatnik, Irentine pattern, ca 1930, 32C, EX 12.00
Mongol, Piatnik, Mongol people, 52+J, M 10.00
Politiker-Skat, caricature cts, 1976, 32+XC, M 7.00
Provence, Piatnik, historic cts/turtle Js, 1959, 52+JJ, M...............50.00
Stralsunder, Werk-Altenburg, Anspach pattern, ca 1925, M.........25.00
Wheel of Fortune, Piatnik, 1961, 52+JJ, M 15.00

Great Britain

Beggar's Opera, words/music, 1978 repro of 1730 deck, M.............15.00

Chess, brd/game-pc bks, ca 1935, 52+J, rare, VG 95.00
Edward VII & Alexandria Coronation, portrait bks, '02, OB, VG..85.00
Nat'l Emblems, Waddington, unicorn kings, 52+JJ, M 11.00
Old Curiosity Shop, narrow, dbl deck, 104C, OB, EX....................15.00
Queen Elizabeth Silver Jubilee, brn/cream portrait bks, M 10.00
Queen Victoria Golden Jubilee, DeLaRue, 1887, 52C, VG 90.00
Victoria Dmn Jubilee, rulers on gray, 1897, 52C, NM 140.00

Italy, Spain, and Latin America

Circus, Massenghini, circus theme cts, ca 1975, 52+JJ+XC, M 15.00
Discoverers & Colonizers of Am, Fournier, 1954, 52+JJ+XC, M...25.00
El Navio, La Cubana, 1947, 40C, M 25.00
El Turco, La Cubana, Turkish cts, 1955, 40C, EX............................75.00
Napoletane Telate #81, Dal Negro, photo bks, 40C, M 12.00
Pasquins Windkaart, Solleone, 1970, 52+2XC, M 15.00
Real Fabrica de Madrid #950, 1936, sq corners, 40C, M 20.00

Miniatures and Patience

Dondorf #190 Patience Karten, Swiss costume cts, 52+J, M..........22.00
Glamour Magazine's 52 Beauty Tricks, ca 1950, 52C, M 25.00
Miss World, nude color photo cts, ca 1950, 52+J, M...................... 6.00
Patience Deluxe #50, Handa, Rococo photo cts, 1952, 52+J, M....10.00
Wust, scenic aces/gold borders, ca 1895, 52C, M 45.00

Souvenir and Expositions

Am Indian, corn dancer clown J, 1900, 52+J, rpr OB, M cards......95.00
Boy's Town, scenic, ca 1955, M 25.00
Montreal & Quebec, wide, Caughnawaga J, 52+J, OB, VG...........20.00
Rocky Mtns Concessions, man on mule J, 1889, 52+J+XC, M......50.00
TX, wide, scenic cts/J, ca 1900, 52+J, M......................................75.00
WI, scenic cts/Js, ca 1960, 104+4 J, OB, EX 15.00

Tarot and Fortune Telling

Cartes Le Normand, Gibson, ca 1900, 36+booklet, OB, EX 35.00
Deutches Original Tarot, Bauer, ca 1930, 78C, M 75.00
Dondorf #1 Fortunes, ca 1900, 36C, VG 30.00
Gypsy Witch Fortunes, 1903, M 20.00
Psychic Development Prediction, 1972, 45+2XC+booklet, M 18.00
Tarot Arista, Grimaud, 1964, 78+booklet, M................................18.00
Zodiac Circle, Whitman, 1931, 45C, M 6.00
Zodiac Fortunes, Ingalls, ca 1920, 30+booklet, OB, EX 8.00

Transformations

Carte Comiche, Arienti, 1982 repo of ca 1850, 52+2XC, M 25.00
Hustling Joe II, USPC, 1895, 52+J, OB, NM 200.00
Joan of Arc, Merrimak, 1965, 52+JJ, M 7.00
Tiffany Harlequin, Carryl, red bks, 1879, 52+XC, NM................475.00

Transportation: Airline, Steamship, Railroad

C&O RR, wide, scenic, ca 1900, 52+J, OB, VG 65.00
CIE GIE Transatlantique, bl bk w/logo, ca 1920, 52, OB, EX........20.00
Flying Tiger Line, 2nd issue, M 15.00
French Line, wide, red/bl Deco bks, ca 1925, 52+J+XC, M 25.00
Grand Trunk RR, wide, scenic, ca 1905, 52+J, OB, M..................30.00
Internat'l Mercantile Marine, red bk w/logo, 52, OB, VG 20.00
Japan Air Lines, ¾-sz, M.. 5.00
Korean Air Lines, 52+J, M 9.00
Pullman, special aces/J, 1942, bridge, 52+J+XC, OB, VG............10.00
Red Star Line, wide, Santa Maria bks, 1942, 52, OB, EX..............25.00

Singapore, men in boat, 52+J, M 10.00
TIA (Trans International Airlines), M 12.00

Political

The most valuable political items are those from any period which relate to a political figure whose term was especially significant or marked by an important event or one whose personality was particularly colorful. Posters, ribbons, badges, photographs, and pin-back buttons are but a few examples of the items popular with collectors of political memorabilia.

Political campaign pin-back buttons were first mass-produced and widely distributed in 1896 for the president-to-be William McKinley and for the first of three unsuccessful attempts by William Jennings Bryan. Pin-back buttons have been used during each presidential campaign ever since and are collected by many people. The most scarce are those used in the presidential campaigns of James Davis in 1924 and James Cox in 1920. Our advisor for this category is Paul J. Longo; he is listed in the Directory under Massachusetts. See also Autographs; Broadsides; Historical Glass; Watch Fobs.

Badge, Cleveland/Stevenson inauguration, 1893, 2x4½" 85.00
Badge, mourning; McKinley, eagle w/blk ribbon, 1901 ....40.00
Badge, Republican Phila Convention photographer, bronze, '48...30.00
Ballot, sample; McKinley, Hobart & MA slate, 1896 campaign 25.00
Banner, FD Roosevelt Our Next president, portrait, 11x12", EX ..50.00
Banner, Happy Days Are Here Again, prohibition ends, 13x17"...85.00
Broadside, Gen Wm H Harrison, printed silk, 1841, 18x12" 350.00
Cabinet photo, Gen Winfield S Hancock...for President, 1880.....35.00
Cabinet photo, JG Blaine campaign, sepia, 1884, 6½x4" 45.00
Cube, McKinley/Hobart jugate, glass, brass eagle hanger, ½" 85.00
Cup plate, Harrison portrait, Sandwich glass, 1840 campaign 68.00

Flag, Wm. H. Harrison, 1840 campaign, fading, 28" x 28", $3,000.00.

Game, Watergate...Political Intrigue, Neal, 1973, EX in box 25.00
Key chain, Eisenhower inauguration, brass, 1⅛" 10.00
Match holder, Grant w/stars, flags, cannon, metal, 1872, 6¼".....150.00
Match safe, Benjamin Harrison, Pat 1888, EX 200.00
Medal, James A Garfield, May 30, 1890, silver 20.00
Money clip, Ike on center of $ form, silvered brass..........................18.00
Mug, McKinley portrait & florals on glass, 3½" 55.00
Pamphlet, Landon/Knox jugate, Finnish, 12-pg, 4x9", EX 10.00
Pamphlet, McKinley's acceptance of nomination, 16-pg, EX.........15.00
Pass, Democratic convention, June 1924, unused...........................22.00
Pillowcase, FD Roosevelt portrait, pk silk w/fringe, 16" 25.00
Pin-bk, Alfred E Smith for President, gray/wht, EX........................30.00
Pin-bk, Bryan/Stevenson jugate, blk/wht photos on bl, EX...........50.00
Pin-bk, Burn Pot Not People, brn on tan, 1¼", EX 10.00
Pin-bk, Coolidge College Clubs, portrait, celluloid, ⅞" 60.00
Pin-bk, Goldwater 64, brass diecut of US, EX.................................. 7.50

Pin-bk, Let's Back Jack, cartoon portrait, 1960, 3", EX 65.00
Pin-bk, MacArthur campaign, celluloid, 1¼", EX 12.50
Pin-bk, Willkie, brass die-cut elephant, red enameling, EX 12.50

Plaque, U.S. Grant and S. Colfax, metal, mounted on engraved steel plate, R. H. Morris Co., 1868 and 1872, 13" x 12" plus frame, $5,000.00.

Post card, photo: Alice Roosevelt & Nicholas Longworth, NM 10.00
Post card, Taft & Sherman portraits, 1908, EX 15.00
Post card, Wm Howard Taft & JS Sherman, Nation's Choice, EX ..15.00
Poster, Earl Warren portrait, cb, 24x18", EX 45.00
Poster, Hoover/Curtis, Keep Them on the Job, paper, 22x16".......65.00
Poster, Humphrey campaign, bl/wht cb w/red letters, 11x17", EX .15.00
Poster, McGovern 72, by Sam Francis, 38x25", EX.......................100.00
Poster, Thomas Dewey portrait, cb, 24x18", EX 50.00
Print, Fremont/Cochrane, Grand Banner, Currier & Ives, sm 500.00
Record, graphophone; Hoover/Smith campaign, Domino, 1928 ...25.00
Ribbon, Harrison...Deeply Lamented..., silk, 1840, 5¾", VG 65.00
Ribbon, I Am for Bryan & American Manhood, 6", EX 50.00
Scarf, Repeal 18th Amendment, textile, EX 100.00
Stereoview, T Roosevelt campaign speech before crowd, M 10.00
Sticker, Hoover/Curtis jugate, red/wht/bl paper, 5x7" 30.00
Sticker, I Like Ike, blk on metallic yel, 1⅜" sq 10.00
Stickpin, Bryan, sepia portrait, oval, 1908, EX 35.00
Stickpin, Cleveland/Thurman jugate, enamel on brass, 1888 ....60.00
Stickpin, Hoover on bl, brass, 1928, ⅜x1¼", M 5.00
Stickpin, US Grant ferrotype, ca 1868, ⅝" (w/brass rim) 110.00
Stickpin, Wm H Taft profile & name, pewter, EX 18.00
Tab, Hoover, brass 5.00
Textile, Harrison/Reid jugate, 1892, 18x19", EX...........................95.00
Ticket, Democratic Nat'l Convention, FDR eng, Phila, 1936 ......15.00
Ticket, Democratic Nat'l Convention, 1948, +envelope...............15.00
Ticket, Republican Nat'l Convention, Lincoln eng, 1940.............15.00
Token, Geo Washington's funeral, silver, lt wear, w/hole..........320.00
Token, WH Harrison campaign, wht metal, 1840, 1¾", EX 40.00
Tray, McKinley/T Roosevelt jugate, aluminum, 3x5", EX 55.00

Pomona

Pomona glass was patented in 1885 by the New England Glass Works. Its characteristics are an etched background of crystal lead glass often decorated with simple designs painted with metallic stains of amber or blue. The etching was first achieved by hand cutting through an acid resist. This method, called first grind, resulted in an uneven feather-like frost effect. Later, to cut production costs, the hand-cut process was discontinued in favor of an acid bath which effected an even frosting. This method is called second grind. Our advisors for this category are Betty and Clarence Maier; they are listed in the Directory under Pennsylvania.

Bowl, mint; 2nd grind, folded-in crimped rim, 3-ftd, 4" 100.00
Bowl, 1st grind, spherical, 3" 265.00
Bowl, 2nd grind, cornflowers, ruffled, scalloped ft, 5½" 125.00
Bowl, 2nd grind, Invt T'print, ruffled, scalloped ft, 8" 200.00
Bowl, 2nd grind, Rivulet w/bl stain, fluted, 2⅝x5" 80.00
Creamer, 2nd grind, bl cornflowers, ruffled, worn, 3x6" 225.00
Creamer & sugar bowl (open), 1st grind, wishbone ft, ea 4" 650.00
Cruet, 2nd grind, pansy/butterfly, no stain, 7" 365.00
Finger bowl, 2nd grind, Rivulet, bl stain, fluted, 2½x6" 145.00
Nappy, 2nd grind, ruffled, hdld, 5½" 100.00
Pitcher, 1st grind, acanthus leaves, ftd, long neck, 9" 450.00

Pitcher, second grind,
gold leaves, 5½",
$280.00.

Punch cup, 1 grind, bl cornflowers 60.00
Toothpick holder, 1st grind, rigaree at waist, scalloped...............325.00
Tumbler, 2nd grind, blberries, gold leaves/amber stain, 3¾" 175.00
Tumbler, 2nd grind, cornflowers, amber & bl stain, 3¾" 150.00
Tumbler, 2nd grind, Dmn Quilt w/bl cornflowers, 4" 95.00

Post Cards

Post cards are distinguished from almost any other collectible due to the fact that nearly any topic can be found represented on cards! For this reason, post card collecting is considered the 'all-encompassing hobby'! A German by the name of Emmanuel Herrman is credited for inventing the post card, first printed in Austria in 1869. They were eagerly accepted by the Continentals and the English alike, who saw them as a more economical way to send written messages.

The first to be printed in the United States were on U.S. government postals. The Columbian Exposition of 1892-1893 served as the spark that ignited the post card phenomenon. Souvenir cards by the thousands were sent to folks back home — expo scenes, transportation themes, animals, birds, and advertising messages became popular. There were patriotic themes, Black themes, and cards for every occasion and holiday. Scenics, cards with small-town railroad depots, and views of U.S. towns (especially photos) are very sought-after.

Some of the earliest post card publishers were Raphael Tuck, Nister and Gabriel. Early 20th-century illustrators such as Frances Brundage, Rose O'Neill, and Ellen Clapsaddle designed cards that are especially sought after today.

Although the post card rage waned at the onset of WWI, they rank today among the most sought-after paper collectibles, second only to stamps.

Even though post cards may be sixty to ninety years old, they must be in excellent condition. As a worth-accessing factor, condition is second only to subject matter. When no condition is indicated, the items listed below are assumed to be in excellent condition whether used or unused. Our advisor for this category is Mrs. Sally Carver; she is listed in the Directory under Massachusetts.

Key:
p/ — publisher   s/ — signed

Real hair, embroidered flowers, hand painted, dated 1908,
PFB in diamond mark, unused, $25.00.

Animal, chimney sweep w/shamrocks & 4 pigs, ca 1930, #2619....**14.00**
Animal, Mrs Hoppin Frog, s/Rose Clark, p/Rotograph, #FL382.....**28.00**
Animal, pig in yel clown suit w/uke, ca 1930, #8665/1, VG **12.00**
Animal, Twice One Are Two, owl/frog/mouse, p/Salmon, #4615... **8.00**
Boileau, When Dreams Come True, p/Reinthal-Newman, #826 ...**15.00**
Brundage, Ever Welcome, girl in brn/gr dress, p/Tuck, EX.............**25.00**
Brundage, Glad Times, Dutch girl/Delft border, p/Tuck, EX **22.00**
Brundage, Pansies Are for Thoughts, couple, p/Gabriel, VG **10.00**
Buchanan, Red Riding Hood, w/6 insets, p/Knight, #874, VG **15.00**
Canada, Cartier & His Two Daughters, 1863, VG **10.00**
Carter, For City Wear, p/Valentine, VG **14.00**
Christy, Cornell University Girl, p/Tuck, #2625, VG...................**20.00**
Christy, Princeton University Girl, p/Ullman, #97, 1907, EX **12.00**
Christy, Worth Waiting For, p/Reinthal-Newman, #946, VG.......**15.00**
Clapsaddle, A Merry Halloween, girl/blk cat on blk, VG.............**28.00**
Clapsaddle, Christmas Greetings, girl in red, p/Wolf, G **10.00**
Clapsaddle, Happy Thanksgiving, lady in plaid, p/Wolf, VG **7.50**
Clapsaddle, Love's Message to My Valentine, boy/heart, VG **12.00**
Clapsaddle, mechanical, Jolly Halloween, #1236, VG **75.00**
Clapsaddle, New Year's Greeting, boy in yel slicker, EX...............**10.00**
Clapsaddle, Remember Green Erin, p/Wolf, #100, VG **10.00**
Clapsaddle, St Valentine Greeting, Queen of Hearts, VG.............**25.00**
Clapsaddle, 4th Birthday Greeting, boy w/dog, #8, VG **12.00**
Coin & Currency, Norwegian, 16 coins, p/MH Berlin, VG **15.00**
Drayton, Joyous Easter/Load of Easter Greetings, p/Tuck...............**32.00**
Dwig, Tis Halloween, Come Fly w/Me, p/mk, VG **20.00**
Dwig, Toasts for Occasions, lady w/hourglass, p/Tuck, VG...........**18.00**
Ebner, wht-robed Santa/3 children in red, p/Munk, VG................**32.00**
Fisher, A Ripening Bud, p/Reinthal-Newman, #868, VG.............**20.00**
Gibson, Halloween Greetings, witch/jack-o'-lantern, VG **8.00**
Gibson, Rubicon, man writing, p/Henderson **9.00**
Golliwog, golli/stick doll in roadster, p/BB London, EX...............**30.00**
Golliwog, golliwog in Bois de Boulogne, p/Tuck, VG **25.00**
Golliwog, Still They Come, s/Attwell, p/Carlton, VG..................**16.00**
Golliwog, Two's Company, girl cuddles golli, p/Photochrom **16.00**
Hayes, cutout/paper doll, Letty & Betty, EX................................**90.00**
Hayes, I love You Darling, p/Nister, #2776, VG............................**15.00**
HBG, With Best Wishes...New Year, Art Nouveau lady, #2276 ....**9.00**
Hold-to-light/cutout, child w/Thanksgiving newspaper, VG.......**125.00**
Hold-to-light/cutout, King's Chapel, Boston MA, VG **28.00**
Hold-to-light/cutout, purple-robed Santa in roadster, EX............**125.00**

Hold-to-light/cutout, Steeplechase...Atlantic City, #2205 ....**35.00**
Kirchner, Temptation, p/Reinthal-Newman, #992, VG **60.00**
Langsdorf, A Cotton Picker, alligator border, #S640, VG.............**32.00**
Langsdorf, Harvard University Girl, in red dress, VG **14.00**
Langsdorf, Pineapple Grove, FL, alligator border, #S615, VG **25.00**
Langsdorf, Yale University Girl, in bl silk dress/hat, VG **28.00**
Map, Europe, insert lithos, p/Remy, VG **12.00**
Map, State of Texas, p/Flying Eagle, VG **8.00**
Mechanical, Happy Hooligan's Hard Luck, squeeze to move **15.00**
Mechanical, kaleidoscope, Butterfly/Happy Easter, EX **25.00**
Mechanical, Mischievous Katzenjammers, kids hit coolie, EX.......**15.00**
Mechanical, swimming man hits lady's rear, ca 1940s, EX **15.00**
Mechanical shutter, dress to bathing suit, p/Post Card Dist **22.00**
Nash, All Hallow's Eve, girl bobbing for apples, Series #30 ....**15.00**
Noury, Gaston; nude w/raised arm & butterfly wings, VG **50.00**
Photo, Harley-Davidson motorcycle racing team, VG **20.00**
Photo, Joseph Nicolas & Family, in front of teepee, VG................**15.00**
Photo, Mexican border, pup tents in field, troops dressing.............. **6.00**
Photo, Navajo Indian Squaw w/Baby, papoose on bk, NM, VG **15.00**
Photo, WJ Bryan/Billy Sunday on train steps, p/Forward, VG **22.00**
Political, He's Good Enough for Me, Uncle Sam/Roosevelt **30.00**
Real hair, Santa w/hair whiskers & eyebrows, scarce, VG..............**75.00**
Rotograph, blk-robed Santa holds apple, girl begs, scarce, EX **45.00**
Russell, Scattering the Riders, p/Glacier, EX **22.00**
Shearer, In War, bears in naval battle, p/Albert Hahn, VG **10.00**
Sowerby, King-Cups, child drinks, p/Humphrey Milford, VG........**10.00**
Sports, Golf Girl, carries golf clubs, p/Gordon, 1908, VG **8.00**
Sports, Hit Hard but Play Fair, boys play ice hockey, VG **15.00**
Stamp, Austria, 17 stamps, p/Ottmar-Zieher, #5, VG **12.00**
Stevens, woven-in-silk, RMS Cedric, ship going left, VG **55.00**
Thiele, I Came, I Saw, I..., dressed dog, p/German-Am, #806 ....**15.00**
Thiele, 6 dogs in school gym, p/TSN, #1013, VG **15.00**
Tuck, A Caquot-Type Kite Balloon, army balloon, EX.................**17.00**
Tuck, Alabama State Belle, #2669, EX... **7.00**
Tuck, Bleak House (Dickens series), Phiz, set of 6, EX...................**25.00**
Tuck, Little Boy Blue, s/Barnes, #9301, VG **10.00**
Tuck, Mary, Mary Quite Contrary, Mary in garden, #3328, VG....**15.00**
Tuck, Monte Carlo, #7053, set of 6, w/orig envelope, EX **25.00**
Tuck, Old Mother Hubbard, cat holds puppy, s/Barnes, VG..........**10.00**
Tuck, Prayer in Stonewall Jackson's Camp, #2510, VG.................**25.00**
Tuck, red-robed Santa uses tire pump/gold car, #C304, VG **25.00**
Tuck, Spherical Balloons, s/Clarkson, #3246, VG.........................**20.00**
Wain, Din Din Please, 3 cats at table, p/Salmon, #874, VG **33.00**
Wain, Father Christmas Caught in the Snow, p/Ettlinger, VG ...**110.00**
Wain, Run a Muck, German cat soldier w/sword, VG **42.00**
Wall, Ain't Man Generous? Everything But That Vote!, #6342....**18.00**
Winsch, A Joyful Christmas, red-coated Santa in plane, VG **20.00**
Winsch, Best New Year's Wishes, Father Time/baby, 1910, VG ...**25.00**
Winsch, Halloween Witch's Wand, owl on pumpkin, 1914, VG ..**50.00**
Winsch, mechanical, My Heart's Gift, boy/heart, 1912, VG **25.00**
Winsch, mechanical, Valentine Thoughts, 1912, VG **12.00**
Woehler, Happy Halloween, couple w/jack-o'-lantern, EX............**20.00**
101 Ranch, Indian Chiefs, p/Gale-Polden, VG **17.00**

Posters

Advertising posters by such French artists as Cheret and Toulouse-Lautrec were used as early as the mid-1800s. Color lithography spurred their popularity. Circus posters by the Strobridge Lithograph Co. are considered to be the finest in their field, though Gibson and Co. Litho, Erie Litho, and Enquirer Job Printing Co. printed fine examples as well. Posters by noted artists such as Mucha, Parrish, and Hohlwein bring high prices. Other considerations are good color, interesting subject

matter and, of course, condition. The WWII posters listed below are among the more expensive examples; 80% of those on the market bring less than $50.00. See also Movie Memorabilia; Political Entourage; Rockwell, Norman.

Key:
B&B — Barnum and Bailey   RB — Ringling Bros.

Advertising

Adriance Buckeye...Machinery, barefoot girl, 1897, 28x21", EX ...**200.00**
Adriance Plows, children on wht horse, 1902, 28x21", G............**225.00**
Allen's Root Beer Extracts, lady & 3 cherubs, 20x14", NM.........**650.00**
Anheuser-Busch, lady w/eagle on finger, fr, 27x37", VG.............**950.00**
Arrow Beer, Matchless Body, nude, fr, 25x14", EX **250.00**
Dr Meyer's Foot Soap, many different people, 38x25", NM.........**150.00**
Dupont Powder, men & dogs, 1917, 31x20", G............................**350.00**
Eureka Mowers, farmer & horse-drawn equipment, 26x20", G....**175.00**
Flirt Biscuits, Mucha, 1900, 25x12".. **2,400.00**
Granite Iron Ware, lady w/pail & cow, 28x12½", G....................**525.00**
Griffith & Boyd Fertilizers, Asti girl, 19x15", VG......................**150.00**
Hay Press, machine w/2-horse team, 18x24", G **125.00**
Hercules Powder, Blk boy hunts in winter, 1920s, 25x16", EX **850.00**
Hoyt's German Cologne, child & flowers, 23x17", VG **250.00**
Internat'l Stock Food, Three Feeds, hogs/corn, 28x22" **130.00**
Internat'l Stock Food, Three Feeds, pig/horse/bull, 29x18", G ...**175.00**
Launbenheimer, cavalier w/stein on horsebk, 1920, 47x32" **70.00**
Lawrence Machine Shope Locomotives, 1853, lg folio, G **2,000.00**
Madison Cigars, Indian princess, 1906, fr, 34x19", EX **300.00**
McCormick Harvester, Battle of Gettysburg/machine, 24x35", G ..**275.00**
Mecca Cigarettes, lady in lg hat, cb, 1912, 40x22", VG..............**300.00**
Missouri Pacific Railway, US Grant's cabin, 26x20", G **50.00**
Nat'l Hay Rake, raking machine, bold graphics, 13x16", VG **125.00**
New Home Sewing Machines, girl at machine, 20x15", EX **150.00**
Ohio Rakes, Statue of Liberty, Krebs, 22x28", VG.....................**275.00**
Old Virginia Cherrots, female graduate, 20x15", VG..................**275.00**
Pabst Malt Extract, knight astride swan, 14x22", EX....................**95.00**
Pacific Enamel Paint, French, ca 1900, 40x28", EX **225.00**
Pillsbury Flour, eagle, men loading ships, 30x24", VG **1,000.00**
Putnam Horse Shoe Nails, horses & carriage, 1888, 21x28", G...**200.00**
Remington Game Load, animals/#d index, 1923, 26x19", EX **45.00**
Seagram's Whiskey, horse & jockey, 1905, 43x29", EX **800.00**
Swift's Washing Powder, Blk family/donkey/cart, 42x28", G .. **6,250.00**
Waterman's Fountain Pens, Uncle Sam, 1900s, 20x42", EX ... **1,250.00**
Wilbur's Stock Tonic, 6 horses/wagon/running dog, 15x32", G.....**60.00**
Wolf Co Flour Mill Machine, Red Riding Hood/Wolf, 14x22" ...**500.00**

Circus

B&B, Greatest Show on Earth, Dble Menagerie, 1901, 64x29"...**900.00**
B&B, smiling clown, 106x80", EX..**660.00**
Christy Bros, tiger family, 28x41", EX......................................**275.00**
Col Tim McCoy's Indian Village, 20x27" **250.00**
Cole Bros, laughing clown, Erie, 80x138", EX..........................**650.00**
Cole Bros, laughing clown, Erie, 80x47", EX............................**400.00**
Cole Bros, Quarter Million Pounds of Elephants, 28x41" **165.00**
Downie Bros, Teddy (Hippodrome elephant), 27x28" **200.00**
Elks All Professional Circus, Erie, 41x27", EX...........................**250.00**
Forepaugh & Sells Bros, ...Trained Animals..., 1907, 29x40".. **1,200.00**
G Barnes Wild Animal Circus, tiger on elephant, 39x26" **450.00**
Heir Granada, high-wire act, Calhoun, muslin, 39x27", EX **325.00**
Jack Hoxie, 3-ring, 4 chiefs, Riverside, 42x28", EX.....................**250.00**
Miller Bros, Miss Bonro...Shot from Cannon, Temple, 28x42" ...**200.00**
Pallenburg's Wonder Bears, muslin, Strobridge, 1915, 20x20" **500.00**

Professor Harry de Rosa, muslin, Donaldson, 28x41", EX 300.00
PT Barnum & JA Bailey pictured, Strobridge, 1909, 38x28"... 1,000.00
RB, Circus Sideshow, Erie, 17x26", EX 450.00
RB, Mr Mistin Jr, Child Wonder of World, 30x28" 300.00
RB B&B, clown & animals, Erie Litho, 106x88", EX.....................500.00
RB B&B, Colleano, high-wire act, Strobridge, 79x42", EX 500.00
RB B&B, Gargantua the Great, gorilla & native, 54x80", EX ...1,250.00
Sell Bros, ...Menagerie of Wild Animals, Strobridge, 40x29" 440.00
Silvan-Drew Circus, tiger roars, Riverside, 42x28", EX...............200.00
Skippy & Bum, elephant & clown, Erie, 41x28", EX 125.00

Magic

Alexander the Man Who Knows, stone litho, 1920, 40x27", EX...600.00
Ask Alexander, stone litho, linen-bk, 1920, 41x27", EX 700.00
Carter the Great Condemned ..., stone litho, 105x80", EX 700.00
Carter the Great...Wonderful Wizard, Otis, 74x38", EX 660.00
Chang & Fak-Hong's United Magicians, Hari Kiri, 24x16", EX..330.00
Chang & Fak-Hong's United Magicians, Noe Ark, 41x28", EX..165.00
George, Supreme Master, stone litho, 24x18", EX 330.00
Germain, Master of Magic, stone litho, 40x26", EX 400.00
Germain the Wizard, spirit in fire w/witch, 79x40", EX 1,210.00
Gordon Master Magician, Nat'l Printing, 26x29", EX 220.00
Great Chang & Fak-Hong's United Magicians' Show, 23x15"....165.00
Great Kar-Mi Troup, stone litho, Donaldson, 1912, 40x26".......385.00
Harry Blackstone, EX color, autographed, fr, 22x14" 100.00
Heany & Co, Donaldson, sm rprs, 79x39", EX 700.00
Houdini in Amsterdam (Holland) Prison, 1902, 29½x19½" ... 7,500.00
Irving the Magician, Oriental Oddities, 42x14", EX 55.00
Kar-Mi Swallows Loaded Gun Barrel, Nat'l Printing, 26x39" 330.00
Kassner, Zaubermeister, Friedlander, 1930, 24x16", EX 1,750.00
Nelson Downs King of Koins, linen bk, Carqueville, 11x28" 220.00
Sorcar, World's Greatest Magician, 1952, 29x18½" 200.00
Thurston, All of a Hat, stone litho, 26x39", EX 385.00
Willard the Wizard, Night of Enchantment, Hunter's, 24x8" 165.00

Minstrel

Vogel's Big City Minstrels, 30" x 43", NM, $1,000.00.

Hilson's Famous..., Donaldson, 21x29", EX 225.00
Primrose & Dockstader Minstrels, Blk man w/chickens, 1901 ....400.00
Primrose & Dockstader Minstrels, Strobridge, NY......................412.00
William West's, Lew Scully, Strobridge, 1900, 81x39", EX 300.00

Theatrical

Cendrillon (Cinderella), Bertrand, Devambez, Paris, 1899..........200.00
Donga, Germaine Kerjean, Paris, linen bk, 63x47", EX 200.00

Girbal, C'est la Rebue, linen bk, 1930, 60x45", EX.....................165.00
John Sheridan, Strobridge, 30x20", EX 80.00
Ripley, Believe It or Not, Snookie...Chimpanzee, 108x82" 175.00
Ripley, Believe It or Not, Snookie...Chimpanzee, 81x82"............55.00
Secret Service, Strobridge, 1896, 30x20", VG 125.00
Theater de Cluny, Delanchy, Paris, ca 1895, fr, 30x22", VG.......250.00

Travel

Amelie-Les-Bains, Pyrenees Orientales, Paris, 41x25", EX 400.00
Batumi, Russian scene, 40x24½", VG 90.00
Bezombes, Cote D'Azur, French Railways, 1972, 40x25", EX 300.00
Cote D'Azur, after Picasso, Deschamps, 41x27", EX 330.00
Eastern Airlines, Mickey Mouse, 1983, fr, NM..........................40.00
Le Tour du Mt Blanc, France, 1927, 42x31" 600.00
Mountains of France, Nathan, France, 38x24½", G...................150.00
Station et Centre du Tourisme, Paris, 1940, 39x24", EX 165.00

War

James Montgomery Flagg, I Want You..., 1917, first printing with red, white and blue stripes, 40" x 30", NM, $1,600.00.

Help Him Win, Gen Pershing & children, WWI, 20x30", EX......65.00
Holland Will Rise Again, bombed city, WWII, 17x22", EX..........20.00
Knights of Columbus (school), We'll Help You..., WWI, 20x13"..60.00
Le Presidente, Grande Illusion, Vietnam, 1968, 24x28", EX 16.00
Lend the Way They Fight..., Powers, WWII, 40x27", EX.............125.00
Monument a la Victoire..., Verdun monument, WWI, 1-sheet...250.00
Navy Rifle Range Learn To Shoot..., WWI, 20x30", EX 65.00
Swat the Pest, Uncle Sam swats German flies, WWI, 28x35". 2,000.00
We've Made Monkey...of You, Uncle Sam/Hitler, '43, 20x15" 15.00
Yugoslavia's Merchant Seamen Fight, 11 ships, WWII, 27x11" 18.00

Miscellaneous

Cabaret Artistique, EX colors, Paris, 1904, 52x39" 660.00
Little Rascals, Fishy Tales, 1950s, 42x26", EX 50.00
Mucha, Au Quartier Latin, color litho, 1897, fr, 18x12" 850.00
Mucha, Gismonda, from Les Maitres de L'Affiche, 1900, 14x6"..950.00
Mucha, Leslie Carter, color litho, 1908, 81x32" 7,100.00
Mucha, Monaco, Monte Carlo, color litho, 1897, 42x30" 12,000.00
Mucha, Salammbo, color litho, 1897, fr, 15x9" 1,950.00
Mucha, Salome, color litho, L'Estampe Moderne, fr, 14x10" . 1,300.00

Pot Lids

Pot lids were pottery covers for containers that were used for hair dressing, potted meats, etc. The most desirable were decorated with colorful transfer prints under the glaze in a variety of themes, animal and scenic. The first and probably the largest company to manufacture these lids was F & R Pratt of Fenton, Staffordshire, established in the early 1800s. The name or initials of Jesse Austin, their designer, may sometimes be found on exceptional designs. Although few pot lids were made after the 1880s, the firm continued into the 20th century.

American pot lids are very rare. Most have been dug up by collectors searching through sites of early gold rush mining towns in California. Minor rim chips are expected and normally do not detract from listed values.

American

Jules Hauel (The Three Choristers) Wholesale Perfumer, Philadelphia, black transfer, rare, 3⅛", $825.00.

Amandine...Chapped Hands, blk transfer, Bazin & Sargent, 3¼" .75.00
Amandine...Chapped Hands, blk transfer, Hauel, 2¾", M 240.00
Bazin's...Premium Shaving Cream, blk transfer, 3", M 80.00
Bear, Bears Grease, blk transfer, Hauel, 2⅞", EX..........................125.00
Burdell's Tooth Powder, mc transfer, Wakelee, rare, 3" 135.00
Bust of Franklin, blk transfer, Hauel Perfumer, 3½", VG 35.00
Cold Cream, mc transfer, HP Wakelee, sm chip, rare, 3" 130.00
Compound for Shaving by Glenn & Co, blk transfer, 3¾", NM .400.00
Eugene Rousell Odontine..., blk transfer, early, 2¾", M..............210.00
House of Parliament in London, blk transfer, Hauel, 4⅛", EX.....475.00
Improved Cold Cream of Roses, blk transfer, X Bazin, 2", EX 220.00
Jules Hauel Wholesale Perfumer Phila, blk transfer, 3⅛" 825.00
Man shaving, blk transfer, Wrights...Shaving Compound, 3½" ..600.00
Man shaving, Taylor's...Compound, blk transfer, 3⅜", EX 195.00
Odonto Oak Bark...Tooth Paste, purple transfer, Choate, 3", M ..450.00
Rousell's...Premium Shaving Cream, blk transfer, 4", NM...........170.00
Roussel's Unrivalled Premium..., red transfer, 3", EX 30.00
Steer, Beef Marrow, blk transfer, Hauel Perfumer, 3", EX............170.00
Superior Rose Tooth Paste, red transfer, X Bazin, 2¼", EX..........220.00
Williams Swiss Violet Shaving Cream, mc transfer, 3⅝", EX 250.00
2 cows, Liston's Extract of Beef, blk transfer, 1⅞", M 110.00
7 Highest Premiums...World's Fair 1851, HP&WC Taylor, 3½" .120.00

English

Ambrosial Shaving Cream, blk transfer, John Gosnell, 3½" 95.00
Battle of the Nile, minor crazing, 3¾" 200.00
Bellevue Tavern, Pratt, 4½" 165.00
Cherry Tooth Paste, Cleansing/Preserving, blk transfer, 3"............70.00
Dutch Battle Scene..125.00
Enthusiast, old man fishing in tub, Pratt, 4" 200.00
Girls on a Swing, minor crazing, 3¾"..250.00
Holburn Village, minor crazing, 3¾" 135.00
Letter from Diggings, Fenton, rnd fr, 4" 195.00
New Blackfriars Bridge, minor crazing, 3¾" 135.00
Pegwell Bay, minor crazing, 3¾" 135.00
Preparing for the Ride, 3¾" 125.00
Pretty Kettle of Fish, Fenton, rnd fr, 4" 265.00
Rimmel (cherries) Cherry Tooth Paste, yel/brn transfer, 3" 70.00
Rivals, 3¾", M 200.00
Shakespeare's House, 3¾" 335.00
Skewbald Horse 115.00
Trafalgar Square, minor crazing, 3¾" 150.00
Uncle Toby, fr 195.00
Village Wedding 88.00
Wimbledon July 1860, Victoria firing shot, 1860s, 4⅛", EX 100.00
Wolf & Lamb 95.00

Potschappel

In the town of Potschappel in 1872, Carl Thieme began a porcelain factory called the Saxonian Porcelain Factory. His work was of excellent quality and consisted of figures, vases, urns, lamp bases, birds, bowls, and animals, the work being similar to Dresden-Meissen and Sitzendorf. After World War II, the company was incorporated and became Saxonian Porcelain Factory Dresden. There are four or five marks assigned to his work. Our advisor for this category is Donald Penrose; he is listed in the Directory under Ohio.

Couple with flower baskets, 9½", $650.00 for the pair.

Figurine, man & lady w/flower baskets, rnd plinth, mk, 9" 695.00
Figurine, pug dogs, tan & wht, male & female, 7x7", pr...............570.00
Lamp base, figural reserves/encrusted florals, w/shade, 30" 1,500.00
Urn, appl florals, bird finial, w/lid, 19" 2,750.00
Urn, appl florals, figural reserve, ornate hdls, w/lid, 14"...............750.00
Vase, figures in garden reserve, floral panels, 1880s, 12" 450.00

Powder Horns and Shot Flasks

Though powder horns had already been in use for hundreds of years, collectors usually focus on those made after the expansion of the United States westward in the very early 1800s. While some are basic and very simple, others were scrimshawed and highly polished. Especially nice carvings can quickly escalate the value of a horn that has survived intact to as high as $400.00. Those with detailed maps, historical scenes, etc. bring even higher prices.

Metal flasks were introduced in the 1830s; by the middle of the century they were produced in quantity and at prices low enough that they became a viable alternative to the powder horn. Today's collector regards the smaller flasks as the more desirable and valuable, and those made for specific companies bring premium prices.

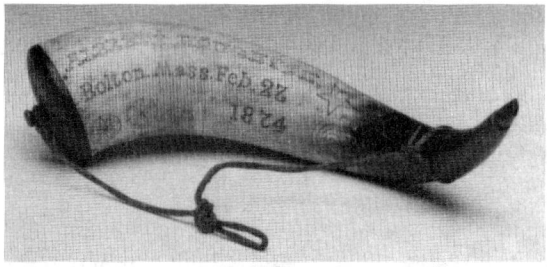

Engraved powder horn, geometric decoration, signed and dated 1874, minor chips, 15", $400.00.

Flask, brass, circle & stars emb, bag form, 7", EX 132.00
Flask, brass, for gun stock, 8", VG...275.00
Flask, brass, horses' heads in panel, Hawksley, 8½" 285.00
Flask, brass, hunter by gate w/dogs, 8½", EX..............................60.00
Flask, brass, hunter/dogs/1776 emb, 8", EX.................................145.00
Flask, brass, shells & scrolls emb, lt wear, lg..............................65.00
Flask, brass, wreath border, bag form, 7½", NM 300.00
Flask, copper, brass spout, Pease, dtd 1856, EX............................235.00
Flask, copper, Colt, eagle emb, brass spout, 4¼"..........................95.00
Flask, copper, Colt's Navy, London 1851, Sheffield, 7", EX 500.00
Flask, German silver, shells emb, 4½", EX...................................220.00
Horn, belt hook near center, brass spout, 1600s, 12" 400.00
Horn, cvd wooden end, 24" along outside curve, EX 45.00
Horn, eng map/name/dtd 1756, sm hole/rpr plug/cleaned, 10" 950.00
Horn, geometrics/name/1723 – 1746, 9"..800.00
Horn, hearts & scallops cvgs, wood cap, 1850s, 15", EX 100.00
Horn, leaves emb on silver mts, 13", +chain................................525.00
Horn, lion/unicorn/hunter/dogs/deer, crack, 12" 1,900.00
Horn, riders/lady/animals cvgs, 1700s, 8", VG 550.00
Horn, riders/lady/floral cvgs, 1600s, 8", EX.................................600.00

Pratt

Prattware is a type of relief-molded earthenware with polychrome decoration. Scenic motifs with figures were popular; sometimes captions were added. Jugs are most common; but teapots, tableware, even figurines were made. The term 'Pratt' refers to Wm. Pratt of Lane Delph, who is credited with making the first of this type, though similar wares were made later by other Staffordshire potters.

Rare 'Faces' pitcher, merman handle, marked Wedgwood & Co., 12", $950.00.

Bank, house, figures at sides, faces in windows, rpr, 5" 600.00
Creamer, children at play in heart reserve, 4¾", EX....................250.00
Creamer, hunt scenes, prof rpr, 5"..175.00
Figurine, bear, mc, edge chips, 3½" L..600.00
Figurine, pearlware, woman/child, imp Virgin Mary, 9½", VG ...400.00
Pipe, Admiral Nelson in tall hat bowl, loop stem, 8", EX........ 1,300.00
Pipe, coiled snake w/head of man in turban, 1800s, 7½" 1,600.00
Pitcher, bust of man in hat/florals, 6-color, 7½", NM 400.00
Sugar bowl, swan finial, woman/child reserve, 5¾", EX 400.00
Vase, quintal; leaves/flowers, 4-color, 7", NM, pr.......................950.00
Watch stand, figure ea side clock, 1820s, chips/rstr, 11" 1,200.00

Precious Moments

Known as 'America's Hummels,' Precious Moments are a line of well-known collectibles created by Samuel J. Butcher and produced by Enesco, Inc. These pieces have endeared themselves to many because of the inspirational messages they portray. The collection is approximately twelve years old and is produced in bisque porcelain in the Orient. Each piece is produced with a different mark each year. This mark, not the date, is usually the link to the value of the piece. Most mold changes result in increased values; and, when a piece is retired or suspended, its price increases as well. As an example, 'God Loveth a Cheerful Giver' retailed for $9.50 in 1980; it was retired in 1981 and has a secondary market price now of $650.00.

Rosie Wells Enterprises, Inc., our advisor for this category, has published the Precious Moments collector magazine, *Precious Collectibles*, as well as a secondary market price guide. Her address is in the Directory under Clubs, Newsletters, and Catalogs. Items listed below are assumed to be in mint condition with the original box.

Bless You Two, E-9255, dove mk 30.00
Bride & Groom, E-7179, bell, no mk 40.00
Bride & Groom, E-7267 B&G, no mk, pr...950.00
Dawn's Early Light, PM-831, Club pc, fish mk 65.00
Drummer Boy, E-2358, bell, no mk, 1982...45.00
Joy to the World, E-2343, ornament, fish mk, suspended...............35.00
Katie Lynne, E-0539, doll, cross mk...180.00
Leopard, 109479, Birthday Series, cedar tree mk............................25.00
Love Is Kind, E-1379A, triangle mk, suspended 85.00
Love Lifted Me, E-5201, triangle mk, suspended 70.00
Mother Sew Dear, E-0514, ornament, fish mk.................................22.00
Peace on Earth, E-2804, hourglass mk..95.00
Press On, E-9265, fish mk...60.00
Purr-fect Grandma, E-7184, no mk...75.00
Rejoicing w/You, E-7172, plate, no mk, 1985 ....40.00
Seek & Ye Shall Find, E-0105, charter member pc, cross mk 50.00
Silent Night, 15814, musical tree, dove mk.....................................55.00
Summer's Joy, 12114, plate, dove mk...55.00
To God Be the Glory, E-2823, fish mk 65.00

Pre-Columbian Artifacts

The term 'Pre-Columbian' loosely refers to some time prior to 1492, when Columbus arrived in America. In particular, it indicates pre-1492 artifacts of Central and South America, some of which can be dated as early as 4000 B.C. Artifacts representing the cultures of the Inca, Maya, and Aztec Indians are avidly sought by the collector. These may be made of precious metals, hardstones, or pottery. Some were used in rituals and religious rites; some such as bowls and other utensils, though strictly utilitarian, nevertheless convey through form and decoration the craftsmanship of these early tribes.

Key: tc — terra cotta

Figurine, pottery, female nursing baby, mc motif, 1890, 6" 200.00
Idol, pottery, seated w/eagle on its bk, 11" 150.00
Necklace, eng blk pottery beads, w/hanging figurine, 31" 85.00
Pitcher, Anasazi, blk/wht Pueblo III Period, as found, 6" 175.00
Pot, Panamanian, pottery, 3 fish-form rattle legs, 5x5" 125.00
Stirrup vessel, Mochica, seated human figure, 8x6" 300.00

Primitives

Like the mouse that ate the grindstone, so has collectible interest in primitives increased, a little bit at a time, until demand is taking bites instead of nibbles into their availability. Although the term 'primitives' once referred to those survival essentials contrived by our American settlers, it has recently been expanded to include objects needed or desired by succeeding generations — items representing the cabin-n'-cornpatch existence as well as examples of life on larger farms and in towns. Through popular usage, it also respectfully covers what are actually 'country collectibles.'

From the 1600s into the latter 1800s, factories employed carvers, blacksmiths, and other artisans whose handwork contributed to turning out quality items. When buying, 'touchmarks,' a company's name and/or location and maker's or owner's initials, are exciting discoveries.

Primitives are uniquely individual. Following identical forms, results more often than not show typically personal ideas. Using this as a guide (combined with circumstances of age, condition, desire to own, etc.) should lead to a reasonably accurate evaluation. For items not listed, consult comparable examples. Authority Kathryn McNerney has compiled several lovely books on primitives and related topics: *Primitives, Our American Heritage; Collectible Blue and White Stoneware*; and *Antique Tools, Our American Heritage*. You will find her address in the Directory under Florida. See also Butter Molds and Stamps; Boxes; Copper; Farm Collectibles; Fireplace Implements; Kitchen Collectibles; Molds; Tinware; Weaving; Woodenware; and Wrought Iron.

Apple corer/slicer, homemade, well made, 18" 65.00
Bed warmer, brass, eng foliage, trn hdl, polished/rfn, 45" 275.00
Bed warmer, brass, floral piercing, trn wood hdl, 49" 225.00
Bed warmer, brass, foliate piercing, grpt hdl, polished..................325.00
Bed warmer, brass, tooled starflower, trn wood hdl, 42" 300.00
Bed warmer, copper lid w/tooled pinwheel, trn hdl, 42", EX 160.00
Candle box, pine, arched top, sq nails, 1830s, EX 265.00
Candle mold, 10-tube, tin, 11" 95.00
Candle mold, 12-tube, tin, divided into 2 segments, ftd, 11" 130.00
Candle mold, 12-tube, tin, lantern finial w/ring hdl, EX..............450.00
Candle mold, 24-tube, pewter, floor style, ca 1800s, 17½" 1,100.00
Candle mold, 24-tube, pnt pine fr/tin top, makes 2 lengths 1,250.00
Candle mold, 24-tube, tin, battered/soldered rpr, 11" 125.00
Candle mold, 5-tube, tin, miniature, 5" 250.00
Candle mold, 6-tube, tin, 19", EX 250.00
Candle mold, 8-tube, tin, minor battering, 10" 95.00
Candle mold, 9-tube, tin, tray top & base, side hdl, 10" 190.00
Candlestand, oak/pine, ratchet, 2 sockets w/push-ups, 22" 1,900.00
Candlestand, wood w/red traces, sawtooth rod w/ratchet, 20". 2,000.00
Churn, New Style Wht Cedar Cylinder, ca 1895, 15x12x10" 135.00
Churn, staved wood/CI, rocking keg form, ca 1900, 33" 135.00
Churn, tin, wooden dasher, bail hdl, 1900s, 19x9" 135.00
Cookie peel, wrought, heart shape, ring hdl, ca 1800, 19" 300.00
Cranberry scoop, all wood, long hdl, 44" 125.00
Cranberry scoop, tin, 10½" 45.00
Cranberry scoop, wood/sheet metal, stencil: CR King, late 90.00
Cranberry scoop, wood/tin, branded: Budd & Co, varnish, 15" 85.00

Foot warmer, cherry fr, trn corner posts, punched tin, 9" 225.00
Foot warmer, wood w/CI top plate w/heart cutout, 13x11"..........225.00

Foot warmer, tinned iron with pierced heart motif in wooden frame, candle holder within, unusual upright rectangular form, 1850s, 6½", $425.00.

Fruit, cvd stone, orig pnt, 3 pcs, 2½" to 3" 100.00
Hat-blocking form, wooden, 10" 45.00
Ironing brd, poplar w/gr-pnt base, trn legs/1-brd 60" top 150.00
Kraut cutter, walnut, cut-out crest, wear, 8x26" 95.00
Quilting clamp, wooden, well made, 33" L, 4 for...........................60.00
Reel, wooden, w/string, knob end hdls, 18" L 75.00
Scouring brd, yel pine, slide-lid base compartment, 14" L 65.00
Sieve, horsehair bottom, wrapped bentwood, ca 1800s, 8¾".........42.00
Sifter, flour or sugar; cedar, pegged, ca 1864, rare.......................275.00
Smoothing brd, birch, horse-shaped hdl, 1800s, 5x30½" 695.00
Smoothing brd, cvd/3-color rpt decor, horse hdl, 25", EX...........500.00
Smoothing brd, gr pnt w/3-color floral & heart, rpl hdl, 25" 125.00
Smoothing brd, 5-color rpt, rstr horse hdl, sgn/1801, 23" 350.00
Soft soap scoop & dish, hewn pine, 1800s, 4" hdl, 8" overall.......175.00
Sugar nippers, steel, EX hand-wrought detail, 9"..........................150.00
Sugar nippers, wrought steel, well shaped/tooled, 8½" 80.00
Wafer iron, iron w/wrought hdls, 8-sided, bldgs/etc, 28" 400.00
Wagon jack, wood/wrought iron, simple tooling/1855, 19" 125.00
Washboard, CI, starflowers on crest, 22x12" 475.00
Washboard, cvd w/corrugated sides, soap pocket, 22x13", EX 95.00
Washboard, pine, whittled ribs, cut-out hdl, 3¼x6⅝" 40.00
Washboard, pine w/Rockingham insert, wear, 26x13" 525.00
Washboard, redware insert in poplar fr, 13½x7" 325.00
Whisk broom, cvd ivory hdl, 11"...40.00

Prints

The term 'print' may be defined today as almost any image printed on paper by any available method. Examples of collectible old 'prints' are Norman Rockwell magazine covers and Maxfield Parrish posters and calendars. 'Original print' refers to one achieved through the efforts of the artist or under his direct supervision. A 'reproduction' is a print produced by an accomplished print maker who reproduces another artist's print or original work. Thorough study is required on the part of the collector to recognize and appreciate the many variable factors to be considered in evaluating a print. Prices vary from one area of the country to another and are dependent upon new findings regarding the scarcity or abundance of prints as such information may arise. Although each collector of old prints may have their own varying criteria by which to judge condition, for those who deal only rarely in this area or newer collectors, a few guidelines may prove helpful. Staining, though unquestionably detrimental, is nearly always present in some degree and should be weighed against the rarity of the print. Professional cleaning should improve its appearance and at the same time help preserve it. Avoid tears that affect the image; minor margin tears are another matter, especially if the print is a rare one. Moderate 'foxing' (brown spots caused by mold or the fermentation of the rag content of old paper) and light stains from the old frames are not serious unless present in excess. Margin trimming was a common practice; but look for at least ½" to 1½" margins, depending on print size.

For further study see *Huxford's Fine Art Value Guide*, available from your local bookstore or Collector Books. When no condition is indicated, the items listed below are assumed to be in very good to excellent condition. See also Parrish, Maxfield; Rockwell, Norman.

Audubon, John J.

Audubon is the best known of American and European wildlife artists. His first series of prints, 'Birds of America,' was produced by Robert Havell of London. They were printed on Whitman watermarked paper bearing dates of 1826 to 1838. The Octavo Edition of the same series was printed in seven editions, the first by J.T. Bowen under Audubon's direction. There were seven volumes of text and prints, each 10" x 7", the first five bearing the J.J. Audubon and J.B. Chevalier mark, the last two, J.J. Audubon. They were produced from 1840 through 1844. The second and other editions were printed up to 1871. The Bien Edition prints were full size, made under the direction of Audubon's sons in the late 1850s. Due to the onset of the Civil War, only 105 plates were finished. These are considered to be the most valuable of the reprints of the 'Birds of America Series.'

In 1971 the complete set was reprinted by Johnson Reprint Corp. of New York and Theaturm Orbis Terrarum of Amsterdam. Examples of the latter bear the watermark G. Schut and Zonen. In 1985 a second reprint was done by Abbeville Press for the National Audubon Society.

Although Audubon is best known for his portrayal of birds, one of his less-familiar series, 'Viviparous Quadrupeds of North America,' portrayed various species of animals. Assembled in corroboration with John Bachman from 1839 until 1851, these prints are 28" x 22" in size. Several octavo editions were published in the 1850s.

American Beaver, #46, Bowen, 16x24"	880.00
American Sparrow Hawk, #142, Havell, 38x25"	3,500.00
American White Pelican, #311, Havell, 38x25"	14,000.00
Barn Swallow, #173, Havell, 38x25"	2,200.00
Barred Owl, #46, Havell, ca 1828, 39x27"	8,500.00
Black-Billed Cuckoo, #32, Havell, 19x26"	3,850.00
Blue Jay, #231, Bien, 27x40"	4,500.00
Brown Pelican, #421, Havell, 26x37"	18,000.00
Canvas-Backed Duck, #301, 25x38"	16,000.00
Cardinal Grosbeak, #154, Havell, 1833, 26x37"	12,000.00
Cayenne Tern, #273, Havell, 1835, 25x39"	3,000.00
Chestnut-Crowned Titmouse, #353, Havell, 1837, 21x15"	2,100.00
Cinnamon Bear (Male & Female), #127, Bowen, 18x25"	4,000.00
Common Crossbill, #198, Havell, 38x26"	3,000.00
Gray Fox, #21, Bowen, 18x24"	6,500.00
Great Footed Hawk, #20, Bien, 27x40"	3,000.00
Ground Dove, #182, Havell, 26x37"	3,500.00
Hooded Merganser, #232, Havell, 1834, 25x38"	7,500.00
Hutchin's Barnacle Goose, #277, Havell, 1836, 39x25"	2,800.00
Ivory-Billed Woodpecker, #66, Havell, 39x26"	14,000.00
Key West Dove, #167, Havell, 25x36"	6,000.00
Long-Billed Curlew, #231, 25x35"	20,900.00
Long-Tailed Duck, #312, Havell, 26x38"	6,500.00
Marsh Hawk, #356, Havell, 38x26"	3,300.00
Mocking Bird, Havell, 38x25"	12,000.00
Nuttalls Lesser-Marsh Hen, #125, Havell, 39x25"	1,200.00

Passenger Pigeon, #62, Havell, 25x38"	12,000.00
Pileated Woodpecker, Bien, 1860, 37x24"	6,000.00
Pin-Tailed Duck, #227, Havell, 1834, 25x39"	6,500.00
Plumed Partridge, #423, Havell, 26x39"	2,900.00
Prairie Starling, #420, Havell, 38x25"	1,900.00
Red-Breasted Merganser, #401, Havell, 1836, 25x38"	6,500.00
Red-Headed Woodpecker, #27, Havell, 38x26"	4,500.00

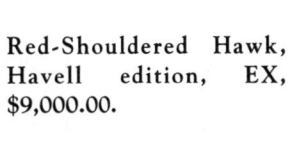

Red-Shouldered Hawk, Havell edition, EX, $9,000.00.

Roscoe's Yellow Throat, 1827, 37x26"	1,900.00
Ruby-Crowned Wren, #195, Havell, 37x25"	1,500.00
Scolopaceus Courlan, #377, Havell, 1838, 26x37"	2,500.00
Sharp-Tailed Finch, #149, Havell, 1832, 38x25"	2,900.00
Snow Goose, #381, Havell, 1837, 25x38"	8,500.00
Snowy Owl, #121, Havell, ca 1833, 38x25"	25,000.00
Swallow-Tailed Hawk, #72, Havell, 29x35"	3,500.00
Swift Fox (Male), #52, Bowen, ca 1845, 19x24"	2,900.00
Tree Sparrow, #188, Havell, 38x26"	1,500.00
Tropic Bird, #262, Havell, 1831, 25x38"	3,300.00
Velvet Duck, #247, Havell, ca 1835, 25x37"	2,800.00
Virginia Partridge, #76, Havell, 26x39"	10,000.00
White-Eyed Flycatcher or Vireo, #63, Havell, 26x38"	2,000.00
White-Headed Pigeon, #36, 1833, elephant folio	6,500.00
White-Winged Silvery Gull, #282, Havell, 26x33"	1,540.00
Yellow-Breasted Chat, #244, 1860, Bien	1,800.00
Yellow-Crowned Warbler, #153, Havell, 38x25"	1,500.00
Zenaida Dove, #162, Havell, 25x37"	3,000.00

Currier and Ives

Nathaniel Currier was in business by himself until the late 1850s when he formed a partnership with James Merrit Ives. Currier is given credit for being the first to use the medium to portray newsworthy subjects, and the Currier and Ives views of 19th-century American culture are familiar to us all. Values are given for prints in very good condition; all are colored unless indicated black and white. Unless noted 'NC' (Nathaniel Currier), all prints are published by Currier and Ives.

A Home on Mississippi, sm folio	500.00
American Choice Fruits, lg folio	1,500.00
American Country Life, May Morning; NC, lg folio	2,500.00
American Country Life, October Afternoon; NC, lg folio	2,500.00
American Country Life, Pleasures of Winter; NC, lg folio	2,700.00
American Field Sports, Chance for Both Barrels; lg folio	3,000.00

American Field Sports, Retrieving; lg folio 3,000.00
American Forest Scene, Maple Sugaring; NC, lg folio 10,000.00
American Frontier Life, On the War-Path; lg folio 6,500.00
American Homestead, Winter; sm folio 600.00
American Nat'l Game of Baseball, lg folio 25,000.00
American Winter Scenes, Morning; NC, lg folio 6,000.00
American Winter Sports, Deer Shooting; NC, lg folio............. 6,000.00
Barefoot Boy, sm folio..150.00
Battle of Gettysburg PA, July 3rd, 1863; sm folio 225.00
Beauties of Billiards, Carom on the Dark Red; 1869, lg folio.... 1,500.00
Benjamin Franklin, Statesman & Philosopher; NC, sm folio 600.00
Black Duck Shooting, sm folio..195.00
Bombardment & Capture of Ft Henry, sm folio 250.00
Bouquet of Fruit, sm folio 125.00
Brook Trout, Just Caught; med folio 650.00
Brush on the Homestretch, lg folio.. 1,900.00
Burning of Chicago, 1871, sm folio..400.00
Cares of a Family, NC, lg folio...4,000.00
Cherry Time, 1866, med folio...500.00
City of New York, NC, lg folio 3,000.00
Clipper Ship Dreadnought, NC, lg folio................................. 3,000.00
Coming from Trot, Sports on Home Stretch; 1869, lg folio 2,200.00
Crack Sloop in the Race to Windward, lg folio 2,000.00
Cutter Yacht Genesta, lg folio 1,500.00
Darktown Trotter Ready for the Word, 1892, sm folio 225.00
Daughter of the Regiment, NC, sm folio 125.00
Death of Gen Zachary Taylor, NC, sm folio 75.00
Death of Tecumseh, NC, sm folio...110.00
Dutchman & Hiram Woodruff, sm folio...............................700.00
English Winter Scene, sm folio..600.00
Fall of Richmond VA, sm folio..250.00
Falls of the Ottawa River, Canada; sm folio............................275.00
Farmer's Home, Autumn; lg folio 2,000.00
Four Seasons of Life, Middle Age; lg folio 1,175.00
Fruit Piece, sm folio 125.00
Fruits, Summer Varieties; sm folio 150.00
Fruits & Flowers of Summer, med folio 350.00
Gem of the Atlantic, NC, sm folio 800.00
Gen Franklin Pierce, NC, sm folio 100.00
Gen Lewis Cass, NC, sm folio...80.00
Gen Stoneman's Great Cavalry Raid, sm folio.........................175.00
George M Dallas, NC, sm folio 65.00
Going to the Trot, Good Day & Good Track; lg folio............. 2,200.00
Good Times on the Old Plantation, sm folio...........................700.00
Grand Nat'l Democratic Banner, Cass & Butler; NC, sm folio....225.00
Grand Nat'l Whig Banner, Henry Clay; NC, sm folio 225.00
Great Bartholdi Statue, Liberty; lg folio 1,200.00
Great Pacer Sorrel Dan, sm folio...350.00
Happy Little Chicks, 1866, med folio 250.00
Harvesting, The Last Load; sm folio.......................................325.00
Haunted Castle, sm folio..75.00
Henry Clay Nominated for Eleventh President, NC, sm folio 100.00
Henry Clay of KY, NC, sm folio...100.00
Home in the Wilderness, 1870, sm folio.................................675.00
Home of Washington, med folio 350.00
In the Mountains, sm folio 250.00
In the Northern Wilds, Trapping Beaver; sm folio....................500.00
Ingleside Winter, sm folio 600.00
James K Polk, NC, sm folio..100.00
John C Fremont, Republican Candidate; NC, sm folio............125.00
Lafayette at the Tomb of Washington, NC, sm folio 100.00
Landing of the Pilgrims, NC, sm folio 200.00
Lexington of 1861, sm folio..225.00
Life in the Woods, Returning to Camp; lg folio.......................3,000.00

Life of a Fireman, New Era System, Steam & Muscle; lg folio. 3,500.00
Life of a Fireman, Night Alarm; NC, lg folio 3,000.00

Life of a Fireman: The Race, Jump Her Boys, large folio, $3,000.00.

Life of a Fireman, Ruins; NC, lg folio....................................... 3,000.00
Life of a Sportsman, Camping in Woods; sm folio.......................450.00
Life of a Sportsman, Going Out; sm folio 450.00
Life on the Prairie, The Buffalo Hunt; lg folio 5,500.00
Little Brother & Sister, sm folio...100.00
Little More Grape, Capt Bragg; NC, sm folio...........................100.00
Little Sisters, sm folio..100.00
Little Snowbird, sm folio 225.00
Low Water in the Mississippi, lg folio...................................... 4,500.00
Maiden's Rock, Mississippi River, sm folio 475.00
Mayflower Saluted by the Fleet, lg folio 1,500.00
Midnight Race on the Mississippi, sm folio.............................. 1,000.00
Mink Trapping, Prime; lg folio...12,500.00
Minnehaha Falls, Minnesota; med folio 400.00
Moosehead Lake, sm folio..295.00
Mountain Ramble, sm folio 195.00
Mrs JK Polk, NC, sm folio 95.00
Mt Spring, West Point Near Cozzen's Dock; 1862, med folio 800.00
My Boyhood's Home, sm folio...250.00
New Palace Steamer Pilgrim, of Fall River Line; med folio 800.00
Niagara Falls, from the Canada Side; sm folio 225.00
Noah's Ark, sm folio..200.00
Noontide, a Shady Spot; sm folio..200.00
Old Farm Gate, lg folio 1,300.00
Old Oaken Bucket, sm folio..250.00
On the St Lawrence, Indian Encampment; sm folio...................325.00
Peaceful River, sm folio..175.00
Pigeon Shooting, Playing the Decoy; lg folio 3,000.00
Preparing for Market, NC, lg folio.. 3,000.00
Presidents of the United States, NC, sm folio 175.00
Rising Family, lg folio 5,000.00
Roadside Cottage, med folio..400.00
Roadside Mill, 1870, sm folio 350.00
Sale of the Pet Lamb, sm folio...225.00
Saratoga Lake, sm folio..225.00
Scenery of the Catskills, sm folio 300.00
Scenery of the Wissahickon near Philadelphia, sm folio.............325.00
See My New Boots, NC, sm folio..150.00
See Saw, NC, sm folio..200.00
Sinking of the Cumberland by Iron-Clad Merrimac, sm folio 400.00
Snowshoe Dance, med folio 1,500.00
Soldier's Adieu, 1847, NC, sm folio..150.00
Sperm Whale in a Flurry, 1852, NC, sm folio 1,300.00
Spirit of 61, lg folio...300.00

Squirrel Shooting, sm folio	500.00
Steamer Penobscot, lg folio	1,500.00
Stopping Place on the Road, lg folio	3,500.00
Summer Fruits, med folio	350.00
Sunday in the Olden Time, sm folio	195.00
Sunny-Side on the Hudson, sm folio	250.00
Three Little White Kitties, Their First Mouse; sm folio	150.00
Tree of Life, NC, sm folio	125.00
Trial of Patience, med folio	400.00
Trotting Cracks at the Forge, lg folio	9,000.00
Trotting Stallion Phallas, lg folio	1,500.00
View of Harper's Ferry, Virginia; lg folio	1,200.00
View on the Housatonic, lg folio	1,500.00
Vigilant & Valkyrie, lg folio	2,000.00
Village Blacksmith, med folio	700.00
Village Street, 1855, med folio	500.00
Washington at Mt Vernon, NC, sm folio	450.00
Washington Crossing the Delaware, NC, sm folio	250.00
Water Rail Shooting, sm folio	700.00
Wedding Day, NC, sm folio	125.00
Western River Scenery, 1866, med folio	1,000.00
Wild Duck Shooting, on the Wing; 1870, sm folio	600.00
William Penn's Treaty w/the Indians, NC, sm folio	250.00
Windsor Castle & Park, med folio	200.00
Winter in the Country, Cold Morning; lg folio	10,000.00
Winter in the Country, Getting Ice; lg folio	10,000.00
Winter Morning, 1861, med folio	2,100.00
Wonderful Albino Family, sm folio	100.00
Wooding Up on the Mississippi, lg folio	10,000.00
Yacht Henrietta, sm folio	400.00
Yacht Squadron at Newport, 1872, lg folio	5,500.00

Erte (Romain de Tirtoff)

Flowered Cape, 1981, Circle Fine Art,
27" x 21", $1,320.00.

After the Rain, sgn, 1979, 31x23"	660.00
Angry Steed, artist proof, ca 1917, 16x10"	1,100.00
Apache Dance, blindstamp, 1929, 21x14"	1,430.00
Arctic Sea, artist proof, sgn, 19x25"	3,300.00
Bird Seller, sgn/blindstamp, #270, ca 1929, 19x24"	1,210.00
Carmen, sgn/blindstamp, #48, ca 1929, 20x13"	1,210.00
Clasp, sgn, 1982, 43x26"	2,200.00

Coming of Spring, sgn, 1982, 30x24"	825.00
Compact Vanities, sgn, 1974, 30x24"	660.00
Conchita, sgn/blindstamp, 1929, 21x14"	1,000.00
Dear Friends, sgn/blindstamp, ca 1929, 14x11"	1,210.00
Eyes of Jealousy, sgn, 1983, 25x40"	880.00
French Rooster, sgn, 1980, 31x23"	3,190.00
Gay Senorita, sgn/blindstamp, ca 1939, 18x22"	1,200.00
Goddess Diana, sgn, 20x14"	825.00
Golden Cloak, sgn, 1979, 24x17"	825.00
Heat, sgn, 1980, 31x24"	1,650.00
Helen of Troy, sgn, 1985, 36x31"	1,210.00
Japanese Garden, sgn, #260, ca 1931, 21x18"	1,430.00
Laziness, artist proof, sgn, ca 1925, 15x19"	1,650.00
Longe de Theatre, sgn, 1984, 33x27"	2,090.00
Make-Up, sgn, 1978, 18x14"	600.00
Mardi Gras, sgn/blindstamp, 1936, 20x19"	3,025.00
Mystique, 32x20"	1,000.00
Orange Seller, sgn/blindstamp, ca 1929, 19x14"	935.00
Printemps, sgn, 1975, 29x23"	495.00
Rigoletto, sgn, 1985, 38x31"	3,300.00
Seville, sgn/blindstamp, #52, ca 1928, 20x13"	990.00
Spilled Milk, sgn, 1928, 16x21"	1,300.00
Summer Breeze, sgn, 1982, 31x23"	1,650.00
Sweet Mystery, sgn/blindstamp, ca 1935, 21x16"	3,080.00
Tosca, sgn/blindstamp, #111, 1928, 21x13"	1,320.00
Traviata, artist proof, sgn, ca 1987, 24x18"	850.00
Waltz Dream, sgn, 1931, 15x17"	7,425.00
Winter Resorts, sgn, 21x16"	750.00
Woman w/Doves, sgn, #228, 19x11"	1,320.00
Z, From the Alphabet; sgn, 1977, 16x11"	1,320.00
Zest, sgn/blindstamp, #211, 19x14"	4,400.00

Fox, R. Atkinson

A Canadian who worked as an artist in the 1880s, R. Atkinson Fox moved to New York about ten years later, where his original oils were widely sold at auction and through exhibitions. Today he is best known, however, for his prints, published by as many as twenty print-makers. More than thirty examples of his work appeared on Brown and Bigelow calendars, and it was used in many other forms of advertising as well. Though he was an accomplished artist able to interpret any subject well, he is today best known for his landscapes. Fox died in 1935. Our advisor for Fox prints is Pat Gibson whose address is listed in the Directory under California.

Cottage by the Sea, sgn, #412, 10½x14"	155.00
Discovery of the Mississippi, sgn, #395, 12x16", EX	300.00
Fallen Monarch, train w/logs, #98, 9x12"	60.00
Garden of Love, fountain, #42, orig fr, 9x13"	75.00
Moonlight at the Camp, #560, 10x8"	100.00
Mount Rainier, #524, 16x10½"	130.00
Mountain Lake, #301, 8x11"	60.00
Nature's Sublime Grandeur, #64, 5½x7½"	50.00
Rosy Glow of the Land of Promise, mountains, #331, 21x16"	120.00
Sentry, bear, sgn, #373, 16x12"	170.00
Silent Rockies, bear, #318, 9x12"	75.00
Trusty Guardian, dog & lamb, #11, 11x14"	170.00
Where Peace Abides, mountains, #445, 9x7"	65.00

Gutmann, Bessie Pease

Delicately tinted prints of appealing children sometimes accompanied by their pets, sometimes asleep, often captured at some childhood activity are typical of the work of Gutmann; she painted lovely ladies as well and was a successful illustrator of children's books. Her career spanned the earlier decades of this century. Our advisor for this category is Earl MacSorley; he is listed in the Directory under Connecticut.

Always, #774, 1913, 18½x13½"	950.00
Buddies, child w/puppy on bench, #779, 17½x13½"	525.00
Chip Off the Old Block, #728	200.00
Chuckles, #216, 1937, 11x14", EX	50.00
Contentment, #781, 1929, oval, 4½x8"	90.00
Daddy's Coming, #644, 1915, 9½x12½"	190.00
Double Blessing, #232, sepia, 1915, 15x10½"	225.00
Excuse My Back, 1911, oval, 8x4", VG	40.00
Feeling, baby w/toy lamb, #19, 1909, 11½x8¾"	100.00
Great Love, #678, 1919, 17x13"	325.00
Harmony, #802, 1940, 13x10"	110.00
Home Builders, #655, matted, 19x15"	100.00
In Disgrace, #792, 1935, 10¼x13¾"	100.00
In Port of Dreams, #214, 1937, 10¾x13¾"	75.00
Little Boy Blue, #206, 1930, 11x14"	70.00
Little Mother, #803, 1940, 12x9½"	120.00
Love's Blossom, #223, 1927, 13½x10½"	60.00
May We Come In?, #808, 1943, 14x10½"	120.00
Message of the Roses, #641, 1915, 15¼x11"	250.00
Mighty Like a Rose, #642, 1915, 10½x15"	80.00
Mischief, #122, 1924, 10½" dia	150.00
New Love, #107, 1907, 9½x13½"	130.00
On Dreamland's Border, #692, 1921, 13¾x16½"	100.00
On the Up & Up, #796, 1938, 10½x14"	75.00
Reward, #794, 1936, 13¼x10¼"	100.00
Seeing, #211, 11x14", EX	50.00
Sunbeam, #730, 1924, 10½" dia	150.00
Tasting, child w/cup, #21, sepia, 1909, 11½x8½"	100.00
Thank You God, #822, full color, 21x14", EX	65.00
To Love & To Cherish, #615, 1911, 13x8¼"	150.00
Tommy, #788, sepia, 14x21", EX	75.00
Winged Aureole, #700, 1921, 10¼x14"	150.00

Homer, Winslow

Baggage Train, sgn, 1863, 13x19"	800.00
Bathe at Newport, on newsprint, 1858	125.00
Bell Time, on newsprint, 1868	80.00
Boston Common, on newsprint, 1858	150.00
Gloucester Harbor, on newsprint, 1873	175.00
Letter from Home, sgn, 1863, 13x9"	800.00
Our Women & the War, on newsprint, 1862	135.00
Picnic Excursion, on newsprint, 1869	150.00
Sharpshooter on Picket Duty, on newsprint, 1862	200.00
Ship Building, Gloucester Harbor; on newsprint, 1873	225.00
Skating on Jamaica Pond near Boston, on newsprint, 1859	150.00
Snap the Whip, on newsprint, 1873	600.00

Icart, Louis

Louis Icart was a Parisian artist who immortalized the women of France through his etchings, which were widely produced in the 1920s. During the '30s and '40s, his popularity waned, and etchings from this period are harder to find. He also produced a few lithographs and about four hundred oils. Most etchings made after 1925 have Icart's embossed 'windmill' seal at the lower left. Be skeptical of watercolors and sketches that look similar in subject to one of the etchings. Prices appear to be stabilizing, as the art market adjusts to American recession and Japanese lethargy. Our Icart advisor is William Holland; he is listed in the Directory under Pennsylvania.

Wishing Well, 1925, 18" x 12", EX, $825.00.

After the Raid, sgn, ca 1927, 17x20"	2,200.00
Backstage, sgn/blindstamp, #11, ca 1926, 12x8"	2,750.00
Basket of Apples, sgn, 1924, 17x12"	1,900.00
Beauty Mark, 1919, 10x7"	1,300.00
Bird of Prey, sgn, #46, ca 1928	1,200.00
Black Mask, sgn/blindstamp, 1933, 13x9"	1,800.00
Blue Alcove, sgn/blindstamp, 1929, 11x13"	1,320.00
Broken Jug, sgn, #69, 17x12"	1,210.00
Chinese Mask, sgn, #66, 15x11"	1,760.00
Cuddling, sgn/blindstamp, #109, 12x17"	1,800.00
Ecstasy, ca 1935, 17x15"	4,000.00
Feathered Shawl, sgn, 1923, 14x12"	1,430.00
Game of Cards, artist proof, sgn, 16x20"	1,400.00
Golden Veil, sgn/blindstamp, 1930, 20x15"	300.00
Hiding Place, sgn/blindstamp, #24, 1927, 18x15"	1,650.00
Leda & the Swan, sgn/blindstamp, 1928, 16x19"	9,000.00
Little Butterflies, sgn, #263, ca 1926, 14x19"	1,800.00
Love's Blossom, sgn/blindstamp, 1927, 18x26"	5,500.00
Mimi, sgn/blindstamp, #84, 1927, 20x13"	1,400.00
On the Beach, sgn/blindstamp, 1925, 11x16"	1,600.00
Pink Lady, sgn/blindstamp, 1933, 8x11"	1,050.00
Rain, the Shower; sgn/blindstamp, 1925, 19x15"	2,200.00
Sea Gulls, sgn/blindstamp, 1926, 21x17"	2,420.00
Solitaire, artist proof, sgn/blindstamp, 1926, 14x18"	1,650.00
Spilled Apples, sgn/blindstamp, 1928, 20x13"	2,350.00
Swing, sgn/blindstamp, ca 1928, 20x14"	9,000.00
Symphony in Blue, sgn/blindstamp, ca 1936, 23x20"	2,800.00
Tosca, sgn, ca 1928, 13x21"	2,300.00
Venetian Night, sgn, #271, 1926, 21x14"	900.00
Venus, sgn/blindstamp, #26, 1928, 14x19"	2,090.00
White Underwear, sgn/blindstamp, 1925, 16x20"	2,400.00
Winsome, sgn/blindstamp, 1935, 18x16"	2,400.00
Woman w/Doves, sgn, ca 1926, 19x12"	2,400.00
Woman w/Grapes, sgn/blindstamp, 1926, 13x10"	1,760.00
Youth, sgn/blindstamp, ca 1930, 24x16"	8,250.00

Kellogg

Abraham Lincoln, Sixteenth President; sm folio	170.00
James Madison, 13x17"	85.00
John Tyler, 1841, 11x14"	220.00
Lt-Gen Ulysses S Grant, 16x12"	45.00
Stephen A Douglas, 10x14"	85.00
Storming of Ft Donelson, Feb 16, 1862; 10x13"	125.00

Kurz and Allison

Louis Kurz founded the Chicago Lithograph Company in 1833. Among his most notable works were a series of thirty-six Civil War scenes and one hundred illustrations of Chicago architecture. His company was destroyed in the Great Fire of 1871, and in 1880 Kurz formed a partnership with Alexander Allison, an engraver. Until both retired in 1903, they produced hundreds of lithographs in color as well as black and white.

Battle Between Monitor & Merrimac, 1889, orig fr, 18x25"........400.00
Battle of La Quasina, 1899, lg folio................200.00
Battle of Nashville, 1891, 19x26" 190.00
Battle of Shiloh, 1862, lg folio 270.00
Battle of Tippecanoe, lg folio 220.00
De Soto's Discovery of the Mississippi, lg folio............170.00
Entrance of Cortez into Mexico, 1892, 18x25" 300.00
George Washington at Mt Vernon, 1889, 20x24" 70.00
John Paul Jones Captures Countess & Serapis, med folio..............50.00
Last Charge & Capture of Port Arthur, lg folio 200.00
Siege of Vicksburg, lg folio 240.00

McKenney and Hall

Ca-Ta-He-Cassa, Shawnee Chief, Greenough, 1838, 14x20"......200.00
Lap-Pa-Win-Soe, Delaware Chief, Biddle, 1837, 10x14".............140.00
Ongewae, Chippewa Chief, Rice & Clark, 1843, 10x14" 200.00
Push-Ma-Ta-Ha, Choctaw Chief, Campbell & Burns, 10x14" ...230.00
Sha-Ha-Ka, Mandan, Bowen, 1841, 10x14"..................140.00
Wa-Baun-See, Pottawatomi Chief, Greenough, 1838, 10x14" 325.00
Weshcubb, Chippewa Chief, Biddle, 1836, 14x20"..............160.00
Yoholo Micco, Creek Chief, 1838, 14x20" 90.00

Mucha, Alphonse

Cycles Perfecta, linen bk, 59x42" 6,300.00
Dusk, sgn in plate, linen bk, 1895, 24x39" 110.00
Emerald, sgn in plate, 1900, 38x15" 5,280.00
Gismonda, sgn in plate, 1894, 85x29" 3,850.00
L'Iris, sgn in plate, 1897, 40x16" 3,400.00
Leslie Carter, linen bk, 1908, 81x30" 5,720.00
Lorenzaccio, 1896, 82x30" 8,350.00
Medee, 1898, 28x80" 6,050.00
Plume, sgn in plate, 1897, 25x19" 13,200.00
Rose, Les Fleurs, 1898, 42x18".................7,150.00
Sara Bernhardt, American Tour; linen bk, 78x30" 6,600.00
Vin des Incas, linen bk, 33x81" 7,500.00

Nutting, Wallace

Born in 1862, Nutting pursued many careers. His hand-tinted photographs of landscapes and interior scenes are prized by collectors today. He was also a writer, minister, farmer, and a furniture maker, designing reproductions of early American pieces. Collectors of his prints should be aware of rosy-hued, inconsistently bright or dark examples — especially large prints of *An Elaborate Dinner* and *A Chair for John*; these have been reproduced. Prices for large interior prints have recently been on the increase. Those with animals have risen at least 50% in the past few years, and prints with men are commanding extremely high prices. Those with babies and/or adolescent children bring very high prices as well. Our advisor for this category is Milt Steinfeld; he is listed in the Directory under New Jersey.

Afternoon Tea, 13x16" 200.00

Sip of Tea, copyright 1907, 7" x 9", $200.00.

All in a Garden Fair, 14x17" 140.00
Autumn Ripples, 10x12" 70.00
Bit of Sewing, 11x14" 110.00
Breakfast Hour, 11x17" 110.00
Budding Years, 14x17" 70.00
Cluster of Zinnias, 8x10" 250.00
Cosmos & Larkspur, 13x16" 875.00
Cottages on the Old Sod, 11x14"..................625.00
Dog-On-It, rare, 7x11" 1,050.00
Dutch Knitting Lesson, 10x14" 850.00
Dutch Sails, 10x16" 250.00
Front, Graves-Redfield House; 13x16" 450.00
Going for the Doctor, 14x17" 650.00
Green Mountain Range, 15x22" 65.00
Home Room, 13x16" 100.00
Jersey Blossoms, 18x22" 90.00
Lambs at Rest, 11x14" 300.00
Larkspur, 10x7½"..............................125.00
Leaf-Strewn Brook, 11x14" 90.00
Living Pillars, 12x16" 130.00
Mary's Little Lamb, 11x13" 260.00
Off for the Legislature, 1904, rare, 13x16" 1,850.00
Patti's Favorite Walk, 7x9".....................240.00
Prudence Drawing Tea, 13x16"..................150.00
Rural Sweetness, 13x16".........................85.00
Spring Pageant, 11x17" 70.00
Thanksgiving Goodies, 9x11" 75.00
Under the Elm, 10x12" 45.00
Where Bees Are Humming, 13x17".................110.00

Prang, Louis

Battle of Antietam, Prang's Litho Co, lg folio 100.00
Battle of Manila, Muller & Luchsinger, lg folio............130.00
Battle of Shiloh, Prang's Litho Co, lg folio 130.00
Robert Burns, 1898, 22x17"......................85.00
Sheridan's Final Charge, Prang's Litho Co, lg folio..............150.00
Ulysses S Grant, 1885, 25x20" 130.00

Yard Longs

Values for yard-longs are given for examples in very good to excellent condition, full length, nicely framed, and with the original glass.

To learn more about this popular area of collector interest, we recommend *Those Wonderful Yard-Long Prints and More* by our advisors W.D. and M.J. Keagy, and C.G. and J.M. Rhoden. They are listed in the Directory under Indiana and Illinois respectively. A word of caution: watch for reproductions; know your dealer.

American Beauty Roses, sgn Paul DeLongpre 175.00
Assorted Fruit, sgn Joseph Hoover & Sons, dtd 1897..................150.00
Battle of the Chicks, sgn Ben Austrian...175.00
Carnations w/Violin...125.00
Pompeian, Honeymooning in Venice, sgn G Pressler, 1922 ....225.00
Pompeian by Forbes, Mary Pickford, 1916-17............................250.00
Selz Shoe, mother & child swinging, 1915 calendar 200.00
Study of Chrysanthemums, sgn Paul DeLongpre, 1900 ....175.00
Study of Voilets, sgn Mary E Hart, ca 1900 ....150.00
Swallows, J Hoover & Sons, 1897, 36" L 135.00
Vertical Roses, sgn Dam Gam, A&P Co, 1892 ....175.00
Yard of Baby's Breath & Roses 135.00
Yard of Cherries, sgn Guy Bedford 200.00
Yard of Chickens, sgn CL Van Vredenburgh, 1905....................150.00
Yard of Kittens, sgn CL Van Vredenburgh 150.00
Yard of Roses, sgn V Jones, 1891..150.00
Yard of Show Dogs, sgn CL Van Vredenburgh 175.00

Purinton

Founded in 1936 in Wellsville, Ohio, Purinton Pottery relocated in 1941 in Shippenville, Pennsylvania, and began producing hand-painted wares that are today attracting the interest of collectors of 'country-type' dinnerware. Using bold brush strokes of vivid color, simple yet attractive patterns such as Apple, Fruits, Tea Rose, and Pennsylvania Dutch were manufactured in tableware sets and accessory pieces. The pottery closed in 1959. Our advisor for this category is Pat Dole; she is listed in the Directory under Alabama. Pat is the editor of *The Glaze;* see Clubs, Newsletters, and Catalogs.

Bowl, dessert; Chartreuse 8.00
Bowl, salad; Plaid, 11"...30.00
Bowl, soup/creal; Plaid.. 7.50
Bowl, spaghetti; Intaglio, 14½" 60.00
Bowl, vegetable; Chartreuse, 8"...12.00
Bowl, vegetable; Plaid, 8" 12.00
Butter dish, Chartreuse, ¼-lb 35.00
Candle holders, Peasant Lady, artist sgn, pr.............................500.00
Canisters, Apple & Pear, 4-pc set 125.00
Canisters, Palm Tree, 4-pc set..300.00
Canisters, Pennsylvania Dutch, 4-pc set.....................................160.00
Child's set, plate, mug, & cereal bowl..100.00
Coffeepot, Apple, 8-cup 30.00
Creamer, Rose 12.00
Creamer & sugar bowl, Apple, w/lid 17.50
Creamer & sugar bowl, Apple & Pear, w/lid 25.00
Creamer & sugar bowl, Turquoise Intaglio, w/lid 40.00
Cup & saucer, Apple 10.00
Cup & saucer, Plaid 10.00
Honey jug, Ivy..12.00
Honey jug, Palm Tree 25.00
Jam/jelly dish, Ivy..20.00
Jug, Apple, Kent, 1-pt...12.00
Jug, Intaglio, 5-pt...32.00
Jug, Rose, Dutch, 2-pt..20.00
Mug, juice; Rose, 6-oz...12.00
Pickle dish, Intaglio, 6" 10.00

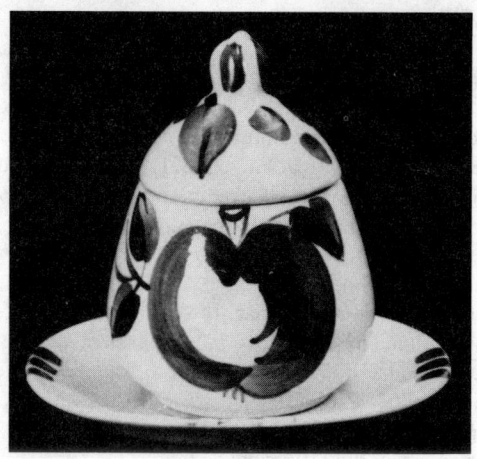

Marmalade, Apple, 5½", $20.00.

Plate, Palm Tree, 9¾" 30.00
Plate, Pennsylvania Dutch, dinner sz 25.00
Plate, Plaid, 6¾".. 7.50
Plate, Plaid, 9¾"..12.50
Platter, Intaglio, 11" 25.00
Platter, Plaid, 11" 16.00
Range set, Ivy, drippings jar+shakers, 3-pc 40.00
Range shakers, Palm Tree..40.00
Roll tray, Peasant 75.00
Teapot, Intaglio, 6-cup...25.00
Teapot, Plaid, 2-cup...12.00
Tumbler, Ivy, 10-oz..12.00

Purses

Beaded purses and bags represent an area of collecting interest that is very popular today. Purses from the early 1800s are often decorated with small, brightly, colored glass beads. Cut steel beads were popular in the 1840s and remained stylish until about 1930. Mesh purses are also popular. In the 1820s mesh was woven. Chain-link mesh came into usage in the 1890s, followed by the enamel mesh bags carried by the flappers in the 1920s. Purses are divided into several categories by (a) construction techniques — whether beaded, embroidered, or a type of needlework; (b) material — fabric or metal; and (c) design and style. Condition is very important. Watch for dry, brittle leather or fragile material. For those interested in learning more, we recommend *Antique Purses, A History, Identification, and Value Guide, Second Edition,* by Richard Holiner; *More Beautiful Purses,* and *Combs and Purses,* both by Evelyn Haertigi of Carmel, California. Our advisor for this category is Veronica Trainer; she is listed in the Directory under Ohio.

Acrylic, pearlized gold/tan, box form, dbl hdl, ca 1955 ....60.00
Bakelite top, hdl, & snap w/rose in center, EX 70.00
Beaded, bl/blk checkerbrd, heavy metal fr, 6¾x8¾".....................110.00
Beaded, bl/red floral on wht, fringe, heavy fr, 7x10¾" 225.00
Beaded, butterflies/rose, blk/wht fringe, drawstring, 7x11"..........150.00
Beaded, fine glass, floral, 7x11", M 250.00
Beaded, fine glass, rug pattern, jeweled fr, 6x11", M 300.00
Beaded, fine glass, rug pattern, 6x11", M 250.00
Beaded, fine glass, scenic/figural, jeweled fr, 7x10", M...............400.00
Beaded, geometric floral, loop fringe, curved fr, 6x9".................110.00
Beaded, glass, floral, celluloid fr, 6½x12", M 170.00
Beaded, gold, dmn form, fringe, V-form fr, 6¾x12" 150.00
Beaded, gold/silver Deco, celluloid fr/chain-link hdl, 9½" 150.00

Beaded, gr/blk check on wht, blk/wht fringe, Czech, 7x9" 70.00
Beaded, mc floral, heavy fringe, German silver fr, 7x11½" 195.00
Beaded, mc floral, relief cherub sterling fr, 8½x13" 350.00
Beaded, mc floral, rnd bottom, bl stone clasp, 5½x7½" 90.00
Beaded, mc flower vase, chain hdl, 8½x7", EX............................150.00
Beaded, mc landscape, fringe, stone-set fr, German, 8x12¾" 200.00
Beaded, mc landscape, sq German silver fr, ca 1900, 7¼x7" 170.00
Beaded, petit point, garden, heavy stone-set fr, 7½x12"..............250.00
Beaded, red dbl fringe at drawstring top, beaded hdl, 6"..............90.00
Beaded, silhouette couple in oval, sq metal fr, 7x12½" 170.00
Beaded, steel, floral, mc, French, 7x12", M..............................180.00
Beaded, steel, geometric, 6x10", M...140.00
Beaded, stylized peacock on blk, silver filigree fr, 10½"..............150.00
Cotton, wht-on-wht embr florals/name/1819, fragile, 6x7"...........85.00
Crochet, ecru, rust lining, heavy emb fr, 6½x8¼" 65.00
Dresden, fringe cut bottom, HP Whiting & Davis fr, 5x6½", M..160.00

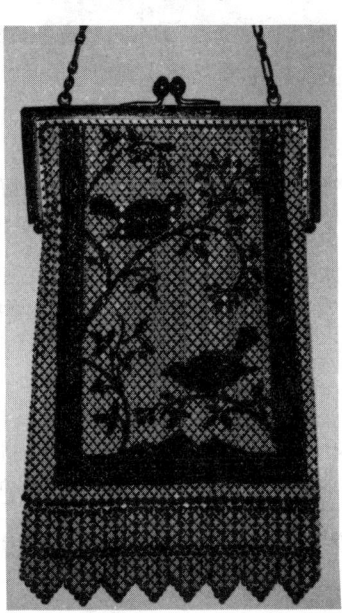

Mandalian Mfg. Co., enameled bird scene, 5" x 8", stones in clasp, $250.00.

Enameled compact type, Whiting & Davis, M 300.00
Enameled scene, Whiting & Davis, 4x6", M 200.00
Enameled top w/compact, gold body, Evans, M..........................275.00
Fringe cut bottom, HP Whiting & Davis fr, 5x7", M 140.00
Fringe cut bottom, Whiting & Davis fr, 5x7", M 140.00
Leather, alligator, dbl-compartment, strap adjusts, 12x9" 135.00
Leather, alligator ft & claws, metal strap, 3x8", EX....................125.00
Leather, alligator paw, sq metal fr, 5¾x7¾" 50.00
Leather, emb floral, sq fr, Jemco, 5¾x6½"..................................75.00
Leather, snakeskin, lt brn, clutch type, 9x4½", EX 50.00
Leather, snakeskin, red w/brass trim, Bass, 1940s, EX 95.00
Leather, 2-tone floral, clutch type, Meeker, 5¼x9¼" 55.00
Mesh, bl/brn/wht, bl drop-bead fringe, Mandalian, 4x8".............145.00
Mesh, enameled, fringe cut, jeweled fr, Mandalian, 6x9", M 270.00
Mesh, enameled, fringe cut bottom, Mandalian Mfg, 4x7", M 150.00
Mesh, enameled, tear-drop bottom, Mandalian, 4½x9", M..........230.00
Mesh, geometric floral, Whiting & Davis, 3½x6" 130.00
Mesh, gold, flat, Whiting & Davis, 4x6", M...............................55.00
Mesh, pewter, blk/bl enameling at bottom, W&D, EX 95.00
Mesh, yel/bl floral, bl enamel fr, Whiting & Davis, 3x4¾" 130.00
Needlepoint, floral, 7x6", M...125.00
Petit point, floral, 7x6", M 170.00
Reticule, beaded, floral pattern, 6x10", M 110.00
Reticule, beaded, floral pattern, 8x11", M 75.00
Reticule, beaded, scene or figural, 6x10", M..............................225.00

Rhinestones allover, silk lining, France, 1930s, EX 185.00
Satin, blk, clutch style w/pearl clasp, EX.....................................30.00
Taffeta, blk w/gathered top, 800 silver fr, German, 9½x9"..........150.00
Tapestry, floral w/birds, sterling fr, 7x7¼" 150.00

Quezal

The Quezal Art Glass and Decorating Company of Brooklyn, New York, was founded in 1901 by Martin Bach. A former Tiffany employee, Bach's glass closely resembled that of his former employer. Most pieces were signed 'Quezal,' a name taken from a Central American bird. After Bach's death in 1920, his son-in-law, Conrad Vohlsing, continued to produce a Quezal-type glass in Elmhurst, New York, which he marked 'Lustre Art Glass.' See also that particular category. Examples listed here are signed unless noted otherwise.

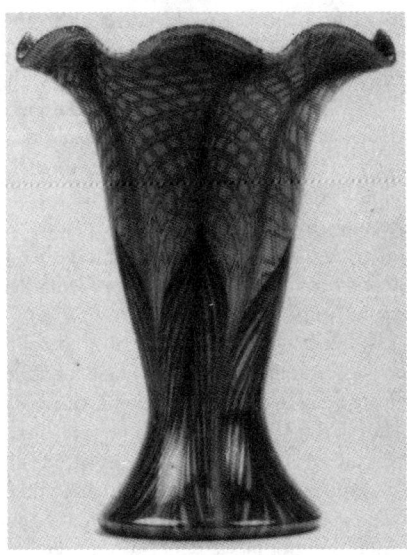

Vase, gold lapets on ivory, green feathering at base, gold within, 9", $1,800.00.

Bottle, scent; gold, 4-sided cone form, 8" 250.00
Bowl, bl irid, ftd, lt int wear, 5½x7½" 500.00
Bowl, feathers, gr/gold/opal, +opal/gold 6" plate 600.00
Bowl, feathers, gr/gold/wht, gold int, 3 gold scroll ft, 6" . 1,700.00
Compote, gold, EX color, 2x6" 225.00
Compote, gold int, wht stem w/gr feathers, amber base, 5x5" . 1,100.00
Jar, gold, squat/bulbous, 2" 250.00
Lamp, 3 yel fishnet-on-opal gold-lined 4" shades; 60" std 1,000.00
Night light, gold ribbed shade, gold metal base, 9½", pr 300.00
Shade, leaves, gold/gr on gold, 5½"..175.00
Vase, bl irid w/gold highlights, 8" 465.00
Vase, bl-gold, squat, stretched/flared/ruffled rim, 9½" 800.00
Vase, feathers, gold/gr on amber, long teardrop form, 10" 1,300.00
Vase, feathers, gold/gr on ivory, compressed w/wide rim, 4" ... 1,200.00
Vase, feathers, gold/gr on ivory, shouldered, 10" 1,500.00
Vase, feathers, gr/gold on ivory, gold int, petal top, 9" 1,800.00
Vase, feathers, gr/gold on opal, gold int, ruffled, ftd, 6"...............900.00
Vase, feathers, gr/gold/opal, petal rim/bun ft, 9½"................... 1,500.00
Vase, feathers, gr/wht/gold, gold int, 4-lobe rim, slim, 9" 800.00
Vase, feathers/floral band, gold int, sgn/#437, 12x9" 6,500.00
Vase, gold w/purple & gr irid, ruffled trumpet form, 9x6" 400.00
Vase, gold w/silver o/l floral scrolls, pinched rim, 2" 1,100.00
Vase, hearts/vines at shoulder on opal irid, gold int, 6" 500.00
Vase, jack-in-pulpit; feathers/chains, gold/gr/wht, 15"............ 3,850.00
Vase, King Tut, bulbous w/flared rim, sgn, 6" 1,200.00
Vase, King Tut, gold on wht opal, ovoid, 7" 770.00
Vase, mc irid, 6-petal flaring top, bun base, 9x6½" 1,300.00
Vase, swirls, gold on gr irid, squat w/trumpet neck, 4" 1,800.00

Quilts

Quilts, while made of necessity, nevertheless represent an art form which expresses the character and the personality of the designer. During the 17th and 18th centuries, quilts were considered a necessary part of a bride's hope chest; the traditional number required to be properly endowed for marriage was a 'baker's dozen'! Quilts were used not only for bed coverings but for curtains, extra insulation, and mattresses as well. The early quilts were made from pieces salvaged from cloth items that had outlived their original usefulness and from bits left over from sewing projects. Regardless of shape, these scraps were fitted together following no organized lines. The resulting hodge-podge design was called a crazy quilt.

In 1793 Eli Whitney developed the cotton gin; as a result, textile production in America became industrialized. Soon inexpensive fabrics were readily available, and ladies were able to choose from colorful prints and solids to add contrast to their work. Both pieced and appliqued work became popular. Pieced quilts were considered utilitarian, while appliqued work was shown with pride of accomplishment at the fair. Today many collectors prize pieced quilts and their intricate geometric patterns above all other types. Many of these designs were given names: Daisy and Oak Leaf, Grandmother's Flower Garden, Log Cabin, and Ocean Wave are only a few. Appliqued quilts involved stitching one piece — carefully cut into a specific form such as a leaf, a flower, or a stylized device — onto either a large one-piece ground fabric or an individual block. Often the background fabric was quilted in a decorative pattern.

Amish women scorned printed calicos as 'worldly' and instead used colorful blocks set with black fabrics to produce a stunning pieced effect. During the Victorian era, the crazy quilt was revived, but the ladies of the 1870s used plush velvets, brocades, silks, and linen patches and embroidered along the seams with feather or chain stitches.

Another type of quilting, highly prized and rare today, is trapunto. These quilts were made by first stitching the outline of the design onto a solid sheet of fabric which was backed with a second having a much looser weave. White was often favored, but color was sometimes used for accent. The design (grapes, flowers, leaves, etc.) was padded through openings made by separating the loose weave of the underneath fabric; a backing was added and the three layers quilted as one.

Besides condition, value is judged on intricacy of pattern, color effect, and craftsmanship. In the listings that follow, examples rated excellent have minor defects. Values given here are auction results; retail may be somewhat higher.

Key:
dmn — diamond   ms — machine sewn
embr — embroidered   X — cross
hs — hand sewn

Amish

Bars, wine on bl, EX quilting: stars/birds/etc, 48x49", EX 2,000.00
Bl sateen w/pk-lav border, mc, EX quilting w/lg star 400.00
Bl/blk/gray sqs, solid wide border, contemporary, ms, 30x45".. 1,200.00
Dmn in Sq, 5 solid colors, EX quilting w/stars etc, EX............. 2,500.00
Pinwheels, bl/blk, ms/hand quilted, contemporary................... 2,500.00
Sunshine & Shadow, solid colors, ms/hand quilted, NM........ 1,800.00
Tartan pattern, pk/gr on wht, ms/hand quilted, VG 2,500.00
12 stars, lav/yel/lt gr, ms/hand quilted, ms binding, EX........... 2,500.00

Appliqued

Album, different flower in every pot, calico, 88x90", EX.............900.00
Butterflies in sqs, mc w/blk quilting, 1930s, 96x78", NM............450.00

Amish crib quilt in the Streak of Lightning pattern, fabric wear, 32" x 42", $695.00 at auction.

English Tea Rose, fine quilting, 73x74", EX 350.00
Feather Wreath (pcd), red/navy, EX work, brn/wht bk, 1800s ..3,000.00
Floral, bl calico w/red calico grid on wht, rpr/minor wear 350.00
Floral medallions, red/teal bl, stains/wear, 80x80" 575.00
Floral w/eagle center, bl/yel/red on wht, wear/stains/faded.........275.00
Flowerpot & Blue Birds, mc on yel, 1930s, 108x84", EX 450.00
Flowers in sqs, tree/flower borders, red/gr on wht, 86x102".........825.00
Sunbursts/cherries, 2 shades of red/gr/yel on wht, 70x80" 350.00
Tulip & Oak Leaf, teal/red on wht, EX work, stains, 90x92"... 1,700.00
16 sqs w/tulips, birds/trees/stars in border, fragile, EX 800.00
16 tulip medallions, red/yel/gr calico on wht, red border 900.00
4 eagles, red/gr/goldenrod, EX work, sm burn/stains................. 1,050.00
4 floral medallions/vine border, red/bl/pk on wht, EX work 1,000.00
9 floral medallions, red/gr/on wht, initialed, EX work, NM 975.00
9 floral medallions+4 circles, zigzag border, calico, VG................850.00
9 maple leaf medallions, solid border, med gr/wht, unused 650.00
9 sqs w/florals, 1854 appl in vine border, EX quilting, EX 3,500.00

Pieced

Baskets, pk & bl on wht, 1890s, full sz, VG 650.00
Bear Paws, red & wht, ca 1900, lg, EX 850.00
Dbl Irish Chain, red on wht, ca 1920, full sz, EX 695.00
Dbl Wedding Ring, French bl, scalloped, 1935, full sz, M...........695.00
Dbl Wedding Ring, mc prints/solids on orange, 1930s, 84x84" ...350.00
Dresden Plate, bright colors, 90x72", EX 650.00
Drunkard's Path, gr & red, ca 1900, full sz, EX...........................750.00
Drunkard's Path, med bl polka dot print, wht, EX work, EX 695.00
Hole in Barn Door, gr & bl, 1890s, sm, VG 350.00
House, shades of bl w/mc floral borders, 78x79" 695.00
Interlocking Circles, gr calico on wht, crib sz, 37x37" 500.00
Irish Chain, ivory & blk, ca 1900, 69x63", NM 450.00
Irish Chain, mc prints/solid red, stains, 70x106" 275.00
Irish Chain, red/gr/goldenrod on wht, 78x91" 475.00
Jackson Star, fuchsia on wht, 1920s, full sz, EX 425.00
Jacob's Ladder & Devil's Sq, indigo on wht, 1880s, lg, EX 595.00
Joseph's Coat, mc calico/orange, 1880s, 79x76", EX 325.00
Log Cabin, mc prints/solid red, embr inscription & 1928 ....495.00
Log Cabin, pastels, 1930s, twin sz 350.00
Lone Star, mc, lt fading, 92x94"...750.00
Lone Star, rust/goldenrod/yel on wht, scalloped, 82x82" 350.00
Mariner's Compass, bl/wht print on wht, rebound/wear, lg 1,250.00
Peter/Paul, wht/brn, 78x90" 410.00
Pineapple, bl/wht calico, machine quilted, 76x78" 495.00

Pineapple Log Cabin, slight fading, 1880s, full sz 375.00
Pinwheel, bl print on wht, overall wear/stains, 74x84" 275.00
Pinwheel, floral prints/polished cotton, 1840s, 101x88", EX 750.00
Pinwheel Star, navy/saffron/wht, ca 1900, lg, EX 695.00
Rolling Stone, navy/wht, Goose Chase border, 1900, lg, EX 625.00
Rolling Stone, red/wht/tan on pk calico, bl binding...................395.00
Simple Pleasures, calicos, EX quilting, 1800s, 61x73", VG 350.00
Snowflakes, red/brn on wht, 86x128" 600.00
Sqs in Dmns, brns/bls on wht alternate w/pk calico, lt stain........395.00
Star, med bl/wht, EX feather quilted circles, ms/hs, 80x82" 550.00
Star (bold), red/bl/wht calico, homespun bk, 71x71" 900.00
Stars/suns/rising suns, calico/floral prints, PA, 101x101"......... 2,300.00
Sunshine & Shadow, solid colors, ms binding, 72x70" 695.00
Triangles, bl/wht calico on wht, stains/lt wear, 82x90" 550.00
Tumbling Block, mc prints, blk/wht check border, 74x86".........850.00
Tumbling Block, red/wht on dk bl w/tiny wht stars 695.00
Wild Goose Chase, pk/wht, ms binding, 74x90" 695.00
Zigzags, bl/wht, overall wear/stains, 74x86" 595.00
16 stars, brn/bl/wht on pk print, lt wear/stains, 87x87" 295.00
30 medallions, sawtooth border, yel/pk/wht calico, NM 395.00
4-Point Stars, red/yel calico on ivory, red calico border 350.00
4-Sq, pk/yel/gr calico, bl/wht homespun bk, 78x78".................495.00
42 baskets, bright solid colors, 42x49" 450.00
9-Patch, sm Xs in brn/bl/red prints on wht, lt stain.....................425.00

Trapunto

Baskets of flowers, Ohio (4X), pieced stars & flowers 10,500.00
Bride's, intricate details, sgn twice, possible rpr/stains..................900.00
Mariner's Compass (pcd), feather wreaths/border, EX work.... 1,850.00

Quimper

Quimper is a type of pottery produced in Quimper, France. A tin enamel-glazed earthenware pottery with hand-painted decoration, it was first produced in the 1600s by the Bousquet and Caussy Factories. Little of this early ware was marked. By the late 1700s, three factories were operating in the area, all manufacturing the same type of pottery. The Grande Maison de HB, a company formed as a result of a marriage joining the Hubaudiere and Bousquet families, was a major producer of Quimper pottery. They marked their wares with various forms of the 'HB' logo; but of the pottery they produced, collectors value examples marked with the 'HB' within a triangle most highly.

Francois Eloury established another pottery in Quimper in the late 1700s. Under the direction of Charles Porquier, the ware was marked simply 'P.' Adolph Porquier replaced Charles in the 1850s, marking the ware produced during that period with an 'AP' logo.

Jule HenRiot began operations in 1886, using molds he had purchased from Porquier. His mark was 'HR,' and until the twentieth century he was in competition with The Grande Maison de HB. In 1926 he began to mark his wares 'HenRiot Quimper.' In 1968 the two factories merged. They are still in operation under the name Les Faenceries de Quimper. The factory sold in the fall of 1983 to Sarah and Paul Janssens from the United States, making it the first time the owners were not French. For those interested in learning more about Quimper, we recommend *Quimper Pottery: A French Folk Art Faience* by Sandra V. Bondhus, our advisor for this category, whose address can be found in the Directory under Connecticut.

Bannette, man's portrait, ivoire corbeille decor, HQ, 8⅝" 90.00
Bookends, girl/boy, Berthe Savigny, HBQ, pr.............................455.00
Bookends, goose girl/biniou player, HBQF, 7¼", pr 350.00
Bowl, Breton broderie banding, HBQ, 1½x3¾".............................70.00

Box, lady w/flowing skirts figural, Maillard, HQF, 5x6¾" 190.00
Candy dish, man/lady, inverted Celtic heart hdl, HBQ, 7x5¼"...100.00

Charger, Breton lady and leafy sprays, signed HBQF, 13½", $110.00.

Cup & saucer, Breton broderie variant, HBQ, 2¾", 7½"...............70.00
Cup & saucer, Deco florals, dragonfly hdl, Fouillen, Quimper.....135.00
Figurine, biniou players, Micheau-Vernez, HQ, 11½" 100.00
Figurine, dancing couple, Micheau-Vernez, HQ, 13" 175.00
Figurine, Saint Anne La Palud w/child, HQ, 9x3x4¼" 50.00
Figurine, Saint Corentin, yel/gold/bl/wht, HBQ, 8½" 110.00
Gravy boat, Breton man, 2-spout, 1930s, HBQF, 4x8" 235.00
Jardiniere, floral, classic scalloped form, HBQ, 7x7½" 300.00
Nut dish, Breton man, trefoil form, hdl, HQ, 4x5½" 80.00
Oyster tray, flower baskets, 10-shell form, HQF, 10¾"...............240.00
Pitcher, Breton broderie sprays on paneled body, HBQ, 4½" 60.00
Pitcher, Breton lady, La Touche decor bk, Odetta, HBQ, 4⅜" ...135.00
Pitcher, Deco florals, dragonfly hdl, Fouillen, Quimper, 6"..........215.00
Pitcher, Deco portrait, bl & blk bands, HBQ, 8x7" 55.00
Pitcher, florals & sponging, ca 1980, HQ, 7x7½" 30.00
Pitcher, lady in tall wht hat, ivoire corbeille, HQ, 6"...................135.00
Pitcher, lady's face figural, hat forms top, HQF, 8½"...................185.00
Plate, Breton man, La Touche border, HQF, 11⅛" 90.00
Plate, Breton portrait, circle fr on sq form, HBQ, 7¼", pr 160.00
Plate, floral sprays w/croisille, canted corners, HBQF, 10" 75.00
Plate, Revolutionary drummer boy, HBQ, 9¾" 180.00
Plate, sailor, lady w/bk turned, Fouillen series, HBQ, 9½" 230.00
Plate, 2-tone bl decor riche border w/gold, ca 1940s, 9¾"............45.00
Platter, fish; Breton couple, HBQF, 24½x11¾".............................275.00
Quintal, Mayflower ship, 5-fingered shape, HQF, 5", EX............170.00
Salt cellar, dbl; Breton man/lady, HBQF, 1920s, 2½x4"................80.00
Salt cellar, dbl; donkey w/baskets pulled by man, HQ, 4x7½" 150.00
Salt cellar, dbl; man/lady, swan form, HQF, 3½x3½" 50.00
Serving dish, trefoil shape w/Baroque curves, HBQF, 11" dia......235.00
Shakers, Breton man/lady, 1930s, HBQF, 3½", pr 85.00
Snuff bottle, lady & florals, early 1900s, HRQ, 3x2½" 195.00
Snuff box, Breton lady/rooster, book form, 19th C, 2⅞x2¼" 150.00
Tile, Breton lady, strong colors, HBQ, 8¾" 150.00
Tile, Breton man, unglazed bottom cuff, QF/Macy star, 6¼" 110.00
Tray, stylized deer, Odetta, HBQ, 10¼x7¾"................................475.00
Tureen, Breton lady, bold colors, w/lid, 1930s, HBQ, 8x10".........230.00
Vase, Breton man's portrait, artist sgn, bulbous, HBQ, 8½" 145.00
Vase, ivoire corbeille decor, squat ewer form, HQ, 4½" 30.00
Wall pocket, Breton lady, slipper shape, HQF, 7¾x2¾" 325.00

Radford

The Jasperware listed below was made in Zanesville, Ohio, at the

A. Radford Pottery Company incorporated there in 1903. This type of ware was first designed and produced in 1896 when Albert Radford worked in Tiffin, Ohio. The Zanesville Jasper, in contrast to the original line, was decorated with Wedgwood-type cameos in relief that were not applied but were formed within the general mold. The only mark found on the ware is a two-digit shape number. The Tiffin Jasper, though not always marked, is sometimes impressed 'Radford Jasper.' After only a few months, Radford sold the plant to Arc-En-Ciel and moved his works to West Virginia. In addition to the regular line of utility wares, several artware lines were also produced there. Among them were Ruko, a standard brown underglaze decorated line; Thera, matt glazed with slip decoration; and Radura, usually done in matt green glazes.

Vase, winged figures with instruments, #14, 7", $310.00.

Jasper

Mug, floral relief, lt bl, 4½" 150.00
Vase, angels in relief, bl & blk, 7"....................................250.00
Vase, bust of Washington, reverse: eagle, bark trim, #12, 7"........265.00
Vase, cupids on flying eagles, #23, 9½" 475.00
Vase, cupids w/instruments, column aside, bark trim, #14, 7"......310.00
Vase, eagle & shield, 7½" 295.00
Vase, lady sits, trees & dog, bark trim, #22, 9"......................475.00
Vase, lady w/dog, bk: Roman kneels, bark trim, #18, 7"...............350.00
Vase, man's head ea side, twisted form, 3" 125.00
Vase, 2 children & lion, wht & lt brn, #15, 7" 225.00
Vase, 3 horses in clouds pull chariot, bark trim, #16, 7" 295.00

Miscellaneous

Candle holder, Ruko, floral, sgn/mk, rare, 7" 175.00
Jardiniere, Ruko, tulips, 8½x9" 250.00
Jardiniere & ped, eagles/foliage, sgn, 41½" 3,000.00
Jardiniere & ped, winged creatures/foliage, streaky gr, 34"...........500.00
Vase, Radura, gr, Nouveau form, 4 long in-mold hdls, rare, 9" ...350.00
Vase, Radura, matt gr, 10"...275.00
Vase, Thera, floral, red on gr matt, rare, 12"........................450.00

Radios

Vintage radios are becoming very collectible. There were thousands of styles and types produced, the most popular of which today are the breadboard and the cathedral. Consoles are usually considered less saleable, since their size makes them hard to display and store. For those wishing to learn more about antique radios, we recommend *The Collector's Guide to Antique Radios* by Sue and Marty Bunis, available from your local bookstore or Collector Books.

Admiral #6T01, plastic, horizontal louvers, table model, '46.........30.00
Admiral #79-PG, leatherette, fold-down front, portable, 1941......30.00
Admiral #990-5Z, blk Bakelite/chrome, table model, '37, EX........85.00
Air Castle #5024, burl veneer, table model, 1948, EX...................40.00
Air Castle #5035, leatherette, horseshoe dial, 1948, EX 22.00
Air Castle #651, plastic, 2 knobs, table model, 1947, EX..............30.00
Air King A-450, plastic, checkered grill, half-rnd dial, M..............40.00
Airline #62-376, wood, 4 knobs, table model, 1939, EX 45.00
American Bosch #27 Amberada, wood console, 1926, EX...........185.00
American Bosch #510 Tombstone, wood, sm case, 1935, EX 50.00
Arvin #242T, metal, oblong cutouts, portable, 1949, M 30.00
Arvin #950T2, plastic, checkered grill, table model, 1958, NM ...27.50

Atwater Kent #90 Cathedral, wood cabinet, 1931, $325.00.

Atwater Kent #155, wood, cloth grill w/cutouts, 1933...................75.00
Atwater Kent #56, metal console, cut-out legs, 1929, EX 85.00
Atwater Kent #627 Cathedral, wood, 3 knobs, 1932, EX...........285.00
Atwater Kent #9A Breadboard, 4 tubes, battery, 1923, M 650.00
Bendix #416A, wood, sm base, 2 knobs, table model, 1948, M......35.00
Bendix #79M7, wood, pull-out phonograph, console, 1949, NM ..65.00
Coronado #43-8576, wood, cloth grill, table model, 1946, NM.....30.00
Coronado #675 Tombstone, wood, airplane dial, 1934, NM 75.00
Crosley #141 Library Universal, book shape, 1932, EX...............185.00
Crosley #31, metal, cast dial, Deco table model, 1929, M............95.00
Crosley #51, wood, blk Bakelite panel, table model, 1924, EX 115.00
Crosley Prestotone #11, walnut, console, 1937, M......................150.00
Crosley Widget Cathedral, pressed wood case, 1931, EX 195.00
Dewald #708, 2-tone wood, lower grill, table model, 1941, EX......30.00
Emerson #CV-316, walnut, rnded sides, table model, 1939, NM...55.00
Emerson #363, bl leatherette, portable, 1940, M.........................25.00
Emerson #520, Catalin, aqua dial, table model, 1946, EX...........400.00
Emerson #745B, leatherette, plaid grill, portable, 1954, M 30.00
Emerson #855, leather case, front grill, transister, 1957, EX 35.00
Fada #115 Bullet, Catalin, 2 knobs, 1941, EX 450.00
Fada #175-A Neutroceiver, mahog, battery, 1924, EX 95.00
Fada #652 Temple, Catalin, rnd corners, table model, 1946 ....450.00
Farnsworth #GK-141, wood, knobs/push buttons, console, '47, M ...80.00
Firestone #4-A-89, plastic, half-moon dial, 1950, EX...................20.00
Freed-Eisemann #29-D, walnut, tuning eye, table model, 1937 .....35.00
General Electric #K-60 Cathedral, wood, hdl, 1933, EX 185.00
General Electric #T-12 Cathedral, wood, 1931, NM 175.00

General Electric #180, wood, cloth grill, 1947, EX..........................27.50
General Electric #220, plastic, table model, 1946, M.....................30.00
General Electric #510, plastic, alarm, table model, 1951, EX........18.00
General Electric #66, plastic, alarm, table model, 1949, M............25.00
Hallicrafters #5R14, plastic, table model, 1951, M.......................30.00
Motorola #3A5 Playboy, maroon metal & crome, 1941, EX 32.00
Motorola #5L1, 2-tone plastic, hdl, portable, 1950, EX................22.00
Motorola #57A, plastic, center M logo, table model, NM.............22.50
Motorola #62C1, plastic, alarm, table model, 1952, NM 18.00
Packard-Bell #471, leatherette, portable, 1947, M 20.00
Philco #F752-124, gr plastic, alarm, table model, 1958, EX 15.00
Philco #17 Cathedral, wood, cloth grill, 4 knobs, NM.................195.00
Philco #37-611K, wood, cloth grill, console, 1937, NM 115.00
Philco #37-93 Cathedral, wood, cloth grill, 1937, EX.................150.00
Philco #38-12C, 2-tone wood, Deco table model, 1938, M...........45.00
Philco #39-72T, striped cloth cover, portable, 1939, EX...............20.00
Philco #40-81T, striped cloth cover, portable, EX 20.00
Philco #46-250 Transitone, plastic, table model, 1946, M.............35.00
Philco #48-1264, walnut, tilt-out phonograph, 1948, M 75.00
Philco #52-544I Transitone, plastic, table model, 1952, M 30.00
Philco #610 Tombstone, wood, shouldered front, 1936, NM.......100.00
Philco #96, wood, lowboy console, cloth grill, NM 125.00
RCA #103 Tombstone, wood, cloth grill, fluting, 1934, NM.........65.00
RCA #15X, plastic, 3 knobs, table model, 1940, M.......................30.00
RCA #2US7, wood, inner phonograph, table model, 1952, EX.....20.00
RCA #55U, wood, lift top, table model, 1946, EX 20.00
RCA #811K, wood, push buttons, console, 1937, NM.................135.00
RCA 5T Tombstone, wood, cloth grill, 1936, NM........................75.00
Sentinel #11, walnut lowboy, Deco console, 1930, NM..............150.00
Sentinel #249-I, ivory plastic, wraparound louvers, '41, EX 30.00
Silvertone #18, plastic, S logo, table model, 1951, NM 28.00
Silvertone #1911, wood, cloth grill, console, 1936, EX...............100.00
Silvertone #4486, wood, tuning eye, console, 1937, M...............130.00
Silvertone #6053 Tombstone, walnut w/inlays, 1939, EX 50.00
Silvertone #8210, wood, lift top, crank phonograph, 1949, EX 28.00
Sonora #KF, 2-tone plastic, vertical bars, 1941, M.......................45.00
Sonora #401, wood, w/phonograph, sm cabinet console, '48, NM ...50.00
Sparton, rnd face of bl mirror/3 chrome bands, 15x14", VG ... 1,700.00
Sparton #7-46, wood, tilt-out phonograph, console, 1946, M........95.00
Stromberg-Carlson #231-F Chairside, wood, Deco, 1937, NM....225.00
Stromberg-Carlson #64, wood, Deco console, 1934, EX 135.00
Stromberg-Carlson #641, walnut, 5-tube, table model, 1929, M....95.00
Truetone #D1840, wood, phonograph, storage, console, '48, EX ..45.00
Truetone #D3615, leatherette, portable, 1947, EX.......................25.00
Westinghouse #H-124 Little Jewel, plastic, portable, 1945, M 75.00
Westinghouse #H-210, plastic, 2 knobs, portable, 1949, EX 25.00
Westinghouse #H-557P4, 2-tone gr plastic, portable, 1957, EX.....20.00
Westinghouse #WR-305, wood, cloth grill, console, 1935, NM..130.00
Zenith #H-500 Transoceanic, blk leatherette, portable, NM 75.00
Zenith #J-514, plastic, alarm, oval case, table model, 1952, M 40.00
Zenith #U-723, plastic, checkered grill, table model, EX...............20.00
Zenith #5-C-01 Consoltone, plastic, table model, 1946, EX 35.00
Zenith #5808, wood, push buttons, 1940, EX 195.00
Zenith #6-D-117, blk & walnut, table model, 1936, NM...............75.00
Zenith #7-D-148 Chairside, wood, Deco style, 1936, NM 110.00
Zenith G-500 Transoceanic, leatherette, portable, 1950, NM.......55.00

Railroadiana

Collecting railroad-related memorabilia has become one of America's most popular hobbies. The range of collectible items available is almost endless, considering the fact that more than 175 different railroad lines are represented. Some collectors prefer to specialize in only one, while others attempt to collect at least one item from every railway line known to have existed. For the advanced collector, there is the challenge of locating rarities from short-lived railroads; for the novice there are abundant keys, buttons, passes, and playing cards. Among the most popular specializations are dining-car collectibles — flatware, glassware, dinnerware, etc., in a wide variety of patterns and styles.

For a more thorough study, we recommend *Railroad Collectibles, Third Revised Edition*, by Stanley L. Baker, available at your local library or bookstore. Some of our listings were provided by Shrader's Antiques (see Directory, California).

Key:
BL — bottom logo   SM — side marked
BS — bottom stamped   TL — top logo
SL — side logo   TM — top marked

Dinnerware

Ash tray, C&O, Chessie, rnd, 3½"...65.00
Ash tray, GN, Glory of the West, 4¼" 125.00
Bowl, bouillon; ATSF, dbl hdl 49.50
Bowl, bouillon; C&O, Geo Washington, SL...........................150.00
Bowl, bouillon; CMStP&P, Traveler 26.50
Bowl, bouillon; CRI&P, Golden State, SL...............................165.00
Bowl, bouillon; MKT, Katy Ornaments 25.00
Bowl, bouillon; Reading, Stotesbury, BS..................................75.00
Bowl, bouillon; SRR, Peach Blossom 25.00
Bowl, bouillon; WP, Feather River, SL 49.00
Bowl, cereal; ACL, Flora of the South, BS, 5½".......................59.00
Bowl, cereal; ATSF, Adobe, TM, 6" 45.00
Bowl, cereal; B&O, Centenary, BS, 6¼"...................................45.00
Bowl, cereal; CMStP&P, Peacock, 6½".....................................42.00
Bowl, cereal; GN, Glacier, BS, 6½"..100.00
Bowl, cereal; NYC, Mercury, TL, 6"...45.00
Bowl, cereal; PRR, Mountain Laurel, 6"...................................20.00
Bowl, cereal; Pullman, Indian Tree, TM, 6½"...........................85.00
Bowl, cereal; UP, Desert Flower, BS, 6½" 38.00
Bowl, soup; B&O, Centenary, BS, 9¼".....................................160.00
Bowl, soup; CB&Q, Violets & Daisies, BS, 9"..........................125.00
Bowl, soup; GN, Glory of the West, BS, 7½".............................75.00
Bowl, soup; MStP&SSM, Logan, 9"...87.00
Bowl, soup; NYC, DeWitt Clinton, TM, 8½".............................42.00
Bowl, soup; PRR, Keystone, TL, 7½" 75.00
Bowl, soup; Pullman, Indian Tree, TM, 8½".............................225.00
Bowl, soup; UP, Harriman Blue, BS, 9"......................................45.00
Bowl, soup; UP, Portland Rose, 9"..210.00
Bowl, vegetable; SP, Prairie-Mountain Wildflowers, 9¼" 325.00
Butter pat, ACL, Flora of the South, BS....................................95.00
Butter pat, ATSF, California Poppy..29.00
Butter pat, ATSF, California Poppy, BS......................................95.00
Butter pat, ATSF, Mimbreno 45.00
Butter pat, B&A, Aroostook 22.50
Butter pat, B&O, Centenary, BS..55.00
Butter pat, C&NW, Depot Ornaments 45.00
Butter pat, CB&Q, Violets & Daisies, BS 110.00
Butter pat, CMStP&P, Galatea...110.00
Butter pat, CMStP&P, Traveler, BS 70.00
Butter pat, D&H, Canterbury...28.00
Butter pat, D&RGW, Blue Adam..33.00
Butter pat, GN, Empire 110.00
Butter pat, GTW, City of Grand Rapids, TL 135.00
Butter pat, KCS, Roxbury..25.00
Butter pat, L&N, Green Leaf 45.00
Butter pat, N&W, Cavalier 95.00

Butter pat, PRR, Keystone, BS 85.00
Butter pat, SL&SF, Denmark 42.00
Butter pat, SP, Prairie-Mountain Wildflowers, BS 88.50
Butter pat, UP, Historical...145.00
Butter pat, UP, Winged Streamliner 29.00
Creamer, ATSF, California Poppy, ind. 150.00
Creamer, CP, Empress, BS, ind, 2¼" 62.00
Creamer, NYNH&H, Platinum Blue, SL, ind 110.00
Creamer, PRR, Keystone, SL, ind, 2¼" 67.50
Creamer, Pullman, Calumet, SL, ind 95.00
Creamer, UP, Harriman Blue, ind............................55.00
Cup & saucer, ATSF, California Poppy 80.00
Cup & saucer, ATSF, Mimbreno, BS 135.00
Cup & saucer, B&O, Centenary, BS.........................95.00
Cup & saucer, CB&Q, Spider Mums, Haviland 175.00
Cup & saucer, CMStP, Olympian, TM on c/s, Haviland......135.00
Cup & saucer, CMStP, Olympian, TM on c/s, Lenox......145.00
Cup & saucer, demitasse; B&O, Centenary, BS 55.00
Cup & saucer, demitasse; CMStP&P, Traveler 75.00
Cup & saucer, demitasse; CP, Bows & Leaves 65.00
Cup & saucer, demitasse; CP, Vancouver..................55.00
Cup & saucer, demitasse; GN, Mountains & Flowers 195.00
Cup & saucer, demitasse; SP, Prairie-Mountain Wildflowers, BS .225.00
Cup & saucer, demitasse; SP, Sunset, SL, BS 275.00
Cup & saucer, demitasse; UP, Desert Flower, BS 50.00
Cup & saucer, demitasse; UP, Winged Streamliner 65.00
Cup & saucer, Fred Harvey, Encanto.........................22.00
Cup & saucer, Fred Harvey, Trend 25.00
Cup & saucer, Fred Harvey, Webster 18.00
Cup & saucer, GN, Oriental, BS on saucer 195.00
Cup & saucer, MP, The Eagle, TM, SL 35.00
Cup & saucer, N&W, Coach & Four 125.00
Cup & saucer, PRR, Broadway, BS 110.00
Cup & saucer, PRR, Keystone, TL 175.00
Cup & saucer, PRR, Purple Laurel, BS 110.00
Cup & saucer, Pullman, Indian Tree, TM 225.00
Cup & saucer, Reading, Stotesbury 125.00
Cup & saucer, SP, Imperial, SL, BS 135.00
Cup & saucer, SP, Prairie-Mountain Wildflowers, BS 77.50
Cup & saucer, SP&S, Red Leaves 22.50
Cup & saucer, StL&SF, Denmark 45.00
Cup & saucer, UP, Challenger 45.00
Cup & saucer, UP, Harriman Blue, BS 75.00
Cup & saucer, UP, Historical, TM............................375.00
Cup & saucer, UP, Winged Streamliner 50.00
Egg cup, B&O, Sweetbrier, lg...................................38.00
Egg cup, CB&Q, Aristocrat, SM 250.00
Egg cup, FEC, Mistic, lg..35.00
Egg cup, GN, Mountains & Flowers, sm 75.00
Egg cup, MP, Eagle, SL, lg 68.00
Egg cup, Pullman, Calumet, lg 185.00
Egg cup, UP, Desert Flower, BS, sm 45.00
Egg cup, UP, Desert Flower, lg 55.00
Egg cup, UP, Streamliner, sm 42.00
Gravy boat, ATSF, Mimbreno, BS 160.00
Gravy boat, CMStP&P, Traveler, sm 65.00
Gravy boat, CN, Vancouver 48.00
Gravy boat, KCS, Roxbury, sm 28.00
Gravy boat, NYC, DeWitt Clinton, BS 85.00
Gravy boat, NYNH&H, Platinum Blue, BS, sm 110.00
Gravy boat, SP, Prairie-Mountian Wildflowers, sm......110.00
Gravy boat, UP, Streamliner, lg 80.00
Hot food cover, CMStP&P, Traveler 65.00
Ice cream shell, ATSF, Adobe, BS.............................75.00

Ice cream shell, CN, Bonaventure, TM 35.00
Ice cream shell, MStP&SStM, Logan, BS 135.00
Ice cream shell, NYC, DeWitt Clinton, TM, BS...........75.00
Matchbox holder, SP, Del Monte, SL 45.00
Mustard, KCS, Roxbury, w/lid, 2⅞" 45.00
Mustard, Pullman, Calumet, w/lid, SL 175.00
Mustard, SP&S, Red Leaves, w/lid, 3¼" 42.50
Pitcher, SP, Del Monte, SL, 6" 175.00
Plate, ACL, Flora of the South, notched corners, 7" 150.00
Plate, ATSF, Adobe, TL, 9½" 72.00
Plate, ATSF, California Poppy, 9½" 35.00
Plate, ATSF, Mimbreno, BS, 9½" 95.00
Plate, ATSF, Turquoise Room, TL, BS, 10¼" 650.00
Plate, B&O, Centenary, BS, 8¼" 75.00
Plate, B&O, Centenary, divided, BS, 10½" 195.00
Plate, C&O, Geo Washington, BS, 8" 85.00
Plate, CN, Quetico, 8" 22.50
Plate, CN, Truro, 7" 25.00
Plate, D&RGW, Prospector, TM, 9" 100.00
Plate, GN, Glory of the West, BS, 9½" 225.00
Plate, GN, Mountains & Flowers, BS, 9½"..................195.00
Plate, L&N, Regent, 9" 195.00
Plate, MP, State Flowers, BS, 10½" 225.00
Plate, N&W, Cavalier, TL, 9½" 210.00
Plate, N&W, Coach & Four, 10½" 125.00
Plate, N&W, Dogwood, legend on reverse, BS, 10" 135.00
Plate, NP, Monad, TL, 7" 70.00
Plate, NYC, Mercury, 6½", BS 22.50
Plate, NYC, Mercury, 9", BS 35.00
Plate, NYNH&H, Merchants, BS, 8½" 110.00
Plate, NYNH&H, Merchants, BS, 9½" 145.00
Plate, NYNH&H, Platinum Blue, BS, 9¼" 150.00
Plate, PRR, Broadway, TM, 8" 45.00
Plate, PRR, Keystone, TM, 9" 85.00
Plate, PRR, Purple Laurel, BS, 9" 98.00
Plate, SAL, Palmbeach, 6¼" 55.00
Plate, service; D&H, Adirondack, TM, 10½"................110.00
Plate, SP, Harriman Blue, BS, 8½"..............................95.00
Plate, SP, Prairie-Mountain Wildflowers, BS, 5½"..........35.00
Plate, SP, Prairie-Mountain Wildflowers, BS, 9½"..........85.00
Plate, SP, Sunset, TM, 8" 135.00
Plate, StL&SF, Denmark, 9" 65.00
Plate, UP, Desert Flower, BS, 10" 85.00
Plate, UP, Historical, TL, 6" 150.00
Plate, UP, Winged Streamliner, 7½" 42.00
Plate, WP, Feather River, TM, 7¼" 65.00
Plate, WP, Feather River, TM, 9½" 225.00
Platter, ATSF, California Poppy, 6x8" 45.00
Platter, ATSF, Mimbreno, BS, 6½x9½" 185.00
Platter, B&O, Centenary, BS, 5½x8" 110.00
Platter, B&O, Centenary, 13½x9½" 365.00
Platter, B&O, Derby, BS, 7x5" 75.00
Platter, C&O, Geo Washington, TL, 9x6" 185.00
Platter, CB&Q, Galatea, 7½x5½" 50.00
Platter, CMStP&P, Peacock, 8x6" 38.00
Platter, CMStP&P, Traveler, 8x6"................................35.00
Platter, CRI&P, Golden State, TM, 8½x5½" 185.00
Platter, CRI&P, LaSalle, TM, 9x6" 200.00
Platter, GN, Hill, TM, 10x8½"....................................200.00
Platter, L&N, Regent, 12x8½"....................................165.00
Platter, MKT, Katy Ornaments, 8½x6" 125.00
Platter, NP, Garnet, BS, 10½x7" 300.00
Platter, PRR, Keystone, TM, 11x8" 100.00
Platter, SP, Sunset, TM, 9½x7" 125.00

Platter, SP&S, Red Leaves, 9½x7" 25.00
Platter, UP, Harriman Blue, BS, 9x7" 49.00
Platter, UP, Historical, TL, BS, 8x6" 175.00
Platter, UP, Winged Streamliner, 8x6" 42.00
Platter, WP, Feather River, TM, 11x9" 225.00
Relish, ATSF, California Poppy, 9½x6½" 85.00
Relish, CB&Q, Violets & Daisies, 3½x7½" 55.00
Relish, CB&Q, Violets & Daisies, 4½x9½" 65.00
Relish, CMStP&P, Traveler, 4½x9½" 45.00
Relish, GN, Mountains & Flowers, BS, 4½x9½" 75.00
Relish, KCS, Roxbury, 3½x7" 22.00
Sherbet, L&N, Regent 85.00
Sherbet, PRR, Purple Laurel 35.00
Sherbet, UP, Winged Streamliner 45.00
Teapot, ATSF, Mimbreno, BS 195.00
Teapot, B&O, Centenary, BS 225.00
Teapot, NYNH&H, Platinum Blue, BS 125.00
Teapot, UP, Winged Streamliner 135.00
Toothpick holder, B&A, Aroostook 45.00

Glassware

Ash tray, Alaska RR, ARR over Mt McKinley Park Hotel, 3½"....25.00
Ash tray, ATSF, Santa Fe in script, oval, 4" 35.00
Ash tray, McCloud RR, logo in red, 3½" dia 16.00

Silverplated castor stand marked Sheffield, three glass bottles, Pullman Car Co. Ltd. on crest, 4¾", $75.00.

Champagne, ATSF, cut banner w/Santa Fe, 3½" 145.00
Cocktail set, UP, logo, pitcher+2½" roly-polys 38.00
Cordial, ATSF, Santa Fe in script, 3½" 24.00
Cruet, SP, Daylight w/ball & wing logo.........................175.00
Goblet, CN, etched logo, 5½" 42.00
Goblet, UP, etched logo in shield, 5½" 17.50
Mug, ATSF, Santa Fe in wht script, 3½" 12.50
Shot glass, D&H in shield, 2¾" 11.00
Shot glass, Erie in bl & wht dmn logo, 2½" 12.00
Tumbler, C&NW, blk & gold logo, 5½" 18.00
Tumbler, D&H, cut D&H inside shield logo, 4½" 18.00
Tumbler, juice; NYC, wht enameling, 3" 28.00
Tumbler, PRR, logo cast in base, 3½" 48.00
Wine, CN, etched logo, 4½" 37.00
Wine, NYC, gold logo, 4½" 27.00

Lamps

Backhead gauge, N&W, Dietz, ca 1930, M.....................45.00

Berth, Pullman, steel/porc, egg shape, NM, pr 45.00
Caboose, Adlake, sq top/oil, 1 red/3 amber lenses, EX 135.00
Caboose bunk, UP, pebbled top globe, brass/steel, hanging 40.00
Carbide, B&O, Oxweld, mk Pat Pend, 5⅞x10⅞", NM 55.00
Inspector's, Star Headlight & Lantern Co, ornate, NM 65.00
Marker, NYCS, Adlake, sq top, oil, complete, NM, pr 195.00
Semaphore, UP, Adlake, electric, dbl bull's-eye lens, NM 85.00
Switch, Adlake, sq top, non-sweating, red/amber/2 gr lenses....125.00

Lanterns

BR&P, Dietz #39 Standard, clear mk globe, Pat 1910............245.00
C&C, Armspear, pot insert, clear unmk Globe, Pat 1913, NM 95.00
CH&D, Adlake, insert pot/burner, red globe, 1909, EX 135.00
CTA, Adlake Kero, red unmk globe, dtd 4-49, NM 65.00
DL&W, Dietz Vesta 1951, unmk red globe, EX.........................45.00
IC, Adlake Reliable, clear mk 5⅜" globe, #300 burner, EX...........75.00
MP, Handlan-Buck, bell bottom, clear globe, lg, M 175.00

Linens

Apron, cook's, D&RGW, wht w/brass grommets, NM..................12.00
Blanket, Canadian Nat'l, maple leaf logo, Pendleton wool, EX 40.00
Blanket, Canadian Pacific, maple leaf logo, Pendleton wool 45.00
Blanket, Pullman, interwoven logo in center, older style, EX........45.00
Blanket, Pullman, wool, pk w/dk pk logo in center, EX 70.00
Blanket, UP, Las Vegas Club, twin sz, EX.................................50.00
Headrest cover, ATSF interwoven in bl stripe on wht, M.............. 7.50
Headrest cover, NYC, gray vertical stripes, EX..........................15.00
Headrest cover, SR, Southern Serves the South 12.50
Headrest cover, UP, Streamliner...12.50
Laundry bag, UP, brass grommets at top, canvas, 30x28", EX 15.00
Napkin, Amtrak, 18x18", EX 5.00
Napkin, CA Zephyr, logo interwoven in center, 21x16", M..........12.00
Napkin, D&RG, red embr on wht, lg, M 5.00
Napkin, RI, wht bearskin logo on wht, 1962, 20"....................10.00
Napkin, Rio Grande, 'speed' letters, wht on wht, 17x17", M 7.50
Napkin, UP, woven letters on pk, 17x17", M 6.00
Pillowcase, BR logo, Pillow Rental 50¢, regular....................... 5.00
Pillowcase, CA Zephyr, over-stamp on Pullman logo, pk 15.00
Pillowcase, Santa Fe, pressed paper, 50¢ rental...................... 2.50
Sheet, BN, stamped logo, twin sz... 8.00
Sheet, Burlington Rte, stamped logo, twin sz, NM 8.00
Sheet, RI, bearskin logo stamp, EX 9.00
Sheet, UP, embr red script, M 12.50
Tablecloth, Burlington Rte, wht on wht, NM 17.50
Tablecloth, C&N, logo interwoven on yel, 53" sq, EX 42.50
Tablecloth, CA Zephyr, wht, interwoven logo, 40x36" 20.00
Tablecloth, CB&Q, Burlington Rte sq logo, 50x36" 20.00
Tablecloth, D&RGW, wht, Rio Grande 'speed' letters, 36x36" 15.00
Tablecloth, GN, center logo, wht on wht, belt/buckle motif.........50.00
Tablecloth, MP Lines, linen, wht on wht, 48x33", EX 45.00
Tablecloth, Soo Line center box logo, wht on wht, 31x52", VG ...22.00
Tablecloth, SP&S oval center logo, wht on wht, 54x54" 27.50
Tablecloth, Sunset logo woven in center on wht, M 22.50
Tablecloth, UP, name near hem, roses on rose pk, 50x42" 22.00
Towel, dish; CA Zephyr, Safety Is Our Dish, red on wht, 30x17"..10.00
Towel, hand; Lehigh Valley, red center stripe, EX 15.00
Towel, PRR, red stripe on wht, Cannon, 15x20", EX 5.00
Towel, UP, all wht, 14x31", EX 4.50
Towel, UP, stamped logo on wht or yel, 17x12", M 10.00

Locks

Signal, ACL, brass, w/chain, NM..16.00

Signal, ACL, Corbin, cleaned, EX 22.00
Signal, B&O, Fraim, brass, dbl stamp, no post, VG 35.00
Signal, L&N, screw type, w/chain, EX 20.00
Signal, N&W, Yale, brass, no chain, EX 15.00
Switch, ATSF, Slaymaker, iron w/brass rivets, 1967, EX 15.00
Switch, ATSF, Slaymaker, steel, 1964, w/chain, M.....................17.50
Switch, Frisco, Adlake, brass, w/chain, EX 36.00
Switch, KCS, T Edwards, brass, incised logo, EX........................75.00
Switch, MoPac Lines, Adlake, CI, w/chain, EX 17.50
Switch, NYCS, Fraim, steel, 1968, unmk brass key w/chain 22.00
Switch, NYCS, Moon, steel, early, w/heavy chain, EX 22.50

Silverplate

Bowl, condiment; Pullman, curved ends, 1928, 4½x7½" 78.00
Bowl, grapefruit; Pullman, 1925, 2½x6½" 88.00
Bowl, ice cream; MP, ped ft, ca 1930, worn 32.00
Bread basket, MP, BS, 1924, 9", EX...65.00
Butter pat, Santa Fe, rnded corners, Internat'l, 2⅝" sq................55.00
Butter pat, UP, BS, 1914, 3½"..32.00
Casserole, NYNH&H, Reed & Barton, w/lid, pre-1928, 1-pt, EX .75.00
Coffeepot, CA Zephyr, BM, worn, 14-oz.....................................95.00
Coffeepot, CB&Q, SL, Reed & Barton, 14-oz, EX 45.00
Coffeepot, GN, insulated, Stanley, worn.....................................50.00
Coffeepot, MP & Iron Mtn, high finial, ornate, Wallace, 10-oz ...80.00
Coffeepot, Rio Grande, Curecanti logo, SM, 12-oz...................265.00
Coffeepot, San Diego Short Line, ornate, lt wear, 10-oz.............165.00
Coffeepot, UP, Internat'l, BS, 1947, 8-oz, VG 85.00
Cover, hot food; IC, SM, fancy Louisiane logo, 7½x10½" 75.00
Creamer, Fred Harvey in script, fancy lip, ⅝-pt 75.00
Creamer, Metropolitan Line, Reed & Barton, SM, 2-oz, EX.........20.00
Creamer, WAB, w/hdl, sm 60.00
Crumber, Canadian Pacific, oval, Elkington, TM, M 88.00
Finger bowl, Rio Grande, 'speed' letters, BM, 1941, 3" 32.00
Fork, dinner; UP, Zephyr, Internat'l...17.50
Fork, pickle; Fred Harvey, Albany, early......................................20.00
Gravy boat, SP, winged ball, Reed & Barton, SL, BS, EX.............35.00
Horseradish holder, NYC, complete w/glass jar, BM 90.00
Ice bowl, NYC, SM, 1946, 4½x7¼", EX 165.00
Knife, dinner; ATSF, Albany, Internat'l......................................17.50
Knife, steak; ATSF, Cromwell, 1912 ....17.50
Menu holder, IC, Wallace, NM 75.00
Menu holder, UP, winged train, BS, 1951, EX 45.00
Mustard, CP, cobalt insert, flip lid, TM, NM..............................95.00
Pitcher, PRR, glass w/cut Keystone, SP fr, 1951, lg 80.00
Platter, RI, dome cover, 1929, 10", EX 195.00
Platter, steak; UP, Overland shield TM, BS, 1925, 11x7½"..........85.00
Platter, UP, Overland shield, Internat'l, 1914, 12".......................88.00
Sauce boat, RI, BM, Wallace, 1921, 3-oz, NM............................115.00
Spoon, bouillon; NYC, Century, Internat'l 18.50
Spoon, cheese; B&O, Columbia, fluted, Reed & Barton................22.50
Spoon, iced tea; Century, Internat'l..17.50
Spoon, iced tea; Paisley, BS..17.50
Spoon, place; C&N, Windsor, 1884, TM 15.00
Spoon, place; NP Monad, Rte of...Big Baked Potato, NM 45.00
Spoon, place; RI, Cromwell, TM, BS, Wallace 17.50
Sugar bowl, Rio Grand, w/lid, 1948, 12-oz, EX 78.00
Sugar bowl, Santa Fe, hinged lid, Gorham, SM, BS, 10-oz...........50.00
Sugar tongs, C&NW, spoon shape, Internat'l, TM in script 62.50
Sugar tongs, NYC, Commonwealth, Reed & Barton 60.00
Sugar tongs, SRR, spoon shape, SM, Internat'l 70.00
Syrup, Rio Grande, attached tray, SM, 1947, EX 45.00
Syrup, UP, Reed & Barton, w/lid & attached undertray, NM........90.00
Tablespoon, Fred Harvey, Cromwell, Internat'l, 1912 ....15.00

Tablespoon, NYC, Vermont, Victor...17.50
Teapot, C&NW, pagoda style, Internat'l, BS, 1925, 8-oz.............75.00
Thermos, Canadian Pacific, Stanley of Toronto, SM, 10", M 40.00
Toast cover, Pullman, 1933...72.50
Tray, MP, fancy appl edge, BM, 1930s, 9x5¾".............................88.00
Tureen, soup; B&O, TM, Reed & Barton, 1-pt, 3-pc..................220.00
Tureen, soup; C&O, w/lid, Reed & Barton, ca 1920, 1-pt............75.00
Tureen, soup; Santa Fe, #3400 series, Reed & Barton, 3-pc 125.00
Vase, bud; WAB, BS, 1948...135.00

Wax Sealers and Accessories

Am Express, Rossville IN, brass, oval head, EX 25.00
Am Ry Express #3557, Messenger, oval brass head, wood hdl 50.00
Rapid City, SD, For Public Use, NP brass hdl.............................35.00
Ry Express Agency, Public, oval brass head, wood hdl 35.00
Wells Fargo Express, Saxman KS, brass, rnd head, EX 135.00

Miscellaneous

Agreement of right of way, C&S, 5 typed pgs, 1926, EX 6.00
Air horn, Leslie Tyfon #125, brass, 20-lb, 20", EX.....................150.00
Application, employment; PRR, telegraph operator, 1906, 8x14" . 5.00
Ash tray, glass, clear, bias corners, 5" 5.00
Ash tray, WP, glass, clear w/bias corners, 5" 5.00
Axe, L&A, long wood hdl, EX...32.00
Badge, Burlington Rte, passenger agent, metal bk, early 4.00
Badge, C&O, sleeping car porter, plastic, 1½x3½" 5.00
Badge, Canadian Pacific Dept Investigation, beaver 40.00
Badge, hat; ACL, fireman, NP, 3½" L...42.50
Badge, hat; ACL, gateman, brass, 3½" 65.00
Badge, hat; IC, porter, blk emb letters on silver, M.....................60.00
Badge, hat; N&W, brakeman, silver skeleton letters, M 58.00
Badge, hat; New Haven, ticket collector, brass, 4" 78.00
Badge, hat; porter, blk enameling on NP brass, 3½" L.................55.00
Badge, IC, waiter, plastic, 1¼", M... 2.50
Bag, Am Ry Express, courier's, leather & canvas, 12x14" 45.00
Bag, money; PRR, canvas, 2 grommets on end, 13x6", EX 17.50
Book, Fire Rules for Denver Round House & Coach Yards, 1930s...22.50
Book, Future of Our Rys, Armstrong, 1920, EX...........................22.00
Book, Iron Horses. . .Locomotives 1829-1900, Alexander, '41, EX..40.00
Book, promo; Georgetown Loop, pictures, '10, 22-pg, 11x13" 45.00
Book, Ry Engineering & Maintenance Cyclopedia, 1939, EX.......55.00
Book, telegraph code, leatherette emb cover, 1928, 73-pg, M......... 5.00
Book, Train Wrecks, Reed, hard cover, M...................................10.00
Book, UP operating rules, blk leather cover, 1972, NM 5.00
Book, Western Union, telegraph blanks, unused, 6x9" 7.50
Booklet, CM, Through Hellgate, red cover, EX............................95.00
Booklet, D&RG, Rhymes of the Rockies, 1895, worn cover, 7x9"...27.50
Box, first aid; CSX Transportation, metal, w/contents, M 8.00
Box, strong; Adams Express, steel, 10x14x10½", EX...................245.00
Box, Western Union Telegraph & Cable blanks, wall mt, EX.......65.00
Brochure, ACL, Tropical Trips, 1923, 31-pg, EX 12.50
Brochure, B&O, Century of Progress Expo, 1934, EX 28.00
Brochure, Hotels & Resorts of UP, red cover, 1911, 4x9", EX......17.50
Brochure, IC, homesteaders & land seekers, 1901, EX 17.50
Brochure, SP Sunset Rte, maps, 1946, 15-pg 7.50
Brush, Pullman, porter's, wood hdl, blk horsehair, NM 18.00
Builder's plate, Fairbanks-Morse, steel, 1956, 5x8" 65.00
Builder's plate, stainless, dtd 1977, 15x4", EX 32.00
Bulletin board, FW&DC, wooden, 62x78", EX............................85.00
Button, uniform; Pullman, silver.. 3.00
Calendar, GN, Indian portrait, 1942, EX....................................75.00
Calendar, Maine Central, passenger train, 1949, pocket sz 3.50

Call card, Ry Express Agency, blk/red, early, EX........................115.00
Cap, Amtrak, asst conductor, bl twill, M....................................40.00
Cap, Pullman, conductor's, gold badge & braid, NM 125.00
Card, Christmas; NYC, Niagara snow scene, unused, 5x7"............ 2.00
Card, conductor's coach record; Pullman, 3x6¾", M......................2.50
Catalog, Kuhlman Car Co, illus, hard bk, ca 1905, EX.............120.00
Cigar, UP, shield cigar band, cello wrap, M................................ 7.50
Cigarette lighter, MoPac, modern logo, red on wht, Bic...............17.50
Clip board, CSS&SB, metal, gold w/red mkings, 9", VG..............45.00
Coat, UP, waiter's, collarless, pearl buttons, EX..........................15.00
Coin, UP, Chicago World's Fair, aluminum...............................30.00
Contract, shipping, Adams Express, rubber stamped, 1890, 5x8" ... 6.00
Cuff protectors, Chessie System, elastic, M, pr...........................12.00
Cup, NYC, paper, folded, bl logo, folded, 2½x3½"....................... 3.00
Cup, PRR, tin, emb Keystone, 2½x3¾", EX...............................65.00
Curtain, RI, canvas, covered berths, 96x48", VG.......................55.00
Decal, N&W, red & blk, ¾" dia, M 1.50
Emblem, lapel; CB&Q, braided gold, screw bk, pr, M..................47.50
Flashlight, PRR, 2-cell, worn chrome finish, SM, EX..................32.50
Fuel pot, NW, Aladdin burner & mantle, 3-pc, EX.....................48.00
Gauge, Ashton Standard Test, NP brass, 7⅜", EX......................35.00
Globe, N&W, clear cast, Corning, 5⅜", M.................................60.00
Guide, B&O, brochure of New York City, 1926, EX....................12.00
Hammock, Pullman, for berth, gr, string ties, NM......................50.00
Hard hat, UP, w/shell & suspension system, EX 18.00

Hat, C.&.O. RY Conductor, $125.00.

Hat, N&W, chef's, paper, ca 1950, unused, M 3.50
Key, switch; C&S, Adlake, #4420 on reverse, EX 55.00
Key, switch; CL&W, Adams & Westlake, EX................................85.00
Key, switch; IC, Adlake, 1948, lt wear......................................17.50
Key, switch; SMStP&P, Adlake, EX patina................................22.50
Key, switch; T&BV, Slaymaker, lt wear 45.00
Kit, first aid; UP, contents in clear zipper bag, M 5.00
Letter opener, RI, red plastic, Century of Progress, EX.................12.00
Lever, reverse control key; unmk, steel, rubber hdl, 6"..................15.00
Magazine, Burlington Bulletin, 1962, 7-pg, 9x12" 3.50
Magazine, Railway Conductor, Roosevelt cover, May 1945, EX..... 5.00
Manual, Moody's Transportation, 1970, M..................................22.50
Map, Atlantic & E Carolina Ry, color, system, 1940s, 11x14" 17.50
Map, Canadian Pacific, 1929, 32x19", EX.................................. 5.00
Marker, SR Post Office, steel head, brass ferrule, 1⅞" 95.00
Matchbook cover, Tennessee Central, early, EX 10.00
Matches, Frisco, yel cb box, freight car shape, 6½" L.................... 5.00
Medallion, RI 70 Yr Commemorative, M...................................35.00
Memo pad, SR, kangaroo on cover, 3x5", M.............................. 2.50
Menu, B&O, child's, bl, train form, opens to 4x18", EX...............15.00

Menu, Burlington Rte, Chuckwagon/Denver Zephyr, '70, 6x9", M ... 8.00
Menu, C&N, single card, 1942, 5x8" 5.00
Menu, D&O, oyster shape, early 1930s, EX................................24.00
Menu, IC, beverages, dbl fold, 1961, 5x7", M............................. 7.50
Menu, NP, Yellowstone Park logo on woodgrain cover, 6x11" 4.00
Menu, Santa Fe (Fred Harvey), supper: 65¢, 6x9".......................16.00
Oiler, bench; Eagle, unused, minor scuffs 22.50
Oiler, long spout, missing spring, Pat 1896, 31", EX...................32.00
Pants, Ft Worth & Denver, waiter's, stamped in waist, EX 6.00
Pants, UP, waiter's, purple stripe ea leg, EX 12.00
Pass, annual; CA Zephyr, 1951, M.. 2.50
Photo, UP RR Streamlined Train, 1934, +booklet & folder..........15.00
Pin, I'm a Burlington Wheel, metal, pinch-bk, 1" dia 2.50
Pin, lapel; Amtrak, gold, half-rnd w/logo, EX............................32.00
Pin, lapel; Brotherhood of...Trainmen, 25 Yrs, wht/brass/gold 22.00
Pin, lapel; Burlington Rte, Safety First, screw bk.........................12.00
Pin, lapel; Clinchfield Rte, blk on gold, ltd ed, EX........................ 4.00
Pin, lapel; New England Veterans, enamel on gold, early 27.50
Pin, lapel; Pullman, gold triangle w/car atop, 25 yrs 42.50
Playing cards, C&O, Chessie, sealed in clear plastic case 20.00
Scuttle, Rio Grande, galvanized metal, iron bail, 13x14x18".........55.00
Scuttle, Soo Line, EX tin, little wear...45.00
Sheet music, Pullman Porter Blues, Blk cover, 1921, EX 27.50
Shovel, AT&SF in hdl, coal hod sz, 15", G 20.00
Sign, Amtrak, Tickets/Tours Sold Here, stand-up, 4x12", VG 45.00
Sign, Santa Fe, Removable Gate, pnt steel, 1915, 3x10", EX.........27.50
Sign, Ship From Here, porc on steel, 12" sq, VG........................25.00
Sign, Train Fare: 10¢, etc, pnt steel, 4x16", EX.........................27.50
Sign, Watch Your Step, porc on steel, 3¼x21", EX......................45.00
Spittoon, Pullman, NP brass, compact passenger style, EX 45.00
Stationery, Burlington Rte, lt gr, 1 sheet+envelope 2.00
Stationery, NP, N Coast Ltd, Yellowstone, 1 sheet+envelope 3.50
Stationery, Wabash Banner Limited, 1 sheet............................... 3.00
Step box, WAB, conductor's, Morton, steel, rfn...........................195.00
Step stool, C&O, emb letters, yel pnt, safety top, 17x13" 165.00
Swizzle stick, Fred Harvey, blk & gold arrow, M......................... 2.00
Tag, baggage; RI, brass, Wilcox, Pat 1880, 1¾x2"......................42.50
Tag, luggage; Omaha, brass, cloverleaf shape, 1½" 27.50
Tag, pillow; C&O, Chessie kitten on bl, 3x4½" 2.00
Telephone, Northern Electric, wood box, handset, wall 75.00
Telephone, Western Electric 1915P model, scissors style, EX......165.00
Thermometer, Pullman, Taylor, inside car, brass, 7½", EX 20.00
Ticket case, Nat'l Ticket Case Co, desk top, oak, roll front.........230.00
Timetable, D&SL, yel, 1944, 3x6", EX.....................................20.00
Timetable, employee; C&O, Cincinnati-Chicago, 1969................12.00
Timetable, employee; CN, British Columbia, 1966......................13.00
Timetable, employee; CP, Laurentian/Farnham, 1953 ....16.00
Timetable, employee; GN, Kalispell Division, 1964 ....16.00
Timetable, employee; IC, Chicago Terminal Division, 1957.........13.00
Timetable, employee; KCS, Northern Terminal Division, 1945....15.00
Timetable, employee; SP, LA Division, 1957 ....15.00
Timetable, employee; SP, San Joaquin, 1942 ....20.00
Timetable, employee; T&P, Eastern Division, 1939.....................19.00
Timetable, employee; White Pass & Yukon System, 1958.............15.00
Timetable, employee; Wisconsin Central, 1947 ....21.00
Timetable, employees; Sumpter Valley RR, 1936, M 4.50
Timetable, Los Angeles & Salt Lake, Way to CA, 1917, 6x9" 17.50
Timetable, public; ACL, full system, 1932 ....22.00
Timetable, public; C&NW System, 1931 ....25.00
Timetable, public; C&O System, Chessie, 1939..........................15.00
Timetable, public; C&O System, map, 1914..............................39.00
Timetable, public; CN, Sept 1926, 152-pg 29.50
Timetable, public; DRGW, Rio Grand System, 1939 ....13.00
Timetable, public; Erie System, Scenic Rt...Chicago WF, 1936 .....18.00

Timetable, public; FEC System, 1932, 32-pg **22.50**
Timetable, public; GN System, Empire Builder, 1939 ....**18.00**
Timetable, public; NP System, Northern Coast Ltd, 1939 ....**17.00**
Timetable, public; SP System, 4 Great Routes, 1932 ....**22.50**
Timetable, public; UP System, maps, 1917 ....**32.00**
Timetable, public; UP System, 1939 ....**16.00**
Timetable, public; WP, Feather River, 1932 ....**23.00**
Timetable, RDG, Bethlehem branch, 1895, VG **25.00**
Timetable, Rio Grand, blk/wht, 1923, EX **17.50**
Timetable, WAB, flag logo, blk/wht, St Louis Union Station **45.00**
Token, UP, aluminum, Lucky Piece, Alco, 1934, NM **12.00**
Torch, flambeau style, early lid w/chain attachment, EX **27.50**
Trust plate, SR Equipment, sheet metal, 1968, 6x17½", EX **30.00**
Uniform, C&O brakeman's, 3-pc suit+hat/buttons/badges, EX ...**100.00**
Voucher, UP, rent for cook's room, 1913, 7x9" **9.50**
Waste basket, NEMCO, wire, unmk, 12¼x12x9", EX **18.00**
Water can, Soo Line at shoulder, tin, 7½-qt, EX **37.50**
Whistle, police; B&O, brass, EX **10.00**
Whistle, steam, brass, Crane #125 emb on valve, 14", EX **75.00**
Whistle, steam, brass, single chamber, #19 on valve, 10" **75.00**
Wrench, monkey; MoPac RR **12.50**
Wrench, SRY, dbl end, heavy steel, strong mk **12.00**

Razors

As straight razors gain in popularity, prices increase. And with the
lure of investment appreciation, the novice or the speculator sometimes
find themselves making purchases that later prove to be unwise. It is
important to be able to recognize the material of which the handle is
made. This has a great bearing on value, and imitations abound. Learn
to distinguish between celluloid and genuine ivory. Razors with plain
celluloid handles are practically worthless unless the blade carries a
desirable trademark. Those with decorations of scrollwork, leaves and
vines, or decorative metal on each end fall into the $8 to $12 price
range. Even plain ivory-handled razors are not especially valuable
unless the blade is well marked and from a good manufacturer. On a
more positive note, celluloid-handled razors with designs such as castles, windmills, nudes, deer, alligators, automobiles, horses, cowboys,
peacocks, and various kinds of birds, etc., are very desirable (some more
than others) and are usually worth from $25 to $50 to collectors. Those
with a figural handle such as a fish, shotgun, eagle, or a barber pole
might be worth in excess of $100 for an especially nice example. Ivory,
on the other hand, is rarely found; if the carvings are well done, clean,
undamaged specimens should start at about $100 and escalate accord-
ing to the intricacy of the design.

Buffalo horn is sometimes mistakenly called bone. It is usually
black, translucent tan, or gray. Though plain handles are worth very little, the early heat-molded examples with a motif such as mentioned
above often sell for more than $100. In the same range are mother-of-
pearl and stag (deer horn) handles; very elaborate designs go even
higher, but watch for imitations.

There is one imitation, however, that is highly desirable. That is
jigged bone made to look like stag. This material is rough textured and
dyed a handsome tan or brown; usually examples with these handles
sell in the $40 to $75 range. Razors with wooden handles are very rare,
but even those from the 1800s are worth only about $35, since they are
usually very plain. 20th-century examples are only valued at around
$15. Don't be fooled by buffalo horn colored in imitation of tortoise —
and you'll find celluloid imitations, too. Genuine tortoise handles are
worth from $25 to $100 depending on age, condition, and workmanship. Sterling razors are valued at $75 and up, but make sure they are
marked 'sterling.' Even if you were to mistake aluminum for silver,
those with relief-cast designs are worth $50 to $75, but only $20 or so if
the design is incised.

Corn razors were made to pare troublesome corns on the feet.
They are a bit smaller and if plain worth a little more than plain full-
size razors. Fancy examples are generally not worth as much as their
full-size couterparts.

The older blades are wedge-shaped (flat-sided) in cross-section;
hollow-ground blades (made after 1880) are concave. Generally speaking, those etched with words are only worth a little more than a plain,
common blade. Try to find those with people, places, and things — the
more famous, the better.

Key:
bd — blade   gw — gold washed
cell — celluloid

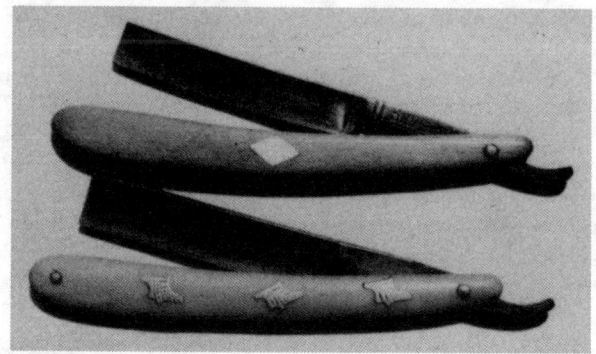

**Top: Wood handle with inlaid mother-of-pearl, $35.00;
Bottom: Celluloid handle with three inlaid metal leaves,
$28.00.**

AF Bannister, gr hdl: Nouveau nude, etch bd: Manganese, EX **98.00**
Bayside Cutlery, hollow-ground bd, MOP 3-panel hdl w/silver ...**250.00**
Case Bros, stamped tang: Tested XX, striped brn hdl, EX **50.00**
Cattaraugus, hollow-ground bd, faux ivory hdl: lizard **15.00**
Challenge Works, hdl: fishscale & scroll, bd: Our Reliable............**15.00**
Clauss Fremont Ohio, beaded ivory cell hdl, NM **27.50**
Clements, Sheffield, hollow-ground bd, ivory hdl **30.00**
Cooper Ceyx, wedge bd, sm tang, blk horn hdl w/pewter inlay......**28.00**
Crown & Castle, wht hdl: emb portrait/vines, etched bd..............**22.50**
Curtin & Clark Cutlery, gr-yel hdl: owl & scroll, EX **30.00**
DePews Patent June 6 1882, etch bd, blk hdl, curved tang **35.00**
Eisemann's 1900, brn cell hdl w/blk stripes, fancy bolsters.............**18.00**
Ellis, Sheffield, hollow-ground bd, blk horn hdl, 1810s.................**88.00**
Fair & Square, plain bd, faux ivory hdl: wrapped rope decor..........**25.00**
Fein Stahl Solinger, cell hdl w/inlay, etch gw bd, NM **35.00**
Geo Fleissner...NY, spotted horn hdl, EX **12.00**
Groesbeeck, Chinese symbols on tang, horn hdl, 1860s, EX..........**45.00**
Henry Sears & Son 1865, brn hdl: emb Queen, etch bd **18.00**
Hope Cutlery, blk hdl: alligator in water, bk: scales **80.00**
Imperial Warranted, faux ivory hdl, etch bd: eagle, VG................**30.00**
Imperial...Warranted, bamboo pattern hdl, etch bd, EX **25.00**
J Smith & Sons, etch bd, clear horn hdl, 1850s..............................**45.00**
Joseph Rodgers & Sons Sheffield, MOP hdl: German silver inlay ...**95.00**
JR Torrey, gr cell hdl, Our Beauty etch on bd, MIB **20.00**
Kinfolks Bl Steel Special, mk wht hdl, NM **22.50**
King...Indiana PA, striped hdl w/silver caps, EX............................**27.50**
Krusius Bros Germany, wht hdl: lady w/flowing hair, EX **45.00**
Northfield Cutlery, faux tortoise hdl w/scrolls, EX **30.00**
Old Forge, plain bd, faux ivory hdl: bamboo w/orange **17.50**
Packwood, etch bd: 3 symbols, blk horn hdl, ca 1810....................**60.00**
Pride of Solingen, faux ivory hdl: nude picks grapes, EX................**65.00**
R Imperial, etch bd: Safety/bicycle for 2, cell hdl: stork **17.50**
Robeson Premier, yel mottled cell hdl, EX **27.50**

Robeson Shuredge, gr/blk stripe hdl, etch bd: Pilot, EX **37.50**
Robeson Shuredge, hollow-ground hdl, blk cell hdl **24.00**
Rogers, blk compo hdl w/inlaid bird, etch bd, Germany **37.50**
Shumate, faux jibbed bone hdl, EX **22.00**
Simmons, Keen Kutter logo on bl steel bd, blk hdl, EX **22.50**
Simmons Hardware, etch bd: Lilliputian, jigged bone hdl, EX **125.00**
Simmons HDLV...St Louis MO, cell hdl, Keen Kutter on bd **32.00**
Simon Pure Cutlery, hollow-ground bd, faux ivory hdl: nude **65.00**
SR Droescher, scroll hdl, etch bd: Our Star, EX **40.00**
Vom Cleff & Co NY, scrolled yel hdl, etch bd, VG **18.00**
Wade & Butcher, Sheffield, hdl: goddess pattern w/gr, NM **37.50**
Warranted Sheffield, horn hdl: eagle in gold, bd: American..........**20.00**
Wilbert Cutlery, gr cracked ice hdl/tang, etch Silver King bd **32.00**
Wm Elliot & Co Germany, cell hdl: emb windmill & boat, EX ...**30.00**
Wm Greaves & Sons Sheaf Works, steel bd, bone hdl, 1840s **32.00**
WR Case, Preparedness, faux ivory hdl: Case Tested XX **40.00**
WR Case & Sons, beaded brn & yel hdl, pearl tang, etch bd, G ...**45.00**
Yankee Cutlery...Magnetized, bamboo pattern hdl, EX..................**22.50**

Reamers

Reamers have been made in hundreds of styles and colors and by as many manufacturers. Their purpose is to extract the juices from lemons, oranges, and grapefruits. The largest producer of glass reamers was McKee, who pressed their products from many types of glass — custard; delphite and Chalaine blue; opaque white; Skokie green; black; caramel and white opalescent; Seville yellow; and transparent pink, green, and clear. Among these, the black and the caramel opalescents are the most valuable.

The Fry Glass Company also made reamers that are today very collectible. The Hazel Atlas Crisscross orange reamer in pink often brings in excess of $225; the same in blue, $200. Hocking produced a light blue orange reamer and, in the same soft hue, a two-piece reamer and measuring cup combination. Both are considered rare and very valuable with currently-quoted estimates at $400 and up for the former and $800 and up for the latter. In addition to the colors mentioned, red glass examples — transparent or slag — are rare and costly.

Among the most valuable ceramic reamers are those made by American potteries. The Spongeband reamer by Red Wing is valued in excess of $500; Coorsite reamers with gold or silver trim are worth $200 and up. Figurals are popular — Mickey Mouse and John Bull may bring $300 to $400. Others range from $45 to $150. Fine china one- and two-piece reamers are also very desirable and command very respectable prices.

A word about reproductions: A series of limited edition reamers is being made by Edna Barnes of Uniontown, Ohio. These are all marked with a 'B' in a circle. Other repoductions have been made from old molds. The most important of these are: Anchor Hocking 2-piece 2-cup measure and top, Gillespie 1-cup measure with reamer top, Westmoreland N-365 with flattened handle, Westmoreland 4-cup measure embossed with orange and lemons, Duboe (hand held), Easley's diamonds 1-piece, and spiral 1-piece #202.

Our advisor for this category is Dee Long; she is listed in the Directory under Illinois. For more information concerning reamers and reproductions, contact our advisor or the National Reamer Collectors Association (see Clubs, Newsletters, and Catalogs). Be sure to include an SASE when requesting information. Reference numbers in the ceramic reamer listings correspond with *200 Years of Reamers* by Mary Walker, available at your local library or from the National Reamer Collectors Association.

Ceramic

Bees, Japan, 2-pc **55.00**
Clown form, C-29, 7½" **90.00**

Clown, marked Mikoai Japan, $45.00.

Clown form, gr/wht/orange, C-36, 6½" **45.00**
Germany, HP, 2-pc, 3⅜" **70.00**
Germany, wht w/gold, 2-pc, 3⅝" **45.00**
Japan, baby's, dog & cat, 2-pc **50.00**
Japan, cottage form, gr/wht/orange/blk, C-29, 7½" **55.00**
Japan, duck form, 2-pc, 2¾" **40.00**
Japan, elephant form, 2-pc, 4¼" **150.00**
Japan, floral, mc on wht, T-89, 3¾" **40.00**
Japan, floral, 3-sided, D-54, 3½" **42.50**
Japan, frog w/geese form, 1-pc, 1¾" **65.00**
Japan, Mexican w/cactus form...**115.00**
Japan, pitcher form, mc florals, P-15, 7" **50.00**
Japan, pitcher form w/clown reamer, 5¾" **45.00**
Japan, saucer w/floral...**25.00**
Japan, saucer w/Negro head reamer, 3½" **275.00**
Nippon, china, 2-pc **120.00**
Pear form, wht w/gr & gold, L-39, 4½" **45.00**
Puddinhead, gr hat, F-32, 6¼"..**135.00**
Royal Rudolstadt, china, 2-pc **160.00**
Shelly, china, 2-pc **100.00**
Tan w/gr leaves, brn hdl, D-40, 4¼" **32.50**

Glass

Fry, opalescent, $45.00.

Clambroth, wht, boat-shaped, ribbed, loop hdl **170.00**
Crystal, Baby's Orange, 2-pc, 2-hdl..**45.00**
Crystal, Easley Pat July 10, 1888; Sept 10, 1889 ....**20.00**
Crystal, emb: Orange Juice Extractor **25.00**
Federal, amber, ribbed, tab hdl, seed dam, N-238..........................**20.00**
Federal, gr, paneled, loop hdl, N-350 ....**22.00**
Federal, pk, ribbed, loop hdl **24.00**

Federal, vaseline, ruffled top............................135.00
Fleur, amberina opal.......................................365.00
Fry, Re-Go, wht opal.......................................420.00
Hazel Atlas, cobalt, tab hdl, N-246.................250.00
Hazel Atlas, gr, tab hdl, lemon reamer.............10.00
Hazel Atlas, wht w/trim, pitcher+reamer, N-129, 2-cup 32.50
Hazel Atlas Crisscross, pk, tab hdl.................250.00
Hobnail, bl opal, saucer form, tabl hdl.............130.00
Hocking, gr, ribbed, orange reamer, N-247 ....15.00
Hocking, gr w/decal, fruit juice, 2-qt................22.00
Hocking, Mayfair bl, pitcher form, N-130, 2-cup......850.00
Indiana, crystal, horizontal hdl.......................12.50
Jeannette, Delphite bl, Jennyware 78.00
Jeannette, ultramarine, Jennyware, N-310.........65.00
Jeannette, yellowish jadite, loop hdl, lg............28.00
Lindsay (or Lindsey), pk..................................420.00
McKee, custard, pointed cone, unemb, 5¼"......28.00
McKee, Skokie gr, grapefruit reamer, N-358.....155.00
Milk glass, saucer form, tab hdl, 5"..................40.00
Paden City, gr, etched, pitcher form 225.00
Sunkist, chocolate, emb letters.......................450.00
Sunkist, dk Chalaine bl, emb letters................135.00
Sunkist, jadite, loop hdl..................................30.00
Sunkist, Seville yel, emb letters......................55.00
US Glass, crystal w/flowers, N-119, 2-pc 35.00
US Glass, gr, 2-cup, +top 35.00
US Glass, pk, pitcher+reamer, N-135, 32-oz.....150.00
US Glass, pk, tub+reamer, wire stand 65.00
Valencia, pk-amber, unemb 180.00
Westmoreland, blk or vaseline, flattened loop hdl, repro.............20.00
Westmoreland, frosted crystal, child's sz 55.00
Westmoreland, gr, Jenkins, baby's 100.00
Westmoreland, pk frosted, baby's.....................120.00
Westmoreland, red or cobalt, flattened loop hdl, repro.............20.00

Records

Records of interest to collectors are often not the million-selling hits by 'superstars.' Very few records by Bing Crosby, for example, are of any more than nominal value, and those that are valuable usually don't even have his name on the label! Collectors today are most interested in records that were made in limited quantities, early works of a performer who later became famous, and those issued in special series or aimed at a limited market. Vintage records are judged desirable by their recorded content as well; those that lack the quality of music that makes a record collectible will always be 'junk' records in spite of their age, scarcity, or the obsolescence of their technology.

Condition plays a critical factor in establishing values for records. In the listings that follow, values in these subcategories: LPs, EPs, and 45s are for records in mint condition. LPs must be in their original jackets; EPs (each has four songs, play at 45 rpm) are priced with their covers which must be free of defects such as writing, stickers, etc.; values for 45s do not include any picture sleeves that may accompany the record. Prices for records in all other subcategories are suggested for examples in excellent condition.

Records are usually graded visually rather than by audio quality, since it is seldom if ever possible to first play the records you buy at shows, by mail, at flea markets, etc. Condition is one of the most important value-assessing factors. For example, a truly mint-condition Elvis Presley 45 of Milk Cow Blues (Sun 215) has a potential value of over $1,000.00. If that same 45 had a sticker on it that was one-eighth of an inch square, it could lose up to half of that value! To be judged mint, a record and sleeve must be in original, unsealed condition. It

may have been played but has no visual or audible deterioration. Excellent condition is a rating applied to a record that may show slight signs of wear and use but will have almost no audible defect. Sleeves may show marginal deterioration but no repairs, pen or pencil marks, stickers, or physical damage. A good record has both visual and audible distractions; but it is still playable. Sleeves will show ring wear but will not be physically damaged, and Fair indicates a record that is both visually and audibly distracting, one that has obvious damage — no skips, but possible 'play through' scratches. It can still be usable. Sleeves will show heavy ring wear and some minor physical damage. A Poor record may or may not play. Sleeves are faded, torn, marked, or otherwise damaged beyond pleasurable viewing.

Many promo records being discarded by radio stations today are finding their way into collections. These may say 'Not for Sale,' 'Audition Copy,' 'D.J.,' etc. These radio station versions are sometimes different than commercial issue and usually more sought after than their commercial twins.

One of our advisors for this category is L.R. Docks, author of *American Premium Record Guide*, which lists 60,000 records by over 7,000 artists, now in its fourth edition. Some of our listings were provided by Mark Phillips, associate editor for the international record collectors' magazine, *DISCoveries*, part-owner of Sunrise Records in Beaumont, Texas, and a member of the board of advisors for the *Rockin' Records* price guide for used and collectible records. You will find both listed in the Directory under Texas.

Key:
Bru — Brunswick   PS — picture sleeve
Ch — Champion   Orch — Orchestra
Col — Columbia   Vi — Victor
Edi — Edison   Vo — Vocalion
Para — Paramount

Blues, Rhythm and Blues, Rock 'N Roll, Rockabilly

Alabama Slim, Boar Hog Blues, Savoy 5553, 78 rpm 8.00
Anderson, Jimmie; Ko Ko Mo Blues, Broadway 5111, 78 rpm.....250.00
Arnold, Kokomo; Bad Luck Blues, Decca 7540, 78 rpm..............20.00
Bailey, De Ford; Pan-American Blues, Bru 146, 78 rpm.............17.50
Barbecue Bob, Brown-Skin Gal, Col 14257-D, 78 rpm............30.00
Barton, Tippy; High Brown Cheater, Vo 1742, 78 rpm.............60.00
Big Richard, Pig Meat Mama, Varsity 6063, 78 rpm.....................10.00
Blind Blake, Skeedle Loo Doo Blues, Para 12413, 78 rpm..............80.00
Bradley, Marie; Down Home Moan, Para 12456, 78 rpm............100.00
Burleson, Hattie; Superstitious Blues, Bru 7042, 78 rpm............100.00
Campbell, Gene; Western Plain Blues, Bru 7154, 78 rpm 80.00
Collins, Sam; The Jail House Blues, Blk Patti 8025, 78 rpm........300.00
Davis, Walter; Santa Claus, Bluebird 6125, 78 rpm 30.00
Domino, Fats; Don't Lie to Me, Imperial 5123, 78 rpm.................20.00
Gordon, Roscoe; Weeping Blues, Flip 227, 78 rpm 12.50
Grant & Wilson, Ducks, Cameo 9015, 78 rpm 30.00
Harris, Mary; Happy New Year Blues, Champion 50045, 78 rpm ..25.00
Henderson, Rosa; Hard-Hearted Hannah, Ajax 17060, 78 rpm.....35.00
Jackson, Lillian; Cow Cow Blues, Supertone 9294, 78 rpm............60.00
James, Skip; Devil Got My Woman, Para 13088, 78 rpm 250.00
Johnson, Margaret; Absent Minded Blues, Okeh 8162, 78 rpm 75.00
Jones, Clint; Blue Valley Blues, Okeh 8587, 78 rpm 35.00
Kansas City Kitty; Scronchin', Vo 1632, 78 rpm............................80.00
Kirkman, Lillie Mae; Hop Head Blues, Vo 04951, 78 rpm 10.00
Liston, Virginia; Bed Time Blues, Okeh 8092, 78 rpm.................15.00
Manning, Leola; He Fans Me, Vo 1446, 78 rpm...........................80.00
McClennan, Tommy; My Little Girl, Bluebird 8605, 78 rpm 12.50
Memphis Slim, Empty Room Blues, Bluebird 8615, 78 rpm 10.00
Mississippi Sheiks, I Am the Devil, Bluebird 5516, 78 rpm 40.00

Nelson, Red; Sweetest Thing Born, Decca 7155, 78 rpm.............30.00
Patton, Charley; It Won't Be Long, Para 12854, 78 rpm 250.00
Poor Bill, A Hundred Women, Varsity 6020, 78 rpm..................15.00
Ross, Ted; Mother-In-Law Blues, Ch 15859, 78 rpm..................150.00
Scruggs, Irene; Borrowed Love, Ch 16102, 78 rpm....................150.00
Smith, Trixie; Trixie's Blues, Blk Swan 2039, 78 rpm..............25.00
St Louis Red Mike, Red Mike Blues, Bluebird 7744, 78 rpm.........15.00
Stowers, Freeman; Railroad Blues, Gennett 6814, 78 rpm 75.00
Stykes, Roosevelt; Candy Man Blues, Bullet 319, 78 rpm.............15.00
Tarpley, Slim; Alabama Hustler, Para 13062, 78 rpm 175.00
Taylor, Sallie; Seven Men Blues, Supertone 9365, 78 rpm 100.00
Townsend, Jesse; No Home Blues, Vi 23322, 78 rpm...................200.00
Wallace, Sippie; The Man I Love, Okeh 8251, 78 rpm.................60.00
Washington, Louis; Standin' on a Rock, Vo 02658, 78 rpm 80.00
Wheatstraw, Peetie; Good Hustler Blues, Decca 7123, 78 rpm......20.00
White, Grace; Friendless Blues, Silvertone 3542, 78 rpm 20.00
Wilkins, Tim; Dirty Deal Blues, Vo 03223, 78 rpm...................70.00
Williamson, Sonny Boy; Sunny Land, Bluebird 7500, 78 rpm.......20.00

Country and Western

Autry, Gene; Wild Cat Mama, Vi 23642, 78 rpm 75.00
Baltzell, John; Turkey in the Straw, Banner 2151, 78 rpm...............8.00
Blake, Charley; Daddy & Home, Supertone 9476, 78 rpm............10.00
Blue Ridge Highballers, Darned, Col 15132-D, 78 rpm..............10.00
Bowers, Earl; The Contented Hobo, Superior 2607, 78 rpm..........15.00
Caplinger, Warren; Chicken Reel, Vo 5222, 78 rpm 35.00
Carlisle, Clifford; Crazy Blues, Ch 16140, 78 rpm 20.00
Carson, Fiddlin' John; John Henry Blues, Okeh 7004, 78 rpm.......50.00
Carter Family, Coal Miner's Blues, Decca 5596, 78 rpm...............10.00
Dalhart, Vernon; Barbara Allen, Blk Patti 8028, 78 rpm...............80.00
Delmore Brothers, Alabama Lullaby, Bluebird 6034, 78 rpm........10.00
Farm Hands, The Old Hayloft Waltz, Para 3294, 78 rpm.............25.00
Fleming & Townsend, Ramblin' Boy, Vi 23557, 78 rpm...............30.00
Frady, Duel; Leavenworth, Vi 20930, 78 rpm 10.00
Georgia Pot Lickers, Up Jumped the Rabbit, Bru 595, 78 rpm.......15.00
Goodson, Price; Lonesome Road Blues, Gennett 6154, 78 rpm 35.00
Gregory, Bobby; Runaway Boys, Okeh 45350, 78 rpm 15.00
Hail, Ewen; Cowboy's Lament, Bru 141, 78 rpm 8.00
Hanson, William; Stop & Listen Blues, Okeh 45506, 78 rpm.......35.00
Harrell, Kelly; New River Train, Vi 20103, 78 rpm 8.00
Helton, Ernest; Royal Clog, Okeh 45010, 78 rpm.....................20.00
Hopkins, Al; Bristol Tennessee Blues, Bru 104, 78 rpm 10.00
Horton, Johnny; Happy Millionaire, Abbott 101, 78 rpm.............10.00
Irby, Jerry; Nails in My Coffin, Globe 113, 78 rpm 8.00
Johnson, Earl; Shortenin' Bread, Okeh 45112, 78 rpm................20.00
Kessinger Brothers, Dill Pickle, Bru 315, 78 rpm......................10.00
Kirby, Fred; My Heavenly Sweetheart, Bluebird 6597, 78 rpm 8.00
Landers, Lee; Lullaby Yodel, Ch 15767, 78 rpm 15.00
Leaders, Bennie; Naggin' Woman, Freedom 5029, 78 rpm.............8.00
Lone Star Cowboys, Deep Elm Blues, Vi 23846, 78 rpm.............30.00
Luther, Frank; Memphis Yodel, Broadway 8102, 78 rpm...............8.00
Macon, Uncle Dave; Diamond in the Rough, Vo 5012, 78 rpm......20.00
Mainer, JE; Great Reaping Day, Bluebird 7965, 78 rpm................8.00
McGhee, John; Hard Luck Jim, Gennett 6546, 78 rpm 15.00
Monroe Brothers, The Old Crossroad, Bluebird 6676, 78 rpm 10.00
Newman, Charlie; The Old Traveling Man, Okeh 45431, 78 rpm..10.00
Noles, Flora; Little Mohee, Okeh 45037, 78 rpm 8.00
North Carolina Ramblers, Blue Eyes, Para 3072, 78 rpm 40.00
Oakdale, Slim; Cowboy's Heaven, Crown 3503, 78 rpm..............10.00
Owens, Tom; Ocean Waves, Challenge 104, 78 rpm 8.00
Owens Brothers, Harvest Field, Vi V-40309, 78 rpm 15.00
Parker, Chubby; Uncle Ned, Ch 15393, 78 rpm..........................8.00
Peterson, Walter; Over the Waves, Superior 349, 78 rpm..............8.00

Pierce, Webb; In the Jailhouse, Pacemaker 1015, 78 rpm 10.00
Puckett, Holland; He Lives on High, Gennett 6206, 78 rpm.........15.00
Ray Brothers, Jake Leg Wobble, Vi V-40291, 78 rpm 40.00
Reed, Blind Alfred; Money Cravin' Folks, Vi V-40236, 78 rpm ...40.00
Reneau, George; Red Wing, Vo 5049, 78 rpm 10.00
Ritter, Tex; The Hills of Old Wyomin', Ch 45198, 78 rpm...........10.00
Rodgers, Jimmie; Old Love Letters, Bluebird 6198, 78 rpm..........20.00
Scottsdale String Band, Carolina Glide, Okeh 45142, 78 rpm.......12.00
Shelor Family, Big Bend Gal, Vi 20865, 78 rpm........................15.00
Stanton, Frank; Creole Girl, Superior 2521, 78 rpm 30.00
Tanner, Arthur; Two Little Children, Col 15180-D, 78 rpm.........12.00
Tew, Norwood; My Old Crippled Daddy, Bluebird 6892, 78 rpm..10.00
Thompkins, Jed; Mississippi Sawyer, Harmony 5099-H, 78 rpm.....6.00
Three Musketeers, Chattanooga Mama, Bluebird 8129, 78 rpm 8.00
Tommie & Willie, By the Old Oak Tree, Ch 16034, 78 rpm........10.00
Toomey, Welby; Little Brown Jug, Gennett 6025, 78 rpm 15.00
Tubb, Ernest; My Mother Is Lonely, Bluebird 8966, 78 rpm.........75.00
Tweedy Brothers, Dixie, Gennett 6734, 78 rpm 10.00
Walker's Corbin Ramblers, I Had a Dream, Vo 02719, 78 rpm 15.00
Washboard Wonders, Roll Your Own, Bluebird 6671, 78 rpm........8.00
Whitter, Henry; Poor Lost Boy, Vi V-40061, 78 rpm 15.00
Williams, Hank; I Wish I Had a Nickel, MGM 12244, 78 rpm.....10.00
Yellow Jackets, Medley, Gennett 7262, 78 rpm..........................12.50
Young, Jess; Lovin' Henry, Col 15431-D, 78 rpm......................15.00
Young Brothers, Are You From Dixie?, Col 15219-D, 78 rpm 12.50

Jazz, Dance Bands, Personalities

Aaronson, Irving; An Evening in June, Col 3037-D, 78 rpm........12.50
Alabama Washboard Stompers, Pepper Steak, Vo 1546, 78 rpm ..25.00
Allen, Henry Jr; Lost in My Dreams, Vo 3340, 78 rpm 8.00
Ammons, Albert; Boogie Woogie Stomp, Decca 749, 78 rpm......10.00
Badgers, It All Depends on You, Broadway 1058, 78 rpm 7.50
Blue Rhythm Band, Blue Flame, Bru 6143, 78 rpm 35.00
Bucktown Five, Mobile Blues, Gennett 5405, 78 rpm 80.00
Cantor, Eddie; Dixie Volunteers, Vo 1233, 78 rpm 15.00
Chicago Footwarmers, Ballin' the Jack, Okeh 8533, 78 rpm.........60.00
Choo Choo Jazzers, Snuggle Up a Bit, Ajex 17038, 78 rpm..........15.00
Cotton Pickers, Rampart Street Blues, Bru 4325, 78 rpm............10.00
Count Basie, Honeysuckle Rose, Decca 1141, 78 rpm 10.00
Dixie Jazz Band, Makin' Friends, Challenge 999, 78 rpm............10.00
Dorsey, Jimmy; Oodles of Noodles, Bru 6352, 78 rpm 8.00
Duerson, Herve; Avenue Strut, Gennett 7009, 78 rpm 150.00
Ellington, Duke; Misty Mornin', Okeh 8662, 78 rpm.................17.50
Fenton, Carl; Delirium, Bru 3519, 78 rpm 7.50
Galveston Serenaders, Twin Blues, Ch 15266, 78 rpm...............175.00
Gibbons, Irene; Longing, Col 14296-D, 78 rpm.........................25.00
Goldkette, Jean; Hoosier Sweetheart, Vi 20471, 78 rpm 6.00
Goodman, Benny; A Jazz Holiday, Vo 15656, 78 rpm.................150.00
Handy, Katherine; Loveless Love, Para 12011, 78 rpm................35.00
Henderson, Bertha; Jamboree Blues, Okeh 8265, 78 rpm.............60.00
Herman, Woody; I Can't Pretend, Decca 1057, 78 rpm 8.00
Hill, Alex; Southbound, Vo 1465, 78 rpm 150.00
Holiday, Billie; All of Me, Okeh 6214, 78 rpm 7.50
Hot Dogs, Carolina Shuffle, Silvertone 3572, 78 rpm................100.00
Hughes, Phil; Just a Crazy Song, Harmony 1313-H, 78 rpm.........12.50
Hunter's Serenaders, Sensational Mood, Vo 1621, 78 rpm...........175.00
Jazz-O-Harmonists, The Cat's Whiskers, Edi 51168, 78 rpm........12.50
Johnson, James P; Go Harlem, Col 2248-D, 78 rpm...................25.00
Jolson, Al; You Are Too Beautiful, Bru 6500, 78 rpm 15.00
Jungle Kings, Friars Point Shuffle, Para 12654, 78 rpm..............250.00
Katz, Al; Ace in the Hole, Vi 20081, 78 rpm............................7.50
Kirk, Andy; Casey Jones Special, Bru 4653, 78 rpm 30.00
Kruger, Jerry; The Bed Song, Variety 666, 78 rpm....................10.00

Lanin, Sam; My Pet, Perfect 14978, 78 rpm **7.50**

Lee, Julia; He's Tall & Dark & Handsome, Bru 4761, 78 rpm **80.00**

Louisiana Rhythm Kings, Swanee, Bru 4845, 78 rpm......................**15.00**

Lytell, Jimmy; Messin' Around, Pathe-Actuelle 36584, 78 rpm.....**15.00**

Mannone, Joe; Cat's Head, Col 14282-D, 78 rpm **80.00**

Markel, Mike; Lulu Belle, Bru 3189, 78 rpm **7.50**

McCoy, Clyde; Nobody's Sweetheart, Col 2808-D, 78 rpm **15.00**

Melody Sheiks, Sob Sister Sadie, Okeh 40326, 78 rpm...................**10.00**

Michall, Ernest; Sidewalk Blues, Blk Patti 8046, 78 rpm **250.00**

Miller, Glenn; I Got Rhythm, Bru 7915, 78 rpm **10.00**

Moonlight Revelers, Memphis Stomp, Gray Gull 1786, 78 rpm ...**35.00**

Morton, Fred (Jelly Roll); London Blues, Okeh 8105, 78 rpm.....**150.00**

Nappi, William; I'll Dream of You, Col 1042-D, 78 rpm **12.50**

Nelson, Ozzie; Dream Little Dream of Me, Bru 6060, 78 rpm **10.00**

Nichols, Red; Mean Dog Blues, Bru 3597, 78 rpm......................**10.00**

Old Southern Jug Band, Hatchet Head Blues, Vo 14958, 78 rpm..**100.00**

Olsen, George; Bless Your Heart, Col 2803-D, 78 rpm **10.00**

Original Dixieland Five, Tiger Rag, Vi 25524, 78 rpm..................**9.00**

Pettis, Jack; Ain't She Sweet?, Banner 1942, 78 rpm **8.00**

Pollack, Ben; Got the Jitters, Col 2870-D, 78 rpm **15.00**

Powell, Tommy; That Cat Is High, Decca 7231, 78 rpm...............**10.00**

Purvis, Jack; Down Georgia Way, Okeh 8782, 78 rpm..................**50.00**

Rich, Fred; Piccolo Pete, Banner 6508, 78 rpm **7.50**

Richardson, Inez; My June Love, Blk Swan 2023, 78 rpm............**30.00**

Robinson, Elzadie; Houston Bound, Para 12420, 78 rpm.............**125.00**

Rose, David; Jig-Saw Rhythm, Bluebird 5708, 78 rpm................**12.50**

Savoy Bearcats, Senegalese Stomp, Vi 20182, 78 rpm..................**25.00**

Selvin, Ben; Young & Healthy, Col 2731-D, 78 rpm...................**12.50**

Simms, Howard, Pensacola Joe, Harmograph 841, 78 rpm............**35.00**

Smith, Willie (The Lion); Knock Wood, Decca 1366, 78 rpm....... **9.00**

Specht, Paul; Roll Up the Carpets, Col 1186-D, 78 rpm **10.00**

Sylvester, Johnny; Indiana Butterfly, Gennett 6056, 78 rpm **12.50**

Taylor, Jasper; Stomp Time Blues, Para 12409, 78 rpm.................**300.00**

Tennessee Music Men, Loveless Love, Clarion 5446-C, 78 rpm...**25.00**

Tin Pan Paraders, Clowning, Gennett 7012, 78 rpm.....................**12.50**

Travelers, Sweet & Hot, Melotone 12113, 78 rpm........................**10.00**

University Orchestra, Lady Luck, Gennett 7042, 78 rpm **10.00**

Valentine, Syd; Asphalt Walk, Gennett 7071, 78 rpm.................**200.00**

Venuti, Joe; There's No Other Girl, Col 2535-D, 78 rpm.............**12.50**

Wade, Jimmy; Someday Sweetheart, Para 20295, 78 rpm.............**125.00**

Waldman, Herman; Cocktails for Two, Bluebird 5437, 78 rpm **7.50**

Webb, Chick; Blues in My Heart, Bru 6156, 78 rpm....................**20.00**

Williams, Clarence; Slow River, Bru 3580, 78 rpm......................**15.00**

Wolverine Orchestra, Copenhagen, Gennett 5453, 78 rpm **100.00**

Yale Collegians, You'll Do It Someday, Edi 52018........................**20.00**

Yankee Six, Jimtown Blues, Okeh 40348......................................**35.00**

Zenith Knights, Congratulations, QRS 1021................................**12.50**

Zon-O-Phone Orchestra, Noodles, Zon-O-Phone 5285.................**20.00**

Long Playing

ADC Band, Brother Luck, Cotillion, promo, M **6.00**

Adrenalin, American Heart, Rocshire **30.00**

Allen, Dave & the Arrows; Wild Angels, Tower **80.00**

Alliance, Alliance, Handshake **30.00**

Anderson, Laurie; United States Live, boxed set of 5....................**50.00**

Angel, Live w/o a Net, Casablanca **30.00**

Angel, Sinful, Casablanca **14.00**

Annette, Sings Anka, Spartan **60.00**

Apple Pie, Mother Hood, Apple Pie, Atlantic **50.00**

Astronauts, Orbit Kampus, RCA LPM-2903 ....**40.00**

Autosalvage, Autosalvage...**20.00**

Avalon, Frankie; Swinging on a Rainbow **30.00**

Avalon & Fabian, The Greatest, MCA **19.00**

Axis, Circus World, RCA **24.00**

Ayers, Roy; Center of the World, Polydor, M................................ **6.00**

Ayers, Roy; Change Up the Groove, Polydor, EX **4.00**

Ayers, Roy; Everybody Loves the Sunshine, Polydor, VG **3.00**

Ayers, Roy; Feeling Good, Polydor, EX **5.00**

Ayers, Roy; Let's Do It, Polydor, EX **4.50**

Ayers, Roy; No Stranger to Love, Polydor, M............................... **5.00**

Ayers, Roy; Step into Our Lives, Polydor, M................................ **6.00**

Ayers, Roy; Ubiquity Lifeline, Polydor, VG **5.00**

Ayers, Roy; Ubiquity Starbooty, Elektra, VG **5.00**

Ayers, Roy; You Might Be Surprised, Col, M................................ **6.00**

Ayers, Roy; You Send Me, Polydor, VG **3.00**

Badfinger, Airwaves, Elektra 6E135 ....**36.00**

Badfinger, Ass, Apple SW3411 ....**22.00**

Badfinger, Straight Up, Apple **90.00**

Band, Rock of Ages, tri-fold cover **30.00**

Bangles, Interchords, promo...**60.00**

Bar-Kays, Too Hot To Stop, Mercury, G **3.00**

Barbarians, Barbarians, Laurie **90.00**

Beatles, A Hard Day's Night, United Artists **40.00**

Beatles, Let It Be, Apple **30.00**

Beck, Jeff; Live, K&S, mc vinyl..**40.00**

Bennett, Duster; 12 DBs, Blue Horizon **30.00**

Benson, George; Collection, Warner Bros, M **9.00**

Benson, George; Give Me the Night, Warner Bros, EX **4.00**

Berry, Claudia; Sweet Dynamite, Salsoul, M **6.00**

Black Cat Bones, Barbed Wire Sandwich, Pip..............................**30.00**

Black Widow, Sacrifice, United Artists...**36.00**

Blackbyrds, Blackbyrds, Fantasy, EX **5.50**

Blackbyrds, City Life, Fantasy, EX.. **5.50**

Blackbyrds, Flying Start, Fantasy, EX.. **5.50**

Bley, Carla; Escalator Over the..., JCOA, boxed set **60.00**

Bloodrock, Bloodrock 3, Capitol...**20.00**

Bloom, Bobby; Clean Sweep, Arista, VG **3.00**

Blue, David; David Blue, Elektra...**30.00**

Blue Cheer, Oh Pleasant Hope, Philips **40.00**

Blue Cheer, Original Human Being, Philips **40.00**

Blue Cheer, Vincebus Eruptus, Philips **30.00**

Blue Magoos, Electric Comic Book, Mercury, w/book **60.00**

Blues Project, Projections, Verve **20.00**

Bohannon, Alive, Phase II, VG **3.50**

Bohannon, Summertime Groove, Mercury, VG............................ **3.50**

Bon Jovi, Slippery When Wet, picture disc **40.00**

Bond, Graham; We Put Our Magic On, Mercury.........................**20.00**

Brewer & Shipley, Down in LA, A&M, SP4154 ....**24.00**

Brick, Brick, Bang, VG **4.00**

Brothers Johnson, Blam, A&M, VG **4.00**

Brown, Bobby; The Wall I Built..., Stormy Forest **60.00**

Brown, James; Payback, Polydor, VG.. **6.00**

Browne, Jackson; Saturate **36.00**

BT Express, Do It Till You're Satisfied, Sceptor, VG **3.00**

Buckley, Tim; Sefronia, Discreet...**55.00**

Bullseye, On Target, Col **30.00**

Buman Beinz, Nobody But Me, Capitol.......................................**44.00**

Burden, Eric & War; Eric Is Here, MGM **40.00**

Bush, Stan; Stan Bush, Columbia **36.00**

Byrd, Donald; Thank You For..., Elektra, M **5.00**

Byrd, Donald; World Sounds, Colors, Elektra, SS **8.00**

Byrds, Preflyte...**50.00**

Canned Heat, Boogie w/..., Liberty LST-7541 ....**36.00**

Canned Heat, Canned Heat, Liberty LST-7526 ....**36.00**

Canned Heat, Living the Blues **50.00**

Captain Beyond, Dawn Explosion, Capricorn..............................**36.00**

Captain Beyond, Sufficiently Breathless, Capricorn.....................**36.00**

Cash, Johnny; Call Aboard the Blue, Sun 30.00
Chad & Jeremy, Before & After, Col...................................36.00
Chairman of the Board, In Session, Invictus, VG......................7.00
Chaka, Chaka, Warner Bros, VG 3.00
Channel, Channel, Epic 24.00
Chapin, Harry; Portrait Gallery, Elektra............................20.00
Checker, Chubby; Twist Party 36.00
Chi-Lites, A Lovely Man, Brun, VG 4.50
Chi-Lites, Give It Away, Brun, promo, VG 5.50
Chi-Lites, Give More Power, Brun, EX 5.00
Children, Rebirth, Atco...50.00
Chocolate Milk, Blue Jeans, RCA, EX 5.00
Chocolate Milk, Milky Way, RCA, EX 6.00
Cinderella, Night Songs, picture disk...............................20.00
Clapton, Eric; Eric Clapton, Polydor................................30.00
Clark, Michael; Free as a Breeze, Capitol 24.00
Clark, Stanley; Let Me Know, Epic, M 5.00
Commodores, In the Pocket, Motown, VG 3.50
Commodores, Machine Gun, Motown, VG.................................3.50
Confunk Shun, Spirit of Love, Mercury, VG 4.00
Confunk Shun, 7, Polygram, VG 5.00
Conley, Arthur; Soul Directions, Atco, VG 7.00
Cooke, Sam; Hits of the '50s..50.00
Cooper, Alice; Easy Action 40.00
Cooper, Alice; Pretties for You, Straight 60.00
Count Five, Psychotic Reaction, Double Shot 50.00
Country Joe & the..., Feel Like I'm Flying 60.00
Country Joe & the..., Together, Vanguard............................20.00
Cowsills, Best of the Cowsills......................................20.00
Crack the Sky, Crack the Sky Live, Lifesong, promo 70.00
Cramps, Bad Music 20.00
Crewcuts, Music a La Carte 40.00
Curtis, King; Soul Serenade, Capitol, VG 6.00
Curtis, King; Water Melon Man, Pickwick, VG 3.50
Darin, Bobby; If I Were a Carpenter 70.00
Darin, Bobby; Oh Look at Me Now 40.00
Day Blindness, Day Blindness, Studio 10.............................56.00
Dells, Always Together, Cadet, EX 5.00
Dells, Dells Vs the Dramatics, Cadet, VG 2.50
Dells, Face to Face, ABC, EX 4.50
Dells, No Way Back, Mercury, promo, EX 5.00
Dells, The Dells, Cadet, cut corner, sealed 10.50
Diamond Reo, Ruff Cuts, Picadilly 36.00
Doc Holliday, Doc Holliday, A&M.....................................24.00
Dolenz, Jones & Boyce, Dolenz, Jones & Boyce, Capitol 40.00
Doobie Brothers, Captain & Me, quadraphonic 40.00
Doors, Waiting for the Sun, gatefold................................40.00
Douglas Fir, Hard Heart Singing, quadraphonic 70.00
Dramatics, Watcha See Is Whatcha Get, Volt, VG 4.50
Dreamies, Auragraphic Entertainment, Stone Theatre.................120.00
Duke, George; Dream On, CBS, sealed 9.00
Duke, George; Dream On, CBS, VG 4.00
Duke, George; Dream On, Epic, VG 3.50
Duke, George; Guardian of the Light, Epic, M 6.00
Duke, George; Guardian of the Light, Epic, VG 5.00
Dust, Hard Attack, Kama Sutra 30.00
Dynamics, What a Shame, Black Gold, EX 8.00
Earth, Wind & Fire, I Am, ARC, VG 4.00
Earth, Wind & Fire, Raise, ARC (Col), VG 4.50
Easy Beats, Friday on My Mind, United Artists 60.00
Eden's Children, Sure Looks Real, ABC 44.00
Electric Prunes, Release or an Oath, Reprise 36.00
Electric Prunes, Underground, Reprise 50.00
Elusion, All Toys Break, Cotillion, promo, M 6.00

Everly, Phil; Living Alone, promo 40.00
Everly Brothers, Everly Brothers Sing 50.00
Everly Brothers, Hits Sounds of the Everly Brothers 50.00
Fair Warning, Fair Warning, MCA.....................................24.00
Fantasy, Fantasy, Pavillion, VG 6.00
Fat Mattress, Fat Mattress, Atco....................................14.00
Fatback, Brite Lites, Big City, Spring, VG 3.00
Fatback, Fired Up & Kicking, Spring, VG 3.00
Ferlinghetti, Lawrence; Ferlinghetti, Fantasy 56.00
Fields, Dawnrazer 20.00
Fillmore, Last Days of the Fillmore, 3 LP boxed set................100.00
Firesign Theatre, Anthology 12.00
Flack, Roberta; Roberta Flack, Atlantic, cut corner, sealed 4.50
Flakes, 1980, Magic Disk, VG 8.00
Flamin' Groovies, Sneakers, Snazz (Private), 10"...................130.00
Flint, Flint, Col...36.00
FM, Surveillance, Passport 24.00
Fortune, Fortune, MCA...30.00
Francis, Connie; At the Copa 24.00
Frankie & the Knockouts, Below the Belt 20.00
Fraternity of Man, Fraternity of Man, ABC...........................30.00
Fraternity of Man, Get It On, Dot 30.00
Freidman, Kinky; Sold American, Vanguard 20.00
Frijid Pink, Defrosted, London 40.00
Fugs, It Crawled into My..., Reprise 30.00
Funkadelic, One Nation, Warner Bros.................................22.00
Gants, Gants Again, Liberty 40.00
Gary O, Gary O, Capitol...24.00
Gary's Gang, Gangbusters, Col 6.00
Gary's Gang, Keep on Dancing, Col, promo, VG 6.00
Gates, David; Never Let Her Go, quadraphonic 30.00
Gaye, Marvin; I Want You, Tamala, EX 4.50
Gaye, Marvin; Midnight Love, Col, EX 3.50
Godmoma, Here, Elektra, sealed 8.00
Grey & Hanks, You Fooled Me, RCA, M 6.00
Griffin, The World Filled w/..., ABC...............................55.00
Groundhogs, Crosscut Hogs, United Artists 16.00
Guns & Roses, Live Like a Suicide, Uzi Suicide.....................200.00
Hammil, Peter; Modern, Roxy Club 30.00
Hancock, Herbie; Feets Don't Fail Me Now, Col, VG 5.00
Hancock, Herbie; Herbie Hancock, Col, VG 5.00
Hancock, Herbie; Lite Me Up, CBS, sealed............................8.00
Hanover, Hungry Eyes, MCA 24.00
Hardin, Tim; Tim Hardin, Verve......................................24.00
Hatchet, Molly; Molly Hatchet, picture disk, promo, CBS............60.00
Hayes, Isaac; Chocolate Chip, ABC, VG 5.00
Headpins, Turn It Loud, Atco..24.00
Heatwave, Too Hot To Handle, Epic, VG 3.50
Heavy Cruiser, Lucky Dog, Family....................................36.00
Henderson, Michael; Wide Receiver, Arista, VG 3.00
Henderson, Michael; Wide Receiver, Stang, M 8.00
Henske, Judy; Judy Henske, Elektra EKS-7231 ....90.00
Hester, Carolyn; That's My Song, Dot................................60.00
Hollies, Beat Group, Imperial LP 9312, mono 60.00
Hollies, Bus Stop, Imperial 50.00
Holman, Eddie; I Love You, ABC, VG 4.50
Hopkins, Mary; Postcard, Apple 20.00
Hour Glass, Hour Glass, Liberty.....................................40.00
Hudson, Al; Spreading Love, ABC, cut corner, VG.....................3.00
Hunter, Dreams of Ordinary..., Polydor 24.00
Huskey, Ferlin; Hits of Ferlin Huskey 16.00
Hyman, Phyllis; Phyllis Hyman, Buddha, cut corner, M 6.00
Ian, Janis; Present Company, Capitol 14.00
Idle Cure, Idle Cure, Frontline.....................................24.00

Imaginations, Imaginations, 20th Century, promo, M................ 7.00
Impressions, Greatest Hits, ABC Para, VG 10.50
Impressions, One By One, ABC Para, VG 10.00
Impressions, People Get Ready, ABC Para, VG 10.00
In Transit, In Transit, RCA 30.00
Ingram, Luther; If Loving You Is Wrong, Koko, VG 4.50
Invisible Man's Band, Invisible Man's Band, M 8.00
Jackson, Jermaine; Let's Get Serious, Motown, VG 3.00
James Gang, Miami, Atco, quadraphonic 60.00
Jamul, Jamul, Lizard 60.00
Jay & the Americans, Greatest Hits Volume 2, UA................30.00
Jay & the Americans, Wax Museum, UA................................20.00
Jones, Grace; Fame, Island, EX 6.00
Jones, Grace; Muse, Island, VG 3.00
Jones, Grace; Night Clubbing, Island, EX 6.00
Jones, Grace; Portfolio, Island, EX 6.00
Jones, Quincy; The Dude, A&M, VG....................................4.00
Joplin, Janis; Pearl..40.00
Juicy, It Takes Two, Private (CBS), sealed 7.00
Kaleidoscope, A Beacon from Mars, Epic 80.00
Kaleidoscope, Incredible, Epic, gatefold 40.00
Kaleidoscope, Side Trips, Epic...30.00
Kaleidoscope, Side Trips, Epic, promo 80.00
Kasim Sultan, Kasim Sultan, EMI 30.00
Kaukone, Jorma; Quah, RCA AYI-3747, promo 36.00
King, Evelyn, Get Loose, RCA, VG.......................................3.00
Kingston Trio, Kingston Trio, Capitol 20.00
Kinks, Great Lost Kinks, Reprise...70.00
Klique, Let's Wear It Out, MCA, VG 4.00
Kool & the Gang, Good Times, Delite, EX 5.00
Kool & the Gang, In the Heat, Delite, EX.............................3.50
Lakeside, Fantastic Voyage, Solar, VG 3.00
Lakeside, Lakeside, ABC, EX 6.00
Lakeside, Rough Riders, Solar, EX 4.50
Landslide, Two-Sided Fantasy, Capitol 50.00
Law, Breakin' It, cut corner, sealed 5.00
Led Zepplin, Led Zepplin II, promo.....................................40.00
Legs Diamond, Fire Power, Cream 24.00
Liberman, Jeffery; Jeffery Liberman, Librah 200.00
Lightfoot, Gordon; Sundown, Warner Bros, MS-2177.........30.00
Lofgren, Nils; Night After Night, promo 30.00
London, Julie; You Don't Have To Be..., Liberty..................30.00
London, Julie; Your Number Please 40.00
Look Up, Look Up, CBS 30.00
Love, Forever Changes, Elektra Gold Label 40.00
Love, Four Sails, Elektra 40.00
Love, Love, Elektra Gold Label..40.00
LTD, Togetherness, A&M, VG 3.00
Lynn, Cheryl; Cheryl Lynn, Col, VG.....................................3.50
Lynn, Cheryl; In Love, Col, promo, EX 6.00
MacLeod, Phillips; Le Partie du Cocktails, Polydor.............20.00
Madonna, You Can Dance, picture disk, promo...................140.00
Mahogany Rush, Maxroom..25.00
Mahogany Rush, Novelty..25.00
Mahogany Rush, Strange Universe 25.00
Manhattans, Manhattans, Col, promo, VG 6.00
Marillion, Script for a Jester, promo 50.00
Mayall, John; Empty Rooms, Polydor...................................10.00
Maypole, Maypole, Colossus...70.00
McClain, Alton & Destiny; More of You, Polydor, M 6.00
MC5, High Time, Atlantic 30.00
MC5, Kick Out the Jams, uncensored orig version................70.00
Melvin, Harold; Black & Blue, Phil Intl, EX 6.00
Meters, Rejuvenation, Warner Bros, VG 3.50

Midler, Bette; Live at Last, promo..30.00
Monkees, Pisces, Aquarius, mono, Colgems Com-104 ....40.00
Morgen, Morgen, Preobe, promo 90.00
Morning Dew, Morning Dew, Roulette 110.00
Morning Star, Venus, Col 39.00
Morrison, Junie; Evacuate Your Seats, Island, M 6.00
Mountain, Best of..., Windfall...40.00
Mountain, Twin Peaks, Col 20.00
Muldaur, Maria; Sweet Potatoes..12.00
Munion, Pugsley; Just Like You, J&S...................................90.00
Music Machine, Turn On, Original Sound, mono..................5.00
Musique, Keep on Jumping, Prelude, sealed 8.00
Myers, Alicia; Alicia, MCA, VG 6.00
Neighborhood Children, Neighborhood Children, Atco.............80.00
Nelson, Ricky; Ricky Sings Again 48.00
Nuggets, Original Artyfacts..., Elektra, promo 80.00
O'Jays, Identify Yourself, Phil Intl, VG..................................5.00
O'Jays, Ship Ahoy, Phil Intl, VG 5.00
O'Jays, Year 2000, taped seams, EX.......................................3.00
Ocean, Billy; Nights I Feel Like Getting..., Epic, M 6.00
Ocean, Billy; Suddenly, Arista, EX 3.50
Off Broadway, Quick Turns, Atlantic 24.00
Ohio Players, Fire, Mercury, VG 4.00
Ohio Players, Gold, Mercury, VG 3.50
Ohio Players, Greatest Hits, West Bound, VG 4.50
Ohio Players, Honey, Mercury, VG 4.00
Ohio Players, Skin Tight, Mercury, M 9.00
Ono, Yoko; Feeling Space, w/lyrics.......................................40.00
Ono, Yoko; Feeling Space, w/sticker & lyrics 40.00
Orang-Utan, Orang-Utan, Bell 60.00
Orbison, Roy; Sings Don Gibson, MGM 30.00
Orbison, Roy; There's Only One, MGM 30.00
Orion the Hunter, Orion the Hunter, Portrait 30.00
Orphan, Salute, Portrait 20.00
Other Half, Other Half, Atco..70.00
Pearls Before Swine, Beautiful Lies You..., Reprise 20.00
Pearls Before Swine, Use of Ashes 70.00
Pendergrass, Teddy; Teddy Pendergrass, Phil Intl, VG..........3.50
Phillips, Shawn; Contribution, A&M, SP4241......................28.00
Phillips, Shawn; Second Contribution, A&M 28.00
Pink Floyd, Saucerfull of Secrets, Tower..............................90.00
Pitney, Gene; Liberty Valance 20.00
Presley, Elvis; Burbank Sessions Vol 80.00
Presley, Elvis; Elvis Presley, 1st Issue 50.00
Presley, Elvis; Elvis's Gold Records 80.00
Presley, Elvis; He Walks Beside Me......................................20.00
Presley, Elvis; Legendary Performer, picture disks...............40.00
Presley, Elvis; Loving You, RCA LPM-1515...........................90.00
Presley, Elvis; Speedway, RCA LSP-3989 ....40.00
Presley, Elvis; Today, quadraphonic 90.00
Preston, Billy; Most Exciting..., Sue 50.00
Prism, Live Tonight, Ariloa, promo 50.00
Quicksilver Messenger, Happy Trails, Capitol 57120............30.00
Raspberries, Fresh, Capitol 16.00
Reynolds, Debbie; Raise a Ruckus, Metro............................20.00
Richards, Cliff; His Land 90.00
Ripperton, Minnie; Perfect Angel, CBS, VG 5.00
Ripple, Sons of the Gods, Salsoul, promo, VG 8.00
Roger, Many Faces, Warner Bros, VG....................................6.00
Ross, Diana; Diana, Motown, EX 4.50
Roy C, More Sex More Soul, Mercury, M 6.00
Ruby & the Romantics, Our Day Will Come, Kapp, VG 9.00
Rush, Hold Your Fire, promo..20.00
Rushen, Patrice; Shout It Out, Prestige, M...........................6.00

Sacred Mushroom, Sacred Mushroom, Parallex 120.00
Salem, Freddie; Cat Dance, Epic 20.00
Salsoul Orchestra, Street Sense, Salsoul, promo, EX 10.00
Seawind, Seawind, A&M, M 5.00
Seeds, Future, gatefold, GNP 40.00
Shadows of Knight, Back Door Men, Dunwich 60.00
Shadows of Knight, Gloria 70.00
Shalamar, Three for Love, Solar, EX 4.00
Shivas Headband, Take Me to the Mountain, Capitol 70.00
Shotgun, III, ABC, VG 3.50
Sigler, Bunny; Let Good Times Roll, Parkway, VG 8.00
Sigler, Bunny; My Music, Phil Intl, EX 8.00
Silk, Fuse One, CTI, EX 5.00
Silk, Silk, Prelude, cut corner, VG 6.00
Simple Minds, Reel to Reel Cacapho, Arista 50.00
Sinatra, Nancy; Boots 20.00
Sister Sledge, We Are Family, Atlantic, VG 2.50
Sly, Slick & Wicked Sly, Slick &..., Ju-Par, M 6.00
Sly & the Family Stone, Fresh, Epic, VG 3.50
Sly & the Family Stone, Life, Epic, VG 3.50
Smith, Sonny Liston; Exotic Mysteries, Chicago Sound, EX 4.00
Smith, Sonny Liston; Love Is the Answer, Col, VG 6.00
Spinners, Dancin' & Lovin', Atlantic, EX 3.00
Spinners, Labour of Love, Atlantic, M 8.00
Spolestra, Mike; State of Mind, Elektra 36.00
Spooky Tooth, The Mirror, Island 12.00
Springfield, Dusty; Brand New Me, Atlantic 20.00
Springsteen, Bruce; Born in the USA, picture disk 60.00
Springsteen, Bruce; Darkness, picture disk, promo 180.00
Spys, Spys, EMI 24.00
SRC, Milestones, Capitol 40.00
Stepson, Stepson, ABC 40.00
Stone Poneys, Stoney End, Pickwick 20.00
Stranger, Stranger, Epic 40.00
Sun, Force of Nature, Capitol, M 6.00
Sun, Let There Be Sun, Capitol, M 6.00
Sun, Sunburn, Capitol, EX 4.00
Surfaris, Hit City 65, Decca 40.00
Surrender, Surrender, Capitol 50.00
Suzy Q, Get on Up & Do It, Atlantic, M 5.00
Syeretta, One to One, Tamala, cut corner, M 6.00
T Rex, Beard of Stars, Blue Thumb 30.00
T-Connection, Pure & Natural, Capitol, EX 5.00
T-Connection, T-Connection, Dash, EX 4.00
Taylor, BE; Inner Mission, MCA 24.00
Tea Company, Have Some More Tea, Smash 60.00
Tempest, Tempest, Bronze, promo 70.00
Temptation, Reunion, Gordy, EX 5.00
Tex, Joe; Best of Joe Tex, Atlantic, VG 6.00
Tex, Joe; Hold What You Got, Atlantic, VG 5.00
Tex, Joe; I Gotcha, Dial, VG 4.00
Tex, Joe; Live & Lively, Atlantic, stereophonic, VG 5.50
Tex, Joe; Soul Country, Atlantic, stereophonic, VG 5.00
Three Dog Night, Captured Live at the..., Dunhill 12.00
Thurston, Bobby; Main Attraction, cut corner, Prelude, M 6.00
Tillotson, Johnny; Sings 40.00
Tillotson, Johnny; Tillotson Touch 30.00
Tragically Hip, Road Apples 18.00
Tripsichord Music Box, Tripsichord Music Box, Janus 150.00
Tryth & Janey, No Rest for the Wicked, Montros 150.00
Twitty, Conway; It's Only Make Believe, MGM 40.00
Twitty, Conway; You Can't Take..., MGM 30.00
Urgent, Cast the First Stone, Manhattan 24.00
Ursa Major, Ursa Major, RCA 40.00

Valentine, Hilton; All in Your Mind, Capitol 80.00
Van Wilks, Bombay Tears, Mercury 24.00
Vanilla Fudge, Beat Goes On, Atco 40.00
Vaughn, Billy; Blue Hawaii, stereophonic 24.00
Vinton, Bobby; Blue Velvet 24.00
Vinton, Bobby; Live at the Copa 20.00
Wade, Adam; Very Good Year for Girls, stereophonic, M 10.00
Walden, Narada M; Dance of Life, Atlantic, EX 4.00
Walker, Scott; Scott 3, Smash 40.00
Washington, Grover; Winelight, Elektra, G 3.00
Washington, Grover; Winelight, Elektra, promo, VG 4.00
Whispers, Whispers, Solar, EX 4.00
Wiggly Bits, Wiggly Bits, Polydor 40.00
Winchester, Jesse; Third Down, 110 To Go, Bearsville 16.00
Wireless, Positively Human, Mercury 30.00
Wonder K Frog, Out of the Frying Pan 30.00
Yes, Time & a Word 10.00
Young, Steve; Seven Bridges Road, Capitol 30.00
Yuro, Timi; Hurt 30.00
Zappa, Frank; Apostrophe 30.00
Zappa, Frank; Freakout, Verve 80.00
Zappa, Frank; Hot Rats 20.00
Zappa, Frank; Mothermania 70.00
Zephyr, Zephyr 60.00
Zombies, Odyssey & Oracle, Date 40.00
1994, Please Stand By, A&M 20.00
7th Wonder, Words Don't Say Enough, Parachute, EX 3.00
707, Megaforce, Boardwalk 30.00

45 rpm

Abdul, Paula; Way You Love Me, promo w/PS 14.00
AC/DC, Flick of the Switch, promo, no PS 12.00
AC/DC, That's the Way, promo, no PS 10.00
Aerosmith, Angel, promo w/PS 10.00
B 52s, Deep Sleep, promo w/PS 16.00
Bauhaus, Ziggy Stardust, promo w/PS 30.00
Blue Oyster Cult, In Thee, promo w/PS 14.00
Bolton, Michael; Wait on Love, promo w/PS 12.00
Cash, Johnny; Belshazah, Sun 12.00
CCR, Up Around the Bend 10.00
Charms, Bazoom, Deluxe 16.00
Cheap Trick, Ain't That a Shame, Epic 12.00
Cher, I Found Someone, promo w/PS 12.00
Cher, Skin Deep, promo w/PS 12.00
Cher, We All Sleep Alone, promo w/PS 12.00
Church, Reptile, promo w/PS 12.00
Clapton, Eric; Crossroads, Atco 8.00
Cooper, Alice; Department of Youth, promo w/PS 16.00
Crests, I Do, Co-Ed 12.00
Crosby, Stills & Nash, American Dream, promo, no PS 5.00
Crosby, Stills & Nash, American Dream, promo w/PS 8.00
De Burgh, Chris; Fatal Hesitation, promo w/PS 12.00
Deacon Blue, Dignity, promo w/PS 12.00
Deacon Blue, Real Gone, promo w/PS 12.00
Deacon Blue, When Will You, promo w/PS 12.00
Def Leppard, Bringin' On, promo w/PS 24.00
Diamond, Neil; Front Page Story, promo, no PS 5.00
Diamond, Neil; Front Page Story, promo w/PS 8.00
Earle, Steve; Six Days on the Road, promo w/PS 12.00
Earle, Steve; Sweet Little 66, promo w/PS 12.00
Estefan, Gloria; Anything for You, promo w/PS 16.00
Estefan, Gloria; Can't Stay Away From..., promo w/PS 14.00
Estefan, Gloria; Rhythm Is Gonna Get..., promo w/PS 14.00

Eurythmics, You Placed a Call, promo w/PS 12.00
Everly, Phil; Dare To Dream Again, promo w/PS 16.00
Fogerty, John; Rock & Roll Girls, promo w/PS 12.00
Frey, Glenn; Sexy Girl, promo, no PS 5.00
Frey, Glenn; Sexy Girl, promo w/PS 8.00
Garfunkle, Art; This Is the Moment, promo, no PS......................... 5.00
Garfunkle, Art; This Is the Moment, promo w/PS 8.00
Georgia Satellites, Battleship, promo w/PS..................................12.00
Georgia Satellites, Open All Night, promo w/PS 10.00
Go-Go's, We Got the Beat, promo w/PS 8.00
Guns & Roses, Patience, promo w/PS...12.00
Guns & Roses, Welcome to the Jungle, promo, no PS 12.00
Guns & Roses, Welcome to the Jungle, promo w/PS 30.00
Hall & Oates, Everything Your Heart Desires, promo, no PS 5.00
Hall & Oates, Everything Your Heart Desires, promo w/PS............ 8.00
Heart, How Can I Refuse, promo w/PS...14.00
Heart, These Dreams, promo w/PS 10.00
Henley, Don; Not Enough Love, promo, no PS 5.00
Henley, Don; Not Enough Love, promo w/PS 8.00
Houston, Whitney; Greatest Love of All, promo, no PS.................. 5.00
Houston, Whitney; Greatest Love of All, promo w/PS 8.00
Incredibles, Crying Heart, Audio Art, promo w/PS......................32.00
Iron Maiden, Flight of Icarus, promo w/PS 40.00
Jackson, Michael, This Girl Is Mine, promo w/PS......................10.00
Joel, Billy; Tell Her About It, promo, no PS................................ 8.00
John, Elton; Mama Can't Buy Your..., promo w/PS....................24.00
Lewis, Huey & News; Now Here's You..., promo, no PS 5.00
Lewis, Huey & News; Now Here's You, promo w/PS.................... 8.00
Loverboy, Heaven in My Eye, promo w/PS..................................... 5.00
Manilow, Barry; One That Got Away, promo w/PS 12.00
Manilow, Barry; When I Wanted You, promo w/PS 12.00
Marillion, Kayleigh, promo w/PS...10.00
Marx, Richard; Don't Mean Nothing, promo w/PS 12.00
Marx, Richard; Endless Summer Nights, promo w/PS 13.00
Marx, Richard; Hold on to the Night, promo w/PS.....................16.00
Marx, Richard; Satisfied, promo w/PS..17.00
Marx, Richard; Should've Known Better, promo w/PS 14.00
Mellencamp, John C; Hand To Hold on To, promo w/PS............12.00
Mellencamp, John C; Jack & Diane, promo w/PS.......................12.00
Mellencamp, John C; Lonely Ol' Night 8.00
Mellencamp, John C; Rooty Toot Toot, promo w/PS...................10.00
Mellencamp, John C; Rumble Seat, promo w/PS.........................11.00
Mellencamp, John C; Small Town, promo w/PS..........................11.00
Moore, Gary; Parisienne Walkways, promo w/PS.........................16.00
Motley Crue, All I Need, promo, no PS 10.00
Motley Crue, Too Young To Fall 12.00
New Edition, Earth Angel, promo, no PS 5.00
New Edition, Earth Angel, promo w/PS... 8.00
New Kids on the Block, Please Don't Go Girl, promo w/PS 12.00
Nugent, Ted; Bound & Gagged, promo, no PS 10.00
Oldfield, Mike; Magic Touch, promo w/PS..................................20.00
Osborne, Ozzy; Bark at the Moon, promo, no PS 10.00
Osborne, Ozzy; Bark at the Moon, promo w/PS 13.00
Osborne, Ozzy; Crazy Babies, promo w/PS...................................10.00
Poison, Every Rose, promo, no PS..10.00
Poison, I Want Action, promo w/PS 15.00
Poison, I Won't Forget You, promo w/PS......................................12.00
Poison, Your Mama, promo w/PS...10.00
Prince, Little Red Corvette, picture disk 50.00
Prince, When Doves Cry, purple vinyl w/PS 70.00
Roxette, Dressed for Success, promo w/PS....................................12.00
Slade, How Does It Feel, promo, no PS 14.00
Smile, Earth/Smile, Mercury 72977 ....100.00
Spector, Ronnie; Love on a Rooftop, promo w/PS......................12.00

Strawberry Alarm Clock, Paxton's Back Street 12.00
Sweet, Blockbusters, promo w/PS..24.00
Thin Lizzy, Showdown Vertigo, promo, no PS 24.00
Transvision Vamp, I Want Your Love, promo w/PS......................10.00
Wet Wet Wet, Angel Eyes, promo w/PS 12.00
Wet Wet Wet, Wishing I Was Lucky, promo w/PS........................12.00
Who, Behind Blue Eyes 8.00
Wonder, Stevie; Kiss Me Baby, Tamala 12.00
ZZ Top, It's Only Love, Vertigo, promo, no PS 30.00

Red Wing

The Red Red Wing Stoneware Company, founded in 1878, took its name from its location in Red Wing, Minnesota. In 1906 the name was changed to the Red Wing Union Stoneware Company after a merger with several of the other local potteries. For the most part they produced utilitarian wares such as flowerpots, crocks, and jugs. Their early 1930s catalogs offered a line of art pottery vases in colored glazes, some of which featured handles modeled after swan's necks, snakes, or female nudes. Other examples were quite simple, often with classic styling. After the addition of their dinnerware lines in the 1935, 'Stoneware' was dropped from the name, and the company became known as Red Wing Potteries, Inc. They closed in 1967. For further study we recommend *Red Wing Stoneware, An Identification and Value Guide*, and *Red Wing Collectibles* by Dan and Gail DePasquale and Larry Peterson, available at your bookstore or Collector Books.

Key:
MN — Minnesota   RW — Red Wing
NS — North Star   RWUS — Red Wing Union
                                     Stoneware

Commercial Art Ware

Ash receiver, donkey figural w/open mouth, bl 32.00
Ash tray, magnolia, #1019 ....10.00
Ash tray, red wing form, emb Indian maiden 165.00
Bowl, floral relief on gun-metal brn, lime int, 13½" 25.00
Bust, President McKinley, sgn bk..275.00
Candlestick, magnolia, wht, #1226, pr 28.00
Clock, Mammy, electric, M 125.00
Figurine, cow w/nursing calf on base, brn 455.00
Planter, glossy speckled gold, fluted, #1561, 12" L 12.00
Sewer pipe, advertising, pottery...35.00
Urn, Grecian motif, #159, 9"...45.00
Vase, cherub, Brushware, 1931, tall 75.00
Vase, elephant-head hdls, mustard gloss, 6x6" 20.00
Vase, fish figural, open mouth, bl, #879 ....38.00
Vase, HP flowers, gray, #1152 ....22.00
Vase, lt gr semi-gloss, ribbed flared top, bulb bottom, 6" 7.50
Vase, Roman scene emb, gr gloss, 2-hdl jug shape, 10" 57.50
Wall pocket, tan, Red Wing Potteries, #1004................................18.00

Cookie Jars

Bob White 65.00
Bunch of Bananas, bl..40.00
Bunch of Bananas, pk...40.00
Carousel...250.00
Crock, wht 25.00
Dutch girl, yel w/brn trim..58.00
French Baker, tan & brn, mk..65.00
Grapes...65.00

Jack Frost 300.00
Jack Frost on Pumpkin, short 395.00
King of Tarts, no mk 250.00
Monk, bl, EX 65.00
Monk, yel w/brn trim 65.00
Pineapple, yel 40.00

Dinnerware

Bob White, bowl, salad; lg 30.00
Bob White, bowl, vegetable; divided, hdls 25.00
Bob White, casserole, w/lid & stand, 4-qt 65.00
Bob White, creamer 20.00
Bob White, cup & saucer 17.50
Bob White, hors d'oeuvres bird 45.00
Bob White, pitcher, water; 60-oz. 35.00
Bob White, plate, 10" 10.00
Bob White, plate, 6½" 6.00
Bob White, platter, 13" 20.00
Bob White, server, center metal hdl 10.00
Bob White, shakers, bird form, pr 35.00
Brittany, bowl, buffet 12.50
Brittany, plate, dinner 7.50
Brittany, shakers, pr 10.00
Capistrano, bowl, divided vegetable 15.00
Capistrano, plate, dinner; 10" 10.00
Capistrano, platter, 13½" 13.00
Capistrano, platter, 15" 15.00
Driftwood, bowl, divided vegetable 12.00
Driftwood, butter dish 25.00
Driftwood, creamer 10.00
Driftwood, cup & saucer 10.00
Driftwood, nappy, 6½" 12.00
Driftwood, plate, bread & butter 5.00
Driftwood, plate, salad 7.00
Driftwood, platter, 13" 15.00
Frontenac, bowl, cereal 5.00
Frontenac, butter dish 16.00
Frontenac, creamer 7.50
Frontenac, plate, dessert 3.00
Frontenac, plate, dinner 7.50
Frontenac, plate, salad 5.00
Frontenac, saucer 2.50
Frontenac, trivet 48.00
Hearthside, plate, 10" 10.00
Hearthside, shakers, tall, pr 15.00
Lanterns, bowl, fruit; 5¼" 4.00
Lanterns, plate, bread & butter; 6½" 3.00
Lanterns, plate, 10½" 8.00
Lotus, bowl, divided vegetable 17.50
Lotus, creamer 8.00
Lotus, plate, grill 20.00
Lotus, plate, 10½" 8.00
Lotus, plate, 6" 3.50
Lotus, plate, 7½" 6.50
Lotus, platter, 13" 17.50
Lotus, relish, 3-part 17.50
Lotus, shakers, pr 18.00
Lotus, teacup 6.50
Lupine, plate, bread & butter 4.00
Lute Song, bowl, berry; 5" 6.50
Lute Song, bowl, cereal; 6¾" 7.50
Lute Song, bowl, divided vegetable 18.00
Lute Song, bowl, nappy 15.00

Lute Song, cup & saucer 8.50
Lute Song, plate, bread & butter; 6½" 6.50
Lute Song, plate, dinner; 10½" 8.50
Lute Song, platter, 13" 20.00
Lute Song, rim soup, 8¼" 15.00
Magnolia, rim soup 8.00
Morning-Glory, creamer & sugar bowl 7.50
Morning-Glory, cup & saucer 6.00
Morning-Glory, gravy boat, w/attached underplate 10.00
Morning-Glory, plate, bread & butter; 6½" 4.50
Morning-Glory, plate, 10¼" 7.50
Morning-Glory, platter, 13" 15.00
Pepe, cup & saucer 10.00
Pepe, plate, 6½" 3.00
Provincial Oomphware, bowl, 11½" 45.00
Provincial Oomphware, shakers, pr 8.00
Random Harvest, casserole, w/lid 25.00
Random Harvest, coffeepot, tall 25.00
Random Harvest, cup & saucer 8.00
Random Harvest, plate, bread & butter; 6½" 4.00
Random Harvest, plate, 10" 7.50
Random Harvest, plate, 8½" 5.00
Random Harvest, platter, 13" 12.50
Random Harvest, relish, 13¼" 15.00
Round-Up, bowl, cereal 40.00
Round-Up, cup & saucer 40.00
Round-Up, gravy boat 95.00
Round-Up, plate, 6" 16.00
Round-Up, platter, 13" 125.00

Round Up, soup/cereal, $40.00; 6" plate, $16.00.

Smart Set, beverage server 45.00
Smart Set, bowl, divided vegetable 20.00
Smart Set, gravy boat 25.00
Smart Set, plate, 7½" 7.00
Tampico, bowl, cereal 10.00
Tampico, bowl, rim soup 15.00
Tampico, cup & saucer 12.00
Tampico, plate, 10½" 10.00
Tampico, platter, 13¼" 18.00
Tampico, sugar bowl, w/lid 15.00
Tip Toe, bowl, fruit 3.00
Town & Country, shaker, lg 6.00
Two Step, creamer 3.00
Two Step, plate, 10" 6.00
Zinnia, chop plate, 12½x11" 6.00
Zinnia, plate, 10" 8.00

Stoneware

Bean pot, Boston style, Albany slip, RW, ½-gal 120.00
Bowl, bl bands on salt glaze, RW, 1930s, 12" 75.00
Bowl, red & bl sponging, paneled body, 11" 110.00
Casserole, sponge band on salt glaze, RWUS, lg 165.00
Chamber pot, Albany slip, fancy hdl, MN 165.00
Chamber pot, bl bands on salt glaze, MN 65.00
Chamber pot, bl sponging, unmk 135.00
Chamber pot, salt glaze, fancy hdl, RW 80.00
Churn, birch leaf/#10 on salt glaze, RWUS, 10-gal 465.00
Churn, dbl leaf/#8 on salt glaze, unmk, 8-gal 300.00

Churn, elephant-ear leaves and #3 in cobalt, Minnesota Stoneware Co., very rare, 3-gallon, $500.00.

Churn, leaf/#4 on salt glaze, RW, 4-gal 575.00
Churn, molded, birch leaf/#3 on salt glaze, MN, 3-gal 600.00
Churn, red wing/#10 on salt glaze, RWUS, 10-gal 465.00
Churn, red wing/#3 on salt glaze, RWUS, 3-gal 140.00
Combinette, emb lily & bl bands on salt glaze, unmk 195.00
Cooler, birch leaves/#25/Ice Water on wht, RWUS, 25-gal 220.00
Cooler, butterfly/#6 on salt glaze, RW, 5-gal 1,550.00
Cooler, daisy/#4 on salt glaze, RW, 4-gal 1,250.00
Cooler, dbl leaves/#4 on salt glaze, RW, 4-gal...................... 1,500.00
Cooler, dbl leaves/#4 on salt glaze, unmk, 4-gal........................385.00
Cooler, flower/#5/Ice Water on salt glaze, RW, 6-gal 2,800.00
Crock, birch leaves/#25 on salt glaze, unmk, 25-gal 185.00
Crock, butter; low style, Albany slip, RW, 1-lb 75.00
Crock, butter; low style, Albany slip, RW, 10-lb 65.00
Crock, butter; low style, salt glaze, RW, 10-lb 65.00
Crock, butter; tall style, bl sponging, unmk 185.00
Crock, butterfly/#6 on salt glaze, RW, 6-gal 275.00
Crock, dbl P/#4 on salt glaze, MN, 4-gal....................................275.00
Crock, drop '8'/#3 on salt glaze, RW, 3-gal 275.00
Crock, red wing/#12 on wht, RWUS, 12" 65.00
Crock, single leaf/#10 on salt glaze, M, 1-gal.............................285.00
Crock, 2 elephant-ear leaves/#6 on wht, MN, 6-gal 50.00
Crock, 4 birch leaves/#20 on wht, rare MSWCo mk, 20-gal........400.00
Crock, 4 leaves stamped on wht, HP #25, RWUS, 25-gal 150.00
Cuspidor, brn & salt glaze, MN...300.00
Cuspidor, mold seam, bl & wht sponging, unmk, lg 325.00
Cuspidor, mold seam, brn & salt glaze, unmk 95.00
Custard cup, bl to wht shaded, unmk 48.00
Flowerpot, Albany slip, MN, 7" 200.00
Hot water bottle, emb leaves, Albany slip, RWUS 200.00

Hot water bottle, emb leaves, bl on wht, RWUS 600.00
Jar, fruit; Stone Mason bl label, Pat Jan 24 1899, 1-gal...............300.00
Jar, pantry; bl bands/red wing on wht, RW, 5-lb 265.00
Jug, beehive; #5 etched on Albany slip, RW, 5-gal 575.00
Jug, beehive; birch leaves/#4 on wht, RWUS, 4-gal 275.00
Jug, beehive; red wing/#4 on wht, RWUS, 4-gal 265.00
Jug, common, Albany slip, ball top, MN, 1-gal.............................48.00
Jug, common, Albany slip, cone top, MN, 1-qt.............................68.00
Jug, common, wht, MN, 1-gal..70.00
Jug, molded seam, Albany slip, bail hdl, RW, 1-gal....................220.00
Jug, molded seam, Albany slip, bird mk/RW, 2-gal 165.00
Jug, molded seam, bl mottled, bail hdl, MN, 1-gal 585.00
Jug, molded seam, wht, bail hdl, MN, 1-gal 100.00
Jug, molded seam, wht, bail hdl, RW, ½-gal 95.00
Jug, shoulder; birch leaves/#4, standard top, MN, 4-gal 145.00
Jug, shoulder; bl bands on wht, standard top, MN, 1-qt 385.00
Jug, shoulder; brn & salt glaze, ball top, RW, 1-gal 185.00
Jug, shoulder; brn & salt glaze, cone top, RW, 2-gal 265.00
Jug, shoulder; brn & salt glaze, dome top, MN, ½-gal 120.00
Jug, shoulder; brn & salt glaze, funnel top, MN, 2-gal...............120.00
Jug, shoulder; brn & salt glaze, pear top, NS, 1-gal 145.00
Jug, shoulder; brn & salt glaze, pear top, NS, 2-gal....................335.00
Jug, shoulder; brn & salt glaze, standard top, RW, 1-gal 125.00
Jug, shoulder; red wing on wht, brn standard top, RW, 2-gal.......300.00
Jug, shoulder; wht, cone top, RW, ½-gal 90.00
Jug, shoulder; wht, standard top, MN, 1-qt.................................75.00
Jug, shoulder; wht, standard top, MN, ½-gal..............................30.00
Jug, shoulder; wht, standard top, RW, 1-qt.................................75.00
Jug, syrup; wht, cone top, pour spout, MN, ½-gal 70.00
Jug, syrup; wht, pour spout, MN, 1-gal 60.00
Jug, threshing; birch leaf/#5 on wht, hole for spigot, 5-gal 350.00
Jug, wide mouth; Albany slip, MN, ½-gal 50.00
Jug, wide mouth; wht, middle mold seam, MN, ½-gal 60.00
Pan, milk; bl, RW, 7"...120.00
Pan, milk; salt glaze, MN, 7" 65.00
Pipkin, Albany slip, unmk, 2-pt..55.00
Pipkin, Albany slip & wht, MN, ca 1900, 1-pt............................175.00
Pitcher, barrel form, Albany slip, RWUS 115.00
Pitcher, Cherryband, bl on wht, ca 1915....................................135.00
Pitcher, milk; Albany slip, Russian style, ½-gal 60.00
Pitcher, mustard; Albany slip, NS 200.00
Pitcher, mustard; salt glaze, MN, 1-qt 80.00
Pitcher, Spongeband & Saffron, RWUS, sm sz............................95.00
Spittoon, bl bands on salt glaze, German style, MN....................550.00
Spittoon, bl bands on salt glaze, MN 550.00
Spittoon, bl bands on salt glaze, unsgn RW 285.00
Spittoon, salt glaze, RW wall stamp...575.00
Umbrella stand, red & bl sponging 585.00
Wax sealer, Albany slip, NS, 1-gal...220.00
Wax sealer, Albany slip, str sides, RW, 1-qt...............................165.00

Redware

The term redware refers to a type of simple earthenware produced by the Colonists as early as the 1600s. The red clay used in its production was abundant throughout the country, and during the 18th and 19th centuries redware was made in great quantities. Intended for utilitarian purposes such as everyday tableware or use in the dairy, redware was simple in design and decoration. Glazes of various colors were used, and a liquid clay referred to as 'slip' was sometimes applied in patterns such as zigzag lines, daisies, or stars. In the following listings, EX (excellent condition) indicates only minor damage. Our advisor for this category is Barbara Rosen; she is listed in the Directory under New Jersey.

Bowl, brn-flecked, appl hdls, 2x3½", EX....95.00
Bowl, brn-sponged lt gr, tooled band, 1½x2", EX....135.00
Bowl, milk; dk brn daubs in glazed int, 12", EX....150.00
Bowl, milk; gr-amber int, worn/flaking, 3x17"....150.00
Bowl, milk; yel slip bands/waves, brn/gr glaze, 13½", EX....1,200.00
Bowl, milk; yel slip stripes/gr waves, rpr/chips, 11"....400.00
Bowl, yel slip comb decor, sieve holes, sgn/1752, rpr, 14"....1,250.00
Bowl, yel slip int w/brn-dotted bird, prof rpr/chips, 14"....2,300.00
Charger, yel slip 'tulips' on brn glaze, 11", NM....2,100.00
Charger, yel slip waves/zigzags, coggled, hairline, 12"....700.00
Charger, yel/orange slip 'feathers,' coggled, 11", NM....1,200.00
Cradle, wht slip designs/1733, tooled, EX detail, rpr, 8"....1,400.00
Cup, brn splotches, 2¾"....50.00
Cup, brn splotches on deep red color, strap hdl, 3" dia, EX....85.00
Cuspidor, brn splotches on deep red, miniature, 4" dia....175.00

Covered dish in brown glaze with 3-color slip decoration, bird and '1852' on lid, 10" diameter, $1,150.00.

Dish, yel slip 3-line X, 5½", EX....375.00
Flowerpot, gr w/wht slip, tooled, saucer base, 5", EX....200.00
Flowerpot, saucer base, mk John Bell, minor wear, 6"....300.00
Jar, brn splotches, tooled lines, ovoid, hdls, 10", VG....325.00
Jar, dk sponging, tooled line at midpoint, 5", NM....125.00
Jar, int glaze, ovoid, 1¾"....75.00
Jar, int glaze, ovoid, 7"....55.00
Jar, tooled shoulder, strap hdl, ovoid w/side spout, 6¾"....225.00
Jug, brn mottle, ribbed strap hdl, sm edge flakes, 8"....150.00
Jug, dk mottle, tooled lines, rib strap hdl, ovoid, 11½"....525.00
Jug, dk running glaze, strap hdl, ovoid, Lyndeboro, 7", EX....350.00
Lamp, grease; lt gr, appl hdl, edge chips, 3¾"....525.00
Lighting stand, dk glaze, simple tooled lip, 3½"....300.00
Loaf pan, yel slip squiggles/waves, 3½x14x17", EX....485.00
Loaf pan, yel slip stylized bird, staple rpr/chips, 13x16"....5,200.00
Mold, butter; tulip, unglazed, worn/edge chips, 4" dia....450.00
Mold, coiled fish, gr-amber, edge chips, 11x11"....225.00
Mold, Turk's head, brn sponged, swirled sides, 4x9¼"....78.00
Mold, Turk's head, dk brn, sm edge chips, mini, 5" dia....65.00
Mug, brn splotches, ovoid, appl hdl, wear/flakes, 4x5"....25.00
Mug, brn-sponged, ribbed strap hdl, sm chips, 6½"....80.00
Mug, strap hdl, 4½", EX....110.00
Pie plate, yel slip crow's ft (3), coggled, 7¾", EX....250.00
Pie plate, yel slip crow's ft (7), coggled, hairline, 9½"....400.00
Pie plate, yel slip waves (3), minor wear/hairline, 8"....275.00
Pie plate, yel slip zigzags (3), coggled, 11", VG....150.00
Pie plate, yel slip zigzags (3), coggled, 9½", NM....625.00
Pitcher, bl-gr mottle, glaze wear/chips, 10"....150.00
Pitcher, brn Albany slip, 11¾"....45.00
Pitcher, brn flecks, tooled, ribbed strap hdl, 3¼", EX....165.00
Pitcher, brn splotches, strap hdl, ovoid, 4", NM....150.00
Pitcher, brn splotches, tooling, ribbed hdl, w/lid, 6"....250.00
Pitcher, brn-splotched yel slip, ribbed hdl, wear/chips, 8"....350.00
Pitcher, gr/amber mottle, appl hdl, ovoid, 5", NM....250.00
Plate, yel slip dots (16), coggled, minor wear/hairline, 8½"....250.00
Plate, yel slip S-curves, coggled, sm rpr rim chip, 6"....400.00
Plate, yel slip 3-line crow's ft, coggled, 7¾", EX....225.00
Slip cup, int glaze, 3 holes for quills, 2¾"....575.00
Tub, gr w/brn flecks, emb band, rim hdls, 7½" dia, NM....200.00

Religious Items

Altar stick, solid brass, 3-arm, repolished, 14", pr....110.00
Chalice, gold-plated silver, filigree & wrought decor, 9½"....145.00
Chalice, gold-plated silver, simple form, unmk, 7¼"....115.00
Crucifix, cast brass, corpus separately attached, rpr, 20"....98.00
Paten, SP metal, inscribed mk ea hdl, 7" dia, NM....32.00
Santos, St Mary, cvd/pnt, tin halo, worn, 17"....285.00
Santos, St Mary w/crown, cvd/pnt, added base, 9½", VG....85.00
Santos, St Rochus, w/sm figure & dog, cvd, worn pnt, 14"....225.00

Restraints

Since the beginning of time, many things from animals to treasures have been held in bondage by hemp, bamboo, chests, chains, shackles, and other constructed devices. Many of these devices were used to hold captives who awaited further torture, as if the restraint wasn't torturous enough. The study and collecting of restraints enables one to learn much about the advancement of civilization in the country or region from which they originated. Such devices at various times in history were made of very heavy metals — so heavy that the wearer could scarcely move about. It has only been in the last sixty years that vast improvements have been made in design and construction that afford the captive some degree of comfort. Our advisor for this category is Joseph Tanner; he is listed in the Directory under Washington.

Key:

bbl — barrel	lc — lock case
d-lb — double lock button	NST — non-swing through
K — key	ST — swing through
Kd — keyed	stp — stamped

Foreign Handcuffs

Adams, teardrop lc, bbl Kd, NST, usually not stp....170.00
Australian, Saf Lock, ST, takes pin-tumbler K in side, stp....110.00
Deutsche Polizei, ST, middle hinge, folds, takes bbl-bit K....80.00
English, Chubb, NST, hi-security 10-slider lock mechanism....250.00
English, Chubb Arrest, steel, ST, multi-bit solid K....200.00
English, Latrobe, aluminum alloy, center chain, ST, dbl-bit K....80.00
French Lapegy, ST, aluminum alloys, takes flat bitted K....65.00
German, 3-lb steel set, 2⅝" thick, center chain, bbl K....150.00
German Clejuso, oval design, ST, dbl-cuff weight, 22-oz....100.00
German Clejuso, sq lc, adjusts/NST, d-lb on side, bbl K....100.00
German Darby, adjusts, well finished, sm....120.00
German Hamburg 8, non-adjust NST, center bar/post w/K-way....250.00
Hiatt, English Darby, like US CW Darby, stp Hiatt & #d....65.00
Hiatt, solid state, 2 separate cuffs joined bk to bk, stp/#d....150.00
Hiatt English non-adjust screw K Darby style, uses screw K....100.00
Hiatt Figure 8, swings open to insert/withdraw wrists....125.00
Italian, stp New Police, modern Peerless type, ST, sm bbl K....30.00
Plug 8, remove plug before inserting external threaded K....200.00

Spanish, stp Alcyon/Star, modern Peerless type, ST, flat K **65.00**
Spanish, stp Alcyon/Star, modern Peerless type, ST, sm bbl K **45.00**

Foreign Leg Shackles

German Clejuso, sq lc, adjusts/NST, d-bl on side, bbl K **125.00**
German Clejuso Darby type, adjusts/NST/plated, uses screw K ...**140.00**
Hiatt English combo manacles, handcuff/leg irons w/chain **225.00**
Hiatt English non-adjust screw K Darby style, uses screw K.........**100.00**
Hiatt Plug leg irons, same K-ing as Plug-8 cuffs, w/chain **225.00**

U.S. Handcuffs

American Munitions, modern/rnd, sm bbl Kd, ST bow, stp...........**45.00**
Bean Giant, sideways figure 8, solid center lc, dbl-bit K **400.00**
Bean Patrolman, kidney-bean form, d-lb on lc, NST, stp T **90.00**
Bean-Cobb, sm rnd lc, removable cylinder, d-lb, NST, 1899 ....**80.00**
Cavenay, looks like Marlin Daley but w/screw K, NST.................**150.00**
Civil War padlocking type, various designs w/loop for lock **135.00**
Colt, modern ST bow, sm bbl Kd, stp w/Colt & co name **100.00**
Flash Action Manacle, like Bean Giant w/ST, K-way center **200.00**
Flexibles, steel segmented bows, NST Darby type, screw K **150.00**
H&R Super, NST, shaft-hinge connector takes hollow titted K....**90.00**
Harvard, takes sm bbl K, ST, stp Harvard Lock Co **65.00**
Judd, NST, used rnd/internally triangular K, stp Mattatuck **100.00**
Lilly Hand Iron, 2" strap iron (8" L), oval bands, NST, sq K **400.00**
Marlin Daley, NST, bottle-neck form, neck stp, dbl-titted K **150.00**
Mattatuck, NST, propeller-like K-way, stp Mattatuck/etc **85.00**
Palmer, 2" steel bands, 2 K-ways (top & center), NST, stp **300.00**
Peerless, ST, takes sm bbl K, stp Mfg'ered by Peerless Co **40.00**
Peerless, ST, takes sm bbl K, stp Mfg'ered by S&W Co **75.00**
Phelps, NST, twist chain between cuffs, Tower Look-alike **200.00**
Pratt combo, 1 cuff connects w/nipper/claw, ST, mk Pratt **225.00**
Rankin, steel NST, mk screw K **200.00**
Romer, NST, takes flat K, resembles padlock, stp Romer Co **225.00**
S&W 94 Maximum Security, ST, takes Ace-type K, stp S&W **65.00**
Strauss, ST, takes lg solid bitted K, stp Strauss Eng Co **85.00**
Tower, NST, bottom K, solid/flat fitted K goes in cuff edge.........**100.00**
Tower bar cuffs, cuffs separate by 10-12" steel bar **120.00**
Tower Dbl Lock, NST, takes bbl-bitted K, usually stp Tower **50.00**
Tower Detective Pinkerton, NST, sq lc, bbl-bitted K, no stp **110.00**
Tower Single Lock, NST, bbl-bit K, K-way slanted on lc, sm **70.00**
Tower-Bean, NST, sm rnd lc, takes tiny bbl-bitted K, stp..............**70.00**
Walden 'Lady Cuff,' NST, takes sm bbl K, lightweight, stp **250.00**

U.S. Leg Shackles

American Munitions, as handcuffs..**55.00**
Civil War or prison ball & chain, padlocking or rivet type..........**225.00**
Clog spike, 30" L opening for ankle w/padlock & 2 spikes...........**500.00**
H&R Supers, as handcuffs...**300.00**
Harvard, as handcuffs **75.00**
Judd, as handcuffs **110.00**
Leg lock brace, metal brace, ankle to knee, lever locked..............**225.00**
Oregon boot, break-apart shackle on above ankle support...........**400.00**
Palmer, as handcuffs but w/detachable chain, NST......................**400.00**
Strauss, as handcuffs **90.00**
Tower, bottom K, as handcuffs **90.00**
Tower ball & chain, leg iron w/chain & 6-lb to 50-lb ball **200.00**
Tower Dbl-Lock, as handcuffs..**75.00**
Tower Detective, as handcuffs **135.00**

Various Other Restraining Devices

African slave Darby-style cuffs, heavy iron/chain, handmade.......**120.00**

African slave Darby-style leg shackles, heavy/hand forged **150.00**
African slave padlocking or riveted forged iron shackles **125.00**
Darby neck collar, rnd steel loop opens w/screw K **150.00**
English figure-8 nipper, claws open by lifting top lock tab **65.00**
Gale finger cuff, knuckle duster, non-K, mk GFC........................**125.00**
German nipper, twist hdl opens/closes cuff, stp Germany/etc **75.00**
Jay Pee, thumb cuffs, mk solid body, bbl K....................................**15.00**
Mighty-Mite, thumb cuffs, solid body, ST, mk, bbl K....................**65.00**
Tower Lyon, thumb cuffs, solid body, NST, dbl-bit center K.......**125.00**

Reverse Painting on Glass

Verre eglomise is the technique of painting on the underside of glass. Dating back to the early 1700s, this art became popular in the 19th century when German immigrants chose historical figures and beautiful women as subjects for their reverse glass paintings. Advertising mirrors of this type came into vogue at the turn of the century.

Bride, bust portrait, orig fr, 12x10" **550.00**
Equestrian w/angel & castle, faux marble fr, 17x14" **900.00**
Poetus & Arria by post, Chinese export, 1800s, 26x19" **4,500.00**

Rooster painted on oval glass (paint losses), tramp art frame, 5" diameter, $200.00.

Silhouette of man, on convex glass, 3-color, 4½" dia...................**200.00**
Vase of flowers, mc/tinsel on blk, rpt gold fr, 19x22½" **235.00**
Washington bust in oval reserve, 7-color, orig fr, 12x10" **1,400.00**

Richard

Richard, who at one time worked for Galle, made cameo art glass in France during the 1920s. His work was often multilayered and acid cut with florals and scenics in lovely colors. The ware was marked with his name in relief. Our advisor for this category is Don Williams; he is listed in the Directory under Missouri.

Cameo

Bowl, floral, dk bl on yel, boat form, 2¾x3¾" **250.00**
Goblet, boat scenic in rich bls, 8" **895.00**
Vase, floral clusters/leaves, cobalt on red, ftd, 4½" **600.00**
Vase, landscape, red on orange, baluster, 23" **2,750.00**
Vase, lg bldgs/figures/boats/mtns, blk on fire orange, 20" **3,500.00**

Vase, mtns/house/trees, red/bk bl on yel, shouldered, 10" **1,300.00**
Vase, trees/house, cut/HP, bulbous, 3½" 450.00

Ridgway

As early as 1792, the Ridgway brothers, Job and George, produced fine quality earthenwares in Shelton, Staffordshire, marking their products 'Ridgway, Smith, & Ridgway' and later 'Job & George Ridgway.' Around 1800 the brothers split and each had his own firm, both in Shelton. They were joined in the business by various members of the Ridgway family, and in fact their descendants still operate there today.

The two firms created by the split were the Bell Works and the Cauldon Pottery. Bell produced stone china and earthenware decorated with blue transfer printing. Their mark was 'J. & W. Ridgway' or 'J. & W.R.' (John and William) until 1848 when 'William Ridgway' was used. The Cauldon Pottery made earthenware, stone china, and high-quality porcelains fine enough to win them the distinction of being appointed potters to the Queen. From 1830 their wares attest to this fact, bearing the Royal Arms mark with 'J.R.' within the crest. In 1840 '& Co.' was added. Most examples of Ridgway's wares found today are transfer-printed historical scenes. See also Staffordshire, Historical; and Flow Blue.

Biscuit jar, Coaching Days, brn rattan hdl, 6½" 230.00
Bowl, Oriental, bl transfer, ftd, 5½x10" 115.00
Cup & saucer, Coaching Days...35.00
Cup & saucer, Royal Vista..20.00
Mug, Coaching Days, silver lustre trim, 2-hdl, mk, 3⅞" 40.00
Mug, Mormon Sq, Salt Lake City, 4½"....................................45.00
Pitcher, Coaching Days, silver lustre trim, 4⅛" 45.00
Pitcher, stoneware, bl w/emb band, HP flowers, 1835, 11" 160.00
Pitcher, tankard; Coaching Days, 12⅝x6⅛" 150.00
Plaque, Taking Up the Mails, yel, 12" 130.00

Plate, Pickwick, Dickens, black transfer on brown glaze, 10", $40.00.

Plate, Coaching Days, 9" 40.00
Teapot, Coaching Days, 5½" 165.00
Tray, Coaching Days, Christmas Visitor, 12½" dia 125.00
Vase, Coaching Days, 5"...65.00

Riviera

Riviera was a line of dinnerware introduced by the Homer Laughlin China Company in 1938. It was sold exclusively by the Murphy Company through their nationwide chain of dime stores. Riviera was unmarked, lightweight, and inexpensive. It was discontinued sometime prior to 1950. Colors are mauve blue, red, yellow, light green, and ivory. On rare occasions, dark blue pieces are found, but this was not a standard color. For further information we recommend *Collector's Encyclopedia of Fiesta* by Sharon and Bob Huxford, available from Collector Books.

Batter set, complete...185.00
Batter set, ivory, w/decals..135.00
Bowl, baker; 9"...16.00
Bowl, cream soup; w/liner, ivory...40.00
Bowl, fruit; 5½"... 8.00
Bowl, nappy, 9¼"...14.00
Bowl, oatmeal; 6"..16.00
Butter dish, cobalt, ¼-lb...190.00
Butter dish, colors other than cobalt & turq, ¼-lb 85.00
Butter dish, turq, ¼-lb...175.00
Butter dish, ½-lb..75.00
Casserole..65.00
Creamer.. 7.50
Cup & saucer, demi; ivory 45.00
Jug, w/lid...85.00
Pitcher, juice; mauve bl..125.00
Pitcher, juice; yel..60.00
Plate, 10"...20.00
Plate, 6".. 5.50
Plate, 7".. 7.50
Plate, 9"...12.00
Platter, cobalt, 12"..28.00
Platter, w/closed hdls, 11¼"..15.00
Platter, 11½"...12.00
Sauce boat..15.00
Saucer... 3.00
Shakers, pr...12.00
Sugar bowl, w/lid..12.00
Syrup, w/lid..85.00
Teacup... 8.50
Teapot..75.00
Tidbit, ivory, 2-tier 60.00
Tumbler, hdld...50.00
Tumbler, juice...32.00

Robj Bottles

Robj was the name of a retail store that operated in Paris for only a few years, from about 1925 to 1931. Robj solicited designs from the best French artisans of the period to produce decorative objects for the home. These objects were produced mostly in porcelain but also in glass and earthenware. The most well known are the figural bottles which were particularly popular in the United States. However, Robj also produced tea sets, perfume lamps, chess sets, ash trays, bookends, humidors, powder jars, cigarette boxes, figurines, lamps, and milk pitchers. Robj objects tend to be whimsical, and all embody the Art Deco style. Our advice for this category comes from Randall Monsen and Rod Baer; they are listed in the Directory under Virginia.

Bottle, French priest figural, blk hat stopper, 10½x4" 335.00
Bottle, Napoleon figural, blk hat stopper, 10½x4" 335.00
Cocktail shaker, golfer figural, bl & wht 1,200.00
Decanter, juice; Carmen Miranda figural.................................850.00
Inkwell, Boy Scout figural 325.00

Roblin

In the late 1800s, Alexander W. Robertson and Linna Irelan

established a pottery in San Francisco, combining parts of their respective names to coin the name Roblin. Robertson was responsible for potting and firing the ware, which often reflected his taste for classic styling. Mrs. Irelan did much of the decorating, utilizing almost every method but favoring relief modeling. Mushrooms and lizards were her favorite subjects. Vases were a large part of their production, all of which was made from native California red, buff, and white clays. The ware was well marked with the firm name or the outline of a bear. Roblin Pottery was destroyed in the earthquake of 1906.

Vase, bsk, ftd bulb body w/short neck collar, 3¼" 275.00
Vase, buff, cvd rings, 2½" 250.00
Vase, red bsk, RAPC mk, 4x3¼"..235.00
Vase, wht bsk, cylindrical w/ridges, sgn AWR, mk, 2" 135.00

Rock 'n Roll Memorabilia

Memorabilia from the early days of Rock 'n Roll recalls an era that many of us experienced firsthand; these listings are offered to demonstrate the many and various aspects of this area of collecting. Values are for mint condition examples. Some are one-of-a-kind items that have sold at specialty auctions and are included as a reference guide to demonstrate price range and rarity. Our advisor for this category is Mark Phillips; he is listed in the Directory under Texas.

Record sleeve, Elvis Presley, Jailhouse Rock, $50.00.

Autographs (on 8" x 10" photograph)

Abdul, Paula; color 35.00
Black, Clint, color..35.00
Brooks, Garth; color 50.00
Cash, Rosanne; color 25.00
Cher, color 60.00
Clapton, Eric; color..60.00
Davis, Sammy Jr..100.00
Domino, Fats; color..40.00
Gayle, Crystal 50.00
Heart (Ann & Nancy), color 50.00
Heart (Nancy Wilson), color 30.00
Liberace...125.00
Martin, Dean...60.00
Miller, Roger; color..15.00

Nelson, Willie; color 25.00
Perkins, Carl 50.00
Presley, Elvis...300.00
Preston, Billy...15.00
Reddy, Helen 10.00
Ross, Diana; color 50.00
Severinson, Doc 10.00
Sheppard, TG; color 10.00
Simon, Carley 25.00
Sinatra, Frank 100.00
Spector, Phil 125.00
Springsteen, Bruce..100.00
Stewart, Rod; color 50.00
Strait, George; color 50.00
Taylor, James 50.00
Travis, Randy; color..30.00
Tull, Jethro (Ian Anderson) 35.00
Twitty, Conway 10.00
West, Dottie...55.00
Williams, Hank Jr; color 15.00
Wilson, Brian; color 140.00
Zappa, Frank; color 65.00

Concert Posters

Bowie, David; German Sounds & Visions Tour, 1990 ....25.00
McEntire, Reba; June 23, Stockton CA, 17x20" 12.00
New Kids on the Block, Live in Germany, 1990 ....15.00
Page, Jimmy; Cleveland, Oct 19, blimp, 18x24" 15.00
Petty, Tom, broken heart, Sept 22..., 13x21"...............................20.00
Plant, Robert; Cheap Trick, NYC, July 29, 1988, 16x23" 12.00
Steppenwolf, Ohio University, Feb 20, 1971, 13x20" 25.00
Three Dog Night, Stage Shot, 1973 tour 25.00
Vaughn, Stevie Ray, Austin, 1984, 18x12".................................75.00
ZZ Top, Recycler Tour '91 ....15.00

Song Sheets

Beatles, Yes It Is 30.00
Buckinghams, Don't You Care 25.00
Canned Heat, Let's Work Together..15.00
Cryan Shames, Up on the Roof 25.00
Four Tops, If I Was a Carpenter 15.00
Grass Roots, Where Were You When I Needed You 18.00
Platters, Great Pretender 25.00
Presley, Elvis; Don't Ask Me Why 20.00
Presley, Elvis; Don't Be Cruel..25.00
Presley, Elvis; In the Ghetto 12.00
Presley, Elvis; Patch It Up 10.00
Presley, Elvis; The Girl I Never Loved...15.00
Strawberry Alarm Clock, Incense & Peppermints 30.00
Surfaris, Wipe Out, surfing scene on cover 20.00
Young Rascals, A Girl Like You 20.00
Youngbloods, Get Together 20.00

Tour Books

Beatles, US, 1964 orig, 24-pg 18.00
Bee Gees, 1989, 24-pg 5.00
Bowie, David; 1987 Glass Spider Tour, 24-pg...............................8.00
Collins, Phil; 1985 No Jacket Required, 24-pg 5.00
Deep Purple, 1972 Japan Tour..60.00
Duran Duran, 1987 Strange Behavior, 38-pg 12.00
Grand Funk Railroad, 1971 Japan Tour.......................................75.00

Lynard Skynard, 1977 tour, 24-pg 8.00
Madonna, 1990 Blond Ambitions tour, LG book 12.00
Moody Blues, 1974 Japan tour..60.00
Rolling Stones, 1975 Tour of Americas, 28-pg 18.00
Uriah Heap, 1973 Japan tour..60.00
Yes, 1987 Big Tour, 16-pg 7.00

Miscellaneous

Beatles, ticket stub, Sheah Stadium, Aug 23, 1966 ....25.00
Cooper, Alice; Marvel comic: From the Inside........................12.00
Cooper, Alice; promo banner, Hey Stoopid.............................15.00
Hendrix, Jimi; Rainbo Bridge Reel to Reel, NMIB.....................40.00
Kiss, board game, On Tour, M...50.00
Kiss, board game, On Tour, sealed 65.00
Kiss, bubble gum cards, 1st series, unopened pack 5.00
Kiss, bubble gum cards, 1st series set 30.00
Kiss, bubble gum cards, 2nd series set....................................25.00
Kiss, eraser, unused & sealed 10.00
Kiss, KISS radio, 1977, sealed..65.00
Kiss, lunch box w/thermos, M..50.00
Kiss, model van, M, unassembled 45.00
Kiss, remote-control van, 1977, w/box 125.00
Kiss, Rub in Play, 1979, sealed..50.00
Kiss, Teen Star magazine, 1978, w/2 posters 4.00
Kiss, toy guitar, 1977 ....100.00
Kiss, Viewmaster dbl-view cartridge, M 50.00
Kiss, Viewmaster reel, M 30.00
Led Zepplin, blow-up promo Zeppelin, 36x18".....................100.00
Partridge Family, lunch box w/thermos..................................50.00
Pink Floyd, hardbk book, Saucer Full of Secrets....................25.00
Presley, Elvis; jig saw puzzle, 1935-1977, NMIB 15.00
Presley, Elvis; lobby card, Clambake, 11x14".........................10.00
Presley, Elvis; lobby card, Speedway, 11x14".........................15.00
Presley, Elvis; Look magazine, August 7, 1956 ....25.00
Presley, Elvis; Look magazine, May 4, 1971 ....20.00
Presley, Elvis; Look magazine, November 13, 1956................30.00
Presley, Elvis; People magazine, January 13, 1975 .... 5.00
Presley, Elvis; Photoplay magazine, July 1957 ....25.00
Presley, Elvis; Photoplay magazine, November 1974 ....10.00
Presley, Elvis; Teddy Bear perfume, gold cap, 1957 ....25.00
Presley, Elvis; Teddy Bear perfume, wht cap, 1957 ....125.00
Presley, Elvis; Teen Screen magazine, November 1961..................15.00
Presley, Elvis; TV & Movie Screen magazine, February 1960 ....15.00
Presley, Elvis; TV & Movie Screen magazine, June 1959 ....20.00
Presley, Elvis; TV & Movie Screen magazine, March 1959 ....20.00
Presley, Elvis; TV & Movie Screen magazine, October 1958.........24.00
Rolling Stones, fan club kit 8.00
Stryper, promo banner, In God We Trust US 15.00
Zappa, Frank; Waka Jawaka Reel to Reel tape, NMIB 60.00

Rockingham

In the early part of the 19th century, American potters began to favor brown- and buff-burning clays over red because of their durability. The glaze favored by many was Rockingham, which varied from a dark brown mottle to a sponged effect sometimes called tortoise shell. It consisted in part of manganese and various metallic salts and was used by many potters until well into the 20th century. Over the past two years, demand and prices have risen sharply, especially in the east. See also Bennington.

Bank, man clutching pitcher, inscribed on bk, rpr, 4½" 170.00
Bowl, leaves emb, JE Jeffords & Co, Phila, 3x12", EX................250.00
Bowl, 5¾x13", NM..175.00
Dog, seated, Staffordshire style, 10" 375.00
Flask, book form, sm chips, 7" 300.00
Flask, morning-glories emb, ovoid, rpr, 7½"...........................85.00
Flask, shoe form, lip chips, 6½"...100.00
Foot warmer, cylindrical, 13" L..350.00
Inkwell, shoe form, rpr, 3" L, EX..125.00
Lion, recumbent on oval base, 15" L, NM..............................950.00
Lion on rectangular base, sm chips, 9½" L...............................750.00
Mug, 3¾"..100.00
Pie plate, 11"...135.00
Pitcher, arched panels & foliage, 8" 195.00
Pitcher, berries, 8½" 150.00
Pitcher, hanging game, 10", EX..225.00
Pitcher, hanging game, hound hdl, 7½"..................................300.00
Pitcher, hanging game, hound hdl, 9"....................................350.00
Pitcher, hunt scene, 9"...145.00
Pitcher, hunt scene/grapes, hound hdl, Am Pottery, 10", EX .. 1,100.00
Pitcher, hunt scene/grapes, hound hdl, eagle mk, 11", NM 1,700.00
Pitcher, hunt scene/grapes, hound hdl, HB Caire, 10", EX 750.00
Pitcher, medallion portraits, To Mrs John Webb, 10"................225.00
Pitcher, squat, minor hairlines, 3½" 45.00
Pitcher, toby barmaid, rpr arm, 7¾" 65.00
Soap dish, oblong, sm rim chips, 5" 70.00
Sugar bowl, ogee sides, conical lid, 5⅞" 285.00
Teapot, women at table emb, lid: eagle/Am flag, 5½", EX 175.00

Rockwell, Norman

Norman Rockwell began his career in 1911 at the age of seventeen doing illustrations for a children's book entitled *Tell Me Why Stories*. Within a few years he had produced the *Saturday Evening Post* cover that made him one of America's most-beloved artists. Though not well accepted by the professional critics of his day who didn't consider his work to be art but 'merely' commercial illustration, Rockwell's popularity grew to the extent that today there is an overwhelming abundance of examples of his work or pieces related to the theme of one of his illustrations.

Ad, Country Gentleman, Jell-O, 1922......................................10.00
Bell, Garden Girl 38.00
Bell, Looking Out to Sea 90.00
Bell, School Play 70.00
Figurine, Boy Meets His Dog, Gorham................................ 1,500.00
Figurine, Checking Good Deeds, Christmas miniature, Gorham...22.00
Figurine, Fishing Hole, Franklin Mint 170.00
Figurine, Gaily Sharing Vintage Times, Gorham 1,200.00
Figurine, Marbles Champion 95.00
Figurine, Marriage License 380.00
Figurine, Nurse, Franklin Mint 180.00
Figurine, Stilt Walker, Franklin Mint 170.00
Figurine, Tiny Tim 70.00
Figurine, Triple Self Portrait 180.00
Ingot, Favorite Moments Series, Innocents Abroad, sterling.......380.00
Lithograph, Family Tree, artist proof, sgn, 25½x23" 800.00
Lithograph, Jester, #119, sgn, 21x17" 1,200.00
Lithograph, Top Hat & Tails, #63, sgn, 34x28" 1,700.00
Lithograph, Weighing In, #14/100, sgn, 23½x13" 700.00
Magazine, Saturday Evening Post, May 30, 1936, EX 26.00
Magazine cover, Sat Evening Post, Bob Hope, Feb 3, 1954............15.00
Toby mug, Catching the Big One 40.00

Rogers, John

John Rogers (1829-1904) was a machinist from Manchester, New Hampshire, who turned his hobby of sculpting into a financially successful venture. From the originals he meticulously fashioned of red clay, he had bronze master molds made from which plaster copies were cast. He specialized in five different categories: theatrical, Shakespeare, Civil War, everyday life, and horses. His large detailed groupings portrayed the life and times of the period between 1859 and 1892. When no condition is indicated, examples are assumed to be in very good to excellent condition. Our advisor for this category is George Humphrey; he is listed in the Directory under Maryland.

Balcony	1,500.00
Bath	2,000.00
Bubbles	2,000.00
Bushwacker	2,000.00
Charity Patient	650.00
Checkers Players, sm	1,500.00
Chess	825.00
Coming to the Parson, Pat Aug 9, 1870, 21"	425.00
Country Post Office	750.00
Courtship in Sleepy Hollow, Pat date	825.00
Fairy's Whisper, ca 1881	1,400.00
Faust & Marguerite, Leaving the Garden	450.00
Fetching the Doctor	750.00
Fighting Bob, ca 1889	1,100.00
First Ride	725.00
Football, inscribed, 16x11"	1,000.00
Frolic at the Ol' Homestead, 1887, 22½"	800.00
Going for the Cows	450.00
Hide & Seek	2,000.00
Home Guard	800.00
Madam Your Mother Craves a Word	700.00
Mail Day	2,000.00

Matter of Opinion, 21½" x 17", $600.00.

Neighboring Pews	475.00
One More Shot	550.00
Parting Promise	475.00
Peddler at the Fair	825.00
Picket Guard	750.00
Playing Doctor	700.00
Politics	700.00
Referee	600.00
Rip Van Winkle at Home, 18½"	425.00

Rip Van Winkle on the Mountain, Pat July 25, 1871, 21"	450.00
Rip Van Winkle Returned	550.00
School Days	600.00
Slave Auction	2,000.00
Speak for Yourself John	600.00
Taking the Oath & Drawing Rations, sgn, 23"	525.00
Tap on the Window	525.00
Traveling Magician, ca 1877	750.00
Village Schoolmaster	850.00
Washington	1,250.00
Watch for the Santa Maria	700.00
Weighing the Baby, Pat 1875, 21"	600.00
Wounded Scout, ca 1864	750.00
Wrestler	1,250.00

Rookwood

The Rookwood Pottery Company was established in 1879 in Cincinnati, Ohio. Its founder was Maria Longworth Nichols Storer, daughter of a wealthy family who provided the backing necessary to make such an enterprise possible. Mrs. Storer hired competent ceramic workers who through constant experimentation developed many lines of superior art pottery. While in her employ, Laura Fry invented the airbrush-blending process for which she was issued a patent in 1884. From this, several lines were designed that utilized blended backgrounds. One of their earlier lines, Standard, was a brown ware decorated with underglaze slip-painted nature studies, animals, portraits, etc. Iris and Sea Green were introduced in 1894 and Vellum, a transparent mat-glaze line, in 1904. Other lines followed: Ombroso in 1910 and Soft Porcelain in 1915. Many of the early artware lines were signed by the artist. Soon after the turn of the twentieth century, Rookwood manufactured 'production' pieces that relied mainly on molded designs and forms rather than freehand decoration for their esthetic appeal. The Depression brought on financial difficulties from which the pottery never recovered. Though it continued to operate, the quality of the ware deteriorated, and the pottery was forced to close in 1967.

Unmarked Rookwood is only rarely encountered. Many marks may be found, but the most familiar is the reverse 'RP' monogram. First used in 1886, a flame point was added above it for each succeeding year until 1900. After that a Roman numeral added below indicated the year of manufacture. Impressed letters that related to the type of clay utilized for the body were also used — G for ginger, O for olive, R for red, S for sage green, W for white, and Y for yellow. Artware must be judged on an individual basis. Quality of the artwork is a prime factor to consider. Portraits, animals, and birds are worth more than florals; and pieces signed by a particularly renowned artist are highly prized. Our advice for this category comes from Fer-Duc, Inc., whose address is listed in the Directory under New York.

Bisque

Coffeepot, spiders/trees, manner of ML Nichols, 1883, 11"	2,000.00
Ewer, floral, butterfly hdl, AB Sprague, #461, 1889, 4"	375.00
Ewer, floral, wht on bl w/gold, HE Wilcox, #101C, 1887, 9"	300.00
Ewer, mums, Albert Valentien, 1884, 8"	950.00
Jar, lg mums in heavy slip on bl to peach, sgn, 1888, 5"	800.00
Jardiniere, magnolia on wht, Albert Valentien, 1886, 16"	2,400.00
Pitcher, floral/gilt, sage clay, AM Bookprinter, 1887, 9"	400.00
Pitcher, roses/gold on peach to gr, AM Valentien, 1888, 9"	1,300.00
Vase, grasses/sm bird, Anna Bookprinter, #288C, 10½"	1,050.00
Vase, wild roses on lt peach, EX art, unsgn, 1888, 8x7"	900.00

Cameo

Bowl, floral on peach to cream, AM Valentien, fluted, 5"	190.00

Bowl, hollyhocks, pointed/shaped rim, W7/#228, 1887, 3x13"....**300.00**
Coffeepot, floral, no mks, 8" **300.00**
Coffeepot, roses, wht on dk peach, G Young, 1889, 9" **425.00**
Dresser set: pitcher/bowl/waste jar, MA Daly, 1888................ **2,600.00**
Plate, floral, wht on pk to bl, AB Sprague, sqd, 9" **210.00**
Plate, floral on peach, S Toohey, swirl rim, 1887, 9" **210.00**
Plate, grasses/sm bird, Albert Valentien, 1886, 8", NM **375.00**
Plate, roses, H Wilcox, 1890, 8½"..**475.00**
Plate, shepherdess/moon, EP Cranch, 1889, rpr edge, 8" **170.00**
Tray, apple blossoms, S Toohey, scalloped, 1886, 11" L...............**325.00**
Vase, extensive floral, AM Valentien, hdls, 5½x6" **475.00**

Iris

Stein, Geo WA portrait, bk: 1776, McDonald, 1896, 9", NM.. **3,250.00**
Vase, floral, EX art, C Schmidt, 1908, rpr drill hole, 13"......... **3,250.00**
Vase, floral, L Van Briggle, #919E, 1904, 4" **600.00**
Vase, floral, wht on pk to gray to bl, M Nourse, 1904, 6" **400.00**
Vase, landscape band on yel & rust, Shirayamadani, '11, 7" ... **1,800.00**
Vase, lily of the valley on gr to pk, C Schmidt, 1910, 10" **2,800.00**
Vase, peacock feathers on dk bl, Chas Schmidt, 1911, 6" **3,600.00**
Vase, poppies, EX art/color, C Schmidt, drilled/rstr, 13" **3,250.00**
Vase, poppies, wht on gray, Rothenbusch, 1903, 8" **1,200.00**
Vase, poppies (lg/plush), Laura Lindeman, #909, 1904, 8½" .. **1,900.00**
Vase, poppies at neck, wht on mocha, Rothenbusch, 1903, 8".. **1,100.00**
Vase, poppies on ivory/gr/chocolate, Rothenbusch, 1903, 8".. **1,700.00**
Vase, scenic w/lg trees, EX art, E Diers, 1917, 10", M............ **3,250.00**
Vase, thistles, EX art, L Asbury, ovoid, #925C, 1906, 10" **2,300.00**
Vase, tulips, EX art, Bishop, bulbous, #916C, 1904, 7", M **2,300.00**
Vase, violets on beige to cobalt, Rothenbusch, 1904, 6" **1,500.00**

Jewel Porcelain

Vase, fish, wht on butterfat texture, Jens Jenson, 1934, 5"...........**325.00**
Vase, floral, bubbled gr/bl/wine, Shirayamadani, 1929, 10"..... **2,500.00**
Vase, floral, pk/rust on bl butterfat, ET Hurley, 1926, 7" **660.00**
Vase, peacock feathers on cream, Sara Sax, 1917, 7" **875.00**

Limoges

Chocolate pot, frogs/spiders on brn, ML Nichols, 1882, 12" ... **1,200.00**
Jar, tea; grasses/birds, bulbous, M Rettig, 1882, 5"......................**650.00**
Jug, bird/clouds/grasses on turq to gr, AR Valentien, 8" **1,000.00**
Jug, honey; grass/butterfly on gr to turq, AR Valentien, 5" **350.00**
Jug, perfume; cherry blossoms, unknown artist, 1883, 4½"...........**325.00**
Jug, perfume; grasses/butterfly, Hattie Horton, 1882, 5"...............**800.00**
Pitcher, daisies, wht/peach on dk gray, AR Valentien, 8"..............**800.00**
Plate, fish in wht notched reserve on gr, NL Nichols, 1880 .... **3,500.00**
Vase, grasses/birds, pinched sides, Rettig, 1883, 9".....................**850.00**

Mat

Ash tray, lt gr, nude at edge, AM Valentien, 1901, 6" **1,200.00**
Inkwell, Arts & Crafts design, yel/brn w/bl, #2016, 1912 ....**270.00**
Mug, cylindrical form of an owl, gr w/rose, 1905, 5½"..................**200.00**
Vase, cvd Arts & Crafts decor at top, LN Lincoln, 7½".................**260.00**
Vase, cvd decor at top, CA Duell, 3-hdl, #830E, 1909, 5" **300.00**
Vase, cvd grapevines, brn/gr/bl on brn, A Pons, '07, 12" **1,700.00**
Vase, cvd peacock feathers on gr w/brn, #2432, 1921, 9"..............**290.00**
Vase, cvd petals/lines on bulbous base, brn, 1915, 12½" **350.00**
Vase, cvd rnd flowers/leaves, lt/dk gr, E Lincoln, 1918, 7"...........**375.00**
Vase, cvd/rtcl leaf/flower base cup, Shirayamadani, 15", EX ... **2,600.00**
Vase, floral emb on dk brn, wide shoulder/sm ft, 1914, 5x7"........**140.00**
Vase, fruit emb on bl, ovoid, #2122, 1925, 4½" **75.00**

Vase, Grueby-like upright leaves on lt gr, WP McDonald, 12" **900.00**
Vase, leaves/flowers emb on gr, #2108, 1928, 6½" **70.00**
Vase, mistletoe, cvd/rtcl, JD Wareham, 1902, 5" **2,600.00**
Vase, nude male sits aside rim, AM Valentien, 1901, 6" **1,500.00**
Vase, peacock feather emb, pk/yel, #1385, 1913, 5"......................**220.00**
Vase, poppies, red on lt gr, Harriet Wilcox, 1905, 10"............. **2,800.00**
Vase, poppies emb on rose to gr, Shirayamadani, 1928, 12" **500.00**
Vase, poppies form rim, red/gr, Shirayamadani, 1913, 10"....... **1,100.00**
Vase, wide emb shoulder band, yel, #2858, 1925, 9"....................**220.00**
Vase, 2 sculptured nudes at rim, AM Valentien, 1901, 6" **3,250.00**

Porcelain

Bowl, floral band, bl on mauve, incurvate, Rothenbusch, 7" **400.00**
Bowl vase, mum border, bl on wht, pk int, A Conant, 4¾" **1,400.00**
Ginger jar, birds/butterflies on gr, ET Hurley, 1924, 15" **2,600.00**
Vase, floral, mc on yel to lime, L Epply, #389, 1925, 4x6"....... **1,300.00**
Vase, pendant flowers on lav to cream, S Sax, 1930, 19" **2,300.00**
Vase, pk-tan gloss, #1944, 1915, 6½".......................................**350.00**
Vase, poppies, cvd/pnt, blk/red on brn bsk, S Sax, 1921, 9" **4,250.00**
Vase, wht 'clouds' on blk bsq, L Holtkamp, 1952, 6" **225.00**

Sea Green

Vase, daffodils, S Coyne, #927C, 1901, 7" **875.00**
Vase, elk in woodland, MA Daly, 1894, 7" **3,100.00**
Vase, lg egret, ET Hurley, 1901, 8½".................................... **6,750.00**
Vase, pansies, caramel on moss, CA Baker, 1903, 8½x4" **1,500.00**
Vase, silver band w/lg emb bird at top, MA Daly, 1900, 4" **1,850.00**
Vase, 3 goldfish/seaweed, ET Hurley, 1906, 4" **2,450.00**
Vase, 3 lg ducks, MA Daly, 1901, wide body, 10", M **9,500.00**

Standard

Basket, floral, AM Bookprinter, 1886, 4" **425.00**
Box, dragon, red clay body, Ed Abel, 1893, 3x6" dia, VG............**375.00**
Chamberstick, berries, M Fogelson, integral hdl, 1897, 3x6".......**250.00**
Creamer & underplate, clover, Harriet Wilcox, 1899, 4" **400.00**

Standard glaze ewer with silver overlay over clover, Edward Abel, 1890, 10", $2,800.00.

Ewer, floral, EX art, CA Baker, dimpled, #719B, 1894, 10" **650.00**
Ewer, leaves/berries, CJ Dibowski, #462D, 1893, 7" **350.00**
Ewer, rose branches on yel-gr, AR Valentien, 1886, 15½"...........**850.00**
Jug, corn, sgn JES, pointed stopper, #733C, 1900, 9" **425.00**
Jug, grapes, H Wilcox, 1887, 7"..**750.00**
Jug, Indian Wht Swan, Crow; Edward Hurley, 1900, 7½" **2,200.00**

Loving cup, silver o/l hdls etc, 5 satyrs, Horsfall, 8" **15,500.00**
Mug, Curly, Gen Custer's Scout; S Markland, 1897, 5¾" **1,600.00**
Mug, Indian Spotted Jack Rabbit Crow, E Brain, 1899, 3-hdl. **2,000.00**
Mug, lion's head, ET Hurley, #587C, 1900, 4¾" **800.00**
Mug, portrait of Blk girl, H Strafer, 1897, 5½" **2,500.00**
Mug, Rembrandt, Wm P McDonald, 1894, 5¾" **800.00**
Mug, Thos Jefferson, MA Daly, 1896, 9½" **7,000.00**
Vase, berries, EX art, ET Hurley, #803B, 1901, 12" **600.00**
Vase, bird flies over water, Shirayamadani, #762C, 1898, 6"... **3,600.00**
Vase, Brave in War Dress, Kiowa; AD Sehon, 1901, 8" **3,000.00**
Vase, cherries, JD Wareham, wide body, 1893, 4x5" **325.00**
Vase, columbine, AB Sprague, trumpet form, 1894, 10½" **700.00**
Vase, Conquering Bear, Sioux; A Drake Sehon, 1901, 9" **5,100.00**
Vase, daffodils, CA Baker, trumpet neck, #556B, 1900, 13" **650.00**
Vase, floral, M Nourse, wide body w/hdls, #518E, 1900, 9" **375.00**
Vase, fruit, LE Handscom, #927E, 1903, 7" **425.00**
Vase, High Hawk Jr, Sioux; F Sturgis Lawrence, bulbous, 9"... **4,000.00**
Vase, Indian, 4 Bull Assiniboines, #787C, 1988, 11½" **4,500.00**
Vase, iris, S Coyne, ovoid w/hdls, inscribed Xmas 1894, 9" **770.00**
Vase, lg irises, MA Daly, 1902, 13x7" **1,700.00**
Vase, olive branches, AB Sprague, #657, 1892, 7" **350.00**
Vase, Pablino Diaz (Kiowa, standing), G Young, 1901, 14" ...**16,500.00**
Vase, Rocky Bear, Sioux; w/horse, G Young, 1900, 10"........... **7,000.00**
Vase, roses, Matt Daly, cylindrical, 1902, 11½" **1,100.00**
Vase, seashells, OG Reed, sm mouth/wide base, 1894, 3", NM ...**325.00**
Vase, yel roses, AB Sprague, #735DD, 1896, 7½" **300.00**
Vase, 3 Fingers, Cheyenne; E Hurley, 1899, 9" **2,300.00**

Vellum

**Floral Vellum vase, Ed Diers, 1908, 7½",
$1,400.00; Wax Matt vase with bird on flower-
ing branch, E.T. Hurley, 1933, 6", $,1800.00.**

Jar, potpourri; dandelions on lt gr, rtcl lid, 1907, 5" **375.00**
Jar, sailboats in harbor, w/lid, C Schmidt, 1922, 8" **3,400.00**
Plaque, Along the Upper OH, CT McLaughlin, 1914, 6x8" .. **2,300.00**
Plaque, Banks of River, F Rothenbusch, orig fr, 5x7½" **1,800.00**
Plaque, forest scene, Ed Diers, crazed, 11x9" **1,600.00**
Plaque, forest/stream, dk bls/earth tones, Ed Diers, 9x11" **2,800.00**
Plaque, Inlet, ET Hurley, 8x5"... **1,400.00**
Plaque, mtn range/lake/grove of trees, ET Hurley, 8x6" **1,600.00**
Plaque, Olympics..., mtn scene, S Sax, 1913, 6x8" **2,000.00**
Plaque, On the Ohio River, Ed Diers, w/label, 6x8" **2,400.00**
Plaque, Quiet Stream, mtns/flat land/trees, Denzler, 8x11" **1,500.00**

Plaque, river/mtns/trees, L Epply, 1924, 5x8", M **1,000.00**
Plaque, riverbank/trees, Ed Diers, 1913, 8x6" **1,700.00**
Plaque, sailboats/Venetian harbor, C Schmidt, 1925, 12x10" . **9,000.00**
Vase, autumnal riverbank, Ed Diers, slender form, 1921, 9" **1,500.00**
Vase, berries at top, EX art, L Asbury, 1929, 9", M **1,000.00**
Vase, blossoms, gr leaves/shoulder, Shirayamadani, 1904, 6" **900.00**
Vase, carnations, Ed Diers, pear form, 1908, 8½" **900.00**
Vase, dogwood, pk/yel on lt pk, SE Coyne, #1045, 1904, 6" **400.00**
Vase, floral shoulder band, Ed Diers, lt crazing, 8¾" **425.00**
Vase, grasses/swallows, bulbous bottom, ET Hurley, 1908, 9"...**650.00**
Vase, pk dogwood, cream w/bl lower body, Asbury, 1910, 9" .. **1,500.00**
Vase, poppies on pk to ivory to lt gr, LN Lincoln, 1910, 7" **700.00**
Vase, road/trees/pond, EX color, F Rothenbusch, 1921, 9" **1,000.00**
Vase, rocky waterfall/trees, Ed Diers, 1919, 11", Xd/M **1,200.00**
Vase, roses, EX art/color, Ed Diers, bulbous, 1927, 6" **650.00**
Vase, roses, pk on yel to wht to gray, C Schmidt, 1913, 9" **1,400.00**
Vase, scenic, S Coyne, 1922, 5¾" **650.00**
Vase, winter forest in bl/gray, Ed Diers, ovoid, 1915, 9" **2,200.00**

Wax Mat

Vase, crocus, EX art, MH McDonald, #6206F, 1931, 5" **600.00**
Vase, floral, bl/gr on lt lav & pk, K Jones, 1927, 6½" **300.00**
Vase, floral, blk-lined red & gr on yel & gr, CS Todd, 10" **500.00**
Vase, floral, EX art, Shirayamadani, #660, 1936, 7" **850.00**
Vase, floral, red/brn on orange, E Lincoln, #551, 1925, 7" **375.00**
Vase, indistinct floral, red/gr/yel, E Lincoln, hdls, 9" **250.00**
Vase, iris, gold on bl to cream, Shirayamadani, 1934, 6" **1,500.00**
Vase, leaves/berries, EX art, LN Lincoln, bulbous, 1930, 7".........**750.00**
Vase, stylized poppies on gr to bl, OG Reed, 1904, 11" **1,650.00**

Miscellaneous

Bookends, 1922, rook among branches, charcoal, #2275, 5x5"....**200.00**
Bookends, 1927, bouquet of flowers, twist hdl, pk/gr, 6x7" **240.00**
Bowl, 1926, wht mat w/bl gloss lining, petal top, #2886, 6" **55.00**
Bust, 1936, maid, hair framing face, wht mat, #2026, 8" **225.00**
Dish, 1887, Uncle Remus illus, gilt edge, 1887, 6½" **400.00**
Figurine, 1920, rook, gr mat, #1623, 3x4" **190.00**
Jar, 1919, gr/bl butterfat glaze, w/lid, #2301E, 9½", pr.................**500.00**
Mug, 1948, w/eagle logo, pewter lid, G Weidemann Brewing......**375.00**
Ramekin, 1892, floral, wht on peach to rust, G Young, 7" L........**190.00**
Sign, 1924, scrolls ea side, Rookwood/Cincinnati, dtd, 13"..... **1,200.00**
Stein, 1881, 2 men fishing, bl on cream, C Chipman, 12"...........**750.00**
Stein, 1882, dogwood, wht on cobalt, ETK, 1882, 9½"...............**550.00**
Tankard, 1881, fisherman, bl on bsk, tan bands, Newton, 11" . **1,700.00**
Trivet, 1921, windmill, 4-color squeeze-bag, 5½" sq **175.00**
Trivet, 1930, crocus, pk/gr on wht mat, #1631, 6" sq **110.00**
Trivet, 1930, parrot/exotic foliage, pastels, 5½" sq **275.00**
Vase, 1884, neck bands w/medallions, gr/brn gloss, #80B, 7" **240.00**
Vase, 1918, bamboo emb on lt bl vellum, #1895, 6" **100.00**
Vase, 1927, bl mat, beaded top/base, sq, #2762, 4" **80.00**
Vase, 1927, high-glaze w/flower band, L Epply, #2969, 7" **675.00**
Vase, 1928, wht mat, high loop hdls, #6005F, 7"............................**75.00**
Vase, 1933, animals, bl on tan/brn, J Jensen, ped ft, 6" **750.00**
Vase, 1948, leaves emb on gr gloss, #6510, 5" **70.00**
Vase, 1950, water lilies emb on deep caramel gloss, 6½" **70.00**
Vase, 1952, floral emb on dk gr gloss, #6870, 11½" **180.00**

Rorstrand

The Rorstrand Pottery was established in Sweden in 1726 and is
today Sweden's oldest existing pottery. The earliest ware, now mostly

displayed in Swedish museums, was much like old Delft. Later types were hard-paste porcelains that were enameled and decorated in a peasant style. Contemporary pieces are often described as Swedish Modern. Rorstrand is also famous for their Christmas plates.

Beaker, figural sculpted flowers, pk/gray, sgn, 4½" 320.00
Coffeepot, floral sprays emb, lav/gr, 1900s, 9" 500.00
Vase, floral, purple on cream, rose-bowl form, mk, 7" dia 145.00
Vase, leaf/berry clusters at shoulder on bl/wht streaks, 3x5½" 250.00
Vase, turq w/lav & yel specks, elongated ovoid, sgn CHS, 21" 500.00

Rose Mandarin

Similar in design to Rose Medallion, this Chinese Export porcelain features the pattern of a robed mandarin, often separated by florals, ladies, genre scenes, or butterflies in polychrome enamels, often having gold trim. Elaborate in decoration, this pattern was popular from the late 1700s until the early 1840s.

Bowl, cut corners, acorn finial, 9" L, EX 1,200.00
Bowl, figural panels, 4-lobed, deep, 9½" 935.00
Dish, rtcl borders, oval, ca 1830, minor wear, 8x9½", pr 1,500.00
Garden seat, late 1800s, chips/wear, 19", pr 4,750.00
Lamp, kerosene; porc cylinder w/brass base & fixture, 12" 600.00

Hot water platter with cover, ca 1840s, 14", EX, $2,400.00.

Platter, fruit; lg figures, ftd/shaped rim, 16x13" 3,100.00
Platter, 1840s, rstr rim chip, 12" 400.00
Punch bowl, courtyard/floral, Rose Canton rim, lt wear, 12" .. 1,400.00
Punch bowl, scenes w/in & w/out, 1830, wear, 21" 4,250.00
Punch bowl, scenes w/in & w/out, 1840s, gilt wear, 11" 1,000.00
Punch bowl, scenes w/in & w/out, 1840s, rim chips, 13" 1,300.00
Shrimp dish, shaped w/rim extended on 1 side, 1830, 11" W 700.00
Vase, figures/inscriptions, bulbous middle, 1840s, 12", EX...........600.00

Rose Medallion

Rose Medallion is one of the patterns of Chinese export porcelain produced from before 1850 until the second decade of the 20th century. It is decorated in rose colors with panels of florals, birds, and butterflies that form reserves containing Chinese figures. Pre-1850s ware is unmarked and is characterized by quality workmanship and gold trim.

From about 1850 until circa 1860, the kilns in Canton did not operate, and no Rose Medallion was made. Post-1860 examples (still unmarked) can often be recognized by the poor quality of the gold trim or its absence. In the 1890s the ware was often marked 'China'; 'Made in China' was used from 1910 through the 1930s.

Bowl, orange-peel texture, 9x24", +tall wooden stand............. 5,400.00
Bowl, rtcl sides & rim, Made in China, 11" L, w/underplate........425.00
Canister, sq, w/lid, 7" 550.00
Chop plate, panels w/bird & insect border, 1850s, 16" 660.00
Chop plate, 1850s, 15", EX 465.00
Fruit basket, rtcl sides, oval, 1870, 8½", +undertray.....................700.00
Garden seat, emb buttons, rtcl sides/top, 1880s, wear, 19" 2,000.00
Mug, dbl-twist hdl, str sides, 5¾" 425.00
Pitcher, bulbous, 1880s, 7½" 300.00
Punch bowl, 1880s, 11½" 600.00
Sauce tureen, twisted hdls, mushroom finial, 1850s, 8" L 550.00
Spittoon, flaring rim, lt fading, 1880s, 7½" 425.00
Tazza, rtcl border, 1850s, rstr chip/lt wear, 4x9½" 700.00
Temple jar, foo dog finial, 4 masks appl to shoulder, 17" 2,860.00
Tray, raised edges, gilt trim, ca 1875, 15x10", NM....................700.00
Umbrella stand, Made in China, ca 1900, 24".............................660.00
Vase, bulbous bottom, 1850s, hairline/rim roughage, 9½"..........495.00
Vase, bulbous middle, flaring top, 1850s, 13½" 600.00
Vase, cupped-out lotus mold top, 1840, 32" 6,500.00
Vase, gold foo dog hdls, pleated rim, 14", pr 1,950.00
Vase, gold foo dog hdls, 2 appl lizards, 1860, rstr, 24" 1,400.00
Vase, mouse figural hdls, now lamp, 1850s, 18"........................850.00
Vase, shouldered, 1850s, 9", EX, pr..700.00
Water bottle, 1870s, no lid, rim chip, 15" 1,200.00

Rosemeade

Rosemeade was the name chosen by Wahpeton Pottery Company of Wahpeton, North Dakota, to represent their product. The founders of the company were Laura Meade Taylor and R.J. Hughes, who organized the firm in 1940. It is most noted for small bird and animal figurals, either in high gloss or a Van Briggle-like matt glaze. The ware was marked 'Rosemeade' with an ink stamp or carried a 'Prairie Rose' sticker. The pottery closed in 1961.

Ash tray, bear figural, Theodore Roosevelt Park 75.00
Ash tray, deer figural...75.00
Ash tray, dove figural...95.00
Bank, rhino...650.00
Bell, peacock 150.00
Creamer & sugar bowl, corn design 35.00
Creamer & sugar bowl, free-form 30.00
Creamer & sugar bowl, turkeys 180.00
Dealer sign, Prairie Rose design, Rosemeade lettering 750.00
Figurine, bear, lg 275.00
Figurine, bear, walking, mini 50.00
Figurine, buffalo, lg 250.00
Figurine, buffalo, solid 100.00
Figurine, cocker spaniel, mini, pr 500.00
Figurine, frog, solid 85.00
Figurine, pheasant, mini 50.00
Figurine, pheasant rooster, 12½" 220.00
Figurine, pheasent hen, 11½"...260.00
Figurine, seals, mini, set of 3..50.00
Figurine, striped gopher, lg, 4"..85.00
Figurine, trout, realistic, single 100.00
Flower frog, bird 35.00

Flower frog, fish	55.00
Flower frog, pheasant	95.00
Good Luck horseshoe (given at open house)	775.00
Incense burner, elephant	200.00
Lamp, TV; blk panther	650.00
Lamp, TV; horse, 9½"	400.00
Lamp, TV; pheasant rooster, 14¾" L	425.00
Pin tray, Internat'l Peace Gardens, w/dove figurine	75.00
Pitcher, Ewald Dairy advertisement	95.00
Pitcher, Minnesota Centennial	95.00
Planter, bird on log	50.00
Planter, boot, lg	45.00
Planter, boot, sm, 4"	30.00
Planter, dove	125.00
Planter, Dutch shoe	35.00
Planter, lamb	45.00
Planter, moccasin, sm	45.00
Planter, pony	75.00
Planter, squirrel on log	40.00
Plaque, fish, realistic, on gr oval, 3½x5¾"	135.00
Salt cellar, dove	100.00
Shakers, blk bear, pr	50.00
Shakers, buffalo, pr	75.00
Shakers, cattle (bull & cow), pr	150.00
Shakers, cock, fighting, pr	100.00
Shakers, coyote, howling, pr	200.00
Shakers, deer, leaping, pr	60.00
Shakers, dog head, bloodhound, pr	30.00
Shakers, dog head, bull dog, pr	40.00
Shakers, dog head, Chow Chow, pr	30.00
Shakers, dog head, English setter, pr	30.00
Shakers, dog head, fox terrier, pr	40.00
Shakers, dog head, greyhound, pr	30.00
Shakers, dog head, pekingese, pr	40.00
Shakers, dog head, Scottish terrier, pr	30.00
Shakers, elephant, pr	65.00
Shakers, fox, pr	175.00
Shakers, horse head, pr	55.00
Shakers, mallard (drake & hen), pr	45.00
Shakers, oxen, red, pr	45.00
Shakers, parakeet, pr	150.00
Shakers, parrot, pr	85.00
Shakers, pelican, lg, pr	65.00
Shakers, pelican, sm, pr	50.00
Shakers, pheasant (golden, hen & rooster), pr	125.00
Shakers, pheasant (hen & rooster), tail down, pr	100.00
Shakers, pheasant (hen & rooster), tail up, pr	30.00
Shakers, pheasant rooster, lg, pr	125.00
Shakers, quail, pr	40.00
Shakers, quail w/real top feathers, pr	75.00
Shakers, raccoon, pr	95.00
Shakers, roadrunner, pr	250.00
Shakers, rooster, strutting, pr	70.00
Shakers, sailfish, pr	150.00
Shakers, skunk, lg, 3", pr	75.00
Shakers, sunfish, pr	200.00
Shakers, swan, pr	50.00
Shakers, tulip, pr	35.00
Shakers, turkey, mini, pr	75.00
Spoon rest, cactus	75.00
Spoon rest, pheasant	65.00
Vase, dusty pk matt, flared, ruffled rim, 7½"	60.00
Vase, flower arranger, rolled edge	40.00
Vase, koala bear on stump, 8½"	375.00

Vase, peacock	165.00
Vase, turq matt, flared top, bulbous, 5½"	50.00

Rosenthal

In 1879 Phillip Rosenthal established the Rosenthal Porcelain Factory in Selb, Bavaria. Its earliest products were figurines and fine tablewares. The company has continued to operate to the present decade, manufacturing limited edition plates.

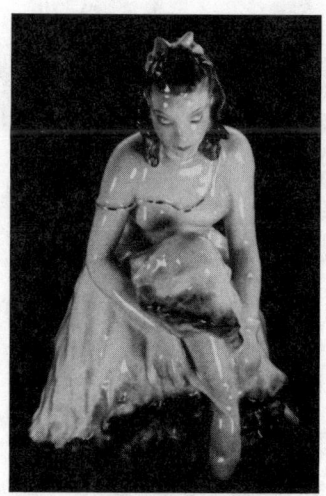

Ballerina, blue and white, 10½", $350.00.

Creamer, Isolde	15.00
Creamer & sugar bowl, Romance, gold trim	25.00
Cup & saucer, Baroque	28.00
Cup & saucer, Romance	18.00
Figurine, angel fish, wht, ca 1963, 16x10"	950.00
Figurine, Blk man playing banjo, 8"	245.00
Figurine, Blk man w/dessert, 7"	295.00
Figurine, boy w/lamb, 6"	195.00
Figurine, colt, blaze face, stocking ft, recumbent, 5½"	65.00
Figurine, dachshund puppy, 3½"	195.00
Figurine, girl kissing clown doll, Claire Weiss, 4"	150.00
Figurine, Princess & Frog, 8½"	250.00
Figurine, rabbit, wht, laughing, 6½"	98.00
Figurine, robin, Selb, Germany, 5"	110.00
Figurine, semi-nude, bl robe, #9123, 8½"	395.00
Mug, HP hens, 5½"	75.00
Rose jar, floral, bl/gr/gold on wht, 8"	330.00
Soup, Springtime, rimmed	15.00
Teapot, Isolde	40.00
Teapot, Romance, gold trim	65.00
Vase, girl w/flower basket, gold rim, tapered, mk, 13½"	250.00
Vase, red storks/bl palms/gilt garlands, sgn Wendler, 11"	660.00

Roseville

The Roseville Pottery Company was established in 1892 by George F. Young in Roseville, Ohio. Finding their facilities inadequate, the company moved to Zanesville in 1898, erected a new building, and installed the most modern equipment available. By 1900 Young felt ready to enter into the stiffly competitive art pottery market. Roseville's first art line was called Rozane. Similar to Rookwood's Standard, Rozane featured dark blended backgrounds with slip-painted underglaze artwork of nature studies, portraits, birds, and animals. Azurean, developed in 1902, was a blue and white underglaze art line on a blue blended background. Egypto (1904) featured a matt glaze in a soft shade of old green and was modeled in low relief after examples of ancient Egyptian pottery. Mongol (1904) was a high-gloss oxblood red line after the fashion of the Chinese Sang de Boeuf. Mara (1904), an iridescent lustre line of magenta and rose with intricate patterns developed on the surface or in low relief, successfully duplicated Sicardo's work. These early lines were followed by many others of highest quality: Fudjiyama and Woodland (1905-06) reflected an Oriental theme; Crystalis (1906) was covered with beautiful frost-like crystals. Della Robbia, their most famous line (introduced in 1906), was decorated with designs ranging from florals, animals, and birds to scenes of Viking warriors and Roman gladiators. These designs were accomplished by sgraffito with slip-painted details. Very limited but of great importance to collectors today, Rozane Olympic (1905) was decorated with scenes of Greek mythology on a red ground. Pauleo (1914) was the last of the artware lines. It was varied — over two hundred glazes were recorded — and some pieces were decorated by hand, usually with florals.

During the second decade of the century until the plant closed forty years later, new lines were continually added. Some of the more popular of the middle-period lines were Donatello, 1915; Futura, 1928; Pine Cone, 1931; and Blackberry, 1933. The floral lines of the later years have become highly collectible. Pottery from every era of Roseville production — even its utility ware — attest to an unwavering dedication to quality and artistic merit.

Examples of the fine art pottery lines present the greatest challenge to evaluate. Scarcity is a prime consideration. The quality of artwork varied from one artist to another. Some pieces show fine detail and good color, and naturally this influences their values. Studies of animals and portraits bring higher prices than the floral designs. An artist's signature often increases the value of any item, especially if the artist is one who is well recognized. For further information consult *The Collector's Encyclopedia of Roseville Pottery, First and Second Series,* by Sharon and Bob Huxford, available at your local library or bookstore. Our advisors for this category are Jeanette and Marvin Stofft; they are listed in the Directory under Indiana.

Apple Blossom, basket, hanging	115.00
Apple Blossom, ewer, #316, 8"	80.00
Apple Blossom, vase, #387, 9"	85.00
Autumn, jardiniere, 9½"	550.00
Autumn, pitcher, no mk, 8½"	365.00
Aztec, pitcher, 5"	250.00
Aztec, vase, cylinder w/wider shoulders, 11½"	375.00
Aztec, vase, no mk, 9"	275.00
Aztec, vase, slim form, 9½"	265.00
Azurean, candlestick, floral, 9"	425.00
Azurean, vase, floral, 9"	325.00
Baneda, jardiniere, 9½"	450.00
Baneda, vase, 6"	200.00
Bank, beehive, no mk, 2½"	165.00
Bank, buffalo, no mk, 3x6"	150.00
Bank, monkey, no mk, 6"	135.00
Bank, pig, no mk, 2½x5"	115.00
Bank, Uncle Sam, no mk, 4"	125.00
Bittersweet, basket, #810, 10"	115.00
Bittersweet, planter, #868, 8"	45.00
Bittersweet, vase, #883, 8"	75.00
Blackberry, bowl, 8"	175.00
Blackberry, candle holder, 4½", pr	300.00
Blackberry, jug, 5"	200.00
Blackberry, vase, 12½"	800.00
Bleeding Heart, ewer, #972, 10"	115.00
Bleeding Heart, pitcher, #1323	150.00
Blue Teapots, teapot, 8"	225.00

Burmese, candle holder/bookend, wht, #80-B, pr	250.00
Bushberry, vase, #29, 6"	50.00
Bushberry, wall pocket, #1291, 8"	175.00
Carnelian I, candle holder, 3", pr	35.00
Carnelian I, flower holder, 6"	30.00
Carnelian II, vase, fan form, ink stamp, 6½"	45.00
Carnelian II, vase, fan form, 6½"	45.00
Carnelian II, vase, squat, hdls, 5"	55.00
Ceramic Design, flower arranger, no mk, 2-pc, 2"	65.00
Ceramic Design, pitcher, no mk, 6½"	285.00
Cherry Blossom, bowl, 6"	225.00
Cherry Blossom, lamp base	415.00
Cherry Blossom, vase, jug form, 7"	225.00
Cherry Blossom, vase, urn form, 8"	315.00
Clemana, candle holder, 4½", pr	125.00
Clematis, candle holder, #11, 4½", pr	60.00
Clematis, ewer, #17, 10"	100.00
Clematis, vase, #188, 6"	47.50
Columbine, bowl, #401, 6"	37.50
Columbine, bowl, #655, 3"	32.50
Corinthian, candlestick, 10", pr	125.00
Corinthian, compote, 10" dia	80.00
Cornelian, cracker jar, w/lid, no mk	300.00
Cornelian, pitcher & bowl, 12", 15½" dia	325.00
Cornelian, shaving mug, no mk, 4"	60.00
Cornelian, soap dish, no mk, 4"	80.00
Cosmos, bowl, #376, 6"	65.00
Creamware, mug, Quaker men, no mk, 5"	165.00
Creamware, mug, strawberry decal, no mk, 5"	85.00
Creamware, tankard, FOE, no mk, 10½"	275.00
Cremona, flower frog	18.00
Cremona, vase, 10"	100.00
Crocus, vase, bulbous, no mk, 7"	375.00
Crystalis, planter, 4"	300.00
Crystalis, vase, 13"	1,300.00
Crystalis, vase, 8½"	425.00
Dahlrose, vase, slim form, angle hdls, 10"	175.00
Dahlrose, vase, sq, 6"	115.00
Dawn, vase, #826, 6"	75.00
Decorated Utility Ware, pitcher, 4"	45.00
Decorated Utility Ware, pitcher, 6"	60.00
Della Robbia, tankard, evergreen trees, 10½"	1,650.00

Della Robbia teapot with Viking ships, $1,100.00.

Dogwood I, wall pocket	135.00
Dogwood II, tub, 4x7"	75.00

Dogwood II, wall pocket, dbl	165.00
Donatello, basket, imp mk, 7½"	125.00
Donatello, compote, stamped, 4"	85.00
Donatello, flower frog	10.00
Donatello, pitcher, mk, 6½"	200.00
Donatello, vase, dbl bud; no mk, 7"	200.00
Dutch, pin tray, no mk, 4"	45.00
Dutch, pitcher, no mk, 9½"	185.00
Dutch, pitcher & bowl, no mk, 9", 12" dia	550.00
Dutch, soap dish, no mk, 3"	215.00
Dutch, tumbler, no mk, 4"	100.00
Earlam, candle holder, 6", pr	60.00
Early Pitcher, Boy, no mk, 7½"	300.00
Early Pitcher, Grapes, 6"	85.00
Early Pitcher, Landscape, 7½"	115.00
Early Pitcher, Tulip, 7½"	115.00
Early Pitcher, Wild Rose, no mk, 9½"	85.00
Egypto, compote, seal mk, 9"	450.00
Egypto, lamp base, 10"	550.00
Egypto, pitcher, 11"	245.00
Egypto, vase, 12½"	325.00
Elsie the Cow, mug, #B-1	115.00
Falline, vase, hdls, 7"	235.00
Falline, vase, urn form, 8"	235.00
Ferella, bowl, ftd, 12"	325.00
Ferella, vase, short neck, angle hdls, 4"	195.00
Florane, vase, urn form, 3½"	48.00
Florentine, bowl, 9"	50.00
Florentine, compote, ftd, 10"	85.00
Florentine, umbrella stand	300.00
Forget-Me-Not, ring tree, no mk, 3½"	75.00
Forget-Me-Not, sugar bowl, no mk, 3"	55.00
Foxglove, conch shell, 3426, 6"	55.00
Foxglove, ewer, #6, 15"	200.00
Foxglove, vase, #659, 3"	27.50
Freesia, bookends, #15, pr	105.00
Freesia, cookie jar, #4, 10"	215.00
Freesia, vase, cornucopia; #198, 8"	50.00
Fuchsia, jardiniere & pedestal	900.00
Fuchsia, vase, #645, 3"	42.50
Fuchsia, vase, #895, 7"	135.00
Futura, bud vase, 6"	175.00
Futura, vase, balloons on spherical body, geometric base, 9"	950.00
Futura, vase, sea gulls, hdls, 10"	685.00
Gardenia, bowl, #600, 4"	35.00
Gardenia, ewer, #616, 6"	55.00
Gold Traced, candlestick, no mk, 9"	100.00
Holland, mug, no mk, 4"	45.00
Holland, pitcher, blended, no mk, 9½"	165.00
Holland, powder jar, no mk, 3"	95.00
Holly, teapot, no mk, 4½"	225.00
Holly, tumbler, no mk, 4"	165.00
Imperial I, basket, #7, 9"	90.00
Imperial I, basket, 6"	85.00
Imperial I, bud vase, 12"	125.00
Imperial I, planter, no mk, 14x16"	100.00
Imperial II, bowl, no mk, 4½"	125.00
Imperial II, wall pocket	250.00
Iris, basket, #354, 8"	175.00
Iris, candle holder, #1135, 4", pr	95.00
Iris, wall shelf, 8"	215.00
Ivory II, vase, 6"	55.00
Ixia, basket, #346, 10"	125.00
Ixia, bowl, #387, 6"	55.00

Jonquil, basket, 9"	175.00
Jonquil, bowl, 5½"	85.00
Jonquil, vase, hdls, 8"	135.00
Juvenile, creamer, bear, no mk, 4"	135.00
Juvenile, creamer, Santa Claus, ink stamp, 3½"	135.00
Juvenile, custard, sitting rabbit, no mk, 2½"	60.00
Juvenile, mug, dog, 2-hdl, ink stamp, 3"	70.00
Juvenile, mug, fat puppy, no mk, 3½"	70.00
Juvenile, plate, pig, ink stamp, 8"	275.00
La Rose, bowl, 6"	50.00
La Rose, vase, 10"	135.00
Landscape, custard cup, no mk, 2½"	55.00
Landscape, planter, sq form, 4½"	70.00
Late Line Florane, bowl, #61	42.50
Late Line Florane, vase, #82, 9"	68.00
Laurel, vase, 6½"	105.00
Laurel, vase, 9"	150.00
Lombardy, jardiniere, paper label, 6½"	150.00
Lotus, vase, #L-3, 10"	125.00
Luffa, bowl, 4"	70.00
Luffa, vase, 13"	275.00
Luffa, vase, 8"	125.00
Lustre, basket, no mk, 10"	125.00
Lustre, candle holder, 8", pr	55.00
Magnolia, basket, #385, 10"	135.00
Magnolia, ewer, #13, 6"	50.00
Magnolia, jardiniere & pedestal	575.00
Magnolia, planter, #389, 8"	85.00
Mara, vase, cylindrical, 13"	1,400.00
Matt Color, vase, silver paper label, 4"	35.00
Matt Green, gate, no mk, 5x8"	37.50
Mayfair, tankard, #1107, 12"	70.00
Medallion, creamer, no mk, 3"	60.00
Ming Tree, candle holder, #551, pr	50.00
Ming Tree, ewer, #516, 10"	80.00
Ming Tree, vase, #582, 8"	55.00
Mock Orange, bowl, #900, 4"	30.00
Mock Orange, ewer, #916, 6"	55.00
Moderne, vase, #794, 7"	55.00
Mongol, mug, 6"	775.00
Mongol, pitcher, seal mk, 6½"	850.00
Mongol, vase, cylindrical, seal mk, 15"	1,000.00
Mongol, vase, 14"	850.00
Monticello, basket, 6½"	215.00
Monticello, vase, 7"	165.00
Morning-Glory, bowl vase, 4"	175.00
Morning-Glory, vase, 12"	400.00
Moss, bowl, console; 13"	150.00
Moss, candle holder, #1107, 4½", pr	85.00
Mostique, comport, no mk, 7"	75.00
Mostique, jardiniere, 10"	150.00
Mostique, umbrella stand	250.00
Mostique, vase, cylindrical, 6"	45.00
Normandy, jardiniere, 7"	165.00
Novelty Stein, ea	225.00
Old Ivory, planter, no mk, 4"	55.00
Olympic, pitcher, Pandora Brought to Earth, 7"	2,000.00
Olympic, vase, ink stamp, 13"	2,750.00
Orian, vase, ftd, w/hdls, 10½"	135.00
Orian, vase, 7"	115.00
Panel, jar, w/lid, ink stamp, 10"	325.00
Panel, lamp base, silver paper label, 10"	215.00
Panel, vase, pillow form, 6"	85.00
Panel, vase, urn form, 8"	175.00

Pasadena, flowerpot, #L-36, 4" 38.00
Pauleo, vase, floral on pearl gray, 14" 850.00
Pauleo, vase, iris on shaded ground, classical form, 19" 1,150.00
Pauleo, vase, trees, leaves cover neck, no mk, 15½" 1,000.00
Peony, basket, #378, 10" 125.00
Peony, ewer, #8, 10" 130.00
Peony, vase, #168, 6" 40.00
Persian, creamer & sugar bowl 135.00
Persian, jardiniere, red ink mk, 5" 165.00
Pine Cone, basket, #339, 9" 350.00
Pine Cone, candle holder, triple, #1106, 5½" 175.00
Pine Cone, pitcher, ice lip, 8" 275.00
Pine Cone, vase, fan form, #472, 6" 115.00
Poppy, basket, #347, 10" 135.00
Poppy, vase, 6½" 70.00
Raymor, bean pot, #195 ....40.00
Raymor, cup & saucer, #151 ....17.50
Raymor, plate, luncheon; #153 ....12.50
Rosecraft Black, vase, 10" 135.00
Rosecraft Hexagon, bowl vase, 4" 150.00
Rosecraft Hexagon, candlestick, ink stamp, 8" 110.00
Rosecraft Vintage, bowl, ink stamp, 3" 45.00
Rosecraft Vintage, candlestick, 8", pr 175.00
Rosecraft Vintage, vase, bulbous, 5" 90.00
Rozane Light, bowl, floral, 3" 165.00
Rozane Light, mug, floral, 5" 235.00
Rozane Light, sugar bowl, floral, lg hdls, 4½" 200.00
Rozane Light, tankard, floral, 10" 375.00
Rozane Light, vase, floral, pillow form, 7" 285.00
Rozane Light, vase, floral, 8½" 315.00
Rozane Royal, bowl, floral, #927, 2½" 100.00
Rozane Royal, chocolate pot, floral, 9½" 375.00
Rozane Royal, jug, floral, #888, 4½" 215.00
Rozane Royal, letter holder, 3½" 185.00
Rozane Royal, tankard, floral, sgn J Imlay, 11½" 475.00
Rozane Royal, vase, floral, #821, RPCo mk, 9½" 300.00
Rozane Royal, vase, Indian portrait, #891, 13" 3,750.00
Rozane 1917, candlestick, 6", pr 65.00
Rozane 1917, champagne bucket 225.00
Russco, vase, matt, 14½" 115.00
Silhouette, basket, #708, 6" 85.00
Silhouette, planter, #731, 14" 55.00
Snowberry, ash tray..42.50
Snowberry, basket, #1BK, 8" 75.00
Snowberry, bowl, #1RB, 5" 50.00
Special, mug, grapes, 5" 135.00
Special, tankard, grapes, 15½" 275.00
Sunflower, jardiniere, 9" 335.00
Sunflower, vase, urn form, 5½" 275.00
Sylvan, jardiniere, no mk, 9" 275.00
Teasel, basket, #349, 10" 150.00
Teasel, vase, #882, 6"...55.00
Thornapple, candle holder, 2½", pr 65.00
Thornapple, vase, cornucopia; 6" 45.00
Topeo, vase, red, 7" 145.00
Topeo, vase, urn form, 6" 120.00
Tourist, window box, no mk, 8½x19" 1,150.00
Tourmaline, ginger jar 275.00
Tourmaline, vase, 8" 65.00
Tuscany, candle holder, 4", pr 45.00
Tuscany, vase, 8" 50.00
Unnamed Line, bowl, #529, 9" 22.50
Unnamed Line, occasional pc, #532, 15" 38.00
Velmoss II, vase, dbl bud; 8" 70.00

Velmoss II, vase, dbl cornucopia; 8½"............................75.00
Velmoss Scroll, candlestick, 11", pr 185.00
Velmoss Scroll, jardiniere & pedestal, 30" 900.00
Velmoss Scroll, vase, classic form, no mk, 8" 115.00
Venetian, bake pan, 7" 30.00
Water Lily, basket, #380, 8" 85.00
Water Lily, cookie jar, #1, 10" 200.00
Water Lily, ewer, #10, 6" 45.00
White Rose, basket, #363, 10" 135.00
White Rose, flower frog, #41 ....27.50
White Rose, vase, urn form, #147, 8" 85.00
Wincraft, basket, #209, 12" 85.00
Wincraft, vase, #285, 10" 65.00
Wincraft, vase, cornucopia; #222, 8" 27.50
Windsor, bowl, console; w/flower frog 165.00
Windsor, candlestick, 4½", pr 185.00
Wisteria, vase, 10" 400.00
Woodland, vase, no mk, 8" 750.00
Woodland, vase, 15" 1,050.00
Woodland, vase, 6½" 565.00
Zephyr Lily, ash tray 37.50
Zephyr Lily, console boat, #475, 10" 80.00
Zephyr Lily, vase, #131, 7" 55.00

Rowland and Marsellus

Though the impressive back stamp seems to suggest otherwise, Rowland and Marsellus were not Staffordshire potters but American importers who commissioned various English companies to supply them with the transfer-printed historical ware that had been a popular import item since the early 1800s. Plates (both flat and with a rolled edge), cups and saucers, pitchers, and platters were sold as souvenirs from 1890 through the 1930s. Though other importers — Bawo & Dotter, and A. C. Bosselman & Co., both of New York City — commissioned the manufacture of similar souvenir items, by far the largest volume carries the R. & M. mark, and Rowland and Marcellus has become a generic term that covers all 20th-century souvenir china of this type. Their mark may be in full or 'R. & M.' in a diamond. Though primarily made with blue transfers on white, other colors may occasionally be found as well. Our advisor for this category is David Ringering; he is listed in the Directory under California.

Key:
r/e — rolled edge   v/o — view of
s/o — souvenir of

Pitcher, Columbia World's Fair, Chicago, blue, $300.00.

Cup & saucer, Minneapolis MN, s/o 65.00
Cup & saucer, Williamsburg VA, s/o 65.00

Plate, Allentown PA, s/o, The Pike, r/e, 10" 50.00
Plate, Bangor ME, s/o, River Front, r/e, 10" 50.00
Plate, Brooklyn NY, s/o, NY & Brooklyn Bridge, r/e, 10" 50.00
Plate, Butte MT, s/o, Bronco Busting, r/e, 10" 60.00
Plate, Cleveland OH, s/o, Garfield Memorial, r/e, 10" 45.00
Plate, coupe; Fresno CA, 5 library scenes, 6" 30.00
Plate, coupe; Minneapolis MN, Minnehaha Falls, s/o, 10"..........48.00
Plate, coupe; San Antonio TX, The Alamo, s/o, 6" 30.00
Plate, East Hampton NY, v/o, Home Sweet Home, r/e, 10" 50.00
Plate, Hartford CT, s/o, State Capital, r/e, 10" 50.00
Plate, Lake George NY, s/o, Paradise Bay, r/e, 10".......................50.00
Plate, Lewis & Clark Centennial, portraits, r/e, 1905, 10" 60.00
Plate, Lookout Mtn TN, s/o, Point Park Entrance, r/e, 10" 50.00
Plate, Mobile AL, s/o, Courthouse & Government St, r/e, 10"......55.00
Plate, Newport RI, s/o, Old Stone Mill, r/e, 10" 50.00
Plate, Philadelphia PA, s/o, City Hall, r/e, 10" 45.00
Plate, Providence RI, s/o, State House, r/e, 10" 50.00
Plate, Robert Burns, portrait, r/e, 10" 55.00
Plate, Sag Harbor LI, NY, s/o, High School, r/e, 10" 55.00
Plate, St Paul's...Church, v/o, Trexlertown...1922, r/e, 10" 55.00
Plate, Toronto Canada, s/o, City Hall, r/e, 10" 50.00
Plate, Vassar College, s/o, general view, r/e, 10".........................50.00
Plate, Wm Shakespeare, portrait, r/e, 10" 50.00
Plate, World's Fair St Louis MO, Jefferson portrait 75.00
Tumbler, Asheville NC, s/o...65.00
Tumbler, New London CT, s/o 65.00
Tumbler, Seattle, v/o 65.00

Royal Bayreuth

Founded in 1794 in Tettau, Bavaria, the Royal Bayreuth firm originally manufactured fine dinnerwares of superior quality. Their figural
items, produced from before the turn of the century until the onset of
WWI, are highly sought after by today's collectors. Perhaps the most
abundantly produced and easily recognized of these are the tomato and
lobster pieces. Fruit, flower, people, animal, bird, and vegetable shapes
were also made. Aside from figural items, pitchers, toothpick holders,
cups and saucers, humidors and the like were decorated in florals and
scenic motifs. Some, such as the very popular Rose Tapestry line, utilized a cloth-like tapestry background. Transfer prints were used as well.
Two of the most popular are Sunbonnet Babies and Nursery Rhymes
(in particular, those decorated with the complete verse).

Caution: Many pieces were not marked; some were marked
'Deponiert' or 'Registered' only. While marked pieces are the most valued, unmarked items are still very worthwhile. Our advisors for this category are Larry Brenner from New Hampshire and Dee Hooks from Illinois; they are listed in the Directory under their home states.

Figurals

Ash tray, eagle, bl mk, 6" 600.00
Ash tray, elk, bl mk 195.00
Bowl, oak leaf, MOP, bl mk, lg 285.00
Bowl, pansy, yel, bl mk, 9"...300.00
Box, Devil & Cards, bl mk, 4x3¼"...260.00
Candlestick, Santa Claus, red, bl mk.......................................4,000.00
Candy dish, murex shell, bl mk 85.00
Celery dish, lobster, bl mk...125.00
Celery dish, tomato, bl mk, 11½x5" 185.00
Chocolate pot, poppy, red, bl mk, +3 cups 700.00
Creamer & sugar bowl, tomato, bl mk, 4"..................................175.00
Cup & saucer, demitasse; Devil & Cards, bl mk 235.00
Cup & saucer, demitasse; Devil & Cards, unmk...........................165.00

Candle holder, Art Nouveau, blue mark, 6½", $1,500.00.

Cup & saucer, demitasse; oyster & pearl, bl mk 150.00
Cup & saucer, poppy, bl mk 125.00
Gravy boat, poppy, bl mk 135.00
Hatpin holder, owl, bl mk 1,000.00
Humidor, Arab, gray turban, bl mk 500.00
Humidor, coachman, bl mk 1,250.00
Humidor, Devil & Cards, bl mk 900.00
Inkwell, Devil, red, full-bodied, bl mk 600.00
Inkwell, elk, bl mk, 2x5" 200.00
Match holder, chimpanzee, bl mk, wall hanging 800.00
Match holder, devil, red, full-bodied, bl mk, wall hanging 3,000.00
Match holder, Santa Claus, red-brn, bl mk 5,250.00
Mustard, grapes, yel, bl mk 120.00
Mustard, poppy, red, Deponiert & gr mk, w/spoon......................115.00
Pitcher, alligator, bl mk, cream sz...325.00
Pitcher, alligator, bl mk, milk sz...600.00
Pitcher, alligator, bl mk, water sz...2,200.00
Pitcher, apple, bl mk, cream sz 225.00
Pitcher, apple, bl mk, lemonade sz 725.00
Pitcher, apple, bl mk, milk sz...325.00
Pitcher, Art Nouveau, deep pk coloring, bl mk, cream sz.............750.00
Pitcher, bell ringer, bl mk, water sz 900.00
Pitcher, bull, brn, bl mk, cream sz..165.00
Pitcher, butterfly, bl mk, closed wings, mc, cream sz 295.00
Pitcher, butterfly, bl mk, closed wings, milk sz 725.00
Pitcher, butterfly, bl mk, open wings, milk sz 425.00
Pitcher, cat, calico, bl mk, cream sz 230.00
Pitcher, cat, gray, bl mk, 5" 225.00
Pitcher, clown, red, bl mk, cream sz 230.00
Pitcher, clown, red, bl mk, water sz 950.00
Pitcher, clown, yel, bl mk, milk sz 550.00
Pitcher, coachman, bl mk, milk sz 325.00
Pitcher, coachman, bl mk, water sz 775.00
Pitcher, cockatoo, bl mk, cream sz 235.00
Pitcher, cow, gray, bl mk, cream sz...245.00
Pitcher, crow, blk, bl mk, cream sz 125.00
Pitcher, dachshund, bl mk, cream sz 195.00
Pitcher, Devil & Cards, bl mk, milk sz.......................................325.00
Pitcher, Devil & Cards, bl mk, water sz 345.00
Pitcher, duck, bl mk, cream sz 150.00
Pitcher, duck, Registered mk, cream sz......................................90.00
Pitcher, eagle, bl mk, cream sz 295.00
Pitcher, eagle, bl mk, milk sz 325.00
Pitcher, elk, unmk, cream sz...65.00
Pitcher, fish head, bl mk, cream sz..150.00
Pitcher, French poodle, bl mk, cream sz.....................................205.00
Pitcher, frog, bl mk, cream sz...225.00
Pitcher, geranium, bl mk, cream sz..425.00
Pitcher, girl w/pitcher, red, bl mk, cream sz 395.00

Pitcher, grapes, gr, bl mk, cream sz 125.00
Pitcher, horse head, bl mk, cream sz 750.00
Pitcher, ladybug, bl mk, water sz, rare...........................1,995.00
Pitcher, lamplighter, bl mk, cream sz 245.00
Pitcher, lemon, bl mk, cream sz, 3½" 200.00
Pitcher, leopard, bl mk, cream sz, rare 1,700.00
Pitcher, lettuce leaf w/lobster hdl, bl mk, cream sz 90.00
Pitcher, lobster, bl mk, cream sz 80.00
Pitcher, lobster, orange w/gr hdl, bl mk, 7¾" 225.00
Pitcher, maple leaf, bl mk, water sz 700.00
Pitcher, melon, bl mk, cream sz 245.00
Pitcher, monkey, gr, bl mk, cream sz 345.00
Pitcher, monkey, gr, bl mk, milk sz 450.00
Pitcher, mountain goat, bl mk, cream sz 250.00
Pitcher, murex shell, MOP, bl mk, cream sz 130.00
Pitcher, owl, bl mk, cream sz 495.00
Pitcher, owl, bl mk, milk sz 600.00
Pitcher, parrot, bl mk, water sz 1,000.00
Pitcher, pear, bl mk, cream sz 325.00
Pitcher, pelican, bl mk, cream sz 200.00
Pitcher, pelican, bl mk, milk sz 450.00
Pitcher, penguin, bl mk, milk sz 450.00
Pitcher, perch, bl mk, water sz 1,395.00
Pitcher, pig, gray, bl mk, cream sz 500.00
Pitcher, poppy, orange, bl mk, 2x3½" 250.00
Pitcher, robin, unmk, cream sz 95.00
Pitcher, rooster, bl mk, water sz 1,495.00
Pitcher, rooster, red top, bl mk, cream sz 250.00
Pitcher, Santa Claus, bl mk, milk sz 2,995.00
Pitcher, Santa Claus, gr, bl mk, cream sz 2,500.00
Pitcher, Santa Claus, red, bl mk, water sz........................5,000.00
Pitcher, seal, bl mk, cream sz 280.00
Pitcher, seal, bl mk, water sz 1,495.00
Pitcher, snake, bl mk, cream sz 525.00
Pitcher, snake, bl mk, water sz 2,995.00
Pitcher, St Bernard, bl mk, cream sz 175.00
Pitcher, St Bernard, bl mk, milk sz 255.00
Pitcher, St Bernard, bl mk, water sz 465.00
Pitcher, strawberry, bl mk, cream sz 155.00
Pitcher, trout, bl mk, cream sz 350.00
Pitcher, trout, bl mk, milk sz 575.00
Pitcher, turtle, bl mk, cream sz 425.00
Pitcher, water buffalo, blk, bl mk, cream sz 165.00
Plate, poppy, bl mk, 7" 85.00
Salt cellar, Devil & Cards, bl mk, master 175.00
Shaker, chili pepper, bl mk 125.00
Shakers, pansy, bl mk, pr 225.00
Shakers, tomato, bl mk, pr 75.00
Sherbet, shell, unmk 70.00
Stein, elk, bl mk, rare 395.00
String holder, rooster, bl mk, wall hanging.........................350.00
Sugar bowl, grapes, purple, w/lid, unmk 75.00
Sugar bowl, horse head, bl mk 750.00
Sugar bowl, poppy, red w/gr vine hdls, bl mk, w/lid............145.00
Teapot, grapes, bl mk 450.00
Teapot, tomato, bl mk, ftd..110.00
Toothpick holder, Art Nouveau, wht satin, bl mk 650.00
Toothpick holder, bell ringer, bl mk 450.00
Toothpick holder, lamplighter, bl mk...................................475.00
Tray, dresser; Devil & Cards, bl mk 350.00
Tureen, rose, oval, bl mk, w/lid, 6" 265.00

Scenics

Ash tray, goose girl, bl mk, spade shape 55.00

Bell, Dutch children playing, mk, orig clapper 225.00
Bell, Sand Babies, bl mk, orig wooden clapper 350.00
Bowl, peacock, jeweled, bl mk, 10" 675.00
Box, Little Jack Horner, bl mk, kidney shape 130.00
Box, stamp; donkey & boy, bl mk, 2x3¾" 88.00
Box, trinket; Sand Babies, bl mk 125.00
Cake plate, Ring Around the Rosie, bl mk, 10½" 160.00
Candle holder, Blk Corinthian, red int, yel trim, bl mk...............210.00
Candlestick, Little Jack Horner, bl mk, shield bk 395.00
Cheese dish, Dutch children, bl mk, slant lid, hdls 95.00
Cheese dish, farmer w/turkeys, bl mk, slant top, 2x2¾x2" 150.00
Flowerpot, Little Jack Horner, bl mk, w/insert 175.00
Hair receiver, Goose Girl, bl mk...135.00
Match holder, sunset sailing scene, bl mk, 3x2½" 55.00
Pitcher, Beach Babies, unmk, 3" 85.00
Pitcher, hunting scene w/moose on red, bl mk, milk sz, 6" 85.00
Pitcher, lady w/basket, sailboat, bl mk, cream sz 65.00
Pitcher, Snowbabies sledding, bl mk, 3" 125.00
Pitcher, 2 musketeers at table, bl mk, cream sz 65.00
Plate, Jack & the Beanstalk, bl mk, 6½" 90.00
Plate, Little Bo Peep, bl mk, 6¼" 75.00
Rose bowl, Jack & the Beanstalk, bl mk 110.00
Tea tile, Snowbabies, bl mk, 6" 115.00
Toothpick holder, Dutch children, bl mk, bbl shape....................225.00
Toothpick holder, man w/dog, bl mk, 3-hdl 260.00
Tray, pin; Dutch children, bl mk, 3¾x5¼" 42.50
Vase, coaching scene, bl mk, hdls, 3⅛x3¼" 65.00
Vase, gazebo, forest & animals, bl mk, 3¾" 195.00
Vase, hunt scene, bl mk, 5" 95.00
Watering can, Little Jack Horner, unmk, mini...............................425.00

Sunbonnet Babies

Bell, babies fishing, bl mk, orig wood clapper 595.00
Bell, babies fishing, unmk...400.00
Box, stamp; babies washing, bl mk, 2½x2x1½" 195.00
Candle holder, babies sweeping, bl mk, shield bk..........................550.00
Candle holder, babies washing, bl mk, shield bk 425.00
Candlestick, babies cleaning, unmk, str, 5¼" 325.00
Compote, babies cleaning, bl mk, 5¾"..395.00
Dish, infant feeding; babies fishing, bl mk, 7½"............................450.00
Match holder, babies sewing, bl mk, wall hanging 495.00
Pitcher, babies cleaning, bl mk, tankard form, 5" 350.00
Pitcher, babies washing, bl mk, cream sz 265.00
Plate, babies hanging clothes, bl mk, 7⅝".......................................125.00
Posey pot, bl mk..295.00
Tea tile, babies washing, bl mk, 5" 200.00
Toothpick holder, babies fishing, bl mk...600.00
Vase, babies cleaning, bl mk, cylindrical, 4" 400.00
Wall pocket, babies cleaning, bl mk 495.00

Tapestries

**Vase, pheasant on tapestry, blue mark, 8",
$700.00.**

Basket, courting couple, bl mk, 5x5½"............................350.00
Basket, Rose Tapestry, bl mk, braided hdl, 5x5"............395.00
Basket, Rose Tapestry, bl mk, scalloped rim, 5" braided hdl 450.00
Bell, Rose Tapestry, 3-color on gr w/gold, orig clapper................495.00
Bottle, scent; floral, bl mk, sterling cap, 1" dia 275.00
Box, jewel; Rose Tapestry, bl mk..................................375.00
Box, lady & man, gr mk, 1½x2½"..................................65.00
Box, powder; mtn/castle/train/water, bl mk...................225.00
Box, trinket; Christmas Cactus Tapestry, bl mk, oval, 2x3½x2"..275.00
Box, trinket; pheasant in woods, bl mk, oval, 2¼x4" 165.00
Chamberstick, 2 men playing instruments, bl mk 210.00
Charger, Rose Tapestry, bl mk, rare, 12" 1,150.00
Hair receiver, Lady & Prince Tapestry, bl mk 275.00
Hair receiver, Rose Tapestry, bl mk 225.00
Hatpin holder, deer & fawn, bl mk, rtcl base w/gold..................235.00
Hatpin holder, Rose Tapestry, bl mk 325.00
Match holder, Rose Tapestry, 3-color roses, bl mk, hanging........395.00
Nappy, Rose Tapestry, 3-color roses, bl mk, clover form.............295.00
Nappy, Rose Tapestry, 3-color roses, bl mk, hdls........................165.00
Pitcher, lady's portrait, bl mk, 3¼"..............................325.00
Pitcher, Rose Tapestry, bl mk, 24-oz, 5" 395.00
Pitcher, Rose Tapestry, pk roses, bl mk, 5¾" 425.00
Posy pot, Rose Tapestry, 3-color, bl mk, w/insert 275.00
Shakers, Rose Tapestry, 3-color, bl mk, pr........................400.00
Stein, Arabs on horses, bl mk, 8" 325.00
Toothpick holder, pastoral scene, bl mk, hdls, 2¾x3¾"..........350.00
Tray, dresser; man w/horses, bl mk, 11½" 325.00
Tumbler, scenic, bl mk 150.00
Vase, cows & trees, bl mk, 5" 125.00
Vase, elk w/3 dogs in river, bl mk, 6" 375.00
Vase, lady w/mauve shawl, bl mk, 9"............................295.00
Vase, musicians, bl mk, silver rim, hdls, 3¼x2½" 50.00
Vase, polar bear, bl mk, gold hdls, 4½".........................255.00
Vase, portrait medallion in gold fr, bl mk, 5¼"................175.00

Royal Bonn

Royal Bonn is a fine-paste porcelain, ornately decorated with scenes, portraits, or florals. The factory was established in the mid-1800s in Bonn, Germany; however, most pieces found today are from the latter part of the century.

Vase, Nouveau florals on organic form, FWB logo, signed Franz Wilhem, #2658, 12", $750.00.

Ewer, HP florals, gold serpent hdls, mk, 12½" 395.00
Vase, floral, U-form w/in leafy Nouveau frwork, Wilhem, 12" 750.00

Vase, lady's portrait, much gold, hdls, mk, 10½x5" 550.00
Vase, purple & yel iris, gold hdls, 7½" 200.00
Vase, roses, mc on shaded ground, mk, 8x3".........................200.00
Vase, roses, sgn FM, 2 animal head hdls, pear form, 14" 350.00

Royal Copenhagen

The Royal Copenhagen Manufactory was established in Denmark in about 1775 by Frantz Henrich Muller. When bankruptcy threatened in 1779, the Crown took charge. The fine dinnerware and objects of art produced after that time carry the familiar logo, the crown over three wavy lines. See also Limited Edition Plates.

Butter pat, Flora Dancia, set of 4...............................425.00
Decanter, Kronberg Castle, #4454, 9½".........................185.00
Dish, Flora Dancia, open lace trim, 10½" L 425.00
Figurine, calf, #1072, 4x7".......................................225.00
Figurine, crow, #365, 15"..525.00
Figurine, faun on goat, #737, 8"...............................575.00
Figurine, fox, #1475, 5½"..235.00
Figurine, girl w/doll, #1938, 5¼"..............................285.00
Figurine, Great Dane, recumbent, #11679, 4½".............175.00
Figurine, Helena, nude, #4639, 10"...........................585.00
Figurine, hunter & dog, #1087, 8½" 565.00
Figurine, koala bear, #5402.....................................575.00
Figurine, lioness, recumbent, #804, 6½x12½".............395.00
Figurine, lovebirds, #402, 5¼" 100.00
Figurine, lynx, crouching, #1329, 5"..........................325.00
Figurine, mare & foal, #4698, 7".............................435.00
Figurine, milkmaid, #899, 11½"...............................450.00
Figurine, owl, #1741, 3½"..85.00
Figurine, panther, #2555, 8½x9"......................... 1,000.00
Figurine, penguin, #3003, 3".....................................65.00
Figurine, pointer puppies, #453, 2"...........................135.00
Figurine, poodle, #14757, 4½"..................................265.00
Figurine, robin, #2238, 1½".......................................75.00
Figurine, scottie, sitting, #3162, 3¼" 165.00
Figurine, Thumbelina, #4374, 4¾".............................220.00
Figurine, turkey, wht, #04784, 3"..............................110.00
Figurine, young girl carries lunch to field, #815, 8½" 135.00
Plate, Flora Dancia, open lace rim, 10¾"......................425.00
Plate, Flora Dancia, open lace rim, 14" 1,100.00
Vase, 2 butterflies, #2390, 3"....................................100.00

Royal Copley

Royal Copley is a decorative type of pottery made by the Spaulding China Company in Sebring, Ohio, from 1942 to 1957. They also produced two other major lines — Royal Windsor and Spaulding. Royal Copley was primarily marketed through five-and-ten cent stores; Royal Windsor and Spaulding were sold through department stores, gift shops, and jobbers. Items trimmed in gold are worth 25% to 50% more than the same item with no gold trim. Our advisor for this category is Joe Devine; he is listed in the Directory under Iowa.

Ash tray, lily pad w/bird, turq & pk, 5" 9.00
Bowl, blossom form, aqua, pk bird at rim, 4".................10.00
Creamer, duck, pk hat, bl wings, 4½".........................14.00
Figurine, hen, #1, 5½" 15.00
Figurine, kingfisher, red & blk, 5" 22.00
Figurine, lark, paper label, 6½" 15.00
Figurine, pheasant, Spaulding 20.00

Figurine, spaniel, brn, 5" 18.00
Figurine, thrush, bl & yel, 6½" 16.00
Figurine, titmouse, paper label, 8" 20.00
Figurine, woodpecker, red, 6¼" 15.00
Figurine, wren, paper label, 6¼" 16.00
Pitcher, daffodil, 8" 26.00
Pitcher, floral, gray & pk, 8" 25.00
Planter, barefoot boy, bl hat, 7½" 18.00
Planter, bear cub clinging to stump, 8¼" 25.00
Planter, blackamoor bust, gray, 8" 25.00
Planter, blk cat & tub 18.00
Planter, blk cat w/pk bow, 8" 28.00
Planter, bunting, 5" 15.00
Planter, Chinese boy w/lg hat, pk, 7½" 18.00
Planter, cocker spaniel w/gr basket.............................15.00
Planter, cocker spaniel's head, 5" 12.50
Planter, Colonial man & lady, 8", pr...........................54.00
Planter, deer & fawn, rectangular, 6" 18.00
Planter, dog & mailbox...18.00
Planter, dog w/right ft raised, 7½" 25.00
Planter, duck & wheelbarrow, paper label, 3¾" 15.00
Planter, duck eating grass, 5" 10.00
Planter, farm girl, bl, 6½" 16.00
Planter, finch on tree stump, 7½"................................37.50
Planter, flowers in row, rose/turq/yel, mk, 7" L 8.00
Planter, girl leaning on barrel......................................15.00
Planter, girl w/pk hat 18.00
Planter, ivy, gr on cream, ftd, 4" 6.50
Planter, kitten & moccasin, 8" 25.00
Planter, kitten w/ball of red yarn, 8¼" 27.50
Planter, Oriental lantern boy 15.00
Planter, puppy w/suitcase, paper label, 7".....................22.00
Planter, rooster, 7¼" 15.00
Planter, rose color w/blk leaves, oval, 4" 8.00
Planter, running horse, 6"..12.50
Planter, tanager by stump, 6¼" 15.00
Planter, water lily, gr, 6¼" 10.00
Plaque/planter, fruit plate, 6¼"....................................15.00
Smoking set, mallards, 3-pc 32.00

**Teddy bear with sucker, 9",
$45.00.**

Vase, bud; parrot beside stump vase, 5"........................10.00
Vase, Carol's Corsage, aqua, 7" 10.00
Vase, dragon, gray & pk, ftd, 5½" 14.00
Vase, fish form, 5" 22.50
Vase, floral decal, floral hdls, gold stamp, 6¼" 10.00
Vase, Floral Elegance, gr shaded, 8" 17.50

Vase, ivy, dk gr on ivory, ftd, 7" 8.00
Vase, mare & foal, 8½" 25.00
Wall pocket, bamboo...25.00
Wall pocket, Blackamoor 24.00
Wall pocket, bonnet w/flowers 18.00
Wall pocket, Chinese girl 18.00
Wall pocket, pirate's head, 8"..32.00
Wall pocket, Tony, 8¼" 34.00

Royal Crown Derby

In the latter 1870s, a new firm, the Derby Crown Porcelain Company Ltd., began operations in Derby, England. Since 1890 when they were appointed Manufacturers of Porcelain to Her Majesty, their fine porcelain wares have been known as Royal Crown Derby. Their earliest wares were marked with a crown over 'Derby'; often a complicated dating code indicated the year of manufacture. After 1890 the 'Royal Crown Derby, England' mark was employed; in 1921 'Made In England' was substituted in the wording. 'Bone China' was added after 1945. See also Derby.

Cup & saucer, bone china, Imari decor 75.00
Ewer, floral on ivory w/gold, #602, 1890, 6¾" 275.00
Ewer, gold florals & arabesques on Chinese red, 7½" ..250.00
Sugar bowl, Imari 135.00
Vase, florals/gilt allover, jeweled neck, w/stopper, 15" ...625.00
Vase, fruit & flower garlands, gold on cobalt, 1890 mk, 6¾" ...450.00
Vase, gilt panels on yel, HP floral, teardrop w/hdls, 20th C, 9" ...165.00

Royal Doulton, Doulton

The range of wares produced by the Doulton Company since its inception in 1815 has been vast and varied. The earliest wares produced in the tiny pottery in Lambeth, England, were salt-glazed pitchers, plain and fancy figural bottles — all utility-type stoneware geared to the practical needs of everyday living. The original partners, John Doulton and John Watts, saw the potential for success in the manufacture of drain and sewage pipes and during the 1840s concentrated on these highly lucrative types of commercial wares. Watts retired from the company in 1854, and Doulton began experimenting with a more decorative style of product. As time went by, many glazes and decorative effects were developed, among them Faience, Impasto, Silicon, Carrara, Marqueterie, Chine, and Rouge Flambe. Tiles and architectural terra cotta were an important part of their manufacture. Late in the nineteenth century at the original Lambeth location, fine artware was decorated by such notable artists as Hannah and Arthur Barlow, George Tinworth, and J.H. McLennan. Stoneware vases with incised animal drawings, gracefully shaped urns with painted scenes, and cleverly modeled figurines rivaled the best of any competitor.

In 1882 a second factory was built in Burslem which continues even yet to produce the famous figurines, character jugs, series ware, and table services so popular with collectors today. Their Kingsware line, made from 1899 to 1946, featured flasks and flagons with drinking scenes, usually on a brown-glazed ground. Some were limited editions, while others were commemorative and advertising items. The Gibson Girl series, twenty-four plates in all, was introduced in 1901. It was drawn by Charles Dana Gibson and is recognized by its blue and white borders and central illustrations, each scene depicting a humorous or poignant episode in the life of 'The Widow and Her Friends.' Dickensware, produced from 1911 through the early 1940s, featured illustrations by Charles Dickens, with many of his famous characters. The Robin Hood series was introduced in 1914; the Shakespeare series #1, portraying scenes from the Bard's plays, was made from 1914 until World War II. The Shakespeare series #2 ran from 1906 until 1974 and was decorated with featured characters. Nursery Rhymes was a series that was first produced in earthenware in 1930 and later in bone china. In 1933 a line of decorated children's ware, the Bunnykins series, was introduced; it continues to be made to the present day. About 150 'bunny' scenes have been devised, the earliest and most desirable being those signed by the artist Barbara Vernon.

Factors contributing to the value of a figurine are age, color, and detail. Those with a limited production run and those signed by the artist or marked 'Potted' (indicating a pre-1939 origin) are also more valuable. After 1920 wares were marked with a lion — with or without a crown — over a circular 'Royal Doulton.' Our advisor for this category is Nicki Budin; she is listed in the Directory under Ohio.

Animals and Birds

Three pups in basket, 3", $65.00.

Antelope, Chatcull	185.00
Cat, Lucky, K-12	125.00
Cat, Persian, #999, blk & wht	145.00
Cat, Siamese, #2655, Chatcull	115.00
Dog, Airedale, #1023, med	150.00
Dog, Boxer, #2643, med	145.00
Dog, Bull Terrier, #1132, med	650.00
Dog, Bulldog, #1043, brindle, med	585.00
Dog, Bulldog, #1047, brn/wht, sm	150.00
Dog, Bulldog, #1072, wht, lg	925.00
Dog, Bulldog, #1074, wht, sm	150.00
Dog, Bulldog, K-1	115.00
Dog, Cairn, #1033, lg	550.00
Dog, Cairn, #1034, med	245.00
Dog, Cocker Spaniel, #1002, liver & wht	300.00
Dog, Cocker Spaniel, #1020, bl roan, med	125.00
Dog, Cocker Spaniel in basket, #2585, 2"	75.00
Dog, Collie, #1057, lg	665.00
Dog, Dachshund, #1140, med	270.00
Dog, Doberman Pinscher, #2645, med	185.00
Dog, English Setter, #1051, sm, 3¾"	165.00
Dog, French Poodle, #2631, med	185.00
Dog, Great Dane, #2601, lg	950.00
Dog, Greyhound, #1065, lg	1,350.00
Dog, Irish Setter, #1055, med	150.00
Dog, Pekingese, #1011, lg	450.00

Dog, Pekingese, K-6	65.00
Dog, Scottish Terrier, #1008, lg	700.00
Dog, Scottish Terrier, K-18	65.00
Dog, Welsh Corgi, #2557, lg	1,150.00
Elephant, #2644, 5½"	95.00
Goat, #1154, gr matt	425.00
Hare, K-37, recumbent	95.00
Kingfisher, #858	165.00
Lamb, #2505	200.00
Mare (Chestnut) & foal, #2522, lg	365.00
Mare (Shire) & foal, #2536, gray, sm	435.00
Owl, #173, red cloak, rare	1,950.00
Penguin & chick, K-20, 2¼"	195.00
Piglet, #2653	225.00
Robin, #2617	175.00

Character Jugs

Apothecary, D6567, lg	95.00
Apothecary, D6574, sm	65.00
Ard of 'Earing, D6588, lg	1,100.00
Ard of 'Earing, D6594, mini	1,195.00
Arriet, D6208, lg	200.00
Arriet, D6236, sm	95.00
Arriet, D6250, mini	85.00
Arry, D6207, lg	200.00
Arry, D6235, sm, A	95.00
Auld Mac, D5823, lg	85.00
Beefeater, D6251, mini	65.00
Blacksmith, D6571, lg	95.00
Blacksmith, D6578, sm	65.00
Bootmaker, D6586, mini	50.00
Cap'n Cuttle, D5842, sm	110.00
Captain Ahab, D6500, 1958, lg	110.00
Captain Hook, D6597, lg	450.00
Captain Hook, D6601, sm	350.00
Captain Hook, D6605, mini	345.00
Cardinal, D5614, lg	150.00
Cardinal, D6033, sm	75.00
Clown, D6322, wht hair, lg, A	950.00
Dick Turpin, D5618, gun hdl, sm	70.00
Dick Turpin, D6528, horse hdl, lg	110.00
Dick Whittington, D6375, lg	385.00
Drake, D6115, lg	145.00
Farmer John, D5788, lg	145.00
Farmer John, D5789, sm	85.00
Fortune Teller, D6497, lg	495.00
Fortune Teller, D6503, sm	285.00
Fortune Teller, D6523, mini	295.00
Friar Tuck, D6321, lg	385.00
Gaoler, D6570, lg	95.00
Gardener, D6630, lg	175.00
Gardener, D6634, sm	60.00
Gladiator, D6550, lg	500.00
Gladiator, D6553, sm	350.00
Gladiator, D6556, mini	350.00
Gondolier, D6589, lg	595.00
Gondolier, D6592, sm	365.00
Gondolier, D6595, mini	375.00
Gone Away, D6531, lg	95.00
Granny, D5521, w/o tooth, lg	650.00
Granny, D5521, w/tooth, lg	95.00
Grant & Lee, D6698, lg	275.00
Gulliver, D6560, lg	625.00

Gulliver, D6566, mini 375.00
Gunsmith of Williamsburg, D6573, lg 95.00
Gunsmith of Williamsburg, D6587, mini 50.00
Jarge, D6288, lg..295.00
Jester, D5556, sm 125.00
Jockey, D6625, lg 375.00
John Peel, D5731, sm...65.00
John Peel, D6130, mini, A 50.00
John Peel, D6259, tiny 225.00
Johnny Appleseed, D6372, lg.............................350.00
Lumberjack, D6610, lg 110.00
Mad Hatter, D6598, 1970, lg...............................150.00
Mad Hatter, D6602, sm 75.00
Mae West, D6688, lg..125.00
Mikado, D6501, lg..550.00
Mikado, D6507, sm 300.00
Mikado, D6525, mini 325.00
Mine Host, D6468, lg..95.00
Mine Host, D6470, sm..55.00
N American Indian, D6611, 1966, lg.....................95.00
N American Indian, D6614, 1966, sm 45.00
Night Watchman, D6576, sm 60.00
Night Watchman, D6583, mini 55.00
Old King Cole, D6036, lg.....................................265.00
Paddy, D5753, lg, A...130.00
Parson Brown, D5486, lg.....................................135.00

Mr. Pickwick, large, $145.00.

Pied Piper, D6403, lg 100.00
Porthos, D6440, lg 95.00
Punch & Judy Man, D6590, lg.............................650.00
Punch & Judy Man, D6593, sm............................375.00
Punch & Judy Man, D6596, mini 355.00
Robin Hood, D6234, plain hdl, sm 60.00
Robinson Crusoe, D6532, lg...................................95.00
Sairey Gamp, D6146, tiny 95.00
Sam Weller, D6064, lg..150.00
Sam Weller, D6140, mini 45.00
Sam Weller, D6147, tiny 95.00
Sancho Panza, D6518, mini 50.00
Santa Claus, D6675, reindeer hdl, lg 150.00
Santa Claus, D6675, Santa doll hdl, lg 150.00
Santa Claus, D6675, Santa toy hdl, lg 175.00
Scaramouche, D6558, lg..650.00
Scaramouche, D6564, mini 345.00

Simple Simon, D6374, lg......................................550.00
Smuggler, D6616, lg..110.00
Tam O'Shanter, D6632, lg 115.00
Tam O'Shanter, D6640, mini..................................45.00
Touchstone, D5613, lg 225.00
Town Crier, D6530, lg 200.00
Town Crier, D6537, sm 95.00
Trapper, D6609, lg...110.00
Ugly Duchess, D6599, lg.......................................450.00
Ugly Duchess, D6607, mini 285.00
Uncle Tom Cobbleigh, D6337, lg..........................475.00
Vicar of Bray, D5615, lg".......................................195.00
Viking, D6496, lg 185.00
Viking, D6502, sm 95.00
Viking, D6526, mini...125.00
Walrus & Carpenter, D6604, sm 65.00
Walrus & Carpenter, D6608, mini...........................50.00
WC Fields, D6674, lg 130.00
Yachtsman, D6622, lg...115.00

Figurines

A Courting, HN2004 ....395.00
A La Mode, HN2544 ....165.00
All Aboard, HN2940 ....150.00
Amy, HN2958 ....120.00
Angelina, HN2013 ....825.00
Annabella, HN1871 ....665.00
Antoinette, HN1850 ....1,100.00
Antoinette, HN2326 ....125.00
At Ease, HN2473..185.00
Baby Bunting, HN2108...250.00
Bachelor, HN2319..225.00
Ballerina, HN2116 ....295.00
Balloon Man, HN1954..250.00
Barbara, HN1421...950.00
Beachcomber, HN2487...180.00
Bess, HN2002 ....225.00
Biddy, HN1513, red dress......................................165.00
Blacksmith of Williamsburg, HN2240 ....145.00
Blue Bird, HN1280 ....675.00
Bluebeard, HN1528, red robe................................850.00
Bo-Peep, HN1810, staff in both hands, 5" 750.00
Bonnie Lassie, HN1626 ....275.00
Bride, HN2166, pk gown..175.00
Bride, HN2873, wht gown, gold trim......................130.00
Bridesmaid, HN2196 ....110.00
Bridesmaid, HN2874 ....75.00
Broken Lance, HN2041...450.00
Camille, HN1586 ....695.00
Captain, HN2260, 9½" 250.00
Captain Cook, HN2889, 8"......................................225.00
Carolyn, HN2112 ....295.00
Carpet Seller, HN1464, hand closed 275.00
Carpet Seller, HN1464, hand open 375.00
Cavalier, HN2716, 2nd version 185.00
Centurion, HN2726 ....175.00
Charlotte, HN2421 ....150.00
Charmian, HN1568...665.00
Chief, HN2892 ....200.00
China Repairer, HN2943 ....140.00
Choir Boy, HN2141 ....125.00
Christmas Parcels, HN2851 ....275.00
Circe, HN1249 ....2,200.00

Circe, HN1250	2,200.00
Clare, HN2793	150.00
Clarinda, HN2724	175.00
Clarissa, HN2345	150.00
Clothilde, HN1598	650.00
Clown, HN2890	225.00
Collinette, HN1999	395.00
Cookie, HN2218	145.00
Coralie, HN2307	135.00
Craftsman, HN2284	475.00
Cup of Tea, HN2322	165.00
Daffy Down Dilly, HN1712	325.00
Daffy Down Dilly, HN1713, bl	850.00
Dainty May, HN1639	550.00
Daisy, HN1575	475.00
Debby, HN2400	70.00
Detective, HN2359, 9½"	225.00
Dimity, HN2169	350.00
Dorcas, HN1491	650.00
Dreamweaver, HN2283	175.00
Drummer Boy, HN2679	350.00
Dulcinea, HN1419	1,575.00
Easter Day, HN2039	295.00
Eliza, HN2543	165.00
Embroidering, HN2855	175.00
Emir, HN1604	850.00
Enchantment, HN2178	150.00
Ermine Coat, HN1981	225.00
Eugene, HN1521	750.00
Fairy, HN1324	965.00
Family Album, HN2321	375.00
Farmer's Wife, HN2069	475.00
Favourite, HN2249	150.00
Fiona, HN2694	140.00
First Dance, HN2803	175.00
First Waltz, HN2862	195.00
Flora, HN2349	265.00
Fortune Teller, HN2159	450.00
Forty Winks, HN1974, 6⅛"	195.00
Francine, HN2422	95.00
Gainesborough Hat, HN47	1,700.00
Geisha, HN1223	815.00
Genie, HN2989	150.00
Gentleman of Williamsburg, HN2227	195.00
Gentlewoman, HN1632	750.00
Georgina, HN2377	120.00
Good Catch, HN2258	140.00
Good Morning, HN2671	175.00
Grace, HN2318	150.00
Grand Manner, HN2723	175.00
Granny's Heritage, HN2031	495.00
Greta, HN1485	285.00
Gwynneth, HN1980	295.00
Gypsy Dance, HN2230, 2nd version	250.00
Helmsman, HN2499	225.00
Hilary, HN2335	150.00
Hostess of Williamsburg, HN2209	185.00
Huntsman, HN2492	185.00
Innocence, HN2842	150.00
Invitation, HN2170	145.00
Jane, HN2806	150.00
Janet, HN1916	250.00
Janice, HN2165	450.00
Jersey Milkmaid, HN2057	195.00

Jolly Sailor, HN2172	600.00
Judge, HN2443, matt	165.00
Julia, HN2705	150.00
Kate, HN2789	150.00
Kathleen, HN1357	650.00
Ko-Ko, HN1266	750.00
Lady Anne Neville, HN2006	675.00

Lady Charmian, green shawl, $295.00.

Lady Fayre, HN1265	665.00
Lady of Georgian Period, HN331	1,900.00
Lady Pamela, HN2718	150.00
Lambing Time, HN1890	195.00
Laurianne, HN2719	165.00
Lavender Woman, HN22	2,225.00
Leisure Hour, HN2055	375.00
Lisa, HN2310, matt	150.00
Love Letter, HN2149	325.00
Lucy, HN2863	125.00
Lucy Ann, HN1502	295.00
Lunchtime, HN2485	150.00
Lydia, HN1908	135.00
Margaret, HN1989	395.00
Marguerite, HN1928	295.00
Marietta, HN1446	665.00
Market Day, HN1991	225.00
Mary Mary, HN2044	165.00
Masque, HN2554	195.00
Meditation, HN2330	295.00
Melanie, HN2271	150.00
Memories, HN1856	625.00
Mendicant, HN1365	275.00
Minuet, HN2019	275.00
Miranda, HN1818	1,500.00
Mirror, HN1852	1,700.00
Modena, HN1846	1,650.00
Monte Carlo, HN2332	225.00
My Pet, HN2238	135.00
Nana, HN1766	465.00
New Companions, HN2770	165.00
Newsboy, HN2244	475.00
Nicola, HN2839, bl	250.00
Nina, HN2347	150.00
Officer of the Line, HN2733	225.00
Old Meg, HN2494	195.00
Once Upon a Time, HN2047	495.00
Orange Lady, HN1953, 8¾"	250.00

Pamela, HN1469, gr gown......................815.00
Pantalettes, HN1412 ....400.00
Parisian, HN2445 ....165.00
Past Glory, HN2484 ....175.00
Pearly Boy, HN2035 ....175.00
Peggy, HN2038 ....110.00
Pensive Moments, HN2704 ....185.00
Phillipine Dancer, HN2439 ....850.00
Phyllis, HN1420 ....625.00
Pied Piper, HN2102 ....225.00
Pillow Fight, HN2270 ....185.00
Pirate King, HN2901 ....750.00
Polka, HN2156 ....250.00
Premiere, HN2343 ....160.00
Prince of Wales, HN1217 .... 1,150.00
Professor, HN2281 ....150.00
Prudence, HN1883 ....885.00
Punch & Judy Man, HN2765..................250.00
Pyjams, HN1942 ....750.00
Rachel, HN2919 ....165.00
Rag Doll, HN2142 ....95.00
Regal Lady, HN2709 ....145.00
Regency Beau, HN1972 ....925.00
Repose, HN2272 ....175.00
Rest Awhile, HN2728 ....175.00
Reverie, HN2306......................................225.00
Rhapsody, HN2267 ....165.00
River Boy, HN2128 ....150.00
Romance, HN2430 ....135.00
Rosabell, HN1620 ....750.00
Roseanna, HN1926 ....325.00
Rustic Swain, HN1746 .... 1,550.00
Ruth the Pirate Maid, HN2900...............725.00
Secret Thoughts, HN2382 ....225.00
Shoreleave, HN2254 ....175.00
Sibell, HN1695..585.00
Simone, HN2378......................................140.00
Sir Walter Raleigh, HN2015....................495.00
Snake Charmer, HN1317 .... 1,450.00
Soiree, HN2312 ....145.00
Sonny, HN1314 ....925.00
Sophie, HN2833.......................................125.00
Southern Belle, HN2229, red overskirt 175.00
Stephanie, HN2807 ....160.00
Stitch in Time, HN2352 ....150.00
Stop Press, HN2683.................................160.00
Suitor, HN2132 ....350.00
Sunday Best, HN2206, yel dress, 7¾" 175.00
Sunday Morning, HN2184 ....285.00
Sweet & Fair, HN1864.............................885.00
Sweet & Twenty, HN1589........................250.00
Sweet Dreams, HN2380 ....135.00
Sweet Suzy, HN1918................................750.00
Sweeting, HN1935 ....125.00
Taking Things Easy, HN2677 ....175.00
Thank You, HN2732 ....150.00
Thanks Doc, HN2731 ....185.00
To Bed, HN1805......................................145.00
Tootles, HN1680......................................115.00
Top o' the Hill, HN1833..........................195.00
Town Crier, HN2119................................295.00
Toymaker, HN2250..................................325.00
Treasure Island, HN2243 ....135.00
Tulips, HN1334 .... 1,565.00

Veronica, HN1517 ....350.00
Wardrobe Mistress, HN2145 ....495.00
Wayfarer, HN2362 ....175.00
Wigmaker of Williamsburg, HN2239 ....175.00
Winsome, HN2220 ....155.00
Young Love, HN2735................................650.00
Young Master, HN2872............................225.00
Young Widow, HN1399 .... 3,000.00

Flambe

Alligator, rare 1,450.00
Bear, Sung, standing, 5x1¾" 765.00
Buddha, standing, 5" 600.00
Dog of Fo, 4¾" 185.00
Elephant, sgn Noke, 9" 425.00
Fish, #666, Veined Sung, 12" 1,150.00
Fox, crouching, lg 550.00
Fox, flat, 5½" L 85.00
Fox, seated, 8" 385.00
Great Horned Owl, perched on limb, mk Flambe Veined, 12¼" .675.00
Hippo, 3¼x6¾" 1,200.00
Monkey, embracing pr, #486, Rouge 285.00
Monkey, embracing pr, #486, Sung.........325.00
Mouse on cube, #1164............................555.00
Pekingese, looking up 465.00
Rhinocerous, half seated, #615, 9x17" .. 1,250.00
Scotty..465.00
Tiger, charging, Veined Flambe, sgn Noke, 6x14" 1,050.00
Tiger, stalking, 6x13" 500.00
Tortoise, #101, 1x3" 525.00

Series Ware

Tankard, Oliver Twist, Old Curiosity Shop, 6", $125.00.

Ash tray, Dickensware, 4" 35.00
Ash tray, Gnomes, bl underglaze..............75.00
Biscuit jar, Coaching Days 350.00
Bowl, Babes in Woods, May Day Children's Procession, 9" 225.00
Bowl, Bobby Burns, 7½" 150.00
Bowl, cereal; Shakespeare, Romeo, mk, 7½" 125.00
Bowl, Gaffers, oval, 11" 150.00
Bowl, Gypsies, 6" 150.00
Bowl, Under the Greenwood Tree, Robin Hood/Friar Tuck, 7¾"..125.00
Candlestick, Dutch People, D1881, pr......195.00
Cheese dish, Coaching Days 365.00
Chop plate, Dickensware, Tony Weller w/whip, mk, 13½" 185.00
Coffeepot, Moorish Gate, merchants, 7x3¾" 145.00

Comport, Sunset Cottage scene, sgn Morrey, porc, 3¾x5⅜" 165.00
Creamer & sugar bowl, Gnomes, w/lid 220.00
Cup & saucer, Don Quixote 50.00
Cup & saucer, Mad Hatter 95.00
Cup & saucer, Nursery Rhymes, Mother Goose 65.00
Cup & saucer, Under the Greenwood Tree, Robin Hood 70.00
Flower bowl, Isaac Walton 150.00
Jardiniere, Babes in Woods, lady & child, 8x9½" 595.00
Jardiniere, Shakespeare, Ophelia/Hamlet, mk, 8¾x10" 300.00
Match holder, Mr Squeers, 2" 95.00
Mug, Dutch People, 3 girls, yel & gr trim, mk, 2x1¾" 40.00
Mug, Kingsware, Drink Wisely 195.00
Mug, Minstrels, mk, 3¼x3½" 65.00
Mug, Moreton Hall, court scene, D1898 ......125.00
Mug, Sir Andrew Aguecheek series, tankard form, mk, 5⅝" 75.00
Pitcher, Cavaliers, Better So Than Worse, 8" 85.00
Pitcher, Coaching Days, 6½" 165.00
Pitcher, Dickensware, Curiosity Shop, sq top 165.00
Pitcher, Dickensware, Oliver, tankard form 225.00
Pitcher, dog, sgn Cecil Alden 125.00
Pitcher, Dutch People, ladies, boy on bk, mk, 2x1¾" 95.00
Pitcher, Egyptian, geometric border, mk, 6⅜" 95.00
Pitcher, Fox Hunting, cream sz 150.00
Pitcher, Fox Hunting, 4" 85.00
Pitcher, Medieval Minstrels, mk, 7½x4½" 125.00
Pitcher, Night Watchman, 8" 105.00
Pitcher, Old English Coaching Scenes, 8¾" 145.00
Pitcher, Polar Bear, D3128 ......95.00
Pitcher, Shakespeare, Portia, mk, 6⅜" 115.00
Pitcher, Shakespeare, Romeo, 4½" 70.00
Pitcher, Ye Canterbury Pilgrims 135.00
Plate, American Views, Pikes Peak, 10½" 60.00
Plate, Arabian Nights, Arrival of Unknown Princess, 10⅜" 85.00
Plate, Automobile, Deaf, scarce, 10⅜" 350.00
Plate, Autumn Glory, landscape, sq 75.00
Plate, Castles & Churches, Pembroke Castle, D3599, 10½" 60.00
Plate, child's feeding; Shakespeare, Shylock, mk, 8¼" 80.00
Plate, Coaching Days, William, Ye Driver, 10" 125.00
Plate, Dickensware, Sam Weller, emb figures, 1938, 10½" 90.00
Plate, Don Quixote, 10" 75.00
Plate, Fairy Tales, Pied Piper 75.00
Plate, Gibson Girl, Miss Babbles Brings Paper 125.00
Plate, Gibson Girl, She Goes into Colors 125.00
Plate, Gibson Girl, They Take a Morning Run 125.00
Plate, Greenaway Almanack, Gemini, May 30.00
Plate, Hiawatha, Wampum Belt, 10" 95.00
Plate, King of Hearts, 10½" 145.00
Plate, Medieval Minstrels, 12-sided, mk, 8½" 65.00
Plate, Old English Inns, Australia, D6072 ......35.00
Plate, Old English Sayings 55.00
Plate, Proverbs, vintage border, 10" 55.00
Plate, Rustic England, D5694, 10" 85.00
Plate, Sir Roger de Coverly, 10" 115.00
Plate, Souter's Cats, 6" 65.00
Platter, Gypsies, D6123 ......55.00
Soap dish, Shakespeare, Shylock, 3-part, mk, 3¾x5¼" 100.00
Teapot, Dutch People, D1884 ......115.00
Teapot, Monks, bl & wht 150.00
Teapot, Reynard the Fox 250.00
Tile, Canterbury Pilgrims 65.00
Tile, Coaching Days, 6½" sq 50.00
Tray, Falconry, hdls, 18" 175.00
Tray, Shakespeare, Katharine, 15½" 150.00
Tray, Under the Greenwood Tree, 11x5" 105.00

Vase, Babes in Woods, flow bl w/gold trim, 6⅜x4⅜" 250.00
Vase, Babes in Woods, lady & child in snow scene, 6½" 425.00
Vase, Babes in Woods, lady picking berries, 5¼" 300.00
Vase, Babes in Woods, 7½" 535.00
Vase, Dickensware, Cap'n Cuttle, early mk, 4⅝" 85.00
Vase, Dickensware, Mr Micawber, 2 hdls, 5" 95.00
Vase, Dunolly Castle, sgn Hughes, mk, 4⅜x2¾" 165.00
Vase, Shakespeare, Romeo & Juliet, 12", facing pr 425.00
Vase, Welsh Ladies, 2 ladies beside fence, mk, 3⅜" 110.00

Stoneware

Beaker, hunt scene, brass rim 60.00
Ducklings, M Marshall, 4½", pr 250.00
Humidor, figures in relief, brn to tan, mk, 5x4¼" 165.00
Lawn fountain, pelican figural, 15", EX 265.00
Pitcher, tan tapestry w/red, gold & wht trim, 3⅜" 45.00

Puzzle jug, inscribed with a verse, ca 1895, 9", $200.00.

Ring dish, owl figural, brn & tan, 4x3¼" 165.00
Teapot, floral tapestry, mk, 5x4½" 145.00
Vase, cows incised, sgn Hanna Barlow, ca 1903, 8" 850.00
Vase, goats incised, sgn Hanna Barlow, dtd 1822, 10" 850.00
Vase, gray mottle, cobalt leaf decor, mk, 5⅞" 135.00
Vase, horses/sheep, fleur-de-lis band, Hanna Barlow, 16" 1,500.00
Vase, hunting scene, Coleman, mini 35.00

Toby Jugs

Best Is None Too Good, D6107, 4½" 275.00
Cap'n Cuttle, D6266, 4½" 185.00
Falstaff, D6020 ......135.00
Fat Boy, D6264, 4½" 225.00
Happy John, D6070 ......85.00
Honest Measure, D6108 ......85.00
Jolly Toby, D6109 ......85.00
Mr Pickwick, D6261 ......195.00
Old Charley, D6030 ......185.00
Sherlock Holmes, D6661 ......105.00
Sir Francis Drake, D6660, 9" 135.00
Squire, D6319 ......265.00

Miscellaneous

Ash pot, Sairey Gamp, D6009 ......95.00

Ash tray, Old Charley, D5599	95.00
Beaker, Wedding, A Princess for Wales, 1981	35.00
Bottle, Zorro, yel	45.00
Bust, Mr Pickwick, D6049	65.00
Bust, Sam Weller, D6052	65.00
Cigarette lighter, Long John Silver, table type	95.00
Decanter, Uncle Sam, Dewars Whiskey, eagle hdl	185.00
Flask, Pied Piper, Dewars Whiskey	230.00
Jug, Old Charley, musical, D5858	450.00
Jug, Pickwick Papers, emb figures, D5756	180.00
Jug, Tony Weller, musical, D5888	450.00
Pitcher, Oliver Twist, emb figures, tankard form, D6286	165.00
Pitcher, Sporting Squire, Dewars Whiskey, 8¼"	275.00
Teapot, Sairey Gamp	1,150.00
Vase, trees/iris, bl on wht w/gold, porc, Burslem, 3⅛x1¾"	100.00
Wall mask, Sweet Anne, HN1590	435.00

Royal Dux

The Duxer Porzellan Manufactur was established by E. Eichler in 1860. Located in what is now Duchcov, Czechoslovakia, the area was known as Dux, Bohemia, until WWI. The war brought about changes in both the style of the ware as well as the mark. Prewar pieces were modeled in the Art Nouveau or Greek Classical manner and marked with 'Bohemia' and a pink triangle containing the letter 'E.' They were usually matt glazed in green, brown, and gold. Better pieces were made of porcelain, while the larger items were of pottery. After the war the ware was marked with the small pink triangle but without the Bohemia designation; 'Made in Czechoslovakia' was added. The style became Art Deco, with cobalt blue a dominant color.

Bowl, cream w/leaves & flowers, appl figure of maid, 14" L	500.00
Bowl, girl pours water, lily form, triangle mk, 9x9½"	650.00
Bust, Caesar, pk toga, wreath on head, triangle mk, 9"	350.00
Centerpc, maid+2 cherubs support shell, girl beside, 20x15"	1,250.00
Compote, leafy, 3-D maid on base/2nd at rim, gray/gold, 18"	750.00
Ewer, leaves & fruits on gr w/gold, stamped gr mks, 4½x5½"	185.00
Figurine, bear (or monkey) w/instrument, triangle mk, 4", pr	110.00
Figurine, boy on donkey, 12"	450.00
Figurine, Colonial couple at fence, triangle mk, 11½", pr	1,150.00
Figurine, couple in classical attire, 19"	425.00
Figurine, dancer in pk flowered skirt & red midriff, 23"	550.00
Figurine, girl, windswept cobalt dress, triangle mk, 10"	450.00
Figurine, girl w/wheat, boy w/sack, ca 1925, 21", pr	895.00
Figurine, harvester & wife, cobalt & wht w/gold, mk, 21"	850.00
Figurine, lady w/flowers, man in toga w/palette, mk, 9", pr	385.00
Figurine, Nouveau lady w/mandolin, sgn Hamdel, 18½"	275.00
Figurine, Rebecca at Well, flower form vase at rear, mk, 17"	950.00
Figurine, seated lady puts roses in hair, child aside, 21"	700.00
Flower bowl, girl w/jug at side, pk triangle mk, 9x9½"	650.00
Vase, floriform, w/2 3-D maids in front, all w/in bowl, 15"	880.00
Vase, girl w/water jug, Baroque floral top, triangle mk, 12"	625.00

Royal Flemish

Royal Flemish was introduced in the late 1880s and was patented in 1894 by the Mt. Washington Glass Company. Transparent glass was enameled with one or several colors and the surface divided by a network of raised lines suggesting leaded glasswork. Some pieces were further decorated with enameled florals, birds, or Roman coins. Our advisors for this category are Betty and Clarence Maier; they are listed in the Directory under Pennsylvania.

Vase, coin medallions on gold-bordered amber, brown and rust-red panels, original label, 7½", $3,000.00.

Bowl, flying ducks/gold stars, scrolled band on frost, 7"	1,500.00
Cracker jar, gold coins on red & amber w/gold lines, 8"	1,300.00
Cracker jar, gold coins/floral on red/brn/frost, rnd, 5½"	1,500.00
Cracker jar, gold griffin on brns/gr/salmon, ovoid, 8"	2,000.00
Cracker jar, gold/mc floral/wine free-forms on frost, 5"	1,900.00
Lamp, banquet; Guba ducks/stars on frost, 3-part, 22"	4,500.00
Rose bowl, asters, wht/bl on lt brn to frost, 8-crimp, lg	1,295.00
Sugar bowl, apple blossoms w/in gold lines, no mk, 2½x6"	400.00
Vase, autumn leaves/berries on frost, wine rim, no mk, 12"	1,850.00
Vase, berries/gold scrolls, bulbous w/tall swirl neck, 8"	1,800.00
Vase, coins/dragons/lions, bulbous w/stick neck & hdls, 14"	2,100.00
Vase, floral, 3-sided, 3 petal hdls at shoulder, ftd, 8"	1,500.00
Vase, gold-traced roses, twist stick neck w/sm hdls, 7"	2,200.00
Vase, gold-traced thistles on frost, stick neck, 13"	1,100.00
Vase, winged dragons, no mk, 8x6"	2,850.00

Royal Haeger, Haeger

In 1871 David Henry Haeger, a young son of German immigrants, purchased a brick factory at Dundee, Illinois, and began an association with the ceramic industry that his descendants have pursued to the present time. Soon their production was expanded to include drainage tile. By 1914 they had ventured into the field of commerical artware. Vases, figurines, lamp bases, and gift items in a pastel matt glaze carried the logo of the company name written over the bar of an 'H.' From 1929 to 1933, they produced a line of dinnerware in solid colors — blue, rose, green, and yellow — which they marketed through Marshall Fields. Royal Haeger, their premium line designed in 1938 by Royal Hickman, and the Flower Ware line (1954 to 1963, marked 'RG' for Royal Garden) are especially desirable with collectors today. Ware produced before the mid-thirties sometimes is found with a paper label; these are also of special interest. A stylized script mark, 'Royal Haeger' in raised lettering, was used during the thirties and forties; later a paper label in the shape of a crown was used. The Macomb plant, built in 1939, primarily made ware for the florist trade. A second plant, built there in 1969, produces lamp bases.

For those interested in learning more about the subject, we recommend *Collecting Royal Haeger* by our advisors, Lee Garmon and Doris Frizzell; both are listed in the Directory under Illinois.

Ash tray, boomerang form, #1006, 12"	4.00
Bookends, calla lily form, R-475, 6", pr	20.00
Bookends, ram form, R-132, 9", pr	36.00
Bowl, console; R-955, 4" H	20.00
Candle holder, block form, R-579, 5", pr	12.00
Covered dish, duck form, R-116	40.00
Figurine, collie, R-734	40.00
Figurine, does (pr), head & neck, R-624, lg & sm	55.00
Figurine, Egyptian cat, orange, 1952, 15"	95.00

Ewer, blue with silver overlay flowers, 9½", $85.00.

Figurine, gypsy girl, R-1224, 16½" **65.00**
Figurine, matador, 11½" **25.00**
Figurine, panther, R-683, 18" **30.00**
Figurine, planter, Bambi, R-1913, 7½" **25.00**
Flower block, jockey, R-788 ....**30.00**
Flower block, sitting frog, R-836 ....**25.00**
Flower holder, colt, R-235, 12½" **25.00**
Lamp, fawns, #5195, 24" **35.00**
Lamp, petal louvre reflectors, #5353, 11¼" **30.00**
Lamp, table; crepe Ginger, #5228, 23¾" **45.00**
Lamp/planter, greyhound form, 13" **35.00**
Pitcher, trout form, R-595, 8" **20.00**
Planter, elephant, R-110, 11½" **35.00**
Planter, fish, R-752, 8½" **12.00**
Planter, gazelle, R-809, 14" **50.00**
Planter, turtle, R-540, 13½" L **25.00**
Swan, open bk, R-310, 13" L **18.00**
Vase, basket form, R-386, 12" **18.00**
Vase, bottle form, #1919, 10" **5.00**
Vase, conch shell form, R-321, 8" **10.00**
Vase, cornucopia; nude aside, R-426, 8" **20.00**
Vase, eagle figural, #3278, 13" **8.00**
Vase, Pegasus, 75th Anniversary sticker, R-393, 11½" **35.00**
Vase, sphere & 3 plumes, R-281, 10½" H **45.00**
Vase, standing colt, R-1531, 15" **25.00**

Royal Rudolstadt

The hard-paste porcelain that has come to be known as Royal Rudolstadt was produced in Thuringia, Germany, in the early 18th century. Various names and marks have been associated with this pottery. One of the earliest was a hay fork symbol associated with Johann Frederich von Schwarzburg-Rudolstadt, one of the first founders. Variations, some that included an 'R,' were also used. In 1854 Earnst Bohne produced wares that were marked with an anchor and the letters 'EB.' Examples commonly found today were made during the late 1800s and early 20th century. These are usually marked with an 'RW' within a shield under a crown and the words 'Crown Rudolstadt.' Items marked 'Germany' were made after 1890.

Chocolate pot, pk roses w/gold, 10" **275.00**
Creamer, Kewpies play leap frog, sgn O'Neill, 4x2", EX **100.00**
Figurine, Athena in toga by column, helmet/sword, 11½" **500.00**
Figurine, beggar girl holds tambourine, wht, 1905, 5½" **150.00**

Figurine, hunchback, brn hat, bl pants, crown mk, 1880s, 5½" ...**125.00**
Plate, maid's portrait, sgn Koller, ca 1900, 9½" **725.00**
Teapot, roses, pk on wht w/gold, mk, ind **115.00**
Vanity set, camellia, pastel w/gold, 2-pc+7x10" tray, mk...........**185.00**
Vase, floral, HP w/gold beads on cobalt, gold hdls, 6½" **165.00**
Vase, mc Baroque floral panels w/gold, draped nude hdls, 14" **450.00**
Vase, tapestry, bl floral on wht, brn loop hdls, 1800, 9" **175.00**

Royal Vienna

In 1719 Claude Innocentius de Paquier established a hard-paste porcelain factory in Vienna where he made highly ornamental wares similar to the type produced at Meissen. Early wares were usually unmarked; but after 1744, when the factory was purchased by the Empress, the Austrian shield (often called 'beehive') was stamped on under the glaze. In the following listings, values are for hand-painted items unless noted otherwise. Decal-decorated items would be considerably lower.

Note: An influx of Japanese reproductions on the market have influenced values to decline on genuine old Royal Vienna. Buyer beware! On new items the beehive mark is over the glaze, the weight of the porcelain is heavier, and the decoration is obviously decaled. Our advisor for this category is Madeleine France; she is listed in the Directory under Florida.

Three-handled cup with paw feet, portrait of 'Rachel' reserved on mottled purple, pink and light blue, signed Rose, blue beehive mark, 7", $1,500.00.

Bowl, Constance, gr & gold border, mk, 2x10x8" **795.00**
Charger, maid on red, Ganz vertieft/Menzler, sgn Seibt, 14" **990.00**
Charger, Mary Queen of Scots, red border, 1900, 17".............. **1,300.00**
Cup, sgn/titled portrait, much gold, 3 gold hdls/paw ft, 7"....... **1,500.00**
Demitasse pot, gods/goddesses/florals, 7", +tray & 4 c/s **350.00**
Plate, Diana, sgn Wagner, 9½"..**350.00**
Plate, fox in forest, cobalt/gold border, hexagonal, mk................**425.00**
Plate, musical scene w/figures, bl w/gold, F Koller, 9½" **440.00**
Plate, mythological scene, Kauffmann, much gold, 8¼"...............**135.00**
Plate, Psyche looks at sleeping Cupid, sgn Keiss, 9½" **1,150.00**
Plate, Waldefle, young woman in grove of trees, 9½" **850.00**
Vase, children as 4 voices of man on bl & gold, ftd, 11"......... **1,000.00**
Vase, Flossie, 3-hdl, 7½"...**475.00**
Vase, Madame LeBrun, sgn Wagner, 8"......................................**895.00**
Vase, portrait reserves, sgn, 3 gold hdls, beehive mk, 9½" **425.00**

Royal Worcester, Worcester

The Worcester Porcelain Company was deeded in 1751. During

the first or Dr. Wall period (so called for one of its proprietors), porcelain with an Oriental influence was decorated in underglaze blue. Useful tablewares represented the largest portion of production, but figurines and decorative items were also made. Very little of the earliest wares were marked and can only be identified by a study of forms, glazes, and the porcelain body, which tends to transmit a greenish cast when held to light. Late in the fifties, a crescent mark was in general use, and rare examples bear a facsimile of the Meissen crossed swords. The first period ended in 1783, and the company went through several changes in ownership during the next eighty years. The years from 1783-1792 are referred to as the Flight period. Marks were a small crescent, a crown with 'Royal,' or an impressed 'Flight.' From 1792-1807 the company was known as Flight and Barr and used the trademark 'F&B' or 'B,' with or without a small cross. From 1807-1813 the company was under the Barr, Flight, and Barr management; this era is recognized as having produced porcelain with the highest quality of artistic decoration. Their mark was 'B.F.B.' From 1813-1840 many marks were used, but the most usual was 'F.B.B.' under a crown to indicate Flight, Barr, and Barr. In 1840 the firm merged with Chamberlain, and in 1852 they were succeeded by Kerr and Binns. The firm became known as Royal Worcester in 1862. Since 1930 Royal Worcester has been considered one of the leaders in the field of limited edition plates and figurines.

Tea set, light green and gold, Pot: #1373, 8½", $750.00; Creamer, 4½", $195.00; Covered sugar bowl, #1575, 5¼", $250.00.

Biscuit jar, HP flowers in relief w/gold, SP trim, mk, 7" 350.00
Bowl, emb weave w/lg leaves, HP int florals, rtcl rim, 5x9" 335.00
Bowl, lattice w/appl flowers, flowers w/in, Dr Wall, 7", EX..........700.00
Bowl, rtcl rim, held between eagle's wings, 7½" 325.00
Bowl, vintage on basketweave, pnt int, #1004, 1884, 9" 335.00
Butter dish, floral, pine cone finial, ca 1890, 5¾x7¼"..................525.00
Candle snuffer, monk, ca 1896, 4½" 185.00
Cup & saucer, Bridal Lace 25.00
Cup & saucer, Gold Chantilly..30.00
Cup & saucer, Oriental florals, mc/gilt, sq bl mk, NM 150.00
Ewer, floral, gold on bl, 4-lobe shape, gold thorn hdl, 1892.........295.00
Ewer, floral sprigs on cream, ovoid, stepped neck, 1885, 7" 175.00
Figurine, Ann Boleyn w/fan, bl dress w/gold trim, 8½" 175.00
Figurine, Audubon's Warbler & Palo Verdi, Doughty, 8", pr ... 1,100.00
Figurine, Bridesmaid, #3224..275.00
Figurine, Cactus Wrens & Prickly Pear, D Doughty, 11", pr .. 1,320.00
Figurine, Corgi, #3243, 3" 375.00
Figurine, English Pointer, #3307, 7½" 395.00
Figurine, Joan (child), 4½x1⅜"..135.00
Figurine, John Bull, ivory, #851, rprs, 7" 300.00

Figurine, Mary Queen of Scots, lav w/gold gown, mk, 8½" 350.00
Figurine, Mid-Eastern lady w/tambourine, sgn Hadley, 12½".......440.00
Figurine, Phoebe & Flame Vine, D Doughty, 11", pr 1,540.00
Figurine, Scarlet Tanagers & Wht Oak, Doughty, 12", VG, pr ...700.00
Figurine, Vermillion Flycatchers & Pussy Willow, 9½", NM, pr..770.00
Figurine, Water Carriers, man/lady, Hadley, 1877, 18", 16".... 2,000.00
Figurine, Yel-Throats & Water Hyacinth, Doughty, 11¾", pr.. 1,320.00
Jardiniere, carnations, ruffled, #1651, 9½x11" 395.00
Jug, floral, mc on cream, dragon hdls, 1887 mk, 9¼" 495.00
Pitcher, floral, melon form w/vine hdl, 1889, 9¾".........................360.00
Pitcher, floral, purple & gold on cream, gold hdl, 10x5½"...........250.00
Plaque, English nobleman portrait, faience, 1865 mk, 17"...........975.00
Plate, floral, scalloped gold rim, 1889, 7⅜" 100.00
Tea caddy, HP bluebells, sgn Sedgley, 4" 295.00
Urn, floral, hdls w/dog heads & face masks, 18", EX............... 2,100.00
Vase, floral, bulbous, #1053, 10" 325.00
Vase, floral on ivory w/gold, hdld bottle form, 1887, 13½" 500.00
Vase, flowers & fruit, ftd, 1909 mk, 4⅛x2⅜" 235.00
Vase, peacock, sgn Watkins, gold trim, mk, dtd 1909, 4⅛".........200.00
Vase, Roman gold & gr trim, ftd shell form, 1888 mk, 8½" 450.00
Vase, Sabrina Ware, trees, gr on bl, hexagonal, 7" 175.00

Roycroft

Near the turn of the century, Elbert Hubbard established the Roycroft Printing Shop in East Aurora, New York. Named in honor of two 17th-century printer-bookbinders, the print shop was just the beginning of a community called Roycroft, which came to be known worldwide. Hubbard became a popular personality of the early 1900s, known for his talents in a variety of areas from writing and lecturing to manufacturing. The Roycroft community became a meeting place for people of various capabilities and included shops for the production of furniture, copper, leather items, and a multitude of other wares which were marked with the Roycroft symbol, an 'R' within a circle below a stylized cross. Hubbard lost his life on the Lusitania in 1915; production in the community continued until the Depression.

Interest is escalating in the field of Arts and Crafts in general, and Roycroft items in particular (along with Stickley, Rolfs, etc.) are rapidly appreciating in value. Copper items are evaluated to a large extent by the condition of the original patina that remains.

Ash stand, hammered copper, match holder on hdl, sgn, 29" 550.00
Bench, Ali Baba #046; oak slab w/bark, orb mk, 42" L, NM ... 5,000.00
Book, Ali Baba, illus Anna Paine, 1899 ....175.00
Book, House of Life, illus Lillie Ess, 1899, leather trim 225.00
Book, King Lear, ¾ levant binding, Japan Vellum, 1904 ....250.00
Book, Rip Van Winkle, ¾ levant binding, 1905 ....225.00
Book, Sonnets from Portuguese, hand-illus, 1898, 12x9" 275.00
Book, Wht Hyacinths, Hubbard, illus Hunter, suede bound, VG ..60.00
Bookends, #309, hammered copper, ring/line decor, 5¼" 175.00
Bookends, #340, open arch, scrolled ends, dk patina, 4x6½" 200.00
Bookends, hammered copper w/tooled owls in reserve, 4x6½" 175.00
Bowl, #208, hammered copper w/brass wash, 1919, 4x10" 200.00
Bowl, copper, 3-ftd, 3x7", +lg oval scoop w/curved hdl...............500.00
Candelabrum, brass, 8 cups on strap w/rolled ends, 3x21" 375.00
Candelabrum, hammered copper, row of 8 cups, 20" L, VG 250.00
Candlestick, #403, dbl supports, lt finish, 8", pr 350.00
Candlestick, copper, pencil std, floral base, 8x3½", pr 550.00
Candlestick, hammered copper, cleaned patina, 1x4" dia..........110.00
Candlestick, Princess, copper, pyramid base, 8", pr 500.00
Card tray, #1104, hammered copper, line/ball design, 7" dia 175.00
Chair, 'Marshall Wilder' #35; rpl seat, orb mk, 35" 500.00
Chair, side; #030, hourglass bk splat, orig leather seat, EX..........650.00

Chair, side; #031, heavy, 3-slat bk, revarnished, sgn, 47" **4,500.00**
Desk, fall front w/strap hinges over 3 drw, script on front........ **6,500.00**
Desk pc, copper tray w/2 sq beveled glass inkwells, 15" L 375.00
Dresser, #108, 2 sm drw over 2, tilt mirror, 61x45", EX........... **3,250.00**
Dressing table, #110, swivel mirror, 1-drw, orb on leg, EX **2,500.00**
Footstool, drop-in leatherette cushion, orb mk, 14x17x12" 500.00
Humidor, brass-washed hammered copper, top/base braid, 8" 230.00
Inkwell, hammered brass, conical w/lid, 2".............................210.00
Lamp, copper/brass/mica, curving 6-sided base/21" shade........ **5,500.00**
Lamp, ldgl 15" cone shade; hammered vasiform base w/hdls ... **8,250.00**
Letter opener, hammered copper, bkward-bent hdl forms arch....140.00
Punch bowl, brn glossy glaze, mk, 10", +8 cups 300.00
Rocker, 5 bk slats, open arms, inset leather seat, 36x24" 450.00

Smoking set, hammered copper with tooled trefoils and geometrics, original dark brown patina, die-stamped, $850.00.

Stand, Little Journey; 2 dbl-keyed shelves, orb, 26", NM 750.00
Stand, Little Journey; 2 dbl-keyed shelves, orig finish, VG..........325.00
Stool, Stool of Repentance cvd into broad apron, rpl, mk 900.00
Table, dining; X-stretchers, 54" sq top, orb on leg, EX **6,000.00**
Table lamp, brass-wash conical shade w/mica panels, 13½" **1,200.00**
Tabouret, 3-slat ends, keyed tenons, orb mk, 20x14"............... **1,700.00**
Telephone, hammered copper, candlestick type, 12½x5"........ **1,600.00**
Tray, emb/tooled int design, oval w/hdls, 22x9", EX...................700.00
Vase, #201, Am Beauty, hammered copper, new patina, 18" .. **1,000.00**
Vase, #202, hammered copper w/brass wash, geometrics, 7" 375.00
Vase, #205, copper w/silver wash, textured, 6", EX......................150.00
Vase, #220, hammered copper, tapering from shoulder, 5", EX ...220.00
Vase, #241, gr matt on copper, long trumpet neck, 16", EX ... **1,000.00**
Wall sconce, hammered copper, concave bk, teardrop form, 8"...280.00

Rozenburg

Some of the most innovative and original Art Nouveau ceramics were created by the Rozenburg factory at The Hague in The Netherlands between 1885 and 1916. Some pieces are similar to Gouda. Rozenburg also made highly prized eggshell ware, so called because of its very thin walls; this is eagerly sought after by collectors. T.A.C. Colenbrander was their artistic leader, with Samuel Schellink and J. Kok designing many of the eggshell pieces.

Key: eg — eggshell

Charger, poppies/daisies/etc, mc on dk brn & gray, sgn, 15".... **1,200.00**
Charger, stylized flowers in earth tones, ca 1890s, 18"............. **1,900.00**
Jar, eg, roses/butterflies, pointed lid w/2 holes, rstr, 16" **2,100.00**
Plaque, thistle flowers, earth tones, coded 1898, 11" dia 700.00

Plate, eg, roses, red/brn/wht/gr on wht, Hartgring, 6½"...............700.00
Vase, bold floral, J van der Vet, integral hdls, rstr, 14" **1,300.00**
Vase, butterfly/floral on bl-gr, basket hdl, Verhoog, 13" **1,600.00**
Vase, eg, freesia on wht, Verhoog, sm neck on teardrop, 6" **2,100.00**
Vase, eg, mushrooms on wht, Verhoog, sqd form, 5" **2,100.00**
Vase, floral/dragons on brn, sqd w/integral hdls, 9½", pr **1,300.00**

Rubena

Rubena glass was made by several firms in the late 1800s. It is a blown art glass that shades from clear to red. See also Art Glass Baskets; Cruets; Sugar Shakers; Salts; specific manufacturers.

Biscuit jar, Dmn Quilt 150.00
Bottle, scent; Dmn Quilt & Drape, silver top, 4x2¼" 110.00
Cruet, Invt T'print, tricorner top, amber cut stopper/hdl.............350.00
Mug, floral, gold & silver trim, 8-sided, 3¾x2¼" 60.00
Pitcher, clear hdl, 7¾" 150.00
Pitcher, lemonade; floral, rib hdl, +2 tumblers 525.00
Rose bowl, gold florals, 4¾x5½" 125.00
Sugar shaker, Invt T'print, 5½" 300.00
Tumble-up, Baby Invt T'print, sq hdl, 6¼"....................................125.00
Tumbler, Invt T'print 65.00
Vase, heavy gold floral, ruffled, trumpet form, 8¾" 225.00
Vase, ribbed, flared, ped ft, 8"...48.00

Rubena Verde

Rubena Verde glass was introduced in the late 1800s by Hobbs, Brockunier, and Company of Wheeling, West Virginia. Its transparent colors shade from red to green. Our advisor for this category is Mike Roscoe; he is listed in the Directory under Michigan. See also Art Glass Baskets; Cruets; Sugar Shakers; Salts.

Cruet, Invt T'print, faceted stopper, att Hobbs, 6¾"...................475.00
Pitcher, Invt T'print, quatrelobe top, 6½" 275.00
Shakers, HP floral, pewter lid, 4½", pr...200.00
Tumbler, floral...95.00
Vase, Drape, bowl form, ped ft, 9¼"..185.00
Vase, reverse colors, scalloped, 6½" 175.00
Vase, ruffled rim, 6" 165.00

Ruby Glass

Produced for over one hundred years by every glasshouse of note in this country, ruby glass has been used to create decorative items such as one might find in gift shops, utilitarian bottles and kitchenware, figurines, and dinnerware lines such as were popular in the Depression era. For further information and study, we recommend *Ruby Glass of the 20th Century* by our advisor, Naomi Over; she is listed in the Directory under Colorado.

Banana boat, Moon & Star, LG Wright, 1974-81, 12" 40.00
Cake plate, Sandwich, Indiana, 1960s-70s, 13" 85.00
Candy dish, Sweetheart, LG Wright, 1974, 3¾" 20.00
Cup, measuring; unknown maker, 16-oz 25.00
Cup, Sweetheart, Macbeth-Evans, 1930-36, rare 100.00
Cup & saucer, Sandwich, Indiana, 1960s-70s................................30.00
Decanter, Blenko, 13" 45.00
Figure, bird, Swedish Glass, ca 1980, 3" 8.00
Lamp, fairy; Sweetheart, LG Wright, 1974-81, 4½".......................25.00

Lamp, oil; Viking, 1976, 9"...20.00
Pitcher, Blenko, #939P, ca 1952, 14"..............................60.00
Pitcher, High Point, Anchor Hocking, 1940s, 80-oz 60.00
Pitcher, hostess; Roly Poly, Macbeth-Evans, 1932, 32-oz.............65.00
Shakers, Mirror & Rose, LG Wright, 1974-81, 3¼", pr.................25.00
Syrup, Moon & Stars, LG Wright, 1981, 4-oz.....................25.00
Tumbler, Hobnail, Anchor Hocking, 1930s, 4½"..........................5.00
Vase, Hoover, Anchor Hocking, 9"................................15.00
Vase, Rachel, Anchor Hocking, 1940s, 10".........................40.00

Ruby-Stained Souvenirs

Ruby-flashed or ruby-stained glass was made through the application of a thin layer of color over clear. It was used in the manufacture of some early pressed tableware and from the Victorian era well into the 20th century for souvenir items which were often engraved on the spot with the date, location, and buyer's name.

Creamer, Arched Ovals, 1908, mini 25.00
Creamer, Invt T'print, mini...32.00
Decanter, Tiny Fine Cut..80.00
Goblet, Bull's Eye Band, dtd..35.00
Mug, Arched Ovals, Boston MA.....................................25.00
Mug, Button Arches, 3¼"...38.00
Mug, Dmn Point Band, 1897 Raymond 30.00
Mug, Heisey Punty Band, Miles Adams.............................40.00
Mug, Sm Corona, St Joseph MO....................................25.00
Punch cup, Button Arches 28.50
Sauce dish, Cathedral 20.00
Toothpick holder, Co-Op's Royal, S Charleston O 1903, 2⅛".......35.00
Tumbler, Lacy Medallion, 1901 ....24.00
Wine, King's Crown, 1893 ....60.00

Rugs, Hooked

Hooked rugs are treasured today for their folk-art appeal. It was a craft that was introduced to this country in about 1830 and flourished its best in the New England states. The prime consideration is not age but artistic appeal. Scenes with animals, buildings, and people; patriotic designs; or whimsical themes are preferred. Condition is, of course, also a factor. Marked examples bearing the stamps of 'Frost and Co.,' 'Abenakee,' 'C.R.,' and 'Ouia' are highly prized. Note: the rugs listed here are rag unless noted otherwise.

Key:
comp — complimentary   mdl — medallion
dmn — diamond   s/a — semi-antique
gb — guard border

Amish, acorns in bl & brn, Lancaster Co PA, 41x24" 145.00
Bright mc sqs in blk grid, unused, 37x21" 85.00
Collie, mtns in bkground, 5-color, 1900s, 35x23" 175.00
Deer, mc border, E Sands Frost pattern maker, rpr, 52x29" 200.00
Dmn design in mc, minor wear, 34x17" 95.00
Dog, mc border, E Sands Frost pattern maker, wool, 45x23" 400.00
Floral, mc on tan, leaf border, cloth bk, 84x50" 850.00
Floral (stylized), leaf border, wear/sm rprs, 61x28" 115.00
Floral (stylized) on tan, lt wear/fading, 54x34"..................250.00
Floral in many colors, dtd 1776-1876, rprs/rpl, 57x37" 375.00
Floral on gray, maroon leaf border, burlap bk, rpr, 49x26".........115.00
Floral/cattails on lg oval, floral spandrels, 25x24", VG...........85.00
Geometrics, red/wht/bl/gr, minor wear, 70x18" 550.00
Geometrics, rich solid colors, 44x29" 325.00

Grenfell, penguin/icebergs, 4-color on burlap, 1900s, 41x40"......550.00
Grenfell, sailboat, 14x11"...200.00
Lighthouse scene, detailed, by JM Bartlette, ME, 35x24" 350.00
Log cabin pattern, red/gr on burlap, 1900s, 144x120"............1,600.00
Man in 1-horse carriage, trees, etc, well done, 39x20" 400.00
Squirrel in oak tree, mc, soiled, 32" dia 200.00
Star/flowers in dmn border, mc on lt ground, 34x21" 85.00
Triangles, dk colors on red, blk/gr borders, 129x19"..............900.00
2 parrots on branches, mc on blk, oval, 1930s, 33x23", EX 45.00

American ship at sea, 58" x 37", 6-color, minor discoloration and wear, $450.00.

Miscellaneous

Braided, hooked panel w/horse on striped ground, 38x30" 195.00
Carpet, American ingrain, mc checks, wool/linen, 110x64"........135.00
Horse, birds in spandrels, yarn X-stitch on burlap, 39x24" 350.00
Loomed, ½" mc felt strips, fringed border, 1900s, 35x24"..............45.00
Penny, wool, mc/blk, wht cotton bk, 37x19", EX.....................200.00

Rumrill

George Rumrill designed and marketed his pottery from 1933 until the early 1940s. During this period at least three different companies produced his works. Today the most popular lines are those made in the 1930s by Red Wing Stoneware and later Red Wing Potteries such as Trumpet Flower, Classica, Manhattan, and of course the Nudes. Rumrill pottery is often recognizable simply by the glaze. A number of two-toned glazes were produced, and these are being avidly sought by today's collectors. It's interesting to note that many Rumrill designs can be found with the Red Wing mark. Our advisors for this category are Wendy and Leo Frese; they are listed in the Directory under Texas.

Vase, elephant handles, $50.00; Vase, Athenian, $275.00; Dealer's sign, $275.00.

Basket, Vintage, gr, #615 ....45.00
Candle holder, Athenian, wht, #576.................................165.00

Cornucopia, dbl; Shell, wht, #452 ....**50.00**
Cornucopia, Empire Line, pk, #684 ....**30.00**
Dealer sign, potter at wheel..**275.00**
Ewer, Vintage, wht, #616 ....**60.00**
Vase, Athenian, gr, #570..**275.00**
Vase, elephant hdls...**50.00**
Vase, not Red Wing, Mammoth Cave, pk, B-5 ....**30.00**
Vase, not Red Wing, pk, H-54 ....**25.00**
Vase, Swan, wht, #443 ....**25.00**
Wall pocket, not Red Wing, gr, I-8............................**15.00**

Rushmore

Ivan Houser studied sculpture and fine arts at the University of Oregon. He gained valuable experience in the potting field, first from the work he did in producing terra cotta architectural sculptures and later through the work he did with the carvers on Mt. Rushmore. In 1933 he purchased a tract of land near Mt. Rushmore where he built his own pottery. Using the especially adaptable clay he found there, he produced a line of decorative items until 1941, after which he went into the teaching field. His wares are characterized by the natural shading of the clay which he allowed to show through the glazes.

Pitcher, gr, water sz **47.50**
Tile, floral, bl, 5", EX..**27.50**
Vase, burnt orange, 1940s, 4" **28.00**
Vase, gold/cream, hand thrown, 4¼" **45.00**
Vase, gr, expansion glaze, mk, 7" **75.00**
Vase, gr drip, 6" **35.00**

Russel Wright Dinnerware

Russel Wright, one of America's foremost industrial designers, also designed several lines of ceramic dinnerware, glassware, and aluminum ware that are now highly sought-after collectibles. His most popular dinnerware then and with today's collectors, American Modern, was manufactured by the Steubenville Pottery Company from 1939 until 1959. It was produced in a variety of solid colors in assortments chosen to stay attune with the times. Casual (his first line sturdy enough to be guaranteed against breakage for ten years from date of purchase) is relatively easy to find today — simply because it has held up so well. During the years of its production, the Casual line was constantly being restyled, some items as many as five times. Early examples were heavily mottled, while later pieces were smoothly glazed and patterned. The ware was marked with Wright's signature and 'China by Iroquois.' It was marketed in fine department stores throughout the country. After 1950 the line was marked 'Iroquois China by Russel Wright.'

To calculate values for items in American Modern, add 100% to the suggested prices in the following listings for examples in these colors: White, Bean Brown, Cantaloupe, and Glacier Blue. In Casual, Brick Red and Aqua items go for around 200% more than any other color, while those in Avocado Yellow are priced lower than suggested values. For those wanting to learn more about the subject, we recommend *The Collector's Encyclopedia of Russel Wright Designs* by our advisor, Ann Kerr. She is listed in the Directory under Ohio.

American Modern

Ash tray, coaster **13.00**
Bowl, lug fruit...**12.00**
Bowl, salad **65.00**
Bowl, vegetable..**17.00**
Butter dish, Coral **175.00**

Butter dish, Wht...**225.00**
Carafe, Gray..**150.00**
Casserole, w/lid, 12"...**45.00**
Celery dish **24.00**

Child's melmac dinner set, $135.00.

Coffee cup lid, Chartreuse..**125.00**
Coffeepot, Chutney, 8x8½" **80.00**
Creamer..**10.00**
Cup & saucer **10.00**
Lug soup **12.00**
Mug (tumbler), Cedar...**50.00**
Pitcher, water..**70.00**
Pitcher, water; w/lid **125.00**
Plate, dinner; 10"...**7.50**
Ramekin, Seafoam, w/lid, ind **125.00**
Refrigerator jar..**115.00**
Salad fork & spoon **85.00**
Shakers, pr...**14.00**
Sugar bowl, w/lid **12.00**
Teapot, Coral, 6x10" **55.00**
Tumbler, Gray, child's...**50.00**

Casual

Bowl, cereal; Charcoal, restyled, 5" **10.00**
Bowl, divided vegetable; 10" **25.00**
Bowl, fruit; restyled, 5¾" **8.00**
Bowl, fruit; 9½-oz, 5½" **8.00**
Bowl, gumbo, 21-oz...**30.00**
Bowl, soup; Aqua, restyled, 18-oz **15.00**
Butter dish, Aqua, ½-lb **150.00**
Butter dish, ½-lb **50.00**
Carafe, Lettuce **125.00**
Carafe, Oyster..**150.00**
Casserole, Oyster, 10" **38.00**
Casserole, 2-qt, 8"...**22.00**
Creamer, lg family sz **16.00**
Cup & saucer, coffee...**12.00**
Cup & saucer, coffee; Wht **18.00**
Gravy bowl, Brick Red, 12-oz, 5¼" **36.00**
Gravy stand, 7½" **7.50**
Pitcher, water; 1½-qt, 5¼"..**40.00**
Plate, luncheon; Canteloupe, 9½" **7.50**
Plate, luncheon; 9½"..**5.00**
Plate, 6½"...**3.00**
Platter, oval, 14½"..**25.00**
Shakers, stacking, pr **12.00**

Glassware

American Modern, bowl, dessert; Smoke	30.00
American Modern, chilling bowl	100.00
American Modern, cocktail, Chartreuse	22.00
American Modern, cocktail, Gray	22.00
American Modern, cocktail, Smoke, 3-oz, 2½"	22.50
American Modern, cordial	40.00
American Modern, cordial, Coral	40.00
American Modern, goblet, Chartreuse	15.00
American Modern, goblet, Smoke	20.00
American Modern, sherbet, Chartreuse	15.00
American Modern, sherbet, Gray	20.00
American Modern, tumbler, iced tea; Coral, 13-oz	25.00
American Modern, tumbler, pilsner; Coral	42.50
American Modern, wine, Chartreuse	17.00
American Modern, wine, Smoke, 4-oz, 3"	22.00
Eclipse, old fashioned	15.00
Eclipse, shot glass	10.00
Flair, tumbler, iced tea; 14-oz	50.00
Flair, tumbler, juice; 6-oz	50.00
Flair, tumbler, water; 11-oz	50.00
Pinch, tumbler, iced tea; 14-oz	30.00
Pinch, tumbler, juice; 6-oz	28.00
Pinch, tumbler, water; 11-oz	30.00
Snow Glass, candle holders, pr	150.00
Snow Glass, tumbler	150.00
Snow Glass, tumbler, iced tea; 14-oz	90.00
Snow Glass, tumbler, juice; 5-oz	90.00
Snow Glass, tumbler, water; 10-oz	90.00

Highlight

Bowl, vegetable; Citron or Nutmeg, oval	50.00
Bowl, vegetable; Wht, Pepper, or Blueberry, rnd	50.00
Butter dish, Wht, Pepper, or Blueberry	125.00
Creamer, Citron or Nutmeg	16.00
Creamer, Wht, Pepper, or Blueberry	20.00
Cup & saucer, AD; high gloss	45.00
Mug, Citron or Nutmeg	30.00
Mug, Wht, Pepper, or Blueberry	35.00
Pitcher, Citron or Nutmeg, w/lid	95.00
Plate, dinner; Wht, Pepper, or Blueberry	16.00
Platter, Citron or Nutmeg, rnd, sm	35.00
Shakers, Wht, Pepper or Blueberry, lg or sm, pr	35.00
Sugar bowl, Citron or Nutmeg	16.00
Sugar bowl, Wht, Pepper, or Blueberry	20.00
Teapot, high gloss	80.00
Teapot, Wht, Pepper, or Blueberry	100.00

Spun Aluminum

Russel Wright's aluminum ware may not have been especially well accepted in its day — it tended to damage easily and seems to have had only limited market appeal — but today's collectors feel quite differently about it, as is apparent in the suggested values noted in the following listings.

Baine Marie, server	400.00
Candelabrum, rare, 18x14"	175.00
Casserole	50.00
Cheese board	40.00
Flower ring	110.00
Gravy boat	125.00

Hot relish server	175.00
Humidor, sandwich	150.00
Humidor, tobacco; 12"	100.00
Ice bucket	50.00
Muffin warmer, wire insert, w/lid	90.00
Old fashioned set, 20-pc	400.00
Peanut scoop	40.00
Pitcher, sherry	225.00
Portable bar/serving cart	1,750.00
Punch set	1,500.00
Relish rosette, sm	75.00
Smoking stand	300.00
Spaghetti set, 3-pc	325.00
Tea set, 4-pc	400.00
Vase, 12"	65.00
Vase or flowerpot, sm, ea	50.00
Waste basket	100.00

Sterling

Bouillon, 7-oz	10.00
Bowl, fruit; 5"	7.00
Bowl, onion soup; 10-oz	16.00
Bowl, salad; 7½"	12.00
Bowl, soup; 6½"	10.00
Creamer, 3-oz	10.00
Cup, 7-oz	10.00
Pitcher, water; restyled	75.00
Pitcher, water; 2-qt	60.00
Plate, service; 11½"	10.00
Plate, 6¼"	4.00
Plate, 9"	7.00
Platter, oval, 13⅝"	18.00
Saucer, demitasse	8.00
Teapot, 10-oz	45.00

Miscellaneous

Bauer, ash tray, sm	175.00
Bauer, vase, pillow form	500.00
Harker White Clover, ash tray	20.00
Harker White Clover, bowl, vegetable; 7½"	18.00
Harker White Clover, clock, General Electric	50.00
Harker White Clover, pitcher, w/lid, 2-qt	65.00
Harker White Clover, platter, 13¼"	25.00
Highlight, fork, stainless steel	55.00
Highlight, knife, stainless steel	75.00
Home Decorator, cup & saucer, plastic	9.00
Home Decorator, platter, plastic	15.00
Ideal, bowl, salad; plastic	13.00
Ideal, tumbler, plastic, lg or sm, ea	25.00
Knowles, bowl, divided vegetable	48.00
Knowles, bowl, 6¼"	7.00
Knowles, Fontaine, teapot	80.00
Knowles, Grass, platter, 13"	25.00
Knowles, Mayfair, shakers, pr	20.00
Knowles, plate, 10¾"	9.00
Knowles, platter, 14¼"	17.50
Meladur, cup, plastic, 7-oz	7.00
Meladur, plate, compartmented, plastic, 9½"	10.00
Meladur, plate, plastic, 9"	8.00

Russian Art

Before the Revolution in 1917, many jewelers and craftsmen created exquisite marvels of their arts, distinctive in the extravagant detail of their enamel work, jeweled inlays, and use of precious metals. These treasures aptly symbolized the glitter and the romance of the glorious days under the reign of the Tsars of Imperial Russia. The most famous of these master jewelers was Carl Faberge (1852-1920), goldsmith to the Romanovs. Following the tradition of his father, he took over the Faberge workshop in 1870. Eventually Faberge employed more than 500 assistants and set up workshops in Moscow, Kiev, and London as well as in St. Petersburg. His specialties were enamel work, clockwork automated figures, carved animal and human figures of precious or semiprecious stones, cigarette cases, small boxes, scent flasks, and his best-known creations, the Imperial Easter Eggs — each of an entirely different design. By the turn of the century, his influence had spread to other countries, and his work was revered by royalty and the very wealthy. The onset of the war marked the end of the era. Very little of his work remains on the market, and items that are available are very expensive. But several of his contemporaries were goldsmiths whose work can be equally enchanting. Among them are Klingert, Ovchinnikov, Smirnov, Ruckert, Loriye, Cheryatov, Kuzmichev, Nevalainen, Adler, Sbitnev, Third Artel, Wakewa, Holmstrom, Britzin, Wigstrom, Orlov, Nichols, and Plincke. Most of them produced excellent pieces similar to those made by Faberge between 1880 and 1910.

Perhaps the most important bronze Russian artist was Eugenie Alexandrovich Lanceray (1847-87). From 1875 until 1887, he modeled many equestrian groups of falconers and soldiers ranging in height from about 20" to 30". Some of them bear the Chopin foundry mark; they are presently worth from $4,000 up. Other excellent artists were Schmidt Felling (19th Century), who specialized in mounted figures of cossacks wearing military uniforms, and Nicholas Leiberich (late 19th Century), who also specialized in equestrian groups. Most of the pieces made by the above artists were signed and had the foundry mark (Chopin, Woerfell, etc.)

Russian porcelain is another field where Imperial connections have undoubtedly added to the interest of collectors and museums worldwide. The most important factories were: Imperial Russian Porcelain, St. Petersburg (or Petrograd or Leningrad, 1744-1917); Gardner, Moscow (1765-1872); Kuznetsoff, St. Petersburg and Moscow (1800-1900); Korniloff, St. Petersburg (1800-1900); and Babunin, St. Petersburg (1800-1900).

Key: lcq — lacquer

Silver gilt and enamel cup, 3½", $500.00; Egg-form box, marks for Klingert, 4¼" long, $1,200.00.

Beaker, silver gilt/niello, eng, mk A Sch, Moscow, 1827, 2⅝".....**750.00**
Beaker, vodka; silver gilt & niello, mk F Ja, Moscow, 3 for **1,200.00**
Bottle, scent; silver/enamel, ovoid, 2-pc, 1900, 3"........................**600.00**
Bowl, silver gilt, shaded enamel, F Ruckert, Faberge, 1900 ....**13,500.00**

Box, silver gilt & enamel, circular, K Faberge, 1910, 2" **3,000.00**
Caddy, lcq papier-mache, Moscow scenes, 1860s, 4½" **2,800.00**
Candelabrum, ormolu w/circular malachite base, 1800s, pr..... **7,500.00**
Champagne flute, silver gilt/niello, eng, J Hendrikson, 1832 .. **1,050.00**
Cigarette case, gold-mtd, silver gilt, enameling, Faberge **15,000.00**
Cigarette case, silver-gilt, chased troika, 1895, 4¼" **235.00**
Cvg, seated pug dog, agate, gold-mt ruby eyes, Faberge, 1900 . **6,000.00**
Dish, HP florals, porc, rnd, Lomonosov, Petrograd, 1921 .... **1,200.00**
Egg, gold, enamel, jeweled beetle form, Faberge, 1900 ....**21,000.00**
Equestrian group, falconer, bronze, after Lanceray, ca 1880s... **6,000.00**
Equestrian group, mtd soldier, bronze, after Lanceray, 1885.... **4,125.00**
Figure, chimney sweep, biscuit, MS Kuznetsov, ca 1900, 11¾"....**900.00**
Figure, coachman, porc, Gardner, early 1800s, 7½" **600.00**
Figure, girl, porc, Gardner, early 1800s, 7½".................................**750.00**
Figure, girl, porc, unmk, 1800s, rstr, 7¾" **600.00**
Figure, Peter the Great, bronze, after BM Mikeshin, 1909 ...... **4,500.00**
Figure, sweeper, porc, Popov, 1800s, 7⅞" **900.00**
Figure (group), porc, Gardner factory, late 1800s, 10" **1,075.00**
Letter opener, silver gilt, enameled florals, 1910, 8¾" **1,025.00**
Pastille burner, pnt biscuit, unmk, 1800s, 8¾" **750.00**
Pitcher, water; silver, Moscow, 1841, 9½" **600.00**
Plate, pnt porc, Lomonosov, Petrograd, 1922, 9⅞" **900.00**
Plate, porc, Imperial, Period of Nicholas I 1825-55, 13", pr **1,350.00**
Plate, porc, Imperial, Period of Nicholas I 1825-55, 9¼" **600.00**
Snuff box, silver, circular, Waechter, Moscow, 1790, 3¾" **900.00**
Snuff box, silver & niello, eng, mk NM, Moscow, mid 1800s **750.00**
Snuff box, silver gilt & niello, mk OB, Moscow, 1834, 2⅝" **750.00**
Spoon, enamel on silver, sgn Faberge, rnd bowl, lg **1,575.00**
Spoon, lcq silver gilt, Ninth Artel, Moscow, 1908-17, 7½" **550.00**
Spoon, serving; silver, P Ovchinnikov, Moscow, 1879, 9"...........**900.00**
Spoon, silver gilt & shaded cloisonne, Faberge, Moscow, 8" ... **2,400.00**
Vase, cobalt glass, ormolu mt, ca 1800, 10⅛", pr **1,650.00**

Sabino

Sabino art glass was produced by Marius-Ernest Sabino in France during the 1920s and '30s. It was made in opalescent, frosted, and colored glass and was designed to reflect the Art Deco style of that era. In 1960, using molds he modeled by hand, Sabino once again began to produce art glass using a special formula he himself developed that was characterized by a golden opalescence. Although the family continued to produce glassware for export after his death in 1971, they were never able to duplicate Sabino's formula.

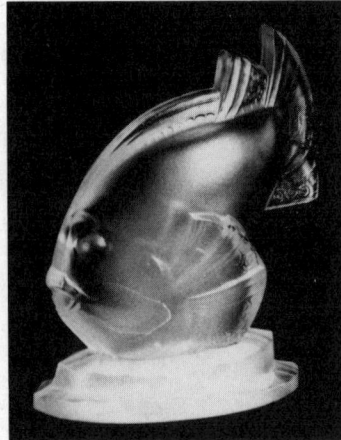

Figure of a fish, 4½", $125.00.

Bottle, scent; Frivolites, women & swans, opal, 6¼" **70.00**
Bowl, shell w/star center, lg **195.00**
Box, powder; Petalia, med sz..**95.00**

Figurine, bird, perched **58.00**
Figurine, bird, teasing, wings down **70.00**
Figurine, butterfly, wings open, sm...........................**32.00**
Figurine, cat **24.00**
Figurine, cherub...**24.00**
Figurine, chick, jumping...................................**55.00**
Figurine, dove, head up, sm...............................**24.00**
Figurine, dragonfly.......................................**120.00**
Figurine, fish, 2x2"......................................**22.50**
Figurine, hand, right or left **200.00**
Figurine, Isadora Duncan.................................**800.00**
Figurine, mockingbird, lg................................**90.00**
Figurine, mouse..**55.00**
Figurine, nude w/long hair, emb/incised mks, 6¾" **195.00**
Figurine, pekingese, sm..................................**24.00**
Figurine, rabbit..**22.50**
Figurine, rooster, lg **465.00**
Figurine, stork group **525.00**
Figurine, Venus de Milo, lg..............................**50.00**
Figurine, woodpecker....................................**55.00**
Knife rest, bee form.....................................**25.00**
Knife rest, fish form **25.00**
Tray, shell, sm...**35.00**
Tray, swallow, sm **28.00**
Vase, Abundance, opal **700.00**
Vase, Colombes, opal **500.00**
Vase, La Danse..**995.00**
Vase, Ovals & Pearls **235.00**

Salesman's Samples and Patent Models

Salesman's samples and patent models are often mistaken for toys or homemade folk art pieces. They are instead actual working models made by very skilled craftsmen who worked as model-makers. Patent models were made until the early 1900s. After that, the patent office no longer required a model to grant a patent. The name of the inventor or the model-maker and the date it was built is sometimes noted on the patent model. Salesman's samples were occasionally made by model-makers, but often they were assembled by an employee of the company. These usually carried advertising messages to boost the sale of the product. Though they are still in use today, the most desirable examples date from the 1800s to about 1945.

Many small stoves are incorrectly termed a 'salesman's sample'; remember that no matter how detailed one may be, it must be considered a toy unless accompanied by a carrying case, the indisputable mark of a salesman's sample.

Clothes wringer, Am Wringer Co, CI/wood, 11x5x3½", EX **135.00**
Coffin & vault, Clark, cast wht metal, 18x21x13", VG **300.00**
Dresser, oak, pressed decor/beading, w/mirror, EX..............**300.00**
Dresser, wood, decal decor, Payne, Vermont, EX **78.00**
Freezer, Gem, wooden, with orig decal, 1891, 7x7x5", VG.........**135.00**
Hammock, woven mc strings w/fringe, wooden base, '30s, 16" **45.00**
Hat, Stetson, M in special Christmas box **45.00**
Heater/furnace, Atlantic Stove Co, #24, 3-pc, 7", G **300.00**
Oil kit, Skelly Oil, 1940s, EX **75.00**
Padlock case, w/21 locks & keys, ca 1929, EX **95.00**
Plow, walking; Oliver Chilled Plow Co, NM **1,850.00**
Street light, Westinghouse, working, 30" **1,250.00**
Table, dressing; decal trim, 3-drw/3 folding mirrors, EX..........**250.00**
Table, hardwood, twin ped, 5½x6x9", EX **75.00**
Table, twin ped, drw w/brass pulls, 5½x18x10", EX **130.00**
Trash can, metal, Chief emb on lid, 4" **45.00**

Vacuum, upright; Hoover, 1930s, 24", NM **90.00**
Wagon jack, Chapman Pat'd Feb 23, 86, heavy steel, 4⅛" **95.00**
Weathervane, gilded, glass case, 19x9", NM **850.00**

Coach, Diamond Tally Ho model, Abbot and Downing Coach Co., NH, wood, canvas, metal, leather, and velvet, 32" long, $4,500.00.

Salt Glaze

As early as the 1600s, potters used common salt to glaze their stoneware. This was accomplished by heating the salt and introducing it into the kiln at maximum temperature. The resulting gray-white glaze was a thin, pitted surface that resembles the peel of an orange.

Basket, rtcl hazelnut motif, 2 hdls, 10" W, EX **465.00**
Charger, basketweave scroll-bordered panels, 18", NM **600.00**
Coffeepot, HP bldgs etc, 2 lion-mask ft, rstr, 8½" **2,860.00**
Creamer, emb floral, Eros in center circle, bl trim, 4" **125.00**
Dish, emb scalloped rim, scroll/weave-emb panels, 8x11" L **400.00**
Dish, intricate molded design w/rtcl rim, rpr, 10½"......................**85.00**
Dish, rtcl trellis panels at shaped rim, 8x9" L, NM.....................**400.00**

Dish, molded border, 1760, hairline, 11" long, $400.00; Basket, molded and reticulated hazelnuts, 10" wide, EX, $465.00; Dish, reticulated trellis panels, 9" long, $400.00.

Jug, hunting scene, cobalt neck, Doulton & Watts, 6½" **135.00**
Plate, emb motif, rtcl rim, 8½", NM **550.00**
Plate, emb motif, rtcl rim, 9¾", EX............................**300.00**
Plate, Success to King of Prussia etc emb on rim, 9", EX.............**880.00**
Sweetmeat, formed as 3 half-melons on leafy tray, rstr, 6" **880.00**
Tall pot, appl scenes, woman/child finial, bl trim, 9½", EX **700.00**
Teapot, acanthus leaves/figures, Castleford type, 6½", VG..........**275.00**
Teapot, appl mc florals, twig spout/hdl, bulbous, rstr, 7" **700.00**
Tureen, allover emb dots, 3 lion-mask ft, 10" W, EX..............**2,970.00**

Salt Shakers

The screw-top salt shaker was invented by John Mason in 1858.

In 1871 when salt became more refined, some ceramic shakers were molded with pierced tops. 'Christmas' shakers, so called because of their December 25, 1877, patent date, were fitted with a rotary agitator designed to break up any lumps in the salt. There are four types: Christmas Barrel (rare in cranberry and amethyst); Christmas Panel (rare in colors); Christmas Pearl (opaque, pearly white with painted decor); and Octagon Waffle (clear, thick glass made in three sizes with a rotary agitator, sometimes having undated tops). The dated top and patented agitator for the Christmas Barrel and Christmas Panel salt shakers were produced by Dana K. Alden of Boston; most of the glass bodies were made by the Boston and Sandwich Glass Co. in the late 1870s and 1880s. Identical shakers which have no agitator or dated top are the companion peppers; these fetch about 30% less than the salts on today's markets.

Today much of the interest in collecting is concentrated on art glass, Wave Crest, and custard glass examples. (See also specific categories.) If you would like to learn more about salt shakers, we recommend *The World of Salt Shakers, Second Edition*, by Mildred and Ralph Lechner; their address may be found in the Directory under Virginia. In the following listings, prices are for single shakers unless noted 'pair.' Values are for old, original shakers. Some of these have been reproduced, and this will be noted in the description.

Lobe Four, pink and white florals with gold on white, $225.00 for the pair.

Annie 45.00
Argus Swirl, cranberry 150.00
Artichoke (Valencia), Fostoria Glass, 1891 ....33.00
Aster & Leaf, bl, pr 125.00
Basket, milk glass, HP decor 25.00
Beaded Dahlia, gr opaque, pr 55.00
Boot on Fan 20.00
Bulging Petal, bl 25.00
Bulging Three-Petal, pigeon blood 45.00
Burmese, ribbed barrel, no decor, Mt WA, pr 400.00
Button Arches, ruby flashed, pr 60.00
Cane & Cable, pr 35.00
Christmas Barrel, amber, w/lid (dtd) & agitator, Dana K Alden ..100.00
Christmas Barrel, apple gr, w/lid & agitator 110.00
Christmas Barrel, cobalt, w/lid & agitator, +pepper, pr ..200.00
Christmas Barrel, cranberry, w/lid & agitator 290.00
Christmas Barrel, cranberry, w/lid & agitator, +pepper, pr ..450.00
Christmas Barrel, dk amethyst, w/lid & agitator 100.00
Christmas Barrel, gr, w/lid & agitator, pr 225.00
Christmas Barrel, peacock bl, w/lid & agitator, +pepper, pr ..250.00
Christmas Panel, amethyst, w/lid & agitator 225.00

Christmas Panel, cranberry, w/lid & agitator 300.00
Christmas Panel, dk amethyst, w/lid & agitator 275.00
Christmas Panel, sapphire bl, w/lid & agitator 225.00
Cord & Tassel, gr 30.00
Cord & Tassel, pk 45.00
Cotton Bale, bl opaque 25.00
Creased Waist, opaque Muranese, New Martinsville, pr ...90.00
Crossroads, amber, pr 35.00
Currier & Ives, bl or vaseline, rare 70.00
Daisy & Fern, cranberry opal, pr 140.00
Diamond w/Peg, custard, pr 85.00
Double Leaf, pk 45.00
Fig, cranberry satin w/floral, Mt WA, 2¾", pr 550.00
Fig, opal w/floral, Mt WA, 2¾", pr 250.00
Fine Cut, yel, pr 50.00
Flower Band, pigeon blood, pr 140.00
Forget-Me-Not, tall, gr, Challinor 25.00
Forget-Me-Not, tall, milk glass, pr 45.00
Geneva, gr w/gold, McKee 95.00
Georgia Gem, custard, souvenir, pr 80.00
Grape w/Vine, pk, rare 55.00
Guttate, pk cased (reproduced), pr 75.00
Heart, milk glass, pr 40.00
Honeycomb, amberina 95.00
Horseshoe, amber, lg, pr 35.00
Intaglio, emerald gr w/gold, Northwood, rare, pr 325.00
Iris w/Meander, gr w/gold, pr 75.00
Jefferson Optic, amethyst, HP, pr 65.00
Leaf & Spear, HP opalware, Wave Crest, pr 165.00
Leaf Mold, cranberry cased, silver flecks, pr 175.00
Leaf Mold, vaseline spatter, pr 125.00
Lobe, Four; shiny Crown Milano w/florals & gilt, pr 225.00
Many Petals, New Martinsville 35.00
National's Eureka, ruby stained, pr 65.00
Nestor, bl, no enamel 35.00
Optic, rubena w/florals, Hobb's, pr 190.00
Owl's head, milk glass, orig top 150.00
Panelled Shell, pk cased (reproduced) 48.00
Panelled Sprig, milk glass w/gr decor, pr 40.00
Peachblow, ribbed, Mt WA 800.00
Pillar, Ribbed; satinized Burmese, HP florals, Mt WA, rare, pr ..900.00
Quilted Phlox, gr cased, Northwood 30.00
Reverse Swirl, cranberry opal, pr 95.00
Roman Rosette, pr 30.00
Sequoia, bl, in stand, pr 85.00
States, glass lid, pr 35.00
Sunset, milk glass 20.00
Thousand Eye, amber 18.00
Thousand Eye, bl 32.00
Torch & Wreath, custard, Dithridge, pr 85.00
Wildflower, apple gr, pr 100.00
Woven Neck, Wave Crest, kitten in grass decor 110.00
Wreath 12-Panel, pk roses, Mt WA, Pairpoint, pr 125.00

Novelty

Those interested in novelty shakers will enjoy *Salt and Pepper Shakers*, an illustrated price guide by Helene Guarnaccia, and *The Collector's Encyclopedia of Salt and Pepper Shakers, Figural and Novelty*, by Melva Davern. Both are available at your local library or from Collector Books. Note: 'Mini' shakers are no taller than 1½". Instead of having a cork, the user was directed to 'use tape to cover hole.'

Elephant, yel & blk pnt chalkware, American, 1920s-50s, pr **7.00**

GE refrigerator shakers, milk glass with paper decal, 3¼", $40.00.

Flamingo, ceramic, Japan, pr 15.00
Hamburger, ceramic, Taiwan, pr 3.00
Hanger, cow w/milk cans, ceramic, Japan, 1940s-50s, 3-pc 10.00
Hanger, Dutch girl w/buckets, ceramic, Japan, ca '35, 3-pc............12.00
Hugger, monkey & coconut, ceramic, Japan, pr 5.00
Hugger, piggybk clowns, ceramic, Japan, 1940s-50s, pr 22.00
Hugger, puppy & garbage can, ceramic, Japan, pr............................ 8.00
Hugger, squirrel w/acorn, ceramic, Japan, pr 6.00
Mini, atomizer & powder box, Arcadia Ceramics, '50s-60s, pr 35.00
Mini, bowling ball & pin, Arcadia Ceramics, '50s-60s, pr..............25.00
Mini, castle & crown, Arcadia Ceramics, 1950s-60s, pr 35.00
Mini, ironing board & washtub, Arcadia Ceramics, '50s, pr 35.00
Mini, lighthouse & sailboat, Arcadia Ceramics, '50s-60s, pr..........25.00
Mini, picnic basket & thermos, Arcadia Ceramics, '50s, pr 35.00
Mini, slice of pie & coffee mug, Arcadia Ceramics, '50s, pr...........20.00
Mini, snake charmer & basket, Arcadia Ceramics, '50s-60s, pr 35.00
Mini, treasure chest & map, Arcadia Ceramics, '50s-60s, pr 30.00
Nester, bear w/beehive, ceramic, Japan, pr.................................... 8.00
Nester, sleeping Mexican, ceramic, Japan, 2-pc.............................15.00
Nester, 2 music notes on treble clef base, ceramic, 3-pc 12.00
One-piece, dachshund, HP ceramic, Japan 8.00
One-piece, Dutch couple, HP ceramic, Japan.................................12.00
One-piece, palm trees, HP ceramic, Japan, 1930-50 ....10.00
Race car, 22k-gold pnt ceramic, Japan, 1940s, pr 18.00
Snuggle, pigs, realistic pnt, Japan, pre-1960, pr 8.00

Salts, Open

Before salt became refined, processed, and free-flowing as we know it today, it was necessary to serve it in a salt cellar. An innovation of the early 1800s, the master salt was placed by the host and passed from person to person. Smaller individual salts were a part of each place setting. A small silver spoon was used to sprinkle it onto the food. If you would like to learn more about the subject of salts, we recommend *5,000 Open Salts*, written by William Heacock and our advisor for this category, Patricia Johnson, with many full-color illustrations and current values. You will find Patricia Johnson's address in the Directory under California.

In the listings below, the numbers refer to *Open Salts* by Johnson and Heacock, and *Pressed Glass Salt Dishes* by L.W. and D.B. Neal. Lines with 'repro' within the description reflect values for reproduced salts.

Key:
EPNS — electroplated nickel silver   HM — hallmarked

Animals, Figurals, and Novelties

Bandmaster's cap, US Glass, H&J-A5013 ....90.00
Bird & Berry, McKee, amber or bl vase, #997, ea 65.00
Bird & Berry, sgn Degenhart, #998 ....25.00
Bird & Berry, unsgn Degenhart, #933...15.00
Chickens, dbl, milk glass, sgn Vallerystahl, #4447.........................55.00
Dog pulling cart, amber, #2102 ....95.00
Dresser, salt & pepper, #4742 ....150.00
Duck, heavy crystal, European, #4677, 2¾" 45.00
Figural hdl, dbl, clear, European, #3777...35.00
Horseshoe, #3741, ind 27.00
Horseshoe, 'Good Luck,' #3742, master 65.00
Rabbit, covered, sgn Vallerystahl, #3750..55.00
Sleigh, amber glass, ca 1900, #3734 ....125.00
Sleigh, Fostoria, ca 1940, #3735..45.00
Squirrel on tree, #3735, ind...45.00
Swan, gr, sgn Cambridge, #935 ....35.00
Turtle, clear, #3758..35.00
Wagon, clear, ca 1890, #3739 ....40.00
Wildflower on turtle base, amber, #506 ....125.00

Art Glass

Cased, pk & wht ruffled top, #126 ....125.00
Cranberry glass, ruffled rigaree, tulip top, SP holder 135.00
Daum, enameled windmills, tub shape..900.00
Daum Nancy, floral, sgn, 7"..800.00
Daum Nancy, windmill scenic, sgn, #10 ....800.00
English, William & Mary, yel vaseline, #69 ....55.00
Legras, floral, sterling gold-washed base, sgn, #12 ....750.00
Monot Stumpf, ormolu holder, stones 350.00
Monot Stumpf, rnd, #19-22 ....95.00
Mt WA, shiny, unsgn, #46 ....135.00
Quezal, #18, 1" dia...140.00
Spatterware, wht cased, clear rigaree, appl ft, HJ-134 ....195.00
Steuben, Calcite, ped ft, #34 ....225.00
Steuben, Jade Gr w/Alabaster ped ft, H&J-2041 ....250.00
Tiffany, bl, ruffled top edge, sgn, #30 ....450.00
Tiffany, ruffled top edge, sgn, #32 ....150.00
Wave Crest, tulip-molded sides, enamel decor, rnd, H&J-47 .....150.00
Webb, cranberry, clear rigaree, berry pontil, SP holder...............275.00
Webb, vaseline, clear rigaree, berry pontil, SP fr, #96.................250.00

China

Austria, HP, rnd, sgn, #1272, ind 12.00
Celery salt, HP, EX quality, #1720..10.00
Elfinware, Germany, basket shape, #1253.....................................15.00
Elfinware, Germany, bird hdls, #1261..25.00
Elfinware, Germany, swan, ornate, #1039......................................35.00
Elfinware, Japan, #1222...10.00
German Dresden, appl flowers, sgn, #1689, ind 45.00
Haviland, pattern decor, #1400, ind 30.00
Japan, HP, #1443, ind 5.00
Limoges, HP china, rnd, sgn, #1275, ind......................................12.00
Meissen, sgn, ca 1890, #1812-1814 ....125.00
Nippon, celery salt, #1714.. 5.00
Nippon, HP, rnd, 3 ft, #1365, ind 10.00
Nippon, HP, rnd, 3 legs, #1423-1425...15.00
Royal Bayreuth, ped ft, HP scenic, sgn, #1666 ....125.00
Royal Copenhagen, ca 1890, #1201...55.00

Cut Glass

Cranberry, etched, ped ft, ca 1890, #123 ....85.00

Diamond Point, #3101 ....**10.00**
Faceted, #2919 ....**10.00**
Heart/club/dmn/spade, #3034-3035, set of 4 ....**200.00**
Ped ft, sgn Clark, #3009 ....**25.00**
Ped ft, sgn Waterford, ca 1970, #3698.................**35.00**
Ped ft, Waterford type, ca 1860, #3699................**100.00**
Ped ft, Waterford type, gr, ca 1860, #601............**125.00**
Sgn Hawkes, #3064 ....**55.00**
Sgn J Hoare, #3166 ....**35.00**
Zippered, #3088 ....**10.00**

Lacy Glass

American, non-flint, repro, ca 1920-40, VG **45.00**
Avon, repro **5.00**
French, amber, non-flint, repro, ca 1920-40, VG **65.00**
Metro Museum of Art, vaseline or bl, sgn, repro **15.00**
Neal-BF-1, basket of flowers, VG **75.00**
Neal-BF-1B, basket of flowers, opal, chip on leg **125.00**
Neal-BT-5, Lafayette boat, med bl **950.00**
Neal-BT-8, Lafayette boat, cobalt, sgn Sandwich, VG ...**950.00**
Neal-CT-1A, scarce, minor chips, 3" L **125.00**
Neal-DI-8, dbl, roughage on bottom **140.00**
Neal-EE-3B, eagles on 4 corners, VG **150.00**
Neal-EE-36, sm edge chips, 3¼" **50.00**
Neal-EE-8, eagle, rnd **280.00**
Neal-GA-2, cathedral windows, cobalt, leg chip **125.00**
Neal-HN-18A, opaline, ftd, VG **250.00**
Neal-NE-1A, wht opaque, sgn NE Glass Co Boston, EX **225.00**
Neal-OL-12A, sm edge chips, 3½" L **50.00**
Neal-OO-7, citron, sm edge chips, very rare, 3" L **500.00**
Neal-SL-8, amber, chips on base, rare, 4" L **350.00**
Neal-WN-1A, wagon, VG **400.00**

Pottery

Chinese Export, bl & wht, trencher, 18th C, EX **400.00**
Figural, condiment w/spoons, Germany, #1119 ....**75.00**
Quimper, ca 1920, #1729..**25.00**
Quimper, dbl, figural hdl, ca 1890, #1129 ....**125.00**
Quimper, dbl, hdl, HP, #1132 ....**65.00**
Royal Doulton, sterling HM rim, ca 1873, #1870.....**95.00**
Royal Doulton, sterling HM rim, ca 1900, #1851 ....**65.00**
Royal Worcester, snail-type shell, ivory stained, M ...**95.00**
Royal Worchester, dbl wall, ca 1862, #1861, ind **125.00**
Wedgwood, gr, sterling HM rim, ca 1897, #1850 .....**165.00**
Wedgwood, sterling HM rim, ca 1897, sgn, #1850.....**125.00**

Pressed Glass, Clear

Alexis, Fostoria, #2631 ....**10.00**
Applied Bands, #2934, ind **25.00**
Arched Leaf, master...**18.00**
Atlanta (Lion), #2758, ind..**45.00**
Atlanta (Lion), master..**45.00**
Beatty Rib, old, #3387 ....**10.00**
Buckle, #3608, master **25.00**
Butterfly & Cattails, #3568 ....**35.00**
Diamond Point Disk, #2930 ....**15.00**
Diamond Rosette, #3407, master................................**25.00**
Diamond Shield, #3600 ....**20.00**
Grasshopper, #3573 ....**35.00**
Harp, #3601, master...**35.00**
Heisey Pillows, sgn, #2697..**35.00**

Illinois, plain, #2760, ind...**15.00**
Jacob's Ladder, #3580 ....**27.00**
King's Crown, plain, #2776 ....**25.00**
Lincoln Drape, #3619 ....**45.00**
Medallion Sunburst, #2543 .... **8.00**
Open Plaid, #3567 ....**12.00**
Plain Band, Heisey, #2560 ....**22.00**
Sawtooth Circle, #3540..**18.00**
Serrated Rib & Fine Cut, #2535, ind **10.00**
Snail #2656, ind...**30.00**
Tree of Life, 'Salt,' #3582, master...............................**75.00**
Washington, #2504, ind...**27.00**
Washington Centennial, #2518, ind **14.00**
Washington State, #1518, ind......................................**14.00**
3-Panel, master **12.00**

Pressed Glass, Colored

Beatty Rib, bl **35.00**
Beatty Rib, opal **30.00**
Boyd, hen on nest, various colors, repro, new **6.00**
English Hobnail, gr, bl, etc, old, ea **15.00**
English Hobnail, repro, Wright, ea **5.00**
Fine Cut & Block, amber flashed, #837, master **65.00**
Fine Cut & Block, bl, pk, etc, flashed-on, ea **45.00**
Heisey Tub, cobalt, sgn **150.00**
Hobnail, opal, amber, or bl, ea **22.00**
Jersey Swirl, bl, #426...**22.00**
King's Crown, cranberry flashed.................................**100.00**
Leaf & Rib (Maple Leaf), vaseline or bl, ea **25.00**
Milk glass, crossed logs, H&J-4473............................**50.00**
Panel w/Diamond Point, apple gr, #372 ....**35.00**
Sowerby's #1350, custard glass, rnd w/sq hdls, H&J-4629 ....**87.00**
Swan, Crown Tuscan, repro **20.00**
Swan, Crown Tuscan, unsgn **50.00**
Wreath & Shell, bl or vaseline, ea **125.00**
3-Panel, bl, vaseline, amber, or gr, #554, ea **18.00**

Silverplate

Clear glass liner, #3918, Victorian **65.00**
Cranberry glass in holder, #4215-4217 ....**200.00**
English, David Hannel, ca 1754, sm dents, pr **250.00**
Oblong, ftd, Meriden Co, #4050, worn......................**15.00**
Overshot glass in holder, #4215-4217 ....**65.00**
Ped ft, Meriden Co, #3948, worn **12.00**
Ruby liner, Derby HM holder, #319 ....**75.00**
Salt & pepper, English, ca 1890, #4134 ....**25.00**

Sterling, Continental Silver, and Enamel

Albert Cole Medallion, ca 1850, #4208 ....**175.00**
American, lattice w/glass liner, ca 1900, ind **20.00**
Cloisonne, Chinese, w/pepper, old **65.00**
English, Dixon & Son, oblong, 4 ft, #3965, ind.........**55.00**
English, gr liner, ca 1920, ind **65.00**
English, rectangular, Birmingham 1911 ....**65.00**
English, shell, 3 ball ft, #4279, ind **20.00**
English, trencher, Rockefeller repro, spoon, #4227 ......**75.00**
English, trencher, 1892, H&J-4161 ....**80.00**
English, tureen shape, heavy Baroque, ca 1890 ....**85.00**
European, cobalt in 800 silver holder, ca 1850, #676............**125.00**
European, reindeer pulling sleigh, #4748 ....**425.00**
French, cobalt, dbl, ped ft, ca 1850, #761 ....**140.00**

French, ornate, ca 1800, master **225.00**
French, ornate, ca 1845, #3935, w/spoon, ind **150.00**
French, ornate, ca 1890, #3937, w/spoon, ind **125.00**
French, oval w/4 hdls, glass liner, H&J-3979.............................**125.00**
French, sq w/glass insert, #3946, w/spoon, ind **95.00**
German, glass insert, ca 1880, #3938, ind **35.00**
German, ped ft, figural hdls, ca 1822, #4286, pr **550.00**
German, swan w/liner, 800 silver, ca 1890, #4294, w/spoon **95.00**
German, wheelbarrow, 800 silver, ca 1800, #4229 ....**150.00**
German, 3 swans hold salt, ca 1890, #714 ....**225.00**
Gorham, Oriental-style etching, ped ft **75.00**
Gorham, ped ft, gold wash, ca 1900, #4248 ....**65.00**
Gorham, rnd bowl supported by 3 griffins..................................**175.00**
Jensen, Georg; acorn design, bl enameling, w/spoon **175.00**
Mexico, simple rnd shape, H&J-4125 ....**20.00**
Pierced holder, w/garlands, ftd, cobalt liner **125.00**
Plique-a-jour filigree rim, enamel bowl, Scandinavia...................**650.00**
Reed & Barton, ca 1890, #4226, master, pr **175.00**
Rnd, plain, #3997-4000, sm..**12.00**
Rnd, plain, HM, ca 1920, #4237 ....**20.00**
Russian, #3936, not old, w/spoon **45.00**
Russian enamel, ca 1896, chipped, #2022...................................**350.00**
Russian enamel, ca 1970, #2008, w/spoon **75.00**
Russian enamel, pastel shaded florals, ca 1900 ....**400.00**
Sheffield, boxed presentation set of 4, matching spoons **250.00**
Shreve & Co holder, Lenox insert, H&J-3856 ....**45.00**
Sleigh on runners, glass insert, H&J-4315 ....**450.00**
Swan, all silver, Germany **80.00**
Swan, glass w/sterling wings, ca 1920, #4289 ....**45.00**
Towle, modern, #4238, w/spoon, ind **35.00**
Viking ship, 830 silver, not old, #4260, w/spoon **45.00**

Other Types

Amethyst glass, grape leaf, Fostoria, ca 1940 ....**35.00**
Amethyst glass, Pairpoint, ca 1880, #416....................................**85.00**
Amethyst glass, tub shape, sgn Sowerby, #413.............................**85.00**
Amethyst glass, tureen shape, Chpndl hdl, sgn Sowerby, #385......**85.00**
Blue glass, rnd, cut & faceted, #3891 ....**15.00**
Blue glass, tub shape, sgn Vallerystahl, #501 ....**55.00**
Blue glass, tureen shape, Chpndl hdl, sgn Sowerby, #385 ....**125.00**
Celluloid, Viking ship, ivory, w/pepper, #207 ....**35.00**
Cobalt glass, ped ft, ca 1860, #629, master **125.00**
Cranberry glass, rnd, 3 clear appl ft, #280, sm.............................**30.00**
Cranberry glass, sterling o/l, #271 ....**125.00**
Green glass, opal, sgn Baccarat, ca 1885, #360 ....**65.00**
Intaglio, cut & beveled, clear, #3418, sm chips **12.00**
Intaglio, cut & beveled, color, #227...**18.00**
Intaglio, pnt animal center, butterfly, sgn, #156 ....**65.00**
Intaglio, pressed, clear, #2462, sm chips **10.00**
Intaglio, pressed, color, #219, sm chips.......................................**14.00**
Mercury glass, cobalt, #655, master...**55.00**

Samplers

American samplers were made as early as the the colonial days; even earlier examples from 17th-century England still exist today. Changes in style and decorative motif are evident down through the years. Verses were not added until the late 17th century. By the 18th century, samplers were used not only for sewing experience but also as an educational tool. Young ladies, who often signed and dated their work, embroidered numbers and letters of the alphabet and practiced fancy stitches as well. Fruits and flowers were added for borders; birds,

animals, and Adam and Eve were popular subjects. Later houses and other buildings were included. By the 19th century, the American Eagle and the little red schoolhouse had made their appearances.

Alphabets, sgn, wool on mesh, unfr, 7x8" **95.00**
Alphabets in blk, sgn/1822, holes/wear/stains, 11x14" **275.00**
Alphabets/bird/vine border, sgn/1785, wear/holes, 18x12" **575.00**
Alphabets/birds/deer/people/etc, sgn/1797, 20x16", VG **600.00**
Alphabets/birds/flowers/verse, sgn/1891, stains/etc, 22x18".........**400.00**
Alphabets/birds/flowers/verse/etc, EX color, 19x16", VG **350.00**
Alphabets/birds/house/trees, minor losses, 18x10" **500.00**
Alphabets/floral border, sgn/1830, darkened/hole, 18x8"............**450.00**
Alphabets/flowerpots/verse/floral border, sgn/1814, 18x14" **1,750.00**
Alphabets/foliage/verse, sgn/1835, in red floss, 18x15", EX **450.00**
Alphabets/motto, wht on gr linen, sgn/1810, 12x13", EX **2,550.00**
Alphabets/trees/dog, sgn/dtd 1812, faded, 17x10" **275.00**
Alphabets/verse, sgn/1828, sm hole, 15x17" **250.00**
Alphabets/verse/vines, sgn/1848, lt stain, 20x20" **450.00**
Alphanumerics, animals, sgn/ca 1870s, 10½x12½", EX **195.00**
Animals/birds/bldgs/verse, wool needlepoint, sgn, 22x22"....... **1,000.00**
Architectural base w/birds & animals, 1817, gilt fr, 18x22" **1,350.00**
Bows/floral vines on appl border, letters, sgn/1807, 18x15"....**10,000.00**
Family record, geometric border, dtd 1831, 22x20", EX **150.00**
Family record/verse/vines, sgn/1827, 22x22" **375.00**
Flowers/stars/parrot/initials/1811, fragile/holes, 10x7".................**300.00**
House/lg bird/girl (paper head)/etc, sgn/1804, 23x21", EX **2,600.00**
Vines/2 lg birds/bldgs/verse/etc, sgn/1822, 19x15" **1,500.00**

Sandwich Glass

The Boston and Sandwich Glass Company was founded in 1820 by Deming Jarves in Sandwich, Massachusetts. Their first products were simple cruets, salts, half-pint jugs, and lamps. They were attributed as being one of the first to perfect a method for pressing glass, a step toward the manufacture of the 'lacy' glass which they made until about 1840. Many other types of glass were made there — cut, colored, snakeskin, hobnail, and opalescent among them. After the Civil War, profits began to dwindle due to the keen competition of the Western factories which were situated in areas rich in natural gas and easily accessible sand and coal deposits. The end came with an unreconcilable wage dispute between the workers and the company, and the factory closed in 1888. Our advisor for this category is Richard Marden; he is listed in the Directory under New Hampshire. See also Cup Plates; Salts, Open; specific types of glass.

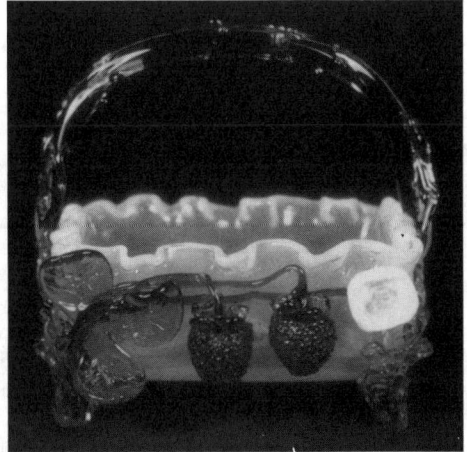

Opalescent basket with applied strawberries, 7" x 6" x 5", $525.00.

Bottle, marbleized cobalt & wht, screw-on cap, 2½" **95.00**
Bowl, lacy, lyre center, shallow, minor chips, 6⅜" **70.00**

Bowl, lacy, Peacock Eye, rim chips, 9" **55.00**
Bowl, lacy, Rose & Thistle, octagonal, minor rim flakes, 8" **75.00**
Candlestick, Crucifix, wht opaque, #4048, 12¾", pr **195.00**
Candlestick, Loop & Petal, canary yel, 7", EX, pr **250.00**
Compote, lacy, Bull's Eye & Nectarine, 5x8", VG......................**200.00**
Dish, lacy, Beehive, octagonal, minor chips/rim check, 9¾" **65.00**
Dish, lacy, Hairpin, oblong, 8½" L **75.00**
Honey dish, lacy, Roman Rosette, fiery opal, sm chips, 4..............**45.00**
Plate, lacy, opal, Roman Rosette, 5½", EX...........................**75.00**
Salt cellar, lacy, Fan w/in Fan.....................................**95.00**
Sauce, Plume & Dmn, yel-amber, flint, 4⅞"...........................**195.00**
Sugar bowl, lacy, clambroth, Gothic Arch, 5", EX.....................**200.00**

Sarreguemines

Sarreguemines, France, is the location of Utzschneider and Company, founded in 1770, producers of majolica, transfer-printed dinnerware, figurines, and novelties which are usually marked 'Sarreguemines.'

Centerpiece, majolica bowl supported by sea nymphs, chips/restorations, 15", $850.00.

Covered dish, hen w/chicks, 5¾" **135.00**
Decanter, man astride potato figural, 9½"...........................**140.00**
Humidor, relief figures in forest, mk, 7½" **145.00**
Pitcher, happy face, bk: frowning, 9" **175.00**
Pitcher, jester holds stomach, seated on stump, mk, 12"..............**395.00**
Pitcher, smiling man, imp mks, 1890s, 8½"...........................**385.00**
Plate, Lincoln portrait **65.00**
Plate, Mars transfer, 7½"...**45.00**
Plate, strawberries w/floral trim on aqua, 8½" **75.00**
Urn, fluted, gilt/dk bl ribs on cream, ped base, 73" **1,750.00**
Urn, vivid colors w/decor simulating cloisonne, 26" **650.00**
Vase, gargoyles & lizards in relief, majolica, mk, 8½" **135.00**
Vase, sang de boeuf, imp mk, 9" **150.00**

Satin Glass

Satin glass is simply glassware with a velvety matt finish achieved through the application of an acid bath. This procedure has been used by many companies since the 20th century, both here and abroad, on many types of colored and art glass. See also Mother-of-Pearl.

Biscuit jar, emb floral panels alternate w/HP panels, 7" **200.00**
Bowl, olive w/wht int & gold floral, 3-lobe rim, 6½" **200.00**
Cookie jar, Fleurette, pk, 6¼x5¾" **225.00**
Creamer & sugar bowl, Fleurette, pk, SP tops, 3¾", 5½"..............**245.00**

Perfume, yel w/gold forget-me-nots, teardrop form, 4" L.............**525.00**
Pitcher, wht w/moss roses, rose int, 9", +6 tumblers.................**375.00**
Rose bowl, bl o/l, emb florals, 8-crimp, 3¼x3½" **125.00**
Rose bowl, bl shaded, HP daisies, red jewels, 4⅜x4⅜" **135.00**
Rose bowl, Indented Swirl, bl o/l, 8-crimp, 3¼x4" **85.00**
Rose bowl, pk shaded o/l, ruffled, 4½" **110.00**
Rose bowl, Shell & Seaweed, yel, HP florals, 8-crimp, 5" **195.00**
Vase, bl, HP birds on branch, frosted hdls, 6½x3¼"..................**110.00**
Vase, bl, ribbed, ruffled top, conical, 6", pr......................**150.00**
Vase, bl o/l, HP florals/jewels, ribbed ewer form, 11" **145.00**
Vase, bl o/l, HP flowers/gold scrolls, ewer form, 9" **95.00**
Vase, cranberry shaded, dbl-gourd, 7" **175.00**
Vase, peach o/l, HP florals, ewer form, 10⅜" **125.00**
Vase, peach o/l, HP florals/scrolls, petal ft, 9¼" **95.00**
Vase, pk o/l, emb florals, melon ribs, frosted hdls, 8".............**95.00**
Vase, pk o/l, HP florals, acid-cut-bk sqs, 7½x3¼"...................**225.00**
Vase, pk o/l, HP florals, melon ribs, ftd, 6⅜x3⅝"...................**95.00**
Vase, pk o/l, HP florals w/gold, melon ribs, hdls, 7⅝" **100.00**
Vase, pk-cased opal, bluebird on branch, scroll hdls, 10" **350.00**

Satsuma

Satsuma is a type of fine cream crackle-glaze pottery or earthenware made in Japan as early as the 17th century. The earliest wares, made at the original kiln in the Satsuma province, were enameled with only simple florals. By the late 18th century, a floral brocade (or nishikide design) was favored, and similar wares were being made at other kilns under the direction of the Lord of Satsuma. In the early part of the 19th century, a diaper pattern was added to the florals. Gold and silver enamels were used for accents by the latter years of the century. During the 1850s, as the quality of goods made for export to the western world increased and the style of decoration began to evolve toward becoming more appealing to the Westerners, human forms such as Arhats, Kannon, geisha girls, and samurai warriors were added. Today the most valuable pieces are those marked 'Kinkozan,' 'Shuzan,' 'Ryuzan,' and 'Kozan.' The genuine Satsuma 'mon' or mark is a cross within a circle — usually in gold on the body or on the lid, or in red on the base of the ware. Character marks may be included.

Caution: Much of what is termed 'Satsuma' comes from the Showa Period (1926 to the present); it is not true Satsuma but a simulated type, a cheaper pottery with heavy enamel. Our advisor for this category is Donald Penrose; he is listed in the Directory under Ohio.

Child's tea set, birds on crackle glaze, pot: 3", $165.00.

Bowl, deities exterior, floral int, floriform, 8⅜x15"................ **2,000.00**
Bowl, finch on snowy branch, bulbous, late 1800s, 4¾"..............**475.00**
Bowl, mc millefiori w/in & w/o, 1910, 10" **200.00**
Buddha, seated on dbl lotus base, sgn, 9" **675.00**
Cookie jar, Kannon & Arhat on brn, gold foo dog hdls, 8½" **350.00**
Cricket cage, birds/flowers, cloisonne style, dmn form, 5" **115.00**
Jardiniere, figure scenes, baluster, late 1800s, 13x11", EX..........**450.00**
Koro, battle scenes & Lohans, pierced lid, 1800s, 9¼"...............**650.00**

Koro, figure reserves, foo dog finial, 1800s, 7½" 400.00	
Kuan Yin, gilt decor, Shimazu mk, 14", EX 1,400.00	
Moon flask, dragons on shoulder, florals & figures, 12", pr 750.00	
Moon flask, samurai battle scene, reserves, 1800s, 6½" 650.00	
Tea set, butterflies & florals, late 1800s, 9-pc 450.00	
Tray, procession beneath Mt Fuji, Meiji period, 7½" 3,500.00	
Urn, warrior/scholar/official ea side, molded hdls, 24" 1,400.00	
Vase, Arhats & Kwan Yin, baluster, old mk, ca 1910, 12½" 450.00	
Vase, figure reserves/diapering, dbl-gourd, 1800s, 3¾", pr 600.00	
Vase, figures & diapering, bottle form, late 1800s, 8⅝" 250.00	
Vase, figures on tan to sage, sgn Kakuzan, 1800s, 9⅝", pr 900.00	
Vase, finches among florals, bottle form, sgn, 1800s, 5½" 200.00	
Vase, floral & fan panels, 4-ftd lobed body, 1800s, 5¾" 1,250.00	
Vase, flowers behind fence, squat, sgn Kate, 1800s, 5" 1,870.00	
Vase, immortals/samurai reserves & diapering, Kinkozan, 15".. 6,500.00	
Vase, samuari & figures in waterfall reserves, 1800s, 11½" 1,000.00	
Vase, scholars/immortals reserves, Kozan, 1800s, 18" 1,250.00	
Vase, serpent & Arhats w/halos encircle body, sgn, 6" 375.00	
Vase, warriors/gilt, horizontal ribs, Miyagawa Kozan, 8½" 750.00	

Scales

In today's world of pre-measured and pre-packaged goods, it is difficult to imagine the days when such products as sugar, flour, soap, and candy first had to be weighed by the grocer. The variety of scales used at the turn of the century was highly diverse; at the Philadelphia Exposition in 1876, one company alone displayed over three hundred different weighing devices. Among those found today, brass and iron models are the most common. Those seeking additional information concerning antique scales are encouraged to contact the International Society of Antique Scale Collectors, whose address can be found in the Directory under Clubs, Newsletters, and Catalogs.

Key:
bal — balance   lb — pound
g — gram   NP — nickel plated

Fairbanks bullion scales, 36" x 40" x 12", 1880s, $1,700.00.

Apothecary, brass pans, marble top, 6x19x5½" 135.00	
Balance, iron, w/brass beam & column, 29x41" 400.00	
Becker Bros, mahog case w/drw, 18x16½x9", EX............95.00	
Chatillon, brass, hanging, wht 13" porc pan, dtd 1884, EX 350.00	
Chatillon, brass face spring bal, 1892, 0-25 lb 25.00	
Christian Becker Chainomatic, gold weighing, glass case 145.00	
Eastman Kodak Rochester NY, 9" wooden base, 6 weights, EX 65.00	
Elmer & Amend, NY, bal, mahog case, 18x20x10", EX 155.00	
Fairbanks, floor, brass w/CI wheels, wood post, 0-500 lb............150.00	

Fairbanks-Morris, candy, iron & brass, 1½-lb, w/scoop 75.00	
Hanson, utility, blk & wht metal, ca 1900s, 25-lb 25.00	
Jacobs Bros, candy, ped ft, 3 weights, EX 98.00	
Jiffy Way, egg grading, tin............18.00	
LE Brown's Pat Dec 3, 1878, solid brass, 12-lb, 10¾" 225.00	
Mancur, mk H Boker & Co Germany, 0-35/20-300 lb, 9½" L 95.00	
Nat'l Specialty #4, confectionary, ornate 175.00	
O'Haus, triple beam, 2610-gram............25.00	
Postal, brass bal type, 3 weights, late Victorian 60.00	
Relouze, candy, CI, Pat 1915, 0-2 lb, +scoop............88.00	
Rheinhart, apothecary, wooden w/marble top, brass pans............125.00	
Salter's Improved, spring bal, EX............45.00	
Seed, Ohaus, 2-qt, 14" scale bar/6" dia seed container, EX 160.00	
Steelyard, iron, complete w/ring, hook & weight, up to 50-lb 20.00	
Tension, enamel on CI, w/weights, EX............78.00	
Triner, confectionary, wht enamel, 0-1 lb, M............38.00	
Troemner, apothecary, oak case, marble platform, EX 120.00	
Troemner #258, chemist, silver pans, label, 2-oz............145.00	
Turnbulls Family Scale, rnd brass face, 0-24 lb, 10", EX............80.00	
W&T Avery Birmingham, brass/CI, central ft, 40x35x12" 475.00	

Schafer and Vater

Established in 1890 by Gustav Schafer and Gunther Vater in the Thuringia district of Germany, by 1913 this firm employed two hundred workers. The original factory burned in 1918, but production and export continued until WWII. Schafer & Vater produced a tremendous variety of products including but not limited to tea sets, dresser sets, flasks, pitchers, humidors, knickknacks, nodders, etc. Items often came in more than one size and in a variety of finishes — glazed and unglazed bisque, jasperware, and twice fired. Most items were incised with a crown over an 'R' within a nine-point star. Collectors should look for pieces with good paint, clean mold lines, and character. They might also consider narrowing their interests to a specific category or type of finish.

Jar, gray jasper with pink trim, blue reserve with profile of lady in white, 6", $80.00.

Box, sphinx in relief, sphinx head finial, 3x3"............100.00	
Box, 2 googly-eyed boys in oval tub, bsk, mk, 3¼x3" 125.00	
Candlestick, lion, yel w/wht eyes, cubist shape, mk, 5¾" 110.00	
Clock, Kewpies, bl & wht jasper, mk S&V & Rose O'Neill 300.00	
Clock, Kewpies, gr & pk jasper, mk S&V & Rose O'Neill...........260.00	
Clock, 2 ladies playing lutes, gr & wht jasper, 7"............200.00	
Figurine, cat dressed as merry widow, mk, 5½x3⅞" 110.00	
Figurine, Cleopatra w/lyre, 4¾x4" 85.00	
Figurine, googly-eyed boy w/dog, gold trim, mk, 3¼x3⅛" 75.00	
Figurine, lady w/book sits on stoop, mk, 4⅛x2" 95.00	

Flask, boy straddles lg urn, bsk, gr & wht, mk, 6½" 150.00
Flask, monk, musical, brn, unmk, 11" 475.00
Flask, Santa holding tree, bag at feet, mk, 4½" 140.00
Flask, skeleton, w/tray & skull shots, brn glaze, mk, 8½"..............300.00
Hatpin holder, lady w/fan, pk jasper 150.00
Hatpin holder, lady's head relief/sphinx base, brn/gr jasper 185.00
Humidor, women holding cigarette, lav jasper 300.00
Incense burner, elephant heads & snake charmer, brn, 4" 100.00
Match holder/striker, chubby Dutchman & wife figural................95.00
Pitcher, classical figures, bl & wht jasper, 5" 70.00
Pitcher, clown figural, pnt overglaze, 4½" 60.00
Pitcher, Mother Goose wearing hat, 4" 125.00
Pitcher, Oriental lady w/howling child, bl & wht glaze, 6" 150.00
Tea set, smiling face, long nose, pk jasper w/gr wash, 3-pc...........400.00
Toothpick holder, sailor w/girl on knee 95.00
Tray, skeleton & coffin..210.00

Scheier

The Scheiers began their ceramics careers in the late 1930s and soon thereafter began to teach their craft at the University of New Hampshire. After WWII they cooperated with the Puerto Rican government in establishing a native ceramics industry, an involvement which would continue to influence their designs. In the fifties they retired and moved to Mexico; they currently reside in Arizona.

Bowl, figures/flowers/sun relief on brn bsk, 1941, 7x9" 2,500.00
Bowl, lt bl-gr, shallow, ca 1950, 2½x11".......................................120.00
Bowl, yel matt, 2¼x6¼" 100.00
Charger, facial features/etc, eggplant glaze, 14½" 210.00

Charger, stylized heads, dark brown over rose-beige, signed, rim hairline, 17", $550.00.

Lamp base, sgraffito figures on bl, elongated pear, 16" 1,100.00
Mug, cows under sunny sky, cvd/pnt, brn on tan, 5" 400.00
Pitcher, cartoon-like animal, gray/wht, 10", +8 5½" mugs....... 1,000.00
Plate, 2 faces stacked in pear-shape reserve, bl/wht, 7" 120.00
Vase, blistered band w/totemic reserves, can neck/ft, 23" 2,750.00
Vase, stylized cvd figures/fish on matt ground, 7x10" 550.00
Vase, 2 bands of cvd abstract heads on brn gloss, 7½", NM 375.00

Schiebe-Alsbach

Founded in Thuringia in the 1840s and still in production today,

the Schiebe-Alsbach factory was the first in the area to make porcelain figures on a large scale. Their earliest were devotional Madonnas, though Rococo figures were soon included in their line as well. In 1890 they added groups such as female dancers and dancing couples. By 1894 they were producing Meissen-style figures, lace figures, and historical figures and groups. Now nationalized and incorporated into a larger firm, the factory is Europe's largest manufacturer of this type of ware. Their mark is an 'S' with superimposed crossed lines, today slightly modified from the original. Our advisor for this category is Donald Penrose; he is listed in the Directory under Ohio.

Bust of Napoleon, gr tunic w/medals, blk hat, N on base, 10½" ..250.00
Dancing Couple, Dutch boy & girl, 6"..160.00
Lovers, lady in gold, Cupid at base, man on knee, 12½", pr 850.00
Marshal DeBeauharnais, in uniform, 10½" 175.00
Marshal Dumoriez, wht pants, long bl coat, 10" 175.00
Marshal Kellerman, bl coat jacket, wht cockade on hat, 10" 175.00
Marshal Lannes, bl coat w/red sash, 10"..175.00
Marshal Murat, long gr coat, red cockade on hat, 10" 175.00
Marshal Murat, on prancing horse, 11x9"......................................450.00
Napoleon, wht uniform, gr jacket, long gray coat, 10" 175.00
Napoleon Coronation Preparation, 3 figures at table, 9x12" 950.00
Napoleon Crossing Alps, gr coat, rearing wht horse, 10½" 325.00
Napoleon Crossing Berezina, rides horse over bridge, 11"............475.00
News Vendor, bl coat/brn hat, papers in arm, 1860s mk, 5½" 95.00
Othello, on balcony before man & lady, 10x15" 1,350.00
Othello, seated girl w/lute, man w/book on stand, 11x15"....... 1,350.00
Pully on Horse, Napoleon aide on wht horse, plumed hat, 11"....450.00
4 children at tea table, Kister, parian, ca 1850, 6½x10" 350.00

Schlegelmilch Porcelain

Authority Mary Frank Gaston, who is our advisor, has completed two volumes of *The Collector's Encyclopedia of R.S. Prussia* with full-color illustrations and current values. Mold numbers appearing in some of the listings refer to these books. You will find Mrs. Gaston's address in the Directory under Texas.

Key:
BM — blue mark   SM — steeple mark
GM — green mark   RM — red mark

E.S. Germany

Fine chinaware marked 'E.S. Germany' or 'E.S. Prov. Saxe' was produced by E.S. Schlegelmilch at his Suhl factory in the Thuringia region of Prussia from the turn of the century until about 1925.

E.S. Germany portrait bowl, burgundy with gold rim, 9", $200.00.

Cake plate, roses reserve on MOP w/gold, open hdls, 11" **198.00**
Chocolate pot, mc roses in 6 circular panels, ftd, 8" **225.00**
Cracker jar, floral tapestry w/pierced o/l, rare mk **800.00**
Cup & saucer, Queen Louise portrait/floral reserves, mk **175.00**
Ewer, portrait medallion, gold ring hdls, crown mk, 7½" **350.00**
Pitcher, maiden w/cupid, emb florals w/gold, 7½" **200.00**
Plate, bird on branch, mk, 6" **40.00**
Plate, Indian transfer on wht, silver trim, mk, 7" **110.00**
Plate, lady w/swallows portrait, roses, hdls, mk, 6" **150.00**
Plate, lady's portrait, scalloped gold rim, hdls, mk, 9½" **170.00**
Vase, Chief Spotted Horse reserve & florals, hdls, mk, 6" **300.00**
Vase, Goddess of Sea reserve, pearl lustre, hdls, mk, 8½".............**400.00**
Vase, lady w/flowers portrait, gold hdls, mk, 11¼" **600.00**

R.S. Germany

In 1869 Reinhold Schlegelmilch began to manufacture porcelain in Tillowitz in upper Silesia. He had formerly worked with his brother, Erdmann, in his factory in Suhl in the German province of Thuringia. Both areas were rich in resources necessary for the production of hard-paste porcelain. Wares marked with the name 'Tillowitz' and the accompanying 'R.S. Germany' phrase are attributed to Reinhold. The most common mark is a wreath and star in a solid color under the glaze. Items marked 'R.S. Germany' are usually more simply decorated than R.S. Prussia. Some reflect the Art Deco trend of the 1920s. Certain hand-painted floral decorations and themes such as 'Sheepherder,' 'Man with Horses,' and 'Cottage' are especially valued by collectors — those with a high-gloss finish or on Art Deco shapes in particular. Not all hand-painted items were painted at the factory. Those with an artist's signature but no 'Hand Painted' mark are indicative of blanks that were decorated outside the factory.

R.S. Germany handled tray with flowers, 12", $85.00.

Bonbon, carnations, pk on gray w/gold, side hdl, mk, 8" **45.00**
Bowl, floral, ftd, mk, 7½" **60.00**
Bowl, tulips w/gold on bl-gr, flanged, mk, 5½" **28.00**
Butter dish, mc florals, heavy gold borders, SM **1,200.00**
Candy dish, hydrangea, grays & pks, GM, 7"..................................**45.00**
Chocolate pot, magnolias on gr, +cr/sug, 6 c/s, BM......................**400.00**
Chocolate pot, robin's egg bl & wht flowers, lg, +4 c/s **325.00**
Coffeepot, floral, wht on gr shaded w/gold, stick hdl, 5½" **200.00**
Creamer & sugar bowl, violets & roses, mk **88.00**
Nappy, pheasant cock & hen, mk **50.00**
Plate, chop; roses, pk & wht w/gold, BM, 12½" **88.00**
Plate, draped woman, leaf border mold, SM, 8¼" **1,200.00**
Plate, floral, gold & blk rim, mk, 11" **75.00**
Plate, parrots, simple gold rim, mk, 8" **400.00**
Plate, poppies on pearl lustre, scalloped, mk, 6½" **45.00**
Spooner, floral, pierced work at ftd base, SM, 5x6"......................**200.00**

Talcum shaker, florals w/gold, pearlized skirt, mk, 5" **185.00**
Teapot, cabbage roses, much gold, steeple finial, mk, 8½" **125.00**
Toothpick holder, roses, red on tan, hdls, GM **60.00**
Tray, dresser; sheepherder & mill scene, hdls, 11½x7¼"..............**285.00**
Tray, mixed fruit, gold trim, mk, 11½x7" **300.00**
Vase, floral, wht on gr shaded, mk, 8½" **88.00**
Vase, lion scenic, up-turned hdls, unmk, 12" **6,000.00**

R.S. Poland

'R.S. Poland' is a mark attributed to Reinhold Schlegelmilch's factory in Tillowitz, Silesia.

Dresser set, roses w/gold trim, 4-pc on 12½x9" tray.....................**550.00**
Planter, pk flower band w/gold, 6¾x6½" **235.00**
Server, lav & pk roses w/gold trim, center hdl, 8x11" dia **500.00**
Tray, bird on floral branch, geometric border, mk, 14x5" **125.00**
Urn, bird of paradise on shaded ground, RM, 11" **2,200.00**
Vase, cottage & shepherdess, ornate gold hdls, mk, 10".............**650.00**
Vase, crowned cranes, mk, salesman's sample, 3½" **800.00**
Vase, roses, yel on tan, salesman's sample, mk, 3⅝" **250.00**
Vase, turkey, salesman's sample, unmk, 3½" **500.00**

R.S. Prussia

Art porcelain bearing the mark 'R.S. Prussia' was manufactured by Erdmann and Reinhold Schlegelmilch from the late 1870s to the early 1900s in a Germanic area known until the end of WWI as Prussia. The vast array of mold shapes in combination with a wide variety of decorations is the basis for R.S. Prussia's appeal. Themes can be categorized as figural (usually based on a famous artist's work), birds, florals, portraits, scenics, and animals.

Bell, gr bridal wreath trim on wht, orig clapper, unmk, 3¼" **195.00**
Bowl, barnyard scene, icicle mold, rtcl hdls, 12" L.....................**550.00**
Bowl, berry; stag w/shadow flowers, scalloped, mk, 5½" **300.00**
Bowl, blown-out carnations, mk, 10½" **175.00**
Bowl, castle scene, iris mold, mk, 9½" **600.00**
Bowl, Countess Patocka portrait, gold lilies on gr, unmk......... **1,500.00**
Bowl, florals w/gold tracing & beading, melon ribs, unmk, 9"........**95.00**
Bowl, Gibson girl portrait, scalloped rim, mk, 11" **1,200.00**
Bowl, lady watering flowers, scalloped, unmk, 10¼" **1,200.00**
Bowl, lady's portrait, lily mold, ftd, mk, 7" **600.00**
Bowl, masted ship, ribbon & jewel mold, mk, 10½" **1,200.00**
Bowl, Old Man of the Mountain, RM, 11"....................................**950.00**
Bowl, poppies, paneled w/red trim, RM, 10"................................**195.00**
Bowl, poppies, pk & ivory on beige & gr, unmk, 10" **175.00**
Bowl, poppies & roses, carnation mold, RM, 9½" **220.00**
Bowl, reflecting poppies & daisies, sq & jewel mold, mk, 11"......**250.00**
Bowl, roses, unmk, 10½" **165.00**
Bowl, roses on bl shaded, gold trim, iris mold, mk, 9½" **350.00**
Bowl, snowballs & roses in panels, gold trim, RM, 10¾" **325.00**
Bowl, summer season, iris mold, RM, 11"................................ **1,400.00**
Bowl, swallows & shadow flowers, medallion mold, mk, 13" L....**400.00**
Bowl, turkey scene, emb gold flowers, unmk, 10" **775.00**
Butter dish, florals, pk on cream, melon ribs, unmk **195.00**
Cake plate, flower basket, roses rim, plume mold, RM, 11" **295.00**
Cake plate, poppies, emb medallions, bl panels, RM, 11½" **225.00**
Cake plate, roses & snowballs, scalloped rim, hdls, mk, 10¼"......**200.00**
Cake plate, swan scene, scalloped rim, RM **450.00**
Cake set, floral on gr irid, 5-pc **90.00**
Celery tray, barnyard animals, swans, swallows, mk, 12½" L .. **2,000.00**
Celery tray, poppies & daisies w/gold, scalloped, RM, 12½" **195.00**
Celery tray, roses on pk, 14x7"...**185.00**

R.S. Prussia chocolate set with roses, pot and six cups and saucers, red mark, $700.00.

Chocolate pot, roses, pk in gr panels, ftd, RM, 8½" 335.00
Chocolate pot, swan & pines, RM, +6 c/s 2,425.00
Chocolate pot, water lilies & reflections, RM 295.00
Coffeepot, bouquets & sprays w/gold, ped ft, RM, 11" 495.00
Coffeepot, demitasse; poppies, plume mold, 9" 650.00
Coffeepot, dogwood & pine, angular hdl, tall spout, mk, 9" 650.00
Coffeepot, roses & urns, serpent spout, RM, 1½-cup 350.00
Cracker jar, fleur-de-lis mold, ring finial, ftd, RM 300.00
Cracker jar, poppies & daises over water, RM 450.00
Cracker jar, roses, ribbed body, dbl hdl, RM...............................295.00
Creamer, cottage, gold trim, RM...225.00
Creamer, cottage on brn & yel, RM 195.00
Creamer, mill scene, paneled, ftd, unmk, tall 90.00
Creamer, sheepherder on stippled ground, unmk 135.00
Creamer & sugar bowl, roses, pk on tan, scalloped base..............165.00
Cup, demitasse; roses & dogwood, swirled body, mk, 3" 60.00
Cup & saucer, chocolate; florals & gold medallion, RM, 3½" 90.00
Cup & saucer, demitasse; cameo portrait, flowers w/gold, mk......140.00
Cup & saucer, lilacs on satin, ped base, RM................................125.00
Cup & saucer, lily, wht w/aqua trim, RM 115.00
Cup & saucer, swans & pines on satin, RM..................................195.00
Ferner, roses & flowers, pk & wht on gr, 4-ftd, RM.....................350.00
Hair receiver, roses & holly, pearl lustre & gold, RM 125.00
Hatpin holder, barnyard animals, 6-sided, mk............................500.00
Hatpin holder, castle scene, bls/grs, mk 275.00
Hatpin holder, cottage scene w/birds, RM...................................450.00
Mug, shaving; Hidden Image, unmk, 3½".....................................300.00
Mug, shaving; mc poppies, 4 emb iris on ivory & bl, RM.............295.00
Mug, shaving; pk roses on bl, carnation mold, RM, 3½".............350.00
Mustard, florals w/gold tracery on cobalt, RM 150.00
Pin dish, Hidden Image, orchids/roses, pk/gold on bl, w/lid.........150.00
Pitcher, poppies, plume mold, mk, 8½"...400.00
Pitcher, tankard; Countess Potocka, much gold, mk, 15" 1,400.00
Pitcher, tankard; roses in irid Tiffany finish, mk, 15"................800.00
Plate, carnations, emb shell rim, shell & leaf mold, RM, 11".......165.00
Plate, castle scene, dk pastels, unmk, 8¼" 295.00
Plate, floral w/gold beads & chain, scalloped, RM, 10" 180.00
Plate, poppies, emb rim w/gold, RM, 8¾" 100.00
Plate, roses & snowballs w/reflections, RM, 5" 80.00
Plate, roses center, 6 scalloped medallions, RM, 8½"...................215.00
Plate, snowbird, icicle mold, mk, 8¼" 875.00
Plate, swans, icicle mold, RM, 8" 395.00
Plate, water lilies, mk, 6¼" 45.00
Relish, roses, 4 emb iris on ivory & turq, hdls, RM, 6x12"...........245.00
Shakers, mill scene, melon ribs, RM, pr.......................................265.00
Sugar bowl, floral, stippled floral mold, mk, w/lid, 5" 150.00
Teapot, poppies on yel, sq ped ft, RM, 6", +cr/sug.......................650.00
Toothpick holder, floral, ruffled rim, 3-hdl, unmk.........................95.00

Toothpick holder, floral, stipple mold, unmk 145.00
Toothpick holder, pk florals w/gold, scalloped, hdls, RM.............125.00
Tray, roses, blown-out carnation mold, RM, 11½"........................285.00
Urn, mill scene, w/lid, RM, 11¾" 1,750.00
Vase, Dice Throwers, ball form, unmk, 6" 500.00
Vase, floral, flared neck, ornate gold hdls, unmk, 10" 295.00
Vase, ladies w/fruit/flowers on gr, Le Brun, unmk, 10¼" 495.00
Vase, Melon Boys on purple irid w/gold, RM, 7⅜" 600.00
Vase, pk roses w/much gold, ornate ped ft, hdls, unmk, 7½" 275.00
Vase, roses, mc on wht stippled, cylindrical, hdls, mk, 9½" 450.00
Vase, roses & snowballs, 8 jewels, hdls, ped ft, RM, 8" 725.00

R.S. Suhl, E.S. Suhl

Porcelains marked with this designation are attributed to Schlegelmich's Suhl factory.

Box, floral, w/beveled mirror, mk 200.00
Cake plate, floral, w/floral border, hdls, 10"................................135.00
Ewer, floral on gr, gold hdl, mk, 13¼" 325.00
Vase, floral on soft gr, gilt stems/centers, 6½"..............................125.00
Vase, Melon Boys, mk, 9"...815.00
Vase, Nightwatch, brn shades, sgn Rembrandt, 7½" 750.00
Wall plaque, daisies, 10½" 125.00

R.S. Tillowitz

R.S. Tillowitz-marked porcelains are attributed to Reinhold Schlegelmilch's factory in Tillowitz, Silesia.

Bowl, pheasants, scalloped, oval, open hdls, mk, 10x6¾" 250.00
Cake set, fuchsia on gr w/tan shadows, open hdls, 7-pc...............325.00
Creamer & sugar bowl, Deco design, mk 145.00
Creamer & sugar bowl, lilies, wht on gr shaded...........................195.00
Plate, poinsettias, pk on ivory to gr, hdls, 9¾" 55.00
Relish, azaleas on yel & brn, hdls, 10½" 40.00
Tray, floral, bl on gr, heavy gold trim, pierced hdls, 4x8".............40.00

Schneider

The Schneider Glass Company was founded in 1914 at Epinay-sur-seine, France. They made many types of art glass, some of which sandwiched designs between layers. Other decorative devices were applique and carved work. These were marked 'Charder' or 'Schneider.' During the twenties commercial artware was produced with Deco motifs cut by acid through two or three layers and signed 'LeVerre Francais' in script or with a section of inlaid filigrane. Our advisor for this category is Don Williams; he is listed in the Directory under Missouri. See also Le Verre Francais.

Bowl, pk/gr to rust, blown in ftd leaf-hdld iron fr, 7x15" 2,400.00
Compote, yel w/appl mc shards & powders, conical, 8½" dia 950.00
Lamp, boudoir; red/purple mottle base & shade, 15" 3,000.00
Lamp, perfume; bl-gray decor, metal floral base, 7"................. 1,300.00
Vase, bl swirl on paperweight millefiori base, 8½" 750.00
Vase, brn & orange in crystal, random bubbles, 8¾x7"................765.00
Vase, bubbly gr-streaked clear, appl purple ft/runs, 11"............ 1,950.00
Vase, clear w/bubbles & pk mottle, rose std, purple ft, 14" 1,650.00
Vase, orange/bl/purple mottle, baluster w/purple hdls, 18" 1,400.00
Vase, orange/red mottle, appl/cvd poppy, trumpet neck, 16"... 4,500.00
Vase, pk/wht mottle, yel/rust/lav splotches, ftd/hdls, 16" 1,500.00
Vase, purple/orange mottle, bulbous rim, cushion ft, 24"......... 2,000.00
Vase, red-purple & wht mottle w/bl spatters, 1920s, 10".............795.00

Vase, mottled red and blue with purple handles, in wrought iron base with leaves and red glass berries, signed, 17", $2,500.00.

Vase, red/bl mottle, wine hdls, red-berried iron base, 17" **2,500.00**
Vase, yel/wht mottle, bulbous rim, cushion ft, 23½" **2,000.00**

Cameo

Compote, floral, wine/pk on wht mottle, Charder, 13" **1,000.00**
Vase, floral panel, brn/rust on mottle, ftd, Charder, 13" **1,000.00**
Vase, fronds, red/bronze on wht, trumpet form, Charder, 18" . **1,900.00**
Vase, grapes, tile band at neck, orange on rust mottle, 18" **1,600.00**

Schoolhouse Collectibles

Schoolhouse collectibles bring to mind memories of a bygone era when the teacher rang her bell to call the youngsters to class in a one-room schoolhouse where often both the 'hickory stick' and an apple occupied a prominent position on her desk. Our advisor for this category is Kenn Norris; he is listed in the Directory under Texas.

Bell, brass, wooden hdl, 1870s, 7¾" **40.00**
Book, Appleton's Standard Elementary Geography, 1880, EX.......**10.00**
Book, Everyday Arithmetic, JB Gifford, 1920, EX..........................**5.00**
Book, Fun w/Dick & Jane, Foresman, 1940, EX **15.00**
Book, McGuffey's Second Eclectic Reader, 1920, EX **5.00**
Book, Palmer Method of Handwriting, c 1930, NM....................**5.00**
Book, Trigonometry, Kenyon & Ingold, 1914, 260-pg, EX **3.00**
Clock, Stromberg master regulator, 1915, 60", EX **575.00**
Desk, pine, mortised base, H stretcher, lift/slant top, drw **400.00**
Globe, CI, paw ft, floor stand, globe: 18" dia, EX **150.00**
Map, pull-down canvas, Universal, NY, 55x48", EX **25.00**
Slate, pegged wooden fr, 9x13" **50.00**

Schoop, Hedi

Swiss-born Hedi Schoop started her ceramics business in North Hollywood in 1940. With a talented crew of about twenty decorators, she produced figurines, figure-vases, console sets, TV lamps, and other decorative housewares — much of which was accented with gold or platinum trim. Schoop's pottery closed after a fire destroyed the building in 1958. Marks are impressed or printed. For further information we recommend *The Collector's Encyclopedia of California Pottery* by our advisor Jack Chipman; he is listed in the Directory under California.

Bowl, formed by lady's skirt, #418, 13" dia.....................................**65.00**

Figurine, boy w/horn, pk & bl, 11"..**48.00**
Figurine, Conchita, Mexican lady w/2 baskets, 12½" **45.00**
Figurine, debutante, 12½"..**40.00**
Figurine, Dutch boy & girl, 11½", pr......................................**75.00**
Figurine, flower girl w/appl flowers, 9" **35.00**
Figurine, girl w/vase in arm, 9"...**30.00**
Figurine, lady w/basket leads lg poodle, 10" **45.00**
Figurine, Margie, southern belle, 12" **42.50**
Figurine, peasant woman dancing, holds bowl over head, 13" **40.00**
Figurine, seated cat, bow w/appl bell **32.00**
Figurine, Siamese dancer, gold trim, male/female, 15", pr **125.00**
Figurine, Tiny & Teeny, flower girls, 7", pr.............................**75.00**
Flower holder, 2 girls w/hands joined, rare, 8" **90.00**
Lamp, TV; jazz combo, #375, rare......................................**175.00**
Planter, geisha w/umbrella, bl, #223......................................**30.00**
Planter, hobby horse, 5"...**30.00**

Kitty, lady with parasol, 12½", $50.00.

Scouting Collectibles

Scouting was founded in England in 1907 by a retired Major General, Lord Robert Baden-Powell. Its purpose is the same today as it was then — to help develop physically strong, mentally alert boys and to teach them basic fundamentals of survival and leadership. The movement soon spread to the United States, and in 1910 a Chicago publisher, William Boyce, set out to establish Scouting in America. The first World Scout Jamboree was held in 1911 in England. Baden-Powell was honored as the Chief Scout of the World. In 1926 he was awarded the Silver Buffalo Award in the United States. He was knighted in 1929 for distinguished military service and for his scouting efforts. Baden-Powell died in 1941. For more information you may contact our advisor, R.J. Sayers, author of *Guide to Scouting Collectables*, whose address (and ordering information regarding his book) may be found in the Directory under North Carolina.

Badge, Eagle, type 2, BSA, 1920s, in coffin box **75.00**
Badge, First Class, Scout, on tan sq cloth, 1920s **10.00**
Badge, GSA, 'thanks' medal, 10k gold w/bl ribbon, 1930 ....**45.00**
Badge, Scoutmaster, tan sq cloth w/gr emblem, 1920s....................**25.00**
Book, BSA Handbook, 1st ed, red linen cover, 1911 ....**50.00**
Book, Cave, Official Boy Scout Hike Book, 1st ed, 1913..............**15.00**
Book, Handbook for Scoutmasters, 1st ed, 1913-14 ....**35.00**
Book, Scouting for Boys, Baden Powell, English, 1908 ....**100.00**
Bracelet, charm; Cub Scout, w/rank charms, sterling.....................**15.00**
Bracelet, charm; GSA, w/10k gold fob....................................**20.00**
Buckle, Be Prepared, 2 slide loops, 1911 ....**35.00**
Buckle, Max Silver, World Jamboree 1953, early issue...................**75.00**

Card, membership; 3-fold, in slipcase, 1920-30 .... 3.00
Card, membership; 4-fold, plastic, ribbon at top, 1915-16 ....10.00
Coin, BSA, Excelsior Shoe, 1910, early................... 7.00
Coin, BSA, scout w/staff, brass, 1915 ....10.00
Compass, camp scene, screw release for needle, 1920...................20.00
Diary, BSA, 1st issue, red linen cover, 1913 ....50.00
Diary, 1-year, any ca 1920-30, ea 6.00
Jacket, high collar, 4-pocket billows type, ca 1915 ....45.00
Jacket, 1953 Jamboree, w/6" patch, wagon train, gr.....................50.00
Neckerchief, 1937 Nat'l Jamboree, red or bl, full sq, ...35.00
Neckerchief, 1950-53-57 Nat'l Jamboree, dmn shape w/logo, ea ...10.00
Pamphlet, Lone Scout Degree, dtd 1918, set of 6 ....50.00
Pamphlet, Lone Scout Handbook, 1918, sm..................15.00
Patch, Eagle, on bl/wht cloth, 1930s-40.....................75.00
Patch, Eagle, type 1, on tan sq, 1920s 35.00
Patch, 1924 World Jamboree, flag, #1-5000, silk, ea................ 1,000.00
Patch, 1935 Nat'l Jamboree, felt, canceled, 3".....................40.00
Patch, 1937 Nat'l Jamboree, wht felt, 3".....................50.00
Patch, 1937 World Jamboree, 16 variations, ea 200.00
Pin, First Class, brass or silver, 1940, 1½", ea...................10.00
Pin, First Class, TH Foley Mfg, 1920, 2" or 3", ea 300.00
Pin, hat; Eagle, 3-color enamel, oval, 1930s-50.....................35.00
Pin, Scoutmaster, gr enamel, rnd, 1940s 20.00
Pin, tie; leader, stick type, sterling, 1920.....................15.00
Poster, Lyendecker, 1918, 20x30".....................50.00
Poster, 1937 Nat'l Jamboree, Rockwell illus w/logo, 24x40" 75.00

Scrimshaw

The most desirable examples of the art of scrimshaw can be traced back to the first half of the 19th century to the heyday of the whaling industry. Some voyages lasted for several years, and conditions on board were often dismal. Sailors filled the long hours by using the tools of their trade to engrave whale teeth and make boxes, pie crimpers (jagging wheels), etc. from the bone and teeth of captured whales. Eskimos also made scrimshaw, sometimes borrowing designs from the sailors who traded with them. Our advisor for this category is John Rinaldi; he is listed in the Directory under Maine. See also Powder Horns.

Jagging wheel, unicorn, minor repair, 7½", $1,300.00; Handle with open hearts and clubs, engraved leaves and berries, 6", $750.00.

Box, wood w/inlays of MOP & ivory (including CCS), 14" L 200.00
Busk, panoramic view of Am ships & bldgs, 15" 465.00
Busk, 4-panel, 2 w/ships, 2 w/florals trees etc, 1800s, 12"............800.00
Calipers, whalebone, naughty Nellie legs form, 3¼" 250.00
Cane, alligator hdl, whalebone shaft w/baleen inlay, 35"............635.00
Cane, trn knob w/ebony & MOP inlay, hardwood shaft, 37" 450.00
Cvg, sperm whale, bone, oak base, 8x9"...........225.00
Fid, openwork heart-shaped hdl, 1850s, 5¾" 265.00

Fid, whalebone, 1850s, 10".....................75.00
Jagging wheel, dbl, w/dbl fork, whale ivory, 1870s, 7" 2,650.00
Jagging wheel, hdl: baleen inlay, bird-head support, fork 1,050.00
Jagging wheel, hdl: C-curve, X-lg wheel, 1875, 5½" 325.00
Jagging wheel, hdl: plain, bird-like support, Nantucket, 6½"....365.00
Pipe, simple form, walrus ivory, 1800s, 4"........................120.00
Ring holder, obelisk, cvd from 2 pcs whale ivory, 1870s.............400.00
Tooth, busts of lady in tiara & man, some mc, 1880s, 5", EX 275.00
Tooth, lady's portrait, floral bk, silver mt, 6"........................400.00
Tooth, patriotic symbols, pinpoint work, 1850s, 4".................365.00
Tooth, whaling scenes, mc ink, early, 5½" 2,450.00
Tooth, women & children all around, 1840s, 7" 2,200.00
Tusk, coastal village scene, 20", EX.....................200.00
Tusk, man & lady, lg group of people beyond, 1870s, 18"............400.00

Seals and Sealing Wax

A seal is used to affix a stamp or embossment either on an official paper or on wax such as was once used on correspondence. The sealing wax was first melted, then allowed to drip on the seam of the envelope or the writing paper. The imprint of the seal on the wax was an easily identifiable device or the writer's monogram.

Brass, bust of George Washington, 2½" 150.00
Brass w/detailed ivory hdl, 2⅝".....................225.00
Cherry amber, faceted, brass mts, lg................135.00
Soapstone, dragon dog/pup cvg, Chinese, 2¼" 75.00
Sterling, full-figure Art Nouveau lady, 5" 75.00
Whalebone, trn, w/brass tip, 3", EX.....................100.00

Sebastians

Sebastian miniatures were first produced in 1938 by Prescott W. Baston in Marblehead, Massachusetts. Since then more than four hundred have been modeled. These figurines have been sold through gift shops all over the country, primarily in the New England states. In 1976 Baston withdrew his Sebastians from production. Under an agreement with the Lance Corporation of Hudson, Massachusetts, one hundred designs were selected to be produced by that company under Baston's supervision. Those remaining were discontinued. In the short time since then, the older figurines have become very collectible. Price is determined by two factors: 1) in production/out of production; 2) labels — color of oval label, i.e. red, blue, green, etc.; Marblehead label, a green and silver palette-shaped label used until 1977; or no label. If there is no label and the varnish coat is quite yellowed, then it is considered to be of the Marblehead era. Dates are merely copyright dates and have no particular significance in regard to value. (Signed) 'P.W. Baston' should only have impact on price when the signature is an actual autograph. Most pieces are manufactured with an imprinted 'P.W. Baston' on the base. Baston died in 1984; the miniatures are now being done by P.W. Baston, Jr.

Abe Lincoln, Marblehead label 85.00
Babe Ruth 725.00
Betsy Ross.....................85.00
Breton Man.....................635.00
Captain Doliber.....................325.00
Cow Hand, Marblehead label........................80.00
Darned Well He Can........................300.00
Davy Crockett 230.00
Doctor, Marblehead label 80.00
Down East 125.00

The Nineties Gibson Girl at Home, 3½", $30.00.

Dutchman's Pipe 200.00
Evangeline 125.00
Gathering Tulips 200.00
George & Martha Washington, Marblehead label, pr 150.00
George Washington w/cannon 75.00
Great Stone Face 700.00
Henry Hudson 130.00
James Madison, pewter 65.00
Jean LaFitte 90.00
Jell-O Giraffe 300.00
Jell-O Santa 500.00
Joan d'Arc 320.00
John Adams, pewter 75.00
Katrina Van Tassel, Marblehead label 75.00
Martha Washington 90.00
Masonic Bible 325.00
Mending Time 650.00
Old Powder House 265.00
Old Salt, Marblehead label 85.00
Paul Bunion 245.00
Pilgrims, Marblehead label 110.00
Princess Elizabeth 235.00
Priscilla Fortescue, w/base 275.00
Romeo & Juliet 385.00
Scuba Diver 445.00
Son of the Desert 235.00
Town Crier, Marblehead label 85.00
Weighing the Baby, Marblehead era 225.00
Williamsburg Lady 115.00

Sevres

Fine-quality porcelains have been made in Sevres, France, since the early 1700s. Rich ground colors were often hand painted with portraits, scenics, and florals. Some pieces were decorated with transfer prints and decalomania; many were embellished with heavy gold. These wares are the most respected of all French porcelains. Their style and designs have been widely copied, and some of the items listed below are Sevres-type wares.

Charger, peacocks medallion w/florals & gold, ca 1895, 16" 795.00
Compote, courting couple, sgn Pajot, ormolu ft/hdls, 10" 275.00
Figurine, dancers, lady w/floral cape, man in gr pants, 11" 1,650.00
Figurine, man sits/2nd stands, lady & harp, bsk/gilt, 9" 650.00
Planter, romantic reserve, sgn Delys, ormolu ft/hdls, 6½" 300.00

Plate, portrait, sgn Perier, bl rim w/floral reserves, 9" 100.00
Urn, figural scenes, ormolu hdls/trim, 1880s, 27", EX, pr 3,500.00
Urn, marriage of Napoleon, after David/sgn Pascault, 61" 15,000.00
Urn, portrait, pearlized gr, ormolu hdls, 8½" 350.00
Vase, battle scene on bl w/gold, now lamp, 1800s, 18", pr 1,700.00
Vase, boy in woods, champleve ft/rim/hdls/lid, 9" 275.00
Vase, courting couple, sgn Pajot, champleve base/rim, 11" 850.00
Vase, streaky bl, ormolu mts, 1910, 11½", EX 150.00
Vase, waisted hexagon w/flared top, ped base, w/label, 10½" 175.00

Sewer Tile

Whimsies, advertising novelties, and other ornamental items were sometimes made in potteries where the primary product was simply tile.

Chest of drawers, losses, 7¾", $195.00.

Bank, seated pig, chips from kiln adhesions, 9" 225.00
Bird on tree stump, sgn EJE, 9½" 425.00
Birdhouse, hut style, tooled surface, 7½" 100.00
Cat, very stylized, simple tooling/CTMW, rpr, 13" 150.00
Dog, reclining, very simple, 8" L, VG 115.00
Dog, seated, tooled detail, dk finish w/wht traces, 7¾" 150.00
Door stop, book shape, 5 incised names/dates/place, 9½", EX 65.00
Fawn, recumbent, amber marble eyes, late, 14" L 75.00
Flowerpot, stump form, tooled, attached deep saucer, 8½" 95.00
Frog, dk brn glaze, mk Superior, 4x8" 185.00
Gorilla torso, open mouth, late, 15" 200.00
Lamp base, stump form, primitive, 8¾" 35.00
Lion, recumbent, primitive, sgn EFE, 6½x9" 95.00
Lion, recumbent on ribbed base, mk Wadsworth, rpt, 9" 350.00
Lion, recumbent on scalloped base, sgn Germain 1890, 9" 200.00
Match holder, lady's high-buttoned shoe form, 1890s, 4½" 145.00
Owl on stump, EX detail, 14", NM 900.00
Spaniel, seated, in Staffordshire style, 11" 125.00
Toothpick holder, devil's head on trunk form, What Cheer, 3¾" .65.00

Sewing Items

Sewing collectibles continue to intrigue collectors, and fine 19th-century and earlier pieces are commanding higher prices due to increased demand and scarcity. Complete needlework boxes and chatelaines in original condition are rare. But even though they may be incomplete, as long as boxes contain fittings of the period and the chains of the chatelaine are intact and contemporary with the style and the individual holders original and matching the brooch, they should be considered prime additions to any collection. As 19th-century items become harder to find, new trends in collecting develop. Among them are needlebooks, many of which were decorated with horses, children, beautiful ladies, etc. Some were giveaways printed with advertisements of products and businesses. Even early pins are collectible; the earliest were made in two parts with the round head attached separately. Pin disks, pin cubes, and other pin holders make interesting additions to a sewing collection as well.

Tape measures are now popular. Victorian figurals command premium prices. Early wooden examples of transferware and Tunbridge ware have gained in popularity as have figurals of vegetable ivory, celluloid, and other early plastics. From the 20th century, tatting shuttles made of plastics as well as bone, brass, sterling, and wood decorated with Art Nouveau, Deco, and more modern designs are in demand; so are darning eggs, stillettos, and thimbles. Because of the decline in the popularity of needlework after the 1920s (due to increased production of machine-made items), many novelty-type items were made in an attempt to regain consumer interest, and many collectors today find them appealing.

Watch for reproductions! Sterling thimbles are being made in Holland and in the U.S. and are available in many designs from the Victorian era. But the originals are usually plainly marked, either in the inside apex or outside on the band. Avoid testing gold and silver thimbles for content; this often destroys the inside marks. Instead, research the manufacturer's mark; this will often denote the material as well. Even though the reproductions are well finished, they do not have the manufacturers' marks. Many thimbles are being made specifically for the collectible market; reproductions of porcelain thimbles are also found. Prices should reflect the age and availability of these thimbles. Our advisor for this cateogry is Marjorie Geddes; she is listed in the Directory under Oregon.

Basket, sweetgrass, made by Maine Indians, 1923, 8½" dia 30.00
Basket, sweetgrass, w/contents, 3½x6½" 24.00
Bodkin, metal, Lord Nelson's Death & Victory, Oct 21, 1805 ....295.00
Bodkin, sterling, alligator shape 65.00
Bodkin, sterling, floral design, graduated set of 3.........................145.00
Booklet, construction hints for 1905, EX 10.00
Box, tramp-art type w/layered cvd wood, drw, 4x16" L 175.00
Button, malachite in gilt mt, Paris label, boxed set of 10.............250.00
Caddy, twined walnut, thread eyelets, trn finial/ftd, 9" 135.00
Crochet hook, brass, sliding retract mechanism 45.00
Crochet hook, ivory, 10" 25.00
Darner, amber blown glass, needle compartment, screw cap..........95.00
Darner, dk gr blown glass, 6" 65.00
Darner, ebony, hollow repousse sterling mk hdl, 4½" 85.00
Darner, Nailsea, pastels in ribbon & spatter, 6¼".......................245.00
Darner, peachblow, rnd form w/hdl, 1890s 295.00
Darner, wood w/emb silver Art Nouveau hdl, 5¾" 65.00
Drafting machine, McDowell Sleeve Machine, brass, Pat'd 1888..95.00
Emery, blk cat's head, plastic, Japan 25.00
Kit, brass w/enameling, glass top, bullet form, EX......................65.00
Kit, ivory, fitted, 5 orig 14k tools.. 2,200.00
Kit, red Bakelite w/thimble cap, M 45.00
Knitting sheath, brass liner, trn decor, scarce 165.00
Ladies' Companion, Shagreen, steel tools....................................250.00
Measure, base metal, straw hat,...Covers the Feet, 2¼" 125.00
Measure, brass, turtle, Pull My Head..., EX...............................145.00
Measure, brass & stainless steel, owl, Germany, common 45.00
Measure, celluloid, basket, Occupied Japan 65.00
Measure, celluloid, bear, Japan...65.00
Measure, celluloid, Blk man w/cigar, Germany, 1¾", EX 145.00

Measure, celluloid, cats playing, rnd 35.00
Measure, celluloid, dog on pillow w/puppy, Germany, EX 75.00
Measure, celluloid, dog w/ball, 2¼" 75.00
Measure, celluloid, dog waving, Japan 65.00
Measure, celluloid, fruit basket, Germany, 1½" dia 95.00
Measure, celluloid, Indian boy's head, Germany 125.00
Measure, celluloid, parrot's head, EX colors, Germany, 1¾" 125.00
Measure, celluloid, penguin, Germany..95.00
Measure, celluloid, pig, Occupied Japan, common 35.00
Measure, celluloid, pig w/winking eye, HP flowers 48.00
Measure, celluloid, strawberry, EX color, 1¼" 75.00
Measure, celluloid, terrier on log, Germany, 2¼" 125.00
Measure, celluloid/metal, Modern Ice Man..., Frigidaire ad 45.00
Measure, ceramic, chicken, mc pnt, 1½" 35.00
Measure, ceramic, gingham dog, 1950s 25.00
Measure, china, rooster, 1960s 35.00
Measure, china, sewing machine, 1970s 20.00
Measure, metal, iron w/wood hdl, cushion top, 1970s 25.00
Measure, plastic, deer, mc pnt, 2" 45.00
Measure, plastic, fish, HP details, common, 4½" 35.00
Measure, plastic, gray house w/red roof, EX details, 1½" 45.00
Measure, plastic, Liberty Bell..55.00
Measure, vegetable ivory, fancy piercing, wind-up knob 60.00
Measure, wood, fishing reel, self-winding hdl, 1" 65.00
Needle book, cb, Century of Progress..12.50
Needle book, cb, horseshoe shape, Czechoslovakia 17.50
Needle book, cb, horseshoe shape, Germany 17.50
Needle book, cb, NY skyline & Statue of Liberty 12.50
Needle book, cb, Piccadilly, picture of airplane 12.50
Needle book, cb, Ralph's (grocery) advertising, 1960s 7.50
Needle book, cb, Victorian ladies sewing, Germany 15.00
Needle book, cb, Von's advertising, Deco building 12.50
Needle case, blk leather, w/scissors, knife, stiletto, EX 30.00
Needle case, celluloid, umbrella form, ivory/blk, 4"....................75.00
Needle case, cvd wood & bone, umbrella form, 4" 100.00
Needle case, felt, basket shape...12.00
Needle case, gold-washed sterling, French, 2¼" 255.00
Needle case, Lydia Pinkham, circular..45.00
Needle case, scrimshaw ivory, perpetual calendar, 4-pc 650.00
Needle case, transferware, Cliffs of Dover, barrel shape 145.00
Needlework box, marbleized metal/velvet, some tools, 1840s .. 3,500.00
Pin cube, cb, blk w/mourning pins 27.50
Pin cube, cb, glass head pins, cupid scrap, 1¼" sq 22.50
Pin cube, cb, pins 4 sides, adv 2 sides, 1¼" sq 35.00
Pincushion, brass, lady's shoe, 3½"...20.00
Pincushion, bsk, doll, glass eyes, on velvet orchid, Germany.........85.00
Pincushion, celluloid, box w/cushion top, 1-drw, 4x4½" 45.00
Pincushion, ceramic, lady beside basket, Occupied Japan 17.50
Pincushion, CI, turtle 35.00
Pincushion, cvd wood, lady's shoe, brass tacks, 1880s, 6¼" 65.00
Pincushion, fabric, dress form, tape in base, thimble atop 55.00
Pincushion, fabric, shoe w/cushion in heel, 1920s 45.00
Pincushion, leather, shoe w/silk bow, EX....................................37.50
Pincushion, silk, apple w/stem, 1900s, 2¼x2½" 40.00
Pincushion, silk, bl & brn high-button shoes, 1870s, NM............65.00
Pincushion, velvet pillow w/theorem-pnt flowers, 5½x4" 95.00
Pincushion, velvet w/theorem-pnt flowers, cb base, 2x2".............50.00
Punch, eyelet; relief/eng floral, mk sterling hdl 47.50
Scissors, embroidery; sterling, repousse finger loops, 4" 75.00
Scissors, folding, celluloid hdls, 2", EX 40.00
Scissors, folding, sterling, repousse finger loops, 2", EX 95.00
Shuttle, tatting; Lydia Pinkham, celluloid, M 125.00
Shuttle, tatting; sterling, oval cartouch/eng floral ea side 165.00
Shuttle, tatting; Tartanware, minor wear 165.00

Spool holder, 10-spindle, treenware w/pincushion, ca 1850 ....**295.00**

Thimble holder, 'From Waterton, NY,' with anchor band on thimble, 3½", $165.00.

Thimble, alloy, floral band, Simons Industrial................................**12.50**
Thimble, brass, floral band **25.00**
Thimble, brass, hearts on band...**27.50**
Thimble, brass, sentiment border, A Gift..**35.00**
Thimble, brass, sentiment border, Good Luck w/horseshoes..........**45.00**
Thimble, ivory, ship scrimshaw, unmk, new **25.00**
Thimble, metal, tailor's, lg knurling, unmk......................................**17.50**
Thimble, sterling, appl cartouch, 8-petal flower cap, Germany **60.00**
Thimble, sterling, appl oak leaf border, red stone top.....................**40.00**
Thimble, sterling, emb feather scroll band, anchor mk, Stern **45.00**
Thimble, sterling, enamel shield, gold inlay, Gabler **75.00**
Thimble, sterling, eng animal band, Simons, child's sz..................**38.00**
Thimble, sterling, eng barnyard scene, shield mk, Simons.............**65.00**
Thimble, sterling, floral band, tailor's **85.00**
Thimble, sterling, floral swag band, Gabler **65.00**
Thimble, sterling, geometric band, Simons **35.00**
Thimble, sterling, wide anchor band, Waite-Thresher....................**65.00**
Thimble, sterling, wide band between scroll borders, Simons........**80.00**
Thimble, sterling, wide gold band, Goldsmith-Stern **110.00**
Thimble box, cb, My Darling, ca 1920...**35.00**
Thimble case, dk bl glass, shoe form, 2¼".....................................**115.00**
Thimble case, transferware, resort scene, casket shape.................**165.00**
Thimble case, transferware, waterfall, barrel shape **125.00**
Thimble case, velvet on metal, shoe form, embr flowers, 2½" **110.00**
Thimble case, wood, bbl form, szd needle openings, Germany.......**95.00**
Thimble case, wood, Tom Mix hat w/feathered brass thimble **85.00**
Thimble case, wooden bbl form w/waterfall transfer, 2", EX **60.00**

Sewing Machines

The fact that Thomas Saint, an English cabinetmaker, invented the first sewing machine in 1790 was unknown until 1874 when Newton Wilson, an English sewing machine manufacturer and patentee, chanced on the drawings included in a patent specification describing methods of making boots and shoes. By the middle of the 19th century, several patents were granted to American inventors, among them Isaac M. Singer, whose machine used a treadle. These machines were ruggedly built, usually of cast iron. By the 1860s and '70s, the sewing machine had become a popular commodity, and the ironwork became more detailed and ornate.

Many of the machines listed below are rare and therefore costly; however, many of the old oak treadle machines (especially these brands: Davis, Home, Household, National, New Home, Singer, Weed, Wheeler & Wilson, and Willcox & Gibbs) have only nominal value. Our advisors for this category are Sandra and Peter Frei; they are listed in the Directory under Massachusetts.

AB Wilson, latest Pat Nov 12, 1850 ....**5,000.00**
Albert H Hook, Pat Nov 30, 1858 & May 17, 1859 ....**3,800.00**
Atwater, Pat May 5, 1857 ....**1,200.00**
Barthol, Pat April 6, 1858..**2,500.00**
Bartlett, Pat Oct 10, 1865 ....**350.00**
Beckwith...**600.00**
Child's, Little Mother, red metal, 8x7¾x4", EX **60.00**
Child's, Stitchwell, treadle/hand crank, on stand, 30", VG **150.00**

Du Laney Little Monitor, Pat 1872, $3,000.00.

DW Clark, latest Pat June 8, 1858 ....**1,400.00**
Fetter & Jones **2,000.00**
FG Folsom, Pat March 1, May 17, 1864.......................................**450.00**
Grover & Baker, latest Pat May 27, 1856...................................**1,200.00**
Hancock...**500.00**
James EA Gibbs, Pat Aug 10, 1858 ....**3,000.00**
Ladd & Webster, Hunt & Webster, Hunt, Pat 1852/1854, any. **3,000.00**
Landfear's, Pat Feb 26, 1856 ....**5,000.00**
Leavitt **1,800.00**
McLean & Hooper..**5,000.00**
Mme Demorest, Pat M **800.00**
National, CI, curved arm, minor pnt chips, 11x9x6", VG **50.00**
Nettleton & Raymond, Pat April 14, 1857 ....**5,000.00**
Pratt's, Ladies' Companion, Pat Feb & March 1857/Feb '58 ... **4,000.00**
Shaw & Clark, CI, fluted column, ped base, 1865, VG..................**75.00**
Shaw & Clark, latest Pat Feb 16, 1864 ....**900.00**
Thompson...**400.00**
Wanamaker Automatic, CI, wooden base, worn pnt, 12x10x6" **50.00**
Watson, Pat March 11, 1856 & Dec 8, 1857................................**850.00**
Willcox & Gibbs, CI, electric motor, 16x10x6", VG **55.00**
Willcox & Gibbs, CI, worn pnt, 11x9x6", VG...............................**50.00**
Willcox & Gibbs, rpl wheel hdl, 11½x8x6", G..............................**40.00**
Woodruff, Pat July 3, 10, 1855 & Sept 7, 1858 ....**3,000.00**

Shaker Items

The Shaker community was founded in America in 1776 at

Niskeyuna, New York, by a small group of English 'Shaking Quakers.' The name referred to a group dance which was part of their religious rites. Their leader was Mother Ann Lee. By 1815 their membership had grown to more than one thousand in eighteen communities as far west as Indiana and Kentucky. But in less than a decade, their numbers began to decline until today only a handful remain. Their furniture is prized for its originality, simplicity, workmanship, and practicality. Few pieces were signed. Some were carefully finished to enhance the natural wood; a few were painted.

Although other methods were used earlier, most Shaker boxes were of oval construction with overlapping 'fingers' at the seams to prevent buckling as the wood aged. Boxes with original paint fetch triple the price of an unpainted box; number of fingers and size should also be considered.

Although the Shakers were responsible for weaving a great number of baskets, their methods are not easily distinguished from those of their outside neighbors, and it is nearly impossible without first-hand knowledge to positively attribute a specific example to their manufacture. They were involved in various commercial efforts other than woodworking — among them sheep and dairy farming, sawmilling, and pipe and brick making. They were the first to raise crops specifically for seed and to market their product commercially. They perfected a method to recycle paper and were able to produce wrinkle-free fabrics. Our advisor for this category is Nancy Winston; she is listed in the Directory under New Hampshire. Standard two-letter state abbreviations have been used throughout the following listings.

Key:
bj — bootjack
CB — Canterbury
EF — Enfield
NL — New Lebanon
PH — Pleasant Hill
ML — Mt. Lebanon
SDL — Sabbathday Lake
WV — Watervliet

Almanac, predictions/medicines/etc, 1886, 32-pg, 8x6", EX 85.00
Apple peeler, pegged maple, mtd on bench, ca 1820s, 8" wheel..375.00
Apple peeler, pine/maple, red pnt, table top, 1850, 11x27x8" 600.00
Apple peeler, wood, brass ferrule, straddle seat, 1850s, 27".........395.00
Basket, ash, cvd hdls, copper nails, EF, 1850, 13½x22" 650.00
Basket, ash, hoop hdl, single-wrapped rim, EF, 8x7¾" 400.00
Basket, gathering; blk ash splint, notched hdls, 17x21"........... 1,300.00
Basket, gathering; maple, dbl-wrapped rim/cvd hdls, SDL, 19"....400.00
Basket, laundry; oak splint, cvd hdls, heavy base, 15x27x19" 350.00
Basket, work; blk ash splint, cvd hdls, EF, 1840, 27x27" 1,100.00
Basket, work; blk ash splint, cvd hdls, 1820s, 18x22", EX 3,800.00
Basket, work; oak splint, cvd hdls, ftd, 16x24" 600.00
Bed, pine/maple, wooden wheels, CI posts, 1840, 30x77x37" 800.00
Bed, poplar/chestnut/cherry/pine, NL, 1840, 24x71x32", pr ... 6,000.00
Bench, yel pine, mortised/splined, bj ends, NL, 1830s, 76".........400.00
Bonnet, woven poplar strips, label inside, #6, 9¼" dia 300.00
Book, Portraiture of Shakerism, Dyer, 1822, 445-pg, EX.............200.00
Bottle, pickle; ED Pettengill Co label, EX 250.00
Bowl, maple, cvd 1-pc, bl pnt, ML, 25" L, +20" iron ladle 500.00
Box, blanket; pine, red pnt, dvtl, SDL, 1801, 15½x42x15" 5,000.00
Box, desk; pine, chrome pnt, dvtl, 1-drw, 1850, 7x21x15" 4,250.00
Box, dough; poplar, mustard pnt, dvtl, EF, 1850, 12x31x14" 800.00
Box, knife; cherry/poplar, red stain, dvtl, 1840s, 5½x13x7" 950.00
Box, maple/pine, 3-finger, orig stain, oval, 1864, 1⅛x3⅜" 3,300.00
Box, maple/pine, 4-finger, blk pnt, copper tacks, 8¾" L...............650.00
Box, pine, bl pnt, lift lid w/finger holes, 15x21x15" 700.00
Box, pine, cherry stain, dvtl, iron hinges, 1840, 24x30x16" 1,500.00
Box, pine, dvtl, 6-brd, Hancock, 1850s, 18x26x18" 900.00
Box, pine/maple, 3-finger, gr pnt, SDL, 1830s, 6" L..................800.00

Box, pine/maple, 3-finger, orig yel pnt, copper nails, 4½" 3,750.00
Box, pine/maple, 4-finger, bl pnt, EF, 2¾x6⅜" 2,000.00
Box, pine/maple, 4-finger, iron tacks, oval, 1830, 4x8¾"............650.00
Box, seed; curly maple, dvtl, 2-part, built w/screws, 28".............450.00
Box, seed; pine, orig red pnt, ML label, 4x23x12", EX 1,000.00
Box, sewing; kid leather/satin trim, 2½x4x4", +contents............150.00
Box, spit; maple/pine, 3-finger, copper nails, NL, 1840s, 10" 800.00
Box, spit; pine/maple, yel pnt, iron tacks, 1840s, 3¼x13" 800.00
Box, wood; pine, dk stain, rpl lift lid, 1850s, 54x43x18" 500.00
Bucket, pine, brass wraps, w/lid, EF, 1860, 7¾x9¾" 450.00
Bucket, pine, orig stain, dmn bail plate, EF, 13x9½" 650.00
Bucket, pine, orig yel pnt, w/lid, 1869, EF, 6x7⅛" 4,000.00
Bucket, pine, 2 blk-pnt bands, EF, 12½x10½" 550.00
Carrier, pine/maple, satin lined, SDL stamp, 6x8" 650.00
Carrier, sewing; maple, hickory hdl, dvtl, 6x6x4" 450.00
Carrier, tiger maple/pine, 4-finger, copper points, 10x15" 650.00
Chair, arm; maple, rstr varnish, tape seat, 41"......................... 1,600.00
Chair, armless rocker #2; maple, tape seat, ML, 1880, 35" 700.00
Chair, armless rocker #4; maple, tape seat, 35"............................800.00
Chair, armless rocker #6; maple, natural, tape seat, 42".......... 1,100.00
Chair, armless rocker #7; maple, tape seat/bk, ML, 1870s, 42" ...800.00
Chair, boudoir; maple, tape seat, ML, 1880, 28"..........................950.00
Chair, rocker #0; maple, tape seat, ML, 1870s, 23" 2,600.00
Chair, rocker #0; maple, tape seat, rfn, 23½" 1,100.00
Chair, rocker #0; maple, velour seat/bk, ML, 23" 1,550.00
Chair, rocker #1; maple, rush seat, rfn, 27"..................................550.00
Chair, rocker #3; maple, padded/covered seat, ML, 1880s, 35"....400.00
Chair, rocker #3; maple, red stain, tape bk/seat, ML, 35" 500.00
Chair, rocker #6; maple, velour seat/bk, ML, 1880s, 41"..............950.00
Chair, rocker #6; maple/bird's-eye maple, tape seat, ML, 41".. 1,000.00
Chair, rocker #6; mushroom arm caps, 4-slat, ML, rpl seat/rfn ...750.00

#7 rocking chairs: in maple with original finish, Mt. Lebanon decal, ca 1880, replaced shawl bar, 42", $1,400.00; in birch and maple with original red paint, split reed seat and back, Mt. Lebanon, ca 1870s, 42½", $1,800.00.

Chair, rocker #7; maple, dk stain, tape seat, ML, 1875, 40" 1,600.00
Chair, rocker #7; maple, tape seat/bk, 1920, 45"..................... 1,300.00
Chair, rocker #7; mushroom arm caps, 4-slat, shawl bar, rfn........750.00
Chair, rocker; maple, orig pnt, rush seat, WV, 1830s, 44" 1,600.00
Chair, rocker; maple/tiger maple, splint seat, 1830s, 44" 6,000.00
Chair, side #21; cherry, orig cane seat, MA, 1850s, 40"........... 5,000.00

Chair, side #3; maple, tape seat, ML, 1880s, 34", set of 4 .... 1,500.00
Chair, side #3; maple, tilters, splint seat, NL, 1850, 39" 1,100.00
Chair, side; birch, rush seat, tilters, EF, 1840s, 41" 1,100.00
Chair, side; maple, orig varnish, tape seat, ML, 41" 600.00
Chair, side; maple, splint oak seat, 1840s, 36½" 500.00
Chair, youth's side; walnut, tape seat, NL, 1830s, 36" 850.00
Chest, apothecary; pine, red pnt, 9-drw, NL, 1830, 60" 2,000.00
Chest, blanket; pine, dvtl drw, NL, 1830, sm rpr, 29x42x18" ..12,000.00
Chest, blanket; poplar, canted ft, dvtl drws, 43x43x19" 3,000.00
Chest, poplar, orig pnt, 4 dvtl drw, OH, 42x40x20" 1,700.00
Chest, sewing; poplar/pine, dvtl, nailed drws, 32x51x24" 3,500.00
Chest, storage; butternut, dbl-pinned, OH, 1830s, 49x36x20" . 3,750.00
Chest, storage; pine, orig stain, dbl lift lid, dvtl, 88" L 4,000.00
Chest, work; pine/poplar, graduated dvtl drws, 35x33x18" 2,500.00
Clamp, sewing; bird's-eye maple, stained cushion, 5½" 300.00
Cloak, child's, red wool, internal pocket, CB, 30" L, EX 250.00
Cloak, rose wool, satin lined, NL, 1890, 48" L 700.00
Cloak, sister's, gray wool, silk-lined hood, 59" L, EX 400.00
Cradle, pine, orig stain, nailed, cut-out edge, 18x44" 350.00
Cupboard, pine, orig pnt, 2 panel doors, 1830s, 73x43x19" 7,000.00
Cupboard, stepbk; pine, old pnt, 3-drw, NL, 79x40x20" 1,000.00
Desk, dbl school; pine/maple/oak, trestle ft, rfn, 31x49x17" 2,600.00
Desk, standing; butternut/poplar, panel doors, WV, 72x36" ... 3,000.00
Diary/day book, handwritten in ink, 1803 .... 2,000.00
Dipper, cvd wood, natural, 5½" L, 3¾" dia 200.00
Doll, pnt compo, orig clothes, poplarware bonnet, 10" 350.00
Dolly, oak/pine, mortise/tenon, porc wheels, WV, 1900, 27" 300.00
Dry sink, pine, 3 sm+3 lg drw, lift top, rfn, 35x66x21" 3,600.00
Duster, maple, blk pnt hdl, dyed wool, 22" 75.00
Engraving, Shakers Near Lebanon, hand colored, fr, 19x22" 600.00
Flax wheel, oak/maple/birch, natural, NL, 1820s, 34x37" 600.00
Footstool, maple, dk stain, ML decal, ca 1880, 5¼x11½" 450.00
Fork, cookery; 1-pc wood, 3-tine, ca 1700s, 33", EX 165.00
Hanger, pine, initialed, 10" L, set of 3 .... 250.00
Ironing board, pine, wool cover w/leather strips, 56" L 150.00
Ladder, pine, gray wash, 4-step, 1860s, 33½" 350.00
Loom, oak/maple, red stain, NL, 1860, 72x54" 3,250.00
Mirror holder, pine, grooved base, brass knobs, 27x15" 800.00
Mortar, birch, natural, EF, 12½x5", +pestle 250.00
Rack, drying; pine, mortised/pegged, WV, 1840, 37x39" 350.00
Rack, drying; pine, mustard stain, mortised, 1830, 34x38x10" . 1,700.00
Rack, drying; pine, orig pnt, mortised, 1850s, 27x21x8" 450.00
Rack, milk; butternut, pine shelves, NY, 72x74x15" 13,000.00
Rug, silk/wool, mc stripes & border, cotton bk, 42x24", EX 250.00
Sconce, pine, orig stain, wall hanging, ca 1850, 15x7x5" 300.00
Shelf, candle; pine/poplar, orig stain, ca 1840, 15x8x5" 650.00
Shelf, clock; pine, lt stain, cut-out brace, 13x21x9" 300.00
Stand, sewing; pine/chestnut/maple, 1-brd top, rpr, 25x24" ... 4,000.00
Stand, work; birch, 2-drw, dvtl, 1830, 29x18x18" 2,250.00
Stand, work; pine, rfn, beveled tapered legs, 39x23x20" 1,400.00
Stool, cherry/maple, khaki plush cover, ML, 5¼x12x11½" 950.00
Stool, pine, ebony stain, trn legs, ML, 1880s, 7x12x12" 800.00
Stool, pine/oak, 2-step, 1890s, sm rpr, 34x15x11½" 250.00
Stool, storage; pine, orig pnt/bj ends, EF, 1850s, 19x13x10" ... 2,500.00
Stove, CI, 4 penny ft, curved sides, EF, 1830s, 19x35x14" 1,000.00
Table, drop leaf; birch, pnt traces, ME, 1850s, 26x42x18" 1,750.00
Table, sewing; poplarware, 3 cherry legs, NL, 1840, 5x10x7" 300.00
Table, work; cherry/pine/butternut, NL, 1857, 26x32x20" 1,000.00
Table, work; pine, rfn, 2-drw, dvtl, NL, 1840s, 26x26x19" 3,000.00
Table, work; pine top, tiger maple drw/skirt, ML, 27x37x23" . 9,000.00
Washstand, pine, old pnt, oak towel rack, nailed, 31x32x20" . 5,000.00
Washstand, pine, orig finish, splashboard, 1830s, 32x27x19" .. 6,000.00
Wool wheel, ash/maple/beech, stamped DM, NL, 1810s, 59x67" ..900.00
Yarn winder, maple/oak, pegged, NL, 1830s, 39x20", EX 1,000.00

Shaving Mugs

In the 1860s it became a popular practice for every man who shaved to have his own special shaving mug. Mugs belonging to men who frequented the barber shop for their tonsorial services were often personalized with their owner's name and kept on display on the barber's shelf. Occupational shaving mugs became the high point of individualism during this period. China mugs, mostly made in France, Germany, and Austria, were imported by American barber-supply companies where artists hand painted the occupation or the fraternal or sports affiliation of its customer on the mug. Often his name was added in gold. Because of sanitary rules and restrictions imposed around 1915, these personalized mugs were eventually taken off the barbers' shelves. Today, occupational shaving mugs are the most valuable. Although some are valued by the excellence of the artist, most are priced by the rarity of the subject matter.

Occupational, two men in blacksmith shop, T. & V. Limoges France, ca 1890, M, $675.00; Farmer standing by cow, Royal China International, ca 1890, M, $500.00.

Florals amid swags at rim, gold name, KPM Germany 185.00
Fraternal, FTL above eye emblem, T&V Limoges 70.00
Fraternal, Knights of Tented Maccabees, HP florals, T&V 110.00
Fraternal/occupational, Masonic emblems, Dr's name, Germany .110.00
Label under glass, gold & blk letters on red, NM 95.00
Milk glass, molded florals, dbl compartment 75.00
Norwich Coat of Arms, scuttle shape, English porc 65.00
Occupational, bartender, customers at bar, Barber Supply 450.00
Occupational, bartender, w/2 customers, much gold, mk 275.00
Occupational, billiards player, men at table, Kern Supply 550.00
Occupational, blacksmith, men in shop, mc w/gold, T&V 675.00
Occupational, brewery wagon driver, horse & wagon, EX gold ... 525.00
Occupational, bricklayer, man at wall, gold trim, T&V 700.00
Occupational, brickmaker, man at workbench, worn gold, 1890s ..450.00
Occupational, buggy driver, man in horse-drawn buggy, EX 325.00
Occupational, craftsman, man at lathe, mc pnt, worn gold 450.00
Occupational, farmer, man w/cow, mc w/gold, Royal China 500.00
Occupational, fireman, fire wagon w/hose, mc w/gold, 1900s 550.00
Occupational, house painter, man at work, Felda 750.00
Occupational, iceman, man w/canvas-covered wagon, T&V 495.00
Occupational, milkman, horse & wagon, Austria, sm rpr 475.00
Occupational, pharmacist, mortar & pestle, NM 220.00
Occupational, plumber, man at sink, mc w/gold, Felda 425.00
Occupational, shoemaker, laced-up boot, name in gold, EX 225.00
Occupational, shoemaker, lady's shoe, EX gold 425.00
Occupational, tailor, man cuts bolt of cloth, much gold 195.00
Occupational, undertaker, calla lilies & name, T&V Limoges 375.00
Owl on limb w/moon beyond, mc pnt, TV Limoges, NM 275.00
Quadruple plate, emb florals, Meriden & Co 50.00

Shawnee

The Shawnee Pottery Company operated in Zanesville, Ohio, from 1937 to 1961. They produced inexpensive novelty ware (vases, flowerpots, and figurines) as well as a very successful line of figural cookie jars, creamers, and salt and pepper shakers.

They also produced three dinnerware lines, the first of which, Valencia, was designed by Louise Bauer in 1937 for Sears & Roebuck. A starter set was given away with the purchase of one of their refrigerators. Second and most popular was the King Corn line. It was produced from 1946 to 1954, when the colors were changed to a lighter yellow for the kernels and darker green for the shucks. This variation was called Queen Corn. Their third dinnerware line, produced after 1954, was called Lobsterware. It was made in either black, brown, or gray; lobsters were usually applied to serving pieces and accessory items.

For further study we recommend these books: *The Collector's Guide to Shawnee Pottery* by our advisors, Janice and Duane Vanderbuilt, who are listed in the Directory under Indiana, and *Collecting Shawnee Pottery, A Pictorial Reference and Price Guide*, by Mark Supnick (see Directory under Florida).

Cookie Jars

Cookie jars, Winnie Pig, gold trim, blue collar, $250.00; Smiley Pig, with clover, $175.00.

Cottage House, USA #6	300.00
Drum Major	150.00
Dutch Boy, #1026, Great Northern	175.00
Dutch Girl, #1025, Great Northern	175.00
Elephant, #60, Kenwood	75.00
Jo Jo the Clown, #12	150.00
Jug, Pennsylvania Dutch, #75	125.00
Little Chef, USA	50.00
Lucky Elephant, gold trim, USA	250.00
Mugsey, gold trim, decals, USA	400.00
Octagon, Fernware, USA	30.00
Puss-N-Boots, tail over ft	160.00
Sailor, gold trim	300.00
Sailor Boy, USA	85.00
Smiley the Pig, w/clover	175.00

Corn Line

Bowl, fruit; 6"	25.00
Bowl, mixing; 5"	22.00
Bowl, mixing; 6½"	25.00
Bowl, mixing; 8"	35.00
Bowl, soup/cereal	30.00
Bowl, vegetable; #95, 9"	35.00
Butter dish	45.00
Casserole, ind	50.00
Casserole, 1½-qt	30.00
Cookie jar	130.00
Creamer	20.00
Cup	30.00
Jug, 1-qt	50.00
Mug, 8-oz	40.00
Plate, luncheon; #68	15.00
Plate, 10"	30.00
Platter, 12"	45.00
Range set, 3-pc	40.00
Relish tray	17.00
Saucer	10.00
Shaker, 3½", pr	12.00
Shaker, 5½", pr	20.00
Sugar bowl	20.00
Teapot, 10-oz	125.00
Teapot, 30-oz	50.00

Kitchenware

Creamer, elephant, w/gold & decals	135.00
Creamer, Smiley w/peach flower	55.00
Creamer, Sunflower	40.00
Lobster, casserole, Kenwood, #904	35.00
Lobster, shakers, claws, pr	17.00
Lobster, spoon holder	100.00
Lobster, sugar bowl, Kenwood, #907	22.00

Bo Peep pitcher, 8½", $65.00.

Pitcher, Charlie Chicken, Pat Chanticleer	45.00
Pitcher, Pennsylvania Dutch, ball jug, USA	90.00
Pitcher, Smiley, Pat Smiley, w/clover bud	80.00
Shakers, ducks, pr	32.00
Shakers, Dutch Boy & Girl, gold & decals, pr	80.00
Shakers, Farmer Pig, pr	20.00
Shakers, Mugsey, sm, pr	30.00
Shakers, Mugsey, w/gold, lg, pr	80.00
Shakers, Puss-N-Boots, pr	30.00
Shakers, Smiley & Winnie, sm, pr	35.00
Teapot, Elephant	80.00
Teapot, Granny Ann, w/gold	135.00

Teapot, Pennsylvania Dutch, #10 ....65.00
Teapot, Tom the Piper's Son...55.00
Valencia, chop plate, 13" 10.00
Valencia, cup 7.00
Valencia, pitcher, ball jug..17.00
Valencia, plate, 10".. 7.00
Valencia, shakers, pr 5.00

Miscellaneous

Ash tray, arrowhead..100.00
Bank, bulldog 95.00
Bank, Howdy Doody 300.00
Bank, tumbling bear..80.00
Bookends, flying geese 40.00

Bookend, potter's wheel,
marked Crafted by Shawnee
Potteries, $250.00.

Cigarette box, Trademk - Arrowhead...175.00
Clock, granddaughter 80.00
Clock, pyramid 100.00
Clock, trellis...50.00
Lamp, deer...65.00
Lamp, native (lt), pr 175.00
Lamp, Spanish dancer, pr 35.00
Lamp, Victorian figure, pr 30.00
Pie bird..25.00
Planter, birds on perch, #502 ....50.00
Planter, canopy bed, #734 ....60.00
Planter, cat on highchair, #727 ....65.00
Planter, frog on lily pad 25.00
Planter, frog playing guitar 15.00
Planter, gazelle w/baby, #840 ....45.00
Planter, red pony, #506...30.00
Planter, trailer, #680...35.00
Planter, truck, #681..35.00
Sock darner...25.00
Vase, Cameo, #2512 ....25.00
Vase, Elegance, #1402 ....25.00
Vase, Touche, #1007 ....20.00
Wall pocket, telephone, USA #529 ....20.00

Shearwater

Since 1928 generations of the Peter, Walter, and James

McConnell Anderson families have been producing figurines and art-wares in their studio at Ocean Springs, Mississippi. Their work is difficult to date. Figures from the twenties and thirties won critical acclaim and have continued to be made to the present time. Early marks include a die-stamped 'Shearwater' in a dime-sized circle, a similar ink stamp, and a half-circle mark. Any older item may still be ordered in the same glazes as it was originally produced, so many pieces on the market today may be relatively new. However, the older marks are not currently in use. Retail sales are available at the pottery or by mail order. Black figures and pirates are usually valued at $35.00 to $50.00.

Vase, orange glaze, thin
walls, 7", $120.00.

Bowl, lt gr/gun metal, rtcl between emb lily pads, 4x8" 775.00
Cup & saucer, Oriental decor, gr...35.00
Figurine, fox, mk 38.00
Pitcher, ochre, bird hdl, sm lid, 6"...55.00
Teapot, dusty gr, hand trn, appl hdl & spout, imp mk, 6" 65.00
Vase, birds/deer/leafy scrolls emb, gr/metallic gray, 6"..................250.00
Vase, cvd fish on bl gloss, sgn Anderson, 1930, rim crack, 9" 800.00
Vase, dk bl mottle, 6½" 32.00
Vase, Ming gr, early mk, 8x6" 80.00
Vase, pelicans emb, Deco style, lav/brn flecks, 7".......................495.00

Sheet Music

Sheet music is often collected more for the colorful lithographed covers rather than for the music itself. Transportation songs which have pictures or illustrations of trains, ships, and planes; ragtime tunes which feature popular entertainers such as Al Jolson; or those with Disney characters are among the most valuable. Much of the sheet music on the market today is valued at under $5.00; some of the better examples are listed here. Our advisor for this category is Jeannie Peters; she is listed in the Directory under Ohio.

All Shook Up, Elvis Presley, EX..15.00
As Time Goes By, Bogart & Bergman cover, EX.........................12.00
Bam, It's Going, Going, Gone; Cincinnati Reds cover, 1939 ....60.00
Bible Tells Me So, Roy Rogers & Dale Evans cover, 1940, VG...... 4.00
Bluebird, Shirley Temple cover, NM 22.50
Come on Pappa, Eddie Cantor cover, EX 20.00
Give a Little Whistle, Pinocchio, Disney, 1940, EX.....................15.00
Hail Prosperity, Roosevelt cover, Shell Oil Co, 1933...................17.50
Here Comes Santa Claus, Gene Autry cover, 1948...................... 6.00
Here's to Your Boy & My Boy, Miss Liberty cover, 1918, EX 3.00
I Didn't Raise My Boy To Be a Soldier, WWI, EX 3.00
If I Was What I Ain't Instead of What I Is, Blk cover, 1922.......... 5.00

Mother O'Mine, Rudyard Kipling, 1903, VG 10.00
My Blossom Bride, Hopi Indian cover, 1928, EX 35.00
My Man, Fanny Brice cover, 1921, EX 25.00
My Prairie Songbird, Indian girl cover, 1909, EX 3.00
On the Atchinson, Topeka & Santa Fe; Garland cover, 1945.......22.50
Over There, service man color cover, 1917, M............................. 5.00
Paul Revere's Ride, ET Paull color cover, 1905, EX...................110.00
Seven Eleven, 2 Blks w/dice, 1929, EX 5.00
Silver Sleigh Bells, ET Paull color illus, 1906, EX 30.00
Some Sunday Morning, Errol Flynn & Alexis Smith cover, EX ...12.00
Tales My Mother Told to Me, W Crane illus cover, 1911, VG 17.50
Then I'll Come Back to You, soldier w/girl cover, 1917, EX 3.00
They Were All Out of Step but Jim, Berlin, 1918, EX 3.00
Three Little Words, Amos & Andy cover, 1930, NM...................22.50
Vassar Girl Waltzes, Lewis/Clark, 1905, 8-pg, 14x11", EX.............25.00
While You're...in No Man's Land..., battle scene/girl knits............ 3.00
Whistle While You Work, Snow White/7 Dwarfs cover, '37, EX ..17.50
Why Can't You?, Al Jolson cover, EX.. 5.00

Shelley

In 1872 Joseph Shelley became partners with James Wileman, owner of Foley China Works, thus creating Wileman & Co. in Stoke-on-Trent. Twelve years later James Wileman withdrew from the company, though the firm continued to use his name until 1925 when it became known as Shelley Potteries, Ltd. Like many successful 19th-century English potteries, this firm continued to produce useful household wares as well as dinnerware of considerable note. In 1896 the beautiful Dainty White shape was introduced, and it is regarded by many as synonymous with the name Shelley. In addition to the original Dainty 6-Flute design, other lovely shapes were produced: 12-Flute, 14-Flute, Leaf, Shell, Queen Anne, and the more modern shapes of Vogue, Regent, and Eve.

Though often overlooked, striking earthenware was produced under the direction of Frederick Rhead and later Walter Slater and his son Eric. Many notable artists contributed their talents in designing unusual, attractive wares: Rowland Morris, Mabel Lucie Attwell (identified by her initials in the following listings), and Hilda Cowham, to name but a few.

In 1966 Allied English Potteries acquired control of the Shelley Company, and by 1967 the last of the exquisite Shelley China had been produced to honor remaining overseas orders. In 1971 Allied English Potteries merged with the Doulton group. The name Shelley China, Ltd., still exists, and it has been reported that Royal Doulton has produced trial wares bearing the Shelley backstamp. Our advisors for this category are Lila and Fred Shrader; they are listed in the Directory under California.

Ash tray, Campanula, 3½" dia....................................22.50
Ash tray, Dainty Pink, 3½" dia 24.00
Ash tray, Harmony Ware, 4½" dia 25.00
Ash tray, Primrose, 5" dia 30.00
Bowl, cereal; Blue Poppy, 6½".....................................35.00
Bowl, cereal; Dainty Blue, 6½" 38.00
Bowl, cereal; Heather, 6½" 32.00
Bowl, cream soup; Bridal Rose, Oleander shape, +underplate........55.00
Bowl, cream soup; Dainty Blue, +underplate 60.00
Bowl, cream soup; wht w/gold, 14-flute, +underplate...................45.00
Bowl, fruit; Festival of Empire, 9"..............................325.00
Bowl, fruit; Harmony Ware, bls, 8½" 95.00
Bowl, sauce; Cape Gooseberry, 5½" 20.00
Bowl, sauce; Daffodil, 5½" 20.00
Bowl, sauce; Dainty Blue, 5½"....................................30.00

Bowl, sauce; Harebell, Oleander shape, 5½" 30.00
Bowl, sauce; Lilac Time, 5½" 32.00
Bowl, sauce; Regency, 5½" 27.00
Bowl, sauce; Sweet Anenome, 5½" 32.50
Bowl, soup; Bridal Rose, rimmed, Oleander shape...................65.00
Bowl, soup; Regency, rimmed, 8" 60.00
Bowl, soup; Wisteria, HP, rimmed, 8" 55.00
Bowl, vegetable; Dainty Blue, oval, 10½" 79.00
Bowl, vegetable; Dainty White, oval, 10½" 60.00
Bowl, vegetable; Heavenly Blue, 6-flute, 10½" 85.00
Bowl, vegetable; Regency, w/lid, 9" dia........................95.00
Bowl, vegetable; Swirl, gr w/gold, w/lid, 9" 95.00
Box, Dainty Blue, w/lid, 4x5½".................................110.00
Butter dish, Begonia, oblong, 6-flute, w/lid 85.00
Butter dish, Lily of the Valley, 6-flute, rnd w/lid........110.00
Butter dish, Regency, oblong, 6-flute, w/lid 80.00
Butter dish, Rosebud, oblong, 6-flute, w/lid 95.00
Butter pat, (Wileman) lt bl floral on wht....................45.00
Butter pat, Bridal Rose, 6-flute 42.00
Butter pat, Dainty Blue, 2¾" 40.00
Butter pat, Dainty Blue, 6-flute 48.00
Butter pat, Maytime, 2¾" 39.00
Butter pat, Rosebud, 6-flute 45.00
Butter pat, Wisteria, HP, 3"...45.00
Cake plate, Bridal Rose, ped ft, 6-ft, 8" 145.00
Cake plate, Dainty White w/sm yel dots, ped, 8" 160.00
Cake plate, Old Sevres, ped ft, 8½" 135.00
Cake plate, Primrose, tab hdls, 6-flute, 9" 65.00
Cake plate, Wisteria, sq w/tab hdls, 9" 50.00
Candle holder, Cloisonne, 5" 65.00
Candle holder, Indian Peony, 5" 65.00
Candle holder, Kingfisher on blk ground 55.00
Candle holder, Rosebud, 6-flute, metal insert 45.00
Candy dish, Begonia, 6-flute, 5" sq.............................24.50
Candy dish, Dainty Pink, 6-flute, 5" dia 35.00
Candy dish, dogs, scalloped, oval, 6" 25.00
Candy dish, Shamrock, 6-flute, 5" sq 26.00
Chamber set, Cloisonne, bowl+pitcher+4 pcs...............125.00
Chamber set, utility ware, bowl+pitcher+2 pcs 125.00
Chamberstick, Harmony Ware, w/finger ring 85.00
Cheese dish, Dainty Blue, 6-flute, w/lid......................175.00
Children's ware, bowl, Baby's Plate, Jack & Jill, 6x9" 110.00
Children's ware, bowl, Baby's Plate, Puff-Puffy, 8½" 95.00
Children's ware, bowl, Baby's Plate, Robinson Crusoe, 6x9" 110.00
Children's ware, chamber pot, Peter Rabbit, 6".............125.00
Children's ware, chamberstick, Jack & Jill, w/finger ring 110.00
Children's ware, cup & saucer, MLA, Boo-Boos on horsie 135.00
Children's ware, cup & saucer, Pussy Cat, Pussy Cat....................95.00
Children's ware, egg cup, MLA, Boo-Boos, sm 75.00
Children's ware, mug, Hansel & Gretel, 3¼"................45.00
Children's ware, mug, MLA, Boo-Boos in boat, 3½" 85.00
Children's ware, mug, MLA, children at play, 4¼" 75.00
Children's ware, plate, Jack & Jill, 5½"........................35.00
Children's ware, plate, MLA, Boo-Boos on horsie, 7" 85.00
Children's ware, plate, Red Riding Hood, 7" 45.00
Children's ware, plate, Teddy Bears marching, 7½" 48.00
Chocolate pot, Bridal Rose, 6-flute, 6" 125.00
Chocolate pot, Violets, 6-flute, 8" 140.00
Cigarette holder, Blue Rock, 6-flute............................34.00
Cigarette holder, Dainty White 27.00
Cigarette holder, Primrose, 6-flute 35.00
Coffeepot, Bridal Rose, 6-flute, med 165.00
Coffeepot, Dainty Blue, 6-flute, sm 165.00
Coffeepot, Glorious Devon, lg 165.00

Coffeepot, Heavenly Blue, 6-flute, lg 195.00
Coffeepot, Rosebud, 6-flute, lg 185.00
Coffeepot, Swirls, grs w/gold, Regent, lg 145.00
Coffeepot, Violets, 6-flute, med 165.00
Coffeepot, Wisteria, HP, Stanley shape, lg................................145.00
Comport, Intarsio, w/ped & 3 curved supports, 8".......................385.00
Creamer & sugar bowl, Blue Rock, 6-flute, w/lid, lg...................110.00
Creamer & sugar bowl, Dainty Blue, med 65.00
Creamer & sugar bowl, Primrose, med sz, +undertray 95.00
Creamer & sugar bowl, Rose, Pansy & Forget-Me-Not, w/lid, lg ...90.00
Creamer & sugar bowl, Rose Spray, 6-flute, w/lid, lg..................90.00
Creamer & sugar bowl, Syringa, Regent shape 55.00
Cup & saucer, alternating blk & gold (6) flutes 55.00
Cup & saucer, Anenome Bunch, Regent shape 52.00
Cup & saucer, Blue Poppy, 6-flute 55.00
Cup & saucer, Blue Rock, 6-flute..52.00
Cup & saucer, Bridal Rose, farmer sz 55.00
Cup & saucer, buff w/gold hdl & base..48.00
Cup & saucer, Celandine, 6-flute...52.00
Cup & saucer, Crystal Cave, Bermuda, 6-flute 45.00
Cup & saucer, Daffodil...50.00
Cup & saucer, Dainty Blue, 6-flute 55.00
Cup & saucer, Dainty Blue, 6-flute, farmer sz 75.00
Cup & saucer, Dainty White, 6-flute 42.00
Cup & saucer, demitasse; Celandine, 6-flute 50.00
Cup & saucer, demitasse; Dainty Blue, 6-flute 52.00
Cup & saucer, demitasse; Harebell, Mocha shape 52.00
Cup & saucer, demitasse; Indian Peony, Mocha shape..................49.00
Cup & saucer, demitasse; Iris, 14-flute.......................................52.00
Cup & saucer, demitasse; Primrose, 6-flute 52.00
Cup & saucer, demitasse; Regency...49.00
Cup & saucer, demitasse; Violet, 14-flute 50.00
Cup & saucer, demitasse; Wildflowers, 6-flute 50.00
Cup & saucer, Diamonds (gold on blk), Vogue shape 59.00
Cup & saucer, DuBarry, Gainsborough..48.00
Cup & saucer, Forget-Me-Nots, 6-flute 54.00
Cup & saucer, Georgian, Mocha shape..47.00
Cup & saucer, Glorious Devon, Oxford shape..............................55.00
Cup & saucer, Green Daisy, Oleander shape 54.00
Cup & saucer, Heather, Henley shape 52.00
Cup & saucer, Heavenly Blue, 6-flute...55.00
Cup & saucer, Heraldic shield on Dainty White 49.50
Cup & saucer, Hibiscus, 6-flute...55.00
Cup & saucer, Indian Peony, farmer sz 50.00
Cup & saucer, Iris, 14-flute...55.00
Cup & saucer, Lilac Time, 6-flute 55.00

Cup & saucer, Meissenette, 14-flute 54.00
Cup & saucer, Morning-Glory, 12-flute 56.00
Cup & saucer, My Garden, Queen Anne shape 58.00
Cup & saucer, pk & wht, floral hdl, 6-flute 56.00
Cup & saucer, Primrose, 12-flute 54.00
Cup & saucer, Rose, Pansy, Forget-Me-Not, Oleander shape 55.00
Cup & saucer, Rose Arches, Queen Anne shape...........................58.00
Cup & saucer, Rosebud, Mocha shape 52.00
Cup & saucer, Scenics, Cambridge shape 50.00
Cup & saucer, Scenics, 6-flute...52.00
Cup & saucer, Shamrock, 14-flute 52.00
Cup & saucer, Souvenir of Bermuda, mini...................................45.00
Cup & saucer, Stocks, 6-flute 54.00
Cup & saucer, Sunset & Flowers, Queen Anne shape....................57.00
Cup & saucer, Swirl, bls w/gold, Regent shape 50.00
Cup & saucer, Thistle, 6-flute..52.00
Cup & saucer, Wild Anenome, 6-flute 54.00
Egg cup, Bridal Rose, 6-flute, lg 57.00
Egg cup, Dainty White, sm 31.00
Egg cup, Lily of the Valley, 6-flute, sm.......................................57.00
Egg cup, pk dots on Dainty White, sm 57.00
Egg cup, Regency, lg 50.00
Egg cup set, Dainty Blue, 4 sm cups on indented tray 220.00
Gravy boat, Dainty Blue, 6-flute, +underplate 165.00
Gravy boat, Dainty White, 6-flute, +underplate 90.00
Gravy boat, Regency, +underplate...125.00
Horseradish container, Lily of the Valley, 6-flute, w/lid 65.00
Horseradish container, Primrose, 6-flute, +underplate 79.00
Jam container, Campanula, 6-flute, +lid & underplate 80.00
Jam container, Old Sevres, +lid & underplate 65.00
Kitchen 'reminder,' vegetable 'people,' 6x8" 75.00
Lamp base, Cloisonne, 9½"...110.00
Lamp base, Harmony Ware, 10½"...165.00
Mug, Bridal Rose, 6-flute, 3¾"...45.00
Mug, Dainty Blue, 6-flute, 4¾"..65.00
Mug, Regency, 4¾"..55.00
Mustard, Bridal Rose, 6-flute, w/lid...60.00
Mustard, Stocks, 6-flute, w/lid..62.00
Mustard, Wisteria, HP, w/lid...55.00
Napkin ring, Harebell 55.00
Napkin ring, Stocks 58.00
Pitcher, Cunard Steamship, cube shape, 4½" 45.00
Pitcher, Dewar's, 7"..55.00
Pitcher, Pansy, 8", sm..55.00
Pitcher, wht utility ware, 7½"...29.00
Plate, Archway of Roses, Queen Anne shape, 8"..........................35.00
Plate, Begonia, 6-flute, 10½"...50.00
Plate, Blue Rock, 6-flute, 10½"..65.00
Plate, Blue Rock, 6-flute, 6"..28.00
Plate, Blue Rock, 6-flute, 8"..35.00
Plate, Bridal Rose, Oleander shape, 10½" 65.00
Plate, Dainty Blue, 6-flute, 10½"..65.00
Plate, Forget-Me-Nots, 14-flute, 8" 38.00
Plate, Glorious Devon, 8" 35.00
Plate, Harebell, Oleander shape, 8"..38.00
Plate, Hunting Scenes, hand-tinted, 10¾" 175.00
Plate, Indian Peony, 10¾"...50.00
Plate, Lilac Time, 6-flute, 8" 38.00
Plate, Melody, notched gr rim, 8" 25.00
Plate, Pansy, 6-flute, 8" 35.00
Plate, Rock Garden, 8" 32.00
Plate, Stocks, 12-flute, 8" 35.00
Plate, Thistle, 6-flute, 8"...35.00
Plate, Wisteria, Regent shape, 7" 32.00

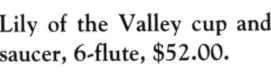
Lily of the Valley cup and saucer, 6-flute, $52.00.

Platter, Begonia, oval, 6-flute, 14" **150.00**
Platter, Bridal Rose, 6-flute, 12" dia...........................**145.00**
Platter, Dainty Blue, oval, 6-flute, 12" **155.00**
Platter, Drifting Leaves, oval, 10" **75.00**
Platter, Harebell, Oleander shape, 12" dia..................**155.00**
Platter, Lily of the Valley, oval, 6-flute, 14" **165.00**
Platter, Regency, oval, 12" **125.00**
Platter, Serenity, 12" dia...**90.00**
Platter, Thistle, oval, 6-flute, 10"...............................**110.00**
Pudding mold, geometric shape, 7½"........................**65.00**
Pudding mold, pyramid shape, 6"...............................**72.50**
Relish dish, Celandine, 6-flute, 5x8" **65.00**
Shakers, Harebell, pear shape, 3½", pr.......................**75.00**
Shakers, Lilac, pear shape, 3½", pr..............................**79.00**
Shakers, Regency, cylindrical, 3½", pr........................**65.00**
Snack set, Blue Rock, 6-flute cup+8" indented sq plate **65.00**
Snack set, Dainty Blue, 6-flute cup+8" indented rnd plate **75.00**
Tea & toast set, Dainty Pink, 6-flute cup+6x9" tray.....................**65.00**
Tea & toast set, Wildflowers, 6-flute cup+6x9" tray......................**72.00**
Teapot, Begonia, 6-flute, lg..**165.00**
Teapot, Blue Iris, Queen Anne shape, lg.....................**165.00**
Teapot, Campanula, 6-flute, sm....................................**165.00**
Teapot, Dog Roses, Regent shape, lg............................**150.00**
Teapot, Heavenly Blue, 6-flute, lg................................**195.00**
Teapot, Lily of the Valley, 6-flute, med......................**175.00**
Teapot, Pansy, 6-flute, sm..**175.00**
Toast rack, Bridal Rose, 6-flute....................................**75.00**
Toast rack, Dainty Mauve, 6-flute................................**85.00**
Toast rack, Harmony Ware, orange shaded **65.00**
Toothpick holder, Pansy, 6-flute..................................**50.00**
Tray, tea; Dainty White, 6-flute, 18" **295.00**
Tureen, Stocks, hdls, 6-flute, w/lid..............................**350.00**
Vase, Indian Peony, cylindrical, 9½"...........................**72.00**
Vase, Moorcroft style, bulbous, 8"..............................**420.00**
Vase, Oriental enamel decor on orange, blk int, 8".......**95.00**

Shenandoah

The Shenandoah Valley, extending from Virginia to Pennsylvania, is well known for the fine pottery made there from the early 1800s until the turn of the century. It is characterized by bright, clear glazes in a variety of colors used alone or in combination. Many small potteries were involved. Items marked 'Bell' indicate one of the large companies.

Eagle on plinth, brn mottle, yel beak, tooled, rpr, 5"...............**525.00**
Flowerpot w/attached saucer, gr on buff clay, mk Bell, 4¾" **700.00**
Pitcher, redware w/brn runs, tooled/emb bands, 11", VG.............**500.00**
Pitcher, wht slip w/gr & brn runs, ornate hdl, 11" **1,350.00**
Wash bowl, wht slip w/gr & brn, appl fancy soap dish, VG **800.00**

Silhouettes

Silhouette portraits were made by positioning the subject between a bright light and a sheet of white drawing paper. The resulting shadow was then traced and cut out, the paper mounted over a contrasting color and framed. The hollow-cut process was simplified by an invention called the Physiognotrace, a device that allowed tracing and cutting to be done in one operation. Experienced silhouette artists could do full-length figures, scenics, ships, or trains freehand. Some of the most famous of these artists were Charles Peale Polk, Charles Wilson Peale, William Bache, Doyle, Edouart, Chamberlain, Brown, and William King. Though not often seen, some silhouettes were drawn or executed in wax. Examples listed here are hollow-cut unless noted.

Key:
bk — backing   p — profile
c/p — cut and pasted   wc — watercolor
fl — full length

Alexander Hamilton (?), p, mk Peale Museum, pine fr, 7x6" **125.00**
Ben Franklin & Paul Jones, p, molded, 5x4", pr **550.00**
DeWitt Clinton, printed textile, matted/fr, 15x12½".................**65.00**
Elderly couple, p, w/inscriptions, dtd 1843, 7x5", pr **350.00**
Family of 7 fl (4 seated), wc int, J Sartain/1864, 16x19" **1,400.00**
Girl, p, pencil detail, identified/1830, emb brass fr, 5x4" **425.00**
Girl w/book, fl, simple gilt detail, soiled, 11x9"..........................**250.00**
Hon Cassius Clay, seated w/book, wc, sgn Brown/1845, 8x7" ..**2,200.00**
Lady, fl, identified, ink on paper w/gilt, wear, 12x8"................**175.00**
Lady, p, Peale Museum, stained, 5¾x4¾".................................**125.00**
Lady, p, pencil bonnet/shawl, flaking rvpt spandrels, 5x6"...........**95.00**
Lady, p in pnt, blk lacquer fr w/gilt liner, 5x4½"......................**85.00**
Lady in bonnet, p, blk reeded fr, 5x4"......................................**150.00**
Lady in bonnet, p, gilt fr, 5½x4½"...**185.00**
Lady w/bouquet, fl, c/p, w/gold, att Hubbard, EX fr, 12x10" **350.00**
Lady w/umbrella, fl, identified, Edouart/1840, 12x10" **1,000.00**
Lady wearing hat, p, mk, 1910, mtd on card, 4"............................**17.50**

Little girl and doll, Edouart, 5" x 5½", 1837, $750.00.

Man, fl, identified, from Edouart's record book, 14x12"...............**175.00**
Man, p, name/1810, emb brass fr, mini, 2¾" dia **300.00**
Man, p, pen/ink detail, att Chamberlain, 4½x5", EX **300.00**
Man, p, pencil detail, gilt fr, 5½x4¾" **150.00**
Man, p, rvpt on convex glass, Gibbs label on fr, 6x5" **125.00**
Man, p, rvpt oval in sq wood fr w/gilt liner, 6x5" **275.00**
Man, p in ink, blk reeded fr, 4¾x3¾"...**175.00**
Man, printed torso, pencil/crayon details, stains, 5x4" **50.00**
Man, wc, identified/born 1801/died 1880, brass fr, 5x4"............**300.00**
Man & woman, ea w/in oval of rvpt mat, gilt fr, 6x9"................**250.00**
Man w/beard, rvpt, emb brass fr, some flaking, 5x4" **200.00**
Mason, p, symbols/JW in ink on mat, 7x4"................................**750.00**
Mother & daughter, p in wc, sgn Adolphe, 1840, 6x6", pr **400.00**
Sailor, hair in queue, p, ink detail, inscribed, 1813, 8x6"............**975.00**

Silver

Coin Silver

The mark 'Coin Silver' was used after the 1830s to indicate items made with 900 parts of silver to every 1000 parts of content.

Abraham Palmer, OH; sugar bowl, emb dome lid, 11" **2,600.00**
American, pitcher, bull's head hdl terminal, eng, 10" **1,700.00**

B Gardinier, NY; tea set, repousse shells, pot: 8", 3-pc 2,200.00
Benjamin Burt, MA; porringer, openwork hdl, initials, 6½" ... 1,600.00
Chas A Burnette, VA; ladle, emb shell on hdl, 1795, 14" 500.00
Christof C Kuchler, New Orleans; sugar bowl, eagle finial 3,300.00
Clark & Anthony, NY; presentation water pitcher, 1835, 12" 800.00
David Kinsey, OH; pitcher, emb classical portrait, 11"........... 1,700.00
Duhme & Co, OH; tablespoon, eng hdls/monogram, 6 for..........120.00
E&D Kinsey, Cincinnati; ladle, eng name.....................................275.00
Edward Kinsey, KY; ladle, fiddle hdl, 1840s, 13" 300.00
Edward Winslow, MA; shaker, scroll hdl, 3¼" 1,650.00
Eli C Garner, KY; julep cup, monogram, 1840s, 3½" 450.00
GD/RG, stuffing spoon, tooled hdl, 'Steady'/flames, 12".............175.00
Gorham, butter dish, cow finial, strainer, ftd/hdls, 1845 ....700.00
H Terlau, teaspoon, monogrammed hdl, 5¾", 4 for......................30.00
Jones/Lows/Ball, Boston; tea set, emb bands, 1839, 3-pc 1,000.00
Jones/Shreve/Brown Co, julep cup, appl threaded bands, 3¾" 400.00
JS Heald, teaspoon, monogrammed, 6 for.....................................150.00
Lincoln & Reed, Boston; ewer, emb acanthus, 12½" 450.00
McFee & Reeder, PA; creamer, ftd helmet form, high hdl, 7" 500.00

Water pitcher, Robert E. Smith, Philadelphia, PA, ca 1820, 13", $1,800.00.

Flatware

Silver flatware is being collected today either to replace missing pieces of heirloom sets or, in lieu of buying new patterns, by those who admire and appreciate the style and quality of the older ware. Prices vary from dealer to dealer; some pieces are harder to find and are therefore more expensive. Items such as olive spoons, cream ladles, lemon forks, etc., once thought a necessary part of a silver service, may today be slow to sell; as a result, dealers may price them low and make up the difference on items that sell more readily. Many factors enter into evaluation. Popular patterns may be high due to demand though easily found, while scarce patterns may be passed over by collectors who find them difficult to reassemble. See also Tiffany, Silver.

Key:
FH — flat handle   HH — hollow handle

Antique Hammered, berry spoon, Shreve 85.00
Antique Hammered, cream soup ladle, Shreve..............................50.00
Antique Hammered, gravy ladle, Shreve 70.00
Antique Hammered, sugar tongs, Shreve 35.00
Baltimore Rose, poultry shears, Schofield, 10⅜" 100.00
Bridal Rose, bouillon, Alvin...35.00

Bridal Rose, dinner fork, Alvin 65.00
Bridal Rose, gumbo, Alvin 50.00
Bridal Rose, ice spoon, Alvin 350.00
Bridal Rose, pickle fork, Alvin 95.00
Bridal Rose, preserve spoon, Alvin 135.00
Bridal Rose, sugar spoon, Alvin..48.00
Bridal Rose, teaspoon, Alvin 20.00
Buttercup, luncheon fork, Gorham 20.00
Buttercup, luncheon knife, Gorham 18.00
Buttercup, salad fork, Gorham 35.00
Candlelight, cold meat fork, Towle 40.00
Candlelight, gravy spoon, Towle 40.00
Candlelight, tablespoon, Towle 32.00
Canterbury, berry spoon, Towle, 9⅜" 90.00
Canterbury, bonbon scoop, Towle 85.00
Canterbury, lettuce spoon, Towle 55.00
Canterbury, olive fork & spoon, Towle, pr 95.00
Canterbury, stuffing spoon, Towle 250.00
Carmel, bouillon, Wallace 25.00
Carmel, butter spreader, Wallace 25.00
Carmel, dinner fork, Wallace 45.00
Carmel, dinner knife, Wallace 40.00
Carmel, salad fork, Wallace 35.00
Chantilly, bonbon, Gorham 28.00
Chantilly, bouillon, Gorham 14.00
Chantilly, luncheon fork, Imperial...18.00
Chantilly, luncheon knife, Imperial 18.00
Charlemagne, cold meat fork, Towle 75.00
Charlemagne, gravy ladle, Towle 75.00
Charlemagne, place spoon, Towle..45.00
Charles II, beef fork, Dominick & Haff, sm 75.00
Charles II, sugar sifter, Dominick & Haff 75.00
Chippendale, cream soup, Towle 22.00
Chippendale, master butter spreader, Towle...................................22.00
Chippendale, tablespoon, Towle..50.00
Chrysanthemum, asparagus server, Durgin 550.00
Chrysanthemum, cheese scoop, Imperial 125.00
Chrysanthemum, luncheon fork, Imperial 23.00
Chrysanthemum, olive fork, Durgin 90.00
Chrysanthemum, pie server, Imperial 175.00
Chrysanthemum, sugar spoon, Durgin 75.00
Chrysanthemum, tablespoon, Imperial 44.00
Craftsman, berry spoon, Towle 32.00
Craftsman, pickle fork, Towle 15.00
Crown Baroque, gravy spoon, Gorham 145.00
Decor, cold meat fork, Gorham 125.00
Decor, cream soup, Gorham 45.00
Decor, gravy spoon, Gorham...120.00
Decor, iced tea spoon, Gorham 45.00
Decor, tablespoon, Gorham 105.00
Diamond, butter spreader, HH, Reed & Barton 25.00
Edgewood, butter knife, Simpson, Hall & Miller............................45.00
Edgewood, dinner knife, Simpson, Hall & Miller............................35.00
El Grandee, bonbon, Towle 30.00
El Grandee, gravy ladle, Towle..50.00
El Grandee, salad fork, Towle 25.00
Eloquence, baby fork & spoon, Lunt 50.00
English Gadroon, jelly server, Gorham 25.00
English Gadroon, salad fork, Gorham 22.00
English Gadroon, tablespoon, Gorham 45.00
Etruscan, bouillon, Gorham 13.00
Etruscan, butter spreader, FH, Gorham 20.00
Etruscan, cocktail fork, Gorham 25.00
Etruscan, fish fork, Gorham 36.00

Etruscan, gravy ladle, Gorham 28.00
Etruscan, ice cream fork, Gorham 30.00
Etruscan, luncheon fork, Gorham 14.00
Etruscan, oyster fork, Gorham 18.00
Etruscan, pastry fork, Gorham 35.00
Etruscan, youth knife, Gorham 20.00
Fashion Lane, iced teaspoon, Durgin 25.00
Fiddle Tip, tablespoon, Kirk 10.15 mk 90.00
Fontainebleau, cheese scoop, Gorham.......................195.00
Fontainebleau, luncheon fork, Gorham 25.00
Fontainebleau, tablespoon, Gorham 50.00
Francis I, infant feeding spoon, Reed & Barton 28.00
Francis I, lasagna server, HH, Reed & Barton 35.00
Francis I, soup ladle, HH, Reed & Barton 35.00
Francis I, steak carving set, Reed & Barton 60.00
Francis I, stuffing spoon, Reed & Barton 260.00
Frontenac, strawberry fork, Internat'l..........................15.00
Georgian, chocolate spoon, Towle...............................55.00
Georgian, cocktail fork, Towle.....................................25.00
Georgian, ice cream fork, Towle...................................65.00
Georgian, lettuce fork, Towle.....................................195.00
Georgian, luncheon fork, Towle...................................25.00
Georgian, teaspoon, Towle...20.00
Grand Duchess, soup spoon, oval, Towle.....................30.00
Grand Duchess, sugar shell, Towle 20.00
Grand Duchess, tablespoon, Towle 50.00
Intaglio, serving spoon, Reed & Barton, 9½"..............250.00
King Albert, salad fork, Whiting...................................20.00
King Edward, butter spreader, Imperial 15.00
King Edward, gravy ladle, Imperial...............................50.00
King Edward, salad fork, Imperial 25.00
King Richard, gravy ladle, Towle 65.00
King Richard, ice cream soup, Towle............................35.00
King Richard, iced teaspoon, Towle.............................28.00
King Richard, master butter spreader, Towle................25.00
King Richard, salad fork, Towle 28.00
King Richard, soup spoon, oval, Towle 38.00
King Richard, teaspoon, Towle 14.00
Lafayette, bouillon, Towle..15.00
Lafayette, butter spreader, Towle, ind 12.00
Lafayette, master butter spreader, Towle......................14.00
Lancaster, bread fork, Imperial...................................195.00
Lancaster, cake saw, Imperial 225.00
Lancaster, cheese scoop, Imperial 150.00
Lancaster, chocolate muddler, Imperial........................95.00
Lancaster, chocolate spoon, Imperial 35.00
Lancaster, dinner fork, Imperial 35.00
Lancaster, fish server, Imperial...................................175.00
Lancaster, ice tongs, Imperial.....................................250.00
Lancaster, sardine fork, Imperial 75.00
Les Six Fleurs, fish slice, 12".....................................550.00
Lily, bouillon, Whiting...35.00
Lily, butter spreader, FH, Whiting 60.00
Lily, grapefruit spoon, Whiting 75.00
Lucerne, claret ladle, Wallace....................................250.00
Lucerne, jelly knife, Wallace 95.00
Lucerne, tablespoon, Wallace.......................................35.00
Madame Royale, asparagus serving fork, 9¾".............295.00
Majestic, bouillon, Alvin 19.00
Majestic, dessert spoon, Alvin 18.00
Majestic, luncheon fork, Alvin 15.00
Marechal Niel, pastry fork..45.00
Marie Antoinette, salad set, Gorham, 8⅞".................250.00
Mary Chilton, ice spoon, Towle.................................150.00

Mary Chilton, sauce ladle, Towle.................................22.00
Mary Chilton, sugar tongs, Towle 30.00
Mary Chilton, tomato server, Towle.............................75.00
Mayflower, berry spoon, repousse strawberries, Kirk, 9⅜" 425.00
Minuet, cold meat fork, Internat'l................................30.00
Minuet, salad fork, Internat'l.......................................20.00
Mythologique, salad fork, Imperial 75.00
Mythologique, serving spoon, Imperial, 8¾" 150.00
Mythologique, sugar tongs, Gorham, 5" 135.00
New Queens, pie server, Gorham, 9¼" 160.00
Old Colonial, chocolate spoon, Towle..........................45.00
Old Colonial, dinner fork, Towle..................................45.00
Old Colonial, gravy ladle, Towle 75.00
Old Colonial, luncheon fork, Towle 25.00
Old Colonial, luncheon knife, Towle 30.00
Old Colonial, master butter spreader 55.00
Old Colonial, sauce ladle, Towle..................................50.00
Old Colonial, soup ladle, gold-washed bowl, Towle 595.00
Old Colonial, tablespoon, Towle...................................50.00
Old Colonial, teaspoon, Towle 12.00
Old Master, dessert spoon, Towle.................................25.00
Old Master, dinner knife, Towle 28.00
Old Master, gravy ladle, Towle.....................................50.00
Old Master, ice cream fork, Towle 25.00
Old Master, iced teaspoon, Towle 22.00
Old Master, lemon fork, Towle 20.00
Old Master, letter opener, Towle 25.00
Old Master, salad fork, Towle 25.00
Old Master, tablespoon, Towle 48.00
Pantheon, place fork, Internat'l....................................18.00
Pantheon, place knife, Internat'l 18.00
Pantheon, salad fork, Internat'l....................................25.00
Paul Revere, pie server, Towle 30.00
Poppy, berry spoon, Gorham, 7⅞"..............................60.00
Raphael, berry spoon, 7⅞"...60.00

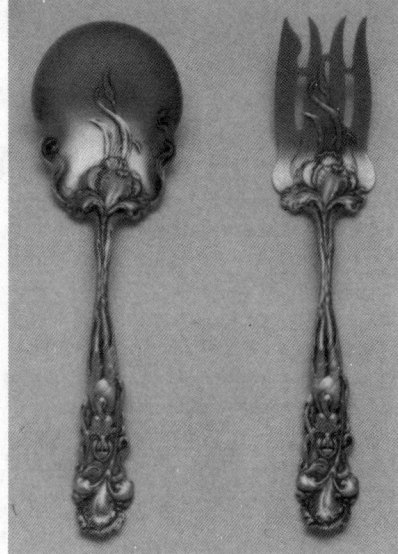

Raphael serving fork and spoon with relief irises, each marked Alvin, 9", $935.00.

Richelieu, butter spreader, FH, Internat'l 23.00
Richelieu, cold meat fork, Internat'l 70.00
Richelieu, gravy spoon, Internat'l 70.00
Richelieu, ice cream fork, Internat'l 25.00
Richelieu, iced teaspoon, Internat'l..............................36.00
Riviera, bouillon, Internat'l..18.00
Riviera, fruit spoon, Internat'l......................................17.00

Riviera, gumbo spoon, Internat'l 20.00
Riviera, ice cream fork, Internat'l 24.00
Riviera, iced teaspoon, Internat'l 20.00
Rose, berry spoon, repousse strawberries, Steiff, 8⅛" 195.00
Rose, tomato server, pierced, Steiff, 7½" 125.00
Rose Tiara, butter spreader, HH, Gorham 16.00
Rose Tiara, sauce ladle, Gorham 42.00
Rosette, master butter spreader, Gorham 35.00
Sculptured Rose, gravy spoon.......................................44.00
Sculptured Rose, tablespoon...40.00
Silver Flutes, bonbon 27.50
Silver Flutes, cold meat fork 52.00
Silver Flutes, iced tea spoon 23.00
Silver Flutes, lemon fork 20.00
Silver Flutes, sauce ladle 38.00
Silver Flutes, sugar tong 30.00
Silver Flutes, tablespoon 50.00
Silver Iris, place spoon, Internat'l...............................38.00
Silver Iris, tablespoon, Internat'l 95.00
Silver Wheat, cream soup, Reed & Barton 25.00
Silver Wheat, salad fork, Reed & Barton 27.00
Southwind, place spoon...25.00
Sovereign/Hispana, place fork, Gorham 35.00
Sovereign/Hispana, salad fork, Gorham 35.00
Sovereign/Hispana, teaspoon, Gorham 18.00
Spanish Baroque, cold meat fork, Reed & Barton 66.00
Spanish Baroque, cream soup, Reed & Barton............30.00
Spanish Baroque, master butter spreader, HH, Reed & Barton......20.00
Spanish Baroque, sugar shell, Reed & Barton 21.00
Spanish Baroque, tablespoon, Reed & Barton 60.00
Spring Glory, butter spreader, HH, Internat'l 17.00
Spring Glory, tablespoon, Internat'l 40.00
Spring Glory, teaspoon, Internat'l...............................12.00
Spring Serenade, cold meat fork, Lunt 44.00
Spring Serenade, tablespoon, Lunt 40.00
St Dunstan, preserve spoon, gilt, Tiffany, 7⅛" 90.00
St James, cream soup spoon, Tiffany, 6¾" 75.00
St James, olive spoon, Tiffany 110.00
Stanton Hall, butter spreader, HH, Oneida 18.00
Stanton Hall, cold meat fork, Oneida.........................50.00
Stanton Hall, cream soup, Oneida 24.00
Stanton Hall, tablespoon, Oneida 44.00
Stanton Hall, teaspoon, Oneida 16.00
Stradivari, cream soup, Wallace 25.00
Stradivari, iced tea spoon, Wallace 27.50
Stradivari, tablespoon, Wallace...................................47.00
Strasbourg, fish fork, Imperial.....................................55.00
Strasbourg, luncheon fork, Gorham 18.00
Strasbourg, sugar shell, Imperial 25.00
Strasbourg, teaspoon, Imperial....................................14.00
Versailles, berry spoon, gold washed, Imperial, 8¾" 190.00
Versailles, demitasse spoon, Imperial 32.00
Versailles, fish server, Imperial 395.00
Versailles, gumbo, Imperial..58.00
Versailles, ice cream slice, Imperial 395.00
Versailles, luncheon fork, Imperial 32.00
Versailles, salad fork, Imperial 150.00
Versailles, tablespoon, Imperial 60.00
Versailles, teaspoon, Imperial......................................26.00
Wedgwood, bouillon, Internat'l 21.00
Wedgwood, butter spreader, FH, Internat'l 20.00
Wedgwood, coffee spoon, Internat'l............................14.00
Wedgwood, ice cream fork, Internat'l.........................25.00
Wedgwood, sauce ladle, Internat'l 44.00

Wedgwood, sugar tongs, Internat'l 30.00
Wedgwood, tablespoon, Internat'l 47.50
Winthrop, cream soup, Tiffany 45.00
Winthrop, ice cream fork, Tiffany 42.00
Winthrop, 5 o'clock spoon, Tiffany 35.00

Hollow Ware

Until the middle of the 19th century, the silverware produced in America was custom made on order of the buyer directly from the silversmith. With the rise of industrialization, factories sprang up that manufactured silverware for retailers who often added their trademark to the ware. Silver ore was mined in abundance, and demand spurred production. Changes in style occurred at the whim of fashion. Repousse decoration (relief work) became popular about 1885, reflecting the ostentatious taste of the Victorian era. Later in the century, Greek, Etruscan, and several classic styles found favor. Today the Art Deco styles of this century are very popular with collectors. In the listings that follow, manufacturer's name or trademark is noted first; in lieu of that information, listings are by item. Weight is given in troy ounces. See also Tiffany, Silver.

Arthur Stone, bowl, simple eng florals/lines, 3½x8" 1,000.00
Austrian, tray, emb/rtcl cherry clusters, hdls, 22".................... 1,200.00

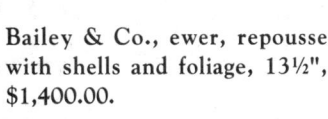
Bailey & Co., ewer, repousse with shells and foliage, 13½", $1,400.00.

Babour, bowl, hand hammered, 4-lobed rim, appl D, 7x10" 150.00
Bigelow/Kennard & Co, compote, ram's head hdls, 1800s, 13". 1,500.00
Black/Starr/Frost, bowl, rim w/appl scrolls & mums, 11".............450.00
Black/Starr/Frost, bowl, rtcl/scalloped rim w/swags, 11".............375.00
Black/Starr/Frost, compote, eng/rtcl mums at rim & ft, 5" 1,000.00
Black/Starr/Frost, vase, hammered w/emb florals, 1900, 15"....2,800.00
Butler Bement, presentation beaker, eng, 1826, 3½" 650.00
Chas Moore/John Ferguson, decanter stand, brite cut, 10x13". 6,000.00
Continental, centerpc, fluted, rtcl floral rim/hdls, 17" 750.00
Crichton Bros, sugar bowl, invt pear form, 1913, 4¼"..................310.00
Dirk Van Erp, tray, simple styling, 12" dia, VG........................260.00
Dominick & Haff, candlestick, eng florals, sq, 10", pr.................500.00
Dominick & Haff, shaped rim, 14½" 550.00
Dominick & Haff, water pitcher, allover repousse mums, 9" .. 2,000.00
Durgin, coffeepot, baluster form w/chased foliage, 11" 350.00
Falick Novick, bowl, fluted w/appl initial, ped ft, 8" dia 605.00
Frank Whiting, candelabra, 3-lite, gadrooned, 1910, 17", pr 600.00
Frederick Smith, fruit bowl, allover repousse, 1889, 9", EX 400.00
Georg Jensen, bowl, ea end scalloped, Denmark, 9½" L 1,000.00

Georg Jensen, coffee set, Blossom, ivory hdls, 7" pot+2 pcs..... 3,300.00
Georg Jensen, compote, grapes/vines under bowl, #263A, 5" 750.00
Georg Jensen, pitcher, hammered w/beaded ft ring, cvd hdl .. 1,600.00
German, cup, 3 repousse portraits, 3 ball ft, Augsburg, 4"...........325.00
German, tray, serpentine oval, 800 std, 20th C, 16" 200.00
Gorham, apple box, appl branch w/fruit, bee as catch, 3⅝"..... 2,800.00
Gorham, basket, chased/rtcl garlands etc, leafy base, 6x10" 1,300.00
Gorham, bread tray, repousse w/foliate spirals, 15" L 250.00
Gorham, cake plate, rtcl rim & ft w/acorns & oak leaves, 9".......450.00
Gorham, decanter, as a wicker-covered Chianti bottle, 1850s.....170.00
Gorham, demitasse set, chased florals, pot+cr/sug, 1894.............750.00
Gorham, hot water kettle+stand, emb panels & florals, 10" 900.00
Gorham, Martele presentation loving cup, twisted snake hdls . 6,500.00
Gorham, pitcher, eng/emb berried vines, 1860, 11½" 1,800.00
Gorham, pitcher, hammered, simple style, 1909, 7¾" 300.00
Gorham, pitcher, scrolled rim, monogram, 1911, 27 troy oz 650.00
Gorham, presentation cup, vasiform, 3 S-hdls, 5½" 400.00
Gorham, shakers, dog form, 1800s, 3", pr 1,200.00
Gorham, tazza, Greek Revival, female figural hdls, 1870, 7".......550.00
Gorham, tea service, Plymouth, 4-pc...................................495.00
Gorham, tea/coffee, plain w/beaded rim, 5-pc, 70 troy oz 800.00
Gorham, tray, serpentine rim w/swags & ribbons, 1900, 20" 900.00
Hester Bateman, teapot, cylindrical, chased flowers, 5" 500.00
J McKay, salver, appl flowers/shells, 3 scallop ft, 11"...................800.00
James Robinson, coffeepot, lighthouse form, wood hdl, 10" 400.00
James T Woolley, bowl, 8 flutes, 5¾".....................................325.00
Japanese, teapot, hammered w/appl eng panels, 1900, 3¾"..........500.00
JB, London; candlestick, fluted w/acanthus leaves, 1821, 14"......550.00
JE Terry, tea tray, Geo III, eng crest, 1820, 125 troy oz 4,200.00
John Ewan, beaker, gadrooned rim, 3¼"................................. 1,200.00
John Schofield, tea caddy, pineapple final, eng arms, 1800..........300.00
John Tanger, pap boat, ca 1794, 5x3" 150.00
John Taylor Jr/Horace Hinsdale, milk jug, coat of arms, 5"..........600.00
Joseph Shoemaker, sugar/cream pot, brite cut, 11"; 7½" 1,900.00
Kalo, bowl, appl rope at rim, short ped base, #130, 3x6"............700.00
Kalo, pitcher, ewer form, raised B on side, dtd 1919, 10" 1,400.00
Kalo, pitcher, hand wrought, bulbous, 6½"..............................900.00
Kalo, pitcher, melon ribs, monogram, 9" 1,800.00
Kalo, tray, ea end scalloped, eng monogram, scratches, 13".........500.00
Kirk, bowl, chased floral, hdls/ftd, 1850s, 3¾x6¼" 400.00
Kirk, cake plate, wide repousse floral rim, monogram, 11" 450.00
Kirk, pitcher, emb village landscape, w/lid, 1850s, 9" 1,800.00
L Huemer, punch bowl, Danish, hammered w/buds, 52 troy oz . 1,000.00
Lebkuecher & Co, bowl, hammered w/Renaissance scrolls, 9½" 450.00
Lebkuecher & Co, tray, hammered w/floral rim, 1925, 12"..........700.00
Lebkuecher & Co, wine cooler, classical style, 1900, 9½"............280.00
Lebolt, basket, hand hammered, bowl form, 4x5" 100.00
Lewis Fueter, waiter, shaped hexagon, gadroon rim, 1775, 7" . 8,800.00
Mappin Bros, creamer/sugar bowl, Regency style, 12 troy oz........200.00
Margot de Mexico, goblet, dome base, baluster stem, 7½" 100.00
Martin Hall & Co, salver, scroll border & ft, 1905, 12½"............800.00
Mauser, bowl, rtcl rim w/Nouveau lilies, oval rim, 12" L 500.00
Mexican, candelabra, 5-lite, rtcl scroll/branch stem, 9" pr...........650.00
Mexican, tray, fluted w/scrolled rim, 1920, 27 troy oz................200.00
P Bruckman & Sohne, tray, appl repousse rim, 1900s, 20" L 550.00
Paul Revere II, cream jug, urn form, strap hdl, 1800, 6½" 18,500.00
Peer Smed, tazza, 2 rtcl leaves as supports, 8" L 700.00
Peter/Anne Bateman, creamer, beaded rim, sq base, dent, 5".......225.00
Peter/Wm Bateman, creamer, brite cut keyfret/leaves, 3¾" 175.00
Randahl, candle snuffer, fluted cup, bun on end of long hdl........150.00
Randahl, flask, hand wrought, 6" 150.00
Redlich, tray, Renaissance-style chasing, 20th C, 15" 200.00
Redlich, tray, shaped rtcl floral/ribbon rim, 28 troy oz 700.00
Reed & Barton, bonbon dish, Francis I, pr 375.00

Reed & Barton, bowl, SP insert, silver-gilt frog, 5x16"............ 1,980.00
Reed & Barton, bread tray, Francis I.....................................350.00
Reed & Barton, chafing dish, cabriole legs/paw ft, '10, 11" 1,400.00
Reed & Barton, tea/coffee, plain ovoid form, 20th C, 5-pc 1,100.00
Samuel Hayne/Dudley Cater, salver, emb Rococo/floral, 16" . 1,400.00
Samuel Minott, str sided, dome lid, thumb lift, 9" 2,200.00
Shreve & Co, bread & butter dish, scroll/floral border, 6" 50.00
Shreve & Co, fruit bowl, ruffled, eng florals, gold-washed....... 1,600.00
Shreve & Co, tea/coffee, 12" pot/hot water kettle+4 pcs......... 8,000.00
Shreve & Co, tea/coffee w/tray, Dolores, 5-pc 8,000.00
Stephen Smith, claret jug, gold-washed, animal/mask frieze ... 2,600.00
Stieff, tray, repousse floral border, 23 troy oz, EX....................750.00
Tennant Co, presentation vase, repousse scrolls/floral, 16" 1,000.00
Wai Kee, sauce boat, eng bamboo, 3 hoof ft, gilt lined, 7"...........220.00
Wallace, bowl, Rose, rtcl scalloped border w/roses, 12" 200.00
Wallace, fruit bowl, shaped rim w/eng poppies, 20th C, 11".......550.00
Wallace Silversmiths, tray, plain w/everted rim, 1950s, 10" 440.00

Whiting Mfg. Co., mug, repousse and chased with putti and acanthus, base inscribed and dated 1892, 4", $1,350.00.

Whiting, bread basket, openwork rim w/loops & scrolls, 12".......300.00
Wm Garret Forbes, creamer/sugar bowl, brite cut band, EX 450.00
Wm Spratling, bowl, 3 bead-trim loop hdls, etched line, 6" 500.00
Wm Vincent, sugar basket, pierced/eng, cobalt liner, 4½"...........500.00

Silver Lustre Ware

Much of the ware known as silver lustre was produced in the early 1800s in Staffordshire, England. This type of earthenware was entirely covered with the metallic silver glaze. It was most popular prior to 1840 when the technique of electroplating was developed, and silverplated wares came into vogue. Later in the century, artisans used silver lustre to develop designs on vases and other decorative ware.

Teapot, ribbed bottom, bird-head handle terminal, 6" x 10", $225.00.

Creamer, Loop Rib base, gadroon top border, 4x5" 70.00
Cuspidor, lady's, minor wear, 5½" dia 90.00
Loving cup, copper lustre int, 4½x5" 75.00
Pitcher, Oriental motif, blk transfer w/mc, 6", EX........................185.00
Shaker, toby figural, minor wear, 5" 85.00
Teapot, ribbed, Queen Anne style, 6" 165.00
Vase, leopards & trees on gr, att De Morgan, 1880s, 8½" 925.00

Silver Overlay

The silver overlay glass made during the 1800s was decorated with a cut-out pattern of sterling silver applied to the surface of the ware.

Bottle, scent; gr, ornate o/l, bulbous, 5" 245.00
Bottle, scent; gr, scrolls/flowers ol, slim, 6" 200.00
Bowl, banana; florals/scrolls o/l, scalloped/ftd, 12½" L 70.00
Bowl, console; gr, Nouveau o/l, rolled rim, 2½x12½" 85.00
Vase, cranberry satin, Nouveau o/l, bulbous/flared, 4¼" 315.00
Vase, gold spangle/dk amber cased in orange, floral o/l, 5" 275.00
Vase, gr, Dmn Optic, wide floral band o/l, 9" 150.00
Vase, gr, dogwood o/l mk sterling, ribbed body, 4" 165.00

Silverplate

Hollow Ware

Silverplated hollow ware is fast becoming the focus of attention for many of today's collectors. See also Pairpoint, Silverplate; Railroadiana, Silverplate.

Key: gw — gold wash

Basket, applied plum blossoms and insects, gilt traces within, Simpson, Hall, & Miller, 1885, 8" x 8", $550.00.

Bowl, covered vegetable; Rococo design, 14½" L 150.00
Candelabrum, 2 scrolling arms, Reed & Barton, 12" 125.00
Candelabrum, 5-lite, beaded bands, Goldfeder, 17", pr 300.00
Candlestick, columnar, Corinthian capital, English, 6", pr..........110.00
Candlestick, Corinthian column form, Italian, 8½", 4 for 375.00
Centerpc, emb scrolls/leaves, shaped mirror, Fr, 7x19" 350.00
Champagne bucket, gadrooned, hdls, Internat'l, 23", pr 300.00
Epergne, cut glass compote on figural std, 3 cherub ft, 26"..........550.00
Figurine, peacock, 12" L, pr...600.00
Hot water kettle on stand, eagle spout, florals, Elkington 325.00
Pitcher, swan finial, dbl-walled, Meriden, 12½", VG...................125.00
Tea urn, chased acanthus, Elkington & Co, 1855, rpr, 22" 1,100.00
Tea urn, repousse flowers, urn finial, curved hdls, 21"..................400.00

Tray, emb floral scrolls, rnded corners, 21" L.............................100.00
Tray, eng florals, chased floral border, scalloped, 29" 275.00
Tray, scrolling dbl border, EX detail, hdls, 27" L.........................185.00

Sheffield

Tureen, Regency style, paw feet, ca 1820, 10", $1,300.00.

Candlestick, emb foliage, 12½", pr 320.00
Candlestick, Geo III, urn-form nozzle, reeding, 1800, 11" 185.00
Honey dish, bee w/red glass body, 3½x7".....................................160.00
Tankard measure, Geo II coin in lid, worn, 7¾" 300.00
Tray, serpentine oval, w/gallery, 24" L.......................................250.00
Tray, tea; appl scroll/shell rim, Smith Sissons & Co, 1850 ....650.00
Wine cooler, Regency style, campagna form, 1820s, 8", pr...... 1,400.00
Wine urn, emb vintage, hdls, ftd, 13" 150.00

Silver Resist

The process for decorating pottery with the silver-resist method involved first coating the design or that portion of the pattern that was to be left unsilvered with a water-soluble solution. The lustre was applied to the entire surface of the vessel and allowed to dry. Before the final firing, the surface was washed, removing only the silver from the coated areas. This type of ware was produced early in the 1800s by many English potteries, Wedgwood included.

Bowl, floral border, 6" 75.00
Mustard pot, ribbed, ftd 80.00
Pitcher, florals, 5¾", EX...75.00
Pitcher, florals & birds, 4⅜", VG 60.00
Pitcher, transfer of Cibb & Molinaux (boxers) on cream, 6".......400.00
Teacup & saucer, red/yel flowers, silver band, Coalport, sm 50.00
Urn, canary yel floral, flared, open, 5½x4⅜" 175.00

Sinclaire

In 1904 H.P. Sinclaire and Company was founded in Corning, New York. For the first sixteen years of production, Sinclaire used blanks from other glassworks for his cut and engraved designs. In 1920 he established his own glass-blowing factory in Bath, New York. His most popular designs utilize fruits, flowers, and other forms from nature. Most of Sinclaire's glass is unmarked; items that are carry his logo: an 'S' within a wreath with two shields.

Bowl, X-mitres/hobstars, very heavy, 2¾x9", NM 165.00
Candlestick, gr, etched florals, 3", pr 175.00
Candlestick, tulip form w/etched florals, prisms, 9", pr 150.00
Console set, amber, garlands/ovals, 14" plate+bowl+sticks 300.00
Pitcher, brilliant cut/floral eng, bulbous on ped ft, 8½"................550.00

Platter, moose medallion, four game birds in rim, silver thread and strawberry diamond cuttings, etched mark, 15", $3,100.00.

Vase, amethyst, int ribbing, sgn, 5½x4" 50.00
Vase, cut, Queen Louise, 15½"..130.00
Wine, cut, Antique & Engraved, sgn, 4½x2½", 5 for...................280.00

Sitzendorf

The Sitzendorf factory began operations in East Germany in the mid-1800s, adopting the name of the city as the name of their company. They produced fine porcelain groups, figurines, etc. in much the same style and quality as Meissen and the Dresden factories. Much of their ware was marked with a crown over the letter 'S' and a horizontal line with two slash marks. Our advisor for this category is Donald Penrose; he is listed in the Directory under Ohio.

Figurine, apple pickers, boy & girl w/dog, 9½x7" 650.00
Figurine, boy & girl, ea w/lamb & flowers, mk, 7½", pr 550.00
Figurine, boy holding Scottie dog, GDR, 3½" 35.00
Figurine, couple w/Russian wolfhounds (lady seated), 9x10" 850.00
Figurine, dancing boy & girl w/lambs, 10", pr 695.00
Figurine, Dutch man & lady w/lambs & flowers, mk, 7½", pr......550.00
Figurine, gardener w/watering can, lady w/flowers, 9", pr 450.00
Figurine, girl holding baby, w/cradle, GDR, 4½" 50.00
Figurine, girl w/flowers, GDR, 3½" 35.00
Figurine, man sewing seed, GDR, 8½"..100.00
Inkstand, Rococo scrolls, appl florals, 2 wells, 9½".......................425.00
Vase, maidens, Kauffmann, floral panels, Voigt, 3-hdld, 8" 225.00

Slag Glass

Slag glass is a marbleized opaque glassware made by several companies from about 1870 until the turn of the century. It is usually found in purple or caramel (see Chocolate Glass), though other colors were also made. Pink is rare and very expensive.

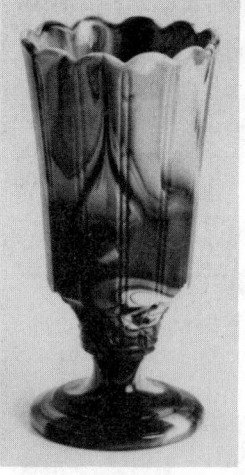

Purple slag vase, paneled sides, 8", $90.00.

Blue, basket, cherries/leaves in relief, crimped/ruffled, 9".............75.00
Green, sugar bowl, w/lid 98.00
Pink, Invt Fan & Feather, bowl, berry 175.00
Pink, Invt Fan & Feather, butter dish 1,000.00
Pink, Invt Fan & Feather, creamer 450.00
Pink, Invt Fan & Feather, cruet...1,250.00
Pink, Invt Fan & Feather, jelly compote 425.00
Pink, Invt Fan & Feather, pitcher, water 1,450.00
Pink, Invt Fan & Feather, punch cup 265.00
Pink, Invt Fan & Feather, sauce dish, ftd, 4" 265.00
Pink, Invt Fan & Feather, shakers, rare, pr..................................1,200.00
Pink, Invt Fan & Feather, spooner 325.00
Pink, Invt Fan & Feather, sugar bowl, w/lid 665.00
Pink, Invt Fan & Feather, toothpick holder..................................650.00
Pink, Invt Fan & Feather, tumbler, 4" 400.00
Purple, Fan & Leaf, tray, shield form, hdls....................................98.00
Purple, Fluted Shell, bowl, pie crust rim, 8½" 75.00
Purple, Jenny Lind, compote 165.00
Purple, Oval Medallion, spooner..90.00
Purple, plate, lattice edge, 10½"..50.00
Purple, plate, lattice edge, 13" 85.00
Purple, Scroll w/Acanthus, creamer & sugar bowl.......................100.00

SMF (Schramberg/Wheelock Black Forest)

Since 1918 the Schramberger Majolica Factory in Schramberg, Wurttemberg, Germany, has produced majolica, stoneware, and porcelain. Various marks were used (Schramberg and Wheelock 'Black Forest' Hand Painted Pottery), but the common link is the SMF insignia. They produced a number of hand-painted pieces, but those of most interest to collectors are painted in gaudy colors in bizarre designs on equally bizarre shapes. As a result it is often referred to as the 'poor man's Clarice Cliff.' Collectors will note that most pieces bear an incised mold number, a painter's number, and the SMF mark. Of special note are the pieces marked Gobelin, followed by a number (or simply G and the number). Gobelin wares have a gray background with as many as ten colors used in the design. The number denotes particular color combinations. For example, Gobelin-3 pieces will be painted in green and orange leaves and yellow eyes, along with other colors specific to that design. Expect to find Gobelin-numbered pottery in various unusual shapes. It is not uncommon to find pieces that are chipped, and a perfect piece should be valued by its owner. Our advisor for this category is Ralph Winslow; he is listed in the Directory under Kansas.

Basket, 4-color, G-5, SMF Wheelock, #2706, 4" 32.00

Candle holder, 3-color, eyes, SMF Wheelock, G-2, 4" 35.00
Inkwell, 3-color, eyes, oblong, G-3, SMF-W, 9" 35.00
Plate/plaque, 3-color, leaf, G-6, SMF-W, 11" 30.00
Vase, gray, hdls, G-4, hdls, SMF Wheelock, 7½" 35.00
Vase, lav & rust, Deco, SMF, 3½" 50.00
Vase, wht, purple ivy, eyes, SMF, 9" 36.00
Vase, 3-color, G-1, SMF, 7½" 38.00
Vase, 3-color, G-7, SMF Wheelock, 8" 40.00
Vase, 3-color, leaves, SMF, 4½" 36.00
Vase, 3-color, linear decor, G-4, SMF, 4½" 30.00

Smith Bros.

Alfred and Harry Smith founded their glassmaking firm in New Bedford, Massachusetts. They had been formerly associated with the Mt. Washington Glass Works, working there from 1871 to 1875 to aid in establishing a decorating department. Smith glass is valued for its excellent enameled decoration on satin or opalescent glass. Pieces were often marked with a lion in a red shield. Our advisors for this category are Betty and Clarence Maier; they are listed in the Directory under Pennsylvania.

Vase with hummingbird and flowers on tan, 8", $140.00; Vase with two round panels, one with mountain scene, one with bird on branch, 5¾", $125.000.

Biscuit jar, gold floral branches, 6-rib melon form, 6" 350.00
Biscuit jar, Persian-style jewels/fans, NM 950.00
Bowl, daisies, yel on bl, melon ribs, 4¼" 265.00
Bowl, lilies/leaves, gold-traced on tan, melon ribs, 4x9" 675.00
Bowl, pansies, bl dotted rim, ribbed, 3" 200.00
Creamer & sugar, gold prunus on tan, melon ribs, SP lid/mts 650.00
Creamer & sugar, pansies on cream, emb rim/bail/lid, 4" dia 250.00
Ferner, wild roses on ribbed wht satin, metal rim, 10" dia 150.00
Humidor, pansies on body & glass lid, 6½x5" 150.00
Jar, carnations/violets on shiny wht, melon ribs, 3½" 325.00
Jar, violets on wht & lt bl, melon ribs, bell form, 4" 375.00
Plate, Santa Maria, mk World's Fair, 1883, 6" dia 325.00
Rose bowl, daisies/beads on cream, lion mk, 4" 225.00
Salt shaker, roses, pk on gr gloss, lay-down style, 2¾" L 90.00
Sugar shaker, daisies, wht on melon ribs, mum-emb lid, 5" 250.00
Sugar shaker, daisies on lt tan, ribbed, silver lid, 5½" 250.00
Sweetmeat, bl florals, ribbed glass lid, mk, 5¼x5¼" 640.00
Vase, dbl pilgrim; lav wisteria w/gold, 7¼x8x2" 1,220.00
Vase, violets, pinched form, beaded rim, mk, 4½" 395.00
Vase, wisteria on pk to wht, gold leaves, flask form, 9x7" 1,250.00

Snow Babies

During the last quarter of the 19th century, snow babies — little figurals in white snowsuits — originated in Germany. They were made of sugar candy and were often used as decorations for Christmas trees. Later on they were made of marzipan, a confection of crushed almonds, sugar, and egg whites. Eventually porcelain manufacturers began making them in bisque. They were popular until WWII. These tiny china figures range in size from just over 1" to the very rare jointed babies sometimes nearly 7" tall. Any example brings a very respectable price on the market today. Beware of reproductions.

Baby, standing with flag, 4½", $350.00.

Babies, 2 stand on lg snowball, 2½" 75.00
Babies slide down brick wall, #6602, 1⅝x2½" 125.00
Baby, jtd, good pnt, impish features, 3" 175.00
Baby climbing tree 150.00
Baby holding baton 110.00
Baby holding camera, 1¾" 125.00
Baby holding picture fr 150.00
Baby in shell, lg 25.00
Baby lying flat on sled, Germany, 1½" 55.00
Baby on ice skates, #3116, Germany, 1¾" 150.00
Baby on red airplane, Germany, 2¼" 175.00
Baby on stomach, googly-eyed, Hertivig & Co, 1915, 2¾" 175.00
Baby riding polar bear, 2¼" 50.00
Baby sits on yel sled, Germany, 1½" 55.00
Baby sits w/arms outstretched, Germany, 1" 45.00
Baby slides down hill on champagne bottle, tree in bkground 145.00
Baby stands on sled, 1¾" 45.00
Bear, Germany, 1½" 40.00
Bear on skis, Germany, 2" 55.00
Carollers, 3 stand in snow, lantern above, Germany, 2¼" 100.00
Girl on sled, #8448, Germany, 1¾" 100.00
Girl w/pk pants on sled, 2½" 90.00
Igloo, baby inside, Santa on roof, Germany 125.00
Penguin, Germany, 4" 65.00
Santa on roof 95.00
Santa sits in gr sleigh, w/reindeer, Germany, 3½" 225.00
Snow pup on skis, mk 110.00
Snowman, 1½" 50.00
Twins, old, G pnt 75.00

Snuff Boxes

As early as the 17th century, the Chinese began using snuff. By the early 19th century, the practice had spread to Europe and America. It was used by both the gentlemen and the ladies alike, and expensive snuff boxes and bottles were the earmark of the genteel. Some were of silver or gold set with precious stones or pearls, while others contained music boxes. In the following listings, the dimension noted is length. See also Orientalia, Snuff Bottles.

Burl, EX figure & color, 3½" dia 175.00
Horn w/ivory & wood inlays on top, 3⅜" L 95.00
Leather, shoe shaped, copper tacks in sole, 4" 165.00
Papier-mache, sled scene, mc on blk, Soviet Union, 3½", EX 100.00
Papier-mache w/pnt eng of woman & parrot, 3", NM 85.00
Pewter, shoe form w/brite-cut eng, hinged lid, 4" 250.00
Silver, eng surface, gold-wash int, rnded ends, English, 3" 275.00
Silver w/enamel faux malachite, inset lapis plaque, 1900............300.00
Silver w/enameling, lobed ends, FR, 950 std, 2½ troy oz.............250.00
Silver w/lg enamel reserve w/boats, 1900, mk, 3½ troy oz...........475.00

Soapstone

Soapstone is a soft talc in rock form with a smooth, greasy feel from whence comes its name. In colonial times it was extracted from out-croppings in large sections with hand saws, carted by oxen to mills, and fashioned into useful domestic articles such as footwarmers, cooking utensils, inkwells, etc. During the early 1800s, it was used to make heating stoves and kitchen sinks. Most familiar today are the carved vases, bookends, and boxes made in China during the Victorian era. Our advisor for this category is Donald Penrose; he is listed in the Directory under Ohio.

Robed Oriental with pipe, 7½", $55.00.

Censer, dragon-mask/ring hdls, dragon finial, 3-leg, 8" 145.00
Cvg, foo lion in clouds before flames, cvd base, 9x8½" 75.00
Cvg, foo lions, female w/pup, male w/ball, 6½" L, pr..................95.00
Cvg, Oriental girl w/arms over head holds fruit tray, 13" 125.00
Cvg, Oriental girl w/basket of fish, detailed, 11" 85.00
Inkwell, dome top, geometrics, 4 quill holders, 2½" sq 155.00
Screen, flower container, oblong base, 5-color, 7½x5".................45.00
Screen, mums & leaves, fan shape, 8½x12½" 45.00
Screen, 2 peacocks w/spread feathers, 5-color, 6½x5½" 40.00
Seal, oxen, head down, brn, rstr, 2½" 145.00
Vase, dbl; peonies/vines/birds, 3-color, 9x7" 140.00
Vase, floral cvg, mottled gray, attached blk base, 5" 35.00

Soda Fountain Collectibles

As the neighborhood ice cream parlor becomes a thing of the past, soda fountain memorabilia from fancy backbars to ice cream advertising is becoming a popular field of collecting. One area of interest is the glassware used to serve the more elaborate ice cream concoctions. A sundae glass is familiar to us all, but there was also a 'lucky mondae' glass, narrow at the bottom and flaring to a top dimension equal to one scoop. There are footed banana split dishes and soda pop glasses with the name or logo of the beverage company painted on them.

Syrup dispensers, especially those from the teens, today command high prices. These had spherical or urn-shaped dispensers and carried names such as Jersey Creme, Buckeye, Cherry Smash, etc.

It is estimated that ice cream dippers may be found in approximately two hundred different styles — some bowl shaped or cylindrical, some for making ice cream sandwiches, and even a very rare heart-shaped dipper. (This one was used along with matching heart-shaped ice cream dishes.)

Glass straw holders are very collectible. Clear is the most common color, but they are also found in green and pink; some are made of frosted glass. Early examples were pattern molded; some had matching glass lids — these are the most desirable. Our advisors for this category are Joyce and Harold Screen; they are listed in the Directory under Maryland. See also Advertising.

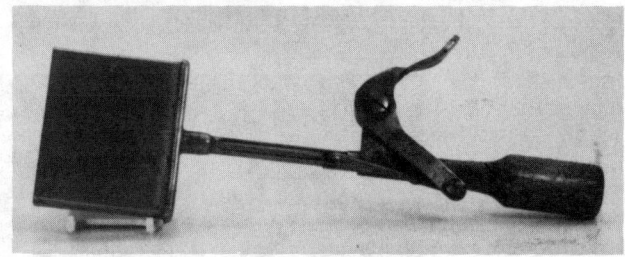

Dipper for ice cream sandwich, Mayer, flat, $250.00.

Bottle, syrup; Cherry Smash, label under glass, 1920, G 300.00
Container, Borden's Malted Milk, aluminum 50.00
Container, Coors Malted Milk, aluminum....................................50.00
Container, Horlick Malted Milk, glass, w/label............................350.00
Container, Thompson's Malted Milk, porc w/NP brass lid 325.00
Cup, Armour's Vigoral 25.00
Cup, Brunham's Clam Bouillon, china 25.00
Cup, Cudahy's Rexsoma, china..25.00
Dipper, banana split; Gilchrist 650.00
Dipper, banana split; United..700.00
Dipper, Benedict, 1¾", EX in orig box 45.00
Dipper, Bohlig, bowl opens 900.00
Dipper, Cold Dog, cylinder 600.00
Dipper, Dover, slicer, single trigger 500.00
Dipper, Gem Trojan 40.00
Dipper, Guaranteed Disher, 'worm' drive 400.00
Dipper, heart shape 3,500.00
Dipper, Icy-Pi, Automatic Cone Co, VG 175.00
Dipper, Kingery Victor, metal hdl 400.00
Dipper, Mosteller, flip-over bowl 1,200.00
Dipper, Pi-Almoder 500.00
Dipper, Sky High Cones..400.00
Dish, banana split; clear, ftd 15.00
Dish, banana split; frosted, flat 5.00
Dish, banana split; gr, ftd..50.00
Dish, banana split; pk, ftd...60.00
Dish, sundae; dbl dip, pebbled finish 25.00
Dish, sundae; triple dip..40.00
Dispenser, Bauer's Orange Julep, 2-part, 16x6x7", EX................300.00
Dispenser, Birchola, orig pump...1,750.00
Dispenser, Buckeye, cola nuts, urn type, w/orig pump 1,600.00
Dispenser, Buckeye, log type, w/orig pump 1,000.00
Dispenser, Buckeye Root Beer, soda glass/nut & leaf, 16", VG.. 1,700.00

Dispenser, Cherri-O, ceramic barrel, w/orig pump 1,000.00
Dispenser, Cherry Smash, glass over cluster 2,500.00
Dispenser, Cherry Smash, orig pump, 16x9", EX 1,300.00
Dispenser, Cherry Smash, red glass, clamp-on counter style 600.00
Dispenser, Cherry Smash, 5 cents on side 1,700.00
Dispenser, Crawford's Cherry Fizz 2,800.00
Dispenser, Daggett's Florida Punch..300.00
Dispenser, Dr Swett's Tree Stump, w/orig pump, M 4,000.00
Dispenser, Fowler's Root Beer, EX 800.00
Dispenser, Ginger-Mint Julep, orig pump, NM 700.00
Dispenser, Grape Kola, figure-8, rear faucet, EX 2,000.00
Dispenser, Grapeola, porc base, 1918, EX................................100.00
Dispenser, Green River, metal base/glass top, 11x8x9", G 100.00
Dispenser, Hires, hourglass, orig pump, 14", EX 400.00
Dispenser, Hires, Muni-Maker, complete............................... 1,800.00
Dispenser, Hires, Muni-Maker, salesman's sample.................10,000.00
Dispenser, Hires, urn style, w/bowl & lid 7,000.00
Dispenser, Howell's Cherry Julip 1,100.00
Dispenser, Howell's Orange Julep, w/orig pump 1,300.00
Dispenser, ice cream cone; glass, orig int & lid, 14½" 300.00
Dispenser, Mission Grapefruit, pk crackle glass........................175.00
Dispenser, Nesbitt's, pk base & top..225.00
Dispenser, Orangeade, tin, Art Deco style, M 500.00
Dispenser, Red Keg, red w/gr bands, 15x8", VG 2,000.00
Dispenser, Ward's Grape Crush, orig pump, EX 1,200.00
Dispenser, Ward's Lemon Crush, w/pump, EX 825.00
Dispenser, Ward's Lime Crush, lime shape, w/pump, VG........ 1,200.00
Dispenser, Ward's Orange Crush, over-sz, EX 1,500.00
Dispenser, Ward's Orange Crush, w/pump, EX..........................850.00
Dispenser, Zipp's Cherri-O, birds sips soda, 16x7½", G 1,500.00
Fountain glass, Dr Brown's Celery Tonic 35.00
Fountain glass, Green River, syrup line......................................20.00
Fountain glass, Hires, Enjoy Nature's Delicious Drink 40.00
Fountain glass, Howell's Root Beer, short, heavy.......................25.00
Fountain glass, ice cream soda; 'soda fountain' pattern, pk...........40.00
Fountain glass, ice cream soda; Tea Room, gr............................60.00
Fountain glass, J Kellenberger's Fruit-Juleps, Durango CO 40.00
Fountain glass, Moxie, Drink, orange band 20.00
Fountain glass, Seven-Up, gr...15.00
Fountain glass, Tiger Brand Ginger Ale, emb tiger head...............50.00
Fountain glass, Zipp's Cherri-O, bird eating berries, flared............35.00
Fountain glass, Zipp's Orangeade 25.00
Ice cream cone holder, glass, emb cones, 3" 30.00
Mixer, Arnold's, wht porc base 75.00
Mixer, Hamilton Beach #10 ....50.00
Mixer, Horlick's, 18x6x8", EX...300.00
Mixer, Walker's Quick & Easy, hand crank, floor model 750.00
Mug, Armour's Veribest Root Beer, crockery 40.00
Mug, Bowey's Old Style Root Beer, w/buoy trademk, pottery 50.00
Mug, Buckeye, plain hdl 50.00
Mug, Lash's Root Beer 50.00
Mug, Miner's Root Beer, bl glaze..125.00
Mug, Modox, emb Indian chief's head, glass, 5x3", EX 50.00
Photo, interior view, front counter service, after 1905 ....10.00
Photo, interior view, wall or cottage fountain, pre-1910................30.00
Shaker, Walker's Imperial, aluminum caps, #48 ....800.00
Sheet music, My Hygrade Sweetie, EX 15.00
Sheet music, Oh My Eskimo Pie 25.00
Sign, Cherry Cheer, cb, 7x11", M..125.00
Sign, Dolbey's Ice Cream, rvpt glass 300.00
Sign, Santa diecut, for ice cream, store hanger, 10x4"...................75.00
Stein, Dr Swett's (Root Beer) 175.00
Stein, Murray's (Root Beer) 125.00
Stein, Simmons & Hammon (Root Beer)....................................50.00

Straw holder, bulbous base, 12", NM 250.00
Straw holder, common, w/lid & insert, 12" 140.00
Straw holder, gr 350.00
Straw holder, Greek Key, Heisey, w/lid 350.00
Straw holder, octagonal, copper lid, 11x4", NM 175.00
Straw holder, Sani-Straw, w/lid & rod 200.00
Straw holder, sq, IL pattern, clear...350.00
Straw holder, sq, IL pattern, gr...500.00
Straw holder, sq, Near Cut 500.00
Thermos, Eskimo Pie, Eskimo figural ft, 9x16", EX 650.00
Tray, Cherry Blossom, narrow rectangle....................................150.00
Tray, Snyder's Ice Cream, mother & child, rnd, M......................400.00
Wafer holder, Reliance...100.00

Soft Paste

Soft paste is a low-fired, granular type of porcelain that must be glazed to retain water.

Bowl, roses, 9¾" 120.00
Creamer, floral band, 3-color stripes, leaf hdl, 3" 105.00
Creamer, gaudy floral in yel+2-tone bl, leaf-end hdl, 3½" 250.00
Creamer, house, 3-color, 3⅜" 125.00
Pitcher, fishermen at river, med bl transfer, 5½" 165.00
Plate, maxim, pk lustre rim, bl transfer, lobed 135.00
Plate, rooster in center in bl-gr & brn, scalloped, 9" 95.00
Shaker, bl feather band, 4½", NM...95.00
Tea bowl & saucer, horses & ruins, bl transfer, EX.......................48.00
Teapot, floral, Gaudy Dutch type w/purple lustre trim, 7", EX ...285.00
Teapot, lt gr bands w/dk brn stripes, 3¾", EX.............................125.00

Southern Folk Pottery

Southern Folk Pottery is vernacular ware produced by a small group of Southern potters, many of whom are descendents of 19th-century potters. Rich alkaline glazes (lustrous greens and browns) are typical, and occasionally shards of glass are applied to the surface of the ware which during firing melts to produce opalescent 'glass runs' over the alkaline. In some locations clay deposits contain elements that result in areas of fluorescent blue or rutile; another varation is swirled or striped ware, reminescent of 18th-century agateware from Staffordshire. The most recognizable form of Southern folk pottery is the face jug. Collector demand for these unique one-of-a-kind jugs is at an all-time high and is still escalating. Choice examples made by Burlon B. Craig and Lanier Meaders often bring over $1,000 on the secondary market. If you're interested in learning more about this type of folk pottery, contact the Southern Folk Pottery Collectors Society; their address is in the Directory under Clubs, Newsletters, and Catalogs. Our advisor for this category is the club's founder, Roy Thompson; he is listed in the Directory under Connecticut.

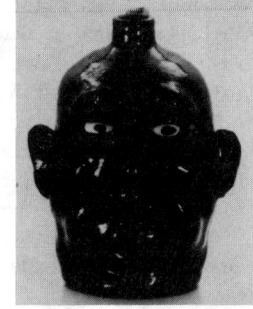

Face jug by Lanier Meaders, dark olive green glaze, 10", $475.00.

John Brock, Virginia

Bank, pig form, alkaline, 6x11" 77.00
Figure, Blk woman, mc glazed earthenware, titled, 9" 275.00
Lady in wide-brim hat figural bank, salt glaze, 9" 137.50

Jerry Brown, Alabama

Face jug, devil, Albany slip, 10" 220.00
Face jug, devil, gray w/bl slip, 10" 132.00

Brown's Pottery, North Carolina

Face jug, cigar in mouth, brn, 8" 176.00
Face jug, cigar in mouth, 9" 220.00
Face jug, devil, brn, 12" 264.00

Burlon Craig, North Carolina

Face jug, alkaline, dbl hdls, stamped BBC, 12" 385.00
Face jug, alkaline, dbl hdls, 10" 247.50
Face jug, alkaline, 8" 148.50
Face jug, 2-color swirl (brn & tan), 8" 137.50
Snake jug, alkaline, 8" 121.00
Snake jug, 2-color swirl, brn & wht dbl hdls, 13" 192.50
Urn, 2-color swirl (lt gray/dk gray), 4-hdl, 17" 192.50
Urn, 3-color swirl (bl/gr/gray), 4-hdl, stamped BBC, 17" 220.00

Chester Hewell, Georgia

Face jug, alkaline, dbl hdls, 14" 110.00
Face jug, alkaline, glass runs, dbl hdls, 16" 165.00
Face jug, salamander atop, alkaline, glass runs, dbl hdls, 14" 148.50
Face wig stand or bust, alkaline, 10" 220.00
Pig bank, alkaline, 7x9" 88.00

Billy Ray Hussey, North Carolina

Face bank, 'Always Keep One Eye on Your Money,' kiln #12, 8"...302.50
Face jug, devil w/snake, dbl hdls, kiln #10, 21" 330.00
Face jug, salt glaze, kiln #13, 10" 270.00
Face jug, salt glaze w/glass runs, kiln #13, 10" 286.00
Face jug, tongue sticking out, Albany slip, 7" 495.00
Figure, lion, standing, salt glaze, kiln #13, 6x6" 286.00
Figure, lion, standing, 8x8" 275.00
Figure, lion standing, 3" 77.00
Figure, Pig Rider, Blk man on pig, mc glaze, 9" 385.00
Figure, Watermelon Eater, mc glaze, 8" 412.50
Snake jug, 2 snakes, 2 hdls, inscr, 22" 330.00

Charles Lisk, North Carolina

Barrel jug, 2-color swirl (brn & wht), 6" 160.00
Face jug, alkaline w/glass runs, dbl hdls, 18" 495.00
Face jug, devil, 2-color (brn & wht), 12" 247.50
Face jug, devil w/fangs, 2-color swirl, inscribed, 12" 275.00
Face jug, 2-color swirl (brn & gr), 2 appl candle arms, 13" 258.50
Face jug, 2-color swirl (brn & wht), dbl hdls, 14" 396.00
Face jug, 2-color swirl (brn & wht), 6 stem holders, 10" 550.00
Face jug, 2-color swirl (gray & wht), 13" 165.00
Face jug, 3-color (bl/wht/brn), dbl hdls, 13" 528.00
Snake jug, 3-color swirl (brn/bl/gr), 13" 247.50

Cleater & Billie Meaders, Georgia

Face buggy jug, alkaline, 7" 385.00

Face chicken waterer, alkaline, 11" 176.00
Face jug, alkaline, dbl hdls, 21" 522.50
Figure, pig, alkaline, 5x6" 132.00
Pitcher, appl grapes, leaves, & snake, alkaline, 12" 247.50
Pitcher, appl grapes & leaves, alkaline, 10" 165.00

Edwin Meaders, Georgia

Figure, rooster w/snake around it, bl, 16" 412.50
Pitcher, appl grapes, leaves & snake, alkaline, 10" 280.50

Lanier Meaders, Georgia

Face jug, alkaline, ca 1988, 9" 330.00
Face jug, melted eyes, alkaline, unknown date, 11" 715.00
Face jug, quartz teeth, alkaline, ca 1975, 10" 880.00
Face jug (dbl face), quartz teeth, alkaline, ca 1970, 11" 3,520.00

Marie Rogers, Georgia

Face buggy jug, 4" 110.00
Face jug, mini, 2" 49.50
Face jug (dbl face), glass runs, 8" 121.00
Figure, dog, brn, mini, 4" L 38.50
Figure, pig, brn, mini, 3" L 38.50
Figure, pig, brn & dk brn, 7" L 121.00
Figure, pig, gray & bl, 7" L 143.00

Spangle Glass

Spangle glass, also known as Vasa Murrhina, is cased art glass characterized by the metallic flakes embedded in its top layer. It was made both abroad and in the United States during the latter years of the 19th century, and it was reproduced in the 1960s by the Fenton Art Glass Company.

Vasa Murrhina was a New England distributor who sold glassware of this type manufactured by a Dr. Flower of Sandwich, Massachusetts. Flower had purchased the defunct Cape Cod Glassworks in 1885 and used the facilities to operate his own company. Since none of the ware was marked, it is very difficult to attribute specific examples to his manufacture. See also Art Glass Baskets; Fenton.

**Vase, cased turquoise with mica, 7",
$150.00.**

Basket, pk & gold w/mica, clear thorn hdl, 6½x6½" 180.00
Bowl, gold w/silver mica, pk int, snail ft, 4⅞x3¾" 235.00
Bowl, gr Dmn Quilt MOP w/mica, melon ribs, 5½x8½x6½" 275.00
Bowl, red w/silver mica, wht int w/mc florals, SP fr, 7x16" 450.00
Finger lamp, mc spatter w/mica, clear reeded hdl, 5½" 195.00
Rose bowl, dk pk w/mica flecks, 3¾x3½" 150.00

Rose bowl, mc spatter w/swirled mica, 8-crimp, 3⅜x3¾" 110.00
Rose bowl, pk shaded w/mica, 8-crimp, 3¾x4⅛" 100.00
Tumbler, Invt T'print, orange & wht spatter w/mica, 3¾" 45.00
Tumbler, mc spatter w/mica, emb swirl, 3¾x2¾" 70.00
Vase, mc spatter w/silver mica, clear ruffle, 9⅛", pr...................135.00
Vase, orange w/mica, clear hdl, ewer form, 8⅜" 125.00
Vase, pk w/mica, clear hdl & rim, ewer form, 9½" 145.00
Vase, yel w/allover silver mica, crystal edge, wht int, 4"................95.00

Spatter Glass

Spatter glass, characterized by its multicolor 'spatters,' has been made from the late 19th century to the present by American glasshouses as well as those abroad. Although it was once thought to have been made entirely by workers at the 'end of the day' from bits and pieces of leftover scrap, it is now known that it was a standard line of production. See also Art Glass Baskets.

Basket, bl/wht/brn, ruffled rim, clear thorn hdl, 7½x4½" 165.00
Basket, yel opaque w/wht, gold trim, clear hdl, 5¼x4½" 55.00
Bottle, rubina & opal, 11" 100.00
Creamer, lg molded droplets, decorative metal spout/hdl 180.00
Cruet, bl/wht, clear hdl, lapidary stopper, Mt WA, 8" 225.00
Pitcher, cranberry/wht frosted, emb swirl, 5½x3½" 145.00
Pitcher, ruby & opal, ribbed, clear hdl, 8½" 200.00
Pitcher, yel opaque w/dk red, yel int, clear hdl, 6½" 225.00
Rolling pin, maroon/cobalt on wht, 15x2" 120.00
Tumbler, maroon/pk/wht/yel/gr swirl, 3¾x2¾" 50.00
Vase, rainbow pastel o/l, clear thorn hdls, 9" 85.00
Vase, yel & wht w/HP florals, 3-petal top, ewer form, 12" 125.00
Vase, yel/pk/wht, flared, 8¾" 85.00

Spatterware

Spatterware is a general term referring to a type of decoration used by English potters beginning in the late 1700s. Using a brush or a stick, brightly-colored paint was dabbed onto the soft-paste earthenware items, achieving a spattered effect which was often used as a border. Because much of this type of ware was made for export to the United States, some of the subjects in the central design — the schoolhouse and the eagle patterns, for instance — reflect American tastes. Yellow, green, and black spatterware is scarce and highly valued by collectors.

In the descriptions that follow, the color listed after the item indicates the color of the spatter. The central design is identified next, and the color description that follows that refers to the design.

Pitcher, yellow spatter with tulip in red with green leaves, 8½", NM, $1,500.00.

Bowl, bl, castle, 4-color, 12-panel, rstr cracks, 14" 225.00
Bowl, bl, thistle, red/gr, 8½", EX 525.00
Bowl, center; bl, rose on 2 sides, red/gr, 11" L 450.00
Bowl, yel, thistle, red/gr, octagonal, 9" L................................. 2,800.00
Coffeepot, bl, ftd, ornate hdl, dome lid, 11" 300.00
Coffeepot, yel, tulip, red w/gr leaves, 8-panel, 8" 2,100.00
Creamer, bl, fort, blk/gr/red, paneled, wear/sm chips, 6" 800.00
Creamer, bl, red dots, 4" 155.00
Creamer, bl, rose & bud, red/bl/gr/blk, 4" 200.00
Creamer, bl, tulip, 4-color, 3½"..285.00
Creamer, red/bl, 4-part flower, red/gr, 4" 250.00
Creamer, red/bl/gr rainbow, 3¾", VG 200.00
Creamer, red/bl/gr t'print, peafowl, 4-color, prof rpr, 4" 150.00
Creamer, red/gr rainbow, leaf emb hdl ends, chips, 3½", EX 325.00
Creamer, red/gr rainbow, leaf emb hdl ends, 3½", VG 215.00
Creamer, yel, tulip, red w/gr leaves, mk J Edwards, 4¾" 900.00
Cup, gr, peafowl, 4-color, & George, prof rpr, 3" 1,025.00
Cup plate, bl, peafowl, 4-color, mk EW & Co, stains, 4" 625.00
Honey pot, bl, pineapple, purple/blk/gr, 5"............................... 5,300.00
Honey pot, bl, schoolhouse, red/yel w/gr tree, cylinder, 6" 6,200.00
Mug, bl, peafowl, 3-color, in gr spatter tree, 5" 600.00
Mug, bl, peafowl, 4-color, hairline/wear, 2½" 425.00
Mug, peafowl, yel/bl/red on gr branch, Present for..., 2½" 925.00
Pitcher, bl, castle, 4-color, 8-panel, str/flaring, 11" 1,700.00
Pitcher, rainbow, 5-color, scalloped rim, faceted, 8" 800.00
Pitcher, rainbow stripes, ornate scroll hdl, 10" 1,900.00
Pitcher, yel, tulip ea side, 1 pk/1 red, rpr spout, 7" 800.00
Plate, bl, acorn & oak leaf, 4-color, stains/wear, 9½" 550.00
Plate, bl, castle, brn/red w/gr trees, paneled, 9⅝"........................800.00
Plate, bl, fort, blk/gr/red, hairline/minor wear, 9¾" 650.00
Plate, bl, peafowl, red/gr/yel ochre, poor rim rpr, 9¾" 225.00
Plate, bl, peafowl, 4-color, 9½" 475.00
Plate, bl, recumbent reindeer on red w/gr trees, 9" 900.00
Plate, bl, schoolhouse, red w/gr tree, 10" 1,700.00
Plate, bl, schoolhouse, red/gr/blk/yel, Pearl, 8", VG 95.00
Plate, bl, 6-point star, red/gr/yel, wear/stains, 9½" 550.00
Plate, bl/gr rainbow, bull's-eye center, pristine, 9½" 600.00
Plate, gr, vine & berry, red/yel, rim hairline, 8" 350.00
Plate, lt bl, peafowl, 4-color, PW&Co Stoneware, 8½", EX.........100.00
Plate, purple, acorn, brn/2 shades gr/blk, 9¾", NM 800.00
Plate, purple, tulip, 4-color, 9½" 450.00
Plate, rainbow, radiating 5-color spikes, 9½" 1,400.00
Plate, red, cowboy & horse, red transfer, 9½", EX 100.00
Plate, red, peafowl, 5-color, 9", NM..450.00
Plate, red, rooster, 4-color, firing flaws/rim rpr, 8" 210.00
Plate, red, schoolhouse, red/brn/gr, rpr chips/stains, 8½" 1,600.00
Plate, red, schoolhouse, red/brn/gr, sm table ring chip, 8½" 1,000.00
Plate, red, tulip, gr/blk/red/bl/yel, 7½" 775.00
Plate, red/bl festoon, floral sprig, red/gr/blk, 8¾", EX 975.00
Plate, red/bl/gr rainbow, rose, red/gr, sm rim rpr, 8" 425.00
Plate, red/gr rainbow, bull's-eye center, wear/stains, 9½" 270.00
Plate, red/gr rainbow, bull's-eye center, 9¾" 550.00
Plate, yel, morning-glory, bl/blk w/gr leaves, 9" 1,100.00
Plate, yel, peafowl, 3-color, 9½" 3,500.00
Plate, yel, tulip, red/gr, paneled rim, 8¾" 1,500.00
Platter, purple, eagle/shield, bl transfer, wear/stain, 16" 250.00
Platter, red/gr stripe, tulip, 3-color, anchor mk, 18"................. 4,400.00
Platter, yel, thistle, red/gr, octagonal, 14½" L 7,600.00
Soup plate, bl/red/gr rainbow, mk Adams, 10¾" 675.00
Sugar bowl, bl, fort, blk/gr/red, paneled, rpr, 9½", VG 275.00
Sugar bowl, bl, parrot, red/gr, rnd w/shallow lid, 7" 900.00
Sugar bowl, bl, windmill, red/blk/gr, tree on bk, 4" 600.00
Sugar bowl, red, rose, red/gr/blk, rim rpr/damage, 4¾" 150.00
Sugar bowl, red, 4-part flower, red/gr, 4", EX................................200.00

Sugar bowl, red/bl/gr rainbow, bulbous, 5", VG............................400.00
Sugar bowl, yel, peafowl, 4-color, rim hairline, 4½"....................750.00
Sugar bowl, yel, thistle, red w/gr leaves, dome lid, 8".............. 3,300.00
Tea bowl, gr, deer in blk on saucer, stapled rpr/damage 275.00
Tea bowl & saucer, bl, fort, 3-color, mismatch, EX.......................175.00
Tea bowl & saucer, bl, fort, 3-color, stains/hairline, mini.............150.00
Tea bowl & saucer, bl, peafowl, gr/yel/red/blk, hairline 195.00
Tea bowl & saucer, bl, schoolhouse, 4-color, NM.........................625.00
Tea bowl & saucer, bl, tulip, red/gr/blk, mini, EX 175.00
Tea bowl & saucer, red, peafowl, bl/yel/gr/blk, EX 235.00
Tea bowl & saucer, red, peafowl, 5-color, lt wear 225.00
Tea bowl & saucer, red, shield w/stars in bl, 6" saucer............. 1,000.00
Tea bowl & saucer, red, thistle, 3-color 75.00
Tea bowl & saucer, red/bl rainbow, sm chips/hairline, mini 200.00
Tea bowl & saucer, red/bl stripes, 3-color star on saucer 375.00
Tea bowl & saucer, red/gr rainbow, tulip, red/bl/gr/blk, NM........750.00
Tea bowl & saucer, red/gr rainbow w/peafowl, mini, NM 275.00
Tea bowl & saucer, yel, eagle in flight in brn 700.00
Tea bowl & saucer, yel, thistle, red/gr, sm flakes 250.00
Teapot, bl, schoolhouse, red w/gr tree, paneled, rpr, 9" 3,100.00
Teapot, gr, tulip, red/bl/blk, paneled, wear/rpr, 7½"....................950.00
Teapot, red/bl/gr rainbow, str flaring sides, 6¾", VG...................500.00
Waste bowl, blk/purple rainbow, tulip, 4-color, 3x6", EX 625.00

Spode-Copeland

The Spode Works was established in 1770 and continued to operate under that title until 1843. Their earliest products were typical
underglaze blue-printed patterns, though basalt was also made. After
1790 a translucent porcelain body was the basis for a line of fine
enamel-decorated dinnerware. Stone china was introduced in 1805,
often in patterns reflecting an Oriental influence. In 1833 Wm Taylor
Copeland purchased the company, continuing business in much the
same tradition. During the last half of the 19th century, Copeland produced excellent parian figures and groups with such success that many
other companies attempted to reproduce his work. He employed famous
painters to decorate plaques, vases, and tablewares, many examples of
which were signed by the artist. Most of the Copeland wares are
marked with one of several variations that incorporate the firm name.
Today the company is owned by Royal Worcester, Ltd., and operates
under the name of Royal Worcester Spode, Ltd. Our advisor for this
category is Don Haase; he is listed in the Directory under Washington.

Bowl, Christmas Tree, gr trim, scalloped, 9" 32.00
Bowl, vegetable; Camellia, oval 45.00
Bowl, vegetable; Florence, oval..45.00
Charger, Gainsborough, 15" dia 65.00
Creamer, Fitzhugh, gr & wht...36.00
Creamer & sugar bowl, Florence, w/lid 85.00
Cruet, Tower, Spode, mini 52.00
Cup & saucer, Chelsea Wicker 29.00
Cup & saucer, Christmas Tree, gr trim 29.00
Cup & saucer, demitasse; Florence 35.00
Cup & saucer, demitasse; Greek, bl...17.00
Cup & saucer, Newburyport 55.00
Cup & saucer, Tower, bl, Spode 35.00
Gravy boat, Gainsborough...45.00
Jug, milk; Tower, pk, Spode...90.00
Mug, Imari floral on ironstone, 1820, Spode, 4½"........................375.00
Pitcher, Chicago..., bl/wht, designed by Burley, Spode, 8½"........300.00
Pitcher, Churchill toby, mc, mk Copeland Spode England, 8½" ...55.00
Plate, dinner; Camellia, bl/pk/gr, 10½" 29.00
Plate, dinner; Chelsea Wicker 29.00

Plate, dinner; Tower, bl w/o wht rim, Spode, 10" 55.00
Plate, pearlware, gaudy 4-color floral, mk Spode, 9", pr 140.00
Platter, Camellia, 12¾" 50.00
Platter, Christmas Tree, gr trim, 14" 60.00
Platter, Florence, 13" 75.00
Platter, Gainsborough, 16½" 135.00
Platter, Tower, pk, Spode, 12" dia 95.00
Punch bowl, Tower, pk, Spode...300.00
Sugar bowl, Christmas Tree, gr trim, w/lid.....................................35.00
Teakettle, Tower, pk, Spode 290.00
Toothpick holder, Royal Jason 20.00
Tray, Florence, hdls, 10x10"..65.00
Vase, gr w/bird reserves, emb shell/scroll ft, Copeland, 7"...........260.00

Spongeware

Spongeware is a type of factory-made earthenware that was popular during the last quarter of the 19th century. It was decorated by dab-
bing color onto the drying ware with a sponge, leaving a splotched
design at random or in simple patterns. Sometimes a solid band of color
was added. The vessel was then covered with a clear glaze and fired at a
high temperature. Blue on white is the most preferred combination, but
green on ivory, orange on white, or those colors in combination may
also occasionally be found.

Bowl, batter; bl on yellowware, bail hdl, 7½" 135.00
Bowl, bl on yellowware, dome lid, bail hdl, glazed int, 13" 150.00
Bowl, bl on yellowware, rim spout, bail hdl, 3½x5½" 85.00
Bowl, bl/wht, 3½x7½" 105.00
Bowl, fruit; bl/wht, pewter-trim ft, ca 1800, 7x11" 175.00
Bowl, mixing; bl/wht, emb exterior, 6¼x13" 175.00
Jar, bl/wht, bail hdl, w/lid, 6"..250.00
Pitcher, bl/brn/wht, cylindrical, crazed/hairline, 11" 55.00
Pitcher, bl/wht, pattern sponging, bbl form, 8"..............................325.00
Pitcher, bl/wht, short can neck, bulbous body, 9", EX 175.00
Pitcher, brn/gr on yel, 4½"..65.00
Plate, bl/wht, gold rim, 8½" 135.00
Plate, bl/wht, 9⅜" 150.00

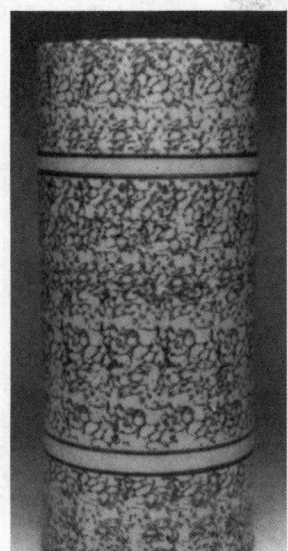

Umbrella stand, two white bands, 21", $500.00.

Wash bowl & pitcher, dk bl/wht, bands at middle of ea pc..........400.00
Waste bowl, bl/wht, 5" dia 100.00

Water cooler, bl/wht, 2-pc, str top/ovoid base, 4-gal, EX **1,025.00**

Spoons

Souvenir spoons have been popular remembrances since the 1890s. The early hand-wrought examples of the silversmith's art are especially sought and appreciated for their fine craftsmanship. Commemorative, personality-related, advertising, and those with Indian busts or floral designs are only a few of the many types of collectible spoons. In the following listings, spoons are entered by city, character, or occasion.

Key:
B — bowl   FF — full figure
BR — bowl reverse   GW — gold wash
emb — embossed   H — handle
eng — engraved   HR — handle reverse

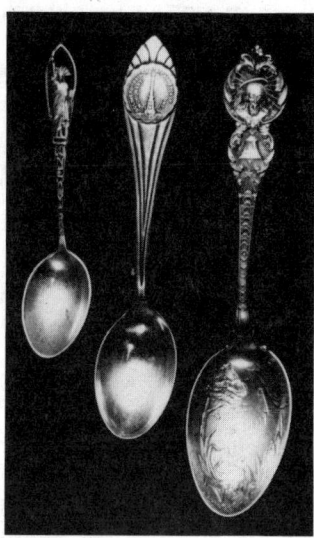

Left to Right: Statue of Liberty, NY, $25.00; Indianapolis, Soldiers' and Sailors' Monument, $25.00; Christmas scene in bowl, saint and bell on handle, $25.00.

Adirondack, elk & Xd rifles emb on H; scalloped B; fruit **60.00**
Alaska scenes on H & HR; plain B **20.00**
Alvarado on H shaft; Church of San Felipe on HR; view in B **40.00**
Annie Russell H; finial plain B; Gorham **135.00**
Asbury Park NJ in B; scenes emb on H & HR **50.00**
Atlanta GA eng in B; ear of corn FF H; teaspoon, EX **17.50**
Belmar emb in B; floral finial H **15.00**
Bermuda on HR; emb onion in B; Shiebler **32.00**
Birmingham Pig Iron eng in B; pig enameled on H **42.50**
Boston & hub on H; Old South Church emb in B **20.00**
Brooklyn Bridge view eng in GW bowl; twist H; Whiting **22.50**
Brooklyn emb on H; City of Churches eng in B; Gorham **70.00**
Buffalo NY eng in B; chameleon FF H **30.00**
Calgary Alberta eng in B; Indian in canoe w/paddle FF H **55.00**
Capitol Building emb in B; Grover Cleveland FF H **20.00**
Capitol Building/statue emb in B; cannon FF H **40.00**
Carlsbad Caverns, totem pole H **28.50**
Carmel Mission emb in B; Junipero Serro on H; Watson **22.50**
Catalina eng in B; Indian head FF H **28.00**
Charleston WV on H; plain B; Dominick & Haff **40.00**
Chicago in gold & silver in B; floral H: Reed & Barton **35.00**
Chicago-Masonic (7 scenes), 6 Masonic symbols **55.00**
Clock w/bl & wht enameling on H; plain B; Watson **48.00**
Colorado on H; cowboy scene on HR; Garden of Gods emb in B.. **60.00**
Columbian Expo symbols on H; ship emb in B; Reed & Barton . **145.00**
Confederate Monument Alexandria LA in B; Louisiana on H.... **120.00**

Denver CO emb in B; Rainbow Falls/waterfall emb on H **48.00**
Denver 1892 emb in B; knight emb on H; Durgin **30.00**
DePauw in B; girl graduate FF H; Watson **40.00**
DeSoto Hotel Savannah GA in B; teepee/canoe on H; Watson.... **30.00**
Detroit skyline FF H; Belle Isle view emb in B **40.00**
Eagle on cactus w/snake in mouth on twisted H; plain B **25.00**
Easter egg on H finial; Easter emb in B **25.00**
Easter eng in B; MOP chick emerging from egg at H finial **37.50**
Ft Pierre SD etched in GW B; miner w/tools emb on H **88.00**
Ft Sumter emb in B; Jasper emb on H **40.00**
General Putnam at H finial; plain B; Gorham, demi **20.00**
Government House Trinidad in B; alligator FF H **42.00**
Hampton VA eng in B; appl crab on H **20.00**
Hannibal Hamlin at H finial; tree & plow emb in B **40.00**
Honolulu in B; pineapple w/cut-out H.. **30.00**
Hope & anchor in finial of twist H: shell forms B; mk **30.00**
Horse head finial twist H; Old KY Home emb in B **42.50**
Hotel Alvarado, Albuquerque NM in B; floral H **12.50**
Independence Hall & Liberty Bell on H; plain B **22.50**
Independence Hall emb in B; Wm Penn FF H **47.50**
Indian head finial w/corn down H; girl w/tray emb in B............. **20.00**
Jacksonville & flag in B; boy in tree FF H; teaspoon **70.00**
Jacksonville FL emb in B; Andrew Jackson H finial; Gorham **60.00**
Knight of Columbus, enameled cross on H; plain B; Watson........ **32.00**
Knights Templar on H; Silver Tricentennial Conclave in B **60.00**
Lake Placid eng in heart-shaped B; cherub FF H; Watson **32.00**
Lakewood emb in B; pine cones & branches emb on H **14.00**
Lenape-Penn Treaty on H; Indian scene emb in B; Simons........... **40.00**
Lewis & Clark Expo Foreign Bldg in B; skyline/salmon FF H **60.00**
Liberty NY, Hotel Wawonda etched in B; scrolled H; mk **30.00**
Los Angeles in GW B; California/florals emb on H; Gorham........ **32.00**
Louisiana, pelican/bales/cane on wavy H; view in B; Shepard **30.00**
Louisiana Purchase Expo on H; Festival Hall & gardens in B........ **45.00**
Luna Park emb in B; floral H.. **22.50**
Madeira eng on H: emb church view in B.................................... **27.50**
Mexican flag enameled in B; scroll H; Wendell **98.00**
Moat Fortress Monroe emb in B; Durgin **25.00**
Mt Hood view eng in B; Columbia River salmon FF H **32.00**
Mt Ranier eng in B; chinook salmon FF H **25.00**
N Point Monument emb in GW B; floral H; Dominick & Haff **25.00**
New Orleans & cotton bale H finial; plain B; Gorham................. **50.00**
New Orleans on H; Cathedral/City Hall on HR; Watson **32.00**
Niagara Falls emb in B; Chief's head H finial; demi **18.00**
Niagara Falls view emb in B; scrolls on H **17.50**
NY skyline FF H; Flat Iron Building emb in B; Watson **70.00**
Obelisk w/hieroglyphics H; rnd GW B.. **38.00**
Our Nat'l Floral Emblem emb in B; goldenrod & flag on H.......... **25.00**
Peoria emb in B; IL state seal/corn/fruit on H; Watson **50.00**
Pharaoh's head at enameled H finial; pyramids in GW B **35.00**
Philadelphia/bell on H; Independence Hall emb in B; Alvin **30.00**
Plattsburgh NY emb in B; Indian FF H; Shepard **40.00**
Pleasant View emb in B; Mary Baker Eddy on H; Durgin **170.00**
Portland in lg emb letters on H; plain B **35.00**
Prospector w/pick FF H; plain B.. **80.00**
Roses cutout on H; plain B; 5¼" **18.00**
Round Oak, World's Fair 1893 in B; shovel shape........................ **70.00**
Santa in chimney H finial; fireplace & stockings in B; Gorham ... **32.00**
Saratoga in B; arrow shaft & Indian H finial; Gorham................. **98.00**
Shamrocks/harp/thistle on H; Liberty & Law emb in B **47.00**
Skagway AK emb in B; totem pole FF H....................................... **28.00**
Soldier H finial; plain B; Howard (old mk), demi........................ **50.00**
St Louis & Indian head emb on H; plain B; Watson, EX **22.50**
Stanley Park, Vancouver BC emb in B; toboggan/leaf/beaver H.... **32.00**
Steamer Robert Fulton emb in B; salmon on H **32.00**

Stevens House, Lake Placid NY in GW B; GW scroll H; demi......**12.50**
Summit Pikes Peak eng in GW B; patterned H **17.50**
Thousand Islands etched in B; fish emb on H; Paye & Baker **20.00**
Trenton NJ emb in B; leaves emb on H **17.00**
University of MO crest held by woman FF H; plain B; Watson **40.00**
US Sub Treasury NY City emb in B; Washington H finial **55.00**
Utah emb on H; Mormon Temple eng in B; mk **25.00**
Vatican emb view in B; Pope Leo portrait on H **22.50**
Washington Monument FF H; Capitol Building emb in B......**45.00**
Washington Monument w/enameling on H; plain B; Watson **47.50**
Washington's cemetery emb in B; Mt Vernon on H; Wallace.......**35.00**
William Penn FF H; Independence Hall emb in B; Shiebler **48.00**
Yellowstone, bear emb on H; plain B; Watson **27.50**
Zanesville eng in B; floral H; Simpson-Hall-Miller......**35.00**
Zodiac September symbols on H; plain B; Gorham......**37.50**

Sporting Goods

Our advisor for this category is Paul Longo; he is listed in the Directory under Massachusetts. See also Target Balls.

Photo folder, Joe DiMaggio's Yacht Club, ca 1940s, $100.00.

Baseball, autographed by Joe DiMaggio **150.00**
Baseball, signed & inscribed by Babe Ruth, dtd 1948......**1,500.00**
Baseball, 1986 World Series, sgn Gooden & Strawberry......**100.00**
Baseball card, Wayne Gretzky Rookie, EX **200.00**
Bat, autographed by Ken Griffey Jr, EX......**75.00**
Bat, autographed by Ken Williams, Spalding, M **25.00**
Bat, autographed by Mickey Mantle, scarce **750.00**
Bicycle, high-wheel, pnt steel, rubber tires, 58", G......**1,300.00**
Bicycle, Keeting Wheel Co, 1920s, orig brn pnt, VG **400.00**
Bicycle, Victoria #30, pnt steel, wood rims/fender, 38", G......**155.00**
Bicycle, Ward Hawthorne, lady's, 1950s, VG......**750.00**
Book, Babe & I, Mrs Babe Ruth, 1959......**30.00**
Button, Babe Ruth Official Baseball Club, EX......**50.00**
Glove, baseball; sgn Willie Stargell......**50.00**
Glove, fielder's; Joe Gordon, Ward's, 1939, MIB......**30.00**
Ice skates, wrought iron, ram's horn curl, gold pnt, 13" **300.00**
License, fishing & hunting; Wht Pine County, Nevada, 1917 ...**100.00**
Loving cup, sterling, OH Golf Championship/1920, 9½" **100.00**
Mask, catcher's; iron, leather & cloth, ca 1920s, 9x8x4", EX......**60.00**
Nodder, NY Yankees, compo, 1960s, M......**75.00**
Photograph, NY Giants baseball team, 1951, EX **45.00**

Program, 1929 Baseball World Series, Cubs vs Athletics......**400.00**
Record book, baseball, Rawlings, 1940 ......**15.00**
Scrapbook, Big Ten Football, 1927, EX **50.00**
Softball, Belknap, 1940s, MIB **12.50**
Yearbook, 1958 Yankees, w/1958 series program, EX **85.00**

St. Clair

The St. Clair Glass Company began as a small family-oriented operation in Elwood, Indiana, in 1941. Most famous for their lamps, the family made numerous small items of carnival, pink and caramel slag, and custard glass as well. Later, paperweights became popular production pieces; many command considerably high prices on today's market. Weights are stamped and usually dated, while small production pieces are often unmarked.

Bell, Liberty; bl carnival, dtd 1776-1976 ......**12.00**
Salt cellar, swan form, bl carnival, unmk **15.00**
Salt cellar, wheelbarrow form, caramel slag **18.00**
Toothpick holder, hobstars, bl......**12.50**
Toothpick holder, Holly Band, caramel slag......**30.00**
Toothpick holder, Indian head, bl carnival **25.00**
Toothpick holder, Indian/Washington/Nixon reliefs, 1976 ......**55.00**
Toothpick holder, Invt Fan & Feather, pk slag, unmk **35.00**
Toothpick holder, President Johnson bust, bl carnival **24.00**
Toothpick holder, ribbed swirl, bl carnival, Bob St Clair **24.00**
Vase, paperweight; 5 flowers, ea different color, label, 7¼"......**35.00**
Vase, pk encased florals & bubbles on gr, early, unmk, 8" **38.00**

Staffordshire

Scores of potteries sprang up in England's Staffordshire district in the early 18th century; several remain to the present time. (See also specific companies.) Figurines and groups were made in great numbers; dogs were favorite subjects. Often they were made in pairs, each a mirror image of the other. They varied in heights from 3" or 4" to the largest, measuring 16" to 18". From 1840 until about 1900, portrait figures were produced to represent specific characters, both real and fictional. As a rule these were never marked.

The Historical Ware listed here was made throughout the district; some collectors refer to it as Staffordshire Blue Ware. It was produced as early as 1820; and, because much was exported to America, it was very often decorated with transfers depicting scenic views of well-known American landmarks. Early examples were printed in a deep cobalt. By 1830 a softer blue was favored, and within the next decade black, pink, red, and green prints were used. Although sometimes careless about adding their trademark, many companies used their own border designs that were as individual as their names.

This ware should not be confused with the vast amounts of modern china (mostly plates) made from early in the century to the present. These souvenir or commemorative items are usually marketed through gift stores and the like. (See Rowland and Marcellus.) Our advisor for Historical Blue Ware is Richard Marden; he is listed in the Directory under New Hampshire. See also specific manufacturers.

Key:
blk — black   l/b — light blue
gr — green   m/b — medium blue
d/b — dark blue   m-d/b — medium dark blue

Historical

Bowl, fisherman & family, d/b, rtcl, +prof rpr 13" tray......**550.00**

Bowl, fruit; West Point Military Academy, d/b, Wood............ **3,450.00**
Bowl, vegetable; Bedford Essex, m/b, Wood, w/lid, EX **365.00**
Bowl, vegetable; East Cowes Isle of Wight, d/b, Wood, 9⅝".......**565.00**
Bowl, vegetable; Hanover Terrace Regents Park, d/b, Adams, 8" .**225.00**
Bowl, vegetable; Quebec, d/b, Wood, sq, w/lid, 9½" **1,600.00**
Bowl, vegetable; Wilkesbarre Vale of WY, l/b, Ridgway, 11".......**165.00**
Coffeepot, Lafayette at Franklin's Tomb, d/b, Wood, rpr, 11". **1,200.00**
Coffeepot, Lafayette at Franklin's Tomb, d/b, Wood, 11" **1,750.00**
Coffeepot, Wadsworth Tower, d/b, Wood, prof rpr, 11" **1,750.00**
Compote, Windsor Castle, d/b, Clews, lg **625.00**
Creamer, American Eagle on Urn, d/b, Clews................................**825.00**
Creamer, Boston Harbor, eagles on sides, d/b, Rogers, rare **1,250.00**
Creamer, English scene of boy fishing, d/b, lt wear, 6" **200.00**
Creamer, Lafayette at Franklin's Tomb, d/b, Stevenson **465.00**
Creamer, Washington...w/Scroll in Hand, d/b, Wood **1,100.00**
Cup, custard; Boston State House, d/b, hdl, Ridgway...................**365.00**
Cup, Franklin's Tomb, d/b, Phillips **200.00**
Cup & saucer, American Eagle on Urn, d/b, Clews **450.00**
Cup & saucer, Lafayette at Franklin's Tomb, d/b, Wood **350.00**
Cup & saucer, Log Cabin, pk, Adams...**485.00**
Cup & saucer, NY from Weehawk, carmine, Adams **225.00**
Cup plate, Andrew Jackson, brick red, Wood **1,350.00**
Cup plate, Arched Stone Bridge, d/b, Wood **220.00**
Cup plate, Battery NY, d/b, no mk, short hairline, 3¾" **250.00**
Cup plate, Cadmus, d/b, Wood, trefoil border **325.00**
Cup plate, Columbus, brn, Adams, 4" **60.00**
Cup plate, Estate View, m/b, stains, 4⅝".......................................**80.00**
Cup plate, Holiday St Theatre Baltimore, d/b, 3½", EX.............**225.00**
Cup plate, Indian Chiefs, brn, emb rim, 3" **125.00**
Cup plate, Lafayette & WA, blk, blk border, Wood, 3¾" **600.00**
Cup plate, NY Battery, d/b, trefoil border....................................**325.00**
Cup plate, River & Castle, d/b, Clews Windsor Castle series **165.00**
Cup plate, Ruggles House, d/b, Wood, trefoil border **225.00**
Cup plate, seashells, d/b, Stubbs, 4" **185.00**
Cup plate, View of Newburgh, purple, Jackson **165.00**
Dish, leaf shape w/emb veins, St Paul's Chapel, d/b, 5", EX **3,500.00**
Gravy ladle, Harvard Hall, blk, rpr **235.00**

Gravy tureen, Chiswick on the Thames, with lid, undertray and ladle, Enoch Wood & Sons, M, $2,000.00.

Pitcher, Lafayette at Franklin's Tomb, d/b, 4¼" **850.00**
Pitcher, Landing of Lafayette, d/b, 5" **2,000.00**
Pitcher, portraits: Lafayette/WA, verse/eagle, 7", EX **1,200.00**
Pitcher, Troy from Mt Ida, blk, Clews, sm rpr **350.00**
Plate, Albany, m-d/b, Clews Cities series, 10" **350.00**
Plate, Arms of S Carolina, d/b, Mayer, 7½" **735.00**
Plate, B&O RR (incline), d/b, Wood, 9¼", NM............................**700.00**
Plate, B&O RR (level), d/b, Wood, 10" **750.00**
Plate, Bakers Falls, brn, Clews, 9" **90.00**
Plate, Battery & C, l/b, Jackson, 7¾" **95.00**

Plates: Baltimore & Ohio (level), Wood & Sons, 10", $750.00; Union Line, Wood, 10", $400.00; Landing of Gen. Lafayette at Castle Garden, Clews, 10", $300.00.

Plate, Blenheim Oxfordshire, d/b, Adams, 10" **145.00**
Plate, Boston Athenaeum, d/b, Ridgway, scarce, 6¼" **400.00**
Plate, Boston State House, brn, Jackson, 10½"...............................**95.00**
Plate, Boston State House, m/b, Wood, 10" **165.00**
Plate, Bunker Hill Monument, mulberry, Jackson, 6⅛" **145.00**
Plate, Caldwell Lake George, blk, Ridgway, 7¾"............................**75.00**
Plate, Capital Washington DC, d/b, Stevenson, 10", EX **305.00**
Plate, Capitol Washington DC, d/b, Stevenson, 10" **475.00**
Plate, Capitol Washington DC, d/b, Wood, 7¾", NM..................**365.00**
Plate, Cathedral & River View, d/b, Stevenson, 10" **145.00**
Plate, Christ Church Oxford, d/b, Ridgway, 10" **120.00**
Plate, City Hall NY, m/b, Ridgway, 10"...**225.00**
Plate, City Hall NY, pk, Stevenson, 10½"......................................**335.00**
Plate, City of Albany State of NY, d/b, Wood, 10" **450.00**
Plate, Columbian Star, brn, Ridgway, 7½" **125.00**
Plate, Columbian Star, brn, Ridgway, 8¾" **135.00**
Plate, Columbian Star, gray, Ridgway, 10⅛" **155.00**
Plate, Columbus, blk, Adams, 10½"..**70.00**
Plate, Columbus, gr, Adams, 10½"...**90.00**
Plate, Constitution & Guerriere, d/b, Wood, 10"..........................**965.00**
Plate, Court House Baltimore, d/b, 8⅝" **425.00**
Plate, Culzean Castle Ayrshire, m/b, Wood, 8½" **100.00**
Plate, Dartmouth, d/b, Wood, 9" **325.00**
Plate, Deer, d/b, Wood's Zoological series, 10" **185.00**
Plate, Erie Canal Inscription, d/b, 6½" **600.00**
Plate, Exchange Baltimore, d/b, Henshall, 10" **500.00**
Plate, Fairmount near Philadelphia, d/b, Stubbs, 10" **325.00**
Plate, Falls of Montmorenci near Quebec, d/b, Wood, 9" **325.00**
Plate, Fort Gansvoort NY, d/b, Stevenson, 6¾" **825.00**
Plate, General Jackson Hero..., blk, pk lustre border, 6½" **185.00**
Plate, Guys Cliff Warwickshire, m/b, Wood, 10" **120.00**
Plate, Hagley Worcestershire, m/b, Wood, 6½" **70.00**
Plate, Harvard College (4 buildings), d/b, RS&W, 10"..............**400.00**
Plate, Insane Hospital Boston, d/b, Ridgway, 7¼", EX **275.00**
Plate, Kent East Indiaman, d/b, Wood, 9¼" **295.00**
Plate, Lafayette & WA w/eagle, red, emb bl edge, 10", NM **700.00**
Plate, Lafayette at Washington's Tomb, d/b, Wood, 8½" **650.00**
Plate, LaGrange Residence of Lafayette, d/b, lt wear, 10" **220.00**
Plate, Landing of Lafayette, d/b, Clews, 10" **300.00**
Plate, Landing of Lafayette, d/b, Clews, 6½" **250.00**
Plate, Landing of Lafayette, d/b, Clews, 7¾" **275.00**
Plate, Landing of Lafayette, d/b, Clews, 8½" **325.00**
Plate, Landing of Lafayette, d/b, Clews, 9" **275.00**
Plate, Landing of Pilgrims, m/b, Wood, 5⅝" **165.00**
Plate, LaPort Romaine a Andernach, d/b, Wood, 6½" **95.00**

Plate, Library Philadelphia, d/b, Ridgway, 8¼" 225.00
Plate, Library Philadelphia, m/b, Ridgway, 8" 225.00
Plate, MacDonnough's Victory, d/b, Wood, 10" 435.00
Plate, Marine Hospital Louisville KY, d/b, Wood, 9¼" 365.00
Plate, Meredith, l/b, Ridgway Catskill Moss series, 9½" 115.00
Plate, Moulin Sur LaMarne a Charenton, d/b, Wood, 9¼" 135.00
Plate, Near Fishkill, d/b, Clews Cities series, 7¾" 325.00
Plate, Near Hudson, Hudson River; brn, Clews, 5¾" 60.00
Plate, New Orleans, pk, Stevenson, 8¼" 165.00
Plate, NY Battery, d/b, Stevenson, 6⅞" 475.00
Plate, NY Battery, d/b, Stevenson, 8", EX 475.00
Plate, NY City Hall, d/b, Ridgway, 10" 220.00
Plate, Oriental Views, d/b, Clews, 10¼" 70.00
Plate, Pains Hill Surrey, d/b, Hall, 10" 165.00
Plate, Peace & Plenty, d/b, Clews, 10" 350.00
Plate, Peace on Earth (Millenium), gr, 10½" 30.00
Plate, Peace on Earth (Millenium), red, 6¾" 85.00
Plate, Penn's Treaty, brn, 7½" 60.00
Plate, Pittsfield Elm, d/b, Clews, 10½" 400.00
Plate, Pittsfield Elm, d/b, Clews, 7½" 300.00
Plate, Pittsfield Elm, d/b, Clews, 8½" 300.00
Plate, Quebec, d/b, retailer's label, scratched, 9" 275.00
Plate, Residence of S Russel, m/b, Wood, 6¾" 185.00
Plate, Residence of...Richard Jordan, mulberry, JH&Co, 8¾" 165.00
Plate, Ruggles House Newburgh Hudson River, blk, 10¼" 90.00
Plate, Shannondale Springs VA, pk, Adams US Views, 8" 88.00
Plate, Sheltered Pheasants, Hall, d/b, 8" 95.00
Plate, Southampton Hampshire, Wood, irreg shell border, 7½" ..300.00
Plate, States, d/b, Clews, 10½" 375.00
Plate, States, d/b, Clews, 6¾" 250.00
Plate, States (curved drive), d/b, sm rpr, 8" 165.00
Plate, States (sheep on lawn), d/b, Clews, 8½" 275.00
Plate, Table Rock Niagara, d/b, Wood, shell border, 10" 500.00
Plate, Taymouth Castle Perthshire, m/b, Wood, 10" 150.00
Plate, Texian Campaign, brn, Shaw, 8" 200.00
Plate, toddy; Am & Independence, d/b, Clews, 4¾" 435.00
Plate, toddy; Am Museum, d/b, Stevenson, 5", NM....................900.00
Plate, toddy; Cadmus, d/b, Wood & Son, hairline, 4½" 150.00
Plate, toddy; Hindu Pagoda, d/b, Rogers, 5" 80.00
Plate, toddy; landscape w/fishermen, d/b, Clews, 4½", NM 125.00
Plate, toddy; winter, Pittsfield MA, d/b, no figures, 4 ½..............500.00
Plate, Transylvania University Lexington KY, d/b, Wood, 9¼" ..400.00
Plate, Trenton Falls, d/b, Wood, 7⅝" 325.00
Plate, Upper Ferry Bridge, d/b, Stubbs, 8¾" 300.00
Plate, Utica Inscription, d/b, 7⅝", EX 435.00
Plate, View near Conway New Hampshire, pk, Adams, 9" 90.00
Plate, View near Liverpool, d/b, Wood, 10" 425.00
Plate, Virginia, brn, Clews, 10½" 100.00
Plate, Virginia, brn, Clews, 9" 80.00
Plate, Washington, d/b, Clews Cities series, 7¾" 375.00
Plate, Waterworks Phila, brn, Jackson, 9" 145.00
Plate, Wellcombe Warwickshire, m/b, Wood, 10" 125.00
Plate, West Point Hudson River, blk, Clews, 7¾" 85.00
Plate, Wistow Hall Leicestershire, d/b, Hall, 8½" 150.00
Plate, Wright's Ferry on Susquehanna, m-d/b, Clews, 9" 485.00
Plate, Young Philosopher, d/b, Wood, 10" 245.00
Plate, Zebra, m/b, Rogers, 8½" 70.00
Platter, American Villa, d/b, BB&B, 14" 485.00
Platter, Arms of N Carolina, d/b, Mayer, prof rpr, 14¾" 2,750.00
Platter, Boston State House, d/b, Stubbs, 14½" 1,000.00
Platter, Boston State House, m/b, Rogers, 12¾" 850.00
Platter, Cape Coast Castle...Africa, d/b, Wood, 16¼" 1,750.00
Platter, Cumberland Terrace Regents Park, d/b, Wood, 18¾" 875.00
Platter, Denton Park Yorkshire, d/b, Adams, 15½" 450.00

Platter, Fort Putnam, l/b, Ridgway, 15½" 235.00
Platter, Hudson River, brn, Clews, 12¼", EX 325.00
Platter, Italian Scenery, Turin; d/b, Wood, 21" 700.00
Platter, Lake George State of NY, d/b, Wood, 16½" 1,200.00
Platter, Landing of Lafayette, d/b, Clews, 9¾" 1,000.00
Platter, Little Falls NY, l/b, Ridgway, 10¾" 365.00
Platter, Mendenhall Ferry, d/b, Stubbs, 16¾" 1,200.00
Platter, Narrows from Fort Hamilton, purple, Ridgway, 17½" 335.00
Platter, Newburgh Hudson River, blk, Clews, 15½" 475.00
Platter, Newburgh Hudson River, brn, Clews, 9½" 500.00
Platter, Niagara Falls from American Side, d/b, Wood, 15" ... 1,950.00
Platter, Oriental Views, d/b, Clews, 14½" 345.00
Platter, Peace & Plenty, d/b, Clews, 15" 825.00
Platter, Ponte de Palazo, d/b, Wood, 16½" 625.00
Platter, Spode Bridge, m/b, well & tree, 20½" 625.00
Platter, States, d/b, Clews, 14½" 1,250.00
Platter, Windsor Castle, l/b, Clews, 19½" 265.00
Sauce boat, Fort Ticonderoga, l/b, Jackson 265.00
Sauce dish, landscape, d/b, Wood & Sons, stains, 4¼" 175.00
Saucer, Eagle on Rock, pk, Wood 110.00
Saucer, Wadsworth Tower, d/b 135.00
Soup, ...Aqueduct Bridge at Little Falls, d/b, Wood, 10" 1,000.00
Soup, Beach at Brighton, d/b, Wood, 10" 525.00
Soup, Boston State House, d/b, Rogers, 9⅞" 175.00
Soup, Bridge of Lucano, d/b, Wood, 10" 145.00
Soup, British Views, d/b, Henshall, 8" 135.00
Soup, Columbian Star, brn, Ridgway, 10¼" 160.00
Soup, Headwaters of Juniata, pk, Adams, 10¼" 100.00
Soup, Octagon Church Boston, d/b, Ridgway, 9¾" 335.00
Soup, States (sheep on lawn), d/b, Clews, 8½" 275.00
Soup, Staughton's Church, d/b, Ridgway, scarce, 8¼" 325.00
Soup, Vue du Chateau de Coucy, d/b, Wood, 10" 175.00
Sugar bowl, American Eagle on Urn, d/b, Clews 725.00
Sugar bowl, Landing of Lafayette, d/b, Clews, EX 825.00
Sugar bowl, MacDonnough's Victory, d/b, Wood, EX....................800.00
Sugar bowl, Wadsworth Tower, d/b, Wood, EX 475.00
Sugar bowl, Washington w/Scroll in Hand, d/b, Wood, EX.........650.00
Teapot, Lafayette at Franklin's Tomb, d/b, Wood, rpr 365.00
Teapot, Landing of Lafayette, d/b, Clews, EX 1,400.00
Tray, Woodlands near Phila, d/b, openwork, Stubbs 1,400.00
Wash bowl, Erie Canal View of Aqueduct..., d/b, Wood, 12"...1,550.00
Waste bowl, Lafayette at Franklin's Tomb, d/b 825.00

Miscellaneous

Will Watch, 15", $295.00.

Bowl, man/lady/bldgs HP on salt glaze, 1750s, 9¾".................6,000.00
Bust of Washington, mc enamel, underglaze bl, 8".....................425.00
Covered dish, hen on basket, mc on wht bsk, 5¾x5½x7"............225.00

Covered dish, hen on basket, mc on wht bsk, 7½x6x8" 325.00
Dog, greyhound, mc detail, lt wear, facing pr, 7" 500.00
Dog, poodle, sanded coat, facing pr, 6" 190.00
Dog, shepherd, standing leg Xd over other, by lamp, 5" 200.00
Dog, spaniel, blk spots/accents, facing pr, 10", EX....................250.00
Dog, spaniel, rust spatter, lg wht/gold locket, 9½" 75.00
Dog, spaniel, wht w/gold, enamel face, facing pr, 1850s, 12" 250.00
Dog, spaniel, wht w/mc features & gilt, facing pr, 10"..................350.00
Dog, spaniel, wht w/pk nose & blk paws, facing pr, 13" 400.00
Dog, spaniel, wht w/red spots, facing pr, 7¾"............................330.00
Dog, spaniel w/basket, mc, facing pr, 9¾"..................................650.00
Dog, spaniel w/flower basket, red spots, facing pr, 8", EX............825.00
Dog, spaniel w/flower basket, wht w/red & mc, 8", EX................500.00
Dog, spaniel w/vase on bk, facing pr, 13¾", EX 270.00
Figurine, Biblical figure seated w/bird, prof rpr, 9½" 250.00
Figurine, bird on rocky perch, minor chips, 4¾"...........................145.00
Figurine, boy sits by dog, lt wear, mini, 2¾" 115.00
Figurine, cat, seated on base, mc detail, facing pr, 7", NM...........700.00
Figurine, cat on pillow, rust/blk spots, facing pr, 1800, 7" 575.00
Figurine, cow feeding calf, oval base, 1850s, rpr, 6" 175.00
Figurine, Dandie, man & woman w/tree, prof rpr, 4⅜" 200.00
Figurine, draped figure, jug at ft, on sq plinth, 9" 250.00
Figurine, Evangelist, facing pr, now lamps, 1800s 350.00
Figurine, Franklin, standing figure, facing pr, 14½"....................500.00
Figurine, Franklin (but mk Washington), gold//mc, 16", EX 450.00
Figurine, lady w/fruit basket, tree, prof rpr, 6½" 175.00
Figurine, lady w/sprinkler, tree, prof rpr, 5¼" 225.00
Figurine, lion, ft on ball/teeth bared, yel, 1825, 9", pr 1,250.00
Figurine, lion, recumbent, cream w/gr spots, 2½", EX 275.00
Figurine, man or lady on horsebk, 12", EX, pr 200.00
Figurine, Minerva, helmet/torch/quiver/etc, 8"...........................250.00
Figurine, ram (& ewe) w/lamb, flowering tree, rpr, 5¾", pr 1,100.00
Figurine, ram & lamb w/tree, prof rpr/minor flaking, 4¾"............300.00
Figurine, Scotsman & lass on clock, 14", NM 175.00
Figurine, St Geo & Dragon, manner of R Wood, rstr, 14" 800.00
Figurine, Widow, prof rpr, minor wear, 9½" 150.00
Figurine, Widow, seated, child 1 side, keg on other, 9"...............300.00
Figurine, Winter, man w/arms folded as if skating, 7½" 235.00
Inkwell, 2 seated dogs w/sanded coats by tree, 5⅜", NM 250.00
Mug, mc on blk transfer: birth inscription, 1834, 3", NM...........100.00
Mug, Precepts That Never Die, mc/blk transfer, NM 145.00
Pastille burner, bldg w/turrets, appl flowers, 1820, 8", EX 275.00
Pastille burner, castle form, clock flanked by towers, 6½" 350.00
Pepper castor, red/gr gaudy floral, blk stripe, 4" 185.00
Pitcher, beehive symbolizing Industry, mc on pearlware, 7" 1,600.00
Pitcher, cottage form, branch hdl, mc details, 6⅜", NM 65.00
Pitcher, floral collar neck/body, 4-color, pearlware, 7".................300.00
Pitcher, gaudy 4-color floral, 8", EX 175.00
Pitcher, lg floral, 5-color on cream, pearlware, ovoid, 8" 500.00
Pitcher, Lord Wellington/Gen Hill, mc/silver lustre, 5", VG.........90.00
Plate, basket of strawberries, berry/flower border, 10" 225.00
Plate, gaudy mc floral, eagle mk, stains, 13" 300.00
Plate, gaudy mc floral, eagle mk, 10", EX 95.00
Plate, spread-wing eagle, bl feather edge, 1820s, 7", EX 600.00
Platter, country squire & dogs, m/b transfer, lt wear, 15" 300.00
Tea bowl & saucer, gaudy 4-color swags, NM.............................155.00

Stained Glass

There are many factors to consider in evaluating a window or panel of stained glass art. Besides the obvious factor of condition, intricacy, jeweling, beveling, and the amount of selenium (red, orange, and yellow) present should all be taken into account. Remember, repair work is itself an art and can be very expensive. Our advisor for this category is Carl Heck; he is listed in the Directory under Colorado.

Transom window with jewels and glue-chipped beveled glass border, ca 1910, 22" x 40", $2,250.00.

Lamps

Allover 6-petal floral wide cone 24" shade; tree std, Suess 8,800.00
Brickwork 18" dome shade w/simple border, Williamson; std 700.00
Chandelier, Prairie School geometrics, shallow, 9x20" sq............300.00
Fleur-de-lis border irregular-edge 16" shade; swirl/rib std............750.00
Geometric w/leaf border 17" shade; vasiform std, 27" 550.00
Geometric 14" shallow shade; cherub std, Chandler, 20" 1,000.00
Geometric 18" cone shade w/appl border band; Nouveau std......650.00
Geometric 18" shade; fluted vase base, Bigelow/Kennard, 24" . 2,650.00
Poppies border on conical 20" dia shade, att Wilkinson, 21" .. 2,800.00

Miscellaneous

Plaque, angel face (pnt details)/wings, 1900, 10" dia 800.00
Window, Arts & Crafts geometrics, pk/gr slag w/amber, 22x40" ..250.00
Window, Prairie School, mc geometrics/etched clear, 48x18".....450.00
Window, Prairie School, simple geometric, 32x12½", EX 200.00

Stanford

The Stanford Company produced a Corn Line, similar to that of the Shawnee Company, that is today becoming very collectible. Most examples are marked, so there should be no difficulty in distinguishing one from the other.

Pitcher, 7½", $55.00.

Corn Line, butter dish 45.00
Corn Line, cookie jar 80.00

Corn Line, creamer & sugar bowl......................**45.00**
Corn Line, relish tray......................**35.00**
Corn Line, shakers, pr......................**25.00**
Corn Line, teapot **60.00**

Stangl

In 1910 Johann Martin Stangl joined the Fulper Pottery Company, working there as ceramic chemist and superintendent of the plant. After a brief absence from 1914 until 1919 when he was employed by the Haeger Pottery, Stangl returned to Fulper. He developed glazes for a new line of cigarette boxes, ash trays, vases, figurines, etc. In 1926 J.M. Stangl became president of the company, and by 1946 he and a partner gained total ownership. The Stangl name first appeared on solid-color dinnerware and novelites in 1926. By 1942 a higher grade of hand-decorated and hand-colored dinnerware was made — Fruit, Yellow Tulip, etc. — which was sold in great abundance. During the war years (1940-1946), bird figures were in great demand, since imports were restricted at that time. Stangl created its famous line of birds; these are very collectible today. Stangl ware continued to be produced after J.M. Stangl died in 1972; soon after 1978 the factory closed. Reference: *The Collector's Handbook of Stangl Pottery* by Norma Rehl, published in 1979. Our advisors for this category are Robert and Nancy Perzel; they are listed in the Directory under New Jersey.

Birds

#3276, Bluebird......................**85.00**
#3276D, Bluebirds, 8½" **150.00**
#3400, Lovebird, 4"......................**65.00**
#3401, Wren......................**65.00**
#3401D, Wrens......................**120.00**
#3402, Oriole, 3¼"......................**65.00**
#3402D, Orioles......................**125.00**
#3404D, Lovebirds, 5½" **95.00**
#3405, Cockatoo, 6"......................**65.00**
#3405D, Cockatoos......................**125.00**
#3406, Kingfisher, 3½"......................**85.00**
#3406D, Kingfishers, 5"......................**150.00**
#3408, Bird of Paradise, 5½"......................**115.00**
#3432, Running Duck......................**325.00**
#3443, Flying Duck, gray, 9"......................**320.00**
#3443, Flying Duck, teal......................**325.00**
#3444, Cardinal, pk, revised male **75.00**
#3444, Cardinal, red matt, 6½"......................**85.00**
#3446, Hen, yel, 7......................**165.00**
#3447, Yel Warbler......................**85.00**
#3448, Bl Headed Vireo, 4¼"......................**85.00**
#3452, Painted Bunting......................**100.00**
#3454, Key West Quail Dove, 9"......................**255.00**
#3456, Cerulean Warbler, 4¼"......................**100.00**
#3490D, Redstarts......................**225.00**
#3491, Hen Pheasant......................**250.00**
#3492, Cock Pheasant, 6¼x11"......................**250.00**
#3580, Cockatoo, 8⅞"......................**185.00**
#3581D, Chickadees......................**200.00**
#3582D, Parakeets, 7"......................**250.00**
#3583, Parula Warbler, 4¾"......................**65.00**
#3584, Cockatoo, 11½"......................**260.00**
#3585, Rufous Hummingbird, 3" **65.00**
#3589, Indigo Bunting......................**75.00**
#3592, Titmouse, 2½"......................**60.00**
#3593, Nuthatch......................**50.00**

#3594, Red-Faced Warbler, 3"......................**85.00**
#3595, Bobolink, 4¾"......................**125.00**
#3596, Gray Cardinal, 4¾"......................**60.00**
#3597, Wilson Warbler, yel, 3½"......................**50.00**
#3598, Kentucky Warbler, 3"......................**55.00**
#3599D, Hummingbirds......................**275.00**
#3627, Rivoli Hummingbird **135.00**
#3629, Broadbill Hummingbird......................**135.00**
#3751, Red-Headed Woodpecker, 6¼"......................**200.00**
#3813, Evening Grosbeak......................**140.00**
#3848, Golden Crown Kinglet, 4"......................**125.00**
#3850, Yel Warbler......................**85.00**

Miscellaneous

Dinnerware, tan with heavy gold mottling, ca 1950s: Plate, 10", $12.00; Plate, 8", $8.00; Cup and saucer, $10.00; Cereal bowl, $7.50.

Antique Gold, ash tray, 9" sq **10.00**
Antique Gold, pitcher, 12"......................**20.00**
Antique Gold, planter, telephone, 2-pc......................**50.00**
Blueberry, cup & saucer......................**12.00**
Blueberry, plate, 10"......................**14.00**
Cup & saucer, AD; w/HP rose......................**25.00**
Fruit, brochure, 1957......................**10.00**
Fruit, cup & saucer......................**15.00**
Fruit, plate, dinner sz......................**14.00**
Golden Grape, creamer......................**6.00**
Golden Grape, shakers, pr **10.00**
Golden Grape, sugar bowl......................**10.00**
Golden Harvest, coffeepot......................**30.00**
Golden Harvest, creamer......................**8.50**
Golden Harvest, gravy boat......................**15.00**
Golden Harvest, pitcher, 2-qt......................**35.00**
Kiddieware, Little Bo Peep, bowl......................**40.00**
Kiddieware, Little Bo Peep, cup **35.00**
Kiddieware, Little Bo Peep, plate **60.00**
Kiddieware, Mealtime Special, plate, divided......................**50.00**
Magnolia, bowl, lug soup......................**10.00**
Magnolia, butter dish **35.00**
Magnolia, casserole, w/lid, 4¼"......................**12.00**
Magnolia, chop plate, 12½"......................**20.00**
Magnolia, creamer & sugar bowl......................**17.00**
Magnolia, cup & saucer......................**10.00**
Magnolia, plate, 10"......................**12.00**
Magnolia, plate, 8"......................**8.00**
Magnolia, relish tray **16.00**

Magnolia, shakers, pr 12.00
Mug, Irish coffee; gr cloverleaf, ftd 25.00
Orchard Song, plate, 10" 9.00
Orchard Song, server, center hdl................................. 6.00
Pitcher & bowl, HP pk rose, lg....................................175.00
Pitcher & bowl, HP violets, sm...................................150.00
Rainbow Ware, vase, red to turq to gr, 3 twist hdls, 9"....120.00
Sportsman, coaster, mallard...20.00
Sportsman, plate, Canada goose, gray, 11½" 40.00
Stoby mug, Archie, 1930s HP colors, w/correct ash tray hat.......225.00
Stoby mug, Archie, 1970s tan & blk stoneware, set 100.00
Terra Rose, cigarette box, Blossom Time......................30.00
Terra Rose, egg cup, yel Tulip 10.00
Terra Rose, sherbet, high std 25.00
Thistle, creamer 8.50
Thistle, cup 7.50
Thistle, pitcher, milk 28.00
Town & Country, baking dish, bl, 2½-qt 65.00
Town & Country, baking dish, gr, 1½-qt 32.00
Town & Country, cup, gr 12.00
Town & Country, mug, brn, lg......................................25.00
Town & Country, pitcher, gr, 2½-pt 40.00
Town & Country, plate, dinner; bl 20.00
Town & Country, plate, dinner; yel 12.00
Town & Country, shakers, gr, hdls, pr 20.00
Wild Rose, plate, 6" 6.00

Statue of Liberty

Long before she began greeting immigrants in 1886, the Statue of Liberty was being honored by craftsmen both here and abroad. Her likeness was etched on blades of the finest straight razors from England, captured in finely detailed busts sold as souvenirs to Paris fairgoers in 1878, and presented on colorfully lithographed trade cards, usually satirical, to American shoppers. Perhaps no other object has been represented in more forms or with such frequency as the universal symbol of America. Liberty's keepsakes are also universally accessible. Delightful souvenir models created in 1885 to raise funds for Liberty's pedestal are frequently found at flea markets, while earlier French bronze and terra cotta Liberties have been auctioned for over $100,000. Some collectors hunt for the countless forms of 19th-century Liberty memorabilia, while many collections were begun in anticipation of the 1986 Centennial with concentration on modern depictions. Our advisor for this category is Mike Brooks; he is listed in the Directory under California.

Bottle, figural, milk glass, sq metal base, 14¾"............595.00
Pocket watch, commemorative, quartz, 1986, MIB w/papers 50.00
Pocket watch, Franco-American, 1876........................300.00

Steamship Collectibles

For centuries, ocean-going vessels with their venturesome officers and crews were the catalyst that changed the unknown aspects of our world to the known. Changing economic conditions, unfortunately, have now placed the North American shipping industry in the same jeopardy as the American passenger train. They are becoming a memory. The surge of interest in railroad collectibles and the railroad-related steamship lines has lead collectors to examine the whole spectrum of steamship collectibles. Our advisors for this category are Lila and Fred Shrader; they are listed in the Directory under California.

Ash tray, Cunard Lines, Catalin blk & wht, 3½" 18.00
Ash tray, Swedish American Line, glass, 2¾" sq 10.00

Booklet, Cunard, Berengaria, color cover, 1920, 8x11" 22.00
Brochure, Alaska SS, cruise & service, 1924 ....16.50
Brochure, Ericksson Line, Phila to Jamestown, 1907.....................28.50
Brochure, R&O, Niagara to the Sea, 1916 ....22.50
Brochure, Wilmington Tran Co, Catalina Island, 1927 ....24.00
Butter Pat, Puerto Rico Line, bl floral border 38.00
Button, uniform; White Star Line, flag on brass 12.00
Cup & saucer, American Mail.....................55.00
Cup & saucer, demitasse; Alaska SS 52.00
Cup & saucer, demitasse; Cunard.....................47.00
Cup & saucer, Eastern SS Lines, Inc 55.00
Deck plan, US Lines, SS United States, 1st class, 1958, M 10.00
Lantern, passageway; brass, glass windows, kerosene, 14"..........195.00
Letter card, Majestic II, portrait 7.50
Letter card, Queen Mary portrait, M..................... 7.50
Match book, Matson 'Hawaii!' 4.00
Menu, American Mail Line, SS President Madison, 1927 ....12.00
Menu, Canadian Pacific, 'To Alaska,' 1930s..................... 9.00
Menu, French Line, Mercier cover, 1970 .... 8.00
Menu, Holland-American Line, pirate cover, 1938.....................14.00
Napkin, Luckenbach Line, damask, woven logo, lg 9.00
Napkin, New England SS Co, damask, emb logo, lg..................... 7.00
Napkin, US Line, linen, woven logo, lg 5.00
Passenger list, Cunard, RMS Caronia, cabin class, 1951, 8-pg 5.00
Passenger list, Leviathan, portrait cover, 1926.....................17.50
Passenger list, Matson Lines, 1939 ....3.50
Plate, Cunard SS Co, tan w/wht & gray stripes, 8" 24.00
Plate, dinner; Georgian Bay Line 60.00
Plate, New England SS Co, New England, top logo, 9½" 65.00
Plate, P&O SS Co, bl & wht stripe+top logo, 9½".....................35.00
Plate, USS Rotterdam round-the-world, Bing & Grondahl, 1980.10.00
Playing cards, Blue Sea Line, dbl deck, MIB.....................24.00
Playing cards, Matson Lines, dbl deck, MIB 15.00
Playing cards, Orient Line, dbl deck, EX in orig box 17.50
Pocket knife, Bremmen 35.00
Teapot, Cunard, Cube, ind 65.00
Tip tray, Cunard, Aquatania chromo litho, ca 1915, M.....................135.00
Towel, SP SS Co, 'Dixie,' 22x40" 35.00

Steins

Steins have been made from pottery, pewter, glass, stoneware, and porcelain, from very small up to the four-liter size. They are decorated by etching, in-mold relief, decals, and occasionally they may be hand painted. Some porcelain steins have lithophane bases. Collectors often specialize in a particular type — faience, regimental, or figural — while others limit themselves to the products of only one manufacturer. Our advisor for this category is Ron Fox; he is listed in the Directory under New York. See also Mettlach.

Key:
L — liter   PUG — print under glaze
POG — print over glaze   tl — thumb lift

Character, Bartmankrug, pewter, Imperial Zinn, dents, 1½-L 285.00
Character, Bismark, porc, Shierholz, ½-L, M 555.00
Character, Bl Hopps Lady, porc, Shierholz, ½-L, NM 1,425.00
Character, bowling pin, porc, Shierholz, ball tl, ½-L, NM...........350.00
Character, cat w/hangover, porc, Shierholz, rpr, ½-L...................425.00
Character, chinaman, pottery, sm chip, ½-L 300.00
Character, drunken monkey, porc, Shierholz, ½-L, M 550.00
Character, Dutch boy, porc, Shierholz, prof lid rpr, ½-L 1,090.00

Character, Frauenkirche Tower, stoneware, ⅛-L, M 300.00
Character, hops lady, pottery, ½-L, M 300.00
Character, hot air balloon, pottery, ¾-L, M 1,400.00
Character, Imperial soldier, porc, ½-L, M 1,750.00
Character, lady w/bustle, stoneware, salt glaze, mk HR, ½-L .. 1,000.00
Character, lion, porc, bsk glaze, Sohne, ½-L, M 3,000.00
Character, man's smiling face, pottery, pewter lid, ½-L, NM 300.00
Character, monk, porc, lithophane, ½-L, M 275.00
Character, monk, pottery, bl salt glaze, ½-L, M 365.00
Character, monk w/hands on tummy, stoneware, ½-L, M 275.00
Character, monkey, pottery, Merkelbach/#661, music box, ½-L .. 450.00
Character, Munich Child, pewter, ½-L, M 355.00
Character, Munich Child, pottery, .3-L, M 155.00
Character, Munich Maid, porc, statue lithophane, ½-L, EX 255.00
Character, Nurnberg Tower, pewter, Perkeo tl, ½-L, NM 300.00
Character, Nurnberg Tower, pottery, mk FMN/#1190, ½-L, NM .. 270.00
Character, Nurnberg Tower, pottery, ⅛-L, M 185.00
Character, ram (seated), porc, Shierholz, ½-L, M 525.00
Character, rooster, porc, Shierholz, sm rpr, ½-L 1,245.00
Character, Scotsman, stoneware, mk LB&C, chip/line, ½-L 440.00
Character, sea captain, porc, bsk glaze, Sohne, ½-L, M 1,900.00
Character, sea captain, porc, Shierholz, rpr, ½-L 800.00
Character, skull, porc, bsk glaze, unmk, strap rpr, ½-L 285.00
Character, skull on book, porc, bsk glaze, Sohne, ½-L, M 600.00
Character, skull on book, porc, E Bohne, .3-L, M 365.00
Character, student, pottery, #805, ½-L, M 355.00
Character, wealthy German, stoneware, sm rpr, ½-L 120.00
Character, 7 electors on Lake Wallen, pottery, 1-L, EX 450.00
Faience, floral, Bayreuth, pewter hdl rpr, ¾-L 135.00
Faience, floral medallions, Bayreuth, 1740s, 1-L, EX 935.00
Glass, bl opaline, pewter lid dtd 1867, 2½", M 220.00
Glass, blown, amber, pnt Munich Maid & keg, ½-L, M 185.00
Glass, blown, cut/faceted, eng stags & trees, ½-L, M 375.00
Glass, blown, eng florals, pewter lid, ca 1800, ½-L, M 475.00
Glass, blown, eng fox in forest, prism in lid, .3-L, M 260.00
Glass, blown, eng leaping stag, pewter lid, 1870s, ½-L, M 235.00
Glass, blown, pk opaline, wht glass hdl, 1850s, 1-L, M 450.00
Glass, blown, porc lady inlay on pewter lid, ½-L, M 110.00
Glass, blown, ruby stained, ruby lid insert, 1840s, ½-L, NM 175.00
Glass, blown, ruby stained w/cut stags scene, postwar, ½-L 88.00
Glass, blown, yel prunts, barmaid pewter lid, ½-L, M 365.00
Glass, blown/enameled: jockey on horse, inlaid glass lid, ½-L, M .. 300.00
Glass, mold blown, Mary Gregory boy on bl, inlay lid, .3-L, M .. 225.00
Glass, mold blown, porc farmer occupational inlay, ½-L, EX 55.00
Glass, pressed, frauleins transfer, pewter lid, ½-L, NM 135.00
Glass, pressed, HP florals, ruby prism in lid, ½-L, M 125.00
Glass, pressed, porc floral inlay lid, ½-L, M 75.00
Glass, pressed, porc inlay of man, minor wear, ½-L 75.00
Glass, pressed, wagon driver occupational inlay, chip, ½-L 105.00
Glass, red cut to clear, cut lid, 1850s, ½-L, NM 475.00
Glass, wheel-cut Warbrunn scene, prism in lid, ½-L, NM 135.00
Military, HP: Iron Cross, stoneware, 1914, ½-L, M 300.00
Military, relief: Bismark & Joseph, stoneware, rpr, 1-L 245.00
Military, relief: Von Hindenburg, pottery, rpl lid, ½-L 185.00
Nazi, Komp 5..., motorized unit, stoneware, ½-L, NM 560.00
Nazi, Pz Jager Abtlg 1939-40, helmet lid, ½-L, M 775.00
Nazi, Rgt Nachr Zug IR 91...1938, porc, ½-L, NM 360.00
Nazi, Uffz Korps 2/Flak Regt...Iserlohn, stoneware, ½-L, M 1,050.00
Nazi, Unteroffz Reiter Rgt 14..., pottery, helmet lid, ½-L 600.00
Occupational, miller, porc w/transfer, ½-L, NM 375.00
Occupational, shoemaker, pewter, rpr, ½-L 400.00
Occupational, trainload of furniture, porc, tang rpr, ½-L 355.00
Pewter, eng relief on lid: Wallhalla, ½-L, M 55.00
Pewter, etched: carpenter scenes, dtd 1855, 1-L, NM 400.00

Pewter, etched: flowers & inscription, dtd 1822, dents, 1-L 300.00
Pewter, relief: eagle & soldiers, dents, .3-L 125.00
Pewter, relief: eagles, eagle finial, dtd 1900, ½-L, EX 200.00
Porc, etched: drinking man w/pipe, mk HR/#219, sm rpr, ½-L ... 187.00
Porc, etched: man in forest, mk HR/#443, flakes, ½-L 300.00
Porc, etched: tavern scene, mk HR/#160, ½-L, M 165.00
Porc, HP: high-wheeler, women reading letter, ½-L, M 610.00
Porc, HP: mtn climber litho, relief pewter lid, 1-L, M 285.00
Porc, transfer: Alpine scene, pewter lid, ½-L, EX 130.00
Porc, transfer: Munster in Ulm, couple lithophane, ½-L, M 185.00
Porc, transfer: Von Hindenburg, helmet lid, ½-L, NM 500.00
Pottery, Bud Man figural, older version, Ceramarte, ½-L, M 235.00
Pottery, etched: Baren, Reinach, pewter lid, ½-L, NM 170.00
Pottery, etched: bicyclist, mk TP/#1453, inlay lid, ½-L, M 935.00
Pottery, etched: cavaliers, #1227, weak tang/chip, ½-L 110.00
Pottery, etched: frogs & gnomes, mk HR/#519, 1-L, M 500.00
Pottery, etched: Liben wir so..., mk HR/#419, ½-L, NM 400.00
Pottery, etched: men toast lady, #1359, .3-L, M 175.00
Pottery, POG: woman & florals, 1-L, M 175.00
Pottery, relief: Boston scenes, postwar, ½-L, M 35.00
Pottery, relief: card game, pewter lid, ½-L, NM 198.00
Pottery, relief: cat, pewter lid, mk Gerz/#1109, ½-L, EX 250.00
Pottery, relief: Heidelberg scenes, metal lid, ⅛-L, M 20.00
Pottery, relief: hunter & game animals, ½-L, M 245.00
Pottery, relief: hunter & target, barmaid as lid, ½-L, EX 75.00
Pottery, relief: monkeys & evolution, monkey hdl, #1402, ½-L .. 550.00
Pottery, relief: Monroe Beer, gr glazed, ½-L, M 40.00
Pottery, relief: skaters, glass inlay lid, mk HR/#460, .5-L 298.00
Pottery, relief: soccer, 3-D soccer ball on shoe, ¾-L, M 155.00
Pottery, transfer & relief: brewery, inlay lid, ½-L, M 400.00

Regimental, 181 Saxon Inft. Regt. Chemnik, 1909-11, roster, M, ½-L, $465.00; 2 Inft. Regt. Munich, 1912-14, roster, ½-L, NM, $385.00.

Regimental, Baden Feld Art Regt...1893-95, porc, ½-L, EX 600.00
Regimental, Bayr Inf Lelb Regt...1905-07, stoneware, M 360.00
Regimental, Bayr Inf Regt Nr 8, pottery, ½-L, NM 375.00
Regimental, Bayr Inf...Metz...1911-13, porc, lion tl, ½-L, M 450.00
Regimental, Bayr Inf...1907-09, porc, lion tl, ½-L, NM 650.00
Regimental, Naval, SMS Turingen 1911-14, pottery, 1-L, NM . 1,200.00
Regimental, Sachs Inf...Chemnitz 1903-05, porc, ½-L, M 775.00
Regimental, Wurtt Feld Artl 49...1912-14, porc, ½-L, M 1,400.00
Regimental, 109th Inf...1903-05, soldier finial/griffin tl, NM 360.00
Regimental, 115 Inf...1897-99, lion tl, porc, M 315.00
Regimental, 138 Inf Regt Dieuz 1911-13, porc, ½-L, M 495.00
Regimental, 16th Bayr Inf...Passeau 1910-12, porc, 12¼", EX 298.00
Regimental, 17 Inf Regt Germersheiv 1909-11, porc, rpr, ½-L 245.00
Regimental, 26th Feld Art...1910-12, pottery, 13½", M 530.00
Regimental, 3 Eisenbahn...1909-11, pottery, ½-L, M 1,045.00

Serpentine, gr w/pewter hdl & bands, 1700s, ½-L, EX 3,000.00
Stoneware, cobalt & scratch decor, 1846, Westerwald, 2-L.........425.00
Stoneware, enameled: couple & tree, Nouveau lid, 1-L, M 400.00
Stoneware, enameled: elk horns & skull, Hohlwein, 2-L, EX 675.00
Stoneware, POG: comic Egyptian scene, sgn AH, 1-L, M 435.00
Stoneware, POG: Kalt Loch..., w/logo, pewter lid, rpr, ½-L...........80.00
Stoneware, POG: Storchen & stork, pewter lid, ½-L, M 200.00
Stoneware, relief: bowling scenes, metal lid, ½-L, M.....................65.00
Stoneware, relief: GR (Georgus Rex), Westerwald, ½-L, EX.......190.00
Stoneware, relief: Munich scenes, band chips, 1-L 45.00
Stoneware, transfer/enamel: Gruss aus Nurnberg, ½-L, M 265.00
Stoneware, transfer: brewery, relief pewter lid, ½-L, M 385.00
Stoneware, transfer: hunter, cavalier relief on lid, ½-L, M 125.00

Steuben

Carder Steuben glass was made by the Steuben Glass Works in Corning, New York, while under the direction of Frederick Carder from 1903 to 1932. A vast variety of types and colors of art glass was produced including gold Aurene, blue Aurene, decorated Aurenes, Cluthra, Verre de Soie, Rosaline, colored Jades, Cintra, Florentia, and a host of others. Carder's leadership ended in 1932, and the production of colored glassware soon ceased. Since 1932 the tradition of fine Steuben art glass has been continued in crystal. Our advisor for this category is Thomas P. Dimitroff; he is listed in the Directory under New York. In the listings that follow, examples are signed unless noted otherwise. See also Aurene; Cluthra.

Key: ACB — acid cut back

Bottle, scent; blk, bl rim/hdls, pk-petal stopper, unmk, 7" 1,500.00
Bottle, scent; Gr Jade, int ribs, wht stopper, Carder, 6" 750.00
Bottle, scent; Verre de Soie, bulbous, gr stopper, unmk, 4"..........375.00
Bowl, ACB, sea holly leaves, blk on Alabaster, bulbous, 7" ... 1,600.00
Bowl, berry; Rosaline, etched swags, Alabaster base, 2¾" 450.00
Bowl, centerpc; bl & Calcite, 3" stretch border, 14½" 650.00
Bowl, Florentia, gr flower center, ped ft, #6785, 12½" 3,500.00
Bowl, gold Aurene on Calcite, flared/shallow, 10" 350.00
Bowl, gold Aurene on Calcite, unsgn, 1⅞x6" 275.00
Bowl, Grotesque, ivory, 4-rib free-form, 7" H.............................600.00
Bowl vase, ACB, Plum Jade, Oriental design, 4½x8" 2,200.00
Candlestick, bl Aurene on Calcite, flare rim, #3581, 6" 1,100.00
Candlestick, ivory & blk, rare shape #7317, 10", pr................. 2,000.00
Candlestick, Rosaline & Alabaster, unsgn, 8½", pr.....................595.00
Candlestick, Verre de Soie, twist stem, #379, 10", pr 350.00
Candy dish, Celeste Bl, swirled, finial, 6½" W 450.00
Champagne, Cerise w/blk rim, clear twist stem, 5¾"...................150.00
Compote, Jade/Alabaster, dbl ACB scroll/floral border, 3½" 500.00
Compote, Topaz, appl fruit finial, 10"..950.00
Compote, Verre de Soie, lt gr w/pk fruit+gr leaf finial, 8".........850.00
Cordial, Selenium Red, knobbed baluster stem, 4¾"...................160.00
Creamer & sugar (open), Pomona Gr w/amber ft & hdls, swirl ...175.00
Goblet, clear w/Celeste Bl threading, lt amber stem/base, 6".......150.00
Goblet, Rosaline bowl, twisted Alabaster stem, 6½" 165.00
Goblet, yel random threads in ribbed bowl, braided stem, 8½"....150.00
Lamp, Oriental Poppy, ribbed gr 7" shaft/sq bronze base 1,500.00
Lamp base, ACB Fircone motif, bl irid to gr, swans on base 1,200.00
Lamp base, ACB stylized pods, gold to blk 13" vasiform, 26" .. 1,600.00
Lamp base, ACB winged horses, blk/yel w/Aurene drips, 19" . 5,000.00
Parfait, Rosaline & Alabaster, stemmed, 6½"..............................150.00
Pitcher, Gr Jade, swirl, Alabaster hdl, fleur-de-lis mk, 11"..........400.00
Plate, Gr Jade, 8½" 65.00
Plate, Oriental Poppy, 8½" 175.00

Rose bowl, Verre de Soie, 10-rib, EX irid, 3½x5½" 175.00
Sculpture, elephant, ivory, 5½"..950.00
Sculpture, nude, Blk Jade, kneels in crystal circle, rare 950.00
Sherbet, Verre de Soie, +underplate, sgn Carder 150.00
Tazza, clear/flat disk on quatreform ped base, 3¾", pr 400.00
Vase, ACB, flowers/webs on clear cylinder, sgn Carder, 10" ... 1,200.00
Vase, ACB, flying ducks on amethyst, hdls 2,900.00
Vase, ACB, Gr Jade & Alabaster, Chinese Pattern, #8558 ..... 1,600.00
Vase, bl, swirled, rectangular, fleur-de-lis mk, 8¾x5¾" 300.00
Vase, Bl Jade on Alabaster base, classical form, 8¾" 1,200.00
Vase, clear w/appl gr threads on dmn texture, 7½".....................250.00
Vase, gold Aurene on Calcite, flattened rim, 10" 660.00
Vase, gold Aurene on Calcite, ruffled, #1409, 6" 400.00
Vase, gold Aurene on Calcite, trumpet form, ftd, 12" 600.00
Vase, Grotesque in Bl Jade, rare, #7277, 6" 3,500.00
Vase, Ivorine, waisted-neck sphere, flared rim, no mk, 11"..........550.00
Vase, Ivory, unsgn, #2683, 10" 650.00
Vase, Gr Jade, Invt Swirl, tapered/bulbous, 6"............................200.00
Vase, Gr Jade, wafer base, 3 thorny prong vases, unmk, 6⅛" 450.00
Vase, Gr Jade fan shape on Alabaster dbl-knob ped ft, 8½".........300.00
Vase, Gr Jade w/Alabaster, 2-prong, Deco style, 9x5" 500.00

Vase, Rose Quartz, acid-cut-back sculptured flowers, 12", $3,500.00.

Vase, Roze Quartz, sculptured, #6766, 11½" 3,500.00
Vase, Selenium Red, ribbed fan form on clear ft, 8½", pr............450.00
Wine, Rosaline bowl, Alabaster stem, 6" 125.00
Wine, Topaz, ribbed, inverted baluster stem, 4¾" 95.00

Stevengraph

A Stevengraph is a small picture made of woven silk resembling an elaborate ribbon, created by Thomas Stevens in England in the latter half of the 1800s. They were matted and framed by Stevens, usually with his name appearing on the mat or, more commonly, the trade announcement on the back of the mat. He also produced silk post cards and bookmarks, all of which have 'Stevens' woven in silk on one of the mitered corners. Anyone wishing to learn more about Stevengraphs is encouraged to contact the Stevengraph Collectors' Association, whose address can be found in the Directory under Clubs, Newsletters, and Catalogs.

Bookmarks

Behold the Man, blk fr, G 50.00
New Year's Gift (child & dog), blk fr 60.00

Old Oaken Bucket, Warner, EX..30.00
Star Spangled Banner, blk fr..40.00
To My Daughter, blk fr, VG..75.00

Silks

Baden Powell, rnded gold fr, G.......................................40.00
Called to the Rescue, maple fr, EX................................150.00
Declaration of Independence, from 1893 Columbian Expo 225.00
Edward VII & Alexandra 100.00
First Set, tennis match, orig mat, 2x6", EX....................325.00
First Train, EX...280.00
For Life or Death, Heroism on Land (2-verse), mat/fr, EX...........250.00
Good Old Days, orig mat & label, EX............................150.00
HRH Prince of Wales (became King Edward VII) 150.00
Kenilworth Castle, rpl fr, EX 70.00
Lady Godiva Procession, maple fr, G.............................100.00
Landing of Columbus, ornate wooden fr, VG 220.00
Last Lap, bicycles (Equal Wheels), VG...........................265.00
Peeping Tom, antique gold fr, EX..................................80.00
Present Time Period 60 Miles an Hour, passenger train, fr, EX ..150.00
Struggle, EX..150.00
Water Jump, antique silver fr, overmtd, VG....................100.00
Windsor Castle, rnded gold fr, EX 125.00

Stevens and Williams

Stevens and Williams glass was produced at the Brierly Hill Glassworks in Stourbridge, England, for nearly a century, beginning in the 1830s. They were credited with being among the first to develop a method of manufacturing a more affordable type of cameo glass. Other lines were also made — silver deposit, alexandrite, and engraved rock crystal, to name but a few. Our advisor for this category is Don Williams; he is listed in the Directory under Missouri.

Pitcher, doce relevio, apple blossoms, aqua and gold on cream, silverplated mounts, 10", $2,900.00.

Bottle, scent; bl swirl w/HP berries & gilt, mk, 13".................325.00
Compote, intaglio poppies/pods, honeycomb stem, 6" 200.00
Salt cellar, clear, wht threading, berry prunt; in fr 145.00
Vase, amber/gold foil, 3 clear loop ft w/berry prunts, 5¾" 265.00
Vase, coral, wht int, clear opal leaves & rim, 12x5".................395.00
Vase, cream opaque, appl pk cherries, ewer form, 6½" 145.00
Vase, mc swirl w/HP florals, pear form, mk, 13" 285.00
Vase, pk, appl leaves, ruffled rim, amber ft, 7½" 225.00
Vase, pk, appl ruffled leaf, 8-crimp top, 6⅝x3¾".................200.00
Vase, pk, wht leaves & grass intaglio, ruffled, 5x3".................395.00
Vase, rose, opal int, ruffled amber leaves, 5¾x3⅞".................165.00

Vase, wht, pk int, amber rim, amber/red leaves, 7½"..................225.00

Cameo

Bowl, apple blossoms, pk on wht satin, ruffled, 4x6" 750.00
Bowl, bamboo/floral, pk w/yel int, 8-crimp, 3½x5⅝" 775.00
Rose bowl, coral branches, pk on custard, yel int 1,000.00
Vase, complex floral/butterfly/border, wht on apricot, 12" 3,000.00
Vase, floral, wht on amber/peach, stick neck w/band, 12" 2,750.00
Vase, foxglove, wht on yel, conical, 12"................................3,000.00
Vase, nasturtiums/beetle, wht on amethyst, 6" 3,200.00
Vase, plums/floral, wht on red, bulbous w/stick neck, 12" 3,000.00

Stickley

Among the leading proponents of the Arts and Crafts Movement, the Stickley brothers — Gustav, Leopold, Charles, Albert, and John George — were at various times and locations involved in designing and producing furniture as well as decorative items for the home. (See Arts and Crafts for further information.) The oldest of the five Stickley brothers was Gustav; his work is the most highly regarded of all. He developed the style of furniture refered to as Mission. It was strongly influenced by the type of furnishings found in the Spanish missions of California — utilitarian, squarely built, and simple. It was made most often of oak, and decoration was very limited or non-existent. The work of his brothers displays adaptations of many of Gustav's ideas and designs. His factory, the Craftsman Shops, operated in Eastwood, New York, from the late 1890s until 1915, when he was forced out of business by larger companies who copied his work and sold it at much lower prices. Among his shopmarks are the early red decal containing a joiner's compass and the words 'Als Ik Kan,' the branded mark with the very similar components, and paper labels.

The firm known as Stickley Brothers was located first in Binghampton, New York, and then Grand Rapids, Michigan. Albert and John made the move to Michigan, leaving Charles in Binghamton (where he and an uncle continued the operation under a different name). After several years John George left the company to rejoin Leopold in New York. (These two later formed their own firm called L. & J.G. Stickley.) The Stickley Brothers Company under Albert's sole direction produced furniture that featured fine inlay work, decorative cutouts, and leaned strongly toward a style of Arts and Crafts with an English influence. It was tagged with a paper label 'Made by Stickley Brothers, Grand Rapids' or with a brass plate or decal with the words 'Quaint Furniture,' an English term he chose to refer to his product. In addition to his furniture, he made metal furnishings as well.

The workshops of the L. & J.G. Stickley Company operated under the name 'Onandaga Shops.' Located in Fayetteville, New York, their designs were often all but copies of Gustav's work. Their products were well made and marketed, and their business was very successful. Their decaled labels contained all or a combination of the words 'Handcraft' or 'Onandaga Shops,' along with the brothers' initials and last name. The firm continues in business today. Our advisor for this category is Bruce Austin; he is listed in the Directory under New York. Note: When only one dimension is given for tables, it is length.

Gustav Stickley

Andirons, #348, iron, post/ball, EX patina, 28", pr 2,100.00
Ash tray, #270, hammered copper, emb at edge, EX patina, 6½"..290.00
Ash tray, hammered copper, match-holder hdl, mk, 5x4", VG ..110.00
Bed, #923, tapered posts, 5 wide slats in head/ft brds, mk........4,620.00
Bed, child's, #919, spindle sides, headbrd takes fabric, EX.......4,500.00
Blanket chest, 2 11-spindle sides, others paneled, mk, 30" 9,000.00

Book rack, 3-shelf, plank sides w/D cutouts at top, mk, EX **2,600.00**
Bookcase, #716, 2 8-pane doors, thru tenons, mk, VG **3,250.00**
Bookcase, #717, gallery over 2 8-pane doors, label, 56" **2,500.00**
Bookcase, 2 12-pane doors, gallery top, label, 60x57" **3,700.00**
Box, waist; cedar lined, copper hdls, branded, 32" L **2,100.00**
Chair, #2607, ca 1902, 37", 4 for **2,200.00**
Chair, #353, designed by Harvey Ellis, 1909, 9 for.................. **3,500.00**
Chair, Morris; #332, 5-slat sides, thru tenons, rpl uphl........... **4,000.00**
Chair, Morris; #367, lady's, 2-spindle sides, str arms, mk........ **6,600.00**
Chair, Morris; #369, 16-spindle sides, drop arms, 42" **10,450.00**
Chair, side; #308, H-bk, slip seat, brand, 39" **275.00**
Chair, side; #345½, V-rail/5-slat bk, reuphl/rnf, 6 for **3,750.00**
Chair, side; #348, rush seats, rare gr finish, set of 8 .... **1,500.00**
Chair, side; #349½, 3 horizontal bk slats, reuphl, 6 for **3,100.00**
Chair, side; #354½, V-groove crest rail, 5-slat, branded.............. **425.00**
Chair set, #340 host, 3 #338 sides, 3-slat bk, decal, EX **2,400.00**
Chamberstick, hammered copper, 7" bobeche, dk patina, 8".......**400.00**
Chandelier, #223, 5 lanterns drop from wide cut-out band **8,250.00**
Chest, #626, 2 short drw over 4, panel sides, label, 53x40" **4,620.00**
Chest, #902, 2 short drw over 4, wood pulls, decal, 52"........... **4,250.00**
China cabinet, #815, 2 8-pane doors, decal, rpl shelves **3,250.00**
China cabinet, #820, 16-pane door, top overhangs, label, EX. **2,600.00**
Desk, #505, chalet; recessed panel drop lid, unsgn, 46x24".........**600.00**
Desk, #709, kneehole shelf, 3-drw, 42" W, EX **650.00**
Desk, #720, letter file+2 sm drws atop, rfn, 37x38"..................**700.00**
Desk, #729, slant lid, gallery top, 1-drw, label, 35x30" **1,000.00**
Desk, drop front, 2 open shelves, decal, nicks/rpr, 52" **6,000.00**
Desk, kneehole; 4 short drw ea side, faceted wood knobs, mk . **2,200.00**
Dinner gong, oak frwork w/hammered copper plate, 37", VG. **1,400.00**
Firescreen, hammered/riveted iron, hdls, 8 screen sections **4,000.00**
Footrest, #300, arched apron, new leather/tacks/rfn, 15x20" **700.00**
Footstool, #299, orig leather/tacks, decal, 9", EX **600.00**
Footstool, #725, tacked leather uphl, arched sides, unsgn **1,200.00**

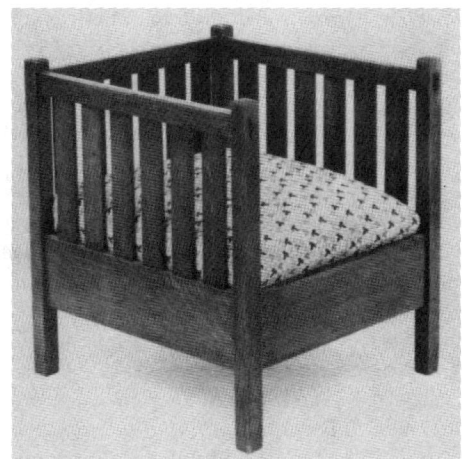

Gustav Stickley slat-sided cube chair #331, branded, $5,250.00.

Hall tree, mirror, umbrella pans both missing, 74x38" **2,100.00**
Lantern, #225, heart cutouts in wrought iron cap, 10", pr **2,000.00**
Lantern, porch; #324, cut-out iron mt, opal glass inserts **1,400.00**
Lantern, porch; #324, iron fr/amber glass panels, unsgn/rpt.........**700.00**
Rocker, #319, open arms, 4-slat bk, 36", VG...............................**700.00**
Rocker, #323, 4-slat bk, 5-slat sides, decal, reuphl, 36" **1,500.00**
Rocker, 4 concave bk slats, flat arms w/curved supports, mk........**400.00**
Rug, Nile pattern, brn/blk/gray, 36x15", VG.................................**200.00**

Sconce, #76, hammered copper/brass, cleaned/varnished, 11" **325.00**
Server, #802, 2-drw/base shelf, Ellis design, rfn, 43" L **2,300.00**
Settle, #171, leatherette cushion, red mk, 78" L **4,900.00**
Settle, #224, recessed panel bk, hinged seat, decal, 48" L........ **4,750.00**
Sidebrd, #800, designed by Harvey Ellis, rfn, 43x54"............... **4,400.00**
Sidebrd, #814, 2 doors flank 3 drw, decal/label, 66" W **4,750.00**
Sidebrd, #814½, 2 doors+3 drws over long drw, 56", EX **5,750.00**
Sidebrd, #816, plate rack, drw over 2 doors, decal, 49", EX **1,500.00**
Stand, magazine; #514, 4-shelf, leather trim/tacks, rfn, 45" **1,600.00**
Stand, magazine; #72, 3 open shelves, 42x22x13", EX **4,250.00**
Stand, magazine; similar to #547, leather trim/tacks, 35" **3,000.00**
Stand, telephone; swing arm w/tray on sq top, brand, 30x16" **425.00**
Table, #439, 30" dia top, offset X-stretchers, decal, EX **1,100.00**
Table, #449, 4-leg, X-stretcher, decal, 24" dia **3,900.00**
Table, #607, 24" dia top w/4 legs & shelf, Craftsman label.........**800.00**
Table, #624, hexagonal, 6-leg, stacked stretchers, 48", EX...... **3,750.00**
Table, #626, 40" dia top, X-stretchers w/finial, label, EX **1,200.00**
Table, center; #609, lower shelf, arched stretchers, decal........ **1,600.00**
Table, dining; #627, arched X-stretchers, decal, NM finish **3,550.00**
Table, dining; #656, ped base w/4 spreading ft, 60" dia **3,850.00**
Table, dining; #656, w/5 leaves, decal/label, 54" dia, VG **2,700.00**
Table, dining; #656, 48" dia top on sq ped, rfn, +4 leaves **2,550.00**
Table, lamp; #644, 30" rnd top, arched stretchers, rfn, VG **1,000.00**
Table, library; #616, 2-drw, oval copper pulls, rfn, 54" L **1,600.00**
Table, library; #619, 3-drw, appl liming over orig, 66", EX...... **2,750.00**
Table, library; #653, 1-drw w/iron V-pulls, decal, EX.................**900.00**
Table, sewing; #630, drop leaves, 2-drw, brand, 18" sq, EX **2,000.00**
Table, tea; #654, 24" dia top, decal, EX orig finish **1,500.00**
Table, trestle; #637, leather top, dbl-key base, label, VG **1,500.00**
Tabouret, #562, 20" sq top, slat sides, arched apron, decal **1,400.00**
Tabouret, #601, 14" dia top, paper label, orig finish **600.00**
Tabouret, #603, 18" dia, X-stretcher, rfn, VG **900.00**
Tabouret, 18½" dia top, arched X-stretcher, decal, 20", pr **1,000.00**
Tabouret, similar to #602, 18" top, str legs, brand, EX **425.00**
Umbrella stand, #54, 4 tapering posts, w/pan, label, rfn...............**500.00**
Vanity, #907, strap hdw, lg mirror atop, 5-drw, label, EX **3,000.00**
Wardrobe, #920, child's, iron hdw, panel doors, 60x33", VG.. **4,250.00**
Wardrobe, 2 panel doors w/copper pulls, decal, 60x35", EX ... **5,000.00**
Wastebasket, #94, wrought iron hoops, 14x12" dia, EX........... **1,700.00**
Wastebasket, #94, 13 slats riveted to metal bands, mk, 14" **850.00**
Window seat, #178, leather/tack uphl, 4-post, decal, 36" L..... **2,860.00**

L. & J.G. Stickley

L. &. J.G. Stickley dinner gong, signed, 34" x 21", $7,000.00.

Armchair, #471, bk adjusts, 6-slat, uphl seat, brand, 35x41" ... **1,100.00**
Bookcase, #643, 16-pane door, dbl keyed, decal, 55x39" **4,000.00**
Bookcase, #653, 1 door w/4 sm panes over lg pane, mk, 55" ... **2,700.00**
Catalog, Work of..., pub Art Press, Syracuse, sm tear **75.00**
Chair, #438, fixed bk, open arms, 4-slat bk, decal **700.00**
Chair, #812, 5 slats in tall bk & lower sides, rfn, 45" ... **1,100.00**
Chair, #830, adjustable bk, open arms, spring seat, label **1,500.00**
Chair, leather seat/bk, open arms, sq legs, no mk, VG **475.00**
Chair, Morris; #412, paddle arms, rpl uphl/bk bar, decal **3,250.00**
Chair, Morris; #830, adjustable bk, open flat arms, decal **2,300.00**
Chair, rocker; #423, concave crest rail, 6-slat bk, brand **400.00**
Chair, side; #332, concave crest rail over 2 slats, decal **165.00**
Chair set, #802 armchair, 5 #800 sides, concave rails, mk **1,850.00**
China closet, #746, 6 sm panes at top of pr glazed doors **4,750.00**
Clock, grandfather's; #91, stepped case, mk, rfn, 79" **8,500.00**
Davenport bed, #285, seat rail slides out for bed, mk, VG **1,600.00**
Desk, #531, 1-drw, lower shelf, dbl-keyed tenons, decal **550.00**
Desk, #660, fall front, 2 sm drw+1, recoated, unmk, 40x29" **600.00**
Desk, panel-sided book shelves, center drw, brand, rpl hdw **200.00**
Desk, 2-drw superstructure, 3 drw ea side, rfn, 60" W **3,000.00**
Frame, V-shape overhanging crest rail w/corbels, 27x22" **700.00**
Magazine stand, #46, 3-slat sides, 4-shelf, decal, 42", VG........ **1,200.00**
Magazine stand, #46, 3-slat sides w/arches top & bottom, mk. **1,750.00**
Pedestal, #28, long corbels under 13" sq top, mk, 42", EX **1,800.00**
Rocker, #413, adjustable 4-slat bk, open arms, no mk, EX.......... **800.00**
Rocker, #475, 6-slat sides, stationary bk, #d cushion, VG **1,700.00**
Rocker, #837, concave crest rail over 4 slats, decal, 39" **475.00**
Rocker, open-arm; V-bk crest rail, 6-slat, decal, 36", pr **550.00**
Rocker, open-arm; 6-slat bk, flat arms, leather uphl, decal **450.00**
Settle, #216, 7-slat bk, 2 ea end, str crest rail, mk, 72" **2,300.00**
Settle, #232, str posts/bk rail, 5 wide slats, decal, 72" **1,500.00**
Settle, #281, even arms, worn orig leather, decal, 34x76" **6,500.00**
Settle, Prairie; #220, 6 inset panels in bk/2 ea side, mk **19,000.00**
Sidebrd, #734, plate rack, 3 drw/2 doors over drw, decal **1,900.00**
Sidebrd, #738, plate rack, 2 doors flank 2 drw, 46" L............... **4,100.00**
Table, dining; #718, 5-leg, 2 leaves, no mk, rfn, 48" dia **1,350.00**
Table, dining; #720, 5-leg, 4 leaves, branded, 48" dia.............. **1,800.00**
Table, dining; #722, X-base, sq legs, 3 leaves, 48" dia.............. **1,300.00**
Table, library; #521, 1-drw, corbeled legs, mk, cleaned................. **700.00**
Table, serving; #752, 2 base shelves, arched gallery, mk......... **2,300.00**
Table, tea; #575, 24" dia top, 9" dia base shelf, rfn, VG **1,100.00**

Stickley Bros.

Bookcase, 2 8-pane doors, Quaint tag, 52x48x12" **1,600.00**
Chair, #917½, open arms, loose cushion, label, 36", VG **400.00**
Chest, #9037, 2 short drw over 3, 46x37", EX......................... **1,000.00**
Chest, swivel mirror, 2 sm drw atop, 2 half drw+3, EX **400.00**
Costumer, #187, sq post, corbelled X-stretcher base, no mk **225.00**
Desk #630, flat top, slant-lid front, 2 half drw, rfn, 38" **200.00**
Jardiniere, hammered copper, relief decor, #300, att, 19" **650.00**
Plant stand, 14" sq overhanging top, X-stretchers, tag, rfn........... **600.00**
Settle, inlaid w/flowers & leaves, 3-part bk, unmk, 52x44" **3,000.00**
Table, center; 4-leg/X-stretcher ftd base, 44" dia, VG **1,500.00**
Wastebasket, thin vertical slats, cut-out hdls, sq, 18" **1,600.00**

Stiegel

Baron Henry Stiegel produced glassware in Pennsylvania as early as 1760, very similar to glass being made concurrently in Germany and England. Without substantiating evidence, it is impossible to positively attribute a specific article to his manufacture. Although he made other types of glass, today the term Stiegel generally refers to any very early

ware made in shapes and colors similar to those he is known to have produced — especially that with etched or enameled decoration. It is generally conceded, however, that most glass of this type is of European origin. Our advisor for this category is Mark Vuono; he is listed in the Directory under Connecticut.

Bottle, fiery opal, mc florals, half-post, 4⅝" **200.00**
Bottle, pocket; amethyst, 12-dmn, minor wear/stain, 5" **3,800.00**
Bottle, pocket; dk amber, 14 swirl ribs, 4¾".............................. **800.00**
Mug, eng floral, appl ribbed hdl, w/lid, 8⅞"............................... **200.00**
Mug, eng hearts, appl hdl, 6⅝" **150.00**
Tumbler, eng bird,w /lid, 10" **225.00**
Tumbler, eng birds, 3*⅜*".. **25.00**
Tumbler, mc bird & florals, 3⅛" **185.00**
Tumbler, mold-blown panels w/eng decor rim, 5"......................... **85.00**
Tumbler, pale gr, eng flower basket, 7⅞" **175.00**

Stocks and Bonds

Scripophily (scrip-awfully), the collecting of 'worthless' old stocks and bonds, gained recognition as an area of serious interest around the mid-1970s. Today there are an estimated 5,000 collectors in the United States and 15,000 worldwide. Collectors who come from numerous business fields mainly enjoy its hobby aspect, though there are those who consider scripophily an investment. Some collectors like the historical significance that certain certificates have. Others prefer the beauty of older stocks and bonds that were printed in various colors with fancy artwork and ornate engravings. Even autograph collectors are found in this field, on the lookout for signed certificates.

Many factors help determine the collector value: autograph value, age of the certificate, the industry represented, whether it is issued or not, its attractiveness, condition, and collector demand. Certificates from the mining, energy, and railroad industries are the most popular with collectors. Other industries or special collecting fields include banking, automobiles, aircraft, and territorials. Serious collectors usually prefer only issued certificates that date from before 1910. Unissued certificates are usually worth one-fourth to one-eighth the value of one that has been issued. Inexpensive issued common stocks and bonds dated between the 1940s and 1980s usually retail between $1.00 to $10.00. Those dating between 1890 and 1930 usually sell for $10.00 to $50.00. Those over one hundred years old retail between $25.00 and $100.00 or more, depending on the quantity found. Autographed stocks normally sell anywhere from $100.00 to $1,000.00. A formal collecting organization for scripophilists is known as The Bond & Share Society with an American chapter located in New York City.

Our advisor for this category is Warren Anderson; he is listed in the Directory under Utah. In many of the following listings, two-letter state abbreviations immediately follow company name. All are in fine condition unless noted otherwise.

Key:
cp — coupon	U — unissued
I/C — issued/cancelled	vgn — vignette
I/U — issued/uncancelled	

Aggwam Canal Co, MA/1875, $500 bond, w/2 cps, U, EX............**70.00**
Amargosa Gold Mining, AZ/1905, sgn Wm Ralston, I/U **75.00**
Automotive Corp, OH/1920, logo vgn, I/U...................................**30.00**
Bl Bird Oil Corp, TX/1922, bird vgns/border, I/U **50.00**
Boston & Albany RR, NY/1904, vgn, 2 pgs cps, $1000 bond, U ...**48.00**
Central Star Gold Mining, NY/1881, star vgn, I/U **65.00**
Chicago, St Louis & Pittsburgh RR, IN/1883, train vgn, I/C.........**25.00**
Cincinnati Insurance, OH/1819, I, sgn, silked, VG **125.00**

Cincinnati RW Tunnel, OH/1872, 100 $50 shares, town vgn, I .**100.00**
Collins Wireless Telephone, District of Columbia/1909, I/U **75.00**
CSA, J Davis/Richmond vgns, 1863, w/7 cp, $1000 bond, EX.......**68.00**
CSA, Montgomery, AL/1861, $500 bond, w/9 cps, VG.................**85.00**
Globe Silver Mining, NY/1873, I/U, 5x9" **70.00**
Gold Cliff Mining, DE/1914, eagle w/shield vgn, I/U....................**17.00**
Golden Anchor Mining, AZ Territory/1907, goddess vgn, I/U **40.00**
Hancock Consolidated Mining, MI/1909, eagle vgn, I/U..............**15.00**
Heuck's Opera House, OH/1895, 3 $100 shares, I/C, sgn Heuck ...**35.00**
Internat'l Mercantile Marine, NJ/1927, ship vgn, I/U...................**10.00**
Las Vegas & Hot Springs Electric RR, NM Territory/1903, I/U..**125.00**
Little Annie Mining, CO/1892, I/U, 5x9" **90.00**
Mutual Gas Light, OH/1899, oil derrick vgn, 2½ #100 shares **55.00**
Nat'l Underground Electric, NJ/1882, state seal vgn, I/U **45.00**
Pacific States Mining, OR/1934, 3 mining vgns, I/U....................**10.00**
Palmer Tire & Rubber, IL/1917, WA capitol building vgn, I/U **15.00**
Pell Lead Mining, OH/1872, miners vgn, 15 $100 shares, I **55.00**
Portland-AZ Mining, OR/1906, 3 mining vgns, I/U.....................**30.00**
Ranger Petroleum Co, AZ/1919, refinery/oil field vgns, I/U **15.00**
Santa Lucia Mining & Milling, NY/1889, men/horse vgn, I/U **50.00**
Stonewall Jackson, 1863, CSA counterfeit $1000 bond, 14x11" ...**52.00**
Swine Breeders Pure Serum, IN/1920, 3 vgns, I/U, 9" L **25.00**
Tucker Automobiles, 100 shares, rare, M **150.00**
Universal Aerial Navigation, CA/1902, I/U, 6x10" **90.00**
Waterloo, Cedar Falls & Northern RR, IA/1951, engine vgn........**15.00**

Stoneware

There are three broad periods of time that collectors of American pottery can look to in evaluating and dating the stoneware and earthenware in their collections. Among the first permanent settlers in America were English and German potters who found a great demand for their individually-turned wares. The early pottery was produced from red and yellow clays scraped from the ground at surface levels. The earthenware made in these potteries was fragile and coated with lead glazes that periodically created health problems for the people who ate or drank from it. There was little stoneware available for sale until the early 1800s, because the clays used in its production were not readily available in many areas and transportation was prohibitively expensive. The opening of the Erie Canal and improved roads brought about a dramatic increase in the accessibility of stoneware clay, and many new potteries began to open in New York and New England.

Collectors have difficulty today locating earthenware and stoneware jugs produced prior to 1840, because few have survived intact. These ovoid or pear-shaped jugs were designed to be used on a daily basis. When cracked or severely chipped, they were quickly discarded. The value of hand-crafted pottery is often determined by the cobalt decoration it carries. Pieces with elaborate scenes (a chicken pecking corn, a bluebird on a branch, a stag standing near a pine tree, a sailing ship, or people) may easily bring $1,000 to $12,000 at auction.

After the Civil War, there was a need and a national demand for stoneware jugs, crocks, canning jars, churns, spittoons, and a wide variety of other pottery items. The competition among the many potteries reached the point where only the largest could survive. To cut costs, most potteries did away with all but the simplest kinds of decoration on their wares. Time-consuming brush-painted birds or flowers quickly gave way to more simply executed swirls or numbers and stenciled designs. The coming of home refrigeration and Prohibition in 1919 effectively destroyed the American stoneware industry. In the following listings, 'c/s' means 'cobalt on salt glaze'; all decoration described before this abbreviation is in cobalt. See also Bennington, Stoneware.

Bottle, 2-tone gray w/bl, J Melvin, 1854, 9¾", NM..................**100.00**

Bowl, stenciled design/#2, c/s, hdls, 7x11" dia **300.00**
Butter crock, brn Albany slip int, FH Cowden, 5x9" **175.00**
Churn, fish, brushed, c/s, ovoid, 16", EX **950.00**
Churn, floral, brushed, c/s, F Woodworth, ca 1860, 16½"...........**385.00**
Churn, Reed & Tyerman Marvel Butter Merger, Chicago, 1-gal.**195.00**
Cooler, woman at wishing well relief, c/s, lid, 17", EX **150.00**

Crock, and cover with floral, John Bell, Waynesburg, signed and dated 1874 under lid, 12", $1,100.00.

Crock, batter; floral spout/front, c/s, Cowden-Wilcox, EX **1,375.00**
Crock, bird on stump, c/s, Adam Caire NY, 13" **275.00**
Crock, brn & wht salt glaze, E Swasey, 1-gal, 7" **95.00**
Crock, butter; foliage, brushed, c/s, w/lid, 6½x11½", EX.............**380.00**
Crock, butter; Hamilton & Jones, stencil/freehand, c/s, 7x11" **375.00**
Crock, floral, brushed, c/s, N Clark Jr, lt stain/chip, 8¾" **200.00**
Crock, floral, lg/quilled, c/s, Ottman Bros, 11", NM...................**175.00**
Crock, flower/cactus, c/s, ES & B Newbright, ca 1890, 12" **250.00**
Crock, leaves, c/s, JF Fisher & Co, ca 1850s, 2-gal, 9¼"...............**185.00**
Crock, lg flourish, quilled, c/s, J Weaver, 14", EX **150.00**
Crock, pickle; salt glaze, ca 1870, 11½" **125.00**
Crock, singing bird on branch, c/s, Lamson & Swasey, 2-gal.......**325.00**
Crock, singing bird on stump, c/s, JA&CW Underwood, #2 ....**475.00**
Crock, singing bird on stump, c/s, Ottman Bros, 5-gal, EX **700.00**
Jar, canning; apples/grapes/#2, brushed, c/s, ovoid, 13" **200.00**
Jar, canning; brn salt glaze, JA Bishop, ca 1800, 9" **125.00**
Jar, canning; foliage, brushed, c/s, 8½", EX **95.00**
Jar, canning; foliage around shoulder, brushed, c/s, 8¾", EX........**175.00**
Jar, canning; simple design, brushed, c/s, hairline, 9" **65.00**
Jar, canning; stencil: Bierbower & Co Stoves..., c/s, 8½" **300.00**
Jar, canning; stencil: Hamilton & Jones, c/s, 9", NM..................**125.00**
Jar, canning; stenciled design, c/s, 6¾", NM...............................**125.00**
Jar, canning; str/wavy lines, brushed, c/s, 6½"..............................**160.00**
Jar, canning; stripes/vining foliage, brushed, c/s, 10", EX **200.00**
Jar, canning; 1881, brushed, c/s, chips, 8½" **170.00**
Jar, cvd swags at shoulder, c/s, Commereau's, hdls, 14", EX.........**750.00**
Jar, flower, c/s, imp Peach, hdls, ovoid, 12½", EX **500.00**
Jar, foliage around shoulder, c/s, tooling, ovoid, 14", EX..............**450.00**
Jar, leaves at shoulder, brushed, c/s, ovoid, 8", NM **150.00**
Jar, stencil & script: Hamilton & Jones/eagle, c/s, hdls, 14".........**700.00**
Jar, stencil: eagle/TF Reppert, c/s, freehand, ovoid, 20" **1,075.00**
Jar, stencil: Hamilton & Jones Star Pottery etc, c/s, 15" **725.00**
Jar, stencil: Wms & Reppert w/eagle, some freehand, c/s, 21". **1,000.00**
Jar, stripe/flower/#2, brushed, c/s, ovoid, 11" **210.00**
Jar, swags, brushed, c/s, C Crolius Mfg NY, ovoid, 12", VG.........**400.00**
Jar, tan Albany slip, lg hdl, SL Pewtress & Co, 8½" **30.00**
Jug, #2, brushed, c/s, J&S Hart, ovoid, 13", EX **250.00**
Jug, basket of flowers, c/s, Ft Edward, rpr neck, 18" **300.00**
Jug, batter; bird on branch, quilled, c/s, no lid, 9", EX **575.00**
Jug, batter; leaves/bk: tulip, c/s, Evan Jones, no lid, 9"............. **1,200.00**
Jug, bird on branch, dotted, c/s, W Roberts, 18", VG...................**800.00**

Jug, bird on branch, dotted/long tail, c/s, White's, 14", EX..........550.00
Jug, brn salt glaze, ovoid, 15"..100.00
Jug, daubs at label/hdl, c/s, Goodwin & Webster, 11", EX ...:......100.00
Jug, dk brn Albany slip, top hdl/spout/air hole, #2, 13"..................45.00
Jug, floral, c/s, S Risley, lip rpr, 14"...150.00
Jug, floral, quilled, c/s, White's Utica, 14" 325.00
Jug, floral/#3, quilled/brushed, c/s, J Shepard, 16", EX 200.00
Jug, flower (4-bloom), quilled, c/s, J Collins, 18", EX...................450.00
Jug, incised bird on branch/ME w/basket & star, c/s, 3⅝".........3,300.00
Jug, J Dearborn & Co, hairline in hdl, 11"....................................35.00
Jug, leopard on leaf, quilled, c/s, W Troy, 14", NM 3,250.00
Jug, lg decorative 2, quilled, c/s, W Troy, 13¾"..........................250.00
Jug, lg floral w/fern-like leaves, c/s, Stetzenmeyer, 2-gal.............650.00
Jug, singing bird on branch, c/s, pouring spout, 2-gal, EX 300.00
Jug, spotted bird on branch, c/s, 2-gal, EX 350.00
Jug, stencil: Hamilton & Jones, c/s, 12".....................................175.00
Jug, tree, bk: wing, c/s, Westwater & Lambright, 19", NM 650.00
Jug, tulip/#2, c/s, Cortland, 13½" 400.00
Jug, tulip/leaf, lg/bold, brn/s, Lyman & Clark, 3-gal 2,250.00
Jug, vintage, c/s, AK Ballard, pouring spout, 12", EX 500.00
Meat tenderizer, wood hdl, Pat 1877, 10", EX 90.00
Mug, emb stripes, hdl decor, c/s, John Wygand NY, 5½" 135.00
Pitcher, c/s brushed at hdl, #4, ovoid, 17"..................................115.00
Pitcher, floral, brushed, c/s, RCR Phila, hairlines, 7½"............ 1,300.00
Pitcher, floral, brushed, c/s, rim hairline, 10½"..........................700.00
Pitcher, floral, brushed, c/s, Sipe Nichols & Co, 13", EX 1,000.00
Pitcher, Hamilton & Jones, stencil/freehand, c/s, 11", NM..... 1,100.00
Pitcher, lines/Wms & Reppert, part stencil, c/s, 13", EX......... 1,400.00
Pitcher, Wms & Reppert, stencil/freehand, c/s, 10½", EX....... 1,200.00
Water cooler, 1863/bands, brushed, c/s, bbl shape, 15", EX 400.00

Store

Perhaps more more than any other yesteryear establishment, the country store evokes the most nostalgic feelings for folks old enough to remember its charms — barrels for coffee, crackers, and big green pickles; candy in a jar for the grocer to weigh on shiny brass scales; beheaded chickens in the meat case outwardly devoid of nothing but feathers. Today mementos from this segment of Americana are being collected by those who 'lived it' as well as those less fortunate! Our advisor for this category is Charles Reynolds; he is listed in the Directory under Virginia. See also Advertising.

Merrick's Spool Cotton display case, Pat 1897 on metal tag, 22", EX, $850.00.

Bag rack, wire, 6 wire shelves, 28"..48.00
Bin, coffee; tin, slant top, orig pnt, ca 1890, 19x16½x13" 355.00
Case, apothecary; pine w/pnt layers, 24-drw, dvtl, 12x28" 1,300.00
Clock, regulator, oak case, 39x18", EX 220.00
Container, tin, self-sealing, stenciled decor, 1880s, 13x8" 90.00
Desk, counter top, slant top, 2-drw, 10½x26x20", EX..................90.00
Dispenser, spice; tin & glass, Jewett & Sherman, 30x24x9" 425.00
Display case, oak fr, cash drw, 1900s, 12x22x52", EX.................450.00
Display case, oak fr, counter top, 1900s, 14x25x72", EX.............200.00
Drw, automatic cash; oak/iron, Whiting, 9x13x14", VG 450.00
Lazy susan, oak, 3-pc, w/spools, Pat 1900, 28" H 250.00
Meat slicer, Sterling #10, CI, EX 30.00
Rack, seed; wire, 6 sm bins, ca 1910, 2½x17¾x2½", M............25.00
Rack, wood w/metal hanger, orig finish, 76x20x3", EX.................90.00
Receipt holder, brass & wood, swivels, 21x14" dia, G 75.00
Receipt spike, Nat'l Cash Register 35.00
Showcase, wood/glass, slant front, CI legs, 70" L, EX 245.00
Whip holder, bent wire, minor pnt loss, 15x16" dia, VG..............65.00

Stoves

Antique stoves' desirability is based on two criteria: their utility and their decorative value. It's the latter that adds an 'antique' premium to the basic functional value that could be served just as well by a modern stove. Sheer age is usually irrelevant. Decorative features that enhance desirability include fancy, embossed ornamentation, nickel-plated trim, mica windows, ceramic tiles, and (in cooking stoves) water reservoirs and high warming closets rather than mere high shelves. The less sheet metal and the more cast iron, the better. Look for crisp, sharp designs in preference to those made from worn or damaged and repaired foundry patterns. Stoves with a pastel porcelain finish can be very attractive; blue is a favorite, white is least desirable. Chrome trim, rather than nickel, is the mark of a stove too recent to be interesting. Among stove types, base burners (with self-feeding coal magazines) are the most desirable. Then come the upright, cylindrical 'oak' stoves, kitchen ranges, and wood parlors. Potbellies approach the margin of undesirability; laundries and gasoline stoves plunge through it.

In judging condition look out for deep rust pits, warped or burnt-out parts, unsound firebricks, poorly fitting parts, poor repairs, and empty mounting holes indicating missing trim. Search meticulously for cracks in the cast iron. Our listings reflect auction prices of completely restored, safe, and functional stoves, unless indicated otherwise.

There's a thin but continuing stream of desirable antique stoves going to the high-priced Pacific Coast market. Interest in antique stoves is least in the Deep South. Demand for wood/coal stoves is strongest in areas where firewood is affordable and storage of it is practical. Demand for antique gas ranges has become strong, especially in metropolitan markets, and interest in antique electric ranges is starting to surface. The market for antique stoves is so limited and the variety so bewildering that a consensus on a going price can hardly emerge. They are only worth something to the right individual, and prices realized depend very greatly on who happens to be in the auction crowd. Even an expert's appraisal will usually miss the realized price by a substantial percent.

Base Burners

Acme Sunburst #112, Wehrle Co, Newark OH, M................. 2,900.00
Art Amherst #15, NP trim, tiles, 11" urn, 50x25x28" 1,500.00
Burdett, Smith & Co #44, Chicago, swivel top, tiles, 38"...........950.00
Detroit Emerald Jewel #14, mica doors, NP trim, 69", EX....... 2,500.00
Favorite #30, Piqua OH, ornate chrome/mica windows, 52" ... 1,600.00
Waverly #12, Thos Caffney & Co, Boston MA, 40x20x22" ... 1,350.00
Weir Glenwood #5, NP trim, mica windows, 1909, 68".............700.00

Box Stoves

A Belanger Barge No 14, scrollwork, CI, 1905, sm 150.00
BF&M Co #1, front load, early legs, 1800s, 17x13x24" 100.00
E Eaton #24, Amherst NH, schoolhouse type, 24x38x16" 350.00
Shaker, 1-pc cast body, wrought latch, 1800s, 21x35x14" 275.00
Unknown, parlor type, reeded column sides, 1830s, 25x32x17" ..400.00

Franklin Stoves

Abendroth Bros NY #13, 3-leg, water urn, dtd 1874 ....75.00
AC Barstow Parlor Franklin #5, ornate CI, 1852, 35x24x38" 300.00
Acme #18 Orient 1890, 6 tiles, mica window, fancy, 43" 300.00
Barstow #137 Orient 1886, CI fireplace, coal, 37"+6" urn...........900.00
Barstow Pat Dec 6, 1886, majolica tiles, 48x24x32" 900.00
C Newcomb & Co, Worcester, fireplace, ca 1800, 38x24x30". 1,250.00
Franklin #214, corner coal fireplace, 1910s, 31x19x24" 150.00
Magee Ideal #3, CI fireplace, 2 side trivets, 1892, 32x28" 150.00
Open Franklin #16, corner style, CI grates, 1890s, 31" 75.00
Orr, Painter & Co Sunshine Franklin #16, 1850s, 35"+9" urn 250.00
Sunny Hearth #2, coal burning, water urn at top, 1850s, 35" 250.00
Walker & Pratt Laconia, ornate CI, NP footrail, 1860s, 35" 100.00
Walker & Pratt Laconia #2, 3-leg, ornate, 1870s, 34x32x25"......150.00
Walker/Pratt Good Cheer, NP trim, 1850s, 32x27x31" 225.00
Werhle Co Newark OH Franklin Gem #16, 1890s, 43"+urn.......275.00

Parlor

AJ Coffin #4, 4 Corinthian columns, 1840s, 47"+10" urn....... 1,200.00
Anthony, Davy & Co Lady Washington, CI, 1848, 26"+7" urn..225.00
Art Amherst No 15, sq, NP trim, 6 tiles, 1880s, 50"+11" urn......750.00
Bangor Foundry & Machine Comfort No 23, CI, 33"+10" urn....150.00
Barstow...Boston MA...NY, cottage type, 1880s, 37"+8" urn 100.00
C Williams Forest No 19, CI, side door, 1870, 26"+7" urn 300.00
Co-Op Foundry Sylvan Red Cross #31, Pat 1888/'89, 37"+urn ...225.00
EG Ruggles Gr Mtn #2, willows decor, Pat 1850, 25"+7" urn 375.00
Favorite #30, ornate scrollwork, mica windows, 52"+14" urn.. 1,600.00
Fuller-Warren-Morrison Floral #2, CI, 1853, 45x22x27" 1,000.00
GH Ransom #3 Gem, ornate CI, Pat 1855, 32"+6" urn 550.00
Johnson-Cox-Fuller Home Parlor #3, CI, Pat 1852, 25+10" urn .300.00
JS&M Peckham Rosedale #23, CI, 1870s, 33"+10" dome............175.00
Low & Hicks #4, Revere Air-Tight, cathedral front, 29"+urn.....275.00
Low & Hicks Gothic #4, CI, 4 front doors, 1840s, 36"+6" urn 350.00
Modern Glenwood Wood Parlor, CI, NP trim, 1900, 42" 275.00
Morison & Manning, ornate CI column, ca 1830, 42x21x32". 2,150.00
Newberry-Filley Oven Parlor No 7, Pat 1855, 34x22x27" 200.00
Perry Stove Co Dandy #12, swivel dome top, 1889, 46"+7" urn..100.00
PP Stewart L'Hiver No 17, sq, 1 tile, NP trim, 1890s, 57" 450.00
Pratt & Perkins Organ #2, CI, slide doors, 1852, 36x22x25" 275.00
Pratt & Wentworth Peerless, tip-up top dome, 1840s, 37"............90.00
Rathbone-Sard Floral Acorn #38, NP trim, ca 1894, 37"+urn.....600.00
SH Ranson Peruvian, ornate CI, Pat 1853, 27"+13" urn 225.00
SH Ranson...Albany, CI, side door, Pat 1848, 31"+13" urn 225.00
Somersworth Machine No 20, tip-up dome top, 1850s, 39".........225.00
Tyson Furnace No 1, 2-column, 2 swing doors, 36x27x25" 250.00
Warnick & Liebrandt Union Airtight, ornate CI, 1851, 26".......200.00

Ranges (Gas)

Cribben-Sexton Univ, 4-burner, gr/cream, high oven, '27, VG ..300.00
Crystal Olive, gray, 4-burner, glass oven door, 1926, VG 400.00
Detroit Jewel, 4-burner, blk/nickel, glass oven door, 1918, VG...400.00
Magic Chef, 6-burner/2-oven, warming closet, wht, 1936, rstr. 3,500.00
Magic Chef, 6-burner/2-oven, warming closet, 1932, EX 2,000.00

Myers & Osborn, 3-burner, no oven, skeleton base, 1880, G 75.00
Weir Insulated Glenwood, 6-burner/2-oven, wht, 1931, rstr .. 3,300.00

Ranges (Wood and Coal)

Noyes & Nutter Star Kineo #8, swing NP trivets, 1906..............600.00
Portland Atlantic Grand, ornate bk shelf, 12x20x18", EX 1,700.00
Portland Ideal Atlantic #8, ornate CI, NP trim, mid-1800s ... 1,250.00
Portland Queen Atlantic, 1-shelf, simple style, 1930s 500.00
Quick Meal, bl graniteware, EX... 2,500.00
Taunton Iron Works Quaker Standard #8, side shelf, 1890s........700.00
Walker & Pratt Village Crawford Royal, NP trim, 1910s 600.00
Weir Glenwood C No 280, 2-shelf, water tank, CI, ca 1900 ....850.00
Weir Glenwood E, ornate CI, ca 1890, oven: 11x20x22" 650.00
Weir Modern Glenwood Home Grand #280, NP trim, 1910s 600.00
Wood/Bishop Home Clarion, CI, 1907, oven: 12x19x19"...........600.00
Wood/Bishop Imperial Clarion #8, 2-shelf, ornate, 1898 .... 1,500.00
Wood/Bishop Modern Clarion #8, side shelf, 1910s...................800.00
Wood/Bishop New Clarion # 8, low closet, 1882, 32x28x46" ..1,500.00
Wood/Bishop Popular Clarion, chrome trim, trivets, 1890s.........850.00

Miscellaneous

Fireplace w/grate, #116, scrollwork/tiles, 1850s, 33x25x32".........200.00
Laundry, Stamford Laundry #20, 4-ring lid, 21½x21x26" 150.00
Laundry, Walker & Pratt #14, Pat 1874, dtd 1883, 25x24x24" ...400.00
Monitor #20, Cleveland 1887, oil burning, 29x21x23"................100.00
Railroad, B&M No 5, potbelly, 1910s, 48x32x32" 300.00
Sears & Roebuck Signal Oak #22, coal burning, 42½" 110.00
Standard Lighting Globe Incandescent, kerosene, 1900, 29" 75.00

Stove Manufacturers' Toy Stoves

Buck's Jr Range, St Louis MO, new body/pnt/recast parts, 26" 850.00
Charter Oak #503, GF Filley, St Louis MO, 14x12x25, EX..... 2,050.00
Dainty, Reading Stove Works, PA, 7x13x8", VG 150.00
Great Majestic Jr, Majestic Mfg, 31x16x23, M 5,650.00
Karr Range, Belleville IL, bl porc, old model, 21½x9x13"....... 3,100.00
Little Eva, T Southard, NYC, 8½x14x11", G 350.00
Little Fanny, CI, minor rust, EX..300.00
Little Willie, CI, EX 75.00
Qualified, bl porc w/nickel, Karr, Belleville IL, 1925, EX........ 2,500.00
Qualified, bl porc w/nickel, 1960s repro, EX 2,500.00
Royal American, Bridgeford, Louisville KY, 14x12x20", G 950.00

Toy Manufacturers' Toy Stoves

Eagle, Hubley, Lancaster PA, nickeled, recast parts 450.00
Eclipse, CI, EX..175.00
Little Giant, unmk/unidentified, 7½x8½x11", EX orig 675.00
Novelty, Kenton Hdwe, bl pnt/nickel trim, rfn, 13x6½x8½".......600.00
Pet, The; Young Bros, Albany NY, 10½x6x8½" 165.00
Queen, The; unmk/unidentified, copper o/l, 23½", M 2,400.00
Rival, J&E Stevens, Cromwell CT, 14x9x16", M, +2 kettles.. 1,350.00
Rival, J&E Stevens, Cromwell CT, 1895, 13x7½x18½", G.........240.00
Triumph, Kenton Hdwe, OH, 14x8½x19", G 195.00

Strawberry Soft Paste and Lustre Ware

Strawberry lustre is a general term for pearlware and semi-porcelain decorated with hand-painted strawberries, vines, tendrils, and pink lustre trim. Strawberry soft paste is decorated creamware without the pink lustre trim. Both were made by many manufactures in England in the 19th century, most of whom never marked their ware.

Creamer, lustre, 3⅜" 200.00
Creamer, vine border, squat, 4 short legs, 3½" 300.00
Plate, pk border, mc floral w/strawberries, lt wear, 7½" 175.00
Tea bowl & saucer, vine border, EX color/design, minor wear.....400.00
Tea bowl & saucer, vine border, minor wear 275.00
Teapot, soft paste, bulbous w/bird's neck spout, Leeds, 7" 400.00
Teapot, vine border, high lip flange, 7¾", NM.............................650.00
Teapot, vine border, ovoid, prof rpr, 7" 350.00
Waste bowl, vine border, crazed/lt hairline, 3x6¼" 450.00

Stretch Glass

Stretch glass, produced from 1916 until after 1930, was made in an effort to emulate the fine art glass of Tiffany and Carder. The glassware was sprayed with a special finish while still hot, and a reheating process caused the coating to contract, leaving a striated, crepe-like iridescence. Northwood, Imperial, Fenton, Diamond, Lancaster, and the United States Glass Company were the largest manufacturers of this type of glass. See also specific companies.

Bowl, bl w/blk rims, ftd, 2¼x4¾" 25.00
Bowl, centerpc; gr, flared, 11"..35.00
Bowl, cupped, bl, 6" 20.00
Bowl, gr, Diamond, w/attached candlesticks..................................55.00
Cake server, gr, center hdl, Fenton 42.00
Candle holder, gr, Northwood, 10", pr 70.00
Candlestick, vaseline, Fenton, 8½", pr..65.00

Candle holders, blue with black base, Fenton, 10", $100.00 for the pair.

Compote, vaseline, bl trim at rim & edge of base, 4½x6½" 25.00
Compote, wht, enamel florals, Lancaster, 3¾x10".........................35.00
Compote, wht satin, knob stem, US Glass, 7" 30.00
Console set, gr w/gold, Central Glass, bowl+2 candlesticks.........135.00
Ferner, vaseline, 3-leg, 3x5" 30.00
Pitcher, lemonade; Celeste Bl, cobalt hdl, Fenton 125.00
Ring holder, yel, enamel florals, 5" dia..25.00
Server, bl, center hdl, Imperial...42.00
Sherbet, bl, ribbed...20.00
Tumbler, lemonade; wht, cobalt hdl 25.00
Vase, pk, dolphin hdls, fan form, 6" 55.00
Vase, red, flared, 7¾" 90.00

String Holders

Today, if you want to wrap and secure a package, you have a variety of products to choose from: cellophane tape, staples, etc. But in the 1800s, string was about the only available binder; thus the string holder, either the hanging or counter type, was a common and practical item found in most homes and businesses. Chalkware and ceramic figurals from the 1930s and 1940s contrast with the cast and wrought iron examples from the 1800s to make for an interesting collection. Our advisor for this category is Charles Reynolds; he is listed in the Directory under Virginia.

Beehive, CI, counter style, 5½x6½", EX orig 65.00
Bell shape, gr glass, counter top, tin bottom, 5¾", EX 145.00
Bird, yel on gr string nest, ceramic 30.00
Boy w/top hat & pipe, chalkware, EX pnt.....................................40.00
Cat's face, ceramic 12.00
CI w/emb leaves, shaped as compote w/lid & tall finial, 10" 75.00
Girl w/hat, chalkware, EX pnt...45.00
SSS for the Blood, CI caldron, 7x5", EX 150.00
Strawberry w/face, chalkware, EX 30.00

Sugar Shakers

Sugar shakers (or muffineers, as they were also called) were used during the Victorian era to sprinkle sugar and spice onto breakfast muffins, toast, etc. They were made of art glass, in pressed patterns, and in china. See also specific types and manufacturers.

Bubble Lattice, blue opalescent, $200.00.

Apollo, etched, orig top..80.00
Apple Blossom, Northwood 145.00
Baby Invt T'print, amberina, SP lid, 8½" 300.00
Beauty, red flashed, orig ornate lid..325.00
Bulging Loops, bl cased..450.00
China, floral spray, pk/wht on wht, no mk 55.00
Chrysanthemum Base Swirl, wht speckled 145.00
Cone, pk cased, tall 175.00
Cone, yel cased, glossy, squatty 150.00
Cranberry, flower/butterfly (EX enamel), ribbed cylinder, 6" 500.00
Flower & Pleat, clear/frosted 135.00
Forget-Me-Not, pk opaque, Challinor 145.00
Quilted Phlox, bl opaque...195.00
Reverse Swirl, canary opal..140.00
Rubena, Invt T'print, 5½"..200.00
Wht satin w/gr shamrocks & bl dots, Dithridge 135.00
Windows, bl opal..235.00

Sunderland Lustre

Sunderland lustre was made by various potters in the Sunderland district of England during the 18th and 19th centuries. It is characterized by a splashed-on application of the pink lustre, which results in an effect sometimes referred to as the 'cloud' pattern. Some pieces are transfer printed with scenes, ships, florals, or portraits.

Bowl, Loss of Gold Is Much/CI Bridge..., Moore, 9", EX..............350.00
Bowl, Sailor's Farewell, blk transfer, Dixon, 7", VG...................145.00
Chamber pot, comic verse, blk transfer, frog w/in, 7x9", EX........700.00

Jug, ode to an English barge, sailing ship transfer, 1842, 9", $650.00.

Jug, Com MacDonnough's Victory, bk: 2nd View, 9½"........... 4,000.00
Jug, Enterprise & Boxer/US & Macedonia in gr, 4⅜".............. 1,800.00
Jug, transfer of ship/ode to English Bark, 1842, 10".....................650.00
Jug, Wasp Boarding Frodic/Constitutions..., 6", EX................. 1,900.00
Jug, West View of Iron Bridge/ship, att Garrison, 9", EX 275.00
Mustard pot, cloud pattern, 4", NM..150.00
Plaque, Prepare To Meet..., blk transfer, CC&Co, 6¾" dia 175.00
Plate, blk transfer verse, pk/copper lustre & mc, late, 8x9".........300.00
Punch bowl, florals/birds of paradise, mk Imperial Faience..........275.00
Vase, emb design w/pk lustre & mc, sm edge flakes, 6¾" 175.00

Surveying Instruments

The practice of surveying offers a wide variety of precision instruments primarily for field use, most of which are associated with the recording of distance and angular measurements. These instruments were primarily made from brass; the larger examples were fitted with tripods and protective cases. These cases also held accessories for the instruments, and these can sometimes play a key part in their evaluation. Instruments in complete condition and showing little use will have much greater values than those that appear to have had moderate or heavy use. Instruments were never polished during use, and those that have been polished as decorator pieces are of little interest to most avid collectors.

Abney level, K&E, top compass, w/case 175.00
Abney level, K&E, w/case, ca 1910 ....75.00
Alidade, folding sight vanes, leather case 45.00
Alidade, telescopic, exploration type, 10".................................225.00
Alidade, telescopic, w/post, ca 1910 ....250.00
Barometer, pocket-watch type, w/case, 1½" dia.............................60.00
Barometer, w/magnifier, 'surveyor's aneroid,' 4" dia 150.00
Chain, Chesterman Sheffield, 100-ft..125.00
Chain, Chesterman Sheffield, 4-pole/66-ft.................................210.00
Chain, Grumann's patent...250.00
Chain, Gurley, 4-pole/66-ft..225.00
Chain, K&E, convertible type, 50- & 100-ft................................200.00
Circumferentor, 4 vanes, ca 1810 .... 1,250.00
Clinometer, leather case, 1890s..75.00
Compass, B Pike & Son, plain 450.00
Compass, B Platt, vernier, 1870s..450.00
Compass, Chandlee, plain, ca 1810 .... 1,250.00

Compass, France, brass housing, 5"..75.00
Compass, geologist's, w/inclinometer needle, 4" sq 100.00
Compass, pocket type, wooden housing, 3" 55.00
Compass, prismatic, leather case, 1900s......................................95.00
Compass, Randolph, telescopic vernier 400.00
Compass, staff, folding sight vanes..110.00
Compass, W&LE Gurley, solar, w/case & tripod, 1890s.......... 2,450.00
Compass, W&LE Gurley, vernier, ca 1880s, 15".........................450.00
Compass, Wm J Young No, railroad type....................................550.00
Compass, wooden, 1810s, 12"..750.00
Cross staff head, simple type w/4 slits, w/case 100.00
Cross staff head, w/top-mt compass..120.00
Drawing instruments, K&E, 12x8" tray, wooden case 150.00
Drawing instruments, leatherette roll, 10" 25.00
Drawing instruments, 8 items in wooden case, 5x8" 75.00
Jacob's staff, oak w/steel tip, octagonal 120.00
Level, Bostrom, unused, w/case & tripod....................................120.00
Level, dumpy, Brunson, blk pnt 125.00
Level, dumpy, K&E, 18"..150.00
Level, farmer's drainage type, simple, 10", w/box & tripod 120.00
Level, hand, peep, w/bubble, 6" L, w/leather case 35.00
Level, wye, architect's convertible, 12"......................................275.00
Level, wye, builder's, 12" telescope 110.00
Level, wye, CG King, ca 1855, 14"...450.00
Level, wye, Gurley, ca 1880, 18"..350.00
Level, wye, Gurley #18345, 22"..350.00
Level, wye, Phelps & Gurley, 24"..950.00
Level, wye, Spencer, London, w/compass 550.00
Level, wye, Stackpole Bros, ca 1870, 16"...................................425.00
Plumb-bob, mining type w/wick & gimbals, in box.......................450.00
Plumb-bob, w/internal reel..110.00
Pocket transit, Brunton, Wm Ainsworth, 1893............................110.00
Semi-circumferentor, Am, all brass, ca 1800............................ 1,250.00
Semi-circumferentor, Am, wooden w/brass sights 950.00
Theodolite, Buff & Buff, 8" horizontal circle 1,250.00
Theodolite, English, 1700s..950.00
Theodolite, Fauth & Co, 16" horizontal circle 3,250.00
Theodolite, Wm Wurdemann #2 —, 12" telescope................... 1,050.00
Transit, blk pnt, ca 1930 ....225.00
Transit, Bostrom, K&E, Leitz, builder's type, ca 1930 ....150.00
Transit, convertible, solar-mining, complete 1,850.00
Transit, exploration type, ca 1890s, 8" H..................................450.00
Transit, K&E, bent-std design, ca 1910 ....550.00
Transit, lt mountain, ca 1900 ....450.00
Transit, mining, w/dbl telescope...750.00
Transit, W&LE Gurley, Troy NY, #1235 ....450.00
Transit, W&LE Gurley, Troy NY, ca 1860................................600.00
Transit, w/Burt solar attachment... 1,200.00
Transit, w/side-mt solar attachment, ca 1910.............................850.00
Transit, w/top-mt solar attachment, ca 1900.............................950.00
Transit, Wm J Young Maker Phila..600.00
Transit, Young & Sons, #9405...375.00
Tripod, compass type, 1-pc legs 75.00
Tripod, transit type, 1-pc legs 75.00
Tripod, transit type, telescopic legs 45.00
Tripod, w/alidade table..150.00

Syracuse

Syracuse was a line of fine dinnerware which was made for nearly a century by the Onondaga Pottery Company of Syracuse, New York. Collectors of American dinnerware are focusing their attention on reassembling some of their many lovely patterns. In 1966 the firm became officially known as the Syracuse China Company in order to better identify with the name of their popular chinaware. By 1971 dinnerware geared for use in the home was discontinued, and the company turned to the manufacture of hotel, restaurant, and other types of commercial tableware.

Apple Blossom, cup & saucer 36.00
Apple Blossom, gravy boat 75.00
Apple Blossom, plate, salad 18.00
Arcadia, bowl, vegetable; w/lid...88.00
Arcadia, cup & saucer 22.00
Arcadia, gravy boat...65.00
Arcadia, plate, dinner...25.00
Arcadia, plate, salad 16.50
Arcadia, platter, 12" 45.00
Arcadia, platter, 16" 65.00
Baroque Gray, bowl, vegetable; w/lid, sm...............................38.00
Baroque Gray, plate, dinner..25.00
Baroque Gray, plate, salad; 8"..18.00
Bombay, coffeepot..98.00
Bombay, cup & saucer 32.00
Bombay, plate, dinner...22.00
Bombay, soup, rimmed..27.50
Bracelet, cup & saucer 42.00
Bracelet, plate, bread & butter 18.00
Bracelet, plate, dinner..35.00
Brantley, gravy boat..65.00
Briarcliff, bowl, vegetable; oval 40.00
Briarcliff, plate, dinner 22.00
Calypso, complete set for 8, MIB 185.00
Carvel, bowl, vegetable...55.00
Carvel, plate, dinner; 10" 28.00
Carvel, platter, 16" 85.00
Celeste, cup & saucer 35.00
Celeste, plate, salad 16.50
Coralbel, cup & saucer, Winchester shape 35.00
Coralbel, gravy boat..55.00
Coralbel, plate, dinner; 10¼" 30.00
Coralbel, platter, 14" 50.00
Countess, bowl, vegetable; rnd..42.00
Countess, gravy boat...45.00
Countess, platter, lg 55.00
Coventry, bowl, vegetable; oval 35.00
Coventry, bowl, vegetable; w/lid 60.00
Coventry, bowl, 6¼" 10.00
Coventry, creamer & sugar bowl 30.00
Coventry, cup & saucer 15.00
Coventry, gravy boat 50.00
Coventry, plate, dinner..20.00
Coventry, plate, luncheon 15.00
Coventry, plate, salad 10.00
Coventry, platter, 12" 36.00
Coventry, platter, 14" 55.00
Edmonton, bowl, vegetable; w/lid 95.00
Governor Clinton, cup & saucer...36.00
Governor Clinton, plate, dinner...22.00
Governor Clinton, platter, 12"..45.00
Jefferson, bowl, vegetable; w/lid 95.00
Jefferson, coffeepot...98.00
Jefferson, cup & saucer 32.00
Jefferson, platter, 12" 65.00
Madame Butterfly, bowl, vegetable; oval 27.50
Madame Butterfly, plate, bread & butter 14.50
Meadow Breeze, plate, bread & butter 15.00

Meadow Breeze, plate, salad 16.50
Monticello, bowl, vegetable 55.00
Monticello, cake plate 45.00
Monticello, cup & saucer 35.00
Monticello, gravy boat...55.00
Monticello, plate, dinner..28.00
Romance Maroon, plate, bread & butter 15.00
Romance Maroon, plate, dinner; 9¾" 30.00
Rose Marie, bowl, salad 16.00
Rose Marie, bowl, vegetable 45.00
Rose Marie, plate, dinner 20.00
Rose Marie, platter, 16" 75.00
Selma, cup & saucer 32.00
Selma, plate, salad...16.00
Sherwood, cup & saucer 35.00
Sherwood, platter, med sz 45.00
Stansbury, bowl, vegetable; 10½x8" 50.00
Stansbury, cup & saucer 32.00
Stansbury, gravy boat...60.00
Suzanne, cup & saucer 35.00
Suzanne, gravy boat, attached tray 50.00
Suzanne, plate, bread & butter 15.00
Suzanne, plate, dinner 28.00
Suzanne, platter, 14" 14.00
Sweetheart, plate, dinner; Silhouette 30.00
Woodbine, bowl, 6½" 14.00
Woodbine, cup & saucer 18.00
Woodbine, plate, dinner...18.00
Woodbine, plate, 8" 8.00
Woodbine, shakers, pr 16.00

Syrups

Values are for old, original syrups. Beware of reproductions! See also various manufacturers and specific types of glass.

Apple Blossom, milk glass 195.00
Banded Portland, rose flashed, very scarce..............................395.00
Block Band, marigold flashed, George Duncan, 1880s................195.00
Bulging Loops, yel cased...750.00
Bulging Midriff, vaseline 165.00
Catherine Anne, milk glass..65.00
Coin Spot, bl opal, ring neck, dtd lid.......................................175.00
Cone, bl 155.00
Cord & Tassel 125.00
Coreopsis, red satin...350.00
Cornell Tarentum..75.00
Crysanthemum Base Swirl, wht speckled 195.00
Dewdrop, Findlay, scarce 95.00
Eyewinker 125.00

**Flat Flower, light blue opaque, 5½",
$245.00.**

French Primrose, milk glass	65.00
Frosted Artichoke, orig spring lid	145.00
Guttage, pk cased, metal lid	295.00
Hexagonal Block, ruby stained	235.00
Hobnail, bl, pewter lid, dtd	245.00
Kokomo, orig spring lid	65.00
Leaf Umbrella, mauve cased, pewter lid, rare	800.00
Lincoln Drape, flint, eagle emb on tin lid	200.00
Millard, plain, ruby stained	195.00
Moon & Star, orig tin lid, rare	135.00
Nail	65.00
Netted Oak, milk glass, gold decor	115.00
Optic, rubena, Hobbs	175.00
Patee Cross	65.00
Pomona, w/fish, pewter lid, 6½"	465.00
Priscilla	135.00
Prize	150.00
Riverside's Brilliant, ruby flashed, EX	275.00
Robin's Nest	125.00
Rubena to clear, ribbed, clear hdl, 6"	145.00
Seneca Loop, appl strap hdl, orig hinged pewter lid	85.00
Seneca Loop, flint, appl strap hdl, dtd pewter lid	145.00
Snail, brass lid	95.00
Star & Punty, wide strap hdl	475.00
States	70.00
Strawberry Patch, milk glass	65.00
Sunburst & Block	50.00
Torpedo	75.00
Torquay, milk glass w/yel stripes	135.00
Torquay, pigeon blood	850.00
Utah, tin lid	78.00
Venetian Dmn, vaseline & wht spatter, rare	185.00
X-Ray, gr w/EX gold, rare	400.00
Zipper, allover cuttings	95.00

Target Balls

Prior to 1880 when the clay pigeon was invented, blown glass target balls were used extensively for shotgun competitions. Approximately 2¾" in diameter, these balls were hand blown into a three-piece mold. All have a ragged hole where the blowpipe was twisted free. Target balls date from approximately 1840 (English) to World War I, although they were most widely used in the 1870-1880 period. Common examples are unmarked except for the blower's code — dots, crude numerals, etc. Some balls are embossed in a dot or diamond pattern so they were more likely to shatter when struck by shot, and some have names and/or patent dates. When evaluating condition, bubbles and other minor manufacturing imperfections are acceptable; cracks are not. The prices below are for mint condition examples.

Black Pitch, CTB Co	250.00
Bogardus' Glass Ball Pat'd April 10 1877, amber	250.00
Bogardus' Glass Ball Pat'd April 10 1877, other than amber	800.00
Emb ribs, amber	150.00
English, shooter emb in 2 rnd panels, clear	300.00
English, shooter emb in 2 rnd panels, gr	300.00
English, shooter emb in 2 rnd panels, purple	300.00
For Hockey's Patent Trap, gr	500.00
Great Western Gun Works, amber	900.00
Gurd & Son, London, Ontario, amber	500.00
Ira Paine's Filled Ball Pat Oct 23 1877, amber	250.00
Ira Paine's Filled Ball Pat Oct 23 1877, amber set of 10	950.00
Ira Paine's Filled Ball Pat Oct 23 1877, other than amber	800.00

NB Glass Works Perth, other than pale gr	300.00
NB Glass Works Perth, pale gr, almost clear	200.00
Plain, amber	65.00
Plain, clear, w/mold marks	1,000.00
Plain, cobalt	150.00
Plain, purple	150.00
WW Greener St Mary's Works Brim/68 Haymarket London	250.00

Related Memorabilia

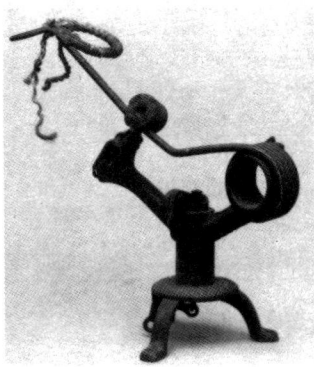

Double glass ball thrower in old red paint, M.E. Card, Pat'd May 7, 78, and April 22, 79, VG, $900.00.

Clay birds, Winchester, Pat May 29 1917, 1 flight in box	100.00
Pitch bird, blk, DUVROCK	1.00
Shell, dummy, w/single window, any brand	25.00
Shell, dummy shotgun, Winchester, window w/powder, 6"	125.00
Shell set, dummy, Gamble Stores, 2 window shells, 3 cut out	125.00
Shell set, dummy, Winchester, 5 window shells	150.00
Shell set, dummy shotgun, Peters, 6 window shells+full box	150.00
Shotshell loader, rosewood/brass, Parker Bros, Pat 1884	50.00
Target, Am sheet metal, rod ends mk Pat Feb 8 '21, set	25.00
Target, blk japanned sheet metal, Bussy Patentee, London	50.00
Target, BUST-O, blk or wht breakable wafer	20.00
Trap, DUVROCK, w/blk pitch birds	150.00
Trap, MO-SKEET-O, w/birds	150.00

Tea Caddies

Because tea was once regarded as a precious commodity, special boxes called caddies were used to store the tea leaves. They were made from various materials: porcelain, carved and inlaid woods, and metals ranging from painted tin or tole to engraved silver. Our advisor for this category is Tina Carter; she is listed in the Directory under California.

Blk lacquer w/much inlaid brass, cut glass bowl w/in, 14"	1,000.00
Burl walnut, coffer form, bracket base, brass liners, 8" L	200.00
Burl walnut w/mc star inlay on lift lid, 1800s, 15" L	200.00
Burled walnut, hinged sloping lid, 1850s, 6x8"	275.00
Elm, grpt, faceted dome lift top, 1800s, 11" L	150.00
Fruitwood, pear form, foil lined, England, 1800s, 7", EX	1,400.00
Ivory w/silver & MOP inlay, 10-sided, Geo III, 1830	1,500.00
Mahog, presentation dtd 1843, 2-compartment, 7" L	150.00
Mahog, 2 lift-out caddies+mixing bowl w/in, 7" L	175.00
Mahog, 3-part, spoon compartment, orig hdw, rpr, 10" L	225.00
Mahog veneer, brass inlay, minor damage/rpr, 5"	150.00
Mahog w/figure, floral inlay lid & int lid, ivory knobs, sm	400.00
Mahog w/line inlay, Chinese export jar w/in, English, 6"	275.00
Quillwork, figured wood/inlay, gilt edge, ivory mts, 7", VG	300.00
Rosewood w/satinwood inlay, paw ft, coffered top, 13" L	750.00
Soft paste w/bl floral, sm flakes/lid rpr, 5¾"	145.00
Tortoise shell w/MOP floral inlay, Oriental form, ivory ft	2,400.00

Tea Leaf Ironstone

Tea Leaf Ironstone became popular in the 1880s when middle-class American housewives became bored with the plain white stone china that English potters had been exporting to this country for nearly a century. The original design has been credited to Anthony Shaw of Longport, who decorated the plain ironstone with a hand-painted copper lustre design of bands and leaves. Originally known as Lustre Band and Sprig, the pattern has since come to be known as Tea Leaf Lustre. It was produced with minor variations by many different firms both in England and the United States. By the early 1900s, it had become so commonplace that it had lost much of its appeal. Our advice for this category comes from Home Place Antiques, whose address is listed in the Directory under Illinois.

Baker, rectangular, Meakin, 8¾x6½" 20.00
Bone dish, Crescent, Meakin...65.00
Bowl, Apple, Shaw, ftd...435.00
Bowl, rectangular, Wedgwood, 9½" 42.00
Bowl, soup; Lily of the Valley..45.00
Bowl, soup; Wedgwood, 9", EX 22.50
Bowl, sq, scalloped, Wedgwood, 9¾" 45.00
Bowl, vegetable; Bamboo, w/lid, Meakin.................................130.00
Bowl, vegetable; Daisy, w/lid, Wilkinson...................................95.00
Bowl, vegetable; Fish Hook, bracket ft, w/lid, Meakin 130.00
Bowl, vegetable; plain, rectangular, w/lid, Wedgwood.............100.00
Bowl, vegetable; sq, pagoda hdls, w/lid, Wedgwood, 11x7".........145.00
Bowl, vegetable; w/lid, Davenport 275.00
Butter dish, Fish Hook, w/lid & drain, Meakin, EX 145.00
Butter dish, sq, w/lid & drain, Wedgwood, 5½", EX................155.00
Butter pat, sq, Meakin, 2¾" 15.00
Cake plate, Bamboo, sq, hdls, Meakin 55.00
Coffeepot, Fish Hook, Meakin, sm..165.00

Coffeepot, Anthony Shaw & Sons, 10",
$185.00.

Creamer, Bamboo, Meakin, 5⅛" 135.00
Creamer, Fish Hook, Meakin, 5x5½".......................................135.00
Creamer, Lily of the Valley blank, child's.................................195.00
Cup & saucer, C-shape hdl, Shaw, 3⅛x3½" 80.00
Cup & saucer, handleless; Lily of the Valley, child sz 125.00
Cup & saucer, handleless; Meakin, 3x3½" 90.00
Doughnut dish, Edge Malkin...435.00
Egg cup, dbl; (Boston) 195.00
Gravy boat, Bamboo, Meakin, EX..65.00

Gravy boat, Fish Hook, Meakin 70.00
Pitcher, Bamboo, Grindley, 7¼" 185.00
Pitcher, milk; Blanket Stitch, Alcock, 8¾" 125.00
Pitcher, Sq Ridged, Wedgwood, 7¾" 140.00
Plate, Meakin, 10" 30.00
Plate, Meakin, 8¾", EX 12.50
Plate, Mellor-Taylor, 9" 22.50
Plate, Wedgwood, 9" 20.00
Plate, Wheat, Elsmore & Forster, 7¾" 22.50
Platter, rectangular, Meakin, 11x8", EX 47.50
Platter, rectangular, Meakin, 12x8½", EX..................................55.00
Platter, rectangular, ribbed, Wedgwood, 12" 60.00
Sauce dish, rnd, Wedgwood, 5" 20.00
Sauce dish, sq, ribbed corners, Meakin, 4¼" 17.50
Sugar bowl, Bamboo, w/lid, Grindley, EX.................................75.00
Sugar bowl, Bamboo, w/lid, Meakin, 6¾" 65.00
Sugar bowl, Fish Hook, w/lid, Meakin, 6½x6".........................85.00
Sugar bowl, Lily of the Valley, Shaw, 5½x6½".........................135.00
Teapot, Chinese shape, paneled, Shaw, late 1850s 250.00
Teapot, Red Cliff 80.00
Teapot, Wedgwood, 8x8½"...185.00
Tureen, sauce; Bamboo, w/lid & underplate, Meakin, 8" 230.00
Tureen, sauce; Fish Hook, w/lid, Meakin.................................135.00

Teapots

The custom of drinking tea has resulted in the production of many tea-related collectibles; the most popular is the teapot. The first teapots were manufactured in the Chinese village of Vi-Hsing during the late 16th century and were no bigger than the tiny cups previously used for tea drinking. Amazingly these same tiny teapots are still being used today.

A wide range of teapots can be found by the avid searcher; those most readily available today were produced from about 1870 to the present. Several books have been written solely devoted to teapots, although most are out of print. An Anthology of British Teapots by Philip Miller and Michael Berthoud is an extensive work with over 2,000 photographs; it is currently available from Micawber Publications, The Lawns, Church Street, Brosely, Shropshire TF12 5DG for £ 24.95. Another is titled The Eccentric Teapot; it is written by Garth Clark and is available at your local bookstore.

Almost every pottery and porcelain manufacturer in Europe as well as in America has produced teapots. Some are purely functional, others decorative and whimsical. Refer to various manufacturers' names for further listings. Our advisor for this category is Tina Carter; she is listed in the Directory under California.

Automobile, gr glaze, no mk, 8" L 300.00
Dbl spout, earthenware, slip decor, ca 1890................................80.00
DM mk, Japan, coralene dragon, 6-cup......................................22.00
Ellgreave, Wood & Sons, England, ironstone w/floral...................35.00
Flow blue, man sits w/legs outstretched, conical hat, 8x9" 60.00
Germany, Royal Hanover, gr lustre, HP, 6½" 75.00
Germany, Royal Honover, gr lustre, HP, 6½", +cr/sug................140.00
Grimwades, Royal Winton, England, cozy set, floral hdls 55.00
H&K England, Old English Sampler, 6-cup, EX.........................45.00
HW&Co England, Wreath, ca 1895-1902....................................98.00
Japan, rooster w/gold specks, head creamer/neck sugar, 9" 28.00
Japan, Tea for Two, man in tux hdl, girl in gown forms pot...........45.00
Ming Tea Co, made in Japan, w/label, 1½-cup............................18.00
Monterey, made in CA, pk spatter, lg..25.00
Noritake, mk M, HP Japan, yel w/flowers, tall, 2-cup.................25.00
Pyrex mk, blown glass, etched flowers, 6-cup............................45.00
S Derbyshire, England, barge, brn, emb mk, lg 75.00

Sadler, pk w/sm flowers, oval, mk, 6-cup...**35.00**
Spode's Tower, England, bl/wht transfer, London shape, VG **45.00**
Sutherland, England, silver lustre, mk, 6-cup **60.00**
SYP, 'Simple Yet Perfect,' brn earthenware, ca 1905....................**95.00**
SYP, Wedgwood, bone china, bl/wht/gold, ca 1905-06.............**110.00**
Tank, gr w/silver details, Made in England, 8½" L **200.00**
US Zone, Germany, cat figural, paw spout, blk/gray/cream, 9" **40.00**
Wade, mk, HP, +matching cr/sug **55.00**
Wales CM, Charles & Diana, brn pottery, 2½" **78.00**
Walt Disney Productions, Snow White w/Dwarfs, musical **50.00**
Wedgwood, Jasperware, bl/wht, ca 1784, 2-cup.........................**210.00**
WS George, yel w/gold, rnd, mk, 6-cup, EX **20.00**

Teco

Teco artware was made by the American Terra Cotta and Ceramic Company, located near Chicago, Illinois. The firm was established in 1886 and until 1901 produced only brick, sewer tile, and other redware. Their early glaze was inspired by the matt green made popular by Grueby. 'Teco Green' was made for nearly ten years. It was similar to Grueby's yet with a subtle silver-gray cast. The company was one of the first in the United States to perfect a true crystalline glaze. The only decoration used was through the modeling and glazing techniques; no hand painting was attempted. Favored motifs were naturalistic leaves and flowers. The company broadened their lines to include garden pottery and faience tiles and panels. New matt glazes (browns, yellows, blue, and rose) were added to the green in 1910. By 1922 the artware lines were discontinued; the company was sold in 1930.

Values are dictated by size and color of glaze with examples in colors other than green bringing the higher prices. High-gloss glaze is seldom seen and expensive. Teco is usually marked with a vertical impressed device comprised of a large 'T' to the left of the remaining three letters.

Bowl, gr, emb floral, #136, 9" **125.00**
Bowl, gr w/charcoal, 2x3" **180.00**
Jardiniere, gr, stylized iris, 4 foliate hdls, ftd, 9¾".................... **1,700.00**
Mug, gr, horizontal ribs, bar-like hdl, 4" **250.00**
Mug, gr w/charcoal, emb woven band, 6" **325.00**
Pitcher, gr, bulbous, flared rim extends to form hdl, 3½" **250.00**
Pitcher vase, gr, waisted cylinder w/side-swept hdl, 8¾" **475.00**
Pot or lamp base, gr, 4 lg buttress ft, #271, 8x10", EX............. **2,300.00**
Vase, dk gray/gr gloss, tulip mold, #423, 11" **800.00**
Vase, dk rust gloss, Moreau design, #420, 13" **900.00**
Vase, gr, angular shoulder, orig label, #366, 4½" **250.00**
Vase, gr, bulbous top on flaring cylinder, #285, 6½" **350.00**
Vase, gr, bulbous w/wide shoulder, #76, 6" **250.00**
Vase, gr, buttress hdls, #441, 6" **1,900.00**
Vase, gr, cylinder flares to wider bottom, 13½x4" **650.00**
Vase, gr, elongated pear w/4 upright buttresses, 7", NM..............**500.00**
Vase, gr, rim-to-shoulder hdls, F Albert design, 9" **600.00**
Vase, gr, rolled-in rim on elongated pear, #392, 7½"....................**400.00**
Vase, gr, short neck on swollen cylinder, #194, 8" **350.00**
Vase, gr, tapered cylinder w/flared rim, #165, 8" **350.00**
Vase, gr, triangular mouth, bulbous body w/rings, #360, 4¾".......**250.00**
Vase, gr, wavy rim, bulbous bottom, #233, 5", NM **170.00**
Vase, gr, 4 top-to-bottom uprights form hdls at neck, 7", NM.. **1,100.00**
Vase, gr, 4 upright straps at slightly recessed neck, 11" **1,800.00**
Vase, gr, 4-lobe mouth & long neck, bulbous base, 17" **1,100.00**
Vase, gr semigloss w/charcoal, thick angle hdls, #425, 3½" **500.00**
Vase, gr w/charcoal, concentric rings, rolled lip, 4x4"..................**290.00**
Vase, gr w/charcoal, 4 t'print sides, #210A, 3x3" **200.00**
Vase, gr w/feathering, waisted cylinder, sm rim, #347, 6" **375.00**

Vase, gray, cylinder w/neck recessed behind 4 uprights, 13".... **1,900.00**
Vase, lt brn crystalline, wht body, experimental, no mk, 3½" **90.00**
Vase, pk, 3 lobes in wide rtcl bottom & neck, 3-ftd, 9".............**600.00**
Vase, pumpkin, 4 upright bars around recessed neck, 8x6"...... **2,000.00**
Wall vase, gr, Oriental-design sq top, disk bottom, 7x6".............**400.00**

Teddy Bear Collectibles

The story of Teddy Roosevelt's encounter with the bear cub has been oft recounted with varying degrees of accuracy, so it will suffice to say that it was as a result of this incident in 1902 that the teddy bear got his name. These appealing little creatures are enjoying renewed popularity with collectors today. To one who has not yet succumbed to their obvious charms, one bear seems to look very much like another. How to tell the older ones? Look for long snouts, jointed limbs, large feet and felt paws, long curving arms, and glass or shoe-button eyes. Most old bears have a humped back and are made of mohair stuffed with straw or excelsior. Cute expressions, original clothes, a nice personality, and, of course, good condition add to their value. Some Steiff bears in mint condition may go as high as $100 per inch. Steiff are easily recognized by the trademark button within the ear. For further information we recommend *Teddy Bears, Annalee's & Steiff Animals* by Margaret Fox Mandel, available from Collector Books. See also Toys, Steiff.

Key: jtd — jointed

Bears

Steiff, fully jointed, glass eyes, embroidered nose, like new condition, 16", $2,500.00.

American, jtd, mohair, button eyes, felt pads, 1900s, 15", G **300.00**
American, jtd, mohair, rpl button eyes/pads, ca 1910, 28", VG ..**500.00**
American, jtd, mohair, straw stuffed, ca 1910, 32", VG **600.00**
American, jtd, mohair, straw stuffed, 1920s, 20", VG **300.00**
American, jtd, red flannel, glass eyes, 1915, 15½", EX **400.00**
Bing, honey mohair, button eyes, rpl pads, 15", EX **1,750.00**
Clemens, fully jtd, tan mohair, glass eyes, 18", EX **325.00**
Fetcher, long mohair, jtd, glass eyes, open mouth, 22", EX..........**100.00**
Fully jtd, beige mohair, hump, straw stuffed, 14", EX **385.00**
Fully jtd, gold mohair, long nose, button eyes, 24" **575.00**
Fully jtd, yel wool, glass eyes, velvet pads, 11", EX **225.00**
German, jtd, hump, button eyes, excelsior, 1900s, 15", EX **375.00**

Growler, jtd, mohair, hump, embr nose/mouth, old, 32" 695.00
Gund, jtd, brn mohair, 85th Anniversary, tags, 8", M................125.00
Hermann, fully jtd, swivel head, long tan mohair, '50s, 16", M ...400.00
Hermann, fully jtd, wht mohair, plastic eyes, 1979, 12", M 125.00
Ideal, fully jtd, gold mohair, button eyes, 1903, 16½" 725.00
Ideal, fully jtd, gold mohair, glass eyes, 1920s, 19", VG 350.00
Ideal, fully jtd, swivel head, gold mohair, 1905, 14", EX 525.00
Japan, jtd, mohair, flannel paws, glass eyes, '20s, 15", G 135.00
Jtd arms, blk mohair, eyes light up, 9-volt battery, 10", NM........235.00
Merrythought, jtd, gold mohair, glass eyes, 1950, 20", NM 300.00
Roosevelt Bear, jtd, growler, glass eyes, Columbia, 26", EX 500.00
Schuco, brassy gold mohair, perfume insert, 5", M 685.00
Schuco, caramel mohair, W Germany tag, 2½", M....................250.00
Schuco, gold mohair, glass eyes, wind-up, 1930s, 14", EX 1,100.00
Schuco, yes/no Bellhop, tan mohair/red/blk felt, 1930s, 9" 435.00
Smokey the Bear, orig hat, belt & badge, 1950s, EX 65.00
Steiff, baby, brn, orig collar/bell, US Zone tag, 12", M.................965.00
Steiff, cinnamon mohair, steel eyes, 1908, 15", EX................1,900.00
Steiff, ginger mohair, hump, embr snout, 1911, 19", EX..........2,700.00
Steiff, gold mohair, button/tag, 3½", M 335.00
Steiff, gold mohair, growler, glass eyes, button, 1920s, 24" 3,000.00
Steiff, mohair, growler, button, on wheels, 14", G 850.00
Steiff, mohair, hump, growler, glass eyes, 20", EX....................500.00
Steiff, mohair, squeaker, button eyes, button, 1905, 10".........2,250.00
Steiff, panda, felt pads, chest tag, orig ribbon, 1948, 6"...............800.00
Steiff, plush mohair, button eyes, button, 1910, 17", M 3,200.00

Related Memorabilia

Book, Roosevelt Bears, Their Travels & Adventures, 1906, EX 85.00
Book, Roosevelt Bears Abroad, 11 color plates, EX 85.00
Cup & saucer, bears write on fence, ceramic 65.00
Puppet, teddy w/blk ears, embr nose, Chad Valley, 10", M..........120.00
Tea set, teddy bears play soccer, Japan, 1920s, 16-pc 575.00
Tip tray, Roosevelt Bears, advertising, 1906, NM 395.00

Telephones

Since Alexander Graham Bell's first successful telephone communication, the phone itself has undergone a complete evolution in style as well as efficiency. Early models, especially those wall types with ornately carved oak boxes, are of special interest to collectors. Also of value are the candlestick phones from the early part of the century and any related memorabilia.

Century double box oak telephone, $475.00; Western Electric dial candlestick, 12", $225.00; Telephone sign, blue/white porcelain, 11" x 12", VG, $200.00; American Electric oak double box phone, 31", EX, $500.00.

American Electric, oak, wall type, swivel mouthpc, G...............500.00
American Telecom, 1972, EX......................................35.00
American Telephone & Telegraph, candlestick, 1915, EX 125.00
Automatic Electric, dial, 1950s 22.50
Automatic Electric, 3-slot coin-op, EX..........................175.00
Bell System, candlestick, operator's issue.......................85.00
Danish French, Bakelite, 1913, EX 65.00
Kellogg, metal, dial wall type..................................85.00
Kellogg, oak, wall type, EX....................................200.00
National Cash Register, EX.....................................125.00
North Electric, Cleveland, oak, wall type 265.00
Stromberg-Carlson, Bakelite, cradle style, 1920s...............37.50
Stromberg-Carlson Mfg, candlestick............................95.00
Utica Fire Alarm, nickeled brass, candlestick 195.00
Vought Berger Co, LaCross WI..................................400.00
Western Electric, brass, candlestick w/dial....................225.00
Western Electric, oval base, non-dial cradle style..............45.00

Blue Bell Paperweights

First issued in the early 1900s, these bell-shaped glass weights were used by telephone company employees to prevent stacks of papers from blowing off their desks in the days of overhead fans. Over the years they have all but vanished — some carried off by retiring employees, others broken. The weights came to be widely used as advertising by individual telephone companies; and as the smaller companies merged to form larger companies, more and more new weights were created. They were widely distributed with the opening of the first transcontinental telephone line in 1915. Note: the weight marked Opening of Trans-Pacific Service, Dec. 23, 1931, in peacock blue glass is very rare, and the price is negotiable. For further study we recommend *Blue Bell Paperweights* by Jacqueline Linscott; she is listed in the Directory under Florida.

Bell System C&P Telephone Co & Assoc Companies, ice bl......225.00
Bell System New York Telephone, peacock.......................95.00
Bell Telephone Company, cobalt...............................150.00
Missouri & Kansas Telephone Company, peacock.................100.00
No embossing, cobalt...50.00
No embossing, ice bl...45.00
Pays 7% Mountain States Telephone, peacock 150.00
Southwestern Bell Telephone Company, peacock 175.00
Southwestern Telegraph & Telephone Company, peacock.........300.00
Western Electric Company, peacock 100.00

Related Memorabilia

Blotter, Bell System Yellow Pages 10.00
Booth, Western Electric, wooden, EX...........................595.00
Lantern, Bell System, red globe................................38.00
Pin, celluloid, long distance logo.............................22.00
Sign, Bell System, porc, flanged, roped bell, 16x16", G 145.00
Sign, Local & Long Distance, porc over steel, flange, 17x18" 225.00
Sign, Western Electric, brass, 4x15"...........................50.00

Telescopes

Old telescopes are still appreciated for the quality of the workmanship and materials that went into their production. Some of the more elaborate styles were covered in leather or ebony and the 'draws' or extensions were often brass.

Bardou & Son for US Navy, 1-draw, 30 power, 27", EX 225.00
Gregory & Wright London, mahog, 10-sided, 1-draw, 26", EX ..500.00

J Chapman London, mahog tube, 1-draw, sliding shutters, EX 100.00
L Casella, brass, cabriole-leg stand, 4 lens, mahog case............ 1,500.00
Mahog, 10-sided, 1-draw, reverse tapered, early, 25", EX.............325.00
Mahog tube, 1-draw, 28", NM...210.00
Ross of London, 1-draw, rpl leather wrap, 25", EX 700.00
US Navy, bronze, 16 power, Wollensak, WWII, 31" 180.00
Wood, brass mts, 1-draw, octagon bbl, 1700s, 33".........................450.00

Televisions

Collectible TV's are becoming popular. Those made prior to WWII (circa 1925-1940) often sell for up to $4,000.00 and more! Unusual wood and Bakelite sets from the '40s are worth $20.00 to $300.00; metal sets and those with square cabinets usually sell for under $100.00. Large screen TV's (over 14") are still poor sellers in most markets. Our advisor for this category is Harry Poster; he is listed in the Directory under New Jersey.

Admiral, wooden, 1950s, 14" sq or larger...40.00
Admiral #20A1, #20X1, or similar 10" set.......................................75.00
Air King #A-2001 or #A-2002, 12" 40.00
Andrea #CO-VK12 or #CO-VJ12, 12" combination 50.00
Ansley, projecting set, end-table style...50.00
Automatic #1649 or similar 16" 40.00
Belmont #18DX21, table top, 7" 125.00
Bendix Model #235, push-button table top, 10" 75.00
CBS-Columbia, blk & wht, 1950s, 12" or larger 40.00
Crosley #307-TA, basically a RCA #630 type 10" table top........175.00
Crosley #9-407, 1949, 12" table top 75.00
DuMont #RA-101, mid-1940s, 15" console.....................................50.00
Emerson #545, wooden 10" table top..125.00
Emerson #654, sq 12" console 40.00
Fada #880, Deco-style projection console.....................................300.00
Fada #899, 10" console 125.00
Garod #1220 or #1230TVP, 12" combo..85.00
Garod #3192, 12" combination 55.00
General Electric #806 or #807, wooden 10" table top 75.00
Hallicrafters #T68, projection console..100.00
Motorola #VT-105, stepped top, 10" table top..............................150.00
Philco #48-1050, 10" console, scarce 200.00
Pilot #TV-37, 1947, 3" table top..125.00

1947 Pilot Radio TV37, 3" screen, $200.00.

Raytheon #M1201, 12" porthole table top 100.00
RCA #8TS30, 10" table top 120.00
Sentinel #412, 10" 35.00
Sparton, sq cabinet, 15" or larger 50.00

Tele Tone #TV-149, 7" W table top 100.00
Westinghouse #H-840-CK15, 1954, 15" color console 375.00
Zenith, porthole combination, ca 1948-50, ea................................75.00

Teplitz

Teplitz, in Bohemia, was an active art pottery center at the turn of the century. The Amphora Pottery Works was only one of the firms that operated there. (See Amphora.) Art Nouveau and Art Deco styles were favored, and much of the ware was hand decorated with the primary emphasis on vases and figurines. Items listed here are marked 'Teplitz' or 'Turn,' a nearby city. Our advisor for this category is Jack Gunsaulus; he is listed in the Directory under Michigan.

Bowl, Deco flower baskets on textured ivory, sgn, 4x7" 650.00
Compote, emb Nouveau florals w/gold, hdls, mk PD, 8x14"........950.00
Ewer, grapes, red on mottle, bulbous, Stellmacher, 10" 95.00
Ewer, HP azaleas, pierced bands/collar, foliate hdl, 9½".............265.00
Vase, appl cupid on gr to lav, dbl hdls, rtcl, 16" 395.00

Vase, bust portrait and flowers on green with gold trim, #468, 11", $1,400.00.

Vase, floral, cobalt & wht on bl, gargoyle on neck, mk, 17" 685.00
Vase, lobster, orange on metallic gray, 3 rim hdls, RSK, 8" 220.00
Vase, poppies, orange on gr w/gold, ewer form, 17", pr 495.00
Vase, portrait, HP bl & wht florals, RS&K mk, 6" 395.00
Vase, 3-D Bacchus bust, rock formation behind, Wahliss, 10" . 1,200.00

Terra Cotta

Terra cotta is a type of earthenware or clay used for statuary, architectural facings, or domestic articles. It is unglazed, baked to durable hardness, and characterized by the color of the body which may range from brick red to buff.

Bust, Louis XIV, verde marble base, 1800s 280.00
Bust of child, after 1700s model, sgn, onyx socle, 12" 175.00
Bust of Salome, HP, sgn F Hartmann, 1900, 19½" 1,225.00
Garden figure, girl w/book, old pnt, metal base, 32"....................950.00
Jardiniere, Oriental dragon relief, 14¼x12¼x7¼" 55.00
Teapot, emb ribbing, ribbed strap hdl w/leaf ends, 6", NM 375.00
Vase, Egyptian motif, WS&S, English, 12" 125.00

Thermometers

The big news in thermometer collecting is the opening of the

American Thermometer Museum in Baker, California, in the Fall of 1992. It will be the largest of its kind in the world.

Though the collecting of advertising thermometers has been popular for years, only recently have decorative thermometers come into their own as bona fide items of interest and value. Indoor and outdoor decorative models have been manufactured for hundreds of years, yet their relative scarcity enhances their value and interest for the collector. Most American thermometers manufactured early in the 20th century were produced by Taylor (Tycos), and today their thermometers remain the most plentiful on the market.

Insofar as sheer beauty, uniqueness, and scientific accuracy, decorative thermometers are far superior to the ordinary and inexpensive versions which carry advertising. Decorative thermometers run the gamut from plain tin household varieties to the highly ornate creations of Tiffany and Bradley and Hubbard. They have been manufactured from nearly every conceivable material — oak, sterling, brass, and glass being the favorites — and have tested the artistry and technical skills of some of America's finest craftsmen. Ornamental models can be found in free-hanging, wall-mounted, or desk/mantel versions.

Thermometer prices are based on age, ornateness, and whether mercury or alcohol is used as the filler in the tube. Thermometers with damaged, missing, or substitute parts bring greatly reduced prices. Paper scales indicate either replacement of a broken metal scale or a device of lower quality.

Virtually all American-made thermometers available today as collectors' items were made between 1875 and 1940. The Golden Age of decoratives ended in the early 1940s as modern manufacturing processes and materials robbed them of their natural distinctiveness. European thermometers, because of their scarcity and fine workmanship, have almost doubled in price over the last eighteen months. Our advisor for this category is Warren Harris; he is listed in the Directory under California.

Key:
br — brass
F & C — Fahrenheit & Celsius
F & R — Fahrenheit & Reamer
mrc — mercury
pmc — permacolor
sc — scales
stl — stainless

Adam Kilt, desk; br portico/scallop roof, F&R sc/mrc, 4½" **95.00**
Alexandre, folding; F&R sc, mrc, 1850s **320.00**
Anonymous, desk; picture fr w/glass, mrc, 1902, 7" **115.00**
B Mumser, desk; cast/cathedral, months rotate/mrc, 12" **2,600.00**
Bargess Reversible Box, br sc, oak case, mrc, 5½" **80.00**
Bearskin Ltd, desk; fluted base, br, br sc, 6" **450.00**
Bearskin Ltd, wall; metal clip, rnd mcr, 1930, 3x4" **300.00**
Blk/Starr/Frost, desk; barometer, stl, F&C sc, mrc, '10, 11" **1,850.00**
BLT-Luce, desk; figural, flared base, br w/br sc, mrc, 6" **220.00**
Bradley & Hubbard, desk; br/ornate lion, br sc/mrc, 9", VG **95.00**
Bradley & Hubbard, scroll bk, steel/cb, Mensh, mrc, 8" **290.00**
Brown Penzance, desk; brn marble, ivory sc, mrc, 6" **210.00**
Capendium, desk; handmade br/porc fr, F&C sc, rnd mrc, 4" **850.00**
Casella London, wall; maxi/minimum, 2 units, wood, plastic sc .**260.00**
CE Lange, kitchen; The Modern Thermometer, tin, pmc **165.00**
Cheshire Silversmiths, desk; br candelabra, mrc, 1875, 10" **4,500.00**
Chester, desk; stl sc, sterling bezel, mrc, 2x6" **140.00**
Clark, desk; ivory ped, crown, mrc, 1904, 7" **295.00**
Cloister, inkwell; stl bk & base w/angels at side, 1901 ....**975.00**
Creswel, travel; ivory case/mirror, removable sc, mrc, 2½" **2,800.00**
CW Wilder...NH, bear & billboard br figural, mrc, 6½" **165.00**
CW Wilder...NH, desk; Deco women, br F sc, mrc, 8" **750.00**
Desk, cvd walrus tusk, 2-tier disk base, inlay sc, 1860, 9" **300.00**
Desk, Spirit of St Louis, dragon, br F sc/mrc, '01, 6" **1,650.00**
Diamond, wall; br F sc on wood, rare, 7½x1½" **400.00**
E Berman Co, desk; br/filigree/top scrollwork, mrc, 8" **180.00**

Freeborn, desk; bronze w/lead decors/br sc, mrc, 8" **75.00**
G Barnes, oak fold-out box, Bakelite sc, mrc, 2½"....................**120.00**
G Cooper, desk; bell shape w/cupola, sterling, dial, 2x3" **100.00**
Gloucester Scientific, stl case, glass front, pmc, 42" **1,200.00**
Golub, hanging; mahog/br bulb cap, lg sc/red spirit, 9x2" **130.00**
H Lauramark, hanging; gold stipple on boxwood, 0-120, mrc **130.00**
Harriman, P, desk; br ped on griffin, mrc, 9" **150.00**
Hiergelsell Bros, indoor; cabinet/oak bk, bl liquid, #159 ....**90.00**
Hohmann Maurer Co, steel F&C sc & bk, mrc, 12" **80.00**
Honeywell, desk; Bakelite bell base, dial sc, 1935, 3" dia............**320.00**
J Needle, desk; figural, calendar, br w/porc sc, mrc, 6" **130.00**
J Waldstein, wall; br R sc on wood, mrc, 1900s, 10½"................**780.00**
Jed Sirrah, hanging; silver, umbrella, mrc, 8".............................**210.00**
Jedseth Ltd, desk; Mercury figure w/base filigree, mrc, 7"............**150.00**
Jockomo IN, desk; sterling face/br sc, mrc, 1904, 6" **140.00**
Nova Products, desk; glass cover over bronze sc, 4" **35.00**
Nova Products, desk; rnd, glass encased, dial sc, Pat 1923............**75.00**
Orchard, iron case, br face, w/glass intact, 14" **75.00**
Pairpoint, desk; sterling picture fr, mrc, 1907, 5"........................**220.00**
Pairpoint, mantel; br, w/angel, sterling sc/mrc, 1904 ....**325.00**
Phila Therm Co, hygrometer; br sc, rotating bezel, 1928 ....**40.00**
Reau, desk; ornate blk bronze, wood F&C sc, mrc **57.00**
Reau, desk; sq incline base, floral top, mrc, 1895 ....**180.00**
S Mitzutani, alabaster ped, candle figural atop, mrc, 15"..............**80.00**
Short & Mason, recording drum; copper case, 1910.......................**75.00**
Slouche, desk; alabaster ped, paper sc inset, mrc, 8x2½"...............**75.00**
Standard, for Fairbanks & Co, rnd, br case, 1886, 7"....................**90.00**
Standard, hanging; rnd, br rim, -40 to 150, dial...........................**40.00**
Standard, wall; br case, dial counterbalance, 1885, 9".................**110.00**
Standard, wall; ivory F sc on ebony, mrc, 9" **375.00**
Taylor, hanging; ornate wood bk, br sc, 10x7" **50.00**
Taylor, hanging; pnt wood, red spirit, 6x24"................................**50.00**
Taylor, lady's profile, cvd wood, emb Art Deco, 20½", EX **195.00**
Taylor, wall; blk enameled case, F&R sc on stl, mrc, 12" **35.00**
Taylor, wall; octagonal wood fr/metal sc, red liquid, 5" **45.00**
Thermindex, Switzerland, desk; Bakelite stand, F sc, 5" **530.00**
Thomas Wright, desk; octagon, pot metal, F&C sc, 5x3" **190.00**
Tiffany, desk; horoscope, bronze, mrc, 1907, 4x7" **86.00**
Tycos, incubator hygrometer; glass reservoir, 4x4"........................**16.00**
Tycos, maxi/minimum, japanned tin/br, mrc, T-5452, 8" **85.00**
Tycos-Taylor, outdoor wall; wood fr, red liquid, 27x5".................**55.00**
VJD Inc, wall; clip, br F sc, mrc tube, 4" **640.00**
Vogue, desk; Victorian, dial, gr, 1931 ....**25.00**
W Pratt, desk; wood inlays, ivory sc, mrc, 1900, 6" **90.00**
Warren Foundries, wall; umbrella w/dragon hdl, br sc, mrc, 12"..**220.00**
WG Loveday, wall; Clearside, metallic F sc, 5" dia......................**400.00**
White & Westall, wall; wht Bakelite F sc, mrc, 7"........................**330.00**
Whitehead & Hoag, Lambrecht's Polymeter, wall; mrc, 9" **890.00**
Wise, desk; Tunbridge, twin columns, mrc, 1870, 5" **1,250.00**
Zeradatha, desk; cast metal, dial w/rotate sc, 1926, 7" **43.00**

Tiffany

Louis Comfort Tiffany was born in 1848 to Charles Lewis and Harriet Young Tiffany of New York. By the time he was eighteen, his father's small dry goods and stationery store had grown and developed into the world-renowned Tiffany and Company. Preferring the study of art to joining his father in the family business, Louis spent the next six years under the tutelage of noted artists. He returned to America in 1870 and until 1875 painted canvases that focused on European and North African scenes. Deciding the more lucrative approach was in the application of industrial arts and crafts, he opened a decorating studio called Louis C. Tiffany and Co., Associated Artists. He began seriously experimenting with glass, and eschewing traditionally painted-on details, he instead learned to produce glass with qualities that could suggest natural textures and effects. His experiments broadened, and he soon concentrated his efforts on vases, bowls, etc. that came to be considered the highest achievements of the art. Peacock feathers, leaves and vines, flowers and abstracts were developed within the plane of the glass as it was blown. Opalescent and metallic lustres were combined with transparent color to produce stunning effects. Tiffany called his glass Favrile, meaning handmade.

In 1900 he established Tiffany Studios and turned his attention full time to producing art glass, leaded-glass lamp shades, and household wares with metal components. He also designed a complete line of jewelry which was sold through his father's store. He became proficiently accomplished in silverwork and produced such articles as hand mirrors embellished with peacock feather designs set with gems and candlesticks with Favrile glass inserts.

Tiffany's work exemplified the Art Nouveau style of design and decoration, and through his own flamboyant personality and business acumen he perpetrated his tastes onto the American market to the extent that his name became a household word. Tiffany Studios continued to prosper until the second decade of this century when due to changing tastes his influence began to diminish. By the early 1930s the company had closed.

Serial numbers were assigned to much of Tiffany's work, and letter prefixes indicated the year of manufacture: A-N for 1896-1900, P-Z for 1901-1905. After that, the letter followed the numbers with A-N in use from 1906-1912; P-Z from 1913-1920. O-marked pieces were made especially for friends of relatives; X indicated pieces not made for sale.

Our listings are primarily from the auction houses in the East where Tiffany sells at a premium. We have recently been advised that the once - uncertain Tiffany market seems to have stabilized. Our advisor for Tiffany lamps is Carl Heck; he is listed in the Directory under Colorado.

Bronze

Ash stand, Artichoke, ash tray cage w/match holder, adjusts **850.00**
Ash stand, overlapping leaves on rnd base, #1651, 17" **800.00**
Ash stand, ribbed disk base, knop std, gold dore, #1695, 32" **750.00**
Blotter ends, Zodiac, #988, EX patina, 19½" L, pr......................**160.00**
Bowl, lobed, everted scalloped rim, gilt patina, 6¾".....................**220.00**
Box, cigar; Byzantine, 12 'malachite' inserts (EX), 7x7".........**1,760.00**
Box, glove; Pine Needle, filigree over gr slag, 13½" L **1,650.00**
Box, Grapevine, filigree over cream slag, gilt patina, 7x7"...........**500.00**
Box, jewelry; Pine Needle, amber slag, worn lining, 9" L............**825.00**
Candelabrum, 3 cups ea side stem w/snuffer, #1290, 15", pr...**5,000.00**
Candelabrum, 6 branch arms, 3-prong cup, snuffer, 16" **2,500.00**
Candlestick, Bamboo, spreading root base, #1205, 10", pr **2,600.00**
Candlestick, Queen Anne's Lace, cup w/appl pulls, 21", EX ..**2,200.00**
Candlestick, rtcl cup w/blown-in gr glass, #1213, 21", pr **1,900.00**
Candlestick, rtcl cup w/blown-in gr glass, #21466, 13", pr **1,400.00**
Candlestick, rtcl cup w/blown-in gr glass, #21466, 17", pr **1,750.00**
Candlestick, rtcl cup w/glass, spiral-ftd 3-leg scd, 10"..............**1,300.00**
Candlestick, slim std w/3 legs, ea w/root ft, 13", pr **3,000.00**
Candlestick, stem w/6 acanthus fronds, gilt, #1210, 10", pr.....**1,750.00**
Clock, desk; Grapevine, w/gilt & cream slag glass, 4¾" **1,200.00**
Clock, desk; Modelled, w/key, #1121, 6"...................................**1,100.00**
Clock, mantel; w/gilt & gr patina in recesses, #1870, 9½".......**1,800.00**
Desk set, Abalone, w/gilt, inkwell/pen tray/box/letter file **850.00**
Desk set, Pine Needle, w/gr glass, letter file/pen tray/box **1,000.00**
Desk set, 9th Century, w/bl & gr jewels, inkwell+7 pcs...........**2,400.00**
Frame, geometric border, w/gilt & burgundy enamel, 12x10" .**3,850.00**
Frame, Gothic motif, w/gilt, #1674, 18x13" **2,400.00**
Frame, Grapevine, w/gr glass, #947, 9½x7¾" **1,650.00**
Frame, Grapevine, w/gr glass, 7½x6½" **1,300.00**

Gilt-bronze 'Gothic' picture frame, #1674, $2,400.00.

Frame, Heraldic, burgundy w/silver trim, #2064, 11½x9" **3,000.00**
Frame, 9th Century, w/bl & gr jewels, #1697, 8x6½" **3,000.00**
Inkwell, leaf relief border, mc irid glass mosaic, 3", VG **3,700.00**
Letter rack, Zodiac, #1030, EX patina, 8x12" **350.00**
Paperweight, figural owl, gilt patina, 3" **1,000.00**
Paperweight, gold irid turtle-bk tile on ftd gold dore fr **935.00**
Pen tray, Grapevine, w/gr glass, 9" L **110.00**

Glass

Bottle, dresser; peacock bl satin, stick neck, 7½" **1,700.00**
Bowl, amber, stretched border, 8" **525.00**
Bowl, amber w/appl yel & gold swirls, shouldered, 5" H **950.00**
Bowl, Bl Pastel, eng grapes, 2x6" **500.00**
Bowl, Bl Pastel, ftd, everted rim, 6" **330.00**
Bowl, feathers, gr/wht opal/gold, flaring sides, 3½x8" **900.00**
Bowl, gold, intaglio leafy vine, ribbed, scalloped, 10" **1,100.00**
Bowl, gold, ribbed, undulating rim, 10½" **770.00**
Bowl, gold, ribbed/ruffled, 6" **220.00**
Bowl, gr/gold irid, wht/gold outer band, 3 shell ft, 10" **850.00**
Bowl, Pk Pastel, quilted wht to pk, folded rim, ftd, 12½" **1,300.00**
Candlestick, enameled cup, bl pencil std, bronze base, 12" **1,200.00**
Compote, dk bl, stretched border, baluster stem, 4x6" **1,400.00**
Compote, gold on amber, EX highlights, tall slim std, 6" H........**650.00**
Cordial, gold, ogee form w/relief 'rattails,' 2¼" **225.00**
Decanter, gold, cut w/swirling facets, ball stopper, 10" **1,100.00**
Dish, Pk Pastel, stretched rim, 6¾" **220.00**
Flower frog, dbl, gold, 3¾"..**175.00**
Liqueur, pulled decor, wht on amber, cut amber stem, 4½".........**110.00**
Medallion, bl, Victory 1918, eagle/bell, bronze rim, 2¾" **700.00**
Plate, Amethyst Pastel, paper label, 8½" **500.00**
Plate, Bl Pastel, octagonal, 10¾"..**350.00**
Punch cup, gold w/lily pads **650.00**
Quill holder, dk bl w/silver flames, metal bud finial, 1¾" **2,400.00**
Salt cellar, gold w/purple highlights, ruffled, 2¾"........................**175.00**
Salt cellar, master; bl irid, 2½" dia **400.00**
Tazza, bl-gold, baluster stem, 3½" **400.00**
Tazza, Tel el Amarna, feathers/zigzag gr/bl band on wht, 6" **2,000.00**
Tumbler, gold, etched vintage wreath at rim................................**700.00**
Vase, amber w/int dots & zippers, 8¾" **1,300.00**
Vase, bl irid, melon-rib bulb base, expanding neck, 3½".............**900.00**
Vase, bl irid, ribbed, ftd, 11¾" **2,000.00**
Vase, bl irid, ribbed gourd form, 4" **825.00**
Vase, bl irid, sm can neck, wide cylinder body, 2¼"....................**425.00**
Vase, bl irid, 12-rib trumpet form, 8½" **1,350.00**

Vase, bl irid w/dk pulled stems, trumpet form, 6" 1,100.00
Vase, bl trumpet form in gilt bronze mt w/pnt feathers, 17" 3,000.00
Vase, bl-gold w/gr irid swirls, 6½" 2,000.00
Vase, blk matt w/4 irid bl feathers, spherical, 3¾" 1,760.00
Vase, bud; bl w/silver irid, invt funnel form, 10" 950.00
Vase, bud; gold, 10 swirl ribs, stick neck, 8½" 700.00
Vase, bud; gold, 23-rib, elongated stick neck, 12½" 1,300.00
Vase, bud; swirls, irid cobalt/gold on gr, stick neck, 9¾" 1,300.00
Vase, cobalt irid, tumpet form, knob above disk ft, 10" 750.00
Vase, Cypriote, bl-blk metallic on gr, gold 'leaves,' 6½" 10,000.00
Vase, dbl feathers, gr/gold on opal, gold int, 3" 1,500.00
Vase, dk burgundy w/appl bl chains, bl int, 3¼x4¾" 2,300.00
Vase, dk/lt pk, wht/gr tulip cup in gilt bronze stem, 18" 7,500.00
Vase, Egyptian, gold loops/feathers over red, blk rim, 10" 18,000.00
Vase, feathers, gold/bl on red, tiny neck, 3½" 4,500.00
Vase, feathers, gr & gold on oyster, trumpet form, 15" 1,695.00
Vase, feathers, gr on amber, 2¾" 1,100.00
Vase, feathers, gr w/amber tips, lt amber swirls, 6½" 900.00
Vase, feathers, silver/rose/aqua irid on dk bl to blk, 3½" 3,000.00
Vase, feathers (top & base) on wht, strong colors, 8¾" 2,700.00
Vase, feathers emb on gold, rnd bottom w/flared rim, 10"...........550.00
Vase, feathers/swags/triangles, gold on yel irid, #A1199, 9"..... 2,800.00
Vase, floriform; amber, pk/silver pulls, elongated cup, 10" 1,100.00
Vase, floriform; bl irid, #531K, 14¾" 3,300.00
Vase, floriform; bl irid, gold int, 10-rib swirl, ftd, 9" 1,300.00
Vase, floriform; bl irid, 8-rib elongated cup, 14¾" 3,300.00
Vase, floriform; Bl Pastel, morning-glory body, 6¾"....................700.00
Vase, floriform; bl w/gr hearts & vines, flat rim, 9" 2,400.00
Vase, floriform; clear/opal/gold/gr ruffled top, 12", EX............. 1,200.00
Vase, floriform; feathered cup & ft, wht/gr on clear, 12" 3,000.00
Vase, floriform; feathers, gr/amber/wht, shallow bowl, 11" 2,300.00
Vase, floriform; feathers, gr/wht/amber, elongated bowl, 18"... 5,500.00
Vase, floriform; gold, flared/scalloped/ribbed bowl, 13" 1,650.00
Vase, floriform; gold on amber, bulb cup, knop stem, 10"........ 1,400.00
Vase, floriform; gold w/gr hearts & vines, flat rim, 8¾" 1,750.00
Vase, gold, dimpled ovoid, 2⅜" 440.00
Vase, gold, dimpled ovoid w/irregular pinched rim, 5¾" 990.00
Vase, gold, elongated/narrow/ftd, 12½" 700.00
Vase, gold, ribbed oval w/8 dimples, scalloped, 3½" 500.00
Vase, gold, trumpet form, on gilt-bronze dome base, 17" 1,400.00
Vase, gold, 12-rib, trumpet form, ped ft, 13½" 1,000.00
Vase, gold on amber, dbl gourd w/vertical ribs, 5" 600.00
Vase, gray irid, reddish int, ribbed cylinder, 7" 850.00

Vase, hearts/vines, gr on gold, bulbous w/can neck, 5¾" 1,300.00
Vase, jack-in-pulpit; gold/orange irid, stretched rim, 19" 6,000.00
Vase, leaves, gr on amber w/EX irid, funnel form, 10" 650.00
Vase, leaves/blossoms, wht/gr on gold, globular, 34" 1,700.00
Vase, loops/waves in purple-bl & gold, gold collar, 5x6" 1,900.00
Vase, medial chain band, gr on gold, wht int, 6" 1,200.00
Vase, millefiori flowers/leaves, red/gr/wht on gold, 7"............. 2,300.00
Vase, pulls/hooks, gr/gold on gold/wht, gilt int, 2" 800.00
Vase, swirls, gold/amber/wht/brn, dbl gourd, early, 9x7" 2,300.00
Vase, 10 vertical gr ribs over wht w/gold, 11x4½" 1,000.00

Lamps

Base, gold w/intaglio gr leaves & vines, rnd ft, 14" 1,600.00
Base, Nasturtium, 2-lite, gourd form, w/finial, 17" 3,500.00
Base, oil canister, spherical on rnd base, 4-ftd, 12" 2,600.00
Base, oil canister, urn form, 3-arm, #9893, 17" 1,100.00
Base, 3-arm, bl pnt floral border, 4-paw ft, #24, 20" 1,800.00
Base, 3-arm, rnd dome base on 5 ball ft, #27420, 19" 2,200.00
Base, 4-arm, ovoid on 4 legs w/rnd beaded base, 14"................ 1,200.00
Bridge, gr irid 10" leaf-cut bowl shade; #425 std, 56" 6,750.00
Candle, bl irid ruffled shade; tall twist std, drilled, 12" 2,300.00
Candle, feathered tube in gold swirl std; gold shade, 15" 1,750.00
Candle, gold, jeweled ball in 3-prong cup in base, 16" 2,400.00
Candle, gold, ruffled shade; tall swirl std, drilled, 18" 850.00
Candle, gold, ruffled shade; twist std, Gorham insert, 13" 880.00
Candle, gold ribbed egg-form shade; bronze bamboo std, 12".. 1,900.00
Candle, pulled feather gold irid shade; sgn/#2412, 17", pr 650.00
Chandelier, ldgl acorn-band dome, 6-light fixture, 21" 7,500.00
Chandelier, ldgl leaf-band crowned dome shade, 24" 8,500.00
Desk, beaded bronze shade w/2 turtlebk tiles; jeweled base 3,500.00
Desk, gold damascene 7" bowl shade w/in harp std #9533, 17". 4,100.00
Desk, gold damascene 7" shade; counterbalance std #417, 22". 7,500.00
Desk, gr damascene 7" bowl shade w/in harp std #419, 13" 3,850.00
Desk, linenfold 10" 12-panel frosted shade; #604 std, 17" 6,500.00
Desk, pulled/hooked 7" irid shade; bronze on pottery std 3,000.00
Desk, Zodiac, turtlebk tile in harp-supported fr, rpl, 14".......... 4,500.00
Desk, Zodiac rondels on gilt base, 6-side mica shade 1,650.00
Desk, 2 pk turtlebk tiles in triangular shade; #9842 std 4,000.00
Floor, counterbalance; irid ripple 10" shade, 5-ftd std, EX....... 5,500.00
Floor, gold damascene 10" shade w/in harp std #428, 55"........ 4,800.00
Floor, ldgl 25" curtain-border shade; std #264, 70" 16,000.00
Floor, sm ball shade w/turtlebk jewels on 55" 4-ftd pole 8,000.00
Floor, tan 10" damascene shade w/in harp; 3-leg #423 std....... 4,500.00
Lily, 10-light, ribbed shades w/EX irid; #381 std, 22"..............30,000.00
Lily, 3-light, gold shades; #319 3-stem base, 13" 3,500.00
Lily, 3-light, gold shades; gold-dore std #310, 13" 4,000.00
Reading, gold 10-rib bell shade w/in harp std #424, 18" 1,650.00
Reading, 5-panel gold shade hangs w/in harp std, 14" 2,250.00
Shade, amber linenfold, 12-panel, #10256, 5x10" 3,000.00
Shade, Arabian, bright gr w/rows of gold dots, conical, 7"....... 1,250.00
Shade, feathers, bl/yel/brn on yel, 4".....................................650.00
Table, damascene 12" gold/wht striated shade; bamboo std..... 4,000.00
Table, ldgl 12" acorn-band shade; Am Indian std #536, 17" .. 4,500.00
Table, ldgl 14" 6-dragonfly shade; std #337....................18,500.00
Table, ldgl 14" 6-dragonfly shade; 12-rib std #617, 1930s 10,000.00
Table, ldgl 16" acorn-band shade; 4-leg canister std #11406 ... 7,100.00
Table, ldgl 16" dogwood shade (EX); 3-arm std #25778, 18" .11,500.00
Table, ldgl 16" Greek Key-border shade; std #534, 22" 11,000.00
Table, ldgl 16" jeweled feather conical shade; unsgn std 5,500.00
Table, ldgl 16" pomegranate-band shade; std #533, 22" 10,500.00
Table, ldgl 18" brickwork shade w/metal tag; turtle bk std 10,000.00
Table, ldgl/turtlebk tile 16" brickwork shade; tiles in std........23,000.00
Table, linenfold 14" shade (EX); 6-arm std #589, 22"............. 8,000.00

Vase, green with vertical black and gold feathered stripes, intaglio rim border, R-1605, 7½", $2,750.00.

Pottery

Ewer, bone bsk, corn mold, 'husk' hdl, rpr/chip, 11x5" 1,100.00
Jar, berry branches, thin moss gr, ovoid, w/lid, 9" 2,200.00
Vase, bands of rings at rim/shoulder/base, grs/yel, 21" 1,650.00
Vase, bl/gr/purple gloss, 6", EX 475.00
Vase, milkweed pods, cylindrical, Bronze Pottery, 7" 1,650.00
Vase, oxidized copper-gr glaze, ribbed ovoid, 16" 2,850.00

Silver

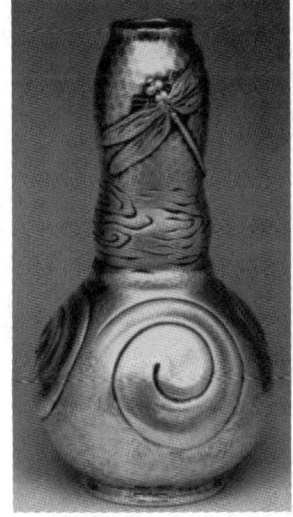

Vase, Japanese style, applied dragon-fly and water beetle, 12", $7,500.00.

Asparagus tongs, arabesque design, monogram, 1855, 10½" 400.00
Bowl, foliage/fruit band, 1900, 4¾", +matching tray....................650.00
Bowl, lengthy inscription dtd 1953, 4¾x11" 800.00
Cake plate, etched Deco florals, 1937, 10½" 350.00
Cigar box, Celtic design, monogram on lid, mahog lined, 7" .. 1,700.00
Coffeepot, fluted w/hammered bottom, appl pendants, 1890 .. 3,500.00
Dish, triangular w/rnded sides, 3-ftd, monogram, 9", EX.............125.00
Dresser set, bl enamel on wavy ground, 1920s, 10-pc.............. 1,100.00
Flask, pocket; eng/emb dog on rocks, leaves ea side, 1875 ...... 1,500.00
Humidor, cut glass w/silver floral-patterned lid, 6"......................900.00
Match safe, appl crab/octopus, eng Jack, 2½x1½" 135.00
Pitcher, repousse flowers/etc on matt finish, 1880, 7" 1,800.00
Plate, bamboo border, octagonal, 11" 275.00
Punch bowl, Colonial Revival style, 1950s, +12" underplate .. 1,600.00
Salver, Japanese style, dragonfly/leaves, copper trim, 12" 13,000.00
Tazza, 8 floral panels, 4 on sq base, etched/emb, 1880s, 6" 3,500.00
Tea/coffee set, pear form w/eng acanthus leaves, 6-pc 1,400.00
Teapot, squat melon form, 1900, 15 troy oz..............................475.00
Tray, serpentine floral-emb rim, hdls, 1900, 30" L.................. 8,000.00
Tureen, soup; mums/leaves ft & hdls, dome lid, 1880s 8,000.00
Vase, chased florals, elongated ovoid, 7½" 350.00
Vase, eng flower on sand-texture, cylindrical, 1880s, 13" 4,000.00

Miscellaneous

Purse, 14k gold mesh, filigree fr w/tiny dmns & sapphires 3,000.00
Vase, magnolias enameled on copper, flared cylinder, 11½".... 5,700.00
Window, ldgl, Venus attended by cherub, 1900, att, 55x44" .. 1,650.00

Tiffin Glass

The Tiffin Glass Company was founded in 1887 in Tiffin, Ohio, one of the many factories composing the U.S. Glass Company. Its early wares consisted of tablewares and decorative items such as lamps and globes. Among the most popular of all Tiffin products was the black satin glass produced there during the 1920s. In 1959 U.S. Glass was sold, and in 1962 the factories closed. The plant was re-opened in 1963 as the Tiffin Art Glass Company. Products from this period were tableware, hand-blown stemware, and other decorative items.

Those interested in learning more about Tiffin glass are encouraged to contact the Tiffin Glass Collectors' Club, whose address can be found in the Directory under Clubs, Newsletters, and Catalogs. See also Black Glass.

Bottle, oil; Flanders, pk, w/stopper...225.00
Bowl, centerpc; Cherokee Rose, 13" 65.00
Bowl, centerpc; Fontaine, Twilight, 13" 95.00
Bowl, Cerise, 9¾", +sterling base...60.00
Bowl, finger; Cherokee Rose, 5" 18.00
Bowl, finger; Flanders, pk, w/liner 35.00
Bowl, pickle; Cadena, pk or yel, 10" 25.00
Bowl, salad; Fuchsia, 11½" 65.00
Bowl, wedding; Grape & Leaf, milk glass w/gold, #1874 ....37.00
Candlestick, Cherokee Rose, 2-light, #5902, pr 60.00
Candlestick, Wisteria, #6037, pr 165.00
Celery, Fuchsia, 11" 35.00
Centerpc, Canterbury, 6-pointed, flame/crystal, 7⅝" 150.00
Champagne, Byzantine 25.00
Champagne, Cadena, yel..30.00
Champagne, Chardonnay 17.00
Champagne, Classic Shawl Dancer..25.00
Champagne, Cordelia, yel, plain stem 18.00
Champagne, Empire 20.00
Champagne, Flanders 18.00
Champagne, Fontaine, Twilight 30.00
Champagne, Fuchsia, hollow stem...22.00
Champagne, June Night, #17392 ....24.00
Champagne, Linda, cut 13.00
Champagne, Medici 24.00
Champagne, Nouvelle 20.00
Champagne, Nymph w/Flute, gr stem & ft 30.00
Champagne, Persian Pheasant..22.50
Champagne, Tiffin Rose, #17399 ....22.00
Champagne, Wisteria 15.00
Cigarette holder, Copen bl...65.00
Claret, Cherokee Rose, 4-oz 30.00
Claret, Flanders, pk..75.00
Claret, Persian Pheasant, #17358, 6⅜" 45.00
Cocktail, Cerise 18.50
Cocktail, Fuchsia 17.00
Cocktail, June Night, #17392, 5¼" 20.00
Cocktail, Paulina, topaz...11.00
Cocktail, Rose, #17399 ....27.00
Compote, Palais Versailles, w/gold...100.00
Cordial, Byzantine 35.00
Cordial, Cherokee Rose, #17399..45.00
Cordial, Flanders 40.00
Cordial, Flanders, yel...55.00
Cordial, Fuchsia 35.00
Cordial, June Night 32.00
Cordial, Palais Versailles, w/gold...95.00
Cordial, Paulina, topaz...28.00
Cordial, Persian Pheasant 40.00
Cordial, Persian Pheasant, amber...50.00
Cordial, Wisteria, #17477 ....45.00
Creamer, Cherokee Rose..28.00
Creamer, Flanders, ftd..35.00

Creamer, Fontaine, twilight, ftd	45.00
Creamer, Fuchsia, ftd	28.00
Creamer & sugar bowl, La Fleur, yel, ftd	125.00
Creamer & sugar bowl, Nymph w/Flute, gr hdl, flat	125.00
Cup, Fuchsia	37.50
Decanter, Byzantine, w/orig stopper	225.00
Decanter, Flanders, pk	250.00
Goblet, water; Beaumont	12.50
Goblet, water; Byzantine	35.00
Goblet, water; Cadena, pk or yel, ftd, 5¼"	27.50
Goblet, water; Camelot	12.50
Goblet, water; Carlyle	25.00
Goblet, water; Cerise, 8"	24.00
Goblet, water; Cherokee Rose, #17399, 8-oz	25.00
Goblet, water; Elyse	25.00
Goblet, water; Flanders	25.00
Goblet, water; Flanders, pk	47.50
Goblet, water; Fuchsia, tall	25.00
Goblet, water; Huntington	15.00
Goblet, water; June Night, #17403	25.00
Goblet, water; Juno, gr pastel	20.00
Goblet, water; La Fleur, topaz w/crystal stem, 8¼"	32.00
Goblet, water; Manchester	22.00
Goblet, water; Montclair	15.00
Goblet, water; Nouvelle	24.00
Goblet, water; Nymph w/Flute, gr stem & ft	37.00
Goblet, water; Renaissance, gold trim	30.00
Goblet, water; Renaissance, platinum trim	27.00
Goblet, water; Riviera	20.00
Goblet, water; Rose Marie	17.00
Goblet, water; Tiffin Rose, cut	15.00
Goblet, water; Wheat	24.00
Goblet, water; Willow	20.00
Goblet, water; Wisteria, #17394	25.00
Lamp, torchere; Santa Maria, sterling on orange	295.00
Mayonnaise, Cadena, yel, 3-pc	40.00
Mayonnaise, Flanders, pk, w/liner	75.00
Mayonnaise, Fuchsia, w/liner	40.00
Mayonnaise, June Night, 3-pc	40.00
Parfait, Flanders, yel	75.00
Pitcher, Cadena, ftd, w/lid	200.00
Pitcher, Cherokee Rose	250.00
Plate, Byzantine, 10½"	35.00
Plate, Cadena, yel, 7¾"	12.00
Plate, Cadena, yel, 9¼"	37.50
Plate, Flanders, pk, 6"	12.00
Plate, Fontaine, Twilight, 6"	12.00
Plate, Fontaine, Twilight, 8"	16.00
Plate, Fuchsia, 8½"	15.00
Plate, sandwich; Cherokee Rose, 14"	45.00
Plate, torte; June Night, 14"	75.00
Relish, Cherokee Rose, 3-part, 12½"	65.00
Relish, Flanders, 3-part	25.00
Relish, Fuchsia, 5-part	35.00
Rose bowl, Swedish Modern, Cerulean bl, #17430	80.00
Shakers, Flanders, yel, pr	100.00
Sherbet, Cadena, 4¾"	15.00
Sherbet, Camelot	7.50
Sherbet, Carlyle, tall	22.00
Sherbet, Cerise, 6"	18.50
Sherbet, Flanders	10.00
Sherbet, Fontaine, Twilight, low	20.00
Sherbet, Fuchsia	12.00
Sherbet, Huntington, tall	12.00

Sherbet, Killarney, gr, ftd	22.00
Sherbet, Montclair	10.00
Sherbet, Wheat, tall	20.00
Sugar bowl, Flanders, pk, flat	95.00
Sugar bowl, Fuchsia, ind	28.00
Tankard, Swedish Modern, #5935, 11½"	65.00

Tazza, crystal with green air twist stem, 9½" x 11", Victor Hendricks, 1930s, $425.00.

Tumbler, iced tea; Byzantine	22.00
Tumbler, iced tea; Cerice	20.00
Tumbler, iced tea; Fontaine, Twilight, tall	40.00
Tumbler, iced tea; Fuchsia	30.00
Tumbler, iced tea; Tiffin Rose, cut	15.00
Tumbler, juice; Cadena, ftd, 4¼"	15.00
Tumbler, juice; Canterbury, amber, flat, 4½"	5.00
Tumbler, juice; Fuchsia, ftd, 5-oz	18.00
Tumbler, juice; Wisteria, #17394	25.00
Vase, bud; Cherokee Rose, #14185, 8"	30.00
Vase, bud; Cherokee Rose, w/sterling base, 10¼"	50.00
Vase, bud; Cherokee Rose, 6"	22.00
Vase, bud; Isabella, #9780, 10"	125.00
Vase, bud; June Night, #14185, 6"	45.00
Vase, bud; June Night, 8"	30.00
Vase, Cadena, pk or yel, 9"	55.00
Vase, Cherokee Rose, urn form, 11"	65.00
Vase, cornucopia; Copen bl, 8¼"	145.00
Vase, Empress, smoke/crystal, 11¾"	150.00
Vase, Flanders, yel, fan form	75.00
Vase, flip; Modern, Copen bl, #5859, 12"	95.00
Vase, Fuchsia, urn form, hdls	95.00
Vase, Modern, #17350, 12¾"	60.00
Vase, Modern, Copen bl, cvd lily of the valley, sgn, 10"	135.00
Vase, Twilight, teardrop form, 8½"	95.00
Wine, Byzantine	27.00
Wine, Cadena, pk or yel, 6"	35.00
Wine, Canterbury, amber	8.00
Wine, Carlyle	25.00
Wine, Cherokee Rose, #17399	30.00
Wine, Elyse	35.00
Wine, Flanders	25.00
Wine, Fontaine, Twilight, 2½-oz	40.00
Wine, June Night	27.00
Wine, Manchester	25.00
Wine, Medici	24.00
Wine, Midnight Mist	20.00
Wine, Persian Pheasant, 6"	35.00

Tiles

Though originally strictly functional, tiles were being produced in various colors and used as architectural highlights as early as the Ancient Roman Empire. By the 18th century, Dutch tiles were decorated with polychrome landscapes and figures. During the 19th century, there were over a hundred companies in England involved in the manufacture of tile. By the Victorian era, the use of decorative tiles had reached its peak. Special souvenir editions, campaign and portrait tiles, and Art Nouveau motifs with lovely ladies and stylized examples from nature were popular. Today all of these are very collectible. See also specific manufacturers.

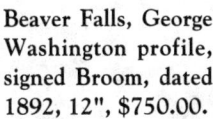

Beaver Falls, George Washington profile, signed Broom, dated 1892, 12", $750.00.

Cambridge Art Tile, floral, mc, 6"	15.00
Franklin, tulips, 4-color matt, 6"	45.00
Hamilton, Roman lady w/vessel, forest gr, 6x12"	250.00
Low, Elizabethan man (brn); lady (turq), wood fr, 8", pr	300.00
Low, floral, stylized, yel-brn, 3⅛"	28.00
Low, geometric florals, yel-gr, 6"	40.00
Low, man w/snuff box, monogram, bl, 5"	115.00
Low, Pedagogue, man's profile, bl-gr gloss, mk AO, 8"	350.00
Low, Roman w/laurels in profile, bl, 6"	115.00
Minton, Anthony or Cleopatra, brn on beige, sgn JM Smith, ea	80.00
Minton, cattle in stream, blk transfer, Wm Wise, 1879, 6"	80.00
Minton, dog by beehive, 1880s, 6"	50.00
Minton, fleur-de-lis, red on beige, 6x5"	30.00
Minton, man w/scythe, bl on wht, Wm Wise, 6"	110.00
Minton, Taming of the Shrew, 6"	55.00
Pardee, duck/frog/pond, cvd/pnt, 3-color, mk, 4⅜"	225.00
Pilkington, Art Nouveau flower, red, Lewis Day design, 6"	80.00
Trenton, HP birds on pine bough, 5½", in walnut fr	90.00

Tinware

In the American household of the 17th and 18th centuries, tinware items could be found in abundance, from food containers to foot warmers and mirror frames. Although the first settlers brought much of their tinware with them from Europe, by 1798 sheets of tin plate were being imported from England for use by the growing number of American tinsmiths. Tinwares were often decorated either by piercing or painted designs which were both freehand and stenciled. (See Toleware.) By the early 1900s, many homes had replaced their old tinware with the more attractive aluminum and graniteware.

In the 19th century, tenth wedding anniversaries were traditionally celebrated by gifts of tin. Couples gave big parties, dressed in their wedding clothes, and reaffirmed their vows before their friends and family who arrived bearing (and often wearing) tin gifts, most of which were quite humorous. Anniversary tin items may include hats, cradles, slippers and shoes, rolling pins, etc. See also Primitives and Kitchen Collectibles.

Box, smoke-pnt dots, wooden lid, 8½" dia	175.00
Candle box, cylindrical, hinged lid, hanging tabs, 14"	175.00
Candle lantern, pierced, Paul Revere type, EX	150.00
Chamber lamp, whale oil burner, 1800s, 11", pr	375.00
Cheese mold, heart-shaped rim, 3 disk ft, 4¾"	125.00
Cheese mold, punched tin, heart shape, 6" L	200.00
Coffeepot, hinged lid, strap hdl, 1860s, 4-cup, 7", EX	55.00
Coffeepot, pewter hdl/lid/spout, mk R Dunham, 9½"	85.00
Coffeepot, punched florals w/tulips, resoldered, 11", EX	1,300.00
Colander, 2" dia mesh drain hole, 1850s, 7x9½" dia	35.00
Drainer, cheese; pierced bottom, 1850s, 1¾x9½" dia	175.00
Egg poacher, 5-compartment, flip-up top, wire hdl, 1900s, 8"	45.00
Funnel, beer filtering; brass screening, 1840s, 8½x5"	32.50
Lamp, bk reflector fixed to rnd base, ring hdl, hanging	85.00
Lamp filler, 5½"	65.00
Map case, cylindrical, rpl leather hdl, 26", EX	38.00
Roaster, 11x7" plus hdls, w/lid, EX	315.00
Sconce, crimped arched crest, 12½x5", pr	650.00
Sconce, crimped crest, worn pnt, 12"	175.00
Sconce, crimped oval bk, 1800s, 15x9"	200.00
Sconce, oval/curved reflectors, crimped edge/pan, 9", pr	1,400.00
Sconce, rectangle bk w/crimped crest & drip pan, 9¾", pr	950.00
Sconce, scalloped/crimped semicircular crest, mirror, 13"	2,250.00
Sconce, tooled bk w/semicircular crest, rust/solder, 10"	150.00
Sconce, 10" dia bk w/7 sm rnd mirrors, 1800s, 12", EX	550.00
Spatula, fish slice; rnded blade, punchwork, wood hdl, EX	75.00
Syrup pitcher, brn japanning, hinged lid, 3½"	65.00

Tobacciana

Tobacciana is the generally accepted term used to cover a field of collecting that includes smoking pipes, cigar molds, cigarette lighters, humidors — in short, any article having to do with the practice of using tobacco in any form. Perhaps the most valuable variety of pipes is the meerschaum, hand carved from hydrous magnesium, an opaque white-gray or cream-colored mineral of the soapstone family. (Much of this is today mined in Turkey which has the largest meerschaum deposit in the world, though there are other deposits of lesser significance around the globe.) These figural bowls often portray an elaborately carved mythological character, an animal, or a historical scene. Amber is sometimes used for the stem. Other collectible pipes are corn cob (Missouri Meerschaum) and Indian peace pipes of clay or catlinite. (See American Indian Art.)

Chosen because it was the Indians who first introduced the white man to smoking, the cigar store Indian was a symbol used to identify tobacco stores in the 19th century. The majority of them were hand carved between 1830 and 1900 and are today recognized as some of the finest examples of early wood sculptures. When found they command very high prices. Our advisor for this category is Chuck Thompson; he is listed in the Directory under Texas. See also Advertising; Snuff Boxes.

Ash tray, bull's head in relief, brass, 4½x5"	50.00
Case, cigarette; silver w/blk/silver/gold scenic, Oriental	135.00
Cigar holder, cvd ivory, 2½", EX	35.00
Cigar holder, meerschaum, girl & pup atop, amber stem, 5½"	200.00
Cigar holder, meerschaum, gnome w/lg face, amber stem, 4" L	500.00
Cigar holder, meerschaum, lg rabbit atop, amber stem, 3¾"	150.00
Cigar holder, meerschaum, lg seated gnome strokes beard, 5"	500.00
Cutter, cigar; antler hdl, sgn in German, 9"	65.00

Cutter, cigar; brass, Pat March 28, 1916, 1½" **25.00**
Cutter, cigar; brass, revolver..**220.00**
Cutter, cigar; brass, w/knife combination, lt wear **20.00**
Cutter, cigar; brass & steel, MOP hdls, scissors type **25.00**
Cutter, cigar; ivory w/metal scissors action, Flor de Lottman **30.00**
Cutter, cigar; silvertone metal, scissors type, Germany **25.00**
Cutter, cigar; steel/copper, Robert Bruce, key wind, 3¾x8" **155.00**
Cutter, cigar; sterling, Pat Dec 09-02, EX **25.00**
Cutter, cigar; 10k gold, dented, 1½", VG.......................................**50.00**
Cutter, plug; Brighton Little Imp **60.00**
Cutter, plug; Brown's Mule, CI, countertop...................................**58.00**
Cutter, plug; cut-out sheet iron horse & rider, rpl hdl..................**275.00**
Cutter, plug; man thumbing nose figural, pnt CI, 7x11x3", G **130.00**
Cutter, plug; Old Star, gilded letters, mk Save the Tags................**90.00**
Cutter, plug; Wilson & McGalley, guillotine model **125.00**
Dispenser, Blk bartender behind bar, Ronson Touch-Tip, 6½" ..**950.00**
Dispenser, crouching monkey faces box, Ronson, 5", EX **750.00**

Ronson cigarette dispenser, Penguin, 5",
$1,150.00; Bartender, $950.00.

Humidor, bulldog w/pipe, majolica, 8" **135.00**
Humidor, ceramic, Oriental lady's head form, mc, 4¾x3½" **95.00**
Humidor, dbl; 2 SP cherubs support match holder, Meriden **350.00**
Humidor, porc, Chinaman's head form, gold skin, 5¼"..................**95.00**
Humidor, pottery, Chinaman w/long braid form, 5¾".................**120.00**
Indian princess, cvd w/EX detail, rpt/filled cracks, 87" **3,200.00**
Lighter, brass, Demley Surelite, Austria..**12.50**
Lighter, glass/sterling, mk Pat Pending F Whiting **20.00**
Lighter, marble & silver decor, Ronson, table sz............................**45.00**
Lighter, metal, donkey figural, sm **25.00**
Lighter, metal, high-top shoe form, 3½", G **35.00**
Lighter, sea horses/shells in clear Lucite, Evans **25.00**
Opener, cigar box; San Felice Cigars emb on hdl, lt rust, 5" **20.00**
Opener, cigar box; stag hdl, etched blade, 6¾" **35.00**
Pipe, clay, Blk man's head, pnt details, C Loph, NY, 7".............**140.00**
Pipe, clay, hand holding pipe, ca 1810, 4½" **325.00**
Pipe, meerschaum, bare-breasted lady, EX, +case.........................**225.00**
Pipe, meerschaum, bearded man in feathered hat, NM in case....**135.00**
Pipe, meerschaum, detailed wolf's head, amber stem, 7" **300.00**
Pipe, meerschaum, lg boar's head, amber stem, 6¾".................**1,200.00**
Pipe, meerschaum, lg reclining nude, amber stem, 9".................**400.00**
Pipe, meerschaum, nude Nouveau-style lady, amber stem, 7" **145.00**
Pipe tamp, bone, lady's leg, 2½"...**85.00**
Smoke set, SP, lg glass-eyed owl humidor, Meriden, 5-pc............**300.00**
Snuff mull, ram's horn w/silver mts, pit bull finial........................**600.00**
Tamp, brass, Georgian nutcracker type, mk Vaun, 1800..............**235.00**
Tamp, brass, Napolean figural, 1840s..**145.00**
Tamp, cast brass/fire gilt, hand w/bird & flowers, 3" **65.00**
Tamp, cvd whalebone, fist w/entwined snake form, 2⅞" **250.00**

Toby Jugs

The delightful jug known as the Toby dates back to the 18th cen-

tury, when factories in England produced them for export to the American colonies. Named for the character Toby Philpots in the song *The Little Brown Jug*, the Toby was fashioned in the form of a jolly fellow, usually holding a jug of beer and a glass. The earlier examples were made with strict attention to details such as fingernails and teeth. Originally representing only a non-entity, a trend developed to portray well-known individuals such as George II, Napoleon, and Ben Franklin. Among the most-valued Tobies are those produced by Ralph Wood I in the late 1700s. By the mid-1830s Tobies were being made in America. See also Doulton, Lenox, and Occupied Japan.

Martha Gunn, att Ralph Wood, ca
1770s, 11", $4,500.00.

Man w/jug, pearlware, yel/gr/bl/brn sponging, lid, 10", NM **1,050.00**
Man w/jug, pearlware, 5-color pnt/sponging, prof rpr, 10" **550.00**
Pratt, Hearty Good Fellow, stands, pitcher/pipe, rstr, 11"........**1,500.00**
Pratt, seated, jug on knee, pipe between ft, rstr/chips, 10" **880.00**
Pratt, seated, sponged overcoat, 1800, chips/rstr, 9" **1,320.00**
Ralph Wood, seated, jug in both hands, pipe aside, 10", EX ... **1,045.00**
Walton, seated, pitcher on knee, ribbon mk, lines/rprs, 10".... **1,045.00**

Toleware

The term 'toleware' originally came from a French term meaning 'sheet iron.' Today it is used to refer to paint-decorated tin items, most popular from 1800 to 1850s. The craft was very popular in Pennsylvania, Connecticut, Maine, and New York state. Early toleware has a very distinctive look. The surface is dull and unvarnished; background colors range from black to cream. Geometrics are quite common, but florals and fruits were also popular motifs. Items made after 1850 were often stenciled, and gold trim was sometimes added.

American toleware is usually found in practical, everyday forms — trays, boxes, and coffeepots are most common — while French examples might include candlesticks, wine coolers, jardinieres, etc. Be sure to note color and design when determining date and value, but condition of the paint is the most important worth-assessing factor. Our advisors for this category are Barbara and Frank Pollack; they are listed in the Directory under Illinois. In the listings that follow, the dimension given for boxes and trays indicates length.

Bowl, floral, 4-color on brn, shallow, 12" **1,000.00**
Box, candle; worn blk pnt, cylindrical, wall mt, 12" L **200.00**
Box, deed; floral, mc on blk, minor wear, 9"..............................**500.00**
Box, deed; floral, 4-color on dk brn, resoldered, 4¼" L **225.00**
Box, deed; gold lid w/stencil: Friendship, gr w/red lines, 7" **200.00**

Box, deed; PA-style flowers on red, dome top, 9½" 1,800.00
Bucket, floral, mc on worn orig red, toy, 2⅝" 75.00

Coffeepot, red with yellow flowers, red berries, and green leaves, 10½", $3,000.00.

Coffeepot, floral, 3-color on dk brn, battered spout, 10½" 700.00
Coffeepot, floral, 3-color on red, str sides/L-spout, 11" 3,000.00
Coffeepot, floral, 4-color on blk, soldered rpr/wear, 11" 1,200.00
Coffeepot, floral, 4-color on blk, tapered sides/spout, 8½" 1,900.00
Coffeepot, floral (lg), 5-color on blk, lt wear, 11" 1,400.00
Coffeepot, floral on blk, str side spout, lt wear, 9" 1,450.00
Creamer, floral on red, lt wear/flaking, hinged lid, 4" 475.00
Creamer, lg floral, 4-color on blk/brn mottle, lid, 4", NM 675.00
Jar, red & yel decor on blk, rpt, ring lid hdl, wear, 6x7" 125.00
Lunch box, floral rpt worn, 3-part int, oval, 12" L 250.00
Matchbox, brn w/floral, crimped trefoil crest, 7", VG 75.00
Mug, floral, red/yel on blk, EX color/worn, 4½" 625.00
Mug, floral, 3-color on dk brn, resoldered/wear, 5¾" 450.00
Mug, floral, 3-color on red, worn, 4⅜" 675.00
Mug, floral, 4-color on dk brn, EX color/lt wear, 6" 700.00
Shaker, simple flower, 3-color on brn, 2¾" 95.00
Sugar bowl, floral, 3-color on 2-tone red, touched up, 4", VG.....200.00
Sugar bowl, floral, 4-color on blk, lt wear, 3¾" 375.00
Sugar bowl, traces of floral on dk brn, wear, 4" 110.00
Tea caddy, floral, 2-color on dk brn, EX color/worn, 4", EX 450.00
Tea caddy, floral, 3-color on red, EX color/lt wear, 5" 2,300.00
Tea caddy, floral, 4-color on blk w/wht band, lt wear, 4" 175.00
Tea canister, floral, 5-color on red, minor wear, 5" 375.00
Tray, Am ship Challenge, 26x19", VG 1,000.00
Tray, apples, red/gr on wht, crystalized center, 13", VG..............450.00
Tray, floral, 4-color floral on dk brn, EX color/wear, 8½" 825.00
Tray, floral in mc, wht band, crystalized center, 12" 900.00
Tray, gold crystalized center/wht band w/4-color motif, 8½" 600.00

Tools

Before the Civil War, tools for the most part were handmade. Some were primitive to the point of crudeness, while others reflected the skill of those who took pride in their trade. Increasing demand for quality tools and the dawning of the age of industrialization resulted in tools that were mass-produced. Factors important in evaluating antique tools are scarcity, usefulness, and portability. Those with a manufac-

turer's mark are worth more than unmarked items. When no condition is indicated, the items listed here are assumed to be in excellent condition. See also Winchester and Keen Kutter. Our advisor for this category is Jim Calison; he is listed in the Directory under New York.

Auger, curly maple hdl, 17" 25.00
Axe, goose-wing; wrought iron, 12" blade, VG 150.00
Beader, Stanley #50, EX 88.00
Bevel, brass & rosewood, IJ Robinson, Pat 1870, 6" 265.00
Bevel, ship builder's; EH Chapin #85 ....30.00
Book press, curly birch, sq legs, dvtl drw, wood press, 52" 550.00
Chisel, bevel-edge; CE Jennings, tang type, EX 8.50
Chisel, flat-edged; L&IJ White, Buffalo NY, EX 20.00
Divider, stamped GWS, curly maple, age crack, 34" 185.00
Drill, folding; Morse Twist Drill & Machine Co, Pat 1906............40.00
Drill, hand; Millers Falls #2, 6 bits in hdl, 14½", EX 22.50
Drill, Stanley #610, hand type, NM 145.00
Gauge, bevel; W Cresson, Phila, 9¾" blade, VG 15.00
Gauge, chisel; Stanley #96 ....135.00
Gauge, clapboard; EW Carpenter, Lancaster, EX 450.00
Gauge, dbl-end marking; Stanley #95, VG 15.00
Gauge, outside-bevel; New Haven Edge Tool Co, EX.......................10.00
Hammer, claw; C Hammond, Phila, VG 18.00
Hammer, tack; CS Osborne & Co #4, rosewood hdl, 11", EX 25.00
Hatchet, T Miller, 3¾" blade, 12½" L, EX 8.00
Knife, cooper's chamfer; 7" blade, 18" L, EX 55.00
Level, Davis Pat 1883, 3-bubble, 6" 375.00
Level, spirit; all brass, decorative detail, 3¼" 105.00
Level, spirit; ebony, brass trim, 12" 65.00
Level, Stanley #237, aluminum w/dbl plumb, 24", EX 37.50
Level, Stanley #36, 9", NM in box 55.00
Level, Universal Star, EX 195.00
Nozzle, brass, w/trn cock valve, dents, 15" 25.00
Panel raiser, EW Carpenter, Lancaster, 3½" cut 395.00
Plane, beading; Gleason/Wood, Watertown NY, VG 25.00
Plane, block; Millers Falls #75, EX 7.50
Plane, block; Stanley #1120, 1936-37, EX 40.00
Plane, bull-nose rabbet; Stanley #75, VG 20.00
Plane, circular; Stanley #20, VG 100.00
Plane, curved stair; I White, Phila, EX 975.00
Plane, fore; M Long, Reading PA, 22", EX 60.00
Plane, hollow; Denison/Saybrook, pre-1845, VG 30.00
Plane, household jack; Stanley, 4-sq, 1930, 11½", VG...................37.50
Plane, joiner; Kellogg, 22x3", VG 17.50
Plane, match; Stanley #148, Pat 1903, VG 50.00
Plane, molding; J&L Denison, pre-1845 mk, G 27.50
Plane, molding; John Bell, Phila, ca 1829-51, 9½", EX 30.00
Plane, plow; E Caldwell, ca 1840s-50s, VG 67.50
Plane, plow; I Hammond, New Haven, ca 1840s, 8½", G 80.00
Plane, plow; Ohio Tool, ivory tipped, EX...............................550.00
Plane, plow; rosewood, brass fittings, 12" 45.00
Plane, plow; Sargent #743, EX 95.00
Plane, rabbet; Stanley #10, early, VG 85.00
Plane, rabbet; Stanley #182, 1910-18, EX 30.00
Plane, Stanley #140, 1936-44, EX..120.00
Plane, Stanley #248-A, w/7 blades, EX 100.00
Plane, Stanley #607-C, VG 72.50
Plane, Stanley #92, EX 65.00
Plane, window mullion; Casey & Co, Auburn NY, beech, 9½" 55.00
Plumb bob, Stanley, brass, w/reel 95.00
Router, close-throated; Stanley #71, VG 55.00
Router, Millers Falls #77, VG 35.00
Rule, Gunter's Slide, Biddle Co, Phila, 2-fold, 24", EX................95.00

Rule, Lufkin #1204, aluminum, zigzag-type, 48" 15.00
Rule, Lufkin #2072, 3-fold w/level, NM 145.00
Rule, Lufkin #372, w/caliper...................................25.00
Rule, Stanley #36, boxwood, folding, w/caliper 20.00
Rule, Stephans #50, boxwood, 4-fold, 24" 22.50
Rule, Upson Nut #78½, boxwood, folding, w/caliper 35.00
Screwdriver, Millers Falls #670, Pat 1926, 11", VG.......12.50
Screwdriver, stamped A, curly maple hdl, age crack, 21" 25.00
Screwdriver, Stanley #1003, EX 8.50
Spokeshave, Stanley #67, NM 100.00
Square, try; Stanley #12, 10" blade, VG.......................10.00
Wrench, alligator; #720554, 7¾", VG 15.00
Wrench, pipe; Stanley #50, w/orig box & 14 blades, NM 75.00

Toothpick Holders

Once common on every table, the toothpick holder was relegated to the china cabinet near the turn of the century. Fortunately, this contributed to their survival; as a result, many are available to collectors today. Because they are small and easily displayed, they are a very popular collectible; and they come in a wide range of prices to fit every budget. The rare ones have been reproduced and, unfortunately, are being offered for sale right along with the originals. (These 'repros' should be priced in the $10.00 to $15.00 range.) So unless you're sure of what you're buying, choose a reputable dealer. In addition to pattern glass, you'll find examples in china, bisque, art glass, and silverplate. In the listings that follow, items are glass unless noted otherwise. Those that have been reproduced are designated with a (+), however values are for the orginals. Our advisor for this category is Judy A. Knauer; she is listed in the Directory under Pennsylvania.

Amberina, Dmn Quilt, sq top 220.00
Amberina, Dmn Quilt, tricorner, NE Glass..................225.00
Atlas, etched leaf & berry....................................30.00
Bassettown...45.00
Beggar's Hand 17.50
Bulging Loops, gr 35.00
Bulging Loops, gr opaque......................................55.00
Burmese, decor, 6-sided top, Mt WA.........................425.00
Champion...28.00
Chute & Ladders...22.00
Coin Dot, amberina, ruffled top 250.00
Colorado, gr w/EX gold, dtd 1911 ....45.00
Cordova, gr 27.50
Cornell, gr 45.00
Creased Bale, pk...65.00
Crocodile Tears, pk..90.00
Croesus, emerald gr, 3-ftd.....................................85.00
Crysanthemum Leaf 55.00
Cut crystal, blk Deco-style pnt bands, 2¼x2" 65.00
Daisy & Button, amberina, ftd, old 275.00
Daisy & Button w/Variant, amber..............................25.00
Delaware, gr w/gold..65.00
Delaware, rose w/EX gold 75.00
Diamond Spearhead, vaseline opal 660.00
Dolphin, amber..60.00
Double Circle, gr 45.00
Double Ring Panel, rose 40.00
Florette, yel satin 110.00
Flower & Pleat, amber stained 110.00
Guttate, pk..110.00
Harvard, custard..35.00
Iris w/Meander, gr opal 55.00

Michigan, ruby stained 80.00
Michigan, yel stained w/rose carnations......................65.00
Michigan (+) 32.00
Nearcut 25.00
Nestor, gr decor..150.00
New Jersey..45.00
Panelled Thistle (+) 35.00
Pansy, bl 45.00
Parallel Greek Key, burmese, Mt WA........................250.00
Pleating, ruby stained..30.00
Pretty Maid (+)..35.00
Quartered Block...45.00
Ribbed Spiral, wht opal 45.00
Rip Van Winkle, gr opaque, sgn Portieux....................95.00
Rising Sun...35.00
Saddle (+) 17.50
Scalloped Swirl, ruby stained 55.00
Shell & Seaweed, gr opaque 70.00
Star in Bull's Eye, gold trim 30.00
Sunflower Patch..55.00

Swag Bracket, amethyst with gold, 3", $65.00.

Swirl & Leaf..65.00
Thousand Eye, amber..25.00
Thumbnail 30.00
Tokyo, bl opal...250.00
US Regal 24.00
W Virginia Optic, gr..35.00
Ward's Regal, gr 25.00
Wheeling Block...45.00
Wreath & Shell, bl opal w/decor 300.00

Torquay 'Devon Motto' Ware

Torquay is a unique type of pottery made in the South Devon area of England as early as 1867. At the height of productivity, at least a dozen companies flourished there, producing simple folk pottery from the area's natural red clay. The ware was both wheel-turned and molded and decorated under the glaze with heavy slip resulting in low-relief nature subjects or simple scrollwork. Three of the best-known of these potteries were: Watcombe (1867-1962); Aller Vale (in operation from the mid-1800s, producing domestic ware and architectural products); and Longpark (1890 until 1957). Watcombe and Aller Vale merged in 1901 and operated until 1962 under the name of Royal Aller Vale and Watcombe Art Pottery.

Perhaps the most famous type of ware potted in this area was Motto

Ware, so called because of the verses, proverbs, and quotations that decorated it. This was achieved by the sgraffito technique — scratching the letters through the slip to expose the red clay underneath. The most popular patterns were Cottage, Black Cockerel, Multi-Cockerel, and a scrollwork design called Scandy. Other popular decorations were Kerswell Daisy, ships, kingfishers, and many other birds on blue ground. Aller Vale ware may sometimes be found marked 'H.H. and Company,' a firm who assumed ownership from 1897 to 1901. 'Watcombe Torquay' was an impressed mark used from 1884 to 1927.

Our advisors for this category are Jerry and Gerry Kline; they are listed in the Directory under Ohio. If you're interested in joining a Torquay club, the address of The North American Torquay Society is given under Clubs, Newsletters, and Catalogs.

Bottle, scent; Devonshire violets, crown stopper, 4" 40.00
Bottle, scent; roses, ink pot shape, pixie stopper.............................75.00
Bowl, Scandy, Longpark, 'There's Maire...,' 6" 85.00
Butter dish, Blk Cockerel, Longpark, 'Elp Yerzel...,' 5" 88.00
Candlestick, Blk Cockerel, Longpark, 'Night Is Long...,' 2½" 75.00
Candlestick, Cottage, Longpark, 'Llanfairfechan...,' 4½" 85.00
Candlestick, Scandy, unmk, 'Happy Be Thy Dreams,' 8"............150.00
Candlestick, Scandy, Watcombe, 'To Bed...Sleepy Head,' 4" 75.00
Coffeepot, Sailing Boats, Longpark, 'Smooth Runs...,' 6½" 135.00
Coffeepot, Scandy, Longpark, 'No Life Can Be...,' 5½" 150.00
Condiment holder, w/shakers, egg cup, & mustard, 3½" 150.00
Creamer, Blk Cockerel, Longpark, motto, 2¾" 55.00
Creamer, Cottage, Longpark, 'From Coniston...,' 3½" 50.00
Creamer, Primrose, 'Canny w/the Cream,' 2½" 40.00
Creamer, Scandy, Watcombe, 'Take a Little Cream,' 3" 40.00
Cup, Blk Cockerel, Longpark, 'Jack & Jill Went...,' 2¾" 75.00
Cup, coffee; Cottage, Watcombe, 'Rolling Stone...,' 3¾"............47.50
Egg cup, Cottage, Longpark, 'Laid Today,' 1¾" 30.00
Egg cup, Cottage, Watcombe, 'Fine Words...,' ped ft, 3" 40.00
Figurine, classical, Watcombe, terra cotta, 11½" 500.00
Hatpin holder, Daffodil, Watcombe, brn ground, 4½" 175.00
Hatpin holder, Scandy, Longpark, 'I'll Take Care...,' 4½" 95.00
Inkwell, Scandy, Longpark, 'Jis a Line Tu...,' 2" 60.00
Jam dish, Blk Cockerel, Longpark, 'Help Yourself...,' 5" dia.........85.00
Jardiniere, Daffodil on gr, Longpark, 5¾" 300.00
Jug, puzzle; Cottage, Watcombe, motto, 4½" 150.00
Jug, puzzle; Scandy, Longpark, w/motto, 3½" 125.00
Mug, Scandy, Watcombe, 'Stitch in Time...,' 2-hdl, 3" 65.00
Mug, shaving; Multi-Cockerel, Longpark, motto 225.00
Mug, toby, MIE, 2" 85.00
Pen tray, Blk Cockerel, Longpark, 'Dunnale Aye...,' 7x8½" 135.00
Pepper pot, Scandy, Allervale, 'Hot & Strong,' 2½" 27.50
Pitcher, Colored Cockerel, Longpark, 'There Would Be...,' 6" 180.00
Pitcher, Cottage, Watcombe, 'Time & Tide...,' 4½" 60.00
Pitcher, Egyptian, no mk, 6½" 250.00
Pitcher, Sailing Boats, Allervale, 'May We Be Kind...,' 5" 70.00
Pitcher, Scandy, Allervale, 'Make Thisen at Hooam,' 3¼" 50.00
Pitcher, tankard, Scandy, Allervale, 'Say Not...,' 4½" 80.00
Plate, Cottage, Dartmouth, 'Us Be Always...,' 6½" 32.00
Plate, Cottage, Watcombe, 'Enough's As Good...,' 5" 50.00
Plate, Scandy, Allervale, 'If at First You...,' 5" 50.00
Salt cellar, Scandy, Longpark, 'Be Aisy w/Tha...,' 1¾x2½" 45.00
Shakers, Cottage, 'Time Ripens.../Hope Well...,' 2½", pr..............60.00
Shakers, Cottage, Watcombe, 'Help Yourself,' pr 50.00
Sugar bowl, Blk Cockerel, Watcombe, 'Take a Little...,' 3" 45.00
Sugar bowl, Colored Cockerel, Longpark, motto, 1¾" 48.00
Sugar bowl, Cottage, MIE, 'Put a Stout Heart...,' 2" 38.00
Sugar bowl, Primrose, 'Help Yersel Tae Sugar,' 2" 40.00
Teapot, appl butterfly, Hele Cross, 5".......................................200.00
Teapot, Blk Cockerel, Longpark, 'Du'ee 'Ave...,' 5" 125.00

Toast rack, Cottage, Watcombe, 'Tak a...,' 5 rails 130.00
Tray, dresser; Scandy, Longpark, 10¾x7½" 175.00
Vase, Blk Cockerel, Longpark, 'Du All Tha...,' 3-hdl, 3½" 70.00
Vase, Blk Cockerel, unmk, 'Wishes Never...,' 2¼" 95.00
Vase, commemorative, Tommy Atkins, Aller Vale, 3-hdld, 4½" ..200.00
Vase, Ladybird on gr ground, Aller Vale, hdls, 8" 275.00

Posy vase, scrolls on blue ground, marked B3, ca 1887-1924, 3½", $65.00.

Vase, Scrolls, Aller Vale, 5-finger funnel, wht clay, 8" 250.00
Vase, Scrolls, Exeter, fan form, 5" 125.00
Vase, udder (posey); peacock on bl, Daison, 6¼" 225.00
Vase, udder; Scandy, Aller Vale, 'Many Are Called...,' 3½" 95.00

Tortoise Shell Glass

By combining several shades of glass — brown, clear, and yellow — glass manufacturers of the 19th century were able to produce an art glass that closely resembled the shell of the tortoise. Some of this type of glassware was manufactured in Germany. In America it was made by several firms, the most prominent of which was the Boston and Sandwich Glass Works.

Finger bowl, scalloped, w/undertray 185.00
Ice bucket, hdls, 8½x7½" 165.00
Pitcher, water; gold flecks, appl hdl 195.00
Tumbler, 3¾x2¾" 125.00
Vase, crimped rim, 9" 135.00

Toys

Toy collecting has grown tremendously in the past few years; toy shows and auctions are common, and the market has broadened. Now toys from the fifties and sixties are as eagerly sought as 19th-century toys. It is important for collectors to become familiar with their areas of interest. Seek out dealers with experience; take advantage of the many fine toy books that are available. These are some of the most helpful: *American Toy Cars and Trucks* by Lillian Gottschalk; *Toy Autos 1890-1939*, the Peter Ottenheimer Collection; *Collecting the Tin Toy Car, 1950-1970*, by Dale Kelley; *Arcade Toys* by Al Aune; *The Art of the Tin Toy* by David Pressland; *Lehmann Toys* by Cieslik; *The History of Martin Mechanical Toys* by Marchand; *Mechanical Toys* by Spilhaus; *American Antique Toys* by Barenholtz, Mc Clintock, and Holland; *American Clockwork Toys* by Whitton; *The George Brown Sketchbook* by Edith Barenholtz; *Toy Dreams* by Kitahara; and *Collecting Toys* by O'Brien.

The Dictionary of Toys Sold in America, Vol. I & II, by Earnest and Ida Long are good for identification and dating. The Longs are our advisors for all toys except Farm Toys, Steiff, Toy Soldiers, and Trains; they are listed in the Directory under California. In the listings that follow, toys are listed by manufacturer's name if possible, otherwise by type. Condition is given when known, since it is one of the major factors in establishing the price of any toy. Measurements are given when appropriate and available; if only one dimension is noted, it is the greater one — height if the toy is vertical, length if it is horizontal. Values given here result from monitoring auctions and checking known retail sales; to some extent, they have been taken from sale lists. See also Children's Things; Personalities. For toy stoves, see Stoves.

Key:
b/o — battery operated   NP — nickel plated
jtd — jointed   w/up — wind-up

Cast Iron

Cast iron toys were made from shortly before the Civil War until the beginning of the 20th century. They are evaluated to a large extent by scarcity, complexity, design, and detail. See next section for examples of cast iron toys listed by company name.

Bellringer, Trick Pony #39, wht/red/blk horse, gr base, 8" 425.00
Blk boy on donkey-drawn cart, worn orig pnt, 1910, 9", EX 770.00
Bus, Century of Progress 1933, 11", EX..175.00
Bus, dbl-decker, w/4 figures, 8", NM...350.00
Car, coupe, rumble seat, 1920s, 5", NM...265.00
Champion motorcycle/driver, worn pnt/wht rubber wheels, 7" ...175.00
Donkey cart, driver nods head, rubber neck, 6½", EX...................225.00
Farm wagon, horse-drawn, 2x5¼", G...75.00
Fire vehicle w/hose & reel, horse-drawn, 18½" L, G...................125.00
Milk wagon, mk Made in USA, worn mc pnt, minor rust............185.00
Studebaker Phaeton, 1920s, M...265.00
Sulky w/driver, ca 1900, 8" L, G...225.00
Sulky w/driver, reins missing, ca 1900, 8", EX 300.00
Sword, ornate hand grip, orig red pnt, 15½" 65.00
Truck, J&B Express, w/driver, G pnt, ca 1915, 15", EX 600.00
UX99 Airplane, single engine, NP wheels/motor/prop, 4¾", EX.125.00
Wagon, 2-wheeled, w/mule & driver, 9½", M 225.00

Company or Country of Manufacturer

AC Williams, racer, CI, early, 6", EX 175.00
Arcade, auto carrier, pnt CI/steel, w/cars, 24½", VG............... 1,400.00
Arcade, Fageol bus, pnt CI, 8", G...165.00
Arcade, Internat'l Harvester dump truck, pnt CI, 11", EX...........750.00
Arcade, Lubrite Gasoline truck, w/driver, pnt CI, 13", EX 2,000.00
Arcade, Mack Coal truck, pnt CI, stains, 9½", G.........................400.00
Arcade, Model-T car, pnt CI, 6¾", NM...500.00
Arcade, Yellow taxicab, CI, orange/blk pnt, 1923, 9", EX 715.00
Arnold, Mac 700 motorcycle, tin litho w/up, 8", EX....................550.00
Bandai, Chevrolet station wagon, tin litho, friction, 9½", EX 95.00
Bandai, Opel Rekord Sedan, tin, friction, 8½", MIB 80.00
Bing, destroyer, tin litho w/up, 10½", VG................................. 2,850.00
Bing, garage w/touring car, tin litho w/up, 6½", G 200.00
Bing, limousine/ambulance, tin litho w/up, 1912, 9½", EX 7,000.00
Bing, ocean liner, tin litho w/up, 4-stack, '20, 15", VG........... 1,760.00
Bing, Royal Mail van, steel, minor rpt, 1929, 22", EX 3,000.00
Bing, Table Railway, tin litho, clockwork, 14", G 300.00
Bing, touring car, tin litho w/up, 1921, 13", EX.......................1,750.00
Bliss, US Cruiser, paper litho on wood, Pat 1877, 31", G 500.00
Bliss, Western Express wagon, paper litho on wood, 8" 150.00

Brimtoy, limousine, tin litho, 1920, 11", NM in box 935.00
Buddy L, aerial ladder truck, pnt steel, NP ladders, 39", VG 850.00
Buddy L, cab, pnt steel, b/o lights, sm nicks, 14", G 75.00
Buddy L, delivery truck, steel, orig pnt, 1930s, 24", EX 1,400.00
Buddy L, dump truck, pnt steel, chain dump, rstr, 24½", EX 375.00
Buddy L, Ford Flivver Delivery, pnt steel, 12", VG 700.00
Buddy L, Ford Huckster truck, pnt steel, rust spots, 14", G 1,900.00
Buddy L, Greyhound bus, pnt steel, b/o lights, w/up, 16", EX......275.00
Buddy L, Hoisting Tower, pnt steel, sm chips, 38½", VG.............375.00
Buddy L, Internat'l Harvester truck, steel, 1935, rstr, 25" 880.00
Buddy L, ladder truck, pnt steel, minor chips, 27", G 325.00
Buddy L, ladder truck, pnt steel, sm scratches, 25", VG..............600.00
Buddy L, Model-T dump truck, pnt metal, 11", EX 1,250.00
Buddy L, Model-T open-bed truck, pnt steel, 1923, 12", VG 450.00
Buddy L, sand loader, pnt steel, minor wear, 17", G......................65.00
Buddy L, tank truck, pnt steel, b/o lights, rstr, 19½", G 350.00
Buddy L, tanker, pnt steel, minor rpt/rust, 24", G 1,100.00
Buddy L, tanker, pnt steel, no tank cap/spigot, 23½", VG 750.00
Burnett, Pullman limousine, tin litho w/up, 1922, 14", EX 3,300.00
Carette, limousine, tin litho w/up, 1908, 16¼", EX 10,450.00
Carette, limousine w/driver, tin litho w/up, 1915, 13½", EX 4,180.00
Carette, ocean liner, tin litho w/up, 4-stack, '08, 20", EX 4,000.00
Carette, warship, pnt tin, w/up, 1915, 13¾", EX 495.00
Carpenter, Depot wagon, horse-drawn, 6 figures, CI, 14", EX 715.00
Carpenter, fire ladder wagon, pnt CI, rpt horses, 24½", VG 475.00
Carpenter, pleasure cart, pnt CI, 2 rpl figures, 12", G 375.00
Carpenter, road cart, pnt CI, rpl driver, 10½", G 110.00
Chein, clown balances on hands, tin litho w/up, G 65.00
Chein, Disneyland Mickey Mouse Ferris wheel, tin w/up, 17" 275.00
Chein, drummer boy, tin litho w/up, 8¾", EX 125.00
Chein, duck, tin litho w/up, 3¾", EX...25.00
Chein, Hercules roller coaster, tin w/up, 1930s, NM in box 250.00
Chein, open stake bed skid truck, tin litho, 1925, 9", EX 525.00
Chein, Popeye jtd figure, pnt wood compo, c 1932, 10", EX 400.00
Chein, Popeye the Pilot, tin litho w/up, 1940, 8", EX 350.00
Chein, Popeye Walker, tin litho w/up, 5", VG.............................325.00
Chein, Raggedy Andy watering can, tin litho, EX........................15.00

Chein, Santa Claus walker, 5½", $295.00.

Chein, See-Saw sand toy, tin litho, ca 1935, 7", EX......................35.00
Chein, top, Snow White & 7 Dwarfs, EX 55.00
Converse, mail wagon, tin litho, pnt chips, 14", VG 325.00
Converse, trolley, pnt steel, clockwork, chips, 16", VG...............425.00
Cragstan, Shaking Antique Car, b/o, NM 95.00
Dayton, American Deluxe bus, tin litho, friction, 25", G............375.00
Dayton, trolley, pnt steel, friction, dents/wear, 14", G 575.00
Decamps, lion, fur-covered w/mane, working tail, 19" L, VG . 1,150.00

Dent, Conestoga wagon, pnt CI, rpr horse, 12", G 225.00
Dent, Hansom cab, pnt CI, rpt body, 14", G 275.00
Dent, Happy Hooligan nodder, pnt CI, wear, 5", G 150.00
Dent, hook & ladder truck, 3-horse-drawn, CI, 1910, 33", EX . 2,300.00
Dent, ice wagon, pnt CI, rpt shaft, rpl driver, 15½", G 220.00
Dent, Landau car, pnt CI, all orig, 15", G.................................600.00
Dent, Public Service bus, w/driver, CI, 13", EX 4,125.00
Dent, Puritan steamboat, pnt CI, lt rust, 11", G 85.00
Dent, summer trolley, pnt CI, lt rust/chips, 8", G.......................450.00
Distler, dbl-decker bus, tin litho w/up, 1910, 7", EX 1,200.00
Fallows, fire pumper, 2-horse-drawn, tin, 1890s, 14", EX......... 5,280.00
Fisher-Price, Bandwagon, #198, EX 450.00
Fisher-Price, Cackling Hen, wood & vinyl, 1966-68, 10", NM......15.00
Fisher-Price, Gold Star Stagecoach, 1954-56, 15½" L, EX.............75.00
Fisher-Price, Granny Doodle, #101 ....700.00
Fisher-Price, Hot Dog Wagon, bellringer, 1940-41, 10¾", M 100.00
Fisher-Price, Humpty Dumpty, pull toy, 1957, 10¼", EX.............75.00
Fisher-Price, Husky Dump Truck, wood/plastic, 1960s, 12", EX 12.00
Fisher-Price, Little Boy Blue TV Radio, 1967, 6x7¼", EX 4.00
Fisher-Price, Looky Fire Truck, pnt wood, 1950-54, 12x4½"..........45.00
Fisher-Price, Mickey Mouse Puddle Jumper, 1953, 6½", EX.........45.00
Fisher-Price, Music Box Iron, plastic, 1966-68, 8", NM 12.50
Fisher-Price, Musical Sweeper, tin litho w/wood hdl, '50, EX........65.00
Fisher-Price, picture disk camera, plastic/paper litho, NM............10.00
Fisher-Price, Snoopy Sniffer, felt ears, 1938-54, 16½", EX...........65.00
Fisher-Price, Tuggy Turtle, inner xylophone, 1960, 9", M............35.00
France, bulldog, papier-mache, pull toy, nodder/barks, 18".........600.00
France, passenger coach, tin w/compo driver, worn pnt, 12", G ..425.00

French, bicycle race, hand painted, felt-lined track, 18", $4,200.00.

Gama, alligator, tin litho, friction, 6½", EX 25.00
Gerard, dump truck, sheet metal, b/o lights, early, EX 120.00
Germany, biplane, tin, w/driver/propeller, 1900, G.....................400.00
Germany, carousel, pnt tin, velvet canopy, w/up, 13", VG...... 2,100.00
Germany, carousel, tin & cb, clockwork, worn pnt, 17", VG . 3,500.00
Germany, castle w/moat & swan, tin litho w/up, 1910, 9" 715.00
Germany, clown hits Blk man in bbl, tin litho clicker, 4½" 70.00
Germany, Ebo Express van, tin litho, clockwork, '07, 8", EX .. 2,400.00
Germany, Esso Gas Pump station, w/tin car, NM in box 750.00
Germany, Felix, pnt tin w/up, worn, 6¾", G 155.00
Germany, Ferris wheel, pnt tin w/up, 1910, 11", EX 1,650.00
Germany, Graf Zeppelin DLZ 127, tin litho w/up, '25, 11", EX ..465.00
Germany, lady w/umbrella & basket, tin litho w/up, 1900, 7", EX .. 1,300.00
Germany, Noah's Ark, pnt wood,1915, 4x14x6", +animals, EX..245.00
Germany, old hag w/umbrella, tin litho w/up, lt rust, G.............250.00

Germany, picture blocks, wooden, landscapes, 1800s, G in box ..100.00
Germany, scottie, tin w/blk felt w/up, glass eyes, 5" 40.00
Germany, spotted bulldog, tin litho w/up, 8", EX.......................100.00
Germany, wagon, goat-drawn, tin litho w/up, 8¼", G 75.00
Germany, waltzing Blk couple, HP tin, ca 1895, 6½", EX 1,850.00
Germany, water wheel, pnt tin w/up, 1910, 7½", EX.................495.00
Gibbs, gas station, tin litho, ca 1930, 11x8¼x7", EX 495.00
Gilbert, erector set, #8, manual, motor, wooden box, VG....... 1,500.00
Gilbert, US Mail truck, steel litho, crank wind, 8", EX................440.00
Gong Bell, Cinderella horse-drawn coach, CI pull toy, 9", VG ...250.00
Gong Bell, Daisy, child w/doll in sleigh, CI pull toy, 8½" 1,000.00
Gong Bell, Ding Dong Bell Pussy's Not in..., CI pull toy, 9", G ..700.00
Gundka (G&K), open touring car, tin litho, 1925, 7½", EX 440.00
Gunthermann, clown & dog, tin litho/pnt, w/up, '15, 8", EX . 1,500.00
Gunthermann, lady w/broom, pnt tin w/up, 1900, 7", EX 1,200.00
Gunthermann, merry-go-round, tin litho w/up, 1915, 7", EX . 1,325.00
Gunthermann, waltzing lady w/muff, tin litho w/up, '05, 8".... 1,760.00
Harris, dog cart, pnt CI, flaking, rpt wheels, 8", G 35.00
Harris, dr's buckboard, pnt CI, recast driver, 14", G 275.00
Harris, firetruck, 3-horse-drawn, HP CI, 1903, 31", EX........... 1,650.00
Harris, goat cart w/driver, pnt CI, 1903, 9½", EX 1,430.00
Hubley, buckboard, rpt CI, rpl driver, 13½", G 200.00
Hubley, chariot, rpt CI, rpl clown, 8", G 195.00
Hubley, Conestoga wagon, pnt CI, 11", G................................120.00
Hubley, general steam shovel, pnt CI, poor tires, 10", G 375.00
Hubley, Harley Davidson motorcycle, pnt CI, 9", EX.............. 1,540.00
Hubley, Huber road roller, pnt CI, lt rust, no driver, 14", G.......450.00
Hubley, ice wagon, pnt CI, all orig, 14½", G............................600.00
Hubley, Indian motorcycle & sidecar w/police, pnt CI, 9" 1,100.00
Hubley, lion wagon, pnt CI, emb panels, 11½", G 125.00
Hubley, Parcel Post motorcycle, CI, worn pnt, 10" 1,650.00
Hubley, Police Patrol truck, orig pnt/lt rust, 12", VG 700.00
Hubley, race car w/removable driver, pnt CI, 5⅜", G.................45.00
Hubley, roadster w/rumble seat, NP radiator, 5", EX..................120.00
Hubley, Roman chariot, 3-horse-drawn, CI, 1917, 10", EX........660.00
Hubley, Royal Circus bandwagon, total rpt CI, 23", VG 950.00
Hubley, Royal Circus cage wagon w/bear, CI, 1920, 9", VG........495.00
Hubley, Santa in sleigh w/reindeer, pnt CI, 1920s, 17", EX 1,000.00
Hubley, seaplane, w/5 motors, pnt CI, 4⅞", EX 200.00
Hubley, sleigh, 1-horse-drawn, rpt CI, 15", EX..........................450.00
Hubley, stake truck, CI, take-apart, 6", EX.................................275.00
Ideal, Bunny Chariot, NP CI, 1930, 9¼", EX 525.00
Ideal, carpet sweeper, plastic, w/dust bag & roller, 4½" 15.00
Ideal, Charlie McCarthy hand puppet, compo face/hat, 13", G.....55.00
Ideal, delivery van, brittle plastic, rubber wheels, 1950, 5" 15.00
Ideal, Hansom cab, rpt CI, 11", G 120.00
Ideal, Phantom Raider, w/torpedos & rockets, 1964, EX in box 85.00
Ideal, Pinocchio, jt wood figure, EX pnt, 1940s, 10½" 225.00
Irwin, Henry figure, pnt vinyl, w/squeaker, 8½", EX...................45.00
Issmayer, train set, tin litho w/up, ca 1900, 15" overall 635.00
Ives, Adams Express, CI, w/2 horses, 1896, 21", EX...................880.00
Ives, balancing horse dray, pnt CI, all orig, 14", VG 850.00
Ives, bandwagon, pnt CI, orig pnt, missing figures, 33", G 2,700.00
Ives, cat cart, CI, worn orig pnt, ca 1885, 6" L 440.00
Ives, coal wagon, CI, w/2 donkeys, 14", EX 800.00
Ives, Dancing Jiggers, clockwork, EX orig 750.00
Ives, fire hose wagon, horse-drawn, pnt CI, 1905, 17", EX 2,650.00
Ives, Flying Artillery, pnt CI, rpl driver, 31", G.......................2,500.00
Ives, Hansom cab, horse-drawn, pnt CI, 14", EX......................825.00
Ives, hook & ladder truck, pnt CI, driver/2 horses, 29", EX........715.00
Ives, hook & ladder truck, pnt CI, recast driver, 34", VG 2,000.00
Ives, pumper, pnt CI, rpl eagle, 23", VG 3,500.00
Ives, Uncle Tom fiddler, tin w/up, 1885, 9¼", EX in box.......15,400.00
J Pressman, Little Orphan Annie knitting outfit, 1930s, EX........100.00

Japan, Atomic Robot Man, tin litho w/up, 1950s, 5", EX **880.00**
Japan, Betty Boop, celluloid w/up figure, metal base, 7", EX........**400.00**
Japan, Buick station wagon, tin litho, b/o, 8", EX **135.00**
Japan, cable car, tin litho, friction, w/box, 6" **65.00**
Japan, Cadillac, tin litho, friction, 12", EX **285.00**
Japan, cat w/tin ball, plastic head/tail, tin w/up, 5", MIB **42.50**
Japan, Chevrolet Secret Agent, tin litho, b/o, 14", VG **65.00**
Japan, clown violinist, tin litho/cloth, 9", EX..............................**85.00**
Japan, cow, plush, on board, moos/walks/milks, b/o, 13", EX **350.00**
Japan, crawling baby, celluloid, w/up, 4½", MIB **65.00**
Japan, Drinking Captain, rubber/cloth, b/o, M **80.00**
Japan, elephant, musical, plays drum & cymbals, 5", MIB **48.00**
Japan, Ford country sedan, tin litho, friction, 12", EX **235.00**
Japan, Ford station wagon, tin litho, friction, 12", VG **400.00**
Japan, hungry cub, tin litho w/up, 5½", MIB **80.00**
Japan, kitchen wagon, tin litho, friction, 13", VG in box **45.00**
Japan, lion, leaps, vinyl face, w/up, 5", MIB **55.00**
Japan, merry-go-round, mtd on truck, 8½", MIB **90.00**
Japan, Oldsmobile, pnt tin, b/o, 7½", VG...................................**55.00**
Japan, parrot, celluloid, w/up, 7", MIB.......................................**85.00**
Japan, racer, tin litho, friction, visible engine, 10", VG **85.00**
Japan, robot, gr w/red tin earmuffs, tin w/up walker, 5"...............**120.00**
Japan, stunt car, pop-up man, tin, friction, 8½", MIB **60.00**
Japan, Sunday Driver, tin litho, b/o, 10", G **65.00**
Japan, trumpet player, rubber/tin w/up, 10½", EX in box............**400.00**
Japan, Uncle Sam plays drum, tin litho w/up, 7½", EX **85.00**
Japan, US Army M50 tank, tin litho, b/o, 4x5x3½", EX...............**27.50**
Japan, Venus motorcycle, tin litho, friction, 9", VG **200.00**
Japan, witch car, tin litho w/up, 3¼", EX in worn box **125.00**
Jones & Bixler, Uncle Sam chariot, rpt CI, 11½", EX...................**990.00**
Kensington, sedan, pnt sheet metal, 11½", G...............................**500.00**
Kenton, Air Cooled Franklin, pnt CI, w/figures, 8½", VG **1,760.00**
Kenton, Alphonse, nodder, pnt CI, 10½", VG **950.00**
Kenton, Army motor truck #807, pnt CI, 14", VG **880.00**
Kenton, Buckeye ditcher, pnt CI, side crank, 12½", G **770.00**
Kenton, Foxy Grandpa, nodder, pnt CI, 10½", VG **950.00**
Kenton, Happy Hooligan, nodder, pnt CI, 10½", VG...................**450.00**
Kenton, Happy Hooligan Police Patrol, rpt CI, 16½", G.........**1,500.00**
Kenton, horseless carriage, CI w/up, 1903, 6¼", EX **2,200.00**
Kenton, Jaeger cement mixer, pnt CI, rust spots, 6½", G...........**145.00**
Kenton, Overland Circus horse-drawn bear cage, CI, 1910, 14"..**550.00**
Kenton, Overland Circus wagon, pnt CI, 14", EX........................**325.00**
Kenton, roadster, pnt CI, no driver, 5¾", VG **300.00**
Kenton, roadster, pnt CI, rpl steering tiller, 5½", VG **175.00**
Kenton, US Mail wagon, pnt CI, lt rust, 6½", G **300.00**
Keystone, Packard Model Army truck, pnt steel, 26½", G **400.00**
Knapp, Electric Automobile, pressed steel, EX pnt, 1903, 11"..**3,575.00**
Kyser & Rex, circus wagon w/animals, CI, worn pnt, 13", EX..**9,900.00**
Lehmann, Adam (porter w/trunk), tin litho w/up, '20, 8", EX..**1,500.00**
Lehmann, Alabama Jigger, tin litho, 1915, 10¼", EX.....**1,650.00**
Lehmann, Autobus, dbl-decker, tin litho, 1910, 8¼", EX **2,400.00**
Lehmann, Blk boy & turtle, tin litho/celluloid w/up, MIB...........**100.00**
Lehmann, bug, tin, w/up, 4" **50.00**
Lehmann, dancing sailor, tin w/up, working, worn, box, 7½" ..**1,500.00**
Lehmann, motor coach, tin litho, 1905, EX in box **1,300.00**
Lehmann, Paddy & his pig, tin litho w/up, 1910, 6¼", EX......**1,100.00**
Lehmann, Quack-Quack, tin litho w/up, 7½", EX **495.00**
Lehmann, Uhu, clockwork, pnt face, non-working, 9" **850.00**
Lehmann, Zick-Zack, tin w/up, working, minor wear, box, 5". **2,300.00**
Lindstrom, motor boat, wood w/metal motor, 15½", G **250.00**
Lindstrom, Sweeping Mammy, tin litho w/up, MIB...................**500.00**
Linemar, Crawling Baby, celluloid/fabric, 10", EX **60.00**
Linemar, duck on skis, tin w/up, 4", MIB.....................................**145.00**
Linemar, Flippo Dog, tin litho w/up, 4", NMIB **120.00**

Linemar, Hot Rod Special, tin litho, friction, 10", G **85.00**
Linemar, Mickey Mouse on roller skates, tin litho w/up, EX........**750.00**
Linemar, Pluto pulls cart, head moves, friction, 1950s, EX..........**225.00**

Linemar, Popeye in airplane, keywind, 6" long, EX, $2,500.00.

Linemar, Popeye & Olive ball toss, tin litho w/up, 19", EX..... **1,000.00**
Linemar, Popeye the Pilot, tin litho w/up, 1940s, rare, 5" **2,500.00**
Linemar, Popeye turnover tank, tin w/up, 4", NM **235.00**
Linemar, Thumper, tin litho friction figure, 1950s, EX.................**90.00**
Linemar, Toytown Dairy milk wagon, tin litho w/up, 10", NM ...**185.00**
Lionel, auto racing set, 2 metal cars w/figures, 1912, EX **2,640.00**
Lionel, rndhouse, terra cotta sides, 1930s, 24", EX **1,100.00**
Marklin, armored car, camouflaged, 1938, complete, 14¾".....**3,000.00**
Martin, drinking man, HP, cotton clothes, w/up, 1890s, 8" **375.00**
Marx, Amos 'N Andy Fresh Air Cab, tin litho, 1932, 8", EX . **1,430.00**
Marx, Amos 'N Andy Fresh Air Cab, tin litho w/up, VG...........**800.00**
Marx, Blondie's Jalopy, tin litho w/up, 16½", EX **500.00**
Marx, BO Plenty walker, tin litho w/up, 8", NM........................**225.00**
Marx, Boat Tail Racer #61, tin litho, wood wheels, 5", EX **65.00**
Marx, Buck Rogers rocket ship, EX in box **1,200.00**
Marx, Bunny Express, 3-pc train set, EX in box **1,250.00**
Marx, Charlie McCarthy car, tin litho w/up, lt rust, 8", G...........**350.00**
Marx, City Sanitation Dept truck, tinplate, 13", EX in box........**250.00**
Marx, cowboy rider, tin litho w/up, 8¼", EX in box **325.00**
Marx, Dick Tracy police station, tin w/up, NM in 6x9x3" box....**245.00**
Marx, Disneyland Express set, tin w/up, on 13x22" brd **125.00**
Marx, Donald Duck & Goofy Duet, tin litho w/up, 10", G.........**325.00**
Marx, Donald the Skier, tin w/up, MIB **175.00**
Marx, drummer boy, tin litho w/up, pnt loss, 9", G **300.00**
Marx, Ferdinand the Bull, tin litho w/up, 7", VG in box.............**325.00**
Marx, fire chief's car, tin litho w/up, b/o lights, 11", VG **175.00**
Marx, Flash Gordon Rocket Fighter, tin litho w/up, 12", VG......**325.00**
Marx, grocery truck, tin plate/plastic, lt wear, 15", EX **150.00**
Marx, Ham & Sam, tin litho w/up, EX **550.00**
Marx, Harold Lloyd walker, tin litho w/up, 10", EX **325.00**
Marx, Here Comes Charlie, tin litho w/up, 1930s, 8⅜", VG **600.00**
Marx, Honeymoon Express, tin litho w/up, 9¼", EX in box **375.00**
Marx, ice truck, tinplate/plastic, 12½", EX in box **160.00**
Marx, Mammy's Boy, tin litho w/up walker, EX **425.00**
Marx, Mickey Mouse convertible, tin litho w/up, 11", VG..........**175.00**
Marx, Milton Berle Funny Car, tin w/up, plastic hat, 6", EX.......**175.00**
Marx, Officer Clancy, tin litho w/up walker, EX **500.00**
Marx, Old Jalopy, tin litho w/up, 7", EX in worn box **195.00**
Marx, Pan Am Clipper Meteor, pnt steel, 22", EX......................**200.00**

Marx, Pinocchio w/bucket in ea hand, tin litho w/up, 8½", G.....**300.00**
Marx, Popeye w/parrots, tin litho w/up, 1930s, 8¼", EX **275.00**
Marx, rabbit in car, plastic w/up, 5", M in box **150.00**
Marx, Ring-A-Ling Circus, tin w/up, wear/non-working, 8"........**400.00**
Marx, Rollover Plane, tin litho w/up, 5", EX in box.................**200.00**
Marx, stove & sink playset, 1950s, MIB **125.00**
Marx, Tidy Tim, tin litho w/up, scratched, 8¾", G....................**250.00**
Marx, tiger, cloth-covered w/up, 11", G......................................**45.00**
Marx, WWI Army Tank #3, tin litho, clockwork, VG **225.00**
Mattel, Cowboy Ge-Tar, plastic, w/up music box, 1952, 14" **15.00**
Mattel, Scarecrow in the Music Box, 1967, M.............................**15.00**
McLoughlin Bros, Magic Picture Puzzles, cb, 1893, +box **115.00**
Meccano, auto construction set #1, ca 1938, NM in box **900.00**
Modern Toys Japan, Old Timers #11, lever-action, box, 10" **85.00**
Motorcade, funeral coach, pnt CI, modern, 10", EX **350.00**
Nat'l Broadcasting, Ding Dong School xylophone, EX **20.00**
Nifty-Nirona (Germany), w/up turntable, w/records, 7", VG **200.00**
Nonpareil, Checker cab, tin litho w/up, sm dents, 6½", VG.......**195.00**
Ohio Art, music box, tin litho, crank hdl, 1948, 6x5½" dia **25.00**
Ohio Art, watering can, tin litho, Indian boy, 1950, 8x5", EX **25.00**
Pratt-Letchworth, Hansom cab, horse-drawn, CI, 1890s, 12", G.**700.00**
Pratt-Letchworth, pumper, horse-drawn, pnt CI, 1895, EX..... **1,500.00**
Rempel, Popeye figure, vinyl squeeze toy, 1950s, 8", NM..............**38.00**
Richter, Anchor Blocks, wooden, 1920, set in litho box..............**200.00**
Schuco, Donald Duck, tin litho w/up, 6", MIB..........................**275.00**
Schuco, Grand Prix racer #1070, tin litho w/up, 6½", EX...........**150.00**
Schuco, Lufthansa plane, 4-engine, tin w/up, '52, 19", EX **1,200.00**
Schuco, Magico car, tin litho w/up, 9¾", EX.............................**400.00**
Schuco, Mercer #1115, tin litho w/up, 7", NM **100.00**
Schuco, pig playing violin, tin litho/cloth, 1938, 4½", EX **600.00**
Schuco, race car, tin plate, 1938, 5½", EX in box **440.00**

Schuco, Yes-No cat, gray tiger stripes, glass eyes, 5½", $400.00.

Shimer, dray wagon, pnt CI, 2 horses, 17", EX **770.00**
Shimer, grocery wagon, NP CI, worn blk finish, 12½", VG.........**825.00**
Smith-Miller, flatbed tractor trailer, pnt steel, 26", VG...............**300.00**
Smith-Miller, Mack lumber truck, pnt wht metal, 19", G............**275.00**
Smith-Miller, Mack truck, pnt wht metal w/aluminum, 20", VG.**350.00**
Sonny, Railway Express truck, steel, EX pnt, 1928, 26", VG **300.00**
Steelcraft, US Mail plane, pnt steel, b/o lights, 22", VG **900.00**
Stevens, delivery wagon, horse-drawn, tin, 1880, 14", EX....... **2,500.00**
Stevens, man rides axle w/2 wheels, CI/tin, 1880, 4¾"............ **2,400.00**
Stevens, pony cart, pnt CI, rpl top, 8½", G.................................**475.00**
Strauss, Inter-State Bus, tin litho w/up, 10½", VG **425.00**
Strauss, Jackie the Hornpiper, tin litho w/up dancer, 9", G ..'......**500.00**

Strauss, Jazzbo Jim, tin litho w/up, '20, 9¾", NM in box **770.00**
Strauss, Knock-Out Prize Fighters, tin litho w/up, 5", EX **400.00**
Strauss, Leaping Lena, tin litho w/up, 8¼", VG **200.00**
Strauss, Santee (sic) Claus, tin litho w/up, sluggish, 11", G **500.00**
Strauss, Santee (sic) Claus, tin w/up, w/sleigh, 11", EX **1,900.00**
Strauss, Tombo Dancer, tin litho w/up, 1915, 10¼", EX............**600.00**
Structo, open roadster, steel, VG pnt, 1922, 15" **600.00**
Tippco, Graf Zeppelin, tin litho w/up, ca 1935, 17", EX.......... **1,300.00**
TootsieToy, battle cruiser, #1032, dtd 1937, 5", EX in box...........**100.00**
TootsieToy, battleship, #1034, M **20.00**
TootsieToy, biwing seaplane, #4650, NM pnt, 1926 ....**25.00**
TootsieToy, Buck Rogers Battlecruiser, EX pnt............................**45.00**
TootsieToy, cement mixer truck, pnt pot metal, 5", NM **50.00**
TootsieToy, Chevy Cameo pickup truck, 1956, 4", NM **24.00**
TootsieToy, Chrysler Windsor convertible, 1941, 4", M **40.00**
TootsieToy, Greyhound bus, #1045, 1937-41, EX.......................**35.00**
TootsieToy, hook & ladder truck, #4652, EX...............................**37.50**
TootsieToy, house trailer, 1935, sm, M.......................................**45.00**
TootsieToy, Internat'l dump truck, K-5, 6", M............................**25.00**
TootsieToy, Jumbo wrecker, #1027, 1941, 6", EX **40.00**
TootsieToy, log car, #1092, NM **12.50**
TootsieToy, Mack B-Line cement truck, 1955, M **18.00**
TootsieToy, Rambler wagon, 1960, 4", M....................................**25.00**
TootsieToy, Torpedo sedan, #1018, M...**45.00**
TootsieToy, Yel Cab sedan, #1629, 1921, NM.............................**22.00**
Tri-Ang, London Transport dbl-decker bus, 1964, 23", EX **450.00**
Unique Art, Dogpatch Band, tin litho w/up, 1945, 8x9½", EX ..**400.00**
Unique Art, Gertie the Galloping Goose, tin litho w/up, MIB....**300.00**
Unique Art, Lincoln Tunnel, tin litho w/up, 24", EX in box.......**375.00**
Unique Art, Rodeo Joe, tin litho w/up, 7", EX in worn box **250.00**
US Zone Germany, sport convertible, w/up, 9½", G....................**110.00**
US Zone Germany, Volkswagen, tin litho w/up, early, 7", EX.....**375.00**
USA, Little Mommies kitchen tool set, 1950s, 8-pc, EX **85.00**
Weeden, Favorite steam engine, pnt tin, alcohol burner, 6"........**500.00**
Weeden, fire pumper, CI/brass, ca 1890s, 18¼", EX **2,000.00**
Wilkins, boy riding bicycle, pnt CI, all orig, 4", G **300.00**
Wilkins, buckboard, pnt CI, minor rprs, 10½", G..........................**75.00**
Wilkins, cart, 1-horse-drawn/2-wheel, CI, 1895, 11", VG **725.00**
Wilkins, clown riding donkey, CI push toy, 1910, 8", EX............**715.00**
Wilkins, dog on base, pnt CI, minor wear, 3½", G.......................**70.00**
Wilkins, dray wagon, pnt CI, steel bed, no driver, 21", G **625.00**
Wilkins, hook & ladder wagon, pnt CI, minor rprs, 28", G **325.00**
Wilkins, horse & rider on platform, pnt CI/steel, 5", G...............**120.00**
Wilkins, locomotive, pnt CI, clockwork, sm rprs, early, 7" **425.00**
Wilkins, ox cart, CI, w/driver, worn pnt, 12", VG **900.00**
Wilkins, Phaeton, 2-horse, pnt CI/steel, 15½", G.......................**300.00**
Wilkins, work wagon, pnt CI, rpl driver, 14", G.........................**300.00**
Wolverine, Little Sweetheart ironing set, 1950s, M **60.00**
Wolverine, refrigerator, pnt metal, 1960s, 15", EX **40.00**
Wolverine, stove & sink set, pnt metal, ca 1950s, 12", pr **70.00**
Wolverine, Zilotone, pnt steel, clockwork, 4¼", EX **255.00**
Wyandotte, dump truck w/front loader, tin litho, 12", EX...........**275.00**
Wyandotte, tow truck, tin litho, 9", NM in orig box **350.00**
Wyandotte, woody convertible, pnt steel, top retracts, 12", G ...**135.00**

Farm Toys

Combine, Case, wht metal, G..**165.00**
Hay rake, CI, 5-pc, EX..**45.00**
Manure spreader, Massey Ferguson, Ertl, metal diecast, NM **12.00**
Manure spreader, TootsieToy, red pnt, 4-wheel, 1970, 4", M **20.00**
Mowing machine, Wilkins, rpt CI, 10½", G **2,200.00**
Pickup truck, Tonka, w/livestock rails, 1960s, NM **115.00**
Plow, Internat'l Harvester, 3-bottom, red pnt, 8", G **15.00**

Oliver diesel tractor, SLIK, 1952, 9", $470.00; Oliver mowing machine, #9986, SLIK, 1952, 4", $225.00.

Plow, Oliver, 2-bottom, ca 1950s, EX 70.00
Thresher, McCormick-Deering, pnt CI, Arcade, 10", G..............200.00
Thresher, McCormick-Deering, unmk, EX 140.00
Tractor, Allis Chalmers, Arcade, w/trailer, EX............................185.00
Tractor, Allis Chalmers, pnt CI, Arcade, 12", VG......................120.00
Tractor, Allis Chalmers type, Japan, friction, 5", EX 25.00
Tractor, Allis Chalmers 4-U Standard, CI, EX red pnt...............195.00
Tractor, Arcadia, CI, orange pnt, steel wheels, 3" 75.00
Tractor, Buddy L, front loader, metal, VG gr pnt, 6" 5.00
Tractor, Case, Ertl, #2590..60.00
Tractor, Ford, Auburn Rubber, ca 1938, EX 65.00
Tractor, Hubley, #500, w/plow 45.00
Tractor, McCormick-Deering, Arcade, +matching thresher 275.00
Tractor, McCormick-Deering, Arcade, rpl driver, 1922 model....475.00
Tractor, McCormick-Deering, CI, w/driver, 8", EX 300.00
Tractor, Minneapolis Moline, cast driver, ca 1956, EX 22.50
Tractor, Oliver, #77...275.00
Tractor, pnt tin w/litho motor, friction, 4¼", EX 25.00
Tractor, True Scale, metal wheels, #401, NM pnt.........................90.00
Wagon, Internat'l Harvester, red pnt, rubber wheels, 4½" 8.00
Wagon, John Deere, CI, removable box, EX 300.00
Wagon, McCormick-Deering, Arcade, EX 175.00

Guns

Though toy guns were patented as early as the 1850s, the cap pistol was not invented until 1870, when paper caps that were primarily developed to detonate muzzleloaders became available. Some of the earlier models were very ornate and were occasionally decorated with figural heads. Most are marked with the name of their manufacturer; Ace, Daisy, Bulldog, Victor, and Excelsior are the most common.

Ace, CI, cap pistol, 5", EX..35.00
Big Bill, CI, lg hammer, cap pistol, 5½", EX...............................22.00
Daisy, stag grips, gray finish, cap pistol, EX...................................30.00
Daisy #25 Pump, BB gun, EX..75.00
Daisy #26, BB gun 70.00
Daisy #71, water pistol, EX...25.00
Daisy Buzz Barton Special No 195, BB gun, M 95.00
Daisy Model H, BB gun 100.00
Echo, cap pistol, 1930, EX..30.00
Hellapin, BB gun, Pat Oct 24, 1893...250.00
Hubley Colt 45, cap pistol, EX...35.00
Hubley Cowboy, gold, cap pistol, worn 40.00
Hubley Ric-o-shay, cap pistol, EX 55.00
Hubley Texan Jr, gold, cap pistol, EX 75.00
Ives, CI, hammer hits head, Pat June 21 1887, 4⅜", NM..............300.00
Kenton Jr Police Chief, CI, automatic cap pistol, 1938, 4", VG 27.50
Kilgore American, CI, cap pistol, 9⅝", NM 100.00
Kilgore Big Chief, CI, cap pistol, 1935, 6", NM 38.00

Kilgore Bigger Bang, CI, lg hammer, cap pistol, 1930, 6", VG.......32.00
Kilgore Billy the Kid, CI, cap pistol, 1930, 6¾", EX.....................55.00
Kilgore Buster, CI, automatic cap pistol, 1910, 5½", VG 50.00
Kilgore G-Man, Bakelite-fr automatic cap pistol, 1940, 6", EX 32.00
King, cap pistol, 1925, EX...40.00
Marx Army #625, tin litho, revolving cylinder, M 18.00
Nichols Stallion Mark II, cap pistol, EX..................................100.00
Nichols Stallion 38, cap pistol, w/bullets, M 90.00

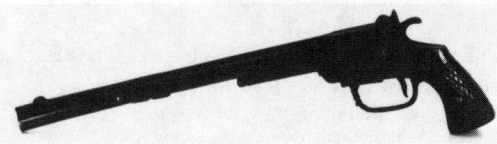

Stevens, cast iron, long barrel, 12", $145.00.

Stevens Bang-O, CI, cap pistol, 1938, 7", EX 27.50
Wyandotte Red Ranger, steel, six-shooter repeater, EX 22.50

Pedal Cars and Ride-On Toys

Am Nat'l, Packard, pnt steel, collapsible top, 53", EX............. 1,700.00
American, car, pnt steel, NP grill, 43", G 4,500.00
Austin Motors, car, steel, EX pnt, 1950, 60", VG 3,850.00
Austin 1940, pnt steel, Dunlop tires, rpt, 60", EX 850.00
Bomb, ride-on, fin tail, 3 metal wheels, 1910s, 36", G 250.00
Buick 1924 Roadster, pnt steel/wood, no windshield, 44", G.......950.00
Buick 1949 Comet, EX orig 750.00
Chrysler Airflow, Steelcraft, EX 1,980.00
Gendron, car, pnt steel, folding windshield, rstr, 38", EX........ 1,500.00
Gendron, 1938 convertible, 2-tone gr, rstr.............................. 2,675.00
Hilman, sports car, electric lights, 1950s, rstr, 58" 5,000.00
John Deere, tractor (2-cylinder), heavy cast metal, EX...............300.00
Keystone, sheet steel/wood, rubber tires, ca 1900, EX 2,250.00
Kirk-Latty, roadster, steel, orig pnt, 1918, 38", EX 325.00
Mors, car, steel plate/wood, maroon pnt, 1907, 45", EX 2,000.00
Steelcraft, car, EX pnt, folding windshield, 36", EX 900.00
Triang, racer, pnt steel, rpt, hand brake, 48", G 750.00

Penny Toys

Airplane, spring activated roundabout, German, 6", EX 275.00
Alligator, jtd neck & tail, Germany, 5" 135.00
Beetle, tin litho, legs move as wheels turn, 1900s, 1⅞" 175.00
Boat, pnt/litho tin, Germany, 4½", EX 500.00
Boxers, animated, clicker, tin litho, Germany, 5¾", EX 160.00
Camel, mc pnt, tin on iron wheels, 6¾x9¼" 275.00
Carousel, pnt/litho tin, Germany, 2½", EX 850.00
Goose, tin, HP, Germany, 4" 110.00
Horses pulling cart w/figure, tin litho, EX pnt 160.00
Limousine, brn pnt, w/driver, GF logo, Germany, 4" 175.00
Tube, pnt tin, blow through & wheel spins, France, 4" 35.00
Wagon, flatbed, horse-drawn, tin litho, Germany, 5"..................75.00
Woman pushes baby carriage, tin litho, 3", EX 290.00

Pipsqueaks

Pipsqueak toys were popular among the Pennsylvania Germans. The earliest had bellows made from sheepskin. Later cloth replaced the sheepskin, and finally paper bellows were used.

Boy on rooster, papier-mache, orig pnt, damage/silent, 3¾" 50.00

Cat, cloth over wood/compo, glass eyes, ribbon, label, 4" 100.00
Cat & kitten, papier-mache, orig pnt, squeaks, 5¾", EX 235.00

Cage with rooster inside, 6", $145.00.

Dog, seated, papier-mache, orig blk/mc pnt, rpl/damage, 4½"........45.00
Duck on nest, papier-mache, orig pnt, rpr, silent, 5¾" 425.00
Elephant, papier-mache, mc pnt, silent, 2¾", VG 55.00
Girl & lamb, animated, papier-mache/pnt/flocking, 4", VG........375.00
Goose on spring legs, squeaks, glued rprs, 7" 165.00
House w/chickens & ducks, wood/cb/papier-mache/bsk, 5", EX..350.00
Peacock, papier-mache, 4-color pnt, silent, minor wear, 5¾" 250.00
Rabbit, haircloth, animated ears, glass eyes, silent, 9".................325.00
Rooster, papier-mache, spring legs, orig pnt/gilt, 8", VG 250.00

Pull Toys

Alligator & boy, pnt CI, w/bell, ca 1900, 7½", EX 3,500.00
Bebe Gloria, bsk on pnt tin platform, w/bell, 1910, 7" 685.00
Clown disk revolves, bellringer, tin, 9½" 95.00
Clown on pig, CI, gong bell, orig pnt, 5¾", EX 1,400.00
Cow on platform, leather over wooden fr, 12" L, G 175.00
Dog, papier-mache, metal bell cart, lt rust, 10½", VG 220.00
Dog, wood, orig mc pnt, minor wear/damage, 5" L 75.00
Donkey, papier-mache nodder, glass eyes, CI wheels, 11"............225.00
Felix the Cat w/2 mice, tin litho, 1930s, 7½", EX 935.00
Horse, hide covered, leather harness/etc, 11", EX 150.00

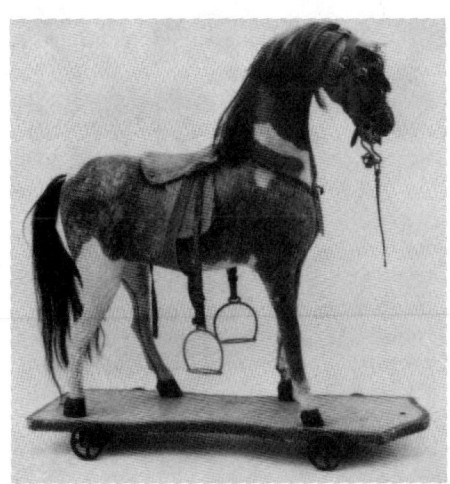

Hide-covered horse, Germany, 1800s, worn pelt, damage, 27" x 24", $500.00.

Horse, mohair over wood, leather ears, ca 1900, 10½", VG.........165.00
Horse/cart, sheet steel/CI legs move, Pat on label, 27", EX..........900.00
Horse/ladder wagon/drivers, tin/CI wheels, All Metal, 23" 8,300.00

Horse/wagon, tin & steel, w/bell, 13½", VG 85.00
Horse/wagon, tin w/worn orig 4-color pnt, Express, 11" L 300.00
Horses (2), pnt tin, Hull & Stafford, late 1800s, 8", EX..............750.00
Horses (2)/buckbrd, tin w/orig 3-color pnt, 12" L, EX 500.00
Jockey & horse, CI & steel, gong bell, 1910, 10" L, EX 850.00
Kicking mule bellringer, pnt CI, ca 1900, 7¾", EX 1,100.00
Liberty Bell Centennial, NP CI, w/bell, Gong Bell Co, 8" 1,400.00
Monkeys on a pole, J&E Stevens, CI, ca 1885, 10½", EX........ 1,450.00
Sailor in boat, tin, Woodette, 12", EX 55.00
Wild Mule Jack, CI, w/bell, orig pnt, ca 1900, 8¼" 700.00

Schoenhut

Buffalo, pnt eyes, regular 395.00
Bulldog, pnt eyes, EX blk & wht pnt, 1903, 5" 280.00
Camel, pnt eyes, 1 hump, regular..335.00
Clown, pnt eyes, reduced 95.00
Dog, glass eyes, wht pnt, 7½", EX..300.00
Donkey, glass eyes, EX pnt, 9", G 110.00
Donkey, pnt eyes, brn, 1903, 9", VG 150.00
Donkey, pnt eyes, reduced 85.00
Elephant, pnt eyes, reduced 85.00
Elephant, pnt eyes, regular 175.00
Geo Washington Coach, wood/compo, brass plaque, 23", VG 175.00
Hippo, pnt eyes, regular, EX 395.00
Horse, Educated; pnt eyes, 1903, 10" L 150.00
Horse, pnt eyes, brn, w/saddle, reduced...................................195.00
Horse, pnt eyes, wht, reduced 175.00
Horse, pnt eyes, 9½", G 150.00
Humpty-Dumpty Circus Set, 1926, complete in orig box, EX ..1,200.00
Ladder 18.00
Lady Circus Rider, pnt eyes, all orig, 8⅛" L 175.00
Lamb, glass eyes, ca 1907, 7¾" 285.00
Lamb, pnt eyes, 7½", EX...335.00
Lion, pnt eyes, gold & brn pnt, 1908, 8", EX............................175.00
Lion, pnt eyes, regular, NM..395.00
Living Picture, man & mouse, paper litho, clockwork, 15" 1,000.00
Piano, mahog finish, 16-note, 8¼x16¾x11¾", EX 275.00
Poodle, pnt eyes, regular, EX 200.00
Poodle, pnt eyes, regular, 7¼", VG 125.00
Ringmaster, bsk head, pnt eyes, orig costume, 8¼", EX.............300.00
Ringmaster, pnt eyes, reduced 175.00
Rubber ball shooting gallery, paper litho, 17", G 500.00
Swinging Golfer, compo head, metal/wood, mechanical, 26" 275.00

Steiff

    Margarete Steiff began making her felt stuffed toys in Germany in the late 1800s. The animals she made were tagged with an elephant in a circle. Her first teddy bear, made in 1903, became such a popular seller that she changed her tag to a bear. Felt stuffing was replaced with excelsior and wool; when it became available, foam was used. In addition to the tag, look for the 'Steiff' ribbon and the button inside the ear. For further information we recommend *Teddy Bears and Steiff Animals*, a full-color identification and value guide by Margaret Fox Mandel, available from Collector Books or your public library. See also Teddy Bears.

Alligator, Gaty, tag/button, 24" L..150.00
Bagheera (from Jungle Book), gold button, 9" 95.00
Bat, Eric, tag/button, 5" 525.00
Bear, Petsy, jtd, glass eyes, tag/button, 1960s, 14", EX................200.00
Bear, Zotty, long frosted mohair, ball jtd, 1950s, 10" 200.00
Bird, mohair & felt, tags/button, 1960s, NM................................60.00

Bison, tag/button, 10", M 250.00
Bison, w/button, 1950s, rare, 5½", M.........................175.00

Steiff, bulldog, 21" long, $795.00.

Camel, tan mohair, tags/button, 1950s, 5", M 75.00
Cat, Tabby, mohair, standing, button, 4"........................60.00
Cat, Topsy, paper tag only, 3" 40.00
Collie, recumbent, tag only, 9" 75.00
Dinosaur, tag/button, 10" L 625.00
Elephant, cloth label only, 6¼"......................................65.00
Elephant on wheels, sound box, ear tag, label, 24" L, VG..........425.00
Fawn, tag/button, 4½" 45.00
Fish, Flossy, tag/button, 26" L 400.00
Froggie, gr amphibian, tag/button, 1960s, 11¼", EX 125.00
Goat, tag/button, 7"..150.00
Goat, tag/button, 8¾"...175.00
Goat, Zicky, tag only, 4" 60.00
Horse, w/saddle, tag/button, 7".....................................65.00
Horse on rocking base, button/label, late, NM 250.00
Kitten, Floppy, tag/button, M 65.00
Kitten, wool pile head & arms, cushion body, dressed, 10", G.......75.00
Koala bear, wool pile, no button, 5", M 45.00
Llama, plush wool, brn glass eyes, w/button, 15", EX 125.00
Llama baby, velvet face & legs, glass eyes, no button, 5", M..........65.00
Monkey, swivel arms/legs/head, squeaker, button, 11", VG...........65.00
Monkey on scooter, straw stuffed, mohair, squeaker, 9", VG.......190.00
Mouse, wool pile, sitting, no button, 3½", M...................35.00
Owl, Wittie, w/button, 1950s, 4" 45.00
Pelican, Piccy, paper label (creased), 9½" 275.00
Penguin, blk & wht plush, glass eyes, tag/button, 29" 400.00
Penguin, tag/button, 4½" 50.00
Polar bear, bl eyes, leather collar & bell, no ID, sm, M.............195.00
Rooster, paper label only, 5¾".....................................115.00
Sled dog, barking jtd head, glass eyes, w/button, 25", EX 250.00
Squirrel, Perri, mohair, tag only, 8" 95.00
Squirrel, Perri, mohair, tag/button, 6" 75.00
Tiger, mohair, standing, w/button, 1950s, 5½x11", NM 85.00
Tiger, mohair, tag/button, 32" L 475.00
Tiger cub, mohair, sitting, w/button, 1950s, 4"...............60.00
Turtle, Slo, mohair, rubber shell, tag/button, 7" L...........55.00
Walrus, pajama bag, no tag...400.00
Walrus, tag/button, 8½" 100.00
Walrus, wool plush, glass eyes, no button, 5", M 45.00
Wild boar, cloth label only, 10½" L.............................150.00

Toy Soldiers

Toy soldiers were popular playthings with children of the 19th cen-

tury. They were made by many European manufacturers in various sizes until 1848 when a standard size of approximately 1⅓" was established. The most collectible of all toy soldiers were made in England by Britains Ltd. from 1893 to 1966. In America some of the important manufacturers were Barclay, Manoil, Grey, and All-Nu. Our advisor for this category is Tim O'Callaghan; he is listed in the Directory under Michigan.

Auburn, A002, marching at port arms.............................10.00
Auburn, A009, officer marching 10.00
Auburn, A014, doctor 27.00
Auburn, A015, nurse, wht..30.00
Auburn, A018, kneeling w/binoculars 15.00
Auburn, A019, signalman 55.00
Auburn, A021, standing, throwing hand grenade 21.00
Auburn, A024, motorcycle w/sidecar..............................50.00
Auburn, A030, sound detector.......................................35.00
Auburn, A034, running w/ammo box 35.00
Barclay, B005, flagbearer w/seperate tin helmet 21.00
Barclay, B007, flagbearer w/cast helmet 18.00
Barclay, B055, naval officer, wht 20.00
Barclay, B058, marine in dress uniform...........................25.00

Barclay, bayonetting, cast helmet, B107a, $275.00; Clubbing with rifle, cast helmet, B109, $100.00.

Barclay, B109, clubbing w/rifle, cast helmet.................100.00
Barclay, B129, standing, firing behind wall.....................50.00
Barclay, B201, flagbearer, WWII helmet........................20.00
Barclay, B213, drum major, WWII helmet 55.00
Barclay, B233, kneeling & firing, WWII, khaki...............10.00
Grey Iron, G010, shoulder arms.....................................14.00
Grey Iron, G018, signaling 25.00
Grey Iron, G021, carrying ammo boxes..........................90.00
Grey Iron, G031, crawling w/pistol 18.00
Grey Iron, G034, cavalryman, sm...................................30.00
Grey Iron, G035, cavalryman, lg.....................................30.00
Grey Iron, G042, Royal Canadian policeman 15.00
Grey Iron, G085, flagbearer..17.00
Grey Iron, G095, litter bearer...28.00
Grey Iron, G105, soldier helping wounded man...........250.00
Jones, J005, prone wire cutter.......................................450.00
Jones, J006, litter bearer 100.00
Jones, J013, officer pointing 225.00
Jones, J014, prone, firing rifle..115.00
Jones, J016, sitting w/anti-tank gun 85.00

Jones, J018, ammo carrier 350.00
Jones, J019, motorcycle rider 100.00
Jones, J020, flag bearer...225.00
Jones, J029, standing & firing rifle 100.00
Jones, J030, wounded, recumbent....................................90.00
Manoil, M003, flag bearer 22.00
Manoil, M024, sailor, wht 17.00
Manoil, M035, doctor, khaki...25.00
Manoil, M036, nurse w/pan 13.00
Manoil, M048, standing & firing rifle 17.00
Manoil, M084, sitting, eating 45.00
Manoil, M086, paymaster...135.00
Manoil, M174, machine gunner, prone WWII, thin sz 95.00
Manoil, M182, tommy gunner, WWII, regular sz 30.00
Manoil, M187, flag bearer, WWII, smaller sz....................30.00

Trains

Electric trains were produced as early as the late 19th century. Names to look for are Lionel, Ives, and American Flyer. The following listings were prepared by our advisor, Bruce C. Greenberg (see the Directory under Maryland), and are taken from his comprehensive publications on Lionel, American Flyer, and Ives trains. The prices presented are the most common versions of each item. In many cases there are several other variations often having a substantially higher value. Identification numbers given in the listings below actually appear on the item.

Key: Std Gauge — Standard Gauge

American Flyer 283, S Gauge engine w/tender, EX.......................60.00
American Flyer 332DC, S Gauge engine w/tender, EX 375.00
American Flyer 332DC, S Gauge engine w/tender, G.................80.00
American Flyer 360, 361 S Gauge diesels, EX 150.00
American Flyer 360, 361 S Gauge diesels, G 35.00
Ives 11, 0 Gauge steam engine w/tender, EX 125.00
Ives 11, 0 Gauge steam engine w/tender, G 75.00
Ives 1118, 0 Gauge steam engine w/tender, EX 150.00
Ives 1118, 0 Gauge steam engine w/tender, G 75.00
Ives 1132, Wide Gauge steam engine w/tender, 1921-26, EX......900.00
Ives 1132, Wide Gauge steam engine w/tender, 1921-26, G........450.00
Ives 3240, 1 Gauge electric engine, 1912-20, EX 800.00
Ives 3240, 1 Gauge electric engine, 1912-20, G 400.00
Ives 3241, Wide Gauge electric engine, 1921-25, EX 200.00
Ives 3241, Wide Gauge electric engine, 1921-25, G 100.00
Ives 3243, Wide Gauge electric engine, 1921-28, EX 600.00
Ives 3243, Wide Gauge electric engine, 1921-28, G 350.00
Lionel 1668, 0 Gauge steam engine w/tender, 1937-41, EX........120.00
Lionel 1668, 0 Gauge steam engine w/tender, 1937-41, G.............60.00
Lionel 2037, 0 Gauge steam engine/tender, 1954-55, 57-63, EX ...90.00
Lionel 2037, 0 Gauge steam engine/tender, 1954-55, 57-63, G 60.00
Lionel 224, 0 Gauge steam engine w/tender, 1938-42, EX..........170.00
Lionel 224, 0 Gauge steam engine w/tender, 1938-42, G 75.00
Lionel 2343, 0 Gauge diesels, 2 units, EX 650.00
Lionel 2343, 0 Gauge diesels, 2 units, G......................................200.00
Lionel 252, 0 Gauge electric engine, 1926-32, EX 140.00
Lionel 252, 0 Gauge electric engine, 1926-32, G 85.00
Lionel 380, Std Gauge electric engine, 1923-27, EX...................400.00
Lionel 380, Std Gauge electric engine, 1923-27, G 200.00
Lionel 400E, Std Gauge steam engine, 1931-40, EX.............. 2,300.00
Lionel 400E, Std Gauge steam engine, 1931-40, G 1,200.00
Lionel 408E, Std Gauge electric engine, 1927-36, EX 1,375.00
Lionel 408E, Std Gauge electric engine, 1927-36, G 600.00
Lionel 42, Std Gauge electric engine, 1913-23, rnd hood, EX.....550.00

Lionel 42, Std Gauge electric engine, 1913-23, rnd hood, G.......225.00
Lionel 50, 027 Gauge gang car, 1954-64, EX..............................50.00
Lionel 50, 027 Gauge gang car, 1954-64, G................................20.00
Lionel 58, 027 Gauge rotary snowplow, 1959-61, EX.................600.00
Lionel 58, 027 Gauge rotary snowplow, 1959-61, G 275.00
Lionel 60, 0 Gauge trolly, 1955-58, EX..125.00
Lionel 60, 0 Gauge trolly, 1955-58, G..50.00
Lionel 700E, 0 Gauge steam engine w/tender, 1937-42, G...... **1,900.00**
Lionel 726, 0 Gauge steam engine w/tender, 1946-49, EX..........325.00
Lionel 726, 0 Gauge steam engine w/tender, 1946-49, G 175.00
Lionel 773, 0 Gauge steam engine w/tender, 1950, 64-66, EX.....775.00
Lionel 773, 0 Gauge steam engine w/tender, 1950, 64-66, G 400.00
Lionel 8, Std Gauge electric engine, 1925-32, EX......................175.00
Lionel 8, Std Gauge electric engine, 1925-32, G.........................90.00

Miscellaneous

Hobby horse, covered mohair, on platform, ca 1900, EX 450.00
Noah's ark, +68 animals, stenciled band on 19" ark, unpnt 450.00
Noah's ark, paper on wood, 1900, 5x20x3¾", +18 figures 150.00
Ox cart & driver, wood w/worn mc pnt, 7", VG 175.00
Rocking horse, pnt wood silhouettes, seat between, rpl 125.00
Rocking horse, pnt wood w/metal brackets, ca 1900, 46", EX......715.00
Rocking horse, wood, head on rockers, sm seat atop, 32"............750.00
Rocking horse, wood, inserted legs, CI stirrups, 46", VG 775.00
Rocking horse, wood w/hide & horsehair, glass eyes, 73", VG.....800.00
Wagon, buckboard style, wooden spoke wheels, old, 22x46x24" .250.00

Trade Signs

Trade signs were popular during the 1800s. They were usually made in an easily recognizable shape that one could mentally associate with the particular type of business it was to represent, especially appropriate in the days when many customers could not read!

Boot, high top, pnt wood figural, 17", VG 210.00
Boot, wood w/gold & silver rpt, 26"...225.00
Butcher, tools/bull atop, CI, dtd 1889, rpt, 20x24" 325.00
Dentist, lg cvd wood tooth, gilt pnt, 14", EX 500.00
Drug (mortar/pestle) Store on ribbon, wood/pnt, rpl, 72"...........700.00
Drugs, lg letters, blk/wht pnt on wood, 12x50", EX.....................225.00
Horse, wood, full figure, ⅔rd-size, laminated, 64x72", EX 1,000.00
Key, 3-D tin key w/'Yale,' metallic/blk pnt, 34" L, VG 800.00
Long Horn Saloon, pnt wood, mug of beer, 1900s, 39½x9" 235.00
Mortar & pestle, pnt tin w/glass jewels, flaking pnt, 36" 650.00
Mortar & pestle, sheet zinc w/gold rpt, dents, 32" 450.00
Optometrist, CI/steel glasses w/pnt-in eyes on banner, 36" 5,000.00
Pawnbroker, 3 copper balls hang from iron fr, 24" 225.00
Pewter teapot w/wood hdl & finial, Richardson, 1800s, 16" ... 3,000.00
Pocket watch, blk/wht pnt sheet metal in CI fr, 21x15", EX 225.00
Pocket watch, pnt CI & tin, dbl-sided, 20", VG 1,600.00
South Bend Watch Co, copper/CI, watch figural, w/chain, 11", G.350.00

Tramp Art

Today considered a type of American folk art, tramp art was primarily made from the end of the Civil War until the 1930s. Often produced by tramps and hobos from wooden materials which could be scavenged (crates and cigar boxes, for instance), articles such as jewelry boxes and picture frames were usually decorated by chip carving and then stained. Some of them were painted; the best were polychromed. Our advisor for this category is Matt Lippa; he is listed in the Directory under Iowa.

Spice box, ca 1870, PA, $395.00; Sewing box, ca 1890, $795.00; Pedestal box, ca 1880, $375.00.

Box, chip cvd, dk gr pnt, hinged top, 1900s, 7x9x5½" 200.00
Box, chip cvd, gold & silver pnt, sgn/dtd 1933, 4x10x8" 175.00
Box, chip cvd, tiered top, inlaid hearts, 6x9x5" 225.00
Box, sewing; chip cvd, dbl ped, 5-drw, 1900s, 18x11x7", EX 745.00
Cabinet, spice; chip cvd, 6-drw w/cvd knobs, 1870, 12x9x4", EX ..400.00
Frame, chip cvd, built in 4 layers, 1920s, 11x7¾", EX 95.00
Frame, chip cvd, heart shapes, fence-like border, 20x18" 350.00
Frame, chip-cvd points, hinged, varnished, 1900s, 15x12x3" 275.00
Frame, oval cvg, Xd corners, lacquered, ca 1880, 13x12", VG 95.00
Frame, teardrop & dmn cvgs in corners, varnished, 10x8½" 195.00
Frame, tiered Vs, circles & rectangles, gold pnt, 14x12" 195.00
Sideboard, chip cvd, 3 doors, gallery, 1880s, 9x8x5½" 350.00
Stool, appl dmn shapes, cloth top, old pnt, 1900s, 8x14x11" 350.00
Wall pocket, chip cvd, scalloped top, 1900s, 8x5x2½" 150.00

Traps

Though of interest to collectors for many years, trap collecting has gained in popularity over the past ten years in particular, causing prices to appreciate rapidly. Traps are usually marked on the pan as to manufacturer, and the condition of these trademarks are important when determining their value. Grading is as follows:

Good: one-half of pan legible.
Very Good: legible in entirety, but light.
Fine: legible in entirety, with strong lettering.
Mint: in like-new, shiny condition.

Our advisor for this category is Boyd Nedry; he is listed in the Directory under Michigan. Prices listed here are for traps in fine condition.

Alaskan, The Wolf Trap, dbl coil spring.................................85.00
Alexander Cosey & Sons, trip wire killer 24.00
Arrow #4, single under spring 80.00
Automatic, The World's Finest, metal mousetrap.....................20.00
Belmont Steel 'Sure Grip,' #1½, single long spring 20.00
Blake Lamb #1, jump, Pat Apr, 28, 56 ....25.00
Bu-ro-des, orchard mouse destroyer, glass 45.00
Champion #2, dbl long spring 15.00
Champion Multi Trigger, Los Angeles Calif, #4 ....120.00
Cobra, Toronto Canada, metal snap mousetrap...................... 4.00
Cooper Humane Killer #2, coil spring.................................45.00
Courtland #1 dogless, plain jaw, single long spring.................75.00
Cush-In-Grip #2, rubber-lined jaws, dbl long spring 25.00
Defiance, Sharpleigh Hdw Co, wood snap mousetrap 25.00
Diamond #1½, single long spring 20.00
Eclipse #2, under spring 40.00
EZ-Set, Clear Lake IA, metal killer, mousetrap 25.00
Family Mouse Trap, live catch, self set..................................45.00
Gibbs #1½, w/sod pan, single under spring 22.00
Gibbs Hawk, dbl coil spring 125.00

Good Luck #1, single long spring 45.00
Half Moon, Canada, tin 2-hole choker.................................65.00
Handforged, w/teeth, beaver trap...125.00
Hector, #0, single long spring 40.00
Hotchkiss & Sons #2, dbl long spring.................................125.00
J Duffis & Sons, English, mole choker 415.00
Jack Frost, Neverlose, coil spring...18.00
Kopper Kat, Aurora IL, metal mousetrap.............................20.00
Kriket #1, single under spring...12.00
Kwik Grip #1, coil spring 6.00
Luna, snap mousetrap 5.00
Magnetic, metal snap mousetrap...20.00
Montgomery #1½, coil spring 5.00
Museum Special, wood snap mousetrap 10.00
Nanco Safe-t-Set, wood snap type...30.00
Newhouse #0, single long spring 50.00
Newhouse #15, bear trap...350.00
Newhouse #3½, single long spring 45.00
Newhouse #4½, wolf trap..150.00
Newhouse #81½, single long spring 85.00
Official Mouse Trap, Animal Trap Co, snap type................... 8.00
Orbeto #400, dbl under spring 20.00
Pioneer #5, dbl long spring 15.00
Reddick, Niles MI, mole trap 15.00
Rice Improved Killer...20.00
Rittenhouse spear type, Pat 1901, mole trap 20.00
Safe Setter, shaped like steel trap, metal mousetrap, rare...........100.00
Sargent #1, sq stamped pan 18.00
Sargent #23, offset jaws w/teeth 150.00
Snappy, Pat 1907, metal mousetrap 20.00
Streeter & Anstice, CI, snap mousetrap 45.00
Taylor, TH Ketchum Mfg Co 30.00
Toms Fly Trap, fits on fruit jar...20.00
Unique, plastic coon trap 20.00
Van Wormer Cast Iron, Pat 1888, mole trap 80.00
Victor, 4-hole, choker mousetrap..18.00
Victor #1, jump & long spring 3.00
Victor #1½, coil spring 3.50
Victor #91½, single long spring 7.00
Vox, mole trap...18.00
Webley #4, coil spring 40.00
Wiggness, gopher trap 32.00
Wilson JR, Pat Oct 11, 21 ....225.00
World's Best Roach Trap Co, Memphis TN 65.00
X-terminator, plastic live mousetrap 4.00
Zip, metal snap mousetrap 10.00

Trivets

Although strictly a decorative item today, the original purpose of the trivet was much more practical. They were used to protect table tops from hot serving dishes, and irons heated on the kitchen range were placed on trivets during use to protect work surfaces. The first patent date was 1869; many of the earliest trivets bore portraits of famous people or patriotic designs. Florals, birds, animals, and fruit were other favored motifs. Watch for remakes of early original designs. Some of these are marked Wilton, Emig, Wright, and Iron Art.

Brass

Cross & crown, Colebrookdale, Pottstown PA..............................50.00
Heart shape, Give Your Heart to God Now in center, 5x8½".......75.00
Home Sweet Home, peg ftd, early...75.00

I Want You, Strause Gas Iron Co, Philadelphia PA **55.00**
Lion & unicorn, rtcl, English, 5½x7x12" **175.00**
Pierced top, bulbous legs, mk WT&S, English, 6½" dia **175.00**
Swans w/rtcl, worn silvering, 11" **85.00**
8-petal center, wrought legs, trn wood hdl, 12½" **125.00**

Cast Iron

Hearts form border, starflower w/in circle center, 13", VG **90.00**
Horseshoe, Good Luck, Pat 1885, 4⅞" L **60.00**
Starflower center, compass circles & arches, 5" dia **65.00**
Tulip (stylized), EX details, 5½" **65.00**
3 hearts & geometrics in openwork, W in center, 9½x5" **65.00**

Wrought Iron

Heart form, 3-leg, rattail hdl, early, 11½" **165.00**
Rnd, circle w/in 4 scrolls, 4 tall legs **195.00**
Rnd w/3 legs & adjustable pot rest, 9" dia........................**175.00**
Triangular strap w/5 curlicues w/in, scroll ft, hdl, 12" L **195.00**

Trolls

The modern-day version of the troll was designed in 1952 by Helena and Marti Kuuskoski of Tampere, Finland. Those made by Dam and those marked with a horseshoe are among the most valuable, since both are made from the original Kuuskoski design. Many copies have been produced, the best of which are the Wishniks, made by the Uneeda Doll Company. These were first marketed in 1979 and are currently still available. Troll animals are scarce, and values are rising. New Dam animals are easily distinguished from the old ones, and though they are popular sellers, it's the old issues that hold their value and collectors' interest. Our advisor for this category is Susan Miller; she is listed in the Directory under Indiana.

Bank, boy or girl, 8", ea **25.00**
Blk, jtd neck, Dam Things, 18" **150.00**
Common type, Dam Things, 16"....................................**75.00**
Common type, Dam Things, 3"......................................**9.00**
Common type, Dam Things, 6"......................................**20.00**
Common type, no mk, 12" **12.00**
Common type, no mk, 3" **5.00**
Common type, Uneeda, 3" **7.00**
Cow, sm **35.00**
Donkey, glassene eyes, all orig, 3" **35.00**
Donkey, 9" **85.00**
Elephant, sm **35.00**
Grandpa, 1977, 13"..**25.00**
Man w/beard, red, 3"..**18.00**
Pattern, McCall's, uncut..**20.00**
Santa Claus, bank, Dam Things, 9" **65.00**
Santa Claus, 3"..**16.00**
Troll House **15.00**
Turtle **55.00**
Viking, glassene eyes, helmet, all orig, 7" **150.00**
Vinyl w/cloth body, Ideal, 14" **75.00**
Vinyl w/cloth body, unmk, 14" **45.00**
2-Headed, 6"..**25.00**

Trunks

In the the days of steamboat voyages, stagecoach journeys, and railroad travel, trunks were used to transport clothing and personal belongings. Some, called 'dome top' or 'turtle backs,' were rounded on top to better accommodate milady's finery. Today some of the more interesting examples are used in various ways in home decorating. For instance, a flat-topped trunk may become a coffee table, while a smaller dome style may be 'home' for antique dolls or a teddy bear collection. In the listings that follow, the dimension given is length.

Camphorwood, brass bound, Chinese, 1850s, 42" **800.00**
Camphorwood, dome top, brass studs, 1800s, 40", EX..................**775.00**
Leather bound, dome top, w/orig label: Sharples Phila 1791 ....**325.00**
Leather covered, gr/tan w/brass-tack trim, 15½"..........................**375.00**
Louis Vuitton, fitted int, 1910, 44"......................................**600.00**
Oak, dome top, dvtl, fancy wrought hinges, 47" **325.00**
Oak, dome top, truncated sides, 50", EX................................**220.00**
Pine, dome top, bl pnt traces, wrought mts, 30", VG **225.00**
Pine, dome top, red pnt & blk grpt, dvtl, 27" **85.00**
Pine, leather trim w/brass tacks, 18x10x9" **125.00**
Tooled leather, dome top, iron lock/hdl, dtd 1650, 11" **250.00**

Tuthill

The Tuthill Glass Company operated in Middletown, New York, from 1902 to 1923. Collectors look for signed pieces and those in an identifiable pattern. Condition is of utmost importance.

Bowl, Rex, hobstars/fans, 8" **1,550.00**
Bowl, step cuttings/stars, canted corners, serrated, 2x7x9"...........**360.00**
Creamer & sugar bowl, intaglio dahlias, notched rims.................**225.00**
Cruet, floral/brilliant cuttings, notched hdl, 7" **150.00**

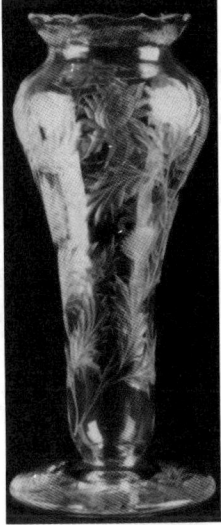

Cut glass vase, chrysanthemum engraving, signed, 18", $2,000.00.

Ferner, stars & fans, brilliant cut, ftd, 4½x7½" **200.00**
Tray, calling card; intaglio florals, scalloped, 8½" L **200.00**
Vase, vintage intaglio, hdls, urn shape, 11" **750.00**
Vase, vintage intaglio allover, slim form, 16½" **395.00**

Typewriters

The first commercially successful typewriter was the Sholes and Glidden, introduced in 1874. By 1882 other models appeared, and by the 1890s dozens were on the market. At the time of the First World War, the ranks of typewriter-makers thinned, and by the 1920s only a few survived.

Collectors informally divide typewriter history into the pioneering period, up to about 1890; the classic period, from 1890 to 1920; and the modern period, since 1920. There are two broad classifications of early typewriters: (1) Keyboard machines, in which depression of a key prints a character and via a shift key prints up to three different characters per key. (2) Index machines, in which a chart of all the characters appears on the typewriter; the character is selected by a pointer or dial and is printed by operation of a lever or other device. Even though index typewriters were simpler and more primitive than keyboard machines, they were none-the-less a later development, designed to provide a cheaper alternative to the standard keyboard models that were selling for upwards of $100. Eventually second-hand keyboard typewriters supplied the low-price customer, and index typewriters vanished except as toys. Both classes of typewriters appeared in a great many designs.

It is difficult, if not impossible, to assign standard market prices to early typewriters. Unlike collectors of postage stamps, carnival glass, etc., few people collect typewriters, so there is no active marketplace from which to draw stable prices. Also, condition is a very important factor, and typewriters can vary infinitely in condition. A third factor to consider is that an early typewriter achieves its value mainly through the skill, effort, and patience of the collector who restores it to its original condition, in which case its purchase price is insignificant. Some unusual-looking early typewriters are not at all rare or valuable, while some very ordinary-looking ones are scarce and could be quite valuable. No general rules apply. When no condition is indicated, the items listed below are assumed to be in excellent, unrestored condition. Our advisor for this category is Mike Brooks; he is listed in the Directory under California.

O'Dell #4, Farquhar and Albrecht, Chicago, with original box, $275.00. (Without box, $200.00.)

Boston, index 1,500.00
Brooks, EX 500.00
Carpenter, EX 500.00
Crary 1,000.00
Dennis Duples, EX 200.00
Fitch, EX 500.00
Hammond Multiplex, early, w/wooden case, EX orig 75.00
Index Visible, EX 300.00
McCool, EX 300.00
Merritt, index, wood cover, instruction label in lid, EX 395.00
Nat'l, curved front, EX 150.00
Niagara, index 700.00
Oliver #5 Standard Visible Writer 75.00
Oliver #9, EX 50.00
Practical #4, oak base 120.00
Royal #5, gold trim, VG 175.00
Sholes & Glidden, 1st mass-produced, ca 1874, EX 1,000.00
Smith-Corona #4, portable, 1920s, EX in case 50.00
Victor, index, rare, EX 500.00

Uhl Pottery

Founded in Evansville, Indiana, in 1849 by German immigrants, the Uhl Pottery was moved to Huntingburg, Indiana, in 1908 because of the more suitable clay available there. They produced stoneware — Acorn Ware jugs, crocks, and bowls — which were marked with the acorn logo and 'Uhl Pottery.' They also made mugs, pitchers, and vases in simple shapes and solid glazes marked with a circular ink stamp containing the name of the pottery and 'Huntingburg, Indiana.' The pottery closed in the mid-1940s. Those seeking additional information about Uhl pottery are encouraged to contact the Uhl Collectors' Society, whose address is listed in the Directory under Clubs, Newsletters, and Catalogs.

Ash tray, Acorn Ware, brn, mk 175.00
Ash tray, Shell Oil, brn 100.00
Bowl, batter; bl, mk, 8" 90.00
Bowl, chili; bl, mk, 12-oz 35.00
Bowl, mixing; Basketweave, brn, 8" 45.00
Bowl, mixing; bl, 4" to 12", set of 9 .... 360.00
Bowl, Pond Lily, bulbous, brn, 7" 45.00
Bowl, salad; pk, mk, 11" 80.00
Candle holder, gr, hand trn, w/hdl, mk, 6" 100.00
Casserole, pk, w/lid, mk, 3-pt 40.00
Churn, Acorn Ware, w/bail, 2-gal 90.00
Churn, Evansville, mk, 3-gal 105.00
Cookie jar, brn, mk, #522 .... 65.00
Cookie jar, globe, bl 120.00
Cookie jar, globe, bl, mini 145.00
Dispenser, ice water; Acorn Ware, 5-gal 180.00
Jug, Acorn Ware, Harvest, stone hdl, 1-gal 275.00
Jug, Acorn Ware, 1-pt 175.00
Jug, Acorn Ware, ½-gal 65.00
Jug, Acorn Ware, 5-gal 50.00
Jug, brn & wht, mk, 1" 90.00
Jug, canteen, Believe-It-Or-Not 285.00
Jug, canteen, pk, mini 45.00
Jug, cat form, bl, mini 90.00
Jug, Egyptian, pk, #133, 12-oz 45.00
Jug, elephant, pk, mini 55.00
Jug, football, brn, mini, 4" 40.00
Jug, horse head, wht, mini 110.00
Jug, Merry Christmas, 1941 .... 220.00
Jug, polar bear, bl, ½-gal, 9" 375.00
Jug, refrigerator; bl, flat, w/stopper, #190 .... 65.00
Jug, softball, wht, 3½" 220.00
Mug, coffee; pk, mk 50.00
Mug, Grape, bl, 12-oz 100.00
Mug, tan, mini, 3-oz 70.00

Pitcher, 8½", $85.00.

Pitcher, bl, bbl form, mk, 1-qt 70.00
Pitcher, Grape, bl, bulbous, #182 ....95.00
Pitcher, Grape, bl, str sides, mk, 3-qt 145.00
Pitcher, Lincoln, bl, 1-pt, 6" 240.00
Pitcher, Lincoln, bl, 2-qt, 10" 350.00
Pitcher, pk, flagon, mk, 5-qt 85.00
Shoe, baby; pk, mk...50.00
Shoe, Dutch; bl, #2 ....50.00
Shoe, Dutch; bl, #6 ....65.00
Teapot, bl, mk, #132, 4-cup 175.00
Teapot, bl, mk, #143, 8-cup 250.00
Vase, bl, #152, 5" 60.00

Unger Brothers

The Art Nouveau silver produced by Unger Brothers, who operated in Newark, New Jersey, from the early 1880s until 1909, is fast becoming very popular with today's collectors. In addition to tableware, they also made brushes, mirrors, powder boxes, and the like for milady's dressing table as well as jewelry and small personal accessories such as match safes and flasks. They often marked their products with a circle seal containing an intertwined 'UB' and '925 fine sterling.' In addition to sterling, a very limited amount of gold was also used. Note: This company made no pewter items; Unger designs may occasionally be found in pewter, but these are copies. Items dated in the mark or signed 'Birmingham' are English (not Unger).

Baby's cup, strainer inside, ornate hdl, 2¾" 350.00
Baby's cup, w/name & dtd 1908, 3" 250.00
Baby's hairbrush, long handle, 5½" 125.00
Baby's rattle, MOP hdl, loop for hanging, 5".....275.00

Belt, poppy forms joined by chain, hallmarked, $300.00.

Bookmark, sterling, monogram, sm...............................30.00
Box, cheroot; repousse nude/waves on rectangle form, 3" L 200.00
Box, cylindrical, lift-off lid, 3⅝".................................275.00
Clothes brush, 7" 160.00
Cream ladle, Duvaine...60.00
Gravy ladle, Duvaine..120.00
Hairbrush, handleless, 4¼x2½".................................190.00
Match safe, repousse angel/nude in waves, sterling, 2¼" L..........150.00
Match safe, repousse floral/scroll/leaves, free-form, 2¾"................90.00
Pickle fork, Duvaine 50.00
Tweezers, 6½" 165.00
Vanity set, repousse lily, hand mirror+2 brushes+buffer 475.00

Universal

Universal Potteries Incorporated operated in Cambridge, Ohio, from 1934 to 1956. Many lines of dinnerware and kitchen items were produced in both earthenware and semi-porcelain. In 1956 the emphasis was shifted to the manufacture of floor and wall tiles, and the name was changed to the Oxford Tile Company, Division of Universal Potteries. The plant closed in 1976. Our advisor for this category is Ted Haun; he is listed in the Directory under Indiana.

Ballerina, bowl, mixing; 3-pc set 55.00
Ballerina, cup 5.00
Ballerina, plate, 6" 2.00
Ballerina, platter, lug hdl, 11½"................................5.00
Ballerina, shakers, pr 8.00
Camwood, utility tray, 13½"..................................12.50
Cattail, bowl, 5¼" 2.75
Cattail, bowl, 8½" 8.00

Cattail butter dish, $30.00.

Cattail, casserole, w/lid, 8¼" 22.00
Cattail, cup & saucer 12.00
Cattail, custard..5.50
Cattail, plate, 6" 2.50
Cattail, plate, 9" 5.00
Cattail, platter, 11½" 12.00
Circus, jug, water; lg, no stopper 12.50
Largo, bowl, 6" 8.00
Poppy, fork 12.00
Poppy, refrigerator jug..18.00
Zinnia, canteen jug 40.00

Val St. Lambert

Since its inception in Belgium at the turn of the 19th century, the Val St. Lambert Cristalleries has been involved in the production of high quality glass, specializing in cameo. The factory is still in production. Our advisor for this category is Don Williams; he is listed in the Directory under Missouri.

Bottle, scent; emb patterning, sapphire bl frost, 5x2" 88.00
Vase, bands of scrolling foliage, gray washed, 7¾" 300.00
Vase, stylized acanthus leaves emb, amber, ovoid, 1940s, 9"........200.00

Cameo

Vase, floral, lt gr on frost, cut/notched collar, 7x3" 650.00
Vase, sailboat, mc on smoky opal, flattened oval, 6"................ 1,100.00

Valentines

Handmade Valentines date back to the mid-1700s in the United States; as time went on, increased interest resulted in other types of Valentine cards being made. Today Valentine collectors are not the only ones who buy; Valentines are often considered a desirable addition to other collections as well — Black memorabilia, advertising, transportation memorabilia, Walt Disney, cartoon and movie characters, etc. Besides examples representing these areas, 3-dimensionals and mechanical Valentines (1860s to the present) are becoming highly prized by many collectors. There are six qualifying specifications to consider when evaluating a Valentine card: age, size, category, manufacturer, artist signature, and condition. Our advisor for this category is Katherine Kreider; she is listed in the Directory under California.

Key: HCPP — honeycomb paper puff

Three-dimensional with Victrola, early 1900s, MIG, 10" long, $175.00.

Airplane, 2-D, chromolitho, MIG, 1920s, 4⅜x3½x3", EX.............30.00
Airplane, 3-D, lobster on wing, MIG, '20, 9x8", NM....................125.00
Angel amid flowers, 2-D, chromolitho, MIG, 1900s, 3x4x2", NM .25.00
Ballerina, chromolitho, HCPP tutu, MIG, 1927, 5¼x4½", EX 30.00
Big-eyed boy, litho, cobweb center, 1900s, EX 75.00
Big-eyed child rides mechanical duck, 5½x7", VG........................35.00
Big-eyed children in 1920s car w/dog, 2-D, 7x8x3", VG 75.00
Big-eyed girl in bonnet, mechanical litho, MIG, '23, 8x5", EX 45.00
Big-eyed kids on HCPP atomizer, tab stand, '20s, 8x7½", NM ...150.00
Black child under sprinkling can, USA, 1940s, 5½x3½", NM.......35.00
Black harmonica player, USA, 1900s, 3¾x2¾", NM 40.00
Brownie & Cub Scout, USA, 1960s, 6x3¼", EX 15.00
Buster Brown, mechanical, chromolitho, MIG, 9¼x6½", NM 175.00
Cagney, James; USA, 1935, 5⅞x3½", EX..45.00
Cherub on HCPP base of 3-D windmill, chromolitho, 5½", NM...35.00
Cherub w/butterfly net, 2-D, litho, MIG, 4x2½x1½", NM 55.00
Choked to Death, dtd 1909, 7½x6", NM in orig box 175.00
Cinderella-type coach, 3-D w/HCPP, 1900s, 11¼x13x6", VG 95.00
Clapsaddle, cherub in cart w/hearts, 3-D, 4¼x6¼x2½", NM 75.00
Dirigible, HCPP top, child in basket, tab stand, MIG, 4", EX........50.00
Dopey, mechanical, Walt Disney Enterprises, 4¼x3", NM 75.00
Drayton, Grace; 3-D, children w/pony, USA, 9⅜x7½", NM 125.00
Elephant w/clown, USA, 1940s, 4½x3½", NM 10.00
Geppetto on raft, mechanical, Walt Disney Productions, '39, EX .65.00
Girl & boy at piano, 2-D, MIG, 3⅜x4x1", EX 45.00
Goat & cart, girl delivers milk, tab stand, USA, 10x7", VG..........35.00
Hanging, litho hearts, 4 tiers w/orig ribbon, 12", EX 75.00
Harp, litho stands w/tab accented w/Victorian scraps, 7", EX........75.00
HCPP, apple core w/2 litho children, USA, '20s, 10¼", NM 125.00
HCPP basket & hearts, litho cherubs, ca 1925, 8½", EX...............85.00

Hold-to-light, 3-D children w/pk flowers, MIG, 8¼", NM 150.00
Hot air balloon, litho w/orig ribbon, MIG, 9½x4", NM..............150.00
Kautz, artist paints portrait, mechanical, '25, 6x4½", EX 35.00
Kautz, boy in winter garb, mechanical, tab stand, 7⅜", EX...........25.00
Kautz, cat, mechanical, tab stand, USA, 1925, 4½x3½", NM........35.00
Kautz, cowboy on horse, mechanical, tab stand, USA, 6¾", EX 45.00
Loverville Telephone Card, cast metal phone, 4x3¼", EX 75.00
Mechanical, airplane, 1940s-50s, 3¼x4½", EX 8.00
Mechanical, baseball player, USA, 1940s, 5½x3", NM 20.00
Mechanical, bear on stump, Stecher Litho, tab stand, 5", EX........25.00
Mechanical, chubby child on scales, MIG, 6¼x3¼", NM 25.00
Mechanical, cow, head & neck moves, USA, '40s, 7¼x4¾", NM .20.00
Mechanical, girl w/slate, litho, tab stand, 1924, 6x4", EX.............20.00
Mechanical, gypsy, USA, 6½x2¼", NM 15.00
Mechanical, lobster, tab stand, MIG, '27, 6¾x4½", EX.................35.00
Mechanical, miner panning for gold, Canada, 5½x3", EX 15.00
Mechanical, parrot, chromolitho, tab stand, MIG, 6¾", EX 35.00
Mechanical, Russian bear & child, tab stand, MIG, 8½", EX 55.00
Native American w/orig feather, USA, 7x4", EX 35.00
Nister, boy & girl, litho, Bavaria, 1900s, 4¾x3", EX 35.00
Nister, mother & children, hanging litho, #114, 13x6½", VG 80.00
Olive Oyl & Popeye, USA, 1940s, 5¾x5", EX................................45.00
Pinocchio, mechanical, Walt Disney Enterprises, 1938, 5", NM ...75.00
St Bernard dog, w/orig chain to doghouse, MIG, 10", VG 75.00
Steamship, 4-D all orig, MIG, 10½x6x3", 1900s, NM 250.00
Tuck, Artistic Series, carriage/Blk child/3-D flowers, 7", VG 95.00
Tuck, girl w/orig ribbon in hair, Series #1557, 5x2", NM..............75.00
Tuck, horse-drawn carriage, 3-D, 6½x10⅜x4½", EX...................175.00
3-D Victorian scene in open heart, To My..., MIG, 3½", NM.......75.00

Van Briggle

The Van Briggle Pottery of Colorado Springs, Colorado, was established in 1901 by Artus Van Briggle, whose early career had been shaped by such notables as Karl Langenbeck and Maria Nichols Storer. His quest for several years had been to perfect a completely flat matt glaze; and, upon accomplishing his goal, he opened his pottery. His wife, Anne, worked with him, and they, along with George Young, were responsible for the modeling of the wares. Their work typified the flow and form of the Art Nouveau movement, and the shapes they designed played as important a part in their success as their glazes. Some of their most famous pieces were Despondency, Lorelei, and Toast Cup. Increasing demand for their work soon made it necessary to add to their quarters as well as their staff. Although much of the ware was eventually made from molds, each piece was carefully trimmed and refined before the glaze was sprayed on. Their most popular colors were Persian Rose, Ming Blue, and Mustard Yellow.

Van Briggle died in 1904, but the work was continued by his wife. New facilities were built; and by 1908, in addition to their artware, tiles, gardenware, and commercial lines were added. By the twenties the emphasis had shifted from art pottery to novelties and commercial wares. As late as 1970, reproductions of some of the early designs continued to be made. Until about 1920 most pieces were marked with the date and shape number; after that the AA mark was used.

Bowl, copper clad, leaves/horizontal ridges, 3½x5" 12.75
Bowl, oak leaf & acorn, Ming Turq, 1920s 75.00
Bowl, stylized floral, bl/turq, post-1920, crazed, 5½" 210.00
Creamer, Persian Rose, paper label, 2½"..35.00
Lamp, ginger jar shape, orig butterfly shade, 6" 225.00
Lamp, girl seated on rock, orig shade, EX 235.00
Lamp, Grecian urn, orig shade, turq, 11½" 55.00
Lamp, kneeling woman, bl, orig butterfly shade, pr......................300.00

Lamp, leopard, Persian Rose, artist sgn, orig shade........................225.00
Lamp, 2 racing deer, Ming Bl, 11" 185.00
Lamp base, Colonial lady figural, turq, 1940s, 17"........................210.00
Lamp base, floral, bl/maroon, bulbous, 18½" 325.00
Plaque, peacock, turq w/red on tail, #807, 1908-11, 7" 260.00
Vase, br striated, narrow elongated neck, ca 1909, 9¾" 225.00
Vase, crocus, dk brn/ochre feathering, #149, dtd 1904, 4x5" 500.00
Vase, daisies at shoulder, bl/turq, #748, ca 1920s, 12½" 235.00
Vase, dk bl w/gr traces, #119, 1908-11, 5" 135.00
Vase, dk brn w/gold-yel overglaze, #496, dtd 1906, 5¼" 850.00
Vase, feathered gr on dk brn clay, slim, #407C, 1907, 7" 270.00
Vase, floral, yel/ochre, bulbous, 8½" 850.00
Vase, Lady of Lily, mulberry, ca 1930s, 10"................................650.00
Vase, lg cranes, turq, post-1920, 17" 550.00
Vase, lg spade leaves, turq w/rose, #438, dtd 1906, 10", EX..... 2,475.00
Vase, long-stemmed poppies, unglazed terra cotta, 1907, 13" 900.00
Vase, Lorelei, dk burgundy over burgundy, 1925, 9½" 600.00
Vase, Lorelei, sea gr, dtd 1902/III, 9¾".................................13,000.00
Vase, narcissi in high relief, gr w/yel, slim, ca 1904, 10" 700.00
Vase, Nouveau floral, veined gr on red clay, 1905-07, 6x4"........500.00
Vase, peacock feather (4X), 2-tone gr, #174, dtd '04, 11x4" ... 3,100.00
Vase, peacock feathers, bl/gr, bulbous neck, 4-hdl, 14" 550.00
Vase, peacock feathers, gr w/wht accent, #231, 1903, 5x7" 1,000.00
Vase, poppy pods, lt gr, wide shoulder, #601, 1908-11, 7" 650.00
Vase, spade leaves/buds, maroon, #278, dtd 1904, 5½x6" 950.00
Vase, spider reserve, lime gr, bulbous, #15, 1902/III, 5" 800.00
Vase, wide upright leaves, thick lt gr, #797, ca 1909, 9" 300.00
Vase buds/whiplash stems, pea-gr crystalline, dtd 1904, 13".... 1,600.00

Vance Avon

Although pottery had been made in Tiltonville, Ohio, since about 1880, the ware manufactured there was of little significance until after the turn of the century when the Vance Faience Company was organized for the purpose of producing quality artware. By 1902 the name had been changed to the Avon Faience Company, and late in the same year it and three other West Virginia potteries incorporated to form the Wheeling Potteries Company. The Avon branch operated in Tiltonville until 1905 when production was moved to Wheeling. Art pottery was discontinued. From the beginning only skilled craftsmen and trained engineers were hired. Wm. P. Jervis and Frederick Hurten Rhead were among the notable artists responsible for designing some of the early artware. Some of the ware was slip decorated under glaze, while other pieces were molded with high-relief designs. Examples with squeeze-bag decoration by Rhead are obviously forerunners of the Jap Birdimal line he later developed for Weller. Ware was marked 'Vance F. Co.'; 'Avon F. Co., Tiltonville'; or 'Avon W. Pts. Co.' Our advisor for this category is Wayne B. Kielsmeier; he is listed in the Directory under Arizona.

Jardiniere, squeeze-bag floral/inscription, Rhead, 9x14" 2,100.00
Jardiniere & pedestal, landscape/pines, squeeze-bag, 39" 2,500.00
Vase, 4 mermaids/fish relief, brn/yel mottle, 12" 650.00

Vaseline

Vaseline, a greenish-yellow colored glass produced by adding uranium oxide to the batch, was made in large quantities during the Victorian era. It was used for pressed glass tablewares, vases, and souvenir items.

Basket, Dmn Quilt, opal, appl florals, ruffled, 7x7".......................225.00
Bowl, Daisy & Button w/Crossbars, 9" 90.00
Bowl, fruit; Daisy & Button, tricorner, 2½x8" 80.00

Candlestick, eng florals, short, pr...65.00
Canoe, Daisy & Button, 13½" L..80.00
Creamer, Daisy & Button w/Crossbars 48.00
Goblet, hexagonal, early, mini...180.00
Honey dish, Thousand Eye, knobbed finial, rectangular 165.00
Tray, Dmn w/Frosted Leaf edge, oval, 13x9½"..........................90.00
Tumbler, Daisy & Button, water sz 45.00
Tumbler, Swag & Brackets 65.00
Vase, Waffle & T'print, 10"..550.00
Waste bowl, Daisy & Button w/Crossbars.................................30.00

Venetian Glass

Venetian glass is a thin, fragile ware usually made in colors, often with internal gold or silver flecks. It was produced on the island of Murano, near Venice, from the 13th century to the early 1900s. 20th-century glassware is always heavier and thicker than the older ware.

Bird, Barovier, 18" 350.00
Blackamoor lady w/basket, gold/blk, 13", pr 875.00
Bowl, latticinio bands, gr/gold ribbons, flower finial, 6½"............175.00
Candle holder, ovoid w/seated female figure beside, 6", pr 1,650.00
Candlestick, dolphin stem, gold flecks w/berry prunts, 5", pr 45.00
Decanter, mc vertical bands, conical stopper, no mk, 20"............275.00
Decanter, silver-specked amber w/3-color star canes, 13" 360.00
Duck, seated, Barbini 250.00
Lamp, caramel/silver/gold swirl 11" shade; 4-arm std, 20" 325.00
Lamp, mushroom 11" millefiori shade on matching base, 20" 200.00
Vase, ruby w/mc spatters, short neck, Murano label, 6"................25.00

Venini Glass

Fine contemporary art glass signed Venini (sometimes with Murano added) has been commanding high prices in some of the Eastern auction galleries. Art Deco items and those from the fifties are the most sought after.

Bird, blown/appl, clear irid, mk Murano Made in Italy, 12" 1,400.00
Bottle, olive gr w/wht lower half & stopper, SA Murano, 13" 400.00
Bottle vase, dk gr w/red & wht 'belt,' Murano, 10" 1,000.00

Bottle vase, emerald green with bright red belt showing white core, stamped Murano, 10", $1,045.00; Vase, clear cased over light amber and taupe, two oval openings, stamped Murano, light scratches, 12", $875.00.

Bowl, clear w/spiral wavy stripes in wht/amethyst/gold, 10" 135.00
Bowl, gold foil pcs in clear-cased bl/wht, high ft, 8" H 1,100.00
Candy dish, lt gr & wht striped 'ribbons,' 2¼x5" 150.00
Decanter, clown form, mc body, cobalt tie & hat, 14" 275.00
Decanter, Inciso, clear-cased amber, incised surface, 14" 1,400.00
Decanter, Inciso, clear-cased amber, incised surface, 8"...........935.00

Hourglass, bl & gr, sgn, 7" 575.00
Lamp base, rope-twist form, acid-stamped Murano Italia, 17" 350.00
Musician, in flowing gown & fancy headpc, 1950, 9", 4 for ... 1,300.00
Sculpture, Tete de Femme, Hans Trugger, 1952, 17½" 1,700.00
Vase, clear, amber/tan int, 2 holes pass through body, 12"..........880.00
Vase, clear cased to wht, sgn, classic form, 24" 550.00
Vase, gr-edged turq uprights on clear, B Fulvio, '53, 10" 950.00
Vase, handkerchief; clear w/bl & wht latticinio, 5¾"....................275.00
Vase, handkerchief; pk & wht latticinio, sgn, 3¾" 275.00
Vase, handkerchief; tan cased to wht, Biaconi, 9" 600.00
Vase, handkerchief; wht w/yel int, Biaconi, 8" 600.00
Vase, sqs of red/bl/gr/clear alternate, Biaconi, 1957, 8" 7,500.00
Vase, swirling red/bl stripes, cylindrical, Italia 81, 14" 495.00
Vase, 3 layers of color, egg form w/2 rim openings, 4x6" 4,800.00

Verlys

Verlys art glass, produced in France after 1931 by the Holophane Company of Verlys, was made in crystal with acid-finished relief work in the Art Deco style. Colored and opalescent glass was also used. In 1935 an American branch was opened in Newark, Ohio, where very similar wares were produced. French Verlys was signed with one of three mold-impressed script signatures, all containing the company name and country of origin. The American-made glassware was signed 'Verlys' only, either scratched with a diamond-tipped pen or impressed in the mold. There is very little if any difference in value between items produced in France and America. Though some seem to feel that the French should be higher priced (assuming it to be scarce), many prefer the American-made product.

In June of 1955, about sixteen Verlys molds were leased to the A.H. Heisey Company. Heisey's versions were not signed with the Verlys name; so if an item is unsigned, it is almost certainly a Heisey piece. The molds were returned to Verlys of America in July 1957. Our advisor for this category is Don Frost; he is listed in the Directory under Oregon.

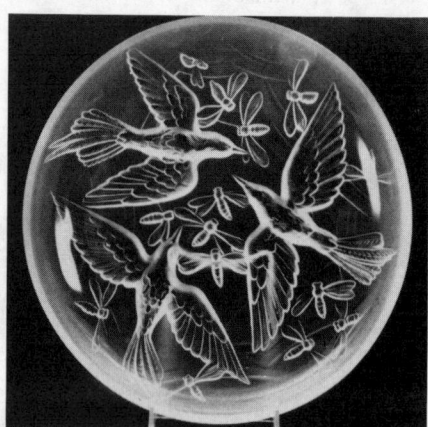

Bowl, Birds (Birds and Bees), etched crystal, engraved mark, 2¼" x 11½", $225.00.

Bowl, Chrysanthemum (known as Casket), crystal etch, 6¼x10"..150.00
Bowl, Chrysanthemum (known as Casket), opal, 6¼x10" 275.00
Bowl, Pine Cone, bl or amber, mk, 1⅞x6¼", ea 95.00
Bowl, Poppy, crystal etch, sgn, 2¾x14" 165.00
Bowl, Wild Duck, Directoire Bl, 2½x13½" 275.00
Box, bouquet of coreopsis emb on lid, opal, 6¾" dia 300.00
Figurine, pigeon, frosted, 4¼" 285.00
Vase, Alpine Thistle, opal, shouldered, 9"....................................600.00
Vase, berries/leaves, ribbed, star base, gray, #1162, 10" 600.00
Vase, Mermaid, shouldered, Directoire Bl, 1 of 2 forms, 11" ... 1,320.00

Vase, rose blossoms/branches on frost, ovoid, 7½" 100.00

Vernon Kilns

Vernon Potteries Ltd. was established by Faye G. Bennison in Vernon, California, in 1931. The name was later changed to Vernon Kilns; until it closed in 1958, dinnerware and figurines were their primary products. Among its wares most sought after by collectors today are items designed by such famous artists as Rockwell Kent, Walt Disney, and Don Blanding. Our advisor for this category is Maxine Nelson; she is listed in the Directory under California.

Anytime, bowl, serving; 9" 8.00
Anytime, creamer 6.00
Anytime, gravy boat 8.00
Anytime, plate, bread & butter 2.00
Anytime, plate, dinner... 5.00
Anytime, plate, salad 3.00
Anytime, platter, 13¼" 12.00
Anytime, platter, 9½" 8.00
Anytime, sugar bowl, w/lid 8.00
Barkwood, carafe 22.50
Barkwood, cup 3.00
Barkwood, gravy boat..10.00
Bel-Air, bowl, 10¼" 20.00
Bel-Air, creamer & sugar bowl 22.00
Bel-Air, gravy boat...16.00
Brown-Eyed Susan, cup & saucer 6.00
Brown-Eyed Susan, plate, bread & butter 3.00
Brown-Eyed Susan, plate, salad 4.00
Brown-Eyed Susan, plate, 9½" 7.00
Brown-Eyed Susan, platter, 12" 12.00
Brown-Eyed Susan, shakers, regular, pr......................................13.00
California Shadows, coffeepot, 10-cup 35.00
California Shadows, cup, coffee; jumbo 15.00
Casual California, mug 15.00
Chatelaine Jade, cup & saucer, ped ft 18.00
Chatelaine Jade, plate, 6½" 5.00
Chatelaine Jade, plate, 7½" 10.00
Dolores, plate, salad; 7½" 8.00
Dreamtime, bowl, chowder... 5.00

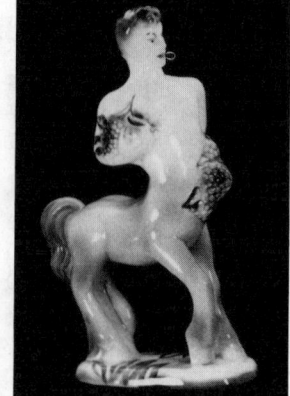

Fantasia, Centaur, 10½", $1,100.00.

Fantasia, bowl, Sprites, cupids in relief, #125, 11½"....................250.00
Fantasia, bowl, Winged Nymph, #122, 2½x12" 275.00
Fantasia, figurine, Ballet Elephant, #27 ....400.00
Fantasia, figurine, Dumbo, sitting 175.00
Fantasia, figurine, Hippo Ballerina, #33, 5" 600.00

Fantasia, figurine, Hyacinth Hippo......................500.00
Fantasia, figurine, Mr Stork................................800.00
Fantasia, figurine, Nubian Centaurette...............700.00
Fantasia, figurine, Satyr, #2...............................225.00
Fantasia, figurine, Satyr, #4, stretching, 4".........300.00
Fantasia, shakers, Milk Weed, pr...........................40.00
Fantasia, shakers, Mushroom, pr..........................135.00
Gingham, creamer, regular....................................10.00
Gingham, pitcher, bulbous, 1-pt............................17.50
Gingham, sugar bowl, w/lid..................................12.00
Homespun, bowl, divided, oval 12.50
Homespun, bowl, rnd..15.00
Homespun, casserole, w/lid...................................30.00
Homespun, coaster, 3⅞"..8.00
Homespun, cup, jumbo..15.00
Homespun, cup & saucer.......................................10.00
Homespun, plate, 10"..7.00
Homespun, plate, 6"..2.50
Homespun, plate, 7"..4.00
Homespun, platter, 10½".......................................12.50
Homespun, shakers, pr...16.00
Lollipop Tree, cup...4.00
Mayflower, plate, 10½"...15.00
Mayflower, plate, 6"..6.00
Mayflower, platter, oval, 14"..................................22.50
Moby Dick, coffeepot, rare...................................200.00
Monterey, bowl, chowder...5.00
Monterey, bowl, 9"...12.00
Monterey, cup & saucer...12.00
Monterey, pitcher, 2-qt..25.00
Monterey, plate, luncheon; 9½"............................12.00
Monterey, shakers, pr..12.00
Monterey, sugar bowl, w/lid..................................10.00
Organdie, bowl, divided vegetable; oval, 11½"......15.00
Organdie, bowl, lug chowder; open, 6" 12.50
Organdie, bowl, 5½"...3.00
Organdie, bowl, 8¾"...12.00
Organdie, casserole, w/lid, ind..............................20.00
Organdie, chop plate, 12".......................................10.00
Organdie, creamer & sugar bowl, w/lid 15.00
Organdie, gravy boat..18.00
Organdie, plate, 6½"..2.50
Organdie, plate, 9½"..8.50
Organdie, platter, 12"..9.00
Organdie, shakers, pr...12.00
Philodendron, bowl, vegetable; oval 15.00
Plate, Battle of Jan Jacinto, 10½".........................20.00
Plate, Bits of the Old South, Southern Mansion 15.00
Plate, Carlsbad Caverns...10.00
Plate, Honolulu, 10½"..15.00
Plate, MacArthur..20.00
Plate, Presidents, through Eisenhower, ea 20.00
Plate, San Juan Capistrano Mission, 10½".............15.00
Plate, Texas Lone Star State, 10½".........................15.00
Plate, Trader Vic, mc...22.00
Plate, Yosemite Nat'l Park, 10½"............................15.00
Raffia, chop plate, 12¾"...15.00
Raffia, pitcher, w/ice lip, 12".................................25.00
Raffia, platter, 13¼"...16.50
Raffia, shakers, pr..16.00
Raffia, syrup, drip-cut top......................................30.00
Rose-a-Day, plate, dinner 8.00
Salamina, cup & saucer..50.00
Salamina, plate, 14"..150.00

Salamina, plate, 9½"..95.00
Salamina, sugar bowl, w/lid, regular.....................35.00
Salamina, tumbler..32.00
Sherwood, creamer & sugar bowl, w/lid 14.00
Tam O' Shanter, bowl, vegetable; divided, oval, 10"...15.00
Tam O' Shanter, carafe...30.00
Tam O' Shanter, chop plate, 14".............................22.00
Tickled Pink, bowl, vegetable; 9"............................8.00
Tickled Pink, bowl, 5¾"...2.50
Tickled Pink, butter dish..12.50
Tickled Pink, creamer & sugar bowl, w/lid............15.00
Tickled Pink, cup & saucer......................................5.00
Tickled Pink, plate, 10"...5.00
Tickled Pink, plate, 6"...2.00
Tickled Pink, platter, 10"...8.00
Tickled Pink, platter, 13¼".....................................14.50
Tickled Pink, shakers, pr...6.00
Ultra California, creamer, pk....................................8.00
Ultra California, plate, 9½".......................................8.00
Ultra California, tumbler..15.00

Villeroy and Boch

The firm of Villeroy and Boch, located in Mettlach, Germany, was brought into being by the 1841 merger of three German factories — the Wallerfangen factory, founded by Nicholas Villeroy in 1787; the Mettlach factory, founded by Jean Francis Boch 1809; and Boch's father's factory in Septfontaines, established in 1767. Villeroy and Boch produced many varieties of wares, including earthenware with printed under-glaze designs which carried the well-known castle mark with the name 'Mettlach.' See also Mettlach.

Bowl, stick spatter w/bl & wht gaudy floral, 8" 55.00
Charger, Meissen castle on Elbe, 12"...195.00
Plaque, bl/wht repro of portrait by Frans Hals, pr 90.00

Plate, scenic tapestry, 8½", $150.00.

Plate, stick spatter, mc floral, 9"..65.00
Platter, snow scene w/house & man, tapestry, 11" L 185.00
Tray, geometrics, in metal fr w/geometric cutouts, hdls, 11"........150.00
Vase, floral, bl/gr on wht, #2694, 11"..70.00

Vase, silver resist, appl berries/leaves on hdl, 7¾" **75.00**

Vistosa

Vistosa was produced from about 1938 through the early forties. It was Taylor, Smith, and Taylor's answer to the very successful Fiesta line of their nearby competitor, Homer Laughlin. Vistosa was made in four solid colors: mango red, cobalt blue, light green, and deep yellow. 'Pie crust' edges and a dainty five-petal flower molded into handles and lid finials made for a very attractive yet nevertheless commercially unsuccessful product. Our advisor for this category is Ted Haun; he is listed in the Directory under Indiana.

Bowl, salad **95.00**
Bowl, 5¾" **10.00**
Bowl, 6⅜" **15.00**
Chop plate, 11" **25.00**
Creamer..**12.00**
Cup & saucer **15.00**
Egg cup..**22.50**
Gravy boat **78.00**
Pitcher, red..**50.00**
Pitcher, yel **40.00**
Plate, 6" **4.00**
Plate, 7" **7.00**
Plate, 9" **10.00**
Shakers, pr...**18.00**
Sugar bowl, w/lid **15.00**
Teapot, red..**80.00**

Volkmar

Charles Volkmar established a workshop in Tremont, New York, in 1882. He produced artware decorated under the glaze in the manner of the early barbotine work done at the Haviland factory in Limoges, France. He relocated in 1888 in Menlo Park, New Jersey, and together with J.T. Smith established the Menlo Park Ceramic Company for the production of art tile. The partnership was dissolved in 1893. From 1895 until 1902, Volkmar located in Corona, New York, first under the name Volkmar Ceramic Company, later as Volkmar and Cory, and for the final six years as Crown Point. During the latter period he made art tile, blue under-glaze Delft-type wares, colorful polychrome vases, etc. The Volkmar Kilns were established in 1903 in Metuchen, New Jersey, by Volkmar and his son. Wares were marked with various devices consisting of the Volkmar name, initials, or 'Crown Point Ware.'

Lamp, blended glaze, Arts & Crafts **255.00**
Plaque, Washington's headquarters, bl/wht, hanging, 11" **185.00**
Tankard, gr & blk, 7¾" **210.00**
Vase, peach/purple mottle, swollen cylinder, 1939, 7½" **200.00**
Vase, robin's egg bl mottle, collar rim, sgn, 3½x5¼" **165.00**

Volkstadt

There were several porcelain factories in and around Volkstadt, Province of Thuringia, the original and earliest one established in 1762 by George Heinrich Macheleid. Others soon followed, producing many fine porcelain figures and groups in the Sheib-Alsbach, Potschappel, and Sitzendorf style. The 'crossed hayforks' mark was used from 1787 to 1800 by Christian Nonne; it was later modified with the addition of a crown by R. Ekhart (1906-08). An 'M' crossed by a 'V' with a crown

was used from 1907-47 by Muller, who used an oval-shaped diamond with an 'M,' 'V' and a crown from 1910-1960. The Greiner Bros. mark was a double crossed 'G' and a crown, in use from 1850-1920. Our advisor for this category is Donald Penrose; he is listed in the Directory under Ohio.

Figurine, ballerina in wht w/appl flowers, brn hair, 5½".............**160.00**
Figurine, couple beside rail watching 2 swans, 9x8½" **550.00**
Figurine, girl in floral dress w/goose, after Canova, 6" **160.00**
Figurine, girl in floral dress w/water jug, after Canova, 6" **160.00**
Figurine, lady in w/red top, torch in hand, Canova, 6" **160.00**
Figurine, lady in wht w/fan, artist w/easel, 7½x9" **650.00**
Figurine, lady sits w/lute, man holds book, 9x9½" **1,050.00**
Figurine, man & lady play chess at table, 6x9" **950.00**
Figurine, 2 cherubs pull shell chariot, 8" L, EX....................**225.00**
Figurine, 2 girls precede bride & groom, page w/train, 9x13" .. **1,250.00**
Figurine, 3 musicians/instruments, appl flowers, rstr, 15"...........**650.00**
Plaque, gr jasper w/wht floral Baroque fr, ca 1874, 9x10½" **450.00**

Wade

The Wade Group of Potteries originated in 1810 with a small, single-oven pottery near Chesterton, just west of Burslem, England. This pottery, first owned by a Henry Hallen, was eventually taken over by George Wade who had opened his own pottery (also in Burslem) in 1867. Both the Hallen pottery and the original Wade pottery specialized in ceramic and pottery items for the textile industry, then booming in northern England. By the early 20th century, the two potteries were merged, taking the name of George Wade Pottery, which in 1919 became George Wade & Son Ltd.

George Wade's brother, Albert, had interests in two potteries, A.J. Wade Ltd. and Wade Heath & Co. Ltd. which manufactured decorative tiles, teapots, and other related dinnerware. In 1938 Wade Heath took over the Royal Victoria Pottery, also in Burslem, and began producing a wide range of figurines and other decorative items. In 1947 a new pottery was opened in Portadown, Northern Ireland, to produce both industrial ceramics and Irish porcelain giftware. In 1958 all the Wade potteries were amalgamated, becoming the Wade group of Potteries. The most recent addition to the group is Wade (PDM) Limited, a marketing arm for the advertising ware made by Wade Heath at the Royal Victoria Pottery. Wade (PDM) Limited was incorporated in 1969. In 1989 the Wade Group of Potteries was bought out by Beauford Engineering. With this takeover, Wade Heath and George Wade & Son Ltd. were combined to form Wade Ceramics. Wade (Ireland) Ltd. and Wade (PDM) Ltd. became subsidiaries of Wade Ceramics. In 1990 Wade (Ireland) Ltd. changed its name to Seagoe Ceramics Limited. For those interested in learning more about Wade pottery, we recommend *The World of Wade* by Ian Warner and Mike Posgay; Mr. Warner is listed in the Directory under Canada.

Bisto Kids cruet set, mid-1970s **250.00**
Disney hat box, Dumbo **85.00**
Disney hat box, girl squirrel **150.00**
Disney hat box, Madame Mim..**140.00**
Guinness promotional figurine, Mad Hatter, ca 1968 ....**160.00**
Guinness promotional figurine, Tony Weller, ca 1968 ....**160.00**
Guinness promotional figurine, Tweedledum/Tweedledee, 1968..**160.00**
Guinness promotional figurine, Wellington Boot, ca 1968..........**160.00**
Irish Porcelain, musical tankard **95.00**
Janny Walker water jug, ca 1960.......................................**35.00**
Lucky Leprechauns, baby Leprechaun on log, 1956-86 ....**24.00**
Lucky Leprechauns, Leprechaun on pig, 1956-86 ....**30.00**
Nat West Panda money box, 1989......................................**30.00**

Noddy series, Big Ears, 1958-60 ....150.00
Noddy series, Noddy, 1958-60 ....250.00
Pearly King or Pearly Queen, 1959, ea 150.00
Red Rose Tea figurine, Doctor Foster, 1971-79 .... 7.00
Red Rose Tea figurine, Little Bo Peep, 1971-79 .... 3.50
Red Rose Tea figurine, Queen of Hearts, 1971-79 ....12.00
Red Rose Tea figurine, Three Bears, 1971-79 ....22.00
San Francisco Painted Ladies, cable car 50.00
San Francisco Painted Ladies, mouse, mini, 1984-86, ea 36.00
Shamrock Pottery, cottage, ca 1959 ....40.00
Shamrock Pottery, cottage & Leprechaun, ca early 1960s 60.00
Thomas the Tank, Engine miniature, 1985-87 ....45.00
Thomas the Tank, Engine money box, 1985-87 ....75.00
Yachts (wall plaque), 1955, set of 3 ....300.00

Walley

The Walley Pottery operated in West Sterling, Massachusetts, from 1898 to 1919. Never more than a one-man operation, Walley himself hand crafted all his wares from local clay. The majority of his pottery was simple and unadorned and usually glazed in matt green. On occasion, however, you may find high- and semi-gloss green, as well as matt glazes in blue, cream, brown, and red. The rarest and most desirable examples of his work are those with applied or relief-carved decorations. Some pieces are marked 'WJW.'

Vase, two embossed trout on mottled green glaze, impressed WJW, paper label, 12", $2,300.00.

Bud vase, ecru gloss, rnd w/elongated neck, 4½" 150.00
Mug, high-relief face in side, gr/brn matt, 5½" 425.00
Vase, gr drip on brn, bulbous w/long neck, WJW, 9½" 700.00
Vase, leaves, cvd/appl, gr-edged on brn, 7x6" 1,300.00

Walrath

Frederick Walrath was a studio potter who worked from around the turn of the century until his death in 1920. He was located in Rochester, New York, until 1918 when he became associated with the Newcomb Pottery in New Orleans, Louisiana.

Candle holder, angel on pedestal, dull-glazed gr ware, 7" 200.00
Flower frog, 2 nude girls, lt gr, 8"; +flat brn bowl, 8" 575.00
Mug, brn, unmk, 3" 80.00
Plate, brn matt, rust abstract tree decor, 5" 165.00
Vase, pine cones/branches, matt glaze, cylindrical, 8¼" 1,800.00
Vase, pk florals on speckled gr, spherical, 5½x5" 2,100.00
Vase, stylized clovers, 5-color matt, mk, 5½x3½" 1,550.00

Walter, A.

Almaric Walter was employed from 1904 through 1914 at Verreries Artistiques des Freres Daum in Nancy, France. After 1919 he opened his own business where he continued to make the same type of quality objects d'art in pate-de-verre glass as he had earlier. His pieces are signed A. Walter, Nancy H. Berge Sc.

Box, gr/bl mottle, stepped rnd pyramid on lid, 6" H 3,000.00
Box, grasshopper on lid, berries/leaves on sides, rnd, 3" 4,800.00
Paperweight, sea nymph rising from surf, sgn Cheret, 10" 6,000.00
Paperweight, sea nymph sleeping on gr leaf, 6¾" L 8,500.00
Paperweight, 2 salamanders/foliage on rock, sgn Berge, 3" 7,400.00
Sparrow on shaped base, Henri Berge, ca 1925, 4" 750.00
Tray, mallard duck faces away from triangular gr tray, 7½" 3,000.00
Tray, roses ea side, red on tan, yel center, Corrette, 6½" 1,600.00
Tray, salamander among yel blossoms & ivy leaves, 7" L.........5,500.00
Vase, floral, red & yel on aqua, sgn, 7x5" 1,850.00
Woman, seated, bk bent, head in hands at ft, yel, 7" 2,000.00

Wannopee

The Wannopee Pottery, established in 1892, developed from the reorganization of the financially insecure New Milford Pottery Company of New Milford, Connecticut. They produced a line of mottled-glazed pottery called 'Duchess' and a similar line in porcelain. Both were marked with the impressed sunburst 'W' with 'porcelain' added to indicate that particular body type.

In 1895 semi-porcelain pitchers in three sizes were decorated with relief medallion cameos of Beethoven, Mozart, and Napoleon. Lettuce-leaf ware was first produced in 1901 and used actual leaves in the modeling. Scarabronze, made in 1895, was their finest artware. It featured simple Egyptian shapes with a coppery glaze. It was marked with a scarab, either impressed or applied. Production ceased in 1903.

Chamberstick, majolica bl & brn, twisted, lg hdl, 12½" 95.00
Ewer, shaded brn & gr, compressed body, 4¾" 50.00
Vase, Scarabronze, appl scarab/emb Egyptian, rstr, 12x6" 200.00
Vase, Scarabronze (metallic), 4 emb buttresses, rpr, 19" 2,000.00

Warwick

The Warwick China Company operated in Wheeling, West Virginia, from 1887 until 1951. They produced both hand-painted and decaled plates, vases, teapots, coffeepots, pitchers, bowls, and jardinieres featuring lovely florals or portraits of beautiful ladies done in luscious colors. Backgrounds were usually blendings of brown and beige, but ivory was also used (and, on rare occasion, pink). Various marks were employed, all of which incorporate the Warwick name. For a more thorough study of the subject, we recommend *Warwick, A to W*, a supplement to *Why Not Warwick* by our advisor, Donald C. Hoffmann; his address can be found in the Directory under Illinois.

Vase, A Beauty, bl w/roses, 15" 265.00
Vase, A Beauty, brn w/roses, 15" 235.00
Vase, A Beauty, gr w/roses, 15" 240.00
Vase, A Beauty, tan w/roses, 15" 235.00
Vase, A Beauty, wht, w/roses, 15" 265.00
Vase, Albany, brn w/hibiscus, 7" 190.00
Vase, Albany, matt, tan w/beechnuts, 7" 195.00
Vase, Alexandria, brn w/hibiscus, 12½" 240.00

Vase, Alexandria, red w/poinsettias, 12½" 250.00
Vase, Bonnie, brn w/hibiscus, 10¼" 255.00
Vase, Bonnie, wht w/roses, 10¼" 255.00
Vase, Bouquet #1, brn w/lady in pearls, 11½" 245.00
Vase, Bouquet #1, brn w/orchid, 11½" 255.00
Vase, Bouquet #1, wht w/egrets 260.00
Vase, Bouquet #2, brn, Countess A Potaka, 10½" 230.00
Vase, Bouquet #2, brn, gypsy w/red turban, 10½" 225.00
Vase, Bouquet #2, brn, lady in pillbox hat, 10½" 265.00

Vase, Bouquet #2, Madame Le Brun on red, 10½", $285.00.

Vase, Bouquet #2, brn, Madame Le Brun as adult, 10½" 225.00
Vase, Bouquet #2, brn, Madame Le Brun as child, 10½" 225.00
Vase, Bouquet #2, brn, Madame Re Camier, 10½" 230.00
Vase, Bouquet #2, brn, nude, sgn Carreno, 10½" 285.00
Vase, Bouquet #2, brn, redheaded lady, 10½" 290.00
Vase, Bouquet #2, brn, redheaded lady w/scarf, 10½" 295.00
Vase, Bouquet #2, brn w/hibiscus, 10½" 220.00
Vase, Bouquet #2, brn w/Madame Re Camier, 10½" ...220.00
Vase, Bouquet #2, gr, Madame Le Brun as child, 10½" 285.00
Vase, Bouquet #2, gr w/roses, 10½" 290.00
Vase, Bouquet #2, red, Countess A Potaka, 10½" 280.00
Vase, Bouquet #2, red, gypsy in bl turban, 10½" 275.00
Vase, Bouquet #2, red, Madame Le Brun as adult, 10½" 285.00
Vase, Bouquet #2, red, Madame Le Brun as child, 10½" 280.00
Vase, Canteen, brn w/dogs, 11½" 325.00
Vase, Canteen, brn w/floral, 11½" 300.00
Vase, Canteen, charcoal w/nude, 11½" 345.00
Vase, Carnation, brn w/floral, paper label, 10½" 130.00
Vase, Carnation, brn w/florals, 10½" 120.00
Vase, Carnation, gr w/roses, 10½" 130.00
Vase, Carnation, pk w/Aunt Hilda type, 10½" 200.00
Vase, Carnation, red, Countess A Potaka, 10½" 130.00
Vase, Carol, brn w/floral, 8" 230.00
Vase, Carol, brn w/nut decor, 8" 230.00
Vase, Carol, pk w/Aunt Hilda type, 8" 295.00
Vase, Chicago, brn w/floral, 8" 300.00
Vase, Chicago, pk w/Aunt Hilda type, 8" 350.00
Vase, Chrys #1, brn w/portrait, 15" 180.00
Vase, Chrys #2, brn w/floral, 13" 170.00
Vase, Clematis, brn w/floral, 10½" 285.00
Vase, Clematis, gr w/roses, 10½" 295.00
Vase, Clematis, red, Countess A Potaka, 10½" 310.00
Vase, Clematis, wht w/egrets, 10½" 300.00
Vase, Cloverleaf, brn w/pine cones, 7½" 295.00
Vase, Cloverleaf, matt w/nut decor, 7½" 285.00

Vase, Cloverleaf, red w/poinsettias, 7½" 295.00
Vase, Clytie, red w/floral point, 6¼" 300.00
Vase, Clytie, red w/portrait, 6¼" 325.00
Vase, Cuba, brn w/pine cones, 7¼" 330.00
Vase, Cuba, brn w/portrait, 7¼" 340.00
Vase, Dahlia, brn w/portrait, 8½" 275.00
Vase, Dahlia, red w/portrait, 8½" 295.00
Vase, Dainty, brn w/floral, 4½" 265.00
Vase, Dainty, red w/floral, 4½" 255.00
Vase, Den, brn w/pine cones, 6½x10" 285.00
Vase, Den, red w/portrait, 6½x10" 290.00
Vase, Duchess, brn w/floral, 8" 200.00
Vase, Duchess, wht w/birds, 8" 220.00
Vase, Egyptian, brn w/floral, 11¾" 325.00
Vase, Egyptian, charcoal w/cosmos, 11¾" 300.00
Vase, Favorite, matt w/floral, 10½" 280.00
Vase, Favorite, pk w/portrait, 10½" 300.00
Vase, Flower, brn w/floral, 12" 145.00
Vase, Flower, brn w/portrait, 10" 155.00
Vase, Flower, pk w/portrait, 12" 160.00
Vase, Flower, red w/floral, 12" 140.00
Vase, Gem, brn w/floral, 12" 200.00
Vase, Gem, red w/floral, 12" 210.00
Vase, Geran, brn w/floral, 11" 225.00
Vase, Geran, charcoal w/cosmos, 11" 235.00
Vase, Grecian, brn w/floral, 8" 230.00
Vase, Grecian, red w/floral, 8" 230.00
Vase, Helene, brn w/floral, 12" 230.00
Vase, Helene, red w/floral, 12" 220.00
Vase, Henrietta, brn w/floral, 10" 215.00
Vase, Henrietta, gr w/roses, 10" 230.00
Vase, Henrietta, red w/portrait, 10" 250.00
Vase, Hyacinth, brn w/floral, 11" 230.00
Vase, Hyacinth, red w/portrait, 11" 240.00
Vase, Iris, brn w/floral, 9¾" 135.00
Vase, Iris, charcoal w/cosmos, 9¾" 145.00
Vase, Iris, red w/poinsettias, 9¾" 145.00
Vase, Lemonade, brn w/floral, 6½" 175.00
Vase, Lemonade, brn w/portrait, 6½" 185.00
Vase, Lemonade, pk w/portrait, 6½" 235.00
Vase, Lemonade, red w/floral, 6½" 170.00
Vase, Lemonade, red w/portrait, 6½" 180.00
Vase, Lemonade, wht w/floral, 6½" 235.00
Vase, Lily, brn, gypsy portrait w/bow in hair, 9½" 210.00
Vase, Lily, brn w/hibiscus, 9½" 190.00
Vase, Lily, brn w/peonies, 9½" 195.00
Vase, Lily, charcoal w/nude, sgn Carreno, 9½" 235.00
Vase, Lily, red, gypsy portrait, 9½" 250.00
Vase, Louise, brn w/sm roses, 9½" 245.00
Vase, Magnolia, brn w/portrait, 10½" 210.00
Vase, Magnolia, red w/portrait, 10½" 230.00
Vase, Magnolia, wht w/birds, 10½" 250.00
Vase, Maria, brn w/floral, 10½" 195.00
Vase, Maria, charcoal w/floral, 10½" 220.00
Vase, Maria, pk w/portrait, 10½" 295.00
Vase, Monroe, brn w/floral, 10½" 215.00
Vase, Monroe, brn w/portrait, 10½" 220.00
Vase, Monroe, red w/portrait, 10½" 250.00
Vase, Monroe, wht w/birds, 10½" 255.00
Vase, Narcis #1, brn w/floral, 8¼" 200.00
Vase, Narcis #1, charcoal w/cosmos, 8½" 235.00
Vase, Narcis #1, charcoal w/nude, 8½" 250.00
Vase, Narcis #2, brn w/floral, 6¾" 230.00
Vase, Narcis #2, brn w/portrait, 8½" 225.00

Vase, Narcis #2, charcoal w/cosmos, 6¾"................................250.00
Vase, Narcis #2, charcoal w/nude, 6¾"..................................260.00
Vase, Narcis #2, red w/portrait, 6¾"......................................235.00
Vase, Narcis #2, wht w/bird, 6¾"...235.00
Vase, Orchid, brn w/floral, 10¼"...210.00
Vase, Orchid, wht w/birds, 10¼"..225.00
Vase, Oriental, brn w/floral, 11"..250.00
Vase, Oriental, red w/floral, 11"..250.00
Vase, Pansy, brn w/floral, 4" 65.00
Vase, Pansy, red w/floral, 4" 75.00
Vase, Parisian, brn w/floral, 4"...215.00
Vase, Parisian, charcoal w/nude, 4"...245.00
Vase, Parisian, pk w/portrait, 4"...255.00
Vase, Peerless, brn w/floral, 9½"...190.00
Vase, Peerless, brn w/portrait, 9½"..220.00
Vase, Peerless, matt brn w/floral, 9½".....................................215.00
Vase, Penn, brn w/floral, 9½"...190.00
Vase, Penn, pk w/portrait, 9½"...225.00
Vase, Poppy, brn w/floral, 10½"..290.00
Vase, Poppy, charcoal w/floral, 10½".......................................295.00
Vase, Queen, charcoal w/nude, 12"..285.00
Vase, Queen, wht w/birds, 12" 275.00
Vase, Regency, brn w/floral, 11½"..275.00
Vase, Regency, charcoal w/cosmos, 11½"...................................280.00
Vase, Roberta, brn w/monk, 10"..290.00
Vase, Roberta, red w/fisherman, 10"...290.00
Vase, Roman, brn w/floral, 11½"..275.00
Vase, Roman, wht w/birds, 11½"..280.00
Vase, Rosalie, brn w/floral, 8"..195.00
Vase, Rosalie, charcoal w/floral, 8"...205.00
Vase, Rosalie, pk w/portrait, 8"..245.00
Vase, Rose, brn w/portrait, 8"...165.00
Vase, Rose, matt w/beechnut, 8"...170.00
Vase, Rose, red w/floral, 8"..155.00
Vase, Royal #1, matt w/portrait, 10"..300.00
Vase, Royal #2, matt w/portrait, 10"..350.00
Vase, Senator #1, brn w/floral, 13¼".......................................195.00
Vase, Senator #2, red w/portrait, 11½" 210.00
Vase, Senator #3, brn w/floral, 9¾"...200.00
Vase, Senator #3, red w/portrait, 9¾".......................................220.00
Vase, Thelma, brn w/floral, 9¼"..210.00
Vase, Thelma, brn w/portrait, 9¼"...215.00
Vase, Tobio Jug #1, gr w/floral, 7¾"..155.00
Vase, Tobio Jug #2, brn w/floral, 7"...160.00
Vase, Tobio Jug #2, brn w/monk, 7¾".......................................135.00
Vase, Tobio Jug #2, red w/floral, 7"...155.00
Vase, Tobio Jug #3, brn w/Indian, 6".......................................185.00
Vase, Verbenia #1, brn w/floral, 9¼".......................................155.00
Vase, Verbenia #1, brn w/portrait, 9½".....................................165.00
Vase, Verbenia #1, charcoal w/cosmos, 9½"...............................180.00
Vase, Verbenia #1, charcoal w/floral, 9½"..................................175.00
Vase, Verbenia #2, brn w/floral, 7¼".......................................160.00
Vase, Verbenia #2, brn w/portrait, 7¼"....................................165.00
Vase, Verbenia #2, charcoal w/cosmos, 7¼"...............................170.00
Vase, Verbenia #2, gr w/roses, 7¼"...170.00
Vase, Verbenia #2, red w/floral, 7¼".......................................145.00
Vase, Verbenia #2, wht w/birds, 7¼".......................................160.00
Vase, Verona, brn w/floral, 11¾"...145.00
Vase, Verona, charcoal w/floral, 11¾"......................................155.00
Vase, Verona, red w/floral, 11¾"...160.00
Vase, Verona, wht w/birds, 11¾"..165.00
Vase, Victoria, brn w/floral, 8¼"..165.00
Vase, Victoria, pk w/portrait, 8¼"..175.00
Vase, Victoria, red w/portrait, 8¼"...185.00

Vase, Violet, brn w/floral, 4"...85.00
Vase, Violet, charcoal w/floral, 4"...100.00
Vase, Violet, matt w/nut decor, 4"...100.00
Vase, Violet, red w/floral, 4"..110.00
Vase, Windsor, brn to yel w/nut decor, 9¼" 210.00
Vase, Windsor, brn w/floral, 9¼"...200.00
Vase, Windsor, pk w/portrait, 9¼"...245.00

Wash Sets

Before the days of running water, bedrooms were standardly equipped with a wash bowl and pitcher as a matter of necessity. A 'toilet set' was comprised of the pitcher and bowl, toothbrush holder, covered commode, soap dish, shaving dish, and mug. Some sets were even more elaborate. Through everyday usage, the smaller items were often broken, and today it is unusual to find a complete set.

Porcelain sets decorated with florals, fruits, or scenics were produced abroad by Limoges in France; some were imported from Germany and England. During the last quarter of the 1800s and until after the turn of the century, American-made toilet sets were manufactured in abundance. Tin and graniteware sets were also made.

Empire, bl/wht windmills, 12" pitcher+bowl+chamber pot..........235.00
English, bl-gr florals, pitcher+bowl+toothbrush holder+pot........350.00
Festoon, med bl transfer, Wedgwood, pitcher+bowl, EX.............125.00
Gilman Collamore & Co, mc florals, pitcher+bowl 165.00
Ironstone, wht w/gold trim, pitcher+bowl 265.00
Knowles-Taylor-Knowles, child's, wht w/gold, pitcher+bowl 50.00
Mandarin, English, 1850s, pitcher+bowl, NM............................125.00
Mercer Pottery, Trenton NJ, wht w/gold trim, 5-pc, EX 415.00
Minton, child's, gr ivy on cream, 7" pitcher+9½" bowl...............250.00

Old Paris pitcher and bowl signed 'Boyer, Guirlandes,' and 'Gerlands' (pattern), ca 1830, $600.00.

Old Paris, floral & scrollwork panels on wht, pitcher+bowl 550.00
Rosetti, Royal Doulton, pitcher+bowl 210.00

Watch Fobs

Watch fobs have been popular since the last quarter of the 19th century. They were often made by retail companies to feature their products. Souvenir, commemorative, and political fobs were also produced. Of special interest today are those with advertising, heavy equipment in particular. Some of the more pricey fobs are listed here, but most of those currently available were produced in such quantities that they are relatively common and should fall into a price range of from $3.00 to $10.00. Our advisor for this category is Tony George; he is listed in the Directory under Washington.

Warco, Riddell Company, Bucyrus, OH, $115.00;
LaPlant-Choate, yellow & blue porcelain inlay,
$95.00

Abraham Fur Co, blk..80.00
Allis Chalmers, harvester 50.00
Alumina Soapalite, celluloid lion's head center 65.00
Aultman Taylor, rooster, brass 65.00
Caterpillar, brass, w/strap, NM 28.00
Dead Shot Powder, celluloid center, NM 250.00
Dead Shot Powder, metal, NM 250.00
DeLaval, enamel 95.00
Fink & Co, overalls & train, BLE logo on celluloid center 85.00
Fred Mueller Saddle Co, Denver, working man's saddle 155.00
Grand Island Horse & Mule Co, Nebraska, dtd 1917...............80.00
Hameley Roundup Saddle, Pendelton, Oregon 125.00
Indianapolis Saddlery Co......................................80.00
Internat'l Harvester, brass, w/strap, NM 28.00
Internat'l Harvester, red & blk 45.00
Jamestown 1907 Expo, Connecticut House 45.00
Kansas Livestock Co, horse & shoe 45.00
Levi Straus Overalls, celluloid, 4-color, w/mirror, EX 175.00
Missouri Livestock Show, buffalo, 1899 ....95.00
Model-T Ford, car w/script wings 125.00
New Mexico 1908 Territorial Fair..............................38.00
Power River Miles City Roundup, 1917..........................45.00
Remington 100th Anniversary..................................195.00
Saddle, copper, old...95.00
Salvet Worm Destroyer 60.00
Samuel Rosenthal & Bros, boy w/trousers, 1890s, EX 30.00
Savage Rifles, facing right, M.................................250.00
Scheaffer Leather Shop, saddle 125.00
Sioux City Stockyards, Indian head 90.00
Standard Horseshoe Co, Boston 70.00
Stanley Motor Carriage, figural 58.00
Trojan Powder, War Service Munitions Mfg.......................150.00
United States Horseshoe Co 40.00
West Cast Steel Motors, truck wheel emb 60.00
West Pennsylvania Volunteer Firemen's Assoc, 1926 ....22.50
Wilson Aldridge Livestock Commission...........................90.00
Wm Springer Denver, importers of draft horses 80.00
Woodbury Whip Co, Rochester, NY 70.00

Watch Stands

Watch stands were decorative articles designed with a hook from which to hang a watch. Some displayed the watch as the face of a grandfather clock or as part of an interior scene with figures in period costumes and contemporary furnishings. They were popular products of Staffordshire potters and silver companies as well.

Chalk, lady stands in glass-enclosed rectangle, 1800s, 14" 550.00
Cherry, box w/heart cutout, urn atop, 1800s, 9½" 735.00
CI, emb helmets/armor, 4 ivory boar tusks, 10½" 95.00

Mc & parcel gilt, putto w/wreath, Germany, 1700s, 16½" 1,100.00
Neoclassical giltwood, lion surmount, Germany, 16" 1,500.00
Oak w/allover cvd punched design, circle fr in top, rpr, 7" 175.00
Parcel gilt, Napoleon on horsebk, Continental, 1800s, 15½" 825.00
Silverplate, cherub holds bird aloft, Meriden, 5" 125.00
Wood, palace w/tower, bricks & gallery, EX pnt, 22x26" 1,300.00

Watches

First made in the 1500s in Germany, early watches were actually small clocks, suspended from the wrist or belt. By 1700 they had become the approximate shape and size we know today. The first watches produced in America were made in 1810. The well-known Waltham Watch Company was established in 1850. Later Waterbury produced inexpensive watches which they sold by the thousands.

Open-face and hunting-case watches of the 1890s were solid gold or gold-filled and were often elaborately decorated in several colors of gold. Gold watches became a status symbol in this decade and were worn by both men and women on chains with fobs or jeweled slides. Ladies sometimes fastened them to their clothing with pins often set with jewels. The chatelaine watch was worn at the waist, only one of several items such as scissors, coin purses, or needle cases, each attached by small chains.

Most turn-of-the-century watch cases were gold-filled; these are plentiful today. Sterling cases, though interest in them is on the increase, are not in great demand. Our advisor for this category is Miles Sandler (Maundy International Watches), an Antiquarian Horologist, collector, dealer, price consultant, and researcher for many watch reference guides and books on Horology. His firm is one of the world's largerst mail order dealers in antique watches of all varieties. He is listed in the Directory under Kansas. For character-related watches, see Personalities.

Key:
adj — adjusted
brg — bridge plate design
d/s — double sunk dial
fbd — finger bridge design
gf — gold-filled
g/j/s — gold jewel setting
h/c — hunter case
HCI#P — heat, cold,
   isochronism & position
   adjusted
j — jewel
k — karat

k/s — key set
k/w — key wind
l/s — lever set
mvt — movement
o/f — open face
p/s — pendant set
r/g/p — rolled gold plate
s — size
s/s — single sunk dial
s/w — stem wind
w/g/f — white gold-filled
y/g/f — yellow gold-filled

Am Watch Co, 10s, 15j, 20-yr, y/g/f, h/c, s/s 140.00
Am Watch Co, 12s, 15j, #1894, 14k, h/c............................395.00
Am Watch Co, 14s, 13j, #1884, 14k, h/c............................550.00
Am Watch Co, 16s, 11-15j, #1872, p/s, silver h/c, Park Road 325.00
Am Watch Co, 16s, 15-16j, #1899, y/g/f, h/c 185.00
Am Watch Co, 16s, 15j, #1883, y/g/f, 2-tone, Railroad King.......440.00
Am Watch Co, 16s, 15j, #1899, silveroid, s/w......................100.00
Am Watch Co, 16s, 16j, #1884, 5-min, coin silver, Repeater . 3,650.00
Am Watch Co, 16s, 17j, #1888, Railroader, rare, NM................875.00
Am Watch Co, 16s, 17j, #1899, y/g/f, s/w..........................90.00
Am Watch Co, 16s, 19j, #1872, Am Watch Co, h/c.............. 1,600.00
Am Watch Co, 16s, 19j, #1872, 14k, ¾-mvt, rare 2,400.00
Am Watch Co, 16s, 21j, #1888, o/f, 14k, Riverside Maximus 1,250.00
Am Watch Co, 16s, 21j, #1899, y/g/f, l/s, o/f, Crescent St..........195.00
Am Watch Co, 16s, 23j, #1908, y/g/f, o/f, adj, RR, Vanguard......240.00
Am Watch Co, 16s, 23j, #1908, y/g/f, o/f, Vanguard Up/Down...450.00
Am Watch Co, 18s, #1857, k/w, silver h/c, Howard/Rice, M.. 1,850.00
Am Watch Co, 18s, #1877, k/w, silver h/c, Excelsior.................225.00

Am Watch Co, 18s, 11j, #1857, k/w, 1st run, PS Barlett	650.00
Am Watch Co, 18s, 11j, #1857, silver h/c, k/w, s/s, Ellery, EX	200.00
Am Watch Co, 18s, 15j, #1857, silverine, o/f, k/w, Fogg's Pat	170.00
Am Watch Co, 18s, 15j, #1877, k/w, RE Robbins	325.00
Am Watch Co, 18s, 17j, #1883, y/g/f, o/f, Crescent Street	100.00
Am Watch Co, 18s, 17j, #1892, HC, Canadian Railway	625.00
Am Watch Co, 18s, 17j, #1892, y/g/f, o/f, Railroader, rare	1,000.00
Am Watch Co, 18s, 17j, #1892, y/g/f, o/f, s/w, AT&Co	110.00
Am Watch Co, 18s, 17j, #1892, y/g/f, s/w, h/c, PS Bartlett	170.00
Am Watch Co, 18s, 17j, 25-yr, y/g/f, o/f, s/s, PS Bartlett	110.00
Am Watch Co, 18s, 21j, #1892, y/g/f, o/f, d/s, Crescent St	275.00
Am Watch Co, 18s, 7j, #1857, k/w, CT Parker, scarce	1,950.00
Auburndale Watch Co, 18s, 7j, k/w, l/s, Lincoln	950.00
Aurora Watch Co, 18s, 11j, o/f, k/w, h/c	425.00
Aurora Watch Co, 18s, 15 ruby j, k/w, h/c	850.00
Ball (Elgin), 18s, 16j, o/f, silver, Official Standard	340.00
Ball (Hamilton), 16s, 21j, #999, g/f, o/f, l/s	275.00
Ball (Hamilton), 18s, 19j, #999, g/f, o/f, l/s	325.00
Ball (Hampden), 18s, 17j, o/f, adj, RR, Superior Grade	1,450.00
Ball (Seth Thomas), 18s, 17j, #3, g/j/s, o/f, l/s, scarce	1,750.00
Ball (Waltham), 16s, 21j, o/f, Offical Standard	265.00
Ball (Waltham), 19j, 16s, o/f, up/down indicator	2,750.00
Columbus Watch Co, 18s, 11-15j, k/w, k/s	440.00
Columbus Watch Co, 18s, 11j, o/f, silveroid case	150.00
Columbus Watch Co, 18s, 15j, o/f, l/s	175.00
Columbus Watch Co, 18s, 15j, y/g/f, o/f, Jay Gould	375.00
Columbus Watch Co, 18s, 15j, 18k, k/w, k/s	1,025.00
Columbus Watch Co, 6s, 15j, 18k, g/j/s, nickel plate	625.00
Cornell, 18s, 15j, s/w, CM Cady	475.00
Dudley, 12s, #1, 14k, o/f, display case, Masonic	2,850.00
Elgin, 10s, 14k, h/c, mc case	585.00
Elgin, 10s, 18k, h/c, k/w, k/s, s/s, Gail Borden	600.00
Elgin, 12s, 15j, 14k, h/c	425.00
Elgin, 12s, 17j, g/f, h/c, Lord Elgin	100.00
Elgin, 12s, 17j, 14k, h/c, GM Wheeler	400.00
Elgin, 12s, 21j, g/f, h/c, Lord Elgin	250.00
Elgin, 16s, 15j, doctor's, 4th model, 14k, 2nd sweep hand	1,350.00
Elgin, 16s, 15j, 14k, h/c	575.00
Elgin, 16s, 17j, g/j/s, o/f, s/w, BW Raymond	180.00
Elgin, 16s, 21j, g/f, 3 fbd, grade #72-91, scarce	1,350.00
Elgin, 16s, 21j, y/g/f, g/j/s, o/f, BW Raymond	175.00
Elgin, 16s, 21j, y/g/f, g/j/s, 3 fbd	320.00
Elgin, 16s, 21j, y/g/f, o/f, l/s, RR, Father Time	225.00
Elgin, 16s, 23j, up/down indicator, BW Raymond	650.00
Elgin, 17s, 7j, k/w, orig silver case, Leader	200.00
Elgin, 18s, 11j, silver, h/c, k/w, gilded, MG Odgen	200.00
Elgin, 18s, 15j, o/f, d/s, k/w, silveroid, RR, BW Raymond	195.00
Elgin, 18s, 15j, y/g/f, l/s, s/w, box hinge case	400.00
Elgin, 18s, 15j, 14k, k/w, k/s, h/c, HL Culver	885.00
Elgin, 18s, 17j, silveroid, BW Raymond	150.00
Elgin, 18s, 21j, g/f, h/c, l/s, s/w	265.00
Elgin, 18s, 21j, y/g/f, o/f, Father Time	275.00
Elgin, 18s, 23j, y/g/f, o/f, 5-position, RR, Veritas	390.00
Elgin, 6s, 11j, 14k, h/c	370.00
Elgin, 6s, 15j, 20-yr, y/g/f, h/c, s/s	125.00
Hamilton, #3992B, 16s, 22j, o/f, steel case	225.00
Hamilton, #904, 12s, 21j, y/g/f, g/j/s, o/f, brg	100.00
Hamilton, #910, 12s, 17j, 20-yr, y/g/f, o/f, s/s	60.00
Hamilton, #912, 12s, 17j, y/g/f, o/f, adj	65.00
Hamilton, #918, presentation, 14k w/20 diamonds, orig box	1,050.00
Hamilton, #920, 12s, 23j, w/g/f, o/f	300.00
Hamilton, #922MP, 12s, 18k case, Masterpiece (sgn)	925.00
Hamilton, #925, 18s, 17j, y/g/f, h/c, s/s, l/s	160.00
Hamilton, #928, 18s, 15j, y/g/f, o/f, s/s	100.00
Hamilton, #933, 18s, 16j, h/c, nickel plate	950.00
Hamilton, #938, 18s, 17j, 10k, y/g/f, adj	525.00
Hamilton, #940, 18s, 21j, nickel plate, coin silver, o/f	200.00
Hamilton, #946, 18s, 23j, y/g/f, o/f, g/j/s, EX	550.00
Hamilton, #947, 18s, 23j, h/c, orig/sgn, EX	6,000.00
Hamilton, #950, 16s, 23j, y/g/f, o/f, l/s, sgn d/s	450.00
Hamilton, #965, 16s, 17j, 14k, p/s, h/c, brg, scarce	925.00
Hamilton, #972, 16s, 17j, y/g/f, g/j/s, o/f, d/s, l/s, adj	120.00
Hamilton, #974, 16s, 17j, 20-yr, y/g/f, o/f, s/s	125.00
Hamilton, #992, 16s, 21j, y/g/f, o/f, adj, d/s, dbl roller	195.00
Hamilton, #992B, 16s, 21j, l/s, o/f, ¾-mvt	250.00
Hampden, 12s, 17j, w/g/f, o/f, thin model, Aviator	95.00
Hampden, 12s, 7j, g/f, o/f, s/w	50.00
Hampden, 16s, 17j, o/f, adj	70.00
Hampden, 16s, 17j, y/g/f, h/c, s/w	135.00
Hampden, 16s, 21j, g/j/s, y/g/f, NP, h/c, Dueber, ¾-mvt	180.00
Hampden, 16s, 21j, o/f, adj, dbl roller, Special Railway	190.00
Hampden, 16s, 7j, gilded, nickel plate, ¾-mvt	60.00
Hampden, 18s, 15j, k/w, mk on mvt, Railway	725.00
Hampden, 18s, 15j, s/w, gilded, JC Perry	125.00
Hampden, 18s, 15j, silver, k/w, h/c, Hayward	200.00
Hampden, 18s, 16j, y/g/f, gilded, damascened, h/c, Dueber	150.00
Hampden, 18s, 17j, adj, h/c, Dueber Grand	150.00
Hampden, 18s, 17j, y/g/f, g/j/s, h/c, adj, Dueber	150.00
Hampden, 18s, 21j, y/g/f, g/j/s, h/c, New Railway	265.00
Hampden, 18s, 21j, y/g/f, o/f, d/s, l/s, N Am Railway	225.00
Hampden, 18s, 23j, y/g/f, d/s, adj, New Railway	325.00
Hampden, 18s, 23j, 14k, h/c, Special Railway	825.00
Hampden, 18s, 7-11j, k/w, gilded, Springfield	110.00
Howard, 12s, 23j, 14k, h/c, brg, Series 8	750.00
Howard, 18s, 17j, 25-yr, y/g/f, o/f, orig case	395.00
Illinois, 0s, 7j, 14k, l/s, h/c	300.00
Illinois, 12s, 17j, y/g/f, o/f, d/s dial	70.00
Illinois, 16s, 17j, silver, h/c, RR King	500.00
Illinois, 16s, 17j, y/g/f, o/f, d/s, Bunn, EX	220.00
Illinois, 16s, 19j, y/g/f, o/f, d/s, 60-hr, Sangamo Special	820.00
Illinois, 16s, 21j, g/j/s, h/c, Burlington	170.00
Illinois, 16s, 21j, h/c, Sangamo Special	1,650.00
Illinois, 16s, 21j, o/f, d/s, Santa Fe Special	190.00
Illinois, 16s, 21j, y/g/f, o/f, s/s, Bunn Special	240.00
Illinois, 16s, 23j, y/g/f, o/f, d/s, RR, Bunn Special	550.00
Illinois, 18s, 11j, #1, silver, k/w, Alleghany	250.00
Illinois, 18s, 11j, #3, o/f, s/w, l/s, Comet	210.00
Illinois, 18s, 11j, Forest City	195.00
Illinois, 18s, 15j, #1, adj, k/w, k/s, Stuart	1,400.00
Illinois, 18s, 15j, #1, y/g/f, k/w, h/c, gilt, Bunn	1,100.00
Illinois, 18s, 15j, k/w, k/s, gilt, Railway Regulator	900.00
Illinois, 18s, 15j, s/w, silveroid	75.00
Illinois, 18s, 17j, g/j/s, adj, B&O RR Special	1,000.00
Illinois, 18s, 17j, o/f, d/s, adj, silveroid case, Lakeshore	240.00
Illinois, 18s, 17j, o/f, s/w, 5th pinion, Miller	365.00
Illinois, 18s, 17j, s/w, nickel plate, coin silver, Bunn	295.00
Illinois, 18s, 21j, g/j/s, adj, B&O RR Special	1,250.00
Illinois, 18s, 21j, g/j/s, g/f, o/f, A Lincoln	290.00
Illinois, 18s, 21j, g/j/s, h/c, Ben Franklin USA	2,450.00
Illinois, 18s, 21j, 14k, g/j/s, h/c, Bunn Special	1,300.00
Illinois, 18s, 23j, g/j/s, Bunn Special	425.00
Illinois, 18s, 24j, g/j/s, adj, Chesapeake & Ohio Special	3,250.00
Illinois, 18s, 24j, g/j/s, Bunn Special	565.00
Illinois, 18s, 26j, Penn Special, orig case	6,450.00
Illinois, 18s, 7j, #3, Interior	180.00
Illinois, 18s, 7j, #3, silveroid, America	135.00
Illinois, 18s, 9-11j, o/f, k/w, s/s, silveroid case, Hoyt	185.00
Illinois, 8s, 13j, ¾-mvt, Rose LeLand, scarce	425.00

Ingersoll, 16s, 7j, wht base metal, Reliance....................................**55.00**
Lancaster, 18s, 7j, o/f, k/w, k/s, eng case **275.00**
Marion US, 18s, h/c, k/w, k/s, ¾-plate, Asa Fuller **495.00**
Marion US, 18s, 15j, nickel plate, h/c, s/w, Henry Randel **575.00**
Melrose Watch Co, 18s, 7j, k/w, k/s..**495.00**
New York Watch Co, 18s, 7j, silver, h/c, k/w, Geo Sam Rice......**325.00**
New York Watch Co, 19j, low sz #, wolf's teeth wind **2,350.00**
Patek Philippe, 12s, 18j, 18k, o/f **2,250.00**
Patek Philippe, 16s, 20j, 18k, h/c **2,675.00**
Rockford, 16s, 17j, y/g/f, h/c, brg, dbl roller **175.00**
Rockford, 16s, 21j, #515, y/g/f..**425.00**
Rockford, 16s, 21j, g/j/s, o/f, grade #537, rare **1,550.00**
Rockford, 16s, 23j, o/f, mk Doll on dial & mvt, rare...............**1,450.00**
Rockford, 18s, 15j, o/f, k/w, silver case **150.00**
Rockford, 18s, 17j, silveroid w/mc dial, fancy mvt/hands............**275.00**
Rockford, 18s, 17j, y/g/f, o/f, Winnebago **270.00**
Rockford, 18s, 21j, o/f, King Edward **350.00**
Seth Thomas, 18s, 17j, #2, g/j/s, adj, Henry Molineux **875.00**
Seth Thomas, 18s, 17j, Edgemere **150.00**
Seth Thomas, 18s, 25j, g/j/s, g/f, Maiden Lane.......................**2,550.00**
Seth Thomas, 18s, 7j, ¾-mvt, bk: eagle/Liberty model................**225.00**
South Bend, 12s, 21j, dbl roller, grade #431 ....**140.00**
South Bend, 12s, 21j, orig o/f, d/s, Studebaker............................**275.00**
South Bend, 18s, 21j, g/j/s, h/c, full plate, grade #328 ....**565.00**
South Bend, 18s, 21j, 14k, h/c **775.00**
Swiss, 18s, 18k, h/c, 1-min, Repeater, High grade **3,650.00**

Waterford

The Waterford Glass Company operated in Ireland from the late 1700s until 1851 when the factory closed. One hundred years later (in 1951) another Waterford glassworks was instituted that produced glass similar to the 18th century wares — crystal glass, usually with cut decoration. Today Waterford is a generic term referring to the type of glass first produced there.

Bowl, Apprentice, 11" **575.00**
Bowl, centerpc; brilliant cuttings, ftd, 1950, 9x7½" **950.00**
Bowl, salad; Lismore, 8" **195.00**
Bowl, turn-over; period pc dmn & wedge cuts, ftd, 7½x10" **1,100.00**
Figure, mallard duck, wedge cut forms feathers, 2½x3¾" **85.00**
Ice bowl, Glandore, 6x6"...**225.00**
Paperweight, shamrock shape, 4" **115.00**
Sugar shaker, Lismore, 8" **65.00**
Symbol, sea horse, 7x4x1½" **225.00**
Tray, dresser; cut base, 8½x4⅝" **115.00**
Vase, brilliant Fancy Cut, 12" **425.00**

Watt Pottery

The Watt Pottery Company was established in Crooksville, Ohio, on July 5, 1922. From approximately 1922 until 1935, they manufactured hand-turned stone containers — jars, jugs, milk pans, preserve jars, and various sizes of mixing bowls, usually marked with a cobalt blue acorn stamp. In 1936 production of these items was discontinued, and the company began to produce kitchen utility ware and ovenware such as mixing bowls, spaghetti bowls and plates, canister sets, covered casseroles, salt and pepper shakers, cookie jars, ice buckets, pitchers, bean pots, and salad and dinnerware sets. Most Watt ware is individually hand-painted with bold brush strokes of red, green, or blue contrasting with the natural buff color of the glazed body. Several patterns were produced: Apple, Autumn Foliage, Cherry, Dutch Tulip, Morn-

ing-Glory, Pansy, Rooster, Tear Drop, Starflower, and Tulip, to name a few. Much of the ware was made for advertising premiums and is often found stenciled with the name of the retail company.

Tragedy struck the Watt Pottery Company on October 4, 1965, when fire completely destroyed the factory and warehouse. Production never resumed, but the ware they made has withstood many years of service in American kitchens and is today highly regarded and prized by collectors. The vivid colors and folk art-like execution of each cheerul pattern create a homespun ambiance that will make Watt pottery a treasure for years to come.

For further study we recommend *Watt Pottery, An Identification and Price Guide,* by our advisors for this category, Sue and Dave Morris, who are listed in the Directory under Iowa. For the address of the *Watt's News* newsletter, see the section on Clubs, Newsletters, and Catalogs.

Tear Drop bean pot, #76, $90.00; Dutch Tulip casserole, individual, $245.00; Apple pitcher, #17, $225.00.

Apple, bean pot, #76..**135.00**
Apple, bowl, #7, w/advertising **45.00**
Apple, bowl, #73, salad..**75.00**
Apple, casserole, #18, French, hdld, ind **225.00**
Apple, creamer, #62..**75.00**
Apple, grease jar, #01..**250.00**
Apple, mug, #121..**175.00**
Apple, pie plate, #33, w/advertising...**150.00**
Apple, pitcher, #15, w/advertising..**55.00**
Apple, plate, dinner; 9½"..**400.00**
Apple, shakers, hourglass form, pr..**200.00**
Apple, tumbler, #56..**325.00**
Autumn Foliage, baker, #96, w/lid **90.00**
Autumn Foliage, bowl, #63, mixing **35.00**
Autumn Foliage, oil & vinegar set, #126, w/lids............................**550.00**
Autumn Foliage, pitcher, #15...**35.00**
Autumn Foliage, sugar bowl, #98, w/lid & advertising................**175.00**
Basketweave, bowl, #8, gr, mixing **25.00**
Cherry, cookie jar, #21..**160.00**
Cherry, platter, #31...**145.00**
Cherry, shaker, barrel shaped **65.00**
Dutch Tulip, bowl, #67, w/lid **175.00**
Dutch Tulip, pitcher, #16..**125.00**
Dutch Tulip, pitcher, #69, sq shape..**325.00**
Eagle, bowl, #6, mixing..**65.00**
Goodies jar, #72..**225.00**
Kathy Kale, apple motif, salad set, 5-pc **250.00**
Morning-Glory, bowl, #6, mixing..**55.00**
Morning-Glory, cookie jar, #95...**275.00**
Pansy, bowl, spaghetti; 13" **70.00**
Pansy, cup & saucer..**75.00**

Pansy, plate, spaghetti; ind, 8½"..................................**40.00**
Pansy, platter, 15"...**100.00**
Rooster, bowl, #58, salad **90.00**
Rooster, canister, 'Flour,' #81, w/lid..........................**425.00**
Rooster, ice bucket, w/lid..**185.00**
Rooster, sugar bowl, #98, w/lid..................................**275.00**
Starflower, bowl, #74, cereal......................................**25.00**
Starflower, casserole, #18, tab hdls, ind........................**150.00**
Starflower, ice bucket, w/lid.....................................**185.00**
Starflower, mug, #501..**85.00**
Starflower, pitcher, #17, w/ice lip...............................**165.00**
Starflower, shakers, barrel shape, pr............................**150.00**
Tear Drop, bean, #75, ind server..................................**25.00**
Tear Drop, bowl, #07, mixing......................................**40.00**
Tear Drop, cheese crock, #80, w/lid..............................**275.00**
Tear Drop, pitcher, #15..**45.00**
Tulip, bowl, #600, w/lid..**200.00**
Tulip, cookie jar, #503...**300.00**
Tulip, creamer, #62..**95.00**
White Daisy, casserole, w/lid **165.00**
White Daisy, cup & saucer **75.00**
Woodgrain, cookie barrel, #617W..................................**250.00**
Woodgrain, pitcher, #615W..**100.00**

Wave Crest

Wave Crest is a line of decorated opal ware (milk glass) patented in 1892 by the C.F. Monroe Co. of Meriden, Connecticut. They made a full line of items for every room of the house, but they are probably best known for their boxes and vases. Most items were hand painted in various levels of decoration, but more transfers were used in the later years prior to the company's demise in 1916. Floral themes are common; items with the scenics and portraits are rarer and more highly prized. Many pieces have ornately scrolled ormolu and brass handles, feet and rims attached. Early pieces were often signed with a black mark; later a red banner mark was used, an occasionally a paper label may be found. However, the glass is quite distinctive and has not been reproduced, so even unmarked items are easy to recognize. Our advisors for this category are Dolli and Wilfred Cohen; they are listed in the Directory under California.

Ash tray, floral on scroll-emb 4½" bowl form...................**125.00**
Atomizer, floral on spherical shape..............................**350.00**
Atomizer, pansies in pastels on sq form, 3¾"....................**500.00**
Atomizer, sm HP floral on bud vase shape, bun base..............**450.00**
Blotter, floral on scroll-emb 5" L rectangle, ormolu mts....**1,000.00**
Bonbon, HP floral, ornate bail, 1½x5¼" dia.....................**300.00**
Bonbon, HP floral, w/metal & glass lid..........................**550.00**
Box, Baroque Shell w/floral, 5½" dia **450.00**
Box, blown-out rose on lid, HP base, hexagonal, 4" W...........**500.00**
Box, clock face in lid, florals, emb blank, 3x5" dia.........**1,200.00**
Box, cobalt w/floral in wht reserve, ormolu ft, 6x5½" dia.....**750.00**
Box, floral on scroll-emb sqd base & lid, 3x3"..................**300.00**
Box, floral on scroll-emb 8x4" oval form........................**350.00**
Box, floral/blown-out shell on lid, ormolu ft/rim, 4" dia......**395.00**
Box, glove; floral on scroll-emb 9½x4½" lid & base.............**750.00**
Box, Rococo, bl w/floral in wht reserve, 7" sq..................**700.00**
Box, Swirl, wht/gold decor on gr transparent, 7" dia...........**850.00**
Bud vase, HP floral, shell emb, hdld ormolu neck, 2¼x3¼"........**450.00**
Butter pat, floral transfer.....................................**150.00**
Card holder, floral in shaped recessed panel, metal rim.........**375.00**
Charger, HP mums on plain rnd form, 11" **500.00**
Charger, transfer floral on plain rnd shape, 11" **350.00**

Cologne, ribbon/floral, swirl-emb neck, str sides, stopper **350.00**
Creamer & sugar, HP floral on plain squat forms, metal mts **400.00**
Ferner, HP ferns, emb scrolls, str sides, rnd, ormolu rim **450.00**
Ferner, HP floral, emb ferns on 6 corners, ormolu rim **450.00**
Hair receiver, floral on scroll-emb rnd form, metal top **325.00**
Humidor, Cigars/floral in scroll-emb front panel **650.00**
Humidor, Egg Crate, floral/Tobacco, ormolu corner mts, 4x5"....**475.00**
Jardiniere, HP floral, str sides, gold trim, ring ft, 7" H.......**550.00**
Mustard jar, floral on plain cylinder, metal lid **400.00**
Plaque, daisies/clover on 10" scroll-emb disk, ormolu fr **1,450.00**
Plaque, scenic in scroll-emb reserve, ormolu fr, 7x10" **1,500.00**
Plate, HP roses, rectangular, scroll edge, 11x8".................**600.00**
Shakers, Billow, HP floral, short/sq form, pr **250.00**
Shakers, Creased Neck, HP floral, pr **225.00**
Shakers, Erie Twist, HP floral on wht opal, pr..................**150.00**
Shakers, Scroll, HP floral, pr **250.00**
Shakers, Tulip, HP floral, pr **125.00**
Sugar shaker, floral on squat swirl-emb form **275.00**
Tray, floral, emb 4" dia bowl, ormolu-mtd rnd mirror **450.00**
Tray, floral, emb 9½x4½" form, ormolu mtd oval mirror **850.00**
Tray, floral on scroll-emb 6" bowl, metal leaf-appl rim **250.00**
Tray, floral/intricate gold work on 7" bowl form, metal rim......**325.00**
Vase, asters on emb scrolls, ormolu hdls/dolphin ft, 14"........**650.00**
Vase, floral, megaphone form w/ornate ormolu hdls, 6x3".........**450.00**
Vase, floral & emb shells, str sides, 5", +ormolu ft **250.00**
Vase, lg floral, unemb classic form, ornate ormolu hdls, 8".....**375.00**
Vase, mums on str-sided form w/emb scrolls, ormolu ft, 11" **800.00**

Weapons

Among the varied areas of specialization within the broad category of weapons, guns are by far the most popular. Muskets are among the earliest firearms; they were large-bore shoulder arms, usually firing black powder with separate loading of powder and shot. Some ignited the charge by flintlock or caplock, while later types used a firing pin with a metallic cartridge. Side arms, referred to as such because they were worn at the side, include pistols and revolvers. Pistols range from early single-shot and multiple barrels to modern types with cartridges held in the handle. Revolvers were supplied with a cylinder that turned to feed a fresh round in front of the barrel breech. Other firearms include shotguns, which fired round or conical bullets and had a smooth inner barrel surface; and rifles, so named because the interior of the barrel contained spiral grooves (rifling) which increased accuracy. For further study we recommend *Modern Guns, Seventh Edition*, by Russell Quertermous and Steve Quertermous, available at your local bookstore. Our advisor for swords is Steve Hess; he is listed in the Directory under Florida. All other weapons are under the advisement of Steve Howard, see the Directory under California. See also Militaria.

Key:
bbl — barrel	hdw — hardware
cal — caliber	h/s — half stock
conv — conversion	mag — magazine
cyl — cylinder	mod — modified
f/l — flintlock	oct — octagon
f/s — full stock	p/b — patch box
ga — gauge	perc — percussion

Carbine

Burnside, 54 cal, inspector's mks on stock, EX **600.00**
Burnside 2nd Model perc, Foster Pat/1860 mks on latch, EX **900.00**
Burnside 4th Model, Civil War perc, eng scenes on bbl, EX **750.00**
Colt Lightning, 44-40 cal, slide action, 20" bbl, EX **1,150.00**

Greene Rifle Works, 50 cal, Warner brass fr, EX............................950.00
Inland WWII M-1, 30 M1 cal, 18" bbl w/carbine front, G 125.00
Joslyn 1862, 54 cal, minor dings to stock, EX 1,000.00
Maynard, 50 cal perc, inspector's mks, label, 36½", VG 700.00
Sharps & Hawkins US Navy M1852, leather-covered bbl, EX....750.00
Sharps Civil War, 50/70 cal, relined 22" rnd bbl, G...................500.00
Smith, Civil War perc, inspection mks, EX 675.00
Spencer Arms, 52 cal, age cracks in stock 500.00
Starr, 54 cal perc, initialed stock, missing ring, G 500.00
Vetterli M1882, 43 cal, bolt action, 18" bbl, EX........................550.00
Winchester 54 Special Order, 30-36, 20" stainless steel bbl, EX...375.00

Musket

Ames, Cavalry officer's, eng hilt, French origin, 42", G...............350.00
Ames US 1850 staff officer's, gilt/eng brass parts, 36", EX 900.00
Ames 1860 enlisted Cavalry, G, +scabbard 225.00
British f/l, 70 cal, f/s, 38½" bbl, VG 650.00
Harper's Ferry 1842 perc, 69 cal, eagle/US 1851 on lock, EX 700.00
Harper's Ferry 1842 perc, 69 cal, 1853 on lock, EX....................575.00
Harper's Ferry 1855 perc, 58 cal, VG 425.00
Hudson Bay perc conv, 60 cal, serpent sideplate, 42" bbl, G... 1,100.00
Lamson-Goodnow-Yale 1861 contract, 58 cal, eagle-mk bbl.......650.00
Rocy US 1840, brass hilt, #87 on crossgard, NP scabbard, VG....600.00
Tower perc, 62 cal, 3-band, 1863 on lock, EX..............................525.00
US 1816 f/l, 69 cal, altered butt stock, 42" rnd bbl, G 700.00
US 1816 f/l, 69 cal, 3 bbl bands, 42" bbl, VG 1,400.00
Winchester high wall, 22 long cal, single shot, 28" bbl, VG.........600.00
Winchester Hotchkiss repeater, bolt action, 45/70 cal, 32" bbl...500.00
Winchester Hotchkiss 1st Military, 45/70 cal, 28" rnd bbl, G 550.00
Winchester 1895 NRA, 30/06 cal, 24" rnd bbl, EX 1,100.00

Pistol

Astra Cub pocket, 25 ACP cal, faux pearl grips, 2⅛" bbl, NM...150.00
ATSTCO Hero perc, fits in boot, 31 cal, single shot, 1860s.........120.00
Beretta 420 pocket, 25 ACP cal, wood grips, 2¼" bbl, EX 250.00
Browning Hi-Power, 9M/M cal, wood grips, 4¾" bbl, NM...........550.00
Colt WWI Commemorative, 45 ACP cal, 5" bbl, M in box 750.00
Colt 1911 Army, conv to 1911-A1, 45 ACP cal, 5" bbl, G 325.00
Colt 2nd Model Derringer, 41 cal, bird grips, 2½" bbl 350.00
English f/l, 45 cal, single shot, eng fr, no wire inlay, VG.............125.00
Fabrique Nat'l (Browning Hi-Power), 9M/M cal, 6" bbl, EX 500.00
Hyde & Goodrich pocket perc, 38 cal, 4¼" oct bbl, G.................145.00
Mauser, 30 cal, broom hdl, 5½" bbl, G 500.00
Mauser pocket semi-auto, 6.35 cal, wood grips, 3" bbl, NM 450.00
Moores, 41 cal, single shot, SP/eng brass fr, 2½" bbl, VG 900.00
Ortgies pocket, 25 ACP cal, wood grips, 2⅝" bbl, EX 75.00
Remington derringer, 41 cal, over/under, blued finish, EX 300.00
Sharps pepperbox, 4-shot, nickeled, molded grips, EX 400.00
Tower 1851 perc, 58 cal, 33" rnd bbl, bayonet lug, G 275.00
US H Aston Military perc, 54 cal, lock dtd 1850, 8½" bbl, G 275.00
US Johnson Military perc, 54 cal, lock dtd 1854, 8½" bbl, G 350.00
Waters 1836 f/l, 54 cal, inspector's mks, 14", EX 800.00
Webley 1906 pocket, 25 ACP cal, rubber grips, 2" bbl, VG 100.00

Revolver

Bacon Arms pocket, 31 cal, eng fr, scene on cyl, 4" bbl, EX 375.00
Brooklyn Firearms pocket, 32 cal, eng brass fr, EX 300.00
Colt Bisley single action, 32/20 cal, 4¾" bbl, VG 1,200.00
Colt Brevete Sq Bk Navy perc, 36 cal, 7½" oct bbl, G................400.00
Colt single action, 45 long cal, ivory grips, 7½" bbl, G 985.00
Colt single action, 45 long cal, rubber grips, 5½" bbl, EX 1,200.00
Colt 1849 London perc, 31 cal, 5-shot cyl, 5" oct bbl, G.............500.00

Colt 1849 pocket, 31 cal, cyl scene, eng grip, 5" bbl, EX 550.00
Colt 1849 pocket, 31 cal, cyl scene, 4" bbl, EX in case 1,000.00
Colt 1849 pocket, 31 cal, cyl scene, 6-shot, 4" bbl, G.................300.00
Colt 1849 Wells Fargo perc, 31 cal, 5-shot, 3" oct bbl, G 750.00
Colt 1851 Navy conv, 38 cal, buffed, EX....................................300.00
Colt 1851 Navy perc, 36 cal, iron trigger guard, 7½" bbl 650.00
Colt 1855 Model 2 perc pocket, 28 cal, 3½" oct bbl, G 350.00
Colt 1860 Army perc, 44 cal, walnut grips, 8" bbl, VG...............525.00
Colt 1862 pocket, conv to cartridge, 38 cal, 4½" bbl, EX............400.00
Colt 1862 Police & pocket perc, 36 cal, 5-shot, 4½" bbl, VG 550.00
Colt 1877 Lightning, 38 cal, 4½" bbl, VG..................................300.00
Marlin XX 1873 pocket, 22 cal, fluted cyl, brass fr, rnd bbl 125.00

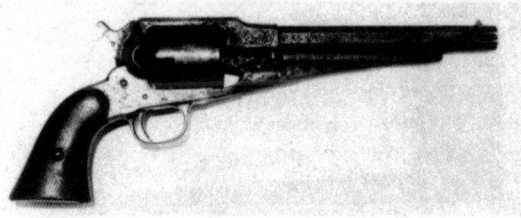

Remington New Model Percussion Army Revolver,
44 caliber, 8" octagon barrel, wood grips with inspector marking on left, #38651, VG, $500.00.

Remington New Model Army, 44 cal, rpl hammer, EX 325.00
Remington-Smoot New Model #1, 30 cal, NP finish, EX 200.00
Smith & Wesson #2 Old Model, 32 cal, w/US stamped holster ...500.00

Rifle

Allin 1865 US breech-loading conv, 58 cal, 31½" bbl, G 600.00
Allin 1866 conv, 40" musket bbl relined to 50 cal, dtd 1864.......700.00
Colt Lightning, pump action, 22 cal, 24" oct bbl, G 325.00
Colt Lightning, slide action, 22 cal, oct bbl, EX 700.00
Hatcher KY perc, 36 cal, maple stock w/silver, 41" bbl, VG.... 1,000.00
KY, 58 cal smooth bore, cherry stock, 39" oct bbl, G 600.00
Remington Mohawk, 22 cal, nylon stock, EX 75.00
Savage NRA target, bolt action, 22 long cal, 25" bbl, VG...........125.00
Savage 6A, 22 cal, w/Weaver scope, EX 175.00
Springfield 1873 trapdoor, 45-70 cal, EX 500.00
Winchester Pre-TR 70 Featherweight, 30/06 cal, 22" bbl, NM ...600.00
Winchester 04 boy's, bolt action, 1-shot, 22 cal, 21" bbl 115.00
Winchester 56 repeater, bolt action, 22 cal, 22" bbl, VG 575.00
Winchester 61 pump, 22 long cal, 24" rare oct bbl, VG 500.00
Winchester 70 STR, bolt action, 22-250 cal, 22" bbl, M 400.00
Winchester 70 Westerner, bolt action, 270 cal, 22" bbl, MIB 600.00
Winchester 86 takedown, 33 cal, ivory sights, 24" bbl, EX...... 1,000.00

Shotgun

Beretta S-685 over/under, 20-ga, 26" vent rib bbls, NM 600.00
Browning Magnum pump, 12-ga, 28" vert rib bbl, NM 300.00
Colt, 12 ga, dbl 26" Damascus bbls, eng locks/hammers, G 350.00
Farmington 1100 Field Grade, 12-ga, 28" mod choke bbl, EX 300.00
Greener, 12-ga, 1½-oz shot, eng lock, 30" bbls, VG 2,000.00
Ithaca Model 200E, 12-ga, 30" full & mod bbls, EX 300.00
Iver/Johnson Deluxe, 12-ga, 26" bbls w/skeet chokes, VG..........500.00
Janssen Sons, 12-ga, dbl Damascus bbls, VG 45.00
LC Smith, 10-ga, dbl Damascus bbls w/eng, EX 350.00
LC Smith, 12-ga, dbl Damascus bbls, eng receiver, EX 350.00
LC Smith, 12-ga, hammerless, dbl 30" Damascus bbls, EX 375.00
Marlin 24 Deluxe, 12-ga, eng doves/ducks, 30" bbl, G.................150.00
Remington Deluxe 870 pump, 28-ga, 25" vent rib bbl, M 350.00

Savage/Fox Special Grade, 12-ga, dbl triggers, 28" bbls, G **300.00**
Winchester 12 pump, 12-ga, 28" full choke bbl, VG **300.00**
Winchester 120, 12-ga, ventilated rib bbl, EX **200.00**
Winchester 1500 XTR, 12-ga, semi-auto, 28" mod choke bbl, M ..**300.00**
Winchester 1893 pump, 12-ga, EX..**250.00**
Winchester 1911, 12-ga, reblued, EX...**165.00**
Winchester 37, 410-ga, single 26" full choke bbl, VG **150.00**
Winchester 50, 20-ga, 28" ventilated rib bbl, EX stock...............**325.00**

Sword

Ames 1840 non-commissioned officer, mk US & 1864, 38", EX ..**150.00**
Ames 1840 US Artillery, eng brass guard, stamped 1848, 37" **175.00**
Ames 1860 Naval cutlass, anchor mk, 1862, 32", EX **450.00**
Cincinnati Regalia...Ohio, helmet pommel, bird guards, 34".........**50.00**
Civil War Cavalry 1860, Providence Tool Co, NP scabbard **275.00**
Civil War Infantry officer, etched blade, brass guard, 38"............**550.00**
Civil War Naval officer, brass hilt w/dolphin/eagle, 34" **400.00**
Engineer's, Ames Cutler Springfield 1838 US on blade, 41" **275.00**
Mansfield & Lamb, Civil War Cavalry, 1864, 43", EX **425.00**
Militia 1840-1850, bone hdl, helmet pommel, 34".........................**65.00**

Weathervanes

The earliest weathervanes were of handmade wrought iron and were generally simple angular silhouettes with a small hole suggesting an eye. Later copper, zinc, and polychromed wood with features in relief were fashioned into more realistic forms. Ships, horses, fish, Indians, roosters, and angels were popular motifs. In the 19th century, silhouettes were often made from sheet metal. Wooden figures became highly carved and were painted in vivid colors. E.G. Washburne and Company in New York was one of the most prominent manufacturers of weathervanes during the last half of the century. Two-dimensional sheet metal weathervanes are increasing in value due to the already heady prices of the full-bodied variety. Originality, strength of line, and patination help to determine value. When no condition is indicated, the items listed below are assumed to be in excellent condition.

Key:
fb — full-bodied   f/fb — flattened full-bodied

Arrow, tin/iron, curvilinear tail, orig pnt, 1900s, 19½x4" **70.00**
Arrow, wooden, old wht pnt, late 1800s, 24x5x1" **125.00**
Bull, f/fb copper/gilt, appl tail, att Howard & Co, 24" **2,000.00**
Cow, f/fb copper, att Cushing/White, VG gilt/shot, 33" L **4,600.00**
Dove, flying; copper cutout, 1800s, 23" W **1,600.00**
Duck w/lady on bk, tin, orig mc pnt, 1900s, 9x18" **175.00**
Fox, fb copper w/gr patina, 14x31" **1,700.00**
Goose, flying; sheet metal, urn-trn wood base, 1800s, 26" W .. **1,600.00**
Grasshopper, fb copper, w/rod & directionals, 20th C, 35" **375.00**
Horse, copper w/orig gold leaf, bullet holes, 1880s, 32" **1,600.00**
Horse, f/fb copper, J Harris & Sons, losses/flaws, 33" L **900.00**
Horse, fb copper/bronze, bronze/wht metal jockey, 31" L, EX......**500.00**
Horse, prancing, sheet metal, silver pnt, 1900, 15x18" **500.00**
Horse, running, brass, pnt, 13½x7½x1", on CI 25" arrow **235.00**
Horse, running, copper/gilt/zinc, dents, 26" **1,000.00**
Horse, running, copper/zinc, att Jewell & Co, 1890s, 16x28".. **1,800.00**
Horse, running, f/fb copper/zinc/gilt, 30", VG **850.00**
Horse, running, f/fb gilded copper, 1880s, no arrow, 28".............**900.00**
Horse, running, sheet metal w/worn pnt, 27" L, VG **245.00**
Horse, running, tin, red pnt, orig iron support rod, 34x26"..........**325.00**
Horse, running, tin, 9½x8½x1", on copper/CI 22" arrow............**165.00**
Horse, sheet iron, rpt, 22x24", EX **1,075.00**
Horse, tied to post, Anno 1887, pnt sheet metal, 20", G **750.00**

Horse, tin, gold pnt, 11x9½", on copper/CI 28" arrow **195.00**
Horse & sulky, f/fb copper w/gr patina, 1875, 19x31"............**12,000.00**
Peacock, f/fb copper on sphere, att Jewell, 1850s **17,500.00**
Pig, molded tin, 9x5", on decorative CI 21" arrow **175.00**
Ram, fb copper w/some gilt, rpl leg, horns missing, 34" L **4,500.00**
Rooster, cast zinc/sheet steel/pnt traces, 24" **1,075.00**
Rooster, copper w/orig gilt, 1880s, 26", EX................................**900.00**
Rooster, hollow copper, EX emb detail, 13", VG **625.00**
Rooster, molded/riveted metal, 13x11x1", on 30" arrow **265.00**
Rooster, sheet iron, pitted, rpr, 30" **400.00**
Rooster, sheet metal, 3-part tail, pine base, 1800s, 35" **1,900.00**
Rooster, well-cut sheet metal, mc rpt, 21" **450.00**
Sailboat w/directionals, copper, 20th C, 37x27" **400.00**
Touring car, man driving, pnt sheet metal, 35" L **1,200.00**

Weaving

Early Americans used a variety of tools and a great amount of time to produce the material from which their clothing was made. Soaked and dried flax was broken on a flax brake to remove waste material. It was then tapped and stroked with a scutching knife. Hackles further removed waste and separated the short fibers from the longer ones. Unspun fibers were placed on the distaff on the spinning wheel for processing into yarn. The yarn was then wound around a reel for measuring. Three tools used for this purpose were the niddy-noddy, the reel yarn winder, and the click reel. After it was washed and dyed, the yarn was transferred to a barrel-cage or squirrel-cage swift and fed onto a bobbin winder.

Today flax wheels are more plentiful than the large wool wheels, since they were small and could be more easily stored and preserved. The distaff, an often-discarded or misplaced part of the wheel, is very scarce. French spinners from the Quebec area painted their wheels. Many have been stripped and refinished by those unaware of this fact. Wheels may be very simple or have a great amount of detail, depending upon the owner's ethnic background and the maker's skill.

Flax comb, hewn & cvd birch, 18th C, 6½x14½" **95.00**
Flax comb, wooden, branded name ea side, 3¾x4¼" **150.00**
Hatchel, decorative bkbrd, cvd compass designs, 30" L **90.00**
Hatchel, tin, punched floral decor, dtd 1809, mtd on brd............**140.00**
Spinning wheel, oak/etc, bobbin damaged, 37" **100.00**
Spinning wheel, trn detail, worn blk pnt, incomplete, 22" **155.00**
Swift, table top, mortised pine, ca 1850, 19" L **185.00**
Wheel, flax; dk stain, ca 1840, 39x40x25½" **525.00**
Wool comb, trn wood hdls, sq nails, ca 1700s, 12x4" base **60.00**
Yarn winder, blk pnt, motised/pinned, age cracks, 24" **155.00**
Yarn winder, chip-cvd detail, dk gr rpt, 42"...............................**100.00**
Yarn winder, floor standing, maple, ca 1880s, 28" dia wheel **195.00**
Yarn winder, mortised & pinned, 12x18½" **75.00**
Yarn winder, red pnt, geared counter w/wood hand, 27" reel.......**175.00**
Yarn winder, wooden, nailed rpr, old rfn, 18" L............................**25.00**
Yarn winder, 18", EX **45.00**

Webb

Thomas Webb and Sons have been making fine art glass in Stourbridge, England, since 1837. Besides their fine cameo glass, they have also made enameled ware and pieces heavily decorated with applied glass ornaments. The butterfly is a motif that has been so often featured that it tends to suggest Webb as the manufacturer. Our advisor for this category is Don Williams; he is listed in the Directory under Missouri. See also specific types of glass such as Alexandrite, Burmese, Mother of Pearl, and Peachblow.

Berry set, wht opaque w/dk red pointed scallops, 5-pc 200.00
Biscuit jar, gold prunus on pk satin cased, floral-emb lid..............350.00
Bottle, scent; mc florals/gold bamboo on ivory satin, 5½".............295.00
Bowl, bamboo/floral intaglio, pk to cream, 3¾x5¾"....................695.00
Ewer, apples/leaves on gr to wht satin, ivory hdl, 9x4".................425.00
Ewer, Rock Crystal, spirals/berry prunts/ferns, 11½" 900.00
Rose bowl, yel to cream satin, wht int, box pleated, 5x6" 325.00
Vase, florals, mc/gold on rainbow swirl, flared top/base, 15" 550.00
Vase, florals, wht w/gold on gr shaded, dimpled, unsgn, 11" 475.00
Vase, florals & bees, gold on coral o/l, 4⅞x2¾" 195.00
Vase, florals/bird/butterfly on bl shaded satin, 8x6" 425.00
Vase, gold florals/drops on brn o/l, 3-petal top, 9¼" 295.00
Vase, yel satin to lt yel, cream int, ftd gourd form, 11" 285.00

Cameo

Bottle, floral/2 insects, wht on yel, cylindrical, 5" 750.00
Bottle, scent; swan's head form, #d, sterling mk cap, 9" 8,500.00
Bowl, intricate floral, wht on cranberry, 2x5"...............................750.00
Creamer, bl Dmn Quilt MOP, bulbous, 5x3⅛" 350.00
Perfume, lay-down; floral, wht on saffron, cut stopper, 4" 1,300.00
Plaque, leafy floral, wht on yel, oval, 5¼" L...............................450.00
Rose bowl, morning-glory/butterfly, 3-color, ftd, 3"..................2,000.00
Vase, apple blossoms/leaves, wht on red, slender, 5"...............1,275.00
Vase, berries/butterfly, wht on dk yel, dbl gourd, 6½" 1,250.00
Vase, blossoms/vines, wht on red, bulbous, 5", NM 2,400.00
Vase, feathers (lg) w/nutmeg stain on faux ivory, 4½x3½" 1,250.00
Vase, floral, wht on citron, conical, 4½"...................................650.00
Vase, floral, wht on peachblow, dbl-gourd stick neck, 9" 5,000.00
Vase, geraniums, wht on amber to rose, ovoid, 6½", EX.......... 1,000.00
Vase, honeysuckle, wht on red, 5" 1,400.00
Vase, leafy branches on faux ivory, silver finial, 6" 935.00
Vase, leaves/flowers, wht on honey amber, gourd form, 6" 1,100.00
Vase, lg floral/insect, wht on bright bl, ovoid, 6"....................1,750.00
Vase, nasturtiums, yel/ruby/wht, flared rim, 6x3¾" 1,600.00
Vase, Nouveau tulips, yel on clear texture, 9x6½".....................675.00
Vase, rose/butterfly, wht on red, no mk, squat/bulbous, 2½" ... 1,000.00
Vase, stylized scrolls/decorative motifs, rose on wht, 7" 1,400.00
Wax seal, floral, wht on turq bl hdl, silver mt, 4½"....................800.00

Wedgwood

Josiah Wedgwood established his pottery in Burslem, England, in 1759. He produced only molded utilitarian earthenwares until 1770 when new facilities were opened at Etruria. It was there he introduced his famous Basalt and Jasperware. Jasperware, an unglazed fine stoneware decorated with classic figures in white relief, was usually produced in blues; but it was also made in ground colors of green, lilac, yellow, black, or white. Occasionally three or more colors were used in combination. It has been in continuous production to the present day and is the most easily recognized of all the Wedgwood lines. (Jasper is a body of solid color or ware with a white body that has been dipped in an overlay color. Jasper-dip, introduced in the late 1700s, is the type most often encountered on today's market.)

Though Wedgwood's Jasperware was highly acclaimed, on a more practical basis his creamware was his greatest success. Due to the ease with which it could be potted and because its lighter weight significantly reduced transportation expenses, Wedgwood was able to offer 'chinaware' at affordable prices. Queen Charlotte was so pleased with the ware that she allowed it to be called 'Queen's Ware.' Most creamware was marked simply 'Wedgwood.' ('Wedgwood & Co.' and 'Wedgewood' are marks of other potters.) From 1769 to 1780, Wedgwood was in partnership with Thomas Bently; artwares of the highest

quality bear the mark indicating this partnership. Moonlight Lustre, an allover splashed-on effect of pink intermingling with gray, brown, or yellow, was made from 1805 to 1815. Porcelain was made, though not to any great extent, from 1812 to 1822. Bone china was produced before 1822 and after 1872. These types of wares were marked 'Wedgwood.' Stone china and Pearlware were made from about 1820 to 1875. Examples of either may be found with a mark to indicate their body type. During the late 1800s, Wedgwood produced some fine parian and majolica. Creamware, hand painted by Emile Lessore, was sold from about 1860 to 1875. From the 20th century, several lines of lustre wares — Butterfly, Dragon, and Fairyland (the latter designed by Miss Makeig-Jones) — have attracted the collector and, as their prices suggest, are highly sought-after and admired.

Nearly all of Wedgwood's wares are clearly marked. 'Wedgwood' was used before 1891, after which time 'England' was added. Most examples marked 'Made In England' were made after 1905. A detailed study of all marks is recommended for accurate dating. See also Majolica.

Key:
WW — Wedgwood   WWE — Wedgwood England

Baker, bsk yellowware, appl grapes/etc, w/insert, 12", NM 495.00
Biscuit jar, Jasper, blk, str-sided bbl form, WWE 450.00
Biscuit jar, Jasper, buff/blk bands, gilt lid/bail, WW, 7" 600.00
Biscuit jar, Jasper, dk bl, resilvered top, WWE, 6½x5½" 285.00
Biscuit jar, Jasper, dk bl, SP trim, WW, 5½x5¼" 265.00
Biscuit jar, Jasper, dk bl, SP trim, WWE, 7½x5½" 275.00
Biscuit jar, Jasper, lav/sage gr/wht, SP lid/hdl, WW, 6x4½".........725.00
Biscuit jar, Jasper, lilac, acorn finial, WW, 6" 595.00
Biscuit jar, Jasper, sage gr, fox hunt, WWE, hallmk band, 7".......400.00
Biscuit jar, Jasper, yel, SP lid, WW, 6".....................................695.00
Biscuit jar, Jasper, 3-color, acanthus leaf trim, WW, 9½" 815.00
Biscuit jar, stoneware, dk gr, ivy, bbl form, WW, rare.................285.00
Bowl, Butterfly Lustre, gold/umber, bl/gr int, WWE, 8"..............500.00
Bowl, Butterfly Lustre, Oriental landscape w/in, 8".....................550.00
Bowl, crater; Jasper, dk bl, 2 lg hdls, WW, ca 1860, 8½" H 650.00
Bowl, Dragon Lustre, bl mottle w/gold, MOP int, WW, 5½".......235.00
Bowl, Dragon Lustre, orange w/bl int, 1910, 9" 425.00
Bowl, Fairyland Lustre, Firbolgs III, 8-sided, 9½" 2,600.00
Bowl, Hummingbird Lustre, geese borders, WW, 4½x10" 525.00
Bowl, Jasper, blk, Dancing Hours, WW, 3x6"............................245.00
Bowl, Jasper, blk, Dancing Hours, WWE, ca 1961, 10" 1,250.00
Bowl, Oriental Lustre, flame, Portland vase mk, 3⅞" 245.00
Bowl, Purple Lustre, shell form, WW, 6½x13" 555.00
Box, Jasper, olive gr, heart shape, WWE, 2x3½x4½".................175.00
Brooch, Jasper, lt bl, sterling fr, WW, 1½" dia...........................235.00
Brooch, Jasper, lt bl, 14k oval fr, WW 365.00
Bust, Basalt, Dwight Eisenhower, WWE, 8½" 280.00
Bust, parian, Milton, EW Wyon, WW, 14¾x8½"........................695.00
Candlestick, Basalt, dolphin std, WW, 8½", pr...........................925.00
Candlestick, Jasper, dk bl, WW, ca 1860, 8", pr.........................450.00
Candy dish, Jasper, dk bl, basket form, WW, ca 1860, 5" 175.00
Cheese dish, Jasper, dk bl, WW, 4⅜x9" dia...............................550.00
Cigarette lighter, Jasper, lt bl, boat shape, WWE, 3½" 80.00
Clock, Jasper, sage gr, British United Clocks, WWE, 11¾".........650.00
Clock, Jasper, 3-color, WW, 8⅜" 1,500.00
Creamer, Drabware, lt brn, WW, 1840s, 2½x5" 225.00
Creamer, Drabware, salt-glazed Egyptian decor, WW, ca 1805 ...465.00
Creamer, Drabware, wht florals, WW, ca 1830 ....200.00
Creamer, Jasper, lt bl, St Louis shape, WWE, 2¼x3½" 80.00
Cup, Basalt, arabesques & foliage, WW, ca 1800, 4½"................475.00
Cup, Fairyland Lustre, elves, Portland vase mk, 3½x4⅞"..............695.00
Cup & saucer, Basalt, Niagara Falls, HP decor, WWE..................110.00
Cup & saucer, Creamware, gr floral, WW, ca 1882....................25.00

Cup & saucer, demitasse; Jasper, terra cotta, WWE, ca 1958 ......235.00
Cup & saucer, handleless; Basalt, no decor, WW, 2¼x3" 50.00

Jasper ferner, white on green, Wedgwood, 6" diameter, $295.00.

Figurine, Basalt, cat, glass eyes, WWE, 4½" 625.00
Flower frog, Creamware, tree trunk form, WWE, ca 1919, 6" dia .80.00
Flowerpot, Jasper, dk bl, WW, 3½", +stand.................................465.00
Hair receiver, Jasper, blk, classical figures, WW, 3½x3¼" 325.00
Honey pot, Jasper, dk bl, WW, 4¾" 165.00
Humidor, Jasper, dk bl, ball finial, WW, 6" 325.00
Humidor, Jasper, lt gr, acorn finial, WWE, ca 1900, 8x5½".........435.00
Jam jar, Jasper, blk w/buff, SP lid, WW, 3⅞x3½", +spoon 295.00
Jam jar, Jasper, dk bl, attached base, SP lid, WW, 4½" 275.00
Jam jar, Jasper, lt bl, SP lid, WW 225.00
Jardiniere, Jasper, dk bl, MIE, 4½x5" 265.00
Jardiniere, Jasper, dk bl, WWE, 6x7" 400.00
Leaf dish, Creamware, dk bl Ferrara decor, 8x10" 235.00
Lemonade set, Creamware, silver lustre, WWE, serves 6 ....385.00
Loving cup, Jasper, lt bl, 3-hdl, WWE, 4½" 170.00
Match holder, Jasper, olive gr, WWE, 2⅜" 85.00
Matchbox holder, Jasper, lt bl, WW, 3¾x6".................................132.00
Medallion, Basalt, Maximinius portrait, WW, 2¼x1½" 125.00
Medallion, Jasper, med bl, brass fr, WW, 2" dia 135.00
Mug, Jasper, dk bl, hallmk silver rim, Elkington, WW, 5x4" 225.00
Pitcher, bone china, Fallow Deer, copper lustre, WWE, 1937.....140.00
Pitcher, bone china, Imari colors, hexagonal, WW, 1880s, 6½"..265.00
Pitcher, Creamware, floral on bl, bulbous, WW, ca 1869, 6½"....335.00
Pitcher, drabware, ladies in relief panels, WW, 6½"....................195.00
Pitcher, Jasper, blk, figures/fretwork, w/lid, WWE, 6" 175.00
Pitcher, Jasper, crimson, bulbous, MIE, 2⅜" 750.00
Pitcher, Jasper, dk bl, WW, 4x3⅜" 150.00
Pitcher, Jasper, lilac, Etruscan shape, MIE, ca 1950 ....235.00
Pitcher, Jasper, sage gr, SP hinged top, WW, 8x3½" 225.00
Pitcher, tankard, Jasper, dk bl, WW, 5½" 125.00
Pitcher, tankard, Jasper, dk bl, WW, 6⅜x3⅞" 145.00
Pitcher, tankard, Jasper, dk bl, WW, 7¾x3½" 165.00
Pitcher, tankard, Jasper, lt gr, WWE, 4⅝" 130.00
Planter, Jasper, dk bl, ftd, w/drainer insert, WW, 3½" 350.00
Plaque, Jasper, lt bl, cherubs, WW, 13½x7½" 665.00
Plaque, Jasper, lt bl, Pegasus, fr, WW, 4" 235.00
Plate, bone china, Alpine Rose, WWE, 8" 80.00
Plate, Creamware, Etruria, WWE, ca 1895 ....137.50
Plate, Creamware, Kruger Park series, Giraffe, WWE, ca 1950......55.00
Plate, Drabware, Capri, WW, ca 1840, 8" 130.00
Plate, Drabware, gold line at rim, WW, ca 1830, 9¾"................125.00
Plate, Gr Glaze, Grapeleaf, WW, 8"...80.00
Plate, Gr Glaze, Sunflower, WW, 8⅝"..100.00
Plate, Gr Glaze, Tremblay, WW, ca 1872 ....140.00
Plate, Jasper, dk bl, Aurora, WW, 8"...155.00
Plate, Jasper, lt bl, WWE, 9½" 75.00

Plate, Pearlware, Moonlight Lustre, shell form, WW, 8¼" 285.00
Platter, Creamware, red & bl floral, WWE, 12¾x10" 130.00
Ring tree, Jasper, dk bl, floral border, WW, 2¾x3⅛" 175.00
Sugar bowl, Basalt, twig hdls, widow finial, WW, ca 1840..........255.00
Syrup, Jasper, dk bl, hinged SP lid, WW, 6x3⅜" 175.00
Tea caddy, Jasper, 3-color, WWE, 5¼" 1,550.00
Tea set, bone china, Liberty, WWE, ca 1919, 11-pc 2,275.00
Tea set, stoneware, platinum over copper, WWE, 3-pc 775.00
Teapot, Basalt, Victoria BC, WWE, 7".......................................125.00
Teapot, Ferrara, dk bl, 5x6¼"...125.00
Teapot, Jasper, dk bl, lacy border, WW, 4½".............................250.00
Teapot, Jasper, dk bl, widow finial, WW, ca 1874, 7" 400.00
Tile, Priscilla & John Alden, bl wht transfer, 1900, 6x6" 125.00
Tray, Jasper, blk, spade form, WW, ca 1890 ....80.00
Tray, Jasper, lilac, WWE, ca 1950, 9¾x7½" 265.00
Urn, Jasper, dk bl, WW, ca 1830, 8¾" dia at top.......................650.00
Vase, Basalt, laurel swags, WW, 6" 335.00
Vase, Butterfly Lustre, 4 butterflies, WW, slim, 5" 275.00
Vase, Fairyland Lustre, maid/fairies, ftd trumpet form, 9" 2,250.00
Vase, Jasper, dk bl, cylindrical, WW, ca 1868, 9⅞", pr 900.00
Vase, Jasper, lt bl, rams' heads & roses, WW, 10⅛x3¾"............275.00
Vase, Jasper, lt gr, Zodiac band, Muse decor, WW, rpr, 13".........465.00
Vase, Keith Murray, cylindrical w/rings, brn matt, 9"................650.00
Vase, Victoria Ware, brn/cream gloss, gold trim, hdls, 7½" 400.00

Weil Ware

Max Weil came to the United States in the 1940s, settling in California. There he began manufacturing dinnerware, figurines, cookie jars, and wall pockets. American clays were used, and the dinnerware was all hand decorated. Weil died in 1954; the company closed two years later. The last backstamp to be used was the outline of a burro with the words 'Weil Ware — Made in California.' Many unmarked pieces found today originally carried a silver foil label; but you'll often find a four-digit handwritten number series, especially on figurines. For further study we recommend *The Collector's Encyclopedia of California Pottery* by our advisor, Jack Chipman. He is listed in the Directory under California.

Bowl, Blossom, rectangular, 8¾" L 15.00
Bowl, vegetable; Rose 10.00
Butter dish, Blossom, ¼-lb 25.00
Coffee server, Bamboo 20.00
Comport, Rose 10.00
Cup & saucer, Blossom 8.00
Cup & saucer, Rose...5.00
Dish, Dogwood, divided, sq, 10½" 7.50
Figurine, Buddy, boy, 7"...15.00
Figurine, girl, lifted chin, sgraffito floral on skirt, lg.....................32.00
Planter, figural girl, artist sgn, #1899, 11" 30.00
Planter, lady's head w/fan, HP flowers, 8" 30.00
Plate, Rose, 10" 6.00
Platter, Blossom, 13" 15.00
Platter, Rose, 10" 10.00
Vase, Ming Tree, w/coralene, 8½" 35.00
Wall pocket, Oriental girl, #4046 ....22.50

Weller

The Weller Pottery Company was established in Zanesville, Ohio, in 1882, the outgrowth of a small one-kiln log cabin works Sam Weller had operated in Fultonham. Through an association with Wm Long, he entered the art pottery field in 1895, producing the Lonhuda Ware Long had perfected in Steubenville six years earlier. His famous Louwelsa line was merely a continuation of Lonhuda and was made in at least five hundred different shapes until 1924. Many fine lines of artware followed under the direction of Charles Babcock Upjohn, Art Director from 1895 to 1904: Dickens Ware (1st Line), under-glaze slip decorations on dark backgrounds; Turada, featuring applied ivory bands of delicate openwork on solid dark brown backgrounds; and Aurelian, similar to Louwelsa, but with a brushed-on rather than blended ground. One of their most famous lines was 2nd Line Dickens, introduced in 1900. Backgrounds, characteristically caramel shading to turquoise matt, were decorated by sgraffito with animals, golfers, monks, Indians, and scenes from Dickens novels. The work is often artist signed. Sicardo, 1903, was a metallic lustre line in tones of rose, blue, green, or purple with flowing Art Nouveau patterns developed within the glaze.

Frederick Hurten Rhead, who worked for Weller in 1903 to 1904, created the prestigious Jap Birdimal line decorated with geisha girls, landscapes, storks, etc., accomplished through application of heavy slip forced through the tiny nozzle of a squeeze bag. Other lines to his credit are L'Art Nouveau, produced both in high-gloss brown and matt pastels, and 3rd Line Dickens, often decorated with Cruikshank's illustrations in relief. Other early artware lines were Eocean, Floretta, Hunter, Perfecto, Dresden, Etched Matt, and Etna.

In 1920 John Lessel was hired as Art Director, and under his supervision several new lines were created. LaSa, LaMar, Marengo, and Besline attest to his expertise with metallic lustres. The last of the artware lines and one of the most sought-after by collectors today is Hudson, first made during the early 1920s. Hudson, a semi-matt glazed ware, was beautifully artist decorated on shaded backgrounds with florals, animals, birds, and scenics. Notable artists often signed their work, among them Hester Pillsbury, Dorothy England Laughead, Ruth Axline, Claude Leffler, Sarah Reid McLaughlin, E.L. Pickens, and Mae Timberlake.

During the thirties, Weller produced a line of gardenware and naturalistic life-sized figures of dogs, cats, swans, geese, and playful gnomes. The depression brought a slow, steady decline in sales, and by 1948 the pottery was closed. For a more thorough study, we recommend *The Collector's Encyclopedia of Weller Pottery* by Sharon and Bob Huxford, available at your local library or from Collector Books.

Alvin, vase, limb hdls, 12"	55.00
Alvin, vase, trunk form, no mk, 8½"	35.00
Animal, cat, 8½x15½"	725.00
Animal, pop-eye dog, 4"	275.00
Animal, Scottie dog, 12x15"	900.00
Animal, Scottie pup, 5x8"	325.00
Ansonia, batter jug, no mk, 14½"	170.00
Ansonia, strawberry pot, 10"	45.00
Arcadia, covered dish, 4½"	45.00
Arcadia, vase, bud; 7½"	18.00
Arcola, planter, experimental, no mk, 5x9"	85.00
Arcola, wall pocket, grape cluster, no mk, 11"	135.00
Ardsley, bowl, console; w/6" iris frog	115.00
Ardsley, bulb bowl, 5"	65.00
Ardsley, vase, bud; 7½"	45.00
Ardsley, vase, corner; floral, 3-ftd, 7"	85.00
Ardsley, wall pocket, dbl, ink stamp, 11½"	120.00
Art Nouveau, ewer, floral, 8"	125.00
Art Nouveau, umbrella stand, floral, glossy, no mk, 26"	725.00
Art Nouveau, vase, corn figural, 4½"	95.00
Art Nouveau, vase, floral, flared cylinder, 13½"	285.00
Art Nouveau, vase, lady, glossy, slim form, no mk, 12½"	375.00
Athens, vase, medallion reserve, no mk, 10"	375.00
Atlas, candle holder, no mk, #C-12, pr	42.50

Atlas, covered dish, 3½"	70.00
Atlas, vase, 6"	55.00
Aurelian, banquet lamp, floral, 27"	1,100.00
Aurelian, jardiniere & pedestal, floral, no mk, 38"	1,350.00
Aurelian, lamp base, oil canister; lilies, 27"	750.00
Aurelian, vase, floral, cylindrical, 16"	875.00
Aurelian, vase, floral, sgn RA, classic form, 13"	425.00
Aurelian, vase, portrait, sgn Fouts, cylindrical, 18"	1,750.00
Auroro, candle holders, floral, sgn W, 9", pr	350.00
Baldin, bowl, apples, no mk, 4"	85.00
Baldin, vase, apples, cylindrical, 9½"	150.00
Barcelona, ewer, floral, 8"	165.00
Barcelona, vase, floral, hdls, 6½"	115.00
Besline, vase, floral, cylindrical, 11"	525.00
Blo Red, vase, 3½"	45.00
Blo Red, vase, 7"	60.00
Blossom, cornucopia, 6"	22.50
Blossom, vase, 14"	120.00
Blue & Decorated, vase, bud; floral, no mk, 10"	135.00
Blue & Decorated, vase, floral, cylindrical, 8½"	175.00
Blue & Decorated, vase, lady, cylindrical, 13½"	1,500.00
Blue Drapery, jardiniere, no mk, 5½"	35.00
Blue Drapery, vase, floral, no mk, 4"	22.50
Blue Ware, comport, fruit swags, 5½"	165.00
Blue Ware, jardiniere, classical figure, 6½"	135.00
Bonito, bowl, floral, sgn CF, 3½"	70.00
Bonito, vase, floral, sgn NC, sm angle hdls, 10"	215.00
Bonito, vase, floral, sm hdls, 4"	55.00
Bonito, vase, floral, upturned hdls, ftd, 6½"	100.00
Bouquet, bowl, console; 5"	30.00
Bouquet, bowl vase, 4½"	17.50
Breton, bowl, 2-tone, 4"	75.00
Brighton, bluebird, #3, 6"	275.00
Brighton, bluebird, #5, 5½"	250.00
Brighton, bud vase, dbl; bird on perch, wall hanging, 12"	185.00
Brighton, cardinal, 5½"	350.00
Brighton, flamingo, no mk, 6"	225.00
Brighton, parrot, 13½"	800.00
Brighton, swan flower frog, 5"	215.00
Brighton, wall vase, bird perched on branch, 9½"	135.00
Brighton, woodpecker, #3X, 6½"	225.00
Burntwood, plaque, bird on branch, no mk, 12"	300.00
Burntwood, vase, grape cluster, no mk, 3½"	85.00
Cactus, boy w/bag, brn, 5"	78.00
Cactus, camel, brn, 4"	70.00
Cactus, Chanticleer Rooster, 7"	125.00
Cactus, frog, tan, 4"	78.00
Cactus, Glouster Woman, 11½"	325.00
Cactus, horse, brn, 5"	78.00
Camelot, lamp, geometrics, no mk, 11½"	300.00
Camelot, vase, funnel neck, squat bulbous base, wht/lime, 8"	275.00
Camelot, vase, geometrics, bulbous, no mk, 8"	225.00
Cameo, flower arranger, 3"	22.50
Cameo, hanging basket, floral, 5"	65.00
Cameo, vase, floral, hdls, 13"	52.50
Cameo Jewell, jardiniere & pedestal, no mk, 34"	900.00
Cameo Jewell, umbrella stand, cameo portrait, 22"	550.00
Candis, candle holder, 1½", pr	35.00
Candis, hanging basket, no mk, 5½"	85.00
Chase, vase, hunt scene, experimental, 7½"	450.00
Chase, vase, hunter on horse w/dog, fan form, 8½"	225.00
Chase, vase, scene in silver, 12"	450.00
Chengtu, vase, bulbous, 11½"	125.00
Chengtu, vase, classic form, 16"	235.00

Claremont, candle holder, 8", pr	165.00
Claremont, candlestick, 10"	95.00
Classic, bowl, gr, 11"	45.00
Classic, bowl, wht, 8"	35.00
Classic, vase, brn, fan form, 5"	50.00
Claywood, bowl, no mk, 2"	30.00
Claywood, candle holder, no mk, 5"	50.00
Claywood, mug, floral, no mk, 5"	85.00
Claywood, spittoon, floral, no mk, 4½"	115.00
Clinton Ivory, window planter, 6x15½"	135.00
Cloudburst, bowl, lustre, 4x9"	95.00
Cloudburst, vase, lustre, 4½"	70.00
Cloudburst, wall pocket, no mk, 5½"	85.00
Coppertone, ash tray, 6½"	145.00
Coppertone, frog, no mk, 11½x15"	850.00
Coppertone, owl, no mk, 9"	275.00
Coppertone, pitcher, frog hdl, 7½"	400.00
Coppertone, vase, fan form, no mk, 8"	300.00
Coppertone, vase, frog hdls, 8"	425.00
Coppertone, vase, hdls, 7"	115.00
Copra, jardiniere, floral, ring hdls, no mk, 10½"	225.00
Corleone, vase, floral, sgn HP, tapered cylinder, 17"	625.00
Cornish, candle holder, 3½", pr	35.00
Cornish, jardiniere, 5"	27.50
Cornish, vase, 7"	27.50
Cretone, vase, brn on tan, 8"	260.00
Darsie, flowerpot, 5½"	25.00
Darsie, vase, cylindrical w/flared rim, 7½"	25.00
Decorated Creamware, mug, floral, hand decorated, no mk, 5"	115.00
Decorated Creamware, teapot, decalcomania, no mk, 5½"	115.00
Decorated Creamware, vase, floral, hand decorated, 11½"	250.00
Delsa, ewer, 7"	26.00
Delsa, vase, 6"	22.50
Delta, vase, floral, sgn Pillsbury, no mk, 7"	350.00
Dickens I, jardiniere, floral, 8"	265.00
Dickens I, loving cup, floral, 3-hdl, 5½"	350.00
Dickens I, mug, floral, 7"	185.00
Dickens I, vase, floral, classic form, 11"	300.00
Dickens II, ewer, fish, sgn EL Pickens, 11½"	500.00
Dickens II, ewer, mermaid, no mk, 10½"	425.00
Dickens II, humidor, captain, 7"	700.00
Dickens II, mug, Black Bird (Indian portrait), sgn UJ, 6"	600.00
Dickens II, tankard, draped nude, sgn/1902, no mk, 12"	2,450.00
Dickens II, vase, Bald Eagle (Indian portrait), sgn, 9"	1,275.00
Dickens II, vase, cavalier, high-gloss bl on bl, 13½"	800.00
Dickens II, vase, Chief Hollowhorn Bear, sgn AD, 13"	1,750.00
Dickens II, vase, Don Quixote & Sancho Setting Out, 16"	1,850.00
Dickens II, vase, fish, sm hdls, 9½"	1,550.00
Dickens II, vase, fisherman, classic form, 15½"	1,350.00
Dickens II, vase, prairie scene, cylindrical, 17"	1,175.00
Dickens II, vase, 2 ladies in country, cylindrical, 17"	2,500.00
Dickens III, carafe w/cup, David Copperfield, 14½"	1,000.00
Dickens III, inkwell, profile portrait, #0038, 2½"	425.00
Dickens III, mug, portrait, no mk, 4"	465.00
Dickens III, teapot, Captain Cuttle, sgn, #5055, 7"	745.00
Dickens III, vase, portrait, sm angular hdls, 6"	285.00
Dresden, mug, windmill scene, 5½"	450.00
Dresden, vase, windmill scene, 10½"	525.00
Dunton, umbrella stand, exotic birds & florals, no mk, 23"	750.00
Dupont, planter, floral, sq form, no mk, 3½"	45.00
Dynasty, vase, ring hdls, no mk, 6"	45.00
Elberta, bowl, 3-part, 3½"	45.00
Elberta, cornucopia, 8"	40.00
Elberta, vase, irregular-shaped top, 5"	22.50

Eocean, basket, floral, no mk, 6½"	250.00
Eocean, Late Line; vase, bud; floral, no mk, 6½"	70.00
Eocean, Late Line; vase, floral, long neck, 10½"	275.00
Eocean, vase, floral, sgn MS, tub hdls, 6"	180.00
Eocean, vase, floral, waisted, hdls, 4½"	100.00
Eocean, vase, floral, 4 sm hdls at rim, slim form, 10½"	350.00
Eocean, vase, sea gulls, wht on dk gr to cream, tapered, 10"	900.00
Etched Matt, vase, floral, bulbous, 6½"	185.00
Etched Matt, vase, lady's profile, 11"	425.00
Ethel, vase, creamware, 11½"	225.00
Ethel, vase, creamware, 9½"	185.00
Etna, bowl, mouse perched on side, 2½"	300.00
Etna, pitcher, floral, 6"	135.00
Etna, vase, frog & snake, 6½"	500.00
Etna, vase, grape cluster, shouldered slim form, 15"	300.00
Euclid, wall pocket, no mk, 10"	85.00
Evergreen, bowl, console; 5"	60.00
Evergreen, candle holder, triple, 7½"	60.00
Evergreen, candlestick, 1½", pr	32.50
Evergreen, pelican, 7½"	100.00
Evergreen, turtle, 5½"	22.50
Evergreen, vase, 4½"	35.00
Fairfield, bowl, cylindrical, no mk, 8"	75.00
Flask, Dust Remover, whisk broom form, no mk, 6"	120.00
Flask, PAP Loyal Order of Moose, no mk, 4½"	100.00
Flemish, Blue; vase, floral, 10"	150.00
Flemish, inkwell, floral, no mk, 4½x7"	385.00
Flemish, jardiniere, floral, 3-ftd, 6"	85.00
Flemish, jardiniere, floral in relief, 8"	175.00
Flemish, tub, floral, hdls, 4½"	80.00
Flemish, umbrella stand, apple trees, 22"	450.00
Fleron, batter pitcher, 11½"	135.00
Fleron, vase, flared rim, sm hdls, 8"	58.00
Fleron, vase, flared rim, 4½"	48.00
Floral, vase, 4½"	17.50
Floral, vase, 6½"	25.00
Florala, bowl, console; floral, no mk, 11"	45.00
Florala, candle holder, floral, hexagonal, 5"	55.00
Florenzo, planter, sq form, ftd, 3½"	30.00
Florenzo, vase, pillow form, 4"	25.00
Floretta, ewer, grape cluster, 10½"	120.00
Floretta, vase, floral on brn to pk shaded, 19"	525.00
Floretta, vase, floral reserve, no mk, 5½"	70.00
Forest, basket, woodland scene, 8½"	175.00
Forest, pitcher, woodland scene, glossy, 5"	175.00
Forest, teapot, woodland scene, 4½"	225.00
Fruitone, vase, sq sides, slim form, 8½"	150.00
Fruitone, vase, 6"	75.00
Fruitone, wall pocket, 5½"	70.00
Garden Ornament, goose, 12½x13"	1,125.00
Garden Ornament, Pan w/fife, 16½"	1,000.00
Garden Ornament, rabbit, 7½x13"	625.00
Garden Ornament, squirrel, no mk, 12"	700.00
Geode, vase, bulbous, 3½"	95.00
Glendale, vase, bird, flared cylinder, no mk, 6½"	235.00
Glendale, vase, bird on nest, classic form, 12"	400.00
Glendale, vase, dbl bud; bird, no mk, 7"	200.00
Glendale, wall pocket, birds on floral branch, 7½"	165.00
Gloria, ewer, #G-12, 9"	35.00
Gloria, vase, floral, 12½"	80.00
Goldenglow, bowl, hdls, no mk, 3½x16"	55.00
Goldenglow, vase, bud; 8½"	30.00
Greenbriar, ewer, no mk, 11½"	155.00
Greenbriar, pitcher, no mk, 10"	150.00

Greenbriar, vase, no mk, 6½" 78.00
Greora, vase, cylindrical, 11½" 125.00
Greora, vase, hdls, 9" 80.00
Greora, vase, 3-ftd, no mk, 4½" 45.00
Hobart, bowl, console; 2½x12", +7½" nudes flower frog.............325.00
Hobart, candle holder, nude beside holder, no mk, 6", pr 225.00
Hudson, vase, birds in flight, sgn Pillsbury, 9½" 1,300.00
Hudson, vase, floral, angle hdls, 13½" 775.00
Hudson, vase, floral, sgn MT, classic form, 16" 1,350.00
Hudson, vase, iris, sgn Axline, cylindrical, 8½"......................325.00
Hudson, vase, landscape, sgn Timberlake, cylindrical, 8½" 675.00
Hudson, vase, mtn scene, sgn Pillsbury, 8" 850.00
Hudson, vase, river scene, sgn Pillsbury, classic form, 15" 1,650.00
Hudson, vase, tiger in grasses, 8" 1,150.00
Hudson, wall pocket, floral on wht, 8".................................185.00
Hudson-Light, vase, floral, bulbous, 4½".............................115.00
Hudson-Light, vase, floral, 15"...850.00
Hudson-Perfecto, vase, floral, sgn DE, no mk, 6½" 200.00
Hudson-Perfecto, vase, floral on tan shaded, 9".....................315.00
Hudson-Perfecto, vase, irises, sgn, bulbous, 13½" 1,100.00
Hudson-Perfecto, vase, pine cones, sgn Leffler, no mk, 10" 425.00
Hunter, vase, deer, hdls, #343, 6½" 650.00
Hunter, vase, duck, ewer form, 7" 500.00
Ivoris, ginger jar, half hdls, 8½"..65.00
Ivoris, pitcher, 6" 40.00
Ivoris, vase, waisted, hdls, 7" 125.00
Ivory, jardiniere, squirrels in tree, no mk, 6½" 90.00
Ivory, jardiniere & pedestal, impressed mk, 36" 675.00
Ivory, vase, floral swags, pillow form, no mk, 5" 60.00
Ivory, wall pocket, eagle, no mk, 9" 215.00
Ivory, wall pocket, stag form, 9" 235.00
Ivory, wall shelf, 9½" 75.00
Ivory, window box, 8x10½"...375.00
Jap Birdimal, mug, geisha w/cat, Rhead Faience mk, 5" 900.00
Jap Birdimal, vase, crane, flared cylinder, 7"........................400.00
Jap Birdimal, vase, fish, bulbous, no mk, 4½" 425.00
Jap Birdimal, vase, geisha, no mk, 4" 575.00
Jap Birdimal, vase, landscape, ftd, 9" 350.00
Jewell, vase, bulbous, 10½"...225.00
Jewell, vase, flared cylinder, 9" 185.00
Juneau, vase, bud; 6" 35.00
Juneau, vase, 8"...80.00
Kenova, vase, floral, bulbous, 5½" 200.00
Kenova, vase, 6½" 225.00
Klyro, basket, floral, no mk, 7"..65.00
Klyro, candle holder, floral, 9½"..45.00
Klyro, planter, floral, sq form, 4" 55.00
Klyro, vase, bud; floral, 8½"..40.00
Klyro, wall pocket, floral, paper label, 7½" 65.00
Knifewood, bowl, floral, 3"...65.00
Knifewood, humidor, dog, no mk, 7" 400.00
Knifewood, vase, dog, flared cylinder, no mk, 3" 115.00
Knifewood, vase, floral, flared cylinder, 7".............................115.00
La Sa, vase, classic form, 6½" 225.00
La Sa, vase, landscape, flared, no mk, 7"...............................375.00
La Sa, vase, palm trees, blk/wht, cylindrical, no mk, 13½" 875.00
La Sa, vase, pyramid form, 6" 225.00
La Sa, vase/lamp base, palms scenic, sgn, 13½".......................475.00
Lamar, lamp, scenic, 15"..400.00
Lamar, vase, scenic, flared cylinder, paper label, 7½" 165.00
Lamar, vase, water scenic, 14½"..500.00
Lavonia, vase, floral, 10" 135.00
Lebanon, vase, bulbous, rnd hdls, no mk, 9"...........................500.00
Lebanon, vase, shouldered form, no mk, 6" 375.00

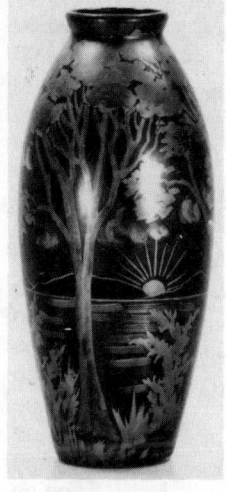

LaSa vase with exceptional decoration, gold and metallic green on dark red, signed, 13", $1,150.00.

Lido, cornucopia, 5"...18.00
Lido, vase, 7"...25.00
Lonhuda, vase, cattle scene, pillow form, #275, 11½" 3,500.00
Lonhuda, vase, floral, integral hdls, #820, 4½".......................185.00
Lorbeek, bowl, console; 3x14", +5" frog................................175.00
Lorbeek, wall pocket, 8½" 85.00
Lorber, vase, mythological creatures, 13" 1,050.00
Loru, vase, 8"..22.50
Louella, bowl, floral, 3" 32.00
Louella, hair receiver, 3"...50.00
Louella, vase, floral, slim form, 4½" 42.50
Louwelsa, Blue; vase, floral, bulbous, 1-hdl, 3"......................350.00
Louwelsa, Blue; vase, floral, cylindrical, 10½" 800.00
Louwelsa, bowl, floral, 2½" 70.00
Louwelsa, candle holder, floral, sgn HL, 9"...........................100.00
Louwelsa, clock, floral, 10½x12½".......................................650.00
Louwelsa, ewer, floral, ornate hdl, 22½"..............................1,300.00
Louwelsa, humidor, floral, sgn CA, 5½" 360.00
Louwelsa, jug, dbl; floral, 6"...150.00
Louwelsa, mug, portrait, sgn Ferrell, #432, 6½" 800.00
Louwelsa, tankard, floral, sgn KK, 12" 275.00
Louwelsa, tankard, monk, sgn LJ Burgess, 12½".....................1,650.00
Louwelsa, vase, dog w/game bird, sgn L Blake, 7" 825.00
Louwelsa, vase, floral, angle hdls, slim form, 11" 245.00
Louwelsa, vase, floral, jug form, 6½" 145.00
Louwelsa, vase, floral, sgn AC, squat pitcher form, 3"..............125.00
Louwelsa, vase, floral, tapered cylinder, 5"...........................100.00
Louwelsa, vase, floral, 3-ftd, integral hdls, 5".......................150.00
Louwelsa, vase, Indian in headdress, sgn Burgess, 11½"..........2,250.00
Louwelsa, vase, Indian maiden's portrait, hdls, 10" 1,550.00
Louwelsa, vase, man's portrait, sgn, pillow form, 7½" 1,300.00
Louwelsa, vase, pansies w/silver o/l, 6½" 1,750.00
Louwelsa, vase, vintage branches, sgn Lybarger, 17" 800.00
Lustre, basket, 6½"...55.00
Lustre, candlestick, 8"...45.00
Lustre, vase, flared rim, 9½" 42.50
Lustre, vase, orange on Glendale shape, experimental, 8½".........275.00
Lustre, wall pocket, 7½"...60.00
Luxor, vase, bud; no mk, 7½"..25.00
Malverne, bowl, console; 2½x11", +2½" frog 75.00
Malverne, circle vase, floral, 8"...50.00
Malverne, jardiniere & pedestal, floral, 34"...........................550.00
Malverne, vase, bud; floral, 8½"..35.00
Malverne, wall pocket, floral, no mk, 11" 55.00
Mammy, creamer, 3½"...225.00
Mammy, sugar bowl, w/lid, 3½" 250.00

Mammy, syrup pitcher, 6"	350.00
Mammy, teapot, 8"	475.00
Manhattan, pitcher, 10"	95.00
Manhattan, vase, leaves, hdls, 8"	65.00
Marbleized, bowl, 1½x5½"	40.00
Marbleized, comport, high std, 8"	85.00
Marbleized, jardiniere, 10"	265.00
Marbleized, vase, hexagonal, 10½"	160.00
Marengo, vase, scenic, hexagonal, no mk, 8"	235.00
Marvo, bowl, console; no mk, 2½x10"	65.00
Marvo, vase, cylindrical, 8½"	55.00
Marvo, vase, dbl bud; no mk, 5"	45.00
Matt Floretta, tankard, fruited branch, sgn CD, no mk, 13½"	400.00
Matt Green, vase, 2 dimensional women at rim, 13x4½"	1,600.00
Melrose, basket, grape cluster, twig hdl, 10"	160.00
Melrose, bowl, console; floral, ruffled rim, hdls, 5x8½"	85.00
Melrose, vase, floral, hdls, scalloped rim, no mk, 5"	65.00
Minerva, planter, mythological figures, 12x16"	450.00
Minerva, vase, woodland scene, classical form, 13½"	325.00
Mirror Black, strawberry jar, 6½"	75.00
Mirror Black, vase, bud; no mk, 5½"	35.00
Mirror Black, vase, long hdls on waisted form, 12"	135.00
Monochrome, comport, 8"	50.00
Monochrome, vase, bud; 7"	47.50
Monochrome, vase, triple bud; 7"	35.00
Montego, vase, sm hdls, 5"	35.00
Muskota, bowl, turtle form, 4½x9½"	275.00
Muskota, dogs, no mk, 7½"	475.00
Muskota, elephant, 7½x12½"	800.00
Muskota, fence, 5"	165.00
Muskota, fishing boy, 6½"	175.00
Muskota, flower frog, geese, no mk, 6"	175.00
Muskota, incense burner, Foxy Grandpa, 4"	185.00
Muskota, kneeling nude, no mk, 3"	135.00
Neiska, bowl, ftd, 4"	27.50
Noval, bowl, fruit, 9½"	55.00
Noval, candle holder, fruit, 9½", pr	100.00
Noval, comport, fruit, no mk, 5½"	55.00
Novelty, ash tray, dog w/bone, 4½"	70.00
Novelty, ash tray, 3 pigs, no mk, 4"	65.00
Novelty, butterfly, 3½"	150.00
Novelty, dragonfly, 3¼"	150.00
Novelty, flower frog, fish, 1½x7"	26.00
Novelty, jar, face form, no mk, 6"	70.00
Novelty, kangaroo & pouch, no mk, 5½"	80.00
Novelty, name card w/blk bird, no mk, 2x3"	85.00
Novelty, red bird, 2½"	150.00
Novelty, wall vase, cup & saucer, 3"	55.00
Oak Leaf, basket, 7½"	55.00
Oak Leaf, planter, 6"	30.00
Panella, cornucopia, 5½"	17.50
Panella, wall pocket, 8"	72.50
Paragon, candle holder, 2", pr	35.00
Paragon, vase, floral, bulbous, 7½"	85.00
Parian, wall pocket, floral, no mk, 10"	135.00
Pastel, planter, #P-5, 4x8"	26.00
Patra, basket, floral, 5½"	85.00
Patra, nut dish, hdl, 3"	30.00
Patra, vase, floral, hdls, 4½"	35.00
Patricia, planter, duck form, 6½"	100.00
Patricia, vase, duck-head hdls, 4"	26.00
Pearl, candle holder, pearls & florals, 8½", pr	115.00
Pearl, wall vase, pearls & florals, 8"	150.00
Perfecto, ewer, floral, #580/2, no mk, 12"	450.00

Perfecto, ewer, floral, sgn HP, 17"	700.00
Perfecto, vase, floral, sgn MH, cylindrical, 14"	500.00
Perfecto, wall pocket, sgn HP, 7"	185.00
Pumilla, bowl, flower form, 3½"	22.50
Pumilla, candle holder, flower form, 3", pr	65.00
Pumilla, plate, console; no mk, 3x12"	45.00
Pumilla, wall pocket, no mk, 7"	55.00
Ragenda, urn, drape swag, 6½"	35.00
Raydance, vase, 7"	30.00
Raydance, vase, 9"	55.00
Regal, birdbath, no mk, 21½"	275.00
Roba, ewer, 6"	40.00
Roba, vase, 12½"	120.00
Rochelle, vase, floral, sgn HP, bulbous, 7"	225.00
Rochelle, vase, floral, sgn HP, 13"	300.00
Roma, bowl, floral, hdls, ftd, 3"	50.00
Roma, candlestick, triple, floral, no mk, 9"	135.00
Roma, comport, floral, 5½"	85.00
Roma, letter pocket, floral, no mk, 4½x7½"	135.00
Roma, vase, bud; grapes on vine, no mk, 6½"	45.00
Roma, vase, pine cones, no mk, 10"	90.00
Roma, wall pocket, floral, 7"	175.00
Rosemont, jardiniere, bird on branch, 7"	175.00
Rosemont, jardiniere, floral, 7"	150.00
Rosemont, jardiniere & pedestal, floral, 25½"	500.00
Rosemont II, jar, w/lid, 7"	70.00
Rudlor, bowl, console; floral, 4½x17½"	45.00
Rudlor, vase, floral, 6"	22.50
Sabrinian, basket, shell form, 7"	225.00
Sabrinian, bowl, console; 3½x11½", +4½" frog	185.00
Sabrinian, candle holder, dolphin std, 6½"	115.00
Sabrinian, planter, shell form, 4½"	115.00
Sabrinian, wall pocket, 8½"	300.00
Scandia, bowl, no mk, 3" H	45.00
Scandia, vase, no mk, 9"	65.00
Senic, vase, 12½"	100.00
Sicardo, bowl, clover/dots, gr/copper irid, lobed, 4x6"	600.00
Sicardo, box, clover blossoms on magenta, lobed, 6x9"	2,200.00
Sicardo, lamp base, floral, 15½"	1,750.00
Sicardo, vase, columbines, hdls at neck, 6"	1,000.00
Sicardo, vase, floral, bowl form, 5"	350.00
Sicardo, vase, floral, gr irid, trilobed, 4"	225.00
Sicardo, vase, floral, gr/purple, lobed/hdld dbl gourd, 8"	1,100.00
Sicardo, vase, floral, gr/purple, 4-lobe top, 11"	2,000.00
Sicardo, vase, floral, long neck, 3½"	325.00
Sicardo, vase, floral, mc irid, swollen cylinder, #66, 6½"	500.00
Sicardo, vase, floral, pillow form, 2½"	275.00
Sicardo, vase, floral/dots, low-waisted body, 9"	1,200.00
Sicardo, vase, leaves/berries, long cylinder neck, 14x5"	800.00
Silhouette, vase, boy fishing, sgn Timberlake, no mk, 15"	1,500.00
Silvertone, basket, grape cluster, twig hdl, 13"	250.00
Silvertone, candle holder, floral, 3", pr	90.00
Silvertone, vase, floral, ruffled rim, hdls, 8½"	225.00
Softone, ewer, 9½"	32.50
Softone, vase, dbl bud; 9"	25.00
Stellar, vase, bulbous, 5½"	100.00
Suevo, humidor, geometrics, 6"	220.00
Suevo, vase, geometrics, flared neck, no mk, 8"	115.00
Sydonia, cornucopia, no mk, 8½"	55.00
Sydonia, planter, bl/gr, 4"	30.00
Sydonia, vase, fan form, 6½"	55.00
Tivoli, vase, flared cylinder, ftd, no mk, 8½"	75.00
Turada, humidor, appl filigree, 5½"	300.00
Turada, lamp, appl filigree, 10"	475.00

Turada, mug, appl filigree, 6" **245.00**
Turkis, vase, angle hdls, 5½" **85.00**
Turkis, vase, sgn DE, 8½" **135.00**
Turkis, vase, upturned hdls, 4" **30.00**
Tutone, vase, floral, no mk, 6" **37.50**
Tutone, vase, floral, 11" **105.00**
Tutone, wall pocket, no mk, 10½" **100.00**
Underglaze Blue Ware, bowl, w/frog **22.50**
Utility Ware, pitcher, 5½" **30.00**
Utility Ware, teapot, pineapple form, 6½" **165.00**
Utility Ware, tumbler, 4" **10.00**
Velva, bowl, floral, half hdls, 12½" **60.00**
Velva, vase, floral, half hdls, 6" **35.00**
Velvetone, pitcher, 10" **125.00**
Voile, jardiniere, fruit trees, no mk, 6" **70.00**
Voile, vase, fruit tree, fan form, 8" **65.00**
Voile, vase, fruit trees, flared cylinder, 9" **90.00**
Warwick, circle vase, 7" **58.00**
Warwick, jardiniere, 7" **115.00**
Warwick, planter, 3½" **55.00**
Warwick, vase, 6½" **60.00**
White & Decorated, bowl, floral, no mk, 4" **115.00**
White & Decorated, vase, birds on branch, 15" **1,050.00**
White & Decorated, vase, floral, hexagonal, 9½" **185.00**
Wild Rose, candle holder, triple; pr **85.00**
Wild Rose, vase, 6½" **22.50**

Woodcraft, whisk broom holder, original broom, $400.00.

Woodcraft, bowl, console; w/frog, ink mk, 11" **175.00**
Woodcraft, hanging basket, floral, no mk, 6" **115.00**
Woodcraft, lamp, owl perched on limb, 16" **550.00**
Woodcraft, planter, foxes, 5½" **200.00**
Woodcraft, vase, floral, fan form, no mk, 8" **60.00**
Woodcraft, wall vase, birds at nest, 14½x12½" **475.00**
Woodrose, jardiniere, 3½" **55.00**
Woodrose, wall pocket, floral, no mk, 6" **57.50**
Woodrose, wall vase, 6½" **85.00**
Xenia, vase, floral, hdls, 9½" **250.00**
Zona, baby plate, duck, 7" **85.00**
Zona, bowl, apples, no mk, 5½" **12.50**
Zona, jardiniere, floral band, no mk, 7" **115.00**
Zona, pitcher, bird, 8" **125.00**
Zona, pitcher, milk; fruit on branch, twig hdl, 3½" **55.00**
Zona, pitcher, no mk, 3" **42.50**
Zona, teapot, floral, 6", +3" sugar bowl & 4" creamer **185.00**
Zona, umbrella stand, ladies w/flowers, glossy, no mk, 20½"........**475.00**

Western Americana

The collecting of Western Americana encompasses a broad spectrum of memorabilia and collectibles. Examples of various areas within
the main stream would include the following fields: weapons, bottles,
photographs, mining/railroad artifacts, cowboy paraphernalia, farm and
ranch implements, maps, barbed wire, tokens, Indian relics,
saloon/gambling items, and branding irons. Some of these areas have
their own separate listings in this book. Western Americana is not only
a collecting field but is also a collecting *era* with specific boundries.
Depending upon which field the collector decides to specialize in,
prices can start at a few dollars and run into the thousands.

Our advisor for this category is Bill Mackin, author of *Cowboy and
Gunfighter Collectibles* (order from the author); he is listed in the Directory under Colorado.

Bit, silver-inlaid California spade, M Morales **800.00**
Branding iron, 3½" letters, 37½" L, EX..**25.00**
Bridle, hitched horsehair, 7-color, Washington prison............ **3,300.00**
Chaps, batwing, work style, outside pockets, ca 1910 ....**250.00**
Conestoga wagon box, worn bl pnt/chip cvg, iron mts, 14" L . **1,025.00**
Conestoga wagon jack, iron/wood, simple tooling/1832, 20" **100.00**
Gauntlets, lady's, fringed leather, Frank Russell Co, EX...............**65.00**
Gun belt, combination money/cartridge, FA Meanea **1,500.00**
Hat, 'Tom Mix' style, Stetson, 1920s...**625.00**
Quirt, braided rawhide, Turk's head knots, 34" **90.00**
Spurs, Hercules bronze/nickel, Indian head medallions, 6½" L....**175.00**

Westmoreland

Originally titled the Specialty Glass Company, Westmoreland
began operations in East Liverpool, Ohio, producing utility items as
well as tableware in milk glass and crystal. When the company moved
to Grapeville, PA, in 1890, lamps, vases, covered animal dishes, and
decorative plates were introduced. Prior to 1920 Westmoreland was a
major manufacturer of carnival glass and soon thereafter added a line of
lovely reproduction art glass items. High-quality milk glass became
their speciality, accounting for about 90% of their production. Black
glass was introduced in the 1940s, and later in the decade ruby-stained
pieces and items decorated in the Mary Gregory style became fashionable. By the 1960s colored glassware was being produced, examples of
which are very popular with collectors today. Early pieces were marked
with a paper label; by the 1960s the ware was embossed with a superimposed 'WG.' The last mark was a circle containing 'Westmoreland'
around the perimeter and a large 'W' in the center. The company
closed in 1985. See also Animal Dishes with Covers; Carnival Glass.

Appetizer, Panelled Grape, milk glass, 2-pc, 9" **42.00**
Ash tray, Beaded Grape, milk glass, 4"...**12.00**
Basket, Panelled Grape, milk glass, oval, 6½" **25.00**
Basket, Panelled Grape, milk glass w/gold trim, oval....................**35.00**
Basket, Princess Feather, 8" **35.00**
Basket, Rose & Trellis, milk glass, nut hdl....................................**30.00**
Bottle, scent; English Hobnail, w/stopper **35.00**
Bottle, toilet; English Hobnail, lime gr **24.00**
Bowl, Beaded Grape, milk glass, sq, high ft, 7" **35.00**
Bowl, Beaded Grape, milk glass, sq, w/lid, 4" **22.00**
Bowl, Beaded Grape, milk glass, sq ftd, 5" **28.00**
Bowl, berry; Panelled Grape, mint gr, 4½"...................................**15.00**
Bowl, Della Robbia, 1-hdl, 7" **40.00**
Bowl, English Hobnail, 4¼" **6.00**
Bowl, nappy, Della Robbia, w/colors, heart shape, loop hdl, 7" **65.00**
Bowl, Panelled Grape, milk glass, lipped, ftd, oval, 9"..................**55.00**
Bowl, Panelled Grape, milk glass, oval, 6½" **22.50**
Bowl, Panelled Grape, milk glass, scalloped rim, 8" **45.00**
Bowl, Panelled Grape, milk glass, scalloped rim, 9¾"...................**45.00**

Bowl, Princess Feather, amber, oval, 11" 35.00
Box, puff; American Hobnail, milk glass, w/lid 25.00
Box, puff; Panelled Grape, milk glass 28.00
Butter dish, Old Quilt, ruby 40.00
Butter dish, Panelled Grape, milk glass, ¼-lb 30.00
Cake salver, Panelled Grape, milk glass, rnd skirt 65.00
Cake stand, Sawtooth 50.00
Canape, Beaded Grape, milk glass, center hdl, 7¼" 35.00
Candelabra, English Hobnail, milk glass, 2-lite, pr 75.00
Candlestick, American Hobnail, milk glass, pr 25.00
Candlestick, Beaded Grape, milk glass, pr, 4" 22.00
Candlestick, Della Robbia, 3½", pr 25.00
Candlestick, Dolphin, milk glass, 4" 25.00
Candlestick, English Hobnail, 8½" 22.00
Candlestick, Lace Edge, #3, pr 20.00
Candlestick, Old Quilt, milk glass, pr 24.00
Candlestick, Panelled Grape, milk glass, 4", pr 24.00
Candy dish, Beaded Grape, milk glass, sq, ftd, w/lid, 5" ...22.00
Candy dish, Cone, purple slag, w/lid 42.00
Candy dish, English Hobnail, milk glass, w/lid, ½-lb 25.00
Candy dish, Old Quilt, milk glass, low ft, w/lid, 5" 18.00
Candy dish, Old Quilt, milk glass, w/lid 25.00
Candy dish, Panelled Grape, milk glass, oval basket form ...22.00
Candy dish, Waterford/Wakefield, ruby stained, w/lid, 7" ...35.00
Candy dish, Waterford/Wakefield, w/lid, 7" 22.00
Candy dish, Waterford/Wakefield, 9½" 45.00
Celery vase, Old Quilt, milk glass 24.00
Champagne, English Hobnail 7.00
Cheese dish, American Hobnail, milk glass 35.00
Cheese dish, Old Quilt, milk glass, rnd 60.00
Cheese dish, Panelled Grape, milk glass 48.00
Chocolate box, Della Robbia, plain, rnd, flat, 8" 45.00
Chocolate box, Della Robbia, w/colors, rnd, flat, 8" 70.00
Chocolate box, Panelled Grape, milk glass, w/lid 45.00
Cocktail, English Hobnail, sq base 7.00
Cocktail, fruit; Old Quilt, milk glass, 3½" 25.00
Cocktail, rooster, milk glass 10.00
Compote, Beaded Grape, milk glass, sq, ftd, 9" 40.00
Compote, English Hobnail, milk glass, hdls, 8" 42.00
Compote, English Hobnail, sq base, 6" 15.00
Compote, Panelled Grape, milk glass, crimped rim, ftd, 7½" ...42.00
Compote, Panelled Grape, milk glass, ftd, rare, 9" 60.00
Compote, Panelled Grape, milk glass, w/lid, 7" 35.00
Compote, Sawtooth, amber, high std, w/lid, 12" 85.00
Compote, Sawtooth, amber, high std, 12" 35.00
Compote, Shell, blk amethyst, #1049, 6" 55.00
Compote, Thousand Eye 22.50
Cordial, Thousand Eye 15.00
Cordial, Waterford/Wakefield 9.00
Cordial, Waterford/Wakefield, ruby stained 20.00
Creamer, Beaded Grape, milk glass 10.00
Creamer, Della Robbia, w/colors 13.00
Creamer, English Hobnail, flat 7.50
Creamer, Old Quilt, milk glass, lg 12.00
Creamer, Panelled Grape, milk glass, lg 14.00
Creamer & sugar bowl, American Hobnail, milk glass 20.00
Creamer & sugar bowl, Beaded Grape, milk glass, sq 22.00
Creamer & sugar bowl, Della Robbia, w/colors 35.00
Creamer & sugar bowl, Della Robbia, milk glass 22.00
Creamer & sugar bowl, English Hobnail, ftd 20.00
Creamer & sugar bowl, Old Quilt, milk glass, sm 25.00
Creamer & sugar bowl, Panelled Grape, milk glass, ftd, w/lid ...30.00
Creamer & sugar bowl, Panelled Grape, milk glass, w/lid, sm ...23.50
Cruet, American Hobnail, milk glass 22.00

Cruet, English Hobnail, w/stopper, lg 35.00
Cruet, English Hobnail, w/stopper, sm 18.00
Cruet, Old Quilt, milk glass, w/stopper 30.00
Cruet, Panelled Grape, milk glass 24.00
Cup & saucer, Beaded Edge, HP fruit on milk glass 18.00
Cup & saucer, Beaded Edge, milk glass 10.00
Cup & saucer, Beaded Grape, milk glass 20.00
Cup & saucer, Panelled Grape, milk glass 16.00
Decanter, Panelled Grape, milk glass, w/stopper 125.00
Epergne, Panelled Grape, mint gr, 3-pc, 14" 200.00
Figurine, owl, amber mist, rhinestone eyes 20.00
Figurine, pistol, blk 48.00
Figurine, rooster, milk glass 38.00
Goblet, Della Robbia, milk glass, #1058, water sz 22.00
Goblet, Della Robbia, milk glass w/gold trim, water sz ...30.00
Goblet, Della Robbia, w/colors, 6" 32.00
Goblet, English Hobnail, milk glass, rnd base, water sz ...14.00
Goblet, Old Quilt, milk glass, water sz 15.00
Goblet, Panelled Grape, milk glass, 8-oz 16.00
Goblet, Princess Feather, amber, 8-oz 9.00
Goblet, Princess Feather, water sz 10.00
Goblet, Thousand Eye, 6½" 12.00
Gravy boat, Panelled Grape, milk glass, w/liner 60.00
Honey jar, Beaded Grape, milk glass, ftd, w/lid, 5" 22.00
Ice tub, English Hobnail 65.00
Jardiniere, Panelled Grape, milk glass, ftd, 5" 25.00
Jug, Panelled Grape, milk glass, 1-qt 35.00
Marmalade, English Hobnail, metal lid, spoon 21.00
Mayonnaise, English Hobnail, milk glass, 6" 10.00
Mayonnaise, Panelled Grape, milk glass, 3-pc set 45.00
Mustard, English Hobnail, milk glass, w/base, +spoon ...25.00
Nappy, Old Quilt, milk glass, flat, 4" 22.50
Parfait, Panelled Grape, milk glass, rare 30.00
Pickle dish, Old Quilt, milk glass, 10" 30.00
Pitcher, American Hobnail, milk glass, ½-gal. 50.00
Pitcher, juice/batter; Old Quilt, milk glass 40.00
Pitcher, Old Quilt, milk glass, 24-oz 35.00
Pitcher, Old Quilt, milk glass, 40-oz 30.00
Pitcher, Panelled Grape, milk glass, 1-pt 38.00
Plate, Beaded Edge, milk glass, 6¼" 12.00
Plate, Beaded Edge, milk glass, 7½" 18.00
Plate, Beaded Edge, milk glass, 8¼" 22.00
Plate, Beaded Grape, milk glass, luncheon sz 22.00
Plate, blackberries, milk glass, beaded rim, 7½" 12.00
Plate, Della Robbia, 10½" 15.00
Plate, English Hobnail, 8½" 6.00
Plate, Lace Edge, blk, #30, 8½" 18.50
Plate, open heart, milk glass, #32 ....15.00
Plate, Panelled Grape, milk glass, bird decal, 8½" 22.00
Plate, Panelled Grape, mint gr, luncheon sz, 8½" 35.00
Plate, Panelled Grape, mint gr, 10½" 22.00
Plate, Panelled Grape, 10½" 38.00
Plate, 3 Kittens, milk glass 32.00
Punch cup, Panelled Grape, milk glass 10.00
Punch cup, Three Fruits, milk glass 10.00
Punch set, English Hobnail, bowl/tray/12 cups 400.00
Punch set, Pineapple & Grape, milk glass, red hooks, 15-pc ...250.00
Relish, Old Quilt, milk glass, 3-part 45.00
Rose bowl, American Hobnail, milk glass, cupped, ftd ...12.00
Rose bowl, Panelled Grape, milk glass, flared, 4" 18.00
Shakers, Beaded Grape, milk glass, pr 18.00
Shakers, Della Robbia, w/colors, pr 45.00
Shakers, Old Quilt, milk glass, pr 18.00
Shakers, Panelled Grape, milk glass, ftd, pr 20.00

Sherbet, Della Robbia, w/colors **28.00**
Sherbet, English Hobnail...**7.00**
Sherbet, Thousand Eye, low **9.00**
Spoon, Old Quilt, milk glass, 6½" **22.00**
Sugar bowl, Della Robbia, w/colors **15.00**
Sugar bowl, Panelled Grape, milk glass, lacy, ftd, w/lid **28.00**
Sugar bowl, Panelled Grape, milk glass, w/lid, sm **15.00**
Syrup, Old Quilt, milk glass...**18.00**
Tidbit tray, Panelled Grape, milk glass, 10½" **45.00**
Toothpick holder, swan, milk glass **15.00**
Tray, dresser; Panelled Grape, milk glass w/22k gold.....................**115.00**
Tumbler, Beaded Edge, HP fruit on milk glass, ftd, 8-oz.................**15.00**
Tumbler, Della Robbia, w/colors, 5¾" **35.00**
Tumbler, English Hobnail, flat, 5" **9.00**
Tumbler, English Hobnail, ftd, 4¾" **8.00**
Tumbler, ginger ale; English Hobnail, sq base, 5-oz.........................**9.00**
Tumbler, iced tea; American Hobnail, milk glass, ftd **10.00**
Tumbler, iced tea; Della Robbia, milk glass **17.00**
Tumbler, iced tea; Old Quilt, milk glass, 5¼" **18.00**
Tumbler, Old Quilt, milk glass, 4½" **15.00**
Tumbler, Panelled Grape, milk glass, 8-oz **19.00**
Urn, Waterford/Wakefield, ruby stained, w/lid, 13" **45.00**
Urn, Waterford/Wakefield, ruby stained w/HP roses, w/lid, 13" .**125.00**
Vase, Beaded Grape, milk glass, bell shape, ftd, 9" **26.00**
Vase, bud; Roses & Bows, 9" **22.00**
Vase, Old Quilt, milk glass, ftd fan form **18.00**
Vase, Panelled Grape, milk glass, belled, ftd, 9" **25.00**
Vase, Panelled Grape, milk glass, 6"..**15.00**

Wheatley, T. J.

In 1880 after a brief association with the Coultry Works, Thomas J. Wheatley opened his own studio in Cincinnati, Ohio, claiming to have been the first to discover the secret of under-glaze slip decoration on an unbaked clay vessel. He applied for and was granted a patent for his process. Demand for his ware increased to the point that several artists were hired to decorate the ware. The company incorporated in 1880 as the Cincinnati Art Pottery, but until 1882 it continued to operate under Wheatley's name. Ware from this period is marked 'T.J. Wheatley' or 'T.J.W. and Co.,' and it may be dated.

Vase, impasto flowers, 9", $650.00.

Lamp base, floral spray, Limoges style, dtd 1880, 9½", NM **325.00**
Vase, appl floral vine, flattened oval on raised ft, 8½" **325.00**
Vase, gr, leaves & buds, bulb w/4 open angled ft, no mk, 11" **450.00**
Vase, gr matt, emb leaves, bulbous top/broad body, 12", EX.... **2,100.00**
Vase, gr matt, 4 bar hdls around recessed coiled neck, 7" **700.00**

Vase, gray & gr, florals, Limoges style, 7" **350.00**
Vase, yel, daisies, 1880, 8"...**385.00**

Whieldon

Thomas Whieldon was regarded as the finest of the Staffordshire potters of the mid-1700s. He produced marbled and black Egyptian wares as well as tortoise shell, a mottled-glazed earthenware accented with touches of color. In 1754 he became a partner of Josiah Wedgwood. Other potters produced similar wares, and today the term Whieldon is used generically.

Creamer, brn/gr tortoise, scalloped lip, rib hdl, 3½", EX **450.00**
Fruit basket, rtcl sides, scalloped rim, rstr chips, 8" L **1,430.00**
Plate, blk tortoise w/gr/bl/brn, emb scalloped rim, 9½", EX **375.00**
Plate, blk tortoise w/gr/bl/brn/yel, emb scalloped rim, 9" **425.00**
Plate, blk/brn tortoise w/gr/bl/brn/yel, emb rim, 9", NM **575.00**
Plate, brn tortoise, emb rim, octagonal, 9"....................................**450.00**
Plate, brn tortoise w/gr & amber, emb/scalloped rim, 9½", NM...**450.00**
Plate, brn/gr/bl tortoise, hairline, 7"..**325.00**
Plate, mc tortoise, emb scalloped rim, 10", NM **600.00**
Plate, 3-color tortoise, lt center+11 sqs, emb rim, 9", NM....... **1,050.00**
Soup plate, blk tortoise w/gr/bl/brn/yel, emb rim, 9", NM **500.00**
Sugar bowl, blk mottled, molded finial, 3½", EX...........................**350.00**
Teapot, brn tortoise, emb vintage, prof rpr/chip, 4" **1,250.00**
Teapot, cauliflower form, wht/gr, prof rpr, sm chips, 4" **475.00**
Teapot, emb floral, twig hdl/spout, bird finial, rstr, 5" **2,530.00**
Tray, blk tortoise w/gr/yel, floral-emb scalloped rim, 8x9"....... **1,375.00**

Wicker

Wicker is the basket-like material used in many types of furniture and accessories. It may be made from bamboo cane, rattan, reed, or artificial fibers. It is airy, lightweight, and very popular in hot regions. Imported from the Orient in the 18th century, it was first manufactured in the United States in about 1850. The elaborate, closely-woven Victorian designs belong to the mid-to-late 1800s, and the simple styles with coarse reedings usually indicate a post-1900 production. Art Deco styles followed in the twenties and thirties. The most important consideration in buying wicker is condition — it can be restored, but only by a professional. Age is an important factor, but be aware that 'Victorian-style' furniture is being manufactured today.

Key:
HB — Heywood Brothers   H-W — Heywood-Wakefield
WR — Wakefield Rattan Co.

Armchair, openwork & serpentine bk & arms, skirted, 1900s **385.00**
Armchair, scrolls & beadwork, serpentine bk & arms, 1890s **335.00**
Baby carriage, simple scrollwork, metal wheels, parasol **450.00**
Basket, fine weave, braided swing hdls, brass clasp, 14x8x14" ...**110.00**
Basket, fine-woven sea grasses, reed braidwork, 1910s, lg **165.00**
Basket, picnic; suitcase type, w/orig utensils, EX **45.00**
Chair, conversation; close-woven bks w/curliques, cane seats ..**1,600.00**
Chair, corner; fancy scrollwork, cane seat, HB, 1890s, EX **725.00**
Chair, curliques & wooden beadwork, Turkish style, 1890s.........**450.00**
Chair, piano; bk/legs ornately woven, H-W #3901, 44"...............**750.00**
Chair, side; scrollwork, cabriole legs, Whitney, 1890s, EX...........**335.00**
Crib, scrolled canopy brace & fr, wooden beadwork, 1890s.........**800.00**
Desk, Bar Harbor style, oak top, center drw, wht pnt, 1910s **600.00**
Desk, wooden shelved superstructure, 1-drw, H-W, 43x75" **800.00**
Divan, fine-woven reed, serpentine arm, cane seat, 1890s....... **1,200.00**

Etagere, 3-shelf, elaborate crest, cabriole legs, HB, 63" **1,200.00**
Highchair, fine-woven bk, wood tray & footrest, 1900s **365.00**
Lamp, floor; fine-woven, fringed shade, 1920s, EX **365.00**
Lamp, floor; sq pyramid shade on sq column, gr stain, 73" **1,100.00**
Lamp, table; machine-woven fiber, wood fr, orig shade, H-W.....**265.00**
Lounge, fine-woven bk & sides, cane seat, HB, 1910s, EX...........**995.00**
Pedestal, sq top, tapered column, H-W, minor breaks, 35" **200.00**
Plant stand, machine-woven fiber w/shelf, trn legs, 1920s **150.00**
Rocker, bbl bk, crest extends to form arms, curlicues **200.00**
Rocker, dmn-patterned panel in serpentine bk, skirted, 1900s **365.00**
Rocker, sewing; curliques & beadwork, natural, 1890s, sm **355.00**
Settee, curlicues low on fine-woven bk & arms, 1900s, NM ... **1,100.00**
Sofa & armchair, trn wood arms/legs, uphl seats, 63", 32" **700.00**
Table, dining; fine-woven skirting under wood top, ped ft, 42"..**500.00**
Table, fine-woven, serpentine edge, skirted, oval, 1900s **385.00**

Willets

The Willets Manufacturing Company of Trenton, New Jersey, produced a type of belleek porcelain during the late 1880s and 1890s. Examples were often marked with a coiled snake that formed a 'W' with 'Willets' below and 'Belleek' above. Not all Willet's is factory decorated. Items painted by amateurs outside the factory are worth considerably less. In the listings below, all items are belleek unless noted otherwise. For more information we recommend *American Belleek* with full-color photos and current market values by Mary Frank Gaston. You will find her address in the Directory under Texas.

Bowl, roses, ruffled rim, shallow, mk, 9½" **295.00**
Centerpiece, 5 pcs joined by shell ft, gold trim, 12½" L **95.00**
Chalice, monk smokes cigar on brn, sgn AHP, mk, 11½" **660.00**
Creamer & sugar bowl, gold Nouveau decor, ped ft, #105..............**85.00**
Creamer & sugar bowl, silver o/l, w/lid **110.00**
Cup & saucer, bouillon; Cactus, yel w/gold cactus hdls **365.00**
Cup & saucer, demi; bl geometrics w/mauve/rust/gold, mk **135.00**
Cup & saucer, demi; purple pansies w/gold, heart shape, mk **325.00**
Egg cup, petal design, gold trim, mk, 2¾" **185.00**
Loving cup, floral, gr on purple, #488, 8"......................................**225.00**
Mug, scenic on dk gr, 7" **95.00**
Pin tray, floral w/gold, flat, crimped rim, mk, 4⅛x4½" **98.00**
Pitcher, tankard; berries, gold dragon hdl, mask spout, 11½".......**250.00**
Plate, floral center, raised gold on rim, mk, 10½" **275.00**
Tea set, rose swags, ft pnt as marble, 5-pc **225.00**
Teapot, bamboo w/mc flowers on gold, 4", +cr/sug **495.00**
Vase, butterflies on gold lustre, ca 1900, 9" **155.00**
Vase, forest scene, bulbous, 6½"...**425.00**
Vase, roses, gold hdls, urn form, snake mk, 14" **770.00**
Vase, roses on dk gr, sgn M Montrose, bulbous, mk, 10" **275.00**
Vase, swans on blk & gray, Deco style, sgn, mk, 16" **450.00**

Willow Ware

Willow Ware, inspired no doubt by the numerous patterns of the blue and white Nanking imports, has been popular since the late 18th century and has been made in as many variations as there were manufacturers. English transfer wares by such notable firms as Allerton and Ridgway are the most sought-after and the most expensive. Japanese potters have been producing Willow-patterned dinnerware since the late 1800s, and American manufacturers have followed suit. Although blue is the color most commonly used, mauve, black, and even multicolor Willow Ware may be found. Complementary glassware, tinware, and linens have also been made. In addition to 'Allerton' and 'Ridgway,' both companies

used the possessive forms of their names in marking their wares (i.e. Allerton's, Ridgway's). For further study we recommend the book *Blue Willow*, with full-color photos and current prices, by Mary Frank Gaston. You will find her address in the Directory under Texas. In the following listings, if no manufacturer is noted, the ware is unmarked.

Covered vegetable bowl, Allerton, 10" long, $235.00.

Bowl, cereal; Allerton, pk, 6½" 12.00
Bowl, cereal; Carr, 6¾" 6.50
Bowl, cereal; Homer Laughlin, 6".. 8.00
Bowl, cereal; Royal, pk, 6⅛" 4.50
Bowl, cereal; Royal, red 7.00
Bowl, cereal; Shenango, 7" 6.50
Bowl, cereal; unmk.. 4.00
Bowl, cereal/soup; Wood 10.00
Bowl, cream soup; Japan 14.00
Bowl, fruit; Allerton, 5½" 6.50
Bowl, fruit; England, 5"... 6.00
Bowl, fruit; Japan, 5½" 5.00
Bowl, fruit; Royal, pk, 5½" 3.00
Bowl, fruit; Shenango, 5¼" 4.00
Bowl, red, Royal, 9¼" 15.00
Bowl, Royal, 10" 15.00
Bowl, Royal, 9¼" 10.00
Bowl, sauce; pk, Walker, 4" 4.00
Bowl, unmk, 8½"..10.00
Butter pat, Buffalo...20.00
Cake plate, Royal, tab hdls, 11¾" 12.50
Carafe, Japan 175.00
Carafe, unmk, w/warmer base..140.00
Casserole, Meakin, w/lid...40.00
Casserole, Royal, red, w/lid...35.00
Casserole, unmk Japan 20.00
Cigarette lighter, Occupied Japan, 4" 25.00
Clock, Seth Thomas, wall hanging, rare.......................................500.00
Coffeepot, demitasse; Japan..40.00
Container, tin, sq bottom, rnd top, w/lid 15.00
Creamer, Royal 6.00
Creamer & sugar bowl, Japan, oval 20.00
Creamer & sugar bowl, Japan, w/lid...30.00
Creamer & sugar bowl, Occupied Japan, w/lid................................40.00
Creamer & sugar bowl, Ridgway, w/lid, lg......................................75.00
Creamer & sugar bowl, Royal, red...12.00
Cup, bouillon; Buffalo, pk, 4¼" 25.00
Cup, Buffalo emb mk 20.00
Cup, demitasse; Buffalo, 1913 ....20.00
Cup & saucer, England, decal inside 9.00
Cup & saucer, Homer Laughlin...10.00

Cup & saucer, Japan 15.00
Cup & saucer, Johnson Bros...15.00
Cup & saucer, Meakin..15.00
Cup & saucer, Royal, angular hdl 5.00
Cup & saucer, Royal, red 6.00
Cup & saucer, USA, stacking 3.50
Fork & spoon, salad; unmk, pattern on hdls 40.00
Gravy boat, Ridgway..30.00
Gravy boat, unmk restaurant ware, 7¾" 15.00
Match safe, Walker...45.00
Mug, Japan, decal inside 25.00
Mug, milk glass, stackable 4.00
Mustard, Japan...50.00
Pepper pot, English..125.00
Pitcher, Japan, 30-oz 45.00
Plate, Allerton, pk, 10" 20.00
Plate, Allerton, pk, 8" 15.00
Plate, Allerton, 10" 18.00
Plate, Allerton, 9" 20.00
Plate, Booth's Real Old..., red, 5" 12.00
Plate, Booth's Real Old..., 6⅝" 15.00
Plate, Buffalo, 6" 12.00
Plate, chop; Royal, 11¼" 15.00
Plate, chop; Shenango 25.00
Plate, England, lt bl, 9" 12.00
Plate, grill; Bailey Walker, 10" 12.00
Plate, grill; Caribe, 9½" 10.00
Plate, grill; child's sz 45.00
Plate, grill; Moriyama, 10¼" 20.00
Plate, grill; Shenango, 9⅝" 15.00
Plate, Homer Laughlin, 6¼" 4.00
Plate, Homer Laughlin, 8¼" 6.50
Plate, Homer Laughlin, 9" 8.00
Plate, Jackson, pk, 7⅛" 6.00
Plate, Japan, pk, 10½" 10.00
Plate, Japan, 6" 5.50
Plate, Japan, 9½" 12.00
Plate, Johnson Bros, 6¼" 6.00
Plate, Maastricht, 6" 8.00
Plate, McNichol, 11¼" 12.00
Plate, Meakin, 9" 12.00
Plate, Ridgeway, 10½" 17.50
Plate, Ridgway, pk, 7¾" 10.00
Plate, Ridgway, 7" 13.00
Plate, Royal, hdls, 10½" 10.00
Plate, Royal, pk, 6" 6.00
Plate, Royal, pk, 7¼" 7.00
Plate, Royal, red, 10" 10.00
Plate, Royal, 10" 10.00
Plate, Royal, 6" 6.00
Plate, Royal, 7¼" 7.00
Plate, snack; Johnson Bros, 10" 15.00
Plate, Sterling, pk, 7⅛" 7.00
Plate, Wood, 10" 12.00
Plate, Wood, 6" 6.00
Plate, Wood, 9" 8.00
Platter, Allerton, 13" 75.00
Platter, Homer Laughlin, oval, 11½" 16.00
Platter, Johnson Bros, oval, 12" 60.00
Platter, unmk, 12" 65.00
Pudding mold, England, 4¼" 55.00
Shakers, Occupied Japan, pr 15.00
Shakers, Royal, red, pr 15.00
Soup, Allerton's, 6"..20.00

Soup, Allerton's, 7½"...24.00
Soup, Buffalo, flat, 1920s, 9"...15.00
Soup, England, flat...18.00
Soup, Japan, pk, 7½"... 8.00
Soup, Maddock, flat...15.00
Soup, Ridgway...22.00
Soup, Royal, flat..10.00
Soup, Wedgwood, flat...25.00
Spice set, 5-pc in wood holder, Japan 115.00
Sugar bowl, Japan, pk, w/lid, lg..15.00
Sugar bowl, Ridgway, w/lid, med 40.00
Sugar bowl, Royal, w/lid 6.00
Sugar shaker, Japan...90.00
Tumbler, ceramic, pk, Jackson, 2¼" 6.00
Tumbler, frosted glass, 12-oz 18.00
Tumbler, juice; ceramic, Japan 16.00
Tumbler, juice; glass, heavy bottom, 3¾"......................... 6.00
Tumbler, water; glass, heavy bottom, 4¾" 10.00
Tumbler, water; glass, Libbey, 4¼" 3.50

Winchester

The Winchester Repeating Arms Company lost their important government contract after WWI and of necessity turned to the manufacture of sporting goods, hardware items, tools, etc. to augment their gun production. Between 1920 and 1931, over 7,500 different items, each marked 'Winchester Trademark U.S.A.,' were offered for sale by thousands of Winchester Hardware stores throughout the country. After 1931 the firm became Winchester-Western. See also Knives. Our advisor for this category is James Anderson; he is listed in the Directory under Minnesota.

Bait casting rod, G 80.00
Booklet, How To Handle Rifle Safety, early......................35.00
Box, Winchester Repeater, 100 count 85.00
Box of ammunition, .56-52 cal, full, NM label 275.00
Bullet mold, 32 WCF, wood hdl, EX 55.00
Calendar, 1916, complete pad, VG..................................750.00
Camp stove 45.00
Chisel, #4993, lg 40.00
Flashlight, VG..18.00
Fly rod, split bamboo, #6080, EX 275.00
Golf club, driver, wood shaft, EX 175.00
Hammer, claw type, VG 85.00
Hockey puck, VG 110.00
Loading tool, 38/55 cal, w/bullet mold, Pat 1880, G 60.00
Pamphlet, guns & ammunition, 1934, 3½x6", 64-pg.......22.50
Pin, lapel 75.00
Plane, metal, #3025, EX 110.00
Plane, wooden, VG 150.00
Plug, 3-hook, rpt, G+ 350.00
Plug, 5-hook, EX+ 500.00
Poster, counter type, 1920s, 9x11", EX 110.00
Poster, paper, 1910s, EX 650.00
Poster, Winchester Western, squirrel, ca 1955, 30x40" 55.00
Reel, #2142 ....90.00
Roller skates, #3831 ....25.00
Saw, EX..125.00
Sharpening stone 45.00
Shipping box, for Jr Rifle Corps kits 30.00
Shot bag, 5-lb, No 6 & logo on front, M............................ 5.00
Sign, About Our Boys in Uniform..., cb, rare 150.00
Sign, Winchester Cartridges, etc, red felt, 14x11", VG.....140.00

Signal cannon, 10-gauge 295.00
Straight razor, MIB 65.00
Toaster, EX 185.00
Waffle iron, VG+ 175.00

Windmill Weights

Windmill weights were used to protect the windmill's plunger rod from damage during high winds by adding weight that slowed down the speed of the blades.

Bull, Fairbury (unmk), CI, wht pnt, 38-lb, 18¼x24½x1⅛" 750.00
Eclipse Moon, Fairbanks Morse, CI, no pnt, 22-lb, 10½" 185.00
Eclipse Moon, Fairbanks Morse, CI, 27-lb, 10x6½x3½" 225.00
Football Monitor Vaneless, cement/CI, 50-lb, 17½" L................165.00
Horse, long-tailed, Dempster, old blk pnt, 37-lb, 21½" 1,000.00
Rooster, Elgin, rainbow-tailed, worn pnt, 63-lb, 18x16x3¾" 950.00
Rooster, Elgin, worn red & wht pnt, 63-lb, 19½x18x1¾"........ 1,400.00
Rooster, Elgin #2, old worn pnt, 34-lb, 15½x16½x4⅜"................950.00
Rooster, Hummer, CI, old mc pnt, ca 1900, 9⅞x8⅞x1¾"..........425.00
Star, Flint & Walling, CI, no pnt, 31-lb, 7½x3½" 550.00
Star, Flint & Walling, pnt CI, 31-lb, 7½x3½" 765.00

Winfield

From 1929 until its closing in the early1960s, the Winfield Pottery operated in Pasadena, California, producing mainly dinnerware for domestic as well as import trade.

Dragon Flower, gravy boat 15.00
Dragon Flower, plate, 10" 7.50
Tiger Iris, bowl, vegetable; divided....................................15.00
Tiger Iris, bowl, vegetable; 9⅛" 10.00
Tiger Iris, butter dish 10.00
Tiger Iris, creamer 6.50
Tiger Iris, cup & saucer.. 4.00
Tiger Iris, gravy boat 10.00
Tiger Iris, plate, 10" 4.00
Tiger Iris, plate, 5½" 2.00
Tiger Iris, shakers, pr... 7.50

Wire Ware

Two thousand years B.C. wire was made by cutting sheet metal into strips which were shaped with mallet and file. By the late 13th century, craftsmen in Europe had developed a method of pulling these strips through progressively smaller holes until the desired gauge was obtained. During the Industrial Revolution of the late 1800s, machinery was developed that could produce wire cheaply and easily; and it became a popular commercial commodity. It was used to produce large items such as garden benches and fencing as well as innumerable small pieces for use in the kitchen or on the farm. Beware of reproductions. Our advisor for this category is Rosella Tinsley; she is listed in the Directory under Kansas.

Basket, fruit; twisted, scalloped rim, 1900s, 3½x11" 45.00
Compote, braided & woven, openwork, 1900s, 4x17"....................85.00
Cream whip, blk tinned wire, spiral base, 1-pc, ca 1890, 16" 28.00
Cruet set, twisted, 3 glass containers, complete...........................125.00
Egg whisk, tinned wire, dmn design, ca 1930s, 9" 8.00
Food/platter cover, screen type, oval w/ring hdl, 14x9"................75.00
Fryer basket, twisted hdl, table rest, ca 1900s, 8" dia 18.00
Lifter, plate; adjustable slide, ca 1890s, rare, 18" 65.00

Lifter, utility; mk Klever Klaw, ca 1920s, 14" 25.00
Napkin holder, twisted, easel bk, stands..65.00
Napkin rings, ornate Victorian design, set of 4............................210.00
Plant stand, 3-tier, 32" 75.00
Plant stand, 3-tier w/trellis top, wht pnt, 73"............................175.00
Settee, dmn woven, iron fr, 37" 215.00
Settee, twisted wire/scrolls, arms, 36" 350.00
Soap dish, twisted, ornate, hanging...65.00

Witch Balls

Witch balls were a Victorian fad touted to be meritorious toward ridding the house of evil spirits, thus warding off sickness and bad luck. Folklore would have it that by wiping the dust and soot from the ball, the spirits were exorcised. It is much more probable, however, considering the fact that such beautiful art glass was used in their making, that the ostensive Victorians perpetrated the myth rather tongue-in-cheek while enjoying them as lovely decorations for their homes.

Aquamarine, alternate opalescent ribs/loops, 1860s, 3" 115.00
Clear, wht loops, on wht opal stand, 14½" 535.00
Cobalt on cobalt stand w/clear base, S Jersey, 14½" 715.00
Cranberry w/opal hobnails, 5", pr 210.00
Dk amber, +matching stand w/folded rim, 12" 465.00
Tortoise shell, lt amber w/red splotches, 1860s, 4" 115.00

Wood Carvings

Wood sculptures represent an important section of American folk art. Wood carvings were made not only by skilled woodworkers such as cabinetmakers, carpenters, etc. but by amateur 'whittlers' as well. They take the form of circus-wagon figures, carousel animals, decoys, busts, figurines, and cigar store Indians. Oriental artists show themselves to have been as proficient with the medium of wood as they were with ivory or hardstone. See also Carousel Animals; Decoys; Tobacciana.

Allegoricals, 1 w/eagle, 1 w/globe, Continental, 11", pr..............450.00
Bird, long-necked/on ball atop plinth, mc rpt, 17".....................525.00
Bird, orig pnt, sq nail legs, wooden base, 1890s, 5" 70.00
Comical man w/guitar & dog, orig pnt, 1920s, 8x7½x4".............135.00
Dog, Schimmel-type, X-hatch coat, orig 4-color pnt, 5" L...........350.00
Eagle w/snake, orig mc pnt, primitive, age cracks, 7" 150.00
Man in suit & tie, burned details, unpnt pine, 7¼" 85.00
Nude on base, 1930s, 16x4¼x4" 275.00
Owl, primitive, rnd base cvd from separate pc, 3¾" 45.00
Parrot, EX detail, orig 3-color pnt, att Schimmel, rpr, 7" 300.00
Parrot on perch, orig mc pnt, sm tail chips, 3½"..........................225.00
Plaque, eagle/shield/banner, att JH Bellamy, 1900s, 28x10".... 2,800.00
Plaque, Indian in relief, sgn/dtd 1938, 6½x5½" 65.00
Rooster, orig mc pnt, att Schimmel, damage/glued, 5".................300.00
Rooster, pine w/5-color pnt, W Schimmel, PA, 1875, 11" 8,000.00
Snake, from twisted branch, inset eyes, 1920s, 45".......................55.00
Squirrel, silhouette form, 2-color pnt, early 20th C, 3½".............150.00

Woodenware

Woodenware (or treenware, as it is sometimes called) generally refers to those wooden items such as spoons, bowls, food molds, etc. that were used in the preparation of food. Common during the 18th and 19th centuries, these wares were designed from a strictly functional viewpoint and were used on a day-to-day basis. With the advent of the Industrial Revolution which brought it new materials and products, many of the old woodenwares were simply discarded. Today original hand-crafted American woodenwares are extremely difficult to find.

Ladle, incised floral in bowl, initialed KLD, 16½", $265.00.

Barrel, staved, old red, iron hdl/lid, 27" 175.00
Bowl, burl, EX figure, end hdls, rim crack, 6x16x19" L............ 2,400.00
Bowl, burl, EX figure, traces of pnt stripes, lid, 4½x6" 1,400.00
Bowl, burl, heavy/irregular form, tab hdls, rfn/cracks, 14" 400.00
Bowl, burl, rfn, 5¾x15" 825.00
Bowl, burl, varnished, blk patina w/in, 4½x11" 275.00
Bowl, burl, wear/minor rim crack, 5¾x11½"...................800.00
Bowl, butter; burl, ca 1800s, 3¾x8½".........................65.00
Bowl, good wear, scrubbed, 4x11" 275.00
Bowl, maple sugar; Peaseware, ped base, w/lid, 4¾x4"...........350.00
Bowl, maple w/some bird's-eye, varnished, 5x17"................100.00
Bowl, poplar, mustard yel rpt, irregular rim, 7x21"..............395.00
Bowl, poplar, rfn, wear/age cracks, 5½x18" 85.00
Bowl, speckled ash burl, 1700s, 6½", EX.......................570.00
Bowl, tiger maple, wide rim band, ca 1845, rare, 17¾"...........210.00
Bowl, trn, red ext, 7½x22" dia 325.00
Bowl, trn, some curl/dk patina, age cracks, 17x17"...............55.00
Bowl, trn poplar, ext: red pnt, rpr age crack, 9x24"..............200.00
Bowl, trn poplar, mustard yel, 7x21" dia 220.00
Box, bulbous, orig James Brown label, 4"......................275.00
Box, trn, minor lid damage, 4" 55.00
Bucket, staved, laced wood bands, swivel bentwood hdl, 11" 150.00
Bucket, staved, trn lid, brass bands, red pnt, Murdock, 4"..........195.00
Bucket, sugar; staved, galvanized metal band, rpt, 8", EX 130.00
Bucket, sugar; staved, w/lid, varnished, 9¾"....................85.00
Busk, chip cvd w/EX detail, cvd initials front/bk, 13½" 425.00
Butter paddle, burl w/EX figure, scrubbed, 9" 375.00
Butter paddle, maple w/curl in bowl, angular hook, rfn, 11" 65.00
Butter scoop, ash burl, 1700s, 9" L, EX 395.00
Butter scoop, maple, deep hook end, 1-pc, ca 1820, 10¼" 115.00
Candle sconce, shield bk, wheel trn, 6½" 350.00
Candy mold, cvd fish, 14½" L................................235.00
Canteen, staved, metal band, worn patina, 7½" 175.00
Churn, staved w/hdl extensions, wood bands renailed, 19".........325.00
Compote, burl, heavy ft, minor rim chips, 5x6" 250.00
Cookie brd, cvd chicken w/EX detail, tin edging, 7x10" 425.00
Cookie brd, heart w/basket of flowers, 10x12" 350.00
Cookie brd, heart w/clasped hands & foliage, 11x8" 275.00
Cookie brd, hen on nest, 3¼x3¾" 85.00
Cookie brd, horse/rider, bk: rooster, minor damage, 10x13" 175.00
Cookie brd, poplar, 18" dia+short hdl 125.00
Cookie brd, Willem & Wilhelmina portraits, 4x10", EX 200.00
Cookie brd, 12 rnd cvgs: train/girl/man on snail/etc, 6x8" 250.00
Cookie brd, 6 cvgs: animals/people/etc, 4x21", VG 110.00
Cookie brd, 6 relief-cvd rnds: man/bird/sheep/etc, 3½x22".........275.00
Cookie brd, 6 sections w/primitive cvgs, 8¾x5" 75.00
Cookie brd, 8 relief cvgs: people/mermaid/etc, 5x28"..............95.00
Cookie brd, 9 animal cvgs, cut down from lg brd, 4x31".............200.00
Cookie brd, 9 cvd segments, scrubbed, minor damage, 2½x3½" 75.00
Cookie roller, cvgs: acorns/vintage/foliage/etc, 12½" L, EX.........500.00
Cutting board, bird's-eye maple, 3" tab hdl, 13x8", EX 145.00

Dipper, maple w/some figure, bird's-eye bowl, 11½", EX 85.00
Dipper, some figure & burl, scrubbed, 11" 125.00
Dough bowl/raiser, pine, ca 1845, 8x39x16"....................255.00
Dough bowl/raiser, pine, ca 1880, 17¾" 110.00
Dough print, flowers & seed pods, 1-pc maple, ca 1860 ....150.00
Egg cup, Lehnware, orig strawberry decor on pk, 2¾", EX 525.00
Garlic press, early hinges, 2-part, 1800s, 10".....................85.00
Herb-drying brd, orig red pnt, sq-headed nails, ca 1900, 14"..........75.00
Jar, Lehnware, staved, red grpt w/florals, w/lid, 9", EX............ 2,000.00
Jar, Lehnware, staved/iron bands, grpt/florals, lid, 9", G...........900.00
Jar, poplar w/traces of red sponging, chipped finial, 6" 425.00
Jar, trn, EX detail, ball finial, age cracks/worn, 6¾" 200.00
Jar, trn, ftd w/dome lid, mk Hand Turned, JC Brown, 5¾" 175.00
Ladle, apple wood, ca 1700s, 11½" 125.00
Ladle, maple, ca 1800s, 11½" 125.00
Lemon squeezer, maple, 2-part, hinged, EX 45.00
Masher, lg mushroom knob, ca 1800s, 19¼" 35.00
Noggin, European, rpr, 11" 45.00
Noggin, gray pnt, 6½" 175.00
Piggin, staved, pnt traces, 5", +hdl...........................250.00
Plate, cherry, 1700s, 10½x11¼" 350.00
Plate, pnt fruit inside, ca 1880, 8" 40.00
Plate, poplar, age crack, 11½" 185.00
Plate, poplar, wear/scratches, 10" 300.00
Plate, serving; rim design, beveled edge, rnd, ca 1920s, 10" 50.00
Pudding stick, shaved blade for batter, hewn hdl, 9½" 12.50
Rolling pin, cherry & maple, dbl bars & posts, 1700s, EX...........285.00
Salt cellar, orig red sponging, 3" 150.00
Salt cellar, some burl, stains, 1¾x1¾" 55.00
Sieve, adjustable, 18" 65.00
Skimmer, cream; pine, 1700s, 5" dia, EX 95.00
Soap dish, trn maple, 1 hdl, 1-pc, 2x7¾"......................165.00
Spoon, eng floral on hdl, well shaped, 7" 45.00
Sugar bowl, trn, mustard pnt, mushroom finial, 1870s, 3x3"........295.00
Trencher, pine, early 1800s, 4x21¾x14½"......................145.00
Trencher, walnut, dk patina, 3x18x9½" 240.00
Tub, staved, split vine bands, cvd lid, 4½", VG...................65.00
Tub, staved w/hdl extensions, wood bands, rfn, 12" dia 85.00
Wall pocket, pine w/bl pnt, late w/wire nails, 21" 450.00
Wax sealer, w/initials MP, dk finish, 4⅝" 80.00

Woodworking Machinery

Vintage cast iron woodworking machines are monuments to the highly skilled engineers, foundrymen, and machinists who devised them, thus making possible the mass production of items ranging from clothespins, boxes, and barrels to decorative moldings and furniture. Though attractive from a nostalgic viewpoint, many of these machines are bought by the hobbyist and professional alike, to be put into actual use — at far less cost than new equipment. Many worth-assessing factors must be considered; but as a general rule, a machine in good condition is worth about 65¢ a pound (excluding motors). A machine needing a lot of restoration is not worth more than 35¢ a pound, while one professionally rebuilt and with a warranty can be calculated at $1.10 a pound. Modern, new machinery averages over $3.00 a pound. Two of the best sources of information on purchasing or selling such machines are *Vintage Machines — Searching for the Cast Iron Classics* by Tom Howell, and *Used Machines and Abused Buyers* by Chuck Seidel from *Fine Woodworking*, November/December 1984. Prices quoted are for machines in good condition, less motors and accessories.

American Saw Mill Machinery Company, 1890s

Planer, Jewel, 16"..475.00

Saw, style D, swing cutoff, 24" 300.00
Table saw, combination, wood fr, 24" 500.00

Blue Star Products, 1939

Band saw, #12, 12" bench model 55.00
Band saw, #1200, 12" floor model 85.00
Drill press, #500, 12" bench model 30.00
Jointer, #66, 6" bench model 65.00
Lathe, #1000, 48" bed, 8" swing 20.00
Lathe, #1002, 72" bed, 10" swing 60.00
Scroll saw, #300, 14" bench model 30.00
Table saw, #800, 8" 95.00

Boice-Crane Power Tools, 1937

Drill press, #1600, 15" 75.00
Jointer, #950, 4" 50.00
Planer, #1000, 12" 250.00
Spindle sander, #504 .... 75.00
Table saw, #1500, tilting arbor, 10" 100.00

Crescent Machine Company, 1921

Jointer, #243, 24" 1,175.00
Jointer, bench; 4" 50.00
Saw, swing cutoff, 18" 300.00
Shaper, single spindle 650.00
Universal Wood-Worker #59, 5 machines in 1 .... 2,050.00

Defiance Machine Works, 1892

Band saw, #6, 36" 1,170.00
Band saw, 28" 520.00
Jointer, 16" 975.00
Lathe, #3, iron bed, 10" swing 1,365.00
Planer, 4-roll, single surface, 24" 1,300.00
Sandpapering machine, #1, horizontal, hand feed, 24" 745.00
Saw, #2, heavy swing, 48" 1,235.00
Shaper, #4, dbl spindle, upright 1,430.00
Table saw, #2, hand feed, 20" 650.00
Table saw, #2, power feed, 20" 1,100.00

G.N. Goodspeed Company, 1876

Planer, New & Improved Pony, 24" 900.00
Sawing & boring machine 200.00

L. Power & Company, 1888

Boring machine, vertical 715.00
Mortiser & borer, #2 .... 780.00
Moulding machine, 7" 1,170.00
Planer, panel; #0, 24" 1,170.00
Planer & matcher (combined), #5, 24" 5,525.00
Rip saw, #2, self feed, 24" 1,040.00
Saw & dado machine, combination 585.00
Shaper, single spindle, reversible 585.00
Surfacer, dbl; endless belt, 26" 3,770.00
Table saw, self feed, 14" 715.00

Oliver Machinery Company, 1912

Jointer, #144, 6" 400.00
Mortiser, #91, vertical hollow chisel 650.00

Rip saw, #45, hand feed, 26" 1,100.00
Saw, #97, heavy swing cutoff, 48" 1,050.00
Scroll saw, #29, Patent 325.00
Table saw, #22, Variety, 20" 1,050.00
Table saw, #60, Universal, 16" 1,300.00

Parks Ball Bearing Machine Company, 1925

Bandsaw, H-62, Jewel, 22" 250.00
Mortising & tenoning machine, H-35, Gem, ft powered 100.00
Planing Mill Special, H-87, 8 machines in 1 .... 1,250.00
Sander, H-160, Model S, self feeding, dbl drum, 36" 900.00
Sanding machine, H-165, Economy, 24" 230.00
Shaper, spindle; H-168, quick reverse 175.00

P.B. Yates Machine Company, 1917

Saw, #232, swing cutoff, 16" 260.00
Saw, trim; Type G-3, 16" 725.00
Table saw, #226, 16" 725.00

S.A. Woods Machine Company, 1876

Moulding machine, #1, 2-roll, 12" 2,275.00
Planer, Patent Improved, endless belt, 30" 1,950.00
Planer, Patent Improved, shop surface, 30" 1,430.00

Sprunger Power Tools, 1950s

Jigsaw, 20" 40.00
Jointer, 6" 80.00
Sander, 12-disk 35.00
Table saw, tilt arbor, 8" 40.00

World's Fairs and Expos

Since 1851 and the Crystal Palace Exhibition in London, World's Fairs and Expositions have taken place at a steady pace. Many of them commemorate historical events. The 1904 Louisiana Purchase Exposition, commonly known as the St. Louis World's Fair, celebrated the 100th anniversary of the Louisiana Purchase agreement between Thomas Jefferson and Napoleon in 1803. The 1893 Columbian Exposition, known as The Chicago World's Fair, commemorated the 400th anniversary of the discovery of America by Columbus in 1492. (Both of these fairs were held one year later than originally scheduled.) The multitude of souvenirs from these and similar events have become a growing area of interest to collectors in recent years. Many items have a 'crossover' interest into other fields: i.e., collectors of post cards and souvenir spoons eagerly search for those from various fairs and expositions. For additional information collectors may contact World's Fairs Collectors Society (WFCS), whose address is in the Directory under Clubs, Newsletters, and Catalogs, or our advisor, D.D. Woollard, Jr. His address is listed in the Directory under Missouri.

Key:
T&P — Trylon & Perisphere   WF — World's Fair

1876 Centennial, Philadelphia

Book, Illus Historical Register, 800 engr, 1879, NY, VG 120.00
Buckle, brass, medallion, 1776-1876, 3½" L 42.00
Catalog, Internat'l Exhibition Official, revised ed, EX 40.00
Napkin ring, wooden, building transfer, Mauchline, 2" 60.00

Pocket watch, NP case, jewel movement, mk w/in cover, EX......300.00

1893 Columbian, Chicago

Ad card, hold-to-light, Uncle Sam views expo/Everett Pianos 50.00
Atlas, Pike's Columbian World's Fair, 180 maps, folio 50.00
Badge, attendant's, NP copper, 1⅛" dia, EX 75.00
Badge, brass, Columbus bust, 400th Anniversary, w/hanger 22.00
Book, Glimpses of WF, Laird & Lee, soft cover, 7x5", EX 22.50
Book, Photographic History of WF, Woodward, emb cover, EX ...48.00
Book, Portfolio of Views, Arnold, hardbk, 34-pg, 10x7" 32.00
Book, Progress of 400 Years, Lossing, 536-pg, 7½x9½"..................45.00
Booklet, MacKinnon Pulleys, WF address 12.00
Buttonhook, Columbus on globe at top, mk Sterling, 3⅛" 40.00
Envelope, angel w/trumpet cachet, globe in ribbon, Sellinger 50.00
Fan, folding, wood spokes, panoramic view, opens to 24", NM ...125.00
Match safe, chrome plated, Administration Building, 2¾" 70.00
Newspaper, Chicago Daily Tribune, Oct 9, 1893, Chicago Day 25.00
Photo, Horticultural Building, Walker, 9x7" on 12x10" mt..........20.00
Photogravure, Mines & Mining Building, 6x14", EX 10.00
Plate, china, Agricultural Building, Wedgwood, 8¼" 50.00
Plate, china, Art Palace, blk on wht, MIE, 6" dia 45.00
Post card, Transportation Building, Zeese, rare, VG 175.00
Purse, rollers at top separate to insert coin, WF mk......................55.00
Razor, Columbian Building on blade, 1492-1892..., Boker, EX......85.00
Ribbon, woven silk, Administration Bldg, 8½x2¾", EX 125.00
Scarf, Manufacturer's Building, silk, sq, 20", EX 75.00
Scarf, 40 nations on border/US flag, silk, sq, 20", EX 65.00
Ticket, Good Only on Day of Sale, 2x4", M 10.00
Ticket, Manhattan Day, w/stub, M 20.00
Tray, SP, Columbus bust, emb floral edge, Simpson, 7" dia 75.00

1901 Pan American

Button, policeman's uniform; brass, bl enamel, silver logo..............22.00
Candy jar, glass, 5½", w/2" metal buffalo finial..............................95.00
Hatchet, glass, Buffalo 1901, Indian bust on reverse 75.00
Match safe, NP, Maid of Mist, WF mk, 1⅜x2⅝", EX 50.00
Medal, brass, 2 continents, Electric Tower on bk, ¾"................... 7.50
Pitcher, ruby-stained glass, Pan Am mk, 7½"..............................50.00
Spoon, buffalo on globe hdl, Niagara Falls in bowl, SP, 6"............20.00
Tray, aluminum, emb buffalo head, 5" dia 22.50
Tumbler, glass, etched Electric Tower, 3⅜" 17.50

1904 St. Louis

Book, Louisiana & Fair, Buel, World's Progress, 405-pg, EX..........40.00
Book, Official History of the Fair, 496-pg, 7x9½", VG..................50.00
Book, Sights & Scenes of LA Purchase Expo, 496-pg, EX 27.50
Booklet, Guide to St Louis & World's Fair, 20-pg, 4x2¾".............. 7.50
Button, pin-bk; Jefferson portrait, Universal Expo..., mc, NM.......15.00
Button, pin-bk; lady w/map, Deed of Pen, mc, EX........................30.00
Dollar, Good Luck, busts of Jefferson & Napoleon, worn................ 7.50
Map, WF grounds, Brown's Business College ads, EX....................12.00
Medal, brass, Napoleon & Jefferson/fleur-de-lis, 1⅛"..................17.50
Newspaper, Youth's Companion, May 19, 1904, opening day, EX.20.00
Post card, hold-to-light, expo buildings/etc, set of 10, NM..........250.00
Post card, hold-to-light/cutout, Grand Lagoon, NM......................25.00
Post card, hold-to-light/cutout, Palace of Liberal Arts, NM..........25.00
Token, aluminum, Palace of Textiles, silver dollar sz 10.00
Tray, copper gilt on metal, eagle/Uncle Sam/Liberty, 2¾x3½" 15.00

1905 Lewis and Clark

Button, pin-bk; 3 figures, Sighting the Pacific, mc, EX 20.00

Dollar, silver-tone metal, Lewis & Clark, EX 32.00
Plate, Lewis & Clark w/Liberty, vignettes, Staffordshire, 10" 78.00
Post card, fair building, unused, NM 5.00
Post card, Statue of Sacajawea & Tower, w/glitter, VG 12.00
Post card, Yew Cedar Sights..., Farran Zerbe, VG.........................15.00

1907 Jamestown

Button, pin-bk; Indian portrait, Official Booster, mc, NM.............22.50
Button, pin-bk; Ohio Day, Sept 11, 1907, ⅞", EX........................15.00
Cent, aluminum, Lucky Penny Pocket Piece, M............................15.00
Napkin ring, copper-plated metal, 3 views, 1¼x2" dia 20.00
Plate, bird's-eye view, bl on wht, Staffordshire, 10" 60.00
Playing cards, by Old Dominion Paper, Pocohantas bk, M 125.00

1909 Alaska Yukon Pacific

Button, pin-bk; children, Children's Day June 5, mc, NM.............15.00
Playing cards, 52+joker, orig box, VG 90.00
Silk, 5 Expo views, blk on brn, mk Souvenir..., 18" sq, EX............60.00
Tumbler, copper gilt on metal, 3 expo scenes & logo, 3½" 15.00

1915 Panama Pacific

Book, Architecture & Landscape Gardening..., Elder, 204-pg, EX...20.00
Book, Jewel City, 32 color views, 4½x6¼", VG..............................22.50
Booklet, Condensed Facts..., bl cover, 4x9" 6.00
Booklet, Official Publication, Reid, 31-pg, 6x9", M 22.50
Box, metal, emb Service Building, hinged lid, 4½x2¼x2"..............17.50
Button, pin-bk; Indian maiden portrait, mc, EX 20.00
Medal, Argentina, Coat of Arms, silver, EX 22.50
Napkin ring, celluloid, Tower of Jewels, 2x2", EX 20.00
Paperweight, metal, golden bear on platform, 1½" 15.00
Print, Festival Hall, c 1913, 6½x8½" 12.50
Ribbon, Closing Day, on celluloid hanger, NM............................45.00
Table cover, bl felt, bird's-eye view & poppies, 16x25" 35.00
View book, 32 color views, 4½x6", EX 17.50

1926 Sesquicentennial

Box, jewelry; wood w/glass top, historical scene, mk, 5x8x3".........37.50
Bust, metal, Geo Washington, medallion on front, 3¾" 16.00
Button, pin-bk; Washington/Betsy Ross House/etc, 1¼" 15.00
Liberty Bell, brass, expo mk, 2¾" 15.00

1933 Chicago

Ash tray, copper, emb Chrysler Building, 3x3" 7.50
Badge, brass, Hall of Science, 2-part, EX 18.00
Bank, tin litho, Am Can, 3½x2" dia 22.00
Booklet, Happy Hours, Pabst Bl Ribbon Casino, 28-pg, 5x5" 10.00
Brochure, Canada from Sea to Sea, colorful, EX........................... 5.00
Coaster, pressed cb w/metallic finish, 3½", EX 10.00
Fan, wood spokes, paper Oriental scene cover, 10x15" 45.00
Plate, china, Carillo Tower, blk on wht, 8½" 40.00
Program, Opening Day, 24-pg, 8x11", EX....................................22.50
Ticket, blk on gr, 4x2¼", EX..12.50
Watch fob, brass, fair overview, advertising, 1¼" dia 35.00

1939 New York

Ash tray, Goodrich tire, expo glass insert, 6"..............................27.50
Book, Official Russian Guide, EX...35.00
Booklet, Nation Tests Its Hearing, 8-pg, EX................................. 5.00
Box, cigarette; Syrocco wood, T&P on top, 6x4x2", EX 25.00

Bracelet, charm; link type, w/attached stanhope & 2 charms 45.00
Button, pin-bk; Order of Golden Chain, 2-color, EX 7.50
Compact, metal w/fabric-covered lid, T&P, 2½", EX....................40.00
Invitation, Opening of British Pavilion reception, VG 15.00
Mailing folder, T&P, 18 views, Trichoner, 4½x6" 12.50
Match book cover, logo/Wrigley's Exhibit Food Building, VG 4.00
Pipe holder, Syrocco wood, T&P medallion at end......................24.00
Ticket, For Peace & Freedom, T&P, mc, 3x2¼" 4.00
Token, brass, face w/T&P, 8-sided, w/attached hanger ring 28.00

1939 San Francisco

Button, pin-bk; I'm Working for a Trip..., bl/wht, EX 7.50
Key, gold-tone metal, w/logo & thermometer, 9", EX 35.00
Pillow, satin rayon, M in orig pkg...25.00
Post card, expo grounds, Oakland/Berkeley, linen, unused, M........ 3.00
Post card, Levi Strauss's Electric Rodeo, color, EX 7.50
Token, Union Pacific, aluminum, NM 5.00

1962 Seattle

Bowl, china, Space Needle, rtcl hearts at rim, heart shape.............12.00
Brochure, Am Home of Immediate Future, EX 2.50
Button, pin-bk; Space Needle, I Was There, M........................... 8.00
Cup & saucer, ceramic, logo on cup, scenic saucer 10.00
Pin, gilt metal, key through heart, Space Needle, EX.................... 5.00
Slides, Official Souvenir; 4 in orig 2x2" sealed package 4.00

1964 New York

Bottle, china, Jim Beam Whiskey, Unisphere form, Regal, 12" 30.00
Dime, silver, encased in 2" bl disk, NM 15.00
Flash card set, 28 mc cards w/info, in 3½x6" mailer, NM.............25.00
Medal, silver, Unisphere form, US Steel, M 12.50
Playing cards, scenic courts w/gold border, M 8.00
Ticket, Special Admission, General Motors, EX 5.00
Tumbler, frosted glass w/mc fair scene, 7", M 7.50

Wrought Iron

Until the middle of the 19th century, almost all the metal hand forged in America was made from a material called wrought iron. When wrought iron rusts it appears grainy, while the mild steel that was used later shows no grain but pits to an orange-peel surface. This is an important aid in determining the age of an ironwork piece.

Broiler, concave fr made to rotate bowl, 18"................................215.00
Broiler, elaborate scrolled detail, pitted, 17x30"...........................375.00
Broiler, rotary, simple bar design, 12" dia, 21" L...........................145.00
Candlestand, tripod base, arm w/socket/pricket, EX form, 42" ..1,050.00
Candlestand, tripod base/penny ft, animal head on arm, 59".......500.00
Coals carrier, sliding lid, 31" 235.00
Fork, plain hdl w/simple copper inlay, 21"................................125.00
Fork, roasting; 3-prong, EX detail, heart cut-out hdl, 28" 250.00
Fork, tooled hdl, 10½" 50.00
Fork, well-shaped hdl w/simple brass inlay, 18" 235.00
Fork, 3-tine, loop hdl end, ca 1700s, 17½" 70.00
Fork, 32" 185.00
Harpoon, 70"...45.00
Hinge, pitted/damage, 27", pr...85.00
Hinge, ram's horn, 7½", EX, pr 75.00
Hinge, scrolled/tooled ram's horn, minor damage, 11", pr............85.00
Hinge, scrolled/tooled ram's horn, 15½", pr 105.00

Hook, 4-prong, ring top, early 1800s, 5½" sq, 9" L 40.00
Hook w/spike, scroll finial w/flat birds, tooled/cut out, 8x6" 175.00
Hook w/spike, scrolled finial, pitted, 7½", pr 70.00
Hook w/spike, 3-D finial w/bird & 2 lilies, pnt, 10x7" 345.00
Ladle, solid bowl, loop hook on hdl end, ca 1700s, 16½" 45.00
Log roller, ram's horn on 1 end, angle on other, 38" 155.00
Meat hook, Dutch crown type w/9 hooks, ring atop, 11x14" dia .395.00
Peel, ram's horn hdl, 3 drilled holes in blade, 40"........................95.00
Roasting rack, adjustable, tripod base w/penny ft, 30"..................550.00
Scraper, twist hdl, 6" L 75.00
Skewer holder, +7 skewers, 15½" overall 1,200.00
Spatula, ca 1840, 12" 65.00
Spatula, simple tooling, heart cutout, 17"................................165.00
Taper jack, EX detail/eng, minor battering, 5 ....850.00
Toaster, EX detail, heart-shaped hdl, pitted/rust, 15x18" 1,025.00
Toaster, well-shaped hdl, 18" 150.00
Tool, shovel shaped, loop in end of twisted hdl, 10"....................140.00
Trammel, sawtooth, adjusts from 26", EX................................100.00
Trammel, sawtooth, ram horn finial/scrolled ratchet, 52", VG....225.00
Wafer iron, eng w/crown etc, 1759, 7½", 34" overall 250.00
Wafer iron, heart shape w/waffle pattern, pitted, 30" 300.00
Wafer iron, 3 figures/church/tree/star/1786, 34" L...................225.00

Yellow Ware

Ranging in color from buff to deep mustard, yellow ware which almost always has a clear glaze can be slip banded, plain, Rockingham decorated, flint enamel glazed, or mocha decorated. Mocha-decorated pieces are usually the most expensive and desirable. The majority of pieces are plain and do not bear a manufacturer's mark. Yellow ware which was primarily produced in the United States, England, and Canada was popular from the mid-19th century to the early 20th century. A utilitarian ware, it was first domestically produced in New York, New Jersey, Pennsylvania, and Vermont. With more than thirty active potteries, East Liverpool, Ohio, became the center for yellow ware production. After experiencing several years of dramatic price increases, the market has begun to stabilize. Watch for a new book on yellow ware to be written by our advisor, John Michel; his address is in the Directory under New York.

Mustard jar, blue seaweed on white band, minor lid chips, 2¼", $350.00.

Bowl, bl seaweed mocha decor, 11" 395.00
Bowl, 1 wide wht band, 10"...95.00
Butter tub, 3 wht bands, stamped Butter, 5" 225.00
Colander, emb w/wht int, 9" dia 145.00
Colander, multi-banded in bl, 13"...695.00
Creamer, cow shaped, plain decor.......................................2,200.00

Master salt, gr mocha decor, 2½" **395.00**
Master salt, 3 wht bands, 2½" **325.00**
Miniature, chamber pot, 1 wht band, 1½" **75.00**
Miniature, mug, 2 bl bands, 2¼" **175.00**
Mold, ear of corn, octagonal, 6" L **95.00**
Mold, heart shaped, mini..**245.00**
Mold, turk's head form, 6" dia **195.00**
Mug, brn mocha seaweed decor, 4½" **395.00**
Mug, 3 wht bands, concave sides, 4½" **175.00**
Mustard pot, bl mocha decor, 4½" **495.00**
Mustard pot, 2 bl incised bands, 4½" **325.00**
Nappy, heart-shaped ft, 6" dia...**155.00**
Pepper pot, bl seaweed mocha decor, 4¾" **550.00**
Pepper pot, blk mocha decor, 4¾" **650.00**
Pepper pot, multi-banded in bl & wht, 4¾" **375.00**
Pie plate, mk JE Jeffords, 12½" **125.00**
Pipkin, ribbed body, plain decor, w/lid, 6¼" **350.00**
Pitcher, bl mocha & multi-banded, 10" **795.00**
Pitcher, brn & wht banded, 4½" **295.00**
Rolling pin, plain decor, 9" **350.00**
Rolling pin, plain w/advertising, 9" **650.00**
Spice jar, emb wheat, 3¾" **185.00**
Tankard, 6 bl bands, str sides, 6½" **395.00**

Zanesville Glass

Glassware was produced in Zanesville, Ohio, from as early as 1815 until 1851. Two companies produced clear and colored hollowware pieces in five characteristic patterns: 1) diamond faceted, 2) broken swirls, 3) vertical swirls, 4) perpendicular fluting, 5) plain, with scalloped or fluted rims and strap handles. The most readily identified product is perhaps the whiskey bottles made in the vertical swirl pattern, often called globular swirls because of their full, round bodies. Their necks vary in width; some have a ringed rim and some are collared. They were made in several colors; amber, light green, and light aquamarine are the most common. Our advisor for this category is Mark Vuono; he is listed in the Directory under Connecticut.

Diamond-patterned bowl in cobalt, 4½" diameter, $600.00;
Creamer with petal foot in cobalt, ca 1820, 5", $400.00.

Bottle, globular; amber, 12 swirl ribs, lt sickness, 7½" **450.00**
Bottle, globular; aqua, 24 swirl ribs, lt stain, 8"...........................**300.00**
Bottle, globular; honey-amber, 24 vertical ribs, 8½", EX **2,100.00**
Bowl, cobalt, dmn pattern, U-form on sm rnd ft, 4½" **600.00**
Creamer, cobalt bl lead glass, trumpet neck, petal ft, 5" **400.00**
Flask, chestnut; aqua, 10-dmn, lt wear, 5½" **700.00**
Flask, chestnut; dk amber, 10-dmn, 5⅜" **2,200.00**
Flask, chestnut; gold-amber, 24-rib broken swirl, lt wear, 5" **300.00**

Whimsey, hat, amber, folded rim, 3¾x10½"...............................**200.00**

Zsolnay

Only until the past decade has the production of the Zsolnay factory become more correctly understood. In the beginning they produced only cement; industrial and kitchenware manufacture began in the 1850s, and in the early 1870s a line of decorative architectural and art pottery was initiated which has continued to the present time.

The city of Pecs (pronounced Paach) is the major provincial city of southwest Hungary close to the Yugoslav border. The old German name for the city was Funfkirchen, meaning 'Five Churches.' (The 'five-steeple' mark became the factory's logo in 1878.)

Although most Americans only think of Zsolnay in terms of the bizarre, reticulated examples of the 1880s and '90s and the small 'Eosine' green figures of animals and children that have been produced since the 1920s, the factory went through all the art trends of major international art potteries and produced various types of forms and decorations. The 'golden period,' circa 1895-1920, is when its Art Nouveau (Sezession in Austro-Hungarian terms) examples were unequaled. Vilmos Zsolnay was a Renaissance man devoted to innovation, and his children carried on the tradition after his death in 1900. Important sculptors and artists of the day were employed (usually anonymously) and married into the family, creating a dynasty.

Nearly all Zsolnay is marked, either impressed 'Zsolnay Pecs' or with the 'five-steeple' stamp. Variations and form numbers can date a piece fairly accurately. For the most part, the earlier ethnic historial-revival pieces do not bring the prices that the later Sezession and second Sezession (Deco) examples do.

Centerpiece, reticulated boat-shaped bowl with blue florals cradled in ormolu chariot pulled by lions, a cherub at either end, 15" long, $1,500.00.

Figurine, eagle perched w/wings folded, EX details, mk, 6½" **75.00**
Figurine, lady pulls dress over head, vase at side, mk, 10" **250.00**
Figurine, standing hooded figure, brn/purple irid, 15" **660.00**
Pitcher, free-form Nouveau flower w/stem hdl, gr, 15" **3,800.00**
Vase, abstract bands in gray/blk/gold, Hamvas, '28, 13", EX........**350.00**
Vase, Islamic style, lg/wide foliate-rtcl hdls, ftd, 20" **1,650.00**
Vase, maiden w/long hair, bulbous w/str neck, 9½x4½"....................**225.00**
Vase, rtcl flower/leaf form, red/gr/gray-gr irid, 1902, 15".........**9,400.00**
Vase, stylized scenic, irid, ovoid w/sq mouth, #6033/M, 4" **450.00**

The editors and staff take this opportunity to express our sincere gratitude and appreciation to each person who has in any way contributed to the preparation of this guide. We believe the credibility of our book is greatly enhanced through their efforts. See each advisor's Directory listing for information concerning their specific areas of expertise.

You will notice that at the conclusion of some of the narratives the advisor's name is given. This is optional and up to the discretion of each individual. Simply because no name is mentioned does not indicate that we have no advisor for that subject. Our board grows with each issue and now numbers over 350; if you care to correspond with any of them or anyone listed in our Directory, you must send a SASE with your letter. If you are seeking an appraisal, first ask about their fee, since many of these people are professionals who must naturally charge for their services. Because of our huge circulation, every person who allows us to publish their name runs the risk of their privacy being invaded by too many phone calls and letters. We are indebted to every advisor and very much regret losing any one of them. By far, the majority of those we lose give this reason. Please help us retain them on our board by observing the simple rules of common courtesy.

Charles & Barbara Adams
Middleboro, Massachusetts

Jay Adams
Washington Township, New Jersey

Geneva D. Addy
Winterset, Iowa

James Anderson
New Brighton, Minnesota

Tim Anderson
Provo, Utah

Warren R. Anderson
Cedar City, Utah

John Apple
Racine, Wisconsin

Dick & Ellie Archer
St. Augustine, Florida

Una Arnbal
Ames, Iowa

Bruce Austin
Fairport, New York

Rod Baer
Arlington, Virginia

Wayne & Gale Bailey
Dacula, Georgia

Mrs. Lillian Baker, Fellow IBA
Cambridge, England
Gardena, California

Roger Baker
Woodside, California

Robert Banks
Brookeville, Maryland

Jim Barker
Hawley, Pennsylvania

Kit Barry
Brattleboro, Vermont

Daniel J. Batchelor
Oswego, New York

Dana Martin Batory
Crestline, Ohio

D.R. Beeks
Coeur d'Alene, Idaho

Scott Benjamin
Lancaster, California

Phyllis & Tom Bess
Tulsa, Oklahoma

Robert Bettinger
Mt. Dora, Florida

John E. Bilane
Union, New Jersey

Dale Blann
Wheatland, Indiana

Clarence H. Bodine, Jr.
New Hope, Pennsylvania

Sandra V. Bondhus
Unionville, Connecticut

Clifford Boram
Monticello, Indiana

Dick & Waunita Bosworth
Kansas City, Missouri

Jeff Bradfield
Dayton, Virginia

Tom Bradshaw
Ventura, California

Larry Brenner
Manchester, New Hampshire

William J. Brinkley
McLeansboro, Illinois

Mike Brooks
Oakland, California

Jim Broom
Effingham, Illinois

David L. Brown
Victoria, British Columbia, Canada

Rick Brown
Newspaper Collector's Society of America
Lansing, Michigan

Nicki Budin
Worthington, Ohio

Robert C. Butz
Newbury Park, California

Jim Calison
Wallkill, New York

Judd Caplovich
Vernon, Connecticut

Carol & Jim Carlton
Englewood, Colorado

Fran Carter
Coos Bay, Oregon

Tina M. Carter
El Cajon, California

Sally S. Carver
Chestnut Hill, Massachusetts

Cerebro
Lancaster, Pennsylvania

Jackie Chamberlain
La Canada, California

Jack Chipman
Redondo Beach, California

Wilfred & Dolli Cohen
Santa Ana, California

Lillian M. Cole
Flemington, New Jersey

J.W. Courter
Simpson, Illinois

Ron Damaska
New Brighton, Pennsylvania

John Danis
Rockford, Illinois

Patricia M. Davis
Wilmington, Delaware

Gael deCourtivron
Sarasota, Florida

Steve DeGenaro
Youngstown, Ohio

Richard Degenhardt
Hendersonville, North Carolina

Mary Delucchi
Stockton, California

Joe Devine
Council Bluffs, Iowa

Thomas P. Dimitroff
Corning, New York

Ginny Distel
Tiffin, Ohio

DLK Nostalgia & Collectibles
Johnstown, Pennsylvania

Rod Dockery
Ft. Worth, Texas

L.R. 'Les' Docks
San Antonio, Texas

Rebecca Dodds
Ft. Lauderdale, Florida

Pat Dole
Birmingham, Alabama

Ron Donnelly
Panama City Beach, Florida

Robert A. Doyle, CAI, ISA
Fishkill, New York

Louise Dumont
Coventry, Rhode Island

Ken & Jackie Durham
Washington, DC

William Durham
Belvidere, Illinois

Rita & John Ebner
Columbus, Ohio

Bill Edwards
Madison, Indiana

J. David Ehrhard
Los Angeles, California

J.M. Ellwood
Scottsdale, Arizona

Adrienne S. Escoe
Los Alamitos, California

Maurice Feinblatt
Wilmette, Illinois

Joseph Ferrara
Newburgh, New York

Steven Fishler
New York, New York

Vicki Flanigan
Winchester, Virginia

Gene Florence
Lexington, Kentucky

Asa P. Forbes, Jr.
Syracuse, New York

Ruth Forsythe
Galena, Ohio

Daniel Fortney
Milwaukee, Wisconsin

Fostoria Glass Society of America, Inc.
Moundsville, West Virginia

Ron Fox
North Babylon, New York

Madeleine France
Ft. Lauderdale, Florida

James Fred
Cutler, Indiana

Sandra & Peter Frei
Brimfield, Massachusetts

Leo & Wendy Frese
Dallas, Texas

Terry Friend
Galax, Virginia

Donald M. Frost
Roseburg, Oregon

John Gacher
Newport, Rhode Island

William Galaway
Belvidere, Illinois

Jerry Gallagher
Plainview, Minnesota

Lee Garmon
Springfield, Illinois

We wish to thank the following auction houses whose catalogs have been used as sources for pricing information. Many have granted us permission to reproduce their photographs as well.

A-1 Auction Service
P.O. Box 540672, Orlando, FL 32854; 407-841-6681. Specializing in American antique sales

America West Archives
Anderson, Warren
P.O. Box 100, Cedar City, UT 84721; 801-586-9497; quarterly 26-page illustrated catalog includes auction section of scarce and historical early western documents, letters, autographs, stock certificates, and other important ephemera. Subscription: $10 per year

Andre Ammelounx
The Stein Auction Company
P.O. Box 136, Palatine, IL 60078; 708-991-5927 or (Fax) 708-991-5947
Specializing in steins

Anthony J. Nard & Co.
US Rt. 220, Milan, PA 18831; 717-888-9404 or (Fax) 717-888-7723

Arman Absentee Auctions
P.O. Box 174, Woodstock, CT 06281; 203-928-5838. Specializing in American glass, Historical Staffordshire, English soft paste, paperweights

Autographs of America
Anderson, Tim
P.O. Box 461, Provo, UT 84603. Free sample catalog of hundreds of autographs for sale

Barrett/Bertoia Auctions & Appraisals
1217 Glenwood Dr., Vineland, NJ 18630; 609-692-4092. Specializing in antique toys and collectibles

Bider's
241 S. Union St., Lawrence, MA 01843; 508-688-4347 or 508-683-3944. Antiques appraised, purchased, and sold on consignment

Brian Riba
Riba Auctions Inc.
P.O. Box 53, Main St., S. Glastonbury, CT 06073; 203-633-3076

C.E. Guarino
Box 49, Denmark, ME 04022

Charles E. Kirtley
P.O. Box 2273, Elizabeth City, NC 27096; 919-335-1262. Specializing in World's Fair, Civil War, political, advertising, and other American collectibles

Col. Doug Allard
P.O. Box 460, St. Ignatius, MT 59865

Collectors Auction Services
326 Seneca St., Oil City, PA 16301; 814-677-6070. Specializing in advertising, oil and gas, toys, rare museum and investment-quality antiques

David Rago
P.O. Box 3592, Station E, Trenton, NJ 08629; 609-397-9374
Gallery: 17 S. Main St., Lambertville, NJ 08530. Specializing in American art pottery and Arts & Crafts

Don Treadway Gallery
2128 Madison Rd., Cincinnati, OH 45208; 513-321-6742 or (Fax) 513-871-7722. Member: National Antique Dealers Association, American Art Pottery Association, International Society of Appraisers, and American Ceramic Arts Society

Doyle, Auctioneers & Appraisers
R.D. 3, Box 137, Osborne Hill Road, Fishkill, NY 12524; 914-896-9492. Thousands of collectibles offered: call for free calendar of upcoming events

Dynamite Auctions
Franklin Antique Mall & Auction Gallery, 1280 Franklin Ave., Franklin, PA 16323; 814-432-8577 or 814-786-9211

Du Mouchelles
409 Jefferson Ave., Detroit, MI 48226

Early Auction Co.
123 Main St., Milford, OH 45150

Garth's Auctions, Inc.
2690 Stratford Rd., Box 369, Delaware, OH 43015; 614-362-4771

Glass Works Auction
James Hagenbuch
102 Jefferson, E. Greenville, PA 18041; 215-679-5849. America's leading auction company in early American bottles and glass

Greenberg Auctions
7566 Main St.
Sykesville, MD 21784. Specializing in trains: Lionel, American Flyer, Ives, Marx, Ho

Guernsey's
136 E. 73rd St., New York, NY 10021; 212-794-2280. Specializing in carousel figures

Gunther's International Auction Gallery
P.O. Box 235, 24 S. Virginia Ave., Brunswick, MD 21716; 301-834-7101 or 800-274-8779. Specializing in political, Oriental rugs, art, bronzes, antiques, the unusual

Hake's Americana & Collectibles
Specializing in character and personality collectibles along with all artifacts of popular culture for over 20 years. To receive a catalog for their next 3,000-item mail/phone bid auction, send $5 to Hake's Americana, P.O. Box 1444M, York, PA 17405

Jack Sellner
Sellner Marketing of California
P.O. Box 308, Fremont, CA 94536; 415-745-9463

James D. Julia
P.O. Box 210, Showhegan Rd., Fairfield, ME 04937

James R. Bakker Antiques, Inc.
James R. Bakker
370 Broadway, Cambridge, MA 02139; 617-864-7067. Specializing in American paintings, prints, and decorative arts

L.R. 'Les' Docks
Box 691035, San Antonio, TX 78269-1035. Providing occasional mail-order record auctions, rarely consigned; the only consignments considered are exceptionally scarce and unusual records

Lloyd Ralston Toys
447 Stratford Rd., Fairfield, CT 06432

Manion's International Auction House, Inc.
P.O. Box 12214, Kansas City, KS 66112

Maritime Auctions
R.R. 2, Box 45A, York, ME 03909; 207-363-4247

Mid-Hudson Auction Galleries
One Idlewild Ave., Cornwall-on-Hudson, NY 12520; 914-534-7828 or (Fax) 914-534-4802

Milwaukee Auction Galleries, Ltd.
4747 W. Bradley Rd., Milwaukee, WI 53223; 414-355-5054

Noel Barrett Antiques & Auctions
P.O. Box 1001, Carversville, PA 18913; 215-297-5109

Nostalgia Co.
21 S. Lake Dr., Hackensack, NJ 07601; 201-488-4536

Nostalgia Galleries
657 Meacham Ave., Elmont, NY 11003; 516-326-9595. Auctioning items from almost every area of the collectible field, catalogs available

Phillips
406 E. 79th St., New York, NY 10021

Rex Stark Auctions
49 Wethersfield Rd., Bellingham, MA 02019

Richard A. Bourne Co., Inc.
Estate Auctioneers & Appraisers
Box 141, Hyannis Port, MA 02647; 617-775-0797

Richard W. Oliver, Inc.
Plaza One, Rt. 1, Kennebunk, ME 04043; 207-985-3600 or (Fax) 207-985-7734. Outside Maine: 800-992-0047

Richard Opfer Auctioneering, Inc.
1919 Greenspring Dr., Timonium, MD 21093; 301-252-5035

Roan, Inc.
Box 118, R.D. 3, Cogan Station, PA 17728

Robert W. Skinner, Inc.
Auctioneers & Appraisers
Rt. 117, Bolton, MA 01740; 617-779-5528

Sotheby Parke Bernet, Inc.
980 Madison Ave., New York, NY 10021

TSACO (The Stein Auction Company)
East
Ron Fox
416 Throop St., N. Babylon, NY 11704.
Telephone and Fax: 516-669-7232

Weschler's, Adam A. Weschler & Son
905 E. St. N.W., Washington, DC 20004

Willis Henry Auctions
22 Main St., Marshfield, MA 02050

When contacting any of the buyers/sellers listed in this part of the Directory, please remember to include an SASE if you are corresponding by mail. If you call and get their answering machine, when you leave your number so that they can return your call, tell them to call back collect. Some of these people are licensed appraisers and may charge a fee for the information they provide. Find out if this is the case before you ask their advice. We need your help. This book sells in such great numbers that allowing their names to be published can create a potential nightmare for each advisor and contributor. Please do you part to alleviate this situation so that we can retain them on our board and in turn pass their experience and knowledge on to you.

Alabama

Dole, Pat
Editor of *The Glaze*
P.O. Box 4782 Birmingham, 35206; 205-833-9853. Specializing in Purinton pottery

Luckey, Carl
Carl F. Luckey Communications
R.R. 4, Box 301, Lingerlost Tr., Killen, 35645. Freelance writer specializing in art, antiques, and collectibles, no telephone calls will be accepted

Arizona

Ellwood, J.M.
7077 E. Main #4, Scottsdale, 85251; 800-435-0455 and 602-947-9679. Specializing in cast iron banks, toys, irons, trivets, doorstops and misc. cast iron

Kielsmeier, Wayne B.
Covington Fine Arts Gallery, Inc.
4951 E. Grant, Rd. 107, Tucson, 85712; 602-326-6111. Specializing in 19th- and 20th-Century American and European art pottery, paintings, prints, watercolors

Arkansas

Gifford, David Edwin
Arkansas Pottery Research
12 Normandy Rd., Little Rock, 72207; 501-664-2846. Historian/author/collector of Arkansas art pottery from 1905 to 1932. Seeking all information and company literature on the Ouachita Pottery, Niloak Pottery, and Camark Pottery companies as well as quality pieces marked 'Ouachita Hot Springs, Niloak Patent Pend'G, LeCamark or Hywood Art Pottery,' will answer queries — LSASE please

Hall, Doris and Burdell
B&B Antiques
P.O. Box 1501, Fairfield Bay, 72088 or 210 W. Sassafras Dr., Morton, IL 61550. Authors of *Morton's Potteries: 99 Years*. Specializing in Morton pottery, American dinnerware, early American pattern glass, historical items, small primitives

Musgrave, Marge
Look Nook Antiques
R.R. 3, Box 352, Mountain Home, 72653; 501-499-5283. Specializing in art glass and colored Victorian glass

Schmidgall, Bob and Judy
Dr. Bob's Antiques
R.R. 1, Box 328, Arkadelphia, 71923; 501-246-2720. Specializing in Depression Glass

Toohey, Marlena
405 Beaconfield, Sherwood, 72116; 501-834-1033. Specializing in black glass

Whysel, Steven
Antique & Art Galleries
101 N. Main, Bentonville, 72712; 501-273-7770. Specializing in Art Nouveau, full line, books and art

Yohe, Darlene
Timberview Antiques
P.O. Box 343, Stuttgart, 72160; 501-673-3437. Specializing in American pattern glass, historical glass, Victorian pattern glass, carnival glass, and custard glass

California

Baker, Mrs. Lillian
15237 Chanera Ave., Gardena, 90249; 213-329-2619. Author Collector Books on antique, collectible, and high-fashion costume jewelry, hatpins and hatpin holders, miniatures

Baker, Roger
Baker's Lady Luck Emporium
Box 620417, Woodside, 94062. Specializing in Saloon Americana — advertising, gambling, bar bottles, cigar lighters, match safes, bowie knives, dirks, daggers, cowboy hats, spurs, chaps, saddles, barber items: bottles, shaving mugs, razors

Benjamin, Scott
2616 Via Madalena, Lancaster, 93535; 805-946-0075. Specializing in gasoline pump globes

Bradshaw, Tom
325 Carol Dr., Ventura, 93003; 805-653-2723 or 310-450-6486. Specializing in antique Bohemian glass

Brooks, Mike
7335 Skyline, Oakland, 94611; 510-339-1751. Specializing in typewriters, early televisions, Statue of Liberty

Butz, Robert C.
Collector's Wedgwood
P.O. Box 462, Newbury Park, 91319; 805-496-7805. Specializing in Wedgwood

Carter, Tina M.
882 S. Mollison, El Cajon, 92020; 619-440-5043. Specializing in teapots, tea-related items, tea tins, children's and toy tea sets, coffeepots, etc.

Chamberlain, Jackie
P.O. Box 594, La Canada, 91012-0594; 818-790-5416. Specializing in holiday collectibles, antique reference books, teddy bears, pewter ice cream molds

Chipman, Jack
California Spectrum
Box 1429, Redondo Beach, 90278. Specializing in California ceramics; author of *Collector's Encyclopedia of California Pottery*, autographed copies available from author for $24.95+$3.50 postage & handling+ (CA) tax of $2.35

Cobabe, John
John Cobabe Antiques
1874 S. Pacific Coast Hwy. #225, Redondo Beach, 90277; 213-373-9956. Specializing in European glass and pottery

Cohen, Wilfred and Dolli
Antiques & Art Glass
P.O. Box 27151, Santa Ana, 92799; 714-545-5673. Specializing in Wave Crest (C.F. Monroe), Victorian era art and pattern glass, shakers, toothpick holders, Moorcroft pottery, art and pattern glass biscuit jars, burmese glass

Ehrhard, J. David
Psycho-Ceramic Restorations
1336 Sutherland St., Los Angeles, 90026; 213-481-3956. Specializing in restoration of ceramics, collects Susie Cooper and British pottery

Enge, Delleen
Franciscan Dinnerware Matching Service
323 E. Matilija, Ste. 112, Ojai, 93023

Escoe, Adrienne S.
Glass Knife Collector's Club
P.O. Box 342, Los Alamitos, 90720; 213-430-6479. Specializing in glass knives

Gibson, Pat
38280 Guava Dr., Newark, 94560; 510-792-0586. Specializing in R.A. Fox

Harris, Warren D.
6130 Rampart Dr., Carmichael, 95608; 916-966-3490. Specializing in decorative (non-advertising) thermometers

Howard, Steve
101 1st St., Suite 404, Los Altos, 94022; 510-484-4488. Specializing in antique American firearms, bowie knives, Western Americana, old advertising and vintage gambling items

Johnson, Patricia A.
Box 1221, Torrance, 90505. Specializing in open salts

Kreider, Katherine
Kingsbury Productions
4555 N. Pershing Ave., Suite 33-138, Stockton, 95207; 209-467-8438. Specializing in Valentines

Long, Earnest and Ida
Long's Americana
P.O. Box 90, Mokelumne Hill, 95245; 209-286-1348. Specializing in children's items: toys, banks, games, etc.; publishers of *Dictionary of Toys, Vol. I & II*; *Dictionary of Still Banks*; and *Penny Lane*, a history of antique mechanical toy banks

MacKie, Jim and Linda
P.O. Box 1419, Soquel, 95073; 408-475-8049. Specializing in all advertising and (Linda's specialty) early lithography citrus and cigar labels

Maurer, Oveda L.
Oveda Maurer Antiques
34 Greenfield Ave., San Anselmo, 94960; 415-454-6439. Specializing in 18th-Century and early 19th-Century American furniture, lighting, pewter, and hearthware

Muller, Jerry
Museum Graphics
P.O. Box 10743, Costa Mesa, 92627; 714-540-0808. Specializing in original comic strips, magazine cartoons, and animation art

Nelson, Maxine
873 Marigold Ct., Carlsbad, 92009. Specializing in Vernon Kilns

Pardini, Dick
3107 N. El Dorado St., Dept. SAPG, Stockton, 95204-3412; 209-466-5550 (recorder may answer). Specializing in California Perfume Company items: buyer and information center. Not interested in items that have Avon or Anniversary Keepsake markings. California Perfume Company offerings must be accompanied by a photo, Xerox copy, or sketching along with a condition report and most important — price wanted. Inquiries require large SASE; not necessary if offering items for sale

Pulati, Evalene
National Valentine Collectors Association
P.O. Box 1404, Santa Ana, 92702; 714-547-1355. Specializing in Valentines and love tokens

Ringering, David
Belle Ringer Antiques
1509 Wilson Terrace, Glendale, 91206; 818-241-8469. Specializing in Rowland & Marsellus, Royal Fenton, Bawo & Dotter, A.C. Bosselman & Co., souvenir china. Feel free to contact David if you have any questions about Rowland & Marsellus china. He will be happy to share any information he has.

Sanford, Steve and Martha
230 Harrison Ave., Campbell, 95088; 408-978-8408. Specializing in Brush McCoy

Shrader, Fred and Lila
Shrader Antiques
2025 Hwy. 199, Crescent City, 95531; 707-458-3525. Specializing in railroad, steamship and other transportation memorabilia; Shelley and select Americana

Stella's Collectibles
Memory Lanes Antique Mall
2451 Frampton St., Harbor City, 90710; Westchester Fair Mall & Farmer's Market Showcase Gallery in Los Angeles; d'Anthony's Antiques and Collectibles, 120 ½ N. Main St., Lake Elsinore, 310-316-7198. Specializing in quality glass and china, paperweights, figurines, plates, jewelry

Yronwode, Catherine
6632 Covey Rd., Forestville, 95436; 707-887-2424. Specializing in pre-1950 collectible plastic

Zeder, Audrey
6755 Coralite St. S, Long Beach, 90808. (Appointment only). Specializing in British Royal Commemorative Souvenirs (mail-order catalog available). Author (Wallace-Homestead) of *British Royal Commemoratives*

Canada

Brown, David L.
Stevengraph Collectors Assn.
2103-2829 Arbutus Rd., Victoria, British Columbia, V8N 5X5; 604-477-9896. Specializing in Stevengraphs

Melis, Mirko
Marcelle Antiques
4589 Longmoor Rd., Mississauga, Ontario, L5M 4H4; 416-820-8066. Specializing in American and European art glass, Russian works of art (enamels, porcelains, silver, etc.), English and Continental glass and china, member of Antique Appraisal Association of America, Inc.

Warner, Ian
P.O. Box 44, Brampton, Ontario, L6V 2K7. Specializing in Wade porcelain and Swankyswigs, author of *The World of Wade*, Co-author: Mike Posgay

Colorado

Carlton, Carol and Jim
8115 S. Syracuse St., Englewood, 80112; 303-773-8616. Specializing in Broadmoor and Coors pottery

Heck, Carl
Carl Heck Decorative Arts
Box 8416, Aspen, 81612; 303-925-8011. Specializing in antique stained, beveled glass, and Tiffany windows; leaded and reverse-painted lamps, Tiffany and French Cameo lamps

Mackin, Bill
Author of *Cowboy and Gunfighter Collectibles*; available from author. P.O. Box 70, Meeker, 81641, clothbound: $29.95, paperback: $19.95; 303-878-4525. Specializing in old and fine spurs, guns, gun leather, cowboy gear, Western Americana (Collection in the Museum of Northwest Colorado, Craig)

Over, Naomi L.
8909 Sharon Lane, Arvada, 80002; 303-424-5922. Specializing in ruby glassware

Winther, Jo Ellen
8449 W. 75th Way, Arvada, 80005; 800-872-2345 or 303-421-2371. Specializing in Coors

Connecticut

Bondhus, Sandra V.
Box 100, Unionville, 06085; 203-678-1808. Author of *Quimper Pottery: A French Folk Art Faience*; specializing in Quimper pottery

Caplovich, Judd
56 Risley Rd., Vernon, 06066; 203-872-7894. Specializing in antique typewriters, sewing machines, telephones, cameras, photos and ephemera, calculators, the unusual

Harned, Denise
P.O. Box 330373, Elmwood, 06133-0373. Author of *Griswold Cast Collectibles*. Specializing in Griswold cast iron and aluminum

Kilbride, Mrs. Richard J.
81 Willard Terrace, Stamford, 06903; 203-322-0568. Has available for sale: *Art Deco Chrome, The Chase Era*, and *Art Deco Chrome, Book 2, A Collector's Guide, Industrial Design in the Chase Era*

MacSorley, Earl
823 Indian Hill Rd., Orange, 06477; 203-387-1793. Specializing in nutcrackers, Bessie Pease Gutmann prints, figural spittoons

Rivera, Ted
Box 163, Torrington, 06790; 203-489-4325. Specializing in inkwells and inkstands; co-author of *Inkstands and Inkwells: A Collector's Guide*

Roenigk, Martin
Mechantiques
26 Barton Hill, E. Hampton, 06424; 203-267-8682. Specializing in mechanical musical instruments, music boxes, band organs, etc.

Thalberg, Bruce
Mountain View Dr., Weston, 06883; 203-227-8175. Specializing in canes and walking sticks: novelty, carved, and Black

Thompson, Roy M., Jr.
Southern Folk Pottery Collectors' Society
1224 Main St., Glastonbury, 06033; 203-633-3121

Van Deusen, Hobart
28 the Green, Watertown, 06795. Specializing in Canton, SASE required when requesting information

Vuono, Mark
306 Mill Rd., Stamford, 06903; 203-329-8744. Specializing in historical flasks, blown 3-mold glass, blown American glass

Delaware

Davis, Patricia M.
700 Greenhill Ave., Wilmington, 19805; 302-658-2992

District of Columbia

Durham, Ken and Jackie
(By appointment)
909 26 St. N.W., Washington, DC 20037; 202-338-1342. Specializing in counter-top arcade machines, trade stimulators, and vending machines; publish *Coin-Op Newsletter*, 16-page illustrated list: $2; Send SASE for free list of books on coin-operated machines

England

Pedel, Alan
Collectibles from England
Marwood Lee, Barnstaple, Devon, EX31 4EB; 011-44-271-75166 (anytime). Specializing in pie birds and most other collectibles

The Crested China Company
Station House, Driffield, E. Yorkshire, Y0257PY; 44-377-47042. Specializing in Goss and other souvenir china; illustrated sales catalogs

Florida

Archer, Dick and Ellie
Antiques
419 Sevilla Dr., St. Augustine, 32086; 904-797-4678. Specializing in Victorian silverplate: figurals, fancy hollow ware, and collectibles

Bettinger, Robert
P.O. Box 333, Mt. Dora, 32757; 904-343-1393. Specializing in American art pottery

deCourtivron, Gael
Cocaholics
4811 Remington Dr., Sarasota, 34234; 813-351-1560. Specializing in Coca-Cola memorabilia. Cocaholics hot line: 813-355-2652 (COLA)

Dodds, Rebecca
Silver Flute
Box 39644, Ft. Lauderdale, 33339. Specializing in jewelry

Donnelly, Ron
Saturday Heroes
Box 7047, Panama City Beach, 32413. Specializing in Big Little Books, movie posters, premiums, western heroes, character collectibles, Gone with the Wind

France, Madeleine
P.O. Box 15555, Ft. Lauderdale, 33318; 305-584-0009. Specializing in top-quality perfume bottles: Rene Lalique, Steuben, Czechoslovakian, DeVilbiss, Baccarat, Commercials

Harry, Pauline
Pauline Harry Paper Collectables
11493 Spring Hill Dr., Spring Hill, 34609; 904-686-9418. Specializing in pinups, illustrators, Rockwell, Leyendecker, etc., old magazines

Hess, Steve
Confederate Swords
P.O. Box 3476; Deland, 32723; 904-254-1809 or 904-736-1067. Specializing in Confederate swords

Hudson, Hardy
Our Antiques Market
5453 Lake Howell Rd., Winter Park, 32792. Specializing in majolica, American art pottery

Lawrence, Judy and Cliff
1169 Overcash Dr., Dunedin, 34698; 813-734-4742. Specializing in fountain pens and mechanical pencils

Linscott, Jacqueline
3557 Nicklaus Dr., Titusville, 32780. Specializing in Blue Bell paperweights; author of *Blue Bell Paperweights*, complete with history, illustrations, and price guide; Available from author for $7 (including postage and handling)

Linscott, Len
Line Jewels
3557 Nicklaus Dr., Titusville, 32780. Specializing in glass insulators (SASE required); Hosted (with wife, Jacqueline) the 23rd National Insulator Association's Convention, Show, and Sale held in Orlando

McNerney, Kathryn
502 Kettering Way, Orange Park, 32073. Author (Collector Books) on blue and white stoneware, primitives, tools

Parker, Alton B.
Box 110, 5030 W. 14 St., Bradenton, 34207; 813-756-0386. Specializing in Azalea china, Depression Glass, Roseville pottery

Supnick, Mark
8524 N.W. 2 St., Coral Springs, 33065; 305-755-3448. Author of *Collecting Hull Pottery's Little Red Riding Hood*. Specializing in American pottery

White, Douglass
Classic Interiors & Antiques
2144 Edgewater Dr., Orlando, 32804; 407-841-6681. Specializing in Fulper, other American art pottery

Georgia

Bailey, Wayne and Gale
P.O. Box 173, Dacula, 30211; 404-963-5736. Specializing in Goebels (Friar Tuck, Santa Claus, Toby pitchers by Goebel)

Glenn, Walter
Geode Ltd.
3393 Peachtree Rd., Atlanta, 30326; 404-261-9346. Specializing in Frankart

Joiner, John R.
245 Ashland Trail, Tyrone, 30290; 404-487-3732. Specializing in commercial aviation collectibles

Idaho

Beeks, D.R.
P.O. Box 2515, Coeur d'Alene 83814; 208-667-0830. Specializing in instruments of early science, technology, and medicine. Also surveying instruments, microscopes

Illinois

Ammelounx, Andre
The Stein Auction Company
P.O. Box 136, Palatine, 60078; 708-991-5927 or (Fax) 708-991-5947. Specializing in steins

Brinkley, Wm. J.
Brinkley Galleries
401 S. Washington Ave., McLeansboro, 62859. Specializing in Meissen, Dresden, European porcelains, American porcelains (Cybis)

Broom, Jim
Box 65, Effingham, 62401. Specializing in opalescent pattern glassware

Courter, J.W.
R.R. 1, Simpson, 62985; 618-949-3884. Specializing in Aladdin lamps; Author of *Aladdin — The Magic Name in Lamps*, softbound, 180 pages; and *Aladdin Electric Lamps*, hardbound, 154 pages

Danis, John
11028 Raleigh Ct., Rockford, 61111; 815-963-0757 or (Fax) 815-877-6042. Specializing in R. Lalique

Feinblatt, Maurice
Wilmette Porcelain Shop
3207 Lake Ave., Wilmette, 60091; 708-251-1170. Specializing in Lladro (since 1973), finer American and European porcelain figurines, western and Art Nouveau bronze recasts

Frizzell, Doris
Doris' Dishes
16 Oakdale Dr., Springfield, 62707; 217-529-3873. Specializing in Royal Haeger, American china and pottery, Depression Glass, co-author (Collector Books) of Royal Haeger book.

Garmon, Lee
1529 Whittier St., Springfield, 62704; 217-789-9574. Specializing in Royal Haeger, Royal Hickman, glass animals; co-author (Collector Books) of *Glass Animals and Figural Flower Frogs of the Depression Era*, co-author (Collector Books) of *Royal Haeger* book.

Griffith, Woody
4107 White Ash Rd., Crystal Lake, 60014; 815-459-7808. Specializing in Jewel Tea, Noritake, Hall

Grist, Everett
3417 Dewitt, Mattoon, 61938. Specializing in marbles

Hall, Doris and Burdell
B&B Antiques
210 W. Sassafras Dr., Morton, 61550 or P.O. Box 1501, Fairfield Bay, AR 72088. Authors of *Morton's Potteries: 99 Years*; specializing in Morton pottery, American dinnerware, early American pattern glass, historical items, small primitives

Haussmann, Richard A., Past President, Aurora Historical Society
Aurora, 60507

Hilst, Randy
1221 Florence #4, Pekin, 61554; 309-346-2710. Specializing in old fishing tackle, duck and goose calls

Hoffmann, Pat and Don, Sr.
1291 N. Elmwood Dr., Aurora, 60506; 312-859-3435. Authors of *Warwick, A to W*, a supplement to *Why Not Warwick? China Collector's Guide*; specializing in Warwick china

The Home Place Antiques
Durham, William; Galaway, William
9633 Beaver Valley Rd., Belvidere, 61008; 815-547-5128. Specializing in Tea Leaf ironstone, and white ironstone

Hooks, Dee
Dee's China Shop
Box 142, Lawrenceville, 62439; 618-943-2741. Specializing in R.S. Prussia, Royal Bayreuth, Haviland, other fine china

Hurney, George and Mary
Glass Connection (mail-order only)
312 Babcock Dr., Palatine, 50067; 708-359-3839. Specializing in Depression Glass

Long, Dee
112 S. Center, Lacon, 61540. Specializing in reamers

Lotton, Charles
Specializing in Lotton art glass; co-author of *Lotton Art Glass*, a comprehensive study with 96 color pages and current values; available from Antique Publications, P.O. Box 553, Marietta, OH, 45750

Miller, Larry; and Strickfaden, Dick
218 Devron Circle, E. Peoria, 61611. Specializing in German and Czechoslovakian Erphila

Owen, Larry & Sally
Specializing in Morten Studio dogs, etc.

Pollack, Frank and Barbara
(Appointment only)
1214 Green Bay Rd., Highland Park, 60035; 708-433-2213. Specializing in American country antiques and art

Randy's Ol' Time Collectibles
Hilst, Randy
1811 Broadway, Pekin, 61554; 309-347-5873. Specializing in outdoor collectibles and general line

Rastello, Lisa
Milkweed Antiques
5N531 Ancient Oak Lane, St. Charles, 60175; 708-377-4612. Specializing in Depression-era collectibles

Rhoden, Joan and Charles
Memories/Rhoden's Antiques
605 N. Main, Georgetown, 61846; 217-662-8046. Specializing in Heisey and other Elegant Glassware, general line antiques. Co-authors of *Those Wonderful Yard-Long Prints and More*, an illustrated value guide

Rodrick, Tammy
Stacey's Treasures
R.R. 2, Box 163, Sumner, 62466; 618-947-2240. Specializing in antiques and collectibles

Spencer, Dick
Glass and More (shows only)
1203 N. Yale, O'Fallon, 62269; 618-632-9067. Specializing in Cambridge, Fenton, Fostoria, Heisey, etc.

Spiess, Greg
230 E. Washington, Joliet, 60433; 815-722-5639. Specializing in Odd Fellows lodge items

Thomsen, Barry
P.O. Box 7066, Westchester, 60154; 708-409-0909. Specializing in cookie jars

Weldi, Frank John
1736 W. Farragut Ave., Chicago, 60640; 312-728-7750. Specializing in American and European art pottery, fine glass, designer collectibles

Weldi-Skinner, Mary
1656 W. Farragut Ave., Chicago, 60640. Specializing in American and European art pottery, designer collectibles

Wells, Rosalie J. 'Rosie'
R.R. 1S, Canton, 61520; 1-800-445-8745. Publishes magazines and annual price guides for Precious Moments Collectibles, Hallmark Ornament Collectibles, Lowell Davis Collectibles, and others! She has hosted the International Convention for Precious Moments Collectors each year since 1984 and hosts the Annual Midwest Collectibles Fest. Write for free literature.

Indiana

Bingaman, Drue
Glenwood
Specializing in Depression Glass and Depression-era dinnerware

Blann, Dale
Vice President of Uhl Collectors' Society, R.R. 1, Box 136, Wheatland, 47597; 812-321-4141. Contact for membership and newsletter information

Blocher, Bob and Debbie
The Antiquarian, Webb's Mall Centerville. Specializing in designer costume jewelry

Boram, Clifford
Antique Stove Information Clearinghouse
Monticello; Phone calls only: 219-583-6465

Cooper, Virgle E.
Cooper's Antiques
Muncie, 47303; 317-289-5172

Edwards, Bill
620 W. 2nd St., Madison 47250. Author (Collector Books) on Carnival Glass

Ervin, Mark A.
P.O. Box 40017, Ft. Wayne, 46804; 219-432-6821. Specializing in Weller Coppertone

Fred, James A.
Antique Radio Labs
R.R. 1, Box 41, Cutler, 46920; 317-268-2214. Specializing in radios made from 1922 to 1950

Garrett, Jerry and Sandi
Jerry's Antiques (shows only)
1807 W. Madison St., Kokomo, 46901; 317-457-5256. Specializing in Greentown glass, old post cards

Haun, Ted
2426 N. 700 East, Kokomo, 46901; 317-628-3640. Specializing in American pottery and china, '50s items, Russel Wright designs

Heiss, Virginia
7777 N. Alton Ave., Indianapolis, 46268; 317-875-6797. Specializing in Muncie, AMACO, Brandt Steele, Marblehead, Kenton Hills

Jennings, Jenny
Futures (in Webbs Antique Mall)
Centerville, 47374; 317-962-9014. Specializing in lunch boxes, banks, and advertising collectibles

Keagy, William and June
P.O. Box 106, Bloomfield 47424; 812-384-3471. Co-authors of *Those Wonderful Yard-Long Prints and More*, an illustrated value guide

Logan, Frank; and Foster, Jerry
Border Line Fools
6724 Means Rd., Centerville, 47303; 317-855-3157. Specializing in fancy cast iron beds

Medd, Terrell
History Haven Antiques
317-825-7479. Specializing in granite, Tea Leaf ironstone, advertising

Michael, Robert L.
R&M Antiques
2789 E. Co. Rd. #67, Anderson, 46017-1858; 317-378-7821. Specializing in pottery, glass, furniture

Miller, Susan
606 E. Wabash Ave., Crawfordsville, 47933; 317-362-0352. Specializing in trolls

Old Storefront Antiques
P.O. Box 357, Dublin, 47335; 317-478-4809. Specializing in country store items, tins, primitives, pharmaceuticals, advertising, etc. Active in mail order with catalogs available. Information requires LSASE

Percell, Ron
Webb's Antiques Mall
106 E. Main St., Centerville, 47330; 317-855-5733 or 317-855-5551. Specializing in folk art and country collectibles

Prentice, Wade
P.O. Box 5100, Ft. Wayne, 46895; 219-484-4863

Robinson Furniture, Antiques, & Coins
9 S. Market St., Liberty, 47353; 317-458-5264. Specializing in art glass

Rough, James
739 W. 5th, Marion, 46953; 317-662-6126. Specializing in art glass, paintings, art pottery

Scowden, Virgil
303 Lincoln, Williamsport, 47993; 317-762-3408 or 317-762-3178. Antiques museum, general line, tours

Slater, Thomas D.
The Political Gallery
1325 W. 86th St., Indianapolis, 46260; 317-257-0863. Specializing in political and sports memorabilia

Stapp, Charles Dennis
7037 Haynes Rd., Georgetown, 47122. Specializing in jack knives, hunting knives, military knives, straight and safety razors

Stofft, Marvin and Jeanette
Marnette Antiques
Tell City, 47586; 812-547-5707. Specializing in Ohio art pottery, buy and sell

Thomas, Roy R.
Common Sense Antiques
(shows or appointment)
23808 Couden Rd., Noblesville, 46060; 317-984-4617. Specializing in American antiques and folk art in original finish

Thompson, Matt and Susie
Farmers Pride
527 W. County Rd., 500 South, New Castle, 47362; 317-987-7935. Specializing in police and other badges, militaria, antique ammunition, general line

Vanderbilt, Duane and Janice
4040 West Over Dr., Indianapolis, 46268; 317-875-8932. Authors (Collector Books) of *Collector's Guide to Shawnee Pottery*

Webb's Antique Mall
Over 400 Quality Dealers
200 W. Union St., Centerville, 47330

Iowa

Addy, Geneva D.
Winterset, 50273; 515-462-3027

Arnbal, Una
Woodland Antiques
236 Trail Ridge Rd., Ames, 50010; 515-292-1005. Specializing in china, glass, Lomonosov figurines

DeGood, Hal and Meredith
The Baggage Car
513 Elm St., West Des Moines, 50265; 515-225-3070. Specializing in Hallmark collectibles; publishers of *Hallmark* newsletter

Devine, Dennis; Norman; and Joe
D&D Antique Mall, 1411 3rd St., Council Bluffs, 51503; 712-323-5233 or 712-328-7305. Specializing in furniture, phonographs, collectibles, general line. Joe Devine: Royal Copley collector

Jaarsma, Ralph
De Pelikaan Antieks
812 Washington St., c/o Red Ribbon Antique Mall, Pella, 50219. Specializing in Dutch antiques

Lippa, Matt; & Schaaf, Elizabeth Artisans
P.O. Box 4902, Davenport, 52808; 319-326-0342. Specializing in folk art, quilts, painted and folky furniture, tramp art, whirligigs, windmill weights

Morris, Dave and Sue
P.O. Box 708, Mason City, 50401. Specializing in Watt pottery; authors of *Watt Pottery — An Identification and Price Guide*; also available: *Watt's News* newsletter. Subscription: $10 per year

Nichols, Harold J.
632 Agg, Ames, 50010; 515-292-9167. Author of *McCoy Cookie Jars from the First to the Last*. Specializing in Roseville, Weller, McCoy

Picek, Louis
Main Street Antiques
110 W. Main St., Box 340, West Branch, 52358. Specializing in folk art, country Americana, the unusual

Kansas

McCormick, John and Marilyn
P.O. Box 3174, Shawnee, 66203; 913-441-0793. Specializing in Gonder pottery

Robison, Joleen A.
502 Lindley Dr., Lawrence, 66044. Author (Collector Books) on advertising dolls

Sandler, Miles
Maundy International Watches
P.O. Box 13028-SA, Overland Park, 66212; 1-800-235-2866. Specializing in watches — antique pocket and vintage wristwatches

Tinsley, Rosella
105 15th St., Osawatomie, 66064; 913-755-3237. Specializing in primitives, kitchen, farm, woodenware, and misc.

Winslow, Ralph
9905 Lee Blvd., Leawood, 66206. Specializing in Dryden and Shramberg pottery

Kentucky

Florence, Gene
Box 7186H, Lexington, 40522. Author (Collector Books) on Depression Glass, Occupied Japan, Elegant Glass, Baseball Cards

Johnson, Wes
1725 Dixie Hwy., Box 169001, Louisville, 40256-0001. Specializing in Cracker Jack: toys, point of sale, packages, etc.; Checkers Confection, Schoenhut toys, Victor Toy Oats, Universal Theatre (Chicago), toys

Willis, Roy M.
Heartland of Kentucky Decanters and Steins
P.O. Box 428, Lebanon Jct., 40150; 502-833-2827. Specializing in most brands of decanters, domestic beer steins, and advertising; open showroom. Include large self-addressed stamped envelope with correspondence

Louisiana

Decker, Dorothy B. and Wade N.
Dottie's Antiques (shows only)
P.O. Box 1141, St. Francisville, 70775; 504-635-3284. Specializing in Elegant and Depression Glass

Maine

Hathaway, John
Hathaway's Antiques
Upper Main St., Bryant Pond, 04219; 207-665-2124. Specializing in fruit jars; mail order a specialty

Rinaldi, John
Nautical Antiques and Related Items
Box 765, Dock Square, Kennebunkport, 04046; 207-967-3218. Specializing in nautical antiques, 19th- & 20th-Century American paintings

Maryland

Banks, Robert
18901 Gold Mine Court, Brookeville, 20833. Specializing in American flags of historical significance and exceptional design

Dennis & George Collectibles
O'Brien, Dennis; and Goehring, George
3407 Lake Montebello Dr., Baltimore, 21218; 301-889-3964. Specializing in upright pocket tobacco tins, advertising items, character collectibles, unusual items

Greenberg, Bruce C., Ph. D.
Greenberg Publishing Company, Inc.
7566 Main St., Sykesville, 21784. Specializing in toy trains; author and publisher of comprehensive publications on Lionel, American Flyer, and Ives trains

Gunther's International Auction Gallery
P.O. Box 235, 24 S. Virginia Ave., Brunswick, 21716; 301-834-7101 or 800-274-8779. Specializing in political, Oriental rugs, bronzes, art, antiques, and the unusual

Humphrey, George C.
4932 Prince George Ave., Beltsville, 20705; 301-937-7899. Specializing in John Rogers groups

Screen, Harold and Joyce
2804 Munster Rd., Baltimore, 21234; 410-661-6765. Specializing in soda fountain 'tools of the trade' and paper: catalogs, *Soda Fountain* magazine, etc.

Massachusetts

Adams, Charles and Barbara
Middleboro, 02346; 508-947-7277. Specializing in Bennington (brown only)

Carver, Mrs. Sally S.
179 South St., Chestnut Hill, 02167; 617-469-9175. Author of *The American Postcard Guide to Tuck;* columnist for *Hobbies; Collector's News; Postcard Collector; Antique Trader Price Guide.* Specializing in all better-quality antique pre-1930 postcards; does not accept consignment material; SASE required with correspondence (questions must be specific); phone calls: M-F, 12 noon to 6 p.m. EST only

Frei, Peter and Sandra
P.O. Box 500, Brimfield, 01010; 1-800-942-8968. Specializing in sewing machines, adding machines, and hand-powered vacuum cleaners; SASE required with correspondence

Hess, John A.
Fine Photographic Americana
P.O. Box 3062, Andover, 01810; 508-470-0327. Specializing in 19th-Century photography

Longo, Paul J.
Paul Longo Americana
Box 490, Chatham Rd., South Orleans, Cape Cod, 02662; 508-255-5482. Specializing in political pins, ribbons, banners, autographs, old stocks and bonds, baseball and sports memorabilia of all types

MacLean, Dale
Dale's
593 High St., Dedham, 02026; 617-326-3010. Specializing in Dedham pottery

Morin, Albert
668 Robbins Ave. #23
Dracut, 01826; 508-454-7907. Specializing in misc. Akro Agate and Westite

Owings, K.C., Jr.
Antiques Americana
Box 19, N. Abington, 02351; 617-857-1655. Specializing in Civil War, Revolutionary War, autographs, documents, books, antiques

Rudisill, John and Barbara
Rudisill's Alt Print Haus
3 Lakewood, Medfield, 02052; 508-359-2261. Specializing in Currier and Ives

Vigue, Norm and Cathy
62 Bailey St., Stoughton, 02072; 617-344-5441. Buying and selling TV, western, and comic character collectibles

Wellman, BA
#106 Cordaville Rd., Ashland, 01721-1002. Specializing in Ceramic Arts Studio and Pennsbury pottery; price guide and videotape identification guides available

Michigan

Brown, Rick
Newspaper Collectors Society of America
Box 19134-S, Lansing, 48901; 517-372-8381 or (Fax) 517-485-9115. Specializing in newspapers

Estes, Linda
Estes Antique Mall
116 & 118 S. Lane, Blissfield, 49228; 517-486-4616. Specializing in oak furniture, cookie jars, trains, old toys, and misc.

Gunsaulus, Jack
Gray's Gallery/Jack's Corner Bookstore
583 W. Ann Arbor Trail, Plymouth, 48170; 313-455-2373. Specializing in porcelain, glass, jewelry, books

Haas, Norman
264 Clizbe Rd., Quincy, 49082; 517-639-8537. Specializing in American art pottery

Marsh, Linda K.
1229 Gould Rd., Lansing, 48917. Specializing in Degenhart glass

Nedry, Boyd W.
728 Buth Dr., Comstock Park, 49321; 616-784-1513. Specializing in traps and trap-related items

Newbound, Betty
4567 Chadsworth, Commerce, 48382. Author (Collector Books) on Blue Ridge dinnerware. Specializing in collectible china and glass

Nickel, Mike
A Nickel's Worth
P.O. Box 456, Portland, 48875; 517-647-7646. Specializing in Roseville, Weller, Rookwood and other important American art pottery, Venetian/Murano glass, Art Deco

O'Callaghan, Tim
46878 Betty Hill, Plymouth, 48170; 313-459-4636. Specializing in dime store soldiers, also Ford Motor Co., and 'Old Ironsides' (USS Constitution) memorabilia

Osentoski, Randy
Lane St. Antiques
106 S. Lane St., Blissfield, 49228; 517-486-4243; Specializing in toys, advertising, coin-operated machines, furniture, and misc.

Oates, Joan
685 S. Washington, Constantine, 49042; 616-435-8353. Specializing in Phoenix Bird chinaware

Ricker, Dawn V.
39145 Marne, Sterling Heights, 48313; 313-566-0891. Schafer & Vater collector

Roscoe, Mike; Smith, Fred
Lane St. Antiques
106 S. Lane St., Blissfield, 49228; 517-486-4243; Specializing in toys, advertising, coin-operated machines, furniture, and misc.

Minnesota

Anderson, James
Box 12704, New Brighton, 55112; 612-484-3198. Specializing in old fishing lures and reels, also tackle catalogs, posters, calendars

Gallagher, Jerry
420 1st Ave. N.W., Plainview, 55964; 507-534-3511. Specializing in Morgantown research; matching service for Morgantown, Heisey, Fostoria, Cambridge, Duncan, and Tiffin. Publisher of Morgantown 1931 Catalog Reprint, Morgantown Colors Placard, and *The Morgantown Newscaster,* quarterly journal of the Morgantown Collectors of America, Inc. (subscription: $15 per year)

Harriman, John
1900 Hennepin, Minneapolis, 55403; 612-872-0226. Specializing in Battersea (English enamel) boxes

Ketcham, Steve
Steve Ketcham Antiques (shows and mail order only)
Box 24114, Edina, 55424; 612-920-4205. Specializing in early American bottles, stoneware, advertising

Podpeskar, Doug
624 Jones St., Eveleth, 55734-1631; 218-744-4854. Specializing in Red Wing dinnerware

Schoneck, Steve
20th Century Art & Design
P.O. Box 56, Newport, 55055; 612-459-2980. Specializing in American art pottery, Arts & Crafts, Handicraft Guild of Minneapolis

Missouri

Bosworth, Dick and Waunita
Kansas City Trade Winds
7307 N.W. 75th St., Kansas City, 64152. Specializing in American art pottery, Parrish prints, art glass

International Rose O'Neill Club
Contact Karen Stewart
P.O. Box 668, Branson, 65616. Dues: $7 (single) or $10 (family) includes newsletter *Kewpiesta Kourier*, published quarterly

Old World Antiques
1715 Summit, Kansas City, 64108
Branch Location: 4436 State Line Rd., Kansas City 66103. Specializing in 18th- and 19th-Century furniture, paintings, accessories, clocks, medical and scientific instruments, chandeliers, sconces, Sabino, and much more

Rhoades, Evelyn
7818 N.E. 54th St., Kansas City, 64119; 816-453-7169. Specializing in Jewel Tea 'Autumn Leaf,' Franciscan dinnerware

Roberts, Brenda
Country Side Antiques
R.R. 2, Marshall, 65340. Specializing in Hull pottery and general line. Author (Collector Books) on Hull pottery; SASE required

Scott, John and Peggy
Scotty's Antiques
4650 S. Leroy, Springfield, 65810; 417-887-2191. Specializing in Depression-era glassware and pottery

Smith, Pat
Independence
Author (Collector Books) of doll book series

Stratton, Bill
Blue Buds
1862 Boonville Ave., Springfield, 65803; 417-862-4212. Specializing in pottery and glassware

Wiesehan, Doug
D&R Farm Antiques
4535 Hwy. H, St. Charles, 63301. Specializing in salesman's samples and patent models, antique toys, farm toys, metal farm signs

Williams, Don
Kirksville 63501. Specializing in art glass

Woollard, D.D., Jr.
11614 Old St. Charles Rd., Bridgeton, 63044. Specializing in world's fair & exposition memorabilia

Nebraska

Larsen, Robert V.
3214 19th St., Columbus, 68601. Specializing in old hatpins and hatpin holders

Nevada

Sakach, Gary L.
S. & S.
316 California Ave., Suite 675, Reno, 89509; 702-825-4840. Specializing in fine American pottery and tiles

New Hampshire

Brenner, Larry
L. Brenner Antiques
1005 Chestnut St., Manchester, 03104; 603-625-8203. Specializing in Royal Bayreuth

Marden, Richard G.
Box 524, Elm St., Wolfeboro, 03894; 603-569-3209

Winston, Nancy
Willow Hollow Antiques
R.F.D. 1, Box 550, Northwood, 03261; 603-942-5739. Specializing in Shaker baskets, primitives, country smalls, paper Americana, toys

New Jersey

Adams, Jay
(Mail order only) 289 Pascack Rd., Washington Twp., 07675; 908-756-6229. Specializing in Depression-era china and glass

Bilane, John E.
(Mail order only, no shop) 2065 Morris Ave., Apt. 109, Union, 07083. Specializing in antique glass cup plates

Cole, Lillian M.
Editor of *Piebirds Unlimited* newsletter
14 Harmony School Rd., Flemington, 08822; 908-782-3198. Specializing in pie birds, pie funnels, pie vents

Litts, Elyce
P.O. Box 394, Morris Plains, 07950; 201-361-4087. Author (Collector Books) of *Collector's Encyclopedia of Geisha Girl Porcelain*

Perzel, Robert and Nancy
Popkorn
4 Mine St. (near Main St.), P.O. Box 1057, Flemington, 08822; 908-782-9631. Specializing in Stangl dinnerware, birds, and artware; Depression Glass

Poster, Harry
Vintage TV's
Box 1883, S. Hackensack, 07606; 201-794-9606 (before 7 p.m.). Publishes *TV/Deco Radio Price Guide*; Specializes in vintage TV's, unusual radios, 1950s items, view master

Rago, David
Box 3592, Station E, Trenton, 08629; 609-397-9374. Specializing in Arts & Crafts, American art pottery

Rosen, Barbara
6 Shoshone Trail, Wayne, 07470. Specializing in figural bottle openers and antique dollhouses

Steinfeld, Milt
633 Westfield Ave., Box 457, Westfield, 07091. Specializing in collectible glass and china, Victorian silverplate, and other small collectibles

Young, Art and Penni
P.O. Box 81, Little Falls, 07424; 201-785-8115. Specializing in Stevengraphs, police and fire badges, police collectibles, photographs

New Mexico

Nelson, Scott H.
Box 6081, Santa Fe, 87502. Specializing in African art

New York

Austin, Bruce A.
40 Selborne Chase, Fairport, 14450; 716-223-0711 (evenings); 716-475-2879 (days). Specializing in clocks and in Arts & Crafts furnishings and accessories

Batchelor, Daniel J.
R.D. 3, Box 10, Oswego, 13126. Specializing in Pairpoint, Handel, Bradley and Hubbard lamps

Calison, Jim
Tools of Distinction
Wallkill, 12589; 914-895-8035. Specializing in antique and collectible tools, buying and selling

Dimitroff, Thomas P.
Dimitroff's Antiques (appointment), 140 E. First St., Corning, 14830; 607-962-6745. Specializing in Steuben and cut glass

Doyle, Robert A.
Doyle Auctioneers & Appraisers
R.D. 3, 109 Osborne Hill Rd., Fishkill, 12524. Thousands of collectibles offered, call for free calendar of upcoming auctions

Fer-Duc Inc.
Ferrara, Joseph
Box 1303, Newburgh, 12550; 914-565-5990. Specializing in American art pottery (Ohr, Rookwood, Zanesville), 19th- and 20th-Century American paintings

Fishler, Stephen
Metropolis Comics
7 W. 18th St., New York City, 10011; 212-627-9691. Specializing in comic books, comic strip original art, and animation art

Forbes, Asa P.
225 Cleveland Ave.
Syracuse, 13208. Specializing in paper goods and general antiques and collectibles

Fox, Ron
TSACO (The Stein Auction Company) East 416 Throop St., N. Babylon, 11704; Telephone and Fax: 516-669-7232. Specializing in steins; auctions with illustrated catalogs and video tapes

Greguire, Helen
Helen's Antiques
103 Trimmer Rd., Hilton, 14468; 716-392-2704. Specializing in graniteware (any color), carnival glass lamps and shades, carnival glass lighting of all kinds; Author (Collector Books) of *The Collector's Encyclopedia of Graniteware, Colors, Shapes & Values*, available from author for $27.95 (including postage and handling); Second book on graniteware in progress. Also available from author is *Carnival in Lights*, featuring Carnival Glass, lamps, shades, etc., available for $11.95+$1.50 postage and handling

Herley, Patrick J.
P.O. Box 606, E. Setauket, 11733; 516-928-6052. Specializing in Goss china

Jordan, Ruth E.
Meridale, 13806; 607-746-2082. Specializing in cut glass, American Brilliant period

Laun, H. Thomas and Patricia
Little Century
215 Paul Ave., Syracuse, 13206; 315-437-4156 Summer residence: Box 69-A, Cape Vincent, 13618, 315-654-3244. Specializing in firefighting collectibles

Meisel, Louis K. and Susan P.;
Bonanno, Joann
Susan P. Meisel Decorative Arts Gallery
133 Prince St., New York City, 10012. Specializing in Clarice Cliff and 20th-Century designs in jewelry, watches, toys, unusual vintage bicycles, and quirky folk art objects

Michel, John and Barbara
Americana Blue
200 E. 78th St., 18E, New York City, 10021; 212-861-6094. Specializing in yellow ware and cast iron

Old China Patterns Limited
P.O. Box 290, Fineview, 13640; 800-525-7390 Ext. 125 or (Fax) 315-482-5827. Specializing in discontinued china dinnerware, matching service (since 1966); charter member I.A.D.M.

Owens, Lowell
Owens' Collectibles
12 Bonnie Ave., New Hartford, 13413. Specializing in beer advertising

Pisello, Faye
577 Lake St., Wilson, 14172. Specializing in Brownies by Palmer Cox

Rifken, Blume J.
Author of *Silhouettes in America — 1790-1840 — a Collector's Guide*. Specializing in American antique silhouettes from 1790 to 1840

Safir, Charlotte F.
1349 Lexington Ave., 9-B, New York City, 10128; 212-534-7933. Specializing in cookbooks, children's books (out-of-print only)

Schleifman, Roselle
Ed's Collectibles
16 Vincent Rd., Spring Valley, 10977; 914-356-2121. Specializing in Duncan & Miller

Steinbock, Nancy
Nancy Steinbock Posters & Prints
518-438-1577. Specializing in posters: travel, war, literary, advertising

Tuggle, Robert
105 W. St., New York City, 10023; 212-595-0514. Specializing in John Bennett, Anglo-Japanese china

Van Kuren, Jean and Dale
Ruth's Antiques, Inc.
9060 Main St., Clarence, 14031; 716-632-1630. Specializing in Buffalo pottery, general line

Van Patten, Joan F.
Box 102, Rexford, 12148. Author (Collector Books) of books on Nippon and Noritake

North Carolina

Degenhardt, Richard K.
Sugar Hollow Farm, 124 Cypress Point, Hendersonville, 28739; 704-696-9750. Author of *Belleek, The Complete Collectors' Guide and Illustrated Reference.* Specializing in Belleek (The only Belleek is the Irish. Established by legal action in 1929)

Kirtley, Charles E.
P.O. Box 2273, Elizabeth City, 27096; 919-335-1262. Specializing in monthly auctions and bid sales dealing with World's Fair, Civil War, political, advertising, and other American collectibles

Ricketts, Bill
Pepper's Deli
126 Cherry St., Black Mountain, 28711. Specializing in items advertising Dr. Pepper

Sayers, R.J.
Southeastern Antiques & Appraisals
P.O. Box 629, Brevard, 28712. Specializing in Boy Scout collectibles, Pisgah Forest pottery, primitive American furniture; Author of *Guide to Scouting Collectibles*, available from author for $19.95+$3.50 postage

North Dakota

Farnsworth, Bryce
1334 14½ St. South, Fargo, 58103. Specializing in Rosemeade pottery

Ohio

Adams, Walt and Linda
Adams Heirlooms
901 Haver Dr., Hicksville, 43526. Specializing in early blown, art, and pattern glass

Batt, Jim and Paulette
Larchmere Antiques
12204 Larchmere Blvd., Cleveland, 44120; 216-231-8181. Specializing in general antiques

Batory, Mr. Dana Martin
402 E. Bucyrus St., Crestline, 44827. Specializing in antique woodworking machinery, old and new woodworking machinery catalogs

Blair, Betty
Golden Apple Antiques
216 Bridge St., Jackson, 45640; 614-286-4817. Specializing in art pottery, Watt, cookie jars, chocolate molds, general line

Bowser, Dale R.
A Passion for Prussia
513-884-7342. Specializing in R.S. Prussia and related china

Briggs, Karen S.
Toledo. Specializing in glass, china, pottery

Budin, Nicki
Curio Cabinet
679 High St., Worthington, 43085; 614-885-1986. Specializing in Royal Doulton

China Specialties, Inc.
19238 Dorchester Circle, Strongsville, 44136; 216-238-2528. Specializing in Autumn Leaf

DeGenaro, Steve
P.O. Box 5662, Youngstown, 44505; 216-759-7151. Specializing in post-mortem photos, mourning collectibles

De Luca, Mary A.
Red Barn Antiques
5510 W. Lakeshore Dr., Port Clinton. 43452; 419-635-2045. Specializing in general line

Distel, Ginny
Distel's Antiques
4041 S.C.R. 22, Tiffin, 44883; 419-447-5832. Specializing in Tiffin glass

Ebner, Rita and John
Cracker Barrel Antiques
4540 Helen Rd., Columbus, 43232. Specializing in door knockers, cast iron bottle openers, doorstops, general line

Ferguson, Maxine
Wayside Antiques
2290 E. Pike, Zanesville, 43701. General line, furniture, dolls, pottery, glass

Forsythe, Ruth A.
Box 327, Galena, 43021. Author of *Made in Czechoslovakia*

Gooder, Mrs. Albert
1149 Spruce St., Sidney, 45365; 513-492-9618. Specializing in glassware

Graff, Shirley
4515 Grafton Rd., Brunswick, 44212. Specializing in Pennsbury pottery

Guenin, Tom
Box 454, Chardon, 44024. Specializing in antique telephones and antique telephone restoration

Hermes, Dianne
5664 W. Harbor Rd., Port Clinton, 43452; General line

Hothem, Lar
Hothem House
Box 458, Lancaster, 43130. Specializing in books about Indians and artifacts

Huffman, Mary
(Shows only) 3143 S. State Rd. 53, Tiffin, 44883; 419-447-5938. Specializing in glass, kitchen items, general line

Kao, Fern
Lustre Pitcher Antiques
Box 312, Bowling Green, 43402; 419-352-5928. Specializing in Shelley china, small antiques

Kerr, Ann
P.O. 437, Sidney, 45365; 513-492-6369. Author (Collector Books) of *Collector's Encyclopedia of Russel Wright Designs.* Specializing in work of Wright, interested in 20th-Century decorative arts

Kitchen, Lorrie
Toledo, 419-478-3815. Specializing in Depression-era glass, Hall china, Fiesta, Blue Ridge, Shawnee

Klender, James and Grace
Town & Country Antiques & Collectibles
P.O. Box 447, Pioneer, 43554; 419-737-2880. Specializing in Depression Glass, and general line

Kline, Mr. & Mrs. Jerry and Gerry
Members of Torquay Pottery Collectors' Society and North America Torquay Society
604 Orchard View Dr., Maumee, 43537; 419-893-1226. Specializing in collecting Torquay pottery

Longnecker, Gale and Deanna
Oleo Acres House of Antiques
P.O. Box 1615, Finzel Rd., Whitehouse, 43571; 419-877-5158. Specializing in Fiesta (old)

Loucks, Walter L.
The Carousel News & Trader
87 Parke Ave. W., Suite 206, Mansfield, 44902. A monthly magazine for the carousel enthusiast. Subscription: $22 per year, sample: $3

Massie, James E.
Cincinnati, 513-251-0320. Specializing in art glass, art pottery, paintings and watercolors

McLaughlin, Harold and Joyce
1403 N. Union St., Fostoria, 44830; 419-435-1262. Specializing in glass, post cards, general line

Michul, Irene
Articles & Old Lace
445 N. Twp. Rd. 165, Tiffin, 44883; 419-448-1511. Specializing in old linens, quilts, dolls, books, and vintage clothing

Moore, Carolyn
445 N. Prospect, Bowling Green, 43402. Specializing in primitives, yellowware, graniteware

National Cambridge Collectors, Inc.
Box 416, Cambridge, 43725
Specializing in Cambridge glass

National Heisey Glass Museum
Heisey Collectors of America, Inc.
6th & Church Sts., P.O. Box 4367, Newark, 43055; 614-345-2932

Nelson, Norman
449 N. Town St., Fostoria, 44830; 419-435-6446. Specializing in jukeboxes

Nitecki, Vicky
Articles & Old Lace
314 Jefferson St., Republic, 44867; 419-585-5151. Specializing in old quilts, linens, glass, and china

Osborne, Ruth
Box 85, Higginsport, 45131. Specializing in vintage clothing, lamps, jewelry

Penrose, Donald M.
(Mail order only) 6351 Garber Rd., Dayton, 45415; 513-890-3728. Specializing in continental porcelains and art glass

Peters, Jeannie L.
Mt. Washington Antiques
3742 Kellogg, Cincinnati, 45226; 513-231-6584. Specializing in sheet music

Pierce, David
27544 Black Road, P.O. Box 248, Danville, 43014. Specializing in Glidden pottery

Piersol, Gary
4558 Eastway, Toledo, 43612; 419-476-7687. Specializing in art glass, pattern, and flint glass

Porter, Mike and Pat
Porterble Collections
P.O. Box 263, Clayton, 45315; 513-836-9720. Specializing in vintage wristwatches, fountain pens, children's items, estate mementos

Radel, Erle and Janice
Rapids Renovations & Antiques
Grand Rapids. Specializing in furniture and fine jewelry, (collectors only) Labino art glass

Rees, Debbie
Zanesville. Specializing in Watt, blue and white stoneware, Steiff, cookie jars, Roseville pottery

Regal Relics
P.O. Box 303, Dayton, 45401; 513-254-2937. Specializing in Elegant Glass: Cambridge, Heisey, Fostoria, and Imperial

Riebel, James; Krause, Terry
Pottery Peregrinators
321 Washington St., Zanesville, 43701; 614-452-7687. Specializing in American art pottery, Nicodemus, and general antiques

Rodgers, Joanne
Stretch Glass Society
P.O. Box 770643, Lakewood, 44107. Specializing in stretch glass

Rouppas, William
Frogtown
Box 822, Toledo, 43601. Specializing in early drugstore, medical, dental, and veterinary items

Sberna, Rosa N.
Rosantiques
634 Barker Rd., Fremont, 43420; 419-332-9876. Specializing in general line, sterling, old Fenton, Fiesta, and jewelry

Sterling, Susan
662 Centerfield Dr., Maumee, 43537; 419-891-0315. General line

Stoma, Rose
Toledo
Specializing in glass, china, and pottery

Trainer, Veronica
Bayhouse
Box 40443, Cleveland, 44140; 216-871-8584. Specializing in beaded and enamelled mesh purses

Tucker, Dan
Toledo, 43612; 419-478-3815. Specializing in Depression-era glass, Hall china, Fiesta, Blue Ridge, Shawnee

Walczak, Mary Jo
Toledo. Specializing in dolls and snow babies

Walker, Bunny
Box 502, Bucyrus, 44820; 419-562-8355. Specializing in Steiff teddy bears, penny toys, pottery

Whitmyer, Margaret and Kenn
Box 30806, Gahanna, 43230. Author (Collector Books) on children's dishes. Specializing in Depression-era collectibles

Wilkins, Juanita
The Bird of Paradise
Lima, 419-227-2163. Specializing in R.S. China, Old Ivory china, colored pattern glass, lamps, and jewelry

Young, Mary
1040 Greenridge Dr., Kettering, 45429. Author (Collector Books) of *Collector's Guide to Paper Dolls*

Oklahoma

Bess, Phyllis and Tom
Authors of *Frankoma Treasures*, 14535 E. 13th St., Tulsa, 74108; 918-437-7776. Specializing in Frankoma pottery

Moore, Art and Shirley
2145 S. Norfolk Ave., Tulsa, 74114; 918-747-4164. Specializing in Lu Ray Pastels, Depression Glass

Willis, Ron L.
2110 Fox Ave., Moore, 73160. Specializing in militaria

Oregon

Bartsch, Henry
Antique Registers
2050 N. Hwy. 101, Rockaway Beach, 97136; 503-355-2932. Specializing in antique cash registers, co-author of *Antique Cash Registers 1880-1920*

Bird, Leah and Walt
Bird's Nest
Medford, 97051; 503-779-9138. Specializing in half-dolls, sewing items, lace

Carter, Fran
(Appointment only)
Box 3220, Coos Bay, 97420; 503-888-5780. Specializing in estate sales

Collins, Harriett and Hank
Harriett's Antiques
(shows and appointments only)192 Janney Lane, Medford, 97501; 503-776-0727. Specializing in children's things

Crandall, Peter
Butte Creek Mill
P.O. Box 561; 503-826-3531.
General line

Fitzpatrick, Sarah
P.O. Box 2025, White City, 97503; 503-826-3748. Specializing in Christmas

Frost, Donald M.
Country Estate Antiques
690 Lower Cleveland Rapids Rd., Roseburg, 97470; 503-672-7613. Specializing in fine glass and porcelain

Geddes, Marjorie
Beaverton, 503-649-1041. Specializing in sewing items, butter pats, egg cups, misc. small and elegant collectibles

Haynes, Carolyn and Jerry
Video-Tiques
Box 1402, Jacksonville, 97530; 503-773-7137. Specializing in complete collections for sale — preview on videotape

Hirshman, Susan and Larry
Everyday Antiques
542 Siskiyou Blvd., Ashland, 97250; 503-482-9411. Specializing in china, glassware, kitchenware

Matthews, Skip and Kathy
Aristocratic Attic
344 S.W. 'K' St., Grants Pass, 97526; 503-474-6660. Specializing in Disneyana, cartoon characters, advertising, books, toys

Miller, Don and Robby
P.O. Box 508, Talent, 97504; 503-535-1231. Specializing in milk bottles, TV Siamese cat lamps, seltzer bottles, red cocktail shakers.

Morris, Thomas G.
Prize Publishers
P.O. Box 8307, Medford, 97504; 503-779-3164. Author of *The Carnival Chalk Prize*, a pictorial price guide on carnival chalkware figures with brief histories and values for each

Travis, Pat
Jayhawker Antiques
2204 Allen Creek Rd., Grants Pass, 97527; 503-479-4704. Specializing in china, glassware, pottery

Worth, Veryl Marie
(25 years in mail order) 76248 Gale St., P.O. Box 601, Oakridge, 97463; 503-782-2703. Specializing in Blue and White China, Blue Onion, Willow, Liberty Blue, Flow Blue

Pennsylvania

Atkinson, Phil and Karol
903 Apache Trail, Mercer, 16137; 412-475-2490. Specializing in antique advertising, country store collectibles

Barker, Jim
Toastermaster Antique Appliances
P.O. Box 592, Hawley, 18428; 717-253-1951. Specializing in electric toasters and appliances

Barrett, Noel
Rosebud Antiques
P.O. Box 1001, Carversville, 18913; 215-297-5109. Specializing in toys

Bodine, Clarence H., Jr., Proprietor
East/West Gallery
41B Ferry St., New Hope, 18938; 908-782-3430. Specializing in antique Japanese woodblock prints, netsuke, inro, tsuba

Cerebro
P.O. Box 1221, Lancaster, 17603; 717-656-7875 or 800-69-LABEL. Specializing in antique advertising labels, especially cigar box labels, cigar bands, food labels

Damaska, Ron
738 9th Ave., New Brighton, 15066; 412-843-1393. Specializing in Fry cut glass, match holders, oil lamps, silver; SASE required when requesting information

DLK Nostalgia & Collectibles
P.O. Box 5112, Johnstown, 15904. Specializing in corkscrews and openers, Art Deco, clocks, toys, breweriana, misc.

Garvin, Joann
P.O. Box 182, Beaver Falls, 15010; 412-843-3999. Specializing in Fiesta

Hagenbuch, James
Glass Works Auction
102 Jefferson, E. Greenville, 18041; 215-679-5849. America's leading auction company in early American bottles and glass

Hain, Henry F., III
Antiques & Collectibles
2623 N. Second St., Harrisburg, 17110; 717-238-0534. Lists available of items for sale

Hinton, Michael C.
Arts & Antiques
R.D. 2, Box 313, Mertztown, 19539; 215-682-7096. Specializing in painting & frame restoration. Catalog of oils, watercolors, decorative arts and frames available

Holland, William
William Holland Fine Arts
1708 E. Lancaster Ave., Paoli, 19301; 215-648-0369 or (Fax) 215-647-4448. Specializing in Louis Icart etchings and oils, Art Nouveau and Art Deco items; Author of *Louis Icart: The Complete Etchings*

Kamm, George
George Kamm Paperweights
24 Townsend Ct., Lancaster, 17603; 717-872-7858. Specializing in paperweights — color brochure published 4-5 times a year; $5 1-time charge

Kelly, Kathy
The Kelly Collection
1621 Princess Ave., Pittsburgh, 15216; 412-561-3379. Buying Phoenix glass and related items, glass company catalogs, trade journals, Monaca PA post cards

Knauer, Judy A.
National Toothpick Holder Collectors' Society
1224 Spring Valley Lane, West Chester, 19380; 215-431-3477. Specializing in toothpick holders and Victorian glass

Krause, Gail
994 Jefferson Ave., Washington, 15301. Author of book on Duncan glass

Lindsay, Ralph
P.O. Box 21, New Holland, 17557. Specializing in target balls

Maier, Clarence and Betty
Mail order: The Burmese Cruet
Box 432, Montgomeryville, 18936; 215-855-5388. Specializing in Victorian art glass. SASE required with correspondence

Marks, Mariann Katz
P.O. Box 750, Honesdale, 18431. Author (Collector Books) of *Majolica Pottery, Second Series*. Specializing in collecting, buying, and selling American and English majolica of the Victorian period; LSASE required for mail order list. Enclose photo and price wanted with offers to sell

Posner, Judy
R.D.1, Box 273, Effort, 18330; 717-629-6583. Specializing in figural pottery, cookie jars, salt and peppers, Black memorabilia, Disneyana

Rosso, Philip J. and Philip Jr.
Wholesale Glass Dealers
1815 Trimble Avenue, Port Vue, 15133; 412-678-7352. Specializing in Westmoreland glass

Weiser, Pastor Frederick S.
55 Kohler School Rd., New Oxford, 17350; 717-624-4106. Specializing in frakturs

Rhode Island

Dumont, Louise
579 Old Main St., Coventry, 02816; 401-828-2799. Specializing in cookie jars, Abington

Gacher, John
The Zsolnay Store
221 Spring St., Newport, 02840; 401-841-5060. Specializing in Zsolnay, Fischer, Amphora, Austro-Hungarian art pottery, and 19th-Century decorative arts

The Occupied Japan Club
c/o Florence Archambault
29 Freeborn St., Newport, 02840. Publishes bimonthly newsletter, *The Upside Down World of an O.J. Collector*. SASE required when requesting information

Tennessee

Price, Gene
Railroad Antiques
Box 278, Erwin, 37650. Specializing in railroadiana

Texas

Dockery, Rod
4600 Kemble St., Ft. Worth, 76103; 817-536-2168. Specializing in milk glass; SASE required with correspondence

Docks, L.R. 'Les'
Shellac Shack; Discollector
Box 691035, San Antonio, 78269-1035. Author of *American Premium Record Guide*. Specializing in vintage records

Frese, Leo and Wendy
Three Rivers Collectibles
Box 551542, Dallas, 75355; 214-341-5165. Specializing in Rumrill, Red Wing pottery and stoneware, Hull

Gaston, Mary Frank
Box 342, Bryan, 77806. Author (Collector Books) on china and metals

Malowanczyk, Abby and Wlodek
Collage-20th Century Classics, 3017-B Routh St., Dallas, 75201; 214-880-0020 or (Fax) 214-241-7445. Specializing in Art Deco and mid-century classic furniture; Scandanavian and Italian art glass and ceramics

Norris, Kenn
Schoolmaster Auctions
P.O. Box 4830, 208 Kerr St., Sanderson, 79848; 915-345-2640. Specializing in school-related items and barbed wire

Phillips, Mark
Sunrise Records
2425 S. 11th St. Beaumont, 77701; 409-835-4438. Specializing in records and Rock 'n Roll memorabilia. SASE a must

Pringle, Joyce M.
Chip & Dale Collectables
3500 S. Cooper St., Arlington, 76015. Specializing in Boyd, Summit, and Mosser glass

Sack, Gordon
4828 Laurel, Bellaire, 77401; 713-665-6577. Specializing in cartoon books (not comics)

Silvermintz, Karen
4837 Cedar Springs #116, Dallas, 75219; 214-528-9364. Specializing in American potter, Russel Wright American dinnerware

Smith, Allan
1806 Shields Dr., Sherman, 75090; 903-893-3626. Specializing in children's lunch boxes and all types of advertising, especially Coca-Cola, Dr. Pepper, Pepsi Cola, RC Cola, Red Goose, Buster Brown Shoes, character tin wind-up toys, and western stars' items

Thompson, Chuck
Chuck Thompson & Associates
P.O. Box 11652, Houston, 77293. Thompson believes all good meals should be followed by an after-dinner cigar (or cigarette). He writes two syndicated food columns: *Food Words* and *Sassy Taste Treats*

Tucker, Richard and Valerie
Argyle Antiques
P.O. Box 262, Argyle, 76226; 817-464-3752. Specializing in windmill weights, shooting gallery targets, and other figural cast iron

Waddell, John W.
2903 Stan Terrace, Mineral Wells, 75067. Specializing in buggy steps

Walker, Jimmy and Carol
The Iron Lady
501 N. 5th, Waelder, 78959; 512-665-7166. Specializing in pressing irons

Utah

Anderson, Tim
Box 461, Provo, 84603; 801-226-1787. Specializing in autographs; Buys single items or collections — historical, movie stars, U.S. Presidents, sports figures, and pre-1860 correspondence

Anderson, Warren R.
America West Archives
P.O. Box 100, Cedar City, 84721; 801-586-9497. Specializing in old stock certificates and bonds, western documents and books, financial ephemera, autographs, maps, prints

Vermont

Barry, Kit
143 Main St., Brattleboro, 05301. Author of *The Advertising Trade Card*. Specializing in advertising trade cards and ephemera in general

Virginia

Bradfield, Jeff
Jeff's Antiques
Corner of Rt. 42 & Rt. 257, Dayton, 22821; 703-879-9961. Also located in Rocky's Antique Mall (I-81), Exit 60, Weyers Cave. Specializing in post cards, candy containers, sugar shakers, toys, pottery, furniture, lamps, and advertising items

Flanigan, Vicki
Flanigan's Antiques
P.O. Box 1662, Winchester, 22601. Specializing in antique dolls and hand fans

Friend, Terry
R.R. 4, Box 152-D, Galax, 24333; 703-236-9027 after 9:30 p.m. EST. Specializing in coffee mills; SASE required

Kenney, Ed
Audubon Prints & Books
9720 Spring Ridge Lane, Vienna, 22182; 703-759-5567. Specializing in Audubon and other natural history antique prints

Lechner, Mildred and Ralph
Box 554, Mechanicsville, 23111; 804-737-3347. Author (Collector Books) on glass salt shakers. Specializing in art and pattern glass salt shakers circa 1870-1940. Directors of Antique and Art Glass Salt Shakers Society Club, 1991-92

Monsen, Randall; Baer, Rod
Monsen & Baer
310 Maple Ave. West, #115, Vienna, 22180; 703-938-2129. Specializing in perfume bottles, Roseville pottery, Art Deco

Reynolds, Charles
Reynolds Toys
2836 Monroe St., Falls Church, 22042; 703-533-1322. Specializing in limited edition mechanical and still banks, figural bottle openers

Tutton, John
R.R. 4, Box 929, Front Royal, 22630; 703-635-7058. Specializing in milk bottles

Washington

George, Tony
16212 Bothell Way S.E. #F215, Mill Creek, 98012; 206-483-6074. Specializing in watch fobs

Haase, Don (Mr. Spode)
D&D Antiques
P.O. Box 818, Mukilteo, 98275; 206-348-7443. Specializing in Spode china

Haynes, Bob
House of Haynes Antiques
P.O. Box 6842, Bellevue, 98008; 206-641-5198. Specializing in Royal Doulton and Moorcroft

Rothe, Linda
P.O. Box 27374, Seattle, 98125-1874. Specializing in Black Americana

Wheeler-Tanner Escapes
Tanner, Joseph and Pamela
3024 E. 35th Ave., Spokane, 99223; 509-448-8457. Specializing in handcuffs, leg shackles, balls and chains, restraints and padlocks of all kinds (including railroad) locking and non-locking devices

West Virginia

Fostoria Glass Society of America, Inc.
Box 826, Moundsville, 26041. Specializing in Fostoria glass

Wisconsin

Apple, John
John Apple Antiques
1720 College Ave., Racine, 53403; 414-633-308. Specializing in brass cash registers and parts

Fortney, Daniel
Suite 713 Chalet at the River, 823 N. 2nd St., Milwaukee, 53203. Specializing in china and glass

Goldmine Magazine
700 E. State St., Iola, 54990; 715-445-2214. Specializing in collectible records

Knapper, Mary
Phoneco, Inc.
207 E. Mill Rd., P.O. Box 70, Galesville, 54630; 608-582-4124. Specializing in telephones, antique to modern

Matzke, Gene
Gene's Badges & Emblems
2345 S. 28th St., Milwaukee, 53215; 414-383-8995. Specializing in police badges, leg irons, old police photos, fire badges (old), patches, old handcuffs, and memorabilia

Rice, Ferill J.
302 Pheasant Run, Kaukauna, 54130. Specializing in Fenton art glass

---

Clubs, Newsletters, and Catalogs

America West Archives
Anderson, Warren
P.O. Box 100, Cedar City, UT 84721; 801-586-9497; 26-page illustrated catalogs issued quarterly. Has both fixed-price and auction sections offering early western documents, letters, stock certificates, autographs, and other important ephemera. Subscription: $10 per year

American Willow Report
Lisa Kay Henze, Editor
P.O. Box 900, Oakridge, OR 97463. Bimonthly newsletter, subscription: $15 per year, out of country add $5 per year

Antique & Art Glass Salt Shaker Collectors' Society (AAGSSCS)
2832 Rapidan Trail, Maitland, FL 32751

Antique & Art Glass Salt Shaker Collectors' Society, c/o Albert Mills, Secretary/Treasurer, 348 N. Hamilton St., Painted Post, NY 14870

Antique Purses catalog: $3.00
Bayhouse, P.O. Box 40443, Cleveland, OH 44140; 216-871-8584

Antique Radio Club of America
81 Steeplechase Rd., Devon, PA 19333

Antique Souvenir Collectors' News
Gary Leveille, Editor
P.O. Box 562, Great Barrington, MA 01230

Antique Stove Association
Clifford Boram, Secretary
Monticello, IN
Phone calls only: 219-583-6465

Antique Wireless Association
Ormiston Rd., Breesport, NY 14816

Arts & Crafts Quarterly
P.O. Box 3592, Station E
Trenton, NJ 08629; 1-800-541-5787

Avon Times (National Newsletter Club)
c/o Dwight or Vera Young
P.O. Box 9868, Dept P., Kansas City, MO 64134. Inquiries should be accompanied by LSASE

Black Memorabilia Catalog
Judy Posner
R.D. 1, Box 273 SC, Effort, PA 18330. Send $2 and LSASE

Boyd's Art Glass Collectors Guild
P.O. Box 52, Hatboro, PA 19040-0052
Books available: *Boyd's Crystal Art Glass, The Tradition Continues*, P.O. Box 127, Cambridge, OH 43725; and *Boyd's Art Glass Production 1978-1991*, P.O. Box 11806, Kansas City, MO 64138

British Royal Commemorative Souvenirs
Mail Order Catalog
Audrey Zeder
6755 Coralite St. S, Long Beach, CA 90808

Butter Pat Collectors' Notebook
c/o 5955 S.W. 179th Ave., Beaverton, OR 97007. Send LSASE for subscription information

California Perfume Company
For information contact Dick Pardini
3107 North El Dorado St., Dept. SAPG,
Stockton, CA 95204-3412. Information
requires LSASE; not necessary when offering items for sale

Candy Container Collectors of America
P.O. Box 1088
Washington, PA 15301

The Cane Collector's Chronicle
Linda Beeman
15 2nd St. N.E., Washington, D.C. 20002;
$30 for 4 issues

The Carousel News & Trader
87 Parke Ave., W., Suite 206, Mansfield,
OH 44902. A monthly magazine for the
carousel enthusiast. Subscription: $22 per
year, sample: $3

Central Florida Insulator Collectors
3557 Nicklaus Dr., Titusville, FL 32780

Character Collectibles Catalog
Judy Posner
R.D. #1, Box 273 SC, Effort, PA 18330.
Send $2 and LSASE

Chicagoland Antique Advertizing
Slot Machine & Jukebox Gazette
Ken Durham, Editor
P.O. Box 2426, Dept. S, Rockville, MD
20852. 20-page newspaper published twice a
year. Subscription: 4 issues for $10; sample: $5

Coin-Op Newsletter
Ken Durham, Publisher
909 26th St. N.W., Washington, DC 20037
Subscription (10 issues): $24, sample: $5

The Cola Clan
Alice Fisher, Treasurer
2084 Continental Drive N.E., Atlanta, GA
30345

Cookie Jar Catalog
Judy Posner
R.D. #1, Box 273 SC, Effort, PA 18330.
Send $2 and LSASE

*Cookie Jarrin' with Joyce: The Cookie Jar
Newsletter*
R.R. 2, Box 504, Walterboro, SC 29488

The Cutting Edge, quarterly publication of
the Glass Knife Collectors Club
Adrienne S. Escoe, Editor
P.O. Box 342, Los Alamitos, CA 90720.
Subscription: $3 per year, sample: 50¢

Depression Glass Daze
Teri Steel, Editor/Publisher
Box 57, Otisville, MI 48463; 313-631-4593.
The nation's market place for glass, china,
and pottery

DISCoveries Magazine
P.O. Box 255, Port Townsend, WA 98368-
2923. Specializing in collectible records,
international distribution

Disneyana Catalog
Judy Posner
R.D. 1, Box 273 SC, Effort, PA 18330.
Send $2 and LSASE

Docks, L.R. 'Les'
Shellac Shack
Box 691035, San Antonio, TX 78269-
1035. Send $2 for a 72-page catalog of 78s
that Docks wants to buy, the prices he will
pay, and shipping instructions

Doyle Auctioneers & Appraisers
Doyle, Robert A.
109 Osborne Hill Rd., Fishkill, NY 12524;
800-551-5161. Newsletter: *Auction Oppor-
tunities, Inc.* for $25 per year

Fenton Art Glass Collectors of America, Inc.
Williamstown, WV 26187

Figural Bottle Opener Collectors
c/o Barbara Rosen
6 Shoshone Trail, Wayne, NJ 07470

Fostoria Glass Society of America, Inc.
P.O. Box 826, Moundsville, WV 26041

George Kamm Paperweights
24 Townsend Court, Lancaster, PA 17603;
717-872-7858. Specializing in paperweights
— color brochure published 4-5 times a
year. $5 (1-time charge)

Glass Knife Collector's Club
Adrienne S. Escoe
P.O. Box 342, Los Alamitos, CA 90270

Glass Works Auction
James Hagenbuch
102 Jefferson, E. Greenville, PA 18041; 215-
679-5849. America's leading auction company in early American bottles and glass

The Glaze, Pottery Collectors' Newsletter
P.O. Box 4782, Birmingham, AL 35706

Gonder Pottery Collectors' Newsletter
c/o John and Marilyn McCormick
P.O. Box 3174, Shawnee, KS 66203; 913-
441-0793

Hake's Americana & Collectibles
Specializing in character and personality
collectibles along with artifacts of popular
culture for over 20 years. To receive a catalog for their next 3,000-item mail/phone
bid auction, send $3 to Hake's Americana,
P.O. Box 1444M, York, PA 17405

Heisey Collectors of America, Inc.
National Heisey Glass Museum
169 W. Church St., Newark, OH 43055;
614-345-2932

Ice Screamer
c/o Ed Marks, Publisher
P.O. Box 5387, Lancaster, PA 17601. Published bimonthly, dues: $15 per year;
annual convention late June

Indiana Historical Radio Society
245 N. Oakland Ave., Indianapolis, IN
46201

International Club for Collectors of Hatpins & Hatpin Holders (ICC of H&HH)
Lillian Baker, Founder
15237 Chanera Ave., Gardena, CA 90249;
213-329-2619. Monthly *Points* newsletter
and *Pictorial Journal*

International Rose O'Neill Club
Contact Karen Stewart
P.O. Box 668, Branson, MO 65616
Publishes quarterly newsletter *Kewpiesta
Kourier*. Dues: (includes newsletter) $7
(single) or $10 (family)

International Society of Antique Scale
Collectors
Bob Stein, President
111 N. Canal St., Suite 380, Chicago, IL
60606. Publishes quarterly magazine

Majolica Mail Order Catalog
Items from the collection of Mariann Katz
Marks P.O. Box 750, Honesdale, PA 18431.
Please send LSASE for majolica listing

Metropolis Quarterly Catalog (comics)
7 W. 18th St., New York, NY 10011. Subscription: $4 per year

Mike's General Store
52 St. Anne's Rd., Winnepeg, Manitoba,
Canada R2M 2Y3; 204-255-3464. Catalog
subscription: $4 per issue or next 3 issues
for $10

Morgantown Collectors of America
Jerry Gallagher and Randy Supplee
420 1st Ave. N.W., Plainview, MN 55964;
507-534-3511; *The Morgantown Newscaster,*
quarterly journal of Morgantown Glass only;
affiliated with no club, no advertising. Subscription: $15 per year. Morgantown 1931
Catalog Reprint: $20 postpaid. Morgantown
Colors Placard: $3 postpaid. SASE required
for answers to queries

Mystic Lights of the Aladdin Knights
bimonthly newsletter
c/o J.W. Courter
R.R. 1, Simpson, IL 62985; 618-949-3883.
Information requires LSASE

National Association of Avon Collectors
c/o Connie Clark
6100 Walnut, Dept. P
Kansas City, MO 64113. Information
requires LSASE

National Association of Miniature Enthusiasts (N.A.M.E.)
Box 2621, Anaheim, CA 92804-0621; 714-
871-NAME

National Autumn Leaf Collectors' Club
c/o Woody Griffith
4107 White Ash Rd., Crystal Lake, IL
60014; 815-459-7808

National Blue Ridge Newsletter
Norma Lilly
144 Highland Dr., Blountville, TN 37617.
Subscription: $12 per year (6 issues)

National Cambridge Collectors, Inc.
P.O. Box 416, Cambridge, OH 43725

National Graniteware Society
P.O. Box 10013, Cedar Rapids, IA 52410

National Greentown Glass Association
1807 W. Madison, Kokomo, IN 46901

National Imperial Glass Collectors' Society
P.O. Box 534, Bellaire, OH 43906. Dues:
$12 per year (plus $1 for each additional
member in same household), quarterly
newsletter, convention every June

National Insulator Association #256
3557 Nicklaus Dr., Titusville, FL 32780

National Milk Glass Collectors' Society
and Quarterly Newsletter
c/o Arlene Johnson, Treasurer
1113 Birchwood Dr, Garland, TX 75043.
Please include SASE

National Reamer Association
c/o Larry Branstad, R.R. 3, Box 67, Frederic, WI 54837

National Toothpick Holder Collectors'
Society
c/o Joyce Ender, Box 246, Sawyer, MI
49125. Dues: $10 (single) or $15 (couple)
per year (includes monthly *Toothpick Bulletin*). Annual convention held in August

National Valentine Collectors Association
Evalene Pulati
P.O. Box 1404, Santa Ana, CA 92702; 714-
547-1355. Specializing in Valentines and
love tokens

New England Society of Open Salt Collectors
Mrs. Ruth Arch, Treasurer
Stoneridge Estates, 9 Casey Circle, Waltham,
MA 02154. Dues: $5 per year

Newspaper Collectors' Society of America
Rick Brown
Box 19134-S, Lansing, MI 48901; 517-372-
8381 or Fax 517-485-9115

North America Torquay Society
Jerry and Gerry Kline, members
604 Orchard View Dr., Maumee, OH
43537. Quarterly newsletter sent to members; Information and membership form
requires #10 SASE

North American Trap Collectors' Association
c/o Tom Parr
P.O. Box 94, Galloway, OH 43119-0094.
Dues: $10.00 per year; Publishes bimonthly
newsletter

The Occupied Japan Club
c/o Florence Archambault
29 Freeborn St., Newport, RI 02840. Publishes *The Upside Down World of an O.J.
Collector,* a bimonthly newsletter. Information requires SASE

Old Storefront Antiques
P.O. Box 357, Dublin, IN 47335; 317-478-
4809. Publishes catalogs on store items,
primitives, advertising, profession-related,
etc. Each is available for $1.50 or all 17 for
$17 postpaid. Include LSASE

Open Salt Collectors of the Atlantic
Regions (O.S.C.A.R.)
Lee Anne Gommer, 56 Northview Dr.,
Lancaster, PA 17601. Dues: $5

Open Salt Seekers of the West, Northern
California Chapter
Verna Boller, 1552 Bicardy, Stockton, CA
95203. Dues: $5

Open Salt Seekers of the West, Southern
California Chapter
Pat Christensen, 1067 Salvador, Costa
Mesa, CA 92626. Dues: $5

Our McCoy Matters
Kathy Lynch, Editor
12704 Lockleven Lane, Woodbridge, VA 22192; 703-590-0274. Subscription: $19 for 6 issues, sample: $4

Paperweight Collectors' Association, Inc
P.O. Box 1059, Easthampton, MA 01027; 413-527-2598. Membership: $15 (single), $25 (couple); bimonthly newsletter; biannual conventions. To promote and study paperweights

Pen Fancier's Club
1169 Overcash Dr., Dunedin, FL 34698. Publishes monthly magazine of pens and mechanical pencils. Subscription: $45 per year, sample: $4

Perfume & Scent Bottle Collectors
Jeane Parris
2022 E. Charleston Blvd., Las Vegas, NV 89104; 702-385-6059. Membership: $15 USA or $30 Foreign (includes quarterly newsletter). Information requires SASE

Phoenix Bird Collectors of America (PBCA)
685 S. Washington, Constantine, MI 49042; 616-435-8353. Membership (payable to Joan Oates): $10 per year includes newsletter, *Phoenix Bird Discoveries*, published 3 times a year

Pie Birds Unlimited Newsletter
Lillian M. Cole, 14 Harmony School Rd., Flemington, NJ 08822; 908-782-3198. Specializing in pie birds, pie funnels, pie vents

The Political Gallery
Thomas D. Slater
1325 W. 86th St., Indianapolis, IN 46260; 317-257-0863. Specializing in political and sports memorabilia

Precious Collectibles magazine for Precious Moments figurine collectors, *The Ornament Collector* magazine for Hallmark ornaments and other ornaments, and the *Collectors' Bulletin* magazine for all Limited Edition collectibles. Rosie Wells Enterprises, Inc. R.R. 1S, Canton, IL 61520. Rosie also has informational secondary market price guides for Lowell Davis collectors, Hallmark Ornament collectors, and Precious Moments collectors

R. Lalique
John Danis
11028 Raleigh Ct., Rockford, IL 61111; 815-963-0757 or (Fax) 815-877-6042

Roseville's of the Past newsletter
Jack Bomm, Editor
P.O. Box 1018, Apopka, FL 32704-1018. $19.95 per year for 6 to 12 newsletters

Salt & Pepper Catalog
Judy Posner
R.D. #1, Box 273 SC, Effort, PA 18330. Send $2 and LSASE

Shawnee Pottery Collectors' Club
P.O. Box 713, New Smyrna Beach, FL 32170-0713. Monthly nationwide newsletter. SASE (c/o Pamela Curran) required when requesting information. Optional: $3 for sample of current newsletter

Slot Machine/Juke Box Collector Magazine, published bimonthly
Jackie Durham, Agent
909 26th St. NW, Washington, DC, 20037. Subscription: $36 per year

Southern Folk Pottery Collectors Society
Roy M. Thompson, Jr., Founder
1224 Main Street, Glastonbury, CT 06033; 203-633-3121

Southern Oregon Antiques & Collectibles Club
P.O. Box 508, Talent, OR 97540; 503-535-1231 Meets 1st Wednesday of the month, promotes 2 shows a year in Medford, OR

The Stein Auction Company
Andre Ammelounx
P.O. Box 136, Palatine, IL 60078; 708-991-5927 or (Fax) 708-991-5947 Specializing in steins

Stevengraph Collectors Assn.
David L. Brown
2103-2829 Arbutus Rd., Victoria, British Columbia, Canada, V8N 5X5; 604-477-9896

Stretch Glass Society
P.O. Box 770643, Lakewood, OH 44107. Membership: $8; quarterly newsletter, annual convention

Surveyors Historical Society Identification Committee
D.R. Beeks
P.O. Box 2515, Coeur d'Alene, ID 83814; 208-667-0830

Susie Cooper Catalogs
J. David Ehrhard
Psycho-Ceramic Restorations
1336 Sutherland St., Los Angeles, CA 90026; 213-481-3956

Table Toppers
1340 West Irving Park Rd., P.O. Box 161, Chicago, 60613; 312-769-3184. Membership: $18 (single) per year, which includes *Table Topics*, a bimonthly newsletter for those interested in table-top collectibles

Tea Leaf Club International
P.O. Box 904, Mt. Prospect, IL 60056. Publishes *Tea Leaf Reading* newsletter for members. Membership: $20 (single) or $25 (couple) per year

Tea Talk
Tina M. Carter, teapot columnist
Diana Rosen and Lucy Roman, Editors
419 N. Larchmont Blvd., Los Angeles, CA 90004; 213-659-9650. Subscription: $17.95 per year, sample: $2

Thermometer Collectors' Club of America
Warren D. Harris, President
6130 Rampart Dr., Carmichael, CA 95608; 916-966-3490

Thimble Collectors International
6411 Montego Rd.
Louisville, KY 40228

Three Rivers Depression Era Glass Society
Meetings held 1st Monday of each month in Pittsburgh, PA; for more information contact Nancy Zamborsky, 4038 Willett Rd., Pittsburgh, PA 15227; 412-882-1989

Tiffin Glass Collectors
P.O. Box 554, Tiffin, OH 44883
Meetings at Seneca Cty. Museum on 2nd Tuesday of each month

Tops & Bottoms Club (Rene Lalique perfumes only)
c/o Madeleine France
P.O. Box 15555, Ft. Lauderdale, FL 33318

Toy Gun Collectors of America Newsletter
Jim Buskirk, Editor & Publisher
312 Starling Way, Anaheim, CA 92807; 714-998-9615. Published quarterly, covers both toy and BB guns. Dues: $15 per year

The Trade Card Journal
Kit Barry
86 High St., Brattleboro, VT 05301. A quarterly publication on the social and historical use of trade cards

UHL Collectors' Society
Steve Brundage, President
80 Tidewater Rd., Hagerstown, IN 47346; 317-489-5815 Dale Blann, Vice President
R.R. 1, Box 136, Wheatland, IN 47597; 812-321-4141. For membership and newsletter information contact either of the above

Vernon Views newsletter
P.O. Box 945, Scottsdale, AZ 85252. Published quarterly beginning with the spring issue, $6 per year

Walking Stick Notes
Cecil Curtis, Editor
4051 E. Olive Rd., Pensacola, FL 32514. Quarterly publication with limited distribution

Watt's News
c/o Susan Morris and Jan Seeck
P.O. Box 708, Mason City, IA 50401. Subscription: $10 per year

Western World (National Avon Collectors Marketplace)
c/o Floyd or Ellen Busby
P.O. Box 23785, Dept. P Pleasant Hill, CA 94523. Information requires LSASE

Wheeler-Tanner Escapes
3024 E. 35th Ave., Spokane, WA 99223; 509-448-8457. 40-page catalog of magician/escape artist equipment from trick and regulation handcuffs, padlocks, leg shackles, straight jackets, to picks and pick sets. Books on all of the above and much more. Catalog: $3

The Whimsey Club
c/o Christopher Davis
522 Woodhill, Newark, NY 14513. *Whimsical Notions*, quarterly newsletter; dues: $5 per year. Annual meeting in Rochester, NY, in April during Genessee Valley Bottle Collectors' Show

World's Fair Collectors' Society, Inc.
Michael R. Pender, Editor of *Fair News* monthly newsletter for members; P.O. Box 20806, Sarasota, FL 34238; 813-923-2590. Dues: $12 per year in U.S.A., $13 in Canada, and $20 for overseas members

Books on Antiques and Collectibles

Most of the following books are available from your local book seller or antique dealer, or on loan from your public library. If you are unable to locate certain titles in your area you may order by mail from COLLECTOR BOOKS, P.O. Box 3009, Paducah, KY 42002-3009. This is only a partial listing of the books on antiques that are available from Collector Books. All books are well illustrated and contain current values. Add $2.00 for postage for the first book ordered and $.30 for each additional book. Include item number, title and price when ordering. Allow 14 to 21 days for delivery.

BOOKS ON GLASS AND POTTERY

1810	American Art Glass, Shuman	$29.95
2016	Bedroom & Bathroom Glassware of the Depression Years	$19.95
1312	Blue & White Stoneware, McNerney	$9.95
1959	Blue Willow, 2nd Ed., Gaston	$14.95
2270	Collectible Glassware from the 40's, 50's, & 60's, Florence	$19.95
3311	Collecting Yellow Ware - Id. & Value Gd., McAllister	$16.95
2352	Collector's Ency. of Akro Agate Glassware, Florence	$14.95
1373	Collector's Ency. of American Dinnerware, Cunningham	$24.95
2272	Collector's Ency. of California Pottery, Chipman	$24.95
3312	Collector's Ency. of Children's Dishes, Whitmyer	$19.95
2133	Collector's Ency. of Cookie Jars, Roerig	$24.95
2273	Collector's Ency. of Depression Glass, 10th Ed., Florence	$19.95
2209	Collector's Ency. of Fiesta, 7th Ed., Huxford	$19.95
1439	Collector's Ency. of Flow Blue China, Gaston	$19.95
1915	Collector's Ency. of Hall China, 2nd Ed., Whitmyer	$19.95
2334	Collector's Ency. of Majolica Pottery, Katz-Marks	$19.95
1358	Collector's Ency. of McCoy Pottery, Huxford	$19.95
3313	Collector's Ency. of Niloak, Gifford	$19.95
1039	Collector's Ency. of Nippon Porcelain I, Van Patten	$19.95
2089	Collector's Ency. of Nippon Porcelain II, Van Patten	$24.95
1665	Collector's Ency. of Nippon Porcelain III, Van Patten	$24.95
1034	Collector's Ency. of Roseville Pottery, Huxford	$19.95
1035	Collector's Ency. of Roseville Pottery, 2nd Ed., Huxford	$19.95
3314	Collector's Ency. of Van Briggle Art Pottery, Sasicki	$24.95
2339	Collector's Guide to Shawnee Pottery, Vanderbilt	$19.95
1425	Cookie Jars, Westfall	$9.95
2275	Czechoslovakian Glass & Collectibles, Barta	$16.95
3315	Elegant Glassware of the Depression Era, 5th Ed., Florence	$19.95
3318	Glass Animals of the Depression Era, Garmon & Spencer	$19.95
2024	Kitchen Glassware of the Depression Years, 4th Ed., Florence	$19.95
2379	Lehner's Ency. of U.S. Marks on Pottery, Porcelain & Clay	$24.95
2394	Oil Lamps II, Thuro	$24.95
3322	Pocket Guide to Depression Glass, 8th Ed., Florence	$9.95
2345	Portland Glass, Ladd	$24.95
1670	Red Wing Collectibles, DePasquale	$9.95
1440	Red Wing Stoneware, DePasquale	$9.95
1958	So. Potteries Blue Ridge Dinnerware, 3rd Ed., Newbound	$14.95
2221	Standard Carnival Glass, 3rd Ed., Edwards	$24.95
1848	Very Rare Glassware of the Depression Years, Florence	$24.95
2140	Very Rare Glassware of the Depression Years, Second Series	$24.95
3326	Very Rare Glassware of the Depression Era, Third Series	$24.95
3327	Watt Pottery - Identification & Value Guide, Morris	$19.95
2224	World of Salt Shakers, 2nd Ed., Lechner	$24.95

BOOKS ON DOLLS & TOYS

2079	Barbie Fashion, Vol. 1, 1959-1967, Eames	$24.95
3310	Black Dolls - 1820-1990 - Id. & Value Guide, Perkins	$17.95
1514	Character Toys & Collectibles 1st Series, Longest	$19.95
1750	Character Toys & Collectibles, 2nd Series, Longest	$19.95
1529	Collector's Ency. of Barbie Dolls, DeWein	$19.95
2338	Collector's Ency. of Disneyana, Longest & Stern	$24.95
2342	Madame Alexander Price Guide #17, Smith	$9.95
1540	Modern Toys, 1930-1980, Baker	$19.95
2343	Patricia Smith's Doll Values Antique to Modern, 8th ed	$12.95
1886	Stern's Guide to Disney	$14.95
2139	Stern's Guide to Disney, 2nd Series	$14.95
1513	Teddy Bears & Steiff Animals, Mandel	$9.95
1817	Teddy Bears & Steiff Animals, 2nd, Mandel	$19.95
2084	Teddy Bears, Annalees & Steiff Animals, 3rd, Mandel	$19.95
2028	Toys, Antique & Collectible, Longest	$14.95
1808	Wonder of Barbie, Manos	$9.95
1430	World of Barbie Dolls, Manos	$9.95

OTHER COLLECTIBLES

1457	American Oak Furniture, McNerney	$9.95
2269	Antique Brass & Copper, Gaston	$16.95
2333	Antique & Collectible Marbles, 3rd Ed., Grist	$9.95
1712	Antique & Collectible Thimbles, Mathis	$19.95
1748	Antique Purses, Holiner	$19.95
1868	Antique Tools, Our American Heritage, McNerney	$9.95
1426	Arrowheads & Projectile Points, Hothem	$7.95
1278	Art Nouveau & Art Deco Jewelry, Baker	$9.95
1714	Black Collectibles, Gibbs	$19.95
1128	Bottle Pricing Guide, 3rd Ed., Cleveland	$7.95
1751	Christmas Collectibles, Whitmyer	$19.95
1752	Christmas Ornaments, Johnston	$19.95
2132	Collector's Ency. of American Furniture, Vol. I, Swedberg	$24.95
2271	Collector's Ency. of American Furniture, Vol. II, Swedberg	$24.95
2338	Collector's Ency. of Disneyana, Longest & Stern	$24.95
2018	Collector's Ency. of Graniteware, Greguire	$24.95
2083	Collector's Ency. of Russel Wright Designs, Kerr	$19.95
2337	Collector's Guide to Decoys, Book II, Huxford	$16.95
2340	Collector's Guide to Easter Collectibles, Burnett	$16.95
1441	Collector's Guide to Post Cards, Wood	$9.95
2276	Decoys, Kangas	$24.95
1629	Doorstops, Id. & Values, Bertoia	$9.95
1716	Fifty Years of Fashion Jewelry, Baker	$19.95
3316	Flea Market Trader, 8th Ed., Huxford	$9.95
3317	Florence's Standard Baseball Card Price Gd., 5th Ed.	$9.95
1755	Furniture of the Depression Era, Swedberg	$19.95
2278	Grist's Machine Made & Contemporary Marbles	$9.95
1424	Hatpins & Hatpin Holders, Baker	$9.95
3319	Huxford's Collectible Advertising - Id. & Value Gd.	$17.95
1181	100 Years of Collectible Jewelry, Baker	$9.95
2023	Keen Kutter Collectibles, 2nd Ed., Heuring	$14.95
2216	Kitchen Antiques - 1790–1940, McNerney	$14.95
3320	Modern Guns - Id. & Val. Gd., 9th Ed., Quertermous	$12.95
1965	Pine Furniture, Our Am. Heritage, McNerney	$14.95
3321	Ornamental & Figural Nutcrackers, Rittenhouse	$16.95
2026	Railroad Collectibles, 4th Ed., Baker	$14.95
1632	Salt & Pepper Shakers, Guarnaccia	$9.95
1888	Salt & Pepper Shakers II, Guarnaccia	$14.95
2220	Salt & Pepper Shakers III, Guarnaccia	$14.95
3323	Schroeder's Antique Price Guide, 11th Ed.	$12.95
3324	Schroeder's Antique & Coll. 1993 Engag. Calendar	$9.95
2346	Sheet Music Ref. & Price Guide, Pafik & Guiheen	$18.95
2096	Silverplated Flatware, 4th Ed., Hagan	$14.95
3325	Standard Knife Collector's Guide, Stewart	$12.95
2348	20th Century Fashionable Plastic Jewelry, Baker	$19.95
2349	Value Guide to Baseball Collectibles, Raycraft	$16.95